Petit Dictionnaire Cassell Français-Anglais Anglais-Français

RÉDIGÉ PAR

J. H. DOUGLAS

B.A.(Lond.), Chevalier dans l'Ordre des Palmes Académiques,
Headmaster, Caldew School, Dalston, Cumberland

DENIS GIRARD

Agrégé de l'Université
Inspecteur de l'Académie de Paris

W. THOMPSON

M.A.(Edin.), Deputy Headmaster,
The White House Grammar School, Brampton, Cumberland

CASSELL & CO. LTD., LONDRES

Cassell's Compact French-English English-French Dictionary

COMPILED BY

J. H. DOUGLAS

B.A.(Lond.), Chevalier dans l'Ordre des Palmes Académiques,
Headmaster, Caldew School, Dalston, Cumberland

DENIS GIRARD

Agrégé de l'Université
Inspecteur de l'Académie de Paris

W. THOMPSON

M.A.(Edin.), Deputy Headmaster,
The White House Grammar School, Brampton, Cumberland

CASSELL & CO. LTD., LONDON

CASSELL & COMPANY LTD.
35 Red Lion Square, London, WC1R 4SJ
and at Sydney · Toronto
Johannesburg · Auckland

CASSELL'S FRENCH-ENGLISH ENGLISH-FRENCH
COMPACT DICTIONARY
First published 1904
Entirely new and revised 33rd Edition 1954
52nd Edition 1967

CASSELL'S COMPACT FRENCH-ENGLISH
ENGLISH-FRENCH DICTIONARY
First published 1968

2nd Impression 1968
3rd Impression 1968
4th Impression 1969
5th Impression 1972

I.S.B.N. 0 304 92492 x (Bookshop edition)
I.S.B.N. 0 304 92590 x (School (non-net) edition)

Printed in Great Britain by Cox & Wyman Ltd.
London, Reading and Fakenham
1271

Contents

This new edition of a work which appeared for the first time in 1904 represents a departure from tradition in that it is not a revised version of its immediate predecessor, but an entirely new work based on 'Cassell's New French Dictionary' compiled by Denis Girard and first published in 1962.

The availability of such a recent publication, and one moreover which has been widely accepted as a reliable work, has made the editors' task much easier than it could ever have been otherwise. The dead wood had already been cut away and many new words had been introduced, but it will come as no surprise that there are entries in the 'Compact' which do not appear in the 'New', e.g. 'escalate', and that others which were included in the 'New' for the first time in 1962 have already been discarded as obsolete, e.g. 'teddy boy'.

It is, of course, the question of selection which poses the greatest problem for anyone concerned with the compilation of a dictionary of limited size. Many uncommon words inevitably fail to find a place, as do the less frequent uses of some which have been included. We have tried wherever possible to illustrate by examples, but we have not attempted to incorporate information which properly belongs to a grammar book rather than a dictionary. It is assumed that the user will have a knowledge not only of parts of speech but also of the essential basic grammar of both languages. Although personal preference may have played a part, we have always tried to regard suitability for this type of dictionary as the primary consideration for or against the inclusion of a word, and we hope that we have, if anything, erred on the safe side.

Several features in the general layout of the 'New French Dictionary' have been incorporated for the first time in the 'Compact'. These include the use of the symbols of the International Phonetic Association throughout, the detailed information given in the 'Advice to the User' and the tables of English and French verbs. Completely new features are the notes at the head of the verb tables and the increased use of French in the explanatory parentheses in the English–French section.

J. H. D.

Advice to the User

Grouping of Words
In both sections of the dictionary alphabetical order has been strictly observed for all entries, including proper nouns.

Numbering of Identical Words
Words which are spelt alike but which differ in origin or pronunciation are numbered separately.

Punctuation
When several translations are given for one word it can generally be assumed that those which are separated by commas have much the same meaning; semi-colons are used where there is a clear difference in meaning or usage.

Words marked with an asterisk (*) are obsolete.

Pronunciation
The phonetic transcription is given in square brackets immediately after the key-word and alternative pronunciations have been given where necessary. The mark (') precedes the syllable which carries the stress.

The symbols of the International Phonetic Association have been used throughout the dictionary, and the user who is unfamiliar with these should refer to the Key to Pronunciation.

Daniel Jones' *English Pronouncing Dictionary* has usually been followed in the English–French section.

Grammatical Information
It is assumed that the user will have a reasonable knowledge of the basic grammar of the two languages. For example, when a noun merely adds **-s** for the plural or an adjective **-e** for the feminine, it has not been considered necessary to show this. Parts of speech are indicated by an abbreviation in italics (*a., n.m., v.t., adv.* etc.) except in the case of proper nouns where in English no indication has been given and in French only the gender. For the meanings of the abbreviations the user is referred to the list on page xiv.

Nouns and Adjectives
In the French–English section French nouns are classed as *n.m.* for the masculine, *n.f.* for the feminine or *n.* for a noun which may be masculine or feminine according to context. In the English–French section the gender of French nouns is shown by the abbreviations *m.* or *f.*; where a noun, without change of form, may be masculine or feminine both genders are given. In a list of nouns the gender is not given after each one and the user should therefore read on to the next gender mentioned, e.g. under **damage** he will find 'dommage; tort,

Groupement des Mots
Dans les deux parties du dictionnaire l'ordre alphabétique a été strictement suivi pour tous les articles, y compris les noms propres.

Numérotage de Mots Identiques
Les mots qui ont la même orthographe sont numérotés séparément lorsqu'ils ont une racine ou une prononciation différente.

Ponctuation
Quand plusieurs traductions sont données pour un même mot, celles qui ne sont séparées que par des virgules ont en règle générale des sens à peu près identiques; le point virgule est utilisé pour indiquer des différences très nettes de sens ou d'emploi.
   Les mots précédés d'un astérisque (*) sont désuets.

Prononciation
La transcription phonétique est donnée entre crochets immédiatement après le mot principal. Lorsqu'il y a d'autres prononciations possibles, elles sont également indiquées. L'accent (') précède la syllabe qui porte l'accent tonique.
   Les signes de l'Association Internationale de Phonétique sont utilisés dans les deux parties du dictionnaire et le lecteur qui n'est pas familiarisé avec ces signes devra consulter la Table de Prononciation.
   Pour la section Anglais–Français, on a généralement suivi le dictionnaire de M. Daniel Jones, *An English Pronouncing Dictionary*.

Indications Grammaticales
Le lecteur est considéré comme ayant une connaissance suffisante de la grammaire de base des deux langues. Par exemple, quand un nom français forme son pluriel en -s et quand un adjectif forme son féminin en -e, il n'a pas paru nécessaire de l'indiquer. La nature des mots est indiquée par une abréviation en italique (*a.*, *n.m.*, *v.t.*, *adv.* etc.) excepté dans le cas des noms propres pour lesquels aucune indication n'a été donnée dans la partie Anglais–Français et seulement le genre dans la partie Français–Anglais. On trouvera la signification des abréviations à la page xiv.

Noms et adjectifs
Dans la partie Français–Anglais, les noms français sont classés en *n.m.* pour les noms masculins, en *n.f.* pour les noms féminins et *n.* pour ceux qui se modifient selon le contexte. Dans la partie Anglais–Français, le genre des noms français est indiqué par les abréviations *m.* ou *f.*; lorsqu'un nom peut, sans changer de forme, être soit du masculin soit du féminin, les deux genres sont donnés. Dans une

dégât; (*fig.*) préjudice, détriment, *m.*' and he will know from this that all these five nouns are masculine. In the English–French section the feminine forms of French adjectives and nouns (where applicable) are not normally given. The user should consult the relevant French word in the French–English section.

Where plurals or feminines of nouns or adjectives are given, abbreviated forms are used. For example the entry **cheval** (pl. **-aux**) means that the full plural word is **chevaux**. Similarly, **acteur** (*fem.* **-trice**) indicates that the feminine form is **actrice**.

Verbs

All Verbs, other than reflexive verbs, form their compound tenses with **avoir** unless there is an indication with the entry that they take **être**. For all further information on verb entries please consult notes on Verb Tables below.

Verb Tables

1. French verbs have been listed in the tables as follows:

    a. A pattern verb for each of the three regular conjugations.
    b. Pattern verbs which may best be described as 'anomalous', i.e. verbs which are basically regular but which, for one reason or another, show slight variations from the normal forms.
    c. An alphabetical list of irregular verbs, some of which are used as a reference for other verbs which show similar irregularities.

Full conjugations have been given for the regular verbs but elsewhere only where it is considered necessary or desirable.

2. An alphabetical list of all irregular English verbs included in this dictionary is given. The user is referred to the Verb Tables for a note on the following:

    a. Verbs ending in **-y** preceded by one or more consonants.
    b. Certain verbs ending in a consonant preceded by a vowel.

3. The following explanation of verb entries in the dictionary may be helpful:

    a. *irr.* See the verb in question in the list of irregular verbs.
    b. *irr.* (*conjug. like* . . . . . .) See the pattern verb in the list of irregular verbs.
    c. (*see Verb Tables*) See the verb in question in the list of anomalous verbs.
    d. (*conjug. like* . . . . . .) See the pattern verb in the list of anomalous verbs.

liste de noms, le genre n'est pas donné après chacun d'eux et le lecteur doit alors se référer au premier genre indiqué, e.g. pour **damage** il trouvera 'dommage; tort, dégât; (*fig.*) préjudice, détriment, *m.*' et il en déduira que ces cinq noms sont du masculin. Dans la partie Anglais–Français, le féminin des mots français, lorsqu'il existe, n'est en principe pas indiqué; on le trouvera dans la partie Français–Anglais.

Lorsque le pluriel ou le féminin des noms ou des adjectifs est indiqué, il est donné en abrégé. Par exemple, **cheval** (*pl.* -aux) signifie que la forme de ce mot au pluriel est **chevaux**. De même, **acteur** (*fem.* -trice) signifie que la forme du féminin est **actrice**.

Verbes

Tous les verbes, autres que les verbes réfléchis, forment leurs temps composés avec l'auxiliaire **avoir**, à moins qu'il soit indiqué qu'ils se conjuguent avec **être**. On trouvera ci-dessous des renseignements complémentaires sur les verbes.

Tables des Verbes

1. Les verbes français sont présentés de la façon suivante:

    a. un verbe-type pour chacune des trois conjugaisons régulières.

    b. des verbes-types 'anomaux', c'est-à-dire, des verbes qui sont fondamentalement réguliers mais qui comportent de légères variations par rapport aux formes normales.

    c. une liste alphabétique des verbes irréguliers dont certains servent de références à d'autres verbes présentant des irrégularités analogues.

La conjugaison des verbes réguliers a été donnée en entier, mais pour les autres verbes elle ne figure que lorsque cela paraît nécessaire.

2. On trouvera une liste alphabétique de tous les verbes irréguliers anglais qui sont donnés dans ce dictionnaire, précédée par des renseignements sur les groupes suivants:

    a. Verbes qui se terminent en **-y** précédé d'une ou plus d'une consonne.

    b. Certains verbes qui se terminent en une consonne précédée d'une voyelle.

3. Les renseignements suivants concernant la présentation des verbes dans le dictionnaire pourront s'avérer utiles:

    a. *irr.* Se reporter à la liste des verbes irréguliers.

    b. *irr.* (*conjug. like* . . . . . .) Voir le verbe-type dans la liste des verbes irréguliers.

    c. (*see Verb Tables*) Voir ce verbe dans la liste des verbes anomaux.

    d. (*conjug. like* . . . . . .) Voir le verbe-type dans la liste des verbes anomaux.

Key to Pronunciation

VOWELS

FRENCH (1)

i	as in	cri [kri], difficile [difi'sil]
i:	,, ,,	écrire [e'kri:r], finir [fi'ni:r]
e	,, ,,	thé [te], mélodie [melɔ'di]
ɛ	,, ,,	réel [re'ɛl], aile [ɛl]
ɛ:	,, ,,	bête [bɛ:t], dentaire [dã'tɛ:r]
a	,, ,,	patte [pat], apparat [apa'ra]
a:	,, ,,	tard [ta:r], barbare [bar'ba:r]
ɑ	,, ,,	pas [pɑ], tailler [tɑ'je]
ɑ:	,, ,,	gaz [gɑ:z], pâte [pɑ:t]
ɔ	,, ,,	coter [kɔ'te], voler [vɔ'le]
ɔ:	,, ,,	confort [kɔ̃'fɔ:r], porc [pɔ:r]
o	,, ,,	côté [ko'te], gros [gro], tôt [to]
o:	,, ,,	dôme [do:m], rôle [ro:l]
u	,, ,,	coup [ku], tourner [tur'ne]
u:	,, ,,	bourre [bu:r], cour [ku:r]
y	,, ,,	cru [kry], salut [sa'ly]
y:	,, ,,	littérature [litera'ty:r]
ø	,, ,,	neveu [nə'vø], rocheux [rɔ'ʃø]
ø:	,, ,,	mitrailleuse [mitrɑ'jø:z]
œ	,, ,,	feuillet [fœ'jɛ]
œ:	,, ,,	faveur [fa'vœ:r]
ə	,, ,,	le [lə], refaire [rə'fɛ:r]

ENGLISH (1)

i:	as in	seat [si:t]
i	,, ,,	finish ['finiʃ], physics ['fiziks]
e	,, ,,	neck [nek], bread [bred]
æ	,, ,,	man [mæn], malefactor ['mælifæktə]
ɑ:	,, ,,	father ['fɑ:ðə], task [tɑ:sk]
ɔ	,, ,,	block [blɔk], waddle [wɔdl]
ɔ:	,, ,,	shawl [ʃɔ:l], tortoise ['tɔ:təs]
o	,, ,,	domain [do'mein]
u	,, ,,	good [gud], July [dʒu'lai]
u:	,, ,,	moon [mu:n], tooth [tu:θ]
ʌ	,, ,,	cut [kʌt], somewhere ['sʌmwɛə]
ə:	,, ,,	search [sə:tʃ], surgeon ['sə:dʒən]
ə	,, ,,	cathedral [kə'θi:drəl], never ['nevə]

NASAL VOWELS

ɛ̃	as in	faim [fɛ̃], vingt [vɛ̃]
ɛ̃:	,, ,,	feindre [fɛ̃:dr], poindre [pwɛ̃:dr]
ã	,, ,,	ensemencement [ãsmãs'mã]
ã:	,, ,,	défendre [de'fã:dr]
õ	,, ,,	son [sõ], fonder [fõ'de]
õ:	,, ,,	contre [kõ:tr], trompe [trõ:p]
œ̃	,, ,,	défunt [de'fœ̃], un [œ̃]
œ̃:	,, ,	humble [œ̃:bl]

DIPHTHONGS

ei	as in	great [greit]
ou	,, ,,	show [ʃou]
ai	,, ,,	high [hai]
au	,, ,,	crowd [kraud]
ɔi	,, ,,	boy [bɔi]
iə	,, ,,	steer [stiə]
ɛə	,, ,,	hair [hɛə]
uə	,, ,,	[moor [muə]

CONSONANTS

FRENCH (1)

p as in peine [pɛn], papier [pa'pje]
b ,, ,, bon [bɔ̃]
t ,, ,, tâter [tɑ'te], thé [te]
d ,, ,, dinde [dɛ̃:d]
k ,, ,, coquelicot [kɔkli'ko]
g ,, ,, gare [gɑ:r]
m ,, ,, maman [ma'mɑ̃], même [mɛ:m]
n ,, ,, nonne [nɔn]

ɲ ,, ,, agneau [a'ɲo], soigner [swa'ɲe]
f ,, ,, fier [fjɛ:r]
v ,, ,, vivre [vi:vr]

s ,, ,, sucre [sykr]
z ,, ,, raser [rɑ'ze]
l ,, ,, lettre [lɛtr], valise [va'li:z]
ʃ ,, ,, charme [ʃarm]
ʒ ,, ,, ronger [rɔ̃'ʒe], joue [ʒu]
r ,, ,, arrière [a'rjɛ:r]

ENGLISH (1)

p as in paper ['peipə]
b ,, ,, ball [bɔ:l]
t ,, ,, tea [ti:], till [til]
d ,, ,, deed [di:d]
k ,, ,, cake [keik]
g ,, ,, game [geim]
m ,, ,, mammoth ['mæməθ]
n ,, ,, nose [nouz], nun [nʌn]
ŋ ,, ,, bring [briŋ], finger ['fiŋgə]
f ,, ,, fair [fɛə], far [fɑ:]
v ,, ,, vine [vain]
θ ,, ,, thin [θin], bath [bɑ:θ]
ð ,, ,, this [ðis], bathe [beið]
s ,, ,, since [sins]
z ,, ,, busy ['bizi]
l ,, ,, land [lænd], hill [hil]
ʃ ,, ,, shield [ʃi:ld], sugar ['ʃugə]
ʒ ,, ,, visionary ['viʒənəri]
r ,, ,, rut [rʌt], brain [brein]
h ,, ,, here [hiə], horse [hɔ:s]
x ,, ,, loch [lɔx]

SEMI-CONSONANTS

j as in rien [rjɛ̃]
w ,, ,, ouate [wat], oui [wi]
ɥ ,, ,, huile [ɥil]

j as in yellow ['jelou], yes [jes]
w ,, ,, wall [wɔ:l]

(1) When the same symbol is used in both English and French it often represents a different sound in each language.

′ denotes that the stress is on the following syllable.
: denotes that the preceding vowel is long.
~ placed over a vowel-symbol shows that the vowel has a nasal sound.

List of Abbreviations

a.	adjective
abbr.	abbreviation
Adm.	Administration
adv.	adverb
adv. phr.	adverbial phrase
affirm.	affirmative
Agric.	Agriculture
Alg.	Algebra
Am.	American
Anat.	Anatomy
Ant.	Antiquities
Arch.	Architecture
Archaeol.	Archaeology
Arith.	Arithmetic
art.	article
Artill.	Artillery
Astron.	Astronomy
aux.	auxiliary
Av.	Aviation
Bibl.	Bible, Biblical
Biol.	Biology
Bookb.	Bookbinding
Bot.	Botany
Box.	Boxing
Build.	Building
(C)	Canadian usage
Carp.	Carpentry
Ch.	Church
Chem.	Chemistry
Cine.	Cinema
Civ. Eng.	Civil Engineering
Coin.	Coinage
collect.	collective
colloq.	colloquially
comb.	combination
comb. form	combining form
Comm.	Commerce
comp.	comparative
Conch.	Conchology
cond.	conditional
conj.	conjunction
conjug.	conjugated
contr.	contraction
Cook.	Cookery
Cost.	Costume
Cycl.	Cycling
dat.	dative
def.	definite
dem.	demonstrative
Dent.	Dentistry
dial.	dialect
dim.	diminutive
Dress.	Dressmaking
Eccles.	Ecclesiastical
Econ.	Economics
Elec.	Electricity
ellipt.	elliptic
emphat.	emphatic
Eng.	Engineering
Engl.	English
Engr.	Engraving
Ent.	Entomology
esp.	especially
Exam.	Examination
f.	feminine
fam.	familiarly
facet.	facetiously
fem.	feminine
Fenc.	Fencing
Feud.	Feudal
fig.	figuratively
Fin.	Financial

foll.	the following
Fort.	Fortification
Fr.	French
Ftb.	Football
fut.	future
Gard.	Gardening
Geog.	Geography
Geol.	Geology
Geom.	Geometry
Gr.	Greek
Gram.	Grammar
Gym.	Gymnastics
Her.	Heraldry
Hist.	History
Horol.	Horology
Hort.	Horticulture
Hunt.	Hunting
Hydr.	Hydrostatics
i.	intransitive
Ichth.	Ichthyology
imp.	imperfect
impers.	impersonal
Ind.	Industry
indec.	indecent
indef.	indefinite
indic.	indicative
inf.	infinitive
int.	interjection
inter.	interrogative
inv.	invariable
iron.	ironical
irr.	irregular (see table of Irregular Verbs, pp. 636–58)
It.	Italian
Jew.	Jewish
Journ.	Journalism
L.	Latin
Lit.	Literature
Log.	Logic
m.	masculine
Mach.	Machinery
Manuf.	Manufacturing
masc.	masculine
Math.	Mathematics
Mech.	Mechanics
Med.	Medicine
Metal.	Metallurgy
Meteor.	Meteorology
Mil.	Military
Min.	Mineralogy
Motor.	Motoring
Mount.	Mountaineering
Mus.	Music
Myth.	Mythology
n.	noun
Nat.	Natural
Naut.	Nautical
neg.	negative
obj.	object
obs.	obsolete
Opt.	Optics
Orn.	Ornithology
Paint.	Painting
Parl.	Parliamentary
part.	participle, participial
Path.	Pathology
pej.	pejorative
perf.	perfect

pers.	person, personal
Pharm.	Pharmacy
Phil.	Philosophy
Philol.	Philology
Phon.	Phonetics
Phot.	Photography
phr.	phrase
Phys.	Physics
Physiol.	Physiology
pl.	plural
poet.	poetical
Polit.	Politics
pop.	popular
poss.	possessive
p.p.	past participle
prec.	the preceding
pref.	prefix
prep.	preposition
pres.	present
pres. p.	present participle
Print.	Printing
pron.	pronoun
prop.	proper, properly
Pros.	Prosody
Psych.	Psychology
Pyro.	Pyrotechnics
r.	reflexive; reciprocal
Rad.	Radio
Rail.	Railway
R.C.	Roman Catholic
reg.	registered
rel.	relative
Relig.	Religion
rhet.	rhetoric
Rom.	Roman
Row.	Rowing
Sc.	Scottish
Sch.	Schools
Sci.	Science
Sculp.	Sculpture
sing.	singular
s.o.'s	someone's
Spt.	Sport
St. Exch.	Stock Exchange
subj.	subjunctive
superl.	superlative
Surg.	Surgery
Surv.	Surveying
Swim.	Swimming
t.	transitive
Tech.	Technical
Tel.	Television
Teleg.	Telegraphy
Teleph.	Telephone
Ten.	Tennis
Tex.	Textiles
Theat.	Theatrical
Theol.	Theological
Trig.	Trigonometry
Univ.	University
U.S.	United States
usu.	usually
v.	verb
Vet.	Veterinary
v.i.	intransitive verb
v.r.	reflexive or reciprocal verb
v.t.	transitive verb
vulg.	vulgar
Zool.	Zoology

A, a [ɑ], *n.m.* in French *a* has two sounds:
(1) as in *part*, shown in this dictionary by
'a'; (2) as in *pas*, shown by 'ɑ'.

à [a], *prep.* [*see also* AU, AUX] to, at, in, into,
on, by, for, from, with.

abaisse [a'bɛ:s], *n.f.* undercrust of pastry.

abaissement [abɛs'mɑ̃], *n.m.* lowering, falling, abatement, depression; humiliation,
abasement.

abaisser [abɛ'se], *v.t.* to let down, to let fall,
to lower; to diminish, to reduce; (*fig.*) to
bring low, to humble, to depress; to roll out
(*paste*). **s'abaisser,** *v.r.* to sink, to subside,
to decrease, to abate, to decline; to humble
oneself, to stoop, to cringe.

abajoue [aba'ʒu], *n.f.* (*Zool.*) cheek-pouch.

abalourdir [abalur'di:r], *v.t.* to make dull *or*
stupid.

abalourdissement [abalurdis'mɑ̃], *n.m.* dullness, stupidity.

abandon [abɑ̃'dɔ̃], *n.m.* relinquishment, surrender, cession; abandonment, forlornness,
destitution; lack of restraint; *à l'abandon,*
at random, in confusion, at sixes and sevens;
(*Naut.*) adrift.

abandonné [abɑ̃dɔ'ne], *a.* abandoned, for-
saken; lost to decency, shameless, profligate.

abandonnement [abɑ̃dɔn'mɑ̃], *n.m.* abandonment; desertion; (*fig.*) dissoluteness, profligacy.

abandonnément [abɑ̃dɔne'mɑ̃], *adv.* freely,
unreservedly.

abandonner [abɑ̃dɔ'ne], *v.t.* to give up, to
hand over, to surrender; to renounce; to
forsake, to desert, to abandon; to leave,
to quit; to neglect. **s'abandonner,** *v.r.* to
give oneself up, to give way (*à*); to indulge
(*à*); to neglect oneself.

abaque [a'bak], *n.m.* (*Arch.*) abacus; (*Arith.*)
abacus.

abasourdir [abazur'di:r], *v.t.* to stun, to
dumbfound; (*fig.*) to astound.

abasourdissant [abazurdi'sɑ̃], *a.* astounding,
overwhelming.

abasourdissement [abazurdis'mɑ̃], *n.m.*
stupefaction, bewilderment.

*abat [a'ba], *n.m.* killing, knocking down;
heavy shower.

abâtardi [abatar'di], *a.* degenerate, corrupt,
debased.

abâtardir [abatar'di:r], *v.t.* to render
degenerate; to debase, to corrupt. **s'abâtardir,** *v.r.* to degenerate.

abâtardissement [abatardis'mɑ̃], *n.m.* degeneracy.

abatée *or* **abattée** [aba'te], *n.f.* swoop (*of
plane*).

abat-jour [aba'ʒu:r], *n.m. inv.* sky-light;
lamp-shade; shade for the eyes.

abat-son [aba'sɔ̃], *n.m.* (*pl. unchanged or* **abat-
sons**) a series of sloping louvres in the
window of a bell-tower for directing the
sound downwards.

abattage [aba'ta:ʒ], *n.m.* cutting down, felling (*of trees*); slaughtering (*of animals*).

abattant [aba'tɑ̃], *n.m.* flap (*of a counter etc.*).

abattée [ABATÉE].

abattement [abat'mɑ̃], *n.m.* weakening; prostration; dejection, despondency, low spirits.

abatteur [aba'tœ:r], *n.m.* one who fells (*trees
etc.*); slaughterer.

abattis [aba'ti], *n.m.* things *or* materials
brought down (*such as houses, walls, trees*);
slaughtered animals, game etc.; killing of
game; giblets (*of poultry*).

abattoir [aba'twa:r], *n.m.* slaughter-house.

abattre [a'batr], *v.t.* (*conjug. like* BATTRE)
to throw *or* hurl down; to knock, beat
or batter down; to pull down; to fell; to
kill, to slaughter; to overthrow, to demolish;
to dishearten, to discourage, to depress.
s'abattre, *v.r.* to throw oneself down, to
fall, to tumble down; to crash (down); to
abate; to be cast down *or* dejected; to
pounce upon; *le vent s'abat,* the wind is
dropping.

abattu [aba'ty], *a.* cast down, depressed,
dejected; humbled, crestfallen.

abat-vent [aba'vɑ̃], *n.m. inv.* louvre-boards
(*of a window*); wind-cowl (*of a chimney*).

abat-voix [aba'vwa], *n.m. inv.* sounding-
board (*of a pulpit*).

abbaye [abe'ji], *n.f.* monastery, abbey.

abbé [a'be], *n.m.* abbot, abbé; *l'abbé
Martin,* Father Martin.

abbesse [a'bɛs], *n.f.* abbess.

A.B.C. [abe'se], *n.m.* alphabet; primer,
spelling-book.

abcéder [apse'de], *v.i.* (*conjug. like* CÉDER) to
turn into an abscess, to gather.

abcès [ap'sɛ], *n.m.* abscess, gathering; *abcès
aux gencives,* gumboil.

abdication [abdika'sjɔ̃], *n.f.* abdication;
renunciation (*of property etc.*); surrender
(*of authority*).

abdiquer [abdi'ke], *v.t.* to abdicate, to resign,
to renounce.

abdomen [abdɔ'mɛn], *n.m.* abdomen.

abdominal [abdɔmi'nal], *a.* abdominal.

abducteur [abdyk'tœ:r], *a.* (*Anat.*) abducent.
—*n.m.* (*Anat.*) abductor.

abduction [abdyk'sjɔ̃], *n.f.* abduction.

abécédaire [abese'dɛ:r], *a.* alphabetical;
ordre abécédaire, alphabetical order.—
n.m. spelling-book; elementary reading-
book; primer.

abecquer [abe'ke], *v.t.* to feed (*a bird*).

abeille [a'bɛ:j], *n.f.* bee; *abeille mère,* queen
bee.

aberration [abera'sjɔ̃], *n.f.* deviation from
the normal *or* the correct course; (*Astron.,
Opt. etc.*) aberration.

abêtir [abe'ti:r], *v.t.* to render stupid; to dull,
to blunt.—*v.i.* to become dull *or* stupid.
s'abêtir, *v.r.* to grow stupid.

abêtissement [abetis'mɑ̃], *n.m.* stultifica-
tion.

abhorrer [abɔ're], *v.t.* to abhor, to hate, to loathe.

abîme [a'biːm], *n.m.* abyss, the deep, chasm; hell.

abîmé [abi'me], *a.* swallowed up, engulfed; ruined; damaged.

abîmer [abi'me], *v.t.* *to engulf, to swallow up; to ruin; to damage. **s'abîmer**, *v.r.* to fall into ruin; to be spoiled.

abject [ab'ʒɛkt], *a.* abject, base.

abjectement [abʒɛktə'mã], *adv.* abjectly.

abjection [abʒɛk'sjɔ̃], *n.f.* abasement, humiliation; vileness.

abjuration [abʒyra'sjɔ̃], *n.f.* solemn renunciation, abjuration.

abjurer [abʒy're], *v.t.* to abjure, to renounce; to foreswear.

ablatif [abla'tif], *a.* (*fem.* **-tive**) ablative. —*n.m.* (*Gram.*) ablative (case).

ablation [ablɑ'sjɔ̃], *n.f.* (*Surg.*) removal (of a part).

able [abl], *n.m.* any small freshwater fish of the bleak family [ABLETTE].

ablette [a'blɛt], *n.f.* bleak [ABLE].

ablution [ably'sjɔ̃], *n.f.* ablution, washing, purification.

abnégation [abnega'sjɔ̃], *n.f.* abnegation, renunciation, sacrifice, self-denial.

aboi [a'bwa], *n.m.* (*dog's*) bark, barking, baying; (*fig.*) desperate condition; *aux abois*, at bay.

aboiement [abwa'mã], *n.m.* barking, baying.

abolir [abɔ'liːr], *v.t.* to abolish, to repeal, to annul, to suppress.

abolissement [abɔlis'mã], *n.m.* abolition.

abolition [abɔli'sjɔ̃], *n.f.* abolition, repeal.

abominable [abɔmi'nabl], *a.* abominable, execrable; heinous.

abominablement [abɔminablə'mã], *adv.* abominably.

abomination [abɔminɑ'sjɔ̃], *n.f.* abomination, detestation, horror.

abominer [abɔmi'ne], *v.t.* to abominate, to detest.

abondamment [abɔ̃da'mã], *adv.* abundantly.

abondance [abɔ̃'dãːs], *n.f.* a great quantity, abundance, plenty; affluence.

abondant [abɔ̃'dã], *a.* abundant, plentiful, copious; exuberant, effusive.

abonder [abɔ̃'de], *v.i.* to abound, to be plentiful, to be in great quantity; *abonder dans le sens de quelqu'un*, to support somebody's views strongly.

abonné [abɔ'ne], *n.m.* (*fem.* **-ée**) subscriber (*to periodicals etc.*); season-ticket holder.

abonnement [abɔn'mã], *n.m.* subscription (*to periodicals, theatres etc.*); agreement; season-ticket; *carte d'abonnement*, season-ticket.

abonner (s') [sabɔ'ne], *v.r.* to become a subscriber.

abonnir [abɔ'niːr], *v.t.* to mend, to improve (*wine*).—*v.i.* to become good. **s'abonnir**, *v.r.* to mend, to grow better.

abonnissement [abɔnis'mã], *n.m.* improvement.

abord [a'bɔːr], *n.m.* landing; arrival; access, approach, meeting; onset, attack; (*pl.*) approaches, surroundings; *d'abord*, at first.

abordable [abɔr'dabl], *a.* accessible, easily approached, affable.

abordage [abɔr'daːʒ], *n.m.* (*Naut.*) boarding; fouling, colliding.

abordée [abɔr'de], *n.f.* the act of meeting, accosting or beginning.

aborder [abɔr'de], *v.t.* to arrive at; to approach, to accost; to enter upon (*a subject etc.*); to grapple (*a vessel*); to run foul of (*a ship*).—*v.i.* to arrive; to land. **s'aborder**, *v.r.* to accost each other; to run foul of each other.

aborigène [abɔri'ʒɛːn], *a.* native, original.— *n.m.* aboriginal, aborigine.

aborner [abɔr'ne], *v.t.* to mark out, to delimit.

abortif [abɔr'tif], *a.* (*fem.* **-tive**) abortive.

abouchement [abuʃ'mã], *n.m.* interview, conference.

aboucher [abu'ʃe], *v.t.* to bring (*things or persons*) together. **s'aboucher**, *v.r.* to have an interview, to confer (*with*); to get in touch (*with*).

aboutement [abut'mã], *n.m.* abutment; placing or fitting end to end.

abouter [abu'te], *v.t.* to join end to end.

aboutir [abu'tiːr], *v.i.* to end at or in, to result (*à*); (*Surg.*) to come to a head (*with aux.* ÊTRE or AVOIR).

aboutissant [abuti'sã], *a.* bordering upon, abutting on, ending in.

aboutissement [abutis'mã], *n.m.* result, issue.

aboyer [abwa'je], *v.i.* (*conjug. like* EMPLOYER) to bark, to bay, to yelp.

abracadabra [abrakada'bra], *n.m.* abracadabra (*magic word*).

abracadabrant [abrakada'brã], *a.* stupendous, amazing, stunning.

abrasif [abra'zif], *n.m.* abrasive.

abrégé [abre'ʒe], *a.* short, summary.—*n.m.* abridgment, résumé, précis, abstract, summary.

abrégement [abreʒ'mã], *n.m.* abridging, abridgment.

abréger [abre'ʒe], *v.t.* (*conjug. like* ASSIÉGER) to abridge, to shorten; to abbreviate.

abreuvage [abrœ'vaːʒ], **abreuvement** [a brœv'mã], *n.m.* watering, soaking, steaming.

abreuver [abrœ've], *v.t.* to water (*animals*); to water (*the ground etc.*). **s'abreuver**, *v.r.* to drink, to be watered (*of animals*).

abreuvoir [abrœ'vwaːr], *n.m.* watering-place, horse-pond; drinking-trough.

abréviation [abrevja'sjɔ̃], *n.f.* abbreviation, shortening.

abri [a'bri], *n.m.* shelter, cover, refuge, dug-out.

abricot [abri'ko], *n.m.* apricot.

abricotier [abrikɔ'tje], *n.m.* apricot-tree.

abriter [abri'te], *v.t.* to shelter, to shade, to protect. **s'abriter**, *v.r.* to take refuge.

abrogation [abrɔga'sjɔ̃], *n.f.* abrogation, repeal, annulment.

abroger [abrɔ'ʒe], *v.t.* (*conjug. like* MANGER) to abrogate, to repeal, to annul. **s'abroger**, *v.r.* to fall into disuse.

abrupt [a'brypt], *a.* abrupt, steep, sheer; (*fig.*) blunt, rugged, rough (*of style etc.*).

abruptement [abryptə'mã], *adv.* abruptly.

abruti [abry'ti], *a.* and *n.m.* (*fem.* **-e**) brutalized, stupid (person).

abrutir [abry'tiːr], *v.t.* to stupefy, to brutalize. **s'abrutir**, *v.r.* to become brutalized or stupid.

2

abrutissant [abryti'sɑ̃], *a.* brutalizing, stupefying.

abrutissement [abrytis'mɑ̃], *n.m.* the act of brutalizing; brutishness, degradation.

absence [ap'sɑ̃:s], *n.f.* absence; want, lack; *absence d'esprit*, absence of mind.

absent [ap'sɑ̃], *a.* absent, away from home; wandering, woolgathering.—*n.m.* (*fem.* -e) absentee.

absentéisme [apsɑ̃te'ism], *n.m.* absenteeism.

absenter (s') [apsɑ̃'te], *v.r.* to absent oneself, to be away; to play truant.

abside [ap'si:d], *n.f.* apse.

absinthe [ap'sɛ̃:t], *n.f.* absinth; wormwood.

absolu [apsɔ'ly], *a.* absolute; despotic, arbitrary; unrestricted; peremptory; positive.

absolument [apsɔly'mɑ̃], *adv.* absolutely; arbitrarily.

absolution [apsɔly'sjɔ̃], *n.f.* absolution, acquittal.

absolutisme [apsɔly'tism], *n.m.* absolutism.

absorbant [apsɔr'bɑ̃], *a.* absorptive, absorbent; engrossing.—*n.m.* absorbent.

absorber [apsɔr'be], *v.t.* to absorb, to imbibe; to eat *or* drink; (*fig.*) to engross. **s'absorber**, *v.r.* to be absorbed; (*fig.*) to be entirely taken up with (*dans*).

absorption [apsɔrp'sjɔ̃], *n.f.* absorption.

absoudre [ap'sudr], *v.t. irr.* to absolve, to acquit; to exonerate, to forgive.

abstenir (s') [apstə'niːr], *v.r. irr.* (*conjug. like* TENIR) to abstain (*from voting*); to refrain, to forbear, to forgo.

abstention [apstɑ̃'sjɔ̃], *n.f.* abstention.

abstinence [apsti'nɑ̃:s], *n.f.* abstinence; temperance, sobriety; (*pl.*) fasts, fasting.

abstinent [apsti'nɑ̃], *a.* abstemious, sober.

abstraction [apstrak'sjɔ̃], *n.f.* abstraction, abstract question *or* idea.

abstraire [aps'trɛːr], *v.t. irr.* (*conjug. like* TRAIRE) to abstract; to separate, to isolate.

abstrait [aps'trɛ], *a.* abstract, abstruse; absent-minded.

abstraitement [apstrɛt'mɑ̃], *adv.* abstractedly; separately; in the abstract.

abstrus [aps'try], *a.* abstruse; obscure.

absurde [ap'syrd], *a.* absurd, nonsensical, stupid, silly, preposterous.

absurdement [apsyrdə'mɑ̃], *adv.* absurdly, nonsensically.

absurdité [apsyrdi'te], *n.f.* absurdity, nonsense.

abus [a'by], *n.m.* abuse; grievance; misuse.

abuser [aby'ze], *v.t.* to deceive, to lead astray, to delude.—*v.i.* to misuse, to make ill use (*de*); to take advantage (*de*). **s'abuser**, *v.r.* to be mistaken, to deceive oneself.

abusif [aby'zif], *a.* (*fem.* -sive) irregular, improper.

abusivement [abyziv'mɑ̃], *adv.* irregularly, improperly.

abyssal [abi'sal], *a.* unfathomable.

abysse [a'bis], *n.m.* abyss, unfathomable gulf *or* depth.

Abyssinie [abisi'ni], l', *f.* Abyssinia.

abyssinien [abisi'njɛ̃] (*fem.* -enne), **abyssin** [abi'sɛ̃], *a.* Abyssinian.—*n.m.* (**Abyssinien**, *fem.* -enne) Abyssinian (*person*).

acabit [aka'bi], *n.m.* quality (*of fruits, vegetables*); character, nature, stamp (*of persons*).

acacia [aka'sja], *n.m.* (*Bot.*) acacia.

académicien [akademi'sjɛ̃], *n.m.* academician.

académie [akade'mi], *n.f.* academy, society of learned men, *esp.* the Académie Française; school (*of dancing, fencing, riding etc.*).

académique [akade'mik], *a.* proper, appropriate *or* belonging to an academy, academic(al).

acagnarder [akaɲar'de], *v.t.* to make lazy. **s'acagnarder**, *v.r.* to drift into an idle, slothful life.

acajou [aka'ʒu], *n.m.* mahogany.

acanthe [a'kɑ̃:t], *n.f.* acanthus.

acariâtre [aka'rjɑːtr], *a.* contrary, crabbed, cross-grained, quarrelsome, shrewish.

acariâtreté [akarjɑtrə'te], *n.f.* crabbedness, peevishness, shrewishness.

accablant [aka'blɑ̃], *a.* oppressive, overwhelming, crushing.

accablement [akɑblə'mɑ̃], *n.m.* prostration, oppression, extreme discouragement *or* dejection.

accabler [aka'ble], *v.t.* to crush, to overpower, to overcome; (*fig.*) to weigh down, to overload, to overwhelm.

accalmie [akal'mi], *n.f.* (*Naut.*) lull.

accaparant [akapa'rɑ̃], *a.* engrossing.

accaparement [akapar'mɑ̃], *n.m.* monopoly, monopolizing.

accaparer [akapa're], *v.t.* to monopolize, to hoard, to engross.

accapareur [akapa'rœːr], *n.m.* (*fem.* -euse) monopolist, monopolizer, hoarder.

accéder [akse'de], *v.i.* (*conjug. like* CÉDER) to arrive, to reach, to have access; to accede, to comply with.

accélérateur [akselera'tœːr], *a.* (*fem.* -trice) accelerative, with increasing speed.—*n.m.* (*Elec., Mech., Phot. etc.*) accelerator; (*fam.*) *appuyer sur l'accélérateur*, to step on the gas.

accélération [akselera'sjɔ̃], *n.f.* acceleration.

accéléré [aksele're], *a.* accelerated.

accélérer [aksele're], *v.t.* (*conjug. like* CÉDER) to accelerate, to quicken, to hasten, to press, to dispatch.

accent [ak'sɑ̃], *n.m.* pitch, accent, stress, tone; pronunciation; expression (*of the voice*).

accentuation [aksɑ̃tɥa'sjɔ̃], *n.f.* accentuation, stressing.

accentuer [aksɑ̃'tɥe], *v.t.* to accent, to accentuate, to stress.

acceptable [aksɛp'tabl], *a.* acceptable, worth accepting.

acceptation [aksɛpta'sjɔ̃], *n.f.* acceptance; acceptation.

accepter [aksɛp'te], *v.t.* to accept, to agree to, to welcome (*what is offered or proposed*).

acception [aksɛp'sjɔ̃], *n.f.* respect, regard, sense, meaning, acceptation.

accès [ak'sɛ], *n.m.* access, opportunity of approach, admittance; attack, fit, paroxysm.

accessibilité [aksɛsibili'te], *n.f.* accessibility.

accessible [aksɛ'sibl], *a.* accessible, approachable; within reach.

accession [aksɛ'sjɔ̃], *n.f.* accession; adhesion, union (*of a country, province etc. to another*).

accessit [aksɛ'sit], *n.m.* award of merit, honourable mention; 'proxime accessit'.

accessoire [aksɛ'swaːr], *a.* accessory, additional, subordinate.—*n.m.* an accessory; (*pl.*) (*Theat.*) properties.

accessoiriste [aksɛswa'rist], *n.m.* props man.

3

accident [aksi'dɑ̃], *n.m.* accident, fortuitous incident; casualty, mishap, mischance; unevenness, irregularity (*in the ground*).

accidenté [aksidɑ̃'te], *a.* varied, unequal (*of style etc.*); rough, uneven, broken, hilly (*of ground*); chequered (*of life, career etc.*).— *n.m.* (*fem.* -ée) one injured by an accident.

accidentel [aksidɑ̃'tɛl], *a.* (*fem.* -elle) accidental, adventitious, fortuitous, unexpected; *signe accidentel*, (*Mus.*) accidental.

accidentellement [aksidɑ̃tɛl'mɑ̃], *adv.* accidentally, casually, by chance.

accidenter [aksidɑ̃'te], *v.t.* to make irregular *or* uneven; to diversify, to chequer, to make picturesque.

accise [ak'si:z], *n.f.* (*Law*) inland duty, excise; *préposé à l'accise*, exciseman.

acclamation [aklɑmɑ'sjɔ̃], *n.f.* acclamation, cheering.

acclamer [aklɑ'me], *v.t.* to acclaim, to applaud, to cheer.

acclimatable [aklima'tabl], *a.* that may be acclimatized.

acclimatation [aklimatɑ'sjɔ̃], *n.f.* acclimatization.

acclimater [aklima'te], *v.t.* to acclimatize. **s'acclimater**, *v.r.* to become acclimatized.

accointance [akwɛ̃'tɑ̃:s], *n.f.* (*used generally in pl. and in a bad sense*) intimacy, familiarity; *avoir des accointances* (*avec*), to have dealings (*with*).

accointer [akwɛ̃'te], *v.t.* to make acquainted.

accolade [akɔ'lad], *n.f.* embrace; kiss; accolade (*in knighting*).

accolader (s') [sakɔla'de], *v.r.* to embrace mutually.

accolage [akɔ'la:ʒ], *n.m.* tying up, training (*branches etc.*).

accolement [akɔl'mɑ̃], *n.m.* joining, uniting.

accoler [akɔ'le], *v.t.* to embrace; to tie up, to fasten, to place against; (*fig.*) to couple, to join together, to bracket.

accommodable [akɔmɔ'dabl], *a.* that may be arranged; adjustable.

accommodage [akɔmɔ'da:ʒ]. *n.m.* preparation *or* dressing (*of meat*).

accommodant [akɔmɔ'dɑ̃], *a.* accommodating, easy-going, courteous.

accommodation [akɔmɔdɑ'sjɔ̃], *n.f.* accommodation.

accommodement [akɔmɔd'mɑ̃], *n.m.* accommodation, arrangement, composition; settlement, reconciliation, compromise.

accommoder [akɔmɔ'de], *v.t.* to adapt, to accommodate, to fit, to adjust; to reconcile; to conciliate; to dress, to trim; to cook, to do up; to suit, to be convenient. **s'accommoder**, *v.r.* to agree, to come to terms; to accommodate oneself, to adapt oneself (*à*); to put up with (*de*).

accompagnateur [akɔ̃paɲa'tœːr], *n.m.* (*fem.* -trice) accompanist (*with instrument or voice*); conductor (*of a tour*).

accompagnement [akɔ̃paɲ'mɑ̃], *n.m.* accompanying; attendance, retinue; an accompaniment, an accessory; (*Mus.*) accompaniment.

accompagner [akɔ̃pa'ɲe], *v.t.* to accompany, to attend on; to go with, to escort; (*Mus.*) to accompany.

accompli [akɔ̃'pli], *a.* accomplished, performed, fulfilled; complete, faultless perfect, out and out.

accomplir [akɔ̃'pli:r], *v.t.* to fulfil, to effect, to perform; to realize, to carry out.

accomplissement [akɔ̃plis'mɑ̃], *n.m.* accomplishment, fulfilment, realization.

accon, acconier [ACON etc.].

accord [a'kɔːr], *n.m.* accord, concurrence, unanimity, harmony; agreement, bargain; convention, settlement; (*Mus.*) chord; *être d'accord*, to agree; *d'accord*, granted, agreed.

accordable [akɔr'dabl], *a.* that may be accorded; reconcilable; (*Mus.*) tunable.

accordage [akɔr'da:ʒ], **accordement** [akɔrdə'mɑ̃], *n.m.* tuning (*of a musical instrument*).

accordailles [akɔr'dɑ:j], *n.f.* (*used only in pl.*) betrothal.

accordant [akɔr'dɑ̃], *a.* accordant, harmonious.

accordé [akɔr'de], *n.m.* (*fem.* -ée) fiancé, fiancée; *les accordés*, the bride and bridegroom.

accordéon [akɔrde'ɔ̃], *n.m.* accordion.

accordéoniste [akɔrdeɔ'nist], *n.* accordionist.

accorder [akɔr'de], *v.t.* to bring into harmony *or* accord, to make agree, to reconcile; to concede, to grant; to admit, to avow; (*Mus.*) to tune, to harmonize; to bestow (*hand in marriage*). **s'accorder**, *v.r.* to agree, to concur; to correspond; to suit, to be suited.

accordeur [akɔr'dœːr], *n.m.* tuner (*of musical instruments*).

accordoir [akɔr'dwaːr], *n.m.* tuning-hammer, -key *or* -cone.

accore [a'kɔːr], *a.* abrupt, sheer, vertical (*of a coast*).

accort [a'kɔːr], *a.* gracious, courteous.

accostable [akɔs'tabl], *a.* easy of access, approachable.

accostage [akɔs'ta:ʒ], *n.m.* the act of accosting, approaching *or* drawing alongside.

accoster [akɔs'te], *v.t.* to accost, to go up to; (*Naut.*) to come alongside.

accotement [akɔt'mɑ̃], *n.m.* (*Civ. Eng.*) roadside; footpath.

accoter [akɔ'te], *v.t.* to prop up, to support, to stay. **s'accoter**, *v.r.* to lean (*contre*).

accotoir [akɔ'twaːr], *n.m.* prop, support, leaning-post.

accouardir [akwar'diːr], *v.t.* to make a coward. **s'accouardir**, *v.r.* to turn coward.

accouchée [aku'ʃe], *n.f.* woman in childbirth, woman who has just had a child.

accouchement [akuʃ'mɑ̃], *n.m.* childbirth, delivery, confinement; *centre d'accouchement*, maternity home.

accoucher [aku'ʃe], *v.t.* to deliver (*a woman*). —*v.i.* to lie in, to be brought to bed, to be delivered.

accoucheur [aku'ʃœːr], *n.m.* male midwife, accoucheur.

accoucheuse [aku'ʃøːz], *n.f.* midwife.

accoudement [akud'mɑ̃], *n.m.* the act of leaning (*on*).

accouder (s') [saku'de], *v.r.* to lean on one's elbow.

accoudoir [aku'dwaːr], *n.m.* elbow-rest; (*Arch.*) rail, balustrade.

accouple [a'kupl], *n.f.* leash (*for tying dogs in couples*).
accouplement [akuplə'mã], *n.m.* coupling; pairing.
accoupler [aku'ple], *v.t.* to couple; to join together in pairs; (*Elec.*) to connect, to group (*batteries etc.*).
accourci [akur'si], *n.m.* abridgement (*of a book*).
accourcir [akur'si:r], *v.t.* to shorten, to abridge, to curtail. **s'accourcir**, *v.r.* to become shorter, to decrease.
accourcissement [akursis'mã], *n.m.* shortening, diminution.
accourir [aku'ri:r], *v.i. irr.* (*conjug. like* COURIR) to run up to, to hasten, to flock.
accoutrement [akutrə'mã], *n.m.* garb, dress, *esp.* as an object of ridicule.
accoutrer [aku'tre], *v.t.* to rig out, to dress. **s'accoutrer**, *v.r.* to dress absurdly, to rig oneself out.
accoutumance [akuty'mã:s], *n.f.* habit, custom, wont, usage.
accoutumé [akuty'me], *a.* ordinary, accustomed, habitual.
accoutumer [akuty'me], *v.t.* to accustom, to habituate, to inure.—*v.i.* (*only in compound tenses*) to use, to be wont. **s'accoutumer**, *v.r.* to be accustomed, to be used (*à*).
accouvage [aku'va:ʒ], *n.m.* hatching (*esp. by artificial means*), incubation.
accouver [aku've], *v.t.* to set (*a hen etc.*).—*v.i.* to sit, to hatch.
accréditation [akredita'sjõ], *n.f.* accreditation, accrediting (*of an ambassador*).
accréditer [akredi'te], *v.t.* to give credit, standing *or* sanction to; to authorize; to accredit (*an ambassador etc.*); to confirm, to spread (*rumours etc.*). **s'accréditer**, *v.r.* to gain credit *or* reputation; to ingratiate oneself; to spread (*of rumours etc.*).
accréditeur [akredi'tœ:r], *n.m.* guarantor, surety.
accroc [a'kro], *n.m.* impediment, hitch; hindrance; rent, tear.
accrochage [akro'ʃa:ʒ], *n.m.* hanging, hooking, hitching; catching, retarding, stopping; grazing (*vehicles*).
accroche-cœur [akroʃ'kœ:r], *n.m. inv.* kiss-curl.
accrochement [akroʃ'mã], *n.m.* hooking, catching (*in something*).
accrocher [akro'ʃe], *v.t.* to hang upon a hook; to hook, to catch, to hitch, to catch and tear; to get hold of; to pick up (*a wireless station*). **s'accrocher**, *v.r.* to catch in, to be caught *or* hooked (*par*); to lay hold of, to cling (*à*).
accroire [a'krwa:r], *v.t. irr.* (*used only in the infinitive after faire*) to believe.
accroissement [akrwas'mã], *n.m.* increase, growth, enlargement, extension.
accroître [a'krwa:tr], *v.t. irr.* (*conjug. like* CROÎTRE *but p.p.* accru, *without circumflex*) to increase, to augment, to enlarge, to amplify. **s'accroître**, *v.r.* to increase, to grow.
accroupi [akru'pi], *a.* crouched, crouching.
accroupir (s') [sakru'pi:r], *v.r.* to sit down on the hams *or* heels, to squat, to crouch.
accroupissement [akrupis'mã], *n.m.* cowering, squatting, crouching.

accru [a'kry], *n.m.* (*Gard.*) sucker, scion.
accrue [a'kry], *n.f.* increase of land through the retreat of waters; encroachment of a forest on adjoining land.
accu [a'ky], *n.m. abbr.* [ACCUMULATEUR].
accueil [a'kœj], *n.m.* reception, welcome, greeting.
accueillir [akœ'ji:r], *v.t. irr.* (*conjug. like* CUEILLIR) to receive (*well or ill*); to receive graciously, to welcome.
acculer [aky'le], *v.t.* to drive into a corner; to bring to a standstill. **s'acculer**, *v.r.* to set one's back against something.
accumulateur [akymyla'tœ:r], *a.* (*fem.*-trice) storing, heaping up, hoarding up.—*n.m.* accumulator (*person or thing*); (*Elec.*) storage cell *or* battery.
accumulation [akymyla'sjõ], *n.f.* accumulation; mass, pile.
accumuler [akymy'le], *v.t.* to accumulate, to pile up, to amass. **s'accumuler**, *v.r.* to accumulate, to increase.
accusable [aky'zabl], *a.* accusable, chargeable.
accusateur [akyza'tœ:r], *a.* (*fem.* -trice) accusing, accusatory.—*n.m.* (*fem.* -trice) accuser, denouncer.
accusatif [akyza'tif], *a.*(*fem.* -tive) and *n.m.* (*Gram.*) accusative (case); *à l'accusatif*, in the accusative.
accusation [akyza'sjõ], *n.f.* accusation, indictment, charge; (*fig.*) prosecution; *mise en accusation*, arraignment.
accusatoire [akyza'twa:r], *a.* accusatory.
accusé [aky'ze], *n.m.* (*fem.* -ée) the accused, prisoner, defendant; *accusé de réception*, acknowledgment of a letter, receipt.
accuser [aky'ze], *v.t.* to impute, to charge with; to reproach, to blame; to indict, to impeach, to prosecute. **s'accuser**, *v.r.* to admit, to avow, to confess.
acéphale [ase'fal], *a.* acephalous, headless.
acérain [ase'rɛ̃], *a.* like *or* pertaining to steel, steely.
acerbe [a'sɛrb], *a.* sour, harsh, sharp, astringent; (*fig.*) bitter, acrimonious.
acerbité [asɛrbi'te], *n.f.* acerbity, harshness; (*fig.*) bitterness, severity.
acéré [ase're], *a.* steely, steeled; sharp, keen; (*fig.*) mordant, trenchant, acute.
acérer [ase're], *v.t.* (*conjug. like* CÉDER) to steel; to sharpen, to render biting, incisive *or* mordant.
acétate [ase'tat], *n.m.* (*Chem.*) acetate.
acéteux [ase'tø], *a.* (*fem.* -euse) acetous, sour, tasting like vinegar.
acétique [ase'tik], *a.* acetic.
acétone [ase'tɔn], *n.m.* acetone.
acétoselle [asetɔ'sɛl], *n.f.* wood-sorrel.
acétylène [aseti'lɛːn], *n.m.* acetylene.
achalandage [aʃalã'da:ʒ], *n.m.* custom, customers; goodwill (*of a shop*).
achalandé [aʃalã'de], *a.* having plenty of custom; *boutique bien achalandée*, a well-frequented shop.
achalander [aʃalã'de], *v.t.* to get custom, to attract customers, to draw trade.
acharné [aʃar'ne], *a.* fleshed, fierce, tenacious, implacable; stubborn, obstinate, intense.
acharnement [aʃarnə'mã], *n.m.* tenacity; rancour, animosity, fury; stubbornness, obstinacy, desperation.

5

acharner [aʃarˈne], *v.t.* to flesh; to set on; to excite, to madden; to embitter, to envenom. **s'acharner**, *v.r.* to be intent, bent *or* obstinately set upon; to set one's heart upon, to persist in; to be infuriated *or* implacable.

achat [aˈʃa], *n.m.* purchasing, buying; purchase; *faire des achats*, to go shopping; *pouvoir d'achat*, purchasing power.

acheminement [aʃminˈmã], *n.m.* progress, advance, conveying.

acheminer [aʃmiˈne], *v.t.* to send on (*towards a place* or *object*); to train (*a horse*). **s'acheminer**, *v.r.* to set out (*pour*), to make one's way towards.

achetable [aʃˈtabl], *a.* purchasable.

acheter [aʃˈte], *v.t.* (*conjug. like* AMENER) to buy, to purchase; (*fig.*) to bribe. **s'acheter**, *v.r.* to be bought; to be for sale, to be venal.

acheteur [aʃˈtœːr], *n.m.* (*fem.* **-euse**) buyer, purchaser.

achevage [aʃˈvaːʒ], *n.m.* completion, finishing; finish (*of a work of art*).

achevé [aʃˈve], *a.* finished, accomplished, perfect, exquisite; absolute, downright, consummate, arrant.

achèvement [aʃɛvˈmã], *n.m.* completion, conclusion.

achever [aʃˈve], *v.t.* (*conjug. like* AMENER) to finish, to terminate; to put the finishing touch to; to complete, to achieve; to consummate, to perfect; (*fig.*) to do for completely, to ruin, to kill.

Achille [aˈʃil], *m.* Achilles.

achoppement [aʃɔpˈmã], *n.m.* obstacle, impediment; unforeseen difficulty, embarrassment; *pierre d'achoppement*, stumbling-block.

achopper [aʃɔˈpe], *v.i.* and **s'achopper**, *v.r.* to stumble, to knock against something; (*fig.*) to come to grief; to fail.

achromatopsie [akrɔmatɔpˈsi], *n.f.* achromatopsy, colour-blindness.

acide [aˈsid], *a.* acid, sour, tart, sharp.—*n.m.* acid.

acidifier [asidiˈfje], *v.t.* to acidify. **s'acidifier**, *v.r.* to become acidified.

acidité [asidiˈte], *n.f.* acidity, sourness, sharpness, tartness.

acidule [asiˈdyl], *a.* subacid, acidulous.

acidulé [asidyˈle], *a.* acidulated; *bonbons acidulés*, acid drops.

aciduler [asidyˈle], *v.t.* to acidulate.

acier [aˈsje], *n.m.* steel; *acier chromé*, chrome steel; *acier coulé* or *fondu*, cast steel; *acier doux*, mild steel; *acier inoxydable*, stainless steel.

aciération [asjeraˈsjõ], *n.f.* steeling, plating with steel.

aciérer [asjeˈre], *v.t.* (*conjug. like* CÉDER) to convert into steel, to cover with steel; to acierate. **s'aciérer**, *v.r.* to steel oneself.

aciéreux [asjeˈrø], *a.* (*fem.* **-euse**) steely, like steel.

aciérie [asjeˈri], *n.f.* steel factory, steelworks.

acné [akˈne], *n.f.* (*Med.*) acne.

acolyte [akɔˈlit], *n.m.* (*Eccles.*) acolyte; (*fig.*) assistant, confederate, associate, accomplice.

acompte [aˈkõːt], *n.m.* instalment, partial payment.

acon or **accon** [aˈkõ], *n.m.* small lighter, punt.

aconier or **acconier** [akɔˈnje], *n.m.* lighterman.

aconit [akɔˈnit], *n.m.* aconite.

acoquinant [akɔkiˈnã], *a.* alluring, engaging, captivating.

acoquiner [akɔkiˈne], *v.t.* to make fond, to allure, to bewitch, to captivate. **s'acoquiner**, *v.r.* (*fam.*) to be bewitched, to be greatly attached to.

Açores [aˈsɔːr], *les*, *f.pl.* the Azores.

à-côté [akoˈte], *n.m.* aside; (*pl.*) little extras.

à-coup [aˈku], *n.m.* jerk, jolt; sudden stop.

acousticien [akustiˈsjɛ̃], *n.m.* (*fem.* **-enne**) acoustician.

acoustique [akusˈtik], *a.* acoustic.—*n.f.* acoustics.

acquéreur [akeˈrœːr], *n.m.* (*fem.* **-euse**) buyer, purchaser.

acquérir [akeˈriːr], *v.t. irr.* to purchase, to buy, to get; to earn, to win, to gain; to acquire, to obtain. **s'acquérir**, *v.r.* to get *or* win for oneself; to be acquired, obtained *or* purchased.

acquiescement [akjɛsˈmã], *n.m.* acquiescence, compliance, consent, willingness.

acquiescer [akjeˈse], *v.i.* (*conjug. like* COMMENCER) to acquiesce, to agree, to assent, to yield, to comply.

acquis [aˈki], *a.* acquired, secured.—*n.m.* acquirements, attainments, experience.

acquisitif [akiziˈtif], *a.* (*fem.* **-tive**) acquisitive.

acquisition [akiziˈsjõ], *n.f.* acquisition, acquiring, attaining, acquirement, attainment; purchase, conquest.

acquisivité [akiziviˈte], *n.f.* acquisitiveness.

acquit [aˈki], *n.m.* receipt, discharge, release, acquittance; (*Billiards*) break (*i.e.* start).

acquittement [akitˈmã], *n.m.* payment, quittance; (*Law*) acquittal.

acquitter [akiˈte], *v.t.* to pay; to discharge, to pay off (*a dependant*); to acquit. **s'acquitter**, *v.r.* to fulfil, to perform; to pay off one's debts, to be quits (*in gambling*); to acquit oneself (*well* or *ill*).

acre [akr], *n.f.* acre.

âcre [ɑːkr], *a.* sour, sharp, tart, acrid; (*fig.*) bitter, pungent, caustic.

âcrement [ɑːkrəˈmã], *adv.* tartly, sourly.

âcreté [ɑːkrəˈte], *n.f.* sourness, acridity, sharpness, tartness, acrimony.

acrimonie [akrimɔˈni], *n.f.* bitterness, sharpness, keenness, acrimony.

acrimonieux [akrimɔˈnjø], *a.* (*fem.* **-euse**) pungent, acrimonious, ill-natured, sharp.

acrobate [akrɔˈbat], *n.* acrobat, rope-dancer.

acrobatie [akrɔbaˈsi], *n.f.* acrobatics; (*Av.*) stunt.

acrobatique [akrɔbaˈtik], *a.* acrobatic.

acrobatisme [akrɔbaˈtism], *n.m.* acrobatics.

acrocéphale [akrɔseˈfal], *a.* having a pointed head, acrocephalic, acrocephalous.—*n.* a person with such a head.

acropole [akrɔˈpɔl], *n.f.* acropolis.

acrostiche [akrɔsˈtiʃ], *a.* and *n.m.* acrostic.

acrotère [akrɔˈtɛːr], *n.m.* (*Arch.*) acroterium, ornamental summit (*of a pediment*).

acte [akt], *n.m.* action, deed; (*Law*) deed, indenture; instrument; document, charter; (*Theat.*) act; (*pl.*) records, public registers, rolls, transactions, proceedings; *acte de naissance*, birth certificate.

acteur [akˈtœːr], *n.m.* (*fem.* **-trice**) actor; actress; player.

actif [akʹtif], *a.* (*fem.* **-tive**) active, busy, energetic, assiduous; nimble, brisk, agile; (*Gram. etc.*) active.—*n.m.* (*Gram.*) active voice; assets, credit balance.

action [akʹsjɔ̃], *n.f.* action, operation, work; activity, motion; deed, feat, performance; fight, engagement, battle; (*Law*) action, law-suit; (*Theat.*) gesture; (*Lit.*) subject, action, plot; (*Comm.*) share, stock.

actionnaire [aksjoʹnɛːr], *n.* shareholder.

actionnariat [aksjonaʹrja], *n.m.* shareholding; **actionnariat ouvrier**, industrial co-partnership.

actionner [aksjoʹne], *v.t.* to bring an action against, to sue at law; to bestir, to rouse up, to set going; to operate, to run, to drive. **s'actionner**, *v.r.* to bestir oneself.

activement [aktivʹmã], *adv.* actively, vigorously.

activer [aktiʹve], *v.t.* to press, to accelerate, to forward, to expedite, to stir up (*a fire, people*).

activisme [aktiʹvism], *n.m.* (*Polit.*) militancy, activism.

activiste [aktiʹvist], *n.m.* activist.

activité [aktiviʹte], *n.f.* activity, full swing; nimbleness, alacrity, promptitude, dispatch.

actrice [akʹtris], [ACTEUR].

actuaire [akʹtɥɛːr], *n.m.* actuary.

actualisation [aktɥalizaʹsjɔ̃], *n.f.* actualization; realization.

actualiser [aktɥaliʹze], *v.t.* to bring up to date. **s'actualiser**, *v.r.* to become real.

actualité [aktɥaliʹte], *n.f.* actuality; event of the moment, present interest; (*Cine.*) **les actualités**, the newsreel.

actuel [akʹtɥɛl], *a.* (*fem.* **-elle**) present, of the present time.

actuellement [aktɥɛlʹmã], *adv.* now, at the present time.

acuité [akɥiʹte], *n.f.* sharpness, acuteness, keenness.

acutangle [akyʹtãːgl], **acutangulaire** [a kytãgyʹlɛːr], *a.* acute-angled (*of triangles etc.*).

acutesse [akyʹtɛs], *n.f.* acuteness, sharpness.

adage [aʹdaːʒ], *n.m.* adage, proverb, saying.

Adam [aʹdã], *m.* Adam.

adamantin [adamãʹtɛ̃], *a.* adamantine.

adaptable [adapʹtabl], *a.* adaptable.

adaptateur [adaptaʹtœːr], *n.m.* adapter, converter.

adaptation [adaptaʹsjɔ̃], *n.f.* adaptation.

adapter [adapʹte], *v.t.* to adapt, to adjust, to apply (*à*); to fit, to make suitable. **s'adapter**, *v.r.* to fit, to suit, to adapt oneself (*to*).

addition [adiʹsjɔ̃], *n.f.* adding up, addition; an addition; bill, reckoning; check.

additionnel [adisjɔ̃ʹnɛl], *a.* (*fem.* **-elle**) additional.

additionner [adisjoʹne], *v.t.* to add up.

Adélaïde [adelaʹid], *f.* Adelaide.

Adèle [aʹdɛl], *f.* Adela.

adénite [adeʹnit], *n.f.* adenitis, inflammation of the glands.

adénoïde [adenoʹid], *a.* adenoid; **végétations adénoïdes**, adenoids.

adent [aʹdã], *n.m.* dovetail, tenon.

adenter [adãʹte], *v.t.* to dovetail, to join with mortise and tenon.

adepte [aʹdɛpt], *n.m.* adept, initiate, follower.

adéquat [adeʹkwa], *a.* adequate; (*Phil.*) equal in content; appropriate.

adhérence [adeʹrãːs], *n.f.* adhesion, adherence; (*fig.*) attachment.

adhérent [adeʹrã], *a.* adherent.—*n.m.* (*fem.* **-e**) adherent, follower, partisan.

adhérer [adeʹre], *v.i.* (*conjug. like* CÉDER) to adhere, to cling; (*fig.*) to hold (*à*), to cleave (*to a sect etc.*).

adhésif [adeʹzif], *a.* (*fem.* **-sive**) adhesive.—*n.m.* (*Phot.*) dry-mounting tissue.

adhésion [adeʹzjɔ̃], *n.f.* adhesion, adherence, union; compliance; joining (*a party*).

adhésivité [adezivi'te], *n.f.* adhesiveness.

adieu [aʹdjø], *int.* adieu, good-bye, farewell. —*n.m.* (*pl.* **-eux**) farewell, parting, leave; **faire ses adieux à**, to take leave of, to say good-bye to.

adipeux [adiʹpø], *a.* (*fem.* **-euse**) adipose, fat.

adiposité [adipoziʹte], *n.f.* adipose or fatty condition.

adjacence [adʒaʹsãːs], *n.f.* adjacency.

adjacent [adʒaʹsã], *a.* adjacent, bordering upon, contiguous.

adjectif [adʒɛkʹtif], *a.* (*fem.* **-tive**) (*Gram.*) adjectival.—*n.m.* adjective.

adjectivement [adʒɛktivʹmã], *adv.* adjectivally.

adjoindre [adʹʒwɛ̃ːdr], *v.t. irr.* (*conjug. like* CRAINDRE) to adjoin, to associate, to add as an assistant. **s'adjoindre**, *v.r.* to join as a partner or associate; to take on.

adjoint [adʹʒwɛ̃], *a.* adjunct, associate.—*n.m.* (*fem.* **-e**) associate, assistant, deputy; **adjoint au maire**, deputy-mayor.

adjonction [adʒɔ̃kʹsjɔ̃], *n.f.* adjunction.

adjudant [adʒyʹdã], *n.m.* company sergeant-major; warrant-officer; **adjudant-major**, adjutant.

adjudicataire [adʒydikaʹtɛːr], *a.* and *n.* contracting party; successful tenderer, highest bidder.

adjudicateur [adʒydikaʹtœːr], *n.m.* (*fem.* **-trice**) adjudicator, awarder; auctioneer.

adjudication [adʒydikaʹsjɔ̃], *n.f.* auction; knocking down; adjudication.

adjuger [adʒyʹʒe], *v.t.* (*conjug. like* MANGER) to adjudge, to adjudicate, to knock down (*to the highest bidder*); to award; **adjugé!** (*at auctions*) gone!

adjuration [adʒyraʹsjɔ̃], *n.f.* adjuration, imprecation.

adjurer [adʒyʹre], *v.t.* to adjure, to conjure; to call upon, to beseech.

admettre [adʹmɛtr], *v.t. irr.* (*conjug. like* METTRE) to admit, to let in; to concede, to allow, to acknowledge.

administrateur [administraʹtœːr], *n.m.* (*fem.* **-trice**) manager, director; administrator, administratrix, trustee (*of an estate*).

administratif [administraʹtif], *a.* (*fem.* **-tive**) administrative.

administration [administraʹsjɔ̃], *n.f.* administration, management, direction, government; (*collect.*) the management, the administration.

administré [adminisʹtre], *n.m.* (*fem.* **-ée**) person under one's administration or jurisdiction.

administrer [adminisʹtre], *v.t.* to manage, to govern, to direct; to administer, to dispense.

admirable [admi'rabl], *a.* admirable; wonderful.

admirablement [admirablə'mã], *adv.* admirably; wonderfully.

admirateur [admira'tœːr], *n.m.* (*fem.* **-trice**) admirer, praiser.

admiratif [admira'tif], *a.* (*fem.* **-tive**) admiring, wondering.

admiration [admira'sjõ], *n.f.* admiration.

admirer [admi're], *v.t.* to admire.

admissibilité [admisibili'te], *n.f.* admissibility.

admissible [admi'sibl], *a.* admittable, admissible.

admission [admi'sjõ], *n.f.* admission, admittance; *soupape d'admission*, inlet valve.

admonestation [admɔnesta'sjõ], *n.f.* admonishment, admonition.

admonester [admɔnes'te], *v.t.* to reprimand, to admonish.

admoniteur [admɔni'tœːr], *n.m.* (*fem.* **-trice**) admonisher.

admonitif [admɔni'tif], *a.* (*fem.* **-tive**) admonitory.

admonition [admɔni'sjõ], *n.f.* (*chiefly R.-C. Ch.*) admonition, advice, reprimand.

adolescence [adɔlɛ'sãːs], *n.f.* adolescence.

adolescent [adɔlɛ'sã], *a.* adolescent.—*n.m.* (*fem.* **-e**) adolescent, youth, teenager.

Adonis [adɔ'niːs], *n.m.* Adonis, beau.

adonné [adɔ'ne], *a.* given to, addicted, devoted. **s'adonner**, *v.r.* to give, devote *or* addict oneself (*à*).

adopté [adɔp'te], *a.* adopted *or* adoptive (*child*).

adopter [adɔp'te], *v.t.* to adopt; to embrace, to espouse; to pass, to carry (*a bill*).

adoptif [adɔp'tif], *a.* (*fem.* **-tive**) adoptive, by adoption.

adoption [adɔp'sjõ], *n.f.* adoption.

adorable [adɔ'rabl], *a.* adorable, charming, delightful, exquisite.

adorablement [adɔrablə'mã], *adv.* adorably, delightfully.

adorateur [adɔra'tœːr], *n.m.* (*fem.* **-trice**) adorer, worshipper.

adoration [adɔra'sjõ], *n.f.* adoration, worship; admiration, respect, reverence.

adorer [adɔ're], *v.t.* to adore, to worship.

adossé [ado'se], *a.* with one's back against.

adosser [ado'se], *v.t.* to set *or* lean with the back against; to put back to back. **s'adosser**, *v.r.* to lean one's back against (*à, contre*).

adoucir [adu'siːr], *v.t.* to soften, to sweeten; to mitigate, to alleviate, to smooth. **s'adoucir**, *v.r.* to grow mild *or* soft; to get milder (*of weather*).

adoucissement [adusis'mã], *n.m.* softening, sweetening; assuaging, appeasing; ease, mitigation, alleviation; consolation.

adrénaline [adrena'lin], *n.f.* adrenalin.

adresse [a'drɛs], *n.f.* address; memorial, a document addressed to an assembly *or* person in authority; skill, dexterity, cleverness.

adresser [adrɛ'se], *v.t.* to direct, to address; to turn, to direct (*one's steps etc.*). **s'adresser**, *v.r.* to be directed; to speak, to address oneself, to make application, to appeal (*à*); *s'adresser ici*, apply within.

Adriatique [adria'tik], **l'**, *f.* the Adriatic.

adroit [a'drwa], *a.* ingenious, clever, skilful; artful.

adroitement [adrwat'mã], *adv.* skilfully, artfully, cleverly.

adulateur [adyla'tœːr], *a.* (*fem.* **-trice**) flattering, adulatory.—*n.m.* (*fem.* **-trice**) adulator, flatterer, sycophant.

adulatif [adyla'tif], *a.* (*fem.* **-tive**) flattering adulatory.

adulation [adyla'sjõ], *n.f.* adulation, flattery sycophancy.

aduler [ady'le], *v.t.* to flatter, to fawn upon.

adulte [a'dylt], *a.* adult, grown-up.—*n.* adult.

adultère [adyl'tɛːr], *a.* adulterous; *femme adultère*, adulteress.—*n.m.* adultery.—*n.* adulterer, adulteress.

adultérer [adylte're], *v.t.* (*conjug. like* CÉDER) (*Pharm.*) to adulterate; (*Law*) to falsify (*money*); (*fig.*) to corrupt, to pervert, to falsify.

adultérin [adylte'rɛ̃], *a.* adulterine.

advenir [advə'niːr], *v.i. irr.* (*used only in inf. and 3rd pers.*) to occur, to happen, to befall.

adventice [advã'tis], *a.* adventitious.

adventif [advã'tif], *a.* (*fem.* **-tive**) (*Bot.*) adventitious, casual.

adverbe [ad'vɛrb], *n.m.* adverb.

adverbial [adver'bjal], *a.* adverbial.

adverbialement [adverbjal'mã], *adv.* adverbially.

adversaire [adver'sɛːr], *n.* adversary, opponent.

adverse [ad'vɛrs], *a.* adverse, opposite, contrary; calamitous.

adversité [adversi'te], *n.f.* adversity, misfortune.

aérage [ae'raːʒ], *n.m.* ventilation, airing.

aérateur [aera'tœːr], *n.m.* ventilator.

aération [aera'sjõ], *n.f.* ventilation, airing.

aéré [ae're], *p.p.* ventilated.—*a.* airy.

aérer [ae're], *v.t.* (*conjug. like* CÉDER) to ventilate, to air, to renew the air of; (*Chem.*) to aerate.

aérien [ae'rjɛ̃], *a.* (*fem.* **-enne**) aerial; living *or* occurring in the air, celestial; (*fig.*) light, airy; *base aérienne*, air-base; *fil aérien*, overhead wire; *ligne aérienne*, airline; *pont aérien*, air-lift; *raid aérien*, air-raid.

aérifère [aeri'fɛːr], *a.* air-conducting.

aérification [aerifika'sjõ], *n.f.* gasification.

aérifier [aeri'fje], *v.t.* to gasify.

aéro-club [aero'klœb], *n.m.* (*pl.* **aéro-clubs**) flying-club.

aérodrome [aero'droːm], *n.m.* aerodrome, airfield.

aérodynamique [aerodina'mik], *a.* aerodynamic, streamlined.—*n.f.* aerodynamics.

aérogare [aero'gaːr], *n.f.* air-terminal

aérographe [aero'graf], *n.m.* aerograph.

aérographie [aerogra'fi], *n.f.* aerography.

aérolithe [aero'lit], *n.m.* aerolite.

aérolithique [aeroli'tik], *a.* aerolitic.

aérologie [aerolɔ'ʒi], *n.f.* aerology.

aéromètre [aero'mɛtr], *n.m.* aerometer, airpoise.

aéronaute [aero'noːt], *n.* aeronaut.

aéronautique [aerono'tik], *a.* aeronautic.—*n.f.* aeronautics, aerial navigation.

aéronef [aero'nɛf], *n.m.* air-ship.

aéroplane [aero'plan], *n.m.* aeroplane.

aéroport [aero'pɔːr], *n.m.* airport.

aéroporté [aeropɔr'te], *a.* airborne (*troops*).

aérosphère [aerɔ'sfɛːr], *n.f.* the mass of air surrounding the globe, atmosphere.

aérostat [aerɔs'ta], *n.m.* aerostat, air-balloon.

aérostation [aerɔsta'sjɔ̃], *n.f.* aerostation, air-navigation.

aérostatique [aerɔsta'tik], *a.* aerostatic.—*n.f.* aerostatics.

aérostier [aerɔs'tje], *n.m.* aeronaut, one directing an aerostat.

aérothérapie [aerotera'pi], *n.f.* aerotherapy.

affabilité [afabili'te], *n.f.* affability, kindness, courtesy.

affable [a'fabl], *a.* affable, courteous.

affadir [afa'diːr], *v.t.* to make unsavoury *or* insipid; (*fig.*) to make flat *or* dull. **s'affadir**, *v.r.* to become insipid.

affadissement [afadis'mã], *n.m.* insipidity, nausea, sickliness.

affaiblir [afɛ'bliːr], *v.t.* to enfeeble, to weaken; to lessen. **s'affaiblir**, *v.r.* to grow weak; to abate.

affaiblissement [afeblis'mã], *n.m.* weakening; allaying, abatement.

affaire [a'fɛːr], *n.f.* affair, business, concern, matter; trouble, scrape; lawsuit; transaction, bargain; *c'est mon affaire*, it is my own concern; *mêlez-vous de vos affaires!*, mind your own business!; *être dans les affaires*, to be in business; *homme d'affaires*, business man, legal adviser.

affairé [afɛ're], *a.* busy.

affairement [afɛr'mã], *n.m.* hurry, bustle, ado.

affaissement [afɛs'mã], *n.m.* depression, subsidence, giving way, collapse.

affaisser [afɛ'se], *v.t.* to cause to sink, to weigh down, to press down; to bear down, to overwhelm. **s'affaisser**, *v.r.* to sink, to subside; to give way; to be bent down (*by age*); to collapse.

affamé [afa'me], *a.* famished, hungry, starving; greedy, craving; *être affamé de*, to be greedy *or* eager for.

affamer [afa'me], *v.t.* to starve, to famish, to deprive of food.

affectation [afɛkta'sjɔ̃], *n.f.* appropriation, destination *or* attribution (*to a certain object*); simulation, show, pretence, affectation; preference; distinction; (*Mil.*) *recevoir une affectation*, to be posted.

affecté [afɛk'te], *a.* affected, assumed, simulated, put on; attributed, destined (*to a certain object*); (*Path.*) affected (*by a disease etc.*); (*Mil.*) posted to.

affecter [afɛk'te], *v.t.* to affect, to make frequent *or* habitual use of, to have a predilection for; to assume (*a certain shape etc.*); to feign, to pretend; to set apart, to earmark, to destine, to appropriate (*to a certain object*); to move, to touch, to impress emotionally. **s'affecter**, *v.r.* to be affected.

affection [afɛk'sjɔ̃], *n.f.* affection, love, attachment; (*Med.*) affection, ailment.

affectionné [afɛksjɔ'ne], *a.* affectionate, loving, attached, loved, liked.

affectionner [afɛksjɔ'ne], *v.t.* to love, to be fond of, to like.

affectueusement [afɛktɥøz'mã], *adv.* affectionately, fondly.

affectueux [afɛk'tɥø], *a.* (*fem.* **-euse**) affectionate, tender, warm-hearted.

afférent [afe'rã], *a.* reverting; relating to; assignable to; accruing to.

affermage [afɛr'maːʒ], *n.m.* farming, renting.

affermataire [afɛrma'tɛːr], *n.m.* tenant farmer.

affermateur [afɛrma'tœːr], *n.m.* (*fem.* **-trice**) lessor.

affermer [afɛr'me], *v.t.* to farm *or* let out by lease; to take a lease of, to rent.

affermir [afɛr'miːr], *v.t.* to strengthen, to make firm; to confirm, to establish, to consolidate. **s'affermir**, *v.r.* to become strong, firm, *or* fast; to become established.

affermissement [afɛrmis'mã], *n.m.* strengthening, consolidation, establishment; support, prop, stay.

affété [afe'te], *a.* affected, prim, finical; canting, mincing, pretty-pretty.

afféterie [afe'tri], *n.f.* affectation, mannerisms, primness.

affichage [afi'ʃaːʒ], *n.m.* bill-sticking; placarding.

affiche [a'fiʃ], *n.f.* placard, bill, poster; *homme affiche*, sandwich-man; *affiche électorale*, election poster.

afficher [afi'ʃe], *v.t.* to post up; to publish, to divulge, to proclaim; to make a show of, to parade; *défense d'afficher*, stick no bills; billposting prohibited. **s'afficher**, *v.r.* to set up (*for*); to attract public notice.

afficheur [afi'ʃœːr], *n.m.* bill-sticker.

affidavit [afida'vit], *n.m.* affidavit.

affidé [afi'de], *a.* trusty, trustworthy, in the know.—*n.m.* (*fem.* **-ée**) confederate, confidential agent; spy.

affilage [afi'laːʒ], **affilement** [afil'mã], *n.m.* whetting, sharpening, setting.

affilé [afi'le], *a.* sharp; nimble, glib (*of the tongue*).

affilée (d') [dafi'le], *adv. phr.* at a stretch; *trois heures d'affilée*, three hours at a stretch.

affiler [afi'le], *v.t.* to sharpen, to set, to put an edge on.

affiliation [afilja'sjɔ̃], *n.f.* affiliation (*to a society, company, plot etc.*).

affilié [afi'lje], *a.* affiliated, admitted a member *or* associate.—*n.m.* (*fem.* **-ée**) affiliated member, associate, confederate.

affilier [afi'lje], *v.t.* to admit, to affiliate, to receive. **s'affilier**, *v.r.* to become admitted *or* affiliated, to join.

affiloir [afi'lwaːr], *n.m.* hone, oilstone, steel, strop.

affinage [afi'naːʒ], **affinement** [afin'mã], *n.m.* refining, fining (*of metals, sugar etc.*); heckling (*of hemp*), maturing (*of a wine*), ripening (*of a cheese*).

affiner [afi'ne], *v.t.* to fine, to refine. **s'affiner**, *v.r.* to be refined, to be fined; to become finer, wittier etc. (*of the mind*).

affinerie [afin'ri], *n.f.* metal refinery.

affineur [afi'nœːr], *n.m.* metal refiner.

affinité [afini'te], *n.f.* affinity, relationship.

affinoir [afi'nwaːr], *n.m.* carding-brush.

affiquet [afi'kɛ], *n.m.* knitting-sheath; (*pl.*) gewgaws, trinkets.

affirmatif [afirma'tif], *a.* (*fem.* **-tive**) affirmative, asserting.—*n.f.* (**-tive**) affirmative statement, answer etc.; asseveration; *répondre par l'affirmative*, to answer in the affirmative.

affirmation [afirma'sjɔ̃], *n.f.* affirmation, assertion.

affirmativement

affirmativement [afirmativ'mã], *adv.* affirmatively.

affirmer [afir'me], *v.t.* to affirm, to assert, to vouch, to declare; to confirm by *or* on oath. **s'affirmer**, *v.r.* to grow stronger, to assert oneself.

affixe [a'fiks], *n.m.* affix.

affleurement [aflœr'mã], *n.m.* levelling, making flush; (*Mining*) outcrop.

affleurer [aflœ're], *v.t.* to make even, to level; (*Arch.*) to make flush.—*v.i.* to be level, to be flush (*with*); (*Mining*) to crop out.

affliction [aflik'sjõ], *n.f.* affliction, trouble, distress; trial, vexation.

affligé [afli'ʒe], *a.* afflicted, grieved, distressed.

affliger [afli'ʒe], *v.t.* (*conjug. like* MANGER) to afflict, to trouble, to distress, to grieve, to vex, to torment; to mortify, to chasten. **s'affliger**, *v.r.* to grieve, to be afflicted, troubled *or* cast down; to take something to heart.

afflouage [aflu'a:ʒ], *n.m.* (*Naut.*) refloating (*of a ship*).

afflouer [aflu'e], *v.t.* to refloat.

affluence [afly'ã:s], *n.f.* affluence, abundance; concourse, crowd; *heures d'affluence*, rush hour.

affluent [afly'ã], *a.* falling into, running into (*of rivers*).—*n.m.* tributary.

affluer [afly'e], *v.i.* to fall, run *or* flow into (*as a tributary*) (*dans*); to abound; to come in great quantity (*à, vers*).

affolant [afɔ'lã], *a.* distracting.

affolé [afɔ'le], *a.* distracted, panic-stricken; (*Mech.*) disconnected, defective.

affolement [afɔl'mã], *n.m.* distraction, panic.

affoler [afɔ'le], *v.t.* to distract; to infatuate; to bewitch; to madden, to drive crazy. **s'affoler**, *v.r.* to fall into a panic, to stampede.

afforestage [afores'ta:ʒ], *n.m.* right of cutting firewood, estovers.

afforestation [af(ɔ)rɛsta'sjõ], *n.f.* afforestation.

affouillable [afu'jabl], *a.* subject *or* liable to undermining.

affouillement [afuj'mã], *n.m.* undermining, washing away.

affouiller [afu'je], *v.t.* to undermine, to wash away.

affouragement *or* **affourragement** [afuraʒ'mã], *n.m.* foraging, foddering.

affourager *or* **affourrager** [afura'ʒe], *v.t.* (*conjug. like* MANGER) to fodder, to give fodder to.

affourcher [afur'ʃe], *v.t.* to seat astride; (*Carp.*) to join a tongue and groove.

affranchi [afrã'ʃi], *a.* set free, freed.—*n.m.* (*fem.* -e) freedman; freedwoman.

affranchir [afrã'ʃi:r], *v.t.* to free, to set free, to enfranchise; to absolve, to exempt; to frank (*a letter*), to stamp. **s'affranchir**, *v.r.* to free oneself; to rid oneself of (*de*), to shake off, to break away from.

affranchissement [afrãʃis'mã], *n.m.* enfranchisement; exemption, discharge; deliverance; payment of postage (*of a letter*).

affranchisseur [afrãʃi'sœ:r], *n.m.* emancipator, liberator.

affres [a:fr], *n.f.* (*used only in pl.*) dread, horror, agony; *les affres de la mort*, the pangs of death, death-throes.

affrètement [afrɛt'mã], *n.m.* chartering freighting.

affréter [afre'te], *v.t.* (*conjug. like* CÉDER) (*Naut.*) to charter, to freight (*a vessel*).

affréteur [afre'tœ:r], *n.m.* charterer, freighter.

affreusement [afrøz'mã], *adv.* frightfully, horribly, dreadfully.

affreux [a'frø], *a.* (*fem.* -euse) frightful, hideous, shocking, horrible, ghastly.

affriander [afriã'de], *v.t.* to allure, to entice to tempt.

affricher [afri'ʃe], *v.t.* to leave fallow.

affrioler [afriɔ'le], *v.t.* to allure, to entice.

affront [a'frõ], *n.m.* affront, insult; disgrace.

affronter [afrõ'te], *v.t.* to face, to confront, to brave; to attack boldly.

affruiter [afrɥi'te], *v.t.* to plant with fruit-trees.—*v.i.* to bear *or* supply fruit. **s'affruiter**, *v.r.* to come into fruit.

affublement [afyblə'mã], *n.m.* grotesque make-up *or* rig-out (*of dress*).

affubler [afy'ble], *v.t.* to dress up, to rig out (*grotesquely*). **s'affubler**, *v.r.* to dress up ridiculously.

affût [a'fy], *n.m.* stand *or* place for lying in wait, watch; gun-carriage; *être à l'affût*, to lie in wait.

affûtage [afy'ta:ʒ], *n.m.* setting *or* sharpening (*of tools*).

affûter [afy'te], *v.t.* to grind, to sharpen.

affûteur [afy'tœ:r], *n.m.* sharpener, setter, grinder; stalker.—*n.f.* (-euse) sharpening machine.

afghan [af'gã], *a.* Afghan.—*n.m.* (**Afghan**, *fem.* -ane) Afghan (*person*).

Afghanistan [afganis'tã], l', *m.* Afghanistan.

afin [a'fɛ̃], *conj.* **afin de** (*with inf.*) to, in order to, so as to; **afin que** (*with subj.*) to, in order that, so that.

africain [afri'kɛ̃], *a.* African.—*n.m.* (**Africain** *fem.* -aine) African (*person*).

Afrique [a'frik], l', *f.* Africa.

agaçant [aga'sã], *a.* irritating, worrying; provoking, provocative; alluring, enticing.

agace *or* **agasse** [a'gas], *n.f.* magpie.

agacement [agas'mã], *n.m.* irritation, setting on edge.

agacer [aga'se], *v.t.* (*conjug. like* COMMENCER) to worry, to irritate, to set on edge; to excite, to provoke; to entice, to allure.

agacerie [aga'sri], *n.f.* allurement, coquetry enticement.

agaillardir [agajar'di:r], *v.t.* to cheer up.

agate [a'gat], *n.f.* agate.

Agathe [a'gat], *f.* Agatha.

âge [ɑ:ʒ], *n.m.* age, years; period, epoch, era, (*pl.*) the ages, time; *Moyen Âge*, Middle Ages; *d'un certain âge*, elderly; *entre deux âges*, of uncertain age.

âgé [a'ʒe], *a.* aged (*so many years*); old, elderly; *âgé de vingt ans*, twenty years old.

agence [a'ʒã:s], *n.f.* agency, bureau, branch office.

agencement [aʒãs'mã], *n.m.* arrangement, grouping, ordering; (*Arch.*) composition, layout.

agencer [aʒã'se], *v.t.* (*conjug. like* COMMENCER) to arrange, to dispose.

agenda [aʒɛ̃'da], *n.m.* note-book; diary; engagement-book.

agenouiller (s') [saʒnuˈje], *v.r.* to kneel down, to fall on one's knees; (*fig.*) to bow down (*devant*).

agenouilloir [aʒnujˈwaːr], *n.m.* hassock.

agent [aˈʒɑ̃], *n.m.* agent; deputy; middleman; broker; *agent de change*, stock-broker; *agent électoral*, canvasser; *agent de liaison*, liaison officer; *agent de police*, policeman.

agglomération [aglɔmeraˈsjɔ̃], *n.f.* agglomeration, built-up area.

aggloméré [aglɔmeˈre], *n.m.* compressed fuel, briquette.

agglomérer [aglɔmeˈre], *v.t.* (*conjug. like* CÉDER) to agglomerate, to mass together, to pile up, to assemble.

agglutinant [aglytiˈnɑ̃], *a.* adhesive.

agglutiner [aglytiˈne], *v.t.* to bind, to cake. **s'agglutiner,** *v.r.* to unite, to cohere; to heal over (*wound*).

aggravant [agraˈvɑ̃], *a.* (*Law*) aggravating, making more heinous.

aggravation [agravaˈsjɔ̃], *n.f.* aggravation, additional penalty; *aggravation de peine,* increase of punishment.

aggraver [agraˈve], *v.t.* to aggravate, to make worse. **s'aggraver,** *v.r.* to worsen (*illness, situation*).

agile [aˈʒil], *a.* agile, nimble.

agilement [aʒilˈmɑ̃], *adv.* nimbly, with agility.

agilité [aʒiliˈte], *n.f.* agility, nimbleness, lightness.

agio [aˈʒjo], *n.m.* stock-jobbing, speculation.

agiotage [aʒjɔˈtaːʒ], *n.m.* stock-jobbing; *faire l'agiotage,* to deal in stocks.

agioter [aʒjɔˈte], *v.i.* to speculate, to job.

agioteur [aʒjɔˈtœːr], *n.m.* speculator, jobber.

agir [aˈʒiːr], *v.i.* to act, to do; to operate; to have an effect (*sur*); to negotiate, to manage a business; to sue, to prosecute, to proceed (*contre*); to behave. **s'agir,** *v.r.* (*impers.*) to be in question, to be the matter; *de quoi s'agit-il?* what is the matter? *il s'agit de votre vie,* your life is at stake.

agissant [aʒiˈsɑ̃], *a.* active, busy; efficacious, effective.

agitateur [aʒitaˈtœːr], *n.m.* (*fem* -trice) agitator.—*n.m.* stirring rod.

agitation [aʒitaˈsjɔ̃], *n.f.* agitation; disturbance, tossing, shaking, tumult; trouble, emotion, uneasiness, restlessness.

agité [aʒiˈte], *a.* restless (*sleep*); rough (*sea*); fretful (*child*).

agiter [aʒiˈte], *v.t.* to agitate, to put in motion, to shake, to stir; to disturb, to trouble; to excite, to perturb; to debate, to discuss. **s'agiter,** *v.r.* to be agitated *or* in movement; to get rough; to be restless, disturbed *or* uneasy; to toss, to wave, to flutter; to be debated.

agneau [aˈɲo], *n.m.* (*fem.* -elle, *pl.* -eaux) lamb.

agnelage [aɲɔˈlaːʒ], **agnèlement** [aɲɛlˈmɑ̃], *n.m.* lambing; lambing-time.

agneler [aɲɔˈle], *v.i.* (*conjug. like* AMENER) to lamb, to yean.

Agnès [aˈɲɛːs], *f.* Agnes.

agnès [aˈɲɛːs], *n.f.* raw young girl.

agnosticisme [agnɔstiˈsism], *n.m.* agnosticism.

agnosticiste [agnɔstiˈsist], **agnostique** [agnɔsˈtik], *a.* and *n.* agnostic.

agonie [agɔˈni], *n.f.* agony, death pangs;

(*fig.*) trouble, anguish, torture; *être à l'agonie,* to be at the point of death.

agonir [agɔˈniːr], *v.t.* to insult grossly.

agonisant [agɔniˈzɑ̃], *a.* dying, in a dying condition.—*n.m.* (*fem.* -e) dying person.

agoniser [agɔniˈze], *v.i.* to be at the point of death.

agoraphobie [agɔrafoˈbi], *n.f.* agoraphobia.

agrafe [aˈgraf], *n.f.* fastener, clasp, clip, staple (*for papers*); *agrafe et porte,* hook and eye.

agrafer [agraˈfe], *v.t.* to hook, to clasp, to fasten with a clasp; to staple.

agrafeuse [agraˈføːz], *n.f.* stapler.

agraire [aˈgrɛːr], *a.* agrarian.

agrandir [agrɑ̃ˈdiːr], *v.t.* to make greater, to enlarge, to augment; to widen; to exaggerate; to promote, to advance; (*fig.*) to elevate. **s'agrandir,** *v.r.* to become greater *or* larger.

agrandissement [agrɑ̃disˈmɑ̃], *n.m.* enlargement, increase; aggrandizement, elevation.

agrandisseur [agrɑ̃diˈsœːr], *n.m.* (*Phot.*) enlarger.

agréable [agreˈabl], *a.* agreeable, pleasing, pleasant, acceptable.

agréablement [agreablˈmɑ̃], *adv.* agreeably, pleasantly.

agréé [agreˈe], *n.m.* solicitor; attorney.

agréer [agreˈe], *v.t.* to accept, to approve, to allow, to receive kindly.—*v.i.* to please, to be agreeable; *veuillez agréer mes salutations,* yours truly.

agrégat [agreˈga], *n.m.* aggregate, composite mass.

agrégation [agregaˈsjɔ̃], *n.f.* (*Phys.*) aggregation, aggregate; (=*concours d'agrégation*) competitive examination for admission on the teaching staff of State secondary schools *or* of faculties of law, medicine, pharmacy.

agrégé [agreˈʒe], *a.* and *n.m. professeur agrégé,* one who has passed the *agrégation.*

agréger [agreˈʒe], *v.t.* (*conjug. like* ASSIÉGER) to admit into a society, to incorporate; (*Phys.*) to aggregate.

agrément [agreˈmɑ̃], *n.m.* consent, approbation; pleasure, charm, gracefulness; amenity; (*pl.*) ornaments, embellishments, amenities (*of life*); *arts d'agrément,* accomplishments.

agrémenter [agremɑ̃ˈte], *v.t.* to set off, to ornament, to adorn.

agrès [aˈgrɛ], *n.m.* (*used only in pl.*) rigging (*of a ship etc.*); apparatus, gear (*of a gymnasium etc.*).

agresseur [agreˈsœːr], *n.m.* aggressor.

agressif [agreˈsif], *a.* (*fem.* -ive) aggressive.

agression [agreˈsjɔ̃], *n.f.* aggression.

agressivité [agresiviˈte], *n.f.* aggressiveness.

agreste [aˈgrɛst], *a.* rustic; countrified (*manners*).

agrestement [agrɛstəˈmɑ̃], *adv.* rustically.

agricole [agriˈkɔl], *a.* agricultural.

agriculteur [agrikylˈtœːr], *n.m.* agriculturist, husbandman, farmer.

agriculture [agrikylˈtyːr], *n.f.* agriculture, husbandry, tillage.

agriffer [agriˈfe], *v.t.* to claw; to clutch, to grip. **s'agriffer,** *v.r.* to claw (*at*).

agrion [agriˈɔ̃], *n.m.* dragon-fly.

agripper [agriˈpe], *v.t.* to grip, to snatch. **s'agripper,** *v.r.* to cling (*to*).

agronome [agrɔ'nɔm], *n.m.* agriculturist.
aguerri [agɛ'ri], *a.* inured to war; disciplined.
aguerrir [agɛ'riːr], *v.t.* to train *or* inure to the hardships of war; to accustom, to inure (*to hardships etc.*). **s'aguerrir**, *v.r.* to inure *or* accustom oneself (*to hardships, abstinence etc.*), to be inured.
aguerrissement [agɛris'mā], *n.m.* inuring to war, hardening.
aguets [a'gɛ], *n.m.* (*used only in pl.*) watch, look-out; **être aux aguets**, to be on the watch.
aheurter (s') [saœr'te], *v.r.* to persist (*in*).
ahuri [ay'ri], *a.* bewildered, perplexed, flurried.
ahurir [ay'riːr], *v.t.* to bewilder, to flurry, to stupefy.
ahurissant [ayri'sā], *a.* bewildering.
ahurissement [ayris'mā], *n.m.* bewilderment, confusion, perplexity.
aï [a'i], *n.m.* (*Zool.*) sloth.
aide [ɛːd], *n.f.* help, relief, assistance; succour, support, protection, rescue; relief (*of the poor etc.*); helper, female assistant, help; *à l'aide de*, with the help of.—*n.m.* a male assistant; *aide de camp* (*pl.* *aides de camp*), aide-de-camp.
aide-mémoire [edme'mwaːr], *n.m. inv.* précis; memorandum.
aider [ɛ'de], *v.t.* to aid, to help, to relieve, to assist, to succour; to abet; to conduce to, to further.—*v.i.* to be helpful, to be of assistance (*à*). **s'aider**, *v.r.* to make use (*de*); to avail oneself.
aïe! [aj], *int.* oh! oh dear!
aïeul [a'jœl], *n.m.* (*fem.* **aïeule**, *pl.* **aïeuls**, **aïeules**) grandfather, grandsire; grandmother, grandam; (*pl.* **aïeux**) forebears, ancestors.
aigle [ɛːgl], *n.* eagle; (*fig.*) clever *or* brilliant person, genius.—*n.m.* reading-desk, lectern (*with effigy of an eagle*).
aiglefin [ɛglə'fɛ̃], **aigrefin** (1) [ɛgrə'fɛ̃], *n.m.* haddock.
aiglon [ɛ'glɔ̃], *n.m.* (*fem.* **-onne**) eaglet.
aigre [ɛgr], *a.* sour, tart; (*fig.*) harsh, bitter, shrill.—*n.m.* sourness, mustiness.
aigre-doux [ɛgrə'du], *a.* (*fem.* **-douce**) sourish, bitter-sweet.
aigrefin (2) [ɛgrə'fɛ̃], *n.m.* sharper, swindler; adventurer; [AIGLEFIN].
aigrelet [ɛgrə'lɛ], *a.* (*fem.* **-ette**) sourish.
aigrement [ɛgrə'mā], *adv.* acrimoniously, sourly, bitterly; roughly, harshly.
aigret [ɛ'grɛ], *a.* (*fem.* **-ette** (1)) sourish.
aigrette (2) [ɛ'grɛt], *n.f.* aigrette, tuft, cluster *or* plume (*of feathers, diamonds etc.*); horn (*of an owl*); crest (*of a peacock*); egret, tufted heron.
aigreur [ɛ'grœːr], *n.f.* sourness, sharpness, tartness; (*fig.*) harshness, bitterness, surliness, animosity, spite.
aigrir [ɛ'griːr], *v.t.* to make sour *or* sharp, to sour; (*fig.*) to irritate, to embitter, to make worse, to incense, to make ill-humoured. **s'aigrir**, *v.r.* to turn sour; (*fig.*) to grow worse, to be exasperated, to be irritated.
aigrissement [ɛgris'mā], *n.m.* souring, embittering.
aigu [ɛ'gy], *a.* (*fem.* **aiguë**) pointed, sharp, keen, acute; (*fig.*) shrill, piercing; *accent aigu*, acute accent.

aiguë [AIGU].
aigue-marine [ɛgma'rin], *n.f.* (*pl.* **aigues-marines**) aquamarine.
aiguière [ɛ'gjɛːr], *n.f.* ewer.
aiguillage [egɥi'jaːʒ], *n.m.* (*Rail.*) shunting, points.
aiguillat [egɥi'ja], *n.m.* dog-fish.
aiguille [ɛ'gɥiːj], *n.f.* needle; index, pointer, hand (*of a dial, watch etc.*); spire (*steeple*); point (*of an obelisk, peak etc.*); rock pinnacle *or* needle-shaped peak; *trou d'une aiguille*, eye of a needle; (*pl., Rail.*) points.
aiguiller [egɥi'je], *v.t.* (*Rail.*) to shunt.
aiguillette [egɥi'jɛt], *n.f.* aglet, point; (*Mil.*) ornamental shoulder-knot.
aiguilleur [egɥi'jœːr], *n.m.* (*Rail.*) pointsman, shunter.
aiguillier [egɥi'je], *n.m.* (*fem.* **-ière**) needle-maker.
aiguillon [egɥi'jɔ̃], *n.m.* goad, sting; (*fig.*) spur, incentive; (*Bot.*) prickle.
aiguillonner [egɥijɔ'ne], *v.t.* to goad, to prick; (*fig.*) to incite, to spur on; to stimulate.
aiguisage [egi'zaːʒ], **aiguisement** [egiz'mā], *n.m.* whetting, sharpening.
aiguisé [egi'ze], *a.* whetted, sharpened.
aiguiser [egi'ze], *v.t.* to whet, to sharpen, to set an edge on; to point; (*fig.*) to make keen, acid, piquant etc.; to excite, to stimulate.
aiguiseur [egi'zœːr], *n.m.* knife-grinder, sharpener.
aiguisoir [egi'zwaːr], *n.m.* sharpening-tool, whetstone.
ail [aːj], *n.m.* (*pl.* (*Cook.*) **aulx** [oː], (*Bot.*) **ails**) garlic.
aile [ɛl], *n.f.* wing; brim (*of a hat*); flipper (*of a penguin*); blade (*of a propeller*); vane, sail (*of a windmill*); flank *or* wing (*of an army, building etc.*); wing, mudguard (*of a car*).
ailé [ɛ'le], *a.* winged.
aileron [ɛl'rɔ̃], *n.m.* pinion (*of a bird*); aileron, balancing flap (*of an aircraft*); fin (*of some fish*).
ailette [ɛ'lɛt], *n.f.* small wing; vane (*of a torpedo etc.*); (*Motor.*) rib, fin, flange.
ailier [ɛ'lje], *n.m.* (*Ftb.*) wing forward, wing three-quarter.
ailleurs [a'jœːr], *adv.* elsewhere, somewhere else; *d'ailleurs*, besides, moreover, in other respects.
aimable [ɛ'mabl], *a.* kind, amiable, obliging.
aimablement [ɛmablə'mā], *adv.* amiably, kindly.
aimant [ɛ'mā], *a.* loving, affectionate.—*n.m.* magnet; (*fig.*) attractiveness.
aimantation [ɛmāta'sjɔ̃], *n.f.* magnetization.
aimanter [ɛmā'te], *v.t.* to magnetize.
Aimée [ɛ'me], *f.* Amy.
aimer [ɛ'me], *v.t.* to love, to be fond of, to be in love with; to like; *aimer mieux*, to prefer. **s'aimer**, *v.r.* to love oneself, to be vain; to love each other.
aine (1) [ɛːn], *n.f.* groin.
aine (2) [ɛːn], *n.f.* herring-stick; leather band on organ-bellows.
aîné [ɛ'ne], *a.* (*fem.* **-ée**) eldest, elder, senior.—*n.m.* (*fem.* **-ée**) eldest son *or* daughter.
aînesse [ɛ'nɛs], *n.f.* seniority, priority by age, primogeniture; *droit d'aînesse*, birthright.

ainsi [ɛ̃'si], *adv.* thus, so, in this *or* that manner; **ainsi de suite,** and so on and so forth; **ainsi soit-il,** so be it, amen; *pour ainsi dire,* so to speak, as it were; *ainsi que,* in the same way (*as*).

air (1) [ɛːr], *n.m.* air; wind; (*Chem. etc.*) gas; (*pl.*) atmosphere; *chambre à air,* inner tube; *courant d'air,* draught; *en plein air,* in the open air.

air (2) [ɛːr], *n.m.* mien, look, expression, air, manner, appearance.

air (3) [ɛːr], *n.m.* (*Mus.*) tune.

airain [ɛ'rɛ̃], *n.m.* bronze; (*Poet.*) cannon, bell.

aire [ɛːr], *n.f.* area, space; threshing-floor; eyrie; *aire d'atterrissage,* (*Av.*) landing area, apron.

airelle [ɛ'rɛl], *n.f.* whortleberry, bilberry.

ais [ɛ], *n.m.* board, plank; stave (*of a barrel*).

aisance [ɛ'zɑ̃ːs], *n.f.* ease, facility; easiness, affluence; competency; (*Mach.*) play; freedom; the comforts *or* conveniences of life; *cabinet* (or *lieu*) *d'aisances,* public convenience.

aisceau [AISSETTE].

aise [ɛːz], *a.* glad, well pleased; *je suis bien aise de vous voir,* I am very glad to see you.—*n.f.* ease, comfort, convenience; (*pl.*) comforts, comfortable circumstances; *à l'aise,* at ease, comfortable; *être à son aise,* to be well off.

aisé [ɛ'ze], *a.* easy; convenient, comfortable; in easy circumstances.

aisément [ɛze'mɑ̃], *adv.* easily, readily, freely; comfortably.

aisseau [ɛ'so], *n.m.* (*pl.* -eaux), aissante [ɛ'sɑ̃ːt], *n.f.* (*Carp.*) shingle, wooden tile.

aisselier [ɛsə'lje], *n.m.* (*Carp.*) tie-beam, brace, strut.

aisselle [ɛ'sɛl], *n.f.* armpit; (*Bot.*) axil.

aissette [ɛ'sɛt], *n.f.,* **aisceau** [ɛ'so] (*pl.* -eaux), *n.m.* adze (*of a cooper*); hooked hammer (*of a tiler*).

Aix-la-Chapelle [ɛkslaʃa'pɛl], *f.* Aachen.

ajointer [aʒwɛ̃'te], *v.t.* to join on to, to fit.

ajonc [a'ʒɔ̃], *n.m.* furze, gorse.

ajournement [aʒurnə'mɑ̃], *n.m.* adjournment, postponement; (*Law*) summons.

ajourner [aʒur'ne], *v.t.* to adjourn; to defer; (*Law*) to summon (*for a specified day*).

ajouter [aʒu'te], *v.t.* to add, to join, to subjoin, to interpolate. **s'ajouter,** *v.r.* to be joined, to attach oneself.

ajusté [aʒys'te], *a.* close-fitting (*clothes*).

ajustement [aʒystə'mɑ̃], *n.m.* adjustment, arranging, fitting, settlement; laying out; attire, apparel.

ajuster [aʒys'te], *v.t.* to adjust, to regulate, to square, to fit, to adapt (*one thing to another*); to take aim at; to set in order; (*Mus.*) to tune; to bedeck; to settle *or* arrange (*a dispute*). **s'ajuster,** *v.r.* to accommodate oneself, to be adapted; to dress, to deck oneself out.

ajusteur [aʒys'tœːr], *n.m.* fitter; weigher (*at the mint*).

alacrité [alakri'te], *n.f.* alacrity, cheerful briskness.

Aladin [ala'dɛ̃], *m.* Aladdin.

Alain [a'lɛ̃], *m.* Alan.

alaise [a'lɛːz], *n.f.* rubber sheet for pram *or* cot.

alambic [alɑ̃'bik], *n.m.* alembic, still.

alambiquer [alɑ̃bi'ke], *v.t.* to distil, to refine.

alangui [alɑ̃'giː], *a.* languid, downcast.

alanguir [alɑ̃'giːr], *v.t.* to enfeeble, to make languid. **s'alanguir,** *v.r.* to languish, to flag, to become languid.

alanguissement [alɑ̃gis'mɑ̃], *n.m.* languor.

alarmant [alar'mɑ̃], *a.* alarming, startling.

alarme [a'larm], *n.f.* alarm, affright, sudden fear, uneasiness.

alarmer [alar'me], *v.t.* to alarm; to startle, to render anxious *or* frightened. **s'alarmer,** *v.r.* to take alarm, to be alarmed.

alarmiste [alar'mist], *a.* and *n.* alarmist.

albanais [alba'ne], *a.* Albanian.—*n.m.* Albanian (*language*); (**Albanais.**—*fem.* -aise) Albanian (*person*).

Albanie [alba'niː], **l',** *f.* Albania.

albâtre [al'baːtr], *n.m.* alabaster; (*fig.*) whiteness.

albatros [alba'tros], *n.m.* albatross.

albinisme [albi'nism], *n.m.* albinism.

albinos [albi'nos], *a.* and *n.* albino.

album [al'bom], *n.m.* album, scrap-book, sketch-book.

albumine [alby'min], *n.f.* albumen.

alcaïque [alka'ik], *a.* alcaic (*verse*).

alcali [alka'li], *n.m.* alkali.

alcalin [alka'lɛ̃], *a.* alkaline.¶

alcalinité [alkalini'te], *n.f.* alkalinity.

alcaliser [alkali'ze], **alcaliniser** [alkalini'ze], *v.t.* to alkalify.

alchimie [alʃi'mi], *n.f.* alchemy.

alchimique [alʃi'mik], *a.* alchemical.

alchimiste [alʃi'mist], *n.m.* alchemist.

alcool [al'kɔl], *n.m.* alcohol; spirit(s); *alcool à brûler, alcool dénaturé,* methylated spirit.

alcoolique [alkɔ'lik], *a.* alcoholic.

alcoolisme [alkɔ'lism], *n.m.* alcoholism.

Alcoran [alkɔ'rɑ̃], [CORAN].

alcôve [al'koːv], *n.f.* alcove, recess.

alcyon [al'sjɔ̃], *n.m.* halcyon; (*Orn.*) kingfisher.

alcyonien [alsjo'njɛ̃], *a.* (*fem.* -enne) halcyon, peaceful.

aléa [ale'a], *n.m.* chance, hazard.

aléatoire [alea'twaːr], *a.* hazardous, uncertain.

alène [a'lɛn], *n.f.* awl.

alentour or **à l'entour** [alɑ̃'tuːr], *adv.* about, around, round about.

alentours [alɑ̃'tuːr], *n.m.* (*used only in pl.*) environs, neighbourhood.

Aléoutiennes [aleu'sjɛn], **les,** *f.pl.* the Aleutian Islands.

alerte [a'lɛrt], *a.* alert, vigilant; active, lively, agile.—*n.f.* alarm, warning; *alerte aérienne,* air-raid warning.

alerter [alɛr'te], *v.t.* to give the alarm to, to warn.

alésage [ale'zaːʒ], *n.m.* boring, drilling; bore (*of cylinder*).

aléser [ale'ze], *v.t.* (*conjug. like* CÉDER) to smooth *or* enlarge the bore of (*a tube, gun etc*); *aléser un canon,* to bore a cannon.

aléseuse [ale'zøːz], *n.f.* boring-machine.

alésoir [ale'zwaːr], *n.m.* borer, boring tool.

alester [alɛs'te], **alestir** [alɛs'tiːr], *v.t.* (*Naut.*) to lighten or disencumber (*a vessel*).

alésure [ale'zyːr], *n.f.* metal turnings *or* filings.

alevin [al'vɛ̃], *n.m.* fry, young fish.

aleviner [alvi'ne], *v.t.* to stock with fry.

alevinier [alvi′nje], *n.m.* breeding-pond.
Alexandre [alɛk′sɑ̃:dr], *m.* Alexander.
Alexandrie [alɛksɑ̃′dri], *f.* Alexandria.
alexandrin [alɛksɑ̃′drɛ̃], *a.* and *n.m.* (*Pros.*) Alexandrine.
alezan [al′zɑ̃], *a.* and *n.m.* chestnut (horse).
alèze or **alèse** [a′lɛ:z], [ALAISE].
alfa [al′fa], *n.m.* esparto-grass.
algarade [alga′rad], *n.f.* insult, affront; rating.
algèbre [al′ʒɛbr], *n.f.* algebra.
algébrique [alʒe′brik], *a.* algebraical.
algébriquement [alʒebrik′mɑ̃], *adv.* algebraically.
Alger [al′ʒe], *m.* Algiers.
Algérie [alʒe′ri], *f.* Algeria.
algérien [alʒe′rjɛ̃], *a.* (*fem.* **-enne**) Algerian.—*n.m.* (**Algérien**, *fem.* **-enne**) Algerian (*person*).
algie [al′ʒi:], *n.f.* ache.
algue [alg], *n.f.* sea-weed, alga.
alibi [ali′bi], *n.m.* (*Law*) alibi.
aliboron [alibɔ′rɔ̃], *n.m.* jackass, stupid or self-conceited fellow.
aliénable [alje′nabl], *a.* alienable, transferable.
aliénation [aljenɑ′sjɔ̃], *n.f.* (*Law*) conveyance of property to another; (*fig.*) alienation, mental derangement; estrangement, aversion.
aliéné [alje′ne], *a.* lunatic, mad.—*n.m.* (*fem.* **-ée**) lunatic.
aliéner [alje′ne], *v.t.* (*conjug. like* CÉDER) to alienate, to give away (*property*); to transfer, to make over; to estrange, to make hostile; to derange (*the mind*). **s′aliéner**, *v.r.* to become estranged (*from*).
aliéniste [alje′nist], *n.m.* alienist.
alignée [ali′ne], *n.f.* line, row.
alignement [aliɲə′mɑ̃], *n.m.* alignment; laying out in line; (*Mil.*) dressing; (*Print.*) ranging.
aligner [ali′ne], *v.t.* to align, to lay out in line; to put in a straight line; (*Mil.*) to dress; (*Print.*) to range. **s′aligner**, *v.r.* (*Mil.*) to dress.
aliment [ali′mɑ̃], *n.m.* aliment, food, nourishment, nutriment; (*Law, pl.*) alimony, maintenance.
alimentaire [alimɑ̃′tɛ:r], *a.* alimental, alimentary; (*Mech.*) **pompe alimentaire**, feed-pump, donkey engine.
alimentateur [alimɑ̃ta′tœ:r], *a.* (*fem.* **-trice**) alimentary.
alimentation [alimɑ̃tɑ′sjɔ̃], *n.f.* alimentation; nourishment, feeding; **rayon d′alimentation**, food department.
alimenter [alimɑ̃′te], *v.t.* to feed, to nourish; to maintain; to supply, to provision; to fuel, to keep up.
alimenteux [alimɑ̃′tø], *a.* (*fem.* **-euse**) nutritive.
alinéa [aline′a], *n.m.* indented line; new paragraph.
alisé [ALIZÉ].
aliter [ali′te], *v.t.* to confine to bed; **être alité**, to be bedridden. **s′aliter**, *v.r.* to take to one′s bed.
alizé or **alisé** [ali′ze], *a.* soft (*said of the trade-winds*); **vents alizés**, trade-winds.—*n.m.* trade-wind.
alkali etc. [ALCALI].
Alkoran [alkɔ′rɑ̃], [CORAN].

Allah [a′la], *m.* Allah.
allaitement [alɛt′mɑ̃], *n.m.* lactation, nursing, suckling; **allaitement artificiel**, bottle feeding.
allaiter [alɛ′te], *v.t.* to suckle, to nurse.
alléchant [ale′ʃɑ̃], *a.* alluring, seductive.
allèchement [aleʃ′mɑ̃], *n.m.* allurement, enticement, seduction, attraction.
allécher [ale′ʃe], *v.t.* (*conjug. like* CÉDER) to allure, to entice, to attract.
allée [a′le], *n.f.* passage, drive, alley, avenue, walk; (*pl.*) goings.
allégation [alega′sjɔ̃], *n.f.* allegation, assertion.
allège [a′lɛ:ʒ], *n.f.* lighter, hopper; (*Arch.*) window basement, sill of window.
allégeance [ale′ʒɑ̃:s], *n.f.* alleviation, relief; allegiance.
allégement [aleʒ′mɑ̃], *n.m.* alleviation, relief; reduction.
alléger [ale′ʒe], *v.t.* (*conjug. like* ASSIÉGER) to ease, to unburden, to lighten; to unload (*a boat*); to alleviate, to relieve, to assuage (*pain or grief*).
allégorie [alegɔ′ri], *n.f.* allegory.
allégorique [alegɔ′rik], *a.* allegorical.
allégoriquement [alegɔrik′mɑ̃], *adv.* allegorically.
allégoriser [alegɔri′ze], *v.t.* to allegorize.
allégoriste [alegɔ′rist], *n.m.* allegorist.
allègre [a′lɛgr], *a.* lively, nimble, sprightly; jolly, cheerful.
allègrement [allegrə′mɑ̃], *adv.* briskly; joyfully, merrily, joyously.
allégresse [alle′grɛs], *n.f.* gaiety, joy, mirth, cheerfulness; sprightliness.
alléguer [alle′ge], *v.t.* (*conjug. like* CÉDER) to allege, to advance; to urge; (*Law*) to quote, to adduce, to cite, to plead.
alléluia [alely′ja], *n.m.* and *int.* Hallelujah.
Allemagne [al′maɲ], *l′*, *f.* Germany.
allemand [al′mɑ̃], *a.* German.—*n.m.* German (*language*); (**Allemand**, *fem.* **-ande**) German (*person*).
aller [a′le], *v.i. irr.* (*with aux.* ÊTRE) to go, to go on, to proceed, to progress (*well, ill etc.*); to be (*in good or ill health*); to act (*in a certain way*); to suit, to fit (*well or ill*); to be going to; **aller au pas**, to go at a walking pace; **aller et venir**, to go up and down; **je ne ferai qu′aller et venir**, I won′t be a minute; **cela va tout seul**, it is plain sailing; **cet enfant ira loin**, this child will go far; **comment allez-vous?** how are you? **je vais bien**, I am well; (*fam.*) **ça va!** all right! **cet habit vous va mal**, this coat does not fit you; **allons!** come on! **allons donc!** surely not! **cela va sans dire**, it stands to reason; **il y va de sa vie**, his life is at stake; **se laisser aller**, to yield, to give way; to abandon oneself to a thing. **s′en aller**, *v.r.* to go away, to run away; to vanish, to disappear; to die, to wear out; **va-t′en! allez-vous-en!** go away! be off with you!—*n.m.* going, course, run; outward voyage, trip, journey; **billet d′aller et retour**, return ticket.
allergie [alɛr′ʒi], *n.f.* allergy.
allergique [alɛr′ʒik], *a.* allergic.
alliage [a′lja:ʒ], *n.m.* alloy, mixture; (*fig.*) impure mixture or combination.

alumine

alliance [a'ljɑ̃:s], *n.f.* alliance; marriage; union, league, coalition, confederacy; compact, covenant; mixture, blending; wedding-ring.

allié [a'lje], *a.* allied; related (*by marriage*); akin, kindred.—*n.m.* (*fem.* **-ée**) ally; connexion (*by marriage*).

allier [a'lje], *v.t.* to mix; to combine; to join, to unite, to ally, to marry; to reconcile; to match. **s'allier,** *v.r.* to be incorporated *or* mixed; to become allied, to join forces (*avec*); to combine (*of metals*).

alligator [aliga'tɔ:r], *n.m.* alligator.

allitération [alitera'sjɔ̃], *n.f.* alliteration.

allo! [a'lo], *int.* (*Teleph.*) hello!

allocataire [aloka'tɛ:r], *n.* recipient of an allowance.

allocation [aloka'sjɔ̃], *n.f.* allocation, allowance; *allocation de chômage,* unemployment benefit; *allocations familiales,* family allowances.

allocution [aloky'sjɔ̃], *n.f.* allocution, short address, speech.

allonge [a'lɔ̃:ʒ], *n.f.* leaf (*of a table*); fly-leaf, addendum; rider (*of a document*); reach (*in boxing*); *allonge de boucher,* meat-hook.

allongé [alɔ̃'ʒe], *a.* lengthened, elongated, out-stretched; downcast, long (*of face*).

allongement [alɔ̃ʒ'mɑ̃], *n.m.* lengthening, elongation, protraction.

allonger [alɔ̃'ʒe], *v.t.* (*conjug. like* MANGER) to lengthen, to elongate, to eke out; to stretch; to drag out, to protract. **s'allonger,** *v.r.* to stretch out, to grow longer; to stretch, to lie down at full length.

allouer [a'lwe], *v.t.* to allow, to grant, to accord; to allocate.

alluchon [aly'ʃɔ̃], *n.m.* cog, tooth (*of a wheel*).

allumage [aly'ma:ʒ], *n.m.* lighting, kindling; ignition; *un raté d'allumage,* misfire; *mettre l'allumage,* to switch on; *couper l'allumage,* to switch off.

allumé [aly'me], *a.* lighted, ignited; (*colloq.*) excited, drunk, lit-up.

allume-feu [alym'fø], *n.m. inv.* firewood, firelighter, kindling.

allume-gaz [alym'gɑ:z], *n.m. inv.* gas-lighter.

allumer [aly'me], *v.t.* to light; to kindle, to set on fire; (*fig.*) to inflame, to incite, to stir up. **s'allumer,** *v.r.* to light, to take *or* catch fire; to blaze, to sparkle, to glare; to flare up, to break out.

allumette [aly'mɛt], *n.f.* match.

allumeur [aly'mœ:r], *n.m.* (*fem.* **-euse**) lighter.

allure [a'ly:r], *n.f.* carriage, gait, pace, way of walking; demeanour; aspect, look; speed; (*pl.*) ways (*of a person*); *à toute allure,* at full speed.

allusion [aly'zjɔ̃], *n.f.* allusion, hint, innuendo.

alluvial [aly'vjal], *a.* (*m. pl.* **-aux**) alluvial.

alluvion [aly'vjɔ̃], *n.f.* alluvium.

almanach [alma'na], *n.m.* almanac, calendar.

aloès [alo'ɛːs], *n.m.* aloe; aloes.

aloi [a'lwa], *n.m.* the statutory degree of purity of gold and silver; (*fig.*) standard (*good* or *bad*), quality, kind (*of persons etc.*).

alors [a'lɔːr], *adv.* then, that time; in that case; *d'alors,* of that time; *alors que,* while, whereas; *jusqu'alors,* up to then,

till that moment; *alors même que,* even though.

alose [a'loːz], *n.f.* shad.

alouette [a'lwɛt], *n.f.* (*Orn.*) lark.

alourdir [alur'diːr], *v.t.* to make heavy, dull or stupid. **s'alourdir,** *v.r.* to grow heavy or dull.

alourdissant [alurdi'sɑ̃], *a.* oppressive, burdensome.

alourdissement [alurdis'mɑ̃], *n.m.* heaviness, dullness.

aloyau [alwa'jo], *n.m.* (*pl.* **-aux**) sirloin.

alpaca [alpa'ka], **alpaga** [alpa'ga], *n.m.* alpaca.

alpenstock [alpɛn'stɔk], *n.m.* alpenstock.

Alpes [alp], **les,** *f.pl.* the Alps.

alpestre [al'pɛstr], *a.* Alpine (*scenery, flora*).

alpha [al'fa], *n.m.* alpha; (*fig.*) beginning.

alphabet [alfa'bɛ], *n.m.* alphabet.

alphabétique [alfabe'tik], *a.* alphabetical.

alphabétiquement [alfabetik'mɑ̃], *adv.* alphabetically.

alpin [al'pɛ̃], *a.* Alpine (*club etc.*).

alpinisme [alpi'nism], *n.m.* mountaineering.

alpiniste [alpi'nist], *n.m.* Alpinist, mountaineer.

Alsace [al'zas], **l',** *f.* Alsace.

alsacien [alza'sjɛ̃], *a.* (*fem.* **-enne**) Alsatian.—*n.m.* (**Alsacien,** *fem.* **-enne**) inhabitant of Alsace.

altérable [alte'rabl], *a.* alterable, corruptible, adulterable.

altérant [alte'rɑ̃], *a.* causing thirst.

altération [altera'sjɔ̃], *n.f.* deterioration; falsification, adulteration, debasing (*of money etc.*); weakening, impairing.

altercation [alterka'sjɔ̃], *n.f.* altercation, wrangle, dispute, quarrel.

altérer [alte're], *v.t.* (*conjug. like* CÉDER) to alter for the worse; to impair, to adulterate, to corrupt, to pervert, to debase, to falsify; to disturb, to trouble, to upset; to make thirsty. **s'altérer,** *v.r.* to be impaired, to degenerate.

alternance [altɛr'nɑ̃:s], *n.f.* alternation, rotation.

alternant [alter'nɑ̃], *a.* alternating, rotating (*as crops*).

alternat [alter'na], *n.m.* rotation (*of crops etc*).

alternatif [alterna'tif], *a.* (*fem.* **-tive**) alternate, alternating, alternative.—*n.f.* (**-tive**) alternation; alternative, choice, option (*between two possible actions*).

alternativement [alternativ'mɑ̃], *adv.* alternately, by turns.

alterne [al'tɛrn], *a.* (*Geom.*) alternate (*of angles*); (*Bot.*) alternate.

alterner [alter'ne], *v.t.* to grow (*crops*) in rotation.—*v.i.* to alternate, to succeed each other alternately.

Altesse [al'tɛs], *n.f.* Highness.

altier [al'tje], *a.* (*fem.* **-ière**) haughty, proud, arrogant, lordly, lofty.

altimètre [alti'mɛtr], *n.m.* altimeter.

altitude [alti'tyd], *n.f.* altitude.

alto [al'to], *n.m.* alto; tenor violin; tenor saxhorn.

altruisme [altry'ism], *n.m.* altruism.

altruiste [altry'ist], *a.* altruistic.—*n.* altruist.

alumine [aly'min], *n.f.* alumina, oxide of aluminium.

15

aluminer [alymi′ne], *v.t.* to aluminate, to aluminize.

aluminium [alymi′njɔm], *n.m.* aluminium.

alun [a′lœ̃], *n.m.* alum.

alunage [aly′na:ʒ], *n.m.* (*Dyeing*) steeping in alum; (*Phot.*) hardening (*negatives etc.*) in an alum-bath.

aluner [aly′ne], *v.t.* (*Dyeing*) to steep in alum-water; (*Phot.*) to harden in an alum-bath.

alunière [aly′njɛːr], *n.f.* alum-pit *or* mine, alum-works.

alunir [aly′niːr], *v.i.* to land on the moon.

alvéole [alve′ɔl], *n.m.* alveolus, cell (*in a honey-comb*); socket (*of a tooth*).

amabilité [amabili′te], *n.f.* amiability, affability, kindness.

amadou [ama′du], *n.m.* amadou, (German) tinder; touchwood.

amadouer [ama′dwe], *v.t.* to coax, to wheedle, to cajole.

amaigrir [ame′griːr], *v.t.* to make lean, meagre *or* thin, to emaciate; to reduce, to lessen (*in bulk etc.*); to impoverish; to exhaust (*soil etc.*).—*v.i.* to fall away, to grow lean *or* thin. **s'amaigrir**, *v.r.* to grow thin, to fall away.

amaigrissant [amɛgri′sɑ̃], *a.* causing emaciation; *régime amaigrissant*, slimming diet.

amaigrissement [amɛgris′mɑ̃], *n.m.* emaciation, wasting away.

amalgamation [amalgama′sjɔ̃], *n.f.* amalgamation.

amalgame [amal′gam], *n.m.* amalgam; (*fig.*) medley, heterogeneous mixture.

amalgamer [amalga′me], *v.t.* to amalgamate, to blend, to combine. **s'amalgamer**, *v.r.* to amalgamate, to blend, to combine.

amande [a′mɑ̃:d], *n.f.* almond; kernel; *amandes lissées*, sugar-plums.

amandier [amɑ̃′dje], *n.m.* almond-tree.

amant [a′mɑ̃], *n.m.* (*fem.* **-e**) lover, suitor; sweetheart, mistress; gallant, paramour; passionate admirer.

amarante [ama′rɑ̃:t], *n.f.* amaranth.

amareilleur *or* **amareyeur** [amarɛ′jœːr], *n.m.* worker on an oyster-bed.

amarinage [amari′na:ʒ], *n.m.* (*Naut.*) manning (*a prize*).

amariner [amari′ne], *v.t.* to man (*a prize*); to inure (*a crew etc.*) to sea. **s'amariner**, *v.r.* to become used to the sea.

amarrage [ama′ra:ʒ], *n.m.* (*Naut.*) mooring; anchorage; lashing.

amarre [a′ma:r], *n.f.* (*Naut.*) cable, rope, hawser.

amarrer [ama′re], *v.t.* to moor, to belay, to make fast.

amaryllis [amari′lis], *n.f.* amaryllis.

amas [a′mɑ], *n.m.* mass, heap, pile, accumulation.

amasser [ama′se], *v.t.* to accumulate, to heap up, to amass; to hoard; to collect, to get together. **s'amasser**, *v.r.* to gather, to get together, to accumulate, to be collected, to crowd, to assemble.

amassette [ama′sɛt], *n.f.* small palette-knife.

amasseur [ama′sœːr], *n.m.* (*fem.* **-euse**) hoarder.

amateur [ama′tœːr], *n.m.* amateur; devotee; connoisseur.

amazone [ama′zo:n], *n.f.* Amazon, female warrior; horse-woman; riding-habit; *habit d'amazone*, riding-habit; *monter en amazone*, to ride side-saddle.

ambages [ɑ̃′ba:ʒ], *n.f.* (*pl.*) circumlocution; *sans ambages*, straight out.

ambassade [ɑ̃ba′sad], *n.f.* embassy, ambassador's staff.

ambassadeur [ɑ̃basa′dœːr], *n.m.* ambassador; (*fig.*) envoy, messenger.

ambassadrice [ɑ̃basa′dris], *n.f.* ambassadress.

ambiance [ɑ̃′bjɑ̃:s], *n.* surroundings, environment; atmosphere.

ambiant [ɑ̃′bjɑ̃], *a.* ambient, surrounding.

ambidextre [ɑ̃bi′dɛkstr], *a.* ambidextrous.— *n.* ambidexter.

ambigu [ɑ̃bi′gy], *a.* (*fem.* **-guë**) ambiguous, equivocal.—*n.m.* heterogeneous mixture, medley.

ambiguïté [ɑ̃bigɥi′te], *n.f.* ambiguity.

ambigument [ɑ̃bigy′mɑ̃], *adv.* ambiguously.

ambitieusement [ɑ̃bisjøz′mɑ̃], *adv.* ambitiously.

ambitieux [ɑ̃bi′sjø], *a.* (*fem.* **-euse**) ambitious.—*n.m.* (*fem.* **-euse**) ambitious person.

ambition [ɑ̃bi′sjɔ̃], *n.f.* ambition.

ambitionner [ɑ̃bisjɔ′ne], *v.t.* to desire earnestly; to be ambitious of, to aspire to.

ambivalence [ɑ̃biva′lɑ̃:s], *n.f.* ambivalence.

ambivalent [ɑ̃biva′lɑ̃], *a.* ambivalent.

amble [ɑ̃:bl], *n.m.* amble.

ambler [ɑ̃′ble], *v.i.* to amble.

ambleur [ɑ̃′blœːr], *a.* (*fem.* **-euse**) ambling.

amblyope [ɑ̃′bljɔp], *a.* amblyopic, weak-sighted.—*n.* weak-sighted person.

ambre [ɑ̃:br], *n.m.* amber; *ambre gris*, ambergris.

ambré [ɑ̃′bre], *a.* amber-coloured.

ambrer [ɑ̃′bre], *v.t.* to perfume with amber.

ambrette [ɑ̃′brɛt], *n.f.* amber-seed; musk-seed.

ambroisie [ɑ̃brwa′zi], *n.f.* ambrosia.

ambulance [ɑ̃by′lɑ̃:s], *n.f.* ambulance; field-hospital; peripatetic clerkship; *chirurgien d'ambulance*, field-surgeon.

ambulancier [ɑ̃bylɑ̃′sje], *n.m.* (*fem.* **-ière**) ambulance-man, stretcher-bearer, nurse.

ambulant [ɑ̃by′lɑ̃], *a.* ambulant, ambulatory, itinerant, peripatetic; travelling (*of a railway post-office*); strolling (*players*).

ambulatoire [ɑ̃byla′twaːr], *a.* ambulatory; (*Law*) movable.

âme (1) [ɑːm], *n.f.* soul, spirit; sentiment, sensibility; (*fig.*) inhabitant, person (*on a lost ship etc.*); core, pith, heart (*of a thing etc.*); *rendre l'âme*, to give up the ghost.

âme (2) [ɑːm], *n.f.* sounding-board (*of a violin etc.*); bore (*of gun*).

amélioration [ameljɔra′sjɔ̃], *n.f.* amelioration, improvement; (*pl.*) repairs, decorations (*of a house etc.*).

améliorer [ameljɔ′re], *v.t.* to ameliorate, to improve, to better. **s'améliorer**, *v.r.* to get better, to mend, to improve.

amen [a′mɛn], *int.* and *n.m.* amen.

aménagement [amenaʒ′mɑ̃], *n.m.* arrangement; disposition (*of a house etc.*); management (*of a forest*).

aménager [amena'ʒe], *v.t.* (*conjug. like* MANGER) to dispose, to arrange, to lay out; to regulate the felling of (*a wood* or *forest*).
amendable [amɑ̃'dabl], *a.* improvable, mendable.
amende [a'mɑ̃ːd], *n.f.* fine, penalty, forfeit, compensation, reparation; *faire amende honorable*, to make a full apology; *mettre* or *condamner à l'amende*, to fine.
amendement [amɑ̃d'mɑ̃], *n.m.* amendment; improvement; manuring (*of land*).
amender [amɑ̃'de], *v.t.* to amend, to better; to manure (*land*). **s'amender**, *v.r.* to mend, to grow better.
amène [a'mɛːn], *a.* agreeable, pleasant (*site*).
amener [am'ne], *v.t.* (*see Verb Tables*) to lead (*hither*), to bring; to induce, prevail upon; to introduce; to bring about; to occasion, to lead to; (*Naut.*) to lower, to strike (*colours, sails etc.*); *mandat d'amener*, warrant.
aménité [ameni'te], *n.f.* amenity, pleasantness, affability; grace, urbanity.
amenuiser [amənɥi'ze], *v.t.* to make thinner or smaller. **s'amenuiser**, *v.r.* to grow thinner or smaller.
amer (1) [a'mɛːr], *a.* (*fem.* **amère**) bitter, harsh; painful, grievous; biting, galling.—*n.m.* something bitter; gall; bitterness; (*pl.*) bitters.
amer (2) [a'mɛːr], *n.m.* (*Naut.*) any landmark or leading mark.
amèrement [amɛr'mɑ̃], *adv.* bitterly, grievously.
américain [ameri'kɛ̃], *a.* American.—*n.m.* (**Américain,** *fem.* **-aine**) American (*person*).
américanisme [amerika'nism], *n.m.* Americanism.
Amérique [ame'rik], *l'*, *f.* America.
amérir or **amerrir** [ame'riːr], *v.i.* (*Av.*) to alight on the water.
amerrissage [ameri'saːʒ], *n.m.* alighting (*on the water*).
amertume [amɛr'tym], *n.f.* bitterness, grief; gall, venom.
améthyste [ame'tist], *n.f.* amethyst.
ameublement [amœblə'mɑ̃], *n.m.* furniture, suite of furniture.
ameublir [amœ'bliːr], *v.t.* (*Agric.*) to make (*soil*) more broken up or lighter.
ameublissement [amœblis'mɑ̃], *n.m.* (*Agric.*) loosening, mellowing.
ameulonner [amœlɔ'ne], *v.t.* to stack (*hay, corn etc.*).
ameuter [amø'te], *v.t.* to train dogs as a pack; (*fig.*) to stir up, to rouse, to excite.
ami [a'mi], *n.m.* (*fem.* **amie**) friend; wellwisher, partisan; lover; *chambre d'ami*, spare room.—*a.* friendly; sympathetic, favourable, kindly-disposed; kind, propitious.
amiable [a'mjabl], *a.* friendly, courteous; amicable, conciliatory; *vente à l'amiable*, sale by private contract.
amiablement [amjablə'mɑ̃], *adv.* amicably.
amiante [a'mjɑ̃ːt], *n.m.* asbestos.
amibe [a'mib], *n.f.* amoeba.
amical [ami'kal], *a.* (*m. pl.* **-aux**) amicable, friendly.
amicalement [amikal'mɑ̃], *adv.* amicably, in a friendly manner.
amidon [ami'dɔ̃], *n.m.* starch.
amidonner [amidɔ'ne], *v.t.* to starch.

amincir [amɛ̃'siːr], *v.t.* to make thinner. **s'amincir**, *v.r.* to become thinner.
amincissement [amɛ̃sis'mɑ̃], *n.m.* thinning.
amiral [ami'ral], *n.m.* (*pl.* **-aux**) admiral; *contre-amiral*, rear-admiral; *grand amiral*, high-admiral; *vice-amiral*, vice-admiral; *vaisseau amiral*, flagship.
Amirauté [amiro'te], **Îles de l'**, *f.* Admiralty Islands.
amirauté [amiro'te], *n.f.* admiralship; admiralty.
amitié [ami'tje], *n.f.* friendship, affection; favour, kindness; (*pl.*) kind regards, compliments; *mes amitiés à tout le monde*, love to all; *par amitié*, out of friendship.
ammoniac [amɔ'njak], *a.* (*fem.* **-iaque**) ammoniac; *sel ammoniac*, sal ammoniac. —*n.f.* (**-iaque**) ammonia.
ammonite [amɔ'nit], *n.f.* ammonite.
amnésie [amne'zi], *n.f.* amnesia.
amnistie [amnis'ti], *n.f.* amnesty, pardon.
amnistier [amnis'tje], *v.t.* to pardon by amnesty.
amoindrir [amwɛ̃'driːr], *v.t.* to lessen, to decrease, to diminish. **s'amoindrir**, *v.r.* to grow less.
amoindrissement [amwɛ̃dris'mɑ̃], *n.m.* lessening, decrease.
amollir [amɔ'liːr], *v.t.* to soften; (*fig.*) to mollify. **s'amollir**, *v.r.* to soften, to grow soft; to grow effeminate or weak.
amollissant [amɔli'sɑ̃], *a.* softening; enervating.
amollissement [amɔlis'mɑ̃], *n.m.* softening, enervation, effeminacy.
amonceler [amɔ̃s'le], *v.t.* (*conjug. like* APPELER) to heap up, to lay in a heap; (*fig.*) to accumulate. **s'amonceler**, *v.r.* to gather; to accumulate, to drift together.
amoncellement [amɔ̃sɛl'mɑ̃], *n.m.* accumulation; heap.
amont [a'mɔ̃], *n.m.* upstream water (*used chiefly in en amont*, up-stream, up-river).
amoral [amɔ'ral], *a.* (*m. pl.* **-aux**) amoral.
amorçage [amɔr'saːʒ], *n.m.* priming (*of pumps, motors, guns etc.*); priming (*of hook*).
amorce [a'mɔrs], *n.f.* bait; (*fig.*) allurement, charm; priming, percussion-cap (*of guns etc.*); priming (*for a pump*).
amorcer [amɔr'se], *v.t.* (*conjug. like* COMMENCER) to bait; (*fig.*) to allure, to entice, to decoy; (*Hydraulics*) to prime; (*Artill.*) to cap (*a shell*).
amorphe [a'mɔrf], *a.* amorphous.
amortir [amɔr'tiːr], *v.t.* to deaden, to allay, to moderate; to weaken, to break (*a fall, shock etc.*); to redeem, to pay off; to cool (*passions*).
amortissable [amɔrti'sabl], *a.* redeemable.
amortissement [amɔrtis'mɑ̃], *n.m.* redemption, buying up; liquidation; deadening (*of a blow etc.*); *fonds d'amortissement*, sinking-fund.
amortisseur [amɔrti'sœːr], *n.m.* shock absorber.
amour [a'muːr], *n.m.* (*usu. fem. in pl.*) love, affection, passion; the object of love, flame, fancy; *l'Amour*, (*Myth.*) Eros, Cupid.
amouracher(s') [samura'ʃe], *v.r.* to be smitten with, to become enamoured (*de*).
amourette [amu'rɛt], *n.f.* passing amour, love-affair.

17

amoureusement [amurøz'mɑ̃], *adv.* amorously, lovingly; tenderly.

amoureux [amu'rø], *a.* (*fem.* **-euse**) loving, in love, smitten, enamoured (*de*); amorous. —*n.m.* (*fem.* **-euse**) lover, sweetheart; fiancé or fiancée.

amour-propre [amur'prɔpr], *n.m.* self-respect; vanity, conceit.

amovibilité [amɔvibili'te], *n.f.* removability, liability to removal; precariousness of tenure.

amovible [amɔ'vibl], *a.* removable, revocable.

ampère [ɑ̃'pɛːr], *n.m.* (*Elec.*) ampere.

amphibie [ɑ̃fi'bi], *a.* amphibious.—*n.m.* amphibian.

amphibiens [ɑ̃fi'bjɛ̃], *n.m. pl.* (*Zool.*) Amphibia.

amphigouri [ɑ̃figu'ri], *n.m.* rigmarole, gibberish.

amphithéâtre [ɑ̃fite'ɑːtr], *n.m.* amphitheatre; the whole body of occupants of this; the gallery in a theatre rising above the boxes and facing the stage; lecture-room; *en amphithéâtre*, in semi-circular tiers.

Amphitryon [ɑ̃fitri'ɔ̃], *n.m.* Amphitryon; host, entertainer.

amphore [ɑ̃'fɔːr], *n.f.* amphora.

ample [ɑ̃:pl], *a.* ample, full; large, vast, spacious; copious.

amplement [ɑ̃plə'mɑ̃], *adv.* amply, fully; largely, plentifully.

ampleur [ɑ̃'plœːr], *n.f.* width, fullness (*of clothes*); abundance; profusion; dignity (*of style etc.*); volume (*of voice*).

amplifiant [ɑ̃pli'fjɑ̃], *a.* magnifying (*of a lens etc.*); amplifying.

amplificateur [ɑ̃plifika'tœːr], *a.* (*fem.* **-trice**) magnifying; amplifying.—*n.m.* (*Phot.*) enlarger.

amplification [ɑ̃plifika'sjɔ̃], *n.f.* amplification; magnification, enlargement; (*fig.*) exaggeration.

amplifier [ɑ̃pli'fje], *v.t.* to amplify, to develop, to enlarge.

amplitude [ɑ̃pli'tyd], *n.f.* extent, amplitude.

ampoule [ɑ̃'pul], *n.f.* blister, swelling; (*Elec.*) bulb; (*Med.*) ampoule.

ampoulé [ɑ̃pu'le], *a.* bombastic, turgid.

amputation [ɑ̃pyta'sjɔ̃], *n.f.* amputation; (*fig.*) curtailment.

amputer [ɑ̃py'te], *v.t.* to amputate, to cut off.

amulette [amy'lɛt], *n.f.* amulet, charm.

amusant [amy'zɑ̃], *a.* amusing, diverting, entertaining.

amusement [amyz'mɑ̃], *n.m.* amusement, entertainment, diversion; fooling, trifling.

amuser [amy'ze], *v.t.* to amuse, to divert, to entertain; to fool, to beguile, to dupe; to detain, to delay. **s'amuser,** *v.r.* to amuse oneself, to divert oneself; to trifle; to have a good time; *s'amuser de quelqu'un*, to make fun of someone; *amusez-vous bien!* enjoy yourselves, have a good time.

amusette [amy'zɛt], *n.f.* petty amusement.

amuseur [amy'zœːr], *n.m.* (*fem.* **-euse**) amuser, entertainer.

amygdale [ami'dal], *n.f.* (*Anat.*) tonsil.

an [ɑ̃], *n.m.* year; (*pl.*) years, time, age; *elle a quinze ans*, she is fifteen; *le jour de l'an*, New Year's day.

anacarde [ana'kard], *n.m.* cashew-nut.

anachorète [anakɔ'rɛt], *n.* anchorite, hermit.

anachronisme [anakrɔ'nism], *n.m.* anachronism.

anaéroïde [ANÉROÏDE].

anagramme [ana'gram], *n.f.* anagram.

analgésie [analʒe'zi], **analgie** [anal'ʒi], *n.f.* (*Med.*) analgesia.

analgésique [analʒe'zik], **analgique** [anal'ʒik], *a.* and *n.m.* analgesic.

analogie [analɔ'ʒi], *n.f.* analogy.

analogique [analɔ'ʒik], *a.* analogous, analogical.

analogue [ana'lɔg], *a.* analogous, similar.

analyse [ana'liːz], *n.f.* analysis; outline, précis, abstract (*of a book etc.*); (*Gram.*) parsing, analysis.

analyser [anali'ze], *v.t.* to analyse.

analyste [ana'list], *n.m.* analyst.

analytique [anali'tik], *a.* analytic, analytical.

analytiquement [analitik'mɑ̃], *adv.* analytically.

ananas [ana'nɑ], *n.m.* pineapple.

anarchie [anar'ʃi], *n.f.* anarchy; (*fig.*) disorder, confusion.

anarchique [anar'ʃik], *a.* anarchical.

anarchiste [anar'ʃist], *n.* anarchist.

anathème [ana'tɛːm], *n.m.* anathema; sentence of reprobation *or* excommunication, ban, curse.

anatomie [anatɔ'mi], *n.f.* anatomy; dissection; (*fam.*) body, figure.

anatomique [anatɔ'mik], *a.* anatomical.

anatomiquement [anatɔmik'mɑ̃], *adv.* anatomically.

anatomiser [anatɔmi'ze], *v.t.* to anatomize, to dissect.

anatomiste [anatɔ'mist], *n.* anatomist.

ancêtre [ɑ̃'sɛːtr], *n.* ancestor, ancestress.—*n.m. pl.* ancestors, forefathers.

anchois [ɑ̃'ʃwa], *n.m.* anchovy.

ancien [ɑ̃'sjɛ̃], *a.* (*fem.* **-ienne**) ancient, old; former, late, ex-; antique; *un ancien élève*, an old boy.—*n.m.* (*fem.* **-ienne**) senior; ancient; (*Eccles.*) elder; (*Mil.*) veteran; (*pl.*) the ancients; our forefathers.

anciennement [ɑ̃sjɛn'mɑ̃], *adv.* formerly; *of yore; in former times.

ancienneté [ɑ̃sjɛn'te], *n.f.* antiquity; seniority.

ancillaire [ɑ̃sil'lɛːr], *a.* ancillary.

ancrage [ɑ̃'kraːʒ], *n.m.* anchorage.

ancre [ɑ̃:kr], *n.f.* anchor; cramp-iron, tie-plate (*of a wall*). *ancre de miséricorde* (or *de salut*), sheet anchor (*fig.*) last resource.

ancrer [ɑ̃'kre], *v.t.* to anchor; (*fig.*) to fix or establish firmly.—*v.i.* to anchor. **s'ancrer,** *v.r.* to establish oneself, to get a footing (*in a place*), to take deep root (*in*).

Andalousie [ɑ̃dalu'zi], l', *f.* Andalusia.

Andes [ɑ̃:d], les, *f. pl.* the Andes.

Andorre [ɑ̃'dɔːr], l', *m.* Andorra.

andouille [ɑ̃'duːj], *n.f.* pork sausage (*made of chitterlings*); (*pop.*) imbecile, duffer.

andouiller [ɑ̃du'je], *n.m.* tine (*of antler*).

André [ɑ̃'dre], *m.* Andrew.

Andromède [ɑ̃drɔ'mɛd], *f.* Andromeda.

âne [ɑːn], *n.m.* ass, donkey; blockhead; stupid, ignorant *or* foolish person, idiot.

anéantir [aneɑ̃'tiːr], *v.t.* to annihilate, to destroy utterly, to abolish; (*fig.*) to overwhelm.

anéantissement [aneãtis'mã], *n.m.* annihilation; destruction, ruin, overthrow; humiliation, prostration.

anecdote [anɛg'dɔt], *n.f.* anecdote.

anecdotique [anɛgdɔ'tik], *a.* anecdotic.

anémie [ane'mi], *n.f.* anaemia.

anémique [ane'mik], *a.* anaemic.

anémone [ane'mɔn], *n.f.* anemone, windflower.

ânerie [ɑn'ri], *n.f.* stupidity; gross ignorance; gross blunder.

anéroïde [anerɔ'id], **anaéroïde** [anaerɔ'id], *a.* aneroid.—*n.m.* aneroid barometer.

ânesse [ɑ'nɛs], *n.f.* she-ass.

anesthésie [anɛste'zi], *n.f.* (*Med.*) anaesthesia.

anesthésier [anɛste'zje], *v.t.* to anaesthetize.

anesthésique [anɛste'zik], *a.* and *n.m.* anaesthetic.

anesthésiste [anɛste'zist], *n.m.* anaesthetist.

anévrisme [ane'vrism], *n.m.* aneurism.

anfractueux [ɑ̃frak'tɥø], *a.* (*fem.* **-euse**) anfractuous, winding, sinuous, craggy.

anfractuosité [ɑ̃fraktɥozi'te], *n.f.* anfractuosity, cragginess, twist, jagged *or* rugged outlines.

ange [ɑ̃:ʒ], *n.m.* angel; (*fig.*) an adorable *or* beloved person.

Angèle [ɑ̃'ʒɛl], *f.* Angela.

angélique [ɑ̃ʒe'lik], *a.* angelic, angelical.

angélus [ɑ̃ʒe'ly:s], *n.m.* angelus.

angevin [ɑ̃ʒə'vɛ̃], *a.* of Anjou.—*n.m.* (**Angevin**, *fem.* **-ine**) native of Anjou.

angine [ɑ̃'ʒin], *n.f.* angina, quinsy, sore throat.

anglais [ɑ̃'glɛ], *a.* English; British.—*n.m.* English (*language*); (**Anglais**, *fem.* **-aise**) Englishman, English girl *or* woman; (*pl.*) the English.

angle [ɑ̃:gl], *n.m.* angle, corner; (*Arch.*) quoin; *angle aigu*, acute angle; *angle droit*, right angle.

Angleterre [ɑ̃glə'tɛ:r], **l'**, *f.* England.

anglican [ɑ̃gli'kɑ̃], *a.* and *n.m.* (*fem.* **-e**) Anglican.

angliciser [ɑ̃glisi'ze], *v.t.* to anglicize. **s'angliciser**, *v.r.* to become anglicized *or* English.

anglicisme [ɑ̃gli'sism], *n.m.* anglicism.

anglomanie [ɑ̃glɔma'ni], *n.f.* Anglomania.

anglo-normand [ɑ̃glɔnɔr'mɑ̃], *a.* and *n.m.* (*fem.* **-e**) Anglo-Norman; *les Îles anglo-normandes*, the Channel Islands.

anglophile [ɑ̃glɔ'fil], *a.* and *n.* Anglophil.

anglo-saxon [ɑ̃glɔsak'sɔ̃], *a.* and *n.m.* (*fem.* **-saxonne**) Anglo-Saxon.

angoisse [ɑ̃'gwas], *n.f.* anguish, agony, great distress; (*Med.*) angor, anguish.

angora [ɑ̃gɔ'ra], *a.* Angora.—*n.m.* Angora cat.

anguille [ɑ̃'giːj], *n.f.* eel; (*pl.*, *Naut.*) launching ways, slips; *il y a anguille sous roche*, I smell a rat.

angulaire [ɑ̃gy'lɛ:r], *a.* angular.

angusture [ɑ̃gys'ty:r], *n.f.* (*Pharm.*) angostura.

anhélation [anelɑ'sjɔ̃], *n.f.* panting.

anhéler [ane'le], *v.i.* (*conjug. like* CÉDER) to pant.

anhydre [a'nidr], *a.* (*Chem.*) anhydrous.

anhydride [ani'drid], *n.m.* anhydride; *anhydride carbonique*, carbon dioxide.

anicroche [ani'krɔʃ], *n.f.* slight obstacle.

animadversion [animadvɛr'sjɔ̃], *n.f.* animadversion, reproof, reprimand, censure.

animal [ani'mal], *n.m.* (*pl.* **-aux**) animal; beast, brute; *société protectrice des animaux*, Royal Society for the Prevention of Cruelty to Animals.—*a.* (*m.pl.* **-aux**) animal; sensual, carnal.

animateur [anima'tœ:r], *a.* (*fem.* **-trice**) animating.

animation [animɑ'sjɔ̃], *n.f.* animation, vitality, life; liveliness; excitement; irritation.

animé [ani'me], *a.* animated; spirited, gay, sprightly; *rue animée*, busy street.

animer [ani'me], *v.t.* to animate, to give life to; to arouse, to excite, to urge on; to enliven, to give force to (*style etc.*). **s'animer**, *v.r.* to become animated *or* lively; to cheer up; to become angry.

animosité [animozi'te], *n.f.* animosity, ill will, spite, rancour.

anis [a'ni], *n.m.* anise, aniseed.

aniser [ani'ze], *v.t.* to flavour with aniseed.

anisette [ani'zɛt], *n.f.* aniseed cordial.

ankylose [ɑ̃ki'loːz], *n.f.* (*Path.*) anchylosis, stiffness in the joints.

annales [a'nal], *n.f.* (*used only in pl.*) annals, public records.

annaliste [ana'list], *n.m.* annalist.

anneau [a'no], *n.m.* (*pl.* **anneaux**) ring; link (*of a chain*); ringlet (*of hair*).

année [a'ne], *n.f.* year, period of twelve months; *année bissextile*, leap-year; *souhaiter la bonne année*, to wish a happy New Year.

année-lumière [anely'mjɛːr], *n.f.* (*pl.* **années-lumière**) light-year.

annelé [an'le], *a.* having *or* arranged in rings, ringed; (*Zool.*) annulated.

annelet [an'lɛ], *n.m.* ringlet, small ring.

annexe [a'nɛks], *n.f.* annex; appendage; appendix, schedule, rider; chapel of ease.

annexer [anɛk'se], *v.t.* to annex, to attach.

annexion [anɛk'sjɔ̃], *n.f.* annexation.

annihilation [aniila'sjɔ̃], *n.f.* annihilation; (*Law*) annulment.

annihiler [anii'le], *v.t.* to annihilate, to destroy; (*Law*) to annul.

anniversaire [anivɛr'sɛːr], *a.* and *n.m.* anniversary, birthday.

annonce [a'nɔ̃:s], *n.f.* announcement, notification; indication, sign, mark; advertisement; *annonce de mariage*, banns of marriage.

annoncer [anɔ̃'se], *v.t.* (*conjug. like* COMMENCER) to announce, to give notice of; to advertise; to announce (*a visitor*), to usher *or* show in; to proclaim; to foretell. **s'annoncer**, *v.r.* to present oneself; to manifest itself.

Annonciation [anɔ̃sja'sjɔ̃], *n.f.* Annunciation; Lady Day (March 25).

annoncier [anɔ̃'sje], *n.m.* publicity manager.

annotateur [anɔta'tœ:r], *n.m.* (*fem.* **-trice**) annotator (*of a book etc.*).

annotation [anɔta'sjɔ̃], *n.f.* annotation.

annoter [anɔ'te], *v.t.* to annotate, to make notes on (*a text etc.*).

annuaire [a'nɥɛːr], *n.m.* annual, year-book; *l'Annuaire des Téléphones*, the telephone directory.

annuel [a'nɥɛl], *a.* (*fem.* **-elle**) annual, yearly.

annuellement [anɥɛl'mã], *adv.* annually, yearly.

T—F.E.D.—B

annuité [anɥi'te], *n.f.* annuity.
annulable [any'labl], *a.* revocable.
annulaire [any'lɛ:r], *a.* annular, ring-shaped. —*n.m.* ring-finger, third finger.
annulation [anyla'sjɔ̃], *n.f.* annulment, cancellation, repeal, abolition.
annuler [any'le], *v.t.* to annul, to rescind, to cancel, to abolish, to set aside, to make void.
anobli [anɔ'bli], *a.* ennobled.—*n.m.* newly created nobleman.
anoblir [anɔ'bli:r], *v.t.* to ennoble, to raise to the rank of the nobility.
anoblissement [anɔblis'mɑ̃], *n.m.* ennoblement.
anode [a'nɔd], *n.f.* (*Elec.*) anode, positive pole.
anodin [anɔ'dɛ̃], *a.* (*Med.*) anodyne, soothing; (*fig.*) harmless, mild, inoffensive, insignificant.
anomal [anɔ'mal], *a.* (*m. pl.* **-aux**) (*Gram.*) anomalous, irregular.
anomalie [anɔma'li], *n.f.* anomaly, irregularity.
ânon [ɑ'nɔ̃], *n.m.* ass's foal, young ass; (*fig.*) a little fool.
ânonnement [ɑnɔn'mɑ̃], *n.m.* faltering, mumbling way of reading a text.
ânonner [anɔ'ne], *v.t.* to mumble and blunder through (*a lesson etc.*).—*v.i.* to read in a faltering way.
anonymat [anɔni'ma], *n.m.* anonymity.
anonyme [anɔ'nim], *a.* anonymous, nameless; *société anonyme*, joint-stock company. —*n.* anonymous person.
anonymement [anɔnim'mɑ̃], *adv.* anonymously.
anorak [anɔ'rak], *n.m.* (*reg. trade mark*) anorak.
anormal [anɔr'mal], *a.* (*m. pl.* **-aux**) abnormal, irregular, mentally deficient.
anormalement [anɔrmal'mɑ̃], *adv.* abnormally.
anse [ɑ̃:s], *n.f.* handle (*of a pot, basket etc.*); creek, cove.
antagonique [ɑ̃tagɔ'nik], *a.* antagonistic.
antagonisme [ɑ̃tagɔ'nism], *n.m.* antagonism.
antagoniste [ɑ̃tagɔ'nist], *a.* antagonistic.— *n.m.* antagonist, adversary, opponent; competitor, rival.
*antan [ɑ'tɑ̃], *n.m.* yesteryear; *les neiges d'antan*, the snows of yesteryear.
antarctique [ɑ̃tark'tik], *a.* Antarctic.
antécédent [ɑ̃tese'dɑ̃], *a.* antecedent, preceding, foregoing, previous.—*n.m.* precedent; (*Gram.*) antecedent.
antéchrist [ɑ̃te'krist], *n.m.* Antichrist.
antédiluvien [ɑ̃tedily'vjɛ̃], *a.* (*fem.* **-ienne**) antediluvian.
antenne [ɑ̃'ten], *n.f.* (*Rad., Tel.*) aerial; (*Ent.*) antenna, (*pl.*) antennae.
antépénultième [ɑ̃tepenyl'tjɛm], *a.* antepenultimate.
antérieur [ɑ̃te'rjœ:r], *a.* anterior, earlier, antecedent, previous, former.
antérieurement [ɑ̃terjœr'mɑ̃], *adv.* previously, before.
antériorité [ɑ̃terjɔri'te], *n.f.* anteriority, priority, precedence.
anthologie [ɑ̃tɔlɔ'ʒi], *n.f.* anthology.
anthracite [ɑ̃tra'sit], *n.m.* anthracite.
anthrax [ɑ̃'traks], *n.m.* (*Med.*) anthrax.
anthropoïde [ɑ̃trɔpɔ'id], *a.* and *n.m.* (*Zool.*) anthropoid.

anthropologie [ɑ̃trɔpɔlɔ'ʒi], *n.f.* anthropology.
anthropologiste [ɑ̃trɔpɔlɔ'ʒist], **anthropologue** [ɑ̃trɔpɔ'lɔg], *n.* anthropologist.
anthropophage [ɑ̃trɔpɔ'fa:ʒ], *n.* cannibal.
anti-aérien [ɑ̃tiae'rjɛ̃], *a.* (*fem.* **-enne**) anti-aircraft.
antibiotique [ɑ̃tibiɔ'tik], *a.* and *n.m.* antibiotic.
anti-brouillard [ɑ̃tibru'ja:r], *n.m.* (*Motor.*) fog-light.
anti-buée [ɑ̃ti'bye], *a.* (*Motor.*) demisting.— *n.m.* demister.
antichambre [ɑ̃ti'ʃɑ̃:br], *n.f.* (*formerly m.*) antechamber, anteroom.
anti-char [ɑ̃ti'ʃa:r], *a.* anti-tank.
antichrétien [ɑ̃tikre'tjɛ̃], *a.* and *n.m.* (*fem.* **-ienne**) antichristian.
anticipation [ɑ̃tisipa'sjɔ̃], *n.f.* anticipation; encroachment, trespass; *par anticipation*, in advance, beforehand.
anticipé [ɑ̃tisi'pe], *a.* done *or* occurring in advance.
anticiper [ɑ̃tisi'pe], *v.t.* to anticipate, to forestall.—*v.i.* to encroach *or* trespass (*sur*).
anticlimax [ɑ̃tikli'maks], *n.m.* anticlimax.
anticommunisme [ɑ̃tikɔmy'nism], *n.m.* anti-communism.
anticonstitutionnellement [ɑ̃tikɔ̃stitysjɔnɛl'mɑ̃], *adv.* (*the longest French word*) anticonstitutionally.
anticorps [ɑ̃ti'kɔ:r], *n.m.* (*Med.*) anti-body.
anticyclone [ɑ̃tisi'klɔ:n], *n.m.* (*Meteor.*) anticyclone.
antidate [ɑ̃ti'dat], *n.f.* antedate.
antidater [ɑ̃tida'te], *v.t.* to antedate.
antidérapant [ɑ̃tidera'pɑ̃], *a.* non-skidding; *pneu antidérapant*, non-skid tyre.
antidote [ɑ̃ti'dɔt], *n.m.* antidote, antitoxin; (*fig.*) cure.
anti-éblouissant [ɑ̃tieblui'sɑ̃], *a.* (*Motor.*) antidazzle.
antienne [ɑ̃'tjen], *n.f.* antiphon; anthem.
antigel [ɑ̃ti'ʒel], *n.m. inv.* anti-freeze.
antillais [ɑ̃ti'je], *a.* West Indian.—*n.m.* (**Antillais**, *fem.* **-aise**) West Indian (*person*).
Antilles [ɑ̃'ti:j], **les**, *f.pl.* the West Indies; *la mer des Antilles*, the Caribbean Sea.
antilope [ɑ̃ti'lɔp], *n.f.* antelope.
anti-mite [ɑ̃ti'mit], *a.* moth-proof.
antimoine [ɑ̃ti'mwan], *n.m.* antimony.
Antioche [ɑ̃'tjɔʃ], *f.* Antioch.
antiparasite [ɑ̃tipara'zit], *n.m.* suppressor.
antiparlementaire [ɑ̃tiparləmɑ̃'tɛ:r], *a.* unparliamentary.
antipathie [ɑ̃tipa'ti], *n.f.* antipathy, aversion.
antipathique [ɑ̃tipa'tik], *a.* antipathetic, repugnant.
antiphonaire [ɑ̃tifɔ'nɛ:r], *n.m.* antiphonal.
antipode [ɑ̃ti'pɔd], *n.m.* the region of the globe diametrically opposite; (*pl.*) antipodes.
antiputride [ɑ̃tipy'trid], *a.* and *n.m.* antiseptic.
antiquaire [ɑ̃ti'kɛ:r], *n.m.* antiquary, antiquarian, antique-dealer.
antique [ɑ̃'tik], *a.* antique, ancient; old-fashioned.—*n.f.* antique, ancient work of art.
antiquité [ɑ̃tiki'te], *n.f.* antiquity; old times; (*pl.*) antiquities; *magasin d'antiquités*, old curiosity shop.
antirouille [ɑ̃ti'ru:j], *n.m.* rust preventive.

antirrhine [ɑ̃ti'rin], *n.f.* (*Bot.*) antirrhinum, snapdragon.
antisémite [ɑ̃tise'mit], *n.* anti-Semite.
antisémitique [ɑ̃tisemi'tik], *a.* anti-Semitic.
antisemitisme [ɑ̃tisemi'tism], *n.m.* anti-Semitism.
antiseptique [ɑ̃tisɛp'tik], *a.* and *n.m.* (*Med.*) antiseptic.
antisocial [ɑ̃tisɔ'sjal], *a.* (*m. pl.* -aux) anti-social.
antisportif [ɑ̃tispɔr'tif], *a.* (*fem.* -ive) unsportsmanlike; opposed to sports.
antithèse [ɑ̃ti'tɛːz], *n.f.* antithesis.
antitoxine [ɑ̃titɔk'sin], *n.f.* (*Med.*) antitoxin.
anti-vol [ɑ̃ti'vɔl], *a. inv.* anti-theft.—*n.m.* burglar-proof device.
antivivisection [ɑ̃tivivisɛk'sjɔ̃], *n.f.* antivivisection.
Antoine [ɑ̃'twan], *m.* Anthony.
antre [ɑ̃ːtr], *n.m.* den, lair; cavern.
anuiter (s') [sanɥi'te], *v.r.* to be benighted.
anus [a'nyːs], *n.m.* anus.
Anvers [ɑ̃'vɛr], *m.* Antwerp.
anxiété [ɑ̃ksje'te], *n.f.* anxiety; uneasiness; (*Med.*) pain in the heart.
anxieusement [ɑ̃ksjøz'mɑ̃], *adv.* anxiously.
anxieux [ɑ̃k'sjø], *a.* (*fem.* -euse) anxious, uneasy, restless.
aorte [a'ɔrt], *n.f.* (*Anat.*) aorta.
août [u(t)], *n.m.* August; (*fig.*) harvest; *la mi-août*, the middle of August.
aoûté [u'te], *a.* ripened by the heat of August.
aoûter (s') [su'te], *v.r.* to ripen (*in August*).
apache [a'paʃ], *n.m.* ruffian of the Paris streets, hooligan.
apaisement [apɛz'mɑ̃], *n.m.* appeasement; abatement, lull.
apaiser [apɛ'ze], *v.t.* to pacify, to calm, to appease; to quiet; to mitigate, to alleviate (*pain, sorrow etc.*); to stay (*hunger*); to quench (*thirst*). **s'apaiser**, *v.r.* to be appeased; to sober down; to grow quiet; to abate, to subside.
Apalaches [apa'laʃ], *m.pl.* Appalachians.
(C) apalachien [apala'ʃjɛ̃], *a.* (*fem.* -chienne) Appalachian.
apanage [apa'naːʒ], *n.m.* apanage; (*fig.*) lot.
apanager [apana'ʒe], *v.t.* (*conjug. like* MANGER) to endow.
aparté [apar'te], *n.m.* aside.
apathie [apa'ti], *n.f.* apathy, indolence, listlessness.
apathique [apa'tik], *a.* apathetic, listless.
apatride [apa'trid], *a.* and *n.* stateless (person).
Apennins [apɛ'nɛ̃], *les, m.pl.* the Apennines.
apepsie [apɛp'si], *n.f.* (*Path.*) apepsy, indigestion.
apeptique [apɛp'tik], *a.* dyspeptic.
apercevable [apɛrsə'vabl], *a.* perceivable, perceptible.
apercevoir [apɛrsə'vwaːr], *v.t.* (*conjug. like* RECEVOIR) to catch sight of, to notice; to perceive, to understand, to comprehend. **s'apercevoir**, *v.r.* (*de quelque chose*) to remark, to notice, to be aware of; to find out, to discover; to be visible.
aperçu [apɛr'sy], *n.m.* rapid view, glance or survey; rough estimate or summary; judgment, idea.
apéritif [aperi'tif], *a.* (*fem.* -ive) aperient, appetizing.—*n.m.* (*Med.*) aperient, laxative; appetizer, aperitif (*e.g. vermouth, bitters*).

à peu près [apø'prɛ], *n.m.* approximation, approach; a word roughly standing for another.—*adv.* nearly, about.
apeuré [apø're], *a.* frightened, scared.
apex [a'pɛks], *n.m.* apex.
aphélie [afe'li], *n.m.* (*Astron.*) aphelion.
aphidé [afi'de], **aphidien** [afi'djɛ̃], *n.m.* (*Ent.*) aphis, greenfly.
aphone [a'fɔn], *a.* voiceless.
aphonie [afɔ'ni], *n.f.* aphony, loss of voice.
aphorisme [afɔ'rism], *n.m.* aphorism.
à-pic [a'pik], *n.m.* steep hill, cliff.
apiculteur [apikyl'tœːr], *n.m.* bee-keeper.
apiculture [apikyl'tyːr], *n.f.* apiculture, bee-keeping.
apitoiement [apitwa'mɑ̃], *n.m.* pity compassion.
apitoyant [apitwa'jɑ̃], *a.* piteous.
apitoyer [apitwa'je], *v.t.* (*conjug. like* EMPLOYER) to move to pity, to soften. **s'apitoyer**, *v.r.* to pity.
aplanir [apla'niːr], *v.t.* to smooth, to level, to make even; (*fig.*) to level down or remove (*obstacles, difficulties etc.*). **s'aplanir**, *v.r.* to grow easy, smooth etc.
aplanissement [aplanis'mɑ̃], *n.m.* smoothing levelling, making even; smoothness, evenness.
aplat [a'pla], *n.m.* flat tint.
aplatir [apla'tiːr], *v.t.* to flatten, to beat flat; (*fig.*) to vanquish, to silence, to floor. **s'aplatir**, *v.r.* to become flat, to be flattened; (*fig.*) to crouch, to cringe.
aplatissement [aplatis'mɑ̃], **aplatissage** [aplati'saːʒ], *n.m.* flattening, flatness; (*fig.*) humiliation.
aplomb [a'plɔ̃], *n.m.* perpendicularity; equilibrium; (*fig.*) assurance, self-possession, steadiness, coolness; impudence, cheek; *d'aplomb*, perpendicularly, upright.
apocalypse [apɔka'lips], *n.f.* Apocalypse, the Book of Revelation.
apocalyptique [apɔkalip'tik], *a.* apocalyptic, obscure.
apocryphe [apɔ'krif], *a.* apocryphal, spurious.
apode [a'pɔd], *a.* (*Zool.*) apodal, footless.
apogée [apɔ'ʒe], *n.m.* apogee; (*fig.*) acme, height, zenith.
apologétique [apɔlɔʒe'tik], *a.* by way of apology, apologetic.
apologie [apɔlɔ'ʒi], *n.f.* apology, vindication, justification.
apologue [apɔ'lɔg], *n.m.* apologue, fable.
apoplectique [apɔplɛk'tik], *a.* and *n.* apoplectic.
apoplexie [apɔplɛk'si], *n.f.* apoplexy.
apostasie [apɔsta'zi], *n.f.* apostasy.
apostat [apɔs'ta], *a.* and *n.m.* (*fem.* -e) apostate.
aposter [apɔs'te], *v.t.* to place in ambush, to station.
apostille [apɔs'tiːj], *n.f.* marginal note, postscript, footnote.
apostiller [apɔsti'je], *v.t.* to add a postscript or marginal recommendation.
apostolat [apɔstɔ'la], *n.m.* apostleship.
apostolique [apɔstɔ'lik], *a.* apostolic; papal.
apostrophe [apɔs'trɔf], *n.f.* (*Rhet. and Gram.*) apostrophe; address; (*fig.*) reprimand, attack.

21

apostropher [apɔstrɔ'fe], *v.t.* to apostrophize, to address; (*fig.*) to reprimand.
apothéose [apɔte'o:z], *n.f.* apotheosis.
apothicaire [apɔti'kɛːr], *n.m.* apothecary.
apôtre [a'poːtr], *n.m.* apostle; (*fig.*) leader of a cause.
apparaître [apa'rɛːtr], *v.i. irr.* (*conjug. like* CONNAÎTRE) to appear, to become visible; to be evident.
apparat [apa'ra], *n.m.* pomp, show, ostentation, parade.
apparaux [apa'ro], *n.m.* (*used only in pl.*) (*Naut.*) gear, tackle, outfit etc.
appareil [apa'rɛːj], *n.m.* formal preparation; pomp, display; appearance, show; apparatus, appliances, machinery, paraphernalia; (*Surg.*) dressing; *appareil (photographique)*, camera; *qui est à l'appareil?* who is speaking?
appareillage [aparɛ'jaːʒ], *n.m.* installation; (*Naut.*) act of getting under sail, weighing.
appareillement [aparɛj'mã], *n.m.* coupling, yoking; pairing (*for breeding*).
appareiller [aparɛ'je], *v.t.* to install equipment; to match; to pair (*animals*).—*v.i.* to get under way, to weigh anchor. **s'appareiller**, *v.r.* to pair (*of birds*).
appareilleur [aparɛ'jœːr], *n.m.* (*Building*) stone dresser; *appareilleur à gaz*, gasfitter.
apparemment [apara'mã], *adv.* apparently.
apparence [apa'rãːs], *n.f.* appearance, look, semblance, likelihood, probability; *en apparence*, seemingly, apparently.
apparent [apa'rã], *a.* visible, prominent.
apparenté [aparã'te], *a.* related; *bien apparenté*, well connected.
apparentement [aparãt'mã], *n.m.* political alliance.
apparenter [aparã'te], *v.t.* to ally, to connect by marriage. **s'apparenter**, *v.r.* to ally oneself (*by marriage*).
appariement or **apparîment** [apari'mã], *n.m.* pairing, matching; coupling, mating; *appariement d'écoles*, school linking.
apparier [apa'rje], *v.t.* to assort by pairs, to pair (*birds etc.*), to match (*horses, gloves etc.*).
apparition [apari'sjõ], *n.f.* apparition, sudden appearance; phantom, ghost; *apparition d'anges*, vision of angels.
appartement [apartə'mã], *n.m.* suite of rooms, flat.
appartenances [apartə'nãːs], *n.f.* (*used in pl.*) appurtenances.
appartenant [apartə'nã], *a.* belonging, appertaining.
appartenir [apartə'niːr], *v.i. irr.* (*conjug. like* TENIR) to belong, to appertain; to relate to, pertain, to concern; to behove, to be the right, privilege, duty etc. of (*à*); *il appartient*, (*v. impers.*) it is meet *or* fit; it behoves, it concerns. **s'appartenir**, *v.r.* to be master of one's own actions, to be free.
appas [a'pɑ], *n.m. pl.* feminine charms, attractions.
appât [a'pɑ], *n.m.* bait; lure, allurement, enticement.
appâter [apa'te] *v.t.* to attract with a bait, to allure; to fatten (*fowls etc.*).
appauvrir [apo'vriːr], *v.t.* to impoverish. **s'appauvrir**, *v.r.* to grow poor, to become impoverished.

appauvrissement [apovris'mã], *n.m.* impoverishment.
appel [a'pɛl], *n.m.* appeal, call, summons; (*Mil.*) roll-call, muster; summoning of conscripts to the colours; (*Law*) appeal to a higher court; *battre* or *sonner l'appel*, (*Mil.*) to sound the fall-in.
appelé [ap'le], *a.* called up.—*n.m.* soldier called up for service.
appeler [ap'le], *v.t.* (*see Verb Tables*) to call, to send for; to call over; to call up, to call together; to summon, to cite, to invoke, to call upon, to invite; to name, to term; to challenge.—*v.i.* to appeal (*to a higher court*). **s'appeler**, *v.r.* to be called, to call oneself.
appellation [apɛla'sjõ], *n.f.* calling; appellation; trade name; *appellation contrôlée*, registered trade-name.
appendice [apã'dis], *n.m.* appendix, appendage, addition.
appendicite [apãdi'sit], *n.f.* (*Path.*) appendicitis.
appendre [a'pãːdr], *v.t.* to hang up, to suspend; to attach.
appentis [apã'ti], *n.m.* shed, lean-to.
appesantir [apəzã'tiːr], *v.t.* to make heavy, to weigh down; (*fig.*) to make dull. **s'appesantir**, *v.r.* to grow heavy and dull, to be weighed down; to dwell on, to expatiate (*sur*).
appesantissement [apəzãtis'mã], *n.m.* heaviness, dullness.
appétissant [apeti'sã], *a.* desirable, appetizing, tempting; dainty, delicious.
appétit [ape'ti], *n.m.* appetite, relish; desire sensuous craving (*usu. in pl.*); appetite (*for food*); (*fig.*) inclination, taste, stomach.
applaudir [aplo'diːr], *v.t.*, *v.i.* to clap the hands, to applaud; to praise, to commend, to approve. **s'applaudir**, *v.r.* to boast, to glory (*in a thing*); to congratulate oneself (*de*); to rejoice (*de*).
applaudissement [aplodis'mã], *n.m.* (*usually pl.*) applause, public praise; cheering.
applicabilité [aplikabili'te], *n.f.* applicability, appositeness.
applicable [apli'kabl], *a.* applicable, apposite, relevant, suitable.
application [aplika'sjõ], *n.f.* application, applying; employment (*of a sum of money*); infliction (*of a penalty*); attention, care, diligence; appliqué lace.
applique [a'plik], *n.f.* ornamental accessories, candelabrum *or* bracket fixed to a wall.
appliqué [apli'ke], *a.* studious; *sciences appliquées*, applied sciences.
appliquer [apli'ke], *v.t.* to apply (*à*), to stick; to apply (*one's mind*); to adapt, to employ; to inflict, to impose (*a penalty etc.*). **s'appliquer**, *v.r.* to apply oneself, to work hard.
appoint [a'pwɛ̃], *n.m.* money paying off an account, balance; change; contribution; *faire l'appoint*, to pay the exact sum.
appointé [apwɛ̃'te], *a.* receiving a salary.
appointement [apwɛ̃t'mã], *n.m.* (*pl.*) salary (*of employee*); emoluments; (*Eccles.*) stipend.
appointer (1) [apwɛ̃'te], *v.t.* to give a salary to.
appointer (2) [apwɛ̃'te], *v.t.* to sharpen to a point, to point.
appontement [apõt'mã], *n.m.* (*Naut.*) bridge-

like structure for loading vessels; (*wooden*) wharf *or* pier.

apport [a'pɔːr], *n.m.* property brought by a husband or wife into the common stock; a shareholder's contribution to the assets of a company.

apporter [apɔr'te], *v.t.* to bring; to furnish, to supply; to bring to bear, to employ (*trouble, pains etc.*); to cause, to produce, to bring about.

apposer [apo'ze], *v.t.* to set, to put, to affix; to insert (*a clause etc.*).

apposition [apozi'sjɔ̃], *n.f.* setting, putting, affixing; (*Gram.*) apposition.

appréciable [apre'sjabl], *a.* appreciable, perceptible.

appréciateur [apresja'tœːr], *n.m.* (*fem.* -trice) valuer.

appréciatif [apresja'tif], *a.* (*fem.* -ive) denoting the value of; *état* or *devis appréciatif,* estimate.

appréciation [apresja'sjɔ̃], *n.f.* appreciation, valuation, estimation; rise in value.

apprécier [apre'sje], *v.t.* to value, to estimate, to appraise, to judge; to appreciate, to esteem.

appréhender [apreɑ̃'de], *v.t.* to arrest, to apprehend; to be apprehensive of, to fear, to dread.

appréhensible [apreɑ̃'sibl], *a.* apprehensible, comprehensible.

appréhensif [apreɑ̃'sif], *a.* (*fem.* -ive) apprehensive, timid.

appréhension [apreɑ̃'sjɔ̃], *n.f.* apprehension, fear, dread.

apprendre [a'prɑ̃ːdr], *v.t. irr.* (*conjug. like* PRENDRE) to learn; to hear of, to be informed of; to acquire (*a habit etc.*); to tell, to inform; to teach, to impart knowledge of (*a subject*).

apprenti [aprɑ̃'ti], *a.* apprenticed, articled.—*n.m.* (*fem.* -e) apprentice; (*fig.*) novice.

apprentissage [aprɑ̃ti'saːʒ], *n.m.* apprenticeship; trial, experiment.

apprêt [a'prɛ], *n.m.* preparation; cooking, dressing (*of food*); manner of preparing cloth, silk, lace etc.; the substance used in this process; (*pl.*) preparations.

apprêtage [aprɛ'taːʒ], *n.m.* dressing, application of the preliminary preparation to cloth, silk etc.

apprêté [aprɛ'te], *a.* studied, affected, stiff.

apprêter [aprɛ'te], *v.t.* to prepare, to get ready; to dress, to cook; to apply the *apprêts* [*q.v.*] to. **s'apprêter,** *v.r.* to prepare oneself, to get ready (*à*).

apprêteur [aprɛ'tœːr], *a.* and *n.m.* (*fem.* -euse) dresser, finisher.—*n.f.* (-euse) hat-trimmer.

apprivoisé [aprivwa'ze], *a.* tame.

apprivoisement [aprivwaz'mɑ̃], *n.m.* taming.

apprivoiser [aprivwa'ze], *v.t.* to tame (*animals*); to win (*people*) over, to make sociable *or* tractable.

apprivoiseur [aprivwa'zœːr], *n.m.* (*fem.* -euse) tamer.

approbateur [aprɔba'tœːr], *a.* (*fem.* -trice) approving.

approbatif [aprɔba'tif], *a.* (*fem.* -tive) approbatory; *geste approbatif,* nod of approbation *or* approval.

approbation [aprɔba'sjɔ̃], *n.f.* approbation, consent, approval.

approbativement [aprɔbativ'mɑ̃], *adv.* approvingly.

approchable [aprɔ'ʃabl], *a.* approachable, easy of access.

approchant [aprɔ'ʃɑ̃], *a.* like, much the same, something like, approximate, bordering on.

approche [a'prɔʃ], *n.f.* approach, coming, advance, nearness; (*pl.*) approaches, access.

approcher [aprɔ'ʃe], *v.t.* to bring, put *or* draw near *or* nearer; to come near *or* nearer; to approach.—*v.i.* to approach, to draw near, to come near; to be something like, to be nearly. **s'approcher,** *v.r.* to approach, to advance.

approfondir [aprɔfɔ̃'diːr], *v.t.* to deepen, to make deeper; to examine thoroughly, to investigate. **s'approfondir,** *v.r.* to become deeper.

approfondissement [aprɔfɔ̃dis'mɑ̃], *n.m.* deepening; fathoming; thorough investigation.

appropriation [aprɔpria'sjɔ̃], *n.f.* adaptation, assimilation; appropriation.

approprier [aprɔpri'e], *v.t.* to make appropriate, to accommodate, to adapt; to clean, to tidy etc.; to suit, to fit, (*style to subject etc.*). **s'approprier,** *v.r.* to appropriate a thing to oneself; to conform, to adapt oneself.

approuver [apru've], *v.t.* to sanction, to consent to, to ratify, to authorize; to approve, to approve of; to pass (*accounts*).

approvisionnement [aprɔvizjɔn'mɑ̃], *n.m.* victualling, supply, stock.

approvisionner [aprɔvizjɔ'ne], *v.t.* to supply with necessaries, to victual, to stock. **s'approvisionner,** *v.r.* to supply oneself; to lay in supplies.

approvisionneur [aprɔvizjɔ'nœːr], *n.m.* (*fem.* -euse) caterer, purveyor.

approximatif [aprɔksima'tif], *a.* (*fem.* -tive) approximate.

approximation [aprɔksima'sjɔ̃], *n.f.* approximation, rough estimate.

approximativement [aprɔksimativ'mɑ̃], *adv.* approximately.

appui [a'pɥi], *n.m.* support, prop, stay; any kind of mechanical support, *as* buttress, rail, handrail, sill (*of windows*); (*Mech.*) fulcrum; (*fig.*) corroboration; (*Gram.*) stress.

appui-main [apɥi'mɛ̃], *n.m.* (*pl.* **appuis-main**) painter's maulstick *or* hand-rest.

appuyer [apɥi'je], *v.t.* (*conjug. like* EMPLOYER) to prop up, to support; to lean (*something against a wall etc.*); (*fig.*) to second, to back up, to uphold, to stand by, to reinforce.—*v.i.* to weigh upon, to lay stress (*sur*); (*fig.*) to insist; *appuyer à droite,* to bear to the right. **s'appuyer,** *v.r.* to lean, to rest (*sur*); to rely upon, to depend (*sur*); to lay stress *or* a stress on, to dwell (*sur*).

âpre [ɑːpr], *a.* hard, rough, harsh, rugged; sharp, tart, sour; bitter, biting, bleak, raw; grating (*of sound*); (*fig.*) austere; crabbed; violent, eager (*in pursuit of something*); *âpre à la curée,* out for the kill (*of animals*); (*fig.*) on the make (*of persons*).

âprement [ɑːprə'mɑ̃], *adv.* harshly, roughly; peevishly, crabbedly; violently, eagerly.

après [a'prɛ], *prep.* after, behind (*in time, order etc.*); next to; in pursuit of; **d'après**, after, according to.—*adv.* afterwards, later; **et après?** (*ellipt.*) what next? what then? so what?—*conj.* **après que**, after, when.

après-demain [aprɛd'mɛ̃], *adv.* the day after tomorrow.

après-midi [apremi'di], *n.m. or f. inv.* afternoon.

âpreté [ɑprə'te], *n.f.* harshness, tartness, sharpness; roughness, ruggedness; (*fig.*) acrimony, asperity; eagerness; keenness; greediness.

à-propos [apro'po], *n.m.* aptness, suitability.

apside [ap'sid], *n.f.* (*Astron.*) apsis.

apte [apt], *a.* apt, fit, proper, suitable.

aptitude [apti'tyd], *n.f.* aptitude, natural disposition *or* capacity (*for*).

apurement [apyr'mɑ̃], *n.m.* verification *or* audit (*of accounts*).

apurer [apy're], *v.t.* to verify, to audit.

aquaplane [akwa'plan], *n.f.* surf-board; **faire de l'aquaplane**, to go surf-riding.

aquarelle [akwa'rɛl], *n.f.* painting in water-colours, aquarelle.

aquarelliste [akwarɛ'list], *n.m.* painter in water-colours.

aquarium [akwa'rjɔm], *n.m.* aquarium.

aquatique [akwa'tik], *a.* aquatic.

aqueduc [akə'dyk], *n.m.* aqueduct, conduit; (*Anat.*) duct.

aqueux [a'kø], *a.* (*fem.* **-euse**) aqueous, watery.

aquilin [aki'lɛ̃], *a.* aquiline, curved, hooked, Roman (*of noses etc.*).

aquilon [aki'lɔ̃], *n.m.* north wind, cold blast.

ara [a'ra], *n.m.* (*Orn.*) ara, macaw.

arabe [a'rab], *a.* Arabic, Arabian.—*n.m.* Arabic (*language*).—*n.* (**Arabe**) Arab, Arabian.

arabesque [ara'bɛsk], *n.f.* arabesque.

Arabie [ara'bi], **l'**, *f.* Arabia; **Arabie Séoudite**, Saudi Arabia.

arabique [ara'bik], *a.* Arabic, Arabian; **gomme arabique**, gum arabic.

arable [a'rabl], *a.* arable, tillable.

arachide [ara'ʃid], *n.f.* pea-nut, ground-nut.

araignée [arɛ'ne], *n.f.* spider; a spider-like implement etc.; (*Mil.*) a series of branching galleries in a mine; (*Naut.*) crowfoot; **toile d'araignée**, cobweb.

arasement [araz'mɑ̃], *n.m.* levelling, making even.

araser [arɑ'ze], *v.t.* to level (*a wall, a building etc.*).

aratoire [ara'twaːr], *a.* pertaining to farming.

arbalète [arba'lɛt], *n.f.* arbalest, cross-bow.

arbalétrier [arbale'trje], *n.m.* cross-bowman; (*Carp.*) principal rafters of a roof; strut (*of plane*); (*Orn.*) (black) swift.

arbitrage [arbi'traːʒ], *n.m.* arbitration; (*Banking*) arbitrage.

arbitraire [arbi'trɛːr], *a.* arbitrary; absolute, despotic.

arbitrairement [arbitrɛr'mɑ̃], *adv.* arbitrarily; despotically.

arbitral [arbi'tral], *a.* (*m. pl.* **-aux**) by arbitration; composed of arbitrators (*of a tribunal etc.*).

arbitralement [arbitral'mɑ̃], *adv.* by arbitration.

arbitre [ar'bitr], *n.m.* arbitrator, umpire, referee; arbiter, disposer; will.

arbitrer [arbi'tre], *v.t.* to arbitrate, to judge, to settle (*a dispute etc.*), to referee *or* umpire (*a match*).

arborer [arbo're], *v.t.* to put up, to hoist, to unfurl (*a flag or as a flag*); (*fig.*) to put on.

arbre [arbr], *n.m.* tree; (*fig.*) anything resembling this (*e.g. a genealogical tree*); (*Mach.*) arbor, shaft, spindle, axle-tree; (*Naut.*) mast; (*Motor.*) **arbre moteur**, mainshaft; **arbre coudé**, crankshaft.

arbrisseau [arbri'so], *n.m.* (*pl.* **-eaux**) shrubby tree.

arbuste [ar'byst], *n.m.* bush, shrub.

arc [ark], *n.m.* bow, long-bow; (*Arch.*) arch; (*Geom., Phys. etc.*) arc.

arcade [ar'kad], *n.f.* arch-shaped opening; (*pl.*) arcade.

arcanes [ar'kan], *n.m. pl.* secrets, mysteries.

arc-boutant [arkbu'tɑ̃], *n.m.* (*pl.* **arcs-boutants**) (*fig.*) buttress, arched flying buttress; supporter, pillar.

arc-bouter [arkbu'te], *v.t.* to strengthen by a flying buttress; (*fig.*) to support, to buttress.

arceau [ar'so], *n.m.* (*pl.* **-eaux**) curved part of a vault *or* arch; anything shaped like an arch; (*croquet*) hoop.

arc-en-ciel [arkɑ̃'sjɛl], *n.m.* (*pl.* **arcs-en-ciel**) rainbow.

archaïque [arka'ik], *a.* archaic.

archaïsme [arka'ism], *n.m.* archaism, obsolete word etc.

archange [ar'kɑ̃ːʒ], *n.m.* archangel.

arche (I) [arʃ], *n.f.* arch (*of a bridge*).

arche (2) [arʃ], *n.f.* ark; **l'arche de Noé**, Noah's ark.

archéologie [arkeɔlɔ'ʒi], *n.f.* archaeology.

archéologique [arkeɔlɔ'ʒik], *a.* archaeological.

archéologue [arkeɔ'lɔg], *n.m.* archaeologist.

archer [ar'ʃe], *n.m.* archer, bowman.

archet [ar'ʃɛ], *n.m.* (*Mus.*) bow, fiddle-stick.

archevêché [arʃəve'ʃe], *n.m.* archbishopric; archiepiscopal diocese; archbishop's residence.

archevêque [arʃə'vɛk], *n.m.* archbishop.

archi- [ar'ʃi *or* ar'ki], *pref.* arch-, archi-, chief; extremely *as in* **archiriche** etc.

archidiacre [arʃi'djakr], *n.m.* archdeacon.

archiduc [arʃi'dyk], *n.m.* archduke.

archiduché [arʃidy'ʃe], *n.m.* archdukedom, archduchy.

archiduchesse [arʃidy'ʃɛs], *n.f.* archduchess.

archiépiscopal [arkiepiskɔ'pal], *a.* (*m. pl.* **-aux**) archiepiscopal.

archière [ar'ʃjɛːr], *n.f.* loophole.

Archimède [arʃi'mɛd], *m.* Archimedes.

archipel [arʃi'pɛl], *n.m.* archipelago.

archiprêtre [arʃi'prɛːtr], *n.ɯ.* arch-priest, high-priest.

architecte [arʃi'tɛkt], *n.m.* architect; **architecte paysagiste**, landscape-gardener.

architectural [arʃitɛkty'ral], *a.* (*m.pl.* **-aux**) architectural.

architecture [arʃitɛk'tyːr], *n.f.* architecture.

architrave [arʃi'traːv], *n.f.* (*Arch.*) architrave.

archives [ar'ʃiːv], *n.f.* (*used only in pl.*) archives; state, civic *or* family records; record-office, muniment-room.

archiviste [arʃi'vist], *n.m.* archivist, keeper of records, registrar; filing clerk.

arçon [ar'sõ], *n.m.* saddle-bow; bow-shaped tool used by hat-makers etc.

arcot [ar'ko], *n.m.* dross, slag.

arctique [ark'tik], *a.* Arctic.

ardemment [arda'mã], *adv.* ardently.

ardent [ar'dã], *a.* burning, hot, fiery, scorching; (*fig.*) violent, intense; ardent, vehement, fervent, earnest, energetic, active; red, reddish (*of hair*); *charbons ardents,* live coals; *buisson ardent,* the burning bush.

ardeur [ar'dœːr], *n.f.* intense heat; ardour, intense activity, fervour, earnestness; fire, spirit, mettle.

ardoise [ar'dwaːz], *n.f.* slate; (*colloq.*) score, account.

ardoisé [ardwa'ze], *a.* slate-coloured.

ardoiser [ardwa'ze], *v.t.* to cover (*a roof*) with slates.

ardoisier [ardwa'zje], *n.m.* owner of or workman in a slate-quarry.

ardoisière [ardwa'zjɛːr], *n.f.* slate-quarry.

ardu [ar'dy], *a.* steep, abrupt; (*fig.*) arduous, difficult.

are [aːr], *n.m.* 100 sq. metres (*approx. 120 sq. yds.*).

arène [a'rɛːn], *n.f.* (*poet.*) sand; arena; (*fig.*) cock-pit, battle-ground, theatre, scene; (*pl.*) the ancient Roman amphitheatres.

arénière [are'njɛːr], *n.f.* sand-pit.

aréomètre [areo'mɛtr], *n.m.* areometer, hydrometer.

aréopage [areo'paːʒ], *n.m.* areopagus.

arête [a'rɛːt], *n.f.* fish-bone; awn *or* beard of wheat etc.; (*Geog. etc.*) ridge; *arête du nez,* bridge of the nose.

argent [ar'ʒã], *n.m.* silver; silver money; money, cash; (*fig.*) wealth, riches; (*Her.*) argent; *argent doré,* silver-gilt; *vif-argent,* quick-silver; *argent comptant,* ready money.

argentage [ARGENTURE].

argenté [arʒã'te], *a.* plated, silvered over; silvery.

argenter [arʒã'te], *v.t.* to silver over, to plate; to give the appearance of silver to.

argenterie [arʒã'tri], *n.f.* plate, silver-plate.

argentin [arʒã'tɛ̃], *a.* silvery, argentine (*tint*); silver-toned (*ringing*); Argentinian, Argentine.—*n.m.* (**Argentin,** *fem.* **-ine** (1)) Argentinian (*person*).

Argentine (2) [arʒã'tin], l', *f.* Argentina, the Argentine.

argenture [arʒã'tyːr], *n.f.,* **argentage** [arʒã'taːʒ], *n.m.* silvering, silver-plating.

argile [ar'ʒil], *n.f.* clay, potter's clay, argil; *argile à porcelaine,* china-clay; *argile réfractaire,* fire-clay.

argileux [arʒi'lø], *a.* (*fem.* **-euse**) clayey, clayish.

argilière [arʒi'ljɛːr], *n.f.* clay-pit.

argon [ar'gõ], *n.m.* (*Chem.*) argon.

argonaute [argo'noːt], *n.m.* argonaut, nautilus.

argot [ar'go], *n.m.* slang, cant.

arguer [ar'gɥe], *v.t.* to infer, to deduce, to argue.

argument [argy'mã], *n.m.* argument, reasoning; proof, evidence; summary; theme, subject.

argumentateur [argymãta'tœːr], *n.m.* (*fem.* **-trice**) habitual arguer *or* disputer.

argumentation, [argymãta'sjõ], *n.f.* argumentation, reasoning.

argumenter [argymã'te], *v.i.* to argue; to quibble.

argutie [argy'si], *n.f.* quibble, hair-splitting, cavil.

aria [a'rja], *n.m.* (*Mus.*) aria; (*pop.*) nuisance; fuss, bother.

arianisme [arja'nism], *n.m.* Arianism.

aride [a'rid], *a.* arid, dry; sterile.

aridité [aridi'te], *n.f.* aridity, dryness, barrenness, sterility.

arien [a'rjɛ̃] *a.* (*fem.* **arienne**) Arian.—*n.m.* (**Arien,** *fem.* **Arienne**) Arian (*person*).

aristocrate [aristo'krat], *a.* aristocratic.—*n.* aristocrat.

aristocratie [aristokra'si], *n.f.* aristocracy.

aristocratique [aristokra'tik], *a.* aristocratic.

aristocratiquement [aristokratik'mã], *adv.* aristocratically.

Aristote [aris'tot], *m.* Aristotle.

arithmétique [aritme'tik], *n.f.* arithmetic.— *a.* arithmetical.

arithmétiquement [aritmetik'mã], *adv.* arithmetically.

arlequin [arlə'kɛ̃], *n.m.* harlequin; (*fig.*) turn-coat; weathercock; *habit d'arlequin,* patchwork, motley.

arlequinade [arləki'nad], *n.f.* harlequinade.

armagnac [arma'nak], *n.m.* brandy (*made in Armagnac, S. of France*).

armateur [arma'tœːr], *n.m.* shipowner; captain of a privateer; privateer.

armature [arma'tyːr], *n.f.* armature, iron braces, stays, casing, gear etc.

arme [arm], *n.f.* arm, weapon; branch *or* arm (*of the service*); (*Her.*) armorial bearings; *arme blanche,* cold steel; *aux armes!* to arms! *un maître d'armes,* a fencing-master.

armé [ar'me], *a.* armed, equipped; (*Her.*) armed (*with claws, horns, teeth etc.*); *béton armé,* reinforced concrete.

armée [ar'me], *n.f.* army; forces, troops, host; (*fig.*) body (*of officials etc.*); *l'Armée du Salut,* the Salvation Army.

armement [armə'mã], *n.m.* arming, raising of forces, warlike preparations; armament, equipment; (*Am.*) ordnance.

Arménie [arme'ni], l', *f.* Armenia.

arménien [arme'njɛ̃], *a.* (*fem.* **-enne**) Armenian.—*n.m.* Armenian (*language*); (**Arménien,** *fem.* **-enne**) Armenian (*person*).

armer [ar'me], *v.t.* to equip, to arm; (*Artill.*) to load, to mount (*guns etc.*); to cock (*a gun etc.*); (*fig.*) to fortify; to strengthen; (*Naut.*) to fit out. **s'armer,** *v.r.* to arm oneself, to take up arms; to protect oneself (*against something*).

armistice [armis'tis], *n.m.* armistice.

armoire [ar'mwaːr], *n.f.* closet, cupboard; clothes-press, wardrobe.

armoiries [armwa'ri], *n.f.* (*used only in pl.*) arms, armorial bearings.

armorial [armo'rjal], *a.* (*m. pl.* **-aux**) armorial, pertaining to heraldry.—*n.m.* armorial, book of heraldry.

armoricain [armori'kɛ̃], *a.* Armorican (*of Brittany*).

armorier [armo'rje], *v.t.* to put *or* paint a coat of arms upon, to blazon.

Armorique

Armorique [armɔ'rik], **l'**, *f.* Armorica.
armoriste [armɔ'rist], *n.m.* armorist, heraldic engraver.
armure [ar'myːr], *n.f.* armour, arms and armour; casing, wrapper; armature (*of a magnet, dynamo etc.*); (*Agric.*) tree-guard; (*Naut.*) fish (*of a mast, yard etc.*); (*fig.*) defence, protection.
armurerie [armyrə'ri], *n.f.* armoury; manufacture of arms; arms factory.
armurier [army'rje], *n.m.* armourer, gunsmith.
arnica [arni'ka], *n.m.* (*Bot.*) arnica.
aromatique [arɔma'tik], *a.* aromatic, fragrant, spicy.
aromatiser [arɔmati'ze], *v.t.* to aromatize, to perfume, to flavour.
arome [a'roːm], *n.m.* aroma, perfume, scent.
aronde [a'rɔ̃ːd], *n.f.* (*Carp.*) dove-tail, tenon.
arpège [ar'pɛːʒ], *n.m.* arpeggio.
arpéger [arpe'ʒe], *v.i.* (*conjug. like* ASSIÉGER) to play arpeggios.
arpent [ar'pɑ̃], *n.m.* acre (*French; about one and a half English acres*).
arpentage [arpɑ̃'taːʒ], *n.m.* land-measurement; survey, measurement.
arpenter [arpɑ̃'te], *v.t.* to survey, to measure (*land*); (*fig.*) to stride up and down.
arpenteur [arpɑ̃'tœːr], *n.m.* land-surveyor.
arpon [ar'pɔ̃], *n.m.* rip-saw, cross-cut saw.
arqué [ar'ke], *a.* bent, curved, arched (*of horses*).
arquebuse [arkə'byːz], *n.f.* arquebus.
arquebusier [arkəby'zje], *n.m.* arquebusier; gunsmith, armourer.
arquer [ar'ke], *v.t., v.i.* to bend, to curve, to arch.
arraché [ara'ʃe], *a.* uprooted.
arrachement [araʃ'mɑ̃], *n.m.* tearing up or away, pulling or rooting up or out; drawing, extraction.
arrache-pied (d') [daraʃ'pje], *adv. phr.* without interruption; *travailler d'arrache-pied,* to work with a will.
arracher [ara'ʃe], *v.t.* to pull or tear away, up or out; to extract, to uproot, to grub up; (*fig.*) to extort. **s'arracher,** *v.r.* to tear oneself away, to get away; to break away or off.
arraisonner [arɛzɔ'ne], *v.t.* (*Naut.*) to hail (*a ship*); to stop and examine (*a ship*).
arrangeant [arɑ̃'ʒɑ̃], *a.* accommodating, easy to deal with or get on with.
arrangement [arɑ̃ʒ'mɑ̃], *n.m.* arrangement, disposition, adjustment, setting in order; order, plan, method; agreement, settlement; (*pl.*) terms; measures; (*Math.*) permutations.
arranger [arɑ̃'ʒe], *v.t.* (*conjug. like* MANGER) to arrange, to put in order; to settle, to compromise, to compose (*a difference etc.*); to manage, to regulate; to make suitable; to fit up (*a house*); to trim up; *cela m'arrange,* that suits me; *comme vous voilà arrangé!* what a sight you look! **s'arranger,** *v.r.* to prepare oneself, to make arrangements (*pour*); to come to an agreement; to be satisfied (*de*); *arrangez-vous,* that is your look-out.
arrérages [are'raːʒ], *n.m.* (*used only in pl.*) arrears.

arrestation [arɛsta'sjɔ̃], *n.f.* arrest, apprehension; custody.
arrêt [a'rɛ], *n.m.* stoppage, stop, check, pause, halt; suspension, cessation; (*Law*) award, judgment; arrest, apprehension; (*fig.*) decree; (*pl.*) imprisonment; *arrêt fixe,* regular (bus) stop; *arrêt facultatif,* request stop; *arrêt de mort,* sentence of death; *chien d'arrêt,* setter, pointer; *robinet d'arrêt,* stop-cock.
arrêté (1) [arɛ'te], *a.* stopped; decreed, agreed upon, resolved; arrested; fastened.
arrêté (2) [arɛ'te], *n.m.* departmental minute, order, decree, decision; *arrêté ministériel,* order in council.
arrêter [arɛ'te], *v.t.* to check, to stop the movement of, to throw out of gear; to delay, to detain, to hinder, to impede, to hold up; to arrest; to decide, to resolve; to settle (*an account*). **s'arrêter,** *v.r.* to stop, to pause, to hesitate; to remain, to loiter; to lag; to leave off; to be concluded, determined or resolved (*of bargains etc.*); to resolve upon; to dwell (*upon*), to insist (*sur*).
arrhes [ar], *n.f. pl.* earnest (*money*), deposit.
arrière [a'rjɛːr], *adv.* behind (*of time and place*); backward; (*Naut.*) aft, abaft; *en arrière,* backward; behindhand, in arrears; at the back, at the rear (*of a train*); *en arrière de,* behind.—*int.* away!—*n.m.* back part, rear; (*Naut.*) stern (*of a vessel*); (*Ftb.*) back.
arriéré [arje're], *a.* in arrears; behindhand, backward, poorly developed.—*n.m.* arrears.

[In *pl.* of all the following compounds *arrière* is *inv.* The *n.* has its normal *pl.*]

arrière-boutique [arjɛrbu'tik], *n.f.* room at the back of a shop.
arrière-cour [arjɛr'kuːr], *n.f.* back-yard.
arrière-cousin [arjɛrku'zɛ̃], *n.m.* (*fem.* **cousine**) distant cousin, cousin several times removed.
arrière-cuisine [arjɛrkɥi'zin], *n.f.* back-kitchen, scullery.
arrière-garde [arjɛr'gard], *n.f.* rear-guard.
arrière-goût [arjɛr'gu], *n.m.* after-taste.
arrière-grand-mère [arjɛrgrɑ̃'mɛːr], *n.f.* (*pl.* **-grand-mères**) great-grand-mother.
arrière-grand-père [arjɛrgrɑ̃'pɛːr], *n.m.* (*pl.* **-grands-pères**) great-grand-father.
arrière-main [arjɛr'mɛ̃], *n.f.* back of the hand; (*Ten.*) backhand (stroke).—*n.m.* hind-quarters (*of a horse*).
arrière-neveu [arjɛrnə'vø], *n.m.* (*pl.* **-eux**) grand-nephew.
arrière-nièce [arjɛr'njɛs], *n.f.* grand-niece.
arrière-pays [arjɛr'pei], *n.m. inv.* hinterland.
arrière-pensée [arjɛrpɑ̃'se], *n.f.* mental reservation, hidden motive, underlying design.
arrière-petite-fille [arjɛrpətit'fiːj], *n.f.* (*pl.* **-petites-filles**) great-grand-daughter.
arrière-petit-fils [arjɛrpəti'fis], *n.m.* (*pl.* **-petits-fils**) great-grandson.
arrière-petits-enfants [arjɛrpətizɑ̃'fɑ̃], *n.m. pl.* great-grandchildren.
arrière-plan [arjɛr'plɑ̃], *n.m.* (*Paint., Cine.*) background.
arrière-point [arjɛr'pwɛ̃], *n.m.* back-stitch.
arrière-port [arjɛr'pɔːr], *n.m.* inner harbour.

arriérer [arjɛ're], *v.t.* (*conjug. like* CÉDER) to defer, to put off; to leave in arrears. **s'arriérer**, *v.r.* to stay behind; to be in arrears.

arrière-saison [arjɛrsɛ'zõ], *n.f.* end of autumn.

arrière-train [arjɛr'trɛ̃], *n.m.* hind-quarters (*of an animal*).

arrimage [ari'ma:ʒ], *n.m.* (*Naut.*) stowage.

arrimer [ari'me], *v.t.* (*Naut.*) to stow (*cargo etc.*).

arrimeur [ari'mœ:r], *n.m.* stower, stevedore.

arrivée [ari've], *n.f.* arrival, moment of landing, coming etc., advent.

arriver [ari've], *v.i.* (*conjug. with* ÊTRE) to arrive, to come; to arrive at, to attain, to get to, to reach (*à*); to make one's way, to succeed; to happen, to occur, to take place; to veer; *quoi qu'il arrive*, come what may.

arrivisme [ari'vism], *n.m.* push, unscrupulous ambition.

arriviste [ari'vist], *n.m.* careerist, unscrupulous person.

arrogamment [arɔga'mã], *adv.* arrogantly, haughtily; insolently.

arrogance [arɔ'gã:s], *n.f.* arrogance, haughtiness, superciliousness.

arrogant [arɔ'gã], *a.* arrogant, haughty, supercilious, overbearing.

arroger (s') [sarɔ'ʒe], *v.r.* (*conjug. like* MANGER) to assume *or* claim presumptuously.

arrondi [arɔ̃'di], *a.* rounded.—*n.m.* curve (*of shoulder, face etc.*).

arrondir [arɔ̃'di:r], *v.t.* to make round; to give a curved shape to, to round off; (*fig.*) to enlarge, to extend. **s'arrondir**, *v.r.* to grow *or* become round; to increase one's estate.

arrondissement [arɔ̃dis'mã], *n.m.* rounding, making round; roundness; division of a (*French*) department; (*in Paris*) one of the 20 wards.

arrosage [arɔ'za:ʒ], **arrosement** [arɔz'mã], *n.m.* watering, sprinkling; irrigation.

arroser [arɔ'ze], *v.t.* to water, to wet, to sprinkle; to irrigate (*land*); to soak, to moisten; to flow through (*of a river*); to bathe (*with tears*).

arrosoir [arɔ'zwa:r], *n.m.* watering-can.

arsenal [arsə'nal], *n.m.* arsenal; *arsenal maritime*, naval dockyard.

arsenic [arsə'nik], *n.m.* arsenic.

arsenical [arsəni'kal], *a.* (*m.pl.* **-aux**) arsenical. —*n.m. pl.* (**-aux**) arsenical compounds.

art [a:r], *n.m.* art; skill, dexterity, artifice; *arts d'agrément*, accomplishments; *les beaux-arts*, the fine arts.

artère [ar'tɛ:r], *n.f.* artery; (*fig.*) thoroughfare (*in a town*).

artériel [arte'rjɛl], *a.* (*fem.* **-elle**) arterial; *tension artérielle*, blood-pressure.

artériole [arte'rjɔl], *n.f.* small artery.

artésien [arte'zjɛ̃], *a.* (*fem.* **-enne**) artesian; *puits artésien*, artesian well.—*n.m.* (**Artésien**, *fem.* **-enne**) inhabitant *or* native of Artois.

arthrite [ar'trit], *n.f.* arthritis.

arthritique [artri'tik], *a.* arthritic.

artichaut [arti'ʃo], *n.m.* globe artichoke.

article [ar'tikl], *n.m.* article (*in all English senses*); clause, provision (*of a treaty etc.*); item; commodity; (*pl.*) goods; *article de fond*, leading article.

articulaire [artiky'lɛ:r], *a.* articular.

articulation [artikyla'sjõ], *n.f.* articulation, pronunciation; (*Bot., Anat.*) joint, articulation; (*Law*) enumeration of facts.

articulé [artiky'le], *a.* articulate, clear, distinct; jointed, articulated.

articuler [artiky'le], *v.t.* to articulate, to put together by the joints; to pronounce distinctly; (*Law*) to enumerate. **s'articuler**, *v.r.* to be connected by joints.

artifice [arti'fis], *n.m.* artifice, contrivance, expedient; dodge, trick, stratagem; craft, ruse; *un feu d'artifice*, fireworks.

artificiel [artifi'sjɛl], *a.* (*fem.* **-elle**) artificial; fictitious, spurious.

artificiellement [artifisjɛl'mã], *adv.* artificially.

artificieusement [artifisjøz'mã], *adv.* cunningly, craftily, artfully, slyly.

artificieux [artifi'sjø], *a.* (*fem.* **-euse**) artful, cunning.

artillerie [artij'ri], *n.f.* artillery, ordnance.

artilleur [arti'jœ:r], *n.m.* artilleryman, gunner.

artimon [arti'mõ], *n.m.* mizen-mast *or* -sail.

artisan [arti'zã], *n.m.* artisan, operative, mechanic; (*fig.*) author, architect, contriver, maker.

artiste [ar'tist], *a.* artistic (*of persons*).—*n.* artist; player, performer.

artistement [artistə'mã], *adv.* in an artistic manner; skilfully, artistically.

artistique [artis'tik], *a.* artistic, pertaining to art.

as [a:s], *n.m.* ace (*at cards, dice*); as (*Roman coin and weight*).

asbeste [az'bɛst], *n.m.* asbestos.

ascendance [asã'dã:s], *n.f.* ascent; ancestry.

ascendant [asã'dã], *n.m.* ascendant; ascendency, influence; (*pl.*) ancestors.—*a.* ascending, ascendant; going upward, rising.

ascenseur [asã'sœ:r], *n.m.* lift, (*Am.*) elevator.

ascension [asã'sjõ], *n.f.* ascent, climbing, rising; upstroke (*of machinery*); (*Jour de*) *l'Ascension*, Ascension Day.

ascète [a'sɛt], *n.* ascetic.

ascétique [ase'tik], *a.* ascetic, rigid, severe.

ascétisme [ase'tism], *n.m.* asceticism.

asepsie [asɛp'si], *n.f.* (*Med.*) asepsis.

aseptique [asɛp'tik], *a.* and *n.m.* aseptic.

aseptiser [asɛpti'ze], *v.t.* to render aseptic.

asexué [asɛk'sɥe], **asexuel** [asɛk'sɥɛl] (*fem.* **-elle**), *a.* asexual.

asiatique [azja'tik], *a.* Asiatic; *grippe asiatique*, Asian flu.—*n.* (**Asiatique**) native of Asia.

Asie [a'zi], *f.* Asia; *Asie Mineure*, Asia Minor.

asile [a'zil], *n.m.* asylum, place of refuge, sanctuary, retreat, home (*for the aged etc.*); (*fig.*) protection, refuge; *asile d'aliénés*, mental hospital.

asine [a'zin], *a.* asinine.

aspect [as'pɛ], *n.m.* aspect, view, look; countenance; phase, bearing; point of view.

asperge [as'pɛrʒ], *n.f.* asparagus (*head of*).

aspergement [aspɛrʒə'mã], *n.m.* sprinkling.

asperger [aspɛr'ʒe], *v.t.* (*conjug. like* MANGER) to sprinkle.

aspergerie [aspɛrʒə'ri], **aspergière** [aspɛr'ʒjɛ:r], *n.f.* asparagus-bed.

aspérité

aspérité [asperi'te], *n.f.* roughness, harshness; unevenness, ruggedness; (*fig.*) asperity.

aspersion [asper'sjɔ̃], *n.f.* aspersion, sprinkling.

aspersoir [asper'swaːr], *n.m.* holy-water sprinkler; rose (*of a watering-can*).

asphaltage [asfal'taːʒ], *n.m.* asphalting.

asphalte [as'falt], *n.m.* bitumen, asphalt.

asphalter [asfal'te], *v.t.* to asphalt.

asphodèle [asfɔ'dɛl], *n.m.* asphodel.

asphyxiant [asfik'sjɑ̃], *a.* asphyxiating, suffocating; **gaz asphyxiant,** poison-gas.

aspyhxie [asfik'si], *n.f.* (*Med.*) asphyxia, suffocation.

asphyxié [asfik'sje], *a.* asphyxiated.—*n.m.* (*fem.* **-ée**) person in a state of asphyxia.

asphyxier [asfik'sje], *v.t.* to asphyxiate, to suffocate. **s'asphyxier,** *v.r.* to commit suicide by suffocation.

aspic [as'pik], *n.m.* asp, viper; (*Bot.*) spike-lavender; (*Cook.*) cold meat *or* fish, in jelly.

aspidistra [aspidis'tra], *n.m.* aspidistra.

aspirail [aspi'raːj], *n.m.* (*pl.* **-aux**) airhole (*in a stove, oven etc.*).

aspirant (1) [aspi'rɑ̃], *a.* suction, sucking (*of pumps*).

aspirant (2) [aspi'rɑ̃], *n.m.* aspirant, candidate; suitor; officer-cadet; midshipman.

aspirateur [aspira'tœːr], *n.m.* ventilator; suction-pump; vacuum cleaner.

aspiration [aspira'sjɔ̃], *n.f.* aspiration (*of the letter* h *etc.*); inhaling, inspiration; (*of pumps*) exhaustion, suction; (*fig.*) yearning, aspiration; (*Motor.*) suction, intake.

aspirer [aspi're], *v.t.* to inspire, to inhale; to draw in, to suck in; (*Gram.*) to aspirate. —*v.i.* to aspire, to aim at.

aspirine [aspi'rin], *n.f.* aspirin.

assagir [asa'ʒiːr], *v.t.* to make wiser, to impart wisdom to. **s'assagir,** *v.r.* to become wiser; to settle down.

assaillant [asa'jɑ̃], *a.* attacking, aggressive. —*n.m.* (*fem.* **-e**) aggressor, assailant, besieger.

assaillir [asa'jiːr], *v.t. irr.* to assault, to assail; to worry, to molest, to beset.

assainir [ase'niːr], *v.t.* to render healthy; (*fig.*) to cleanse, to purify morally etc. **s'assainir,** *v.r.* to become healthy.

assainissement [asɛnis'mɑ̃], *n.m.* purification, sanitation salubrity; drainage.

assaisonnement [asezɔn'mɑ̃], *n.m.* condiment, seasoning, dressing.

assaisonner [asezɔ'ne], *v.t.* to season, to dress, to give a relish to.

assassin [asa'sɛ̃], *a.* killing, murderous. —*n.m.* (*fem.* **-e**) assassin, murderer; ruffian.

assassinat [asasi'na], *n.m.* assassination, wilful murder, homicide.

assassiner [asasi'ne], *v.t.* to assassinate, to murder; (*fig.*) to bore; to tease, to importune.

assaut [a'so], *n.m.* assault, onset, attack.

assèchement [asɛʃ'mɑ̃], *n.m.* drying up, drainage.

assécher [ase'ʃe], *v.t.* (*conjug. like* CÉDER) to drain (*a mine, pond etc.*).—*v.i.* to become dry, to be drained.

assemblage [asɑ̃'blaːʒ], *n.m.* assemblage, collection, union, combination; (*Print.*)

gathering; (*Carp.*) joint, scarf; **chaîne d'assemblage,** assembly line.

assemblée [asɑ̃'ble], *n.f.* assembly, meeting, company, party; convocation, congregation (*of churches*); meet (*of hunters*).

assembler [asɑ̃'ble], *v.t.* to assemble, to call together; to collect, to gather; to bring together; (*Print.*) to gather; (*Carp.*) to trim, to scarf. **s'assembler,** *v.r.* to assemble, to meet, to congregate.

asséner [ase'ne], *v.t.* (*conjug. like* CÉDER) to strike *or* deal (*a blow*).

assentiment [asɑ̃ti'mɑ̃], *n.m.* assent, agreement.

asseoir [a'swaːr], *v.t. irr.* to seat, to put on a seat, to set, to place, to fix, to establish; to pitch (*a camp etc.*). **s'asseoir,** *v.r.* to sit, to sit down, to take a seat, to settle, to perch.

assermenté [asɛrmɑ̃'te], *a.* sworn in, attested.

assermenter [asɛrmɑ̃'te], *v.t.* to swear in.

assertif [asɛr'tif], *a.* (*fem.* **-tive**) assertive.

assertion [asɛr'sjɔ̃], *n.f.* assertion, affirmation.

asservir [asɛr'viːr], *v.t.* to enslave, to reduce to servitude; to subdue, to conquer. **s'asservir,** *v.r.* to obey, to submit (*à*).

asservissant [asɛrvi'sɑ̃], *a.* enslaving, subjecting, coercive.

asservissement [asɛrvis'mɑ̃], *n.m.* bondage, servitude, slavery, subjection.

assez [a'se], *adv.* enough, sufficiently; tolerably, passably, rather.

assidu [asi'dy], *a.* assiduous, diligent, attentive; punctual; regular, constant.

assiduité [asidɥi'te], *n.f.* assiduity, application, diligence, attention.

assidûment [asidy'mɑ̃], *adv.* assiduously, diligently, constantly; punctually.

assiéger [asje'ʒe], *v.t.* (*see Verb Tables*) to besiege; to lay siege to; to surround; to importune.

assiette [a'sjɛt], *n.f.* plate; plateful; attitude *or* posture (*in sitting etc.*), pose, situation, bearing, basis; seat (*in the saddle*); position, site; tone, state, disposition (*of the mind etc.*).

assiettée [asjɛ'te], *n.f.* plateful.

assignation [asiɲa'sjɔ̃], *n.f.* order to pay, transfer; (*Law*) summons, subpoena, writ; appointment, rendezvous, assignation.

assigner [asi'ɲe], *v.t.* to assign (*property in payment of a debt etc.*); to cite, to summon, to subpoena; to appoint, to fix (*a rendezvous etc.*).

assimilation [asimila'sjɔ̃], *n.f.* assimilation.

assimiler [asimi'le], *v.t.* to make like; to liken, to compare, to assimilate.

assis [a'si], *a.* seated, sitting; situated; established.

assise [a'siːz], *n.f.* course (*of stones etc.*), foundation, basis; (*Geol.*) stratum; (*Mining*) measure (*of coal*); (*pl.*) assizes; **cour d'assises,** assize court.

assistance [asis'tɑ̃ːs], *n.f.* audience, company, bystanders; congregation (*in a church*); assistance, help, aid; relief.

assistant [asis'tɑ̃], *n.m.* (*fem.* **-ante**) assistant (*priest, teacher etc.*); person present, bystander, witness etc.; **assistant(e) social(e),** social welfare worker.

assisté [asis'te], *a.* receiving public assistance. —*n.m.* (*fem.* **-ée**) person in receipt of relief.

28

assister [asis'te], *v.t.* to assist, to help, to succour.—*v.i.* to be at, to be present (à), to look on, to be a witness (à).

association [asɔsja'sjɔ̃], *n.f.* association; union; partnership, fellowship, society, order.

associé [asɔ'sje], *a.* associated, admitted (*as a member*).—*n.m.* (*fem.* **-ée**) associate, fellow, member, partner.

associer [asɔ'sje], *v.t.* to associate, to take into partnership etc.; to divide *or* share something with someone; to link together, to connect (*ideas etc.*). **s'associer**, *v.r.* to enter into partnership, to associate oneself, to combine (*with*).

assoiffé [aswa'fe], *a.* thirsty; eager (*for*).

assolement [asɔl'mɑ̃], *n.m.* (*Agric.*) rotation (*of crops*).

assoler [asɔ'le], *v.t.* to vary *or* rotate (*crops*).

assombrir [asɔ̃'briːr], *v.t.* to darken, to throw a gloom over, to cloud. **s'assombrir**, *v.r.* to become dark *or* gloomy; to darken (*of the brow*).

assombrissement [asɔ̃bris'mɑ̃], *n.m.* darkening, gloom.

assommant [asɔ'mɑ̃], *a.* wearisome, tiresome, boring.

assommer [asɔ'me], *v.t.* to beat to death, to knock on the head; to overpower; to overwhelm, to stun; (*fig.*) to bore, to importune, to oppress.

assommeur [asɔ'mœːr], *n.m.* (*fem.* **-euse**) slaughterer (*of oxen etc.*).

assommoir [asɔ'mwaːr], *n.m.* pole-axe; life-preserver.

Assomption [asɔ̃p'sjɔ̃], *n.f.* (*Eccles.*) Assumption of the Blessed Virgin (August 15).

assomption [asɔ̃p'sjɔ̃], *n.f.* assumption.

assonance [asɔ'nɑ̃ːs], *n.f.* assonance.

assonant [asɔ'nɑ̃], *a.* assonant.

assorti [asɔr'ti], *a.* assorted, matched, paired.

assortiment [asɔrti'mɑ̃], *n.m.* suitability, match; assortment, set.

assortir [asɔr'tiːr], *v.t.* to assort, to match, to pair; to stock, to furnish (*with things that go together or match*).—*v.i.* to match, to suit, to go well together. **s'assortir**, *v.r.* to match, to agree, to go well together.

assortissant [asɔrti'sɑ̃], *a.* suitable, matching, going well (*with something else*).

assoupi [asu'pi], *a.* dozing; dormant (*volcano*).

assoupir [asu'piːr], *v.t.* to make drowsy, sleepy, heavy *or* dull; (*fig.*) to assuage, to allay, to deaden. **s'assoupir**, *v.r.* to grow drowsy, sleepy, dull *or* heavy; to doze; (*fig.*) to be assuaged, to be appeased, to be stilled.

assoupissant [asupi'sɑ̃], *a.* making drowsy or sleepy, soporific.

assoupissement [asupis'mɑ̃], *n.m.* drowsiness, sleepiness, heaviness; (*fig.*) carelessness, sloth; (*Med.*) coma.

assouplir [asu'pliːr], *v.t.* to make supple, flexible *or* tractable; to break in (*a horse*). **s'assouplir**, *v.r.* to become supple, tractable *or* manageable.

assouplissement [asuplis'mɑ̃], *n.m.* suppleness, tractability, docility.

assourdir [asur'diːr], *v.t.* to deafen, to stun; to muffle.

assourdissant [asurdi'sɑ̃], *a.* deafening.

assourdissement [asurdis'mɑ̃], *n.m.* deafen-

ing, muffling, deadening; deafening noise; temporary deafness.

assouvir [asu'viːr], *v.t.* to glut, to satiate, to surfeit; to gratify; to cloy. **s'assouvir**. *v.r*, to be satiated, gratified *or* cloyed.

assouvissement [asuvis'mɑ̃], *n.m.* glutting, satiating.

assujettir [asyʒe'tiːr], *v.t.* to subdue, to subjugate; to compel; to fix, to fasten. **s'assujettir**, *v.r.* to subject oneself, to submit.

assujettissant [asyʒeti'sɑ̃], *a.* binding, constraining, fettering, restrictive.

assujettissement [asyʒetis'mɑ̃], *n.m.* subjection, subjugation; obligation, fixing.

assumer [asy'me], *v.t.* to take upon oneself, to assume.

assurance [asy'rɑ̃ːs], *n.f.* confidence, security, assurance; certainty, conviction; warrant, pledge; insurance, underwriting; (*fig.*) boldness; (*les*) **assurances sociales**, national insurance.

assuré [asy're], *a.* assured, confident; sure, secure, positive, certain; trusty; insured.—*n.m.* (*fem.* **-ée**) insured person.

assurément [asyre'mɑ̃], *adv.* assuredly, confidently; surely, undoubtedly; certainly.

assurer [asy're], *v.t.* to fix securely, to fasten, to steady; (*Naut.* and *Mount.*) to belay; to assure, to guarantee; to insure; to underwrite; to assert, to affirm. **s'assurer**, *v.r.* to make sure of, to ascertain.

assureur [asy'rœːr], *n.m.* underwriter, insurer, assurer.

Assyrie [asi'ri], *f.* Assyria.

assyrien [asi'rjɛ̃], *a.* (*fem.* **-enne**) Assyrian.—*n.m.* (**Assyrien,** *fem.* **-enne**) Assyrian (*person*).

aster [as'teːr], *n.m.* (*Bot.*) aster.

astérie [aste'ri], *n.f.* starfish.

astérisque [aste'risk], *n.m.* asterisk.

astéroïde [asterɔ'id], *n.m.* asteroid.

asthmatique [asma'tik], *a.* asthmatic.

asthme [asm], *n.m.* asthma.

asticot [asti'ko], *n.m.* gentle (*bait for fishing*); maggot.

asticoter [astikɔ'te], *v.t.* (*colloq.*) to tease, to worry.

astigmate [astig'mat], *a.* astigmatic.

astigmatisme [astigma'tism], *n.m.* astigmatism.

astiquer [asti'ke], *v.t.* to polish, to furbish, to glaze.

astracan *or* **astrakan** [astra'kɑ̃], *n.m.* astrakhan, Persian lamb (*fur*).

astral [as'tral], *a.* (*m. pl.* **-aux**) astral.

astre [astr], *n.m.* star; (*fig.*) celebrity.

astreindre [as'trɛ̃ːdr], *v.t. irr.* (*conjug. like* CRAINDRE) to oblige, to compel, to subject. **s'astreindre**, *v.r.* to confine oneself, to tie oneself down (à).

astreinte [as'trɛ̃ːt], *n.f.* (*Law*) compulsion; fine for delay in the performance of a contract.

astringence [astrɛ̃'ʒɑ̃ːs], *n.f.* astringency.

astringent [astrɛ̃'ʒɑ̃], *a.* and *n.m.* astringent.

astroïde [astrɔ'id], *a.* star-shaped.

astrologie [astrɔlɔ'ʒi], *n.f.* astrology.

astrologique [astrɔlɔ'ʒik], *a.* astrological.

astrologue [astrɔ'lɔg], *n.m.* astrologer.

astronaute [astrɔ'noːt], *n.m.* astronaut.

astronautique [astronɔ'tik], *n.f.* astronautics.

astronome [astrɔ'nɔm], *n.m.* astronomer.

astronomie [astrɔnɔ'mi], *n.f.* astronomy.
astronomique [astrɔnɔ'mik], *a.* astronomical, astronomic.
astrophysique [astrɔfi'zik], *a.* astrophysical. —*n.f.* astrophysics.
astuce [as'tys], *n.f.* craft, guile; cunning.
astucieusement [astysjøz'mã], *adv.* craftily, cunningly.
astucieux [asty'sjø], *a.* (*fem.* **-euse**) crafty, wily.
Asturies [asty'ri], **les**, *f. pl.* the Asturias.
asymétrie [asime'tri], *n.f.* asymmetry.
asymétrique [asime'trik], *a.* asymmetrical.
atelier [ata'lje], *n.m.* workshop, studio, atelier; (*collect.*) gang of workmen etc.; (*Freemasonry*) lodge, lodge-meeting.
atermoyer [atermwa'je], *v.t.* (*conjug. like* EMPLOYER) to put off, to delay (*a payment*). —*v.i.* (*fig.*) to put off, to make shifts. **s'atermoyer**, *v.r.* to compound with one's creditors.
athée [a'te], *a.* atheistic.—*n.* atheist.
athéisme [ate'ism], *n.m.* atheism.
Athènes [a'tɛːn], *f.* Athens.
athénien [ate'njɛ̃], *a.* (*fem.* **-enne**) Athenian. —*n.m.* (**Athénien**, *fem.* **-enne**) Athenian (*person*).
athlète [a'tlɛt], *n.m.* athlete.
athlétique [atle'tik], *a.* athletic.
athlétisme [atle'tism], *n.m.* athleticism; athletics.
Atlantide [atlã'tid], *f.* Atlantis.
atlantique [atlã'tik], *a.* Atlantic.—*n.m.* (**L'Atlantique**) the Atlantic (Ocean).
atlas [a'tlɑːs], *n.m.* atlas.
atmosphère [atmɔs'fɛːr], *n.f.* atmosphere.
atmosphérique [atmɔsfe'rik], *a.* atmospheric; *pression atmosphérique*, atmospheric pressure.
atoll [a'tɔl], *n.m.* atoll.
atome [a'toːm], *n.m.* atom, corpuscle.
atomicité [atɔmisi'te], *n.f.* (*Chem.*) atomicity, valency.
atomique [atɔ'mik], *a.* atomic(al); *commissariat à l'énergie atomique*, atomic energy authority.
atomiser [atɔmi'ze], *v.t.* to pulverize.
atomiste [atɔ'mist], *n.m.* atomist.
atomistique [atɔmis'tik], *a.* atomic(al).
atone [a'ton], *a.* atonic, debilitated, dull; lack-lustre, expressionless (*of eyes*); (*Gram.*) atonic, unaccentuated.
atonie [atɔ'ni], *n.f.* atony, debility.
atonique [atɔ'nik], *a.* atonic.
atours [a'tuːr], *n.m.* (*used only in pl.*) woman's attire, dress, ornament.
atout [a'tu], *n.m.* trump; trump-card.
atoxique [atɔk'sik], *a.* non-poisonous.
atrabilaire [atrabi'lɛːr], *a.* morose, peevish.
âtre [ɑːtr], *n.m.* hearth; fire-place.
atroce [a'trɔs], *a.* atrocious, cruel, excruciating; heinous, odious, dreadful.
atrocement [atrɔs'mã], *adv.* atrociously, cruelly, outrageously.
atrocité [atrɔsi'te], *n.f.* atrociousness, heinousness; atrocity, cruelty.
atrophie [atrɔ'fi], *n.f.* (*Path.*) atrophy.
atrophié [atrɔ'fje], *a.* atrophied, wasted, withered, stunted.
atrophier [atrɔ'fje], *v.t.* to cause to waste *or* wither. **s'atrophier**, *v.r.* to waste away, to atrophy.

atrophique [atrɔ'fik], *a.* atrophic.
attablé [ata'ble], *a.* seated at table.
attabler (s') [sata'ble], *v.r.* to sit down to *or* take one's place at table.
attachant [ata'ʃã], *a.* engaging, winning, attractive.
attache [a'taʃ], *n.f.* bond, cord, leash, strap; (*fig.*) attachment, affection for.
attaché [ata'ʃe], *n.m.* attaché (*of an embassy*).
attachement [ataʃ'mã], *n.m.* attachment; affection, liaison; eagerness, zeal.
attacher [ata'ʃe], *v.t.* to fasten, to tie, to attach, to fix; (*fig.*) to apply, to affix; to connect, to associate; to engage, to endear.— **s'attacher**, *v.r.* to take hold, to attach *or* fasten oneself; to cling, to adhere; to have an affection for; to apply oneself to.
attaquable [ata'kabl], *a.* assailable; of doubtful validity.
attaquant [ata'kã], *n.m.* assailant.
attaque [a'tak], *n.f.* attack, assault, aggression; fit, stroke.
attaquer [ata'ke], *v.t.* to attack, to assail, to assault; to seize suddenly (*of illness etc.*); to criticize; *attaquer en justice*, to sue for. **s'attaquer**, *v.r.* to make *or* conduct an attack (*à*), to set upon.
attaqueur [ata'kœːr], *n.m.* attacker.
attardé [atar'de], *a.* late, behindhand; mentally retarded (*child*).
attarder [atar'de], *v.t.* to make late, to delay. **s'attarder**, *v.r.* to be belated; to loiter, to linger.
atteindre [a'tɛ̃ːdr], *v.t. irr.* (*conjug. like* CRAINDRE) to reach, to hit, to attain; to arrive at; to overtake, to come up to.—*v.i.* to reach with difficulty, to attain (*à*); *atteindre à la perfection*, to attain to perfection.
atteint [a'tɛ̃], *a.* hit, struck; attacked, seized, affected; reached.
atteinte [a'tɛ̃t], *n.f.* reach, blow, stroke, touch; attack, fit, seizure (*of disease*); injury, damage, harm, wrong.
attelage [at'laːʒ], *n.m.* harnessing, yoking; team, yoke, set, pair; carriage, horses; (*Rail.*) coupling.
atteler [at'le], *v.t.* (*conjug. like* APPELER) to put horses etc. (*to*); to harness, to yoke; (*fig.*) to subjugate. **s'atteler**, *v.r.* to settle down to (*à*); (*fig.*) to apply oneself to, to hitch one's waggon to.
attelle [a'tɛl], *n.f.* hame; (*Surg.*) splint.
attenant [at'nã], *a.* contiguous, adjoining, next door to, close by (*à*).
attendre [a'tãːdr], *v.t.* to await, to wait for, to stay for; to look forward to, to expect; to look for, to count upon. **s'attendre**, *v.r.* to rely upon, to count upon, to trust (*à*); to expect, to look forward (*à*).
attendrir [atã'driːr], *v.t.* to make tender, to soften; to touch, to move. **s'attendrir**, *v.r.* to grow tender; to be moved, to melt, to pity, to relent.
attendrissant [atãdri'sã], *a.* moving, touching.
attendrissement [atãdris'mã], *n.m.* compassion, pity; tears, sensibility; tenderness.
attendu [atã'dy], *prep.* considering, on account of, in consideration of.—*conj. attendu que*, seeing that, as, whereas, since.
attenir [at'niːr], *v.i. irr.* (*conjug. like* TENIR) to adjoin, to be contiguous (*à*); to be related.

aube

attentat [atɑ̃'ta], *n.m.* attempt at crime; crime, attempt; outrage, violation.

attente [a'tɑ̃:t], *n.f.* waiting, expectation; hope; *salle d'attente*, waiting-room.

attenter [atɑ̃'te], *v.i.* to make a criminal attempt.

attentif [atɑ̃'tif], *a.* (*fem.* **-tive**) attentive, heedful; considerate.

attention [atɑ̃'sjɔ̃], *n.f.* attention, notice; heed, care, vigilance; regard, respect, consideration; *attention!* look out! stand by!

attentionné [atɑ̃sjo'ne], *a.* attentive, considerate.

attentivement [atɑ̃tiv'mɑ̃], *adv.* attentively, carefully.

atténuant [ate'nɥɑ̃], *a.* mitigating; (*Law*) extenuating.

atténuation [atenɥa'sjɔ̃], *n.f.* attenuation, extenuation, mitigation.

atténué [ate'nɥe], *a.* attenuated, wasted, emaciated.

atténuer [ate'nɥe], *v.t.* to make smaller, thinner, feebler etc.; to attenuate; to extenuate; to mitigate.

atterrant [ate'rɑ̃], *a.* astounding, startling, overwhelming.

atterrement [ater'mɑ̃], *n.m.* overthrow; prostration, amazement.

atterré [ate're], *a.* horror-stricken, dumb-founded.

atterrer [ate're], *v.t.* to overwhelm; to astound.

atterrir [ate'ri:r], *v.i.* to land, to make land.

atterrissage [ateri'sa:ʒ], *n.m.* landing; *terrain d'atterrissage*, landing-ground.

atterrissement [ateris'mɑ̃], *n.m.* alluvion, accretion, alluvium.

attestation [atɛsta'sjɔ̃], *n.f.* attestation, evidence; certificate, voucher, testimonial; *attestation sous serment*, affidavit.

attester [atɛs'te], *v.t.* to attest, to certify, to avouch, to witness, to testify.

attiédir [atje'di:r], *v.t.* to cool, to make luke-warm; to take the chill off. **s'attiédir**, *v.r.* to grow cool or lukewarm; to cool off.

attiédissement [atjedis'mɑ̃], *n.m.* lukewarmness, coolness; abatement.

attifage [ati'fa:ʒ], **attifement** [atif'mɑ̃], *n.m.* get-up, rig-out.

attifer [ati'fe] (*always in a bad sense*), *v.t.* to dress up. **s'attifer**, *v.r.* to dress up, to rig oneself out.

attique [a'tik], *a.* Attic; (*fig.*) witty, urbane.— *n.m.* (*Arch.*) attic.

attirail [ati'ra:j], *n.m.* (*collect.*) apparatus, implements, utensils, gear, tackle; baggage, paraphernalia; show, pomp.

attirance [ati'rɑ̃:s], *n.f.* attraction (*vers*).

attirant [ati'rɑ̃], *a.* attractive, alluring, enticing, engaging.

attirer [ati're], *v.t.* to attract, to draw; to win or gain over, to lure, to wheedle, to entice; to occasion. **s'attirer**, *v.r.* to draw to or down upon one; to bring upon one; to incur, to win.

attisage [ati'za:ʒ], **attisement** [atiz'mɑ̃], *n.m.* the act of stirring up, poking (*a fire*), fanning (*flame*).

(*C*) **attisée** [ati'ze], *n.f.* a good fire; armful (*of stove-wood*).

attiser [ati'ze], *v.t.* to make or stir up (*a fire*); to poke; (*fig.*) to incense, to stir up.

attisoir [ati'zwa:r], **attisonnoir** [atizɔ'nwa:r], *n.m.* poker (*especially in foundries*), fire-rake.

attitré [ati'tre], *a.* recognized, appointed, regular, ordinary; hired.

attitude [ati'tyd], *n.f.* attitude; (*Paint.*) posture; (*fig.*) attitude of mind etc.

attouchement [atuʃ'mɑ̃], *n.m.* touch, contact.

attracteur [atrak'tœ:r], *a.* (*fem.* **-trice**) attractile.

attractif [atrak'tif], *a.* (*fem.* **-tive**) attractive.

attraction [atrak'sjɔ̃], *n.f.* attraction; (*pl.*) cabaret show.

attractivement [atraktiv'mɑ̃], *adv.* attractively.

attrait [a'trɛ], *n.m.* allurement, attraction, charm; inclination, bent; (*pl.*) attractions, charms; bait.

attrape [a'trap], *n.f.* trap, gin; (*fig.*) trick, take-in, sell, hoax; (*Naut.*) hawser.

attrape-mouche or **attrape-mouches** [atrap'muʃ], *n.m. inv.* fly-catcher.

attrape-nigaud [atrapni'go], *n.m.* (*pl.* **attrape-nigauds**) booby-trap.

attraper [atra'pe], *v.t.* to catch; to entrap, to ensnare; to take in, to trick, to bamboozle; to imitate; (*fam.*) to scold; to hit; to over-take, to catch up; to get accidentally (*a cold etc.*); *attrape!* take that! **s'attraper**, *v.r.* to hit (*against*); to be caught (*in*); to get hold of; to seize, to stick (*à*).

attrapeur [atra'pœ:r], *n.m.* (*fem.* **-euse**) deceiver, cheat, trickster.

attrayant [atrɛ'jɑ̃], *a.* attractive, winning, engaging, charming.

attribuable [atri'bɥabl], *a.* attributable, due to.

attribuer [atri'bɥe], *v.t.* to assign, to confer; to attribute, to ascribe, to impute (*a thing to someone*). **s'attribuer**, *v.r.* to assume, to take upon oneself, to claim.

attribut [atri'by], *n.m.* attribute, prerogative; special symbol or emblem; (*Gram.*) predicate.

attributif [atriby'tif], *a.* (*fem.* **-tive**) (*Gram.*) attributive; predicative; (*Law*) conferring a right.

attribution [atriby'sjɔ̃], *n.f.* attribution, conferment, awarding (*of a grant*); (*usu. in pl.*) privilege, prerogative (*of a person*); province, department, jurisdiction.

attristant [atris'tɑ̃], *a.* saddening, sorrowful, melancholy, grievous.

attrister [atris'te], *v.t.* to grieve, to sadden, to trouble. **s'attrister**, *v.r.* to be sad, to become sorrowful.

attrition [atri'sjɔ̃], *n.f.* attrition, friction.

attroupement [atrup'mɑ̃], *n.m.* riotous assemblage, mob, crowd, gathering of people.

attrouper [atru'pe], *v.t.* to assemble, to gather together in troops or a mob. **s'attrouper**, *v.r.* to flock together, to gather in crowds.

au [o], (*contraction of* À LE) to the.

aubade [o'bad], *n.f.* aubade, dawn song; (*iron.*) hot reception.

aubaine [o'bɛn], *n.f.* (*Law*) escheat; windfall, piece of good luck.

aube [o:b], *n.f.* the dawn; alb (*priest's vestment*).

31

aubépine [obe'pin], *n.f.* hawthorn, white-thorn, may.

aubère [o'bɛːr], *a.* red roan (*horse*).

auberge [o'bɛrʒ], *n.f.* inn, public-house, tavern; *auberge de (la) jeunesse*, youth hostel.

aubergine [obɛr'ʒin], *n.f.* aubergine, egg-plant.

aubergiste [obɛr'ʒist], *n.* innkeeper, publican, landlord, host.

aubour [o'buːr], *n.m.* laburnum; guelder-rose.

aucun [o'kœ̃], *a.* and *pron.* none, no one, not one; not any; anyone; any.

aucunement [okyn'mã], *adv.* in no wise, not at all, not in the least; at all.

audace [o'das], *n.f.* audacity, daring, bold-ness; impudence, insolence; *payer d'audace*, to brazen it out.

audacieusement [odasjøz'mã], *adv.* audaci-ously, daringly, boldly; rashly; impudently.

audacieux [oda'sjø], *a.* (*fem.* **-euse**) audaci-ous, bold, daring; impudent, presumptuous.

au deçà, au dedans, au dehors, au delà [DEÇÀ, DEDANS, DEHORS, DELÀ].

au-dessous [od'su], *prep.* below.

au-dessus [od'sy], *prep.* above.

au-devant d'un danger [od'vã], *prep.* towards; *aller au-devant d'un danger*, to anticipate danger.

audibilité [odibili'te], *n.f.* audibility.

audible [o'dibl], *a.* audible.

audience [o'djãːs], *n.f.* audience, hearing; reception; sitting, session, court, tribunal.

audiomètre [odjo'mɛtr], **audimètre** [odi'mɛtr], *n.m.* audiometer.

audiophone [odjo'fɔn], **audiphone** [odi'fɔn], *n.m.* audiphone.

audio-visuel [odjovi'zɥɛl], *a.* (*fem.* **-elle**) audio-visual; *moyens audio-visuels*, audio-visual aids.

auditeur [odi'tœːr], *n.m.* (*fem.* **-trice**) hearer, listener.

auditif [odi'tif], *a.* (*fem.* **-tive**) auditory.

audition [odi'sjõ], *n.f.* hearing; (*Law*) hearing (*of a case etc.*); audition (*of a singer etc.*).

auditionner [odisjo'ne], *v.t.* to audition.

auditoire [odi'twaːr], *n.m.* auditory; congre-gation (*in church*), audience (*theatre etc.*).

auditrice [odi'tris], [AUDITEUR].

auge [oːʒ], *n.f.* trough (*for drinking etc.*); (*plasterer's*) hod; (*Elec.*) cell.

auget [o'ʒɛ], *n.m.* small trough; seed-box.

augmentation [ogmãta'sjõ], *n.f.* augmenta-tion, increase, addition, rise (*in salary*).

augmenter [ogmã'te], *v.t.* to augment, to increase; to enlarge; to raise the salary of.—*v.i.* to augment, to increase, to grow, to rise (*in price*), to multiply. **s'augmenter**, *v.r.* to increase, to enlarge, to improve.

augural [ogy'ral], *a.* (*m. pl.* **-aux**) augural.

augure [o'gyːr], *n.m.* augur, soothsayer; augury, omen, sign; *de mauvais augure*, ominous, portentous.

augurer [ogy're], *v.t.* to augur; (*fig.*) to con-jecture, to surmise.

Auguste [o'gyst], *m.* Augustus.

auguste [o'gyst], *a.* august, majestic.

augustin [ogys'tɛ̃], *n.m.* (*fem.* **-ine**) Augustin-ian or Austin friar or (*f.*) nun.

aujourd'hui [oʒur'dɥi], *adv.* today, during this day; nowadays, now, at present.

aulnaie [AUNAIE].

aulne [AUNE].

aulx [oː], [AIL].

aumône [o'mon], *n.f.* alms, alms-giving; (*fig.*) charity, favour.

aumônerie [omon'ri], *n.f.* chaplaincy.

aumônier [omo'nje], *n.m.* (*Eccles.*) almoner, chaplain; *aumônier militaire*, army chap-lain, padre.

aunaie or **aulnaie** [o'nɛ], *n.f.* grove of alders.

aune (1) or **aulne** [oːn], *n.m.* alder-tree.

aune (2) [oːn], *n.f.* ell; (*fig.*) measure, standard.

aunée [o'ne], *n.f.* length of an ell.

auparavant [opara'vã], *adv.* before, formerly previously.

auprès [o'prɛ], *adv.* near, by, close by.—*prep. auprès de*, near to, close to; in com-parison with; in the service of; in the opinion of.

auquel [o'kɛl], *contraction of* À LEQUEL (*fem.* **à laquelle**, *pl.* **auxquels, auxquelles**) to whom, to which.

auréole [ore'ɔl], *n.f.* aureole, halo, nimbus; (*fig.*) glory, prestige.

auréoler [oreo'le], *v.t.* to crown with a halo.

auriculaire [oriky'lɛr], *a.* auricular.—*n.m.* the little finger.

auricule [ori'kyl], *n.f.* lower lobe of the ear, auricle; (*Bot.*) auricula.

auriculiste [oriky'list], *n.m.* ear specialist.

aurifère [ori'fɛːr], *a.* auriferous.

auriste [o'rist], *n.m.* ear specialist.

aurore [o'rɔːr], *n.f.* dawn, morn, daybreak; (*fig.*) promise, beginning, the East; (*Astron.*) aurora.

auscultation [oskylta'sjõ], *n.f.* (*Med.*) auscul-tation.

ausculter [oskyl'te], *v.t.* to sound a patient.

auspice [os'pis], *n.m.* auspice, omen, presage; (*pl.*) protection, patronage.

aussi [o'si], *adv.* also, likewise, too, besides; as; so.—*conj.* and so, accordingly, therefore, consequently; but then.

aussière [o'sjɛːr], *n.f.* (*Naut.*) hawser.

aussitôt [osi'to], *adv.* immediately, forthwith.—*conj. aussitôt que*, as soon as.

austère [os'tɛːr], *a.* austere, severe, stern.

austèrement [ostɛr'mã], *adv.* austerely.

austérité [osteri'te], *n.f.* austerity; severity; strictness.

austral [os'tral], *a.* (*m. pl.* **-als** or **-aux**) austral, southern.

Australasie [ostrala'zi], **l'**, *f.* Australasia.

australasien [ostrala'zjɛ̃], *a.* (*fem.* **-enne**) Australasian.

Australie [ostra'li], **l'**, *f.* Australia.

australien [ostra'ljɛ̃], *a.* (*fem.* **-enne**) Austra-lian.—*n.m.* (**Australien**, *fem.* **-enne**) Aus-tralian (*person*).

autant [o'tã], *adv.* as much, so much, as many, so many; *autant de têtes, autant d'avis*, there are as many opinions as there are men; *autant que*, as much as, as many as, as far as, in the same way as; *d'autant*, in the same proportion; *d'autant mieux* or *d'autant plus*, the more, so much the more.—*conj. d'autant que*, seeing that, since, more especially as.

autel [o'tɛl], *n.m.* altar; (*fig.*) ministry, Church, religious life.

auteur [oˈtœːr], *n.m.* author, creator, maker; writer (*of a book etc.*); perpetrator; achiever, contriver, framer; composer, sculptor; informant, authority; *droit d'auteur*, royalty.

authenticité [otãtisiˈte], *n.f.* authenticity genuineness.

authentique [otãˈtik], *a.* authenticated, genuine, incontestable, positive.

authentiquement [otãtikˈmã], *adv.* authentically.

authentiquer [otãtiˈke], *v.t.* to authenticate; (*Law*) to make legal and binding.

auto [oˈto], *n.f. abbr.* [AUTOMOBILE].

auto-allumage [otoalyˈmaːʒ], *n.m.* pinking (*of a car*).

autobiographe [otobjoˈgraf], *n.m.* autobiographer.

autobiographie [otobjograˈfi], *n.f.* autobiography.

autobiographique [otobjograˈfik], *a.* autobiographical.

autobus [otoˈbys], *n.m.* bus.

autocar [otoˈkaːr], *n.m.* motor-coach.

autochenille [otoˈʃniːj], *n.f.* caterpillar tractor; half-track vehicle.

autoclave [otoˈklaːv], *a.* and *n.m.* vacuum-pan, sterilizer; *marmite autoclave*, autoclave, digester; pressure cooker.

autocopie [otokoˈpi], *n.f.* cyclostyling.

autocopier [otokoˈpje], *v.t.* to cyclostyle.

autocopiste [otokoˈpist], *n.m.* duplicator, cyclostyle.

autocrate [otoˈkrat], *n.m.* autocrat.

autocratie [otokraˈsi], *n.f.* autocracy.

autocratique [otokraˈtik], *a.* autocratic.

autocratiquement [otokratikˈmã], *adv.* autocratically.

autocritique [otokriˈtik], *n.f.* self-criticism.

auto-cuiseur [otokɥiˈzœːr], *n.m.* pressure-cooker.

autodidacte [otodiˈdakt], *n.* self-taught person.

autodrome [otoˈdroːm], *n.m.* race-track for motor-cars.

auto-école [otoeˈkɔl], *n.f.* school of motoring.

autogare [otoˈgaːr], *n.f.* bus *or* coach station.

autographe [otoˈgraf], *a.* autographic.—*n.m.* autograph.

autographie [otograˈfi], *n.f.* autography.

autographier [otograˈfje], *v.t.* to autograph.

autogyre [otoˈʒiːr], *n.m.* autogyro.

automate [otoˈmat], *n.m.* automaton, robot.

automation [otomaˈsjõ], *n.f.* automation.

automatique [otomaˈtik], *a.* automatic; *distributeur automatique*, (penny-in-the-) slot machine; *machine à vente automatique*, vending machine.—*n.m.* *l'Automatique*, automatic telephone.

automatiquement [otomatikˈmã], *adv.* automatically.

automatisme [otomaˈtism], *n.m.* automatism, purely mechanical movement.

automitrailleuse [otomitraˈjøːz], *n.f.* light armoured car.

automnal [otoˈnal], *a.* (*m. pl.* -**aux**) autumnal.

automne [oˈtɔn], *n.m.* or *f.* autumn.

automobile [otomoˈbil], *a.* self-moving, self-propelling; *canot automobile*, motor-boat.—*n.f.* motor-car; *salon de l'automobile*, motor show.

automobilisme [otomobiˈlism], *n.m.* automobilism, motoring.

automobiliste [otomobiˈlist], *n.* motorist.

automoteur [otomoˈtœːr], *a.* (*fem.* -**trice**) self-acting, self-moving, self-propelling.

(*C*) **auto-neige** [otoˈnɛːʒ], *n.f.* snowmobile.

autonome [otoˈnɔm], *a.* autonomous.

autonomie [otonoˈmi], *n.f.* autonomy, self-government; cruising range.

autonomiste [otonoˈmist], *n.m.* autonomist.

autoplastie [otoplasˈti], *n.f.* (*Surg.*) plastic surgery.

auto-portrait [otoporˈtrɛ], *n.m.* self-portrait.

auto-propulsé [otopropylˈse], *a.* self-propelled.

auto-propulsion [otopropylˈsjõ], *n.f.* self-propulsion.

autopsie [otopˈsi], *n.f.* autopsy; post-mortem examination.

autorail [otoˈraːj], *n.m.* rail-car.

autorisation [otorizaˈsjõ], *n.f.* authorization; authority, warrant; written consent *or* permission, licence (*of a preacher*).

autoriser [otoriˈze], *v.t.* to authorize, to empower, to commission; to license, to warrant, to permit, to sanction. **s'autoriser**, *v.r.* to have, get *or* assume authority; to act on the authority (*of*), to be warranted by (*de*).

autoritaire [otoriˈtɛːr], *a.* and *n.* authoritative, commanding, arbitrary (person).

autoritairement [otoriterˈmã], *adv.* authoritatively.

autorité [otoriˈte], *n.f.* authority, legal *or* legitimate power; an authority; (*fig.*) control.

autoroute [otoˈrut], *n.f.* motorway; (*Am.*) speedway.

auto-stop [otoˈstop], *n.m.* hitch-hiking; *faire de l'auto-stop*, to hitch-hike.

autostrade [otoˈstrad], *n.f.* special road for motor-cars, motorway.

autosuggestion [otosygʒɛsˈtjõ], *n.f.* auto-suggestion.

autour (1) [oˈtuːr], *adv.* about, round about.—*prep. phr. autour de*, about, round, around.

autour (2) [oˈtuːr], *n.m.* (*Orn.*) goshawk.

autre [oːtr], *a.* other; second; another different, distinct (*but of the same kind*).—*pron. indef.* another person, someone else; (*pl.*) the others, the rest.

autrefois [otrəˈfwa], *adv.* formerly, in former times; of old; *d'autrefois*, former, bygone; *des mœurs d'autrefois*, bygone customs.

autrement [otrəˈmã], *adv.* otherwise, after another manner; else; or else; *autrement dit*, in other words.

Autriche [oˈtriʃ], **l'**, *f.* Austria.

autrichien [otriˈʃjɛ̃], *a.* (*fem.* -**enne**) Austrian. —*n.m.* (**Autrichien**, *fem.* -**enne**) Austrian (*person*).

autruche [oˈtryʃ], *n.f.* ostrich.

autrucherie [otryʃˈri], *n.f.* ostrich-farm.

autrui [oˈtrɥi], *pron. indef. inv.* others, other people, one's *or* our neighbours.

auvent [oˈvã], *n.m.* weather-board, porch roof; *auvent de capot*, bonnet louvre.

aux [o], *pl.* [AU].

auxiliaire [oksiˈljɛːr], *a.* auxiliary, aiding, subsidiary.—*n.* auxiliary; helper, assistant.

auxquels [oˈkɛl], *pl.* (*fem.* -**elles**) [AUQUEL].

avachi [avaˈʃi], *a.* out of shape, worn out; (*fam.*) flabby, floppy, downcast (*of a person*).

avachir

avachir (s') [sava'ʃiːr], *v.r.* to flag; to grow fat and flabby; to get out of shape *or* down at heel.

avachissement [avaʃis'mɑ̃], *n.m.* flabbiness; lack of energy.

aval (1) [a'val], *n.m.* (*pl.* **avals**) guarantee, endorsement.

aval (2) [a'val], *n.m.* down stream; *en aval de*, below.

avalaison [avalɛ'zõ], **avalasse** [ava'las], *n.f.* sudden flood, spate; (*Naut.*) a long-continued wind from the sea.

avalanche [ava'lɑ̃ːʃ], *n.f.* avalanche.

avalasse [AVALAISON].

avalement [aval'mɑ̃], *n.m.* descent, lowering, letting down; swallowing.

avaler [ava'le], *v.t.* to swallow, to swallow down; to drink, to gulp down; to let down, to lower (*things into a cellar*); (*fig.*) to endure (*an affront*); to believe.—*v.i.* to go down (*a river etc. with the stream*).

avaliser [avali'ze], *v.t.* to guarantee, to endorse [AVAL (1)].

avance [a'vɑ̃ːs], *n.f.* part of a building etc. projecting forwards; advance; start, distance in advance; payment of money in advance; (*fig., pl.*) attentions, first steps in an acquaintanceship.

avancé [avɑ̃'se], *a.* advanced, forward, early; late (*of the hour*); over-ripe, tainted, high; liberal, progressive (*of opinions etc.*); paid in advance; put forward, enunciated.

avancement [avɑ̃s'mɑ̃], *n.m.* projection; progress, advancement; preferment, promotion, rise.

avancer [avɑ̃'se], *v.t.* (*conjug. like* COMMENCER) to move, bring, put *or* hold forward, to advance; to pay beforehand *or* in advance; to assert, to bring forward, to urge; to promote, to give promotion to; to advantage, to profit; (*fig.*) to bring nearer, to hasten, to forward; to put on (*a clock*).—*v.i.* to advance, to proceed, to keep on; to project, to jut out; to make progress, to thrive, to get on, to gain ground; to go too fast; *l'horloge avance*, the clock is fast. **s'avancer**, *v.r.* to advance, to go on, to move forward; to get on, to improve; to get promoted, to be successful; to grow old; to project.

avanie [ava'ni], *n.f.* insult, affront; snub.

avant [a'vɑ̃], *prep.* before, in advance of (*of time and order*); *avant J.-C.*, B.C.—*adv.* before, previously; forward, in front; farther in advance.—*conj. avant que*, before; *en avant!* forward!—*n.m.* front; prow, head, bow (*of a ship*); (*Ftb.*) forward.

avantage [avɑ̃'taːʒ], *n.m.* advantage, benefit, profit, superiority, whip-hand; (*Ten.*) 'vantage.

avantager [avɑ̃ta'ʒe], *v.t.* (*conjug. like* MANGER) to advantage, to give an advantage to; to favour. **s'avantager**, *v.r.* to take advantage.

avantageusement [avɑ̃taʒøz'mɑ̃], *adv.* advantageously, to advantage; usefully, favourably.

avantageux [avɑ̃ta'ʒø], *a.* (*fem.* -euse) advantageous, profitable, favourable; conceited, presumptuous; (*of dress*) becoming.

[In *pl.* of the following compounds *avant* is *inv.* The *n.* has its normal *pl.*]

avant-bassin [avɑ̃ba'sɛ̃], *n.m.* outer-dock.

avant-bras [avɑ̃'bra], *n.m. inv.* forearm.

avant-centre [avɑ̃'sɑ̃ːtr], *n.m.* (*Ftb.*) centre-forward.

avant-corps [avɑ̃'kɔːr], *n.m. inv.* (*Arch.*) forepart (*of a building*).

avant-cour [avɑ̃'kuːr], *n.f.* fore-court.

avant-coureur [avɑ̃ku'rœːr], *a.* going in front, preceding, presaging.—*n.m.* forerunner, precursor, harbinger.

avant-courrier [avɑ̃ku'rje], *n.m.* (*fem.* -ière) (*fig.*) herald, forerunner, harbinger.

avant-dernier [avɑ̃dɛr'nje], *a.* and *n.m.* (*fem.* -ière) the last but one.

avant-garde [avɑ̃'gard], *n.f.* vanguard, van.

avant-goût [avɑ̃'gu], *n.m.* foretaste; earnest; anticipation.

avant-guerre [avɑ̃'gɛːr], *n.m.* the pre-war period.

avant-hier [avɑ̃'tjɛːr], *adv.* and *n.m.* the day before yesterday.

avant-main [avɑ̃'mɛ̃], *n.m.* flat of the hand; forehand (*of a horse*); (*Ten.*) forehand (stroke); (*Cards*) lead.

avant-port [avɑ̃'pɔːr], *n.m.* outer harbour, tide-dock.

avant-poste [avɑ̃'post], *n.m.* (*Mil.*) advanced post, outpost; (*fig.*) outer defence.

avant-première [avɑ̃prə'mjɛːr], *n.f.* dress rehearsal; (*Cine.*) preview.

avant-projet [avɑ̃prɔ'ʒɛ], *n.m.* rough draft.

avant-propos [avɑ̃prɔ'po], *n.m. inv.* preface, preamble, introduction, foreword.

avant-scène [avɑ̃'sɛːn], *n.f.* front of the stage (*between curtain and orchestra*), proscenium.

avant-toit [avɑ̃'twa], *n.m.* eaves.

avant-train [avɑ̃'trɛ̃], *n.m.* fore-carriage, limber.

avant-veille [avɑ̃'vɛːj], *n.f.* two days before.

avare [a'vaːr], *a.* avaricious, miserly, covetous, stingy, close-fisted.—*n.m.* miser, niggard.

avarement [avar'mɑ̃], *adv.* stingily.

avariable [ava'rjabl], *a.* perishable, damageable.

avarice [ava'ris], *n.f.* avarice, greed, covetousness; niggardliness, stinginess.

avaricieusement [avarisjøz'mɑ̃], [*adv.* avariciously.

avaricieux [avari'sjø], *a.* (*fem.* -euse) avaricious, covetous, stingy.

avarie [ava'ri], *n.f.* damage (*to a ship* or *cargo*); deterioration.

avarié [ava'rje], *a.* damaged, spoiled, deteriorated.

avarier [ava'rje], *v.t.* to damage, to spoil. **s'avarier**, *v.r.* to become damaged.

avec [a'vɛk], *prep.* with, at the same time as, along *or* together with; by means of, by; regarding; against, in spite of; *avec ça!* (*colloq.*) nonsense!

aveline [a'vlin], *n.f.* filbert, Kentish cob.

avelinier [avli'nje], *n.m.* filbert-tree, hazel-tree.

aven [a'vɛ̃], *n.m.* pot-hole, swallow, chasm (*in mountain limestone*).

avenant [av'nɑ̃], *a.* personable, prepossessing, comely, pleasing, taking.—*adv. phr. à l'avenant*, in keeping, in the same proportions, of a piece.—*n.m.* additional clause (*to an insurance policy*); rider (*to a verdict*); codicil (*to a treaty*).

avènement [avɛn'mɑ̃], *n.m.* coming, advent; accession, succession (*to a throne etc.*).

avenir [av'niːr], *n.m.* future, future ages; posterity; (*fig.*) prospects; **à l'avenir**, in future, henceforth.

Avent [a'vɑ̃], *n.m.* (*Ch.*) Advent.

aventure [avɑ̃'tyːr], *n.f.* surprising *or* unexpected event *or* experience, chance, accident, luck; adventure, daring enterprise, hazardous exploit; love affair *or* intrigue; **à l'aventure**, at random; **d'aventure** or **par aventure**, by chance, perchance.

aventurer [avɑ̃ty're], *v.t.* to venture, to hazard, to risk. **s'aventurer**, *v.r.* to venture, to take one's chance, to take risks.

aventureux [avɑ̃ty'rø], *a.* (*fem.* **-euse**) venturesome, adventurous; left to chance.

aventurier [avɑ̃ty'rje], *n.m.* (*fem.* **-ière**) adventurer, adventuress.

avenue [av'ny], *n.f.* approach; avenue.

avéré [ave're], *a.* authenticated, established by evidence.

avérer [ave're], *v.t.* (*conjug. like* CÉDER) to verify, to confirm, to establish. **s'avérer**, *v.r.* (*used only in inf. and p.p.*) to appear, to be distinctly, to turn out to be, to prove.

avers [a'vɛːr], *n.m.* obverse (*of coins etc.*).

averse [a'vɛrs], *n.f.* sudden and heavy shower of rain, downpour; (*fig.*) flood (*of talk etc.*).

aversion [aver'sjɔ̃], *n.f.* aversion, dislike, detestation.

averti [aver'ti], *a.* warned, informed; wide awake; well-informed, experienced.

avertir [aver'tiːr], *v.t.* to inform, to acquaint with, to give notice, to warn, to admonish (*de*).

avertissement [avɛrtis'mɑ̃], *n.m.* information, notification, advice, warning, caution; **avertissement au lecteur**, foreword (*of a book*).

avertisseur [averti'sœːr], *n.m.* look-out man; (*Theat.*) call-boy; call-bell, hooter; **avertisseur d'incendie**, fire-alarm.

aveu [a'vø], *n.m.* (*pl.* **-eux**) admission, avowal, confession; approbation, consent; **homme sans aveu**, vagrant, vagabond.

aveuglant [avœ'glɑ̃], *a.* blinding, dazzling; (*fig.*) distracting, misleading.

aveugle [a'vœgl], *a.* blind, sightless; blinded by passion etc., deluded.—*n.* blind person.

aveuglement [avœglə'mɑ̃], *n.m.* blindness; (*fig.*) infatuation, delusion.

aveuglément [avœglé'mɑ̃], *adv.* blindly, rashly; implicitly.

aveugle-né [avœglə'ne], *a.* and *n.m.* (*fem.* **-née**, *pl.* **aveugles-nés**) blind from birth.

aveugler [avœ'gle], *v.t.* to blind, to make blind; (*fig.*) to dazzle; to delude. **s'aveugler**, *v.r.* to shut one's eyes (*to*); (*fig.*) to be blinded, to be infatuated.

aveuglette [avœ'glɛt], *n.f.* (*only used in*) **à l'aveuglette**, blindly; **aller à l'aveuglette**, to go groping along, to go blindly *or* rashly; (*Av.*) **voler à l'aveuglette**, to fly blind.

aveulir [avœ'liːr], *v.t.* to render weak, to enfeeble, to enervate. **s'aveulir**, *v.r.* to sink into sloth.

aveulissant [avœli'sɑ̃], *a.* enfeebling, enervating.

aveulissement [avœlis'mɑ̃], *n.m.* enfeeblement, enervation.

aviateur [avja'tœːr], *n.m.* (*fem.* **-trice**) aviator; air-man, air-woman; flyer.

aviation [avja'sjɔ̃], *n.f.* aviation; **terrain d'aviation**, flying ground, air-field.

aviculteur [avikyl'tœːr], *n.m.* one who raises birds *or* poultry; bird fancier.

aviculture [avikyl'tyːr], *n.f.* bird-raising; poultry-farming.

avide [a'vid], *a.* greedy, voracious, rapacious; eager for, grasping.

avidement [avid'mɑ̃], *adv.* greedily, voraciously; eagerly.

avidité [avidi'te], *n.f.* avidity, greediness; eagerness.

avilir [avi'liːr], *v.t.* to debase, to depreciate, to disparage; to lower; to degrade, to disgrace. **s'avilir**, *v.r.* to degrade oneself, to stoop to (*doing something*).

avilissant [avili'sɑ̃], *a.* debasing, degrading, humiliating.

avilissement [avilis'mɑ̃], *n.m.* debasement, degradation; depreciation, disparagement.

avilisseur [avili'sœːr], *a.* (*fem.* **-euse**) debasing, degrading.—*n.m.* (*fem.* **-euse**) one who debases, disparages *or* degrades.

aviné [avi'ne], *a.* drunk, unsteady (*from drink*); wine-soaked (*of a cask*).

aviner [avi'ne], *v.t.* to soak *or* fill with wine. **s'aviner**, *v.r.* to get drunk.

avion [a'vjɔ̃], *n.m.* aeroplane, aircraft; **avion de bombardement**, bomber; **avion de chasse**, fighter; **avion de ligne**, air-liner; **avion à réaction**, jet-plane; **avion-fusée**, rocket-plane; **avion-taxi**, charter-plane; **par avion**, by air, by air mail.

aviron [avi'rɔ̃], *n.m.* oar; (*Spt.*) rowing.

avis [a'vi], *n.m.* opinion, way of thinking, judgment; vote, motion; advice, counsel; information, notice, warning, caution, intelligence; **à mon avis**, in my opinion; **j'ai changé d'avis**, I have changed my mind; **avis au public**, notice.

avisé [avi'ze], *a.* shrewd, clear-sighted, wary, circumspect, prudent.

aviser [avi'ze], *v.t.* to perceive, to espy; to inform, to apprise; (*Comm.*) to advise by letter.—*v.i.* to consider, to think (*about*), to look (*to*). **s'aviser**, *v.r.* to think (*of*), to be minded (*to*); to venture to do.

avivage [avi'vaːʒ], *n.m.* brightening, reviving (*of colours*).

aviver [avi've], *v.t.* to revive, to brighten; to sharpen the edges of, to polish, to burnish; to irritate, to exacerbate (*a wound, resentment etc.*). **s'aviver**, *v.r.* to revive.

avocat (1) [avɔ'ka], *n.m.* (*fem.* **-e**) barrister, advocate, counsel; (*fig.*) pleader, intercessor, champion.

avocat (2) [avɔ'ka], *n.m.* avocado, alligator pear.

avoine [a'vwan], *n.f.* oats.

avoir [a'vwair], *v.t. irr.* to have, to possess; to experience, to feel (*pain, hunger etc.*); to obtain, to get, to buy etc.; to be aged (*so many years*); to have on, to wear; to ail; **avoir à**, to have to, to be under obligation to (*do etc.*); **y avoir** (*impers.*), to be; **avoir faim**, to be hungry; **combien y a-t-il de Paris à Londres?** how far is it from Paris to London? **il a quarante ans**, he is forty; **il n'y a pas de quoi**, don't mention it, no offence taken; **il y a deux mois que je**

suis ici, I have been here two months; *il est arrivé il y a trois semaines*, he arrived three weeks ago; *j'ai à vous parler*, I have something to tell you; *qu'avez-vous donc?* what's the matter? *quel âge avez-vous?* how old are you? *qu'est-ce que vous avez?* what is the matter with you? *la pièce a cinq mètres de large*, the room is fifteen feet wide.—*n.m.* possessions, property, what one is worth.

avoisinant [avwazi'nɑ̃], *a.* neighbouring, adjoining, close by.

avoisiner [avwazi'ne], *v.t.* to border upon, to be contiguous to.

avortement [avɔrtə'mɑ̃], *n.m.* abortion, miscarriage; failure.

avorter [avɔr'te], *v.i.* to miscarry, to have a miscarriage; to fail to develop, ripen etc. (*of plants, fruit etc.*); to prove abortive, to fail.

avorton [avɔr'tɔ̃], *n.m.* abortion; abortive child; (*fig.*) a paltry *or* miserable person *or* thing, a miserable specimen.

avoué [a'vwe], *n.m.* attorney, solicitor; *une étude d'avoué*, a solicitor's office.

avouer [a'vwe], *v.t.* to own, to acknowledge, to confess; to approve; to recognize as one's own, to avow.

avril [a'vril], *n.m.* April.

avunculaire [avõky'lɛːr], *a.* avuncular.

axe [aks], *n.m.* axis; axle, axle-tree, spindle, trunnion; (*Bot., Geol., Anat. etc.*) axis; (*fig.*) central support *or* main axis of a system of ideas etc.; (*Polit.*) the Nazi-Fascist Axis.

axiomatique [aksjɔma'tik], *a.* axiomatic.

axiome [ak'sjoːm], *n.m.* axiom; (*fig.*) an accepted proposition, truism.

ayant [ɛ'jɑ̃], *pres. p.* [AVOIR].

ayant cause [ɛjɑ̃'koːz], *n.m.* (*pl.* ayants cause) (*Law*) trustee, executor, assign.

ayant droit [ɛjɑ̃'drwa], *n.m.* (*pl.* ayants droit) beneficiary, rightful claimant.

azalée [aza'le], *n.f.* azalea.

azotate [azɔ'tat], *n.m.* nitrate.

azote [a'zɔt], *a.* nitric.—*n.m.* nitrogen.

azoté [azɔ'te], *a.* nitrogenized.

azoter [azɔ'te], *v.t.* to charge with nitrogen; to azotize.

azoteux [azɔ'tø], *a.* (*fem.* -euse) nitrous.

azotique [azɔ'tik], *a.* nitric.

azur [a'zyːr], *n.m.* azure, blue, sky-colour; washing blue; *la Côte d'Azur*, the French Riviera.

azuré [azy're], *a.* azure, sky-coloured; *la voûte azurée*, the azure skies.

azyme [a'zim], *a.* azymous, unleavened (*bread*).—*n.m.* azyme, unleavened bread; *fête des azymes*, feast of unleavened bread.

B

B, b [be], *n.m.* the second letter of the alphabet.

baba [ba'ba], *n.m.* a sponge cake, with sultanas, steeped in rum and syrup.

Babel [ba'bɛl], *n.f.* Babel; (*fig.*) uproar, disorder.

babeurre [ba'bœːr], *n.m.* buttermilk.

babil [ba'bi], *n.m.* babble, prattle; chit-chat, tattle; chattering, babbling.

babillage [babij'maʒ], **babillement** [babij'mɑ̃], *n.m.* prattle, babbling, twaddle; tittle-tattle.

babillard [babi'jaːr], *a.* babbling, prattling, talkative, garrulous; gossiping, tell-tale.—*n.m.* (*fem.* -e) chatterer, babbler; tattler, blabber, gossip, tell-tale.

babillement [BABILLAGE].

babiller [babi'je], *v.i.* to babble, to prattle, to chat; to gossip, to chatter; (*fig.*) to blab, to backbite.

babine [ba'bin], **babouine** [ba'bwin], *n.f.* the pendulous lip (*of certain animals*); (*colloq.*) chops.

babiole [ba'bjɔl], *n.f.* bauble, trinket, toy; (*fig.*) trifle, trumpery affair.

bâbord [ba'bɔːr], *n.m.* (*Naut.*) port (*side*).

babouche [ba'buʃ], *n.f.* Turkish heelless slipper, babouche.

babouin [ba'bwɛ̃], *n.m.* baboon, monkey.

Babylone [babi'lon], *f.* Babylon.

babylonien [babilo'njɛ̃], *a.* (*fem.* -enne) Babylonian.—*n.m.* (**Babylonien**, *fem.* -enne) Babylonian (*person*).

bac [bak], *n.m.* ferry, ferry-boat; vat; (*Elec.*) *bac d'accumulateurs*, accumulator-jar.

baccalauréat [bakalɔre'a], *n.m.* baccalaureate, bachelorship (*of arts, science etc.*), school-leaving certificate.

bacchanal [baka'nal], *n.m.* (*colloq.*) racket, uproar.

bacchante [ba'kɑ̃ːt], *n.f.* bacchante, lewd woman.

bâche [baːʃ], *n.f.* cart tilt; awning; tank, cistern; *bâche (goudronnée)*, tarpaulin.

bachelier [baʃə'lje], *n.m.* (*fem.* -ière) Bachelor (*ès Lettres, ès Sciences, of Arts, Science*).

bachique [ba'ʃik], *a.* bacchic, jovial, convivial; *chant bachique*, drinking-song.

bachot [ba'ʃo], *n.m.* wherry, small ferry-boat; (*Univ. slang*) baccalaureate.

bachoteur [baʃo'tœːr], *n.m.* ferryman.

bacille [ba'sil], *n.m.* (*Biol.*) bacillus; *porteur de bacilles*, germ-carrier.

bacillose [basi'loːz], [TUBERCULOSE].

bâclage [ba'klaːʒ], *n.m.* closing of a port by means of chains, booms etc.; line of boats (*in a port*) for the discharge *or* loading of cargo; (*fig.*) hasty, scamped work.

bâcle [baːkl], *n.f.* bar (*for door or gate*).

bâcler [ba'kle], *v.t.* to bar, fasten *or* secure (*a door, window etc.*); to stop, obstruct *or* interrupt (*traffic, navigation etc.*); (*fig.*) to do hastily, to polish off, to scamp (*work*); to bungle.

bactérie [bakte'ri], *n.f.* bacterium, microbe.

bactérien [bakte'rjɛ̃], *a.* (*fem.* -enne) bacterial.

bactériologie [bakterjɔlɔ'ʒi], *n.f.* bacteriology.

bactériologique [bakterjɔlɔ'ʒik], *a.* bacteriological; *guerre bactériologique*, germ warfare.

bactériologiste [bakterjɔlɔ'ʒist], *n.m.* bacteriologist.

bactériothérapie [bakterjɔtera'pi], *n.f.* medical treatment by means of bacteria.

badaud [ba'do], *n.m.* (*fem.* **-e**) ninny, booby star-gazer; lounger, idler, rubber-neck.
badaudage [bado'da:ʒ], *n.m.* star-gazing, lounging, loitering, idling.
badauder [bado'de], *v.i.* to go gaping about; to lounge, to saunter, to loiter.
badauderie [bado'dri], *n.f.* star-gazing, silliness; lounging, idling, sauntering.
Bade [bad], *f.* Baden.
badigeon [badi'ʒɔ̃], *n.m.* badigeon, filling-paste; whitewash; distemper.
badigeonnage [badiʒɔ'na:ʒ], *n.m.* filling up with badigeon, making up; daubing; white-washing.
badigeonner [badiʒɔ'ne], *v.t.* to fill up (*stone-work, sculpture etc.*) with badigeon; to whitewash; (*fig.*) to disguise defects with varnish, rouge etc.; (*Med.*) to anoint.
badigeonneur [badiʒɔ'nœ:r], *n.m.* white-washer; (*pej.*) dauber.
badin [ba'dɛ̃], *a.* waggish, jocular, roguish, droll.—*n.m.* (*fem.* **-e** (1)) wag, joker; buf-foon.
badinage [badi'na:ʒ], *n.m.* badinage, raillery, banter; playfulness, jocularity (*of style*); mere child's-play.
badine (2) [ba'din], *n.f.* switch, light cane, wand; (*pl.*) small tongs.
badiner [badi'ne], *v.i.* to trifle, to dally, to toy; to speak *or* write banteringly *or* play-fully.
badinerie [badin'ri], *n.f.* jesting, foolery, trifling; silliness, childishness.
(C) **bâdrant** [bɑ'drɑ̃], *a.* bothersome.
(C) **bâdrer** [bɑ'dre], *v.t.* to annoy, to bother.
bafouer [ba'fwe], *v.t.* to scoff at, to make game of.
bafouillage [bafu'ja:ʒ], *n.f.* gibberish, rig-marole; spluttering; bad running (*of engine*).
bafouiller [bafu'je], *v.i.* (*colloq.*) to stammer; to splutter; to miss, to chatter (*of engine*).
bafouilleur [bafu'jœ:r], *n.m.* (*fem.* **-euse**) stammerer.
bagages [ba'ga:ʒ], *n.m. pl.* luggage; *bagages enregistrés*, registered luggage.
bagarre [ba'ga:r], *n.f.* riot; uproar; crush, squabble, scuffle.
bagatelle [baga'tɛl], *n.f.* bauble, trinket, trifle, anything frivolous; trifling sum, mere nothing.
bagne [baɲ], *n.m.* convict-prison; penal servitude.
bagnole [ba'nɔl], *n.f.* (*fam.*) (old) motor-car.
bague [bag], *n.f.* ring; ring band (*for birds*).
bague-agrafe [baga'graf], *n.f.* (*d'un stylo*) (fountain-pen) clip.
baguer [ba'ge], *v.t.* to baste, to tack, to stitch; to decorate *or* hang with rings; (*Hort.*) to ring (*trees*); to ring (*a bird*).
baguette [ba'gɛt], *n.f.* switch, rod, wand; pointer; clock (*of stockings*); glove-stretcher; long roll (*French bread*).
baguier [ba'gje], *n.m.* casket for rings, jewels etc., jewel-box, ring-stand.
bah! [bɑ], *int.* pooh! pshaw! nonsense! fudge!
bahut [ba'y], *n.m.* cabinet, trunk, chest; press, cupboard; (*Sch. slang*) grammar school.
bahutier [bay'tje], *n.m.* maker of trunks, chests, cabinets, etc.
bai [bɛ], *a.* bay; *une jument baie*(1), a bay mare.

baie (2) [bɛ], *n.f.* bay, gulf; (*Arch.*) bay, opening.
baie (3) [bɛ], *n.f.* berry.
baignade [bɛ'ɲad], *n.f.* bathing; bathing-place.
baigner [bɛ'ɲe], *v.t.* to bathe, to give a bath to, to dip; (*fig.*) to wash, to water (*a coast etc.*); to wet, to suffuse.—*v.i.* to be plunged into; to welter (*in blood etc.*). **se baigner**, *v.r.* to bathe, to wash.
baigneur [bɛ'ɲœ:r], *n.m.* (*fem.* **-euse**) bather; bathkeeper *or* attendant, bathing-attendant.
baignoire [bɛ'ɲwa:r], *n.f.* bath-tub, bath; (*Theat.*) ground-floor box.
bail [ba:j], *n.m.* (*pl.* **baux** [bo]) lease.
bâillement [bɑj'mɑ̃], *n.m.* yawning, yawn.
bâiller [bɑ'je], *v.i.* to yawn, to gape; to open (*of fissures etc.*); to be ajar (*of doors*).
bailleur [ba'jœ:r], *n.m.* (*fem.* **-eresse**) one who leases, lessor.
bâilleur [bɑ'jœ:r], *n.m.* (*fem.* **-euse**) yawner; gaper.
bailli [ba'ji], *n.m.* (*Fr. Hist.*) bailiff.
bâillon [bɑ'jɔ̃], *n.m.* gag, muzzle.
bâillonnement [bɑjɔn'mɑ̃], *n.m.* gagging.
bâillonner [bɑjɔ'ne], *v.t.* to stop the mouth of, to gag, to muzzle; (*fig.*) to silence.
bain [bɛ̃], *n.m.* bath; bathing-tub; (*pl.*) baths, bathing establishment, watering-place, spa; *la salle de bain(s)*, the bathroom.
bain-douche [bɛ̃'duʃ], *n.m.* shower-bath.
bain-marie [bɛ̃ma'ri], *n.m.* (*pl.* **bains-marie**) (*Cook.*) double saucepan for foods that burn easily; boiler (*in a kitchen-range etc.*).
baïonnette [bajɔ'nɛt], *n.f.* bayonet.
baiser [bɛ'ze], *v.t.* (*of strictly literary use, no longer decent in conversation, practically replaced by* **embrasser**) to kiss.—*n.m.* kiss, kissing; salute.
baisse [bɛ:s], *n.f.* fall, abatement; decline; reduction *or* fall (*of prices etc.*); falling off (*of credit etc.*).
baisser [bɛ'se], *v.t.* to let down, to lower; to reduce the height of; to strike (*a flag etc.*); to bow (*the head etc.*).—*v.i.* (*with aux.* ÊTRE *or* AVOIR) to go down; to ebb; to be on the decline *or* the wane; to flag, to droop; to fail, to diminish. **se baisser**, *v.r.* to stoop; to bow down; to be lowered.
bajoue [ba'ʒu] *n.f.* jowl; chap (*of pigs etc.*).
bakélite [bake'lit], *n.f.* (*reg. trade name*) bakelite.
bal [bal], *n.m.* ball, dance; *bal costumé*, fancy-dress ball.
baladeuse [bala'dø:z], *n.f.* costermonger's barrow; portable lamp; trailer (*for cycle or tram*).
baladin [bala'dɛ̃], *n.m.* (*fem.* **-e**) mounte-bank; buffoon.
balafre [ba'lɑ:fr], *n.f.* gash, slash, cut; scar.
balafrer [balɑ'fre], *v.t.* to gash, to slash.
balai (1) [ba'lɛ], *n.m.* broom, besom; (*Elec.*) brush.
(C) **balai** (2) [ba'lɛ], *n.m.* cedar.
balalaïka [balalai'ka], *n.f.* balalaika.
balance [ba'lɑ:s], *n.f.* balance, scales, pair of scales; (*Comm.*) balance (*of an account*), balance sheet.
balancement [balɑ̃s'mɑ̃], *n.m.* balancing, poising; rocking, see-saw; (*fig.*) fluctuation, wavering, hesitation.

balancer

balancer [balɑ'se], *v.t. (conjug. like* COM-
MENCER) to balance, to poise, to hold in
equilibrium; to swing to and fro, to rock;
(*fig.*) to weigh, to consider; to square (*accounts*); to counterbalance.—*v.i.* to hesitate,
to be in suspense, to waver; to fluctuate, to
oscillate, to remain undecided. **se balancer,**
v.r. to swing, to rock.
balancier [balɑ'sje], *n.m.* maker of weights
and scales; pendulum, balance; balancing-
pole.
balançoire [balɑ̃'swaːr], *n.f.* see-saw; swing.
balandre [ba'lɑ̃ːdr], *n.f.* flat canal boat.
balayage [balɛ'jaːʒ], **balayement** [balɛ
'mɑ̃], *n.m.* sweeping; (*Tel.*) scanning.
balayer [balɛ'je], *v.t. (conjug. like* PAYER) to
sweep, to clean with a broom; (*Tel.*) to scan.
balayette [balɛ'jɛt], *n.f.* small broom, whisk.
balayeur [balɛ'jœːr], *n.m.* (*fem.* -**euse**)
sweeper, scavenger.—*n.f.* (-**euse**) sweeping-
machine.
balayures [balɛ'jyːr], *n.f.* (*used only in pl.*)
sweepings.
balbutier [balby'sje], *v.t.* to pronounce
indistinctly.—*v.i.* to stammer, to stutter;
to mumble.
balbutieur [balby'sjœːr], *n.m.* (*fem.* -**euse**)
stutterer, stammerer.
balcon [bal'kɔ̃], *n.m.* balcony; (*Theat.*) dress-
circle.
baldaquin [balda'kɛ̃], *n.m.* baldachin,
canopy; tester (*of bed*).
Bâle [bɑːl], *f.* Basel, Basle.
Baléares [bale'aːr], **les,** *f. pl.* the Balearic
Isles.
baleine [ba'lɛːn], *n.f.* whale; whalebone; rib
of an umbrella.
baleiné [balɛ'ne], *a.* stiffened with whalebone.
baleineau [balɛ'no], *n.m.* (*pl.* -**eaux**) young
whale.
baleinier [balɛ'nje], *n.m.* (*fem.* -**ière**) whaler.
—*n.f.* (-**ière**) whale-boat.
balisage [bali'zaːʒ], *n.m.* (*Naut.*) buoying,
signalling; (*Av.*) ground-lights.
balise [ba'liːz], *n.f.* sea-mark, buoy, beacon;
(*Av.*) ground-light.
baliser [bali'ze], *v.t.* to buoy; to mark with
beacons *or* ground-lights.
balistique [balis'tik], *a.* ballistic.—*n.f.* bal-
listics.
balivage [bali'vaːʒ], *n.m.* *staddling.
baliveau [bali'vo], *n.m.* (*pl.* -**eaux**) *staddle;
sapling.
baliverne [bali'vɛrn], *n.f.* nonsense, humbug.
baliverner [balivɛr'ne], *v.i.* to talk idly, to
talk twaddle.
balkanique [balka'nik], *a.* Balkan.
ballade [ba'lad], *n.f.* ballade; ballad.
ballant [ba'lɑ̃], *a.* waving, swinging, dangling.
ballast [ba'last], *n.m.* (*Rail.*) ballast.
balle [bal], *n.f.* ball; bullet, shot; bale, pack.
ballerine [bal'rin], *n.f.* ballerina.
ballet [ba'lɛ], *n.m.* ballet.
ballon [ba'lɔ̃], *n.m.* hand-ball; football; balloon; air-balloon (*child's*).
ballonné [balɔ'ne], *a.* distended, swollen.
ballonnier [balɔ'nje], *n.m.* maker *or* vendor of
toy balloons.
ballon-sonde [balɔ̃'sɔ̃ːd], *n.m.* sounding
balloon.
ballot [ba'lo], *n.m.* small pack (*of wares for
sale*).

ballottement [balɔt'mɑ̃], *n.m.* tossing,
shaking.
ballotter [balɔ'te], *v.t.* to toss, to toss about;
to bandy; to keep in suspense.—*v.i.* to
shake, to rattle.
balnéaire [balne'ɛːr], *a.* pertaining to baths
etc.; *station balnéaire,* watering-place;
seaside resort.
balourd [ba'luːr], *a.* dull, heavy, thick-
headed.—*n.m.* (*fem.* -**e**) stupid *or* dull person,
numskull, dunce.
balourdise [balur'diːz], *n.f.* gross blunder;
stupidity.
balsamier [balza'mje], **baumier** [bo'mje],
n.m. balsam-tree.
balsamine [balza'min], *n.f.* balsamine.
Baltique [bal'tik], **la,** *f.* the Baltic (Sea).
balustrade [balys'trad], *n.f.* balustrade; low
railing etc.
balustre [ba'lystr], *n.m.* baluster, hand-rail.
balustrer [balys'tre], *v.t.* to rail in, to surround.
balzane [bal'zan], *n.f.* white stocking (*of a
horse*).
bambin [bɑ̃'bɛ̃], *n.m.|(fem.* -**e**) (*colloq.*) urchin;
brat, tiny tot.
bambou [bɑ̃'bu], *n.m.* bamboo (cane).
ban [bɑ̃], *n.m.* ban, announcement, public
order, edict *or* proclamation; banishment,
proscription; (*pl.*) banns (*of matrimony*).
banal [ba'nal], *a.* (*m. pl.* -**aux**) common,
commonplace, trite.
banalité [banali'te], *n.f.* vulgarity; banality,
commonplace, trite expression.
banane [ba'nan], *n.f.* banana.
bananier [bana'nje], *n.m.* banana-tree;
banana boat.
banc [bɑ̃], *n.m.* bench, settle, form; reef,
sand-bank; shoal (*of fish*); (*Geol.*) layer, bed;
dock, bar; *banc d'essai,* (*Motor.*) test
bench; (*C*) *banc de neige,* heap of snow;
banc d'huîtres, oyster-bed.
bancal [bɑ̃'kal], *a.* (*m. pl.* -**als**) bandy-
legged.—*n.m.* (*fem.* -**e**) bandy-legged person.
bandage [bɑ̃'daːʒ], *n.m.* application of
bandages; bandage; belt; truss; tyre (*of
wheels*).
bande (1) [bɑ̃ːd], *n.f.* band, belt, strip; ribbon;
bandage; *bande de papier,* slip of paper,
wrapper.
bande (2) [bɑ̃ːd], *n.f.* band, troop, company;
gang, crew, set (*of brigands etc.*); flock,
pack.
bandé [bɑ̃'de], *a.* bandaged, taut, stretched.
bandeau [bɑ̃'do], *n.m.* (*pl.* -**eaux**) headband,
bandage (*for the eyes*).
bandelette [bɑ̃'dlɛt], *n.f.* little band, string
fillet.
bander [bɑ̃'de], *v.t.* to bind *or* tie up; to
bandage; to tighten, to bend (*a bow etc.*).—
v.i. to be stretched, to be taut *or* too tight.
banderole [bɑ̃'drɔl], *n.f.* banderole, streamer.
bandit [bɑ̃'di], *n.m.* brigand, bandit; ruffian,
blackguard; scamp.
bandoulière [bɑ̃du'ljɛːr], *n.f.* shoulder-strap,
bandolier; *en bandoulière,* slung across
the back.
banjo [bɑ̃'ʒo], *n.m.* banjo.
banlieue [bɑ̃'ljø], *n.f.* suburbs, outskirts (*of
a town*).
banne [ban], *n.f.* hamper; awning; tilt,
tarpaulin.

banni [ba'ni], *a.* banished, outlawed; (*fig.*) banned, forbidden.—*n.m.* (*fem.* -e) exile, outlaw.

bannière [ba'njɛːr], *n.f.* banner, standard, flag.

bannir [ba'niːr], *v.t.* to banish; (*fig.*) to expel, to dismiss.

bannissement [banis'mã], *n.m.* banishment.

banque [bãːk], *n.f.* bank, banking.

banqueroute [bã'krut], *n.f.* bankruptcy; (*fig.*) failure, collapse.

banqueroutier [bãkru'tje], *n.m.* (*fem.* -ière) bankrupt.

banquet [bã'kɛ], *n.m.* banquet, feast.

banquette [bã'kɛt], *n.f.* bench; towing-path; (*Fort.*) banquette.

banquier [bã'kje], *n.m.* banker.

banquise [bã'kiːz], *n.f.* ice-floe, ice-pack.

bantam [bã'tam], *n.m.* bantam.

baptême [ba'tɛːm], *n.m.* baptism, christening; *nom de baptême*, Christian name.

baptiser [bati'ze], *v.t.* to baptize; (*fig.*) to christen, to give a name *or* nickname to.

baptismal [batiz'mal], *a.* (*m. pl.* -aux) baptismal.

baptistaire [batis'tɛːr], *a.* of baptism; *registre baptistaire*, parish register.

Baptiste [ba'tist], *n.m.* Baptist.

baquet [ba'kɛ], *n.m.* tub; (*Av.*) cockpit.

bar (1) [baːr], *n.m.* (*Ichth.*) bass.

bar (2) [baːr], *n.m.* bar (*of a public-house etc.*).

baragouin [bara'gwɛ̃], *n.m.* gibberish, jargon, lingo.

baragouinage [baragwi'naːʒ], *n.m.* talking, gibberish, jargon etc.

baragouiner [baragwi'ne], *v.t.* to sputter out (*words*).—*v.i.* to talk gibberish; to gabble.

baraque [ba'rak], *n.f.* hut, shed, shanty; (*fam.*) hovel; booth (*at a fair*).

baraquement [barak'mã], *n.m.* (*Mil.*) hutting.

barattage [bara'taːʒ], *n.m.* churning.

baratte [ba'rat], *n.f.* churn.

baratter [bara'te], *v.t.* to churn.

barbacane [barba'kan], *n.f.* (*Fort.*) barbican.

Barbade [bar'bad], *f.* Barbados.

barbare [bar'baːr], *a.* barbarous, barbarian; cruel, inhuman; (*fig.*) uncouth, rude; incorrect, ungrammatical.—*n.m.* (*usu. in pl.*) barbarians.

barbarement [barbar'mã], *adv.* barbarously.

barbaresque [barba'rɛsk], *a.* of *or* pertaining to Barbary.

Barbarie [barba'ri], **la,** *f.* Barbary.

barbarie [barba'ri], *n.f.* barbarity, rudeness; (*fig.*) cruelty.

barbarisme [barba'rism], *n.m.* (*Gram.*) barbarism.

barbe (1) [barb], *n.f.* beard; whiskers (*of cats, dogs etc.*); beard (*of corn etc.*); wattles (*of fowls*).

barbe (2) [barb], *n.m.* barb, barbary horse.

barbeau [bar'bo], *n.m.* (*pl.* -eaux) barbel; (*Bot.*) blue-bottle, cornflower.

barbelé [barbə'le], *a.* barbed, spiked; (*fil de fer*) *barbelé*, barbed wire.

barbiche [bar'biʃ], **barbichette** [barbi'ʃɛt], *n.f.* beard growing only on the chin, goatee.

barbier [bar'bje], *n.m.* barber.

barbiturate [barbity'rat], **barbiturique** [barbity'rik], *n.m.* (*Chem.*) barbiturate.

barboter [barbɔ'te], *v.i.* to dabble about in mud *or* water (*with the beak, like a duck*); to paddle, to flounder about in the mud; (*fig.*) to mumble.

barboteuse [barbɔ'tøːz], *n.f.* rompers.

barbotière [barbɔ'tjɛːr], *n.f.* duck-pond; trough.

barbouillage [barbu'jaːʒ], *n.m.* daubing; daub; scrawl; (*fig.*) twaddle.

barbouiller [barbu'je], *v.t.* to soil, to dirty, to blot; to daub, to besmear; to scrawl, to scribble; to splutter out, to mumble; to bungle.

barbouilleur [barbu'jœːr], *n.m.* (*fem.* -euse) dauber, scribbler; mumbler.

barbu [bar'by], *a.* bearded.

barbue [bar'by], *n.f.* brill.

barcarolle [barka'rɔl], *n.f.* (*Mus.*) barcarolle.

Barcelone [barsə'lɔn], *f.* Barcelona.

bardane [bar'dan], *n.f.* burr, burdock.

barde (1) [bard], *n.m.* bard.

barde (2) [bard], *n.f.* bard (*iron armour for horses*); thin rasher of bacon used for larding poultry etc.

bardé [bar'de], *a.* barded; larded.

barder [bar'de], *v.t.* to barb a horse; to cover with thin slices of bacon, to lard; (*slang*) *ça barde* or *ça va barder*, things are beginning to hum.

bardot *or* **bardeau** (*pl.* -eaux) [bar'do], *n.m.* hinny; pack-mule.

barème [ba'rɛːm], *n.m.* ready-reckoner.

barguignage [bargi'naːʒ], *n.m.* (*colloq.*) hesitation, wavering, dilly-dallying.

barguigner [bargi'ne], *v.i.* to be irresolute, to waver, to shilly-shally.

barguigneur [bargi'nœːr], *n.m.* (*fem.* -euse) waverer, haggler.

baril [ba'ri], *n.m.* small barrel, cask, keg.

bariolage [barjɔ'laːʒ], *n.m.* variegation, odd medley of colours, motley.

bariolé [barjɔ'le], *a.* gaudy, motley, many-coloured.

barioler [barjɔ'le], *v.t.* to streak with several colours, to variegate.

barnache [BERNACLE].

baromètre [barɔ'mɛtr], *n.m.* barometer.

barométrique [barɔme'trik], *a.* barometrical.

baron [ba'rɔ̃], *n.m.* (*fem.* -onne) baron, baroness.

baronnet [barɔ'nɛ], *n.m.* baronet.

baronnial [barɔ'njal], *a.* (*m. pl.* -aux) baronial.

baronnie [barɔ'ni], *n.f.* barony.

baroque [ba'rɔk], *a.* irregular, grotesque odd; baroque.

barque [bark], *n.f.* bark, boat, small craft.

barquerolle [barkə'rɔl], *n.f.* small mastless barge.

barquette [bar'kɛt], *n.f.* small craft; light puff-biscuit.

barrage [ba'raːʒ], *n.m.* barrier; toll-bar; dam, weir, barrage.

barre [baːr], *n.f.* bar (*of metal, wood etc.*); dash, cross, stroke (*of the pen etc.*); bar (*in courts*) of justice; (*Naut.*) helm, tiller, bar; (*Mus.*) bar; bore (*of river*).

barreau [ba'ro], *n.m.* (*pl.* -eaux) small bar (*of wood, metal etc.*); bench reserved for barristers; (*fig.*) lawyers, barristers; rung (*of a ladder*); *être reçu* or *admis au barreau*, to be called to the bar.

barrer [ba're], *v.t.* to bar up, to fence off; to obstruct, to thwart; to cross off, to erase.

barrette (1) or **barette** [ba'rɛt], *n.f.* square flat cap, biretta; cardinal's hat.

barrette (2) [ba'rɛt], *n.m.* axle, pin, bolt, etc. (*in watches, jewellery etc.*); bar (*of medal*).

barreur [ba'rœːr], *n.m.* helmsman, coxswain.

barricade [bari'kad], *n.f.* barricade.

barricader [barika'de], *v.t.* to barricade, to obstruct.

barrière [ba'rjɛːr], *n.f.* railing, barrier; gateway; farm gate.

barrique [ba'rik], *n.f.* large barrel or cask, hogshead.

baryton [bari'tõ], *n.m.* baritone.

baryum [ba'rjɔm], *n.m.* barium.

bas (1) [bɑ], *a.* (*fem.* **basse** (1)) low; in a low situation; inferior; (*fig.*) vile, base, sordid; mean; subdued (*of sounds*); decadent; *la marée est basse*, it is low tide; *les Pays-Bas*, the Netherlands.—*adv.* low, down; in a subdued voice, tone, etc.; *ici bas*, here below; *là-bas*, over there, yonder.—*n.m.* the lower part, bottom or foot (*of something*); *en bas*, below, downstairs; *le bas de l'escalier*, the foot of the stairs.

bas (2) [bɑ], *n.m. inv.* stocking.

basalte [ba'zalt], *n.m.* basalt.

basane [ba'zan], *n.f.* sheepskin.

basané [baza'ne], *a.* sunburnt, bronzed, swarthy, tawny.

bascule [bas'kyl], *n.f.* see-saw; weighing-machine.

basculer [basky'le], *v.i.* to see-saw; to rock, to swing.

base [baːz], *n.f.* base, foundation; lower part, bottom; basis.

base-ball [bes'bɔl], *n.m.* baseball.

baser [bɑ'ze], *v.t.* to found, to base, to ground. **se baser**, *v.r.* to be grounded; to depend, to rely.

bas-fond [bɑ'fõ], *n.m.* (*pl.* **bas-fonds**) low-lying ground, hollow, bottom; shallow, shallow water; (*fig., pl.*) underworld.

basilic [bazi'lik], *n.m.* (*Bot.*) basil, sweet basil; (*Myth.*) basilisk, cockatrice.

basilique [bazi'lik], *n.f.* basilica.

basket-ball [basket'bɔl], *n.m.* basket-ball.

basketteur [baske'tœːr], *n.m.* (*fem.* **-euse**) basket-ball player.

basque (1) [bask], *n.f.* flap, skirt, tail (*of a garment*).

basque (2) [bask], *a.* Basque.—*n.m.* Basque (*language*).—*n.* (**Basque**) Basque (*person*).

bas-relief [bɑrə'ljɛf], *n.m.* (*pl.* **bas-reliefs**) bas-relief.

basse (1) [bɑːs], [BAS (1)].

basse (2) [bɑːs], *n.f.* bass, bass-string; sax-horn.

basse (3) [bɑːs], *n.f.* shallow, reef.

basse-contre [bas'kõːtr], *n.f.* (*pl.* **basses-contre**) (*Mus.*) contra-bass, lower tenor.

basse-cour [bas'kuːr], *n.f.* (*pl.* **basses-cours**) farm-yard, poultry-yard.

bassement [bas'mã], *adv.* basely, meanly, vilely.

bassesse [ba'sɛs], *n.f.* baseness; lowness (*of station etc.*); meanness, vileness; mean or sordid action.

basset [ba'sɛ], *n.m.* basset-hound; *basset allemand*, dachshund.

basse-taille [bas'tɑːj], *n.f.* (*pl.* **basses-tailles**) (*Mus.*) baritone; (*Sculp.*) bas-relief.

bassin [ba'sɛ̃], *n.m.* basin; pond; dock; (*Anat.*) pelvis.

bassine [ba'sin], *n.f.* deep, wide pan.

bassiner [basi'ne], *v.t.* to warm (*a bed etc.*); to bathe (*with warm lotions*), to foment, to steep; to water, to sprinkle (*crops etc.*).

bassinet [basi'nɛ], *n.m.* small basin, pan, bowl.

bassinoire [basi'nwaːr], *n.f.* warming-pan; (*pop.*) bore.

bassiste [ba'sist], *n.m.* saxhorn-player; 'cellist.

basson [ba'sõ], *n.m.* bassoon; bassoonist.

bastide [bas'tid], *n.f.* (*Provence*) country cottage, villa.

bastille [bas'tiːj], *n.f.* bastille, fort.

bastion [bas'tjõ], *n.m.* bastion.

bastionner [bastjo'ne], *v.t.* to bastion, to fortify with bastions.

bastonnade [basto'nad], *n.f.* bastinado; caning.

bastringue [bas'trɛ̃ːg], *n.m.* (*pop.*) dance hall; (*slang*) noise.

bas-ventre [ba'vãːtr], *n.m.* (*pl.* **bas-ventres**) lower part of the belly.

bât [bɑ], *n.m.* pack-saddle.

bataclan [bata'klã], *n.m.* (*fam.*) paraphernalia.

bataille [ba'tɑːj], *n.f.* battle, fight, engagement.

batailler [bata'je], *v.i.* to give battle; to be at war, to fight; to struggle hard, to strive.

batailleur [bata'jœːr], *a.* (*fem.* **-euse**) combative, pugnacious, quarrelsome; disputatious.

bataillon [bata'jõ], *n.m.* battalion; (*fig.*) host; (*pl.*) troops.

bâtard [bɑ'taːr], *a.* and *n.m.* (*fem.* **-e**) bastard, illegitimate or natural (*child*).

bâté [bɑ'te], *a.* saddled with a pack; *c'est un âne bâté*, he is an ignorant lout.

bateau [ba'to], *n.m.* (*pl.* **-eaux**) boat; *bateau mouche*, pleasure steamer (*Paris and Lyons*).

batelage [ba'tlaːʒ], *n.m.* juggling, legerdemain; lighterage charges.

bateleur [ba'tlœːr], *n.m.* (*fem.* **-euse**) juggler, buffoon, mountebank.

batelier [batə'lje], *n.m.* (*fem.* **-ière**) boatman, boatwoman, ferryman, ferrywoman.

bâter [bɑ'te], *v.t.* to load with a pack-saddle.

bathyscaphe [batis'kaf], *n.m.* bathyscape.

bâti [bɑ'ti], *n.m.* framing, structure; basting, tacking (*of a garment*).

batifolage [batifo'laːʒ], *n.m.* romping; cuddling.

batifoler [batifo'le], *v.i.* to play, to romp; to cuddle.

bâtiment [bati'mã], *n.m.* building, structure, edifice; building trade; ship, vessel.

bâtir [bɑ'tiːr], *v.t.* to build, to erect, to construct; *faire bâtir*, to have built, to build; *terrain à bâtir*, building site.

bâtisse [bɑ'tis], *n.f.* masonry, ramshackle building.

batiste [ba'tist], *n.f.* cambric.

bâton [bɑ'tõ], *n.m.* stick, staff, cudgel, cane.

bâtonner [batɔ'ne], *v.t.* to cudgel, to cane.

batracien [batra'sjɛ̃], *n.m.* (*Zool.*) batrachian.

battant (1) [ba'tã], *n.m.* clapper (*of a bell*); leaf (*of a table or door*); fly (*of a flag*); *porte à deux battants*, double door.

40

battant (2) [ba'tɑ̃], *a.* beating, pelting, falling heavily (*of rain etc.*); **mener tambour battant**, to hurry on (*a business*).

batte [bat], *n.f.* long wooden staff *or* beater; *batte de blanchisseuse*, washing-board; *batte* (*de cricket*), (cricket) bat.

battée [ba'te], *n.f.* jamb of door *or* window.

battement [bat'mɑ̃], *n.m.* beating; clapping (*of hands*), stamping (*of feet*), flapping (*of wings*); beating (*of the heart*); shuffling (*of cards*).

batterie [ba'tri], *n.f.* (*Artill.*, *Elec.*, *Cook. etc.*) battery; *batterie de cuisine*, complete set of kitchen utensils.

batteur [ba'tœːr], *n.m.* (*fem.* **-euse**) beater; (*cricket etc.*) batsman; (*jazz*) drummer.—*n.f.* (**-euse**) threshing-machine.

battre [batr], *v.t.* (*see Verb Tables*) to strike upon, against etc.; to beat, to thrash, to whip (*a horse etc.*); to beat up, to mix; to defeat; to shuffle (*cards*); *battre des mains*, to clap; *la fête battait son plein*, the party was in full swing.—*v.i.* to beat, to knock; to pant, to throb. **se battre**, *v.r.* to fight, to combat; to hit oneself (*contre etc.*).

battu [ba'ty], *a.* beaten (*of a path, road etc.*); frequented; (*fig.*) trite, commonplace.

battue [ba'ty], *n.f.* (*Shooting*) wholesale slaughter, battue.

baudet [bo'dɛ], *n.m.* ass; (*fig.*) dolt, donkey; sawyer's trestle.

bauge [boːʒ], *n.f.* lair of a wild boar; squirrel's nest; (*fig.*) a dirty hovel.

baume [boːm], *n.m.* balm; balsam; (*fig.*) consolation.

baumier [BALSAMIER].

baux [BAIL].

bauxite [bo'sit], *n.f.* bauxite.

bavard [ba'vaːr], *a.* prating, talkative, loquacious.—*n.m.* (*fem.* **-e**) prater, babbler, chatterer.

bavardage [bavar'daːʒ], *n.m.* babbling, prattling; (*fig.*) twaddle, nonsense.

bavarder [bavar'de], *v.i.* to babble, to prattle.

bavarois [bava'rwa], *a.* Bavarian.—*n.m.* (**Bavarois**, *fem.* **-oise**) Bavarian (*person*).

bave [baːv], *n.f.* slaver, dribble; foam; (*fig.*) slime.

baver [ba've], *v.i.* to slobber, to dribble.

bavette [ba'vɛt], *n.f.* bib.

baveux [ba'vø], *a.* (*fem.* **-euse**) dribbling, slobbering.

Bavière [ba'vjɛːr], **la**, *f.* Bavaria.

bavure [ba'vyːr], *n.f.* seam (*left by a mould*); smudge (*of a pen*).

bazar [ba'zaːr], *n.m.* bazaar; ill-kept, untidy house; (*fam.*) *mettre tout son bazar dans une malle*, to put all one's belongings in a trunk.

bazooka [bazu'ka], *n.m.* (*Artill.*) bazooka.

béant [be'ɑ̃], *a.* gaping, yawning, wide open.

béat [be'a], *a.* blessed; devout; sanctimonious.

béatement [beat'mɑ̃], *adv.* sanctimoniously.

béatification [beatifika'sjɔ̃], *n.f.* beatification.

béatifier [beati'fje], *v.t.* to beatify.

béatifique [beati'fik], *a.* beatific, blissful.

béatitude [beati'tyd], *n.f.* beatitude, blessedness.

beau [bo], **bel** [bɛl] (*before nouns singular beginning with a vowel or h mute*), *a.* (*fem.* **belle**, *pl.* **beaux, belles**) beautiful, fine, handsome, fair; smart, spruce; glorious; lofty, noble;

seemly, becoming; (*iron.*) nice, precious; *au beau milieu*, in the very middle; *il fait beau*, it is a fine day; *il l'a échappé belle*, he has had a narrow escape.—*adv.* finely, promisingly; in vain; *avoir beau dire*, to speak in vain; *de plus belle*, with renewed ardour, worse than ever; *tout beau*, gently, not so fast.—*n.m.* that which is beautiful, fine, excellent etc.; beauty; beau.—*n.f.* (**belle**) belle; *la Belle et la Bête*, Beauty and the Beast.

beaucoup [bo'ku], *adv.* many, much; a great many, a great deal; *avoir beaucoup d'argent*, to have plenty of money.

beau-fils [bo'fis], *n.m.* (*pl.* **beaux-fils**) stepson.

beau-frère [bo'frɛːr], *n.m.* (*pl.* **beaux-frères**) brother-in-law.

beau-père [bo'pɛːr], *n.m.* (*pl.* **beaux-pères**) father-in-law; step-father.

beaupré [bo'pre], *n.m.* (*Naut.*) bowsprit.

beauté [bo'te], *n.f.* beauty; fineness, loveliness, comeliness, elegance, agreeableness.

beaux-arts [bo'zaːr], *n.m. pl.* fine arts.

beaux-parents [bopa'rɑ̃], *n.m. pl.* father-in-law and mother-in-law.

bébé [be'be], *n.m.* baby; baby-doll.

bec [bɛk], *n.m.* beak, bill; (*fig.*) mouth; snout (*of some fishes*); lip (*of a jug*), spout (*of a kettle etc.*); gas-jet, burner; mouthpiece (*of musical instrument*); nib (*pen*); *avoir bon bec*, to have the gift of the gab.

bécane [be'kan], *n.f.* (*pop.*) bike.

bécarre [be'kaːr], *a.* and *n.m.* (*Mus.*) natural.

bécasse [be'kas], *n.f.* woodcock; (*fam.*) stupid woman.

bécassine [beka'sin], *n.f.* snipe.

bec-de-lièvre [bɛkdə'ljɛːvr], *n.m.* (*pl.* **becs-de-lièvre**) harelip; harelipped person.

bec-fin [bɛk'fɛ̃], *n.m.* (*pl.* **becs-fins**) warbler; pipit.

béchamel [beʃa'mɛl], *n.f.* cream-sauce, béchamel sauce.

bêche [bɛːʃ], *n.f.* spade.

bêcher [be'ʃe], *v.t.* to dig.

becquée [be'ke], **béquée** [be'ke], *n.f.* billful; *donner la becquée*, to feed.

becqueter [bɛk'te], **béqueter** [bek'te], *v.t.* (*conjug. like* AMENER) to peck; (*colloq.*) to eat. **se becqueter**, **se béqueter**, *v.r.* to peck one another.

bedaine [bə'dɛn], *n.f.* (*colloq.*) paunch.

bedeau [bə'do], *n.m.* (*pl.* **-eaux**) beadle, verger.

bedonnant [bədo'nɑ̃], *a.* stout, pot-bellied.

bedonner [bədo'ne], *v.i.* to get *or* grow stout.

bédouin [be'dwɛ̃], *a.* Bedouin.—*n.m.* (**Bédouin**, *fem.* **-e**) Bedouin.

bée [be], *a. only used in* **bouche bée**, gaping, open-mouthed.

beffroi [be'frwa], *n.m.* belfry.

bégaiement [begɛ'mɑ̃], *n.m.*, **bégayant** [begɛ'jɑ̃], *a.* stammering, faltering.

bégayer [begɛ'je], *v.t.* (*conjug. like* PAYER) to stammer out, to stutter, to lisp.—*v.i.* to stammer.

bégayeur [begɛ'jœːr], *n.m.* (*fem.* **-euse**) stammerer, stutterer.

bégonia [bego'nja], *n.m.* begonia.

bègue [bɛg], *a.* stammering, stuttering.—*n.* stammerer, stutterer.

bégueule [be'gœl], *a.* prudish, squeamish; straitlaced.—*n.f.* (*fam.*) prude.

bégueulerie

bégueulerie [begœl′ri], *n.f.* prudery, prudish airs, squeamishness.

béguin [be′gɛ̃], *n.m.* hood, child's cap; *avoir un béguin pour*, to be sweet on; *c'est mon béguin*, he *or* she is my darling.

béguine [be′gin], *n.f.* beguine (*Flemish nun*); nun; bigoted person.

bégum [be′gɔm], *n.f.* begum.

beige [bɛːʒ], *a.* natural, undyed (*of wool*); beige.—*n.f.* unbleached serge.

beignet [bɛ′ɲɛ], *n.m.* fritter.

béjaune [be′ʒoːn], *n.m.* (*Falconry*) eyas, unfledged hawk; (*fig.*) ninny, novice; blunder, silliness, mistake.

bel [BEAU].

bêlant [bɛ′lã], *a.* bleating.

bêlement [bɛl′mã], *n.m.* bleating (*of sheep*).

bêler [bɛ′le], *v.i.* to bleat.

belette [bə′lɛt], *n.f.* weasel.

belge [bɛlʒ], *a.* Belgian.—*n.* (**Belge**) Belgian (*person*).

Belgique [bɛl′ʒik], **la**, *f.* Belgium.

bélier [be′lje], *n.m.* ram; battering-ram; Aries.

bélière [be′ljɛːr], *n.f.* sheep-bell; clapper-ring (*of a bell*); watch-ring; sword-sling.

bélître [be′litr], *n.m.* rascal, cad.

belladone [bɛla′dɔn], *n.f.* belladonna, deadly nightshade.

bellâtre [bɛ′lɑːtr], *a.* having insipid beauty; foppish.—*n.m.* insipid beauty; fop, coxcomb.

belle-fille [bɛl′fiːj], *n.f.* (*pl.* **belles-filles**) daughter-in-law; stepdaughter.

belle-maman [bɛlma′mã], (*colloq.*) [BELLE-MÈRE].

bellement [bɛl′mã], *adv.* prettily, charmingly, softly, gently.

belle-mère [bɛl′mɛːr], *n.f.* (*pl.* **belles-mères**) mother-in-law; stepmother.

belles-lettres [bɛl′lɛtr], *n.f. pl.* polite literature, belles-lettres.

belle-sœur [bɛl′sœːr], *n.f.* (*pl.* **belles-sœurs**) sister-in-law; stepsister.

belligérance [bɛliʒe′rɑ̃ːs], *n.f.* belligerence, belligerency.

belligérant [bɛliʒe′rã], *a.* and *n.m.* (*fem.* -**e**) belligerent.

belliqueux [bɛli′kø], *a.* (*fem.* -**euse**) war-like, martial; bellicose, quarrelsome.

belvédère [bɛlve′dɛːr], *n.m.* turret, terrace, belvedere, gazebo.

bémol [be′mɔl], *a.* and *n.m.* (*Mus.*) flat.

bémoliser [bemɔli′ze], *v.t.* (*Mus.*) to mark flat *or* with a flat.

bénédicité [benedisi′te], *n.m.* grace (*before meals*).

bénédictin [benedik′tɛ̃], *a.* and *n.m.* (*fem.* -**e**) Benedictine.

bénédiction [benedik′sjɔ̃], *n.f.* benediction, blessing, consecration; (*fig.*) expression of thanks.

bénéfice [bene′fis], *n.m.* benefit, gain, profit; privilege, advantage; (*Eccles.*) benefice, living.

bénéficiaire [benefi′sjɛːr], *a.* receiving a benefit *or* benefice.—*n.* beneficiary, recipient.

bénéficial [benefi′sjal], *n.m.* beneficiary (*of ecclesiastical livings*).

bénéficier [benefi′sje], *v.i.* to gain, to profit.—*n.m.* beneficed clergyman, incumbent.

benêt [bə′nɛ], *a.* silly, foolish, simple.—*n.m* booby, fool, simpleton.

bénévole [bene′vɔl], *a.* well-disposed, kindly; unpaid.

bénévolement [benevɔl′mã], *adv.* out of good-will; voluntarily, spontaneously.

Bengale [bɛ̃′gal], **le**, *m.* Bengal.

bengali [bɛ̃ga′li], *a.* Bengali.—*n.m.* Bengali (*language*).—*n.* (**Bengali**) Bengali (*person*).

Béni-oui-oui [beniwi′wi], *n.m. inv.* (*fam.*) yes-man.

bénignement [beniɲ′mã], *adv.* benignly, kindly, graciously.

bénignité [beniɲi′te], *n.f.* benignity, kindness; mildness (*of a disease*).

bénin [be′nɛ̃], *a.* (*fem.* **bénigne**) benign, good-natured, indulgent; mild (*of attacks of disease, remedies etc.*).

bénir [be′niːr], *v.t.* to bless, to hallow, to consecrate; to call down blessings on; to thank; to praise.

bénit [be′ni], *a.* hallowed, consecrated.

bénitier [beni′tje], *n.m.* holy-water basin; fount.

benjamin [bɛ̃ʒa′mɛ̃], *n.m.* favourite (*especially the youngest child*).

benjoin [bɛ̃′ʒwɛ̃], *n.m.* benjamin, benzoin.

benne [bɛn], *n.f.* hamper, basket; (*Mining*) hopper, bucket.

benzine [bɛ̃′zin], *n.f.* benzine.

benzol [bɛ̃′zɔl], *n.m.* benzol.

béquillard [beki′jaːr], *a.* (*pop.*) crippled, going on crutches.—*n.m.* (*fem.* -**e**) cripple.

béquille [be′kiːj], *n.f.* crutch; (*Av.*) tail-skid.

béquiller [beki′je], *v.i.* to walk on crutches.

berbère [bɛr′bɛːr], *a.* Berber.—*n.* (**Berbère**) Berber (*person*).

berbéris [berbe′ris], *n.m.* (*Bot.*) barberry, berberis.

bercail [bɛr′kaːj], *n.m.* (*used only in sing.*) sheepfold, fold.

berce [bɛrs], *n.f.* cow-parsnip.

berceau [bɛr′so], *n.m.* (*pl.* -**eaux**) cradle; (*fig.*) infancy; origin, source; (*Hort.*) arbour, bower.

bercement [bɛrsə′mã], *n.m.* rocking; lulling.

bercer [bɛr′se], *v.t.* (*conjug. like* COMMENCER) to rock, to lull asleep; to lull, to soothe; (*fig.*) to delude *or* flatter with vain hopes. **se bercer**, *v.r.* to rock; (*fig.*) to delude oneself (*de*).

berceuse [bɛr′søːz], *n.f.* woman who rocks an infant; rocking-chair; cradle that rocks; (*Mus.*) lullaby.

béret [be′rɛ], *n.m.* beret, tam-o'-shanter (*worn by the French Alpine regiments*).

berge [bɛrʒ], *n.f.* steep bank (*of a river*); side (*of a canal, ditch, roadway etc.*).

berger [bɛr′ʒe], *n.m.* (*fem.* -**ère** (1)) shepherd, shepherdess; (*poet.*) swain; pastor, guardian (*of the people etc.*); (*Chess*) *le coup du berger*, fool's mate.

bergère (2) [bɛr′ʒɛːr], *n.f.* large and deep arm-chair.

bergerie [bɛrʒə′ri], *n.f.* sheepfold, pen; (*Lit.*) (*chiefly used in the plural*) pastoral.

bergeronnette [bɛrʒərɔ′nɛt], *n.f.* (*Orn.*) wagtail.

berlue [bɛr′ly], *n.f.* dimness of sight.

Bermudes [bɛr′myd], **les**, *f. pl.* the Bermudas.

bernacle [bɛr'nakl], **bernache** [bɛr'naʃ], **barnache** [bar'naʃ], *n.f.* barnacle-goose; barnacle (*shell-fish*).

bernard-l'ermite [bɛrnarlɛr'mit], *n.m.* hermit-crab.

berne (1) [bɛrn], *n.f.* tossing in a blanket.

berne (2) [bɛrn], *n.f.* (*Naut.*) *mettre le pavillon en berne*, to fly the flag at half-mast.

berner [bɛr'ne], *v.t.* to toss in a blanket; (*fig.*) to ridicule, to make a fool of, to deride; to deceive, to hoax.

bernique [bɛr'nik], *int.* (*pop.*) no use; not a bit of it, no go.

berthon [bɛr'tɔ̃], *n.m.* a small collapsible boat.

béryl or **béril** [be'ril], *n.m.* beryl.

besace [bə'zas], *n.f.* beggar's wallet, scrip.

bésigue [be'zig], *n.m.* bezique (*card game*).

besogne [bə'zɔɲ], *n.f.* work, business, labour; job, piece of work.

besogner [bəzɔ'ɲe], *v.i.* to work, to labour.

besogneux [bəzɔ'ɲø], *a.* and *n.m.* (*fem.* -**euse**) necessitous, needy (person).

besoin [bə'zwɛ̃], *n.m.* need, want; necessity; poverty, distress, emergency; *au besoin*, at a pinch, if need be.

Bessarabie [besara'bi], **la**, *f.* Bessarabia.

bestial [bɛs'tjal], *a.* (*m. pl.* -**aux** (1)) bestial, brutish.

bestialement [bɛstjal'mã], *adv.* bestially, brutally, like a beast.

bestialité [bɛstjali'te], *n.f.* bestiality.

bestiaux [BESTIAL, BÉTAIL].

bestiole [bɛs'tjɔl], *n.f.* little animal.

bêta [be'ta], *n.m.* (*fem.* -**asse**) a bit of a blockhead, rather a simpleton.

bétail [be'ta:j], *n.m.* (*pl.* **bestiaux** (2) [bɛs'tjo]) cattle, livestock; *gros bétail*, oxen etc.; *menu bétail*, sheep, goats etc.

bêtasse [be'ta:s], [BÊTA].

bête [bɛːt], *a.* silly, stupid, nonsensical.—*n.f.* animal, beast, brute; fool, blockhead, stupid creature; *bête noire*, pet aversion; *bête sauvage*, wild animal.

bêtement [bɛt'mã], *adv.* like a fool, foolishly, stupidly.

Bethléem [betle'em], *f.* Bethlehem.

bêtise [be'ti:z], *n.f.* silliness, stupidity; tomfoolery, foolish act, suggestion etc., silly thing, absurdity.

béton [be'tɔ̃], *n.m.* (*Masonry*) beton (*a kind of concrete*); *béton armé*, reinforced concrete.

bétonnière [betɔ'njɛːr], **bétonneuse** [betɔ'nøːz], *n.f.* concrete-mixer.

bette [bɛt], **blette** (2) [blɛt], *n.f.* beet.

betterave [bɛ'traːv], *n.f.* beetroot; *betterave à sucre*, sugar-beet; *betterave fourragère*, mangel-wurzel.

beuglement [bøglə'mã], *n.m.* bellowing, lowing (*of cattle*).

beugler [bø'gle], *v.i.* to bellow, to low.

beurre [bœːr], *n.m.* butter.

beurrée [bœ're], *n.f.* slice of bread and butter.

beurrer [bœ're], *v.t.* to butter (*bread etc.*).

beurrerie [bœr'ri], *n.f.* butter factory.

beurrier [bœ'rje], *n.m.* butter-dish.

bévue [be'vy], *n.f.* blunder, oversight, mistake; (*colloq.*) howler.

bey [bɛ], *n.m.* bey.

biais [bjɛ], *a.* slanting, sloping, askew; oblique. —*n.m.* bias, obliquity, slope; (*fig.*) shift, subterfuge.

biaisement [bjɛz'mã], *n.m.* sloping, slanting, shift, evasion.

biaiser [bjɛ'ze], *v.i.* to be oblique, to go obliquely, to slope, to slant, to lean on one side; to use shifts *or* evasions.

bibelot [bi'blo], *n.m.* trinket, knick-knack.

biberon (1) [bi'brɔ̃], *n.m.* (*Med.*) feeding-cup; feeding-bottle (*for infants*).

biberon (2) [bi'brɔ̃], *n.m.* (*fem.* -**onne**) tippler, toper.

Bible [bibl], *n.f.* Bible.

bibliographe [biblio'graf], *n.m.* bibliographer.

bibliographie [bibliogra'fi], *n.f.* bibliography.

bibliographique [bibliogra'fik], *a.* bibliographical.

bibliomane [biblio'man], *n.m.* book-collector.

bibliomanie [biblioma'ni], *n.f.* bibliomania.

bibliophile [biblio'fil], *n.m.* book-lover.

bibliothécaire [bibliote'kɛːr], *n.m.* librarian.

bibliothèque [biblio'tɛk], *n.f.* library; bookcase.

biblique [bi'blik], *a.* Biblical.

bicarbonate [bikarbo'nat], *n.m.* (*Chem.*) bicarbonate.

biceps [bi'sɛps], *n.m.* biceps.

biche [biʃ], *n.f.* hind, doe.

bichon [bi'ʃɔ̃], *n.m.* (*fem.* -**onne**) lap-dog with long, silky hair.

bichonner [biʃɔ'ne], *v.t.* to curl; (*fig.*) to caress. **se bichonner**, *v.r.* to curl one's hair; to make oneself smart.

biconcave [bikɔ̃'kaːv], *a.* bi-concave.

biconvexe [bikɔ̃'vɛks], *a.* bi-convex.

bicoque [bi'kɔk], *n.f.* (*colloq.*) ramshackle house, shanty.

bicorne [bi'kɔrn], *a.* and *n.m.* cocked (hat).

bicyclette [bisi'klɛt], *n.f.* bicycle.

bidet [bi'dɛ], *n.m.* pony, small nag; bidet (*bath*).

bidon [bi'dɔ̃], *n.m.* tin, can (*esp. petrol can*); camp-kettle; soldier's water-bottle.

bidonville [bidɔ̃'vil], *n.m.* shanty town.

bielle [bjɛl], *n.f.* (*Mach.*) connecting-rod.

Biélorussie [bjelory'si], **la**, *f.* Byelorussia, White Russia.

bien [bjɛ̃], *n.m.* good; that which is pleasant, useful *or* advantageous; benefit; welfare, well-being, blessing; wealth, estate, property; gift, boon, mercy; (*pl.*) goods, chattels; fruits (*of the soil etc.*); *biens de consommation*, consumer goods; *biens immobiliers*, real estate.—*adv.* well; rightly, finely; much, very, far, entirely, completely; about, well-nigh; favourably, successfully; well off; on good terms, in favour; certainly, truly, indeed; formally, clearly, expressly; *aussi bien*, anyhow, in any case; *bien de*, plenty of, many; *bien mieux*, far better; *bien plus*, besides, moreover; *bien que*, although; *c'est bien*, that's right; *cette femme est bien*, that woman is good-looking; *eh bien!* well! *or* well? *je vous l'avais bien dit*, I told you so; *ou bien*, or else; *si bien que*, so that; *tant bien que mal*, so-so.—*int.* (*sometimes pronounced colloq.* [bɛ̃]) well!

bien-aimé [bjɛ̃ne'me], *a.* beloved, well-beloved.—*n.m.* (*fem.* -**ée**) darling, dear.

bien-dire [bjɛ̃'diːr], *n.m.* (*no pl.*) fine speaking.

43

bien-être

bien-être [bjɛ̃'nɛːtr], *n.m.* (*no pl.*) well-being, welfare, comfort.
bienfaisance [bjɛ̃fəˈzɑ̃ːs], *n.f.* beneficence, charity, munificence.
bienfaisant [bjɛ̃fəˈzɑ̃], *a.* charitable, beneficent, kind, gracious; beneficial, salutary.
bienfait [bjɛ̃ˈfɛ], *n.m.* good turn, kindness, benefit, favour, courtesy.
bienfaiteur [bjɛ̃fɛˈtœːr], *n.m.* (*fem.* -**trice**) benefactor, benefactress, patron.
bien-fonds [bjɛ̃ˈfɔ̃], *n.m.* (*pl.* **biens-fonds**) real estate.
bienheureux [bjɛ̃nœˈrø], *a.* (*fem.* -**euse**) happy, fortunate; (*Eccles.*) blessed.
biennal [bieˈnal], *a.* (*m. pl.* -**aux**) biennial.
bienséance [bjɛ̃seˈɑ̃ːs], *n.f.* propriety decency, decorum, seemliness.
bienséant [bjɛ̃seˈɑ̃], *a.* decent, becoming, seemly, decorous, fit.
bientôt [bjɛ̃ˈto], *adv.* soon, before long, shortly; *à bientôt!* see you soon!
bienveillance [bjɛ̃vɛˈjɑ̃ːs], *n.f.* benevolence, goodwill, favour, kindness.
bienveillant [bjɛ̃vɛˈjɑ̃], *a.* benevolent, kind, friendly, favourable.
bienvenu [bjɛ̃ˈvny], *a.* welcome; *soyez le bienvenu*, it's nice to have you with us.
bienvenue [bjɛ̃ˈvny], *n.f.* welcome; *souhaiter la bienvenue à quelqu'un*, to greet *or* welcome someone.
bière (1) [bjɛːr], *n.f.* beer.
bière (2) [bjɛːr], *n.f.* coffin.
biffer [biˈfe], *v.t.* to cancel, to blot out, to erase.
biflore [biˈflɔːr], *a.* (*Bot.*) biflorate.
bifocal [bifoˈkal], *a.* (*m. pl.* -**aux**) bifocal.
bifolié [bifoˈlje], *a.* (*Bot.*) bifoliate.
bifteck [bifˈtɛk], *n.m.* beefsteak.
bifurcation [bifyrkaˈsjɔ̃], *n.f.* bifurcation; fork (*of a road*).
bigame [biˈgam], *a.* bigamous.—*n.* bigamist.
bigamie [bigaˈmi], *n.f.* bigamy.
bigarré [bigaˈre], *a.* parti-coloured, streaked.
bigarrer [bigaˈre], *v.t.* to chequer, to streak, to variegate.
bigarrure [bigaˈryːr], *n.f.* medley, mixture, motley, variegation.
bigot [biˈgo], *a.* bigoted.—*n.m.* (*fem.* -**e**) bigot.
bigoterie [bigoˈtri], *n.f.*, **bigotisme** [bigoˈtism], *n.m.* bigotry.
bigoudi [biguˈdi], *n.m.* curling pin *or* curler (*for the hair*).
bijou [biˈʒu], *n.m.* (*pl.* -**oux**) jewel, gem; (*fig.*) darling.
bijouterie [biʒuˈtri], *n.f.* jewellery.
bijoutier [biʒuˈtje], *n.m.* (*fem.* -**ière**) jeweller.
bilan [biˈlɑ̃], *n.m.* balance-sheet.
bilatéral [bilateˈral], *a.* (*m. pl.* -**aux**) bilateral.
bilboquet [bilboˈkɛ], *n.m.* cup-and-ball (*toy*); small weighted figure that balances itself.
bile [bil], *n.f.* bile, spleen, gall; (*fig.*) anger.
bilieux [biˈljø], *a.* (*fem.* -**euse**) bilious; (*fig.*) choleric, passionate.
bilingue [biˈlɛ̃ːg], *a.* bilingual.
billard [biˈjaːr], *n.m.* billiards; billiard-table; billiard-room.
bille [biːj], *n.f.* billiard-ball; marble, taw; log, unworked piece of timber; *roulement à billes*, ball-bearings.
billet [biˈjɛ], *n.m.* note, missive; bill, handbill; ticket, lottery-ticket; promissory note;

billet (*for quartering soldiers*); **billet de banque**, bank-note; **billet d'aller et retour**, return ticket; **billet doux**, love-letter.
billevesée [bilvəˈze], *n.f.* idle story, stuff, nonsense, bunkum.
billion [biˈljɔ̃], *n.m.* (*since* 1948 = 1 *followed by* 12 *ciphers*), billion, one million million(s); (*Am.*) trillion.
billot [biˈjo], *n.m.* block; executioner's block.
bimbelot [bɛ̃ˈblo], *n.m.* plaything, toy, bauble.
bimensuel [bimɑ̃ˈsɥɛl], *a.* (*fem.* -**elle**) twice monthly, fortnightly.
bimoteur [bimoˈtœːr], *a.* and *n.m.* twin-engined (plane).
binaire [biˈnɛːr], *a.* binary.
biner [biˈne], *v.t.* (*Agric.*) to dig again; to hoe.
binette [biˈnɛt], *n.f.* hoe; (*colloq.*) face, phiz.
biniou [biˈnju], *n.m.* Breton bagpipe.
binôme [biˈnoːm], *n.m.* (*Alg.*) binomial.
biochimie [bioʃiˈmi], *n.f.* biochemistry.
biographe [bioˈgraf], *n.m.* biographer.
biographie [biograˈfi], *n.f.* biography.
biographique [biograˈfik], *a.* biographical.
biologie [biolɔˈʒi], *n.f.* biology.
biologique [biolɔˈʒik], *a.* biological.
biologiste [biolɔˈʒist], **biologue** [bioˈlɔg], *n.m.* biologist.
bion [bjɔ̃], *n.m.* sucker, shoot.
bioxyde [biokˈsid], *n.m.* dioxide.
biparti [bipaˈrti], **bipartite** [bipaˈrtit], *a.* bipartite.
bipède [biˈpɛd], *a.* and *n.* (*Zool.*) biped.
biplan [biˈplɑ̃], *n.m.* biplane.
bipolaire [bipoˈlɛːr], *a.* bipolar.
bique [bik], *n.f.* nanny-goat.
biréacteur [bireakˈtœːr], *n.m.* twin-engined jet-plane.
birloir [birˈlwaːr], *n.m.* window-catch.
birman [birˈmɑ̃], *a.* Burmese.—*n.m.* (**Birman,** *fem.* -**ane**) Burmese (*person*).
Birmanie [birmaˈni], **la,** *f.* Burma.
bis (1) [bi], *a.* brown; tawny, swarthy; *du pain bis*, brown bread.
bis (2) [biːs], *adv.* twice.—*int.* encore!
bisaïeul [bizaˈjœl], *n.m.* great-grandfather.
bisaïeule [bizaˈjœl], *n.f.* great-grandmother.
bisannuel [bizaˈnɥɛl], *a.* (*fem.* -**elle**) (*Bot.*) biennial.
bisbille [bizˈbiːj], *n.f.* (*fam.*) petty quarrel, tiff, bickering.
biscornu [biskɔrˈny], *a.* irregular, misshapen; (*fig.*) outlandish, odd, queer.
biscotte [bisˈkɔt], *n.f.* rusk.
biscuit [bisˈkɥi], *n.m.* biscuit; pastry made with flour, eggs, and sugar; (*Am.*) cracker; unglazed porcelain.
bise [biːz], *n.f.* dry and cold north wind; (*colloq.*) kiss.
biseau [biˈzo], *n.m.* (*pl.* -**eaux**) bevel, chamfer; bevelling tool.
biseauter [bizoˈte], *v.t.* to bevel.
bismuth [bisˈmyt], *n.m.* bismuth.
bison [biˈzɔ̃], *n.m.* bison, buffalo.
bisque [bisk], *n.f.* soup made of crayfish, chicken *or* game, fish etc.; (*colloq.*) ill-humour, spite.
bisquer [bisˈke], *v.i.* (*colloq.*) to be vexed *or* riled.
bissac [biˈsak], *n.m.* double wallet, sack *or* bag, haversack.
bissecter [bisɛkˈte], *v.t.* to bisect.

44

bisser [bi'se], v.t. to encore.
bissextile [bisɛks'til], a. *année bissextile*, leap-year.
bissexué [bisɛk'sɥe], **bissexuel** [-sɥɛl] (*fem.* -elle), a. (*Bot.*) bisexual.
bistouri [bistu'ri], n.m. bistoury, lancet.
bistourner [bistur'ne], v.t. to twist, to distort; to castrate.
bistre [bistr], n.m. bistre, sepia.
bistro or **bistrot** [bis'tro], n.m. (*slang*) pub.
bitume [bi'tym], n.m. bitumen.
bituminer [bitymi'ne], v.t. to asphalt.
bitumineux [bitymi'nø], **bitumeux** [bity'mø], a. (*fem.* -euse) bituminous.
bivalent [biva'lɑ̃], a. divalent, bivalent.
bivalve [bi'valv], a. bivalvular.—n.m. bivalve.
bivouac [bi'vwak], n.m. bivouac.
bivouaquer [bivwa'ke], v.i. to bivouac.
bizarre [bi'zaːr], a. queer, strange, whimsical, bizarre.
bizarrement [bizar'mɑ̃], adv. oddly, queerly, whimsically.
bizarrerie [bizar'ri], n.f. singularity, oddness; caprice, whim.
black-out [blak'aut], n.m. black-out.
blafard [bla'faːr], a. pale, wan; livid.
blague [blag], n.f. tobacco pouch; (*slang*) chaff, humbug, hoax, fib; trick, practical joke; *sans blague!* you don't say!
blaguer [bla'ge], v.i. to chaff, to hoax, to humbug.
blagueur [bla'gœːr], n.m. (*fem.* -euse) wag, hoaxer, humbug.
blaireau [blɛ'ro], n.m. (*pl.* -eaux) badger; shaving-brush; badger-hair brush.
blâmable [blɑ'mabl], a. blameworthy.
blâme [blɑːm], n.m. blame; reproach, reprimand.
blâmer [blɑ'me], v.t. to blame, to criticize; to censure, to reprimand.
blanc [blɑ̃], a. (*fem.* **blanche** (1) [blɑ̃ːʃ]) white; hoar, hoary; clean; blank; *gelée blanche*, hoar frost; *passer une nuit blanche*, to have a sleepless night; *vers blancs*, blank verse.—n.m. white; blank; target, mark; *blanc de chaux*, whitewash; *de but en blanc*, point-blank; *en blanc*, left blank.
blanc-bec [blɑ̃'bɛk], n.m. (*pl.* **blancs-becs**) beardless youth, youngster; greenhorn; sucker.
blanchaille [blɑ̃'ʃaːj], n.f. whitebait.
blanchâtre [blɑ̃'ʃɑːtr], a. whitish.
blanche (1) [BLANC].
blanche (2) [blɑ̃ːʃ], n.f. (*Mus.*) minim.
blancheur [blɑ̃'ʃœːr], n.f. whiteness; cleanliness; light; (*fig.*) purity, innocence.
blanchiment [blɑ̃ʃi'mɑ̃], n.m. whitening, bleaching; blanching.
blanchir [blɑ̃'ʃiːr], v.t. to whiten; to whitewash; to wash, to bleach, to clean; to blanch.—v.i. to whiten.
blanchissage [blɑ̃ʃi'saːʒ], n.m. washing; refining (*of sugar etc.*).
blanchissant [blɑ̃ʃi'sɑ̃], a. that whitens or grows white; foaming.
blanchisserie [blɑ̃ʃis'ri], n.f. laundry, washhouse.
blanchisseuse [blɑ̃ʃi'søːz], n.f. washerwoman; laundress.
blanc-manger [blɑ̃mɑ̃'ʒe], n.m. (*pl.* **blancs-mangers**) blancmange.

blaser [blɑ'ze], v.t. to blunt, to cloy, to sicken, to surfeit.
blason [blɑ'zɔ̃], n.m. coat of arms; blazon; heraldry, blazonry.
blasonner [blɑzɔ'ne], v.t. to blazon; to interpret (*coats of arms*).
blasphémateur [blasfema'tœːr], n.m. (*fem.* -trice) blasphemer.
blasphématoire [blasfema'twaːr], a. blasphemous.
blasphème [blas'fɛːm], n.m. blasphemy.
blasphémer [blasfe'me], v.t., v.i. (*conjug. like* CÉDER) to blaspheme, to curse.
blatte [blat], n.f. cockroach, black-beetle.
blé [ble], n.m. corn, wheat; *halle au blé*, corn-exchange; *manger son blé en herbe*, to spend one's money before one has it.
blême [blɛːm], a. sallow, pale, wan; ghastly.
blêmir [ble'miːr], v.i. to turn or grow pale.
blèsement [blɛz'mɑ̃], n.m. lisping.
bléser [ble'ze], v.i. (*conjug. like* CÉDER) to lisp.
blessant [blɛ'sɑ̃], a. wounding; (*fig.*) offensive, mortifying.
blessé [blɛ'se], a. wounded; (*fig.*) offended.—n.m. (*fem.* -ée) (*Mil.*) casualty.
blesser [blɛ'se], v.t. to wound, to hurt; to offend, to injure; to shock. **se blesser**, v.r. to hurt oneself; (*fig.*) to take offence.
blessure [blɛ'syːr], n.f. wound, hurt, injury; offence; *coups et blessures*, assault and battery.
blet [blɛ], a. (*fem.* -ette (1)) over-ripe, sleepy (*of fruit*).
blette (2) [BETTE].
bleu [blø], a. blue, black and blue (*as a bruise*); (*fig.*) amazed; *cordon bleu*, first-rate cook.—n.m. blue, blueness; washing-blue; greenhorn, novice; (C) Conservative, Tory.
bleuâtre [blø'aːtr], a. bluish.
bleuet [BLUET].
bleuir [blø'iːr], v.t. to make blue, to blue (*in washing*).—v.i. to become blue.
blindage [blɛ̃'daːʒ], n.m. iron-plating, armour-plating.
blindé [blɛ̃'de], a. armoured, armour-plated screened; (*slang*) drunk.
blinder [blɛ̃'de], v.t. to armour-plate (*a ship, fort etc.*).
bloc [blɔk], n.m. block, lump, the whole lot.
blocage (1) [blɔ'kaːʒ], n.m. blockading; blocking; block (*of traffic*); obstruction; (*Fin.*) freezing.
blocage (2) [blɔ'kaːʒ], n.m. rubble.
blockhaus [blɔ'koːs], n.m. *inv.* blockhouse.
bloc-note(s) [blɔk'nɔt], n.m. writing-pad.
blocus [blɔ'kyːs], n.m. *inv.* blockade.
blond [blɔ̃], a. blond, fair; light (*ale*); *blond ardent*, auburn; *blond cendré*, ash-blond.—n.f. (-e) (C) sweetheart.
blondin [blɔ̃'dɛ̃], a. fair-haired.—n.m. (*fem.* -e) fair-haired child.—n.m. spark, beau.
blondir [blɔ̃'diːr], v.i. to grow blond or fair.
blondissant [blɔ̃di'sɑ̃], a. growing yellow or golden (*of corn etc.*).
bloquer [blɔ'ke], v.t. to block up, to fill up (*cavities in walls*) with mortar; (*Mil.*) to blockade; (*Fin.*) to freeze; to jam on (*brakes*).
blottir (se) [səblɔ'tiːr], v.r. to curl up, to snuggle, to huddle; to cower, to crouch.
blouse [bluːz], n.f. smock, tunic; blouse; pinafore; overall.

blouser

blouser [blu'ze], v.t. to mislead, to cheat. **se blouser**, v.r. (Billiards) to pocket one's own ball; (fig.) to blunder; to bark up the wrong tree.

blouson [blu'zɔ̃], n.m. lumber-jacket, windcheater.

bluet [bly'ɛ], **bleuet** [blœ'ɛ], n.m. bluebottle, corn-flower; (C) blueberry.

bluette [bly'ɛt], n.f. spark; (fig.) literary trifle, novelette.

bluff [blœf], n.m. bluff.

bluffer [blœ'fe], v.t. to bluff.

blutage [bly'ta:ʒ], n.m. bolting, sifting (of flour).

bluter [bly'te], v.t. to bolt, to sift (flour etc.).

boa [bɔ'a], n.m. boa (snake); boa (of feathers).

bobèche [bɔ'bɛʃ], n.f. socket (of a candlestick); sconce.

bobine [bɔ'bin], n.f. bobbin, spool, reel; (Cine.) reel; **bobine d'induction**, induction-coil.

bobiner [bɔbi'ne], v.t. to wind on a bobbin, to spool.

bobineuse [bɔbi'nø:z], n.f. winder, winding machine.

bobo [bɔ'bo], n.m. (Childish) hurt, sore, bump; **avoir bobo** or **du bobo**, to have a slight pain, sore etc.; **faire bobo**, to hurt.

bocage [bɔ'ka:ʒ], n.m. copse, grove.

bocager [bɔka'ʒe], a. (fem. **-ère**) of groves or woodlands; shady.

bocal [bɔ'kal], n.m. (pl. **-aux**) druggist's short-necked bottle; carboy; glass jar, fishglobe.

boche [bɔʃ] (aphæresis of Alboche), n. (pej.) German, Jerry.

bock [bɔk], n.m. bock or glass (beer).

bœuf [bœf], n.m. (pl. **bœufs** [bø]) ox; beef.

Bohême [bɔ'ɛ:m], la, f. Bohemia.

bohème [bɔ'ɛ:m], a. Bohemian.—n. Bohemian, person of careless, unconventional habits.

bohémien [bɔe'mjɛ̃], a. and n.m. (fem. **-enne**) Bohemian; gipsy.

boire [bwa:r], v.t. irr. to drink; to consume or waste on drink; to absorb; to swallow (an insult etc.).—v.i. to drink (to someone's health); to tipple; to blot (of paper).—n.m. drink; drinking.

bois [bwa], n.m. wood, forest; wood, timber; wooden part or object; horns (of a deer etc.).

boisage [bwa'za:ʒ], n.m. wood-work; timbering (of mines etc.); wainscotting.

(C) **bois-brûlé** [bwabry'le], n.m. half-breed.

(C) **bois-debout** [bwad'bu], n.m. standing timber.

boisé [bwa'ze], a. wooded, well-timbered.

boisement [bwaz'mɑ̃], n.m. planting land with trees.

boiser [bwa'ze], v.t. to put woodwork to; to timber (a mine etc.); to wainscot; to plant with woods.

boiserie [bwaz'ri], n.f. wainscot, wainscotting.

boisseau [bwa'so], n.m. (pl. **-eaux**) bushel.

boisson [bwa'sɔ̃], n.f. drink; beverage; (fig.) drinking, drunkenness; (C) hard liquor; **boisson forte**, strong drink, (Am.) liquor.

boîte [bwat], n.f. box; casket, caddy, chest; case (of a watch, rudder etc.); (pop.) mouth; **boîte à feu**, stoke-hole; (Motor.) **boîte de vitesses**, gear-box; **boîte de nuit**, night-club; (pop.) **ta boîte !** shut your big mouth!

boitement [bwat'mɑ̃], n.m. halting, limping.

boiter [bwa'te], v.i. to limp; to be lame.

boiteux [bwa'tø], a. (fem. **-euse**) lame, halt, limping; rickety (furniture).—n.m. (fem. **-euse**) lame man or woman.

boîtier [bwa'tje], n.m. surgeon's case of instruments; case (of a watch, an electric torch).

bol [bɔl], n.m. bowl, basin.

bolchevik [bɔlʃə'vik], n.m. Bolshevik.

bolchevisme [bɔlʃə'vism], n.m. Bolshevism.

bolée [bɔ'le], n.f. bowlful.

boléro [bɔle'ro], n.m. bolero (dance and garment).

Bolivie [bɔli'vi], la, f. Bolivia.

bolivien [bɔli'vjɛ̃], a. (fem. **-enne**) Bolivian.—n.m. (**Bolivien**, fem. **-enne**) Bolivian (person).

bombance [bɔ̃'bɑ̃:s], n.f. feasting, junketing.

bombardement [bɔ̃barda'mɑ̃], n.m. bombardment, shelling; **bombardement en piqué**, dive-bombing.

bombarder [bɔ̃bar'de], v.t. to bombard, to bomb; **quartier bombardé**, bombed site.

bombardier [bɔ̃bar'dje], n.m. bombardier.

bombe [bɔ̃:b], n.f. bomb; spray flask; bombe atomique, atom bomb; **bombe à hydrogène**, H-bomb; **bombe incendiaire**, incendiary bomb; (colloq.) **faire la bombe**, to be on the razzle.

bombé [bɔ̃'be], a. convex, arched.

bombement [bɔ̃bə'mɑ̃], n.m. convexity, swelling, bulge.

bomber [bɔ̃'be], v.t. to cause (something) to bulge, jut, swell out, arch, curve or barrel.—v.i. to bulge, to jut out.

bombyx [bɔ̃'biks], n.m. (Ent.) bombyx; silkworm.

bon (1) [bɔ̃], a. (fem. **bonne** (1)) good; kind, favourable; fine, convenient, advantageous, profitable, proper; well-executed, cleverly done etc.; easy, good-natured; (iron.) simple, credulous; **à quoi bon tant de peine?** what is the good of so much trouble? **il fait bon dans cette pièce**, this room is nice and warm; **pour de bon**, for good and all.—n.m. that which is good; the best.—adv. well, right, properly; **tout de bon**, seriously, truly.

bon (2) [bɔ̃], n.m. bond, coupon, voucher; **bon du trésor**, treasury bond; **bon d'essence**, petrol coupon.

bonasse [bɔ'nas], a. simple-minded, credulous; soft.

bon-bec [bɔ̃'bɛk], n.m. (pl. **bons-becs**) chatterbox, gossip.

bonbon [bɔ̃'bɔ̃], n.m. sweet, (Am.) candy.

bond [bɔ̃], n.m. bound, leap, jump, caper; **faire faux bond**, to give (someone) the slip.

bonde [bɔ̃:d], n.f. bung-hole, bung; sluice, flood-gate.

bondé [bɔ̃'de], a. chock-full, packed, crammed.

bondir [bɔ̃'di:r], v.i. to bound, to leap, to bounce, to caper, to frisk.

bondissant [bɔ̃di'sɑ̃], a. bounding, skipping.

bondissement [bɔ̃dis'mɑ̃], n.m. bounding, skipping, frisking.

bonheur [bɔ'nœ:r], n.m. happiness, prosperity, welfare; good fortune, good luck, success.

bonhomie [bɔnɔ'mi], *n.f.* good nature; simplicity, credulity.

bonhomme [bɔ'nɔm], *n.m.* (*pl.* **bonshommes** [bɔ̃'zɔm]) simple, good-natured man; foolish *or* credulous person; (*fig.*) rough drawing *or* effigy of a man; *bonhomme de neige*, snowman.

boni [bɔ'ni], *n.m.* bonus.

boniface [bɔni'fas], *a.* and *n.* (*pop.*) simple, artless (person).

bonification [bɔnifika'sjɔ̃], *n.f.* amelioration, improvement (*of land*); (*Fin.*) bonus, discount.

bonifier [bɔni'fje], *v.t.* to better, to improve; (*Fin.*) to pay, to transfer.

boniment [bɔni'mɑ̃], *n.m.* quack's show; (*fig.*) humbug.

bonjour [bɔ̃'ʒuːr], *n.m.* and *int.* good morning, good afternoon, good day.

bonne (1) [BON (1)].

bonne (2) [bɔn], *n.f.* servant-maid; housemaid; *bonne d'enfants*, nursery-maid; *bonne à tout faire*, general maid.

bonnement [bɔn'mɑ̃], *adv.* plainly, simply, honestly; *tout bonnement*, quite frankly.

bonnet [bɔ'ne], *n.m.* cap; *c'est bonnet blanc et blanc bonnet*, it is six of one and half a dozen of the other.

bonneterie [bɔn'tri], *n.f.* hosiery business, hosiery.

bonnetier [bɔn'tje], *n.m.* (*fem.* **-ière**) hosier.

bon-prime [bɔ̃'prim], *n.m.* (*Comm.*) free-gift token.

bonsoir [bɔ̃'swaːr], *n.m.* and *int.* good evening, good night.

bonté [bɔ̃'te], *n.f.* goodness, kindness.

boom [bum], *n.m.* (*Fin.*) boom.

borax [bɔ'raks], *n.m.* borax.

bord [bɔːr], *n.m.* edge, margin, brink, brim, border, rim; shore, bank, side; *au bord de la mer*, at the seaside; *à bord*, on board; *par-dessus bord*, overboard.

bordage [bɔr'daːʒ], *n.m.* bordering, hemming etc.; (*Naut.*) planking, bulwarks.

bordé [bɔr'de], *n.m.* hem, edging, bordering (*of a garment*); (*Naut.*) planking.

bordeaux [bɔr'do], *n.m.* Bordeaux wine; *bordeaux rouge*, claret.

bordée [bɔr'de], *n.f.* (*Naut.*) broadside; volley, salvo; (C) *une bordée de neige*, a snow-fall.

bordelais [bɔrdə'lɛ:], *a.* of Bordeaux.—*n.m.* (**Bordelais**, *fem.* **-aise**) native of Bordeaux.

border [bɔr'de], *v.t.* to border, to edge, to hem, to skirt, to bind; to tuck in (*bedclothes*); (*Naut.*) to haul (*the sheets*).

bordereau [bɔrdə'ro], *n.m.* (*pl.* **-eaux**) memorandum, note, schedule, account.

bordure [bɔr'dyːr], *n.f.* frame, edge, edging; margin, border, kerb; rim.

boréal [bɔre'al], *ʿ.* (*m. pl.* **-aux**) boreal, northern.

borée [bɔ're], *n.m.* Boreas, north wind (*poet.*).

borgne [bɔrɲ], *a.* one-eyed; *rue borgne*, blind alley.—*n.* one-eyed person.

borique [bɔ'rik], *a.* boric.

borne [bɔrn], *n.f.* landmark; boundary, limit, confine; milestone; (*Elec.*) terminal; *borne kilométrique*, milestone.

borné [bɔr'ne], *a.* bounded, limited, confined; narrow, mean, hide-bound.

borne-fontaine [bɔrnfɔ̃'tɛːn], *n.f.* (*pl.* **bornes-fontaines**) street fountain (*like a boundary-post*).

borner [bɔr'ne], *v.t.* to set landmarks to; to bound, to limit, to confine.

Bosphore [bɔs'fɔːr], **le**, *m.* the Bosphorus.

bosquet [bɔs'ke], *n.m.* grove, thicket, arbour.

bosse [bɔs], *n.f.* hump, hunch; bump, bruise; knob, protuberance, lump, boss; (*Arch.*) embossment; (*Sculp.*) relief.

bosselage [bɔs'laːʒ], *n.m.* embossing.

bosseler [bɔs'le], *v.t.* (*conjug. like* APPELER) to dent; to emboss.

bossu [bɔ'sy], *a.* hunch-backed; deformed, crooked; pigeon-breasted.—*n.m.* (*fem.* **-e**) hunch-back; *rire comme un bossu*, to split one's sides with laughter.

bossuer [bɔ'sɥe], *v.t.* to dent, to batter.

boston [bɔs'tɔ̃], *n.m.* boston (*card-game, dance*).

bot [bo], *a.* *pied bot*, club-foot; club-footed.

botanique [bɔta'nik], *a.* botanical.—*n.f.* botany.

botaniser [bɔtani'ze], *v.i.* to botanize.

botaniste [bɔta'nist], *n.* botanist.

botte (1) [bɔt], *n.f.* wellington boot, jack-boot.

botte (2) [bɔt], *n.f.* bunch, truss, bale.

botte (3) [bɔt], *n.f.* (*Fenc.*) pass, thrust

bottelage [bɔt'laːʒ], *n.m.* tying up in bundles.

botteler [bɔt'le], *v.t.* (*conjug. like* APPELER) to put up in bundles, to truss.

botteleur [bɔt'lœːr], *n.m.*, **botteleuse** [bɔt'løːz], *n.f.* sheaf-binding machine, binder.

botter [bɔ'te], *v.t.* to put boots on (*a person*).

bottier [bɔ'tje], *n.m.* bootmaker.

bottin [bɔ'tɛ̃], *n.m.* a directory published by the firm of Didot Bottin.

bottine [bɔ'tin], *n.f.* (ankle) boot.

bouc [buk], *n.m.* billy-goat; *bouc émissaire* scapegoat.

boucanage [buka'naːʒ], *n.m.* smoke-drying.

boucaner [buka'ne], *v.t.* to smoke (*meat, hides etc.*).

boucanier [buka'nje], *n.m.* buccaneer; freebooter.

(C) **boucanière** [buka'nɛːr], *n.f.* smokehouse (*for fish*).

bouchage [bu'ʃaːʒ], *n.m.* stopping, corking.

bouche [buʃ], *n.f.* mouth; lips; tongue; voice; victuals; muzzle (*of a cannon*); *bouche d'eau*, hydrant.

bouchée [bu'ʃe], *n.f.* mouthful.

boucher (1) [bu'ʃe], *v.t.* to stop, to choke.

boucher (2) [bu'ʃe], *n.m.* butcher.

bouchère [bu'ʃɛːr], *n.f.* butcher's wife; woman keeping a butcher's shop.

boucherie [buʃ'ri], *n.f.* butcher's shop; butchery, slaughter.

bouche-trou [buʃ'tru], *n.m.* (*pl.* **bouche-trous**) stopgap.

bouchon [bu'ʃɔ̃], *n.m.* stopper, cork; wisp (*of straw etc.*).

bouchonner [buʃɔ'ne], *v.t.* to rub down (*a horse*).

bouchonnier [buʃɔ'nje], *n.m.* one who cuts or sells corks.

boucle [bukl], *n.f.* buckle; curl, lock (*of hair*); loop (*of a river etc.*).

bouclé [bu'kle], *a.* buckled, curled.

47

boucler [bu'kle], v.t. to buckle; to put a ring to; to curl (hair); *boucler la boucle*, to loop the loop. se **boucler**, v.r. to curl one's hair.

bouclier [bu'klje], n.m. buckler, shield; (fig.) defence.

Bouddha [bu'da], m. Buddha.

bouddhisme [bu'dism], n.m. Buddhism.

bouddhiste [bu'dist], n. Buddhist.

bouder [bu'de], v.i. to sulk, to be sullen, to pout. se **bouder**, v.r. to be cool towards each other.

bouderie [bu'dri], n.f. pouting, sulkiness.

boudeur [bu'dœːr], a. (fem. -euse) sulky, sullen.

boudin [bu'dɛ̃], n.m. black-pudding; spring (of a coach).

boudoir [bu'dwaːr], n.m. boudoir, lady's private room.

boue [bu], n.f. mud, mire, dirt, filth.

bouée [bu'e], n.f. buoy.

boueux [bu'ø], a. (fem. -euse) muddy, dirty, miry; foul.—n.m. scavenger; dustman.

bouffant [bu'fã], a. puffed (sleeve), baggy (trousers).

bouffe [buf], a. comic.—n.m. pl. *Les Bouffes*, the Italian opera (in Paris).

bouffée [bu'fe], n.f. puff, gust, blast, whiff.

bouffette [bu'fɛt], n.f. bow of ribbon; tassel.

bouffi [bu'fi], a. puffed up, swollen, inflated.

bouffir [bu'fiːr], v.t. to puff up, to swell, to bloat.—v.i. to swell.

bouffissure [bufi'syːr], n.f. swelling, puffing up.

bouffon [bu'fɔ̃], a. (fem. -onne) jocose, facetious, comical.—n.m. buffoon, clown, jester.

bouffonner [bufɔ'ne], v.i. to play the buffoon; to be jocose *or* full of jests.

bouffonnerie [bufɔn'ri], n.f. buffoonery, drollery, jesting.

bougainvillée [bugɛ̃vi'le], n.f.; **bougainvillier** [bugɛ̃vi'lje], n.m. bougainvillea.

bouge [buːʒ], n.m. den, dirty hole, hovel.

bougeoir [bu'ʒwaːr], n.m. flat candlestick.

bouger [bu'ʒe], v.i. (conjug. like MANGER) to stir, to budge, to fidget.

bougie [bu'ʒi], n.f. wax-candle; (Elec.) candle-power; *bougie d'allumage*, (Motor.) sparking-plug.

bougran [bu'grã], n.m. buckram.

bouillabaisse [buja'bɛs], n.f. Provençal fish-soup with saffron etc.

bouillant [bu'jã], a. boiling, hot, scalding.

bouilleur [bu'jœːr], n.m. brandy distiller; boiler-tube (of an engine).

bouilli [bu'ji], n.m. boiled beef.

bouillie [bu'ji], n.f. pap (for infants), porridge; pulp.

bouillir [bu'jiːr], v.t. irr. to boil (milk etc.).—v.i. to boil.

bouilloire [buj'waːr], n.f. kettle.

bouillon [bu'jɔ̃], n.m. broth, beef-tea; bubble; ebullition.

bouillonnement [bujɔn'mã], n.m. bubbling up, spouting, gushing.

bouillonner [bujɔ'ne], v.i. to bubble, to boil; (fig.) to be in a state of excitement.

bouillotte [bu'jɔt], n.f. foot-warmer; hot-water bottle; small kettle.

boulanger [bulã'ʒe], n.m. (fem. -ère) baker, baker's wife.—v.t. (conjug. like MANGER) to make, knead *or* bake (bread).

boulangerie [bulã'ʒri], n.f. baking, baker's business; baker's shop.

boule [bul], n.f. ball; bowl; (pop.) face, pate, head.

bouleau [bu'lo], n.m. (pl. -eaux) birch, birch-tree.

bouledogue [bul'dɔg], n.m. bulldog.

boulet [bu'lɛ], n.m. cannon- *or* musket-ball.

boulette [bu'lɛt], n.f. pellet; forcemeat ball.

boulevard [bul'vaːr], n.m. rampart; boulevard.

bouleversement [bulvɛrsə'mã], n.m. overthrow; commotion, confusion; destruction, ruin.

bouleverser [bulvɛr'se], v.t. to overthrow, to throw down; to subvert; (fig.) to agitate, to upset.

boulier [bu'lje], n.m. (Fishing) bag-net; scoring-board (at billiards).

bouline [bu'lin], n.f. (Naut.) bowline.

boulon [bu'lɔ̃], n.m. bolt, large iron pin.

boulonner [bulɔ'ne], v.t. to fasten with iron pins, to bolt.

boulot [bu'lo], a. (fem. -otte) fat, dumpy, squat.

bouquet [bu'kɛ], n.m. bunch (of flowers), nosegay, bouquet; aroma (of wine), perfume.

bouquetier [buk'tje], n.f. flower-vase.

bouquetière [buk'tjɛːr], n.f. flower-girl.

bouquetin [buk'tɛ̃], n.m. ibex.

bouquin (1) [bu'kɛ̃], n.m. (Zool.) old billy-goat; old hare.

bouquin (2) [bu'kɛ̃], n.m. old book; second-hand book; (colloq.) book.

bouquiner [buki'ne], v.i. to hunt after old books; (colloq.) to read.

bouquineur [buki'nœːr], n.m. (colloq.) lover of old books, book-fancier.

bouquiniste [buki'nist], n.m. dealer in second-hand books.

bourbe [burb], n.f. mud, mire, slush.

bourbeux [bur'bø], a. (fem. -euse) miry, muddy, sloshy.

bourbier [bur'bje], n.m. slough, puddle, mire.

bourdaine [bur'dɛn], **bourgène** [bur'ʒɛn], n.f. black alder.

bourdon (1) [bur'dɔ̃], n.m. pilgrim's staff.

bourdon (2) [bur'dɔ̃], n.m. humble-bee; great bell; (Organ) drone.

bourdonnant [burdɔ'nã], a. humming, buzzing.

bourdonnement [burdɔn'mã], n.m. buzz, buzzing; humming.

bourdonner [burdɔ'ne], v.t. to hum.—v.i. to buzz, to hum; to murmur.

bourdonneur [burdɔ'nœːr], a. humming.—n.m. humming-bird, colibri.

bourg [buːr], n.m. borough, market-town.

bourgade [bur'gad], n.f. small market-town.

bourgène [BOURDAINE].

bourgeois [bur'ʒwa], a. middle-class; plain, common, ordinary.—n.m. (fem. -e) citizen, townsman, townswoman; commoner; middle-class person, bourgeois.

bourgeoisie [burʒwa'zi], n.f. bourgeoisie, middle-class.

bourgeon [bur'ʒɔ̃], n.m. (Bot.) bud, shoot; pimple.

bourgeonnement [burʒɔn'mã], n.m. budding.

braise

bourgeonner [burʒɔ'ne], v.i. to bud; to
break out in pimples.
bourgeron [burʒə'rɔ̃], n.m. workman's
blouse, smock-frock.
bourgmestre [burg'mɛstr], n.m. burgomaster.
Bourgogne [bur'gɔɲ], la, f. Burgundy.
bourguignon [burgi'ɲɔ̃], a. (fem. -onne)
Burgundian, of Burgundy.—n.m. (Bourguignon, fem. -onne) native or inhabitant
of Burgundy.
bourrade [bu'rad], n.f. blow, thrust, buffet.
bourrasque [bu'rask], n.f. squall, gust; fit of
anger.
bourre [bu:r], n.f. hair, fluff (of animals); flock
(of wool); floss (of silk); (fig.) stuff, trash.
bourreau [bu'ro], n.m. (pl. -eaux) hangman,
executioner; tyrant.
bourrée [bu're], n.f. brushwood, faggot; an
Auvergne dance.
bourreler [bur'le], v.t. (conjug. like APPELER)
to torment, to rack.
bourrelet [bur'lɛ], n.m. pad, cushion.
bourrelier [burə'lje], n.m. harness-maker.
bourrellerie [burɛl'ri], n.f. harness-maker's
shop.
bourrer [bu're], v.t. to tamp; to stuff, to
cram; (fig.) to ill-treat, to thrash. se
bourrer, v.r. to cram oneself; to thrash
each other.
bourriche [bu'riʃ], n.f. game-basket, basket
of game.
bourrique [bu'rik], n.f. she-ass; (fig.) stupid
person, dolt.
bourriquet [buri'kɛ], n.m. ass's colt or small
ass; hand-barrow.
bourru [bu'ry], a. cross, peevish, moody,
surly.
Bourse [burs], n.f. Stock Exchange; Bourse
du travail, labour exchange.
bourse [burs], n.f. purse, bag; scholarship,
grant, bursary; rabbit-net.
boursier [bur'sje], a. (fem. -ière) pertaining to
the Stock Exchange.—n.m. (fem. -ière) speculator on the Stock Exchange, exchange
broker; purse-maker; (Univ.) exhibitioner.
boursouflage [bursu'flaːʒ], n.m. bombast.
boursouflé [bursu'fle], a. bloated; bombastic,
swollen.
boursouflement [bursuflə'mɑ̃], n.m. bloatedness, puffiness; blister (of paint).
boursoufler [bursu'fle], v.t. to bloat, to puff
up.
boursouflure [bursu'flyːr], n.f. bloatedness
(of face etc.); (fig.) turgidity (of style).
bousculade [busky'lad], n.f. jostling, hust-
ling; scrimmage.
bousculer [busky'le], v.t. to throw into
disorder; to jostle, to hustle. se bousculer,
v.r. to jostle each other.
boussole [bu'sɔl], n.f. compass.
bout [bu], n.m. end, tip, top, point; fragment,
bit; venir à bout de, to succeed, to get
through (something).
boutade [bu'tad], n.f. whim, fit, start,
caprice; witticism.
boute-en-train [butɑ̃'trɛ̃], n.m. inv. one who
promotes gaiety in others, merry-maker;
être le boute-en-train, to be the life and
soul of the party.
boutefeu [but'fø], n.m. (pl. -eux) (fig.)
incendiary, fire-brand.

bouteille [bu'tɛːj], n.f. bottle; bottleful.
bouteillerie [butɛj'ri], n.f. bottle-works.
boutique [bu'tik], n.f. shop; work-shop;
(collect.) tools, implements.
boutiquier [buti'kje], n.m. (fem. -ière) shopkeeper.—a. (fem. -ière) shopkeeping.
bouton [bu'tɔ̃], n.m. bud; pimple; button,
stud, knob; (Elec. etc.) switch.
bouton d'or [butɔ̃'dɔːr], n.m. (pl. boutons
d'or) (Bot.) buttercup.
boutonné [butɔ'ne], a. buttoned; pimpled.
boutonner [butɔ'ne], v.t. to button; (Fenc.) to
touch.—v.i. to bud; to button up. se
boutonner, v.r. to button one's coat.
boutonnière [butɔ'njɛːr], n.f. buttonhole.
bouture [bu'tyːr], n.f. slip; cutting.
bouveau [bu'vo] (pl. -eaux), bouvelet
[buv'lɛ], n.m. young ox.
bouverie [bu'vri], n.f. cattle-shed, byre.
bouvet [bu've], n.m. joiner's grooving-plane.
bouvetage [buv'taːʒ], n.m. grooving and
tonguing.
bouveter [buv'te], v.t. (conjug. like APPELER)
to groove and tongue.
bouvier [bu'vje], n.m. (fem. -ière) cow-herd,
ox-drover.
bouvillon [buvi'jɔ̃], n.m. young bullock, steer.
bouvreuil [bu'vrœːj], n.m. bullfinch.
bovin [bɔ'vɛ̃], a. bovine.
box [bɔks], n.m. (pl. boxes) horse-box, loose
box; lock-up garage; le box des accusés,
the dock.
boxe [bɔks], n.f. boxing.
boxer [bɔk'se], v.i. to box, to spar.
boxeur [bɔk'sœːr], n.m. boxer, prize-fighter.
boy [bɔj], n.m. groom; native servant.
boyau [bwa'jo], n.m. (pl -aux) bowel, gut;
catgut; hose-pipe; (Cycl.) racing tyre.
brabançon [brabɑ̃'sɔ̃], a. (fem. -onne)
Brabantine, Belgian.—n.m. (Brabançon,
fem. -onne) Brabantine, Belgian (person).
bracelet [bras'lɛ], n.m. bracelet, armlet,
bangle.
bracelet-montre [braslə'mɔ̃ːtr], n.m. (pl.
bracelets-montres) wrist-watch.
braconnage [brakɔ'naːʒ], n.m. poaching.
braconner [brakɔ'ne], v.i. to poach, to steal
game.
braconnier [brakɔ'nje], n.m. (fem. -ière)
poacher.—a. (fem. -ière) poaching; pertaining to poaching.
braguette [bra'gɛt], n.f. fly (of trousers).
brahmane [bra'man], brahme [bram], n.m.
Brahmin.
brahmanisme [brama'nism], n.m. Brahmin-
ism.
brahme [BRAHMANE].
brai [brɛ], n.m. resin, rosin, pitch.
braillard [brɑ'jaːr], a. brawling, squalling;
obstreperous.—n.m. (fem. -e) brawler,
squaller.—n.m. small speaking-trumpet.
braille [braːj], n.m. braille.
braillement [brɑj'mɑ̃], n.m. squalling.
brailler [brɑ'je], v.i. to bawl, to shout, to be
noisy.
brailleur [brɑ'jœːr], a. and n.m. (fem. -euse)
[BRAILLARD].
braiment [brɛ'mɑ̃], n.m. braying (of an ass).
braire [brɛːr], v.i. irr. to bray; (fig.) to cry, to
whine.
braise [brɛːz], n.f. wood-embers, live coals.

49

braiser

braiser [brɛ'ze], *v.t.* to braise.
braisier [brɛ'zje], *n.m.* brazier.
braisière [brɛ'zjɛːr], *n.f.* braising-pan.
bramer [bra'me], *v.i.* to bell (*of deer*).
brancard [brɑ̃'kaːr], *n.m.* stretcher, litter; hand-barrow; shaft (*of a cart*).
brancardier [brɑ̃kar'dje], *n.m.* stretcher-bearer, ambulance-man.
branchage [brɑ̃'ʃaːʒ], *n.m.* (*collect.*) branches, boughs.
branche [brɑ̃ːʃ], *n.f.* branch, bough; part, division.
brancher [brɑ̃'ʃe], *v.t.* to divide into branches; (*Elec.*) to connect, to plug in; to tap (*a gas or water pipe*).—*v.i.* to branch off.
branchu [brɑ̃'ʃy], *a.* forked, bifurcated, ramifying.
brande [brɑ̃ːd], *n.f.* heather; heath.
Brandebourg [brɑ̃d'buːr], *m.* Brandenburg.
brandebourgs [brɑ̃d'buːr], *n.m. pl.* braid; frogs and loops (*on a uniform*).
brandillement [brɑ̃dij'mɑ̃], *n.m.* tossing; swinging.
brandiller [brɑ̃di'je], *v.t.* to swing, to shake to and fro.—*v.i.* to swing, to move to and fro. **se brandiller**, *v.r.* to swing.
brandir [brɑ̃'diːr], *v.t.* to brandish, to flourish.
brandissement [brɑ̃dis'mɑ̃], *n.m.* brandishing, flourishing.
brandon [brɑ̃'dɔ̃], *n.m.* torch, fire-brand.
branlant [brɑ̃'lɑ̃], *a.* shaking, loose, tottering.
branle [brɑ̃ːl], *n.m.* oscillation, shaking *or* tossing motion; jog; an old-fashioned dance.
branle-bas [brɑ̃l'bɑ], *n.m. inv.* (*Naut.*) clearing for action; (*fig.*) commotion, disturbance.
branlement [brɑ̃l'mɑ̃], *n.m.* oscillation, shaking, swing.
branler [brɑ̃'le], *v.t.* to shake, to wag.—*v.i.* to shake, to stagger, to rock; to move; to waver.
braquage [bra'kaːʒ], *n.m.* aiming; steering, lock (*of a car*).
braque (1) [brak], *n.m.* French pointer.
braque (2) [brak], *a.* madcap, hare-brained.
braquer [bra'ke], *v.t.* to aim, to level, to point.
bras [brɑ], *n.m.* arm; bracket; branch (*of a stream etc.*); (*fig.*) power, action, assistance.
braser [brɑ'ze], *v.t.* to braze.
brasier [brɑ'zje], *n.m.* quick clear fire; brazier, furnace.
brasiller [brazi'je], *v.t.* to grill, to broil.—*v.i.* to glitter, to shine (*of the sea*).
brassage [brɑ'saːʒ], *n.m.* mashing, brewing.
brassard [brɑ'saːr], *n.m.* brace (*armour*); armlet.
brasse [brɑs], *n.f.* fathom, six feet; armful; stroke (*in swimming*).
brassée [brɑ'se], *n.f.* armful; stroke (*in swimming*).
brassement [brɑs'mɑ̃], *n.m.* brewing; mixing.
brasser [brɑ'se], *v.t.* to mix; to brew, to mash; to stir up.
brasserie [brɑs'ri], *n.f.* brewery; brewing; drinking-saloon, 'pub'.
brasseur [brɑ'sœːr], *n.m.* brewer.
brassière [brɑ'sjɛːr], *n.f.* shoulder-strap (*of a knapsack etc.*); infant's vest *or* bodice.
brassin [brɑ'sɛ̃], *n.m.* brewing-tub; mash-tub; a boiling (*quantity boiled or brewed*).

bravache [bra'vaʃ], *n.m.* bully, swaggerer blusterer.—*a.* blustering, bullying.
bravade [bra'vad], *n.f.* bravado, boast, bluster.
brave [braːv], *a.* brave, courageous, gallant; worthy, honest, good.—*n.m.* brave *or* courageous man; good fellow.
bravement [brav'mɑ̃], *adv.* bravely, stoutly, valiantly; skilfully, finely.
braver [bra've], *v.t.* to defy, to dare; to brave, to beard.
bravo [bra'vo], *n.m.* (*pl.* **bravos**) and *int.* bravo; hear, hear!
bravoure [bra'vuːr], *n.f.* bravery, courage, gallantry; (*pl.*) exploits.
break [brɛk], *n.m.* break (*carriage*).
brebis [brə'bi], *n.f.* ewe; (*fig.*) sheep; (*pl.*) flock.
brèche [brɛʃ], *n.f.* breach, flaw; notch, gap.
bréchet [bre'ʃɛ], *n.m.* (*Orn.*) breast-bone.
bredouillage [brədu'jaːʒ], **bredouillement** [brəduj'mɑ̃], *n.m.* stammering, stuttering, sputtering.
bredouille [brə'duːj], *n.f.* (*Trictrac*) lurch.— *a. inv.* empty-handed; *revenir bredouille*, to return with an empty bag (*of sportsmen*).
bredouillement [BREDOUILLAGE].
bredouiller [brədu'je], *v.t., v.i.* to stammer, to stutter.
bredouilleur [brədu'jœːr], *a.* (*fem.* **-euse**) stammering, stuttering.—*n.m.* (*fem.* **-euse**) stammerer, stutterer.
bref [brɛf], *a.* (*fem.* **brève** (1)) short, brief, concise; brusque.—*adv.* in short, in fine, in a word.
brelan [brə'lɑ̃], *n.m.* brelan (*card game*); gaming-house.
brêler *or* **breller** [brɛ'le], *v.t.* to lash.
breller [BRÊLER].
breloque [brə'lɔk], *n.f.* trinket, gewgaw; charm.
Brême [brɛːm], *m.* Bremen.
brème [brɛːm], *n.f.* bream.
Brésil [bre'zil], **le**, *m.* Brazil.
brésil [bre'zil], *n.m.* Brazil-wood (*for dyeing*).
brésilien [brezi'ljɛ̃], *a.* (*fem.* **-enne**) Brazilian.—*n.m.* (**Brésilien**, *fem.* **-enne**) Brazilian (*person*).
Bretagne [brə'taɲ], **la**, *f.* Brittany; *la Grande-Bretagne*, Great Britain; *la Nouvelle-Bretagne*, New Britain.
bretelle [brə'tɛl], *n.f.* strap; brace; (*pl.*) pair of braces; (*Rail.*) points; (*rifle*) sling.
breton [brə'tɔ̃], *a.* (*fem.* **-onne**) Breton.— *n.m.* Breton (*language*); (**Breton**, *fem.* **-onne**) Breton (*person*).
bretteur [brɛ'tœːr], *n.m.* swashbuckler, duellist.
bretzel [brɛt'sɛl], *n.m.* pretzel.
breuil [brœːj], *n.m.* enclosed coppice, covert.
breuvage [brœ'vaːʒ], *n.m.* beverage, drink, liquor.
brève (1) [brɛːv], [BREF].
brève (2) [brɛːv], *n.f.* short syllable; (*Mus.*) breve.
brevet [brə'vɛ], *n.m.* warrant, brevet, certificate (*school etc.*); diploma, licence (*of printers*); patent; badge (*of boy-scouts*); (*Mil.*) commission.
breveté [brəv'te], *a.* patented; (*Mil.*) certificated—*n.m.* (*fem.* **-ée**) patentee.

50

breveter [brəv'te], *v.t.* (*conjug. like* APPELER) to patent; to license; to certificate.

bréviaire [bre'vjɛːr], *n.m.* breviary.

brévité [brevi'te], *n.f.* shortness (*of syllables*).

bribes [brib], *n.f. pl.* scraps, bits; odds and ends.

bric-à-brac [brika'brak], *n.m. inv.* curios, bric-a-brac; curiosity-shop.

brick [brik], *n.m.* brig.

bricolage [briko'la:ʒ], *n.m.* pottering.

bricoler [briko'le], *v.i.* to potter, to do odds and ends.

bricoleur [briko'lœːr], *n.m.* (*fem.* -euse) odd job man, handyman *or* woman.

bride [brid], *n.f.* bridle, bridle-rein; check, curb; string (*of a woman's cap, bonnet etc.*).

brider [bri'de], *v.t.* to bridle; to restrain, to curb; to truss (*a fowl*); to tie; to check.

bridge [bridʒ], *n.m.* bridge (*card game*); bridge (*in dentistry*).

bridger [bri'dʒe], *v.i.* to play bridge.

bridgeur [bri'dʒœːr], *n.m.* (*fem.* -euse) bridge-player.

bridon [bri'dõ], *n.m.* snaffle-bridle.

brie [bri], *n.m.* Brie cheese.

brièvement [briɛv'mã], *adv.* briefly, succinctly, in short.

brièveté [briɛv'te], *n.f.* brevity, briefness, conciseness.

brigade [bri'gad], *n.f.* brigade; (*fig.*) troop, gang, body.

brigadier [briga'dje], *n.m.* corporal (*in cavalry, artillery*); sergeant (*of police*).

brigand [bri'gã], *n.m.* brigand; (*fig.*) robber, thief.

brigandage [brigã'da:ʒ], *n.m.* brigandage, plunder.

brigander [brigã'de], *v.i.* to rob, to plunder.

brigantin [brigã'tɛ̃], *n.m.* brigantine.

brigantine [brigã'tin], *n.f.* (*Naut.*) spanker; small vessel.

brigue [brig], *n.f.* intrigue, cabal, faction.

briguer [bri'ge], *v.t.* to canvass for, to solicit, to court.

brigueur [bri'gœːr], *n.m.* (*fem.* -euse) intriguer, canvasser.

brillamment [brija'mã], *adv.* brilliantly, in a brilliant manner.

brillance [bri'jɑ̃:s], *n.f.* (*Opt.*) brilliancy.

brillant [bri'jã], *a.* brilliant, sparkling, glittering; radiant.—*n.m.* brilliance, splendour; brilliant (*diamond*).

brillanter [brijã'te], *v.t.* to cut into a brilliant.

brillantine [brijã'tin], *n.f.* brilliantine (*hair-oil*); glossy cotton-cloth.

briller [bri'je], *v.i.* to shine, to glitter, to sparkle; (*fig.*) to distinguish oneself, to stand out.

brimade [bri'mad], *n.f.* ragging; vexation; persecution.

brimborion [brɛ̃bo'rjõ], *n.m.* knick-knack, bauble.

brimer [bri'me], *v.t.* to rag, to bully.

brin [brɛ̃], *n.m.* blade, slender stalk, shoot (*of corn etc.*); (*fig.*) bit, jot.

brindille [brɛ̃'diːj], *n.f.* sprig, twig.

brio [bri'o] [It.], *n.m.* (*Mus. etc.*) dash, spirit, go.

brioche [bri'ɔʃ], *n.f.* brioche, bun; (*fig.*) blunder.

brique [brik], *n.f.* brick; *brique anglaise*, bath brick.

briquet [bri'kɛ], *n.m.* tinder-box; (cigarette) lighter.

briquetage [brik'ta:ʒ], *n.m.* brick-work; imitation brick-work.

briqueter [brik'te], *v.t.* (*conjug. like* APPELER) to brick, to pave with bricks.

briqueterie [brik'tri], *n.f.* brick-field, brick-making; brickworks.

briqueteur [brik'tœːr], *n.m.* bricklayer.

briquetier [brik'tje], *n.m.* brick-maker.

briquette [bri'kɛt], *n.f.* briquette; compressed slack.

brisant [bri'zã], *n.m.* sand-bank, reef, shoal; (*pl.*) breakers.

brise [bri:z], *n.f.* breeze; strong wind.

brisé [bri'ze], *a.* broken to pieces; (*fig.*) harassed.

brise-bise [briz'bi:z], *n.m. inv.* draught excluder; sash curtain.

brisées [bri'ze], *n.f.* (*used only in pl.*) footsteps, wake; *aller* or *marcher sur les brisées de quelqu'un*, to poach on someone's preserves.

brise-glace [briz'glas], *n.m.* (*pl. brise-glace* or -glaces) ice-breaker (*ship*).

brise-jet [briz'ʒɛ], *n.m. inv.* anti-splash tapnozzle.

brise-lames [briz'lam], *n.m. inv.* breakwater.

brisement [briz'mã], *n.m.* breaking, dashing (*of waves*); (*fig.*) trouble, contrition.

briser [bri'ze], *v.t.* to break to pieces, to smash, to break, to shatter; to burst; to crack; to destroy.—*v.i.* to break; to dash (*of waves*).

brise-tout [briz'tu], *n.m. inv.* person who breaks everything; rough, clumsy fellow.

briseur [bri'zœːr], *n.m.* (*fem.* -euse) one who breaks *or* likes to break anything; iconoclast.

brise-vent [briz'vã], *n.m.* (*pl. brise-vent* or *brise-vents*) wind-screen (*for protecting plants*).

brisque [brisk], *n.f.* a card-game; (*Mil.*) stripe; war service chevron.

brisure [bri'zy:r], *n.f.* break; folding-point in a piece of joiner's work; small fragment.

britannique [brita'nik], *a.* British, Britannic; *Les Îles Britanniques*, the British Isles.

broc [bro], *n.m.* large jug *or* quart-pot.

brocantage [brokã'ta:ʒ], *n.m.* dealing in second-hand goods, broker's business; bartering.

brocante [bro'kã:t], *n.f.* second-hand trade; article of trifling value.

brocanter [brokã'te], *v.i.* to deal in second-hand goods; to exchange, to barter.

brocanteur [brokã'tœːr], *n.m.* (*fem.* -euse) dealer in second-hand goods, junk-shop owner.

brocard [bro'ka:r], *n.m.* taunt, jeer; lampoon.

brocarder [brokar'de], *v.t.* to taunt, to ridicule.

brocardeur [brokar'dœːr], *n.m.* (*fem.* -euse) scoffer, jeerer.

brocart or **broquart** [bro'ka:r], *n.m.* brocade.

brochage [bro'ʃa:ʒ], *n.m.* stitching (*of books*).

broche [brɔʃ], *n.f.* spit; spindle; skewer; spigot; knitting-needle; brooch; (*pl.*) tusks (*of wild boars*); (*Elec.*) *fiche à deux broches*, two-pin plug.

broché [brɔ'ʃe], *a.* embossed (*of linen*); brocaded, figured (*of other materials*); *livre broché*, paper-bound book.

brocher [brɔ'ʃe], *v.t.* to stitch (*a book etc.*); to figure (*materials*); to emboss (*linen*).

brochet [brɔ'ʃɛ], *n.m.* pike (*fish*).

brocheter [brɔʃ'te], *v.t.* (*conjug. like* APPELER) to skewer.

brochette [brɔ'ʃɛt], *n.f.* (*Cook.*) small spit.

brocheur [brɔ'ʃœːr], *n.m.* (*fem.* -euse) stitcher, esp. book-stitcher.

brochure [brɔ'ʃyːr], *n.f.* stitching; booklet, brochure, pamphlet, tract; embroidery.

brocoli [brɔkɔ'li], *n.m.* broccoli.

brodequin [brɔd'kɛ̃], *n.m.* buskin, half-boot.

broder [brɔ'de], *v.t.* to embroider; to adorn, to embellish (*a story etc.*).—*v.i.* to romance.

broderie [brɔd'ri], *n.f.* embroidery; (*fig.*) embellishment.

brodeur [brɔ'dœːr], *n.m.* (*fem.* -euse) embroiderer.

broiement or **broîment** [brwa'mɑ̃], **broyage** [brwa'jaːʒ], *n.m.* grinding, powdering.

bromure [brɔ'myːr], *n.m.* bromide.

bronche [brɔ̃ːʃ], *n.f.* (*pl.*) (*Anat.*) bronchial tubes.

bronchement [brɔ̃ʃ'mɑ̃], *n.m.* stumbling; flinching.

broncher [brɔ̃'ʃe], *v.i.* to stumble, to trip, to reel; to falter.

bronchial [brɔ̃'ʃjal], *a.* (*m. pl.* -aux) (*Anat.*) bronchial.

bronchique [brɔ̃'ʃik], *a.* bronchial.

bronchite [brɔ̃'ʃit], *n.f.* (*Path.*) bronchitis.

broncho-pneumonie [brɔ̃kɔpnœmɔ'ni], *n.f.* broncho-pneumonia.

bronze [brɔ̃ːz], *n.m.* bronze; bronze statue *or* medal.

bronzer [brɔ̃'ze], *v.t.* to bronze; to tan (*the face etc.*).

broquart [BROCART].

broquette [brɔ'kɛt], *n.f.* tack, carpet-nail.

brosse [brɔs], *n.f.* brush; painter's brush *or* pencil; *cheveux en brosse*, crew-cut hair.

brosser [brɔ'se], *v.t.* to brush. **se brosser**, *v.r.* to brush oneself.

brosserie [brɔ'sri], *n.f.* brushmaking business; brush factory.

brou [bru], *n.m.* husk or peel (*of nuts, esp. walnuts*); *brou de noix*, walnut stain, walnut liquor.

brouet [bru'ɛ], *n.m.* thin broth.

brouette [bru'ɛt], *n.f.* wheelbarrow.

brouettée [brue'te], *n.f.* barrow-load.

brouetter [brue'te], *v.t.* to wheel in a barrow.

brouetteur [brue'tœːr], **brouettier** [brue'tje], *n.m.* barrowman.

brouhaha [brua'a], *n.m.* hubbub, uproar, hurly-burly.

brouillage [bru'jaːʒ], *n.m.* (*Rad.*) atmospherics, jamming.

brouillard [bru'jaːr], *n.m.* fog, mist, haze; (*Comm.*) rough-book.

brouillasse [bru'jas], *n.f.* drizzle, Scotch mist.

brouillasser [bruja'se], *v.impers.* to drizzle.

brouille [bru:j], **brouillerie** [bruj'ri], *n.f.* quarrel, falling-out.

brouillé [bru'je], *a.* scrambled (*eggs*); blurred; on bad terms.

brouillement [bruj'mɑ̃], *n.m.* mixing together, jumbling.

brouiller [bru'je], *v.t.* to mix together, to jumble up, to shuffle; to embroil, to confuse; (*Rad.*) to jam. **se brouiller**, *v.r.* to fall out (*with someone*).

brouillerie [BROUILLE].

brouillon [bru'jɔ̃], *a.* (*fem.* -onne) mischief-making; blundering.—*n.m.* rough draft, rough copy; blunderer, bungler.

brouillonner [brujɔ'ne], *v.t.* to write in a blundering or confused way, to botch.

brouir [bru'iːr], *v.t.* to blight, to nip, to parch.

brouissure [brui'syːr], *n.f.* blight, scorching.

broussailles [bru'saːj], *n.f.* (*usu. in pl.*) bushes, brushwood, undergrowth.

broussailleux [brusa'jø], *a.* (*fem.* -euse) bushy, covered with bushes.

brousse [brus], *n.f.* brushwood, bush (*Australia etc.*).

brouter [bru'te], *v.t., v.i.* to browse, to graze.

broutilles [bru'tiːj], *n.f. pl.* sprigs; (*fig.*) trifles.

brownien [brɔ'nɛ̃], *a.* *mouvements browniens*, molecular motion.

browning [brɔ'niŋ], *n.m.* automatic pistol.

broyage [brwa'jaːʒ], *n.m.* crushing (*of ore*), grinding (*of colours*).

broyer [brwa'je], *v.t.* (*conjug. like* EMPLOYER) to grind, to pound, to pulverize.

broyeur [brwa'jœːr], *a.* (*fem.* -euse) grinding.—*n.m.* (*fem.* -euse) grinding; grinder, pounder.

bru [bry], *n.f.* daughter-in-law.

brucelles [bry'sɛl], *n.f. pl.* tweezers.

brugnon [bry'nɔ̃], *n.m.* nectarine.

bruine [bruin], *n.f.* light drizzling rain.

bruiner [brui'ne], *v.impers.* to drizzle.

bruineux [brui'nø], *a.* (*fem.* -euse) drizzly, drizzling.

bruire [bruiːr], *v.t. irr.* to make a noise; to rustle, to rattle; to roar, to sough (*of the wind*).

bruissant [brui'sɑ̃], *a.* rustling, rattling; roaring.

bruissement [bruis'mɑ̃], *n.m.* rustling noise, rattling, roaring.

bruit [brui], *n.m.* noise, din, uproar, clamour; fame, renown; report, talk, rumour.

bruitage [brui'taːʒ], *n.m.* sound-effects.

bruiter [brui'te], *v.i.* to make sound-effects.

bruiteur [brui'tœːr], *n.m.* sound-effects specialist.

brûlage [bry'laːʒ], *n.m.* burning (*of rubbish*); singeing (*of hair*); roasting (*of coffee*).

brûlant [bry'lɑ̃], *a.* burning, scorching, hot, torrid; (*fig.*) eager, ardent.

brûlé [bry'le], *n.m.* smell of burning; (*G*) burnt part of wood, burnbeat field.

brûle-gueule [bryl'gœl], *n.m. inv.* (*colloq.*) short pipe, cutty.

brûle-pourpoint, à [abrylpur'pwɛ̃], *adv.* point-blank (*of shooting*).

brûler [bry'le], *v.t.* to burn; to cauterize; to scorch, to parch; to singe (*hair*).—*v.i.* to burn, to be on fire; (*fig.*) to be eager. **se brûler**, *v.r.* to burn oneself, to be burnt.

brûleur [bry'lœːr], *n.m.* (*fem.* -euse) burner; incendiary; *brûleur à gaz*, gas-ring, gas-jet.

brûlis [bry'li], *n.m.* burnt part of a wood *or* field.

brûloir [bry'lwaːr], *n.m.* coffee-burner *or* roaster.

buter

brûlot [bry'lo], *n.m.* fire-ship; (*fig.*) firebrand, incendiary; (*G*) kind of gnat *or* midge.

brûlure [bry'ly:r], *n.f.* burn, frost nip, scald.

brumaire [bry'mɛ:r], *n.m.* Brumaire (*second month of the calendar of the first French Republic, from Oct. 22nd to Nov. 20th*).

brume [brym], *n.f.* haze, mist.

brumeux [bry'mø], *a.* (*fem.* **-euse**) hazy, misty; (*fig.*) sombre.

brun [brœ̃], *a.* brown, dark, dusky.—*n.m.* brown (*colour*); (*fem.* **-e** (1)) dark-complexioned person.

brunâtre [bry'nɑ:tr], *a.* brownish.

brune (2) [bryn], *n.f.* dusk (*of the evening*); dark woman, dark girl, brunette.

brunet [bry'nɛ], *a.* (*fem.* **-ette**) brownish.—*n.f.* (**-ette**) dark woman, dark girl.

brunir [bry'ni:r], *v.t.* to make brown; to burnish.—*v.i.* to turn brown. **se brunir**, *v.r.* to turn dark *or* brown.

brunissage [bryni'sa:ʒ], *n.m.* burnishing.

brunisseur [bryni'sœ:r], *n.m.* (*fem.* **-euse**) burnisher.

brunissoir [bryni'swa:r], *n.m.* burnisher (*tool*).

brunissure [bryni'sy:r], *n.f.* burnishing; polish.

brusque [brysk], *a.* blunt, abrupt, rough; unexpected.

brusquement [bryskə'mɑ̃], *adv.* bluntly, abruptly; uncivilly.

brusquer [brys'ke], *v.t.* to be sharp with (*someone*); to offend; (*fig.*) to precipitate.

brusquerie [bryskə'ri], *n.f.* abruptness, bluntness; hastiness.

brut [bryt], *a.* rough, raw, unhewn; uncultured.—*adv.* (*Comm.*) gross (*as opposed to* net).

brutal [bry'tal], *a.* (*m.pl.* **-aux**) brutal; surly, churlish.—*n.m.* (*fem.* **-e**) brute, brutal person.

brutalement [brytal'mɑ̃], *adv.* brutally.

brutaliser [brytali'ze], *v.t.* to bully; to brutalize.

brutalité [brytali'te], *n.f.* brutality, brutishness.

brute [bryt], *n.f.* brute, brutal person; boor.

Bruxelles [bry'sɛl], *f.* Brussels.

bruyamment [bryja'mɑ̃], *adv.* noisily.

bruyère [bry'jɛ:r], *n.f.* heath, heather.

buanderie [bɥɑ̃'dri], *n.f.* wash-house, laundry.

buandier [bɥɑ̃'dje], *n.m.* (*fem.* **-ière**) bleacher; washerman, washerwoman.

bube [byb], *n.f.* pimple.

bubonique [bybo'nik], *a.* bubonic.

Bucarest [byka'rest], *m.* Bucharest.

buccin [byk'sɛ̃], *n.m.* (*Mus. Ant.*) long trumpet; (*Conch.*) whelk.

bûche [byʃ], *n.f.* log; (*fig.*) blockhead, dolt.

bûcher (1) [by'ʃe], *n.m.* wood-house; funeral-pile, pyre; stake.

bûcher (2) [by'ʃe], *v.t.* to rough-hew.—*v.i.* to cram, to swot.

bûcheron [byʃ'rɔ̃], *n.m.* (*fem.* **-onne**) wood-cutter.

bûchette [by'ʃɛt], *n.f.* stick of dry wood.

bucolique [byko'lik], *a.* bucolic.

budget [byd'ʒɛ], *n.m.* budget.

budgétaire [bydʒe'tɛ:r], *a.* budgetary.

buée [bɥe], *n.f.* steam (*on window-panes*).

buffet [by'fɛ], *n.m.* sideboard; buffet; refreshment-room.

buffetier [byf'tje], *n.m.* (*fem.* **-ière**) refreshment-room manager.

buffle [byfl], *n.m.* buffalo; buffalo hide; buff-leather.

buffleterie [byflɔ'tri], *n.f.* buff belts, straps etc. (*of a soldier*).

bugle [bygl], *n.m.* key-bugle.

buis [bɥi], *n.m.* box; box-tree, box-wood.

buissaie [bɥi'sɛ], **buissière** [bɥi'sjɛ:r], *n.f.* box-grove.

buisson [bɥi'sɔ̃], *n.m.* bush; thicket.

buissoner [bɥiso'ne], *v.i.* to grow into a bush.

buissonnet [bɥiso'nɛ], *n.m.* little bush.

buissonneux [bɥiso'nø], *a.* (*fem.* **-euse**) bushy.

buissonnier [bɥiso'nje], *a.* (*fem.* **-ière**) retiring into the bushes; *faire l'école buissonnière*, to play truant; *lapins buissonniers*, thicket-rabbits.—*n.m.* shrubbery.

bulbe [bylb], *n.m.* bulb.

bulbeux [byl'bø], *a.* (*fem.* **-euse**) bulbous.

bulgare [byl'ga:r], *a.* Bulgarian.—*n.m.* Bulgarian (*language*).—*n.* (**Bulgare**) Bulgarian (*person*).

Bulgarie [bylga'ri], **la**, *f.* Bulgaria.

bulle [byl], *n.f.* bubble; blister; a papal bull.

bullé [by'le], *a.* authenticated with a seal; by papal bull.

bulletin [byl'tɛ̃], *n.m.* bulletin, official report (*school etc.*); certificate; receipt; ballot paper; *bulletin d'information* news bulletin; *bulletin météorologique*, weather forecast.

bulleux [by'lø], *a.* (*fem.* **-euse**) bubbly; blistery.

buraliste [byra'list], *n.* receiver of taxes; tobacconist.

bure [by:r], *n.f.* drugget; fustian, baize.

bureau [by'ro], *n.m.* (*pl.* **-eaux**) writing-table, desk; office; board; committee; *Deuxième Bureau*, Intelligence Service, M.I.5.

bureaucrate [byro'krat],*n.m.*(*pej.*) bureaucrat.

bureaucratie [byrokra'si], *n.f.* bureaucracy; (*fig.*) red tape.

bureaucratique [byrokra'tik], *a.* bureaucratic; formal.

burette [by'rɛt], *n.f.* cruet; oil-can; (*Chem.*) burette.

burin [by'rɛ̃], *n.m.* graver, graving-tool; (*fig.*) pen.

buriner [byri'ne], *v.t.* to engrave; to drill (*a tooth*).

burineur [byri'nœ:r], *n.m.* engraver.

burlesque [byr'lɛsk], *a.* burlesque, ludicrous.—*n.m.* burlesque.

burnous [byr'nus], *n.m.* burnous, hooded Arab cloak.

busard [by'za:r], *n.m.* buzzard.

buse (1) [by:z], *n.f.* buzzard; (*fig.*) blockhead.

buse (2) [by:z], *n.f.* channel, pipe; nozzle; (*Mining*) air-shaft.

busqué [bys'ke], *a.* aquiline (*nose*).

buste [byst], *n.m.* bust, head and shoulders.

but [by(t)], *n.m.* mark; object, end; purpose, design, goal, objective; *de but en blanc*, bluntly; (*Ftb.*) *marquer un but*, to score.

buté [by'te], *a.* stubborn, (*fam.*) dead set on.

buter *or* **butter** (1) [by'te], *v.t.* to support, to prop.—*v.i.* to rest *or* abut (*contre*); to stumble *or* hit (*contre*). **se buter**, *v.r.* to be bent on, to stick (*à*).

53

butin [by'tɛ̃], *n.m.* booty, spoils, prize, plunder.

butiner [byti'ne], *v.t., v.i.* to pillage, to plunder.

butoir [by'twaːr], *n.m.* buffer, buffer-stop (*on railway*); tappet.

butor [by'tɔːr], *n.m.* bittern; (*fig.*) churl, lout, booby.

butte [byt], *n.f.* rising ground; knoll, mound.

butter (1) [BUTER].

butter (2) [by'te], *v.t.* to earth up.

butteur [BUTTOIR].

buttoir [by'twaːr], **butteur** [by'tœːr], *n.m.* ridging-plough.

buvable [by'vabl], *a.* drinkable, fit to drink.

buvard [by'vaːr], *a. papier buvard*, blotting paper.—*n.m.* blotting-pad, blotter.

buvetier [byv'tje], *n.m.* (*fem.* **-ière**) inn-keeper, publican.

buvette [by'vɛt], *n.f.* refreshment-room (*railway station*); pump-room (*at spa*).

buveur [by'vœːr], *n.m.* (*fem.* **-euse**) drinker; toper; *buveur d'eau*, teetotaller.

buvoter [byvɔ'te], *v.i.* to sip, to tipple.

Byzance [bi'zɑ̃ːs], *f.* Byzantium.

byzantin [bizɑ̃'tɛ̃], *a.* Byzantine.—*n.m.* (**Byzantin**, *fem.* **-ine**) Byzantine (*person*).

C

C, c [se], *n.m.* the third letter of the alphabet.

ça [sa], *pron.* [*contraction of* **cela**] that; *comme ci comme ça*, only so-so; *donnez-moi ça*, give me that.

çà [sa], *adv.* here; *çà et là*, here and there. —*int.* now; *çà alors!* well, I never!

cabale [ka'bal], *n.f.* cabal, faction.

cabaler [kaba'le], *v.i.* to cabal, to plot.

cabaleur [kaba'lœːr], *n.m.* (*fem.* **-euse**) caballer, intriguer.

caban [ka'bɑ̃], *n.m.* hooded cloak, oilskins.

cabane [ka'ban], *n.f.* hut, shed, cabin, shanty; central part (*of an aeroplane*).

cabanon [kaba'nõ], *n.m.* small hut; prison-cell; padded room.

cabaret [kaba're], *n.m.* inferior kind of wine-shop, tavern; night-club.

cabaretier [kabar'tje], *n.m.* (*fem.* **-ière**) publican, tavern-keeper.

cabas [ka'bɑ], *n.m.* flat two-handled basket.

cabeliau [CABILLAUD].

cabestan [kabes'tɑ̃], *n.m.* capstan, windlass.

cabillaud [kabi'jo], **cabeliau** [kab'ljo] (*pl.* **-aux**), *n.m.* fresh cod.

cabine [ka'bin], *n.f.* cabin; (*Av.*) *cabine de pilotage*, cockpit; *cabine téléphonique*, call-box.

cabinet [kabi'ne], *n.m.* closet, study; practice (*of a professional man*); office (*of a lawyer, barrister etc.*); (*Polit.*) Cabinet; *cabinet d'aisances* or *les cabinets*, lavatory.

câblage [kɑ'blaːʒ], *n.m.* (*Elec.*) wiring.

câble [kɑːbl], *n.m.* cable.

câbler [kɑ'ble], *v.t.* to twist into a cord; to telegraph by cable.

câblogramme [kɑblɔ'gram], *n.m.* cablegram.

cabochon [kabɔ'ʃõ], *n.m.* fancy brass nail; (*Cycl.*) *cabochon rouge*, red reflector.

cabosse [ka'bɔs], *n.f.* (*pop.*) bruise, bump.

cabosser [kabɔ'se], *v.t.* to bump, to bruise; to dent.

cabotage [kabɔ'taːʒ], *n.m.* coasting, coasting-trade.

caboter [kabɔ'te], *v.i.* to coast.

caboteur [kabɔ'tœːr], **cabotier** [kabɔ'tje], *n.m.* coasting-vessel; coaster.

cabotin [kabɔ'tɛ̃], *n.m.* strolling player; bad actor, mummer.

cabotiner [kaboti'ne], *v.i.* to act badly; (*fig.*) to strut.

cabré [kɑ'bre], *a.* rearing (*of a horse*); tail-down (*of a plane*).

cabrer [kɑ'bre], *v.t.* to make (*a horse, a plane*) rear. **se cabrer**, *v.r.* to prance, to rear; (*fig.*) to revolt, to fly into a passion.

cabri [ka'bri], *n.m.* kid.

cabriole [kabri'ɔl], *n.f.* caper, leap.

cabrioler [kabriɔ'le], *v.i.* to caper, to cut capers.

cabriolet [kabriɔ'lɛ], *n.m.* cabriolet, cab.

cacahouète [kaka'wɛt], **cacahuète** [kaka'ɥɛt], *n.f.* peanut, monkey nut.

cacao [kaka'o], *n.m.* cacao, chocolate-nut.

cacaoyer [kakaɔ'je], **cacaotier** [kakaɔ'tje], *n.m.* cacao-tree.

cacaoyère [kakaɔ'jeːr], **cacaotière** [kakaɔ'tjeːr], *n.f.* cacao-plantation.

cacatois [kaka'twa], **cacatoès** [kakatɔ'ɛːs], *n.m.* cockatoo.

cachalot [kaʃa'lo], *n.m.* sperm whale.

cachalotier [kaʃalɔ'tje], *n.m.* whaler.

cache [kaʃ], *n.f.* hiding-place.

cache-cache [kaʃ'kaʃ], *n.m.* hide-and-seek.

cachemire [kaʃ'miːr], *n.m.* cashmere.

cache-nez [kaʃ'ne], *n.m.* muffler, comforter.

cacher [ka'ʃe], *v.t.* to hide, to conceal; to mask. **se cacher**, *v.r.* to hide, to lurk.

cache-sexe [kaʃ'sɛks], *n.m.* trunks; panties; (*collog.*) G-string.

cachet [ka'ʃe], *n.m.* seal, stamp; signet-ring; ticket; tablet (*of aspirin*); (*fig.*) character, stamp, mark.

cacheter [kaʃ'te], *v.t.* (*conjug. like* APPELER) to seal.

cachette [ka'ʃet], *n.f.* hiding-place.

cachot [ka'ʃo], *n.m.* dungeon, prison.

cachotter [kaʃɔ'te], *v.t.* to make a mystery of, to conceal.

cachotterie [kaʃɔ'tri], *n.f.* mysterious ways; underhand work.

cachottier [kaʃɔ'tje], *a.* (*fem.* **-ière**) mysterious, sly.—*n.m.* (*fem.* **-ière**) one who makes a mystery of things.

cachou [ka'ʃu], *n.m.* cachou.

cacophonie [kakɔfɔ'ni], *n.f.* cacophony.

cacophonique [kakɔfɔ'nik], *a.* cacophonous.

cactier [kak'tje], **cactus** [kak'tyːs], *n.m.* cactus.

cadastral [kadas'tral], *a.* (*m. pl.* **-aux**) cadastral, referring to the register of lands.

cadastre [ka'dastr], *n.m.* cadastre, register of the survey of lands.

cadastrer [kadas'tre], *v.t.* to survey.

cadavéreux [kadave'rø], *a.* (*fem.* **-euse**) cadaverous, corpse-like, ghastly.

cadavérique [kadave'rik], *a.* of or pertaining to a corpse.

cadavre [ka'dɑːvr], *n.m.* corpse, dead body.
cadeau [ka'do], *n.m.* (*pl.* -eaux) present, gift.
cadenas [kad'nɑ], *n.m.* padlock; clasp.
cadenasser [kadna'se], *v.t.* to padlock; to snap, clasp.
cadence [ka'dɑːs], *n.f.* cadence, rhythm, time (*in dancing*).
cadencer [kadɑ̃'se], *v.t.* (*conjug. like* COMMENCER) to cadence, to harmonize.
cadène [ka'dɛːn], *n.f.* chain (*for convicts*); chain-gang.
cadenette [kad'nɛt], *n.f.* tress (*of hair*).
cadet [ka'dɛ], *a.* and *n.m.* (*fem.* -ette) younger, junior (*of two*).
Cadix [ka'diks], *f.* Cadiz.
cadmium [kad'mjɔm], *n.m.* cadmium.
cadrage [ka'drɑːʒ], *n.m.* (*Phot., Cine.*) centring.
cadran [ka'drɑ̃], *n.m.* dial-plate, dial; *cadran solaire*, sun-dial.
cadre [kɑːdr], *n.m.* frame, framework; (*Mil.*) the staff; (*pl.*) the higher staff (*of an administration* or *a firm*).
cadrer [ka'dre], *v.t.* (*Phot., Cine.*) to centre.— *v.i.* to agree, to tally, to square (*à* or *avec*).
caduc [ka'dyk], *a.* (*fem.* -uque) decrepit, decayed; frail, tumble-down; lapsed, null, void (*of legacies*); (*Bot.*) deciduous.
caducité [kadysi'te], *n.f.* caducity, decrepitude.
cafard [ka'faːr], *a.* hypocritical, sanctimonious.— *n.m.* (*fem.* -e) hypocrite, sanctimonious person; humbug; (*Sch.*) sneak.— *n.m.* cockroach.
cafarder [kafar'de], *v.i.* (*fam.*) to sneak, to tell tales (*at school*).
cafarderie [kafar'dri], *n.f.* cant, hypocrisy, sanctimoniousness.
café [ka'fe], *n.m.* coffee; café, coffee-house; coffee-berry.
caféière [kafe'jɛːr], *n.f.* coffee-plantation.
caféine [kafe'iːn], *n.f.* caffeine.
cafetan or caftan [kaf'tɑ̃], *n.m.* caftan.
cafetier [kaf'tje], *n.m.* (*fem.* cafetière (1)) coffee-house keeper.
cafetière (2) [kaf'tjɛːr]ₑ *n.f.* coffee-pot, percolator.
cafouillage [kafu'jaːʒ], *n.m.* floundering.
cafre [kɑːfr], *a.* and *n.* (Cafre) Kaffir, Bantu.
caftan [CAFETAN].
cage [kaːʒ], *n.f.* cage; coop.
cageot [ka'ʒo], *n.m.* little cage, hamper, crate.
cagibi [kaʒi'bi], *n.m.* small hut *or* room.
cagneux [ka'ɲø], *a.* (*fem.* -euse) knock-kneed, pigeon-toed.
cagnotte [ka'ɲot], *n.f.* kitty, pool, jackpot.
cagot [ka'go], *a.* (*fem.* -otte) bigoted, hypocritical.— *n.m.* (*fem.* -otte) bigot, hypocrite.
cagoterie [kago'tri], *n.f.* an act *or* word of hypocrisy *or* bigotry.
cagotisme [kago'tism], *n.m.* hypocrisy, bigotry.
cagoule [ka'gul], *n.f.* monk's cloak; penitent's cowl; hood.
cahier [ka'je], *n.m.* stitched paper-book; exercise-book; quarter of a quire of paper.
cahot [ka'o], *n.m.* jerk, jolt.
cahotage [kao'taːʒ], cahotement [kaot'mɑ̃], *n.m.* jolting, jerking.
cahotant [kao'tɑ̃], *a.* rough, jolting.
cahoter [kao'te], *v.i.* to jolt, to be jerked about.

cahute [ka'yt], *n.f.* hut, hovel.
ciad [ka'id], *n.m.* Arab chief *or* judge.
caïeu or cayeu [ka'jø], *n.m.* (*pl.* -eux) (*Hort.*) offshoot of a bulb, clove.
caillage [ka'jaːʒ], *n.m.* curdling, congealing.
caille [kɑːj], *n.f.* quail.—(C) *a.* piebald.
caillé [ka'je], *n.m.* curdled milk, curds.— *a.* curdled.
caillebottage [kajbo'taːʒ], *n.m.* curdling.
caillebotte [kaj'bot], *n.f.* curds.
caillebotter (se) [səkajbo'te], *v.r.* to curdle.
caille-lait [kaj'lɛ], *n.m. inv.* rennet.
caillement [kaj'mɑ̃], *n.m.* curdling, coagulating.
cailler [ka'je], *v.t.* to curdle, to clot. se cailler, *v.r.* to coagulate, to turn to curds.
cailleteau [kaj'to], *n.m.* (*pl.* -eaux) young quail.
caillette (1) [ka'jɛt], *n.f.* rennet.
caillette (2) [ka'jɛt], *n.f.* (*Orn.*) petrel; flirt.
caillot [ka'jo], *n.m.* clot of blood, coagulum.
caillou [ka'ju], *n.m.* (*pl.* -oux) pebble, small stone, flint, flint-stone.
cailloutage [kaju'taːʒ], *n.m.* gravelling; ballasting; rough-cast, pebble-work.
caillouter [kaju'te], *v.t.* to gravel, to ballast.
caillouteux [kaju'tø], *a.* (*fem.* -euse) pebbly, flinty.
cailloutis [kaju'ti], *n.m.* broken stones, gravel, road metal.
caïman [kai'mɑ̃], *n.m.* American crocodile, cayman.
Caïn [ka'ɛ̃], *m.* Cain.
caïque or caïc [ka'ik], *n.m.* (*Naut.*) caique.
Caire [kɛːr], Le, *m.* Cairo.
caisse [kɛːs], *n.f.* chest, case, box, trunk; till; cash; cashier's office, pay desk; *la grosse caisse*, the (big) drum; *caisse d'épargne*, savings-bank.
caissette [kɛ'sɛt], *n.f.* small box.
caissier [kɛ'sje], *n.m.* (*fem.* -ière) treasurer, cashier.
caisson [kɛ'sɔ̃], *n.m.* ammunition-wagon; (*Naut.*) locker.
cajoler [kaʒo'le], *v.t.* to cajole, to coax.
cajolerie [kaʒol'ri], *n.f.* cajolery, coaxing.
cajoleur [kaʒo'lœːr], *n.m.* (*fem.* -euse) cajoler, coaxer.— *a.* cajoling, coaxing.
cal [kal], *n.m.* callosity, callus.
Calabre [ka'lɑːbr], la, *f.* Calabria.
calage [ka'laːʒ], *n.m.* lowering (*of sails etc.*) propping, wedging (*of furniture*).
calaison [kalɛ'zɔ̃], *n.f.* load-line, sea-gauge.
calaminage [kalami'naːʒ], *n.m.* (*Motor.*) carbonizing.
calamine [kala'min], *n.f.* carbon (*on plugs of a car etc.*).
calamité [kalami'te], *n.f.* calamity, misfortune.
calamiteusement [kalamitøz'mɑ̃], *adv.* calamitously.
calamiteux [kalami'tø], *a.* (*fem.* -euse) calamitous.
calandrage [kalɑ̃'draːʒ], *n.m.* calendering, hot-pressing.
calandre [ka'lɑ̃ːdr], *n.f.* mangle, calender; (*Motor.*) radiator grill.
calandrer [kalɑ̃'dre], *v.t.* to calender, to press, to smooth.
calandrette [kalɑ̃'drɛt], *n.f.* song-thrush.
calcaire [kal'kɛːr], *a.* calcareous.— *n.m.* limestone.
calcéolaire [kalseo'lɛːr], *n.f.* calceolaria.

55

calcination [kalsinɑ'sjõ], *n.f.* calcination.
calciner [kalsi'ne], *v.t.* to calcine, to burn. **se calciner**, *v.r.* to calcine.
calcium [kal'sjɔm], *n.m.* calcium.
calcul [kal'kyl], *n.m.* calculation; arithmetic; reckoning, counting; (*Math.*) calculus; (*fig.*) design, selfish motive; (*Med.*) calculus (*stone*).
calculable [kalky'labl], *a.* computable, calculable.
calculateur [kalkyla'tœːr], *a.* (*fem.* **-trice**) calculating, scheming.—*n.m.* (*fem.* **-trice**) calculator, reckoner; schemer.—*n.f.* (**-trice**) computer.
calculer [kalky'le], *v.t.* to calculate, to compute, to estimate; *machine à calculer*, computer.
cale (1) [kal], *n.f.* hold (*of a ship*); stocks, slip; ducking, keel-hauling (*punishment*); *cale sèche*, dry dock.
cale (2) [kal], *n.f.* wedge, block; prop, strut.
calebasse [kal'bas], *n.f.* calabash, gourd.
calèche [ka'lɛʃ], *n.f.* calash; barouche, open carriage.
caleçon [kal'sõ], *n.m.* (*men's*) drawers, pants; *caleçon de bain*, bathing-trunks.
Calédonie [kaledɔ'ni], **la**, *f.* Caledonia.
calédonien [kaledɔ'njɛ̃], *a.* (*fem.* **-enne**) Caledonian.—*n.m.* (**Calédonien**, *fem.* **-enne**) Caledonian (*person*).
caléfaction [kalefak'sjõ], *n.f.* heating, calefaction.
calembour [kalɑ̃'buːr], *n.m.* pun.
calembourdiste [kalɑ̃bur'dist], *n.m.* punster.
calembredaine [kalɑ̃brə'dɛn], *n.f.* quibble, subterfuge, nonsense.
calendes [ka'lɑ̃:d], *n.f. pl.* (*Ant.*) calends; convocation of the clergy of a diocese.
calendrier [kalɑ̃dri'e], *n.m.* calendar, almanac.
calendule [kalɑ̃'dyl], *n.f.* calendula.
cale-pied [kal'pje], *n.m.* toe clip.
calepin [kal'pɛ̃], *n.m.* notebook, memorandum-book.
caler (1) [ka'le], *v.t.* (*Naut.*) to lower, to strike; to draw, to have a draught of.
caler (2) [ka'le], *v.t.* to prop up, to wedge; to steady; to jam; (*Motor.*) to stall.—*v.i.* (*Motor.*) to stall.
calfeutrage [kalfø'traːʒ], **calfeutrement** [kalføtr'mɑ̃], *n.m.* stopping of chinks.
calfeutrer [kalfø'tre], *v.t.* to stop up the chinks of, to make air-tight. **se calfeutrer**, *v.r.* to shut oneself up.
calibre [ka'libr], *n.m.* calibre, bore (*of a gun*); size (*of a bullet*); (*fig.*) kind, sort.
calibrer [kali'bre], *v.t.* to calibrate; to give the proper calibre to (*bullets etc.*).
calice (1) [ka'lis], *n.m.* chalice, communion-cup; (*fig.*) grief, sacrifice.
calice (2) [ka'lis], *n.m.* (*Bot.*) calyx, flower, cup.
calicot [kali'ko], *n.m.* calico; (*slang*) counter-jumper.
calicule [kali'kyl], *n.m.* calicle, caliculus.
califat [kali'fa], *n.m.* caliphate.
calife [ka'lif], *n.m.* caliph.
Californie [kalifɔr'ni], **la**, *f.* California.
califourchon [kalifur'ʃõ], *n.m. à califourchon*, astride.
câlin [kɑ'lɛ̃], *a.* wheedling, winning, coaxing. —*n.m.* (*fem.* **-e**) wheedler, cajoler.

câliner [kɑ:li'ne], *v.t.* to cajole, to wheedle. **se câliner**, *v.r.* to coddle oneself, to take one's ease.
câlinerie [kɑ:lin'ri], *n.f.* wheedling, cajolery, caressing.
calleux [ka'lø], *a.* (*fem.* **-euse**) callous, horny.
calligraphe [kali'graf], *n.m.* calligrapher, good penman.
calligraphie [kaligra'fi], *n.f.* calligraphy, penmanship.
callisthénie [kaliste'ni], *n.f.* callisthenics.
callosité [kaloži'te], *n.f.* callosity.
calmant [kal'mɑ̃], *a.* calming, soothing, sedative.—*n.m.* (*Med.*) anodyne, sedative.
calme [kalm], *a.* tranquil, quiet, serene, calm; composed, dispassionate.—*n.m.* calm, stillness, quiet; composure.
calmer [kal'me], *v.t.* to calm, to still, to quiet, to allay, to soothe.—*v.i.* (*Naut.*) to lull, to become calm. **se calmer**, *v.r.* to become calm, to compose oneself; to blow over.
calomel [kalɔ'mɛl], *n.m.* calomel.
calomniateur [kalɔmnja'tœːr], *a.* (*fem.* **-trice**) slanderous.—*n.m.* (*fem.* **-trice**) calumniator, slanderer.
calomnie [kalɔm'ni], *n.f.* calumny, slander.
calomnier [kalɔm'nje], *v.t.* to calumniate, to slander.
calomnieusement [kalɔmnjøz'mɑ̃], *adv.* calumniously, slanderously.
calomnieux [kalɔm'njø], *a.* (*fem.* **-euse**) calumnious, slanderous.
calorie [kalɔ'ri], *n.f.* calorie, unit of heat.
calorifère [kalɔri'fɛːr], *n.m.* hot-air stove *or* pipe; central heating.—*a.* heat-conveying.
calorifique [kalɔri'fik], *a.* calorific.
calorifuger [kalɔrify'ʒe], *v.t.* (*conjug. like* MANGER) to insulate, to lag (*pipes*).
calorique [kalɔ'rik], *a.* and *n.m.* caloric, heat.
calotte [ka'lɔt], *n.f.* skull-cap (*esp. that worn by priests*); small dome; box on the ears.
calotter [kalɔ'te], *v.t.* to box the ears of.
calque [kalk], *n.m.* tracing; close copy.—*a. papier calque*, tracing paper.
calquer [kal'ke], *v.t.* to trace; to copy, to imitate closely. **se calquer**, *v.r.* (*sur*) to model oneself (*on*).
calumet [kaly'me], *n.m.* pipe, calumet.
calvados [kalva'dɔs], *n.m.* apple brandy, calvados.
calvaire [kal'vɛːr], *n.m.* calvary; (*fig.*) torture, suffering, tribulation.
calvinisme [kalvi'nism], *n.m.* Calvinism.
calviniste [kalvi'nist], *a.* Calvinistic.—*n.* (**Calviniste**) Calvinist.
calvitie [kalvi'si], *n.f.* baldness.
camaïeu [kama'jø], *n.m.* (*pl.* **-eux**) cameo (*brooch etc.*).
camail [ka'ma:j], *n.m.* (*pl.* **-ails**) hood, capuchin; hackles (*of poultry*).
camarade [kama'rad], *n.* comrade, fellow, mate, chum, playmate.
camaraderie [kamara'dri], *n.f.* comradeship; intimacy.
camard [ka'maːr], *a.* snub-nosed, flat.—*n.m.* (*fem.* **-e**) snub-nosed person.
Cambodge [kɑ̃'bɔdʒ], **le**, *m.* Cambodia.
cambodgien [kɑ̃bɔ'dʒjɛ̃], *a.* (*fem.* **-enne**) Cambodian.—*n.m.* (**Cambodgien**, *fem.* **-enne**) Cambodian (*person*).
cambouis [kɑ̃'bwi], *n.m.* dirty cart-grease, dirty lubricating oil.

cambrage [kã′bra:ʒ], *n.m.* cambering, bending.

cambrai [kã′brɛ], *n.m.* machine-made lace; cambric.

cambré [kã′bre], *a.* bent, cambered.

cambrement [kãbrə′mã], *n.m.* arching, curving.

cambrer [kã′bre], *v.t.* to arch, to bend, to curve. **se cambrer**, *v.r.* to be cambered; to warp; to draw oneself up.

cambriolage [kãbriɔ′la:ʒ], *n.m.* house-breaking, burglary.

cambrioler [kãbriɔ′le], *v.t.* to break into (*a house*), to burgle.

cambrioleur [kãbriɔ′lœ:r], *n.m.* house-breaker, burglar.

cambrure [kã′bry:r], *n.f.* bend, curvature, arch; the arched part in a shoe.

cambuse [kã′by:z], *n.f.* (*Naut.*) store-room, canteen.

came [kam], *n.f.* cam, wiper; *arbre à cames* cam-shaft.

camée [ka′me], *n.m.* cameo.

caméléon [kamele′ɔ̃], *n.m.* chameleon.

camélia [kame′lja], *n.m.* camellia.

camelot [kam′lo], *n.m.* camlet; cheap-jack, pedlar, hawker.

camelote [kam′lɔt], *n.f.* inferior merchandise, shoddy; (*fig.*) trash.

caméra [kame′ra], *n.f.* ciné camera.

camérier [kame′rje], *n.m.* chamberlain (*of the Pope etc.*).

Cameroun [kamə′run], **le**, *m.* Cameroon.

camion [ka′mjɔ̃], *n.m.* dray, low wagon, lorry.

camionnage [kamjɔ′na:ʒ], *n.m.* carting, carriage.

camionner [kamjɔ′ne], *v.t.* to convey on a dray, lorry, truck etc.

camionnette [kamjɔ′nɛt], *n.f.* light motor lorry; van.

camionneur [kamjɔ′nœ:r], *n.m.* drayman; vanman; haulage contractor.

camisole [kami′zɔl], *n.f.* woman's morning jacket; *camisole de force*, strait jacket.

camomille [kamɔ′mi:j], *n.f.* camomile.

camouflage [kamu′fla:ʒ], **camouflement** [kamuflə′mã], *n.m.* disguise; camouflage.

camoufler [kamu′fle], *v.t.* to disguise; to camouflage. **se camoufler**, *v.r.* to disguise or camouflage oneself.

camouflet [kamu′flɛ], *n.m.* whiff of smoke (*in the face*); (*fig.*) affront, snub.

camp [kã], *n.m.* camp; (*fig.*) army; party; (*C*) country cottage.

campagnard [kãpa′na:r], *a.* rustic, countrified, rural.—*n.m.* (*fem.* **-e**) countryman *or* countrywoman, peasant; clodhopper.

campagne [kã′paɲ], *n.f.* the country, the fields, plain; seat, estate, country-house; campaign; (*Naut.*) cruise.

campagnol [kãpa′nɔl], *n.m.* vole, field-mouse.

campanile [kãpa′nil], *n.m.* campanile, bell-tower.

campanule [kãpa′nyl], *n.f.* campanula, bell-flower, bluebell.

campé [kã′pe], *a.* established, firmly planted, well set up.

campement [kãp′mã], *n.m.* encamping; encampment; camp party, billeting party.

camper [kã′pe], *v.t.* to encamp (*troops etc.*); to place, to seat, to clap down.—*v.i.* to live in camp, to encamp. **se camper**, *v.r.* to encamp; to plant oneself.

campeur [kã′pœ:r], *n.m.* (*fem.* **-euse**) camper.

camphre [kã:fr], *n.m.* camphor.

camphré [kã′fre], *a.* camphorated.

camphrier [kãfri′e], *n.f.* camphor-tree.

camus [ka′my], *a.* flat-nosed, snub-nosed.

Canada [kana′da], **le**, *m.* Canada.

canadien [kana′djɛ̃], *a.* (*fem.* **-enne**) Canadian.—*n.m.* (**Canadien**, *fem.* **-enne**) Canadian (*person*).

canaille [ka′nɑ:j], *n.f.* rabble, riffraff, mob.

canaillerie [kanɑ:j′ri], *n.f.* blackguardism; vulgarity.

canal [ka′nal] *n.m.* (*pl.* **-aux**) canal; conduit, drain; pipe, tube, spout; water-course.

canalisation [kanaliza′sjɔ̃], *n.f.* canalization; mains; *canalisation de gaz*, gas mains.

canaliser [kanali′ze], *v.t.* to canalize; to instal pipes (*for gas etc.*).

canamelle [kana′mɛl], *n.f.* sugar-cane.

canapé [kana′pe], *n.m.* sofa, couch.

canapé-lit [kanape′li], *n.m.* divan-bed.

canard [ka′na:r], *n.m.* duck; drake; (*fig.*) hoax.

canardeau [kanar′do], *n.m.* (*pl.* **-eaux**) young duck.

canarder [kanar′de], *v.t.* to shoot from behind a shelter; to snipe.—*v.i.* (*Naut.*) to pitch heavily.

canardière [kanar′dje:r], *n.f.* duck-pond; duck-gun.

canari [kana′ri], *n.m.* canary (*bird*).

Canaries [kana′ri], **les Îles**, *f. pl.* the Canary Islands.

canasta [kanas′ta], *n.f.* canasta.

cancan [kã′kã], *n.m.* tittle-tattle, scandal; French cancan.

cancaner [kãka′ne], *v.i.* to tattle, to invent stories.

cancanier [kãka′nje], *a.* (*fem.* **-ière**) addicted to gossip.—*n.m.* (*fem.* **-ière**) scandal-monger.

cancer [kã′sɛ:r], *n.m.* (*Astron., Geol., Med.*) cancer.

cancéreux [kãse′rø], *a.* (*fem.* **-euse**) cancerous.

cancre [kã:kr], *n.m.* crab; (*fig.*) dunce (*at school*).

cancrelat *or* **cancrelas** [kãkrə′la], *n.m.* cockroach.

candélabre [kãde′la:br], *n.m.* candelabrum, sconce.

candeur [kã′dœ:r], *n.f.* artlessness, guilelessness, ingenuousness.

candi [kã′di], *a.m.* candied; *fruits candis*, crystallized fruits.—*n.m.* sugar-candy.

candidat [kãdi′da], *n.m.* candidate.

candidature [kãdida′ty:r], *n.f.* candidature.

candide [kã′did], *a.* ingenuous, artless.

candidement [kãdid′mã], *adv.* ingenuously.

candir [kã′di:r], *v.i.* or **se candir**, *v.r.* to candy, to crystallize.

cane [kan], *n.f.* (*female*) duck.

canebière [CANNEBIÈRE].

canepetière [kanpə′tje:r], *n.f.* lesser bustard.

caneton [kan′tɔ̃], *n.m.* duckling.

canette (1) *or* **cannette** (1) [ka′nɛt], *n.f.* small duck, duckling; teal.

canette (2) *or* **cannette** (2) [ka′nɛt], *n.f.* measure for beer; spool (*inside shuttle*).

canevas [kan′va], *n.m.* canvas; sail-cloth; outline sketch, rough draft.

caniche [ka′niʃ], *n.m.* poodle.

canichon [kani'ʃõ], *n.m.* small poodle; duckling.

caniculaire [kaniky'lɛːr], *a.* canicular.

canicule [kani'kyl], *n.f.* dog-days; (*Astron.*) dog-star.

canif [ka'nif], *n.m.* penknife.

canin [ka'nɛ̃], *a.* canine.—*n.f.* (*dent*) *canine*, canine (tooth).

canitie [kani'si], *n.f.* whiteness of the hair.

caniveau [kani'vo], *n.m.* (*pl.* **-eaux**) (*Arch.*) channel-stone, gutter.

cannage [ka'naːʒ], *n.m.* cane-work (*in chairs etc.*).

cannaie [ka'nɛ], *n.f.* cane-plantation, cane-field.

canne [kan], *n.f.* cane, reed; walking-stick; glass-blower's pipe.

canneberge [kan'bɛrʒ], *n.f.* cranberry.

cannebière or **canebière** [kan'bjɛːr], *n.f.* (*S.-E. France*) [CHÈNEVIÈRE].

cannelé [kan'le], *a.* fluted (*column*); grooved (*tyre*).—*n.m.* ribbed silk.

canneler [kan'le], *v.t.* (*conjug. like* APPELER) to flute, to channel, to groove.

cannelier [kanə'lje], *n.m.* cinnamon-tree.

cannelle (1) [ka'nɛl], *n.f.* cinnamon bark, cinnamon.

cannelle (2) [ka'nɛl], **cannette** (3) [ka'nɛt], *n.f.* spigot, tap.

cannelure [kan'lyːr], *n.f.* fluting, channelling.

cannette (1) [CANETTE (1)].

cannette (2) [CANETTE (2)].

cannette (3) [CANNELLE (2)].

cannibale [kani'bal], *n.m.* cannibal.

cannibalisme [kaniba'lism], *n.m.* cannibalism; (*fig.*) ferocity.

canon (1) [ka'nõ], *n.m.* cannon, gun; barrel (*of a gun*); cylinder, pipe, tube (*of lock*).

canon (2) [ka'nõ], *n.m.* (*Eccles.*) canon; (*Mus.*) round, canon.

cañon [ka'nõ], *n.m.* canyon.

canonial [kanɔ'njal], *a.* (*m.pl.* **-aux**) canonical.

canonicat [kanɔni'ka], *n.m.* canonry; (*fig.*) sinecure.

canonicité [kanɔnisi'te], *n.f.* canonicity.

canonique [kanɔ'nik], *a.* canonical.

canonisation [kanɔniza'sjõ], *n.f.* canonization.

canoniser [kanɔni'ze], *v.t.* to canonize.

canonnade [kanɔ'nad], *n.f.* cannonading, cannonade.

canonner [kanɔ'ne], *v.t.* to attack with heavy artillery, to cannonade.

canonnier [kanɔ'nje], *n.m.* gunner.

canonnière [kanɔ'njɛːr], *n.f.* pop-gun; gun-boat.

canot [ka'no], *n.m.* small open boat, dinghy; (*C*) Canadian canoe; *canot automobile*, motor-boat; *canot de sauvetage*, lifeboat.

canotage [kanɔ'taːʒ], *n.m.* boating, rowing.

cantate [kã'tat], *n.f.* (*Mus.*) cantata.

cantatrice [kãta'tris], *n.f.* cantatrice, (*classical*) singer.

cantharide [kãta'rid], *n.f.* (*Ent.*) cantharis, Spanish fly.

cantilène [kãti'lɛːn], *n.f.* cantilena, ballad, popular song.

cantine [kã'tin], *n.f.* canteen; kit-case.

cantique [kã'tik], *n.m.* canticle, hymn.

canton [kã'tõ], *n.m.* canton (*district*); (*C*) township.

cantonade [kãtɔ'nad], *n.f.* (*Theat.*) either of the wings; *parler à la cantonade*, to speak to an actor off the stage.

cantonnement [kãtɔn'mã], *n.m.* (*Mil.*) cantonment, billet, quarters.

cantonner [kãtɔ'ne], *v.t.* (*Mil.*) to billet (*troops*). **se cantonner**, *v.r.* to take up a position, quarters *or* abode; to fortify oneself.

cantonnier [kãtɔ'nje], *n.m.* roadman; (*Rail.*) platelayer.

cantonnière [kãtɔ'njɛːr], *n.f.* valance.

canule [ka'nyl], *n.f.* clyster-pipe, injection-tube, douche-tube.

caoutchouc [kau'tʃu], *n.m.* (India-)rubber; mackintosh; (*pl.*) galoshes.

cap [kap], *n.m.* head; bow (*of a ship*); cape, headland, promontory.

capable [ka'pabl], *a.* able, fit, capable; apt; competent.

capacité [kapasi'te], *n.f.* extent, size; ability.

caparaçon [kapara'sõ], *n.m.* caparison, trappings.

caparaçonner [kaparasɔ'ne], *v.t.* to caparison (*a horse*).

cape [kap], *n.f.* cape, mantle *or* cloak with a hood.

capharnaüm [kafarna'ɔm], *n.m.* lumber-room, glory-hole.

capillaire [kapi'lɛːr], *a.* capillary.—*n.m.* capillary; maiden-hair.

capilotade [kapilɔ'tad], *n.f.* hash, ragoût; (*fig.*) thrashing.

capitaine [kapi'tɛn], *n.m.* captain; (*fig.*) eminent commander.

capital [kapi'tal], *a.* (*m.pl.* **-aux**) capital, main, chief, principal.—*n.m.* capital, principal; property, stock.

capitale [kapi'tal], *n.f.* capital, chief city; capital letter.

capitaliser [kapitali'ze], *v.t.* to put at compound interest; to add to the capital; to realize, to capitalize.—*v.i.* to save, to lay by.

capitaliste [kapita'list], *n.* capitalist, moneyed man *or* woman.

capitan [kapi'tã], *n.m.* braggadocio, swaggerer.

capitation [kapita'sjõ], *n.f.* capitation, poll-tax.

capiteux [kapi'tø], *a.* (*fem.* **-euse**) heady, strong.

Capitole [kapi'tɔl], *n.m.* Capitol (*of Rome etc.*).

capitonner [kapitɔ'ne], *v.t.* to stuff, to pad.

capitulaire [kapity'lɛːr], *a.* and *n.m.* capitulary.

capitulation [kapityla'sjõ], *n.f.* capitulation; compromise.

capituler [kapity'le], *v.i.* to capitulate; to compound, to compromise.

capoc [ka'pɔk], *n.m.* kapok.

capon [ka'põ], *a.* (*fem.* **-onne**) cowardly.—*n.m.* (*fem.* **-onne**) mean fellow, sneak; coward.

caponner [kapɔ'ne], *v.i.* to cheat; to be cowardly; to rat.

caporal [kapɔ'ral], *n.m.* (*pl.* **-aux**) corporal; sort of 'shag' (*tobacco*).

capot (1) [ka'po], *n.m.* (*Motor.*) bonnet, (*Am.*) hood.

capot (2) [ka'po], *a. inv.* capot (*at piquet etc.*); flabbergasted.

capote [ka'pɔt], *n.f.* capote, large cloak with a hood; (*soldier's*) great-coat; baby's bonnet.

capoter [kapo'te], *v.i.* (*Naut. etc.*) to capsize; to turn turtle.

câpre [kɑ:pr], *n.f.* (*Bot.*) caper.

caprice [ka'pris], *n.m.* caprice, whim, humour; flight, sally.

capricieusement [kaprisjøz'mã], *adv.* capriciously, whimsically.

capricieux [kapri'sjø], *a.* (*fem.* **-euse**) capricious, whimsical, fickle.

capricorne [kapri'kɔrn], *n.m.* (*Astron.*) Capricorn.

capsule [kap'syl], *n.f.* capsule; pod; percussion-cap (*of firearms*).

captation [kaptɑ'sjɔ̃], *n.f.* captation, inveigling; intercepting.

captatoire [kapta'twa:r], *a.* inveigling.

capter [kap'te], *v.t.* to obtain by underhand methods; to win by bribery etc.

captieusement [kapsjøz'mã], *adv.* insidiously, cunningly, deceitfully.

captieux [kap'sjø], *a.* (*fem.* **-euse**) insidious, cunning, specious.

captif [kap'tif], *a.* and *n.m.* (*fem.* **-tive**) captive.

captivant [kapti'vã], *a.* captivating; enthralling.

captiver [kapti've], *v.t.* to captivate, to charm.

captivité [kaptivi'te], *n.f.* captivity, bondage.

capture [kap'ty:r], *n.f.* capture, prize, booty.

capturer [kapty're], *v.t.* to capture; to arrest.

capuchon [kapy'ʃɔ̃], *n.m.* hood, cowl.

capuchonné [kapyʃo'ne], *a.* cowled; hooded.

capucin [kapy'sɛ̃], *n.m.* (*fem.* **capucine** (1) [kapy'sin]) Capuchin friar *or* nun.

capucine (1) [CAPUCIN]

capucine (2) [kapy'sin], *n.f.* nasturtium.

caque [kak], *n.f.* keg, barrel.

caquet [ka'kɛ], *n.m.* cackle (*of geese etc.*); tittle-tattle, gossip, scandal.

caquetage [kak'ta:ʒ], *n.m.*, **caqueterie** [kak(ə)'tri], *n.f.* babbling, prattling; tattling, gossiping.

caqueter [kak'te], *v.i.* (*conjug. like* APPELER) to cackle, to chatter; to gossip.

car (1) [ka:r], *conj.* for, because.

car (2) [ka:r], *n.m.* (*fam.*) coach, long-distance bus.

carabin [kara'bɛ̃], *n.m.* (*colloq.*) saw-bones, medical student.

carabine [kara'bin], *n.f.* carbine, rifle.

carabiné [karabi'ne], *a.* rifled; (*colloq.*) strong, violent.

carabiner [karabi'ne], *v.t.* to rifle (*a gun-barrel*).

carabinier [karabi'nje], *n.m.* carabinier, rifleman.

caractère [karak'tɛ:r], *n.m.* character, letter; hand-writing; nature, disposition; temper, spirit; stamp; quality.

caractériser [karakteri'ze], *v.t.* to characterize, to describe.

caractéristique [karakteris'tik], *a.* and *n.f.* characteristic.

carafe [ka'raf], *n.f.* carafe, decanter water-bottle.

carafon [kara'fɔ̃], *n.m.* small carafe *or* decanter.

Caraïbes [kara'ib], **les**, *f.pl.* the Caribbean Isles.

carambolage [karãbo'la:ʒ], *n.m.* (*Billiards*) cannon; (*pop.*) affray, shindy; (*fig.*) rebound (*against*).

caramboler [karãbo'le], *v.i.* (*Billiards*) to cannon.

caramel [kara'mɛl], *n.m.* caramel.

carapace [kara'pas], *n.f.* (*Zool.*) carapace, shell.

carat [ka'ra], *n.m.* (*Gold*) carat.

caravane [kara'van], *n.f.* caravan, convoy; caravan (*on wheels*).

carbonate [karbo'nat], *n.m.* (*Chem.*) carbonate.

carbone [kar'bon], *n.m.* carbon.

carboné [karbo'ne], *a.* carbonated, carbonized.

carbonique [karbo'nik], *a.* carbonic.

carboniser [karboni'ze], *v.t.* to carbonize.

carburant [karby'rã], *a.* and *n.m.* motor-fuel.

carburateur [karbyra'tœ:r], *n.m.* carburettor.

carbure [kar'by:r], *n.m.* (*Chem.*) carbide.

carburé [karby're], *a.* carburetted.

carcasse [kar'kas], *n.f.* carcass, skeleton.

cardage [kar'da:ʒ], *n.m.* carding.

cardan [kar'dã], *n.m.* (*Mech.*) universal joint.

carde [kard], *n.f.* (*Bot.*) cardoon.

carder [kar'de], *v.t.* to card, to comb.

cardialgie [kardjal'ʒi], *n.f.* cardialgy, heartburn.

cardiaque [kar'djak], *a.* and *n.* cardiac (case).

cardinal [kardi'nal], *a.* (*m. pl.* **-aux**) cardinal, chief, principal.—*n.m.* (*pl.* **-aux**) (*Eccles.*) cardinal.

cardinalat [kardina'la], *n.m.* cardinalate, cardinalship.

cardiogramme [kardio'gram], *n.m.* cardiogram.

cardiographe [kardio'graf], *n.m.* cardiograph.

cardon [kar'dɔ̃], *n.m.* (*Bot.*) cardoon.

carême [ka're:m], *n.m.* Lent; Lent-sermons.

carénage [kare'na:ʒ], *n.m.* careening.

carence [ka'rã:s], *n.f.* (*Law*) insolvency.

carène [ka're:n], *n.f.* (*Naut.*) bottom (*keel and sides up to water-mark*).

caréné [kare'ne], *a.* (*Bot.*) carinate; keeled; (*Motor.*) stream-lined.

caréner [kare'ne], *v.t.* (*conjug. like* CÉDER) to careen; to stream-line.

caressant [karɛ'sã], *a.* caressing, endearing; tender.

caresse [ka'rɛs], *n.f.* caress, endearment.

caresser [karɛ'se], *v.t.* to caress, to fondle, to stroke.

caret (1) [ka're], *n.m.* rope-maker's reel.

caret (2) [ka're], *n.m.* turtle.

cargaison [kargɛ'zɔ̃], *n.f.* cargo, freight.

cargo [kar'go], *n.m.* (*Naut.*) tramp, cargo-boat.

carguer [kar'ge], *v.t.* to reef (*sails*).

cargueur [kar'gœ:r], *n.m.* (*Naut.*) reefer.

cari [ka'ri], *n.m.* curry-powder.

cariatide [karja'tid], *n.f.* caryatid.

caribou [kari'bu], *n.m.* cariboo.

caricature [karika'ty:r], *n.f.* caricature; (*fam.*) fright (*person*).

caricaturer [karikaty're], *v.t.* to caricature.

caricaturiste [karikaty'rist], *n.* caricaturist.

carie [ka'ri], *n.f.* (*Path.*) caries, decay; (*Bot.*) brown rust; rot (*of timber*).

carier [ka'rje], *v.t.* to make carious, to rot.

carillon [kari'jɔ̃], *n.m.* carillon; chime, peal.

carillonnement [karijon'mã], *n.m.* chiming, jingling.

59

carillonner [karijɔ'ne], *v.i.* to chime; to ring the changes; to jingle.

carillonneur [karijɔ'nœːr], *n.m.* bell-ringer.

carlin [kar'lɛ̃], *a.* pug; turned-up (*nose*).

carlingue [kar'lɛ̃ːg], *n.f.* (*Av.*) cockpit.

carmagnole [karma'ɲɔl], *n.f.* Piedmontese jacket; carmagnole.

carme [karm], *n.m.* Carmelite friar, White friar.

carmélite [karme'lit], *n.f.* Carmelite nun.— *a.* light brown.

carmin [kar'mɛ̃], *a.* and *n.m.* carmine.

carnage [kar'naːʒ], *n.m.* carnage, slaughter.

carnassier [karna'sje], *a.* (*fem.* **-ière**) carnivorous, flesh-eating.—*n.m.* feline animal; flesh-eater.—*n.f.* (**-ière**) game-bag.

carnation [karna'sjɔ̃], *n.f.* complexion; flesh-colour.

carnaval [karna'val], *n.m.* carnival; masquerade, festival; guy.

carné [kar'ne], *a.* flesh-coloured; composed of meat.

carnet [kar'nɛ], *n.m.* notebook, log-book.

carnier [kar'nje], *n.m.* game-bag.

carnivore [karni'vɔːr], *a.* carnivorous.—*n.* carnivore.

carogne [ka'rɔɲ], *n.f.* hag, jade, impudent slut.

carotide [karɔ'tid], *a.* and *n.f.* carotid.

carotte [ka'rɔt], *n.f.* carrot; (*slang*) fake, ruse, hoax; plug outside a tobacconist's shop.—*a.* (*inv.*) ginger (*hair*).

carotter [karɔ'te], *v.t.* to cheat, to diddle.

carotteur [karɔ'tœːr], **carottier** [karɔ'tje], *n.m.* (*fem.* **-euse, -ière**) cheat, trickster; wangler.

carpe (1) [karp], *n.f.* (*Ichth.*) carp.

carpe (2) [karp], *n.m.* (*Anat.*) wrist.

carquois [kar'kwa], *n.m.* quiver.

carrare [ka'raːr], *n.m.* Carrara marble.

carré [ka're], *a.* square; well-set; plain, straightforward.—*n.m.* square; landing, floor; (*Hort.*) plot.

carreau [ka'ro], *n.m.* (*pl.* **-eaux**) small square; square tile or brick, small flag-stone; pane (*of glass*); diamond (*at cards*).

carrefour [kar'fuːr], *n.m.* cross-roads.

carrelage [kar'laːʒ], *n.m.* tile-flooring, paving-squares.

carreler [kar'le], *v.t.* (*conjug. like* APPELER) to pave (*a floor*) with square tiles, bricks, stones etc.; to cobble (*shoes etc.*).

carrelet [kar'lɛ], *n.m.* plaice.

carrelette [kar'lɛt], *n.f.* flat file.

carreleur [kar'lœːr], *n.m.* floor-tiler.

carrément [kare'mã], *adv.* squarely; (*fig.*) bluntly, plainly.

carrer [ka're], *v.t.* to square. **se carrer**, *v.r.* to strut, to pose.

carrier [ka'rje], *n.m.* quarryman.

carrière (1) [ka'rjɛːr], *n.f.* career, course; scope, play, vent; profession, vocation; *la Carrière*, the diplomatic service.

carrière (2) [ka'rjɛːr], *n.f.* quarry.

carriole [ka'rjɔl], *n.f.* light covered cart.

carrossable [karɔ'sabl], *a.* practicable for vehicles (*of roads*).

carrosse [ka'rɔs], *n.m.* state-coach, four-wheeled carriage.

carrosserie [karɔ'sri], *n.f.* coach-building; body (*of motors*).

carrossier [karɔ'sje], *n.m.* coach-maker carriage-builder.

carrousel [karu'zɛl], *n.m.* merry-go-round, roundabout; tournament.

carrure [ka'ryːr], *n.f.* breadth of shoulders.

cartable [kar'tabl], *n.m.* school-satchel.

carte [kart], *n.f.* pasteboard; card, playing-card, postcard; ticket; bill of fare; map, chart; *avoir carte blanche*, to have full power; *carte d'abonnement*, season ticket; *carte d'alimentation*, ration card, ration book; *un jeu de cartes*, a pack of cards.

cartel [kar'tɛl], *n.m.* challenge; cartel; dial-case; wall clock; frieze-panel.

carte-lettre [karts'letr], *n.f.* (*pl.* **cartes-lettres**) letter-card.

carter [kar'tɛr], *n.m.* gear-case (*of bicycle*); crank-case (*of car*).

cartésianisme [kartezja'nism], *n.m.* Cartesian philosophy.

cartésien [karte'zjɛ̃], *a.* and *n.m.* (*fem.* **-ienne**) Cartesian.

cartilage [karti'laːʒ], *n.m.* cartilage, gristle.

cartilagineux [kartilaʒi'nø], *a.* (*fem.* **-euse**) cartilaginous, gristly.

cartographe [kartɔ'graf], *n.m.* cartographer.

cartographie [kartɔgra'fi], *n.f.* cartography.

carton [kar'tɔ̃], *n.m.* cardboard, pasteboard; cardboard box, hat-box; (*Paint.*) cartoon; (*Phot.*) mount.

cartonnage [kartɔ'naːʒ], *n.m.* (*Bookb.*) board-ing.

cartonneur [kartɔ'nœːr], *n.m.* (*fem.* **-euse**) binder (*of books*).

carton-pâte [kartɔ̃'pɑːt], *n.m.* millboard; papier mâché.

carton-pierre [kartɔ̃'pjɛːr], *n.m.* pasteboard for making ornaments.

cartothèque [kartɔ'tɛk], *n.f.* card-index.

cartouche (1) [kar'tuʃ], *n.m.* escutcheon, scroll.

cartouche (2) [kar'tuʃ], *n.f.* cartridge.

cartouchier [kartu'ʃje], *n.m.*, **cartouchière** [kartu'ʃjɛːr], *n.f.* cartridge-pouch or box.

cas [kɑ], *n.m.* case; instance, circumstance, state of things, conjuncture; (*Law*) cause; *c'est le cas ou jamais*, it is now or never; *en tout cas*, at all events.

casanier [kaza'nje], *a.* (*fem.* **-ière**) domestic, stay-at-home, home-loving.

cascade [kas'kad], *n.f.* cascade, waterfall.

case [kɑːz], *n.f.* cabin, hut, small house; division, compartment; box (*for animals*); pigeon-hole; square (*of chess* or *draught-board*); (*Naut.*) berth.

casemate [kaz'mat], *n.f.* (*Fort.*) casemate.

caser [kɑ'ze], *v.t.* to put in order, to file (*documents*), (*fam.*) to provide for; to marry off.—*v.i.* (*backgammon*) to make a point. **se caser**, *v.r.* to take up one's abode, to settle.

caserne [ka'zɛrn], *n.f.* barracks.

caserner [kazɛr'ne], *v.t.* to quarter in barracks.—*v.i.* to be in barracks.

casier [kɑ'zje], *n.m.* rack, card- *or* music-stand, set of pigeon-holes; *casier judiciaire*, police record.

casilleux [kazi'jø], *a.* (*fem.* **-euse**) brittle.

casino [kazi'no], *n.m.* casino, club.

casque [kask], *n.m.* helmet, head-piece; (*Nat. Hist.*) crest; head-phone (*wireless*).

casquette [kasˈkɛt], *n.f.* cap.
cassable [kɑˈsabl], *a.* breakable.
cassage [kɑˈsaːʒ], *n.m.* breakage.
cassant [kɑˈsã], *a.* brittle; crisp; breakable; (*fig.*) abrupt, gruff.
cassation [kɑsɑˈsjõ], *n.f.* (*Law*) cassation, annulment, repeal; *cour de cassation*, the highest court of appeal in France.
casse (1) [kɑːs], *n.f.* breakage(s); damage, losses.
casse (2) [kɑːs], *n.f.* (*Print.*) case; *bas de casse*, lower case.
casse-cou [kɑsˈku], *n.m. inv.* death-trap; rough-rider; dare-devil.
casse-croûte [kɑsˈkrut], *n.m. inv.* quick meal, snack.
casse-noisette [kɑsnwaˈzɛt], *n.m.* (*pl.* **casse-noisettes**) nutcracker; (*Orn.*) nuthatch.
casse-noix [kɑsˈnwɑ], *n.m. inv.* nutcrackers.
casse-pipes [kɑsˈpip], *n.m. inv.* shooting-gallery; (*pop.*) war.
casser [kɑˈse], *v.t.* to break, to smash; to cashier (*an officer*), to reduce to the ranks; to dissolve (*Parliament etc.*); to annul, to rescind. **se casser**, *v.r.* to break, to snap; to break down.
casserole [kɑsˈrɔl], *n.f.* saucepan, stewpan.
casse-tête [kɑsˈtɛːt], *n.m. inv.* life-preserver; (*fig.*) din; conundrum.
cassette [kɑˈsɛt], *n.f.* casket; cash-box.
casseur [kɑˈsœːr], *n.m.* (*fem.* **-euse**) breaker, smasher.
cassis [kɑˈsis], *n.m.* black currant.
casson [kɑˈsõ], *n.m.* piece of broken glass *or* pottery; rough lump (*of sugar*).
cassonade [kɑsoˈnad], *n.f.* moist brown sugar.
cassoulet [kɑsuˈlɛ], *n.m.* stew of beans with mutton and pork.
cassure [kɑˈsyːr], *n.f.* break, crack, fracture; broken piece.
castagnette [kɑstaˈnɛt], *n.f.* castanet.
caste [kast], *n.f.* caste.
castillan [kastiˈjã], *a.* Castilian.—*n.m.* Castilian (*speech*); (**Castillan**, *fem.* **-ane**) Castilian (*person*).
castine [kasˈtin], *n.f.* (*Metal.*) flux.
castor [kasˈtɔːr], *n.m.* beaver.
casuel [kɑˈzɥɛl], *a.* (*fem.* **-uelle**) casual, fortuitous, accidental.—*n.m.* perquisites, fees.
casuiste [kɑˈzɥist], *n.m.* casuist.
cataclysme [kataˈklism], *n.m.* cataclysm; (*fig.*) disaster.
catacombes [kataˈkõːb], *n.f. pl.* catacombs.
catafalque [kataˈfalk], *n.m.* catafalque.
cataire [kaˈtɛːr], *n.f.* (*Bot.*) catmint.
catalan [kataˈlã], *a.* Catalan.—*n.m.* Catalan (*language*); (**Catalan**, *fem.* **-ane**) Catalan (*person*).
catalepsie [katalɛpˈsi], *n.f.* catalepsy.
catalogue [kataˈlɔg], *n.m.* list, catalogue.
cataloguer [kataloˈge], *v.t.* to catalogue.
catalyse [kataˈliːz], *n.f.* (*Chem.*) catalysis.
catalyseur [kataliˈzœːr], *n.m.* catalyst.
catalytique [kataliˈtik], *a.* catalytic.
cataphote [kataˈfɔt], *n.m.* cat's eye (*reflector*).
cataplasme [kataˈplasm], *n.m.* cataplasm, poultice.
cataracte [kataˈrakt], *n.f.* cataract, waterfall; (*Path.*) cataract.
catarrhal [kataˈral], *a.* (*m.pl.* **-aux**) catarrhal.
catarrhe [kaˈtaːr], *n.m.* catarrh.

catastrophe [katasˈtrɔf], *n.f.* catastrophe, calamity.
catastrophique [katastrɔˈfik], *a.* catastrophic.
catéchiser [kateʃiˈze], *v.t.* to catechize; (*fig.*) to reason with; to lecture.
catéchisme [kateˈʃism], *n.m.* catechism.
catégorie [kategoˈri], *n.f.* category.
catégorique [kategoˈrik], *a.* categorical, explicit.
catégoriquement [kategorikˈmã], *adv.* categorically.
catharsis [katarˈsis], *n.f.* (*Med.*) catharsis.
cathédral [kateˈdral], *a.* (*m.pl.* **-aux**) cathedral.
cathédrale [kateˈdral], *n.f.* cathedral.
cathode [kaˈtɔd], *n.f.* cathode.
cathodique [katoˈdik], *a.* cathode.
catholicisme [katoliˈsism], *n.m.* Catholicism.
catholique [katoˈlik], *a.* catholic; moral, orthodox.—*n.* Catholic (*person*).
cati [kaˈti], *n.m.* gloss, lustre.
catir [kaˈtiːr], *v.t.* to give a gloss to.
catissage [katiˈsaːʒ], *n.m.* glossing, pressing.
catisseur [katiˈsœːr], *a.* and *n.m.* (*fem.* **-euse**) presser.
Caucase [koˈkɑːz], **le**, *m.* the Caucasus.
caucasien [kokaˈzjɛ̃], *a.* (*fem.* **-enne**) Caucasian.—*n.m.* (**Caucasien**, *fem.* **-enne**) Caucasian (*person*).
cauchemar [koʃˈmaːr], *n.m.* nightmare.
caudataire [kodaˈtɛːr], *n.m.* train-bearer.
cauri, cauris *or* **coris** [koˈri], *n.m.* cowrie.
causal [koˈzal], *a.* causal.
causant [koˈzã], *a.* chatty, talkative.
causatif [kozaˈtif], *a.* (*fem.* **-tive**) (*Gram.*) causative, causal.
cause [koːz], *n.f.* cause; grounds, motive; interest; case, trial, suit, action; *à cause de*, because of; *mettre en cause*, to sue.
causer (1) [koˈze], *v.t.* to cause, to be the cause of.
causer (2) [koˈze], *v.i.* to chat, to talk; to prate.
causerie [koˈzri], *n.f.* talk, chat, gossip; chatty essay, review etc.
causette [koˈzɛt], *n.f.* chit-chat, small talk.
causeur [koˈzœːr], *a.* (*fem.* **-euse**) talkative, chatty.—*n.m.* (*fem.* **-euse**) talker.—*n.f.* (**-euse**) small sofa, settee for two.
causticité [kostisiˈte], *n.f.* causticity.
caustique [kosˈtik], *a.* caustic, biting, cutting.—*n.m.* caustic.
caustiquement [kostikˈmã], *adv.* caustically.
cauteleusement [kotløzˈmã], *adv.* craftily, slyly.
cauteleux [kotˈlø], *a.* (*fem.* **-euse**) cunning, crafty.
cautère [koˈtɛːr], *n.m.* (*Med.*) cautery; issue.
cautérisation [koterizaˈsjõ], *n.f.* cauterization.
cautériser [koteriˈze], *v.t.* to cauterize.
caution [koˈsjõ], *n.f.* security, bail, surety; (*fig.*) pledge, guarantee; *verser une caution*, to pay a deposit.
cautionnement [kosjonˈmã], *n.m.* bail; security.
cautionner [kosjoˈne], *v.t.* to stand bail for someone.
cavage [kaˈvaːʒ], *n.m.* cellarage.
cavalcade [kavalˈkad], *n.f.* procession; cavalcade.
cavale [kaˈval], *n.f.* mare.
cavalerie [kavalˈri], *n.f.* cavalry.

cavalier [kava'lje], *n.m.* horseman, rider, trooper; (*Dancing*) partner; (*C*) lover, sweetheart; (*Chess*) knight.—*a.* (*fem.* **-ière**) cavalier, unceremonious (*of manners etc.*); off-hand, flippant.

cavalièrement [kavaljɛr'mã], *adv.* cavalierly, bluntly.

cave (1) [ka:v], *a.* hollow.

cave (2) [ka:v], *n.f.* (*wine*) cellar, vault; cellarage.

caveau [ka'vo], *n.m.* (*pl.* **-eaux**) small cellar; burial vault.

caver [ka've], *v.t.* to hollow, to scoop out, to dig under; (*fig.*) to undermine; (*Fenc.*) to lunge. **se caver**, *v.r.* to become hollow *or* sunken.

caverne [ka'vɛrn], *n.f.* cavern, cave, hollow; (*fig.*) retreat, lair.

caverneux [kavɛr'nø], *a.* (*fem.* **-euse**) cavernous, hollow.

caviar [ka'vja:r], *n.m.* caviare.

cavillation [kavila'sjõ], *n.f.* sophistry, cavil.

cavité [kavi'te], *n.f.* cavity, hollow.

ce (1) [sə], *dem. a.* (*before vowels* **cet**, *fem.* **cette**, *pl.* **ces**) this, that, (*pl.*) these, those.

ce (2) [sə], *dem. pron. inv.* it, that (*sometimes* = he, she, *or*, *with plural verb*, they); **c'en est fait**, it is all over, it is done; **c'est-à-dire**, that is to say; **c'est que**, the fact is that; **pour ce qui est de . . .**, as for . . . .

*céans [se'ã], *adv.* within, here within, in this house, at home.

ceci [sə'si], *dem. pron.* this, this thing.

cécité [sesi'te], *n.f.* blindness.

cédant [se'dã], *a.* that grants; (*Law*) that assigns, transfers.—*n.m.* (*fem.* **-e**) (*Law*) grantor, assignor, transferrer.

céder [se'de], *v.t.* (*see Verb Tables*) to give up, to yield, to surrender, to cede; to transfer, to make over.—*v.i.* to give way; to submit.

cédille [se'di:j], *n.f.* cedilla.

cédrat [se'dra], *n.m.* citron-tree; citron.

cèdre [sɛ:dr], *n.m.* cedar.

cédule [se'dyl], *n.f.* schedule, memorandum; notice; (*Law*) notification.

cégétiste [seʒe'tist], *n.m.* a member of the C.G.T. (Confédération Générale du Travail.)

ceindre [sɛ:dr], *v.t. irr.* (*conjug. like* CRAINDRE) to gird, to encircle, to encompass, to surround; to bind *or* gird on. **se ceindre**, *v.r.* to bind round one, to put on (*a scarf etc.*).

ceinture [sɛ'ty:r], *n.f.* sash, girdle, belt, waist-band; waist; enclosure, circle; **ceinture de sauvetage**, life-belt.

ceinturer [sɛty're], *v.t.* to girdle, to surround.

ceinturon [sɛty'rõ], *n.m.* belt, sword-belt.

cela [sə'la, sla], *dem. pron.* that, that thing (*in opposition to this, of which we are speaking*); **c'est cela**, that's it. *In popular speech* **cela** becomes **ça; pas de ça**, none of that; **comme ci comme ça**, middling.

céladon [sela'dõ], *a.* and *n.m.* sea-green (*colour*).

célébrant [sele'brã], *n.m.* celebrant.

célébration [selebra'sjõ], *n.f.* solemn performance, celebration.

célèbre [se'lɛbr], *a.* celebrated, famous, renowned.

célébrer [sele'bre], *v.t.* (*conjug. like* CÉDER) to celebrate, to praise, to extol; to solemnize.

célébrité [selebri'te], *n.f.* celebrity.

*celer [sə'le], *v.t.* (*conjug. like* AMENER) to conceal, to keep secret. ***se celer**, *v.r.* to conceal oneself, to hide.

céleri [sel'ri], *n.m.* celery; **un pied de céleri**, a stick of celery.

célerin [sel'rɛ̃], *n.m.* (*Ichth.*) pilchard.

célérité [seleri'te], *n.f.* celerity, rapidity.

céleste [se'lɛst], *a.* celestial, heavenly, divine.

célibat [seli'ba], *n.m.* celibacy, single life.

célibataire [seliba'tɛ:r], *a.* single.—*n.m.* bachelor.—*n.f.* spinster.

celle [sɛl], [CELUI].

cellérier [sɛle'rje], *n.m.* (*fem.* **-ière**) cellarer.

cellier [sɛ'lje], *n.m.* cellar, store-room.

cellophane [sɛlo'fan], *n.f.* cellophane.

cellulaire [sɛly'lɛ:r], *a.* cellular.

cellule [se'lyl], *n.f.* cell; **cellule photo-électrique**, electric eye.

celluleux [sɛly'lø], *a.* (*fem.* **-euse**) cellular.

celluloïd [sɛlylo'id] *or* **celluloïde** [sɛlylo'id], *n.m.* celluloid.

cellulose [sɛly'lo:z], *n.f.* cellulose.

Celte [sɛlt], *n.* Celt.

celtique [sɛl'tik], *a.* Celtic.—*n.m.* Celtic (*language*).

celui [sə'lɥi], *dem. pron. m.* (*fem.* **celle**, *pl.* **ceux**, **celles**) the one, that, those (*sometimes* = he *or* she). Followed by **-ci** *or* **-là** = this one, that one etc. *or* the latter *and* the former.

cément [se'mã], *n.m.* (*Metal.*) cement.

cémentation [semãta'sjõ], *n.f.* (*Metal.*) cementation.

cémenter [semã'te], *v.t.* (*Metal.*) to cement.

cénacle [se'nakl], *n.m.* (*Ant.*) guest-chamber; (*fig.*) literary society *or* coterie.

cendre [sã:dr], *n.f.* ashes, embers, cinders; dust, ashes (*of the dead*).

cendré [sã'dre], *a.* ashy, ashen.

cendrée [sã'dre], *n.f.* small shot; cinders (*for track*); **piste en cendrée**, dirt track, cinder track.

cendrer [sã'dre], *v.t.* to paint ash-grey; to mix *or* cover with ashes.

cendreux [sã'drø], *a.* (*fem.* **-euse**) ashy.

cendrier [sãdri'e], *n.m.* ash-pan, ash-pit; ash-tray.

cendrière [sãdri'ɛ:r], *n.f.* peat.

Cendrillon [sãdri'jõ], *n.f.* Cinderella, drudge.

Cène [sɛ:n], *n.f.* The Lord's Supper, Holy Communion.

cenelle [sə'nɛl], *n.f.* haw.

cénobite [seno'bit], *n.m.* coenobite.

cénotaphe [seno'taf], *n.m.* cenotaph.

cens [sã:s], *n.m.* census; rating.

censé [sã'se], *a.* accounted, reputed, supposed.

censeur [sã'sœ:r], *n.m.* censor; critic; proctor (*of Engl. Univ.*); assistant headmaster (*in French Lycée*).

censure [sã'sy:r], *n.f.* censorship; criticism, censure; audit (*of accounts*).

censurer [sãsy're], *v.t.* to find fault with, to criticize; to censure.

cent [sã], *a.* one hundred; **faire les cent pas**, to walk up and down.—*n.m.* a hundred; **cinq pour cent**, five per cent.

centaine [sã'tɛn], *n.f.* a hundred; a hundred or so.

centaure [sã'to:r], *n.m.* centaur.

centenaire [sãt'nɛ:r], *a.* a hundred years old. —*n.* centenarian.—*n.m.* centenary.

centième [sã'tjɛm], *a.* hundredth.—*n.m.* hundredth part.

centigrade [sãti'grad], *a.* centigrade.

centigramme [sãti'gram], *n.m.* centigram, the hundredth part of a gram (·1543 grain).

centilitre [sãti'litr], *n.m.* centilitre, hundredth part of a litre (·61028 cubic in.).

centime [sã'tim], *n.m.* centime, hundredth part of a franc.

centimètre [sãti'mɛtr], *n.m.* centimetre, hundredth part of a metre (·39371 in.).

centipède [sãti'pɛd], *n.m.* centipede.

central [sã'tral], *a.* (*m. pl.* **-aux**) central; chief, principal, head.—*n.m. central téléphonique*, telephone exchange.—*n.f. centrale électrique*, electric power station.

centralement [sãtral'mã], *adv.* centrally.

centralisateur [sãtraliza'tœːr], *a.* (*fem.* **-trice**) centralizing.

centralisation [sãtraliza'sjõ], *n.f.* centralization.

centraliser [sãtrali'ze], *v.t.* to centralize.

centre [sã:tr], *n.m.* centre, middle.

centrer [sã'tre], *v.t.* to centre.

centrifuge [sãtri'fyːʒ], *a.* centrifugal.

centripète [sãtri'pɛt], *a.* centripetal.

centuple [sã'typl], *a.* and *n.m.* centuple, hundredfold.

centupler [sãty'ple], *v.t.* to multiply a hundredfold.

centurion [sãty'rjõ], *n.m.* centurion.

cep [sɛp], *n.m.* vine-stock.

cépage [se'paːʒ], *n.m.* vine-plant.

cépée [se'pe], *n.f.* (*Agric.*) tuft of shoots from a pollarded stump; copse of one or two years' growth.

cependant [spã'dã], *adv.* in the meantime, meanwhile.—*conj.* yet, still, however, nevertheless.

céramique [sera'mik], *a.* ceramic.—*n.f.* ceramics.

Cerbère [sɛr'bɛːr], *m.* (*Myth.*) Cerberus.

cerceau [sɛr'so], *n.m.* (*pl.* **-eaux**) hoop, ring; hoop-net.

cerclage [sɛr'klaːʒ], *n.m.* hooping (*of casks*).

cercle [sɛrkl], *n.m.* circle, ring; circumference; club, club-house.

cercler [sɛr'kle], *v.t.* to bind with hoops, to hoop.

cercueil [sɛr'kœːj], *n.m.* coffin; (*fig.*) the tomb.

céréale [sere'al], *n.f.* cereal, corn, grain.

cérébral [sere'bral], *a.* (*m.pl.* **-aux**) cerebral.

cérémonial [seremo'njal], *a.* (*m.pl.* **-aux**) ceremonial.—*n.m.* (*no pl.*) ceremonial, pomp.

cérémonie [seremo'ni], *n.f.* ceremony; pomp; fuss, ado.

cérémonieux [seremo'njø], *a.* (*fem.* **-euse**) ceremonious, formal.

cerf [sɛːr], *n.m.* stag, hart, deer.

cerfeuil [sɛr'fœːj], *n.m.* chervil.

cerf-volant [sɛrvo'lã], *n.m.* (*pl.* **cerfs-volants**) stag-beetle; kite, paper-kite.

cerisaie [sri'zɛ], *n.f.* cherry-orchard.

cerise [sə'riːz], *n.f.* cherry.—*n.m.* cherry-colour, cerise.—*a.* cherry-coloured, cerise.

cerisier [sri'zje], *n.m.* cherry-tree, cherry-wood.

cerner [sɛr'ne], *v.t.* to cut or dig round (*a tree*), to ring (*a tree*); to surround, to encompass, to hem in.

certain [sɛr'tɛ̃], *a.* certain, sure, positive; fixed, determined; *d'un certain âge*, not so young.—*n.m.* certainty; a sure thing.

certainement [sɛrtɛn'mã], *adv.* certainly.

certes [sɛrt], *adv.* indeed, most certainly.

certificat [sɛrtifi'ka], *n.m.* certificate; testimonial; diploma.

certification [sɛrtifika'sjõ], *n.f.* certification.

certifier [sɛrti'fje], *v.t.* to certify, to testify, to vouch for.

certitude [sɛrti'tyd], *n.f.* certitude, certainty.

cerveau [sɛr'vo], *n.m.* (*pl.* **-eaux**) brain; mind, intellect, intelligence.

cervelas [sɛrvə'la], *n.m.* saveloy.

cervelle [sɛr'vel], *n.f.* brains; mind, intelligence.

cervin [sɛr'vɛ̃], *a.* cervine; *le (Mont) Cervin*, the Matterhorn.

César [se'za:r], *m.* Caesar.—*n.m.* Caesar, emperor.

césarien [seza'rjɛ̃], *a.* (*fem.* **-ienne**) Caesarean.—*n.f.* (**-ienne**) Caesarean operation.

cessant [se'sã], *a.* ceasing, suspended.

cessation [sɛsa'sjõ], *n.f.* cessation, suspension, stoppage.

cesse [sɛs], *n.f.* ceasing, intermission, respite.

cesser [se'se], *v.t.* to leave off, to break off, to stop.—*v.i.* to cease, to leave off, to stop.

cession [se'sjõ], *n.f.* transfer, assignment (*of property*).

cessionnaire [sɛsjo'nɛːr], *n.m.* grantee, assignee.

césure [se'zyːr], *n.f.* caesura.

cet, cette [sɛt], [CE].

cétacé [seta'se], *a.* cetaceous.—*n.m.* cetacean.

ceux [sø:], [CELUI].

Ceylan [se'lã], *le, m.* Ceylon.

chablis (1) [ʃa'bli], *n.m.* dead-wood.

chablis (2) [ʃa'bli], *n.m.* Chablis (*white wine*).

chacal [ʃa'kal], *n.m.* jackal.

chacun [ʃa'kœ̃], *pron. indef. sing.* each, each one, every one.

chafouin [ʃa'fwɛ̃], *a.* weasel-faced, mean-looking.

chagrin (1), [ʃa'grɛ̃], *n.m.* grief, chagrin; sorrow.—*a.* gloomy, melancholy, sad.

chagrin (2) [ʃa'grɛ̃], *n.m.* shagreen.

chagrinant [ʃagri'nã], *a.* distressing, sad.

chagriner [ʃagri'ne], *v.t.* to grieve, to afflict; to cross, to vex. **se chagriner**, *v.r.* to fret, to grieve.

chahut [ʃa'y], *n.m.* row, shindy.

chahuter [ʃay'te], *v.i.* to make a row, to kick up a shindy.

chaîne [ʃɛn], *n.f.* chain; shackle, fetters; bonds, bondage; (*Naut.*) cable; (*fig.*) series, range; (*Ind.*) *chaîne de montage*, assembly-line.

chaîner [ʃɛ'ne], *v.t.* (*Surveying*) to measure (*land*) with the chain.

chaînette [ʃɛ'nɛt], *n.f.* little chain; (*Arch.*) catenary arch.

chaînon [ʃɛ'nõ], *n.m.* link.

chaintre [ʃɛ̃tr], *n.m.* (*Agric.*) balk, headland.

chair [ʃɛːr], *n.f.* flesh; meat; (*fig.*) the human body, the flesh; (*Paint.*, *pl.*) naked flesh.

chaire [ʃɛːr], *n.f.* pulpit; professorship; bishop's throne.

chaise [ʃɛːz], *n.f.* chair, seat; post-chaise.

chaland (1) [ʃa'lã], *n.m.* lighter, barge.

chaland (2) [ʃa'lã], *n.m.* (*fem.* **-e**) customer, client.

chalandeau [ʃalɑ̃'do], *n.m.* (*pl.* **-eaux**) lighterman, bargee.

chalcographe [kalko'graf], *n.m.* chalcographer, engraver on metal.

chalcographie [kalkɔgra'fi], *n.f.* chalcography; engraving establishment.

chaldaïque [kalda'ik], *a.* Chaldaic.

Chaldée [kal'de], *f.* Chaldea.

chaldéen [kalde'ɛ̃], *a.* (*fem.* **-éenne**) Chaldean. —*n.m.* (**Chaldéen**, *fem.* **-éenne**) Chaldean (*person*).

châle [ʃɑːl], *n.m.* shawl.

chalet [ʃa'lɛ], *n.m.* chalet, Swiss cottage.

chaleur [ʃa'lœːr], *n.f.* heat; warmth, warm weather; (*fig.*) glow; zeal, ardour; *'craint la chaleur'*, 'store in a cool place'.

chaleureusement [ʃalœrøz'mɑ̃], *adv.* cordially, warmly.

chaleureux [ʃalœ'rø], *a.* (*fem.* **-euse**) warm, cordial.

chalicose [ʃali'koːz], *n.f.* silicosis.

châlit [ʃɑ'li], *n.m.* bedstead.

chaloupe [ʃa'lup], *n.f.* ship's boat, launch.

chalumeau [ʃaly'mo], *n.m.* (*pl.* **-eaux**) stalk of corn, drinking-straw; flute, pipe.

chalut [ʃa'ly], *n.m.* drag-net, trawl.

chalutier [ʃaly'tje], *n.m.* trawler.

chamaillard [ʃama'jaːr], *a.* squabbling, quarrelsome.

chamailler [ʃama'je], *v.i.* to bicker, to squabble. **se chamailler**, *v.r.* to squabble, to wrangle.

chamaillis [ʃama'ji], *n.m.* fray; squabble; uproar.

chamarrer [ʃama're], *v.t.* to bedizen, to bedeck.

chambellan [ʃɑ̃bɛ'lɑ̃], *n.m.* chamberlain.

chambranle [ʃɑ̃'brɑ̃ːl], *n.m.* door-frame, window-frame.

chambre [ʃɑ̃ːbr], *n.f.* chamber, room; apartment; House (*of Parliament*); court (*of justice*); **chambre à air**, inner tube (*bicycle etc.*); **chambre à un (deux) lit(s)**, single (double) room; **chambre d'ami**, spare bedroom; **chambre d'écluse**, lock; **chambre noire**, camera obscura.

chambrée [ʃɑ̃'bre], *n.f.* barrack-room; roomful; (*Theat. etc.*) house.

chambrer [ʃɑ̃'bre], *v.t.* to keep (*someone*) confined; to bring wine to room temperature.—*v.i.* to lodge (*together*). **se chambrer**, *v.r.* to become pitted.

chambrette [ʃɑ̃'brɛt], *n.f.* little room.

chameau [ʃa'mo], *n.m.* (*pl.* **-eaux**) camel; (*pop.*) nasty, evil-minded person.

chamelier [ʃamə'lje], *n.m.* camel-driver.

chamelle [ʃa'mɛl], *n.f.* female camel.

chamelon [ʃamə'lɔ̃], *n.m.* young camel.

chamois [ʃa'mwa], *n.m.* chamois; chamois leather.—*a.* chamois-coloured, buff.

chamoiseur [ʃamwa'zœːr], *n.m.* chamois- or leather-dresser.

champ [ʃɑ̃], *n.m.* field, piece of ground; scope, range; (*poet.*) land; (*fig.*) space; *sur-le-champ*, at once, immediately.

champagne [ʃɑ̃'paɲ], *n.m.* champagne; *champagne frappé*, iced champagne; *champagne mousseux*, sparkling champagne; *fine champagne*, liqueur brandy.

champenois [ʃɑ̃pə'nwa], *a.* of Champagne. —*n.m.* (**Champenois**, *fem.* **-oise**) inhabitant of Champagne.

champêtre [ʃɑ̃'pɛːtr], *a.* rural, rustic; *garde champêtre*, village policeman.

champignon [ʃɑ̃pi'ɲɔ̃], *n.m.* mushroom, fungus.

champion [ʃɑ̃'pjɔ̃] *n.m.* (*fem.* **-onne**) champion.

championnat [ʃɑ̃pjo'na], *n.m.* championship.

chançard [ʃɑ̃'saːr], *a.* and *n.m.* (*fem.* **-e**) (*fam.*) lucky (person).

chance [ʃɑ̃ːs], *n.f.* chance; luck, good luck, good fortune; (*pl.*) chances, (*fam.*) odds.

chancelant [ʃɑ̃s'lɑ̃], *a.* staggering, tottering.

chanceler [ʃɑ̃s'le], *v.i.* (*conjug. like* APPELER) to stagger, to totter; to reel.

chancelier [ʃɑ̃sə'lje], *n.m.* chancellor.

chancellement [ʃɑ̃sɛl'mɑ̃], *n.m.* tottering, staggering.

chancellerie [ʃɑ̃sɛl'ri], *n.f.* chancellery.

chanceux [ʃɑ̃'sø], *a.* (*fem.* **-euse**) lucky, fortunate; risky, doubtful (*of things*).

chanci [ʃɑ̃'si], *a.* mouldy.

chancir [ʃɑ̃'siːr], *v.i.* to grow musty *or* mouldy.

chancissure [ʃɑ̃si'syːr], *n.f.* mustiness, mouldiness.

chancre [ʃɑ̃ːkr], *n.m.* ulcer, tumour; canker.

chancreux [ʃɑ̃'krø], *a.* (*fem.* **-euse**) ulcerous; cankered.

chandail [ʃɑ̃'daːj], *n.m.* jersey, sweater.

Chandeleur [ʃɑ̃'dlœːr], *n.f.* Candlemas.

chandelier [ʃɑ̃də'lje], *n.m.* candlestick.

chandelle [ʃɑ̃'dɛl], *n.f.* (*tallow*) candle; (*fig.*) light; (*Tennis*) lob.

change [ʃɑ̃ːʒ], *n.m.* exchange; exchange of money; exchange office; agio; (*Hunt.*) wrong scent; *agent de change*, stockbroker; *cours du change*, rate of exchange.

changeant [ʃɑ̃'ʒɑ̃], *a.* changeable, fickle; unstable; unsettled (*of the weather*).

changement [ʃɑ̃ʒ'mɑ̃], *n.m.* change, alteration; (*Law*) amendment.

changer [ʃɑ̃'ʒe], *v.t.*, *v.i.* (*conjug. like* MANGER) to change, to exchange; to alter.

changeur [ʃɑ̃'ʒœːr], *n.m.* (*fem.* **-euse**) money-changer.

chanoine [ʃa'nwan], *n.m.* canon.

chanson [ʃɑ̃'sɔ̃], *n.f.* song, ballad; (*fig.*) idle story, stuff, trash; *chansons que tout cela!* humbug!

chansonner [ʃɑ̃so'ne], *v.t.* to lampoon.

chansonnette [ʃɑ̃so'nɛt], *n.f.* little song, ditty.

chansonneur [ʃɑ̃so'nœːr], *n.m.* lampooner.

chansonnier [ʃɑ̃so'nje], *n.m.* (*fem.* **-ière**) song-writer, ballad-writer; singer of satirical songs.

chant [ʃɑ̃], *n.m.* singing; song; air, tune; poem; canto; chant, hymn.

chantable [ʃɑ̃'tabl], *a.* fit to be sung, worth singing.

chantage [ʃɑ̃'taːʒ], *n.m.* extortion of hush-money, blackmail.

chantant [ʃɑ̃'tɑ̃], *a.* easily sung; tuneful, harmonious.

chanteau [ʃɑ̃'to], *n.m.* (*pl.* **-eaux**) hunk (*of bread*), bit (*of material etc.*), remnant; (*Dress.*) gore.

chantepleure [ʃɑ̃t'plœːr], *n.f.* funnel with a rose.

chanter [ʃɑ̃'te], v.t. to extol, to praise, to celebrate; to sing.—v.i. to sing; to chirp, to warble, to crow; *cela vous chante-t-il?* how do you like the idea? se chanter, v.r. to be sung.

chanterelle [ʃɑ̃'trɛl], n.f. first string of a violin etc.; decoy-bird.

chanteur [ʃɑ̃'tœ:r], a. (fem. -euse) singing.— n.m. (fem. -euse) singer, vocalist.

chantier [ʃɑ̃'tje], n.m. timber-yard, wood-yard; stone-yard; dock-yard; site; (C) shanty, lumber camp.

chantonner [ʃɑ̃tɔ'ne], v.t., v.i. to hum.

chantourner [ʃɑ̃tur'ne], v.t. to cut in profile; *scie à chantourner*, bow saw.

chantre [ʃɑ̃:tr], n.m. singer, esp. a chorister; precentor, lay-clerk; (fig.) songster (of birds).

chanvre [ʃɑ̃:vr], n.m. hemp.

chanvreux [ʃɑ̃'vrø], a. (fem. -euse) hempen.

chaos [ka'o], n.m. chaos; (fig.) confusion, disorder.

chaotique [kaɔ'tik], a. chaotic.

chaparder [ʃapar'de], v.t. (slang) to steal, to scrounge.

chape [ʃap], n.f. cope (ecclesiastical vestment); tread (of a tyre).

chapeau [ʃa'po], n.m. (pl. -eaux) hat; (Mech. etc.) cap; *un coup de chapeau*, a bow.

chapelain [ʃa'plɛ̃], n.m. chaplain.

chapelet [ʃa'plɛ], n.m. rosary, beads; (Arch. etc.) chaplet; *chapelet de bombes*, stick of bombs; *chapelet d'oignons*, string of onions.

chapelier [ʃapə'lje], n.m. (fem. -ière) hatter.

chapelle [ʃa'pɛl], n.f. chapel; coterie, school (of literature etc.); church plate; living.

chapellenie [ʃapɛl'ni], n.f. chaplaincy.

chapellerie [ʃapɛl'ri], n.f. hat-making; hat trade, shop or business.

chapelure [ʃa'ply:r], n.f. grated bread-crumbs.

chaperon [ʃa'prɔ̃], n.m. hood; (fig.) chaperon; *Le Petit Chaperon Rouge*, Little Red Riding Hood.

chaperonner [ʃaprɔ'ne], v.t. to cope (a wall); (fig.) to chaperon.

chapiteau [ʃapi'to], n.m. (pl. -eaux) capital (of column etc.); cornice (of a wardrobe etc.); big top (circus).

chapitre [ʃa'pitr], n.m. chapter (of a book, of knights, of a cathedral); subject-matter of discourse.

chapitrer [ʃapi'tre], v.t. to reprimand, to rebuke.

chapon [ʃa'pɔ̃], n.m. capon; sop in broth.

chaponner [ʃapɔ'ne], v.t. to caponize.

chaque [ʃak], a. each, every.

char [ʃa:r], n.m. chariot, carriage, vehicle; *char d'assaut*, (Mil.) tank.

charabia [ʃara'bja], n.m. gibberish.

charade [ʃa'rad], n.f. charade.

charançon [ʃarɑ̃'sɔ̃], n.m. weevil.

charbon [ʃar'bɔ̃], n.m. coal, charcoal; (pl.) embers; (Path.) anthrax; (Chem.) carbon.

charbonnée [ʃarbɔ'ne], n.f. piece of grilled meat; charcoal-drawing.

charbonner [ʃarbɔ'ne], v.t. to char; to black with coal. se charbonner, v.r. to be charred, to burn black.

charbonnerie [ʃarbɔn'ri], n.f. coal depot.

charbonneux [ʃarbɔ'nø], a. (fem. -euse) coaly; affected or infected with anthrax.

charbonnier [ʃarbɔ'nje], n.m. (fem. -ière) charcoal-burner; coal-man.—n.m. coal-heaver; coal-hole; (Naut.) collier.—n.f. (-ière) charcoal-kiln; coal-scuttle; (Orn.) great tit.

charcuter [ʃarky'te], v.t. to hack and hew (meat); to hack, to butcher (of a surgeon).

charcuterie [ʃarky'tri], n.f. pork-butcher's meat; pork-butcher's business or shop.

charcutier [ʃarky'tje], n.m. (fem. -ière) pork-butcher; (colloq.) sawbones.

chardon [ʃar'dɔ̃], n.m. thistle; spikes (on a wall or railing).

chardonneret [ʃardɔn're], n.m. goldfinch.

charge [ʃarʒ], n.f. pack; load; expense, cost; accusation; post, employment; care, custody; charge, onset; *à charge de revanche*, provided that I may return the favour.

chargé [ʃar'ʒe], a. loaded, burdened.

chargement [ʃarʒə'mɑ̃], n.m. cargo, freight; bill of lading; load; charging (of a battery).

charger [ʃar'ʒe], v.t. (conjug. like MANGER) to load, to charge; to burden; to charge with; to register (a letter). se charger, v.r. to take upon oneself, to saddle oneself with (de).

chargeur [ʃar'ʒœ:r], n.m. loader, shipper; stoker; (Phot., Cine.) cassette.

chariot [ʃa'rjo], n.m. waggon, go-cart; (Mach.) truck, trolley.

charitable [ʃari'tabl], a. charitable.

charitablement [ʃaritablə'mɑ̃], adv. charitably.

charité [ʃari'te], n.f. charity; benevolence, alms.

charivari [ʃariva'ri], n.m. rough music; hubbub, clatter.

charlatan [ʃarla'tɑ̃], n.m. charlatan, mountebank, quack.

charlatanisme [ʃarlata'nism], n.m. quackery, charlatanism.

charlot [ʃar'lo], n.m. (Orn.) curlew.

charmant [ʃar'mɑ̃], a. charming, delightful.

charme (1) [ʃarm], n.m. charm; spell; enchantment.

charme (2) [ʃarm], n.m. (Bot.) hornbeam.

charmer [ʃar'me], v.t. to charm, to enchant, to bewitch; to fascinate, to captivate, to delight.

charmeur [ʃar'mœ:r], n.m. (fem. -euse) charmer, enchanter; bewitching woman, enchantress.

charmille [ʃar'mi:j], n.f. hedge of young hornbeam; bower, arbour.

charnel [ʃar'nɛl], a. (fem. -elle) carnal; sensual (person).

charnellement [ʃarnɛl'mɑ̃], adv. carnally.

charnier [ʃar'nje], n.m. charnel-house.

charnière [ʃar'njɛ:r], n.f. hinge; joint, articulation.

charnu [ʃar'ny], a. fleshy, plump; pulpy (of fruits).

charogne [ʃa'rɔɲ], n.f. carrion; (pop.) blackguard; slut.

charpente [ʃar'pɑ̃:t], n.f. frame, framework.

charpenter [ʃarpɑ̃'te], v.t. to square (timber); (fig.) to frame, to construct.

charpenterie [ʃarpɑ̃'tri], n.f. carpentry, carpenter's work or trade.

charpentier [ʃarpɑ̃'tje], *n.m.* carpenter.
charpie [ʃar'pi], *n.f.* lint.
charretée [ʃar'te], *n.f.* cart-load.
charretier [ʃar'tje], *n.m.* (*fem.* **-ière**) carter, waggoner.—*a.* passable for carts etc.
charrette [ʃa'rɛt], *n.f.* cart; *charrette à bras*, hand-cart.
charriage [ʃa'ria:ʒ], *n.m.* cartage; haulage.
charrier [ʃa'rje], *v.t.* to cart.—*v.i.* to drift (*of ice*).
charroi [ʃa'rwa], *n.m.* cartage.
charron [ʃa'rɔ̃], *n.m.* wheelwright.
charroyer [ʃarwa'je], *v.t.* (*conjug. like* EM-PLOYER) to cart (*heavy things*).
charrue [ʃa'ry], *n.f.* plough.
charte [ʃart], *n.f.* charter.
chartreuse [ʃar'trøːz], *n.f.* Carthusian monastery *or* convent; Carthusian nun; isolated country-house; chartreuse (*liqueur*).
chartreux [ʃar'trø], *n.m.* Carthusian friar; cat of a bluish-grey colour.
chartrier [ʃartri'e], *n.m.* keeper of charters; archives; muniment room.
Charybde [ka'ribd], *n.m.* Charybdis.
chas [ʃɑ], *n.m.* eye (*of a needle*).
chasme [kasm], *n.m.* chasm.
châsse [ʃɑːs], *n.f.* reliquary, shrine; frame.
chasse [ʃas], *n.f.* hunting, shooting, fowling; the hunt, the chase; game preserve; play (*of machinery etc.*); flush (*of lavatory*).
chassé [ʃa'se], *n.m.* chassé (*a step in dancing*).
chassé-croisé [ʃasekrwa'ze], *n.m.* (*pl. chassés-croisés*) (*Dancing*) a dance step; (*fig.*) *faire un chassé-croisé*, to exchange places.
chasselas [ʃas'la], *n.m.* table grapes.

[In the following compounds chasse is *inv.*]

chasse-marée [ʃasma're], *n.m.* fish-cart.
chasse-mouches [ʃas'muʃ], *n.m.* a form of fan; fly-swatter.
chasse-neige [ʃas'nɛːʒ], *n.m.* snow-plough.
chasse-pierre(s) [ʃas'pjeːr], *n.m.* (*Rail.*) guard-iron, cow-catcher.
chasser [ʃa'se], *v.t.* to hunt; to chase, to pursue; to drive in (*a nail etc.*); to expel, to turn out, to discharge; to propel.—*v.i.* to go shooting *or* hunting; to glide along; (*Motor.*) to skid.
chasseresse [ʃas'rɛs], *n.f.* huntress.
chasseur [ʃa'sœːr], *n.m.* (*fem.* **-euse**) hunter *or* huntress, sportsman *or* sportswoman.— *n.m.* page-boy; light infantry soldier; (*Av.*) fighter.
chassie [ʃa'si], *n.f.* gum on the edge of the eyelids.
chassieux [ʃa'sjø], *a.* (*fem.* **-euse**) blear-eyed.
châssis [ʃa'si], *n.m.* case, frame; window-sash; garden-frame; printer's chase; (*Motor.*) chassis; (*Theat.*) flat for scenery.
chaste [ʃast], *a.* chaste; pure, virtuous.
chastement [ʃastə'mɑ̃], *adv.* chastely, purely, virtuously.
chasteté [ʃastə'te], *n.f.* chastity, purity.
chasuble [ʃa'zybl], *n.f.* chasuble.
chat [ʃa], *n.m.* (*fem.* **chatte**) cat; darling, dear little thing; *à bon chat bon rat*, set a thief to catch a thief; (C) *chat sauvage*, raccoon; *Le Chat Botté*, Puss in Boots.
châtaigne [ʃa'tɛɲ], *n.f.* chestnut.
châtaignier [ʃatɛ'ɲje], *n.m.* chestnut-tree.

châtain [ʃa'tɛ̃], *a. inv.* chestnut, nut-brown, auburn.
chat-cervier [ʃaser'vje], *n.m.* (*pl. chats-cerviers*) lynx.
château [ʃa'to], *n.m.* (*pl.* **-eaux**) castle, fortress; country-seat, mansion, hall, palace.
châteaubriant [ʃatobri'ɑ̃], *n.m.* large grilled rump-steak.
châtelain [ʃa'tlɛ̃], *n.m.* (*fem.* **-aine**) lord *or* lady of a manor, squire *or* squire's wife.
chat-huant [ʃa'ɥɑ̃], *n.m.* (*pl. chats-huants*) tawny owl.
châtiable [ʃa'tjabl], *a.* chastisable, punishable.
châtier [ʃa'tje], *v.t.* to chastise, to punish; (*fig.*) to correct.
chatière [ʃa'tjɛːr], *n.f.* cat's hole (*in door etc.*).
châtiment [ʃati'mɑ̃], *n.m.* chastisement, punishment.
chatoiement *or* **chatoîment** [ʃatwa'mɑ̃], *n.m.* play of colours, changing lustre (*as of shot-silk, opals etc.*).
chaton (1) [ʃa'tɔ̃], *n.m.* kitten; catkin.
chaton (2) [ʃa'tɔ̃], *n.m.* setting of a gem; stone in a setting.
chatouillant [ʃatu'jɑ̃], *a.* tickling.
chatouillement [ʃatuj'mɑ̃], *n.m.* tickling, titillation.
chatouiller [ʃatu'je], *v.t.* to tickle, to titillate; (*fig.*) to please, to gratify, to flatter.
chatouilleux [ʃatu'jø], *a.* (*fem.* **-euse**) ticklish; (*fig.*) delicate, touchy.
chatoyant [ʃatwa'jɑ̃], *a.* shot, glistening (*of colours etc.*).
chatoyer [ʃatwa'je], *v.i.* (*conjug. like* EM-PLOYER) to shimmer, to glisten.
châtrer [ʃa'tre], *v.t.* to castrate, to geld; (*Hort.*) to lop, to prune; (*fig.*) to expurgate.
chattée [ʃa'te], *n.f.* litter of kittens.
chatte [ʃat], [CHAT].
chatterie [ʃat'ri], *n.f.* playfulness, pretty *or* coaxing way; wheedling caress; (*pl.*) titbits.
chatterton [ʃater'tɔn], *n.m.* insulating tape.
chaud [ʃo], *a.* hot, warm, burning, glowing.— *n.m.* heat, warmth; *il fait chaud*, it is hot. —*adv.* hot, warm.
chaudeau [ʃo'do], *n.m.* (*pl.* **-eaux**) egg-flip.
chaudement [ʃod'mɑ̃], *adv.* warmly; (*fig.*) quickly, eagerly, fiercely, hotly.
chaud-froid [ʃo'frwa], *n.m.* cold jellied chicken *or* game with mayonnaise.
chaudière [ʃo'djɛːr], *n.f.* copper; boiler (*of a steam-engine etc.*); (C) pail.
chaudron [ʃo'drɔ̃], *n.m.* cauldron.
chaudronnerie [ʃodrɔn'ri], *n.f.* boiler works.
chaudronnier [ʃodrɔ'nje], *n.m.* brazier, coppersmith, tinker.
chauffage [ʃo'faːʒ], *n.m.* heating, warming; stoking; fuel, firewood; *chauffage central*, central heating.
chauffard [ʃo'faːr], *n.m.* (*pop.*) road-hog.
chauffe [ʃoːf], *n.f.* furnace.
chauffe-bain [ʃof'bɛ̃], *n.m.* (*pl.* **chauffe-bains**) geyser.
chauffe-eau [ʃof'o], *n.m. inv.* water-heater.
chauffelinge [ʃof'lɛːʒ], *n.m. inv.* clothes-horse, airing cupboard.
chauffer [ʃo'fe], *v.t.* to heat, to warm; (*fig.*) to excite.—*v.i.* to grow hot; to be brewing; (*fig.*) to be urgent *or* pressing. se **chauffer**, *v.r.* to warm oneself.
chaufferette [ʃo'frɛt], *n.f.* foot-warmer.

chauffeur [ʃoˈfœːr], *n.m.* fireman; (*fem.* **-euse**)(*Motor.*) driver, chauffeur, chauffeuse.

chaufour [ʃoˈfuːr], *n.m.* lime-kiln.

chaulage [ʃoˈlaːʒ], *n.m.* (*Agric.*) liming.

chauler [ʃoˈle], *v.t.* to lime (*soil*).

chaume [ʃoːm], *n.m.* stubble; stubble-field; thatch.

chaumer [ʃoˈme], *v.t., v.i.* (*Agric.*) to cut stubble.

chaumière [ʃoˈmjɛːr], *n.f.* thatched house, cottage.

chausse [ʃoːs], *n.f.* shoulder-band (*worn in universities etc.*); **(pl.)* hose (*covering the body from waist to foot*).

chaussée [ʃoˈse], *n.f.* embankment, dike; causeway; roadway, (*Am.*) pavement; *le rez-de-chaussée*, the ground floor.

chausse-pied [ʃosˈpje], *n.m.* (*pl.* **chausse-pieds**) shoe-horn.

chausser [ʃoˈse], *v.t.* to put on (*footwear*); to shoe, to make (*the shoes etc.*) for; (*colloq.*) to fit, to suit.—*v.i. chausser du* 40, to take a 7 (*in shoes*). **se chausser**, *v.r.* to put on one's shoes etc.

chausse-trape [ʃosˈtrap], *n.f.* (*pl.* **chausse-trapes**) snare, trap.

chaussette [ʃoˈsɛt], *n.f.* sock.

chausseur [ʃoˈsœːr], *n.m.* footwear dealer.

chausson [ʃoˈsɔ̃], *n.m.* slipper; gym shoe; bootee (*for infants*).

chaussure [ʃoˈsyːr], *n.f.* foot-wear.

chauve [ʃoːv], *a.* bald.

chauve-souris [ʃovsuˈri], *n.f.* (*pl.* **chauves-souris**) bat, flittermouse.

chauvin [ʃoˈvɛ̃], *n.m.* fanatical patriot.—*a.* chauvinistic, jingoistic.

chaux [ʃo], *n.f.* lime; limestone.

chavirage [ʃaviˈraːʒ], **chavirement** [ʃavirˈmã], *n.m.* capsizing, upsetting.

chavirer [ʃaviˈre], *v.t., v.i.* to capsize, to upset.

chef [ʃɛf], *n.m.* chief, commander, conductor, master, principal, ringleader; chef.

chef-d'œuvre [ʃɛˈdœːvr], *n.m.* (*pl.* **chefs-d'œuvre**) chef-d'œuvre, masterpiece.

chef-lieu [ʃɛfˈljø], *n.m.* (*pl.* **chefs-lieux**) chief town, county town.

cheik [SCHEIK].

chelem or **schelem** [ʃlɛm], *n.m. inv.* slam (*at cards*).

chemin [ʃəˈmɛ̃], *n.m.* way, road, path, track; (*fig.*) means; course; *chemin de fer*, railway, (*Am.*) railroad.

chemineau [ʃəmiˈno], *n.m.* (*pl.* **-eaux**) tramp.

cheminée [ʃəmiˈne], *n.f.* chimney; funnel; fire-place; mantelpiece; nipple (*of a percussion-gun*).

cheminer [ʃəmiˈne], *v.i.* to walk, to tramp; to proceed.

cheminot [ʃəmiˈno], *n.m.* railwayman; plate-layer.

chemise [ʃəˈmiːz], *n.f.* shirt; wrapper, cover.

chemiserie [ʃəmiˈzri], *n.f.* shirt-factory; shirt-making.

chemisette [ʃəmiˈzɛt], *n.f.* short-sleeved shirt (*men*).

chemisier [ʃəmiˈzje], *n.m.* (*fem.* **-ière**) shirt-maker *or* seller.

chênaie [ʃeˈnɛ], *n.f.* oak-plantation.

chenal [ʃəˈnal], *n.m.* channel, fairway.

chenapan [ʃənaˈpã], *n.m.* vagabond, good-for-nothing, scamp.

chêne [ʃɛːn], *n.m.* oak.

chêneau [ʃeˈno], *n.m.* (*pl.* **-eaux**) young oak.

chéneau [ʃeˈno], *n.m.*(*pl.*-**eaux**)(*eaves*)gutter.

chenet [ʃəˈnɛ], *n.m.* fire-dog.

chènevière [ʃɛnˈvjɛːr], *n.f.* hemp-field.

chènevis [ʃɛnˈvi], *n.m.* hemp-seed.

chènevotte [ʃɛnˈvot], *n.f.* stalk (*of hemp*).

chenil [ʃəˈni], *n.m.* dog-kennel; kennels; dirty hovel.

chenille [ʃəˈniːj], *n.f.* caterpillar; kind of silk cord, chenille; *tracteur à chenille*, (*reg. trade name*) caterpillar tractor.

chenillère [ʃəniˈjɛːr], *n.f.* nest of caterpillars.

chenillette [ʃəniˈjɛt], *n.f.* (*Mil.*) half-track.

chenu [ʃəˈny], *a.* grey-headed; snow-capped.

cheptel [ʃəˈtɛl, ʃɛpˈtɛl], *n.m.* live-stock (*of a country*).

chèque [ʃɛk], *n.m.* cheque, (*Am.*) check.

chéquier [ʃeˈkje], *n.m.* cheque-book.

cher [ʃɛːr], *a.* (*fem.* **chère** (1)) dear, beloved; precious; expensive.—*adv.* dear, dearly, expensively.

chercher [ʃɛrˈʃe], *v.t.* to seek, to look for, to search for; to endeavour, to try, to attempt; *aller chercher*, to go for; to fetch.

chercheur [ʃɛrˈʃœːr], *n.m.* (*fem.* **-euse**) seeker, searcher; research worker.

chère (1) [ʃɛːr], [CHER].

chère (2) [ʃɛːr], *n.f.* entertainment, fare; *bonne chère*, good cheer, good living.

chèrement [ʃɛrˈmã], *adv.* dearly, tenderly; dear, at a high price.

chéri [ʃeˈri], *a.* beloved; cherished.—*n.m.* (*fem.* **-e**) darling, dearest.

chérif [ʃeˈrif], *n.m.* shereef (*Arabian prince*).

chérir [ʃeˈriːr], *v.t.* to love dearly, to cherish.

cherté [ʃɛrˈte], *n.f.* dearness, high price.

chérubin [ʃeryˈbɛ̃], *n.m.* cherub.

chérubique [ʃeryˈbik], *a.* cherubic.

chester [ʃɛsˈtɛr], *n.m.* Cheshire cheese.

chétif [ʃeˈtif], *a.* (*fem.* **-tive**) puny, pitiful; worthless.

chétivement [ʃetivˈmã], *adv.* meanly, pitifully, poorly, feebly.

chétiveté [ʃetivˈte], *n.f.* puniness, paltriness.

cheval [ʃəˈval], *n.m.* (*pl.* **-aux**) horse; nag, steed; *aller à cheval*, to ride; *cheval d'arçons, cheval de bois*, (*Gym.*) vaulting horse; *cheval à bascule*, rocking-horse; *chevaux de bois*, merry-go-round; *cheval marin*, sea-horse; walrus.

chevaleresque [ʃəvalˈrɛsk], *a.* chivalrous, knightly.

chevaleresquement [ʃəvalrɛskˈmã], *adv.* chivalrously.

chevalerie [ʃəvalˈri], *n.f.* knighthood, chivalry.

chevalet [ʃəvaˈlɛ], *n.m.* easel; bridge (*of a stringed instrument*); sawing-trestle; buttress, prop; clothes-horse.

chevalier (1) [ʃəvaˈlje], *n.m.* knight.

chevalier (2) [ʃəvaˈlje], *n.m.* (*Orn.*) sand-piper; redshank.

chevalière [ʃəvaˈljɛːr], *n.f.* knight's lady; signet-ring.

chevalin [ʃəvaˈlɛ̃], *a.* equine; *boucherie chevaline*, horse butcher's shop.

cheval-vapeur [ʃəvalvaˈpœːr], *n.m.* (*pl.* **chevaux-vapeur**) horse-power.

chevauchant [ʃəvoˈʃã], *a.* overlapping.

chevauchée [ʃəvoˈʃe], *n.f.* ride, excursion on horseback; cavalcade.

chevauchement [ʃəvoʃˈmɑ̃], *n.m.* overlap *or* crossing (*tiles, wires*).

chevaucher [ʃəvoˈʃe], *v.i.* to ride on horseback; to be astride; to overlap.

chevaucheur [ʃəvoˈʃœːr], *n.m.* rider, horseman.

chevauchure [ʃəvoˈʃyːr], *n.f.* overlapping.

chevelu [ʃəˈvly], *a.* hairy, long-haired; (*Bot.*) fibrous.

chevelure [ʃəˈvlyːr], *n.f.* hair, head of hair.

chevesne [ʃəˈvɛn], *n.m.* (*Ichth.*) chub.

chevet [ʃəˈvɛ], *n.m.* head (*of a bed*); bolster; pillow; bedside.

cheveu [ʃəˈvø], *n.m.* (*pl.* **-eux**) a single hair; *pl.* the hair (*of the head*).

chevillage [ʃəviˈjaːʒ], *n.m.* fastening, bolting, dowelling.

cheville [ʃəˈviːj], *n.f.* ankle; peg, pin, dowel, bolt; plug.

cheviller [ʃəviˈje], *v.t.* to dowel, to peg, to bolt.

cheviotte [ʃəˈvjɔt], *n.f.* cheviot (*tweed*).

chèvre [ʃɛːvr], *n.f.* goat, nanny-goat.

chevreau [ʃəˈvro], *n.m.* (*pl.* **-eaux**) kid (*animal or skin*).

chèvrefeuille [ʃɛvrəˈfœːj], *n.m.* honeysuckle.

chèvrerie [ʃɛvrəˈri], *n.f.* goat-pen.

chevrette [ʃəˈvrɛt], *n.f.* small goat; young roe.

chevreuil [ʃəˈvrœːj], *n.m.* roe, roe-deer.

chevrier [ʃəvriˈe], *n.m.* (*fem.* **-ière**) goatherd.

chevron [ʃəˈvrɔ̃], *n.m.* rafter; chevron, stripe.

chevronnage [ʃəvrɔˈnaːʒ], *n.m.* rafters, raftering.

chevronné [ʃəvrɔˈne], *a.* (*fam.*) experienced

chevrotain *or* chevrotin [ʃəvrɔˈtɛ̃], *n.m.* chevrotain, musk-deer.

chevrotant [ʃəvrɔˈtɑ̃], *a.* quavering, tremulous.

chevrotement [ʃəvrɔtˈmɑ̃], *n.m.* tremulous motion, trembling (*of the voice etc.*).

chevroter [ʃəvrɔˈte], *v.i.* to sing *or* speak in a tremulous voice.

chevrotin (1) [CHEVROTAIN].

chevrotin (2) [ʃəvrɔˈtɛ̃], *n.m.* fawn of roedeer; kid (*leather*).

chevrotine [ʃəvrɔˈtin], *n.f.* buck-shot.

chez [ʃe], *prep.* at, to, in (*the house, family or country of*); in, with, among; in the works of, (*on letters*) care of.

chiasse [ʃjas], *n.f.* dross, scum.

chibouque *or* chibouk [ʃiˈbuk], *n.f.* chibouk (*Turkish pipe*).

chic [ʃik], *n.m.* style, chic; aplomb, ease and elegance.—*a. inv.* stylish, smart.

chicane [ʃiˈkan], *n.f.* cavil, evasion, quibble; chicanery.

chicaner [ʃikaˈne], *v.t.* to quarrel *or* wrangle with.—*v.i.* to cavil, to quibble.

chicanerie [ʃikanˈri], *n.f.* chicanery, quibbling, cavilling.

chicaneur [ʃikaˈnœːr], *n.m.* (*fem.* **-euse**) *or* chicanier [ʃikaˈnje], *n.m.* (*fem.* **-ière**) caviller, pettifogger.—*a.* litigious, cavilling, wrangling.

chiche (1) [ʃiʃ], *a.* niggardly, stingy.

chiche (2) [ʃiʃ], *a.* **pois chiches**, chick-peas.

chichement [ʃiʃˈmɑ̃], *adv.* stingily.

chicorée [ʃikɔˈre], *n.f.* endive; chicory.

chicot [ʃiˈko], *n.m.* stub *or* stump (*of tree or tooth*).

chicotin [ʃikɔˈtɛ̃], *n.m.* bitter juice of aloes.

chien [ʃjɛ̃], *n.m.* (*fem.* **chienne**) dog; hammer, cock (*of a gun or pistol*); **chien de mer**, dog-fish.

chiendent [ʃjɛ̃ˈdɑ̃], *n.m.* couch-grass.

chiennée [ʃjɛˈne], *n.f.* litter of pups.

chiffe [ʃif], *n.f.* poor stuff, rag; (*fig.*) weakling; spineless person.

chiffon [ʃiˈfɔ̃], *n.m.* rag, scrap, bit; frippery.

chiffonnage [ʃifɔˈnaːʒ], *n.m.* rumpled drapery, rumpling, crumpling.

chiffonner [ʃifɔˈne], *v.t.* to rumple, to crumple; (*colloq.*) to ruffle, to tease, to vex. —*v.i.* to be a rag-collector.

chiffonnier [ʃifɔˈnje], *n.m.* (*fem.* **-ière**) rag-picker; chiffonnier.

chiffrage [ʃiˈfraːʒ], chiffrement [ʃifrˈmɑ̃], *n.m.* figuring, figures; calculation; writing in cipher, coding.

chiffre [ʃifr], *n.m.* figure, number; total amount; cipher; monogram.

chiffrer [ʃiˈfre], *v.t.* to calculate, to tot up; to code.—*v.i.* to cipher.

chiffreur [ʃiˈfrœːr], *n.m.* (*fem.* **-euse**) reckoner, cipherer.

chignole [ʃiˈɲɔl], *n.f.* ratchet drill.

chignon [ʃiˈɲɔ̃], *n.m.* chignon, coil of hair.

Chili [ʃiˈli], le, *m.* Chile.

chilien [ʃiˈljɛ̃], *a.* (*fem.* **-enne**) Chilean.—*n.m.* (**Chilien**, *fem.* **-enne**) Chilean (*person*).

chimère [ʃiˈmɛːr], *n.f.* chimera; myth, idle fancy.

chimérique [ʃimeˈrik], *a.* chimerical, visionary.

chimériquement [ʃimerikˈmɑ̃], *adv.* chimerically.

chimie [ʃiˈmi], *n.f.* chemistry.

chimique [ʃiˈmik], *a.* chemical.

chimiquement [ʃimikˈmɑ̃], *adv.* chemically.

chimiste [ʃiˈmist], *n.m.* chemist (*not pharmaceutical chemist*).

chimpanzé [ʃɛ̃pɑ̃ˈze], *n.m.* chimpanzee.

chinchilla [ʃɛ̃ʃiˈla], *n.m.* chinchilla.

Chine [ʃin], la, *f.* China.

chiner [ʃiˈne], *v.t.* to colour differently; to figure (*stuffs*).

chinois [ʃiˈnwa], *a.* Chinese.—*n.m.* Chinese (*language*); **un chinois**, a small green orange preserved in brandy; (**Chinois**, *fem.* **-oise**) Chinese (*person*).

chinoiserie [ʃinwaˈzri], *n.f.* Chinese thing, curio; (*fig.*) trick; red tape.

chiot [ʃjo], *n.m.* puppy.

chiourme [ʃjurm], *n.f.* convict-gang.

chipolata [ʃipɔlaˈta], *n.f.* onion stew; small sausage.

chipotage [ʃipɔˈtaːʒ], *n.m.* dawdling; haggling.

chipoter [ʃipɔˈte], *v.i.* to dally, to dawdle; to haggle; to peck at a dish.

chipotier [ʃipɔˈtje], *n.m.* (*fem.* **-ière**) trifler dallier, shuffler.

chique [ʃik], *n.f.* quid of tobacco.

chiquement [ʃikˈmɑ̃], *adv.* smartly.

chiquenaude [ʃikˈnoːd], *n.f.* flick.

chiquenauder [ʃiknoˈde], *v.t.* to flick.

chiquer [ʃiˈke], *v.i.* to chew tobacco.

chiquet [ʃiˈkɛ], *n.m.*, chiquette [ʃiˈkɛt], *n.f.* driblet, bit, shred.

chiqueur [ʃiˈkœːr], *n.m.* chewer of tobacco; pretender.

chiromancie [kirɔmɑ̃'si], *n.f.* chiromancy, palmistry.

chiromancien [kirɔmɑ̃'sjɛ̃], *n.m.* (*fem.* **-ienne**) chiromancer, palmist.

chirurgical [ʃiryrʒi'kal], *a.* (*m.pl.* **-aux**) surgical.

chirurgicalement [ʃiryrʒikal'mɑ̃], *adv.* surgically.

chirurgie [ʃiryr'ʒi], *n.f.* surgery.

chirurgien [[ʃiryr'ʒjɛ̃], *n.m.* surgeon.

chirurgique [ʃiryr'ʒik], *a.* surgical.

chiure [ʃjy:r], *n.f.* fly-speck.

chlorate [klɔ'rat], *n.m.* chlorate.

chlore [klɔ:r], *n.m.* (*Chem.*) chlorine.

chloré [klɔ're], *a.* containing chlorine.

chlorhydrate [klɔri'drat], *n.m.* (*Chem.*) hydrochlorate.

chlorhydrique [klɔri'drik], *a.* hydrochloric.

chloroforme [klɔrɔ'fɔrm], *n.m.* chloroform.

chloroformer [klɔrɔfɔr'me], *v.t.* to chloroform.

chlorure [klɔ'ry:r], *n.m.* (*Chem.*) chloride.

choc [ʃɔk], *n.m.* shock; impact; clash, encounter.

chocolat [ʃɔkɔ'la], *n.m.* chocolate.—*a.* chocolate-coloured.

chocolaterie [ʃɔkɔla'tri], *n.f.* chocolate-making; chocolate-factory.

chocolatier [ʃɔkɔla'tje], *n.m.* (*fem.* **-ière**) chocolate-maker *or* seller.—*n.f.* (**-ière**) chocolate-pot.

chœur [kœ:r], *n.m.* choir; chancel; (*Ant. and fig.*) chorus.

choir [ʃwa:r], *v.i. irr.* to fall, to drop.

choisir [ʃwa'zi:r], *v.t.* to choose, to single out, to select.

choix [ʃwa], *n.m.* choice, alternative; selection; distinction.

choléra [kɔle'ra], *n.m.* cholera.

cholérique [kɔle'rik], *a.* choleraic.—*n.* person affected with cholera.

chômable [ʃo'mabl], *a.* (*of days, fêtes etc.*) to be kept as a holiday.

chômage [ʃo'ma:ʒ], *n.m.* unemployment, enforced idleness; stoppage; *allocation de chômage,* unemployment benefit, 'dole'.

chômer [ʃo'me], *v.i.* to be doing nothing; to be unemployed.

chômeur [ʃo'mœ:r], *n.m.* (*fem.* **-euse**) idle *or* unemployed person.

chope [ʃɔp], *n.f.* large beer-glass; mug of beer.

chopper [ʃɔ'pe], *v.i.* to stumble, to trip (*contre*).

choquant [ʃɔ'kɑ̃], *a.* offensive, unpleasant, improper.

choquer [ʃɔ'ke], *v.t.* to shock, to strike *or* dash against; to displease, to offend.—*v.i.* to clink glasses; to be offensive, to be shocking. **se choquer,** *v.r.* to take offence; to come into collision with each other.

choral [kɔ'ral], *a.* choral.—*n.m.* (*pl.* **-als**) choral(e).—*n.f.* (**chorale**) choir, choral society.

chorée [kɔ're], *n.f.* chorea, St. Vitus's dance.

chorégraphe [kɔre'graf], *n.m.* choreographer.

chorégraphie [kɔregra'fi], *n.f.* choreography.

choriste [kɔ'rist], *n.m.* chorister; (*Theat.*) member of the chorus.

chorus [kɔ'ry:s], *n.m.* chorus.

chose [ʃo:z], *n.f.* thing; matter, business, affair; (*Law*) chattel, property.

chou [ʃu], *n.m.* (*pl.* **choux**) cabbage, kale; (*colloq.*) puff-paste; darling, dear; bow, rosette; *choux de Bruxelles,* Brussels sprouts.

chouan [ʃwɑ̃], *n.m.* Chouan, Breton royalist insurgent (*during the French Revolution*).

choucas [ʃu'ka], *n.m.,* **chouchette** [ʃu'ʃet] *n.f.* jackdaw.

choucroute [ʃu'krut], *n.f.* sauerkraut.

chouette (1) [ʃwet], *n.f.* owl.

chouette (2) [ʃwet] *int.* (*pop.*) fine, marvellous.—*a.* nice, fine, good of its kind.

chou-fleur [ʃu'flœ:r], *n.m.* (*pl.* **choux-fleurs**) cauliflower.

chou-rave [ʃu'ra:v], *n.m.* (*pl.* **choux-raves**) kohl-rabi, turnip-cabbage.

choyer [ʃwa'je], *v.t.* (*conjug. like* EMPLOYER) to take great care of, to be fond of, to pamper, to pet. **se choyer,** *v.r.* to pamper oneself.

chrême [krɛ:m], *n.m.* chrism, holy oil.

chrémeau [kre'mo], *n.m.* (*pl.* **-eaux**) chrism-cloth.

chrétien [kre'tjɛ̃], *a. and n.m.* (*fem.* **-enne**) Christian.

chrétiennement [kretjɛn'mɑ̃], *adv.* like a Christian.

chrétienté [kretjɛ̃'te], *n.f.* Christendom.

christ [krist], *n.m.* crucifix; representation of Christ crucified; *le Christ,* Jesus Christ.

christianisme [kristja'nism], *n.m.* Christianity.

Christophe [kris'tɔf], *m.* Christopher.

chromage [krɔ'ma:ʒ], *n.m.* chromium plating.

chromate [krɔ'mat] *n.m.* (*Chem.*) chromate.

chromatique [krɔma'tik], *a.* (*Chem., Mus.*) chromatic.—*n.f.* (*Mus., Paint.*) chromatics.

chrome [kro:m], *n.m.* chromium, chrome.

chromé [kro'me], *a.* chromium-plated.

chromer [kro'me], *v.t.* to chrome.

chromique [kro'mik], *a.* chromic.

chromosome [kromo'zo:m], *n.m.* chromosome.

chronique (1) [kro'nik], *n.f.* chronicle, history; news-summary.

chronique (2) [kro'nik], *a.* (*Med.*) chronic.

chroniqueur [kroni'kœ:r], *n.m.* (*fem.* **-euse**) chronicler; newswriter, columnist.

chronologie [kronolo'ʒi], *n.f.* chronology.

chronologique [kronolo'ʒik], *a.* chronological.

chronomètre [krono'mɛ:tr], *n.m.* chronometer.

chronométrer [kronome'tre], *v.t.* (*conjug. like* CÉDER) to time.

chronométreur [kronome'trœ:r], *n.m.* timekeeper.

chrysalide [kriza'lid], *n.f.* chrysalis.

chrysanthème [krizɑ̃'tɛ:m], *n.m.* chrysanthemum.

chuchotement [ʃyʃɔt'mɑ̃], *n.m.* whispering, whisper, rustling.

chuchoter [ʃyʃɔ'te], *v.t., v.i.* to whisper.

chuchoterie [ʃyʃɔ'tri], *n.f.* whispering.

chuchoteur [ʃyʃɔ'tœ:r], *n.m.* (*fem.* **-euse**) whisperer.

chuinter [ʃɥɛ̃'te], *v.i.* to hoot (*of owls*); to hiss (*of gas*).

chut [ʃt], *int. and n.m.* hush!

69

chute

chute [ʃyt], *n.f.* fall, tumble; collapse, ruin, downfall; disaster.

chuter [ʃyˈte], *v.i.* (*fam.*) to fall, to fail.

Chypre [ʃipr], *f.* Cyprus.

ci [si], *adv.* here.

cible [sibl], *n.f.* target, mark; (*fig.*) purpose.

ciboire [siˈbwaːr], *n.m.* sacred vase, pyx.

ciboule [siˈbul], *n.f.* Welsh onion, scallion.

ciboulette [sibuˈlɛt], *n.f.* chive.

cicatrice [sikaˈtris], *n.f.* scar, seam, mark.

cicatrisant [sikatriˈzɑ̃], *a.* cicatrizing.

cicatrisation [sikatrizaˈsjɔ̃], *n.f.* cicatrization.

cicatriser [sikatriˈze], *v.t.* to cicatrize; to close, to heal up. **se cicatriser**, *v.r.* to skin over, to heal up.

Cicéron [siseˈrɔ̃], *m.* Cicero.

cicérone [siseˈron], *n.m.* cicerone, guide.

cicéronien [siseroˈnjɛ̃], *a.* (*fem.* **-enne**) Ciceronian.

cidre [sidr], *n.m.* cider.

cidrerie [sidrəˈri], *n.f.* cider making; cider-factory.

ciel [sjɛl], *n.m.* (*pl.* **cieux**) the heavens, the firmament, the sky; heaven.

cierge [sjɛrʒ], *n.m.* taper, church candle.

cigale [siˈgal], *n.f.* cicada.

cigare [siˈgaːr], *n.m.* cigar.

cigarette [sigaˈrɛt], *n.f.* cigarette.

cigogne [siˈgɔɲ], *n.f.* stork.

cigogneau [sigoˈɲo], *n.m.* (*pl.* **-eaux**) young stork.

ciguë [siˈgy], *n.f.* hemlock (*plant or poison*).

cil [sil], *n.m.* eyelash.

cilice [siˈlis], *n.m.* cilice, hair-shirt.

cillement [sijˈmɑ̃], *n.m.* blink, winking.

ciller [siˈje], *v.t., v.i.* to wink, to blink (*the eyes*).

cimaise or **cymaise** [siˈmɛːz], *n.f.* cyma, ogee; dado-rail, picture rail.

cime [sim], *n.f.* top, summit, peak.

ciment [siˈmɑ̃], *n.m.* cement.

cimenter [simɑ̃ˈte], *v.t.* to cement; to strengthen, to consolidate.

cimentier [simɑ̃ˈtje], *n.m.* cement-maker.

cimeterre [simˈtɛːr], *n.m.* scimitar.

cimetière [simˈtjɛːr], *n.m.* cemetery, churchyard.

cimier [siˈmje], *n.m.* crest (*of a helmet*); buttock (*of beef*).

cinéaste [sineˈast], *n.m.* film producer.

cinéma [sineˈma], *n.m.* cinema.

cinémascope [sinemasˈkɔp], *n.m.* cinemascope.

cinémathèque [sinemaˈtɛk], *n.f.* film library.

cinématographier [sinematɔgraˈfje], *v.t.* to film.

cinérama [sineraˈma], *n.m.* cinerama.

cinétique [sineˈtik], *n.f.* kinetics.—*a.* kinetic, motive (*energy*).

cinétiquement [sinetikˈmɑ̃], *adv.* kinetically.

cingalais [sɛ̃gaˈlɛ], *a.* Sin(g)halese *or* Cingalese.—*n.m.* Sin(g)halese *or* Cingalese (*language*); (**Cingalais,** *fem.* **-aise**) Sin(g)halese *or* Cingalese (*person*).

cinglage [sɛ̃ˈglaːʒ], *n.m.* sailing, ship's course, run of a ship in twenty-four hours.

cinglement [sɛ̃glˈmɑ̃], *n.m.* lashing, slashing.

cingler (1) [sɛ̃ˈgle], *v.i.* to sail before the wind.

cingler (2) [sɛ̃ˈgle], *v.t.* to lash; (*fig.*) to chastize.

cinname [siˈnam], **cinnamome** [sinaˈmɔm], *n.m.* cinnamon.

cinq [sɛ̃ːk], *a.* five.—*n.m.* five.

cinquantaine [sɛ̃kɑ̃ˈtɛn], *n.f.* about fifty.

cinquante [sɛ̃ˈkɑ̃ːt], *a.* fifty.

cinquantenaire [sɛ̃kɑ̃tˈnɛːr], *a.* and *n.* quinquagenarian.—*n.m.* fiftieth anniversary, jubilee.

cinquantième [sɛ̃kɑ̃ˈtjɛm], *a.* fiftieth.—*n.m.* fiftieth part.

cinquième [sɛ̃ˈkjɛm], *a.* fifth.—*n.m.* fifth part; fifth floor.

cintrage [sɛ̃ˈtraːʒ], *n.m.* arching, curving (*of arches etc.*).

cintre [sɛ̃ːtr], *n.m.* curve of an arch; coat-hanger.

cintrer [sɛ̃ˈtre], *v.t.* to arch, to curve.

cipaye [siˈpaːj], **cipahi** [siˈpai], *n.m.* sepoy.

cipolin [sipoˈlɛ̃], *n.m.* cipollino, cipolin marble.

cippe [sip], *n.m.* cippus (*half-column*).

cirage [siˈraːʒ], *n.m.* waxing; blacking (*composition or process*); boot-polish.

circoncire [sirkɔ̃ˈsiːr], *v.t. irr.* (*conjug. like* CONFIRE *except for p.p.* **circoncis**) to circumcise.

circoncis [sirkɔ̃ˈsi], *a.* circumcised.—*n.m.* one who is circumcised.

circoncision [sirkɔ̃siˈzjɔ̃], *n.f.* circumcision.

circonférence [sirkɔ̃feˈrɑ̃ːs], *n.f.* circumference.

circonflexe [sirkɔ̃ˈflɛks], *a.* and *n.m.* circumflex.

circonlocution [sirkɔ̃lɔkyˈsjɔ̃], *n.f.* circumlocution.

circonscription [sirkɔ̃skripˈsjɔ̃], *n.f.* circumscription; district; constituency.

circonscrire [sirkɔ̃ˈkriːr], *v.t. irr.* (*conjug. like* ÉCRIRE) to circumscribe, to encircle; to limit.

circonspect [sirkɔ̃sˈpɛkt, -spɛ], *a.* circumspect, wary, discreet, reserved.

circonspection [sirkɔ̃spɛkˈsjɔ̃], *n.f.* circumspection, wariness, caution.

circonstance [sirkɔ̃sˈtɑ̃ːs], *n.f.* circumstance; occurrence, event.

circonstanciel [sirkɔ̃stɑ̃ˈsjɛl], *a.* (*fem.* **-elle**) circumstantial.

circonstancier [sirkɔ̃stɑ̃ˈsje], *v.t.* to state circumstantially, to particularize.

circonvenir [sirkɔ̃vˈniːr], *v.t. irr.* (*conjug. like* TENIR) to circumvent, to outwit.

circonvention [sirkɔ̃vɑ̃ˈsjɔ̃], *n.f.* circumvention, fraud.

circonvoisin [sirkɔ̃vwaˈzɛ̃], *a.* circumjacent, neighbouring, adjoining.

circonvolution [sirkɔ̃vɔlyˈsjɔ̃], *n.f.* circumvolution.

circuit [sirˈkɥi], *n.m.* circuit, circumference; detour; lap; (*Elec.*) **court circuit**, short circuit; **en circuit**, switched on.

circulaire [sirkyˈlɛːr], *a.* circular, round.—*n.f.* circular.

circulation [sirkylaˈsjɔ̃], *n.f.* circulation; currency; traffic.

circulatoire [sirkylaˈtwaːr], *a.* circulatory, circulating.

circuler [sirkyˈle], *v.i.* to circulate, to revolve, to move round; to be current.

cire [siːr], *n.f.* beeswax; wax; taper.

ciré [siˈre], *n.m.* (*Naut.*) (suit of) oilskins.

cirer [siˈre], *v.t.* to wax; to black *or* to polish (*boots*).

70

cireur [si'rœːr], *n.m.* (*fem.* **cireuse** (1)) polisher; *cireuse électrique*, electric polisher.
cireux [si'rø], *a.* (*fem.* **cireuse** (2)) waxy.
ciron [si'rɔ̃], *n.m.* mite.
cirque [sirk], *n.m.* circus.
cirrus [sir'ryːs], *n.m.* cirrus (*curl-cloud*).
cirure [si'ryːr], *n.f.* prepared wax.
cisaille [si'zɑːj], *n.f.* clipping *or* shearing of metals; (*pl.*) shears; (*Bookb.*) guillotine.
cisailler [sizɑ'je], *v.t.* to pare, to clip (*coins etc.*); to cut with shears.
cisalpin [sizal'pɛ̃], *a.* Cisalpine.
ciseau [si'zo], *n.m.* (*pl.* **-eaux**) chisel; (*pl.*) scissors.
ciseler [siz'le], *v.t.* (*conjug. like* AMENER) to chisel; to chase.
ciselet [siz'lɛ], *n.m.* small chisel, graver.
ciseleur [siz'lœːr], *n.m.* chaser; carver, sculptor.
ciselure [siz'lyːr], *n.f.* chasing, sculpture, carving.
cisoires [si'zwaːr], *n.f.* (*used only in pl.*) big bench-shears (*to cut sheet iron*).
ciste [sist], *n.m.* cistus, rock-rose.
citadelle [sita'dɛl], *n.f.* citadel; (*fig.*) stronghold.
citadin [sita'dɛ̃], *n.m.* (*fem.* **-e**) citizen, townsman *or* -woman.
citation [sita'sjɔ̃], *n.f.* citation, quotation; summons.
cité [si'te], *n.f.* city; town.
citer [si'te], *v.t.* to cite, to quote; to summon.
citérieur [site'rjœːr], *a.* (*Geog.*) nearer, hithermost.
citerne [si'tɛrn], *n.f.* cistern, reservoir; (*Naut.*) tanker.
cithare [si'taːr], *n.f.* zither.
citoyen [sitwa'jɛ̃], *n.m.* (*fem.* **-enne**) citizen, burgess; (*fig.*) patriot.
citrate [si'trat], *n.m.* citrate.
citrin [si'trɛ̃], *a.* citrine, lemon-coloured.
citrique [si'trik], *a.* citric.
citron [si'trɔ̃], *a.* lemon-coloured.—*n.m.* lemon, citron.
citronnade [sitro'nad], *n.f.* lemon-squash.
citronnat [sitro'na], *n.m.* candied lemon-peel.
citronné [sitro'ne], *a.* lemon-flavoured.
citronnier [sitro'nje], *n.m.* citron-tree.
citrouille [si'truːj], *n.f.* pumpkin, gourd.
cive [siːv], **civette** (1) [si'vɛt], [CIBOULETTE].
civet [si'vɛ], *n.m.* wine stew (*of venison*); *civet de lièvre*, jugged hare.
civette (2) [si'vɛt], *n.f.* civet-cat; civet.
civière [si'vjɛːr], *n.f.* hand-barrow; stretcher; bier.
civil [si'vil], *a.* civil; private; plain; polite.—*n.m.* civilian.
civilement [sivil'mã], *adv.* civilly; courteously.
civilisable [sivili'zabl], *a.* civilizable.
civilisateur [siviliza'tœːr], *a.* (*fem.* **-trice**) civilizing.
civilisation [siviliza'sjɔ̃], *n.f.* civilization.
civiliser [sivili'ze], *v.t.* to civilize. **se civiliser**, *v.r.* to become civilized.
civilité [sivili'te], *n.f.* civility, good manners; (*pl.*) compliments.
civique [si'vik], *a.* civic.
civisme [si'vism], *n.m.* good citizenship.

clabaudage [klabo'daːʒ], *n.m.* barking, bawling.
clabauder [klabo'de], *v.i.* to clamour, to bawl out.
clabaudeur [klabo'dœːr], *n.m.* (*fem.* **-euse**) brawler, scandalmonger.
claie [klɛ], *n.f.* wattle, hurdle; screen (*of a sieve*).
clair [klɛːr], *a.* clear, bright, luminous; light-coloured, pure, cloudless; thin (*of liquids etc.*); plain, intelligible, obvious.—*adv.* clearly, distinctly, plainly.—*n.m.* light, clearness; (*Paint.*) highlight.
Claire [klɛːr], *f.* Clara, Cla(i)re.
clairement [klɛr'mã], *adv.* clearly, plainly, distinctly.
clairet [klɛ'rɛ], *a.* (*fem.* **clairette** (1)) palish, lightish (*of wines*).—*n.m.* light-red wine.
clairette (2) [klɛ'rɛt], *n.f.* white grape.
claire-voie [klɛr'vwa], *n.f.* (*pl.* **claires-voies**) wooden fencing; opening (*in garden wall*), wicket; skylight.
clairière [klɛ'rjɛːr], *n.f.* clearing, glade.
clair-obscur [klɛrɔps'kyːr], *n.m.* (*pl.* **clairs-obscurs**) chiaroscuro; light and shade.
clairon [klɛ'rɔ̃], *n.m.* clarion, bugle; bugler.
clairsemé [klɛrsə'me], *a.* thin, thinly sown, scattered.
clairvoyance [klɛrvwa'jãːs], *n.f.* sharpness, perspicacity; clairvoyance.
clairvoyant [klɛrvwa'jã], *a.* clear-sighted, discerning; clairvoyant.
clamer [klɑ'me], *v.t.* to cry out, to shout.
clameur [klɑ'mœːr], *n.f.* clamour, outcry.
clan [klã], *n.m.* clan.
clandestin [klãdɛs'tɛ̃], *a.* clandestine, secret.
clandestinement [klãdestin'mã], *adv.* clandestinely, secretly.
clapement [CLAPPEMENT].
clapet [kla'pɛ], *n.m.* valve, clapper.
clapier [kla'pje], *n.m.* hutch (*for rabbits*).
clapir [kla'piːr], *v.i.* to squeak (*of rabbits*). **se clapir**, *v.r.* to hide in a hole, to squat, to cower.
clapotage [klapo'taːʒ], *n.m.* rippling, plashing; lapping.
clapotement [klapot'mã], *n.m.* [CLAPOTAGE].
clapoter [klapo'te], *v.i.* to plash, to chop.
clapoteux [klapo'tø], *a.* (*fem.* **-euse**) plashing, choppy, rough.
clapotis [klapo'ti], *n.m.* [CLAPOTAGE].
clappement *or* **clapement** [klap'mã], *n.m.* clacking, smacking.
clapper [kla'pe], *v.i.* to clack, to smack (*of the tongue*).
claque (1) [klak], *n.f.* slap, smack; claque (*paid applauders at theatres*); (*pl.*) (C) clogs, galoshes.
claque (2) [klak], *n.m.* opera-hat, crush-hat.
claquebois [klak'bwa], *n.m.* xylophone.
claquement [klak'mã], *n.m.* clapping, clap; snapping; cracking; chattering; slamming.
claquemurer [klakmy're], *v.t.* to coop up, to imprison. **se claquemurer**, *v.r.* to shut oneself up.
claquer [kla'ke], *v.t.* to slap, to crack, to slam.—*v.i.* to snap, to crack, to clap, to clack; to slam, to bang.
claqueter [klak'te], *v.i.* (*conjug. like* APPELER) to cackle (*of a hen*); to cry (*of the stork*).
claquette [kla'kɛt], *n.f.* clapper, rattle; *danseur à claquettes*, tap-dancer.

71

claquoir

claquoir [kla'kwaːr], *n.m.* [CLAQUETTE].
clarification [klarifika'sjõ], *n.f.* clarification.
clarifier [klari'fje], *v.t.* to clarify; to purify, to fine. **se clarifier**, *v.r.* to clarify, to settle.
clarine [kla'rin], *n.f.* bell (*attached to cattle*).
clarinette [klari'nɛt], *n.f.* clarinet.
clarinettiste [klarine'tist], *n.* clarinetist.
clarté [klar'te], *n.f.* light, splendour; clearness.
classe [klɑːs], *n.f.* class, order, rank; kind, tribe; class *or* form (*in a school*); classroom; lesson; (*pl.*) school-hours; school-time.
classement [klɑs'mã], *n.m.* classing, classification, filing.
classer [klɑ'se], *v.t.* to class, to classify, to sort; to file.
classeur [klɑ'sœːr], *n.m.* card-index; file.
classification [klasifika'sjõ], *n.f.* classification.
classifier [klasi'fje], *v.t.* to classify.
classique [kla'sik], *a.* classic, classical; standard (*of authors, books etc.*); conventional.—*n.m.* classic (*author, book etc.*).
claudicant [klodi'kã], *a.* lame, limping.
claudication [klodika'sjõ], *n.f.* lameness, limping, halting.
clause [kloːz], *n.f.* clause.
claustral [klos'tral], *a.* (*m. pl.* **-aux**) claustral; monastic.
claustration [klostra'sjõ], *n.f.* claustration, confinement.
claustrer [klos'tre], *v.t.* to cloister, to confine.
claustrophobie [klostrofo'bi], *n.f.* claustrophobia.
clavecin [klav'sɛ̃], *n.m.* harpsichord, clavecin.
clavette [kla'vɛt], *n.f.* (*Tech.*) peg, pin; key, cotter.
claviculaire [klaviky'lɛːr], *a.* clavicular.
clavicule [klavi'kyl], *n.f.* clavicle, collar-bone.
clavier [kla'vje], *n.m.* clavier, key-board (*piano, typewriter*), key-frame.
clayère [klɛ'jɛːr], *n.f.* oyster bed *or* breeding-ground.
clayon [klɛ'jõ], *n.m.* wattle; stand (*for draining cheese*).
clef *or* **clé** [kle], *n.f.* key; plug (*of a cock*); spanner; keystone (*of arch*); (*Mus.*) clef, tuning-key.
clématite [klema'tit], *n.f.* (*Bot.*) clematis.
clémence [kle'mãːs], *n.f.* clemency, mercy.
clément [kle'mã], *a.* clement, merciful, lenient; mild (*of the weather*).
Clémentine [klemã'tin], *f.* Clementine.
clenche [klãːʃ], **clenchette** [klã'ʃɛt], *n.f.* catch *or* latch (*of a lock*).
cleptomane [klɛpto'man], *n.* kleptomaniac.
cleptomanie [klɛptoma'ni], *n.f.* kleptomania.
clerc [klɛːr], *n.m.* clergyman; (*fig.*) scholar.
clergé [klɛr'ʒe], *n.m.* clergy.
clérical [kleri'kal], *a.* (*m. pl.* **-aux**) clerical.
cléricalisme [klerika'lism], *n.m.* clericalism.
cléricaliste [klerika'list], *n.* clericalist.
clic-clac [klik'klak], *n.m.* cracking (*of a whip*).
clichage [kli'ʃaːʒ], *n.m.* stereotyping, stereotype.
cliché [kli'ʃe], *n.m.* stereotype plate, cliché; (*fig.*) stereotyped phrase; (*Phot.*) negative; (*Sculp.*) cast.
clicher [kli'ʃe], *v.t.* to stereotype.
client [kli'ã], *n.m.* (*fem.* **-e**) client (*of law-*

yers etc.); patient (*of physicians*); customer (*of tradesmen*).
clientèle [kliã'tɛl], *n.f.* clientele; practice; connection; custom; goodwill (*of a business*).
clignement [kliɲ'mã], *n.m.* winking, blinking, wink.
cligner [kli'ɲe], *v.t., v.i.* to wink, to blink.
clignotant [kliɲo'tã], *a.* winking, blinking.—*n.m.* (*Motor.*) winker, flashing indicator.
clignotement [kliɲot'mã], *n.m.* winking, blinking.
clignoter [kliɲo'te], *v.i.* to wink, to blink.
climat [kli'ma], *n.m.* climate; region, country.
climatérique [klimate'rik], **climatique** [klima'tik], *a.* climatic.
climatisation [klimatiza'sjõ], *n.f.* air conditioning.
climatisé [klimati'ze], *a.* air-conditioned.
climatiser [klimati'ze], *v.t.* to air-condition.
clin [klɛ̃], *n.m.* wink (*of an eye*).
clinicien [klini'sjɛ̃], *a.m.* clinical.—*n.m.* clinical physician.
clinique [kli'nik], *a.* clinical.—*n.f.* clinical surgery; clinic, nursing-home.
clinquant [klɛ̃'kã], *a.* showy, gaudy, trumpery.—*n.m.* tinsel; (*fig.*) glitter, affectation.
clip [klip], *n.m.* clip-fastened jewel.
clipper [kli'pɛr], *n.m.* (*Naut.* and *Av.*) clipper.
clique [klik], *n.f.* set, coterie, party, clique.
cliquet [kli'kɛ], *n.m.* catch, pawl.
cliqueter [klik'te], *v.i.* (*conjug. like* APPELER) to click *or* jingle; (*Motor.*) to 'pink'.
cliquetis [klik'ti], *n.m.* clanking, clash.
cliquette [kli'kɛt], *n.f.* sinker (*of net*); (*usu. pl.*) bones (*a kind of castanets*).
clissage [kli'saːʒ], *n.m.* wickering.
clisse [klis], *n.f.* wicker mat for draining cheese; basket-work cover for a bottle; (*Surg.*) splint.
clisser [kli'se], *v.t.* to wicker, to cover with wicker-work etc.
clivage [kli'vaːʒ], *n.m.* (*Min.*) cleavage; cleaving.
cliver [kli've], *v.t.* to cleave (*diamonds etc.*). **se cliver**, *v.r.* to split, to be cleft.
cloaque [klo'ak], *n.m.* drain, sewer, sink, cesspool; (*fig.*) filthy hole.
clochage [klo'ʃaːʒ], *n.m.* cultivation under cloches.
clochard [klo'ʃaːr], *n.m.* (*fam.*) tramp, vagrant; (*Am.*) hobo.
cloche [klɔʃ], *n.f.* bell; dish-cover; blister; stew-pan; (*Gard.*) cloche.
clochement [klɔʃ'mã], *n.m.* hobbling, halting.
cloche-pied [klɔʃ'pje], *n.m.* hopping on one leg.
clocher (1) [klɔ'ʃe], *n.m.* steeple, belfry; (*fig.*) parish, native place.
clocher (2) [klɔ'ʃe], *v.t.* (*Gard.*) to cover with a cloche.
clocher (3) [klɔ'ʃe], *v.i.* to limp, to hobble; (*fig., fam.*) to go wrong somewhere, to be defective.
clocheton [klɔʃ'tõ], *n.m.* bell-turret.
clochette [klɔ'ʃɛt], *n.f.* small bell, hand-bell; bell-flower.
cloison [klwa'zõ], *n.f.* partition, division; compartment; (*Naut.*) bulkhead.
cloisonnage [klwazo'naːʒ], **cloisonnement** [klwazon'mã], *n.m.* partition-work, wainscoting.

cloisonner [klwazɔ'ne], v.t. to partition.
cloître [klwɑ:tr], n.m. cloister; cathedral close.
cloîtrer [klwɑ'tre], v.t. to shut up in a cloister, to immure. **se cloîtrer**, v.r. to enter a monastery or convent.
cloîtrier [klwɑ'trie], n.m. (fem. **-ière**) cloistered monk or nun.
clopin-clopant [klɔpɛ̆klɔ'pɑ̃], adv. limpingly, hobbling along.
clopiner [klɔpi'ne], v.i. to limp, to halt, to hobble.
cloporte [klɔ'pɔrt], n.m. woodlouse.
cloque [klɔk], n.f. blister (on skin, paint etc.); blight, rust (of plants).
cloquer [klɔ'ke], v.i. to blister (of paint).
clore [klɔ:r], v.t. irr. (chiefly used in p.p.) to close, to shut; to enclose; to end.—v.i. to close, to shut. **se clore**, v.r. to close, to be closed; to end.
clos [klo], a. closed, sealed; completed; à huis clos, in camera.—n.m. close; enclosure, field.
closeau [klo'zo], n.m. (pl. **-eaux**) small garden.
closerie [kloz'ri], n.f. small enclosed farm or garden.
clôture [klo'ty:r], n.f. enclosure, fence; closing, close; closure; (Relig.) enclosure (of nuns etc.).
clôturer [kloty're], v.t. to close.
clou [klu], n.m. nail, spike, stud; (Path.) carbuncle, boil; clou de girofle, clove.
clouage [klu'a:ʒ], **clouement** [klu'mɑ̃] n.m. nailing.
clouer [klu'e], v.t. to nail; to fix; (fig.) to detain.
clouter [klu'te], v.t. to adorn with nails, to stud; passage clouté, pedestrian crossing.
clouterie [klu'tri], n.f. nail-factory; nail trade.
cloutier [klu'tje], n.m. nail-maker, nail-dealer.
cloutière [klu'tjɛ:r], n.f. nail-box.
clovisse [klɔ'vis], n.f. winkle; cockle.
clown [klun], n.m. clown.
cloyère [klwa'jɛ:r], n.f. oyster-basket.
club [klʌb, klyb], n.m. club (sporting or political).
clystère [klis'tɛ:r], n.m. clyster, injection, enema.
coaccusé [koaky'ze], n.m. (fem. **-ée**) fellow-prisoner; co-defendant.
coacquéreur [koake'rœ:r], n.m. (fem. **-euse**) co-purchaser, joint buyer.
coacquisition [koakizi'sjɔ̃], n.f. joint purchase.
coactif [koak'tif], a. (fem. **-tive**) coactive.
coaction [koak'sjɔ̃], n.f. coercion, compulsion.
coadjuteur [koadʒy'tœ:r], n.m. coadjutor.
coadjutrice [koadʒy'tris], n.f. coadjutrix.
coagulant [koagy'lɑ̃], a. coagulant.
coagulation [koagyla'sjɔ̃], n.f. coagulation.
coaguler [koagy'le], v.t. to coagulate. **se coaguler**, v.r. to coagulate.
coaliser [koali'ze], v.t. to unite in a coalition. **se coaliser**, v.r. to coalesce, to league, to unite, to combine.
coalition [koali'sjɔ̃], n.f. coalition, union, league.
coassement [koas'mɑ̃], n.m. croaking (of frogs).
coasser [koa'se], v.i. to croak (of frogs).

coassocié [koasɔ'sje], n.m. (fem. **-ée**) co-partner.
coauteur [koo'tœ:r], n.m. co-author.
cobalt [kɔ'balt], n.m. cobalt.
cobaye [kɔ'ba:j], n.m. guinea-pig.
cobra [kɔ'bra], n.m. cobra, hooded-snake.
cocagne [kɔ'kaɲ], n.f. mât de cocagne, greasy pole; pays de cocagne, land of plenty.
cocaïne [kɔka'in], n.f. cocaine.
cocarde [kɔ'kard], n.f. cockade; rosette.
cocasse [kɔ'kas], a. (fam.) odd, laughable, comical.
cocasserie [kɔkas'ri], n.f. drollery, foolery, farce.
coccinelle [kɔksi'nɛl], n.f. lady-bird.
coche (1) [kɔʃ], n.m. coach; c'est la mouche du coche, he is a busy-body.
coche (2) [kɔʃ], n.f. notch, score.
coche (3) [kɔʃ], n.f. sow.
cochenille [kɔʃ'ni:j], n.f. cochineal.
cocher (1) [kɔ'ʃe], n.m. coachman, driver.
cocher (2) [kɔ'ʃe], v.t. to notch.
cochère [kɔ'ʃɛ:r], a.f. for carriages; porte cochère, carriage-entrance, gateway.
cochet [kɔ'ʃɛ], n.m. young cock, cockerel.
cochon [kɔ'ʃɔ̃], n.m. hog, pig; pork; cochon d'Inde, guinea-pig.
cochonnée [kɔʃɔ'ne], n.f. litter (of pigs).
cochonner [kɔʃɔ'ne], v.i. to farrow, to pig.
cochonnerie [kɔʃɔn'ri], n.f. nastiness, filth.
cochonnet [kɔʃɔ'nɛ], n.m. young pig; jack (at bowls).
cocktail [kɔk'tɛl], n.m. cocktail; cocktail party.
coco [kɔ'ko], n.m. coco-nut.
cocon [kɔ'kɔ̃], n.m. cocoon.
cocotier [kɔkɔ'tje], n.m. coco-nut palm.
coction [kɔk'sjɔ̃], n.f. coction, boiling; digestion (of food).
code [kɔd], n.m. code (digest or collection of laws); law, rule.
codemandeur [kɔdəmɑ̃'dœ:r], n.m. (fem. **-eresse**) co-plaintiff.
coder [kɔ'de], v.t. to code (telegram).
codétenteur [kodetɑ̃'tœ:r], n.m. (fem. **-trice**) joint-holder.
codétenu [kodet'ny], n.m. (fem. **-e**) fellow-prisoner.
codicillaire [kɔdisi'lɛ:r], a. contained in a codicil.
codicille [kɔdi'sil], n.m. codicil, rider.
codifier [kɔdi'fje], v.t. to codify.
codirecteur [kodirɛk'tœ:r], n.m. (fem. **-trice**) joint manager.
codonataire [kɔdɔna'tɛ:r], n. joint donee.
codonateur [kɔdɔna'tœ:r], n.m. (fem. **-trice**) joint donor.
coéquipier [koeki'pje], n.m. fellow member (of a crew, team etc.).
coercer [kɔɛr'se], v.t. to coerce.
coercition [kɔɛrsi'sjɔ̃], n.f. coercion.
cœur [kœ:r], n.m. heart; (fig.) bosom, mind, soul; courage; core, middle; love, affection; hearts (cards).
coexistant [kɔɛgzis'tɑ̃], a. coexistent.
coexistence [kɔɛgzis'tɑ̃:s], n.f. coexistence.
coexister [kɔɛgzis'te], v.i. to coexist.
coffre [kɔfr], n.m. chest, trunk; coffer; (Naut.) mooring-buoy; boot (of a car).
coffre-fort [kɔfrə'fɔ:r], n.m. (pl. **coffres-forts**) strong-box, safe.

73

coffret

coffret [kɔ'frɛ], *n.m.* little chest, casket.
cogitation [kɔʒita'sjɔ̃], *n.f.* cogitation, reflection.
cognac [kɔ'nak], *n.m.* Cognac brandy.
cognasse [kɔ'nas], *n.f.* wild quince.
cognassier [kɔna'sje], *n.m.* quince-tree.
cognée [kɔ'ne], *n.f.* axe, hatchet.
cogner [kɔ'ne], *v.t.* to knock in, to drive in; to thump.—*v.i.* to hit, to bump (*contre*); to knock (*engine*). **se cogner,** *v.r.* to knock (*against*).
cohabitant [koabi'tɑ̃], *a.* cohabiting (*with*).
cohabitation [koabita'sjɔ̃], *n.f.* cohabitation.
cohabiter [koabi'te], *v.i.* to cohabit.
cohérence [kɔe'rɑ̃ːs], *n.f.* coherence.
cohérent [kɔe'rɑ̃], *a.* coherent.
cohériter [koeri'te], *v.i.* to inherit conjointly.
cohéritier [koeri'tje], *n.m.* (*fem.* **-ière**) co-heir, co-heiress.
cohésif [kɔe'zif], *a.* (*fem.* **-sive**) cohesive.
cohésion [kɔe'zjɔ̃], *n.f.* cohesion.
cohorte [kɔ'ɔrt], *n.f.* cohort; (*poet.*) troop, host; (*colloq.*) crew, gang.
cohue [kɔ'y], *n.f.* throng, mob, crush.
coi [kwa], *a.* (*fem.* **coite** (1)) quiet, calm, still.
coiffe [kwaf], *n.f.* hood, head-dress.
coiffer [kwa'fe], *v.t.* to put on the head of; to dress the hair of; (*fig.*) to infatuate.—*v.i.* to dress hair; to become; to suit. **se coiffer,** *v.r.* to put one's hat on; to do one's hair.
coiffeur [kwa'fœːr], *n.m.* (*fem.* **-euse**) hair-dresser.—*n.f.* (**-euse**) lady's dressing-table.
coiffure [kwa'fyːr], *n.f.* head-dress, hairstyle.
coin [kwɛ̃], *n.m.* corner, angle, nook; (*Coin. etc.*) stamp.
coincer [kwɛ̃'se], *v.t.* (*conjug. like* COMMENCER) to wedge. **se coincer,** *v.r.* to jam (*of machines*).
coïncidence [kɔɛ̃si'dɑ̃ːs], *n.f.* coincidence.
coïncident [kɔɛ̃si'dɑ̃], *a.* coincident.
coïncider [kɔɛ̃si'de], *v.i.* to coincide, to be coincident.
coing [kwɛ̃], *n.m.* quince.
coïntéressé [kɔɛ̃tere'se], *a.* jointly interested.—*n.m.* (*fem.* **-ée**) associate, partner.
coite (1) [kwat], [COI].
coite (2), **coitte** [COUETTE].
cojouissance [kɔʒwi'sɑ̃ːs], *n.f.* (*Law*) joint use.
coke [kɔk], *n.m.* coke.
cokéfier [kɔke'fje], *v.t.* to coke.
col [kɔl], *n.m.* neck (*of a bottle, dress etc.*); collar; pass, col (*of mountain*).
colback [kɔl'bak], *n.m.* busby.
colchique [kɔl'ʃik], *n.m.* (*Bot.*) meadow-saffron, colchicum.
colégataire [kolega'tɛːr], *n.* co-legatee.
coléoptère [kɔleɔp'tɛːr], *a.* coleopterous.—*n.m.* beetle.
colère [kɔ'lɛːr], *n.f.* anger, wrath, rage, fury.
colérique [kɔle'rik], *a.* choleric, irascible.
colibri [kɔli'bri], *n.m.* humming-bird.
colifichet [kɔlifi'ʃɛ], *n.m.* trinket, knick-knack.
colimaçon [kɔlima'sɔ̃], *n.m.* snail; *escalier en colimaçon,* spiral staircase.
colin-maillard [kɔlɛ̃ma'jaːr], *n.m. inv.* blind-man's-buff.
colique [kɔ'lik], *n.f.* colic, stomach-ache.
colis [kɔ'li], *n.m.* package, parcel, case.
collaborateur [kɔlabɔra'tœːr], *n.m.* (*fem.* **-trice**) collaborator.

collaboration [kɔlabɔra'sjɔ̃], *n.f.* collaboration.
collaborer [kɔlabɔ're], *v.i.* to collaborate.
collage [kɔ'laːʒ], *n.m.* pasting, gluing; paper-hanging; (*Art*) collage.
collant [kɔ'lɑ̃], *a.* sticky; tight, close-fitting.
collatéral [kɔllate'ral], *a.* (*m. pl.* **-aux**) collateral.
collatéralement [kɔllateral'mɑ̃], *adv.* collaterally.
collation [kɔlla'sjɔ̃], *n.f.* light meal; comparison (*of documents etc.*).
collationnement [kɔllasjɔn'mɑ̃], *n.m.* collating, comparing.
collationner [kɔllasjɔ'ne], *v.t.* to collate, to compare.—*v.i.* to have a snack.
colle [kɔl], *n.f.* paste, gum; poser; sham, fib.
collecte [kɔ'lɛkt], *n.f.* collection (*of money etc.*); collect (*prayer*).
collecteur [kɔlɛk'tœːr], *n.m.* (*fem.* **-trice**) collector.
collectif [kɔlɛk'tif], *a.* (*fem.* **-tive**) collective.
collection [kɔlɛk'sjɔ̃], *n.f.* collection; set.
collectionner [kɔlɛksjɔ'ne], *v.t.* to collect, to make collections of things.
collectionneur [kɔlɛksjɔ'nœːr], *n.m.* (*fem.* **-euse**) collector.
collectivement [kɔlɛktiv'mɑ̃], *adv.* collectively.
collectivisme [kɔlɛkti'vism], *n.m.* collectivism.
collectiviste [kɔlɛkti'vist], *n.* collectivist.
collectivité [kɔlɛktivi'te], *n.f.* collectivity; common ownership.
collège [kɔ'lɛːʒ], *n.m.* college; grammar-school.
collégien [kɔle'ʒjɛ̃], *n.m.* (*fem.* **-enne**) high-school boy or girl.
collègue [kɔl'lɛg], *n.* colleague.
coller [kɔ'le], *v.t.* to paste, to glue; to stick together.—*v.i.* to stick, to adhere. **se coller,** *v.r.* to stick to.
collerette [kɔl'rɛt], *n.f.* collar (*for ladies*).
collet [kɔ'lɛ], *n.m.* collar (*of gown etc.*); cape; flange; snare.
colleter [kɔl'te], *v.t.* (*conjug. like* APPELER) to collar, to seize by the neck.—*v.i.* to set snares. **se colleter,** *v.r.* to come to grips (*with someone*).
colleur [kɔ'lœːr], *n.m.* (*fem.* **-euse**) gluer, paster, paper-hanger; bill-sticker.
collier [kɔ'lje], *n.m.* necklace; gold chain (*of knightly orders etc.*); collar (*for animals*).
colline [kɔ'lin], *n.f.* hill, hillock.
collision [kɔli'zjɔ̃], *n.f.* collision.
collocation [kɔlloka'sjɔ̃], *n.f.* classification.
colloque [kɔl'lɔk], *n.m.* colloquy, conference.
collusion [kɔlly'zjɔ̃], *n.f.* collusion.
collusoire [kɔlly'zwaːr], *a.* collusory, collusive.
Colomb [kɔ'lɔ̃], *m.* Columbus.
colombe [kɔ'lɔ̃:b], *n.f.* (*poet.*) pigeon, dove.
Colombie [kɔlɔ̃'bi], **la,** *f.* Colombia.
colombien [kɔlɔ̃'bjɛ̃], *a.* (*fem.* **-enne**) Colombian.—*n.m.* (**Colombien,** *fem.* **-enne**) Colombian (*person*).
colombier [kɔlɔ̃'bje], *n.m.* dove-cot, pigeon-house.
colombin [kɔlɔ̃'bɛ̃], *a.* columbine; dove-colour.
colombophile [kɔlɔ̃bɔ'fil], *a.* and *n.* pigeon-fancier.

colon [kɔ'lɔ̃], *n.m.* colonist, planter; settler.
côlon [ko'lɔ̃], *n.m.* (*Anat.*) colon.
colonel [kɔlɔ'nɛl], *n.m.* colonel; (*Av.*) group captain.
colonial [kɔlɔ'njal], *a.* (*m. pl.* **-aux**) colonial. —*n.m.* (*fem.* **-e**) colonial.
colonie [kɔlɔ'ni], *n.f.* colony, settlement; *colonie de vacances*, holiday camp.
colonisation [kɔlɔniza'sjɔ̃], *n.f.* colonization.
coloniser [kɔlɔni'ze], *v.t.* to colonize.
colonnade [kɔlɔ'nad], *n.f.* (*Arch.*) colonnade.
colonne [kɔ'lɔn], *n.f.* column, pillar; column (*of units, tens etc.*).
colonnette [kɔlɔ'nɛt], *n.f.* little column.
colorant [kɔlɔ'rɑ̃], *a.* colouring.—*n.m.* dye.
coloration [kɔlɔra'sjɔ̃], *n.f.* coloration, staining.
colorer [kɔlɔ're], *v.t.* to colour, to dye; to varnish. **se colorer**, *v.r.* to colour (*of a thing*).
coloriage [kɔlɔ'rjaːʒ], *n.m.* (*Paint.*) colouring.
colorier [kɔlɔ'rje], *v.t.* to colour, to stain (*a drawing etc.*).
coloris [kɔlɔ'ri], *n.m.* colouring, art of colouring.
coloriste [kɔlɔ'rist], *n.* colourer; colourist.
colossal [kɔlɔ'sal], *a.* (*m. pl.* **-aux**) colossal.
colosse [kɔ'los], *n.m.* colossus, giant.
colportage [kɔlpɔr'taːʒ], *n.m.* hawking, peddling.
colporter [kɔlpɔr'te], *v.t.* to hawk about; to spread.
colporteur [kɔlpɔr'tœːr], *n.m.* hawker, pedlar.
coltiner [kɔlti'ne], *v.t.* to carry heavy loads (*on head and back*).
coltineur [kɔlti'nœːr], *n.m.* coal-heaver, load-porter.
colza [kɔl'za], *n.m.* colza, rape, rape-seed.
coma [kɔ'ma], *n.m.* coma.
comateux [kɔma'tø], *a.* (*fem.* **-euse**) comatose.
combat [kɔ̃'ba], *n.m.* combat, fight, battle, contest; struggle; *hors de combat*, disabled.
combattant [kɔ̃ba'tɑ̃], *n.m.* combatant; champion; *anciens combattants*, ex-service men.
combattre [kɔ̃'batr], *v.t.* (*conjug. like* BATTRE) to fight, to combat, to wage war against; to strive against.—*v.i.* to fight, to vie, to struggle. **se combattre**, *v.r.* to combat; to contend with each other.
combien [kɔ̃'bjɛ̃], *adv.* how much, how many; how; how far; how long.
combinaison [kɔ̃bine'zɔ̃], *n.f.* combination; contrivance, scheme; overalls; slip (*woman's undergarment*).
combiné [kɔ̃bi'ne], *n.m.* (*Chem.*) compound; (*Rad.*) radiogram.
combiner [kɔ̃bi'ne], *v.t.* to combine; (*fig.*) to contrive.
comble [kɔ̃bl], *n.m.* heaping up above a full measure; summit; (*fig.*) zenith; (*pl.*) roof-timbers.—*a.* full, heaped up, full to the top; *salle comble*, house full.
comblement [kɔ̃blə'mɑ̃], *n.m.* filling up, heaping up.
combler [kɔ̃'ble], *v.t.* to heap up, to fill up; to complete; to overwhelm.
comburant [kɔ̃by'rɑ̃], *a.* (*Chem.*) causing burning (*of oxygen etc.*).—*n.m.* fuel.
combustibilité [kɔ̃bystibili'te], *n.f.* combustibility.

combustible [kɔ̃bys'tibl], *a.* combustible.—*n.m.* combustible; fuel, firing.
combustion [kɔ̃bys'tjɔ̃], *n.f.* combustion, flame.
comédie [kɔme'di], *n.f.* comedy; theatre; players.
comédien [kɔme'djɛ̃], *n.m.* (*fem.* **-enne**) comedian, actor, actress, player; (*fig.*) hypocrite.
comestible [kɔmes'tibl], *a.* edible, eatable.—*n.m.* eatable; (*pl.*) eatables.
comète [kɔ'mɛt], *n.f.* comet.
comice [kɔ'mis], *n.m.* meeting; electoral meeting; *comice agricole*, agricultural show.
comique [kɔ'mik], *a.* comic; comical, ludicrous.—*n.m.* comic art, comedy.
comiquement [kɔmik'mɑ̃], *adv.* comically.
comité [kɔmi'te], *n.m.* committee, board.
commandant [kɔmɑ̃'dɑ̃], *a.* commanding.—*n.m.* (*fem.* **-e**) commander, commanding officer, commandant; major.
commande [kɔ'mɑ̃ːd], *n.f.* order; (*Mach.*) driving-wheel.
commandement [kɔmɑ̃d'mɑ̃], *n.m.* command; authority, control; order; commandment, law.
commander [kɔmɑ̃'de], *v.t.* to command, to order; to govern; to overlook.—*v.i.* to command, to have authority. **se commander**, *v.r.* to control oneself.
commandeur [kɔmɑ̃'dœːr], *n.m.* commander (*in orders of knighthood*).
commanditaire [kɔmɑ̃di'tɛːr], *n.* sleeping partner.
commandite [kɔmɑ̃'dit], *n.f.* limited partnership.
commanditer [kɔmɑ̃di'te], *v.t.* to finance (*a commercial undertaking*).
commando [kɔmɑ̃'do], *n.m.* commando.
comme [kɔm], *adv.* as; like, such as; almost, nearly, as if; how, in what way; to what extent.—*conj.* as, since, because.
commémoraison [kɔmemɔre'zɔ̃], *n.f.* (*R.-C. Ch.*) commemoration, remembrance.
commémoratif [kɔmemɔra'tif], *a.* (*fem.* **-tive**) commemorative.
commémoration [kɔmemɔra'sjɔ̃], *n.f.* commemoration.
commémorer [kɔmemɔ're], *v.t.* to commemorate, to remember.
commençant [kɔmɑ̃'sɑ̃], *n.m.* (*fem.* **-e**) beginner, novice.
commencement [kɔmɑ̃s'mɑ̃], *n.m.* beginning, commencement.
commencer [kɔmɑ̃'se], *v.t., v.i.* (*see Verb Tables*) to begin, to commence; to initiate.
commensal [kɔmɑ̃'sal], *n.m.* (*m. pl.* **-aux**) habitual guest; fellow-boarder, messmate.
commensurable [kɔmɑ̃sy'rabl], *a.* commensurable.
comment [kɔ'mɑ̃], *adv.* how, in what manner; why, wherefore.—*int.* what! indeed!—*n.m.* the why and wherefore.
commentaire [kɔmɑ̃'tɛːr], *n.m.* commentary, exposition; (*fig.*) unfavourable comment.
commentateur [kɔmɑ̃ta'tœːr], *n.m.* (*fem.* **-trice**) commentator, annotator.
commenter [kɔmɑ̃'te], *v.t.* to comment on, to explain; to annotate.—*v.i.* to criticize adversely.

commérage [kɔme'raːʒ], *n.m.* gossip, tittle-tattle.

commerçant [kɔmɛr'sɑ̃], *a.* commercial, mercantile, trading.—*n.m.* (*fem.* -e) merchant, tradesman, shopkeeper.

commerce [kɔ'mɛrs], *n.m.* commerce, trade, trading, traffic; intercourse, dealings.

commercer [kɔmɛr'se], *v.i.* (*conjug. like* COMMENCER) to trade, to deal.

commercial [kɔmɛr'sjal], *a.* (*m. pl.* -aux) commercial.

commercialement [kɔmɛrsjal'mɑ̃], *adv.* commercially.

commercialisation [kɔmɛrsjaliza'sjɔ̃], *n.f.* commercialization.

commercialiser [kɔmɛrsjali'ze], *v.t.* to commercialize.

commère [kɔ'mɛr], *n.f.* godmother; gossip.

commettre [kɔ'mɛtr], *v.t. irr.* (*conjug. like* METTRE) to commit, to perpetrate; to appoint, to empower; to entrust. **se commettre**, *v.r.* to commit oneself.

commis (1) [kɔ'mi], *n.m.* (*fem.* **commise**) clerk; *commis voyageur*, commercial traveller.

commis (2) [kɔ'mi], *a.* committed, appointed.

commisération [kɔmizera'sjɔ̃], *n.f.* commiseration, compassion, pity.

commissaire [kɔmi'sɛr], *n.m.* commissioner; manager, steward, trustee; purser (*of a vessel*).

commissaire-priseur [kɔmisɛrpri'zœːr], *n.m.* auctioneer, valuer.

commissariat [kɔmisa'rja], *n.m.* commissaryship, trusteeship; (*Mil., Navy*) commissariat; police station.

commission [kɔmi'sjɔ̃], *n.f.* commission, charge; errand; power; (*Comm.*) percentage; warrant.

commissionnaire [kɔmisjɔ'nɛr], *n.m.* commission agent, commissionnaire; messenger, porter.

commissioner [kɔmisjɔ'ne], *v.t.* to empower, to commission; to order (*goods*).

commode [kɔ'mɔd], *a.* convenient, commodious, handy; comfortable, suitable; easy.—*n.f.* chest of drawers, commode.

commodément [kɔmɔde'mɑ̃], *adv.* commodiously, conveniently; comfortably, suitably.

commodité [kɔmɔdi'te], *n.f.* convenience, accommodation.

commotion [kɔmo'sjɔ̃], *n.f.* commotion; shock; concussion.

commotionné [kɔmosjɔ'ne], *a.* suffering from concussion.

commuable [kɔ'mɥabl], *a.* commutable.

commun [kɔ'mœ̃], *a.* common; usual, ordinary; mean, vulgar; *le bien commun*, the common weal; *lieux communs*, commonplaces.—*n.m.* common people.

communal [kɔmy'nal], *a.* (*m. pl.* -aux) communal, parochial; common.—*n.m. pl.* (*biens*) *communaux*, communal property.

communauté [kɔmyno'te], *n.f.* community, society, corporation.

commune [kɔ'myn], *n.f.* commune (*parish, township, in France*).

communément [kɔmyne'mɑ̃], *adv.* commonly, usually.

communiant [kɔmy'njɑ̃], *n.m.* (*fem.* -e) communicant.

communicatif [kɔmynika'tif], *a.* (*fem.* -tive) communicative, open.

communication [kɔmynika'sjɔ̃], *n.f.* intercourse, communication; (*Teleph.*) call.

communicativement [kɔmynikativ'mɑ̃], *adv.* communicatively.

communier [kɔmy'nje], *v.i.* to communicate, to receive the sacrament.

communion [kɔmy'njɔ̃], *n.f.* communion, fellowship; persuasion; sacrament.

communiqué [kɔmyni'ke], *n.m.* statement, communiqué.

communiquer [kɔmyni'ke], *v.t.* to communicate, to impart; to tell, to acquaint.—*v.i.* to be in contact *or* correspondence (*with*).

communisant [kɔmyni'zɑ̃], *a.* communistic.—*n.m.* (*fem.* -e) fellow-traveller.

communisme [kɔmy'nism], *n.m.* communism.

communiste [kɔmy'nist], *n.* communist.

commutable [kɔmy'tabl], [COMMUABLE].

commutateur [kɔmyta'tœːr], *n.m.* (*Elec.*) switch.

compact [kɔ̃'pakt], *a.* compact, dense.

compagne [kɔ̃'paɲ], *n.f.* female companion, consort; playmate.

compagnie [kɔ̃pa'ɲi], *n.f.* society, companionship; company; (*Comm.*) company.

compagnon [kɔ̃pa'ɲɔ̃], *n.m.* companion, comrade; playmate; mate; (*Bot.*) campion.

comparable [kɔ̃pa'rabl], *a.* comparable.

comparablement [kɔ̃parablə'mɑ̃], *adv.* in comparison (*with*).

comparaison [kɔ̃parɛ'zɔ̃], *n.f.* comparison; similitude.

comparaître [kɔ̃pa'rɛːtr], *v.i. irr.* (*conjug. like* CONNAÎTRE) to appear (*before a tribunal*).

comparant [kɔ̃pa'rɑ̃], *n.m.* (*fem.* -e) person appearing in court on a summons.

comparatif [kɔ̃para'tif], *a.* (*fem.* -tive) comparative.—*n.m.* comparative degree.

comparativement [kɔ̃parativ'mɑ̃], *adv.* comparatively.

comparer [kɔ̃pa're], *v.t.* to compare. **se comparer**, *v.r.* to be compared.

compartiment [kɔ̃parti'mɑ̃], *n.m.* compartment, division.

compas [kɔ̃'pa], *n.m.* pair of compasses; mariner's compass.

compassé [kɔ̃pa'se], *a.* formal, stiff, starchy.

compasser [kɔ̃pa'se], *v.t.* to measure, set out; to proportion, to regulate; (*fig.*) to weigh, to consider.

compassion [kɔ̃pa'sjɔ̃], *n.f.* compassion, pity, mercy.

compatibilité [kɔ̃patibili'te], *n.f.* compatibility.

compatible [kɔ̃pa'tibl], *a.* compatible, consistent.

compatir [kɔ̃pa'tiːr], *v.i.* to sympathize; to agree, to be compatible (*with*).

compatissant [kɔ̃pati'sɑ̃], *a.* compassionate, tender.

compatriote [kɔ̃patri'ɔt], *n.* compatriot, fellow-countryman.

compendium [kɔ̃pɛn'djɔm], *n.m.* summary.

compensable [kɔ̃pɑ̃'sabl], *a.* that may be compensated.

compensation [kɔ̃pɑ̃sa'sjɔ̃], *n.f.* compensation, amends, reparation.

compensatoire [kɔ̃pɑ̃sa'twaːr], *a.* compensatory.

compenser [kɔ̃pɑ̃'se], *v.t.* to counterbalance, to compensate, to make up for. **se compenser,** *v.r.* to compensate each other; to be set off against.

compère [kɔ̃'pɛːr], *n.m.* godfather; (*fig.*) gossip, crony; confederate.

compétence [kɔ̃pe'tɑ̃ːs], *n.f.* competence, cognizance; (*fig.*) department, province; proficiency.

compétent [kɔ̃pe'tɑ̃], *a.* competent, qualified; (*fig.*) suitable, requisite.

compétiteur [kɔ̃peti'tœːr], *n.m.* (*fem.* **-trice**) competitor, candidate.

compétitif [kɔ̃peti'tif], *a.* (*fem.* **-tive**) competitive.

compétition [kɔ̃peti'sjɔ̃], *n.f.* competition, rivalry.

compilateur [kɔ̃pila'tœːr], *n.m.* compiler.

compilation [kɔ̃pila'sjɔ̃], *n.f.* compilation.

compiler [kɔ̃pi'le], *v.t.* to compile.

complainte [kɔ̃'plɛ̃ːt], *n.f.* tragic *or* plaintive ballad, lament; (*fig.*) lamentation.

complaire [kɔ̃'plɛːr], *v.i. irr.* (*conjug. like* PLAIRE) to be pleasing (**à**). **se complaire,** *v.r.* to delight (*dans* or **à**).

complaisamment [kɔ̃plɛza'mɑ̃], *adv.* complaisantly, obligingly.

complaisance [kɔ̃plɛ'zɑ̃ːs], *n.f.* complaisance, good-nature; complacency.

complaisant [kɔ̃plɛ'zɑ̃], *a.* affable, civil, obliging, kind.—*n.m.* (*fem.* **-e**) flatterer; go-between.

complément [kɔ̃ple'mɑ̃], *n.m.* complement; (*Gram.*) object; extension (*of subject*).

complémentaire [kɔ̃plemɑ̃'tɛːr], *a.* complementary, completing.

complet [kɔ̃'plɛ], *a.* (*fem.* **-plète**) complete, whole; full, filled.—*n.m.* complement, full number; suit (*of clothes*).

complètement [kɔ̃plɛt'mɑ̃], *adv.* completely, entirely, thoroughly.

complétement [kɔ̃plet'mɑ̃], *n.m.* finishing, completion.

compléter [kɔ̃ple'te], *v.t.* (*conjug. like* CÉDER) to complete, to perfect; to fill up.

complexe [kɔ̃'plɛks], *a.* complex, complicated.—*n.m.* **complexe d'infériorité,** inferiority complex.

complexion [kɔ̃plɛk'sjɔ̃], *n.f.* constitution; disposition, humour, temper.

complexité [kɔ̃plɛksi'te], *n.f.* complexity.

complication [kɔ̃plika'sjɔ̃], *n.f.* complication, intricacy.

complice [kɔ̃'plis], *a.* accessory, privy to.—*n.* accomplice, accessory.

complicité [kɔ̃plisi'te], *n.f.* complicity, participation.

compliment [kɔ̃pli'mɑ̃], *n.m.* compliment; (*pl.*) regards, congratulations.

complimenter [kɔ̃plimɑ̃'te], *v.t.* to compliment, to congratulate.

complimenteur [kɔ̃plimɑ̃'tœːr], *a.* and *n.m.* (*fem.* **-euse**) over-complimentary; obsequious (person).

compliqué [kɔ̃pli'ke], *a.* complicated, intricate.

compliquer [kɔ̃pli'ke], *v.t.* to complicate, to entangle. **se compliquer,** *v.r.* to become complicated

complot [kɔ̃'plo], *n.m.* plot, conspiracy; *chef du complot,* ringleader.

comploter [kɔ̃plo'te], *v.t.* to plot.

comploteur [kɔ̃plo'tœːr], *n.m.* plotter, schemer.

componction [kɔ̃pɔ̃k'sjɔ̃], *n.f.* compunction; solemn manners *or* expression.

comportement [kɔ̃pɔrtə'mɑ̃], *n.m.* demeanour, deportment, behaviour.

comporter [kɔ̃pɔr'te], *v.t.* to permit, to allow; to require; to comprise. **se comporter,** *v.r.* to behave; to act, to manage.

composant [kɔ̃po'zɑ̃], *n.m.* (*Chem.*) component, constituent.

composé [kɔ̃po'ze], *a.* composed, compound. —*n.m.* compound.

composer [kɔ̃po'ze], *v.t.* to compose, to compound, to make up; to form, to create; to adjust, to regulate; *composer un numéro,* to dial a number.—*v.i.* to compound, to compromise, to make up.

composeuse [kɔ̃po'zøːz], *n.f.* type-setting machine.

composite [kɔ̃po'zit], *a.* composite.

compositeur [kɔ̃pozi'tœːr], *n.m.* (*fem.* **-trice**) composer (*of music*); (*Print.*) compositor.

composition [kɔ̃pozi'sjɔ̃], *n.f.* composition; chemical composition; settlement; (*fig.*) disposition; (*Print.*) composing.

compost [kɔ̃'post], *n.m.* (*Agric.*) compost.

composter [kɔ̃pos'te], *v.t.* to compost; to date *or* obliterate (*ticket etc.*).

compote [kɔ̃'pot], *n.f.* stewed fruit, compote.

compotier [kɔ̃po'tje], *n.m.* fruit-dish.

compréhensibilité [kɔ̃preɑ̃sibili'te], *n.f.* comprehensibility.

compréhensible [kɔ̃preɑ̃'sibl], *a.* understandable, intelligible.

compréhensif [kɔ̃preɑ̃'sif], *a.* (*fem.* **-sive**) comprehensive; broadminded.

compréhension [kɔ̃preɑ̃'sjɔ̃], *n.f.* comprehension; (*fig.*) understanding, intelligence.

compréhensivité [kɔ̃preɑ̃sivi'te], *n.f.* comprehensiveness, faculty of comprehending.

comprendre [kɔ̃'prɑ̃ːdr], *v.t. irr.* (*conjug. like* PRENDRE) to include, to comprise; to understand, to conceive, to realize.

compresse [kɔ̃'prɛːs], *n.f.* (*Surg.*) compress, pledget.

compresseur [kɔ̃prɛ'sœːr], *a.* compressive.— *n.m.* compressor, roller.

compressif [kɔ̃prɛ'sif], *a.* (*fem.* **-ssive**) compressive, repressive.

compression [kɔ̃prɛ'sjɔ̃], *n.f.* compression; (*fig.*) constraint.

comprimable [kɔ̃pri'mabl], *a.* compressible.

comprimé [kɔ̃pri'me], *a.* compressed, condensed; kept under.—*n.m.* (*Pharm.*) tabloid, tablet.

comprimer [kɔ̃pri'me], *v.t.* to compress, to condense; to repress, to restrain.

compris [kɔ̃'pri], *a.* understood; included.

compromettant [kɔ̃promɛ'tɑ̃], *a.* compromising; damaging.

compromettre [kɔ̃pro'mɛtr], *v.t. irr.* (*conjug. like* METTRE) to expose, to commit, to compromise, to jeopardize.—*v.i.* to compromise; to submit to arbitration. **se compromettre,** *v.r.* to compromise oneself.

compromis [kɔ̃pro'mi], *n.m.* mutual agreement, compromise.

comptabilité [kɔ̃tabili'te], *n.f.* accountancy, book-keeping; accountant's department.

comptable [kɔ̃'tabl], *a.* responsible for accounts; accountable, responsible.—*n.m.* accountant, book-keeper; (*Naut.*) purser.

comptant [kɔ̃'tɑ̃], *a.m.* (*of money*) ready; (*of payment*) in cash.—*n.m.* ready money, cash.

compte [kɔ̃:t], *n.m.* reckoning; account, score, statement, report; (*fig.*) profit; esteem, value; *se rendre compte de*, to realize.

compte-gouttes [kɔ̃t'gut], *n.m. inv.* (*Med.*) drop-tube, dropper; filler; (*fig.*) *au compte-gouttes*, sparingly.

compte-pas [kɔ̃tə'pa], *n.m.* pedometer.

compter [kɔ̃'te], *v.t.* to count, to calculate, to compute; to pay down; to comprise.—*v.i.* to reckon, to count; to be reckoned; to expect; to intend; to rely (*sur*). **se compter**, *v.r.* to be reckoned *or* included.

compteur [kɔ̃'tœːr], *a.* and *n.m.* (*fem.* **-euse**) that counts; computer.—*n.m.* meter; (*C*) *compteur de stationnement*, parking meter.

comptoir [kɔ̃'twaːr], *n.m.* counter; cashier's desk; counting-house; branch bank; factory.

compulser [kɔ̃pyl'se], *v.t.* to inspect (*documents etc.*).

computation [kɔ̃pyta'sjɔ̃], *n.f.* computation.

computer [kɔ̃py'te], *v.t.* to compute.

comtal [kɔ̃'tal], *a.* (*m. pl.* **-aux**) pertaining to an earl *or* a countess.

comte [kɔ̃:t], *n.m.* count; earl.

comté [kɔ̃'te], *n.m.* county, shire; earldom.

comtesse [kɔ̃'tɛs], *n.f.* countess.

concassage [kɔ̃ka'sa:ʒ], *n.m.* pounding, crushing.

concasser [kɔ̃ka'se], *v.t.* to pound, to crush.

concasseur [kɔ̃ka'sœːr], *n.m.* crushing-mill; steam-roller.

concave [kɔ̃'kaːv], *a.* concave.

concavité [kɔ̃kavi'te], *n.f.* concave; concavity.

concéder [kɔ̃se'de], *v.t.* (*conjug. like* CÉDER) to grant, to concede, to allow.

concentration [kɔ̃sɑ̃tra'sjɔ̃], *n.f.* concentration; condensation; *camp de concentration*, concentration camp.

concentré [kɔ̃sɑ̃'tre], *a.* concentrated; (*fig.*) silent, reserved.—*n.m.* extract.

concentrer [kɔ̃sɑ̃'tre], *v.t.* to concentrate, to focus; (*fig.*) to repress, to smother (*anger etc.*). **se concentrer**, *v.r.* to concentrate; to withdraw within oneself.

concentrique [kɔ̃sɑ̃'trik], *a.* concentric.

concentriquement [kɔ̃sɑ̃trik'mɑ̃], *adv.* concentrically.

concept [kɔ̃'sɛpt], *n.m.* concept.

conceptibilité [kɔ̃sɛptibili'te], *n.f.* conceivability.

conceptible [kɔ̃sɛp'tibl], *a.* conceivable.

conceptif [kɔ̃sɛp'tif], *a.* (*fem.* **-tive**) conceptive.

conception [kɔ̃sɛp'sjɔ̃], *n.f.* conception; thought, notion; understanding.

concernant [kɔ̃sɛr'nɑ̃], *prep.* concerning, relating to.

concerner [kɔ̃sɛr'ne], *v.t.* to relate (*to*), to concern, to regard.

concert [kɔ̃'sɛːr], *n.m.* harmony; concert; (*fig.*) concord.

concertant [kɔ̃sɛr'tɑ̃], *a.* in concert (*of a piece of music*).—*n.m.* (*fem.* **-e**) performer in a concert.

concerté [kɔ̃sɛr'te], *a.* concerted, united; studied, stiff.

concerter [kɔ̃sɛr'te], *v.t.* to contrive, to concert; to plan, to devise; to compose (*one's demeanour etc.*). **se concerter**, *v.r.* to plan together, to concert.

concertiste [kɔ̃sɛr'tist], *n.* performer (*at a concert*).

concerto [kɔ̃sɛr'to], *n.m.* concerto.

concession [kɔ̃sɛ'sjɔ̃], *n.f.* concession, privilege.

concessionnaire [kɔ̃sɛsjɔ'nɛːr], *a.* concessionary.—*n.* grantee.

concevable [kɔ̃s'vabl], *a.* conceivable, imaginable.

concevoir [kɔ̃sə'vwaːr], *v.t. irr.* (*conjug. like* RECEVOIR) to become pregnant, to conceive; to imagine, to understand; to comprehend.

concierge [kɔ̃'sjɛrʒ], *n.* concierge, hall-porter, caretaker.

conciergerie [kɔ̃sjɛrʒə'ri], *n.f.* caretaker's lodge; *La Conciergerie*, a prison in Paris (*during French Revolution*).

concile [kɔ̃'sil], *n.m.* an assembly of prelates and doctors, council, synod.

conciliable [kɔ̃si'ljabl], *a.* reconcilable.

conciliabule [kɔ̃silja'byl], *n.m.* conventicle, secret meeting.

conciliaire [kɔ̃si'ljɛːr], *a.* of *or* belonging to a council.

conciliant [kɔ̃si'ljɑ̃], *a.* conciliating, reconciling.

conciliateur [kɔ̃silja'tœːr], *a.* (*fem.* **-trice**) conciliatory.—*n.m.* (*fem.* **-trice**) conciliator.

conciliation [kɔ̃silja'sjɔ̃], *n.f.* reconciliation.

conciliatoire [kɔ̃silja'twaːr], *a.* conciliatory.

concilier [kɔ̃si'lje], *v.t.* to conciliate, to reconcile; to gain, to win, to procure. **se concilier**, *v.r.* to gain, to win.

concis [kɔ̃'si], *a.* concise, brief, short.

concision [kɔ̃si'zjɔ̃], *n.f.* brevity, conciseness.

concitoyen [kɔ̃sitwa'jɛ̃], *n.m.* (*fem.* **-enne**) fellow-citizen.

conclave [kɔ̃'klaːv], *n.m.* conclave, assembly of all the cardinals.

concluant [kɔ̃kly'ɑ̃], *a.* conclusive, decisive.

conclure [kɔ̃'klyːr], *v.t. irr.* to conclude; to infer; to judge.

conclusif [kɔ̃kly'zif], *a.* (*fem.* **-sive**) conclusive.

conclusion [kɔ̃kly'zjɔ̃], *n.f.* conclusion, upshot.

concombre [kɔ̃'kɔ̃:br], *n.m.* cucumber.

concomitance [kɔ̃komi'tɑ̃:s], *n.f.* concomitance.

concomitant [kɔ̃komi'tɑ̃], *a.* concomitant.

concordance [kɔ̃kor'dɑ̃:s], *n.f.* agreement; (*Bibl. etc.*) concordance.

concordant [kɔ̃kor'dɑ̃], *a.* concordant.

concordat [kɔ̃kor'da], *n.m.* concordat, agreement; bankrupt's certificate.

concordataire [kɔ̃korda'tɛːr], *n.m.* certificated bankrupt.

concorde [kɔ̃'kord], *n.f.* concord, agreement, harmony; good understanding.

concorder [kɔ̃kor'de], *v.i.* to be in accord, to agree, to concur.

concourir [kɔ̃ku'riːr], *v.i. irr.* (*conjug. like* COURIR) to concur; to contribute to; to co-operate; to compete; to converge.

concours [kɔ̃'kuːr], n.m. concourse, meeting; coincidence; competition; co-operation; competitive examination; assistance.

concret [kɔ̃'krɛ], a. (fem. -crète) concrete, solid.

concubine [kɔ̃ky'bin], n.f. concubine.

concupiscence [kɔ̃kypi'sɑ̃s], n.f. concupiscence, lust.

concurremment [kɔ̃kyra'mɑ̃], adv. concurrently; jointly, together.

concurrence [kɔ̃ky'rɑ̃ːs], n.f. competition; rivalry, opposition.

concurrent [kɔ̃ky'rɑ̃], n.m. (fem. -e) competitor, rival.

concussion [kɔ̃ky'sjɔ̃], n.f. extortion, embezzlement.

concussionnaire [kɔ̃kysjo'nɛːr], a. guilty of peculation, of bribery or of extortion.—n.m. extortioner, peculator, embezzler.

condamnable [kɔ̃da'nabl], a. condemnable, blamable.

condamnation [kɔ̃dana'sjɔ̃], n.f. condemnation, judgment, sentence; penalty.

condamné [kɔ̃da'ne], a. condemned, convicted.—n.m. (fem. -ée) convict.

condamner [kɔ̃da'ne], v.t. to condemn, to sentence, to convict; (fig.) to blame, to censure.

condensateur [kɔ̃dɑ̃sa'tœːr], n.m. (Phys.) condenser.

condensation [kɔ̃dɑ̃sa'sjɔ̃], n.f. condensation.

condensé [kɔ̃dɑ̃'se], a. condensed.—n.m. digest.

condenser [kɔ̃dɑ̃'se], v.t. to condense.

condenseur [kɔ̃dɑ̃'sœːr], n.m. condenser.

condescendance [kɔ̃desɑ̃'dɑ̃ːs], n.f. condescension.

condescendant [kɔ̃desɑ̃'dɑ̃], a. condescending, complying.

condescendre [kɔ̃de'sɑ̃ːdr], v.i. to condescend, to comply.

condiment [kɔ̃di'mɑ̃], n.m. condiment, seasoning.

condisciple [kɔ̃di'sipl], n.m. schoolfellow.

condit [kɔ̃'di], n.m. candied fruit.

condition [kɔ̃di'sjɔ̃], n.f. condition; rank, station; domestic service; situation, circumstances; terms; à condition or sous condition, on condition, on approval.

conditionné [kɔ̃disjo'ne], a. conditioned (bien or mal); well-conditioned, sound.

conditionnel [kɔ̃disjo'nɛl], a. conditional.—n.m. (Gram.) conditional.

conditionnellement [kɔ̃disjonɛl'mɑ̃], adv. conditionally, on condition.

conditionner [kɔ̃disjo'ne], v.t. to condition; to dry (silk); to season (wood).

condoléance [kɔ̃dole'ɑ̃ːs], n.f. condolence.

condominium [kɔ̃domi'njɔm], n.m. condominium.

condor [kɔ̃'dɔːr], n.m. condor.

conductance [kɔ̃dyk'tɑ̃ːs], n.f. (Elec.) conductance.

conducteur [kɔ̃dyk'tœːr], n.m. (fem. -trice) conductor, conductress, leader, guide; driver, drover.—a. (Phys.) conducting.

conductibilité [kɔ̃dyktibili'te], n.f. conductibility.

conductible [kɔ̃dyk'tibl], a. conductible.

conduction [kɔ̃dyk'sjɔ̃], n.f. (Phys.) conduction; (Civic Law) hiring.

conduire [kɔ̃'dɥiːr], v.t. irr. to conduct, to lead, to guide; to drive; to accompany; to bring, to take; to be at the head of.—v.i. to lead (à); to drive. se conduire, v.r. to conduct or behave oneself.

conduit [kɔ̃'dɥi], n.m. conduit, duct, pipe, passage, tube, canal.

conduite [kɔ̃'dɥit], n.f. conducting, leading, driving, steering; management, direction, administration; conveyance, distribution; scheme, plan; water-pipe, conduit; behaviour, demeanour; prudence, discretion.

cône [koːn], n.m. cone; en cône, conical.

confection [kɔ̃fɛk'sjɔ̃], n.f. preparation, making; making of ready-made clothes; (Pharm.) confection; vêtements de confection, ready-made clothes.

confectionner [kɔ̃fɛksjo'ne], v.t. to make, to manufacture, to finish.

confectionneur [kɔ̃fɛksjo'nœːr], n.m. (fem. -euse) maker, finisher (of wearing apparel), clothier, outfitter.

confédération [kɔ̃federa'sjɔ̃], n.f. confederation, confederacy; la Confédération Générale du Travail (abbr. C.G.T.), the French equivalent of the T.U.C.

confédéré [kɔ̃fede're], a. and n.m. (fem.-ée) confederate, associate.

confédérer (se) [səkɔ̃fede're], v.r. (conjug. like CÉDER) to combine, to enter into confederation.

conférence [kɔ̃fe'rɑ̃ːs], n.f. conference; lecture.

conférencier [kɔ̃ferɑ̃'sje], n.m. (fem. -ière) lecturer.

conférer [kɔ̃fe're], v.t. (conjug. like CÉDER) to confer, to bestow, to grant; to compare.—v.i. to consult together, to confer.

confesse [kɔ̃'fɛs], n.f. (always used with à or de) aller à confesse, to go to confession; venir de confesse, to come from confession.

confesser [kɔ̃fe'se], v.t. to confess; to acknowledge, to admit; to shrive. se confesser, v.r. to confess one's sins, to confess (to a priest).

confesseur [kɔ̃fe'sœːr], n.m. (father) confessor.

confession [kɔ̃fe'sjɔ̃], n.f. confession, acknowledgment, avowal.

confessionnal [kɔ̃fɛsjo'nal], n.m. confessional.

confetti [kɔ̃fɛt'ti], n.m. pl. confetti.

confiance [kɔ̃'fjɑ̃ːs], n.f. confidence, reliance, trust.

confiant [kɔ̃'fjɑ̃], a. confident, unsuspecting, sanguine; self-conceited.

confidemment [kɔ̃fida'mɑ̃], adv. confidentially.

confidence [kɔ̃fi'dɑ̃ːs], n.f. confidence; secret.

confident [kɔ̃fi'dɑ̃], n.m. (fem. -ente) confidant, confidante.

confidentiel [kɔ̃fidɑ̃'sjɛl], a. confidential.

confidentiellement [kɔ̃fidɑ̃sjɛl'mɑ̃], adv. confidentially.

confier [kɔ̃'fje], v.t. to confide, to entrust, to commit (à). se confier, v.r. to trust in; to unbosom oneself (à).

configuration [kɔ̃figyra'sjɔ̃], n.f. configuration, form, shape, lie (of the land).

confinement [kɔ̃fin'mɑ̃], n.m. confinement; overcrowding.

confiner

confiner [kɔ̃fi'ne], v.t. to confine, to imprison; *air confiné*, stuffy atmosphere.—v.i. to border upon, to be adjoining. **se confiner**, v.r. to confine or to limit oneself.

confins [kɔ̃'fɛ̃], n.m. (*used only in pl.*) confines, borders, limits.

confire [kɔ̃'fiːr], v.t. irr. to preserve; to candy, to pickle.

confirmatif [kɔ̃firma'tif], a. (*fem.* -tive) confirmative.

confirmation [kɔ̃firma'sjɔ̃], n.f. confirmation, ratification.

confirmer [kɔ̃fir'me], v.t. to strengthen, to corroborate; to confirm; to ratify. **se confirmer**, v.r. to be confirmed.

confiscable [kɔ̃fis'kabl], a. confiscable, forfeitable.

confiscation [kɔ̃fiska'sjɔ̃], n.f. confiscation, forfeiture.

confiserie [kɔ̃fiz'ri], n.f. confectionery; confectioner's shop.

confiseur [kɔ̃fi'zœːr] n.m. (*fem.* -euse) confectioner.

confisquer [kɔ̃fis'ke], v.t. to confiscate, to forfeit, to impound; to seize.

confit (1) [kɔ̃'fi], p.p. [CONFIRE].

confit (2) [kɔ̃'fi], n.m. meat, poultry etc. preserved in fat; bran-mash (*for pigs etc.*).

confiture [kɔ̃fi'tyːr], n.f. preserve, jam.

conflagration [kɔ̃flagra'sjɔ̃], n.f. conflagration.

conflit [kɔ̃'fli], n.m. conflict, collision, encounter; contention, strife, contest, rivalry; jar, clash.

confluent [kɔ̃fly'ã], n.m. confluence, junction (*of rivers*).

confluer [kɔ̃fly'e], v.i. to meet, to unite (*of streams etc.*).

confondre [kɔ̃'fɔ̃ːdr], v.t. to confound, to confuse; to mix, to mingle; (*fig.*) to amaze, to astound. **se confondre**, v.r. to mingle, to be lost in; to be confounded, to be abashed.

conformation [kɔ̃fɔrma'sjɔ̃], n.f. conformation, structure.

conforme [kɔ̃'fɔrm], a. conformable; congenial, consistent; *pour copie conforme*, certified true copy.

conformé [kɔ̃fɔr'me], a. formed, shaped (*bien* or *mal*).

conformément [kɔ̃fɔrme'mã], adv. suitably; according to.

conformer [kɔ̃fɔr'me], v.t. to give form to. **se conformer**, v.r. to conform, to comply (*with*).

conformisme [kɔ̃fɔr'mism], n.m. conformity, orthodoxy.

conformité [kɔ̃fɔrmi'te], n.f. likeness, conformity, compliance.

confort [kɔ̃'fɔːr], n.m. comfort, ease.

confortable [kɔ̃fɔr'tabl], a. cosy, comfortable.

confortablement [kɔ̃fɔrtablə'mã], adv. comfortably.

confraternité [kɔ̃fratɛrni'te], n.f. fraternity, brotherhood.

confrère [kɔ̃'frɛːr], n.m. colleague; fellow-member.

confrérie [kɔ̃fre'ri], n.f. brotherhood, fraternity.

confrontation [kɔ̃frɔ̃ta'sjɔ̃], n.f. confrontation; comparing.

confronter [kɔ̃frɔ̃'te], v.t. to confront; to compare.

confus [kɔ̃'fy], a. confused, muddled, vague, indistinct, obscure; abashed, crest-fallen.

confusément [kɔ̃fyze'mã], adv. confusedly, vaguely, dimly.

confusion [kɔ̃fy'zjɔ̃], n.f. confusion, disorder; bewilderment; embarrassment, shame, blush; misunderstanding.

congé [kɔ̃'ʒe], n.m. leave, permission; leave of absence, holiday; discharge, dismissal; notice (to quit); permit.

congédier [kɔ̃ʒe'dje], v.t. to discharge, to dismiss, to pay off; to disband.

congélateur [kɔ̃ʒela'tœːr], n.m. refrigerator.

congeler [kɔ̃ʒ'le], v.t., **se congeler**, v.r. (*conjug. like* AMENER) to congeal, to freeze; to coagulate.

congénère [kɔ̃ʒe'nɛːr], a. congeneric; of same species; (*Philol.*) cognate.

congénial [kɔ̃ʒe'njal], a. (*m. pl.* -aux) congenial, of the same nature.

congénital [kɔ̃ʒeni'tal], a. (*m. pl.* -aux) congenital, hereditary.

congère [kɔ̃'ʒɛːr], n.f. snow-drift.

congestion [kɔ̃ʒɛs'tjɔ̃], n.f. congestion.

conglomération [kɔ̃glɔmera'sjɔ̃], n.f. conglomeration.

conglomérer [kɔ̃glɔme're], v.t. (*conjug. like* CÉDER) to conglomerate.

congolais [kɔ̃gɔ'lɛ], a. Congolese.— (**Congolais**, *fem.* -aise) Congolese (*person*).

congratulation [kɔ̃gratyla'sjɔ̃], n.f. congratulation.

congratulatoire [kɔ̃gratyla'twaːr], a. congratulatory.

congratuler [kɔ̃gratyle], v.t. to congratulate.

congre [kɔ̃ːgr], n.m. conger, conger-eel.

congrégation [kɔ̃grega'sjɔ̃], n.f. fraternity, brotherhood, general body (*of an order etc.*).

congrès [kɔ̃'grɛ], n.m. congress.

congressiste [kɔ̃grɛ'sist], n.m. (*Am.*) congressman.

congru [kɔ̃'gry], a. suitable, consistent, congruous, proper.

congruité [kɔ̃gryi'te], n.f. congruity, consistency, propriety.

congrûment [kɔ̃gry'mã], adv. congruously, properly.

conifère [kɔni'fɛːr], a. coniferous.—n.m. conifer.

conique [kɔ'nik], a. conical.

conjecture [kɔ̃ʒɛk'tyːr], n.f. conjecture, surmise, guess.

conjecturer [kɔ̃ʒɛkty're], v.t. to conjecture, to guess, to surmise.

conjoindre [kɔ̃'ʒwɛ̃ːdr], v.t. irr. (*conjug. like* CRAINDRE) to conjoin, to unite together; to marry.

conjoint [kɔ̃'ʒwɛ̃], a. conjoined, united, joint. —n.m. (*fem.* -e) spouse.

conjointement [kɔ̃ʒwɛ̃t'mã], adv. conjointly, unitedly.

conjoncteur [kɔ̃ʒɔ̃k'tœːr], n.m. (*Elec.*) circuit-breaker, switch key.

conjonctif [kɔ̃ʒɔ̃k'tif], a. (*fem.* -tive) conjunctive.

conjonction [kɔ̃ʒɔ̃k'sjɔ̃], n.f. conjunction; union, connexion; coition.

conjoncture [kɔ̃ʒɔ̃k'tyːr], n.f. conjuncture, juncture.

conjugaison [kɔ̃ʒygɛ'zɔ̃], n.f. conjugation.

conjugal [kɔ̃ʒyˈgal], a. (m. pl. **-aux**) conjugal.
conjugalement [kɔ̃ʒygalˈmã], adv. conjugally.
conjugué [kɔ̃ʒyˈge], a. (Mech.) twin.
conjuguer [kɔ̃ʒyˈge], v.t. (Gram.) to conjugate.
conjuration [kɔ̃ʒyrɑˈsjɔ̃], n.f. conspiracy, plot.
conjuré [kɔ̃ʒyˈre], a. confederate, sworn.—n.m. (fem. **-ée**) conspirator, plotter.
conjurer [kɔ̃ʒyˈre], v.t. to implore; to conspire; to swear; to conjure up, to exorcize, to ward off.
connaissable [kɔnɛˈsabl], a. recognizable.
connaissance [kɔnɛˈsãːs], n.f. knowledge, learning; consciousness (de); acquaintance; intercourse; (Law) cognizance; (pl.) attainments.
connaisseur [kɔnɛˈsœːr], a. (fem. **-euse**) expert, skilled.—n.m. connoisseur, expert.
connaître [kɔˈnɛːtr], v.t. irr. to know, to perceive; to understand; to be acquainted with.—v.i. to have or take cognizance of; to deal with (a matter). **se connaître**, v.r. to know oneself; to know each other; to be a connoisseur.
connecter [kɔnɛkˈte], v.t. to connect; (Elec.) to couple (up), to group.
connétable [kɔneˈtabl], n.m. high constable.
connexion [kɔnɛkˈsjɔ̃], n.f. connexion, affinity.
connexité [kɔnɛksiˈte], n.f. connexion.
connivence [kɔniˈvãːs], n.f. connivance.
connotation [kɔnɔtaˈsjɔ̃], n.f. connotation.
connu [kɔˈny], a. known, understood.—n.m. that which is known.
conque [kɔ̃ːk], n.f. conch, sea-shell.
conquérant [kɔ̃keˈrã], a. conquering.—n.m. (fem. **-e**) conqueror.
conquérir [kɔ̃keˈriːr], v.t. irr. (conjug. like ACQUÉRIR) to conquer, to subdue (a country); (fig.) to gain, to win over.
conquête [kɔ̃ˈkɛːt], n.f. conquest, acquisition.
conquis [kɔ̃ˈki], a. conquered.
consacrant [kɔ̃saˈkrã], a. consecrating, officiating.—n.m. consecrator, officiant.
consacrer [kɔ̃saˈkre], v.t. to consecrate, to dedicate, to sanctify; to sanction; to authorize. **se consacrer**, v.r. to devote oneself.
consciemment [kɔ̃sjaˈmã], adv. consciously, knowingly.
conscience [kɔ̃ˈsjãːs], n.f. consciousness, perception; conscience, conscientiousness.
consciencieusement [kɔ̃sjãsjøzˈmã], adv. conscientiously.
consciencieux [kɔ̃sjãˈsjø], a. (fem. **-euse**) conscientious.
conscient [kɔ̃ˈsjã], a. conscious (de); self-conscious.
conscription [kɔ̃skripˈsjɔ̃], n.f. enlistment; conscription.
conscrit [kɔ̃ˈskri], a. conscript.—n.m. conscript; (raw) recruit.
consécrateur [kɔ̃sekraˈtœːr], a. [CONSACRANT].
consécration [kɔ̃sekraˈsjɔ̃], n.f. consecration; ordination.
consécutif [kɔ̃sekyˈtif], a. (fem. **-tive**) consecutive, following.
consécutivement [kɔ̃sekytivˈmã], adv. consecutively.
conseil [kɔ̃ˈsɛːj], n.m. counsel, advice; resolution; council, board; (Law) counsel;

conseil d'administration, board of directors; **Conseil d'État**, Council of State; **Conseil de Sécurité (de l'O.N.U.)**, (U.N.) Security Council; **conseil judiciaire**, guardian; **conseil de guerre**, court-martial; council of war; **conseil municipal**, town council, corporation.
conseiller [kɔ̃sɛˈje], v.t. to advise, to counsel; to recommend.—n.m. (fem. **-ère**) counsellor, adviser, councillor.
consensus [kɔ̃sãˈsyːs], n.m. consent, consensus.
consentant [kɔ̃sãˈtã], a. consenting, willing.
consentement [kɔ̃sãtˈmã], n.m. consent, assent.
consentir [kɔ̃sãˈtiːr], v.i. irr. (conjug. like SENTIR) to consent, to agree, to acquiesce (à).
conséquemment [kɔ̃sekaˈmã], adv. consequently, accordingly.
conséquence [kɔ̃seˈkãːs], n.f. consequence, sequel; issue, result; inference, conclusion.
conséquent [kɔ̃seˈkã], a. rational, consistent.—n.m. (Log., Math.) consequent; **par conséquent**, consequently.
conservateur [kɔ̃sɛrvaˈtœːr], a. (fem. **-trice**) preserving, conservative.—n.m. (fem. **-trice**) Conservative, Tory.—n.m. guardian, keeper, curator.
conservatif [kɔ̃sɛrvaˈtif], a. (fem. **-tive**) conservative, preservative.—n.m. preservative.
conservation [kɔ̃sɛrvaˈsjɔ̃], n.f. conservation, preservation; registration (of mortgages etc.).
conservatisme [kɔ̃sɛrvaˈtism], n.m. conservatism.
Conservatoire [kɔ̃sɛrvaˈtwaːr], n.m. academy of music and school of elocution in Paris.
conserve [kɔ̃ˈsɛrv], n.f. preserve; tinned (Am. canned) food.
conserver [kɔ̃sɛrˈve], v.t. to preserve; to keep. **se conserver**, v.r. to be preserved; to bear one's age well; to keep (of meat, fruit etc.).
considérable [kɔ̃sideˈrabl], a. considerable, notable, eminent; **peu considérable**, of little importance.
considérablement [kɔ̃siderabləˈmã], adv. considerably.
considérant [kɔ̃sideˈrã], conj. phr. **considérant que**, whereas.
considération [kɔ̃sideraˈsjɔ̃], n.f. consideration, attention; motive, grounds; regard, respect.
considérément [kɔ̃sidereˈmã], adv. considerately, prudently.
considérer [kɔ̃sideˈre], v.t. (conjug. like CÉDER) to consider, to look at, to view; to ponder; to value, to esteem; to pay attention to. **se considérer**, v.r. to esteem oneself.
consignataire [kɔ̃siɲaˈtɛːr], n. trustee, depositary.
consignateur [kɔ̃siɲaˈtœːr], n.m. (fem. **-trice**) (Comm.) consignor, shipper.
consignation [kɔ̃siɲaˈsjɔ̃], n.f. (Comm.) deposit, consignment.
consigne [kɔ̃ˈsiɲ], n.f. (Mil.) order, password; (fig.) strict command, prohibition; (Rail.) left-luggage office, cloak-room; (sch.) gating, detention.

consigner

consigner [kɔ̃siɲe], v.t. to deposit; to consign; to record, to register; to keep in; to refuse admittance to.

consistance [kɔ̃sistɑ̃:s], n.f. consistency; firmness, stability; (fig.) credit, consideration.

consistant [kɔ̃sistɑ̃], a. consisting of; consistent, firm, solid.

consister [kɔ̃siste], v.i. to consist; to be composed of.

consistoire [kɔ̃sistwa:r], n.m. consistory.

consolable [kɔ̃sɔlabl], a. consolable.

consolant [kɔ̃sɔlɑ̃], a. consoling, comforting.

consolateur [kɔ̃sɔlatœ:r] a. (fem. -trice) consoling.—n.m. (fem. -trice) comforter, consoler.

consolation [kɔ̃sɔlasjɔ̃], n.f. consolation, comfort, solace.

console [kɔ̃sɔl], n.f. console, bracket.

consoler [kɔ̃sɔle], v.t. to console, to comfort. **se consoler**, v.r. to console oneself.

consolidation [kɔ̃sɔlidasjɔ̃], n.f. consolidation; strengthening; funding (of interest).

consolidé [kɔ̃sɔlide], a. funded.—n.m. (Fin., used only in pl.) consols.

consolider [kɔ̃sɔlide], v.t. to consolidate; to strengthen. **se consolider**, v.r. to consolidate, to grow firm.

consommable [kɔ̃sɔmabl], a. consumable, edible.

consommateur [kɔ̃sɔmatœ:r], n.m. (fem. -trice) consumer (as opposed to producer), eater, drinker.

consommation [kɔ̃sɔmasjɔ̃], n.f. consumption; consummation; food, drinks, refreshments.

consommé [kɔ̃sɔme], a. consumed; consummated; consummate; accomplished.—n.m. clear soup.

consommer [kɔ̃sɔme], v.t. to consume, to use; (fig.) to consummate, to accomplish.—v.i. (pop.) to have a drink.

consomption [kɔ̃sɔ̃psjɔ̃], n.f. consumption, using up; (Path.) phthisis, decline.

consonance [kɔ̃sɔnɑ̃:s], n.f. consonance; (fig.) concord.

consonant [kɔ̃sɔnɑ̃], a. consonant.

consonne [kɔ̃sɔn], n.f. consonant.

consort [kɔ̃sɔ:r], a. consort (of the husband or wife of a sovereign).—n.m. (used only in pl.) consorts, confederates; (Law) associates.

consortium [kɔ̃sɔrsjɔm], n.m. consortium.

conspirateur [kɔ̃spiratœ:r], n.m. (fem. -trice) conspirator.—a. conspiring.

conspiration [kɔ̃spirasjɔ̃], n.f. conspiracy, plot.

conspirer [kɔ̃spire], v.t. to plot.—v.i. to conspire, to concur; to plot.

conspuer [kɔ̃spɥe], v.t. to despise, to spurn; to boo, to barrack.

constamment [kɔ̃stamɑ̃] adv. steadily, continually, constantly.

constance [kɔ̃stɑ̃:s], n.f. constancy; perseverance.

constant [kɔ̃stɑ̃], a. constant, faithful, unshaken; persevering.

constatation [kɔ̃statasjɔ̃], n.f. authentication; statement; findings.

constater [kɔ̃state], v.t. to prove, to verify; to ascertain; to state, to declare.

constellation [kɔ̃stelasjɔ̃], n.f. constellation.

constellé [kɔ̃stele], a. constellated; studded.

consteller [kɔ̃stele], v.t. to constellate, to stud.

consternation [kɔ̃sternasjɔ̃], n.f. consternation, dismay.

consterné [kɔ̃sterne], a. dismayed, overwhelmed.

consterner [kɔ̃sterne], v.t. to dismay, to dishearten; to astound, to amaze.

constipation [kɔ̃stipasjɔ̃], n.f. constipation, costiveness.

constipé [kɔ̃stipe], a. costive, constipated.

constiper [kɔ̃stipe], v.t. to constipate, to bind.

constituant [kɔ̃stitɥɑ̃], a. constituent.

constituer [kɔ̃stitɥe], v.t. to constitute; to establish; to appoint; to settle, to assign. **se constituer**, v.r. to constitute oneself.

constitution [kɔ̃stitysjɔ̃], n.f. constitution; establishment; settlement (of an annuity etc.); temperament.

constitutionnel [kɔ̃stitysjɔnel], a. (fem. -elle) constitutional.

constitutionnellement [kɔ̃stitysjɔnɛl'mɑ̃], adv. constitutionally.

constriction [kɔ̃striksjɔ̃], n.f. constriction.

constringent [kɔ̃strɛ̃ʒɑ̃], a. constringent.

constructeur [kɔ̃stryktœ:r], n.m. constructor, builder; shipbuilder, shipwright.

construction [kɔ̃stryksjɔ̃], n.f. building, construction; erection, structure.

constructivité [kɔ̃stryktivite], n.f. constructiveness.

construire [kɔ̃strɥi:r], v.t. irr. (conjug. like CONDUIRE) to construct, to build, to erect.

consul [kɔ̃syl], n.m. consul.

consulaire [kɔ̃syle:r], a. consular.

consulat [kɔ̃syla], n.m. consulate, consulship.

consultant [kɔ̃syltɑ̃], a. consulting.—n.m. (fem. -e) consultant, consulting physician.

consultatif [kɔ̃syltatif], a. (fem. -tive) consultative, deliberative.

consultation [kɔ̃syltasjɔ̃], n.f. consultation; opinion, advice; **cabinet de consultation**, surgery.

consulter [kɔ̃sylte], v.t. to consult; to refer to.—v.i. to deliberate, to take counsel (together). **se consulter**, v.r. to consider, to reflect, to deliberate.

consumable [kɔ̃symabl], a. consumable.

consumant [kɔ̃symɑ̃], a. consuming, devouring, burning.

consumer [kɔ̃syme], v.t. to consume; to destroy, to wear out, to wear away, to squander, to waste. **se consumer**, v.r. to decay, to waste away, to wear out; to undermine one's health.

contact [kɔ̃takt], n.m. contact; touch; connexion; (Motor.) **clé de contact**, ignition key; (Opt.) **verres de contact**, contact lenses.

contagieux [kɔ̃taʒjø], a. (fem. -euse) contagious, infectious.

contagion [kɔ̃taʒjɔ̃], n.f. contagion, infection.

contamination [kɔ̃taminasjɔ̃], n.f. contamination, pollution.

contaminé [kɔ̃tamine], a. polluted, contaminated.

contaminer [kɔ̃tamine], v.t. to contaminate.

conte [kɔ̃:t], n.m. story, tale; (fig.) fib, fairytale.

contemplateur [kɔ̃tɑ̃pla'tœːr], *n.m.* (*fem.* -**trice**) contemplator.

contemplatif [kɔ̃tɑ̃pla'tif], *a.* (*fem.* -**tive**) contemplative.

contemplation [kɔ̃tɑ̃plɑ'sjɔ̃], *n.f.* contemplation, meditation.

contempler [kɔ̃tɑ̃'ple], *v.t.* to contemplate, to survey, to gaze on.—*v.i.* to contemplate, to meditate, to reflect.

contemporain [kɔ̃tɑ̃pɔ'rɛ̃], *a.* and *n.m.* (*fem.* -**e**) contemporary.

contempteur [kɔ̃tɑ̃p'tœːr], *a.* (*fem.* -**trice**) contemptuous, scornful, insolent, disdainful.—*n.m.* contemner, despiser, scorner.

contenance [kɔ̃t'nɑːs], *n.f.* capacity; volume; (*fig.*) countenance, air, bearing.

contenant [kɔ̃t'nɑ̃], *a.* holding, containing.—*n.m.* holder, container.

contenir [kɔ̃t'niːr], *v.t. irr.* (*conjug. like* TENIR) to contain, to comprise, to hold, to include; to restrain. **se contenir**, *v.r.* to keep within bounds, to be moderate; to control oneself.

content [kɔ̃'tɑ̃], *a.* content, satisfied; pleased, glad, gratified.

contentement [kɔ̃tɑ̃t'mɑ̃], *n.m.* contentment, satisfaction; comfort, pleasure.

contenter [kɔ̃tɑ̃'te], *v.t.* to content, to satisfy; to please, to gratify. **se contenter**, *v.r.* to be satisfied, to be content.

contentieusement [kɔ̃tɑ̃sjøz'mɑ̃], *adv.* contentiously, litigiously.

contentieux [kɔ̃tɑ̃'sjø], *a.* (*fem.* -**euse**) contentious, disputable; litigious; in dispute; quarrelsome. — *n.m.* debatable matter; *bureau du contentieux*, legal department.

contention [kɔ̃tɑ̃'sjɔ̃], *n.f.* application, vehemence; contention, contest, debate, strife.

contenu [kɔ̃t'ny], *a.* contained; (*fig.*) kept in control.—*n.m.* contents; enclosure; terms (*of a letter etc.*).

conter [kɔ̃'te], *v.t.* to tell, to relate; *en conter*, to tell fibs.

contestable [kɔ̃tɛs'tabl], *a.* disputable, debatable.

contestant [kɔ̃tɛs'tɑ̃], *a.* contending (*at law*).—*n.m.* (*fem.* -**e**) contesting party, litigant.

contestation [kɔ̃tɛsta'sjɔ̃], *n.f.* contestation, contest; dispute, debate; litigation.

contester [kɔ̃tɛs'te], *v.t.* to dispute, to contest; to contend, to debate.—*v.i.* to quarrel; to be contentious.

conteur [kɔ̃'tœːr], *a.* (*fem.* -**euse**) who tells stories.—*n.m.* (*fem.* -**euse**) story-teller; (*fig.*) fibber.

contexte [kɔ̃'tɛkst], *n.m.* context; text (*of a deed*).

contexture [kɔ̃tɛks'tyːr], *n.f.* contexture (*of the muscles etc.*); texture (*of materials*).

contigu [kɔ̃ti'gy], *a.* (*fem.* -**ë**) contiguous, adjoining.

contiguïté [kɔ̃tigɥi'te], *n.f.* contiguity.

continence [kɔ̃ti'nɑ̃ːs], *n.f.* continency, chastity.

continent (1) [kɔ̃ti'nɑ̃], *a.* chaste, continent.

continent (2) [kɔ̃ti'nɑ̃], *n.m.* continent, mainland.

continental [kɔ̃tinɑ̃'tal], *a.* (*m. pl.* -**aux**) continental.

contingence [kɔ̃tɛ̃'ʒɑ̃ːs], *n.f.* contingency, casualty.

contingent [kɔ̃tɛ̃'ʒɑ̃], *a.* contingent, accidental, casual.—*n.m.* quota; contingent.

continu [kɔ̃ti'ny], *a.* continuous, continual, uninterrupted; incessant.

continuation [kɔ̃tinɥa'sjɔ̃], *n.f.* continuation.

continuel [kɔ̃ti'nɥɛl], *a.* (*fem.* -**elle**) continual, perpetual.

continuellement [kɔ̃tinɥɛl'mɑ̃], *adv.* continually, perpetually.

continuer [kɔ̃ti'nɥe], *v.t.* to continue, to proceed with; to lengthen.—*v.i.* to continue, to keep on. **se continuer**, *v.r.* to be continued, to last.

continuité [kɔ̃tinɥi'te], *n.f.* continuity; continuance.

continûment [kɔ̃tiny'mɑ̃], *adv.* unremittingly, continuously, without cessation.

contorsion [kɔ̃tɔr'sjɔ̃], *n.f.* contortion; grimace.

contorsionniste [kɔ̃tɔrsjɔ'nist], *n.* contortionist.

contour [kɔ̃'tuːr], *n.m.* circuit, circumference; contour, outline.

contourné [kɔ̃tur'ne], *a.* distorted, bizarre.

contournement [kɔ̃turnə'mɑ̃], *n.m.* outlining, tracing; winding, convolution; *route de contournement*, by-pass (*road*).

contourner [kɔ̃tur'ne], *v.t.* to outline; to distort, to twist; to twist, turn, go *or* wind round. **se contourner**, *v.r.* to grow crooked, to become bent.

contractant [kɔ̃trak'tɑ̃], *a. partie contractante*, contracting party.—*n.m.* (*fem.* -**e**) stipulator.

contracté [kɔ̃trak'te], *a.* contracted, shortened.

contracter [kɔ̃trak'te], *v.t.* to contract; to covenant, to stipulate, to bargain; to make a contract; to acquire. **se contracter**, *v.r.* to contract, to shrink; to shorten; to be settled by contract.

contraction [kɔ̃trak'sjɔ̃], *n.f.* contraction.

contractuel [kɔ̃trak'tɥɛl], *a.* (*fem.* -**elle**) stipulated, done by contract.

contractuellement [kɔ̃traktɥɛl'mɑ̃], *adv.* by contract.

contradicteur [kɔ̃tradik'tœːr], *n.m.* contradictor; (*Law*) adversary.

contradiction [kɔ̃tradik'sjɔ̃], *n.f.* contradiction, denial; opposition; discrepancy.

contradictoire [kɔ̃tradik'twaːr], *a.* contradictory, inconsistent, conflicting; *examen contradictoire*, cross-examination.

contraindre [kɔ̃'trɛ̃ːdr], *v.t. irr.* (*conjug. like* CRAINDRE) to constrain, to compel, to coerce; to restrain; to squeeze. **se contraindre**, *v.r.* to restrain oneself, to refrain.

contraint [kɔ̃'trɛ̃], *a.* constrained, forced.

contrainte [kɔ̃'trɛ̃ːt], *n.f.* constraint, compulsion, coercion; restraint; uneasiness.

contraire [kɔ̃'trɛːr], *a.* contrary, opposite, inconsistent; adverse; prejudicial.—*n.m.* contrary, opposite, reverse.

contrairement [kɔ̃trɛr'mɑ̃], *adv.* contrarily, in opposition.

contralte [kɔ̃'tralt], **contralto** [kɔ̃tral'to], *n.m.* contralto, counter-tenor.

contrariant [kɔ̃tra'rjɑ̃], *a.* thwarting, annoying.

contrarier [kɔ̃tra'rje], *v.t.* to thwart, to counteract, to baffle; to annoy; to disappoint.

contrariété

contrariété [kɔ̃trarje'te], *n.f.* contrariety, contradiction; annoyance; hindrance, disappointment; *quelle contrariété !* how annoying!
contrastant [kɔ̃tras'tɑ̃], *a.* contrasting.
contraste [kɔ̃'trast], *n.m.* contrast, opposition.
contraster [kɔ̃tras'te], *v.t.*, *v.i.* to contrast.
contrat [kɔ̃'tra], *n.m.* contract, deed; agreement, bargain.
contravention [kɔ̃travɑ̃'sjɔ̃], *n.f.* contravention.
contre [kɔ̃:tr], *prep.* against, versus, contrary to; close up against, near; in exchange for; *ci-contre,* opposite, in the margin; *par contre,* on the other hand; *pour et contre,* pro and con.—*adv.* against.—*n.m.* the opposite side of the question; *le pour et le contre,* the pros and cons.
contre-allée [kɔ̃tra'le], *n.f.* side-walk, side-alley.
contre-amiral [kɔ̃trami'ral], *n.m.* (*pl.* **contre-amiraux**) rear-admiral.
contre-attaque [kɔ̃tra'tak], *n.f.* (*Mil.*) counter-attack.
contre-avions [kɔ̃tra'vjɔ̃], *a.* anti-aircraft.
contrebalancer [kɔ̃trəbalɑ̃'se], *v.t.* (*conjug. like* COMMENCER) to counterbalance, to counterpoise.
contrebande [kɔ̃trə'bɑ̃:d], *n.f.* contraband, smuggling; smuggled goods.
contrebandier [kɔ̃trəbɑ̃'dje], *n.m.* smuggler, gunrunner; smuggling vessel.
contre-bas (en) [kɔ̃trə'ba], *adv.* downwards.
contrebasse [kɔ̃trə'ba:s], *n.f.* double-bass.
contre-bord (à) [akɔ̃trə'bɔ:r], *adv.* (*Naut.*) on the opposite tack.
contre-boutant [kɔ̃trəbu'tɑ̃], **contre-boutement** [kɔ̃trəbut'mɑ̃], *n.m.* abutment, buttress.
contre-bouter [kɔ̃trəbu'te], *v.t.* to buttress; to shore up.
contrecarrer [kɔ̃trəka're], *v.t.* to thwart, to oppose.
contre-cœur [kɔ̃trə'kœ:r], *n.m.* chimney-back; *à contre-cœur,* reluctantly.
contre-coup [kɔ̃trə'ku], *n.m.* rebound, repercussion; (*fig.*) consequence, result; *par contre-coup,* as a consequence.
contredanse [kɔ̃trə'dɑ̃:s], *n.f.* quadrille.
contredire [kɔ̃trə'di:r], *v.t. irr.* (*conjug. like* MÉDIRE) to contradict, to gainsay; (*Law*) to disprove. **se contredire,** *v.r.* to contradict oneself; to be contradictory.
contredisant [kɔ̃trədi'zɑ̃], *a.* contradicting.
contredit [kɔ̃trə'di], *n.m.* contradiction; answer, reply; *sans contredit,* incontestably.
contrée [kɔ̃'tre], *n.f.* country, region, district.
contre-échange [kɔ̃tre'ʃɑ̃:ʒ], *n.m.* mutual exchange.
contre-écrou [kɔ̃tre'kru], *n.m.* lock-nut.
contre-épreuve [kɔ̃tre'prœ:v], *n.f.* (*Engraving*) counter-proof; (*fig.*) feeble imitation.
contre-espionnage [kɔ̃trespjɔ'na:ʒ], *n.m.* counter-espionage.
contrefaçon [kɔ̃trəfa'sɔ̃], *n.f.* counterfeiting, forgery.
contrefacteur [kɔ̃trəfak'tœ:r], *n.m.* counterfeiter (*of coins etc.*); forger (*of bills etc.*); infringer (*of patents etc.*).
contrefaire [kɔ̃trə'fɛ:r], *v.t. irr.* (*conjug. like* FAIRE) to counterfeit, to imitate; to copy; to forge; to mimic; to disguise. **se contrefaire,** *v.r.* to dissemble, to sham.
contrefaiseur [kɔ̃trəfɔ'zœ:r], *n.m.* (*fem.* **-euse**) counterfeiter, mimic, imitator.
contrefait [kɔ̃trə'fɛ], *a.* counterfeit; deformed.
contre-fiche [kɔ̃trə'fiʃ], *n.f.* (*Carp.*) prop, strut.
contre-haut (en) [ɑ̃kɔ̃trə'o], *adv.* upwards.
contre-jour [kɔ̃trə'ʒu:r], *n.m.* (*Phot.*) low light; *à contre-jour,* against the light.
contremaître [kɔ̃trə'mɛ:tr], *n.m.* overseer, foreman.
contremander [kɔ̃trəmɑ̃'de], *v.t.* to countermand.
contremarche [kɔ̃trə'marʃ], *n.f.* counter-march.
contremarcher [kɔ̃trəmar'ʃe], *v.i.* to counter-march.
contremarque [kɔ̃trə'mark], *n.f.* counter-mark; (*Theat.*) check ticket.
contre-mesure [kɔ̃trəmə'zy:r], *n.f.* counter-measure.
contre-offensive [kɔ̃trɔfɑ̃'si:v], *n.f.* counter-attack.
contre-partie [kɔ̃trəpar'ti], *n.f.* counterpart; (*fig.*) opposite, contrary; return match.
contre-pédaler [kɔ̃trəpeda'le], *v.i.* to back-pedal.
contre-pied [kɔ̃trə'pje], *n.m.* (*Hunt.*) back-scent; (*fig.*) reverse way, contrary.
contre-plaqué [kɔ̃trəpla'ke], *a.* laminated.—*n.m.* two- (*or* three-) ply wood.
contrepoids [kɔ̃trə'pwa], *n.m. inv.* counter-poise, counter-balance; (*fig.*) equilibrium.
contre-poil [kɔ̃trə'pwal], *n.m.* wrong way of the hair *or* of the nap; *à contre-poil,* against the grain.
contrepoint [kɔ̃trə'pwɛ̃], *n.m.* counterpoint.
contrepoison [kɔ̃trəpwa'zɔ̃], *n.m.* antidote, counter-poison.
contre-poser [kɔ̃trəpo'ze], *v.t.* to misplace; (*Comm.*) to set down wrong.
contrer [kɔ̃'tre], *v.t.* (*Bridge*) to double.
contre-ressort [kɔ̃trərə'sɔ:r], *n.m.* shock-absorber.
contre-révolution [kɔ̃trərevɔly'sjɔ̃], *n.f.* counter-revolution.
contre-saison (à) [akɔ̃trəsɛ'zɔ̃], *adv. phr.* (*flower*) produced out of season; ill-timed.
contresens [kɔ̃trə'sɑ̃:s], *n.m.* contrary sense; wrong construction *or* meaning; mistranslation; wrong side (*of material*).
contresigner [kɔ̃trəsi'ɲe], *v.t.* to countersign.
contretemps [kɔ̃trə'tɑ̃], *n.m. inv.* untoward accident, disappointment, mishap; (*Mus.*) syncopation; *à contretemps,* at the wrong time.
contre-torpilleur [kɔ̃trətɔrpi'jœ:r], *n.m.* torpedo-boat destroyer.
contrevenant [kɔ̃trəv'nɑ̃], *n.m.* (*fem.* -e) contravener, infringer, offender, transgressor.
contrevenir [kɔ̃trəv'ni:r], *v.i. irr.* (*conjug. like* TENIR) to contravene, infringe.
contrevent [kɔ̃trə'vɑ̃], *n.m.* outside window-shutter.
contribuable [kɔ̃tri'bɥabl], *a.* taxable, rate-able.—*n.* tax-payer, rate-payer.
contribuer [kɔ̃tri'bɥe], *v.i.* to contribute, to pay; (*fig.*) to conduce, to be an accessory (*à*).

84

contributaire [kɔ̃triby'tɛːr], *a.* contributory.
contribution [kɔ̃triby'sjɔ̃], *n.f.* contribution; tax; share, portion; *contribution foncière*, land tax.
contrister [kɔ̃tris'te], *v.t.* to grieve, to vex, to sadden.
contrit [kɔ̃'tri], *a.* contrite, penitent; afflicted.
contrition [kɔ̃tri'sjɔ̃], *n.f.* contrition.
contrôlable [kɔ̃tro'labl], *a.* that may be checked, verified.
contrôle [kɔ̃'troːl], *n.m.* control-register; roll, list; controller's office; stamp, hallmark; (*Theat.*) ticket-checking counter; (*fig.*) control, censure.
contrôler [kɔ̃tro'le], *v.t.* to register; to stamp; to check, to verify; to audit; to censure.
contrôleur [kɔ̃tro'lœːr], *n.m.* (*fem.* **-euse**) controller; (*Taxes, Theat., Rail.*) inspector; time-keeper; ticket-collector; (*fig.*) critic.
controuver [kɔ̃tru've], *v.t.* to forge, to fabricate.
controversable [kɔ̃trɔvɛr'sabl], *a.* controvertible, controversial.
controverse [kɔ̃trɔ'vɛrs], *n.f.* controversy, discussion, dispute.
controverser [kɔ̃trɔvɛr'se], *v.t.* to dispute, to discuss.
contumace [kɔ̃ty'mas], *n.f.* contumacy, nonappearance *or* default, contempt of court; obstinacy.—*a.* contumacious.—*n.* defaulter.
contus [kɔ̃'ty], *a.* bruised, contused.
contusion [kɔ̃ty'zjɔ̃], *n.f.* contusion, bruise.
contusionner [kɔ̃tyzjɔ'ne], *v.t.* to contuse, to bruise.
convaincant [kɔ̃vɛ̃'kã], *a.* convincing.
convaincre [kɔ̃'vɛ̃ːkr], *v.t. irr.* (*conjug. like* VAINCRE) to convince; to persuade. **se convaincre**, *v.r.* to convince oneself.
convaincu [kɔ̃vɛ̃'ky], *a.* convinced; sincere; convicted.
convalescence [kɔ̃valɛ'sãːs], *n.f.* convalescence.
convalescent [kɔ̃valɛ'sã], *a.* and *n.m.* (*fem.* **-e**) convalescent (person).
convection [kɔ̃vɛk'sjɔ̃], *n.f.* convection.
convenable [kɔ̃v'nabl], *a.* suitable, fit, proper; convenient; becoming.
convenablement [kɔ̃vənablə'mã], *adv.* suitably, becomingly, decently.
convenance [kɔ̃v'nãːs], *n.f.* fitness, propriety; seasonableness (*of time*); decency, seemliness; (*pl.*) propriety, decorum; *mariage de convenance*, marriage of convenience.
convenir [kɔ̃v'niːr], *v.i. irr.* (*conjug. like* TENIR, *but with aux.* ÊTRE) to agree; to admit, to own, to acknowledge (*de*); (*with aux.* AVOIR) to suit, to fit, to match; (*impers.*) to be fitting. **se convenir**, *v.r.* to suit each other, to agree.
convention [kɔ̃vã'sjɔ̃], *n.f.* agreement, treaty; (*social and other*) convention; (*pl.*) conditions (*of an agreement*).
conventionnel [kɔ̃vãsjɔ'nɛl], *a.* (*fem.* **-elle**) conventional.
conventionnellement [kɔ̃vãsjɔnɛl'mã], *adv.* by agreement.
convenu [kɔ̃v'ny], *a.* agreed; conventional, banal.
convergent [kɔ̃vɛr'ʒã], *a.* convergent.
converger [kɔ̃vɛr'ʒe], *v.i.* (*conjug. like* MANGER) to converge.

conversation [kɔ̃vɛrsɑ'sjɔ̃], *n.f.* conversation, converse, talk.
converse [kɔ̃'vɛrs], *a.* and *n.f.* (*Log.*) converse; (*Math.*) inverted.
converser [kɔ̃vɛr'se], *v.i.* to converse, to discourse.
conversible [kɔ̃vɛr'sibl], [CONVERTIBLE].
conversion [kɔ̃vɛr'sjɔ̃], *n.f.* conversion; transformation; change.
converti [kɔ̃vɛr'ti], *n.m.* (*fem.* **-e**) convert.
convertible [kɔ̃vɛr'tibl], *a.* convertible.
convertir [kɔ̃vɛr'tiːr], *v.t.* to convert, to transform, to change, to turn. **se convertir**, *v.r.* to be converted, to turn.
convertissement [kɔ̃vɛrtis'mã], *n.m.* conversion.
convexe [kɔ̃'vɛks], *a.* convex.
convexité [kɔ̃vɛksi'te], *n.f.* convexity.
conviction [kɔ̃vik'sjɔ̃], *n.f.* conviction, convincing proof.
convié [kɔ̃'vje], *a.* invited.—*n.m.* (*fem.* **-ée**) guest.
convier [kɔ̃'vje], *v.t.* to invite, to bid; (*fig.*) to urge.
convive [kɔ̃'viv], *n.* guest; fellow diner.
convocation [kɔ̃vɔkɑ'sjɔ̃], *n.f.* convocation; summons.
convoi [kɔ̃'vwa], *n.m.* (*Mil., Navy*) convoy; (*Rail. etc.*) train; *convoi funèbre*, funeral procession.
convoiter [kɔ̃vwa'te], *v.t.* to covet, to hanker after.
convoitise [kɔ̃vwa'tiːz], *n.f.* covetousness; lust.
convolution [kɔ̃vɔly'sjɔ̃], *n.f.* convolution.
convolvulus [kɔ̃vɔlvy'lyːs], *n.m.* (*Bot.*) convolvulus.
convoquer [kɔ̃vɔ'ke], *v.t.* to convoke, to convene; to summon.
convoyer [kɔ̃vwa'je], *v.t.* (*conjug. like* EMPLOYER) to convoy, to escort.
convoyeur [kɔ̃vwa'jœːr], *n.m.* convoy (*ship*); (*Mech.*) conveyor.
convulser [kɔ̃vyl'se], *v.t.* to convulse. **se convulser**, *v.r.* to be *or* become convulsed.
convulsif [kɔ̃vyl'sif], *a.* (*fem.* **-sive**) convulsive.
convulsion [kɔ̃vyl'sjɔ̃], *n.f.* convulsion.
convulsionner [kɔ̃vylsjɔ'ne], *v.t.* (*Med.*) to convulse.
convulsivement [kɔ̃vylsiv'mã], *adv.* convulsively.
coolie *or* **coulis** [ku'li], *n.m.* coolie.
coopérateur [kɔɔpera'tœːr], *n.m.* (*fem.* **-trice**) co-operator, fellow-workman.—*a.* (*fem.* **-trice**) co-operating.
coopératif [kɔɔpera'tif], *a.* (*fem.* **-tive**) co-operative.
coopération [kɔɔpera'sjɔ̃], *n.f.* co-operation.
coopérer [kɔɔpe're], *v.i.* (*conjug. like* CÉDER) to co-operate.
coopter [kɔɔp'te], *v.t.* to co-opt.
coordination [kɔɔrdinɑ'sjɔ̃], *n.f.* co-ordination.
coordonné [kɔɔrdɔ'ne], *a.* co-ordinate.—*n.f. pl.* (**-ées**) (*Gram., Geom.*) co-ordinates.
coordonner [kɔɔrdɔ'ne], *v.t.* to co-ordinate.
copain [kɔ'pɛ̃], *n.m.* (*colloq.*) pal, mate.
copal [kɔ'pal], *n.m.* copal.
copeau [kɔ'po], *n.m.* (*pl.* **-eaux**) shaving, chip (*of wood*).
Copenhague [kɔpə'nag], *f.* Copenhagen.

cophte [COPTE].

copie [kɔ'pi], n.f. copy, transcript; reproduction; (*Print.*) 'copy'; candidate's paper.

copier [kɔ'pje], v.t. to copy; to imitate; to
mimic.

copieusement [kɔpjøz'mɑ̃], adv. copiously,
heartily (*of drinking, eating*).

copieux [kɔ'pjø], a. (*fem.* -euse) copious,
plentiful.

co-pilote [kɔpi'lɔt], n.m. second pilot.

copiste [kɔ'pist], n. copier, transcriber,
copyist.

copte or cophte [kɔpt], a. Coptic.—n. (Copte,
Cophte) Copt.

coq [kɔk], n.m. cock, rooster; cock- (*as opposed
to hen*); weathercock; *au chant du coq*, at
cock-crow; *coq de bruyère*, grouse; *coq
d'Inde*, turkey-cock; *poids coq*, (*Box.*)
bantam weight.

coq-à-l'âne [kɔka'lɑːn], n.m. inv. nonsense,
cock-and-bull story.

coque [kɔk], n.f. shell (*of eggs, walnuts, fruits,
snails etc.*); cocoon; cockle-shell (*small
boat*); (*Naut.*) hull.

coquelicot [kɔkli'ko], n.m. corn-poppy.

coqueluche [kɔ'klyʃ], n.f. the rage, favourite;
(*Med.*) whooping-cough.

coquerico [kɔkri'ko], n.m. cock-a-doodle-doo.

coqueriquer [kɔkri'ke], v.i. to crow.

coquet [kɔ'kɛ], a. (*fem.* -ette) coquettish,
stylish, smart.—n.m. (*fem.* -ette) coquette,
flirt; dandy.

coqueter [kɔk'te], v.i. (*conjug. like* APPELER)
to coquet, to flirt.

coquetier [kɔk'tje], n.m. egg-merchant,
poulterer; egg-cup.

coquetterie [kɔkɛ'tri], n.f. coquettishness,
flirtation; affectation (*in dress etc.*).

coquillage [kɔki'jaːʒ], n.m. shell-fish; shell.

coquille [kɔ'kiːj], n.f. shell (*of shell-fish, egg,
fruits etc.*); (*Cook.*) Dutch oven; pat (*of
butter*); (*Print.*) wrong letter; thumb (*of a
latch*); (*Ornament*) conch.

coquin [kɔ'kɛ̃], a. roguish; rascally.—n.m.
knave, rascal, rogue, scamp.—n.f. (-e)
slut, hussy, jade.

coquinerie [kɔkin'ri], n.f. knavery, rascality
roguery.

coquinet [kɔki'ne], n.m. little rascal.

cor (1) [kɔːr], n.m. horn, hunting-horn.

cor (2) [kɔːr], n.m. corn (*on the foot*).

cor (3) [kɔːr], n.m. tine (*of antler*).

corail [kɔ'raːj], n.m. (*pl.* -aux) coral.

corailleur [kɔra'jœːr], n.m. coral-fisher;
coral-fishing boat.

Coran [kɔ'rɑ̃], n.m. Koran.

corbeau [kɔr'bo], n.m. (*pl.* -eaux) crow;
raven.

corbeille [kɔr'bɛːj], n.f. flat, wide basket.

corbillard [kɔrbi'jaːr], n.m. hearse.

corbillon [kɔrbi'jɔ̃], n.m. small basket;
crambo (*game*).

corbin [kɔr'bɛ̃], n.m. crow.

corbine [kɔr'bin], n.f. carrion-crow.

corbleu! [kɔr'blø], int. by Jove!

cordage [kɔr'daːʒ], n.m. cord, rope, cordage,
rigging.

corde [kɔrd], n.f. cord, rope; twine, twist;
string (*musical instrument, racquet*); line;
(*Mus., Geom. etc.*) chord; tone, note; *corde
à boyau*, catgut.

cordé (1) [kɔr'de], a. twisted, corded.

cordé (2) [kɔr'de], a. cordate, heart-shaped.

cordeau [kɔr'do], n.m. (*pl.* -eaux) cord; line;
fuse; tape.

cordée [kɔr'de], n.f. fishing-line; line of
roped mountaineers.

cordeler [kɔrdə'le], v.t. (*conjug. like* APPELER)
to twist, to twine.

cordelette [kɔrdə'lɛt], n.f. small cord; string.

cordelier [kɔrdə'lje], n.m. Franciscan friar.

cordelière [kɔrdə'ljɛːr], n.f. girdle (*of
dressing-gown etc.*).

cordelle [kɔr'dɛl], n.f. towline, tow-rope.

corder [kɔr'de], v.t. to twist (*into cord*); to
cord; to bind with a cord; to string (*racquet*).
se corder, v.r. to be corded; to become
stringy (*of plants etc.*).

corderie [kɔr'dri], n.f. rope-walk.

cordial [kɔr'djal], a. (*m. pl.* -aux) cordial,
hearty, sincere.—n.m. cordial.

cordialement [kɔrdjal'mɑ̃], adv. cordially,
heartily, sincerely.

cordialité [kɔrdjali'te], n.f. cordiality, heartiness.

cordier [kɔr'dje], n.m. rope-maker.

Cordillères [kɔrdi'jɛːr], les, f.pl. the Cor-
dilleras.

cordite [kɔr'dit], n.f. cordite.

cordon [kɔr'dɔ̃], n.m. strand (*of a rope*); twist,
string; cord; ribbon (*of an order*); border,
edging; *cordon bleu*, blue-ribbon, first-
rate cook.

cordonner [kɔrdɔ'ne], v.t. to twist, to twine,
to braid; to mill (*coins*).

cordonnerie [kɔrdɔn'ri], n.f. shoe-making;
cobbler's shop.

cordonnet [kɔrdɔ'nɛ], n.m. twist; milled edge
(*of coins*).

cordonnier [kɔrdɔ'nje], n.m. shoe-maker.

Corée [kɔ're], la, f. Korea.

coréen [kɔre'ɛ̃], a. (*fem.* -enne) Korean.—
n.m. Korean (*language*); (Coréen, *fem.*
-enne) Korean (*person*).

coriace [kɔ'rjas], a. tough, leathery; (*fig.*)
close, niggardly; dogged.

coricide [kɔri'sid], n.m. corn cure.

corinthien [kɔrɛ̃'tjɛ̃], a. (*fem.* -enne)
Corinthian.—n.m. (Corinthien, *fem.* -enne)
Corinthian.

coris [CAURI].

corli [kɔr'li], courlis [kur'li], corlieu
[kɔr'ljø], n.m. curlew.

cormoran [kɔrmɔ'rɑ̃], n.m. cormorant.

cornac [kɔr'nak], n.m. elephant-driver,
mahout; mentor.

corne [kɔrn], n.f. horn, hoof; shoe-horn;
dog's-ear (*on books, leaves*); *chapeau à
trois cornes*, three-cornered hat.

corné [kɔr'ne], a. corneous, horny.

cornée [kɔr'ne], n.f. cornea.

corneille [kɔr'nɛːj], n.f. crow, rook, jackdaw.

cornement [kɔrnə'mɑ̃], n.m. buzzing in the
ears.

cornemuse [kɔrnə'myːz], n.f. bagpipes.

corner (1) [kɔr'ne], v.t. to blurt out, to
trumpet; to dog's-ear (*a leaf*).—v.i. to blow,
wind *or* sound a horn; to tingle (*of the ears*).

corner (2) [kɔr'nɛr], n.m. (*Ftb.*) corner (-kick).

cornet [kɔr'nɛ], n.m. horn, hooter; ink-horn;
cone.

cornette [kɔr'nɛt], n.f. mob-cap; pennant
of cavalry.

corniche [kɔr'niʃ], n.f. cornice; ledge.

cornichon [kɔrni'ʃɔ̃], *n.m.* gherkin; *(fig.)* greenhorn.

corniste [kɔr'nist], *n.* horn-player.

Cornouaille [kɔr'nwɑ:j], **la**, *f.* Cornwall.

cornu [kɔr'ny], *a.* horned; angular, cornered; *(fig.)* absurd.

cornue [kɔr'ny], *n.f.* (*Chem.*) retort.

corollaire [kɔro'lɛːr], *n.m.* corollary.

corolle [kɔ'rɔl], *n.f.* corolla.

coronaire [kɔro'nɛːr], *a.* (*Anat.*) coronary.

coronal [kɔro'nal], *a.* (*m. pl.* -aux) (*Anat.*) coronal.

corporation [kɔrpɔra'sjɔ̃], *n.f.* corporation, corporate body.

corporel [kɔrpɔ'rɛl], *a.* (*fem.* -elle) corporal, bodily.

corps [kɔːr], *n.m.* body; matter, substance; thickness, consistence; chief part; corporation, company; society, college; corps; fellow-creature; *à corps perdu*, desperately; *à son corps défendant*, (*fig.*) reluctantly; *corps à corps*, hand to hand, (*Box.*) in-fight(ing); *corps morts*, (*Naut.*) fixed moorings; *garde du corps*, lifeguard; *sombrer corps et biens*, to founder with all hands.

corpulence [kɔrpy'lɑ̃ːs], *n.f.* corpulence, stoutness.

corpulent [kɔrpy'lɑ̃], *a.* corpulent, stout.

corpuscule [kɔrpys'kyl], *n.m.* corpuscule, corpuscle.

correct [kɔ'rɛkt], *a.* correct, accurate.

correctement [kɔrɛkt'mɑ̃], *adv.* correctly, accurately.

correctif [kɔrɛk'tif], *a.* (*fem.* -tive) corrective. —*n.m.* corrective.

correction [kɔrɛk'sjɔ̃], *n.f.* correction; correctness, accuracy; (*Print.*) reading, alteration (*of a proof etc.*); (*fig.*) reprimand, reproof; punishment; thrashing.

correctionnel [kɔrɛksjɔ'nɛl], *a.* (*fem.* -elle) within the jurisdiction of the *tribunal de police correctionnelle*, court of petty sessions.

corrélation [kɔrela'sjɔ̃], *n.f.* correlation.

correspondance [kɔrɛspɔ̃'dɑ̃ːs], *n.f.* correspondence; connexion; intercourse; conformity; (*Rail.*) connexion.

correspondant [kɔrɛspɔ̃'dɑ̃], *a.* correspondent, corresponding.—*n.m.* (*fem.* -e) correspondent, corresponding member.

correspondre [kɔrɛs'pɔ̃:dr], *v.i.* to correspond, to communicate, to be in correspondence; to agree.

corridor [kɔri'dɔːr], *n.m.* corridor, gallery, passage.

corrigé [kɔri'ʒe], *n.m.* corrected (*schoolboy's*) exercise; key (*book*), crib.

corriger [kɔri'ʒe], *v.t.* (*conjug. like* MANGER) to correct, to rectify; to repair, to amend; to reprove, to chide, to chastise. **se corriger**, *v.r.* to correct oneself, to amend, to reform.

corroboration [kɔrɔbɔra'sjɔ̃], *n.f.* corroboration, strengthening.

corroborer [kɔrɔbɔ're], *v.t.* to strengthen; to corroborate.

corrodant [kɔrɔ'dɑ̃], *a.* corroding, corrosive.

corroder [kɔrɔ'de], *v.t.* to corrode.

corrompre [kɔ'rɔ̃:pr], *v.t.* (*conjug. like* ROMPRE) to corrupt; to infect; to spoil; to taint (*meat*); (*fig.*) to pervert; to bribe. **se**

corrompre, *v.r.* to grow corrupt; to become tainted.

corrompu [kɔrɔ̃'py], *a.* corrupted, unsound; bribed.

corrosif [kɔro'zif], *a.* (*fem.* -sive) and *n.m.* corrosive.

corrosion [kɔro'zjɔ̃], *n.f.* corrosion.

corroyer [kɔrwa'je], *v.t.* (*conjug. like* EMPLOYER) to curry (*leather*); to plane (*wood*).

corroyeur [kɔrwa'jœːr], *n.m.* currier.

corrupteur [kɔryp'tœːr], *a.* (*fem.* -trice) corrupting, perverting, infectious.—*n.m.* (*fem.* -trice) corrupter, seducer; briber.

corruptibilité [kɔryptibili'te], *n.f.* corruptibility.

corruptible [kɔryp'tibl], *a.* corruptible.

corruptif [kɔryp'tif], *a.* (*fem.* -tive) corruptive.

corruption [kɔryp'sjɔ̃], *n.f.* corruption; rottenness; (*fig.*) depravity; (*Polit.*) bribery.

corsage [kɔr'saːʒ], *n.m.* chest (*of the body*); corsage, bodice.

corsaire [kɔr'sɛːr], *n.m.* privateer, corsair; (*fig.*) shark.

Corse [kɔrs], **la**, *f.* Corsica.—*n.* Corsican (*person*).

corse [kɔrs], *a.* Corsican.

corsé [kɔr'se], *a.* rich, full-bodied; (*colloq.*) strong, thick; (*of stories etc.*) spicy.

corser [kɔr'se], *v.t.* to stiffen, to thicken; to complicate.

corset [kɔr'sɛ], *n.m.* corset, stays.

corsetier [kɔrsə'tje], *n.m.* (*fem.* -ière) corset-maker.

cortège [kɔr'tɛ:ʒ], *n.m.* train, retinue, suite, procession.

corvée [kɔr've], *n.f.* (*Feud.*) forced *or* statute labour; fatigue party; (*fig.*) drudgery.

corvette [kɔr'vɛt], *n.f.* corvette, sloop of war.

Cosaque [kɔ'zak], *n.m.* Cossack.

cosinus [kɔsi'nyːs], *n.m.* cosine.

cosmétique [kɔsme'tik], *a.* and *n.m.* cosmetic.

cosmique [kɔs'mik], *a.* cosmic.

cosmographie [kɔsmɔgra'fi], *n.f.* cosmography.

cosmopolite [kɔsmɔpɔ'lit], *n.* cosmopolite. —*a.* cosmopolitan.

cosmos [kɔs'mos], *n.m.* cosmos.

cosse [kɔs], *n.f.* pod, shell, husk, rind.

cossu [kɔ'sy], *a.* substantial, wealthy.

costume [kɔs'tym], *n.m.* costume, dress; uniform.

costumer [kɔsty'me], *v.t.* to dress (*in a certain style etc.*). **se costumer**, *v.r.* to dress (*oneself*) up.

costumier [kɔsty'mje], *n.m.* (*fem.* -ière) costumier.

cote [kɔt], *n.f.* quota, share; letter, number, figure (*to indicate order etc.*); (*St. Exch.*) quotation; (*Comm.*) price-list; odds.

côte [koːt], *n.f.* rib (*of the body, cloth, fruit etc.*); slope, hill; shore, sea-coast; *à mi-côte*, half-way up.

côté [ko'te], *n.m.* side; part, quarter, hand, way, direction; face, aspect; *à côté de*, by, near; *d'à côté*, adjoining, next.

coté [kɔ'te], *a.* marked; classed; backed; *point coté*, (*on a map*) trig-point; *cheval bien coté*, well-backed horse.

coteau [kɔ'to], *n.m.* (*pl.* -eaux) slope; little hill.

côtelette [koˈtlɛt], *n.f.* cutlet, chop.
coter [koˈte], *v.t.* to number; to price; *(St. Exch.)* to quote.
coterie [kɔˈtri], *n.f.* coterie, set, circle, clique.
cothurne [kɔˈtyrn], *n.m.* buskin.
côtier [koˈtje], *a. (fem.* **-ière**) coasting.—*n.m.* coaster *(ship).*
cotillon [kɔtiˈjɔ̃], *n.m.* under-petticoat; cotillion.
cotisation [kɔtizaˈsjɔ̃], *n.f.* assessment, quota, share; subscription.
cotiser [kɔtiˈze], *v.t.* to assess, to rate. **se cotiser**, *v.r.* to club together; to get up a subscription, to subscribe.
coton [kɔˈtɔ̃], *n.m.* cotton; fluff, down *(of fruit, and hair on the face)*; cotton wool.
cotonnade [kɔtɔˈnad], *n.f.* cotton-cloth.
cotonné [kɔtɔˈne], *a.* covered with *or* full of cotton; downy; woolly *(of hair)*; padded.
cotonner [kɔtɔˈne], *v.t.* to fill *or* to stuff with cotton; to pad. **se cotonner**, *v.r.* to be covered with down.
cotonneux [kɔtɔˈnø], *a. (fem.* **-euse**) cottony, downy; spongy, mealy.
cotonnier [kɔtɔˈnje], *n.m.* cotton-bush.
côtoyer [kotwaˈje], *v.t. (conjug. like* EMPLOYER) to go by the side of, to skirt; to coast; *(fig.)* to keep close to.
cotre [koːtr], *n.m.* cutter *(vessel).*
cotret [kɔˈtrɛ], *n.m.* faggot; stick.
cottage [kɔˈtaːʒ], *n.m.* cottage.
cotte [kɔt], *n.f.* short petticoat; *(engineer's)* overalls.
cotuteur [kɔtyˈtœːr], *n.m. (fem.* **-trice**) joint-guardian.
cou [ku], *n.m.* neck.
couac [kwak], *n.m.* false note; squawk.
couard [kwaːr], *a.* coward, cowardly.—*n.m. (fem.* **-e**) coward.
couardise [kwarˈdiːz], *n.f.* cowardice.
couchage [kuˈʃaːʒ], *n.m.* act of lying in bed; bed, night's lodging; bedding.
couchant [kuˈʃɑ̃], *a.* setting; lying; *(fig.)* fawning; **un chien couchant**, a setter.—*n.m.* west; *(fig.)* decline.
couche [kuʃ], *n.f.* bed, couch; confinement; nappy; layer, row; *(Min.)* seam; *(Gard.)* hotbed, bed; coat *(of varnish or colour)*; *(fig.)* social stratum.
couché [kuˈʃe], *a.* in bed, gone to bed, lying down, recumbent; *(Her.)* couchant.
couchée [kuˈʃe], *n.f.* act of lying down; sleeping place; night's lodging.
coucher [kuˈʃe], *v.t.* to put to bed; to lay down; to knock down; to lay on; to stake.—*v.i.* to sleep, to lie (down), to rest; *coucher à la belle étoile*, to sleep in the open air. **se coucher**, *v.r.* to go to bed; to lie down; to set, to go down *(of the sun etc.)*.—*n.m.* going to bed; bed-time; setting *(of the sun etc.)*.
couchette [kuˈʃɛt], *n.f.* small bed, crib; berth; bunk *(on a ship)*; **wagon à couchettes**, second-class sleeper.
coucou [kuˈku], *n.m.* cuckoo; cuckoo-clock; *(Bot.)* cowslip.
coude [kud], *n.m.* elbow; bend, angle; turning.
coudé [kuˈde], *a.* bent, elbowed, cranked.
coudée [kuˈde], *n.f.* length of arm from elbow to tip of middle finger, cubit.
cou-de-pied [kudˈpje], *n.m. (pl.* **cous-de-pied**) instep.
couder [kuˈde] *v.t.* to bend, to make an

elbow in. **se couder**, *v.r.* to elbow, to form an elbow.
coudoyer [kudwaˈje], *v.t. (conjug. like* EMPLOYER) to elbow, to jostle. **se coudoyer**, *v.r.* to elbow *or* jostle each other.
coudraie [kuˈdrɛ], *n.f.* hazel-copse; filbert-orchard.
coudre [kudr], *v.t. irr.* to sew, to stitch; *(fig.)* to attach, to connect.
coudrier [kuˈdrje], *n.m.* hazel-tree.
couenne [kwan], *n.f.* scraped pig-skin; crackling *(of pork)*; rind; *(Med.)* birth-mark.
couette [kwɛt], **coît(t)e** (2) [kwat], *n.f.* feather-bed; sea-gull; *(hare's)* scut.
couguar [kuˈgaːr], *n.m.* cougar, puma.
coulage [kuˈlaːʒ], *n.m.* flow *(of metal in fusion)*; melting, casting; leakage, waste; pilferage.
coulant [kuˈlɑ̃], *a.* flowing, smooth, natural *(of style etc.)*; *(fig.)* easy; **nœud coulant**, slip knot.—*n.m.* sliding ring *(for a necktie, umbrella etc.).*
coulé [kuˈle], *n.m. (Mus.)* slur; *(Billiards)* follow through; *(Swim.)* plunge.
coulée [kuˈle], *n.f.* running-hand *(of writing)*; *(Metal.)* tapping; flow, rush *(of a torrent etc.)*; *(Hunt.)* track, path.
couler [kuˈle], *v.t.* to cast; to strain; to slip *(dans)*; to sink, to run down; *(Mus.)* to slur.—*v.i.* to flow; to glide; to trickle; to leak; to slip away *(of time etc.)*; to founder *(of a ship etc.)*. **se couler**, *v.r.* to slip, to creep, to steal, to glide; to be cast *(of metals).*
couleur [kuˈlœːr], *n.f.* colour; colouring-matter, paint; colouring; *(fig.)* appearance; pretence; suit *(at cards).*
couleuvre [kuˈlœːvr], *n.f.* *(grass)* snake.
coulis [kuˈli], *n.m.* strained juice from meat etc. slowly stewed.
coulisse [kuˈlis], *n.f.* groove, channel; running string; *(Theat.)* wing; *(fig.)* behind the scenes; *porte à coulisse*, sliding door; *faire les yeux en coulisse*, to make sheep's eyes.
coulissé [kuliˈse], *a.* grooved.
coulissier [kuliˈsje], *n.m.* stock-jobber outside broker.
couloir [kuˈlwaːr], *n.m.* passage, corridor, lobby, gangway.
couloire [kuˈlwaːr], *n.f.* colander, strainer.
coup [ku], *n.m.* blow, stroke, hit, thump, knock, stab, thrust; beat *(of a drum)*; draught *(of liquids)*; clap *(of thunder)*; *(Artill.)* charge; gust *(of wind)*; throw; shot; moment; bout; attempt; deed; event; *à coup sûr*, unquestionably; *(Ftb.) coup d'envoi*, kick-off; *coup d'œil*, glance; *coup de téléphone*, telephone call; *le coup de grâce*, the finishing stroke; *tout à coup*, all of a sudden; *tout d'un coup*, all at once.
coupable [kuˈpabl], *a.* culpable, guilty.—*n.* guilty person, culprit.
coupage [kuˈpaːʒ], *n.m.* cutting; diluting *(of wine)*; blending *(of spirits).*
coupant [kuˈpɑ̃], *a.* cutting, sharp.—*n.m.* edge *(of a sword etc.).*
coupe (1) [kup], *n.f.* cutting, felling *(of wood)*; wood felled; the cut end; cut *(clothes etc.)*; shape; *(Pros.)* cadence; *(Swim.)* overarm stroke.

coupe (2) [kup], *n.f.* cup, goblet, chalice; basin (*of a fountain etc.*).

coupé (1) [ku'pe], *a.* intersected; diluted; (*fig.*) laconic.

coupé (2) [ku'pe], *n.m.* coupé (*kind of brougham*); a dance step.

[In the following compounds *coupe* is *inv.*]

coupe-circuit [kupsir'kɥi], *n.m. inv.* cut-out, circuit-breaker; fuse.

coupée [ku'pe], *n.f.* (*Naut.*) gangway; *échelle de coupée*, accommodation ladder.

coupe-file [kup'fil], *n.m. inv.* police pass.

coupe-gorge [kup'gɔrʒ], *n.m. inv.* cut-throat place, den.

coupe-jarret [kupʒa'rɛ], *n.m.* cut-throat, assassin, ruffian.

coupe-papier [kuppa'pje], *n.m. inv.* paper-knife.

couper [ku'pe], *v.t.* to cut; to dock. to strike off; to clip, to pare; to geld; (*Mil.*) to intercept; to dilute (*milk, wine, with water*); to intersect; to interrupt.—*v.i.* to make an incision; to cut, to trump (*at cards*). **se couper**, *v.r.* to cut oneself; to intersect.

couperet [ku'prɛ], *n.m.* (*butcher's*) chopper; knife (*of guillotine*).

couperose [ku'pro:z], *n.f.* copperas.

couperosé [kupro'ze], *a.* blotched.

coupeur [ku'pœːr], *n.m.* (*fem.* **-euse**) cutter.—*n.f.* (**-euse**) cutting machine.

(*C*) **coupe-vent** [kup'vɑ̃], *n.m.* wind breaker.

couplage [ku'plaːʒ], *n.m.* coupling.

couple [kupl], *n.f.* brace, couple.—*n.m.* married couple; pair (*of animals, male and female*); (*Naut.*) frame.

coupler [ku'ple], *v.t.* to couple, to link.

couplet [ku'plɛ], *n.m.* couplet; verse of song; (*fig.*) tirade; (*Tech.*) hinge.

coupleur [ku'plœːr], *n.m.* (*Elec.*) make-and-break.

coupoir [ku'pwaːr], *n.m.* cutter (*instrument*).

coupole [ku'pɔl], *n.f.* cupola; (*Naut.*) revolving gun-turret.

coupon [ku'pɔ̃], *n.m.* remnant; coupon; dividend-warrant, cheque; (*Theat.*) ticket.

coupure [ku'pyːr], *n.f.* cut, incision, slit; cutting; suppression; drain; (*Banking*) small note.

cour [kuːr], *n.f.* court (*of a prince, of justice etc.*); yard, courtyard; (*fig.*) courtship, suit.

courage [ku'raːʒ], *n.m.* courage, daring; spirit, mettle; fortitude, greatness of soul.

courageusement [kuraʒøz'mɑ̃], *adv.* courageously, bravely, resolutely.

courageux [kura'ʒø], *a.* (*fem.* **-euse**) courageous, daring, fearless, plucky.

couramment [kura'mɑ̃], *adv.* fluently, readily.

courant [ku'rɑ̃], *a.* running; current, present; usual; fair, middling (*of goods*); lineal (*of measures*).—*n.m.* stream, current, tide; course (*of time etc.*); routine; present price; present (*time*).

courbage [kur'baːʒ], *n.m.* bending, curving.

courbatu [kurba'ty], *a.* foundered (*of horses*); stiff in the joints; (*Med.*) affected with lumbago.

courbature [kurba'tyːr], *n.f.* foundering, lameness; (*Path.*) stiffness in the limbs, lumbago.

courbaturer [kurbaty're], *v.t.* to make (*someone*) feel stiff all over.

courbe [kurb], *a.* curved, bent, crooked.—*n.f.* curve; (*Naut., Carp.*) knee; (*Vet.*) curb; (*Math.*) graph.

courber [kur'be], *v.t.* to curve, to bend, to warp, to make crooked.—*v.i.* to bend, to sag. **se courber**, *v.r.* to bend, to stoop; to bow down.

courbette [kur'bɛt], *n.f.* curvet; (*pl.*) bowing and scraping, cringing.

courbetter [kurbɛ'te], *v.i.* to curvet.

courbure [kur'byːr], *n.f.* curvature, curve; bend; sagging.

coureur [ku'rœːr], *a.* (*fem.* **-euse**) swift.—*n.m.* runner, racer; hunter (*horse*); light porter; rover; rake, libertine; (*Mil.*) scout.

courge [kurʒ], *n.f.* gourd; *courge à la moelle*, vegetable marrow.

courir [ku'riːr], *v.t. irr.* to pursue; to travel over; to hunt; to frequent; to expose oneself to.—*v.i.* to run; to hasten; to ramble, to rove; to flow; to stretch; to circulate.

courlis [kur'li], **courlieu** [kur'ljø], *n.m.* curlew.

couronne [ku'rɔn], *n.f.* crown; coronet; wreath; crown (*a coin*).

couronnement [kurɔn'mɑ̃], *n.m.* crowning, coronation; completion.

couronner [kurɔ'ne], *v.t.* to crown; to award a prize, to honour (*avec*); to consummate; to wreathe.

courre [kuːr], *v.t. only used in chasse à courre*, hunting.

courrier [ku'rje], *n.m.* messenger, courier; mail, post; letters, correspondence.

courriériste [kurje'rist], *n.m.* columnist.

courroie [ku'rwa], *n.f.* strap, thong; driving belt or band.

courroucer [kuru'se], *v.t.* (*conjug. like* COMMENCER) to provoke, to anger, to incense, to irritate. **se courroucer**, *v.r.* to become angry, to rage.

courroux [ku'ru], *n.m.* wrath, anger, rage.

cours [kuːr], *n.m.* course, stream, current, flow; lapse; path, orbit; vent, scope; public drive or walk; vogue; currency; series of lectures; (*pl.*) classes; (*St. Exch.*) market price, rate.

course [kurs], *n.f.* running, run; course; drive, walk, excursion; career; race; errand; privateering; cruise; length of the stroke (*of a piece of machinery*).

coursier [kur'sje], *n.m.* charger; (*poet.*) steed; (*Naut.*) bow-gun.

coursive [kur'siːv], *n.f.* (*Naut.*) gangway.

court (1) [kuːr], *a.* short; brief; concise, curt; limited, scanty; fleeting.—*adv.* short, abruptly; *demeurer court*, to stop short; *être à court d'argent*, to be short of money.

court (2) [kɔrt, kuːr], *n.m.* tennis court.

courtage [kur'taːʒ], *n.m.* brokerage, commission.

courtaud [kur'to], *a.* thick-set, dumpy, docked, crop-eared.—*n.m.* (*fem.* **-e**) short, thick-set person; docked or crop-eared horse.

courtauder [kurto'de], *v.t.* to dock, to crop (*horses etc.*).

court-circuit [kursir'kɥi], *n.m.* (*pl.* **courts-circuits**) short-circuit.

court-circuiter [kursirkɥi'te], *v.t.* to short-circuit.

courtement [kurtə'mã], *adv.* shortly, briefly.

courtepointe [kurtə'pwɛ̃:t], *n.f.* counterpane, quilt.

courtier [kur'tje], *n.m.* (*fem.* **-ière**) broker, agent.

courtil [kur'til], *n.m.* *small garden; garth.

courtisan [kurti'zã], *n.m.* courtier; fawner.

courtisane [kurti'zan], *n.f.* courtesan.

courtisanerie [kurtizan'ri], *n.f.* court flattery, toadyism.

courtisanesque [kurtiza'nɛsk], *a.* courtier-like.

courtiser [kurti'ze], *v.t.* to court; to woo; to flatter.

courtois [kur'twa], *a.* courteous, polite.

courtoisement [kurtwaz'mã], *adv.* courteously.

courtoisie [kurtwa'zi], *n.f.* courtesy; kindness, good turn.

couseur [ku'zœr], *n.m.* (*fem.* **-euse**) sewer, stitcher (*of books*).

cousin [ku'zɛ̃], *n.m.* (*fem.* **-e**) cousin; (*fig.*) friend, crony.

cousinage [kuzi'na:ʒ], *n.m.* cousinhood; cousins; relationship.

cousiner [kuzi'ne], *v.t.* to call cousin; to hob-nob with.—*v.i.* to live on others; to be friends *or* cronies.

coussin [ku'sɛ̃], *n.m.* cushion, hassock; pad.

coussiner [kusi'ne], *v.t.* to pad, to cushion.

coussinet [kusi'ne], *n.m.* small cushion, pad; iron wedge; pillion.

cousu [ku'zy], *a.* sewn, stitched.

coût [ku], *n.m.* costs, charge; *le coût de la vie*, the cost of living.

coûtant [ku'tã], *a.* costing; *à prix coûtant*, at cost price.

couteau [ku'to], *n.m.* (*pl.* **-eaux**) knife.

coutelas [kut'la], *n.m.* cutlass.

coutelier [kutə'lje], *n.m.* cutler.

coutelière [kutə'ljɛːr], *n.f.* knife-case; cutler's wife.

coutellerie [kutɛl'ri], *n.f.* cutler's shop *or* business; cutlery.

coûter [ku'te], *v.i.* to cost, to cause, to occasion.—*v.i.* to cost (*cher etc.*); to be expensive; (*fig.*) to be painful, troublesome.

coûteusement [kutøz'mã], *adv.* expensively.

coûteux [ku'tø], *a.* (*fem.* **-euse**) expensive, costly.

coutil [ku'ti], *n.m.* tick, ticking; (*Tex.*) drill.

coutre [kutr], *n.m.* plough-share, coulter, axe.

coutume [ku'tym], *n.f.* custom, habit, practice.

coutumier [kuty'mje], *a.* (*fem.* **-ière**) customary, common, ordinary; habitual.

couture [ku'tyːr], *n.f.* sewing, needlework; seam, suture; scar.

couturer [kuty're], *v.t.* to seam.

couturier [kuty'rje], *n.m.* ladies' tailor.—*a.* sartorial.

couturière [kuty'rjɛːr], *n.f.* dressmaker, seamstress.

couvage [ku'va:ʒ], **couvaison** [kuvɛ'zõ], *n.f.* brooding-time, sitting, incubation.

couvée [ku've], *n.f.* sitting (*of eggs*); brood, covey.

couvent [ku'vã], *n.m.* convent, monastery, nunnery; convent school.

couver [ku've], *v.t.* to sit on, to incubate, to hatch; to brood, to prepare in secret (*a plot etc.*); to brood over.—*v.i.* to lie hidden, to lurk; to smoulder.

couvercle [ku'vɛrkl], *n.m.* cover, lid, cap, shutter.

couvert [ku'vɛːr], *a.* covered; clad, clothed; cloudy, overcast; obscure, ambiguous (*of words*).—*n.m.* cover (*plate, spoon, knife, fork*); shelter; cover, wrapper; covert, thicket; *le vivre et le couvert*, board and lodging.

couverte [ku'vɛrt], *n.f.* glaze, glazing.

couverture [kuvɛr'tyːr], *n.f.* covering, wrapper; blanket, rug, counterpane, quilt; cover (*of a book*); (*Comm.*) guaranty, security; *couverture chauffante*, electric blanket.

couveuse [ku'vøːz], *n.f.* broody hen; *couveuse artificielle*, incubator.

couvi [ku'vi], *a.* addled, rotten (*egg*).

couvoir [ku'vwaːr], *n.m.* incubator.

[In the following compounds **couvre** is *inv.*]

couvre-chef [kuvrə'ʃɛf], *n.m.* headgear.

couvre-feu [kuvrə'fø], *n.m. inv.* curfew; curfew-bell; fire-cover, fire-plate; black-out.

couvre-plat [kuvrə'pla], *n.m.* dish-cover.

couvre-théière [kuvrəte'jɛːr], *n.m.* tea-cosy.

couvreur [ku'vrœːr], *n.m.* roofer.

couvrir [ku'vriːr], *v.t. irr.* (*conjug. like* OUVRIR) to cover; to wrap up; to roof; to overwhelm; to clothe; to defend, to protect; to overrun, to overflow; to excuse; to disguise; to defray (*expenses etc.*). **se couvrir**, *v.r.* to cover oneself, to put on (*one's hat*); to get under cover; to be overcast (*of the weather*); (*Comm.*) to reimburse oneself.

coyote [ko'jɔt], *n.m.* prairie wolf.

crabe [kra:b], *n.m.* crab.

crac! [krak], *int.* crack! pop!

crachat [kra'ʃa], *n.m.* spittle, expectoration.

crachement [kraʃ'mã], *n.m.* spitting.

cracher [kra'ʃe], *v.t.* to spit; (*fig.*) to spit out, to come out with.—*v.i.* to spit, to splutter; (*Mach. etc.*) to spark, to backfire.

crachoir [kra'ʃwaːr], *n.m.* spittoon.

crachoter [kraʃo'te], *v.i.* to spit often.

Cracovie [krako'vi], *f.* Cracow.

craie [krɛ], *n.f.* chalk.

craillement [kraj'mã], *n.m.* cawing (*of crows*).

crailler [kra'je], *v.i.* to caw.

craindre [krɛ̃:dr], *v.t. irr.* to fear; to dread; to dislike.

crainte [krɛ̃:t], *n.f.* fear, apprehension; dread, awe.

craintif [krɛ̃'tif], *a.* (*fem.* **-tive**) fearful, apprehensive, timid.

craintivement [krɛ̃tiv'mã], *adv.* fearfully timorously.

cramoisi [kramwa'zi], *a.* and *n.m.* crimson.

crampe [krã:p], *n.f.* cramp; crampon.

crampon [krã'põ], *n.m.* crampon, cramp-iron, grappling-iron.

cramponner [krãpo'ne], *v.t.* to cramp, to fasten with a cramp-iron. **se cramponner**, *v.r.* to hold fast, to cling like grim death.

cramponnet [krãpɔ'nɛ], *n.m.* small cramp, tack; staple (*of a lock*).

cran (1) [krã], *n.m.* notch; cog; (*Print.*) nick; (*fam.*) pluck.

cran (2) [krã], *n.m.* horse-radish.

crâne [krɑ:n], *a.* bold, plucky.—*n.m.* skull, cranium.

crânement [krɑn'mã], *adv.* pluckily; in style, famously.

craner [kra'ne], *v.t.* to notch, to indent (*a clock wheel*).

crâner [krɑ'ne], *v.i.* to swagger.

cranologie [kranɔlɔ'ʒi], **craniologie** [kranjɔlɔ'ʒi], *n.f.* craniology.

crapaud [kra'po], *n.m.* toad; jumping cracker; (*fig.*) urchin, brat.

crapaudière [krapo'djɛ:r], *n.f.* nest of toads; (*fig.*) low, swampy place.

crapaudine [krapo'din], *n.f.* toadstone; grating (*of an escape-pipe*); **à la crapaudine**, cut open and broiled.

crapouillot [krapu'jo], *n.m.* trench-mortar.

crapule [kra'pyl], *n.f.* low vulgar debauchery, gluttony, drunkenness; blackguards.

crapuleusement [krapyløz'mã], *adv.* dissolutely.

crapuleux [krapy'lø], *a.* (*fem.* **-euse**) low, debauched, vicious, dissolute.

craque [krak], *n.f.* fib, humbug.

craqueler [kra'kle], *v.t.* (*conjug. like* APPELER) to crackle (*china*).

craquelot [kra'klo], *n.m.* bloater.

craquelure [kra'kly:r], *n.f.* crack (*in china*).

craquement [krak'mã], *n.m.* cracking noise, creaking, snapping (*boughs*).

craquer [kra'ke], *v.i.* to crack, to crackle, to snap, to creak, to crunch.

craquètement [krakɛt'mã], *n.m.* crackling; chattering (*of the teeth*); gabbling (*of a stork and other birds*).

craqueter [krak'te], *v.i.* (*conjug. like* APPELER) to crackle, to crepitate; to gabble (*birds*).

crasse (1) [kras], *a.* gross, thick, coarse, crass.

crasse (2) [kras], *n.f.* dirt, filth, squalor; stinginess; dross.

crasser [kra'se], *v.t.* to foul, to dirty (*fire-arms etc.*). **se crasser**, *v.r.* to become foul (*of fire-arms etc.*).

crasseux [kra'sø], *a.* (*fem.* **-euse**) dirty, filthy, nasty, squalid, sordid; stingy, mean.—*n.m.* (*fem.* **-euse**) sloven, slut; skinflint.

crassier [kra'sje], *n.m.* slag heap; rubbish dump.

cratère [kra'tɛ:r], *n.m.* crater (*mouth of volcano*); (*Gr. or Rom.*) bowl or cup.

cravache [kra'vaʃ], *n.f.* riding-whip.

cravacher [krava'ʃe], *v.t.* to horsewhip.

cravate [kra'vat], *n.f.* cravat, (neck-)tie.

cravater (se) [səkrava'te], *v.r.* to put on one's (neck-)tie.

cravatier [krava'tje], *n.m.* maker or vendor of neckties.

crawl [krol], *n.m.* (*Swim.*) crawl.

crawleur [kro'lœ:r], *n.m.* crawl-swimmer.

crayer [krɛ'je], *v.t.* (*conjug. like* PAYER) to chalk, to mark up etc. with chalk.

crayère [krɛ'jɛ:r], *n.f.* chalk-pit.

crayeux [krɛ'jø], *a.* (*fem.* **-euse**) chalky.

crayon [krɛ'jõ], *n.m.* pencil; drawing or portrait in crayon; (*fig.*) style; sketch; **crayon à bille**, ball-point pen.

crayonnage [krɛjɔ'na:ʒ], *n.m.* pencil-drawing.

crayonner [krɛjɔ'ne], *v.t.* to draw with a pencil; to mark with a pencil; (*fig.*) to sketch.

crayonneux [krɛjɔ'nø], *a.* (*fem.* **-euse**) chalky.

créance [kre'ã:s], *n.f.* credence, trust, belief; credit; money owing; (*Hunt.*) command.

créancier [kreã'sje], *n.m.* (*fem.* **-ière**) creditor.

créateur [krea'tœ:r], *a.* (*fem.* **-trice**) creative, inventive.—*n.m.* (*fem.* **-trice**) creator, maker, author.

création [krea'sjõ], *n.f.* creation; universe; establishment; (*Dress.*) design.

créature [krea'ty:r], *n.f.* creature; man, as opposed to God.

crécelle [kre'sɛl], *n.f.* child's or hand rattle.

crécerelle [kres'rɛl], *n.f.* (*Orn.*) kestrel.

crèche [krɛ:ʃ], *n.f.* manger; crib; crèche.

crédence [kre'dã:s], *n.f.* credence-table; side-board.

crédibilité [kredibili'te], *n.f.* credibility.

crédit [kre'di], *n.m.* credit; trust; authority, influence; esteem; vogue; parliamentary grant.

créditer [kredi'te], *v.t.* to credit.

créditeur [kredi'tœ:r], *a.* credit.—*n.m.* (*fem.* **-trice**) creditor.

credo [kre'do], *n.m.* (*no pl.*) creed, belief.

crédule [kre'dyl], *a.* credulous.

crédulement [kredyl'mã], *adv.* credulously.

crédulité [kredyli'te], *n.f.* credulity.

créer [kre'e], *v.t.* to create; to produce; to invent; to imagine; to establish.

crémaillère [krema'jɛ:r], *n.f.* pot-hook.

crémation [krema'sjõ], *n.f.* cremation.

crématorium [krematɔ'rjɔm], *n.m.* (*pl.* **-ia**) crematorium.

crème [krɛ:m], *n.f.* cream; custard; sweet liqueur; the best part of a thing.

crémer (1) [kre'me], *v.t.* (*conjug. like* CÉDER) to dye cream colour.—*v.i.* to cream.

crémer (2) [kre'me], *v.t.* (*conjug. like* CÉDER) to cremate.

crémerie [krem'ri], *n.f.* creamery, dairy.

crémeux [kre'mø], *a.* (*fem.* **-euse**) creamy.

crémier [kre'mje], *n.m.* (*fem.* **-ière**) milkman, dairyman or -woman.—*n.f.* (**-ière**) cream-jug.

créneau [kre'no], *n.m.* (*pl.* **-eaux**) battlement.

crénelage [kren'la:ʒ], *n.m.* milling, milled edge (*on coins*), crenellation.

créneler [kren'le], *v.t.* (*conjug. like* APPELER) to embattle; to indent, to notch.

crénelure [kren'ly:r], *n.f.* crenellation; notching.

créole [kre'ɔl], *a.* Creole.—*n.* (**Créole**) Creole.

créosote [kreɔ'zɔt], *n.f.* creosote.

créosoter [kreɔzɔ'te], *v.t.* to creosote.

crêpe (1) [krɛ:p], *n.m.* crape; (*fig.*) veil; crêpe-rubber.

crêpe (2) [krɛ:p], *n.f.* pancake.

crêpelu [krɛ'ply], *a.* frizzy (*hair*).

crêper [krɛ'pe], *v.t.* to crisp, to frizz.

crépi [kre'pi], *n.m.* rough-cast, parget.

crépir [kre'pi:r], *v.t.* to rough-cast, to plaster.

crépissage [krepi'sa:ʒ], **crépissement** [krepis'mã], *n.m.* plastering, pargeting, rough-casting.

crépissure [krepi'sy:r], *n.m.* parget; rough-casting.

crépitant [krepi'tā], *a.* crepitating; crackling.
crépitation [krepita'sjō], *n.f.*, **crépitement** [krepit'mā], *n.m.* crepitation; crackling.
crépiter [krepi'te], *v.i.* to crackle; to crepitate.
crépu [kre'py], *a.* crisped, frizzy; woolly.
crépure [krɛ'py:r], *n.f.* crisping; craping.
crépusculaire [krepysky'lɛ:r], *a.* crepuscular, twilight.
crépuscule [krepys'kyl], *n.m.* twilight; dawn.
créquier [kre'kje], *n.m.* sloe-tree.
cresson [krɛ'sō], *n.m.* cress.
cressonnière [krɛso'njɛ:r], *n.f.* water-cress bed.
Crésus [kre'zy:s], Croesus.
crésus [kre'zy:s], *n.m. inv.* very rich man.
crétacé [kreta'se], *a.* cretaceous, chalky.
Crète [krɛ:t], la, *f.* Crete.
crête [krɛ:t], *n.f.* crest, comb (*of a cock or hen*); tuft; ridge; coping.
crêté [krɛ'te], *a.* crested, tufted.
crêteler [krɛ'tle], *v.i.* (*conjug. like* APPELER) to cackle (*of hens*).
crétin [kre'tɛ̃], *a.* cretinous; idiotic.—*n.m.* (*fem.* **-e**) cretin; idiot, dunce.
crétinerie [kretin'ri], *n.f.* idiotic behaviour; foolishness.
crétiniser [kretini'ze], *v.t.* to make cretinous, to brutalize, to make an idiot of.
crétinisme [kreti'nism], *n.m.* cretinism.
crétois [kre'twa], *a.* Cretan.—*n.m.* (**Crétois**, *fem.* **-oise**) Cretan (*person*).
cretonne [krə'ton], *n.f.* cretonne.
creusage [krø'za:ʒ], **creusement** [krøz'mā], *n.m.* deepening, hollowing; excavation.
creuser [krø'ze], *v.t.* to dig, to hollow, to excavate, to scoop out; to sink, to drive (*a well, shaft etc.*); to make hollow *or* empty. **se creuser,** *v.r.* to become hollow.
creuset [krø'ze], *n.m.* crucible, melting-pot; (*fig.*) test, trial.
creux [krø], *a.* (*fem.* **creuse**) hollow; cavernous; deep; empty; (*fig.*) airy, extravagant. —*n.m.* hollow, cavity; pit, hole, chasm; mould, mortar, trough.—*adv.* hollow; **sonner creux,** to sound hollow.
crevaison [krəvɛ'zō], *n.f.* puncture (*of a tyre*).
crevant [krə'vā], *a.* (*vulg.*) tiresome; killing (*toil etc.*); killing (*funny*).
crevasse [krə'vas], *n.f.* crevice, rift, crack, chink, crevasse; gap, cranny; chap (*in the hands etc.*).
crevasser [krəva'se], *v.t.* to split; to crack; to chap. **se crevasser,** *v.r.* to crack, to become chapped.
crevé [krə've], *n.m.* (*Dress.*) opening, slash (*in sleeves*).
crève-cœur [krɛv'kœ:r], *n.m. inv.* heart-break; heart-breaking thing.
crever [krə've], *v.t.* (*conjug. like* AMENER) to burst, to split, to break open; to rend; to stave in; to puncture.—*v.i.* to burst; to die (*animals*); (*vulg.*) to die (*human beings*). **se crever,** *v.r.* to burst; to kill oneself.
crevette [krə'vɛt], *n.f.* shrimp, prawn.
cri [kri], *n.m.* cry; scream, roar, yell, shriek, screech, wail, outcry, clamour.
criaillement [kriaj'mā], *n.m.* shouting, wrangling, brawling; scolding.

criailler [kria'je], *v.i.* to bawl, to cry, to clamour; to scold; to brawl; to gabble (*of geese*).
criaillerie [kriaj'ri], *n.f.* brawling, clamouring, wrangling.
criailleur [kria'jœ:r], *n.m.* (*fem.* **-euse**) brawler, wrangler; shrew, scold.
criant [kri'ā], *a.* crying; (*fig.*) glaring, shocking.
criard [kri'a:r], *a.* crying, noisy, clamorous; scolding; (*fig.*) shrill, discordant, crude.— *n.m.* (*fem.* **-e**) bawler, clamourer; scold, shrew.
criblage [kri'bla:ʒ], *n.m.* sifting, screening (*of coals etc.*).
crible [kribl], *n.m.* sieve, riddle.
cribler [kri'ble], *v.t.* to sift, to riddle; to pierce all over, to riddle (*with wounds etc.*); (*fig.*) to overwhelm.
cric [kri], *n.m.* jack, screw-jack, hand-screw.
cri-cri [kri'kri], *n.m. inv.* (*fam.*) cricket (*insect*); chirping.
criée [kri'e], *n.f.* (*public*) auction.
crier [kri'e], *v.t.* to cry, to proclaim, to put up for sale; to publish; to announce.—*v.i.* to cry out; to shout, to scream, to shriek; to call out; to whine; to complain loudly, to exclaim; to chirp; to creak.
crieur [kri'jœ:r], *n.m.* (*fem.* **-euse**) bawler; crier; (*Theat.*) call-boy; auctioneer; hawker; **crieur public,** town-crier; **crieur de journaux,** newsboy.
crime [krim], *n.m.* crime, offence.
Crimée [kri'me], la, *f.* the Crimea.
criminel [krimi'nɛl], *a.* (*fem.* **-elle**) criminal, felonious, guilty.—*n.m.* (*fem.* **-elle**) criminal, felon, culprit, offender.
criminellement [kriminɛl'mā], *adv.* criminally, culpably, guiltily.
crin [krɛ̃], *n.m.* horse-hair, bristles, fibres, mane.
crinière [kri'njɛ:r], *n.f.* mane (*of animal*).
crinoline [krino'lin], *n.f.* crinoline.
crique [krik], *n.f.* creek, cove; flaw, crack.
criquet [kri'kɛ], *n.m.* locust; (*fig.*) bad horse.
criqueter [krik'te], *v.i.* (*conjug. like* APPELER) to rasp, to grate.
crise [kri:z], *n.f.* crisis; fit, convulsion; slump.
crispation [krispa'sjō], *n.f.* shrivelling, crispation; fidgets.
crisper [kris'pe], *v.t.* to shrivel; to irritate (*the nerves*), to give (*someone*) the fidgets. **se crisper,** *v.r.* to shrivel, to contract.
crissement [kris'mā], *n.m.* grating (*of teeth, of brakes etc.*).
crisser [kri'se], *v.i.* to grate, to squeak.
cristal [kris'tal], *n.m.* (*pl.* **-aux**) crystal, cut glass; (*fig.*) limpidity; **cristal de mine,** quartz; **cristal de roche,** rock-crystal.
cristallerie [kristal'ri], *n.f.* glass-cutting; crystal-manufactory, glass-works.
cristallier [krista'lje], *n.m.* glass-cutter; glass-cupboard.
cristallière [krista'ljɛ:r], *n.f.* rock-crystal mine; machine for glass-cutting.
cristallin [krista'lɛ̃], *a.* crystalline; pellucid. —*n.m.* (*Anat.*) crystalline lens (*of the eye*); (*Astron.*) crystalline heaven.
cristallisant [kristali'zā], *a.* crystallizing.
cristallisation [kristaliza'sjō], *n.f.* crystallization.

cristalliser [kristali'ze], *v.t.*, *v.i.* to crystallize. **se cristalliser**, *v.r.* to crystallize; to candy.

critère [kri'tɛːr], **critérium** [krite'rjɔm], *n.m.* criterion, standard, test.

critiquable [kriti'kabl], *a.* open to criticism, censurable, exceptionable.

critique [kri'tik], *a.* critical; censorious, carping; ticklish, momentous; critical (*in the literary sense*).—*n.m.* critic; censor, carper.—*n.f.* criticism, science of criticism; review.

critiquer [kriti'ke], *v.t.* to criticize unfavourably; to censure, to find fault with.

critiqueur [kriti'kœːr], *n.m.* (*fem.* **-euse**) criticizer, fault-finder, carper.

croassement [krɔas'mã], *n.m.* croak, croaking, cawing (*of rooks*).

croasser [krɔa'se], *v.i.* to croak, to caw (*of crows, rooks etc.*).

croate [krɔ'at], *a.* Croatian.—*n.m.* Croatian (*language*).—*n.* (**Croate**) Croat.

Croatie [krɔa'si], la, *f.* Croatia.

croc [kro], *n.m.* hook; fang (*of dog*), tusk (*of walrus*).

croc-en-jambe [krɔkã'ʒã:b], *n.m.* (*pl.* **crocs-en-jambe**) trip up; dirty trick.

croche [krɔʃ], *a.* crooked, bent.—*n.f.* (*Mus.*) quaver; (*pl.*) smith's tongs; **double croche**, semi-quaver; **triple croche**, demi-semi-quaver.

crocher [krɔ'ʃe], *v.t.* to hook; to bend like a hook.

crochet [krɔ'ʃɛ], *n.m.* small hook; knitting-needle, crochet-hook; (*Print.*) square bracket; teeth of certain animals.

crochetable [krɔʃ'tabl], *a.* pickable (*of locks*).

crochetage [krɔʃ'ta:ʒ], *n.m.* lock-picking.

crocheter [krɔʃ'te], *v.t.* (*conjug. like* AMENER) to pick (*a lock*); to crochet.

crochetier [krɔʃ'tje], *n.m.* hook-maker, clasp-maker.

crochu [krɔ'ʃy], *a.* crooked, hooked.

crocodile [krɔkɔ'dil], *n.m.* crocodile; (*Rail.*) automatic stop.

crocus [krɔ'kyːs], *n.m.* (*Bot.*) crocus.

croire [krwaːr], *v.t. irr.* to believe; to have faith in; to think, to deem.—*v.i.* to believe, to have faith (à); to be a believer. **se croire**, *v.r.* to believe or think oneself, to consider oneself; to be believed, to be credible.

croisade [krwa'zad], *n.f.* crusade.

croisé [krwa'ze], *a.* crossed; twilled, double-milled (*of cloth*); cross (*of breeds of animals*); **mots croisés**, a crossword.—*n.m.* crusader; twill; crossing (*a step in dancing*).

croisée [krwa'ze], *n.f.* crossing point; casement window (*opening inside*).

croisement [krwaz'mã], *n.m.* crossing (*of two roads etc.*); meeting; cross-breeding (*of animals*).

croiser [krwa'ze], *v.t.* to cross; to lay across; to cross (*breeds of animals*); to pass (*a person*); to thwart.—*v.i.* to overlap; to cruise. **se croiser**, *v.r.* to cross or pass each other; to be crossed; to thwart one another.

croiseur [krwa'zœːr], *n.m.* cruiser.

croisière [krwa'zjɛːr], *n.f.* cruise, cruising; (*Rail.*) crossing.

croissance [krwa'sãːs], *n.f.* growth, increase.

croissant [krwa'sã], *a.* growing, increasing.—*n.m.* the moon in her increase; crescent; pruning-hook, hedging-bill; crescent roll.

croît [krwa], *n.m.* increase (*from breeding*).

croître [krwaːtr], *v.i. irr.* to grow; to increase; to wax (*moon*); to spring up, to sprout; to lengthen; to swell.

croix [krwa], *n.f.* cross; the Holy Rood; (*fig.*) affliction; (*Coin.*) obverse.

cromlech [krɔm'lɛk], *n.m.* (*Archaeol.*) stone circle.

crône [kroːn], *n.m.* crane (*on a wharf*).

croquade [krɔ'kad], *n.f.* rough sketch.

croquant [krɔ'kã], *a.* crisp, crackling, short.—*n.m.* poor wretch; clodhopper.—*n.f.* crisp almond-cake.

croque-au-sel (à la) [krɔkɔ'sɛl], *adv. phr.* with salt only.

croque-mitaine [krɔkmi'tɛn], *n.m.* (*pl.* **croque-mitaines**) bogy-man.

croquer [krɔ'ke], *v.t.* to crunch; to devour; to draft, to sketch.—*v.i.* to crackle between the teeth, to make a scrunching noise.

croquet [krɔ'kɛ], *n.m.* crisp biscuit; croquet (*game*).

croquette [krɔ'kɛt], *n.f.* croquette.

croquignole [krɔki'nɔl], *n.f.* cracknel; fillip; (*C*) doughnut.

croquis [krɔ'ki], *n.m.* first sketch, rough draft, outline.

cross [krɔs], *n.m.* (*Box.*) cross-counter; cross-country running.

crosse [krɔs], *n.f.* crooked stick, crosier (*of bishops*); butt (*of rifle*); stock; hockey-stick, golf-club) etc.; (*C*) **jeu de crosse**, lacrosse.

crossé [krɔ'se], *a.* crosiered, mitred.

crosser [krɔ'se], *v.t.* to strike (*a ball etc.*).

crosseur [krɔ'sœːr], *n.m.* hockey-player, lacrosse-player.

crotale [krɔ'tal], *n.m.* rattlesnake.

crotte [krɔt], *n.f.* dung; dirt, mud, mire.

crotté [krɔ'te], *a.* dirty, muddy; (*fig.*) squalid.

crotter [krɔ'te], *v.t.* to dirty; to draggle, to bespatter. **se crotter**, *v.r.* to get dirty.

crottin [krɔ'tɛ̃], *n.m.* dung.

croulant [kru'lã], *a.* sinking, crumbling, tottering, tumbledown.

croulement [krul'mã], *n.m.* sinking, falling in, collapse.

crouler [kru'le], *v.i.* to give way, to fall in, to collapse.

croup [krup], *n.m.* (*Path.*) croup, diphtheria.

croupal [kru'pal], *a.* (*m. pl.* **-aux**) pertaining to the croup; laryngitic.

croupe [krup], *n.f.* croup, crupper, buttocks (*of a horse*), rump; top or brow (*of a hill*); **monter en croupe**, to ride pillion.

croupé [kru'pe], *a.* with a rump or crupper.

croupi [kru'pi], *a.* stagnant, putrid; **de l'eau croupie**, ditch-water.

croupier [kru'pje], *n.m.* croupier (*at a gaming-table*); partner (*of a financier etc.*).

croupière [kru'pjɛːr], *n.f.* saddle-tie, crupper.

croupion [kru'pjɔ̃], *n.m.* rump; **le croupion** (*d'une volaille*), the parson's nose.

croupir [kru'piːr], *v.i.* to stagnate; to wallow.

croupissant [krupi'sã], *a.* stagnant, putrescent.

croupon [kru'põ], *n.m.* square hide, butt.

croustillant [krusti'jã], *a.* crisp, crusty.

croustille [krus'tiːj], *n.f.* little crust; (*fig.*) snack.

croustiller

croustiller [krusti′je], *v.i.* to bite, eat, crunch a crust, to munch.

croûte [krut], *n.f.* crust; pie-crust; scab; *casser la croûte,* to have a snack; *(C)* crust *(of the snow)*; *(fig.)* bad painting, daub.

croûton [kru′tɔ̃], *n.m.* bit of crust, crusty end; sippet.

croyable [krwɑ′jabl], *a.* credible, likely.

croyance [krwɑ′jɑ̃ːs], *n.f.* belief; creed, faith.

croyant [krwɑ′jɑ̃], *a.* believing.—*n.m.* *(fem.* **-e)** believer.

cru (1) [kry], *n.m.* growth; production *(esp. of wine).*

cru (2) [kry], *a.* raw, uncooked; unwrought; *(fig.)* crude, coarse, indecent; *à cru,* on the bare skin.

cruauté [kryo′te], *n.f.* cruelty, inhumanity.

cruche [kryʃ], *n.f.* pitcher, jar, jug; *(colloq.)* blockhead.

cruchée [kry′ʃe], *n.f.* pitcherful, jugful, jarful.

cruchon [kry′ʃɔ̃], *n.m.* little pitcher; *(stone)* hot-water bottle.

crucial [kry′sjal], *a.* *(m. pl.* **-aux)** cross-shaped, crucial; *(fig.)* decisive.

crucifiement [krysifi′mɑ̃], *n.m.* crucifixion.

crucifier [krysi′fje], *v.t.* to crucify.

crucifix [krysi′fi], *n.m.* crucifix.

crucifixion [krysifik′sjɔ̃], *n.f.* crucifixion.

cruciforme [krysi′fɔrm], *a.* cruciform, cross-shaped.

crudité [krydi′te], *n.f.* crudity, rawness; coarse expression; *(pl.)* raw vegetables *or* fruit.

crue [kry], *n.f.* growth, increase; rise, swelling *(of river etc.);* flood.

cruel [kry′ɛl], *a.* *(fem.* **-elle)** cruel, merciless; bloodthirsty; hard; grievous, sad.

cruellement [kryɛl′mɑ̃], *adv.* cruelly; unmercifully; severely.

crûment [kry′mɑ̃], *adv.* roughly, coarsely; crudely.

crustacé [krysta′se], *a.* crustaceous.—*n.m.* crustacean; shell-fish.

crypte [kript], *n.f.* crypt.

cryptogramme [kriptɔ′gram], *n.m.* cryptogram, cipher.

cryptographe [kriptɔ′graf], *n.* cryptographer.

cryptographie [kriptɔgra′fi], *n.f.* cryptography.

cryptographique [kriptɔgra′fik], *a.* cryptographic.

cubage [ky′baːʒ], *n.m.* cubage, cubature; cubic content.

cubain [ky′bɛ̃], *a.* Cuban.—*n.m.* **(Cubain,** *fem.* **-aine)** Cuban *(person).*

cubature [kyba′tyːr], *n.f.* cubature.

cube [kyb], *a.* cubic.—*n.m.* cube *(shape and measure).*

cuber [ky′be], *v.t.* to cube.

cubique [ky′bik], *a.* cubic; cubical.

cubisme [ky′bism], *n.m.* *(Art)* cubism.

cubiste [ky′bist], *a.* and *n.* cubist.

cueillage [kœ′jaːʒ], *n.m.,* **cueillaison** [kœjɛ′zɔ̃], **cueille** [kœːj], *n.f.* gathering-time, gathering.

cueillette [kœ′jɛt], *n.f.* gathering of a crop; harvesting time.

cueilleur [kœ′jœːr], *n.m.* *(fem.* **-euse)** gatherer, picker.

cueillir [kœ′jiːr], *v.t. irr.* to gather, to cull, to pick, to pluck; to acquire.

cueilloir [kœj′waːr], *n.m.* fruit-basket; implement for picking fruit.

cuiller [kɥi′je], **cuillère** [kɥi′jɛːr], *n.f.* spoon; scoop.

cuillerée [kɥij′re], *n.f.* spoonful.

cuilleron [kɥij′rɔ̃], *n.m.* bowl of a spoon.

cuir [kɥiːr], *n.m.* hide; leather; strop.

cuirasse [kɥi′ras], *n.f.* cuirass, breast-plate.

cuirassé [kɥira′se], *a.* armed with a cuirass; armour-plated; hardened; secret.—*n.m.* *(Naut.)* battleship.

cuirassement [kɥiras′mɑ̃], *n.m.* armour-plating.

cuirasser [kɥira′se], *v.t.* to arm with a cuirass; to armour-plate; *(fig.)* to steel, to harden. **se cuirasser,** *v.r.* to put on a cuirass; to harden *or* fortify oneself.

cuirassier [kɥira′sje], *n.m.* cuirassier.

cuire [kɥiːr], *v.t. irr. (conjug. like* CONDUIRE*)* to cook; to burn *(of the sun);* to ripen.—*v.i.* to cook, to be cooked, to be done; to bake, boil etc.; to smart.

cuisage [kɥi′zaːʒ], *n.m.* burning *(of charcoal),* charring.

cuisant [kɥi′zɑ̃], *a.* sharp, smarting, piercing.

cuiseur [kɥi′zœːr], *n.m.* pressure cooker.

cuisine [kɥi′zin], *n.f.* kitchen; cookery; cooks; fare, living; *(Naut.)* galley.

cuisiner [kɥizi′ne], *v.t., v.i.* to cook.

cuisinier [kɥizi′nje], *n.m.* *(fem.* **-ière)** cook.—*n.f.* **(-ière)** Dutch oven.

cuisse [kɥis], *n.f.* thigh; quarter *(of venison);* leg *(of poultry).*

cuisseau [kɥi′so], *n.m.* *(pl.* **-eaux)** leg *(of veal).*

cuisson [kɥi′sɔ̃], *n.f.* cooking *(baking, boiling, roasting etc.);* smart *(pain).*

cuissot [kɥi′so], *n.m.* haunch *(of venison).*

cuit [kɥi], *a.* cooked, done *(roasted, boiled, baked etc.);* *(fig.)* done for, dished.

cuite [kɥit], *n.f.* baking; burning *(of bricks etc.);* ovenful, kilnful; *(slang)* intoxication.

cuivrage [kɥi′vraːʒ], *n.m.* coppering; copper-plating.

cuivre [kɥiːvr], *n.m.* copper; copper money; copper-plate; *cuivre battu,* wrought copper; *cuivre jaune,* brass; *cuivre rouge,* copper.

cuivré [kɥi′vre], *a.* copper-coloured; *(fig.)* bronzed *(complexion);* ringing, clear.

cuivrer [kɥi′vre], *v.t.* to cover with copper.

cuivrerie [kɥivrə′ri], *n.f.* copper-works; copper wares.

cuivreux [kɥi′vrø], *a.* *(fem.* **-euse)** coppery.

cul [ky], *n.m.* *(indec.)* backside, posterior; bottom *(of bottle or bag);* stern *(of ship).*

culasse [ky′las], *n.f.* breech *(of a cannon etc.);* cylinder-head *(of car engine).*

culbute [kyl′byt], *n.f.* somersault; fall, tumble; *(fig.)* ruin, bankruptcy.

culbuter [kylby′te], *v.t.* to throw over, to upset violently; to overthrow.—*v.i.* to fall head over heels.

culbutis [kylby′ti], *n.m.* confused heap, jumble.

cul de bouteille [kydbu′tɛj], *a.* bottle-green.—*n.m.* bottom of bottle.

cul-de-jatte [kyd′ʒat], *n.m.* *(pl.* **culs-de-jatte)** legless cripple.

cul-de-lampe [kyd′lɑ̃p], *n.m.* *(Print.)* tail-piece.

cul-de-sac [kyd′sak], *n.m.* *(pl.* **culs-de-sac)** blind alley, cul-de-sac; *(fig.)* deadlock.

culée [ky'le], n.f. abutment (of bridges); (Naut.) stern-way.

culer [ky'le], v.i. to go backwards; to fall astern.

culière [ky'ljɛːr], n.f. hind girth, crupper (of harness); gutter-stone.

culinaire [kyli'nɛːr], a. culinary.

culminance [kylmi'nɑ̃:s], n.f. culmination, highest point.

culminant [kylmi'nɑ̃], a. culminating; prominent.

culmination [kylminɑ'sjɔ̃], n.f. culmination.

culminer [kylmi'ne], v.i. to culminate.

culot [ky'lo], n.m. bottom (of lamps, crucibles etc.); residuum, (fam.) dottle (in a pipe).

culottage [kylo'ta:ʒ], n.m. colouring, seasoning (of pipes).

culotte [ky'lɔt], n.f. breeches; (pl.) shorts; tights; (Cook.) rump (of an ox).

culotter [kylo'te], v.t. to breech, to put in breeches; to colour (pipes). se culotter, v.r. to put on one's breeches; to become coloured (of pipes).

culottier [kylo'tje], n.m. (fem. -ière) breeches-maker.

culpabilité [kylpabili'te], n.f. culpability; guilt.

culte [kylt], n.m. worship, adoration; (fig.) cult, religion, creed; veneration, love.

cultivable [kylti'vabl], a. cultivable, arable.

cultivateur [kyltiva'tœːr], a. agricultural.— n.m. (fem. -trice) cultivator, farmer, agriculturist; cultivator (implement).

cultivé [kylti've], a. cultivated; (of the mind) cultured.

cultiver [kylti've], v.t. to cultivate; to till; to improve (the mind); to study, to practise; to cultivate the acquaintance of.

cultural [kylty'ral], a. (m. pl. -aux) cultural (in relation to agriculture).

culture [kyl'ty:r], n.f. culture, cultivation, tillage, husbandry; education, improvement.

culturel [kylty'rɛl], a. (fem. -elle) cultural (in relation to intellectual culture).

cumulatif [kymyla'tif], a. (fem. -tive) cumulative.

cumulativement [kymylativ'mɑ̃], adv. by accumulation.

cumuler [kymy'le], v.t. to accumulate; to hold several (offices, salaries etc.).

cumulus [kymy'ly:s], n.m. cumulus.

cupide [ky'pid], a. covetous, greedy, grasping.

cupidement [kypid'mɑ̃], adv. greedily, covetously.

cupidité [kypidi'te], n.f. cupidity, covetousness, greed.

Cupidon [kypi'dɔ̃], n.m. (Myth.) Cupid, Love.

curable [ky'rabl], a. curable.

curaçao [kyra'so], n.m. curaçao (liqueur).

curage [ky'ra:ʒ], curement [kyr'mɑ̃], n.m. cleansing.

curatelle [kyra'tɛl], n.f. guardianship, trusteeship.

curateur [kyra'tœːr], n.m. (fem. -trice) guardian, trustee.

curatif [kyra'tif], a. (fem. -tive) curative.— n.m. curative agent.

cure [ky:r], n.f. medical treatment, cure, healing; living, rectorship; vicarage, rectory.

curé [ky're], n.m. parish priest; parson, rector, vicar.

cure-dent [kyr'dɑ̃], n.m. (pl. cure-dents) tooth-pick.

curée [ky're], n.f. (Hunt.) quarry, chase; (fig.) prey, booty.

curement [CURAGE].

cure-môle [kyr'moːl], n.m. (pl. cure-môles) dredging-machine.

cure-ongles [kyr'ɔ̃gl], n.m. inv. nail-file.

curer [ky're], v.t. to cleanse, to clean out (harbours, sewers etc.); to pick (teeth, ears etc.).

curial (1) [ky'rjal], a. (m. pl. -aux) vicarial, rectorial.

curial (2) or curiale [ky'rjal], a. (Rom. Ant.) curial.

curie [ky'ri], n.f. (Rom. Ant.) curia.

curieusement [kyrjøz'mɑ̃], adv. curiously; inquisitively; carefully; quaintly.

curieux [ky'rjø], a. (fem. -euse) curious; inquisitive, prying; inquiring; careful; dainty; particular; strange.—n.m. (fem. -euse) interested person; inquisitive person; sightseer, looker-on.—n.m. curious fact.

curiosité [kyrjozi'te], n.f. curiosity; inquisitiveness; curio, rarity; quaintness.

cursif [kyr'sif], a. (fem. -sive) cursive, running; cursory.

cursivement [kyrsiv'mɑ̃], adv. cursively; cursorily.

curure [ky'ry:r], n.f. dirt, sewage.

cussonné [kyso'ne], a. worm-eaten (of wood).

custode [kys'tɔd], n.m. warden (among monks); custodian, inspector.

cutané [kyta'ne], a. cutaneous.

cuticule [kyti'kyl], n.f. cuticle.

cuvage [ky'va:ʒ], n.m., cuvaison [kyvɛ'zɔ̃], n.f. fermenting (of wine).

cuve [ky:v], n.f. tub, vat.

cuvée [ky've], n.f. tubful; vatful.

cuvelage [ky'vla:ʒ], cuvellement [kyvɛl'mɑ̃], n.m. lining, casing (of mine-shafts).

cuveler [ky'vle], v.t. (conjug. like APPELER) to line, to case (mine shafts etc.).

cuver [ky've], v.t. to ferment; (fam.) to sleep off the effects of (wine).—v.i. to work, to ferment, to settle.

cuvette [ky'vɛt], n.f. shallow basin; wash-hand basin; lavatory bowl.

cuvier [ky'vje], n.m. wash-tub.

cyanure [sja'ny:r], n.m. (Chem.) cyanide.

cybernétique [siberne'tik], n.f. cybernetics.

cyclamen [sikla'mɛn], n.m. cyclamen, sowbread.

cycle [sikl], n.m. cycle (of events); cycle à 4 temps (d'un moteur), 4-stroke cycle (of an engine).

cyclique [si'klik], a. cyclical.

cyclisme [si'klism], n.m. cycling.

cycliste [si'klist], n. cyclist.

cyclomoteur [siklomo'tœːr], n.m. auto-cycle.

cyclonal [siklo'nal], a. (m. pl. -aux) cyclonic.

cyclone [si'klo:n], n.m. cyclone.

cyclonique [siklo'nik], a. cyclonic.

Cyclope [si'klɔp], n.m. Cyclops.

cygne [siɲ], n.m. swan.

cylindrage [silɛ̃'dra:ʒ], n.m. mangling (of linen etc.); rolling (of roads).

cylindre [si'lɛ̃:dr], n.m. cylinder; roller; garden-roller; mangle, calender.

cylindrée [silɛ̃'dre], *n.f.* cubic capacity of an engine.
cylindrer [silɛ̃'dre], *v.t.* to calender; to roll.
cylindrique [silɛ̃'drik], *a.* cylindrical.
cymaise [CIMAISE].
cymbale [sɛ̃'bal], *n.f.* (*Mus.*) cymbal.
cymbalier [sɛ̃ba'lje], *n.m.* cymbal-player.
cynancie [sinã'si], [ESQUINANCIE].
cynégétique [sineʒe'tik], *a.* relating to hunting and dogs.—*n.f.* the art of hunting with dogs, cynegetics.
cynique [si'nik], *a.* cynical; snarling, snappish; impudent.—*n.* cynic.
cyniquement [sinik'mã], *adv.* cynically.
cynisme [si'nism], *n.m.* cynicism; impudence.
cynodrome [sinɔ'dro:m], *n.m.* greyhound racing track.
cynosure [sinɔ'sy:r], *n.f.* (*Astron.*) Cynosure, Little Bear.
cyprès [si'prɛ], *n.m.* cypress, cypress-tree.
cyprière [si'prjɛ:r], *n.f.* cypress-grove.
cypriote [si'prjɔt], *a.* Cypriot.—*n.* (**Cypriote**) Cypriot (*person*).
cytise [si'ti:z], *n.m.* cytisus, laburnum.
czar [tsa:r], [TZAR].

D

D, d [de], *n.m.* the fourth letter of the alphabet.
d', *abbr.* [DE].
da [da], *particle* (*used after* **oui, non**) truly, indeed; *oui-da*, yes indeed.
d'abord [da'bɔ:r], [ABORD].
dactylo [dakti'lo], *n.f. abbr. of* [DACTYLO-GRAPHE].
dactylographe [daktilɔ'graf], *n.f.* typist.
dactylographie [daktilɔgra'fi], *n.f.* typewriting.
dactylographier [daktilɔgra'fje], *v.t.* to type(write).
dactylographique [daktilɔgra'fik], *a.* typewritten (*report*); typewriting (*material*).
dactyloptère [daktilɔp'tɛ:r], *n.m.* flying-fish.
dada [da'da], *n.m.* (*childish*) horse, cockhorse; gee-gee.
dadais [da'dɛ], *n.m.* booby, clown, ninny.
dague [dag], *n.f.* dagger, dirk.
daguerréotype [dagɛreɔ'tip], *n.m.* daguerreotype.
dahlia [da'lja], *n.m.* dahlia.
daigner [dɛ'ne], *v.i.* to deign, to condescend.
d'ailleurs [da'jœ:r], [AILLEURS].
daim [dɛ̃], *n.m.* deer, fallow-deer; buck.
daine [dɛn], *n.f.* doe.
dais [dɛ], *n.m.* canopy.
dallage [da'la:ʒ], *n.m.* paving with flagstones.
dalle [dal], *n.f.* flag, flagstone; slab.
daller [da'le], *v.t.* to pave with flagstones, to flag.
dalleur [da'lœ:r], *n.m.* pavior.
dalmate [dal'mat], *a.* Dalmatian.—*n.* (**Dalmate**) Dalmatian (*person*).
dalmatique [dalma'tik], *n.f.* dalmatic.
daltonisme [daltɔ'nism], *n.m.* colour-blindness.

damas [da'ma], *n.m.* damask; damson; Damascus blade.
damasquiner [damaski'ne], *v.t.* to damascene.
damassé [dama'se], *n.m.* damask linen, damask cloth.
damasser [dama'se], *v.t.* to damask.
damassin [dama'sɛ̃], *n.m.* figured linen cloth, diaper.
damassure [dama'sy:r], *n.f.* damasking (*of linen*); damask work.
dame (1) [dam], *n.f.* (*married*) lady, dame; rowlock; beetle, rammer; (*Cards*, and *Chess*) queen.
dame (2) [dam], *int.* **dame oui!** why, yes!
dame-jeanne [dam'ʒɑ:n], *n.f.* (*pl.* **dames-jeannes**) demijohn, carboy.
damer [da'me], *v.t.* (*Draughts*) to crown (*a man*); (*Chess*) to queen; to ram (*earth etc.*).
damier [da'mje], *n.m.* draught-board.
damnable [dɑ'nabl], *a.* damnable.
damnablement [dɑnablɑ'mã], *adv.* damnably.
damnation [dɑnɑ'sjõ], *n.f.* damnation.
damné [dɑ'ne], *a.* and *n.m.* (*fem.* **-ée**) damned (person).
damner [dɑ'ne], *v.t.* to damn. **se damner**, *v.r.* to damn oneself.
dancing [dã'siŋ], *n.m.* dance-hall, palais de danse.
dandin [dã'dɛ̃], *n.m.* ninny.
dandinement [dãdin'mã], *n.m.* swinging (*of the body*); rolling gait.
dandiner [dãdi'ne], *v.i.* to swing (*of the body*), to dandle (*of a baby*). **se dandiner**, *v.r.* to waddle.
dandy [dã'di], *n.m.* dandy.
dandysme [dã'dism], *n.m.* dandyism.
Danemark [dan'mark], **le**, *m.* Denmark.
danger [dã'ʒe], *n.m.* danger, peril, risk, hazard.
dangereusement [dãʒrøz'mã], *adv.* dangerously.
dangereux [dã'ʒrø], *a.* (*fem.* **-euse**) dangerous.
danois [da'nwa], *a.* Danish.—*n.m.* Danish (*language*); Great Dane (*dog*); (**Danois**, *fem.* **-oise**) Dane (*person*).
dans [dã], *prep.* in, within; into; with, according to; during; out of.
danse [dã:s], *n.f.* dance; dancing; (*fig.*) beating, hiding; **danse de Saint-Guy**, St. Vitus's dance.
danser [dã'se], *v.t., v.i.* to dance.
danseur [dã'sœ:r], *n.m.* (*fem.* **-euse**) dancer, ballet-girl.
dard [da:r], *n.m.* dart; sting; forked tongue (*of a snake*); pistil.
darder [dar'de], *v.t.* to hurl; to spear; to shoot forth, to beam, to dart.
dardillon [dardi'jõ], *n.m.* small dart; barb (*of a fish-hook*).
dare-dare [dar'da:r], *adv.* (*fam.*) in great haste, in double-quick time.
darne [darn], *n.f.* slice (*of fish*).
dartre [dartr], *n.f.* slight and dry eruption (*of the skin*); scurf.
dartreux [dar'trø], *a.* (*fem.* **-euse**) herpetic, scurfy.
date [dat], *n.f.* date.
dater [da'te], *v.t.* to date (*a letter etc.*).—*v.i.* to date (*de*); to reckon.
datif [da'tif], *n.m.* (*Gram.*) dative, dative case

débordé

datte [dat], *n.f.* date.
dattier [da'tje], *n.m.* date-palm.
datura [daty'ra], *n.m.* datura, thorn-apple.
daube [do:b], *n.f.* stew.
dauber [do'be], *v.t.* to cuff, to drub; (*fig.*) to banter, to jeer at; (*Cook.*) to stew.
daubeur [do'bœ:r], *n.m.* (*fem.* **-euse**) jeerer, banterer, sneerer.
daubière [do'bjɛ:r], *n.f.* stew-pan.
dauphin [do'fɛ̃], *n.m.* dolphin; dauphin (*eldest son of the king of France*).
dauphine [do'fin], *n.f.* wife of the dauphin.
dauphinelle [dofi'nɛl], *n.f.* (*Bot.*) larkspur, delphinium.
daurade [do'rad], *n.f.* gilt-head (*fish*).
davantage [davɑ̃'ta:ʒ], *adv.* more, any more; any longer, any further.
davier [da'vje], *n.m.* dentist's forceps; cramp; (*Naut.*) davit.
de [də], *prep.* of; out of, made of, composed of, from; by, with; at, for; concerning, about.
dé (1) [de], *n.m.* die (*for playing*); (*fig.*) throw, hazard.
dé (2) [de], *n.m.* thimble.
débâcher [debɑ'ʃe], *v.t.* to uncover, to untilt.
débâcle [de'bɑ:kl], *n.f.* breaking up (*of ice*); (*fig.*) downfall, collapse.
débâcler [debɑ'kle], *v.i.* to break up (*of ice*).
débâcleur [debɑ'klœ:r], *n.m.* water or portbailiff.
déballage [deba'la:ʒ], *n.m.* unpacking.
déballer [deba'le], *v.t.* to unpack.
débandade [debɑ̃'dad], *n.f.* rout, stampede; *à la débandade*, in confusion.
débander [debɑ̃'de], *v.t.* to unbind; to loosen, to remove a bandage from. se **débander**, *v.r.* to slacken, to relax; to disband.
débaptiser [debati'ze], *v.t.* to change the name of.
débarbouillage [debarbu'ja:ʒ], *n.m.* washing, cleansing.
débarbouiller [debarbu'je], *v.t.* to wash, to cleanse. se **débarbouiller**, *v.r.* to wash one's face etc.; (*fig.*) to extricate oneself.
débarcadère [debarka'dɛ:r], *n.m.* landing-place, wharf; (*Rail.*) station; arrival platform.
débardage [debar'da:ʒ], *n.m.* unloading (*of wood etc.*).
débarder [debar'de], *v.t.* to unload (*wood etc.*); to clear (*a wood etc.*) of felled trees.
débardeur [debar'dœ:r], *n.m.* stevedore, lighterman, docker.
débarquement [debarkə'mɑ̃], *n.m.* landing, disembarkation (*of persons*); unloading (*of goods*).
débarquer [debar'ke], *v.t.*, *v.i.* to disembark, to land.
débarras [deba'ra], *n.m.* riddance, disencumbrance; *chambre de débarras*, lumber-room, box-room.
débarrasser [debara'se], *v.t.* to disencumber, to rid; to disentangle, to extricate; to clear (*the table*). se **débarrasser**, *v.r.* to extricate oneself, to rid oneself of; to shake off; to get clear.
débarrer [deba're], *v.t.* to unbar.
débat [de'ba], *n.m.* dispute, contest; debate, discussion; (*pl.*) parliamentary debates.
débateler [debatə'le], *v.t.* (*conjug. like* APPELER) to unlade (*boats etc.*).

débâter [debɑ'te], *v.t.* to unsaddle; to take a packsaddle off.
débâtir [debɑ'ti:r], *v.t.* to pull down, to demolish; to unbaste, to untack (*garments*).
débattre [de'batr], *v.t. irr.* (*conjug. like* BATTRE) to debate, to discuss, to argue. se **débattre**, *v.r.* to struggle, to strive; to flounder, to flutter.
débauche [de'bo:ʃ], *n.f.* debauchery; dissoluteness.
débauché [debo'ʃe], *n.m.* debauchee, rake.
débaucher [debo'ʃe], *v.t.* to debauch; to corrupt; to lead astray. se **débaucher**, *v.r.* to become debauched.
débet [de'bɛ], *n.m.* debit.
débile [de'bil], *a.* weak, feeble.
débilement [debil'mɑ̃], *adv.* feebly, weakly.
débilité [debili'te], *n.f.* debility, weakness.
débiliter [debili'te], *v.t.* to debilitate, to enfeeble.
débit [de'bi], *n.m.* sale; market; retail; retail shop; (*fig.*) delivery, utterance; (*Book-keeping*) debit.
débitage [debi'ta:ʒ], *n.m.* cutting up (*of stones, timber etc.*).
débitant [debi'tɑ̃], *n.m.* (*fem.* **-e**) retailer, dealer.
débiter [debi'te], *v.t.* to sell; to retail; to supply; to debit; to cut up (*wood, stone etc.*); (*fig.*) to spread, to report, to utter.
débiteur (1) [debi'tœ:r], *n.m.* (*fem.* **-trice**) debtor.
débiteur (2) [debi'tœ:r], *n.m.* (*fem.* **-euse**) prattler, newsmonger.
déblai [de'blɛ], *n.m.* clearing; excavation; (*pl.*) earth, stones etc. cleared away.
déblaiement or **déblayement** [deblɛ'mɑ̃], *n.m.* clearance; cutting, excavation, digging.
déblatérer [deblate're], *v.i.* (*conjug. like* CÉDER) to utter violent abuse, to rail (*contre*).
déblayement [DÉBLAIEMENT].
déblayer [deblɛ'je], *v.t.* (*conjug. like* PAYER) to clear away; to clear; (*fig.*) to sweep away (*obstacles etc.*).
déblocage [deblo'ka:ʒ], *n.m.* (*Print.*) turning letters.
débloquer [deblo'ke], *v.t.* to raise the blockade from; (*Print.*) to turn letters; to unlock; to release.
débobiner [debobi'ne], *v.t.* to unwind.
déboire [de'bwa:r], *n.m.* after-taste; (*fig.*) disappointment, vexation.
déboisement [debwaz'mɑ̃], *n.m.* clearing of trees, deforestation.
déboiser [debwa'ze], *v.t.* to clear of trees.
déboîtement [debwat'mɑ̃], *n.m.* dislocation.
déboîter [debwa'te], *v.t.* to put out of joint, to dislocate; (*Elec.*) to disconnect. se **déboîter**, *v.r.* to be dislocated.
débonder [debɔ̃'de], *v.t.* to unplug, to unstopper; to loosen, to unbind.—*v.i.* or se **débonder**, *v.r.* to gush, to break out, to burst forth; to be relaxed (*of a person*).
débonnaire [debo'nɛ:r], *a.* good-natured, easy-tempered.
débonnairement [debonɛr'mɑ̃], *adv.* compliantly, easily.
débonnaireté [debonɛr'te], *n.f.* compliance, good-nature.
débordé [debor'de], *a.* overflowing (*river*); overwhelmed (*man*); outflanked (*troops*).

97

débordement

débordement [debɔrdə'mã], *n.m.* overflowing, flood; outburst; (*fig.*) dissoluteness.

déborder [debɔr'de], *v.t.* to take off the border from; to go beyond; to outrun.—*v.i.* to overflow, to run over; to project, to jut out. **se déborder**, *v.r.* to overflow; to run over, to burst forth.

débordoir [debɔr'dwaːr], *n.m.* edging-tool; spoke-shave.

débosseler [debɔs'le], *v.t.* (*conjug. like* APPELER) to take the dents out of.

débotté or **débotter** (1) [debɔ'te], *n.m.* the moment of taking boots off; (*fig.*) *au débotté*, at once.

débotter (2) [debɔ'te], *v.t.* to pull off (*someone's*) boots. **se débotter**, *v.r.* to take off one's boots.

débouché [debu'ʃe], *n.m.* outlet, issue; waterway; (*Comm.*) market, sale.

débouchage [debu'ʃaːʒ], **débouchement** [debuʃ'mã], *n.m.* uncorking; outlet; market, sale.

déboucher [debu'ʃe], *v.t.* to open, to clear; to uncork; to unplug.—*v.i.* to emerge; to empty itself (*of rivers*); (*Mil.*) to debouch.

déboucler [debu'kle], *v.t.* to unbuckle; to uncurl.

débouler [debu'le], *v.i.* to roll down (*like a ball*); to start off suddenly (*like a hare*).

déboulonner [debulɔ'ne], *v.t.* to unrivet, to unbolt.

débourrer [debu're], *v.t.* to draw the wad *or* wadding out of (*fire-arms*); to empty the tobacco out of (*a pipe*); (*fig.*) to polish (*a person's manners*).

débours [de'buːr], **déboursé** [debur'se], *n.m.* disbursement, outlay.

déboursement [deburs'mã], *n.m.* outlay, expenditure.

débourser [debur'se], *v.t.* to disburse, to expend, to lay out.

debout [də'bu], *adv.* upright, on end, standing up; out of bed, up; in existence; (*Naut.*) ahead (*of the wind*).

déboutonner [debutɔ'ne], *v.t.* to unbutton. **se déboutonner**, *v.r.* to unbutton oneself; (*colloq.*) to unbosom oneself.

débraillé [debra'je], *a.* loosely dressed, in disorder.—*n.m.* disorder, untidiness; (*fig.*) licence.

débrailler (se) [sədebra'je], *v.r.* to uncover one's breast, to be untidy *or* disordered.

débrancher [debrã'ʃe], *v.t.* (*Elec.*) to disconnect.

débrayage [debrɛ'jaːʒ], **désembrayage** [dezãbrɛ'jaːʒ], *n.m.* disengaging gear (*of motors etc.*); declutching.

débrayer [debrɛ'je], *v.t.* (*conjug. like* PAYER) to throw out of gear, to disengage, to declutch.

débridement [debrid'mã], *n.m.* unbridling; (*fig.*) dispatch, hurry.

débrider [debri'de], *v.t. v.i.* to unbridle (*horse*); to halt.

débris [de'bri], *n.m.* (*usu. in pl.*) remains, debris, rubbish.

débrouillard [debru'jaːr], *a.* and *n.m.* (*fem.* **-e**) (*colloq.*) resourceful (person).

débrouiller [debru'je], *v.t.* to disentangle, to unravel; (*fig.*) to explain. **se débrouiller**, *v.r.* to be cleared up; to get out of difficulties, to manage.

débusquement [debyskə'mã], *n.m.* driving out, dislodging.

débusquer [debys'ke], *v.t.* to turn out, to oust, to expel; (*Hunt.*) to start.

début [de'by], *n.m.* lead; outset; début.

débutant [deby'tã], *n.m.* (*fem.* **-e**) actor *or* actress appearing for the first time; beginner.

débuter [deby'te], *v.i.* to lead, to play first; to open; to start; to make one's début.

deçà [də'sa], *prep.* on this side of; short of, well within.—*adv.* here, on this side; *deçà* (*et*) *delà*, here and there.

décachetage [dekaʃ'taːʒ], *n.m.* unsealing, opening.

décacheter [dekaʃ'te], *v.t.* (*conjug. like* APPELER) to unseal, to open.

décadaire [deka'deːr], *a.* decadal.

décade [de'kad], *n.f.* decade, group of ten.

décadenasser [dekadna'se], *v.t.* to unpadlock.

décadence [deka'dãːs], *n.f.* decadence, decline, wane.

décadent [deka'dã], *a.* and *n.m.* (*fem.* **-e**) decadent (person).

décaèdre [deka'ɛdr], *a.* decahedral.—*n.m.* decahedron.

décagonal [dekagɔ'nal], *a.* (*pl.* **-aux**) decagonal (*ten-sided*).

décagone [deka'gɔn], *n.m.* decagon.

décagramme [deka'gram], *n.m.* decagramme, ten grammes.

décaissement [dekɛs'mã], **décaissage** [dekɛ'saːʒ], *n.m.* uncasing, unpacking.

décaisser [dekɛ'se], *v.t.* to unpack; to pay out.

décaler [deka'le], *v.t.* to unwedge.

décalaminage [dekalami'naːʒ], *n.m.* (*Motor.*) decarbonizing.

décalaminer [dekalami'ne], *v.t.* to decarbonize.

décalitre [deka'litr], *n.m.* decalitre (2·2 *gallons*).

décalquer [dekal'ke], *v.t.* to transfer (*a tracing*), to countertrace.

décamètre [deka'mɛtr], *n.m.* decametre.

décamper [dekã'pe], *v.i.* to decamp; (*fig.*) to bolt.

décanter [dekã'te], *v.t.* to decant, to pour off gently.

décapitation [dekapita'sjɔ̃], *n.f.* decapitation, beheading.

décapiter [dekapi'te], *v.t.* to behead, to decapitate.

décapotable [dekapɔ'tabl], *a.* (*Motor.*) convertible.

décarboniser [dekarbɔni'ze], *v.t.* to decarbonize.

décarburation [dekarbyra'sjɔ̃], *n.f.* decarbonization.

décarburer [dekarby're], *v.t.* to decarburize, to decarbonize.

décastère [deka'stɛːr], *n.m.* measure of 10 steres *or* cubic metres (13·1 cubic yards).

décathlon [dekat'lɔ̃], *n.m.* (*spt.*) decathlon.

decauville [dəkɔ'vil], *n.m.* narrow gauge railway.

décaver [deka've], *v.t.* to win the whole of the stakes from, (*fam.*) to clean out; (*fig.*) to ruin, to beggar.

décédé [dese'de], *n.m.* (*fem.* **-ée**) deceased (*person*).

décéder [dese'de], *v.i.* (*conjug. like* CÉDER) to die, to decease.

décèlement [desɛl'mã], *n.m.* disclosure, exposure, discovery.

déceler [des'le], *v.t.* (*conjug. like* AMENER) to disclose, to reveal, to betray. **se déceler**, *v.r.* to betray oneself.

déceleur [des'lœːr], *n.m.* (*fem.* **-euse**) betrayer, revealer.

décembre [de'sãːbr], *n.m.* December.

décemment [desa'mã], *adv.* decently.

décence [de'sãːs], *n.f.* decency, propriety.

décent [de'sã], *a.* decent, becoming; modest.

décentralisation [desãtraliza'sjõ], *n.f.* decentralization.

décentraliser [desãtrali'ze], *v.t.* to decentralize.

déception [desɛp'sjõ], *n.f.* disappointment; deception, deceit.

décernement [desɛrnə'mã], *n.m.* awarding.

décerner [desɛr'ne], *v.t.* to decree, to enact; to award, to confer (*an honour*); to issue (*a summons etc.*).

décès [de'sɛ], *n.m.* decease, demise, death.

décevant [des'vã], *a.* deceptive; disappointing.

décevoir [desə'vwaːr], *v.t. irr.* (*conjug. like* RECEVOIR) to deceive; to disappoint.

déchaînement [deʃɛn'mã], *n.m.* unbridling, bursting (*of storm*); outburst (*of passion*); fury, rage; invective.

déchaîner [deʃɛ'ne], *v.t.* to unchain, to let loose; to give vent to (*passion*). **se déchaîner**, *v.r.* to break loose; to burst out; to run wild (*of passions etc.*).

déchaler [deʃa'le], *v.i.* to ebb; to lie dry.

déchanter [deʃã'te], *v.i.* to lower one's key (*in singing*); (*fig.*) to lower one's pretensions, to sing another tune.

déchaperonner [deʃaprɔ'ne], *v.t.* to unhood (*a hawk etc.*); to uncope (*a wall*).

décharge [de'ʃarʒ], *n.f.* unloading; rebate (*on a tax*); outlet, discharge (*of water etc.*); (*Law*) discharge, acquittal; (*Mil.*) volley.

déchargement [deʃarʒə'mã], *n.m.* unloading, unlading.

décharger [deʃar'ʒe], *v.t.* (*conjug. like* MANGER) to unload; to empty; to disburden; to discharge; to fire (*fire-arms*); to acquit (*de*). **se décharger**, *v.r.* to be unloaded, to discharge; to give vent (*to*); to unburden oneself.

déchargeur [deʃar'ʒœːr], *n.m.* unloader, wharf-porter, heaver, lumper.

décharné [deʃar'ne], *a.* fleshless; lean, emaciated.

décharnement [deʃarnə'mã], *n.m.* emaciation.

décharner [deʃar'ne], *v.t.* to strip the flesh off; to emaciate.

déchaumage [deʃo'maːʒ], *n.m.* (*Agric.*) ploughing up fallow ground.

déchaumer [deʃo'me], *v.t.* to plough up the stubble on; to break up (*fallow land*).

déchaussé [deʃo'se], *a.* barefooted.

déchausser [deʃo'se], *v.t.* to pull off (*some-one's*) shoes and stockings; to lay bare the root *or* base (*of trees, buildings, teeth etc.*). **se déchausser**, *v.r.* to take off one's shoes and stockings.

déchéance [deʃe'ãːs], *n.f.* forfeiture; disgrace; deposition.

déchet [de'ʃɛ], *n.m.* loss, waste, offal.

décheveler [deʃə'vle], *v.t.* (*conjug. like* APPELER) to dishevel [ÉCHEVELER].

déchevêtrer [deʃəvɛ'tre], *v.t.* to unhalter (*a beast of burden*).

décheviller [deʃəvi'je], *v.t.* to unpeg, to unpin.

déchiffrable [deʃi'frabl], *a.* legible.

déchiffrement [deʃifrə'mã], *n.m.* deciphering; reading *or* playing at sight.

déchiffrer [deʃi'fre], *v.t.* to decipher, to unravel; to read *or* play at sight. **se déchiffrer**, *v.r.* to be deciphered.

déchiffreur [deʃi'frœːr], *n.m.* (*fem.* **-euse**) decipherer; sight-reader; *déchiffreur de radar*, radar scanner.

déchiqueté [deʃik'te], *a.* jagged, indented.

déchiqueter [deʃik'te], *v.t.* (*conjug. like* APPELER) to cut, to slash, to hack; to cut into long pieces.

déchiqueture [deʃik'tyːr], *n.f.* tear, slash.

déchirage [deʃi'raːʒ], *n.m.* ripping up, breaking up (*of a ship etc.*).

déchirant [deʃi'rã], *a.* heart-rending, piercing; excruciating.

déchirement [deʃir'mã], *n.m.* rending, tearing, laceration; (*fig.*) heart-break.

déchirer [deʃi're], *v.t.* to tear to pieces, to rend; (*fig.*) to torture; to revile. **se déchirer**, *v.r.* to tear, to be torn; to defame each other.

déchirure [deʃi'ryːr], *n.f.* rent, tear; fissure.

déchoir [de'ʃwaːr], *v.i. irr.* to decay, to fall off, to decline; to sink.

déchouer [deʃu'e], *v.t.* to get off, to set afloat.

déchu [de'ʃy], *a.* fallen, decayed; sunken; *ange déchu*, fallen angel.

décidé [desi'de], *a.* decided, determined, resolved.

décidément [deside'mã], *adv.* decidedly, positively; firmly; definitely.

décider [desi'de], *v.t.* to decide, to determine, to settle; to induce, to persuade.—*v.i.* to decide. **se décider**, *v.r.* to decide, to determine, to make up one's mind.

décigramme [desi'gram], *n.m.* decigram (*one-tenth of a gramme*, 1·54 *grains*).

décilitre [desi'litr], *n.m.* decilitre (*one-tenth of a litre*).

décimal [desi'mal], *a.* (*m.pl.* **-aux**) decimal.—*n.f.* (**-e**) a decimal.

décimalisation [desimaliza'sjõ], *n.f.* decimalization.

décimaliser [desimali'ze], *v.t.* to decimalize.

décimateur [desima'tœːr], *n.m.* tithe-owner.

décime [de'sim], *n.f.* tithe.

décimer [desi'me], *v.t.* to decimate, to destroy, to annihilate.

décimètre [desi'mɛtr], *n.m.* decimetre (3·937 *inches*).

décimo [desi'mo], *adv.* tenthly.

décintrer [desɛ'tre], *v.t.* to remove the centerings from (*arches*).

décisif [desi'zif], *a.* (*fem.* **-sive**) decisive, conclusive.

décision [desi'zjõ], *n.f.* decision, determination; resolution.

décisivement [desiziv'mã], *adv.* decisively; peremptorily, positively.

décistère [desi'stɛːr], *n.m.* tenth of a stere (3·53 *cubic feet*).

déciviliser [desivili'ze], *v.t.* to decivilize.

99

déclamateur

déclamateur [deklama'tœːr], *n.m.* (*fem.* **-trice**) declaimer; (*fig.*) tub-thumper.—*a.* (*fem.* **-trice**) declamatory, bombastic.

déclamation [deklama'sjɔ̃], *n.f.* declamation, elocution.

déclamatoire [deklama'twaːr], *a.* declamatory.

déclamer [dekla'me], *v.t., v.i.* to declaim; to spout, to mouth.

déclarant [dekla'rɑ̃], *n.m.* (*Law*) informant.

déclaration [deklara'sjɔ̃], *n.f.* declaration, proclamation; disclosure; notification; *déclaration sous serment*, affidavit.

déclaratoire [deklara'twaːr], *a.* declaratory.

déclarer [dekla're], *v.t.* to declare, to make known; to proclaim; to certify. **se déclarer**, *v.r.* to speak one's mind; to declare oneself *or* itself; to show oneself *or* itself.

déclassé [dekla'se], *a.* come down in the world.—*n.m.* (*fem.* **-ée**) one who has come down in the world; one rejected by his own class *or* sphere.

déclassement [deklɑs'mɑ̃], *n.m.* loss of social position.

déclasser [dekla'se], *v.t.* to alter the classing of; to transfer from one class to another (*on trains, boats etc.*); to strike off the rolls, to dismiss from the service.

déclencher [deklɑ̃'ʃe], *v.t.* to unlatch (*a door*); to unhook, to detach; to release; (*Mil.*) to launch (*an attack*).

déclic [de'klik], *n.m.* pawl, catch.

déclin [de'klɛ̃], *n.m.* decline; decay; wane (*of the moon*); ebb; close (*of day etc.*).

déclinaison [dekline'zɔ̃], *n.f.* (*Gram.*) declension.

déclinant [dekli'nɑ̃], *a.* declining.

décliner [dekli'ne], *v.t.* to refuse; (*Gram.*) to decline; to state.—*v.i.* to decline, to be on the wane, to fall off.

déclive [de'kliːv], *a.* declivous, sloping.

déclivité [deklivi'te], *n.f.* declivity, slope.

décloîtrer (se) [sədeklwa'tre], *v.r.* to leave the cloister, to return to the world.

déclore [de'klɔːr], *v.t. irr.* (*conjug. like* CLORE) to unclose, to throw open.

décochement [dekoʃ'mɑ̃], *n.m.* discharge, shooting (*of arrows, shafts etc.*).

décocher [deko'ʃe], *v.t.* to discharge, to dart (*arrows etc.*); to let fly (*insults etc.*).

décoiffer [dekwa'fe], *v.t.* to remove *or* undo the coiffure of, to undress the hair of. **se décoiffer**, *v.r.* to undo one's head-dress; to take off one's hat.

décoincer (se) [sədekwɛ̃'se], *v.r.* (*conjug. like* COMMENCER) to work loose.

décollage [deko'laːʒ], *n.m.* (*Av.*) taking off.

décollement [dekol'mɑ̃], *n.m.* ungluing, unpasting; coming off; detachment (*of retina*).

décoller [deko'le], *v.t.* to unglue.—*v.i.* (*Av.*) to take off. **se décoller**, *v.r.* to become unglued, to come off.

décolletage [dekɔl'taːʒ], *n.m.* lowness in the neck (*of dresses*); baring the neck and shoulders.

décolleté [dekɔl'te], *a.* (*Dress.*) low-necked.

décolleter [dekɔl'te], *v.t.* (*conjug. like* APPELER) to uncover the neck, shoulders etc., of; to cut (*a dress*) low. **se décolleter**, *v.r.* to bare one's shoulders; to wear a low dress.

décoloration [dekolora'sjɔ̃], *n.f.* discoloration.

décoloré [dekolo're], *a.* discoloured, faded.

décolorer [dekolo're], *v.t.* to discolour. **se décolorer**, *v.r.* to become discoloured, to fade.

décombres [de'kɔ̃br], *n.m.* (*used only in pl.*) rubbish, debris, ruins.

décommander [dekomɑ̃'de], *v.t.* to countermand; to cancel.

décomposé [dekɔ̃po'ze], *a.* decomposed.

décomposer [dekɔ̃po'ze], *v.t.* to decompose; to break up; to distort. **se décomposer**, *v.r.* to decompose, to rot; (*fig.*) to be distorted (*of the face etc.*).

décomposition [dekɔ̃pozi'sjɔ̃], *n.f.* decomposition, analysis.

décompresseur [dekɔ̃prɛ'sœːr], *n.m.* (*Motor.*) exhaust-valve.

décompte [de'kɔ̃t], *n.m.* deduction, discount, allowance; deficit; balance due; (*fig.*) drawback; disappointment.

décompter [dekɔ̃'te], *v.t.* to deduct.—*v.i.* (*fig.*) to be disappointed.

déconcertant [dekɔ̃sɛr'tɑ̃], *a.* disconcerting.

déconcerter [dekɔ̃sɛr'te], *v.t.* to disconcert; to baffle. **se déconcerter**, *v.r.* to be disconcerted *or* put out.

déconfiture [dekɔ̃fi'tyːr], *n.f.* discomfiture; break-down; insolvency.

décongeler [dekɔ̃'ʒle], *v.t.* (*conjug. like* AMENER) to thaw (*chilled meat*).

déconseiller [dekɔ̃sɛ'je], *v.t.* to dissuade.

déconsidération [dekɔ̃sidera'sjɔ̃], *n.f.* disrepute, discredit.

déconsidérer [dekɔ̃side're], *v.t.* (*conjug. like* CÉDER) to bring into disrepute, to discredit. **se déconsidérer**, *v.r.* to fall into disrepute.

décontenancement [dekɔ̃tnɑ̃s'mɑ̃], *n.m.* mortification, embarrassment.

décontenancer [dekɔ̃tnɑ̃'se], *v.t.* (*conjug. like* COMMENCER) to abash, to put out of countenance. **se décontenancer**, *v.r.* to be put out of countenance, to be abashed.

déconvenue [dekɔ̃v'ny], *n.f.* discomfiture; disappointment, set-back.

décor [de'kɔːr], *n.m.* decoration; (*Theat., pl.*) scenery.

décorateur [dekora'tœːr], *n.m.* (*fem.* **-trice**) ornamental painter, decorator; scene-painter.

décoratif [dekora'tif], *a.* (*fem.* **-tive**) decorative, ornamental.

décoration [dekora'sjɔ̃], *n.f.* decoration, embellishment; medal, insignia (*of an order*).

décorder [dekor'de], *v.t.* to untwist, to untwine (*a cord etc.*); to untie the rope (*of a box*).

décoré [deko're], *a.* decorated; wearing the insignia of some order *or* its ribbon in one's buttonhole.

décorer [deko're], *v.t.* to decorate; to set off; to confer the Legion of Honour etc. upon.

décorner [dekor'ne], *v.t.* to dishorn.

décortiquer [dekorti'ke], *v.t.* to decorticate, to bark, to husk, to shell, to peel.

décorum [deko'rɔm], *n.m.* decorum, propriety.

découcher [deku'ʃe], *v.i.* to sleep away from home; to stay out all night.

100

découdre [de'kudr] *v.t. irr.* (*conjug. like* COUDRE) to unsew, to unstitch; to rip up. **se découdre,** *v.r.* to come unstitched.

découler [deku'le], *v.i.* to trickle, to flow; to spring, to proceed (*from*).

découpage [deku'pa:ʒ], *n.m.* cutting out, carving out.

découpé [deku'pe], *a.* (*Bot.*) cut, denticulated.

découper [deku'pe] *v.t.* to cut up; to pink, to cut out; to punch. **se découper,** *v.r.* to stand out, to show up (*against*).

découpeur [deku'pœːr], *n.m.* (*fem.* **-euse**) carver; pinker, cutter.

découplé [deku'ple], *a.* strapping.

découpler [deku'ple], *v.t.* to uncouple, to unleash, to let loose (*in pursuit*).

découpoir [deku'pwaːr], *n.m.* punch, stamping-machine, stamping-press.

découpure [deku'pyːr], *n.f.* cutting out, pinking, work cut out; cut paper-work; indentation.

décourageant [dekura'ʒã], *a.* discouraging, disheartening.

découragement [dekuraʒ'mã], *n.m.* discouragement.

décourager [dekura'ʒe], *v.t.* (*conjug. like* MANGER) to discourage, to dishearten. **se décourager,** *v.r.* to be disheartened.

décours [de'kuːr], *n.m.* decrease; wane (*of the moon*).

décousu [deku'zy], *a.* unsewn, unstitched; (*fig.*) desultory (*of style etc.*).

décousure [deku'zyːr], *n.f.* unpicked stitching.

découvert [deku'vɛːr], *a.* uncovered; discovered; open, unguarded; bare, bareheaded.—*n.m.* (*Comm.*) overdraft, deficit.

découverte [deku'vɛrt], *n.f.* discovery, detection; (*Mil.*) reconnoitring; (*Naut.*) look out.

découvreur [deku'vrœːr], *n.m.* (*fem.* **-euse**) discoverer.

découvrir [deku'vriːr], *v.t.* (*conjug. like* OUVRIR) to uncover, to expose; to discover, to disclose, to detect. **se découvrir,** *v.r.* to uncover oneself, to take off one's hat; to unbosom oneself; to expose oneself; to lie open *or* bare; to clear up (*of the sky*).

décramponner (se) [sədekrãpɔ'ne], *v.r.* to let go one's hold.

décrasser [dekra'se], *v.t.* to take the dirt off, to scour; (*fig.*) to make presentable. **se décrasser,** *v.r.* to wash, to clean oneself; to become polished.

décrassoir [dekra'swaːr], *n.m.* fine toothcomb.

décréditement [dekredit'mã], *n.m.* discrediting.

décrépi [dekre'pi], *a.* unplastered.

décrépir (se) [sədekre'piːr], *v.r.* to lose its plaster (*of a wall etc.*).

décrépit [dekre'pi], *a.* decrepit, brokendown.

décrépitude [dekrepi'tyd], *n.f.* decrepitude.

décret [de'krɛ], *n.m.* decree, order, enactment; (*Law*) writ, warrant.

décret-loi [dekrɛ'lwa], *n.m.* Order in Council.

décréter [dekre'te], *v.t.* (*conjug. like* CÉDER) to decree, to order, to enact.

décri [de'kri], *n.m.* official crying down *or* depreciation (*of coinage*); (*fig.*) discredit.

décrier [dekri'e], *v.t.* to decry, to run down;

(*fig.*) to discredit. **se décrier,** *v.r.* to bring oneself into disrepute; to decry one another.

décrire [de'kriːr], *v.t. irr.* (*conjug. like* ÉCRIRE) to describe, to depict. **se décrire,** *v.r.* to be described.

décrocher [dekrɔ'ʃe], *v.t.* to unhook, to take down, to disconnect.

décroiser [dekrwa'ze], *v.t.* to uncross (*the legs etc.*).

décroissant [dekrwa'sã], *a.* decreasing, diminishing; subsiding.

décroissement [dekrwas'mã], *n.m.*, **décroissance** [dekrwa'sãːs], *n.f.* decrease.

décroît [de'krwa], *n.m.* wane (*of the moon*).

décroître [de'krwaːtr], *v.i. irr.* (*conjug. like* CROÎTRE *but p.p.* **décru,** *without circumflex*) to decrease, to diminish, to wane.

décrottage [dekrɔ'ta:ʒ], *n.m.* cleaning (*of boots, trousers etc.*).

décrotter [dekrɔ'te], *v.t.* to rub the dirt off; (*fig.*) to improve the manners of. **se décrotter,** *v.r.* to clean oneself; to clean one's boots etc.

décrotteur [dekrɔ'tœːr], *n.m.* (*fem.* **-euse**) shoe-black.

décrottoir [dekrɔ'twaːr], *n.m.* scraper (*for shoes*).

décrottoire [dekrɔ'twaːr], *n.f.* shoe-brush.

décrue [de'kry], *n.f.* decrease; fall (*of water*).

décrypter [dekrip'te], *v.t.* to decipher.

déculotter [dekylɔ'te], *v.t.* to take off (*s.o.'s*) breeches, (*a child's*) pants; (*colloq.*) to debag.

décuple [de'kypl], *a.* and *n.m.* tenfold.

décupler [deky'ple], *v.t.* to increase tenfold.

décuvage [deky'va:ʒ], *n.m.*, **décuvaison** [dekyvɛ'zõ], *n.f.* tunning (*of wine*).

décuver [deky've], *v.t.* to tun.

dédaigner [dedɛ'ɲe], *v.t.* to disdain, to scorn, to despise.

dédaigneusement [dedɛɲøz'mã], *adv.* disdainfully, scornfully.

dédaigneux [dedɛ'ɲø], *a.* (*fem.* **-euse**) disdainful, scornful.

dédain [de'dɛ̃], *n.m.* disdain, scorn, disregard.

dédale [de'dal], *n.m.* labyrinth, maze.

dedans [də'dã], *adv.* within, in, inside; at home.—*n.m.* inside, interior.

dédicace [dedi'kas], *n.f.* dedication, consecration (*of a church etc.*).

dédication [dedika'sjõ], *n.f.* (*Law*) dedication (*of a temple etc.*).

dédier [de'dje], *v.t.* to dedicate, to consecrate; to devote; to inscribe (*a book etc.*).

dédire [de'diːr], *v.t. irr.* (*conjug. like* MÉDIRE) to disown; gainsay, to contradict. **se dédire,** *v.r.* to recant, to retract, to go back on one's word.

dédit [de'di], *n.m.* retraction; forfeit.

dédommagement [dedɔmaʒ'mã], *n.m.* indemnification; compensation; damages.

dédommager [dedɔma'ʒe], *v.t.* (*conjug. like* MANGER) to make amends for; to compensate, to make up for. **se dédommager,** *v.r.* to indemnify oneself.

dédorer [dedɔ're], *v.t.* to ungild. **se dédorer,** *v.r.* to lose its gilt (*of metal etc.*).

dédouanement [dedwan'mã], *n.m.* (*customs*) clearance.

dédouaner [dedwa'ne], *v.t.* to clear (*goods*) from the custom house.

dédoublement

dédoublement [dedublə'mã], **dédoublage** [dedu'bla:ʒ], *n.m.* dividing into two; unlining (*of a garment*); diluting.

dédoubler [dedu'ble], *v.t.* to take out the lining of; to divide into two; *dédoubler un autocar* (*un train*), to run a relief coach (train). **se dédoubler**, *v.r.* to be divided into two.

déductif [dedyk'tif], *a.* (*fem.* **-tive**) deductive.

déduction [dedyk'sjõ], *n.f.* deduction, allowance; inference.

déduire [de'dɥi:r], *v.t. irr.* (*conjug. like* CONDUIRE) to deduct, to subtract; to deduce, to infer.

déesse [de'ɛs], *n.f.* goddess, female deity.

défâcher [defa'ʃe], *v.t.* to pacify. **se défâcher**, *v.r.* to be pacified, to cool down.

défaillance [defa'jã:s], *n.f.* fainting fit, swoon, faintness; exhaustion; extinction (*of a family etc.*).

défaillant [defa'jã], *a.* failing, falling off; decaying; without heirs; weak, feeble.—*n.m.* (*fem.* **-e**) (*Law*) defaulter.

défaillir [defa'ji:r], *v.i. irr.* (*conjug. like* ASSAILLIR) to fail, to default; to decay; to swoon, to faint away.

défaire [de'fɛ:r], *v.t. irr.* (*conjug. like* FAIRE) to undo, to unmake; to defeat; to emaciate; to embarrass; to rid. **se défaire**, *v.r.* to come undone; *se défaire de*, to get rid of, to give up.

défait [de'fɛ], *a.* undone, defeated; meagre, wasted; worn out.

défaite [de'fɛt], *n.f.* defeat, overthrow; evasion, pretence, excuse.

défaitisme [defɛ'tism], *n.m.* defeatism.

défaitiste [defɛ'tist], *a.* and *n.* defeatist.

défalcation [defalka'sjõ], *n.f.* deduction.

défalquer [defal'ke], *v.t.* to take off, to deduct.

défausser [defo'se], *v.t.* to straighten.

défaut [de'fo], *n.m.* absence, lack, default; defect, fault, flaw; (*Law*) non-appearance; *à défaut de*, instead of, for want of; *faire défaut*, to be wanting, to be missing.

défaveur [defa'vœ:r], *n.f.* disfavour, discredit.

défavorable [defavo'rabl], *a.* unfavourable.

défavorablement [defavorablə'mã], *adv.* unfavourably.

défectif [defɛk'tif], *a.* (*fem.* **-tive**) (*Gram.*) defective.

défection [defɛk'sjõ], *n.f.* defection, falling off, disloyalty.

défectueux [defɛk'tɥø], *a.* (*fem.* **-euse**) defective, imperfect.

défectuosité [defɛktɥozi'te], *n.f.* defect, imperfection, flaw.

défendable [defã'dabl], *a.* defensible, tenable.

défendeur [defã'dœ:r], *n.m.* (*fem.* **-eresse**) defendant; respondent.

défendre [de'fã:dr], *v.t.* to defend, to protect; to shield; to support; to forbid. **se défendre**, *v.r.* to defend oneself; to clear oneself; to deny.

défense [de'fã:s], *n.f.* defence, protection; prohibition; apology, plea; (*Law*) the defence; (*Fort., pl.*) outworks; tusk, fang (*of animals*); (*Naut.*) fender; *défense de fumer*, no smoking.

défenseur [defã'sœ:r], *n.m.* defender, supporter; advocate, counsel.

défensif [defã'sif], *a.* (*fem.* **-sive**) defensive. —*n.f.* (**-sive**) defensive.

déféquer [defe'ke], *v.t.* (*conjug. like* CÉDER) to purify.—*v.i.* to defecate.

déférence [defe'rã:s], *n.f.* deference, regard, respect.

déférent [defe'rã], *a.* deferential, compliant.

déférer [defe're], *v.t.* (*conjug. like* CÉDER) * to confer, to bestow; to tender; to accuse, to inform against.—*v.i.* to defer, to yield, to comply.

déferler [defɛr'le], *v.t.* (*Naut.*) to unfurl.— *v.i.* to break into foam (*of the sea*).

déferrer [defe're], *v.t.* to unshoe (*a horse*). **se déferrer**, *v.r.* to come unshod, to lose a shoe.

défeuiller [defœ'je], *v.t.* to take the leaves off. **se défeuiller**, *v.r.* to shed its leaves.

défi [de'fi], *n.m.* defiance, challenge.

défiance [de'fjã:s], *n.f.* distrust, mistrust; caution.

défiant [de'fjã], *a.* distrustful, suspicious.

déficeler [defis'le], *v.t.* (*conjug. like* APPELER) to untie; to undo.

déficient [defi'sjã], *a.* deficient.

déficit [defi'sit], *n.m.* deficit, deficiency.

défier [de'fje], *v.t.* to defy, to challenge; to brave, to face; to set at defiance. **se défier**, *v.r.* to defy *or* to challenge each other; to distrust, to beware (*de*).

défiger [defi'ʒe], *v.t.* (*conjug. like* MANGER) to liquefy.

défiguration [defigyra'sjõ], *n.f.*, **défigurement** [defigyr'mã], *n.m.* disfigurement, defacement.

défigurer [defigy're], *v.t.* to disfigure, to mar; to distort. **se défigurer**, *v.r.* to disfigure oneself; to become deformed.

défilade [defi'lad], *n.f.* filing off *or* past, marching past; succession.

défilé [defi'le], *n.m.* defile, narrow pass, gorge; (*fig.*) strait, difficulty; (*Mil.*) filing past; *un défilé de mannequins*, a mannequin parade.

défiler [defi'le], *v.t.* to unstring, to unthread; to untwist.—*v.i.* to file off, to march past. **se défiler**, *v.r.* to come unthreaded *or* unstrung; (*Mil.*) to take cover; to slip away.

défini [defi'ni], *a.* definite, determined, defined.

définir [defi'ni:r], *v.t.* to define; to determine; to describe.

définissable [defini'sabl], *a.* definable.

définitif [defini'tif], *a.* (*fem.* **-tive**) definitive, final; ultimate, eventual.

définition [defini'sjõ], *n.f.* definition.

définitivement [definitiv'mã], *adv.* definitively, positively, decidedly; eventually.

déflation [defla'sjõ], *n.f.* deflation.

défléchir [defle'ʃi:r], *v.t., v.i.* to turn from *or* aside, to deflect.

déflecteur [deflɛk'tœ:r], *n.m.* (*Motor.*) ventilating window; deflector.

défleuraison [DÉFLORAISON].

défleurir [deflœ'ri:r], *v.t.* to nip *or* strip off blossoms.—*v.i.* to lose its flowers.

déflexion [deflɛk'sjõ], *n.f.* deviation; (*Gram.*) deflection.

défloraison [deflɔrɛ'zõ], **défleuraison** [deflœrɛ'zõ], *n.f.* fall *or* withering of the blossom.

déflorer [deflɔ're], *v.t.* to deflower, to seduce.

dégradant

défonçage [defõ'sa:ʒ], **défoncement** [defõs'mã], *n.m.* staving in (*of the head of casks*), breaking *or* smashing in; (*Agric.*) deep trenching.

défoncer [defõ'se], *v.t.* (*conjug. like* COMMENCER) to stave in, to bilge (*a cask*); to dig deeply, to trench (*ground*). **se défoncer**, *v.r.* to give way; to break up (*of roads*); to get battered.

défonceuse [defõ'sø:z], *n.f.* trenching plough.

déforestation [deforesta'sjõ], *n.f.* deforestation.

déformant [defor'mã], *a.* distorting (*mirror etc.*).

déformation [deforma'sjõ], *n.f.* distortion, buckling.

déformer [defor'me], *v.t.* to deform, to distort. **se déformer**, *v.r.* to lose its shape.

défortifier [deforti'fje], *v.t.* to dismantle the fortifications of.

défourner [defur'ne], *v.t.* to draw out of an oven *or* kiln.

défourrer [defu're], *v.t.* to unwrap, to take out of his cover; to thresh (*corn*).

défraîchir [defre'ʃi:r], *v.t.* to tarnish, to take away the brilliancy, gloss *or* freshness of. **se défraîchir**, *v.r.* to lose its brilliancy, freshness etc., to tarnish.

défrayer [defre'je], *v.t.* (*conjug. like* PAYER) to defray, to bear the cost of; to amuse.

défriche [de'friʃ], *n.f.*, **défriché** [defri'ʃe], *n.m.* piece of cleared land.

défrichement [defriʃ'mã], **défrichage** [defri'ʃa:ʒ], *n.m.* clearing, breaking up (*of land for tillage*).

défricher [defri'ʃe], *v.t.* to clear, to break up (*ground*) for tillage; to reclaim.

défricheur [defri'ʃœ:r], *n.m.* clearer; settler.

défriper [defri'pe], *v.t.* to smooth out.

défrisement [defriz'mã], *n.m.* uncurling.

défriser [defri'ze], *v.t.* to uncurl; (*fam.*) to disappoint; to ruffle.

défroque [de'frok], *n.f.* the effects left by a dying monk; *hence*, old things, effects, castoff clothes, etc.

défroqué [defro'ke], *a.* and *n.m.* unfrocked (*priest*).

défroquer [defro'ke], *v.t.* to unfrock. **se défroquer**, *v.r.* to renounce one's order (*of monks*).

défunt [de'fœ̃], *a.* defunct, deceased, late.—*n.m.* (*fem.* -**e**) the deceased.

dégagé [dega'ʒe], *a.* free, easy, unconstrained; flippant; bold; slender, graceful.

dégagement [degaʒ'mã], *n.m.* disengagement, redemption; clearance; discharge (*of gas etc.*); (*fig.*) unconcern.

dégager [dega'ʒe], *v.t.* (*conjug. like* MANGER) to disengage, to extricate; to clear; to deliver, to rescue; to release, to emit (*fumes etc.*); to redeem, to take out of pawn. **se dégager**, *v.r.* to be liberated (*de*); to extricate, disengage *or* disentangle oneself; to get away; (*Chem.*) to be emitted.

dégaine [de'gɛ:n], *n.f.* (*colloq.*) awkward gait.

dégainer [dege'ne], *v.t.* to unsheathe (*one's sword etc.*).

déganter [degã'te], *v.t.* to unglove. **se déganter**, *v.r.* to take off one's gloves.

dégarnir [degar'ni:r], *v.t.* to strip; to dismantle; to thin (*trees, woods etc.*). **se dégarnir**, *v.r.* to strip oneself (*de*); to

become empty; to grow thin; to lose branches etc.

dégât [de'gɑ], *n.m.* havoc, damage, ravage.

dégauchir [dego'ʃi:r], *v.t.* to smooth, to plane, to level, to straighten; (*fig.*) to polish.

dégauchissement [degoʃis'mã], **dégauchissage** [degoʃi'sa:ʒ], *n.m.* planing, straightening, levelling, smoothing.

dégazonner [degazo'ne], *v.t.* to remove the turf from.

dégel [de'ʒel], *n.m.* thaw.

dégeler [de'ʒle], *v.t.*, *v.i.* (*conjug. like* AMENER) to thaw. **se dégeler**, *v.r.* to thaw (*of persons*).

dégénération [deʒenera'sjõ], *n.f.* degeneration, degeneracy.

dégénéré [deʒene're], *a.* and *n.m.* (*fem.* -**ée**) degenerate (person).

dégénérer [deʒene're], *v.i.* (*conjug. like* CÉDER) to decline, to degenerate.

dégénérescence [deʒenere'sã:s], *n.f.* degeneracy, degeneration.

dégénérescent [deʒenere'sã], *a.* degenerating.

dégingandé [deʒɛ̃gã'de], *a.* ungainly, gawky, awkward in one's gait; clumsy, disjointed, irregular.

dégivrer [deʒi'vre], *v.t.* to de-ice.

dégivreur [deʒi'vrœ:r], *n.m.* (*Motor.*, *Av.*) de-icer.

déglutir [degly'ti:r], *v.t.* to swallow.

déglutition [deglyti'sjõ], *n.f.* deglutition, swallowing.

dégommer [dego'me], *v.t.* to wash the gum out of; (*slang*) to sack.

dégonflement [degõflə'mã], *n.m.* deflating (*of tyre, balloon*); collapse; reduction.

dégonfler [degõ'fle], *v.t.* to cause to collapse; to deflate; to reduce (*a swelling*). **se dégonfler**, *v.r.* to go down, to be reduced; to subside; (*pop.*) to sing small.

dégorgement [degorʒ'mã], *n.m.* breaking out, overflow; unstopping.

dégorger [degor'ʒe], *v.t.* (*conjug. like* MANGER) to disgorge; to unstop, to clear; to cleanse.—*v.i.* to discharge, to overflow. **se dégorger**, *v.r.* to discharge *or* empty itself *or* oneself, to be unstopped, to be cleared.

dégourdi [degur'di], *a.* quick, sharp, acute, smart; tepid (*of water*).—*n.m.* (*fem.* -**e**) a shrewd *or* forward person.

dégourdir [degur'di:r], *v.t.* to revive, to quicken; to take the chill off; (*fig.*) to sharpen, to render shrewd; to polish. **se dégourdir**, *v.r.* to lose numbness, to feel warmer; to brighten up.

dégourdissement [degurdis'mã], *n.m.* return of circulation; quickening, reviving.

dégoût [de'gu], *n.m.* dislike, distaste; disgust, aversion; mortification.

dégoûtant [degu'tã], *a.* disgusting, distasteful, nauseous; loathsome; unpleasant.

dégoûté [degu'te], *a.* disgusted; fastidious.—*n.m.* (*fem.* -**ée**) fastidious person.

dégoûter [degu'te], *v.t.* to disgust. **se dégoûter**, *v.r.* to take a dislike to.

dégouttant [degu'tã], *a.* dripping.

dégouttement [degut'mã], *n.m.* dripping, falling in drops.

dégoutter [degu'te], *v.i.* to drip, to fall in drops, to trickle.

dégradant [degra'dã], *a.* degrading, debasing.

103

dégradation [degradɑ'sjõ], *n.f.* degradation; debasement; (*Paint.*) gradation of light and shade; (*Law*) *dégradation nationale* or *civile*, loss of civil rights; *dégradation militaire*, cashiering.

dégrader [degra'de], *v.t.* to degrade, to debase; to deface; (*Mil.*) to reduce to the ranks; to cashier; (*Paint.*) to graduate the light and shade. **se dégrader**, *v.r.* to degrade, debase or disgrace oneself; to become damaged *or* defaced.

dégrafer [degra'fe], *v.t.* to unclasp, to unhook. **se dégrafer**, *v.r.* to come unfastened (*of garments etc.*); to unfasten one's clothes.

dégraissage [degrɛ'sa:ʒ], **dégraissement** [degrɛs'mã], *n.m.* dry-cleaning (*garments*); scouring (*wool*).

dégraisser [degrɛ'se], *v.t.* to remove greasy stains from.

dégraisseur [degrɛ'sœ:r], *n.m.* (*fem.* **-euse**) scourer (*of wool*); dry-cleaner (*of clothes etc.*).

dégraissoir [degrɛ'swa:r], *n.m.* scraper.

degré [də'gre], *n.m.* step, stair; stage, grade, degree; point, extent, height, pitch.

dégréer [degre'e], *v.t.* to unrig, to strip a mast.

dégrèvement [degrɛv'mã], *n.m.* reduction; tax allowance, relief.

dégrever [degra've], *v.t.* (*conjug. like* AMENER) to diminish, to reduce (*a tax etc.*); to relieve (*someone of a tax*); to disencumber (*an estate etc.*); to pay off (*a mortgage*).

dégringolade [degrẽgɔ'lad], *n.f.* (*fam.*) fall, tumble.

dégringoler [degrẽgɔ'le], *v.i.* to tumble down, to topple over.

dégrisement [degriz'mã], *n.m.* (*colloq.*) sobering, getting sober; (*fig.*) cooling down.

dégriser [degri'ze], *v.t.* to sober; (*fig.*) to cool down, to bring to one's senses. **se dégriser**, *v.r.* to sober down; (*fig.*) to come to one's senses; to lose one's illusions.

dégrossir [degro'si:r], *v.t.* to rough-hew; (*fig.*) to make a rough sketch of.

dégrossissage [degrosi'sa:ʒ], **dégrossissement** [degrosis'mã], *n.m.* roughhewing; (*Carp.*) dressing, trimming.

déguenillé [degəni'je], *a.* tattered, ragged.— *n.m.* (*fem.* **-ée**) ragamuffin.

déguerpir [deger'pi:r], *v.i.* to move off; to be gone.

déguerpissement [degɛrpis'mã], *n.m.* quitting, giving up, abandonment.

dégueuler [degœ'le], *v.t.* (*vulg.*) to spew.

déguignonner [degiɲɔ'ne], *v.t.* to lift a curse from, to bring better luck to.

déguisable [degi'zabl], *a.* disguisable.

déguisement [degiz'mã], *n.m.* disguise, concealment; *parlez sans déguisement*, speak openly.

déguiser [degi'ze], *v.t.* to disguise, to cloak; to misrepresent. **se déguiser**, *v.r.* to disguise oneself, to put on fancy dress.

dégustateur [degysta'tœ:r], *n.m.* (*fem.* **-trice**) taster (*of wines etc.*).

dégustation [degysta'sjõ], *n.f.* tasting (*of wines etc.*).

déguster [degys'te], *v.t.* to taste; to sip, to savour.

déhaler [dea'le], *v.t.* (*Naut.*) to tow out; to haul off.

déhâler [dea'le], *v.t.* to take away sun-burn, freckles, tan etc. from. **se déhâler**, *v.r.* to clear one's complexion.

déhanché [deã'ʃe], *a.* having the hip dislocated; (*fig.*) ungainly.

déhanchement [deãʃ'mã], *n.m.* waddling gait, waddle.

déhancher (se) [sədeã'ʃe], *v.r.* to sway one's hips; to have a waddling, loose gait.

déharnachement [dearnaʃ'mã], *n.m.* unharnessing.

déharnacher [dearna'ʃe], *v.t.* to unharness.

dehors [də'ɔ:r], *adv.* out, *without, outside; out of doors; abroad; externally; (*Naut.*) at sea; *au dedans et au dehors*, at home and abroad; *au dehors*, outwardly; *de dehors*, from without; *en dehors*, outside, *without; *mettre quelqu'un dehors*, to turn someone out.— *n.m. inv.* outside, exterior; (*pl.*) appearances; (*Fort.*) outworks; dependencies, approaches, grounds (*of a house*); *sauver les dehors*, to save appearances.

déification [deifika'sjõ], *n.f.* deification.

déifier [dei'fje], *v.t.* to deify.

déisme [de'ism], *n.m.* deism.

déiste [de'ist], *a.* deistic.—*n.* deist.

déité [dei'te], *n.f.* deity (*god, goddess*), divinity.

déjà [de'ʒa], *adv.* already, before, previously.

déjection [deʒɛk'sjõ], *n.f.* (*Med.*) dejection, ejection, evacuation.

déjeté [deʒ'te], *a.* awry, lopsided, off the straight.

déjeter [deʒ'te], *v.t.* (*conjug. like* APPELER) to warp. **se déjeter**, *v.r.* to warp (*of wood etc.*); (*Path.*) to deviate.

déjettement [deʒɛt'mã], *n.m.* warping; deviation.

déjeuner [deʒœ'ne], *n.m.* lunch; *petit déjeuner*, breakfast; *un déjeuner de porcelaine*, a china breakfast-set.—*v.i.* to breakfast, to lunch.

déjouer [de'ʒwe], *v.t.* to baffle, to frustrate, to foil; (*Mil.*) to outmanœuvre.

déjucher [deʒy'ʃe], *v.t.* to dislodge.—*v.i.* to come down from the roost *or* from one's perch.

déjuger (se) [sədeʒy'ʒe], *v.r.* (*conjug. like* MANGER) to reverse one's opinion *or* decision.

delà [də'la], *prep.* on the other side of; beyond; *au delà, de delà, par delà*, or *en delà*, beyond; *deçà et delà*, both here and there, both this and that; *l'au-delà*, the hereafter.

délabré [dela'bre], *a.* tattered, shabby (*garments*); tumbledown, ramshackle (*building*).

délabrement [delɑbrə'mã], *n.m.* decay, dilapidation; shabbiness.

délabrer [dela'bre], *v.t.* to shatter, to ruin, to tear to tatters. **se délabrer**, *v.r.* to fall to pieces, to go to ruin.

délacer [dela'se], *v.t.* (*conjug. like* COMMENCER) to unlace (*shoes etc.*). **se délacer**, *v.r.* to unlace oneself; to come undone (*of shoes, strings etc.*).

délai [de'lɛ], *n.m.* delay; respite.

délaissé [delɛ'se], *a.* abandoned, friendless.

délaissement [delɛs'mã], *n.m.* desertion; destitution, helplessness.
délaisser [dele'se], *v.t.* to forsake, to abandon; to neglect.
délassant [dela'sã], *a.* refreshing, diverting.
délassement [delas'mã], *n.m.* relaxation; repose.
délasser [dela'se], *v.t.* to refresh, to relax, to divert. **se délasser**, *v.r.* to refresh oneself, to rest.
délateur [dela'tœ:r], *n.m.* (*fem.* **-trice**) informer, accuser.
délation [dela'sjõ], *n.f.* informing.
délavage [dela'va:ʒ], *n.m.* diluting of colour; soaking.
délaver [dela've], *v.t.* to dilute *or* wash (*colour*); to soak into. **se délaver**, *v.r.* to become soaked; to lose colour.
délayable [delɛ'jabl], *a.* dilutable.
délayage [delɛ'ja:ʒ], *n.m.* diluting, dilution.
délayé [delɛ'je], *a.* watery.
délayer [delɛ'je], *v.t.* (*conjug. like* PAYER) to dilute; (*fig.*) to spin out.
délectable [delɛk'tabl], *a.* delectable, delightful.
délecter (se) [sədelɛk'te], *v.r.* to take delight.
délégation [delega'sjõ], *n.f.* delegation, assignment.
délégatoire [delega'twa:r], *a.* a delegatory.
délégué [dele'ge], *n.m.* (*fem.* **-ée**) delegate, deputy; proxy.
déléguer [dele'ge], *v.t.* (*conjug. like* CÉDER) to delegate; to assign. **se déléguer**, *v.r.* to be delegated.
délester [delɛs'te], *v.t.* to unballast.
délétère [dele'tɛ:r], *a.* deleterious.
délibérant [delibe'rã], *a.* deliberative.
délibératif [delibera'tif], *a.* (*fem.* **-tive**) deliberative.
délibération [delibera'sjõ], *n.f.* deliberation; resolution.
délibéré [delibe're], *a.* deliberate, determined, resolute.
délibérément [delibere'mã], *adv.* deliberately, resolutely.
délibérer [delibe're], *v.i.* (*conjug. like* CÉDER) to deliberate; to resolve.
délicat [deli'ka], *a.* delicate, dainty; nice, fastidious, frail.—*n.m.* (*fem.* **-e**) fastidious person.
délicatement [delikat'mã], *adv.* delicately, daintily, tenderly.
délicatesse [delika'tɛs], *n.f.* delicacy, fragility; tenderness; daintiness, fastidiousness; refinement, squeamishness; nicety (*of language etc.*); considerateness; (*pl.*) dainties.
délice [de'lis], *n.m. in sing.* (*used chiefly in f.pl.*) delight, pleasure.
délicieusement [delisjøz'mã], *adv.* deliciously, delightfully.
délicieux [deli'sjø], *a.* (*fem.* **-euse**) delicious, delightful.
délié [de'lje], *a.* slender, fine; sharp, shrewd; glib, flowing (*of style etc.*); untied, loose.
délier [de'lje], *v.t.* to unbind, to untie; to liberate, to release; to absolve. **se délier**, *v.r.* to come untied, to get loose.
délimitation [delimita'sjõ], *n.f.* delimitation, fixing of boundaries.
délimiter [delimi'te], *v.t.* to delimit, to settle the boundaries of.

délinéation [delinea'sjõ], *n.f.* delineation.
délinéer [deline'e], *v.t.* to delineate.
délinquance [delɛ̃'kã:s], *n.f.* delinquency.
délinquant [delɛ̃'kã], *n.m.* (*fem.* **-e**) delinquent, offender.—*a.* **enfance délinquante**, juvenile delinquents.
délirant [deli'rã], *a.* delirious, frenzied, frantic; rapturous, ecstatic.—*n.m.* (*fem.* **-e**) a delirious *or* ecstatic person.
délire [de'li:r], *n.m.* delirium, frenzy, folly.
délirer [deli're], *v.i.* to be delirious, to rave, to wander.
délit [de'li], *n.m.* misdemeanour, offence; **en flagrant délit**, in the very act, redhanded.
délivrance [deli'vrã:s], *n.f.* rescue, deliverance; issue (*of tickets*); delivery (*of certificates etc.*); accouchement.
délivre [de'livr], *n.m.* (*Anat.*) after-birth, placenta.
délivrer [deli'vre], *v.t.* to deliver, to release, to set free; to hand over; to issue; to deliver (*a woman of a baby*).
délogement [delɔʒ'mã], *n.m.* removal, change of quarters, decamping.
déloger [delɔ'ʒe], *v.t.* (*conjug. like* MANGER) to turn out (*of house etc.*), to oust; to drive away; (*Mil.*) to dislodge.—*v.i.* to remove, to go (*from one's house etc.*), to go away, to march off.
déloyal [delwa'jal], *a.* (*m.pl.* **-aux**) disloyal, false, treacherous, unfair; foul.
déloyalement [delwajal'mã], *adv.* disloyally, unfairly.
déloyauté [delwajo'te], *n.f.* disloyalty, treachery.
delta [dɛl'ta], *n.m.* delta.
déluge [de'ly:ʒ], *n.m.* deluge, flood.
déluré [dely're], *a.* wide-awake, sharp.
délustrer [delys'tre], *v.t.* to take the lustre *or* gloss from.
démagnétiser [demaɲeti'ze], *v.t.* to demagnetize.
démagogue [dema'gɔg], *n.* demagogue.
démailler [dema'je], *v.t.* to undo the meshes of (*a net etc.*).
demain [də'mɛ̃], *adv.* and *n.m.* tomorrow; **à demain !** see you tomorrow!
démancher [demã'ʃe], *v.t.* to take off the handle of; (*fig.*) to dislocate. **se démancher**, *v.r.* to lose its handle; to go wrong.
demande [də'mã:d], *n.f.* question; request, application, petition; claim; (*Comm.*) demand; order.
demander [dəmã'de], *v.t.* to ask, to beg, to request; to desire, to wish; to require, to call for; to need, to want; to inquire about; to ask to see; to seek in marriage; (*Comm.*) to order. **se demander**, *v.r.* to ask oneself, to wonder.
demandeur [dəmã'dœ:r], *a.* (*fem.* **-euse**) always asking.—*n.m.* (*fem.* **-eresse**) asker, applicant; (*Law*) plaintiff.
démangeaison [demãʒɛ'zõ], *n.f.* itching; longing.
démanger [demã'ʒe], *v.i.* (*conjug. like* MANGER) to itch; to long.
démantibuler [demãtiby'le], *v.t.* to break, to dislocate.
démaquiller [demaki'je], *v.t.* to take off someone's make-up. **se démaquiller**, *v.r.* to take off one's make-up.

démarcation [demarkɑ'sjɔ̃], *n.f.* demarcation; *ligne de démarcation*, line of demarcation.

démarche [de'marʃ], *n.f.* gait, walk, bearing; proceeding, measure, step, course.

démarcheur [demar'ʃœːr], *n.m.* canvasser.

démarier [dema'rje], *v.t.* (*fam.*) to annul the marriage of; (*Hort.*) to thin out. **se démarier**, *v.r.* to be divorced.

démarrer [dema're], *v.t.* to cast off; to unfasten.—*v.i.* to leave, to slip her moorings (*of a ship*); to move, to get away, to start.

démarreur [dema'rœːr], *n.m.* (*Motor.*) self-starter.

démasquer [demas'ke], *v.t.* to unmask; to show up.

démâter [demɑ'te], *v.t.* to dismast.—*v.i.* to lose her masts (*of a ship*).

démêlage [demɛ'laːʒ], *n.m.* combing (*of wool*).

démêlé [demɛ'le], *n.m.* strife, contest, quarrel.

démêler [demɛ'le], *v.t.* to unravel, to disentangle, to separate; to clear up; to distinguish, to discern; to comb out (*hair*), to tease (*wool*). **se démêler**, *v.r.* to be disentangled; to extricate oneself; to stand out (*clearly*); to comb out one's hair.

démembrement [demɑ̃brə'mɑ̃], *n.m.* dismemberment; breaking up.

démembrer [demɑ̃'bre], *v.t.* to tear limb from limb, to dismember; to break up.

déménagement [demenaʒ'mɑ̃], *n.m.* (*household*) removal.

déménager [demena'ʒe], *v.t.* (*conjug. like* MANGER) to remove (*one's furniture*).—*v.i.* to (re)move.

déménageur [demena'ʒœːr], *n.m.* furniture-remover.

démence [de'mɑ̃ːs], *n.f.* insanity, madness.

démener (se) [sədem'ne], *v.r.* (*conjug. like* AMENER) to stir, to struggle, to make a great fuss, to strive hard.

démenti [demɑ̃'ti], *n.m.* denial, flat contradiction; lie.

démentir [demɑ̃'tiːr], *v.t.* (*conjug. like* SENTIR) to give the lie to, to contradict; to deny; to belie, to refute. **se démentir**, *v.r.* to contradict oneself; to fall off, to flag.

démérite [deme'rit], *n.m.* demerit.

démériter [demeri'te], *v.i.* to lose esteem *or* favour.

démesuré [demezy're], *a.* inordinate, excessive, enormous.

démesurément [demezyre'mɑ̃], *adv.* inordinately, excessively.

démettre [de'mɛtr], *v.t. irr.* (*conjug. like* METTRE) to put out of joint, to dislocate; to dismiss; (*Law*) to overrule. **se démettre**, *v.r.* to be put out of joint; to resign.

démeubler [demœ'ble], *v.t.* to strip of furniture.

demeurant [dəmœ'rɑ̃], *a.* dwelling, living.—*n.m.* remainder; *au demeurant*, after all, nevertheless.

demeure [də'mœːr], *n.f.* abode, home, dwelling; stay; (*Law*) delay.

demeurer [dəmœ're], *v.i.* to live, to lodge, to reside; to stop, to stand; to continue, to stay.

demi [də'mi], *a.* and *adv.* half.—*n.m.* (*Arith.*) half; (*Ftb. etc.*) half-back; glass of beer.—*n.f.* (-e) (the) half-hour.

[In the following compounds *demi* is *inv.* The noun has its regular plural, unless otherwise indicated.]

demi-bain [dəmi'bɛ̃], *n.m.* hip-bath.

demi-bas [dəmi'bɑ], *n.m. inv.* knee-length stocking.

demi-botte [dəmi'bɔt], *n.f.* Wellington boot.

demi-cercle [dəmi'sɛrkl], *n.m.* semicircle.

demi-finale [dəmifi'nal], *n.f.* (*Spt.*) semi-final.

demi-fond [dəmi'fɔ̃], *n.m. inv.* middle distance (*race*).

demi-heure [dəmi'œːr], *n.f.* half-hour; *une demi-heure*, half an hour.

demi-jour [dəmi'ʒuːr], *n.m.* twilight.

demi-mot [dəmi'mo], *adv. phr. comprendre à demi-mot*, to take the hint.

déminage [demi'naːʒ], *n.m.* mine clearing.

déminer [demi'ne], *v.t.* to clear of mines.

demi-pension [dəmipɑ̃'sjɔ̃], *n.f.* half-board.

demi-pensionnaire [dəmipɑ̃sjo'nɛːr], *n.* day-boarder.

demi-place [dəmi'plas], *n.f.* half-fare.

demi-saison [dəmisɛ'zɔ̃], *n.f.* autumn *or* spring.

demi-sang [dəmi'sɑ̃], *n.m. inv.* half-bred horse.

demi-sel [dəmi'sɛl], *n.m.* slightly salted cream-cheese.

demi-solde [dəmi'sold], *n.f.* half-pay.

démission [demi'sjɔ̃], *n.f.* resignation.

démissionnaire [demisjo'nɛːr], *a.* who has resigned *or* vacated his seat, outgoing.

démissionner [demisjo'ne], *v.i.* to resign.

demi-tour [dəmi'tuːr], *n.m.* half-turn; (*Mil.*) about turn; *faire demi-tour*, to turn back.

démobilisation [demobiliza'sjɔ̃], *n.f.* demobilization.

démobiliser [demobili'ze], *v.t.* to demobilize.

démocrate [demo'krat], *a.* democratic.—*n.* democrat.

démocratie [demokra'si], *n.f.* democracy.

démocratique [demokra'tik], *a.* democratic.

démocratiquement [demokratik'mɑ̃], *adv.* democratically.

démocratiser [demokrati'ze], *v.t.* to democratize.

démodé [demo'de], *a.* old-fashioned, antiquated.

demoiselle [dəmwa'zɛl], *n.f.* young lady; unmarried woman, spinster; young girl; dragon-fly; *demoiselle d'honneur*, bridesmaid.

démolir [demo'liːr], *v.t.* to demolish, to pull down.

démolisseur [demoli'sœːr], *n.m.* (*fem.* **-euse**) demolisher.

démolition [demoli'sjɔ̃], *n.f.* demolition; (*pl.*) old building materials.

démon [de'mɔ̃], *n.m.* demon; (*good or evil*) genius; devil, fiend.

démonétisation [demonetiza'sjɔ̃], *n.f.* withdrawal from circulation (*of money*).

démonétiser [demoneti'ze], *v.t.* to withdraw from circulation, to call in (*money*).

démoniaque [demo'njak], *a.* demoniac(al).—*n.* demoniac, demon, devil.

démonstrateur [demɔ̃stra'tœːr], *n.m.* (*fem.* **-euse**) demonstrator, lecturer.

démonstratif [demɔ̃stra'tif], *a.* (*fem.* **-tive**) demonstrative.

démonstration [demɔ̃stra'sjɔ̃], n.f. demonstration, proof; exhibition.

démontable [demɔ̃'tabl], a. that can be taken to pieces; collapsible (canoe).

démontage [demɔ̃'ta:ʒ], n.m. taking to pieces, dismantling.

démonte-pneu [demɔ̃t'pnø], n.m. tyre lever.

démonter [demɔ̃'te], v.t. to unhorse, to dismount; to take to pieces, to dismantle; (fig.) to nonplus, to baffle; mer démontée, very rough sea. se démonter, v.r. to take or come to pieces (of machinery); to lose countenance, to be nonplussed; to be getting out of order (of machinery etc.).

démontrer [demɔ̃'tre], v.t. to demonstrate, to prove.

démoralisant [demɔrali'zɑ̃], a. demoralizing.

démoralisateur [demɔraliza'tœːr], a. (fem. -trice) corrupting, demoralizing.

démoralisation [demɔraliza'sjɔ̃], n.f. demoralization.

démoraliser [demɔrali'ze], v.t. to demoralize; to corrupt.

démordre [de'mɔrdr], v.i. to let go one's hold; to desist, to yield, to give in.

démoucheter [demuʃ'te], v.t. (conjug. like APPELER) to take off the button from (a foil), to uncap.

démoulage [demu'la:ʒ], n.m. taking from the mould.

démouler [demu'le], v.t. to take from the mould.

démunir [demy'niːr], v.t. to strip (of ammunition), to leave unprovided. se démunir, v.r. to deprive oneself, to leave oneself unprovided for.

démuseler [demyz'le], v.t. (conjug. like APPELER) to unmuzzle; (fig.) to let loose.

dénatalité [denatali'te], n.f. fall in the birthrate.

dénationalisation [denasjɔnaliza'sjɔ̃], n.f. denationalization.

dénationaliser [denasjɔnali'ze], v.t. to denationalize.

dénatter [dena'te], v.t. to unplait (hair etc.).

dénaturé [denaty're], a. unnatural, barbarous, cruel.

dénaturer [denaty're], v.t. to alter the nature of; to misrepresent, to distort; to disfigure; to methylate (alcohol).

dénégation [denega'sjɔ̃], n.f. denial, denegation.

déni [de'ni], n.m. denial, refusal.

déniaiser [denjɛ'ze], v.t. to sharpen the wits of; to initiate; to seduce. se déniaiser, v.r. to learn to be sharp, to grow cunning; (fam.) to lose one's innocence.

dénicher [deni'ʃe], v.t. to take out of the nest; to hunt out, to find out.—v.i. to forsake its nest (of a bird); to make off, to run away.

dénicheur [deni'ʃœːr], n.m. bird's-nester.

denier [də'nje], n.m. (Rom. Ant.) denarius; (Fr. Ant.) denier; penny; farthing, mite; (pl.) state revenues.

dénier [de'nje], v.t. to deny, to refuse.

dénigrant [deni'grɑ̃], a. disparaging.

dénigrement [denigrə'mɑ̃], n.m. disparagement.

dénigrer [deni'gre], v.t. to disparage; to vilify.

dénivellation [denivɛlla'sjɔ̃], n.f., dénivellement [denivɛl'mɑ̃], n.m. difference of level; unevenness.

dénombrement [denɔ̃brə'mɑ̃], n.m. enumeration; census.

dénombrer [denɔ̃'bre], v.t. to number, to enumerate.

dénominateur [denɔmina'tœːr], n.m. (Arith.) denominator.

dénomination [denɔmina'sjɔ̃], n.f. denomination, name.

dénommer [denɔ'me], v.t. to designate.

dénoncer [denɔ̃'se], v.t. (conjug. like COMMENCER) to denounce, to inform against; to give notice of, to declare (war etc.). se dénoncer, v.r. to own up; to give oneself up.

dénonciateur [denɔ̃sja'tœːr], n.m. (fem. -trice) informer, accuser.

dénonciation [denɔ̃sja'sjɔ̃], n.f. denunciation, declaration.

dénoter [denɔ'te], v.t. to denote, to betoken.

dénouement or dénoûment [denu'mɑ̃], n.m. dénouement, unravelling (esp. of a play etc.).

dénouer [denu'e], v.t. to untie, to loosen; to solve (difficulties etc.); to unravel (plots). se dénouer, v.r. to come untied, to be unravelled; to be solved.

denrée [dɑ̃'re], n.f. commodity, produce, provisions.

dense [dɑ̃:s], a. dense, close, thick.

densité [dɑ̃si'te], n.f. density, thickness.

dent [dɑ̃], n.f. tooth; fang; notch; cog; prong; faire ses dents, to cut one's teeth.

dentaire [dɑ̃'tɛːr], a. dental.

dental [dɑ̃'tal], a. (m.pl. -aux) (Phon.) dental.

dent-de-lion [dɑ̃də'ljɔ̃], n.m. (pl. dents-de-lion) dandelion.

denté [dɑ̃'tje], a. toothed; (Bot.) dentate; roue dentée, cogged wheel.

dentelé [dɑ̃'tle], a. notched, denticulated, indented, jagged.

denteler [dɑ̃'tle], v.t. (conjug. like APPELER) to indent, to notch.

dentelle [dɑ̃'tɛl], n.f. lace, lace-work.

dentellier [dɑ̃tɛ'lje], n.m. (fem. -ière) lace-maker.

dentelure [dɑ̃'tlyːr], n.f. denticulation, indenting; scallop.

denticule [dɑ̃ti'kyl], n.m. denticle.

dentier [dɑ̃'tje], n.m. set of teeth (esp. artificial), denture.

dentifrice [dɑ̃ti'fris], n.m. toothpaste.

dentiste [dɑ̃'tist], n.m. dentist.

denture [dɑ̃'tyːr], n.f. set of teeth; (Horol.) teeth of a wheel.

dénudation [denyda'sjɔ̃], n.f. denudation.

dénuder [deny'de], v.t. to denude; to lay bare.

dénuement or dénûment [deny'mɑ̃], n.m. destitution, penury, want.

dénuer [de'nɥe], v.t. to strip, to leave destitute. se dénuer, v.r. to strip oneself; to leave oneself destitute.

dépannage [depa'na:ʒ], n.m. (Mach., Elec.) repairing; service de dépannage, breakdown or repair service.

dépanner [depa'ne], v.t. (Mach., Elec.) to repair (a breakdown).

dépanneuse [depa'nøːz], n.f. breakdown vehicle.

dépaqueter [depak'te], v.t. (conjug. like APPELER) to unpack.

dépareillé

dépareillé [depare'je], *a.* unmatched, odd.
déparer [depa're], *v.t.* to strip (*of ornaments*); (*fig.*) to mar, to disfigure.
déparier [depa'rje], *v.t.* to take away one (*of a pair*); to separate (*a pair of animals*).
départ [de'pa:r], *n.m.* departure, start, setting out.
départager [departa'ʒe], *v.t.* (*conjug. like* MANGER) to settle by a casting-vote.
département [departə'mã], *n.m.* department; line, business.
départemental [departəmã'tal], *a.* (*m. pl.* **-aux**) departmental.
départir [depar'ti:r], *v.t. irr.* (*conjug. like* SENTIR) to separate; to distribute, to divide, to endow, to bestow. **se départir**, *v.r.* to desist; to deviate (*from*).
dépassement [depɑs'mã], *n.m.* overstepping (*of credit etc.*); (*Motor.*) overtaking.
dépasser [depa'se], *v.t.* to go beyond, to pass, to overtake; to exceed, to surpass; to be taller etc. than; to show; *son jupon dépasse*, her slip is showing.
dépaver [depa've], *v.t.* to unpave, to take up the pavement of.
dépaysé [depei'ze], *a.* away from home, out of one's element.
dépayser [depei'ze], *v.t.* to send away from home; to remove from his natural sphere etc.; (*fig.*) to bewilder. **se dépayser**, *v.r.* to leave one's home; to go abroad; to get out of one's element.
dépècement [depɛs'mã], **dépeçage** [depə'sa:ʒ], *n.m.* cutting up, carving, dismemberment.
dépecer [dep'se], *v.t.* (*see Verb Tables*) to cut up (*a carcass*), to carve.
dépêche [de'pɛ:ʃ], *n.f.* dispatch (*letter on affairs of State*); communication (*esp. a telegram*).
dépêcher [depɛ'ʃe], *v.t.* to dispatch, to do quickly; to send quickly, to send by messenger; to kill. **se dépêcher**, *v.r.* to hurry, to make haste; *dépêchez-vous*, hurry up.
dépeigner [depɛ'ɲe], *v.t.* to ruffle (*hair*).
dépeindre [de'pɛ̃:dr], *v.t. irr.* (*conjug. like* CRAINDRE) to depict, to describe; to portray, to paint.
dépelotonner [deplətɔ'ne], *v.t.* to unwind. **se dépelotonner**, *v.r.* to come unwound; to uncurl (*of cat*).
dépenaillé [depnɑ'je], *a.* tattered, ragged.
dépendance [depã'dã:s], *n.f.* subordination; dependence; appendage, annexe, outhouse, (*pl.*) out-buildings.
dépendant [depã'dã], *a.* dependent.
dépendre (1) [de'pã:dr], *v.t.* to take down; to unhang.
dépendre (2) [de'pã:dr], *v.i.* to depend, to be dependent (*de*).
dépens [de'pã], *n.m.* (*used only in pl.*) expense, cost.
dépense [de'pã:s], *n.f.* expense; expenditure, outlay; waste, flow.
dépenser [depã'se], *v.t.* to spend, to consume; to waste.
dépensier [depã'sje], *a.* (*fem.* **-ière**) extravagant.—*n.m.* (*fem.* **-ière**) extravagant person, spend-thrift; bursar.
déperdition [deperdi'sjõ], *n.f.* loss, waste.
dépérir [depe'ri:r], *v.i.* to decline, to pine away, to wither, to dwindle, to waste away.

dépérissement [deperis'mã], *n.m.* decay, withering, wasting away.
dépêtrer [depɛ'tre], *v.t.* to disentangle, to extricate. **se dépêtrer**, *v.r.* to get clear of.
dépeuplement [depœplə'mã], *n.m.* depopulation; thinning (*of forests etc.*).
dépeupler [depœ'ple], *v.t.* to depopulate; to thin. **se dépeupler**, *v.r.* to become depopulated, to be unstocked (*of river*).
dépilage [depi'la:ʒ], *n.m.* removal of hairs, bristles, etc. (*from hides etc.*).
dépilation [depila'sjõ], *n.f.* depilation.
dépiquage [depi'ka:ʒ], *n.m.* threshing *or* treading out (*corn etc.*).
dépiquer (1) [depi'ke], *v.t.* to unquilt, to unstitch.
dépiquer (2) [depi'ke], *v.t.* to tread out (*corn*).
dépister [depis'te], *v.t.* to track down; to hunt out; (*fig.*) to throw off the scent.
dépit [de'pi], *n.m.* spite; vexation.
dépiter [depi'te], *v.t.* to vex, to spite. **se dépiter**, *v.r.* to be vexed, to fret.
déplacé [depla'se], *a.* displaced, misplaced, ill-timed, unbecoming.
déplacement [deplas'mã], *n.m.* removal; displacement; *frais de déplacement*, travelling expenses.
déplacer [depla'se], *v.t.* (*conjug. like* COMMENCER) to displace; to remove, to change; to misplace. **se déplacer**, *v.r.* to move, to change one's place, to leave one's residence; to be displaced (*of things*).
déplaire [de'plɛ:r], *v.i. irr.* (*conjug. like* PLAIRE) to displease, to offend; to be disagreeable, to give offence. **se déplaire**, *v.r.* to be displeased *or* dissatisfied (*with*).
déplaisant [deplɛ'zã], *a.* unpleasant, disagreeable.
déplaisir [deplɛ'zi:r], *n.m.* displeasure, annoyance; grief.
déplanter [deplã'te], *v.t.* to dig *or* take up (*a plant*).
déplantoir [deplã'twa:r], *n.m.* garden trowel.
dépliant [depli'ã], *n.m.* folding page; folder, prospectus, leaflet.
déplier [depli'e], *v.t.* to unfold, to open out; to lay out.
déplisser [depli'se], *v.t.* to unpleat. **se déplisser**, *v.r.* to come unpleated; to lose its pleats (*of a skirt etc.*).
déploiement *or* **déploîment** [deplwa'mã], *n.m.* unfolding; display, show; (*Mil.*) deployment.
déplombage [deplõ'ba:ʒ], *n.m.* unsealing, unstopping.
déplomber [deplõ'be], *v.t.* to take the custom-house seal off (*goods*); to unstop (*a tooth*).
déplorable [deplɔ'rabl], *a.* deplorable, lamentable.
déplorablement [deplɔrablə'mã], *adv.* deplorably, wretchedly.
déplorer [deplɔ're], *v.t.* to deplore, to bewail, to lament, to mourn.
déployer [deplwa'je], *v.t.* (*conjug. like* EMPLOYER) to unfold, to unroll, to unfurl, to spread out; to display, to show; (*Mil.*) to deploy; *à gorge déployée*, at the top of one's voice. **se déployer**, *v.r.* to unroll; to display oneself; (*Mil.*) to deploy.
déplumer [deply'me], *v.t.* to pluck; (*fig.*) to despoil; to tear the hair from. **se déplumer**, *v.r.* to moult, to shed feathers.

dérégler

dépolariser [depɔlari'ze], *v.t.* to depolarize.
dépolir [depɔ'liːr], *v.t.* to make the surface (*of metal etc.*) dull, to frost (*glass*).
dépopulation [depɔpylɑ'sjɔ̃], *n.m.* depopulation.
déportation [depɔrtɑ'sjɔ̃], *n.f.* deportation.
déporté [depɔr'te], *n.m.* (*fem.* **-ée**) deported person.
déportements [depɔrtə'mɑ̃], *n.m. pl.* misconduct, evil-doings.
déporter [depɔr'te], *v.t.* to deport, to transport for life; to swerve; to carry away, to drift. **se déporter**, *v.r.* (*Law*) to desist (*from*).
déposant [depo'zɑ̃], *a.* giving evidence; depositing.—*n.m.* (*fem.* **-e**) witness; depositor.
déposer [depo'ze], *v.t.* to lay down *or* aside; to divest oneself of; to depose; to deposit; to lodge (*a complaint etc.*); **marque déposée**, registered trademark.—*v.i.* to give evidence; to settle, to leave a sediment.
dépositaire [depozi'tɛːr], *n.m.* depositary, trustee; agent.
déposition [depozi'sjɔ̃], *n.f.* deposition, evidence.
dépositoire [depozi'twaːr], *n.m.* depository, mortuary.
déposséder [depose'de], *v.t.* (*conjug. like* CÉDER) to dispossess, to oust.
dépossession [depose'sjɔ̃], *n.f.* dispossession, deprivation.
dépôt [de'po], *n.m.* depositing; deposit; sediment; depository, warehouse; (*Mil.*) depot; (*Med.*) tumour, abscess; **dépôt d'essence**, petrol station; **en dépôt**, as a deposit in trust, (*Comm.*) on sale; **mandat de dépôt**, writ of imprisonment.
dépotage [depo'taːʒ], **dépotement** [depot'mɑ̃], *n.m.* unpotting; decanting.
dépoter [depo'te], *v.t.* to take out of a pot; to decant.
dépouille [de'puːj], *n.f.* slough, cast-off skin *or* hide; spoil; remains, wardrobe (*of persons deceased*); (*pl.*) spoils, booty; **dépouille mortelle**, mortal remains.
dépouillement [depuj'mɑ̃], *n.m.* spoliation, despoiling; scrutiny (*of a ballot-box*); abstract (*of an account*).
dépouiller [depu'je], *v.t.* to strip, to skin; to unclothe; to despoil; to throw off; to cast (*of insects*); to reap (*crops*); to inspect, to count up (*a ballot-box*); to present an abstract (*of accounts*). **se dépouiller**, *v.r.* to shed its skin (*of insects and animals*), to moult; *se dépouiller de*, to divest oneself of, to strip oneself of, to renounce (*possessions etc.*).
dépourvoir [depur'vwaːr], *v.t. irr.* (*conjug. like* POURVOIR) to leave unprovided (*with*) *or* destitute (*of*). **se dépourvoir**, *v.r.* to leave oneself unequipped.
dépourvu [depur'vy], *a.* destitute, unprovided; **au dépourvu**, unawares, unexpectedly.
dépravation [depravɑ'sjɔ̃], *n.f.* vitiation, depravity.
dépravé [depra've], *a.* vitiated, depraved, corrupt.
dépraver [depra've], *v.t.* to deprave, to corrupt, to pervert. **se dépraver**, *v.r.* to become depraved *or* corrupted.

dépréciation [depresjɑ'sjɔ̃], *n.f.* depreciation.
déprécier [depre'sje], *v.t.* to depreciate, to undervalue, to underrate; to disparage. **se déprécier**, *v.r.* to underrate oneself; to fall in value (*of things*).
déprédateur [depreda'tœːr], *n.m.* (*fem.* **-trice**) depredator, plunderer.
déprédation [depredɑ'sjɔ̃], *n.f.* plundering, depredation.
déprendre [de'prɑ̃ːdr], *v.t. irr.* (*conjug. like* PRENDRE) to loosen, to detach. **se déprendre**, *v.r.* to get loose; to detach oneself (*de*).
dépression [depre'sjɔ̃], *n.f.* depression, hollow; (*fig.*) recession, slump (*of business*); **dépression nerveuse**, nervous breakdown.
déprimer [depri'me], *v.t.* to press down, to depress; (*fig.*) to discourage.
depuis [də'pɥi], *prep.* since, for; from, after; **depuis longtemps**, for a long time; **depuis peu**, lately; **depuis quand?** since when?—*adv.* since (then), afterwards, since that time.—*conj. phr.* **depuis que**, since.
députation [depytɑ'sjɔ̃], *n.f.* deputation, deputyship.
député [depy'te], *n.m.* deputy, delegate; Member of Parliament.
députer [depy'te], *v.t.* to send as representative, to depute.
déracinement [derasin'mɑ̃], *n.m.* uprooting, eradication.
déraciner [derasi'ne], *v.t.* to uproot; to eradicate, to extirpate.
déraidir [dere'diːr], *v.t.* to unstiffen; to make pliant. **se déraidir**, *v.r.* to grow soft *or* supple; to unbend.
déraillement [deraj'mɑ̃], *n.m.* derailment.
dérailler [dera'je], *v.i.* to run off the rails.
déraison [dere'zɔ̃], *n.f.* unreasonableness, folly.
déraisonnable [derezɔ'nabl], *a.* unreasonable, senseless.
déraisonnablement [derezɔnablə'mɑ̃], *adv.* unreasonably, irrationally.
déraisonner [derezɔ'ne], *v.i.* to reason falsely, to talk nonsense; to rave.
dérangement [derɑ̃ʒ'mɑ̃], *n.m.* derangement; trouble; disorder, disturbance.
déranger [derɑ̃'ʒe], *v.t.* (*conjug. like* MANGER) to derange, to put out of place *or* order; to discompose, to disconcert; to disturb, to upset; to unsettle. **se déranger**, *v.r.* to move; to be deranged, to get out of order; to trouble *or* disturb oneself, to put oneself out.
déraper [dera'pe], *v.i.* to skid, to side-slip (*bicycle, car etc.*).
dératé [dera'te], *n.m. only used in* **courir comme un dératé**, to run like a greyhound.
derechef [dər'ʃɛf], *adv.* over again, afresh, anew.
déréglé [dere'gle], *a.* out of order; irregular; intemperate, (*fig.*) unruly, dissolute.
déréglement [dereglə'mɑ̃], *n.m.* irregularity, disorder; dissoluteness, licentiousness.
dérégler [dere'gle], *v.t.* (*conjug. like* CÉDER) to put out of order. **se dérégler**, *v.r.* to get out of order, to be deranged; to lead a disorderly life.

109

dérider

dérider [deri'de], *v.t.* to unwrinkle, to smooth; to brighten, to cheer up. **se dérider**, *v.r.* to smooth one's brow; to cheer up.

dérision [deri'zjõ], *n.f.* derision, mockery, ridicule.

dérisoire [deri'zwa:r], *a.* derisive, mocking.

dérivatif [deriva'tif], *a.* (*fem.* **-tive**) derivative.—*n.m.* (*Med.*) derivative, counter-irritant.

dérivation [deriva'sjõ], *n.f.* derivation; diversion (*of water etc.*); (*Elec.*) branching, shunting; (*Naut.*) drift, leeway; (*Av.*) windage; (*Elec.*) *circuit en dérivation,* branch-circuit.

dérive [de'ri:v], *n.f.* (*Naut.*) drift, leeway; (*Av.*) fin.

dérivé [deri've], *a.* drifted.—*n.m.* (*Gram.*) derivative.

dériver [deri've], *v.t.* to divert; to derive.—*v.i.* to be turned from its proper course; (*Naut.*) to drift (*from the shore*), to go adrift.

dermatite [derma'tit], *n.f.* dermatitis.

dernier [dɛr'nje], *a.* (*fem.* **-ière**) last, latest; vilest, meanest; extreme (*highest, greatest etc.*); the one just past; youngest (*of a family of children*).—*n.m.* (*fem.* **-ière**) the last; the highest, lowest etc.

dernièrement [dɛrnjɛr'mã], *adv.* lately, recently.

dérobé [derɔ'be], *a.* stolen, hidden, secret; *à la dérobée,* stealthily.

dérober [derɔ'be], *v.t.* to steal; to remove; to conceal; to protect, to screen. **se dérober,** *v.r.* to steal away, to escape, to disappear.

dérogation [derɔga'sjõ], *n.f.* derogation.

dérogatoire [derɔga'twa:r], *a.* derogatory.

déroger [derɔ'ʒe], *v.i.* (*conjug. like* MANGER) to derogate; to detract; to condescend, to stoop.

dérouillement [deruj'mã], *n.m.* removal of rust.

dérouiller [deru'je], *v.t.* to remove the rust from; (*fig.*) to polish. **se dérouiller,** *v.r.* to lose its *or* one's rust; to brighten up; to read a subject up again.

déroulement [derul'mã], *n.m.* unrolling, unfolding.

dérouler [deru'le], *v.t.* to unroll; to spread out, to display. **se dérouler,** *v.r.* to unroll; to open to the view; to roll in (*of the waves*); to take place (*of events*).

déroutant [deru'tã], *a.* baffling, confusing.

déroute [de'rut], *n.f.* rout, overthrow; ruin; disorder, confusion.

dérouter [deru'te], *v.t.* to lead astray; to embarrass, to disconcert; to baffle; to divert (*ship, train etc.*).

derrière [dɛ'rjɛ:r], *prep.* behind, on the other side of.—*adv.* behind, after.—*n.m.* back, hinder part; posterior; behind; *pattes de derrière,* hind legs; *porte de derrière,* back-door.

derviche [dɛr'viʃ], **dervis** [dɛr'vi], *n.m.* dervish.

des [de], [*contr. of* DE LES].

dès [de], *prep.* from, since, as early as.—*conj. phr.* **dès que,** when, as soon as, since.

désabonnement [dezabɔn'mã], *n.m.* withdrawal of subscription.

désabonner (se) [sədezabɔ'ne], *v.r.* to with-

draw one's subscription (*to a magazine etc.*).

désabuser [dezaby'ze], *v.t.* to disabuse, to undeceive. **se désabuser,** *v.r.* to be undeceived, to face the facts.

désaccord [deza'kɔ:r], *n.m.* disagreement, discord.

désaccorder [dezakɔr'de], *v.t.* to untune; (*fig.*) to set at variance. **se désaccorder,** *v.r.* to get out of tune.

désaccouplement [dezakuplə'mã], *n.m.* uncoupling.

désaccoupler [dezaku'ple], *v.t.* to uncouple. **se désaccoupler,** *v.r.* to become uncoupled; to come asunder.

désaccoutumer [dezakuty'me], *v.t.* to disaccustom. **se désaccoutumer,** *v.r.* to break oneself of, to lose the habit of.

désaffecter [dezafɛk'te], *v.t.* to secularize (*a church*); (*Mil.*) to transfer; to put a building to another use.

désaffection [dezafɛk'sjõ], *n.f.* loss of affection.

désaffectionner [dezafɛksjɔ'ne], *v.t.* to cause (*someone*) to lose his *or* her affection; to disaffect. **se désaffectionner,** *v.r.* to lose affection.

désagencement [dezaʒãs'mã], *n.m.* throwing out of gear.

désagencer [dezaʒã'se], *v.t.* (*conjug. like* COMMENCER) to throw out of gear, to disarrange.

désagréable [dezagre'abl], *a.* disagreeable, unpleasant.

désagréablement [dezagreablə'mã], *adv.* disagreeably, unpleasantly.

désagréger [dezagre'ʒe], *v.t.* (*conjug. like* ASSIÉGER) to disaggregate, to break up, to separate.

désagrément [dezagre'mã], *n.m.* disagreeableness, unpleasantness; annoyance, discomfort.

désaimanter [dezɛmã'te], *v.t.* to demagnetize.

désajustement [dezaʒystə'mã], *n.m.* disarrangement, disorder.

désajuster [dezaʒys'te], *v.t.* to disarrange, to disturb, to put out of order. **se désajuster,** *v.r.* to become disarranged, to get out of order.

désaltérant [dezalte'rã], *a.* thirst-quenching.

désaltérer [dezalte're], *v.t.* (*conjug. like* CÉDER) to quench the thirst of, to refresh. **se désaltérer,** *v.r.* to quench one's thirst.

désamorcer [dezamɔr'se], *v.t.* (*conjug. like* COMMENCER) to unprime, to uncap (*fire-arms etc.*). **se désamorcer,** *v.r.* to run down (*dynamo*); to run dry (*pump*).

désappointement [dezapwɛ̃'mã], *n.m.* disappointment.

désappointer [dezapwɛ̃'te], *v.t.* to disappoint.

désapprendre [deza'prã:dr], *v.t. irr.* (*conjug. like* PRENDRE) to unlearn, to forget.

désapprobateur [dezaprɔba'tœ:r], *a.* (*fem.* **-trice**) disapproving, censuring, carping.—*n.m.* (*fem.* **-trice**) censurer, fault-finder.

désapprobation [dezaprɔba'sjõ], *n.f.* disapprobation, disapproval.

désappropriation [dezaprɔpria'sjõ], *n.f.* renunciation (*of property*).

désapprouver [dezapru've], *v.t.* to disapprove of, to blame.

désarçonner [dezarsɔ'ne], *v.t.* to unhorse; (*fig.*) to baffle, to floor.
désarmement [dezarmə'mã], *n.m.* disarming, disarmament; (*Naut.*) laying up.
désarmer [dezar'me], *v.t.* to disarm, to unarm; (*fig.*) to appease, to calm; to uncock (*a gun*); (*Naut.*) to lay up (*a vessel*).—*v.i.* to disarm; to give up maintaining troops.
désarroi [deza'rwa], *n.m.* disorder, disarray, confusion.
désarticulation [dezartikylɑ'sjɔ̃], *n.f.* disarticulation.
désarticuler [dezartiky'le], *v.t.* to disarticulate, to disjoint.
désassemblage [dezasɑ̃'bla:ʒ], **désassemblement** [dezasɑ̃blə'mã], *n.m.* dismantling.
désassembler [dezasɑ̃'ble], *v.t.* to take to pieces, to separate, to dismantle.
désassocier [dezasɔ'sje], *v.t.* to disassociate, to dissociate.
désassortiment [dezasɔrti'mã], *n.m.* unmatching, ill-assortment; unstocking.
désastre [de'zastr], *n.m.* disaster.
désastreusement [dezastrøz'mã], *adv.* disastrously.
désastreux [dezas'trø], *a.* (*fem.* **-euse**) disastrous, unfortunate, very sad.
désavantage [dezavɑ̃'ta:ʒ], *n.m.* disadvantage; detriment, prejudice; drawback, handicap.
désavantager [dezavɑ̃ta'ʒe], *v.t.* (*conjug. like* MANGER) to disadvantage, to handicap.
désavantageusement [dezavɑ̃taʒøz'mã], *adv.* disadvantageously; disparagingly.
désavantageux [dezavɑ̃ta'ʒø], *a.* (*fem.* **-euse**) disadvantageous; detrimental, prejudicial, unfavourable.
désaveu [deza'vø], *n.m.* (*pl.* **-eux**) disavowal; denial; retractation.
désavouer [deza'vwe], *v.t.* to disown, to disclaim, to disavow; to retract.
désaxé [deza'kse], *a.* offset, out of true (*of a wheel, etc.*); (*fig.*) out of joint.
descellement [desɛl'mã], *n.m.* loosening, unsealing.
desceller [desɛ'le], *v.t.* to unseal; to loosen (*masonry etc.*). **se desceller**, *v.r.* to become loose or unsealed.
descendance [desɑ̃'dã:s], *n.f.* descent, lineage.
descendant [desɑ̃'dã], *a.* descending, going down; (*Mil.*) coming off duty.—*n.m.* (*fem.* **-e**) descendant, offspring, issue.
descendre [de'sɑ̃:dr], *v.t.* (*with aux.* AVOIR) to take down, bring or let down; to go or come down (*a staircase etc.*); to set down (*of a cab etc.*); to land.—*v.i.* (*with aux.* ÊTRE) to descend, to go down; to go downstairs; to alight, to land; to slope, to incline; to fall, to subside.
descente [de'sɑ̃:t], *n.f.* descent; taking down; subsidence (*of waters etc.*); dismounting; disembarkation; declivity; raid; (*pop.*) rupture; **descente de lit**, bedside rug; **descente de bain**, bath-mat.
descriptif [deskrip'tif], *a.* (*fem.* **-tive**) descriptive.
description [deskrip'sjɔ̃], *n.f.* description; inventory.
désemballage [dezɑ̃ba'la:ʒ], *n.m.* unpacking.
désemballer [dezɑ̃ba'le], *v.t.* to unpack.

désembarquement [dezɑ̃barkə'mã], *n.m.* disembarkation, landing.
désembarquer [dezɑ̃bar'ke], *v.t.* to disembark, to land; to unship, to unload.
désemboîter [dezɑ̃bwa'te], *v.t.* to dislocate. **se désemboîter**, *v.r.* to become disjointed.
désembourber [dezɑ̃bur'be], *v.t.* to draw out of the mire.
désemparé [dezɑ̃pa're], *a.* in distress, helpless.
désemparer [dezɑ̃pa're], *v.t.* (*Naut.*) to disable.—*v.i.* to quit, to go away; *sans désemparer*, on the spot, at once.
désempeser [dezɑ̃pə'ze], *v.t.* (*conjug. like* AMENER) to unstarch. **se désempeser**, *v.r.* to become limp.
désemplir [dezɑ̃'pli:r], *v.t.* to make less full, to empty in part.—*v.i.* to become less full (*used only in negative*). **se désemplir**, *v.r.* to become less full.
désenchaîner [dezɑ̃ʃɛ'ne], *v.t.* to unchain.
désenchantement [dezɑ̃ʃãt'mã], *n.m.* disenchantment, disillusion.
désenchanter [dezɑ̃ʃã'te], *v.t.* to disenchant, to disillusion.
désenchanteur [dezɑ̃ʃã'tœ:r], *a.* (*fem.* **-eresse**) disenchanting.
désencombrement [dezɑ̃kɔ̃brə'mã], *n.m.* disencumbrance; dispersal.
désencombrer [dezɑ̃kɔ̃'bre], *v.t.* to disencumber, to clear (*a road etc.*).
désenfiler [dezɑ̃fi'le], *v.t.* to unthread, to unstring. **se désenfiler**, *v.r.* to come unthreaded or unstrung.
désenfler [dezɑ̃'fle], *v.t.* to reduce the swelling of.—*v.i.* and **se désenfler**, *v.r.* to become less swollen.
désenflure [dezɑ̃'fly:r], *n.f.*, **désenflement** [dezɑ̃flə'mã], *n.m.* diminution or disappearance of a swelling.
désengager [dezɑ̃ga'ʒe], *v.t.* (*conjug. like* MANGER) to disengage, to release from an engagement.
désengrener [dezɑ̃grə'ne], *v.t.* (*conjug. like* AMENER) to throw out of gear.
désenivrer [dezɑ̃ni'vre], *v.t.*, to make sober again.—*v.i.* to sober. **se désenivrer**, *v.r.* to become sober (*again*), to sober up.
désenlaidir [dezɑ̃lɛ'di:r], *v.t.* to render less ugly.—*v.i.* to become less ugly.
désennuyer [dezɑ̃nɥi'je], *v.t.* (*conjug. like* EMPLOYER) to enliven, to cheer. **se désennuyer**, *v.r.* to find amusement, to kill time.
désenrayer [dezɑ̃rɛ'je], *v.t.* (*conjug. like* PAYER) to unlock or unskid (*a wheel etc.*).
désenrhumer [dezɑ̃ry'me], *v.t.* to cure (*someone*) of a cold. **se désenrhumer**, *v.r.* to get rid of a cold.
désenrôlement [dezɑ̃rol'mã], *n.m.* (*Mil.*) discharge.
désenrôler [dezɑ̃ro'le], *v.t.* to discharge.
désensevelir [dezɑ̃sə'vli:r], *v.t.* to unshroud; to exhume.
désensevelissement [dezɑ̃səvlis'mã], *n.m.* unshrouding, exhumation, disinterment.
désentortiller [dezɑ̃tɔrti'je], *v.t.* to untwist to unravel.
désentraver [dezɑ̃tra've], *v.t.* to untrammel, to unhobble (*a horse etc.*).
déséquilibre [dezeki'libr], *n.m.* lack of balance, unbalance; imbalance.

déséquilibré

déséquilibré [dezekili'bre], *a.* and *n.m.* (*fem.* **-ée**) unbalanced (person).

déséquilibrer [dezekili'bre], *v.t.* to unbalance.

désert [de'zɛːr], *a.* uninhabited, solitary; wild, waste, deserted.—*n.m.* desert, wilderness; solitary place; (*C*) clearing in a forest.

déserter [dezɛrte], *v.t.* to desert, to abandon, to forsake; to quit, to leave; (*C*) to clear land, to break up (*ground*) for tillage.—*v.i.* to desert, to go over to the enemy.

déserteur [dezɛr'tœːr], *n.m.* deserter.

désertion [dezɛr'sjɔ̃], *n.f.* desertion.

désespérance [dezɛspe'rãːs], *n.f.* despair.

désespérant [dezɛspe'rã], *a.* desperate, hopeless; disheartening, distressing.

désespéré [dezɛspe're], *a.* hopeless, desperate; disconsolate.—*n.m.* (*fem.* **-ée**) person in despair; madman, madwoman.

désespérément [dezɛspere'mã], *adv.* desperately, despairingly.

désespérer [dezɛspe're], *v.t.* (*conjug. like* CÉDER) to drive to despair; to dishearten; to distress.—*v.i.* to despair. **se désespérer**, *v.r.* to be in despair.

désespoir [dezɛs'pwaːr], *n.m.* despair, hopelessness, despondency, grief; *en désespoir de cause,* as a last resource.

déshabiliter [dezabili'te], *v.t.* to disqualify.

déshabillé [dezabi'je], *n.m.* deshabille, undress; *en déshabillé,* partly *or* scantily dressed.

déshabiller [dezabi'je], *v.t.* to undress, to strip. **se déshabiller**, *v.r.* to undress oneself.

déshabituer [dezabi'tɥe], *v.t.* to disaccustom, to break off. **se déshabituer**, *v.r.* to lose the habit of; to break oneself of.

déshérence [deze'rãːs], *n.f.* (*Law*) escheat.

déshériter [dezeri'te], *v.t.* to disinherit.

déshonnête [dezɔ'nɛːt], *a.* immodest, indecent, unseemly.

déshonnêtement [dezɔnɛt'mã], *adv.* indecently, immodestly.

déshonnêteté [dezɔnɛt'te], *n.f.* indecency, unseemliness.

déshonneur [dezɔ'nœːr], *n.m.* dishonour, disgrace, shame.

déshonorable [dezɔnɔ'rabl], *a.* dishonourable.

déshonorablement [dezɔnɔrablə'mã], *adv.* dishonourably.

déshonorant [dezɔnɔ'rã], *a.* dishonourable, disgraceful.

déshonorer [dezɔnɔ're], *v.t.* to dishonour, to disgrace. **se déshonorer**, *v.r.* to dishonour *or* disgrace oneself.

déshydrater [dezidra'te], *v.t.* to dehydrate.

désignatif [deziɲa'tif], *a.* (*fem.* **-tive**) indicative.

désignation [deziɲa'sjɔ̃], *n.f.* designation, indication.

désigner [dezi'ɲe], *v.t.* to designate, to denote; to appoint, to nominate, to point out; (*Mil.*) to detail.

désillusion [dezily'zjɔ̃], *n.f.*, **désillusionnement** [dezilyzjɔn'mã], *n.m.* disillusion.

désillusionner [dezilyzjɔ'ne], *v.t.* to disillusion, to disappoint.

désinfectant [dezɛ̃fɛk'tã], *a.* disinfecting.—*n.m.* disinfectant.

désinfecter [dezɛ̃fɛk'te], *v.t.* to disinfect, to decontaminate.

désinfection [dezɛ̃fɛk'sjɔ̃], *n.f.* disinfection.

désintégration [dezɛ̃tegra'sjɔ̃], *n.f.* disintegration; fission.

désintégrer [dezɛ̃te'gre], *v.t.* (*conjug. like* CÉDER) to disintegrate; to split (*atom*).

désintéressé [dezɛ̃tere'se], *a.* disinterested, unselfish, unbiased.

désintéressement [dezɛ̃terɛs'mã], *n.m.* disinterestedness.

désintéresser [dezɛ̃tere'se], *v.t.* to indemnify.

désinvestir [dezɛ̃vɛs'tiːr], *v.t.* (*Mil.*) to raise the siege of.

désinvolte [dezɛ̃'vɔlt], *a.* free, easy; offhand.

désinvolture [dezɛ̃vɔl'tyːr], *n.f.* casual, easy bearing *or* gait; offhandedness.

désir [de'ziːr], *n.m.* desire, wish, longing.

désirable [dezi'rabl], *a.* desirable.

désirer [dezi're], *v.t.* to desire, to wish for, to long for, to want.

désireux [dezi'rø], *a.* (*fem.* **-euse**) desirous, anxious, eager (*to*).

désistement [dezistə'mã], *n.m.* desistance, withdrawal.

désister (se) [sədezis'te], *v.r.* to desist from, to renounce, to withdraw.

désobéir [dezɔbe'iːr], *v.i.* to disobey.

désobéissance [dezɔbei'sãːs], *n.f.* disobedience.

désobéissant [dezɔbei'sã], *a.* disobedient.

désobligeamment [dezɔbliʒa'mã], *adv.* disobligingly; unkindly.

désobligeance [dezɔbli'ʒãːs], *n.f.* lack of complaisance; unkindness.

désobligeant [dezɔbli'ʒã], *a.* disobliging; uncivil.

désobliger [dezɔbli'ʒe], *v.t.* (*conjug. like* MANGER) to disoblige, to displease.

désodorisant [dezɔdɔri'zã], *a.* and *n.m.* deodorant.

désœuvré [dezœ'vre], *a.* unoccupied, idle.

désœuvrement [dezœvrə'mã], *n.m.* want of occupation, idleness.

désolant [dezɔ'lã], *a.* grievous, distressing.

désolation [dezɔla'sjɔ̃], *n.f.* desolation, ruin; deep affliction, grief.

désolé [dezɔ'le], *a.* afflicted, broken-hearted; very sorry, grieved; dreary, desolate (*place*).

désoler [dezɔ'le], *v.t.* to devastate, to desolate, to lay waste; to afflict, to grieve; to annoy, to torment. **se désoler**, *v.r.* to grieve, to be disconsolate.

désolidariser [desɔlidari'ze], *v.t.* to break the ties which keep together (*a party, friends etc.*).

désopilant [dezɔpi'lã], *a.* very funny, side-splitting.

désopiler [dezɔpi'le], *v.t.* (*Med.*) to clear of obstruction; (*fig.*) to cheer up, to enliven.

désordonné [dezɔrdɔ'ne], *a.* disorderly; (*fig.*) dissolute, unruly; inordinate.

désordonner [dezɔrdɔ'ne], *v.t.* to disturb; to throw into confusion.

désordre [de'zɔrdr], *n.m.* disorder, confusion; disorderly life; perturbation; (*pl.*) disturbances, riots.

désorganisation [dezɔrganiza'sjɔ̃], *n.f.* disorganization.

désorganiser [dezɔrgani'ze], *v.t.* to disorganize. **se désorganiser**, *v.r.* to become disorganized.

désorienter [dezɔrjɑ̃'te], v.t. to lead astray, to mislead, to bewilder; to put out, to disconcert.

désormais [dezɔr'mɛ], adv. henceforth, hereafter.

désossé [dezo'se], a. boneless, flabby.

désosser [dezo'se], v.t. to bone. **se désosser**, v.r. to become disjointed, limp, flabby etc.

despote [dɛs'pɔt], n.m. despot.

despotique [dɛspo'tik], a. despotic.

despotiquement [dɛspotik'mɑ̃], adv. despotically.

despotisme [dɛspo'tism], n.m. despotism.

desquels [de'kɛl], m.pl. (fem. **-elles**) [DUQUEL].

dessaisir [desɛ'ziːr], v.t. to let go; to dispossess. **se dessaisir**, v.r. to give up, to part with.

dessaisissement [deseziz'mɑ̃], n.m. parting with, abandonment.

dessalé [desa'le], a. unsalted, free from salt; (fam.) sharp.—n.m. (fem. **-ée**) sharp person.

dessaler [desa'le], v.t. to remove salt from (meat etc.); (fig.) to make sharp, cunning etc.

dessangler [desɑ̃'gle], v.t. to loosen the girth of (a horse etc.).

desséchant [dese'ʃɑ̃], a. drying, parching.

dessèchement [deseʃ'mɑ̃], n.m. drying up; dryness.

dessécher [dese'ʃe], v.t. to dry up; to parch; (fig.) to wither (the heart etc.); to emaciate. **se dessécher**, v.r. to become dry, to dry up; (fig.) to wither, to waste away.

dessein [de'sɛ̃], n.m. design, plan, scheme; intention, resolution.

desseller [dese'le], v.t. to unsaddle.

desserrer [dese're], v.t. to loosen, to relax; to ease. **se desserrer**, v.r. to become loose, to relax.

dessert [de'sɛːr], n.m. dessert.

desserte [de'sɛrt], n.f. leavings, remains (of a meal); small sideboard; parochial duty; railway service.

desservant [desɛr'vɑ̃], n.m. officiating minister (of a parish etc.).

desservir [desɛr'viːr], v.t. irr. (conjug. like SENTIR) to clear (a table); to officiate (of clergymen); to ply between (of boats etc.); (fig.) to do someone a disservice.

dessiller or **déciller** [desi'je], v.t. to open (someone's eyes); to undeceive.

dessin [de'sɛ̃], n.m. drawing; sketch; pattern, design; **dessin animé**, (Cine.) cartoon.

dessinateur [desina'tœːr], n.m. (fem. **-trice**) draughtsman; designer.

dessiner [desi'ne], v.t. to draw, to sketch; to set off, to indicate; to lay out. **se dessiner**, v.r. to be delineated, to be visible, to stand out.

dessous [də'su], adv. under, underneath, below.—n.m. lower part; under, hidden or wrong side; worst; lee (of the wind); (pl.) underclothing (of women).—prep. phr. **au-dessous de**, beneath.

dessus [də'sy], adv. on, upon, over, above; **là-dessus**, thereupon; **par-dessus**, over, besides; **sens dessus dessous**, upside down.—n.m. top, upper part; right side; upper hand, advantage.—prep. phr. **au-dessus de**, above.

destin [dɛs'tɛ̃], n.m. destiny, fate; career.

destinataire [dɛstina'tɛːr], n. addressee; recipient; (Comm.) consignee; payee.

destination [dɛstina'sjɔ̃], n.f. destination; object, end.

destinée [dɛsti'ne], n.f. fate, destiny, doom.

destiner [dɛsti'ne], v.t. to destine, to purpose; to reserve (for a particular fate etc.). **se destiner**, v.r. to be destined.

destituer [dɛsti'tɥe], v.t. to dismiss, to discharge.

destitution [dɛstity'sjɔ̃], n.f. dismissal, removal (from office).

destroyer [dɛstrwa'jœːr], n.m. (Navy) destroyer.

destructeur [dɛstryk'tœːr], a. (fem. **-trice**) destructive, deadly, ruinous.—n.m. (fem. **-trice**) ravager, spoiler.

destructif [dɛstryk'tif], a. (fem. **-tive**) destructive, destroying.

destruction [dɛstryk'sjɔ̃], n.f. destruction.

désuet [desɥ'ɛ], a. (fem. **-ète**) obsolete, out-of-date.

désuétude [desɥe'tyd], n.f. disuse, desuetude.

désunion [dezy'njɔ̃], n.f. disunion; disjunction.

désunir [dezy'niːr], v.t. to disunite, to disjoin, to part. **se désunir**, v.r. to disunite, to come asunder.

détachage [deta'ʃaːʒ], n.m. cleaning, scouring.

détachant [deta'ʃɑ̃], n.m. cleaner, stain-remover.

détachement [detaʃ'mɑ̃], n.m. indifference, unconcern; (Mil.) detachment, draft.

détacher (1) [deta'ʃe], v.t. to remove stains, spots etc.

détacher (2) [deta'ʃe], v.t. to detach, to untie, to unfasten, to undo; to cut off; (Mil.) to detail. **se détacher**, v.r. to come unfastened, to come undone; to disengage oneself; to break away; to stand out clearly.

détail [de'taːj], n.m. detail, small matter, trifle; retail.

détaillant [deta'jɑ̃], n.m. (fem. **-e**) retailer, small dealer.

détailler [deta'je], v.t. to cut in pieces; to retail; to relate minutely.

détaxation [detaksa'sjɔ̃], n.f. decontrol (of prices).

détaxer [detak'se], v.t. to reduce or take off a tax; to decontrol.

détecter [detɛk'te], v.t. to detect.

détecteur [detɛk'tœːr], n.m. detector.

détection [detɛk'sjɔ̃], n.f. detection.

détective [detɛk'tiːv], n.m. detective.

déteindre [de'tɛ̃dr], v.t. irr. (conjug. like CRAINDRE) to take the dye or colour out of.—v.i. to lose colour, to run, to fade.

dételage [de'tlaːʒ], n.m. unharnessing.

dételer [de'tle], v.t. (conjug. like APPELER) to unharness, to unyoke.

détendre [de'tɑ̃dr], v.t. to slacken, to relax; to reduce the pressure of; to take down. **se détendre**, v.r. to slacken, to unbend, to become easier, to relax.

détenir [det'niːr], v.t. irr. (conjug. like TENIR) to detain, to withhold; to confine.

détente [de'tɑ̃t], n.f. trigger (of a gun etc.); cut-off (of an engine); relaxation, easing.

détenteur [detɑ̃'tœːr], n.m. (fem. **-trice**) holder, detainer.

détention

détention [detɑ̃'sjɔ̃], *n.f.* detention; imprison-ment.

détenu [det'ny], *a.* detained, imprisoned.—*n.m.* (*fem.* -**e**) prisoner.

détergent [deter'ʒɑ̃], *a.* (*Med.*) detergent.—*n.m.* detergent.

déterger [deter'ʒe], *v.t.* (*conjug. like* MANGER) to cleanse, to purify.

détérioration [deterjɔrɑ'sjɔ̃], *n.f.* deteriora-tion; wear and tear.

détériorer [deterjɔ're], *v.t.* to impair, to make worse. se **détériorer**, *v.r.* to deterio-rate.

déterminable [detɛrmi'nabl], *a.* determin-able.

déterminant [detɛrmi'nɑ̃], *a.* determinative, decisive.—*n.m.* (*Math.*) determinant.

détermination [detɛrminɑ'sjɔ̃], *n.f.* deter-mination, resolution.

déterminé [detɛrmi'ne], *a.* determined, decided, fixed; resolute, firm.

déterminer [detɛrmi'ne], *v.t.* to determine, to settle; to ascertain; to decide; to cause to take a resolution. se **déterminer**, *v.r.* to resolve, to determine.

déterré [detɛ're], *n.m.* exhumed body.

déterrer [detɛ're], *v.t.* to dig up, to disinter; to unearth, to bring to light.

détestable [detɛs'tabl], *a.* detestable, hateful, odious; wretched.

détestablement [detɛstablə'mɑ̃], *adv.* detest-ably, abominably.

détestation [detɛstɑ'sjɔ̃], *n.f.* detestation, abhorrence.

détester [detɛs'te], *v.t.* to detest, to hate.

détirer [deti're], *v.t.* to draw out, to stretch.

détisser [deti'se], *v.t.* to unweave.

détonateur [detɔnɑ'tœːr], *n.m.* detonator.

détonation [detɔnɑ'sjɔ̃], *n.f.* detonation, report.

détoner [detɔ'ne], *v.t.*, *v.i.* to detonate.

détonneler [detɔn'le], *v.t.* (*conjug. like* APPELER) to draw from a cask.

détonner [detɔ'ne], *v.i.* to be out of tune; to jar.

détordre [de'tɔrdr], *v.t.* to untwist; to unravel. se **détordre**, *v.r.* to come un-twisted.

détors [de'tɔːr], *a.* untwisted.

détortiller [detɔrti'je], *v.t.* to untwist; to unravel. se **détortiller**, *v.r.* to become un-twisted; to be unravelled.

détour [de'tuːr], *n.m.* turning, change of direction; roundabout way; (*fig.*) shift, evasion, trick.

détourné [detur'ne], *a.* out of the way, un-frequented; indirect.

détournement [deturnə'mɑ̃], *n.m.* turning aside; embezzlement; *détournement de mineur*, (*Law*) abduction.

détourner [detur'ne], *v.t.* to turn away; to lead astray; to divert; to ward off; to em-bezzle; to deter.—*v.i.* to turn, to turn off. se **détourner**, *v.r.* to turn aside; to abandon (*de*).

détracteur [detrak'tœːr], *a.* (*fem.* -**trice**) de-tractive, detracting.—*n.m.* (*fem.* -**trice**) detractor, disparager.

détraqué [detra'ke], *a.* out of order; de-ranged, (*colloq.*) crazy.—*n.m.* (*fem.* -**ée**) person shattered in mind or body.

détraquement [detrak'mɑ̃], *n.m.* breakdown (*of mechanism, mind, health*).

détraquer [detra'ke], *v.t.* to spoil (*a horse's*) paces; (*fig.*) to put out of order. se **détra-quer**, *v.r.* to lose its paces (*of a horse*); (*fig.*) to be disordered.

détrempe [de'trɑ̃p], *n.f.* distemper (*paint*).

détremper [detrɑ̃'pe], *v.t.* to dilute, to dis-solve.

détresse [de'trɛs], *n.f.* distress, grief, trouble.

détresser [detrɛ'se], *v.t.* to unravel; to un-plait.

détriment [detri'mɑ̃], *n.m.* detriment, injury, prejudice.

détritus [detri'tys], *n.m.* residue, refuse; offal.

détroit [de'trwa], *n.m.* strait, channel, sound, narrow firth.

détromper [detrɔ̃'pe], *v.t.* to undeceive. se **détromper**, *v.r.* to be undeceived.

détrônement [detron'mɑ̃], *n.m.* dethrone-ment.

détrôner [detro'ne], *v.t.* to dethrone.

détrousser [detru'se], *v.t.* to untruss, to let down; (*fig.*) to rob.

détrousseur [detru'sœːr], *n.m.* (*fem.* -**euse**) highwayman, robber.

détruire [de'trɥiːr], *v.t. irr.* (*conjug. like* CONDUIRE) to destroy, to demolish, to ruin; to exterminate, to do away with, to efface, to suppress. se **détruire**, *v.r.* to fall into ruin or decay; to destroy each other.

dette [dɛt], *n.f.* debt; obligation.

deuil [dœːj], *n.m.* mourning; grief, sorrow; gloom; period of mourning; bereavement; mourning clothes; funeral cortège.

Deutéronome [døterɔ'nɔm], *n.m.* Deutero-nomy.

deux [dø], *a.* two, both; second.—*n.m.* two; second (*of the month*); (*Cards, Dice etc.*) deuce.

deuxième [dø'zjɛm], *a.* second.—*n.m.* second; second floor.

deuxièmement [døzjɛm'mɑ̃], *adv.* secondly.

deux-pièces [dø'pjɛs], *n.m. inv.* (*women's*) two-piece (*suit*).

deux-points [dø'pwɛ̃], *n.m. inv.* (*Print.*) colon.

dévaler [deva'le], *v.t.* to descend; to lower.—*v.i.* to descend, to slope; to go *or* rush down (*of streams etc.*).

dévaliser [devali'ze], *v.t.* to rifle, to strip, to rob.

dévaliseur [devali'zœːr], *n.m.* (*fem.* -**euse**) thief, burglar.

dévaluation [devalɥɑ'sjɔ̃], *n.f.* devaluation.

dévaluer [deva'lɥe], *v.t.* to devalue.

devancer [devɑ̃'se], *v.t.* (*conjug. like* COM-MENCER) to precede; to outstrip; to forestall, to anticipate; to surpass.

devancier [devɑ̃'sje], *n.m.* (*fem.* -**ière**) pre-decessor; (*pl.*) ancestors, forefathers.

devant [də'vɑ̃], *prep.* before; in front of, over against.—*adv.* in front, ahead.—*n.m.* front, forepart.

devanture [dəvɑ̃'tyːr], *n.f.* front(age) (*of a building*); shop-front.

dévaser [deva'ze], *v.t.* to dredge.

dévastateur [devasta'tœːr], *a.* (*fem.* -**trice**) devastating, destructive.—*n.m.* (*fem.* -**trice**) devastator.

114

dévastation [devasta'sjɔ̃], *n.f.* devastation, ravage, havoc.

dévaster [devas'te], *v.t.* to devastate, to lay waste.

développement [devlɔp'mã], *n.m.* unfolding, opening; development, progress; (*Mil.*) deployment.

développer [devlɔ'pe], *v.t.* to open, to unwrap; to expand, to explain; to develop. **se développer**, *v.r.* to expand, to unfold; to be unravelled; to extend; to develop.

devenir [dəv'niːr], *v.i. irr.* (*conjug. like* TENIR) to become, to grow, to get, to turn into.— *n.m.* gradual development (*of beings or of things*).

dévergondage [devɛrgɔ̃'da:ʒ], *n.m.* shamelessness; profligacy, dissoluteness.

dévergonder (se) [sədevɛrgɔ̃'de], *v.r.* to become dissolute.

déverrouillement [devɛruj'mã], *n.m.* unbolting.

déverrouiller [devɛru'je], *v.t.* to unbolt; (*fig.*) to set free.

devers [də'vɛːr], *prep.* towards; **par devers**, in the presence of.

dévers [de'vɛːr], *a.* inclined; out of alignment. —*n.m.* inclination; warping.

déverser [devɛr'se], *v.t.* to bend; to dump; to pour out (*water etc.*).—*v.i.* to lean, to jut out; to warp. **se déverser**, *v.r.* to empty (*of rivers, canals etc.*).

déversoir [devɛr'swaːr], *n.m.* overflow (*of a canal etc.*); outfall.

dévêtir [deve'tiːr], *v.t. irr.* (*conjug. like* VÊTIR) to undress, to strip of clothes; (*Law*) to divest. **se dévêtir**, *v.r.* to take off one's clothes, to undress.

déviation [devja'sjɔ̃], *n.f.* deviation, curvature; diversion (*of a road*).

déviationnisme [devjasjɔ'nism], *n.m.* (*Polit.*) deviationism.

déviationniste [devjasjɔ'nist], *n.* deviationist.

dévidage [devi'da:ʒ], *n.m.* winding *or* reeling off.

dévider [devi'de], *v.t.* to wind off (*into skeins etc.*); (*fig.*) to explain.

dévideur [devi'dœːr], *n.m.* (*fem.* **-euse**) winder, reeler.

dévidoir [devi'dwaːr], *n.m.* reel, skein-winder, spool.

dévier [de'vje], *v.i.* and **se dévier**, *v.r.* to deviate; to swerve.

devin [də'vɛ̃], *n.m.* (*fem.* **devineresse**) diviner, augur; fortune-teller.

deviner [dəvi'ne], *v.t.* to divine, to predict; to guess. **se deviner**, *v.r.* to understand each other.

devinette [dəvi'nɛt], *n.f.* poser, riddle, conundrum.

devineur [dəvi'nœːr], *n.m.* (*fem.* **-euse**) guesser.

devis [də'vi], *n.m.* estimate; specification.

dévisager [deviza'ʒe], *v.t.* (*conjug. like* MANGER) to disfigure; to stare out.

devise [də'viːz], *n.f.* device, emblem; motto, slogan; (*Fin.*) currency; *des devises étrangères*, foreign currency.

deviser [dəvi'ze], *v.i.* to talk casually, to chat.

dévissage [devi'sa:ʒ], **dévissement** [devis'mã], *n.m.* unscrewing.

dévisser [devi'se], *v.t.* to unscrew. **se dévisser**, *v.r.* to come unscrewed.

dévitaliser [devitali'ze], *v.t.* to kill the nerve (*of a tooth etc.*).

dévoiement [devwa'mã], *n.m.* looseness (*of the bowels*); (*Arch.*) inclination, slope; (*fig.*) departure from the normal path.

dévoilement [devwal'mã], *n.m.* unveiling, disclosure.

dévoiler [devwa'le], *v.t.* to unveil, to reveal, to disclose. **se dévoiler**, *v.r.* to be revealed.

dévoîment [DÉVOIEMENT].

devoir [də'vwaːr], *v.t. irr.* to owe (*money, gratitude*); to be obliged to, to be bound to, to have to, must. **se devoir**, *v.r.* to owe oneself; to owe it to oneself.—*n.m.* duty; (*Sch.*) work set, homework; (*pl.*) respects, compliments.

dévoltage [devɔl'ta:ʒ], *n.m.* (*Elec.*) reduction of voltage.

dévolter [devɔl'te], *v.t.* to reduce the voltage, to step down (*current*).

dévolteur [devɔl'tœːr], *n.m.* reducing transformer.

dévolu [devɔ'ly], *a.* (*Law*) devolved, vested.— *n.m.* choice, preference.

dévolution [devɔly'sjɔ̃], *n.f.* devolution; escheat.

dévorant [devɔ'rã], *a.* devouring, ravenous; (*fig.*) wasting.

dévorateur [devɔra'tœːr], *a.* (*fem.* **-trice**) devouring.—*n.m.* (*fem.* **-trice**) devourer, destroyer.

dévorer [devɔ're], *v.t.* to devour; to destroy; to squander; to gaze at eagerly.

dévot [de'vo], *a.* devout, pious; sanctimonious; holy (*of books etc.*).—*n.m.* (*fem.* **-e**) devout person, devotee; bigot.

dévotement [devɔt'mã], *adv.* devoutly, piously.

dévotion [devɔ'sjɔ̃], *n.f.* devotion, piety; disposal; devoutness.

dévouement or **dévoûment** [devu'mã], *n.m.* self-sacrifice; devotion, devotedness; zeal.

dévouer [de'vwe], *v.t.* to devote, to dedicate. **se dévouer**, *v.r.* to devote oneself; to dedicate oneself.

dévoyé [devwa'je], *a.* stray, gone astray.—*n.m.* (*fem.* **-ée**) (*fig.*) black sheep.

dévoyer [devwa'je], *v.t.* (*conjug. like* EMPLOYER) to corrupt; to lead astray. **se dévoyer**, *v.r.* to become corrupted.

dextérité [deksteri'te], *n.f.* dexterity, skill.

dextrine [dɛks'trin], *n.f.* dextrin.

dextrose [dɛks'tro:z], *n.f.* dextrose, glucose.

diabète [dja'bɛt], *n.m.* diabetes.

diabétique [djabe'tik], *a.* and *n.* diabetic.

diable [dja:bl], *n.m.* devil; wayward child; jack-in-the-box; luggage-truck; drag; *un bon diable*, a good-natured fellow; *un pauvre diable*, a poor wretch.—*int.* the devil! the deuce! confound it! hang it!

diablement [djablə'mã], *adv.* devilishly.

diablerie [djablə'ri], *n.f.* devilry, witchcraft; mischief.

diablesse [dja'blɛs], *n.f.* she-devil; shrew, vixen.

diablotin [djablɔ'tɛ̃], *n.m.* imp; (Christmas) cracker.

diabolique [djabɔ'lik], *a.* diabolical, devilish.

diaboliquement [djabɔlik'mã], *adv.* diabolically, devilishly.

diaconal [djakɔ'nal], *a.* (*m. pl.* **-aux**) diaconal.

diaconat [djakɔ'na], *n.m.* diaconate, deaconry.

diaconesse

diaconesse [djakɔ'nɛs], *n.f.* deaconess.
diacre [djakr], *n.m.* deacon.
diadème [dja'dɛːm], *n.m.* diadem; coronet.
diagnose [djag'noːz], *n.f.* (*art of*) diagnosis.
diagnostic [djagnɔs'tik], *n.m.* diagnosis.
diagnostique [djagnɔs'tik], *a.* diagnostic.
diagnostiquer [djagnɔsti'ke], *v.t.* to diagnose.
diagonal [djago'nal], *a.* (*m. pl.* **-aux**) diagonal.—*n.f.* (**-e**) diagonal.
diagonalement [djagonal'mɑ̃], *adv.* diagonally.
diagramme [dja'gram], *n.m.* diagram.
dialecte [dja'lɛkt], *n.m.* dialect.
dialecticien [djalɛkti'sjɛ̃], *n.m.* dialectician.
dialectique [djalɛk'tik], *a.* dialectical.—*n.f.* dialectics, logic.
dialogue [dja'lɔg], *n.m.* dialogue, colloquy.
dialoguer [djalɔ'ge], *v.t.* to write in dialogue form.—*v.i.* to converse, to chat.
dialoguiste [djalɔ'gist], *n.m.* (*Cine.*) scriptwriter.
diamant [dja'mɑ̃], *n.m.* diamond.
diamantaire [djamɑ̃'tɛːr], *a.* of diamond brilliancy.—*n.m.* diamond-cutter *or* seller.
diamanter [djamɑ̃'te], *v.t.* to set with diamonds; to tinsel, to frost.
diamétral [djame'tral], *a.* (*m. pl.* **-aux**) diametrical.
diamétralement [djametral'mɑ̃], *adv.* diametrically.
diamètre [dja'mɛtr], *n.m.* diameter.
diane [djan], *n.f.* reveille.
diantre [djɑ̃:tr], *int.* the deuce! dash! blast!
diapason [djapa'zɔ̃], *n.m.* diapason, pitch; tuning-fork.
diaphane [dja'fan], *a.* diaphanous, transparent.
diaphragme [dja'fragm], *n.m.* diaphragm, midriff.
diapositive [djapozi'tiːv] *n.f.* transparency, slide.
diapré [dja'pre], *a.* dappled, variegated.
diaprer [dja'pre], *v.t.* to dapple, to variegate, to mottle.
diarrhée [dja're], *n.f.* diarrhoea.
diatribe [dja'trib], *n.f.* diatribe, bitter criticism *or* dissertation.
dictamen [dikta'mɛn], *n.m.* dictate (*of one's conscience*).
dictateur [dikta'tœːr], *n.m.* dictator.
dictatorial [diktatɔ'rjal], *a.* (*m.pl.* **-aux**) dictatorial.
dictature [dikta'tyːr], *n.f.* dictatorship.
dictée [dik'te], *n.f.* act of dictating, dictation.
dicter [dik'te], *v.t.* to dictate; (*fig.*) to suggest, to inspire.
diction [dik'sjɔ̃], *n.f.* diction; delivery.
dictionnaire [diksjɔ'nɛːr], *n.m.* dictionary.
dicton [dik'tɔ̃], *n.m.* common saying, saw, proverb.
didactique [didak'tik], *a.* didactic.—*n.f.* didactic art.
didactiquement [didaktik'mɑ̃], *adv.* didactically.
dièse [djɛːz], *n.m.* (*Mus.*) sharp.
diesel [djeˈzɛl], *n.m.* diesel (*engine*).
diète (1) [djɛt], *n.f.* diet (*regimen*).
diète (2) [djɛt], *n.f.* (*Hist.*) diet.
diététicien [djeteti'sjɛ̃], *n.m.* (*fem.* **-enne**) dietician, dietist.

diététique [djete'tik], *a.* dietetical.—*n.f.* dietetics.
Dieu [djø], *n.m.* God.
dieu [djø], *n.m.* (*pl.* **dieux**) god.
diffamant [difa'mɑ̃], *a.* defamatory, libellous, slanderous.
diffamateur [difama'tœːr], *n.m.* (*fem.* **-trice**) defamer, slanderer.
diffamation [difama'sjɔ̃], *n.f.* defamation, aspersion, calumny.
diffamatoire [difama'twaːr], *a.* defamatory, libellous, slanderous.
diffamer [difa'me], *v.t.* to defame, to slander, to libel.
différemment [difera'mɑ̃], *adv.* differently.
différence [dife'rɑ̃ːs], *n.f.* difference, diversity, contrast.
différenciation [diferɑ̃sja'sjɔ̃], *n.f.* differentiation.
différencier [diferɑ̃'sje], *v.t.* to make a difference, to distinguish; (*Math.*) to differentiate.
différend [dife'rɑ̃], *n.m.* difference, quarrel, dispute.
différent [dife'rɑ̃], *a.* different, dissimilar, unlike.
différentiel [diferɑ̃'sjɛl], *a.* (*fem.* **-elle**) differential.—*n.m.* (*Motor.*) differential.
différer [dife're], *v.t.* (*conjug. like* CÉDER) to defer, to postpone, to adjourn.—*v.i.* to defer, to put off; to differ, to disagree.
difficile [difi'sil], *a.* difficult; hard, trying; hard to please, particular.
difficilement [difisil'mɑ̃], *adv.* with difficulty.
difficulté [difikyl'te], *n.f.* difficulty; obstacle; rub; objection.
difficultueux [difikyl'tɥø], *a.* (*fem.* **-euse**) prone to raise difficulties; hard to please.
difforme [di'fɔrm], *a.* deformed, misshapen.
difformité [difɔrmi'te], *n.f.* deformity; hideousness.
diffus [di'fy], *a.* diffuse, prolix, verbose.
diffusément [difyze'mɑ̃], *adv.* diffusely, wordily.
diffuser [dify'ze], *v.t.* to diffuse; (*Rad. Tel.*) to broadcast.
diffuseur [dify'zœːr], *n.m.* diffuser, spray cone; loudspeaker.
diffusion [dify'zjɔ̃], *n.f.* diffusion; diffusiveness, wordiness; propagation; broadcasting.
digérer [diʒe're], *v.t.* (*conjug. like* CÉDER) to digest; to ponder, to discuss; to put up with.
digestible [diʒɛs'tibl], *a.* digestible.
digestif [diʒɛs'tif], *a.* (*fem.* **-tive**) and *n.m.* digestive.
digestion [diʒɛs'tjɔ̃], *n.f.* digestion.
digital [diʒi'tal], *a.* (*m. pl.* **-aux**) digital; *empreinte digitale*, finger-print.
digitale [diʒi'tal], *n.f.* foxglove.
digitaline [diʒita'lin], *n.f.* (*Pharm.*) digitalis.
digne [diɲ], *a.* deserving, worthy; dignified.
dignement [diɲ'mɑ̃], *adv.* worthily, deservedly; with dignity.
dignitaire [diɲi'tɛːr], *n.m.* dignitary.
dignité [diɲi'te], *n.f.* dignity, nobility, seriousness; self-respect.
digresser [digre'se], *v.i.* to digress, to depart from the main subject.
digressif [digre'sif], *a.* (*fem.* **-ive**) digressive.
digression [digre'sjɔ̃], *n.f.* digression.

116

digressivement [digrɛsiv'mã], *adv.* digressively.

digue [dig], *n.f.* dike, dam, embankment; (*fig.*) limit; security.

diguer [di'ge], *v.t.* to dam, to embank.

dilacération [dilaserɑ'sjõ], *n.f.* tearing, rending.

dilacérer [dilase're], *v.t.* (*conjug. like* CÉDER) to tear to pieces.

dilapidateur [dilapida'tœːr], *a.* (*fem.* -**trice**) wasteful, extravagant.—*n.m.* (*fem.* -**trice**) squanderer.

dilapidation [dilapidɑ'sjõ], *n.f.* waste; embezzlement.

dilapider [dilapi'de], *v.t.* to waste, to squander (*a fortune*); to embezzle.

dilatation [dilatɑ'sjõ] *n.f.* dilatation, expansion, distension.

dilater [dila'te], *v.t.* to dilate, to distend, to expand. **se dilater**, *v.r.* to dilate, to be dilated.

dilatoire [dila'twaːr], *a.* (*Law*) dilatory.

dilemme [di'lɛm], *n.m.* dilemma.

dilettante [dile'tãːt], *n.* dilettante.

dilettantisme [diletã'tism], *n.m.* dilettantism, amateurism.

diligemment [diliʒa'mã], *adv.* diligently, promptly.

diligence [dili'ʒãːs], *n.f.* diligence; dispatch, application; stage-coach.

diligent [dili'ʒã], *a.* diligent, assiduous, active.

diluer [di'lɥe], *v.t.* to dilute.

dilution [dily'sjõ], *n.f.* dilution.

diluvien [dily'vjɛ̃], *a.* (*fem* -**enne**) diluvian.

dimanche [di'mãːʃ], *n.m.* Sunday, Sabbath.

dîme [dim], *n.f.* tithe; (U.S.) dime.

dimension [dimã'sjõ], *n.f.* dimension, size.

dîmer [di'me], *v.t.* to tithe.—*v.i.* to levy a tithe.

diminuer [dimi'nɥe], *v.t.* to diminish, to lessen; to impair.—*v.i.* to diminish, to abate, to fall (*in price etc.*); to draw in (*of days*).

diminutif [diminy'tif], *a.* (*fem.* **ive**) and *n.m.* diminutive.

diminution [diminy'sjõ], *n.f.* diminution, reduction, abatement.

dinde [dɛ̃ːd], *n.f.* turkey-hen; turkey.

dindon [dɛ̃'dõ], *n.m.* turkey-cock.

dindonneau [dɛ̃dɔ'no], *n.m.* (*pl.* -**eaux**) young turkey.

dindonner [dɛ̃dɔ'ne], *v.t.* to dupe, to take in.

dindonnier [dɛ̃dɔ'nje], *n.m.* (*fem.* -**ière**) turkey-keeper.

dîné [DÎNER].

dîner [di'ne], *v.i.* to dine, to have dinner.—*n.m.* or **dîné** [di'ne], dinner; dinner-party.

dînette [di'nɛt], *n.f.* child's *or* doll's dinner.

dîneur [di'nœːr], *n.m.* (*fem.* -**euse**) diner; diner-out.

diocésain [djɔse'zɛ̃], *a.* diocesan.

diocèse [djɔ'sɛːz], *n.m.* diocese.

diphasé [difa'ze], *a.* (*Elec.*) two-phase, diphasic.

diphtérie [difte'ri], *n.f.* diphtheria.

diphtongue [dif'tõːg], *n.f.* diphthong.

diplomate [diplɔ'mat], *a.* diplomatic.—*n.* diplomatist, diplomat.

diplomatie [diplɔma'si], *n.f.* diplomacy; diplomatic service.

diplomatique [diplɔma'tik], *a.* diplomatic; tactful.

diplomatiquement [diplɔmatik'mã], *adv.* diplomatically.

diplôme [di'plo:m], *n.m.* diploma.

diplômé [diplo'me], *a.* (*fem.* -**ée**) qualified. —*n.m.* (*fem.* -**ée**) qualified person.

dipsomane [dipsɔ'man], *n.m.* dipsomaniac.

dipsomanie [dipsɔma'ni], *n.f.* dipsomania.

dire [diːr], *v.t. irr.* to say, to speak; to tell; to recite; to order; to express. **se dire**, *v.r.* to call oneself, to be called; to say to oneself; to be said.—*n.m.* what one says, statement; (*Law*) allegation.

direct [di'rɛkt], *a.* direct, straight, immediate. —*n.m.* (*Box.*) straight blow; **un direct du gauche**, a straight left.

directement [dirɛktə'mã], *adv.* directly, point-blank.

directeur [dirɛk'tœːr], *n.m.* (*fem.* -**trice**) director, manager, superintendent, head; principal, head master, head mistress; conductor (*of orchestra*).

direction [dirɛk'sjõ], *n.f.* directing, direction; management; directorship; (*Motor.*) steering.

directives [dirɛk'tiːv], *n.f. pl.* general rules, directives.

directoire [dirɛk'twaːr], *n.m.* (*Eccles.*) directory.

directorat [dirɛktɔ'ra], *n.m.* directorship, directorate.

dirigeable [diri'ʒabl], *n.m.* dirigible balloon *or* airship.

dirigeant [diri'ʒã], *a.* directing, leading.—*n.* ruler, leader.

diriger [diri'ʒe], *v.t.* (*conjug. like* MANGER) to direct; to control; to steer, to manage, to govern; to send, to aim. **se diriger**, *v.r.* to make for, to go (*towards*); to govern oneself.

dirigisme [diri'ʒism], *n.m.* (*Polit.*) state planning *or* controls.

discernement [disɛrnə'mã], *n.m.* discernment; discrimination; judgment.

discerner [disɛr'ne], *v.t.* to discern; to distinguish, to discriminate.

disciple [di'sipl], *n.m.* disciple, follower.

disciplinaire [disipli'nɛːr], *a.* disciplinary.

discipline [disi'plin], *n.f.* discipline; education, training; (*sch.*) subject.

discipliner [disipli'ne], *v.t.* to discipline. **se discipliner**, *v.r.* to be disciplined.

discontinu [diskõti'ny], *a.* discontinuous.

discontinuation [diskõtinɥɑ'sjõ], *n.f.* discontinuance, discontinuation.

discontinuer [diskõti'nɥe], *v.t.* to discontinue, to interrupt, to suspend.—*v.i.* to cease, to leave off.

discontinuité [diskõtinɥi'te], *n.f.* discontinuity, discontinuance, interruption.

disconvenance [diskõv'nãːs], *n.f.* incongruity, unsuitability; dissimilarity.

disconvenir [diskõv'niːr], *v.i. irr.* (*conjug. like* TENIR) to deny, to disown; to disagree.

discord [dis'kɔːr], *a.* (*Mus.*) out of tune, discordant.

discordance [diskɔr'dãːs], *n.f.* discordancy, dissonance.

discordant [diskɔr'dã], *a.* discordant, dissonant, out of tune; inharmonious, incongruous.

discorde [dis'kɔrd], *n.f.* discord, disagreement, strife.

117

discorder

discorder [diskɔr'de], v.i. (Mus.) to be out of tune; to be in a state of dissension.
discothèque [disko'tɛk], n.f. record library; discothèque.
discoureur [disku'rœːr], n.m. (fem. -euse) talker, chatterer.
discourir [disku'riːr], v.i. irr. (conjug. like COURIR) to discourse; to descant (sur); to babble.
discours [dis'kuːr], n.m. discourse; speech, address; diction; treatise.
discourtois [diskur'twa], a. discourteous.
discourtoisement [diskurtwaz'mã], adv. discourteously.
discourtoisie [diskurtwa'zi], n.f. discourtesy, incivility.
discrédit [diskre'di], n.m. discredit, disrepute.
discréditer [diskredi'te], v.t. to discredit.
discret [dis'krɛ], a. (fem. -ète) discreet; cautious, shy; secret, close.
discrètement [diskrɛt'mã], adv. discreetly, warily.
discrétion [diskre'sjõ], n.f. circumspection, prudence; discretion; reserve; *pain à discrétion*, bread ad lib.
discrétionnaire [diskresjɔ'nɛːr], a. discretionary.
discrimination [diskrimina'sjõ], n.f. discrimination.
discriminer [diskrimi'ne], v.t. to discriminate.
disculper [diskyl'pe], v.t. to exculpate, to vindicate, to exonerate.
discursif [diskyr'sif], a. (fem. -sive) discursive.
discussion [disky'sjõ], n.f. discussion, debate; altercation, dispute.
discutable [disky'tabl], a. debatable, disputable, contestable.
discuter [disky'te], v.t. to discuss, to debate, to argue; to examine, to inquire into, to sift.
discuteur, [disky'tœːr] n.m. (fem. -euse) disputant.
disert [di'zɛːr], a. copious, fluent, eloquent.
disertement [dizɛrtə'mã], adv. copiously, fluently.
disette [di'zɛt], n.f. scarcity, dearth, famine; poverty, penury.
diseur [di'zœːr], n.m. (fem. -euse) sayer, teller; diseuse.
disgrâce [diz'grɑːs], n.f. disfavour; disgrace; misfortune; plainness (of features).
disgracié [dizgra'sje], a. out of favour; (fig.) ill-favoured, deformed.
disgracier [dizgra'sje], v.t. to disgrace, to put out of favour.
disgracieusement [dizgrasjøz'mã], adv. awkwardly, ungracefully.
disgracieux [dizgra'sjø], a. (fem. -euse) awkward, uncouth, disagreeable.
disjoindre [diz'ʒwɛ̃:dr], v.t. irr. (conjug. like CRAINDRE) to disjoin, to disunite. se disjoindre, v.r. to come apart, to disunite.
disjoncteur [dizʒɔ̃k'tœːr], n.m. (Elec.) circuit breaker.
disjonction [dizʒɔ̃k'sjõ], n.f. disjunction, separation.
dislocation [dislɔka'sjõ], n.f. dislocation, dismemberment.
disloquement [dislɔk'mã], n.m. dislocation.

disloquer [dislɔ'ke], v.t. to dislocate, to dismember; to take to pieces (machines etc.); (Mil.) to break up (an army). se disloquer, v.r. to dislocate one's arm etc.; to be taken to pieces; to come apart.
dispache [dis'paʃ], n.f. (Maritime Insurance) assessment; average adjustment.
dispacheur [dispa'ʃœːr], dispatcheur [dispa'tʃœːr], n.m. assessor, average adjuster.
disparaître [dispa'rɛːtr], v.i. irr. (conjug. like CONNAÎTRE) to vanish, to disappear; to abscond; to die.
disparate [dispa'rat], a. dissimilar, incongruous, unlike, ill-matched.—n.f. incongruity, dissimilarity.
disparité [dispari'te], n.f. disparity, dissimilarity.
disparition [dispari'sjõ], n.f. disappearance.
dispendieusement [dispãdjøz'mã], adv. expensively.
dispendieux [dispã'djø], a. (fem. -euse) expensively, costly.
dispensaire [dispã'sɛːr], n.m. dispensary; out-patients' department.
dispensateur [dispãsa'tœːr], n.m. (fem. -trice) dispenser; bestower, giver.
dispensation [dispãsa'sjõ], n.f. dispensation; distribution; dispensing.
dispense [dis'pãːs], n.f. dispensation (from fasting); exemption (from military service).
dispenser [dispã'se], v.t. to dispense, to bestow; to exempt; to dispense (with). se dispenser, v.r. to dispense with; to exempt or excuse oneself (from); to spare oneself.
disperser [disper'se], v.t. to disperse, to scatter. se disperser, v.r. to be dispersed, to break up, to be scattered.
dispersion [disper'sjõ], n.f. dispersion, breaking up.
disponibilité [disponibili'te], n.f. (Law) state of being disposable, disposal (of property); (Mil.) state of being unattached.
disponible [dispo'nibl], a. disposable, available; disengaged.—n.m. realizable assets.
dispos [dis'po], a. fit and well, in good fettle, nimble; cheerful.
disposer [dispo'ze], v.t. to dispose, to arrange, to prepare; to incline, to prevail upon.—v.i. to dispose (de); to prescribe; to ordain. se disposer, v.r. to dispose oneself, to be disposed; to get ready.
disposition [dispozi'sjõ], n.f. disposition, arrangement; inclination, frame of mind; mind, intention.
disproportion [disprɔpɔr'sjõ], n.f. disproportion.
disproportionné [disprɔpɔrsjɔ'ne], a. disproportionate, inadequate.
disproportionnel [disprɔpɔrsjɔ'nɛl], a. (fem. -elle) disproportional.
disputable [dispy'tabl], a. disputable, debatable, doubtful.
dispute [dis'pyt], n.f. dispute, debate, controversy, wrangle; quarrel.
disputer [dispy'te], v.t. to contend for; to dispute, to call in question.—v.i. to discuss, to argue, to dispute; to contend, to wrangle. se disputer, v.r. to dispute; to contend, to quarrel.
disputeur [dispy'tœːr], a. (fem. -euse) contentious, quarrelsome.—n.m. (fem. -euse) wrangler.

distributaire

disqualification [diskalifikɑ'sjɔ̃], *n.f.* disqualification.
disqualifier [diskali'fje], *v.t.* to disqualify.
disquaire [dis'kɛːr], *n.* gramophone record seller.
disque [disk], *n.m.* discus, quoit; disk; (*Rail.*) signal-disk; gramophone record; *disque longue durée* or *microsillon*, long-playing record.
disruptif [disryp'tif], *a.* (*fem.* **-tive**) disruptive.
disrupteur [disryp'tœːr], *n.m.* (*Elec.*) interrupter.
dissecteur [disɛk'tœːr], *n.m.* dissector.
dissection [disɛk'sjɔ̃], *n.f.* dissection.
dissemblable [disɑ̃'blabl], *a.* dissimilar, unlike.
dissemblablement [disɑ̃blablə'mɑ̃], *adv.* dissimilarly.
dissemblance [disɑ̃'blɑ̃ːs], *n.f.* dissimilarity, difference.
dissemblant [disɑ̃'blɑ̃], *a.* dissimilar, different.
dissémination [diseminɑ'sjɔ̃], *n.f.* dissemination, scattering (*of seeds etc.*).
disséminer [disemi'ne], *v.t.* to disseminate, to scatter.
dissension [disɑ̃'sjɔ̃], *n.f.* dissension, discord, strife.
dissentiment [disɑ̃ti'mɑ̃], *n.m.* dissent, disagreement.
disséquer [dise'ke], *v.t.* (*conjug. like* CÉDER) to dissect; to analyse.
disséqueur [dise'kœːr], [DISSECTEUR].
dissertation [disɛrtɑ'sjɔ̃], *n.f.* dissertation, treatise; essay (*in schools*).
disserter [disɛr'te], *v.i.* to dissert.
dissidence [disi'dɑ̃ːs], *n.f.* dissidence, difference of opinion, dissent.
dissident [disi'dɑ̃], *a.* dissident.—*n.m.* (*fem.* **-e**) dissenter, rebel.
dissimilaire [disimi'lɛːr], *a.* dissimilar, different, unlike.
dissimilarité [disimilari'te], *n.f.* dissimilarity.
dissimilitude [disimili'tyd], *n.f.* dissimilitude, difference.
dissimulateur [disimyla'tœːr], *n.m.* (*fem.* **-trice**) dissembler; hypocrite.
dissimulation [disimylɑ'sjɔ̃], *n.f.* dissimulation; double-dealing.
dissimulé [disimy'le], *a.* two-faced, artful.—*n.m.* (*fem.* **-ée**) dissembler; hypocrite.
dissimuler [disimy'le], *v.t.* to dissemble, to conceal. **se dissimuler**, *v.r.* to hide oneself, to pass unnoticed.
dissipateur [disipa'tœːr], *a.* (*fem.* **-trice**) lavish, extravagant.—*n.m.* (*fem.* **-trice**) squanderer, spendthrift.
dissipation [disipɑ'sjɔ̃], *n.f.* dissipation, waste; idleness.
dissipé [disi'pe], *a.* dissipated, profligate; inattentive.
dissiper [disi'pe], *v.t.* to dissipate, to dispel; to scatter, to squander. **se dissiper**, *v.r.* to be dispersed; to vanish; to be squandered; to be inattentive (*in class-room*).
dissolu [diso'ly], *a.* dissolute, profligate, licentious.
dissolubilité [disɔlybili'te], *n.f.* dissolubility.
dissoluble [diso'lybl], *a.* dissoluble, dissolvable.

dissolution [disɔly'sjɔ̃], *n.f.* dissolution; solution; dissoluteness.
dissolvant [disɔl'vɑ̃], *a.* and *n.m.* dissolvent, solutive, solvent.
dissonance [diso'nɑ̃ːs], *n.f.* dissonance, discord.
dissonant [diso'nɑ̃], *a.* dissonant, discordant.
dissoudre [di'sudr], *v.t. irr.* (*conjug. like* ABSOUDRE) to dissolve; to break up; to annul. **se dissoudre**, *v.r.* to dissolve, to be dissolved; to break up.
dissous [di'su], *a.* (*fem.* **-oute**) dissolved; broken up.
dissuader [disɥa'de], *v.t.* to dissuade.
dissuasif [disɥa'zif], *a.* (*fem.* **-sive**) dissuasive.
dissymétrique [disime'trik], *a.* assymetric(al).
distance [dis'tɑ̃ːs], *n.f.* distance; interval (*of place or time*).
distancer [distɑ̃'se], *v.t.* (*conjug. like* COMMENCER) to out-distance, to outrun; (*fig.*) to surpass, to outdo.
distant [dis'tɑ̃], *a.* distant, remote; aloof, stand-offish.
distendre [dis'tɑ̃ːdr], *v.t.* to distend.
distension [distɑ̃'sjɔ̃], *n.f.* distension, strain.
distillable [disti'labl], *a.* distillable.
distillateur [distila'tœːr], *n.m.* distiller.
distillation [distilɑ'sjɔ̃], *n.f.* distillation.
distiller [disti'le], *v.t.* to distil; to discharge; to vent.—*v.i.* to drop, to distil, to trickle.
distillerie [distil'ri], *n.f.* distillery; distilling.
distinct [dis'tɛ̃], *a.* distinct, different, separate.
distinctement [distɛ̃ktə'mɑ̃], *adv.* distinctly, clearly, plainly.
distinctif [distɛ̃k'tif], *a.* (*fem.* **-tive**) distinctive, characteristic.
distinction [distɛ̃k'sjɔ̃], *n.f.* distinction; division, difference; eminence; refinement.
distinctivement [distɛ̃ktiv'mɑ̃], *adv.* distinctively.
distingué [distɛ̃'ge], *a.* distinguished, eminent, noted; elegant, well-bred.
distinguer [distɛ̃'ge], *v.t.* to distinguish, to discern; to discriminate; to honour. **se distinguer**, *v.r.* to be conspicuous; to gain distinction.
distique [dis'tik], *n.m.* distich; couplet.
distordre [dis'tɔrdr], *v.t.* to distort; to sprain. **se distordre**, *v.r.* to become distorted.
distorsion [distɔr'sjɔ̃], *n.f.* distortion; sprain.
distraction [distrak'sjɔ̃], *n.f.* separation; absence of mind, inattention; diversion, hobby.
distraire [dis'trɛːr], *v.t. irr.* (*conjug. like* TRAIRE) to separate; to distract, to disturb; to entertain. **se distraire**, *v.r.* to be disturbed; to be diverted (*de*); to amuse oneself.
distrait [dis'trɛ], *a.* absent-minded, heedless; vacant (*person*).—*n.m.* (*fem.* **-e**) absent-minded person.
distraitement [distrɛt'mɑ̃], *adv.* absent-mindedly.
distrayant [distre'jɑ̃], *a.* diverting, pleasing.
distribuable [distri'bɥabl], *a.* distributable.
distribuer [distri'bɥe], *v.t.* to distribute, to divide; to dispose; to arrange.
distributaire [distriby'tɛːr], *n.* recipient, receiver; sharer.

119

distributeur

distributeur [distriby'tœːr], *a.* (*fem.* **-trice**) distributing.—*n.m.* (*fem.* **-trice**) distributer, bestower, dispenser; *distributeur automatique*, slot machine.

distributif [distriby'tif], *a.* (*fem.* **-tive**) distributive.

distribution [distriby'sjɔ̃], *n.f.* distribution; division; disposition; delivery (*of mail*).

district [dis'trikt], *n.m.* (administrative) district; region.

dit [di], *a.* said, spoken; surnamed, called; *aussitôt dit, aussitôt fait,* no sooner said than done; *autrement dit,* in other words. —*n.m.* maxim; saying.

dito [di'to], *adv.* (*Comm.*) ditto, (*abbr.*) do.

diurnal [djyr'nal], *a.* (*m. pl.* **-aux**) diurnal.—*n.m.* diurnal, daily prayer-book.

diurne [djyrn], *a.* diurnal, daily.—*n.m.* diurnal insect.

divagant [diva'gɑ̃], *a.* wandering, rambling.

divagateur [divaga'tœːr], *a.* (*fem.* **-trice**) desultory, rambling.—*n.m.* (*fem.* **-trice**) rambling speaker.

divagation [divagɑ'sjɔ̃], *n.f.* divagation, wandering.

divaguer [diva'ge], *v.i.* to ramble, to wander from the question; to be incoherent (*in writing or speaking*).

divan [di'vɑ̃], *n.m.* divan; couch.

divergence [diver'ʒɑ̃ːs], *n.f.* divergence.

divergent [diver'ʒɑ̃], *a.* divergent; different.

diverger [diver'ʒe], *v.i.* (*conjug. like* MANGER) to diverge, to branch off.

divers [di'vɛːr], *a.* diverse, miscellaneous; changing; (*pl.*) various, divers, sundry.

diversement [diversə'mɑ̃], *adv.* diversely, variously.

diversifier [diversi'fje], *v.t.* to diversify; to variegate. **se diversifier,** *v.r.* to be varied *or* diversified.

diversion [diver'sjɔ̃], *n.f.* diversion; change.

diversité [diversi'te], *n.f.* diversity, variety, difference.

divertir [diver'tiːr], *v.t.* to amuse, to delight; to divert; to embezzle. **se divertir**, *v.r.* to amuse oneself.

divertissant [diverti'sɑ̃], *a.* diverting, entertaining.

divertissement [divertis'mɑ̃], *n.m.* diversion, amusement, entertainment; (*Law*) embezzlement.

divette [di'vet], *n.f.* musical comedy actress.

dividende [divi'dɑ̃ːd], *n.m.* dividend.

divin [di'vɛ̃], *a.* divine, heavenly; (*fig.*) admirable, exquisite.

divinateur [divina'tœːr], *a.* (*fem.* **-trice**) prophetic.—*n.m.* (*fem.* **-trice**) diviner, seer.

divination [divina'sjɔ̃], *n.f.* divination.

divinatoire [divina'twaːr], *a.* divinatory divining.

divinement [divin'mɑ̃], *adv.* divinely; (*fig.*) admirably, exquisitely.

diviniser [divini'ze], *v.t.* to deify; to laud to the skies.

divinité [divini'te], *n.f.* divinity, godhead, deity.

diviser [divi'ze], *v.t.* to divide, to portion out; to disunite. **se diviser,** *v.r.* to be divided; to fall (*into*), to break up (*into*).

diviseur [divi'zœːr], *a.* divisive, dividing.— *n.m.* (*Arith.*) divisor; divider.

divisibilité [divizibili'te], *n.f.* divisibility.

divisible [divi'zibl], *a.* divisible.

division [divi'zjɔ̃], *n.f.* division, partition, dividing; (*Mil.*) division.

divisionnaire [divizjo'nɛːr], *a.* divisional, divisionary.

divorce [di'vɔrs], *n.m.* divorce; (*fig.*) variance.

divorcer [divɔr'se], *v.i.* (*conjug. like* COMMENCER) to divorce oneself (*de*); to break with; to divorce *or* get a divorce from someone (*d'avec quelqu'un*).

divulgation [divylgɑ'sjɔ̃], *n.f.* divulgence; revelation.

divulguer [divyl'ge], *v.t.* to divulge, to reveal, to make public. **se divulguer,** *v.r.* to leak out (*secret*).

dix [dis], *when other words follow* [di] *or* [diz], *a.* ten; tenth.—*n.m.* ten.

dix-huit [di'zɥit], *a.* and *n.m.* eighteen.

dix-huitième [dizɥi'tjɛm], *a.* and *n.* eighteenth.

dixième [di'zjɛm], *a.* and *n.* tenth.

dixièmement [dizjɛm'mɑ̃], *adv.* tenthly.

dix-neuf [diz'nœf], *a.* and *n.m.* nineteen; nineteenth.

dix-neuvième [diznœ'vjɛm], *a.* and *n.* nineteenth.

dix-sept [dis'sɛt], *a.* and *n.m.* seventeen; seventeenth.

dix-septième [dissɛ'tjɛm], *a.* and *n.* seventeenth.

dizaine [di'zɛn], *n.f.* half a score; about ten.

djinn [dʒin], *n.m.* jinn(ee).

do [do], *n.m.* (*Mus.*) do *or* ut; (the note) C.

docile [dɔ'sil], *a.* docile, tractable, submissive.

docilement [dɔsil'mɑ̃], *adv.* with docility.

docilité [dɔsili'te], *n.f.* docility, tractability.

dock [dɔk], *n.m.* dock; warehouse.

docker [dɔ'kɛːr], *n.m.* docker.

docte [dɔkt], *a.* erudite, learned.

doctement [dɔktə'mɑ̃], *adv.* learnedly; pedantically.

docteur [dɔk'tœːr], *n.* doctor.

doctoral [dɔktɔ'ral], *a.* (*m. pl.* **-aux**) doctoral.

doctorat [dɔktɔ'ra], *n.m.* doctorate, doctor's degree.

doctrinaire [dɔktri'nɛːr], *a.* stiff, formal, pedantic.—*n.m.* doctrinaire.

doctrinairement [dɔktrinɛr'mɑ̃], *adv.* stiffly, formally, pedantically.

doctrine [dɔk'trin], *n.f.* doctrine.

document [dɔky'mɑ̃], *n.m.* document; (*pl.*) records.

documentaire [dɔkymɑ̃'tɛːr], *a.* documentary.—*n.m.* (*Cine.*) documentary film.

documentation [dɔkymɑ̃tɑ'sjɔ̃], *n.f.* documentation.

documenter [dɔkymɑ̃'te], *v.t.* to give information. **se documenter,** *v.r.* to gather evidence.

dodelinement [dɔdlin'mɑ̃], *n.m.* wagging, nodding (*of head*); dandling.

dodeliner [dɔdli'ne], *v.t.* to dandle, to rock (*a child*).—*v.i.* to wag, nod (*head*).

dodiner [dɔdi'ne], *v.t.* to rock, to dandle.— *v.i.* to oscillate. **se dodiner,** *v.r.* to rock one's body; to nurse *or* coddle oneself.

dodo [dɔ'do], *n.m.* (*Infantile*) bye-bye; (*fig.*) sleep, bed.

dodu [dɔ'dy], *a.* plump.

dogaresse [dɔga'rɛs], *n.f.* dogaressa, wife of a doge.

doge [dɔːʒ], *n.m.* doge.

dogmatique [dɔgma'tik], *a.* dogmatic.
dogmatiquement [dɔgmatik'mɑ̃], *adv.* dogmatically.
dogmatiser [dɔgmati'ze], *v.t.* to state dogmatically.—*v.i.* to dogmatize.
dogmatisme [dɔgma'tism], *n.m.* dogmatism.
dogmatiste [dɔgma'tist], *n.* dogmatist.
dogme [dɔgm], *n.m.* dogma, tenet.
dogue [dɔg], *n.m.* mastiff; (*fig.*) bull-dog (*of a man*).
doguin [dɔ'gɛ̃], *n.m.* pug.
doigt [dwa], *n.m.* finger, digit; toe.
doigté [dwa'te], *n.m.* (*Mus.*) fingering, touch; (*fig.*) tact, adroitness.
doigtier [dwa'tje], *n.m.* finger-stall.
dol [dɔl], *n.m.* deceit, fraud.
dolage [dɔ'la:ʒ], *n.m.* planing.
doléances [dɔle'ɑ̃:s], *n.f. pl.* complaints; grievances.
dolemment [dɔla'mɑ̃], *adv.* dolefully.
dolent [dɔ'lɑ̃], *a.* doleful, piteous, plaintive.
doler [dɔ'le], *v.t.* to smooth with the adze; to plane.
dolmen [dɔl'mɛn], *n.m.* dolmen.
doloir [dɔ'lwa:r], *n.m.* paring-knife, parer.
doloire [dɔ'lwa:r], *n.f.* cooper's adze; mason's axe.
dolosif [dɔlo'zif], *a.* (*fem.* -**sive**) fraudulent.
domaine [dɔ'mɛːn], *n.m.* domain, estate, property; province, sphere.
dôme [do:m], *n.m.* dome; canopy, vault.
domestication [dɔmestika'sjɔ̃], *n.f.* domestication.
domesticité [dɔmestisi'te], *n.f.* domesticity; (*collect.*) domestic servants.
domestique [dɔmes'tik], *a.* domestic; tame, domesticated.—*n.* servant, domestic.—*n.m.* household.
domestiquer [dɔmesti'ke], *v.t.* to domesticate, to tame.
domicile [dɔmi'sil], *n.m.* domicile, residence.
domiciliaire [dɔmisi'ljɛːr], *a.* domiciliary.
domicilié [dɔmisi'lje], *a.* resident, domiciled.
domicilier (se) [sədɔmisi'lje], *v.r.* to settle down in a place.
dominance [dɔmi'nɑ̃:s], *n.f.* dominance.
dominant [dɔmi'nɑ̃], *a.* dominant, predominant, prevalent.
dominateur [dɔmina'tœːr], *a.* (*fem.* -**trice**) ruling, domineering, arrogant.—*n.m.* (*fem.* -**trice**) dominator, ruler, tyrant.
domination [dɔmina'sjɔ̃], *n.f.* domination; dominion, rule, sway.
dominer [dɔmi'ne], *v.t.* to dominate; to rule; to prevail over; to overlook; to tower over.—*v.i.* to rule, to control; to dominate, to prevail; to lord it; to tower. **se dominer**, *v.r.* to control oneself.
dominicain [dɔmini'kɛ̃], *a.* (*Relig., Polit.*) Dominican.—*n.m.* (**Dominicain**, *fem.* -**aine**) (*Polit.*) Dominican (*person*), Dominican friar *or* nun; **la République Dominicaine**, the Dominican Republic.
dominical [dɔmini'kal], *a.* (*m. pl.* -**aux**) dominical.
dominicale [dɔmini'kal], *n.f.* Sunday sermon.
dominion [dɔmi'njɔ̃], *n.m.* dominion.
domino [dɔmi'no], *n.m.* domino.
dommage [dɔ'ma:ʒ], *n.m.* damage, injury, loss; *c'est dommage*, it is a pity.

dommageable [dɔma'ʒabl], *a.* hurtful, prejudicial, injurious; damageable (*goods*).
domptable [dɔ̃'tabl], *a.* tamable, manageable.
dompter [dɔ̃'te], *v.t.* to subdue, to subjugate, to tame. **se dompter**, *v.r.* to quell *or* overcome one's passions.
dompteur [dɔ̃'tœːr], *n.m.* (*fem.* -**euse**) subduer; tamer; breaker-in.
don [dɔ̃], *n.m.* gift, donation; (*fig.*) aptitude, talent.
donataire [dɔna'tɛːr], *n.* donee, recipient.
donateur [dɔna'tœːr], *n.m.* (*fem.* -**trice**) donor, giver.
donation [dɔna'sjɔ̃], *n.f.* donation, free gift.
donc [dɔ̃:k, dɔ̃], *conj.* then, therefore, accordingly, hence; consequently; of course, to be sure.
donjon [dɔ̃'ʒɔ̃], *n.m.* keep, castle-keep; turret.
donnant [dɔ'nɑ̃], *a.* open-handed, generous; *donnant donnant*, give and take.
donne [dɔn], *n.f.* deal (*at cards*).
donnée [dɔ'ne], *n.f.* given fact, datum; notion; (*Math.*) known quantity; (*pl.*) data.
donner [dɔ'ne], *v.t.* to give, to bestow; to grant; to present (*a play etc.*); to deal (*at cards*).—*v.i.* to give way; to hit, to stumble (*dans*); to be addicted to (*dans*); to attack (*of troops etc.*); to yield; to overlook. **se donner**, *v.r.* to procure; to take place (*of battles etc.*); to give oneself out (*pour*).
donneur [dɔ'nœːr], *n.m.* (*fem.* -**euse**) giver, donor; dealer (*of cards*); *donneur de sang*, blood donor.
don Quichotte [dõki'ʃɔt], *n.m.* Don Quixote, quixotic person.
dont [dɔ̃], *pron.* whose, of which, of whom, from whom etc.
doper [dɔ'pe], *v.t.* (*Spt.*) to dope (*a horse etc.*).
doping [dɔ'piŋ], *n.m.* dope; doping.
dorade [dɔ'rad], *n.f.* (*Ichth.*) sea-bream.
doré [dɔ're], *a.* gilt, gilded, golden.
dorénavant [dɔrena'vɑ̃], *adv.* henceforth, hereafter.
dorer [dɔ're], *v.t.* to gild; to glaze (*pastry*). **se dorer**, *v.r.* to gild; to become yellow.
doreur [dɔ'rœːr], *n.m.* (*fem.* -**euse**) gilder.
dorien [dɔ'rjɛ̃], *a.* and *n.m.* (*fem.* -**enne**) Dorian; Doric.
dorique [dɔ'rik], *a.* and *n.m.* Doric.
dorloter [dɔrlɔ'te], *v.t.* to fondle, to pamper, to coddle, to pet. **se dorloter**, *v.r.* to coddle oneself; to indulge oneself.
dormant [dɔr'mɑ̃], *a.* sleeping, asleep; dormant, stagnant.—*n.m.* fixed frame (*of window etc.*).
dormeur [dɔr'mœːr], *a.* (*fem.* -**euse** (1)) sleepy, drowsy, sluggish.—*n.m.* (*fem.* -**euse** (1)) sleeper; sluggard.—*n.f.* (-**euse** (2)) sort of chaise-longue.
dormeuse (3) [dɔr'møːz], *n.f.* stud ear-ring.
dormir [dɔr'miːr], *v.i. irr.* (*conjug. like* SENTIR) to sleep, to be asleep; to lie still; to lie dormant (*of money*); to be stagnant (*of water*).
dormitif [dɔrmi'tif], *a.* (*fem.* -**tive**) soporific, dormitive.
Dorothée [dɔrɔ'te], *f.* Dorothy.
dorsal [dɔr'sal], *a.* dorsal.
dortoir [dɔr'twaːr], *n.m.* dormitory.
dorure [dɔ'ryːr], *n.f.* gilding; glazing (*of pastry*).

doryphore

doryphore [dɔri'fɔːr], *n.m.* Colorado beetle.
dos [do], *n.m. inv.* back; rear; top, ridge.
dosable [do'zabl], *a.* measurable.
dosage [do'zaːʒ], *n.m.* dosage; titration.
dose [doːz], *n.f.* dose; quantity; portion.
doser [do'ze], *v.t.* to dose; to proportion.
dossier [do'sje], *n.m.* back (*of chair etc.*); brief (*of a barrister*); record, file, dossier.
dossière [do'sjɛːr], *n.f.* back-band, ridge-band (*of harness*); back-plate (*of a cuirass*).
dot [dɔt], *n.f.* marriage portion, dowry.
dotal [do'tal], *a.* (*m. pl.* **-aux**) of *or* concerning dowry.
dotation [dɔta'sjɔ̃], *n.f.* endowment.
doter [do'te], *v.t.* to endow; to make a grant.
douaire [dwɛːr], *n.m.* (*widow's*) dower; jointure, marriage-settlement.
douairière [dwɛ'rjɛːr], *n.f.* dowager.
douane [dwan], *n.f.* customs; custom-house; custom-duty.
douanier [dwa'nje], *a.* relating to the custom-house, of customs.—*n.m.* customs officer.
doublage [du'blaːʒ], *n.m.* lining, plating; (*Cine.*) dubbing.
double [dubl], *a.* twofold, double, duplicate; (*fig.*) deceitful, downright.—*n.m.* double; carbon copy, duplicate, replica; (*Ten.*) doubles.—*adv.* double; *voir double*, to see double.
doublé [du'ble], *n.m.* gold- *or* silver-plated ware; (*Billiards*) cannon off the cushion.
doubleau [du'blo], *n.m.* (*pl.* **-eaux**) ceiling-beam.
doublement [dublə'mɑ̃], *n.m.* doubling.—*adv.* doubly.
doubler [du'ble], *v.t.* to double; to line (*clothes etc.*); to overtake, to pass; (*Theat.*) to understudy; (*Cine.*) to dub.
doublet [du'blɛ], *n.m.* doublet.
doubleur [du'blœːr], *n.m.* (*fem.* **-euse**) doubler, twister.
doublure [du'blyːr], *n.f.* lining; (*Theat.*) understudy.
douce-amère [dusa'mɛːr], *n.f.* (*pl.* **douces-amères**) woody nightshade, bitter-sweet.
douceâtre [du'saːtr], *a.* sweetish, sickly.
doucement [dus'mɑ̃], *adv.* gently, tenderly; slowly, quietly; mildly, calmly; so-so.
doucereux [du'srø], *a.* (*fem.* **-euse**) sweetish; mawkish, mealy-mouthed.
doucet [du'sɛ], *a.* and *n.m.* (*fem.* **-ette** (1)) demure, mild, affected (person).
doucette (2) [du'sɛt], *n.f.* corn salad.
doucette (3) [du'sɛt], *n.f.* Venus's looking-glass.
douceur [du'sœːr], *n.f.* sweetness, softness; fragrance; kindness; peacefulness; gentleness; (*pl.*) sweets; gallantries.
douche [duʃ], *n.f.* shower-bath.
doucher [du'ʃe], *v.t.* to give someone a shower-bath; to cool down (*excitement etc.*). **se doucher**, *v.r.* to take a shower.
doucir [du'siːr], *v.t.* to polish (*looking-glasses etc.*).
doucissage [dusi'saːʒ], *n.m.* polishing.
doucisseur [dusi'sœːr], *n.m.* polisher.
doué [dwe], *a.* gifted.
douer [dwe], *v.t.* to endow, to bestow upon.
douille [duːj], *n.f.* socket; case *or* shell (*of cartridges*); *douille d'embrayage*, clutch casing; *douille de lampe*, lamp-socket, lamp-holder.

douillet [du'jɛ], *a.* effeminate, delicate; sensitive; soft.
douillettement [dujɛt'mɑ̃], *adv.* softly; delicately; cosily.
douleur [du'lœːr], *n.f.* pain, suffering, ache; anguish, grief, sorrow.
douloureusement [dulurøz'mɑ̃], *adv.* painfully; grievously.
douloureux [dulu'rø], *a.* (*fem.* **-euse**) painful, smarting, sore; grievous, afflicting, sad.
doute [dut], *n.m.* doubt, irresolution; suspicion; scepticism; fear; *sans doute*, no doubt.
douter [du'te], *v.i.* (**de**) to doubt, to question; to hesitate; to distrust, to fear. **se douter**, *v.r.* (**de, que**) to suspect, to conjecture.
douteur [du'tœːr], *a.* (*fem.* **-euse** (1)) doubting.—*n.m.* (*fem.* **-euse**) doubter.
douteusement [dutøz'mɑ̃], *adv.* doubtfully.
douteux [du'tø], *a.* (*fem.* **-euse** (2)) doubtful, questionable.
douve [duːv], *n.f.* stave (*for casks*); trench, moat.
Douvres [du:vr], *m.* Dover.
doux [du], *a.* (*fem.* **douce**) sweet; fragrant; kindly, charming; easy; gentle; calm; fresh (*of water*).—*adv.* gently; submissively.
douzaine [du'zɛn], *n.f.* dozen.
douze [du:z], *a.* twelve, twelfth.—*n.m.* twelve.
douzième [du'zjɛm], *a.* and *n.* twelfth.
douzièmement [duzjɛm'mɑ̃], *adv.* twelfthly.
doyen [dwa'jɛ̃], *n.m.* (*fem.* **-enne**) senior, oldest member; dean.
doyenné [dwaje'ne], *n.m.* deanship, deanery.
drachme [drakm], *n.f.* drachma; (*Pharm.*) dram.
draconien [drako'njɛ̃], *a.* (*fem.* **-enne**) draconian, harsh, severe.
dragage [dra'gaːʒ], *n.m.* dredging, dragging (*of a river etc.*).
dragée [dra'ʒe], *n.f.* sugar-almond, sugar-plum; small shot.
drageoir [dra'ʒwaːr], *n.m.* comfit-dish.
drageon [dra'ʒɔ̃], *n.m.* sucker.
drageonner [draʒɔ'ne], *v.i.* to put forth suckers.
dragon [dra'gɔ̃], *a.* dragonish—*n.m.* dragon; (*fig.*) vixen; dragoon.
dragonne [dra'gɔn], *n.f.* sword-knot.
drague [drag], *n.f.* dredger; dredge-net; grappling-iron.
draguer [dra'ge], *v.t.* to drag, to dredge.
dragueur [dra'gœːr], *n.m.* dredger; *dragueur de mines*, minesweeper.
drain [drɛ̃], *n.m.* drain, drain-pipe.
drainage [drɛ'naːʒ], *n.m.* drainage.
drainer [drɛ'ne], *v.t.* to drain.
dramatique [drama'tik], *a.* dramatic.
dramatiser [dramati'ze], *v.t.* to dramatize.
dramaturge [drama'tyrʒ], *n.m.* dramatist, playwright.
drame [dram], *n.m.* drama.
drap [dra], *n.m.* cloth; (*bed*) sheet; pall.
drapeau [dra'po], *n.m.* (*pl.* **-eaux**) flag, standard, ensign, streamer, colours.
draper [dra'pe], *v.t.* to cover with cloth; to drape. **se draper**, *v.r.* to wrap oneself up; to make a show, to parade.
draperie [dra'pri], *n.f.* drapery; cloth-trade, cloth-making.
drapier [dra'pje], *n.m.* draper, clothier.

drastique [dras'tik], *a.* and *n.m.* (*Med.*) drastic.

(*C*) **drave** [drav], *n.f.* drive, log-running.

(*C*) **draver** [dra've], *v.t.* to drive, to drift.

(*C*) **draveur** [dra'vœːr], *n.m.* wood-floater, rafter.

drayage [drɛ'jaːʒ], *n.m.* fleshing (*of hides*).

drayer [drɛ'je], *v.t.* (*conjug. like* PAYER) to flesh (*hides*).

dressage [drɛ'saːʒ], *n.m.* erection; training (*of animals*); pitching (*of a tent*).

dresser [drɛ'se], *v.t.* to erect, to set up, to raise; to straighten; to lay out; to lay (*a snare*); to pitch (*a tent*); to draw up (*a report*); to prick up (*the ears*); to train (*animals*). se **dresser**, *v.r.* to stand on end (*of hair*); to stand erect; to rear.

dresseur [drɛ'sœːr], *n.m.* (*fem.* **-euse**) trainer (*of dogs etc.*).

dressoir [drɛ'swaːr], *n.m.* dresser, sideboard.

drille [dri:j], *n.f.* hand-drill, borer.

driller [dri'je], *v.t.* to drill, to bore.

drive [driv], *n.m.* (*Ten.*) drive.

drogue [drɔg], *n.f.* drug; rubbish; dope.

droguer [drɔ'ge], *v.t.* to drug, to physic. se **droguer**, *v.r.* to physic *or* doctor oneself, to dope oneself.

droguerie [drɔ'gri], *n.f.* drug-store; drug-trade, drysaltery.

droguiste [drɔ'gist], *n.* retailer in drugs and chemicals.

droguet [drɔ'gɛ], *n.m.* (*Tex.*) drugget.

droit [drwa], *a.* straight, right, direct; vertical, upright; just, sincere; right (*opposed to* left).—*adv.* straight, straight on.—*n.m.* right, equity; law; right (*to*), claim, title; fee; due (*tax*), duty, customs duty.

droite [drwat], *n.f.* right hand, right.

droitement [drwat'mɑ̃], *adv.* rightly; sincerely, straightforwardly.

droitier [drwa'tje], *a.* and *n.m.* (*fem.* **-ière**) right-handed (person).

droiture [drwa'tyːr], *n.f.* equity, justice; uprightness, integrity.

drolatique [drɔla'tik], *a.* amusing, laughable, facetious.

drôle [dro:l], *a.* funny, droll, ludicrous; strange, curious.—*n.* rogue, rascal, scoundrel.

drôlement [drol'mɑ̃], *adv.* comically, facetiously, jocosely.

drôlerie [drol'ri], *n.f.* drollery; buffoonery.

drôlesse [dro'lɛs], *n.f.* jade, hussy.

dromadaire [drɔma'dɛːr], *n.m.* dromedary.

dru [dry], *a.* sturdy; dense (*of rain*); brisk, lively; close-planted; fledged (*of birds*).—*adv.* thick, fast, hard.

druide [drɥid], *n.m.* Druid.

druidesse [drɥi'dɛs], *n.f.* Druidess.

druidique [drɥi'dik], *a.* druidical.

druidisme [drɥi'dism], *n.m.* druidism.

dryade [dri'ad], *n.f.* dryad; (*Bot.*) dryas.

du [dy], (*contraction of* DE LE) of the, from the, by the; some, any.

dû [dy], *n.m.* due, what is owed, what is owing.

dualisme [dɥa'lism], *n.m.* dualism.

dualiste [dɥa'list], *a.* and *n.* dualist.

dualité [dɥali'te], *n.f.* duality.

duc [dyk], *n.m.* duke; horned owl.

ducal [dy'kal], *a.* (*m. pl.* **-aux**) ducal.

ducat [dy'ka], *n.m.* ducat.

duché [dy'ʃe], *n.m.* dukedom, duchy.

duchesse [dy'ʃɛs], *n.f.* duchess.

ductile [dyk'til], *a.* ductile, malleable.

ductilité [dyktili'te], *n.f.* ductility.

duègne [dɥɛɲ], *n.f.* duenna, chaperon.

duel [dɥɛl], *n.m.* duel; struggle.

duelliste [dɥɛ'list], *n.* duellist.

dulcifier [dylsi'fje], *v.t.* to dulcify.

dulcinée [dylsi'ne], *n.f.* sweetheart.

dûment [dy'mɑ̃], *adv.* duly, properly.

dumping [dãm'piŋ], *n.m.* dumping, unfair competition.

dune [dyn], *n.f.* dune, sand-hill.

dunette [dy'nɛt], *n.f.* poop-deck.

duo [dɥo], *n.m.* duet.

duodécimal [dɥodesi'mal], *a.* (*m. pl.* **-aux**) duodecimal.

duodénal [dɥode'nal], *a.* (*m. pl.* **-aux**) duodenal.

duodénum [dɥode'nɔm], *n.m.* duodenum.

dupe [dyp], *n.f.* dupe.

duper [dy'pe], *v.t.* to dupe, to gull, to take in.

duperie [dy'pri], *n.f.* dupery, trickery.

dupeur [dy'pœːr], *n.m.* (*fem.* **-euse**) cheat, trickster.

duplicata [dyplika'ta], *n.m.* duplicate.

duplicateur [dyplika'tœːr], *n.m.* (*Elec.*) duplicator; duplicating machine.

duplicité [dyplisi'te], *n.f.* duplicity, double-dealing, deceit.

duquel [dy'kɛl], (*contraction of* DE LEQUEL) of whom, of which.

dur [dyːr], *a.* hard; tough; (*fig.*) unyielding, harsh, unkind; difficult.—*adv.* hard; firmly; *travailler dur*, to work hard.

durabilité [dyrabili'te], *n.f.* durability.

durable [dy'rabl], *a.* durable, lasting, solid.

durablement [dyrablə'mɑ̃], *adv.* durably, lastingly.

duralumin [dyraly'mɛ̃], *n.m.* duralumin.

durant [dy'rɑ̃], *prep.* during.

durcir [dyr'siːr], *v.t.* to harden.—*v.i.* to harden, to stiffen. se **durcir**, *v.r.* to harden.

durcissement [dyrsis'mɑ̃], *n.m.* hardening, stiffening, induration.

dure [dyːr], *n.f.* hard ground *or* floor *in coucher sur la dure*.

durée [dy're], *n.f.* duration; continuance.

durement [dyr'mɑ̃], *adv.* hard; harshly, roughly.

durer [dy're], *v.i.* to last, to remain; to endure.

dureté [dyr'te], *n.f.* hardness; harshness, austerity, unkindness; (*pl.*) harsh *or* offensive words.

durillon [dyri'jɔ̃], *n.m.* callosity, corn.

duvet [dy'vɛ], *n.m.* down; wool, nap; fluff.

duveté [dyv'te], *a.* downy (*of birds etc.*); like down.

duveteux [dyv'tø], *a.* (*fem.* **-euse**) downy, fluffy.

dynamique [dina'mik], *a.* dynamic.—*n.f.* dynamics.

dynamisme [dina'mism], *n.m.* dynamism.

dynamiste [dina'mist], *n.* dynamist.

dynamitage [dinami'taːʒ], *n.m.* blasting, blowing up.

dynamite [dina'mit], *n.f.* dynamite.

dynamiter [dinami'te], *v.t.* to dynamite, to blow up.

dynamo [dina'mo], *n.f.* dynamo.

dynastie [dinas'ti], *n.f.* dynasty.

dynastique [dinas'tik], *a.* dynastic.
dysenterie [disɑ̃'tri], *n.f.* dysentery.
dyspepsie [dispɛp'si], *n.f.* dyspepsia.
dyspepsique [dispɛp'sik], **dyspeptique** [dispɛp'tik], *a.* dyspeptic.

E

E, e [ə], *n.m.* the fifth letter of the alphabet.
eau [o], *n.f.* water; rain, flood; (*pl.*) mineral *or* thermal waters; watering-place; stream; track; gloss; *à fleur d'eau*, on a level with the water; (*Chem.*) *eau lourde*, heavy water.
eau-de-vie [o'dvi], *n.f.* (*pl.* **eaux-de-vie**) brandy.
ébahi [eba'i], *a.* astonished, dumbfounded.
ébahir (s') [seba'i:r], *v.r.* to wonder (at), to be amazed.
ébahissement [ebais'mɑ̃], *n.m.* amazement, astonishment.
ébats [e'ba], *n.m. pl.* pastime, sport, gambol, frolic.
ébattre (s') [se'batr], *v.r.* (*conjug. like* BATTRE) to sport, to gambol, to frolic.
ébauchage [ebo'ʃa:ʒ], *n.m.* sketching.
ébauche [e'bo:ʃ], *n.f.* rough draft, outline.
ébaucher [ebo'ʃe], *v.t.* to make the first draft of, to draw an outline of, to sketch.
ébauchoir [ebo'ʃwa:r], *n.m.* (*Sculp.*) roughing-chisel; (*Carp.*) mortise-chisel.
ébène [e'bɛːn], *n.f.* ebony, ebony work.
ébéner [ebe'ne], *v.t.* (*conjug. like* CÉDER) to ebonize.
ébénier [ebe'nje], *n.m.* ebony-tree.
ébéniste [ebe'nist], *n.* cabinet-maker.
ébénisterie [ebenis'tri], *n.f.* cabinet-work.
ébiseler [ebi'zle], *v.t.* (*conjug. like* APPELER) to chamfer, to bevel.
éblouir [eblu'i:r], *v.t.* to dazzle; (*fig.*) to fascinate, to amaze. **s'éblouir**, *v.r.* to be dazzled *or* fascinated.
éblouissant [eblui'sɑ̃], *a.* dazzling, resplendent.
éblouissement [ebluis'mɑ̃], *n.m.* dazzle, daze; (*fig.*) bewilderment.
ébonite [ebo'nit], *n.f.* ebonite; vulcanite.
ébouage [ebu'a:ʒ], *n.m.* scavenging.
ébouer [ebu'e], *v.t.* to scavenge.
éboueur [ebu'œ:r], *n.m.* (*fem.* **-euse**) road-sweeper, scavenger.—*n.f.* (**-euse**) road-sweeping machine.
ébouillanter [ebujɑ̃'te], *v.t.* to dip in hot water, to scald.
éboulement [ebul'mɑ̃], *n.m.* falling in, fall; caving in, collapse; landslide, landslip.
ébouler [ebu'le], *v.i.* to fall in, to fall down, to sink. **s'ébouler**, *v.r.* to fall in, to cave in.
éboulis [ebu'li], *n.m. inv.* debris, fallen rocks.
ébourgeonner [eburʒɔ'ne], *v.t.* to disbud.
ébouriffé [eburi'fe], *a.* disordered, ruffled, in disorder; (*fig.*) in a flutter.
ébouriffer [eburi'fe], *v.t.* to ruffle, to disorder; (*fig.*) to startle, to amaze.
ébouter [ebu'te], *v.t.* to cut off (*the end*).

ébranchage [ebrɑ̃'ʃa:ʒ], **ébranchement** [ebrɑ̃ʃ'mɑ̃], *n.m.* (*Hort.*) pruning, lopping, trimming.
ébrancher [ebrɑ̃'ʃe], *v.t.* to prune, to lop, to trim.
ébranlement [ebrɑ̃l'mɑ̃], *n.m.* shock, shaking; (*fig.*) perturbation, disturbance.
ébranler [ebrɑ̃'le], *v.t.* to shake; to disturb, to unsettle. **s'ébranler**, *v.r.* to get under way, to move off.
ébrécher [ebre'ʃe], *v.t.* (*conjug. like* CÉDER) to notch, to indent; to crack, to chip; (*fig.*) to impair.
ébriété [ebrie'te], *n.f.* drunkenness, inebriety.
ébrouement [ebru'mɑ̃], *n.m.* snorting.
ébrouer (s') [sebru'e], *v.r.* to snort from fear (*of horses*).
ébruiter [ebrɥi'te], *v.t.* to make known, to spread about. **s'ébruiter**, *v.r.* to spread, to be noised abroad.
ébullition [ebyli'sjɔ̃], *n.f.* boiling, ebullition.
écaille [eka:j], *n.f.* scale; shell.
écaillé [eka'je], *a.* scaly.
écailler (1) [eka'je], *v.t.* to scale. **s'écailler** *v.r.* to peel off, to scale.
écailler (2) [eka'je], *n.m.* (*fem.* **-ère**) oysterman, oyster-woman.
écailleux [eka'jø], *a.* (*fem.* **-euse**) scaly, squamous.
écale [e'kal], *n.f.* shell, pod (*of peas etc.*); hull, husk (*of walnut*).
écaler [eka'le], *v.t.* to shell (*beans, peas etc.*); to hull, to husk (*almonds, nuts etc.*). **s'écaler**, *v.r.* to come out of the shell.
écarlate [ekar'lat], *a.* and *n.f.* scarlet; hectic red.
écarquillement [ekarkij'mɑ̃], *n.m.* spreading out, opening wide (*of one's eyes, legs etc.*).
écarquiller [ekarki'je], *v.t.* to spread out, to open wide.
écart [e'ka:r], *n.m.* stepping aside, swerving; fault; deviation; *à l'écart*, aside; *faire un écart*, to step aside.
écarté (1) [ekar'te], *n.m.* écarté (*game of cards*).
écarté (2) [ekar'te], *a.* remote, lonely, secluded.
écartelé [ekartə'le], *a.* (*of mind, heart etc.*) divided, torn asunder; (*Her.*) quartered.
écartèlement [ekartɛl'mɑ̃], *n.m.* tearing to pieces, quartering.
écarteler [ekartə'le], *v.t.* (*conjug. like* AMENER) to tear to pieces; (*Her.*) to quarter.
écartement [ekartə'mɑ̃], *n.m.* putting aside; removal; spacing; spread.
écarter [ekar'te], *v.t.* to open, to throw wide apart; to set aside; to avert; to dispel, to deviate; to spread. **s'écarter**, *v.r.* to turn aside, to swerve; to stray; to make way.
ecchymose [ɛki'mo:z], *n.f.* (*Med.*) ecchymosis.
ecclésiastique [ɛklezjas'tik], *a.* ecclesiastic; clerical.—*n.m.* clergyman, ecclesiastic.
écervelé [esɛrvə'le], *a.* hare-brained, rash, giddy.—*n.m.* (*fem.* **-ée**) madcap; scatter-brain.
échafaud [eʃa'fo], *n.m.* scaffold.
échafaudage [eʃafo'da:ʒ], *n.m.* scaffolding; (*fig.*) structure.
échafauder [eʃafo'de], *v.t.* to pile up; (*fig.*) to lay out (*a plan*).—*v.i.* to erect scaffolding.

échalas [eʃɑ'lɑ], *n.m.* vine-prop; hop-pole.
échalassage [eʃɑlɑ'sa:ʒ], **échalassement** [eʃɑlɑs'mã], *n.m.* propping.
échalasser [eʃɑlɑ'se], *v.t.* to prop (*vines etc.*).
échalier [eʃɑ'lje], **échalis** [eʃɑ'li], *n.m.* stile; wooden fence.
échalote [eʃɑ'lɔt], *n.f.* (*Bot.*) shallot.
échancrer [eʃɑ̃'kre], *v.t.* to make a crescent-shaped cut; to indent.
échancrure [eʃɑ̃'kry:r], *n.f.* notch, cut, indentation; opening.
échandole [eʃɑ̃'dɔl], *n.f.* shingle (*for roofing*).
échange [e'ʃɑ̃:ʒ], *n.m.* exchange, barter; *libre échange*, free trade.
échangeable [eʃɑ̃'ʒabl], *a.* exchangeable.
échanger [eʃɑ̃'ʒe], *v.t.* (*conjug. like* MANGER) to exchange, to barter; to interchange.
échanson [eʃɑ̃'sɔ̃], *n.m.* cup-bearer; butler.
échantillon [eʃɑ̃ti'jɔ̃], *n.m.* sample, pattern, specimen; (*fig.*) model.
échantillonner [eʃɑ̃tijɔ'ne], *v.t.* to sample.
échappatoire [eʃapa'twa:r], *n.f.* shift, subterfuge, loop-hole, evasion.
échappé [eʃa'pe], *a.* runaway.—*n.m.* (*fem.* -ée* (1)) one who has escaped, runaway.
échappée (2) [eʃa'pe], *n.f.* escapade, prank; short space of time.
échappement [eʃap'mã], *n.m.* escape; leakage; (*Horol.*) escapement; exhaust.
échapper [eʃa'pe], *v.t.* to escape, to avoid; *l'échapper belle*, to have a narrow escape. —*v.i.* to escape, to make good one's escape; to be overlooked. **s'échapper,** *v.r.* to escape; to vanish.
écharde [e'ʃard], *n.f.* prickle (*of a thistle etc.*); splinter.
écharner [eʃar'ne], *v.t.* to flesh or scrape (*hides*).
écharnoir [eʃar'nwa:r], *n.m.* fleshing-knife.
écharpe [e'ʃarp], *n.f.* scarf, sash; arm-sling.
écharper [eʃar'pe], *v.t.* to slash, to cut.
échasse [e'ʃa:s], *n.f.* stilt; long-legged plover.
échassier [eʃa'sje], *n.m.* (*fem.* -ière) stilt-walker; (*colloq.*) long-legged person.—*n.m.* (*Orn.*) wader.
échauboulure [eʃobu'ly:r], *n.f.* pimple, blotch.
échaudage [eʃo'da:ʒ], *n.m.* whitewash; white-washing; scalding.
échaudé (1) [eʃo'de], *n.m.* simnel, cracknel.
échaudé (2) [eʃo'de], *a.* scalded.
échauder [eʃo'de], *v.t.* to scald. **s'échauder,** *v.r.* to burn oneself.
échaudoir [eʃo'dwa:r], *n.m.* scalding-house; scalding-tub.
échaudure [eʃo'dy:r], *n.f.* scald.
échauffant [eʃo'fã], *a.* heating; binding (*food*).
échauffement [eʃof'mã], *n.m.* heating; over-excitement.
échauffer [eʃo'fe], *v.t.* to warm, to heat, to over-heat; to excite, to irritate. **s'échauffer,** *v.r.* to grow warm, to overheat oneself; to grow angry, to chafe.
échauffourée [eʃofu're], *n.f.* rash or blundering enterprise; brush, scuffle.
échauffure [eʃo'fy:r], *n.f.* red rash.
échauguette [eʃo'gɛt], *n.f.* (*Mil.*) watch-tower.
échéable [eʃe'abl], *a.* due, payable.
échéance [eʃe'ã:s], *n.f.* falling due (*of bill*); date (*of payment, of maturity*); expiration (*of tenancy*).

échéant [eʃe'ã], *a.* falling due; *le cas échéant*, in that case, if need be.
échec [e'ʃek], *n.m.* check, defeat, blow, loss.
échecs [e'ʃek], *n.m. pl.* chess; chess-men.
échelle [e'ʃɛl], *n.f.* ladder; scale; gradation.
échelon [eʃ'lɔ̃], *n.m.* round, rung, step (*of a ladder*); degree; (*Mil.*) echelon.
échelonner [eʃlɔ'ne], *v.t.* to draw up in echelon; to arrange according to gradation; to spread (*over a period of time*); to place (*at regular intervals*); *vacances échelonnées*, staggered holidays. **s'échelonner,** *v.r.* to be graduated; to slope gradually; to be arranged in echelon.
écheniller [eʃni'je], *v.t.* to rid (*plants, trees etc.*) of caterpillars.
écheveau [eʃ'vo], *n.m.* (*pl.* -eaux) hank, skein.
échevelé [eʃə'vle], *a.* dishevelled; (*fig.*) wild, extravagant.
écheveler [eʃə'vle], *v.t.* (*conjug. like* APPELER) to dishevel.
***échevin** [eʃ'vɛ̃], *n.m.* sheriff; alderman; (*C*) municipal magistrate.
échine [e'ʃin], *n.f.* spine, backbone, chine.
échiner [eʃi'ne], *v.t.* to beat unmercifully; to tire out. **s'échiner,** *v.r.* (*pop.*) to work oneself to death.
échiqueté [eʃik'te], *a.* chequered.
échiquier [eʃi'kje], *n.m.* chess-board; exchequer; square net.
écho [e'ko], *n.m.* echo.
échoir [e'ʃwa:r], *v.i. irr.* (*aux.* ÊTRE) to expire, to fall due, to lapse; to happen, to befall.
échoppe [e'ʃɔp], *n.f.* booth, covered stall.
échopper [eʃɔ'pe], *v.t.* to gouge.
échotier [eko'tje], *n.m.* (*fem.* -ière) gossip-writer, columnist.
échouage [e'ʃwa:ʒ], **échouement** [eʃu'mã], *n.m.* (*Naut.*) beaching, running aground.
échouer [e'ʃwe], *v.t.* to run (*a vessel*) aground. —*v.i.* to run aground, to be stranded; (*fig.*) to miscarry, to fail.
écimer [esi'me], *v.t.* to top (*plants etc.*), to pollard (*trees*).
éclaboussement [eklabus'mã], *n.m.* splashing, bespattering.
éclabousser [eklabu'se], *v.t.* to splash, to bespatter.
éclaboussure [eklabu'sy:r], *n.f.* splash.
éclair [e'klɛ:r], *n.m.* lightning, flash of lightning; variety of chocolate cake.
éclairage [eklɛ'ra:ʒ], *n.m.* lighting, illumination, light.
éclaircie [eklɛr'si], *n.f.* opening, rift (*in clouds etc.*); glade, clearing; (*fig.*) favourable change of affairs.
éclaircir [eklɛr'si:r], *v.t.* to make clear or clearer, to brighten; to clarify; to make thin or thinner; to elucidate, to explain. **s'éclaircir,** *v.r.* to become clear, bright or fine; to grow light; to be explained.
éclaircissement [eklɛrsis'mã], *n.m.* clearing up, explanation, solution; hint, light.
éclaire [e'klɛ:r], *n.f.* celandine.
éclairé [eklɛ're], *a.* lighted; well-lighted; (*fig.*) well-informed; intelligent; enlightened.
éclairer [eklɛ're], *v.t.* to light, to give light to, to illuminate; to enlighten; to observe; (*Mil.*) to reconnoitre.—*v.i.* to sparkle, to shine, to glitter. **s'éclairer,** *v.r.* to become enlightened; to instruct or enlighten one another; to light up.

éclaireur

éclaireur [eklɛ'rœːr], *n.m.* (*Mil.*) scout; boy-scout.

éclanche [e'klɑ̃ːʃ], *n.f.* shoulder of mutton.

éclat [e'kla], *n.m.* burst; crash, peal; splinter (*of wood, stone, brick etc.*); brightness, glare, glitter; lustre, pomp; renown; gaudiness (*of colours*); rumour, scandal; *un éclat de rire*, a burst of laughter; *un grand éclat de voix*, a loud shout; *voler en éclats*, to fly into a thousand pieces.

éclatant [ekla'tɑ̃], *a.* bright, sparkling, brilliant; striking; piercing, shrill.

éclatement [eklat'mɑ̃], *n.m.* bursting, explosion.

éclater [ekla'te], *v.i.* to split, to burst, to explode; to cry out; to shine, to sparkle, to flash; to break out (*war etc.*); *éclater de rire*, to burst out laughing.

éclectique [eklɛk'tik], *a.* and *n.* eclectic; dilettante.

éclectisme [eklɛk'tism], *n.m.* eclecticism.

éclipse [e'klips], *n.f.* eclipse; (*fig.*) disappearance.

éclipser [eklip'se], *v.t.* to eclipse, (*fig.*) to surpass. **s'éclipser**, *v.r.* (*fig.*) to disappear, to vanish.

écliptique [eklip'tik], *a.* and *n.f.* ecliptic.

éclisse [e'klis], *n.f.* (*Surg.*) splint.

éclisser [ekli'se], *v.t.* (*Surg.*) to splint.

éclopé [eklɔ'pe], *a.* crippled, footsore, lame.— *n.m.* (*fem.* **-ée**) cripple.

écloper [eklɔ'pe], *v.t.* to lame, to disable.

éclore [e'klɔːr], *v.i. irr.* (*conjug. like* CLORE, *but with aux.* ÊTRE) to hatch; to open, to bloom (*of flowers*); (*fig.*) to show itself.

éclosion [eklo'zjɔ̃], *n.f.* hatching; (*fig.*) opening, blooming; appearance.

écluse [e'klyːz], *n.f.* lock (*on canals etc.*); dam, weir; *porte d'écluse*, sluice, flood-gate.

écluser [ekly'ze], *v.t.* to furnish with locks; to take (*a boat etc.*) through a lock.

éclusier [ekly'zje], *n.m.* (*fem.* **-ière**) lock-keeper.

écœurant [ekœ'rɑ̃], *a.* disgusting, nauseating.

écœurement [ekœr'mɑ̃], *n.m.* disgust; nausea.

écœurer [ekœ're], *v.t.* to disgust, to sicken; (*fig.*) to shock, to dishearten.

école [e'kɔl], *n.f.* school, college; scholastic philosophy; sect; (*Mil.*) training; (*fig.*) manner, practice.

écolier [ekɔ'lje], *n.m.* (*fem.* **-ière**) schoolboy, schoolgirl, pupil, student.

éconduire [ekɔ̃'dɥiːr], *v.t. irr.* (*conjug. like* CONDUIRE) to show out, to dismiss; to refuse.

économat [ekɔnɔ'ma], *n.m.* stewardship, bursarship.

économe [ekɔ'nɔm], *a.* economical, saving, thrifty.—*n.* steward, housekeeper, bursar, treasurer (*of colleges, hospitals etc.*).

économie [ekɔnɔ'mi], *n.f.* economy; thrift, saving.

économique [ekɔnɔ'mik], *a.* (*applied to things only*) economic, economical, cheap.—*n.f.* economics.

économiquement [ekɔnɔmik'mɑ̃], *adv.* economically.

économiser [ekɔnɔmi'ze], *v.t., v.i.* to economize, to save (up).

économiste [ekɔnɔ'mist], *n.* economist.

écope [e'kɔp], *n.f.* scoop, ladle; (*Naut.*) bailer.

écorce [e'kɔrs], *n.f.* bark, rind, peel; shell; (*Geol.*) crust (*of the earth*).

écorcement [ekɔrs'mɑ̃], **écorçage** [ekɔr'saːʒ], *n.m.* barking *or* stripping (*of trees etc.*); peeling.

écorcer [ekɔr'se], *v.t.* (*conjug. like* COMMENCER) to bark, to strip (*trees etc.*), to peel.

écorchement [ekɔrʃə'mɑ̃], *n.m.* excoriation, flaying, skinning.

écorcher [ekɔr'ʃe], *v.t.* to flay, to skin; to graze (*skin*); to peel, to bark; (*fig.*) to strip, to fleece. **s'écorcher**, *v.r.* to graze oneself.

écorcheur [ekɔr'ʃœːr], *n.m.* (*fem.* **-euse**) knacker, flayer; (*fig.*) fleecer.

écorchure [ekɔr'ʃyːr], *n.f.* scratch, graze.

écorner [ekɔr'ne], *v.t.* to break the horns of; to break the corners of, to dog-ear; to curtail, to impair.

écornifler [ekɔrni'fle], *v.t.* to sponge upon.

écornure [ekɔr'nyːr], *n.f.* broken-off corner, chip.

écossais [ekɔ'sɛ], *a.* Scottish.—*n.m.* Scots (*language*); plaid, tartan cloth; (**Écossais**, *fem.* **-aise**) Scot, Scotsman, Scotswoman.

Écosse [e'kɔs], **l'**, *f.* Scotland; *La Nouvelle Écosse*, *f.* Nova Scotia.

écosser [ekɔ'se], *v.t.* to shell, to husk (*peas or beans*).

écosseur [ekɔ'sœːr], *n.m.* (*fem.* **-euse**) sheller.

écot (1) [e'kɔ], *n.m.* share (*of a reckoning*); bill, reckoning, score (*usually in the expression payer son écot*, to pay one's share).

écot (2) [e'kɔ], *n.m.* stump of a tree.

écoulement [ekul'mɑ̃], *n.m.* flowing, flow, running; outlet; (*Comm.*) sale, disposal; export.

écouler [eku'le], *v.t.* to dispose of, to sell. **s'écouler**, *v.r.* to run *or* flow away, to pass, to slip away; (*Comm.*) to be disposed of.

écourter [ekur'te], *v.t.* to shorten, to dock, to crop.

écoutant [eku'tɑ̃], *a.* listening; *avocat écoutant*, briefless barrister.

écoute (1) [e'kut], *n.f.* hiding-place for listening; *être aux écoutes*, to be on the watch.

écoute (2) [e'kut], *n.f.* (*Naut.*) sheet (*of sail*).

écouter [eku'te], *v.t.* to listen to, to hearken to; to pay attention to. **s'écouter**, *v.r.* to like the sound of one's own voice; to indulge oneself.

écouteur [eku'tœːr], *n.m.* (*fem.* **-euse**) listener, listener-in; (*Teleph.*) receiver; (*Teleg.*) ear-phone.

écoutille [eku'tiːj], *n.f.* (*Naut.*) hatchway.

écran [e'krɑ̃], *n.m.* screen; *vedette de l'écran*, film-star.

écrasant [ekra'zɑ̃], *a.* crushing; (*fig.*) humiliating, excessive; overwhelming.

écrasé [ekra'ze], *a.* crushed, ruined.

écrasement [ekraz'mɑ̃], *n.m.* crushing, bruising; (*fig.*) overwhelming.

écraser [ekra'ze], *v.t.* to crush; to bruise; to overwhelm, to ruin; to run over.

écraseur [ekra'zœːr], *n.m.* crusher; (*Motor.*) road-hog; steam-roller.

écrémer [ekre'me], *v.t.* (*conjug. like* CÉDER) to take the cream off, to skim.

écrémeuse [ekre'møːz], *n.f.* separator.

écrevisse [ekrə'vis], *n.f.* crayfish; (*Am.*) crawfish; (*Astron.*) Cancer.

écrier (s') [sekri'je], *v.r.* to cry out, to exclaim.

écrin [e'krɛ̃], *n.m.* casket, jewel-box *or* case.
écrire [e'kriːr], *v.t. irr.* to write; to spell. **s'écrire**, *v.r.* to be written; to be spelled; to write to each other.
écrit [e'kri], *n.m.* writing; pamphlet.
écriteau [ekri'to], *n.m.* (*pl.* **-eaux**) bill (*poster*); board.
écritoire [ekri'twaːr], *n.f.* writing-desk; ink-stand.
écriture [ekri'tyːr], *n.f.* writing, hand-writing; scripture; (*pl.*) accounts, documents.
écrivain [ekri'vɛ̃], *n.m.* writer, author; *femme écrivain*, authoress, woman writer.
écrivassier [ekriva'sje], *n.m.* (*fem.* **-ière**) (*colloq.*) scribbler.
écrou [e'kru], *n.m.* screw-nut; *écrou à oreilles*, wing-nut.
écrouelles [ekru'ɛl], *n.f. pl.* king's evil, scrofula.
écrouelleux [ekruɛ'lø], *a.* (*fem.* **-euse**) scrofulous.
écrouer [ekru'e], *v.t.* to imprison, to lock up.
écroulement [ekrul'mɑ̃], *n.m.* falling in, collapse; wreck, ruin.
écrouler (s') [sekru'le], *v.r.* to fall in, to fall to pieces, to collapse.
écru [e'kry], *a.* raw, unbleached; *toile écrue*, (brown) holland.
ectoplasme [ɛkto'plasm], *n.m.* ectoplasm.
écu [e'ky], *n.m.* shield; crown (*coin*); (*fig.*) money, cash.
écueil [e'kœːj], *n.m.* reef, rock; (*fig.*) danger, stumbling-block.
écuelle [e'kɥɛl], *n.f.* porringer, bowl, basin.
écuellée [ekɥe'le], *n.f.* bowlful.
éculer [eky'le], *v.t.* to tread down at heel; *des souliers éculés*, down-at-heel shoes.
écumage [eky'ma:ʒ], *n.m.* skimming.
écumant [eky'mɑ̃], *a.* foaming, frothing, seething.
écume [e'kym], *n.f.* foam, froth; lather; (*fig.*) scum, dregs.
écumer [eky'me], *v.t.* to skim; to scour; *écumer la marmite*, to be a sponger.—*v.i.* to foam, to froth.
écumeur [eky'mœːr], *n.m.* (*fem.* **écumeuse** (1)) skimmer; hanger-on, parasite.
écumeux [eky'mø], *a.* (*fem.* **écumeuse** (2)) frothy, foaming.
écumoire [eky'mwaːr], *n.f.* skimmer.
écurage [eky'ra:ʒ], *n.m.* scouring, cleaning.
écurer [eky're], *v.t.* to scour, to cleanse.
écureuil [eky'rœːj], *n.m.* squirrel.
écurie [eky'ri], *n.f.* stable, mews; stud.
écusson [eky'sɔ̃], *n.m.* escutcheon; shield.
écuyer [ekɥi'je], *n.m.* squire; equerry; riding-master; rider; wall hand-rail (*of a staircase*).
écuyère [ekɥi'jɛːr], *n.f.* horsewoman; female equestrian performer; *bottes à l'écuyère*, top-boots, riding-boots.
eczéma [ɛgze'ma], *n.m.* eczema.
édenté [edɑ̃'te], *a.* toothless.
édenter [edɑ̃'te], *v.t.* to break the teeth of (*combs, saws etc.*).
édicter [edik'te], *v.t.* to enact, to decree.
édicule [edi'kyl], *n.m.* small building (*pavilion, kiosk etc.*).
édifiant [edi'fjɑ̃], *a.* edifying.
édification [edifika'sjɔ̃], *n.f.* building, erection; (*fig.*) edification.
édifice [edi'fis], *n.m.* edifice, building, pile.

édifier [edi'fje], *v.t.* to build, to erect, to construct; (*fig.*) to edify, to improve; to instruct, to enlighten; to satisfy.
édile [e'dil], *n.m.* ædile; town councillor.
Édimbourg [edɛ̃'buːr], *m. or f.* Edinburgh.
édit [e'di], *n.m.* edict.
éditer [edi'te], *v.t.* to publish; to edit.
éditeur [edi'tœːr], *n.m.* (*fem.* **-trice**) publisher.
édition [edi'sjɔ̃], *n.f.* edition.
éditorial [edito'rjal], *n.m.* (*pl.* **-aux**) leading article, leader.
éditorialiste [editorja'list], *n.* leader-writer.
Édouard [e'dwaːr], *m.* Edward.
édredon [edrǝ'dɔ̃], *n.m.* eider-down; eider-down quilt.
éducateur [edyka'tœːr], *a.* (*fem.* **-trice**) educative, instructing.—*n.m.* (*fem.* **-trice**) educator; breeder.
éducatif [edyka'tif], *a.* (*fem.* **-tive**) educational.
éducation [edyka'sjɔ̃], *n.f.* education; training; rearing (*of animals*); breeding, manners.
éduquer [edy'ke], *v.t.* to bring up, to educate (*children*).
effacement [efas'mɑ̃], *n.m.* effacement, obliteration; disappearance; humility, self-effacement.
effacer [efa'se], *v.t.* (*conjug. like* COMMENCER) to efface, to erase, to rub out; to blot out, to obliterate, **s'effacer**, *v.r.* to become obliterated; to wear away; to draw aside, to give way.
effaçure [efa'syːr], *n.f.* erasure, blotting out, obliteration.
effaré [efa're], *a.* wild, scared, bewildered; astounded.
effarement [efar'mɑ̃], *n.m.* bewilderment, terror, affright.
effarer [efa're], *v.t.* to frighten, to scare. **s'effarer**, *v.r.* to be scared, to take fright.
effarouchant [efaru'ʃɑ̃], *a.* startling, disquieting; shocking; annoying.
effaroucher [efaru'ʃe], *v.t.* to startle, to frighten away. **s'effaroucher**, *v.r.* to be scared, to be startled.
effectif [efɛk'tif], *a.* (*fem.* **-tive**) actual, real, positive.—*n.m.* effective force (*of troops etc.*); size (*of a class*).
effectivement [efɛktiv'mɑ̃], *adv.* in effect, actually, indeed, in fact; (*in answer*) that is so.
effectuer [efɛk'tɥe], *v.t.* to effect, to accomplish, to carry out. **s'effectuer**, *v.r.* to be accomplished, to take place.
effémination [efemina'sjɔ̃], *n.f.* effeminacy.
efféminé [efemi'ne], *a.* effeminate, womanish.
effervescence [efɛrve'sɑ̃:s], *n.f.* effervescence; (*fig.*) agitation, ferment.
effervescent [efɛrve'sɑ̃], *a.* effervescent; (*fig.*) excitable, irascible.
effet [e'fɛ], *n.m.* effect, result; performance; impression; power (*transmitted by machinery etc.*); (*Comm.*) bill of exchange; (*pl.*) belongings; *en effet*, indeed, in fact.
effeuillaison [efœjɛ'zɔ̃], *n.f.*, **effeuillement** [efœj'mɑ̃], *n.m.* fall of the leaves.
effeuiller [efœ'je], *v.t.* to strip off leaves, to pick (*a flower*) to pieces. **s'effeuiller**, *v.r.* to lose *or* shed its leaves.
efficace [efi'kas], *a.* efficacious, effective.

127

efficacité [efikasi'te], *n.f.* efficacy, effectiveness; efficiency.

effigie [efi'ʒi], *n.f.* effigy.

effilé [efi'le], *a.* slender, slim; sharp, keen, trenchant.—*n.m.* fringe.

effiler [efi'le], *v.t.* to unweave, to unravel; to taper. **s'effiler**, *v.r.* to unravel; to taper, to become sharp; to fray.

effiloche [efi'lɔʃ], **effiloque** [efi'lɔk], *n.f.* floss silk, light refuse silk.

effilocher [efilɔ'ʃe], **effiloquer** [efilɔ'ke], *v.t.* to unravel, to undo.

efflanqué [eflɑ̃'ke], *a.* lean, thin, lank.

efflanquer [eflɑ̃'ke], *v.t.* to make lean, to emaciate.

effleurer [eflœ're], *v.t.* to graze, to skim the surface of, to touch lightly; (*fig.*) to touch upon.

efflorescence [eflɔre'sɑ̃:s], *n.f.* efflorescence.

efflorescent [eflɔre'sɑ̃], *a.* efflorescent.

effluent [efly'ɑ̃], *a.* effluent.

effluve [e'fly:v], *n.m.* effluvium.

effondrement [efɔ̃drə'mɑ̃], *n.m.* (*Agric.*) trenching; falling in, sinking; collapse.

effondrer [efɔ̃'dre], *v.t.* to dig deeply; to break in; to overwhelm. **s'effondrer**, *v.r.* to fall in, to collapse.

efforcer (s') [efɔr'se], *v.r.* (*conjug. like* COMMENCER) to exert oneself, to strain, to strive.

effort [e'fɔ:r], *n.m.* effort, exertion, endeavour; stress; (*Med.*) strain, rupture.

effraction [efrak'sjɔ̃], *n.f.* breaking into, house-breaking; **vol avec effraction**, burglary.

effraie [e'frɛ], *n.f.* barn-owl, screech owl.

effrayant [efre'jɑ̃], *a.* frightful, dreadful.

effrayer [efre'je], *v.t.* (*conjug. like* PAYER) to frighten, to alarm, to terrify. **s'effrayer**, *v.r.* to be frightened, to be startled.

effréné [efre'ne], *a.* unrestrained; lawless; wild.

effritement [efrit'mɑ̃], *n.m.* crumbling into dust.

effriter (s') [sefri'te], *v.r.* to crumble.

effroi [e'frwa], *n.m.* fright, terror, dread.

effronté [efrɔ̃'te], *a.* and ⊞*n.m.*⊞(*fem.* **-ée**) shameless, brazen, impudent (person).

effrontément [efrɔ̃te'mɑ̃], *adv.* impudently, shamelessly.

effronterie [efrɔ̃'tri], *n.f.* effrontery, impudence.

effroyable [efrwa'jabl], *a.* frightful, dreadful, hideous.

effroyablement [efrwajablə'mɑ̃], *adv.* frightfully, horribly, dreadfully.

effusion [efy'zjɔ̃], *n.f.* effusion; overflowing.

égal [e'gal], *a.* (*m. pl.* **-aux**) equal, alike; even, level, smooth; all the same.—*n.m.* (*fem.* **-e**) equal.

également [egal'mɑ̃], *adv.* equally, alike.

égaler [ega'le], *v.t.* to equal; to make equal; to compare. **s'égaler**, *v.r.* to equal; to compare oneself (*à*).

égalisation [egaliza'sjɔ̃], *n.f.* equalization.

égaliser [egali'ze], *v.t.* to equalize; to level.

égalitaire [egali'tɛ:r], *a.* and *n.* egalitarian.

égalité [egali'te], *n.f.* equality, parity; uniformity.

égard [e'ga:r], *n.m.* regard, consideration, respect.

égaré [ega're], *a.* wandering, strayed; misled; mislaid; distracted.

égarement [egar'mɑ̃], *n.m.* straying, losing one's way; mistake; ill-conduct.

égarer [ega're], *v.t.* to mislead; to lose; to lead astray; to bewilder; to impair (*intellect*). **s'égarer**, *v.r.* to lose one's way, to stray; to err.

égayer [ege'je], *v.t.* (*conjug. like* PAYER) to enliven, to cheer up; (*Hort.*) to prune (*trees*). **s'égayer**, *v.r.* to brighten up; to make merry.

églantier [eglɑ̃'tje], *n.m.* eglantine, briar, dog-rose (*bush*).

églantine [eglɑ̃'tin], *n.f.* eglantine, dog-rose (*flower*).

église [e'gli:z], *n.f.* church.

églogue [e'glɔg], *n.f.* eclogue.

égocentrique [egosɑ̃'trik], *a.* egocentric, self-centred.

égoïsme [egɔ'ism], *n.m.* egoism, selfishness.

égoïste [egɔ'ist], *a.* egoistic, selfish.—*n.* egoist, selfish person.

égorger [egɔr'ʒe], *v.t.* (*conjug. like* MANGER) to cut the throat of, to slaughter.

égorgeur [egɔr'ʒœ:r], *n.m.* (*fem.* **-euse**) slaughterer, murderer.

égosiller (s') [segozi'je], *v.r.* to make oneself hoarse; to bawl.

égotisme [egɔ'tism], *n.m.* egotism.

égotiste [egɔ'tist], *a.* egotistic(al).—*n.* egotist.

égout [e'gu], *n.m.* running *or* falling of water; sink, drain, sewer.

égouttage [egu'ta:ʒ], **égouttement** [egut 'mɑ̃], *n.m.* drainage, draining; dripping.

égoutter [egu'te], *v.t., v.i.* to drain, to drip. **s'égoutter**, *v.r.* to drip, to drain.

égouttoir [egu'twa:r], *n.m.* drainer (*plate-rack etc.*).

égrapper [egra'pe], *v.t.* to pick (*grapes, currants etc.*) from the bunch.

égratigner [egrati'ɲe], *v.t.* to scratch.

égratignure [egrati'ɲy:r], *n.f.* scratch; slight wound.

égrenage [egrə'na:ʒ], *n.m.* picking off (*of grapes etc.*).

égrener [egrə'ne], *v.t.* (*conjug. like* AMENER) to tell (*beads*); to unstring (*beads etc.*); to pick off (*grapes etc.*) from the bunch. **s'égrener**, *v.r.* to fall from the stalk, to drop one by one.

égrillard [egri'ja:r], *a.* lewd, broad, naughty; **propos égrillards**, spicy talk.

égrilloir [egri'jwa:r], *n.m.* weir; grate (*to confine fish in a pond*).

égrisé, *n.m.* or **égrisée** [egri'ze], *n.f.* diamond-dust.

égriser [egri'ze], *v.t.* to grind, to polish (*diamonds etc.*).

égrugeoir [egry'ʒwa:r], *n.m.* mortar.

égruger [egry'ʒe], *v.t.* (*conjug. like* MANGER) to pound, to grind in a mortar.

égueuler [egœ'le], *v.t.* to break off the mouth *or* neck (*of glass and other vessels*).

Égypte [e'ʒipt], **l'**, *f.* Egypt.

égyptien [eʒip'sjɛ̃], *a.* (*fem.* **-enne**) Egyptian.—*n.m.* (**Égyptien**, *fem.* **-enne**) Egyptian (*person*).

eh! [e], *int.* ah! well! hey! **eh bien !** well!

éhonté [eɔ̃'te], *a.* shameless.

éjaculation [eʒakylɑ'sjɔ̃], *n.f.* throwing out with force, discharge; ejaculation.

éjaculer [eʒaky'le], *v.t.* to discharge, to ejaculate.

éjecter [eʒɛk'te], *v.t.* to eject.

éjecteur [eʒɛk'tœːr], *a.* (*fem.* **-trice**) ejecting; (*Av.*) **siège éjecteur**, ejector seat.—*n.m.* ejector (*of firearm*).

élaboration [elabɔrɑ'sjɔ̃], *n.f.* elaboration.

élaboré [elabɔ're], *a.* wrought; elaborate.

élaborer [elabɔ're], *v.t.* to elaborate, to work out.

élaguer [ela'ge], *v.t.* to lop, to prune; (*fig.*) to curtail, to cut down.

élagueur [ela'gœr], *n.m.* (*Hort.*) pruner.

élan (1) [e'lɑ̃], *n.m.* start, spring, bound; flight; burst; dash.

élan (2) [e'lɑ̃], *n.m.* elk; moose, wapiti (*Canada*), eland (*S. Africa*).

élancé [elɑ̃'se], *a.* slender, slim.

élancement [elɑ̃s'mɑ̃], *n.m.* darting forward; shooting pain, twinge; (*pl.*) transports.

élancer [elɑ̃'se], *v.t.* (*conjug. like* COMMENCER) to dart, to hurl.—*v.i.* to shoot, to twitch (*of pain*). **s'élancer**, *v.r.* to bound, to shoot *or* dart forth, to rush, to dash; to soar up.

élargir [elar'ʒiːr], *v.t.* to widen, to enlarge; to release. **s'élargir**, *v.r.* to widen; to stretch; to enlarge one's estate.

élargissement [elarʒis'mɑ̃], *n.m.* widening, enlarging; discharge (*from prison etc.*).

élasticité [elastisi'te], *n.f.* elasticity, springiness.

élastique [elas'tik], *a.* elastic, springy.—*n.m.* india-rubber; elastic band.

électeur [elɛk'tœːr], *n.m.* (*fem.* **-trice**) (*Hist.*) elector, electress; (*Polit.*) voter.

élection [elɛk'sjɔ̃], *n.f.* election, polling; choice; appointment.

électoral [elɛktɔ'ral], *a.* (*m. pl.* **-aux**) electoral.

électorat [elɛktɔ'ra], *n.m.* electorate.

électricien [elɛktri'sjɛ̃], *n.m.* electrician.

électricité [elɛktrisi'te], *n.f.* electricity.

électrification [elɛktrifikɑ'sjɔ̃], *n.f.* electrification.

électrifier [elɛktri'fje], *v.t.* to provide with current, to electrify.

électrique [elɛk'trik], *a.* electric; *secousse électrique*, electric shock.

électriquement [elɛktrik'mɑ̃], *adv.* electrically.

électriser [elɛktri'ze], *v.t.* to electrify.

électro-aimant [elɛktroɛ'mɑ̃], *n.m.* (*pl.* **électro-aimants**) electro-magnet.

électrocuter [elɛktrɔky'te], *v.t.* to electrocute.

électrocution [elɛktrɔky'sjɔ̃], *n.f.* electrocution.

électron [elɛk'trɔ̃], *n.m.* electron.

électronique [elɛktrɔ'nik], *a.* electronic.

élégamment [elega'mɑ̃], *adv.* elegantly, stylishly.

élégance [ele'gɑ̃ːs], *n.f.* elegance, style.

élégant [ele'gɑ̃], *a.* elegant, smart, fashionable, stylish.—*n.m.* (*fem.* **-ée**) gentleman *or* lady of fashion.

élégiaque [ele'ʒjak], *a.* elegiac.—*n.* elegist.

élégie [ele'ʒi], *n.f.* elegy.

élément [ele'mɑ̃], *n.m.* element, component part.

élémentaire [elemɑ̃'tɛːr], *a.* elementary, elemental.

éléphant [ele'fɑ̃], *n.m.* elephant.

éléphantin [elefɑ̃'tɛ̃], *a.* elephantine.

élevage [el'vaːʒ], *n.m.* breeding, rearing (*of cattle*); stud.

élévateur [eleva'tœːr], *a.* (*fem.* **-trice**) raising, lifting.—*n.m.* elevator, lift, hoist.

élévation [eleva'sjɔ̃], *n.f.* elevation, raising; eminence, height; promotion; greatness (*of soul*); rise (*in prices etc.*).

élève [e'lɛːv], *n.* pupil; student, disciple; apprentice.

élevé [el've], *a.* raised, grand; reared; heroic, eminent; high (*of prices etc.*); exalted; *bien élevé*, well-bred; *mal élevé*, ill-bred.

élever [el've], *v.t.* (*conjug. like* AMENER) to raise, to lift up; to erect; to exalt; to run up (*accounts etc.*); to bring up, to rear; to educate; to foster. **s'élever**, *v.r.* to rise, to ascend, to go up; to be constructed; to increase; to break out.

éleveur [el'vœːr], *n.m.* (*fem.* **-euse**) raiser; cattle-breeder.—*n.f.* (**-euse**) incubator.

elfe [ɛlf], *n.m.* elf, brownie.

élider [eli'de], *v.t.* (*Gram.*) to cut off, to elide. **s'élider**, *v.r.* to be elided.

éligibilité [eliʒibili'te], *n.f.* eligibility.

éligible [eli'ʒibl̩], *a.* eligible.

élimer [eli'me], *v.t.* to wear out. **s'élimer**, *v.r.* to wear threadbare (*of clothes etc.*).

élimination [eliminɑ'sjɔ̃], *n.f.* elimination.

éliminatoire [elimina'twaːr], *a.* and *n.f.* (*Spt.*) eliminating (heat); disqualifying.

éliminer [elimi'ne], *v.t.* to eliminate; to expel; to remove.

élire [e'liːr], *v.t. irr.* (*conjug. like* LIRE) to elect, to choose; to return, to appoint.

élision [eli'zjɔ̃], *n.f.* elision.

élite [e'lit], *n.f.* choice, pick, select few, élite.

élixir [elik'siːr], *n.m.* elixir.

elle [ɛl], *pron.* (*pl.* **elles**) she, her, it; (*pl.*) they.

ellébore [ele'bɔːr], *n.m.* hellebore.

ellipse [ɛ'lips], *n.f.* ellipse; (*Gram.*) ellipsis.

elliptique [elip'tik], *a.* elliptical.

élocution [elɔky'sjɔ̃], *n.f.* elocution.

éloge [e'lɔːʒ], *n.m.* eulogy, praise; panegyric.

élogieux [elɔ'ʒjø], *a.* (*fem.* **-euse**) laudatory, eulogistic, flattering.

éloigné [elwa'ɲe], *a.* removed, distant, remote; absent.

éloignement [elwaɲ'mɑ̃], *n.m.* removal; remoteness; dislike; unwillingness.

éloigner [elwa'ɲe], *v.t.* to remove; to dismiss; to set aside, to repudiate; to waive; to banish; to put off; to alienate. **s'éloigner**, *v.r.* to go away, to withdraw; to digress; to deviate; to be alienated.

éloquemment [elɔka'mɑ̃], *adv.* eloquently.

éloquence [elɔ'kɑ̃ːs], *n.f.* eloquence, oratory.

éloquent [elɔ'kɑ̃], *a.* eloquent.

élu [e'ly], *a.* elected, chosen, elect; appointed. —*n.m.* (*fem.* **-e**) elected *or* chosen person.

élucidation [elysidɑ'sjɔ̃], *n.f.* elucidation.

élucider [elysi'de], *v.t.* to elucidate, to clear up.

éluder [ely'de], *v.t.* to elude, to evade.

Élysée [eli'ze], *n.m.* Elysium; *l'Élysée*, the residence (*in Paris*) of the President of the Republic.

émaciation [emasjɑ'sjɔ̃], *n.f.* emaciation.

émacié [ema'sje], *a.* emaciated.

émail

émail [e'maːj], *n.m.* (*pl.* émaux) enamel.
émaillage [ema'jaːʒ], *n.m.* enamelling.
émailler [ema'je], *v.t.* to enamel; (*fig.*) to adorn.
émailleur [ema'jœr], *n.m.* enameller.
émaillure [ema'jyːr], *n.f.* enamelling.
émanation [emana'sjɔ̃], *n.f.* emanation.
émancipation [emɑ̃sipa'sjɔ̃], *n.f.* emancipation.
émanciper [emɑ̃si'pe], *v.t.* to emancipate. s'émanciper, *v.r.* to gain one's liberty; to overstep the mark, to forget oneself.
émaner [ema'ne], *v.i.* to emanate.
émargement [emarʒə'mɑ̃], *n.m.* writing in the margin, marginal note; signature in the margin.
émarger [emar'ʒe], *v.t.* (*conjug. like* MANGER) to write *or* sign in the margin, *esp. on receipt*; *hence*, to draw one's salary.
embâcle [ɑ̃'baːkl], *n.m.* ice-pack (*in a river etc.*).
emballage [ɑ̃ba'laːʒ], *n.m.* packing up, packing; package; (*Spt.*) spurt.
emballement [ɑ̃bal'mɑ̃], *n.m.* excitement; flying into a temper; burst of enthusiasm.
emballer [ɑ̃ba'le], *v.t.* to pack up, to wrap up; (*colloq.*) to pack off; to arrest; to tell (*someone*) off. s'emballer, *v.r.* to bolt (*of a horse etc.*); to wrap oneself up; to be carried away (*by rage, enthusiasm etc.*), to race (*of an engine*).
emballeur [ɑ̃ba'lœr], *n.m.* packer.
embarbouiller [ɑ̃barbu'je], *v.t.* to besmear. s'embarbouiller, *v.r.* to get muddled.
embarcadère [ɑ̃barka'dɛːr], *n.m.* wharf, pier, landing-stage.
embarcation [ɑ̃barka'sjɔ̃], *n.f.* small boat, craft.
embardée [ɑ̃bar'de], *n.f.* lurch (*of a boat, a car etc.*); faire une embardée, to lurch (*of boat*); to swerve, to skid (*of car*).
embargo [ɑ̃bar'go], *n.m.* embargo.
embarquement [ɑ̃barkə'mɑ̃], *n.m.* embarkation, embarking; shipment.
embarquer [ɑ̃bar'ke], *v.t.* to embark, to take on board; to ship (*water etc.*). s'embarquer, *v.r.* to embark, to go on board; s'embarquer dans, (*fig.*) to embark upon.
embarras [ɑ̃ba'ra], *n.m.* encumbrance, hindrance; difficulty, fuss; (*pl.*) embarrassing circumstances; trouble, nervousness.
embarrassant [ɑ̃bara'sɑ̃], *a.* embarrassing, puzzling, awkward; troublesome.
embarrassé [ɑ̃bara'se], *a.* embarrassed, perplexed.
embarrasser [ɑ̃bara'se], *v.t.* to embarrass, to obstruct; to trouble, to confound, to puzzle. s'embarrasser, *v.r.* to entangle oneself; to be embarrassed; to concern oneself (*with*).
embâter [ɑ̃ba'te], *v.t.* to put a pack-saddle on, to saddle.
embauchage [ɑ̃bo'ʃaːʒ], *n.m.*, embauche [ɑ̃'boʃ], *n.f.* hiring, engaging (*of workmen*); enlisting, recruiting (*soldiers*).
embaucher [ɑ̃bo'ʃe], *v.t.* to hire, to engage, to sign on (*workmen*); to enlist (*soldiers*).
embaucheur [ɑ̃bo'ʃœr], *n.m.* (*fem.* -euse) hirer, recruiting officer.
embauchoir [ɑ̃bo'ʃwaːr], *n.m.* boot-tree, boot-last.

embaumement [ɑ̃bom'mɑ̃], *n.m.* embalming.
embaumer [ɑ̃bo'me], *v.t.* to embalm; to perfume.—*v.i.* to smell sweet.
embaumeur [ɑ̃bo'mœːr], *n.m.* embalmer.
embecquer [ɑ̃be'ke], *v.t.* to feed (*a bird*); to bait (*a hook*).
embéguiner [ɑ̃begi'ne], *v.t.* to muffle up. s'embéguiner, *v.r.* to wrap oneself up; (*fig.*) to be infatuated with.
embellir [ɑ̃be'liːr], *v.t.* to embellish, to beautify.—*v.i.* to grow more beautiful. s'embellir, *v.r.* to grow more beautiful; to enhance one's looks.
embellissement [ɑ̃belis'mɑ̃], *n.m.* embellishment; improvement.
embêtant [ɑ̃be'tɑ̃], *a.* (*colloq.*) boring, annoying.
embêtement [ɑ̃bet'mɑ̃], *n.m.* (*colloq.*) annoyance; nuisance, bore.
embêter [ɑ̃be'te], *v.t.* to bore; to annoy, to rile; to worry. s'embêter, *v.r.* to feel dull *or* bored.
emblée (d') [dɑ̃'ble], *adv.* at the first, at the first attempt, directly.
emblématique [ɑ̃blema'tik], *a.* emblematical.
emblème [ɑ̃'blɛːm], *n.m.* emblem.
emboîtage [ɑ̃bwa'taːʒ], *n.m.* boards, cover (*book*).
emboîtement [ɑ̃bwat'mɑ̃], *n.m.* fitting in, jointing, clamping.
emboîter [ɑ̃bwa'te], *v.t.* to fit in, to put (*a book*) into its boards; to clamp. s'emboîter, *v.r.* to fit, to fit in; (*fig.*) to model oneself upon.
emboîture [ɑ̃bwa'tyːr], *n.f.* socket, clamp.
embolie [ɑ̃bɔ'li], *n.f.* (*Path.*) embolism.
embonpoint [ɑ̃bɔ̃'pwɛ̃], *n.m.* plumpness, stoutness, obesity.
emboucher [ɑ̃bu'ʃe], *v.t.* to put to one's mouth, to sound (*wind-instruments*); to bit (*a horse*).
embouchure [ɑ̃bu'ʃyːr], *n.f.* mouth (*of a river, harbour etc.*); mouth-piece (*of wind-instruments*); opening (*of a receptacle*).
embourber [ɑ̃bur'be], *v.t.* to put in the mire; (*fig.*) to implicate in a dirty affair. s'embourber, *v.r.* to stick in the mire, to get bogged down; (*fig.*) to be involved (*in some trouble*); to put one's foot in it.
embourser [ɑ̃bur'se], *v.t.* to receive, to pocket (*affronts etc.*).
embout [ɑ̃'bu], *n.m.* ferrule.
embouteillage [ɑ̃bute'jaːʒ], *n.m.* bottling; traffic-jam.
embouteiller [ɑ̃bute'je], *v.t.* to bottle; to bottle up; to block up.
emboutir [ɑ̃bu'tiːr], *v.t.* to beat out (*coppersmith's work etc.*); to scoop out, to stamp; (*fam.*) to bump into. s'emboutir, *v.r.* to crash, to cannon into.
embranchement [ɑ̃brɑ̃ʃ'mɑ̃], *n.m.* branching off; branch-road, branch-line etc.; junction.
embrancher [ɑ̃brɑ̃'ʃe], *v.t.* to put together, to join up (*roads, railways, pipes etc.*). s'embrancher, *v.r.* to join (*of a minor road or line joining a major one*).
embrasement [ɑ̃braz'mɑ̃], *n.m.* conflagration; illumination.

130

embraser [ãbrɑ'ze], v.t. to fire, to set on fire; (fig.) to inflame; to illuminate. s'embraser, v.r. to kindle, to catch fire; to glow.

embrassade [ãbrɑ'sad], n.f. embrace, hug; kissing, kiss.

embrasse [ã'bras], n.f. curtain-loop.

embrassement [ãbras'mã], n.m. embrace, embracing.

embrasser [ãbra'se], v.t. to embrace, to clasp; to kiss; (fig.) to encircle; to comprise. s'embrasser, v.r. to embrace or kiss one another; to be included.

embrassure [ãbras'syːr], n.f. band of iron.

embrasure [ãbrɑ'zyːr], n.f. embrasure, recess.

embrayage [ãbrɛ'jaːʒ], n.m. (Motor.) coupling-gear, clutch.

embrayer [ãbrɛ'je], v.t. (conjug. like PAYER) to connect up, to throw into gear.—v.i. to let in the clutch.

embrèvement [ãbrɛv'mã], n.m. (Carp.) mortise.

embrocation [ãbrɔkɑ'sjõ], n.f. embrocation.

embrocher [ãbrɔ'ʃe], v.t. to put on the spit.

embrouillement [ãbruj'mã], n.m. embroilment, entanglement, perplexity.

embrouiller [ãbru'je], v.t. to embroil, to confuse; to perplex; to obscure. s'embrouiller, v.r. to become intricate or entangled; to get confused or muddled.

embrouilleur [ãbru'jœːr], n.m. (fem. -euse) muddler, blunderer.

embrumer (s') [sãbry'me], v.r. to be covered with fog etc; to become misty or hazy; (fig.) to grow sombre or gloomy.

embrun [ã'brœ̃], n.m. (usu. pl.) spray, spindrift.

embrunir [ãbry'niːr], v.t. to brown.

embryon [ãbri'jõ], n.m. embryo; germ; (fig.) dwarf, shrimp.

embryonnaire [ãbrijɔ'nɛːr], a. embryonic, in embryo.

embûche [ã'byʃ], n.f. ambush, snare.

embuscade [ãbys'kad], n.f. ambuscade, ambush.

embusqué [ãbys'ke], n.m. (Mil. slang) shirker, scrimshanker.

embusquer [ãbys'ke], v.t. to place in ambuscade, to post. s'embusquer, v.r. to lie in wait.

émender [emã'de], v.t. (Law) to amend, to correct.

émeraude [em'roːd], n.f. emerald.

émergence [emɛr'ʒãːs], n.f. emergence, emersion.

émergent [emɛr'ʒã], a. emergent.

émerger [emɛr'ʒe], v.i. (conjug. like MANGER) to emerge, to rise out.

émeri [em'ri], n.m. emery.

émerillon [emri'jõ], n.m. (Orn.) merlin.

émeriser [emri'ze], v.t. to cover with emery; papier émerisé, emery-paper.

émérite [eme'rit], a. emeritus; practised, perfect; eminent.

émersion [emɛr'sjõ], n.f. emersion.

émerveillement [emɛrvɛj'mã], n.m. wonder, astonishment.

émerveiller [emɛrvɛ'je], v.t. to astonish, to amaze. s'émerveiller, v.r. to marvel, to be astonished.

émétique [eme'tik], a. and n.m. emetic.

émetteur [emɛ'tœːr], a. (fem. -trice)

(Rad., Tel.) poste émetteur or station émettrice, broadcasting station.—n.m. transmitter; émetteur-récepteur, transmitter-receiver, (fam.) walkie-talkie.

émettre [e'mɛtr], v.t. irr. (conjug. like METTRE) to emit, to give out; to utter, to express; (Rad., Tel.) to broadcast.

émeu [e'mø], n.m. (Orn.) emu.

émeute [e'møːt], n.f. riot, disturbance, tumult, rising; chef d'émeute, ringleader.

émeuter [emø'te], v.t. to rouse, to stir up, to excite.

émeutier [emø'tje], n.m. (fem. -ière) rioter.

émiettement [emjɛt'mã], n.m. crumbling.

émietter [emjɛ'te], v.t. to crumble. s'émietter, v.r. to crumble.

émigrant [emi'grã], a. emigrating.—n.m. (fem. -e) emigrant.

émigration [emigrɑ'sjõ], n.f. emigration, migration.

émigré [emi'gre], n.m. (fem. -ée) emigrant; refugee.

émigrer [emi'gre], v.i. to emigrate; to migrate.

émincé [emɛ̃'se], n.m. (Cook.) thin slices (of meat).

émincer [emɛ̃'se], v.t. (conjug. like COMMENCER) to slice (meat).

éminemment [emina'mã], adv. eminently.

éminence [emi'nãːs], n.f. eminence, elevation, rising ground, height.

éminent [emi'nã], a. eminent, high, lofty.

émissaire [emi'sɛːr], n.m. emissary, messenger; bouc émissaire, scapegoat.

émission [emi'sjõ], n.f. emission; issue, uttering; broadcasting.

emmagasinage [ãmagazi'naːʒ], n.m. storage, warehousing.

emmagasiner [ãmagazi'ne], v.t. to warehouse, to store.

emmaillotement [ãmajɔt'mã], n.m. swaddling, swathing.

emmailloter [ãmajo'te], v.t. to swaddle, to swathe.

emmanchement [ãmãʃ'mã], n.m. hafting, helving (putting a handle on); (fig.) joining.

emmancher [ãmã'ʃe], v.t. to put a handle to, to haft, to helve. s'emmancher, v.r. to fit on a handle; (fig.) to start (of an affair).

emmanchure [ãmã'ʃyːr], n.f. armhole.

emmarchement [ãmarʃo'mã], n.m. tread (of stair).

emmêlement [ãmɛl'mã], n.m. tangle, muddle.

emmêler [ãmɛ'le], v.t. to entangle. s'emmêler, v.r. to get entangled.

emménagement [ãmena'ʒmã], n.m. moving into (a new house), installation.

emménager [ãmena'ʒe], v.t. (conjug. like MANGER) to move in; to fit out (a ship etc.).—v.i. and s'emménager, v.r. to move in.

emmener [ãm'ne], v.t. (conjug. like AMENER) to take away, to lead away, to fetch away, to convey away.

emmenotter [ãmnɔ'te], v.t. to handcuff.

emmeuler [ãmø'le], v.t. to stack (hay etc.).

emmiellé [ãmjɛ'le], a. honeyed, sweet.

emmieller [ãmjɛ'le], v.t. to honey, to sweeten with or as with honey.

emmitoufler [ãmitu'fle], v.t. to wrap up warmly.

émoi

émoi [e'mwa], *n.m.* emotion, anxiety, flutter.
émollient [emɔ'ljã], *a.* emollient, softening. —*n.m.* emollient.
émolument [emɔly'mã], *n.m.* emolument, fee; (*pl.*) salary.
émondage [emɔ̃'da:ʒ], *n.m.* pruning, lopping, trimming.
émonder [emɔ̃'de], *v.t.* to prune, to lop.
émondeur [emɔ̃'dœ:r], *n.m.* (*fem.* -euse) pruner, trimmer.
émotion [emo'sjɔ̃], *n.f.* emotion; stir, commotion.
émotter [emo'te], *v.t.* to break up (*soil, a field etc.*).
émoucher [emu'ʃe], *v.t.* to drive flies away from. s'émoucher, *v.r.* to whisk away the flies.
émouchet [emu'ʃɛ], *n.m.* sparrow-hawk.
émouchet [emu'ʃɛt], *n.f.* fly-net (*for horses etc.*).
émouchoir [emu'ʃwa:r], *n.m.* fly-whisk.
émoudre [e'mudr], *v.t. irr.* (*conjug. like* MOUDRE) to grind, to sharpen.
émouleur [emu'lœ:r], *n.m.* knifegrinder.
émoulu [emu'ly], *a.* sharpened, sharp.
émousser [emu'se], *v.t.* to blunt, to take the edge off; (*fig.*) to dull; to deaden. s'émousser, *v.r.* to get blunt; to become dull.
émoustiller [emusti'je], *v.t.* (*colloq.*) to exhilarate, to put into good spirits; (*fam.*) to ginger up. s'émoustiller, *v.r.* to bestir oneself.
émouvant [emu'vã], *a.* touching, moving, stirring.
émouvoir [emu'vwa:r], *v.t. irr.* (*conjug. like* MOUVOIR) to move, to affect; to excite, to rouse. s'émouvoir, *v.r.* to be roused *or* moved; to be agitated.
empaillage [ãpa'ja:ʒ], empaillement [ãpaj'mã], *n.m.* bottoming (*with straw*); stuffing (*of animals*).
empaillé [ãpa'je], *a.* stuffed; (*fam.*) avoir l'air empaillé, to be slow *or* dull-witted.
empailler [ãpa'je], *v.t.* to pack in [straw; to straw-bottom; to stuff (*birds etc.*).
empailleur [ãpa'jœ:r], *n.m.* (*fem.* -euse) chair-mender; bird- *or* animal-stuffer, taxidermist.
empaler [ãpa'le], *v.t.* to impale.
empanacher [ãpana'ʃe], *v.t.* to adorn with a plume; (*colloq.*) to touch up.
empaquetage [ãpak'ta:ʒ], *n.m.* packing.
empaqueter [ãpak'te], *v.t.* (*conjug. like* APPELER) to pack up, to make up into a bundle, to do up. s'empaqueter, *v.r.* to wrap oneself up.
emparer (s') [sãpa're], *v.r.* to possess oneself (*of*), to get hold (*of*); to seize, to secure.
empâtement [ãpat'mã], *n.m.* stickiness, clamminess.
empâter [ãpa'te], *v.t.* to make clammy *or* sticky; to cram (*fowls*).
empattement [ãpat'mã], *n.m.* footing, foundation, base; (*Motor. etc.*) wheel-base.
empaumer [ãpo'me], *v.t.* to catch *or* strike (*tennis-ball etc.*) in *or* with the palm of the hand; (*fig.*) to get hold of, to grasp, to take possession of.
empêchement [ãpɛʃ'mã], *n.m.* hindrance, obstacle, impediment, objection.
empêcher [ãpɛ'ʃe], *v.t.* to oppose, to prevent; to hinder. s'empêcher *v.r.* (*always in the*

negative) to forbear, to refrain from; *je ne peux m'empêcher de rire*, I cannot help laughing.
empeigne [ã'pɛɲ], *n.f.* upper (leather) (*of shoe*).
empenner [ãpɛ'ne], *v.t.* to feather (*arrows*); to fit on (*fins*).
empereur [ã'prœ:r], *n.m.* emperor.
empesage [ãpə'za:ʒ], *n.m.* starching.
empesé [ãpə'ze], *a.* starched; stiff (*of style etc.*), formal.
empeser [ãpə'ze], *v.t.* (*conjug. like* AMENER) to starch.
empester [ãpɛs'te], *v.t.* to infect, to taint; to cause to stink horribly; (*fig.*) to corrupt.
empêtrer [ãpɛ'tre], *v.t.* to entangle; to embarrass. s'empêtrer, *v.r.* to become entangled.
emphase [ã'fa:z], *n.f.* grandiloquence; emphasis, stress.
emphatique [ãfa'tik], *a.* bombastic, affected; emphatic.
empiècement [ãpjɛs'mã], *n.m.* yoke (*of blouse*).
empierrement [ãpjɛr'mã], *n.m.* stoning, metalling (*a road etc.*).
empierrer [ãpjɛ're], *v.t.* to stone, to metal (*roads etc.*).
empiétement [ãpjet'mã], *n.m.* encroaching, infringement.
empiéter [ãpje'te], *v.t.* (*conjug. like* CÉDER) to encroach upon, to invade, to trespass upon.—*v.i.* to encroach (*sur*).
empilement [ãpil'mã], *n.m.* piling, stacking.
empiler [ãpi'le], *v.t.* to pile up, to stack.
empire [ã'pi:r], *n.m.* empire, sovereignty, control, authority, dominion; (*fig.*) prestige, sway, mastery.
empirer [ãpi're], *v.t.* to make worse.—*v.i.* to grow worse.
empirique [ãpi'rik], *a.* empiric(al).
empirisme [ãpi'rism], *n.m.* empiricism.
emplacement [ãplas'mã], *n.m.* site, place, piece of ground.
emplâtre [ã'pla:tr], *n.m.* plaster, ointment; (*fig.*) palliative; (*colloq.*) helpless creature.
emplette [ã'plɛt], *n.f.* purchase; *faire des emplettes*, to go shopping.
emplir [ã'pli:r], *v.t.* to fill. s'emplir, *v.r.* to fill; to be filled.
emploi [ã'plwa], *n.m.* employ, employment; use, function; situation, post.
employé [ãplwa'je], *a.* employed.—*n.m.* (*fem.* -ée) employee, assistant, clerk.
employer [ãplwa'je], *v.t.* (*see Verb Tables*) to employ, to use; to give employment to; to spend, to invest. s'employer, *v.r.* to employ oneself, to exert *or* busy oneself; to use one's interest; to be used.
employeur [ãplwa'jœ:r], *n.m.* (*fem.* -euse) employer.
emplumer (s') [sãply'me], *v.r.* to become fledged.
empocher [ãpo'ʃe], *v.t.* to pocket.
empoignade [ãpo'ɲad, ãpwa'ɲad], *n.f.* (*colloq.*) dispute, row, set-to.
empoignant [ãpo'ɲã, ãpwa'ɲã], *a.* thrilling, poignant.
empoigner [ãpo'ɲe, ãpwa'ɲe], *v.t.* to grasp, to seize. s'empoigner, *v.r.* to lay hold of each other, to grapple.
empois [ã'pwɑ], *n.m.* starch.

empoisonné [ãpwazɔ'ne], *a.* poisoned; (*fig.*) poisonous.

empoisonner [ãpwazɔ'ne], *v.t.* to poison; (*fig.*) to infect; to corrupt; to embitter; (*slang*) to bore to death. **s'empoisonner**, *v.r.* to poison oneself.

empoisonneur [ãpwazɔ'nœːr], *a.* (*fem.* **-euse**) poisonous; (*fig.*) corrupting.—*n.m.* (*fem.* **-euse**) poisoner; (*fig.*) corrupter.

empoissonner [ãpwasɔ'ne], *v.t.* to stock with fish.

emporté [ãpɔr'te], *a.* fiery, passionate, hot-headed; runaway, unmanageable.

emportement [ãpɔrtə'mã], *n.m.* transport, fit of passion, outburst (*of anger, rage etc.*).

emporte-pièce [ãpɔrtə'pjɛs], *n.m.* punch (*instrument*), cutting-out machine; *c'est une réponse à l'emporte-pièce*, it is a very cutting answer.

emporter [ãpɔr'te], *v.t.* to carry away, to take away; to remove (*stains etc.*); to transport (*of emotion etc.*); to entail, to involve; to gain, to obtain. **s'emporter**, *v.r.* to fly into a passion, to flare up; to declaim (*contre*); to bolt (*of horses*).

empotage [ãpɔ'taːʒ], *n.m.* potting (*of plants*).

empoter [ãpɔ'te], *v.t.* to pot (*plants*).

empourpré [ãpur'pre], *a.* crimson.

empourprer [ãpur'pre], *v.t.* to colour red *or* purple. **s'empourprer**, *v.r.* to turn red *or* purple; to flush, to blush.

empreindre [ã'prɛ̃ːdr], *v.t. irr.* (*conjug. like* CRAINDRE) to imprint, to stamp, to impress. **s'empreindre**, *v.r.* to become tinged.

empreinte [ã'prɛ̃ːt], *n.f.* stamp, print, impression; mark; *empreintes digitales*, finger-prints.

empressé [ãprɛ'se], *a.* eager, earnest; assiduous.

empressement [ãprɛs'mã], *n.m.* alacrity, eagerness; haste, hurry.

empresser (s') [sãprɛ'se], *v.r.* to be eager (*to*); to crowd, to press.

emprisonnement [ãprizɔn'mã], *n.m.* imprisonment.

emprisonner [ãprizɔ'ne], *v.t.* to imprison, to confine.

emprunt [ã'prœ̃], *n.m.* borrowing; loan.

emprunter [ãprœ̃'te], *v.t.* to borrow; to assume.

emprunteur [ãprœ̃'tœːr], *a.* (*fem.* **-euse**) borrowing.—*n.m.* (*fem.* **-euse**) borrower.

empuantir [ãpɥã'tiːr], *v.t.* to give an ill smell to, to infect.

ému [e'my], *a.* moved, affected.

émulation [emyla'sjɔ̃], *n.f.* emulation, rivalry.

émule [e'myl], *n.* rival, competitor.

émulgent [emyl'ʒã], *a.* (*Physiol.*) emulgent.

émulsif [emyl'sif], *a.* (*fem.* **-sive**) emulsive.

émulsion [emyl'sjɔ̃], *n.f.* emulsion.

en (1) [ã], *prep.* in; to; within; into; at; like, in the form of, as; out of, by, through, from; for, on.

en (2) [ã], *pron. inv.* of him, of her, of it, its, of them, their; from him, by him, about him etc.; thence, from thence; some of it, any.

enamourer (s') [sãnamu're], *v.r.* to fall in love; to be enamoured (*de*).

encadrement [ãkadrə'mã], *n.m.* framing, frame; border; (*fig.*) environment.

encadrer [ãka'dre], *v.t.* to frame; to surround; to insert; (*Mil.*) to bracket (*target*);

to officer (*troops*). **s'encadrer**, *v.r.* to be inserted *or* enclosed.

encadreur [ãka'drœːr], *n.m.* (*fem.* **-euse**) picture-frame maker.

encager [ãka'ʒe], *v.t.* (*conjug. like* MANGER) to cage, to put in a cage.

encaissage [ãkɛ'saːʒ], *n.m.* encasing.

encaisse [ã'kɛs], *n.f.* cash in hand, cash-balance.

encaissé [ãkɛ'se], *a.* encased; sunk, hollow; steeply *or* deeply embanked.

encaissement [ãkɛs'mã], *n.m.* packing, putting in boxes etc.; embankment; paying in (*of money*).

encaisser [ãkɛ'se], *v.t.* to encase, to pack; to bank, pay in; to collect, to receive (*money*).

encaisseur [ãkɛ'sœːr], *n.m.* (*fem.* **-euse**) cashier.

encan [ã'kã], *n.m.* public auction.

encapuchonner (s') [sãkapyʃɔ'ne], *v.r.* to put on a cowl; to wrap one's head up; to arch the neck (*of horses*).

encarter [ãkar'te], *v.t.* to card-index.

en-cas [ã'ka], *n.m. inv.* anything kept for use in emergency; small umbrella; light meal prepared in case of need.

encastrement [ãkastrə'mã], *n.m.* fitting, fitting in.

encastrer [ãkas'tre], *v.t.* to fit in, to imbed.

encaustiquage [ãkosti'ka:ʒ], *n.m.* wax-polishing.

encavement [ãkav'mã], *n.m.* storing (*in cellar*), cellaring.

encaver [ãka've], *v.t.* to put *or* store in a cellar.

enceindre [ã'sɛ̃ːdr], *v.t. irr.* (*conjug. like* CRAINDRE) to surround, to enclose.

enceinte [ã'sɛ̃ːt], *n.f.* circuit, enclosure; (*Fort.*) enceinte. *a.* pregnant

encens [ã'sã], *n.m.* incense; (*fig.*) fragrance; flattery.

encensement [ãsãs'mã], *n.m.* incensing; (*fig.*) flattery.

encenser [ãsã'se], *v.t.* to incense; (*fig.*) to flatter.

encenseur [ãsã'sœːr], *n.m.* (*fem.* **-euse**) burner of incense; (*fig.*) flatterer.

encensoir [ãsã'swaːr], *n.m.* censer; (*fig.*) flattery.

encerclement [ãsɛrklə'mã], *n.m.* encircling; (*Polit.*) encirclement.

encercler [ãsɛr'kle], *v.t.* to encircle.

enchaînement [ãʃɛn'mã], *n.m.* chaining, linking; series, connexion.

enchaîner [ãʃɛ'ne], *v.t.* to chain up, to bind in chains; (*Cine.*) to fade in; (*fig.*) to restrain; to captivate; to link. **s'enchaîner**, *v.r.* to be connected *or* linked together.

enchanté [ãʃã'te], *a.* enchanted; (*fig.*) charmed, delighted.

enchantement [ãʃãt'mã], *n.m.* enchantment, magic; (*fig.*) charm, delight.

enchanter [ãʃã'te], *v.t.* to enchant; (*fig.*) to fascinate, to charm.

enchanteur [ãʃã'tœːr], *a.* (*fem.* **-eresse**) enchanting, entrancing, captivating.—*n.m.* (*fem.* **-eresse**) enchanter, enchantress, charmer.

enchâsser [ãʃã'se], *v.t.* to enchase; to enshrine; to insert.

enchâssure [ãʃã'syːr], *n.f.* setting, mount; insertion.

enchère [ã′ʃɛːr], *n.f.* bid (*at an auction*); auction.

enchérir [ãʃe′riːr], *v.t.* to bid for, to outbid; to raise (*prices etc.*).—*v.i.* to rise (*in price*); (*fig.*) to surpass, to outdo; to bid, to outbid (*sur*).

enchérissement [ãʃeris′mã], *n.m.* rise, increase.

enchérisseur [ãʃeri′sœːr], *n.m.* bidder (*at an auction*).

enchevêtrement [ãʃvɛtrə′mã], *n.m.* entanglement.

enchevêtrer [ãʃve′tre], *v.t.* to halter (*a horse etc.*); to entangle. **s'enchevêtrer,** *v.r.* to get entangled, confused *or* embarrassed.

enclave [ã′klaːv], *n.f.* enclave, piece of enclosed land.

enclaver [ãkla′ve], *v.t.* to enclose, to hem in.

enclenchement [ãklãʃ′mã], *n.m.* throwing into gear; automatic clutch.

enclin [ã′klɛ̃], *a.* inclined; prone, addicted, apt, given to.

enclore [ã′klɔːr], *v.t. irr.* (*conjug. like* CLORE) to enclose, to fence in, to take in, to shut in.

enclos [ã′klo], *n.m.* enclosure, close; paddock; fencing, wall.

enclume [ã′klym], *n.f.* anvil.

encoche [ã′kɔʃ], *n.f.* notch.

encoffrer [ãkɔ′fre], *v.t.* to shut in a coffer; (*fig.*) to cage.

encoignure [ãkɔ′ɲyːr], *n.f.* corner, angle (*of a street*); corner-piece; corner-cupboard.

encollage [ãkɔ′laːʒ], *n.m.* sizing, gluing; glue, size.

encoller [ãkɔ′le], *v.t.* to size, to glue.

encolure [ãkɔ′lyːr], *n.f.* neck and shoulders (*of a horse*); neck-line (*of a garment*); size (*of collars*); (*fig.*) appearance (*of a person*).

encombrant [ãkɔ̃′brã], *a.* cumbersome.

encombre [ã′kɔ̃:br], *n.m.* (*now only used after* **sans**) impediment, hindrance.

encombrement [ãkɔ̃brə′mã], *n.m.* obstruction; crowding, congestion (*of traffic*).

encombrer [ãkɔ̃′bre], *v.t.* to obstruct; to crowd, to throng.

encontre (à l' . . . de) [alã′kɔ̃:trdə], *prep. phr.* against, counter to.

encore [ã′kɔːr], *adv.* yet, still, as yet; anew, again, once more; further, moreover, besides; even, but, only.

encorner [ãkɔr′ne], *v.t.* to gore, to toss.

encourageant [ãkura′ʒã], *a.* encouraging, cheering.

encouragement [ãkuraʒ′mã], *n.m.* encouragement.

encourager [ãkura′ʒe], *v.t.* (*conjug. like* MANGER) to encourage, to stimulate. **s'encourager,** *v.r.* to encourage each other, to take courage.

encourir [ãku′riːr], *v.t. irr.* (*conjug. like* COURIR) to incur (*disgrace, reproach*), to fall under.

encrasser [ãkra′se], *v.t.* to make dirty, to foul. **s'encrasser,** *v.r.* to become dirty.

encre [ãːkr], *n.f.* ink.

encrier [ãkri′e], *n.m.* ink-stand, ink-pot.

encroûté [ãkru′te], *a.* covered with a crust; (*fig.*) full of prejudices.—*n.m.* (*fem.* **-ée**) 'Blimp'.

encroûter (s') [sãkru′te], *v.r.* to crust, to get hard; to become dull, stupid *or* hide-bound.

encuvage [ãky′va:ʒ], **encuvement** [ãkyv′mã], *n.m.* tubbing.

encuver [ãky′ve], *v.t.* to put into a vat, to tub.

encyclopédie [ãsiklɔpe′di], *n.f.* encyclopaedia.

endémique [ãde′mik], *a.* endemic.

endenté [ãdã′te], *a.* indented.

endenter [ãdã′te], *v.t.* to cog, to tooth.

endetter [ãdɛ′te], *v.t.* to get (*a person*) into debt. **s'endetter,** *v.r.* to run into debt.

endeuiller [ãdœ′je], *v.t.* to put into mourning; to sadden.

endiablé [ãdja′ble], *a.* possessed; (*fig.*) devilish.

endiabler [ãdja′ble], *v.i.* to be furious; *faire endiabler,* to torment.

endiguement [ãdig′mã], *n.m.* damming up.

endiguer [ãdi′ge], *v.t.* to dam up, to embank.

endimancher (s') [sãdimã′ʃe], *v.r.* to put on one's Sunday best.

endive [ã′diːv], *n.f.* (*broad-leaved*) chicory.

endoctrinement [ãdɔktrin′mã], *n.m.* indoctrination.

endoctriner [ãdɔktri′ne], *v.t.* to indoctrinate.

endolorir [ãdɔlɔ′riːr], *v.t.* to make sore; to make (*the heart etc.*) ache. **s'endolorir,** *v.r.* to become sore.

endolorissement [ãdɔlɔris′mã], *n.m.* pain, soreness.

endommagement [ãdɔmaʒ′mã], *n.m.* loss, injury, damage.

endommager [ãdɔma′ʒe], *v.t.* (*conjug. like* MANGER) to damage, to injure.

endormeur [ãdɔr′mœːr], *n.m.* (*fem.* **-euse**) cajoler, flatterer; bore.

endormi [ãdɔr′mi], *a.* asleep; sleepy; benumbed.—*n.m.* (*fem.* **-e**) sleepy-head.

endormir [ãdɔr′miːr], *v.t. irr.* (*conjug. like* SENTIR) to send to sleep, to rock to sleep; to anaesthetize; to wheedle, to deceive; to benumb; to bore. **s'endormir,** *v.r.* to fall asleep.

endos [ã′do], **endossement** [ãdɔs′mã], *n.m.* endorsement.

endosser [ãdɔ′se], *v.t.* to put on one's back, to put on; to saddle oneself with (*an obligation etc.*); to endorse.

endroit [ã′drwa], *n.m.* place, spot; point; right side (*of a material*); part, passage (*of a book etc.*).

enduire [ã′dɥiːr], *v.t. irr.* (*conjug. like* CONDUIRE) to do over, to coat, to smear.

enduit [ã′dɥi], *n.m.* coating, layer, plaster, glaze, varnish, polish.

endurance [ãdy′rãːs], *n.f.* endurance, fortitude; *épreuve d'endurance,* endurance *or* reliability test.

endurant [ãdy′rã], *a.* patient, tolerant.

endurci [ãdyr′si], *a.* hardened; inured, callous.

endurcir [ãdyr′siːr], *v.t.* to harden, to toughen, to inure; to render callous. **s'endurcir,** *v.r.* to harden, to grow hard; to become callous.

endurcissement [ãdyrsis′mã], *n.m.* hardening, obduracy; callousness.

endurer [ãdy′re], *v.t.* to endure, to bear; to put up with.

énergie [enɛr′ʒi], *n.f.* energy, strength, vigour, power.

énergique [enɛr′ʒik], *a.* energetic, vigorous.

énergiquement [enɛrʒik'mɑ̃], *adv.* energetically, vigorously.

énervant [enɛr'vɑ̃], *a.* enervating; debilitating, nerve-racking.

énervé [enɛr've], *a.* nerveless; nervy, fidgety.

énervement [enɛrv'mɑ̃], *n.m.* nervous tension.

énerver [enɛr've], *v.t.* to enervate, to debilitate; to weaken; to unnerve; (*fam.*) to get on the nerves. **s'énerver**, *v.r.* to become enervated, unnerved, irritable *or* fidgety.

enfance [ɑ̃'fɑ̃:s], *n.f.* infancy, childhood; childishness.

enfant [ɑ̃'fɑ̃], *n.* child; infant, baby; descendant; citizen, native.

enfantement [ɑ̃fɑ̃t'mɑ̃], *n.m.* childbirth.

enfanter [ɑ̃fɑ̃'te], *v.t.* to bring forth, to bear; (*fig.*) to beget, to give birth to.

enfantillage [ɑ̃fɑ̃ti'ja:ʒ], *n.m.* child's-play, childishness.

enfantin [ɑ̃fɑ̃'tɛ̃], *a.* infantile, childish.

enfariner [ɑ̃fari'ne], *v.t.* to flour, to sprinkle with flour.

enfer [ɑ̃'fɛ:r], *n.m.* hell; (*fig.*) torment, misery.

enfermer [ɑ̃fɛr'me], *v.t.* to shut in *or* up; to lock up; to enclose; to conceal; to comprise. **s'enfermer**, *v.r.* to lock oneself in.

enficeler [ɑ̃fis'le], *v.t.* (*conjug. like* APPELER) to tie with string etc.

enfièvrement [ɑ̃fjɛvrə'mɑ̃], *n.m.* feverishness.

enfilade [ɑ̃fi'lad], *n.f.* suite (*of chambers etc.*); string (*of phrases etc.*); (*Mil.*) enfilade.

enfiler [ɑ̃fi'le], *v.t.* to thread (*a needle*); to string (*beads*); to pierce; to pass through; (*Mil.*) to enfilade; to slip on (*clothes*). **s'enfiler**, *v.r.* to be threaded; to be pierced; to get involved in.

enfin [ɑ̃'fɛ̃], *adv.* at last, finally, at length, after all, lastly; in short, in a word.

enflammé [ɑ̃flɑ'me], *a.* on fire, in flames, ignited.

enflammer [ɑ̃flɑ'me], *v.t.* to set on fire, to kindle; (*fig.*) to incense, to provoke. **s'enflammer**, *v.r.* to catch fire, to blaze; (*fig.*) to be incensed.

enflé [ɑ̃'fle], *a.* swollen, puffed up; (*fig.*) bombastic, high-flown (*style etc.*).

enfler [ɑ̃'fle], *v.t.* to swell out, to puff up, to distend; (*fig.*) to excite; to exaggerate. **s'enfler**, *v.r.* to swell; (*fig.*) to be puffed up.

enflure [ɑ̃'fly:r], *n.f.* bloatedness, swelling; bombast.

enfoncé [ɑ̃fɔ̃'se], *a.* broken open; sunken; (*pop.*) done for.

enfoncement [ɑ̃fɔ̃s'mɑ̃], *n.m.* breaking in; sinking; recess; (*Paint.*) background.

enfoncer [ɑ̃fɔ̃'se], *v.t.* (*conjug. like* COMMENCER) to push *or* drive in, down etc.; to sink; to break in; to get the better of.— *v.i.* to sink, to founder. **s'enfoncer**, *v.r.* to sink; to bury oneself; to plunge; (*fig.*) to fail.

enfonçure [ɑ̃fɔ̃'sy:r], *n.f.* cavity, hole, hollow.

enforcir [ɑ̃for'si:r], *v.t.* to strengthen.—*v.i.* and **s'enforcir**, *v.r.* to gather strength; to grow stronger.

enfouir [ɑ̃'fwi:r], *v.t.* to put *or* bury in the ground; (*fig.*) to hide. **s'enfouir**, *v.r.* to bury oneself (*in an out-of-the-way place etc.*).

enfourcher [ɑ̃fur'ʃe], *v.t.* to bestride, to straddle; to pierce with a pitch-fork etc.

enfourchure [ɑ̃fur'ʃy:r], *n.f.* fork; crotch.

enfourner [ɑ̃fur'ne], *v.t.* to put in the oven. **s'enfourner**, *v.r.* to get into a blind alley, a scrape etc.

enfreindre [ɑ̃'frɛ̃:dr], *v.t. irr.* (*conjug. like* CRAINDRE) to infringe, to break, to violate.

enfuir (s') [sɑ̃'fɥi:r], *v.r. irr.* (*conjug. like* FUIR) to run away, to escape.

enfumer [ɑ̃fy'me], *v.t.* to smoke, to fill with smoke, to smoke (*vermin etc.*) out.

enfûtage [ɑ̃fy'ta:ʒ], *n.m.* casking.

enfutailler [ɑ̃fyta'je], **enfuter** [ɑ̃fy'te], *v.t.* to cask, to barrel, to tun (*wine etc.*).

engagé [ɑ̃ga'ʒe], *a.* pledged; engaged, enlisted; in action; (*Naut.*) water-logged.

engageant [ɑ̃ga'ʒɑ̃], *a.* engaging, winning.

engagement [ɑ̃gaʒ'mɑ̃], *n.m.* engagement, commitment; pledging; mortgage; appointment; (*Mil.*) enlisting; action; entry (*for a sporting event*); (*pl.*) liabilities.

engager [ɑ̃ga'ʒe], *v.t.* (*conjug. like* MANGER) to pledge, to pawn; to engage; to begin; to invite, to induce, to urge; to involve. **s'engager**, *v.r.* to engage oneself, to undertake, to promise; to stand security; to begin; to enter; to enlist; to get involved.

engeance [ɑ̃'ʒɑ̃:s], *n.f.* breed; brood (*esp. of poultry*).

engelure [ɑ̃ʒ'ly:r], *n.f.* chilblain.

engendrer [ɑ̃ʒɑ̃'dre], *v.t.* to beget, to engender; (*fig.*) to produce.

engin [ɑ̃'ʒɛ̃], *n.m.* machine, engine; snare; tool; *engin téléguidé*, guided missile.

englober [ɑ̃glɔ'be], *v.t.* to unite, to put together; (*fig.*) to include, to embrace.

engloutir [ɑ̃glu'ti:r], *v.t.* to swallow, to devour. **s'engloutir**, *v.r.* to be swallowed up.

engloutissement [ɑ̃glutis'mɑ̃], *n.m.* engulfing, swallowing up.

engoncé [ɑ̃gɔ̃'se], *a. avoir l'air engoncé*, to look awkward and stiff.

engorgement [ɑ̃gɔrʒə'mɑ̃], *n.m.* obstruction, stopping up (*of a pipe etc.*); (*Med.*) congestion; (*Econ.*) glut.

engorger [ɑ̃gɔr'ʒe], *v.t.* (*conjug. like* MANGER) to obstruct, to block. **s'engorger**, *v.r.* to be obstructed *or* choked up.

engouement *or* **engoûment** [ɑ̃gu'mɑ̃], *n.m.* (*Med.*) choking, obstruction; (*fig.*) infatuation.

engouer [ɑ̃'gwe], *v.t.* to obstruct (*the throat etc.*); (*fig.*) to infatuate. **s'engouer**, *v.r.* to half choke oneself; (*fig.*) to be infatuated.

engouffrer [ɑ̃gu'fre], *v.t.* to engulf; (*fig.*) to swallow up. **s'engouffrer**, *v.r.* to be engulfed; to be swallowed up; to blow hard (*of the wind*).

engourdi [ɑ̃gur'di], *a.* torpid; benumbed.

engourdir [ɑ̃gur'di:r], *v.t.* to benumb; to dull, to enervate. **s'engourdir**, *v.r.* to get benumbed; to become sluggish.

engourdissement [ɑ̃gurdis'mɑ̃], *n.m.* numbness; torpor, enervation.

engrais [ɑ̃'grɛ], *n.m.* manure, fertilizer; fattening (*cattle*).

engraissant [ɑ̃grɛ'sɑ̃], *a.* fattening.

engraissement [ɑ̃grɛs'mɑ̃], *n.m.* fattening.

engraisser [ɑ̃grɛ'se], *v.t.* to fatten; to manure; (*fig.*) to enrich.—*v.i.* to grow fat; (*fig.*) to thrive. **s'engraisser**, *v.r.* to grow fat *or* stout.

engrenage [ãgrə'naːʒ], *n.m.* gear, gearing etc.; action of these; (*fig.*) correlation (*of circumstances etc.*).

engrener (1) [ãgrə'ne], *v.t.* (*conjug. like* AMENER) to put corn into (*the mill-hopper*); to feed with corn.

engrener (2) [ãgrə'ne], *v.t.* (*conjug. like* AMENER) (*Mach.*) to throw into gear. **s'engrener**, *v.r.* to work into each other (*of toothed wheels*); to be put in gear.

engrenure [ãgrə'nyːr], *n.f.* engagement of teeth, cogs etc.

engrumeler (s') [sãgrym'le], *v.r.* (*conjug. like* APPELER) to clot, to coagulate.

enhardir [ãar'diːr], *v.t.* to embolden, to encourage. **s'enhardir**, *v.r.* to grow bold.

enherber [ãnɛr'be], *v.t.* to put land under grass.

énigmatique [enigma'tik], *a.* enigmatical.

énigmatiquement [enigmatik'mã], *adv.* enigmatically.

énigme [e'nigm], *n.f.* enigma, riddle.

enivrant [ãni'vrã], *a.* intoxicating.

enivrement [ãnivrə'mã], *n.m.* intoxication; (*fig.*) elation.

enivrer [ãni'vre], *v.t.* to intoxicate, to inebriate; (*fig.*) to elate. **s'enivrer**, *v.r.* to get intoxicated; (*fig.*) to be elated.

enjambée [ãʒã'be], *n.f.* stride.

enjambement [ãʒãb'mã], *n.m.* (*Pros.*) run-on line, enjambment.

enjamber [ãʒã'be], *v.t.* to skip *or* leap over; to stride; (*fig.*) to encroach upon; (*Pros.*) to make enjambment.

enjeu [ã'ʒø], *n.m.* (*pl.* **-eux**) stake (*gaming and fig.*).

enjoindre [ã'ʒwɛːdr], *v.t. irr.* (*conjug. like* CRAINDRE) to enjoin, to charge, to direct, to prescribe.

enjôlement [ãʒol'mã], *n.m.* wheedling, coaxing, cajoling.

enjôler [ãʒo'le], *v.t.* to coax, to wheedle.

enjôleur [ãʒo'lœːr], *n.m.* (*fem.* **-euse**) wheedler, coaxer.

enjolivement [ãʒoliv'mã], *n.m.* embellishment, decoration, ornament.

enjoliver [ãʒoli've], *v.t.* to embellish, to set off.

enjoliveur [ãʒoli'vœːr], *n.m.* (*fem.* **-euse**) embellisher.

enjolivure [ãʒoli'vyːr], *n.f.* (small) embellishment.

enjoué [ã'ʒwe], *a.* playful, sprightly, lively, jovial, sportive.

enjouement or **enjoûment** [ãʒu'mã], *n.m.* playfulness, sportiveness, sprightliness.

enlacement [ãlas'mã], *n.m.* lacing, interlacing, entwining.

enlacer [ãla'se], *v.t.* (*conjug. kile* COMMENCER) to lace; to entwine; to clasp. **s'enlacer**, *v.r.* to entwine, to be interlaced.

enlaidir [ãlɛ'diːr], *v.t.* to make ugly; to disfigure.—*v.i.* to grow ugly, to be disfigured.

enlaidissement [ãlɛdis'mã], *n.m.* disfigurement.

enlèvement [ãlɛv'mã], *n.m.* carrying off; removal; wiping off; kidnapping.

enlever [ãlə've], *v.t.* (*conjug. like* AMENER) to remove, to take off; to carry off; to kidnap; to wipe off; to charm. **s'enlever**, *v.r.* to rise, to be lifted; to come off, to peel off; to come

out; to be snapped up (*of goods on sale*); to get into a passion.

enlève-taches [ãlɛv'taʃ], *n.m. inv.* stain remover.

enliasser [ãlja'se], *v.t.* to tie up in a bundle.

enlignement [ãliɲ'mã], *n.m.* alignment.

enligner [ãli'ne], *v.t.* to put in line.

enlisement [ãliz'mã], *n.m.* sinking, swallowing up (*in quicksand*).

enliser [ãli'ze], *v.t.* to engulf. **s'enliser**, *v.r.* to be engulfed *or* swallowed up.

enluminer [ãlymi'ne], *v.t.* to colour; to illuminate. **s'enluminer**, *v.r.* to rouge, to paint; to flush.

enlumineur [ãlymi'nœːr], *n.m.* (*fem.* **-euse**) colourer of maps, prints etc.

enluminure [ãlymi'nyːr], *n.f.* colouring; coloured print; tinsel (*of style*).

enneigé [ãnɛ'ʒe], *a.* snow-covered.

ennemi [ɛn'mi], *a.* hostile; injurious.—*n.m.* (*fem.* **-e**) enemy, foe.

ennoblir [ãno'bliːr], *v.t.* to dignify, to exalt. **s'ennoblir**, *v.r.* to be ennobled *or* exalted.

ennoblissement [ãnoblis'mã], *n.m.* ennoblement, exaltation.

ennui [ã'nɥi], *n.m.* trouble, worry; nuisance; boredom.

ennuyer [ãnɥi'je], *v.t.* (*conjug. like* EMPLOYER) to bore, to weary; to pester; (*fig.*) to annoy. **s'ennuyer**, *v.r.* to be bored, to feel dull; to miss.

ennuyeusement [ãnɥijøz'mã], *adv.* tediously, irksomely.

ennuyeux [ãnɥi'jø], *a.* (*fem.* **-euse**) boring, tedious, dull, tiresome; annoying.—*n.m.* (*fem.* **-euse**) tiresome person, bore.

énoncé [enõ'se], *n.m.* statement.

énoncer [enõ'se], *v.t.* (*conjug. like* COMMENCER) to state, to express, to enunciate. **s'énoncer**, *v.r.* to be worded *or* expressed.

éconciatif [enõsja'tif], *a.* (*fem.* **-tive**) enunciative.

énonciation [enõsjɑ'sjõ], *n.f.* enunciation, delivery; statement; wording.

enorgueillir [ãnorgœ'jiːr], *v.t.* to make proud, to elate. **s'enorgueillir**, *v.r.* to be *or* grow proud of, to be elated, to glory in (*de*).

énorme [e'nɔrm], *a.* enormous, huge.

énormément [enɔrme'mã], *adv.* enormously, beyond measure.

énormité [enɔrmi'te], *n.f.* hugeness, vastness; enormity.

enquérir (s') [sãke'riːr], *v.r. irr.* (*conjug. like* ACQUÉRIR) to inquire, to make inquiries.

enquête [ã'kɛːt], *n.f.* inquiry, investigation; inquest.

enquêter [ãkɛ'te], *v.i.* to inquire into a matter (*sur*), to conduct an inquiry.

enquêteur [ãkɛ'tœːr], *n.m.* (*fem.* **-euse**) investigator.

enraciner [ãrasi'ne], *v.t.* to root; (*fig.*) to implant. **s'enraciner**, *v.r.* to take root.

enragé [ãra'ʒe], *a.* mad, rabid; (*fig.*) enthusiastic.—*n.m.* (*fem.* **-ée**) madman, mad woman; desperate person.

enrageant [ãra'ʒã], *a.* maddening, vexing.

enrager [ãra'ʒe], *v.i.* (*conjug. like* MANGER) to be mad, to go mad; to be enraged, to fume.

enrayage [ãrɛ'jaːʒ], *n.m.* (*Mil.*) jam (*in rifle*).

enrayement or **enraiement** [ãrɛj'mã], *n.m.* skidding, locking.

enrayer (1) [ãrɛ'je], *v.t.* (*conjug. like* PAYER) to put spokes to (*a wheel*); to skid (*a wheel*), to apply brakes to; (*fig.*) to check, to slow up (*an attack*); to stem (*an epidemic*); to jam (*a machine-gun*).

enrayer (2) [ãrɛ'je], *v.t.* (*conjug. like* PAYER) (*Agric.*) to plough the first furrow in.

enrayure (1) [ãrɛ'jyːr], *n.f.* drag, skid, lock-chain.

enrayure (2) [ãrɛ'jyːr], *n.m.* (*Agric.*) first furrow.

enrégimenter [ãreʒimã'te], *v.t.* to form into regiments; (*fig.*) to enrol.

enregistrement [ãrəʒistrə'mã], *n.m.* registration, recording; booking (*of luggage*).

enregistrer [ãrəʒis'tre], *v.t.* to register, to record; to book (*luggage*).

enregistreur [ãrəʒis'trœːr], *n.m.* registrar; recording machine.

enrêner [ãrɛ'ne], *v.t.* to rein in; to tie up by the reins.

enrhumer [ãry'me], *v.t.* to give a cold to (*someone*). **s'enrhumer**, *v.r.* to catch a cold.

enrichi [ãri'ʃi], *n.m.* (*fem.* **-e**) upstart, parvenu, new rich.

enrichir [ãri'ʃiːr], *v.t.* to enrich; (*fig.*) to embellish. **s'enrichir**, *v.r.* to enrich oneself, to thrive.

enrichissement [ãriʃis'mã], *n.m.* enrichment; (*fig.*) embellishment.

enrôlement [ãrol'mã], *n.m.* enrolment; (*Mil.*) enlistment.

enrôler [ãro'le], *v.t.* to enlist; to enrol. **s'enrôler**, *v.r.* to enrol oneself, to enlist.

enroué [ã'rwe], *a.* hoarse, husky.

enrouement [ãru'mã], *n.m.* hoarseness, huskiness.

enrouer [ã'rwe], *v.t.* to make hoarse. **s'enrouer**, *v.r.* to become hoarse *or* husky.

enroulement [ãrul'mã], *n.m.* rolling up; (*Arch.*) scroll.

enrouler [ãru'le], *v.t.* to roll up, to coil. **s'enrouler**, *v.r.* to roll oneself up; to twine (*of plants etc.*).

enrubanner [ãryba'ne], *v.t.* to deck out with ribbons. **s'enrubanner**, *v.r.* to beribbon oneself.

ensablement [ãsablə'mã], *n.m.* sand-bank; ballasting; stranding (*of a ship*).

ensabler [ãsa'ble], *v.t.* to ballast; to run aground, to strand. **s'ensabler**, *v.r.* to run aground; to sink in sand; to silt up.

ensacher [ãsa'ʃe], *v.t.* to put in bags *or* sacks.

ensanglanter [ãsãglã'te], *v.t.* to make bloody, to stain with blood.

enseignant [ãsɛ'ɲã], *a.* teaching.—*n.m.* (*pl.*) teachers.

enseigne [ã'sɛɲ], *n.f.* sign, signboard; mark, token; ensign, flag.—*n.m.* (*Navy*) sub-lieutenant; (*U.S.*) ensign.

enseignement [ãsɛɲ'mã], *n.m.* teaching, education; teaching profession.

enseigner [ãsɛ'ɲe], *v.t.* to teach, to instruct; to inform, to direct.

ensemble [ã'sãːbl], *adv.* together, at the same time.—*n.m.* whole, general effect, mass; two- *or* three-piece (*clothing*); suite (*furniture*); (*Math.*) set.

ensemencement [ãsmãs'mã], *n.m.* sowing.

ensemencer [ãsmã'se], *v.t.* (*conjug. like* COMMENCER) to sow.

enserrer [ãsɛ're], *v.t.* to enclose; to lock up; to hem in.

ensevelir [ãsə'vliːr], *v.t.* to shroud; (*fig.*) to bury; to swallow up, to entomb; to absorb. **s'ensevelir**, *v.r.* to bury oneself.

ensevelissement [ãsəvlis'mã], *n.m.* putting in a shroud; burial.

ensoleillé [ãsɔlɛ'je], *a.* sunny.

ensoleiller [ãsɔlɛ'je], *v.t.* to light up with sunshine; (*fig.*) to brighten.

ensommeillé [ãsɔmɛ'je], *a.* heavy with sleep; (*fig.*) torpid.

ensorceler [ãsɔrsə'le], *v.t.* (*conjug. like* APPELER) to bewitch.

ensorceleur [ãsɔrsə'lœːr], *a.* (*fem.* **-euse**) bewitching.—*n.m.* (*fem.* **-euse**) enchanter, enchantress.

ensorcellement [ãsɔrsɛl'mã], *n.m.* bewitchment.

ensuite [ã'sɥit], *adv.* after, afterwards, then, in the next place; what then? what next? well!

ensuivre (s') [sã'sɥiːvr], *v.r. irr.* (*conjug. like* SUIVRE) to follow, to result, to ensue.

entacher [ãta'ʃe], *v.t.* to sully; to taint, to cast a slur on.

entaille [ã'taːj], *n.f.* notch; cut; gash; groove.

entailler [ãta'je], *v.t.* to notch, to cut.

entamer [ãta'me], *v.t.* to make the first cut in; to make an incision in; to broach; to break into.

entartrer (s') [sãtar'tre], *v.r.* to scale, to become furred.

entassement [ãtas'mã], *n.m.* accumulation; heap, pile; crowding together.

entasser [ãta'se], *v.t.* to heap *or* pile up, to accumulate; to hoard up; to pack together. **s'entasser**, *v.r.* to heap up; to crowd together.

entendement [ãtãd'mã], *n.m.* understanding; judgment, sense.

entendre [ã'tãːdr], *v.t.* to hear; to understand; to know; to intend; to mean. **s'entendre**, *v.r.* to hear each other; to hear one's own voice; to be heard; to be understood; to understand one another; to act in concert; to come to terms (*avec*) to agree with; to be skilful in.

entendu [ãtã'dy], *a.* heard; understood; agreed; skilful.

enténébrer [ãtene'bre], *v.t.* (*conjug. like* CÉDER) to plunge *or* wrap in darkness.

entente [ã'tãːt], *n.f.* meaning; skill, judgment; understanding, agreement.

enter [ã'te], *v.t.* to graft upon, to engraft; to join.

entériner [ãteri'ne], *v.t.* to ratify, to confirm.

entérique [ãte'rik], *a.* enteric.

entérite [ãte'rit], *n.f.* enteritis.

enterrement [ãtɛr'mã], *n.m.* burial, interment, funeral.

enterrer [ãtɛ're], *v.t.* to bury, to inter; (*fig.*) to survive, to outlive; to end. **s'enterrer**, *v.r.* to bury oneself.

en-tête [ã'tɛːt], *n.m.* (*pl.* **-têtes**) heading, headline.

entêté [ãtɛ'te], *a.* stubborn, obstinate.—*n.m.* (*fem.* **-ée**) stubborn person.

entêtement [ătɛt'mă], *n.m.* stubbornness, obstinacy; infatuation.

entêter [ătɛ'te], *v.t.* to give a headache to; to make giddy, to intoxicate. **s'entêter,** *v.r.* to be stubborn, to persist (*in*); to be infatuated (*de*).

enthousiasme [ătu'zjasm], *n.m.* enthusiasm, rapture, ecstasy.

enthousiasmer [ătuzjas'me], *v.t.* to render enthusiastic, to enrapture. **s'enthousiasmer,** *v.r.* to be enthusiastic, to be in raptures (*de*).

enthousiaste [ătu'zjast], *a.* enthusiastic.—*n.* enthusiast.

entiché [ăti'ʃe], *a.* infatuated, keen on.

entichement [ătiʃ'mă], *n.m.* infatuation, addiction.

enticher [ăti'ʃe], *v.t.* to infatuate. **s'enticher,** *v.r.* to be infatuated with (*de*).

entier [ă'tje], *a.* (*fem.* **-ière**) entire, whole; total; positive.—*n.m.* entirety, totality; (*Arith.*) integral.

entièrement [ătjɛr'mă], *adv.* entirely, wholly.

entité [ăti'te], *n.f.* entity.

entonner (1) [ătɔ'ne], *v.t.* to tun, to put into casks.

entonner (2) [ătɔ'ne], *v.t.* to begin to sing, to strike up.

entonnoir [ătɔ'nwa:r], *n.m.* funnel; shell-hole.

entorse [ă'tɔrs], *n.f.* sprain; strain, twist.

entortillage [ătɔrti'ja:ʒ], **entortillement** [ătɔrtij'mă], *n.m.* entanglement; winding, coiling; abstruseness; subterfuge; equivocation.

entortiller [ătɔrti'je], *v.t.* to wrap, to roll round; to distort; to entangle. **s'entortiller,** *v.r.* to twist oneself round; to twine; to be obscure.

entour [ă'tuir], *n.m.* (*used only in pl. except in the adverbial expression* **à l'entour,** around) environs, adjacent parts.

entourage [ătu'ra:ʒ], *n.m.* frame; entourage, friends, relations, circle, attendants.

entourer [ătu're], *v.t.* to surround; to gather round.

entournure [ătur'ny:r], *n.f.* arm-hole.

entracte [ă'trakt], *n.m.* interval (*between acts*); interlude.

entraide [ă'trɛd], *n.f.* (*no pl.*) mutual aid.

entraider (s') or **entr'aider (s')** [sătrɛ'de], *v.r.* to help one another.

entrailles [ă'tra:j], *n.f. pl.* intestines, entrails, bowels; (*fig.*) feelings, tenderness, pity.

entrain [ă'trɛ̃], *n.m.* warmth, heartiness; spirit, animation, life, go.

entraînant [ătrɛ'nă], *a.* captivating, seductive.

entraînement [ătrɛn'mă], *n.m.* enthusiasm, rapture; impulse, temptation; (*Spt.*) coaching, training.

entraîner [ătrɛ'ne], *v.t.* to drag along; to carry away; to win over; to involve; to train.

entraîneur [ătrɛ'nœ:r], *n.m.* (*fem.* **-euse**) trainer (*esp. of horses*); pace-maker; coach (*of teams*).

entrant [ă'tră], *a.* ingoing, incoming.—*n.m.* (*fem.* **-e**) person going *or* coming in.

entr'apercevoir [ătrapɛrsə'vwa:r], *v.t. irr.* (*conjug. like* RECEVOIR) to catch a quick glimpse of.

entr'appeler (s') [sătra'ple], *v.r.* (*conjug. like* APPELER) to call one another.

entrave [ă'tra:v], *n.f.* clog, fetter, hobble; (*fig.*) hindrance, impediment.

entraver [ătra've], *v.t.* to shackle; to hinder, to thwart.

entre [ă:tr], *prep.* between, betwixt; among, amongst; into.

entrebâillé [ătrəba'je], *a.* ajar, half-open.

entrebâillement [ătrəbaj'mă], *n.m.* small opening, gap, chink.

entrebâiller [ătrəba'je], *v.t.* to half-open.

entrechat [ătrə'ʃa], *n.m.* caper in dancing, entrechat.

entrechoquement [ătrəʃɔk'mă], *n.m.* clash, collision, conflict.

entrechoquer (s') [sătrəʃɔ'ke], *v.r.* to knock, to run *or* dash against each other.

entre-clos [ătrə'klo], *a.* half-closed; half-drawn.

entr'éclos [ătrə'klo], *a.* half-opened (*flower*).

entrecôte [ătrə'ko:t], *n.f.* steak cut from between the ribs.

entrecoupé [ătrəku'pe], *a.* broken (*of words, speech etc.*).

entrecouper [ătrəku'pe], *v.t.* to intersect; to interrupt; to intersperse.

entrecroisement [ătrəkrwaz'mă], *n.m.* intersection, crossing.

entrecroiser [ătrəkrwa'ze], *v.t.* to intersect. **s'entrecroiser,** *v.r.* to cross one other, to intersect.

entre-deux [ătrə'dø], *n.m. inv.* partition; insertion (*of lace etc.*).

entrée [ă'tre], *n.f.* entry, entrance; mouth; reception; beginning; first course.

entrefaites [ătrə'fɛt], *n.f. pl.* interval, meantime; *sur ces entrefaites,* meanwhile.

entrefilet [ătrəfi'lɛ], *n.m.* (short) paragraph, note (*in a newspaper*).

entregent [ătrə'ʒă], *n.m.* tact, cleverness (*in dealing with people*).

entrelacement [ătrəlas'mă], *n.m.* interlacing, interweaving, intertwining.

entrelacer [ătrəla'se], *v.t.* (*conjug. like* COMMENCER) to interlace, to intertwine. **s'entrelacer,** *v.r.* to entwine, to twist round each other.

entrelardé [ătrəlar'de], *a.* interlarded, streaky.

entrelarder [ătrəlar'de], *v.t.* to lard.

entremêlement [ătrəmɛl'mă], *n.m.* intermixing, intermingling.

entremêler [ătrəmɛ'le], *v.t.* to intermingle, to intermix. **s'entremêler,** *v.r.* to intermingle, to meddle.

entremets [ătrə'mɛ], *n.m. inv.* side-dish, sweet.

entremetteur [ătrəmɛ'tœ:r], *n.m.* (*fem.* **-euse**) go-between, mediator.

entremettre (s') [sătrə'mɛtr], *v.r. irr.* (*conjug. like* METTRE) to interpose; to interfere, to meddle.

entremise [ătrə'mi:z], *n.f.* intervention, mediation.

entrepont [ătrə'põ], *n.m.* (*Naut.*) between decks; *passagers d'entrepont,* steerage passengers.

entreposer [ătrəpo'ze], *v.t.* to store, to warehouse; to put in bond.

entrepositaire [ătrəpozi'tɛ:r], *n.* bonder; depositor (*of goods*).

entrepôt [ătrə'po], *n.m.* bonded warehouse, store; mart, emporium, depot.

entreprenant [ătrəprə'nă], *a.* enterprising, adventurous; daring, bold.

entreprendre [ătrə'prã:dr], *v.t. irr. (conjug. like* PRENDRE) to undertake, to attempt; to contract for *or* to; to venture.—*v.i.* to encroach, to infringe (*sur*).

entrepreneur [ătrəprə'nœ:r], *n.m.* (*fem.* **-euse**) contractor; master-builder; *entrepreneur de pompes funèbres*, undertaker.

entreprise [ătrə'pri:z], *n.f.* enterprise, undertaking; concern, company.

entrer [ă'tre], *v.i. (with aux.* ÊTRE) to enter, to come *or* go in; to run into.

entre-rail [ătrə'rɑ:j], *n.m.* (*pl.* **-rails**) (*Rail.*) gauge.

entresol [ătrə'sɔl], *n.m.* mezzanine, entresol (*rooms between the ground floor and the first floor*).

entre-temps [ătrə'tã], *n.m. inv.* interval; *dans l'entre-temps*, meanwhile.—*adv.* meanwhile.

entretenir [ătrət'ni:r], *v.t. irr. (conjug. like* TENIR) to hold together, to keep up, to keep in good order; to maintain, to support; to entertain. **s'entretenir**, *v.r.* to be kept up, to be maintained; to subsist; to converse.

entretien [ătrə'tjɛ̃], *n.m.* maintenance, servicing (*of car etc.*); preservation; living, livelihood; conversation, interview, conference.

entrevoir [ătrə'vwa:r], *v.t. irr. (conjug. like* VOIR) to catch a glimpse of; to foresee confusedly.

entrevue [ătrə'vy], *n.f.* interview.

entr'ouvert [ătru'vɛ:r], *a.* partly open, ajar; gaping.

entr'ouvrir [ătru'vri:r], *v.t. irr. (conjug. like* OUVRIR) to open a little, to half-open. **s'entr'ouvrir**, *v.r.* to be ajar; to open up.

énumérateur [enymera'tœ:r], *n.m.* (*fem.* **-trice**) enumerator.

énumératif [enymera'tif], *a.* (*fem.* **-tive**) enumerative.

énumération [enymera'sjɔ̃], *n.f.* enumeration.

énumérer [enyme're], *v.t. (conjug. like* CÉDER) to enumerate, to count, to reckon.

envahir [ăva'i:r], *v.t.* to invade, to overrun; to encroach upon.

envahissant [ăvai'sã], *a.* invading, encroaching.

envahissement [ăvais'mã], *n.m.* invasion, overrunning; encroachment.

envahisseur [ăvai'sœ:r], *a.* (*fem.* **-euse**) invading, encroaching.—*n.m.* (*fem.* **-euse**) invader.

envaser [ăva'ze], *v.t.* to fill up *or* choke with silt. **s'envaser**, *v.r.* to stick fast in the mud; to silt up.

enveloppe [ă'vlɔp], *n.f.* wrapper, cover; envelope; exterior; (*Motor.*) outer cover.

enveloppement [ăvlɔp'mã], *n.m.* enveloping, wrapping up.

envelopper [ăvlɔ'pe], *v.t.* to envelop, to wrap up, to cover; to surround; to disguise. **s'envelopper**, *v.r.* to cover *or* wrap oneself up.

envenimement [ăvnim'mã], *n.m.* poisoning; aggravation (*of a quarrel*).

envenimer [ăvni'me], *v.t.* to poison; to inflame, to exasperate. **s'envenimer**, *v.r.* to be envenomed; to fester, to rankle.

envergure [ăver'gy:r], *n.f.* spread (*of sail*); spread, span (*of a bird's wings, of an aeroplane*).

envers [ă've:r], *prep.* towards, to (*in respect of*).—*n.m.* wrong side, reverse side, back; *à l'envers*, on the wrong side, inside out.

envi (à l') [ală'vi], *adv. phr.* emulously, vying with each other.

enviable [ă'vjabl], *a.* enviable, to be envied.

envie [ă'vi], *n.f.* envy; desire, longing; birthmark; *avoir envie de*, to have a mind to, to long for, to feel like.

envier [ă'vje], *v.t.* to envy; to long for; to grudge.

envieux [ă'vjø], *a. and n.m.* (*fem.* **-euse**) envious, jealous (person).

environ [ăvi'rɔ̃], *adv.* about, nearly, thereabouts.—*n.m.* (*pl.*) environs, vicinity, neighbourhood.

environnant [ăviro'nã], *a.* surrounding.

environner [ăviro'ne], *v.t.* to surround, to stand round, to encircle, to enclose.

envisager [ăviza'ʒe], *v.t. (conjug. like* MANGER) to look, to stare in the face, to face; to consider, to envisage.

envoi [ă'vwa], *n.m.* sending (*of thing sent*); packet, parcel, consignment, shipment; (*Pros.*) envoy.

envol [ă'vɔl], *n.m.* taking wing (*of birds*), taking off (*of aeroplanes*), start; *piste d'envol*, runway.

envolée [ăvɔ'le], *n.f.* flight; (*fig.*) élan.

envoler (s') [săvɔ'le], *v.r.* to fly away; to take off; (*fig.*) to be carried off (*by the wind etc.*); (*fig.*) to disappear.

envoûtement [ăvut'mã], *n.m.* spell, magical charm.

envoûter [ăvu'te], *v.t.* to cast a spell on (*someone*).

envoyé [ăvwa'je], *n.m.* (*fem.* **-ée**) envoy, delegate, messenger; *envoyé spécial (of a paper)*, special correspondent.

envoyer [ăvwa'je], *v.t. irr.* to send, to forward, to dispatch.

envoyeur [ăvwa'jœ:r], *n.m.* (*fem.* **-euse**) sender.

enzyme [ă'ʒim], *n.f.* enzyme.

éon [e'ɔ̃], *n.m.* aeon.

épagneul [epa'nœl], *n.m.* spaniel.

épais [e'pɛ], *a.* thick, dense; thickset; (*fig.*) dull, gross.—*adv.* thick, thickly.

épaisseur [epɛ'sœ:r], *n.f.* thickness, density; stoutness; dullness.

épaissir [epɛ'si:r], *v.t.* to thicken.—*v.i.* and **s'epaissir**, *v.r.* to become thick, to grow big; to become heavy.

épaississement [epɛsis'mã], *n.m.* thickening.

épanchement [epãʃ'mã], *n.m.* pouring out, discharge; (*fig.*) outpouring (*emotion etc.*).

épancher [epã'ʃe], *v.t.* to pour out, to shed; to discharge. **s'épancher**, *v.r.* to be discharged, to overflow; to open one's heart.

épanchoir [epã'ʃwa:r], *n.m.* outlet, overflow.

épandre [e'pã:dr], *v.t.* to scatter, to strew; to shed (*light etc.*). **s'épandre**, *v.r.* to spread; (*fig.*) to stretch (*of a sheet of water etc.*).

épanoui [epa'nwi], *a.* in full bloom; (*fig.*) beaming.

épanouir [epa'nwi:r], *v.t.* to cause to open *or* expand; (*fig.*) to gladden. **s'épanouir**, *v.r.* to blossom, to open (*of flowers*); to brighten up (*of the face etc.*).

épanouissement [epanwis'mã], *n.m.* blossoming, opening (*of flowers*); (*fig.*) brightness, glow.

épargnant [epar'nã], *a.* sparing, saving; parsimonious.—*n.m.* (*fem.* **-e**) small investor.

épargne [e'parɲ], *n.f.* saving, thrift; parsimony; *caisse d'épargne*, savings bank.

épargner [epar'ɲe], *v.t.* to save; to spare; to economize.

éparpillement [eparpij'mã], *n.m.* scattering, dispersion.

éparpiller [eparpi'je], *v.t.* to scatter, to spread, to disperse; to squander.

épars [e'paːr], *a.* scattered, dispersed, sparse; dishevelled (*of hair*).

épaté [epa'te], *a.* flat (*of noses*); (*fam.*) amazed.

épaule [e'poːl], *n.f.* shoulder.

épaulement [epol'mã], *n.m.* shoulder; (*Naut.*) bows; (*Fort.*) breast-work.

épauler [epo'le], *v.t.* to splay the shoulder (*a horse etc.*); to bring (*a rifle*) to the shoulder.

épaulette [epo'let], *n.f.* shoulder-strap; epaulet.

épave [e'paːv], *n.f.* wreck; flotsam, jetsam; waif.

épée [e'pe], *n.f.* sword; (*fig.*) brand, steel.

épeler [e'ple], *v.t.* (*conjug. like* APPELER) to spell.

épellation [epɛla'sjõ], *n.f.* spelling.

éperdu [epɛr'dy], *a.* distracted, bewildered.

éperdument [epɛrdy'mã], *adv.* madly, distractedly.

éperon [e'prõ], *n.m.* spur; (*Arch.*) buttress, starling (*of a bridge etc.*); (*Naut.*) prow.

éperonné [epro'ne], *a.* spurred.

éperonner [epro'ne], *v.t.* to spur; to urge forward.

éperonnière [epro'njɛːr], *n.f.* larkspur.

épervier [epɛr'vje], *n.m.* sparrow-hawk; cast-net.

épeuré [epø're], *a.* scared.

éphélide [efe'lid], *n.f.* sunburn; freckle.

éphémère [efe'mɛːr], *a.* ephemeral, short-lived.—*n.m.* ephemera, may-fly.

épi [e'pi], *n.m.* ear of corn; (*Rail.*) system of marshalling tracks.

épice [e'pis], *n.f.* spice.

épicé [epi'se], *a.* spiced; seasoned.

épicer [epi'se], *v.t.* (*conjug. like* COMMENCER) to spice.

épicerie [epi'sri], *n.f.* spices; grocery.

épicier [epi'sje], *n.m.* (*fem.* **-ière**) grocer.

épicurien [epiky'rjɛ̃], *a.* (*fem.* **-enne**) epicurean, voluptuous.—*n.m.* (*fem.* **-enne**) epicure.

épicurisme [epiky'rism], *n.m.* epicureanism, epicurism.

épidémie [epide'mi], *n.f.* epidemic.

épidémique [epide'mik], *a.* epidemic.

épiderme [epi'dɛrm], *n.m.* epidermis, cuticle.

épidermique [epidɛr'mik], *a.* epidermic, epidermal.

épier (1) [e'pje], *v.i.* to ear (*of grain*).

épier (2) [e'pje], *v.t.* to watch; to spy upon; to lie in wait for.

épieu [e'pjø], *n.m.* (*pl.* **-eux**) boar-spear, hunting-pole.

épigrammatique [epigrama'tik], *a.* epigrammatical.

épigrammatiste [epigrama'tist], *n.* epigrammatist.

épigramme [epi'gram], *n.f.* epigram.

épigraphe [epi'graf], *n.f.* epigraph.

épilation [epila'sjõ], *n.f.* depilation.

épilatoire [epila'twaːr], *a.* depilatory.

épilepsie [epilɛp'si], *n.f.* epilepsy.

épileptique [epilɛp'tik], *a.* and *n.* epileptic.

épiler [epi'le], *v.t.* to depilate. **s'épiler**, *v.r.* to pluck out one's hairs.

épileur [epi'lœːr], *n.m.* (*fem.* **-euse**) depilator (*person*).

épilogue [epi'lɔg], *n.m.* epilogue.

épiloguer [epilɔ'ge], *v.t.* to censure, to criticize.—*v.i.* to carp, to find fault.

épilogueur [epilɔ'gœːr], *a.* (*fem.* **-euse**) fault-finding.—*n.m.* (*fem.* **-euse**) critic, fault-finder, carper.

épiloir [epi'lwaːr], *n.m.* tweezers.

épinaie [epi'nɛ], *n.f.* brake, thorny thicket.

épinard [epi'naːr], *n.m.* spinach.

épine [e'pin], *n.f.* thorn, prickle; (*fig.*) obstacle, difficulty; (*Anat.*) spine.

épinette [epi'nɛt], *n.f.* *spinet; (*Bot.*) spruce.

épineux [epi'nø], *a.* (*fem.* **-euse**) thorny prickly; (*fig.*) irritable; ticklish, intricate.

épingle [e'pɛ̃gl], *n.f.* pin; scarf-pin, breast-pin.

épinglé [epɛ̃'gle], *a.* pinned; corded, terry.—*n.m.* terry velvet.

épingler [epɛ̃'gle], *v.t.* to pin.

épinglier [epɛ̃'glje], *n.m.* pin-tray; (*fem.* **-ière**) pin-maker.

épinière [epi'njɛːr], *a.* (*Anat.*) spinal.

Épiphanie [epifa'ni], *n.f.* Epiphany.

épique [e'pik], *a.* epic(al).

épiscopal [episkɔ'pal], *a.* (*m.pl.* **-aux**) episcopal.

épiscopalien [episkɔpa'ljɛ̃], *a.* and *n.m.* (*fem.* **-enne**) episcopalian.

épiscopat [episkɔ'pa], *n.m.* episcopate, episcopacy.

épisode [epi'zɔd], *n.m.* episode.

épistolaire [epistɔ'lɛːr], *a.* epistolary.

épitaphe [epi'taf], *n.f.* epitaph.

épithète [epi'tɛt], *n.f.* epithet.

épitomé [epitɔ'me], *n.m.* epitome, abridgment.

épître [e'piːtr], *n.f.* epistle, letter, missive.

éploré [eplɔ're], *a.* in tears, distressed.

épluchage [eply'ʃaːʒ], *n.m.* cleaning; picking; peeling.

éplucher [eply'ʃe], *v.t.* to pick; to clean; to peel; (*fig.*) to sift.

éplucheur [eply'ʃœːr], *n.m.* (*fem.* **-euse**) picker; fault-finder, hair-splitter.

épluchures [eply'ʃyːr], *n.f. pl.* parings, peelings.

épointé [epwɛ̃'te], *a.* blunt (*pencil, needle*).

épointement [epwɛ̃t'mã], *n.m.* bluntness.

épointer [epwɛ̃'te], *v.t.* to break the point off, to blunt. **s'épointer**, *v.r.* to have its point broken off.

éponge [e'põːʒ], *n.f.* sponge.

épongeage [epõ'ʒaːʒ], *n.m.* sponging.

éponger [epõ'ʒe], *v.t.* (*conjug. like* MANGER) to sponge.

épopée [epɔ'pe], *n.f.* epic.

époque [e'pɔk], *n.f.* epoch, period, era; time.

époumoner [epumɔ'ne], *v.t.* to tire the lungs of, to exhaust. **s'époumoner**, *v.r.* to tire one's lungs; (*fig.*) to shout oneself hoarse.

épouse [e'puːz], *n.f.* spouse, bride, wife.

épouser [epu'ze], *v.t.* to marry, to wed; (*fig.*) to take up. **s'épouser**, *v.r.* to marry (*each other*).

époussetage [epus'ta:ʒ], *n.m.* dusting.
épousseter [epus'te], *v.t.* (*conjug. like* AP-PELER) to dust.
époussette [epu'sɛt], *n.f.* dusting-brush, duster.
épouvantable [epuvɑ̃'tabl], *a.* frightful, dreadful, horrible, appalling.
épouvantablement [epuvɑ̃tablə'mɑ̃], *adv.* frightfully; dreadfully.
épouvantail [epuvɑ̃'ta:j], *n.m.* scarecrow; (*fig.*) bugbear.
épouvante [epu'vɑ̃:t], *n.f.* terror, fright; dismay.
épouvanter [epuvɑ̃'te], *v.t.* to terrify, to frighten. **s'épouvanter**, *v.r.* to be frightened *or* terrified.
époux [e'pu], *n.m.* husband, bridegroom; (*pl.*) married couple.
épreindre [e'prɛ̃:dr], *v.t. irr.* (*conjug. like* CRAINDRE) to squeeze out, to press.
éprendre (s') [se'prɑ̃:dr], *v.r. irr.* (*conjug. like* PRENDRE) to fall in love (*de*).
épreuve [e'prœ:v], *n.f.* proof, test; ordeal; examination; (*Print.*) proof-sheet; (*Phot.*) print.
épris [e'pri], *a.* in love, taken with.
éprouvé [epru've], *a.* tried, tested; stricken with misfortune.
éprouver [epru've], *v.t.* to try, to test; to put to the proof; (*fig.*) to feel, to experience.
éprouvette [epru'vɛt], *n.f.* gauge; test-tube; eprouvette (*for testing gunpowder*); (*Surg.*) probe.
épuisable [epɥi'zabl], *a.* exhaustible.
épuisement [epɥiz'mɑ̃], *n.m.* exhaustion, draining; enervation.
épuiser [epɥi'ze], *v.t.* to exhaust, to drain; to use up; to tire out, to wear out. **s'épuiser**, *v.r.* to be exhausted; to use up one's strength.
épuisette [epɥi'zɛt], *n.f.* landing-net; scoop.
épurateur [epyra'tœ:r], *a.* (*fem.* **-trice**) purifying.—*n.m.* purifier.
épuratif [epyra'tif], *a.* (*fem.* **-tive**) purifying, refining.
épuration [epyra'sjɔ̃], *n.f.* purification; refining; (*Polit.*) purge.
épuratoire [epyra'twa:r], *a.* purifying.
épurement [epyr'mɑ̃], *n.m.* purifying.
épurer [epy're], *v.t.* to purify, to clarify; to refine; to purge. **s'épurer**, *v.r.* to be purified, to become pure.
équanime [ekwa'nim], *a.* even-tempered.
équanimité [ekwanimi'te], *n.f.* equanimity.
équarrir [eka'ri:r], *v.t.* to square; to cut up (*a carcass*).
équarrissage [ekari'sa:ʒ], **équarrissement** [ekaris'mɑ̃], *n.m.* squaring; squareness; flaying and cutting up (*of horses etc.*).
équarrisseur [ekari'sœ:r], *n.m.* knacker.
Équateur [ekwa'tœ:r], **l'**, *m.* Ecuador.
équateur [ekwa'tœ:r], *n.m.* equator.
équation [ekwa'sjɔ̃], *n.f.* equation.
équatorial [ekwatɔ'rjal], *a.* (*m. pl.* **-aux**) equatorial.
équatorien [ekwatɔ'rjɛ̃], *a.* (*fem.* **-enne**) Ecuadorean.—*n.m.* (**Équatorien**, *fem.* **-enne**) Ecuadorean (*person*).
équerre [e'kɛ:r], *n.f.* square, set-square.
équerrer [eke're], *v.t.* to square, to bevel.
équestre [e'kɛstr], *a.* equestrian.

équilibre [eki'libr], *n.m.* equilibrium, poise, balance; (*Hist.*) balance of power.
équilibrer [ekili'bre], *v.t.* to equilibrate, to balance.
équilibriste [ekili'brist], *n.* tight-rope walker, acrobat.
équin [e'kɛ̃], *a.* equine; *pied équin*, club foot.
équinoxe [eki'nɔks], *n.m.* equinox.
équinoxial [ekinɔk'sjal], *a.* (*m. pl.* **-aux**) equinoctial.
équipage [eki'pa:ʒ], *n.m.* equipage; carriage; dress; gear, tackle; personnel, crew.
équipe [e'kip], *n.f.* train of boats; gang (*of workmen etc.*); team (*of sportsmen*).
équipement [ekip'mɑ̃], *n.m.* outfit, fitting out; equipment.
équiper [eki'pe], *v.t.* to equip, to fit out; to furnish; to man. **s'équiper**, *v.r.* to fit oneself out; to rig oneself out.
équitable [eki'tabl], *a.* equitable, just, fair.
équitablement [ekitablə'mɑ̃], *adv.* equitably, justly, fairly.
équitation [ekita'sjɔ̃], *n.f.* horsemanship, riding.
équité [eki'te], *n.f.* equity, fairness.
équivalence [ekiva'lɑ̃:s], *n.f.* equivalence.
équivalent [ekiva'lɑ̃], *a.* equivalent; tantamount (to).—*n.m.* equivalent.
équivaloir [ekiva'lwa:r], *v.i. irr.* (*conjug. like* VALOIR) to be equivalent, to be tantamount (*à*).
équivoque [eki'vɔk], *a.* equivocal, ambiguous; doubtful.—*n.f.* equivocation, ambiguity; evasion.
équivoquer [ekivɔ'ke], *v.t.* to equivocate, to speak ambiguously, to quibble.
érable [e'rabl], *n.m.* maple, maple-tree.
éradication [eradika'sjɔ̃], *n.f.* eradication.
érafler [era'fle], *v.t.* to scratch slightly, to graze.
éraflure [era'fly:r], *n.f.* slight scratch, graze.
éraillé [era'je], *a.* frayed; wrinkled; bloodshot (*of the eyes*); raucous, hoarse (*of the voice*).
éraillement [eraj'mɑ̃], *n.m.* eversion of the eyelids; fraying; huskiness.
érailler [era'je], *v.t.* to unravel; to fray. **s'érailler**, *v.r.* to fray; to become bloodshot (*of the eyes*); to become husky (*of the voice*).
éraillure [era'jy:r], *n.f.* fret, fraying; scratch.
ère [ɛ:r], *n.f.* era, epoch.
érection [erɛk'sjɔ̃], *n.f.* erection, erecting.
éreinter [erɛ̃'te], *v.t.* to break the back (*of*); to tire out; to beat unmercifully; (*fig.*) to slate, to lash (*satire etc.*). **s'éreinter**, *v.r.* to break one's back, to tire oneself out, to drudge.
érésipèle [ERYSIPÈLE].
ergot [ɛr'go], *n.m.* spur (*of certain birds etc.*); catch, stop (*of machine*).
ergotage [ɛrgɔ'ta:ʒ], **ergotement** [ɛrgɔt'mɑ̃], *n.m.*, **ergoterie** [ɛrgɔ'tri], *n.f.* cavilling, quibbling.
ergoter [ɛrgɔ'te], *v.i.* (*colloq.*) to cavil; to wrangle.
ergoteur [ɛrgɔ'tœ:r], *a.* (*fem.* **-euse**) cavilling.—*n.m.* (*fem.* **-euse**) caviller, quibbler.
ériger [eri'ʒe], *v.t.* (*conjug. like* MANGER) to erect, to raise, to rear; to set up; to exalt. **s'ériger**, *v.r.* to set up for, to pose (*en*); to be erected.
ermitage [ɛrmi'ta:ʒ], *n.m.* hermitage.

ermite

ermite [ɛrˈmit], *n.* hermit, recluse.
éroder [eroˈde], *v.t.* to erode.
érosif [eroˈzif], *a.* (*fem.* **-sive**) erosive.
érosion [eroˈzjɔ̃], *n.f.* erosion.
érotique [eroˈtik], *a.* erotic.
errant [ɛˈrɑ̃], *a.* wandering, roving, errant; erring; *chevalier errant*, knight-errant.
erratique [ɛraˈtik], *a.* erratic.
erre [ɛːr], *n.f.* course, way; (*pl.*) track (*of a stag etc.*).
errements [ɛrˈmɑ̃], *n.m.* (*used only in pl.*) manner, way; vagaries, follies.
errer [ɛˈre], *v.i.* to wander, to stray; to range to rove; to err, to go astray.
erreur [ɛˈrœːr], *n.f.* error, mistake.
erroné [ɛroˈne], *a.* erroneous, mistaken, false.
erronément [eroneˈmɑ̃], *adv.* erroneously.
érudit [eryˈdi], *a.* erudite, learned.—*n.m.* (*fem.* **-e**) scholar, learned person.
érudition [erydiˈsjɔ̃], *n.f.* erudition, scholarship.
éruptif [erypˈtif], *a.* (*fem.* **-tive**) eruptive.
éruption [erypˈsjɔ̃], *n.f.* eruption; cutting (*of teeth*); breaking out (*of a rash*).
érysipèle [eriziˈpɛl], **érésipèle** [ereziˈpɛl], *n.m.* erysipelas.
ès [ɛs], *contraction of* EN (I) LES (*survives only in a few set expressions*) in, of; *licencié ès lettres*, bachelor of arts.
escabeau [ɛskaˈbo], *n.m.* (*pl.* **-eaux**) stool; step-ladder.
escabelle [ɛskaˈbɛl], *n.f.* three-legged stool.
escadre [ɛsˈkaːdr], *n.f.* (*Naut.*) squadron; (*Av.*) wing.
escadrille [ɛskaˈdriːj], *n.f.* small squadron, flotilla.
escadron [ɛskaˈdrɔ̃], *n.m.* squadron (*of horse*).
escalade [ɛskaˈlad], *n.f.* scaling (*a wall*); rock-climbing; escalation (*of a war etc.*).
escalader [ɛskalaˈde], *v.t.* to scale, to climb over.
escale [ɛsˈkal], *n.f.* port of call, stopping-place.
escalier [ɛskaˈlje], *n.m.* staircase, stairs, steps; *escalier roulant*, escalator.
escalope [ɛskaˈlɔp], *n.f.* escalope, collop (*of veal*); steak (*of fish*).
escamotable [ɛskamoˈtabl], *a.* which can be tucked away; (*Av.*) *train escamotable*, retractable landing-gear.
escamotage [ɛskamoˈtaːʒ], *n.m.* juggling, sleight of hand; (*fig.*) filching.
escamoter [ɛskamoˈte], *v.t.* to conjure away; to pilfer, to make away with; (*Av.*) to retract (*the undercarriage*).
escamoteur [ɛskamoˈtœːr], *n.m.* (*fem.* **-euse**) juggler, conjurer; pilferer, pickpocket.
escapade [ɛskaˈpad], *n.f.* escapade, prank.
escarbille [ɛskarˈbiːj], *n.f.* cinder (*of coal*).
escarboucle [ɛskarˈbukl], *n.f.* carbuncle (*precious stone*).
escargot [ɛskarˈgo], *n.m.* snail (*edible*).
escarmouche [ɛskarˈmuʃ], *n.f.* skirmish; brush; (*fig.*) bickering.
escarmoucher [ɛskarmuˈʃe], *v.i.* to skirmish; (*fig.*) to bicker.
escarpé [ɛskarˈpe], *a.* scarped, steep, precipitous; (*fig.*) difficult.
escarpement [ɛskarpəˈmɑ̃], *n.m.* escarpment; steep face *or* slope.
escarpin [ɛskarˈpɛ̃], *n.m.* pump, dancing-shoe.

escarpolette [ɛskarpoˈlɛt], *n.f.* (*child's*) swing.
escarre or **eschare** [ɛsˈkaːr], *n.f.* scab.
escient [ɛˈsjɑ̃], *n.m.* used *only in à bon escient*, wittingly, knowingly.
esclaffer (s') [sɛsklaˈfe], *v.r.* to laugh noisily, to guffaw.
esclandre [ɛsˈklɑ̃ːdr], *n.m.* scandal, exposure, scene.
esclavage [ɛsklaˈvaːʒ], *n.m.* slavery; bondage.
esclave [ɛsˈklaːv], *a.* slavish.—*n.* slave, bondsman; drudge.
escogriffe [ɛskoˈgrif], *n.m.* (*colloq.*) tall, lanky, ungainly fellow.
escompte [ɛsˈkɔ̃ːt], *n.m.* discount, rebate.
escompter [ɛskɔ̃ˈte], *v.t.* to discount; (*fig.*) to anticipate; *escompter un billet*, to cash a bill.
escorte [ɛsˈkɔrt], *n.f.* escort; (*Navy*) convoy; (*fig.*) retinue, attendants.
escorter [ɛskɔrˈte], *v.t.* to escort, to accompany, to attend.
escorteur [ɛskɔrˈtœːr], *n.m.* escort vessel.
escouade [ɛsˈkwad], *n.f.* squad, small party (*of soldiers*); gang (*of workmen*).
escrime [ɛsˈkrim], *n.f.* fencing.
escrimer [ɛskriˈme], *v.i.* to fence; (*fig.*) to have a trial of skill etc. **s'escrimer**, *v.r.* (*colloq.*) to strive; to try hard.
escrimeur [ɛskriˈmœːr], *n.m.* (*fem.* **-euse**) fencer.
escroc [ɛsˈkro], *n.m.* sharper, swindler.
escroquer [ɛskroˈke], *v.t.* to swindle out of; to cheat.
escroquerie [ɛskroˈkri], *n.f.* swindling.
espace [ɛsˈpaːs], *n.m.* space, room; duration.—*n.f.* (*Print.*) space.
espacement [ɛspasˈmɑ̃], *n.m.* interval; (*Print.*) spacing.
espacer [ɛspaˈse], *v.t.* (*conjug. like* COMMENCER) to leave a space between; to separate. **s'espacer**, *v.r.* to become less frequent *or* numerous.
espadrille [ɛspaˈdriːj], *n.f.* canvas shoe with cord soles.
Espagne [ɛsˈpaɲ], **l'**, *f.* Spain.
espagnol [ɛspaˈɲɔl], *a.* Spanish.—*n.m.* Spanish (*language*); (**Espagnol**, *fem.* **-ole**) Spaniard.
espagnolette [ɛspaɲoˈlɛt], *n.f.* bolt of french window.
espalier [ɛspaˈlje], *n.m.* espalier (*tree or wall*).
espèce [ɛsˈpɛs], *n.f.* species; sort, nature; (*pl.*) ready money, hard cash.
espérance [ɛspeˈrɑ̃ːs], *n.f.* hope, trust, expectation.
espéranto [ɛsperɑ̃ˈto], *n.m.* Esperanto.
espérer [ɛspeˈre], *v.t.* (*conjug. like* CÉDER) to hope for; to expect; to trust.—*v.i.* to hope; to put one's trust in.
espiègle [ɛsˈpjɛgl], *a.* and *n.* mischievous, roguish (person).
espièglerie [ɛspjɛgləˈri], *n.f.* frolic, roguish trick, prank.
espion [ɛsˈpjɔ̃], *n.m.* (*fem.* **-onne**) spy.
espionnage [ɛspjoˈnaːʒ], *n.m.* espionage.
espionner [ɛspjoˈne], *v.t.* to spy, to pry into.
esplanade [ɛsplaˈnad], *n.f.* esplanade, parade.
espoir [ɛsˈpwaːr], *n.m.* hope.
esprit [ɛsˈpri], *n.m.* spirit, ghost; soul; mind, sense, intellect; wit; humour, character.
esquif [ɛsˈkif], *n.m.* small boat.
esquille [ɛsˈkiːj], *n.f.* splinter (*of a bone*).

esquimau [ɛski'mo], _a._ (_pl._ **-aux**) and _n._ (**Esquimau** or **Eskimo**) Eskimo.

esquinancie [eskinɑ̃'si], **cynancie** [sinɑ̃'si], _n.f._ quinsy.

esquisse [ɛs'kis], _n.f._ sketch, outline, rough draft _or_ plan.

esquisser [ɛski'se], _v.t._ to sketch, to outline.

esquiver [ɛski've], _v.t._ to avoid, to elude; to duck; to dodge. **s'esquiver**, _v.r._ to escape; to give the slip.

essai [ɛ'sɛ], _n.m._ trial; attempt; experiment, testing; (_Rugby_) try; (_Lit._) essay.

essaim [ɛ'sɛ̃], _n.m._ swarm; (_fig._) crowd, host.

essaimer [ɛsɛ'me], _v.i._ to swarm; to hive off.

essarter [ɛsar'te], _v.t._ to clear, to grub (_land_).

essayage [ɛsɛ'jaːʒ] _n.m._ trying, testing; trying-on (_of clothes_).

essayer [ɛsɛ'je], _v.t._ (_conjug. like_ PAYER) to try; to try on; to attempt; to assay.—_v.i._ to try, to make an attempt. **s'essayer**, _v.r._ to try one's strength or skill.

essayeur [ɛsɛ'jœːr], _n.m._ (_fem._ **-euse**) assayer; (_cloth_) fitter.

essayiste [ɛsɛ'jist], _n._ essayist.

essence [ɛ'sɑ̃ːs], _n.f._ essence; petrol; attar (_of roses_).

essentiel [ɛsɑ̃'sjɛl], _a._ (_fem._ **-elle**) essential, material.—_n.m._ essential, main point.

essentiellement [ɛsɑ̃sjɛl'mɑ̃], _adv._ essentially, absolutely, above all.

essieu [ɛ'sjø], _n.m._ (_pl._ **-eux**) axle-tree; spindle; pin (_of a block_); **écartement des essieux**, wheel base (_motor_); **essieu moteur**, driving-shaft.

essor [ɛ'sɔːr], _n.m._ flight, soaring; (_fig._) impulse, vigour.

essorer [ɛsɔ're], _v.t._ to hang in the air to dry, to wring out (_washing_).

essoreuse [ɛsɔ'røːz], _n.f._ wringer; _essoreuse_ (_rotative_), spin dryer.

essoriller [ɛsɔri'je], _v.t._ to cut the ears (_of a dog etc._); to crop.

essoufflement [ɛsuflə'mɑ̃], _n.m._ panting, breathlessness.

essouffler [ɛsu'fle], _v.t._ to wind (_horses etc._). **s'essouffler**, _v.r._ to be out of breath; to be winded.

essuie-glaces [ɛsɥi'glas], _n.m. pl._ windscreen wipers.

essuie-main(s) [ɛsɥi'mɛ̃], _n.m. inv._ hand-towel.

essuie-pieds [ɛsɥi'pje], _n.m. inv._ doormat.

essuyage [ɛsɥi'jaːʒ], _n.m._ wiping, drying.

essuyer [ɛsɥi'je], _v.t._ (_conjug. like_ EMPLOYER) to wipe; to dry; to sustain, to endure, to undergo. **s'essuyer**, _v.r._ to dry oneself; **s'essuyer les mains, la figure etc.**, to dry one's hands, one's face etc.

est [ɛst], _n.m._ east.

estacade [ɛsta'kad], _n.f._ breakwater; pier _or_ boom made of timbers.

estafette [ɛsta'fɛt], _n.f._ courier, express messenger; dispatch rider.

estafilade [ɛstafi'lad], _n.f._ cut, gash; rent.

estaminet [ɛstami'nɛ], _n.m._ coffee-house or room; tavern.

estampage [ɛstɑ̃'paːʒ], _n.m._ stamping (_of metal etc._).

estampe [ɛs'tɑ̃ːp], _n.f._ print, engraving.

estamper [ɛstɑ̃'pe], _v.t._ to stamp, to punch.

estampeur [ɛstɑ̃'pœːr], _a._ (_fem._ **-euse**) stamp-ing.—_n.m._ (_fem._ **-euse**) stamper.—_n.f._ (**-euse**) stamping-machine.

estampillage [ɛstɑ̃pi'jaːʒ], _n.m._ stamping, marking.

estampille [ɛstɑ̃'piːj], _n.f._ stamp, mark, trade-mark.

estampiller [ɛstɑ̃pi'je], _v.t._ to stamp, to mark.

esthétique [ɛste'tik], _a._ aesthetic.—_n.f._ aesthetics.

Esthonie [ɛstɔ'ni], l', _f._ Estonia.

esthonien [ɛstɔ'njɛ̃], _a._ (_fem._ **-enne**) Estonian.—_n.m._ Estonian (_language_); (**Esthonien,** _fem._ **-enne**) Estonian (_person_).

estimable [ɛsti'mabl], _a._ estimable.

estimateur [ɛstima'tœːr], _n.m._ (_fem._ **-trice**) appraiser, valuer.

estimation [ɛstimɑ'sjɔ̃], _n.f._ estimation, appraising, valuation, estimate.

estime [ɛs'tim], _n.f._ esteem, regard, estimation; (_Naut._) reckoning.

estimer [ɛsti'me], _v.t._ to estimate, to value, to assess; to esteem; to deem. **s'estimer**, _v.r._ to esteem oneself; to deem oneself.

estival [ɛsti'val], _a._ (_m. pl._ **-aux**) aestival, summer (_plant, resort etc._).

estivant [ɛsti'vɑ̃], _n.m._ (_fem._ **-e**) summer visitor.

estomac [ɛstɔ'ma], _n.m._ stomach; (_fig._) pluck.

estompe [ɛs'tɔ̃ːp], _n.f._ (_Drawing_) stump.

estomper [ɛstɔ̃'pe], _v.t._ (_Drawing_) to stump; to shade off, to blur. **s'estomper**, _v.r._ to become blurred.

Estonie [ESTHONIE].

estonien [ESTHONIEN].

estrade [ɛs'trad], _n.f._ platform, stand, stage.

estragon [ɛstra'gɔ̃], _n.m._ (_Bot._) tarragon.

estropié [ɛstrɔ'pje], _a._ crippled, lame, disabled.—_n.m._ (_fem._ **-ée**) cripple.

estropier [ɛstrɔ'pje], _v.t._ to cripple, to maim, to disable; (_fig._) to distort, to mangle.

estuaire [ɛs'tɥɛːr], _n.m._ estuary.

esturgeon [ɛstyr'ʒɔ̃], _n.m._ sturgeon.

et [e], _conj._ and.

étable [e'tabl], _n.f._ shed (_for oxen, sheep, goats etc._); stall; pigsty, sty.

établi [eta'bli], _n.m._ bench (_joiner's etc._).

établir [eta'bliːr], _v.t._ to fix, to erect, to set up; to establish, to found; to assert. **s'établir**, _v.r._ to establish oneself; to take up one's residence; to settle down; to set up in business.

établissement [etablis'mɑ̃], _n.m._ establishment, setting up; placing, erecting; proving; imposition (_of taxes_).

étage [e'taːʒ], _n.m._ storey, floor, flight (_of stairs_); (_fig._) stage; tier; (_Geol., Mining_) layer, stratum.

étager [eta'ʒe], _v.t._ (_conjug. like_ MANGER) to dispose in tiers. **s'étager**, _v.r._ to rise tier upon tier.

étagère [eta'ʒɛːr], _n.f._ whatnot, set of shelves, shelf.

étai [e'tɛ], _n.m._ stay, shore, prop, strut.

étaiement [ÉTAYAGE].

étain [e'tɛ̃], _n.m._ tin; pewter.

étal [e'tal], _n.m._ (_pl._ **-aux** or **-als**) butcher's stall, butcher's shop.

étalage [eta'laːʒ], _n.m._ laying out of goods for sale; goods exposed for sale; shop window, frontage; (_fig._) showing off.

143

étalager

étalager [etala'ʒe], *v.t.* (*conjug. like* MANGER) to display (*goods*) for sale.

étalagiste [etala'ʒist], *n.* stall-keeper; window-dresser.

étale [e'tal], *a.* slack (*of water or wind*).

étalement [etal'mɑ̃] *n.m.* display, parade; staggering (*of holidays*).

étaler [eta'le], *v.t.* to expose for sale; to spread out; to display; (*Naut.*) to stem (*current*); to weather (*gale*). **s'étaler,** *v.r.* to stretch oneself out, to sprawl; to show off.

étalon (1) [eta'lɔ̃], *n.m.* stallion.

étalon (2) [eta'lɔ̃], *n.m.* standard (*of weights and measures*).

étalonnage [etalɔ'naːʒ], **étalonnement** [etalɔn'mɑ̃], *n.m.* standardization; stamping (*of weights etc.*); gauging.

étalonner [etalɔ'ne], *v.t.* to standardize; to gauge.

étalonneur [etalɔ'nœːr], *n.m.* inspector of weights and measures.

étamage [eta'maːʒ], *n.m.* tinning; quick-silvering (*of glass*).

étamer [eta'me], *v.t.* to tin; to quicksilver.

étameur [eta'mœːr], *n.m.* tinner; silverer (*of mirrors*).

étamine (1) [eta'min], *n.f.* sieve, strainer; (*Naut.*) bunting.

étamine (2) [eta'min], *n.f.* (*Bot.*) stamen.

étampe [e'tɑ̃ːp], *n.f.* die; punch.

étamper [etɑ̃'pe], *v.t.* to punch (*horse-shoes etc.*); to stamp (*sheet metal etc.*).

étanche [e'tɑ̃ːʃ], *a.* water-tight, air-tight etc.

étanchement [etɑ̃ʃ'mɑ̃], *n.m.* stanching, stopping; slaking; quenching.

étancher [etɑ̃'ʃe], *v.t.* to stanch, to stop; to render water-tight; (*fig.*) to quench.

étang [e'tɑ̃], *n.m.* pond, mere, pool.

étape [e'tap], *n.f.* halting-place, stage, station; day's march.

état [e'ta], *n.m.* state, case, condition; circumstance, predicament; statement; list, estimate; profession.

étatique [eta'tik], *a.* nationalized.

étatiser [etati'ze], *v.t.* to nationalize.

étatisme [eta'tism], *n.m.* State-socialism, State control, nationalization.

état-major [etama'ʒɔːr], *n.m.* (*pl.* **états-majors**) (*Mil.*) staff, general staff.

étau [e'to], *n.m.* (*pl.* **-aux**) (*Tech.*) vice.

étayage [etɛ'jaːʒ], **étayement** [etɛj'mɑ̃], **étaiement** [etɛ'mɑ̃], *n.m.* staying, shoring, supporting.

étayer [etɛ'je], *v.t.* (*conjug. like* PAYER) to stay, to shore; to support (*a theory etc.*).

été [e'te], *n.m.* summer; (*C*) *Été des Sauvages,* Indian summer.

éteignoir [etɛ'ɲwaːr], *n.m.* extinguisher (*for candles*).

éteindre [e'tɛ̃ːdr], *v.t. irr.* (*conjug. like* CRAINDRE) to put out, to extinguish; to appease; to destroy. **s'éteindre,** *v.r.* to be extinguished, to be put out; to die out; to become extinct.

éteint [e'tɛ̃], *a.* extinguished; extinct; (*fig.*) dull.

étendard [etɑ̃'daːr], *n.m.* standard, banner, flag.

étendre [e'tɑ̃ːdr], *v.t.* to extend; to spread out; to stretch; to dilute; to prolong; to lay (down) (*a person*). **s'étendre,** *v.r.* to stretch oneself out; to reach, to extend; to dwell on.

étendu [etɑ̃'dy], *a.* outstretched, outspread; extensive; diluted.

étendue [etɑ̃'dy], *n.f.* extent; scope, length.

éternel [etɛr'nɛl], *a.* (*fem.* **-elle**) eternal, everlasting.—*n.m.* (**l'Eternel**) God, the Eternal.

éternellement [etɛrnɛl'mɑ̃], *adv.* eternally.

éterniser [etɛrni'ze], *v.t.* to perpetuate. **s'éterniser,** *v.r.* to be perpetuated, to last forever.

éternité [etɛrni'te], *n.f.* eternity.

éternuement or **éternûment** [etɛrny'mɑ̃], *n.m.* sneezing, sneeze.

éternuer [etɛr'nɥe], *v.i.* to sneeze.

éternueur [etɛr'nɥœːr], *n.m.* (*fem.* **-euse**) sneezer.

éteule [e'tœːl], *n.f.* stubble.

éther [e'tɛːr], *n.m.* ether.

éthéré [ete're], *a.* ethereal.

éthériser [eteri'ze], *v.t.* to etherize.

Éthiopie [etjo'pi], **l'**, *f.* Ethiopia.

éthiopien [etjo'pjɛ̃], *a.* (*fem.* **-enne**) Ethiopian.—*n.m.* (**Éthiopien,** *fem.* **-enne**) Ethiopian (*person*).

éthique [e'tik], *a.* ethic(al).—*n.f.* ethics, morals.

ethnique [ɛt'nik], *a.* ethnic(al).

ethnographe [ɛtnɔ'graf], *n.* ethnographer.

ethnographie [ɛtnɔgra'fi], *n.f.* ethnography.

ethnographique [ɛtnɔgra'fik], *a.* ethnographic.

ethnologie [ɛtnɔlɔ'ʒi], *n.f.* ethnology.

ethnologique [ɛtnɔlɔ'ʒik], *a.* ethnological.

ethnologue [ɛtnɔ'lɔg], **ethnologiste** [ɛtnɔlɔ'ʒist], *n.* ethnologist.

éthologie [etɔlɔ'ʒi], *n.f.* ethology.

éthyle [e'tiːl], *n.m.* ethyl.

étiage [e'tjaːʒ], *n.m.* low-water mark; (*fig.*) level.

Étienne [e'tjɛn], *m.* Stephen.

étincelant [etɛ̃s'lɑ̃], *a.* sparkling, glittering, glistening.

étinceler [etɛ̃s'le], *v.i.* (*conjug. like* APPELER) to sparkle, to flash, to gleam, to glitter.

étincelle [etɛ̃'sɛl], *n.f.* spark, flash; brilliance.

étincellement [etɛ̃sɛl'mɑ̃], *n.m.* sparkling, twinkling, scintillation.

étiolement [etjɔl'mɑ̃], *n.m.* etiolation, sickliness (*of plants etc.*); paleness, emaciation.

étioler [etjɔ'le], *v.t.* to etiolate (*plants*); (*fig.*) to enervate. **s'étioler,** *v.r.* to become etiolated (*of plants*); (*fig.*) to waste away.

étique [e'tik], *a.* consumptive; emaciated.

étiqueter [etik'te], *v.t.* (*conjug. like* APPELER) to label, to ticket.

étiquette [eti'kɛt], *n.f.* ticket, label, tag; etiquette.

étirage [eti'raːʒ], *n.m.* stretching.

étirer [eti're], *v.t.* to stretch; to lengthen. **s'étirer,** *v.r.* to stretch one's limbs.

étisie [eti'zi], *n.f.* consumption.

étoffe [e'tɔf], *n.f.* material; stuff, cloth; quality, worth; (*C*) *étoffe du pays,* homespun.

étoffé [etɔ'fe], *a.* stuffed full; upholstered; stout, substantial.

étoffer [etɔ'fe], *v.t.* to stuff; to upholster.

étoile [e'twal], *n.f.* star; (*fig.*) fate, destiny; blaze (*on horse's head*); star (*crack in glass*).

étoilé [etwa'le], *a.* starry; star-shaped.

étoiler [etwa'le], *v.t.* to star, to stud with stars; to crack (*of glass*). **s'étoiler,** *v.r.* to star, to crack (*of glass*).

étole [e'tal], *n.f.* stole.
étonnamment [etɔna'mã], *adv.* astonishingly, wonderfully, amazingly.
étonnant [etɔ'nã], *a.* astonishing, wonderful, marvellous.
étonnement [etɔn'mã], *n.m.* astonishment, amazement; wonder; crack, fissure.
étonner [etɔ'ne], *v.t.* to astonish, to amaze, to astound; to shock; to cause to crack. **s'étonner,** *v.r.* to be astonished, to wonder; to become cracked.
étouffant [etu'fã], *a.* suffocating, sultry, close.
étouffement [etuf'mã], *n.m.* suffocation.
étouffer [etu'fe], *v.t.* to suffocate, to choke, to smother; (*fig.*) to stifle, to hush up; to deaden (*sound etc.*).—*v.i.* to choke, to suffocate. **s'étouffer,** *v.r.* to be choking, to be suffocated; to swelter.
étoupe [e'tup], *n.f.* tow, oakum.
étouper [etu'pe], *v.t.* to stop (*with tow or oakum*]; to caulk.
étoupiller [etupi'je], *v.t.* to prime (*a friction tube*).
étourderie [eturdə'ri], *n.f.* heedlessness, thoughtlessness; blunder.
étourdi [etur'di], *a.* giddy, thoughtless, heedless.—*n.m.* (*fem.* -e) madcap.
étourdiment [eturdi'mã], *adv.* heedlessly, thoughtlessly.
étourdir [etur'di:r], *v.t.* to stun, to deafen, to make giddy; to din; to astound. **s'étourdir,** *v.r.* to divert one's thoughts; to try to forget something.
étourdissant [eturdi'sã], *a.* deafening; stunning, astounding.
étourdissement [eturdis'mã], *n.m.* dizziness, giddiness; stupefaction; shock.
étourneau [etur'no], *n.m.* (*pl.* -eaux) starling; (*fig.*) giddyfellow.
étrange [e'trã:ʒ], *a.* strange, odd, queer.
étrangement [etrãʒ'mã], *adv.* strangely, queerly, extraordinarily.
étranger [etrã'ʒe], *a.* (*fem.* -ère) foreign; strange; unknown; irrelevant.—*n.m.* (*fem.* -ère) foreigner, alien; stranger; *a l'etranger,* abroad.
étrangeté [etrãʒ'te], *n.f.* strangeness, oddness.
étranglé [etrã'gle], *a.* strangled; restricted, scanty, too narrow.
étranglement [etrãglə'mã], *n.m.* strangling; garotting; constriction.
étrangler [etrã'gle], *v.t.* to strangle, to choke, to stifle; to constrict, to confine; (*fig.*) to smother, to suppress.—*v.i.* to be choked, to be short of breath. **s'étrangler,** *v.r.* to strangle oneself; to choke.
étrangleur [etrã'glœ:r], *n.m.* (*fem.* -euse) strangler; garotter.
être [ɛ:tr], *v.i. irr.* to be, to exist; to belong (*à*); to stand; to take part (*à*); to be a member (*de*).—*n.m.* being, existence; creature.
étreindre [e'trɛ̃:dr], *v.t. irr.* (*conjug. like* CRAINDRE) to embrace, to clasp, to grip.
étreinte [e'trɛ̃:t], *n.f.* embrace, hug; grip.
étrenne [e'trɛn], *n.f.* New Year's gift (*usually in pl.*); gift, present.
étrenner [etrɛ'ne], *v.t.* to give a New Year's gift; to handsel; to try *or* put on for the first time; to buy the first lot from.
étrier [etri'e], *n.m.* stirrup; (*Surg.*) caliper.
étrille [e'tri:j], *n.f.* curry-comb.

étriller [etri'je], *v.t.* to curry, to comb (*a horse*); (*fig.*) to fleece; to drub.
étriper [etri'pe], *v.t.* to gut (*an animal*).
étriqué [etri'ke], *a.* scanty, narrow, curtailed.
étriquer [etri'ke], *v.t.* to shorten, to curtail, to make too small.
étrivière [etri'vjɛ:r], *n.f.* stirrup-leather.
étroit [e'trwa], *a.* narrow, tight, strait; limited; (*fig.*) strict, rigorous.
étroitement [etrwat'mã], *adv.* narrowly, tightly; intimately, closely.
étroitesse [etrwa'tɛs], *n.f.* narrowness, straitness; tightness, closeness.
Étrurie [etry'ri], l', *f.* Etruria.
étrusque [e'trysk], *a.* Etruscan.—*n.m.* Etruscan (*language*).—*n.* (**Étrusque**) Etruscan (*person*).
étude [e'tyd], *n.f.* study; room for study; time of preparation; office, practice (*of attorneys*); essay, article.
étudiant [ety'djã], *n.m.* (*fem.* -e) student; undergraduate.
étudié [ety'dje], *a.* studied; affected.
étudier [ety'dje], *v.t.* to study, to learn; to practise (*music*); to rehearse (*a play*); to observe.—*v.i.* to study, to learn; to practise (*music*). **s'étudier,** *v.r.* to make (*it*) one's study, to school oneself.
étui [e'tɥi], *n.m.* case, box, sheath.
étuve [e'ty:v], *n.f.* sweating-room; stove; drying room; incubator.
étuvée [ety've], *n.f.* stew.
étuver [ety've], *v.t.* to stew; (*Med.*) to bathe, to foment.
étymologie [etimɔlɔ'ʒi], *n.f.* etymology.
étymologique [etimɔlɔ'ʒik], *a.* etymological.
étymologiste [etimɔlɔ'ʒist], *n.* etymologist.
eucharistie [økaris'ti], *n.f.* eucharist.
eucharistique [økaris'tik], *a.* eucharistic.
eugénique [øʒe'nik], *n.f.*, **eugénisme** [øʒe'nism], *n.m.* eugenics.
euh [ø], *int.* aha! oh! hum!
eunuque [ø'nyk], *n.m.* eunuch.
euphémique [øfe'mik], *a.* euphemistic.
euphémisme [øfe'mism], *n.m.* euphemism.
euphonie [øfɔ'ni], *n.f.* euphony.
euphonique [øfɔ'nik], *a.* euphonious.
Euphrate [ø'frat], l', *m.* the Euphrates.
euphuïsme [øfy'ism], *n.m.* euphuism.
eurasien [øra'zjɛ̃], *a.* (*fem.* -enne) Eurasian.—*n.m.* (**Eurasien**, *fem.* -enne) Eurasian (*person*).
Euripide [øri'pid], *m.* Euripides.
Europe [ø'rɔp], *f.* (*Myth.*) Europa; *l'Europe* (*Geog.*) Europe.
européaniser [ørɔpeani'ze], *v.t.* to Europeanize.
européen [ørɔpe'ɛ̃], *a.* (*fem.* -éenne) European.—*n.m.* (**Européen**, *fem.* -éenne) European (person).
euthanasie [øtana'zi], *n.f.* euthanasia.
eux [ø], *pron. pers. m. pl.* (*fem.* -elles) they; them.
évacuant [eva'kɥã], **évacuatif** [evakɥa'tif] (*fem.* -tive), *a.* and *n.m.* evacuant.
évacuation [evakɥa'sjɔ̃], *n.f.* evacuation; ejection.
évacué [eva'kɥe], *n.m.* (*fem.* -ée) evacuee.
évacuer [eva'kɥe], *v.t.* to evacuate; to throw off, to eject, to clear. **s'évacuer,** *v.r.* to discharge (*into*).

évadé [eva'de], *a.* and *n.m.* (*fem.* **-ée**) escaped (*person*); escapee.

évader (s') [seva'de], *v.r.* to escape; to get away *or* out of (*de*).

évaluable [eva'lɥabl], *a.* rateable, appraisable.

évaluateur [evalɥa'tœːr], *n.m.* (*fem.* **-trice**) valuer, appraiser.

évaluation [evalɥa'sjɔ̃], *n.f.* valuation, estimate.

évaluer [eva'lɥe], *v.t.* to value, to estimate, to appreciate.

évangélique [evɑ̃ʒe'lik], *a.* evangelical.

évangéliser [evɑ̃ʒeli'ze], *v.t.* to evangelize, to preach the Gospel to.

évangélisme [evɑ̃ʒe'lism], *n.m.* evangelism.

évangéliste [evɑ̃ʒe'list], *n.m.* evangelist.

évangile [evɑ̃'ʒil], *n.m.* Gospel.

évanouir (s') [seva'nwiːr], *v.r.* to faint, to swoon, to lose consciousness; (*fig.*) to vanish, to disappear.

évanouissement [evanwis'mɑ̃], *n.m.* swoon, fainting fit; disappearance; (*Math.*) cancelling out.

évaporatif [evapora'tif], *a.* (*fem.* **-tive**) evaporative.

évaporation [evapora'sjɔ̃], *n.f.* evaporation.

évaporé [evapo're], *a.* and *n.m.* (*fem.* **-ée**) frivolous, thoughtless (person).

évaporer [evapo're], *v.t.* to evaporate; (*fig.*) to exhale, to give vent to; *évaporer son chagrin,* to give vent to one's grief. **s'évaporer,** *v.r.* to evaporate; (*fig.*) to get giddy.

évasé [eva'ze], *a.* wide, bell-shaped; flared (*skirt*).

évasement [evɑz'mɑ̃], *n.m.* width, widening (*at the mouth of a vase etc.*); flare (*of a skirt*).

évaser [eva'ze], *v.t.* to widen (*an opening*); to flare (*a skirt*). **s'évaser,** *v.r.* to be widened; to extend, to spread.

évasif [eva'zif], *a.* (*fem.* **-sive**) evasive.

évasion [eva'zjɔ̃], *n.f.* escape, flight; evasion; escapism.

évasivement [evaziv'mɑ̃], *adv.* evasively.

évêché [evɛ'ʃe], *n.m.* bishopric, episcopate, see; bishop's palace.

éveil [e'vɛːj], *n.m.* awakening; warning, hint, alarm.

éveillé [evɛ'je], *a.* wide-awake; lively, sprightly; sharp, intelligent.

éveiller [evɛ'je], *v.t.* to awaken, to rouse; to excite, to enliven. **s'éveiller,** *v.r.* to wake up; to become animated.

événement [even'mɑ̃], *n.m.* event, occurrence; result; climax; emergency.

évent [e'vɑ̃], *n.m.* open air; vent-hole, air-hole; (*fig.*) flatness, vapidness.

éventail [evɑ̃'taːj], *n.m.* (*pl.* **éventails**) fan; fan-light.

éventaire [evɑ̃'tɛːr], *n.m.* flat tray (*carried by hawkers*); street stall.

éventé [evɑ̃'te], *a.* fanned, aired; flat, stale (*beer etc.*); (*fig.*) giddy, thoughtless.

éventer [evɑ̃'te], *v.t.* to fan; to winnow (*corn*); to air; to let (*wine etc.*) get flat; to get wind of; to divulge. **s'éventer,** *v.r.* to fan oneself; to evaporate; to become flat; to be divulged.

éventrer [evɑ̃'tre], *v.t.* to disembowel, to gut (*fish etc.*); to rip up, to break open. **s'éventrer,** *v.r.* to rip one's bowels open; to commit hara-kiri.

éventualité [evɑ̃tɥali'te], *n.f.* contingency, eventuality.

éventuel [evɑ̃'tɥɛl], *a.* (*fem.* **-elle**) contingent, possible.

éventuellement [evɑ̃tɥɛl'mɑ̃], *adv.* possibly; on occasion.

évêque [e'vɛːk], *n.m.* bishop.

évertuer (s') [sever'tɥe], *v.r.* to strive, to exert *or* bestir oneself.

éviction [evik'sjɔ̃], *n.f.* eviction, ejectment.

évidemment [evida'mɑ̃], *adv.* evidently.

évidence [evi'dɑːs], *n.f.* obviousness, clearness; conspicuousness.

évident [evi'dɑ̃], *a.* evident, plain, clear, obvious.

évider [evi'de], *v.t.* to hollow, to groove, to scoop out.

évier [e'vje], *n.m.* sink.

évincer [evɛ̃'se], *v.t.* (*conjug. like* COMMENCER) to evict, to eject, to oust.

éviscérer [evise're], *v.t.* (*conjug. like* CÉDER) to disembowel.

évitable [evi'tabl], *a.* avoidable.

évitement [evit'mɑ̃], *n.m.* (*Rail.*) siding, shunting; by-pass.

éviter [evi'te], *v.t.* to shun, to avoid, to evade; to abstain from.

évocateur [evɔka'tœːr], *a.* (*fem.* **-trice**) evocative.

évocation [evɔka'sjɔ̃], *n.f.* evocation; recollection.

évolué [evɔ'lɥe], *a.* highly civilized.

évoluer [evɔ'lɥe], *v.i.* to evolve; to develop.

évolution [evɔly'sjɔ̃], *n.f.* evolution.

évoquer [evɔ'ke], *v.t.* to evoke; to allude to.

exacerbation [egzasɛrba'sjɔ̃], *n.f.* exacerbation.

exacerber [egzasɛr'be], *v.t.* to exacerbate.

exact [eg'zakt], *a.* exact, correct; punctual.

exactement [egzakta'mɑ̃], *adv.* exactly, accurately; punctually.

exaction [egzak'sjɔ̃], *n.f.* exaction, impost, extortion.

exactitude [egzakti'tyd], *n.f.* exactness, accuracy; punctuality.

exagération [egzaʒera'sjɔ̃], *n.f.* exaggeration; overrating.

exagérer [egzaʒe're], *v.t.* (*conjug. like* CÉDER) to exaggerate, to magnify.

exaltation [ɛgzalta'sjɔ̃], *n.f.* exaltation; extolling.

exalté [egzal'te], *a.* exalted, feverish.—*n.m.* (*fem.* **-ée**) enthusiast, fanatic.

exalter [egzal'te], *v.t.* to exalt, to magnify; to excite, to inflame. **s'exalter,** *v.r.* to become excited, to be elated.

examen [egza'mɛ̃], *n.m.* examination; inspection; research.

examinateur [ɛgzamina'tœːr], *n.m.* (*fem.* **-trice**) examiner.

examiner [ɛgzami'ne], *v.t.* to examine, to inspect, to survey; to discuss, to investigate. **s'examiner,** *v.r.* to examine *or* search oneself; to observe each other attentively.

exaspération [ɛgzaspera'sjɔ̃], *n.f.* exasperation, aggravation.

exaspérer [egzaspe're], *v.t.* (*conjug. like* CÉDER) to exasperate, to incense, to inflame; to aggravate (*pain etc.*). **s'exaspérer,** *v.r.* to become exasperated *or* incensed; to become aggravated (*pain etc.*).

exaucer [εgzo'se], *v.t.* (*conjug. like* COM-
MENCER) to hearken to, to grant.
excavateur [εkskava'tœ:r], *n.m.* excavator,
digging-machine.
excavation [εkskava'sjɔ̃], *n.f.* excavation.
excaver [εkska've], *v.t.* to excavate, to hollow
out.
excédant [εkse'dɑ̃], *a.* exceeding, excessive;
unbearable.
excédent [εkse'dɑ̃], *n.m.* surplus, excess.
excéder [εkse'de], *v.t.* (*conjug. like* CÉDER)
to exceed, to surpass, to rise above (*in level,
price etc.*); (*fig.*) to wear out, to tire out.
excellemment [εksεla'mɑ̃], *adv.* excellently,
surpassingly.
Excellence [εksε'lɑ̃:s], *f.* (*title*) Excellency.
excellence [εksε'lɑ̃:s], *n.f.* excellence; *par
excellence*, pre-eminently, above all.
excellent [εksε'lɑ̃], *a.* excellent; delightful.
excellentissime [εksεlɑ̃ti'sim], *a.* most
excellent.
exceller [εksε'le], *v.i.* to excel, to be eminent;
to surpass.
excentricité [εksɑ̃trisi'te], *n.f.* eccentricity.
excentrique [εksɑ̃'trik], *a.* eccentric, odd.
excepté [εksεp'te], *prep.* except, excepting, but.
excepter [εksεp'te], *v.t.* to except.
exception [εksεp'sjɔ̃], *n.f.* exception.
exceptionnel [εksεpsjɔ'nεl], *a.* (*fem.* **-elle**)
exceptional; rare, infrequent.
excès [εk'sε], *n.m. inv.* excess; (*pl.*) riot, out-
rages, violence.
excessif [εksε'sif], *a.* (*fem.* **-ive**) excessive,
exorbitant; intemperate.
excessivement [εksεsiv'mɑ̃], *adv.* excessively, to excess.
excise [εk'si:z], *n.f.* excise; excise-office.
excitabilité [εksitabili'te], *n.f.* excitability.
excitable [εksi'tabl], *a.* excitable.
excitant [εksi'tɑ̃], *a.* exciting.—*n.m.* (*Med.*)
excitant.
excitateur [εksita'tœ:r], *a.* (*fem.* **-trice**)
provocative.—*n.m.* (*fem.* **-trice**) instigator.
excitation [εksita'sjɔ̃], *n.f.* exciting, excitation; excitement.
exciter [εksi'te], *v.t.* to excite, to stir up, to
rouse; to stimulate, to animate; to instigate,
to prompt; to irritate. **s'exciter**, *v.r.* to
excite oneself, to work oneself up; to
encourage each other; to be excited.
exclamation [εksklama'sjɔ̃], *n.f.* exclamation;
point d'exclamation, exclamation mark.
exclamer (s') [sεksklα'me], *v.r.* to exclaim, to
cry out; to protest.
exclure [εks'kly:r], *v.t. irr.* (*conjug. like*
CONCLURE) to exclude, to debar, to shut out;
to bar; to be incompatible with.
exclusif [εkskly'zif], *a.* (*fem.* **-sive**) exclusive;
intolerant.
exclusion [εkskly'zjɔ̃], *n.f.* exclusion.
exclusivement [εksklyziv'mɑ̃], *adv.* exclu-
sively.
excommunication [εkskɔmynika'sjɔ̃], *n.f.*
excommunication.
excommunié [εkskɔmy'nje], *a.* excom-
municated.—*n.m.* (*fem.* **-ée**) excommuni-
cated person.
excommunier [εkskɔmy'nje], *v.t.* to excommunicate.
excrément [εkskre'mɑ̃], *n.m.* excrement.
excréter [εkskre'te], *v.t.* (*conjug. like* CÉDER)
to excrete.

excrétion [εkskre'sjɔ̃], *n.f.* excretion.
excroissance [εkskrwɑ'sɑ̃:s], *n.f.* excrescence
(*tumour etc.*).
excursion [εkskyr'sjɔ̃], *n.f.* excursion, ramble,
tour, trip; raid; (*fig.*) digression.
excursionniste [εkskyrsjɔ'nist], *n.* tripper.
excusable [εksky'zabl], *a.* excusable, pardonable.
excuse [εks'ky:z], *n.f.* excuse, (*pl.*) apology.
excuser [εksky'ze], *v.t.* to excuse, to pardon;
to bear with; to apologize for. **s'excuser**,
v.r. to excuse *or* exculpate oneself; to
apologize; to decline; *qui s'excuse,
s'accuse*, excuses indicate a guilty conscience.
exécrable [egze'krabl], *a.* execrable; abominable.
exécrablement [egzekrablɑ'mɑ̃], *adv.* exe-
crably.
exécration [egzεkra'sjɔ̃], *n.f.* execration.
exécrer [egze'kre], *v.t.* (*conjug. like* CÉDER)
to execrate, to abhor.
exécutable [egzeky'tabl], *a.* feasible, practicable.
exécutant [egzeky'tɑ̃], *n.m.* (*fem.* **-e**) performer, player (*esp. of music*).
exécuter [egzeky'te], *v.t.* to execute, to perform, to accomplish; to carry out, to fulfil.
s'exécuter, *v.r.* to be performed, to be
done, to take place; to yield, to comply, to
submit; *allons, exécutez-vous*, come, do
the needful.
exécuteur [egzeky'tœ:r], *n.m.* (*fem.* **-trice**)
executor, executrix; *exécuteur (des
hautes œuvres)*, executioner.
exécutif [egzeky'tif], *a.* (*fem.* **-tive**) executive.—*n.m.* the executive.
exécution [egzeky'sjɔ̃], *n.f.* execution, accomplishment, performance, fulfilment; (*St.
Exch.*) hammering (*of defaulter*).
exemplaire [egzɑ̃'plε:r], *a.* exemplary.—
n.m. model, pattern; copy (*of printed books,
engravings etc.*); specimen.
exemplairement [egzɑ̃plεr'mɑ̃], *adv.* in an
exemplary manner.
exemple [eg'zɑ̃:pl], *n.m.* example, pattern,
model; precedent, parallel, instance; *à
l'exemple de*, in imitation of; *par
exemple*, for instance; upon my word!
sans exemple, unparalleled.
exempt [eg'zɑ̃], *a.* exempt, free (*from*).
exempté [egzɑ̃'te], *a.* and *n.m.* (*fem.* **-ée**)
exempt(ed) (person).
exempter [egzɑ̃'te], *v.t.* to exempt, to free;
to dispense, to exonerate.
exemption [egzɑ̃'sjɔ̃], *n.f.* exemption, immunity; dispensation.
exercer [egzεr'se], *v.t.* (*conjug. like* COM-
MENCER) to exercise, to train; to fulfil (*an
office etc.*); to follow, to practise (*a trade or
profession*); (*fig.*) to try (*one's patience etc.*).
s'exercer, *v.r.* to exercise, to practise; to
exert oneself.
exercice [egzεr'sis], *n.m.* exercise, practice,
use; (*Customs*) inspection; (*Administration*)
financial year; (*Mil.*) drill.
exerciseur [egzεrsi'zœ:r], *n.m.* (*Gym.*) chest
expander.
exhalaison [egzalε'zɔ̃], *n.f.* exhalation,
effluvium.
exhalation [egzalɑ'sjɔ̃], *n.f.* exhalation.

exhaler

exhaler [εgza'le], *v.t.* to send forth, to exhale; to give vent to, to emit. **s'exhaler**, *v.r.* to be emitted, to be exhaled; to give vent to.

exhausser [εgzo'se], *v.t.* to raise, to make higher.

exhaustif [εgzos'tif], *a.* (*fem.* **-tive**) exhaustive.

exhaustion [εgzos'tjõ], *n.f.* exhaustion.

exhiber [εgzi'be], *v.t.* to exhibit (*in a law-court*); to produce, to show. **s'exhiber**, *v.r.* (*pej.*) to show off.

exhibition [εgzibi'sjõ], *n.f.* producing, show, exhibiting, exhibition.

exhilarant [εgzila'rã], *a.* exhilarating.

exhortation [εgzorta'sjõ], *n.f.* exhortation.

exhorter [εgzor'te], *v.t.* to exhort, to encourage.

exhumation [εgzyma'sjõ], *n.f.* exhumation, disinterment.

exhumer [εgzy'me], *v.t.* to exhume, to disinter; (*fig.*) to rake up.

exigeant [εgzi'ʒã], *a.* exacting, hard to please.

exigence [εgzi'ʒã:s], *n.f.* unreasonableness; exigency; demand, requirement.

exiger [εgzi'ʒe], *v.t.* (*conjug. like* MANGER) to exact, to require, to demand.

exigu [εgzi'gy], *a.* (*fem.* **-uë**) very small; scanty, slender, slight.

exiguïté [εgzigui'te], *n.f.* scantiness, slenderness, slightness.

exil [εg'zil], *n.m.* exile, banishment.

exilé [εgzi'le], *a.* exiled.—*n.m.* (*fem.* **-ée**) exile.

exiler [εgzi'le], *v.t.* to exile, to banish. **s'exiler**, *v.r.* to go into exile.

existant [εgzis'tã], *a.* existing, in being, existent; extant.

existence [εgzis'tã:s], *n.f.* existence; subsistence, living; (*pl.*) (*Comm.*) stock on hand.

existentialisme [εgzistãsja'lism], *n.m.* existentialism.

exister [εgzis'te], *v.i.* to exist, to live; to be extant.

exocet [εgzo'sε], *n.m.* flying-fish.

exode [εg'zod], *n.m.* exodus.

exonération [εgzonera'sjõ], *n.f.* exoneration.

exonérer [εgzone're], *v.t.* (*conjug. like* CÉDER) to exonerate, to discharge.

exorable [εgzo'rabl], *a.* lenient, merciful.

exorbitant [εgzorbi'tã], *a.* exorbitant.

exorciser [εgzorsi'ze], *v.t.* to exorcize.

exorde [εg'zord], *n.m.* exordium, beginning (*of a speech etc.*).

exotique [εgzo'tik], *a.* exotic; foreign, outlandish.

expansif [εkspã'sif], *a.* (*fem.* **-sive**) expansive; (*fig.*) unreserved, open-hearted.

expansion [εkspã'sjõ], *n.f.* expansion; (*fig.*) unreservedness.

expatriation [εkspatria'sjõ], *n.f.* expatriation; self-banishment.

expatrier [εkspatri'e], *v.t.* to expatriate, to exile. **s'expatrier**, *v.r.* to leave one's country.

expectant [εkspεk'tã], *a.* expectant.

expectative [εkspεkta'ti:v], *n.f.* expectation, hope, expectancy.

expectoration [εkspεktora'sjõ], *n.f.* expectoration; sputum.

expectorer [εkspεkto're], *v.t.* to expectorate, to spit.

expédient [εkspe'djã], *a.* expedient, fit, meet.—*n.m.* expedient, device; shift.

expédier [εkspe'dje], *v.t.* to dispatch, to send off, to forward; to do quickly; to clear (*at the customs*); to draw up (*a deed etc.*).

expéditeur [εkspedi'tœ:r], *n.m.* (*fem.* **-trice**) sender (*by post*); shipper, consigner.

expéditif [εkspedi'tif], *a.* (*fem.* **-tive**) expeditious, quick.

expédition [εkspedi'sjõ], *n.f.* expedition, dispatch; shipment; thing sent; performance; (*Law*) copy (*of a deed etc.*).

expéditionnaire [εkspedisjo'nε:r], *a.* expeditionary.—*n.* sender, shipper; commission-agent; copying-clerk.

expérience [εkspe'rjã:s], *n.f.* experience; experiment, test.

expérimental [εksperimã'tal], *a.* (*m.pl.* **-aux**) experimental.

expérimenté [εksperimã'te], *a.* experienced.

expérimenter [εksperimã'te], *v.t.* to try out, to test; to experience.

expert [εks'pε:r], *a.* expert, skilful.—*n.m.* connoisseur; valuer, surveyor; expert; **expert comptable**, chartered accountant.

expertement [εkspεrtə'mã], *adv.* expertly skilfully.

expertise [εkspεr'ti:z], *n.f.* survey, valuation; appraisal.

expertiser [εkspεrti'ze], *v.t.* to make a survey of; to appraise, to value, to assess.

expiation [εkspja'sjõ], *n.f.* expiation, atonement.

expiatoire [εkspja'twa:r], *a.* expiatory.

expier [εks'pje], *v.t.* to expiate, to atone for.

expirant [εkspi'rã], *a.* expiring, dying.

expiration [εkspira'sjõ], *n.f.* expiration.

expirer [εkspi're], *v.t.* to breathe out; exhale. —*v.i.* to expire, to die; to come to an end.

explicable [εkspli'kabl], *a.* explicable.

explicatif [εksplika'tif], *a.* (*fem.* **-tive**) explicative, explanatory.

explication [εksplika'sjõ], *n.f.* explanation; interpretation; meaning.

explicite [εkspli'sit], *a.* explicit, clear, express.

explicitement [εksplisit'mã], *adv.* explicitly, clearly.

expliquer [εkspli'ke], *v.t.* to explain, to expound; to interpret; to make known. **s'expliquer**, *v.r.* to explain oneself; to be explained.

exploit [εks'plwa], *n.m.* exploit, achievement, feat; (*Law*) writ, process.

exploitable [εksplwa'tabl], *a.* workable; (*Law*) distrainable.

exploitant [εksplwa'tã], *n.m.* operator (*of mines etc.*); farmer, grower.

exploitation [εksplwata'sjõ], *n.f.* working, improving (*of lands etc.*); employing, using; taking advantage of, exploitation.

exploiter [εksplwa'te], *v.t.* to work, to improve, to cultivate; to use; to exploit, to take (*unfair*) advantage of.

exploiteur [εksplwa'tœ:r], *n.m.* (*fem.* **-euse**) exploiter, person who takes advantage (*of others*).

explorateur [εksplora'tœ:r], *a.* (*fem.* **-trice**) exploratory.—*n.m.* (*fem.* **-trice**) explorer.

exploration [ɛksplɔrɑ'sjɔ̃], *n.f.* exploration.
explorer [ɛksplɔ're], *v.t.* to explore.
exploser [ɛksplo'ze], *v.i.* to explode, to blow up.
explosible [ɛksplo'zibl], *a.* explosive.
explosif [ɛksplo'zif], *a.* (*fem.* -**sive**) and *n.m.* explosive.
explosion [ɛksplo'zjɔ̃], *n.f.* explosion; (*fig.*) outbreak.
exportateur [ɛkspɔrta'tœːr], *a.* (*fem.* -**trice**) exporting.—*n.m.* (*fem.* -**trice**) exporter.
exportation [ɛkspɔrta'sjɔ̃], *n.f.* exportation, export.
exporter [ɛkspɔr'te], *v.t.* to export.
exposant [ɛkspo'zɑ̃], *n.m.* (*fem.* -**e**) exhibitor; (*Law*) petitioner.—*n.m.* (*Math.*) exponent.
exposé [ɛkspo'ze], *a.* exposed, on view; dangerous (*position*).—*n.m.* statement, explanation; account, report.
exposer [ɛkspo'ze], *v.t.* to expose, to show, to exhibit; to lay bare; to state, to explain; to endanger.—*v.i.* to explain; to exhibit.
s'exposer, *v.r.* to expose oneself; to be liable.
exposition [ɛkspozi'sjɔ̃], *n.f.* exhibition; exposure; situation, aspect; explanation; account.
exprès [ɛks'prɛs], *a.* (*fem.* -**presse**) express, formal, positive.—[ɛks'prɛ], *adv.* expressly, on purpose.—*n.m.* express (*messenger*).
express [ɛks'prɛs], *a.* (*Rail.*) express.—*n.m.* express train.
expressément [ɛksprɛse'mɑ̃], *adv.* expressly, positively.
expressif [ɛksprɛ'sif], *a.* (*fem.* -**ive**) expressive.
expression [ɛksprɛ'sjɔ̃], *n.f.* expression; expressiveness.
exprimer [ɛkspri'me], *v.t.* to express; to press *or* squeeze out; to utter; to betoken.
s'exprimer, *v.r.* to express oneself.
expropriation [ɛksprɔpria'sjɔ̃], *n.f.* expropriation, dispossession, compulsory purchase.
exproprier [ɛksprɔpri'e], *v.t.* to expropriate, to dispossess; to requisition (*buildings*).
expulser [ɛkspyl'se], *v.t.* to expel, to turn out; to evict.
expulsion [ɛkspyl'sjɔ̃], *n.f.* expulsion; (*Law*) ejection.
expurger [ɛkspyr'ʒe], *v.t.* (*conjug. like* MANGER) to expurgate, to bowdlerize (*a book*).
exquis [ɛks'ki], *a.* exquisite, nice, refined.
exquisement [ɛkskiz'mɑ̃], *adv.* exquisitely.
exsangue [ɛk'sɑ̃ːg], *a.* bloodless, anaemic.
extase [ɛks'taːz], *n.f.* ecstasy, rapture.
extasier (s') [sɛksta'zje], *v.r.* to be enraptured, to go into raptures.
extatique [ɛksta'tik], *a.* ecstatic, rapturous.
extenseur [ɛkstɑ̃'sœːr], *a.* extensor.—*n.m.* (*Anat.*) extensor; chest-expander.
extension [ɛkstɑ̃'sjɔ̃], *n.f.* extension, stretching; extent; increase.
exténuant [ɛkste'nɥɑ̃], *a.* extenuating.
exténuation [ɛkstenɥa'sjɔ̃], *n.f.* extenuation, debility.
exténuer [ɛkste'nɥe], *v.t.* to extenuate, to enfeeble.

extérieur [ɛkste'rjœːr], *a.* exterior, external, outward; foreign.—*n.m.* exterior; outward appearance; abroad.
extérieurement [ɛksterjœr'mɑ̃], *adv.* externally, outwardly.
exterminateur [ɛkstɛrmina'tœːr], *a.* (*fem.* -**trice**) exterminating, destroying.—*n.m.* (*fem.* -**trice**) destroyer, exterminator.
extermination [ɛkstɛrmina'sjɔ̃], *n.f.* extermination.
exterminer [ɛkstɛrmi'ne], *v.t.* to exterminate, to destroy.
externat [ɛkstɛr'na] *n.m.* day-school.
externe [ɛks'tɛrn], *a.* external, exterior, outer.—*n.* day-scholar.
extincteur [ɛkstɛ̃k'tœːr], *a.* (*fem.* -**trice**) extinguishing (*fire*).—*n.m.* fire-extinguisher.
extinction [ɛkstɛ̃k'sjɔ̃], *n.f.* extinction, destruction; liquidation; quelling; quenching (*of thirst*); slaking (*of lime*).
extinguible [ɛkstɛ̃'gibl], *a.* extinguishable.
extirpateur [ɛkstirpa'tœːr], *n.m.* extirpator, destroyer; (*Agric.*) scarifier.
extirpation [ɛkstirpa'sjɔ̃], *n.f.* extirpation.
extirper [ɛkstir'pe], *v.t.* to extirpate.
extorquer [ɛkstor'ke], *v.t.* to extort, to wrest.
extorsion [ɛkstor'sjɔ̃], *n.f.* extortion.
extra [ɛks'tra], *n.m. inv.* extra.
extra-conjugal [ɛkstrakɔ̃ʒy'gal], *a.* (*m.pl.* -**aux**) extra-marital.
extracteur [ɛkstrak'tœːr], *n.m.* extractor.
extraction [ɛkstrak'sjɔ̃], *n.f.* extraction; origin, descent.
extrader [ɛkstra'de], *v.t.* to extradite.
extradition [ɛkstradi'sjɔ̃], *n.f.* extradition.
extraire [ɛks'trɛːr], *v.t. irr.* (*conjug. like* TRAIRE) to extract, to take out; to make extracts from.
extrait [ɛks'trɛ], *n.m.* extract; selection; abstract; certificate.
extraordinaire [ɛkstraɔrdi'nɛːr], *a.* extraordinary, unusual.—*n.m.* extraordinary thing.
extraordinairement [ɛkstraɔrdiner'mɑ̃], *adv.* extraordinarily, unusually; oddly.
extrapolation [ɛkstrapɔlɑ'sjɔ̃], *n.f.* (*Math.*) extrapolation.
extra-scolaire [ɛkstrasko'lɛːr], *a.* out-of-school (*activities*).
extravagamment [ɛkstravaga'mɑ̃], *adv.* extravagantly, unreasonably.
extravagance [ɛkstrava'gɑ̃ːs], *n.f.* extravagance, folly.
extravagant [ɛkstrava'gɑ̃], *a.* and *n.m.* (*fem.* -**e**) extravagant (person).
extravaguer [ɛkstrava'ge], *v.i.* to talk wildly.
extrême [ɛks'trɛːm], *a.* extreme, utmost; excessive.—*n.m.* extreme *or* utmost point.
extrêmement [ɛkstrɛm'mɑ̃], *adv.* extremely.
Extrême-Orient [ɛkstremo'rjɑ̃], l', *m.* Far East.
extrémiste [ɛkstre'mist], *n.* extremist, die-hard.
extrémité [ɛkstremi'te], *n.f.* extremity, end; last moment; (*fig.*) border, brink.
exubérance [ɛgzybe'rɑ̃ːs], *n.f.* exuberance.
exubérant [ɛgzybe'rɑ̃], *a.* exuberant, luxuriant.
exultation [ɛgzyltɑ'sjɔ̃], *n.f.* exultation, rapture.

F, f

F

F, f (1) [εf], *n.m.* the sixth letter of the alphabet.
f. (2) or **fr.**, (*abbr.*) franc.
fa [fa], *n.m.* (*Mus.*) fa; F.
fable [faːbl], *n.f.* fable; story, tale; (*fig.*) untruth; byword.
fablier [fabliˈe], *n.m.* book of fables; fabulist.
fabricant [fabriˈkã], *n.m.* (*fem.* **-e**) manufacturer, maker.
fabricateur [fabrikaˈtœːr], *n.m.* (*fem.* **-trice**) fabricator; coiner, forger.
fabrication [fabrikaˈsjɔ̃], *n.f.* fabrication, manufacture.
fabrique [faˈbrik], *n.f.* building, fabric (*esp. of churches*); factory; fabrication.
fabriquer [fabriˈke], *v.t.* to manufacture, to make; to fabricate.
fabuleusement [fabyløzˈmã], *adv.* fabulously; (*fig.*) incredibly.
fabuleux [fabyˈlø], *a.* (*fem.* **-euse**) fabulous, fictitious; (*fig.*) incredible.
fabuliste [fabyˈlist], *n.* fabulist.
façade [faˈsad], *n.f.* façade, front (*of an edifice*); (*fig.*) appearance.
face [fas], *n.f.* face; front; side (*of a record*); (*fig.*) state, appearance; turn (*of affairs*); **en face de**, opposite.
facétie [faseˈsi], *n.f.* facetiousness; jest, joke.
facétieusement [fasesjøzˈmã], *adv.* facetiously.
facétieux [faseˈsjø], *a.* (*fem.* **-euse**) facetious, humorous.
facette [faˈsɛt], *n.f.* facet, face.
fâcher [faˈʃe], *v.t.* to anger, to offend, to displease; **être fâché avec**, to be on bad terms with; **fâché (contre)**, angry (*with*); **fâché (de)**, sorry. **se fâcher**, *v.r.* to get angry, to be offended.
fâcherie [faˈʃri], *n.f.* angry feeling; quarrel.
fâcheusement [faʃøzˈmã], *adv.* unfortunately, unpleasantly; inopportunely, disagreeably; awkwardly.
fâcheux [faˈʃø], *a.* (*fem.* **-euse**) troublesome, vexatious; unfortunate; cross.—*n.m.* (*fem.* **-euse**) troublesome *or* disagreeable person *or* thing, pesterer, bore.
facial [faˈsjal], *a.* (*m. pl.* **-aux**) (*Anat.*) facial.
facile [faˈsil], *a.* easy; facile; fluent; ready, quick; weak.
facilement [fasilˈmã], *adv.* easily, readily.
facilité [fasiliˈte], *n.f.* facility, ease; readiness; (*pl.*) easy terms (*for payment*).
faciliter [fasiliˈte], *v.t.* to facilitate, to make easy.
façon [faˈsɔ̃], *n.f.* make, shape, fashion; making, workmanship; (*fig.*) manner; appearance; sort; affectation; fuss; (*pl.*) ceremony.
faconde [faˈkɔ̃ːd], *n.f.* talkativeness, loquacity.
façonné [fasɔˈne], *a.* figured (*of materials*); wrought.
façonnement [fasɔnˈmã], **façonnage** [fasɔˈnaːʒ], *n.m.* fashioning, making.
façonner [fasɔˈne], *v.t.* to make, to fashion, to form; to work, to mould; to accustom, to use (*to discipline etc.*).
façonnier [fasɔˈnje], *a.* (*fem.* **-ière**) ceremonious, affected.—*n.m.* bespoke tailor.
fac-similé [faksimiˈle], *n.m.* facsimile.

150

factage [fakˈtaːʒ], *n.m.* porterage, carriage.
facteur [fakˈtœːr], *n.m.* (*fem.* **-trice**) maker (*of musical instruments*); agent; postman; railway porter; (*Math., Biol.*) factor.
factice [fakˈtis], *a.* factitious, artificial; unnatural.
factieux [fakˈsjø], *a.* (*fem.* **-euse**) factious, mutinous.—*n.m.* (*fem.* **-euse**) rebel.
faction [fakˈsjɔ̃], *n.f.* watch, sentry-duty; faction.
factionnaire [faksjɔˈnɛːr], *n.m.* sentry.
factorerie [faktɔrˈri], *n.f.* trading depot, factory (*in a colony etc.*).
facture [fakˈtyːr], *n.f.* composition, workmanship (*of music, verse etc.*); (*Comm.*) bill (*of sale*), invoice.
facturer [faktyˈre], *v.t.* to invoice.
facultatif [fakyltaˈtif], *a.* (*fem.* **-tive**) optional; **arrêt facultatif**, request stop.
faculté [fakylˈte], *n.f.* faculty, ability, power; quality; option, right; (*pl.*) mental faculties.
fadaise [faˈdɛːz], *n.f.* trifle, stuff, nonsense, twaddle.
fade [fad], *a.* insipid, tasteless, dull; (*fig.*) flat, stale.
fadement [fadˈmã], *adv.* insipidly, tastelessly; mawkishly.
fadeur [faˈdœːr], *n.f.* insipidity, tastelessness; (*fig.*) pointlessness.
fagot [faˈgo], *n.m.* faggot, bundle of sticks etc.
fagoter [fagɔˈte], *v.t.* to tie into faggots; (*fig.*) to jumble together; to dress in a slovenly manner; **comme le voilà fagoté**, what a sight he looks. **se fagoter**, *v.r.* to dress in a slovenly manner.
faible [fɛːbl], *a.* and *n.* weak, feeble (person). —*n.m.* weak part; defect, failing; partiality, weakness (*for*).
faiblement [fɛblˈmã], *adv.* weakly, feebly.
faiblesse [fɛˈblɛs], *n.f.* weakness, feebleness; faintness; deficiency; backwardness; defect; partiality.
faiblir [fɛˈbliːr], *v.i.* to become weak, to flag, to yield; to abate; to relax.
faïence [faˈjãːs], *n.f.* crockery, earthenware.
faïencier [fajãˈsje], *n.m.* (*fem.* **-ière**) dealer in *or* maker of crockery.
faille [faːj], *n.f.* (*Geol.*) fault.
failli [faˈji], *a.* and *n.m.* (*fem.* **-e**) bankrupt, insolvent (person).
faillibilité [fajibiliˈte], *n.f.* fallibility.
faillible [faˈjibl], *a.* fallible.
faillir [faˈjiːr], *v.i. irr.* to err, to transgress; to yield; to fail; to be on the point of; **j'ai failli tomber**, I nearly fell.
faillite [faˈjit], *n.f.* bankruptcy, insolvency; **faire faillite**, to become bankrupt.
faim [fɛ̃], *n.f.* hunger, appetite; (*fig.*) longing; **avoir faim**, to be hungry.
faine [fɛːn], *n.f.* beechnut; beechmast.
fainéant [fɛneˈã], *a.* idle, lazy.—*n.m.* (*fem.* **-e**) idler.
fainéanter [fɛneãˈte], *v.i.* (*colloq.*) to be idle, to loaf.
fainéantise [fɛneãˈtiːz], *n.f.* idleness, laziness, sloth.
faire (1) [fɛːr], *v. irr.* (*The most frequently used verb in the language; faire not only translates* to do *or* to make, *but, followed by a noun or an infinitive, it may take the place of practically any verb; followed by an adjective*

or an adverb it forms many current idioms.)

I. *v.t.* to do; to make; to form; to be; *cela fait mon affaire*, this is exactly what I want; *cela fait beaucoup*, that makes a great difference; *cela ne fait rien*, that makes no difference; *faire accueil à*, to welcome; *faire attention*, to pay attention; *faire bâtir*, to have built; *faire cas de*, to have a high opinion of; (*Motor.*) *faire du 50 à l'heure*, to do 50 kilometres an hour; *faire le mort*, to sham dead; *faire part de*, to inform, to announce; *faire peu de cas de*, to set little store by; *faire ses dents*, to cut one's teeth; *faire une promenade*, to take a walk; *faire venir*, to send for; *faire voir*, to show; *faites-le entrer*, show him in; *il ne fait que d'arriver*, he has only just arrived; *je n'ai que faire de lui*, I am in no way interested in him; *qu'est-ce que cela vous fait?* what is that to you? *que faire?* what is to be done? *se laisser faire*, to offer no resistance.

II. *v.i.* to do; to mean, to signify, to look; to fit, to suit; to deal (*at cards*); to arrange, to manage; *avoir à faire*, to have work to do; *c'en est fait de*, it is all up with.

III. *v. impers.* to be; *il fait beau*, it is fine; *quel temps fait-il?* what sort of weather is it?

IV. *se faire*, *v.r.* to be done, to be made; to happen, to become; to pretend to be; to have, make *or* get oneself; to be used (*à*), to accustom oneself (*à*); to improve; *cela ne se fait pas*, that is not done.

faire (2) [fɛːr], *n.m.* doing, making; (*Paint. etc.*) execution, style.

faire-part [fɛr'paːr], *n.m. inv.* *un faire-part* *or* *une lettre de faire-part de décès* *or* *de mariage*, notification of death, wedding-card.

faisable [fə'zabl], *a.* practicable, feasible.

faisan [fə'zɑ̃], *n.m.* pheasant.

faisandé [fəzɑ̃'de], *a.* gamy, high.

faisandeau [fəzɑ̃'do], *n.m.* (*pl.* -eaux) young pheasant.

faisceau [fɛ'so], *n.m.* (*pl.* -eaux) bundle; sheaf (*of arrows etc.*); pile (*of arms etc.*); (*fig.*) union; (*Elec.*) beam; (*Antiq., pl.*) fasces.

faiseur [fə'zœːr], *n.m.* (*fem.* -euse) maker; doer; charlatan, quack.

fait [fɛ, fɛt], *a.* made; done; fit, qualified; dressed, got up; full grown; mature.—*n.m.* act, deed; fact, actual event; case, matter, point in business; *tout à fait*, quite.

faîte [fɛːt], *n.m.* top, pinnacle; ridge, coping (*of a building*); (*fig.*) zenith, height.

faits divers [fɛdi'vɛr], *n.m. pl.* news items, news in brief.

faix [fɛ], *n.m. inv.* weight, burden, load.

falaise [fa'lɛːz], *n.f.* cliff.

fallacieusement [falasjøz'mɑ̃], *adv.* fallaciously, falsely.

fallacieux [fala'sjø], *a.* (*fem.* -euse) fallacious, deceptive.

falloir [fa'lwaːr], *v. impers. irr.* to be necessary, to be obligatory, proper *or* expedient (*should, must*); to be needful, to be wanting *or* lacking; *comme il faut*, properly, well-bred (*of people*); *peu s'en*

---

faut, very nearly; *tant s'en faut*, far from it.

falot [fa'lo], *n.m.* large hand-lantern.

falsification [falsifika'sjɔ̃], *n.f.* falsification; adulteration, debasement.

falsifier [falsi'fje], *v.t.* to falsify; to alter (*texts etc.*); to adulterate (*milk, metals*); to tamper with.

faluche [fa'lyʃ], *n.f.* student's beret.

famé [fa'me], *a. used only in bien* or *mal famé*, of good *or* evil repute.

famélique [fame'lik], *a.* starving.—*n.* starveling.

fameux [fa'mø], *a.* (*fem.* -euse) famous, celebrated; first-rate; (*iron. adj. before noun*) perfect.

familial [fami'ljal],⸰*a.* (*m. pl.* -aux) pertaining to family.

familiariser [familjari'ze], *v.t.* to accustom to, to familiarize. se **familiariser**, *v.r.* to familiarize oneself (*avec*), to become accustomed; to grow familiar.

familiarité [familjari'te], *n.f.* familiarity, familiar terms, intimacy; (*pl.*) liberties.

familier [fami'lje], *a.* (*fem.* -ière) familiar, intimate; free; homely.—*n.m.* familiar.

familièrement [familjɛr'mɑ̃], *adv.* familiarly.

famille [fa'miːj], *n.f.* family, kindred, kin; race, tribe; (*fig.*) set.

famine [fa'min], *n.f.* famine, dearth.

fanal [fa'nal], *n.m.* (*pl.* -aux) signal-light; ship's lantern.

fanatique [fana'tik], *a.* fanatical.—*n.* fanatic, enthusiast.

fanatiquement [fanatik'mɑ̃], *adv.* fanatically.

fanatisme [fana'tism], *n.m.* fanaticism.

faner [fa'ne], *v.t.* to toss *or* ted (*hay*); to cause to fade; to tarnish. se **faner**, *v.r.* to fade, to droop, to wither; to tarnish.

faneur [fa'nœːr], *n.m.* (*fem.* -euse) haymaker. —*n.f.* (-euse) haymaking machine.

fanfare [fɑ̃'faːr], *n.f.* flourish (*of trumpets*), fanfare; brass band.

fanfaron [fɑ̃fa'rɔ̃], *a.* (*fem.* -onne) blustering, swaggering, boasting.—*n.m.* (*fem.* -onne) blusterer, swaggerer; braggart.

fanfreluche [fɑ̃frə'lyʃ], *n.f.* bauble, gewgaw.

fange [fɑ̃ːʒ], *n.f.* mire, mud, dirt; vileness.

fangeux [fɑ̃'ʒø], *a.* (*fem.* -euse) miry, muddy, dirty.

fanon [fa'nɔ̃], *n.m.* dewlap (*oxen*); fetlock (*horse*); horny strip (*in whales*); (*Mil.*) pennon (*of lance*).

fantaisie [fɑ̃tɛ'zi], *n.f.* imagination; fancy; whim, caprice; (*Mus.*) fantasia.

fantaisiste [fɑ̃tɛ'zist], *a.* whimsical, fantastic. —*n.* whimsical painter, writer *or* other artist.

fantasmagorie [fɑ̃tasmago'ri], *n.f.* phantasmagoria.

fantasque [fɑ̃'task], *a.* fantastic, whimsical; strange, odd.

fantassin [fɑ̃ta'sɛ̃], *n.m.* foot-soldier, infantryman.

fantastique [fɑ̃tas'tik], *a.* fantastic, fanciful. —*n.m.* uncanny.

fantastiquement [fɑ̃tastik'mɑ̃], *adv.* fantastically.

fantoche [fɑ̃'tɔʃ], *n.m.* marionette, puppet.

fantôme [fɑ̃'toːm], *n.m.* phantom, spectre, ghost.

faon [fɑ̃], *n.m.* fawn, calf of deer.
faquin [fa'kɛ̃], *n.m.* cad, rascal.
farandole [farɑ̃'dɔl], *n.f.* farandole (*Provençal dance*).
farce [fars], *n.f.* stuffing, force-meat; farce; buffoonery; practical joke; prank.
farceur [far'sœːr], *a.* (*fem.* **-euse**) waggish, facetious.—*n.m.* (*fem.* **-euse**) practical joker; humbug.
farcir [far'siːr], *v.t.* to stuff with force-meat etc.; to cram.
fard [faːr], *n.m.* paint (*for the complexion*), rouge, make-up; (*fig.*) varnish, disguise; *sans fard*, plainly, frankly.
fardeau [far'do], *n.m.* (*pl.* **-eaux**) burden, load; mash (*for brewing*); (*Mining*) mass.
farder [far'de], *v.t.* to paint (*the face*), to make up; (*fig.*) to varnish, to gloss over. **se farder**, *v.r.* to paint one's face, to make up.
(C) **fardoches** [far'dɔʃ], *n.f. pl.* brushwood.
farfadet [farfa'dɛ], *n.m.* goblin, elf.
farfouiller [farfu'je], *v.i.* (*fam.*) to rummage.
faribole [fari'bɔl], *n.f.* idle story; trifle.
farine [fa'rin], *n.f.* flour; meal.
farineux [fari'nø], *a.* (*fem.* **-euse**) mealy, farinaceous; white with flour.
farouche [fa'ruʃ], *a.* wild; fierce; sullen; shy.
fascicule [fasi'kyl], *n.m.* fascicle.
fascinateur [fasina'tœːr], *a.* (*fem.* **-trice**) fascinating.
fascination [fasina'sjɔ̃], *n.f.* fascination.
fasciner [fasi'ne], *v.t.* to fascinate.
fascisme [fa'fism], *n.m.* Fascism.
fasciste [fa'fist], *a.* and *n.* Fascist.
faste [fast], *a.* favourable, lucky.—*n.m.* (*used only in sing.*) pomp, ostentation.
fastidieusement [fastidjøz'mɑ̃], *adv.* tediously.
fastidieux [fasti'djø], *a.* (*fem.* **-euse**) irksome, tedious.
fastueusement [fastɥøz'mɑ̃], *adv.* ostentatiously, pompously; splendidly.
fastueux [fas'tɥø], *a.* (*fem.* **-euse**) ostentatious, pompous, showy; stately.
fat [fat], *a.* conceited, vain, foppish.—*n.m.* fop, coxcomb.
fatal [fa'tal], *a.* fatal; inevitable; *une femme fatale*, a vamp.
fatalement [fatal'mɑ̃], *adv.* fatally; inevitably.
fatalisme [fata'lism], *n.m.* fatalism.
fataliste [fata'list], *n.* fatalist.
fatalité [fatali'te], *n.f.* fatality.
fatigant [fati'gɑ̃], *a.* fatiguing, tiring, wearisome.
fatigue [fa'tig], *n.f.* fatigue, weariness; toil, hardship; *habits de fatigue*, working clothes.
fatigué [fati'ge], *a.* fatigued, tired; (*fig.*) worn out.
fatiguer [fati'ge], *v.t.* to fatigue; to tire.—*v.i.* to tire; to be fatiguing. **se fatiguer**, *v.r.* to tire oneself out, to get tired, to be jaded.
fatras [fa'trɑ], *n.m.* jumble; rubbish, trash.
fatuité [fatɥi'te], *n.f.* fatuity, self-conceit.
faubourg [fo'buːr], *n.m.* outskirts, suburb.
faubourien [fobu'rjɛ̃], *a.* (*fem.* **-enne**) suburban, working-class; common.—*n.m.* (*fem.* **-enne**) person living in the suburbs; (*pej.*) common person.
fauchage [fo'ʃaːʒ], *n.m.* mowing.
fauchaison [foʃɛ'zɔ̃], *n.f.* mowing-time.
fauché [fo'ʃe], *a.* mown; (*slang*) broke.

faucher [fo'ʃe], *v.t.* to mow, to reap.
faucheur [fo'ʃœːr], *n.m.* (*fem.* **-euse**) mower, reaper.—*n.f.* (**-euse**) (*mechanical*) mower.
faucille [fo'siːj], *n.f.* sickle, reaping-hook.
faucon [fo'kɔ̃], *n.m.* falcon, hawk.
fauconnerie [fokɔn'ri], *n.f.* falconry.
fauconnier [fokɔ'nje], *n.m.* falconer.
faufiler [fofi'le], *v.t.* to tack, to baste (*needlework*). **se faufiler**, *v.r.* to insinuate oneself, to sneak in; to find a way in.
faune (1) [foːn], *n.m.* faun.
faune (2) [foːn], *n.f.* (*Zool.*) fauna.
faussaire [fo'sɛːr], *n.* forger.
fausse [fos], [FAUX].
faussement [fos'mɑ̃], *adv.* falsely, wrongfully.
fausser [fo'se], *v.t.* to bend; to falsify, to pervert; to break, to force or strain (*a lock*).
fausset [fo'sɛ], *n.m.* (*Mus.*) falsetto.
fausseté [fos'te], *n.f.* falsity, falsehood; duplicity.
faute [foːt], *n.f.* want; defect; fault, mistake, error; *faute de*, for want of.
fauteuil [fo'tœːj], *n.m.* arm-chair; chair (*speaker's, president's seat*).
fauteur [fo'tœːr], *n.m.* abettor, favourer.
fautif [fo'tif], *a.* (*fem.* **-tive**) faulty, at fault, defective.
fauve [foːv], *a.* fawn-coloured, tawny.—*n.m.* wild animal; *Les Fauves*, group of French painters at the beginning of this century.
fauvette [fo'vɛt], *n.f.* warbler.
faux (1) [fo], *n.f. inv.* scythe.
faux (2) [fo], *a.* (*fem.* **fausse**) false, untrue, wrong; base, counterfeit, forged (*coinage*); sham; insincere; (*Mus.*) out of tune; *faire un faux pas*, to stumble; (*fig.*) to make a slip.—*n.m.* falsehood; error; forgery.—*adv.* falsely, erroneously; (*Mus.*) out of tune.
faux-filet [fofi'lɛ], *n.m.* sirloin.
faux-fuyant [fofɥi'jɑ̃], *n.m.* subterfuge, evasion.
faux-monnayeur [fomɔne'jœːr], *n.m.* coiner, counterfeiter.
faveur [fa'vœːr], *n.f.* favour, boon; grace; vogue; (*narrow*) silk ribbon; *à la faveur de*, by means of; *en faveur de*, on behalf of.
favorable [favo'rabl], *a.* favourable, propitious.
favorablement [favorablə'mɑ̃], *adv.* favourably.
favori [favo'ri], *a.* and *n.m.* (*fem.* **-ite**) favourite.—*n.m.* (*pl.*) side-whiskers.
favoriser [favori'ze], *v.t.* to favour, to befriend; to assist, to protect.
favoritisme [favori'tism], *n.m.* favouritism.
fébrile [fe'bril], *a.* febrile, feverish.
fécond [fe'kɔ̃], *a.* fruitful, prolific; copious, abundant, fertile.
fécondation [fekɔ̃da'sjɔ̃], *n.f.* impregnation; fertilization.
féconder [fekɔ̃'de], *v.t.* to make fruitful, to fertilize.
fécondité [fekɔ̃di'te], *n.f.* fecundity, fruitfulness, fertility.
fécule [fe'kyl], *n.f.* faecula, starch.
féculent [feky'lɑ̃], *a.* feculent.—*n.m.* starchy food.
fédéral [fede'ral], *a.* (*m. pl.* **-aux**) federal.
fédéralisme [federa'lism], *n.m.* federalism.
fédéraliste [federa'list], *a.* and *n.* federalist.

fédération [federɑ'sjɔ̃], *n.f.* federation, alliance.

fédéré [fede're], *a.* federate, confederate; amalgamated.

fédérer (se) [səfede're], *v.r.* (*conjug. like* CÉDER) to federate, to band together.

fée [fe], *n.f.* fairy, fay.

féerie [feə'ri], *n.f.* enchantment; fairy scene; fairy-land.

féerique [feə'rik], *a.* fairy-like; wonderful.

feindre [fɛ̃:dr], *v.t. irr* (*conjug. like* CRAINDRE) to feign, to simulate, to sham, to pretend.— *v.i.* to feign, to sham.

feint [fɛ̃], *a.* feigned, pretended, sham.

feinte [fɛ̃:t], *n.f.* feint; pretence, dissimulation.

feld-maréchal [fɛldmare'ʃal], *n.m.* (*pl.* **-aux**) field-marshal.

feldspath [fɛls'pat], *n.m.* feldspar.

fêlé [fɛ'le], *a.* cracked (*of glass*); (*fig.*) crack-brained.

fêler [fɛ'le], *v.t. and* **se fêler**, *v.r.* to crack (*of glass etc.*).

félicitation [felisitɑ'sjɔ̃], *n.f.* felicitation, congratulation.

félicité [felisi'te], *n.f.* felicity, bliss.

féliciter [felisi'te], *v.t.* to congratulate, to felicitate. **se féliciter**, *v.r.* to congratulate oneself.

félin [fe'lɛ̃], *a. and n.m.* (*fem.* **-e**) feline.

félon [fe'lɔ̃], *a.* (*fem.* **-onne**) disloyal, traitorous.—*n.m.* (*fem.* **-onne**) traitor, caitiff.

félonie [felo'ni], *n.f.* (*Feud.*) felony, treason.

fêlure [fɛ'ly:r], *n.f.* crack, fissure.

femelle [fə'mɛl], *a.* female, feminine, she-.— *n.f.* female, (*pej.*) woman.

féminin [femi'nɛ̃], *a.* feminine, female, womanish, womanly, effeminate.—*n.m.* (*Gram.*) feminine.

femme [fam], *n.f.* woman; married woman; wife; female attendant; lady.

femme-agent [fama'ʒɑ̃], *n.f.* police-woman.

femmelette [fam'lɛt], *n.f.* silly, weak woman; effeminate man.

femme-soldat [famsɔl'da], *n.f.* service-woman.

fémur [fe'my:r], *n.m.* femur, thigh-bone.

fenaison [fənɛ'zɔ̃], *n.f.* hay-time, hay-making.

fendiller (se) [səfɑ̃di'je], *v.r.* to be covered with small cracks, to crack, to split.

fendre [fɑ̃:dr], *v.t.* to cleave, to split, to crack, to cut open; to plough (*the sea*). **se fendre**, *v.r.* to burst asunder, to split, to be ready to burst.

fendu [fɑ̃'dy], *a.* cleft, split, cloven.

fenêtre [fə'nɛ:tr], *n.f.* window, casement.

fenil [fə'ni], *n.m.* hayloft.

fenouil [fə'nu:j], *n.m.* fennel.

fente [fɑ̃:t], *n.f.* slit, chink, cleft; gap, crevice.

féodal [feo'dal], *a.* (*m. pl.* **-aux**) feudal.

féodalisme [feoda'lism], *n.m.* feudalism.

fer [fɛːr], *n.m.* iron; iron tool; horseshoe; head, point, etc.; (*fig.*) sword, brand; (*Golf*) club; (*pl.*) irons, chains, fetters; *fer battu* or *forgé*, wrought-iron; *fil de fer*, wire.

fer-blanc [fɛr'blɑ̃], *n.m.* (*pl.* **fers-blancs**) tin, tin-plate.

férié [fe'rje], *a.* holiday; *jour férié*, holiday, general holiday, bank-holiday.

férir [fe'rir], *v.t. used only in* **sans coup férir**, without striking a blow.

ferler [fɛr'le], *v.t.* to furl (*sails*).

fermage [fɛr'ma:ʒ], *n.m.* rent (*of a farm*).

fermail [fɛr'ma:j], *n.m.* clasp, buckle.

ferme (1) [fɛrm], *a.* firm; fixed, stable; strong, stout, stiff, steady; resolute.—*adv.* firmly, fast, hard.

ferme (2) [fɛrm], *n.f.* farm, farmhouse, farmstead; farming (*of taxes*); letting out on lease.

ferme (3) [fɛrm], *n.f.* framework of beams.

fermement [fɛrmə'mɑ̃], *adv.* firmly, steadily; resolutely.

ferment [fɛr'mɑ̃], *n.m.* ferment, leaven.

fermentation [fɛrmɑ̃tɑ'sjɔ̃], *n.f.* fermentation, working; (*fig.*) ferment.

fermenter [fɛrmɑ̃'te], *v.i.* to ferment, to rise, to work.

fermer [fɛr'me], *v.t.* to shut, to close; to fasten; to turn off (*water, gas etc.*); to put an end to (*a discussion etc.*); to enclose.— *v.i.* to shut, to be shut. **se fermer**, *v.r.* to shut, to close, to be closed; to lock.

fermeté [fɛrmə'te], *n.f.* firmness; steadiness; resolution.

fermeture [fɛrmə'ty:r], *n.f.* closing, shutting; *fermeture à glissière*, zip fastener.

fermier [fɛr'mje], *n.m.* (tenant) farmer.

fermière [fɛr'mjɛ:r], *n.f.* farmer's wife.

fermoir [fɛr'mwa:r], *n.m.* clasp, fastener.

féroce [fe'rɔs], *a.* ferocious, fierce, savage.

férocement [ferɔs'mɑ̃], *adv.* ferociously.

férocité [ferɔsi'te], *n.f.* ferocity, fierceness.

ferraille [fɛ'ra:j], *n.f.* old iron, scrap-iron.

ferrailler [fɛra'je], *v.i.* (*Spt.*) to fence clumsily; (*fig.*) to squabble.

ferrailleur [fɛra'jœ:r], *n.m.* dealer in old iron, scrap merchant; (*Spt.*) clumsy fencer.

ferrant [fɛ'rɑ̃], *a.* *maréchal ferrant*, farrier, shoeing-smith.

ferré [fɛ're], *a.* bound, shod etc., with iron; metalled; (*colloq.*) skilled; *voie ferrée*, railway.

ferrer [fɛ're], *v.t.* to bind, hoop, etc., with iron; to shoe (*a horse etc.*).

ferret [fɛ'rɛ], *n.m.* tag (*of a lace*).

ferronnerie [fɛrɔn'ri], *n.f.* iron-foundry; ironmongery; wrought iron.

ferronnier [fɛrɔ'nje], *n.m.* (*fem.* **-ière**) ironmonger, iron-worker.

ferroviaire [fɛrɔ'vjɛ:r], *a.* pertaining to railways.

ferrure [fɛ'ry:r], *n.f.* iron-work; shoeing (*of a horse etc.*).

fertile [fɛr'til], *a.* fertile, fruitful.

fertilement [fɛrtil'mɑ̃], *adv.* fertilely, abundantly.

fertilisant [fɛrtili'zɑ̃], *a.* fertilizing.

fertiliser [fɛrtili'ze], *v.t.* to fertilize, to manure.

fertilité [fɛrtili'te], *n.f.* fertility, fruitfulness.

féru [fe'ry], *a.* smitten; keen on (*something or someone*).

férule [fe'ryl], *n.f.* (*Sch.*) cane, ferule, rod; stroke, cut.

fervent [fɛr'vɑ̃], *a.* fervent.—*n.m.* (*fem.* **-e**) enthusiast, devotee, fan.

ferveur [fɛr'vœ:r], *n.f.* fervour, ardour.

fesse [fɛs], *n.f.* buttock, rump; (*pl.*) bottom.

fessée [fɛ'se], *n.f.* spanking.

fesse-mathieu [fɛsma'tjø], *n.m.* (*pl.* **fesse-mathieux**) miser, skinflint.

fesser [fɛ'se], *v.t.* to spank, to smack.

153

fessier [fɛ'sje], *n.m.* buttocks, bottom.
festin [fɛs'tɛ̃], *n.m.* feast, banquet.
***festiner** [fɛsti'ne], *v.i.* to banquet, to carouse.
festival [fɛsti'val], *n.m.* festival.
festivité [fɛstivi'te], *n.f.* festivity.
feston [fɛs'tɔ̃], *n.m.* festoon; scallop.
festonner [fɛstɔ'ne], *v.t.* to festoon; to cut in festoons, to scallop.
festoyer [fɛstwa'je], *v.t.* (*conjug. like* EM-PLOYER) to entertain, to feast.
fête [fɛːt], *n.f.* holiday, festival; saint's day; feast; birthday; festivity, merry-making.
fête-Dieu [fɛːt'djø], *n.f.* Corpus Christi day.
fêter [fɛ'te], *v.t.* to keep (as a holiday); to entertain, to feast.
fétiche [fe'tiʃ], *n.m.* fetish.
fétide [fe'tid], *a.* fetid, rank, offensive.
fétidité [fetidi'te], *n.f.* fetidity, offensive smell.
fétu [fe'ty], *n.m.* straw; (*fig.*) pin, rap.
feu (1) [fø], *n.m.* (*pl.* **feux**) fire; burning; heat; discharge of fire-arms; fire-place; (*fig.*) light; brilliancy; passion; vivacity; **crier 'au feu'**, to cry 'fire!'; **faire feu**, to fire; **feu d'artifice**, fireworks; **feu de joie**, bonfire; **feux de position**, (*Motor.*) parking lights; **le coin du feu**, the fireside; **prendre feu**, to catch fire.
feu (2) [fø], *a.* late, deceased.
feuillage [fœ'jaːʒ], *n.m.* foliage, leaves.
feuille [fœːj], *n.f.* leaf; sheet (*of paper, metal etc.*); newspaper; list; foil (*of mirrors*).
feuillet [fœ'jɛ], *n.m.* leaf (*of a book*).
feuilleter [fœj'te], *v.t.* (*conjug. like* APPELER) to turn over; to peruse rapidly; **gâteau feuilleté**, flaky puff.
feuillu [fœ'jy], *a.* leafy.
feutrage [fø'traːʒ], *n.m.* felting.
feutre [føːtr], *n.m.* felt; felt hat.
feutrer [fø'tre], *v.t.* to felt; to pad, to pack.
feutrier [føtri'e], *n.m.* (*fem.* **-ière**) felt-maker.
fève [fɛːv], *n.f.* bean, broad bean.
février [fevri'e], *n.m.* February.
fez [fɛːz], *n.m. inv.* fez (*Turkish cap*).
fi! [fi], *int.* fie!
fiacre [fjakr], *n.m.* hackney-coach, cab.
fiançailles [fjã'saːj], *n.f.* (*used only in pl.*) betrothal, engagement.
fiancé [fjã'se], *n.m.* (*fem.* **-ée**) betrothed, fiancé, fiancée.
fiancer [fjã'se], *v.t.* (*conjug. like* COMMENCER) to betroth, to affiance. **se fiancer**, *v.r.* to become engaged to each other.
fiasco [fjas'ko], *n.m. inv.* fiasco, failure.
fibre [fibr], *n.f.* fibre, filament; (*fig.*) feeling.
fibreux [fi'brø], *a.* (*fem.* **-euse**) fibrous, stringy.
ficeler [fis'le], *v.t.* (*conjug. like* APPELER) to bind *or* tie up with string; to do up; to dress up.
ficeleur [fis'lœːr], *n.m.* (*fem.* **-euse**) packer.
ficelle [fi'sɛl], *n.f.* string, packthread, twine; (*fig.*) dodge.
fiche [fiʃ], *n.f.* peg, pin (*for a hinge etc.*); (*Teleph.*) plug; small card; (*Whist*) booby prize; (*colloq.*) slip of paper, memo.
ficher [fi'ʃe], *v.t.* to drive in, to fasten in. **se ficher**, *v.r.* (*colloq.*) to laugh at (*de*).
fichier [fi'ʃje], *n.m.* card-index (*cabinet*).
fichoir [fi'ʃwaːr], *n.m.* peg, clothes-peg.
fichtre! [fiʃtr], *int.* (*colloq.*) dash it! hang it!
fichu (1) [fi'ʃy], *n.m.* neckerchief.

fichu (2) [fi'ʃy], *a.* sorry, pitiful; got up (*dressed*); (*slang*) done for.
fictif [fik'tif], *a.* (*fem.* **-tive**) supposed, fictitious.
fiction [fik'sjɔ̃], *n.f.* fiction; fable.
fictivement [fiktiv'mã], *adv.* fictitiously.
fidèle [fi'dɛl], *a.* faithful, loyal, true.—*n.* faithful friend etc.; (*pl.*) worshippers, faithful.
fidèlement [fidɛl'mã], *adv.* faithfully, truly.
fidélité [fideli'te], *n.f.* fidelity, faithfulness, loyalty; accuracy.
fief [fjɛf], *n.m.* fief, fee.
fieffé [fjɛ'fe], *a.* (*colloq.*) arrant, downright.
fiel [fjɛl], *n.m.* gall; (*fig.*) hatred, bitterness, rancour.
fier [fje], *v.t.* to trust, to entrust. **se fier**, *v.r.* to trust to *or* in, to depend upon (*à*).
fier [fjɛːr], *a.* (*fem.* **fière**) proud, haughty; bold; (*colloq.*) fine, capital.
fièrement [fjɛr'mã], *adv.* proudly, arrogantly, haughtily; boldly.
fierté [fjɛr'te], *n.f.* pride, arrogance; dignity.
fièvre [fjɛːvr], *n.f.* fever, feverishness; (*fig.*) restlessness, excitement.
fiévreux [fje'vrø], *a.* (*fem.* **-euse**) feverish; (*fig.*) restless.—*n.m.* (*fem.* **-euse**) fever-patient.
fifre [fifr], *n.m.* fife; fifer.
figé [fi'ʒe], *a.* stiff, cold, set (*features, smile etc.*).
figement [fiʒ'mã], *n.m.* congealment, coagulation, curdling.
figer [fi'ʒe], *v.t.* and **se figer**, *v.r.* (*conjug. like* MANGER) to congeal, to coagulate, to curdle.
figue [fig], *n.f.* fig.
figuier [fi'gje], *n.m.* fig-tree.
figurant [figy'rã], *n.m.* (*fem.* **-e**) (*Theat., Cine.*) figurant; extra.
figuratif [figyra'tif], *a.* (*fem.* **-tive**) figurative.
figurativement [figyrativ'mã], *adv.* figuratively.
figure [fi'gyːr], *n.f.* figure, shape; face, appearance; symbol, type.
figuré [figy're], *a.* figured; figurative.
figurer [figy're], *v.t.* to figure, to represent.—*v.i.* to figure, to appear. **se figurer**, *v.r.* to imagine, fancy *or* picture to oneself.
figurine [figy'rin], *n.f.* figurine, statuette.
fil [fil], *n.m.* thread; wire; yarn; (*cutting*) edge; grain, vein (*in stones etc.*); course (*of a stream etc.*); chain, series; **de fil en aiguille**, one thing leading to another; **donner un coup de fil**, to give a ring; **être au bout du fil**, to be speaking (*on the phone*); **fil à coudre**, sewing-thread; **fil de la Vierge**, gossamer; **laine deux fils**, two-ply wool.
filage [fi'laːʒ], *n.m.* spinning.
filament [fila'mã], *n.m.* filament, thread.
filamenteux [filamã'tø], *a.* (*fem.* **-euse**) thready, stringy.
filandière [filã'djɛːr], *n.f.* spinner.
filandreux [filã'drø], *a.* (*fem.* **-euse**) fibrous, stringy, thready.
filant [fi'lã], *a.* flowing; ropy; shooting (*of stars*).
filasse [fi'las], *n.f.* harl, tow (*of flax, hemp etc.*); oakum.
filateur [fila'tœːr], *n.m.* spinning-mill owner; spinner.

filature [fila'ty:r], *n.f.* spinning-mill; spinning; shadowing (*by a detective*).
file [fil], *n.f.* file; *à la file*, one after another; *prendre la file*, to take one's place in the queue.
filé [fi'le], *a.* drawn out, sustained.—*n.m.* gold *or* silver thread.
filer [fi'le], *v.t.* to spin; (*fig.*) to carry on; to spin out (*a story etc.*); (*Naut.*) to pay out (*a rope*); to trail, to shadow.—*v.i.* to become ropy; to go, to travel; to shoot (*of stars*); to flare (*of a lamp etc.*); to take oneself off; *filer à l'anglaise*, to take French leave; *filer doux*, to sing small.
filet [fi'lɛ], *n.m.* slender thread, string; net; (*Rail.*) rack; filament, fibre; (*Bot., Arch. etc.*) fillet; drop (*of water etc.*); (*fig.*) streak; trickle, streamlet; snaffle-bridle; (*fig.*) snare.
fileur [fi'lœ:r], *n.m.* (*fem.* **-euse**) spinner; wire-drawer.
filial [fi'ljal], *a.* (*m. pl.* **-aux**) filial.
filiale [fi'ljal], *n.f.* subsidiary company, branch.
filiation [filja'sjɔ̃], *n.f.* filiation; (*fig.*) connexion, relationship.
filière [fi'ljɛ:r], *n.f.* draw-plate; screw-plate; (*Carp.*) purlin; (*fig.*) channel, series.
filigrane [fili'gran], *n.m.* filigree, filigree-work; water-mark (*in paper*); embossing.
filigraner [filigra'ne], *v.t.* to work in filigree; to emboss.
fille [fi:j], *n.f.* daughter; girl, young unmarried woman; maiden; servant-maid; *arrière-petite-fille*, great-granddaughter; *belle-fille*, daughter-in-law, stepdaughter; *jeune fille*, girl; *petite-fille*, granddaughter; *vieille fille*, old maid.
fillette [fi'jɛt], *n.f.* little girl; lass.
filleul [fi'jœ:l], *n.m.* godson.
filleule [fi'jœ:l], *n.f.* goddaughter.
film [film], *n.m.* film; *film fixe*, film strip.
filmer [fil'me], *v.t.* to film.
filon [fi'lɔ̃], *n.m.* metallic vein; (*fig.*) good job; tip.
filou [fi'lu], *n.m.* pickpocket, thief; swindler.
filouter [filu'te], *v.t.* to steal; to cheat, to swindle.
filouterie [filu'tri], *n.f.* picking pockets; swindling, cheating.
fils [fis], *n.m. inv.* son, male child; offspring; *arrière-petit-fils*, great-grandson; *beau-fils*, stepson, son-in-law; *petit-fils*, grandson.
filtrage [fil'tra:ʒ], *n.m.* filtering, straining.
filtrant [fil'trɑ̃], *a.* filtering, straining; *bout filtrant*, filter-tip.
filtration [filtra'sjɔ̃], *n.f.* filtration, straining; percolation.
filtre (1) [filtr], *n.m.* filter; cup of filtered coffee; *filtre à café*, percolator.
filtre (2) [PHILTRE].
filtrer [fil'tre], *v.t.* to filter, to strain.—*v.i.* and **se filtrer**, *v.r.* to filter; to percolate.
filure [fi'ly:r], *n.f.* texture of a spun fabric.
fin (1) [fɛ̃], *n.f.* end, conclusion, close; death; destination; aim, design.
fin (2) [fɛ̃], *a.* fine, thin, slender; delicate; refined, polite; acute; cunning.—*n.m.* sharp fellow; main point.—*n.f.* (**-e**) type of liqueur brandy.
final [fi'nal], *a.* final, last, ultimate.

finale [fi'nal], *n.m.* (*Mus.*) finale.—*n.f.* (*Spt.*) final.
finalement [final'mɑ̃], *adv.* finally, lastly.
finalité [finali'te], *n.f.* finality.
finance [fi'nɑ̃:s], *n.f.* ready money; (*pl.*) (*public*) finances, exchequer, treasury.
financer [finɑ̃'se], *v.t.* (*conjug. like* COMMENCER) to finance; (*fig.*) to lay out money.
financier [finɑ̃'sje], *a.* (*fem.* **-ière**) financial. —*n.m.* financier.
financièrement [finɑ̃sjɛr'mɑ̃], *adv.* financially.
finaud [fi'no], *a.* sly, artful, cunning.—*n.m.* (*fem.* **-e**) sly, artful person.
fine [fin], [FIN (2)].
finement [fin'mɑ̃], *adv.* finely, delicately; ingeniously; artfully.
finesse [fi'nɛs], *n.f.* fineness; delicacy; ingenuity; finesse, artifice, slyness.
finette [fi'nɛt], *n.f.* thin material of wool *or* cotton, flannelette.
fini [fi'ni], *a.* finished, ended.—*n.m.* finish, high finish, perfection.
finir [fi'ni:r], *v.t.* to finish, to complete; to end, to terminate.—*v.i.* to end, to conclude, to be over; to expire.
finissage [fini'sa:ʒ], *n.m.* finishing touches.
finissant [fini'sɑ̃], *a.* declining, dying.
finlandais [fɛ̃lɑ̃'dɛ], *a.* Finnish.—*n.m.* Finnish (*language*); (**Finlandais**, *fem.* **-aise**) Finn.
Finlande [fɛ̃'lɑ̃:d], **la**, *f.* Finland.
finnois [fi'nwa], *a.* Finnish.—*n.m.* Finnish (*language*); (**Finnois**, *fem.* **-oise**) Finn.
fiole [fjol], *n.f.* phial.
firmament [firma'mɑ̃], *n.m.* firmament, sky.
fisc [fisk], *n.m.* public treasury, fisc.
fiscal [fis'kal], *a.* (*m. pl.* **-aux**) fiscal, financial.
fissible [fi'sibl], *a.* fissile (*of radio-active materials*).
fission [fi'sjɔ̃], *n.f.* fission, splitting (*of atom*); *fission de l'atome*, nuclear fission.
fissure [fi'sy:r], *n.f.* fissure, crack, rent.
fissurer (**se**) [səfisy're], *v.r.* to become fissured.
five-o'clock [faivo'klɔk], *n.m.* afternoon tea.
fixation [fiksa'sjɔ̃], *n.f.* fixation, fixing; settlement; rating, assessment.
fixe [fiks], *a.* fixed; settled; appointed, regular. —*n.m.* fixed salary.—*int.* (*Mil.*) eyes front! steady!
fixement [fiksə'mɑ̃], *adv.* fixedly, steadily.
fixer [fik'se], *v.t.* to fix, to fasten; to settle; to establish; to stare at; to attract. **se fixer**, *v.r.* to be fixed; to settle down.
fixité [fiksi'te], *n.f.* fixity, stability.
flac [flak], *int.* slap! bang! plop!—*n.m.* anti-aircraft gunfire, flak.
flaccidité [flaksidi'te], *n.f.* flaccidity.
flacon [fla'kɔ̃], *n.m.* bottle; decanter; phial.
flagellant [flaʒɛ'lɑ̃], *n.m.* flagellant.
flagellation [flaʒɛla'sjɔ̃] *n.f.* flagellation, flogging.
flageller [flaʒɛ'le], *v.t.* to flagellate, to scourge, to flog; (*fig.*) to lash with words.
flageoler [flaʒɔ'le], *v.i.* to tremble, to shake (*of legs*).
flageolet [flaʒɔ'lɛ], *n.m.* flageolet (*music*); (*small*) green kidney bean.
flagorner [flagɔr'ne], *v.t.* to flatter servilely, to toady to.

flagornerie

flagornerie [flagɔrnə'ri], *n.f.* sycophancy, base flattery.

flagorneur [flagɔr'nœːr], *n.m.* (*fem.* **-euse**) sycophant, toady.

flagrant [fla'grã], *a.* flagrant, gross; *en flagrant délit*, red-handed.

flair [flɛːr], *n.m.* (*Hunt.*) nose; (*fig.*) perspicacity.

flairer [flɛ're], *v.t.* to smell, to scent; (*colloq.*) to smell of; to find out.

flamand [fla'mã], *a.* Flemish.—*n.m.* Flemmish (*language*); (**Flamand**, *fem.* **-ande**) Fleming.

flamant (rose) [fla'mã(roːz)], *n.m.* flamingo.

flambant [flã'bã], *a.* blazing, flaming; (*pop.*) smart, flashy; *flambant neuf*, brand new.

flambeau [flã'bo], *n.m.* (*pl.* **-eaux**) torch, link; candle, candlestick.

flambée [flã'be], *n.f.* blaze.

flamber [flã'be], *v.t.* to singe; to fumigate, to disinfect.—*v.i.* to blaze, to flame, to flare.

flamboiement [flãbwa'mã], *n.m.* flaming, blaze.

flamboyant [flãbwa'jã], *a.* flaming, blazing; flashing.

flamboyer [flãbwa'je], *v.i.* (*conjug. like* EMPLOYER) to flame, to blaze, to flare.

flamme [flaːm], *n.f.* flame; (*fig.*) fire; glow; ardour, passion.

flammèche [fla'mɛʃ], *n.f.* flake of fire, spark.

flammer [fla'me], *v.t.* to singe (*material*).

flan [flã], *n.m.* (*baked*) custard tart; flan.

flanc [flã], *n.m.* flank, side; (*fig.*) womb, bowels.

flancher [flã'ʃe], *v.i.* (*fam.*) to give in, to rat, to jib; (*Motor.*) to stop, to break down.

flandrin [flã'drɛ̃], *n.m.* (*colloq.*) *un grand flandrin*, a long, lanky fellow.

flanelle [fla'nɛl], *n.f.* flannel.

flâner [flã'ne], *v.i.* to lounge, to stroll, to loaf.

flânerie [flã'nri], *n.f.* lounging; stroll; loafing.

flâneur [flã'nœːr], *n.m.* (*fem.* **-euse**) stroller; lounger, loafer.

flanquer [flã'ke], *v.t.* to flank; (*Mil.*) to defend, to guard; (*colloq.*) to deal (*a blow*); to fling. **se flanquer**, *v.r. se flanquer par terre*, to throw oneself down.

flaque [flak], *n.f.* small pool, puddle.

flash [flaʃ], *n.m.* (*Phot.*) flash-light; (*Cine.*) flash.

flasque (1) [flask], *a.* limp, slack, flabby, flaccid.

flasque (2) [flask], *n.f.* powder-horn.

flatter [fla'te], *v.t.* to stroke, to caress; to flatter; to soothe; to cajole. **se flatter**, *v.r.* to flatter oneself; to pride oneself; to hope, to expect.

flatterie [fla'tri], *n.f.* flattery, adulation.

flatteur [fla'tœːr], *a.* (*fem.* **-euse**) flattering, complimentary.—*n.m.* (*fem.* **-euse**) flatterer.

flatteusement [flatøz'mã], *adv.* flatteringly.

flatulence [flaty'lãːs], *n.f.* flatulence, wind.

flatulent [flaty'lã], *a.* flatulent, windy.

fléau [fle'o], *n.m.* (*pl.* **fléaux**) flail; (*fig.*) scourge, plague; beam (*of a balance*).

flèche [flɛʃ], *n.f.* arrow, dart; shaft; (*Arch.*) slender spire; *faire flèche de tout bois*, to leave no stone unturned.

fléchette [fle'ʃɛt], *n.f.* dart (*game*).

fléchir [fle'ʃiːr], *v.t.* to bend, to bow; (*fig.*) to move, to persuade.—*v.i.* to bend, to bow, to yield; to stagger.

fléchissement [fleʃis'mã], *n.m.* bending, giving way.

flegmatique [flɛgma'tik], *a.* (*Med.*) phlegmatic; (*fig.*) stolid, sluggish.

flegme [flɛgm], *n.m.* phlegm; (*fig.*) coolness, impassivity.

flet [flɛ], **flétan** [fle'tã], *n.m.* **grand flétan**, halibut; *petit flétan* or *flet*, flounder.

flétrir [fle'triːr], *v.t.* to wither; (*fig.*) to blight, to tarnish, to blemish. **se flétrir**, *v.r.* to fade, to wither.

flétrissant [fletri'sã], *a.* dishonouring, blighting.

flétrissure [fletri'syːr], *n.f.* fading, withering; stigma, disgrace.

fleur [flœːr], *n.f.* flower, blossom; bloom; (*fig.*) best, pick; surface; *à fleur d'eau*, at water level; *à fleur de peau*, superficially; *yeux à fleur de tête*, prominent or goggle eyes.

fleurer [flœ're], *v.i.* to smell, to exhale.

fleuret [flœ'rɛ], *n.m.* (*Fenc.*) foil; miner's drill.

fleurette [flœ'rɛt], *n.f.* little flower, floweret; amorous discourse, gallant speech.

fleuri [flœ'ri], *a.* flowery; florid.

fleurir [flœ'riːr], *v.t.* to decorate with flowers.—*v.i.* to flower, to blossom; to flourish. **se fleurir**, *v.r.* to adorn oneself with flowers.

fleurissant [flœri'sã], *a.* blossoming, blooming.

fleuriste [flœ'rist], *a.* and *n.* florist; artificial flower-maker or seller.

fleuron [flœ'rɔ̃], *n.m.* carved or painted flower; (*fig.*) flower-work; jewel.

fleuve [flœːv], *n.m.* river (*flowing into the sea*), large stream.

flexibilité [flɛksibili'te], *n.f.* flexibility, pliancy.

flexible [flɛk'sibl], *a.* flexible, pliable, supple.

flexion [flɛk'sjɔ̃], *n.f.* flexion, bending.

flibuster [flibys'te], *v.i.* to buccaneer, to filibuster, to freeboot.

flibusterie [flibys'tri], *n.f.* filibustering; robbery, theft.

flibustier [flibys'tje], *n.m.* buccaneer, pirate; filibuster.

flirt [flœrt], *n.m.* flirtation, flirting.

flirter [flœr'te], *v.i.* to flirt.—*int.* flop!

floc [flɔk], *n.m.* tuft, tassel.—*int.* flop!

floche [flɔʃ], *a.* flossy, shaggy.

flocon [flɔ'kɔ̃], *n.m.* flock, tuft; flake (*of snow*).

floconneux [flɔkɔ'nø], *a.* (*fem.* **-euse**) flaky.

floraison [flɔrɛ'zɔ̃], *n.f.* efflorescence, flowering.

floral [flɔ'ral], *a.* (*m. pl.* **-aux**) floral.

flore [flɔːr], *n.f.* flora.

florentin [flɔrã'tɛ̃], *a.* Florentine.

florin [flɔ'rɛ̃], *n.m.* florin.

florir [flɔ'riːr], [FLEURIR].

florissant [flɔri'sã], *a.* prosperous, flourishing.

floriste [flɔ'rist], *n.* florist.

flot [flo], *n.m.* wave, billow; (*fig.*) tide, flood; crowd; (*pl.*) sea, stream, torrent.

flottage [flɔ'taːʒ], *n.m.* floating of wood, rafting.

flottaison [flɔtɛ'zɔ̃], *n.f.* floating.

flottant [flɔ'tã], *a.* floating, waving; (*fig.*) irresolute.

flotte [flɔt], *n.f.* fleet; navy.

flottement [flɔt'mã], *n.m.* floating; (*fig.*) wavering, irresolution.

flotter [flɔ'te], _v.i._ to float; to flutter (_of flag_); to be irresolute.

flotteur [flɔ'tœːr], _n.m._ raftsman; fishing-float; cable-buoy.

flottille [flɔ'tiːj], _n.f._ flotilla.

flou [flu], _a._ hazy, soft, blurred, out of focus. —_n.m._ softness, haziness (_of outlines_); (_Dress._) looseness.

fluctuation [flyktɥa'sjɔ̃], _n.f._ fluctuation.

fluctuer [flyk'tɥe], _v.i._ to fluctuate.

fluctueux [flyk'tɥø], _a._ (_fem._ **-euse**) fluctuating, agitated, boisterous.

fluet [flɥ'ɛ], _a._ (_fem._ **-ette**) slender, thin, slim.

fluide [flɥ'id], _a._ fluid (_liquid_).—_n.m._ fluid.

fluidité [flɥidi'te], _n.f._ fluidity.

fluorescence [flyɔrɛ'sãːs], _n.f._ fluorescence.

fluorescent [flyɔrɛ'sã], _a._ fluorescent.

fluorure [flyɔ'ryːr], _n.m._ fluoride.

flûte [flyt], _n.f._ flute; long French roll; tall glass (_for champagne_).

flûté [fly'te], _a._ soft, fluted, fluty (_of a voice_).

flûtiste [fly'tist], _n._ flautist, flute-player.

fluvial [fly'vjal], _a._ (_m. pl._ **-aux**) fluvial.

flux [fly], _n.m._ flux, flow, flood, rising.

fluxion [flyk'sjɔ̃], _n.f._ inflammation, swelling.

foc [fɔk], _n.m._ (_Naut._) jib.

focal [fɔ'kal], _a._ (_m. pl._ **-aux**) focal.

foi [fwa], _n.f._ faith, belief; trust; fidelity, honour; proof, testimony.

foie [fwa], _n.m._ liver.

foin [fwɛ̃], _n.m._ hay.

foire [fwaːr], _n.f._ fair (_market_); fairing.

fois [fwa], _n.f. inv._ time (_turn, occasion_); **une fois**, once; **trois fois**, three times.

foison [fwa'zɔ̃], _n.f._ plenty, abundance.

foisonner [fwazɔ'ne], _v.i._ to abound, to increase, to multiply.

fol [fɔl], [FOU].

folâtre [fɔ'laːtr], _a._ playful, gay, frolicsome.

folâtrer [fɔla'tre], _v.i._ to play, to sport, to frolic.

folâtrerie [fɔlatrə'ri], _n.f._ frolic, prank, gambol.

foliacé [fɔlja'se], _a._ (_Bot._) foliaceous.

foliation [fɔlja'sjɔ̃], _n.f._ foliation.

folichon [fɔli'ʃɔ̃], _a._ (_fam._) frolicsome, waggish, wanton.

folie [fɔ'li], _n.f._ madness, distraction, folly; foolery, jest; mania; hobby.

folio [fɔ'ljo], _n.m._ folio.

folle [fɔl], [FOU].

follement [fɔl'mã], _adv._ madly, foolishly.

follet [fɔ'lɛ], _a._ (_fem._ **-ette**) wanton, playful, frolicsome; _feu follet_, will o' the wisp.

fomentation [fɔmãta'sjɔ̃], _n.f._ fomentation.

fomenter [fɔmã'te], _v.t._ to foment, (_fig._) to feed, to excite.

foncé [fɔ̃'se], _a._ dark, deep (_of colour_).

foncer [fɔ̃'se], _v.t._ (_conjug. like_ COMMENCER) to fit a bottom to (_a cask etc._); to sink (_wells etc._); to deepen (_colours_).—_v.i._ to dash, to swoop (_sur_).

foncier [fɔ̃'sje], _a._ (_fem._ **-ière**) landed; based on _or_ derived from land; (_fig._) thorough.—_n.m._ land-tax.

foncièrement [fɔ̃sjɛr'mã], _adv._ thoroughly, completely, fundamentally.

fonction [fɔ̃k'sjɔ̃], _n.f._ function, office; occupation.

fonctionnaire [fɔ̃ksjɔ'nɛːr], _n.m._ civil servant, officer, official.

fonctionnel [fɔ̃ksjɔ'nɛl], _a._ (_fem._ **-elle**) functional.

fonctionnement [fɔ̃ksjɔn'mã], _n.m._ operation, working, action.

fonctionner [fɔ̃ksjɔ'ne], _v.i._ to work, to act, to operate.

fond [fɔ̃], _n.m._ bottom; bed, ground; farther end; foundation; (_fig._) essence; basis; subject matter; (_Paint._) background; (_Theat._) back-cloth.

fondage [fɔ̃'daːʒ], _n.m._ casting, smelting.

fondamental [fɔ̃damã'tal], _a._ (_m. pl._ **-aux**) fundamental, essential.

fondamentalement [fɔ̃damãtal'mã], _adv._ fundamentally, essentially, radically.

fondant [fɔ̃'dã], _a._ melting, dissolving, luscious.—_n.m._ fondant (_sweetmeat_); flux (_for metals_).

fondateur [fɔ̃da'tœːr], _n.m._ (_fem._ **-trice**) founder; promoter.

fondation [fɔ̃da'sjɔ̃], _n.f._ foundation; groundwork; founding; endowment.

fondé [fɔ̃'de], _a._ founded; well-founded; (_Fin._) consolidated.—_n.m._ proxy.

fondement [fɔ̃d'mã], _n.m._ foundation; basis, ground, cause.

fonder [fɔ̃'de], _v.t._ to lay the foundation of, to establish; to institute; to base; to endow. **se fonder**, _v.r._ to rely or rest (_upon_), to be founded (_sur_).

fonderie [fɔ̃'dri], _n.f._ foundry; smelting-house; casting.

fondeur [fɔ̃'dœːr], _n.m._ founder, caster, smelter.

fondre [fɔ̃:dr], _v.t._ to melt; to dissolve; to smelt; to cast.—_v.i._ to melt; to pounce (_sur_); to vanish; to blow (_of a fuse_); _fondre en larmes_, to burst into tears. **se fondre**, _v.r._ to melt; to dissolve; to be cast; to blend; to diminish, to melt away.

fondrière [fɔ̃dri'ɛːr], _n.f._ bog, quagmire; rut, pothole; slough.

fonds [fɔ̃], _n.m._ land, soil; landed property; funds, capital; business assets; (_pl._) funds, stocks etc.

fondue [fɔ̃'dy], _n.f._ dish of melted cheese and eggs.

fongicide [fɔ̃ʒi'sid], _a._ fungicide.

fongoïde [fɔ̃gɔ'id], _a._ fungoid.

fongueux [fɔ̃'gø], _a._ (_fem._ **-euse**) fungous.

fongus [fɔ̃'gys], _n.m._ (_Med._) fungus.

fontaine [fɔ̃'tɛːn], _n.f._ fountain, spring; cistern.

fonte [fɔ̃:t], _n.f._ melting, smelting; cast-iron; casting; holster (_of saddles_).

fonts [fɔ̃], _n.m. pl._ (_no sing._) font.

football [fut'bɔl], _n.m._ Association Football.

footballeur [futbɔ'lœːr], _n.m._ footballer.

footing [fu'tiŋ], _n.m._ walking (_for training_ or _exercise_).

forage [fɔ'raːʒ], _n.m._ boring, drilling; sinking (_of well_).

forain [fɔ'rɛ̃], _a._ non-resident, travelling, itinerant; _marchand forain_, hawker, pedlar.

forban [fɔr'bã], _n.m._ pirate, corsair, free-booter.

forçat [fɔr'sa], _n.m._ convict.

force [fɔrs], _n.f._ strength, might, power; authority; violence, constraint; vigour; resolution; skill; (_pl._) troops, forces.— *_adv._ a great deal, a great many.

forcé [fɔr'se], *a.* forced, compulsory; unnatural, strained, far-fetched.

forcément [fɔrse'mã], *adv.* forcibly; necessarily, inevitably.

forcené [fɔrsə'ne], *a.* mad, furious; passionate, infuriated.—*n.m.* (*fem.* **-ée**) mad person.

forceps [fɔr'sɛps], *n.m. inv.* forceps.

forcer [fɔr'se], *v.t.* (*conjug. like* COMMENCER) to force; to compel; to impel; to strain; to break open; to storm; to outrage. **se forcer**, *v.r.* to strain oneself; to do violence to one's feelings.

forer [fɔ're], *v.t.* to bore, to drill, to perforate.

forestier [fɔrɛs'tje], *a.* (*fem.* **-ière**) pertaining to forests.—*n.m.* ranger, keeper, forester.

foret [fɔ'rɛ], *n.m.* borer, drill.

forêt [fɔ'rɛ], *n.f.* forest; woodland.

forfaire [fɔr'fɛːr], *v.t. irr.* to forfeit (*a fief*).—*v.i.* (*used only in inf., p.p.* (**forfait** (1) *and compound tenses*) to fail (*in one's duty*); to trespass, to be false to.

forfait (2) [fɔr'fɛ], *n.m.* crime, heinous offence.

forfait (3) [fɔr'fɛ], *n.m.* contract.

forfaiture [fɔrfɛ'tyːr], *n.f.* forfeiture; breach of duty.

forfanterie [fɔrfɑ̃'tri], *n.f.* romancing, bragging, boasting.

forge [fɔrʒ], *n.f.* forge, smithy; iron-works.

forger [fɔr'ʒe], *v.t.* (*conjug. like* MANGER) to forge, to hammer; (*fig.*) to invent, to fabricate. **se forger**, *v.r.* to imagine, to conjure up, to fancy.

forgeron [fɔrʒə'rɔ̃], *n.m.* smith, blacksmith.

formaliser (se) [səfɔrmali'ze], *v.r.* to take exception *or* offence (*de*).

formalisme [fɔrma'lism], *n.m.* formalism.

formaliste [fɔrma'list], *a.* formal, precise.—*n.* formalist; quibbler.

formalité [fɔrmali'te], *n.f.* formality; form, ceremony.

format [fɔr'ma], *n.m.* format (*size, shape etc., of a book*).

formateur [fɔrma'tœːr], *a.* (*fem.* **-trice**) formative, creative.

formation [fɔrma'sjɔ̃], *n.f.* formation; education; (*Geol.*) structure.

forme [fɔrm], *n.f.* form, shape, figure; etiquette; crown (*of a hat*).

formé [fɔr'me], *a.* formed, mature.

formel [fɔr'mɛl], *a.* (*fem.* **-elle**) formal; express, precise.

formellement [fɔrmɛl'mã], *adv.* formally; expressly, precisely, strictly.

former [fɔr'me], *v.t.* to form, to frame; to make up; to bring up; to train; to mould. **se former**, *v.r.* to be formed; to take shape.

formidable [fɔrmi'dabl], *a.* formidable, fearful; (*fam.*) terrific.

Formose [fɔr'moːz], la, *f.* Formosa, Taiwan.

formule [fɔr'myl], *n.f.* formula, form; model; recipe.

formuler [fɔrmy'le], *v.t.* to formulate; to detail; (*Med.*) to write (*a prescription*).

fort [fɔːr], *a.* strong, sturdy; powerful; clever; plentiful; shocking; painful; high (*wind*); heavy (*ground, rain*).—*n.m.* strong part; stronghold, fort; strength; depth, heat, height; centre.—*adv.* very, very much, extremely; hard.

fortement [fɔrtə'mã], *adv.* strongly, vigorously; much, exceedingly.

forteresse [fɔrtə'rɛs], *n.f.* fortress, stronghold.

fortifiant [fɔrti'fjã], *a.* strengthening, bracing.—*n.m.* (*Med.*) tonic.

fortification [fɔrtifika'sjɔ̃], *n.f.* fortification; fort, redoubt.

fortifier [fɔrti'fje], *v.t.* to strengthen, to invigorate; to fortify; to confirm. **se fortifier**, *v.r.* to fortify oneself, to grow strong.

fortuit [fɔr'tɥi], *a.* fortuitous, casual.

fortuitement [fɔrtɥit'mã], *adv.* fortuitously, casually, by chance.

fortune [fɔr'tyn], *n.f.* fortune, chance, hazard, risk; success, luck; wealth.

fortuné [fɔrty'ne], *a.* fortunate, lucky; happy; well-to-do.

fosse [foːs], *n.f.* hole, pit; grave; (*Hort.*) trench.

fossé [fo'se], *n.m.* ditch, drain, trench; moat.

fossette [fo'sɛt], *n.f.* dimple.

fossile [fo'sil], *a.* fossilized.—*n.m.* fossil.

fossiliser [fɔsili'ze], *v.t.* to fossilize. **se fossiliser**, *v.r.* to become fossilized.

fossoyage [foswa'jaːʒ], *n.m.* ditching; gravedigging.

fossoyer [foswa'je], *v.t.* (*conjug. like* EMPLOYER) to ditch, to dig a trench round.

fossoyeur [foswa'jœːr], *n.m.* grave-digger; sexton beetle.

fou [fu], *a.* (*before vowels* **fol**, *fem.* **folle**) mad, demented; wild, foolish; tremendous.—*n.m.* (*fem.* **folle**) madman, madwoman.—*n.m* jester, fool; (*Chess*) bishop.

foudre (1) [fudr], *n.f.* lightning; thunder, thunderbolt; (*fig.*) sudden calamity; *coup de foudre*, clap of thunder.—*n.m.* (*fig.*) *un foudre de guerre*, a great captain; *un foudre d'éloquence*, a mighty speaker.

foudre (2) [fudr], *n.m.* large cask, tun.

foudroiement [fudrwa'mã], *n.m.* striking, blasting (*by thunder or lightning*); (*fig.*) destruction.

foudroyant [fudrwa'jã], *a.* thundering, terrible, crushing (*news*).

foudroyer [fudrwa'je], *v.t.* (*conjug. like* EMPLOYER) to strike (*thunder or lightning*); to riddle with shot; (*fig.*) to blast, to crush.—*v.i.* to thunder; (*fig.*) to fulminate.

fouet [fwɛ], *n.m.* whip; lash; whipping, slating (*criticism*).

fouetter [fwɛ'te], *v.t.* to whip, to flog; to whisk (*eggs etc.*); to flick; (*fig.*) to excite.—*v.i.* to beat, to patter (*of hail, rain*).

fougeraie [fuʒ'rɛ], *n.f.* fern-patch, fernery.

fougère [fu'ʒɛːr], *n.f.* fern.

fougue [fug], *n.f.* ardour, impetuosity; fire, spirit, mettle; (*Naut.*) mizzen-top.

fougueux [fu'gø], *a.* (*fem.* **-euse**) fiery, impetuous, ardent, passionate, high-mettled.

fouille [fuːj], *n.f.* excavation, digging; search.

fouiller [fu'je], *v.t.* to excavate; (*fig.*) to pry into, to rummage, to ransack; to search; to think out (*problems etc.*).—*v.i.* to dig, to search; (*fig.*) to rummage.

fouillis [fu'ji], *n.m.* medley, jumble; confused mass (*of foliage etc.*).

fouine (1) [fwin], *n.f.* marten.

fouine (2) [fwin], *n.f.* pitchfork; fish-spear.
fouiner [fwi'ne], *v.i.* (*colloq.*) to nose about, to ferret; to slink off.
fouir [fwi:r], *v.t.* to dig; to burrow.
fouissement [fwis'mɑ̃], *n.m.* digging; burrowing.
fouisseur [fwi'sœr], *a.* (*fem.* **-euse**) burrowing (*animal*).
foulage [fu'la:ʒ], *n.m.* fulling; treading, pressing (*of grapes*).
foulant [fu'lɑ̃], *a.* pressing; forcing; *pompe foulante*, force-pump.
foulard [fu'la:r], *n.m.* silk neckerchief; scarf.
foule [ful], *n.f.* crowd, throng, multitude; mob.
foulée [fu'le], *n.f.* tread (*of steps*); stride (*of a horse or runner*).
fouler [fu'le], *v.t.* to tread; to trample down; to press; to oppress; to sprain (*ankle*).—*v.i.* (*Print.*) to press. **se fouler**, *v.r. se fouler le pied*, to sprain one's foot.
fouleur [fu'lœr], *n.m.* (*fem.* **-euse**) fuller; wine-presser.
foulure [fu'ly:r], *n.f.* sprain, wrench, strain.
four [fu:r], *n.m.* oven; bakehouse; furnace; kiln; *des petits fours*, fancy biscuits, small cakes.
fourbe [furb], *a.* cheating, deceitful.—*n.* cheat, swindler, impostor.
fourberie [furbə'ri], *n.f.* cheating, knavery, imposture, deceit.
fourbir [fur'bi:r], *v.t.* to furbish, to polish.
fourbisseur [furbi'sœr], *n.m.* furbisher; sword-cutler.
fourbissure [furbi'sy:r], *n.f.* furbishing, polishing.
fourbu [fur'by], *a.* foundered, run down (*of horses*); dead tired (*of persons*).
fourbure [fur'by:r]. *n.f.* foundering, inflammation of the feet.
fourche [furʃ], *n.f.* pitchfork, (garden) fork, fork (*of roads*).
fourchée [fur'ʃe], *n.f.* pitchforkful.
fourcher [fur'ʃe], *v.i.* to fork; to divide. **se fourcher**, *v.r.* to fork, to branch off.
fourchetée [furʃ'te], *n.f.* table-forkful.
fourchette [fur'ʃɛt], *n.f.* table-fork; breast-bone (*of birds*).
fourchu [fur'ʃy], *a.* forked; cloven; furcate.
fourgon (1) [fur'gɔ̃], *n.m.* van, wagon, guard's van.
fourgon (2) [fur'gɔ̃], *n.m.* poker, fire-iron (*for ovens etc.*).
fourgonner [furgɔ'ne], *v.i.* to poke the fire (*of an oven*); (*colloq.*) to poke, to rummage.
fourmi [fur'mi], *n.f.* ant.
fourmilière [furmi'ljɛ:r], *n.f.* ant-hill, ants' nest; (*fig.*) swarm; crowd.
fourmillement [furmij'mɑ̃], *n.m.* tingling, pins and needles; swarming.
fourmiller [furmi'je], *v.i.* to swarm, to be full (*de*); to have pins and needles (*in one's limbs etc.*).
fournaise [fur'nɛ:z], *n.f.* (*Lit.*) furnace; (*fig.*) oven.
fourneau [fur'no], *n.m.* (*pl.* **-eaux**) stove, cooker, cooking-range; furnace.
fournée [fur'ne], *n.f.* batch, baking; kilnful (*of bricks*).
fournil [fur'ni], *n.m.* bakehouse.
fourniment [furni'mɑ̃], *n.m.* (*Mil.*) equipment.

fournir [fur'ni:r], *v.t.* to furnish, to supply, to stock, to provide; to make up (*a sum of money*).—*v.i.* to contribute (*à*); to suffice.
fournisseur [furni'sœr], *n.m.* army contractor; purveyor; tradesman.
fourniture [furni'ty:r], *n.f.* furnishing; supply, provision; equipment.
fourrage [fu'ra:ʒ], *n.m.* fodder; forage; foraging-party.
fourrager [fura'ʒe], *v.t.* (*conjug. like* MANGER) to ravage; to upset.—*v.i.* to forage; to plunder, to ravage; (*fig.*) to rummage.
fourrageur [fura'ʒœr], *n.m.* forager; (*fig.*) marauder; rummager.
fourré [fu're], *a.* thick, furry; wooded; (*fig.*) underhand (*of a blow etc.*).—*n.m.* thicket, brake.
fourreau [fu'ro], *n.m.* (*pl.* **-eaux**) sheath, case; scabbard; cover; tight-fitting *or* sheath dress.
fourrer [fu're], *v.t.* to line with fur; to poke; to cram, to stuff. **se fourrer**, *v.r.* to thrust oneself in, to intrude; to wrap oneself up warmly.
fourreur [fu'rœr], *n.m.* furrier.
fourrier [fu'rje], *n.m.* quartermaster-sergeant; (*fig.*) harbinger.
fourrière [fu'rjɛ:r], *n.f.* pound (*for vehicles, strayed animals*).
fourrure [fu'ry:r], *n.f.* fur, furred gown.
fourvoyer [furvwa'je], *v.t.* (*conjug. like* EMPLOYER) to lead astray, to mislead; (*fig.*) to baffle. **se fourvoyer**, *v.r.* to go astray, to lose one's way; (*fig.*) to blunder badly.
fox (1) [fɔks], *n.m.* fox-terrier.
fox (2) [fɔks], *n.m.* foxtrot.
foyer [fwa'je], *n.m.* hearth; fire; fire-box (*of an engine*); (*fig.*) home, family; (*Theat.*) foyer; focus, source.
frac [frak], *n.m.* frock-coat.
fracas [fra'kɑ], *n.m.* noise, din; disturbance; fuss.
fracasser [fraka'se], *v.t.* to break into pieces, to shatter. **se fracasser**, *v.r.* to crash to pieces.
fraction [frak'sjɔ̃], *n.f.* breaking; fraction, portion.
fractionnaire [fraksjɔ'nɛ:r], *a.* fractional.
fracture [frak'ty:r], *n.f.* breaking (*with violence*), rupture; (*Surg.*) fracture.
fracturer [frakty're], *v.t.* to break, to smash; (*Surg.*) to fracture. **se fracturer**, *v.r.* to fracture oneself; to be fractured.
fragile [fra'ʒil], *a.* fragile, brittle; frail.
fragilité [fraʒili'te], *n.f.* fragility, brittleness; frailty.
fragment [frag'mɑ̃], *n.m.* fragment, piece, remnant.
fragmentaire [fragmɑ̃'tɛ:r], *a.* fragmentary.
fragmentation [fragmɑ̃ta'sjɔ̃], *n.f.* fragmenting, fragmentation.
fragmenter [fragmɑ̃'te], *v.t.* to reduce to fragments.
fragrance [fra'grɑ̃:s], *n.f.* fragrance.
fragrant [fra'grɑ̃], *a.* fragrant.
frai [frɛ], *n.m.* fraying; spawning (*of fish*).
fraîche [frɛʃ], [FRAIS (1).]
fraîchement [frɛʃ'mɑ̃], *adv.* coolly, freshly; newly, recently.
fraîcheur [frɛ'ʃœr], *n.f.* coolness, freshness, coldness; ruddiness; brilliancy.
fraîchir [frɛ'ʒi:r], *v.i.* to freshen; to get cool.

frais

frais (1) [frɛ], *a.* (*fem.* **fraîche**) cool; fresh; new; youthful; ruddy; new-laid (*of eggs*).— *n.m.* coolness, freshness; cool spot.—*adv.* freshly, newly, recently, just.

frais (2) [frɛ], *n.m.* (*used only in pl.*) expense, expenses; charge, charges, cost, outlay; *menus frais*, petty expenses; *sans frais*, free of charge.

fraise (1) [frɛːz], *n.f.* strawberry; strawberry-mark; ruff.

fraise (2) [frɛːz], *n.f.* fraise (*tool for enlarging a drill hole etc.*); (dentist's) drill.

fraiser [frɛ'ze], *v.t.* to plait, to ruffle; to countersink.

fraisier [frɛ'zje], *n.m.* strawberry-plant; strawberry grower.

framboise [frɑ̃'bwaːz], *n.f.* raspberry.

framboiser [frɑ̃bwa'ze], *v.t.* to give a raspberry flavour to.

framboisier [frɑ̃bwa'zje], *n.m.* raspberry-bush.

franc (1) [frɑ̃], *n.m.* franc (*French coin*); new franc (*of 1960*).

franc (2) [frɑ̃], *a.* (*fem.* **franche**) free; exempt; frank, candid, sincere; clear.— *adv.* frankly, openly, sincerely; clean; quite, completely.

franc (3) [frɑ̃], *a.* (*fem.* **franque**) Frankish.— *n.m.* Frankish (*language*); (**Franc**, *fem.* **Franque**) Frank.

français [frɑ̃'sɛ], *a.* French.—*n.m.* French (*language*); (**Français**, *fem.* **-aise**) Frenchman, Frenchwoman.

France [frɑ̃ːs], **la**, *f.* France.

franche [frɑ̃ʃ], [FRANC (2)].

franchement [frɑ̃ʃ'mɑ̃], *adv.* frankly, sincerely; plainly; boldly.

franchir [frɑ̃'ʃiːr], *v.t.* to leap, to jump over; to clear; to pass over; to surmount.

franchise [frɑ̃'ʃiːz], *n.f.* exemption, immunity; freedom (*of a city*); (*fig.*) frankness, sincerity.

franchissable [frɑ̃ʃi'sabl], *a.* passable, capable of being crossed.

franchissement [frɑ̃ʃis'mɑ̃], *n.m.* leaping over, crossing.

francisation [frɑ̃siza'sjɔ̃], *n.f.* gallicizing of foreign word; registration as a French ship.

franciscain [frɑ̃sis'kɛ̃], *a.* and *n.m.* (*fem.* **-e**) Franciscan, grey friar, Franciscan nun.

franciser [frɑ̃si'ze], *v.t.* to gallicize; to Frenchify. **se franciser**, *v.r.* to become French *or* Frenchified.

franc-maçon [frɑ̃ma'sɔ̃], *n.m.* (*pl.* **francs-maçons**) freemason.

franc-maçonnerie [frɑ̃masɔn'ri], *n.f.* freemasonry.

franco [frɑ̃'ko], *adv.* free of charge; prepaid.

François [frɑ̃'swa], *m.* Francis.

Françoise [frɑ̃'swaːz], *f.* Frances.

francophile [frɑ̃ko'fil], *a.* and *n.* Francophile.

francophobe [frɑ̃ko'fob], *a.* and *n.* Francophobe.

franc-parler [frɑ̃par'le], *n.m.* frankness *or* freedom of speech.

franc-tireur [frɑ̃ti'rœːr], *n.m.* franc-tireur; sniper.

frange [frɑ̃ːʒ], *n.f.* fringe.

franger [frɑ̃'ʒe], *v.t.* (*conjug. like* MANGER) to fringe.

franque [frɑ̃k], [FRANC (3)].

frappant [fra'pɑ̃], *a.* striking, impressive.

frappé [fra'pe], *a.* struck, astounded; iced (*of liquids etc.*); (*fig.*) powerful.

frappement [frap'mɑ̃], *n.m.* striking, stamping; clapping (*of hands*).

frapper [fra'pe], *v.t.* to strike, to slap, to hit; to make an impression on, to affect; to surprise, to frighten; to ice (*liquids*).—*v.i.* to knock, to rap. **se frapper**, *v.r.* to strike oneself; to strike each other; to be impressed.

frappeur [fra'pœːr], *a.* (*fem.* **-euse**) striking, rapping.—*n.m.* (*fem.* **-euse**) beater, striker.

frasque [frask], *n.f.* prank, escapade.

fraternel [fratɛr'nɛl], *a.* (*fem.* **-elle**) fraternal, brotherly.

fraternellement [fratɛrnɛl'mɑ̃], *adv.* fraternally.

fraternisation [fratɛrniza'sjɔ̃], *n.f.* fraternization.

fraterniser [fratɛrni'ze], *v.t.* to fraternize.

fraternité [fratɛrni'te], *n.f.* fraternity, brotherhood.

fratricide [fratri'sid], *a.* fratricidal.—*n.m.* fratricide.

fraude [froːd], *n.f.* fraud, deceit.

frauder [fro'de], *v.t.* to defraud.—*v.i.* to smuggle.

fraudeur [fro'dœːr], *n.m.* (*fem.* **-euse**) defrauder; smuggler.

frauduleusement [frodyløz'mɑ̃], *adv.* fraudulently.

frauduleux [frody'lø], *a.* (*fem.* **-euse**) fraudulent.

frayer [frɛ'je], *v.t.* to trace out, to open out; to make (*a way etc.*); to rub against, to graze.—*v.i.* to wear away; to spawn (*of fish*); (*fig.*) to frequent, to be on good terms (*avec*). **se frayer**, *v.r.* to open for oneself; to prepare *or* carve out (*a way*) for oneself.

frayeur [frɛ'jœːr], *n.f.* fright, terror, fear.

fredaine [frɔ'dɛn], *n.f.* (*colloq.*) frolic, prank; freak.

Frédéric [frede'rik], *m.* Frederick.

Frédérique [frede'rik], *f.* Frederica.

fredon [frɔ'dɔ̃], *n.m.* song, refrain.

fredonnement [frɔdɔn'mɑ̃], *n.m.* humming.

fredonner [frɔdɔ'ne], *v.t.*, *v.i.* to hum.

frégate [fre'gat], *n.f.* frigate; frigate bird; (*Navy*) *capitaine de frégate*, commander.

frein [frɛ̃], *n.m.* bit, bridle; curb, check; brake.

freinage [frɛ'naːʒ], *n.m.* braking.

freiner [frɛ'ne], *v.t.* to brake; to curb.

frelatage [frɔla'taːʒ], *n.m.*, **frelatement** [frɔlat'mɑ̃], *n.m.*, **frelaterie** [frɔla'tri], **frelatation** [frɔlata'sjɔ̃], *n.f.* adulteration.

frelater [frɔla'te], *v.t.* to adulterate.

frêle [frɛːl], *a.* frail, fragile, weak.

frelon [frɔ'lɔ̃], *n.m.* hornet.

freluquet [frɔly'kɛ], *n.m.* conceited young man, puppy.

frémir [fre'miːr], *v.i.* to quiver, to shudder, to tremble; to vibrate; to rustle.

frémissant [fremi'sɑ̃], *a.* quivering, trembling.

frémissement [fremis'mɑ̃], *n.m.* quivering, trembling, shuddering; thrill, vibration; rustling.

frênaie [frɛ'nɛ], *n.f.* ash-grove.

frêne [frɛːn], *n.m.* ash, ash-tree.

frénésie [frene'zi], *n.f.* frenzy, madness.

frénétique [frene′tik], *a.* frantic, frenzied.—*n.* raving, frantic person.

frénétiquement [frenetik′mɑ̃], *adv.* frantically.

fréquemment [freka′mɑ̃], *adv.* frequently.

fréquence [fre′kɑ̃ːs], *n.f.* frequency.

fréquent [fre′kɑ̃], *a.* frequent.

fréquentation [frekɑ̃tɑ′sjɔ̃], *n.f.* frequentation, company.

fréquenter [frekɑ̃′te], *v.t.* to frequent, to keep company with; to haunt.—*v.i.* to associate (*chez*); to be a frequent caller (*at*).

frère [frɛːr], *n.m.* brother; fellow-member; monk.

fresque [frɛsk], *n.f.* fresco.

fret [frɛ], *n.m.* freight, cargo.

fréter [fre′te], *v.t.* (*conjug. like* CÉDER) to charter; to freight; to hire (*a car*).

fréteur [fre′tœːr], *n.m.* freighter, charterer.

frétillant [freti′jɑ̃], *a.* wriggling, lively; frisky.

frétillement [fretij′mɑ̃] *n.m.* wriggling; frisking.

frétiller [freti′je], *v.i.* to wriggle, to jump about; to frisk.

fretin [frə′tɛ̃], *n.m.* fry, young fish; (*fig.*) trash.

freudien [frə′djɛ̃], *a.* (*fem.* **-enne**) Freudian.

freux [frø], *n.m. inv.* (*Orn.*) rook.

friable [fri′abl], *a.* friable; crisp, short.

friand [fri′ɑ̃], *a.* dainty, nice; partial to; appetizing.

friandise [friɑ̃′diːz], *n.f.* daintiness; dainty, titbit.

fricassée [frika′se], *n.f.* hash.

fricasser [frika′se], *v.t.* to fricassee.

friche [friʃ], *n.f.* waste *or* fallow land.

fricot [fri′ko], *n.m.* (*colloq.*) ragout, stew.

fricoter [friko′te], *v.t.* to squander.—*v.i.* to cook.

fricoteur [friko′tœːr], *n.m.* (*fem.* **-euse**) feaster; fast liver.

friction [frik′sjɔ̃] *n.f.* friction, rubbing.

frictionner [friksjo′ne], *v.t.* to rub.

frigide [fri′ʒid], *a.* frigid.

frigidité [friʒidi′te], *n.f.* frigidity.

frigorifier [frigori′fje], *v.t.* to chill, to freeze (*meat etc.*).

frileux [fri′lø], *a.* (*fem.* **-euse**) chilly; susceptible to cold.—*n.m.* redbreast, robin.

frimas [fri′ma], *n.m.* *rime, hoar-frost.

frime [frim], *n.f.* (*pop.*) show, pretence, sham.

fringant [frɛ̃′gɑ̃], *a.* brisk, frisky, smart.

fringuer [frɛ̃′ge], *v.i.* to skip; to prance (*of a horse*).

fripe [frip], *n.f.* rag, scrap (*of cloth etc.*).

friper [fri′pe], *v.t.* to crumple, to rumple. se **friper**, *v.r.* to become rumpled *or* shabby.

friperie [fri′pri], *n.f.* frippery, old clothes; junk shop.

fripier [fri′pje], *n.m.* (*fem.* **-ière**) dealer in old clothes, furniture etc.

fripon [fri′pɔ̃], *a.* (*fem.* **-onne**) cheating, rascally.—*n.m.* (*fem.* **-onne**) rogue, cheat.

friponnerie [fripon′ri], *n.f.* cheating, roguery, knavery.

friquet [fri′kɛ], *n.m.* tree-sparrow.

frire [friːr], *v.t., v.i. irr.* to fry.

frisage [fri′zaːʒ], *n.m.* curling, frizzing (*of hair etc.*).

frise [friːz], *n.f.* (*Arch. etc.*) frieze.

friser [fri′ze], *v.t.* to curl, to frizz (*hair*); to graze; to border upon.—*v.i.* to curl. se **friser**, *v.r.* to curl; to curl one's hair.

frisson [fri′sɔ̃], *n.m.* shiver, shudder; thrill.

frissonnant [friso′nɑ̃], *a.* shuddering, shivering.

frissonnement [frison′mɑ̃], *n.m.* shivering, shudder; thrill.

frissonner [friso′ne], *v.i.* to shiver, to shudder; to feel a thrill; to tremble.

frisure [fri′zyːr], *n.f.* crisping; curling.

frit [fri], *a.* fried.—*n.f. pl.* **des frites**, chips.

friture [fri′tyːr], *n.f.* frying; fried fish etc.; grease (*for frying*).

frivole [fri′vɔl], *a.* frivolous, trifling; futile.

frivolité [frivoli′te], *n.f.* frivolity; trifle.

froc [frɔk], *n.m.* cowl, monk's gown.

froid [frwa], *a.* cold; (*fig.*) indifferent, lifeless; reserved.—*n.m.* cold, coldness; chilliness; (*fig.*) unconcern, dullness; reserve.

froidement [frwad′mɑ̃], *adv.* coldly, frigidly; dispassionately.

froideur [frwa′dœːr], *n.f.* coldness; chilliness; (*fig.*) indifference, coolness.

froidure [frwa′dyːr], *n.f.* coldness (*of the weather*); cold; (*fig.*) winter.

froissement [frwas′mɑ̃], *n.m.* rumpling; bruising; (*fig.*) clash; slight, affront, annoyance.

froisser [frwa′se], *v.t.* to rumple; to crease; to bruise slightly; (*fig.*) to offend, to wound. se **froisser**, *v.r.* to become bruised (*of a muscle*); to take offence.

froissure [frwa′syːr], *n.f.* crease; bruise.

frôlement [frol′mɑ̃], *n.m.* grazing; rustle.

frôler [fro′le], *v.t.* to graze, to touch slightly in passing; to brush past.

fromage [frɔ′maːʒ], *n.m.* cheese; (*fig.*) **un** (**bon**) **fromage**, a nice soft job.

fromagerie [frɔmaʒ′ri], *n.f.* cheese farm *or* dairy; cheese-trade.

fromageux [frɔma′ʒø], *a.* (*fem.* **-euse**) cheesy.

froment [frɔ′mɑ̃], *n.m.* wheat.

fronce [frɔ̃ːs], *n.f.* gather, pucker (*in needlework etc.*); crease (*in paper*).

froncement [frɔ̃s′mɑ̃], *n.m.* contraction, knitting (*of the brows etc.*); (*fig.*) frowning, frown.

froncer [frɔ̃′se], *v.t.* (*conjug. like* COMMENCER) to contract; to wrinkle; to purse (*the lips*); to gather (*needlework*); **froncer les sourcils**, to frown. se **froncer**, *v.r.* to contract, to pucker; to wrinkle.

frondaison [frɔ̃de′zɔ̃], *n.f.* foliation; foliage.

fronde [frɔ̃ːd], *n.f.* sling; frond; (*Surg.*) bandage.

fronder [frɔ̃′de], *v.t.* to sling, to fling with a sling; to banter; to jeer at.

frondeur [frɔ̃′dœːr], *n.m.* (*fem.* **-euse**) slinger; censurer, fault-finder; rioter.

front [frɔ̃], *n.m.* forehead, brow; face; (*fig.*) boldness, impudence; (*Polit.*) **Front populaire**, Popular Front.

frontal [frɔ̃′tal], *a.* (*m. pl.* **-aux**) (*Anat.*) frontal.—*n.m.* headband.

frontière [frɔ̃′tjɛːr], *n.f.* frontier, border.

frontispice [frɔ̃tis′pis], *n.m.* frontispiece; title-page.

fronton [frɔ̃′tɔ̃], *n.m.* (*Arch.*) fronton, pediment.

frottage [frɔ′taːʒ], *n.m.* rubbing; polishing.

frottée [frɔ'te], *n.f.* (*colloq.*) drubbing.
frottement [frɔt'mã], *n.m.* rubbing, friction; (*fig.*) interaction.
frotter [frɔ'te], *v.t.* to rub; to polish; (*fig.*) to pommel, to warm (*the ears of*).—*v.i.* to rub. **se frotter**, *v.r.* to rub oneself; to provoke, to meddle (*à*).
frotteur [frɔ'tœːr], *n.m.* (*fem.* **-euse**) rubber; scrubber; floor-polisher.
frottoir [frɔ'twaːr], *n.m.* rubbing-cloth; (*Elec.*) brush (*of dynamo*).
frou-frou [fru'fru], *n.m.* (*pl.* **-frous**) rustling (*of silk etc.*).
fructification [fryktifika'sjõ], *n.f.* fructification.
fructifier [frykti'fje], *v.i.* to fructify, to bear fruit; (*fig.*) to thrive.
fructueusement [fryktɥøz'mã], *adv.* fruitfully, profitably.
fructueux [fryk'tɥø], *a.* (*fem.* **-euse**) fruitful, profitable.
frugal [fry'gal], *a.* (*m. pl.* **-aux**) frugal.
frugalement [frygal'mã], *adv.* frugally.
frugalité [frygali'te], *n.f.* frugality.
fruit [frɥi], *n.m.* fruit; (*fig.*) offspring; advantage, utility; (*pl.*) fruits; result.
fruiterie [frɥi'tri], *n.f.* fruit-loft; fruit-trade.
fruitier [frɥi'tje], *a.* (*fem.* **-ière**) fruit-bearing.—*n.m.* (*fem.* **-ière**) fruiterer, green-grocer.
fruste [fryst], *a.* worn, defaced; unpolished (*person*).
frustration [frystra'sjõ], *n.f.* frustration.
frustrer [frys'tre], *v.t.* to defraud; to frustrate, to disappoint, to baffle.
fuchsia [fyk'sja], *n.m.* fuchsia.
fugace [fy'gas], *a.* fugitive, fleeting, transient.
fugitif [fyʒi'tif], *a.* (*fem.* **-tive**) fugitive, fleeting.—*n.m.* (*fem.* **-tive**) fugitive, runaway.
fugue [fyg], *n.f.* fugue; (*colloq.*) flight, escapade.
fuir [fɥiːr], *v.t. irr.* to fly, to avoid; to shun.—*v.i.* to fly, to flee, to run away; to elude; to leak. **se fuir**, *v.r.* to fly from oneself; to shun *or* avoid each other.
fuite [fɥit], *n.f.* flight, escaping; avoiding; evasion, shift; leakage.
fulgurant [fylgy'rã], *a.* flashing, vivid, sharp.
fulguration [fylgyra'sjõ], *n.f.* (*Chem.*) fulguration, lightning.
fuligineux [fyliʒi'nø], *a.* (*fem.* **-euse**) fuliginous.
fulminant [fylmi'nã], *a.* fulminant, fulminating.
fulminer [fylmi'ne], *v.t.* to fulminate, to send forth (*maledictions* or *religious decrees*).—*v.i.* to explode; (*fig.*) to storm, to thunder, to inveigh (*against*).
fumage [fy'maːʒ], *n.m.*, **fumaison** [fyme'zõ], **fumure** [fy'myːr], *n.f.* manuring, spreading of dung on land.
fumant [fy'mã], *a.* smoking, reeking, fuming.
fumé [fy'me], *a.* smoked; manured.
fumée [fy'me], *n.f.* smoke; steam; fume, reek; phantom, dream.
fumer [fy'me], *v.t.* to smoke (*a cigarette etc.*); to smoke-dry; to manure.—*v.i.* to smoke; to reek, to steam; (*fig.*) to fret, to fume.
fumerolle [fym'rɔl], *n.f.* fumarole.
fumet [fy'me], *n.m.* flavour (*of meat*); bouquet (*of wines*); (*fig.*) raciness; (*Hunt.*) scent.

fumeur [fy'mœːr], *n.m.* (*fem.* **-euse** (1)) smoker.
fumeux [fy'mø], *a.* (*fem.* **-euse** (2)) smoky, fumy; hazy (*of brain, ideas etc.*).
fumier [fy'mje], *n.m.* manure, dung, dung-hill; (*fig.*) trash.
fumigateur [fymiga'tœːr], *n.m.* fumigator.
fumigation [fymiga'sjõ], *n.f.* fumigation.
fumiger [fymi'ʒe], *v.t.* (*conjug. like* MANGER) to fumigate.
fumiste [fy'mist], *n.m.* stove- *or* chimney-repairer; (*fig.*) practical joker; humbug, trickster.
fumisterie [fymis'tri], *n.f.* (*fig.*) practical joke.
fumoir [fy'mwaːr], *n.m.* smoking-shed (*for curing fish etc.*); smoking-room.
fumure [FUMAGE].
funèbre [fy'nɛbr], *a.* funeral, funereal, mournful; dismal.
funérailles [fyne'raːj], *n.f. pl.* funeral ceremonies, obsequies.
funéraire [fyne'rɛːr], *a.* funeral, funereal.
funeste [fy'nɛst], *a.* fatal, deadly; (*fig.*) disastrous; distressing.
funestement [fynɛst'mã], *adv.* fatally, disastrously.
funiculaire [fyniky'lɛːr], *a.* funicular.—*n.m.* funicular railway.
fur [fyːr], *n.m.*, *used only in the expression* **au fur et à mesure (que)**, gradually (as), in proportion (as).
furet [fy'rɛ], *n.m.* ferret; **jouer au furet**, to hunt the slipper.
fureter [fyr'te], *v.i.* (*conjug. like* AMENER) to ferret, to hunt with a ferret; (*fig.*) to rummage.
fureteur [fyr'tœːr], *n.m.* (*fem.* **-euse**) ferreter; (*fig.*) Nosey Parker.
fureur [fy'rœːr], *n.f.* rage, fury; passion, frenzy.
furibond [fyri'bõ], *a.* furious, raging, wild.—*n.m.* (*fem.* **-e**) furious person.
furie [fy'ri], *n.f.* fury, rage; ardour, intensity.
furieusement [fyrjøz'mã], *adv.* furiously.
furieux [fy'rjø], *a.* (*fem.* **-euse**) furious; mad, fierce, impetuous; (*colloq.*) monstrous.—*n.m.* (*fem.* **-euse**) mad person.
furoncle [fy'rõːkl], *n.m.* (*Med.*) furuncle, boil.
furtif [fyr'tif], *a.* (*fem.* **-tive**) furtive, stealthy, secret.
furtivement [fyrtiv'mã], *adv.* furtively.
fusain [fy'zɛ̃], *n.m.* spindle-tree; charcoal (*for drawing*).
fuseau [fy'zo], *n.m.* (*pl.* **-eaux**) spindle; distaff.
fusée [fy'ze], *n.f.* spindleful; spindle (*of axle*); (*Motor.*) stub axle; (*Mil. etc.*) fuse; rocket; (*Vet.*) splint.
fuselage [fyz'laːʒ], *n.m.* framework, fuselage (*of an aeroplane*).
fuselé [fyz'le], *a.* slender, tapering (*fingers*); streamlined.
fuser [fy'ze], *v.i.* to spirt; to liquefy, to dissolve, to fuse.
fusibilité [fyzibili'te], *n.f.* fusibility.
fusible [fy'zibl], *a.* fusible.—*n.m.* (*Elec.*) fuse.
fusil [fy'zi], *n.m.* gun, rifle; steel (*for sharpening knives*).
fusilier [fyzi'lje], *n.m.* fusilier; *fusilier marin*, marine.
fusillade [fyzi'jad], *n.f.* discharge of musketry, fusillade; execution by shooting.

fusiller [fyzi'je], *v.t.* to shoot (down); to execute by shooting.

fusil-mitrailleur [fyzimitra'jœːr], *n.m.* sub-machine-gun.

fusion [fy'zjɔ̃], *n.f.* fusion, melting; (*fig.*) blending, merger.

fusionner [fyzjɔ'ne], *v.t., v.i.* to amalgamate, to unite, to merge; to blend.

fustigation [fystiga'sjɔ̃], *n.f.* fustigation, whipping, flogging.

fustiger [fysti'ʒe], *v.t.* (*conjug. like* MANGER) to flog, to whip.

fût [fy], *n.m.* stock (*of a gun* or *pistol*); shaft (*of a column*); cask; barrel (*of a drum*).

futaie [fy'tɛ], *n.f.* forest of high trees; high forest tree.

futaille [fy'taːj], *n.f.* cask, barrel.

futaine [fy'tɛːn], *n.f.* fustian.

futé [fy'te], *a.* (*colloq.*) sharp, cunning, sly.

futile [fy'til], *a.* futile, frivolous, trifling.

futilité [fytili'te], *n.f.* futility; trifle.

futur [fy'tyːr], *a.* future.—*n.m.* (*Gram.*) future. —*n.m.* (*fem.* **-e**) intended husband *or* wife.

futurisme [fyty'rism], *n.m.* futurism.

futuriste [fyty'rist], *a.* futuristic.—*n.* futurist.

fuyant [fɥi'jɑ̃], *a.* flying, fleeing, retreating; receding (*of the forehead etc.*); fleeting.— *n.m.* perspective.

fuyard [fɥi'jaːr], *a.* and *n.m.* (*fem.* **-e**) fugitive, runaway.

G

G, g [ʒe], *n.m.* the seventh letter of the alphabet.

gabardine [gabar'din], *n.f.* gabardine.

gabare [ga'baːr], *n.f.* lighter, flat-bottomed barge; store-ship.

gabarier [gaba'rje], *n.m.* lighterman.

gabelle [ga'bɛl], *n.f.* gabelle, salt-tax.

gâche (1) [gaːʃ], *n.f.* staple, wall-hook.

gâche (2) [gaːʃ], *n.f.* trowel; (baker's) spatula.

gâcher [ga'ʃe], *v.t.* to mix (*mortar*); (*fig.*) to bungle, to botch.

gâchette [ga'ʃɛt], *n.f.* tumbler, sear (*of a gun-lock*); follower, catch (*of a lock*); (*fam.*) trigger.

gâcheur [ga'ʃœːr], *n.m.* mason's labourer; (*fig.*) bungler.

gâchis [ga'ʃi], *n.m.* wet mortar; sludge; (*fig.*) mess.

gaélique [gae'lik], *a.* Gaelic.—*n.m.* Gaelic (*language*).

gaffe [gaf], *n.f.* boat-hook, gaff; (*fam.*) gross blunder, howler.

gaffer [ga'fe], *v.t.* to hook with a gaff.—*v.i.* (*fam.*) to blunder; (*Row.*) to catch a crab.

gage [gaːʒ], *n.m.* pawn, pledge; security, deposit; stake, token; (*pl.*) wages.

gager [ga'ʒe], *v.t.* (*conjug. like* MANGER) to wager, to bet, to stake; to pay wages to; to engage.

gageur [ga'ʒœːr], *n.m.* (*fem.* **-euse**) bettor, one who wagers, punter.

gageure [ga'ʒyːr], *n.f.* wager, stake.

gagnant [ga'ɲɑ̃], *a.* winning.—*n.m.* (*fem.* **-e**) winner.

gagne-pain [gaɲ'pɛ̃], *n.m. inv.* livelihood, daily bread; bread-winner.

gagner [ga'ɲe], *v.t.* to gain, to earn; to win; to deserve; to prevail upon, to gain over; to allure; to seize; to overtake.—*v.i.* to spread; to gain (*à*); to improve. **se gagner**, *v.r.* to be gained; to be contagious.

gai [ge], *a.* gay, merry; exhilarating; vivid (*of colours*).

gaiement or **gaîment** [ge'mɑ̃], *adv.* gaily, merrily, cheerfully; briskly, willingly.

gaieté or **gaîté** [ge'te], *n.f.* gaiety, cheerfulness, good humour.

gaillard (1) [ga'jaːr], *n.m.* (*Naut.*) castle; *gaillard d'arrière*, quarter-deck; *gaillard d'avant*, forecastle.

gaillard (2) [ga'jaːr], *a.* strong; jolly, lively; wanton; gallant.—*n.m.* (*fem.* **-e**) lively, merry, strapping fellow *or* girl.

gaillardement [gajardə'mɑ̃], *adv.* joyously, merrily; boldly.

gaillardise [gajar'diːz], *n.f.* sprightliness, liveliness, jollity; broad language, risky story.

gaîment [GAIEMENT].

gain [gɛ̃], *n.m.* gain, profit; earnings; winnings.

gaine [gɛːn], *n.f.* sheath; foundation garment; case (*of a clock etc.*).

gaîté [GAIETÉ].

gala [ga'la], *n.m.* gala.

galamment [gala'mɑ̃], *adv.* gallantly, courteously; gracefully, handsomely.

galant [ga'lɑ̃], *a.* attentive to ladies; elegant, correct, courteous; complimentary, flattering; *c'est un galant homme*, he is a man of honour; *femme galante*, courtesan.— *n.m.* gallant; sweetheart, suitor; *faire le galant*, to court the ladies.

galanterie [galɑ̃'tri], *n.f.* politeness; gallantry (*towards the ladies*); intrigue, love-affair.

galantin [galɑ̃'tɛ̃], *n.m.* fop, coxcomb.

galbe [galb], *n.m.* graceful curve *or* contour.

gale [gal], *n.f.* scabies; itch; scab; mange.

galène [ga'lɛːn], *n.f.* galena; *poste à galène*, crystal set.

galère [ga'lɛːr], *n.f.* galley; (*pl.*) galleys, imprisonment with hard labour.

galerie [gal'ri], *n.f.* gallery; corridor; picture-gallery; (*Theat.*) upper circle, gallery; (*fig.*) spectators; (*Mining*) drift.

galérien [gale'rjɛ̃], *n.m.* galley-slave, convict.

galet [ga'lɛ], *n.m.* pebble, shingle; friction-roller.

galetas [gal'ta], *n.m. inv.* garret, attic; (*fig.*) hole, hovel.

galette [ga'lɛt], *n.f.* broad thin cake; sea-biscuit.

galeux [ga'lø], *a.* (*fem.* **-euse**) itchy; scabby; mangy; *brebis galeuse*, (*fig.*) black sheep.

Galilée [gali'le], *m.* Galileo.

Galilée [gali'le], *f.* Galilaea, Galilee.

galimatias [galima'tja], *n.m.* balderdash; rigmarole.

galion [ga'ljɔ̃], *n.m.* galleon.

galiote [ga'ljɔt], *n.f.* galliot, half-galley.

galle [gal], *n.f.* gall.

Galles, le Pays de [ləpeidə'gal], *m.* Wales.

163

gallican [gali′kã], *a.* gallican.
gallicisme [gali′sism], *n.m.* gallicism, French idiom.
gallois [ga′lwa], *a.* Welsh.—*n.m.* Welsh (*language*); (**Gallois**, *fem.* -**oise**) Welshman, Welshwoman.
galoche [ga′lɔʃ], *n.f.* clog.
galon [ga′lõ], *n.m.* braid; lace; (*pl.*) (*Mil.*) bands *or* stripes (*officers and N.C.O.s*).
galonner [galɔ′ne], *v.t.* to lace, to adorn with gold- *or* silver-lace.
galonnier [galɔ′nje], *n.m.* gold- *or* silver-lace maker.
galop [ga′lo], *n.m.* gallop, galloping.
galopade [galɔ′pad], *n.f.* galloping, gallop.
galoper [galɔ′pe], *v.t.* to gallop (*a horse etc.*); to run after.—*v.i.* to gallop; (*fig.*) to run on.
galopin [galɔ′pɛ̃], *n.m.* errand-boy; (*fig.*) urchin, rogue, imp.
galvanique [galva′nik], *a.* galvanic.
galvaniser [galvani′ze], *v.t.* to galvanize; (*fig.*) to stimulate.
galvanisme [galva′nism], *n.m.* galvanism.
galvanomètre [galvanɔ′mɛtr], *n.m.* galvanometer.
galvanoplastie [galvanɔplas′ti], *n.f.* electroplating.
galvauder [galvo′de], *v.t.* to muddle; to lower, to dishonour.
gambade [gã′bad], *n.f.* skip, gambol.
gambader [gãba′de], *v.i.* to skip, to gambol, to romp, to frisk about.
Gambie [gã′bi], **la**, *f.* Gambia.
gambit [gã′bi], *n.m.* gambit.
gamelle [ga′mɛl], *n.f.* (*Mil.*, *Naut.*) mess-tin, dixie; (*fig.*) company-mess.
gamète [ga′mɛt], *n.m.* (*Biol.*) gamete.
gamin [ga′mɛ̃], *n.m.* boy, youngster, urchin.
gamine [ga′min], *n.f.* hoyden, chit of a girl.
gamme [gam], *n.f.* gamut, scale.
gammée [ga′me], *a.* *used in* '*croix gammée*', swastika.
ganache [ga′naʃ], *n.f.* lower jaw (*of a horse*); (*colloq.*) booby, blockhead.
gandin [gã′dɛ̃], *n.m.* dandy, swell.
gang [gãg], *n.m.* gang (*of thieves*).
Gange [gã:ʒ], **le**, *m.* Ganges.
gangrène [gã′grɛ:n], *n.f.* gangrene; (*fig.*) corruption.
gangrené [gãgrə′ne], *a.* gangrened; (*fig.*) cankered, corrupt.
gangrener [gãgrə′ne], *v.t.* (*conjug. like* AMENER) to gangrene, to mortify; (*fig.*) to corrupt.
gangreneux [gãgrə′nø], *a.* (*fem.* -**euse**) gangrenous, cankered.
gangster [gãgs′tɛːr], *n.m.* gangster.
ganse [gã:s], *n.f.* braid; cord, twist; edging; string.
gant [gã], *n.m.* glove, gauntlet.
gantelet [gã′tlɛ], *n.m.* gauntlet; hand-leather; (*Surg.*) glove-bandage.
ganter [gã′te], *v.t.* to glove, to put gloves on; (*fig.*) to fit, to suit. **se ganter**, *v.r.* to put on one's gloves.
ganterie [gã′tri], *n.f.* glove-making; glove-trade; glove-shop.
gantier [gã′tje], *n.m.* (*fem.* -**ière**) glover.
garage [ga′ra:ʒ], *n.m.* parking, storing away; (*Rail.*) shunting; siding; (*on rivers, canals etc.*) putting into wet dock; (*Motor. etc.*) garage; (*Row.*) boat-house.

garagiste [gara′ʒist], *n.m.* garage keeper; garage mechanic *or* owner.
garance [ga′rã:s], *a.* madder-coloured.—*n.f.* madder; madder-root.
garant [ga′rã], *n.m.* (*fem.* -**e**) guarantor, surety.—*n.m.* guaranty, voucher, proof.
garanti [garã′ti], *a.* guaranteed, warranted.
garantie [garã′ti], *n.f.* guarantee, guaranty; indemnity; security; voucher, pledge.
garantir [garã′tiːr], *v.t.* to guarantee, to vouch for; to ensure; to indemnify; to protect, to shield. **se garantir**, *v.r.* to secure oneself, to preserve oneself.
garantisseur [garãti′sœːr], *n.m.* warranter.
garçon [gar′sõ], *n.m.* boy, lad; bachelor; workman; porter; waiter; stable-boy; steward (*on ship*).
garçonnet [garsɔ′ne], *n.m.* little boy.
garçonnière [garsɔ′njɛːr], *n.f.* bachelor's flat.
garde [gard], *n.f.* keeping; defence, guard; custody, watch; heed; nurse; hilt (*of sword*).—*n.m.* guard, guardsman, keeper, warder; watchman.
garde-à-vous [garda′vu], *n.m. inv.* (*Mil.*) position at attention.
garde-barrière [gardba′rjɛːr], *n.m.* (*pl. unchanged* or **gardes-barrières**) (*Rail.*) signalman at level-crossing.
garde-boue [gard′bu], *n.m. inv.* mudguard.
garde-cendre(s) [gard′sã:dr], *n.m. inv.* fender, fire-guard.
garde-chasse [gard′ʃas], *n.m.* (*pl. unchanged* or **gardes-chasses**) game-keeper.
garde-chiourme [gard′ʃjurm], *n.m.* (*pl. unchanged* or **gardes-chiourme**) overseer of convict-gangs; warder.
garde-corps [gard′kɔːr], *n.m. inv.* rail, hand-rail; (*Naut.*) life-line.
garde-côte(s) [gard′kot], *n.m.* (*pl.* **garde-côtes** or **gardes-côtes**) guard-ship, coast-guard.
garde-crotte [gard′krɔt], *n.m. inv.* mud-guard.
garde-feu [gard′fø], *n.m.* (*pl. unchanged* or **garde-feux**) fire-guard; fender.
garde-fou [gard′fu], *n.m.* (*pl.* -**fous**) parapet; railings.
garde-frein [gard′frɛ̃], *n.m.* (*pl.* **garde-freins** or **gardes-freins**) brakesman.
garde-magasin [gardmaga′zɛ̃], *n.m.* (*pl. unchanged* or **gardes-magasins**) warehouse-keeper, storekeeper.
garde-malade [gardma′lad], *n.* (*pl. unchanged* or **gardes-malades**) sick-nurse, attendant.
garde-manger [gardmã′ʒe], *n.m. inv.* larder, pantry, meat safe.
garde-meuble(s) [gard′mœbl], *n.m. inv.* furniture repository.
garde-pêche [gard′pɛːʃ], *n.m.* (*pl.* **gardes-pêche**) river-keeper, water-bailiff.
garde-port [gard′pɔːr], *n.m.* (*pl.* **gardes-port** or **gardes-ports**) harbour-master.
garder [gar′de], *v.t.* to keep, to preserve; to retain; to watch over, to take care of, to nurse; to guard, to defend; to observe (*silence etc.*); to keep up. **se garder**, *v.r.* to keep, to last; to beware, to take care not to; to refrain (*de*); to guard.
garderie [gardə′ri], *n.f.* day nursery.

gaz

garde-robe (1) [gard'rɔb], *n.m.* (*pl.* **-robes**) apron; overall.
garde-robe (2) [gard'rɔb], *n.f.* (*pl.* **-robes**) wardrobe (*cupboard for clothes*).
gardeur [gar'dœːr], *n.m.* (*fem.* **-euse**) herd-boy *or* -girl, keeper.
gardien [gar'djɛ̃], *a.* (*fem.* **-enne**) tutelary, guardian.—*n.m.* (*fem.* **-enne**) guardian, keeper, door-keeper; trustee; *gardien de but*, goalkeeper.
gardon [gar'dɔ̃], *n.m.* roach.
gare! (1) [gaːr], *int.* beware! take care! look out!
gare (2) [gaːr], *n.f.* railway-station, terminus; (*wet*) dock; *gare routière*, coach station.
garenne [ga'rɛn], *n.f.* warren.
garer [ga're], *v.t.* to side-track (*a train*); to garage, to park. **se garer**, *v.r.* to keep *or* get out of the way; to take cover; to park.
Gargantua [gargɑ̃'tɥa], *n.m.* Gargantua; glutton.
gargantuesque [gargɑ̃'tɥɛsk], *a.* gluttonous.
gargariser (se) [səgargari'ze], *v.r.* to gargle.
gargarisme [garga'rism], *n.m.* gargle, gargling.
gargote [gar'gɔt], *n.f.* cheap eating-house, cook-shop.
gargotier [gargo'tje], *n.m.* (*fem.* **-ière**) keeper of a cook-shop; bad cook.
gargouille [gar'guːj], *n.f.* gargoyle, water-spout.
gargouillement [garguj'mɑ̃], *n.m.* rumbling (*in the stomach*); gurgling, bubbling (*of water*).
gargouiller [gargu'je], *v.i.* to rumble, to gurgle.
gargouillis [gargu'ji], *n.m.* gurgling (*of water*).
gargousse [gar'gus], *n.f.* cannon-cartridge; *papier à gargousse*, cartridge-paper.
garnement [garnə'mɑ̃], *n.m.* scapegrace, scamp, (*young*) rogue.
garni [gar'ni], *a.* furnished; trimmed, garnished.—*n.m.* furnished lodgings *or* house.
garnir [gar'niːr], *v.t.* to furnish, to stock; to trim, to garnish, to adorn; to fill. **se garnir**, *v.r.* to furnish *or* provide oneself (*with*).
garnison [garni'zɔ̃], *n.f.* garrison, station.
garnissage [garni'saːʒ], **garnissement** [garnis'mɑ̃], *n.m.* trimming (*of clothes etc.*).
garnisseur [garni'sœːr], *n.m.* (*fem.* **-euse**) trimmer.
garniture [garni'tyːr], *n.f.* furniture, trimmings; ornaments.
garrot (1) [ga'ro], *n.m.* withers (*of a horse etc.*).
garrot (2) [ga'ro], *n.m.* tightener, garrot; (*Surg.*) tourniquet.
garrotte [ga'rɔt], *n.f.* garrotting, strangulation.
garrotter [garo'te], *v.t.* to tie down, to pinion; to strangle.
gars [gɑ], *n.m.* lad, stripling, young fellow.
Gascogne [gas'kɔɲ], **la**, *f.* Gascony; **le Golfe de Gascogne**, the Bay of Biscay.
gascon [gas'kɔ̃], *a.* (*fem.* **-onne**) Gascon.—*n.m.* Gascon (*dialect*); (**Gascon**, *fem.* **-onne**) Gascon (*person*); (*fig.*) boaster, braggart.
gasconnade [gaskɔ'nad], *n.f.* gasconade, boast, brag.

gasconner [gaskɔ'ne], *v.i.* to speak with a Gascon accent; to brag.
gaspillage [gaspi'jaːʒ], *n.m.* waste, squandering.
gaspiller [gaspi'je], *v.t.* to waste, to squander.
gaspilleur [gaspi'jœːr], *a.* (*fem.* **-euse**) wasting, squandering.—*n.m.* (*fem.* **-euse**) waster, squanderer, spendthrift.
gastrique [gas'trik], *a.* gastric.
gastrite [gas'trit], *n.f.* gastritis.
gastro-entérite [gastroɑ̃te'rit], *n.f.* gastro-enteritis.
gâté [gɑ'te], *a.* marred, damaged, tainted; (*fig.*) spoiled.
gâteau [gɑ'to], *n.m.* (*pl.* **-eaux**) cake.
gâte-métier [gɑtme'tje], *n.m.* (*pl. unchanged or* **gâte-métiers**) underseller.
gâte-papier [gɑtpa'pje], *n. inv.* scribbler, poor writer.
gâter [gɑ'te], *v.t.* to spoil, to damage, to injure, to mar; to corrupt. **se gâter**, *v.r.* to taint, to spoil, to get spoiled; to break up (*of weather*).
gâterie [gɑ'tri], *n.f.* spoiling (*of children*), foolish indulgence.
gâte-sauce [gɑt'soːs], *n.m.* (*pl. unchanged or* **gâte-sauces**) scullion; (*colloq.*) bad cook.
gâteux [gɑ'tø], *a.* and *n.m.* (*fem.* **-euse**) idiot.
gauche [goːʃ], *a.* left; (*fig.*) crooked, ugly; clumsy.—*n.f.* left hand, left side; (*Mil.*) left wing, left flank.
gauchement [goʃ'mɑ̃], *adv.* awkwardly, clumsily.
gaucher [go'ʃe], *a.* and *n.m.* (*fem.* **-ère**) left-handed (person).
gaucherie [go'ʃri], *n.f.* awkwardness, clumsiness.
gauchir [go'ʃiːr], *v.t.* to warp.—*v.i.* to turn aside; to flinch; to become warped; (*fig.*) to dodge.
gaudriole [godri'ɔl], *n.f.* broad joke, coarse jest.
gaufrage [go'fraːʒ], *n.m.* goffering.
gaufre [goːfr], *n.f.* wafer, waffle (*thin cake*); honeycomb.
gaufrer [go'fre], *v.t.* to goffer.
gaufrette [go'frɛt], *n.f.* small wafer.
gaufreur [go'frœːr], *n.m.* (*fem.* **-euse**) gofferer.
gaufrier [gofri'e], *n.m.* waffle-iron.
gaufrure [go'fryːr], *n.f.* goffering.
Gaule [goːl], **la**, *f.* Gaul.
gaule [goːl], *n.f.* pole, switch, long stick.
gauler [go'le], *v.t.* to beat (*trees*) with a long pole; to knock down (*fruit*).
gaullisme [go'lism], *n.m.* policy *or* partisanship of General de Gaulle.
gaulliste [go'list], *a.* and *n.* follower of General de Gaulle.
gaulois [go'lwa], *a.* Gaulish, Gallic; (*fig.*) free.—*n.m.* Gallic (*language*); (**Gaulois**, *fem.* **-oise**) Gaul (*person*).
gausser (se) [səgo'se], *v.r.* (*colloq.*) to banter, to chaff.
Gauthier [go'tje], *m.* Walter.
gave (1) [gaːv], *n.m.* torrent, mountain stream (*in the Pyrenees*).
gave (2) [gaːv], *n.f.* crop (*of birds*).
gaver [ga've], *v.t.* (*colloq.*) to cram, to gorge.
gavotte [ga'vɔt], *n.f.* gavotte (*dance*).
gavroche [ga'vrɔʃ], *n.m.* Parisian urchin.
gaz [gɑːz], *n.m.* gas; *bec de gaz*, gas-burner.

165

gaze

gaze [gɑːz], *n.f.* gauze.
gazé [gɑ'ze], *a.* covered with gauze, veiled; softened, toned down; (*Mil.*) gassed (*soldier*).
gazelle [gɑ'zɛl], *n.f.* gazelle.
gazer (1) [gɑ'ze], *v.t.* to cover with gauze; (*fig.*) to veil, to tone down.
gazer (2) [gɑ'ze], *v.t.* (*Mil.*) to gas (*men*).
gazette [gɑ'zɛt], *n.f.* gazette, newspaper; (*fig.*) newsmonger.
gazeux [gɑ'zø], *a.* (*fem.* **-euse**) gaseous; aerated.
gazier (1) [gɑ'zje], *n.m.* gas-fitter.
gazier (2) [gɑ'zje], *n.m.* (*fem.* **-ière**) gauze-maker.
gazolène [gɑzɔ'lɛn], **gazoléine** [gɑzɔle'in], **gazoline** [gɑzɔ'lin], *n.f.* gasolene.
gazomètre [gɑzɔ'mɛtr], *n.m.* gasometer.
gazon [gɑ'zɔ̃], *n.m.* grass; sod, turf; lawn.
gazonnant [gɑzɔ'nɑ̃], *a.* producing grass; grassy.
gazonner [gɑzɔ'ne], *v.t.* to cover with turf, to turf.
gazonneux [gɑzɔ'nø], *a.* (*fem.* **-euse**) turfy, swarded.
gazouillement [gɑzuj'mɑ̃], *n.m.* chirping, warbling (*of birds*); babbling (*of a brook etc.*); prattle.
gazouiller [gɑzu'je], *v.i.* to chirp, to warble; to twitter; to prattle; to babble.
gazouillis [gɑzu'ji], *n.m.* warbling, twittering.
geai [ʒe], *n.m.* jay.
géant [ʒe'ɑ̃], *a.* gigantic.—*n.m.* (*fem.* **-e**) giant.
geignard [ʒɛ'naːr], *a.* always whining, querulous.
geignement [ʒɛɲ'mɑ̃], *n.m.* moan, whine.
geindre [ʒɛ̃:dr], *v.i. irr.* (*conjug. like* CRAINDRE) to moan, to whine, to fret, to complain.
gel [ʒɛl], *n.m.* frost, freezing.
gélatine [ʒelɑ'tin], *n.f.* gelatine.
gélatiner [ʒelɑti'ne], *v.t.* to gelatinize.
gélatineux [ʒelɑti'nø], *a.* (*fem.* **-euse**) gelatinous.
gelé [ʒə'le], *a.* frozen, cold.
gelée [ʒə'le], *n.f.* frost; jelly; aspic.
geler [ʒə'le], *v.t., v.i.* (*conjug. like* AMENER) and **se geler**, *v.r.* to freeze.
gélignite [ʒeli'nit], *n.f.* gelignite.
gelinotte [ʒəli'nɔt], *n.f.* grouse (*bird*).
gémir [ʒe'miːr], *v.i.* to groan, to moan; to lament; (*fig.*) to suffer.
gémissant [ʒemi'sɑ̃], *a.* groaning, moaning; lamenting.
gémissement [ʒemis'mɑ̃], *n.m.* groan, moan; (*fig.*) lament, cooing.
gemme [ʒɛm], *n.f.* gem; resin; (*Bot.*) bud.
gemmer [ʒɛ'me], *v.i.* to bud.
gênant [ʒɛ'nɑ̃], *a.* troublesome, inconvenient, embarrassing.
gencive [ʒɑ̃'siːv], *n.f.* gum (*of the teeth*).
gendarme [ʒɑ̃'darm], *n.m.* gendarme (*armed policeman*); constable; virago (*woman*).
gendarmerie [ʒɑ̃darm'ri], *n.f.* gendarmery (*armed police*); constabulary; barracks (*of gendarmes*).
gendre [ʒɑ̃:dr], *n.m.* son-in-law.
gêne [ʒɛ:n], *n.f.* constraint, uneasiness, annoyance; difficulty; financial difficulties, penury.
gêné [ʒɛ'ne], *a.* constrained, ill at ease; hard up.

généalogie [ʒenealɔ'ʒi], *n.f.* genealogy; pedigree.
généalogique [ʒenealɔ'ʒik], *a.* genealogical.
généalogiste [ʒenealɔ'ʒist], *n.m.* genealogist.
gêner [ʒɛ'ne], *v.t.* to constrain, to constrict; to impede; to obstruct; to thwart, to restrain; to inconvenience, to embarrass; to annoy. **se gêner**, *v.r.* to constrain oneself, to put oneself out.
général [ʒene'ral], *a.* (*m. pl.* **-aux**) general, universal; vague.—*adv. phr.* **en général**, in general.—*n.m.* (*Mil.*) general.
générale [ʒene'ral], *n.f.* general's wife; drumbeat (*to give alarm of fire etc.*).
généralement [ʒeneral'mɑ̃], *adv.* generally, in general.
généralisation [ʒeneraliza'sjɔ̃], *n.f.* generalization.
généraliser [ʒenerali'ze], *v.t.* to generalize.
généralissime [ʒenerali'sim], *n.m.* generalissimo, commander-in-chief of allied armies.
généralité [ʒenerali'te], *n.f.* generality.
générateur [ʒenera'tœːr], *a.* (*fem.* **-trice**) generating, generative.—*n.m.* generator.
génératif [ʒenera'tif], *a.* (*fem.* **-tive**) generative.
génération [ʒenera'sjɔ̃], *n.f.* generation; procreation.
générer [ʒene're], *v.t.* (*conjug. like* CÉDER) to generate.
généreusement [ʒenerøz'mɑ̃], *adv.* generously, bountifully; nobly, bravely.
généreux [ʒene'rø], *a.* (*fem.* **-euse**) generous, liberal, bountiful; noble; courageous.
générique [ʒene'rik], *a.* generic.—*n.m.* (*Cine.*) credits.
générosité [ʒenerozi'te], *n.f.* generosity, liberality; magnanimity.
Gênes [ʒɛːn], *f.* Genoa.
genèse [ʒə'nɛːz], *n.f.* genesis.
genêt [ʒə'ne], *n.m.* (*Bot.*) broom.
genette [ʒə'nɛt], *n.f.* genet, civet cat.
gêneur [ʒɛ'nœːr], *n.m.* (*fem.* **-euse**) intruder; spoil-sport.
Genève [ʒə'nɛv], *f.* Geneva.
genevois [ʒən'vwa], *a.* Genevese.
genévrier [ʒənevri'e], *n.m.* juniper-tree.
génie [ʒe'ni], *n.m.* genius; spirit, nature, bent, talent; (*Mil.*) corps of engineers.
genièvre [ʒə'njɛːvr], *n.m.* juniper-berry; juniper-tree; gin.
génisse [ʒe'nis], *n.f.* heifer.
génital [ʒeni'tal], *a.* (*m. pl.* **-aux**) genital.
génitif [ʒeni'tif], *n.m.* (*Gram.*) genitive.
génocide [ʒeno'sid], *n.m.* genocide.
génois [ʒe'nwa], *a.* Genoese.
genou [ʒə'nu], *n.m.* (*pl.* **-oux**) knee; (*Mech.*) ball and socket; (*pl.*) lap.
genouillère [ʒənu'jɛːr], *n.f.* knee-piece (*of armour*); top (*of a high boot*); knee-cap; ball-and-socket joint.
genre [ʒɑ̃:r], *n.m.* genus; species, kind, sort; fashion, style; (*Gram.*) gender.
gens [ʒɑ̃], *n.m. pl.* (*but adjectives directly preceding the word take the feminine form*) people, persons, folk; men, hands; servants.
gent [ʒɑ̃], *n.f.* brood, race, tribe.
gentiane [ʒɑ̃'sjan], *n.f.* (*Bot.*) gentian.
gentil (1) [ʒɑ̃'til], *n.m.* Gentile.
gentil (2) [ʒɑ̃'ti], *a.* (*fem.* **-ille**) noble, gentle; pretty, nice, graceful; amiable, pleasing.

gentilhomme [ʒãti'jɔm], *n.m.* (*pl.* **gentils-hommes**) nobleman, gentleman.
gentillesse [ʒãti'jɛs], *n.f.* kindness, sweetness (*of temperament*); prettiness, gracefulness; pretty thing, thought etc.
gentiment [ʒãti'mã], *adv.* prettily, gracefully, like a good boy *or* girl.
génuflexion [ʒenyflɛk'sjõ], *n.f.* genuflexion.
géocentrique [ʒeosã'trik], *a.* geocentric.
Geoffroy [ʒo'frwɑ], *m.* Geoffrey, Jeffrey.
géographe [ʒeo'graf], *n.m.* geographer.
géographie [ʒeogra'fi], *n.f.* geography.
géographique [ʒeogra'fik], *a.* geographical.
geôle [ʒo:l], *n.f.* gaol, prison.
geôlier [ʒo'lje], *n.m.* gaoler.
géologie [ʒeolɔ'ʒi], *n.f.* geology.
géologique [ʒeolɔ'ʒik], *a.* geological.
géologue [ʒeo'lɔg], *n.m.* geologist.
géométral [ʒeome'tral], *a.* (*m. pl.* **-aux**) geometrical.
géomètre [ʒeo'mɛtr], *n.m.* geometrician; geometer.
géométrie [ʒeome'tri], *n.f.* geometry.
géométrique [ʒeome'trik], *a.* geometrical.
Georges [ʒɔrʒ], *m.* George.
gérance [ʒe'rã:s], *n.f.* management, managership; editorship.
géranium [ʒera'njɔm], *n.m.* geranium.
gérant [ʒe'rã], *n.m.* (*fem.* **-e**) manager; editor; *rédacteur gérant*, managing editor.
gerbe [ʒɛrb], *n.f.* sheaf, bundle; bunch of flowers.
gerber [ʒɛr'be], *v.t.* to make up *or* bind into sheaves.
gerbier [ʒɛr'bje], *n.m.* cornstack.
gerce [ʒɛrs], *n.f.* chap, crack.
gercé [ʒɛr'se], *a.* chapped (*hands*).
gercer [ʒɛr'se], *v.t., v.i., (conjug. like* COMMENCER) and **se gercer**, *v.r.* to chap, to crack.
gerçure [ʒɛr'sy:r], *n.f.* chap, crack; chink, cleft.
gérer [ʒe're], *v.t. (conjug. like* CÉDER) to manage, to administer.
gerfaut [ʒɛr'fo], *n.m.* gerfalcon.
germain [ʒɛr'mɛ̃], *a.* german, first (*of cousins etc.*); (*Law*) full (*brother etc.*).
germanique [ʒɛrma'nik], *a.* Germanic.
germe [ʒɛrm], *n.m.* germ, embryo; seed; bud, sprout, shoot; (*fig.*) origin.
germer [ʒɛr'me], *v.i.* to shoot, to sprout, to germinate.
germination [ʒɛrmina'sjõ], *n.f.* germination.
gésier [ʒe'zje], *n.m.* gizzard.
*****gésir** [ʒe'zi:r], *v.i. irr.* to lie; *ci-gît*, here lies.
gestation [ʒɛsta'sjõ], *n.f.* gestation.
gestatoire [ʒɛsta'twa:r], *a.* gestatory.
geste [ʒɛst], *n.m.* gesture, action; sign.
gesticulateur [ʒɛstikyla'tœːr], *n.m.* (*fem.* **-trice**) gesticulator.
gesticulation [ʒɛstikyla'sjõ], *n.f.* gesticulation.
gesticuler [ʒɛstiky'le], *v.i.* to gesticulate.
gestion [ʒɛs'tjõ], *n.f.* management, administration.
geyser [ge'zɛːr], *n.m.* geyser.
Ghana [ga'na], **le**, *m.* Ghana.
ghetto [ge'to], *n.m.* Jewish quarter, ghetto.
gibbeux [ʒi'bø], *a.* (*fem.* **-euse**) gibbous, hump-backed.
gibbon [ʒi'bõ], *n.m.* gibbon (*ape*).
gibbosité [ʒibozi'te], *n.f.* gibbosity; hump.

gibecière [ʒib'sjeːr], *n.f.* game-bag, satchel; juggler's pocket.
gibelet [ʒi'blɛ], *n.m.* gimlet.
giberne [ʒi'bɛrn], *n.f.* cartridge-box *or* pouch.
gibet [ʒi'bɛ], *n.m.* gibbet, gallows.
gibier [ʒi'bje], *n.m.* (*Hunt.*) game.
giboulée [ʒibu'le], *n.f.* sudden shower, hailshower.
gibus [ʒi'by:s], *n.m. inv.* gibus (*crush-hat, opera-hat*).
giclage [ʒi'kla:ʒ], *n.m.* spraying; *carburateur à giclage*, jet carburettor.
giclée [ʒi'kle], *n.f.* squirt, spirt.
gicleur [ʒi'klœːr], *n.m.* spray nozzle, jet.
gicler [ʒi'kle], *v.i.* to spout, to squirt.
gifle [ʒifl], *n.f.* slap in the face, box on the ear.
gifler [ʒi'fle], *v.t.* to slap in the face, to box the ears of.
gigantesque [ʒigã'tɛsk], *a.* gigantic, colossal.
gigot [ʒi'go], *n.m.* leg of mutton.
gigue [ʒig], *n.f.* shank, leg, haunch (*of venison*); jig (*dance*).
gilet [ʒi'lɛ], *n.m.* waistcoat; vest.
Gilles [ʒil], *m.* Giles.
gingembre [ʒɛ̃'ʒãːbr], *n.m.* ginger.
gingivite [ʒɛ̃ʒi'vit], *n.f.* gingivitis.
ginguet [ʒɛ̃'gɛ], *a.* (*fem.* **-ette**) (*colloq.*) weak, worthless, scanty.—*n.m.* thin wine.
girandole [ʒirã'dɔl], *n.f.* girandole, epergne.
giration [ʒira'sjõ], *n.f.* gyration.
giratoire [ʒira'twaːr], *a.* gyratory.
girofle [ʒi'rɔfl], *n.m.* clove.
giroflée [ʒiro'fle], *n.f.* gillyflower, stock; *giroflée jaune*, wallflower.
giron [ʒi'rõ], *n.m.* lap; (*fig.*) bosom.
girouette [ʒi'rwɛt], *n.f.* weathercock, vane.
gisant [ʒi'zã], *a.* lying (*ill, dead etc.*); outstretched [GÉSIR].
gisement [ʒiz'mã], *n.m.* (*Geol. etc.*) lie (*of strata*); layer, bed; (*Naut.*) bearing (*of coast etc.*).
gitan [ʒi'tã], *n.m.* (*fem.* **-e**) gipsy.
gîte [ʒit], *n.m.* home, lodging; refuge; lair (*of deer*); (*Min.*) seam, layer.—*n.f.* (*Naut.*) list.
gîter [ʒi'te], *v.t.* to lodge, to house, to put up, to shelter.—*v.i.* to lie, to lodge; (*Naut.*) to list; to run aground. **se gîter**, *v.r.* to lodge, to sleep.
givrage [ʒi'vra:ʒ], *n.m.* (*Av.*) frosting, icing.
givre [ʒi:vr], *n.m.* hoar-frost, *rime.
givré [ʒi'vre], *a.* rimed, rimy.
glabre [glɑ:br], *a.* (*Bot.*) glabrous, smooth, without down; hairless.
glaçage [gla'sa:ʒ], *n.m.* frosting, glazing.
glaçant [gla'sã], *a.* freezing; icy, chilling.
glace [glas], *n.f.* ice; ice-cream; glass, plate-glass; mirror; carriage window; flaw (*in a diamond etc.*); icing (*on cakes etc.*).
glacé [gla'se], *a.* frozen, freezing; icy-cold; iced; glazed; glossy (*paper*); candied.
glacer [gla'se], *v.t. (conjug. like* COMMENCER) to freeze; to ice; (*fig.*) to paralyse; to glaze.—*v.i.* and **se glacer**, *v.r.* to freeze.
glaciaire [gla'sjɛːr], *a.* of glaciers, glacial.
glacial [gla'sjal], *a.* frozen, glacial, icy.
glaciale [gla'sjal], *n.f.* (*Bot.*) ice-plant.
glacier [gla'sje], *n.m.* glacier, field of ice; ice-cream vendor.
glaçon [gla'sõ], *n.m.* block of ice; floe; ice-cube; *petit glaçon*, icicle.
gladiateur [gladja'tœːr], *n.m.* gladiator.

glaïeul

glaïeul [gla'jœl], *n.m.* gladiolus; iris.
glaire [glɛːr], *n.f.* glair, white of egg; phlegm, mucus.
glaise [glɛːz], *a.* clayey.—*n.f.* clay, loam; potter's earth.
glaiseux [glɛ'zø], *a.* (*fem.* **-euse**) clayey, loamy.
glaisière [glɛ'zjɛːr], *n.f.* clay-pit.
glaive [glɛːv], *n.m.* sword, blade, steel.
gland [glɑ̃], *n.m.* acorn; tassel.
glande [glɑ̃ːd], *n.f.* (*Anat.*) gland; (*pop.*) tumour; kernel.
glanduleux [glɑ̃dy'lø], *a.* (*fem.* **-euse**) glandulous, glandular.
glaner [gla'ne], *v.t., v.i.* to glean.
glaneur [gla'nœːr], *n.m.* (*fem.* **-euse**) gleaner.
glapir [gla'piːr], *v.i.* to yelp (*of puppies etc.*); to screech, to scream (*of persons*).
glapissant [glapi'sɑ̃], *a.* yelping; screeching, shrill.
glapissement [glapis'mɑ̃], *n.m.* yelping; screeching.
glas [glɑ], *n.m.* knell.
glauque [gloːk], *a.* glaucous, sea-green.
glèbe [glɛb], *n.f.* glebe; land, soil.
glissade [gli'sad], *n.f.* sliding, slide; slipping.
glissant [gli'sɑ̃], *a.* slippery; (*fig.*) ticklish, delicate.
glissement [glis'mɑ̃], *n.m.* slipping, sliding, gliding; (*Polit.*) landslide.
glisser [gli'se], *v.t.* to slip, to slide; to insinuate.—*v.i.* to slip, to slide; to glide. **se glisser**, *v.r.* to slip, to slide, to creep, to steal, to insinuate oneself (*dans*).
glissière [gli'sjɛːr], *n.f.* slide; *porte à glissière*, sliding door.
glissoire [gli'swaːr], *n.f.* slide on ice.
global [glɔ'bal], *a.* (*m. pl.* **-aux**) in a mass, entire; *somme globale*, lump sum.
globe [glɔb], *n.m.* globe, sphere, orb; glass-shade.
globulaire [glɔby'lɛːr], *a.* globular.
globule [glɔ'byl], *n.m.* globule.
gloire [glwaːr], *n.f.* glory, fame.
gloriette [glɔ'rjɛt], *n.f.* arbour, summer-house.
glorieusement [glɔrjøz'mɑ̃], *adv.* gloriously.
glorieux [glɔ'rjø], *a.* (*fem.* **-euse**) glorious; vainglorious.—*n.m.* braggart, boaster.
glorification [glɔrifika'sjɔ̃], *n.f.* glorification.
glorifier [glɔri'fje], *v.t.* to glorify, to honour. **se glorifier**, *v.r.* to glory in, to boast (*de*).
gloriole [glɔ'rjɔl], *n.f.* vainglory, petty vanity.
glose [gloːz], *n.f.* gloss; criticism; comment; parody.
gloser [glo'ze], *v.t.* to gloss; to criticize.—*v.i.* to carp, to find fault.
gloseur [glo'zœːr], *n.m.* (*fem.* **-euse**) carper, fault-finder.
glossaire [glɔ'sɛːr], *n.m.* glossary, vocabulary.
glouglou [glu'glu], *n.m.* gurgling, gurgle.
glouglouter [gluglu'te], *v.i.* to gurgle.
gloussement [glus'mɑ̃], *n.m.* clucking.
glousser [glu'se], *v.i.* to cluck (*of hens*).
glouton [glu'tɔ̃], *a.* (*fem.* **-onne**) gluttonous, greedy.—*n.m.* (*fem.* **-onne**) glutton.
gloutonnement [gluton'mɑ̃], *adv.* gluttonously, greedily.
gloutonnerie [gluton'ri], *n.f.* gluttony, greediness.
glu [gly], *n.f.* bird-lime, glue.
gluant [gly'ɑ̃], *a.* glutinous, sticky; slimy.

glucose [gly'koːz], *n.m.* glucose.
glutineux [glyti'nø], *a.* (*fem.* **-euse**) glutinous, viscous.
glycérine [glise'rin], *n.f.* glycerine.
glycine [gli'sin], *n.f.* wistaria.
gnome [gno:m], *n.m.* (*fem.* **gnomide**) gnome.
gnou [gnu], *n.m.* gnu.
gobelet [gɔ'blɛ], *n.m.* goblet, mug; dice-box; *tour de gobelet*, juggler's trick.
gobelin [gɔ'blɛ̃], *n.m.* goblin, imp.
gobe-mouches [gɔb'muʃ], *n.m. inv.* fly-catcher (*bird*); fly-trap (*plant*); (*fig.*) simpleton.
gober [gɔ'be], *v.t.* to gulp down, to swallow; (*colloq.*) to believe easily; to have a liking for (*a person*).
(*C*) **godendard** [gɔdɑ̃'daːr], *n.m.* cross-cut saw, whip-saw, two-handle saw.
goder [gɔ'de], *v.i.* to crease, to bag (*of clothes*), to pucker (*of needlework etc.*).
godiche [gɔ'diʃ], *a.* clumsy, boobyish, simple.
godille [gɔ'diːj], *n.f.* stern-oar; scull.
goéland [gɔe'lɑ̃], *n.m.* gull, sea-gull.
goélette [gɔe'lɛt], *n.f.* schooner.
goémon [gɔe'mɔ̃], *n.m.* seaweed.
gogo [gɔ'go], (*in adv. phr.*) *à gogo*, galore.
goguenard [gɔg'naːr], *a.* bantering, jeering, mocking, scoffing.—*n.m.* (*fem.* **-e**) banterer, jeerer, chaffer.
goguenarder [gɔgnar'de], *v.i.* to jeer, to banter, to chaff.
goguette [gɔ'gɛt], *n.f.* *être en goguette*, to be in a merry mood, to be on the spree.
goinfre [gwɛ̃:fr], *n.m.* (*fam.*) guzzler, gormandizer.
goinfrer [gwɛ̃'fre], *v.i.* to gorge, to gormandize.
goinfrerie [gwɛ̃frɔ'ri], *n.f.* gluttony.
goître [gwaːtr], *n.m.* goitre, wen.
goîtreux [gwa'trø], *a.* (*fem.* **-euse**) goitrous.—*n.m.* (*fem.* **-euse**) goitrous person, (*colloq.*) imbecile, idiot.
golfe [gɔlf], *n.m.* gulf, bay.
gommage [gɔ'maːʒ], *n.m.* gumming.
gomme [gɔm], *n.f.* gum; rubber, eraser.
gommer [gɔ'me], *v.t.* to gum; to rub out.
gommeux [gɔ'mø], *a.* (*fem.* **-euse**) gummy.
gommier [gɔ'mje], *n.m.* gum-tree.
gond [gɔ̃], *n.m.* hinge; *hors des gonds*, unhinged, (*fig.*) enraged, beside oneself.
gondole [gɔ̃'dɔl], *n.f.* gondola; car *or* gondola (*of a balloon etc.*); eye-bath.
gondoler [gɔ̃dɔ'le], *v.i.* to bulge; to warp (*of wood*); to buckle.
gondolier [gɔ̃dɔ'lje], *n.m.* gondolier.
gonflement [gɔ̃flə'mɑ̃], *n.m.* swelling, inflation.
gonfler [gɔ̃'fle], *v.t.* to swell, to inflate; to pump up (*a tyre*); to puff up.—*v.i.* to swell, to be swollen. **se gonfler**, *v.r.* to swell, to be swollen, to be puffed up; (*fig.*) to swank.
gonfleur [gɔ̃'flœːr], *n.m.* air-pump, inflator.
gong [gɔ̃:g], *n.m.* gong.
gorge [gɔrʒ], *n.f.* throat, gullet; bosom, neck; defile, strait; (*Bot.*) mouth; (*Arch., Fort.*) gorge; *avoir mal à la gorge*, to have a sore throat; *avoir la gorge serrée*, to have a lump in one's throat; *rendre gorge*, to refund, to stump up; *faire des gorges chaudes*, to gloat over.
gorge-de-pigeon [gɔrʒdəpi'ʒɔ̃], *a. inv.* iridescent, shot (*of colours*).

168

gorgée [gɔr'ʒe], *n.f.* draught, gulp; *petite gorgée*, sip.
gorger [gɔr'ʒe], *v.t.* (*conjug. like* MANGER) to gorge, to cram. **se gorger**, *v.r.* to gorge oneself.
gorille [gɔ'riːj], *n.m.* gorilla.
gosier [go'zje], *n.m.* throat, gullet; (*fig.*) voice.
gosse [gos], *n.* (*fam.*) brat, urchin, kid.
gothique [go'tik], *a.* Gothic.—*n.f.* (*Print.*) Old English.
gouache [gwaʃ], *n.f.* gouache, body-colour; painting in this.
goudron [gu'drɔ̃], *n.m.* tar.
goudronnage [gudro'naːʒ], *n.m.* tarring.
goudronner [gudro'ne], *v.t.* to tar.
goudronneux [gudro'nø], *a.* (*fem.* -euse) tarry.
gouffre [gufr], *n.m.* gulf, abyss, pit.
gouge [guːʒ], *n.f.* gouge.
goujat [gu'ʒa], *n.m.* (*fig.*) cad, vulgar fellow.
goujon [gu'ʒɔ̃], *n.m.* gudgeon (*pin or fish*).
goule [gul], *n.f.* ghoul.
goulet [gu'lɛ], *n.m.* narrow entrance (*to a harbour etc.*); inlet; mouth, neck (*of a bottle etc.*); gully, gorge (*between mountains etc.*).
goulot [gu'lo], *n.m.* neck (*of a bottle etc.*).
goulu [gu'ly], *a.* gluttonous, greedy.—*n.m.* (*fem.* -e) glutton, greedy person.
goulûment [guly'mɑ̃], *adv.* greedily.
goupille [gu'piːj], *n.f.* pin, peg, bolt.
goupiller [gupi'je], *v.t.* to pin, to bolt.
gourd [guːr], *a.* benumbed, numb.
gourde [gurd], *n.f.* gourd; flask, wineskin.
gourdin [gur'dɛ̃], *n.m.* cudgel, club, thick stick.
gourmade [gur'mad], *n.f.* smack in the face.
gourmand [gur'mɑ̃], *a.* greedy.—*n.m.* (*fem.* -e) glutton.
gourmander [gurmɑ̃'de], *v.t.* to chide, to reprimand; to prune (*trees*).
gourmandise [gurmɑ̃'diːz], *n.f.* gluttony, greediness; (*pl.*) sweetmeats.
gourmé [gur'me], *a.* stiff, stuck-up, formal, solemn.
gourmer [gur'me], *v.t.* to box, to thump; to curb (*a horse*). **se gourmer**, *v.r.* to thump, to pummel each other.
gourmet [gur'mɛ], *n.m.* connoisseur in wines etc.; epicure.
gourmette [gur'mɛt], *n.f.* curb, curb-chain.
gousse [gus], *n.f.* shell, pod, husk; *gousse d'ail*, clove of garlic.
gousset [gu'sɛ], *n.m.* armpit; fob, (waistcoat-) pocket; gusset (*of a shirt etc.*); bracket.
goût [gu], *n.m.* taste, flavour, relish; savour; inclination, liking; style, manner; *chacun à son goût*, every man to his taste; *chacun son goût*, tastes differ; *viande de haut goût*, highly seasoned meat.
goûter [gu'te], *v.t.* to taste, to try; to like; to enjoy; to feel.—*v.i.* to taste; to try; to have a snack.—*n.m.* a snack taken between lunch and dinner (*the equivalent of English tea*).
goutte (1) [gut], *n.f.* drop, small quantity; sip, dram; (*Arch., Pharm.*) drop.—*adv. phr. ne . . . goutte; n'entendre goutte*, not to hear *or* understand in the least; *n'y voir goutte*, not to make it out at all.
goutte (2) [gut], *n.f.* gout.
gouttelette [gu'tlɛt], *n.f.* small drop, drip.
goutter [gu'te], *v.i.* to drip.

goutteux [gu'tø], *a.* and *n.m.* (*fem.* -euse) gouty (person).
gouttière [gu'tjɛːr], *n.f.* gutter of a roof; shoot, spout (*for rain-water*); cradle splint.
gouvernable [guver'nabl], *a.* governable, manageable.
gouvernail [guver'naːj], *n.m.* rudder, helm.
gouvernant [guver'nɑ̃], *a.* governing, ruling.—*n.m.* governor, ruler.—*n.f.* (-e) governor's wife; governess; housekeeper (*of bachelor*).
gouverne [gu'vɛrn], *n.f.* guidance, guide, direction; (*pl.*) (*Av.*) rudders and ailerons.
gouvernement [guvɛrnə'mɑ̃], *n.m.* government, rule, sway; management; governorship.
gouvernemental [guvɛrnəmɑ̃'tal], *a.* (*m. pl.* -aux) governmental.
gouverner [guvɛr'ne], *v.t.* to control, to govern, to direct, to steer; to rule, to command, to manage, to regulate.—*v.i.* to steer, to answer the helm.
gouverneur [guvɛr'nœːr], *n.m.* governor; manager; tutor.
grabat [gra'ba], *n.m.* pallet, litter (*of straw etc.*), truckle-bed.
grabuge [gra'byːʒ], *n.m.* (*fam.*) wrangling, squabble, brawl.
grâce [graːs], *n.f.* grace, favour, mercy, forgiveness; gracefulness, elegance; (*pl.*) thanks; (*Myth.*) *les Grâces*, the Graces.
graciable [gra'sjabl], *a.* pardonable.
gracier [gra'sje], *v.t.* to pardon, to reprieve.
gracieusement [grasjøz'mɑ̃], *adv.* graciously, kindly, gracefully.
gracieuseté [grasjøz'te], *n.f.* graciousness, kindness; act of courtesy; gratuity.
gracieux [gra'sjø], *a.* (*fem.* -euse) graceful, gracious, obliging.
gracilité [grasili'te], *n.f.* slimness, slenderness.
gradation [grada'sjɔ̃], *n.f.* gradation; climax.
grade [grad], *n.m.* grade, rank; degree; *monter en grade*, to be promoted.
gradé [gra'de], *n.m.* (*Mil.*) non-commissioned officer.
gradin [gra'dɛ̃], *n.m.* step; tier.
graduation [gradqa'sjɔ̃], *n.f.* graduation; scale.
gradué [gra'dqe], *a.* graduated; progressive (*exercises*).—*n.m.* (*fem.* -ée) graduate (*of a university*).
graduel [gra'dqel], *a.* (*fem.* -elle) gradual.
graduellement [gradqɛl'mɑ̃], *adv.* gradually.
graduer [gra'dqe], *v.t.* to graduate, to proportion.
graillon [grɑ'jɔ̃], *n.m.* smell of burnt meat *or* fat; (*pl.*) scraps (*of meat etc.*) from a meal.
grain (1) [grɛ̃], *n.m.* grain, berry; bead; jot, bit; *avoir un grain*, to have a bee in one's bonnet; *grain de beauté*, mole, beauty-spot; *grain de café*, coffee bean; *grain de poivre*, peppercorn; *grain de raisin*, grape.
grain (2) [grɛ̃], *n.m.* (*Naut.*) squall.
graine [grɛn], *n.f.* seed; breed; *c'est une mauvaise graine*, he is a bad lot.
grainetier [grɛn'tje], **grainier** [grɛ'nje], *n.m.* (*fem.* -ière) seedsman, seedswoman; corn-chandler.
graissage [grɛ'saːʒ], *n.m.* greasing, oiling, lubrication.

169

graisse [grɛ:s], *n.f.* fat, grease.
graisser [grɛ'se], *v.t.* to grease; to make greasy; to lubricate, to oil.
graisseur [grɛ'sœ:r], *n.m.* greaser, oiler.
graisseux [grɛ'sø], *a.* (*fem.* **-euse**) greasy; oily; fatty.
grammaire [gra'mɛːr], *n.f.* grammar.
grammairien [gramɛ'rjɛ̃], *n.m.* (*fem.* **-enne**) grammarian.
grammatical [gramati'kal], *a.* (*m. pl.* **-aux**) grammatical.
grammaticalement [gramatikal'mɑ̃], *adv.* grammatically.
gramme [gram], *n.m.* gramme *or* gram.
grand [grɑ̃], *a.* great; large, big; high, tall; wide, spacious; grown-up; capital (*of letters*); broad (*of daylight*); grand, noble.— *adv. voir grand*, to have big ideas; *en grand*, on a large scale; (*of portraits*) full length.—*n.m.* the grand, the sublime.— *n.m.* (*fem.* **-e**) great person; grown-up person; *grand d'Espagne*, Spanish grandee; (*pl.*) the great, great people; (*sch.*) the big (*or* senior) boys *or* girls.
(C) **grand-bois** [grɑ̃'bwɑ], *n.m.* virgin forest.
grand-duc [grɑ̃'dyk], *n.m.* (*pl.* **grands-ducs**) grand duke; eagle-owl.
grand-duché [grɑ̃dy'ʃe], *n.m.* (*pl.* **grands-duchés**) grand-duchy.
grande-duchesse [grɑ̃ddy'ʃɛs], *n.f.* (*pl.* **grandes-duchesses**) grand-duchess.
grandement [grɑ̃d'mɑ̃], *adv.* greatly, extremely, very much; grandly, nobly, handsomely.
grandeur [grɑ̃'dœːr], *n.f.* extent, size; height; length; breadth; bulk; greatness, magnitude; tallness; grandeur, magnificence; grace, highness (*titles*).
grandiose [grɑ̃'djoːz], *a.* grandiose.
grandir [grɑ̃'diːr], *v.t.* to increase; to magnify.—*v.i.* to grow; to grow (tall, big, up etc.). **se grandir,** *v.r.* to make oneself appear taller; to grow taller; to raise oneself, to rise.
grandissement [grɑ̃dis'mɑ̃], *n.m.* growth, increase; rise; (*Opt.*) magnification.
grand-maman [grɑ̃ma'mɑ̃], *n.f.* (*pl.* **-mamans**) granny.
grand-mère [grɑ̃'mɛːr], *n.f.* (*pl.* **-mères**) grandmother.
grand-père [grɑ̃'pɛːr], *n.m.* (*pl.* **grands-pères**) grandfather.
grand-route [grɑ̃'rut], *n.f.* (*pl.* **-routes**) high-road, main road.
grand-rue [grɑ̃'ry], *n.f.* (*pl.* **-rues**) high street, main street.
grange [grɑ̃ːʒ], *n.f.* barn.
granit [gra'nit, gra'ni], **granite** [gra'nit], *n.m.* granite.
granulaire [grany'lɛːr], *a.* granular.
granule [gra'nyl], *n.m.* granule.
granulé [grany'le], *a.* granulated, granular.
graphique [gra'fik], *a.* graphic.—*n.m.* diagram; graph.
graphiquement [grafik'mɑ̃], *adv.* graphically.
graphite [gra'fit], *n.m.* graphite; plumbago.
grappe [grap], *n.f.* bunch (*of grapes, currants etc.*); cluster (*of fruit etc.*); (*Artill.*) grape-shot.
grappillage [grapi'jaːʒ], *n.m.* vine-gleaning *or* pickings.

grappiller [grapi'je], *v.t.* to glean.—*v.i.* to glean; to get pickings, to make a little profit.
grappilleur [grapi'jœːr], *n.m.* (*fem.* **-euse**) gleaner; petty thief, profiteer.
grappin [gra'pɛ̃], *n.m.* grapnel, grappling-iron; grab.
gras [grɑ], *a.* (*fem.* **grasse**) fat; fleshy, corpulent; greasy, oily, unctuous; rich; broad, indecent; *eaux grasses*, dishwater; *faire la grasse matinée*, to get up late; *mardi gras*, Shrove Tuesday; *matières grasses*, fats.—*n.m.* fat, fat part (*of meat etc.*); meat, flesh; meat diet.
gras-double [grɑ'dubl], *n.m.* tripe.
grassement [grɑs'mɑ̃], *adv.* plentifully, liberally; in affluence.
grasseyement [grasɛj'mɑ̃], *n.m.* exaggerated rolling of uvular r.
grasseyer [grasɛ'je], *v.i.* to roll one's r's.
grassouillet [grasu'jɛ], *a.* (*fem.* **-ette**) (*fam.*) plump, chubby.
gratification [gratifika'sjɔ̃], *n.f.* gratuity, extra pay, reward.
gratifier [grati'fje], *v.t.* to confer (*a favour*) on; to ascribe.
gratin [gra'tɛ̃], *n.m.* burnt part; *au gratin*, (*Cook.*) dressed with crust of bread-crumbs.
gratis [gra'tis], *adv.* gratis, for nothing.
gratitude [grati'tyd], *n.f.* gratitude.
gratte-ciel [grat'sjɛl], *n.m. inv.* skyscraper.
grattelle [gra'tɛl], *n.f.* rash, itching.
gratte-papier [gratpa'pje], *n.m. inv.* scribbler, pen-pusher.
gratter [gra'te], *v.t.* to scratch; to scrape. **se gratter,** *v.r.* to scratch oneself.
grattoir [gra'twaːr], *n.m.* scraper; eraser, paint-scraper.
gratuit [gra'tɥi], *a.* free (of charge); gratuitous.
gratuité [gratɥi'te], *n.f.* gratuitousness.
gratuitement [gratɥit'mɑ̃], *adv.* for nothing; gratuitously.
gravats [gra'va], *n.m. pl.* rubbish, debris (*of a building*).
grave [graːv], *a.* heavy, grave, serious; weighty; dangerous; low, deep (*of voice*); (*Mus.*) low-pitched.
gravé [gra've], *a.* pitted; engraved.
graveleux [gra'vlø], *a.* (*fem.* **-euse**) gravelly, sandy, gritty; (*fig.*) smutty.
gravelle [gra'vɛl], *n.f.* (*Path.*) gravel.
gravement [grav'mɑ̃], *adv.* gravely, seriously.
graver [gra've], *v.t.* to engrave; to impress, to imprint. **se graver,** *v.r.* to be engraved, to be impressed *or* imprinted.
graveur [gra'vœːr], *n.m.* engraver.
gravier [gra'vje], *n.m.* gravel, grit; (*Path.*) gravel.
gravir [gra'viːr], *v.t.* to clamber up, to climb, to ascend.
gravitation [gravita'sjɔ̃], *n.f.* gravitation.
gravité [gravi'te], *n.f.* gravity; seriousness, solemnity; weight, importance.
graviter [gravi'te], *v.i.* to gravitate.
gravure [gra'vyːr], *n.f.* engraving, print; illustration (*in book*).
gré [gre], *n.m.* will; liking, pleasure; mind, taste; accord, consent *bon gré mal gré* or *de gré ou de force*, willy nilly; *de bon gré*, willingly; *de mauvais gré*, unwillingly; *savoir (bon) gré*, to be thankful; *vendre de gré à gré*, to sell by private contract.

grèbe [grɛb], *n.m.* (*Orn.*) grebe.
grec [grɛk], *a.* (*fem.* **grecque**) Greek; Grecian.—*n.m.* Greek (*language*); (**Grec**, *fem.* **Grecque**) Greek (*person*).
Grèce [grɛs], **la**, *f.* Greece.
gredin [grə'dɛ̃], *n.m.* rascal, scoundrel.
gréer [gre'e], *v.t.* to rig.
greffe (1) [grɛf], *n.m.* (*Law*) registry, record-office.
greffe (2) [grɛf], *n.f.* graft; grafting.
greffer [grɛ'fe], *v.t.* to graft.
greffier [grɛ'fje], *n.m.* registrar, recorder, clerk of the court.
greffoir [grɛ'fwaːr], *n.m.* grafting-knife.
greffon [grɛ'fɔ̃], *n.m.* graft, scion, slip.
grégaire [gre'gɛːr], **grégarien** [grega'rjɛ̃] (*fem.* **-enne**), *a.* gregarious.
grêle (1) [grɛ:l], *a.* slender, slim; shrill.
grêle (2) [grɛ:l], *n.f.* hail; hailstorm.
grêlé [grɛ'le], *a.* ravaged by hail; pock-marked.
grêler [grɛ'le], *v. impers.* to hail.—*v.t.* to ravage, ruin *or* spoil by hail.
grêlon [grɛ'lɔ̃], *n.m.* hailstone.
grelot [grə'lo], *n.m.* small (*round*) bell.
grelotter [grələ'te], *v.i.* to tremble, to shake, to shiver (*with cold, fear*); to tinkle.
grenade [grə'nad], *n.f.* pomegranate; (*Mil.*) grenade.
grenadier [grəna'dje], *n.m.* pomegranate-tree; (*Mil.*) grenadier.
grenadine [grəna'din], *n.f.* grenadine (*silk* or *syrup*).
grenat [grə'na], *n.m.* garnet.—*a.* garnet-red.
grener [grə'ne], *v.t.* (*conjug. like* AMENER) to granulate; to grain (*leather etc.*); (*Engr.*) to stipple.—*v.i.* to seed, to run to seed.
grènetis [grɛn'ti], *n.m.* milling, milled edge.
grenier [grə'nje], *n.m.* loft; attic; corn-loft, granary.
grenouille [grə'nuːj], *n.f.* frog.
grenu [grə'ny], *a.* full of corn; rough-grained.
grès [grɛ], *n.m.* sandstone, stoneware.
grésil [gre'zil], *n.m.* sleet.
grésillement [grezij'mɑ̃], *n.m.* pattering (*like* *sleet*); shrivelling, crackling; chirping.
grésiller [grezi'je], *v. impers.* to sleet, to patter.—*v.t.* to shrivel up.—*v.i.* to crackle.
grève [grɛːv], *n.f.* strand, beach of sand *or* shingle; strike of workmen; **grève du zèle**, working to rule.
grever [grə've], *v.t.* (*conjug. like* AMENER) to wrong, to injure; to burden; to encumber (*with debt etc.*).
gréviste [gre'vist], *n.* striker.
gribouillage [gribu'jaːʒ], **gribouillis** [gribu'ji], *n.m.* (*Paint.*) daub; scrawl.
gribouiller [gribu'je], *v.t., v.i.* to daub; to scrawl, to scribble.
gribouilleur [gribu'jœːr], *n.m.* (*fem.* **-euse**) dauber; scrawler, scribbler.
grief [gri'ɛf], *n.m.* wrong, injury, grievance.
grièvement [griɛv'mɑ̃], *adv.* grievously, gravely.
grièveté [griɛv'te], *n.f.* gravity, seriousness.
griffade [gri'fad], *n.f.* clawing, scratch.
griffe [grif], *n.f.* claw, talon; (*pl.*) clutches; paper-clip, clamp; **griffe d'asperge**, root of asparagus.
griffer [gri'fe], *v.t.* to claw, to scratch (*of cats etc.*); to stamp (*with signature etc.*).

griffon [gri'fɔ̃], *n.m.* griffin; griffon.
griffonnage [grifɔ'naːʒ], *n.m.* scrawl, scribble.
griffonner [grifɔ'ne], *v.t.* to scrawl, to scribble.
griffonneur [grifɔ'nœːr], *n.m.* (*fem.* **-euse**) scrawler, scribbler.
grignoter [griɲɔ'te], *v.t.* to nibble; (*fig.*) to get pickings out of.
gril [gri], *n.m.* gridiron, grill.
grillade [gri'jad], *n.f.* grilling, broiling; grill, grilled steak.
grillage [gri'jaːʒ], *n.m.* grilling, broiling, toasting; wire guard *or* mesh; light iron railing.
grille [griːj], *n.f.* railing, grating, grill; iron gate *or* bars; (*Elec.*) grid.
grille-pain [grij'pɛ̃], *n.m. inv.* toaster.
griller (1) [gri'je], *v.t.* to broil, to grill (*meat*); to roast (*coffee*); to toast (*bread*).—*v.i.* to broil, to be burned up *or* scorched; to burn out (*electric bulbs*); (*fig.*) to be itching (*to do something*). **se griller**, *v.r.* to be scorched, to be parched.
griller (2) [gri'je], *v.t.* to enclose with iron rails.
grillon [gri'jɔ̃], *n.m.* cricket.
grimaçant [grima'sɑ̃], *a.* grimacing, grinning; (*fig.*) gaping, ill-fitting.
grimace [gri'mas], *n.f.* grimace, wry face; (*fig.*) (*pl.*) affectations, airs and graces.
grimacer [grima'se], *v.i.* (*conjug. like* COMMENCER) to make faces, to grimace, to grin; to simper; to pucker.
grimer (se) [səgri'me], *v.r.* to make up.
grimpant [grɛ̃'pɑ̃], *a.* climbing, creeping (*of plants*).
grimper [grɛ̃'pe], *v.i.* to climb, to clamber up; to creep up (*of plants*).
grimpeur [grɛ̃'pœːr], *a.* (*fem.* **-euse**) climbing, twining.—*n.m.* (*fem.* **-euse**) (*Orn.*) climber.
grincement [grɛ̃s'mɑ̃], *n.m.* gnashing, grinding (*of the teeth etc.*); grating.
grincer [grɛ̃'se], *v.i.* (*conjug. like* COMMENCER) to grind, to gnash, to grate.
grincheux [grɛ̃'ʃø], *a.* (*fem.* **-euse**) ill-tempered, peevish, crabbed, surly.—*n.m.* (*fem.* **-euse**) grumbler.
gringalet [grɛ̃ga'lɛ], *n.m.* weak, puny man.
griotte [gri'ɔt], *n.f.* morello cherry.
grippage [gri'paːʒ], **grippement** [grip'mɑ̃], *n.m.* friction (*of two surfaces*); seizing, jamming (*of bearing*).
grippe [grip], *n.f.* influenza, 'flu; (*colloq.*) dislike.
grippé [gri'pe], *a.* shrunk, contracted (*of the face*); ill with influenza; run hot, seized up (*of motors*).
gripper [gri'pe], *v.t.* to pounce upon, to clutch, to seize.—*v.i.* to run hot, to seize up, to jam. **se gripper**, *v.r.* to shrivel, to shrink.
grippe-sou [grip'su], *n.m.* (*pl. unchanged* or **grippe-sous**) miser, money-grubber.
gris [gri], *a.* grey; grey-haired; dull (*of the weather*); (*fig.*) tipsy; **papier gris**, brown paper.—*n.m.* grey.
grisaille [gri'zaːj], *n.f.* sketch *or* painting in tones of grey; greyness (*of weather*).
grisâtre [gri'zaːtr], *a.* greyish.
griser [gri'ze], *v.t.* to give a grey tint to; to intoxicate; **se griser**, *v.r.* to get tipsy.
grisette [gri'zɛt], *n.f.* grey gown; (*Orn.*) whitethroat.

171

grison

grison [gri′zõ], *a.* (*fem.* **-onne**) grey, grey-haired.—*n.m.* (*colloq.*) grey-beard (*old man*); donkey.

grisonnant [grizo′nã], *a.* turning grey.

grisonner [grizo′ne], *v.i.* to grow grey (*of hair etc.*).

grisou [gri′zu], *n.m.* fire-damp.

grive [gri:v], *n.f.* thrush.

grivelé [gri′vle], *a.* speckled.

grivois [gri′vwa], *a.* loose, broad, obscene.

grivoiserie [grivwaz′ri], *n.f.* smutty story.

Groenland [groen′lãd], **le**, *m.* Greenland.

groenlandais [groenlã′de], *a.* of Greenland.—*n.m.* (**Groenlandais**, *fem.* **-aise**) Greenlander.

grognard [gro′na:r], *a.* grumbling, growling.—*n.* grumbler, grouser; veteran of Napoleon's Old Guard.

grognement [groɲ′mã], *n.m.* grunt, grunting; growling, grumbling.

grogner [gro′ɲe], *v.i.* to grunt; to growl, to grumble, to grouse.

grognon [gro′nõ], *a.* (*fem.* **-onne**, *but usu. unchanged*) grumbling, querulous.—*n.m.* (*fem.* **-onne**) grumbler, growler.

groin [grwɛ̃], *n.m.* snout (*of a hog*).

grommeler [grom′le], *v.t., v.i.* (*conjug. like* APPELER) to mutter, to grumble.

grondant [grõ′dã], *a.* scolding; roaring, rumbling.

grondement [grõd′mã], *n.m.* rumbling, growling, snarling; roar.

gronder [grõ′de], *v.t.* to chide, to scold.—*v.i.* to growl, to mutter; to snarl, to rumble, to roar.

gronderie [grõ′dri], *n.f.* scolding, chiding.

grondeur [grõ′dœ:r], *a.* (*fem.* **-euse**) grumbling, scolding.—*n.m.* (*fem.* **-euse**) scold; grumbler.

grondin [grõ′dɛ̃], *n.m.* (*Ichth.*) gurnard, gurnet.

groom [grum], *n.m.* page, (*U.S.*) bell-boy; stable lad.

gros [gro], *a.* (*fem.* **grosse** (1)) big, large, bulky; stout; coarse; pregnant; loud (*of laughter*); gruff (*of the voice*); substantial; foul (*of the weather*); high (*of the sea etc.*); dark, deep (*in colour*); (*Cine.*) **gros plan**, close-up.—*n.m.* large or main part; bulk, mass; main body (*of an army*); **en gros et en détail**, wholesale and retail.—*adv.* much.

groseille [gro′zɛ:j], *n.f.* currant; **groseille à maquereau**, gooseberry.

groseillier [groze′je], *n.m.* currant-bush.

grosse (1) [gros], [GROS].

grosse (2) [gros], *n.f.* gross (*twelve dozen*).

grossement [gros′mã], *adv.* grossly, coarsely.

grossesse [gro′sɛs], *n.f.* pregnancy.

grosseur [gro′sœ:r], *n.f.* size, bulk; bigness; swelling, tumour.

grossier [gro′sje], *a.* (*fem.* **-ière**) gross, coarse, thick; plain, common; rough, rude, unpolished, unmannerly, boorish.

grossièrement [grosjɛr′mã], *adv.* coarsely, rudely, roughly, uncouthly.

grossièreté [grosjɛr′te], *n.f.* coarseness, grossness; rudeness; coarse language.

grossir [gro′si:r], *v.t.* to make bigger or greater.—*v.i.* to grow bigger; to put on weight.

grossissant [grosi′sã], *a.* magnifying.

grossissement [grosis′mã], *n.m.* magnifying, magnifying-power; increase; exaggeration.

grosso-modo [grosomo′do], *adv.* summarily.

grotesque [gro′tɛsk], *a.* and *n.m.* grotesque.

grotte [grot], *n.f.* grotto, cave.

grouillant [gru′jã], *a.* stirring, swarming, crawling.

grouillement [gruj′mã], *n.m.* stirring, swarming; rumbling (*of the intestines*).

grouiller [gru′je], *v.i.* to stir, to move; to swarm; to rumble (*of the intestines*).

groupe [grup], *n.m.* group, party (*of people*); cluster (*of stars*); clump (*of trees etc.*).

groupement [grup′mã], *n.m.* grouping.

grouper [gru′pe], *v.t.* to group. **se grouper**, *v.r.* to form groups, to gather.

gruau [gry′o], *n.m.* flour of wheat; **gruau d'avoine**, groats; oatmeal; **tisane de gruau**, gruel.

grue [gry], *n.f.* (*Orn., Eng.*) crane.

gruger [gry′ʒe], *v.t.* (*conjug. like* MANGER) to crunch; to eat, to devour.

grume [grym], *n.f.* bark (*of tree*); **bois de** or **en grume**, wood with the bark on.

grumeau [gry′mo], *n.m.* (*pl.* **-eaux**) clot, small lump.

grumeler (se) [səgry′mle], *v.r.* (*conjug. like* APPELER) to clot.

grumeleux [gry′mlø], *a.* (*fem.* **-euse**) clotted, rough.

gruyère [gry′jɛ:r], *n.m.* Gruyère cheese.

guano [gwa′no], *n.m.* guano.

Guatémala [gwatema′la], **le**, *m.* Guatemala.

guatémaltèque [gwatemal′tɛk], *a.* Guatemalan.—*n.* (**Guatémaltèque**) Guatemalan (*person*).

gué [ge], *n.m.* ford.

guéable [ge′abl], *a.* fordable.

guéer [ge′e], *v.t.* to ford.

guenille [gə′ni:j], *n.f.* rag, tatter; (*pl.*) tattered clothes.

guenilleux [gəni′jø], *a.* (*fem.* **-euse**) tattered, ragged.

guenon [gə′nõ], *n.f.* monkey, ape; she-monkey; (*fig.*) fright, ugly woman.

guépard [ge′pa:r], *n.m.* cheetah.

guêpe [gɛ:p], *n.f.* wasp.

guêpier [gɛ:′pje], *n.m.* wasps' nest; bee-eater (*bird*); scrape, difficulty.

guère [gɛ:r], *adv.* but little, not much, not very; not long; hardly, scarcely.

guères (*poet.*) [GUÈRE].

guéret [ge′rɛ], *n.m.* ploughed but unsown land; fallow-land; (*pl., poet.*) fields.

guéridon [geri′dõ], *n.m.* (small) round table.

guérilla [geri′ja], *n.f.* guerrilla war or troops.

guérir [ge′ri:r], *v.t.* to heal, to cure.—*v.i.* to heal, to heal up; to recover, to be cured.

guérison [geri′zõ], *n.f.* recovery, healing, cure.

guérissable [geri′sabl], *a.* curable.

guérisseur [geri′sœ:r], *n.m.* (*fem.* **-euse**) healer, faith-healer; quack.

guérite [ge′rit], *n.f.* sentry-box; look-out turret.

Guernesey [gɛrnə′ze], *f.* Guernsey.

guerre [gɛ:r], *n.f.* war; warfare, hostilities; strife.

guerrier [gɛ′rje], *a.* (*fem.* **-ière**) warlike, martial.—*n.m.* (*fem.* **-ière**) warrior, fighting man or woman.

172

habilleur

guerroyant [gɛrwa'jɑ̃], *a.* bellicose, pugnacious.
guerroyer [gɛrwa'je], *v.i. (conjug. like* EMPLOYER) to make war, to wage war.
guet [gɛ], *n.m.* watch; watching; *au guet,* on the look-out.
guet-apens [gɛta'pɑ̃], *n.m. (pl.* guets-apens) ambush; trap.
guêtre [gɛ:tr], *n.f.* gaiter; *grandes guêtres,* leggings; *petites guêtres,* spats.
guetter [gɛ'te], *v.t.* to lie in wait for, to watch for, to waylay.
guetteur [gɛ'tœ:r], *n.m.* signalman, look-out man.
gueulard [gœ'la:r], *a. (pop.)* bawling, mouthing; gluttonous; hard-mouthed *(of horses).*—*n.m. (fem.* -e) bawler; glutton.—*n.m.* furnace-mouth.
gueule [gœl], *n.f.* mouth *(of animals); (vulg.)* mouth, face, mug *(of human).*
gueule-de-lion [gœldə'ljɔ̃], *n.f. (pl.* gueules-de-lion) antirrhinum.
gueule-de-loup [gœldə'lu], *n.f. (pl.* gueules-de-loup) snapdragon; chimney cowl.
gueuler [gœ'le], *v.i. (pop.)* to bawl.
gueuse [gø:z], *n.f.* pig-iron.
gueuser [gø'ze], *v.t., v.i.* to beg.
gueuserie [gø'zri], *n.f.* beggary; destitution; *(fig.)* trash.
gueux [gø], *a. (fem.* -euse) poor, destitute; wretched.—*n.m.* beggar, tramp; knave, rascal.—*n.f.* (-euse (2)) wench, bitch.
gui [gi], *n.m.* mistletoe.
guichet [gi'ʃɛ], *n.m.* wicket-gate *(of prison);* spyhole *(of door);* position at counter *(banks, post-office),* pay-desk; booking-office *(railways).*
guichetier [giʃ'tje], *n.m.* turnkey.
guide [gid], *n.m.* guide; guide-book.—*n.f.* girl-guide; rein.
guider [gi'de], *v.t.* to guide, to lead; to direct.
guidon [gi'dɔ̃], *n.m. (Mil.)* guidon; *(Navy)* burgee; (fore)sight, bead *(of fire-arms);* reference-mark *(in a book);* handle-bar *(of bicycle).*
guigner [gi'ne], *v.t.* to peer *or* peep at; to ogle; to covet.—*v.i.* to peep, to peer.
guignol [gi'nɔl], *n.m.* Punch; puppet-show, Punch and Judy show.
guignolet [gino'lɛ], *n.m.* cherry-brandy.
guignon [gi'nɔ̃], *n.m.* bad luck, ill-luck.
Guillaume [gi'jo:m], *m.* William.
guillemet [gij'mɛ], *n.m.* quotation mark, inverted comma.
guillemot [gij'mo], *n.m. (Orn.)* guillemot.
guilleret [gij'rɛ], *a. (fem.* -ette) brisk, lively.
guilleri [gij'ri], *n.m.* chirping *(of sparrows).*
guillotine [gijo'tin], *n.f.* guillotine; *fenêtre à guillotine,* sash-window.
guillotiner [gijoti'ne], *v.t.* to guillotine.
guimauve [gi'mo:v], *n.f.* marsh-mallow.
guimbarde [gɛ̃'bard], *n.f.* Jew's-harp; *(colloq.)* rickety old vehicle, boneshaker.
guimpe [gɛ̃p], *n.f.* stomacher; wimple *(for nuns etc.).*
guindé [gɛ̃'de], *a.* stiff, forced, unnatural; formal *(of style).*
guindeau [gɛ̃'do], *n.m. (pl.* -eaux) windlass.
guinder [gɛ̃'de], *v.t.* to hoist; to strain, to force. se **guinder,** *v.r.* to hoist oneself up; to be strained, to be forced.

Guinée [gi'ne], **la,** *f.* Guinea.
guinéen [gine'ɛ̃], *a. (fem.* -éenne) Guinean.—*n.m.* (**Guinéen,** *fem.* -éenne) Guinean *(person).*
guingan [gɛ̃'gɑ̃], *n.m.* gingham.
guingois [gɛ̃'gwa], *n.m.* crookedness; *de guingois,* awry, askew.
guinguette [gɛ̃'gɛt], *n.f.* small suburban tavern *(usually with pleasure garden).*
guirlande [gir'lɑ̃:d], *n.f.* garland, wreath.
guise [gi:z], *n.f.* manner, way, guise; fancy; *en guise de,* by way of.
guitare [gi'ta:r], *n.f.* guitar.
guitariste [gita'rist], *n.* guitarist, guitar-player.
gustatif [gysta'tif], *a. (fem.* -tive) gustatory.
gustation [gysta'sjɔ̃], *n.f.* tasting, gustation.
guttural [gyty'ral], *a. (m. pl.* -aux) guttural.
guyanais [gɥija'nɛ], *a. (fem.* -aise) Guyanese.—*n.m.* (**Guyanais,** *fem.* -aise) Guyanese *(person).*
Guyane [gɥi'jan], **la,** *f.* Guyana.
gymnase [ʒim'nɑ:z], *n.m.* gymnasium.
gymnaste [ʒim'nast], *n.* gymnast.
gymnastique [ʒimnas'tik], *a.* gymnastic.—*n.f.* gymnastics.
gynécologie [ʒinekɔlɔ'ʒi], *n.f.* gynaecology.
gynécologiste [ʒinekɔlɔ'ʒist], **gynécologue** [ʒinekɔ'lɔg], *n.* gynaecologist.
gypse [ʒips], *n.m.* gypsum; plaster of Paris.
gyroscope [ʒirɔs'kɔp], *n.m.* gyroscope.

H

[In words marked thus † the *h* is 'aspirated'.]

H, h [aʃ], *n.m. or f.* the eighth letter of the alphabet. *H* is mute *or* aspirated. The so-called aspirated *h* is a graphic symbol which indicates that there is neither elision nor liaison; *e.g.* **la halle** [la'al], *les halles* [lɛ'al]; *l'heure H,* (*Mil.*) zero hour.
habile [a'bil], *a.* able, clever; capable; skilful; sharp, cunning.
habilement [abil'mɑ̃], *adv.* cleverly, skilfully.
habileté [abil'te], *n.f.* ability, skill, cleverness.
habilité [abili'te], *a.* entitled, qualified.—*n.f.* (*Law*) competency, qualification.
habiliter [abili'te], *v.t.* to qualify, to enable, to entitle.
habillage [abi'ja:ʒ], *n.m.* dressing; trussing *(poultry).*
habillant [abi'jɑ̃], *a.* dressy *or* suiting well *(of clothes etc.).*
habillé [abi'je], *a.* dressed, clad, decked out.
habillement [abij'mɑ̃], *n.m.* clothes, dress, attire.
habiller [abi'je], *v.t.* to dress; to make clothes for; to become, to fit; to wrap up; (*Cook.*) to truss *(fowls, fish etc.);* (*fig.*) to adorn. **s'habiller,** *v.r.* to dress; to have one's clothes made.
habilleur [abi'jœ:r], *n.m. (fem.* -euse) (*Theat.*) dresser.

habit [a'bi], *n.m.* clothes; dress-coat; *habit complet*, suit of clothes.
habitable [abi'tabl], *a.* habitable.
habitànt [abi'tã], *n.m.* (*fem.* **-e**) inhabitant, resident; occupier; denizen; (*C*) farmer.
habitation [abita'sjõ], *n.f.* habitation, residence, abode.
habiter [abi'te], *v.t.* to inhabit, to dwell in, to live in; to frequent; *habiter un lieu*, to live in a place.—*v.i.* to inhabit, to dwell, to reside; *habiter avec*, (*Law*) to cohabit.
habitude [abi'tyd], *n.f.* habit, custom, practice; *d'habitude*, usually.
habitué [abi'tɥe], *n.m.* (*fem.* **-ée**) frequenter, customer.
habituel [abi'tɥɛl], *a.* (*fem.* **-elle**) habitual, usual.
habituellement [abitɥɛl'mã], *adv.* habitually usually.
habituer [abi'tɥe], *v.t.* to accustom. **s'habituer**, *v.r.* to accustom oneself; to get used (*à*).
†**hâbler** [ɑ'ble], *v.i.* to brag, to boast.
†**hâblerie** [ablə'ri], *n.f.* bragging, boasting.
†**hâbleur** [ɑ'blœːr], *n.m.* (*fem.* **-euse**) braggart, boaster.
†**hache** [aʃ], *n.f.* axe, hatchet.
†**haché** [a'ʃe], *a.* chopped up; mixed; (*fig.*) abrupt.
†**hacher** [a'ʃe], *v.t.* to chop, to cut to pieces; to hash, to mince; to hack; to cross-hatch.
†**hachis** [a'ʃi], *n.m.* minced meat, hash.
†**hachoir** [a'ʃwaːr], *n.m.* chopping-board; chopping-knife; mincer.
†**hachure** [a'ʃyːr], *n.f.* (*Engr.*) hatching, hachure.
†**hagard** [a'gaːr], *a.* wild-looking, haggard.
†**haie** [ɛ], *n.f.* hedge, hedgerow; hurdle; row, line.
†**haillon** [a'jõ], *n.m.* rag, tatter.
†**haine** [ɛːn], *n.f.* hate, hatred; dislike; spite.
†**haineusement** [ɛnøz'mã], *adv.* hatefully, spitefully.
†**haineux** [ɛ'nø], *a.* (*fem.* **-euse**) hating, spiteful.
†**haïr** [a'iːr], *v.t. irr.* to hate, to detest, to loathe.
†**haire** [ɛːr], *n.f.* hair-shirt.
†**haïssable** [ai'sabl], *a.* hateful, odious.
Haïti [ai'ti], *m.* or *f.* Haiti.
†**haïtien** [ai'sjɛ̃], *a.* (*fem.* **-enne**) Haitian.—*n.m.* (**Haïtien**, *fem.* **-enne**) Haitian (*person*).
†**halage** [a'laːʒ], *n.m.* towage, hauling.
†**hale** [aːl], *n.m.* tow-line, tow-rope.
†**hâle** [ɑːl], *n.m.* heat of the sun; sunburn.
†**hâlé** [ɑ'le], *a.* sunburnt; tanned; swarthy.
haleine [a'lɛn], *n.f.* breath, wind.
†**haler** [a'le], *v.t.* (*Naut.*) to haul, to tow.
†**hâler** [ɑ'le], *v.t.* to tan, to burn (*of the sun*). **se hâler**, *v.r.* to become sunburnt *or* tanned.
†**haletant** [al'tã], *a.* out of breath, panting.
†**haleter** [al'te], *v.i.* (*conjug. like* AMENER) to pant, to gasp for breath.
†**hall** [ɔl], *n.m.* large entrance hall (*of hotel, station*).
†**halle** [al], *n.f.* market; market-hall, market-place.
†**hallebarde** [al'bard], *n.f.* halberd; *pleuvoir des hallebardes*, to rain cats and dogs.
†**hallebardier** [albar'dje], *n.m.* halberdier.
†**hallier** [a'lje], *n.m.* thicket, coppice.

hallucination [alysina'sjõ], *n.f.* hallucination, delusion.
halluciné [alysi'ne], *a.* hallucinated; (*fig.*) deluded.—*n.m.* (*fem.* **-ée**) person suffering from delusions.
halluciner [alysi'ne], *v.t.* to hallucinate; (*fig.*) to delude.
†**halo** [a'lo], *n.m.* halo; (*Phot.*) halation.
†**halot** [a'lo], *n.m.* rabbit-burrow.
†**halte** [alt], *n.f.* halt; stand, stop; halting-place.—*int.* halt! stop!
haltère [al'tɛːr], *n.m.* dumb-bell.
†**hamac** [a'mak], *n.m.* hammock.
†**hameau** [a'mo], *n.m.* (*pl.* **-eaux**) hamlet.
hameçon [am'sõ], *n.m.* hook, fish-hook; bait.
†**hampe** [ɑ̃ːp], *n.f.* staff (*of a lance, flag etc.*); stem, flower-stalk.
†**hamster** [ams'tɛːr], *n.m.* hamster.
†**hanche** [ɑ̃ːʃ], *n.f.* hip; haunch (*of horse*).
†**handicap** [ɑ̃di'kap], *n.m.* handicap.
†**hangar** [ɑ̃'gaːr], *n.m.* outhouse, shed, cart-shed; hangar (*for aeroplanes*).
†**hanneton** [an'tõ], *n.m.* May-bug, cockchafer; (*fig.*) thoughtless person.
†**hanter** [ɑ̃'te], *v.t.* to haunt; to frequent.
†**hantise** [ɑ̃'tiːz], *n.f.* obsession.
†**happer** [a'pe], *v.t.* to snap up, to snatch; to seize.
†**happeur** [a'pœːr], *n.m.* paper-clip.
†**haquenée** [ak'ne], *n.f.* hack, quiet horse; (*fig.*) ungainly woman.
†**haquet** [a'kɛ], *n.m.* dray.
†**harangue** [a'rɑ̃ːg], *n.f.* harangue, speech; (*boring*) address.
†**haranguer** [arɑ̃'ge], *v.t., v.i.* to harangue.
†**harangueur** [arɑ̃'gœːr], *n.m.* (*fem.* **-euse**) haranguer, orator, speechifier.
†**haras** [a'rɑ], *n.m.* stud, breeding-stud.
†**harasser** [ara'se], *v.t.* to harass, to tire out, to weary.
†**harceler** [arsə'le], *v.t.* (*conjug. like* APPELER) to worry, to pester, to torment, to harass.
†**harde** [ard], *n.f.* herd (*of deer etc.*); leash (*for hounds*).
†**hardes** [ard], *n.f.* (*used only in pl.*) wearing apparel, attire; worn clothes.
†**hardi** [ar'di], *a.* bold, daring, fearless; rash; impudent.
†**hardiesse** [ar'djɛs], *n.f.* boldness, daring; rashness; assurance, impudence.
†**hardiment** [ardi'mã], *adv.* boldly, daringly; impudently.
†**harem** [a'rɛm], *n.m.* harem.
†**hareng** [a'rɑ̃], *n.m.* herring.
†**harengère** [arɑ̃'ʒɛːr], *n.f.* fish-wife.
†**harenguet** [arɑ̃'ge], *n.m.* sprat.
†**hargneux** [ar'nø], *a.* (*fem.* **-euse**) cross, cross-grained, peevish, surly.
†**haricot** [ari'ko], *n.m.* kidney-bean; *haricot de mouton*, Irish stew; *haricots d'Espagne*, scarlet runners; *haricots verts*, French beans.
†**haridelle** [ari'dɛl], *n.f.* jade, hack; (*fig.*) gawky woman.
†**harle** [arl], *n.m.* (*Orn.*) merganser.
harmonica [armoni'ka], *n.m.* harmonica; mouth-organ.
harmonie [armɔ'ni], *n.f.* harmony; concord; (*Mus.*) harmonics.
harmonieusement [armɔnjøz'mã], *adv.* harmoniously.

harmonieux [armɔ'njø], *a.* (*fem.* **-euse**) harmonious; musical, melodious; in keeping; blending (*of colours*).

harmonique [armɔ'nik], *a.* harmonic.—*n.f.* harmonics.

harmoniser [armɔni'ze], *v.t.* and **s'harmoniser**, *v.r.* to harmonize.

harmonium [armɔ'njɔm], *n.m.* harmonium.

†**harnachement** [arnaʃ'mɑ̃], *n.m.* harness, trappings.

†**harnacher** [arna'ʃe], *v.t.* to harness; to rig out.

†**harnais** [ar'nɛ], *n.m.* harness; horse-trappings; armour; equipment, tackle.

†**haro** [a'ro], *n.m.* hue and cry.

†**harpagon** [arpa'gɔ̃], *n.m.* miser, skinflint.

†**harpe** [arp], *n.f.* harp.

†**harper** [ar'pe], *v.t.* to grasp, to clutch.

†**harpie** [ar'pi], *n.f.* harpy, vixen, shrew.

†**harpiste** [ar'pist], *n.* harpist.

†**harpon** [ar'pɔ̃], *n.m.* harpoon.

†**harponner** [arpɔ'ne], *v.t.* to harpoon.

†**hasard** [a'zaːr], *n.m.* chance; hazard; risk, danger; *à tout hasard*, on the off chance; *au hasard*, at random; *par hasard*, by chance.

†**hasardé** [azar'de], *a.* hazarded, ventured; hazardous, bold.

†**hasarder** [azar'de], *v.t.* to hazard, to risk, to venture. **se hasarder**, *v.r.* to hazard, to venture, to take the risk.

†**hasardeusement** [azardøz'mɑ̃], *adv.* hazardously.

†**hasardeux** [azar'dø], *a.* (*fem.* **-euse**) venturesome, daring; hazardous, unsafe.

†**hâte** [aːt], *n.f.* hurry, haste; *à la hâte*, in a hurry.

†**hâter** [a'te], *v.t.* to hasten, to forward, to hurry, to urge on; to expedite; to force (*fruit*). **se hâter**, *v.r.* to make haste, to hurry.

†**hâtif** [a'tif], *a.* (*fem.* **-tive**) forward; precocious, premature; (*Hort.*) early.

†**hâtivement** [ativ'mɑ̃], *adv.* early, prematurely; hastily.

†**hauban** [o'bɑ̃], *n.m.* (*Naut.*) shroud, guy, stay.

†**hausse** [oːs], *n.f.* lift, block (*for raising anything*); (*Comm.*) rise, advance; (back) sight (*of a rifle*).

†**haussement** [os'mɑ̃], *n.m.* raising, lifting; *haussement d'épaules*, shrugging of the shoulders.

†**hausser** [o'se], *v.t.* to raise, to lift up; to increase; to shrug; (*Comm.*) to advance.—*v.i.* to rise; to get higher; to increase. **se hausser**, *v.r.* to be raised, to rise; to raise oneself; to clear up (*of the weather*); to increase.

†**haussier** [o'sje], *n.m.* (*St. Exch.*) bull.

†**haussière** [o'sjɛːr], *n.f.* hawser.

†**haut** [o], *a.* high, tall, lofty; elevated; upper; principal; eminent; haughty; loud (*of sound*); *lire à haute voix*, to read aloud; *pousser les hauts cris*, to complain loudly.—*n.m.* height; top, summit; upper part; *d'en haut*, from above.—*n.f.* (*colloq.*) *la haute*, the wealthy, the upper crust.—*adv.* high; loud, aloud, loudly; haughtily; *ainsi qu'il a été dit plus haut*, as has already been said; *parlez plus haut*, speak louder.—*adv. phr.* **en haut**, upstairs.

†**hautain** [o'tɛ̃], *a.* haughty, proud.

†**hautainement** [otɛn'mɑ̃], *adv.* haughtily, superciliously, proudly.

†**hautbois** [o'bwa], *n.m.* hautboy, oboe; oboe-player.

†**haut-de-forme** [od'fɔrm], *n.m.* (*pl.* **hauts-de-forme**) top-hat.

†**hautement** [ot'mɑ̃], *adv.* boldly, resolutely, proudly; aloud.

†**hauteur** [o'tœːr], *n.f.* height, elevation, altitude; depth; rising ground; haughtiness, arrogance; pitch (*of the voice etc.*); (*Naut.*) bearing; *être à la hauteur de quelqu'un*, to be a match for someone; *être à la hauteur d'une tâche*, to be equal to a task.

†**haut-fond** [o'fɔ̃], *n.m.* (*pl.* **hauts-fonds**) shoal, shallow.

†**haut-le-corps** [ol'kɔːr] *n.m. inv.* spring, bound; start.

†**haut-le-pied** [ol'pje], *a. inv. cheval haut-le-pied*, spare horse; *locomotive haut-le-pied*, engine running light.

†**haut-parleur** [opar'lœːr], *n.m.* (*pl.* **-parleurs**) loud-speaker; amplifier.

†**Havane** [a'van], **la**, *f.* Havana.

†**havane** [a'van], *a.* brown, tan.—*n.m.* Havana cigar.

†**hâve** [aːv], *a.* pale, wan, emaciated.

†**havre** [aːvr], *n.m.* haven, harbour, port.

†**havresac** [avrə'sak], *n.m.* knapsack, pack.

†**Haye** [ɛ], **La**, *f.* the Hague.

†**hé!** [e], *int.* hoy! (*for calling, warning etc.*); why! well! I say! (*emphat.*).

†**heaume** [oːm], *n.m.* helmet.

hebdomadaire [ɛbdɔma'dɛːr], *a.* weekly.—*n.m.* weekly newspaper.

hébergement [ɛbɛrʒə'mɑ̃], *n.m.* lodging.

héberger [ebɛr'ʒe], *v.t.* (*conjug. like* MANGER) to lodge.

hébété [ebe'te], *a.* dazed, stupid, bewildered.

hébéter [ebe'te], *v.t.* (*conjug. like* CÉDER) to make stupid, to besot.

hébraïque [ebra'ik], *a.* Hebrew, Hebraic.

hébreu [e'brø], *a.* (*fem.* **hébraïque**)Hebrew.—*n.m.* Hebrew (*language*); (**Hébreu**, *fem.* **Juive**, *pl.* **Hébreux**) Hebrew (*person*).

hécatombe [eka'tɔ̃:b], *n.f.* hecatomb.

hectare [ɛk'taːr], *n.m.* hectare (*2 acres, 1 rood 35 perches or* 2·4711 *acres*).

hectogramme [ɛktɔ'gram], **hecto** [ɛk'to], *n.m.* hectogramme (3·527 *oz. avoirdupois*).

hectolitre [ɛktɔ'litr], *n.m.* hectolitre (22·009668 *imperial gallons*).

hectomètre [ɛktɔ'mɛtr], *n.m.* hectometre (*109·936 yds.*).

hégire [e'ʒiːr], *n.f.* Hegira (*Mohammedan era*).

†**hein!** [ɛ], *int.* (*before a sentence*) hey! what! (*after a sentence* = *n'est-ce pas*) isn't it etc. ?

†**hélas!** [e'laːs], *int.* alas!

Hélène [e'lɛn], *f.* Helen.

†**héler** [e'le], *v.t.* (*conjug. like* CÉDER) to hail, to call (*a taxi, a boat etc.*).

hélice [e'lis], *n.f.* screw; propeller.

hélicoptère [elikɔp'teːr], *n.m.* helicopter.

héliport [eli'pɔːr], *n.m.* heliport, helicopter landing-ground.

hélium [e'ljɔm], *n.m.* helium.

helvétique [ɛlve'tik], *a.* Helvetic, Helvetian, Swiss.

hémisphère [emis'fɛːr], *n.m.* hemisphere.

hémisphérique [emisfe′rik], *a.* hemispheric.
hémistiche [emis′tiʃ], *n.m.* hemistich.
hémoglobine [emɔglɔ′bin], *n.f.* haemoglobin.
hémophylie [emɔfi′li], *n.f.* haemophilia.
hémorragie [emɔra′ʒi], *n.f.* haemorrhage.
hémorroïdes [emɔrɔ′id], *n.f. pl.* haemorrhoids, piles.
†**henné** [ɛ′ne], *n.m.* (*Bot.*) henna.
†**hennir** [ɛ′niːr], *v.i.* to neigh, to whinny.
†**hennissement** [ɛnis′mã], *n.m.* neighing.
Henri [ã′ri], *m.* Henry.
hépatique [epa′tik], *a.* hepatic.—*n.f.* (*Bot.*) liverwort.
hépatite [epa′tit], *n.f.* hepatitis (*inflammation of the liver*); (*Min.*) hepatite (*liver-stone*).
heptagone [ɛpta′gɔn], *a.* heptagonal.—*n.m.* heptagon.
héraldique [ɛral′dik], *a.* heraldic.—*n.f.* heraldry.
†**héraut** [e′ro], *n.m.* herald.
herbacé [ɛrba′se], *a.* (*Bot.*) herbaceous.
herbage [ɛrba′ʒe], *n.m.* herbage, grass-land; pasture.
herbager [ɛrba′ʒe] *v.t.* (*conjug. like* MANGER) to graze (*cattle*).
herbe [ɛrb], *n.f.* herb, grass, wort; *blé en herbe*, corn in the blade; *brin d'herbe*, blade of grass; *fines herbes*, herbs for seasoning; *mauvaise herbe*, weed; (*fig.*) scamp.
herbette [ɛr′bɛt], *n.f.* (*Poet.*) short grass, green-sward.
herbeux [ɛr′bø], *a.* (*fem.* **-euse**) grassy, herbous.
herbicide [ɛrbi′sid], *a.* weed-killing.—*n.m.* weed-killer.
herbivore [ɛrbi′vɔːr], *a.* herbivorous.—*n.m.* herbivore.
herboriste [ɛrbɔ′rist], *n.* herbalist, dealer in medicinal herbs.
herbu [ɛr′by], *a.* grassy, covered with grass.
Hercule [ɛr′kyl], *m.* Hercules.
hercule [ɛr′kyl], *n.m.* man of herculean strength; strong-arm man.
herculéen [ɛrkyle′ɛ̃], *a.* (*fem.* **-éenne**) herculean.
†**hère** [ɛːr], *n.m.* *un pauvre hère*, a sorry fellow, a poor devil.
héréditaire [eredi′tɛːr], *a.* hereditary.
hérédité [eredi′te], *n.f.* hereditary transmission, inheritance *or* succession, hereditary right; heredity.
hérésie [ere′zi], *n.f.* heresy.
hérétique [ere′tik], *a.* heretical.—*n.* heretic.
†**hérissé** [eri′se], *a.* bristling, on end; rough, shaggy; (*Bot.*) hairy, prickly.
†**hérissement** [eris′mã], *n.m.* bristling, shagginess.
†**hérisser** [eri′se], *v.t.* to bristle, to erect; **se hérisser**, *v.r.* to stand on end, to bristle up; to be bristling with.
†**hérisson** [eri′sõ], *n.m.* hedgehog; (*fig.*) cross-grained person; *hérisson de mer*, sea-urchin.
héritage [eri′taːʒ], *n.m.* heritage, inheritance, legacy.
hériter [eri′te], *v.t.* to inherit.—*v.i.* to inherit, to be heir (*de*); to succeed.
héritier [eri′tje], *n.m.* (*fem.* **-ière**) heir, heiress.
hermétique [ɛrme′tik], *a.* hermetic, air-tight, water-tight.

hermétiquement [ɛrmetik′mã], *adv.* hermetically.
hermine [ɛr′min], *n.f.* ermine.
hermitage [ɛrmi′taːʒ], [ERMITAGE].
†**herniaire** [ɛr′njɛːr], *a.* hernial; *bandage herniaire*, truss.
†**hernie** [ɛr′ni], *n.f.* hernia, rupture.
héroïne [erɔ′in], *n.f.* heroine; (*Chem.*) heroin.
héroïque [erɔ′ik], *a.* heroic.
héroïquement [erɔik′mã], *adv.* heroically.
héroïsme [erɔ′ism], *n.m.* heroism.
†**héron** [e′rõ], *n.m.* heron.
†**héros** [e′ro], *n.m.* hero.
†**hersage** [ɛr′saːʒ], *n.m.* harrowing.
†**herse** [ɛrs], *n.f.* harrow; portcullis, herse; (*pl.*) (*Theat.*) battens, lights (*above stage*).
†**hersé** [ɛr′se], *a.* harrowed; (*Her.*) represented with a herse.
†**herser** [ɛr′se], *v.t.* to harrow.
hésitant [ezi′tã], *a.* hesitating, wavering.
hésitation [ezita′sjõ], *n.f.* hesitation.
hésiter [ezi′te], *v.i.* to hesitate, to falter, to pause, to waver.
†**hessois** [ɛ′swa], *a.* Hessian.—*n.m.* (**Hessois**, *fem.* **-oise**) Hessian (*person*).
hétéroclite [eterɔ′klit], *a.* heteroclite, anomalous; irregular.
hétérodoxe [eterɔ′dɔks], *a.* heterodox.
hétérodyne [eterɔ′din], *a.* and *n.f.* (*Rad.*) heterodyne.
hétérogène [eterɔ′ʒɛːn], *a.* heterogeneous; incongruous.
†**hêtre** [ɛːtr], *n.m.* beech, beech-tree.
heure [œːr], *n.f.* hour; o'clock; time of day; moment; (*pl.*) primer (*prayer-book*); *heures d'affluence* or *de pointe*, rush hours, peak periods; (*nouvelles de la*) *dernière heure*, latest news; *quelle heure est-il?* what time is it? *tout à l'heure*, in a few minutes, just now; *de bonne heure*, early.
heureusement [œrøz′mã], *adv.* happily, luckily, fortunately; successfully.
heureux [œ′rø], *a.* (*fem.* **-euse**) happy, blissful; blessed, lucky; successful; pleasing; delighted.
†**heurt** [œːr], *n.m.* blow; knock, shock, collision; bruise.
†**heurté** [œr′te], *a.* abrupt, harsh, jerky (*of style*).
†**heurtement** [œrtə′mã], *n.m.* clash, collision; hiatus.
†**heurter** [œr′te], *v.t.* to knock against, to strike against; to jostle; to shock, to offend; to jar with.—*v.i.* to strike, to knock, to hit. **se heurter**, *v.r.* to strike *or* hit oneself; to strike against each other; to jostle each other, to clash.
hiatus [ja′tyːs], *n.m.* hiatus; gap.
hibernal [ibɛr′nal], *a.* (*m. pl.* **-aux**) hibernal.
hibernant [ibɛr′nã], *a.* hibernating.
hibernation [ibɛrna′sjõ], *n.f.* hibernation.
hiberner [ibɛr′ne], *v.i.* to hibernate.
†**hibou** [i′bu], *n.m.* (*pl.* **-oux**) owl; (*fig.*) moper.
†**hic** [ik], *n.m.* knot, difficulty, rub.
†**hideur** [i′dœːr], *n.f.* hideousness.
†**hideusement** [idøz′mã], *adv.* hideously.
†**hideux** [i′dø], *a.* (*fem.* **-euse**) hideous, frightful, shocking.
hier [jɛːr], *adv.* yesterday; *avant-hier*, the day before yesterday; *hier matin*, yesterday morning; *hier (au) soir*, last night.

†hiérarchie [jerarʹʃi], *n.f.* hierarchy.
†hiérarchique [jerarʹʃik], *a.* hierarchical.
hiératique [jeraʹtik], *a.* hieratic.
hiéroglyphe [jeroʹglif], *n.m.* hieroglyph.
hiéroglyphique [jerɔgliʹfik], *a.* hieroglyphical.
Hilaire [iʹlɛːr], *m.* Hilary.
hilarant [ilaʹrã], *a.* screamingly funny, rollicking; *gaz hilarant*, laughing-gas.
hilare [iʹlaːr], *a.* hilarious.
hilarité [ilariʹte], *n.f.* hilarity, mirth, laughter.
hindou [ɛ̃ʹdu], *a.* Hindu; Indian (*of India*).—*n.m.* (**Hindou**, *fem.* **-oue**) Hindu; Indian (*of India*).
hindouisme [ɛ̃duʹism], *n.m.* Hinduism.
hindoustani [ɛ̃dustaʹni], *n.m.* Hindustani, Urdu (*language*).
hippique [iʹpik], *a.* hippic; *concours hippique*, horse-show.
hippodrome [ipɔʹdrom], *n.m.* hippodrome, circus; race-course.
hippopotame [ipɔpɔʹtam], *n.m.* hippopotamus.
hirondelle [irõʹdɛl], *n.f.* swallow.
hirsute [irʹsyt], *a.* hirsute, hairy; shaggy, dishevelled; (*fig.*) boorish.
†hisser [iʹse], *v.t.* to hoist, to lift, to run up, to raise. **se hisser**, *v.r.* to raise, hoist *or* lift oneself up.
histoire [isʹtwaːr], *n.f.* history; tale, story; idle story, untruth, falsehood; trifle; (*pl.*) fuss.
historien [istɔʹrjɛ̃], *n.m.* historian.
historier [istɔʹrje], *v.t.* to illustrate, to embellish, to adorn.
historiette [istɔʹrjɛt], *n.f.* little story, short tale.
historiographe [istɔriɔʹgraf], *n.* historiographer.
historique [istɔʹrik], *a.* historic(al).—*n.m.* historical account.
historiquement [istɔrikʹmã], *adv.* historically.
histrion [istriʹjõ], *n.m.* histrion, actor; mountebank.
histrionique [istriɔʹnik], *a.* histrionic.
hitlérien [itleʹrjɛ̃], *a.* (*fem.* **-enne**) Hitlerite.
hitlérisme [itleʹrism], *n.m.* Hitlerism.
hiver [iʹvɛːr], *n.m.* winter.
hivernage [ivɛrʹnaːʒ], *n.m.* winter season, winter-time; wintering place.
hivernal [ivɛrʹnal], *a.* (*m. pl.* **-aux**) wintry.
hiverner [ivɛrʹne], *v.t.* (*Agric.*) to winterfallow.—*v.i.* to winter.
†hobereau [ɔʹbro], *n.m.* (*pl.* **-eaux**) hobby (*bird*); country squire, squireen.
†hochement [ɔʃʹmã], *n.m.* shaking, tossing, wagging (*of the head*).
†hochequeue [ɔʃʹkø], *n.m.* (*Orn.*) wagtail.
†hocher [ɔʹʃe], *v.t.* to shake, to toss; to wag (*the tail etc.*).
†hochet [ɔʹʃɛ], *n.m.* rattle (*for children*); (*fig.*) toy, bauble, plaything.
†hockey [ɔʹkɛ], *n.m.* hockey; (*C*) hockey, hockey stick; *hockey sur glace,* icehockey.
†holà! [ɔʹla], *int.* stop! hold on! hallo, there!—*n.m.* stop, end; *mettre le holà,* to put a stop to (*a quarrel*).
†hollandais [ɔlãʹdɛ], *a.* Dutch.—*n.m.* Dutch (*language*), (**Hollandais**, *fem.* **-aise**) Dutchman, Dutchwoman.

†Hollande [ɔʹlãːd], **la,** *f.* Holland, the Netherlands.
holocauste [ɔlɔʹkoːst], *n.m.* holocaust, burntoffering; sacrifice.
†homard [ɔʹmaːr], *n.m.* lobster.
homélie [ɔmeʹli], *n.f.* homily, familiar sermon.
homéopathe [ɔmeɔʹpat], *a.* homoeopathic.—*n.* homoeopath.
homéopathie [ɔmeɔpaʹti], *n.f.* homoeopathy.
homéopathique [ɔmeɔpaʹtik], *a.* homoeopathic.
Homère [ɔʹmɛːr], *m.* Homer.
homérique [ɔmeʹrik], *a.* Homeric.
homicide [ɔmiʹsid], *a.* murderous.—*n.m.* homicide, manslaughter.—*n.* murderer.
hommage [ɔʹmaːʒ], *n.m.* homage; respect; service; acknowledgment; token, gift; (*pl.*) respects.
homme [ɔm], *n.m.* man; (*colloq.*) husband, old man.
homme-grenouille [ɔmgrəʹnuːj], *n.m.* (*pl.* **hommes-grenouilles**) frogman.
homme-sandwich [ɔmsãʹdwitʃ], *n.m.* (*pl.* **hommes-sandwich(e)s**) sandwich man.
homogène [ɔmɔʹʒɛːn], *a.* homogeneous.
homogénéité [ɔmɔʒeneiʹte], *n.f.* homogeneity.
homonyme [ɔmɔʹnim], *a.* homonymous.—*n.m.* homonym; namesake.
†Honduras [õdyʹras], **le,** *m.* Honduras.
†hondurien [õdyʹrjɛ̃], *a.* (*fem.* **-enne**) Honduran.—*n.m.* (**Hondurien**, *fem.* **-enne**) Honduran (*person*).
†hongre [õːgr], *a.* gelded.—*n.m.* gelding.
†hongrer [õʹgre], *v.t.* to geld (*a horse*).
†Hongrie [õʹgri], **la,** *f.* Hungary.
†hongrois [õʹgrwa], *a.* Hungarian.—*n.m.* Hungarian (*language*); (**Hongrois**, *fem.* **-oise**) Hungarian (*person*).
honnête [ɔʹnɛːt], *a.* honest, upright; modest (*of women*); respectable; decorous; proper; handsome; reasonable.—*n.m.* honesty, probity.
honnêtement [ɔnɛtʹmã], *adv.* honestly, honourably; virtuously; becomingly; handsomely; suitably; reasonably.
honnêteté [ɔnɛtʹte], *n.f.* honesty, integrity; modesty, chastity, virtue; propriety; respectability.
honneur [ɔʹnœːr], *n.m.* honour; virtue; integrity; repute; credit; distinction; respect; (*Cards*) honour.
†honnir [ɔʹniːr], *v.t.* to dishonour, to disgrace, to cover with shame.
honorabilité [ɔnɔrabiliʹte], *n.f.* honour, respectability.
honorable [ɔnɔʹrabl], *a.* honourable; respectable, creditable; suitable.
honorablement [ɔnɔrabləʹmã], *adv.* honourably, respectably, creditably; nobly.
honoraire [ɔnɔʹrɛːr], *a.* honorary, titular.—*n.m.* (*pl.*) honorarium, fee.
honorer [ɔnɔʹre], *v.t.* to honour; to do credit to, to be an honour to; *honorer une traite,* to meet a bill. **s'honorer,** *v.r.* to do oneself honour; to acquire honour; to deem it an honour; to pride oneself.
honorifique [ɔnɔriʹfik], *a.* honorary, titular, gratuitous.

honte

†**honte** [ɔ̃:t], *n.f.* shame; disgrace, infamy; reproach; scandal; *avoir honte de*, to be ashamed of; *mauvaise honte* or *fausse honte*, self-consciousness, bashfulness.

†**honteusement** [ɔ̃tøz'mɑ̃], *adv.* shamefully, disgracefully; infamously.

†**honteux** [ɔ̃'tø], *a.* (*fem.* **-euse**) ashamed; bashful, shy; shameful, disgraceful.

hôpital [ɔpi'tal], *n.m.* (*pl.* **-aux**) hospital.

†**hoquet** [ɔ'kɛ], *n.m.* hiccup.

hoqueter [ɔk'te], *v.i.* (*conjug. like* APPELER) to hiccup.

horaire [ɔ'rɛ:r], *a.* hourly; horary, horal.— *n.m.* time-table, schedule.

†**horde** [ɔrd], *n.f.* horde; pack; rabble.

horizon [ɔri'zɔ̃], *n.m.* horizon, sky-line.

horizontal [ɔrizɔ̃'tal], *a.* (*m. pl.* **-aux**) horizontal.

horizontalement [ɔrizɔ̃tal'mɑ̃], *adv.* horizontally.

horloge [ɔr'lɔ:ʒ], *n.f.* clock; time-keeper.

horloger [ɔrlo'ʒe], *a.* (*fem.* **-ère**) pertaining to clock-making.—*n.m.* (*fem.* **-ère**) clockmaker, watch-maker.

horlogerie [ɔrlo'ʒri], *n.f.* watch- and clockmaking; clocks and watches.

hormis [ɔr'mi], *prep.* except, excepting, but.

hormone [ɔr'mɔn], *n.f.* hormone.

horoscope [ɔrɔs'kɔp], *n.m.* horoscope.

horreur [ɔ'rœ:r], *n.f.* horror, dread; detestation; enormity.

horrible [ɔ'ribl], *a.* horrible, dreadful; hideous, frightful, shocking.

horriblement [ɔribla'mɑ̃], *adv.* horribly, awfully.

horrifier [ɔri'fje], *v.t.* to horrify.

horrifique [ɔri'fik], *a.* hair-raising.

horripilant [ɔripi'lɑ̃], *a.* exasperating.

horripiler [ɔripi'le], *v.t.* to horripilate; to exasperate.

†**hors** [ɔ:r], *prep.* out of, outside of; beyond, past; but, except, save; *hors d'affaire*, out of danger; *hors de combat*, disabled; *hors de doute*, beyond doubt; *hors d'ici!* away with you! out of my sight! *hors de prix*, exorbitant; *hors de service*, unserviceable, out of order; *hors la loi*, outlawed.

†**hors-bord** [ɔr'bɔr], *n.m. inv.* outboard; speed-boat.

†**hors-caste** [ɔr'kast], *a.* and *n. inv.* outcaste, untouchable.

†**hors-d'œuvre** [ɔr'dœ:vr], *n.m. inv.* (*Arch.*) outwork, outbuilding; (*Lit.*) digression, episode; (*Cook.*) dish served at the beginning of a meal.

†**hors-jeu** [ɔr'ʒø], *n.m. inv.* (*Ftb.*) off-side.

†**hors-la-loi** [ɔrla'lwa], *n.m. inv.* outlaw.

hortensia [ɔrtɑ̃'sja], *n.m.* hydrangea.

horticulteur [ɔrtikyl'tœ:r], *n.m.* horticulturist.

horticultural [ɔrtikylty'ral], *a.* (*m. pl.* **-aux**) horticultural.

horticulture [ɔrtikyl'tyr], *n.f.* horticulture.

hospice [ɔs'pis], *n.m.* refuge; asylum; almshouse.

hospitalier [ɔspita'lje], *a.* (*fem.* **-ière**) hospitable.—*n.m.* (*fem.* **-ière**) hospitaller.

hospitalièrement [ɔspitaljɛr'mɑ̃], *adv.* hospitably.

hospitalité [ɔspitali'te], *n.f.* hospitality.

hostellerie [ɔstɛl'ri], *n.f.* inn.

hostie [ɔs'ti], *n.f.* (*Jewish Ant.*) offering, victim, sacrifice; (*R.-C. Ch.*) host.

hostile [ɔs'til], *a.* hostile, adverse.

hostilement [ɔstil'mɑ̃], *adv.* hostilely, adversely.

hostilité [ɔstili'te], *n.f.* hostility, enmity.

hôte [o:t], *n.m.* (*fem.* **-esse**) host, hostess; landlord, innkeeper; guest; lodger; occupier, inmate.

hôtel [o'tɛl], *n.m.* town mansion, large house; hotel, inn; *hôtel de ville*, town hall; *hôtel des ventes*, auction mart; *hôtel meublé*, furnished lodgings, lodging-house.

hôtelier [otə'lje], *n.m.* (*fem.* **-ière**) innkeeper, host, hostess.

hôtellerie [otɛl'ri], *n.f.* inn, hotel; hotel trade.

hôtesse [o'tɛs], [HÔTE].

†**hotte** [ɔt], *n.f.* basket (*carried on the back*); dosser, hod.

†**hottée** [ɔ'te], *n.f.* basketful.

†**hottentot** [ɔtɑ̃'to], *a.* Hottentot.—*n.m.* (**Hottentot**, *fem.* **-e**) Hottentot (*person*).

†**houage** [wa:ʒ], *n.m.* hoeing.

†**houblon** [u'blɔ̃], *n.m.* (*Bot.*) hop.

†**houblonnière** [ublɔ'njɛ:r], *n.f.* hop-field.

†**houe** [u], *n.f.* hoe.

†**houer** [u'e], *v.t.* to hoe.

†**houille** [u:j], *n.f.* coal, pit-coal.

†**houiller** [u'je], *a.* (*fem.* **-ère**) coal-bearing. —*n.f.* (**-ère**) coal-mine, colliery.

†**houilleur** [u'jœ:r], *n.m.* collier, coal-miner.

†**houilleux** [u'jø], *a.* (*fem.* **-euse**) containing coal.

†**houle** [ul], *n.f.* swell, surge.

†**houlette** [u'lɛt], *n.f.* (shepherd's) crook; crosier.

†**houleux** [u'lø], *a.* (*fem.* **-euse**) swelling, rough (*of sea*).

†**houppe** [up], *n.f.* tuft; top-knot; tassel.

†**houppé** [u'pe], *a.* tufted, crested.

†**houppelande** [u'plɑ̃:d], *n.f.* great-coat, cloak.

†**houpper** [u'pe], *v.t.* to tuft; to comb (*wool*).

†**houppette** [u'pɛt], *n.f.* powder-puff.

†**hourdage** [ur'da:ʒ], †**hourdis** [ur'di], *n.m.* rough-walling; pugging.

†**hourder** [ur'de], *v.t.* to rough-wall; to pug.

†**hourdis** [HOURDAGE].

†**hourra** [u'ra], *n.m.* hurrah.

†**houspiller** [uspi'je], *v.t.* to manhandle, to rough-house; to abuse.

†**housse** [us], *n.f.* housing, horse-cloth; dust-sheet, loose cover.

†**housser** [u'se], *v.t.* to cover up.

†**houssine** [u'sin], *n.f.* switch, riding-switch.

†**houssiner** [usi'ne], *v.t.* to switch; to beat.

†**houx** [u], *n.m.* holly, holly-tree.

†**hoyau** [wa'jo], *n.m.* (*pl.* **-aux**) mattock, grubbing-hoe.

†**huard** [ɥa:r], *n.m.* osprey; sea-eagle.

†**hublot** [y'blo], *n.m.* (*Naut.*) side-light, port-hole.

†**huche** [yʃ], *n.f.* kneading-trough; bread-pan.

†**hue!** [y], *int.* gee! gee-up!

†**huée** [ɥe], *n.f.* whoop, shouting; hooting, booing.

†**huer** [ɥe], *v.t.* to shout after; to hoot at, to boo.—*v.i.* to boo.

†**huguenot** [yg'no], *a.* Huguenot.—*n.m.* (**Huguenot**, *fem.* **-e**) Huguenot (*person*).
huilage [ɥi'la:ʒ], *n.m.* oiling.
huile [ɥil], *n.f.* oil.
huiler [ɥi'le], *v.t.* to oil; to anoint with oil; to lubricate.—*v.i.* (*Bot.*) to exude oil.
huilerie [ɥil'ri], *n.f.* oil-works.
huileux [ɥi'lø], *a.* (*fem.* **-euse**) oily, greasy.
huilier [ɥi'lje], *n.m.* cruet-stand; oil-merchant.
†**huis** [ɥi], *n.m.* door; *à huis clos*, behind closed doors, in camera.
huisserie [ɥis'ri], *n.f.* door-frame.
huissier [ɥi'sje], *n.m.* usher; gentleman-usher; door-keeper; sheriff's officer, bailiff.
†**huit** [ɥit], *a.* and *n.m.* eight; eighth.
†**huitaine** [ɥi'tɛn], *n.f.* eight days, week.
†**huitième** [ɥi'tjɛm], *a.* eighth.—*n.m.* eighth, eighth part.
†**huitièmement** [ɥitjɛm'mɑ̃], *adv.* eighthly.
huître [ɥitr], *n.f.* oyster; (*fig.*) blockhead, dunce.
huîtrier [ɥi'trje], *n.m.* (*Orn.*) oyster-catcher.
huîtrière [ɥitri'ɛ:r], *n.f.* oyster-bed.
hululer [ULULER].
humain [y'mɛ̃], *a.* human; humane, benevolent.—*n.m.* humanity, mankind.
humainement [ymɛn'mɑ̃], *adv.* humanly; humanely.
humaniser [ymani'ze], *v.t.* to humanize, to civilize. **s'humaniser**, *v.r.* to become humanized.
humanisme [yma'nism], *n.m.* humanism.
humaniste [yma'nist], *a.* and *n.* humanist; classical scholar.
humanitaire [ymani'tɛ:r], *a.* and *n.* humanitarian.
humanité [ymani'te], *n.f.* humanity; human nature; mankind.
humble [œ̃:bl], *a.* humble, meek, modest.
humblement [œ̃mblə'mɑ̃], *adv.* humbly, meekly.
humectant [ymɛk'tɑ̃], *a.* refreshing, moistening.—*n.m.* humectant.
humectation [ymɛkta'sjɔ̃], *n.f.* moistening.
humecter [ymɛk'te], *v.t.* to damp, to moisten, to refresh. **s'humecter**, *v.r.* to be moistened; to refresh oneself.
†**humer** [y'me], *v.t.* to inhale.
humeur [y'mœ:r], *n.f.* humour; temperament, disposition; mood, fancy; ill-humour.
humide [y'mid], *a.* damp, wet, moist, humid.
humidité [ymidi'te], *n.f.* humidity, moisture, dampness.
humiliant [ymi'ljɑ̃], *a.* humiliating, degrading.
humiliation [ymilja'sjɔ̃], *n.f.* humiliation, abasement.
humilier [ymi'lje], *v.t.* to humble, to humiliate. **s'humilier**, *v.r.* to humble or abase oneself.
humilité [ymili'te], *n.f.* humility, meekness, lowliness.
humoriste [ymo'rist], *a.* humorous.—*n.* humorist.
humoristique [ymoris'tik] *a.* humorous (*writer etc.*).
humour [y'mur], *n.m.* humour.
humus [y'mys], *n.m.* humus, mould.
†**hune** [yn], *n.f.* (*Naut.*) top.
†**hunier** [y'nje], *n.m.* topsail.
†**huppe** [yp], *n.f.* hoopoe; tuft, crest.

†**huppé** [y'pe], *a.* tufted, crested (*of birds*); (*colloq.*) well off, smartly dressed.
†**hurlement** [yrlə'mɑ̃], *n.m.* howling; howl, roar, yell.
†**hurler** [yr'le], *v.i.* to howl, to yell; to roar; *hurler avec les loups*, to do as others do.
†**hurleur** [yr'lœ:r], *a.* (*fem.* **-euse** howling.—*n.m.* (*fem.* **-euse**) howler.
hurluberlu [yrlyber'ly], *n.* hare-brained person, harum-scarum.
†**hussard** [y'sa:r], *n.m.* hussar.
†**hutte** [yt], *n.f.* hut, cabin, shanty.
hyacinthe [ja'sɛ̃:t], *n.f.* jacinth; hyacinth.
hybride [i'brid], *a.* and *n.m.* hybrid, mongrel.
hydrangée [idrɑ̃'ʒe], *n.f.* (*Bot.*) hydrangea.
hydrater [idra'te], *v.t.* to hydrate.
hydraulique [idro'lik], *a.* hydraulic.—*n.f.* hydraulics.
hydravion [idra'vjɔ̃], *n.m.* flying-boat, sea-plane.
hydre [idr], *n.f.* hydra.
hydro-électrique [idroelɛk'trik], *a.* hydroelectric.
hydrogène [idro'ʒɛ:n], *n.m.* hydrogen.
hydrophobe [idro'fob], *a.* and *n.* hydrophobic (person).
hydrophobie [idrofo'bi], *n.f.* hydrophobia, rabies.
hydropique [idro'pik], *a.* and *n.* dropsical (person).
hydropisie [idropi'zi], *n.f.* dropsy.
hydroplane [idro'plan], *n.m.* hydroplane.
hydroscope [idros'kɔp], *n.m.* water-diviner.
hyène [jɛ:n], *n.f.* hyena.
hygiène [i'ʒjɛ:n], *n.f.* hygiene.
hygiénique [iʒje'nik], *a.* hygienic; sanitary.
hymen [i'mɛn], **hyménée** [ime'ne], *n.m.* hymen, marriage, wedlock.
hymnaire [im'nɛ:r], *n.m.* hymn-book, hymnal.
hymne [imn], *n.m.* (*patriotic*) song, anthem.—*n.f.* hymn.
hyperbole [ipɛr'bol], *n.f.* hyperbole, exaggeration; (*Math.*) hyperbola.
hyperbolique [ipɛrbo'lik], *a.* hyperbolic.
hypermétrope [ipɛrme'trɔp], *a.* long-sighted.
hypersensible [ipɛrsɑ̃'sibl], *a.* over-sensitive.
hypertension [ipɛrtɑ̃'sjɔ̃], *n.f.* high blood-pressure.
hypnose [ip'no:z], *n.f.* hypnosis.
hypnotique [ipno'tik], *a.* and *n.m.* hypnotic.
hypnotiser [ipnoti'ze], *v.t.* to hypnotize; to fascinate.
hypnotiseur [ipnoti'zœ:r], *n.m.* (*fem.* **-euse**) hypnotist.
hypnotisme [ipno'tism], *n.m.* hypnotism.
hypocondriaque [ipokɔ̃'driak], *a.* and *n.* hypochondriac.
hypocondrie [ipokɔ̃'dri], *n.f.* hypochondria.
hypocrisie [ipokri'zi], *n.f.* hypocrisy.
hypocrite [ipo'krit], *a.* hypocritical.—*n.* hypocrite.
hypodermique [ipoder'mik], *a.* hypodermic, under the skin.
hypotension [ipotɑ̃'sjɔ̃], *n.f.* low blood-pressure.
hypothécaire [ipote'kɛ:r], *a.* on mortgage.
hypothèque [ipo'tɛk], *n.f.* mortgage.
hypothéquer [ipote'ke], *v.t.* (*conjug. like* CÉDER) to mortgage.
hypothèse [ipo'tɛ:z], *n.f.* hypothesis, supposition.

hypothétique [ipɔte'tik], *a.* hypothetical.
hystérie [iste'ri], *n.f.* hysteria.
hystérique [iste'rik], *a.* hysteric, hysterical.

I

I, i [i], *n.m.* the ninth letter of the alphabet.
iceberg [is'bɛrg], *n.m.* iceberg.
ici [i'si], *adv.* here, in this place; hither; now, this time.
iconoclaste [ikɔnɔ'klast], *a.* iconoclastic.— *n.* iconoclast.
iconolâtre [ikɔnɔ'lɑːtr], *n.m.* image-worshipper.
iconolâtrie [ikɔnɔla'tri], *n.f.* image-worship.
idéal [ide'al], *a.* (*m. pl.* **-aux**) ideal; unreal, imaginary.—*n.m.* (*pl.* **-als** or **-aux**) ideal.
idéalement [ideal'mɑ̃], *adv.* ideally.
idéaliser [ideali'ze], *v.t.* to idealize.
idéalisme [idea'lism], *n.m.* idealism.
idéaliste [idea'list], *a.* idealistic.—*n.* idealist.
idée [i'de], *n.f.* idea; notion; conception; opinion; plan; fancy; sketch, suggestion.
idem [i'dɛm], *adv.* idem, ditto.
identification [idɑ̃tifika'sjɔ̃], *n.f.* identification.
identifier [idɑ̃ti'fje], *v.t.* to identify. **s'identifier**, *v.r.* to identify oneself.
identique [idɑ̃'tik], *a.* identical, the same.
identiquement [idɑ̃tik'mɑ̃], *adv.* identically.
identité [idɑ̃ti'te], *n.f.* identity.
idéologie [ideɔlɔ'ʒi], *n.f.* ideology.
idéologique [ideɔlɔ'ʒik], *a.* ideological.
idéologue [ideɔ'lɔg], *n.m.* ideologist.
ides [id], *n.f. pl.* Ides (15 March etc.).
idiomatique [idjɔma'tik], *a.* idiomatic.
idiome [i'djoːm], *n.m.* idiom, dialect.
idiosyncrasie [idjɔsɛ̃kra'zi], *n.f.* idiosyncrasy.
idiot [i'djo], *a.* idiotic, absurd.—*n.m.* (*fem.* **-e**) idiot, imbecile, fool.
idiotie [idjɔ'si], *n.f.* idiocy, imbecility.
idiotisme [idjɔ'tism], *n.m.* (*Gram.*) idiom; (*Path.*) idiocy.
idolâtre [idɔ'lɑːtr], *a.* idolatrous.—*n.* idolater.
idolâtrer [idɔla'tre], *v.t.* to idolize, to dote upon.
idolâtrie [idɔla'tri], *n.f.* idolatry.
idole [i'dɔl], *n.f.* idol.
idylle [i'dil], *n.f.* idyll.
idyllique [idi'lik], *a.* idyllic.
if [if], *n.m.* yew, yew-tree.
igloo or **iglou** [i'glu], *n.m.* igloo.
ignare [i'naːr], *a.* illiterate, ignorant.—*n.* dunce, ignoramus.
igné [ig'ne], *a.* igneous.
ignifuge [igni'fyːʒ], *a.* fire-resisting, fire-proof; **grenade ignifuge**, fire-extinguisher.
ignifuger [ignify'ʒe], *v.t.* (*conjug. like* MANGER) to fireproof.
ignition [igni'sjɔ̃], *n.f.* ignition.
ignoble [i'nɔbl], *a.* ignoble; vile, base; beastly, filthy.
ignoblement [inɔblə'mɑ̃], *adv.* ignobly, vilely, basely.

ignominie [inɔmi'ni], *n.f.* ignominy, shame, dishonour.
ignominieusement [inɔminjøz'mɑ̃], *adv.* ignominiously.
ignominieux [inɔmi'njø], *a.* (*fem.* **-euse**) ignominious.
ignorance [inɔ'rɑ̃ːs], *n.f.* ignorance; error, mistake, blunder.
ignorant [inɔ'rɑ̃], *a.* ignorant, illiterate, unlearned.—*n.m.* (*fem.* **-e**) ignoramus.
ignorer [inɔ're], *v.t.* to be ignorant of, not to know, not to be aware of. **s'ignorer**, *v.r.* not to know oneself; to be ignorant of one's own capabilities.
iguane [i'gwan], *n.m.* iguana.
il [il], *pron. m.* (*pl.* **ils**) he; it; there; (*pl.*) they.
île [il], *n.f.* island, isle.
illégal [ille'gal], *a.* (*m. pl.* **-aux**) illegal, unlawful.
illégalement [illegal'mɑ̃], *adv.* illegally.
illégalité [illegali'te], *n.f.* illegality.
illégitime [illeʒi'tim], *a.* illegitimate; unlawful, unjust.
illégitimement [illeʒitim'mɑ̃], *adv.* illegitimately, unlawfully.
illégitimité [illeʒitimi'te], *n.f.* illegitimacy; unlawfulness; spuriousness.
illettré [ille'tre], *a.* and *n.m.* (*fem.* **-ée**) illiterate, unlettered (person).
illicite [illi'sit], *a.* illicit, unlawful.
illicitement [illisit'mɑ̃], *adv.* illicitly, unlawfully.
illimitable [illimi'tabl], *a.* illimitable.
illimité [illimi'te], *a.* unlimited, unbounded, boundless.
illisibilité [illizibili'te], *n.f.* illegibility.
illisible [illi'zibl], *a.* illegible.
illisiblement [illiziblə'mɑ̃], *adv.* illegibly.
illogique [illɔ'ʒik], *a.* illogical.
illogiquement [illɔʒik'mɑ̃], *adv.* illogically.
illuminant [illymi'nɑ̃], *a.* illuminating.— *n.m.* illuminant.
illuminateur [illymina'tœːr], *n.m.* illuminator, enlightener.
illumination [illymina'sjɔ̃], *n.f.* illumination.
illuminé [illymi'ne], *a.* illuminated, enlightened.—*n.m.* (*fem.* **-ée**) visionary, fanatic.
illuminer [illymi'ne], *v.t.* to illuminate, to illumine, to light up; to enlighten (*the mind etc.*). **s'illuminer**, *v.r.* to light or brighten up.
illusion [illy'zjɔ̃], *n.f.* illusion, self-deception, delusion; fallacy, chimera.
illusionner [illyzjɔ'ne], *v.t.* to delude, to deceive.
illusionniste [illyzjɔ'nist], *n.m.* conjurer.
illusoire [illy'zwaːr], *a.* illusive, illusory, delusive.
illusoirement [illyzwar'mɑ̃], *adv.* illusively.
illustration [illystra'sjɔ̃], *n.f.* illustriousness, renown; explanation; illustration.
illustre [il'lystr], *a.* illustrious, famous.
illustrer [illys'tre], *v.t.* to do honour to; to illustrate, to make clear. **s'illustrer**, *v.r.* to win fame.
illustrissime [illystri'sim], *a.* most illustrious.
îlot [i'lo], *n.m.* islet (*in sea*); holm (*in river*); block (*of houses*).
ilote [i'lɔt], *n.m.* helot.
ils [il], *pl. pron.* [IL].
image [i'maːʒ], *n.f.* image; likeness; picture; statue.

imaginable [imaʒi'nabl], *a.* imaginable.
imaginaire [imaʒi'nɛːr], *a.* imaginary, visionary, unreal, fantastic.
imaginatif [imaʒina'tif], *a.* (*fem.* **-tive**) imaginative.
imagination [imaʒina'sjɔ̃], *n.f.* imagination; conception, thought; fancy.
imaginer [imaʒi'ne], *v.t.* to imagine, to conceive; to fancy, to suppose; to devise. **s'imaginer**, *v.r.* to imagine oneself; to imagine, to fancy, to surmise.
imbécile [ɛ̃be'sil], *a.* imbecile; foolish, idiotic.—*n.* imbecile, idiot; fool.
imbécilement [ɛ̃besil'mɑ̃], *adv.* foolishly.
imbécillité [ɛ̃besili'te], *n.f.* imbecility, idiocy; stupidity.
imberbe [ɛ̃'bɛrb], *a.* beardless; (*fig.*) green.
imbiber [ɛ̃bi'be], *v.t.* to imbibe; to imbue; to steep. **s'imbiber**, *v.r.* to imbibe, to drink in.
imbroglio [ɛ̃brɔ'ljo], *n.m.* imbroglio, intricacy.
imbu [ɛ̃'by], *a.* imbued, saturated.
imbuvable [ɛ̃by'vabl], *a.* undrinkable.
imitable [imi'tabl], *a.* imitable.
imitateur [imita'tœːr], *a.* (*fem.* **-trice**) imitative.—*n.m.* (*fem.* **-trice**) imitator.
imitatif [imita'tif], *a.* (*fem.* **-tive**) imitative.
imitation [imita'sjɔ̃], *n.f.* imitation.
imiter [imi'te], *v.t.* to imitate, to copy; to mimic; to resemble.
immaculé [immaky'le], *a.* immaculate, spotless.
immanent [imma'nɑ̃], *a.* immanent.
immangeable [ɛ̃mɑ̃'ʒabl, imɑ̃'ʒabl], *a.* uneatable.
immanquable [ɛ̃mɑ̃'kabl], *a.* infallible, certain, sure.
immanquablement [ɛ̃mɑ̃kablə'mɑ̃], *adv.* infallibly, certainly, without fail.
immatériel [immate'rjɛl], *a.* (*fem.* **-elle**) immaterial, incorporeal.
immatriculation [immatrikyla'sjɔ̃], *n.f.* matriculation; registering; enrolment; (*Motor.*) *plaque d'immatriculation*, number plate.
immatriculé [immatriky'le], *a.* registered; matriculated.
immatriculer [immatriky'le], *v.t.* to matriculate; to register.
immaturité [immatyri'te], *n.f.* unripeness, immaturity.
immédiat [imme'dja], *a.* immediate.
immédiatement [immedjat'mɑ̃] *adv.* immediately.
immémorial [immemo'rjal], *a.* (*m. p.* **-aux**) immemorial.
immense [im'mɑ̃ːs], *a.* immense, immeasurable; boundless, huge.
immensément [immɑ̃se'mɑ̃], *adv.* immensely.
immensité [immɑ̃si'te], *n.f.* immensity.
immerger [immɛr'ʒe], *v.t.* (*conjug. like* MANGER) to immerse, to plunge.
immérité [immeri'te], *a.* undeserved, unmerited, unjust.
immersion [immɛr'sjɔ̃], *n.f.* immersion; submergence; committal to the deep.
immesurable [immǝzy'rabl], *a.* unmeasurable, immeasurable.
immeuble [im'mœbl], *a.* fixed, real (*of estate*).—*n.m.* real estate; property; premises.

immigrant [immi'grɑ̃], *a.* and *n.m.* (*fem.* **-e**) immigrant.
immigration [immigra'sjɔ̃], *n.f.* immigration.
immigrer [immi'gre], *v.i.* to immigrate.
imminence [immi'nɑ̃ːs], *n.f.* imminence.
imminent [immi'nɑ̃], *a.* imminent, impending.
immiscer (s') [simmi'se], *v.r.* (*conjug. like* COMMENCER) to interfere.
immobile [immɔ'bil], *a.* motionless, still; (*fig.*) firm, immovable, unshaken.
immobilier [immɔbi'lje], *a.* (*fem.* **-ière**) real, landed (*of estate*); *agent immobilier*, estate agent; *société immobilière*, building society.
immobilisation [immɔbiliza'sjɔ̃], *n.f.* immobilization; (*Law*) conversion of movable property into real estate.
immobiliser [immɔbili'ze], *v.t.* to immobilize; to convert into real estate, to tie up (*capital*).
immobilité [immɔbili'te], *n.f.* immobility, immovability.
immodération [immɔdera'sjɔ̃], *n.f.* immoderation.
immodéré [immɔde're], *a.* immoderate, excessive, violent.
immodérément [immɔdere'mɑ̃], *adv.* immoderately, intemperately; excessively.
immodeste [immɔ'dɛst], *a.* immodest, indecent.
immodestement [immɔdestǝ'mɑ̃], *adv.* immodestly.
immodestie [immɔdes'ti], *n.f.* immodesty.
immolation [immɔla'sjɔ̃], *n.f.* immolation; (*fig.*) sacrifice.
immoler [immɔ'le], *v.t.* to immolate, to sacrifice; to slay. **s'immoler**, *v.r.* to immolate *or* sacrifice oneself.
immonde [im'mɔ̃ːd], *a.* unclean, impure.
immondice [immɔ̃'dis], *n.f.* (*usu. in pl.*) filth, dirt; rubbish.
immoral [immɔ'ral], *a.* (*m. pl.* **-aux**) immoral.
immoralité [immɔrali'te], *n.f.* immorality.
immortaliser [immɔrtali'ze], *v.t.* to immortalize. **s'immortaliser**, *v.r.* to immortalize oneself.
immortalité [immɔrtali'te], *n.f.* immortality.
immortel [immɔr'tɛl], *a.* (*fem.* **-elle**) immortal, everlasting.
immuable [im'mɥabl], *a.* immutable, unalterable, unchangeable.
immuablement [immɥablǝ'mɑ̃], *adv.* immutably, unalterably, unchangeably.
immunisation [immyniza'sjɔ̃], *n.f.* (*Med.*) immunization.
immuniser [immyni'ze], *v.t.* to immunize.
immunité [immyni'te], *n.f.* immunity; privilege; exemption.
immutabilité [immytabili'te], *n.f.* immutability, unchangeableness, fixity.
impact [ɛ̃'pakt], *n.m.* impact; hit.
impaction [ɛ̃pak'sjɔ̃], *n.f.* (*Surg.*) impaction.
impair [ɛ̃'pɛːr], *a.* odd, uneven.—*n.m.* blunder, bloomer.
impalpabilité [ɛ̃palpabili'te], *n.f.* impalpability.
impalpable [ɛ̃pal'pabl], *a.* impalpable.
impardonnable [ɛ̃pardɔ'nabl], *a.* unpardonable, unforgivable.

imparfait [ɛ̃par'fɛ], a. imperfect, incomplete, defective.—n.m. (Gram.) imperfect (tense).

imparfaitement [ɛ̃parfɛt'mã], adv. imperfectly.

imparité [ɛ̃pari'te], n.f. imparity, inequality; oddness.

impartageable [ɛ̃parta'ʒabl], a. indivisible.

impartial [ɛ̃par'sjal], a. (m. pl. -aux) impartial.

impartialement [ɛ̃parsjal'mã], adv. impartially, even-handedly.

impartialité [ɛ̃parsjali'te], n.f. impartiality.

impasse [ɛ̃'pɑːs], n.f. blind alley, cul-de-sac; deadlock, dilemma.

impassibilité [ɛ̃pɑsibili'te], n.f. impassibility, insensibility.

impassible [ɛ̃pɑ'sibl], a. impassive, unmoved.

impassiblement [ɛ̃pɑsiblə'mã], adv. impassively, impassibly.

impatiemment [ɛ̃pasja'mã], adv. impatiently, eagerly.

impatience [ɛ̃pa'sjɑːs], n.f. impatience; restlessness; eagerness, longing.

impatient [ɛ̃pa'sjã], a. impatient; anxious, restless, eager.

impatientant [ɛ̃pasjã'tã], a. provoking, vexing, tiresome.

impatienter [ɛ̃pasjã'te], v.t. to make impatient, to put out of patience; to provoke. s'impatienter, v.r. to lose one's patience; to fret, to worry.

impayable [ɛ̃pe'jabl], a. invaluable, priceless; inimitable, extraordinarily funny.

impayé [ɛ̃pe'je], a. unpaid.

impeccabilité [ɛ̃pɛkabili'te], n.f. impeccability.

impeccable [ɛ̃pɛ'kabl], a. impeccable, faultless.

impécunieux [ɛ̃peky'njø], a. (fem. -euse) impecunious.

impénétrabilité [ɛ̃penetrabili'te], n.f. impenetrability, imperviousness.

impénétrable [ɛ̃pene'trabl], a. impenetrable, impervious; inscrutable.

impénitence [ɛ̃peni'tãːs], n.f. impenitence, obduracy.

impénitent [ɛ̃peni'tã], a. and n.m. (fem. -e) impenitent, obdurate (person).

impératif [ɛ̃pera'tif], a. (fem. -tive) imperative, peremptory.—n.m. (Gram.) imperative.

impérativement [ɛ̃perativ'mã], adv. imperatively.

impératrice [ɛ̃pera'tris], n.f. empress.

imperceptible [ɛ̃pɛrsɛp'tibl], a. imperceptible, unperceivable.

imperceptiblement [ɛ̃pɛrsɛptiblə'mã], adv. imperceptibly.

imperfectible [ɛ̃pɛrfɛk'tibl], a. imperfectible.

imperfection [ɛ̃pɛrfɛk'sjɔ̃], n.f. imperfection, defect, flaw.

impérial [ɛ̃pe'rjal], a. (m. pl. -aux) imperial.

impériale [ɛ̃pe'rjal], n.f. top, outside (of a coach); imperial (small beard under the lip).

impérieusement [ɛ̃perjøz'mã], adv. imperiously.

impérieux [ɛ̃pe'rjø], a. (fem. -euse) imperious, supercilious, haughty, lordly.

impérissable [ɛ̃peri'sabl], a. imperishable.

impérissablement [ɛ̃perisablə'mã], adv. imperishably.

impéritie [ɛ̃peri'si], n.f. incapacity, incompetence.

imperméabilité [ɛ̃pɛrmeabili'te], n.f. impermeability.

imperméable [ɛ̃pɛrme'abl], a. impermeable, impervious.—n.m. raincoat, mackintosh.

impersonnalité [ɛ̃pɛrsɔnali'te], n.f. impersonality.

impersonnel [ɛ̃pɛrsɔ'nɛl], a. (fem. -elle) impersonal.—n.m. (Gram.) impersonal verb.

impersonnellement [ɛ̃pɛrsɔnɛl'mã], adv. impersonally.

impertinemment [ɛ̃pɛrtina mã], adv. impertinently.

impertinence [ɛ̃pɛrti'nãːs], n.f. impertinence, insolence; silliness.

impertinent [ɛ̃pɛrti'nã], a. impertinent, insolent, pert.—n.m. (fem. -e) impertinent, saucy person.

imperturbabilité [ɛ̃pɛrtyrbabili'te], n.f. imperturbability.

imperturbable [ɛ̃pɛrtyr'babl], a. imperturbable.

imperturbablement [ɛ̃pɛrtyrbablə'mã], adv. imperturbably.

impétigo [ɛ̃peti'go], n.m. (Med.) impetigo.

impétueusement [ɛ̃petɥøz'mã], adv. impetuously.

impétueux [ɛ̃pe'tɥø], a. (fem. -euse) impetuous, vehement, violent.

impétuosité [ɛ̃petɥozi'te], n.f. impetuosity, vehemence; impetus.

impie [ɛ̃'pi], a. impious, godless; irreligious. —n. impious, ungodly or irreligious person.

impiété [ɛ̃pje'te], n.f. impiety, godlessness.

impitoyable [ɛ̃pitwa'jabl], a. pitiless, merciless, ruthless; unrelenting.

impitoyablement [ɛ̃pitwajablə'mã], adv. pitilessly.

implacabilité [ɛ̃plakabili'te], n.f. implacability.

implacable [ɛ̃pla'kabl], a. implacable.

implacablement [ɛ̃plakablə'mã], adv. implacably.

implantation [ɛ̃plãta'sjɔ̃], n.f. implantation.

implanter [ɛ̃plã'te], v.t. to implant; to plant. s'implanter, v.r. to be implanted, fixed, rooted or lodged.

implication [ɛ̃plika'sjɔ̃], n.f. implication, involving; discrepancy.

implicite [ɛ̃pli'sit], a. implicit.

implicitement [ɛ̃plisit'mã], adv. implicitly.

impliquer [ɛ̃pli'ke], v.t. to implicate, to involve, to entangle; to imply.

implorateur [ɛ̃plɔra'tœːr], n.m. (fem. -trice) implorer, supplicant.

imploration [ɛ̃plɔra'sjɔ̃], n.f. supplication, imploration.

implorer [ɛ̃plɔ're], v.t. to implore, to entreat, to beseech; to crave.

imployable [ɛ̃plwa'jabl], a. unbending.

impoli [ɛ̃pɔ'li], a. impolite, discourteous, uncivil, rude.

impoliment [ɛ̃pɔli'mã], adv. impolitely, discourteously.

impolitesse [ɛ̃pɔli'tɛs], n.f. impoliteness, incivility; rudeness.

impolitique [ɛ̃pɔli'tik], a. impolitic, ill-advised.

impolitiquement [ɛ̃pɔlitik'mã], *adv.* unwisely.

impopulaire [ɛ̃pɔpy'lɛːr], *a.* unpopular.

impopularité [ɛ̃pɔpylari'te], *n.f.* unpopularity.

importable [ɛ̃pɔr'tabl], *a.* importable.

importance [ɛ̃pɔr'tãːs], *n.f.* importance, consequence; authority, credit; self-conceit.

important [ɛ̃pɔr'tã], *a.* important, of consequence, weighty.—*n.m.* the essential, the main point; (*fem.* **-e**) person of importance.

importateur [ɛ̃pɔrta'tœːr], *a.* (*fem.* **-trice**) importing.—*n.m.* (*fem.* **-trice**) importer.

importation [ɛ̃pɔrta'sjɔ̃], *n.f.* importation; (*pl.*) imports.

importer [ɛ̃pɔr'te], *v.t.* to import; (*fig.*) to introduce.—*v.i.* to import, to be of moment, to matter; *n'importe*, no matter, never mind; *n'importe où*, anywhere; *n'importe qui*, anyone; *n'importe quoi*, anything; *peu importe*, it does not much matter; *venez n'importe quand*, come when you like.

importun [ɛ̃pɔr'tœ̃], *a.* importunate, tiresome, obtrusive, irksome.—*n.m.* (*fem.* **-e**) tiresome person; intruder, bore.

importuner [ɛ̃pɔrty'ne], *v.t.* to importune, to pester; to inconvenience; to tease.

importunité [ɛ̃pɔrtyni'te], *n.f.* importunity.

imposable [ɛ̃po'zabl], *a.* taxable.

imposant [ɛ̃po'zã], *a.* imposing, impressive, striking.

imposer [ɛ̃po'ze], *v.t.* to lay on (*hands*); to impose, to tax; to force (*à*).—*v.i.* or **en imposer**, to awe, to overawe. **s'imposer**, *v.r.* to assert oneself; to thrust oneself (*upon somebody*); to be indispensable.

imposition [ɛ̃pozi'sjɔ̃], *n.f.* imposition, laying on (*of hands*); tax, assessment.

impossibilité [ɛ̃pɔsibili'te], *n.f.* impossibility.

impossible [ɛ̃pɔ'sibl], *a.* impossible.—*n.m.* one's utmost, a great deal.

imposte [ɛ̃'pɔst], *n.f.* (*Arch.*) impost, fanlight.

imposteur [ɛ̃pɔs'tœːr], *n.m.* impostor, cheat.

imposture [ɛ̃pɔs'tyːr], *n.f.* imposture, deception.

impôt [ɛ̃'po], *n.m.* tax, duty, impost; *percevoir les impôts*, to collect the taxes.

impotence [ɛ̃pɔ'tãːs], *n.f.* helplessness, infirmity.

impotent [ɛ̃pɔ'tã], *a.* infirm, crippled.—*n.m.* (*fem.* **-e**) cripple, helpless invalid.

impraticabilité [ɛ̃pratikabili'te], *n.f.* impracticability.

impraticable [ɛ̃prati'kabl], *a.* impracticable; impassable; unmanageable.

imprécation [ɛ̃preka'sjɔ̃], *n.f.* imprecation, curse.

imprécatoire [ɛ̃preka'twaːr], *a.* imprecatory.

imprécis [ɛ̃pre'si], *a.* unprecise, indefinite (*words*); (*Mil.*) inaccurate (*fire*).

imprécision [ɛ̃presi'zjɔ̃], *n.f.* lack of precision, vagueness (*of statement*); looseness (*of terms*); (*Mil.*) inaccuracy (*in firing*).

imprégnation [ɛ̃preɲa'sjɔ̃], *n.f.* impregnation.

imprégner [ɛ̃pre'ɲe], *v.t.* (*conjug. like* CÉDER) to impregnate; (*fig.*) to imbue. **s'imprégner**, *v.r.* to become impregnated; to be imbued.

imprenable [ɛ̃prə'nabl], *a.* impregnable.

impressif [ɛ̃prɛ'sif], *a.* (*fem.* **-ive**) impressive, striking.

impression [ɛ̃prɛ'sjɔ̃], *n.f.* impression; mark, stamp; print; edition; *faute d'impression*, misprint.

impressionnable [ɛ̃prɛsjɔ'nabl], *a.* impressionable, sensitive.

impressionnant [ɛ̃prɛsjɔ'nã], *a.* impressive.

impressionner [ɛ̃prɛsjɔ'ne], *v.t.* to move, to affect, to impress.

impressionnisme [ɛ̃prɛsjɔ'nism], *n.m.* impressionism.

impressionniste [ɛ̃prɛsjɔ'nist], *a.* and *n.* impressionist.

imprévisible [ɛ̃previ'zibl], *a.* unforeseeable.

imprévoyance [ɛ̃prevwa'jãːs], *n.f.* want of foresight, improvidence.

imprévoyant [ɛ̃prevwa'jã], *a.* improvident.

imprévu [ɛ̃pre'vy], *a.* unforeseen, unexpected.

imprimable [ɛ̃pri'mabl], *a.* fit to be printed.

imprimé [ɛ̃pri'me], *n.m.* printed book, paper, document etc.; *service des imprimés*, book-post.

imprimer [ɛ̃pri'me], *v.t.* to imprint, to impress, to stamp; to print; to instil; to impart. **s'imprimer**, *v.r.* to be printed.

imprimerie [ɛ̃prim'ri], *n.f.* printing; printing-office, printing establishment.

imprimeur [ɛ̃pri'mœːr], *n.m.* printer; (*Print.*) press-man.

improbabilité [ɛ̃prɔbabili'te], *n.f.* improbability, unlikelihood.

improbable [ɛ̃prɔ'babl], *a.* improbable, unlikely.

improbablement [ɛ̃prɔbablə'mã], *adv.* improbably.

improbité [ɛ̃prɔbi'te], *n.f.* improbity, dishonesty.

improductible [ɛ̃prɔdyk'tibl], *a.* unproducible.

improductif [ɛ̃prɔdyk'tif], *a.* (*fem.* **-tive**) unproductive, idle.

impromptu [ɛ̃prɔ̃p'ty], *a. inv.* impromptu, extemporary.—*n.m.* impromptu.—*adv.* off-hand, extempore.

imprononçable [ɛ̃prɔnɔ̃'sabl], *a.* unpronounceable (*word*).

impropre [ɛ̃'prɔpr], *a.* improper, wrong; unfit.

improprement [ɛ̃prɔprə'mã], *adv.* improperly.

impropriété [ɛ̃prɔprie'te], *n.f.* impropriety; unfitness.

improvisateur [ɛ̃prɔviza'tœːr], *n.m.* (*fem.* **-trice**) improviser, extemporary speaker.

improvisation [ɛ̃prɔviza'sjɔ̃], *n.f.* improvisation; (*Mus.*) voluntary.

improviser [ɛ̃prɔvi'ze], *v.t.* to improvise, to extemporize.

improviste (à l') [alɛ̃prɔ'vist], *adv. phr.* all of a sudden, unawares, unexpectedly.

imprudemment [ɛ̃pryda'mã], *adv.* imprudently, indiscreetly.

imprudence [ɛ̃pry'dãːs], *n.f.* imprudence, rashness; indiscretion.

imprudent [ɛ̃pry'dã], *a.* imprudent, foolhardy, unwise, incautious.

impudemment [ɛ̃pyda'mã], *adv.* impudently, shamelessly.

impudence [ɛ̃py'dãːs], *n.f.* impudence, shamelessness.

impudent

impudent [ɛ̃py'dɑ̃], *a.* impudent, shameless, saucy.—*n.m.* (*fem.* **-e**) impudent person.
impudeur [ɛ̃py'dœːr], *n.f.* immodesty, indecency; effrontery.
impudicité [ɛ̃pydisi'te], *n.f.* impudicity, immodesty, lewdness.
impudique [ɛ̃py'dik], *a.* unchaste, lewd, immodest.
impudiquement [ɛ̃pydik'mɑ̃], *adv.* immodestly, unchastely, lewdly.
impuissance [ɛ̃pɥi'sɑ̃ːs], *n.f.* impotence, incapacity, powerlessness.
impuissant [ɛ̃pɥi'sɑ̃], *a.* impotent, powerless, unable.
impulsif [ɛ̃pyl'sif], *a.* (*fem.* **-sive**) impulsive.
impulsion [ɛ̃pyl'sjɔ̃], *n.f.* impulsion, impulse; impetus; motive.
impunément [ɛ̃pyne'mɑ̃], *adv.* with impunity.
impuni [ɛ̃py'ni], *a.* unpunished.
impunité [ɛ̃pyni'te], *n.f.* impunity.
impur [ɛ̃'pyːr], *a.* impure, foul; unchaste, immodest; unclean.
impurement [ɛ̃pyr'mɑ̃], *adv.* impurely; immodestly.
impureté [ɛ̃pyr'te], *n.f.* impurity, foulness; immodesty; obscenity.
imputabilité [ɛ̃pytabili'te], *n.f.* imputability.
imputable [ɛ̃py'tabl], *a.* imputable, chargeable; to be deducted.
imputation [ɛ̃pyta'sjɔ̃], *n.f.* imputation, charge; deduction.
imputer [ɛ̃py'te], *v.t.* to impute, to attribute; to deduct.
imputrescible [ɛ̃pytrɛ'sibl], *a.* not liable to putrefaction; rot-proof.
inabordable [inabor'dabl], *a.* inaccessible, unapproachable.
inabrité [inabri'te], *a.* unsheltered, open.
inabrogé [inabrɔ'ʒe], *a.* unrepealed.
inacceptable [inaksɛp'tabl], *a.* unacceptable.
inaccessibilité [inaksɛsibili'te], *n.f.* inaccessibility.
inaccessible [inaksɛ'sibl], *a.* inaccessible.
inaccordable [inakɔr'dabl], *a.* irreconcilable; unallowable, inadmissible.
inaccoutumé [inakuty'me], *a.* unaccustomed, unusual.
inachevé [inaʃ've], *a.* unfinished.
inactif [inak'tif], *a.* (*fem.* **-tive**) inactive; inert, indolent.
inaction [inak'sjɔ̃], *n.f.* inaction; indolence, inertness.
inactivement [inaktiv'mɑ̃], *adv.* inactively.
inactivité [inaktivi'te], *n.f.* inactivity.
inadaptation [inadapta'sjɔ̃], *n.f.* maladjustment.
inadapté [inadap'te], *a.* maladjusted.—*n.m.* (*fem.* **-ée**) social misfit.
inadmissible [inadmi'sibl], *a.* inadmissible.
inadmission [inadmi'sjɔ̃], *n.f.* non-admission.
inadvertance [inadvɛr'tɑ̃ːs], *n.f.* inadvertence, oversight.
inaliénable [inalje'nabl], *a.* inalienable.
inaliéné [inalje'ne], *a.* unalienated.
inalliable [ina'ljabl], *a.* that cannot be alloyed; incompatible.
inaltérable [inalte'rabl], *a.* unalterable, invariable.
inamical [inami'kal], *a.* (*m. pl.* **-aux**) unfriendly.

inamovibilité [inamɔvibili'te], *n.f.* irremovability, fixity of tenure.
inamovible [inamɔ'vibl], *a.* irremovable, permanent; built in.
inanimé [inani'me], *a.* inanimate, lifeless.
inanité [ɪnani'te], *n.f.* inanity, emptiness.
inanition [inani'sjɔ̃], *n.f.* inanition, starvation.
inapaisé [inapɛ'ze], *a.* unappeased; unquenched.
inaperçu [inapɛr'sy], *a.* unperceived, unobserved, unnoticed.
inapparent [inapa'rɑ̃], *a.* unapparent; inconspicuous.
inapplicable [inapli'kabl], *a.* inapplicable.
inappliqué [inapli'ke], *a.* inattentive, heedless.
inappréciable [inapre'sjabl], *a.* inappreciable; invaluable.
inappréciablement [inapresjablə'mɑ̃], *adv.* inappreciably.
inapprécié [inapre'sje], *a.* unappreciated.
inapprêté [inaprɛ'te], *a.* unprepared, undressed, uncooked.
inapprochable [inaprɔ'ʃabl], *a.* unapproachable.
inapte [i'napt], *a.* inapt, unfit, unqualified.
inaptitude [inapti'tyd], *n.f.* inaptitude, unfitness; disqualification.
inarticulé [inartiky'le], *a.* inarticulate.
inassouvi [inasu'vi], *a.* unsatiated.
inassouvissable [inasuvi'sabl], *a.* insatiable.
inattaquable [inata'kabl], *a.* unassailable; (*fig.*) unimpeachable, irreproachable.
inattendu [inatɑ̃'dy], *a.* unexpected, unforeseen; unhoped for.
inattentif [inatɑ̃'tif], *a.* (*fem.* **-tive**) inattentive, unmindful.
inattention [inatɑ̃'sjɔ̃], *n.f.* inattention, carelessness; *faute d'inattention*, slip.
inaudible [ino'dibl], *a.* inaudible.
inaugural [inogy'ral], *a.* (*m. pl.* **-aux**) inaugural.
inauguration [inogyra'sjɔ̃], *n.f.* inauguration.
inaugurer [inogy're], *v.t.* to inaugurate, to open; to usher in.
inavouable [ina'vwabl], *a.* unavowable; shameful.
incalculable [ɛ̃kalky'labl], *a.* incalculable, numberless.
incandescence [ɛ̃kɑ̃dɛ'sɑ̃ːs], *n.f.* incandescence.
incandescent [ɛ̃kɑ̃dɛ'sɑ̃], *a.* incandescent.
incapable [ɛ̃ka'pabl], *a.* incapable, unable (*de*); unfit, incompetent.
incapacité [ɛ̃kapasi'te], *n.f.* incapacity, incapability; inability, unfitness; incompetence, disability; disqualification, (*Mil.*) disablement; *frapper d'incapacité* to incapacitate.
incarcération [ɛ̃karsera'sjɔ̃], *n.f.* incarceration.
incarcérer [ɛ̃karse're], *v.t.* (*conjug. like* CÉDER) to incarcerate, to imprison.
incarnat [ɛ̃kar'na], *a.* flesh-coloured, rosy.—*n.m.* carnation, flesh-colour.
incarnation [ɛ̃karna'sjɔ̃], *n.f.* incarnation.
incarné [ɛ̃kar'ne], *a.* incarnate; ingrowing (*nail*).

incarner [ɛ̃kar'ne], *v.t.* to incarnate, to embody. **s'incarner**, *v.r.* to become incarnate; to grow in (*of nails*).

incartade [ɛ̃kar'tad], *n.f.* thoughtless insult; prank, folly.

incassable [ɛ̃ka'sabl], *a.* unbreakable.

incendiaire [ɛ̃sɑ̃'djɛːr], *a.* and *n.* incendiary.

incendie [ɛ̃sɑ̃'di], *n.m.* fire, conflagration.

incendié [ɛ̃sɑ̃'dje], *a.* burnt-out, gutted.—*n.m.* (*fem.* **-ée**) sufferer by fire.

incendier [ɛ̃sɑ̃'dje], *v.t.* to set fire to, to burn down.

incertain [ɛ̃sɛr'tɛ̃], *a.* uncertain; unsettled, inconstant; vague.

incertitude [ɛ̃sɛrti'tyd], *n.f.* uncertainty, doubt, suspense; instability, fickleness.

incessamment [ɛ̃sɛsa'mɑ̃], *adv.* immediately, at once; incessantly.

incessant [ɛ̃sɛ'sɑ̃], *a.* incessant, ceaseless, unremitting.

inceste [ɛ̃'sɛst], *a.* incestuous.—*n.m.* incest. —*n.* incestuous person.

incestueusement [ɛ̃sɛstɥœz'mɑ̃], *adv.* incestuously.

incestueux [ɛ̃sɛs'tɥø], *a.* (*fem.* **-euse**) incestuous.—*n.m.* (*fem.* **-euse**) incestuous person.

incidemment [ɛ̃sida'mɑ̃], *adv.* incidentally.

incidence [ɛ̃si'dɑ̃ːs], *n.f.* incidence.

incident [ɛ̃si'dɑ̃], *a.* incidental; incident.—*n.m.* incident, occurrence.

incinération [ɛ̃sinerɑ'sjɔ̃], *n.f.* incineration; cremation.

incinérer [ɛ̃sine're], *v.t.* (*conjug. like* CÉDER) to incinerate; to cremate.

inciser [ɛ̃si'ze], *v.t.* to make an incision in, to notch, to gash; to tap (*a tree*).

incisif [ɛ̃si'zif], *a.* (*fem.* **-sive**) sharp, cutting, incisive.—*n.f.* (**-sive**) incisive tooth, incisor.

incision [ɛ̃si'zjɔ̃], *n.f.* incision.

incitation [ɛ̃sita'sjɔ̃], *n.f.* incitement, instigation; (*Med.*) stimulus.

inciter [ɛ̃si'te], *v.t.* to incite; to instigate, to induce.

incivil [ɛ̃si'vil], *a.* uncivil, unmannerly.

incivilement [ɛ̃sivil'mɑ̃], *adv.* uncivilly.

incivilisé [ɛ̃sivili'ze], *a.* uncivilized.

incivilité [ɛ̃sivili'te], *n.f.* incivility; rude remark.

inclémence [ɛ̃kle'mɑ̃ːs], *n.f.* inclemency.

inclément [ɛ̃kle'mɑ̃], *a.* inclement.

inclinaison [ɛ̃kline'zɔ̃], *n.f.* inclination; incline, gradient; pitch, slant.

inclination [ɛ̃klina'sjɔ̃], *n.f.* bow, bending; proneness, propensity; attachment, passion.

incliner [ɛ̃kli'ne], *v.t.* to incline, to slope; to bow; to bend; (*fig.*) to dispose, to turn.—*v.i.* to incline, to lean; to be inclined (*à* or *vers*). **s'incliner**, *v.r.* to incline, to lean; to bow, to bend, to yield.

inclure [ɛ̃'klyːr], *v.t. irr.* (*conjug. like* CON-CLURE *but p.p.* **inclus**) to include, to enclose, to insert.

inclus [ɛ̃'kly], *a.* enclosed, included.

inclusif [ɛ̃kly'zif], *a.* (*fem.* **-sive**) inclusive.

inclusion [ɛ̃kly'zjɔ̃], *n.f.* enclosing; inclusion.

inclusivement [ɛ̃klyziv'mɑ̃], *adv.* inclusively.

incognito [ɛ̃kɔɲi'to], *adv.* incognito.

incohérence [ɛ̃kɔe'rɑ̃ːs], *n.f.* incoherence.

incohérent [ɛ̃kɔe'rɑ̃], *a.* incoherent.

incolore [ɛ̃kɔ'lɔːr], *a.* colourless.

incomber [ɛ̃kɔ̃'be], *v.i.* to be incumbent (*on anyone*).

incombustible [ɛ̃kɔ̃bys'tibl], *a.* incombustible, fire-proof.

incomestible [ɛ̃kɔmɛs'tibl], *a.* inedible.

incommode [ɛ̃kɔ'mɔd], *a.* inconvenient, uncomfortable; annoying, disagreeable.

incommodé [ɛ̃kɔmɔ'de], *a.* indisposed, unwell, poorly.

incommodément [ɛ̃kɔmɔde'mɑ̃], *adv.* incommodiously, inconveniently.

incommoder [ɛ̃kɔmɔ'de], *v.t.* to inconvenience, to trouble; to disturb, to annoy; to make unwell.

incommodité [ɛ̃kɔmɔdi'te], *n.f.* inconvenience, incommodiousness; annoyance; indisposition.

incommunicable [ɛ̃kɔmyni'kabl], *a.* incommunicable.

incomparable [ɛ̃kɔpa'rabl], *a.* incomparable, unequalled, peerless.

incomparablement [ɛ̃kɔ̃parablə'mɑ̃], *adv.* incomparably.

incompatibilité [ɛ̃kɔ̃patibili'te], *n.f.* incompatibility.

incompatible [ɛ̃kɔ̃pa'tibl], *a.* incompatible, inconsistent.

incompétence [ɛ̃kɔ̃pe'tɑ̃ːs], *n.f.* incompetence.

incompétent [ɛ̃kɔ̃pe'tɑ̃], *a.* incompetent.

incomplet [ɛ̃kɔ̃'plɛ], *a.* (*fem.* **-ète**) incomplete.

incomplètement [ɛ̃kɔ̃plɛt'mɑ̃], *adv.* incompletely.

incompréhensible [ɛ̃kɔ̃preɑ̃'sibl], *a.* incomprehensible, inscrutable.

incompréhension [ɛ̃kɔ̃preɑ̃'sjɔ̃], *n.f.* lack of understanding, obtuseness.

incompressible [ɛ̃kɔ̃prɛ'sibl], *a.* incompressible.

incompris [ɛ̃kɔ̃'pri], *a.* and *n.m.* (*fem.* **-e**) misunderstood, unappreciated (person).

inconcevable [ɛ̃kɔ̃s'vabl], *a.* inconceivable, unthinkable.

inconcevablement [ɛ̃kɔ̃svablə'mɑ̃], *adv.* inconceivably.

inconciliable [ɛ̃kɔ̃si'ljabl], *a.* irreconcilable, incompatible.

inconduite [ɛ̃kɔ̃'dɥit], *n.f.* misconduct.

inconfort [ɛ̃kɔ̃'fɔːr], *n.m.* discomfort, lack of comfort.

inconfortable [ɛ̃kɔ̃fɔr'tabl], *a.* uncomfortable.

incongru [ɛ̃kɔ̃'gry], *a.* incongruous, improper, unseemly.

incongruité [ɛ̃kɔ̃gryi'te], *n.f.* incongruity, impropriety.

incongrûment [ɛ̃kɔ̃gry'mɑ̃], *adv.* incongruously, improperly.

inconnu [ɛ̃kɔ'ny], *a.* unknown.—*n.m.* the unknown.—*n.m.* (*fem.* **-e**) stranger. —*n.f.* (**-e**) (*Math.*) unknown quantity.

inconquis [ɛ̃kɔ̃'ki], *a.* unconquered.

inconsciemment [ɛ̃kɔ̃sja'mɑ̃], *adv.* unconsciously, unawares.

inconscience [ɛ̃kɔ̃'sjɑ̃ːs], *n.f.* unconsciousness; failure to realize.

inconscient [ɛ̃kɔ̃'sjɑ̃], *a.* unconscious.—*n.m.* the unconscious.

inconséquemment [ɛ̃kɔ̃seka'mɑ̃], *adv.* inconsistently, inconsequentially.

inconséquence [ɛ̃kɔ̃se'kɑ̃ːs], *n.f.* inconsistency, inconsequence.

inconséquent [ɛ̃kɔ̃se'kɑ̃], *a.* inconsistent; inconsequential.

inconsidéré

inconsidéré [ɛ̃kõside're], *a.* inconsiderate, thoughtless.

inconsistance [ɛ̃kõsis'tɑ̃:s], *n.f.* inconsistency.

inconsistant [ɛ̃kõsis'tɑ̃], *a.* inconsistent.

inconsolable [ɛ̃kõsɔ'labl], *a.* disconsolate; inconsolable.

inconsolablement [ɛ̃kõsɔlablə'mɑ̃], *adv.* disconsolately, inconsolably.

inconsolé [ɛ̃kõsɔ'le], *a.* unconsoled, uncomforted.

inconstamment [ɛ̃kõsta'mɑ̃], *adv.* inconstantly; unsteadily.

inconstance [ɛ̃kõs'tɑ̃:s], *n.f.* inconstancy, fickleness; instability.

inconstant [ɛ̃kõs'tɑ̃], *a.* inconstant, fickle; changeable; unsettled, unsteady.—*n.m.* (*fem.* **-e**) fickle person.

inconstitutionnel [ɛ̃kõstitysjɔ'nɛl], *a.* (*fem.* **-elle**) unconstitutional.

incontestable [ɛ̃kõtɛs'tabl], *a.* incontestable, indisputable.

incontestablement [ɛ̃kõtɛstablə'mɑ̃], *adv.* incontestably.

incontesté [ɛ̃kõtɛs'te], *a.* uncontested, unquestioned, undisputed.

incontinence [ɛ̃kõti'nɑ̃:s], *n.f.* incontinence.

incontinent (1) [ɛ̃kõti'nɑ̃], *a.* incontinent, unchaste.

incontinent (2) [ɛ̃kõti'nɑ̃], *adv.* at once, immediately, forthwith.

incontrôlable [ɛ̃kõtro'labl], *a.* that cannot be checked *or* verified.

inconvenance [ɛ̃kõv'nɑ̃:s], *n.f.* impropriety, unseemliness; indecorum; *quelle inconvenance!* how very improper!

inconvenant [ɛ̃kõv'nɑ̃], *a.* improper, unbecoming, unseemly.

inconvénient [ɛ̃kõve'njɑ̃], *n.m.* inconvenience, harm; drawback, objection.

inconvertible [ɛ̃kõvɛr'tibl], *a.* unconvertible.

incorporation [ɛ̃kɔrpɔrɑ'sjõ], *n.f.* incorporation.

incorporer [ɛ̃kɔrpɔ're], *v.t.* to incorporate, to embody; to fuse. **s'incorporer,** *v.r.* to be embodied; to unite, to be blended.

incorrect [ɛ̃kɔ'rɛkt], *a.* incorrect, inaccurate.

incorrectement [ɛ̃kɔrɛktə'mɑ̃], *adv.* incorrectly, inaccurately.

incorrection [ɛ̃kɔrɛk'sjõ], *n.f.* incorrectness, inaccuracy.

incorrigible [ɛ̃kɔri'ʒibl], *a.* incorrigible.

incorrigiblement [ɛ̃kɔriʒiblə'mɑ̃], *adv.* incorrigibly.

incorruptible [ɛ̃kɔryp'tibl], *a.* incorruptible, unbribable.

incrédibilité [ɛ̃kredibili'te], *n.f.* incredibility.

incrédule [ɛ̃kre'dyl], *a.* incredulous, unbelieving.—*n.* unbeliever, infidel.

incrédulité [ɛ̃kredyli'te], *n.f.* incredulity, unbelief.

incriminer [ɛ̃krimi'ne], *v.t.* to incriminate, to accuse.

incroyable [ɛ̃krwa'jabl], *a.* incredible, past belief.

incroyablement [ɛ̃krwajablə'mɑ̃], *adv.* incredibly.

incroyance [ɛ̃krwa'jɑ̃:s], *n.f.* unbelief.

incroyant [ɛ̃krwa'jɑ̃], *a.* unbelieving.—*n.m.* (*fem.* **-e**) unbeliever.

incruster [ɛ̃krys'te], *v.t.* to encrust, to inlay. **s'incruster,** *v.r.* to become encrusted.

incubateur [ɛ̃kyba'tœ:r], *a.* (*fem.* **-trice**) incubating.—*n.m.* incubator.

incubation [ɛ̃kyba'sjõ], *n.f.* incubation, hatching.

incuber [ɛ̃ky'be], *v.t.* to incubate.

inculcation [ɛ̃kylka'sjõ], *n.f.* inculcation.

inculpation [ɛ̃kylpa'sjõ], *n.f.* indictment, charge.

inculpé [ɛ̃kyl'pe], *n.m.* (*fem.* **-ée**) defendant, accused.

inculper [ɛ̃kyl'pe], *v.t.* to indict, to inculpate, to charge.

inculquer [ɛ̃kyl'ke], *v.t.* to inculcate, to impress.

inculte [ɛ̃'kylt], *a.* uncultivated; untilled; unpolished; unkempt.

incultivable [ɛ̃kylti'vabl], *a.* untillable, uncultivable.

incultivé [ɛ̃kylti've], *a.* uncultivated; (*fig.*) uncultured.

incurable [ɛ̃ky'rabl], *a.* and *n.* incurable.

incurablement [ɛ̃kyrablə'mɑ̃], *adv.* incurably.

incurie [ɛ̃ky'ri], *n.f.* carelessness, heedlessness; negligence.

incursion [ɛ̃kyr'sjõ], *n.f.* incursion, inroad, irruption; expedition.

incurver [ɛ̃kyr've], *v.t.* to curve (*something*) inwards.

Inde [ɛ̃:d], l', *f.* India; **les Indes,* the Indies; *les Indes occidentales,* the West Indies.

indécemment [ɛ̃desa'mɑ̃], *adv.* indecently.

indécence [ɛ̃de'sɑ̃:s], *n.f.* indecency, impropriety.

indécent [ɛ̃de'sɑ̃], *a.* indecent; unseemly.

indéchiffrable [ɛ̃deʃi'frabl], *a.* undecipherable, illegible; obscure, incomprehensible.

indéchirable [ɛ̃deʃi'rabl], *a.* untearable.

indécis [ɛ̃de'si], *a.* undecided, doubtful; irresolute.

indécision [ɛ̃desi'zjõ], *n.f.* indecision, irresolution.

indécrottable [ɛ̃dekrɔ'tabl], *a.* uncleanable; (*fig.*) incorrigible.

indéfendable [ɛ̃defɑ̃'dabl], *a.* indefensible, untenable.

indéfini [ɛ̃defi'ni], *a.* indefinite, unlimited.

indéfiniment [ɛ̃defini'mɑ̃], *adv.* indefinitely.

indéfinissable [ɛ̃defini'sabl], *a.* undefinable; nondescript.

indéfrichable [ɛ̃defri'ʃabl], *a.* unclearable (*of land*).

indéfrisable [ɛ̃defri'zabl], *n.f.* permanent wave.

indélébile [ɛ̃dele'bil], *a.* indelible, ineffaceable.

indélicat [ɛ̃deli'ka], *a.* indelicate; unhandsome.

indélicatement [ɛ̃delikat'mɑ̃], *adv.* indelicately; unhandsomely.

indélicatesse [ɛ̃delika'tɛs], *n.f.* tactlessness; unscrupulousness; objectionable action.

indémaillable [ɛ̃dema'jabl], *a.* ladder-proof (*stocking*).

indemne [ɛ̃'dɛmn], *a.* uninjured.

indemnisation [ɛ̃dɛmniza'sjõ], *n.f.* indemnification, compensation.

indemniser [ɛ̃dɛmni'ze], *v.t.* to indemnify; to make good.

186

indemnité [ɛ̃dɛmni'te], *n.f.* indemnity; *indemnité de charges de famille,* family allowance; *indemnité de chômage,* unemployment benefit; *indemnité de vie chère,* cost of living bonus.

indéniable [ɛ̃de'njabl], *a.* undeniable; self-evident.

indépendamment [ɛ̃depɑ̃da'mɑ̃], *adv.* independently.

indépendance [ɛ̃depɑ̃'dɑ̃ːs], *n.f.* independence.

indépendant [ɛ̃depɑ̃'dɑ̃], *a.* independent.

indescriptible [ɛ̃dɛskrip'tibl], *a.* indescribable.

indésirable [ɛ̃dezi'rabl], *a.* and *n.* undesirable.

indestructible [ɛ̃dɛstryk'tibl], *a.* indestructible.

indéterminable [ɛ̃dɛtɛrmi'nabl], *a.* indeterminable.

indétermination [ɛ̃dɛtɛrmina'sjɔ̃], *n.f.* indetermination, irresolution.

indéterminé [ɛ̃dɛtɛrmi'ne], *a.* undetermined, irresolute.

index [ɛ̃'dɛks], *n.m. inv.* fore-finger; index.

indicateur [ɛ̃dika'tœːr], *a.* (*fem.* **-trice**) indicating, indicatory.—*n.m.* indicator, guide; time-table; (*fem.* **-trice**) (*fig.*) informer.

indicatif [ɛ̃dika'tif], *a.* (*fem.* **-tive**) indicative.—*n.m.* (*Gram.*) indicative mood; call-sign; signature-tune.

indication [ɛ̃dika'sjɔ̃], *n.f.* indication, information; sign, mark.

indice [ɛ̃'dis], *n.m.* indication, sign, mark, clue.

indicible [ɛ̃di'sibl], *a.* inexpressible, unspeakable, indescribable.

indiciblement [ɛ̃disibla'mɑ̃], *adv.* inexpressibly.

indien [ɛ̃'djɛ̃], *a.* (*fem.* **-enne**) Indian.—*n.m.* (**Indien**, *fem.* **-enne**) Indian (*person*).—*n.f.* (**-enne**) printed calico, printed cotton.

indifféremment [ɛ̃difera'mɑ̃], *adv.* indifferently; alike.

indifférence [ɛ̃dife'rɑ̃ːs], *n.f.* indifference, unconcern.

indifférent [ɛ̃dife'rɑ̃], *a.* indifferent, immaterial; unconcerned, heedless.—*n.m.* (*fem.* **-e**) indifferent person.

indigence [ɛ̃di'ʒɑ̃ːs], *n.f.* indigence, poverty, need.

indigène [ɛ̃di'ʒɛːn], *a.* indigenous, native.—*n.* native.

indigent [ɛ̃di'ʒɑ̃], *a.* indigent, needy.—*n.m.* (*fem.* **-e**) pauper, destitute person.

indigéré [ɛ̃diʒe're], *a.* undigested, crude.

indigeste [ɛ̃di'ʒɛst], *a.* indigestible; undigested.

indigestion [ɛ̃diʒɛs'tjɔ̃], *n.f.* indigestion, surfeit.

indignation [ɛ̃dina'sjɔ̃], *n.f.* indignation.

indigne [ɛ̃'diɲ], *a.* unworthy; infamous, worthless.

indigné [ɛ̃di'ɲe], *a.* indignant; shocked.

indignement [ɛ̃diɲa'mɑ̃], *adv.* unworthily; scandalously.

indigner [ɛ̃di'ɲe], *v.t.* to render indignant; to shock. **s'indigner,** *v.r.* to be indignant; to be shocked.

indignité [ɛ̃diɲi'te], *n.f.* unworthiness, worthlessness; indignity; infamy.

indigo [ɛ̃di'go], *a. inv.* and *n.m.* indigo.

indigotier [ɛ̃digo'tje], *n.m.* indigo plant *or* manufacturer.

indiquer [ɛ̃di'ke], *v.t.* to indicate, to point out; to mention; to denote; to appoint, to recommend; to outline.

indirect [ɛ̃di'rɛkt], *a.* indirect; circumstantial (*of evidence*); collateral (*of heirs*).

indirectement [ɛ̃dirɛkta'mɑ̃], *a.* indirectly.

indiscipline [ɛ̃disi'plin], *n.f.* indiscipline, insubordination.

indiscipliné [ɛ̃disipli'ne], *a.* undisciplined.

indiscret [ɛ̃dis'krɛ], *a.* (*fem.* **-ète**) indiscreet, inconsiderate; inquisitive; tell-tale.—*n.m.* (*fem.* **-ète**) babbler.

indiscrètement [ɛ̃diskrɛt'mɑ̃], *adv.* indiscreetly, inconsiderately.

indiscrétion [ɛ̃diskre'sjɔ̃], *n.f.* indiscretion; unwariness.

indiscutable [ɛ̃disky'tabl], *a.* incontestable, indisputable, obvious.

indispensable [ɛ̃dispɑ̃'sabl], *a.* indispensable.

indispensablement [ɛ̃dispɑ̃sabla'mɑ̃], *adv.* indispensably.

indisponible [ɛ̃dispo'nibl], *a.* unavailable.

indisposé [ɛ̃dispo'ze], *a.* unwell; unfriendly.

indisposer [ɛ̃dispo'ze], *v.t.* to indispose, to make unwell; to disincline, to set against (*contre*).

indisposition [ɛ̃dispozi'sjɔ̃], *n.f.* indisposition; disinclination.

indisputé [ɛ̃dispy'te], *a.* unquestioned.

indissoluble [ɛ̃diso'lybl], *a.* indissoluble.

indissolublement [ɛ̃disolybla'mɑ̃], *adv.* indissolubly.

indistinct [ɛ̃dis'tɛ̃kt], *a.* indistinct.

indistinctement [ɛ̃distɛ̃kta'mɑ̃], *adv.* indistinctly.

individu [ɛ̃divi'dy], *n.m.* individual; (*colloq.*) fellow.

individualisme [ɛ̃dividɥa'lism], *n.m.* individualism.

individualiste [ɛ̃dividɥa'list], *a.* individualistic.—*n.* individualist.

individualité [ɛ̃dividɥali'te], *n.f.* individuality.

individuel [ɛ̃divi'dɥɛl], *a.* (*fem.* **-elle**) individual.

individuellement [ɛ̃dividɥɛl'mɑ̃], *adv.* individually.

indivisé [ɛ̃divi'ze], *a.* undivided.

indivisément [ɛ̃divize'mɑ̃], *adv.* jointly.

indivisibilité [ɛ̃divizibili'te], *n.f.* indivisibility.

indivisible [ɛ̃divi'zibl], *a.* indivisible.

indivisiblement [ɛ̃divizibla'mɑ̃], *adv.* indivisibly.

indivision [ɛ̃divi'zjɔ̃], *n.f.* joint-possession.

Indochine [ɛ̃do'ʃin], **l',** *f.* Indo-China.

indochinois [ɛ̃doʃi'nwa], *a.* Indo-Chinese.—*n.m.* (**Indochinois**, *fem.* **-oise**) Indo-Chinese (*person*).

indocile [ɛ̃do'sil], *a.* indocile, unmanageable.

indocilité [ɛ̃dosili'te], *n.f.* indocility, intractability.

indolemment [ɛ̃dola'mɑ̃], *adv.* indolently.

indolence [ɛ̃do'lɑ̃ːs], *n.f.* indolence, sloth.

indolent [ɛ̃do'lɑ̃], *a.* indolent, slothful.—*n.m.* (*fem.* **-e**) sluggard.

indolore [ɛ̃do'loːr], *a.* painless.

indomptable [ɛ̃dɔ̃'tabl], *a.* indomitable, untamable; unmanageable.

indompté [ɛ̃dɔ̃'te], *a.* untamed, wild; unsubdued.
Indonésie [ɛ̃dɔnɛ'zi], l', *f.* Indonesia.
indonésien [ɛ̃dɔnɛ'zjɛ̃], *a.* Indonesian.—*n.m.* Indonesian (*language*); (**Indonésien**, *fem.* **-enne**) Indonesian (*person*).
indou [HINDOU].
indu [ɛ̃'dy], *a.* undue, unseasonable, late.
indubitable [ɛ̃dybi'tabl], *a.* indubitable, certain.
indubitablement [ɛ̃dybitablə'mɑ̃], *adv.* undoubtedly.
inductif [ɛ̃dyk'tif], *a.* (*fem.* **-tive**) inductive.
induction [ɛ̃dyk'sjɔ̃], *n.f.* induction, inference.
induire [ɛ̃'dɥiːr], *v.t. irr.* (*conjug. like* CONDUIRE) to induce, to lead; to infer.
indulgence [ɛ̃dyl'ʒɑ̃ːs], *n.f.* indulgence, leniency.
indulgent [ɛ̃dyl'ʒɑ̃], *a.* indulgent, forbearing.
indûment [ɛ̃dy'mɑ̃], *adv.* unduly.
industrialiser [ɛ̃dystriali'ze], *v.t.* to industrialize.
industrialisme [ɛ̃dystria'lism], *n.m.* industrialism.
industrie [ɛ̃dys'tri], *n.f.* skill, ingenuity; business; manufacturing; industry, work; *chevalier d'industrie*, swindler, sharper; *industrie de base* or *industrie clef*, key industry.
industriel [ɛ̃dystri'ɛl], *a.* (*fem.* **-elle**) industrial, manufacturing.—*n.m.* manufacturer, mill-owner.
industrieusement [ɛ̃dystriøz'mɑ̃], *adv.* ingeniously, skilfully; industriously.
industrieux [ɛ̃dystri'ø], *a.* (*fem.* **-euse**) ingenious, skilful; industrious.
inébranlable [inebrɑ̃'labl], *a.* immovable; firm, resolute.
inébranlablement [inebrɑ̃lablə'mɑ̃], *adv.* immovably, steadily; resolutely.
inédit [ine'di], *a.* unpublished; new.
ineffable [inɛ'fabl], *a.* ineffable, inexpressible, unutterable.
ineffaçable [inɛfa'sabl], *a.* indelible, ineffaceable.
inefficace [inɛfi'kas], *a.* ineffectual, ineffective.
inefficacité [inɛfikasi'te], *n.f.* inefficacy, ineffectiveness.
inégal [ine'gal], *a.* (*m. pl.* **-aux**) unequal; rough; (*fig.*) ill-matched; irregular.
inégalement [inegal'mɑ̃], *adv.* unequally, unevenly.
inégalité [inegali'te], *n.f.* inequality; unevenness; irregularity.
inélégance [inele'gɑ̃ːs], *n.f.* inelegance.
inélégant [inele'gɑ̃], *a.* inelegant.
inéligible [ineli'ʒibl], *a.* ineligible.
inéluctable [inelyk'tabl], *a.* unavoidable; unescapable.
inénarrable [inena'rabl], *a.* untellable; incredible.
inepte [i'nɛpt], *a.* foolish, silly, inept, absurd.
ineptie [inɛp'si], *n.f.* ineptitude, foolishness, absurdity.
inépuisable [inepɥi'zabl], *a.* inexhaustible.
inépuisablement [inepɥizablə'mɑ̃], *adv.* inexhaustibly.
inéquitable [ineki'tabl], *a.* unfair.
inerte [i'nɛrt], *a.* inert, sluggish, inactive.
inertie [inɛr'si], *n.f.* inertia; indolence.

inespéré [inɛspe're], *a.* unhoped for, unexpected.
inestimable [inɛsti'mabl], *a.* inestimable.
inévitable [inevi'tabl], *a.* inevitable, unavoidable.
inévitablement [inevitablə'mɑ̃], *adv.* inevitably, unavoidably.
inexact [inɛg'zakt], *a.* inexact, inaccurate, incorrect.
inexactement [inɛgzaktə'mɑ̃], *adv.* inaccurately, incorrectly.
inexactitude [inɛgzakti'tyd], *n.f.* incorrectness; inaccuracy, slip.
inexcusable [inɛksky'zabl], *a.* inexcusable, unwarrantable.
inexécutable [inɛgzeky'tabl], *a.* impracticable.
inexercé [inɛgzɛr'se], *a.* untrained.
inexistant [inɛgzis'tɑ̃], *a.* non-existent.
inexorable [inɛgzɔ'rabl], *a.* inexorable, inflexible; pitiless.
inexorablement [inɛgzɔrablə'mɑ̃], *adv.* inexorably.
inexpérience [inɛkspe'rjɑ̃ːs], *n.f.* inexperience.
inexpérimenté [inɛksperimɑ̃'te], *a.* inexperienced; untried (*of things*).
inexplicable [inɛkspli'kabl], *a.* inexplicable, unaccountable.
inexpliqué [inɛkspli'ke], *a.* unexplained.
inexploitable [inɛksplwa'tabl], *a.* unworkable, useless.
inexploité [inɛksplwa'te], *a.* uncultivated (*of land*); unworked (*of mines etc.*); untapped (*resources*).
inexploré [inɛksplɔ're], *a.* unexplored.
inexplosible [inɛksplo'zibl], *a.* unexplosive.
inexpressible [inɛkspre'sibl], *a.* inexpressible.
inexpressif [inɛkspre'sif], *a.* (*fem.* **-ive**) inexpressive, lacking expression.
inexprimable [inɛkspri'mabl], *a.* inexpressible, unspeakable.
inextinguible [inɛkstɛ̃'gibl], *a.* inextinguishable; unquenchable (*thirst, fire*); irrepressible (*laughter*).
inextricable [inɛkstri'kabl], *a.* inextricable.
inextricablement [inɛkstrikablə'mɑ̃], *adv.* inextricably.
infaillibilité [ɛ̃fajibili'te], *n.f.* infallibility.
infaillible [ɛ̃fa'jibl], *a.* infallible.
infailliblement [ɛ̃fajiblə'mɑ̃], *adv.* infallibly.
infaisable [ɛ̃fə'zabl], *a.* impracticable.
infamant [ɛ̃fa'mɑ̃], *a.* infamous, ignominious.
infâme [ɛ̃'faːm], *a.* infamous; squalid, sordid.—*n.* infamous person, wretch.
infamie [ɛ̃fa'mi], *n.f.* infamy, ignominy; baseness.
infant [ɛ̃'fɑ̃], *n.m.* (*fem.* **-e**) infante, infanta (*Spanish prince* or *princess*).
infanterie [ɛ̃fɑ̃'tri], *n.f.* infantry.
infanticide [ɛ̃fɑ̃ti'sid], *n.m.* infanticide.—*n.* child-murderer.
infantile [ɛ̃fɑ̃'til], *a.* infantile.
infatigable [ɛ̃fati'gabl], *a.* indefatigable, untiring.
infatuation [ɛ̃fatɥa'sjɔ̃], *n.f.* infatuation.
infatuer [ɛ̃fa'tɥe], *v.t.* to infatuate. **s'infatuer**, *v.r.* to become infatuated.
infécond [ɛ̃fe'kɔ̃], *a.* unfruitful, barren, sterile.

infécondité [ɛ̃fekõdi'te], *n.f.* unfruitfulness, barrenness, sterility.

infect [ɛ̃'fɛkt], *a.* infected, foul, noisome, stinking.

infectant [ɛ̃fɛk'tɑ̃], *a.* infecting.

infecter [ɛ̃fɛk'te], *v.t.* to infect, to contaminate; to taint.—*v.i.* to stink.

infectieux [ɛ̃fɛk'sjø], *a.* (*fem.* **-euse**) infectious.

infection [ɛ̃fɛk'sjõ], *n.f.* infection; infectious disease; stench; *foyer d'infection*, hotbed of disease.

inférence [ɛ̃fe'rɑ̃:s], *n.f.* conclusion, inference.

inférer [ɛ̃fe're], *v.t.* (*conjug. like* CÉDER) to infer, to conclude.

inférieur [ɛ̃fe'rjœ:r], *a.* inferior, lower.—*n.m.* (*fem.* **-e**) inferior; subordinate.

infériorité [ɛ̃ferjori'te], *n.f.* inferiority.

infernal [ɛ̃fɛr'nal], *a.* (*m. pl.* **-aux**) infernal, hellish.

infernalement [ɛ̃fɛrnal'mɑ̃], *adv.* infernally.

infertile [ɛ̃fɛr'til], *a.* infertile, unfruitful; sterile, barren.

infertilité [ɛ̃fɛrtili'te], *n.f.* unfruitfulness.

infester [ɛ̃fɛs'te], *v.t.* to infest, to overrun; to haunt.

infidèle [ɛ̃fi'dɛl], *a.* unfaithful, disloyal; unbelieving.—*n.* unfaithful person; infidel.

infidèlement [ɛ̃fidɛl'mɑ̃], *adv.* unfaithfully; inaccurately.

infidélité [ɛ̃fideli'te], *n.f.* infidelity; unbelief; dishonesty.

infiltration [ɛ̃filtra'sjõ], *n.f.* infiltration.

infiltrer (s') [sɛ̃fil'tre], *v.r.* to infiltrate, to percolate.

infime [ɛ̃'fim], *a.* lowest (*of ranks*); tiny.

infini [ɛ̃fi'ni], *a.* infinite, boundless.—*n.m.* infinite, infinity.

infiniment [ɛ̃fini'mɑ̃], *adv.* infinitely, without end; exceedingly, extremely.

infinité [ɛ̃fini'te], *n.f.* infinity, infiniteness; (*fig.*) crowd; no end.

infinitif [ɛ̃fini'tif], *a.* (*fem.* **-tive**) and *n.m.* infinitive (mood).

infirme [ɛ̃'firm], *a.* crippled, invalid; infirm; feeble.—*n.* invalid, cripple.

infirmerie [ɛ̃firm'ri], *n.f.* infirmary, sickward; (*sch.*) sanatorium, sick-bay.

infirmier [ɛ̃fir'mje], *n.m.* (*fem.* **-ière**) hospital-attendant; nurse.

infirmité [ɛ̃firmi'te], *n.f.* infirmity, weakness, failing.

inflammable [ɛ̃fla'mabl], *a.* inflammable.

inflammation [ɛ̃flama'sjõ], *n.f.* inflammation.

inflammatoire [ɛ̃flama'twa:r], *a.* inflammatory.

inflation [ɛ̃fla'sjõ], *n.f.* inflation, swelling.

inflexible [ɛ̃flɛk'sibl], *a.* inflexible; unyielding, unbending.

inflexiblement [ɛ̃flɛksiblə'mɑ̃], *adv.* inflexibly.

inflexion [ɛ̃flɛk'sjõ], *n.f.* inflexion; modulation, variation.

infliction [ɛ̃flik'sjõ], *n.f.* infliction.

infliger [ɛ̃fli'ʒe], *v.t.* (*conjug. like* MANGER) to inflict, to impose.

influence [ɛ̃fly'ɑ̃:s], *n.f.* influence; sway, power, authority.

influencer [ɛ̃flyɑ̃'se], *v.t.* (*conjug. like* COMMENCER) to influence, to sway, to bias.

influent [ɛ̃fly'ɑ̃], *a.* influential.

influenza [ɛ̃flyɑ̃'za], *n.f.* influenza.

influer [ɛ̃fly'e], *v.i.* to have an influence (*sur, on*).

informateur [ɛ̃forma'tœ:r], *n.m.* (*fem.* **-trice**) informant.

information [ɛ̃forma'sjõ], *n.f.* inquiry; information; (*pl.*) news (bulletin).

informe [ɛ̃'form], *a.* shapeless; misshapen; crude, imperfect.

informer [ɛ̃for'me], *v.t.* to inform, to acquaint, to apprise. **s'informer**, *v.r.* to inquire, to make inquiries, to investigate.

infortune [ɛ̃for'tyn], *n.f.* misfortune, adversity.

infortuné [ɛ̃forty'ne], *a.* unfortunate, unhappy, ill-fated, wretched.—*n.m.* (*fem.* **-ée**) unfortunate, unhappy *or* wretched person.

infraction [ɛ̃frak'sjõ], *n.f.* infringement, breach, violation.

infranchissable [ɛ̃frɑ̃ʃi'sabl], *a.* insurmountable, insuperable.

infra-rouge [ɛ̃fra'ruʒ], *a.* infra-red.

infréquenté [ɛ̃freka'te], *a.* unfrequented.

infructueusement [ɛ̃fryktɥøz'mɑ̃], *adv.* fruitlessly, to no purpose, in vain.

infructueux [ɛ̃fryk'tɥø], *a.* (*fem.* **-euse**) unfruitful, vain, unavailing.

infus [ɛ̃'fy], *a.* infused, innate, native (*of knowledge etc.*).

infuser [ɛ̃fy'ze], *v.t.* to infuse, to instil; to steep.

infusion [ɛ̃fy'zjõ], *n.f.* infusion, decoction.

ingambe [ɛ̃'gɑ̃:b], *a.* nimble, brisk, active.

ingénier (s') [sɛ̃ʒe'nje], *v.r.* to tax one's ingenuity, to contrive.

ingénieur [ɛ̃ʒe'njœ:r], *n.m.* engineer.

ingénieusement [ɛ̃ʒenjøz'mɑ̃], *adv.* ingeniously.

ingénieux [ɛ̃ʒe'njø], *a.* (*fem.* **-euse**) ingenious, clever, witty.

ingéniosité [ɛ̃ʒenjozi'te], *n.f.* ingenuity; cleverness.

ingénu [ɛ̃ʒe'ny], *a.* ingenuous; guileless, unsophisticated; simple, artless.—*n.m.* (*fem.* **-e**) ingenuous person artless *or* simple-minded person.

ingénuité [ɛ̃ʒenɥi'te], *n.f.* ingenuousness.

ingénument [ɛ̃ʒeny'mɑ̃], *adv.* ingenuously.

ingérence [ɛ̃ʒe'rɑ̃:s], *n.f.* interference, meddling.

ingérer (s') [sɛ̃ʒe're], *v.r.* (*conjug. like* CÉDER) to meddle with, to interfere, to obtrude.

inglorieux [ɛ̃glo'rjø], *a.* (*fem.* **-euse**) inglorious.

ingouvernable [ɛ̃guvɛr'nabl], *a.* ungovernable, uncontrollable.

ingrat [ɛ̃'gra], *a.* unthankful, ungrateful; thankless, unprofitable.

ingratitude [ɛ̃grati'tyd], *n.f.* ingratitude, thanklessness.

ingrédient [ɛ̃gre'djɑ̃], *n.m.* ingredient.

inguérissable [ɛ̃geri'sabl], *a.* incurable.

inhabile [ina'bil], *a.* unskilful, unskilled, inexpert.

inhabilement [inabil'mɑ̃], *adv.* unskilfully.

inhabileté [inabil'te], *n.f.* unskilfulness, incompetence, inability.

inhabitable [inabi'tabl], *a.* uninhabitable.

inhabité [inabi'te], *a.* uninhabited.

inhabitué [inabi'tɥe], *a.* unaccustomed, unused.

inhalation

inhalation [inala'sjɔ̃], *n.f.* inhalation.
inhaler [ina'le], *v.t.* to inhale.
inharmonieux [inarmɔ'njø], *a.* (*fem.* **-euse**) inharmonious, unmusical.
inhérent [ine'rɑ̃], *a.* inherent.
inhospitalier [inɔspita'lje], *a.* (*fem.* **-ière**) inhospitable; (*fig.*) unfriendly, forbidding.
inhumain [iny'mɛ̃], *a.* inhuman, cruel.
inhumainement [inymɛn'mɑ̃], *adv.* inhumanly.
inhumanité [inymani'te], *n.f.* inhumanity, cruelty.
inhumation [inyma'sjɔ̃], *n.f.* inhumation, interment.
inhumer [iny'me], *v.t.* to bury, to inter.
inimaginable [inimaʒi'nabl], *a.* unimaginable, inconceivable.
inimitable [inimi'tabl], *a.* inimitable.
inimitié [inimi'tje], *n.f.* enmity, antipathy, aversion.
ininflammable [inɛ̃fla'mabl], *a.* non-inflammable, fire-proof.
inintelligemment [inɛ̃teliʒa'mɑ̃], *adv.* unintelligently.
inintelligence [inɛ̃teli'ʒɑ̃:s], *n.f.* lack of intelligence.
inintelligent [inɛ̃teli'ʒɑ̃], *a.* unintelligent.
inintelligible [inɛ̃teli'ʒibl], *a.* unintelligible.
inintéressant [inɛ̃tere'sɑ̃], *a.* uninteresting.
ininterrompu [inɛ̃terɔ̃'py], *a.* uninterrupted.
inique [i'nik], *a.* iniquitous; unrighteous.
iniquement [inik'mɑ̃], *adv.* iniquitously.
iniquité [iniki'te], *n.f.* iniquity, unrighteousness; injustice.
initial [ini'sjal], *a.* (*m. pl.* **-aux**) initial.
initiale [ini'sjal], *n.f.* initial.
initialement [inisjal'mɑ̃], *adv.* initially.
initiateur [inisja'tœ:r], *n.m.* (*fem.* **-trice**) initiator.
initiation [inisja'sjɔ̃], *n.f.* initiation.
initiative [inisja'ti:v], *n.f.* initiative.
initier [ini'sje], *v.t.* to initiate, to admit.
injecté [ɛ̃ʒɛk'te], *a.* injected; bloodshot; creosoted.
injecter [ɛ̃ʒɛk'te], *v.t.* to inject.
injection [ɛ̃ʒɛk'sjɔ̃], *n.f.* injection.
injonction [ɛ̃ʒɔ̃k'sjɔ̃], *n.f.* injunction, order.
injudicieux [ɛ̃ʒydi'sjø], *a.* (*fem.* **-euse**) injudicious.
injure [ɛ̃'ʒyːr], *n.f.* injury; insult; (*pl.*) abuse, abusive language; slander.
injurier [ɛ̃ʒy'rje], *v.t.* to abuse, to insult.
injurieux [ɛ̃ʒy'rjø], *a.* (*fem.* **-euse**) wrongful; abusive, insulting.
injuste [ɛ̃'ʒyst], *a.* unjust, unfair, wrong.
injustement [ɛ̃ʒystə'mɑ̃], *adv.* unjustly, wrongly.
injustice [ɛ̃ʒys'tis], *n.f.* injustice; wrong.
injustifiable [ɛ̃ʒysti'fjabl], *a.* unjustifiable.
injustifié [ɛ̃ʒysti'fje], *a.* unjustified, groundless.
inlassable [ɛ̃la'sabl], *a.* untirable.
inné [in'ne], *a.* innate, inborn.
innocemment [inɔsa'mɑ̃], *adv.* innocently.
innocence [inɔ'sɑ̃:s], *n.f.* innocence; inoffensiveness; simplicity.
innocent [inɔ'sɑ̃], *a.* innocent; harmless, inoffensive; guileless, simple.—*n.m.* (*fem.* **-e**) simpleton; idiot.
innocenter [inɔsɑ̃'te], *v.t.* to acquit.
innombrable [innɔ̃'brabl], *a.* innumerable, numberless.

innombrablement [inɔ̃brablə'mɑ̃], *adv.* innumerably.
innovateur [innɔva'tœːr], *n.m.* (*fem.* **-trice**) innovator.
innovation [innɔva'sjɔ̃], *n.f.* innovation.
innover [inno've], *v.i.* to make innovations.
inobservable [inɔpsɛr'vabl], *a.* inobservable.
inobservation [inɔpsɛrva'sjɔ̃], *n.f.* non-observance.
inobservé [inɔpsɛr've], *a.* unobserved, unnoticed.
inoccupé [inɔky'pe], *a.* unoccupied; idle; vacant.
inoculateur [inɔkyla'tœːr], *n.m.* (*fem.* **-trice**) inoculator.
inoculation [inɔkyla'sjɔ̃], *n.f.* inoculation.
inoculer [inɔky'le], *v.t.* to inoculate.
inodore [inɔ'dɔːr], *a.* odourless.
inoffensif [inɔfɑ̃'sif], *a.* (*fem.* **-sive**) inoffensive; innocuous.
inoffensivement [inɔfɑ̃siv'mɑ̃], *adv.* inoffensively.
inofficiel [inɔfi'sjɛl], *a.* (*fem.* **-elle**) unofficial.
inofficiellement [inɔfisjɛl'mɑ̃], *adv.* unofficially.
inondation [inɔ̃da'sjɔ̃], *n.f.* inundation, flood, deluge.
inonder [inɔ̃'de], *v.t.* to inundate, to overflow; (*fig.*) to overrun.
inopérant [inɔpe'rɑ̃], *a.* inoperative; inefficient.
inopiné [inɔpi'ne], *a.* unforeseen, unexpected, sudden.
inopinément [inɔpine'mɑ̃], *adv.* unawares, unexpectedly, suddenly.
inopportun [inɔpɔr'tœ̃], *a.* inopportune, untimely.
inorganique [inɔrga'nik], *a.* inorganic.
inoubliable [inu'bljabl], *a.* unforgettable.
inoublié [inu'blje], *a.* unforgotten, well-remembered.
inouï [i'nwi], *a.* unheard of, unprecedented.
inoxydable [inɔksi'dabl], *a.* rustless, stainless.
inqualifiable [ɛ̃kali'fjabl], *a.* unspeakable.
inquiet [ɛ̃'kjɛ], *a.* (*fem.* **-ète**) anxious; restless.
inquiétant [ɛ̃kje'tɑ̃], *a.* disquieting, alarming.
inquiéter [ɛ̃kje'te], *v.t.* (*conjug. like* CÉDER) to disquiet; to worry; to disturb. **s'inquiéter**, *v.r.* to be anxious, to be uneasy; to worry.
inquiétude [ɛ̃kje'tyd], *n.f.* anxiety, uneasiness, concern.
inquisiteur [ɛ̃kizi'tœːr], *a.* inquisitorial; inquisitive.—*n.m.* inquisitor.
inquisitif [ɛ̃kizi'tif], *a.* (*fem.* **-tive**) inquisitive.
inquisition [ɛ̃kizi'sjɔ̃], *n.f.* inquisition.
insaisissable [ɛ̃sɛzi'sabl], *a.* unseizable, imperceptible.
insalubre [ɛ̃sa'lybr], *a.* insalubrious, unhealthy, unwholesome.
insalubrement [ɛ̃salybrə'mɑ̃], *adv.* insalubriously, unhealthily.
insalubrité [ɛ̃salybri'te], *n.f.* insalubrity, unhealthiness.
insanité [ɛ̃sani'te], *n.f.* insanity.
insatiabilité [ɛ̃satjabili'te], *n.f.* insatiability.
insatiable [ɛ̃sa'sjabl], *a.* insatiable.
insciemment [ɛ̃sja'mɑ̃], *adv.* unwittingly.
inscription [ɛ̃skrip'sjɔ̃], *n.f.* inscription; registration, enrolment; matriculation.

institution

inscrire [ɛ̃s'kriːr], *v.t. irr. (conjug. like* ÉCRIRE) to inscribe, to set down, to register. **s'inscrire,** *v.r.* to inscribe oneself; to enter one's name; to register, to enrol.
inscrutable [ɛ̃skry'tabl], *a.* inscrutable, unfathomable.
insecte [ɛ̃'sɛkt], *n.m.* insect.
insecticide [ɛ̃sɛkti'sid], *a.* insecticidal.—*n.m.* insecticide.
insectivore [ɛ̃sɛkti'vɔːr], *a.* insectivorous.
insécurité [ɛ̃sekyri'te], *n.f.* insecurity.
insémination [ɛ̃semina'sjɔ̃], *n.f.* insemination (*cows, ewes etc.*).
inséminer [ɛ̃semi'ne], *v.t.* to inseminate.
insensé [ɛ̃sɑ̃'se], *a.* insane, mad; foolish, senseless.—*n.m.* (*fem.* **-ée**) madman, mad woman, maniac.
insensibiliser [ɛ̃sɑ̃sibili'ze], *v.t.* to anaesthetize.
insensibilité [ɛ̃sɑ̃sibili'te], *n.f.* insensibility; callousness.
insensible [ɛ̃sɑ̃'sibl], *a.* insensible, unconscious; hard-hearted, insensitive.
insensiblement [ɛ̃sɑ̃siblə'mɑ̃], *adv.* insensibly; gradually, imperceptibly.
inséparable [ɛ̃sepa'rabl], *a.* inseparable.—*n.m.* (*pl.*) (*Orn.*) love-birds.
inséparablement [ɛ̃separablə'mɑ̃], *adv.* inseparably.
insérer [ɛ̃se're], *v.t.* (*conjug. like* CÉDER) to insert, to put in.
insertion [ɛ̃sɛr'sjɔ̃], *n.f.* insertion.
insidieusement [ɛ̃sidjøz'mɑ̃], *adv.* insidiously.
insidieux [ɛ̃si'djø], *a.* (*fem.* **-euse**) insidious.
insigne [ɛ̃'siɲ], *a.* distinguished; conspicuous; notorious.—*n.m.* badge, mark; (*pl.*) insignia.
insignifiance [ɛ̃siɲi'fjɑ̃ːs], *n.f.* insignificance.
insignifiant [ɛ̃siɲi'fjɑ̃], *a.* insignificant, trivial.
insincère [ɛ̃sɛ̃'sɛːr], *a.* insincere.
insinuant [ɛ̃si'nɥɑ̃], *a.* insinuating; ingratiating.
insinuation [ɛ̃sinɥa'sjɔ̃], *n.f.* insinuation, hint, innuendo.
insinuer [ɛ̃si'nɥe], *v.t.* to insinuate; to hint, to suggest. **s'insinuer,** *v.r.* to insinuate oneself (*dans*), to creep or worm one's way (*into*).
insipide [ɛ̃si'pid], *a.* insipid, tasteless; dull.
insipidité [ɛ̃sipidi'te], *n.f.* insipidity.
insistance [ɛ̃sis'tɑ̃ːs], *n.f.* insistence, persistence.
insister [ɛ̃sis'te], *v.i.* to insist, to lay stress (*sur*).
insociable [ɛ̃sɔ'sjabl], *a.* unsociable; difficult to live with.
insolation [ɛ̃sɔla'sjɔ̃], *n.f.* insolation, sun-stroke.
insolemment [ɛ̃sɔla'mɑ̃], *adv.* insolently.
insolence [ɛ̃sɔ'lɑ̃ːs], *n.f.* insolence, impertinence.
insolent [ɛ̃sɔ'lɑ̃], *a.* insolent, impudent, rude. —*n.m.* (*fem.* **-e**) insolent person.
insolite [ɛ̃sɔ'lit], *a.* unusual, unwonted.
insolubilité [ɛ̃sɔlybili'te], *n.f.* insolubility.
insoluble [ɛ̃sɔ'lybl], *a.* insoluble.
insolvabilité [ɛ̃sɔlvabili'te], *n.f.* insolvency.
insolvable [ɛ̃sɔl'vabl], *a.* insolvent.
insomnie [ɛ̃sɔm'ni], *n.f.* insomnia.
insondable [ɛ̃sɔ̃'dabl], *a.* unfathomable.
insonore [ɛ̃sɔ'nɔːr], *a.* sound-proof.

insouciance [ɛ̃su'sjɑ̃ːs], *n.f.* carelessness, thoughtlessness.
insouciant [ɛ̃su'sjɑ̃], **insoucieux** [ɛ̃su'sjø] (*fem.* **-euse**), *a.* careless, thoughtless; unconcerned, easy-going.
insoumis [ɛ̃su'mi], *a.* unsubdued; refractory, unruly.—*n.m.* (*Mil.*) defaulter.
insoumission [ɛ̃sumi'sjɔ̃], *n.f.* insubordination.
insoutenable [ɛ̃sut'nabl], *a.* indefensible; unbearable.
inspecter [ɛ̃spɛk'te], *v.t.* to inspect, to survey, to scan.
inspecteur [ɛ̃spɛk'tœːr], *n.m.* (*fem.* **-trice**) inspector, superintendent, surveyor.
inspection [ɛ̃spɛk'sjɔ̃], *n.f.* inspection, survey; superintendence; *faire l'inspection de,* to inspect; *passer à l'inspection,* to undergo inspection.
inspirateur [ɛ̃spira'tœːr], *a.* (*fem.* **-trice**) inspiring; (*Anat.*) inspiratory.—*n.m.* (*fem.* **-trice**) inspirer.
inspiration [ɛ̃spira'sjɔ̃], *n.f.* inspiration; suggestion; inhaling.
inspiré [ɛ̃spi're], *a.* and *n.m.* (*fem.* **-ée**) inspired (person).
inspirer [ɛ̃spi're], *v.t.* to inspire, to breathe in; (*fig.*) to suggest, to instil. **s'inspirer,** *v.r.* to draw one's inspiration (*de*).
instabilité [ɛ̃stabili'te], *n.f.* instability, fickleness.
instable [ɛ̃'stabl], *a.* unstable; unsteady, wobbly.
installation [ɛ̃stala'sjɔ̃], *n.f.* installation; equipment.
installer [ɛ̃sta'le], *v.t.* to install; to inaugurate, to establish. **s'installer,** *v.r.* to install oneself; to settle.
instamment [ɛ̃sta'mɑ̃], *adv.* earnestly, urgently.
instance [ɛ̃s'tɑ̃ːs], *n.f.* entreaty; urgency, earnestness; (*Law*) instance; (*pl.*) entreaties.
instant (1) [ɛ̃s'tɑ̃], *n.m.* instant, moment; *à l'instant,* in an instant, immediately.
instant (2) [ɛ̃s'tɑ̃], *a.* pressing, urgent; imminent.
instantané [ɛ̃stɑ̃ta'ne], *a.* instantaneous.—*n.m.* snapshot.
instantanément [ɛ̃stɑ̃tane'mɑ̃], *adv.* instantaneously.
instar (à l') [alɛ̃s'taːr], *prep. phr. à l'instar de,* in imitation of.
instigateur [ɛ̃stiga'tœːr], *n.m.* (*fem.* **-trice**) instigator.
instigation [ɛ̃stiga'sjɔ̃], *n.f.* instigation.
instiller [ɛ̃sti'le], *v.t.* to instil.
instinct [ɛ̃s'tɛ̃], *n.m.* instinct.
instinctif [ɛ̃stɛ̃k'tif], *a.* (*fem.* **-tive**) instinctive.
instinctivement [ɛ̃stɛ̃ktiv'mɑ̃], *adv.* instinctively.
instituer [ɛ̃sti'tɥe], *v.t.* to institute, to establish.
institut [ɛ̃sti'ty], *n.m.* institution; institute; order (*of monks*).
instituteur [ɛ̃stity'tœːr], *n.m.* (*fem.* **-trice**) teacher, schoolmaster, schoolmistress (*in primary schools*); *institutrice (particulière),* governess.
institution [ɛ̃stity'sjɔ̃], *n.f.* institution; establishment; (*Law*) appointment.

instructeur

instructeur [ɛ̃stryk'tœːr], *n.m.* instructor, drill-master.

instructif [ɛ̃stryk'tif], *a.* (*fem.* **-tive**) instructive.

instruction [ɛ̃stryk'sjɔ̃], *n.f.* instruction, tuition, education, learning; (*Law*) inquiry, examination; (*pl.*) directions.

instruire [ɛ̃s'trɥiːr], *v.t. irr.* (*conjug. like* CONDUIRE) to instruct, to teach, to educate; to inform (*de*). **s'instruire**, *v.r.* to instruct, inform *or* improve oneself.

instruit [ɛ̃s'trɥi], *a.* instructed, informed; aware; educated.

instrument [ɛ̃stry'mã], *n.m.* instrument, tool; document.

instrumental [ɛ̃strymã'tal], *a.* (*m. pl.* **-aux**) instrumental.

instrumentiste [ɛ̃strymã'tist], *n.* instrumentalist.

insu [ɛ̃'sy], *prep. phr.* **à l'insu de**, unknown to; **à mon insu**, unknown to me.

insubmersible [ɛ̃sybmɛr'sibl], *a.* unsinkable.

insubordination [ɛ̃sybɔrdina'sjɔ̃], *n.f.* insubordination.

insubordonné [ɛ̃sybɔrdɔ'ne], *a.* insubordinate.

insuccès [ɛ̃syk'sɛ], *n.m. inv.* failure, lack of success.

insuffisamment [ɛ̃syfiza'mã], *adv.* insufficiently.

insuffisance [ɛ̃syfi'zãːs], *n.f.* insufficiency.

insuffisant [ɛ̃syfi'zã], *a.* insufficient, inadequate.

insulaire [ɛ̃sy'lɛːr], *a.* insular.—*n.* islander.

insularité [ɛ̃sylari'te], *n.f.* insularity.

insuline [ɛ̃sy'lin], *n.f.* insulin.

insultant [ɛ̃syl'tã], *a.* insulting.

insulte [ɛ̃'sylt], *n.f.* insult.

insulter [ɛ̃syl'te], *v.t.* to insult, to affront.

insupportable [ɛ̃sypɔr'tabl], *a.* intolerable, unbearable.

insupportablement [ɛ̃sypɔrtablə'mã], *adv.* intolerably, unbearably.

insurgé [ɛ̃syr'ʒe], *a. and n.m.* (*fem.* **-ée**) rebel, insurgent.

insurger (s') [sɛ̃syr'ʒe], *v.r.* (*conjug. like* MANGER) to revolt, to rebel.

insurmontable [ɛ̃syrmɔ̃'tabl], *a.* insurmountable, insuperable.

insurrection [ɛ̃syrɛk'sjɔ̃], *n.f.* insurrection, rising.

intact [ɛ̃'takt], *a.* intact, entire, whole.

intangible [ɛ̃tã'ʒibl], *a.* intangible.

intarissable [ɛ̃tari'sabl], *a.* inexhaustible.

intégral [ɛ̃te'gral], *a.* (*m. pl.* **-aux**) integral, whole, entire.

intégrale [ɛ̃te'gral], *n.f.* (*Math.*) integral.

intégralement [ɛ̃tegral'mã], *adv.* integrally, entirely, in full.

intègre [ɛ̃'tɛgr], *a.* honest, upright, just.

intègrement [ɛ̃tɛgrə'mã], *adv.* honestly, uprightly.

intégrer [ɛ̃te'gre], *v.t.* (*conjug. like* CÉDER) to integrate. **s'intégrer**, *v.r.* to combine into; to form an integral part of.

intégrité [ɛ̃tegri'te], *n.f.* integrity, uprightness, probity.

intellect [ɛ̃te'lɛkt], *n.m.* intellect, understanding.

intellectuel [ɛ̃telɛk'tɥɛl], *a.* (*fem.* **-elle**) and *n.m.* (*fem.* **-elle**) intellectual.

intellectuellement [ɛ̃telɛktɥɛl'mã], *adv.* intellectually.

intelligemment [ɛ̃teliʒa'mã], *adv.* intelligently.

intelligence [ɛ̃teli'ʒãːs], *n.f.* intelligence, intellect; clear comprehension; cleverness, skill, ability; mutual understanding; *avec intelligence*, skilfully, cleverly; *en bonne intelligence avec*, on good terms with; *être d'intelligence avec*, to be in collusion with.

intelligent [ɛ̃teli'ʒã], *a.* intelligent; bright, clever, sharp.

intelligible [ɛ̃teli'ʒibl], *a.* intelligible; distinct, clear.

intelligiblement [ɛ̃teliʒiblə'mã], *adv.* intelligibly, clearly.

intempérance [ɛ̃tãpe'rãːs], *n.f.* intemperance, insobriety.

intempérant [ɛ̃tãpe'rã], *a.* intemperate.

intempérie [ɛ̃tãpe'ri], *n.f.* (*usu. in pl.*) inclemency (*of the weather*).

intempestif [ɛ̃tãpes'tif], *a.* (*fem.* **-tive**) unseasonable, untimely.

intenable [ɛ̃tə'nabl], *a.* untenable, insufferable.

intendance [ɛ̃tã'dãːs], *n.f.* stewardship (*of an estate*); (*Mil.*) commissariat; the Army Service Corps.

intendant [ɛ̃tã'dã], *n.m.* intendant, steward; major-domo; (*Mil.*) administrative officer (*having the rank of a general*).

intense [ɛ̃'tãːs], *a.* intense, violent; severe.

intensité [ɛ̃tãsi'te], *n.f.* intensity, violence, severity.

intensivement [ɛ̃tãsiv'mã], *adv.* intensively.

intenter [ɛ̃tã'te], *v.t.* (*Law*) *intenter une action* or *un procès à* or *contre quelqu'un*, to enter or bring an action against someone.

intention [ɛ̃tã'sjɔ̃], *n.f.* intention; (*Law*) intent; purpose; *à l'intention de*, for the sake of; *avec intention*, on purpose; *avoir l'intention de*, to intend to; *sans intention*, unintentionally.

intentionné [ɛ̃tãsjɔ'ne], *a.* intentioned, disposed, meaning.

intentionnel [ɛ̃tãsjɔ'nɛl], *a.* (*fem.* **-elle**) intentional.

inter [ɛ̃'tɛr], *n.m.* (*Ftb.*) inside-forward.

interaction [ɛ̃tɛrak'sjɔ̃], *n.f.* interaction.

intercaler [ɛ̃tɛrka'le], *v.t.* to intercalate; to interpolate; (*Elec.*) to switch in.

intercéder [ɛ̃tɛrse'de], *v.i.* (*conjug. like* CÉDER) to intercede, to plead.

intercepter [ɛ̃tɛrsɛp'te], *v.t.* to intercept.

intercession [ɛ̃tɛrse'sjɔ̃], *n.f.* intercession; mediation.

intercontinental [ɛ̃tɛrkɔ̃tinã'tal], *a.* (*m. pl.* **-aux**) intercontinental.

interdépartemental [ɛ̃tɛrdepartəmã'tal], *a.* (*m. pl.* **-aux**) interdepartmental.

interdiction [ɛ̃tɛrdik'sjɔ̃], *n.f.* interdiction, prohibition.

interdire [ɛ̃tɛr'diːr], *v.t. irr.* (*conjug. like* MÉDIRE) to interdict, to prohibit; to forbid; to suspend; (*fig.*) to confound, to nonplus.

interdit [ɛ̃tɛr'di], *a.* forbidden, prohibited; (*fig.*) abashed, confused; *entrée interdite*, no admittance; *passage interdit*, no thoroughfare.—*n.m.* interdict.—*n.m.* (*fem.* **-e**) person interdicted.

intéressant [ɛ̃terɛ'sɑ̃], *a.* interesting; attractive (*price*).

intéressé [ɛ̃terɛ'se], *a.* interested; selfish.—*n.m.* (*fem.* **-ée**) interested party.

intéresser [ɛ̃tere'se], *v.t.* to interest; to concern, to affect. **s'intéresser,** *v.r.* to take an interest in, to be interested (*à*).

intérêt [ɛ̃te're], *n.m.* interest, concern; share.

interférence [ɛ̃tɛrfe'rɑ̃:s], *n.f.* interference; (*pl.*) (*Rad., Tel.*) interference.

interférer [ɛ̃tɛrfe're], *v.i.* (*conjug. like* CÉDER) to interfere.

intérieur [ɛ̃te'rjœːr], *a.* inner, inward, internal, interior; inland.—*n.m.* interior; home, private life; *à l'intérieur,* inside; *Ministre de l'Intérieur,* Home Secretary.

interlocuteur [ɛ̃tɛrlɔky'tœːr], *n.m.* (*fem.* **-trice**) speaker (*in a conversation*).

interloquer [ɛ̃tɛrlɔ'ke], *v.t.* to nonplus, to disconcert.

intermède [ɛ̃tɛr'mɛd], *n.m.* interlude.

intermédiaire [ɛ̃tɛrme'djɛːr], *a.* intermediate, intervening.—*n.m.* medium, agency; intermediary, middleman, agent.

interminable [ɛ̃tɛrmi'nabl], *a.* interminable, endless.

intermission [ɛ̃tɛrmi'sjɔ̃], *n.f.* intermission, pause.

intermittence [ɛ̃tɛrmi'tɑ̃:s], *n.f.* intermission, cessation.

intermittent [ɛ̃tɛrmi'tɑ̃], *a.* intermittent.

internat [ɛ̃tɛr'na], *n.m.* boarding-school; house-surgeonship (*of hospitals*).

international [ɛ̃tɛrnasjo'nal], *a.* (*m. pl.* **-aux**) international.

interne [ɛ̃'tɛrn], *a.* internal, inward, resident. —*n.* boarder (*in schools*).

interné [ɛ̃tɛr'ne], *a.* interned.—*n.m.* (*fem.* **-ée**) internee.

interner [ɛ̃tɛr'ne], *v.t.* to intern.

interpellation [ɛ̃tɛrpɛla'sjɔ̃], *n.f.* interpellation.

interpeller [ɛ̃tɛrpɛ'le], *v.t.* to hail, to call upon, to challenge; (*Polit.*) to interpellate.

interplanétaire [ɛ̃tɛrplane'tɛːr], *a.* interplanetary.

interpoler [ɛ̃tɛrpɔ'le], *v.t.* to interpolate.

interposer [ɛ̃tɛrpo'ze], *v.t.* to interpose. **s'interposer,** *v.r.* to interpose, to come between.

interprétation [ɛ̃tɛrpreta'sjɔ̃], *n.f.* interpretation; rendering (*of a play*).

interprète [ɛ̃tɛr'prɛt], *n.* interpreter, expounder; artist, actor, actress.

interpréter [ɛ̃tɛrpre'te], *v.t.* (*conjug. like* CÉDER) to interpret, to explain; to construe.

interrègne [ɛ̃tɛr'rɛɲ], *n.m.* interregnum.

interrogateur [ɛ̃tɛrɔga'tœːr], *n.m.* (*fem.* **-trice**) interrogator, questioner, examiner.

interrogatif [ɛ̃tɛrɔga'tif], *a.* (*fem.* **-tive**) interrogative.

interrogation [ɛ̃tɛrɔga'sjɔ̃], *n.f.* interrogation, question; *point d'interrogation,* question mark.

interrogatoire [ɛ̃tɛrɔga'twaːr], *n.m.* examination.

interroger [ɛ̃tɛrɔ'ʒe], *v.t.* (*conjug. like* MANGER) to interrogate, to question; to examine.

interrompre [ɛ̃tɛ'rɔ̃:pr], *v.t.* (*conjug. like* ROMPRE) to interrupt, to break off; to stop.

interrupteur [ɛ̃tɛryp'tœːr], *a.* and *n.m.* (*fem.* **-trice**) interrupting; interrupter.—*n.m.* (*Elec.*) switch, cut-out.

interruption [ɛ̃tɛryp'sjɔ̃], *n.f.* interruption; (*Elec.*) disconnection.

interscolaire [ɛ̃tɛrskɔ'lɛːr], *a.* inter-school (*competition etc.*).

intersection [ɛ̃tɛrsɛk'sjɔ̃], *n.f.* intersection.

interstice [ɛ̃tɛr'stis], *n.m.* interstice, chink, crack.

intervalle [ɛ̃tɛr'val], *n.m.* interval; distance, gap; *dans l'intervalle,* in the meantime.

intervenir [ɛ̃tɛrvə'niːr], *v.i. irr.* (*conjug. like* TENIR) to intervene, to interfere; to happen.

intervention [ɛ̃tɛrvɑ̃'sjɔ̃], *n.f.* intervention, interference.

interversion [ɛ̃tɛrvɛr'sjɔ̃], *n.f.* inversion.

intervertir [ɛ̃tɛrvɛr'tiːr], *v.t.* to invert, to reverse.

intestin [ɛ̃tɛs'tɛ̃], *a.* intestine; internal, domestic, civil.—*n.m.* intestine.

intimation [ɛ̃tima'sjɔ̃], *n.f.* notification.

intime [ɛ̃'tim], *a.* intimate, inmost secret; close.—*n.* intimate.

intimement [ɛ̃tim'mɑ̃], *adv.* intimately.

intimider [ɛ̃timi'de], *v.t.* to intimidate, to frighten.

intimité [ɛ̃timi'te], *n.f.* intimacy, closeness.

intitulé [ɛ̃tity'le], *a.* entitled.—*n.m.* title (*of deeds, books etc.*).

intituler [ɛ̃tity'le], *v.t.* to entitle, to call, to name. **s'intituler,** *v.r.* to entitle or call oneself.

intolérable [ɛ̃tɔle'rabl], *a.* intolerable, insufferable.

intolérablement [ɛ̃tɔlerablə'mɑ̃], *adv.* unbearably.

intolérance [ɛ̃tɔle'rɑ̃:s], *n.f.* intolerance.

intolérant [ɛ̃tɔle'rɑ̃], *a.* intolerant.

intonation [ɛ̃tɔna'sjɔ̃], *n.f.* intonation; pitch.

intoxicant [ɛ̃tɔksi'kɑ̃], *a.* poisonous.

intoxication [ɛ̃tɔksika'sjɔ̃], *n.f.* poisoning.

intoxiquer [ɛ̃tɔksi'ke], *v.t.* to poison.

intraduisible [ɛ̃tradɥi'zibl], *a.* untranslatable.

intraitable [ɛ̃trɛ'tabl], *a.* intractable, unmanageable.

intransigeant [ɛ̃trɑ̃zi'ʒɑ̃], *a.* intransigent, uncompromising.—*n.m.* (*fem.* **-e**) intransigent, diehard.

intransitif [ɛ̃trɑ̃zi'tif], *a.* (*fem.* **-tive**) (*Gram.*) intransitive.

intraversable [ɛ̃travɛr'sabl], *a.* impassable.

intrépide [ɛ̃tre'pid], *a.* intrepid, dauntless, fearless.

intrigant [ɛ̃tri'gɑ̃], *a.* intriguing.—*n.m.* (*fem.* **-e**) intriguer, schemer.

intrigue [ɛ̃'trig], *n.f.* intrigue; plot (*of a novel etc.*).

intrigueur [ɛ̃tri'gœːr], *n.m.* (*fem.* **-euse**) intriguer, plotter.

intrinsèque [ɛ̃trɛ̃'sɛk], *a.* intrinsic.

introduction [ɛ̃trodyk'sjɔ̃], *n.f.* introduction; preamble.

introductoire [ɛ̃trodyk'twaːr], *a.* introductory, preliminary.

introduire [ɛ̃tro'dɥiːr], *v.t. irr.* (*conjug. like* CONDUIRE) to show or bring in, to introduce. **s'introduire,** *v.r.* to get in, to find one's way in; to intrude.

introniser [ɛ̃trɔni'ze], *v.t.* to install, to enthrone; (*fig.*) to establish (*a fashion*).

introspectif [ɛ̃trɔspɛk'tif], *a.* (*fem.* **-tive**) introspective.

introuvable [ɛ̃tru'vabl], *a.* not to be found; matchless.

introverti [ɛ̃trovɛr'ti], *a.* introverted.—*n.m.* (*fem.* **-e**) introvert.

intrus [ɛ̃'try], *a.* intruding, intruded.—*n.m.* (*fem.* **-e**) intruder.

intrusion [ɛ̃try'zjɔ̃], *n.f.* intrusion.

intuitif [ɛ̃tɥi'tif], *a.* (*fem.* **-tive**) intuitive.

intuition [ɛ̃tɥi'sjɔ̃], *n.f.* intuition.

inusable [iny'zabl], *a.* durable, everlasting.

inusité [inyzi'te], *a.* unused; unusual; obsolete.

inutile [iny'til], *a.* useless, unnecessary.

inutilement [inytil'mã], *adv.* uselessly, to no purpose, needlessly.

inutilisable [inytili'zabl], *a.* that cannot be utilized, worthless.

inutilité [inytili'te], *n.f.* uselessness; useless thing.

invaincu [ɛ̃vɛ̃'ky], *a.* unvanquished, unconquered.

invalidation [ɛ̃valida'sjɔ̃], *n.f.* invalidation.

invalide [ɛ̃va'lid], *a.* disabled, crippled, infirm, invalid; (*Law*) not valid.—*n.* invalid, pensioner; *Hôtel des Invalides*, the Chelsea Hospital of France.

invalider [ɛ̃vali'de], *v.t.* to invalidate, to annul.

invariable [ɛ̃va'rjabl], *a.* invariable, unchangeable.

invariablement [ɛ̃varjablə'mã], *adv.* invariably.

invasion [ɛ̃va'zjɔ̃], *n.f.* invasion; inroad.

invective [ɛ̃vɛk'ti:v], *n.f.* invective, (*pl.*) abuse.

invectiver [ɛ̃vɛkti've], *v.t.* to abuse.—*v.i.* to inveigh against, to revile (**contre**).

inventaire [ɛ̃vã'tɛ:r], *n.m.* inventory; stocktaking.

inventer [ɛ̃vã'te], *v.t.* to invent, to devise; to find out; to imagine; to forge.

inventeur [ɛ̃vã'tœ:r], *n.m.* (*fem.* **-trice**) inventor.

inventif [ɛ̃vã'tif], *a.* (*fem.* **-tive**) inventive.

invention [ɛ̃vã'sjɔ̃], *n.f.* invention; inventiveness; device, trick; falsehood; *brevet d'invention*, patent.

inventorier [ɛ̃vãto'rje], *v.t.* to draw up an inventory of; to schedule, to catalogue.

inversable [ɛ̃vɛr'sabl], *a.* that cannot be upset.

inverse [ɛ̃'vɛrs], *a.* inverse, inverted.—*n.m.* reverse, contrary.

inversement [ɛ̃vɛrs'mã], *adv.* inversely.

invertébré [ɛ̃vɛrte'bre], *a.* and *n.m.* (*fem.* **-ée**) invertebrate.

inverti [ɛ̃vɛr'ti], *a.* inverted, reversed.

investigateur [ɛ̃vɛstiga'tœ:r], *a.* (*fem.* **-trice**) searching, inquiring.—*n.m.* (*fem.* **-trice**) investigator.

investigation [ɛ̃vɛstiga'sjɔ̃], *n.f.* investigation, inquiry.

investir [ɛ̃vɛs'ti:r], *v.t.* to invest; to surround, to lay siege to.

investiture [ɛ̃vɛsti'ty:r], *n.f.* investiture.

invétéré [ɛ̃vete're], *a.* inveterate.

invincibilité [ɛ̃vɛ̃sibili'te], *n.f.* invincibility.

invincible [ɛ̃vɛ̃'sibl], *a.* invincible, unconquerable.

inviolable [ɛ̃vjo'labl], *a.* inviolable.

inviolé [ɛ̃vjo'le], *a.* inviolate.

invisible [ɛ̃vi'zibl], *a.* invisible.

invisiblement [ɛ̃viziblə'mã], *adv.* invisibly.

invitation [ɛ̃vita'sjɔ̃], *n.f.* invitation.

invité [ɛ̃vi'te], *n.m.* (*fem.* **-ée**) guest.

inviter [ɛ̃vi'te], *v.t.* to invite, to request; to incite, to tempt.

invocation [ɛ̃voka'sjɔ̃], *n.f.* invocation.

involontaire [ɛ̃volɔ̃'tɛ:r], *a.* involuntary, unwilling.

involontairement [ɛ̃volɔ̃tɛr'mã], *adv.* involuntarily.

invoquer [ɛ̃vo'ke], *v.t.* to invoke, to call upon; to appeal to.

invraisemblable [ɛ̃vrɛsã'blabl], *a.* unlikely, improbable.

invraisemblablement [ɛ̃vrɛsãblablə'mã], *adv.* improbably.

invraisemblance [ɛ̃vrɛsã'blã:s], *n.f.* unlikelihood, improbability.

invulnérable [ɛ̃vylne'rabl], *a.* invulnerable.

iode [jod], *n.m.* iodine.

ion [jɔ̃], *n.m.* (*Phys.*) ion.

ionisation [jɔniza'sjɔ̃], *n.f.* ionization.

ionosphère [jɔnɔs'fɛ:r], *n.f.* ionosphere.

iota [jo'ta], *n.m.* iota, jot, tittle.

Irak [i'rak], *l'*, *m.* Iraq.

irakien [ira'kjɛ̃], *a.* (*fem.* **-enne**) Iraqi.—*n.m.* (**Irakien**, *fem.* **-enne**) Iraqi (*person*).

Iran [i'rã], *l'*, *m.* Iran.

iranien [ira'njɛ̃], *a.* (*fem.* **-enne**) Iranian.—*n.m.* (**Iranien**, *fem.* **-enne**) Iranian (*person*).

irascibilité [irasibili'te], *n.f.* irascibility.

irascible [ira'sibl], *a.* irascible, irritable.

iridescence [iridɛ'sã:s], *n.f.* iridescence.

iridescent [iridɛ'sã], *a.* iridescent.

iris [i'ris], *n.m. inv.* iris; rainbow.

irisé [iri'ze], *a.* rainbow-coloured, iridescent.

irlandais [irlã'dɛ], *a.* Irish.—*n.m.* Irish (*language*); (**Irlandais**, *fem.* **-aise**) Irishman, Irishwoman.

Irlande [ir'lãd], *l'*, *f.* Ireland.

ironie [iro'ni], *n.f.* irony, mockery, raillery.

ironique [iro'nik], *a.* ironical.

irradiation [irradja'sjɔ̃], *n.f.* irradiation.

irradier [irra'dje], *v.t.* to radiate through; (*C*) to broadcast.

irraisonnable [irrɛzo'nabl], *a.* irrational.

irraisonnablement [irrɛzonablə'mã], *adv.* irrationally.

irrationnel [irrasjo'nɛl], *a.* (*fem.* **-elle**) irrational.

irrationnellement [irrasjonɛl'mã], *adv.* irrationally.

irréalisable [irreali'zabl], *a.* impossible, impracticable.

irréconciliable [irrekõsi'ljabl], *a.* irreconcilable.

irrécusable [irreky'zabl], *a.* unexceptionable, unimpeachable.

irréductible [irredyk'tibl], *a.* irreducible; (*fig.*) unyielding.

irréel [irre'ɛl], *a.* (*fem.* **-éelle**) unreal.—*n.m.* unreality.

irréfléchi [irrefle'ʃi], *a.* thoughtless, inconsiderate.

irréflexion [irreflɛk'sjɔ̃], *n.f.* thoughtlessness, heedlessness.

irréfutable [irrefy'tabl], *a.* irrefutable.

irrégularité [irregylari'te], *n.f.* irregularity.

irrégulier [irregy'lje], *a.* (*fem.* **-ière**) irregular.

irrégulièrement [irregyljɛr'mã], *adv.* irregularly.

irréligieux [irreli'ʒjø], *a.* (*fem.* **-euse**) irreligious.

irrémédiable [irreme'djabl], *a.* irremediable, irreparable, irretrievable.

irrémédiablement [irremedjablə'mã], *adv.* irremediably, irreparably.

irrémissible [irremi'sibl], *a.* irremissible, unpardonable.

irremplaçable [irrãpla'sabl], *a.* irreplaceable.

irréparable [irrepa'rabl], *a.* irreparable.

irrépressible [irrepre'sibl], *a.* irrepressible.

irréprochable [irreprɔ'ʃabl], *a.* irreproachable.

irrésistible [irrezis'tibl], *a.* irresistible.

irrésistiblement [irrezistiblə'mã], *adv.* irresistibly.

irrésolu [irrezɔ'ly], *a.* irresolute, wavering.

irrésolument [irrezɔly'mã], *adv.* irresolutely.

irrésolution [irrezɔly'sjõ], *n.f.* irresolution, indecision.

irrespectueusement [irrɛspɛktɥøz'mã], *adv.* disrespectfully.

irrespectueux [irrɛspɛk'tɥø], *a.* (*fem.* **-euse**) disrespectful.

irresponsabilité [irrɛspõsabili'te], *n.f.* irresponsibility.

irresponsable [irrɛspõ'sabl], *a.* irresponsible.

irrétrécissable [irretresi'sabl], *a.* unshrinkable.

irrévérence [irreve'rã:s], *n.f.* irreverence, disrespect.

irrévocable [irrevɔ'kabl], *a.* irrevocable.

irrévocablement [irrevɔkablə'mã], *adv.* irrevocably.

irrigateur [irriga'tœ:r], *n.m.* wateringengine; garden-hose.

irrigation [irriga'sjõ], *n.f.* irrigation.

irriguer [irri'ge], *v.t.* to irrigate, to water.

irritabilité [irritabili'te], *n.f.* irritability.

irritable [irri'tabl], *a.* irritable.

irritant [irri'tã], *a.* irritating, provoking.

irritation [irrita'sjõ], *n.f.* irritation, exasperation.

riter [irri'te], *v.t.* to irritate, to incense, to anger; to provoke, to excite. **s'irriter**, *v.r.* to grow angry; to become irritated.

irruption [irryp'sjõ], *n.f.* irruption, raid; overflow, flood; *faire irruption dans,* to invade.

Isaïe [iza'i], *m.* Isaiah.

Islam [is'lam], *n.m.* Islam.

islandais [islã'dɛ], *a.* Icelandic.—*n.m.* Icelandic (*language*); (**Islandais**, *fem.* **-aise**) Icelander.

Islande [is'lãd], **l'**, *f.* Iceland.

isobare [izɔ'bar], *n.f.* isobar.

isocèle or **isoscèle** [izɔ'sɛl], *a.* (*Geom.*) isosceles.

isolant [izɔ'lã], *a.* insulating; *bouteille isolante,* vacuum flask.

isolateur [izɔla'tœ:r], *a.* (*fem.* **-trice**) insulating.—*n.m.* insulator.

isolation [izɔla'sjõ], *n.f.* insulation; isolation.

isolé [izɔ'le], *a.* isolated; lonely, solitary; detached; insulated; apart.

isolement [izɔl'mã], *n.m.* loneliness, isolation; insulation.

isolément [izɔle'mã], *adv.* separately.

isoler [izɔ'le], *v.t.* to isolate; to insulate; to detach; to separate.

isotope [izɔ'tɔp], *n.m.* isotope.

Israël [isra'ɛl], **l'**, *m.* Israel.

israélien [israe'ljɛ̃], *a.* (*fem.* **-enne**) Israel(i). —*n.m.* (**Israélien**, *fem.* **-enne**) Israeli (*person*).

issu [i'sy], *a.* born, descended, sprung from.

issue [i'sy], *n.f.* issue, outlet; escape; (*fig.*) end, event.

isthme [ism], *n.m.* isthmus.

Italie [ita'li], **l'**, *f.* Italy.

italien [ita'ljɛ̃], *a.* (*fem.* **-enne**) Italian.— *n.m.* Italian (*language*); (**Italien**, *fem.* **-enne**) Italian (*person*).

italique [ita'lik], *a.* and *n.m.* italic.

itinéraire [itine'rɛ:r], *a.* pertaining to roads etc.—*n.m.* itinerary, route; guide-book.

itinérant [itine'rã], *a.* itinerant.

ivoire [i'vwa:r], *n.m.* ivory; (*fig.*) whiteness; *la Côte d'Ivoire,* Ivory Coast.

ivraie [i'vrɛ], *n.f.* darnel, tare.

ivre [i:vr], *a.* drunk; intoxicated; (*fig.*) transported; *ivre mort,* dead-drunk.

ivresse [i'vrɛs], *n.f.* drunkenness, intoxication; (*fig.*) frenzy, rapture.

ivrogne [i'vrɔɲ], *a.* drunken.—*n.* drunkard.

ivrognerie [ivrɔ'ɲri], *n.f.* habitual drunkenness.

J

J, j [ʒi], *n.m.* the tenth letter of the alphabet.

jabot [ʒa'bo], *n.m.* crop (*of a bird*); frill (*of a shirt* or *blouse*); jabot.

jaboter [ʒabo'te], *v.i.* (*colloq.*) to prattle, to chatter.

jacasser [ʒaka'se], *v.i.* to chatter (*of the magpie*); (*fig.*) to chatter, to jabber.

jachère [ʒa'ʃɛːr], *n.f.* fallow.

jacinthe [ʒa'sɛ̃:t], *n.f.* jacinthe; hyacinth.

Jacques [ʒɑːk], *m.* James.

jade [ʒad], *n.m.* jade.

jadis [ʒa'dis], *adv.* of old, formerly.

jaguar [ʒa'gwaːr], *n.m.* jaguar.

jaillir [ʒa'jiːr], *v.i.* to spout, to gush; to shoot out or up.

jaillissant [ʒaji'sã], *a.* spouting, gushing.

jaillissement [ʒajis'mã], *n.m.* gushing, spouting, flashing.

jais [ʒɛ], *n.m.* jet.

jalon [ʒa'lõ], *n.m.* levelling-staff, surveyingstaff; (*fig.*) landmark, beacon.

jalonnement [ʒalon'mã], *n.m.* (*Land-surveying*) staking-out, marking-out.

jalonner [ʒalo'ne], *v.t.* to mark or stake out.—*v.i.* to place land marks etc.

jalousement [ʒaluz'mã], *adv.* jealously.

jalouser [ʒalu'ze], *v.t.* to be jealous of, to envy.

jalousie [ʒalu'zi], *n.f.* jealousy, envy; Venetian blind; (*Bot.*) sweet-william.

jaloux [ʒa'lu], *a.* (*fem.* **-ouse**) jealous; envious; desirous, anxious.—*n.m.* (*fem.* **-ouse**) jealous person.

jamaïquain [ʒamai'kɛ̃], a. Jamaican.—n.m.
(**Jamaïquain**, fem. **-aine**) Jamaican (person).
Jamaïque [ʒama'ik], **la**, f. Jamaica.
jamais [ʒa'mɛ], adv. (neg.) never, (affirm.)
ever; à jamais, for ever; jamais de la
vie, not on your life!; mieux vaut tard
que jamais, better late than never.
jambage [ʒɑ̃'baːʒ], n.m. jamb (of a door etc.);
down-stroke, pot-hook (in writing).
jambe [ʒɑ̃ːb], n.f. leg; shank; courir à
toutes jambes, to run as fast as one can;
prendre ses jambes à son cou, to take to
one's heels.
jambière [ʒɑ̃'bjɛːr], n.f. legging, leg-guard.
jambon [ʒɑ̃'bɔ̃], n.m. ham.
jamboree [ʒɑ̃bo'ri], n.m. jamboree.
jante [ʒɑ̃ːt], n.f. felloe, rim (of a wheel).
janvier [ʒɑ̃'vje], n.m. January.
Japon [ʒa'pɔ̃], **le**, m. Japan.
japonais [ʒapo'nɛ], a. Japanese.—n.m.
Japanese (language); (**Japonais**, fem. **-aise**)
Japanese (person).
japper [ʒa'pe], v.i. to yelp, to yap.
jaquette [ʒa'kɛt], n.f. morning coat, tail-
coat; woman's jacket; dust-cover (of book).
jardin [ʒar'dɛ̃], n.m. garden.
jardinage [ʒardi'naːʒ], n.m. gardening;
garden-produce.
jardiner [ʒardi'ne], v.i. to garden.
jardinier [ʒardi'nje], a. (fem. **-ière**) (of the)
garden.—n.m. (fem. **-ière**) gardener.—n.f.
(**-ière**) flower-stand, jardinière.
jardiniste [ʒardi'nist], n. landscape-
gardener.
jargon [ʒar'gɔ̃], n.m. jargon, gibberish; lingo.
jarre [ʒaːr], n.f. jar.
jarret [ʒa'rɛ], n.m. ham (of man); hough,
hock (of horse).
jarretière [ʒar'tjɛr], n.f. garter.
jars (1) [ʒaːr], n.m. gander.
jars (2) [ʒaːr], n.m. (another form of **jargon**)
slang.
jaser [ʒa'ze], v.i. to chatter, to gossip.
jaserie [ʒaz'ri], n.f. chatter; gossip.
jaseur [ʒa'zœːr], a. (fem. **-euse**) talkative.—
n.m. (fem. **-euse**) chatterer, chatterbox.
jasmin [ʒas'mɛ̃], n.m. jasmine.
jaspe [ʒasp], n.m. jasper.
jasper [ʒas'pe], v.t. to marble, to vein, to
variegate.
jaspure [ʒas'pyːr], n.f. marbling, veining.
jatte [ʒat], n.f. bowl, platter; dog's bowl.
jauge [ʒoːʒ], n.f. gauge; (Naut.) tonnage.
jaugeage [ʒo'ʒaːʒ], n.m. gauging.
jauger [ʒo'ʒe], v.t. (conjug. like MANGER) to
gauge, to measure the capacity of; (Naut.)
to draw (so many feet of water).
jaunâtre [ʒo'naːtr], a. yellowish.
jaune [ʒoːn], a. yellow; rire jaune, to give a
sickly smile.—n.m. yellow; jaune d'œuf,
egg-yolk.
jaunir [ʒo'niːr], v.t. to make yellow, to dye
yellow.—v.i. to grow yellow, to turn yellow.
jaunissant [ʒoni'sɑ̃], a. turning yellow,
yellowing; ripening.
jaunisse [ʒo'nis], n.f. jaundice.
javanais [ʒava'nɛ], a. Javanese.—n.m.
(**Javanais**, fem. **-aise**) Javanese (person).
javeau [ʒa'vo], n.m. (pl. **-eaux**) sandbank.
javeline [ʒa'vlin], n.f. javelin.
javelle [ʒa'vɛl], n.f. swathe, loose sheaf.
javelot [ʒa'vlo], n.m. javelin.

jazz [(d)ʒaːz], n.m. jazz.
je [ʒə], (**j'**, before a vowel sound), pron. I.
Jean [ʒɑ̃], m. John [JEANNOT].
Jeanne [ʒa(ː)n], f. Joan, Jane, Jean.
Jeannot [ʒa'no], m. Johnny, Jock.
jeep [(d)ʒip], n.f. jeep.
jésuite [ʒe'zɥit], a. Jesuit.—n.m. (**Jésuite**)
Jesuit.
Jésus [ʒe'zy], m. Jesus.
jet [ʒɛ], n.m. casting, cast, throw; jet, gush,
spurt (of water); sudden ray (of light);
casting (of metal); shoot, sprout (of plants);
spout (of pump etc.); new swarm (of bees);
arme de jet, missile weapon.
jetée [ʒə'te], n.f. jetty, pier; breakwater.
jeter [ʒə'te], v.t. (conjug. like APPELER) to
throw, to fling, to hurl; to throw up; to
throw down, to knock down; to throw out;
to mould; to shoot out; to send forth; to
empty; to discharge. se jeter, v.r. to throw
oneself, to fling oneself; to fall upon (attack);
to flow (of rivers etc.).
jeton [ʒə'tɔ̃], n.m. token, counter; voucher.
jeu [ʒø], n.m. (pl. **jeux**) play, sport; game;
fun; gambling; (fig.) stake; manner of
playing; performance (of players); (Mach.)
working; clearance; play.
jeudi [ʒø'di], n.m. Thursday.
jeun (à) [a'ʒœ̃], adv. fasting, sober, on an
empty stomach.
jeune [ʒœn], a. youthful, young; junior; new;
early, unripe, green.—n. young person or
animal.
jeûne [ʒøːn], n.m. fasting; fast, abstinence.
jeûner [ʒø'ne], v.i. to fast.
jeunesse [ʒœ'nɛs], n.f. youth, young days;
youthfulness; freshness; prime; young
people.
jeunet [ʒœ'nɛ], a. (fem. **-ette**) (colloq.) very
young.
jiu-jitsu [(d)ʒyʒi'tsy], n.m. ju-jitsu.
joaillerie [ʒwaj'ri], n.f. jeweller's trade or
business; jewellery, jewels.
joaillier [ʒwa'je], n.m. (fem. **-ière**) jeweller.
jobard [ʒo'baːr], n.m. (colloq.) sucker, mug,
fool.
jockey [ʒo'kɛ], n.m. jockey.
jocrisse [ʒo'kris], n.m. dolt, simpleton.
joie [ʒwa], n.f. joy, happiness, joyfulness,
gladness; glee, mirth.
joignant [ʒwa'nɑ̃], a. and prep. next to,
adjoining.
joindre [ʒwɛ̃:dr], v.t. irr. (conjug. like
CRAINDRE) to join, to put together, to unite,
to combine; to add; to meet; to overtake.—
v.i. to join, to meet. se joindre, v.r. to join,
to be joined, to be united; to be adjoining,
to be adjacent; to be added.
joint [ʒwɛ̃], a. joined, united; added.—n.m.
joint; seam, junction.
jointé [ʒwɛ̃'te], a. jointed.
jointure [ʒwɛ̃'tyːr], n.f. joint, jointing, articulation.
joli [ʒo'li], a. pretty, pleasing, neat; fine; nice.
—n.m. what is pretty; le joli de la chose
c'est que . . . , the best of the thing is
that . . . .
joliment [ʒoli'mɑ̃], adv. prettily; (iron.)
nicely, finely; (colloq.) awfully, jolly, much,
very.
jonc [ʒɔ̃], n.m. (Bot.) rush; cane, Malacca
cane; keeper, guard (ring).

jonchée [ʒɔ̃'ʃe], *n.f.* strewing (*of flowers*).

joncher [ʒɔ̃'ʃe], *v.t.* to strew; to heap; to scatter.

jonction [ʒɔ̃k'sjɔ̃], *n.f.* junction, joining.

jongler [ʒɔ̃'gle], *v.i.* to juggle.

jonglerie [ʒɔ̃glə'ri], *n.f.* juggling.

jongleur [ʒɔ̃'glœːr], *n.m.* juggler; (*fig.*) trickster.

jonque [ʒɔ̃:k], *n.f.* junk (*Chinese vessel*).

jonquille [ʒɔ̃'ki:j], *n.f.* jonquil.—*a. inv.* and *n.m.* pale yellow, jonquil (*colour*).

Jordanie [ʒɔrda'ni], **la,** *f.* Jordan.

jordanien [ʒɔrda'njɛ̃], *a.* Jordanian.—*n.m.* (**Jordanien,** *fem.* **-enne**) Jordanian (*person*).

Joseph [ʒɔ'zef], *m.* Joseph.

jouable [ʒwabl], *a.* playable.

joue [ʒu], *n.f.* cheek; **coucher** or **mettre en joue,** to take aim at.

jouer [ʒwe], *v.t.* to play; to stake; to gamble away; to move (*a piece*); to perform, to act; to pretend to be, to imitate; to ridicule; to deceive.—*v.i.* to play, to amuse oneself; to gambol, to frolic; to gamble, to run the risk; to speculate (*on the funds*); to work, to work loose (*of machinery etc.*); to act, to perform. **se jouer,** *v.r.* to sport, to play; to make game (*of*); to make light of.

jouet [ʒwe], *n.m.* plaything, toy; laughing-stock, jest, sport.

joueur [ʒwœːr], *n.m.* (*fem.* **-euse**) player; gambler; speculator; performer (*on an instrument*).

joufflu [ʒu'fly], *a.* chubby, chubby-cheeked.

joug [ʒu(g)], *n.m.* yoke; bondage, slavery.

jouir [ʒwiːr], *v.i.* to enjoy, to revel; to be in possession (**de**).

jouissance [ʒwi'sɑ̃:s], *n.f.* enjoyment; possession, use; delight; interest payable.

jouissant [ʒwi'sɑ̃], *a.* enjoying, in possession (**de**).

joujou [ʒu'ʒu], *n.m.* (*pl.* **-oux**) plaything, toy.

jour [ʒuːr], *n.m.* day, daylight; light; day-break; day-time; opening, gap; **broderie à jours,** open-work embroidery; **donner le jour à,** to give birth to; **plat du jour,** today's special; **se faire jour,** to force one's way through; **un jour de fête,** a holiday.

Jourdain [ʒur'dɛ̃], **le,** *m.* Jordan (*river*).

journal [ʒur'nal], *n.m.* (*pl.* **-aux**) journal, diary; newspaper; (*Comm.*) day-book.

journalier [ʒurna'lje], *a.* (*fem.* **-ière**) daily, diurnal.—*n.m.* journeyman, day-labourer.

journalisme [ʒurna'lism], *n.m.* journalism.

journaliste [ʒurna'list], *n.* journalist.

journée [ʒur'ne], *n.f.* day (time), day's work or wages; day's journey; battle; historic day; **toute la journée,** all day (long).

journellement [ʒurnɛl'mɑ̃], *adv.* daily, every day.

joute [ʒut], *n.f.* joust, tilting-match; contest; (*C*) game.

jouter [ʒu'te], *v.i.* to joust, to tilt.

jouteur [ʒu'tœːr], *n.m.* tilter; (*fig.*) antagonist, adversary.

jovial [ʒɔ'vjal], *a.* (*m. pl.* **-aux**) jovial, jolly, merry.

jovialement [ʒɔvjal'mɑ̃], *adv.* jovially.

jovialité [ʒɔvjali'te], *n.f.* joviality, jollity.

joyau [ʒwa'jo], *n.m.* (*pl.* **-aux**) jewel.

joyeusement [ʒwajøz'mɑ̃], *adv.* cheerfully, joyfully.

joyeuseté [ʒwajøz'te], *n.f.* (*fam.*) joke, jest.

joyeux [ʒwa'jø], *a.* (*fem.* **-euse**) joyful, merry; cheerful.

jubilaire [ʒybi'lɛːr], *a.* jubilee; (*fig.*) of fifty years' standing (*of persons etc.*).

jubilant [ʒybi'lɑ̃], *a.* jubilant, delighted.

jubilation [ʒybila'sjɔ̃], *n.f.* jubilation, rejoicing.

jubilé [ʒybi'le], *n.m.* jubilee; (*fig.*) golden wedding.

jubiler [ʒybi'le], *v.i.* to jubilate, to exult.

jucher [ʒy'ʃe] *v.i.* to roost, to perch; to lodge (*at the top of a house etc.*). **se jucher,** *v.r.* to go to roost; to perch (*oneself*).

juchoir [ʒy'ʃwaːr], *n.m.* roosting-place, perch.

judaïque [ʒyda'ik], *a.* Judaical, Jewish.

judaïsme [ʒyda'ism], *n.m.* Judaism.

judas [ʒy'dɑ], *n.m.* Judas, traitor; peep-hole (*in a door etc.*).

Judée [ʒy'de], **la,** *f.* Judaea.

judicature [ʒydika'tyːr], *n.f.* judicature, magistracy.

judiciaire [ʒydi'sjɛːr], *a.* judiciary, judicial; legal.

judiciairement [ʒydisjɛr'mɑ̃], *adv.* judicially, by authority of justice.

judicieusement [ʒydisjøz'mɑ̃], *adv.* judiciously, discreetly.

judicieux [ʒydi'sjø], *a.* (*fem.* **-euse**) judicious, wise, discreet.

juge [ʒy:ʒ], *n.m.* judge; magistrate, justice; (*pl.*) bench.

jugé [ʒy'ʒe], *a.* judged.—*n.m. au jugé,* at a guess.

jugement [ʒyʒ'mɑ̃], *n.m.* judgment; opinion; trial; sentence; good sense; **jugement arbitral,** award; **jugement provisoire,** decree nisi; **jugement définitif,** decree absolute.

juger [ʒy'ʒe], *v.t.* (*conjug. like* MANGER) to judge; to try; to pass sentence on; to consider, to think.—*v.i.* to judge (**de**), to give judgment, to deem. **se juger,** *v.r.* to judge oneself; to deem oneself; to be judged.

jugulaire [ʒygy'lɛːr], *a.* (*Anat.*) jugular.—*n.f.* jugular vein; chin-strap.

juguler [ʒygy'le] *v.t.* to strangle; (*fig.*) to torment; to fleece.

juif [ʒɥif], *a.* (*fem.* **juive**) Jewish.—*n.m.* (**Juif,** *fem.* **Juive**) Jew, Jewess.

juillet [ʒɥi'jɛ], *n.m.* July.

juin [ʒɥɛ̃], *n.m.* June.

juiverie [ʒɥi'vri], *n.f.* Jewry (*Jews' quarter*).

jujube [ʒy'ʒyb]. *n.f.* jujube (*fruit*).—*n.m.* or **pâte de jujube,** jujube (*lozenge*).

julep [ʒy'lɛp], *n.m.* julep.

julienne [ʒy'ljɛn], *n.f.* julienne (*vegetable soup*).

jumeau [ʒy'mo], *a.* (*fem.* **-elle,** *m. pl.* **-eaux**) twin; double (*of fruit etc.*).—*n.m.* twin (brother).

jumelage [ʒym'la:ʒ], *n.m.* twinning (*of towns etc.*).

jumelé [ʒym'le], *a.* twin, in couples; **maison jumelée,** semi-detached house; (*horse-racing*) **pari jumelé,** each-way bet.

jumelle [ʒy'mɛl], *n.f.* twin (sister); (*pl.*) binoculars; **jumelles de campagne,** field-glasses; **jumelles de théâtre,** opera-glasses; **jumelles de manchettes,** cuff-links.

jument [ʒy'mɑ̃], *n.f.* mare.

jungle [ʒɔ̃:gl], *n.f.* jungle.

jupe [ʒyp], *n.f.* skirt.

Jupiter [ʒypi'tɛr], *m.* Jupiter, Jove.

jupon [ʒy'pɔ̃], *n.m.* petticoat.

juré [ʒy're], *a.* sworn.—*n.m.* juror, juryman.

jurement [ʒyr'mɑ̃], *n.m.* oath; swearing.

jurer [ʒy're], *v.t.* to swear by; to swear, to vow, to take an oath that; to blaspheme.—*v.i.* to swear, to take an oath; to blaspheme; (*fig.*) to contrast, to jar, to clash (*of colours etc.*).

juridiction [ʒyridik'sjɔ̃], *n.f.* jurisdiction; department, province.

juridique [ʒyri'dik], *a.* juridical, judicial, legal.

juridiquement [ʒyridik'mɑ̃], *adv.* juridically, judicially.

jurisprudence [ʒyrispry'dɑ̃:s], *n.f.* jurisprudence.

juriste [ʒy'rist], *n.m.* jurist.

juron [ʒy'rɔ̃], *n.m.* oath, curse, swear-word.

jury [ʒy'ri], *n.m.* jury; board, committee.

jus [ʒy], *n.m.* juice; gravy.

jusque or *jusques** [ʒysk], *prep.* even to, as far as; till, until; down to; up to.

juste [ʒyst], *a.* just, equitable; fair, legitimate, lawful; proper, fit; exact; well-fitting; tight; *au plus juste prix*, at the lowest price; *un homme juste*, a righteous man.—*n.m.* upright man, virtuous man; what is just.—*adv.* just, exactly, precisely; (*Mus.*) true.

justement [ʒystə'mɑ̃], *adv.* justly, precisely; justifiably.

justesse [ʒys'tɛs], *n.f.* justness, exactness, precision, accuracy; appropriateness.

justice [ʒys'tis], *n.f.* justice; righteousness, probity; fairness, impartiality; reason; courts of justice, judges; *palais de justice*, law-court.

justifiable [ʒysti'fjabl], *a.* justifiable; warrantable.

justification [ʒystifika'sjɔ̃], *n.f.* justification, vindication, proof.

justifier [ʒysti'fje], *v.t.* to justify, to vindicate, to make good. **se justifier**, *v.r.* to justify, clear *or* vindicate oneself.

jute [ʒyt], *n.m.* jute.

juteux [ʒy'tø], *a.* (*fem.* **-euse**) juicy.

juvénile [ʒyve'nil], *a.* juvenile, youthful.

juvénilement [ʒyvenil'mɑ̃], *adv.* boyishly, in a juvenile manner.

juxtaposer [ʒykstapo'ze], *v.t.* to place side by side. **se juxtaposer**, *v.r.* to be in juxtaposition.

juxtaposition [ʒykstapozi'sjɔ̃], *n.f.* juxtaposition.

K

K, k [kɑ], *n.m.* the eleventh letter of the alphabet; *Échelle K* (*viz. Kelvin*), absolute scale (*of temperature*).

kakatoès [kakato'ɛs], [CACATOIS].

kaki [ka'ki], *a. inv.* khaki (*colour*).

kaléidoscope [kaleidɔs'kɔp], *n.m.* kaleidoscope.

kangourou [kɑ̃gu'ru], *n.m.* kangaroo.

kaolin [kao'lɛ̃], *n.m.* kaolin, porcelain clay, china-clay.

kapok or **kapoc** [ka'pɔk], *n.m.* kapok.

kascher or **kacher** [ka'ʃɛr], **kachir** [ka'ʃir], *a.* (*Jew. Relig.*) kosher.

kayac [ka'jak], *n.m.* kayak.

Kénia [ke'nja], **le**, *m.* Kenya.

képi [ke'pi], *n.m.* kepi, military cap; peak cap.

kermesse [kɛr'mɛs], *n.f.* kermis (*in the Netherlands*); kermesse; village fair.

kérosène [kero'zɛ:n], *n.m.* kerosene paraffin-oil.

kidnapper [kidna'pe], *v.t.* to kidnap.

kilo [ki'lo], *n.m.* (*abbr.*) kilogramme.

kilocycle [kilo'sikl], *n.m.* kilocycle.

kilogramme [kilo'gram], *n.m.* kilogramme (*2·2 lb. avoirdupois*).

kilomètre [kilo'mɛtr], *n.m.* kilometre (*1093·6 yards*).

kilowatt [kilo'wat], *n.m.* kilowatt.

kimono [kimo'no], *n.m.* kimono.

kiosque [kjɔsk], *n.m.* kiosk; (*Naut.*) house; *kiosque à journaux*, newspaper kiosk; *kiosque à musique*, bandstand.

klakson or **klaxon** [klak'sɔ̃], *n.m.* klaxon, hooter, horn.

kleptomane [klɛpto'man], *a.* and *n.* kleptomaniac.

kleptomanie [klɛptoma'ni], *n.f.* kleptomania.

kola or **cola** [kɔ'la], *n.m.* kola.

Kominform [kɔmɛ̃'form], *n.m.* Cominform.

Komintern [kɔmɛ̃'tɛrn], *n.m.* Comintern.

Koweit [kɔ'weit], **le**, *m.* Kuwait.

kyrielle [ki'rjɛl], *n.f.* litany; (*fig.*) long string (*of words etc.*), long tedious story.

kyste [kist], *n.m.* (*Path.*) cyst.

L

L 1 [ɛl], *n.m.* or *f.* the twelfth letter of the alphabet.

l', *art.* and *pron.* (*by elision of* **le** *or* **la**) the; him, her, it.

la (1) [la], *art.* and *pron. f.* the; her, it.

la (2) [la], *n.m.* (*Mus.*) la; the note A.

là [la], *adv.* and *int.* there, thither; then (*of time*); *çà et là*, here and there; *là là*, now now! there! there now! *là où*, where; *par là*, that way.

là-bas [la'ba], *adv.* there, over there.

labbe [lab], *n.m.* (*Orn.*) skua.

label [la'bɛl], *n.m.* (*Ind.*) label; brand, mark.

labeur [la'bœ:r], *n.m.* labour, work, toil.

laboratoire [labora'twa:r], *n.m.* laboratory.

laborieusement [labɔrjøz'mɑ̃], *adv.* laboriously; painfully.

laborieux [labɔ'rjø], *a.* (*fem.* **-euse**) laborious, hard-working.

labour [la'bu:r], *n.m.* ploughing, tillage; arable land.

labourable [labu'rabl], *a.* arable.

labourage [labu'ra:ʒ], *n.m.* tillage, ploughing; dressing.

labourer [labu're], *v.t.* to plough, to till; to dig, to turn up; to dress; to toil through.

laboureur [labu'rœːr], *n.m.* husbandman, ploughman.

laboureuse [labu'røːz], *n.f.* tractor plough.

laburne [la'byrn], *n.m.* laburnum.

labyrinthe [labi'rɛ̃ːt], *n.m.* labyrinth, maze.

lac [lak], *n.m.* lake.

laçage [la'saːʒ], *n.m.* lacing.

lacer [la'se], *v.t.* (*conjug. like* COMMENCER) to lace.

lacération [lasera'sjõ], *n.f.* laceration.

lacérer [lase're], *v.t.* (*conjug. like* CÉDER) to lacerate, to tear.

lacet [la'sɛ], *n.m.* lace, shoe-lace; noose; bow-string (*for strangling*); winding, hairpin bend (*of road etc.*); (*pl.*) toils.

lâche [lɑːʃ], *a.* loose, slack; faint-hearted, cowardly; base, mean, shameful.—*n.* coward, craven; dastard.—*adv.* loosely.

lâché [lɑ'ʃe], *a.* slovenly, slipshod.

lâchement [laʃ'mɑ̃], *adv.* in a dastardly *or* cowardly manner; loosely; shamefully.

lâcher [lɑ'ʃe], *v.t.* to loosen, to slacken; to let go, to release; to unbind; to blurt out; to let fly, to discharge; to let down (*someone*).—*v.i.* to slacken, to become loose; to slip; (*Spt.*) to give up.

lâcheté [laʃ'te], *n.f.* cowardice; baseness, meanness.

lacis [la'si], *n.m.* network.

laconique [lakɔ'nik], *a.* laconic.

laconiquement [lakɔnik'mɑ̃], *adv.* laconically.

lacs [la], *n.m. inv.* string; noose; trap; *lacs d'amour*, love-knot.

lacté [lak'te], *a.* lacteous, milky; *la voie lactée*, the Milky Way.

lacune [la'kyn], *n.f.* gap, break, hiatus, blank.

là-dedans [lada'dɑ̃], *adv.* in there.

là-dehors [lada'ɔːr], *adv.* outside.

là-dessous [la'tsu], *adv.* under there.

là-dessus [la'tsy], *adv.* on that; thereupon.

ladite [la'dit], [LEDIT].

ladre [lɑːdr], *a.* leprous; (*fig.*) mean, sordid, stingy; unfeeling.—*n.m.* (*fem.* **-esse**) leper; (*fig.*) sordid person.

ladrerie [lɑdrə'ri], *n.f.* sordid avarice, stinginess.

lagune [la'gyn], *n.f.* lagoon.

là-haut [la'o], *adv.* up there; upstairs.

lai [lɛ], *n.m.* lay (*poem, song*).

laïc [LAÏQUE].

laid [lɛ], *a.* ugly, unsightly; unseemly, unbecoming.—*n.m.* ugliness; (*fem.* **-e**) ugly person, creature etc.; naughty boy *or* girl.

laidement [lɛd'mɑ̃], *adv.* in an ugly way.

laideron [lɛd'rõ], *n.m.* (*fem.* **-onne**) ugly creature.

laideur [lɛ'dœːr], *n.f.* ugliness, uncomeliness; unseemliness.

laie [lɛ], *n.f.* path (*in a forest*).

lainage [lɛ'naːʒ], *n.m.* woollens, woollen goods.

laine [lɛn], *n.f.* wool; *laine filée*, yarn; *laine peignée*, worsted; *tapis de haute laine*, thick-pile carpet; *tout laine*, pure wool.

lainerie [lɛn'ri], *n.f.* woollen goods, woollens; wool trade, shop etc.

laineux [lɛ'nø], *a.* (*fem.* **-euse**) woolly, fleecy.

lainier [lɛ'nje], *a.* (*fem.* **-ière**) of wool, woollen.—*n.m.* (*fem.* **-ière**) wool-merchant; wool-worker.

laïque *or* **laïc** [la'ik], *a.* lay, secular.—*n.* layman, lay person.

laisse [lɛːs], *n.f.* string, leash, lead.

laisser [lɛ'se], *v.t.* to leave, to quit; to leave behind, to part with; to bequeath; to permit, to let, to allow; to let alone; to leave off; to give up. **se laisser**, *v.r.* to allow oneself, to let oneself.

laisser-aller [lɛsea'le], *n.m.* unconstraint, negligence; slovenliness; indolence.

laisser-faire [lɛse'fɛːr], *n.m.* non-interference.

laissez-passer [lɛsepa'se], *n.m. inv.* permit, leave, pass.

lait [lɛ], *n.m.* milk; *au lait*, with milk; *lait de chaux*, whitewash; *lait de poule*, egg-flip; *petit-lait* *or* *lait clair*, whey.

laitage [lɛ'taːʒ], *n.m.* milk puddings; milk products.

laiterie [lɛ'tri], *n.f.* dairy, dairy-farm.

laiteux [lɛ'tø], *a.* (*fem.* **-euse**) lacteous, milky.

laitier [lɛ'tje], *a.* (*fem.* **-ière**) pertaining to milk; having milk, milch (*of cows*).—*n.m.* (*fem.-ière*) milkman; milkmaid, dairy-maid.—*n.f.* (*-ière*) milch cow; milk-lorry *or* -cart.

laiton [lɛ'tõ], *n.m.* brass, latten.

laitue [lɛ'ty], *n.f.* lettuce.

lama [la'ma], *n.m.* lama (*priest*); llama.

lambeau [lɑ̃'bo], *n.m.* (*pl.* **-eaux**) shred; rag; fragment, scrap.

lambin [lɑ̃'bɛ̃], *a.* slow, dawdling.—*n.m.* (*fem.* **-e**) dawdler, slowcoach.

lambiner [lɑ̃bi'ne], *v.i.* to dawdle, to dilly-dally.

lambrequin [lɑ̃brə'kɛ̃], *n.m.* valance, cut-out, pelmet.

lambris [lɑ̃'bri], *n.m.* panelling; wainscot; ceiling; (*fig.*) mansion, palace; canopy.

lambrissage [lɑ̃bri'saːʒ], *n.m.* wainscoting, panelling.

lambrisser [lɑ̃bri'se], *v.t.* to panel, to wainscot.

lame [lam], *n.f.* thin plate, leaf of metal; foil; knife (*of mower etc.*), blade; (*fig.*) sword; wave, billow.

lamé [la'me], *a.* spangled with gold *or* silver.

lamentable [lamɑ̃'tabl], *a.* lamentable, sad, distressing; pitiful.

lamentablement [lamɑ̃tablə'mɑ̃], *adv.* woefully.

lamentation [lamɑ̃ta'sjõ], *n.f.* lamentation, wailing; lament; whining.

lamenter (se) [sǝlamɑ̃'te], *v.r.* to lament, to bewail.

laminage [lami'naːʒ], *n.m.* laminating; rolling (*of gold etc.*).

laminer [lami'ne], *v.t.* to laminate, to roll.

laminoir [lami'nwaːr], *n.m.* flattening-mill; rolling-mill.

lampe [lɑ̃ːp], *n.f.* lamp; (*Rad. Tel.*) valve; *lampe de bord*, (*Motor.*) dashboard light; *lampe de poche*, electric torch.

lampion [lɑ̃'pjõ], *n.m.* illumination-lamp, fairy-light; Chinese lantern; (*slang*) cocked hat.

lampiste [lɑ̃'pist], *n.m.* lamp-maker; lamplighter.

lampisterie [lɑ̃pis'tri], *n.f.* lamp-room.

lamproie [lɑ̃'prwa], *n.f.* lamprey.

lance [lɑ̃ːs], *n.f.* lance, spear; staff, flagstaff; nozzle (*of a fire-hose*).

199

lance-flammes

lance-flammes [lɑ̃s'flam], *n.m.* *inv.* flame-thrower.

lancement [lɑ̃s'mɑ̃], *n.m.* throwing, darting; launching, launch.

lance-pierres [lɑ̃s'pjɛːr], *n.m.* *inv.* catapult.

lancer [lɑ̃'se], *v.t.* (*conjug. like* COMMENCER) to fling, to hurl, to throw; to launch; to shoot forth, to dart; to issue (*a warrant etc.*). **se lancer**, *v.r.* to dart, to spring; to rush, to fly; to launch out; (*fig.*) to make a start.

lancette [lɑ̃'sɛt], *n.f.* lancet.

lancier [lɑ̃'sje], *n.m.* lancer.

lancinant [lɑ̃si'nɑ̃], *a.* shooting (*of pains*).

lande [lɑ̃ːd], *n.f.* waste land, moor, heath.

langage [lɑ̃'gaːʒ], *n.m.* language; speech, diction.

lange [lɑ̃ːʒ], *n.m.* napkin; swaddling-cloth; (*pl.*) swaddling-clothes.

langoureusement [lɑ̃gurøz'mɑ̃], *adv.* languishingly, languidly.

langoureux [lɑ̃gu'rø], *a.* (*fem.* **-euse**) languishing, languid.

langouste [lɑ̃'gust], *n.f.* spiny lobster.

langoustine [lɑ̃gus'tin], *n.f.* large Brittany prawn; Dublin Bay prawn.

langue [lɑ̃ːg], *n.f.* tongue; language; strip (*of land*); **avoir la langue bien pendue** or **bien affilée**, to have the gift of the gab; **avoir la langue liée**, to be tongue-tied.

languette [lɑ̃'gɛt], *n.f.* small tongue; tongue-like strip; partition; tongue (*of instruments*); index (*of a balance*); tongue (*of shoe*).

langueur [lɑ̃'gœːr], *n.f.* apathy, languor; weakness, weariness; debility.

languir [lɑ̃'giːr], *v.i.* to languish, to pine away, to droop; to linger; to flag.

languissant [lɑ̃gi'sɑ̃], *a.* languid, languishing, pining; (*Comm.*) dull, inactive.

lanière [la'njɛːr], *n.f.* thong, lash.

lanoline [lano'lin], *n.f.* lanoline.

lanterne [lɑ̃'tɛrn], *n.f.* lantern; street-lamp; (*Arch.*) skylight; dawdler; **lanterne vénitienne**, Chinese lantern.

lanterner [lɑ̃tɛr'ne], *v.i.* to dawdle, to trifle away one's time.

Laos [laos], **le**, *m.* Laos.

laotien [lao'sjɛ̃], *a.* (*fem.* **-enne**) Laotian.—*n.m.* (**Laotien**, *fem.* **-enne**) Laotian (*person*).

lapement [lap'mɑ̃], *n.m.* lapping.

laper [la'pe], *v.t.*, *v.i.* to lap (up).

lapidaire [lapi'dɛːr], *a.* and *n.m.* lapidary.

lapidation [lapida'sjɔ̃], *n.f.* lapidation, stoning.

lapider [lapi'de], *v.t.* to lapidate, to stone to death; (*fig.*) to pelt, to abuse.

lapin [la'pɛ̃], *n.m.* rabbit.

lapis [la'piːs], **lapis lazuli** [lapislazy'li], *n.m. inv.* lapis lazuli.

lapon [la'pɔ̃], *a.* (*fem.* **-onne**) Lapp.—*n.m.* Lappish (*language*); (**Lapon**, *fem.* **-onne**) Laplander.

Laponie [lapo'ni], **la**, *f.* Lapland.

laps (1) [laps], *n.m.* lapse (*of time*).

laps (2) [laps], *a.* *lapsed, fallen into heresy.

lapsus [lap'syːs], *n.m. inv.* slip, mistake.

laquais [la'kɛ], *n.m. inv.* lackey, footman.

laque [lak], *n.f.* lacquer, lac, lake (*paint*).—*n.m.* lacquer.

laquelle [la'kɛl], [LEQUEL].

laquer [la'ke], *v.t.* to lacquer, to japan.

larcin [lar'sɛ̃], *n.m.* larceny, pilfering; petty theft; **larcin littéraire**, plagiarism.

lard [laːr], *n.m.* fat (*esp. of pigs*); bacon; **flèche de lard**, flitch of bacon; **tranche de lard**, rasher of bacon.

larder [lar'de], *v.t.* to lard; to pink, to run through, to pierce.

lardon [lar'dɔ̃], *n.m.* thin slice of bacon; (*fam.*) child, kid, brat.

large [larʒ], *a.* broad, wide; large, great, extensive; generous, liberal; lax, loose.—*n.m.* breadth, width; offing, open sea; **au large!** keep off! sheer off! **au large de Dieppe**, off Dieppe.

largement [larʒ'mɑ̃], *adv.* largely, abundantly; fully; liberally.

largesse [lar'ʒɛs], *n.f.* largess, bounty, munificence.

largeur [lar'ʒœːr], *n.f.* breadth, width; amplitude.

larme [larm], *n.f.* tear; drop; **fondre en larmes**, to burst into tears.

larmoiement [larmwa'mɑ̃], *n.m.* watering of the eyes.

larmoyant [larmwa'jɑ̃], *a.* weeping, in tears; tearful, whining.

larmoyer [larmwa'je], *v.i.* (*conjug. like* EMPLOYER) to shed tears; to whine, to snivel; to water (*of the eyes*).

larron [la'rɔ̃], *n.m.* thief.

larve [larv], *n.f.* larva, grub.

laryngite [larɛ̃'ʒit], *n.f.* laryngitis.

larynx [la'rɛ̃ːks], *n.m. inv.* larynx.

las! (1) [lɑ], *int.* alas!

las (2) [lɑ], *a.* (*fem.* **lasse**) tired, weary, fatigued; bored; disgusted.

lascif [la'sif], *a.* (*fem.* **-cive**) lascivious, lewd, wanton.

lascivement [lasiv'mɑ̃], *adv.* lasciviously.

lassant [lɑ'sɑ̃], *a.* tiresome, wearisome, tedious.

lasser [lɑ'se], *v.t.* to tire, to weary, to fatigue, to wear out. **se lasser**, *v.r.* to tire, to grow tired, to be wearied.

lassitude [lɑsi'tyd], *n.f.* lassitude, weariness.

lasso [la'so], *n.m.* lasso.

latent [la'tɑ̃], *a.* latent, concealed, secret.

latéral [late'ral], *a.* (*m. pl.* **-aux**) lateral, side.

latéralement [lateral'mɑ̃], *adv.* laterally.

latin [la'tɛ̃], *a.* Latin.—*n.m.* Latin (*language*); **latin de cuisine**, dog Latin.—*n.m.* (**Latin**, *fem.* **-ine**) Latin (*person*).

latitude [lati'tyd], *n.f.* latitude; room, space, margin.

latte [lat], *n.f.* lath.

latter [la'te], *v.t.* to lath.

lattis [la'ti], *n.m.* lathing, lath-work; laths.

laudanum [loda'nɔm], *n.m.* laudanum.

laudatif [loda'tif], *a.* (*fem.* **-tive**) laudatory.

lauréat [lore'a], *a.* laureate.—*n.m.* (*fem.* **-e**) prize-winner.

laurier [lo'rje], *n.m.* laurel, bay-tree; (*fig.*) glory, honour.

lavable [la'vabl], *a.* washable.

lavabo [lava'bo], *n.m.* wash-basin; wash-stand; (*pl.*) conveniences.

lavage [la'vaːʒ], *n.m.* washing; dilution.

lavande [la'vɑ̃ːd], *n.f.* lavender.

lavandière [lavɑ̃'djɛːr], *n.f.* laundress, washerwoman; (*Orn.*) grey wagtail.

lavasse [la'vas], *n.f.* washy soup *or* wine.

lave [laːv], *n.f.* lava.

lavé [la've], *a.* washed out, faint.

200

lave-dos [lav'do], *n.m. inv.* back-brush.
lavement [lav'mã], *n.m.* (*Med.*) enema.
laver [la've], *v.t.* to wash, to cleanse; to purify; to expiate; *laver à grande eau*, to swill; *laver la vaisselle*, to wash up; *machine à laver*, washing machine. **se laver**, *v.r.* to wash, to wash oneself; to clear oneself (*of an accusation*).
lavette [la'vɛt], *n.f.* dish-mop.
laveur [la'vœːr], *n.m.* (*fem.* **-euse**) washer, scourer; *laveuse de vaisselle*, scullery-maid.
lavoir [la'vwaːr], *n.m.* wash-house.
laxatif [laksa'tif], *a.* (*fem.* **-tive**) laxative, opening.—*n.m.* laxative.
layette [lɛ'jɛt], *n.f.* box; baby's trousseau *or* outfit.
le [lə], *art.* and *pron. m.* the; him, it; so; *je le crois*, I think so.
lécher [le'ʃe], *v.t.* (*conjug. like* CÉDER) to lick; to lick up; (*fig.*) to labour, to polish, to elaborate, to overdo; *lécher les vitrines*, to go window-shopping.
leçon [lə'sɔ̃], *n.f.* lesson; reading (*of a text*).
lecteur [lɛk'tœːr], *n.m.* (*fem.* **-trice**) reader, lector.
lecture [lɛk'tyːr], *n.f.* reading; perusal.
ledit [lə'di], *a.* (*fem.* **ladite**, *pl.* **lesdit(e)s**) the (afore)said, the same.
légal [le'gal], *a.* (*m. pl.* **-aux**) legal, lawful, legitimate.
légalement [legal'mã], *adv.* legally, lawfully.
légaliser [legali'ze], *v.t.* to legalize.
légalité [legali'te], *n.f.* legality, lawfulness.
légataire [lega'tɛːr], *n.* legatee.
légation [lega'sjɔ̃], *n.f.* legateship; legation.
légendaire [leʒã'dɛːr], *a.* and *n.m.* legendary.
légende [le'ʒã:d], *n.f.* legend; inscription; caption; key (*to map etc.*).
léger [le'ʒe], *a.* (*fem.* **-ère**) light; slight; buoyant; fleet, fast; nimble; fickle; faint; thoughtless.
légèrement [leʒɛr'mã], *adv.* lightly, slightly; swiftly; thoughtlessly.
légèreté [leʒɛr'te], *n.f.* lightness; swiftness; fickleness, frivolity; thoughtlessness.
légiférer [leʒife're], *v.i.* (*conjug. like* CÉDER) to legislate.
légion [le'ʒjɔ̃], *n.f.* legion; great number, host.
légionnaire [leʒjɔ'nɛːr], *n.m.* legionary; member of the Legion of Honour; soldier of the Foreign Legion.
législateur [leʒisla'tœːr], *a.* (*fem.* **-trice**) legislative, lawgiving.—*n.m.* (*fem.* **-trice**) legislator.
législatif [leʒisla'tif], *a.* (*fem.* **-tive**) legislative.
législation [leʒisla'sjɔ̃], *n.f.* legislation.
législature [leʒisla'tyːr], *n.f.* legislature.
légitime [leʒi'tim], *a.* lawful, legitimate, rightful; justifiable.
légitimement [leʒitim'mã], *adv.* legitimately, lawfully; justifiably.
légitimer [leʒiti'me], *v.t.* to legitimate; to justify; to recognize.
légitimité [leʒitimi'te], *n.f.* legitimacy, lawfulness.
legs [lɛ], *n.m.* legacy, bequest.
léguer [le'ge], *v.t.* (*conjug. like* CÉDER) to leave by will, to bequeath.
légume [le'gym], *n.m.* vegetable.—*n.f. pl.* (*fam.*) *les grosses légumes*, the bigwigs.

légumier [legy'mje], *a.* (*fem.* **-ière**) of vegetables.—*n.m.* vegetable-dish.
lendemain [lãd'mɛ̃], *n.m.* morrow, next day, day after.
lent [lã], *a.* slow, tardy; backward; sluggish, slack.
lentement [lãt'mã], *adv.* slowly, tardily; sluggishly.
lenteur [lã'tœːr], *n.f.* slowness; tardiness.
lenticulaire [lãtiky'lɛːr], **lenticulé** [lãtiky'le] *a.* lenticular.
lentille [lã'tiːj], *n.f.* lentil; lens; (*pl.*) freckles; *lentille d'eau*, duckweed.
léonin [leo'nɛ̃], *a.* leonine.
léopard [leo'paːr], *n.m.* leopard.
lèpre [lɛpr], *n.f.* leprosy.
lépreux [le'prø], *a.* (*fem.* **-euse**) leprous.—*n.m.* (*fem.* **-euse**) leper.
léproserie [lepro'zri], *n.f.* leper-hospital.
lequel [lə'kɛl], *pron. m.* (*fem.* **laquelle**, *m. pl.* **lesquels**, *f. pl.* **lesquelles**) who, whom, that, which; (*inter.*) which one, which?
les [le], *art.* and *pron. pl.* the; them.
lèse-majesté [lɛzmaʒɛs'te], *n.f.* high treason, lese-majesty.
léser [le'ze], *v.t.* (*conjug. like* CÉDER) to wrong; to injure, to hurt.
lésine [le'zin], *n.f.* niggardliness, stinginess.
lésiner [lezi'ne], *v.i.* to be stingy *or* mean; to haggle.
lésinerie [lezin'ri], *n.f.* stinginess, meanness.
lésion [le'zjɔ̃], *n.f.* (*Law*) wrong, injury; (*Surg.*) lesion.
lessive [le'siːv], *n.f.* wash, linen washed *or* to be washed, washing.
leste [lɛst], *a.* brisk, nimble, active; light; smart; sharp; improper, free.
lestement [lɛst'mã], *adv.* briskly; cleverly; flippantly; freely.
lester [lɛs'te], *v.t.* to ballast. **se lester**, *v.r.* (*fam.*) to take in ballast; to line one's stomach.
léthargie [letar'ʒi], *n.f.* lethargy.
léthargique [letar'ʒik], *a.* lethargic.
lette [lɛt], **letton** [le'tɔ̃] (*fem.* **-onne**), *a.* Latvian.—*n.m.* Latvian (*language*); (**Lette, Letton**, *fem.* **-onne**) Latvian (*person*).
Lettonie [lɛtɔ'ni], **la**, *f.* Latvia.
lettre [lɛtr], *n.f.* letter, note; (*Print.*) character, type; (*pl.*) literature, letters; *les belles-lettres*, humanities; *lettre de change*, bill of exchange; *lettre d'envoi*, covering letter; *lettre de voiture*, way-bill.
lettré [lɛ'tre], *a.* cultured, literate, well-read; literary.—*n.m.* (*fem.* **-ée**) scholar.
leur [lœːr], *a. poss.* their.—*poss. pron. le leur, la leur* or *les leurs*, theirs.—*pers. pron.* to them, them.
leurre [lœːr], *n.m.* lure, decoy; bait; snare, trap.
leurrer [lœ're], *v.t.* to lure, to entice, to decoy; to ensnare. **se leurrer**, *v.r.* to delude oneself.
levage [lə'va:ʒ], *n.m.* raising, lifting.
levain [lə'vɛ̃], *n.m.* leaven; (*fig.*) germ.
levant [lə'vã], *a.* rising.—*n.m.* east; rising sun; Levant.
levantin [ləvã'tɛ̃], *a.* Levantine.—*n.m.* (**Levantin**, *fem.* **-ine**) Levantine (*person*).
levé [lə've], *a.* lifted up, raised; up, out of bed.

levée

levée [lə′ve], *n.f.* raising, lifting; levying; gathering (*crop, fruit etc.*); collection (*post-office*); embankment; swell (*of the sea*); (*Cards*) trick.

lever [lə′ve], *v.t.* (*conjug. like* AMENER) to lift, to lift up, to raise; to heave; to pull up; to weigh (*anchor*); to take away; to take out; to collect; to levy.—*v.i.* to come up; to spring up, to rise. **se lever**, *v.r.* to rise, to get up; to stand up; to heave (*of the sea*); to clear up (*of the weather*).

lever [lə′ve], *n.m.* rising, getting up; levee (*of king*).

levier [lə′vje], *n.m.* lever; crowbar, hand-spike.

levraut [lə′vro], *n.m.* leveret, young hare.

lèvre [lɛːvr], *n.f.* lip; rim.

lévrier [levri′e], *n.m.* greyhound.

levure [lə′vyːr], *n.f.* yeast.

lexique [lɛk′sik], *n.m.* lexicon; abridged dictionary.

lézard [le′zaːr], *n.m.* lizard.

lézarde [le′zard], *n.f.* crevice, crack, chink.

lézardé [lezar′de], *a.* cracked (*of walls etc.*).

lézarder [lezar′de], *v.t.* to crack (*walls etc.*). **se lézarder**, *v.r.* to crack, to become cracked.

liais [ljɛ], *n.m.* lias; blue limestone.

liaison [ljɛ′zɔ̃], *n.f.* joining; connexion, acquaintance; intimacy; (*Mil.*) liaison.

liane [ljan], *n.f.* liana, tropical creeper.

liant [ljɑ̃], *a.* supple, flexible; affable, sociable. —*n.m.* suppleness; sociability; gentleness.

liard [ljaːr], *n.m.* liard (*half-farthing*).

liasse [ljas], *n.f.* bundle, file (*of papers*); wad (*of banknotes*).

Liban [li′bɑ̃], **le**, *m.* Lebanon.

libanais [liba′nɛ], *a.* Lebanese.—*n.m.* (**Libanais**, *fem.* **-aise**) Lebanese (*person*).

libation [liba′sjɔ̃], *n.f.* libation; (*fig.*) potation.

libelle [li′bɛl], *n.m.* libel, lampoon.

libellé [libɛl′le], *a.* drawn up, specified.—*n.m.* wording, contents.

libellule [libɛl′lyl], *n.f.* dragon-fly.

libéral [libe′ral], *a.* (*m. pl.* **-aux**) liberal, generous, bountiful; (*Polit.*) Liberal.

libéralement [liberal′mɑ̃], *adv.* liberally, bountifully, generously.

libéralisme [libera′lism], *n.m.* liberalism.

libéralité [liberali′te], *n.f.* generosity, open-handedness.

libérateur [libera′tœːr], *n.m.* (*fem.* **-trice**) deliverer, liberator, rescuer.

libération [libera′sjɔ̃], *n.f.* liberation, deliverance; rescue, discharge.

libéré [libe′re], *a.* liberated, discharged.

libérer [libe′re], *v.t.* (*conjug. like* CÉDER) to liberate, to free; to discharge. **se libérer**, *v.r.* to free oneself, to clear oneself (*de*); to pay off one's debts.

Libéria [libe′rja], **le**, *m.* Liberia.

libérien [libe′rjɛ̃], *a.* (*fem.* **-enne**) Liberian. —*n.m.* (**Libérien**, *fem.* **-enne**) Liberian (*person*).

liberté [liber′te], *n.f.* liberty, freedom, ease.

libertin [liber′tɛ̃], *a.* libertine, licentious; dissolute.—*n.m.* (*fem.* **-e**) libertine, rake.

libertinage [liberti′naːʒ], *n.m.* libertinism, debauchery.

libraire [li′brɛːr], *n.* bookseller; **libraire-éditeur**, publisher and bookseller.

librairie [librɛ′ri], *n.f.* book-trade; book-seller's shop.

libre [libr], *a.* free; at liberty; independent; undisciplined, unconfined; bold, broad; exempt; irregular (*of verse*).

libre-échange [librɛ′ʃɑ̃ːʒ], *n.m.* free trade.

libre-échangiste [librɛʃɑ̃′ʒist], *n.m.* (*pl.* **libre-échangistes**) free-trader.

librement [libro′mɑ̃], *adv.* freely, without restraint; boldly.

librettiste [librɛ′tist], *n.m.* librettist.

Libye [li′bi], **la**, *f.* Libya.

libyen [li′bjɛ̃], *a.* (*fem.* **-enne**) Libyan.—*n.m.* (**Libyen**, *fem.* **-enne**) Libyan (*person*).

lice [lis], *n.f.* lists, tilt-yard.

licence [li′sɑ̃ːs], *n.f.* licence, leave, permission; licentiousness; licentiate's degree.

licencié [lisɑ̃′sje], *a.* licentiate; (*C*) **épicier licencié**, licensed grocer.—*n.m.* (*fem.* **-ée**) licenciate.

licenciement [lisɑ̃si′mɑ̃], *n.m.* disbanding.

licencier [lisɑ̃′sje], *v.t.* to disband (*troops*); to declare redundant, to lay off; to dismiss.

licencieusement [lisɑ̃sjøz′mɑ̃], *adv.* licentiously, dissolutely.

licencieux [lisɑ̃′sjø], *a.* (*fem.* **-euse**) licentious, dissolute.

licite [li′sit], *a.* licit, lawful, allowable.

licitement [lisit′mɑ̃], *adv.* lawfully, licitly.

licol [LICOU].

licorne [li′kɔrn], *n.f.* unicorn.

licou [li′ku], **licol** [li′kɔl], *n.m.* halter.

licteur [lik′tœːr], *n.m.* (*Rom. Ant.*) lictor.

lie [li], *n.f.* lees, dregs; (*fig.*) scum, refuse.

liège [ljɛːʒ], *n.m.* cork; cork-tree.

lien [ljɛ̃], *n.m.* bond, tie, link; (*pl.*) bonds, shackles.

lier [lje], *v.t.* to fasten, to tie; to bind, to tie up; to join, to connect (*avec*); to engage in; (*Mus.*) to slur; to thicken (*a sauce etc.*). **se lier**, *v.r.* to become acquainted; to thicken (*of sauce etc.*).

lierre [ljɛːr], *n.m.* ivy.

lieu [ljø], *n.m.* (*pl.* **lieux**) place, spot; position; cause; (*pl.*) premises, apartments; **au lieu de**, instead of; **avoir lieu**, to take place; **lieu commun**, commonplace.

lieue [ljø], *n.f.* league (*4 kilometres, 2½ miles*).

lieur [ljœːr], *n.m.* (*fem.* **-euse**) (*Agric.*) binder (*person*).—*n.f.* (**-euse**) binder (*machine*).

lieutenance [ljøt′nɑ̃ːs], *n.f.* lieutenancy.

lieutenant [ljøt′nɑ̃], *n.m.* lieutenant; right-hand man.

lièvre [ljɛːvr], *n.m.* hare.

liftier [lif′tje], *n.m.* (*fem.* **-ière**) lift-boy *or* girl, lift-attendant.

ligament [liga′mɑ̃], *n.m.* ligament.

ligature [liga′tyːr], *n.f.* ligature.

ligaturer [ligaty′re], *v.t.* to ligature, to splice.

lignage [li′naːʒ], *n.m.* lineage.

ligne [liɲ], *n.f.* line; row; path, way; cord; fishing-line; order.

lignée [li′ɲe], *n.f.* issue, progeny, offspring.

ligoter [ligo′te], *v.t.* to bind, to tie up.

ligue [lig], *n.f.* league, confederacy.

liguer [li′ge], *v.t.* to unite in a league; **se liguer**, *v.r.* to league, to combine.

ligueur [li′gœːr], *n.m.* (*fem.* **-euse**) leaguer; plotter.

lilas [li′la], *a. inv.* lilac-coloured.—*n.m.* lilac.

lilliputien [lilipy′sjɛ̃], *a.* (*fem.* **-enne**) Lilliputian.

limace [li′mas], *n.f.* slug; Archimedean screw.

limaçon [lima′sɔ̃], *n.m.* snail.

limbe [lɛ̃:b], *n.m.* (*Math., Bot. etc.*) limb; (*Astron.*) border, halo; (*pl.*) limbo.

lime (1) [lim], *n.f.* file.

lime (2) [lim], *n.f.* lime, citron.

limer [li′me], *v.t.* to file, to smooth.

limeur [li′mœːr], *n.m.* (*fem.* **-euse**) filer.— *n.f.* (**-euse**) finishing-tool *or* machine.

limier [li′mje], *n.m.* bloodhound; (*fig.*) police-spy, detective.

liminaire [limi′nɛːr], *a.* prefatory.

limitatif [limita′tif], *a.* (*fem.* **-tive**) limiting, restrictive.

limitation [limitɑ′sjɔ̃], *n.f.* limitation.

limite [li′mit], *n.f.* limit, boundary; border; landmark.

limiter [limi′te], *v.t.* to limit, to bound; to confine.

limitrophe [limi′trɔf], *a.* neighbouring, bordering.

limon [li′mɔ̃], *n.m.* silt, ooze, mud; shaft (*of a carriage*); sour lime (*fruit*).

limonade [limɔ′nad], *n.f.* lemonade.

limonadier [limɔnɑ′dje], *n.m.* (*fem.* **-ière**) seller of lemonade.

limoneux [limɔ′nø], *a.* (*fem.* **-euse**) muddy, turbid, slimy; alluvial.

limonier [limɔ′nje], *n.m.* shaft-horse; lime-tree.

limonière [limɔ′njɛːr], *n.f.* pair of shafts (*of wagon etc.*); wagon with two shafts.

limousin [limu′zɛ̃], *n.m.* stonemason.

limousine [limu′zin], *n.f.* limousine (*car*); coarse woollen cloak.

limpide [lɛ̃′pid], *a.* limpid, clear.

limpidité [lɛ̃pidi′te], *n.f.* limpidity.

lin [lɛ̃], *n.m.* flax; *graine de lin*, linseed; *huile de lin*, linseed oil; *toile de lin*, linen-cloth.

linceul [lɛ̃′sœl], *n.m.* winding-sheet, shroud.

linéaire [line′ɛːr], *a.* linear.

linéal [line′al], *a.* (*m. pl.* **-aux**) lineal, in a direct line.

linéament [linea′mɑ̃], *n.m.* lineament, feature; (*fig.*) trace, vestige.

linge [lɛ̃:ʒ], *n.m.* linen; piece, rag.

linger [lɛ̃′ʒe], *n.m.* (*fem.* **-ère**) linen-draper; maker of linen goods; seamstress (*of same*).—*n.f.* (**-ère**) wardrobe woman.

lingerie [lɛ̃′ʒri], *n.f.* linen-trade, linen-drapery; linen goods.

lingot [lɛ̃′go], *n.m.* ingot; bullion.

lingue [lɛ̃:g], *n.f.* (*Ichth.*) ling.

linguiste [lɛ̃′gɥist], *n.* linguist.

linguistique [lɛ̃gɥis′tik], *a.* linguistic.—*n.f.* linguistics.

linier [li′nje], *a.* (*fem.* **-ière**) of flax *or* linen.—*n.f.* (**-ière**) flax-field.

linoléum [linɔle′ɔm], *n.m.* linoleum.

linon [li′nɔ̃], *n.m.* lawn (*fine linen*).

linot [li′no], *n.m.*, **linotte** [li′nɔt], *n.f.* linnet.

linotype [linɔ′tip], *n.f.* linotype.

linotypiste [linɔti′pist], *n.* linotype operator.

linteau [lɛ̃′to], *n.m.* (*pl.* **-eaux**) lintel.

lion [ljɔ̃], *n.m.* (*fem.* **lionne**) lion, lioness; (*fig.*) a bold, brave fellow.

lionceau [ljɔ̃′so], *n.m.* (*pl.* **-eaux**) young lion, lion's cub.

lippe [lip], *n.f.* thick lower lip; pouting lip.

lippu [li′py], *a.* thick-lipped.

liquéfaction [likefak′sjɔ̃], *n.f.* liquefaction.

liquéfiable [like′fjabl], *a.* liquefiable.

liquéfier [like′fje], *v.t.* and **se liquéfier**, *v.r.* to liquefy.

liqueur [li′kœːr], *n.f.* liquid; liqueur, cordial; (*Chem.*) spirit.

liquidateur [likida′tœːr], *n.m.* liquidator.

liquidation [likidɑ′sjɔ̃], *n.f.* liquidation; settlement (*of debts etc.*); winding up (*of a business*); clearance sale.

liquide [li′kid], *a.* liquid; clear, net (*of money*).—*n.m.* liquid, fluid; drink.

liquider [liki′de], *v.t.* to liquidate, to settle; to wind up; to sell off; (*fam.*) to get rid of.

liquidité [likidi′te], *n.f.* liquidity, fluidity.

liquoreux [likɔ′rø], *a.* (*fem.* **-euse**) luscious, sweet.

liquoriste [likɔ′rist], *n.m.* wine and spirit merchant.

lire [liːr], *v.t. irr.* to read, to peruse, to study.

lis [lis], *n.m.* lily.

liseré [lizə′re], *n.m.* piping; border, edge.

lisérer [lize′re], *v.t.* (*conjug. like* CÉDER) to trim (*a dress etc.*) with piping.

liseron [liz′rɔ̃], **liset** [li′zɛ], *n.m.* (*Bot.*) convolvulus.

liseur [li′zœːr], *n.m.* (*fem.* **-euse**) reader.

lisibilité [lizibili′te], *n.f.* legibility, readableness.

lisible [li′zibl], *a.* legible, readable.

lisiblement [lizibla′mɑ̃], *adv.* legibly.

lisière [li′zjɛːr], *n.f.* selvedge, edge (*of cloth etc.*); border, verge, outskirts.

lissage [li′saːʒ], *n.m.* smoothing, glossing.

lisse (1) [lis], *a.* smooth; sleek; glossy.—*n.m.* smoothness, gloss.

lisse (2) [lis], *n.f.* rail, railing (*of ship*).

lisser [li′se], *v.t.* to smooth, to polish.

lisseur [li′sœːr], *n.m.* (*fem.* **-euse**) polisher.

liste [list], *n.f.* list, roll; catalogue; schedule.

lit [li], *n.m.* bed; layer (*of clay, mortar*); direction, set (*of tide, current*); (*fig.*) marriage.

litanie [lita′ni], *n.f.* (*fig.*) rigmarole; (*pl.*) litany.

litée [li′te], *n.f.* litter (*of animals*).

literie [li′tri], *n.f.* bedding.

lithographe [litɔ′graf], *n.m.* lithographer.

lithographie [litɔgra′fi], *n.f.* lithography; lithograph.

lithographier [litɔgra′fje], *v.t.* to lithograph.

lithographique [litɔgra′fik], *a.* lithographic.

Lithuanie [LITUANIE].

lithuanien [LITUANIEN].

litière [li′tjɛːr], *n.f.* stable-litter; litter (*for carrying sick persons etc.*).

litigant [liti′gɑ̃], *a.* litigant.

litige [liti:ʒ], *n.m.* litigation, legal dispute; (*fig.*) strife.

litigieux [liti′ʒjø], *a.* (*fem.* **-euse**) litigious, given to lawsuits.

litre [litr], *n.m.* litre (*1·76 pints*).

littéraire [lite′rɛːr], *a.* literary; *propriété littéraire*, copyright.

littérairement [literɛr′mɑ̃], *adv.* in a literary manner *or* way.

littéral [lite′ral], *a.* (*m. pl.* **-aux**) literal.

littéralement [literal′mɑ̃], *adv.* literally, word for word.

littérateur [litera′tœːr], *n.m.* literary man, author, man of letters.

littérature [litera′tyːr], *n.f.* literature.

littoral [litɔ'ral], *a.* (*m. pl.* **-aux**) littoral, coastal.—*n.m.* littoral, seaboard.

Lituanie [litɥa'ni], **la**, *f.* Lithuania.

lituanien [litɥa'njɛ̃], *a.* Lithuanian.—*n.m.* Lithuanian (*language*); (**Lituanien**, *fem.* **-enne**) Lithuanian (*person*).

liturgie [lityr'ʒi], *n.f.* liturgy.

liturgique [lityr'ʒik], *a.* liturgic, liturgical.

liturgiste [lityr'ʒist], *n.* liturgist.

livide [li'vid], *a.* livid, ghastly.

lividité [lividi'te], *n.f.* lividness.

livrable [li'vrabl], *a.* deliverable.

livraison [livrɛ'zɔ̃], *n.f.* delivery (*of goods*); part, number, issue (*of a magazine etc.*).

livre (1) [li:vr], *n.m.* book; register, account-book.

livre (2) [li:vr], *n.f.* pound (*1·1 lb. avoirdupois*); **livre sterling**, pound sterling.

livrée [li'vre], *n.f.* livery; livery-servants.

livrer [li'vre], *v.t.* to deliver; to give up, to hand over; to betray (*a secret*). **se livrer**, *v.r.* to give oneself up (*à*); to surrender; to devote oneself; to entrust oneself to; to indulge in (*a vice*).

livret [li'vrɛ], *n.m.* little book; memorandum-book; libretto.

livreur [li'vrœ:r], *n.m.* (*fem.* **-euse**) deliverer (*of goods*); delivery-man, van-man.—*n.f.* (**-euse**) delivery-van.

lobe [lɔb], *n.m.* lobe (*of ear, liver etc.*).

lobélie [lɔbe'li], *n.f.* (*Bot.*) lobelia.

local [lɔ'kal], *a.* (*m. pl.* **-aux**) local.—*n.m.* place, premises; quarters.

localement [lɔkal'mɑ̃], *adv.* locally.

localisation [lɔkaliza'sjɔ̃], *n.f.* localization.

localiser [lɔkali'ze], *v.t.* to localize. **se localiser**, *v.r.* to become localized.

localité [lɔkali'te], *n.f.* locality.

locataire [lɔka'tɛ:r], *n.* tenant, lodger, occupier.

location [lɔka'sjɔ̃], *n.f.* letting out; hiring, renting; (*Theat.*) booking of seat.

lock-out [lɔ'kaut], *n.m. inv.* lock-out.

lock-outer [lɔkau'te], *v.t.* to lock-out.

locomoteur [lɔkɔmɔ'tœ:r], *a.* (*fem.* **-trice**) locomotor.

locomotif [lɔkɔmɔ'tif], *a.* (*fem.* **-tive**) locomotive.—*n.f.* (**-tive**) locomotive, engine.

locomotion [lɔkɔmɔ'sjɔ̃], *n.f.* locomotion.

locomotive [LOCOMOTIF].

locuste [lɔ'kyst], *n.f.* locust.

locution [lɔky'sjɔ̃], *n.f.* locution, expression, form of speech; term, phrase.

logarithme [lɔga'ritm], *n.m.* logarithm.

loge [lɔ:ʒ], *n.f.* hut; lodge; (*Theat.*) box, dressing-room; stand, stall; kennel; booth.

logeable [lɔ'ʒabl], *a.* a tenantable, fit to live in.

logement [lɔʒ'mɑ̃], *n.m.* lodgings; dwelling; house-room, accommodation; quarters.

loger [lɔ'ʒe], *v.t.* (*conjug. like* MANGER) to lodge; to put up, to accommodate, to house; to quarter; to stable.—*v.i.* to lodge, to live; to put up. **se loger**, *v.r.* to lodge, to take up one's abode; to lodge itself.

logette [lɔ'ʒet], *n.f.* small lodge.

logeur [lɔ'ʒœ:r], *n.m.* (*fem.* **-euse**) lodging-house keeper.

logicien [lɔʒi'sjɛ̃], *n.m.* (*fem.* **-enne**) logician.

logique [lɔ'ʒik], *a.* logical.—*n.f.* logic.

logiquement [lɔʒik'mɑ̃], *adv.* logically.

logis [lɔ'ʒi], *n.m.* (*rare*) house, dwelling.

loi [lwa], *n.f.* law, statute, act; rule.

loin [lwɛ̃], *adv.* far, at a distance; remote, distant; *au loin*, far away, far and wide; *de loin*, from afar, from a distance; *de loin en loin*, at long intervals.

lointain [lwɛ̃'tɛ̃], *a.* remote, far off, distant.—*n.m.* distance, distant prospect.

loir [lwa:r], *n.m.* dormouse.

loisible [lwa'zibl], *a.* optional, lawful, allowable.

loisir [lwa'zi:r], *n.m.* leisure, spare time.

lombes [lɔ̃:b], *n.m. pl.* (*Anat.*) lumbar region, loins.

londonien [lɔ̃dɔ'njɛ̃], *a.* (*fem.* **-enne**) of *or* pertaining to London.—*n.m.* (**Londonien**, *fem.* **-enne**) Londoner.

Londres ['lɔ̃drə], *f.* London.

long [lɔ̃], *a.* (*fem.* **longue**) long; slow, tedious; diffuse, drawn out.—*n.m.* length; extent; (*tout*) *au long*, in full; *de long en large*, up and down, to and fro.—*n.f.* *à la longue*, in the long run.—*adv.* much, great deal.

longanimité [lɔ̃ganimi'te], *n.f.* longanimity, forbearance, long-suffering.

long-courrier [lɔ̃ku'rje], *n.m.* (*pl.* **-courriers**) ocean-going ship.

longe (1) [lɔ̃:ʒ], *n.f.* tether, leading-rein; thong.

longe (2) [lɔ̃:ʒ], *n.f.* *longe de veau*, loin of veal.

longer [lɔ̃'ʒe], *v.t.* (*conjug. like* MANGER) to go, to run along; to skirt; to extend along.

longévité [lɔ̃ʒevi'te], *n.f.* longevity.

longitude [lɔ̃ʒi'tyd], *n.f.* longitude.

longitudinal [lɔ̃ʒitydi'nal], *a.* (*m. pl.* **-aux**) longitudinal.

longitudinalement [lɔ̃ʒitydinal'mɑ̃], *adv.* lengthwise.

longtemps [lɔ̃'tɑ̃], *adv.* long, a long while.

longuement [lɔ̃g'mɑ̃], *adv.* long, a long time, for a great while.

longueur [lɔ̃'gœ:r], *n.f.* length, extent in time; slowness; prolixity.

longue-vue [lɔ̃g'vy], *n.f.* (*pl.* **longues-vues**) telescope, spy-glass.

lopin [lɔ'pɛ̃], *n.m.* small piece *or* share; *lopin de terre*, plot of ground.

loquace [lɔ'kwas], *a.* loquacious, talkative.

loquacement [lɔkwas'mɑ̃], *adv.* talkatively, loquaciously.

loquacité [lɔkwasi'te], *n.f.* loquacity, talkativeness.

loque [lɔk], *n.f.* rag, tatter.

loquet [lɔkɛ], *n.m.* latch; *fermé au loquet*, on the latch.

loqueteau [lɔk'to], *n.m.* (*pl.* **-eaux**) small latch.

loqueteux [lɔk'tø], *a.* (*fem.* **-euse**) in rags.—*n.m.* (**-euse**) ragged person.

lorgner [lɔr'ɲe], *v.t.* to leer at, to ogle.

lorgnette [lɔr'ɲet], *n.f.* field *or* opera-glasses.

lorgnon [lɔr'ɲɔ̃], *n.m.* (*sometimes pl.*) eye-glasses; lorgnette.

lorry [lɔ'ri], *n.m.* (*Rail.*) lorry, trolley (*of platelayer*).

lors [lɔ:r], *adv.* then; *depuis* or *dès lors*, from that time, since then; *lors de*, at the time of; *lors même que*, even though; *pour lors*, then, at the time; so, therefore.

lorsque [lɔrsk, 'lɔrskə], *conj.* when; at the time *or* moment of.

losange [lɔ'zã:ʒ], *n.m.* diamond-shape, lozenge.
losangé [lɔzã'ʒe], *a.* in lozenges.
lot [lo], *n.m.* lot; portion, share; prize (*in a lottery*); (*fig.*) fate.
loterie [lɔ'tri], *n.f.* lottery, raffle.
lotion [lo'sjɔ̃], *n.f.* lotion; ablution.
lotir [lɔ'ti:r], *v.t.* to divide into lots, to portion off.
lotissement [lɔtis'mã], *n.m.* dividing into lots; building plot.
loto [lɔ'to], *n.m.* lotto (*game of chance*); housey-housey, bingo.
lotus [lɔ'ty:s], *n.m. inv.* lotus.
louable [lwabl], *a.* laudable, praiseworthy, commendable.
louablement [lwablə'mã], *adv.* commendably.
louage [lwa:ʒ], *n.m.* letting out, hiring, renting; hire.
louange [lwã:ʒ], *n.f.* praise, commendation, eulogy.
louanger [lwã'ʒe], *v.t.* (*conjug. like* MANGER) to praise, to flatter, to extol.
louangeur [lwã'ʒœ:r], *a.* (*fem.* **-euse**) laudatory, eulogistic.—*n.m.* (*fem.* **-euse**) praiser, flatterer.
louche (1) [luʃ], *n.f.* (*soup*) ladle; scoop; countersink bit.
louche (2) [luʃ], *a.* squint-eyed; dubious, ambiguous; suspicious, shady.
loucher [lu'ʃe], *v.i.* to squint.
loucheur [lu'ʃœ:r], *a.* (*fem.* **-euse**) squinting. —*n.m.* (*fem.* **-euse**) squinter.
louer (1) [lwe], *v.t.* to let *or* hire out; to lease, to rent, to hire; to book. **se louer** (1), *v.r.* to hire oneself out; to be let *or* rented.
louer (2) [lwe], *v.t.* to praise, to commend, to extol. **se louer** (2), *v.r.* to praise oneself; to rejoice.
loueur [lwœ:r], *n.m.* (*fem.* **-euse**) hirer, letter-out.
lougre [lugr], *n.m.* lugger.
Louis [lwi], *m.* Lewis.
louis [lwi], *n.m. inv.* louis (*a French coin worth 20 gold francs*).
loup [lu], *n.m.* wolf; black velvet mask.
loup-cervier [luser'vje], *n.m.* (*pl.* **loups-cerviers**) lynx; (*fig.*) profiteer.
loupe (1) [lup], *n.f.* magnifying-glass.
loupe (2) [lup], *n.f.* wen; gnarl (*on trees*).
louper [lu'pe], *v.t.* (*pop.*) to botch (*a piece of work*); (*Exam.*) to fail; to miss (*train*).
loupeux [lu'pø], *a.* (*fem.* **-euse**) wenny, knobby.
loup-garou [luga'ru], *n.m.* (*pl.* **loups-garous**) wer(e)wolf; bugbear.
lourd [lu:r], *a.* heavy, clumsy; stupid; sultry.
lourdaud [lur'do], *a.* loutish.—*n.m.* (*fem.* **-e**) blockhead.
lourdement [lurdə'mã], *adv.* heavily, clumsily.
lourdeur [lur'dœ:r], *n.f.* heaviness; clumsiness; stupidity; sultriness.
loutre [lutr], *n.f.* otter; otter-fur.
louve [lu:v], *n.f.* she-wolf.
louveteau [luv'to], *n.m.* (*pl.* **-eaux**) wolf-cub.
louveterie [luv'tri], *n.f.* wolf-hunting equipage; wolf-hunting.
louvetier [luv'tje], *n.m.* wolf-hunter.
louvoyer [luvwa'je], *v.i.* (*conjug. like* EM-

PLOYER) to tack, to tack about; (*fig.*) to manœuvre; to dodge.
lover [lɔ've], *v.t.* to coil (*rope etc.*). **se lover**, *v.r.* to coil up (*of snakes*).
loyal [lwa'jal], *a.* (*m. pl.* **-aux**) fair, honest, upright; loyal; (*Comm.*) unadulterated.
loyalement [lwajal'mã] *adv.* fairly, honestly; loyally.
loyauté [lwajo'te], *n.f.* honesty, fairness; loyalty, faithfulness.
loyer [lwa'je], *n.m.* hire, rent.
lubie [ly'bi] *n.f.* crotchet, whim, fad.
lubrifiant [lybri'fjã], *a.* lubricating.—*n.m.* lubricant.
lubrification [lybrifika'sjɔ̃], *n.f.* lubrication.
lubrifier [lybri'fje], *v.t.* to lubricate.
Luc [lyk], *m.* Luke.
lucarne [ly'karn], *n.f.* dormer-window, skylight.
lucide [ly'sid], *a.* lucid, clear.
lucidement [lysid'mã], *adv.* lucidly.
lucidité [lysidi'te], *n.f.* lucidity, clearness.
luciole [ly'sjɔl], *n.f.* (*Ent.*) fire-fly; winged glow-worm.
lucratif [lykra'tif], *a.* (*fem.* **-tive**) lucrative.
lucre [lykr], *n.m.* lucre, gain.
lueur [lɥœ:r], *n.f.* glimmer, gleam; flash.
luffa [ly'fa], *n.m.* or *f.* loofah.
lugubre [ly'gybr], *a.* lugubrious, doleful, dismal.
lugubrement [lygybrə'mã], *adv.* ominously; dismally.
lui [lɥi], *pers. pron.* he, it; to him, to her, to it.
luire [lɥi:r], *v.i. irr.* to shine; to glitter, to gleam, to glisten; to dawn.
luisant [lɥi'zã], *a.* glistening, glittering, bright; glossy.—*n.m.* gloss, shine.
lumbago [lœ̃ba'go], *n.m.* lumbago.
lumière [ly'mjɛ:r], *n.f.* light; daylight, day; (*fig.*) enlightenment; knowledge, wisdom.
luminaire [lymi'nɛ:r], *n.m.* luminary, light.
lumineux [lymi'nø], *a.* (*fem.* **-euse**) luminous; bright.
lunaire [ly'nɛ:r], *a.* lunar.
lunatique [lyna'tik], *a.* fantastical, whimsical. —*n.* incalculable *or* whimsical person.
lundi [lœ̃'di], *n.m.* Monday.
lune [lyn], *n.f.* moon.
lunetier [lyn'tje], *n.m.* (*fem.* **-ière**) spectacle-maker; optician.
lunette [ly'nɛt], *n.f.* telescope, field-glass; (*pl.*) spectacles.
lupin [ly'pɛ̃], *n.m.* (*Bot.*) lupin(e).
lupus [ly'py:s], *n.m.* lupus.
luron [ly'rɔ̃], *n.m.* (*fem.* **-onne**) jolly fellow, gay dog; carefree type of girl.
lustrage [lys'tra:ʒ], *n.m.* glossing.
lustral [lys'tral], *a.* (*m. pl.* **-aux**) lustral.
lustration [lystra'sjɔ̃], *n.f.* lustration.
lustre (1) [lystr], *n.m.* lustre, brilliancy, brightness; (*fig.*) distinction; chandelier.
lustre (2) [lystr], *n.m.* (*Rom. Ant.*) lustrum, space of five years.
lustré [lys'tre], *a.* glossy, shiny.
lustrer [lys'tre], *v.t.* to give a lustre *or* gloss to, to glaze.
lustrine [lys'trin], *n.f.* lustring, cotton lustre.
luth [lyt], *n.m.* lute.
luthérien [lyte'rjɛ̃], *a.* Lutheran.—*n.m.* (**Luthérien**, *fem.* **-enne**) Lutheran (*person*)

lutin

lutin [ly'tɛ̃], *a.* roguish, sprightly.—*n.m.* goblin, sprite elf, imp.

lutiner [lyti'ne], *v.t.* to plague, to tease, to pester.—*v.i.* to be mischievous, to play the imp.

lutrin [ly'trɛ̃], *n.m.* music-lectern *or* desk; choir.

lutte [lyt], *n.f.* wrestling; struggle, contest, strife; *de bonne lutte*, by fair play; *de haute lutte*, by force.

lutter [ly'te], *v.i.* to wrestle; to struggle, to contend.

lutteur [ly'tœːr], *n.m.* (*fem.* **-euse**) wrestler.

luxation [lyksa'sjɔ̃], *n.f.* luxation, dislocation.

luxe [lyks], *n.m.* luxury; profusion; extravagance, excess.

Luxembourg [lyksɑ̃'buːr], **le**, *m.* Luxembourg.

luxembourgeois [lyksɑbur'ʒwa], *a.* (of) Luxembourg.—*n.m.* (**Luxembourgeois**, *fem.* **-oise**) citizen of Luxembourg.

luxer [lyk'se], *v.t.* to luxate, to dislocate.

luxueusement [lyksɥøz'mɑ̃], *a.* luxuriously, sumptuously, richly.

luxueux [lyk'sɥø], *a.* (*fem.* **-euse**) luxurious; magnificent, rich, sumptuous.

luxure [lyk'syːr], *n.f.* lust.

luxuriance [lyksy'rjɑ̃ːs], *n.f.* luxuriance.

luxuriant [lyksy'rjɑ̃], *a.* luxuriant.

luxurieux [lyksy'rjø], *a.* (*fem.* **-euse**) lustful, lecherous.

lycée [li'se], *n.m.* French grammar- *or* high-school.

lycéen [lise'ɛ̃], *n.m.* (*fem.* **-éenne**) grammar-school pupil.

lymphatique [lɛ̃fa'tik], *a.* lymphatic.

lymphe [lɛ̃ːf], *n.f.* lymph; (*Bot.*) sap.

lynchage [lɛ̃'ʃaːʒ], *n.m.* lynching.

lyncher [lɛ̃'ʃe], *v.t.* to lynch.

lynx [lɛ̃ːks], *n.m. inv.* lynx.

Lyon [ljɔ̃], *m.* Lyons.

lyre [liːr], *n.f.* lyre; (*fig.*) poetry.

lyrique [li'rik], *a.* lyric, lyrical.

lyrisme [li'rism], *n.m.* lyric poetry; poetic fire.

M

M m [ɛm], *n.m. or f.* the thirteenth letter of the alphabet; *M*, 1000; *M.*, *MM.*, abbr. of *Monsieur, Messieurs.*

m' [ME].

ma [ma], *a. poss. f.* [MON].

macabre [ma'kɑːbr], *a.* gruesome, macabre, deathly, ghastly; *la danse macabre*, the dance of death.

macadam [maka'dam], *n.m.* macadam.

macadamiser [makadami'ze], *v.t.* to macadamize.

macaque [ma'kak], *n.m.* macaco (*monkey*).

macaron [maka'rɔ̃], *n.m.* macaroon.

macaroni [makaro'ni], *n.m.* macaroni.

Macédoine [mase'dwan], **la**, *f.* Macedonia.

macédoine [mase'dwan], *n.f.* vegetable hotchpotch; fruit salad; (*fig.*) medley, hotchpotch.

macédonien [masedɔ'njɛ̃], *a.* Macedonian.—*n.m.* (**Macédonien**, *fem.* **-enne**) Macedonian (*person*).

macération [masera'sjɔ̃], *n.f.* maceration.

macérer [mase're], *v.t.* (*conjug. like* CÉDER) to macerate; (*fig.*) to mortify.—*v.i.* to soak, se **macérer**, *v.r.* to macerate one's body; (*fig.*) to mortify oneself.

mâcher [mɑ'ʃe], *v.t.* to chew, to masticate; *ne pas mâcher ses mots*, not to mince matters.

machiavélique [makjave'lik], *a.* Machiavellian.

machiavélisme [makjave'lism], *n.m.* Machiavellism.

machiavéliste [makjave'list], *n.* Machiavellian.

machinal [maʃi'nal], *a.* (*m. pl.* **-aux**) mechanical. automatic, instinctive.

machinalement [maʃinal'mɑ̃], *adv.* mechanically, automatically, instinctively.

machinateur [maʃina'tœːr], *n.m.* (*fem.* **-trice**) plotter, schemer.

machination [maʃina'sjɔ̃], *n.f.* machination, plot, scheme.

machine [ma'ʃin], *n.f.* machine, engine, piece of machinery; apparatus; scheme, plot; *machine à coudre*, sewing-machine; *machine à écrire*, typewriter; *machine à laver*, washing machine; *machine pneumatique*, air-pump.

machine-outil [maʃinu'ti], *n.f.* (*pl.* **machines-outils**) machine-tool.

machiner [maʃi'ne], *v.t.* to contrive, to plot.

machiniste [maʃi'nist], *n.m.* machinist, engine-man; (*Theat.*) scene-shifter.

mâchoire [mɑ'ʃwaːr], *n.f.* jaw; jawbone.

mâchonner [maʃɔ'ne], *v.t.* to chew with difficulty; to munch; to mumble; to champ (*the bit*).

mâchurer [mɑʃy're], *v.t.* to daub, to smudge; to bruise.

maçon [ma'sɔ̃], *n.m.* mason, bricklayer; free-mason.

maçonnage [masɔ'naːʒ], *n.m.* mason's work, stonework.

maçonner [masɔ'ne], *v.t.* to build; to wall up.

maçonnerie [masɔn'ri], *n.f.* masonry, mason's work, stone-work; freemasonry.

maçonnique [masɔ'nik], *a.* masonic.

macule [ma'kyl], *n.f.* stain, spot.

maculer [maky'le], *v.t.* to blot. to spot.

Madagascar [madagas'kaːr], **le**, *n.m.* Malagasy Republic.

madame [ma'dam], *n.f.* (*pl.* **mesdames**) madam, ma'am; Mrs.; your ladyship.

madécasse [made'kas], *a.* Madagascan.—*n.* (**Madécasse**) Madagascan (*person*).

madeleine [ma'dlɛn], *n.f.* shell-shaped sponge-cake; early pear.

Madelon [ma'dlɔ̃], *f.* Maud.

mademoiselle [madmwa'zɛl], *n.f.* (*pl.* **mesdemoiselles**) Miss; young lady.

Madère [ma'dɛːr], **la**, *f.* Madeira.

madère [ma'dɛːr], *n.m.* Madeira wine.

madone [ma'dɔn], *n.f.* Madonna.

madré [mɑ'dre], *a.* veined, mottled; (*fig.*) cunning, sly, sharp.—*n.m.* (*fem.* **-ée**) cunning, sharp *or* sly person.

madrier [madri'e], *n.m.* thick plank.

maestria [maɛs'tria], *n.f.* masterliness; *avec maestria*, in a masterly manner.

magasin [maga'zɛ̃], *n.m.* warehouse, storehouse; shop, store; magazine (*of fire-arm, camera etc.*).

(C) **magasiner** [magazi'ne], *v.i.* to shop.

magasinier [magazi'nje], *n.m.* warehouse-keeper, storeman.

magazine [maga'zin], *n.m.* magazine (*usu. illustrated*).

mage [ma:ʒ], *n.m.* mage, magus; seer; *les rois mages*, the three wise men.

magicien [maʒi'sjɛ̃], *n.m.* (*fem.* **-enne**) magician, wizard, sorcerer, sorceress.

magie [ma'ʒi], *n.f.* magic.

magique [ma'ʒik], *a.* magic(al).

magister [maʒis'tɛːr], *n.m.* village schoolmaster; pedant.

magistral [maʒis'tral], *a.* (*m. pl.* **-aux**) magisterial; masterly, authoritative, sovereign.

magistralement [maʒistral'mɑ̃], *adv.* magisterially; in a masterly fashion.

magistrat [maʒis'tra], *n.m.* magistrate, justice; civic officer.

magistrature [maʒistra'tyːr], *n.f.* magistracy; bench.

magnanime [maɲa'nim], *a.* magnanimous, high-minded.

magnanimement [maɲanim'mɑ̃], *adv.* magnanimously.

magnanimité [maɲanimi'te], *n.f.* magnanimity.

magnat [mag'na], *n.m.* magnate.

magnésie [maɲe'zi], *n.f.* magnesia.

magnétique [maɲe'tik], *a.* magnetic.

magnétiser [maɲeti'ze], *v.t.* to magnetize.

magnétiseur [maɲeti'zœːr], *n.m.* magnetizer.

magnétisme [maɲe'tism], *n.m.* magnetism; (*fig.*) attraction.

magnétophone [maɲeto'fɔn], *n.m.* (*Reg. trade mark*) tape-recorder.

magnificence [maɲifi'sɑ̃:s], *n.f.* magnificence, splendour.

magnifier [maɲi'fje], *v.t.* to magnify, to glorify.

magnifique [maɲi'fik], *a.* magnificent, splendid; gorgeous.

magnifiquement [maɲifik'mɑ̃], *adv.* magnificently.

magot [ma'go], *n.m.* magot, ape; grotesque figure (*of china*); (*fig.*) ugly person; (*fam.*) hoard, hidden savings.

Mahomet [mao'mɛ], *m.* Mohammed.

mahométan [maome'tɑ̃], *a.* Mohammedan. —*n.m.* (**Mahométan**, *fem.* **-ane**) Mohammedan (*person*).

mahométisme [maome'tism], *n.m.* Mohammedanism.

mai [mɛ], *n.m.* May; maypole.

maigre [mɛːgr], *a.* meagre, lean, thin; poor, scanty; barren; fasting; *repas maigre*, meatless meal; *maigre repas*, slender meal.

maigrement [mɛgrə'mɑ̃], *adv.* meagrely; poorly, sparingly.

maigreur [mɛ'grœːr], *n.f.* leanness, meagreness; thinness, poorness, barrenness.

maigrir [mɛ'griːr], *v.i.* to grow thin, to lose weight.

mail [ma:j], *n.m.* mall (*game, promenade, avenue of trees*).

maille [ma:j], *n.f.* mesh; ring of cable; link of mail; stitch.

maillé [mɑ'je], *a.* stitched; mailed.

mailler [mɑ'je], *v.t.* to make with meshes, to lattice; to mail.

maillet [ma'jɛ], *n.m.* mallet.

maillon [mɑ'jɔ̃], *n.m.* link (*of chain*).

maillot [ma'jo], *n.m.* swaddling-band; swaddling-clothes; pair of tights (*for theatre*); bathing costume; (*Spt.*) jersey, vest; *enfant au maillot*, baby in arms.

main [mɛ̃], *n.f.* hand; handwriting; lead, deal (*at cards*); handle; quire (*of paper*); *à la main*, in his *or* her hand, by hand; *à la portée de la main*, within reach; *à main armée*, by force of arms, armed; *à pleines mains*, by handfuls, liberally; *vol à main armée*, armed robbery.

main-d'œuvre [mɛ̃'dœːvr], *n.f.* (*pl.* **mains-d'œuvre**) man-power, labour; workmanship.

main-forte [mɛ̃'fɔrt], *n.f.* assistance, help.

maint [mɛ̃], *a.* many; *maintes fois*, many a time.

maintenant [mɛ̃t'nɑ̃], *adv.* now, at this moment, at present, nowadays.

maintenir [mɛ̃t'niːr], *v.t. irr.* (*conjug. like* TENIR) to uphold, to sustain; to maintain; to enforce. **se maintenir**, *v.r.* to keep up; to subsist; to hold out, to stand one's ground; to remain in force.

maintien [mɛ̃'tjɛ̃], *n.m.* maintenance, keeping up; deportment; attitude.

maire [mɛːr], *n.m.* mayor.

mairesse [mɛ'rɛs], *n.f.* mayoress.

mairie [mɛ'ri], *n.f.* mayoralty; town hall.

mais [mɛ], *conj.* but; why.

maïs [ma'is], *n.m.* maize, Indian corn.

maison [mɛ'zɔ̃], *n.f.* house; home; housekeeping; family; (*Comm.*) firm; *à la maison*, at home.

maisonnée [mɛzo'ne], *n.f.* (*fam.*) whole house *or* family, household.

maisonnette [mɛzo'nɛt], *n.f.* small house, cottage, lodge.

maître [mɛːtr], *n.m.* master; ruler, lord; proprietor, landlord; teacher, tutor; (*Naut.*) chief petty officer; *coup de maître*, masterly stroke; *maître chanteur*, blackmailer.

maître-autel [mɛtro'tɛl], *n.m.* (*pl.* **maîtres-autels**) high altar.

maîtresse [mɛ'trɛs], *a.* chief, leading, main. —*n.f.* mistress; ruler, lady; proprietress; teacher; sweetheart.

maîtrise [mɛ'triːz], *n.f.* mastery; control; music-school (*in a cathedral*).

maîtriser [metri'ze], *v.t.* to master, to control; to lord (it) over.

majesté [maʒes'te], *n.f.* majesty; stateliness.

majestueusement [maʒestɥøz'mɑ̃], *adv.* majestically.

majestueux [maʒes'tɥø], *a.* (*fem.* **-euse**) majestic.

majeur [ma'ʒœːr], *a.* major, greater; superior, main, chief, most important; of full age. —*n.m.* (*fem.* **-e**) a male *or* female of full age, major.—*n.m.* middle finger.

majolique [maʒo'lik], *n.f.* majolica.

major [ma'ʒɔːr], *n.m.* major; medical officer.

majordome [maʒor'dɔm], *n.m.* major-domo.

majorer [maʒo're], *v.t.* to raise (*the price*).

majorité [maʒori'te], *n.f.* majority.

majuscule [maʒys'kyl], *a.* capital, large.—*n.f.* capital letter.

mal

mal [mal], *n.m.* (*pl.* maux) evil, ill; harm; pain, ache, sickness; hardship, misfortune; trouble; repugnance.—*adv.* wrong, badly; *mal à propos*, improperly.

malade [ma'lad], *a.* sick, ill; unhealthy.—*n.* sick person, invalid; patient.

maladie [mala'di], *n.f.* illness, sickness, malady.

maladif [mala'dif], *a.* (*fem.* -dive) sickly, puny, ailing, unhealthy.

maladivement [maladiv'mã], *adv.* morbidly.

maladresse [mala'drɛs], *n.f.* awkwardness, clumsiness; blunder.

maladroit [mala'drwa], *a.* and *n.m.* (*fem.* -e) awkward, clumsy, stupid (person).

maladroitement [maladrwat'mã], *adv.* clumsily.

malais [ma'lɛ], *a.* Malay, Malayan, Malaysian.—*n.m.* Malay (*language*); (Malais, *fem.* -aise) Malay, Malayan, Malaysian (*person*).

malaise [ma'lɛːz], *n.m.* uneasiness, discomfort; indisposition.

malaisé [malɛ'ze], *a.* hard, difficult, rough, arduous.

malaisément [malɛze'mã], *adv.* with difficulty, painfully.

Malaisie [malɛ'zi], la, *f.* Malaysia.

malappris [mala'pri], *a.* unmannerly ill-bred.—*n.m.* (*fem.* -e) ill-bred person, lout.

malard [ma'laːr], *n.m.* mallard, wild drake.

malaria [mala'rja], *n.f.* malaria.

malart [MALARD].

malavisé [malavi'ze], *a.* ill-advised, imprudent, unwise, indiscreet.

malaxer [malak'ze], *v.t.* to mix, knead *or* work up; to massage.

malbâti [malba'ti], *a.* ill-shaped, gawky.—*n.m.* (*fem.* -e) ill-favoured person.

malchance [mal'ʃãːs], *n.f.* ill-luck, mishap mischance.

malchanceux [malʃã'sø], *a.* (*fem.* -euse) unlucky.

mâle [maːl], *a.* male; manly, virile; masculine.—*n.m.* male; cock.

malédiction [maledik'sjõ], *n.f.* malediction, curse.

maléfice [male'fis], *n.m.* evil spell, sorcery.

maléfique [male'fik], *a.* harmful, malefic, baleful.

malencontre [malã'kõːtr], *n.f.* mishap, mischance.

malencontreusement [malãkõtrøz'mã], *adv.* unluckily, untowardly.

malencontreux [malãkõ'trø], *a.* (*fem.* -euse) unlucky, untoward.

mal-en-point [malã'pwɛ̃], *adv.* badly off; in a sorry plight.

malentendu [malãtã'dy], *n.m.* misunderstanding, misapprehension, mistake.

malfaçon [malfa'sõ], *n.f.* bad work; malpractice, illicit profit.

malfaire [mal'fɛːr], *v.i.* (*used only in the inf.*) to do evil.

malfaisant [malfɛ'zã], *a.* mischievous; spiteful, malevolent.

malfaiteur [malfɛ'tœːr], *n.m.* (*fem.* -trice) malefactor, evil-doer; offender; thief.

malfamé [malfa'me], *a.* ill-famed, of bad repute.

malformation [malfɔrma'sjõ], *n.f.* malformation.

malgache [mal'gaʃ], *a.* Madagascan.—*n.* (Malgache) Malagasy, Madagascan.

malgracieusement [malgrasjøz'mã], *adv.* ungraciously, rudely, uncivilly.

malgracieux [malgra'sjø], *a.* (*fem.* -euse) rude, ungracious, uncivil.

malgré [mal'gre], *prep.* in spite of, notwithstanding.

malhabile [mala'bil], *a.* unskilled, awkward.

malhabilement [malabil'mã], *adv.* unskilfully, awkwardly.

malhabileté [malabil'te], *n.f.* unskilfulness, awkwardness, clumsiness.

malheur [ma'lœːr], *n.m.* unhappiness, misfortune, bad luck; mischance; calamity disaster; woe, adversity; poverty.

malheureusement [malœrøz'mã], *adv.* unfortunately.

malheureux [malœ'rø], *a.* (*fem.* -euse) unfortunate, unlucky; unsuccessful; unpleasant; unhappy, miserable, wretched.—*n.m.* (*fem.* -euse) unhappy person.

malhonnête [malɔ'nɛːt], *a.* dishonest; uncivil, rude.—*n.* rude person.

malhonnêtement [malɔnɛt'mã], *adv.* dishonestly; rudely.

malhonnêteté [malɔnɛt'te], *n.f.* rudeness, incivility; dishonesty.

malice [ma'lis], *n.f.* malice, spite; mischievousness; prank, trick.

malicieusement [malisjøz'mã], *adv.* maliciously; mischievously; slyly.

malicieux [mali'sjø], *a.* (*fem.* -euse) malicious, spiteful; mischievous; roguish.

malignement [malin'mã], *adv.* malignantly; maliciously.

malignité [malini'te], *n.f.* malignity, spite.

malin [ma'lɛ̃], *a.* (*fem.* maligne) malicious, mischievous; malignant; waggish, roguish; cunning, clever.—*n.m.* (*fem.* maligne) malignant *or* malicious person.—*n.m.* devil, evil spirit, fiend.

maline [ma'lin], *n.f.* spring tide.

malingre [ma'lɛ̃ːgr], *a.* sickly, weakly, puny.

malintentionné [malɛ̃tãsjo'ne], *a.* evil-minded, ill-disposed.

malle [mal], *n.f.* trunk, box; mail-coach, mail boat.

malléabilité [maleabili'te], *n.f.* malleability; pliability.

malléable [male'abl], *a.* malleable.

malle-poste [mal'pɔst], *n.f.* (*pl.* malles-poste(s)) mail-coach.

mallette [ma'lɛt], *n.f.* small case, suitcase, attaché-case.

malmener [malmə'ne], *v.t.* (*conjug. like* AMENER) to ill-treat, to handle roughly; to abuse.

malodorant [malɔdɔ'rã], *a.* malodorous, ill-smelling.

malotru [malɔ'try], *a.* coarse, uncouth, vulgar.—*n.m.* (*fem.* -e) ill-bred person; lout.

Malouines [ma'lwin], les Îles, *f. pl.* the Falkland Islands.

malpeigné [malpɛ'ne], *a.* unkempt.—*n.m.* (*fem.* -ée) unkempt *or* dirty person.

malplaisant [malplɛ'zã], *a.* unpleasant, disagreeable.

malpropre [mal'prɔpr], *a.* slovenly, dirty; dishonest; unfit (à).

malproprement [malprɔprə'mã], *adv.* in a slovenly way, dirtily; improperly.

malpropreté [malprɔprə'te], *n.f.* dirtiness.
malsain [mal'sɛ̃], *a.* unhealthy; unwholesome, injurious.
malséant [malse'ã], *a.* unbecoming, unseemly, improper.
malsonnant [malsɔ'nã], *a.* ill-sounding; offensive.
malt [malt], *n.m.* malt.
maltais [mal'tɛ], *a.* Maltese.—*n.m.* Maltese (*language*); (**Maltais,** *fem.* **-aise**) Maltese (*person*).
Malte [malt], **la,** *f.* Malta.
maltraiter [maltrɛ'te], *v.t.* to ill-use, to maltreat, to abuse.
malveillamment [malvɛja'mã], *adv.* malevolently.
malveillance [malvɛ'jãːs], *n.f.* malevolence, ill-will, malice.
malveillant [malvɛ'jã], *a.* malevolent, malignant, ill-disposed, spiteful.—*n.m.* (*fem.* **-e**) evil-minded person.
malversation [malvɛrsa'sjɔ̃], *n.f.* malversation, peculation, embezzlement.
maman [ma'mã], *n.f.* mamma, mummy.
mamelle [ma'mɛl], *n.f.* breast; udder.
mamelon [mam'lɔ̃], *n.m.* nipple, teat; dug (*of animals*); pap, hillock, knoll.
mameluk [mam'luk], *n.m.* mameluke.
mammouth [ma'mut], *n.m.* mammoth.
manant [ma'nã], *n.m.* peasant, clodhopper.
manche (1) [mãːʃ], *n.m.* handle; neck (*of violin etc.*).
manche (2) [mãːʃ], *n.f.* sleeve; hose(-pipe); channel; (*Spt.*) rubber, game, heat.
Manche [mãːʃ], **la,** *f.* The (English) Channel. *Les Îles de la Manche,* the Channel Islands.
manchette [mã'ʃɛt], *n.f.* cuff; ruffle; wristband.
manchon [mã'ʃɔ̃], *n.m.* muff.
manchot [mã'ʃo], *a.* one-handed, one-armed.—*n.m.* penguin; (*fem.* **-e**) one-handed, one-armed person.
mandarin [mãda'rɛ̃], *a.* and *n.m.* (*fem.* **-ine** (1)) mandarin.
mandarine (2) [mãda'rin], *n.f.* tangerine.
mandat [mã'da], *n.m.* mandate, authority; warrant, writ; money-order, order.
mandataire [mãda'tɛːr], *n.m.* mandatory; proxy, attorney, agent.
mandchou [mãt'ʃu], *a.* Manchu(rian).—*n.m.* Manchu(rian) (*language*); (**Mandchou,** *fem.* **-oue**) Manchu(rian) (*person*).
Mandchourie [mãtʃu'ri], **la,** *f.* Manchuria.
mandement [mãd'mã], *n.m.* mandate; bishop's letter.
mander [mã'de], *v.t.* to write, to send word, to inform; to send for.
mandoline [mãdɔ'lin], *n.f.* mandolin.
mandoliniste [mãdɔli'nist], *n.* mandolin-player.
manège [ma'nɛːʒ], *n.m.* horsemanship; riding-school; merry-go-round; (*fig.*) trick, intrigue.
mânes [mɑːn], *n.m. pl.* manes, shades.
manette [ma'nɛt], *n.f.* hand-lever, grip; (*Hort.*) trowel.
mangeable [mã'ʒabl], *a.* eatable, edible.
mangeoire [mã'ʒwaːr], *n.f.* manger, crib.
manger [mã'ʒe], *v.t.* (*see Verb Tables*) to eat; (*fig.*) to squander, to run through.—*v.i.* to eat; to feed.—*n.m.* eating; victuals, food.

se manger, *v.r.* to eat each other; to hurt each other; to be edible.
mangeur [mã'ʒœːr], *n.m.* (*fem.* **-euse**) eater; spendthrift.
mangouste [mã'gust]. *n.f.* mongoose.
maniable [ma'njabl], *a.* easy to handle; tractable, supple, pliable.
maniaque [ma'njak], *a.* eccentric, having a mania.—*n.* crank, faddist.
manicure [mani'kyːr], [MANICURE].
manie [ma'ni], *n.f.* mania; fad, hobby; inveterate habit. craze.
maniement [mani'mã], *n.m.* handling; management, use.
manier [ma'nje], *v.t.* to handle; to touch; to use, to wield; to manage, to govern.
manière [ma'njɛːr], *n.f.* manner, way, style; sort; affectation; (*pl.*) manners; *de manière à,* so as to; *de quelle manière,* how; *manière d'être,* bearing, attitude.
maniéré [manje're], *a.* affected, unnatural, forced.
maniérisme [manje'rism], *n.m.* mannerism.
manifestation [manifɛsta'sjɔ̃], *n.f.* manifestation; (*Polit.*) demonstration.
manifeste [mani'fɛst], *a.* manifest, obvious.—*n.m.* manifesto.
manifestement [manifɛstə'mã], *adv.* manifestly.
manifester [manifɛs'te], *v.t.* to manifest, to display, to show.—*v.i.* to attend a (*political*) demonstration. **se manifester,** *v.r.* to manifest oneself, to make oneself known.
manigance [mani'gãːs], *n.f.* (*fam.*) manœuvre, intrigue.
manigancer [manigã'se], *v.t.* (*conjug. like* COMMENCER) to contrive, to plot.
Manille [ma'niːj], **la,** *f.* Manila.
manipulateur [manipyla'tœːr]. *n.m.* (*fem.* **-trice**) manipulator.
manipulation [manipyla'sjɔ̃]. *n.f.* manipulation.
manipuler [manipy'le], *v.t.* to manipulate; (*Teleg.*) to operate.
manivelle [mani'vɛl], *n.f.* crank; handle.
manne (1) [maːn], *n.f.* manna.
manne (2) [maːn]. *n.f.* hamper, flat basket.
mannequin (1) [man'kɛ̃], *n.m.* small hamper.
mannequin (2) [man'kɛ̃], *n.m.* lay figure; tailor's dummy; model girl; mannequin.
manœuvre [ma'nœːvr], *n.f.* working; drilling (*of soldiers*); manœuvre; scheme; move; (*Rail.*) marshalling.—*n.m.* unskilled workman, labourer, navvy.
manœuvrer [manœ'vre], *v.t.* to manœuvre; to work (*a machine*); to shunt (*trains*).
manœuvrier [manœvri'e], *a.* (*fem.* **-ière**) highly trained.—*n.m.* expert seaman; tactician.
manoir [ma'nwaːr], *n.m.* manor; country-house.
manouvrier [manuvri'e], *n.m.* (*fem.* **-ière**) day-labourer.
manquant [mã'kã], *a.* missing, absent, wanting.—*n.m.* (*fem.* **-e**) absentee, defaulter.—*n.m.* (*pl.*) shortages deficiencies.
manque [mãːk]. *n.m.* want, lack; defect; deficiency.
manqué [mã'ke], *a.* missed; defective; unsuccessful, abortive.
manquement [mãkə'mã], *n.m.* omission, oversight; failure; breach.

manquer

manquer [mã′ke], *v.t.* to miss, to lose; to spoil.—*v.i.* to miss, to fail; to be wanting; to be deficient; to slip; to misfire; to go bankrupt; to miscarry.

mansarde [mã′sard], *n.f.* roof-window, dormer; garret.

mansardé [mãsar′de], *a.* with attics.

mansuétude [mãsɥe′tyd], *n.f.* mildness, gentleness, forbearance.

mante (1) [mã:t], *n.f.* mantle (*woman's*).

mante (2) [mã:t], *n.f.* mantis; *mante religieuse*, praying mantis.

manteau [mã′to], *n.m.* (*pl.* **-eaux**) cloak, mantle; overcoat; (*fig.*) pretence.

mantille [mã′ti:j], *n.f.* mantilla.

manucure [many′ky:r], **manicure** [mani′ky:r], *n.* manicure (*person*); manicurist.

manuel [ma′nɥel], *a.* (*fem.* **-elle**) manual, portable.—*n.m.* manual, textbook.

manuellement [manɥel′mã], *adv.* by hand, manually.

manufacture [manyfak′ty:r], *n.f.* manufacture, making; factory, mill, works.

manufacturer [manyfakty′re], *v.t.* to manufacture.

manufacturier [manyfakty′rje], *a.* (*fem.* **-ière**) manufacturing.—*n.m.* manufacturer.

manuscrit [manys′kri], *a.* handwritten.—*n.m.* manuscript.

manutention [manytã′sjõ], *n.f.* management, administration; manipulation; handling (*of goods etc.*); army bakery.

mappemonde [map′mõ:d], *n.f.* map of the world, planisphere.

maquereau [ma′kro], *n.m.* (*pl.* **-eaux**) mackerel.

maquette [ma′kɛt], *n.f.* (*Sculp.*) small rough model (*in clay, wax etc.*); (*Paint.*) rough sketch; lay figure; (*Theat., Cine.*) model.

maquignon [maki′nõ], *n.m.* (*fem.* **-onne**) horse-dealer, jobber.

maquignonnage [makinɔ′na:ʒ], *n.m.* horse-dealing; underhand work, jobbery.

maquignonner [makinɔ′ne], *v.t.* to jockey, to bishop (*a horse for sale*); to job.

maquillage [maki′ja:ʒ], *n.m.* make-up.

maquiller [maki′je], *v.t.* to make up; to fake up. **se maquiller**, *v.r.* to make up *or* paint oneself.

maquilleur [maki′jœ:r], *n.m.* (*fem.* **-euse**) (*Theat.*) maker-up; faker (*of paintings etc.*).

maquis [ma′ki], *n.m. inv.* scrub (*in Corsica*); (*1941-44*) underground forces.

maquisard [maki′za:r], *n.m.* free fighter in the maquis.

maraîcher [marɛ′ʃe], *a.* (*fem.* **-ère**) of market-gardening.—*n.m.* market-gardener.

marais [ma′rɛ], *n.m.* marsh, fen, bog, swamp.

marasme [ma′rasm], *n.m.* emaciation; (*fig.*) depression; stagnation, slump.

marâtre [ma′rɑ:tr], *n.f.* stepmother; (*fig.*) harsh mother.

maraudage [maro′da:ʒ], *n.m.* marauding.

maraude [ma′ro:d], *n.f.* pilfering.

marauder [maro′de], *v.i.* to pilfer, to go scrounging.

maraudeur [maro′dœ:r], *n.m.* (*fem.* **-euse**) marauder; plunderer.

marbre [marbr], *n.m.* marble.

marbré [mar′bre], *a.* marbled.

marbrer [mar′bre], *v.t.* to marble, to vein.

marbrerie [marbrə′ri], *n.f.* marble-cutting; marble-works.

marbrier [marbri′e], *a.* (*fem.* **-ière**) of marble.—*n.m.* marble-cutter, marble-polisher; dealer in marble.—*n.f.* (**-ière**) marble-quarry.

marbrure [mar′bry:r], *n.f.* marbling; mottling (*on the skin*).

marc [ma:r], *n.m.* residuum (*of fruit etc. squeezed, boiled* or *strained*); dregs, grounds.

Marc [mark], *m.* Mark.

marchand [mar′ʃã], *a.* saleable, trading.—*n.m.* (*fem.* **-e**) dealer, tradesman, shopkeeper; merchant; *marchand des quatre saisons*, costermonger, barrow-boy; *marchand au détail*, retail merchant; *marchand en gros*, wholesale dealer.

marchandage [marʃã′da:ʒ], *n.m.* bargaining, haggling; piece-work.

marchander [marʃã′de], *v.t.* to bargain for; to haggle over; (*fig.*) to spare; to grudge.—*v.i.* to haggle; to hesitate.

marchandeur [marʃã′dœ:r], *n.m.* (*fem.* **-euse**) bargainer, haggler; contractor on small scale.

marchandise [marʃã′di:z], *n.f.* merchandise; goods, wares, commodities.

marche (1) [marʃ], *n.f.* walk; gait; march, journey; procession; movement; conduct; *marche arrière*, reversing (*of a car*); *mettre en marche*, to set going.

marche (2) [marʃ], *n.f.* step, stair; treadle.

marché [mar′ʃe], *n.m.* market; market-place; bargain, purchase; price, rate; contract; *à bon marché*, cheaply; *bon marché*, cheap, cheapness.

marchepied [marʃə′pje], *n.m.* step (*of a coach, altar etc.*); step-ladder; running-board.

marcher [mar′ʃe], *v.i.* to walk; to progress; to step, to tread; to march; to run, to ply; to work (*of a machine*).

marcheur [mar′ʃœ:r], *n.m.* (*fem.* **-euse**) walker.

mardi [mar′di], *n.m.* Tuesday; *mardi gras*, Shrove Tuesday.

mare [ma:r], *n.f.* pool, pond.

marécage [mare′ka:ʒ], *n.m.* marsh, bog, fen, swamp.

marécageux [mareka′ʒø], *a.* (*fem.* **-euse**) marshy, swampy, boggy.

maréchal [mare′ʃal], *n.m.* (*pl.* **-aux**) marshal, field-marshal.

maréchalerie [mareʃal′ri], *n.f.* farriery, smithy.

maréchal-ferrant [mareʃalfɛ′rã], *n.m.* (*pl.* **maréchaux-ferrants**) farrier, shoeing-smith.

marée [ma′re], *n.f.* tide, flood; fresh sea-fish.

marelle [ma′rɛl], *n.f.* hopscotch.

mareyeur [marɛ′jœ:r], *n.m.* fish-factor, fish-salesman.

margarine [marga′rin], *n.f.* margarine.

marge [marʒ], *n.f.* margin, border, edge; (*fig.*) freedom, latitude, scope; means.

margelle [mar′ʒɛl], *n.f.* curb, edge (*of a well etc.*).

Marguerite [margə′rit], *f.* Margaret.

marguerite [margə′rit], *n.f.* daisy.

marguillier [margi′je], *n.m.* churchwarden.

mari [ma′ri], *n.m.* husband.

mariable [ma′rjabl], *a.* marriageable.

mariage [ma'rjaːʒ], n.m. marriage; matrimony; wedding; union, blending.

Marie [ma'ri], f. Mary, Maria.

marié [ma'rje], a. married.—n.m. (fem. -ée) married man; bridegroom; married woman; bride.

marier [ma'rje], v.t. to give in marriage, to marry off; to match. **se marier,** v.r. to marry, to get married (avec).

marieur [ma'rjœːr], n.m. (fem. -euse) matchmaker.

marin [ma'rɛ̃], a. marine; sea-going.—n.m. sailor.

marinade [mari'nad], n.f. pickle, souse.

marine [ma'rin], n.f. sea-service; Admiralty; navy.

mariner [mari'ne], v.t. to pickle, to souse.

marinier [mari'nje], a. (fem. -ière (1)) officiers mariniers, petty officers.—n.m. bargeman, lighter-man.—n.f. (-ière) (Swim.) side-stroke.

marinière (2) [mari'njɛːr], n.f. (Cook.) onion sauce.

marionnette [marjɔ'nɛt], n.f. puppet, marionette; (pl.) puppet-show.

marital [mari'tal], a. (m. pl. -aux) marital.

maritalement [marital'mã], adv. maritally, as man and wife.

maritime [mari'tim], a. maritime, naval.

marmaille [mar'maːj], n.f. (collog.) brats.

marmelade [marmə'lad], n.f. compote; (fig.) jelly, soup.

marmite [mar'mit], n.f. cooking-pot.

marmiteux [marmi'tø], a. (fem. -euse) pitiful, wretched, miserable.—n.m. (fem. -euse) poor devil.

marmiton [marmi'tɔ̃], n.m. scullion.

marmonner [marmɔ'ne], v.t. to mutter.

marmoréen [marmɔre'ɛ̃], a. (fem. -éenne) marmorean.

marmot [mar'mo], n.m. kid, brat, urchin.

marmotte [mar'mɔt], n.f. marmot.

marmotter [marmɔ'te], v.t., v.i. to mutter, to mumble.

marmouset [marmu'zɛ], n.m. grotesque figure; young monkey (little boy); fire-dog.

marne [marn], n.f. marl, chalk, clay.

marner [mar'ne], v.t. to marl.

marneux [mar'nø], a. (fem. -euse) marly.

marnière [mar'njɛːr], n.f. marlpit.

Maroc [ma'rɔk], le, m. Morocco.

marocain [marɔ'kɛ̃], a. Moroccan.—n.m. (**Marocain,** fem. **-aine**) Moroccan (person).

maroquin [marɔ'kɛ̃], n.m. morocco leather.

maroquiner [marɔki'ne], v.t. to morocco.

maroquinerie [marɔkin'ri], n.f. moroccoleather manufacture or factory.

maroquinier [marɔki'nje], n.m. moroccoleather tanner.

marotte [ma'rɔt], n.f. cap and bells; hairdresser's dummy head; (fig.) fancy, hobby.

marquant [mar'kã], a. conspicuous, striking.

marque [mark], n.f. mark, imprint, stamp; cipher, trade-mark, make; badge, sign, token; proof; distinction.

marqué [mar'ke], a. marked, conspicuous, obvious; determined.

marquer [mar'ke], v.t. to mark; to stamp; to brand; to indicate; to denote; to testify; to score.—v.i. to mark, to be remarkable; to show off.

marqueter [markə'te], v.t. (conjug. like APPELER) to speckle, to spot; to inlay.

marqueterie [markə'tri], n.f. marquetry, inlaid-work, inlaying.

marqueur [mar'kœːr], n.m. (fem. -euse) marker; scorer.

marquis [mar'ki], n.m. marquess, marquis.

marquise [mar'kiːz], n.f. marchioness; marquee, glass porch or roof.

marraine [ma'rɛn], n.f. godmother; sponsor.

marron (1) [ma'rɔ̃], a. inv. maroon, chestnutcolour.—n.m. chestnut; cracker (fireworks); marron d'Inde, horse-chestnut.

marron (2) [ma'rɔ̃], a. (fem. -onne) fugitive, runaway (of slaves); (Comm.) unlicensed; unqualified (doctor etc.).

marronnier [marɔ'nje], n.m. chestnut-tree; marronnier d'Inde, horse-chestnut-tree.

mars [mars], n.m. March.

Marseillaise [marsɛ'jɛːz], n.f. Marseillaise (French national anthem).

marsouin [mar'swɛ̃], n.m. porpoise.

marte [MARTRE].

marteau [mar'to], n.m. (pl. -eaux) hammer; marteau de porte, knocker; marteau pneumatique, pneumatic drill.

marteau-pilon [martopi'lɔ̃], n.m. (pl. marteaux-pilons) steam-hammer.

martelage [martə'laːʒ], n.m. hammering; marking (of trees).

martelé [martə'le], a. hammered; (Mus.) brilliant and distinct.

marteler [martə'le], v.t. (conjug. like AMENER) to hammer; to mark (trees).

Marthe [mart], f. Martha.

martial [mar'sjal], a. (m. pl. -aux) martial, warlike, soldierly.

martinet (1) [marti'nɛ], n.m. (Orn.) swift, martlet.

martinet (2) [marti'nɛ], n.m. tilt-hammer; cat-o'-nine-tails.

martingale [martɛ̃'gal], n.f. martingale; jouer la martingale, to play double or quits.

martin-pêcheur [martɛpɛ'ʃœːr], n.m. (pl. martins-pêcheurs) kingfisher; martinpêcheur d'Australie, laughing jackass.

martre [martr], **marte** [mart], n.f. marten.

martyr [mar'tiːr], n.m. (fem. **martyre** (1)) martyr.

martyre (2) [mar'tiːr], n.m. martyrdom.

martyriser [martiri'ze], v.t. to martyrize; to torment, to torture.

marxisme [mark'sism], n.m. Marxism.

marxiste [mark'sist], a. and n. Marxist.

mascarade [maska'rad], n.f. masquerade.

mascotte [mas'kɔt], n.f. mascot, charm.

masculin [masky'lɛ̃], a. masculine, male.—n.m. (Gram.) masculine.

masculiniser [maskylini'ze], v.t. to make masculine.

masculinité [maskylini'te], n.f. masculinity.

masque [mask], n.m. mask; (fig.) blind, cloak, pretence; masquerader, mummer; (Fenc.) face-guard.

masqué [mas'ke], a. masked; disguised; concealed; virage masqué, blind corner.

masquer [mas'ke], v.t. to mask; to cloak, to disguise; to conceal.

massacrant [masa'krã], a. used chiefly in être d'une humeur massacrante, to be in an awful temper.

massacre

massacre [ma'sakr], *n.m.* massacre, butchery, slaughter; (*fig.*) havoc, waste.
massacrer [masa'kre], *v.t.* to massacre, to butcher, to murder, to slaughter; (*fig.*) to bungle.
massacreur [masa'krœːr], *n.m.* (*fem.* **-euse**) slaughterer, slayer; (*fig.*) bungler.
massage [ma'saːʒ], *n.m.* massage.
masse (1) [mas], *n.f.* mass, heap, lump; mob; stock; (*Elec.*) earth.
masse (2) [mas], *n.f.* sledge-hammer.
massepain [mas'pɛ̃], *n.m.* marzipan.
masser [ma'se], *v.t.* to mass (*troops etc.*); to massage.
masseur [ma'sœːr], *n.m.* (*fem.* **-euse**) masseur, masseuse.
massier [ma'sje], *n.m.* mace-bearer.
massif [ma'sif], *a.* (*fem.* **-ive**) massive, bulky, massy, solid; lumpish, heavy.—*n.m.* clump (*of trees, flowers etc.*); solid mass *or* block (*of masonry*); (*Geog.*) massif.
massivement [masiv'mɑ̃], *adv.* massively, heavily, solidly.
massiveté [masiv'te], *n.f.* massiveness.
massue [ma'sy], *n.f.* club (*weapon*).
mastic [mas'tik], *n.m.* mastic; cement; putty; stopping (*for teeth, tyres*); plastic wood.
masticage [masti'kaːʒ], *n.m.* cementing, puttying, filling.
mastication [mastikɑ'sjɔ̃], *n.f.* mastication, chewing.
mastiquer (1) [masti'ke], *v.t.* to masticate.
mastiquer (2) [masti'ke], *v.t.* to putty, to cement.
mastodonte [mastɔ'dɔ̃ːt], *n.m.* mastodon.
mastoïde [mastɔ'id], *a.* mastoid.
masure [ma'zyːr], *n.f.* hovel, tumbledown cottage.
mat (1) [mat], *n.m.* (*Chess*) mate.
mat (2) [mat], *a.* mat, dull, unpolished; dull-sounding; heavy, sodden.
mât [mɑ], *n.m.* mast; pole.
matador [matɑ'dɔːr], *n.m.* matador.
matamore [mata'mɔːr], *n.m.* blusterer, braggart.
match [matʃ], *n.m.* (*pl.* **matches**) (*Spt.*) match; *match nul*, draw.
matelas [ma'tlɑ], *n.m.* mattress; pad, cushion; *toile à matelas*, ticking.
matelasser [matla'se], *v.t.* to stuff, to pad.
matelot [ma'tlo], *n.m.* sailor, seaman.
matelote [ma'tlɔt], *n.f.* sailor's wife; fish-stew.
mater (1) [ma'te], *v.t.* to checkmate; to bring down, to subdue.
mater (2) [ma'te], *v.t.* to make mat *or* dull, to deaden.
matérialiser [materjali'ze], *v.t.* to materialize.
matérialisme [materja'lism], *n.m.* materialism.
matérialiste [materja'list], *a.* materialistic.—*n.* materialist.
matériaux [mate'rjo], *n.m. pl.* materials.
matériel [mate'rjɛl], *a.* (*fem.* **-elle**) material; gross, rough; heavy, dull.—*n.m.* material, working-stock, implements, plant.
matériellement [materjɛl'mɑ̃], *adv.* materially; positively; sensually.
maternel [mater'nɛl], *a.* (*fem.* **-elle**) maternal, motherly; *école maternelle*, nursery school.
maternité [materni'te], *n.f.* maternity.

mathématicien [matemati'sjɛ̃], *n.m.* (*fem.* **-enne**) mathematician.
mathématique [matema'tik], *a.* mathematical.—*n.f.* (*usu. in pl.*) mathematics.
mathématiquement [matematik'mɑ̃], *adv.* mathematically.
matière [ma'tjɛːr], *n.f.* matter; material; subject-matter; cause, motive; contents; *matière première*, raw material.
matin [ma'tɛ̃], *n.m.* morning, forenoon; prime, dawn.—*adv.* early, early in the morning.
mâtin [mɑ'tɛ̃], *n.m.* mastiff; big mongrel dog.
matinal [mati'nal], *a.* (*m. pl.* **-aux**) morning, early; early-rising.
matinée [mati'ne], *n.f.* morning, forenoon; afternoon performance, matinée.
matines [ma'tin], *n.f. pl.* matins.
matineux [mati'nø], *a.* (*fem.* **-euse**) rising early.
matois [ma'twa], *a.* cunning, artful, sly.—*n.m.* (*fem.* **-e**) cunning person, sly dog.
matoisement [matwaz'mɑ̃], *adv.* cunningly, slyly.
matoiserie [matwaz'ri], *n.f.* cunning; wile.
matou [ma'tu], *n.m.* tom-cat; (*fam.*) curmudgeon.
matraque [ma'trak], *n.f.* bludgeon; truncheon.
matriarcal [matriar'kal], *a.* (*m. pl.* **-aux**) matriarchal.
matriarcat [matriar'ka], *n.m.* matriarchy.
matrice [ma'tris], *n.f.* womb, matrix.
matricide [matri'sid], *a.* matricidal.—*n.* matricide (*person*).—*n.m.* matricide (*crime*).
matricule [matri'kyl], *n.f.* register, roll; matriculation.—*n.m.* regimental number (*of a soldier*); number (*of a rifle etc.*).
matrimonial [matrimɔ'njal], *a.* (*m. pl.* **-aux**) matrimonial.
Matthieu [ma'tjø], *m.* Matthew.
maturation [matyrɑ'sjɔ̃], *n.f.* maturation.
mâture [mɑ'tyːr], *n.f.* masting, masts and spars.
maturité [matyri'te], *n.f.* maturity, ripeness.
maudire [mo'diːr], *v.t. irr.* to curse; to detest.
maudissable [modi'sabl], *a.* execrable, detestable.
maudit [mo'di], *a.* cursed, accursed; wretched.
maugréer [mogre'e], *v.i.* to fret and fume, to curse and swear.
maure [MORE].
Maurice [mɔ'ris], *m.* Maurice; *l'île Maurice*, Mauritius.
Mauritanie [mɔrita'ni], **la**, *f.* Mauritania.
mauritanien [mɔrita'njɛ̃], *a.* (*fem.* **-enne**) Mauritanian.—*n.m.* (**Mauritanien**, *fem.* **-enne**) Mauritanian (*person*).
mausolée [mozo'le], *n.m.* mausoleum.
maussade [mo'sad], *a.* sulky sullen, cross; disagreeable, dull.
maussadement [mosad'mɑ̃], *adv.* disagreeably, sullenly, peevishly.
maussaderie [mosa'dri], *n.f.* sullenness, sulkiness.
mauvais [mɔ'vɛ], *a.* bad, ill, evil; naughty mischievous; hurtful, wrong; unpleasant; wretched; nasty.—*n.m.* bad.—*adv.* bad, badly, wrong.
mauve [moːv] *a.* mauve.—*n.f.* (*Bot.*) mallow.

212

maxillaire [maksi'lɛːr], *a.* maxillary.—*n.m.* jaw-bone.

maxime [mak'sim], *n.f.* maxim.

maximum [maksi'mɔm], *a.* (*fem.* **maxima**) maximum.—*n.m.* (*pl.* **maxima** or **maximums**) maximum; acme.

mayonnaise [majɔ'nɛːz], *n.f.* mayonnaise.

mazout [ma'ʒut], *n.m.* fuel oil.

me [mə], *pron. pers.* me; to me.

méandre [me'ãːdr], *n.m.* meander, winding.

mécanicien [mekani'sjɛ̃], *n.m.* mechanic; engine-driver, (*Am.*) engineer; *ingénieur mécanicien*, mechanical engineer.

mécanique [meka'nik], *a.* mechanical.—*n.f.* mechanics; mechanism, machinery; machine.

mécaniquement [mekanik'mã], *adv.* mechanically.

mécanisation [mekaniza'sjɔ̃], *n.f.* mechanization.

mécaniser [mekani'ze], *v.t.* to mechanize.

mécanisme [meka'nism], *n.m.* mechanism, machinery.

méchamment [meʃa'mã], *adv.* wickedly; maliciously.

méchanceté [meʃãs'te], *n.f.* wickedness; spitefulness; naughtiness.

méchant [me'ʃã], *a.* wicked, evil, bad; spiteful, malicious; naughty; paltry; vicious (*of an animal*); nasty.—*n.m.* (*fem.* **-e**) wicked person, evil-doer; naughty child.

mèche [mɛːʃ], *n.f.* wick (*of candle*); fuse; bit, drill; worm (*of screws*); lock (*of hair*).

mécompte [me'kɔ̃ːt], *n.m.* miscalculation; mistake; disappointment.

méconnaissable [mekɔnɛ'sabl], *a.* unrecognizable.

méconnaissance [mekɔnɛ'sãːs], *n.f.* misappreciation, misreading; ingratitude.

méconnaître [mekɔ'nɛːtr], *v.t. irr.* (*conjug. like* CONNAÎTRE) not to recognize; to disown; to disregard, to ignore; to misjudge. **se méconnaître**, *v.r.* to forget oneself.

méconnu [mekɔ'ny], *a.* unrecognized, unacknowledged; ignored, disowned.

mécontent [mekɔ̃'tã], *a.* displeased, dissatisfied.—*n.m.* (*fem.* **-e**) malcontent.

mécontentement [mekɔ̃tãt'mã], *n.m.* dissatisfaction, discontent.

mécontenter [mekɔ̃tã'te], *v.t.* to displease.

Mecque [mɛk], **la**, *f.* Mecca.

mécréant [mekre'ã], *n.m.* (*fem.* **-e**) unbeliever, infidel.

médaille [me'daːj], *n.f.* medal; (*Arch.*) medallion.

médaillé [meda'je], *a.* with a medal as a reward; having a badge (*of hawker, porter etc.*).—*n.m.* (*fem.* **-ée**) holder of a medal.

médaillon [meda'jɔ̃], *n.m.* medallion; locket.

médecin [med'sɛ̃], *n.m.* physician, doctor; *faire venir le médecin*, to send for the doctor.

médecine [med'sin], *n.f.* medicine.

médiateur [medja'tœːr], *a.* (*fem.* **-trice**) mediatory.—*n.m.* (*fem.* **-trice**) mediator.

médiation [medja'sjɔ̃], *n.f.* mediation.

médical [medi'kal], *a.* (*m. pl.* **-aux**) medical.

médicament [medika'mã], *n.m.* medicine, drug.

médicamenter [medikamã'te], *v.t.* to physic, to doctor.

médication [medika'sjɔ̃], *n.f.* medication.

médicinal [medisi'nal], *a.* (*m. pl.* **-aux**) medicinal.

médiéval [medje'val], *a.* (*m. pl.* **-aux**) medi(a)eval.

médiocre [me'djɔkr], *a.* mediocre, middling; moderate.—*n.m.* mediocrity.

médiocrement [medjɔkrə'mã], *adv.* middlingly, indifferently; poorly; barely.

médiocrité [medjɔkri'te], *n.f.* mediocrity.

médire [me'diːr], *v.i. irr.* to slander, to speak ill of, to traduce.

médisance [medi'zãːs], *n.f.* slander, scandal.

médisant [medi'zã], *a.* slanderous, scandalous.—*n.m.* (*fem.* **-e**) slanderer, scandalmonger.

méditatif [medita'tif], *a.* (*fem.* **-tive**) meditative, pensive.

méditation [medita'sjɔ̃], *n.f.* meditation.

méditer [medi'te], *v.t.* to meditate, to think over; to plan.—*v.i.* to meditate, to muse.

méditerrané [meditɛra'ne], *a.* inland; *la* (*Mer*) *Méditerranée* the Mediterranean (Sea).

méditerranéen [meditɛrane'ɛ̃], *a.* (*fem.* **-enne**) Mediterranean.

médium [me'djɔm], *n.m.* medium.

médoc [me'dɔk], *n.m.* or *vin de Médoc*, Médoc (*claret*).

meeting [mi'tiŋ], *n.m.* (*Polit., Spt.*) meeting.

méfait [me'fɛ], *n.m.* misdeed, crime.

méfiance [me'fjãːs], *n.f.* mistrust, distrust, suspicion.

méfiant [me'fjã], *a.* distrustful, suspicious.

méfier (**se**) [səme'fje], *v.r.* to mistrust, to distrust, to be suspicious of (*de*).

mégaphone [mega'fɔn], *n.m.* megaphone.

mégarde [me'gard], *n.f.* inadvertence; *par mégarde*, inadvertently.

mégère [me'ʒɛːr], *n.f.* shrew, vixen.

mégot [me'go], *n.m.* (*pop.*) cigar-stump, cigarette-end.

meilleur [me'jœːr], *a.* better; preferable; *le meilleur*, the best; *meilleur marché*, cheaper; *de meilleure heure* earlier.—*n.m.* best.

mélancolie [melãkɔ'li], *n.f.* melancholy, sadness, gloom, dejection.

mélancolique [melãkɔ'lik], *a.* melancholy; dismal, gloomy.

mélancoliquement [melãkɔlik'mã], *adv.* gloomily.

mélange [me'lãːʒ], *n.m.* mixture, mingling; blending (*of tea*); medley, mash (*for brewing*).

mélanger [melã'ʒe], *v.t.* and **se mélanger**, *v.r.* (*conjug. like* MANGER) to mix, to mingle, to blend.

mélasse [me'las], *n.f.* molasses treacle.

mêlé [mɛ'le], *a.* mixed; miscellaneous.

mêlée [mɛ'le], *n.f.* conflict, fray; scramble, scuffle, free-fight; (*Rugby*) scrum.

mêler [mɛ'le], *v.t.* to mingle, to mix; to blend; to jumble; to entangle, to involve; to shuffle (*cards*). **se mêler**, *v.r.* to mingle to blend, to intermingle; to trouble oneself (*de*); to interfere (*de*); to have a hand in; to get entangled, to get mixed up (*dans*); *mêlez-vous de vos affaires*, mind your own business.

mélèze [me'lɛːz], *n.m.* larch.

mélodie [melɔ'di], *n.f.* melody; melodiousness.

mélodieusement

mélodieusement [melədjøz′mã], *adv.* tunefully.

mélodieux [melə′djø], *a.* (*fem.* **-euse**) melodious, musical, tuneful.

mélodramatique [melədrama′tik], *a.* melodramatic.

mélodrame [melə′dram], *n.m.* melodrama.

melon [mə′lɔ̃], *n.m.* melon; bowler (hat).

membrane [mã′bran], *n.f.* membrane; web (*of duck's foot etc.*).

membraneux [mãbra′nø], *a.* (*fem.* **-euse**) membranous.

membre [mã:br], *n.m.* limb; member.

membrure [mã′bry:r], *n.f.* limbs, frame (*of a person etc.*); ribs, timbers (*of a ship*).

même [mɛːm], *a.* same; self, self-same, very same; *moi-même*, myself.—*adv.* even, also; *à même de*, in a position to, able to; *de même*, likewise; *quand même*, even though; *tout de même*, all the same.

mémoire (1) [me′mwa:r], *n.f.* memory; remembrance; commemoration; fame; *de mémoire*, from memory; *de mémoire d'homme*, within living memory.

mémoire (2) [me′mwa:r], *n.m.* memorandum, bill, statement of account; (*Sci., Lit.*) treatise; memorial; (*pl.*) memoirs.

mémorable [memo′rabl], *a.* memorable.

mémorandum [memɔrã′dɔm], *n.m.* memorandum; notebook.

mémorial [memɔ′rjal], *n.m.* (*pl.* **-aux**) memorial; memoirs; (*Comm.*) waste-book.

menaçant [məna′sã], *a.* menacing, threatening.

menace [mə′nas], *n.f.* menace, threat.

menacer [məna′se], *v.t.* (*conjug. like* COMMENCER) to threaten, to menace; to forebode; to impend.

ménage [me′na:ʒ], *n.m.* housekeeping; household, family, married couple; household equipment; economy; *faire bon ménage*, to live happily together; *faire des ménages*, to go out charring; *femme de ménage*, charwoman.

ménagement [menaʒ′mã], *n.m.* regard, circumspection, caution, discretion.

ménager [mena′ʒe], *v.t.* (*conjug. like* MANGER) to be sparing of, to save; to be careful of, to treat with caution, to humour; to procure; to contrive. **se ménager**, *v.r.* to take care of oneself; to spare oneself.—*a.* (*fem.* **-ère**) thrifty, sparing, frugal; household.—*n.f.* (**-ère**) housewife, housekeeper; cruetstand; canteen (*of cutlery*).

ménagerie [menaʒ′ri], *n.f.* menagerie.

mendiant [mã′djã], *n.m.* (*fem.* **-e**) beggar, mendicant.

mendicité [mãdisi′te], *n.f.* begging, mendicity.

mendier [mã′dje], *v.t.* to beg for.—*v.i.* to beg.

mener [mə′ne], *v.t.* (*conjug. like* AMENER) to guide, to conduct, to lead; to drive (*a carriage*); to steer (*a boat etc.*); to bring, to take; to manage.—*v.i.* to lead, to conduct, to go.

ménestrel [menɛs′trɛl], *n.m.* minstrel.

meneur [mə′nœ:r], *n.m.* (*fem.* **-euse**) driver, leader; agitator, ringleader.

méningite [menɛ̃′ʒit], *n.f.* meningitis.

menotte [mə′nɔt], *n.f.* (*colloq.*) little hand (*of a child*); (*pl.*) handcuffs.

menotter [mənɔ′te], *v.t.* to handcuff.

mensonge [mã′sɔ̃:ʒ], *n.m.* lie, falsehood, untruth.

mensonger [mãsɔ̃′ʒe], *a.* (*fem.* **-ère**) lying, untrue, false.

menstruation [mãstrɥa′sjɔ̃], *n.f.* menstruation.

menstrues [mã′stry], *n.f. pl.* menstrua, periods.

mensualité [mãsɥali′te], *n.f.* monthly payment.

mensuel [mã′sɥɛl], *a.* (*fem.* **-elle**) monthly.

mensuellement [mãsɥɛl′mã], *adv.* monthly.

mensuration [mãsɥra′sjɔ̃], *n.f.* measurement.

mental [mã′tal], *a.* (*m. pl.* **-aux**) mental.

mentalement [mãtal′mã], *adv.* mentally.

mentalité [mãtali′te], *n.f.* mentality.

menteur [mã′tœ:r], *a.* (*fem.* **-euse**) lying, false, deceitful.—*n.m.* (*fem.* **-euse**) liar, story-teller.

menthe [mã:t], *n.f.* mint.

mention [mã′sjɔ̃], *n.f.* mention; (*sch.*) *reçu avec mention*, passed with distinction.

mentionner [mãsjɔ′ne], *v.t.* to mention, to name.

mentir [mã′ti:r], *v.i. irr.* (*conjug. like* SENTIR) to lie, to tell a lie *or* untruth.

menton [mã′tɔ̃], *n.m.* chin.

mentor [mã′tɔ:r], *n.m.* mentor, guide, tutor.

menu [mə′ny], *a.* slender, spare, thin, small; petty.—*n.m.* minute detail, particulars; menu, bill of fare; *par le menu*, in detail.—*adv.* small, fine, minutely, in small pieces; *hacher menu*, to mince.

menuet [mə′nɥɛ], *n.m.* minuet.

menuiser [mənɥi′ze], *v.t.* to saw, cut etc. (*wood*).—*v.i.* to do joiner's work.

menuiserie [mənɥi′zri], *n.f.* woodwork, joinery, joiner's work.

menuisier [mənɥi′zje], *n.m.* joiner, carpenter.

méprendre (se) [səme′prã:dr], *v.r. irr.* (*conjug. like* PRENDRE) to mistake, to be mistaken.

mépris [me′pri], *n.m.* contempt, scorn.

méprisable [mepri′zabl], *a.* contemptible, despicable.

méprisant [mepri′zã], *a.* contemptuous, scornful.

méprise [me′pri:z], *n.f.* mistake, misunderstanding.

mépriser [mepri′ze], *v.t.* to despise, to scorn.

mer [mɛ:r], *n.f.* sea; *aller au bord de la mer*, to go to the seaside; *en pleine mer*, on the open sea; *mal de mer*, seasickness.

mercantile [mɛrkã′til], *a.* mercantile, commercial; (*fig.*) mercenary.

mercenaire [mɛrsə′nɛ:r], *a.* mercenary, venal.—*n.m.* mercenary, hireling.

mercerie [mɛrsə′ri], *n.f.* haberdashery.

merci [mɛr′si], *n.f.* (*no pl.*) mercy, discretion, will.—*n.m.* thanks.—*int.* thank you, thanks.

mercier [mɛr′sje], *n.m.* (*fem.* **-ière**) haberdasher.

mercredi [mɛrkra′di], *n.m.* Wednesday; *mercredi des Cendres*, Ash Wednesday.

mercure [mɛr′ky:r], *n.m.* mercury, quicksilver.

mercuriel [mɛrky′rjɛl], *a.* (*fem.* **-elle**) mercurial.

mère [mɛ:r], *n.f.* mother; dam (*of animals*); (*fig.*) cause, reason.

méridien [meri′djɛ̃], *a.* (*fem.* **-enne**) and *n.m.* meridian.—*n.f.* (**-enne**) siesta.

méridional [meridjo'nal], *a.* (*m. pl.* **-aux**) meridional, southern.—*n.m.* (*fem.* **-e**) person of the Midi, southerner.

meringue [mə'rɛ̃:g], *n.f.* meringue (*confection*).

mérinos [meri'no:s], *n.m.* merino sheep; merino wool; merino (*material*).

merise [mə'ri:z], *n.f.* wild cherry.

merisier [mori'zje], *n.m.* wild cherry-tree.

méritant [meri'tɑ̃], *a.* meritorious, worthy.

mérite [me'rit], *n.m.* merit, worth; desert.

mériter [meri'te], *v.t.* to deserve, to merit; to earn.—*v.i.* to be deserving (*de*).

méritoire [meri'twa:r], *a.* meritorious.

méritoirement [meritwar'mɑ̃], *adv.* meritoriously, deservingly.

merlan [mɛr'lɑ̃], *n.m.* whiting.

merle [mɛrl], *n.m.* blackbird.

merluche [mɛr'lyʃ], *n.f.* hake; dried cod.

merveille [mɛr'vɛ:j], *n.f.* wonder, marvel, prodigy; *à merveille*, wonderfully well.

merveilleusement [mɛrvejøz'mɑ̃], *adv.* wonderfully, admirably.

merveilleux [mɛrvɛ'jø], *a.* (*fem.* **-euse**) wonderful, marvellous.—*n.m.* the wonderful the marvellous part.

mes [me], *pl.* [MON].

mésalliance [meza'ljɑ̃:s], *n.f.* misalliance, bad match.

mésallier [meza'lje], *v.t.* to marry off (*somebody*) badly; (*fig.*) to disparage. **se mésallier,** *v.r.* to marry beneath one.

mésange [me'zɑ̃:ʒ], *n.f.* (*Orn.*) tit.

mésangette [mezɑ̃'ʒɛt], *n.f.* bird-trap.

mésaventure [mezavɑ̃'ty:r], *n.f.* mischance, misadventure, misfortune.

mésentente [mezɑ̃'tɑ̃:t], *n.f.* misunderstanding; disagreement.

mésestime [mezɛs'tim], *n.f.* low esteem.

mésestimer [mezɛsti'me], *v.t.* to underestimate, to underrate.

mésintelligence [mezɛ̃tɛli'ʒɑ̃:s], *n.f.* misunderstanding, variance, disagreement.

mesmérisme [mɛsme'rism], *n.m.* mesmerism.

mesquin [mɛs'kɛ̃], *a.* shabby; paltry; mean.

mesquinement [mɛskin'mɑ̃], *adv.* shabbily, meanly.

mesquinerie [mɛskin'ri], *n.f.* meanness, shabbiness.

mess [mɛs], *n.m. inv.* (*Mil.*) mess.

message [mɛ'sa:ʒ], *n.m.* message.

messager [mɛsa'ʒe], *n.m.* (*fem.* **-ère**) messenger; carrier; (*fig.*) forerunner.

messagerie [mɛsa'ʒri], *n.f.* shipping office; carriage of goods; goods department; parcels office; *messageries maritimes*, shipping service.

messe [mɛs], *n.f.* (*R.-C. Ch.*) mass.

messéance [mɛse'ɑ̃:s], *n.f.* unseemliness, impropriety.

messéant [mɛse'ɑ̃], *a.* unseemly, unbecoming, improper.

messeigneurs [mɛse'nœːr], *pl.* [MONSEIGNEUR].

Messie [mɛ'si], *m.* Messiah.

messieurs [mɛ'sjø], *pl.* [MONSIEUR].

mesurable [məzy'rabl], *a.* measurable.

mesurage [məzy'ra:ʒ], *n.m.* measurement, measuring.

mesure [mə'zy:r], *n.f.* measure; gauge; standard; measurement, extent, limit; (*fig.*)

moderation; dimension; (*Mus.*) bar; (*Pros.*) metre; *à mesure que*, in proportion as, as; *outre mesure*, excessively; *se mettre en mesure de*, to prepare to, to get ready to.

mesuré [məzy're], *a.* measured, regular; cautious.

mesurer [məzy're], *v.t.* to measure; to proportion; to calculate; to compare, to consider. **se mesurer,** *v.r.* to try one's strength; (*fig.*) to vie, to contend, to cope.

mesureur [məzy'rœːr], *n.m.* measurer; meter.

mésusage [mezy'za:ʒ], *n.m.* misuse, abuse.

mésuser [mezy'ze], *v.i.* to misuse, to abuse (*de*).

métabolisme [metabo'lism], *n.m.* metabolism.

métairie [metɛ'ri], *n.f.* land, small farm.

métal [me'tal], *n.m.* (*pl.* **-aux**) metal.

métallique [meta'lik], *a.* metallic.

métallurgie [metalyr'ʒi], *n.f.* metallurgy.

métallurgiste [metalyr'ʒist], *n.m.* metallurgist.

métamorphose [metamor'fo:z], *n.f.* metamorphosis, transformation.

métaphore [meta'fo:r], *n.f.* metaphor.

métaphorique [metafo'rik], *a.* metaphorical.

métaphoriquement [metaforik'mɑ̃], *adv.* metaphorically.

métaphysique [metafi'zik], *a.* metaphysical, —*n.f.* metaphysics.

métatarse [meta'tars], *n.m.* (*Anat.*) metatarsus.

métayage [metɛ'ja:ʒ], *n.m.* metayage.

métayer [metɛ'je], *n.m.* (*fem.* **-ère**) small farmer.

météo [mete'o], *n.f.* (*fam.*) meteorology; weather-report; meteorological office.

météore [mete'o:r], *n.m.* meteor.

météorique [meteo'rik], *a.* meteoric.

météorite [meteo'rit], *n.m.* or *f.* meteorite.

météorologie [meteorolo'ʒi], *n.f.* meteorology.

météorologique [meteorolo'ʒik], *a.* meteorological.

météorologiste [meteorolo'ʒist], **météorologue** [meteoro'log], *n.* meteorologist.

méthane [me'tan], *n.m.* marsh gas, methane.

méthode [me'tod], *n.f.* method, system; way.

méthodique [meto'dik], *a.* methodical, systematic.

méthodiquement [metodik'mɑ̃], *adv.* methodically.

méthodisme [meto'dism], *n.m.* Methodism.

méthodiste [meto'dist] *a. and n.* Methodist.

méticuleusement [metikyløz'mɑ̃], *adv.* meticulously.

méticuleux [metiky'lø], *a.* (*fem.* **-euse**) meticulous, fastidious.

méticulosité [metikylozi'te], *n.f.* meticulousness.

métier [me'tje], *n.m.* trade, business, calling, craft, profession; loom, frame; *arts et métiers*, arts and crafts; *corps de métier*, corporation, guild; *gens de métier*, professionals; *homme de métier*, craftsman; *métier manuel*, handicraft.

métis [me'ti:s], *a.* (*fem.* **-isse**) half-caste, cross-bred; hybrid (*plant*); mongrel (*dog*).—*n.m.* (*fem.* **-isse**) half-caste; mongrel (*dog*).

métissage [meti'sa:ʒ], *n.m.* cross-breeding.

métisser [meti'se], *v.t.* to cross-breed.

métrage

métrage [me′tra:ʒ], *n.m.* measurement *(in metres)*; *(Cine.)* **court métrage**, short film.

mètre [mɛtr], *n.m.* metre *(1.09 yards)*; rule, measure *(of 1 metre)*; *(Pros.)* metre.

métrer [me′tɛ], *v.t. (conjug. like* CÉDER) to measure *(by the metre)*.

métreur [me′trœːr], *n.m.* quantity-surveyor.

métrique [me′trik], *a.* metric *(system etc.)*; *(Pros.)* metrical.—*n.f.* scansion.

métro [me′tro], *n.m. (colloq. abbr. of* **chemin de fer métropolitain**) the underground (railway), the tube *(in Paris)*, *(Am.)* the subway.

métropole [metro′pɔl], *n.f.* mother country; metropolis.

métropolitain [metropoli′tɛ̃], *a.* metropolitan.—*n.m.* metropolitan, archbishop; underground railway.

mets [mɛ], *n.m.* dish, food, viands.

mettable [mɛ′tabl], *a.* fit to be worn, wearable.

metteur [me′tœːr], *n.m.* **metteur en scène,** *(Theat.)* producer, *(Cine.)* director.

mettre [mɛtr], *v.t. irr.* to put, to set, to place; to put on, to wear; to employ; to contribute, to expend; to suppose, to imagine; *mettre en marche* or *en mouvement,* to start up, to set going; *mettre quelqu'un en état de,* to enable someone to; *mettre un habit,* to put on a coat. **se mettre,** *v.r.* to put or place oneself; to dress; to begin *(à)*; to take to; *se mettre à parler,* to begin to speak; *se mettre à table,* to sit down to table; *se mettre bien,* to dress well; *se mettre en route,* to start.

meuble [mœbl], *a.* movable; *biens meubles,* *(Law)* personal property.—*n.m.* piece of furniture; *(pl.)* furniture.

meublé [mœ′ble], *a.* furnished.—*n.m.* a furnished room *or* flat.

meubler [mœ′ble], *v.t.* to furnish; to stock, to store. **se meubler,** *v.r.* to furnish one's home.

meule [mø:l], *n.f.* millstone, grindstone; *(Agric.)* stack, rick *(of corn, hay etc.)*; *(Hort.)* hotbed.

meunerie [møn′ri], *n.f.* miller's trade; *(collect.)* millers.

meunier [mø′nje], *n.m.* miller; chub *(fish)*.

meunière [mø′njɛːr], *n.f.* miller's wife.

meurtre [mœrtr], *n.m.* murder.

meurtrier [mœrtri′e], *a. (fem.* **-ière)** murdering, murderous, deadly; killing.—*n.m. (fem.* **-ière** (1)) murderer, murderess.

meurtrière (2) [mœrtri′ɛːr], *n.f. (Fort.)* loophole.

meurtrir [mœr′triːr], *v.t.* to bruise, to make black and blue.

meurtrissure [mœrtri′syːr], *n.f.* bruise.

meute [mø:t], *n.f.* pack *(of hounds etc.)*.

mévendre [me′vãːdr], *v.t.* to sell at a loss.

mévente [me′vãːt], *n.f.* selling at a loss; slump.

mexicain [mɛksi′kɛ̃], *a.* Mexican.—*n.m.* **(Mexicain,** *fem.* **-aine)** Mexican *(person)*.

Mexico [mɛksi′ko], *m.* Mexico City.

Mexique [mɛk′sik], **le,** *m.* Mexico.

mi [mi], *n.m. (Mus.)* mi; the note E.

mi- [mi], *comb. form.* half, demi-, semi-; mid, middle; *à mi-chemin,* half-way; *à mi-corps,* up to the waist; *à mi-côte,* half-way

up the hill; *à mi-jambe,* half-way up the leg; *la mi-août,* the middle of August.

miaou [mjau], *n.m. inv. (fam.)* mew, miaow; cat.

miaulement [mjol′mã], *n.m.* mewing.

miauler [mjo′le], *v.i.* to mew; to caterwaul.

mica [mi′ka], *n.m.* mica.

miche [miʃ], *n.f.* round loaf.

Michel [mi′ʃɛl], *m.* Michael; *la Saint-Michel,* Michaelmas.

Michel-Ange [mikɛl′ãːʒ], *m.* Michelangelo.

micheline [miʃ′lin], *n.f.* rail-car.

micro [mi′kro], *n.m. (fam. abbr. of* **microphone)** mike.

microbe [mi′krɔb], *n.m.* microbe.

microcosme [mikro′kɔsm], *n.m.* microcosm.

microfilm [mikro′film], *n.m.* microfilm.

micromètre [mikro′mɛtr], *n.m.* micrometer.

micro-organisme [mikroorga′nism], *n.m.* micro-organism.

microphone [mikro′fɔn], *n.m.* microphone.

microscope [mikros′kɔp], *n.m.* microscope.

microscopique [mikrosko′pik], *a.* microscopic.

midi [mi′di], *n.m.* noon, midday, twelve o'clock *(in the day)*; meridian; south; *le Midi (de la France),* the South of France.

midinette [midi′nɛt], *n.f. (fam.)* young dressmaker *or* milliner in Paris.

mie [mi], *n.f.* crumb; soft part of loaf.

miel [mjɛl], *n.m.* honey; *lune de miel,* honeymoon.

miellé [mjɛ′le], *a.* honeyed; like honey; *(fig.)* sweet, bland.

miellée [mjɛ′le], **miellure** [mjɛ′lyːr], *n.f.* honeydew.

mielleusement [mjɛløz′mã], *adv.* sweetly, blandly, honey-like.

mielleux [mjɛ′lø], *a. (fem.* **-euse)** honeyed; sweet, bland.

mien [mjɛ̃], **a. poss.* and *pron. poss. (fem.* **mienne)** mine; *le mien, la mienne, les miens, les miennes,* mine, my own.

miette [mjɛt], *n.f.* crumb, bit, morsel.

mieux [mjø], *adv.* better; correctly; more agreeably, more comfortably etc.; rather, more; *faute de mieux,* for want of better; *mieux vaut tard que jamais,* better late than never; *tant mieux,* so much the better; *valoir mieux,* to be better, to be worth more.—*n.m.* best thing; improvement.

mièvre [mjɛːvr], *a.* finical, affected; delicate *(child)*, fragile.

mièvrerie [mjɛvrə′ri], **mièvreté** [mjɛvrə′te], *n.f.* affectation.

mignard [mi′naːr], *a.* delicate, pretty, dainty; mincing, affected.

mignardement [minardə′mã], *adv.* delicately, daintily; mincingly.

mignarder [minar′de], *v.t.* to fondle, to pet, to indulge.

mignardise [minar′diːz], *n.f.* delicacy, prettiness, daintiness; affectation, mincing ways.

mignon [mi′nɔ̃], *a. (fem.* **-onne)** delicate, pretty, dainty; sweet; neat, tiny.—*n.m. (fem.* **-onne)** darling, pet, favourite.

mignonnement [minɔn′mã], *adv.* daintily, prettily.

migraine [mi′grɛːn], *n.f.* sick headache; migraine.

migrateur [migra'tœːr], *a.* (*fem.* -**trice**) migratory.

migration [migra'sjɔ̃], *n.f.* migration.

migratoire [migra'twaːr], *a.* migratory.

mijoter [miʒo'te], *v.t., v.i.* to cook slowly to stew; to simmer; (*fig.*) to plot, to brew.

mil (1) [MILLE (2)].

mil (2) [mil], *n.m.* millet.

milan [mi'lɑ̃], *n.m.* kite (*bird*).

milice [mi'lis], *n.f.* militia; (*fig.*) troops, soldiery.

milicien [mili'sjɛ̃], *n.m.* militiaman.

milieu [mi'ljø], *n.m.* (*pl.* -**eux**) middle, midst; heart, centre; mean; environment, surroundings; *au beau milieu*, in the very middle.

militaire [mili'tɛːr], *a.* military.—*n.m.* soldier.

militairement [militɛr'mɑ̃], *adv.* in a soldier-like manner.

militant [mili'tɑ̃], *a.* militant.

militer [mili'te], *v.i.* to militate (*pour* or *contre*).

(*C*) **millage** [mi'laːʒ], *n.m.* mileage.

mille (1) [mil], *n.m.* mile (*English mile, 1609·3 metres*).

mille (2) [mil], *a. inv.* and *n.m. inv.* (**mil** *in dates of the Christian era*) thousand, a thousand, one thousand.

millénaire [mille'nɛːr], *a.* millenary.—*n.m.* millennium.

mille-pattes [mil'pat], *n.m. inv.* centipede.

millésime [mille'zim], *n.m.* date (*on a coin, monument etc.*).

millet [mi'jɛ], *n.m.* millet, millet grass.

milliard [mi'ljaːr], *n.m.* one thousand millions, (*Am.*) one billion.

milliardaire [miljar'dɛːr], *a.* and *n.* multi-millionaire(ss).

millibar [milli'bar], *n.m.* (*Meteor.*) millibar.

millième [mi'ljɛm], *a.* and *n.m.* thousandth.

millier [mi'lje], *n.m.* thousand.

milligramme [milli'gram], *n.m.* milligramme (·*0154 grain*).

millimètre [milli'mɛtr], *n.m.* millimetre (·*03937 in.*).

million [mi'ljɔ̃], *n.m.* million.

millionième [miljo'njɛːm], *a.* and *n.m.* millionth.

millionnaire [miljo'nɛːr], *a.* and *n.* millionaire(ss).

mime [mim], *n.m.* mime; mimic.

mimer [mi'me], *v.t., v.i.* to mimic, to mime.

mimi [mi'mi], *n.m.* (*Childish*) cat, pussy, darling, ducky.

mimique [mi'mik], *a.* mimic, mimetic.—*n.f.* art of mimicry.

mimosa [mimo'za], *n.m.* mimosa.

minable [mi'nabl], *a.* (*colloq.*) seedy, shabby.

minaret [mina'rɛ], *n.m.* minaret.

minauder [mino'de], *v.i.* to smirk, to simper.

minauderie [mino'dri], *n.f.* affected or mincing manners, simpering, smirking.

minaudier [mino'dje], *a.* (*fem.* -**ière**) affected, lackadaisical.—*n.m.* (*fem.* -**ière**) affected person.

mince [mɛ̃ːs], *a.* thin, slender, slim; puny, slight, trivial; scanty, small.—*int.* (*pop.*) *ah! mince!* or *mince alors!* my word! well, I never!

minceur [mɛ̃'sœːr], *n.f.* slenderness, slimness.

mine (1) [min], *n.f.* look, bearing; face, expression; appearance, aspect; (*pl.*) airs.

mine (2) [min], *n.f.* (*Min.*) mine; (*fig.*) source, store.

mine (3) [min], *n.f.* (*Mil., Pyro.*) mine.

miner [mi'ne], *v.t.* to mine, to undermine, to sap; to wear away.

minerai [min'rɛ], *n.m.* ore.

minéral [mine'ral], *a.* (*m. pl.* -**aux**) mineral. —*n.m.* (*pl.* -**aux**) mineral; ore.

minéralogie [mineralɔ'ʒi], *n.f.* mineralogy.

minéralogique [mineralɔ'ʒik], *a.* mineralogical.

minéralogiste [mineralɔ'ʒist], *n.* mineralogist.

Minerve [mi'nɛrv], *f.* Minerva.

minet [mi'ne], *n.m.* (*fem.* -**ette**) (*colloq.*) puss, kitten.

mineur (1) [mi'nœːr], *n.m.* miner, pitman; (*Mil.*) sapper.

mineur (2) [mi'nœːr], *a.* lesser, minor; under age.—*n.m.* (*fem.* -e) minor; (*Law*) infant.

miniature [minja'tyːr], *n.f.* miniature.

miniaturiste [minjaty'rist], *a.* of miniatures. —*n.* miniature-painter.

minier [mi'nje], *a.* (*fem.* -**ière**) pertaining to mines, mining.—*n.f.* (-**ière**) open mine.

minime [mi'nim], *a.* very small, trifling.

minimum [mini'mɔm], *a.* (*usu. inv.*) minimum.—*n.m.* (*pl.* **minimums** or **minima**) minimum.

ministère [minis'tɛːr], *n.m.* ministry; department; minister's office; offices, services; administration.

ministériel [ministe'rjɛl], *a.* (*fem.* -**elle**) ministerial.

ministre [mi'nistr], *n.m.* (*Polit., Ch.*) minister; clergyman.

minois [mi'nwa] *n.m. inv.* pretty face; looks, appearance.

minoritaire [minɔri'tɛːr], *a.* minority.

minorité [minɔri'te], *n.f.* minority; (*Law*) infancy.

Minorque [mi'nɔrk], *f.* Minorca.

minoterie [minɔ'tri] *n.f.* flour-mill; flour trade.

minotier [minɔ'tje], *n.m.* flour-dealer, corn-factor.

minuit [mi'nɥi], *n.m.* midnight.

minuscule [minys'kyl], *a.* small (*of letters*), minute, tiny.—*n.f.* small letter.

minute [mi'nyt], *n.f.* minute (*of time*), moment, instant; rough draft; minute, record; *minute!* (*fam.*) just a moment!

minuter [miny'te], *v.t.* to record; to time.

minuterie [minyt'ri], *n.f.* time-switch.

minutie [miny'si], *n.f.* trifle, (*pl.*) minutiae.

minutieusement [minysjøz'mɑ̃], *adv.* minutely.

minutieux [miny'sjø], *a.* (*fem.* -**euse**) minute; meticulous.

mioche [mjɔʃ], *n.* (*colloq.*) brat, urchin.

mi-parti [mipar'ti], *a.* bipartite, half and half.

mirabelle [mira'bɛl], *n.f.* yellow variety of plum.

miracle [mi'raːkl], *n.m.* miracle; (*fig.*) wonder; *à miracle*, wonderfully well.

miraculeusement [mirakyløz'mɑ̃], *adv.* miraculously; wonderfully.

miraculeux [miraky'lø], *a.* (*fem.* -**euse**) miraculous; wonderful, marvellous.

mirage [mi'ra:ʒ], *n.m.* mirage; (*Naut.*) looming; (*fig.*) shadow.

mire [mi:r], *n.f.* land-surveyor's pole; (*Artill.*) aim; sight (*of fire-arms*).

mirer [mi're], *v.t.* to aim at; to have in view, to look at; to covet. **se mirer**, *v.r.* to look at oneself; to admire oneself; to be reflected.

mirliton [mirli'tɔ̃], *n.m.* reed-pipe.

mirobolant [mirobɔ'lɑ̃], *a.* (*colloq.*) wonderful, prodigious.

miroir [mi'rwa:r], *n.m.* mirror, looking-glass.

miroitant [mirwa'tɑ̃], *a.* reflecting (*like a mirror*), glistening.

miroité [mirwa'te], *a.* shot, shiny; dappled (*of horses*).

miroitement [mirwat'mɑ̃], *n.m.* reflection of the light by polished surfaces; sheen, brilliancy.

miroiter [mirwa'te], *v.i.* to reflect light, to shine, to glisten, to shimmer.

mis [mi], *p.p.* [METTRE] *bien* or *mal mis*, well or badly dressed.

misaine [mi'zɛ:n], *n.f. mât de misaine*, foremast; *voile de misaine*, foresail.

misanthrope [mizɑ̃'trɔp], *n.* misanthrope.

misanthropie [mizɑ̃trɔ'pi], *n.f.* misanthropy.

misanthropique [mizɑ̃trɔ'pik], *a.* misanthropic.

miscellanées [misɛla'ne], *n.f. pl.* miscellanea, miscellany.

mise [mi:z], *n.f.* placing; stake; investment; bidding (*at auctions*); capital; dress; *mise en marche*, starting; starting-handle; *mise en marche automatique*, self-starter; *mise en scène*, (*Theat.*) production, (*Cine.*) direction.

misérable [mize'rabl], *a.* miserable, pitiable; worthless; despicable.—*n.* wretch, miserable person; miscreant.

misérablement [mizerablə'mɑ̃], *adv.* miserably.

misère [mi'zɛ:r], *n.f.* misery, wretchedness, distress; poverty; trouble; trifling thing.

miséreux [mize'rø], *a.* and *n.m.* (*fem.* **-euse**) poor, destitute; seedy looking (person).

miséricorde [mizeri'kɔrd], *n.f.* mercy, pardon, grace.

miséricordieux [mizerikɔr'djø], *a.* (*fem.* **-euse**) merciful, compassionate.

missel [mi'sɛl], *n.m.* missal, mass-book.

mission [mi'sjɔ̃], *n.f.* mission.

missionnaire [misjɔ'nɛ:r], *n.* missionary.

missive [mi'si:v], *a.f.* and *n.f.* missive.

mistral [mis'tral], *n.m.* mistral (*cold north wind in southern France*).

mitaine [mi'tɛn], *n.f.* mitten.

mite [mit], *n.f.* mite; moth; *mangé des mites*, moth-eaten.

mité [mi'te], *a.* moth-eaten, maggoty.

mi-temps [mi'tɑ̃], *n.f.* (*Ftb.*) half-time.

miteux [mi'tø], *a.* (*fem.* **-euse**) full of mites; (*fig.*) shabby, poverty-stricken.

mitigation [mitiga'sjɔ̃], *n.f.* mitigation.

mitiger [miti'ʒe], *v.t.* (*conjug. like* MANGER) to mitigate, to alleviate, to modify.

mitonner [mitɔ'ne], *v.t.* to coddle, to fondle; to nurse.—*v.i.* to let slices of bread simmer in the broth, to simmer.

mitoyen [mitwa'jɛ̃], *a.* (*fem.* **-enne**) middle; intermediate; party, joint; *mur mitoyen*, party-wall.

mitraille [mi'trɑ:j], *n.f.* grape-shot.

mitrailler [mitra'je], *v.t., v.i.* to machine-gun.

mitraillette [mitra'jet], *n.f.* tommy-gun.

mitrailleuse [mitra'jø:z], *n.f.* machine-gun.

mitre [mitr], *n.f.* mitre.

mitré [mi'tre], *a.* mitred.

mitron [mi'trɔ̃], *n.m.* journeyman baker; pastry-cook's boy.

mixte [mikst], *a.* mixed.

mixture [miks'ty:r], *n.f.* mixture.

mobile [mɔ'bil], *a.* mobile, movable; unsteady, variable.—*n.m.* body in motion; mover, motive power.

mobilier [mɔbi'lje], *a.* (*fem.* **-ière**) movable; personal (*of property*).—*n.m.* furniture.

mobilisation [mɔbiliza'sjɔ̃], *n.f.* mobilization; liquidation (*of capital*).

mobiliser [mɔbili'ze], *v.t.* (*Law*) to liquidate; (*Mil.*) to mobilize.

mobilité [mɔbili'te], *n.f.* mobility; variability; instability.

mode (1) [mɔd], *n.f.* fashion; manner, way, custom; (*pl.*) millinery.

mode (2) [mɔd], *n.m.* (*Mus. etc.*) mode; (*Gram.*) mood; method; *mode d'emploi*, directions for use.

modelage [mɔ'dla:ʒ], *n.m.* modelling.

modèle [mɔ'dɛl], *a.* exemplary.—*n.m.* model; pattern, design.

modelé [mɔ'dle], *n.m.* (*Sculp., Paint.*) relief; reproduction.

modeler [mɔ'dle], *v.t.* (*conjug. like* AMENER) to model; to shape; to mould (*clay*). **se modeler**, *v.r.* to model oneself (*sur*).

modeleur [mɔ'dlœ:r], *n.m.* modeller.

modérateur [mɔdera'tœ:r], *a.* (*fem.* **-trice**) moderating.—*n.m.* (*fem.* **-trice**) moderator.—*n.m.* (*Mech.*) regulator.

modération [mɔdera'sjɔ̃], *n.f.* moderation; abatement.

modéré [mɔde're], *a.* moderate, reasonable. —*n.m.* (*fem.* **-e**) (*Polit.*) moderate.

modérément [mɔdere'mɑ̃], *adv.* moderately, in moderation.

modérer [mɔde're], *v.t.* (*conjug. like* CÉDER) to moderate, to mitigate; to restrain. **se modérer**, *v.r.* to keep one's temper; to restrain oneself.

moderne [mɔ'dɛrn], *a.* modern, up-to-date. —*n.m.* modern style.

modernisation [mɔderniza'sjɔ̃], *n.f.* modernization.

moderniser [mɔderni'ze], *v.t.* to modernize.

modeste [mɔ'dɛst], *a.* modest, unassuming; quiet; simple.

modestement [mɔdɛstə'mɑ̃], *adv.* modestly, quietly, simply.

modestie [mɔdɛs'ti], *n.f.* modesty, simplicity.

modicité [mɔdisi'te], *n.f.* smallness; modicum.

modification [mɔdifika'sjɔ̃], *n.f.* modification.

modifier [mɔdi'fje], *v.t.* to modify, to change, to alter. **se modifier**, *v.r.* to become modified.

modique [mɔ'dik], *a.* moderate; small.

modiquement [mɔdik'mɑ̃], *adv.* moderately.

modiste [mɔ'dist], *n.* modiste, milliner.

modulation [mɔdyla'sjɔ̃], *n.f.* modulation; (*Rad.*) *modulation de fréquence*, very high frequency, V.H.F.

moduler [mɔdy'le], *v.t.* to modulate.
moelle [mwal], *n.f.* marrow (*of bone*); (*Bot.*) pith.
moelleusement [mwaløz'mã], *adv.* softly; (*Paint.*) with mellowness.
moelleux [mwa'lø], *a.* (*fem.* **-euse**) full of marrow; pithy; soft; mellow.—*n.m.* softness; mellowness.
moellon [mwa'lɔ̃], *n.m.* rubble; building stone.
mœurs [mœrs], *n.f. pl.* morals; manners, habits, ways, customs; *certificat de bonne vie et mœurs*, certificate of good character.
Mogol [mɔ'gɔl], *m.* Mogul.
moi [mwa], *pron. pers.* I; me, to me; *moi-même*, myself.—*n.m.* self, ego.
moignon [mwa'ɲɔ̃], *n.m.* stump (*of limbs, trees etc.*).
moindre [mwɛ̃:dr], *a.* lesser; least.
moine [mwan], *n.m.* monk, friar; bed-warmer.
moineau [mwa'no], *n.m.* (*pl.* **-eaux**) sparrow.
moins [mwɛ̃], *adv.* less; fewer (*de* or *que*); not so; *à moins de* (or *que*), unless; *du moins*, at least, at any rate; *les moins de seize ans*, the under sixteens.—*prep.* less, minus.—*n.m.* (*Math.*) minus sign; (*Print.*) dash.
moire [mwar], *n.f.* watering; moire, watered silk.
moiré [mwa're], *a.* watered, moiré.—*n.m.* watered effect.
moirer [mwa're], *v.t.* to moiré, to give a watered appearance to.
mois [mwa], *n.m.* month; monthly allowance, month's pay.
Moïse [mɔ'iːz], *m.* Moses.
moisi [mwa'zi], *a.* mouldy, musty.—*n.m.* mouldiness, mustiness.
moisir [mwa'ziːr], *v.t.* to make mouldy *or* musty.—*v.i.* and **se moisir**, *v.r.* to grow mouldy *or* musty.
moisissure [mwazi'syːr], *n.f.* mouldiness, mustiness, mildew.
moisson [mwa'sɔ̃], *n.f.* harvest, harvest-time.
moissonner [mwasɔ'ne], *v.t.* to reap, to gather in, to mow.
moissonneur [mwasɔ'nœːr], *n.m.* (*fem.* **-euse**) reaper, harvester.—*n.f.* (**-euse**) reaping-machine.
moissonneuse-batteuse [mwasɔ'nøzba'tøːz], *n.f.* (*pl.* **moissonneuses-batteuses**) combine harvester.
moite [mwat], *a.* moist, damp; clammy.
moiteur [mwa'tœːr], *n.f.* moistness, dampness.
moitié [mwa'tje], *n.f.* half; (*colloq.*) better half, wife.—*adv.* half; *à moitié fait*, half done; *trop cher de moitié*, too dear by half.
moka [mɔ'ka], *n.m.* mocha (*coffee* or *cake*).
mol [mɔl], [MOU].
molaire [mɔ'lɛːr], *a.* molar.—*n.f.* molar-tooth.
môle [moːl], *n.m.* mole, pier.
moléculaire [mɔleky'lɛːr], *a.* molecular.
molécule [mɔle'kyl], *n.f.* molecule.
molestation [mɔlɛsta'sjɔ̃], *n.f.* molestation, annoyance.
molester [mɔlɛs'te], *v.t.* to molest, to trouble.

mollasse [mɔ'las], *a.* flabby; spineless.
molle [mɔl], [MOU].
mollement [mɔl'mã], *adv.* softly; feebly; indolently.
mollesse [mɔ'lɛs], *n.f.* softness; flabbiness; slackness; indolence.
mollet [mɔ'lɛ], *a.* (*fem.* **-ette**) soft; light (*of bread*).—*n.m.* calf (*of the leg*).
molletière [mɔl'tjɛːr], *n.f.* legging, puttee.
molleton [mɔl'tɔ̃], *n.m.* thick flannel, duffel.
mollir [mɔ'liːr], *v.i.* to soften; to mellow (*of fruit*); to slacken, to give way.
mollusque [mɔ'lysk], *n.m.* mollusc.
molosse [mɔ'lɔs], *n.m.* mastiff, watch-dog.
môme [moːm], *n.* (*pop.*) brat, urchin.
moment [mɔ'mã], *n.m.* moment, instant; favourable occasion; *au moment de*, just as; *du moment que*, since.
momentané [mɔmãta'ne], *a.* momentary.
momentanément [mɔmãtane'mã], *adv.* momentarily.
momie [mɔ'mi], *n.f.* mummy; (*fig.*) old fogy.
momifier [mɔmi'fje], *v.t.* to mummify.
mon [mɔ̃], *a.poss.m.* (*fem.* **ma**, *pl.* **mes**) my.
monarchie [mɔnar'ʃi], *n.f.* monarchy.
monarchique [mɔnar'ʃik], *a.* monarchical.
monarchiste [mɔnar'ʃist], *a.* and *n.* monarchist.
monarque [mɔ'nark], *n.m.* monarch.
monastère [mɔnas'tɛːr], *n.m.* monastery, convent.
monastique [mɔnas'tik], *a.* monastic.
monceau [mɔ̃'so], *n.m.* (*pl.* **-eaux**) heap, pile.
mondain [mɔ̃'dɛ̃], *a.* worldly, mundane.—*n.m.* (*fem.* **-e**) worldly person.
mondanité [mɔ̃dani'te], *n.f.* worldliness; (*pl.*) social events.
monde [mɔ̃:d], *n.m.* world; universe; mankind; people; society; company, set; men; customers; *tout le monde*, everybody.
monder [mɔ̃'de], *v.t.* to cleanse; to hull (*barley*), to blanch (*almonds*).
mondial [mɔ̃'djal], *a.* (*m. pl.* **-aux**) world, world-wide.
monétaire [mɔne'tɛːr], *a.* monetary.
mongol [mɔ̃'gɔl], *a.* Mongolian.—*n.m.* Mongolian (*language*) or (**Mongol**, *fem.* **-ole**) Mongol(ian) (*person*).
Mongolie [mɔ̃gɔ'li], **la**, *f.* Mongolia.
Monique [mɔ'nik], *f.* Monica.
moniteur [mɔni'tœːr], *n.m.* (*fem.* **-trice**) (*sch.*) prefect, monitor; instructor.
monnaie [mɔ'nɛ], *n.f.* coin, money; change; mint; *monnaie forte*, hard currency; *monnaie légale*, legal tender.
monnayage [mɔnɛ'jaːʒ], *n.m.* coining, minting.
monnayer [mɔnɛ'je], *v.t.* (*conjug. like* PAYER) to coin into money, to mint; (*fig.*) to make money out of, to sell.
monnayeur [mɔnɛ'jœːr], *n.m.* coiner, minter; *faux monnayeur*, counterfeiter, forger.
monochrome [mɔnɔ'krɔm], *a.* monochrome.
monocle [mɔ'nɔkl], *n.m.* monocle, eyeglass.
monogramme [mɔnɔ'gram], *n.m.* monogram.
monologue [mɔnɔ'lɔg], *n.m.* monologue, soliloquy.
monopole [mɔnɔ'pɔl], *n.m.* monopoly.
monopoliser [mɔnɔpɔli'ze], *v.t.* to monopolize.
monorail [mɔnɔ'raːj], *a.* and *n.m.* monorail.

monosyllabe [mɔnɔsil'lab], *a.* monosyllabic. —*n.f.* monosyllable.
monosyllabique [mɔnɔsilla'bik], *a.* monosyllabic.
monotone [mɔnɔ'tɔn], *a.* monotonous.
monotonie [mɔnɔtɔ'ni], *n.f.* monotony.
monseigneur [mɔ̃sɛ'nœːr], *n.m.* (*pl.* **messeigneurs** or **nosseigneurs**) my lord; your Grace; your Royal *or* Imperial Highness.
monsieur [mə'sjø, msjø], *n.m.* (*pl.* **messieurs**) sir; gentleman; Mr.
monstre [mɔ̃:str], *a.* (*fam.*) huge.—*n.m.* monster.
monstrueusement [mɔ̃strɥøz'mɑ̃], *adv.* monstrously, prodigiously.
monstrueux [mɔ̃s'trɥø], *a.* (*fem.* **-euse**) monstrous, prodigious.
monstruosité [mɔ̃strɥozi'te], *n.f.* monstrosity.
mont [mɔ̃], *n.m.* hill, mount, mountain.
montage [mɔ̃'ta:ʒ], *n.m.* carrying up; mounting, setting; assembling; (*Cine.*) editing (*of film*); (*Ind.*) **châine de montage,** assembly line.
montagnard [mɔ̃ta'na:r], *a.* mountain, highland.—*n.m.* (*fem.* **-e**) mountaineer, highlander.
montagne [mɔ̃'tan], *n.f.* mountain; hill.
montagneux [mɔ̃ta'nø], *a.* (*fem.* **-euse**) mountainous, hilly.
montant (1) [mɔ̃'tɑ̃], *n.m.* upright (*of a ladder etc.*); post (*of door etc.*); (*Naut.*) stanchion; amount, sum total; rising tide; high flavour, pungency; (*Ftb.*) goal-post.
montant (2) [mɔ̃'tɑ̃], *a.* rising; ascending; flowing, coming in; high-necked (*of dresses*).
monte [mɔ̃:t], *n.f.* mounting, mount (*of a jockey*); serving (*of animals*), covering season.
monte-charge [mɔ̃t'ʃarʒ], *n.m. inv.* hoist, goods lift; (*Am.*) freight elevator.
montée [mɔ̃'te], *n.f.* gradient, slope; ascent; (*Arch. etc.*) height.
monter [mɔ̃'te], *v.t.* to mount, to ascend, to go up; to walk, ride, row etc. up; to get up on, to ride; to raise; to wind up; to equip; to make up; to rouse.—*v.i.* (*with aux.* AVOIR *or* ÊTRE *according as action or condition is meant*) to go up (*or* come) up, to mount; to climb; to rise; to increase; to amount. **se monter,** *v.r.* to amount, to rise; to get excited; to supply oneself with (*en*).
monteur [mɔ̃'tœːr], *n.m.* (*fem.* **-euse**) setter, mounter (*of jewels, machinery etc.*); (*Cine.*) (film-)editor.
monticule [mɔ̃ti'kyl], *n.m.* hillock, knoll.
montoir [mɔ̃'twaːr], *n.m.* horse-block; **côté du montoir,** near side; **côté hors montoir,** off side.
montre (1) [mɔ̃:tr], *n.f.* show-case; shop-window; show, display, exhibition.
montre (2) [mɔ̃:tr], *n.f.* watch.
montre-bracelet [mɔ̃trəbras'le], *n.f.* (*pl.* **montres-bracelets**) wrist-watch.
montrer [mɔ̃'tre], *v.t.* to show, to display; to demonstrate; to teach; to indicate. **se montrer,** *v.r.* to show oneself; to appear; to prove oneself to be, to turn out.
montreur [mɔ̃'trœːr], *n.m.* (*fem* **-euse**) showman, exhibitor.
montueux [mɔ̃'tɥø], *a.* (*fem.* **-euse**) hilly.

monture [mɔ̃'tyːr], *n.f.* animal for riding, mount; setting (*of gems etc.*); frame.
monument [mɔny'mɑ̃], *n.m.* monument; memorial.
monumental [mɔnymɑ̃'tal], *a.* (*m. pl.* **-aux**) monumental.
moquer (se) [sǝmɔ'ke], *v.r.* (*de*) to mock, to jeer, to laugh at; to make fun of.
moquerie [mɔ'kri], *n.f.* mockery, derision; jest.
moquette [mɔ'kɛt], *n.f.* carpet; fitted carpet; velvet pile.
moqueur [mɔ'kœːr], *a.* (*fem.* **-euse**) mocking, jeering, derisive.—*n.m.* (*fem.* **-euse**) mocker, scoffer; wag.
moral [mɔ'ral], *a.* (*m. pl.* **-aux**) moral; mental.—*n.m.* mind, mental faculties, spirit, morale.
morale [mɔ'ral], *n.f.* ethics, moral philosophy; morals, morality; rebuke, lecture; moral (*of a story etc.*).
moralement [mɔral'mɑ̃], *adv.* morally.
moraliste [mɔra'list], *a.* and *n.* moralist.
moralité [mɔrali'te], *n.f.* morality; morals.
morbide [mɔr'bid], *a.* morbid.
morbleu! [mɔr'blø], *int.* the devil! hang it!
morceau [mɔr'so], *n.m.* (*pl.* **-eaux**) bit, piece, morsel, fragment.
morceler [mɔrsə'le], *v.t.* (*conjug. like* APPELER) to parcel out; to cut up.
mordant [mɔr'dɑ̃], *a.* biting; cutting, sarcastic.—*n.m.* mordant; pungency, keenness.
mordiller [mɔrdi'je], *v.t.* to nibble, to bite at.
mordoré [mɔrdɔ're], *a.* and *n.m.* reddish brown.
mordre [mɔrdr], *v.t.* to bite; to gnaw; to eat into.—*v.i.* to bite, to nibble; to take hold; to succeed; to criticize. **se mordre,** *v.r.* to bite oneself; **s'en mordre les doigts,** to repent of a thing.
more [mɔːr], **moresque** [mɔ'rɛsk], *a.* Moorish.—*n.* (**More**) Moor; Negro.
morfondre [mɔr'fɔ̃:dr], *v.t.* to chill. **se morfondre,** *v.r.* to be chilled, to shiver; to kick one's heels; (*fig.*) to mope.
morfondu [mɔrfɔ̃'dy], *a.* chilled, shivering, benumbed.
morganatique [mɔrgana'tik], *a.* morganatic.
morgue (1) [mɔrg], *n.f.* haughtiness, arrogance.
morgue (2) [mɔrg], *n.f.* morgue, mortuary.
moribond [mɔri'bɔ̃], *a.* moribund, dying.—*n.m.* (*fem.* **-e**) person in a dying state.
moricaud [mɔri'ko], *a.* dark, darkish.—*n.m.* (*fem.* **-e**) (*pej.*) blackamoor, (*pej.*) nigger.
morigéner [mɔriʒe'ne], *v.t.* (*conjug. like* CÉDER) to scold; to reprimand.
mormon [mɔr'mɔ̃], *a.* Mormon.—*n.m.* (**Mormon,** *fem.* **-e**) Mormon (*person*).
morne [mɔrn], *a.* gloomy, dejected, dreary.
morose [mɔ'roːz], *a.* morose, sullen, surly.
morosité [mɔrozi'te], *n.f.* moroseness, sullenness, surliness.
Morphée [mɔr'fe], *m.* Morpheus.
morphine [mɔr'fin], *n.f.* morphia.
morphologie [mɔrfɔlɔ'ʒi], *n.f.* morphology.
mors [mɔr], *n.m. inv.* bit (*of a bridle*); (*fig.*) curb, check.
morse (1) [mɔrs], *n.m.* morse, walrus.
morse (2) [mɔrs], *n.m.* Morse (code).
morsure [mɔr'syːr], *n.f.* bite, biting.

mort [mɔːr], *a.* dead; lifeless, inanimate; dormant; stagnant; out (*of a candle etc.*); *nature morte*, still life; *au point mort*, at a standstill, in neutral (gear) (*of a car*).— *n.m.* (*fem.* **-e**) dead person, corpse.—*n.m.* dummy (*at cards*).—*n.f.* death; *à mort*, mortally, to the death.

mortalité [mɔrtali'te], *n.f.* mortality.

mort-bois [mɔr'bwa], *n.m.* (*no pl.*) brushwood, undergrowth.

morte-eau [mɔr'to], *n.f.* (*pl.* **mortes-eaux**) neap tide.

mortel [mɔr'tɛl], *a.* (*fem.* **-elle**) mortal, deadly; grievous.—*n.m.* (*fem.* **-elle**) mortal, deadly.

mortellement [mɔrtɛl'mɑ̃], *adv.* fatally, deadly.

morte-saison [mɔrtsɛ'zɔ̃], *n.f.* (*pl.* **mortes-saisons**) slack time, off season.

mortier [mɔr'tje], *n.m.* mortar (*cement, artillery, vessel*).

mortifiant [mɔrti'fjɑ̃], *a.* mortifying, humiliating.

mortification [mɔrtifika'sjɔ̃], *n.f.* mortification, humiliation.

mortifier [mɔrti'fje], *v.t.* to mortify; to humiliate. **se mortifier**, *v.r.* to mortify oneself.

mort-né [mɔr'ne], *a.* and *n.m.* (*fem.* **mort-née**, *pl.* **mort-nés, mort-nées**) stillborn (child).

mortuaire [mɔr'tɥɛːr], *a.* mortuary; *drap mortuaire*, pall.

morue [mɔ'ry], *n.f.* cod, codfish; *huile de foie de morue*, cod-liver oil.

morveux [mɔr'vø], *a.* (*fem.* **-euse**) snotty; *qui se sent morveux se mouche*, if the cap fits, wear it.

mosaïque [mɔza'ik], *a.* and *n.f.* mosaic.

Moscou [mɔs'ku], **le**, *m.* Moscow.

mosquée [mɔs'ke], *n.f.* mosque.

mot [mo], *n.m.* word; remark, saying, sentence; motto; note; (*Mil.*) parole, watchword; *au bas mot*, at the least; *bon mot*, witticism; *mots croisés*, crossword.

motel [mɔ'tɛl], *n.m.* motel.

moteur [mɔ'tœːr], *a.* (*fem.* **-trice**) motive, driving.—*n.m.* mover; motor, engine; motive power.

motif [mɔ'tif], *a.* (*fem.* **-tive**) moving, inciting.—*n.m.* motive, incentive; cause; (*Mus. etc.*) motif, design.

motion [mɔ'sjɔ̃], *n.f.* (*Polit.*) motion.

motiver [mɔti've], *v.t.* to justify; to allege as a motive; to be the cause of, to bring about.

moto [mɔ'to], *n.f.* (*fam.*) motor bike.

motocyclette [mɔtosi'klɛt], *n.f.* motor-cycle.

motte [mɔt], *n.f.* clod; *motte de beurre*, pat of butter.

motus! [mɔ'tyːs], *int.* (*colloq.*) mum's the word!

mou [mu], *a.* (**mol** before vowel or *h* mute, *fem.* **molle**) soft; limp; flabby; weak; slack, sluggish, indolent.—*n.m.* soft part of thing; slack (*of a rope*); lights (*of animals*).

mouchard [mu'ʃaːr], *n.m.* sneak, *esp.* policespy, nark, informer.

moucharder [muʃar'de], *v.t., v.i.* to inform (*on*), to spy (*on*); to sneak.

mouche [muʃ], *n.f.* fly; patch (*on the face*), beauty-spot; button (*of foil*); bull's-eye (*of a target*); river passenger-steamer.

(*C*) **mouche à feu** [muʃa'fø], *n.f.* firefly.

moucher [mu'ʃe], *v.t.* to wipe the nose of; to snuff. **se moucher**, *v.r.* to blow one's nose.

moucheron [muʃ'rɔ̃], *n.m.* gnat, very small fly.

moucheté [muʃ'te], *a.* spotted, speckled, flecked; capped (*of foils*).

moucheter [muʃ'te], *v.t.* (*conjug. like* APPELER) to spot, to speckle, to fleck; to cap (*foils*).

mouchoir [mu'ʃwaːr], *n.m.* handkerchief.

moudre [mudr], *v.t. irr.* to grind, to crush.

moue [mu], *n.f.* pout; *faire la moue*, to pout.

mouette [mwɛt], *n.f.* gull, sea-mew.

moufle [mufl], *n.f.* mitten; tackle-block.

mouillage [mu'jaːʒ], *n.m.* soaking, wetting; anchorage.

mouillé [mu'je], *a.* wet, watery; liquid (*of the letter l*); at anchor.

mouiller [mu'je], *v.t.* to wet, to moisten.— *v.i.* to drop anchor; to moor.

moulage [mu'laːʒ], *n.m.* moulding, casting; mould, cast; grinding, milling.

moule (I) [mul], *n.m.* mould, matrix; pattern.

moule (2) [mul], *n.f.* mussel.

moulé [mu'le], *a.* moulded, cast; well-formed; *lettre moulée*, block letter.

mouler [mu'le], *v.t.* to cast, to mould; to shape. **se mouler**, *v.r.* to model oneself (*sur*).

mouleur [mu'lœːr], *n.m.* moulder.

moulin [mu'lɛ̃], *n.m.* mill; grinder; (*Geol.*) pothole; *jeter son bonnet par-dessus les moulins*, to throw off all restraint.

moulinet [muli'nɛ], *n.m.* small mill; winch; turnstile; fishing reel.

moulu [mu'ly], *a.* ground; bruised.

moulure [mu'lyːr], *n.f.* (*Arch.*) moulding.

mourant [mu'rɑ̃], *a.* dying, expiring; fading. —*n.m.* (*fem.* **-e**) dying person.

mourir [mu'riːr], *v.i. irr.* (*with aux.* ÊTRE) to die, to expire; to perish; to stop; to go out (*of fire*); to be out (*at play*). **se mourir**, *v.r.* (*Poet., only used in pres. and imp. indic.*) to be dying.

mouron [mu'rɔ̃], *n.m.* (*Bot.*) *mouron rouge*, scarlet pimpernel; *mouron des oiseaux*, chickweed.

mousquet [mus'kɛ], *n.m.* musket; *mousquet à pierre*, flintlock.

mousquetaire [muskə'tɛːr], *n.m.* musketeer.

mousse (I) [mus], *a.* blunt (*of tools*).

mousse (2) [mus], *n.f.* moss; froth, foam; lather; whipped cream.

mousse (3) [mus], *n.m.* ship's boy.

mousseline [mus'lin], *n.f.* muslin.

mousser [mu'se], *v.i.* to froth, to foam; to sparkle (*of wine*).

mousseux [mu'sø], *a.* (*fem.* **-euse**) foaming, frothy; sparkling (*of wine etc.*).

mousson [mu'sɔ̃], *n.f.* monsoon.

moussu [mu'sy], *a.* mossy.

moustache [mus'taʃ], *n.f.* moustache; whiskers (*of animals*).

moustiquaire [musti'kɛːr], *n.f.* mosquito-net.

moustique [mus'tik], *n.m.* mosquito.

moût [mu], *n.m.* must (*wine not fermented*); wort (*of beer*).

moutarde [mu'tard], *n.f.* mustard.

221

moutardier [mutar′dje], *n.m.* mustard-pot; mustard-maker.

mouton [mu′tõ], *n.m.* sheep; mutton; sheepskin (*leather*); ram; (*fig.*) ninny; (*slang*) decoy, prison-spy; (*pl.*) white-crested waves; *revenons à nos moutons*, let us return to the subject.

moutonné [muto′ne], *a.* fleecy, curled; white with foam (*of the sea*).

moutonner [muto′ne], *v.t.* to make woolly *or* fleecy; to curl, to frizzle.—*v.i.* to be ruffled, to foam.

moutonneux [muto′nø], *a.* (*fem.* **-euse**) fleecy; foaming (*of waves*).

moutonnier [muto′nje], *a.* (*fem.* **-ière**) sheep-like.

mouvant [mu′vã], *a.* moving, shifting; unstable.

mouvement [muv′mã], *n.m.* movement, motion; march; animation, bustle; emotion, commotion; spirit, impulse; (*Mus.*) time; (*Mil.*) manœuvre.

mouvementé [muvmã′te], *a.* animated, lively; undulating (*ground*).

mouvoir [mu′vwaːr], *v.t. irr.* to move, to stir; to prompt. **se mouvoir**, *v.r.* to move, to stir.

moyen [mwa′jɛ̃], *a.* (*fem.* **-enne**) mean, middle, medium; average.—*n.m.* means; way, manner, medium; (*pl.*) resources; talents.

moyennant [mwajɛ′nã], *prep.* by means of; in consideration of.—*conj. phr. moyennant que*, on condition that.

moyenne [mwa′jen], *n.f.* average; (*sch.*) pass-mark.

moyeu [mwa′jø], *n.m.* (*pl.* **-eux**) nave (*of cartwheel*); hub (*of bicycle*).

muable [mɥabl], *a.* mutable, changeable.

mucosité [mykozi′te], *n.f.* mucus.

mucus [my′kyːs], *n.m.* mucus.

mue [my], *n.f.* moulting; skin, slough; mew, coop (*cage*).

muer [mɥe], *v.i.* to moult, to cast *or* slough horns etc.; to break (*of the voice*).

muet [mɥɛ], *a.* (*fem.* **muette**) dumb, mute; silent (*of letters*); blank (*of maps*).—*n.m.* (*fem.* **muette** (I)) dumb man *or* woman.

muette (2) [mɥɛt], *n.f.* mews; hunting-lodge.

mufle [myfl], *n.m.* snout, muzzle (*of animals*); (*pop.*) beast, cad.

muflier [myfli′e], *n.m.* (*Bot.*) antirrhinum.

mugir [my′ʒiːr], *v.i.* to bellow, to low; (*fig.*) to roar; to sough (*of the wind*).

mugissement [myʒis′mã], *n.m.* bellowing, lowing, roaring; soughing (*of the wind*).

muguet [my′gɛ], *n.m.* lily of the valley.

mulâtre [my′laːtr], *a.* and *n.m.* (*fem. inv.* or **-esse**) mulatto, half-caste.

mule [myl], *n.f.* mule, slipper; she-mule.

mulet [my′lɛ], *n.m.* he-mule; mullet.

muletier [myl′tje], *a.* (*fem.* **-ière**) pertaining to mules.—*n.m.* muleteer.

mulot [my′lo], *n.m.* field-mouse.

multicolore [myltiko′loːr], *a.* many-coloured; motley, variegated.

multiforme [multi′fɔrm], *a.* multiform.

multilatéral [myltilate′ral], *a.* (*m. pl.* **-aux**) multilateral.

multiple [myl′tipl], *a.* multiple; multifarious. —*n.m.* multiple.

multiplicateur [myltiplika′tœːr], *a.* (*fem.* **-trice**) multiplying.—*n.m.* (*Arith.*) multiplier, multiplicator.

multiplication [myltiplika′sjõ], *n.f.* multiplication; gearing (-ratio).

multiplicité [myltiplisi′te], *n.f.* multiplicity.

multiplié [myltipli′e], *a.* multiplied; manifold; frequent.

multiplier [myltipli′e], *v.t., v.i.* to multiply; to gear up to. **se multiplier**, *v.r.* to multiply; to be repeated.

multitude [mylti′tyd], *n.f.* multitude; crowd.

muni [my′ni], *a.* supplied, provided (*de*); fortified.

municipal [mynisi′pal], *a.* (*m. pl.* **-aux**) municipal.—*n.m.* soldier of the municipal guard.

municipalité [mynisipali′te], *n.f.* municipality; town council and staff.

munificence [mynifi′sãːs], *n.f.* bounty, munificence.

munificent [mynifi′sã], *a.* bountiful.

munir [my′niːr], *v.t.* to provide, to supply; to arm, to secure. **se munir**, *v.r.* to provide oneself, to be provided (*de*).

munitions [myni′sjõ], *n.f. pl.* ammunition, munitions; military stores.

muqueux [my′kø], *a.* (*fem.* **-euse** (I)) mucous.

muqueuse (2) [my′køːz], *n.f.* mucous membrane.

mur [myːr], *n.m.* wall; *le mur du son*, the sound barrier.

mûr [myːr], *a.* ripe, mature, matured.

murage [my′raːʒ], *n.m.* walling.

muraille [my′raːj], *n.f.* thick, high wall; (*pl.*) ramparts.

mural [my′ral], *a.* (*m. pl.* **-aux**) mural; *peinture murale*, mural.

mûre [myːr], *n.f.* mulberry.

mûrement [myr′mã], *adv.* maturely.

murer [my′re], *v.t.* to wall in, to brick up; (*fig.*) to screen.

mûrier [my′rje], *n.m.* mulberry-tree, bramble bush.

mûrir [my′riːr], *v.t.* to ripen, to mature.— *v.i.* to ripen, to grow ripe, to mature.

murmurant [myrmy′rã], *a.* murmuring; babbling; grumbling.

murmure [myr′myːr], *n.m.* murmur; grumbling; whispering, babbling; soughing (*of the wind*).

murmurer [myrmy′re], *v.t.* to mutter, to whisper.—*v.i.* to murmur, to whisper; to grumble; to gurgle, to prattle, to babble; to sough.

musard [my′zaːr], *a.* loitering, dawdling.— *n.m.* (*fem.* **-e**) (*colloq.*) loiterer, dawdler.

musarder [myzar′de], *v.i.* to dawdle.

musarderie [myzar′dri], **musardise** [myzar′diːz], *n.f.* loitering, dawdling, trifling.

musc [mysk], *n.m.* musk-deer, musk.

muscade [mys′kad], *n.f.* nutmeg; juggler's ball.

muscadier [myska′dje], *n.m.* nutmeg-tree.

muscat [mys′ka], *a.* and *n.m.* muscat (grape), muscadine; dried muscatel wine; variety of pear.

muscle [myskl], *n.m.* muscle.

musculaire [mysky′lɛːr], *a.* muscular.

musculeux [mysky′lø], *a.* (*fem.* **-euse**) muscular, brawny.

muse [myːz], *n.f.* muse.

museau [my'zo], *n.m.* (*pl.* **-eaux**) muzzle, snout, nose.

musée [my'ze], *n.m.* museum, art gallery.

museler [myz'le], *v.t.* (*conjug. like* APPELER) to muzzle; (*fig.*) to gag, to silence.

muselière [myz'ljɛːr], *n.f.* muzzle.

musellement [myzɛl'mã], *n.m.* muzzling; (*fig.*) gagging, silencing.

muser [my'ze], *v.i.* to loiter, to moon, to dawdle.

musette [my'zɛt], *n.f.* bagpipe; (*Mil.*) haversack; nosebag (*for horses*).

muséum [myze'ɔm], *n.m.* natural history museum.

musical [myzi'kal], *a.* (*m. pl.* **-aux**) musical.

musicalement [myzikal'mã], *adv.* musically.

musicien [myzi'sjɛ̃], *n.m.* (*fem.* **-enne**) musician.

musique [my'zik], *n.f.* music; band, musicians.

musoir [my'zwaːr], *n.m.* pier-head, jettyhead.

musqué [mys'ke], *a.* musked, perfumed; (*fig.*) affected (*language etc.*).

musquer [mys'ke], *v.t.* to perfume with musk.

musulman [myzyl'mã], *a.* Moslem.—*n.m.* (**Musulman**, *fem.* **-ane**) Moslem (*person*).

mutabilité [mytabili'te], *n.f.* mutability, changeableness.

mutation [myta'sjɔ̃], *n.f.* change; (*Biol.*) mutation.

muter [my'te], *v.t.* (*Mil., Adm.*) to transfer.

mutilateur [mytila'tœːr], *n.m.* (*fem.* **-trice**) mutilator, maimer, defacer.

mutilation [mytila'sjɔ̃], *n.f.* mutilation, maiming.

mutiler [myti'le], *v.t.* to mutilate, to maim; (*fig.*) to disfigure.

mutin [my'tɛ̃], *a.* obstinate; fractious; pert.—*n.m.* (*fem.* **-e**) mutineer, rebel.

mutiné [myti'ne], *a.* mutinous, riotous.

mutiner (se) [səmyti'ne], *v.r.* to mutiny.

mutinerie [mytin'ri], *n.f.* unruliness; mutiny, riot; pertness.

mutisme [my'tism], *n.m.* dumbness; speechlessness.

mutualité [mytɥali'te], *n.f.* mutuality.

mutuel [my'tɥɛl], *a.* (*fem.* **-elle**) mutual, reciprocal; *société de secours mutuels*, friendly society.

mutuellement [mytɥɛl'mã], *adv.* mutually.

myope [mjɔp], *a.* myopic, short-sighted.—*n.* short-sighted person.

myopie [mjɔ'pi], *n.f.* myopia, short-sightedness.

myosotis [mjozo'tiːs], *n.m.* myosotis, forget-me-not.

myriade [mi'rjad], *n.f.* myriad.

myrrhe [miːr], *n.f.* myrrh.

myrte [mirt], *n.m.* myrtle.

myrtille [mir'tiːj], *n.f.* bilberry.

mystère [mis'tɛːr], *n.m.* mystery; secret; (*fig.*) fuss.

mystérieusement [misterjøz'mã], *adv.* mysteriously.

mystérieux [miste'rjø], *a.* (*fem.* **-euse**) mysterious.

mysticisme [misti'sism], *n.m.* mysticism.

mystificateur [mistifika'tœːr], *a.* (*fem.*

-trice) mystifying, hoaxing.—*n.m.* (*fem.* **-trice**) mystifier, hoaxer.

mystification [mistifika'sjɔ̃], *n.f.* hoax.

mystifier [misti'fje], *v.t.* to mystify; to hoax.

mystique [mis'tik], *a.* mystical, mystic.—*n.* mystic.

mythe [mit], *n.m.* myth; fable, fiction.

mythique [mi'tik], *a.* mythical.

mythologie [mitolo'ʒi], *n.f.* mythology.

mythologique [mitolo'ʒik], *a.* mythological.

mythologiste [mitolo'ʒist], **mythologue** [mito'lɔg], *n.* mythologist.

myxomatose [miksoma'toːz], *n.f.* myxomatosis.

N

N, n [ɛn], *n.m.* the fourteenth letter of the alphabet.

nabab [na'bab], *n.m.* nabob.

nacelle [na'sɛl], *n.f.* wherry, skiff; gondola (*of airship etc.*).

nacre [nakr], *n.f.* mother-of-pearl.

nacré [na'kre], *a.* nacreous, pearly.

nage [naːʒ], *n.f.* swimming; rowing, sculling; (*fam.*) *être en nage*, to be bathed in perspiration.

nageoire [na'ʒwaːr], *n.f.* fin (*of a fish*).

nager [na'ʒe], *v.i.* (*conjug. like* MANGER) to swim; to float; to row.

nageur [na'ʒœːr], *a.* (*fem.* **-euse**) swimming.—*n.m.* (*fem.* **-euse**) swimmer; rower, oarsman.

naguère [na'gɛːr], *adv.* lately, not long ago.

naïade [na'jad], *n.f.* naiad, water-nymph.

naïf [na'if], *a.* (*fem.* **naïve**) naïve, artless, ingenuous, unaffected; simple.

nain [nɛ̃], *a.* dwarfish.—*n.m.* (*fem.* **-e**) dwarf.

naissance [nɛ'sãːs], *n.f.* birth; descent; (*fig.*) beginning, dawn, rise.

naissant [nɛ'sã], *a.* new-born, in its infancy; beginning, rising.

naître [nɛːtr], *v.i. irr.* (*with aux.* ÊTRE) to be born, (*fig.*) to originate; to dawn.

naïvement [naiv'mã], *adv.* naïvely, ingenuously, artlessly.

naïveté [naiv'te], *n.f.* artlessness, simplicity naïvety.

nantir [nã'tiːr], *v.t.* to give as a pledge, to secure; (*fig.*) to furnish. **se nantir**, *v.r.* to provide oneself (*de*); to take possession (*de*).

nantissement [nãtis'mã], *n.m.* security, pledge.

naphte [naft], *n.m.* naphtha.

napolitain [napoli'tɛ̃], *a.* Neapolitan.—*n.m.* (**Napolitain**, *fem.* **-aine**) Neapolitan (*person*).

nappe [nap], *n.f.* table-cloth, cover; sheet (*of water etc.*).

napperon [na'prɔ̃], *n.m.* tray-cloth; doily.

narcisse [nar'sis], *n.m.* (*Bot.*) narcissus.

narcotique [narko'tik], *a.* and *n.m.* narcotic.

narcotisme [narko'tism], *n.m.* narcotism.

narguer [nar'ge], *v.t.* to defy, to flout.

narine [na'rin], *n.f.* nostril.
narquois [nar'kwa], *a.* cunning, sly; chaffing.
narquoisement [narkwaz'mã], *adv.* slyly, quizzingly.
narrateur [nara'tœ:r], *n.m.* (*fem.* **-trice**) narrator, relater.
narratif [nara'tif], *a.* (*fem.* **-tive**) narrative.
narration [nara'sjõ], *n.f.* narration, narrative.
narrer [na'rɛ], *v.t.* to narrate, to tell.
nasal [na'zal], *a.* (*m. pl.* **-aux**) nasal.
nasalement [nazal'mã], *adv.* nasally, with a nasal sound.
naseau [na'zo], *n.m.* (*pl.* **-eaux**) nostril (*of animals*).
nasillant [nazi'jã], *a.* speaking through the nose.
nasillard [nazi'ja:r], *a.* snuffling, nasal.
nasillement [nazij'mã], *n.m.* speaking through the nose, snuffling; twang.
nasiller [nazi'je], *v.i.* to speak through the nose, to snuffle.
nasse [na:s], *n.f.* bow-net, weir, eel-pot.
natal [na'tal], *a.* (*m. pl.* **-als** (*rare*)) natal, native.
natalité [natali'te], *n.f.* birth-rate.
natation [nata'sjõ], *n.f.* swimming.
natif [na'tif], *a.* (*fem.* **-tive**) native; natural.—*n.m.* native.
nation [na'sjõ], *n.f.* nation.
national [nasjo'nal], *a.* (*m. pl.* **-aux**) national.
nationalement [nasjonal'mã], *adv.* nationally.
nationalisation [nasjonaliza'sjõ], *n.f.* nationalization.
nationaliser [nasjonali'ze], *v.t.* to nationalize.
nationaliste [nasjona'list], *n.* nationalist.
nationalité [nasjonali'te], *n.f.* nationality.
nativité [nativi'te], *n.f.* nativity, birth.
natte [nat], *n.f.* mat, matting (*of straw*); plait.
natter [na'te], *v.t.* to mat; to plait, to twist.
naturalisation [natyraliza'sjõ], *n.f.* naturalization; taxidermy.
naturaliser [natyrali'ze], *v.t.* to naturalize; to stuff (*animal*).
naturalisme [natyra'lism], *n.m.* naturalness; naturalism.
naturaliste [natyra'list], *a.* naturalistic.—*n.* naturalist; taxidermist.
nature [na'ty:r], *n.f.* nature; kind, sort; temperament; life, life-size; *de nature à*, likely to; *dessiner d'après nature*, to draw from life; *nature morte*, still life; *payer en nature*, to pay in kind.
naturel [naty'rɛl], *a.* (*fem.* **-elle**) natural; native, innate; artless, plain; *enfant naturel*, illegitimate child.—*n.m.* (*fem.* **-elle**) native (*of a country*).—*n.m.* disposition, nature; genuineness, simplicity.
naturellement [natyrɛl'mã], *adv.* naturally.—*int.* of course!
naturiste [naty'rist], *a.* naturistic.—*n.* naturist.
naufrage [no'fra:ʒ], *n.m.* shipwreck.
naufragé [nofra'ʒe], *a.* shipwrecked, wrecked.—*n.m.* (*fem.* **-ée**) shipwrecked person, castaway.
nauséabond [nozea'bõ], *a.* nauseating, loathsome, disgusting.
nausée [no'ze], *n.f.* nausea, sickness; (*fig.*) loathing, disgust.
nauséeux [noze'ø],ʳ*a.* (*fem.* **-éeuse**) nauseating.

nautique [no'tik], *a.* nautical.
naval [na'val] *a.* (*m. pl.* **-als**) naval, nautical.
navet [na'vɛ], *n.m.* turnip.
navette [na'vɛt], *n.f.* incense-box; weaver's shuttle; (*Bot.*) rape; *faire la navette*, to run a shuttle-service.
navigabilité [navigabili'te], *n.f.* airworthiness, seaworthiness.
navigable [navi'gabl], *a.* navigable; seaworthy, airworthy.
navigateur [naviga'tœ:r], *n.m.* navigator.—*a.m.* seafaring; swimming (*birds etc.*).
navigation [naviga'sjõ], *n.f.* navigation; voyage, sailing.
naviguer [navi'ge], *v.i.* to navigate; to row, to sail etc.
navire [na'vi:r], *n.m.* vessel, ship.
navrant [nɑ'vrã], *a.* heartrending, harrowing, distressing.
navrer [nɑ'vre], *v.t.* to distress, to rend (*the heart*).
nazaréen [nazare'ɛ], *a.* (*fem.* **-éenne**) of Nazareth.—*n.m.* (**Nazaréen**, *fem.* **-éenne**) Nazarene; Nazarite.
nazi [na'zi], *a.* Nazi.—*n.* (**Nazi**) Nazi.
nazisme [na'zism], *n.m.* Nazism.
ne [nə], *adv.* no, not.
né [ne], *a.* born.
néanmoins [neã'mwɛ], *adv.* nevertheless, however, for all that.
néant [ne'ã], *n.m.* naught, nothingness; nil.
nébuleux [neby'lø], *a.* (*fem.* **-euse**) cloudy, misty; nebulous; (*fig.*) obscure.—*n.f.* (**-euse**) nebula.
nébulosité [nebylozi'te], *n.f.* patch of haze.
nécessaire [nesɛ'sɛ:r], *a.* necessary; inevitable.—*n.m.* the needful; necessities (*of life etc.*); dressing-case, work-box.
nécessairement [nesɛsɛr'mã], *adv.* necessarily; inevitably, of course.
nécessité [nesɛsi'te], *n.f.* necessity; need, want.
nécessiter [nesɛsi'te], *v.t.* to necessitate; to compel, to oblige.
nécessiteux [nesɛsi'tø], *a.* (*fem.* **-euse**) necessitous, needy.—*n.m.* (*fem.* **-euse**) pauper.
nécrologe [nekrɔ'lɔ:ʒ], *n.m.* obituary list; death roll.
nécrologie [nekrɔlɔ'ʒi], *n.f.* necrology, obituary.
nécrologique [nekrɔlɔ'ʒik], *a.* necrological.
nécromancie [nekrɔmã'si], *n.f.* necromancy.
nécromancien [nekrɔmã'sjɛ], *n.m.* (*fem.* **-enne**) necromancer.
nécropole [nekrɔ'pɔl], *n.f.* necropolis.
nectar [nɛk'ta:r], *n.m.* nectar.
néerlandais [neɛrlã'dɛ], *a.* Dutch.—*n.m.* Dutch (*language*); (**Néerlandais**, *fem.* **-aise**) Dutchman, Dutchwoman.
nef [nɛf], *n.f.* nave (*of a church*).
néfaste [ne'fast], *a.* inauspicious; disastrous.
nèfle [nɛfl], *n.f.* medlar.
néflier [ne'flje], *n.m.* medlar-tree.
négatif [nega'tif], *a.* (*fem.* **-tive**) negative.—*n.m.* (*Phot.*) negative.—*n.f.* (**-tive**) negative, refusal.
négation [nega'sjõ], *n.f.* negation; (*Gram.*) negative.
négativement [negativ'mã], *adv.* negatively.

nitrique

négligé [negli'ʒe], *a.* neglected, unnoticed; careless; slovenly.—*n.m.* undress, negligee.

négligeable [negli'ʒabl], *a.* negligible; trifling, unimportant.

négligemment [negliʒa'mã], *adv.* nonchalantly; negligently.

négligence [negli'ʒã:s], *n.f.* negligence, neglect, oversight.

négligent [negli'ʒã], *a.* negligent, careless.—*n.m. (fem. -e)* negligent person.

négliger [negli'ʒe], *v.t. (conjug. like* MANGER) to neglect; to omit. **se négliger**, *v.r.* to neglect oneself; to be careless.

négoce [ne'gɔs], *n.m.* trade, business; trafficking.

négociabilité [negɔsjabili'te], *n.f.* negotiability.

négociable [negɔ'sjabl], *a.* negotiable, transferrable.

négociant [negɔ'sjã], *n.m. (fem. -e)* merchant *(wholesale)*.

négociateur [negɔsja'tœ:r], *n.m. (fem. -trice)* negotiator, transactor.

négociation [negɔsja'sjɔ̃], *n.f.* negotiation, transaction.

négocier [negɔ'sje], *v.t.* to negotiate.—*v.i.* to trade.

nègre [nɛ:gr], *a.* and *n.m. (fem. négresse) (pej.)* Negro; *(pl.) (pej.)* blacks.

négrier [negri'e], *n.m.* slave-ship; slaver; slave-dealer.

négrillon [negri'jɔ̃], *n.m. (fem. -onne) (pej.)* little Negro, Negro boy *or* girl.

neige [nɛ:ʒ], *n.f.* snow; **boule de neige**, snowball.

neiger [nɛ'ʒe], *v. impers. (conjug. like* MANGER) to snow.

neigeux [nɛ'ʒø], *a. (fem. -euse)* snowy, snow-covered.

nénuphar [neny'fa:r], *n.m.* water-lily.

néon [ne'ɔ̃], *n.m.* neon.

néo-zélandais [neozelã'dɛ], *a.* New Zealand *(butter, cheese etc.).*—*n.m. (Néo-Zélandais, fem. -aise)* New Zealander.

Népal [ne'pal], **le**, *m.* Nepal.

népalais [nepa'lɛ], *a.* Nepalese.—*n.m. (Népalais, fem. -aise)* Nepalese *(person).*

népotisme [nepɔ'tism], *n.m.* nepotism.

nerf [nɛ:r], *n.m.* nerve; sinew; fortitude, strength.

nerveusement [nɛrvøz'mã], *adv.* impatiently; nervously.

nerveux [nɛr'vø], *a. (fem. -euse)* nervous; excitable; muscular.

nervosité [nɛrvozi'te], *n.f.* nervousness.

nervure [nɛr'vy:r], *n.f. (Bot. etc.)* nervure, nerve; *(Arch.)* moulding; *(Carp.)* rib, fillet; *(Bookb.)* tapes, cording; *(Needlework)* piping.

net [nɛt], *a. (fem. nette)* clean; pure; clear, distinct; flat, frank, pointblank; net *(of prices).*—*n.m.* fair copy; **mettre au net**, to make a fair copy.—*adv.* clean off, at once; flatly, point-blank.

nettement [nɛt'mã], *adv.* cleanly; clearly; plainly, flatly.

netteté [nɛt'te], *n.f.* cleanness; clearness, distinctness.

nettoiement [nɛtwa'mã], **nettoyage** [nɛtwa'ja:ʒ], *n.m.* cleaning; clearing; wiping.

nettoyer [nɛtwa'je], *v.t. (conjug. like* EMPLOYER) to clean; to wipe; to rid *(de).*

neuf (1) [nœf], *a.* and *n.m.* nine, ninth.

neuf (2) [nœf], *a. (fem. neuve)* new, brand-new; young, raw.—*n.m.* something new.

neurologie [nørɔlɔ'ʒi], *n.f.* neurology.

neutralisation [nøtraliza'sjɔ̃], *n.f.* neutralization.

neutraliser [nøtrali'ze], *v.t.* to neutralize. **se neutraliser**, *v.r.* to neutralize each other.

neutralité [nøtrali'te], *n.f.* neutrality.

neutre [nø:tr], *a.* and *n.m.* neuter; neutral.

neutron [nø'trɔ̃], *n.m.* neutron.

neuvième [nœ'vjɛm], *a.* and *n.* ninth.

neveu [nə'vø], *n.m. (pl. -eux)* nephew; *(pl. poet.)* descendants.

névralgie [nevral'ʒi], *n.f.* neuralgia.

névralgique [nevral'ʒik], *a.* neuralgic.

névrite [ne'vrit], *n.f.* neuritis.

névritique [nevri'tik], *a.* neuritic.

névrose [ne'vro:z], *n.f.* neurosis, nervous disorder.

névrosé [nevro'ze], *a.* and *n.m. (fem. -ée)* neurotic.

nez [ne], *n.m. inv.* nose; face; scent *(of dogs etc.).*

ni [ni], *conj.* nor, neither . . . nor; *(after sans, sans que, etc.)* either . . . or.

niable [njabl], *a.* deniable.

niais [njɛ], *a.* silly, foolish.—*n.m. (fem. -e)* ninny, simpleton.

niaisement [njɛz'mã], *adv.* foolishly.

niaiser [njɛ'ze], *v.i.* to play the fool.

niaiserie [njɛz'ri], *n.f.* foolishness; nonsense.

Nicaragua [nikara'gwa], **le**, *m.* Nicaragua.

nicaraguayen [nikaragwa'jɛ̃], *a. (fem. -enne)* Nicaraguan.—*n.m. (Nicaraguayen, fem. -enne)* Nicaraguan *(person).*

niche [niʃ], *n.f.* niche, nook; recess; kennel; *(fam.)* prank.

nichée [ni'ʃe], *n.f.* nestful *(of young birds);* brood *(of animals, children etc.).*

nicher [ni'ʃe], *v.t.* to lodge, to put.—*v.i.* to build a nest; to nestle. **se nicher**, *v.r.* to nest, to nestle; to hide oneself.

nickel [ni'kɛl], *n.m.* nickel.

nickelage [ni'kla:ʒ], *n.m.* nickel-plating.

nickeler [ni'kle], *v.t. (conjug. like* APPELER) to nickel-plate.

Nicolas [nikɔ'la], *m.* Nicholas.

nicotine [nikɔ'tin], *n.f.* nicotine.

nid [ni], *n.m.* nest; berth, post.

nièce [njɛs], *n.f.* niece.

nier [nje], *v.t.* to deny; to repudiate, to disown.

nigaud [ni'go], *a. (colloq.)* silly, simple.—*n.m. (fem. -e)* booby, simpleton.

Nigéria [niʒe'rja], **le**, *m.* Nigeria.

nigérien [niʒe'rjɛ̃], *a. (fem. -enne)* Nigerian.—*n.m. (Nigérien, fem. -enne)* Nigerian *(person).*

nihilisme [nii'lism], *n.m.* nihilism.

nihiliste [nii'list], *a.* nihilistic.—*n.* nihilist.

Nil [nil], **le**, *m.* the Nile.

nimbe [nɛ̃:b], *n.m.* nimbus, halo.

nippe [nip], *n.f. usu. pl. (colloq.)* old clothes, togs.

nipper [ni'pe], *v.t. (colloq.)* to fit out, to rig out. **se nipper**, *v.r.* to rig oneself out.

nippon [ni'pɔ̃], *a.* Japanese.—*n.m. (Nippon, fem. -one)* Japanese *(person).*

nitrate [ni'trat], *n.m.* nitrate.

nitre [nitr], *n.m.* nitre, saltpetre.

nitrique [ni'trik], *a.* nitric.

225

nitrogène [nitrɔ'ʒɛn], *n.m.* nitrogen.
niveau [ni'vo], *n.m.* (*pl.* -eaux) level; standard; *passage à niveau*, level crossing.
niveler [ni'vle], *v.t.* (*conjug. like* APPELER) to level, to flatten (out).
niveleur [ni'vlœːr], *a.* (*fem.* -euse) levelling. —*n.m.* (*fem.* -euse) leveller.
nivellement [nivɛl'mã], *n.m.* levelling.
nobiliaire [nɔbi'ljɛːr], *a.* of the nobility, nobiliary.
noble [nɔbl], *a.* noble; great, high, exalted.— *n.* noble, nobleman, noblewoman.
noblement [nɔblə'mã], *adv.* nobly; honourably.
noblesse [nɔ'blɛs], *n.f.* nobility; nobleness, loftiness.
noce [nɔs], *n.f.* wedding; wedding-party; (*colloq.*) jollification.
noceur [nɔ'sœːr], *n.m.* (*fem.* -euse) gay dog, gay woman, rake.
nocif [nɔ'sif], *a.* (*fem.* -cive) injurious, noxious.
noctambule [nɔktã'byl], *a.* noctambulant, noctambulous.—*n.* sleep-walker.
noctambulisme [nɔktãby'lism], *n.m.* noctambulism, sleep-walking.
nocturne [nɔk'tyrn], *a.* nocturnal, nightly.— *n.m.* (*Mus.*) nocturne.
Noël [nɔ'ɛl], *n.m.* Christmas, Yule-tide; (*noël*) Christmas carol.
nœud [nø], *n.m.* knot; bow; difficulty, intricacy; (*fig.*) tie; bond.
noir [nwaːr], *a.* black; swarthy; gloomy, dismal; foul; *bête noire*, pet aversion.— *n.m.* black (*fem.* -e (1)); Negro.
noirâtre [nwa'rɑːtr], *a.* blackish.
noiraud [nwa'ro], *a.* dark, swarthy-looking.
noirceur [nwar'sœːr], *n.f.* blackness; baseness; foul deed.
noircir [nwar'siːr], *v.t.* to blacken; to sully; to defame; to darken.—*v.i.* and *se noircir*, *v.r.* to blacken, to darken, to grow black or dark.
noircissure [nwarsi'syːr], *n.f.* black spot, smudge.
noire (2) [nwaːr], *n.f.* (*Mus.*) crotchet.
noisetier [nwaz'tje], *n.m.* hazel (*tree or bush*).
noisette [nwa'zɛt], *n.f.* hazel-nut.
noix [nwa], *n.f. inv.* walnut; nut.
nom [nɔ̃], *n.m.* name; fame, celebrity; noun.
nomade [nɔ'mad], *a.* nomad, nomadic, wandering.—*n.* nomad.
nombre [nɔ̃ːbr], *n.m.* number; quantity; numbers.
nombrer [nɔ̃'bre], *v.t.* to number, to reckon.
nombreux [nɔ̃'brø], *a.* (*fem.* -euse) numerous; harmonious (*prose, style*).
nombril [nɔ̃'bri], *n.m.* navel.
nomenclature [nɔmãkla'tyːr], *n.f.* nomenclature; list catalogue.
nominal [nɔmi'nal], *a.* (*m. pl.* -aux) nominal.
nominalement [nɔminal'mã], *adv.* nominally.
nominatif [nɔmina'tif], *a.* (*fem.* -tive) and *n.m.* nominative.
nomination [nɔmina'sjɔ̃], *n.f.* nomination; appointment.
nominativement [nɔminativ'mã], *adv.* by name.
nommé [nɔ'me], *a.* named, called; appointed.
nommément [nɔme'mã], *adv.* namely; particularly, especially.

nommer [nɔ'me], *v.t.* to name, to call; to mention; to nominate, to appoint. *se nommer*, *v.r.* to state one's name; to be called.
non [nɔ̃], *adv.* no, not.
non-activité [nɔ̃nakti̇vi'te], *n.f.* state of being unattached *or* unemployed.
nonagénaire [nɔnaʒe'nɛːr], *a.* ninety years of age.—*n.* nonagenarian.
non-agression [nɔ̃nagre'sjɔ̃], *n.f.* non-aggression.
nonce [nɔ̃ːs], *n.m.* nuncio.
nonchalamment [nɔ̃ʃala'mã], *adv.* nonchalantly, carelessly, heedlessly.
nonchalance [nɔ̃ʃa'lãːs], *n.f.* carelessness, heedlessness, nonchalance.
nonchalant [nɔ̃ʃa'lã], *a.* nonchalant, careless; listless.—*n.m.* (*fem.* -e) such a person.
non-lieu [nɔ̃'ljø], *n.m.* (*Law*) no true bill.
nonne [nɔn], *n.f.* nun.
nonobstant [nɔnɔps'tã], *prep.* notwithstanding, in spite of.—*adv.* nevertheless.
nonpareil [nɔ̃pa'rɛːj], *a.* (*fem.* -eille) nonpareil, matchless.
non-sens [nɔ̃'sãːs], *n.m.* meaningless sentence, translation, or action.
nord [nɔːr], *a. inv.* north; *Pôle nord*, North Pole.—*n.m.* north; north-wind; *nord-est*, north-east; *nord-ouest*, north-west.
nordique [nɔr'dik], *a.* Nordic, Scandinavian. —*n.* (**Nordique**) Nordic, Scandinavian (*person*).
normal [nɔr'mal], *a.* (*m. pl.* -aux) normal; (*Geom.*) perpendicular.
normalement [nɔrmal'mã], *adv.* normally.
normalien [nɔrma'ljɛ̃], *n.m.* (*fem.* -enne) training-college student *or* ex-student.
normalité [nɔrmali'te], *n.f.* normality.
normand [nɔr'mã], *a.* Norman.—*n.m.* (**Normand**, *fem.* -**ande**) Norman (*person*).
Normandie [nɔrmã'di], **la**, *f.* Normandy.
norme [nɔrm], *n.f.* norm, average.
Norvège [nɔr'vɛːʒ], **la**, *f.* Norway.
norvégien [nɔrve'ʒjɛ̃], *a.* (*fem.* -enne) Norwegian.—*n.m.* Norwegian (*language*); (**Norvégien**, *fem.* -**enne**) Norwegian (*person*).
nos [no], *pl.* [NOTRE].
nostalgie [nɔstal'ʒi], *n.f.* nostalgia, homesickness.
nostalgique [nɔstal'ʒik], *a.* nostalgic; sad.
notabilité [nɔtabili'te], *n.f.* respectability; person of note.
notable [nɔ'tabl], *a.* notable, of influence.— *n.* notable, person of note.
notablement [nɔtablə'mã], *adv.* notably.
notaire [nɔ'tɛːr], *n.m.* notary; solicitor.
notamment [nɔta'mã], *adv.* specially; more particularly.
notariat [nɔta'rja], *n.m.* profession, business *or* function of notary.
notation [nɔta'sjɔ̃], *n.f.* notation.
note [nɔt], *n.f.* note, memorandum; mark; statement; bill.
noter [nɔ'te], *v.t.* to note; to mark; to note down; to observe, to notice.
notice [nɔ'tis], *n.f.* notice, account; review (*of a book*); notification.
notification [nɔtifika'sjɔ̃], *n.f.* notification, notice, intimation.
notifier [nɔti'fje], *v.t.* to notify; to intimate.
notion [nɔ'sjɔ̃], *n.f.* notion, idea; (*pl.*) elements, rudiments.

ô!

notoire [nɔ'twaːr], *a.* notorious; well-known.
notoirement [nɔtwar'mɑ̃], *adv.* notoriously.
notoriété [nɔtɔrje'te], *n.f.* notoriety (*of fact*); repute (*of person*).
notre [nɔtr], *a. poss.* (*pl.* **nos**) our.
nôtre [no:tr], *pron. poss.* (*pl.* **nôtres**) ours; our own: our things, friends, relatives etc.
noué [nwe], *a.* knotty, tied; rickety.
nouer [nwe], *v.t.* to tie, to knot; (*fig.*) to devise; to establish. **se nouer**, *v.r.* to be twisted *or* tied; to fasten oneself.
noueux [nu'ø], *a.* (*fem.* **-euse**) knotty, gnarled.
nougat [nu'ɡɑ], *n.m.* nougat; almond-cake.
nouilles [nuːj], *n.f. pl.* noodles, spaghetti.
nourri [nu'ri], *a.* nourished, fed; full, rich, copious; brisk (*fire*).
nourrice [nu'ris], *n.f.* nurse; wet-nurse; (*Motor., Av.*) feed-tank.
nourricier [nuri'sje], *a.* (*fem.* **-ière**) life-giving, nourishing; producing food.—*n.m.* (*fem.* **-ière**) foster-parent.
nourrir [nu'riːr], *v.t.* to nourish, to feed; to keep, to maintain; to nurse; to foster; to rear; to cherish. **se nourrir**, *v.r.* to feed, to live upon.
nourrissage [nuri'saːʒ], *n.m.* rearing, feeding (*of cattle*).
nourrissant [nuri'sɑ̃], *a.* nutritious; nourishing; sustaining.
nourrisseur [nuri'sœːr], *n.m.* cow-keeper; stock-raiser.
nourrisson [nuri'sɔ̃], *n.m.* (*fem.* **-onne**) infant; foster-child; nursling.
nourriture [nuri'tyːr], *n.f.* nourishment, food; livelihood.
nous [nu], *pers. pron.* we; us; to us; ourselves; each other.
nouveau [nu'vo] (*before a vowel or unaspirated* h **nouvel**), *a.* (*fem.* **-elle** (1)) new; recent, novel; additional; inexperienced.—*n.m.* (*pl.* **-eaux**) new, something new; *à nouveau*, afresh; *de nouveau*, again.
nouveau-né [nuvo'ne], *n.m.* (*fem.* **nouveau-née**, *pl.* **nouveau-né(e)s**) new-born child.
nouveauté [nuvo'te], *n.f.* novelty; change, innovation; (*pl.*) fancy articles; (*fig.*) new book, new play.
nouvelle (2) [nu'vɛl], *n.f.* (*often in pl.*) news, tidings; short story, short novel.
nouvellement [nuvɛl'mɑ̃], *adv.* newly, lately, recently.
Nouvelle-Zélande [nuvɛlze'lɑ̃:d], la, *f.* New Zealand.
nouvelliste [nuvɛ'list], *n.* newswriter; short story writer.
novateur [nɔva'tœːr], *a.* (*fem.* **-trice**) innovating.—*n.m.* (*fem.* **-trice**) innovator.
novembre [nɔ'vɑ̃:br], *n.m.* November.
novice [nɔ'vis], *a.* novice, inexperienced.—*n.* novice, probationer.
noviciat [nɔvi'sja], *n.m.* noviciate.
noyade [nwa'jad], *n.f.* drowning.
noyau [nwa'jo], *n.m.* (*pl.* **-aux**) stone (*of fruit*), nucleus; core (*of statues, casts etc.*).
noyé [nwa'je], *a.* drowned.—*n.m.* (*fem.* **-ée**) drowned person.
noyer (1) [nwa'je], *n.m.* walnut-tree; walnut (*wood*).
noyer (2) [nwa'je], *v.t.* (*conjug. like* EMPLOYER) to drown; to swamp; to deluge. **se noyer**, *v.r.* to be drowned; to be plunged (*dans*).

nu [ny], *a.* naked, nude, bare; uncovered; unadorned; destitute.—*n.m.* the nude, nudity.
nuage [nɥa:ʒ], *n.m.* cloud; mist; (*fig.*) gloom, dejection.
nuageux [nɥa'ʒø], *a.* (*fem.* **-euse**) cloudy, overcast.
nuance [nɥɑ̃:s], *n.f.* shade, hue; gradation; tinge.
nuancer [nɥɑ̃'se], *v.t.* (*conjug. like* COMMENCER) to shade; to vary slightly.
nubile [ny'bil], *a.* nubile, marriageable.
nubilité [nybili'te], *n.f.* nubility, marriageable age.
nucléaire [nykle'ɛːr], *a.* nuclear.
nudité [nydi'te], *n.f.* nudity, nakedness.
nuée [nɥe], *n.f.* cloud; (*fig.*) swarm, host, multitude, flock.
nues [ny], *n.f. pl.* (*Poet.*) skies.
nuire [nɥiːr], *v.i. irr.* to be hurtful, to jeopardize, to harm (*à*).
nuisible [nɥi'zibl], harmful, noxious, prejudicial.
nuit [nɥi], *n.f.* night, night-time; darkness; *il fait nuit*, it is dark; *nuit blanche*, sleepless night.
nuitamment [nɥita'mɑ̃], *adv.* by night, in the night.
nul [nyl], *a.* (*fem.* **nulle**) no, not any; void, null.—*pron.* no one, nobody, not one.
nullement [nyl'mɑ̃], *adv.* not at all, by no means.
nullifier [nyli'fje], *v.t.* to nullify.
nullité [nyli'te], *n.f.* nullity; nonentity; (*fig.*) incapacity.
numéraire [nyme'rɛːr], *a.* legal (*of coin*).—*n.m.* metallic currency, cash.
numéral [nyme'ral], *a.* (*m. pl.* **-aux**) numeral.
numérateur [nymera'tœːr], *n.m.* (*Arith.*) numerator.
numération [nymera'sjɔ̃], *n.f.* numeration, notation.
numérique [nyme'rik], *a.* numerical.
numériquement [nymerik'mɑ̃], *adv.* numerically.
numéro [nyme'ro], *n.m.* number.
numérotage [nymero'ta:ʒ], *n.m.*, **numérotation** [nymerota'sjɔ̃], *n.f.* numbering.
numéroter [nymero'te], *v.t.* to number.
numismate [nymis'mat], **numismatiste** [nymisma'tist], *n.* numismatist.
numismatique [nymisma'tik], *a.* numismatic.—*n.f.* numismatics.
nuptial [nyp'sjal], *a.* (*m. pl.* **-aux**) nuptial, bridal.
nuque [nyk], *n.f.* nape (*of the neck*).
nutritif [nytri'tif], *a.* (*fem.* **-tive**) nutritious, nourishing.
nutrition [nytri'sjɔ̃], *n.f.* nutrition.
nylon [ni'lɔ̃], *n.m.* nylon; *des bas nylon*, nylon stockings.
nymphe [nɛ̃:f], *n.f.* nymph.

O

O, o [o], *n.m.* the fifteenth letter of the alphabet.
ô! [o] *int.* oh!

227

oasis [oaˈziːs], n.f. inv. oasis.
obéir [ɔbeˈiːr], v.i. to obey; to comply, to yield, to submit (à).
obéissance [ɔbeiˈsãːs], n.f. obedience; allegiance.
obéissant [ɔbeiˈsã], a. obedient; docile.
obélisque [ɔbeˈlisk], n.m. obelisk, needle.
obérer [ɔbeˈre], v.t. (conjug. like CÉDER) to encumber or involve in debt.
obèse [ɔˈbɛːz], a. obese, stout.
obésité [ɔbeziˈte], n.f. obesity, stoutness.
obituaire [ɔbitɥˈɛːr], a. and n.m. obituary, register of deaths; mortuary.
objecter [ɔbʒɛkˈte], v.t. to object; to allege.
objecteur [ɔbʒɛkˈtœːr], n.m. objector.
objectif [ɔbʒɛkˈtif], a. (fem. -tive) objective. —n.m. objective, aim; lens; (Mil.) target.
objection [ɔbʒɛkˈsjõ], n.f. objection.
objectivement [ɔbʒɛktivˈmã], adv. objectively.
objectivité [ɔbʒɛktiviˈte], n.f. objectivity.
objet [ɔbˈʒɛ], n.m. object; subject, matter; aim; (pl.) articles, goods.
obligation [ɔbligaˈsjõ], n.f. obligation; (Law) bond; (Comm.) debenture.
obligatoire [ɔbligaˈtwaːr], a. compulsory, obligatory, incumbent.
obligatoirement [ɔbligatwarˈmã], adv. compulsorily.
obligeamment [ɔbliʒaˈmã], adv. obligingly.
obligeance [ɔbliˈʒãːs], n.f. obligingness; kindness.
obligeant [ɔbliˈʒã], a. obliging, kind, helpful.
obliger [ɔbliˈʒe], v.t. (conjug. like MANGER) to oblige, to bind; to compel; to gratify. s'obliger, v.r. to put oneself under an obligation.
oblique [ɔˈblik], a. oblique, slanting; (fig.) indirect, underhand.
obliquement [ɔblikˈmã], adv. obliquely, indirectly; unfairly.
obliquer [ɔbliˈke], v.i. to slant, to swerve.
obliquité [ɔblikiˈte], n.f. obliquity.
oblitération [ɔbliteraˈsjõ], n.f. obliteration.
oblitérer [ɔbliteˈre], v.t. (conjug. like CÉDER) to obliterate; to cancel (stamps).
oblong [ɔˈblõ], a. (fem. -ue) oblong.
obole [ɔˈbɔl], n.f. obolus; (fig.) farthing, mite.
obscène [ɔpˈsɛːn], a. obscene.
obscénité [ɔpseniˈte], n.f. obscenity, lewdness.
obscur [ɔpsˈkyːr], a. obscure; dark, gloomy; (fig.) humble; mean.
obscurcir [ɔpskyrˈsiːr], v.t. to obscure, to darken, to dim; to tarnish. s'obscurcir, v.r. to grow dim.
obscurcissement [ɔpskyrsisˈmã], n.m. darkening; (Mil.) black-out.
obscurément [ɔpskyreˈmã], adv. obscurely, dimly.
obscurité [ɔpskyriˈte], n.f. obscurity, darkness.
obséder [ɔpseˈde], v.t. (conjug. like CÉDER) to beset; to haunt, to importune, to obsess.
obsèques [ɔpˈsɛk], n.f. pl. obsequies, funeral.
obséquieusement [ɔpsekjøzˈmã], adv. obsequiously.
obséquieux [ɔpseˈkjø], a. (fem. -euse) obsequious, fawning.
observable [ɔpsɛrˈvabl], a. observable.
observance [ɔpsɛrˈvãːs], n.f. observance.

observateur [ɔpsɛrvaˈtœːr], a. (fem. -trice) observant.—n.m. (fem. -trice) observer, onlooker.
observation [ɔpsɛrvaˈsjõ], n.f. observation; observance; remark.
observatoire [ɔpsɛrvaˈtwaːr], n.m. observatory; look-out.
observer [ɔpsɛrˈve], v.t. to observe, to notice; to watch; to remark; to perform. s'observer, v.r. to be circumspect, to be on one's guard; to observe each other.
obsession [ɔpsɛˈsjõ], n.f. obsession.
obstacle [ɔpsˈtakl], n.m. obstacle, bar, hindrance.
obstination [ɔpstinaˈsjõ], n.f. obstinacy, stubbornness, wilfulness.
obstiné [ɔpstiˈne], a. obstinate, self-willed, stubborn; persistent.
obstinément [ɔpstineˈmã], adv. obstinately, stubbornly.
obstiner (s') [sɔpstiˈne], v.r. to be obstinately resolved (à), to insist, to persist.
obstructif [ɔpstrykˈtif], a. (fem. -tive) obstructive.
obstruction [ɔpstrykˈsjõ], n.f. obstruction; stoppage.
obstruer [ɔpstrɥˈe], v.t. to obstruct, to block.
obtempérer [ɔptãpeˈre], v.i. (conjug. like CÉDER) to obey, to comply (à).
obtenir [ɔptəˈniːr], v.t. irr. (conjug. like TENIR) to obtain, to procure, to get. s'obtenir, v.r. to be obtained; to be obtainable.
obtention [ɔptãˈsjõ], n.f. obtaining, getting.
obturer [ɔptyˈre], v.t. to seal, to obturate; to fill (gap), to stop (a tooth etc.).
obtus [ɔpˈty], a. obtuse; dull, blunt.
obus [ɔˈby], n.m. (Artill.) shell.
obusier [ɔbyˈzje], n.m. howitzer.
obvier [ɔbˈvje], v.i. to obviate, to prevent (à).
occasion [ɔkaˈzjõ], n.f. opportunity, occasion; cause; bargain, job lot; livres d'occasion, second-hand books.
occasionnel [ɔkazjoˈnɛl], a. (fem. -elle) occasional.
occasionnellement [ɔkazjonɛlˈmã], adv. occasionally.
occasionner [ɔkazjoˈne], v.t. to occasion, to cause.
occident [ɔksiˈdã], n.m. west.
occidental [ɔksidãˈtal], a. (m. pl. -aux) occidental, western.
Occidentaux [ɔksidãˈto], n.m. pl. natives or inhabitants of the western countries, members of the western bloc.
occulte [ɔˈkylt], a. occult.
occupant [ɔkyˈpã], a. occupying.—n.m. (fem. -e) occupant, occupier.
occupation [ɔkypaˈsjõ], n.f. occupation; occupancy; capture.
occupé [ɔkyˈpe], a. occupied, busy, engaged; seized.
occuper [ɔkyˈpe], v.t. to occupy; to employ; to inhabit. s'occuper, v.r. to occupy oneself; to be busy; to look after; to see to (de).
occurrence [ɔkyˈrãːs], n.f. occurrence; event; en l'occurrence, under the circumstances.
océan [ɔseˈã], n.m. ocean, high sea.
océanique [ɔseaˈnik], a. oceanic.
ocre [ɔkr], n.f. ochre.
octane [ɔkˈtan], n.m. octane.
octave [ɔkˈtaːv], n.f. octave.

octavo [ɔkta'vo], *adv.* eighthly.—*n.m.* octavo.
octobre [ɔk'tɔbr], *n.m.* October.
octogénaire [ɔktɔʒe'nɛːr], *a.* and *n.* octogenarian.
octogone [ɔktɔ'gɔn], *a.* octagonal, eight-sided.—*n.m.* octagon.
octroi [ɔk'trwa], *n.m.* grant, concession; town dues, toll; toll-house *or* office.
octroyer [ɔktrwa'je], *v.t.* (*conjug. like* EMPLOYER) to grant, to concede.
oculaire [ɔky'lɛːr], *a.* ocular; *témoin oculaire,* eyewitness.—*n.m.* eye-piece.
oculiste [ɔky'list], *n.m.* oculist.
odalisque [ɔda'lisk], *n.f.* odalisque.
ode [ɔd], *n.f.* ode.
odeur [ɔ'dœːr], *n.f.* odour, smell; scent.
odieusement [ɔdjøz'mã], *adv.* odiously, hatefully.
odieux [ɔ'djø], *a.* (*fem.* -**euse**) odious, hateful, loathsome.—*n.m.* odiousness, hatefulness.
odorant [ɔdɔ'rã], *a.* fragrant, sweet-smelling.
odorat [ɔdɔ'ra], *n.m.* smell, sense of smell.
odoriférant [ɔdɔrife'rã], *a.* sweet-smelling.
Odyssée [ɔdi'se], *n.f.* Odyssey.
œil [œːj], *n.m.* (*pl.* **yeux**) eye; look; lustre; bud; dint, hole (*in bread, cheese*); *des yeux à fleur de tête,* prominent eyes; *d'un coup d'œil,* at a glance; *en un clin d'œil,* in the twinkling of an eye.
œil-de-bœuf [œjdə'bœf], *n.m.* (*pl.* **œils-de-bœuf**) round *or* oval window.
œillade [œ'jad], *n.f.* glance; ogle, leer; wink.
œillère [œ'jɛːr], *n.f.* blinker; canine tooth; eye-bath.
œillet [œ'jɛ], *n.m.* eyelet; (*Bot.*) dianthus, pink; *œillet des fleuristes,* carnation; *œillet de poète,* sweet william; *petit œillet d'Inde,* French marigold.
œuf [œf], *n.m.* (*pl.* **œufs**) egg; ovum; spawn, roe (*of fish*).
œuvre [œːvr], *n.f.* work; performance; production; (*pl.*) works (*of an author*).—*n.m.* (*no pl.*) work (*of an author, painter, musician etc.*)
œuvrer [œ'vre], [OUVRER].
offensant [ɔfã'sã], *a.* offensive, insulting.
offense [ɔ'fãːs], *n.f.* offence; injury, wrong, trespass.
offensé [ɔfã'se], *n.m.* (*fem.* -**ée**) offended party.
offenser [ɔfã'se], *v.t.* to offend; to sin against; to hurt, to injure (*feelings*); to shock. **s'offenser,** *v.r.* to be offended, to take offence.
offenseur [ɔfã'sœːr], *n.m.* offender.
offensif [ɔfã'sif], *a.* (*fem.* -**sive**) offensive.—*n.f.* (-**sive**) offensive (*attack*).
offensivement [ɔfãsiv'mã], *adv.* offensively.
office [ɔ'fis], *n.m.* office; duty; employment; service; Divine worship.—*n.f.* servants' hall, pantry, larder.
officiant [ɔfi'sjã], *a.* officiating.—*n.m.* officiating priest.
officiel [ɔfi'sjɛl], *a.* (*fem.* -**elle**) official, formal.
officiellement [ɔfisjɛl'mã], *adv.* officially.
officier (1) [ɔfi'sje], *v.i.* to officiate (*at divine service*).
officier (2) [ɔfi'sje], *n.m.* officer.
officieusement [ɔfisjøz'mã], *adv.* officiously.
officieux [ɔfi'sjø], *a.* (*fem.* -**euse**) officious; semi-official; obliging.—*n.m.* (*fem.* -**euse**) busybody.

offrande [ɔ'frãːd], *n.f.* offertory; offering.
offre [ɔfr], *n.f.* offer, tender.
offrir [ɔ'friːr], *v.t.* (*conjug. like* OUVRIR) to offer, to tender; to present, to give. **s'offrir,** *v.r.* to offer oneself; to present itself.
offusquer [ɔfys'ke], *v.t.* to obscure; to dazzle; to offend. **s'offusquer,** *v.r.* (*rare*) to become darkened; (*fig.*) to take offence.
ogival [ɔʒi'val], *a.* (*m. pl.* -**aux**) (*Arch.*) pointed; gothic.
ogive [ɔ'ʒiːv], *n.f.* ogive, pointed arch; nose (*of missile, rocket*).
ogre [ɔgr], *n.m.* (*fem.* -**esse**) ogre, ogress.
oh! [o], *int.* O! ho!
ohm [om], *n.m.* ohm.
oie [wa], *n.f.* goose; (*fig.*) simpleton.
oignon [ɔ'ɲõ], *n.m.* onion; bulb; bunion.
oindre [wɛ̃dr], *v.t. irr.* to anoint.
oiseau [wa'zo], *n.m.* (*pl.* -**eaux**) bird; hod; (*colloq.*) fellow, chap; *à vol d'oiseau,* as the crow flies.
oiseau-mouche [wazo'muʃ], *n.m.* (*pl.* **oiseaux-mouches**) humming-bird.
oiselet [wa'zlɛ], *n.m.* small bird.
oiseleur [wa'zlœːr], *n.m.* bird-catcher; fowler.
oiselier [waz'lje], *n.m.* bird-seller; bird-fancier.
oiseux [wa'zø], *a.* (*fem.* -**euse**) idle; useless; trifling.
oisif [wa'zif], *a.* (*fem.* -**sive**) idle, unoccupied; lying dead (*money*).—*n.m.* (*fem.* -**sive**) idler.
oisillon [wazi'jõ], *n.m.* young bird, fledg(e)ling.
oisivement [waziv'mã], *adv.* idly.
oisiveté [waziv'te], *n.f.* idleness; hours of ease.
oison [wa'zõ], *n.m.* gosling; (*fig.*) simpleton.
oléagineux [ɔleaʒi'nø], *a.* (*fem.* -**euse**) oleaginous, oily.
oléoduc [ɔleo'dyk], *n.m.* pipeline.
oligarchie [ɔligar'ʃi], *n.f.* oligarchy.
oligarchique [ɔligar'ʃik], *a.* oligarchical.
oligarque [ɔli'gark], *n.* oligarch.
olivâtre [ɔli'vaːtr], *a.* olivaceous, olive-hued; sallow.
olive [ɔ'liːv], *a. inv.* olive-coloured.—*n.f.* olive.
Olivier [ɔli'vje], *m.* Oliver.
olivier [ɔli'vje], *n.m.* olive-tree; olive-wood.
olographe [ɔlɔ'graf], *a.* holograph(ic) (*will*).
Olympe [ɔ'lɛ̃ːp], *n.m.* Olympus; (*fig.*) heaven.
olympien [ɔlɛ̃'pjɛ̃], *a.* (*fem.* -**enne**) Olympian.—*n.m.* (**Olympien,** *fem.* -**enne**) Olympian.
olympique [ɔlɛ̃'pik], *a.* Olympic.
ombrage [õ'braːʒ], *n.m.* shade; umbrage, suspicion.
ombrager [õbra'ʒe], *v.t.* (*conjug. like* MANGER) to shade; (*fig.*) to protect.
ombrageux [õbra'ʒø], *a.* (*fem.* -**euse**) skittish (*of horses*); suspicious, touchy.
ombre [õːbr], *n.f.* shadow; shade; darkness; ghost; *à l'ombre,* in the shade.
ombré [õ'bre], *a.* tinted, shaded.
ombrelle [õ'brɛl], *n.f.* parasol, sunshade.
ombrer [õ'bre], *v.t.* to shade; to darken.
ombreux [õ'brø], *a.* (*fem.* -**euse**) shady.
omelette [ɔm'lɛt], *n.f.* omelet(te).
omettre [ɔ'mɛtr], *v.t. irr.* (*conjug. like* METTRE) to omit.
omission [ɔmi'sjõ], *n.f.* omission.
omnibus [ɔmni'byːs], *a.* suitable for all; *train omnibus,* slow train, stopping train. —*n.m. inv.* omnibus, bus.

omnipotence [ɔmnipɔ'tɑ̃:s], *n.f.* omnipotence.

omnipotent [ɔmnipɔ'tɑ̃], *a.* omnipotent.

omnivore [ɔmni'vɔːr], *a.* omnivorous.—*n.m.* omnivore.

omoplate [ɔmɔ'plat], *n.f.* shoulder-blade; scapula.

on [ɔ̃], *indef. pron.* one, they, we, you, people, men, somebody.

once (1) [ɔ̃:s], *n.f.* ounce (*weight*).

once (2) [ɔ̃:s], *n.f.* ounce, snow leopard.

oncle [ɔ̃:kl], *n.m.* uncle.

onction [ɔ̃k'sjɔ̃], *n.f.* unction, anointing; (*fig.*) unctuousness.

onctueusement [ɔ̃ktɥøz'mɑ̃], *adv.* unctuously.

onctueux [ɔ̃k'tɥø], *a.* (*fem.* **-euse**) unctuous, oily.

onctuosité [ɔ̃ktɥɔzi'te], *n.f.* unctuousness; smoothness.

onde [ɔ̃:d], *n.f.* wave, billow; (*fig.*) sea.

ondé [ɔ̃'de], *a.* undulating, wavy; watered (*of silk etc.*).

ondée [ɔ̃'de], *n.f.* shower (*of rain*).

ondoyant [ɔ̃dwa'jɑ̃], *a.* undulating; (*fig.*) changeable.

ondoyer [ɔ̃dwa'je], *v.t.* (*conjug. like* EMPLOYER) to baptize privately.—*v.i.* to undulate; to ripple (*water*).

ondulant [ɔ̃dy'lɑ̃], *a.* undulating; waving, flowing.

ondulation [ɔ̃dyla'sjɔ̃], *n.f.* undulation; wave (*of hair*).

ondulé [ɔ̃dy'le], *a.* rolling, undulating; waved (*hair*); corrugated (*iron*).

onduler [ɔ̃dy'le], *v.t.* to wave (*hair*).—*v.i.* to undulate; to ripple.

onduleux [ɔ̃dy'lø], *a.* (*fem.* **-euse**) sinuous, wavy.

onéreux [ɔne'rø], *a.* (*fem.* **-euse**) burdensome, onerous; expensive.

ongle [ɔ̃:gl], *n.m.* nail (*of fingers, claws etc.*); claw, talon; hoof.

onglée [ɔ̃'gle], *n.f.* numbness of the fingers (*from cold*).

onglet [ɔ̃'glɛ], *n.m.* mitre, mitre-joint.

onglier [ɔ̃'glje], *n.m.* manicure-case; (*pl.*) (*curved*) nail-scissors.

onguent [ɔ̃'gɑ̃], *n.m.* ointment, salve.

ongulé [ɔ̃gy'le], *a.* hoofed, ungulate.

onyx [ɔ'niks], *a.* and *n.m. inv.* onyx.

onze [ɔ̃:z], *a.* and *n.m.* eleven, eleventh.

onzième [ɔ̃'zjɛm], *a.* and *n.m.* eleventh.

onzièmement [ɔzjɛm'mɑ̃], *adv.* eleventhly, in the eleventh place.

opacité [ɔpasi'te], *n.f.* opacity; (*fig.*) darkness.

opale [ɔ'pal], *n.f.* opal.

opalescence [ɔpalɛ'sɑ̃:s], *n.f.* opalescence.

opalescent [ɔpalɛ'sɑ̃], *a.* opalescent.

opaque [ɔ'pak], *a.* opaque.

opéra [ɔpe'ra], *n.m.* opera; opera-house.

opéra-bouffe [ɔpera'buf], *n.m.* comic opera; musical comedy.

opérateur [ɔpera'tœːr], *n.m.* (*fem.* **-trice**) operator; operative.

opératif [ɔpera'tif], *a.* (*fem.* **-tive**) operative.

opération [ɔpera'sjɔ̃], *n.f.* operation, working, performance; (*Comm.*) transaction.

opératoire [ɔpera'twaːr], *a.* operative, surgical.

opérer [ɔpe're], *v.t.* (*conjug. like* CÉDER) to operate, to bring about, to perform; to

operate upon.—*v.i.* to work, to operate.

s'opérer, *v.r.* to take place, to be brought about.

opérette [ɔpe'rɛt], *n.f.* operetta, light opera.

ophtalmie [ɔftal'mi], *n.f.* ophthalmia.

ophtalmique [ɔftal'mik], *a.* ophthalmic.

opiner [ɔpi'ne], *v.i.* to opine, to give *or* be of opinion; to speak.

opiniâtre [ɔpi'njɑːtr], *a.* stubborn, obstinate.—*n.* stubborn person.

opiniâtrement [ɔpinjɑtrə'mɑ̃], *adv.* doggedly.

opiniâtrer (s') [sɔpinjɑ'tre], *v.r.* to be obstinate, to insist.

opiniâtreté [ɔpinjɑtrə'te], *n.f.* obstinacy.

opinion [ɔpi'njɔ̃], *n.f.* opinion; judgment, view; (*pl.*) votes.

opium [ɔ'pjɔm], *n.m.* opium.

opossum [ɔpɔ'sɔm], *n.m.* opossum.

opportun [ɔpɔr'tœ̃], *a.* opportune, timely; expedient.

opportunément [ɔpɔrtyne'mɑ̃], *adv.* seasonably.

opportunisme [ɔpɔrty'nism], *n.m.* opportunism.

opportuniste [ɔpɔrty'nist], *a.* and *n.* opportunist.

opportunité [ɔpɔrtyni'te], *n.f.* opportuneness, expediency.

opposant [ɔpo'zɑ̃], *a.* opposing, adverse.—*n.m.* (*fem.* **-e**) opponent, adversary.

opposé [ɔpo'ze], *a.* opposite, contrary.—*n.m.* the opposite, the reverse, the contrary.

opposer [ɔpo'ze], *v.t.* to oppose; to object; to urge. **s'opposer**, *v.r.* to be opposed *or* contrary (*à*), to set oneself against, to resist.

opposition [ɔpozi'sjɔ̃], *n.f.* opposition, resistance; contrast.

oppresser [ɔprɛ'se], *v.t.* (*fig.*) to depress; *to oppress.

oppresseur [ɔprɛ'sœːr], *a.m.* oppressive.—*n.m.* oppressor.

oppressif [ɔprɛ'sif], *a.* (*fem.* **-ive**) oppressive.

oppression [ɔprɛ'sjɔ̃], *n.f.* oppression.

oppressivement [ɔprɛsiv'mɑ̃], *adv.* tyrannically, oppressively (*person*).

opprimant [ɔpri'mɑ̃], *a.* oppressing.

opprimé [ɔpri'me], *a.* oppressed.—*n.m.* (*fem.* **-ée**) the oppressed.

opprimer [ɔpri'me], *v.t.* to oppress, to crush.

opprobre [ɔ'prɔbr], *n.m.* opprobrium, shame, disgrace.

opter [ɔp'te], *v.i.* to choose, to decide.

opticien [ɔpti'sjɛ̃], *n.m.* optician.

optimisme [ɔpti'mism], *n.m.* optimism.

optimiste [ɔpti'mist], *a.* optimistic.—*n.* optimist.

option [ɔp'sjɔ̃], *n.f.* option, choice.

optique [ɔp'tik], *a.* optic, optical.—*n.f.* optics; perspective.

opulence [ɔpy'lɑ̃:s], *n.f.* opulence, wealth.

opulent [ɔpy'lɑ̃], *a.* opulent, wealthy.

or (1) [ɔːr], *n.m.* gold; (*Her.*) or.

or (2) [ɔːr], *conj.* but, now; well.

oracle [ɔ'rɑːkl], *n.m.* oracle.

orage [ɔ'raːʒ], *n.m.* storm; thunder-storm; (*fig.*) tumult, disorder.

orageusement [ɔraʒøz'mɑ̃], *adv.* tempestuously; boisterously.

orageux [ɔra'ʒø], *a.* (*fem.* **-euse**) stormy, tempestuous; restless.

oraison [ɔrɛ'zɔ̃], *n.f.* speech, oration; prayer.

oral [ɔ'ral], *a.* (*m. pl.* **-aux**) oral, by word of mouth.

oralement [ɔral'mã], *adv.* orally, by word of mouth.

orange [ɔ'rãːʒ], *n.f.* orange (*fruit*).—*a. inv.* and *n.m.* orange (*colour*).

orangé [ɔrã'ʒe], *a.* orange(-coloured).

orangeade [ɔrã'ʒad], *n.f.* orangeade, orange squash.

oranger [ɔrã'ʒe], *n.m.* orange-tree.

orangerie [ɔrã'ʒri], *n.f.* orange-house; orange-grove, orangery.

orang-outan(g) [ɔrãu'tã], *n.m.* (*pl.* **orangs-outans**) orang-utan.

orateur [ɔra'tœːr], *n.m.* (*fem.* **-trice**) orator, speaker.

oratoire [ɔra'twaːr], *a.* oratorical; oratorial.—*n.m.* oratory; private chapel.

orbe [ɔrb], *n.m.* orb, orbit; globe; sphere; coil (*snake*).

orbite [ɔr'bit], *n.f.* orbit; (*Anat.*) socket; (*fig.*) sphere (*of action*).

Orcades [ɔr'kad], **les**, *f. pl.* the Orkneys.

orchestral [ɔrkɛs'tral], *a.* (*m. pl.* **-aux**) orchestral.

orchestration [ɔrkɛstra'sjɔ̃], *n.f.* scoring, orchestration.

orchestre [ɔr'kɛstr], *n.m.* orchestra; band.

orchestrer [ɔrkɛs'tre], *v.t.* to score, to orchestrate.

orchidée [ɔrki'de], *n.f.* orchid; (*pl.*) Orchidaceae.

ordinaire [ɔrdi'nɛːr], *a.* ordinary, common, usual.—*n.m.* ordinary practice; usual fare.

ordinairement [ɔrdinɛr'mã], *adv.* usually.

ordinal [ɔrdi'nal], *a.* (*m. pl.* **-aux**) ordinal.

ordination [ɔrdina'sjɔ̃], *n.f.* ordination.

ordonnance [ɔrdɔ'nãːs], *n.f.* order, ordinance, regulation; disposition, arrangement; (*Med.*) prescription.—*n.* (*usu. fem.*) (*Mil.*) batman.

ordonnateur [ɔrdɔna'tœːr], *a.* (*fem.* **-trice**) ordaining, ordering.—*n.m.* (*fem.* **-trice**) organizer, manager; master of ceremonies.

ordonné [ɔrdɔ'ne], *a.* ordered; tidy; ordained (*priest*).

ordonner [ɔrdɔ'ne], *v.t.* to order, to regulate; to direct, to command; to ordain; (*Med.*) to prescribe.

ordre [ɔrdr], *n.m.* order, command; class, tribe; (*pl.*) holy orders.

ordure [ɔr'dyːr], *n.f.* filth, dirt; (*pl.*) sweepings, refuse, garbage.

ordurier [ɔrdy'rje], *a.* (*fem.* **-ière**) filthy, ribald, lewd.

oreille [ɔ'rɛːj], *n.f.* ear; hearing; flange; handle (*of a vase etc.*); **avoir l'oreille basse**, to be crestfallen; **avoir mal aux oreilles**, to have ear-ache; **faire la sourde oreille**, to turn a deaf ear; **prêter l'oreille à**, to listen to.

oreiller [ɔrɛ'je], *n.m.* pillow.

oreillons [ɔrɛ'jɔ̃], *n.m. pl.* mumps.

orfèvre [ɔr'fɛːvr], *n.m.* goldsmith, silversmith.

orfraie [ɔr'frɛ], *n.f.* osprey.

organdi [ɔrgã'di], *n.m.* organdie.

organe [ɔr'gan], *n.m.* organ; voice; agent, agency; spokesman.

organique [ɔrga'nik], *a.* organic.

organisateur [ɔrganiza'tœːr], *a.* (*fem.* **-trice**) organizing.—*n.m.* (*fem.* **-trice**) organizer.

organisation [ɔrganiza'sjɔ̃], *n.f.* organization; (*fig.*) set-up; constitution.

organisé [ɔrgani'ze], *a.* organized.

organiser [ɔrgani'ze], *v.t.* to organize; to get up, to arrange. **s'organiser**, *v.r.* to become organized.

organisme [ɔrga'nism], *n.m.* organism.

organiste [ɔrga'nist], *n.* organist.

orge [ɔrʒ], *n.f.* barley; (*masc. in* **orge mondé**, hulled barley, *and* **orge perlé**, pearl barley).

orgelet [ɔrʒ'lɛ], *n.m.* sty (*in the eye*).

orgie [ɔr'ʒi], *n.f.* orgy; (*fig.*) profusion.

orgue [ɔrg], *n.m.* (*fem. in pl.*) (*Mus.*) organ.

orgueil [ɔr'gœːj], *n.m.* pride; arrogance.

orgueilleusement [ɔrgœjøz'mã], *adv.* proudly, haughtily.

orgueilleux [ɔrgœ'jø], *a.* (*fem.* **-euse**) proud, haughty, arrogant.—*n.m.* (*fem.* **-euse**) proud and haughty person.

orient [ɔ'rjã], *n.m.* East, Orient; rise; water (*of pearls*).

oriental [ɔrjã'tal], *a.* (*m. pl.* **-aux**) oriental, eastern.—*n.m.* (*fem.* **-e**) oriental (*person*).

orientation [ɔrjãta'sjɔ̃], *n.f.* orientation.

orienter [ɔrjã'te], *v.t.* to orientate; to set (*a map*) by the compass; (*fig.*) to guide; (*Naut.*) to trim (*sails*). **s'orienter**, *v.r.* to take one's bearings, to ascertain one's position; (*fig.*) to see what one is about.

orifice [ɔri'fis], *n.m.* orifice, aperture, hole.

originaire [ɔriʒi'nɛːr], *a.* originally (*coming*) from; native (*de*); primitive.

originairement [ɔriʒinɛr'mã], *adv.* originally, primitively.

original [ɔriʒi'nal], *a.* (*m. pl.* **-aux**) original; singular, odd, peculiar, quaint.—*n.m.* original manuscript, drawing etc. (*not a copy*).—*n.m.* (*fem.* **-e**) queer person, character, oddity.

originalement [ɔriʒinal'mã], *adv.* originally; singularly, oddly.

originalité [ɔriʒinali'te], *n.f.* originality; eccentricity.

origine [ɔri'ʒin], *n.f.* origin, source; descent, derivation, extraction; **d'origine**, authentic; vintage (*wine*).

originel [ɔriʒi'nɛl], *a.* (*fem.* **-elle**) original, primitive.

originellement [ɔriʒinɛl'mã], *adv.* originally.

orignal [ɔri'nal], *n.m.* elk (*of Canada*), moose.

Orion [ɔ'rjɔ̃], *n.m.* (*Astron.*) Orion.

oripeau [ɔri'po], *n.m.* (*pl.* **-eaux**) tinsel; foil; (*pl.*) tawdry finery; (*more usually*) rags.

orme [ɔrm], *n.m.* elm.

ormeau [ɔr'mo], *n.m.* (*pl.* **-eaux**) young elm.

orné [ɔr'ne], *a.* ornate.

ornement [ɔrnə'mã], *n.m.* ornament, embellishment.

ornemental [ɔrnəmã'tal], *a.* (*m. pl.* **-aux**) ornamental.

ornementation [ɔrnəmãta'sjɔ̃], *n.f.* ornamentation.

orner [ɔr'ne], *v.t.* to adorn, to decorate, to deck, to embellish. **s'orner**, *v.r.* to adorn oneself; to be adorned.

ornière [ɔr'njɛːr], *n.f.* rut.

ornithologie [ɔrnitɔlɔ'ʒi], *n.f.* ornithology.

ornithologiste [ɔrnitɔlɔ'ʒist], **ornithologue** [ɔrnitɔ'lɔg], *n.m.* ornithologist.

Orphée [ɔr'fe], *m.* Orpheus.
orphelin [ɔrfə'lɛ̃], *a.* and *n.m.* (*fem.* -e) orphan.
orphelinat [ɔrfəli'na], *n.m.* orphanage.
orphéon [ɔrfe'ɔ̃], *n.m.* male-voice choir.
ort [ɔːr], *a. inv.* and *adv.* (*Comm.*) gross, gross weight.
orteil [ɔr'tɛːj], *n.m.* toe, *esp.* the big toe.
orthodoxe [ɔrtɔ'dɔks], *a.* orthodox.
orthodoxie [ɔrtɔdɔk'si], *n.f.* orthodoxy.
orthographe [ɔrtɔ'graf], *n.f.* orthography, spelling.
orthopédie [ɔrtɔpe'di], *n.f.* orthopedics.
ortie [ɔr'ti], *n.f.* nettle.
orvet [ɔr've], *n.m.* slow-worm.
os [ɔs; *pl.* o], *n.m. inv.* bone.
oscillant [ɔsi'lɑ̃], *a.* oscillating.
oscillation [ɔsila'sjɔ̃], *n.f.* oscillation, vibration.
oscillatoire [ɔsila'twaːr], *a.* oscillatory.
osciller [ɔsi'le], *v.i.* to oscillate, to swing, to vibrate; (*fig.*) to fluctuate.
oscillographe [ɔsilɔ'graf], *n.m.* (*Elec.*) oscillograph.
osé [o'ze], *a.* bold, daring.
oseille [o'zɛːj], *n.f.* sorrel.
oser [o'ze], *v.t., v.i.* to dare, to venture.
oseraie [oz'rɛ], *n.f.* osier-bed.
osier [o'zje], *n.m.* osier, withy, wicker.
osselet [ɔs'lɛ], *n.m.* knuckle-bone (*of sheep*); ossicle (*of ear*).
ossements [ɔs'mɑ̃], *n.m. pl.* bones (*of the dead*).
osseux [ɔ'sø], *a.* (*fem.* -euse) bony, osseous.
ossification [ɔsifika'sjɔ̃], *n.f.* ossification.
ossifier [ɔsi'fje], *v.t.* to ossify. **s'ossifier**, *v.r.* to become ossified.
ossuaire [ɔ'sɥɛːr], *n.m.* ossuary, charnel-house.
ostensible [ɔstɑ̃'sibl], *a.* open; above-board.
ostensiblement [ɔstɑ̃siblə'mɑ̃], *adv.* openly, publicly.
ostensoir [ɔstɑ̃'swaːr], *n.m.* monstrance.
ostentateur [ɔstɑ̃ta'tœːr], *a.* (*fem.* -trice) ostentatious.
ostentation [ɔstɑ̃ta'sjɔ̃], *n.f.* ostentation, show.
ostraciser [ɔstrasi'ze], *v.t.* to ostracize.
ostracisme [ɔstra'sism], *n.m.* ostracism.
ostréiculture [ɔstreikyl'tyːr], *n.f.* oyster-culture.
otage [ɔ'taːʒ], *n.m.* hostage; pledge.
ôter [o'te], *v.t.* to take away; to remove; to take off; to deprive of; to deduct; to rid of. **s'ôter**, *v.r.* to remove oneself, to get away; to rid oneself; *ôtez-vous de mon chemin*, stand aside.
ou [u], *conj.* or, either, else; *ou bien*, or else; *ou . . . ou*, either . . . or.
où [u], *adv.* where; whither; at which, in which, to which, through which; when, that; *par où?* which way?
ouais! [wɛ], *int.* well now! my word!
ouate [wat], *n.f.* *l'ouate* or *la ouate*, wadding, padding; cotton-wool.
ouater [wa'te], *v.t.* to wad, to pad; to coddle.
oubli [u'bli], *n.m.* forgetfulness; oblivion; oversight, slip; pardon.
oubliable [u'bljabl], *a.* liable *or* deserving to be forgotten.
oublier [u'blje], *v.t.* to forget, to omit, to

neglect; to pardon. **s'oublier**, *v.r.* to forget oneself; to be forgotten.
oubliettes [u'bljɛt], *n.f. pl.* oubliette, trap-dungeon.
oublieux [u'bljø], *a.* (*fem.* -euse) forgetful, unmindful.
ouest [wɛst], *a. inv.* westerly, western.—*n.m.* west.
ouf! [uf], *int.* oh! (*of relief*).
Ouganda [ugɑ̃'da], l', *m.* Uganda.
oui [wi], *adv.* yes.—*n.m.* yes.
ouï [wi] *p.p.* [OUÏR].
ouï-dire [wi'diːr], *n.m. inv.* hearsay.
ouïe [wi], *n.f.* *hearing; hole (*of a violin etc.*); (*pl.*) gills (*of fish*).
ouïr [wiːr], *v.t. irr.* (*rarely used except in the infinitive and compound tenses*) to hear; *j'ai ouï dire*, I have heard say.
ouragan [ura'gɑ̃], *n.m.* hurricane; (*fig.*) storm.
ourdir [ur'diːr], *v.t.* to warp (*cloth*); (*fig.*) to weave, to plot, to concoct.
ourdissage [urdi'saːʒ], *n.m.* warping.
ourdou [ur'du], *n.m.* Urdu (*language*), Hindustani.
ourler [ur'le], *v.t.* to hem; *ourler à jour*, to hemstitch.
ourlet [ur'lɛ], *n.m.* hem.
ours [urs], *n.m.* bear.
ourse [urs], *n.f.* she-bear.
oursin [ur'sɛ̃], *n.m.* sea-urchin.
ourson [ur'sɔ̃], *n.m.* bear cub.
outil [u'ti], *n.m.* tool, implement.
outillage [uti'jaːʒ], *n.m.* stock of tools equipment.
outillé [uti'je], *a.* furnished with tools.
outiller [uti'je], *v.t.* to furnish with tools; to equip.
outrage [u'traːʒ], *n.m.* outrage, gross insult; injury, wrong.
outrageant [utra'ʒɑ̃], *a.* outrageous; insulting, abusive.
outrager [utra'ʒe], *v.t.* (*conjug. like* MANGER) to outrage; to insult, to offend.
outrageusement [utraʒøz'mɑ̃], *adv.* insultingly.
outrageux [utra'ʒø], *a.* (*fem.* -euse) outrageous.
outrance [u'trɑ̃s], *n.f.* extreme; excess; *à outrance*, to the death.
outre (1) [utr], *n.f.* goatskin *or* leather bottle.
outre (2) [utr], *adv.* further, beyond; *en outre*, besides; *passer outre*; to go on, to take no notice of a thing.—*prep.* beyond; besides, in addition to; *outre que*, besides.
outré [u'tre], *a.* exaggerated, strained, excessive; incensed.
outrecuidance [utrəkɥi'dɑ̃s], *n.f.* presumption.
outrecuidant [utrəkɥi'dɑ̃], *a.* presumptuous, bumptious.
outre-Manche [utrə'mɑ̃ːʃ], *adv.* across the Channel.
outremer [utrə'mɛːr], *n.m.* ultramarine (*colour*).
outre-mer [utrə'mɛːr], *adv.* overseas.
outrepasser [utrəpa'se], *v.t.* to go beyond, to transgress.
outrer [u'tre], *v.t.* to overdo; to exaggerate.
ouvert [u'vɛːr], *a.* open; unfortified (*of towns*); (*fig.*) frank.

ouvertement [uvɛrtə'mɑ̃] *adv.* openly, frankly.

ouverture [uver'ty:r], *n.f.* opening; aperture, gap, hole; (*Mus.*) overture; (*Arch.*) span, width (*of a doorway etc.*); (*Av.*) (parachute) drop.

ouvrable [u'vrabl], *a.* working, workable; *jour ouvrable*, working-day.

ouvrage [u'vra:ʒ], *n.m.* work, piece of work; performance, workmanship.

ouvragé [uvra'ʒe], *a.* wrought, figured.

ouvrager [uvra'ʒe], *v.t.* (*conjug. like* MANGER) to work, to figure.

ouvrant [u'vrɑ̃], *a.* opening.

ouvré [u'vre], *a.* wrought; diapered, figured.

ouvre-boîte [uvrə'bwaːt], *n.m.* (*pl.* **-boîtes**) tin-opener.

ouvrer [u'vre], *v.t.* to work (*material*); to diaper (*linen*).—*v.i.* to work.

ouvrier [uvri'e], *a.* (*fem.* **-ière**) operative, working.—*n.m.* (*fem.* **-ière**) workman, (female) worker, hand, operative; labourer.

ouvrir [u'vri:r], *v.t. irr.* to open, to unlock; to sharpen (*the appetite*); to broach (*opinions etc.*).—*v.i.* to open; to expand. **s'ouvrir**, *v.r.* to open; to open for oneself; to open one's mind.

ouvroir [u'vrwaːr], *n.m.* charity workshop; workroom.

ovaire [ɔ'vɛːr], *n.m.* ovary.

ovalaire [ɔva'lɛːr], *a.* (*Anat.*) oval.

ovale [ɔ'val], *a.* and *n.m.* oval.

ovation [ɔva'sjɔ̃], *n.f.* ovation.

ovoïde [ɔvɔ'id], *a.* ovoid, egg-shaped.

ovule [ɔ'vyl], *n.m.* ovule.

oxalique [ɔksa'lik], *a.* oxalic.

oxyacétylénique [ɔksiasetile'nik], *a.* oxyacetylene (*welding etc.*).

oxyde [ɔk'sid], *n.m.* oxide.

oxyder [ɔksi'de], *v.t.* to oxidize.

oxygène [ɔksi'ʒɛːn], *n.m.* oxygen.

oxygéné [ɔksiʒe'ne], *a. eau oxygénée*, peroxide of hydrogen.

ozone [ɔ'zɔn], *n.m.* ozone.

P

P, p [pe], *n.m.* the sixteenth letter of the alphabet.

pacage [pa'ka:ʒ], *n.m.* pasture-land; *droit de pacage*, grazing rights.

pacificateur [pasifika'tœːr], *a.* (*fem.* **-trice**) pacifying, peace-making.—*n.m.* (*fem.* **-trice**) pacifier, peacemaker.

pacification [pasifika'sjɔ̃], *n.f.* pacification.

pacifier [pasi'fje], *v.t.* to pacify, to appease.

pacifique [pasi'fik], *a.* pacific, peaceful.

pacifiquement [pasifik'mɑ̃], *adv.* peaceably, quietly.

pacifisme [pasi'fism], *n.m.* pacifism.

pacifiste [pasi'fist], *a.* and *n.* pacifist.

pacotille [pako'tiːj], *n.f.* goods carried free of charge by passengers *or* seamen; shoddy goods; pack, bale.

pacte [pakt], *n.m.* compact, contract, pact, agreement; *pacte de préférence*, preference clause.

pactiser [pakti'ze], *v.i.* to covenant, to make a compact (*avec*).

paf! [paf], *int.* slap! bang!

pagaie [pa'gɛ], *n.f.* paddle (*for canoe etc.*).

pagaie or **pagaille** [pa'gaj], *n.f.* hurry; disorder; *en pagaie*, (*pop.*) higgledy-piggledy.

paganisme [paga'nism], *n.m.* paganism.

pagayer [pagɛ'je], *v.t.*, *v.i.* (*conjug. like* PAYER) to paddle.

page (1) [pa:ʒ], *n.m.* page (boy).

page (2) [pa:ʒ], *n.f.* page (*of a book*).

pagode [pa'gɔd], *n.f.* pagoda.

paiement [PAYEMENT].

païen [pa'jɛ̃], *a.* and *n.m.* (*fem.* **-enne**) pagan, heathen.

paillard [pa'jaːr], *a.* lecherous, lewd.—*n.m.* (*fem.* **-e**) wanton, sensual person, bawd.

paillasse (1) [pa'jas], *n.f.* straw mattress.

paillasse (2) [pa'jas], *n.m.* clown, buffoon.

paillasson [paja'sɔ̃], *n.m.* straw-mat; door-mat.

paille [pa:j], *a. inv.* straw-coloured.—*n.f.* straw; flaw (*in gems, metals etc.*); *botte de paille*, bale of straw.

paillé [pa'je], *a.* straw-coloured; faulty (*of metals etc.*).

pailler (1) [pa'je], *n.m.* farm-yard; heap *or* stack of straw.

pailler (2) [pa'je], *v.t.* to mulch (*plants*).

pailleter [paj'te], *v.t.* (*conjug. like* APPELER) to spangle.

paillette [pa'jɛt], *n.f.* spangle; flaw (*in a gem*); *savon en paillettes*, soap flakes.

paillis [pa'ji], *n.m.* mulch.

paillon [pa'jɔ̃], *n.m.* large spangle, tinsel; wisp of straw; straw wrapper (*for bottle*).

pain [pɛ̃], *n.m.* bread; loaf; cake (*of soap etc.*); (*pop.*) blow, punch; *pain grillé*, toast; *un pain*, a loaf; *un petit pain*, a roll.

pair [pɛːr], *a.* equal, even (*of numbers*).—*n.m.* peer; equal; mate (*of birds*); par, equality; *au pair*, at par, even (*with*), 'au pair'; *de pair*, on a par; *hors* (*de*) *pair*, beyond comparison.

paire [pɛːr], *n.f.* pair, brace, couple.

pairesse [pɛ'rɛs], *n.f.* peeress.

pairie [pɛ'ri], *n.f.* peerage.

paisible [pɛ'zibl], *a.* peaceful, quiet, calm.

paisiblement [pɛzibla'mɑ̃], *adv.* peacefully.

paître [pɛːtr], *v.t.*, *v.i. irr.* to graze, to feed.

paix [pɛ], *n.f.* peace; quiet; stillness; rest.—*int.* be quiet!

Pakistan [pakis'tɑ̃], le, *m.* Pakistan.

pakistanais [pakista'nɛ], *a.* Pakistani.—*n.m.* (**Pakistanais**, *fem.* **-aise**) Pakistani (*person*).

paladin [pala'dɛ̃], *n.m.* paladin, champion.

palais (1) [pa'lɛ], *n.m.* palace; (*fig.*) the Bar; the law; *palais de justice*, law-courts.

palais (2) [pa'lɛ], *n.m.* palate, roof (*of the mouth*).

palan [pa'lɑ̃], *n.m.* tackle, pulley-block.

pale [pal], *n.f.* blade (*of oar, propeller etc.*); sluice, flood-gate.

pâle [paːl], *a.* pale, wan, pallid, ghastly.

palefrenier [palfrə'nje], *n.m.* groom, ostler.

palefroi [pal'frwa], *n.m.* palfrey.

Palestine [palɛs'tin], la, *f.* Palestine.

palestinien [palɛsti'njɛ̃], *a.* (*fem.* **-enne**) Palestinian.

palet [pa'lɛ], *n.m.* quoit.
palette [pa'lɛt], *n.f.* paddle (*of paddle-wheel*); bat (*ping-pong*); palette (*of painter*).
pâleur [pɑ'lœːr], *n.f.* pallor, wanness.
pâli [pɑ'li], *a.* grown pale.
palier [pa'lje], *n.m.* landing (*on a staircase*), floor; stage, degree; level stretch; *vitesse en palier*, speed on the flat.
pâlir [pɑ'liːr], *v.t.* to make pale, to bleach.— *v.i.* to (grow, turn *or* become) pale; to grow dim.
palis [pa'li], *n.m.* stake, pale; paling, enclosure.
palissade [pali'sad], *n.f.* palisade, paling; wooden fence; hedgerow; stockade.
palissader [palisa'de], *v.t.* to palisade; to stockade; to fence in.
pâlissant [pali'sɑ̃], *a.* turning pale, fading.
pallier [pa'lje], *v.t.* to palliate, to excuse.
palmarès [palma'rɛːs], *n.m. inv.* prize-list, list of honours.
palme [palm], *n.f.* palm, palm-branch; palm-tree; (*fig.*) victory, triumph.
palmé [pal'me], *a.* palmate; web-footed.
palmier [pal'mje], *n.m.* palm-tree, palm.
palombe [pa'lɔ̃ːb], *n.f.* wood-pigeon, ring-dove.
palonnier [palɔ'nje], *n.m.* pole (*of a coach*); (*Motor.*) compensator (*of brake*); (*Av.*) rudder-bar.
pâlot [pɑ'lo], *a.* (*fem.* **-otte**) palish, rather pale.
palourde [pa'lurd], *n.f.* clam.
palpable [pal'pabl], *a.* palpable.
palpablement [palpablə'mɑ̃], *adv.* palpably.
palper [pal'pe], *v.t.* to feel, to touch; (*colloq.*) to pocket.
palpitant [palpi'tɑ̃], *a.* palpitating; thrilling.
palpitation [palpita'sjɔ̃], *n.f.* palpitation; throbbing; thrill, flutter.
palpiter [palpi'te], *v.i.* to palpitate, to throb; to quiver, to flutter.
paludéen [palyde'ɛ̃], *a.* (*fem.* **-éenne**) paludal, marshy.
pâmer [pɑ'me], *v.i.* and **se pâmer**, *v.r.* to swoon.
pâmoison [pɑmwa'zɔ̃], *n.f.* swoon, fainting fit.
pamphlet [pɑ'flɛ], *n.m.* satirical booklet, lampoon.
pamphlétaire [pɑfle'tɛːr], *n.* pamphleteer.
pamplemousse [pɑplə'mus], *n.m. or f.* grape-fruit.
pampre [pɑ̃ːpr], *n.m.* vine-branch.
pan (1) [pɑ̃], *n.m.* flap, coat-tails, panel (*of dress*); side, section (*of a wall etc.*); *pan de ciel*, stretch *or* patch of sky; *pan de mur*, bare wall, piece of wall.
pan! (2) [pɑ̃], *int.* slap! bang! smack!
panacée [pana'se], *n.f.* panacea.
panache [pa'naʃ], *n.m.* plume, bunch of feathers etc.; (*fig.*) show, swagger.
panaché [pana'ʃe], *a.* plumed, tufted; striped; (*colloq.*) variegated, motley; *glace panachée*, mixed ice-cream.
panacher [pana'ʃe], *v.t.* to plume; to streak, to variegate, to mix.
panais [pa'nɛ], *n.m.* parsnip.
Panama [pana'ma], **le**, *m.* Panama.
panama [pana'ma], *n.m.* panama-hat.
panamien [pana'mjɛ̃], *a.* (*fem.* **-enne**) Panama(nian).—*n.m.* (**Panamien**, *fem.* **-enne**) Panamanian (*person*).

panaris [pana'ri], *n.m.* whitlow.
pancarte [pɑ̃'kart], *n.f.* large placard *or* bill.
pancréas [pɑ̃kre'ɑːs], *n.m. inv.* pancreas; sweetbread.
panda [pɑ̃'da], *n.m.* panda.
pandémonium [pɑ̃demɔ'njɔm], *n.m.* pandemonium.
pandit [pɑ̃'di], *n.m.* pundit.
Pandore [pɑ̃'dɔːr], *f.* Pandora.
pané [pa'ne], *a.* covered, *or* fried, in bread-crumbs.
panégyrique [panezi'rik], *n.m.* panegyric.
paner [pa'ne], *v.t.* to cover with breadcrumbs.
panier [pa'nje], *n.m.* basket, hamper, pannier; hoop-petticoat; *le dessus du panier*, the pick of the basket; *panier à salade*, (*wire*) salad washer; (*slang*) black Maria; *panier percé*, spendthrift.
panique [pa'nik], *a.* and *n.f.* panic.
panne [pan], *n.f.* plush; fat, lard; purlin; breakdown, mishap; *panne d'allumage*, (*Motor.*) ignition trouble; *rester en panne* (*Motor.*) to have a breakdown.
panneau [pa'no], *n.m.* (*pl.* **-eaux**) panel; snare, trap; (*Naut.*) hatch; (*Hort.*) glass-frame.
panoplie [panɔ'pli], *n.f.* panoply; trophy (*of arms*).
panorama [panɔra'ma], *n.m.* panorama.
panoramique [panɔra'mik], *a.* panoramic.
pansage [pɑ̃'saːʒ], *n.m.* grooming (*of horses etc.*).
panse [pɑ̃ːs], *n.f.* belly, paunch.
pansement [pɑ̃s'mɑ̃], *n.m.* dressing (*of wounds*); *pansement sommaire*, first aid; dressing.
panser [pɑ̃'se], *v.t.* to dress (*wounds*); to groom (*a horse*).
pansu [pɑ̃'sy], *a.* and *n.m.* (*fem.* **-e**) pot-bellied (person); bulging.
pantalon [pɑ̃ta'lɔ̃], *n.m.* (pair of) trousers; *pantalon de femme*, women's knickers, panties.
pantelant [pɑ̃'tlɑ̃], *a.* panting, gasping.
panteler [pɑ̃'tle], *v.i.* (*conjug. like* APPELER) to gasp, to pant.
panthère [pɑ̃'tɛːr], *n.f.* panther.
pantin [pɑ̃'tɛ̃], *n.m.* nonentity, puppet; (*fig.*) jumping-jack.
pantois [pɑ̃'twa], *a.* (*fig.*) astonished, flabbergasted.
pantomime [pɑ̃tɔ'mim], *a.* pantomimic.— *n.f.* dumb-show, pantomime.—*n.m.* pantomime (*actor*).
pantoufle [pɑ̃'tufl], *n.f.* slipper; *en pantoufles*, slipshod.
paon [pɑ̃], *n.m.* peacock; emperor-moth; (*fig.*) vain person.
paonne [pan], *n.f.* peahen.
papa [pa'pa], *n.m.* papa, daddy.
papal [pa'pal], *a.* (*m. pl.* **-aux**) papal.
papauté [papo'te], *n.f.* papacy.
pape [pap], *n.m.* pope.
paperasse [pa'pras], *n.f.* useless papers, documents; red-tape; paper-work.
paperasser [papra'se], *v.i.* to rummage among old papers; to scribble.
paperasserie [papras'ri], *n.f.* red-tape.
paperassier [papra'sje], *a.* (*fem.* **-ière**) red-tape, formal.—*n.m.* (*fem.* **-ière**) everlasting scribbler; rummager through old papers.

papeterie [pap'tri], *n.f.* paper-mill, paper-trade; stationery; stationer's shop; stationery case.

papetier [papə'tje], *a.* (*fem.* **-ière**) paper (*industry etc.*).—*n.m.* (*fem.* **-ière**) papermaker; stationer.

papier [pa'pje], *n.m.* paper; *papier buvard*, blotting paper; *papier d'emballage*, brown paper; *papier de verre*, glass-paper, sand-paper; *papier hygiénique*, lavatory paper.

papillon [papi'jɔ̃], *n.m.* butterfly.

papillonner [papijɔ'ne], *v.i.* to flutter about, to hover; (*fig.*) to trifle, to flirt.

papillotage [papijɔ'ta:ʒ], *n.m.* blinking (*of the eyes*); dazzle, glitter, tinsel (*of style*).

papillote [papi'jɔt], *n.f.* curl-paper; bonbon; *fer à papillotes*, curling-irons; *papillotes à pétard*, Christmas crackers.

papilloter [papijɔ'te], *v.t.* to put (*hair etc.*) in paper.—*v.i.* to blink; to dazzle, to be gaudy.

papisme [pa'pism], *n.m.* papism, popery.

papiste [pa'pist], *a.* popish.—*n.* papist.

papou [pa'pu], *a.* Papuan.—*n.m.* (**Papou,** *fem.* **-oue**) Papuan (*person*).

Papouasie [papwa'zi], **la,** *f.* Papua.

papyrus [papi'ry:s], *n.m.* papyrus.

pâque [pɑ:k], *n.f.* Passover (*among Jews*).

paquebot [pak'bo], *n.m.* packet-boat, steamer, liner.

pâquerette [pɑ'krɛt], *n.f.* daisy.

Pâques [pɑ:k], *n.m.* Easter.

paquet [pa'kɛ], *n.m.* package, bundle, parcel; packet; (*fig.*) clumsy lout.

paqueter [pak'te], *v.t.* (*conjug. like* APPELER) to make into a packet, parcel etc.

par [pa:r], *prep.* by, through, out of; from; about, in, into; for, for the sake of.

parabole [para'bol], *n.f.* parabola; parable.

parabolique [parabɔ'lik], *a.* parabolic.

parachutage [paraʃy'ta:ʒ], *n.m.* parachuting; parachute landing.

parachute [para'ʃyt], *n.m.* parachute; *sauter en parachute*, to bale out.

parachuter [paraʃy'te], *v.t., v.i.* to parachute, to drop (by parachute).

parachutiste [paraʃy'tist], *n.* parachutist, paratrooper.

parade [pa'rad], *n.f.* parade, show, display; pageantry; (*Fenc.*) parry.

parader [para'de], *v.i.* to show off.

paradis [para'di], *n.m.* paradise; (*Theat.*) upper gallery, the gods.

paradoxal [paradɔk'sal], *a.* (*m. pl.* **-aux**) paradoxical.

paradoxe [para'dɔks], *n.m.* paradox.

parafe or **paraphe** [pa'raf], *n.m.* paraph; flourish (*after one's signature*); initials and flourish.

parafer or **parapher** [para'fe], *v.t.* to paraph, to put one's flourish, dash or initials to.

paraffine [para'fin], *n.f.* paraffin, paraffin wax; *huile de paraffine*, liquid paraffin.

parage [pa'ra:ʒ], *n.m.* extraction, descent, lineage; (*usually in pl.*) localities, latitudes, waters; *dans ces parages*, in these parts.

paragraphe [para'graf], *n.m.* paragraph.

Paraguay [para'gwɛ], **le,** *m.* Paraguay.

paraguayen [paragwɛ'jɛ̃], *a.* (*fem.* **-enne**)

Paraguayan.—*n.m.* (**Paraguayen,** *fem.* **-enne**) Paraguayan (*person*).

paraître [pa'rɛ:tr], *v.i. irr.* (*conjug. like* CON-NAÎTRE) to appear, to come into sight; to make a show, to seem, to look like; to come out, to be published; *à ce qu'il paraît*, as it would seem.

parallèle [para'lɛl], *a.* parallel.—*n.f.* parallel line.—*n.m.* parallel, comparison; (*Geog.*) parallel of latitude.

parallèlement [paralɛl'mɑ̃], *adv.* in a parallel way or direction.

parallélogramme [paralelɔ'gram], *n.m.* parallelogram.

paralysateur [paraliza'tœ:r] (*fem.* **-trice**), **paralysant** [parali'zɑ̃], *a.* paralysing.

paralyser [parali'ze], *v.t.* to paralyse.

paralysie [parali'zi], *n.f.* paralysis, palsy.

paralytique [parali'tik], *a.* and *n.* paralytic.

parangon [parɑ̃'gɔ̃], *n.m.* model, paragon; comparison; flawless precious stone.

paranoïa [paranɔ'ja], *n.f.* (*Med.*) paranoia.

parapet [para'pɛ], *n.m.* parapet.

paraphrase [para'fra:z], *n.f.* paraphrase, amplification.

paraphraser [parafrɑ'ze], *v.t.* to paraphrase; to amplify.

parapluie [para'plɥi], *n.m.* umbrella.

parasite [para'zit], *a.* parasitic; superfluous; extraneous.—*n.m.* parasite; (*fig.*) hanger-on; (*pl.*) (*Rad.*) atmospherics.

parasol [para'sɔl], *n.m.* sunshade.

paratonnerre [paratɔ'nɛ:r], *n.m.* lightning-conductor.

paratyphoïde [paratifɔ'id], *a.* and *n.f.* (*Med.*) paratyphoid (fever).

paravent [para'vɑ̃], *n.m.* folding-screen; (*fig.*) screen.

parbleu! [par'blø], *int.* by Jove! why, of course!

parc [park], *n.m.* park; pen; *parc à huîtres*, oyster-bed; *parc d'attractions*, fun fair.

parcage [par'ka:ʒ], *n.m.* folding (*of sheep*); penning (*of cattle*); parking (*of cars*).

parcellaire [parsɛ'lɛ:r], *a.* by small portions, by lots, in detail.

parcelle [par'sɛl], *n.f.* portion; particle; piece (*of land*).

parceller [parsɛ'le], *v.t.* to portion or parcel out.

parce que [parsə'kə, pars'kə], *conj.* because, as.—*n.m. inv. les pourquoi et les parce que*, the whys and the wherefores.

parchemin [parʃə'mɛ̃], *n.m.* parchment; (*fam.*) diploma; (*pl.*) titles of nobility.

parcimonie [parsimɔ'ni], *n.f.* parsimony.

parcimonieusement [parsimɔnjøz'mɑ̃], *adv.* parsimoniously.

parcimonieux [parsimɔ'njø], *a.* (*fem.* **-euse**) parsimonious, stingy.

(C) parcomètre [parko'mɛtr], *n.m.* parking-meter.

parcourir [parku'ri:r], *v.t. irr.* (*conjug. like* COURIR) to travel through; to run over or through, to scour; to look over; to peruse, to glance through (*a book*).

parcours [par'ku:r], *n.m.* line, course, road, way; route (*of bus*); distance; course (*golf*).

par-dessous [pardə'su], *prep.* and *adv.* under, beneath, underneath.

par-dessus [pardə'sy], *prep.* and *adv.* over, above.

235

pardessus [pardə'sy], *n.m.* overcoat.
pardon [par'dɔ̃], *n.m.* pardon, forgiveness; pilgrimage (*in Brittany*); *pardon !* excuse me!
pardonnable [pardɔ'nabl] *a.* pardonable, excusable.
pardonner [pardɔ'ne], *v.t.* to pardon, to forgive; to overlook; to excuse.
paré [pa're], *a.* adorned, got up; dressed.
pare-boue [par'bu], *n.m. inv.* mud-guard.
pare-brise [par'bri:z], *n.m. inv.* wind-screen (*of motor-car*).
pare-chocs [par'ʃɔk], *n.m. inv.* bumper (*of car*).
pare-étincelles [paretɛ̃'sɛl], *n.m. inv.* fire-screen, fire-guard.
pareil [pa'rɛːj], *a.* (*fem.* -**eille**) like, equal, similar; such, like that; same, identical.—*n.m.* (*fem.* -**eille**) similar *or* equal person.—*n.m.* equal, fellow.—*n.f.* (-**eille**) the like, tit for tat.
pareillement [parɛj'mã], *adv.* in like manner; likewise, also.
parement [par'mã], *n.m.* ornament; facing (*of dress*); cuff (*of sleeves*); (*Build.*) kerb-stone.
parent [pa'rã], *n.m.* (*fem.* -**e**) relative, kinsman, kinswoman; (*pl.*) parents, relations, relatives; *être parent*, to be related; *parents par alliance*, related by marriage.
parenté [parã'te], *n.f.* relationship, kinship; relatives, kith and kin.
parenthèse [parã'tɛːz], *n.f.* parenthesis, digression; (*Print.*) bracket.
parer [pa're], *v.t.* to adorn, to set off, to embellish; to attire, to trim; (*Box.*) to parry; to shelter, to guard.—*v.i.* to fend, to guard (*against*). **se parer**, *v.r.* to adorn oneself; to deck oneself out; to screen *or* guard oneself, to ward off.
pare-soleil [parsɔ'lɛːj], *n.m. inv.* (*Motor.*) sun-visor.
paresse [pa'rɛs], *n.f.* idleness, sloth, laziness, indolence.
paresser [parɛ'se], *v.i.* to idle, to fritter away one's time.
paresseusement [parɛsøz'mã], *adv.* lazily, idly.
paresseux [parɛ'sø], *a.* (*fem.* -**euse**) lazy, idle, slothful.—*n.m.* (*fem.* -**euse**) sluggard, lazy person.—*n.m.* (*Zool.*) sloth.
parfaire [par'fɛːr], *v.t. irr.* (*conjug. like* FAIRE) to complete, to perfect.
parfait [par'fɛ], *a.* perfect, faultless; complete, full.—*n.m.* perfection; (*Gram.*) perfect; *un parfait au café*, a coffee ice-cream.
parfaitement [parfɛt'mã], *adv.* perfectly, completely; exactly, just so, decidedly.
parfilage [parfi'la:ʒ], *n.m.* unravelling.
parfois [par'fwa], *adv.* sometimes, occasionally.
parfum [par'fœ̃], *n.m.* perfume, odour, scent.
parfumer [parfy'me], *v.t.* to perfume, to sweeten; to scent; to fumigate. **se parfumer** *v.r.* to use perfume, to scent oneself.
parfumerie [parfym'ri], *n.f.* perfumery.
pari [pa'ri], *n.m.* bet, wager, stake; *pari mutuel*, totalizator, (*fam.*) tote.
paria [pa'rja], *n.m.* pariah, outcast.

parier [pa'rje], *v.t.* to bet, to stake.
parieur [pa'rjœːr], *n.m.* (*fem.* -**euse**) punter; backer.
parisien [pari'zjɛ̃], *a.* (*fem.* -**enne**) Parisian.—*n.m.* (**Parisien**, *fem.* -**enne**) Parisian (*person*).
parité [pari'te], *n.f.* parity, likeness, equality; (*Fin.*) par.
parjure [par'ʒyːr], *a.* perjured.—*n.m.* perjury, false oath.—*n.* perjurer.
parjurer (se) [səparʒy're], *v.r.* to perjure oneself.
parking [par'kiŋ], *n.m.* parking place, car park.
parlant [par'lã], *a.* speaking; (*colloq.*) talkative.
parlement [parlə'mã], *n.m.* parliament.
parlementaire [parləmã'tɛːr], *a.* parliamentary.—*n.m.* bearer of a flag of truce; parliamentarian.
parlementer [parləmã'te], *v.i.* to parley, to come to terms.
parler [par'le], *v.t.* to speak, to talk.—*v.i.* to speak, to talk; to discourse, to converse, to treat (*de*); (*pop.*) *tu parles !* you're telling me! **se parler**, *v.r.* to be spoken; to talk to oneself; to talk to each other.—*n.m.* speech.
parleur [par'lœːr], *n.m.* (*fem.* -**euse**) glib talker.
parloir [par'lwaːr], *n.m.* parlour (*of convent, school, prison*).
parmentier [parmã'tje], *a.* and *n.m.* *potage parmentier*, thick potato soup.
parmesan [parmə'zã], *n.m.* Parmesan (*cheese*).
parmi [par'mi], *prep.* among, amongst, amid, amidst.
parodie [parɔ'di], *n.f.* parody.
parodier [parɔ'dje], *v.t.* to parody, to burlesque.
paroi [pa'rwa], *n.f.* wall; partition; inner surface; lining; (*Theat.*) flat.
paroisse [pa'rwas], *n.f.* parish; (*collect.*) parishioners.
paroissial [parwa'sjal], *a.* (*m. pl.* -**aux**) parochial, parish.
paroissien [parwa'sjɛ̃], *n.m.* (*fem.* -**enne**) parishioner.—*n.m.* prayer-book.
parole [pa'rɔl], *n.f.* (spoken) word; speech, utterance, voice; eloquence; promise; parole; *engager sa parole*, to pledge one's word; *manquer à sa parole*, to break one's word; *tenir parole*, to keep one's word.
paroxysme [parɔk'sism], *n.m.* paroxysm; culminating point.
parpaing [par'pɛ̃], *n.m.* (*Build.*) breeze-block.
parquer [par'ke], *v.t.* to fold, to pen; to enclose; (*Motor.*) to park.—*v.i.* to be penned up (*of cattle etc.*). **se parquer**, *v.r.* to be placed in an enclosure.
parquet [par'kɛ], *n.m.* well (*of a court of justice*); prosecuting magistrates; (inlaid) floor.
parquetage [parkə'ta:ʒ], *n.m.* making a floor; flooring.
parqueter [parkə'te], *v.t.* (*conjug. like* AP-PELER) to floor, to lay a floor.
parqueterie [parkə'tri], *n.f.* floor-making; inlaid flooring.

parrain [pa'rɛ̃], *n.m.* godfather, sponsor; proposer.

parricide [pari'sid], *a.* parricidal.—*n.* parricide (*person*).—*n.m.* parricide crime).

parsemer [parsə'me], *v.t.* (*conjug. like* AMENER) to strew, to sprinkle; to be strewn on, to stud, to spangle.

parsi [par'si], *a.* Parsee.—*n.m.* (**Parsi,** *fem.* **-ie**) Parsee (*person*).

part [pa:r], *n.f.* share, part; concern, interest; place (*where*); *à part,* aside; apart from; *de part en part,* through and through; *de toutes parts,* on all sides; *dites-lui de ma part,* tell him from me; *nulle part,* nowhere; *quelque part,* somewhere (or other).

partage [par'ta:ʒ], *n.m.* sharing; share; partition.

partageable [parta'ʒabl], *a.* divisible into shares.

partageant [parta'ʒɑ̃], *n.m.* (*fem.* **-e**) (*Law*) sharer.

partager [parta'ʒe], *v.t.* (*conjug. like* MANGER) to divide, to share out; to participate in; to endow.—*v.i.* to share, to receive a share. **se partager,** *v.r.* to divide, to be divided.

partance [par'tã:s], *n.f.* (*Naut.*) sailing, departure; *en partance pour,* bound for.

partant [par'tã], *adv.* consequently, hence, therefore.—*n.m.* (*Turf*) starter.

partenaire [partə'nɛ:r], *n.* (*Spt. etc.*) partner.

parterre [par'tɛ:r], *n.m.* flower-bed; (*Theat.*) pit.

parti [par'ti], *n.m.* (*Polit.*) party; part, cause; resolution, course; profit, advantage; match (*marriage*); (*Mil.*) detachment; *parti pris,* set purpose; rank prejudice; *le parti conservateur,* the Conservative party; *le parti travailliste,* the Labour party.

partial [par'sjal], *a.* (*m. pl.* **-aux**) partial, biased.

partialement [parsjal'mã], *adv.* partially, with partiality.

partialité [parsjali'te], *n.f.* partiality, bias.

participant [partisi'pã], *a.* participating.—*n.m.* (*fem.* **-e**) participant, sharer.

participation [partisipa'sjõ], *n.f.* participation, share.

participe [parti'sip], *n.m.* (*Gram.*) participle.

participer [partisi'pe], *v.i.* to participate in, to share in; to be a party to (*à*); to partake of (*de*).

particularité [partikylari'te], *n.f.* peculiarity; particular circumstance.

particule [parti'kyl], *n.f.* particle.

particulier [partiky'lje], *a.* (*fem.* **-ière**) particular, peculiar; private; special; singular; personal.—*n.m.* (*fem.* **-ière**) private person, individual; (*colloq.*) fellow.

particulièrement [partikyljɛr'mã], *adv.* particularly, especially.

partie [par'ti], *n.f.* part (*of a whole*); line of business; party, amusement; game, match; client; opponent; (*Law*) party; (*Comm.*) parcel; *partie nulle,* drawn game.

partiel [par'sjɛl], *a.* (*fem.* **-elle**) partial.

partiellement [parsjɛl'mã], *adv.* partially, in part.

partir [par'ti:r], *v.i. irr.* (*with aux.* ÊTRE) to set out, to start, to depart, to leave; to rise (*of birds*); to proceed, to emanate (*from*); to go off (*of firearms*); *à partir d'aujourd'hui,* from this day forward.

partisan [parti'zã], *n.m.* (*fem.* **-e**) partisan.

partition [parti'sjõ], *n.f.* (*Her.*) partition; (*Mus.*) score.

partout [par'tu], *adv.* everywhere, on all sides.

parure [pa'ry:r], *n.f.* attire, dress, finery, ornament.

parvenir [parvə'ni:r], *v.i. irr.* (*conjug. like* TENIR *but with aux.* ÊTRE) to attain, to reach; to succeed; to get; to arrive; to rise in the world.

parvenu [parvə'ny], *n.m.* (*fem.* **-e**) upstart, self-made person.

parvis [par'vi], *n.m.* parvis, open space (*in front of a church*); (*Poet.*) hall, temple.

pas (1) [pa], *n.m. inv.* step, pace; footprint; gait; dance; precedence; threshold; step of stair; strait, pass; thread (*of screw*); *aller à pas mesurés,* to proceed with circumspection; *au pas,* at a walking pace; in step; *faire un faux pas,* to stumble, (*fig.*) to blunder; *le pas de Calais,* the Straits of Dover; *pas à pas,* slowly, little by little.

pas (2) [pa], *adv.* no; not; *pas du tout,* not at all.

pascal [pas'kal], *a.* (*m. pl.* **-aux**) paschal.

passable [pa'sabl], *a.* passable, tolerable; (*fig.*) middling, so-so.

passablement [pasablə'mã], *adv.* fairly, passably.

passade [pa'sad], *n.f.* short stay; (*fig.*) passing fancy.

passage [pa'sa:ʒ], *n.m.* passage, transit; thoroughfare; arcade; crossing (*on railway etc.*); *passage clouté,* pedestrian crossing.

passager [pasa'ʒe], *a.* (*fem.* **-ère**) passing, transitory, short-lived; migratory.—*n.m.* (*fem.* **-ère**) passenger (*by sea or air*); passer-by.

passagèrement [pasaʒɛr'mã], *adv.* transiently.

passant [pa'sã], *a.* much-frequented.—*n.m.* (*fem.* **-e**) passer-by, wayfarer.

passavant [pasa'vã], *n.m.* pass, permit; (*Naut.*) gangway.

passe [pas], *n.f.* passing, passage; permit, pass; situation, state; (*Fenc.*) thrust; channel, narrow passage (*of harbours, rivers etc.*); stake (*at play*); (*Ftb.*) pass; *être dans une mauvaise passe,* to be in a fix; *en passe de,* in a fair way to.

passé [pa'se], *a.* past, bygone; faded, worn, withered.—*n.m.* past, past life, time past.—*prep.* after, beyond.

passée [pa'se], *n.f.* (*Hunt.*) flight, passage (*of woodcock etc.*).

passefiler [pasfi'le], *v.t.* to darn.

passement [pas'mã], *n.m.* lace (*of gold, silk etc.*).

passe-partout [paspar'tu], *n.m. inv.* master-key; latch-key; passe-partout (*frame*); cross-cut saw.

passeport [pas'po:r], *n.m.* passport.

passer [pa'se], *v.t.* (*takes the auxiliary* AVOIR *or* ÊTRE *according as action or condition is implied*) to pass; to cross, to go over; to transport; to strain (*liquids*); to sift (*flour*); to put on (*wearing apparel*); to omit; to waive; to allow; to spend (*time*); to take (*an examination*).—*v.i.* to pass to pass on;

to pass away; to die; to pass for; to fade. **se passer**, *v.r.* to pass, to pass away; to fade; to happen; to do without (*de*).

passereau [pas'ro], *n.m.* (*pl.* **-eaux**) sparrow.

passerelle [pas'rɛl], *n.f.* foot-bridge; (*Naut.*) bridge, gangway.

passe-temps [pas'tã], *n.m. inv.* pastime, hobby.

passeur [pa'sœːr], *n.m.* (*fem.* **-euse**) ferryman, ferrywoman.

passibilité [pasibili'te], *n.f.* liability.

passible [pa'sibl], *a.* passible; liable (*to*).

passif [pa'sif], *a.* (*fem.* **-ive**) passive; (*Comm.*) on debit side.—*n.m.* (*Gram.*) passive; (*Comm.*) liabilities.

passion [pa'sjõ], *n.f.* suffering, agony; passion, *esp.* love; (*fig.*) fondness.

passionnant [pasjo'nã], *a.* exciting, thrilling.

passionné [pasjo'ne], *a.* passionate, impassioned, very fond of (*de*).

passionnel [pasjo'nɛl], *a.* (*fem.* **-elle**) *crime passionnel*, crime due to jealous love.

passionnément [pasjone'mã], *adv.* passionately, fondly.

passionner [pasjo'ne], *v.t.* to impassion, to interest deeply. **se passionner**, *v.r.* to be passionately fond of; to become enamoured of.

passivement [pasiv'mã], *adv.* passively.

passiveté [pasiv'te], **passivité** [pasivi'te], *n.f.* passivity.

passoire [pa'swaːr], *n.f.* strainer.

pastel [pas'tel], *n.m.* pastel, crayon.

pastèque [pas'tek], *n.f.* water-melon.

pasteur [pas'tœːr], *n.m.* pastor, (*Protestant*) minister; clergyman.

pasteurisation [pastœriza'sjõ], *n.f.* pasteurization.

pasteuriser [pastœri'ze], *v.t.* to pasteurize.

pastiche [pas'tiʃ], *n.m.* pastiche; (*Mus.*) medley.

pastille [pas'tiːj], *n.f.* pastille; lozenge; rubber patch (*for tubes of tyre*).

pastoral [pasto'ral], *a.* (*m. pl.* **-aux**) pastoral. —*n.f.* (**-e**) pastoral (*play or poem*).

patapouf [pata'puf], *int. faire patapouf*, to fall flop.—*n.m. gros patapouf*, fat fellow, fatty.

patate [pa'tat], *n.f.* sweet potato.

patati [pata'ti], *only used in the phrase, et patati et patata*, and so on and so forth.

patatras! [pata'tra], *int.* crack! slap! bang!

pataud [pa'to], *a.* awkward, clumsy.—*n.m.* (*fem.* **-e**) pup with large paws; (*fig.*) lout, clumsy person.

patauger [pato'ʒe], *v.i.* (*conjug. like* MANGER) to splash, to flounder.

pâte [paːt], *n.f.* paste; dough, batter; (*fig.*) kind, sort; (*Print.*) pie.

pâté [pa'te], *n.m.* pie, pasty, patty; blot (*of ink*); block (*of buildings*); (*Print.*) pie.

pâtée [pa'te], *n.f.* mash (*to fatten poultry*); mess (*for dogs or cats*).

patelin [pa'tlɛ̃], *a.* smooth-tongued, wheedling.—*n.m.* (*fem.* **-e**) wheedler.—*n.m.* (*fam.*) village.

patent [pa'tã], *a.* patent; obvious, manifest.

patenté [patã'te], *a.* licensed.—*n.m.* (*fem.* **-ée**) licensed dealer.

patenter [patã'te], *v.t.* to license.

patère [pa'tɛːr], *n.f.* coat-hook; curtain-hook.

paternel [patɛr'nɛl], *a.* (*fem.* **-elle**) paternal, fatherly.

paternité [patɛrni'te], *n.f.* paternity, fatherhood.

pâteux [pa'tø], *a.* (*fem.* **-euse**) pasty, clammy, sticky.

pathétique [pate'tik], *a.* pathetic, moving.— *n.m.* pathos.

pathétiquement [patetik'mã], *adv.* pathetically.

pathologie [patolo'ʒi], *n.f.* pathology.

pathologiste [patolo'ʒist], *n.m.* pathologist.

pathos [pa'toːs], *n.m.* bathos; (*fig.*) bombast.

patiemment [pasja'mã], *adv.* patiently.

patience [pa'sjãːs], *n.f.* patience, endurance.

patient [pa'sjã], *a.* patient, enduring, forbearing.—*n.m.* (*fem.* **-e**) sufferer; (*Med.*) patient.

patienter [pasjã'te], *v.i.* to be patient.

patin [pa'tɛ̃], *n.m.* skate; flange (*of rail*); skid (*of aeroplane*); shoe (*of brake*); *patins à roulettes*, roller skates.

patinage [pati'naːʒ], *n.m.* skating; skidding (*of locomotive, car etc.*).

patine [pa'tin], *n.f.* patina (*of bronze*).

patiner [pati'ne], *v.i.* to skate; to skid (*of wheels*).

patinette [pati'net], *n.f.* scooter.

patineur [pati'nœːr], *n.m.* (*fem.* **-euse**) skater.

patinoire [pati'nwaːr], *n.f.* skating-rink.

pâtir [pa'tiːr], *v.i.* to suffer; to be in distress.

pâtisser [pati'se], *v.t.*, to knead (*flour*).—*v.i.* to knead; to make pastry.

pâtisserie [patis'ri], *n.f.* pastry, fancy cake; pastry-cook's shop or business.

pâtissier [pati'sje], *n.m.* (*fem.* **-ière**) pastry-cook.—*a.f.*(**-ière**) *crème patissière*, custard.

patois [pa'twa], *n.m. inv.* patois, provincial dialect; brogue; jargon.

patouiller [patu'je], [PATAUGER].

patraque [pa'trak], *a.* seedy, broken-down.— *n.f.* old crock.

pâtre [paːtr], *n.m.* herdsman, shepherd.

patriarcal [patriar'kal], *a.* (*m. pl.* **-aux**) patriarchal.

patriarche [patri'arʃ], *n.m.* patriarch.

Patrice [pa'tris], *m.* Patrick.

patrice [pa'tris], *n.m.* patrician.

patricien [patri'sjɛ̃], *a.* and *n.m.* (*fem.* **-enne**) patrician.

patrie [pa'tri], *n.f.* native land, fatherland.

patrimoine [patri'mwan], *n.m.* patrimony, inheritance.

patriote [patri'ɔt], *a.* patriotic (*person*).—*n.* patriot.

patriotique [patrio'tik], *a.* patriotic (*song, speech etc.*).

patriotisme [patrio'tism], *n.m.* patriotism.

patron (1) [pa'trõ], *n.m.* pattern, model.

patron (2) [pa'trõ], *n.m.* (*fem.* **-onne**) patron; master, mistress, employer; proprietor; (*colloq.*) boss; (*Naut.*) skipper, coxswain.

patronage [patro'naːʒ], *n.m.* patronage.

patronat [patro'na], *n.m.* management.

patronner [patro'ne], *v.t.* to patronize; to support.

patrouille [pa'truːj], *n.f.* patrol.

patrouiller [patru'je], *v.i.* to patrol.

patrouilleur [patru'jœːr], *n.m.* (*Naut.*) patrol-boat.

patte [pat], *n.f.* paw (*of quadruped*); foot (*of bird*); leg (*of insect*); bracket, cramp; flap (*of pocket etc.*); tab, strap (*of clothes*); (*fig.*) claws, clutches.

pêle-mêle

pâturage [pɑty'ra:ʒ], *n.m.* pasture.
pâture [pɑ'ty:r], *n.f.* food (*for animals*); pasture; fodder.
pâturer [pɑty're], *v.t.* to graze on.—*v.i.* to pasture, to graze, to feed.
pâturon or **paturon** [pɑty'rɔ̃], *n.m.* pastern.
paume [po:m], *n.f.* palm (*of the hand*); *jeu de paume*, (*court*) tennis, 'real' tennis.
paupérisme [pope'rism], *n.m.* pauperism.
paupière [po'pjɛ:r], *n.f.* eyelid; (*fig.*) eye(s).
pause [po:z], *n.f.* pause, stop; (*Mus.*) rest.
pauser [po'ze], *v.i.* to pause.
pauvre [po:vr], *a.* poor, needy; wretched, paltry, mean.—*n.m.* poor person pauper; beggar.
pauvrement [povrə'mɑ̃], *adv.* poorly, wretchedly.
pauvresse [po'vrɛs], *n.f.* poor woman, beggar-woman.
pauvret [po'vrɛ], *n.m.* (*fem.* **-ette**) poor creature, poor little thing.
pauvreté [povrə'te], *n.f.* poverty; wretchedness; sorry thing.
pavage [pa'va:ʒ], *n.m.* paving; pavement.
pavane [pa'van], *n.f.* pavan (*dance*).
pavaner (se) [səpava'ne], *v.r.* to strut, to stalk proudly.
pavé [pa've], *a.* paved.—*n.m.* paving-stone; paved part of road; (*fig.*) road, street(s).
pavement [pav'mɑ̃], *n.m.* paving; flooring.
paver [pa've], *v.t.* to pave.
paveur [pa'vœ:r], *n.m.* paviour.
pavillon [pavi'jɔ̃], *n.m.* pavilion, tent; summerhouse; detached house; wing (*of a house*), outhouse, lodge; (*Naut.*) flag.
pavoiser [pavwa'ze], *v.t.* to deck with flags, to dress (*ship*).
pavot [pa'vo], *n.m.* poppy.
payable [pɛ'jabl], *a.* payable.
payant [pɛ'jɑ̃], *a.* paying; to be paid for.—*n.m.* (*fem.* **-e**) payer.
paye [pɛ:j], **paie** [pɛ], *n.f.* pay, wages.
payement or **paiement** [pɛ'mɑ̃], *n.m.* payment.
payer [pɛ'je], *v.t.* (*see Verb Tables*) to pay (for); to reward; to expiate, to atone for. **se payer**, *v.r.* to be paid or satisfied; to treat oneself to.
payeur [pɛ'jœ:r], *n.m.* (*fem.* **-euse**) payer; pay-clerk; (*Mil.*) pay-master.
pays [pe'i], *n.m. inv.* country, land; region, district; fatherland, home; *avoir le mal du pays*, to be home-sick; *pays perdu*, out-of-the-way place.
paysage [pei'za:ʒ], *n.m.* landscape, scenery.
paysagiste [peiza'ʒist], *a.* and *n.m.* landscape (-painter).
paysan [pei'zɑ̃], *a.* (*fem.* **-anne**) rustic.—*n.m.* (*fem.* **-anne**) peasant, countryman, countrywoman; farmer.
paysannerie [peizan'ri], *n.f.* rusticity; peasantry.
Pays-Bas [pei'bɑ], **les**, *m.pl.* the Netherlands.
péage [pe'a:ʒ], *n.m.* toll; toll-house.
péan or **pæan** [pe'ɑ̃], *n.m.* pæan, song of triumph or joy.
peau [po] *n.f.* (*pl.* **peaux**) skin; hide; peel, rind.
Peau-Rouge [po'ru:ʒ], *n.* (*pl.* **Peaux-Rouges**) Redskin, Red Indian.
peccadille [pɛka'di:j], *n.f.* peccadillo.
pêche (1) [pɛ:ʃ], *n.f.* peach.

pêche (2) [pɛ:ʃ], *n.f.* fishing, angling.
péché [pe'ʃe], *n.m.* sin, transgression.
pécher [pe'ʃe], *v.i.* (*conjug. like* CÉDER) to sin, to transgress; to offend; to be deficient.
pêcher (1) [pe'ʃe], *n.m.* peach-tree.
pêcher (2) [pe'ʃe], *v.t.* to fish for; to drag out; (*fig.*) to get hold of.—*v.i.* to fish, to angle.
pêcheresse [peʃ'rɛs], [PÊCHEUR].
pêcherie [pɛʃ'ri], *n.f.* fishing-ground, fishery.
pêcheur [pe'ʃœ:r], *n.m.* (*fem.* **-eresse**) sinner.
pêcheur [pe'ʃœ:r], *n.m.* (*fem.* **-euse**) fisher, fisherman, fisherwoman.
pécore [pe'kɔ:r], *n.f.* stupid creature, blockhead; *esp.* silly girl.
pécule [pe'kyl], *n.m.* savings; earnings (*of a prisoner*).
pécuniaire [peky'njɛ:r], *a.* pecuniary.
pédagogie [pedagɔ'ʒi], *n.f.* pedagogy.
pédagogue [peda'gɔg], *n.* pedagogue.
pédale [pe'dal], *n.f.* pedal; treadle.
pédaler [peda'le], *v.i.* to pedal; (*colloq.*) to cycle.
pédant [pe'dɑ̃], *a.* pedantic.—*n.m.* (*fem.* **-e**) pedant.
pédanterie [pedɑ̃'tri], *n.f.* pedantry.
pédantesque [pedɑ̃'tɛsk], *a.* pedantic.
pédantisme [pedɑ̃'tism], *n.m.* pedantry.
pédestre [pe'dɛstr], *a.* pedestrian, on foot.
pédestrement [pedɛstrə'mɑ̃], *adv.* on foot.
pédicure [pedi'ky:r], *n.* chiropodist.
Pégase [pe'gɑ:z], *m.* Pegasus.
peignage [pe'na:ʒ], *n.m.* combing, wool-combing.
peigne [pɛɲ], *n.m.* comb.
peigné [pe'ɲe], *a.* combed; (*fig.*) arranged.—*n.m.* worsted.
peigner [pe'ɲe], *v.t.* to comb; to card; (*fig.*) to polish (*style*). **se peigner**, *v.r.* to comb one's hair.
peignoir [pe'ɲwa:r], *n.m.* dressing-gown; (*Am.*) bath-robe.
peindre [pɛ̃:dr], *v.t. irr.* (*conjug. like* CRAINDRE) to paint, to portray; to represent, to express; *se faire peindre*, to sit for one's portrait. **se peindre**, *v.r.* to paint oneself; to be represented.
peine [pɛn], *n.f.* punishment, penalty; pain, grief, sorrow; anxiety; trouble; difficulty; reluctance; *à peine*, hardly, scarcely; *un homme de peine*, an unskilled labourer.
peiné [pe'ne], *a.* pained, grieved; laboured; elaborate.
peiner [pe'ne], *v.t.* to pain, to trouble, to grieve; (*fig.*) to elaborate.—*v.i.* to labour, to toil; to be reluctant.
peintre [pɛ̃:tr], *n.m.* painter.
peinture [pɛ̃'ty:r], *n.f.* painting; picture; description, appearance; paint, colour.
péjoratif [peʒɔra'tif], *a.* (*fem.* **-tive**) pejorative.
Pékin [pe'kɛ̃], *m.* Peking.
pékinois [peki'nwa], *a.* Pekinese.—*n.m.* Pekinese (*dog*); (**Pékinois**, *fem.* **-oise**) Pekinese (*person*).
pelage [pə'la:ʒ], *n.m.* hair, fur, coat (*of animal*).
pelé [pə'le], *a.* bald; which has lost its hair (*animals*).—*n.m.* (*fem.* **-ée**) bald-headed person.
pêle-mêle [pɛl'mɛl], *adv.* pell-mell, higgledy-piggledy.—*n.m. inv.* disorder, jumble.

peler [pə'le], *v.t.* (*conjug. like* AMENER) to skin, to peel.—*v.i.* to peel off (*of the skin etc.*). se **peler,** *v.r.* to come off, to peel.

pèlerin [pɛl'rɛ̃], *n.m.* (*fem.* **-ine** (1)) pilgrim; peregrine falcon; basking shark.

pèlerinage [pɛlri'naːʒ], *n.m.* pilgrimage.

pèlerine (2) [pɛl'rin], *n.f.* tippet, cape (*with hood*).

pélican [peli'kɑ̃], *n.m.* pelican.

pelisse [pə'lis], *n.f.* pelisse; fur-lined coat.

pelle [pɛl], *n.f.* shovel, scoop, blade (*of an oar*); (*fam.*) spill, cropper.

pelletée [pɛl'te], *n.f.* shovelful.

pelleter [pɛl'te], *v.t.* (*conjug. like* APPELER) to shovel.

pelletier [pɛl'tje], *n.m.* (*fem.* **-ière**) furrier.

pellicule [peli'kyl], *n.f.* pellicle; (*Phot.*) film; (*pl.*) scurf (*of scalp*), dandruff.

pelotage [pələ'taːʒ], *n.m.* winding skeins into balls; (*Billiards, Ten.*) knock-up.

pelote [pə'lɔt], *n.f.* ball; ball of thread; pellet; pin-cushion; (*Spt.*) **pelote basque,** pelota.

peloter [pələ'te], *v.t.* to make *or* wind into a ball.—*v.i.* (*Spt.*) to knock up.

peloton [pələ'tɔ̃], *n.m.* ball; cluster (*of bees*); (*Mil.*) squad; (*Racing*) bunch (*of runners*).

pelotonner [pələtɔ'ne], *v.t.* to wind into balls. se **pelotonner,** *v.r.* to roll oneself up; to curl up.

pelouse [pə'luːz], *n.f.* lawn, greensward.

peluche [pə'lyʃ], *n.f.* plush.

peluché [pəly'ʃe], *a.* shaggy.

pelucher [pəly'ʃe], *v.i.* to become shaggy, to wear rough.

pelucheux [pəly'ʃø], *a.* (*fem.* **-euse**) shaggy; fluffy.

pelure [pə'lyːr], *n.f.* paring; peel, skin; rind.

pénal [pe'nal], *a.* (*m. pl.* **-aux**) penal.

pénaliser [penali'ze], *v.t.* to penalize.

pénalité [penali'te], *n.f.* penal law; penalty.

pénates [pe'nat], *n.m. pl.* penates, household gods; (*fig.*) home.

penaud [pə'no], *a.* abashed, sheepish, crest-fallen.

penchant [pɑ̃'ʃɑ̃], *a.* inclined, sloping, leaning.—*n.m.* declivity; slope; inclination, bent.

pencher [pɑ̃'ʃe], *v.t.* to incline, to bend.—*v.i.* to lean; to tilt, to slope. se **pencher,** *v.r.* to bend, to stoop; to slope, to be inclined.

pendable [pɑ̃'dabl], *a.* deserving hanging, abominable.

pendaison [pɑ̃dɛ'zɔ̃], *n.f.* hanging (*on the gallows*), death by hanging.

pendant [pɑ̃'dɑ̃], *a.* pendent, hanging; pending; depending.—*n.m.* thing hanging, pendant; counterpart.—*prep.* during; for; *pendant que,* while, whilst.

pendard [pɑ̃'daːr], *n.m.* (*fem.* **-e**) (*colloq.*) rascal, rogue, jade.

pendeloque [pɑ̃'dlɔk], *n.f.* ear-drop; pendant.

pendiller [pɑ̃di'je], *v.i.* to hang loose, to dangle.

pendre [pɑ̃ːdr], *v.t.* to hang, to hang up, to suspend.—*v.i.* to hang; to dangle, to droop. se **pendre,** *v.r.* to hang oneself.

pendu [pɑ̃'dy], *a.* hanging; hanged; hung.—*n.m.* (*fem.* **-e**) one that has been hanged.

pendule [pɑ̃'dyl], *n.f.* clock, time-piece.—*n.m.* pendulum.

pêne [pɛːn], *n.m.* bolt (*of a lock*).

pénétrabilité [penetrabili'te], *n.f.* penetrability.

pénétrable [pene'trabl], *a.* penetrable.

pénétrant [pene'trɑ̃], *a.* penetrating; piercing, keen; acute; impressive.

pénétration [penetra'sjɔ̃], *n.f.* penetration; acuteness, shrewdness.

pénétré [pene'tre], *a.* penetrated; moved, impressed.

pénétrer [pene'tre], *v.t.* (*conjug. like* CÉDER) to penetrate, to go through; to pierce; to pervade; to fathom; to impress, to affect.—*v.i.* to penetrate (*dans*); to reach (*à*). se **pénétrer,** *v.r.* to penetrate each other; to be impressed.

pénible [pe'nibl], *a.* painful, laborious; troublesome.

péniblement [peniblə'mɑ̃], *adv.* laboriously.

pénicilline [penisi'lin], *n.f.* penicillin.

péninsulaire [penɛ̃sy'lɛːr], *a.* peninsular.

péninsule [penɛ̃'syl], *n.f.* peninsula.

pénitence [peni'tɑ̃ːs], *n.f.* penitence, repentance; penance; punishment.

pénitencier [penitɑ̃'sje], *a.* penitentiary.—*n.m.* penitentiary, reformatory.

pénitent [peni'tɑ̃], *a.* penitent, repentant.—*n.m.* (*fem.* **-e**) penitent.

pénitentiaire [penitɑ̃'sjɛːr], *a.* penitentiary.

penne [pɛn], *n.f.* tail-feather, wing-feather.

penniforme [pɛni'fɔrm], *a.* penniform.

pennon [pɛ'nɔ̃], *n.m.* pennon.

pénombre [pe'nɔ̃ːbr], *n.f.* penumbra; semi-darkness, half-light.

pensée [pɑ̃'se], *n.f.* thought; opinion; idea, conception; meaning; (*Bot.*) pansy.

penser [pɑ̃'se], *v.t.* to think, to think of (*à* or *de*).—*v.i.* to think, to reflect, to consider; to expect; to take heed, to take care.—*n.m.* (*poet.*) inward reasoning, thought.

penseur [pɑ̃'sœːr], *a.* (*fem.* **-euse**) thinking, thoughtful.—*n.m.* (*fem.* **-euse**) thinker.

pensif [pɑ̃'sif], *a.* (*fem.* **-sive**) pensive, thoughtful.

pension [pɑ̃'sjɔ̃], *n.f.* board and lodging; boarding-house; boarding-school; pension, allowance, annuity.

pensionnaire [pɑ̃sjɔ'nɛːr], *n.* boarder; school-boy *or* -girl; pensioner, resident.

pensionnat [pɑ̃sjɔ'na], *n.m.* private boarding-school.

pensionné [pɑ̃sjɔ'ne], *a.* pensioned.—*n.m.* (*fem.* **-ée**) pensioner.

pensionner [pɑ̃sjɔ'ne], *v.t.* to pension, to grant a pension to.

pensum [pɛ̃'sɔm], *n.m.* imposition, extra task (*at school*).

pente [pɑ̃ːt], *n.f.* declivity, slope; acclivity, ascent; gradient; pitch (*of roofs*); (*fig.*) propensity, bent.

Pentecôte [pɑ̃t'koːt], *n.f.* Pentecost, Whitsuntide.

pénultième [penyl'tjɛm], *a.* last but one, penultimate.

pénurie [peny'ri], *n.f.* scarcity, dearth; penury, want.

pépier [pe'pje], *v.i.* to chirp, to cheep.

pépin [pe'pɛ̃], *n.m.* pip (*of apple etc.*); stone (*of grape*).

pépinière [pepi'njɛːr], *n.f.* nursery (*of trees*).

pépiniériste [pepinje'rist], *n.m.* nurseryman.

pépite [pe'pit], *n.f.* nugget (*of gold*).

pepsine [pɛp'sin], *n.f.* pepsine.

peptique [pɛp'tik], a. peptic.
percale [pɛr'kal], n.f. cotton cambric, percale.
percaline [pɛrka'lin], n.f. glazed calico or lining, percaline.
perçant [pɛr'sã], a. piercing; sharp; shrill, acute.
perce [pɛrs], n.f. piercer, borer.
percé [pɛr'se], a. pierced, bored, in holes.
percée [pɛr'se], n.f. opening, cutting (in a wood), vista, glade; (fig.) break-through.
percement [pɛrsə'mã], n.m. piercing, boring, perforation.
perce-neige [pɛrs'nɛːʒ], n.f. inv. snowdrop.
perce-oreille [pɛrsə'rɛːj], n.m. (pl. -oreilles) earwig.
percepteur [pɛrsɛp'tœːr], n.m. collector of taxes.
perceptible [pɛrsɛp'tibl], a. collectible; perceptible.
perceptiblement [pɛrsɛptiblə'mã], adv. perceptibly.
perceptif [pɛrsɛp'tif], a. (fem. -tive) perceptive.
perception [pɛrsɛp'sjõ], n.f. perception; collecting, receipt; collectorship, collector's office.
percer [pɛr'se], v.t. (conjug. like COMMENCER) to pierce, to bore, to drill; to make an opening; to tunnel; to wet through (of rain etc.).—v.i. to pierce through, to come through; to transpire; to manifest itself. **se percer**, v.r. to pierce oneself, to be pierced.
perceur [pɛr'sœːr], n.m. (fem. -euse) borer.—n.f. (-euse) boring-machine, drill.
percevoir [pɛrsə'vwaːr], v.t. irr. (conjug. like RECEVOIR) to collect (taxes etc.); (Phil.) to perceive.
perche [pɛrʃ], n.f. perch, pole; (Ichth.) perch.
perché [pɛr'ʃe], a. perched, perched up, roosting.
percher [pɛr'ʃe], v.i. and **se percher**, v.r. to perch, to roost.
percheur [pɛr'ʃœːr], a. (fem. -euse) perching, roosting (of birds).
perchoir [pɛr'ʃwaːr], n.m. roost.
perclus [pɛr'kly], a. crippled, impotent.
percolateur [pɛrkola'tœːr], n.m. percolator.
percussion [pɛrky'sjõ], n.f. percussion.
percutant [pɛrky'tã], a. producing percussion; (colloq.) fabulous.
percuter [pɛrky'te], v.t. to strike; to percuss. —v.i. to crash.
perdable [pɛr'dabl], a. losable.
perdant [pɛr'dã], a. losing.—n.m. (fem. -e) loser.
perdition [pɛrdi'sjõ], n.f. perdition.
perdre [pɛrdr], v.t. to lose, to be deprived of; to waste, to ruin, to corrupt, to lead astray. —v.i. to lose, to be a loser; to leak. **se perdre**, v.r. to be lost; to lose one's way, to be bewildered; to disappear.
perdreau [pɛr'dro], n.m. (pl. -eaux) young partridge.
perdrix [pɛr'dri], n.f. inv. partridge.
perdu [pɛr'dy], a. lost; ruined; spoilt; stray; obsolete; out of the way; bewildered; *salle des pas perdus*, waiting hall (in courts of law).
père [pɛːr], n.m. father; sire.

pérégrination [peregrinɑ'sjõ], n.f. peregrination.
péremptoire [perãp'twaːr], a. peremptory.
péremptoirement [perãptwar'mã], adv. peremptorily.
pérennité [perɛni'te], n.f. perpetuity.
perfectibilité [pɛrfɛktibili'te], n.f. perfectibility.
perfectible [pɛrfɛk'tibl], a. perfectible.
perfection [pɛrfɛk'sjõ], n.f. perfection; faultlessness; completeness.
perfectionnement [pɛrfɛksjon'mã], n.m. improvement, perfecting.
perfectionner [pɛrfɛksjo'ne], v.t. to perfect; to improve. **se perfectionner**, v.r. to perfect oneself; to improve.
perfide [pɛr'fid], a. perfidious, treacherous, false.—n. perfidious or treacherous person.
perfidement [pɛrfid'mã], adv. perfidiously, falsely, treacherously.
perfidie [pɛrfi'di], n.f. perfidy, treachery.
perforage [pɛrfo'raːʒ], n.m. boring, perforation.
perforant [pɛrfo'rã], a. perforating, penetrating.
perforateur [pɛrfora'tœːr], a. (fem. -trice (1)) perforative.—n.m. perforator.
perforation [pɛrforɑ'sjõ], n.f. perforation.
perforatrice (2) [pɛrfora'tris], n.f. drilling-machine.
perforer [pɛrfo're], v.t. to perforate, to bore, to drill.
péricliter [perikli'te], v.i. to be in jeopardy.
péril [pe'ril], n.m. peril, danger, hazard, risk.
périlleusement [perijøz'mã], adv. perilously.
périlleux [peri'jø], a. (fem. -euse) perilous, dangerous.
périmé [peri'me], a. out-of-date, no longer valid.
période [pe'rjod], n.f. period of time, era; (Gram.) period, sentence; (Mus.) phrase.— n.m. pitch, summit, degree, acme.
périodicité [perjodisi'te], n.f. periodicity.
périodique [perjo'dik], a. periodic, periodical.—n.m. periodical.
périodiquement [perjodik'mã], adv. periodically.
péripétie [peripe'si], n.f. sudden turn of fortune; (pl.) vicissitudes.
périr [pe'riːr], v.i. to perish, to die; to be wrecked; to decay.
périscope [peris'kop], n.m. periscope.
périssable [peri'sabl], a. perishable.
péristyle [peris'til], a. and n.m. peristyle.
péritoine [peri'twan], n.m. peritoneum.
péritonite [perito'nit], n.f. peritonitis.
perle [pɛrl], n.f. pearl; bead, bugle (for bracelets, necklaces etc.); (fig.) gem, jewel, the best.
perlé [pɛr'le], a. pearled, set with pearls; pearly.
perler [pɛr'le], v.t. to bead, to form into beads; to pearl.—v.i. to form beads (of sweat etc.).
perlier [pɛr'lje], a. (fem. -ière) of pearl.
permanence [pɛrma'nãːs], n.f. permanence; headquarters (of a political party).
permanent [pɛrma'nã], a. permanent, lasting.
permanente [pɛrma'nãːt], n.f. (Hairdressing) permanent wave.

perméabilité

perméabilité [pɛrmeabili'te], *n.f.* permeability.

perméable [pɛrme'abl], *a.* permeable, pervious (*to*).

permettre [pɛr'mɛtr], *v.t. irr.* (*conjug. like* METTRE) to permit, to allow; to enable, to afford room for. **se permettre**, *v.r.* to permit oneself; to indulge, to venture, to take the liberty (*de*).

permis [pɛr'mi], *a.* allowed, permitted, lawful.—*n.m.* permission, leave; permit, licence, pass.

permission [pɛrmi'sjɔ̃], *n.f.* permission, leave, permit.

permutant [pɛrmy'tɑ̃], *n.m.* permuter, exchanger.

permutation [pɛrmyta'sjɔ̃], *n.f.* permutation, exchange; (*Mil.*) transfer.

permuter [pɛrmy'te], *v.t.* to exchange, to permute, to transpose.

pernicieusement [pɛrnisjøz'mɑ̃], *adv.* perniciously, mischievously, injuriously.

pernicieux [pɛrni'sjø], *a.* (*fem.* **-euse**) pernicious, mischievous, hurtful.

péronnelle [pero'nɛl], *n.f.* pert hussy, saucy baggage.

péroraison [perore'zɔ̃], *n.f.* peroration.

pérorer [pero're], *v.i.* to hold forth, to speechify.

péroreur [pero'rœːr], *n.m.* (*fem.* **-euse**) speechifier, spouter.

Pérou [pe'ru], **le**, *m.* Peru.

perpendiculaire [pɛrpɑ̃diky'lɛːr], *a.* and *n.f.* perpendicular.

perpendiculairement [pɛrpɑ̃dikylɛr'mɑ̃], *adv.* perpendicularly.

perpétration [pɛrpetra'sjɔ̃], *n.f.* perpetration.

perpétrer [pɛrpe'tre], *v.t.* (*conjug. like* CÉDER) to perpetrate, to commit.

perpétuation [pɛrpetɥa'sjɔ̃], *n.f.* perpetuation.

perpétuel [pɛrpe'tɥɛl], *a.* (*fem.* **-elle**) perpetual, permanent; for life.

perpétuellement [pɛrpetɥɛl'mɑ̃], *adv.* perpetually; everlastingly.

perpétuer [pɛrpe'tɥe], *v.t.* to perpetuate. **se perpétuer**, *v.r.* to be perpetuated, to continue.

perpétuité [pɛrpetɥi'te], *n.f.* perpetuity; *à perpétuité*, for ever, for life.

perplexe [pɛr'plɛks], *a.* perplexed, embarrassed, irresolute; perplexing.

perplexité [pɛrplɛksi'te], *n.f.* perplexity.

perquisition [pɛrkizi'sjɔ̃], *n.f.* perquisition, search; investigation.

perquisitionner [pɛrkizisjo'ne], *v.i.* to make a search.

perron [pɛ'rɔ̃], *n.m.* steps (*before a house*).

perroquet [pero'kɛ], *n.m.* parrot.

perruche [pɛ'ryʃ], *n.f.* parakeet, budgerigar; (*pop.*) hen-parrot.

perruque [pɛ'ryk], *n.f.* wig, periwig.

perruquier [pɛry'kje], *n.m.* wig-maker; (*obs.*) hair-dresser, barber.

persan [pɛr'sɑ̃], *a.* Persian.—*n.m.* Persian (*language*); (**Persan**, *fem.* **-ane**) Persian (*person*).

Perse [pɛrs], **la**, *f.* Persia.

perse [pɛrs], *n.f.* chintz.

persécuter [pɛrseky'te], *v.t.* to persecute; (*fig.*) to bore, to dun.

persécuteur [pɛrseky'tœːr], *a.* (*fem.* **-trice**) persecuting; troublesome.—*n.m.* (*fem.* **-trice**) persecutor; troublesome person.

persécution [pɛrseky'sjɔ̃], *n.f.* persecution; annoyance, importunity.

persévérance [pɛrseve'rɑːs], *n.f.* perseverance; firmness, steadiness.

persévérant [pɛrseve'rɑ̃], *a.* persevering; steady, resolute.

persévérer [pɛrseve're], *v.i.* (*conjug. like* CÉDER) to persevere; to be steadfast; to persist.

persienne [pɛr'sjɛn], *n.f.* Venetian shutter.

persiflage [pɛrsi'flaːʒ], *n.m.* banter, chaff, persiflage.

persifler [pɛrsi'fle], *v.t., v.i.* to rally, to banter, to chaff.

persifleur [pɛrsi'flœːr], *a.* (*fem.* **-euse**) bantering, chaffing.—*n.m.* (*fem.* **-euse**) banterer, quiz.

persil [pɛr'si], *n.m.* parsley.

persillé [pɛrsi'je], *a.* spotted; blue-moulded, (*cheese*).

persique [pɛr'sik], *a.* ancient Persian; *le Golfe Persique*, Persian Gulf.

persistance [pɛrsis'tɑːs], *n.f.* persistence.

persistant [pɛrsis'tɑ̃], *a.* persistent.

persister [pɛrsis'te], *v.i.* to persist.

personnage [pɛrso'naːʒ], *n.m.* personage, person; (*Theat.*) character, part.

personnalité [pɛrsonali'te], *n.f.* personality, personal character; person; selfishness.

personne [pɛr'son], *n.f.* person; own self; appearance.—*pron. indef.* anyone, no one, nobody.

personnel [pɛrso'nɛl], *a.* (*fem.* **-elle**) personal; selfish.—*n.m.* personnel, staff.

personnellement [pɛrsonɛl'mɑ̃], *adv.* personally.

personnification [pɛrsonifika'sjɔ̃], *n.f.* personification.

personnifier [pɛrsoni'fje], *v.t.* to personify; to embody.

perspectif [pɛrspɛk'tif], *a.* (*fem.* **-tive**) perspective.—*n.f.* (**-tive**) perspective; view, prospect, distance, vista.

perspicace [pɛrspi'kas], *a.* perspicacious, shrewd.

perspicacité [pɛrspikasi'te], *n.f.* perspicacity, insight.

persuader [pɛrsɥa'de], *v.t.* to persuade; to convince, to satisfy. **se persuader**, *v.r.* to persuade *or* convince oneself; to be persuaded.

persuasible [pɛrsɥa'zibl], *a.* persuadable.

persuasif [pɛrsɥa'zif], *a.* (*fem.* **-sive**) persuasive; convincing.

persuasion [pɛrsɥa'zjɔ̃], *n.f.* persuasion; conviction, belief, opinion.

persuasivement [pɛrsɥaziv'mɑ̃], *adv.* persuasively.

perte [pɛrt], *n.f.* loss; waste; ruin, fall, doom; *à perte*, at a loss; *en pure perte*, in vain.

pertinemment [pɛrtina'mɑ̃], *adv.* pertinently.

pertinence [pɛrti'nɑːs], *n.f.* pertinence.

pertinent [pɛrti'nɑ̃], *a.* pertinent, relevant.

pertuis [pɛr'tɥi], *n.m.* opening, sluice; straits.

perturbateur [pɛrtyrba'tœːr], *a.* (*fem.* **-trice**) disturbing.—*n.m.* (*fem.* **-trice**) disturber.

perturbation [pɛrtyrba'sjɔ̃], *n.f.* perturbation, disturbance.

perturber [pɛrtyr'be], *v.t.* to perturb, to disturb.

péruvien [pery'vjɛ̃], *a.* (*fem.* -enne) Peruvian.—*n.m.* (**Péruvien**, *fem.* -enne) Peruvian (*person*).

pervenche [pɛr'vɑ̃:ʃ], *n.f.* (*Bot.*) periwinkle.

pervers [pɛr'vɛ:r], *a.* perverse, wicked, depraved.—*n.m.* (*fem.* -e) perverse person; wrongdoer.

perversion [pɛrvɛr'sjɔ̃], *n.f.* perversion.

perversité [pɛrvɛrsi'te], *n.f.* perverseness.

pervertir [pɛrvɛr'ti:r], *v.t.* to pervert.

pervertissement [pɛrvɛrtis'mɑ̃], *n.m.* perversion.

pervertisseur [pɛrvɛrti'sœ:r], *a.* (*fem.* -euse) perverting.—*n.m.* (*fem.* -euse) perverter, corrupter.

pesage [pə'za:ʒ], *n.m.* weighing; (*Turf.*) weighing-in room; paddock (*on race-course*), the enclosure.

pesamment [pəza'mɑ̃], *adv.* heavily, ponderously; clumsily.

pesant [pə'zɑ̃], *a.* heavy, ponderous; unwieldy; sluggish.—*n.m.* weight.—*adv.* in weight.

pesanteur [pəzɑ̃'tœ:r], *n.f.* weight; heaviness; unwieldiness, dullness, ponderousness; (*Phys.*) gravity.

pesée [pə'ze], *n.f.* weighing.

pèse-lettre [pɛz'lɛtr], *n.m.* (*pl.* -lettres) letter-scales.

peser [pə'ze], *v.t.* (*conjug. like* AMENER) to weigh; (*fig.*) to ponder, to estimate.—*v.i.* to weigh; to be heavy; to be of importance; to lie heavy; to dwell (*sur*).

peseur [pə'zœ:r], *n.m.* (*fem.* -euse) weigher.

pessimisme [pɛsi'mism], *n.m.* pessimism.

pessimiste [pɛsi'mist], *a.* pessimistic.—*n.* pessimist.

peste [pɛst], *n.f.* plague, pestilence; (*fig.*) pest, bore, nuisance.—*int.* the deuce! hang it!

pester [pɛs'te], *v.i.* to inveigh, to storm, to rave.

pestiféré [pɛstife're], *a.* and *n.m.* (*fem.* -ée) plague-stricken (person).

pestilence [pɛsti'lɑ̃:s], *n.f.* pestilence.

pestilent [pɛsti'lɑ̃], *a.* pestilent.

pestilentiel [pɛstilɑ̃'sjɛl], *a.* (*fem.* -elle) pestilential.

pétale [pe'tal], *n.m.* petal.

pétarade [peta'rad], *n.f.* cracking (*noise*); back-fire (*of car*).

pétard [pe'ta:r], *n.m.* petard; cracker (*firework*); (*Rail.*) detonator, fog-signal.

pétaudière [peto'djɛ:r], *n.f.* bear-garden, noisy *or* disorderly assembly.

pétillant [peti'jɑ̃], *a.* crackling; sparkling.

pétillement [petij'mɑ̃], *n.m.* crackling; sparkling.

pétiller [peti'je], *v.i.* to crackle (*of burning wood*); to sparkle.

petiot [pə'tjo], *a.* (*fam.*) tiny, wee.—*n.m.* (*fem.* -e) little one; darling.

petit [pə'ti], *a.* little, small; short; very young; petty, slight; shabby; humble.—*n.m.* (*fem.* -e) little child, little one; young one; whelp, pup, kitten, cub.

petite-fille [pətit'fij], *n.f.* (*pl.* petites-filles) grand-daughter.

petitement [pətit'mɑ̃], *adv.* in small quantity; not much, poorly, meanly.

petitesse [pəti'tɛs], *n.f.* smallness, littleness; insignificance; meanness; narrowness.

petit-fils [pəti'fis], *n.m.* (*pl.* petits-fils) grandson.

pétition [peti'sjɔ̃], *n.f.* petition, request.

pétitionnaire [petisjɔ'nɛ:r], *n.* petitioner.

pétitionnement [petisjɔn'mɑ̃], *n.m.* petitioning.

pétitionner [petisjɔ'ne], *v.i.* to make a request, to petition.

petit-lait [pəti'lɛ], *n.m.* whey.

petits-enfants [pətizɑ̃'fɑ̃], *n.m. pl.* grand-children.

pétrel [pe'trɛl], *n.m.* petrel.

pétri [pe'tri], *a.* kneaded.

pétrifiant [petri'fjɑ̃], *a.* petrifying.

pétrification [petrifika'sjɔ̃], *n.f.* petrifaction.

pétrifier [petri'fje], *v.t.* to petrify. **se pétrifier**, *v.r.* to turn into stone.

pétrin [pe'trɛ̃], *n.m.* kneading-trough; (*fig.*) scrape.

pétrir [pe'tri:r], *v.t.* to knead; (*fig.*) to mould, to form.

pétrissable [petri'sabl], *a.* that can be kneaded; (*fig.*) yielding, pliant.

pétrissage [petri'sa:ʒ], **pétrissement** [petris'mɑ̃], *n.m.* kneading; (*fig.*) forming.

pétrisseur [petri'sœ:r], *n.m.* (*fem.* -euse) kneader.—*n.f.* (-euse) kneading-machine.

pétrole [pe'trɔl], *n.m.* petroleum, (mineral) oil; paraffin.

pétrolier [petrɔ'lje], *a.* (*fem.* -ière) pertaining to oil.—*n.m.* oil-tanker.

pétulance [pety'lɑ̃:s], *n.f.* liveliness, ebulliency; friskiness.

pétulant [pety'lɑ̃], *a.* lively, ebullient, frisky.

pétunia [pety'nja], *n.m.* petunia.

peu [pø], *adv.* little, not much; few, not many; not very.—*n.m.* little; bit.

peuplade [pœ'plad], *n.f.* clan, tribe, horde.

peuple [pœpl], *a.* plebeian, common, vulgar.—*n.m.* people, nation; the people, the multitude, the lower classes.

peuplé [pœ'ple], *a.* heavily populated, populous.

peuplement [pœplə'mɑ̃], *n.m.* peopling; stocking of a poultry-yard, pond etc.

peupler [pœ'ple], *v.t.* to people; to stock with animals etc.; to populate; to throng.—*v.i.* to multiply, to breed. **se peupler**, *v.r.* to become peopled; to be populated.

peuplier [pœ'plje], *n.m.* poplar.

peur [pœ:r], *n.f.* fear, dread, terror; apprehension; **avoir peur**, to be afraid; **de peur de**, for fear of.

peureusement [pœrøz'mɑ̃], *adv.* timorously.

peureux [pœ'rø], *a.* (*fem.* -euse) fearful, timid, timorous.—*n.m.* (*fem.* -euse) timid person.

peut-être [pø'tɛ:tr], *adv.* perhaps, maybe.

phalange [fa'lɑ̃:ʒ], *n.f.* phalanx; (*poet.*) army, host.

phalène [fa'lɛ:n], *n.f.* moth.

pharaon [fara'ɔ̃], *n.m.* Pharaoh.

phare [fa:r], *n.m.* lighthouse; beacon; (*Motor.*) head-light.

pharisien [fari'zjɛ̃], *n.m.* Pharisee; (*fig.*) hypocrite; self-righteous person.

pharmaceutique [farmasø'tik], *a.* pharmaceutical.—*n.f.* pharmaceutics.

pharmacie

pharmacie [farma'si], *n.f.* pharmacy, chemist and druggist's shop, dispensary; medicine chest.

pharmacien [farma'sjɛ̃], *n.m.* (*fem.* **-enne**) chemist, pharmacist.

phase [faːz], *n.f.* phasis (*of planet*); phase; aspect, period.

phénicien [feni'sjɛ̃], *a.* (*fem.* **-enne**) Phoenician.—*n.m.* (**Phénicien**, *fem.* **-enne**) Phoenician (*person*).

phénix [fe'niks], *n.m.* phoenix; paragon.

phénoménal [fenɔme'nal], *a.* (*m. pl.* **-aux**) phenomenal; (*colloq.*) extraordinary.

phénomène [fenɔ'mɛːn], *n.m.* phenomenon; (*colloq.*) remarkable person *or* thing; freak.

philanthrope [filɑ̃'trɔp], *n.* philanthropist.

philanthropie [filɑ̃trɔ'pi], *n.f.* philanthropy.

philanthropique [filɑ̃trɔ'pik], *a.* philanthropic.

philatélie [filate'li], *n.f.* philately, stamp-collecting.

philatéliste [filate'list], *n.* stamp collector.

Philippe [fi'lip], *m.* Philip.

philippin [fili'pɛ̃], *a.* Philippine, Filipino. —*n.* (**Philippin**) Filipino (*person*).

Philippines [fili'pin], **les**, *f. pl.* Philippines, Philippine Islands.

Philistin [filis'tɛ̃], *n.m.* (*fem.* **-e**) Philistine, person of vulgar taste.

philosophale [filɔzɔ'fal], *a. la pierre philosophale*, the philosopher's stone.

philosophe [filɔ'zɔf], *a.* philosophical.—*n.* philosopher.

philosopher [filɔzɔ'fe], *v.i.* to philosophize.

philosophie [filɔzɔ'fi], *n.f.* philosophy; class in French school roughly equivalent to English sixth.

philosophique [filɔzɔ'fik], *a.* philosophical.

philosophiquement [filɔzɔfik'mɑ̃], *adv.* philosophically.

philtre *or* **filtre** [filtr], *n.m.* philtre.

phlébite [fle'bit], *n.f.* phlebitis.

phlegmatique [FLEGMATIQUE].

phobie [fɔ'bi], *n.f.* phobia, morbid dread.

phonétique [fɔne'tik], *a.* phonetic.—*n.f.* phonetics.

phonique [fɔ'nik], *a.* phonic.

phonographe [fɔnɔ'graf], *n.m.* phonograph, gramophone.

phonographie [fɔnɔgra'fi], *n.f.* phonography, sound recording.

phonographique [fɔnɔgra'fik], *a.* phonographic.

phoque [fɔk], *n.m.* (*Zool.*) seal.

phosphate [fɔs'fat], *n.m.* phosphate.

phosphore [fɔs'fɔːr], *n.m.* phosphorus.

phosphorescence [fɔsfɔre'sɑ̃ːs], *n.f.* phosphorescence.

phosphorescent [fɔsfɔre'sɑ̃], *a.* phosphorescent.

phosphoreux [fɔsfɔ'rø], *a.m.* phosphorous.

phosphorique [fɔsfɔ'rik], *a.* phosphoric.

photo [fɔ'to], *n.f. abbr.* [PHOTOGRAPHIE].

photocopie [fɔtokɔ'pi], *n.f.* photocopy, photostat.

photogénique [fɔtoʒe'nik], *a.* photogenic.

photographe [fɔto'graf], *n.* photographer.

photographie [fɔtogra'fi], *n.f.* photography; photograph.

photographier [fɔtogra'fje], *v.t.* to photograph.

photographique [fɔtogra'fik], *a.* photographic; *appareil photographique*, camera.

photogravure [fɔtogra'vyːr], *n.f.* photogravure.

phrase [fraːz], *n.f.* sentence; (*Mus.*) phrase; *phrase toute faite*, commonplace, stock phrase.

phraséologie [frazeɔlɔ'zi], *n.f.* phraseology.

phraser [fra'ze], *v.t.* to express in phrases; (*Mus.*) to phrase.—*v.i.* to phrase.

phraseur [fra'zœːr], *n.m.* (*fem.* **-euse**) (*fam.*) verbose writer *or* talker.

phtisie [fti'zi], *n.f.* phthisis, consumption.

phtisique [fti'zik], *a.* consumptive.—*n.* consumptive person.

physicien [fizi'sjɛ̃], *n.m.* (*fem.* **-enne**) physicist.

physionomie [fizjɔnɔ'mi], *n.f.* physiognomy, countenance, aspect, look.

physionomiste [fizjɔnɔ'mist], *n.* physiognomist.

physiothérapie [fizjotera'pi], *n.f.* (*Med.*) physiotherapy.

physiothérapiste [fizjotera'pist], *n.* physiotherapist.

physique [fi'zik], *a.* physical, material bodily.—*n.f.* physics.—*n.m.* physique, natural constitution; outward appearance.

physiquement [fizik'mɑ̃], *adv.* physically.

piaffer [pja'fe], *v.i.* to paw the ground, to prance (*of horses*).

piaffeur [pja'fœːr], *a.* (*fem.* **-euse**) pawing, prancing.—*n.m.* (*fem.* **-euse**) pawer, prancer.

piailler [pja'je], *v.i.* to cheep (*of small birds*); (*fig.*) to squall; to rant.

piaillerie [pjaj'ri], *n.f.* cheeping; squealing.

piailleur [pja'jœːr], *n.m.* (*fem.* **-euse**) cheeper; squaller.

pianiste [pja'nist], *n.* pianist.

piano [pja'no], *n.m.* piano, pianoforte; *piano à queue*, grand piano.

piaulement [pjol'mɑ̃], *n.m.* whining, puling; cheeping (*of chickens*).

piauler [pjo'le], *v.i.* to cheep (*of chickens etc.*); (*fig.*) to pule, to whine.

pic [pik], *n.m.* pick, pickaxe; gaff; peak (*of a mountain*); woodpecker.

pick-up [pi'kœp], *n.m. inv.* record player.

picoté [piko'te], *a.* pricked, marked.

picotement [pikot'mɑ̃], *n.m.* pricking, tingling.

picoter [piko'te], *v.t.* to cause to tingle; to prick; to peck (*of birds*).

picvert *or* **pivert** [pi'vɛːr], *n.m.* green woodpecker.

pie [pi], *a. inv.* and *n.* piebald (horse).—*n.f.* magpie.

pièce [pjɛs], *n.f.* piece; patch; cask (*of wine etc.*); head (*of cattle, poultry etc.*); apartment, room; piece of ordnance, cannon; (*Theat.*) play; coin; joint (*of meat*).

pied [pje], *n.m.* foot; footing; footprint; track; leg (*of furniture*); stand, rest; stalk (*of plants*).

pied-à-terre [pjeta'tɛːr], *n.m. inv.* occasional lodging.

pied-de-biche [pjed'biʃ], *n.m.* (*pl.* **pieds-de-biche**) bell-pull; (*Surg.*) forceps; nail-clench.

piédestal [pjedɛs'tal], *n.m.* (*pl.* **-aux**) pedestal.

piège [pjɛ:ʒ], *n.m.* trap, snare.
piéger [pje'ʒe], *v.t.* (*conjug. like* CÉDER) to trap (*animals*); (*Mil.*) to set a booby trap.
pie-grièche [pigri'ɛʃ], *n.f.* (*pl.* **pies-grièches**) (*Orn.*) shrike; (*fig.*) shrew.
pierraille [pjɛ'rɑ:j], *n.f.* rubble, ballast.
Pierre [pjɛ:r], *m.* Peter.
pierre [pjɛ:r], *n.f.* stone; (*Path.*) calculus.
pierreries [pjɛr'ri], *n.f. pl.* precious stones, gems.
pierreux [pjɛ'rø], *a.* (*fem.* **-euse**) stony, flinty, gritty, gravelly; calculous.
pierrot [pjɛ'ro], *n.m.* pierrot, merry-andrew; house-sparrow.
piété [pje'te], *n.f.* piety, godliness; affection.
piétinement [pjetin'mɑ̃], *n.m.* stamping, trampling.
piétiner [pjeti'ne], *v.t.* to tread or trample under foot.—*v.i.* to stamp; to paw the ground (*of horses*).
piéton [pje'tɔ̃], *n.m.* (*fem.* **-onne**) pedestrian.
piètre [pjɛtr], *a.* poor, paltry, pitiful.
piètrement [pjetrə'mɑ̃], *adv.* pitifully, wretchedly.
pieu [pjø], *n.m.* (*pl.* **pieux** (1)) stake, pile, post.
pieusement [pjøz'mɑ̃], *adv.* piously, devoutly; obediently; reverently.
pieuvre [pjœ:vr], *n.f.* octopus, poulpe.
pieux (2) [pjø], *a.* (*fem.* **pieuse**) pious, godly.
pigeon [pi'ʒɔ̃], *n.m.* pigeon, dove; (*slang*) dupe, gull.
pigeonneau [piʒɔ'no], *n.m.* (*pl.* **-eaux**) young pigeon, squab.
pigeonnier [piʒɔ'nje], *n.m.* pigeon-house, dove-cot.
pigment [pig'mɑ̃], *n.m.* (*Anat.*) pigment.
pignon [pi'ɲɔ̃], *n.m.* gable end; pinion; kernel (*of fir-cone*).
pilaire [pi'lɛ:r], *a.* pilous, pilose.
pilastre [pi'lastr], *n.m.* (*Arch.*) pilaster.
pilchard [pil'ʃa:r], *n.m.* pilchard.
pile [pil], *n.f.* pile, heap; pier (*of a bridge etc.*); mole (*masonry*); (*Elec.*) battery; reverse (*of coins*); **pile atomique**, atomic pile.
piler [pi'le], *v.t.* to pound, to crush, to powder.
pileur [pi'lœ:r], *n.m.* (*fem.* **-euse** (1)) pounder, beater.
pileux [pi'lø], *a.* (*fem.* **-euse** (2)) pilous, hairy.
pilier [pi'lje], *n.m.* pillar, column, post; (*fig.*) supporter, prop.
pillage [pi'ja:ʒ], *n.m.* pillage, plunder; (*fig.*) pilfering.
pillard [pi'ja:r], *a.* plundering; predatory.—*n.m.* (*fem.* **-e**) pillager, plunderer.
piller [pi'je], *v.t.* to pillage, to plunder; to ransack; to pilfer.
pillerie [pij'ri], *n.f.* pillage plunder; extortion.
pilleur [pi'jœ:r], *n.m.* (*fem.* **-euse**) pillager, plunderer, pilferer.
pilon [pi'lɔ̃], *n.m.* pestle; rammer, stamper; wooden leg.
pilonnage [pilɔ'na:ʒ], *n.m.* ramming, pounding, stamping, milling.
pilonner [pilɔ'ne], *v.t.* to ram, to pound, to mill; to stamp (*ore*).
pilori [pilɔ'ri], *n.m.* pillory.
pilorier [pilɔ'rje], *v.t.* to pillory.
pilotage [pilɔ'ta:ʒ], *n.m.* (*Civ. Eng.*) pile-driving; (*Naut.*) piloting.
pilote [pi'lɔt], *n.m.* pilot; guide; pilot-fish.

piloter [pilɔ'te], *v.t.* to pile, to drive piles into; (*Naut., Av.*) to pilot; (*fig.*) to guide.
pilotis [pilɔ'ti], *n.m.* pilework.
pilule [pi'lyl], *n.f.* pill.
pimbêche [pɛ̃'bɛʃ], *n.f.* uppish and impertinent woman.
piment [pi'mɑ̃], *n.m.* pimento, allspice.
pimenter [pimɑ̃'te], *v.t.* to flavour with pimento.
pimpant [pɛ̃'pɑ̃], *a.* natty, spruce, smart.
pin [pɛ̃], *n.m.* pine-tree; *pomme de pin*, fir-cone.
pinacle [pi'nakl], *n.m.* pinnacle.
pince [pɛ̃:s], *n.f.* pinching, nipping; hold, grip; pincers, pliers, forceps; tongs, clip; crowbar (*lever*); toe (*of a horse's foot*); claw (*of a lobster etc.*).
pincé [pɛ̃'se], *a.* affected, stiff, prim.
pinceau [pɛ̃'so], *n.m.* (*pl.* **-eaux**) paint-brush.
pincée [pɛ̃'se], *n.f.* pinch (*of snuff, salt etc.*).
pince-nez [pɛ̃s'ne], *n.m. inv.* pince-nez, (*folding*) eye-glasses.
pince-notes [pɛ̃s'nɔt], *n.m. inv.* paper-clip.
pincer [pɛ̃'se], *v.t.* (*conjug. like* COMMENCER) to pinch, to nip; to grip; to bite (*of cold etc.*); to pluck (*a musical instrument*); (*Naut.*) to hug (*the wind*).
pince-sans-rire [pɛ̃ssɑ̃'ri:r], *n.m. inv.* sly or malicious person, dry joker.
pincette(s) [pɛ̃'sɛt], *n.f.* (*pl.*) tongs; tweezers, nippers.
pinçure [pɛ̃'sy:r], *n.f.* pinching; crease in cloth.
pingouin [pɛ̃'gwɛ̃], *n.m.* auk.
pingre [pɛ̃:gr], *a.* avaricious, stingy.—*n.* miser, skinflint.
pinson [pɛ̃'sɔ̃], *n.m.* finch, chaffinch.
pintade [pɛ̃'tad], *n.f.* guinea-fowl.
piochage [pjɔ'ʃa:ʒ], *n.m.* digging; (*fig.*) working, fagging.
pioche [pjɔʃ], *n.f.* pickaxe.
piocher [pjɔ'ʃe], *v.t.* to dig.—*v.i.* to dig; (*fig.*) to fag, to work hard, to swot.
piocheur [pjɔ'ʃœ:r], *n.m.* (*fem.* **-euse**) digger; (*slang*) hard-working student, swotter.—*n.f.* (**-euse**) (*Civ. Eng.*) excavator.
piolet [pjɔ'lɛ], *n.m.* piolet, ice-axe.
pion [pjɔ̃], *n.m.* pawn (*at chess*); piece (*at draughts*); (*Sch. slang*) usher.
pionnier [pjɔ'nje], *n.m.* pioneer.
pipe [pip], *n.f.* pipe; tobacco-pipe; pipe (*cask*).
pipeau [pi'po], *n.m.* (*pl.* **-eaux**) pipe, reed-pipe; bird-call; limed twig, snare.
pipée [pi'pe], *n.f.* bird-catching (*with a bird-call*); (*fig.*) deceit, trickery.
piper [pi'pe], *v.t.* to catch (*birds*) with a bird-call etc.; (*fig.*) to trick, to decoy.
pipeur [pi'pœ:r], *a.* (*fem.* **-euse**) cheating, deceitful.—*n.m.* (*fem.* **-euse**) one who decoys birds; cheat, trickster (*at play*).
piquant [pi'kɑ̃], *a.* prickling, stinging; pungent; biting; cutting, keen; piquant, pointed; smart.—*n.m.* prickle; quill (*of porcupine*); pungency, point, piquancy.
pique [pik], *n.f.* pike (*weapon*); pique, spite, quarrel.—*n.m.* (*Cards*) spade(s).
piqué [pi'ke], *a.* quilted, pinked; worm-eaten; sour (*wine*).—*n.m.* quilting; piqué; nose-dive; *bombardement en piqué*, dive-bombing.

pique-nique [pik′nik], *n.m.* (*pl.* **-niques**) picnic.

piquer [pi′ke], *v.t.* to prick; to sting; to goad, to spur; to puncture; to bite (*of insects*); to quilt; to lard; to prick off; to excite, to stimulate; to nettle, to rouse; (*Med.*) to inject.—*v.i.* to turn sour (*of wine etc.*). **se piquer**, *v.r.* to prick oneself; to be offended, to be piqued; to pride oneself; to turn sour.

piquet [pi′kɛ], *n.m.* peg, stake; (*Mil.*) picket; piquet (*card game*).

piqueter [pik′te], *v.t.* (*conjug. like* APPELER) to mark out with stakes *or* pegs; to mark with little points.

piquette [pi′kɛt], *n.f.*, **piqueton** [pik′tɔ̃], *n.m.* thin wine.

piqueur (1) [pi′kœːr], *n.m.* outrider; overseer (*of workmen*); stud-groom; huntsman.

piqueur (2) [pi′kœːr], *n.m.* (*fem.* **-euse**) stitcher.

piqûre [pi′kyːr], *n.f.* prick; sting; bite; puncture; (*Needlework*) quilting, stitching; (*Med.*) injection, shot.

pirate [pi′rat], *n.m.* pirate; (*fig.*) extortioner, plagiarist.

pirater [pira′te], *v.i.* to commit piracy.

piraterie [pira′tri], *n.f.* piracy; act of piracy *or* plagiarism.

pire [piːr], *a.* and *n.m.* worse; the worst.

pirogue [pi′rɔg], *n.f.* pirogue, dug-out, canoe.

pirouette [pi′rwɛt], *n.f.* pirouette, whirligig.

pirouetter [pirwɛ′te], *v.i.* to pirouette, to whirl about.

pis (1) [pi], *n.m.* udder, dug (*of cow*).

pis (2) [pi], *adv.* and *n.m.* worse.—*n.m. inv.* **pis aller**, the worst, last resource, makeshift.

pisciculture [pisikyl′tyːr], *n.f.* fish-culture.

piscine [pi′sin], *n.f.* piscina; swimming-pool.

pissenlit [pisɑ̃′li], *n.m.* dandelion.

pistache [pis′taʃ], *n.f.* pistachio, pistachionut.

pistachier [pista′ʃje], *n.m.* pistachio-tree.

piste [pist], *n.f.* track, footprint, trail, scent; course, race-course.

pistolet [pisto′lɛ], *n.m.* pistol; spray gun.

piston [pis′tɔ̃], *n.m.* piston; sucker (*of a pump*); press button; (*Mus.*) cornet.

pitance [pi′tɑ̃ːs], *n.f.* pittance; allowance (*of food*), dole.

piteusement [pitøz′mɑ̃], *adv.* piteously, woefully, sadly.

piteux [pi′tø], *a.* (*fem.* **-euse**) piteous, pitiable, woeful.

pitié [pi′tje], *n.f.* pity, compassion; object of pity.

piton [pi′tɔ̃], *n.m.* eye-bolt, screw-ring, ringbolt; peak (*of mountain*).

pitoyable [pitwa′jabl], *a.* pitiful, piteous, paltry.

pitoyablement [pitwajablə′mɑ̃], *adv.* pitifully.

pittoresque [pitɔ′rɛsk], *a.* picturesque; graphic.—*n.m.* the picturesque, picturesqueness.

pittoresquement [pitɔrɛsk′mɑ̃], *adv.* picturesquely.

pivert [PICVERT].

pivoine [pi′vwan], *n.m.* bullfinch.—*n.f.* peony.

pivot [pi′vo], *n.m.* pivot, pin spindle, hinge.

pivoter [pivo′te], *v.i.* to pivot, to turn on a pivot, to revolve, to turn.

placage [pla′kaːʒ], *n.m.* plating (*metal-work*); veneering (*of wood*); (*Lit.*) patchwork.

placard [pla′kaːr], *n.m.* placard, poster, bill; (*Print.*) slip; cupboard (*in a wall*).

placarder [plakar′de], *v.t.* to placard, to post up.

place [plas], *n.f.* place; room; seat; stead; post, job, situation; town; public square; **faire place**, to make room; **retenir des places**, to book seats; **sur place**, on the spot.

placement [plas′mɑ̃], *n.m.* placing; sale; employment; investment.

placer [pla′se], *v.t.* (*conjug. like* COMMENCER) to place, to put; to find a place *or* situation for; to invest; to deposit; to sell. **se placer**, *v.r.* to place oneself; to find a job.

placet [pla′sɛ], *n.m.* petition, address.

placide [pla′sid], *a.* placid, calm.

placidement [plasid′mɑ̃], *adv.* placidly, calmly.

placidité [plasidi′te], *n.f.* placidity.

plafond [pla′fɔ̃], *n.m.* ceiling.

plafonnage [plafɔ′naːʒ], *n.m.* ceiling (*action, work*); (*Av.*) visibility.

plafonner [plafɔ′ne], *v.t.* to ceil, to put a ceiling to.—*v.i.* to reach the highest point (*of prices etc.*); (*Av.*) to fly at the ceiling, the (*Motor.*) to travel at maximum speed.

plafonneur [plafɔ′nœːr], *n.m.* plasterer.

plafonnier [plafɔ′nje], *n.m.* ceiling-light.

plage [plaːʒ], *n.f.* beach, shore; sea-side resort.

plagiaire [pla′ʒjɛːr], *a.* and *n.* plagiarist.

plagiat [pla′ʒja], *n.m.* plagiarism.

plagier [pla′ʒje], *v.t.* to plagiarize.

plaid [plɛd], *n.m.* plaid, travelling rug.

plaidant [plɛ′dɑ̃], *a.* pleading, litigant.

plaider [plɛ′de], *v.t.* to defend; to allege.—*v.i.* to go to law, to litigate; to plead, to argue.

plaideur [plɛ′dœːr], *n.m.* (*fem.* **-euse**) litigant, suitor.

plaidoirie [plɛdwa′ri], *n.f.* pleading; counsel's speech.

plaidoyer [plɛdwa′je], *n.m.* speech for the defence, counsel's address.

plaie [plɛ], *n.f.* wound; sore; (*fig.*) plague; evil.

plaignant [plɛ′nɑ̃], *a.* complaining; *la partie plaignante*, the plaintiff.—*n.m.* (*fem.* **-e**) plaintiff, prosecutor.

plain [plɛ̃], *a.* plain, even, flat, level.

plaindre [plɛ̃ːdr], *v.t. irr.* (*conjug. like* CRAINDRE) to pity, to be sorry for. **se plaindre**, *v.r.* to complain; to grumble.

plaine [plɛn], *n.f.* plain; flat country.

plain-pied (de) [dəplɛ̃′pje], *adv. phr.* on a level; (*fig.*) without difficulty.

plainte [plɛ̃ːt], *n.f.* complaint, plaint; lamentation, wail; plaint at law.

plaintif [plɛ̃′tif], *a.* (*fem.* **-tive**) plaintive, complaining; querulous.

plaintivement [plɛ̃tiv′mɑ̃], *adv.* dolefully, querulously.

plaire [plɛːr], *v.i. irr.* to please; to be pleasant *or* agreeable (*à*); *s'il vous plaît*, please. **se plaire**, *v.r.* to delight, to take pleasure; to like.

plaisamment [plɛza'mã], *adv.* humorously, amusingly; ludicrously.

plaisance [plɛ'zã:s], *n.f.* pleasure.

plaisant [plɛ'zã], *a.* humorous, amusing, funny; (*iron.*) odd, strange.—*n.m.* jester, wag; the funny side; *un mauvais plaisant*, a practical joker.

plaisanter [plɛzã'te], *v.t.* to chaff, to banter. —*v.i.* to jest, to joke.

plaisanterie [plɛzã'tri], *n.f.* jest, joke, witticism; mockery, trifle.

plaisir [plɛ'zi:r], *n.m.* pleasure; delight; diversion, entertainment; favour.

plan [plã], *a.* even, level, flat.—*n.m.* plane; plan; drawing; scheme, project; (*Paint.*) ground.

planche [plã:ʃ], *n.f.* board, plank; shelf; (*Engr.*) plate; (*Gard.*) bed, border.

planchéiage [plãʃe'ja:ʒ], *n.m.* boarding, planking; flooring.

planchéier [plãʃe'je], *v.t.* to board over, to floor.

plancher [plã'ʃe], *n.m.* floor, deck planking.

planchette [plã'ʃɛt], *n.f.* small board; (*Math.*) plane-table.

plancton [plãk'tõ], *n.m.* plankton.

plane [plan], *n.f.* drawing-knife; planisher.

plané [pla'ne], *a.* soaring, gliding; *un vol plané*, gliding descent.

planer [pla'ne], *v.t.* to make smooth, to plane. —*v.i.* to hover, to soar; to look down (*on*) (*sur*); (*Av.*) to glide.

planétaire [plane'tɛ:r], *a.* planetary.

planète [pla'nɛ:t], *n.f.* planet.

planeur [pla'nœ:r], *n.m.* planisher; glider (*aeroplane*).

planeuse [pla'nø:z], *n.f.* planing-machine.

planification [planifika'sjõ], *n.f.* (*Polit. Econ.*) planning.

planifier [plani'fje], *v.t.* to plan.

plant [plã], *n.m.* young plant, seedling; slip; sapling; plantation.

plantation [plãta'sjõ], *n.f.* planting; plantation.

plante [plã:t], *n.f.* plant; *la plante du pied*, (*Anat.*) the sole of the foot.

planter [plã'te], *v.t.* to plant; to set, to drive in; to set up, to erect. **se planter**, *v.r.* to station oneself.

planteur [plã'tœ:r], *n.m.* planter.

planteuse [plã'tø:z], *n.f.* potato-planting machine.

plantoir [plã'twa:r], *n.m.* dibble.

planton [plã'tõ], *n.m.* (*Mil.*) orderly.

plantureusement [plãtyrøz'mã], *adv.* copiously, abundantly, luxuriantly.

plantureux [plãty'rø], *a.* (*fem.* **-euse**) plentiful, copious; fertile.

plaquage [pla'ka:ʒ], *n.m.* (*Ftb.*) rugby tackle.

plaque [plak], *n.f.* plate, slab; plaque; badge, star; *plaque tournante*, (*Rail.*) turn-table.

plaqué [pla'ke], *a.* plated, covered with.

plaquer [pla'ke], *v.t.* to plate (*metal*); to veneer (*wood*); (*Ftb.*) to tackle.

plaquette [pla'kɛt], *n.f.* small thin book; small plate; thin slab.

plasticité [plastisi'te], *n.f.* plasticity.

plastique [plas'tik], *a.* plastic.—*n.m.* plastics. —*n.f.* plastic art; figure.

plastron [plas'trõ], *n.m.* breast-plate; fencing-pad; shirt-front.

plastronner [plastrɔ'ne], *v.i.* to strut, to swagger.

plat (1) [pla], *a.* flat; level; regular, (*fig.*) dull, insipid.—*n.m.* flat part, side; flat racing.

plat (2) [pla], *n.m.* dish (*the vessel and the food*), (*Naut.*) mess; course (*of a meal*).

platane [pla'tan], *n.m.* plane-tree, platan.

plateau [pla'to], *n.m.* (*pl.* **-eaux**) scale (*of a balance*); tray; table-land, plateau; turn-table (*of gramophone*).

plate-bande [plat'bã:d], *n.f.* (*pl.* **plates-bandes**) border, flower-bed.

plate-forme [plat'form], *n.f.* (*pl.* **plates-formes**) platform (*of a bus etc.*).

platement [plat'mã], *adv.* flatly, dully.

platine [pla'tin], *n.f.* lock (*of fire-arms*); plate (*of lock, watch, machine*); platen (*of type-writer*).—*n.m.* platinum.

platiné [plati'ne], *a.* platinum plated; platinum coloured (*of hair*).

platitude [plati'tyd], *n.f.* platitude; flatness, dullness.

Platon [pla'tõ], *m.* Plato.

platonique [plato'nik], *a.* Platonic.

platonisme [plato'nism], *n.m.* Platonism.

plâtrage [pla'tra:ʒ], *n.m.* plaster-work, plastering.

plâtras [pla'tra], *n.m.* debris of plaster-work; rubbish.

plâtre [pla:tr], *n.m.* plaster.

plâtré [pla'tre], *a.* plastered.

plâtrer [pla'tre], *v.t.* to plaster; (*fig.*) to patch up, to disguise.

plâtreux [pla'trø], *a.* (*fem.* **-euse**) chalky.

plâtrier [platri'je], *n.m.* plasterer.

plâtrière [platri'jɛ:r], *n.f.* chalk pit; plaster-kiln.

plâtroir [pla'trwa:r], *n.m.* plasterer's trowel.

plausibilité [plozibili'te], *n.f.* plausibility.

plausible [plo'zibl], *a.* plausible (*never of person*).

plausiblement [plozibl∂'mã], *adv.* plausibly.

plèbe [plɛb], *n.f.* common people.

plébéien [plebe'jɛ̃], *a.* and *n.m.* (*fem.* **-enne**) plebeian.

plébiscite [plebi'sit], *n.m.* plebiscite.

plein [plɛ̃], *a.* full; fraught (*de*); filled, replete; entire, whole; thorough; copious; solid; *en plein air*, in the open air; *en plein hiver*, in the heart of winter.—*n.m.* full part; plenum.—*adv.* full.

pleinement [plɛn'mã], *adv.* fully, entirely, thoroughly.

plénier [ple'nje], *a.* (*fem.* **-ière**) plenary; full, complete.

plénipotentiaire [plenipotã'sjɛ:r], *a.* and *n.m.* plenipotentiary.

plénitude [pleni'tyd], *n.f.* plenitude, fullness.

pleur [plœ:r], *n.m.* (*poet.*) tear; lament.

pleurard [plœ'ra:r], *a.* whimpering, tearful.— *n.m.* (*fem.* **-e**) whimperer, blubberer.

pleurer [plœ're], *v.t.* to weep, to bewail, to mourn, to deplore the loss of.—*v.i.* to weep, to cry, to shed tears; to mourn; to run (*of the eyes*); to drip (*of a tap*).

pleurésie [plœre'zi], *n.f.* pleurisy.

pleureur [plœ'rœ:r], *a.* (*fem.* **-euse**) whimpering, tearful; *saule pleureur*, weeping willow.—*n.m.* (*fem.* **-euse**) whimperer, weeper.—*n.f.* (**-euse**) paid mourner.

pleurnichement

pleurnichement [plœrniʃ'mã], *n.m.* whimpering, snivelling.

pleurnicher [plœrni'ʃe], *v.i.* to whimper, to snivel.

pleurnicheur [plœrni'ʃœːr], *a.* (*fem.* **-euse**) whimpering, snivelling.—*n.m.* (*fem.* **-euse**) whimperer, sniveller.

pleutre [pløːtr], *n.m.* contemptible fellow.

pleuvoir [plœ'vwaːr], *v. impers. irr.* to rain; *il pleut à verse* or *à seaux*, it is pouring in buckets; *pleuvoir des hallebardes*, to rain cats and dogs.

pli [pli], *n.m.* fold; wrinkle; coil; bend; undulation, depression; cover, envelope; habit; (*Cards*) trick; *mise en pli*, setting (*the hair*); *sous pli recommandé*, in a registered envelope; *un faux pli*, a crease.

pliable [pli'jabl], *a.* pliable, flexible, supple.

pliage [pli'jaːʒ], **pliement** [pli'mã], *n.m.* folding.

pliant [pli'jã], *a.* pliant, docile; folding, collapsible.—*n.m.* folding-chair, deck-chair.

plie [pli], *n.f.* plaice.

plier [pli'je], *v.t.* to fold, to fold up; to bend.—*v.i.* to bend, to bow; to give way. **se plier**, *v.r.* to bow, to bend, to yield.

plieur [pli'jœːr], *n.m.* (*fem.* **-euse**) folder.—*n.f.* (**-euse**) folding-machine.

plinthe [plɛ̃ːt], *n.f.* plinth; skirting-board.

plissage [pli'saːʒ], *n.m.* pleating, kilting.

plissé [pli'se], *a.* kilted, pleated.—*n.m.* kilting, pleats.

plissement [plis'mã], *n.m.* folding, doubling over; crumpling.

plisser [pli'se], *v.t.* to fold; to crumple, to wrinkle; to pleat.—*v.i.* and **se plisser**, *v.r.* to be wrinkled, to pucker.

plissure [pli'syːr], *n.f.* pleating; pleats.

ploiement [plwa'mã], *n.m.* folding, bending.

plomb [plɔ̃], *n.m.* lead; bullet, shot; plumbline; sinker; custom-house seal; fuse; *à plomb*, vertically.

plombage [plɔ̃'baːʒ], *n.m.* leading, plumbing; filling (*of teeth*).

plombagine [plɔ̃ba'ʒin], *n.f.* plumbago, blacklead, graphite.

plomber [plɔ̃'be], *v.t.* to cover with lead, to seal; to fill (*a tooth*); to plumb.

plomberie [plɔ̃'bri], *n.f.* plumber's shop; plumbing; lead-making; lead-works.

plombier [plɔ̃'bje], *n.m.* lead-worker; plumber.

plongée [plɔ̃'ʒe], *n.f.* slope; dive.

plongeoir [plɔ̃'ʒwaːr], *n.m.* diving-board.

plongeon [plɔ̃'ʒɔ̃], *n.m.* plunge, dive; (*Orn.*) diver.

plonger [plɔ̃'ʒe], *v.t.* (*conjug. like* MANGER) to plunge, to dip, to immerse; to throw, to involve.—*v.i.* to dive, to plunge; to submerge (*of submarine*); to pitch (*of ships*). **se plonger**, *v.r.* to be plunged; to immerse oneself (*in*).

plongeur [plɔ̃'ʒœːr], *a.* (*fem.* **-euse**) plunging, diving (*bird*).—*n.m.* (*fem.* **-euse**) diver; dish-washer (*in hotels etc.*).

ploutocrate [pluto'krat], *n.m.* plutocrat.

ploutocratie [plutokra'si], *n.f.* plutocracy.

ploutocratique [plutokra'tik], *a.* plutocratic.

ployable [plwa'jabl], *a.* pliable, flexible.

ployer [plwa'je], *v.t.* (*conjug. like* EMPLOYER) to bend; to fold up.—*v.i.* and **se ployer**, to bend, to be folded; to yield, to give way.

pluie [plɥi], *n.f.* rain; (*fig.*) shower.

plumage [ply'maːʒ], *n.m.* plumage, feathers.

plumassier [plyma'sje], *n.m.* (*fem.* **-ière**) feather merchant *or* dresser.

plume [plym], *n.f.* feather; plume; quill, pen; nib.

plumeau [ply'mo], *n.m.* (*pl.* **-eaux**) featherbroom; feather-duster.

plumée [ply'me], *n.f.* penful (*of ink*); plucking (*of poultry*).

plumer [ply'me], *v.t.* to pluck, to plume; (*fig.*) to fleece.

plumet [ply'mɛ], *n.m.* plume.

plumetis [plym'ti], *n.m.* feather-stitch.

plumier [ply'mje], *n.m.* pen-box, pen-tray.

plupart [ply'paːr], *n.f.* *la plupart*, most, most part, the majority (*de*), most people.

pluralité [plyrali'te], *n.f.* plurality; pluralism.

pluriel [ply'rjɛl], *a.* (*fem.* **-elle**) plural.—*n.m.* plural.

plus [ply], *adv.* more, -er (*que*, than); -est, the most; also, moreover, further, besides; (*with ne*) no more, no longer, never again; *de plus*, besides, moreover.—*n.m.* the most, the maximum; the more.

plusieurs [ply'zjœːr], *a. pl.* and *pron. indef.* several, some.

plus-que-parfait [plyskəpar'fɛ], *n.m.* pluperfect.

plutonium [plytɔ'njɔm], *n.m.* plutonium.

plutôt [ply'to], *adv.* rather, sooner (*que*).

pluvial [ply'vjal], *a.* (*m. pl.* **-aux**) pluvial, of rain, rainy.

pluvier [ply'vje], *n.m.* plover.

pluvieux [ply'vjø], *a.* (*fem.* **-euse**) rainy, wet, pluvious.

pluviomètre [plyvjo'mɛtr], *n.m.* rain-gauge.

pluviosité [plyvjozi'te], *n.f.* rainfall.

pneu [pnø], *n.m.* (*pl.* **pneus**) *fam. abbr.* [PNEUMATIQUE].

pneumatique [pnøma'tik], *a.* pneumatic.—*n.m.* tyre; express letter (*in Paris*).—*n.f.* pneumatics.

pneumonie [pnømɔ'ni], *n.f.* pneumonia.

pochade [po'ʃad], *n.f.* rough sketch; (*fig.*) hurried piece of writing etc.

poche [poʃ], *n.f.* pocket; pouch; sack, bag; wrinkle (*in clothes*); crop (*of a bird*).

pocher [po'ʃe], *v.t.* to poach (*eggs*); to give a black eye to; to stencil; to make a rough sketch of.—*v.i.* to become baggy, to bag.

pochet [po'ʃe], *n.m.* nosebag (*of horse*).

pochette [po'ʃɛt], *n.f.* small pocket; small net; folder, jacket (*containers*); fancy handkerchief.

pochoir [po'ʃwaːr], *n.m.* stencil.

podagre [po'dagr], *a.* gouty.—*n.f.* gout.—*n.* gouty person.

podomètre [pɔdo'mɛtr], *n.m.* pedometer.

poêle [pwaːl], *n.f.* frying-pan.—*n.m.* stove; pall (*at a funeral*).

poêlée [pwa'le], *n.f.* panful.

poêlon [pwa'lɔ̃], *n.m.* small saucepan.

poème [po'ɛm], *n.m.* poem.

poésie [poe'zi], *n.f.* poetry, verse; poem.

poète [po'ɛt], *n.m.* poet.

poétesse [poe'tɛs], *n.f.* poetess.

poétique [poe'tik], *a.* poetical.—*n.f.* poetics.

poétiquement [poetik'mã], *adv.* poetically.

248

polisson

poétiser [pɔeti'ze], *v.t.* to make poetical, to idealize, to poeticize.

pogrom [pɔ'grɔm], *n.m.* pogrom.

poids [pwɑ], *n.m. inv.* weight; heaviness; gravity; load; (*fig.*) importance, consequence; *les poids lourds,* heavy vehicles.

poignant [pwa'nɑ̃], *a.* poignant; sharp, acute, keen.

poignard [pwa'naːr], *n.m.* dagger.

poignarder [pwaɲar'de], *v.t.* to stab; to knife; (*fig.*) to grieve to the heart.

poigne [pwaɲ], *n.f.* (*colloq.*) grasp, grip; (*fig.*) strength.

poignée [pwa'ɲe], *n.f.* handful; handle, hilt; shake (*of the hand*).

poignet [pwa'ɲɛ], *n.m.* wrist; wristband, cuff.

poil [pwal], *n.m.* hair (*of animals*); hair (*of persons, other than that of the head*); (*fig.*) beard; nap (*of cloth, of hats etc.*); *à contre-poil,* against the grain.

poilu [pwa'ly], *a.* hairy, shaggy.

poinçon [pwɛ̃'sɔ̃], *n.m.* punch; point, stiletto; awl, stamp, die.

poinçonnage [pwɛ̃sɔ'naːʒ], **poinçonnement** [pwɛ̃sɔn'mɑ̃], *n.m.* stamping, punching.

poinçonner [pwɛ̃sɔ'ne], *v.t.* to punch, to stamp.

poinçonneuse [pwɛ̃sɔ'nøːz], *n.f.* stamping-*or* punching-machine.

poindre [pwɛ̃ːdr], *v.i. irr.* to dawn, to break; (*fig.*) to appear.

poing [pwɛ̃], *n.m.* fist, hand; (*fig.*) force, brute strength; (*fig.*) *dormir à poings fermés,* to sleep like a log.

point [pwɛ̃], *adv.* (*used with negative*) no, not at all; none (*more emphatic than* pas).—*n.m.* point; speck; dot, mark; (*Sch.*) mark; full stop; hole (*of a strap etc.*); (*Needlework*) stitch; matter, question; particular; state, case; degree; place; *à point,* in the nick of time; well done (*of meat*); *en tout point,* in every respect; *sur ce* or *en ce point,* on that score.

pointage [pwɛ̃'taːʒ], **pointement** [pwɛ̃t'mɑ̃], *n.m.* pointing, levelling (*of guns*); checking; scrutiny (*of votes*), tally.

pointe [pwɛ̃ːt], *n.f.* point (*sharp end*); tip, head (*of an arrow etc.*); nose (*of a bullet*); cape; peak; etching-needle; nail, tack; (*Print.*) bodkin; (*fig.*) dash, flavour; pungency, sharpness; witticism.

pointement [POINTAGE].

pointer [pwɛ̃'te], *v.t.* to point, to aim (*a gun etc.*); to pierce, to stab; to prick; to mark; to tally, to scrutinize (*votes*); to prick up (*ears etc.*); to sharpen.—*v.i.* to point; to spring, to soar; to rear; to sprout.

pointeur [pwɛ̃'tœːr], *n.m.* (*fem.* **-euse**) pointer, marker, checker; (*Artill.*) gun-layer.

pointillage [pwɛ̃ti'jaːʒ], **pointillement** [pwɛ̃tij'mɑ̃], *n.m.* dotting, stippling; dotted line.

pointillé [pwɛ̃ti'je], *n.m.* stipple drawing *or* engraving; dotted line.

pointiller [pwɛ̃ti'je], *v.t.* to dot, to stipple; (*fig.*) to tease.—*v.i.* to bicker, to cavil.

pointilleux [pwɛ̃ti'jø], *a.* (*fem.* **-euse**) cavilling, captious; fastidious.

pointu [pwɛ̃'ty], *a.* pointed, sharp; (*fig.*) subtle, captious.

pointure [pwɛ̃'tyːr], *n.f.* (*Print.*) point; size, number (*of shoes, gloves etc.*).

poire [pwaːr], *n.f.* pear; bulb (*rubber*).

poiré [pwa're], *n.m.* perry.

poireau [pwa'ro], **porreau** [pɔ'ro], *n.m.* (*pl.* **-eaux**) leek; wart.

poirée [pwa're], *n.f.* white beet.

poirier [pwa'rje], *n.m.* pear-tree.

pois [pwa], *n.m. inv.* pea, peas.

poison [pwa'zɔ̃], *n.m.* poison.

poissard [pwa'saːr], *a.* vulgar, low.

poisser [pwa'se], *v.t.* to pitch; to make sticky.

poisseux [pwa'sø], *a.* (*fem.* **-euse**) pitchy, gluey, sticky.

poisson [pwa'sɔ̃], *n.m.* fish; *poisson d'avril,* April fool.

poissonnerie [pwasɔn'ri], *n.f.* fishmarket; fish-shop.

poissonneux [pwasɔ'nø], *a.* (*fem.* **-euse**) abounding in fish.

poissonnier [pwasɔ'nje], *n.m.* (*fem.* **-ière**) fishmonger, fishwife.—*n.f.* (**-ière**) fishkettle.

poitrail [pwa'traːj], *n.m.* breast (*of a horse*); breast-piece (*of harness*).

poitrinaire [pwatri'nɛːr], *a. and n.* consumptive.

poitrine [pwa'trin], *n.f.* chest, breast; breasts; lungs; brisket.

poivrade [pwa'vrad], *n.f.* pepper-sauce.

poivre [pwaːvr], *n.m.* pepper.

poivrer [pwa'vre], *v.t.* to pepper.

poivrier [pwavri'je], *n.m.* pepper-plant; pepper-box.

poivrière [pwavri'jɛːr], *n.f.* pepper-plantation; (*Fort.*) corner turret; pepper-box.

poix [pwa], *n.f.* pitch; shoemakers' wax.

polaire [pɔ'lɛːr], *a.* polar.

polariser [pɔlari'ze], *v.t.* to polarize.

pôle [poːl], *n.m.* (*Astron., Geog.*) pole.

polémique [pɔle'mik], *a.* polemical.—*n.f.* polemics, controversy.

poli [pɔ'li], *a.* polished, glossy, sleek; polite, civil; refined.—*n.m.* polish, finish, gloss.

police [pɔ'lis], *n.f.* police; police-regulations; insurance policy; *agent de police,* police-constable.

policer [pɔli'se], *v.t.* (*conjug. like* COMMENCER) to establish law and order in; to civilize, to polish, to refine.

polichinelle [pɔliʃi'nɛl], *n.m.* Punch; buffoon; Punch and Judy show.

policier [pɔli'sje], *a.* (*fem.* **-ière**) pertaining to the police; *roman policier,* detective story.—*n.m.* policeman; detective.

policlinique [pɔlikli'nik], *n.f.* out-patients' department.

poliment [pɔli'mɑ̃], *adv.* politely.

poliomyélite [pɔljomje'lit], *n.f.* poliomyelitis.

polir [pɔ'liːr], *v.t.* to polish, to burnish; (*fig.*) to civilize, to refine. **se polir,** *v.r.* to become polished; to become refined.

polissage [pɔli'saːʒ], **polissement** [pɔlis'mɑ̃], *n.m.* polishing, finishing.

polisseur [pɔlisœːr], *n.m.* (*fem.* **-euse**) polisher.

polissoir [pɔli'swaːr], *n.m.* polisher (*tool*).

polisson [pɔli'sɔ̃], *a.* (*fem.* **-onne**) loose, naughty, licentious, smutty.—*n.m.* (*fem.* **-onne**) mischievous child, scamp; loose person.

249

polissonner [pɔlisɔ'ne], *v.i.* to run about the streets (*of children*).
polissonnerie [pɔlisɔn'ri], *n.f.* smutty joke, lewd act.
polissure [pɔli'syːr], *n.f.* polishing.
politesse [pɔli'tɛs], *n.f.* politeness, civility, polite attention; compliment.
politicien [pɔliti'sjɛ̃], *n.m.* (*fem.* **-enne**) (*usu. pej.*) politician.
politique [pɔli'tik], *a.* political; (*fig.*) politic, prudent, wise.—*n.f.* politics; policy, discretion.—*n.m.* politician, statesman.
politiquement [pɔlitik'mɑ̃], *adv.* politically; (*fig.*) shrewdly.
polka [pɔl'ka], *n.f.* polka.
pollen [pɔl'lɛn], *n.m.* pollen.
pollinisation [pɔlliniza'sjɔ̃], *n.f.* pollinization.
polluer [pɔl'lɥe], *v.t.* to pollute; to defile; to profane.
pollution [pɔly'sjɔ̃], *n.f.* pollution; profanation.
polo [pɔ'lo], *n.m.* polo.
Pologne [pɔ'lɔɲ], **la**, *f.* Poland.
polonais [pɔlɔ'nɛ], *a.* Polish.—*n.m.* Polish (*language*); (**Polonais**, *fem.* **-aise**) Pole.—*n.f.* (**-aise**) Polonaise (*dress, dance, tune*).
poltron [pɔl'trɔ̃], *a.* (*fem.* **-onne**) cowardly, chicken-hearted.— *n.m.* (*fem.* **-onne**) coward, poltroon.
poltronnerie [pɔltrɔn'ri], *n.f.* cowardice, poltroonery.
polycopier [pɔlikɔ'pje], *v.t.* to cyclostyle.
polygamie [pɔliga'mi], *n.f.* polygamy.
polyglotte [pɔli'glɔt], *a.* and *n.* polyglot.
polytechnique [pɔlitɛk'nik], *a.* polytechnic.
pommade [pɔ'mad], *n.f.* pomade; ointment.
pomme [pɔm], *n.f.* apple; ball, knob; head (*of a cabbage, lettuce, walking-stick etc.*); (*pop.*) head, nut; *pomme de pin*, fir-cone; *pomme de terre*, potato.
pommé [pɔ'me], *a.* grown to a round head; (*colloq.*) complete, downright.
pommeau [pɔ'mo], *n.m.* (*pl.* **-eaux**) pommel (*of a saddle, sword etc.*); head, knob.
pommelé [pɔm'le], *a.* dappled, mottled.
pommeler (se) [səpɔm'le], *v.r.* (*conjug. like* APPELER) to become dappled.
pommer [pɔ'me], *v.i.* and **se pommer**, *v.r.* to grow to a firm round head (*of cabbage, lettuce etc.*).
pommette [pɔ'mɛt], *n.f.* apple-like ball or knob; cheek-bone; (*C*) crab-apple.
pommier [pɔ'mje], *n.m.* apple-tree.
pompe [pɔ̃ːp], *n.f.* pomp, ceremony; display; pump, inflator; *pompe à incendie*, fire-engine.
pomper [pɔ̃'pe], *v.t.* to pump; (*fig.*) to suck up.—*v.i.* to pump.
pompeusement [pɔ̃pøz'mɑ̃], *adv.* solemnly, with pomp.
pompeux [pɔ̃'pø], *a.* (*fem.* **-euse**) stately, solemn; pompous.
pompier [pɔ̃'pje], *a. inv.* conventional (*art, style*).—*n.m.* fireman.
pompiste [pɔ̃'pist], *n.* pump-attendant (*at petrol-pump etc.*).
pompon [pɔ̃'pɔ̃], *n.m.* pompon, top-knot.
pomponner [pɔ̃pɔ'ne], *v.t.* to ornament with pompons to deck out. **se pomponner**, *v.r.* to dress oneself up.
ponce [pɔ̃ːs] *n.f.* pumice; (*Drawing*) pounce.
ponceau (1) [pɔ̃'so], *n.m.* (*pl.* **-eaux**) small bridge, culvert.

ponceau (2) [pɔ̃'so], *a.* poppy-red.—*n.m.* (*pl.* **-eaux**) corn-poppy.
Ponce Pilate [pɔ̃spi'lat], *m.* Pontius Pilate.
poncer [pɔ̃'se], *v.t.* (*conjug. like* COMMENCER) to pumice; (*Drawing*) to pounce.
poncif [pɔ̃'sif], *n.m.* pounced drawing; (*fig.*) commonplace piece of work.
ponctualité [pɔ̃ktɥali'te], *n.f.* punctuality.
ponctuation [pɔ̃ktɥa'sjɔ̃], *n.f.* punctuation.
ponctué [pɔ̃k'tɥe], *a.* punctuated; dotted; *ligne ponctuée*, dotted line.
ponctuel [pɔ̃k'tɥɛl], *a.* (*fem.* **-elle**) punctual, exact.
ponctuellement [pɔ̃ktɥɛl'mɑ̃], *adv.* punctually.
ponctuer [pɔ̃k'tɥe], *v.t.* to punctuate; to point.
pondéré [pɔ̃de're], *a.* poised, calm, self-controlled.
pondérer [pɔ̃de're], *v.t.* (*conjug. like* CÉDER) to poise, to balance.
pondeur [pɔ̃'dœːr], *a.* (*fem.* **-euse**) good laying (*of poultry etc.*); (*colloq.*) productive. —*n.f.* (**-euse**) good layer.
pondre [pɔ̃:dr], *v.t.* to lay (*eggs*).
poney [pɔ'ne], *n.m.* pony.
pont [pɔ̃], *n.m.* bridge; deck; *Ponts et Chaussées*, (*France*) Department of Bridges and Highways.
ponte (1) [pɔ̃:t], *n.f.* laying of eggs.
ponte (2) [pɔ̃:t], *n.m.* punter; (*fam.*) V.I.P.
ponté [pɔ̃'te], *a.* decked (*of ship*); *non ponté*, open (*boat*).
ponter [pɔ̃'te], *v.i.* to punt, to gamble.
pontet [pɔ̃'te], *n.m.* trigger-guard; saddle-tree.
pontife [pɔ̃'tif], *n.m.* pontiff.
pontifier [pɔ̃ti'fje], *v.i.* (*fam.*) to act or speak solemnly or pompously; to pontificate, to lay down the law.
pont-levis [pɔ̃l'vi], *n.m.* (*pl.* **ponts-levis**) drawbridge.
ponton [pɔ̃'tɔ̃], *n.m.* bridge of boats; pontoon.
popeline [pɔ'plin], *n.f.* poplin.
populace [pɔpy'las], *n.f.* populace, mob, rabble.
populacier [pɔpyla'sje], *a.* (*fem.* **-ière**) low, vulgar.
populaire [pɔpy'lɛːr], *a.* popular; common. —*n.m.* populace, rabble.
populairement [pɔpylɛr'mɑ̃], *adv.* popularly.
populariser [pɔpylari'ze], *v.t.* to popularize.
popularité [pɔpylari'te], *n.f.* popularity.
population [pɔpyla'sjɔ̃], *n.f.* population.
populeux [pɔpy'lø], *a.* (*fem.* **-euse**) populous.
porc [pɔːr], *n.m.* pig; swine; pork.
porcelaine [pɔrsə'lɛn], *n.f.* porcelain, china, chinaware.
porcelet [pɔrsə'lɛ], *n.m.* young pig, piglet.
porc-épic [pɔrke'pik], *n.m.* (*pl.* **porcs-épics**) porcupine; (*Am.*) hedgehog.
porche [pɔrʃ], *n.m.* porch.
porcher [pɔr'ʃe], *n.m.* (*fem.* **-ère**) swineherd.
porcherie [pɔrʃ'ri], *n.f.* pigsty, piggery.
porcin [pɔr'sɛ̃], *a.* porcine.—*n.m.* (*pl.*) pigs.
pore [pɔːr], *n.m.* pore.
poreux [pɔ'rø], *a.* (*fem.* **-euse**) porous.
pornographie [pɔrnɔgra'fi], *n.f.* pornography.
pornographique [pɔrnɔgra'fik], *a.* pornographic.

porphyre [pɔrˈfiːr], *n.m.* porphyry.
porphyriser [pɔrfiriˈze], *v.t.* to porphyrize; to pulverize.
porreau [POIREAU].
port (1) [pɔːr], *n.m.* haven, harbour, port; sea-port town; *arriver à bon port*, to arrive safely; (*fig.*) to end happily; *port d'escale*, port of call.
port (2) [pɔːr], *n.m.* carrying, carriage; postage; bearing, gait; (*Naut.*) tonnage.
portable [pɔrˈtabl], *a.* portable; wearable.
portage [pɔrˈtaːʒ], *n.m.* carriage, transport.
portail [pɔrˈtaːj], *n.m.* (*pl.* -s) portal, front gate (*of a church etc.*).
portant [pɔrˈtɑ̃], *a.* bearing, carrying; *être bien portant*, to be in good health.
portatif [pɔrtaˈtif], *a.* (*fem.* -tive) portable.
porte [pɔrt], *n.f.* doorway, gateway; door; gate; entrance; eye (*of hooks etc.*); defile.
porté [pɔrˈte], *a.* carried; inclined, prone, disposed (*à*); projected (*of shadows*).
porte-à-faux [pɔrtaˈfo], *n.m. inv.* overhang; *en porte-à-faux*, overhanging; unsteady.
porte-affiches [pɔrtaˈfiʃ], *n.m. inv.* advertising-board.
porte-avions [pɔrtaˈvjɔ̃], *n.m. inv.* aircraft carrier.
porte-bagages [pɔrtbaˈgaːʒ], *n.m. inv.* luggage-rack.
porte-billets [pɔrtbiˈjɛ], *n.m. inv.* note-case; (*Am.*) bill-fold.
porte-bonheur [pɔrtbɔˈnœːr], *n.m. inv.* good-luck charm; mascot.
porte-bouteilles [pɔrtbuˈtɛːj], *n.m. inv.* bottle-rack, wine-bin.
porte-chapeaux [pɔrtʃaˈpo], *n.m. inv.* hat-stand.
porte-cigarettes [pɔrtsigaˈrɛt], *n.m. inv.* cigarette case.
porte-clefs [pɔrtəˈkle], *n.m. inv.* key-ring.
porte-couteau [pɔrtkuˈto], *n.m. inv.* knife-rest.
porte-crayon [pɔrtəkrɛˈjɔ̃], *n.m. inv.* pencil-case.
porte-documents [pɔrtdɔkyˈmɑ̃], *n.m. inv.* dispatch-case.
porte-drapeau [pɔrtdraˈpo], *n.m. inv.* ensign, colour-bearer.
portée [pɔrˈte], *n.f.* brood, litter; reach (*of the hand, arm etc.*); hearing; range, shot; scope; capacity; import, significance; bearing; resting-point; (*Mus.*) stave.
porte-étendard [pɔrtetɑ̃ˈdaːr], *n.m. inv.* standard-bearer.
porte-fenêtre [pɔrtfəˈnɛːtr], *n.f.* (*pl.* portes-fenêtres) French window.
portefeuille [pɔrtəˈfœːj], *n.m.* wallet; (*fig.*) portfolio; office.
porte-flambeau [pɔrtflɑ̃ˈbo], *n.m. inv.* torch-bearer, linkman.
porte-jupe [pɔrtəˈʒyp], *n.m. inv.* skirt-hanger.
porte-livres [pɔrtəˈliːvr], *n.m. inv.* book-rest.
porte-malheur [pɔrtmaˈlœːr], *n.m. inv.* bird of ill-omen, bearer of ill-luck.
portemanteau [pɔrtmɑ̃ˈto], *n.m.* (*pl.* -eaux) coat-stand, coat-rail; peg.
porte-masse [pɔrtəˈmas], *n.m. inv.* mace-bearer.
porte-mine(s) [pɔrtəˈmin], *n.m. inv.* propelling pencil.

porte-monnaie [pɔrtmɔˈnɛ], *n.m. inv.* purse.
porte-musique [pɔrtmyˈzik], *n.m. inv.* music-case.
porte-parapluies [pɔrtparaˈplɥi], *n.m. inv.* umbrella-stand.
porte-parole [pɔrtpaˈrɔl], *n.m. inv.* mouthpiece, spokesman.
porte-plume [pɔrtəˈplym], *n.m. inv.* penholder.
porte-queue [pɔrtəˈkø], *n.m. inv.* train-bearer; swallowtail butterfly.
porter [pɔrˈte], *v.t.* to carry, to bear, to support; to endure; to bring, to take; to wear; to deal (*blows etc.*); to turn (*the eyes etc.*); to entertain (*affection etc.*); to incline; to produce; to declare, to show.—*v.i.* to bear; to rest, to lie; to take effect; to hit; to reach; to carry (*of a gun etc.*); (*Naut.*) to stand, to bear off; to be with young (*of animals*). **se porter,** *v.r.* to go, to repair, to move; to resort, to flock; to be inclined *or* disposed, to tend; to be, to do (*of health*); to be worn; to present oneself, to stand forth; to turn, to be directed.
porte-rame [pɔrtˈram], *n.m. inv.* rowlock.
porte-serviette(s) [pɔrtsɛrˈvjɛt], *n.m. inv.* towel-rail.
porteur [pɔrˈtœːr], *n.m.* (*fem.* -euse) porter, carrier, bearer; holder; sleeper (*on railway track*).
porte-voix [pɔrtˈvwa], *n.m. inv.* megaphone.
portier [pɔrˈtje], *n.m.* (*fem.* -ière (1)) porter, door-keeper.
portière (2) [pɔrˈtjɛːr], *n.f.* door-curtain, door (*of vehicle*).
portion [pɔrˈsjɔ̃], *n.f.* portion, part, share, allowance.
portionner [pɔrsjɔˈne], *v.t.* to share out.
portique [pɔrˈtik], *n.m.* portico; porch.
porto [pɔrˈto], *n.m.* port (*wine*).
portrait [pɔrˈtrɛ], *n.m.* portrait, likeness, picture.
portraitiste [pɔrtrɛˈtist], *n.* portrait painter.
portugais [pɔrtyˈgɛ], *a.* Portuguese.—*n.m.* Portuguese (*language*); (**Portugais,** *fem.* -aise) Portuguese (*person*).
Portugal [pɔrtyˈgal], **le,** *m.* Portugal.
pose [poːz], *n.f.* laying, setting; pose, posture, attitude; posing, affectation; sitting (*for one's portrait etc.*); hanging (*of bells*); (*Mil.*) posting (*of sentries*); (*Phot.*) (time) exposure.
posé [poˈze], *a.* laid, set, poised; bearing, resting; sedate, staid, sober; *cela posé*, this being granted.
posément [pozeˈmɑ̃], *adv.* calmly; sedately.
poser [poˈze], *v.t.* to put, to put in (*a lock, a window-pane*); to place, to lay down; to hang; to suppose, to grant; to post (*sentries etc.*); to lay down, to state; (*Mus.*) to pitch; to sit (*for portrait*); *poser une question*, to ask a question.—*v.i.* to rest (*sur*); to stand, to pose, to sit (*for one's portrait*); to show off. **se poser,** *v.r.* to perch (*of birds etc.*); to come down, to land (*plane*); to set up (*en*), to play the part (*en*).
poseur [poˈzœːr], *n.m.* (*Rail.*) plate-layer.—*n.m.* (*fem.* -euse) (*colloq.*) poseur, snob, prig.
positif [poziˈtif], *a.* (*fem.* -tive) positive, certain; practical, actual, matter-of-fact.—*n.m.* positive reality; certainty, fact; (*Phot., Cine., Gram.*) positive.

position [pozi'sjɔ̃], *n.f.* position, situation; status, standing; case, state, circumstances.
positivement [pozitiv'mɑ̃], *adv.* positively, exactly.
possédé [pose'de], *a.* possessed.—*n.m.* (*fem.* **-ée**) person possessed, madman, maniac.
posséder [pose'de], *v.t.* (*conjug. like* CÉDER) to possess, to be possessed of, to own; to be master of; to be conversant with; to dominate (*a person*); (*pop.*) to deceive. **se posséder**, *v.r.* to master one's passions, to contain oneself.
possesseur [pose'sœːr], *n.m.* possessor, owner, occupier.
possessif [pose'sif], *a.* (*fem.* **-ive**) possessive. —*n.m.* (*Gram.*) possessive adjective *or* pronoun.
possession [pose'sjɔ̃], *n.f.* possession; property.
possibilité [posibili'te], *n.f.* possibility; (*pl.*) facilities.
possible [po'sibl], *a.* possible.—*n.m.* possibility; *au possible*, extremely; *je ferai tout mon possible*, I'll do the best I can.
postal [pos'tal], *a.* (*m. pl.* **-aux**) postal, of the post.
poste (1) [post], *n.m.* post, station; guard-house; place, employment, post; (*Naut.*) berth; (*Teleph.*) extension; entry (*in books*); *poste de radio*, wireless set; *poste d'incendie*, fire-station.
poste (2) [post], *n.f.* post (*relay*); post-stage; postal service; post-office, mail; *bureau de poste*, post-office.
poster [pos'te], *v.t.* to station, to post (*sentry or letter*).
postérieur [poste'rjœːr], *a.* posterior, later; behind.—*n.m.* (*colloq.*) posterior.
postérieurement [posterjœr'mɑ̃], *adv.* subsequently.
postérité [posteri'te], *n.f.* posterity.
posthume [pos'tym], *a.* posthumous.
postiche [pos'tiʃ], *a.* superadded; false, artificial.—*n.m.* wig.
postier [pos'tje], *n.m.* (*fem.* **-ière**) post-office employee.
postillon [posti'jɔ̃], *n.m.* postilion; post-boy.
postscolaire [postsko'lɛːr], *a.* continuation (*class*); *enseignement postscolaire*, adult education.
post-scriptum [postskrip'tom] (*abbr.* **P.S.**), *n.m. inv.* postscript.
postulant [posty'lɑ̃], *n.m.* (*fem.* **-e**) candidate, applicant; postulant.
postuler [posty'le], *v.t.* to solicit, to apply for.—*v.i.* (*Law*) to act on behalf of a client.
posture [pos'tyːr], *n.f.* posture, attitude; situation.
pot [po], *n.m.* pot; jug, tankard, flagon, can, jar; (*C*) half a gallon.
potable [po'tabl], *a.* drinkable (*water*).
potage [po'taːʒ], *n.m.* soup.
potager (1) [pota'ʒe], *n.m.* kitchen-garden; kitchen-stove.
potager (2) [pota'ʒe], *a.* (*fem.* **-ère**) culinary; *jardin potager*, kitchen-garden.
potasse [po'tas], *n.f.* potash.
potassium [pota'sjom], *n.m.* potassium.
pot-au-feu [poto'fø], *n.m. inv.* beef boiled with carrots etc.; broth of this.
pot-de-vin [pod'vɛ̃], *n.m.* (*pl.* **pots-de-vin**) gratuity; bribe; hush-money.

poteau [po'to], *n.m.* (*pl.* **-eaux**) post, stake.
potée [po'te], *n.f.* potful; (*colloq.*) swarm (*of children etc.*); putty; (*Metal.*) moulding.
potelé [po'tle], *a.* plump, chubby.
potence [po'tɑ̃ːs], *n.f.* gallows, gibbet; bracket; crutch; *gibier de potence*, jail-bird.
potentat [potɑ̃'ta], *n.m.* potentate.
potentiel [potɑ̃'sjɛl], *a.* (*fem.* **-elle**) potential, —*n.m.* potentialities.
potentiellement [potɑ̃sjɛl'mɑ̃], *adv.* potentially.
poterie [po'tri], *n.f.* pottery, earthenware.
poterne [po'tɛrn], *n.f.* postern.
potiche [po'tiʃ], *n.f.* China *or* Japan porcelain vase.
potier [po'tje], *n.m.* potter.
potin [po'tɛ̃], *n.m.* pinchbeck; (*pl.*) gossip.
potion [po'sjɔ̃], *n.f.* potion, draught.
potiron [poti'rɔ̃], *n.m.* pumpkin.
pou [pu], *n.m.* (*pl.* **poux**) louse.
pouah! [pwa], *int.* ugh! disgusting!
poubelle [pu'bel], *n.f.* dustbin; (*Am.*) ash-can.
pouce [pus], *n.m.* thumb; big toe; inch; *un morceau sur le pouce*, a snack; (*C*) *faire du pouce*, to hitch-hike.
poucet [pu'sɛ], *n.m.* **le petit Poucet**, Tom Thumb.
pouding [pu'diŋ], *n.m.* plum-pudding.
poudre [pudr], *n.f.* powder; gunpowder; dust; *sucre en poudre*, castor sugar.
poudrer [pu'dre], *v.t.* to powder, to sprinkle with powder.
poudrerie [pudrə'ri], *n.f.* gunpowder-factory; (*C*) blizzard.
poudreux [pu'drø], *a.* (*fem.* **-euse**) dusty, powdery.
poudrier [pudri'e], *n.m.* (powder) compact.
poudrière [pudri'ɛːr], *n.f.* powder-mill, magazine; sand-box.
poudroyer [pudrwa'je], *v.i.* (*conjug. like* EMPLOYER) to rise in dust; to be dusty (*of roads etc.*).
pouf! (1) [puf], *int.* plop! flop! phew!
pouf (2) [puf], *n.m.* ottoman (*seat*), pouf; puff (*advertisement*).
pouffer [pu'fe], *v.i. pouffer de rire*, to burst out laughing, to guffaw.
pouilleux [pu'jø], *a.* and *n.m.* (*fem.* **-euse**) lousy; wretched, mean (person).
poulailler [pula'je], *n.m.* hen-house; (*of persons*) poulterer; (*Theat.*) gods.
poulain [pu'lɛ̃], *n.m.* foal, colt.
poularde [pu'lard], *n.f.* fat pullet.
poulbot [pul'bo], *n.m.* Paris street urchin.
poule [pul], *n.f.* hen; fowl; pool (*at games*); eliminating round (*in a competition*).
poulet [pu'lɛ], *n.m.* chicken; love-letter.
poulette [pu'lɛt], *n.f.* pullet.
pouliche [pu'liʃ], *n.f.* filly.
poulie [pu'li], *n.f.* pulley; (*Naut.*) block.
pouliner [puli'ne], *v.i.* to foal (*of mares*).
poulinière [puli'njɛːr], *a.f.* and *n.f.* (*jument*) *poulinière*, brood mare.
poulpe [pulp], *n.m.* octopus, devil-fish.
pouls [pu], *n.m.* pulse; *se tâter le pouls*, to feel one's pulse.
poumon [pu'mɔ̃], *n.m.* lung; *poumon d'acier*, iron lung.

poupard [pu'pa:r], *a.* chubby.—*n.m.* baby; doll.

poupe [pup], *n.f.* stern, poop.

poupée [pu'pe], *n.f.* doll; puppet; tailor's dummy.

poupin [pu'pɛ̃], *a.* fresh-coloured; rosy.

poupon [pu'põ], *n.m.* (*fem.* **-onne**) baby; plump, chubby-cheeked boy *or* girl.

pouponnière [pupo'njɛːr], *n.f.* (*public*) day-nursery.

pour [puːr], *prep.* for; on account of; on behalf of; as regards, as for; in order; although.—*n.m.* for, pro.

pourboire [pur'bwaːr], *n.m.* tip, gratuity.

pourceau [pur'so], *n.m.* (*pl.* **-eaux**) hog, pig, swine.

pour-cent [pur'sɑ̃], **pourcentage** [pursɑ̃'ta:ʒ], *n.m.* percentage.

pourchasser [purʃa'se], *v.t.* to pursue, to chase, to badger.

pourfendre [pur'fɑ̃:dr], *v.t.* to cleave asunder.

pourlécher [purle'ʃe], *v.t.* (*conjug. like* CÉDER) to lick all over. **se pourlécher,** *v.r.* to lick one's lips.

pourparler [purpar'le], *n.m.* (*usu. in pl.*) parley, negotiations; talks.

pourpoint [pur'pwɛ̃], *n.m.* doublet.

pourpre [purpr], *a.* purple, dark red.—*n.f.* purple (*stuff*); (*fig.*) sovereign dignity; cardinalate.—*n.m.* purple, crimson (*colour*).

pourpré [pur'pre], *a.* purple.

pourquoi [pur'kwa], *adv.* and *conj.* why, wherefore; **pourquoi pas?** why not?—*n.m. inv.* the reason why.

pourri [pu'ri], *a.* rotten; **temps pourri,** muggy weather.—*n.m.* the rotten part; rottenness.

pourrir [pu'ri:r], *v.t.* to make rotten, to corrupt.—*v.i.* to rot; (*fig.*) to perish. **se pourrir,** *v.r.* to become rotten, to go bad.

pourrissable [puri'sabl], *a.* perishable.

pourrissant [puri'sɑ̃], *a.* rotting, causing rot.

pourriture [puri'ty:r], *n.f.* rot, rottenness, putrefaction; (*fig.*) corruption.

poursuite [pur'sɥit], *n.f.* pursuit, chase; prosecution; (*Law*) suit, proceedings.

poursuivable [pursɥi'vabl], *a.* actionable.

poursuivant [pursɥi'vɑ̃], *a.* suing, prosecuting.—*n.m.* suitor.—*n.m.* (*fem.* **-e**) prosecutor, plaintiff.

poursuivre [pur'sɥi:vr], *v.t. irr.* (*conjug. like* SUIVRE) to pursue; to seek; to persecute; to haunt; to go on with; to follow up; (*Law*) to sue, to prosecute.—*v.i.* to pursue, to go on, to continue. **se poursuivre,** *v.r.* to continue, to follow its course.

pourtant [pur'tɑ̃], *adv.* however, yet, still, nevertheless.

pourtour [pur'tu:r], *n.m.* periphery, circumference; gangway (*in a theatre etc.*); precincts (*of cathedral*).

pourvoi [pur'vwa], *n.m.* (*Law*) appeal.

pourvoir [pur'vwa:r], *v.t. irr.* to invest with, to appoint; to provide, to supply, to endow.—*v.i.* (*followed by* à) to see to, to attend to, to provide for; to make an appointment to. **se pourvoir,** *v.r.* to provide oneself; to appeal.

pourvoyeur [purvwa'jœ:r], *n.m.* (*fem.* **-euse**) purveyor, provider, caterer.

pourvu que [pur'vykə], *conj. phr.* provided that, provided.

pousse [pus], *n.f.* shoot, sprout.

pousse-café [puska'fe], *n.m. inv.* (*fam.*) liqueur (*after coffee*).

poussée [pu'se], *n.f.* pushing; shove; thrust (*of arches etc.*); pressure (*of business etc.*).

pousse-pousse [pus'pus], *n.m. inv.* rickshaw (*carriage* or *man*).

pousser [pu'se], *v.t.* to push, to thrust, to shove; to drive on; to carry on, to extend; to grow, to send forth (*of plants etc.*); to urge, to provoke; to assist, to help on; to utter, to heave (*a sigh etc.*); to deal (*a blow etc.*).—*v.i.* to sprout, to shoot (*of plants*); to grow (*of the hair, nails etc.*); to push on, to go on; to bulge; to be broken-winded (*of horses*). **se pousser,** *v.r.* to push forward, to push oneself forward; to push each other, to jostle.

poussette [pu'sɛt], *n.f.* push-chair; movement in dancing.

poussier [pu'sje], *n.m.* coal-dust, screenings.

poussière [pu'sjɛ:r], *n.f.* dust; spray (*of water*).

poussiéreux [pusje'rø], *a.* (*fem.* **-euse**) dusty.

poussif [pu'sif], *a.* (*fem.* **-ive**) shortwinded.

poussin [pu'sɛ̃], *n.m.* chick, chicken just hatched.

poussinière [pusi'njɛ:r], *n.f.* chicken-coop; incubator.

poutre [putr], *n.f.* beam; girder.

poutrelle [pu'trɛl], *n.f.* small beam.

pouvoir [pu'vwa:r], *v.t. irr.* to be able to do.—*v.i.* to be able (*can etc.*); to have power; to be allowed (*may etc.*); (*impers.*) to be possible; **il peut arriver que,** it may happen that; **il se peut que,** it is possible that; **on ne peut plus,** (*followed by adj.*) exceedingly; **sauve qui peut,** every man for himself.—*n.m.* power; might; authority; command, government.

prairie [prɛ'ri], *n.f.* meadow, grass-land, grass-field; (*U.S.*) prairie.

praline [pra'lin], *n.f.* burnt almond.

praliner [prali'ne], *v.t.* to brown in sugar (*like burnt almonds*).

praticabilité [pratikabili'te], *n.f.* practicability, feasibility.

praticable [prati'kabl], *a.* practicable, feasible; passable (*of roads*); accessible; (*Theat.*) real.

praticien [prati'sjɛ̃], *a.* (*fem.* **-enne**) practising.—*n.m.* (*fem.* **-enne**) practitioner.

pratiquant [prati'kɑ̃], *a.* church-going.—*n.m.* (*fem.* **-e**) church-goer.

pratique [pra'tik], *a.* practical; experienced.—*n.f.* practice; execution; method; experience; usage; custom (*of tradesman*), practice (*of attorneys, physicians etc.*); customer; (*pl.*) dealings.

pratiquement [pratik'mɑ̃], *adv.* in actual fact, practically; in a practical way.

pratiquer [prati'ke], *v.t.* to practise, to exercise; to frequent; to tamper with, to bribe; to obtain; (*Arch.*) to contrive. **se pratiquer,** *v.r.* to be in use, to be practised.

pré [pre], *n.m.* meadow.

préalable [prea'labl], *a.* preliminary; previous.—*n.m. au préalable,* previously, first of all.

préalablement [prealablə'mɑ̃], *adv.* previously, first, to begin with.

préambule

préambule [preɑ̃'byl], *n.m.* preamble, preface.

préau [pre'o], *n.m.* (*pl.* **-aux**) courtyard (*of a convent* or *prison*); (*sch.*) covered playground.

préavis [prea'vi], *n.m. inv.* (previous) notice.

précaire [pre'kɛːr], *a.* precarious; uncertain.

précairement [prekɛr'mɑ̃], *adv.* precariously.

précaution [preko'sjɔ̃], *n.f.* precaution; caution, care.

précautionner [prekosjɔ'ne], *v.t.* to warn, to caution. **se précautionner**, *v.r.* to take precautions.

précédemment [preseda'mɑ̃], *adv.* before, previously.

précédent [prese'dɑ̃], *a.* preceding, former.— *n.m.* precedent.

précéder [prese'de], *v.t.* (*conjug. like* CÉDER) to precede, to go before; to take precedence (*of*).

précepte [pre'sɛpt], *n.m.* precept, rule.

précepteur [presɛp'tœːr], *n.m.* (*fem.* **-trice**) tutor, teacher.

prêche [prɛːʃ], *n.m.* sermon (*Protestant*); Protestant church.

prêcher [prɛ'ʃe], *v.t.* to preach; to exhort; to extol, to praise.—*v.i.* to preach.

prêcheur [prɛ'ʃœːr], *n.m.* (*fem.* **-euse**) preacher.

précieusement [presjøz'mɑ̃], *adv.* preciously; carefully; affectedly.

précieux [pre'sjø], *a.* (*fem.* **-euse**) precious, valuable; affected.—*n.m.* affectation.—*n.m.* (*fem.* **-euse**) affected person.

préciosité [presjozi'te], *n.f.* affectation.

précipice [presi'pis], *n.m.* precipice.

précipitamment [presipita'mɑ̃], *adv.* precipitately, hurriedly, rashly.

précipitation [presipita'sjɔ̃], *n.f.* haste, hurry; (*Chem.*) precipitation.

précipité [presipi'te], *a.* precipitated, hurled; precipitate, hasty, sudden.—*n.m.* (*Chem.*) precipitate.

précipiter [presipi'te], *v.t.* to precipitate, to hurl; to hasten, to accelerate; (*Chem.*) to precipitate. **se précipiter**, *v.r.* to precipitate, throw *or* hurl oneself; to rush forward, to spring forth, to dart.

précis [pre'si], *a.* fixed, precise, exact; formal, terse, concise.—*n.m.* summary, abstract.

précisément [presize'mɑ̃], *adv.* precisely, exactly; quite; just so.

préciser [presi'ze], *v.t.* to state precisely, to specify.

précision [presi'zjɔ̃], *n.f.* precision, preciseness.

précité [presi'te], *a.* afore-mentioned.

précoce [pre'kɔs], *a.* precocious, early, forward.

précocité [prekɔsi'te], *n.f.* precocity.

préconçu [prekɔ̃'sy], *a.* preconceived.

préconiser [prekɔni'ze], *v.t.* to advocate, to recommend.

préconnaissance [prekɔnɛ'sɑ̃ːs], *n.f.* fore-knowledge.

précurseur [prekyr'sœːr], *n.m.* forerunner, precursor, harbinger.

prédateur [preda'tœːr], *a.* (*fem.* **-trice**) (*Ent.*) predatory.

254

prédécéder [predese'de], *v.i.* (*conjug. like* CÉDER) to predecease (*someone*).

prédestination [predɛstina'sjɔ̃], *n.f.* predestination.

prédestiné [predɛsti'ne], *a.* predestined; predetermined.—*n.m.* (*fem.* **-ée**) one of the elect.

prédicateur [predika'tœːr], *n.m.* (*fem.* **-trice**) preacher.

prédiction [predik'sjɔ̃], *n.f.* prediction, forecast.

prédilection [predilɛk'sjɔ̃], *n.f.* predilection, preference.

prédire [pre'diːr], *v.t. irr.* (*conjug. like* MÉDIRE) to predict, to foretell.

prédisposer [predispo'ze], *v.t.* to predispose.

prédisposition [predispozi'sjɔ̃], *n.f.* predisposition.

prédominance [predɔmi'nɑ̃ːs], *n.f.* predominance, ascendancy.

prédominant [predɔmi'nɑ̃], *a.* predominant.

prédominer [predɔmi'ne], *v.i.* to prevail over.—*v.i.* to predominate.

prééminence [preemi'nɑ̃ːs], *n.f.* pre-eminence.

prééminent [preemi'nɑ̃], *a.* pre-eminent.

préemption [preɑ̃p'sjɔ̃], *n.f.* pre-emption.

préfabriqué [prefabri'ke], *a.* prefabricated.

préface [pre'fas], *n.f.* preface; foreword.

préfecture [prefɛk'tyːr], *n.f.* prefecture; *préfecture de police*, Paris police headquarters.

préférable [prefe'rabl], *a.* preferable.

préférablement [preferablə'mɑ̃], *adv.* preferably.

préféré [prefe're], *a.* favourite.

préférence [prefe'rɑ̃ːs], *n.f.* preference.

préférer [prefe're], *v.t.* (*conjug. like* CÉDER) to prefer.

préfet [pre'fɛ], *n.m.* prefect; chief administrator of a department in France; *préfet de police*, chief commissioner of Parisian police.

préhensile [preɑ̃'sil], *a.* prehensile.

préhistorique [preisto'rik], *a.* prehistoric.

préjudice [preʒy'dis], *n.m.* detriment, injury, damage, prejudice.

préjudiciable [preʒydi'sjabl], *a.* prejudicial, detrimental.

préjudicier [preʒydi'sje], *v.i.* to be prejudicial *or* detrimental.

préjugé [preʒy'ʒe], *n.m.* presumption, prejudice; (*Law*) precedent.

préjuger [preʒy'ʒe], *v.t.* (*conjug. like* MANGER) to prejudge.

prélasser (se) [səprelɑ'se], *v.r.* to strut, to stalk along.

prélat [pre'la], *n.m.* prelate.

prélèvement [prelɛv'mɑ̃], *n.m.* deduction; sample; (*Med.*) swab.

prélever [prelə've], *v.t.* (*conjug. like* AMENER) to deduct; to appropriate.

préliminaire [prelimi'nɛːr], *a.* and *n.m.* preliminary.

prélude [pre'lyd], *n.m.* prelude.

prématuré [prematy're], *a.* premature, untimely.

prématurément [prematyre'mɑ̃], *adv.* prematurely.

préméditation [premedita'sjɔ̃], *n.f.* premeditation.

préméditer [premedi'te], *v.t.* to premeditate.

prémices [pre'mis], *n.f. pl.* first-fruits; *(fig.)* beginning.

premier [prə'mje], *a.* *(fem.* **-ière)** first; foremost, best, chief; former *(of two)*; early, pristine, primeval; *(Arith.)* prime; *au premier abord*, at first sight; *le premier rang*, the front rank; *matières premières*, raw materials.—*n.m.* *(fem.* **-ière)** chief, head, leader.—*n.m.* first floor; first of the month etc.—*n.f.* **(-ière)** *(Theat.)* first night; *(Sch.)* sixth form.

premièrement [prəmjɛr'mɑ̃], *adv.* firstly, in the first place.

prémonition [premɔni'sjɔ̃], *n.f.* premonition.

prémunir [premy'ni:r], *v.t.* to forewarn, to caution, to secure beforehand. **se prémunir,** *v.r.* to provide **(contre).**

prenant [prə'nɑ̃], taking, prehensile; *(fig.)* fascinating; *partie prenante*, payee.

prendre [prɑ̃:dr], *v.t. irr.* to take; to take up; to snatch; to seize; to capture; to contract, to catch *(a cold etc.)*; to choose; to fetch; to assume; to collect *(votes etc.)*; to help oneself to; to conduct *(an affair etc.)*; to entertain *(a feeling etc.)*; **en prendre à son aise,** to take it easy; *prendre pour dit*, to take for granted; *que je t'y prenne un peu!* just let me catch you at it!—*v.i.* to take; to take root; to congeal, to freeze; to curdle *(of milk etc.)*; to succeed; to begin to burn. **se prendre,** *v.r.* to be taken; to be caught; to catch; to freeze, to congeal *(of liquids)*; to begin.

preneur [prə'nœ:r], *n.m.* *(fem.* **-euse)** taker; lessee; purchaser; catcher *(of animals)*.

prénom [pre'nɔ̃], *n.m.* Christian name.

prénommé [prenɔ'me], *a.* and *n.m.* *(fem.* **-ée)** (the) above-named, aforesaid; named.

préoccupation [preɔkypɑ'sjɔ̃], *n.f.* preoccupation; anxiety, concern.

préoccupé [preɔky'pe], *a.* preoccupied, absorbed; worried.

préoccuper [preɔky'pe], *v.t.* to engross, to preoccupy; to worry. **se préoccuper,** *v.r.* to see to, to be engaged in *(de)*, to be anxious about.

préparateur [prepara'tœ:r], *n.m.* *(fem.* **-trice)** preparer, assistant *(in laboratory or in a dispensing chemist's)*.

préparatif(s) [prepara'tif], *n.m. sing.* or *pl.* preparation.

préparation [preparɑ'sjɔ̃], *n.f.* preparation; *sans préparation*, extempore.

préparatoire [prepara'twa:r], *a.* preparatory.

préparer [prepa're], *v.t.* to prepare, to make ready; to fit; to make up, to manufacture. **se préparer,** *v.r.* to prepare, to prepare oneself, to get ready.

prépondérance [prepɔ̃de'rɑ̃:s], *n.f.* preponderance.

prépondérant [prepɔ̃de'rɑ̃], *a.* preponderant; *voix prépondérante*, casting-vote.

préposé [prepo'ze], *n.m.* *(fem.* **-ée)** officer in charge, superintendent, agent.

préposer [prepo'ze], *v.t.* to set over, to appoint to, to put in charge of.

préposition [prepozi'sjɔ̃], *n.f.* preposition.

prérogative [preroga'ti:v], *n.f.* prerogative.

près [prɛ], *adv.* by, near, hard by; nearly, almost, about; on the point of; *à beaucoup près*, by a great deal; *à cela près*, with that exception; *à peu près*, pretty near, nearly so; *de près*, close, near; *tout près*, very near.—*prep.* *(usu.* **près de)** near, close to.

présage [pre'za:ʒ], *n.m.* presage, omen, foreboding.

présager [preza'ʒe], *v.t. (conjug. like* MANGER) to presage, to portend.

pré-salé [presa'le], *n.m.* *(pl.* **prés-salés)** salt-marsh sheep *or* mutton.

presbyte [prɛz'bit], *a.* long-sighted.—*n.* long-sighted person.

presbytère [prɛzbi'tɛ:r], *n.m.* parsonage, vicarage, rectory; presbytery *(R.-C. Ch.)*.

presbytérien [prɛzbite'rjɛ̃], *a.* and *n.m.* *(fem.* **-enne)** Presbyterian.

presbytie [prɛzbi'si], *n.f.* far- *or* long-sightedness.

prescience [pre'sjɑ̃:s], *n.f.* prescience, foreknowledge.

prescription [prɛskrip'sjɔ̃], *n.f.* prescription; regulation.

prescrire [prɛs'kri:r], *v.t. irr. (conjug. like* ÉCRIRE) to prescribe, to stipulate; *(Law)* to bar.

préséance [prese'ɑ̃:s], *n.f.* precedence.

présence [pre'zɑ̃:s], *n.f.* presence, attendance, appearance; *mettre en présence*, to bring face to face.

présent [pre'zɑ̃], *a.* present; *présent !* here! —*n.m.* present, present time; gift; *dès à présent*, from now on.

présentable [prezɑ̃'tabl], *a.* presentable, fit to be seen.

présentation [prezɑ̃tɑ'sjɔ̃], *n.f.* presentation, introduction.

présentement [prezɑ̃t'mɑ̃], *adv.* now, a present.

présenter [prezɑ̃'te], *v.t.* to present, to offer; to show; to introduce. **se présenter,** *v.r.* to present oneself, to appear.

préservateur [prezɛrva'tœ:r], *a.* *(fem.* **-trice)** preservative.

préservatif [prezɛrva'tif], *a.* *(fem.* **-tive)** preservative.

préservation [prezɛrva'sjɔ̃], *n.f.* preservation.

préserver [prezɛr've], *v.t.* to preserve; to defend, to keep safe; *le ciel m'en préserve !* heaven forbid! **se préserver,** *v.r.* to preserve oneself, to guard against.

présidence [prezi'dɑ̃:s], *n.f.* presidency, chairmanship.

président [prezi'dɑ̃], *n.m.* president *(of tribunal)*, presiding judge; speaker *(of the House of Commons)*, chairman.

présidente [prezi'dɑ̃:t], *n.f.* lady president; president's wife.

présider [prezi'de], *v.t.* to preside over, to be president *or* chairman of.—*v.i.* to preside, to be president, to be in the chair.

présomptif [prezɔ̃p'tif], *a.* *(fem.* **-tive)** presumptive, apparent, presumed *(of heirs)*.

présomption [prezɔ̃p'sjɔ̃], *n.f.* presumption, self-conceit.

présomptueusement [prezɔ̃ptɥøz'mɑ̃], *adv.* presumptuously.

présomptueux [prezɔ̃p'tɥø], *a.* *(fem.* **-euse)** presumptuous.

presque [prɛsk], *adv.* almost, nearly, all but; hardly, scarcely; *presque jamais*, hardly ever; *presque plus (de)*, scarcely any left; *presque rien*, hardly anything.

presqu'île [prɛs'kil], *n.f.* peninsula.

pressage [prɛ'sa:ʒ], *n.m.* pressing.

pressant [prɛ'sɑ̃], *a.* pressing, urgent, earnest.

presse [prɛs], *n.f.* throng, crowd; hurry; urgency; (*Navy*) press-gang; press (*newspapers*); printing-press.

pressé [prɛ'se], *a.* pressed; crowded; close, thick; in haste, hurried; urgent; eager; very busy; (*fig.*) condensed, concise.

presse-citron [prɛssi'trɔ̃], *n.m.* (*pl. unchanged* or **-citrons**) lemon-squeezer.

pressée [prɛ'se], *n.f.* pressing, pressure; pressful (*of print etc.*).

pressentiment [prɛsɑ̃ti'mɑ̃], *n.m.* presentiment; foreboding.

pressentir [prɛsɑ̃'ti:r], *v.t. irr.* (*conjug. like* SENTIR) to have a presentiment of; to sound.

presse-papiers [prɛspa'pje], *n.m. inv.* paperweight.

presse-purée [prɛspy're], *n.m. inv.* potato masher.

presser [prɛ'se], *v.t.* to press, to squeeze; to tread down; to crowd; to hasten; to entreat, to urge.—*v.i.* to be urgent. **se presser,** *v.r.* to press, to squeeze, to crowd; to make haste, to hurry.

pression [prɛ'sjɔ̃], *n.f.* pressure.

pressoir [prɛ'swa:r], *n.m.* press (*wine etc.*).

pressurer [prɛsy're], *v.t.* to press (*grapes, apples etc.*); (*fig.*) to squeeze money etc. out of; to oppress.

pressureur [prɛsy'rœ:r], *n.m.* (*fem.* **-euse**) presser (*of fruit etc.*); (*fig.*) squeezer, sponger; oppressor.

prestance [prɛs'tɑ̃:s], *n.f.* commanding appearance, fine presence.

prestation [prɛsta'sjɔ̃], *n.f.* taking (*of an oath*); prestation (*payment of toll etc.*).

preste [prɛst], *a.* agile, nimble; smart.

prestement [prɛstə'mɑ̃], *adv.* nimbly, quickly.

prestesse [prɛs'tɛs], *n.f.* agility, quickness.

prestidigitateur [prɛstidiʒita'tœ:r], *n.m.* conjurer, juggler.

prestidigitation [prɛstidiʒita'sjɔ̃], *n.f.* conjuring, sleight of hand.

prestige [prɛs'ti:ʒ], *n.m.* marvel; illusion, magic spell; prestige.

prestigieux [prɛsti'sjø], *a.* (*fem.* **-euse**) marvellous, amazing.

(*C*) **presto** [prɛs'to], *n.m.* pressure cooker.

présumer [prezy'me], *v.t.* to presume, to suppose.

présure [pre'zy:r], *n.f.* rennet.

prêt (1) [prɛ], *a.* ready, prepared.

prêt (2) [prɛ], *n.m.* loan; (*Mil.*) pay.

prétantaine [pretɑ̃'tɛn], *n.f.* **courir la prétantaine,** to gad about.

prêté [prɛ'te], *a.* lent.

prétendant [pretɑ̃'dɑ̃], *n.m.* (*fem.* **-e**) claimant.—*n.m.* suitor; pretender (*to the throne*).

prétendre [pre'tɑ̃:dr], *v.t.* to claim, to lay claim to; to mean; affirm.—*v.i.* to lay claim (*to*); to aspire (*à*).

prétendu [pretɑ̃'dy], *a.* pretended, supposed, sham, so-called, would-be.—*n.m.* (*fem.* **-e**) future husband or wife.

prétentieux [pretɑ̃'sjø], *a.* (*fem.* **-euse**) pretentious, assuming.

prétention [pretɑ̃'sjɔ̃], *n.f.* pretension, claim; intention, wish; expectation.

prêter [prɛ'te], *v.t.* to lend; to impart; to attribute; to bestow.—*v.i.* to give, to stretch; to invite, to give rise to. **se prêter,** *v.r.* to give way; to lend oneself *or* itself; to countenance, to favour.

prêteur [prɛ'tœ:r], *n.m.* (*fem.* **-euse**) lender.

prétexte [pre'tɛkst], *n.m.* pretext, pretence; plea.

prétexter [pretɛks'te], *v.t.* to allege (*as pretext*), to pretend, to feign.

prétoire [pre'twa:r], *n.m.* (*Rom. Ant.*) praetorium.

prétorien [preto'rjɛ̃], *a.* (*fem.* **-enne**) praetorian.

prêtre [prɛ:tr], *n.m.* priest.

prêtresse [prɛ'trɛs], *n.f.* priestess.

prêtrise [prɛ'tri:z], *n.f.* priesthood.

preuve [prœ:v], *n.f.* proof; evidence, testimony.

preux [prø], *a. inv.* gallant, doughty, valiant.—*n.m.* valiant knight.

prévaloir [preva'lwa:r], *v.i. irr.* (*conjug. like* VALOIR) to prevail. **se prévaloir,** *v.r.* to take advantage, to avail oneself; to boast.

prévaricateur [prevarika'tœ:r], *a.* (*fem.* **-trice**) dishonest, unjust.—*n.m.* (*fem.* **-trice**) betrayer of trust.

prévarication [prevarika'sjɔ̃], *n.f.* betrayal of trust, maladministration of justice.

prévariquer [prevari'ke], *v.i.* to betray one's trust.

prévenance [prev'nɑ̃:s], *n.f.* (*pl.*) kind attentions.

prévenant [prev'nɑ̃], *a.* obliging, kind; prepossessing, engaging.

prévenir [prev'ni:r], *v.t. irr.* (*conjug. like* TENIR) to precede; to forestall; to prevent; to prepossess; to predispose; to warn. **se prévenir,** *v.r.* to be prejudiced.

préventif [prevɑ̃'tif], *a.* (*fem.* **-tive**) preventive.

prévention [prevɑ̃'sjɔ̃], *n.f.* prepossession, prejudice; suspicion; accusation.

préventivement [prevɑ̃tiv'mɑ̃], *adv.* by way of prevention; while awaiting trial.

prévenu [prev'ny], *a.* forestalled, anticipated; prejudiced; accused.—*n.m.* (*fem.* **-e**) the accused.

prévisible [previ'zibl], *a.* foreseeable.

prévision [previ'zjɔ̃], *n.f.* forecast; estimate, expectation.

prévoir [pre'vwa:r], *v.t. irr.* to foresee, to anticipate.

prévôt [pre'vo], *n.m.* provost.

prévôté [prevo'te], *n.f.* provostship; military police.

prévoyance [prevwa'jɑ̃:s], *n.f.* foresight, forethought, prudence.

prévoyant [prevwa'jɑ̃], *a.* provident, prudent, careful.

prié [pri'je], *a.* invited (*to a feast etc.*).

prie-Dieu [pri'djø], *n.m. inv.* praying-stool.

prier [pri'je], *v.t.* to pray, to beseech; to request; to invite.

prière [pri'jɛ:r], *n.f.* prayer; request, entreaty; invitation.

prieur [pri'jœ:r], *n.m.* prior (*superior of a convent*).

prieure [pri'jœ:r], *n.f.* prioress.

prieuré [prijœ're], *n.m.* priory.

primaire [pri'mɛ:r], *a.* primary.

procuration

primat [pri'ma], *n.m.* primate, metropolitan.
primauté [primo'te], *n.f.* primacy, priority, pre-eminence; the lead (*at cards, dice etc.*).
prime [prim], *a.* first.—*n.f.* premium; subsidy; (*Mil.*) bounty; bonus, prize; (*Fenc.*) prime; (*Comm.*) free gift; *certificat de primes*, debenture; *faire prime*, to be at a premium.
primer [pri'me], *v.t.* to surpass, to excel.—*v.i.* to play first, to lead (*at games*); to excel.
primeur [pri'mœːr], *n.f.* early vegetables, fruit, flowers, etc.; early sentiment, love etc.; freshness, bloom.
primevère [prim'vɛːr], *n.f.* (*Bot.*) primula, primrose, cowslip.
primitif [primi'tif], *a.* (*fem.* **-tive**) first, early, primitive, aboriginal; pristine.—*n.m.* (*Gram., Paint.*) primitive.
primitivement [primitiv'mã], *adv.* primitively, originally.
primo [pri'mo], *adv.* first, in the first place.
primordial [primor'djal], *a.* (*m. pl.* **-aux**) primordial.
prince [prɛ̃ːs], *n.m.* prince.
princeps [prɛ̃'sɛps], *a. inv. édition princeps*, first edition.
princesse [prɛ̃'sɛs], *n.f.* princess.
princier [prɛ̃'sje], *a.* (*fem.* **-ière**) princely, like a prince.
principal [prɛ̃si'pal], *a.* (*m. pl.* **-aux**) principal, chief, most important.—*n.m.* chief thing, principal point; principal, capital (*money*); headmaster (*of a collège*); (*pl.*) chief personages (*of a town etc.*).
principalement [prɛ̃sipal'mã], *adv.* principally, chiefly.
principauté [prɛ̃sipo'te], *n.f.* principality, princedom.
principe [prɛ̃'sip], *n.m.* beginning, source, basis; principle; (*pl.*) principles, rudiments; *dès le principe*, from the very first; *en principe*, as a rule.
printanier [prɛ̃ta'nje], *a.* (*fem.* **-ière**) spring-like, vernal; (*fig.*) youthful, early.
printemps [prɛ̃'tã], *n.m.* spring, spring-time; (*fig.*) prime, bloom.
priorité [priori'te], *n.f.* priority.
pris [pri], *a.* taken, caught, seized; frozen.
prisable [pri'zabl], *a.* estimable, worthy of esteem.
prise [priːz], *n.f.* taking, capture; prize; hold, purchase; grip; quarrel; dose; pinch (*of snuff etc.*); (*pl.*) fighting.
priser (1) [pri'ze], *v.t., v.i.* to (take) snuff.
priser (2) [pri'ze], *v.t.* to appraise, to estimate; to esteem.
priseur [pri'zœːr], *n.m.* *commissaire priseur*, auctioneer, valuer.
prismatique [prisma'tik], *a.* prismatic.
prisme [prism], *n.m.* prism.
prison [pri'zɔ̃], *n.f.* prison, gaol; imprisonment.
prisonnier [prizo'nje], *n.m.* (*fem.* **-ière**) prisoner.
privation [priva'sjɔ̃], *n.f.* privation; want, need.
privauté [privo'te], *n.f.* extreme familiarity *or* liberty.
privé [pri've], *a.* and *n.m.* (*fem.* **-ée**) private; familiar, intimate; tame (*of animals*).

priver [pri've], *v.t.* to deprive, to bereave; to tame (*animals etc.*). **se priver**, *v.r.* to deprive *or* stint oneself; to abstain (*de*).
privilège [privi'lɛːʒ], *n.m.* privilege; licence; prerogative, grant.
privilégié [privile'ʒje], *a.* privileged; licensed; entitled to preference (*of creditors*); preference (*of shares*).—*n.m.* (*fem.* **-ée**) privileged person.
privilégier [privile'ʒje], *v.t.* to privilege; to license.
prix [pri], *n.m. inv.* price, cost, value; rate, return; reward, prize; stakes (*race for prize*); *à prix d'argent*, for money; *à vil prix*, dirt-cheap; *prix coûtant*, cost price; *prix de gros*, wholesale price; *remporter le prix*, to carry off the prize.
probabilité [probabili'te], *n.f.* probability, likelihood.
probable [pro'babl], *a.* probable, likely, credible.
probablement [probablə'mã], *adv.* probably.
probant [pro'bã], *a.* convincing, conclusive.
probation [proba'sjɔ̃], *n.f.* (*Eccles.*) probation.
probe [prob], *a.* honest, upright.
probité [probi'te], *n.f.* probity, honesty, integrity.
problématique [problema'tik], *a.* problematical; questionable, doubtful.
problématiquement [problematik'mã], *adv.* problematically.
problème [pro'blɛm], *n.m.* problem.
procédé [prose'de], *n.m.* behaviour, proceeding, conduct; process, operation; (*Billiards*) cue-tip.
procéder [prose'de], *v.i.* (*conjug. like* CÉDER) to proceed, to arise, to originate (*de*); to behave.
procédure [prose'dyːr], *n.f.* procedure; proceedings.
procès [pro'sɛ], *n.m.* lawsuit, action, trial; (*Anat.*) process.
procession [prose'sjɔ̃], *n.f.* procession.
processionnel [prosesjo'nɛl], *a.* (*fem.* **-elle**) processional.
procès-verbal [prosɛvɛr'bal], *n.m.* (*pl.* **-verbaux**) official report; minute of proceedings; police report.
prochain [pro'ʃɛ̃], *a.* near, nearest, next.—*n.m.* neighbour, fellow-creature.
prochainement [proʃɛn'mã], *adv.* shortly, soon.
proche [proʃ], *a.* near, neighbouring; nigh, approaching.—*prep.* and *adv.* near, nigh; *de proche en proche*, gradually.—*n.m.* (*usu. in pl.*) near relation, kin, kindred.
proclamation [proklama'sjɔ̃], *n.f.* proclamation.
proclamer [prokla'me], *v.t.* to proclaim, to announce; to publish; to disclose.
proclivité [prokivi'te], *n.f.* proclivity, slope.
procréateur [prokrea'tœːr], *a.* (*fem.* **-trice**) procreative.—*n.m.* (*fem.* **-trice**) procreator.
procréation [prokrea'sjɔ̃], *n.f.* procreation.
procréer [prokre'e], *v.t.* to procreate, to beget.
procurateur [prokyra'tœːr], *n.m.* (*Hist.*) procurator.
procuration [prokyra'sjɔ̃], *n.f.* procuration, power of attorney, proxy (*deed*).

257

procurer

procurer [prɔky're], *v.t.* to procure, to obtain.
se procurer, *v.r.* to procure, to get for
oneself.

procureur [prɔky'rœːr], *n.m.* (*fem.* procuratrice) attorney, procurator, proxy.

prodigalement [prɔdigal'mɑ̃], *adv.* prodigally, extravagantly.

prodigalité [prɔdigali'te], *n.f.* prodigality, lavishness.

prodige [prɔ'diːʒ], *n.m.* prodigy, marvel.

prodigieusement [prɔdiʒjøz'mɑ̃], *adv.* prodigiously.

prodigieux [prɔdi'ʒjø], *a.* (*fem.* -euse) prodigious, wonderful; stupendous.

prodigue [prɔ'dig], *a.* prodigal, lavish; wasteful.—*n.* prodigal, spendthrift.

prodiguer [prɔdi'ge], *v.t.* to be prodigal of; to waste, to squander. se prodiguer, *v.r.* to make oneself cheap; not to spare oneself.

prodrome [prɔ'droːm], *n.m.* introduction, preface, preamble.

producteur [prɔdyk'tœːr], *a.* (*fem.* -trice) productive.—*n.m.* (*fem.* -trice) producer.

productif [prɔdyk'tif], *a.* (*fem.* -tive) productive.

production [prɔdyk'sjɔ̃], *n.f.* production; produce, product (*of nature*); yield, output.

productivité [prɔdyktivi'te], *n.f.* productivity; productiveness.

produire [prɔ'dɥiːr], *v.t. irr.* (*conjug. like* CONDUIRE) to produce; to bear; to exhibit; to introduce. se produire, *v.r.* to put oneself forward; to occur, to happen.

produit [prɔ'dɥi], *n.m.* produce, product, production; proceeds.

proéminence [prɔemi'nɑ̃ːs], *n.f.* prominence; protuberance.

proéminent [prɔemi'nɑ̃], *a.* prominent, protuberant.

profanateur [prɔfana'tœːr], *n.m.* (*fem.* -trice) profaner.

profanation [prɔfana'sjɔ̃], *n.f.* profanation.

profane [prɔ'fan], *a.* profane; secular.—*n.* profane person; outsider; layman.

profaner [prɔfa'ne], *v.t.* to profane, to desecrate; to defile.

proférer [prɔfe're], *v.t.* (*conjug. like* CÉDER) to utter, to pronounce.

professer [prɔfɛ'se], *v.t.* to profess; to exercise, to practise; to teach, to lecture on. —*v.i.* to lecture, to teach.

professeur [prɔfɛ'sœːr], *n.m.* (*fem.* femme professeur) professor, lecturer (*at university*); teacher in secondary schools.

profession [prɔfɛ'sjɔ̃], *n.f.* profession, declaration; calling, business.

professionnel [prɔfesjɔ'nɛl], *a.* and *n.m.* (*fem.* -elle) (*Spt. etc.*) professional.

professoral [prɔfesɔ'ral], *a.* (*m. pl.* -aux) professorial.

professorat [prɔfesɔ'ra], *n.m.* professorship, lectureship; mastership (*of lycée or collège*).

profil [prɔ'fil], *n.m.* profile, side-view; outline; (*Drawing*) section.

profiler [prɔfi'le], *v.t.* to represent *or* show in profile. se profiler, *v.r.* to appear in profile, to be outlined.

profit [prɔ'fi], *n.m.* profit, gain; benefit, utility, use; (*pl.*) perquisites.

profitable [prɔfi'tabl], *a.* profitable, advantageous.

profiter [prɔfi'te], *v.i.* to profit, to gain, to benefit; to take advantage of (*de*).

profiteur [prɔfi'tœːr], *n.m.* (*fem.* -euse) (*pej.*) profiteer.

profond [prɔ'fɔ̃], *a.* deep; profound; vast; sound (*of sleep etc.*); downright; dark (*of night etc.*).—*n.m.* depth, abyss.

profondément [prɔfɔ̃de'mɑ̃], *adv.* deeply, profoundly, greatly; soundly.

profondeur [prɔfɔ̃'dœːr], *n.f.* depth; profundity; penetration; extent.

profus [prɔ'fy], *a.* profuse.

profusément [prɔfyze'mɑ̃], *adv.* profusely.

profusion [prɔfy'zjɔ̃], *n.f.* profusion.

progéniture [prɔʒeni'tyːr], *n.f.* progeny.

prognostique [prɔgnɔs'tik], *a.* (*Med.*) prognostic.

programmation [prɔgrama'sjɔ̃], *n.f.* programming.

programme [prɔ'gram], *n.m.* (*Theat. etc.*) programme; (*sch.*) curriculum, syllabus.

progrès [prɔ'grɛ], *n.m.* progress; advancement, improvement, development.

progresser [prɔgrɛ'se], *v.i.* to progress, to get on.

progressif [prɔgrɛ'sif], *a.* (*fem.* -ive) progressive.

progression [prɔgrɛ'sjɔ̃], *n.f.* progression.

progressiste [prɔgrɛ'sist], *a.* progressive.— *n.* progressist, progressive.

progressivement [prɔgresiv'mɑ̃], *adv.* progressively.

prohiber [prɔi'be], *v.t.* to forbid, to prohibit.

prohibitif [prɔibi'tif], *a.* (*fem.* -tive) prohibitive, exorbitant.

prohibition [prɔibi'sjɔ̃], *n.f.* prohibition.

proie [prwa], *n.f.* prey, prize, booty.

projecteur [prɔʒɛk'tœːr], *n.m.* searchlight; projector; floodlight.

projectile [prɔʒɛk'til], *a.* and *n.m.* projectile, missile.

projection [prɔʒɛk'sjɔ̃], *n.f.* projection; (*Cine.*) **appareil de projection**, projector.

projectionniste [prɔʒɛksjɔ'nist], *n.* (*Cine.*) projectionist.

projet [prɔ'ʒɛ], *n.m.* project, plan, idea; rough draft; **homme à projets**, schemer.

projeter [prɔʒ'te], *v.t.* (*conjug. like* APPELER) to project, to throw; to delineate, to plan, to design; to contemplate, to intend.—*v.i.* to scheme, to form projects. se projeter, *v.r.* to project, to stand out.

prolétaire [prɔle'tɛːr], *a.* and *n.m.* proletarian.

prolétariat [prɔleta'rja], *n.m.* proletariat.

prolifique [prɔli'fik], *a.* prolific.

prolixe [prɔ'liks], *a.* verbose.

prologue [prɔ'lɔg], *n.m.* prologue.

prolongation [prɔlɔ̃ga'sjɔ̃], *n.f.* prolongation; extension.

prolongement [prɔlɔ̃ʒ'mɑ̃], *n.m.* prolongation, extension.

prolonger [prɔlɔ̃'ʒe], *v.t.* (*conjug. like* MANGER) to prolong, to lengthen, to protract; to draw out. se prolonger, *v.r.* to be protracted; to extend; to continue.

promenade [prɔm'nad], *n.f.* walk; walking; promenade; drive, excursion, pleasure-trip.

promener [prɔm'ne], *v.t.* to take out for a walk, for a drive, for a ride, for an airing; to cast (*one's eyes*) over; to run or pass (*one's hand, fingers*) over. se promener, *v.r.* to walk, to go for a walk, ramble, drive, row, sail etc.; to stroll.

promeneur [prɔm'nœːr], *n.m. (fem. -euse)* walker; rider; person taking a drive.

promenoir [prɔm'nwaːr], *n.m.* covered walk; promenade (*in a concert-hall etc.*).

promesse [prɔ'mɛs], *n.f.* promise; promissory note.

promettre [prɔ'mɛtr], *v.t. irr. (conjug. like* METTRE) to promise; to forebode.—*v.i.* to be promising. **se promettre,** *v.r.* to promise oneself; to purpose; to promise each other.

promis [prɔ'mi], *a.* promised; intended, engaged.—*n.m. (fem. -e)* fiancé *or* fiancée.

promiscuité [prɔmiskɥi'te], *n.f.* promiscuity.

promontoire [prɔmɔ̃'twaːr], *n.m.* promontory, headland.

promoteur [prɔmɔ'tœːr], *n.m. (fem. -trice)* promoter.

promotion [prɔmo'sjɔ̃], *n.f.* promotion, preferment.

promouvoir [prɔmu'vwaːr], *v.t. irr. (conjug. like* MOUVOIR) to promote, to advance.

prompt [prɔ̃], *a.* prompt, quick, active; sudden, swift; hasty.

promptement [prɔ̃t'mã], *adv.* promptly.

promptitude [prɔ̃ti'ty:d], *n.f.* promptitude, promptness; suddenness; hastiness.

promulgation [prɔmylga'sjɔ̃], *n.f.* promulgation.

promulguer [prɔmyl'ge], *v.t.* to promulgate.

prône [proːn], *n.m.* sermon (*at Mass*); (*fig.*) lecture, rebuke.

prôner [pro'ne], *v.t.* to lecture, to sermonize; to extol.—*v.i.* to sermonize.

prôneur [pro'nœːr], *n.m. (fem. -euse)* long-winded preacher.

pronom [prɔ'nɔ̃], *n.m. (Gram.)* pronoun.

prononçable [prɔnɔ̃'sabl], *a.* pronounceable.

prononcé [prɔnɔ̃'se], *a.* pronounced, decided, marked; (*Paint. etc.*) prominent; broad (*of speech*).—*n.m.* judgment delivered, sentence.

prononcer [prɔnɔ̃'se], *v.t. (conjug. like* COMMENCER) to pronounce, to utter, to say, to declare; to pass (*a verdict etc.*).—*v.i.* to declare one's sentiments, to decide with authority. **se prononcer,** *v.r.* to declare oneself, to express one's opinion, to give a verdict; to be pronounced.

prononciation [prɔnɔ̃sja'sjɔ̃], *n.f.* pronunciation; utterance.

pronostic [prɔnɔs'tik], *n.m.* prognostic; prognostication; (*Med.*) prognosis; weather forecast; (*racing*) tip.

propagande [prɔpa'gãːd], *n.f.* propaganda.

propagandiste [prɔpagã'dist], *n.* propagandist.

propagateur [prɔpaga'tœːr], *a. (fem. -trice)* propagating, spreading.—*n.m. (fem -trice)* propagator.

propagation [prɔpaga'sjɔ̃], *n.f.* propagation, spreading, diffusion.

propager [prɔpa'ʒe], *v.t. (conjug. like* MANGER) to propagate, to spread abroad, to diffuse. **se propager,** *v.r.* to be propagated, to spread.

propension [prɔpã'sjɔ̃], *n.f.* propensity, tendency.

prophète [prɔ'fɛːt], *n.m.* prophet, seer.

prophétesse [prɔfe'tɛs], *n.f.* prophetess.

prophétie [prɔfe'si], *n.f.* prophecy, prophesying.

prophétique [prɔfe'tik], *a.* prophetic.

prophétiser [prɔfeti'ze], *v.t.* to prophesy, to foretell.

propice [prɔ'pis], *a.* propitious, favourable.

propitiation [prɔpisja'sjɔ̃], *n.f.* propitiation.

propitiatoire [prɔpisja'twaːr], *a.* propitiatory.

proportion [prɔpɔr'sjɔ̃], *n.f.* proportion, ratio.

proportionné [prɔpɔrsjɔ'ne], *a.* proportioned, suited.

proportionnel [prɔpɔrsjɔ'nɛl], *a. (fem. -elle)* proportional.

proportionner [prɔpɔrsjɔ'ne], *v.t.* to proportion, to adjust, to adapt.

propos [prɔ'po], *n.m.* talk, words; remark; purpose, resolution; (*pl.*) idle remarks, tittle-tattle; *à propos,* apt, to the purpose; by the way; *à propos de,* with respect to; *à quel propos?* what about? *de propos délibéré,* of set purpose; *mal à propos,* ill-timed; *propos de table,* table-talk; *venir fort à propos,* to come in the nick of time.

proposer [prɔpo'ze], *v.t.* to propose; to propound, to move; to designate, to set up.—*v.i.* to propose. **se proposer,** *v.r.* to propose oneself; to intend, to have in view.

proposeur [prɔpo'zœːr], *n.m. (fem. -euse)* proposer, propounder.

proposition [prɔpozi'sjɔ̃], *n.f.* proposal; proposition; motion; (*Gram.*) clause.

propre [prɔpr], *a.* own; very, same, selfsame; proper; appropriate, suitable; good, right, correct; clean, neat, tidy; *le mot propre,* the right word; *peu propre,* inappropriate; dirty.—*n.m.* characteristic, property; proper sense; (*Law*) real property.

propre à rien [prɔpra'rjɛ̃], *n. inv.* good for nothing.

proprement [prɔprə'mã], *adv.* properly correctly; cleanly, neatly.

propret [prɔ'prɛ], *a. (fem. -ette)* spruce, neat, tidy.

propreté [prɔprə'te], *n.f.* cleanliness; neatness.

propriétaire [prɔprie'tɛːr], *n.* owner, proprietor, proprietress; landlord, householder.

propriété [prɔprie'te], *n.f.* property; estate; characteristic; *propriété littéraire,* copyright.

propulser [prɔpyl'se], *v.t. (Naut., Av.)* to propel.

propulseur [prɔpyl'sœːr], *n.m.* propeller.

propulsif [prɔpyl'sif], *a. (fem. -sive)* propelling, propellent.

propulsion [prɔpyl'sjɔ̃], *n.f.* propulsion.

prorogation [prɔrɔga'sjɔ̃], *n.f.* adjournment, prorogation (*of Parliament etc.*); extension.

proroger [prɔrɔ'ʒe], *v.t. (conjug. like* MANGER) to prolong the time of; to prorogue (*Parliament etc.*).

prosaïque [prɔza'ik], *a.* prosaic; banal; prosy.

prosaïquement [prɔzaik'mã], *adv.* prosaically.

prosateur [prɔza'tœːr], *n.m.* prose-writer.

proscription [prɔskrip'sjɔ̃], *n.f.* proscription.

proscrire [prɔs'kriːr], *v.t. irr. (conjug. like* ÉCRIRE) to proscribe, to outlaw; to banish.

proscrit

proscrit [prɔs'kri], *a.* proscribed, forbidden. —*n.m.* (*fem.* **-e**) proscribed person, outlaw; exile.

prose [proːz], *n.f.* prose.

prosodie [prɔzɔ'di], *n.f.* prosody.

prospecter [prɔspɛk'te], *v.t.* to prospect (*for oil, minerals*).

prospecteur [prɔspɛk'tœːr], *n.m.* prospector.

prospectus [prɔspɛk'tyːs], *n.m. inv.* prospectus; handbill.

prospère [prɔs'pɛːr], *a.* prosperous, thriving.

prospérer [prɔspe're], *v.i.* (*conjug. like* CÉDER) to prosper, to be prosperous, to thrive.

prospérité [prɔsperi'te], *n.f.* prosperity.

prostate [prɔs'tat], *n.f.* (*Anat.*) prostate.

prosternation [prɔstɛrna'sjɔ̃], *n.f.*, **prosternement** [prɔstɛrnə'mã], *n.m.* prostration, ʋbeisance.

prosterner [prɔstɛr'ne], *v.t.* to prostrate. **se prosterner,** *v.r.* to prostrate oneself, to bow low.

prostituée [prɔsti'tɥe], *n.f.* prostitute.

prostituer [prɔsti'tɥe], *v.t.* to prostitute. **se prostituer,** *v.r.* to prostitute oneself.

prostitution [prɔstity'sjɔ̃], *n.f.* prostitution.

prostration [prɔstra'sjɔ̃], *n.f.* prostration.

protagoniste [prɔtagɔ'nist], *n.m.* protagonist.

protecteur [prɔtɛk'tœːr], *a.* (*fem.* **-trice**) protective; patronizing.—*n.m.* (*fem.* **-trice**) protector, protectress; patron, patroness.—*n.m.* (*Eng.*) guard (*for machine tool*).

protection [prɔtɛk'sjɔ̃], *n.f.* protection, shelter; support, patronage.

protectorat [prɔtɛktɔ'ra], *n.m.* protectorate.

protégé [prɔte'ʒe], *n.m.* (*fem.* **-ée**) favourite, dependant.

protéger [prɔte'ʒe], *v.t.* (*conjug. like* ASSIÉGER) to protect, to defend; to patronize, to favour.

protège-vue [prɔtɛʒ'vy], *n.m. inv.* eye-shade.

protéine [prɔte'in], *n.f.* protein.

protestant [prɔtɛs'tã], *a.* and *n.m.* (*fem.* **-e**) Protestant.

protestantisme [prɔtɛstã'tism], *n.m.* Protestantism.

protestation [prɔtɛsta'sjɔ̃], *n.f.* protestation, protest.

protester [prɔtɛs'te], *v.t.* to protest, to affirm.—*v.i.* to protest.

protocole [prɔtɔ'kɔl], *n.m.* protocol.

proton [prɔ'tɔ̃], *n.m.* proton.

protoplasma [prɔtɔplas'ma], **protoplasme** [prɔtɔ'plasm], *n.m.* protoplasm.

prototype [prɔtɔ'tip], *n.m.* prototype.

protubérance [prɔtybe'rãːs], *n.f.* protuberance.

protubérant [prɔtybe'rã], *a.* protuberant.

proue [pru], *n.f.* prow, stem, bows (*of ship*).

prouesse [pru'ɛs], *n.f.* prowess, valour; feat.

prouver [pru've], *v.t.* to prove; to substantiate; to show.

provenance [prɔv'nãːs], *n.f.* origin, source; (*pl.*) produce, commodities.

provençal [prɔvã'sal], *a.* (*m. pl.* **-aux**) Provençal.—*n.m.* Provençal (*language*); (**Provençal,** *fem.* **-ale**) Provençal (*person*).

provenir [prɔv'niːr], *v.i. irr.* (*conjug. like* TENIR *but with aux.* ÊTRE) to issue, proceed, spring, originate *or* come from (*de*).

proverbe [prɔ'vɛrb], *n.m.* proverb, saying.

proverbial [prɔvɛr'bjal], *a.* (*m. pl.* **-aux**) proverbial.

providence [prɔvi'dãːs], *n.f.* providence.

providentiel [prɔvidã'sjɛl], *a.* (*fem.* **-elle**) providential.

provigner [prɔvi'ɲe], *v.t.* to layer (*vines*).

provin [prɔ'vɛ̃], *n.m.* layer (*of a vine*).

province [prɔ'vɛ̃ːs], *n.f.* province, shire; country; **en province,** in the country, in the provinces.

provincial [prɔvɛ̃'sjal], *a.* (*m. pl.* **-aux**) provincial; countrified.—*n.m.* (*fem.* **-e**) provincial, country person.

proviseur [prɔvi'zœːr], *n.m.* headmaster (*of a lycée*).

provision [prɔvi'zjɔ̃], *n.f.* provision, stock, store, supply; deposit; (*Comm.*) reserve funds.

provisionnel [prɔvizjɔ'nɛl], *a.* (*fem.* **-elle**) provisional.

provisoire [prɔvi'zwaːr], *a.* provisional, temporary.—*n.m.* provisional nature (*of something*).

provisoirement [prɔvizwar'mã], *adv.* provisionally, temporarily.

provocant [prɔvɔ'kã], *a.* provoking, provocative; exciting.

provocateur [prɔvɔka'tœːr], *a.* (*fem.* **-trice**) provoking, provocative; **agent provocateur,** agent hired to instigate a riot etc.—*n.m.* (*fem.* **-trice**) provoker; aggressor.

provocation [prɔvɔka'sjɔ̃], *n.f.* provocation.

provoquer [prɔvɔ'ke], *v.t.* to provoke, to incite, to call forth; to instigate.

proximité [prɔksimi'te], *n.f.* proximity, nearness.

prude [pryd], *a.* prudish.—*n.f.* prude.

prudemment [pryda'mã], *adv.* prudently, discreetly, cautiously.

prudence [pry'dãːs], *n.f.* carefulness, prudence.

prudent [pry'dã], prudent, discreet; advisable.

pruderie [pry'dri], *n.f.* prudery, prudishness.

prud'homme [pry'dɔm], *n.m.* upright, honest man; (*Ind.*) arbitrator.

pruine [prɥin], *n.f.* bloom (*on fruits*).

prune [pryn], *n.f.* plum.

pruneau [pry'no], *n.m.* (*pl.* **-eaux**) prune.

prunelle (1) [pry'nɛl], *n.f.* sloe; sloe-gin.

prunelle (2) [pry'nɛl], *n.f.* pupil, apple (*of the eye*), eyeball.

prunellier [prynɛ'lje], *n.m.* sloe-tree, blackthorn.

prunier [pry'nje], *n.m.* plum-tree.

Prusse [prys], **la**, *f.* Prussia.

prussien [pry'sjɛ̃], *a.* (*fem.* **-enne**) Prussian.—*n.m.* (**Prussien,** *fem.* **-enne**) Prussian (*person*).

prussique [pry'sik], *a.* (*Chem.*) prussic.

psalmiste [psal'mist], *n.m.* psalmist.

psalmodie [psalmɔ'di], *n.f.* psalmody, intoning; (*fig.*) sing-song.

psalmodier [psalmɔ'dje], *v.t., v.i.* to recite, to chant (*as the psalms*); to read *or* recite in a sing-song manner.

psaume [psoːm], *n.m.* psalm.

psautier [pso'tje], *n.m.* psalter, psalm-book.

pseudonyme [psødɔ'nim], *a.* pseudonymous. —*n.m.* pseudonym, nom-de-plume.

psychanalyse [psikana'liːz], *n.f.* psychoanalysis.

psychanalyste [psikana'list], *n.m.* psycho-analyst.
psychiatre [psi'kjaːtr], *n.m.* psychiatrist.
psychiatrie [psikja'tri], *n.f.* psychiatry.
psychologie [psikɔlɔ'ʒi], *n.f.* psychology.
psychologique [psikɔlɔ'ʒik], *a.* psychological.
psychologue [psikɔ'lɔg], *n.* psychologist.
puant [pɥɑ̃], *a.* stinking; foul.
puanteur [pɥɑ̃'tœːr], *n.f.* stench, stink.
pubère [py'bɛːr], *a.* pubescent, puberal.
puberté [pybɛr'te], *n.f.* puberty.
public [py'blik], *a.* (*fem.* **-ique**) public; notorious; *la chose publique*, the common weal, the State.—*n.m.* public.
publication [pyblika'sjɔ̃], *n.f.* publication; publishing, proclamation.
publiciste [pybli'sist], *n.m.* publicist, journalist.
publicité [pyblisi'te], *n.f.* publicity; advertising.
publier [py'blje], *v.t.* to publish, to make public, to proclaim; to issue.
publiquement [pyblik'mɑ̃], *adv.* in public.
puce (1) [pys], *a. inv.* puce, puce-coloured.
puce (2) [pys], *n.f.* flea.
puceron [pys'rɔ̃], *n.m.* plant-louse, greenfly.
pudeur [py'dœːr], *n.f.* modesty; bashfulness, shame; reserve.
pudibond [pydi'bɔ̃], *a.* bashful; prudish.
pudicité [pydisi'te], *n.f.* modesty, chastity.
pudique [py'dik], *a.* chaste, modest, bashful.
pudiquement [pydik'mɑ̃], *adv.* modestly.
puer [pɥe], *v.t.* (*fam.*) to smell of, to reek of.—*v.i.* to stink.
puéril [pɥe'ril], *a.* juvenile, childish, puerile.
puérilement [pɥeril'mɑ̃], *adv.* childishly.
puérilité [pɥerili'te], *n.f.* puerility, childishness.
pugilat [pyʒi'la], *n.m.* pugilism, boxing.
pugiliste [pyʒi'list], *n.m.* pugilist, boxer.
pugnace [pyg'nas], *a.* pugnacious.
pugnacité [pygnasi'te], *n.f.* pugnacity.
puîné [pɥi'ne], *a.* (*fem.* **-ée**) younger (*brother or sister*).
puis [pɥi], *adv.* then, afterwards, after that, next; besides.
puisage [pɥi'zaːʒ], **puisement** [pɥiz'mɑ̃], *n.m.* drawing up; drawing water.
puisard [pɥi'zaːr], *n.m.* cesspool; sump, water-sump.
puisatier [pɥiza'tje], *n.m.* well-sinker; shaft-sinker (*in mining*).
puisement [PUISAGE].
puiser [pɥi'ze], *v.t.* to draw, to fetch up (*a liquid*); (*fig.*) to imbibe.
puisque [pɥisk], *conj.* since, as, seeing that.
puissamment [pɥisa'mɑ̃], *adv.* powerfully; extremely, very.
puissance [pɥi'sɑ̃ːs], *n.f.* power; force; dominion, sway; influence.
puissant [pɥi'sɑ̃], *a.* powerful, mighty; lusty, stout; strong.
puits [pɥi], *n.m. inv.* well; pit, shaft.
pullulation [pylyla'sjɔ̃], *n.f.*, **pullulement** [pylyl'mɑ̃], *n.m.* pullulation, swarming.
pulluler [pyly'le], *v.i.* to multiply, to pullulate, to swarm.
pulmonaire [pylmɔ'nɛːr], *a.* pulmonary; *phthisie pulmonaire*, consumption.
pulmonique [pylmɔ'nik], *a.* and *n.* consumptive.
pulpe [pylp], *n.f.* pulp.

pulper [pyl'pe], *v.t.* to pulp.
pulpeux [pyl'pø], *a.* (*fem.* **-euse**) pulpous, pulpy.
pulsatif [pylsa'tif], *a.* (*fem.* **-tive**) pulsatory, throbbing.
pulsation [pylsa'sjɔ̃], *n.f.* beating of the pulse, pulsation, throbbing.
pulvérin [pylve'rɛ̃], *n.m.* spray (*from water-falls*).
pulvérisateur [pylveriza'tœːr], *n.m.* pulverizator, vaporizer; spray, atomiser.
pulvérisation [pylveriza'sjɔ̃], *n.f.* pulverization.
pulvériser [pylveri'ze], *v.t.* to reduce to powder *or* dust, to pulverize; to atomize; (*fig.*) to annihilate.
pulvérulent [pylvery'lɑ̃], *a.* pulverulent, powdery.
puma [py'ma], *n.m.* puma, cougar.
pumicin [pymi'sɛ̃], *n.m.* palm-oil.
punaise [py'nɛːz], *n.f.* bug; drawing-pin.
punch [pɔ̃ːʃ], *n.m.* (*Box.*) punch; punch (*beverage*).
punique [py'nik], *a.* Punic.
punir [py'niːr], *v.t.* to punish, to chastise.
punissable [pyni'sabl], *a.* punishable.
punisseur [pyni'sœːr], *a.* (*fem.* **-euse**) punishing, avenging.—*n.m.* (*fem.* **-euse**) punisher; avenger.
punitif [pyni'tif], *a.* (*fem.* **-tive**) punitive.
punition [pyni'sjɔ̃], *n.f.* punishment.
pupille [py'pil], *n.* ward, minor in charge of guardian.—*n.f.* pupil (*of the eye*).
pupitre [py'pitr], *n.m.* desk; music-stand.
pur [pyːr], *a.* pure, unalloyed; unadulterated; unblemished; innocent, chaste; mere, sheer; neat (*of liquor*); *en pure perte*, to no purpose.
purée [py're], *n.f.* mash, purée, thick soup.
purement [pyr'mɑ̃], *adv.* purely; merely.
pureté [pyr'te], *n.f.* purity, guilelessness, innocence; chastity.
purgatif [pyrga'tif], *a.* (*fem.* **-tive**) purgative, purging.—*n.m.* (*Med.*) purgative.
purgation [pyrga'sjɔ̃], *n.f.* purgation, purge.
purgatoire [pyrga'twaːr], *n.m.* purgatory.
purge [pyrʒ], *n.f.* purge; cleansing; disinfection.
purger [pyr'ʒe], *v.t.* (*conjug. like* MANGER) to purge; to cleanse, to purify. **se purger**, *v.r.* to purge oneself; to clear oneself (*of.*).
purificateur [pyrifika'tœːr], *a.* (*fem.* **-trice**) purifying.—*n.m.* (*fem.* **-trice**) purifier.
purification [pyrifika'sjɔ̃], *n.f.* purification.
purifier [pyri'fje], *v.t.* to purify, to cleanse; to refine (*metals etc.*). **se purifier**, *v.r.* to purify oneself, to become refined.
puritain [pyri'tɛ̃], *a.* and *n.m.* (*fem.* **-e**) Puritan.
puritanisme [pyrita'nism], *n.m.* puritanism.
purpurin [pyrpy'rɛ̃], *a.* purplish.
pur-sang [pyr'sɑ̃], *n.m. inv.* thoroughbred.
pus [py], *n.m.* pus, matter.
pusillanime [pyzila'nim], *a.* pusillanimous, faint-hearted.
pusillanimité [pyzilanimi'te], *n.f.* pusillanimity.
pustule [pys'tyl], *n.f.* pustule, pimple, blotch.
putatif [pyta'tif], *a.* (*fem.* **-tive**) putative reputed, supposed.
putativement [pytativ'mɑ̃], *adv.* reputedly.
putois [py'twa], *n.m.* polecat, skunk.

putréfaction

putréfaction [pytrefak'sjɔ̃], *n.f.* putrefaction; putrescence.
putréfier [pytre'fje], *v.t.* to putrefy; to rot. **se putréfier**, *v.r.* to putrefy; to rot; to decompose.
putride [py'trid], *a.* putrid.
pygmée [pig'me], *n.m.* pygmy.
pyjama [piʒa'ma], *n.m.* pyjamas.
pylône [pi'loːn], *n.m.* pylon; mast.
pyorrhée [pio're], *n.f.* pyorrhœa.
pyramidal [pirami'dal], *a.* (*m. pl.* -aux) pyramidal.
pyramide [pira'mid], *n.f.* pyramid.
python [pi'tɔ̃], *n.m.* python (*snake*).

Q

Q, q [ky] *n.m.* the seventeenth letter of the alphabet.
qu' [k], *elision* [QUE].
quadragénaire [kwadraʒe'nɛːr], *a.* forty years of age.—*n.* person forty years old.
quadrangle [kwa'drɑ̃:gl], *n.m.* quadrangle.
quadrangulaire [kwadrɑ̃gy'lɛːr], *a.* quadrangular, four-cornered.
quadrillage [kadri'jaːʒ], *n.m.* chequer-work, pattern in squares; map grid.
quadrille [ka'driːj], *n.m.* quadrille (*card game*); quadrille (*dance*); check (*in tapestry*).
quadrillé [kadri'je], *a.* chequered (*of cloth*); ruled in squares (*of paper*).
quadriréacteur [kwadrireak'tœːr], *n.m.* four-engined jet plane.
quadrupède [kwadry'pɛd], *a.* and *n.m.* quadruped.
quadruple [kwa'drypl], *a.* quadruple, fourfold.
quadruplé [kwadry'ple], *n.m.* (*fem.* -ée) quadruplet, (*fam.*) quad.
quadrupler [kwadry'ple], *v.t., v.i.* to quadruple, to increase fourfold.
quai [ke], *n.m.* quay, wharf, pier; embankment (*along river*); platform (*railway*).
qualifiable [kali'fjabl], *a.* qualifiable, characterized (*as*).
qualification [kalifika'sjɔ̃], *n.f.* title; designation, qualification.
qualifié [kali'fje], *a.* qualified; named.
qualifier [kali'fje], *v.t.* to qualify; to style. **se qualifier**, *v.r.* to style oneself; to qualify (*for*).
qualité [kali'te], *n.f.* quality; property; excellence; talent; qualification; title; *en qualité de*, in the capacity of.
quand [kɑ̃], *adv.* when, whenever, what time; while.—*conj.* though; *quand même*, even though; all the same.
quant [kɑ̃], *adv.* (*followed by à*) as for, with regard to.
quant-à-soi [kɑ̃ta'swa], *n.m.* reserve, dignity.
quantième [kɑ̃'tjɛm], *n.m.* which (*day of the month etc.*).
quantité [kɑ̃ti'te], *n.f.* quantity; abundance, plenty; variety.

quarantaine [karɑ̃'tɛn], *n.f.* about forty; age of forty; quarantine.
quarante [ka'rɑ̃t], *a.* and *n.m.* forty.
quarantième [karɑ̃'tjɛm], *a.* and *n.* fortieth.
quart [kaːr], *a.* fourth.—*n.m.* quarter, fourth part; point (*of the compass*); quart (*measure*); (*Mil.*) tin cup; (*Naut.*) watch.
quarte [kart], *n.f.* (*Mus.*) fourth; (*Fenc., Piquet*) carte.
quartier [kar'tje]. *n.m.* quarter, fourth part; piece, part; ward, district; gammon; (*Mil.*) quarters, barracks.
quartier-maître [kartje'mɛːtr], *n.m.* (*pl.* **quartiers-maîtres**) (*Naut.*) leading seaman.
quarto [kwar'to], *adv.* fourthly, in the fourth place.
quartz [kwaːrts], *n.m.* quartz.
quasi [ka'zi], *adv.* almost, as if, quasi.
quasiment [kazi'mɑ̃], *adv.* (*dial.*) almost, nearly, as you might say.
quaternaire [kwater'nɛːr], *a.* quaternary.
quatorze [ka'tɔrz], *a.* and *n.m.* fourteen; fourteenth.
quatorzième [katɔr'zjɛm], *a.* and *n.* fourteenth.
quatrain [ka'trɛ̃], *n.m.* quatrain.
quatre ['katrə, katr], *a.* and *n.m. inv.* four, fourth.
quatre-temps [katrə'tɑ̃], *n.m. pl.* ember-days.
quatre-vingtième [katrəvɛ̃'tjɛm], *a.* and *n.m.* eightieth.
quatre-vingt(s) [katrə'vɛ̃], *a.* and *n.m.* eighty.
quatrième [kat'rjɛm], *a.* and *n.* fourth.—*n.m.* fourth floor, fourth storey.—*n.f.* third form (*of upper school*); (*Piquet*) quart.
quatrièmement [katrjɛm'mɑ̃], *adv.* fourthly.
quatuor [kwaty'ɔr], *n.m.* (*Mus.*) quartet.
que (1) [kə, k], *pron. rel.* whom, that; which; what? on which; *qu'est-ce que c'est?* what is it?
que (2) [kə, k], *conj.* that; than; than that; as, if, whether; when; without; yet; lest; in order that; oh that, may; let; before; so; only, but; *afin que*, in order that; *attendez qu'il vienne*, wait till he comes; *de sorte que*, so that.—*adv.* how, how much, how many; why, wherefore?
quel [kɛl], *a.* (*fem.* **quelle**) what, which, what sort of.
quelconque [kɛl'kɔ̃:k], *a. indef.* any; any whatsoever; mediocre.
quelque ['kɛlkə, kɛlk], *adj.* some, any; a few; whatever, whatsoever.—*adv.* however, howsoever; some, about.
quelquefois [kɛlkə'fwa], *adv.* sometimes.
quelqu'un [kɛl'kœ̃], *pron. indef. m.* someone, somebody; anyone, anybody.—*n.m.* (*fem.* **quelqu'une**, *pl.* **quelques-uns, quelques-unes,** one (or other), some.
quémander [kemɑ̃'de], *v.t. v.i.* to beg, to solicit.
quémandeur [kemɑ̃'dœːr], *n.m.* (*fem.* -euse) importunate beggar.
qu'en-dira-t-on [kɑ̃dira'tɔ̃], *n.m. inv.* public talk, tittle-tattle.
quenelle [kə'nɛl], *n.f.* forcemeat *or* fish ball.
quenotte [kə'nɔt], *n.f.* (*colloq.*) tooth (*of young children*).
quenouille [kə'nuːj], *n.f.* distaff; bed-post.

querelle [kə'rɛl], *n.f.* quarrel; row, brawl; feud; cause of dispute; *chercher querelle à*, to pick a quarrel with.

quereller [kərɛ'le], *v.t.* to quarrel with; to scold. **se quereller**, *v.r.* to quarrel, to wrangle, to have words.

querelleur [kərɛ'lœːr], *a.* (*fem.* **-euse**) quarrelsome.—*n.m.* (*fem.* **-euse**) quarreller, wrangler.

quérir [ke'riːr], *v.t.* to fetch; (*employed only in the infinitive with aller, envoyer, venir*).

questeur [kɥɛs'tœːr], *n.m.* quaestor.

question [kɛs'tjõ], *n.f.* question, interrogation; query, point, issue; rack, torture.

questionnaire [kɛstjɔ'nɛːr], *n.m.* questionnaire; book of questions.

questionner [kɛstjɔ'ne], *v.t.* to question, to interrogate.

questionneur [kɛstjɔ'nœːr], *a.* (*fem.* **-euse**) inquisitive.—*n.m.* (*fem.* **-euse**) questioner.

questure [kɥɛs'tyːr], *n.f.* quaestorship; quaestors' office.

quête [kɛːt], *n.f.* quest, search; collection, offertory; (*Hunt.*) beating about.

quêter [kɛ'te], *v.t.* to look for, to seek, to go in quest of, to gather.—*v.i.* to beg.

quêteur [kɛ'tœːr], *n.m.* (*fem.* **-euse**) collector; mendicant (friar).

queue [kø], *n.f.* tail; stalk; stem; end; rear; billiard-cue; handle; train (*of robes etc.*); queue.

queue-d'aronde [køda'rõːd], *n.f.* (*pl.* **queues-d'aronde**) dovetail.

qui [ki], *pron. rel.* and *inter.* who, that, whom, which; whoever, whomsoever, whatever; what; some.

quiconque [ki'kõːk], *pron. indef.* whoever, whosoever; whomsoever, whichever.

quiétude [kɥie'tyd], *n.f.* quietude.

quignon [ki'ɲõ], *n.m.* hunch, chunk, hunk (*of bread*).

quille [kiːj], *n.f.* keel; skittle, ninepin.

quiller [ki'je], *v.i.* to throw for partners *or* for first play (*at skittles*).

quillier [ki'je], *n.m.* skittle-alley.

quincaillerie [kɛ̃kaj'ri], *n.f.* ironmongery, hardware.

quincaillier [kɛ̃ka'je], *n.m.* ironmonger.

quinconce [kɛ̃'kõːs], *n.m.* quincunx.

quine [kin], *n.m.* two fives (*at trictrac*); five winning numbers (*in a lottery*).

quinine [ki'nin], *n.f.* quinine.

quinquagénaire [kɥɛ̃kwaʒe'nɛːr], *a.* fifty years old.—*n.* person of fifty.

quinquennal [kɥɛ̃kɥe'nal], *a.* (*m. pl.* **-aux**) quinquennial.

quinquet [kɛ̃'kɛ], *n.m.* argand lamp.

quinquina [kɛ̃ki'na], *n.m.* Peruvian bark.

quintal [kɛ̃'tal], *n.m.* (*pl.* **-aux**) quintal, hundredweight; 100 kilogr.

quinte [kɛ̃t], *n.f.* (*Mus.*) fifth; (*Piquet*) quint; (*fig.*) freak, whim; (*Fenc.*) quinte; *quinte de toux*, fit of coughing.

quintessence [kɛ̃tɛ'sɑ̃ːs], *n.f.* quintessence; (*fig.*) pith, essential part.

quintette [kɛ̃'tɛt], *n.m.* quintet.

quinteux [kɛ̃'tø], *a.* (*fem.* **-euse**) whimsical, crotchety; jibbing (*of a horse*).

quintuple [kɛ̃'typl], *a.* and *n.m.* quintuple.

quintuplé [kɛ̃ty'ple], *n.m.* quintuplet.

quintupler [kɛ̃ty'ple], *v.t.* to quintuple.

quinzaine [kɛ̃'zɛn], *n.f.* about fifteen; fortnight.

quinze [kɛ̃ːz], *a.* and *n.m.* fifteen; fifteenth.

quinzième [kɛ̃'zjɛm], *a.* and *n.* fifteenth.

quinzièmement [kɛ̃zjɛm'mɑ̃], *adv.* fifteenthly, in the fifteenth place.

quiproquo [kipro'ko], *n.m.* mistake; quid pro quo.

quittance [ki'tɑ̃ːs], *n.f.* receipt, discharge.

quittancer [kitɑ̃'se], *v.t.* (*conjug. like* COMMENCER) to receipt.

quitte [kit], *a.* discharged (*from debt*); clear, free.

quitter [ki'te], *v.t.* to leave; to discharge; to give up; to leave off, to lay aside; to depart (*life*); *ne quittez pas !* (*Teleph.*) hold the line! **se quitter**, *v.r.* to part company, to separate.

qui va là? [kiva'la], *inter. phr.* who goes there?

qui-vive? [ki'viːv], *n.m.* who goes there? (*challenge of a sentry*); *être sur le qui-vive*, to be on the alert.

quoi [kwa], *pron. rel.* and *inter.* which; what; *il n'y a pas de quoi*, don't mention it! *le je ne sais quoi*, the indefinable something; *quoi que*, whatever.—*int.* what!

quoique ['kwakə], *conj.* although, though.

quolibet [kɔli'bɛ], *n.m.* gibe, jeer.

quote-part [kɔt'paːr], *n.f.* (*pl.* **quotes-parts**) quota, portion, share.

quotidien [kɔti'djɛ̃], *a.* (*fem.* **-enne**) daily, quotidian.—*n.m.* daily (newspaper).

quotidiennement [kɔtidjɛn'mɑ̃], *adv.* daily.

quotient [kɔ'sjɑ̃], *n.m.* quotient.

quotité [kɔti'te], *n.f.* (*Fin.*) quota, share; proportion.

R

R, r [ɛːr], *n.m.* the eighteenth letter of the alphabet.

rabâchage [rabɑ'ʃaːʒ], *n.m.* tiresome repetition; drivel.

rabâcher [rabɑ'ʃe], *v.t.*, *v.i.* to repeat (*the same thing*) over and over again.

rabâcheur [rabɑ'ʃœːr], *n.m.* (*fem.* **-euse**) eternal repeater, twaddler.

rabais [ra'bɛ], *n.m. inv.* abatement, reduction; discount.

rabaissement [rabɛs'mɑ̃], *n.m.* lowering, depreciation; (*fig.*) humiliation.

rabaisser [rabɛ'se], *v.t.* to lower; to abate, to lessen; to depreciate; to humble, to disparage.

rabat [ra'ba], *n.m.* clerical *or* academic band; beating (*for game*).

rabat-joie [raba'ʒwa], *n.m. inv.* damper, wet blanket, spoil-sport.

rabattage [raba'taːʒ], *n.m.* cutting down, diminution; beating (*for game*).

rabattre [ra'batr], *v.t.* (*conjug. like* BATTRE) to beat down, to bring *or* cut down; to smooth down; to humble; (*Hunt.*) to beat up; to abate.—*v.i.* to reduce one's pretensions. **se**

rabattre, *v.r.* to turn off, to change one's road; to come down; to fall back on.
rabbin [ra'bɛ̃], *n.m.* rabbi.
rabbinique [rabi'nik], *a.* rabbinical.
rabique [ra'bik], *a.* rabid, rabic.
râble [rɑ:bl], *n.m.* back (*of hare, rabbit etc.*); fire-rake.
râblé [rɑ'ble], *a.* broad-backed; (*fig.*) vigorous, strapping.
rabonnir [rabo'ni:r], *v.t., v.i.* to improve (*wine*).
rabot [ra'bo], *n.m.* plane.
rabotage [rabo'ta:ʒ], **rabotement** [rabɔt 'mã], *n.m.* planing.
raboter [rabo'te], *v.t.* to plane; (*fig.*) to polish; (*slang*) to pilfer, to filch.
raboteur [rabo'tœ:r], *n.m.* planer.
raboteuse (1) [rabo'tø:z], *n.f.* planing-machine.
raboteux [rabo'tø], *a.* (*fem.* **-euse** (2)) knotty; rough, rugged, uneven; (*fig.*) harsh (*of style*).
rabougri [rabu'gri], *a.* stunted, dwarfed.
rabougrir [rabu'gri:r], *v.t.* to stunt.
raboutir [rabu'ti:r], **rabouter** [rabu'te], *v.t.* to join end to end, to join on.
rabrouer [rabru'e], *v.t.* to snub, to rebuke sharply.
rabroueur [rabru'œ:r], *n.m.* (*fem.* **-euse**) snappish person, scold.
racaille [ra'kɑ:j], *n.f.* rabble, riffraff; rubbish, trash.
raccommodage [rakomo'da:ʒ], *n.m.* mending, repairing; darning.
raccommodement [rakomod'mã], *n.m.* reconciliation.
raccommoder [rakomo'de], *v.t.* to mend, to repair; to darn; to patch; to set right, to correct; to reconcile. **se raccommoder**, *v.r.* to be reconciled.
raccommodeur [rakomo'dœ:r], *n.m.* (*fem.* **-euse**) mender.
raccompagner [rakõpa'ɲe], *v.t.* to accompany back.
raccord [ra'kɔ:r], *n.m.* joining, fitting; joint, connection.
raccordement [rakordə'mã], *n.m.* joining, union, junction; levelling; *voie de raccordement*, loop line.
raccorder [rakor'de], *v.t.* to join, to unite, to connect. **se raccorder**, *v.r.* to fit together, to blend.
raccourci [rakur'si], *a.* shortened, abridged. —*n.m.* abridgment, epitome; short cut.
raccourcir [rakur'si:r], *v.t.* to shorten, to curtail, to abridge.—*v.i.* to become shorter; to take a short cut. **se raccourcir**, *v.r.* to grow shorter, to contract, to shrink.
raccourcissement [rakursis'mã], *n.m.* shortening, abridgment, shrinking.
raccoutrage [raku'tra:ʒ], **raccoutrement** [rakutrə'mã], *n.m.* mending (*of clothes etc.*).
raccoutrer [raku'tre], *v.t.* to mend, to repair (*garment*).
raccoutumer (se) [sərakuty'me], *v.r.* to re-accustom oneself, to get used to again.
raccroc [ra'kro], *n.m.* chance, lucky stroke (*esp. at billiards*), fluke.
raccrocher [rakro'ʃe], *v.t.* to hook up again, to hang up again; (*colloq.*) to recover.—*v.i.* to make flukes (*at play*); (*Teleph.*) to ring off. **se raccrocher**, *v.r.* to cling; to retrieve one's losses; to grasp *or* snatch at.

race [ras], *n.f.* race; stock, breed; family, ancestry; generation; *un cheval de race*, a thoroughbred horse.
rachat [ra'ʃa], *n.m.* repurchase, redemption.
rachetable [raʃ'tabl], *a.* redeemable.
racheter [raʃ'te], *v.t.* (*conjug. like* AMENER) to buy back, to repurchase; to redeem; to ransom; to compensate; to atone for. **se racheter**, *v.r.* to redeem oneself; to be made up for.
rachitique [raʃi'tik], *a.* rachitic, rickety.—*n.* rickety person.
rachitis [raʃi'tis], **rachitisme** [raʃi'tism], *n.m.* rachitis, rickets; (*Bot.*) blight.
racial [ra'sjal], *a.* (*m. pl.* **-aux**) racial.
racine [ra'sin], *n.f.* root; (*fig.*) principle, origin.
racisme [ra'sism], *n.m.* racialism.
raciste [ra'sist], *a.* racial.—*n.* racialist.
raclage [ra'kla:ʒ], *n.m.* scraping, raking.
racle [rɑ:kl], *n.f.* scraper.
raclée [rɑ'kle], *n.f.* (*fam.*) thrashing, hiding.
racler [rɑ'kle], *v.t.* to scrape, to rake; to rasp.
racleur [rɑ'klœ:r], *n.m.* (*fem.* **-euse**) scraper; (*fam.*) bad violinist.
racloir [rɑ'klwa:r], *n.m.* scraper, road-scraper.
raclure [rɑ'kly:r], *n.f.* scrapings.
racolage [rako'la:ʒ], *n.m.* impressing; recruiting.
racoler [rako'le], *v.t.* to enlist.
racoleur [rako'lœ:r], *n.m.* tout.
racontable [rakõ'tabl], *a.* relatable.
racontar [rakõ'ta:r], *n.m.* gossip, tittle-tattle.
raconter [rakõ'te], *v.t.* to relate, to tell, to narrate.
raconteur [rakõ'tœ:r], *n.m.* (*fem.* **-euse**) story-teller, narrator, raconteur.
racornir [rakor'ni:r], *v.t.* to harden; to dry up, to shrivel up. **se racornir**, *v.r.* to grow hard; to shrivel up; to grow callous.
racornissement [rakornis'mã], *n.m.* hardening.
racquit [ra'ki], *n.m.* winning back.
racquitter [raki'te], *v.t.* to indemnify, to recoup. **se racquitter**, *v.r.* to retrieve one's losses.
radar [ra'dar], *n.m.* radar.
radariste [rada'rist], *n.* radar operator.
rade [rad], *n.f.* (*Naut.*) roads, roadstead.
radeau [ra'do], *n.m.* (*pl.* **-eaux**) raft.
radiance [ra'djã:s], *n.f.* radiance, lustre.
radiant [ra'djã], *a.* radiant.
radiateur [radja'tœ:r], *a.* (*fem.* **-trice**) radiating.—*n.m.* radiator.
radiation [radja'sjõ], *n.f.* radiation, irradiation; obliteration.
radical [radi'kal], *a.* (*m. pl.* **-aux**) radical; complete.—*n.m.* radical; root.
radicalement [radikal'mã], *adv.* radically.
radicalisme [radika'lism], *n.m.* radicalism.
radier (1) [ra'dje], *n.m.* floor *or* apron (*of docks, locks, basins etc.*); invert (*of tunnel*).
radier (2) [ra'dje], *v.t.* to strike out, to erase.—*v.i.* to radiate, to beam (*with satisfaction*).
radieux [ra'djø], *a.* (*fem.* **-euse**) radiant, beaming, shining.
radio [ra'djo], *n.f.* broadcasting, radio; wireless set; radiography.—*n.m.* wireless message; wireless-operator.
radio-actif [radjoak'tif], *a.* (*fem.* **-tive**) radio-active.

radio-activité [radjoaktivi′te], *n.f.* radio-activity.

radiodiffuser [radjɔdify′ze], *v.t.* to broadcast.

radiodiffusion [radjɔdify′zjõ], *n.f.* broadcasting.

radiographie [radjɔgra′fi], *n.f.* radiography.

radio-reporter [radjɔrɛpɔr′tɛːr], *n.m.* commentator.

radio-thérapie [radjɔtera′pi], *n.f.* X-ray treatment, radio-therapy.

radis [ra′di], *n.m.* radish.

radium [ra′djɔm], *n.m.* radium.

radotage [radɔ′taːʒ], *n.m.* nonsense, drivel; dotage.

radoter [radɔ′te], *v.i.* to talk idly, to talk drivel; to dote.

radoteur [radɔ′tœːr], *n.m.* (*fem.* **-euse**) driveller; dotard.

radoucir [radu′siːr], *v.t.* to soften; to appease, to pacify. **se radoucir,** *v.r.* to grow milder; to soften, to be appeased, to relent, to relax.

radoucissement [radusis′mã], *n.m.* softening; getting milder (*of the weather*); mitigation, appeasement.

rafale [ra′fal], *n.f.* squall; gust of wind; (*Mil.*) burst of fire.

raffermir [rafɛr′miːr], *v.t.* to make firm, to secure, to strengthen; to confirm. **se raffermir,** *v.r.* to grow stronger; to be established; to improve in strength *or* health.

raffermissement [rafɛrmis′mã], *n.m.* hardening; securing; strengthening; confirmation.

raffinage [rafi′naːʒ], *n.m.* refining.

raffiné [rafi′ne], *a.* refined, delicate; subtle, clever; polished.—*n.m.* (*fem.* **-ée**) exquisite; sophisticated person.

raffinement [rafin′mã], *n.m.* refinement, affectation.

raffiner [rafi′ne], *v.t.* to refine.—*v.i.* to split hairs. **se raffiner,** *v.r.* to become refined.

raffinerie [rafin′ri], *n.f.* refinery.

raffineur [rafi′nœːr], *n.m.* (*fem.* **-euse**) refiner.

raffoler [rafɔ′le], *v.i.* to dote, to be passionately fond (*de*).

rafistolage [rafistɔ′laːʒ], *n.m.* (*colloq.*) patching up, mending.

rafistoler [rafistɔ′le], *v.t.* to mend, to patch up.

rafle [rɑːfl], *n.f.* clean sweep (*by thieves*); raid, round-up in the streets by police.

rafler [rɑ′fle], *v.t.* to sweep off, to carry off; to round up (*of police*).

rafraîchir [rafrɛ′ʃiːr], *v.t.* to cool; to refresh, to restore, to renew; to rub up; to trim.—*v.i.* to cool; to freshen. **se rafraîchir,** *v.r.* to cool, to take refreshment; to be refreshed, to rest.

rafraîchissant [rafrɛʃi′sã], *a.* cooling, refreshing; laxative.

rafraîchissement [rafrɛʃis′mã], *n.m.* cooling; (*pl.*) cool drinks.

ragaillardir [ragaiar′diːr], *v.t.* to enliven, to cheer up, to buck up.

rage [raːʒ], *n.f.* rabies; hydrophobia; violent pain; rage, fury; passion; mania.

rager [ra′ʒe], *v.i.* (*conjug. like* MANGER) (*colloq.*) to be in a passion; to be angry, to fume.

rageur [ra′ʒœːr], *a.* and *n.m.* (*fem.* **-euse**) ill-tempered (person).

ragot [ra′go], *a.* thick-set.—*n.m.* tittle-tattle.

ragoût [ra′gu], *n.m.* ragout; stew; (*fig.*) relish.

ragoûtant [ragu′tã], *a.* relishing, savoury, (*fig.*) inviting, tempting.

ragoûter [ragu′te], *v.t.* to restore the appetite of; to stimulate, to stir up.

ragrafer [ragra′fe], *v.t.* to reclasp, to hook again.

ragréer [ragre′e], *v.t.* to give the finishing touch to (*wall, building*); to renovate (*building*).

ragrément *or* **ragréement** [ragre′mã], *n.m.* finishing; restoration, renovation.

rai [RAIS].

raid [rɛd], *n.m.* long-distance run *or* flight; raid; *un raid aérien,* an air-raid.

raide [rɛd], *a.* stiff, rigid; taut; steep; firm; rapid.—*adv.* quickly, swiftly, suddenly.

raideur [rɛ′dœːr], *n.f.* stiffness; inflexibility; steepness; harshness.

raidillon [redi′jõ], *n.m.* stiff ascent.

raidir [rɛ′diːr], *v.t.* to stiffen; to tighten; to make inflexible.—*v.i.* and **se raidir,** *v.r.* to stiffen; to be inflexible; (*fig.*) to harden oneself (*contre*).

raidissement [redis′mã], *n.m.* stiffening, tautening.

raie [rɛ], *n.f.* line, stroke; stripe; parting (*of hair*); (*Ichth.*) ray, skate.

raifort [rɛ′fɔːr], *n.m.* horse-radish.

rail [rɑːj, raːjl], *n.m.* (*Rail.*) rail.

railler [rɑ′je], *v.t.* to chaff; to scoff at.—*v.i.* to banter, to jest. **se railler,** *v.r.* to jest, to mock, to make game (*de*).

raillerie [rɑj′ri], *n.f.* raillery, bantering; jesting.

railleur [rɑ′jœːr], *a.* (*fem.* **-euse**) bantering, joking; jeering, scoffing.—*n.m.* (*fem.* **-euse**) banterer, joker; scoffer.

rainette [rɛ′nɛt], *n.f.* (*Zool.*) tree-frog.

rainure [rɛ′nyːr], *n.f.* groove, rabbet, slot.

rais *or* **rai** [rɛ], *n.m.* spoke (*of a wheel*); ray (*of light*).

raisin [rɛ′zɛ̃], *n.m.* grapes; *des raisins secs,* raisins.

raisiné [rɛzi′ne], *n.m.* grape jam.

raison [rɛ′zõ], *n.f.* reason; sense, judgment; satisfaction; justice, right; proof, ground; motive; *avoir raison,* to be right.

raisonnable [rɛzɔ′nabl], *a.* rational, reasonable, sensible; just, right; adequate, moderate, fair.

raisonnablement [rɛzɔnablə′mã], *adv.* reasonably, sensibly; fairly, justly; moderately; tolerably.

raisonné [rɛzɔ′ne], *a.* rational, intelligent; systematic; classified, analytical.

raisonnement [rɛzɔn′mã], *n.m.* reasoning, argument.

raisonner [rɛzɔ′ne], *v.t.* to study; to talk *or* discourse upon.—*v.i.* to reason; to argue; to answer, to murmur. **se raisonner,** *v.r.* to reason with oneself.

raisonneur [rɛzɔ′nœːr], *a.* (*fem.* **-euse**) reasoning; argumentative.—*n.m.* (*fem.* **-euse**) reasoner, logician; argufier, pertinacious answerer.

rajeunir [raʒœ′niːr], *v.t.* to rejuvenate; to make look young *or* younger; to renew; to modernize.—*v.i.* to grow young again. **se**

rajeunir, *v.r.* to make oneself look young again.

rajeunissant [raʒœni'sɑ̃], *a.* that makes one look younger, rejuvenating.

rajeunissement [raʒœnis'mɑ̃], *n.m.* rejuvenation; renewal, renovation.

rajouter [raʒu'te], *v.t.* to add again; to add more of.

rajustement [raʒystə'mɑ̃], *n.m.* readjustment, setting in order; (*fig.*) reconciliation.

rajuster [raʒys'te], *v.t.* to readjust; (*fig.*) to settle, to reconcile. **se rajuster**, *v.r.* to readjust *or* straighten one's dress; to be reconciled.

râle (1) [rɑːl], **râlement** [rɑːl'mɑ̃], *n.m.* rattling in the throat; death-rattle.

râle (2) [rɑːl], *n.m.* (*Orn.*) rail.

ralenti [ralɑ̃'ti], *a.* slower.—*n.m.* (*Cine.*) slow motion; *tourner au ralenti*, (*Motor.*) to tick over.

ralentir [ralɑ̃'tiːr], *v.t., v.i.* to slow down, to ease up; to lessen, to moderate. **se ralentir**, *v.r.* to slacken, to slow up; to abate, to relax.

ralentissement [ralɑ̃tis'mɑ̃], *n.m.* slackening; decrease; cooling (*of zeal*).

râler [rɑ'le], *v.i.* to be at one's last gasp.

ralliement [rali'mɑ̃], *n.m.* rallying, rally; winning over; *mot de ralliement*, (*Mil.*) password.

rallier [ra'lje], *v.t.* to rally; to rejoin; to win over. **se rallier**, *v.r.* to rally; to join.

rallonge [ra'lɔ̃ːʒ], *n.f.* lengthening-piece, leaf; *table à rallonges*, draw-table.

rallongement [ralɔ̃ʒ'mɑ̃], *n.m.* lengthening, extension.

rallonger [ralɔ̃'ʒe], *v.t.* (*conjug. like* MANGER) to lengthen; to let out (*skirt*).

rallumer [raly'me], *v.t.* to relight; to rekindle; to revive. **se rallumer**, *v.r.* to light again; (*fig.*) to rekindle.

rallye [ra'li], *n.m.* (*Motor.*) race meeting, rally.

ramage [ra'maːʒ], *n.m.* floral pattern (*on materials*); chirping, warbling (*of birds*); (*fig.*) prattle (*of children*).

ramaigrir [rame'griːr], *v.t.* to make lean *or* thin again.—*v.i.* to grow thin again.

ramaigrissement [ramegris'mɑ̃], *n.m.* emaciation, leanness.

ramas [ra'mɑ], *n.m. inv.* heap, disorderly collection; set, troop, lot, rabble.

ramassé [rama'se], *a.* thick-set, stocky, compact.

ramasser [rama'se], *v.t.* to collect, to gather; to pick up, to take up. **se ramasser**, *v.r.* to assemble, to gather together; to roll itself up (*of an animal*); to crouch; to pick oneself up (*after a spill*).

ramasseur [rama'sœːr], *n.m.* (*fem.* **-euse**) gatherer, collector.

ramassis [rama'si], [RAMAS].

rame [ram], *n.f.* scull, oar; (*Hort.*) stick, prop; (*Manuf.*) tenter frame; ream (*of paper*); made-up train *or* portion of train; *une rame de Métro*, an Underground train.

ramé [ra'me], *a.* supported with sticks (*of peas*), staked (*of plants*).

rameau [ra'mo], *n.m.* (*pl.* **-eaux**) bough, small branch (*of a tree*); subdivision.

ramée [ra'me], *n.f.* green boughs, green arbour.

ramener [ram'ne], *v.t.* (*conjug. like* AMENER) to bring back; to take home; to restore; to reclaim; to recall.

ramer (1) [ra'me], *v.t.* to stick (*peas*) to stake (*plants*).

ramer (2) [ra'me], *v.i.* to row, to scull.

rameur [ra'mœːr], *n.m.* (*fem.* **-euse**) rower.

ramier [ra'mje], *n.m.* wood-pigeon, ring-dove.

ramification [ramifika'sjɔ̃], *n.f.* ramification.

ramifier [rami'fje], *v.t.* to ramify. **se ramifier**, *v.r.* to ramify, to divide.

ramille [ra'miːj], *n.f.*, **ramillon** [rami'jɔ̃], *n.m.* twig.

ramollir [ramɔ'liːr], *v.t.* to soften, (*fig.*) to enervate, to unman. **se ramollir**, *v.r.* to soften; (*fig.*) to relent.

ramollissant [ramɔli'sɑ̃], *a.* softening, emollient.

ramollissement [ramɔlis'mɑ̃], *n.m.* softening.

ramonage [ramɔ'naːʒ], *n.m.* chimney sweeping.

ramoner [ramɔ'ne], *v.t.* to sweep (*a chimney*).

ramoneur [ramɔ'nœːr], *n.m.* chimney-sweeper, sweep.

rampant [rɑ̃'pɑ̃], *a.* creeping, crawling; (*fig.*) cringing, servile.

rampe [rɑ̃ːp], *n.f.* banister; flight of stairs; slope, ramp, incline, gradient; (*Theat.*) footlights.

rampement [rɑ̃p'mɑ̃], *n.m.* creeping, crawling.

ramper [rɑ̃'pe], *v.i.* to creep, to crawl; (*fig.*) to crouch, to grovel.

ramure [ra'myːr], *n.f.* branches, boughs; antlers (*of a stag*).

rancart [rɑ̃'kaːr], *n.m. mettre au rancart*, to throw aside, to cast off; to put on the shelf.

rance [rɑ̃ːs], *a.* rancid, rank.—*n.m.* rancidness.

ranci [rɑ̃'si], *a.* rancid.

rancidité [rɑ̃sidi'te], **rancissure** [rɑ̃si'syːr], *n.f.*, **rancissement** [rɑ̃sis'mɑ̃], *n.m.* rancidity.

rancir [rɑ̃'siːr], *v.i.* to grow rancid.

rancœur [rɑ̃'kœːr], *n.f.* rancour, bitterness.

rançon [rɑ̃'sɔ̃], *n.f.* ransom.

rançonnement [rɑ̃sɔn'mɑ̃], *n.m.* ransoming; (*fig.*) extortion.

rançonner [rɑ̃sɔ'ne], *v.t.* to ransom; (*fig.*) to fleece.

rancune [rɑ̃'kyn], *n.f.* rancour, spite, grudge, malice.

rancunier [rɑ̃ky'nje], *a. and n.m.* (*fem.* **-ière**) rancorous, spiteful (person).

randonnée [rɑ̃dɔ'ne], *n.f.* outing, run, ramble, tour.

rang [rɑ̃], *n.m.* row, line; order, class; rank.

rangé [rɑ̃'ʒe], *a.* tidy; steady; *en bataille rangée*, in a pitched battle.

rangée [rɑ̃'ʒe], *n.f.* row, range, line, tier, set.

rangement [rɑ̃ʒ'mɑ̃], *n.m.* arranging, putting in order.

ranger [rɑ̃'ʒe], *v.t.* (*conjug. like* MANGER) to put in order, to set to rights; to draw up; to arrange; to range; to rank; to reduce, to subdue. **se ranger**, *v.r.* to make room, to make way (*for*); to draw up (*of carriages*, *troops etc.*), to pull up (*at kerb*); to fall in (*of soldiers*).

ranimer [rani'me], *v.t.* to restore to life, to revive; to rouse, to enliven; to cheer up. **se ranimer**, *v.r.* to revive, to brighten up, to be enlivened; to cheer up.

Raoul [ra'ul], *m.* Ralph.

rapace [ra'pas], *a.* rapacious; grasping (*of person*).—*n.m.* rapacious bird, bird of prey.

rapacement [rapas'mã], *adv.* rapaciously.

rapacité [rapasi'te], *n.f.* rapacity; cupidity.

râpage [rɑ'pa:ʒ], *n.m.* rasping; grating.

rapatriement [rapatri'mã], *n.m.* repatriation.

rapatrier [rapatri'je], *v.t.* to repatriate; (*dial.*) to reconcile.

râpe [rɑ:p], *n.f.* grater; rasp; stalk (*of grapes*).

râpé [rɑ'pe], *a.* grated; rasped; threadbare (*of clothes*).

râper [rɑ'pe], *v.t.* to grate (*cheese*), to rasp; to make threadbare.

rapetassage [rapta'sa:ʒ], *n.m.* patching up, mending, cobbling.

rapetasser [rapta'se], *v.t.* to patch, to mend, to cobble.

rapetasseur [rapta'sœ:r], *n.m.* (*fem.* **-euse**) piecer, patcher; cobbler; (*fig.*) compiler, adapter.

rapetissement [raptis'mã], *n.m.* shortening, shrinking; (*fig.*) belittling.

rapetisser [rapti'se], *v.t.* to shorten, to make smaller; (*fig.*) to belittle.—*v.i.* to grow less, to shorten, to shrink.

raphia [ra'fja], *n.m.* raffia.

rapide [ra'pid], *a.* rapid, quick, fast; sudden; steep.—*n.m.* rapid; fast train.

rapidement [rapid'mã], *adv.* rapidly, swiftly, steeply.

rapidité [rapidi'te], *n.f.* rapidity; speed; steepness.

rapiéçage [rapje'sa:ʒ], **rapiècement** [rapjɛs'mã], *n.m.* piecing, patching.

rapiécer [rapje'se] (*see Verb Tables*), **rapiéceter** [rapjes'te] (*conjug. like* AMENER), *v.t.* to piece, to patch.

rapière [ra'pjɛ:r], *n.f.* rapier.

rapin [ra'pɛ̃], *n.m.* art student; (*fig.*) dauber.

rapine [ra'pin], *n.f.* rapine, robbery; plunder; graft.

rapiner [rapi'ne], *v.t., v.i.* to pillage, to plunder.

rapineur [rapi'nœ:r], *n.m.* (*fem.* **-euse**) plunderer, pillager, pilferer.

rappareiller [rapare'je], **rapparier** [rapa'rje], *v.t.* to match, to complete.

rappel [ra'pɛl], *n.m.* recall, reminder, call (*to order*); tattoo, assembly; revocation; back pay; (*Theat.*) curtain-call.

rappeler [ra'ple], *v.t.* (*conjug. like* APPELER) to call back, to recall; to restore (*to life etc.*); to muster; to retract; to recall to mind; to remind. **se rappeler**, *v.r.* to recollect, to remember.

rapport [ra'po:r], *n.m.* revenue, profit; produce; productiveness; report, account, information, tale; return, statement; resemblance, conformity; agreement; connexion; communication; proportion; reimbursement; *faire un rapport,* to draw up a report; *maison de rapport,* tenement house; *sous tous les rapports,* in every respect.

rapporter [rapor'te], *v.t.* to bring back; to bring home; to yield; to retrieve (*of dog*); to refund; to recall; to give an account of; to attribute.—*v.i.* to retrieve (*of dog*); (*sch.*) to tell tales; to be profitable. **se rapporter**, *v.r.* to agree, to correspond, to tally; to be related.

rapporteur [rapor'tœ:r], *n.m.* (*fem.* **-euse**) tale-bearer; reporter.—*n.m.* (*Geom.*) protractor.

rapprendre [ra'prã:dr], *v.t. irr.* (*conjug. like* PRENDRE) to learn anew; to teach again.

rapprochement [raproʃ'mã], *n.m.* drawing closer, bringing together; reconciliation; junction; comparison.

rapprocher [rapro'ʃe], *v.t.* to bring near again; to bring together; to reconcile; to compare. **se rapprocher**, *v.r.* to come near again; to draw nearer; to be brought together; to become reconciled; to approximate (*de*).

rapsodie [rapso'di], *n.f.* rhapsody.

rapt [rapt], *n.m.* abduction; kidnapping.

raquette [ra'kɛt], *n.f.* racket, battledore; snow-shoe.

rare [ra:r], *a.* rare, uncommon; scarce; thin, scanty.

raréfaction [rarefak'sjõ], *n.f.* rarefaction.

raréfiant [rare'fjã], *a.* rarefying.

raréfier [rare'fje], *v.t.* to rarefy. **se raréfier** *v.r.* to become rare; to become rarefied.

rarement [rar'mã], *adv.* rarely, seldom.

rareté [rar'te], *n.f.* rarity; scarcity.

rarissime [rari'sim], *a.* very rare, most rare.

ras [rɑ], *a.* close-shaven, shorn; bare, smooth; open, flat, low; *faire table rase,* to sweep away all preconceptions; *rase campagne,* open country.—*n.m.* short-nap cloth; level; raft; race (*of a mill*) [RAZ].

rasade [rɑ'zad], *n.f.* brimful glass (*of wine*).

rasant [rɑ'zã], *a.* shaving, grazing; sweeping; (*fam.*) boring.

raser [rɑ'ze], *v.t.* to shave; to demolish; to graze, to skim over; (*fam.*) to bore. **se raser**, *v.r.* to shave, to be shaved.

rasoir [rɑ'zwa:r], *n.m.* razor; (*fam.*) bore.

rassasiant [rasa'zjã], *a.* satiating, filling (*food*).

rassasiement [rasazi'mã], *n.m.* satiety.

rassasier [rasa'zje], *v.t.* to satisfy, to fill; to satiate; to surfeit. **se rassasier**, *v.r.* to be cloyed; to take one's fill.

rassemblement [rasãblə'mã], *n.m.* assembly, muster, crowd, mob; political group.

rassembler [rasã'ble], *v.t.* to gather together, to collect; to put together; to assemble. **se rassembler**, *v.r.* to assemble, to congregate, to muster.

rasseoir [ra'swa:r], *v.t. irr.* (*conjug. like* ASSEOIR) to seat again, to reseat; to replace; to calm, to compose. **se rasseoir**, *v.r.* to sit down again; to settle (*of liquids*); to become composed again.

rasséréner [rasere'ne], *v.t.* (*conjug. like* CÉDER) to clear up; to restore serenity to. **se rasséréner**, *v.r.* to clear up; to recover one's serenity.

rassis [ra'si], *a.* settled; calm, staid, sedate; stale.

rassortiment [rasorti'mã], **réassortiment** [reasorti'mã], *n.m.* rematching (*of colours, materials etc.*), resorting; restocking.

rassortir [rasɔr'tiːr], **réassortir** [reasɔr'tiːr], v.t. to sort or match again; to stock (a shop etc.).

rassurant [rasy'rã], a. tranquillizing; encouraging, reassuring.

rassurer [rasy're], v.t. to make firm; to strengthen; to tranquillize, to reassure. **se rassurer**, v.r. to be reassured; to reassure oneself; to clear up (of the weather); **rassurez-vous**, set your mind at rest.

rat [ra], n.m. rat; **rat des champs**, fieldmouse; **rat d'hôtel**, hotel thief.

ratafia [rata'fja], n.m. ratafia.

ratatiné [ratati'ne], a. shrivelled, shrunken.

ratatiner (se) [səratati'ne], v.r. to shrink, to shrivel up.

rate (1) [rat], n.f. spleen.

rate (2) [rat], n.f. female rat.

râteau [ra'to], n.m. (pl. **-eaux**) rake.

râtelage [rɑt'laːʒ], n.m. raking.

râtelée [rɑt'le], n.f. rakeful, raking.

râteler [rɑt'le], v.t. (conjug. like APPELER) to rake.

râteleur [rɑt'lœːr], n.m. (fem. **-euse**) raker.

râtelier [rɑtə'lje], n.m. rack; set of teeth, denture.

rater [ra'te], v.t. to miss; (fig.) to fail to obtain.—v.i. to misfire, to miss (one's shot); (fig.) to miscarry.

ratière [ra'tjeːr], n.f. rat-trap.

ratification [ratifika'sjɔ̃], n.f. ratification.

ratifier [rati'fje], v.t. to ratify.

ratine [ra'tin], n.f. ratteen, petersham (cloth).

ration [ra'sjɔ̃], n.f. ration, allowance.

rationaliser [rasjɔnali'ze], v.t. to rationalize.

rationalisme [rasjɔna'lism], n.m. rationalism.

rationaliste [rasjɔna'list], a. and n. rationalist.

rationalité [rasjɔnali'te], n.f. rationality.

rationnel [rasjɔ'nɛl], a. (fem. **-elle**) rational.

rationnement [rasjɔn'mã], n.m. rationing.

rationner [rasjɔ'ne], v.t. to ration.

ratissage [rati'saːʒ], n.m. scraping; raking.

ratisser [rati'se], v.t. to rake; to scrape.

ratissoire [rati'swaːr], n.f. scraper, light rake, hoe.

ratissure [rati'syːr], n.f. scrapings.

raton [ra'tɔ̃], n.m. little rat; (fig.) little pet, darling.

rattacher [rata'ʃe], v.t. to refasten; to attach; (fig.) to link. **se rattacher**, v.r. to be attached or connected; to be linked up (with).

ratteindre [ra'tɛ̃ːdr], v.t. irr. (conjug. like CRAINDRE) to retake, to catch again; to overtake.

rattendrir [ratɑ̃'driːr], v.t. to soften again.

rattraper [ratra'pe], v.t. to catch again, to retake; to overtake; to recover. **se rattraper**, v.r. to catch hold (à); to be caught again; to make up for one's losses.

rature [ra'tyːr], n.f. erasure.

raturer [raty're], v.t. to erase.

raucité [rosi'te], n.f. raucity, hoarseness.

rauque [roːk], a. hoarse, raucous, rough.

ravage [ra'vaːʒ], n.m. ravage, havoc.

ravager [rava'ʒe], v.t. (conjug. like MANGER) to ravage, to lay waste; to spoil, to ruin.

ravageur [rava'ʒœːr], n.m. (fem. **-euse**) ravager, spoiler.

ravalement [raval'mã], n.m. scraping and pointing (of a wall); rough-casting; repainting.

ravaler [rava'le], v.t. to swallow again; (fig.) to disparage; to point (stonework); to roughcast (wall). **se ravaler**, v.r. to debase oneself, to lower oneself.

ravaudage [ravo'daːʒ], n.m. mending (of old clothes etc.).

ravauder [ravo'de], v.t. to mend, to darn; (dial.) to scold.

ravaudeur [ravo'dœːr], n.m. (fem. **-euse**) mender (of stockings, old clothes etc.).

rave [raːv], n.f. (Bot.) **grosse rave**, French turnip; **petite rave**, radish.

ravenelle [rav'nɛl], n.f. wallflower.

ravi [ra'vi], a. carried away, enraptured, delighted.

ravier [ra'vje], n.m. radish-dish.

ravière [ra'vjeːr], n.f. radish-bed.

ravigote [ravi'gɔt], n.f. ravigote-sauce.

ravigoter [ravigɔ'te], v.t. to revive, to refresh, to buck up. **se ravigoter**, v.r. to recover one's spirits, to perk up.

ravilir [ravi'liːr], v.t. to degrade, to lower.

ravin [ra'vɛ̃], n.m. ravine; gully.

ravine [ra'viːn], n.f. mountain torrent; small gully.

ravinement [ravin'mã], n.m. hollowing out or furrowing (by waters).

raviner [ravi'ne], v.t. to channel, to furrow.

ravir [ra'viːr], v.t. to carry off, to ravish; (fig.) to charm, to enrapture.

raviser (se) [səravi'ze], v.r. to change one's mind; to think better of it.

ravissant [ravi'sã], a. ravishing, delightful, charming.

ravissement [ravis'mã], n.m. carrying off; *rape; rapture, delight.

ravisseur [ravi'sœːr], n.m. (fem. **-euse**) ravisher; kidnapper.

ravitaillement [ravitaj'mã], n.m. revictualling; supplying; supplies; food.

ravitailler [ravitɑ'je], v.t. to provision; to supply.

raviver [ravi've], v.t. to revive, to cheer; to freshen up (colours).

ravoir [ra'vwaːr], v.t. (usu. in infin.) to get back again, to recover.

rayé [rɛ'je], a. striped (garment); rifled (gun); scratched (glass); struck off (a list).

rayer [rɛ'je], v.t. (conjug. like PAYER) to scratch (dishes etc.); to streak, to stripe; to erase; (Artill.) to rifle.

rayon [rɛ'jɔ̃], n.m. ray; beam, gleam; radius; spoke (of a wheel); shelf; department (of a shop); **rayon de miel**, honeycomb.

rayonnant [rɛjɔ'nã], a. radiant, beaming.

rayonne [rɛ'jɔn], n.f. rayon.

rayonnement [rɛjɔn'mã], n.m. radiance; radiation.

rayonner [rɛjɔ'ne], v.i. to radiate; to shine, to beam; to sparkle.

rayure [rɛ'jyːr], n.f. stripe; streak, scratch; rifling (of fire-arms); erasure.

raz or **ras** [ra], n.m. inv. race (a violent current); **raz de marée**, tidal wave.

razzia [ra'zja], n.f. (Algerian) razzia, raid, inroad, foray.

ré [re], n.m. (Mus.) re, D.

réabonnement [reabɔn'mã], n.m. renewed subscription.

réabonner (se) [səreabɔ'ne], *v.r.* to renew one's subscription.
réacteur [reak'tœːr], *n.m.* reactor; (*Av.*) jet-engine.
réaction [reak'sjɔ̃], *n.f.* reaction; *les avions à réaction*, jet-aircraft.
réactionnaire [reaksjɔ'nɛːr], *a.* and *n.* reactionary.
réactionner [reaksjɔ'ne], *v.t.* to sue again.—*v.i.* (*St. Exch.*) to react against a rise.
réadmettre [read'mɛtr], *v.t. irr.* (*conjug. like* METTRE) to admit again, to readmit.
réadmission [readmi'sjɔ̃], *n.f.* readmission.
réagir [rea'ʒiːr], *v.i.* to react.
réajourner [reaʒur'ne], *v.t.* to readjourn.
réalisable [reali'zabl], *a.* realizable; feasible.
réalisateur [realiza'tœːr], *n.m.* (*Cine.*) film director.
réalisation [realiza'sjɔ̃], *n.f.* realization; achievement; conversion into money; clearance sale.
réaliser [reali'ze], *v.t.* to realize; to achieve; to convert into money. **se réaliser**, *v.r.* to be realized, to come true.
réalisme [rea'lism], *n.m.* realism.
réaliste [rea'list], *a.* realistic.—*n.* realist.
réalité [reali'te], *n.f.* reality.
réapparaître [reapa'rɛːtr], *v.i. irr.* (*conjug. like* CONNAÎTRE) to reappear.
réapparition [reapari'sjɔ̃], *n.f.* reappearance.
réarmement [rearmə'mɑ̃], *n.m.* rearmament.
réarmer [rear'me], *v.t.* to rearm; (*Navy*) to refit.
réassortiment [RASSORTIMENT].
rebaisser [rəbɛ'se], *v.t.* to lower again.
rébarbatif [rebarba'tif], *a.* (*fem.* **-tive**) stern, surly, forbidding.
rebâtir [rəbɑ'tir], *v.t.* to rebuild.
rebattre [rə'batr], *v.t.* (*conjug. like* BATTRE) to beat again; to repeat; to shuffle (*cards*) again.
rebattu [rəba'ty], *a.* hackneyed, trite.
rebelle [rə'bɛl], *a.* rebellious; disobedient; unyielding; refractory.—*n.* rebel.
rebeller (se) [sərəbɛ'le], *v.r.* to rebel, to revolt.
rébellion [rebɛ'ljɔ̃], *n.f.* rebellion; resistance.
rebiffer (se) [sərəbi'fe], *v.r.* (*fam.*) to bridle up, to kick over the traces.
reblanchir [rəblɑ'ʃiːr], *v.t.* to bleach again; to whitewash again.
reboire [rə'bwaːr], *v.t. irr.* (*conjug. like* BOIRE) to drink again.
reboisement [rəbwaz'mɑ̃], *n.m.* retimbering, reafforestation.
reboiser [rəbwa'ze], *v.t.* to retimber, to reafforest.
rebond [rə'bɔ̃], *n.m.* rebound; bounce (*of ball*).
rebondi [rəbɔ̃'di], *a.* plump, chubby.
rebondir [rəbɔ̃'diːr], *v.i.* to rebound; to bounce.
rebondissement [rəbɔ̃dis'mɑ̃], *n.m.* rebounding; bounce.
rebord [rə'bɔːr], *n.m.* edge, brink; sill (*of window*); border, hem.
reborder [rəbɔr'de], *v.t.* to border again, to re-hem.
rebouillir [rəbu'jiːr], *v.i. irr.* (*conjug. like* BOUILLIR) to boil again.
rebours [rə'buːr], *a.* cross-grained (*wood*); intractable (*horse*).—*n.m.* wrong side (*of*

material *etc.*); wrong way (*of the grain*); contrary, reverse; *à rebours* or *au rebours* the wrong way, against the grain, backwards.
reboutage [rəbu'taːʒ], *n.m.* bone-setting.
rebouter [rəbu'te], *v.t.* to set (*bones*).
rebouteur [rəbu'tœːr], **rebouteux** [rəbu'tø], *n.m.* (*fem.* **-euse**) bone-setter.
reboutonner [rəbutɔ'ne], *v.t.* to rebutton. **se reboutonner**, *v.r.* to button up one's clothes again.
rebroussement [rəbrus'mɑ̃], *n.m.* turning back, turning up.
rebrousse-poil (à) [arəbrus'pwal], *adv. phr.* against the grain; the wrong way.
rebrousser [rəbru'se], *v.t.* to turn up (*the hair*); *rebrousser chemin*, to turn back.
rebuffade [rəby'fad], *n.f.* rebuff, repulse; snub.
rébus [re'byːs], *n.m.* rebus; riddle.
rebut [rə'by], *n.m.* repulse, rebuff; refuse; rubbish; scum.
rebutant [rəby'tɑ̃], *a.* repulsive, disgusting, forbidding.
rebuter [rəby'te], *v.t.* to repulse, to rebuff, to reject, to snub; to disgust. **se rebuter**, *v.r.* to become discouraged.
récalcitrant [rekalsi'trɑ̃], *a.* refractory, recalcitrant; rebellious.
récalcitrer [rekalsi'tre], *v.i.* to kick (*of horses*); (*fig.*) to be refractory.
recaler [rəka'le], *v.t.* to wedge up again, to refix; (*Sch.*) to plough (*at an examination*).
récapitulation [rekapityla'sjɔ̃], *n.f.* recapitulation, summing up; summary.
récapituler [rekapity'le], *v.t.* to recapitulate, to sum up; (*colloq.*) to recap.
recel [rə'sɛl], **recèlement** [rəsɛl'mɑ̃], *n.m.* receiving of stolen goods.
receler [rəs'le] (*conjug. like* AMENER), **recéler** [rəse'le] (*conjug. like* CÉDER), *v.t.* to receive (*stolen goods*); to embezzle; to conceal from justice; to contain.
receleur [rəs'lœːr], *n.m.* (*fem.* **-euse**) receiver of stolen goods, fence.
récemment [resa'mɑ̃], *adv.* recently, newly.
recensement [rəsɑ̃s'mɑ̃], *n.m.* census; return, inventory; verification.
recenser [rəsɑ̃'se], *v.t.* to take the census of; to record; to verify.
recenseur [rəsɑ̃'sœːr], *n.m.* (*fem.* **-euse**) census-taker; enumerator.
recension [rəsɑ̃'sjɔ̃], *n.f.* recension; collation (*of books etc.*).
récent [re'sɑ̃], *a.* recent, new, fresh, late.
receper [rəsə'pe] (*conjug. like* AMENER), **recéper** [rəse'pe] (*conjug. like* CÉDER), *v.t.* to cut back; to clear (*a wood*).
récépissé [resepi'se], *n.m.* receipt, acknowledgment (*for documents, papers etc.*).
réceptacle [resɛp'takl], *n.m.* receptacle; repository.
récepteur [resɛp'tœːr], *a.* (*fem.* **-trice**) receiving; *poste récepteur*, receiving set.—*n.m.* receiver; reservoir (*in a machine, etc.*); receiving instrument (*of telegraphs*).
réception [resɛp'sjɔ̃], *n.f.* receiving; receipt; admission; (*hotel*) reception desk; reception, party.
réceptionnaire [resɛpsjɔ'nɛːr], *a.* receiving.—*n.* receiver, receiving clerk; consignee.
réceptionniste [resɛpsjɔ'nist], *n.* receptionist.

recette [rə'sɛt], *n.f.* receipts, returns; takings; (*Cook.*) recipe; receiver's office; *faire recette*, to be a draw (*of a play*).

recevable [rəsə'vabl], *a.* receivable, admissible.

receveur [rəsə'vœːr], *n.m.* (*fem.* **-euse**) receiver, collector (*of taxes etc.*); (*bus*-) conductor.

recevoir [rəsə'vwaːr], *v.t. irr.* to receive, to accept, to take, to let in, to admit; to welcome; to entertain.—*v.i.* to receive, to be at home to visitors.

rechange [rə'ʃɑ̃ːʒ], *n.m.* change (*of anything*), replacement; spare things; (*Comm.*) re-exchange; *roue de rechange*, spare-wheel.

rechanter [rəʃɑ̃'te], *v.t.* to sing again; to retell.

rechaper [rəʃa'pe], *v.t.* to retread (*a tyre*).

réchapper [reʃa'pe], *v.i.* to escape; *réchapper d'une maladie*, to recover from an illness.

recharge [rə'ʃarʒ], *n.f.* fresh *or* second charge.

rechargement [rəʃarʒə'mɑ̃], *n.m.* reloading, relading; reballasting.

recharger [rəʃar'ʒe], *v.t.* (*conjug. like* MANGER) to load again; to recharge.

réchaud [re'ʃo], *n.m.* small portable stove; chafing-dish; dish-warmer.

réchauffage [reʃo'faːʒ], *n.m.* warming up again, reheating.

réchauffé [reʃo'fe], *n.m.* dish *or* food warmed up again; rehash, stale stuff *or* news.

réchauffer [reʃo'fe], *v.t.* to warm up, to reheat; to reanimate, to stir up. **se réchauffer**, *v.r.* to warm oneself, to get warm.

réchauffoir [reʃo'fwaːr], *n.m.* plate-warmer, hot-plate.

rechausser [rəʃo'se], *v.t.* to put shoes *or* stockings on (*a person*) again; (*Build.*) to underpin.

rêche [rɛːʃ], *a.* rough (*to the taste, touch etc.*); (*fig.*) sour, crabbed (*of persons*).

recherche [rə'ʃɛrʃ], *n.f.* search, pursuit; inquiry, investigation; research; (*fig.*) studied elegance *or* refinement, affectation.

recherché [rəʃɛr'ʃe], *a.* choice, exquisite; affected; far-fetched; in great demand.

rechercher [rəʃɛr'ʃe], *v.t.* to seek again; to seek, to search for; to investigate, to pry into; to desire; to court, to woo.

rechigné [rəʃi'ɲe], *a.* sour-faced, surly, crabbed.

rechignement [rəʃiɲə'mɑ̃], *n.m.* sulking, sullenness.

rechigner [rəʃi'ɲe], *v.i.* to look sulky, sullen, grim etc; to balk (*at something*).

rechute [rə'ʃyt], *n.f.* relapse, set-back.

rechuter [rəʃy'te], *v.i.* to have a relapse; to backslide.

récidive [resi'diːv], *n.f.* recidivism; second offence.

récidiver [residi've], *v.i.* to repeat the offence; to relapse; to recur (*of disease*).

récidiviste [residi'vist], *n.* recidivist, old lag.

récif [re'sif], *n.m.* reef (*of rocks*).

récipé [resi'pe], *n.m.* recipe, prescription.

récipient [resi'pjɑ̃], *n.m.* container, receptacle; reservoir.

réciprocité [resiprɔsi'te], *n.f.* reciprocity, reciprocation.

réciproque [resi'prɔk], *a.* reciprocal, mutual.

réciproquement [resiprɔk'mɑ̃], *adv.* reciprocally, mutually; vice versa.

récit [re'si], *n.m.* recital, account, story narrative, report.

récital [resi'tal], *n.m.* (*pl.* **-als**) musical recital.

récitant [resi'tɑ̃], *a.* (*Mus.*) solo (*instrument, voice*).—*n.m.* (*fem.* **-e**) soloist; narrator.

récitateur [resita'tœːr], *n.m.* (*fem.* **-trice**) reciter, repeater.

récitatif [resita'tif], *n.m.* (*Mus.*) recitative.

récitation [resita'sjɔ̃], *n.f.* recitation, reciting; repetition.

réciter [resi'te], *v.t.* to recite, to rehearse; to repeat, to say; to tell, to relate, to recount.

réclamant [rekla'mɑ̃], *a.* claiming.—*n.m.* (*fem.* **-e**) claimant.

réclamation [reklama'sjɔ̃], *n.f.* claim, request, demand; complaint.

réclame [re'klaːm], *n.f.* advertisement; publicity; (*Print.*) catch-word; puff.

réclamer [rekla'me], *v.t.* to crave, to entreat; to beseech; to claim.—*v.i.* to object, to complain; to protest (*contre*). **se réclamer**, *v.r.* to refer to.

reclus [rə'kly], *a.* shut up, secluded.—*n.m.* (*fem.* **-e**) recluse; monk, nun.

reclusion [rəkly'zjɔ̃], **réclusion** [rekly'zjɔ̃], *n.f.* reclusion, confinement; (*Law*) solitary confinement (*with hard labour*).

recoin [rə'kwɛ̃], *n.m.* corner, nook; *coins et recoins*, nooks and crannies.

récolte [re'kɔlt], *n.f.* harvest, crop, vintage.

récolter [rekɔl'te], *v.t.* to reap, to gather in; to get in.

recommandable [rəkɔmɑ̃'dabl], *a.* respectable; commendable.

recommandation [rəkɔmɑ̃dɑ'sjɔ̃], *n.f.* recommendation; reference; (*fig.*) esteem; (*Post*) registration.

recommander [rəkɔmɑ̃'de], *v.t.* to recommend; to enjoin; to request; to commend; (*Post*) to register. **se recommander**, *v.r.* to recommend oneself; to refer to.

recommencement [rəkɔmɑ̃s'mɑ̃], *n.m.* recommencement, fresh start.

recommencer [rəkɔmɑ̃'se], *v.t., v.i.* (*conjug. like* COMMENCER) to recommence, to begin again; to do (*it*) again.

récompense [rekɔ̃'pɑ̃ːs], *n.f.* reward, recompense; prize; compensation; *en récompense de*, in return for.

récompenser [rekɔ̃pɑ̃'se], *v.t.* to reward; to compensate; to repay.

recomposer [rəkɔ̃po'ze], *v.t.* to recompose.

recomposition [rəkɔ̃pozi'sjɔ̃], *n.f.* recomposition.

réconciliable [rekɔ̃si'ljabl], *a.* reconcilable.

réconciliateur [rekɔ̃silja'tœːr], *n.m.* (*fem.* **-trice**) reconciler.

réconciliation [rekɔ̃silja'sjɔ̃], *n.f.* reconciliation.

réconcilier [rekɔ̃si'lje], *v.t.* to reconcile. **se réconcilier**, *v.r.* to be(come) reconciled; (*colloq.*) to make it up.

reconduire [rəkɔ̃'dɥiːr], *v.t. irr.* (*conjug. like* CONDUIRE) to lead back, to see home; to show out.

reconduite [rəkɔ̃'dɥit], *n.f.* showing out, seeing out, seeing home.

réconfort [rekɔ̃'fɔːr], *n.m.* comfort, relief.

réconforter [rekɔ̃fɔr'te], *v.t.* to comfort, to cheer up; to fortify.

reconnaissable [rəkɔnɛ'sabl], *a.* recognizable.

reconnaissance [rəkɔnɛ'sɑ̃ːs], *n.f.* recognition; discovery; gratitude, thankfulness; survey; acknowledgment, confession; reward; recognizance; pawn-ticket; (*Mil.*) reconnaissance.

reconnaissant [rəkɔnɛ'sɑ̃], *a.* grateful, thankful.

reconnaître [rəkɔ'nɛːtr], *v.t. irr.* (*conjug. like* CONNAÎTRE) to recognize, to identify; to discover; to acknowledge, to admit; to be grateful for; to reconnoitre. **se reconnaître,** *v.r.* to recognize oneself; to be recognizable; to make out where one is.

reconquérir [rəkɔ̃ke'riːr], *v.t. irr.* (*conjug. like* ACQUÉRIR) to reconquer; to regain.

reconstituer [rəkɔ̃sti'tɥe], *v.t.* to reconstitute, to restore.

reconstitution [rəkɔ̃stity'sjɔ̃], *n.f.* reconstitution, reorganization; reconstruction (*of a murder*).

reconstruction [rəkɔ̃stryk'sjɔ̃], *n.f.* reconstruction, rebuilding.

reconstruire [rəkɔ̃s'trɥiːr], *v.t. irr.* (*conjug. like* CONDUIRE) to rebuild, to reconstruct; to rehabilitate.

recopier [rəkɔ'pje], *v.t.* to make a copy of.

recoquillement [rəkɔkij'mɑ̃], *n.m.* curling up, dog('s)-earing (*of pages of book*).

recoquiller [rəkɔki'je], *v.t.* to turn up *or* back. **se recoquiller,** *v.r.* to curl up, to shrivel.

record [rə'kɔːr], *n.m.* record (*in sports etc.*).

recorder [rəkɔr'de], *v.t.* to learn by heart; to tie up again.

recors [rə'kɔːr], *n.m.* bailiff's man.

recoucher [rəku'ʃe], *v.t.* to put to bed again; to lay down again. **se recoucher,** *v.r.* to go to bed again, to lie down again.

recoudre [rə'kudr], *v.t. irr.* (*conjug. like* COUDRE) to sew again, to sew up.

recoupement [rəkup'mɑ̃], *n.m.* (*Build.*) offset; cross-checking.

recouper [rəku'pe], *v.t.* to cut again; to cross-check.

recourbé [rəkur'be], *a.* curved, bent (back).

recourber [rəkur'be], *v.t.* to bend back, to bend round. **se recourber,** *v.r.* to be curved, to bend.

recourir [rəku'riːr], *v.i. irr.* (*conjug. like* COURIR) to run again; to resort (*à*); (*Law*) to appeal

recours [rə'kur], *n.m.* recourse; (*fig.*) resource, remedy; (*Law*) appeal.

recousu [rəku'zy], *a.* sewn *or* stitched again.

recouvrement [rəkuvrə'mɑ̃], *n.m.* recovery, regaining; recovering (*of debts etc.*); covering up, overlapping; cap (*of a watch*).

recouvrer [rəku'vre], *v.t.* to recover, to retrieve, to collect.

recouvrir [rəku'vriːr], *v.t. irr.* (*conjug. like* OUVRIR) to cover up, to cover over, to overlay; to hide. **se recouvrir,** *v.r.* to cover oneself again; to cloud over.

recracher [rəkra'ʃe], *v.t.* to spit out again; to disgorge.—*v.i.* to spit again.

récréatif [rekrea'tif], *a.* (*fem.* **-tive**) recreative, entertaining.

récréation [rekrea'sjɔ̃], *n.f.* recreation, amusement; (*Sch.*) playtime, break.

recréer [rəkre'e], *v.t.* to re-create, to create again.

récréer [rekre'e], *v.t.* to entertain; to amuse. **se récréer,** *v.r.* to amuse oneself, to take recreation.

recrépir [rəkre'piːr], *v.t.* to give a fresh coat of plaster to; to repoint (*a wall*); (*fig.* and *fam.*) to paint (*one's face*); to recast.

recrépissement [rəkrepis'mɑ̃], **recrépissage** [rəkrepi'saːʒ], *n.m.* replastering; repatching.

récrier (se) [sərekri'je], *v.r.* to exclaim, to cry out; to protest (*contre*); to be amazed.

récrimination [rekrimina'sjɔ̃], *n.f.* recrimination.

récriminatoire [rekrimina'twaːr], *a.* recriminatory.

récriminer [rekrimi'ne], *v.i.* to recriminate.

récrire [re'kriːr], *v.t. irr.* (*conjug. like* ÉCRIRE) to rewrite; to write back.

recroqueviller (se) [sərəkrɔkvi'je], *v.r.* to curl up, to shrivel.

recru [rə'kry], *a.* tired out, worn out.

recrudescence [rəkryde'sɑ̃ːs], *n.f.* recrudescence.

recrudescent [rəkryde'sɑ̃], *a.* recrudescent.

recrue [rə'kry], *n.f.* recruiting; recruit.

recrutement [rəkryt'mɑ̃], *n.m.* recruiting, recruitment.

recruter [rəkry'te], *v.t.* to recruit; to enrol. **se recruter,** *v.r.* to be recruited.

recruteur [rəkry'tœːr], *n.m.* recruiter; recruiting officer.

rectangle [rɛk'tɑ̃ːgl], *n.m.* rectangle.

rectangulaire [rɛktɑ̃gy'lɛːr], *a.* rectangular, right-angled.

recteur [rɛk'tœːr], *n.m.* rector, vice-chancellor (*of a University*); parish priest (*in Brittany*).

rectifiable [rɛkti'fjabl], *a.* rectifiable.

rectification [rɛktifika'sjɔ̃], *n.f.* rectification; adjustment.

rectifier [rɛkti'fje], *v.t.* to rectify; to adjust; to reform.

rectiligne [rɛkti'liɲ], *a.* rectilinear.

rectitude [rɛkti'tyd], *n.f.* rectitude, uprightness.

recto [rɛk'to], *n.m.* first page of a leaf, right-hand page.

rectorat [rɛkto'ra], *n.m.* rectorship.

reçu [rə'sy], *a.* received; admitted, recognized; *être reçu* (*à un examen*), to pass (an examination).—*n.m.* receipt.

recueil [rə'kœːj], *n.m.* collection, selection; anthology.

recueillement [rəkœj'mɑ̃], *n.m.* meditation; peaceful contemplation.

recueilli [rəkœ'ji], *a.* meditative, calm, rapt.

recueillir [rəkœ'jiːr], *v.t. irr.* (*conjug. like* CUEILLIR) to gather, to collect; to reap; to receive; to shelter. **se recueillir,** *v.r.* to collect one's thoughts; to be plunged in meditation.

recuire [rə'kɥiːr], *v.t. irr.* (*conjug. like* CONDUIRE) to cook again.

recuit [rə'kɥi], *a.* cooked, baked *or* roasted again.

recul [rə'kyl], *n.m.* recoil (*of cannon*), kick (*of rifle*); backing (*of horse, car*).

reculade [rəky'lad], *n.f.* falling back, retreat.

reculé [rəky'le], *a.* distant, remote.

reculement

reculement [rəkyl'mã], *n.m.* drawing back, backing (*of carriages etc.*); breech (*of saddles*).

reculer [rəky'le], *v.t.* to draw back, to move back, to back; (*fig.*) to put off, to defer.— *v.i.* to go back, to draw back, to retreat; to recoil; to give way. **se reculer**, *v.r.* to draw back, to become more remote.

reculons (à) [arəky'lõ], *adv. phr.* backwards.

récupérage [rekype'ra:ʒ], *n.m.*, **récupération** [rekypera'sjõ], *n.f.* recovery, recuperation.

récupérer [rekype're], *v.t.* (*conjug. like* CÉDER) to recover, to retrieve, to recuperate.

récurer [reky're], *v.t.* to scour, to clean.

récusable [reky'zabl], *a.* (*Law*) exceptionable, doubtful (*of witnesses etc.*).

récusation [rekyza'sjõ], *n.f.* (*Law*) challenge; exception.

récuser [reky'ze], *v.t.* to challenge, to object to (*witnesses, jurors etc.*); to reject. **se récuser**, *v.r.* to excuse oneself, to decline; to decline, to give a decision (*of judges, jurors etc.*).

rédacteur [redak'tœːr], *n.m.* (*fem.* **-trice**) writer, inditer (*of deed*); clerk (*in public office*); *rédacteur en chef*, editor.

rédaction [redak'sjõ], *n.f.* drawing up (*deeds etc.*); wording; editing (*periodicals*); essay.

reddition [rɛdi'sjõ], *n.f.* surrender; rendering (*of accounts*).

rédempteur [redãp'tœːr], *a.* (*fem.* **-trice**) redeeming, redemptory.—*n.m.* redeemer, saviour.

rédemption [redãp'sjõ], *n.f.* redemption; redeeming.

redescendre [rədɛ'sãːdr], *v.t.* (*with aux.* AVOIR) to carry or take down again.—*v.i.* (*with aux.* ÊTRE) to come, go or step down again.

redevable [rəd'vabl], *a.* indebted, owing.

redevance [rəd'vãːs], *n.f.* rent, due, tax.

redevenir [rədəv'niːr], *v.i. irr.* (*conjug. like* TENIR, *but with aux.* ÊTRE) to become again.

redevoir [rəd(ə)'vwaːr], *v.t. irr.* (*conjug. like* DEVOIR) to owe still.

rédiger [redi'ʒe], *v.t.* (*conjug. like* MANGER) to draw up, to draft; to edit.

redingote [rədɛ̃'gɔt], *n.f.* frock-coat.

redire [rə'diːr], *v.t. irr.* (*conjug. like* DIRE) to repeat, to reveal.—*v.i.* to criticize; *trouver à redire à*, to find fault with.

redondance [rədõ'dãːs], *n.f.* superfluity of words, redundancy.

redondant [rədõ'dã], *a.* redundant.

redonner [rədɔ'ne], *v.t.* to give back again, to restore.—*v.i.* to fall again; to begin again; to charge again.

redoublé [rədu'ble], *a.* redoubled, increased.

redoublement [rədublə'mã], *n.m.* redoubling, increase; (*Med.*) paroxysm.

redoubler [rədu'ble], *v.t.* to redouble, to reiterate; to increase; to reline (*dress*).—*v.i.* to increase, to redouble.

redoutable [rədu'tabl], *a.* formidable, redoubtable.

redoute [rə'dut], *n.f.* redoubt.

redouter [rədu'te], *v.t.* to dread, to fear.

redressement [rədrɛs'mã], *n.m.* straightening; rectification, redress.

redresser [rədrɛ'se], *v.t.* to make straight; to set up again; to put right; (*colloq.*) to rebuke. **se redresser**, *v.r.* to become

straight again; to right itself (*of a ship etc.*); to be redressed; *redressez-vous*, sit up.

redû [rə'dy], *n.m.* balance due.

réducteur [redyk'tœːr], *a.* (*fem.* **-trice**) reducing.—*n.m.* (*Chem.*) reducer.

réductible [redyk'tibl], *a.* reducible.

réduction [redyk'sjõ], *n.f.* reduction; subjugation; allowance.

réduire [re'dɥiːr], *v.t. irr.* (*conjug. like* CONDUIRE) to reduce, to diminish; to subdue; to compel, to oblige. **se réduire**, *v.r.* to be reduced, to diminish, to abate, to vanish; to be subdued; to amount to.

réduit [re'dɥi], *a.* reduced; dimmed (*of light*).—*n.m.* retreat, nook; hovel; (*Fort.*) keep.

réédification [reedifika'sjõ], *n.f.* rebuilding.

réédifier [reedi'fje], *v.t.* to rebuild.

rééducatif [reedyka'tif], *a.* (*fem.* **-tive**) *thérapie rééducative*, occupational therapy.

réel [re'ɛl], *a.* (*fem.* **-elle**) real, actual; genuine.—*n.m.* reality.

réélection [reelɛk'sjõ], *n.f.* re-election.

réélire [ree'liːr], *v.t. irr.* (*conjug. like* LIRE) to re-elect.

réellement [reɛl'mã], *adv.* really, in reality.

réembobiner [reãbobi'ne], *v.t.* to rewind.

réemploi [reã'plwa], *n.m.* re-employment.

réexpédier [reɛkspe'dje], *v.t.* to send on, to (re)forward; to send back.

refaçonner [rəfasɔ'ne], *v.t.* to make again, to refashion.

réfaction [refak'sjõ], *n.f.* rebate, allowance.

refaire [rə'fɛːr], *v.t. irr.* (*conjug. like* FAIRE) to do again, to remake; to recommence; to do up; to deal again (*at cards*); to revive; (*slang*) to diddle. **se refaire**, *v.r.* to recover one's strength; to recoup oneself.

refait [rə'fɛ], *a.* set up, done again; (*slang*) *j'ai été refait(e)*, I have been had.—*n.m.* drawn game.

réfection [refɛk'sjõ], *n.f.* repairs (*to buildings etc.*).

réfectoire [refɛk'twaːr], *n.m.* refectory, dining-room or -hall (*in college, convent etc.*).

refend [rə'fã], *n.m.* splitting, sawing, dividing; *mur de refend*, partition wall.

refendre [rə'fãːdr], *v.t.* to cleave or split again; to quarter (*timber*); to saw (*stone*) into slabs.

référence [refe'rãːs], *n.f.* reference.

referendum [rəfərã'dom], **référendum** [referã'dom], *n.m.* referendum.

référer [refe're], *v.t.* (*conjug. like* CÉDER) to refer; to ascribe.—*v.i.* to refer; *en référer à*, to refer to. **se référer**, *v.r.* to refer, to have reference; to leave it (*à*); to trust (*à*).

refermer [rəfɛr'me], *v.t.* to shut again; to close up. **se refermer**, *v.r.* to shut itself; to close up; to heal up (*of wound*).

réfléchi [refle'ʃi], *a.* reflected; deliberate; reflective, thoughtful; wary; (*Gram.*) reflexive.

réfléchir [refle'ʃiːr], *v.t.* to reflect, to throw back; to reverberate.—*v.i.* to reflect, to consider, to ponder. **se réfléchir**, *v.r.* to be reflected.

réfléchissant [refleʃi'sã], *a.* reflecting.

réflecteur [reflɛk'tœːr], *a.* reflecting.—*n.m.* reflector.

reflet [rə'flɛ], *n.m.* reflection, reflex; reflected light.

refléter [rəfle'te], *v.t.* (*conjug. like* CÉDER) to reflect (*light etc.*).—*v.i.* and **se refléter**, *v.r.* to be reflected.

refleurir [rəflœ'riːr], *v.i.* to blossom again.

réflexe [re'flɛks], *a.* and *n.m.* reflex.

réflexion [reflɛk'sjɔ̃], *n.f.* reflection; thought, consideration.

refluer [rə'flɥe], *v.i.* to reflow, to ebb; (*fig.*) to swing back.

reflux [rə'fly], *n.m.* reflux, ebb; flowing back.

refondre [rə'fɔ̃:dr], *v.t.* to refound (*metal*), to melt down again, to cast again; (*fig.*) to remodel.

refonte [rə'fɔ̃:t], *n.f.* refounding, recasting; recoining; remodelling.

réformateur [reforma'tœːr], *a.* (*fem.* **-trice**) reforming.—*n.m.* (*fem.* **-trice**) reformer.

réformation [reforma'sjɔ̃], *n.f.* reformation.

réforme [re'form], *n.f.* reform, reformation, amendment; (*Mil.*) reduction, discharge.

réformé [refor'me], *a.* reformed; (*Mil.*) invalided out of the service.

réformer [refor'me], *v.t.* to reform, to improve; (*Mil.*) to invalid. **se réformer**, *v.r.* to reform, to mend one's ways.

reformer [rəfor'me], *v.t.* to form again. **se reformer**, *v.r.* to form anew, to re-form (*of troops etc.*).

réformiste [refor'mist], *a.* and *n.* reformist.

refoulement [rəful'mɑ̃], *n.m.* driving back; (*Psych.*) inhibition, repression.

refouler [rəfu'le], *v.t.* to drive back; to compress; to suppress; to expel (*aliens*); to stem (*the tide*).—*v.i.* to ebb, to flow back; *la marée refoule*, the tide is ebbing.

réfractaire [refrak'tɛːr], *a.* refractory, obstinate, rebellious; *terre réfractaire*, fireproof clay.—*n.m.* defaulter.

réfracter [refrak'te], *v.t.* to refract. **se réfracter**, *v.r.* to be refracted.

réfraction [refrak'sjɔ̃], *n.f.* refraction.

refrain [rə'frɛ̃], *n.m.* refrain, chorus; (*fig.*) constant theme.

réfréner [refre'ne], *v.t.* (*conjug. like* CÉDER) to curb, to control (*passions*); to bridle, to restrain.

réfrigérant [refriʒe'rɑ̃], *a.* refrigerant, cooling.—*n.m.* refrigerator.

réfrigérateur [refriʒera'tœːr], *n.m.* refrigerating chamber; refrigerator, (*colloq.*) fridge; (*Am.*) icebox.

réfrigération [refriʒera'sjɔ̃], *n.f.* refrigeration.

réfrigérer [refriʒe're], *v.t.* (*conjug. like* CÉDER) to chill, to freeze (*food etc.*).

refroidir [rəfrwa'diːr], *v.t.* to cool, to chill.—*v.i.* to cool, to become cold. **se refroidir**, *v.r.* to cool, to grow cold; to catch cold; to slacken, to relax.

refroidissement [rəfrwadis'mɑ̃], *n.m.* cooling, refrigeration; coldness; chill, cold.

refuge [rə'fy:ʒ], *n.m.* refuge, shelter; (street-)island; lay-by.

réfugié [refy'ʒje], *n.m.* (*fem.* **-ée**) refugee.

réfugier (se) [sərefy'ʒje], *v.r.* to take refuge; (*fig.*) to have recourse (*to*) (**dans**).

refus [rə'fy], *n.m. inv.* refusal, denial.

refuser [rəfy'ze], *v.t.* to refuse, to deny, to decline to reject.—*v.i.* to refuse; to decline.

se refuser, *v.r.* to deny oneself; to shun; to resist.

réfuter [refy'te], *v.t.* to refute, to disprove.

regagner [rəga'ɲe], *v.t.* to regain, to recover, to retrieve; to rejoin, to reach.

regain [rə'gɛ̃], *n.m.* aftermath; second crop; (*fig.*) revival, new lease (*of life*).

régal [re'gal], *n.m.* feast, entertainment, treat.

régalade [rega'lad], *n.f.* giving a treat, regaling; blazing fire.

régalant [rega'lɑ̃], *a.* pleasant, entertaining.

régaler [rega'le], *v.t.* to regale, to treat, to entertain. **se régaler**, *v.r.* to regale oneself; to enjoy oneself; to entertain *or* treat each other.

regard [rə'gaːr], *n.m.* look; glance; gaze, notice, attention; inspection-hole; (*pl.*) eyes; *au regard de*, in comparison with; *d'un seul regard*, at one glance; *en regard*, opposite; *un regard de côté*, a sidelong glance.

regardant [rəgar'dɑ̃], *a.* particular, meticulous; stingy, niggardly.

regarder [rəgar'de], *v.t.* to look at, to behold; to look into, to consider; to face, to be opposite; to concern; *cela vous regarde*, that concerns you.—*v.i.* to look; to mind, to pay heed. **se regarder**, *v.r.* to look at oneself; to look at each other; to look upon oneself (*comme*); to consider one another (*comme*); to face each other.

regarnir [rəgar'niːr], *v.t.* to furnish again; to retrim (*dress*); to re-cover (*furniture*) etc.

régate [re'gat], *n.f.* regatta, boat-race.

régence [re'ʒɑ̃:s], *n.f.* regency.

régénérateur [reʒenera'tœːr], *a.* (*fem.* **-trice**) regenerating.—*n.m.* regenerator.

régénération [reʒenera'sjɔ̃], *n.f.* regeneration; reclamation (*of land*).

régénérer [reʒene're], *v.t.* (*conjug. like* CÉDER) to regenerate.

régent [re'ʒɑ̃], *a.* and *n.m.* (*fem.* **-e**) regent.

régenter [reʒɑ̃'te], *v.t.* to domineer, to lord it over.

régie [re'ʒi], *n.f.* administration; (*public*) corporation; excise.

regimbement [rəʒɛ̃bə'mɑ̃], *n.m.* kicking (*of horses*); resistance, recalcitrance.

regimber [rəʒɛ̃'be], *v.i.* to kick (*of horses*); (*fig.*) to resist, to jib.

régime [re'ʒim], *n.m.* regimen; diet; form of government; rules, regulations; régime, system; speed (*of motor etc.*); bunch (*of bananas etc.*).

régiment [reʒi'mɑ̃], *n.m.* regiment.

régimentaire [reʒimɑ̃'tɛːr], *a.* regimental.

région [re'ʒjɔ̃], *n.f.* region; district.

régional [reʒjo'nal], *a.* (*m. pl.* **-aux**) local.

régir [re'ʒiːr], *v.t.* to govern, to rule; to administer.

régisseur [reʒi'sœːr], *n.m.* manager, steward; (*Theat.*) stage manager.

registre [rə'ʒistr], *n.m.* register; account-book; damper (*in chimneys*).

réglable [re'glabl], *a.* adjustable.

réglage [re'glaːʒ], *n.m.* ruling (*of paper*); regulating, adjusting, tuning.

règle [rɛgl], *n.f.* ruler, rule; order, regularity; model.

réglé [re'gle], *a.* regular, steady; ruled; paid.

règlement

règlement [rɛglə'mã], *n.m.* regulation; settlement (*of accounts*).

réglementaire [rɛgləmã'tɛːr], *a.* according to regulations, lawful; usual.

réglementer [rɛgləmã'te], *v.t.* to regulate.—*v.i.* to make regulations.

régler [re'gle], *v.t.* (*conjug. like* CÉDER) to rule (*paper etc.*); to regulate, to order, to adjust, to time (*a watch etc.*); to settle (*an account*). **se régler**, *v.r.* to regulate oneself, to be regulated; to be guided (*sur*).

régleur [re'glœːr], *n.m.* (*fem.* -**euse**) regulator (*of clocks etc.*).

réglisse [re'glis], *n.f.* liquorice.

réglure [re'glyːr], *n.f.* ruling (*of paper*).

régnant [re'nã], *a.* reigning; (*fig.*) prevailing, predominant.

règne [rɛɲ], *n.m.* reign; prevalence, vogue; (*Nat. Hist.*) kingdom.

régner [re'ɲe], *v.i.* (*conjug. like* CÉDER) to reign, to rule; to prevail, to be in fashion.

regonfler [rəgõ'fle], *v.t.* to swell again; to pump up (*tyre*).—*v.i.* to swell again.

regorgeant [rəgɔr'ʒã], *a.* overflowing; abounding.

regorger [rəgɔr'ʒe], *v.t.* (*conjug. like* MANGER) to regurgitate, to disgorge.—*v.i.* to overflow, to run over; to be crammed (*with*); to be plentiful, to abound.

régressif [regrɛ'sif], *a.* (*fem.* -**ive**) regressive, retrogressive.

régression [regrɛ'sjõ], *n.f.* regression, recession; retrogression; (*fig.*) decline.

regret [rə'grɛ], *n.m.* regret; *à regret*, with reluctance.

regrettable [rəgrɛ'tabl], *a.* regrettable, deplorable.

regrettablement [rəgrɛtablə'mã], *adv.* regrettably.

regretter [rəgrɛ'te], *v.t.* to regret; to grieve; to be sorry for, to repent; to miss.

régularisation [regylariza'sjõ], *n.f.* putting in order, regularization.

régulariser [regylari'ze] *v.t.* to put in order, to regularize.

régularité [regylari'te], *n.f.* regularity.

régulateur [regyla'tœːr], *a.* (*fem.* -**trice**) regulating.—*n.m.* regulator; (*Eng. etc.*) governor.

régulier [regy'lje], *a.* (*fem.* -**ière**) regular; steady, exact.—*n.m.* regular (*monk, soldier etc.*).

régulièrement [regyljɛr'mã], *adv.* regularly.

régurgitation [regyrʒita'sjõ], *n.f.* regurgitation.

régurgiter [regyrʒi'te], *v.t.* to regurgitate.

réhabilitation [reabilita'sjõ], *n.f.* rehabilitation.

réhabiliter [reabili'te], *v.t.* to rehabilitate; to reinstate. **se réhabiliter**, *v.r.* to rehabilitate oneself, to recover one's good name.

rehaussement [rəos'mã], *n.m.* raising; heightening, enhancing; increase of value (*of coin*).

rehausser [rəo'se], *v.t.* to raise; to heighten, to enhance; to raise the value of; to enrich; to set off.

réimposer [reɛ̃po'ze], *v.t.* to reassess (*tax*); (*Print.*) to reimpose.

réimpression [reɛ̃prɛ'sjõ], *n.f.* reprinting; reprint.

réimprimer [reɛ̃pri'me], *v.t.* to print again, to reprint.

rein [rɛ̃], *n.m.* kidney; (*pl.*) loins, back.

réincarnation [reɛ̃karna'sjõ], *n.f.* reincarnation.

reine [rɛn], *n.f.* queen.

reine-claude [rɛn'kloːd], *n.f.* (*pl.* **reines-claude**) greengage.

reine-des-prés [rɛ̃nde'pre], *n.f.* (*pl.* **reines-des-prés**) meadowsweet.

réinstallation [reɛ̃stala'sjõ], *n.f.* reinstalment, re-establishment.

réinstaller [reɛ̃sta'le], *v.t.* to reinstall.

réintégration [reɛ̃tegra'sjõ], *n.f.* reinstatement.

réintégrer [reɛ̃te'gre], *v.t.* (*conjug. like* CÉDER) to reinstate.

réitératif [reitera'tif], *a.* (*fem.* -**tive**) reiterative.

réitération [reitera'sjõ], *n.f.* reiteration, repetition.

réitérer [reite're], *v.t.* (*conjug. like* CÉDER) to reiterate, to repeat.

rejaillir [rəʒa'jiːr], *v.i.* to gush, to spurt out; to spring, to spout; (*fig.*) to flash; to reflect; to rebound.

rejaillissement [rəʒajis'mã], *n.m.* gushing out; spouting, springing; reflection, flashing; rebound.

réjection [reʒɛk'sjõ], *n.f.* rejection.

rejet [rə'ʒɛ], *n.m.* rejection; throwing out; young shoot, sprout.

rejeter [rəʒ'te], *v.t.* (*conjug. like* APPELER) to throw again; to throw back; to tilt back (*one's hat*); to repel; to throw away; to throw up (*of plants*); to reject; to deny.—*v.i.* to shoot (*of plants*). **se rejeter**, *v.r.* to have recourse to; to fall back (*upon*).

rejeton [rəʒ'tõ], *n.m.* shoot, sprout; (*fig.*) scion.

rejoindre [rə'ʒwɛ̃ːdr], *v.t. irr.* (*conjug. like* CRAINDRE) to rejoin, to join; to reunite; to overtake, to catch up. **se rejoindre**, *v.r.* to reunite; to meet; to catch each other up again.

rejouer [rə'ʒwe], *v.t., v.i.* to play again, to replay.

réjoui [re'ʒwi], *a.* and *n.m.* (*fem.* -**e**) jovial, joyous, merry (person).

réjouir [re'ʒwiːr], *v.t.* to rejoice, to delight, to cheer. **se réjouir**, *v.r.* to be *or* to make merry; to rejoice, to be delighted (*de*).

réjouissance [reʒwi'sãːs], *n.f.* rejoicing; (*pl.*) merry-making.

réjouissant [reʒwi'sã], *a.* cheering; diverting; amusing.

relâchant [rəla'ʃã], *a.* relaxing; laxative, loosening.—*n.m.* (*Med.*) laxative.

relâche (1) [rə'laːʃ], *n.m.* intermission, discontinuance, respite; relaxation; (*Theat.*) suspension of performance; *relâche ce soir*, no performance this evening.

relâche (2) [rə'laːʃ], *n.f.* (*Naut.*) putting into a port; port of call.

relâché [rəla'ʃe], *a.* lax, relaxed; loose, remiss.

relâchement [rəlaʃ'mã], *n.m.* slackening; slackness; laxity (*of morals*); looseness (*of bowels*).

relâcher [rəla'ʃe], *v.t.* to slacken, to loosen, to relax; to release; to unbend (*the mind etc.*); to yield, to abate.—*v.i.* (*Naut.*) to **put**

into port. se **relâcher**, v.r. to grow slack or loose; to abate; to relax, to unbend.

relais [rə'lɛ], n.m. relay (fresh horses); stage; shift (of workmen).

relancer [rəlɑ̃'se], v.t. (conjug. like COMMENCER) to throw back; (Ten.) to return (the ball); (Cards) to raise (a bid); (fig.) to harry (someone).

relaps [rə'laps], a. relapsed, relapsed into heresy.—n.m. (fem. -e) relapsed heretic.

rélargir [relar'ʒiːr], v.t. to widen, to let out (clothes etc.).

relater [rəla'te], v.t. to state, to tell.

relatif [rəla'tif], a. (fem. -tive) relative; relating (à).

relation [rəla'sjɔ̃], n.f. relation, account; statement; respect; connexion; communication, correspondence; (pl.) connexions.

relativement [rəlativ'mɑ̃], adv. relatively.

relativité [rəlativi'te], n.f. relativity.

relaxation [rəlaksa'sjɔ̃], n.f. release; relaxation (of muscles).

relaxer [rəlak'se], v.t. to release (a prisoner); to relax (muscles).

relayer [rəlɛ'je] v.t. (conjug. like PAYER) to take the place of, to relieve; (Elec. Eng., Rad., Teleg. etc.) to relay.—v.i. to change horses. se **relayer**, v.r. to relieve each other; to work in shifts.

relégation [rəlega'sjɔ̃], n.f. relegation; transportation (of convict).

reléguer [rəle'ge], v.t. (conjug. like CÉDER) to transport (for life), to shut up; to relegate, to consign (à). se **reléguer**, v.r. to shut oneself up.

relent [rə'lɑ̃], a. mouldy, musty.—n.m. mustiness, mouldiness.

relève [rə'lɛːv], n.f. (Mil.) relief.

relevé [rəl've], a. raised, erect; exalted, lofty; refined; highly seasoned.—n.m. abstract; statement, return; survey.

relèvement [rəlɛv'mɑ̃], n.m. raising again; recovery (of business); relieving (of sentry); rise, increase (of salary); (Naut.) bearing.

relever [rəl've], v.t. (conjug. like AMENER) to raise again, to lift up again; to turn up; to restore; to relieve (troops), to change (sentry); to raise (prices, salary); to set off, to enhance; to extol; to remark; to note, take down (name, address etc.); to release (from vows, oath); to survey; (Naut.) to take the bearings of.—v.i. to recover; to turn up; to depend. se **relever**, v.r. to rise again; to get up, to pick oneself up; to recover; to be raised; to relieve each other.

relief [rə'ljɛf], n.m. relief, embossment; enhancement; (pl.) scraps (from the table).

relier [rə'lje], v.t. to connect; to hoop (casks); to bind (books).

relieur [rə'ljœːr], n.m. (fem. -euse) binder, book-binder.

religieusement [rəliʒjøz'mɑ̃], adv. religiously; scrupulously.

religieux [rəli'ʒjø], a. (fem. -euse) religious, strict.—n.m. (fem. -euse) monk, nun.

religion [rəli'ʒjɔ̃], n.f. religion.

reliquaire [rəli'kɛːr], n.m. reliquary, shrine.

reliquat [rəli'ka], n.m. balance, remainder (of an account); after-effects (of a disease etc.).

relique [rə'lik], n.f. relic (of a saint).

relire [rə'liːr], v.t. irr. (conjug. like LIRE) to re-read.

reliure [rə'ljyːr], n.f. binding (of books).

relouer [rəlu'e], v.t. to relet, to sub-let.

reluire [rəlɥi'iːr], v.i. irr. (conjug. like LUIRE) to shine, to glitter.

reluisant [rəlɥi'zɑ̃], a. gleaming, shining, glittering.

reluquer [rəly'ke], v.t. (colloq.) to ogle, to leer at; (fig.) to have an eye on.

remâcher [rəmɑ'ʃe], v.t. to chew again; (fig.) to turn over in one's mind.

remailler [rəma'je], v.t. to repair the meshes (of fishing-nets etc.); to mend a ladder (in stocking).

remaniement or **remanîment** [rəmani'mɑ̃], n.m. (Polit.) reshuffle; handling again, touching up; repairing; changing.

remanier [rəma'nje], v.t. to handle again; to remodel; to adapt, to revise.

remariage [rəma'rjaːʒ], n.m. re-marriage.

remarier [rəma'rje], v.t. to remarry. se **remarier**, v.r. to marry again, to remarry.

remarquable [rəmar'kabl], a. remarkable, notable.

remarquablement [rəmarkablə'mɑ̃], adv. remarkably.

remarque [rə'mark], n.f. remark; notice.

remarquer [rəmar'ke], v.t. to mark again; to notice; to distinguish; faire **remarquer**, to point out. se **remarquer**, v.r. to be remarked.

remballer [rɑ̃ba'le], v.t. to pack up again.

rembarquement [rɑ̃barkə'mɑ̃], n.m. re-embarkation.

rembarquer [rɑ̃bar'ke], v.t. to re-embark, to ship again. se **rembarquer**, v.r. to go on board again.

rembarrer [rɑ̃ba're], v.t. to repulse; to snub; (fam.) to tick someone off.

remblai [rɑ̃'blɛ], n.m. filling up; embankment.

remblayer [rɑ̃blɛ'je], v.t. (conjug. like PAYER) to embank, to fill up (with earth).

remboîter [rɑ̃bwa'te], v.t. to fit in again; to reassemble; to reset (a bone).

rembourrage [rɑ̃bu'raːʒ], **rembourrement** [rɑ̃bur'mɑ̃], n.m. stuffing, padding.

rembourrer [rɑ̃bu're], v.t. to stuff, to pad; to upholster.

remboursable [rɑ̃bur'sabl], a. repayable; redeemable.

remboursement [rɑ̃bursə'mɑ̃], n.m. reimbursement, repayment.

rembourser [rɑ̃bur'se], v.t. to repay; to reimburse; to redeem (an annuity etc.).

rembruni [rɑ̃bry'ni], a. dark, gloomy.

rembrunir [rɑ̃bry'niːr], v.t. to darken; to cloud over; (fig.) to sadden. se **rembrunir**, v.r. to grow darker; to become cloudy or gloomy.

remède [rə'mɛd], n.m. remedy, medicine.

remédiable [rəme'djabl], a. remediable.

remédier [rəme'dje], v.i. to remedy, to cure (à).

remêler [rəmɛ'le], v.t. to mix again, to reshuffle.

remembrement [rəmɑ̃brə'mɑ̃], n.m. consolidation (of land).

remémoratif [rəmemɔra'tif], a. (fem. -tive) commemorative.

remémorer [rəmemɔ're], v.t. to bring (a thing) to someone's mind. se **remémorer**, v.r. to recollect.

T—F.E.D.—K

remerciement

remerciement or **remercîment** [rəmɛrsi'mā], *n.m.* thanking; (*pl.*) thanks; *faire des remerciements*, to thank.

remercier [rəmɛr'sje], *v.t.* to thank; to dismiss; *non, je vous remercie*, no, thank you.

remettre [rə'mɛtr], *v.t. irr.* (*conjug. like* METTRE) to put back; to put on again; to lay down again; to make well again; to deliver; to postpone; to entrust; to forgive; to remember; (*Ten.*) (*balle*) *à remettre*, let (ball); *je vous remets*, I remember your face; *remettre dans l'esprit*, to remind. **se remettre**, *v.r.* to recover (*oneself*); to resume, to start again; to recollect; to refer; to improve (*of weather*).

réminiscence [remini'sā:s], *n.f.* reminiscence.

remis [rə'mi], *a.* put back, put off, postponed.

remisage [rəmi'za:ʒ], *n.m.* housing, putting away (*vehicle*).

remise [rə'mi:z], *n.f.* delivery; remittance; discount; commission; delay; coach-house, mews, shed.

remiser [rəmi'ze], *v.t.* to put up, to put away (*vehicle*); to house; (*colloq.*) to put by.

rémissible [remi'si:bl], *a.* remissible, pardonable.

rémission [remi'sjō], *n.f.* remission, forgiveness.

remmener [rām'ne], *v.t.* (*conjug. like* AMENER) to take back, to lead back.

remodeler [rəmo'dle], *v.t.* (*conjug. like* AMENER) to remodel.

remontage [rəmō'ta:ʒ], *n.m.* going up; winding up (*of clock etc.*); assembling; refitting (*of parts of machinery*); restocking (*of shop*).

remonte [rə'mō:t], *n.f.* remounting, going upstream; run (*of fish*); (*Mil.*) remount.

remonter [rəmō'te], *v.t.* (*with aux.* AVOIR *or* ÊTRE *according as action or condition is meant*) to go up again; to take up again; to raise; to stock; to wind up (*clock etc.*); to re-string (*instruments*).—*v.i.* to go up again; to go back; to rise or increase (*in value etc.*); to date back; to remount (*cavalry*). **se remonter**, *v.r.* to take in a fresh supply (*de*); to be wound up (*of watches etc.*); to recover one's strength or spirits.

remontoir [rəmō'twa:r], *n.m.* winder, key (*of clock, watch*).

remontrance [rəmō'trā:s], *n.f.* remonstrance.

remontrer [rəmō'tre], *v.t.* to show again; to point out; to represent.—*v.i. en remontrer*, (*fig.*) to give advice.

remordre [rə'mordr], *v.t.* to bite again.—*v.i.* to try again.

remords [rə'mo:r], *n.m.* remorse.

remorquage [rəmor'ka:ʒ], *n.m.* towing, hauling.

remorque [rə'mork], *n.f.* towing; tow; towline; trailer (*car*).

remorquer [rəmor'ke], *v.t.* to tow, to haul.

remorqueur [rəmor'kœ:r], *a.* (*fem.* -euse) towing, hauling.—*n.m.* tug-boat, tug.

rémoulade [remu'lad], *n.f.* sharp sauce.

rémouleur [remu'lœ:r], *n.m.* knife-grinder.

remous [rə'mu], *n.m.* eddy; back-wash (*of ship*); slip-stream.

rempailler [rāpa'je], *v.t.* to re-seat (*a straw-bottomed chair*); to re-stuff with straw.

rempailleur [rāpa'jœ:r], *n.m.* (*fem.* -euse) chair-mender.

rempaqueter [rāpak'te], *v.t.* (*conjug. like* APPELER) to pack up again.

rempart [rā'pa:r], *n.m.* rampart; (*fig.*) bulwark.

remplaçable [rāpla'sabl], *a.* replaceable.

remplaçant [rāpla'sā], *n.m.* (*fem.* -e) substitute; locum.

remplacement [rāplas'mā], *n.m.* replacing, replacement.

remplacer [rāpla'se], *v.t.* (*conjug. like* COMMENCER) to take the place of, to replace; to reinvest. **se remplacer**, *v.r.* to be replaced.

rempli [rā'pli], *a.* filled, full.—*n.m.* tuck, take-up.

remplier [rāpli'je], *v.t.* to make a tuck in; to turn in.

remplir [rā'pli:r], *v.t.* to refill, to replenish; to fill, to fill up; to fill in (*form*); to cram; to supply; to occupy (*time etc.*); to fulfil. **se remplir**, *v.r.* to fill oneself; to become full.

remplissage [rāpli'sa:ʒ], *n.m.* filling, filling up (*of casks etc.*); (*fig.*) rubbish, padding.

remploi [rā'plwa], *n.m.* reinvestment.

remployer [rāplwa'je], *v.t.* (*conjug. like* EMPLOYER) to use again; to reinvest.

remplumer [rāply'me], *v.t.* to feather again. **se remplumer**, *v.r.* to get new feathers; (*fig.*) to retrieve one's losses; to get plump again.

rempocher [rāpo'ʃe], *v.t.* to put (*something*) back in one's pocket.

remporter [rāpor'te], *v.t.* to carry or take back; to carry off, to take away with one; to get; to win.

rempoter [rāpo'te], *v.t.* to repot.

remuant [rə'mɥā], *a.* restless; bustling; (*fam.*) on the go.

remue-ménage [rəmyme'na:ʒ], *n.m. inv.* stir, disturbance, bustle.

remuement or **remûment** [rəmy'mā], *n.m.* stir, stirring; removal; disturbance.

remuer [rə'mɥe], *v.t.* to move, to stir; to rouse; to turn up; to shake.—*v.i.* and **se remuer**, *v.r.* to stir, to move; to fidget.

rémunérateur [remynera'tœ:r], *a.* (*fem.* -trice) remunerative, profitable.—*n.m.* (*fem.* -trice) rewarder.

rémunération [remynera'sjō], *n.f.* remuneration, reward.

rémunératoire [remynera'twa:r], *a.* remunerative.

rémunérer [remyne're], *v.t.* (*conjug. like* CÉDER) to remunerate; to reward.

renâcler [rənɑ'kle], *v.i.* to snort; (*fam.*) to turn up one's nose; to jib (*at something*).

renaissance [rənɛ'sā:s], *n.f.* rebirth; renaissance.

renaissant [rənɛ'sā], *a.* springing up again, reviving.

renaître [rə'nɛ:tr], *v.i. irr.* (*conjug. like* NAÎTRE, *but no p.p.*) to be born again; to grow again; to spring up again; to revive.

rénal [re'nal], *a.* (*m. pl.* -aux) (*Anat.*) renal.

renard [rə'na:r], *n.m.* fox; (*fig.*) sly fellow; (*pop.*) blackleg.

renarde [rə'nard], *n.f.* vixen.

renardeau [rənar'do], *n.m.* (*pl.* -eaux) fox-cub.

Renaud [rə'no], *m.* Reginald.

renchéri [rɑ̃ʃe'ri], *a.* particular, over-nice (*of a person*).—*n.m.* (*fem.* -e) fastidious person; *faire le renchéri*, to put on airs.

renchérir [rɑ̃ʃe'ri:r], *v.i.* to raise the price of. —*v.i.* to get dearer, to rise in price; *renchérir sur*, to improve upon.

renchérissement [rɑ̃ʃeris'mɑ̃], *n.m.* rise in price.

rencogner (se) [sərɑ̃kɔ'ɲe], *v.r.* to retreat, to crouch in a corner.

rencontre [rɑ̃'kɔ̃:tr], *n.f.* meeting, encounter; duel; accidental meeting, discovery etc.; collision; chance, coincidence.

rencontrer [rɑ̃kɔ̃'tre], *v.t.* to meet, to meet with; to light upon, to encounter. **se rencontrer**, *v.r.* to meet, to meet each other; to be met with; to agree, to coincide.

rendement [rɑ̃d'mɑ̃], *n.m.* produce, yield, output; efficiency (*of a machine etc.*); (*Spt.*) handicap; (*Comm.*) return, profit.

rendez-vous [rɑ̃de'vu], *n.m. inv.* rendezvous, appointment; engagement; place of meeting.

rendormir [rɑ̃dɔr'mi:r], *v.t. irr.* (*conjug. like* SENTIR) to send to sleep again. **se rendormir**, *v.r.* to fall asleep again.

rendre [rɑ̃:dr], *v.t.* to return, to restore, to give back; to repay; to deliver; to give up; to pay; to produce; to reward; to carry; to eject, to emit; to express; to translate; *rendre visite*, to pay a visit.—*v.i.* to lead (*of roads*); to be lucrative; to function, to work. **se rendre**, *v.r.* to go; to resort; to make oneself, to render oneself; to become; to surrender, to give up; to be worn out.

rendu [rɑ̃'dy], *a.* rendered, delivered; exhausted, tired out; arrived.—*n.m.* return, tit for tat.

rendurcir [rɑ̃dyr'si:r], *v.t.* to make harder. **se rendurcir**, *v.r.* to become harder.

rêne [rɛ:n], *n.f.* rein.

renégat [rəne'ga], *a.* and *n.m.* (*fem.* -e) renegade, turncoat.

rêner [rɛ'ne], *v.t.* to bridle (*a horse*).

renfermé [rɑ̃fɛr'me], *a. personne renfermée*, close, uncommunicative person.— *n.m. odeur de renfermé*, fustiness; musty smell; *sentir le renfermé*, to smell close, fusty or stuffy.

renfermer [rɑ̃fɛr'me], *v.t.* to shut up; to contain; to include, to comprise; to conceal. **se renfermer**, *v.r.* to shut oneself up; to confine oneself.

renfiler [rɑ̃fi'le], *v.t.* to thread, to string again.

renflammer [rɑ̃fla'me], *v.t.* to rekindle. **se renflammer**, *v.r.* to flare up again.

renflé [rɑ̃'fle], *a.* swollen, swelling; (*Bot.*) inflated.

renflement [rɑ̃flə'mɑ̃], *n.m.* swelling, bulge.

renfler [rɑ̃'fle], *v.t., v.i.* to swell.

renflouage [rɑ̃flu'a:ʒ], **renflouement** [rɑ̃flu'mɑ̃], *n.m.* refloating (*a ship*).

renflouer [rɑ̃flu'e], *v.t.* to refloat, to raise (*a ship*); (*fig.*) to salvage (*firm, company etc.*).

renfoncement [rɑ̃fɔ̃s'mɑ̃], *n.m.* cavity, hollow, recess.

renfoncer [rɑ̃fɔ̃'se], *v.t.* (*conjug. like* COMMENCER) to drive deeper; to pull (*a hat etc.*) further on.

renforçage [rɑ̃fɔr'sa:ʒ], *n.m.* strengthening.

renforcé [rɑ̃fɔr'se], *a.* downright, regular; reinforced.

renforcement [rɑ̃fɔrsə'mɑ̃], *n.m.* strengthening; reinforcement.

renforcer [rɑ̃fɔr'se], *v.t.* (*conjug. like* COMMENCER) to strengthen, to reinforce; to increase. **se renforcer**, *v.r.* to gather strength, to grow stronger; (*Mil.*) to be reinforced.

renfort [rɑ̃'fɔ:r], *n.m.* reinforcement; (*fig.*) help, aid, relief; strengthening-piece.

renfrogné [rɑ̃frɔ'ɲe], *a.* frowning, scowling, surly.

renfrognement [rɑ̃frɔɲə'mɑ̃], *n.m.* frown, scowl.

renfrogner (se) [sərɑ̃frɔ'ɲe], *v.r.* to frown.

rengagement [rɑ̃gaʒ'mɑ̃], *n.m.* re-engagement; (*Mil.*) re-enlistment.

rengager [rɑ̃ga'ʒe], *v.t.* (*conjug. like* MANGER) to re-engage.—*v.i.* (*Mil.*) to re-enlist. **se rengager**, *v.r.* to re-engage; to begin afresh; to re-enlist.

rengaine [rɑ̃'gɛ:n], *n.f.* catch-phrase; (*fam.*) hackneyed story; popular tune.

rengainer [rɑ̃gɛ'ne], *v.t.* to sheathe, to put up (*one's sword*); to withdraw, to put away.

rengorgement [rɑ̃gɔrʒə'mɑ̃], *n.m.* swaggering, puffing out the neck (*of peacock*).

rengorger (se) [sərɑ̃gɔr'ʒe], *v.r.* to carry one's head high; (*fig.*) to give oneself airs.

reniable [rə'njabl], *a.* deniable.

reniement or **reniment** [rəni'mɑ̃], *n.m.* denying, disowning.

renier [rə'nje], *v.t.* to disown (*son, friend etc.*); to deny (*God, doctrine*).

reniflement [rəniflə'mɑ̃], *n.m.* sniffing, snuffing, snivelling.

renifler [rəni'fle], *v.i.* to sniff, to snivel; (*fig.*) to turn up one's nose (*sur*); to hang back.

renne [rɛn], *n.m.* reindeer.

renom [rə'nɔ̃], *n.m.* renown, fame, reputation.

renommé [rənɔ'me], *a.* renowned, famed.

renommée [rənɔ'me], *n.f.* renown, fame, reputation; rumour.

renommer [rənɔ'me], *v.t.* to name again, to re-elect; to make famous, to praise.

renoncement [rənɔ̃s'mɑ̃], *n.m.* renouncement; renunciation.

renoncer [rənɔ̃'se], *v.t.* (*conjug. like* COMMENCER) to renounce, to disclaim, to disown.—*v.i.* to give up, to renounce (*à*).

renonciation [rənɔ̃sja'sjɔ̃], *n.f.* renunciation, self-denial.

renoncule [rənɔ̃'kyl], *n.f.* (*Bot.*) ranunculus, buttercup, crowfoot.

renouer [rənu'e], *v.t.* to tie again, to knot again; to put together; to resume.—*v.i.* to resume relations (*avec*).

renouveau [rənu'vo], *n.m.* (*pl.* -eaux) (*poet.*) spring.

renouvelable [rənu'vlabl], *a.* renewable.

renouveler [rənu'vle], *v.t.* (*conjug. like* APPELER) to renew; to renovate; to revive; to recommence, to repeat. **se renouveler**, *v.r.* to be renewed; to be revived, to occur again.

renouvellement [rənuvɛl'mɑ̃], *n.m.* renewal, revival, renovation; increase.

rénovateur [renova'tœ:r], *a.* (*fem.* -trice) renovating.—*n.m.* (*fem.* -trice) renovator, restorer.

rénovation [renɔvɑ'sjɔ̃], *n.f.* renovation, renewal.

renseignement [rɑ̃sɛɲ'mɑ̃], *n.m.* (piece of) information, (piece of) intelligence, account; (*pl.*) information; references; *bureau de renseignements*, information bureau, inquiry-office.

renseigner [rɑ̃sɛ'ɲe], *v.t.* to give information to; to direct. **se renseigner**, *v.r.* to seek information, to make inquiries.

rente [rɑ̃:t], *n.f.* yearly income; revenue; stock, funds.

renté [rɑ̃'te], *a.* of independent means; endowed (*of hospital etc.*).

renter [rɑ̃'te], *v.t.* to allow a yearly income to, to endow (*public services etc.*).

rentier [rɑ̃'tje], *n.m.* (*fem.* **-ière**) stockholder; person of independent means.

rentrant [rɑ̃'trɑ̃], *a.* re-entering, returning; (*Av.*) retractable.—*n.m.* recess (*in a wall*); (*fem.* **-e**) new player.

rentré [rɑ̃'tre], *a.* returned; suppressed; depressed.

rentrée [rɑ̃'tre], *n.f.* re-entrance; return, home-coming; reopening (*of schools etc.*); reappearance; ingathering (*of crops etc.*); receipt, collection.

rentrer [rɑ̃'tre], *v.t.* (*aux.* AVOIR) to take in, to bring in; to suppress.—*v.i.* (*aux.* ÊTRE) to re-enter, to go in again; to return home; to join again; to reopen (*of schools etc.*).

renversable [rɑ̃vɛr'sabl], *a.* liable to be upset; reversible.

renversant [rɑ̃vɛr'sɑ̃], *a.* (*colloq.*) amazing, stunning.

renverse [rɑ̃'vɛrs], *n.f. à la renverse*, backwards.

renversé [rɑ̃vɛr'se], *a.* thrown down, thrown back; upside-down.

renversement [rɑ̃vɛrsə'mɑ̃], *n.m.* reversing; overturning, overthrow; turning upside down; confusion; subversion.

renverser [rɑ̃vɛr'se], *v.t.* to turn upside down, to upset; to reverse; to knock over; to spill (*a liquid*); to destroy; to confuse; to turn (*the brain*); (*fam.*) to astound; to rout; (*Arith., Mus.*) to invert. **se renverser**, *v.r.* to fall back; to fall down; to capsize; to be spilt.

renvoi [rɑ̃'vwa], *n.m.* sending back, return; dismissal; referring (*to a committee etc.*).

renvoyer [rɑ̃vwa'je], *v.t. irr.* (*conjug. like* ENVOYER) to send again; to send back, to return; to dismiss; to refer; to postpone; to throw back; to reflect (*light, heat etc.*); to reverberate (*sound*). **se renvoyer**, *v.r.* to be sent back *or* returned; to send from one to the other.

réoccupation [reɔkypa'sjɔ̃], *n.f.* reoccupation.

réoccuper [reɔky'pe], *v.t.* to reoccupy.

réorganisation [reɔrganiza'sjɔ̃], *n.f.* reorganization.

réorganiser [reɔrgani'ze], *v.t.* to reorganize.

réouverture [reuvɛr'ty:r], *n.f.* reopening (*of a theatre*).

repaire (1) [rə'pɛ:r], *n.m.* haunt (*of criminals*); den, lair (*of animals*).

repaire (2) [REPÈRE].

repaître [rə'pɛ:tr], *v.t. irr.* (*conjug. like* PAÎTRE) to feed, to nourish. **se repaître**, *v.r.* to feed on, to feast on; to delight in, to indulge in.

répandre [re'pɑ̃:dr], *v.t.* to pour out, to shed; to spill; to scatter; to distribute; to exhale; to spread abroad. **se répandre**, *v.r.* to be poured out, to be shed, to be spilt; to be spread; to be exhaled; to be spread abroad; to be current; to go into society.

répandu [repɑ̃'dy], *a.* spilt, shed; widespread.

réparable [repa'rabl], *a.* reparable; rectifiable.

reparaître [rəpa'rɛ:tr], *v.i. irr.* (*conjug. like* CONNAÎTRE) to reappear.

réparateur [repara'tœ:r], *a.* (*fem.* **-trice**) restorative, refreshing.—*n.m.* (*fem.* **-trice**) repairer, restorer.

réparation [repara'sjɔ̃], *n.f.* repairing, mending; amends; compensation; *en réparation*, under repair.

réparer [repa're], *v.t.* to repair, to mend; to make amends for, to make up for.

répareur [repa'rœ:r], *n.m.* (*fem.* **-euse**) repairer.

reparler [rəpar'le], *v.i.* to speak again.

repartie [rəpar'ti], *n.f.* repartee, retort.

repartir (1) [rəpar'ti:r], *v.t., v.i.* (*conjug. like* SENTIR) to answer, to retort.

repartir (2) [rəpar'ti:r], *v.i. irr.* (*conjug. like* SENTIR, *but with aux.* ÊTRE) to set out again, to go away again.

répartir [repar'ti:r], *v.t.* to divide, to distribute; to assess.

répartissable [reparti'sabl], *a.* divisible; assessable.

répartiteur [reparti'tœ:r], *n.m.* (*fem.* **-trice**) distributor; assessor (*of taxes etc.*).

répartition [reparti'sjɔ̃], *n.f.* distribution; assessment.

repas [rə'pa], *n.m. inv.* meal, repast.

repassage [rəpa'sa:ʒ], *n.m.* repassing; grinding, sharpening (*of cutlery*); ironing (*of linen etc.*).

repasser [rəpa'se], *v.t.* (*aux.* AVOIR) to pass again; to cross again; to think over; to sharpen, to grind (*tools*); to iron; to repeat; to look over again.—*v.i.* (*aux.* ÊTRE) to pass again; to go, come, call etc., again.

repasseur [rəpa'sœ:r], *n.m.* (*fem.* **-euse**) (*Ind.*) examiner; grinder.—*n.f.* (**-euse**) ironer (*person* or *machine*).

repavage [rəpa'va:ʒ], **repavement** [rəpav'mɑ̃], *n.m.* repaving.

repaver [rəpa've], *v.t.* to repave.

repêchage [rəpe'ʃa:ʒ], *n.m.* rescuing; (*Spt.*) *épreuve de repêchage*, supplementary heat; (*Sch.*) second chance (*for candidate who has failed an examination*).

repêcher [rəpe'ʃe], *v.t.* to fish up *or* out again; (*fig.*) to recover, to retrieve.

repeindre [rə'pɛ̃:dr], *v.t. irr.* (*conjug. like* CRAINDRE) to repaint.

repenser [rəpɑ̃'se], *v.t., v.i.* to think over; to think again (of).

repentance [rəpɑ̃'tɑ̃:s], *n.f.* repentance, contrition.

repentant [rəpɑ̃'tɑ̃], *a.* repentant.

repenti [rəpɑ̃'ti], *a.* penitent.

repentir [rəpɑ̃'ti:r], *n.m.* repentance, contrition, regret.

repentir (se) [sərəpɑ̃'ti:r], *v.r. irr.* (*conjug. like* SENTIR) to repent; to rue (*de*).

repérage [rəpe'ra:ʒ], *n.m.* locating; (*Cine.*) synchronization; (*Mil.*) spotting.

répercussion [repɛrky'sjɔ̃], *n.f.* repercussion, reverberation.

répercuter [repɛrky'te], *v.t.* to reverberate, to echo; to reflect. **se répercuter**, *v.r.* to be reflected (*light*); to reverberate (*sound*); (*fig.*) to have repercussions.

repère or **repaire** [rə'pɛːr], *n.m.* mark; benchmark; (*fig.*) landmark.

repérer [rəpe're], *v.t.* (*conjug. like* CÉDER) to locate, to spot; to make a guiding mark upon. **se repérer**, *v.r.* to find one's bearings.

répertoire [repɛr'twaːr], *n.m.* table, list, catalogue; repertory.

répéter [repe'te], *v.t.* (*conjug. like* CÉDER) to repeat, to tell again; to rehearse; to reflect; (*Law*) to demand back. **se répéter**, *v.r.* to be repeated; to repeat oneself.

répétiteur [repeti'tœːr], *n.m.* (*fem.* **-trice**) private teacher, tutor.

répétition [repeti'sjɔ̃], *n.f.* repetition; recurrence; private lesson; (*Theat.*) rehearsal.

repétrir [rəpe'triːr], *v.t.* to remould; to re-fashion.

repeupler [rəpœ'ple], *v.t.* to repeople; to restock. **se repeupler**, *v.r.* to be repeopled; to be restocked.

repiquage [rəpi'kaːʒ], *n.m.* transplanting, pricking *or* planting out (again); repairing (*of road*).

repiquer [rəpi'ke], *v.t.* to prick again; to prick out, to transplant; to repair (*road*).

répit [re'pi], *n.m.* respite; (*fig.*) rest, breathing space.

replacement [rəplas'mã], *n.m.* replacing, putting *or* setting again; reinvestment (*of funds*).

replacer [rəpla'se], *v.t.* (*conjug. like* COMMENCER) to replace, to put in place again; to bring back; to reinvest (*funds*). **se replacer**, *v.r.* to find oneself a new situation.

replanir [rəpla'niːr], *v.t.* to plane down (*wood*).

replanter [rəplã'te], *v.t.* to replant.

replâtrer [rəpla'tre], *v.t.* to replaster; to patch up (*temporarily*).

replet [rə'plɛ], *a.* (*fem.* **-ète**) obese, stout; (*fam.*) podgy.

réplétion [reple'sjɔ̃], *n.f.* stoutness; repletion, surfeit.

repli [rə'pli], *n.m.* fold, crease; (*fig.*) winding, coil, meander (*of river*); (*Mil.*) withdrawal.

repliable [rəpli'jabl], *a.* folding, collapsible.

replier [rəpli'je], *v.t.* to fold again, to fold up; to bend back; to coil (*a rope etc.*). **se replier**, *v.r.* to twist oneself, to writhe, to wind, to coil; (*Mil.*) to retreat.

réplique [re'plik], *n.f.* reply, answer, retort; (*Mus.*) repeat; (*Theat.*) cue.

répliquer [repli'ke], *v.t.*, *v.i.* to reply, to retort.

replonger [rəplɔ̃'ʒe], *v.t.* (*conjug. like* MANGER) to plunge again, to dip again.— *v.i.* **se replonger**, *v.r.* to plunge again; to dive again.

répondant [repɔ̃'dã], *n.m.* candidate (*at an examination*); bail, surety.

répondre [re'pɔ̃ːdr], *v.t.* to answer, to reply. —*v.i.* to answer, to reply; to write back; to come up (*à*); to correspond; to re-echo; to be answerable (*de*); to pledge oneself (*pour*); *je vous en réponds*, take my word for it.

répons [re'pɔ̃], *n.m.* response (*in church*).

réponse [re'pɔ̃ːs], *n.f.* answer, reply, response.

report [rə'pɔːr], *n.m.* (*Book-keeping*) carrying forward, bringing forward; amount brought forward.

reportage [rəpɔr'ta:ʒ], *n.m.* (*Journ.*) reporting; feature article.

reporter (1) [rəpɔr'tɛːr], *n.m.* (*Journ.*) reporter.

reporter (2) [rəpɔr'te], *v.t.* to carry back; to take back; (*Book-keeping*) to carry forward. **se reporter**, *v.r.* to go back; to refer; *se reporter à*, please refer to.

repos [rə'po], *n.m.* rest, repose; sleep; quiet; resting-place; *en repos*, at rest; (*Mil.*) *repos !* stand at ease!

reposant [rəpo'zã], *a.* restful, refreshing.

reposé [rəpo'ze], *a.* rested, refreshed; quiet, calm, cool.

reposer [rəpo'ze], *v.t.* to place again, to lay again, to replace; to rest (*on anything*); to refresh.—*v.i.* to rest, to lie down; to sleep; to be at rest. **se reposer**, *v.r.* to rest, to lie down; to settle down; to alight again (*of birds*); *se reposer sur*, to rely on.

reposoir [rəpo'zwaːr], *n.m.* resting-place; pause.

repoussant [rəpu'sã], *a.* repulsive, loathsome.

repoussé [rəpu'se], *a.* chased (*silver*), embossed.

repousser [rəpu'se], *v.t.* to push back, to repel; to spurn, to reject; to rebuff; to shoot out (*branches etc.*) again; *repousser du cuir*, to emboss leather;—*repousser du cuivre*, to chase copper.—*v.i.* to recoil; to spring up again (*of plants etc.*); to grow again (*of hair*); to be repulsive.

repoussoir [rəpu'swaːr], *n.m.* (*Paint.*) foil.

répréhensible [repreã'sibl], *a.* reprehensible.

répréhension [repreã'sjɔ̃], *n.f.* reprehension, reproof.

reprendre [rə'prãːdr], *v.t. irr.* (*conjug. like* PRENDRE) to recover, to recapture; to take up again; to reprove; to repair.—*v.i.* to take root again; to freeze again; to close up again (*of wounds etc.*); to begin again, to return to; to improve; to reply; to resume. **se reprendre**, *v.r.* to correct oneself; to be caught again; to begin again.

représaille [repre'zaːj], *n.f.* (*usu. pl.*) reprisal; *user de représailles*, to retaliate.

représentant [rəprezã'tã], *n.m.* (*fem.* **-e**) representative.

représentatif [rəprezã'tif], *a.* (*fem.* **-tive**) representative.

représentation [rəprezãta'sjɔ̃], *n.f.* representation; performance; show; remonstrance; agency.

représenter [rəprezã'te], *v.t.* to present again; to show, to produce; to represent; to resemble; to act (*a play*); to be the representative of.—*v.i.* to have an imposing appearance; to make a good show. **se représenter**, *v.r.* to present oneself again; to picture to oneself; to occur.

répressible [repre'sibl], *a.* repressible.

répressif [repre'sif], *a.* (*fem.* **-ive**) repressive.

répression [repre'sjɔ̃], *n.f.* repression.

réprimande [repri'mɑ̃:d], *n.f.* reprimand, rebuke.

réprimander [reprimɑ̃'de], *v.t.* to reprimand, to reprove.

réprimant [repri'mɑ̃], *a.* repressive.

réprimer [repri'me], *v.t.* to repress, to restrain.

repris [rə'pri], *a.* retaken, taken up again; reset (*of a bone*).—*n.m. repris de justice*, old offender, (*fam.*) old lag.

reprisage [rəpri'za:ʒ], *n.m.* darn; darning.

reprise [rə'pri:z], *n.f.* resumption; recapture, recovery; revival; darn; (*Mus.*) repetition; refrain (*of a song*); (*Ftb. etc.*) second half; (*Fenc.*) bout; (*Box.*) round; *à plusieurs reprises*, several times, repeatedly.

repriser [rəpri'ze], *v.t.* to darn.

réprobateur [reprɔba'tœ:r], *a.* (*fem.* -**trice**) reproving.

réprobation [reprɔba'sjɔ̃], *n.f.* reprobation.

reprochable [rəprɔ'ʃabl], *a.* reproachable.

reproche [rə'prɔʃ], *n.m.* reproach.

reprocher [rəprɔ'ʃe], *v.t.* to reproach, to upbraid; to taunt. **se reprocher**, *v.r.* to reproach oneself; to blame oneself.

reproducteur [rəprɔdyk'tœ:r], *a.* (*fem.* -**trice**) reproductive.

reproductif [rəprɔdyk'tif], *a.* (*fem.* -**tive**) reproductive.

reproduction [rəprɔdyk'sjɔ̃], *n.f.* reproduction; copy.

reproduire [rəprɔ'dɥi:r], *v.t. irr.* (*conjug. like* CONDUIRE) to reproduce; to reprint. **se reproduire**, *v.r.* to reproduce; to breed; to recur.

réprouvable [repru'vabl], *a.* censurable, reprehensible.

réprouvé [repru've], *a.* and *n.m.* (*fem.* -**ée**) reprobate.

réprouver [repru've], *v.t.* to disapprove of; (*Theol.*) to condemn.

reps [rɛps], *n.m.* rep (*silk or woollen fabric*).

reptile [rɛp'til], *a.* creeping, crawling.—*n.m.* reptile.

repu [rə'py], *a.* and *p.p.* of *repaître*, full, satiated.

républicain [repybli'kɛ̃], *a.* and *n.m.* (*fem.* -**e**) republican.

republier [repybli'je], *v.t.* to republish.

république [repy'blik], *n.f.* republic; commonwealth.

répudiation [repydja'sjɔ̃], *n.f.* repudiation.

répudier [repy'dje], *v.t.* to repudiate.

répugnance [repy'nɑ̃:s], *n.f.* repugnance; reluctance.

répugnant [repy'nɑ̃], *a.* repugnant.

répugner [repy'ne], *v.i.* to be repugnant; to feel repugnance; to clash with.

répulsif [repyl'sif], *a.* (*fem.* -**sive**) repulsive, repellent; (*fig.*) disgusting.

répulsion [repyl'sjɔ̃], *n.f.* repulsion; (*fig.*) aversion, disgust.

réputation [repyta'sjɔ̃], *n.f.* reputation, character; fame.

réputé [repy'te], *a.* well-known.

réputer [repy'te], *v.t.* to repute, to consider, to deem.

requérant [rəke'rɑ̃], *n.m.* (*fem.* -**e**) plaintiff, petitioner.

requérir [rəke'ri:r], *v.t. irr.* (*conjug. like* ACQUÉRIR) to request; to require; to claim; to requisition.

requête [rə'kɛ:t], *n.f.* request, petition, demand.

requiem [rekɥi'ɛm], *n.m.* requiem.

requin [rə'kɛ̃], *n.m.* shark.

requis [rə'ki], *a.* required, requisite, necessary.

réquisition [rekizi'sjɔ̃], *n.f.* requisition; summons; levy.

réquisitionner [rekizisjɔ'ne], *v.t.* to requisition, to commandeer.

rescapé [rɛska'pe], *a.* and *n.m.* (*fem.* -**ée**) survivor of a disaster.

rescousse [rɛs'kus], *n.f. venir (aller) à la rescousse*, to come (to go) to the rescue.

réseau [re'zo], *n.m.* (*pl.* -**eaux**) net; network; (*fig.*) web, tangle; (*Rail., Elec. etc.*) network, system.

réséda [reze'da], *n.m.* reseda; mignonette.

réservation [rezɛrva'sjɔ̃], *n.f.* reservation, reserving; booking (*of seats*).

réserve [re'zɛrv], *n.f.* reserve; reservation, caution; modesty; stock, store; preserve (*for game*).

réservé [rezɛr've], *a.* reserved; cautious.

réserver [rezɛr've], *v.t.* to reserve; to keep (*pour*). **se réserver**, *v.r.* to reserve for oneself; to reserve oneself, to wait.

réserviste [rezɛr'vist], *n.m.* (*Mil.*) reservist.

réservoir [rezɛr'vwa:r], *n.m.* reservoir; tank, cistern, well.

résidant [rezi'dɑ̃], *a.* resident.

résidence [rezi'dɑ̃:s], *n.f.* residence, dwelling.

résident [rezi'dɑ̃], *n.m.* (*fem.* -**e**) resident.

résidentiel [rezidɑ̃'sjɛl], *a.* (*fem.* -**elle**) residential.

résider [rezi'de], *v.i.* to reside, to dwell.

résidu [rezi'dy], *n.m.* residue; remainder.

résiduaire [rezi'dɥɛ:r], *a.* waste.

résignation [rezina'sjɔ̃], *n.f.* resignation.

résigné [rezi'ne], *a.* resigned, submissive.

résigner [rezi'ne], *v.t.* to resign, to give up. **se résigner**, *v.r.* to resign oneself to submit.

résiliation [rezilja'sjɔ̃], *n.f.*, **résiliement** or **résiliment** [rezili'mɑ̃], *n.m.* cancelling, annulment.

résilience [rezi'ljɑ̃:s], *n.f.* resilience (*in metals*).

résilier [rezi'lje], *v.t.* to cancel, to annul.

résille [re'zi:j], *n.f.* hair-net.

résine [re'zin], *n.f.* resin, rosin.

résineux [rezi'nø], *a.* (*fem.* -**euse**) resinous.

résistance [rezis'tɑ̃:s], *n.f.* resistance, opposition; *la Résistance*, the Resistance Movement (1940–45).

résistant [rezis'tɑ̃], *a.* unyielding; resistant, tough.—*n.m.* (*fem.* -**e**) member of the Resistance Movement.

résister [rezis'te], *v.i.* to resist, to withstand (*à*).

résistible [rezis'tibl], *a.* resistible.

résistivité [rezistivi'te], *n.f.* (*Elec.*) resistivity.

résolu [rezo'ly], *a.* resolved, resolute, determined; solved.

résoluble [rezo'lybl], *a.* soluble.

résolument [rezoly'mɑ̃], *adv.* resolutely, boldly.

résolution [rezoly'sjɔ̃], *n.f.* resolution, solution; decision, determination; resolve.

résonance [rezo'nɑ̃:s], *n.f.* resonance.

résonnant [rezo'nɑ̃], *a.* resonant, resounding, sonorous.

résonnement [rezɔn'mɑ̃], *n.m.* resounding, re-echoing.
résonner [rezɔ'ne], *v.i.* to resound, to reverberate, to re-echo.
résoudre [re'zuːdr], *v.t. irr.* to resolve; to dissolve; to solve; to decide upon; to cancel; to persuade. **se résoudre**, *v.r.* to resolve, to determine; to be resolved, to be solved; to dissolve.
respect [rɛs'pɛ], *n.m.* respect, regard, reverence.
respectabilité [rɛspɛktabili'te], *n.f.* respectability.
respectable [rɛspɛk'tabl], *a.* respectable.
respectablement [rɛspɛktablə'mɑ̃], *adv.* respectably.
respecter [rɛspɛk'te], *v.t.* to respect, to revere; to spare.
respectif [rɛspɛk'tif], *a.* (*fem.* **-tive**) respective.
respectivement [rɛspɛktiv'mɑ̃], *adv.* respectively.
respectueusement [rɛspɛktɥøz'mɑ̃], *adv.* respectfully, deferentially.
respectueux [rɛspɛk'tɥø], *a.* (*fem.* **-euse**) respectful, deferential.
respirable [rɛspi'rabl], *a.* respirable, breathable.
respirateur [rɛspira'tœːr], *a.m.* respiratory. —*n.m.* respirator.
respiration [rɛspira'sjɔ̃], *n.f.* respiration, breathing.
respiratoire [rɛspira'twaːr], *a.* respiratory, breathing.
respirer [rɛspi're], *v.t.* to breathe; (*fig.*) to express; to long for.—*v.i.* to breathe; to take breath, to rest.
resplendir [rɛsplɑ̃'diːr], *v.i.* to shine brightly; to glitter.
resplendissant [rɛsplɑ̃di'sɑ̃], *a.* resplendent, glittering.
resplendissement [rɛsplɑ̃dis'mɑ̃], *n.m.* splendour, refulgence.
responsabilité [rɛspɔ̃sabili'te], *n.f.* responsibility, liability.
responsable [rɛspɔ̃'sabl], *a.* responsible, accountable.
resquillage [rɛski'jaːʒ], *n.m.*, **resquille** [rɛs'kiːj], *n.f.* (*slang*) queue-crashing; **entrer à la resquille**, to gate-crash.
resquiller [rɛski'je] *v.i.* to gate-crash; to wangle.
ressac [rə'sak], *n.m.* surf.
ressaisir [rəsɛ'ziːr], *v.t.* to seize again. **se ressaisir**, *v.r.* to regain one's self-control.
ressasser [rəsa'se], *v.t.* (*fig.*) to scrutinize; (*fig.*) to repeat tediously, to harp on.
ressaut [rə'so], *n.m.* projection; abrupt fall, dip.
ressauter [rəso'te], *v.t.* to leap over again.—*v.i.* to leap again; (*Arch.*) to project.
ressemblance [rəsɑ̃'blɑ̃ːs], *n.f.* resemblance, likeness.
ressemblant [rəsɑ̃'blɑ̃], *a.* like, similar.
ressembler [rəsɑ̃'ble], *v.i.* to look like, to resemble (*à*). **se ressembler**, *v.r.* to be like each other; to look alike.
ressemelage [rəsəm'laːʒ], *n.m.* resoling (*of boots*).
ressemeler [rəsə'mle], *v.t.* (*conjug. like* APPELER) to re-sole (*boots etc.*).
ressenti [rəsɑ̃'ti], *a.* felt; (*Paint.*) strongly expressed.

ressentiment [rəsɑ̃ti'mɑ̃], *n.m.* resentment.
ressentir [rəsɑ̃'tiːr], *v.t. irr.* (*conjug. like* SENTIR) to feel, to experience; to manifest; to resent. **se ressentir**, *v.r.* to feel the effects (*de*); to be felt.
resserrement [rəsɛr'mɑ̃], *n.m.* contraction, tightening; restriction.
resserrer [rəsɛ're], *v.t.* to tighten; to pen in; to restrain; to abridge; to close up; to lock up again. **se resserrer**, *v.r.* to contract, to be contracted; to confine oneself; to curtail one's expenses.
ressort (1) [rə'soːr], *n.m.* spring; elasticity; energy, activity, strength; means.
ressort (2) [rə'soːr], *n.m.* extent of jurisdiction; (*fig.*) department, line.
ressortir (1) [rəsɔr'tiːr], *v.i. irr.* (*conjug. like* SENTIR, *but with aux.* ÊTRE) to go or come out again; (*fig.*) to stand out; to result (*de*); **faire ressortir**, to throw into relief.
ressortir (2) [rəsɔr'tiːr], *v.i.* to be under the jurisdiction of, to be dependent on.
ressortissant [rəsɔrti'sɑ̃], *n.m.* (*fem.* **-e**) national.
ressource [rə'surs], *n.f.* resource, resort, expedient, shift; (*pl.*) resources; **il n'y a point de ressource**, there's no help for it; **ressources personnelles**, private means.
ressouvenir [rəsuv'niːr], *n.m.* remembrance, recollection, reminiscence.
ressouvenir (se) [sərəsuv'niːr], *v.r. irr.* (*conjug. like* TENIR, *but with aux.* ÊTRE) to recollect, to remember.
ressuscitation [resysita'sjɔ̃], *n.f.* resuscitation, revival.
ressusciter [resysi'te], *v.t.* to resuscitate; to revive (*a custom etc.*).—*v.i.* to come to life again.
restant [rɛs'tɑ̃], *a.* remaining, left.—*n.m.* remainder, rest.
restaurant [rɛsto'rɑ̃], *n.m.* restaurant; restorative.
restaurateur [rɛstora'tœːr], *n.m.* (*fem.* **-trice**) restorer; restaurant keeper.
restauration [rɛstora'sjɔ̃], *n.f.* restoration, repair.
restaurer [rɛsto're], *v.t.* to restore; to refresh. **se restaurer**, *v.r.* to take refreshment; to build up one's strength (*after illness*).
reste [rɛst], *n.m.* rest, remainder; trace, vestige; (*pl.*) remnants, relics; remains; **au reste** or **du reste**, besides, moreover; **de reste**, over and above; **et le reste**, and so on, and so forth; **être en reste**, to be in arrears; **les restes**, remnants (*of meal*); mortal remains.
rester [rɛs'te], *v.i.* (*aux.* ÊTRE) to remain; to stay; to last; to pause; **rester court**, to stop short.
restituable [rɛsti'tɥabl], *a.* repayable returnable.
restituer [rɛsti'tɥe], *v.t.* to restore; to return, to refund.
restitution [rɛstity'sjɔ̃], *n.f.* restitution; restoration.
restreindre [rɛs'trɛ̃ːdr], *v.t. irr.* (*conjug. like* CRAINDRE) to restrict; to limit; to restrain. **se restreindre**, *v.r.* to restrain oneself; to curtail one's expenses.
restreint [rɛs'trɛ̃], *a.* restricted, limited.
restrictif [rɛstrik'tif], *a.* (*fem.* **-tive**) restrictive.

restriction [rɛstrik'sjõ], *n.f.* restriction, restraint; *restriction mentale*, mental reservation.

restringent [rɛstrɛ̃'ʒã], *a.* and *n.m.* (*Med.*) astringent.

résultant [rezyl'tã], *a.* resulting.

résultat [rezyl'ta], *n.m.* result.

résulter [rezyl'te], *v.i.* to result.

résumé [rezy'me], *n.m.* recapitulation, summary; *en résumé*, to sum up.

résumer [rezy'me], *v.t.* to summarize. **se résumer**, *v.r.* to recapitulate, to sum up.

résurrection [rezyrɛk'sjõ], *n.f.* resurrection; revival.

rétablir [reta'bliːr], *v.t.* to re-establish, to restore; to repair; to recover; to retrieve. **se rétablir**, *v.r.* to recover one's health; to be restored.

rétablissement [retablis'mã], *n.m.* re-establishment, restoration; repair; recovery.

retailler [rətɑ'je], *v.t.* to cut again, to prune again.

rétamer [reta'me], *v.t.* to tin over again; to resilver.

rétameur [reta'mœːr], *n.m.* tinker.

retaper [rətɑ'pe], *v.t.* (*collog.*) to do up (*a hat etc.*), to straighten (*bedclothes*). **se retaper**, *v.r.* (*fam.*) to buck up.

retard [rə'taːr], *n.m.* delay; slowness (*of a clock etc.*); *être en retard*, to be late.

retardataire [rətardɑ'tɛːr], *a.* in arrears, late; backward.—*n.* late-comer; defaulter.

retardement [rətardə'mã], *n.m.* delay, retardment.

retarder [rətar'de], *v.t.* to retard, to delay; to defer (*payment*); to put back (*clocks and watches*).—*v.i.* to lose time; to be slow (*of clocks and watches*); to be behind the times.

retenir [rət'niːr] *v.t. irr.* (*conjug. like* TENIR) ber; to reserve; to hold in, to restrain; to to hold back; to retain; to detain; to remem-engage; to prevent; to get hold of again; (*Arith.*) to carry. **se retenir**, *v.r.* to control oneself; to refrain; to catch hold.

retenteur [rətã'tœːr], *a.* (*fem.* **-trice**) retaining.

rétentif [retã'tif], *a.* (*fem.* **-tive**) retentive.

rétention [retã'sjõ], *n.f.* reservation.

etentir [rətã'tiːr], *v.i.* to resound, to re-echo; to ring.

retentissant [rətãti'sã], *a.* resounding, echoing; ringing, loud; (*fig.*) famous.

retentissement [rətãtis'mã], *n.m.* resounding, echo; ringing; (*fig.*) fame, celebrity.

retenu [rət'ny], *a.* reserved, cautious, wary.

retenue [rət'ny], *n.f.* discretion, circum-spection, caution; detention; (*Comm.*) deduction; guy-rope.

réticence [reti'sãːs], *n.f.* reserve, silence; concealment (*of some particular*).

rétif [re'tif], *a.* (*fem.* **-tive**) restive; stubborn.

rétine [re'tin], *n.f.* retina (*of the eye*).

retirable [rəti'rabl], *a.* withdrawable.

retiré [rəti're], *a.* retired, secluded; in retire-ment.

retirement [rətir'mã], *n.m.* contraction; shrinking.

retirer [rəti're], *v.t.* to draw again; to pull back, to withdraw; to take away; to retract; to derive. **se retirer**, *v.r.* to retire, to with-draw; to subside (*of waters*); to contract.

retombée [rətõ'be], *n.f.* fall, fall-out;

retombée de particules radioactives, radio-active fall-out.

retomber [rətõ'be], *v.i.* (*aux.* ÊTRE) to fall again; to have a relapse; to subside.

retordre [rə'tordr], *v.t.* to twist again; to twist (*silk, thread etc.*).

rétorquer [retor'ke], *v.t.* to retort.

retors [rə'tɔːr], *a.* twisted; artful, cunning, crafty.—*n.m.* twisted thread; crafty person.

retouche [rə'tuʃ], *n.f.* retouching, touching up.

retoucher [rətu'ʃe], *v.t.* to retouch; to touch up.

retour [rə'tuːr], *n.m.* return; repetition, recur-rence; sending back; (*fig.*) change; reverse; turning, winding; (*Law*) reversion; *billet d'aller et retour*, return ticket.

retourne [rə'turn], *n.f.* trump-card.

retourner [rətur'ne], *v.t.* (*aux.* AVOIR) to turn, to turn up, to turn over, round, about etc.; to send back.—*v.i.* (*aux.* ÊTRE) to return, to go again, to go back (again); to recoil upon; to turn up (*cards*). **se retourner**, *v.r.* to turn, to turn round, to look round.

retracer [rətra'se], *v.t.* (*conjug. like* COM-MENCER) to trace again, to retrace; to relate. **se retracer**, *v.r.* to recall to mind; to recur, to be retraced (*in mind*).

rétracter [retrak'te], *v.t.* and **se rétracter**, *v.r.* to retract; to recant.

retrait [rə'trɛ], *a.* shrunk (*of grain, wood etc.*).—*n.m.* shrinkage; recess (*in wall*), closet; withdrawal.

retraite [rə'trɛt], *n.f.* retreat, retiring; privacy; refuge; haunt; retirement (*from office*); superannuation; retiring pension; *battre en retraite*, to beat a retreat.

retraité [rətrɛ'te], *a.* superannuated, retired, pensioned off.

retraiter [rətrɛ'te], *v.t.* to retire, to pension off.

retranchement [rətrãʃ'mã], *n.m.* retrench-ment, curtailment; (*Mil.*) entrenchment.

retrancher [rətrã'ʃe], *v.t.* to retrench, to curtail, to cut short; to cut out; to abridge; (*Arith.*) to subtract; (*Mil.*) to entrench. **se retrancher**, *v.r.* to restrain oneself; to curtail one's expenses; (*Mil.*) to entrench oneself; (*fig.*) to fall back upon.

rétrécir [retre'siːr], *v.t.* to take in, to con-tract; to narrow, to limit.—*v.i.* and **se rétrécir**, *v.r.* to grow narrower; to shrink, to contract.

rétrécissement [retresis'mã], *n.m.* narrow-ing; shrinking.

retremper [rətrã'pe], *v.t.* to soak again; to temper again; (*fig.*) to strengthen. **se retremper**, *v.r.* to be strengthened *or* invigorated.

rétribuer [retri'bɥe], *v.t.* to remunerate.

rétribution [retriby'sjõ], *n.f.* payment, reward.

rétroactif [retroak'tif], *a.* (*fem.* **-tive**) retro-active.

rétroaction [retroak'sjõ], *n.f.* retroaction; (*Rad. Teleg.*) feed-back.

rétrograde [retro'grad], *a.* retrograde; back-ward.

rétrograder [retrogra'de], *v.i.* to retrograde; to go back, (*Mil.*) to fall back.

rétrogressif [retrogrɛ'sif], *a.* (*fem.* **-ive**) retrogressive.

rétrogression [retrɔgrɛ'sjɔ̃], *n.f.* retrogression.

rétrospectif [retrɔspɛk'tif], *a.* (*fem.* **-tive**) retrospective.

retroussé [rətru'se], *a.* turned up; tucked up; *nez retroussé*, turned-up nose, snub nose.

retrousser [rətru'se], *v.t.* to turn up, to roll up (*trousers*); to tuck up; to cock (*one's hat*). **se retrousser**, *v.r.* to tuck up one's skirt *or* other garment.

retroussis [rətru'si], *n.m.* cock (*of a hat*); top (*of a boot*); facing (*of a uniform*).

retrouver [rətru've], *v.t.* to find again, to regain, to recover. **se retrouver**, *v.r.* to find each other again; to be oneself again.

rétroviseur [retrɔvi'zœːr], *n.m.* (*Motor.*) driving mirror.

rets [rɛ], *n.m. inv.* net; (*fig.*) snare, toils.

réunion [rey'njɔ̃], *n.f.* reunion; reconciliation; junction; meeting, assembly, gathering; reception.

réunir [rey'niːr], *v.t.* to reunite, to join again, to bring together again, to reconcile; to connect; to collect. **se réunir**, *v.r.* to assemble again, to reunite; to meet; to amalgamate.

réussi [rey'si], *a.* successful, brilliant.

réussir [rey'siːr], *v.t.* to carry out well, to accomplish, to perform successfully.—*v.i.* to succeed, to be successful, to prosper, to thrive; to pass (*Exam*).

réussite [rey'sit], *n.f.* success; (*happy*) issue *or* result; (*Cards*) patience.

revaloir [rəva'lwaːr], *v.t. irr.* (*conjug. like* VALOIR) to return like for like, to be even with.

revanche [rə'vãːʃ], *n.f.* revenge; return match.

rêvasser [rɛva'se], *v.i.* to day-dream, to muse.

rêvasserie [rɛvas'ri], *n.f.* day-dreams; idle musing.

rêvasseur [rɛva'sœːr], *n.m.* (*fem.* **-euse**) (*colloq.*) dreamer, muser.

rêve [rɛːv], *n.m.* dream; day-dream, illusion.

revêche [rə've:ʃ], *a.* rough; cross, ill-natured, cantankerous.

réveil [re'vɛːj], *n.m.* waking, awaking; alarm-clock; (*Mil.*) reveille.

réveille-matin [revɛjma'tɛ̃], *n.m. inv.* alarm-clock.

réveiller [revɛ'je], *v.t.* to awake, to arouse; to recall. **se réveiller**, *v.r.* to awake, to wake up; to be roused; to revive.

réveillon [revɛ'jɔ̃], *n.m.* midnight repast, *esp.* Christmas Eve revel.

réveillonner [revɛjɔ'ne], *v.i.* to take part in a *réveillon*.

révélateur [revela'tœːr], *a.* (*fem.* **-trice**) revealing, tell-tale.—*n.m.* (*fem.* **-trice**) revealer, informer.—*n.m.* (*Phot.*) developer.

révélation [revela'sjɔ̃], *n.f.* revelation, disclosure.

révéler [reve'le], *v.t.* (*conjug. like* CÉDER) to reveal, to disclose; to betray; (*Phot.*) to develop. **se révéler**, *v.r.* to reveal oneself; to prove (to be).

revenant [rəv'nã], *a.* pleasing, prepossessing. —*n.m.* ghost.

revendeur [rəvã'dœːr], *n.m.* (*fem.* **-euse**) retail dealer, dealer in old clothes etc.

revendicable [rəvãdi'kabl], *a.* claimable.

revendicateur [rəvãdika'tœːr], *n.m.* (*fem.* **-trice**) claimant.

revendication [rəvãdika'sjɔ̃], *n.f.* claim, demand.

revendiquer [rəvãdi'ke], *v.t.* to claim.

revendre [rə've:dr], *v.t.* to sell again, to resell.

revenir [rəv'niːr], *v.i. irr.* (*conjug. like* TENIR *but with aux.* ÊTRE) to come again, to come back, to return; to reappear, to haunt, to walk (*of ghosts*); to recur; to recover; to amount, to cost; to retract; to please.

revente [rə'vã:t], *n.f.* resale.

revenu [rəv'ny], *n.m.* revenue, income.

revenue [rəv'ny], *n.f.* young wood, after-growth.

rêver [rɛ've], *v.t.* to dream, to dream of.—*v.i.* to dream; to have day-dreams; to muse.

réverbérant [reverbe'rã], *a.* reverberating.

réverbération [reverbera'sjɔ̃], *n.f.* reverberation; reflection (*of light, heat*).

réverbère [rever'bɛːr], *n.m.* reflector; street lamp.

réverbérer [reverbe're], *v.t., v.i.* (*conjug. like* CÉDER) to reverberate; to reflect (*light, heat*).

reverdir [rəver'diːr], *v.t.* to make green again, to revive.—*v.i.* to become green again; (*fig.*) to grow young again.

reverdissement [rəverdis'mã], *n.m.* growing green again.

révéremment [revera'mã], *adv.* reverently.

révérence [reve'rã:s], *n.f.* reverence; bow, curtsy.

révérenciel [reverã'sjɛl], *a.* (*fem.* **-elle**) reverential.

révérencieusement [reverãsjøz'mã], *adv.* reverentially.

révérencieux [reverã'sjø], *a.* (*fem.* **-euse**) ceremonious, obsequious.

révérend [reve'rã], *a.* a reverend.

révérendissime [reverãdi'sim], *a.* most reverend, right reverend.

révérer [reve're], *v.t.* (*conjug. like* CÉDER) to revere.

rêverie [rɛ'vri], *n.f.* reverie, musing, dreaming.

revers [rə'vɛːr], *n.m.* back, reverse; facing (*of clothes*); lapel (*of a coat*); turn-up (*of trousers*); top (*of boots*); (*Ten.*) back-hand stroke; misfortune, set back.

reverser [rəver'se], *v.t.* to pour out again; to pour back; to transfer; to pay back.

réversible [rever'sibl], *a.* reversible; revertible.

réversion [rever'sjɔ̃], *n.f.* reversion.

reversoir [rəver'swaːr], *n.m.* weir.

revêtement [rəvɛt'mã], *n.m.* facing (*of masonry etc.*); surface (*of road*).

revêtir [rəve'tiːr], *v.t. irr.* (*conjug. like* VÊTIR) to give clothes to, to dress; to put on; to assume; to cover; (*fig.*) to invest *or* endow with. **se revêtir**, *v.r.* to clothe oneself, to array oneself; to put on, to assume.

rêveur [rɛ'vœːr], *a.* (*fem.* **-euse**) dreaming; (*fig.*) pensive, dreamy.—*n.m.* (*fem.* **-euse**) dreamer; muser.

revient [rə'vjɛ̃], *n.m. prix de revient*, net cost.

revirement [rəvir'mã], *n.m.* tacking about; (*fig.*) sudden change.

revirer [rəvi're], *v.i.* to tack, to put about; (*fig.*) to change sides.

revisable [rəvi'zabl], révisable [revi'zabl], a. revisable.

reviser [rəvi'ze], réviser [revi'ze], v.t. to revise, to review, to examine; to overhaul (*engine*).

reviseur [rəvi'zœːr], réviseur [revi'zœːr], n.m. reviser, examiner; auditor; proof-reader.

revision [rəvi'zjõ], révision [revi'zjõ], n.f. revision, review; overhaul (*of engine*).

revivifier [rəvivi'fje], v.t. to revivify, to regenerate, to revive.

revivre [rə'viːvr], v.t. irr. (*conjug. like* VIVRE) to relive.—v.i. to come to life again, to live again.

révocable [revo'kabl], a. revocable; removable (*of an official*).

révocation [revoka'sjõ], n.f. revocation (*of will*), repeal; dismissal (*of an official*).

revoici [rəvwa'si], revoilà [rəvwa'la], adv. (*colloq.*) me revoici, here I am again; le revoilà, there he is again.

revoir [rə'vwaːr], v.t. irr. (*conjug. like* VOIR) to see again; to meet again; to revise, to review. se revoir, v.r. to see or meet each other again.—n.m. inv. au revoir, good-bye (*for the present*).

revoler (1) [rəvo'le], v.t. to steal again.

revoler (2) [rəvo'le], v.i. to fly again; to fly back.

révoltant [revol'tã], a. revolting, shocking.

révolte [re'volt], n.f. revolt, rebellion.

révolté [revol'te], n.m. (*fem.* -ée) rebel, mutineer.

révolter [revol'te], v.t. to stir up, to rouse; to shock, to disgust. se révolter, v.r. to revolt, to rebel; to be indignant, to be shocked.

révolu [revo'ly], a. accomplished, completed; elapsed.

révolution [revoly'sjõ], n.f. revolution.

révolutionnaire [revolysjo'nɛːr], a. revolutionary.—n. revolutionary; revolutionist.

révolutionner [revolysjo'ne], v.t. to revolutionize.

revolver [revol'vɛːr], n.m. revolver.

révoquer [revo'ke], v.t. to dismiss (*an official etc.*); to recall (*an ambassador etc.*); to repeal, to cancel.

revue [rə'vy], n.f. review, survey; revision; magazine; review (*critical article*); (*Mil.*) review; (*Theat.*) revue.

révulsion [revyl'sjõ], n.f. revulsion.

rez [re], prep. on a level with, even with.

rez-de-chaussée [redʃo'se], n.m. inv. ground-level; ground floor.

rhabillage [rabi'jaːʒ], n.m. mending, over-haul.

rhabiller [rabi'je], v.t. to dress again; to mend.

rhétoricien [retori'sjɛ̃], n.m. rhetorician.

rhétorique [reto'rik], n.f. rhetoric.

Rhin [rɛ̃], le, m. the Rhine.

rhinocéros [rinose'ros], n.m. inv. rhinoceros.

rhododendron [rododɛ̃'drõ], n.m. rhododendron.

rhombe [rõːb], a. rhombic.—n.m. rhomb; rhombus.

rhubarbe [ry'barb], n.f. rhubarb.

rhum [rɔm], n.m. rum.

rhumatisant [rymati'zã], a. suffering from rheumatism, rheumatic.—n.m. (*fem.* -e) sufferer from rheumatism.

rhumatismal [rymatis'mal], a. (*m. pl.* -aux) rheumatic.

rhumatisme [ryma'tism], n.m. rheumatism.

rhume [rym], n.m. cold (*illness*).

riant [ri'jã], a. smiling, cheerful, pleasant, pleasing.

ribambelle [ribã'bɛl], n.f. (*colloq.*) swarm, string, lot.

ribaud [ri'bo], a. and n.m. (*fem.* -e) ribald.

ribauderie [ribod'ri], n.f. ribaldry.

ricanement [rikan'mã], n.m. sneering, sneer; mocking laughter.

ricaner [rika'ne], v.i. to sneer, to snigger.

ricaneur [rika'nœːr], a. (*fem.* -euse) sneering, derisive.—n.m. (*fem.* -euse) sneerer.

Richard [ri'ʃaːr], m. Richard.

richard [ri'ʃaːr], n.m. (*fam. and pej.*) moneyed person, capitalist.

riche [riʃ], a. rich, wealthy; copious; valuable. —n. rich person.

richement [riʃ'mã], adv. richly; splendidly.

richesse [ri'ʃɛs], n.f. riches, wealth; copious-ness; richness.

richissime [riʃi'sim], a. (*colloq.*) rolling in money.

ricin [ri'sɛ̃], n.m. castor-oil plant.

ricocher [riko'ʃe], v.i. to rebound; to rico-chet.

ricochet [riko'ʃɛ], n.m. rebound (*on the water*); (*Artill.*) ricochet; (*fig.*) chain (*of events*).

rictus [rik'tyːs], n.m. inv. grin; rictus.

ride [rid], n.f. wrinkle; ripple.

ridé [ri'de], a. wrinkled; rippling; corru-gated.

rideau [ri'do], n.m. (*pl.* -eaux) curtain; screen (*of trees etc.*).

rider [ri'de], v.t. to wrinkle; to corrugate; to shrivel; to ruffle (*water*). se rider, v.r. to be wrinkled; to shrivel up; to ripple (*of water*).

ridicule [ridi'kyl], a. ridiculous.—n.m. ridi-cule; ridiculousness.

ridiculement [ridikyl'mã], adv. ridiculously.

ridiculiser [ridikyli'ze], v.t. to ridicule, to make fun of.

rien [rjɛ̃], n.m. trifle, mere nothing.—indef. pron. nothing, nought, not anything; any-thing.

rieur [ri'jœːr], a. (*fem.* rieuse) laughing, joking.

rigide [ri'ʒid], a. rigid, stiff; strict, severe.

rigidement [riʒid'mã], adv. rigidly, strictly.

rigidité [riʒidi'te], n.f. rigidity, stiffness; strictness, severity.

rigole [ri'gol], n.f. trench, small ditch or channel; gutter.

rigoler [rigo'le], v.i. (*pop.*) to laugh; to have fun; to joke.

rigorisme [rigo'rism], n.m. rigorism, aus-terity.

rigoriste [rigo'rist], a. over-severe.—n. rigor-ist, stickler.

rigoureusement [rigurøz'mã], adv. rigor-ously, severely, strictly.

rigoureux [rigu'rø], a. (*fem.* -euse) rigorous, harsh; strict; stern; inclement.

rigueur [ri'gœːr], n.f. rigour, strictness; pre-cision; severity; inclemency; à la rigueur, at a pinch; if necessary; de rigueur, in-dispensable, compulsory.

rimailler [rima'je], v.i. to write doggerel.

rimailleur [rimɑ'jœːr], *n.m.* (*fem.* **-euse**) sorry rhymer, rhymester.

rime [rim], *n.f.* rhyme; (*fig.*) verse.

rimer [ri'me], *v.i.* to rhyme; to write verses.

rimeur [ri'mœːr], *n.m.* rhymer, versifier.

rinçage [rɛ̃'saːʒ], *n.m.* rinsing, washing.

rincer [rɛ̃'se], *v.t.* (*conjug. like* COMMENCER) to rinse, to wash. **se rincer,** *v.r.* to rinse.

ripaille [ri'pɑːj], *n.f.* feasting, junketing.

riposte [ri'pɔst], *n.f.* (*Fenc.*) ripost, return; (*fig.*) retort, repartee.

riposter [ripɔs'te], *v.i.* (*Fenc.*) to ripost, to parry and thrust; (*fig.*) to make a smart reply.

rire [riːr], *v.i. irr.* to laugh; to smile; to be favourable; to joke; to mock. **se rire,** *v.r.* to make sport, to scoff (*de*).—*n.m.* laughter, laughing.

ris [ri], *n.m. inv.* laugh, smile, laughter; (*Naut.*) reef (*of sails*); sweetbread.

risée [ri'ze], *n.f.* laugh, laughter; mockery; laughing-stock.

risette [ri'zɛt], *n.f.* pleasant little laugh, smile.

risible [ri'zibl], *a.* comical, laughable; ridiculous.

risiblement [rizible'mã], *adv.* laughably, ludicrously.

risque [risk], *n.m.* risk, hazard.

risqué [ris'ke], *a.* risky; **une plaisanterie risquée,** a doubtful joke.

risquer [ris'ke], *v.t.* to risk, to venture; (*fam.*) to chance. **se risquer,** *v.r.* to risk, to venture.

risque-tout [riskə'tu], *n.m. inv.* (*colloq.*) dare-devil.

rissole [ri'sɔl], *n.f.* rissole.

rissoler [risɔ'le], *v.t.* (*Cook.*) to brown.

ristourne [ris'turn], *n.f.* refund; rebate.

rit or **rite** [rit], *n.m.* rite.

ritournelle [ritur'nɛl], *n.f.* (*Mus.*) ritornello, flourish.

rituel [ri'tɥɛl], *a.* (*fem.* **-elle**) ritual.—*n.m.* ritual (*prayer-book*).

rivage [ri'vaːʒ], *n.m.* shore, strand, beach; bank, waterside.

rival [ri'val], *a.* (*m. pl.* **-aux**) rival, competitive.—*n.m.* (*fem.* **-e,** *m. pl.* **-aux**) rival.

rivaliser [rivali'ze], *v.i.* to rival, to vie, to compete.

rivalité [rivali'te], *n.f.* rivalry, emulation.

rive [riːv], *n.f.* bank, shore (*of rivers, lakes etc.*); (*fig.*) seashore; border.

rivement [riv'mã], *n.m.* riveting.

river [ri've], *v.t.* to clinch, to rivet.

riverain [ri'vrɛ̃], *a.* riparian; bordering (*on rivers* or *woods*).—*n.m.* (*fem.* **-e**) riverside resident; borderer.

rivet [ri'vɛ], *n.m.* rivet; clinch.

rivetage [riv'taːʒ], *n.m.* riveting.

riveter [riv'te], *v.t.* (*conjug. like* APPELER) to rivet.

riveteur [riv'tœːr], **riveur** [ri'vœːr], *n.m.* riveter.

rivière [ri'vjɛːr], *n.f.* river, stream.

rivoir, *n.m.* or **rivoire** [ri'vwaːr], *n.f.* riveting-hammer *or* machine.

rivure [ri'vyːr], *n.f.* clinching, riveting.

rixe [riks], *n.f.* fight, scuffle; brawl, affray.

riz [ri], *n.m.* rice.

rizière [ri'zjɛːr], *n.f.* rice-field, paddy-field, rice-plantation; rice-swamp.

robe [rɔb], *n.f.* gown, dress, frock; robe; long robe (*lawyers*), the cloth (*clergy*); coat (*of certain animals*); skin, husk, peel (*of certain fruits etc.*).

robinet [rɔbi'nɛ], *n.m.* tap; cock; **ouvrir** (**fermer**) **le robinet,** to turn on (off) the tap.

robot [rɔ'bo], *a. inv.* **avion robot,** pilotless plane; **fusée, satellite robot,** unmanned rocket, satellite.—*n.m.* automaton, robot.

robuste [rɔ'byst], *a.* robust, sturdy; hardy, strong.

robustement [rɔbystə'mã], *adv.* robustly, athletically.

robustesse [rɔbys'tɛs], *n.f.* robustness, strength, vigour.

roc [rɔk], *n.m.* rock.

rocaille [rɔ'kaːj], *n.f.* rock-work, grotto-work.

rocailleux [rɔkɑ'jø], *a.* (*fem.* **-euse**) pebbly, stony; rugged, rough.

roche [rɔʃ], *n.f.* rock; boulder; stony mass.

rocher [rɔ'ʃe], *n.m.* rock, crag.

rochet [rɔ'ʃɛ], *n.m.* rochet (*surplice*); ratchet.

rocheux [rɔ'ʃø], *a.* (*fem.* **-euse**) rocky, stony.

rococo [rɔkɔ'ko], *a. inv.* rococo; antiquated.—*n.m.* rococo, antiquated style.

rodage [rɔ'daːʒ], *n.m.* grinding in; polishing; **en rodage,** running in (*engine*).

roder [rɔ'de], *v.t.* to run in (*car*); to grind, to polish.

rôder [rɔ'de], *v.i.* to prowl.

rôdeur [rɔ'dœːr], *a.* (*fem.* **-euse**) prowling.—*n.m.* (*fem.* **-euse**) prowler; vagrant.

rodomontade [rɔdɔmɔ̃'tad], *n.f.* bluster, swagger.

Rodrigue [rɔ'drig], *m.* Roderick.

rogaton [rɔgɑ'tɔ̃], *n.m.* (*pl.*) scraps, odds and ends.

Roger [rɔ'ʒe], *m.* Roger; **c'est un vrai Roger Bontemps,** he is a happy-go-lucky sort of chap.

rogner [rɔ'ɲe], *v.t.* to cut, to pare, to crop; to clip, to prune.

rogneux [rɔ'ɲø], *a.* (*fem.* **-euse**) mangy, scabby.

rognon [rɔ'ɲɔ̃], *n.m.* kidney (*as food*).

rognure [rɔ'ɲyːr], *n.f.* a paring, a clipping; (*pl.*) scraps, refuse, leavings.

rogue [rɔg], *a.* arrogant, haughty.

roi [rwa], *n.m.* king.

roitelet [rwa'tlɛ], *n.m.* petty king; wren.

rôle [roːl], *n.m.* roll; list, roster, catalogue; (*Theat.*) part, character.

romain [rɔ'mɛ̃], *a.* Roman.—*n.m.* (**Romain,** *fem.* **-aine**) Roman (*person*).

roman (1) [rɔ'mã], *a.* Romance, Romanic.

roman (2) [rɔ'mã], *n.m.* novel, romance, fiction.

romance [rɔ'mãːs], *n.f.* (*Mus.*) ballad, sentimental song.

romancier [rɔmã'sje], *n.m.* (*fem.* **-ière**) novelist.

romanesque [rɔma'nɛsk], *a.* romantic.—*n.m.* the romantic.

roman-feuilleton [rɔmãfœj'tɔ̃], *n.m.* (*pl.* **romans-feuilletons**) newspaper serial (story).

romantique [rɔmã'tik], *a.* romantic.—*n.* romanticist.

romantiquement [rɔmãtik'mã], *adv.* romantically.

romantisme [rɔmã'tism], *n.m.* (*Lit. Hist.*) romanticism.

romarin

romarin [rɔma'rɛ̃], n.m. rosemary.
rompre [rɔ̃:pr], v.t. (see Verb Tables) to break, to snap; to break off; to rout; to dissolve; to break in; to divert; to interrupt. —v.i. to break; to fall out. se rompre, v.r. to break off, to snap.
rompu [rɔ̃'py], a. broken, snapped; broken in.
romsteck [rɔm'stɛk], n.m. rump-steak.
ronce [rɔ̃:s], n.f. bramble, blackberry-bush.
ronceraie [rɔ̃s'rɛ], n.f. brake, brambly ground.
ronchonner [rɔ̃ʃɔ'ne], v.i. (fam.) to grumble.
rond [rɔ̃], a. round; plump, rotund; frank; even (of money or accounts).—adv. normally, true (of motor).—n.m. round, ring, orb, circle, disk.
ronde [rɔ̃:d], n.f. round; patrol; beat; (Mus.) semibreve; roundelay; round-hand (writing).
rondeau [rɔ̃'do], n.m. (pl. -eaux) rondeau (French poem); (Mus.) rondo; roller.
rondelet [rɔ̃'dlɛ], a. (fem. -ette) roundish, plump, podgy.
rondelle [rɔ̃'dɛl], n.f. rondelle, washer; rundle, ring.
rondement [rɔ̃d'mɑ̃], adv. roundly; briskly; frankly, bluntly.
rondeur [rɔ̃'dœ:r], n.f. roundness, rotundity; fullness; plain dealing.
rondin [rɔ̃'dɛ̃], n.m. round log; cudgel.
rond-point [rɔ̃'pwɛ̃], n.m. (pl. ronds-points) (Arch.) apsis; circus (place where several roads etc. meet), roundabout.
ronflant [rɔ̃'flɑ̃], a. snoring; humming, whirring; sonorous.
ronflement [rɔ̃flə'mɑ̃], n.m. snoring; roaring, rumbling; boom; snorting (of horses).
ronfler [rɔ̃'fle], v.i. to snore; to snort (of horses); to roar (cannon, thunder etc.); to boom; to peal (organs); to hum (spinning-tops).
ronfleur [rɔ̃'flœ:r], n.m. (fem. -euse) snorer.
rongeant [rɔ̃'ʒɑ̃], a. gnawing, corroding; (fig.) tormenting.
ronger [rɔ̃'ʒe], v.t. (conjug. like MANGER) to gnaw, to nibble; to consume, to corrode; to prey upon (the mind etc.); ronger son frein, to champ the bit. se ronger, v.r. to fret.
rongeur [rɔ̃'ʒœ:r], a. (fem. -euse) gnawing, biting; corroding; consuming.—n.m. (Zool.) rodent.
ronron [rɔ̃'rɔ̃], n.m. purr, purring.
ronronner [rɔ̃rɔ'ne], v.i. to purr, to hum.
roquet [rɔ'kɛ], n.m. pug-dog; cur, mongrel.
rosace [ro'zas], n.f. (Arch.) rose; rose-window.
rosage [ro'za:ʒ], n.m. rhododendron; azalea.
rosaire [ro'zɛ:r], n.m. (R.-C. Ch.) rosary.
rosâtre [ro'zɑ:tr], a. pinkish.
rosbif [rɔs'bif], n.m. roast beef.
rose [ro:z], a. rosy; pink, rose-coloured.—n.f. rose; rose-window; rose trémière, hollyhock.—n.m. rose-colour, pink.
rosé [ro'ze], a. rosy, roseate; vin rosé, light-red wine.
roseau [ro'zo], n.m. (pl. -eaux) reed.
rosée [ro'ze], n.f. dew.
roselière [rozə'ljɛ:r], n.f. reed-bed.
roséole [roze'ɔl], n.f. scarlet rash; German measles.
roser [ro'ze], v.t. to make pink.

roseraie [roz'rɛ], n.f. rosery, rose garden.
rosette [ro'zet], n.f. small rose; rosette.
rosier [ro'zje], n.m. rose-tree, rose-bush.
rosière [ro'zjɛ:r], n.f. rose-queen; queen of the May.
rosiériste [rozje'rist], n. rose-grower.
rosse [rɔs], a. bad, malicious.—n.f. jade, screw; (fig. and fam.) worthless or nasty person.
rossée [ro'se], n.f. shower of blows, thrashing.
rosser [ro'se], v.t. (colloq.) to thrash, to beat up.
rossignol [rosi'ɲɔl], n.m. nightingale; picklock, skeleton key; (Carp.) wedge; (fig.) unsaleable article (in a shop).
rot [ro], n.m. (pop.) belch, eructation.
rôt [ro], n.m. roast, roast meat.
rotarien [rɔta'rjɛ̃], n.m. member of a Rotary Club.
rotateur [rɔta'tœ:r], a. (fem. -trice) (Anat.) rotatory.—n.m. (Anat.) rotator.
rotatif [rɔta'tif], a. (fem. -tive) rotary.
rotation [rɔta'sjɔ̃], n.f. rotation.
rotatoire [rɔta'twa:r], a. rotatory.
roter [ro'te], v.i. to belch.
rôti [ro'ti], n.m. roast, roast meat.
rôtie [ro'ti], n.f. slice of toast.
rôtir [ro'ti:r], v.t., v.i. to roast; to broil; to toast (bread etc.); (fig.) to parch.
rôtissage [roti'sa:ʒ], n.m. roasting.
rôtisserie [rotis'ri], n.f. cook-shop.
rôtisseur [roti'sœ:r], n.m. (fem. -euse) cook-shop keeper.
rôtissoire [roti'swa:r], n.f. roaster, Dutch oven.
rotonde [ro'tɔ̃:d], n.f. rotunda; long sleeveless cloak.
rotondité [rotɔ̃di'te], n.f. rotundity; plumpness.
rotor [ro'tɔ:r], n.m. rotor.
roturier [roty'rje], a. (fem. -ière) plebeian; vulgar, mean.—n.m. (fem. -ière) commoner.
rouage [rwa:ʒ], n.m. wheelwork; cog-wheel; machinery; (Horol.) movement.
rouan [rwɑ̃], a. (fem. rouanne) roan (of horses, cattle etc.).—n.m. roan horse.
roublard [ru'bla:r], a. and n.m. (fem. -e) (fam.) wily, crafty (person).
rouble [rubl], n.m. rouble (Russian coin).
roucoulement [rukul'mɑ̃], n.m. cooing; gurgling (of babies).
roucouler [ruku'le], v.t., v.i. to coo.
roue [ru], n.f. wheel; paddle-wheel; faire la roue, to spread (out) its tail (of peacocks etc.); to show off; mettre or jeter des bâtons dans les roues, to put spokes into the wheel (of).
roué [rwe], a. cunning, sharp, artful; exhausted.—n.m. rake, profligate; (fem. -ée) cunning or unscrupulous person.
rouelle [rwɛl], n.f. round slice (meat).
rouer [rwe], v.t. to break upon the wheel; rouer de coups, to beat unmercifully.
rouerie [ru'ri], n.f. piece of knavery, trick, sharp practice.
rouet [rwɛ], n.m. spinning-wheel.
rouge [ru:ʒ], a. red; red-hot; bloodshot.—n.m. rouge; redness.—n. (fam.) left-winger, communist.
rougeâtre [ru'ʒa:tr], a. reddish.
rougeaud [ru'ʒo], a. (colloq.) red-faced, ruddy.—n.m. (fem. -e) red-faced person.

286

rouge-gorge [ruʒ'gɔrʒ], *n.m.* (*pl.* **rouges-gorges**) red-breast, robin redbreast.

rougeole [ru'ʒɔl], *n.f.* measles.

rougeoyer [ruʒwa'je], *v.i.* (*conjug. like* EMPLOYER) to turn red; to glow.

rouget [ru'ʒɛ], *a.* (*fem.* **-ette**) reddish.—*n.m.* (*Ichth.*) red mullet.

rougeur [ru'ʒœːr], *n.f.* redness; flush, glow, blush.

rougir [ru'ʒiːr], *v.t.* to redden, to tinge with red.—*v.i.* to redden, to grow red, to colour, to blush.

rouille [ruːj], *n.f.* rust, rustiness; (*Agric.*) mildew, blight.

rouillé [ru'je], *a.* rusty; blighted (*of corn*).

rouiller [ru'je], *v.t., v.i.* to rust; to blight; to impair. **se rouiller**, *v.r.* to rust; to grow rusty; to be impaired.

rouilleux [ru'jø], *a.* (*fem.* **-euse**) rust-coloured.

rouillure [ru'jyːr], *n.f.* rustiness; (*Agric.*) rust.

rouir [rwiːr], *v.t.* to steep, to soak, to ret.

rouissage [rwi'saːʒ], *n.m.* steeping, retting.

roulade [ru'lad], *n.f.* roll, rolling down; (*Mus.*) trill.

roulage [ru'laːʒ], *n.m.* rolling; haulage, carriage (*in wagons etc.*); road traffic.

roulant [ru'lɑ̃], *a.* rolling; travelling (*crane*); easy (*of roads*); (*Print.*) at work.

rouleau [ru'lo], *n.m.* (*pl.* **-eaux**) roll; roller; rolling-pin; coil (*rope*).

roulement [rul'mɑ̃], *n.m.* rolling, roll; rumbling, rattle; rotation; **par roulement**, in rotation; **roulement à billes**, ball-bearing.

rouler [ru'le], *v.t.* to roll; to roll up; to wind up; to revolve; (*colloq.*) to cheat; (*Golf*) **coup roulé**, putt.—*v.i.* to roll, to roll along; to revolve; to ride (*en*); to ramble; to keep going. **se rouler**, *v.r.* to roll; to tumble, to wallow.

roulette [ru'lɛt], *n.f.* small wheel; roller, castor, truckle; roulette (*game*).

roulier [ru'lje], *a.* carrying (*trade*).—*n.m.* wagoner, carter, carrier.

roulis [ru'li], *n.m.* rolling, roll (*waves or ships*), lurch.

roulotte [ru'lot], *n.f.* gipsy-van; (*Motor.*) caravan.

roumain [ru'mɛ̃], *a.* Rumanian.—*n.m.* Rumanian (*language*); (**Roumain**, *fem.* **-aine**) Rumanian (*person*).

Roumanie [ruma'ni], **la**, *f.* Rumania.

roupie [ru'pi], *n.f.* rupee.

roupiller [rupi'je], *v.i.* (*colloq.*) to doze, to snooze.

rouquin [ru'kɛ̃], *a.* (*pop.*) ginger-haired, carroty-haired.

roussâtre [ru'saːtr], *a.* reddish, russet.

rousseur [ru'sœːr], *n.f.* redness.

roussi [ru'si], *a.* browned, scorched.—*n.m.* burnt smell; burning.

roussir [ru'siːr], *v.t., v.i.* to redden; to singe, to scorch; **faire roussir**, to brown (*meat etc.*).

roussissage [rusi'saːʒ], **roussissement** [rusis'mɑ̃], *n.m.* reddening; browning; scorching.

routage [ru'taːʒ], *n.m.* sorting (*of mail*).

route [rut], *n.f.* road, way; route, path, course; track (*of a ship etc.*); highway.

router [ru'te], *v.t.* to sort (*mail*).

routier [ru'tje], *a.* (*fem.* **-ière**) of roads;

carte routière, road-map.—*n.m.* lorry-driver; (*fig.*) old hand; road racer (*cyclist*).

routine [ru'tin], *n.f.* routine, habit, practice.

routinier [ruti'nje], *a.* (*fem.* **-ière**) routine, following a routine.—*n.m.* (*fem.* **-ière**) person following a routine; stick-in-the-mud.

rouvrir [ru'vriːr], *v.t., v.i. irr.* (*conjug. like* OUVRIR) to reopen.

roux [ru], *a.* (*fem.* **rousse**) reddish; red-haired, sandy.—*n.m.* (*fem.* **rousse**) red-haired *or* sandy person.—*n.m.* reddish colour.

royal [rwa'jal], *a.* (*m. pl.* **-aux**) royal, regal, kingly.

royalement [rwajal'mɑ̃], *adv.* royally; regally.

royalisme [rwaja'lism], *n.m.* royalism.

royaliste [rwaja'list], *a.* and *n.* royalist.

royaume [rwa'joːm], *n.m.* kingdom, realm; **le Royaume-Uni**, the United Kingdom.

royauté [rwajo'te], *n.f.* royalty, kingship, monarchy.

ruade [rɥad], *n.f.* kick (*by horse etc.*); lashing out.

Ruanda [RWANDA].

ruban [ry'bɑ̃], *n.m.* ribbon; (*fig.*) strip; tape.

rubané [ryba'ne], *a.* covered with ribbons.

rubaner [ryba'ne], *v.t.* to trim with ribbons; to cut into ribbons.

rubanerie [ryban'ri], *n.f.* ribbon-weaving; ribbon-trade.

rubéole [rybe'ɔl], *n.f.* rubeola, German measles.

rubescent [rybɛ'sɑ̃], *a.* reddish; growing red.

rubicond [rybi'kɔ̃], *a.* rubicund.

rubis [ry'bi], *n.m. inv.* ruby.

rubrique [ry'brik], *n.f.* red chalk; (*pl.*) rubric; (*fig.*) heading (*of article*).

ruche [ryʃ], *n.f.* hive; (*Needlework*) frilling, ruche.

ruchée [ry'ʃe], *n.f.* hiveful.

rucher (1) [ry'ʃe], *n.m.* stand *or* shed for bee-hives; apiary.

rucher (2) [ry'ʃe], *v.t.* (*Needlework*) to ruche, to frill.

rude [ryd], *a.* harsh, rough, rugged; violent; severe; uncouth; churlish; arduous, difficult.

rudement [ryd'mɑ̃], *adv.* roughly, harshly, severely, violently; (*pop.*) awfully, very.

rudesse [ry'dɛs], *n.f.* roughness, coarseness; ruggedness, uncouthness; harshness; unkindness.

rudiment [rydi'mɑ̃], *n.m.* rudiment; primer.

rudimentaire [rydimɑ̃'tɛːr], *a.* rudimentary.

rudoiement [rydwa'mɑ̃], *n.m.* bullying, brow-beating.

rudoyer [rydwa'je], *v.t.* (*conjug. like* EMPLOYER) to treat roughly; to bully, to ill-treat.

rue [ry], *n.f.* street; rue (*plant*).

ruée [rɥe], *n.f.* rush; onslaught.

ruelle [rɥɛl], *n.f.* lane, alley.

ruer [rɥe], *v.i.* to kick (*of horses etc.*). **se ruer**, *v.r.* to throw oneself, to rush (*sur*).

rugby [ryg'bi], *n.m.* rugby football, rugger.

rugir [ry'ʒiːr], *v.i.* to roar, to bellow.

rugissant [ryʒi'sɑ̃], *a.* roaring.

rugissement [ryʒis'mɑ̃], *n.m.* roaring, roar.

rugosité [rygozi'te], *n.f.* rugosity, roughness.

rugueux [ry'gø], *a.* (*fem.* **-euse**) rugose, rough.

ruine [rɥin], *n.f.* ruin; decay, destruction.
ruiner [rɥi'ne], *v.t.* to ruin, to lay waste; to destroy; to spoil. **se ruiner**, *v.r.* to ruin oneself; to fall into decay.
ruineux [rɥi'nø], *a.* (*fem.* **-euse**) ruinous.
ruisseau [rɥi'so], *n.m.* (*pl.* **-eaux**) brook, stream; gutter.
ruisselant [rɥi'slɑ̃], *a.* streaming, dripping.
ruisseler [rɥi'sle], *v.i.* (*conjug. like* APPELER) to run, to be very wet, to stream (with) (*de*).
rumeur [ry'mœːr], *n.f.* clamour, uproar; (*fig.*) report, rumour.
ruminant [rymi'nɑ̃], *a.* ruminant, ruminating.—*n.m.* ruminant.
rumination [rymina'sjɔ̃], *n.f.* rumination (*chewing the cud*).
ruminer [rymi'ne], *v.t.* to ruminate on; (*fig.*) to think over.—*v.i.* to ruminate, to chew the cud; (*fig.*) to ponder, to muse.
rupture [ryp'tyːr], *n.f.* breaking, rupture; annulment; hernia.
rural [ry'ral], *a.* (*m. pl.* **-aux**) rural, rustic.
ruse [ryːz], *n.f.* guile, cunning; trick, wile, ruse.
rusé [ry'ze], *a.* artful, crafty, sly.—*n.m.* (*fem.* **-ée**) artful, crafty *or* sly person.
ruser [ry'ze], *v.i.* to use deceit, craft *or* guile.
russe [rys], *a.* Russian.—*n.m.* Russian (*language*).—*n.* (**Russe**) Russian (*person*).
Russie [ry'si], **la**, *f.* Russia.
rustaud [rys'to], *a.* rustic, boorish, uncouth.—*n.m.* (*fem.* **-e**) rustic, clodhopper.
rusticité [rystisi'te], *n.f.* rusticity, simplicity.
rustique [rys'tik], *a.* rustic, rural; homely, simple.
rustiquement [rystik'mɑ̃], *adv.* rustically; boorishly, uncouthly.
rustre [rystr], *a.* boorish, rude.—*n.m.* boor, lout.
rutabaga [rytaba'ga], *n.m.* swede, Swedish turnip.
rutilant [ryti'lɑ̃], *a.* glowing, gleaming, rutilant.
rutiler [ryti'le], *v.i.* to glow, to gleam (*red*).
Rwanda, Ruanda [rwɑ̃'da], **le**, *m.* Rwanda.
rythme [ritm], *n.m.* rhythm.
rythmique [rit'mik], *a.* rhythmical.

S

S, s [ɛs], *n.m.* the nineteenth letter of the alphabet.
s' [s], *elision*, [SE].
sa [sa], [SON (1)].
sabbat [sa'ba], *n.m.* Sabbath.
sable [saːbl], *n.m.* sand; gravel; (*Zool., Her.*) sable.
sablé [sa'ble], *a.* covered with sand *or* gravel.
sabler [sa'ble], *v.t.* to sand, to gravel; (*fig.*) to drink off.
sableux [sa'blø], *a.* (*fem.* **-euse**) sandy.
sablier [sabli'je], *n.m.* sand-glass, hour-glass; egg-timer.
sablière [sabli'jɛːr], *n.f.* sand-pit; gravel-pit.

sablon [sa'blɔ̃], *n.m.* fine sand, scouring sand.
sablonner [sablɔ'ne], *v.t.* to scour with sand.
sablonneux [sablɔ'nø], *a.* (*fem.* **-euse**) sandy, gritty.
sablonnière [sablɔ'njɛːr], *n.f.* sand-pit.
sabord [sa'bɔːr], *n.m.* (*Naut.*) port-hole.
saborder [sabɔr'de], *v.t.* to scuttle.
sabot [sa'bo], *n.m.* sabot, clog; hoof (*of horse etc.*); drag (*of carriages*); **dormir comme un sabot**, to sleep like a top.
sabotage [sabɔ'taːʒ], *n.m.* sabotage.
saboter [sabɔ'te], *v.t.* (*colloq.*) to bungle; to damage wilfully, to sabotage.
saboteur [sabɔ'tœːr], *n.m.* (*fem.* **-euse**) bungler; saboteur.
sabotier [sabɔ'tje], *n.m.* (*fem.* **-ière**) sabot maker.
sabre [saːbr], *n.m.* sabre; broadsword.
sabrer [sa'bre], *v.t.* to strike *or* cut with a sabre, to sabre; (*colloq.*) to hurry over, to botch.
sabreur [sa'brœːr], *n.m.* swashbuckler; (*colloq.*) botcher.
sac (1) [sak], *n.m.* sack, bag; pouch (*of certain animals*).
sac (2) [sak], *n.m.* sack (*plunder*), pillage.
saccade [sa'kad], *n.f.* jerk, jolt.
saccadé [saka'de], *a.* jerky, broken, abrupt; irregular.
saccader [saka'de], *v.t.* to jerk.
saccage [sa'kaːʒ], *n.m.* upset, confusion; pillage.
saccager [saka'ʒe], *v.t.* (*conjug. like* MANGER) to sack, to plunder; (*fig.*) to play havoc with.
saccharine [saka'rin], *n.f.* saccharine.
sacerdoce [sasɛr'dɔs], *n.m.* priesthood.
sacerdotal [sasɛrdɔ'tal], *a.* (*m. pl.* **-aux**) sacerdotal.
sachée [sa'ʃe], *n.f.* sackful, bagful.
sachet [sa'ʃɛ], *n.m.* small bag, sachet.
sacoche [sa'kɔʃ], *n.f.* (*Mil.*) saddle-bag; money-bag; tool-bag.
sacramental [sakramɑ̃'tal] (*m. pl.* **-aux**), **sacramentel** [sakramɑ̃'tɛl] (*fem.* **-elle**), *a.* sacramental.
sacre [sakr], *n.m.* anointing and coronation of a king; consecration of a bishop.
sacré [sa'kre], *a.* holy, consecrated; sacred, inviolable.
sacrebleu! [sakrə'blø], *int.* confound it! curse it!
sacrement [sakrə'mɑ̃], *n.m.* sacrament, *esp.* matrimony.
sacrer [sa'kre], *v.t.* to anoint, to crown; to consecrate.—*v.i.* to curse and swear.
sacrificateur [sakrifika'tœːr], *n.m.* (*fem.* **-trice**) sacrificer.
sacrificatoire [sakrifika'twaːr], *a.* sacrificial.
sacrifice [sakri'fis], *n.m.* sacrifice; renunciation.
sacrifier [sakri'fje], *v.t.* to sacrifice; to devote; to give up.—*v.i.* to sacrifice.
sacrilège [sakri'lɛːʒ], *a.* sacrilegious.—*n.m.* sacrilege.
sacrilègement [sakrilɛʒ'mɑ̃], *adv.* sacrilegiously.
sacripant [sakri'pɑ̃], *n.m.* rascal, scoundrel.
sacristain [sakris'tɛ̃], *n.m.* sacristan, sexton.
sacristie [sakris'ti], *n.f.* sacristy, vestry; church plate.
sacristine [sakris'tin], *n.f.* vestry-nun, sacristine.

sacro-saint [sakrɔ'sɛ̃], *a.* sacrosanct.
sadique [sa'dik], *a.* sadistic.—*n.* sadist.
sadisme [sa'dism], *n.m.* sadism.
saducéen [sadyse'ɛ̃], *a.* (*fem.* **-éenne**) Sadducean.—*n.m.* (*fem.* **-éenne**) Sadducee.
safran [sa'frɑ̃], *n.m.* saffron; crocus.
safrané [safra'ne], *a.* saffron-coloured.
saga [sa'ga], *n.f.* saga.
sagace [sa'gas], *a.* sagacious, shrewd.
sagacité [sagasi'te], *n.f.* sagacity.
sage [sa:ʒ], *a.* wise; sage, sensible, prudent; sober, well-behaved, good; virtuous, modest; gentle (*of animals*).—*n.m.* wise man, sage.
sage-femme [saʒ'fam], *n.f.* (*pl.* **sages-femmes**) midwife.
sagement [saʒ'mɑ̃] *adv.* wisely; prudently; soberly, steadily.
sagesse [sa'ʒɛs], *n.f.* wisdom; prudence; steadiness; chastity; good behaviour (*of children*); gentleness (*of animals*).
sagittaire [saʒi'tɛːr], *n.m.* (*Rom. Ant.*) archer; (*Astron.*) Sagittarius.
sagou [sa'gu], *n.m.* sago.
sagouier [sagu'je] *or* (*preferably*) **sagoutier** [sagu'tje], *n.m.* sago-tree.
sagouin [sa'gwɛ̃], *n.m.* squirrel-monkey; (*fem.* **-e**) (*fig.*) slovenly fellow *or* woman.
Sahara [saa'ra], **le**, *m.* the Sahara.
saignant [sɛ'nɑ̃], *a.* bleeding, bloody; underdone (*of meat*).
saignée [sɛ'ne] *n.f.* blood-letting, phlebotomy; small of the arm; (*fig.*) drain on the purse.
saignement [sɛɲə'mɑ̃], *n.m.* bleeding.
saigner [sɛ'ne], *v.t.* to bleed; to stick (*an animal*); (*fig.*) to drain.—*v.i.* to bleed. **se saigner**, *v.r.* to bleed oneself; to drain oneself *or* one's purse.
saigneux [sɛ'nø], *a.* (*fem.* **-euse**) bloody.
saillant [sa'jɑ̃], *a.* jutting out, projecting; (*fig.*) striking, remarkable.—*n.m.* (*Fort.*) salient.
saillie [sa'ji], *n.f.* start, sudden spurt; sally; (*fig.*) witticism; projection.
saillir [sa'jiːr], *v.i.* to gush (*of liquids*); to ripple (*of muscles*).
sain [sɛ̃], *a.* hale, healthy; sound; sane; *sain et sauf*, safe and sound.
saindoux [sɛ̃'du], *n.m. inv.* lard.
sainement [sɛn'mɑ̃], *adv.* wholesomely; healthily, soundly; judiciously.
sainfoin [sɛ̃'fwɛ̃], *n.m.* sainfoin.
saint [sɛ̃], *a.* holy, sacred; godly, saintly; sanctified, consecrated.—*n.m.* (*fem.* **-e**) saint; patron saint.
saintement [sɛ̃t'mɑ̃], *adv.* sacredly; piously, religiously.
sainteté [sɛ̃tə'te], *n.f.* holiness, sanctity, sacredness, saintliness; *Sa Sainteté le Pape*, His Holiness the Pope.
saisi [sɛ'zi], *a.* seized, possessed, struck (*de*).
saisie [sɛ'zi], *n.f.* (*Law*) seizure; distraint, execution.
saisir [sɛ'ziːr], *v.t.* to seize, to take hold of; to understand; (*fig.*) to impress, to shock, to startle; to distrain. **se saisir**, *v.r.* to seize, to catch hold (*de*); to take possession (*de*); to arrest.
saisissable [sɛzi'sabl], *a.* distrainable, seizable.
saisissant [sɛzi'sɑ̃], *a.* keen, sharp, piercing (*of cold*); striking, impressive.

saisissement [sɛzis'mɑ̃], *n.m.* shock, violent impression, seizure.
saison [sɛ'zɔ̃], *n.f.* season; *marchand des quatre saisons*, costermonger, barrowboy.
saisonnier [sɛzɔ̃'nje], *a.* (*fem.* **-ière**) seasonal.
salade [sa'lad], *n.f.* salad, herb grown for salad; (*fig.*) medley, confusion.
saladier [sala'dje], *n.m.* salad-bowl.
salage [sa'laːʒ], *n.m.* salting.
salaire [sa'lɛːr], *n.m.* wages, pay, hire; reward.
salaison [salɛ'zɔ̃], *n.f.* salting; salt provisions; curing (*of bacon etc.*).
salamalec [salama'lɛk], *n.m.* (*used chiefly in pl.*) salaam; (*fig.*) exaggerated politeness.
salamandre [sala'mɑ̃ːdr], *n.f.* salamander; slow-combustion stove.
salant [sa'lɑ̃], *a.m.* *marais salant*, salt-marsh.
salarié [sala'rje], *a.* paid, wage-earning.—*n.m.* (*fem.* **-ée**) wage-earner.
salarier [sala'rje], *v.t.* to pay, to give wages to.
salaud [sa'lo], *n.m.* (*fem.* **-e**) (*pop.* and *rude*) sloven, dirty person, slut; *quel salaud!* dirty beast! dirty dog! bastard!
sale [sal], *a.* dirty; nasty, foul; coarse, obscene; squalid.
salé [sa'le], *a.* salted, salt; briny; (*fig.*) keen, biting; coarse; spicy.—*n.m.* salt pork; *du petit salé*, pickled pork.
salement [sal'mɑ̃], *adv.* dirtily; nastily.
saler [sa'le], *v.t.* to salt; (*fig.*) to overcharge for; to fleece (*customers*).
saleté [sal'te], *n.f.* dirtiness, filthiness; filth, dirt; dirty trick; obscenity.
saleur [sa'lœːr], *n.m.* (*fem.* **-euse**) salter, curer.
salière [sa'ljɛːr], *n.f.* salt-cellar; salt-box; eye-pit (*in horses*).
salin [sa'lɛ̃], *a.* salt, saline, briny.—*n.m.* salt-works; salt-marsh.
saline [sa'lin], *n.f.* salt-marsh, salt-mine, salt-pit.
salinier [sali'nje], *n.m.* owner of salt-works; salt-worker *or* -vendor.
salique [sa'lik], *a.* *loi salique*, Salic law.
salir [sa'liːr], *v.t.* to dirty, to soil; to taint, to sully. **se salir**, *v.r.* to get dirty; to sully one's reputation.
salissant [sali'sɑ̃], *a.* that soils *or* gets dirty easily; dirty (*of job, work etc.*).
salive [sa'liːv], *n.f.* saliva, spittle.
saliver [sali've], *v.i.* to salivate.
salle [sal], *n.f.* hall; large room; gallery (*of museum*); ward (*in hospitals*); (*Theat.*) house; *salle à manger*, dining-room; *salle d'attente*, waiting-room; *salle de bain(s)*, bathroom; *salle de spectacle*, playhouse.
saloir [sa'lwaːr], *n.m.* salt-box; salting-tub.
salon [sa'lɔ̃], *n.m.* drawing-room, parlour; lounge; saloon; exhibition (*art*); (*pl.*) world of fashion.
salopette [salɔ'pɛt], *n.f.* overall, dungarees.
salpêtrage [salpɛ'traːʒ], *n.m.* saltpetre-making; nitrification.
salpêtre [sal'pɛːtr], *n.m.* saltpetre.
salpêtrer [salpɛ'tre], *v.t.* to cover with saltpetre.
salpêtrerie [salpɛtrə'ri], *n.f.* saltpetre-works.

salpêtreux

salpêtreux [salpɛ'trø], *a.* (*fem.* **-euse**) saltpetrous.

salpêtrière [salpɛtri'jɛːr], *n.f.* saltpetreworks.

salsepareille [salspa'rɛːj], *n.f.* sarsaparilla.

saltimbanque [saltɛ̃'bãːk], *n.m.* mountebank, buffoon; (*fig.*) humbug.

salubre [sa'lybr], *a.* salubrious, healthy (*climate*).

salubrité [salybri'te], *n.f.* salubrity, healthfulness, wholesomeness.

saluer [sa'lɥe], *v.t.* to salute, to bow to; to greet; to cheer; to proclaim. **se saluer,** *v.r.* to bow to *or* salute each other.

salure [sa'lyːr], *n.f.* saltness, salinity.

salut [sa'ly], *n.m.* safety; salvation; welfare; escape; salutation, greeting; hail, cheers.

salutaire [saly'tɛːr], *a.* salutary, advantageous, beneficial.

salutairement [salytɛr'mã], *adv.* beneficially.

salutation [salytɑ'sjɔ̃], *n.f.* salutation, greeting; (*pl.*) compliments.

Salvador [salva'dɔr], **le,** *m.* El Salvador.

salvadorègne [salvadɔ'rɛɲ], *a.* Salvadorean. —*n.* (**Salvadorègne**) Salvadorean (*person*).

salve [salv], *n.f.* salvo, volley; salute (*of artillery*).

samedi [sam'di], *n.m.* Saturday.

sanatorium [sanatɔ'rjɔm], *n.m.* sanatorium.

sanctifiant [sãkti'fjã], *a.* sanctifying.

sanctificateur [sãktifika'tœːr], *a.* (*fem.* **-trice**) sanctifying.—*n.m.* sanctifier.

sanctification [sãktifika'sjɔ̃], *n.f.* sanctification.

sanctifier [sãkti'fje], *v.t.* to sanctify, to hallow.

sanction [sãk'sjɔ̃], *n.f.* sanction; approbation; penalty.

sanctionner [sãksjɔ'ne], *v.t.* to sanction, to approve; to penalize.

sanctuaire [sãk'tɥɛːr], *n.m.* sanctuary (*of the temple etc.*), shrine; chancel (*of church*).

sandale [sã'dal], *n.f.* sandal; fencing-shoe.

sandalier [sãda'lje], *n.m.* sandal-maker.

sandow [sã'dɔf], *n.m.* chest-expander; rubber shock-absorber.

sandwich [sã'dwitʃ], *n.m.* (*pl.* **sandwichs** or **sandwiches**) sandwich.

sang [sã], *n.m.* blood; race; kindred; *pur sang,* thoroughbred.

sang-froid [sã'frwɑ], *n.m.* coolness, composure, sang-froid.

sanglade [sã'glad], *n.f.* lash, cut (*with a whip*).

sanglant [sã'glã], *a.* bloody, bleeding; (*fig.*) biting, outrageous.

sangle [sãːgl], *n.f.* strap, belt; saddle-girth; *lit de sangle,* camp-bed.

sangler [sã'gle], *v.t.* to girth, to strap; to lace too tightly; to deal (*a slashing blow*). **se sangler,** *v.r.* to lace oneself tightly.

sanglier [sã'glje], *n.m.* wild boar.

sanglot [sã'glo], *n.m.* sob.

sangloter [sãglɔ'te], *v.i.* to sob.

sang-mêlé [sãme'le], *n.m. inv.* half-caste.

sangsue [sã'sy], *n.f.* leech; (*fig.*) extortioner.

sanguin [sã'gɛ̃], *a.* of blood; full-blooded; blood-red.

sanguinaire [sãgi'nɛːr], *a.* sanguinary, bloody, blood-thirsty.

sanitaire [sani'tɛːr], *a.* sanitary.

sans [sã], *prep.* without; free from; but for; had it not been for, were it not for; *cela va sans dire,* of course; *sans abri, sans gîte, sans logis,* homeless; *sans cela,* otherwise; *sans quoi,* otherwise.

sans-atout [sãza'tu], *n.m.* no trumps.

sans-cœur [sã'kœːr], *n. inv.* heartless, unfeeling person.

sanscrit [sãs'kri], *n.m.* Sanskrit.

sans-façon [sãfa'sɔ̃], *n.m.* bluntness; offhandedness.

sans-gêne [sã'ʒɛːn], *n.m.* unceremoniousness, coolness; (*fam.*) cheek.

sansonnet [sãsɔ'nɛ], *n.m.* (*Orn.*) starling.

sans-patrie [sãpa'tri], *n. inv.* stateless person.

sans-souci [sãsu'si], *a.* carefree, happy-go-lucky.—*n. inv.* (*colloq.*) carefree, easy-going person.—*n.m. inv.* free-and-easy manners.

sans-travail [sãtra'vaj], *n.m. inv. les sans-travail,* the unemployed.

santal [sã'tal], *n.m.* (*pl.* **-als**) sandalwood, santal.

santé [sã'te], *n.f.* health, healthiness; state of health. ∧

saoul [SOUL].

sape [sap], *n.f.* sapping, undermining; mine; trench.

saper [sa'pe], *v.t.* to sap, to undermine.

sapeur [sa'pœːr], *n.m.* sapper.

sapeur-pompier [sapœrpɔ̃'pje], *n.m.* (*pl.* **sapeurs-pompiers**) fireman.

sapeur-télégraphiste [sapœrtelegra'fist], *n.m.* (*pl.* **sapeurs-télégraphistes**) soldier of the signal corps; (*pl.*) (*fam.*) signals.

saphir [sa'fiːr], *n.m.* sapphire.

sapin [sa'pɛ̃], *n.m.* fir, fir-tree; (*bois de*) *sapin,* deal.

sapinette [sapi'nɛt], *n.f.* spruce.

sapinière [sapi'njɛːr], *n.f.* fir wood, fir plantation.

sarabande [sara'bãːd], *n.f.* saraband (*dance*); (*fam.*) song-and-dance.

sarcasme [sar'kasm], *n.m.* sarcasm, sarcastic remark.

sarcastique [sarkas'tik], *a.* sarcastic.

sarcelle [sar'sɛl], *n.f.* (*Orn.*) teal.

sarclage [sar'klaːʒ], *n.m.* weeding.

sarcler [sar'kle], *v.t.* to weed; to hoe; (*fig.*) to extirpate.

sarcleur [sar'klœːr], *n.m.* (*fem.* **-euse**) weeder.

sarcloir [sar'klwaːr], *n.m.* hoe.

sarcophage (1) [sarkɔ'faːʒ], *n.m.* sarcophagus.

sarcophage (2) [sarkɔ'faːʒ], *n.f.* (*Ent.*) blowfly.

Sardaigne [sar'dɛɲ], **la,** *f.* Sardinia.

sarde [sard], *a.* Sardinian.—*n.* (**Sarde**) Sardinian (*person*).

sardine [sar'din], *n.f.* sardine.

sardinerie [sardin'ri], *n.f.* sardine packing and curing factory.

sardinier [sardi'nje], *n.m.* (*fem.* **-ière**) sardine fisher; sardine packer *or* curer. —*n.m.* sardine-net; sardine-boat.

sardoine [sar'dwan], *n.f.* sardonyx.

sardonique [sardɔ'nik], *a.* sardonic.

sarigue [sa'rig], *n.* sarigue (*opossum*).

sarment [sar'mã], *n.m.* vine-shoot, vine-branch.

sarmenteux [sarmã'tø], *a.* (*fem.* **-euse**) branchy, climbing; rambling (*of roses*).

sarrasin [sara'zɛ̃], *n.m.* buckwheat.

290

sauvetage

sarrau [sa'ro], *n.m.* (*pl.* -aux) smock-frock; child's blouse.
sas [sɑ], *n.m. inv.* sieve, screen; (*Naut.*) floating chamber (*of submarine*).
Satan [sa'tɑ̃], *m.* Satan.
satané [sata'ne], *a.* (*colloq.*) devilish, confounded.
satanique [sata'nik], *a.* satanic, diabolical.
sataniquement [satanik'mɑ̃], *adv.* fiendishly, diabolically.
satellite [satɛ'lit], *a.* satellite.—*n.m.* satellite.
satiété [sasje'te], *n.f.* satiety, repletion.
satin [sa'tɛ̃], *n.m.* satin.
satiné [sati'ne], *a.* satin-like, satiny; glazed (*of paper etc.*).
satiner [sati'ne], *v.t.* to satin; to glaze (*paper etc.*).—*v.i.* to look like satin.
satire [sa'tiːr], *n.f.* satire; lampoon.
satirique [sati'rik], *a.* satirical.—*n.m.* satirist.
satiriquement [satirik'mɑ̃], *adv.* satirically.
satiriser [satiri'ze], *v.t.* to satirize.
satisfaction [satisfak'sjɔ̃], *n.f.* satisfaction; gratification; atonement.
satisfaire [satis'fɛːr], *v.t. irr.* (*conjug. like* FAIRE) to satisfy; to gratify; to answer; to give satisfaction to, to make amends to.—*v.i.* to be satisfactory (*à*); to fulfil (*à*). se satisfaire, *v.r.* to satisfy oneself, to indulge oneself.
satisfaisant [satisfə'zɑ̃], *a.* satisfactory.
satisfait [satis'fɛ], *a.* satisfied, contented, pleased.
saturant [saty'rɑ̃], *a.* saturating.
saturation [satyra'sjɔ̃], *n.f.* saturation.
saturer [saty're], *v.t.* to saturate; (*fig.*) to surfeit.
saturnales [satyr'nal], *n.f. pl.* saturnalia.
Saturne [sa'tyrn], *m.* Saturn.
satyre [sa'tiːr], *n.m.* satyr.
sauce [soːs], *n.f.* sauce; *sauce hollandaise*, egg yolks and melted butter.
saucé [so'se], *a.* soused, wet through.
saucer [so'se], *v.t.* (*conjug. like* COMMENCER) to dip in sauce; to sop, to souse.
saucière [so'sjɛːr], *n.f.* sauce-boat.
saucisse [so'sis], *n.f.* (*fresh*) sausage.
saucisson [sosi'sɔ̃], *n.m.* large dry sausage; salami.
sauf (1) [sof], *a.* (*fem.* sauve) safe; unhurt, unscathed; *sain et sauf*, safe and sound.
sauf (2) [sof], *prep.* save, except; unless.
sauf-conduit [sofkɔ̃'dɥi], *n.m.* (*pl.* -conduits) safe-conduct.
sauge [soːʒ], *n.f.* sage (*herb*).
saugrenu [sogrə'ny], *a.* absurd, ridiculous, preposterous.
saulaie [so'lɛ], *n.f.* willow-grove.
saule [soːl], *n.m.* willow.
saumâtre [so'mɑːtr], *a.* brackish, briny.
saumon [so'mɔ̃], *n.m.* salmon.
saumoné [somɔ'ne], *a.* salmon-coloured; *truite saumonée*, salmon-trout.
saumurage [somy'raːʒ], *n.m.* pickling (*in brine*), brining.
saumure [so'myːr], *n.f.* brine, pickle.
saumuré [somy're], *a.* pickled, brined.
saunage [so'naːʒ], *n.m.*, saunaison [sonɛ'zɔ̃], *n.f.* salt-making, salt-trade.
sauner [so'ne], *v.i.* to make salt.
saunerie [son'ri], *n.f.* saltworks.

saunier [so'nje], *n.m.* salt-maker; salt-merchant.
saunière [so'njɛːr], *n.f.* salt-bin.
saupoudrage [supu'draːʒ], *n.m.* salting; sprinkling, powdering.
saupoudrer [supu'dre], *v.t.* to sprinkle with salt, pepper etc.; to powder, to sprinkle.
saur or sor [soːr], *a.m.* smoked and salted; red (*of herrings*).
saure [soːr], *a.* yellowish-brown; sorrel (*of horses*); red, smoked (*of herrings*).
saurer [so're], *v.t.* to smoke (*herrings*).
saurin [so'rɛ̃], *n.m.* freshly smoked herring, bloater.
saurisserie [soris'ri], *n.f.* kippering factory.
saut [so], *n.m.* leap, jump, hop, bound; *de plein saut*, at once, suddenly; *saut périlleux*, somersault.
sautage [so'taːʒ], *n.m.* exploding (*mines*).
saut-de-mouton [sodmu'tɔ̃], *n.m.* (*pl.* sauts-de-mouton*) fly-over crossing.
saute [soːt], *n.f.* (*Naut.*) sudden shift or change (*of wind*).
sauté [so'te], *a.* fried, tossed in the pan.
saute-mouton [sotmu'tɔ̃], *n.m.* leap-frog (*game*).
sauter [so'te], *v.t.* to leap over; to leave out, to skip; to toss in the pan.—*v.i.* to leap, to jump; to explode; to spring; to blow out (*of fuse*).
sauterelle [so'trɛl], *n.f.* grasshopper, locust.
sauterie [sot'ri], *n.f.* (*fam.*) informal dance, hop.
saute-ruisseau [sotrɥi'so], *n.m. inv.* messenger-boy (*in offices*).
sauteur [so'tœːr], *a.* (*fem.* -euse) jumping, leaping.—*n.m.* (*fem.* -euse) leaper, jumper; vaulter.
sautillant [soti'jɑ̃], *a.* hopping, skipping.
sautiller [soti'je], *v.i.* to hop, to skip, to jump about.
sautoir [so'twaːr], *n.m.* Saint Andrew's cross; watch-guard.
sauvage [so'vaːʒ], *a.* savage, wild; uncivilized; brutal; shy; unsociable.—*n.* savage; unsociable person.
sauvagement [sovaʒ'mɑ̃], *adv.* wildly, savagely; barbarously, fiercely.
sauvageon [sova'ʒɔ̃], *n.m.* (*Agric.*) wild stock (*for grafting*); briar (*of roses*).
sauvagerie [sova'ʒri], *n.f.* unsociableness; shyness; wildness.
sauvagesse [sova'ʒɛs], *n.f.* uncivilized woman; hoyden.
sauvagin [sova'ʒɛ̃], *a.* fishy (*in taste, smell, etc.*).—*n.m.* fishy taste or smell.—*n.f.* (-e) wild waterfowl.
sauvegarde [sov'gard], *n.f.* safe-keeping, safeguard; safe-conduct; (*Naut.*) life-line.
sauvegarder [sovgar'de], *v.t.* to watch over, to protect, to safeguard.
sauve-qui-peut [sovki'pø], *n.m. inv.* headlong flight, stampede; every man for himself.
sauver [so've], *v.t.* to save, to rescue; to preserve; to exempt; to conceal. se sauver, *v.r.* to escape, to make off; (*fam.*) to abscond; to take refuge.
sauvetage [sov'taːʒ], *n.m.* salvage; life-saving, rescue; *appareil de sauvetage*, rescue apparatus, fire-escape; *bouée de*

291

sauvetage, life-buoy; *canot de sauvetage*, life-boat; *ceinture de sauvetage*, life-belt.
sauveteur [sov'tœːr], *n.m.* rescuer, lifeboatman.
sauveur [so'vœːr], *a.* saving, redeeming.—*n.m.* saver, deliverer; Saviour.
savamment [sava'mã], *adv.* learnedly; knowingly.
savane [sa'van], *n.f.* savanna; (*C*) swamp.
savant [sa'vã], *a.* learned, expert (*en*); scholarly; clever.—*n.m.* (*fem.* **-e**) scholar, scientist.
savarin [sava'rɛ̃], *n.m.* round, hollow cake.
savate [sa'vat], *n.f.* old shoe; clumsy person.
savetier [sav'tje], *n.m.* cobbler; (*fig.*) bungler.
saveur [sa'vœːr], *n.f.* savour, flavour, relish.
savoir [sa'vwaːr], *v.t. irr.* to know, to be aware of; to understand; to know how (*can*), to be able. **se savoir**, *v.r.* to get known.—*n.m.* knowledge, learning, scholarship.
savoir-faire [savwar'fɛːr], *n.m.* tact; savoir-faire; cleverness.
savoir-vivre [savwar'viːvr], *n.m.* good manners, good breeding.
savon [sa'võ], *n.m.* soap; (*colloq.*) scolding.
savonnage [savo'naːʒ], *n.m.* soaping, washing with soap.
savonner [savo'ne], *v.t.* to soap; to lather; (*colloq.*) to scold. **se savonner**, *v.r.* to be washable, to wash (*of fabrics*); to lather (*oneself*).
savonnerie [savon'ri], *n.f.* soap-manufacture; soap-trade; soap-works.
savonnette [savo'nɛt], *n.f.* cake of toilet soap.
savonneux [savo'nø], *a.* (*fem.* **-euse**) soapy.
savourer [savu're], *v.t.* to savour, to relish; (*fig.*) to enjoy.
savoureusement [savurøz'mã], *adv.* with relish.
savoureux [savu'rø], *a.* (*fem.* **-euse**) savoury, tasty (*dish*); racy (*story*).
savoyard [savwa'jaːr], *a.* of Savoy.—*n.m.* (**Savoyard**, *fem.* **-arde**) Savoyard (*person*); *petit Savoyard*, little chimney-sweep.
saxifrage [saksi'fraːʒ], *a.* saxifragous.—*n.f.* saxifrage.
saxon [sak'sõ], *a.* (*fem.* **-onne**) Saxon.—*n.m.* (**Saxon**, *fem.* **-onne**) Saxon (*person*).
saxophone [sakso'fon], *n.m.* saxophone.
saynète [sɛ'nɛt], *n.f.* playlet, sketch.
scabieux [ska'bjø], *a.* (*fem.* **-euse**) scabious, scabby.—*n.f.* (**-euse**) scabious (*plant*).
scabreux [ska'brø], *a.* (*fem.* **-euse**) scabrous, rugged, rough; (*fig.*) dangerous, difficult, ticklish; improper.
scalp [skalp], *n.m.* scalp (*of an enemy*).
scalpel [skal'pɛl], *n.m.* scalpel.
scalper [skal'pe], *v.t.* to scalp.
scandale [skã'dal], *n.m.* scandal; shame, dismay, disgust.
scandaleusement [skãdaløz'mã], *adv.* scandalously.
scandaleux [skãda'lø], *a.* (*fem.* **-euse**) scandalous.
scandaliser [skãdali'ze], *v.t.* to scandalize, to shock. **se scandaliser**, *v.r.* to be shocked.
scander [skã'de], *v.t.* to scan; to stress (*a phrase*).
scandinave [skãdi'naːv], *a.* Scandinavian.—*n.* (**Scandinave**) Scandinavian (*person*).
Scandinavie [skãdina'vi], **la**, *f.* Scandinavia.

scansion [skã'sjõ], *n.f.* scansion.
scaphandre [ska'fãːdr], *n.m.* diving-suit.
scaphandrier [skafãdri'je], *n.m.* diver.
scapulaire [skapy'lɛːr], *a.* and *n.m.* scapular.
scarabée [skara'be], *n.m.* scarabaeus (*beetle*); scarab.
scarlatine [skarla'tin], *a.* and *n.f.* (*fièvre*) *scarlatine*, scarlet fever.
sceau [so], *n.m.* (*pl.* **sceaux**) seal; (*fig.*) sanction; *mettre le sceau à*, to seal, (*fig.*) to complete.
scélérat [sele'ra], *a.* wicked, villainous, criminal, vile.—*n.m.* (*fem.* **-e**) scoundrel, villain, miscreant, jade.
scélératesse [selera'tɛs], *n.f.* villainy.
scellé [sɛ'le], *n.m.* seal.
scellement [sɛl'mã], *n.m.* sealing; fastening.
sceller [se'le], *v.t.* to put an official seal on, to seal; (*Build.*) to fasten; (*fig.*) to ratify.
scénario [sena'rjo], *n.m.* (*pl.* **scénarios** or **scénarii**) scenario (*of ballet etc.*); film script.
scénariste [sena'rist], *n.* script-writer, scenario-writer.
scène [sɛːn], *n.f.* stage; scenery; (*colloq.*) scene, quarrel.
scénique [se'nik], *a.* scenic, theatrical; *indications scéniques*, stage directions.
scepticisme [sɛpti'sism], *n.m.* scepticism.
sceptique [sɛp'tik], *a.* sceptical.—*n.* sceptic.
sceptre [sɛptr], *n.m.* sceptre; (*fig.*) sway, dominion.
schah [ʃa], *n.m.* shah (*of Persia*).
scheik or **cheik** [ʃɛk], *n.m.* sheik.
schéma [ʃe'ma], **schème** [ʃɛm], *n.m.* diagram; rough sketch.
schématique [ʃema'tik], *a.* diagrammatic; *dessin schématique*, draft, diagram.
schibboleth [ʃibo'lɛt], *n.m.* catchword, shibboleth.
schisme [ʃism], *n.m.* schism.
schiste [ʃist], *n.m.* schist, slaty rock, shale.
schizophrène [skizo'frɛn], *a.* and *n.* schizophrenic.
schizophrénie [skizofre'ni], *n.f.* schizophrenia.
schnorkel [ʃnɔr'kɛl], *n.m.* schnorkel, submarine's air-tube.
schooner [sku'nœːr], *n.m.* schooner.
sciage [sja:ʒ], *n.m.* sawing.
sciatique [sja'tik], *a.* sciatic.—*n.m.* sciatic nerve.—*n.f.* sciatica.
scie [si], *n.f.* saw; (*pop.*) bore, nuisance.
sciemment [sja'mã], *adv.* wittingly, knowingly.
science [sjã:s], *n.f.* science, knowledge, learning; skill.
scientifique [sjãti'fik], *a.* scientific.
scientifiquement [sjãtifik'mã], *adv.* scientifically.
scier [sje], *v.t.* to saw; to cut down.—*v.i.* (*Row.*) to back water.
scierie [si'ri], *n.f.* sawmill.
scieur [sjœːr], *n.m.* sawyer.
scinder [sɛ̃'de], *v.t.* to divide, to split up.
scintillant [sɛ̃ti'jã], *a.* scintillating; twinkling.
scintillation [sɛ̃tija'sjõ], *n.f.*, **scintillement** [sɛ̃tij'mã], *n.m.* scintillation, sparkling; twinkling.
scintiller [sɛ̃ti'je], *v.i.* to scintillate, to sparkle; to twinkle (*of star*); to flicker.

scion [sjø], n.m. scion, shoot.
scission [si'sjõ], n.f. scission; split, secession.
scissure [si'syːr], n.f. fissure, crack, cleft.
sciure [sjyːr], n.f. sciure de bois, sawdust.
sclérose [skle'roːz], n.f. sclerosis.
scolaire [skɔ'lɛːr], a. of schools; année scolaire, school year.
scolarité [skɔlari'te], n.f. course of study; school attendance.
scolastique [skɔlas'tik], a. scholastic.—n.m. scholastic; schoolman.—n.f. scholasticism.
scolastiquement [skɔlastik'mã], adv. scholastically.
scooter [sku'tɛːr], n.m. motor-scooter; autos scooters, dodgems.
scorbut [skɔr'byt], n.m. scurvy.
scorbutique [skɔrby'tik], a. and n. scorbutic.
scorie [skɔ'ri], n.f. scoria, slag, dross.
scorifier [skɔri'fje], v.t. to scorify.
scorpion [skɔr'pjõ], n.m. scorpion.
scout [skut], a. of scouting.—n.m. (boy) scout.
scoutisme [sku'tism], n.m. scouting, boy-scout movement.
scratch [skratʃ], n.m. (Spt.) être or partir scratch, to start at scratch.
scratcher [skra'tʃe], v.t. (Spt.) to scratch (horse, competitor etc.).
scribe [skrib], n.m. scribe; copyist.
script [skript], n.m. script (film or play).
scriptural [skripty'ral], a. (m. pl. -aux) scriptural.
scrofule [skrɔ'fyl], n.f. scrofula, king's evil.
scrofuleux [skrɔfy'lø], a. and n.m. (fem. -euse) scrofulous (person).
scrupule [skry'pyl], n.m. scruple, qualm, doubt; scrupulousness.
scrupuleusement [skrypyløz'mã], adv. scrupulously.
scrupuleux [skrypy'lø], a. (fem. -euse) scrupulous, strict, punctilious.
scrutateur [skryta'tœːr], a. (fem. -trice) searching, scrutinizing.—n.m. (fem. -trice) investigator, scrutinizer; scrutineer; teller (of a ballot etc.).
scruter [skry'te], v.t. to scrutinize, to investigate.
scrutin [skry'tɛ̃], n.m. ballot, balloting, poll.
sculpter [skyl'te], v.t. to sculpture, to carve.
sculpteur [skyl'tœːr], n.m. sculptor, carver.
sculptural [skylty'ral], a. (m. pl. -aux) sculptural.
sculpture [skyl'tyːr], n.f. sculpture, carving.
se [sə], s' [s], pron. inv. oneself, himself, herself, itself, themselves; to oneself etc.; one another, each other; cela se peut, that may be.
séance [se'ãːs], n.f. seat (right to sit); session, duration, meeting; sitting (for one's portrait etc.); seance; être en séance, to be in session; lever la séance, to close the meeting; séance tenante, there and then, forthwith.
séant [se'ã], a. sitting; fitting, seemly, becoming.—n.m. sitting posture; seat.
seau [so], n.m. (pl. seaux) pail, bucket.
sébile [se'bil], n.f. small wooden bowl (used by beggars); pan (in gold-mining).
sec [sɛk], a. (fem. sèche) dry, arid; withered; lean; plain; unfeeling, sharp; à pied sec, dry-shod; coup sec, sharp stroke; perte

sèche, dead loss.—n.m. dryness.—adv. dryly, sharply.
sécateur [seka'tœːr], n.m. (Gard.) pruning-shears; secateurs.
seccotine [sɛkɔ'tin], n.f. (reg. trade mark) Seccotine.
sécession [sesɛ'sjõ], n.f. secession.
séchage [se'ʃaːʒ], n.m. drying.
sèchement [sɛʃ'mã], adv. dryly; curtly.
sécher [se'ʃe], v.t. (conjug. like CÉDER) to dry; to dry up; to cure.—v.i. to dry; to wither; to pine away. se sécher, v.r. to dry oneself; to dry (of a thing).
sécheresse [se'ʃrɛs], n.f. dryness; drought; (fig.) sharpness.
séchoir [se'ʃwaːr], n.m. drying-room; clothes-horse; clothes-airer; hair-dryer.
second [sə'gõ, zgõ], a. second.—n.m. (fem. -e) second, assistant.—n.m. second floor.—n.f. (-e) second class; (Sch.) fifth form; second (of time).
secondaire [səgõ'dɛːr], a. secondary; accessory.
secondairement [səgõdɛr'mã], adv. secondarily.
secondement [səgõd'mã], adv. secondly.
seconder [səgõ'de], v.t. to second, to assist; to back (up), to support; to promote.
secouement [səku'mã], secouage [sə'kwaːʒ], n.m. shaking, jogging, jolting.
secouer [sə'kwe], v.t. to shake, to jolt; to shake off; to shock; to rouse. se secouer, v.r. to shake oneself, to bestir oneself.
secourable [səku'rabl], a. helpful, helping; relievable.
secourir [səku'riːr], v.t. irr. (conjug. like COURIR) to succour, to assist, to help, to relieve.
secourisme [səku'rism], n.m. first-aid.
secouriste [səku'rist], n. qualified first-aider.
secours [sə'kuːr], n.m. help, assistance, aid, succour; rescue; appeler police secours, to dial 999; au secours! help!
secousse [sə'kus], n.f. shake, shock; blow, concussion; jerk, jolt.
secret [sə'krɛ], a. (fem. -ète) secret, private, hidden; reserved.—n.m. secret; secrecy, privacy, mystery.
secrétaire [səkre'tɛːr], n. secretary.—n.m. writing-desk.
secrétariat [səkreta'rja], n.m. secretaryship; secretary's office; secretariat.
secrètement [səkrɛt'mã], adv. secretly, in secret, inwardly.
sécréter [sekre'te], v.t. (conjug. like CÉDER) to secrete (of glands etc.).
sécréteur [sekre'tœːr], a. (fem. -euse or -trice) secretory.
sécrétion [sekre'sjõ], n.f. secretion.
sectaire [sɛk'tɛːr], a. sectarian.—n. sectary.
sectateur [sɛkta'tœːr], n.m. (fem. -trice) follower, votary.
secte [sɛkt], n.f. sect.
secteur [sɛk'tœːr], n.m. sector, section; district.
section [sɛk'sjõ], n.f. section; division.
sectionnement [sɛksjɔn'mã], n.m. division into parts.
sectionner [sɛksjɔ'ne], v.t. to divide into sections; to cut off.
séculaire [seky'lɛːr], a. secular, coming once in a century; ancient; time-honoured.

293

séculier

séculier [seky'lje], *a.* (*fem.* **-ière**) secular, lay; temporal, worldly.—*n.m.* layman.

secundo [səgɔ̃'do], *adv.* secondly.

sécurité [sekyri'te], *n.f.* security, safety.

sédatif [seda'tif], *a.* (*fem.* **-tive**) and *n.m.* sedative.

sédentaire [sedɑ̃'tɛ:r], *a.* sedentary; settled, stationary.

sédiment [sedi'mɑ̃], *n.m.* sediment.

sédimentaire [sedimɑ̃'tɛ:r], *a.* sedimentary.

séditieusement [sedisjøz'mɑ̃], *adv.* seditiously.

séditieux [sedi'sjø], *a.* (*fem.* **-euse**) seditious; mutinous.—*n.m.* rebel, mutineer.

sédition [sedi'sjɔ̃], *n.f.* sedition, mutiny, riot.

séducteur [sedyk'tœ:r], *a.* (*fem.* **-trice**) seductive; enticing, alluring.—*n.m.* (*fem.* **-trice**) seducer, enticer.

séduction [sedyk'sjɔ̃], *n.f.* seduction; allurement; bribing.

séduire [se'dɥi:r], *v.t.* irr. (*conjug. like* CONDUIRE) to seduce; to beguile; to charm; to fascinate; to bribe.

séduisant [sedɥi'zɑ̃], *a.* seductive, alluring; fascinating; tempting.

segment [sɛg'mɑ̃], *n.m.* segment.

ségrégation [segrega'sjɔ̃], *n.f.* segregation.

seigle [sɛgl], *n.m.* rye.

seigneur [sɛ'nœ:r], *n.m.* lord; lord of the manor, squire; nobleman; *le Seigneur*, the Lord.

seigneurial [sɛnœ'rjal], *a.* (*m. pl.* **-aux**) manorial; lordly.

seigneurie [sɛnœ'ri], *n.f.* lordship; manor.

sein [sɛ̃], *n.m.* breast, bosom; (*fig.*) heart, midst; womb.

seine [sɛ:n], *n.f.* seine, (fishing-) net.

séisme [se'ism], *n.m.* earthquake.

seize [sɛ:z], *a.* and *n.m.* sixteen, sixteenth.

seizième [sɛ'zjɛm], *a.* and *n.* sixteenth.

séjour [se'ʒu:r], *n.m.* stay, abode, sojourn; place where one sojourns.

séjourner [seʒur'ne], *v.i.* to stay, to sojourn.

sel [sɛl], *n.m.* salt; (*fig.*) wit, pungency; (*pl.*) smelling-salts.

sélecteur [selɛk'tœ:r], *a.* (*fem.* **-trice**) selecting; selective.

sélection [selɛk'sjɔ̃], *n.f.* selection.

sélectivité [selɛktivi'te], *n.f.* selectivity.

sellage [sɛ'la:ʒ], *n.m.* saddling.

selle [sɛl], *n.f.* saddle; motion of the bowels.

seller [sɛ'le], *v.t.* to saddle.

sellerie [sɛl'ri], *n.f.* saddlery; harness-room.

sellette [sɛ'lɛt], *n.f.* stool of repentance; shoeblack's box; (*Naut.*) slung cradle.

sellier [sɛ'lje], *n.m.* saddler.

selon [sə'lɔ̃], *prep.* according to; *c'est selon*, that depends; *selon moi*, in my opinion; *selon que*, according as.

semailles [sə'mɑ:j], *n.f. pl.* seeds; sowing; sowing-time.

semaine [sə'mɛn], *n.f.* week; week's work; week's money.

semainier [səmɛ'nje], *n.m.* (*fem.* **-ière**) person on duty for the week.—*n.m.* (*Ind.*) time-sheet; weekly output.

sémaphore [sema'fɔ:r], *n.m.* semaphore, signal-post.

semblable [sɑ̃'blabl], *a.* like, similar, alike.—*n.* like; fellow, match, equal.—*n.m.* fellow-creature.

semblablement [sɑ̃blablə'mɑ̃], *adv.* likewise, also.

semblant [sɑ̃'blɑ̃], *n.m.* appearance, semblance, look; pretence; *faire semblant*, to pretend.

sembler [sɑ̃'ble], *v.i.* to seem, to appear.

semé [sə'me], *a.* sowed, sown; strewn (*de*).

semelle [sə'mɛl], *n.f.* sole (*of boots, shoes etc.*); foot (*of stockings*); length of a foot.

semence [sə'mɑ̃:s], *n.f.* seed; semen; (*fig.*) cause.

semer [sə'me], *v.t.* (*conjug. like* AMENER) to sow; to scatter, to strew, to sprinkle.

semestre [sə'mɛstr], *n.m.* half-year, six months.

semestriel [səmɛstri'ɛl], *a.* (*fem.* **-elle**) half-yearly.

semeur [sə'mœ:r], *n.m.* (*fem.* **-euse**) sower; (*fig.*) disseminator.

semi-circulaire [səmisirky'lɛ:r], *a.* semi-circular.

sémillance [semi'jɑ̃:s], *n.f.* sprightliness, liveliness.

sémillant [semi'jɑ̃], *a.* brisk, lively, sprightly.

semi-mensuel [səmimɑ̃'sɥɛl], *a.* (*fem.* **-elle**) fortnightly.

séminaire [semi'nɛ:r], *n.m.* seminary, theological college; specialized course.

semis [sə'mi], *n.m.* sowing; seed-bed; seedlings.

sémitique [semi'tik], *a.* Semitic.

sémitisme [semi'tism], *n.m.* Semitism.

semi-ton [səmi'tɔ̃], *n.m.* (*pl.* **-tons**) semitone.

semoir [sə'mwa:r], *n.m.* seed-bag; seed-drill.

semonce [sə'mɔ̃:s], *n.f.* rebuke, reprimand, lecture.

semoncer [səmɔ̃'se], *v.t.* (*conjug. like* COMMENCER) to reprimand, to lecture.

semoule [sə'mul], *n.f.* semolina.

sempiternel [sɛ̃pitɛr'nɛl], *a.* (*fem.* **-elle**) sempiternal, everlasting.

sénat [se'na], *n.m.* senate; senate-house.

sénateur [sena'tœ:r], *n.m.* senator.

sénatorial [senatɔ'rjal], *a.* (*m. pl.* **-aux**) senatorial.

séné [se'ne], *n.m.* senna.

seneçon [sən'sɔ̃], *n.m.* groundsel.

Sénégal [sene'gal], **le**, *m.* Senegal.

sénégalais [senega'lɛ], *a.* Senegalese.—*n.m.* (**Sénégalais**, *fem.* **-aise**) Senegalese (*person*).

Sénèque [se'nɛk], *m.* Seneca.

*__senestre** [se'nɛstr], **senestre** [sə'nɛstr], *a.* left, (*Her.*) sinister.

sénile [se'nil], *a.* senile.

sénilité [senili'te], *n.f.* senility, old age.

senne [sɛn], [SEINE].

sens [sɑ̃:s], *n.m. inv.* sense; senses, feelings; intelligence; consciousness; meaning; opinion; way, direction; *à contre-sens*, in a wrong sense; *à double sens*, with double meaning; *sens dessus dessous*, upside down; *sens interdit*, no entry.

sensation [sɑ̃sa'sjɔ̃], *n.f.* sensation, feeling.

sensationnel [sɑ̃sasjɔ'nɛl], *a.* (*fem.* **-elle**) sensational.

sensé [sɑ̃'se], *a.* sensible, intelligent.

sensément [sɑ̃se'mɑ̃], *adv.* sensibly, judiciously.

sensibilité [sɑ̃sibili'te], *n.f.* sensibility, sensitiveness, feeling; compassion.

sensible [sɑ̃'sibl], *a.* sensitive, susceptible, sympathetic; tender, sore (*skin etc.*); perceptible, noticeable, tangible.

sensiblement [sɑ̃siblə'mɑ̃], *adv.* appreciably; feelingly, deeply; obviously; considerably.

sensiblerie [sɑ̃siblə'ri], *n.f.* sentimentality; (*fam.*) sob-stuff.

sensitif [sɑ̃si'tif], *a.* (*fem.* **-tive**) sensitive; sensory.—*n.f.* (**-tive**) sensitive plant.

sensitivité [sɑ̃sitivi'te], *n.f.* sensitivity.

sensualiste [sɑ̃sɥa'list], *a.* sensual.—*n.* sensualist.

sensualité [sɑ̃sɥali'te], *n.f.* sensuality.

sensuel [sɑ̃'sɥɛl], *a.* (*fem.* **-elle**) sensual.—*n.m.* (*fem.* **-elle**) sensualist.

sensuellement [sɑ̃sɥɛl'mɑ̃], *adv.* sensually.

sentence [sɑ̃'tɑ̃:s], *n.f.* maxim; sentence, judgment, verdict.

sentencieusement [sɑ̃tɑ̃sjøz'mɑ̃], *adv.* sententiously.

sentencieux [sɑ̃tɑ̃'sjø], *a.* (*fem.* **-euse**) sententious.

senteur [sɑ̃'tœ:r], *n.f.* smell; scent, perfume; *pois de senteur,* sweet pea.

senti [sɑ̃'ti], *a.* felt, experienced.

sentier [sɑ̃'tje], *n.m.* path, footpath; *sentier battu,* beaten track.

sentiment [sɑ̃ti'mɑ̃], *n.m.* feeling; sensation; sentiment; affection, *esp.* love; perception, sense; opinion.

sentimental [sɑ̃timɑ̃'tal], *a.* (*m. pl.* **-aux**) sentimental.

sentimentalement [sɑ̃timɑ̃tal'mɑ̃], *adv.* sentimentally.

sentimentaliste [sɑ̃timɑ̃ta'list], *n.* sentimentalist.

sentimentalité [sɑ̃timɑ̃tali'te], *n.f.* sentimentality.

sentinelle [sɑ̃ti'nɛl], *n.f.* sentinel, sentry.

sentir [sɑ̃'ti:r], *v.t. irr.* to feel; to guess; to perceive; to smell; to savour of; to seem.—*v.i.* to smell. **se sentir,** *v.r.* to feel oneself, to feel; to be conscious; to feel the effects (*de*); to be perceived, felt etc.

seoir (1) [swa:r], *v.i. irr.* (*only used in pres. p.* **séant** *and p.p.* **sis**) to sit, to be sitting.

seoir (2) [swa:r], *v.i. irr.* (*pres. p.* **seyant**, *no p.p.*) to suit, to become.

Séoudite [seu'dit], [ARABIE].

séparable [sepa'rabl], *a.* separable.

séparation [separa'sjɔ̃], *n.f.* separation, parting.

séparé [sepa're], *a.* separate; distinct.

séparément [separe'mɑ̃], *adv.* separately; apart.

séparer [sepa're], *v.t.* to separate, to part; to sever. **se séparer,** *v.r.* to separate, to part; to divide.

sépia [se'pja], *n.f.* sepia.

sept [sɛt], *a.* and *n.m. inv.* seven; seventh.

septembre [sɛp'tɑ̃:br], *n.m.* September.

septénaire [sɛpte'nɛ:r], *a.* and *n.m.* septenary.

septennal [sɛpte'nal], *a.* (*m. pl.* **-aux**) septennial.

septentrion [sɛptɑ̃tri'ɔ̃], *n.m.* north.

septentrional [sɛptɑ̃trio'nal], *a.* (*m. pl.* **-aux**) north, northern.

septicémie [sɛptise'mi], *n.f.* (*Med.*) septicaemia, blood poisoning.

septième [se'tjɛm], *a.* and *n.* seventh.

septique [sɛp'tik], *a.* septic.

septuagénaire [sɛptɥaʒe'nɛ:r], *a.* and *n.* septuagenarian.

sépulcral [sepyl'kral], *a.* (*m. pl.* **-aux**) sepulchral.

sépulcre [se'pylkr], *n.m.* sepulchre.

sépulture [sepyl'ty:r], *n.f.* burial, interment; burial place, tomb.

séquelle [se'kɛl], *n.f.* (*pl.*) after-effects (*of illness*).

séquence [se'kɑ̃:s], *n.f.* sequence.

séquestration [sekɛstra'sjɔ̃], *n.f.* sequestration.

séquestre [se'kɛstr], *n.m.* sequestration; sequestrator; depository.

séquestrer [sekɛs'tre], *v.t.* to sequester, to sequestrate; to shut up illegally. **se séquestrer,** *v.r.* to sequester oneself.

sequin [sə'kɛ̃], *n.m.* sequin (*gold coin*).

sérail [se'ra:j], *n.m.* seraglio.

séraphin [sera'fɛ̃], *n.m.* seraph.

séraphique [sera'fik], *a.* seraphic.

serbe [sɛrb], *a.* Serbian.—*n.* (**Serbe**) Serb.

Serbie [sɛr'bi], **la**, *f.* Serbia.

serein [sə'rɛ̃], *a.* serene, placid, calm.—*n.m.* (*poet.*) night-dew.

sérénade [sere'nad], *n.f.* serenade.

sérénité [sereni'te], *n.f.* serenity, calmness; equanimity.

séreux [se'rø], *a.* (*fem.* **-euse**) serous, watery.

serf [sɛrf], *a.* (*fem.* **serve**) in bondage, servile.—*n.m.* (*fem.* **serve**) serf, bondsman, bondswoman.

serge [sɛrʒ], *n.f.* serge.

sergent [sɛr'ʒɑ̃], *n.m.* sergeant; *sergent de ville,* police constable.

séricicole [serisi'kɔl], *a.* silk-producing.

sériciculteur [serisikyl'tœ:r], *n.m.* silk-grower.

sériciculture [serisikyl'ty:r], *n.f.* silk-culture.

série [se'ri], *n.f.* series; succession; run; (*Spt.*) heat; *fabrication en série,* mass-production.

sérieusement [serjøz'mɑ̃], *adv.* seriously, gravely.

sérieux [se'rjø], *a.* (*fem.* **-euse**) serious, grave; earnest; real, true.—*n.m.* seriousness, importance, gravity.

serin [sə'rɛ̃], *n.m.* canary; (*fig.*) duffer, fool.

seriner [səri'ne], *v.t.* to din (*something*) into someone.

seringue [sə'rɛ̃:g], *n.f.* syringe, squirt.

seringuer [sərɛ̃'ge], *v.t.* to syringe, to squirt; to inject.

serment [sɛr'mɑ̃], *n.m.* oath, promise, solemn declaration; (*pl.*) swearing.

sermon [sɛr'mɔ̃], *n.m.* sermon; lecture.

sermonner [sɛrmɔ'ne], *v.t., v.i.* to sermonize, to lecture, to reprimand.

sermonneur [sɛrmɔ'nœ:r], *n.m.* (*fem.* **-euse**) sermonizer, preacher, fault-finder.

sérosité [serozi'te], *n.f.* serosity, wateriness.

serpe [sɛrp], *n.f.* bill-hook.

serpent [sɛr'pɑ̃], *n.m.* serpent, snake; *serpent à sonnettes,* rattlesnake.

serpenter [sɛrpɑ̃'te], *v.i.* to meander, to wind.

serpentin [sɛrpɑ̃'tɛ̃], *a.* serpentine.—*n.m.* paper streamer.

serpette [sɛr'pɛt], *n.f.* pruning-knife.

serpolet [sɛrpɔ'lɛ], *n.m.* wild thyme.

serrage [sɛ'ra:ʒ], *n.m.* tightening, pressing.

295

serre

serre [sɛːr], *n.f.* squeeze, pressure; talon, claw (*of birds*); clip; hot-house, greenhouse, conservatory.

serré [sɛ're], *a.* close; compact; tight; clenched; (*fam.*) close-fisted.

serre-frein(s) [sɛr'frɛ̃], *n.m. inv.* (*Rail.*) brakesman.

serre-livres [sɛːr'livr], *n.m. inv.* book-ends.

serrement [sɛr'mɑ̃], *n.m.* pressing, squeezing; **serrement de cœur**, pang (*of grief*); **serrement de main**, handshake.

serre-papiers [sɛrpa'pje], *n.m. inv.* paper-clip; file (*for papers*); set of pigeon-holes (*for papers*).

serrer [sɛ're], *v.t.* to press, to squeeze; to fasten, to lock; to grip; to condense, to put close together; to press; to close (*the ranks*); to clench (*one's fist, teeth etc.*). **se serrer**, *v.r.* to press each other close; to sit, lie *or* stand close together; to stint oneself.

serre-tête [sɛr'tɛːt], *n.m. inv.* headband; crash-helmet.

serrure [sɛ'ryːr], *n.f.* lock.

serrurier [sɛry'rje], *n.m.* locksmith.

sérum [se'rom], *n.m.* serum.

servage [sɛr'vaːʒ], *n.m.* servitude, bondage.

servant [sɛr'vɑ̃], *a.m.* serving; in waiting.—*n.m.* (*Artill.*) gunner.

servante [sɛr'vɑ̃ːt], *n.f.* maid-servant; servant-girl; dinner-wagon.

serveur [sɛr'vœːr], *n.m.* (*fem.* **-euse**) (*Ten.*) server; waiter, barman; (*Cards*) dealer.

serviable [sɛr'vjabl], *a.* willing, obliging.

service [sɛr'vis], *n.m.* service; attendance; duty; function; divine service.

serviette [sɛr'vjɛt], *n.f.* napkin, serviette; towel; briefcase.

servile [sɛr'vil], *a.* servile, menial; slavish.

servilement [sɛrvil'mɑ̃], *adv.* servilely, slavishly.

servir [sɛr'viːr], *v.t. irr.* (*conjug. like* SENTIR) to serve, to attend; to serve up; to be of service to; to assist.—*v.i.* to serve, to be of use; to serve up a meal. **se servir**, *v.r.* to serve oneself; to be served up (*of dishes*); **servez-vous**, help yourself.

serviteur [sɛrvi'tœːr], *n.m.* servant, man-servant.

servitude [sɛrvi'tyd], *n.f.* servitude, slavery.

ses [sɛ], [SON].

session [sɛ'sjɔ̃], *n.f.* session, sitting; term (*of law courts etc.*).

seuil [sœːj], *n.m.* threshold; door-step; shelf (*of ocean bed*).

seul [sœl], *a.* alone; single, only, sole; mere, bare.—*n.m.* one only, the only one.

seulement [sœl'mɑ̃], *adv.* only; but; solely, merely.

sève [sɛːv], *n.f.* sap; (*fig.*) pith, vigour, strength.

sévère [se'vɛːr], *a.* severe, stern, austere; strict.

sévèrement [sevɛr'mɑ̃], *adv.* severely, sternly; strictly.

sévérité [severi'te], *n.f.* severity; strictness; purity.

séveux [se'vø], *a.* (*fem.* **-euse**) (*Bot.*) sappy; (*fig.*) vigorous.

sévices [se'vis], *n.m. pl.* (*Law*) cruelty, ill-treatment.

sévir [se'viːr], *v.i.* to deal severely (*contre*); to rage (*of war etc.*).

sevrage [sə'vraːʒ], *n.m.* weaning.

sevrer [sə'vre], *v.t.* (*conjug. like* AMENER) to wean; (*fig.*) to deprive (*de*).

sexagénaire [sɛksaʒe'nɛːr], *a.* and *n.* sexagenarian.

sexe [sɛks], *n.m.* sex.

sextant [sɛks'tɑ̃], *n.m.* sextant.

sextuple [sɛks'typl], *a.* and *n.m.* sextuple, six-fold.

sexualité [sɛksɥali'te], *n.f.* sexuality.

sexuel [sɛk'sɥel], *a.* (*fem.* **-elle**) sexual.

shampooing [ʃɑ̃'pwɛ̃], *n.m.* shampoo, hair-wash.

shérif [ʃe'rif], *n.m.* sheriff.

short [ʃɔrt], *n.m.* (*Cost.*) shorts.

shunt [ʃœ̃t], *n.m.* (*Elec.*) shunt.

shunter [ʃœ̃'te], *v.t.* to shunt.

si (1) [si], *conj.* if; whether; supposing, what if.

si (2) [si], *adv.* so, so much, however much; yes.

si (3) [si], *n.m. inv.* (*Mus.*) si; the note B.

Siam [sjam], **le**, *m.* Thailand, Siam.

siamois [sja'mwa], *a.* Siamese.—*n.m.* Siamese (*language*); (**Siamois**, *fem.* **-oise**) Siamese (*person*).

Sibérie [sibe'ri], **la**, *f.* Siberia.

sibérien [sibe'rjɛ̃], *a.* (*fem.* **-enne**) Siberian.—*n.m.* (**Sibérien**, *fem.* **-enne**) Siberian (*person*).

sibilant [sibi'lɑ̃], *a.* sibilant, hissing.

siccatif [sika'tif], *a.* (*fem.* **-tive**) siccative, drying.

Sicile [si'sil], **la**, *f.* Sicily.

sicilien [sisi'ljɛ̃], *a.* (*fem.* **-enne**) Sicilian.—*n.m.* (**Sicilien**, *fem.* **-enne**) Sicilian (*person*).

sidérurgie [sideryr'ʒi], *n.f.* iron and steel industry.

siècle [sjɛkl], *n.m.* century; age, period.

siège [sjɛːʒ], *n.m.* seat; bench (*of a court of justice*); headquarters (*of society etc.*); (*Eccles.*) see; siege.

siéger [sje'ʒe], *v.i.* (*conjug. like* ASSIÉGER) to sit (*of assemblies, courts etc.*); to hold one's see (*of bishops*); to be seated; (*fig.*) to lie (*of a thing*); to have one's headquarters (*of business, society*).

sien [sjɛ̃], *pron. poss. 3rd pers. sing.* (*fem.* **sienne**) his, hers, its, one's.—*n.m.* one's own (*property, work etc.*).

Sienne [sjɛn], *f.* Sienna.

Sierra-Leone [sjɛrale'on], **le**, *m.* Sierra Leone.

sieste [sjɛst], *n.f.* siesta.

sifflant [si'flɑ̃], *a.* hissing; whistling; wheezing.

sifflement [siflə'mɑ̃], *n.m.* hissing, hiss; whistling, whistle; whizzing; wheezing.

siffler [si'fle], *v.t.* to whistle; to hiss.—*v.i.* to hiss; to whistle; to whizz; to wheeze.

sifflet [si'flɛ], *n.m.* whistle (*instrument and sound*); catcall; hiss; (*colloq.*) windpipe.

siffleur [si'flœːr], *a.* (*fem.* **-euse**) whistling, piping (*of birds*); wheezing (*of horses*).—*n.m.* (*fem.* **-euse**) whistler; hisser.

sigle [sigl], *n.m.* initial letter; group of initial letters used as abbreviation of phrase (*U.N. etc.*).

signal [si'ɲal], *n.m.* (*pl.* **-aux**) signal.

signalé [siɲa'le], *a.* signal, remarkable, conspicuous.

signalement [siɲal'mɑ̃], *n.m.* description (*of a man etc.*), particulars.

signaler [siɲa'le], *v.t.* to signal; to give the description of; to point out, to mark out; to signalize. **se signaler**, *v.r.* to signalize *or* distinguish oneself.

signaleur [siɲa'lœːr], *n.m.* signalman; (*Mil.*) signaller.

signalisateur [siɲaliza'tœːr], *n.m.* traffic indicator, trafficator.

signataire [siɲa'tɛːr], *n.* signer, subscriber, signatory.

signature [siɲa'tyːr], *n.f.* signature; signing.

signe [siɲ], *n.m.* sign; mark, indication; badge; omen; *faire signe de la main*, to beckon; *signe de la tête*, nod.

signer [si'ɲe], *v.t., v.i.* to sign, to subscribe. **se signer**, *v.r.* to cross oneself.

signet [si'ɲɛ], *n.m.* signet; book-mark; signet-ring.

significatif [siɲifika'tif], *a.* (*fem.* **-tive**) significant.

signification [siɲifika'sjɔ̃], *n.f.* signification, meaning; (*Law*) legal notice.

significativement [siɲifikativ'mã], *adv.* significantly.

signifier [siɲi'fje], *v.t.* to signify, to mean; to notify, to intimate; (*Law*) to serve.

silence [si'lãːs], *n.m.* silence; stillness; secrecy; (*Mus.*) rest.

silencieusement [silãsjøz'mã], *adv.* silently.

silencieux [silã'sjø], *a.* (*fem.* **-euse**) silent; still.—*n.m.* (*Motor.*) silencer.

silex [si'lɛks], *n.m.* silex, flint.

silhouette [si'lwɛt], *n.f.* silhouette; outline, profile.

silice [si'lis], *n.f.* (*Chem.*) silica, flint.

sillage [si'jaːʒ], *n.m.* wake, wash; slip-stream.

sillon [si'jɔ̃], *n.m.* furrow made by plough; seed-drill; (*fig.*) track, wake (*of a ship etc.*); wrinkle.

sillonner [sijo'ne], *v.t.* to furrow; to streak.

silo [si'lo], *n.m.* silo (*pit* or *tower for preserving fodder*).

silotage [silo'taːʒ], *n.m.* silage.

simagrée [sima'gre], *n.f.* pretence, affectation; (*pl.*) fuss.

simiesque [si'mjɛsk], *a.* ape-like, apish (*face*).

similaire [simi'lɛːr], *a.* similar.

similarité [similari'te], *n.f.* similarity, likeness.

similitude [simili'tyd], *n.f.* similitude, resemblance; simile.

simoun [si'muːn], *n.m.* simoom, simoon.

simple [sɛ̃ːpl], *a.* simple, single; easy; only, mere; common, plain; private (*soldier*); simple-minded, silly; natural.—*n.m.* that which is simple; (*Ten.*) singles; *simple dames*, women's singles.

simplement [sɛ̃plə'mã], *adv.* simply.

simplet [sɛ̃'plɛ], *a.* (*fem.* **-ette**) naïve, simple; (*fam.*) a bit daft; (*Am.*) green.—*n.m.* (*fem.* **-ette**) simpleton, silly.

simplicité [sɛ̃plisi'te], *n.f.* simplicity; artlessness; silliness.

simplification [sɛ̃plifika'sjɔ̃], *n.f.* simplification.

simplifier [sɛ̃pli'fje], *v.t.* to simplify.

simulacre [simy'lakr], *n.m.* image; phantom; semblance, sham.

simulé [simy'le], *a.* feigned, sham.

simuler [simy'le], *v.t.* to feign, to sham.

simultané [simylta'ne], *a.* simultaneous.

simultanément [simyltane'mã], *adv.* simultaneously.

sincère [sɛ̃'sɛːr], *a.* sincere, frank; honest.

sincèrement [sɛ̃sɛr'mã], *adv.* sincerely, honestly.

sincérité [sɛ̃seri'te], *n.f.* sincerity.

sinécure [sine'kyːr], *n.f.* sinecure.

Singapour [sɛ̃ga'puːr], *m.* Singapore.

singe [sɛ̃ːʒ], *n.m.* ape, monkey; hoist; (*Mil. slang*) bully beef.

singer [sɛ̃'ʒe], *v.t.* (*conjug. like* MANGER) to ape, to mimic.

singerie [sɛ̃'ʒri], *n.f.* monkey-house; grimace; antic; mimicry.

singeur [sɛ̃'ʒœːr], *a.* (*fem.* **-euse**) aping, mimicking.—*n.m.* (*fem.* **-euse**) ape, mimic.

singulariser [sɛ̃gylari'ze], *v.t.* to singularize; to make conspicuous. **se singulariser**, *v.r.* to make oneself conspicuous.

singularité [sɛ̃gylari'te], *n.f.* singularity; peculiarity.

singulier [sɛ̃gy'lje], *a.* (*fem.* **-ière**) singular; peculiar; odd.—*n.m.* (*Gram.*) singular.

singulièrement [sɛ̃gyljɛr'mã], *adv.* singularly, oddly.

sinistre [si'nistr], *a.* sinister; dismal; evil.—*n.m.* disaster, calamity.

sinistré [sinis'tre], *a.* affected by disaster (*shipwreck, fire etc.*).—*n.m.* (*fem.* **-ée**) victim of disaster; casualty.

sinon [si'nɔ̃], *conj.* otherwise, if not, else; except, unless; *sinon que*, except that.

sinueux [si'nɥø], *a.* (*fem.* **-euse**) sinuous, winding.

sinuosité [sinɥozi'te], *n.f.* sinuosity, winding.

sinus [si'nyːs], *n.m. inv.* sine; (*Anat.*) sinus.

sinusite [siny'zit], *n.f.* sinusitis.

siphon [si'fɔ̃], *n.m.* siphon; (*Naut.*) water-spout.

sire [siːr], *n.m.* sire (*title of kings and emperors*).

sirène [si'rɛn], *n.f.* siren, mermaid; hooter, fog-horn.

sirocco [siro'ko], *n.m.* sirocco.

sirop [si'ro], *n.m.* syrup.

siroter [siro'te], *v.t.* to sip; (*pop.*) to tipple.

sirupeux [siry'pø], *a.* (*fem.* **-euse**) syrupy.

sis [si], *a.* seated, situated (SEOIR (I)].

Sisyphe [si'zif], *m.* Sisyphus.

site [sit], *n.m.* site (*situation with regard to scenery etc.*); *un beau site*, a beauty spot.

sitôt [si'to], *adv.* so soon, as soon; *sitôt dit, sitôt fait*, no sooner said than done; *sitôt que*, as soon as.

situation [sitɥa'sjɔ̃], *n.f.* situation, site, position; state of affairs, predicament.

situé [si'tɥe], *a.* situated, lying.

situer [si'tɥe], *v.t.* to place.

six [si *before a consonant*, siz *before a vowel* sis *at the end of a sentence*], *a.* six; sixth.— [sis], *n.m.* six; sixth; sixth day.

sixième [si'zjɛm], *a.* and *n.* sixth.—*n.m.* sixth (part); sixth floor.—*n.f.* (*in France*) sixth class, (*in England*) first form (*of upper school*).

ski [ski], *n.m.* ski; *faire du ski*, to go in for ski-ing; *ski nautique*, water-ski-ing.

slave [slav], *a.* Slav, Slavonic.—*n.* (**Slave**) Slav (*person*).

slip [slip], *n.m.* (*Cost.*) trunks, briefs; *slip de bain*, (swimming) trunks.

slovène

slovène [slɔ'vɛn], *a.* Slovenian.—*n.* (**Slovène**) Slovene.

smoking [smɔ'kiŋ], *n.m.* dinner-jacket.

snob [snɔb], *a.* (*fam.*) swanky.—*n.m.* person who tries to be always in the swim.

snobisme [snɔ'bism], *n.m.* affected up-to-dateness.

sobre [sɔbr], *a.* (*of persons*) abstemious, temperate, moderate; (*of colours, style etc.*) sober, quiet, unadorned.

sobrement [sɔbrə'mã], *adv.* soberly, moderately.

sobriété [sɔbrie'te], *n.f.* sobriety; abstemiousness (*in food and drink*).

sobriquet [sɔbri'kɛ], *n.m.* nickname.

soc [sɔk], *n.m.* ploughshare.

sociabilité [sɔsjabili'te], *n.f.* sociability, good fellowship.

sociable [sɔ'sjabl], *a.* sociable, companionable.

sociablement [sɔsjablə'mã], *adv.* sociably.

social [sɔ'sjal], *a.* (*m. pl.* **-aux**) social; *siège social*, registered office; head office.

socialement [sɔsjal'mã], *adv.* socially.

socialisme [sɔsja'lism], *n.m.* socialism.

socialiste [sɔsja'list], *a.* and *n.* socialist.

sociétaire [sɔsje'tɛːr], *n.* associate, member; partner; shareholder.

société [sɔsje'te], *n.f.* society, association; community; firm; partnership; *société anonyme*, private company.

sociologie [sɔsjɔlɔ'ʒi], *n.f.* sociology.

sociologiste [sɔsjɔlɔ'ʒist], **sociologue** [sɔsjɔ'lɔg], *n.* sociologist.

socle [sɔkl], *n.m.* socle, pedestal, stand, base.

socque [sɔk], *n.m.* clog, patten.

Socrate [sɔ'krat], *m.* Socrates.

sœur [sœːr], *n.f.* sister; nun.

sœurette [sœ'rɛt], *n.f.* (*colloq.*) little sister, sis(s).

sofa [sɔ'fa], *n.m.* sofa, settee.

soi [swa], **soi-même** [swa'mɛm], *impers. pron. 3rd pers. sing.* oneself, itself; self.

soi-disant [swadi'zã], *a. inv.* self-styled, would-be, so-called.

soie [swa], *n.f.* silk; silken hair; bristle (*of hogs*); *papier de soie*, tissue paper.

soierie [swa'ri], *n.f.* silks, silk goods; silk-trade; silk-factory.

soif [swaf], *n.f.* thirst; *avoir soif*, to be thirsty.

soigné [swa'ne], *a.* carefully done; neat, smart; (*colloq.*) first-rate.

soigner [swa'ne], *v.t.* to take care of, to look after; to nurse. **se soigner**, *v.r.* to take care of oneself.

soigneusement [swaɲøz'mã], *adv.* carefully.

soigneux [swa'nø], *a.* (*fem.* **-euse**) careful; solicitous.

soi-même [sɔɪ].

soin [swɛ̃], *n.m.* care; attendance; (*pl.*) attentions, pains, trouble.

soir [swaːr], *n.m.* evening; night.

soirée [swa're], *n.f.* evening (*duration*); evening party.

soit [swat, swa], *adv.* be it so, well and good, granted; let us say.—*conj.* either, or; whether.

soixantaine [swasã'tɛn], *n.f.* about sixty.

soixante [swa'sãːt], *a.* and *n.m.* sixty.

soixantième [swasã'tjɛːm], *a.* and *n.* sixtieth.

298

sol [sɔl], *n.m.* ground; soil; earth.

solaire [sɔ'lɛːr], *a.* solar.

soldat [sɔl'da], *n.m.* soldier; *simple soldat*, private; *les simples soldats*, the rank and file.

soldatesque [sɔlda'tɛsk], *n.f.* (*usu. pej.*) soldiery.

solde (1) [sɔld], *n.f.* (*Mil.*) pay.

solde (2) [sɔld], *n.m.* balance (*between debit and credit*); clearance sale; (*pl.*) sale bargains, reductions.

solder (1) [sɔl'de], *v.t.* to pay (*soldiers*); to have in one's pay.

solder (2) [sɔl'de], *v.t.* to settle (*an account*); to sell off, to clear.

sole [sɔl], *n.f.* sole (*of animal's foot*); sole (*fish*).

solécisme [sɔle'sism], *n.m.* solecism.

soleil [sɔ'lɛj], *n.m.* sun; sunshine; (*fig.*) star; catherine-wheel (*firework*); sunflower.

solennel [sɔla'nɛl], *a.* (*fem.* **-elle**) solemn.

solennellement [sɔlanɛl'mã], *adv.* solemnly.

solenniser [sɔlani'ze], *v.t.* to solemnize.

solennité [sɔlani'te], *n.f.* solemnity.

solénoïde [sɔlenɔ'id], *n.m.* solenoid.

solidaire [sɔli'dɛːr], *a.* jointly and separately liable.

solidairement [sɔlidɛr'mã], *adv.* jointly and severally.

solidariser [sɔlidari'ze], *v.t.* to render jointly liable.

solidarité [sɔlidari'te], *n.f.* joint and separate liability; solidarity, fellowship.

solide [sɔ'lid], *a.* solid; strong; substantial; sound; reliable.—*n.m.* solid, solid body.

solidement [sɔlid'mã], *adv.* solidly; firmly; soundly.

solidification [sɔlidifika'sjõ], *n.f.* solidification.

solidifier [sɔlidi'fje], *v.t.* and **se solidifier**, *v.r.* to solidify.

solidité [sɔlidi'te], *n.f.* solidity; strength; stability; soundness.

soliloque [sɔli'lɔk], *n.m.* soliloquy.

soliste [sɔ'list], *a.* solo.—*n.* soloist.

solitaire [sɔli'tɛːr], *a.* solitary, single, alone; lonely, desert.—*n.m.* lonely person, recluse; solitaire (*diamond or game*).

solitairement [sɔlitɛr'mã], *adv.* solitarily, alone.

solitude [sɔli'tyd], *n.f.* solitude, loneliness; desert.

solive [sɔ'liːv], *n.f.* joist.

soliveau [sɔli'vo], *n.m.* (*pl.* **-eaux**) small joist.

sollicitation [sɔlisita'sjõ], *n.f.* solicitation; pull (*of magnet*).

solliciter [sɔlisi'te], *v.t.* to incite; to solicit, to entreat; to call into action; to attract (*of magnet*).

sollicitude [sɔlisi'tyd], *n.f.* solicitude, care; concern.

solo [sɔ'lo], *a. inv.* solo.—*n.m.* (*pl.* **solos** or **soli**) solo.

solstice [sɔls'tis], *n.m.* solstice.

solubilité [sɔlybili'te], *n.f.* solubility.

soluble [sɔ'lybl], *a.* soluble.

solution [sɔly'sjõ], *n.f.* solution; resolution; (*Law*) discharge; *solution de continuité*, interruption, break, fault.

solvabilité [sɔlvabili'te], *n.f.* solvency.

solvable [sɔl'vabl], *a.* solvent.

solvant [sɔl'vã], *n.m.* solvent.

somali [sɔmaˈli], *a.* Somali.—*n.m.* Somali (*language*).—*n.* (**Somali**) Somali (*person*); *Côte Française des Somalis*, French Somaliland.

Somalie [sɔmaˈli], **la**, *f.* Somalia, Somaliland.

sombre [sɔ̃:br], *a.* dark, sombre, gloomy; dim; overcast; melancholy.

sombrer [sɔ̃ˈbre], *v.i.* (*Naut.*) to founder.

sombrero [sɔ̃breˈro], *n.m.* sombrero.

sommaire [sɔˈmɛ:r], *a.* summary, concise; scanty.—*n.m.* summary, abstract.

sommairement [sɔmɛrˈmɑ̃], *adv.* summarily; hastily.

sommation [sɔmaˈsjɔ̃], *n.f.* summons, demand; (*Mil.*) challenge.

somme [sɔm], *n.f.* sum, total; amount; summary; burden.—*n.m.* nap; *faire un somme*, to have forty winks.

sommeil [sɔˈmɛ:j], *n.m.* sleep; *avoir sommeil*, to be sleepy.

sommeiller [sɔmɛˈje], *v.i.* to slumber; to doze.

sommelier [sɔmɛˈlje], *n.m.* butler, cellarman, wine-waiter.

sommellerie [sɔmɛlˈri], *n.f.* butler's pantry.

sommer [sɔˈme], *v.t.* to summon, to call upon; to sum up.

sommet [sɔˈmɛ], *n.m.* top, summit; acme; crown (*of the head etc.*).

sommier (1) [sɔˈmje], *n.m.* pack-horse; box-mattress; wind-chest (*of organ*); (*Arch.*) cross-beam.

sommier (2) [sɔˈmje], *n.m.* cash-book, register.

sommité [sɔmiˈte], *n.f.* summit, top; head, principal; chief point; prominent person.

somnambule [sɔmnɑ̃ˈbyl], *a.* somnambulistic.—*n.* sleepwalker.

somnambulisme [sɔmnɑ̃byˈlism], *n.m.* somnambulism, sleep-walking.

somnolence [sɔmnɔˈlɑ̃:s], *n.f.* somnolence.

somnolent [sɔmnɔˈlɑ̃], *a.* somnolent, sleepy.

somptuaire [sɔ̃pˈtɥɛ:r], *a.* sumptuary.

somptueusement [sɔ̃ptɥøzˈmɑ̃], *adv.* sumptuously.

somptueux [sɔ̃pˈtɥø], *a.* (*fem.* **-euse**) sumptuous; magnificent.

somptuosité [sɔ̃ptɥoziˈte], *n.f.* sumptuousness.

son (1) [sɔ̃], *a.* (*fem.* **sa**, *pl.* **ses**) his, her, its; one's.

son (2) [sɔ̃], *n.m.* sound.

son (3) [sɔ̃], *n.m.* bran; *tache de son*, freckle.

sonate [sɔˈnat], *n.f.* sonata.

sondage [sɔ̃ˈda:ʒ], *n.m.* sounding; (*Mining*) boring.

sonde [sɔ̃:d], *n.f.* sounding-line, lead; (*Surg. etc.*) probe; (*Mining*) drill, boring machine.

sonder [sɔ̃ˈde], *v.t.* to sound; to taste; to search, to fathom, to investigate.

sondeur [sɔ̃ˈdœ:r], *n.m.* (*Naut.*) leadsman; (*Mining*) driller, borer.

songe [sɔ̃:ʒ], *n.m.* dream; dreaming.

songe-creux [sɔ̃ʒˈkrø], *n.m. inv.* dreamer, visionary.

songer [sɔ̃ˈʒe], *v.t.* (*conjug. like* MANGER) to dream; (*fig.*) to imagine; to think of.—*v.i.* to dream; (*fig.*) to day-dream; to think; to mean, to intend, to propose.

songerie [sɔ̃ˈʒri], *n.f.* dreaming; musing; day-dreaming.

songeur [sɔ̃ˈʒœ:r], *a.* (*fem.* **-euse**) thoughtful, dreamy.—*n.m.* (*fem.* **-euse**) dreamer.

sonique [sɔˈnik], *a.* sonic.

sonnant [sɔˈnɑ̃], *a.* sounding; sonorous.

sonner [sɔˈne], *v.t., v.i.* to sound; to ring, to toll, to strike (*of clocks etc.*).

sonnerie [sɔnˈri], *n.f.* ring, ringing (*of bells*); bells, chimes; striking part (*of a clock etc.*); (*Mil.*) bugle-call.

sonnet [sɔˈne], *n.m.* sonnet.

sonnette [sɔˈnɛt], *n.f.* small bell; hand-bell.

sonneur [sɔˈnœ:r], *n.m.* bell-ringer.

sonore [sɔˈnɔ:r], *a.* resonant; clear; *ondes sonores*, sound waves.

sonorité [sɔnɔriˈte], *n.f.* resonance.

sophisme [sɔˈfism], *n.m.* sophism, fallacy.

sophiste [sɔˈfist], *a.* sophistical.—*n.* sophist.

sophistiqué [sɔfistiˈke], *a.* sophisticated; affected.

soporifique [sɔpɔriˈfik], *a.* soporific; (*fig.*) tedious.—*n.m.* soporific.

soprano [sɔpraˈno], *n.* (*pl.* **soprani** or **sopranos**) soprano, treble.

sorbet [sɔrˈbe], *n.m.* sherbet.

sorbier [sɔrˈbje], *n.m.* mountain-ash, rowan tree.

sorcellerie [sɔrsɛlˈri], *n.f.* sorcery, witchcraft.

sorcier [sɔrˈsje], *n.m.* (*fem.* **-ière**) sorcerer, wizard, sorceress, witch.

sordide [sɔrˈdid], *a.* sordid, filthy; mean, vile.

sordidement [sɔrdidˈmɑ̃], *adv.* sordidly.

Sorlingues [sɔrˈlɛ̃:g], **les**, *f. pl.* the Scilly Isles.

sornette [sɔrˈnɛt], *n.f.* (*usu. in pl.*) idle talk, small talk.

sort [sɔ:r], *n.m.* fate, destiny; lot; condition; fortune; chance; spell, charm; *au sort*, by lot; *le sort en est jeté*, the die is cast; *tirer au sort*, to draw lots; to toss.

sortable [sɔrˈtabl], *a.* suitable.

sortablement [sɔrtabləˈmɑ̃], *adv.* suitably.

sortant [sɔrˈtɑ̃], *a.* outgoing, retiring, leaving (*office etc.*); drawn (*of numbers in lotteries*).—*n.m.* person going out; person leaving office etc.; *les entrants et les sortants*, the incomers and outgoers.

sorte [sɔrt], *n.f.* sort, kind, species; manner, way; *de la sorte*, thus, in that way; *de sorte que* or *en sorte que*, so that.

sortie [sɔrˈti], *n.f.* going or coming out; exit, way out; outing, trip; exportation; sortie; (*colloq.*) outburst, attack; *droit de sortie*, export duty; *jour de sortie*, day out.

sortilège [sɔrtiˈlɛ:ʒ], *n.m.* sorcery, magic; spell, charm.

sortir [sɔrˈti:r], *v.t. irr.* (*conjug. like* SENTIR *with aux.* AVOIR) to bring out, to take out; to pull out, to extricate.—*v.i.* (*with aux.* ÊTRE) to go out, to come out, to come forth, to emerge; to make one's exit; to leave, to depart; to swerve; to wander (*from a subject*); to proceed, to result; to spring, to come up; to sally forth; to burst forth; to escape; (*Paint. etc.*) to stand out; to be in relief.—*n.m.* going out, leaving; rising.

sosie [sɔˈzi], *n.m.* double, counterpart.

sot [so], *a.* (*fem.* **sotte**) stupid, silly, foolish; (*fig.*) embarrassed, sheepish.—*n.m.* (*fem.* **sotte**) fool, ass, idiot.

sottement [sɔtˈmɑ̃], *adv.* stupidly; foolishly.

299

sottise [sɔ'tiːz], *n.f.* silliness, folly; foolish trick, nonsense; insult; (*pl.*) abusive language.

sou [su], *n.m.* sou (*copper coin worth 5 centimes*); copper, halfpenny.

soubresaut [subrə'so], *n.m.* sudden leap *or* bound; plunge (*of a horse*); start; jolt.

soubresauter [subrə'sote], *v.i.* to start, to jump, to plunge.

soubrette [su'brɛt], *n.f.* lady's maid, waiting-woman.

souche [suʃ], *n.f.* stump, stock, stub, stem; (*fig.*) blockhead; founder (*of a family etc.*); origin; chimney-stack; counterfoil; tally; *faire souche*, to found a family.

souci (1) [su'si], *n.m.* care, anxiety.

souci (2) [su'si], *n.m.* (*Bot.*) marigold.

soucier (se) [səsu'sje], *v.r.* to care, to mind, to be concerned, to be anxious (*de*).

soucieux [su'sjø], *a.* (*fem.* **-euse**) anxious, full of care; pensive, thoughtful.

soucoupe [su'kup], *n.f.* saucer.

soudage [su'daːʒ], *n.m.* soldering, welding; (*fig.*) reconciliation.

soudain [su'dɛ̃], *a.* sudden, unexpected.—*adv.* suddenly.

soudainement [sudɛn'mɑ̃], *adv.* suddenly, all of a sudden.

soudaineté [sudɛn'te], *n.f.* suddenness.

Soudan [su'dɑ̃], **le**, *n.m.* the Sudan.

soudanais [suda'nɛ], *a.* Sudanese.—*n.m.* (**Soudanais**, *fem.* **-aise**) Sudanese (*person*).

soude [sud], *n.f.* soda.

souder [su'de], *v.t.* to solder, to braze, to weld; (*fig.*) to unite. **se souder**, *v.r.* to be soldered *or* welded; to knit (*of bones*).

soudeur [su'dœːr], *n.m.* welder.

soudoyer [sudwa'je], *v.t.* (*conjug. like* EMPLOYER) to keep in one's pay; to hire; to bribe.

soudure [su'dyːr], *n.f.* solder; soldering, welding; *soudure autogène*, oxyacetylene welding.

soue [su], *n.f.* pigsty.

soufflage [su'flaːʒ], *n.m.* glass-blowing.

soufflant [su'flɑ̃], *a.* blowing.

souffle [sufl], *n.m.* breath, breathing; puff (*of wind etc.*); (*fig.*) inspiration, influence.

soufflé [su'fle], *a.* soufflé (*of pastry etc.*); exaggerated (*reputation*).—*n.m.* soufflé (*light dish*).

soufflement [suflə'mɑ̃], *n.m.* blowing.

souffler [su'fle], *v.t.* to blow, to blow out; to inflate; to whisper; (*Theat.*) to prompt; to huff (*at draughts*); (*Naut.*) to sheathe.—*v.i.* to blow, to breathe; to pant, to puff; (*fig.*) to breathe a word etc.; *souffler aux oreilles de quelqu'un*, to whisper in someone's ear.

soufflerie [suflə'ri], *n.f.* bellows (*of an organ*); wind-tunnel.

soufflet [su'flɛ], *n.m.* pair of bellows; box on the ear, slap in the face; affront.

souffleter [sufla'te], *v.t.* (*conjug. like* APPELER) to slap in the face, to box the ears of; (*fig.*) to insult.

souffleur [su'flœːr], *a.* (*fem.* **-euse**) blowing, puffing.—*n.m.* (*fem.* **-euse**) blower; (*Theat.*) prompter.—(*C*) *n.f.* (**-euse**) snow blower.

souffrance [su'frɑ̃ːs], *n.f.* suffering, pain; suspense; (*Law*) sufferance; *en souffrance*, awaiting delivery; in abeyance.

souffrant [su'frɑ̃], *a.* suffering; unwell; long-suffering.

souffre-douleur [sufrədu'lœːr], *n.m. inv.* drudge; butt, laughing-stock.

souffreteux [sufrə'tø], *a.* (*fem.* **-euse**) needy; poorly, sickly, weakly.

souffrir [su'friːr], *v.t. irr.* (*conjug. like* OUVRIR) to suffer; to bear, to endure, to undergo, to sustain; to stand, to tolerate; to admit of; *faire souffrir*, to pain, to grieve.—*v.i.* to suffer, to be in pain; to be pained; to be injured.

soufre [sufr], *n.m.* sulphur, brimstone.

souhait [swe], *n.m.* wish, desire; *à souhait*, to one's heart's content, as one would have it.

souhaitable [swɛ'tabl], *a.* desirable.

souhaiter [swɛ'te], *v.t.* to desire, to wish for.

souiller [su'je], *v.t.* to soil, to dirty; to stain, to blemish, to sully; to defile. **se souiller**, *v.r.* to soil oneself, to get dirty; to tarnish one's good name.

souillon [su'jɔ̃], *n.* sloven, slut; scullion.

souillure [su'jyːr], *n.f.* spot, stain; blot, blemish; contamination.

soûl *or* **saoul** [su], *a.* glutted, surfeited (*de*); drunk; satiated, heartily sick (*de*).—*n.m.* fill, bellyful; *tout son soûl*, to one's heart's content.

soulagement [sulaʒ'mɑ̃], *n.m.* relief, alleviation; solace, help.

soulager [sula'ʒe], *v.t.* (*conjug. like* MANGER) to relieve, to ease; to alleviate, to allay; to soothe, to comfort. **se soulager**, *v.r.* to relieve oneself; to help each other.

soûlard [su'laːr], *a.* drunken.—*n.m.* (*fem.* **-e**) drunkard, sot.

soûler [su'le], *v.t.* to fill, to glut; to make drunk. **se soûler**, *v.r.* to gorge; to get drunk.

soûlerie [sul'ri], *n.f.* drinking bout, 'binge'.

soulèvement [sulɛv'mɑ̃], *n.m.* heaving; swelling (*of sea waves etc.*); rising (*of the stomach*); (*fig.*) insurrection, revolt.

soulever [sul've], *v.t.* (*conjug. like* AMENER) to raise, to lift up; to heave; to take up; (*fig.*) to excite, to stir up; to sicken; to rouse the indignation of. **se soulever**, *v.r.* to raise oneself, to rise; to heave, to swell; to rise in insurrection.

soulier [su'lje], *n.m.* shoe; *être dans ses petits souliers*, to be ill at ease; *souliers ferrés*, hobnailed boots.

soulignement [sulinj'mɑ̃], *n.m.* underlining.

souligner [suli'ne], *v.t.* to underline; (*fig.*) to emphasize.

soumettre [su'mɛtr], *v.t. irr.* (*conjug. like* METTRE) to subdue, to subject; to submit; to refer; to subordinate. **se soumettre**, *v.r.* to submit, to yield; to comply, to assent (*à*).

soumis [su'mi], *a.* submissive.

soumission [sumi'sjɔ̃], *n.f.* submission, compliance, obedience; subjection; mark of respect; tender for a contract etc.

soumissionner [sumisjo'ne], *v.t.* to tender for.

soupape [su'pap], *n.f.* valve; *soupape de sûreté*, safety-valve.

soupçon [sup'sɔ̃], *n.m.* suspicion; surmise, conjecture; (*fig.*) slight taste, dash, touch.

soupçonner [supsɔ'ne], *v.t.* to suspect; to surmise.

soupçonneux [supsɔ'nø], _a._ (_fem._ **-euse**) suspicious.

soupe [sup], _n.f._ soup; sop; _c'est une soupe au lait_, he has a quick temper; _trempé comme une soupe_, drenched to the skin.

soupente [su'pãːt], _n.f._ straps (_of a horse_); loft, garret.

souper [su'pe], _v.i._ to sup, to have supper. —_n.m._ supper.

soupeser [supə'ze], _v.t._ (_conjug. like_ AMENER) to weigh in one's hand, to try the weight of.

soupière [su'pjɛːr], _n.f._ soup-tureen.

soupir [su'piːr], _n.m._ sigh; breath, gasp; (_Mus._) crotchet-rest.

soupirail [supi'raːj], _n.m._ (_pl._ **-aux**) air-hole, ventilator.

soupirant [supi'rã], _a._ sighing.—_n.m._ wooer, lover.

soupirer [supi're], _v.t._ to breathe forth, to sigh out.—_v.i._ to sigh; to gasp; to long.

souple [supl], _a._ a supple, pliant, flexible, yielding; docile.

souplesse [su'plɛs], _n.f._ suppleness, flexibility; compliance, pliancy; versatility; toughness.

souquenille [suk'niːj], _n.f._ smock-frock; (shabby) old garment.

source [surs], _n.f._ spring, source, fountain.

sourcier [sur'sje], _n.m._ (_fem._ **-ière**) water-diviner.

sourcil [sur'si], _n.m._ eyebrow, brow; _froncer le sourcil_, to frown.

sourciller [sursi'je], _v.i._ to knit one's brows, to frown; to wince.

sourcilleux [sursi'jø], _a._ (_fem._ **-euse**) haughty, proud, supercilious; frowning; uneasy.

sourd [suːr], _a._ deaf; (_fig._) dull; insensible; hollow, muffled (_of sound_); underhand.— _n.m._ (_fem._ **-e**) deaf person.

sourdement [surdə'mã], _adv._ indistinctly; with a hollow voice; in an underhand manner.

sourdine [sur'din], _n.f._ sordine (_of a musical instrument_); damper (_of a piano etc._); _en sourdine_, secretly, on the sly.

sourd-muet [sur'mɥɛ], _a._ and _n.m._ (_fem._ **sourde-muette**) deaf-and-dumb (person), deaf-mute.

sourdre [surdr], _v.i._ to spring, to gush, to well; (_fig._) to result.

souriant [su'rjã], _a._ smiling.

souricière [suri'sjɛːr], _n.f._ mouse-trap.

sourire [su'riːr], _v.i._ _irr._ (_conjug. like_ RIRE) to smile; to be agreeable, to delight, to please; to be propitious.—_n.m._ smile; _large sourire_, grin; _sourire affecté_, smirk.

souris [su'ri], _a._ _inv._ mouse-coloured.— _n.f._ mouse; mouse-colour; knuckle (_of a leg of mutton_).

sournois [sur'nwa], _a._ artful, cunning, sly.— _n.m._ (_fem._ **-e**) sneak.

sournoisement [surnwaz'mã], _adv._ cunningly, slyly.

sournoiserie [surnwaz'ri], _n.f._ slyness, cunning; underhand trick.

sous [su], _prep._ under, beneath, below; on, upon; with; in; by; _affirmer sous serment_, to swear on oath; _sous dix jours_, within ten days; _sous peu_, in a short time.

sous-alimentation [suzalimãta'sjõ], _n.f._ malnutrition.

sous-alimenté [suzalimã'te], _a._ underfed.

sous-chef [su'ʃɛf], _n.m._ deputy head-clerk; assistant manager.

souscripteur [suskrip'tœːr], _n.m._ subscriber; (_Comm._) underwriter.

souscription [suskrip'sjõ], _n.f._ subscription; signature.

souscrire [sus'kriːr], _v.t._ _irr._ (_conjug. like_ ÉCRIRE) to subscribe, to sign.—_v.i._ to consent, to agree (_à_).

sous-développé [sudevlɔ'pe], _a._ underdeveloped (_country_).

sous-dit [su'di], _a._ undermentioned.

sous-entendre [suzã'tãːdr], _v.t._ not to express fully, to hint, to imply.

sous-entendu [suzãtã'dy], _n.m._ thing understood, implication.

sous-entente [suzã'tãːt], _n.f._ mental reservation.

sous-lieutenant [suljøt'nã], _n.m._ second-lieutenant; _sous-lieutenant aviateur_, pilot officer.

sous-louer [su'lwe], _v.t._ to sub-let.

sous-main [su'mɛ̃], _n.m._ _inv._ writing-pad; _en sous-main_, behind the scenes.

sous-marin [suma'rɛ̃], _a._ and _n.m._ submarine.

sous-off [su'zɔf], _abbr. fam._ of **sous-officier** [suzofi'sje], _n.m._ non-commissioned officer, N.C.O.

sous-ordre [su'zɔrdr], _n.m._ _inv._ subordinate.

sous-préfet [supre'fɛ], _n.m._ subprefect, under-sheriff.

sous-produit [suprɔ'dɥi], _n.m._ by-product.

sous-secrétaire [susəkre'tɛːr], _n._ under-secretary.

soussigné [susi'ne], _a._ undersigned; _nous soussignés certifions_, we, the undersigned, certify.

sous-sol [su'sɔl], _n.m._ subsoil; basement.

sous-titre [su'titr], _n.m._ sub-title.

soustraction [sustrak'sjõ], _n.f._ taking away, subtraction.

soustraire [sus'trɛːr], _v.t._ _irr._ (_conjug. like_ TRAIRE) to take away, to withdraw, to screen; (_Arith._) to subtract. **se soustraire**, _v.r._ to escape, to flee, to avoid; to withdraw oneself; to be subtracted.

sous-traitant [sutrɛ'tã], _n.m._ subcontractor.

soutache [su'taʃ], _n.f._ braid.

soutane [su'tan], _n.f._ cassock; (_fig._) the cloth.

soute [sut], _n.f._ (_Naut._) store-room; (_Av._) luggage-bay, bomb-bay.

soutenable [sut'nabl], _a._ sustainable; tenable.

soutènement [sutɛn'mã], _n.m._ (_Arch._) support.

soutenir [sut'niːr], _v.t._ _irr._ (_conjug. like_ TENIR) to hold up, to support, to sustain, to keep up, to prop up; (_fig._) to maintain, to uphold; to countenance; to afford (_an expense_); to endure. **se soutenir**, _v.r._ to support oneself; to hold oneself up; to bear up, to hold out; to stand firm; to succeed; to continue; to sustain one another.

soutenu [sut'ny], _a._ sustained; unremitting, unceasing, constant; lofty, elevated.

souterrain [sutɛ'rɛ̃], _a._ underground; (_fig._) underhand.—_n.m._ underground vault, cavern; (_Rail._) tunnel; subway.

soutien [su'tjɛ̃], *n.m.* support, prop, stay, staff.

soutien-gorge [sutjɛ̃'gɔrʒ], *n.m. inv.* brassière.

soutirer [suti're], *v.t.* to draw off, to rack (*liquors*); (*fig.*) to worm out (*à*), to extract (*money, information*).

souvenir [suv'ni:r], *n.m.* recollection; reminder, souvenir, keepsake.—*v. impers. irr.* (*conjug. like* TENIR *but with aux.* ÊTRE) to occur to the mind; *il m'en souvient*, I remember it. **se souvenir**, *v.r.* to remember, to call to mind, to recollect.

souvent [su'vɑ̃], *adv.* often, frequently.

souverain [su'vrɛ̃], *a.* sovereign, supreme; highest, extreme; infallible.—*n.m.* (*fem.* **-e**) sovereign (*monarch*).—*n.m.* sovereign (*coin*).

souverainement [suvrɛn'mɑ̃], *adv.* in the extreme; supremely.

souveraineté [suvrɛn'te], *n.f.* sovereignty, dominion.

soviet [sɔ'vjɛt], *n.m.* Soviet.

soviétique [sɔvje'tik], *a. l'Union des Républiques socialistes soviétiques* (*U.R.S.S.*), the Union of Soviet Socialist Republics (*U.S.S.R.*).—*n.* (**Soviétique**) Soviet citizen.

soyeux [swa'jø], *a.* (*fem.* **-euse**) silky, silken.

spacieusement [spasjøz'mɑ̃], *adv.* spaciously.

spacieux [spa'sjø], *a.* (*fem.* **-euse**) spacious, wide, roomy.

spahi [spa'i], *n.m.* spahi (*Algerian native trooper*).

sparadrap [spara'dra], *n.m.* sticking plaster.

Sparte [spart], **la,** *f.* Sparta.

spartiate [spar'sjat], *a.* Spartan.—*n.* (**Spartiate**) Spartan (*person*).

spasme [spasm], *n.m.* spasm.

spasmodique [spasmɔ'dik], *a.* spasmodic.

spasmodiquement [spasmɔdik'mɑ̃], *adv.* spasmodically.

spatule [spa'tyl], *n.f.* spatula.

speaker [spi'kœ:r], *n.m.* (*fem.* **speakerine**) (*Rad.*) announcer.

spécial [spe'sjal], *a.* (*m. pl.* **-aux**) special, especial, particular; professional.

spécialement [spesjal'mɑ̃], *adv.* especially, particularly.

spécialisation [spesjaliza'sjɔ̃], *n.f.* specialization.

spécialiser [spesjali'ze], *v.t.* to specialize.

spécialiste [spesja'list], *n.* specialist, expert.

spécialité [spesjali'te], *n.f.* peculiarity, speciality; patent medicine.

spécieux [spe'sjø], *a.* (*fem.* **-euse**) specious, plausible.

spécification [spesifika'sjɔ̃], *n.f.* specification.

spécifier [spesi'fje], *v.t.* to specify.

spécifique [spesi'fik], *a.* and *n.m.* specific.

spécifiquement [spesifik'mɑ̃], *adv.* specifically.

spécimen [spesi'mɛn], *n.m.* specimen.

spectacle [spɛk'takl], *n.m.* spectacle, scene, sight; theatre; play, performance; show; *se donner en spectacle*, to make an exhibition of oneself.

spectaculaire [spɛktaky'lɛːr], *a.* spectacular.

spectateur [spɛkta'tœːr], *n.m.* (*fem.* **-trice**) spectator, looker-on.

spectral [spɛk'tral], *a.* (*m. pl.* **-aux**) spectral.

spectre [spɛktr], *n.m.* spectre, ghost; spectrum.

spéculateur [spekyla'tœːr], *n.m.* (*fem.* **-trice**) speculator.

spéculatif [spekyla'tif], *a.* (*fem.* **-tive**) speculative.

spéculation [spekyla'sjɔ̃], *n.f.* speculation.

spéculativement [spekylativ'mɑ̃], *adv.* in a speculative manner.

spéculer [speky'le], *v.i.* to speculate.

sperme [spɛrm], *n.m.* sperm, seed.

sphaigne [sfɛ:ɲ], *n.f.* sphagnum moss.

sphère [sfɛːr], *n.f.* sphere, orb, globe; (*fig.*) circle.

sphérique [sfe'rik], *a.* spherical.

sphinx [sfɛ̃:ks], *n.m.* sphinx.

spinal [spi'nal], *a.* (*m. pl.* **-aux**) spinal.

spiral [spi'ral], *a.* (*m. pl.* **-aux**) spiral.—*n.m.* hair-spring (*of watch*).

spirale [spi'ral], *n.f.* spiral.

spirite [spi'rit], *a.* spiritualistic.—*n.* spiritualist.

spiritisme [spiri'tism], *n.m.* spiritualism.

spiritualisme [spiritɥa'lism], *n.m.* spiritualism.

spiritualiste [spiritɥa'list], *a.* and *n.* spiritualist.

spirituel [spiri'tɥɛl], *a.* (*fem.* **-elle**) spiritual; intellectual; witty, shrewd, lively, intelligent.

spirituellement [spiritɥɛl'mɑ̃], *adv.* spiritually; wittily, cleverly.

spiritueux [spiri'tɥø], *a.* (*fem.* **-euse**) spirituous.—*n.m.* spirit, spirituous liquor.

spleen [splin], *n.m.* spleen; (*fam.*) *avoir le spleen*, to be in the dumps.

splendeur [splɑ̃'dœːr], *n.f.* splendour, brilliance; magnificence.

splendide [splɑ̃'did], *a.* sumptuous, magnificent.

splendidement [splɑ̃did'mɑ̃], *adv.* splendidly.

spoliateur [spɔlja'tœːr], *a.* (*fem.* **-trice**) despoiling.—*n.m.* (*fem.* **-trice**) spoiler, despoiler.

spoliation [spɔlja'sjɔ̃], *n.f.* spoliation.

spolier [spɔ'lje], *v.t.* to despoil, to plunder.

spongieux [spɔ̃'ʒjø], *a.* (*fem.* **-euse**) spongy.

spontané [spɔ̃ta'ne], *a.* spontaneous.

spontanéité [spɔ̃tanei'te], *n.f.* spontaneity.

spontanément [spɔ̃tane'mɑ̃], *adv.* spontaneously.

sporadique [spɔra'dik], *a.* sporadic.

spore [spɔ:r], *n.f.* spore.

sport [spɔːr], *n.m.* games, outdoor games; *faire du sport*, to play games.

sportif [spɔr'tif], *a.* (*fem.* **-tive**) sporting; *réunion sportive*, athletics meeting.—*n.m.* (*fem.* **-tive**) athlete; devotee of out-door games; sportsman, sportswoman.

spumeux [spy'mø], *a.* (*fem.* **-euse**) spumy.

square [skwa:r], *n.m.* residential square with enclosed garden.

squelette [skə'lɛt], *n.m.* skeleton; carcass, frame (*of a ship*).

squelettique [skəle'tik], *a.* lanky.

stabilisateur [stabiliza'tœːr], *a.* (*fem.* **-trice**) stabilizing.—*n.m.* (*Av., Naut.*) stabilizer.

stabiliser [stabili'ze], *v.t.* to stabilize.

stabilité [stabili'te], *n.f.* stability, durability.

stable [sta:bl], *a.* stable, firm; durable, lasting, permanent.

stade [stad], *n.m.* sports ground, stadium; (*fig.*) stage, period.

stage [staːʒ], *n.m.* term of probation, study, residence etc.; training course; (*fig.*) probation.

stagiaire [sta'ʒjɛːr], *n.* probationer, trainee.

stagnant [stag'nɑ̃], *a.* stagnant, at a standstill.

stagnation [stagna'sjɔ̃], *n.f.* stagnation.

stagner [stag'ne], *v.i.* to stagnate.

stalactite [stalak'tit], *n.f.* stalactite.

stalagmite [stalag'mit], *n.f.* stalagmite.

stalle [stal], *n.f.* stall; box (*for horses*) (*Theat.*) stall, seat.

stance [stɑ̃ːs], *n.f.* stanza.

stand [stɑ̃ːd], *n.m.* rifle-range; shooting-gallery; stall, stand (*at exhibitions etc.*).

standard [stɑ̃'daːr], *n.m.* (*in house or office*) switchboard; standard (*of living*).

standardiser [stɑ̃dardi'ze], *v.t.* to standardize.

standardiste [stɑ̃dar'dist], *n.* switchboard operator.

star [staːr], *n.f.* (*Cine.*) star.

starlette [star'lɛt], *n.f.* starlet.

starter [star'tɛːr], *n.m.* (*Motor.*) choke; (*Racing*) starter.

station [sta'sjɔ̃], *n.f.* station, standing; stage (*of bus, trams*), taxi-rank; resort.

stationnaire [stasjɔ'nɛːr], *a.* stationary.

stationnement [stasjɔn'mɑ̃], *n.m.* stationing, standing; parking; *stationnement interdit*, no parking, no waiting.

stationner [stasjɔ'ne], *v.i.* to stop, to stand, to park (*of cars*).

statique [sta'tik], *a.* static.—*n.f.* statics.

statisticien [statisti'sjɛ̃], *n.m.* statistician.

statistique [statis'tik], *a.* statistical.—*n.f.* statistics.

statuaire [sta'tɥɛːr], *a.* statuary.—*n.* sculptor. —*n.f.* statuary (*art*).

statue [sta'ty], *n.f.* statue.

statuer [sta'tɥe], *v.t.* to decree, to resolve, to ordain.—*v.i.* to give a ruling.

statuette [sta'tɥɛt], *n.f.* statuette.

stature [sta'tyːr], *n.f.* stature, height.

statut [sta'ty], *n.m.* statute, ordinance, by-law; status.

statutaire [staty'tɛːr], *a.* statutory.

stellaire [stɛl'lɛːr], *a.* stellar, starry.

stencil [stɛn'sil], *n.m.* stencil.

sténo [ste'no], *abbr. of* **sténographe** or **sténographie.**

sténo-dactylo(graphe) [stenodakti'lo('graf)], *n.* shorthand typist.

sténographe [stenɔ'graf], *n.* stenographer, shorthand writer.

sténographie [stenɔgra'fi], *n.f.* stenography, shorthand.

sténographier [stenɔgra'fje], *v.t.* to take down in shorthand.

stentor [stɑ̃'tɔːr], *n.m.* Stentor; *d'une voix de stentor*, in a stentorian voice.

steppe [stɛp], *n.f.* steppe.

stéréoscope [stereɔs'kɔp], *n.m.* stereoscope.

stéréotypé [stereɔti'pe], *a.* stereotyped, hackneyed.

stérile [ste'ril], *a.* sterile, barren; (*fig.*) fruitless, vain.

stérilisant [sterili'zɑ̃], *a.* sterilizing.—*n.m.* sterilizing agent.

stérilisation [steriliza'sjɔ̃], *n.f.* sterilization.

stériliser [sterili'ze], *v.t.* to sterilize.

stérilité [sterili'te], *n.f.* sterility, barrenness.

sterling [stɛr'liŋ], *a. inv.* and *n.m.* sterling.

stéthoscope [stetɔs'kɔp], *n.m.* stethoscope.

stigmate [stig'mat], *n.m.* scar, stigma, stain; brand.

stigmatiser [stigmati'ze], *v.t.* to stigmatize, to brand.

stimulant [stimy'lɑ̃], *a.* stimulating.—*n.m.* stimulant; stimulus; incentive.

stimulation [stimyla'sjɔ̃], *n.f.* stimulation.

stimuler [stimy'le], *v.t.* to stimulate; to excite, to rouse.

stipendiaire [stipɑ̃'djɛːr], *a.* and *n.m.* stipendiary, mercenary.

stipendié [stipɑ̃'dje], *a.* hired.—*n.m.* stipendiary, hireling.

stipendier [stipɑ̃'dje], *v.t.* to hire, to keep in pay.

stipulation [stipyla'sjɔ̃], *n.f.* stipulation.

stipuler [stipy'le], *v.t.* to stipulate; to contract.

stock [stɔk], *n.m.* (*Comm.*) stock.

stocker [stɔ'ke], *v.t.* to stock; to stockpile.

stockiste [stɔ'kist], *n.m.* warehouseman; stockist; agent (*for a certain make of car*); service-station (*with spare parts*).

stoïcien [stɔi'sjɛ̃], *a.* Stoic, stoical.—*n.m.* (*fem.* **-enne**) Stoic.

stoïcisme [stɔi'sism], *n.m.* stoicism.

stoïque [stɔ'ik], *a.* Stoic, stoical.—*n.* Stoic.

stoïquement [stɔik'mɑ̃], *adv.* stoically.

stop [stɔp], *int.* stop!—*n.m.* (*Motor.*) stop-light.

stoppage [stɔ'paːʒ], *n.m.* invisible mending; stoppage (*of motion, current*).

stopper [stɔ'pe], *v.t.* to mend invisibly; to stop.—*v.i.* to stop (*of a train, steamboat etc.*).

store [stɔːr], *n.m.* (*spring-roller*) blind.

strabisme [stra'bism], *n.m.* squinting.

strangulation [strɑ̃gyla'sjɔ̃], *n.f.* strangulation.

strapontin [strapɔ̃'tɛ̃], *n.m.* folding-seat, tip-up seat.

strass or **stras** [stras], *n.m.* strass, paste jewels.

stratagème [strata'ʒɛm], *n.m.* stratagem.

strate [strat], *n.f.* stratum.

stratégie [strate'ʒi], *n.f.* strategy.

stratégique [strate'ʒik], *a.* strategic.

stratégiquement [strateʒik'mɑ̃], *adv.* strategically.

stratégiste [strate'ʒist], *n.m.* strategist.

stratosphère [stratɔs'fɛːr], *n.f.* stratosphere.

strict [strikt], *a.* strict, precise; severe.

strictement [striktə'mɑ̃], *adv.* strictly; severely.

strident [stri'dɑ̃], *a.* strident, jarring.

strié [stri'e], *a.* striate, streaked; corrugated; scored.

strontium [strɔ̃'sjɔm], *n.m.* strontium.

strophe [strɔf], *n.f.* strophe; stanza.

structural [strykty'ral], *a.* (*m. pl.* **-aux**) structural.

structure [stryk'tyːr], *n.f.* structure; form, make.

strychnine [strik'nin], *n.f.* strychnin(e).

stuc [styk], *n.m.* stucco.

stucage [sty'kaːʒ], *n.m.* stucco-work.

studieusement [stydjøz'mɑ̃], *adv.* studiously.

studieux [sty'djø], *a.* (*fem.* **-euse**) studious.

studio [sty'djo], *n.m.* (*Cine.*) film-studio; (*Rad.*, *Tel.*) broadcasting studio; one-roomed flat.

stupéfaction

stupéfaction [stypefak'sjō], n.f. stupefaction, amazement.

stupéfait [stype'fɛ], a. amazed, dumbfounded.

stupéfiant [stype'fjā], a. stupefactive; amazing, astounding.—n.m. narcotic.

stupéfier [stype'fje], v.t. to stupefy, to astound, to dumbfound.

stupeur [sty'pœːr], n.f. stupor; amazement.

stupide [sty'pid], a. stunned; stupid, foolish, dull.

stupidement [stypid'mā], adv. stupidly.

stupidité [stypidi'te], n.f. stupidity.

style (1) [stil], n.m. style.

style (2) [stil], n.m. stylus.

stylé [sti'le], a. stylate; (colloq.) trained, taught, clever.

styler [sti'le], v.t. to train, to form, to school.

stylet [sti'lɛ], n.m. stiletto; (Surg.) probe.

stylo [sti'lo], abbr. of stylographe [stilo'graf], n.m. fountain-pen; stylo à bille, ball-point pen.

stylomine [stilo'min], n.m. propelling pencil.

styptique [stip'tik], a. and n.m. styptic.

su (1) [sy], n.m. knowledge; au vu et au su de tout le monde, as everybody knows.

su (2) [sy], p.p. [SAVOIR].

suaire [sɥɛːr], n.m. winding-sheet, shroud.

suant [sɥā], a. sweating, in a sweat.

suave [sɥaːv], a. sweet, agreeable; suave, bland; soft.

suavement [sɥav'mā], adv. suavely; sweetly.

suavité [sɥavi'te], n.f. suavity; sweetness.

subalterne [sybal'tɛrn], a. and n. subaltern, subordinate; inferior.

subdiviser [sybdivi'ze], v.t. to subdivide. se subdiviser, v.r. to be subdivided.

subdivision [sybdivi'zjō], n.f. subdivision.

subir [sy'biːr], v.t. to support; to go through, to undergo, to suffer; to submit to.

subit [sy'bit], a. sudden, unexpected.

subitement [sybit'mā], adv. suddenly, all of a sudden.

subjectif [sybʒɛk'tif], a. (fem. -tive) subjective.

subjection [sybʒɛk'sjō], n.f. subjection.

subjectivement [sybʒɛktiv'mā], adv. subjectively.

subjonctif [sybʒɔ̃k'tif], a. (fem. -tive) and n.m. subjunctive.

subjugation [sybʒyga'sjō], n.f. subjugation.

subjuguer [sybʒy'ge], v.t. to subjugate, to subdue.

sublimation [syblima'sjō], n.f. sublimation.

sublime [sy'blim], a. lofty, sublime, splendid. —n.m. the sublime.

sublimement [syblim'mā], adv. sublimely.

submerger [sybmɛr'ʒe], v.t. (conjug. like MANGER) to submerge, to swamp, to flood; (fig.) to overwhelm.

submersible [sybmɛr'sibl], a. submersible. —n.m. submarine (boat).

submersion [sybmɛr'sjō], n.f. submersion.

subordination [sybordina'sjō], n.f. subordination.

subordonné [sybordo'ne], a. and n.m. (fem. -ée) subordinate, dependent.

subordonner [sybordo'ne], v.t. to subordinate.

suborner [sybor'ne], v.t. to suborn, to bribe.

suborneur [sybor'nœːr], a. (fem. -euse) suborning, bribing.—n.m. (fem. -euse) suborner, briber.

subreptice [sybrɛp'tis], a. surreptitious.

subrepticement [sybrɛptis'mā], adv. surreptitiously.

subséquemment [sybseka'mā], adv. subsequently.

subséquent [sybse'kā], a. subsequent.

subside [syb'sid], n.m. subsidy; (colloq.) aid.

subsidiaire [sybsi'djɛːr], a. subsidiary, auxiliary.

subsidiairement [sybsidjɛr'mā], adv. further, also, additionally.

subsistance [sybzis'tāːs], n.f. subsistence, sustenance, maintenance; (pl.) provisions.

subsistant [sybzis'tā], a. subsisting, existing.

subsister [sybzis'te], v.i. to subsist, to stand; to hold good; to exist, to live.

substance [sybs'tāːs], n.f. substance.

substantiel [sybstā'sjɛl], a. (fem. -elle) substantial.

substantiellement [sybstāsjɛl'mā], adv. substantially.

substantif [sybstā'tif], a. (fem. -tive) substantive.—n.m. (Gram.) noun.

substituer [sybsti'tɥe], v.t. to substitute; (Law) to entail.

substitut [sybsti'ty], n.m. substitute, deputy (to someone).

substitution [sybstity'sjō], n.f. substitution; (Law) entail.

subterfuge [sybtɛr'fyːʒ], n.m. subterfuge, evasion, shift.

subtil [syb'til], a. subtile, tenuous; penetrating; acute, keen, sharp; cunning; fine-spun, subtle.

subtilement [sybtil'mā], adv. subtly, craftily.

subtiliser [sybtili'ze], v.t. to subtilize, to refine; (colloq.) to sneak, to steal.

subtilité [sybtili'te], n.f. subtlety, fineness; acuteness; shrewdness.

suburbain [sybyr'bē], a. suburban.

subvenir [sybvə'niːr], v.i. irr. (conjug. like TENIR) to be helpful; to supply, to provide.

subvention [sybvā'sjō], n.f. subsidy, aid.

subventionner [sybvāsjo'ne], v.t. to subsidize, to make a grant to.

subversif [sybvɛr'sif], a. (fem. -sive) subversive.

subversion [sybvɛr'sjō], n.f. subversion, overthrow.

suc [syk], n.m. juice; (fig.) essence, quintessence.

succéder [sykse'de], v.i. (conjug. like CÉDER) to succeed, to follow after (à). se succéder, v.r. to succeed each other.

succès [syk'sɛ], n.m. success.

successeur [sykse'sœːr], n.m. successor.

successif [sykse'sif], a. (fem. -ive) successive, in succession.

succession [sykse'sjō], n.f. succession; inheritance; heritage, estate.

successivement [syksesiv'mā], adv. successively, in succession.

succinct [syk'sɛ̃], a. succinct, concise.

succinctement [syksɛ̃t'mā], adv. succinctly, briefly.

succion [syk'sjō], n.f. suction.

succomber [sykō'be], v.i. to sink, to faint; to yield, to succumb; to fail; to die.

succulence [syky'lāːs], n.f. succulence.

succulent [syky'lā], a. succulent, juicy; rich.

succursale [sykyr'sal], *n.f.* branch (*of a bank etc.*).
sucement [sys'mɑ̃], *n.m.* sucking, suck.
sucer [sy'se], *v.t.* (*conjug. like* COMMENCER) to suck, to suck in; to imbibe.
sucette [sy'sɛt], *n.f.* lollipop; comforter (*for baby*).
suceur [sy'sœːr], *a.* (*fem.* **-euse**) sucking.— *n.m.* sucker; nozzle (*of a vacuum cleaner*).
suçoir [sy'swaːr], *n.m.* sucker.
sucre [sykr], *n.m.* sugar; *sucre cristallisé*, granulated sugar; *sucre d'orge*, barley-sugar; *sucre en poudre*, castor-sugar.
sucré [sy'kre], *a.* sugared, sweet, sugary; (*fig.*) demure, prim.
sucrer [sy'kre], *v.t.* to sugar, to sweeten.
sucrerie [sykrə'ri], *n.f.* sugar-refinery; (*pl.*) sweets.
sucrier [sykri'e], *n.m.* sugar-basin; sugar-maker.
sud [syd], *a. inv.* south, southerly (*of the wind*).—*n.m.* south; south wind.
sud-est [sy'dɛst], *a. inv.* and *n.m.* south-east.
Sudètes [sy'dɛt], **les**, *m. pl.* Sudetenland.
sud-ouest [sy'dwɛst], *a. inv.* and *n.m.* south-west.
Suède [sɥɛd], **la**, *f.* Sweden.
suède [sɥɛd], *n.m.* suède (*glove leather*).
suédois [sɥe'dwa], *a.* Swedish.—*n.m.* Swedish (*language*); (**Suédois**, *fem.* **-oise**) Swede.
suée [sɥe], *n.f.* sweating.
suer [sɥe], *v.t.* to sweat.—*v.i.* to sweat, to perspire; (*fig.*) to toil, to drudge; to ooze (*of walls*).
sueur [sɥœːr], *n.f.* sweat, perspiration; (*pl.*) labour, toil.
suffire [sy'fiːr], *v.i. irr.* to suffice, to be sufficient; to be adequate; *cela suffit*, that's enough. **se suffire**, *v.r.* to provide for oneself.
suffisamment [syfiza'mɑ̃], *adv.* sufficiently.
suffisance [syfi'zɑ̃ːs], *n.f.* sufficiency, adequacy; conceit, self-sufficiency.
suffisant [syfi'zɑ̃], *a.* sufficient; conceited.— *n.m.* (*fem.* **-e**) conceited person.
suffixe [sy'fiks], *n.m.* suffix.
suffocant [syfɔ'kɑ̃], *a.* suffocating, choking.
suffocation [syfɔka'sjɔ̃], *n.f.* suffocation.
suffoquer [syfɔ'ke], *v.t.* to suffocate, to choke. —*v.i.* to choke.
suffrage [sy'fraːʒ], *n.m.* suffrage, vote; approbation, commendation.
suggérer [sygʒe're], *v.t.* (*conjug. like* CÉDER) to suggest.
suggestif [sygʒɛs'tif], *a.* (*fem.* **-tive**) suggestive; erotic.
suggestion [sygʒɛs'tjɔ̃], *n.f.* suggestion, hint, instigation.
suicide [sɥi'sid], *n.m.* suicide.
suicidé [sɥisi'de], *n.m.* (*fem.* **-ée**) suicide.
suicider (**se**) [səsɥisi'de], *v.r.* to commit suicide.
suie [sɥi], *n.f.* soot.
suif [sɥif], *n.m.* tallow.
suintement [sɥɛ̃t'mɑ̃], *n.m.* oozing, sweating.
suinter [sɥɛ̃'te], *v.i.* to ooze, to sweat (*of walls etc.*); to leak, to run (*of vessels*).
Suisse [sɥis], **la**, *f.* Switzerland.
suisse [sɥis], *a.* Swiss.—*n.m.* porter (*of a mansion*); church officer; (**Suisse**, *fem.* **Suissesse**) Swiss (*person*).

suite [sɥit], *n.f.* the rest; retinue, attendants; sequel, continuation; series; set; connexion; result; *à la suite*, after, behind; *de suite*, consecutively; *et ainsi de suite*, and so on; *tout de suite*, immediately.
suivant [sɥi'vɑ̃], *prep.* according to; in the direction of; *suivant que*, as, according as. —*a.* next, following, subsequent.—*n.m.* (*fem.* **-e**) follower, attendant.—*n.f.* (**-e**) lady's maid.
suivi [sɥi'vi], *a.* followed; connected; consistent; popular.
suivre [sɥiːvr], *v.t. irr.* to follow; to be next to; to attend; to observe; to pursue; to practise (*a profession etc.*).—*v.i.* to follow; to come after; to result; to ensue; *à faire suivre*, to be forwarded; *à suivre*, to be continued. **se suivre**, *v.r.* to follow each other, to be continuous.
sujet [sy'ʒɛ], *a.* (*fem.* **-ette**) subject, subjected, liable, exposed; apt, addicted, inclined (*à*).—*n.m.* subject; topic; cause.
sujétion [syʒe'sjɔ̃], *n.f.* subjection, servitude; constraint.
sulfate [syl'fat], *n.m.* sulphate.
sulfureux [sylfy'rø], *a.* (*fem.* **-euse**) sulphurous, sulphureous.
sulfurique [sylfy'rik], *a.* sulphuric (*acid*).
sultan [syl'tɑ̃], *n.m.* sultan.
sultane [syl'tan], *n.f.* sultana, sultaness.
sumac [sy'mak], *n.m.* sumac.
superbe [sy'pɛrb], *a.* proud, arrogant; superb; stately; lofty; vainglorious.—*n.* proud person.—*n.f.* arrogance; vainglory.
superbement [sypɛrbə'mɑ̃], *adv.* haughtily, superbly.
supercarburant [sypɛrkarby'rɑ̃], *n.m.* high-octane petrol.
supercherie [sypɛrʃə'ri], *n.f.* deceit, fraud.
superficie [sypɛrfi'si], *n.f.* area, surface; (*fig.*) superficiality.
superficiel [sypɛrfi'sjɛl], *a.* (*fem.* **-elle**) superficial; shallow.
superficiellement [sypɛrfisjɛl'mɑ̃], *adv.* superficially.
superfin [sypɛr'fɛ̃], *a.* superfine, of superior quality.
superflu [sypɛr'fly], *a.* superfluous; unnecessary.—*n.m.* superfluity, excess.
superfluité [sypɛrflɥi'te], *n.f.* superfluity.
supérieur [sype'rjœːr], *a.* superior; upper, higher.—*n.m.* (*fem.* **-e**) superior.
supérieurement [syperjœr'mɑ̃], *adv.* in a superior manner; surpassingly.
supériorité [syperjori'te], *n.f.* superiority.
superlatif [sypɛrla'tif], *a.* (*fem.* **-tive**) superlative.—*n.m.* (*Gram.*) superlative.
superlativement [sypɛrlativ'mɑ̃], *adv.* superlatively.
superposer [sypɛrpo'ze], *v.t.* to superpose; to superimpose.
superposition [sypɛrpozi'sjɔ̃], *n.f.* superposition; superimposition.
supersonique [sypɛrsɔ'nik], *a.* supersonic.
superstitieusement [sypɛrstisjøz'mɑ̃], *adv.* superstitiously.
superstitieux [sypɛrsti'sjø], *a.* (*fem.* **-euse**) superstitious.
superstition [sypɛrsti'sjɔ̃], *n.f.* superstition.
superstructure [sypɛrstryk'tyːr], *n.f.* superstructure; permanent way (*of railway*).
supin [sy'pɛ̃], *n.m.* (*Gram.*) supine.

supplantation

supplantation [syplᾱta'sjõ], *n.f.* supplantation; supersession.

supplanter [syplᾱ'te], *v.t.* to supplant, to oust, to supersede.

suppléance [syple'ᾱːs], *n.f.* substitution, deputyship.

suppléant [syple'ᾱ], *a.* and *n.m.* (*fem.* -e) substitute, assistant, deputy, understudy.

suppléer [syple'e], *v.t.* to supply, to fill up; to take the place of.—*v.i.* to make up the deficiency, to compensate for (*à*).

supplément [syple'mᾱ], *n.m.* supplement; additional price, excess fare.

supplémentaire [syplemᾱ'teːr], *a.* supplementary, supplemental, additional, extra.

suppliant [sypli'ᾱ], *a.* suppliant, beseeching. —*n.m.* (*fem.* -e) suppliant, supplicant, petitioner.

supplication [syplika'sjõ], *n.f.* supplication, entreaty.

supplice [sy'plis], *n.m.* corporal punishment; torture; (*fig.*) torment, ordeal; *être au supplice*, to be upon the rack.

supplicié [sypli'sje], *n.m.* (*fem.* -ée) executed criminal.

supplicier [sypli'sje], *v.t.* to put to death, to execute.

supplier [sypli'e], *v.t.* to beseech, to entreat, to beg.

supplique [sy'plik], *n.f.* petition, entreaty.

support [sy'poːr], *n.m.* support, prop; rest, stand, bracket.

supportable [sypɔr'tabl], *a.* supportable, bearable, tolerable.

supportablement [sypɔrtablə'mᾱ], *adv.* tolerably.

supporter (1) [sypɔr'tœːr], *n.m.* (*Spt.*) supporter, partisan.

supporter (2) [sypɔr'te], *v.t.* to support, to uphold; to endure, to suffer; to stand. **se supporter**, *v.r.* to be borne; to bear with each other.

supposable [sypo'zabl], *a.* supposable.

supposé [sypo'ze], *a.* pretended, forged, assumed; reputed.

supposer [sypo'ze], *v.t.* to suppose; to admit, to imply; to conjecture; to forge (*a will*).

supposition [sypozi'sjõ], *n.f.* supposition; substitution; forgery.

suppôt [sy'po], *n.m.* agent, tool, abettor.

suppressif [sypre'sif], *a.* (*fem.* -ive) suppressive.

suppression [sypre'sjõ], *n.f.* suppression; cancelling (*of passage*); concealment.

supprimer [sypri'me], *v.t.* to suppress; to omit; to abolish, to cancel.

suppuration [sypyra'sjõ], *n.f.* suppuration.

suppurer [sypy're], *v.i.* to suppurate, to run.

supputation [sypyta'sjõ], *n.f.* computation, calculation.

supputer [sypy'te], *v.t.* to calculate, to compute, to reckon.

suprématie [syprema'si], *n.f.* supremacy.

suprême [sy'preːm], *a.* supreme, highest; last.

suprêmement [syprɛmə'mᾱ], *adv.* supremely.

sur (1) [syr], *prep.* on, upon; over; in; towards; about; concerning; out of.

sur (2) [syːr], *a.* sour, tart.

sûr [syːr], *a.* sure, certain; safe, secure; firm, steady; trustworthy; *à coup sûr*, for certain; *en lieu sûr*, in a place of safety; *je suis sûr de vous*, I can depend on you; *sûr et certain*, positive.

surabondamment [syrabõda'mᾱ], *adv.* superabundantly.

surabondance [syrabõ'dᾱːs], *n.f.* superabundance; glut.

surabondant [syrabõ'dᾱ], *a.* superabundant.

surabonder [syrabõ'de], *v.i.* to superabound; to be glutted (*de*).

suraigu [syre'gy], *a.* (*fem.* -ë) overshrill; very acute (*inflammation*).

suralimenté [syralimᾱ'te], *a.* overfed.

suralimenter [syralimᾱ'te], *v.t.* to overfeed, to feed up; (*Motor.*) to supercharge.

suranné [syra'ne], *a.* expired; superannuated, antiquated.

surcharge [syr'ʃarʒ], *n.f.* overloading; (*stamp*) surcharge; excess.

surcharger [syrʃar'ʒe], *v.t.* (*conjug. like* MANGER) to overload, to overtax; (*fig.*) to overwhelm; to oppress; *surcharger d'impôts*, to overtax.

surchauffer [syrʃo'fe], *v.t.* to overheat.

surclasser [syrkla'se], *v.t.* to outclass.

surcompresseur [syrkõpre'sœːr], *n.m.* supercharger.

surcompression [syrkõpre'sjõ], *n.f.* supercharging.

surcomprimé [syrkõpri'me], *a.* supercharged.

surcroît [syr'krwa], *n.m.* addition, increase; surplus, excess.

surcuit [syr'kɥi], *a.* overdone.

surdité [syrdi'te], *n.f.* deafness.

sureau [sy'ro], *n.m.* (*pl.* -eaux) elder(-tree).

surélever [syrel've], *v.t.* (*conjug. like* AMENER) to raise higher; (*Golf*) to tee.

sûrement [syr'mᾱ], *adv.* surely, certainly, to be sure; safely.

surenchère [syrᾱ'ʃɛːr], *n.f.* higher bid, outbidding.

surenchérir [syrᾱʃe'riːr], *v.i.* to overbid, to bid higher.

surestimation [syrɛstima'sjõ], *n.f.* overestimate, overvaluation.

surestimer [syresti'me], *v.t.* to overestimate; to overrate.

sûreté [syr'te], *n.f.* safety, security; warranty; *la Sûreté*, Criminal Investigation Department.

surexcitation [syrɛksita'sjõ], *n.f.* excitement, overexcitement.

surexciter [syrɛksi'te], *v.t.* to overexcite.

surexposer [syrɛkspo'ze], *v.t.* (*Phot.*) to overexpose.

surexposition [syrɛkspozi'sjõ], *n.f.* (*Phot.*) overexposure.

surface [syr'fas], *n.f.* surface; outside.

surfaire [syr'fɛːr], *v.t. irr.* (*conjug. like* FAIRE) to ask too much for; to overrate, to overpraise.

surfin [syr'fɛ̃], *a.* (*Comm.*) superfine.

surgir [syr'ʒiːr], *v.i.* to rise, to surge; to loom up.

surgissement [syrʒis'mᾱ], *n.m.* upheaval.

surhomme [sy'rom], *n.m.* superman.

surhumain [syry'mɛ̃], *a.* superhuman.

surintendant [syrɛ̃tᾱ'dᾱ], *n.m.* superintendent, overseer; steward (*of large estate*).

surintendante [syrɛ̃tᾱ'dᾱːt], *n.f.* woman superintendent; superintendent's wife.

surir [sy'riːr], *v.i.* to turn sour.

sur-le-champ [syrlə'ʃᾱ], *adv.* at once.

surlendemain [syrlɑ̃d'mɛ̃], *n.m.* two days after.

surmenage [syrmə'naːʒ], *n.m.* excess fatigue; overworking.

surmener [syrmə'ne], *v.t.* (*conjug. like* AMENER) to overwork, to overtire. **se surmener,** *v.r.* to overwork.

surmontable [syrmɔ̃'tabl], *a.* surmountable, superable.

surmonter [syrmɔ̃'te], *v.t.* to surmount; to overcome, to surpass.

surmultiplication [syrmyltiplika'sjɔ̃], *n.f.* (*Motor.*) overdrive.

surnager [syrna'ʒe], *v.i.* (*conjug. like* MANGER) to float on the surface; (*fig.*) to survive.

surnaturel [syrnaty'rɛl], *a.* (*fem.* **-elle**) supernatural.—*n.m.* supernatural.

surnaturellement [syrnatyrɛl'mɑ̃], *adv.* supernaturally.

surnom [syr'nɔ̃], *n.m.* nickname.

surnommer [syrnɔ'me], *v.t.* to nickname.

surnuméraire [syrnyme'rɛːr], *a.* and *n.m.* supernumerary.

surpasser [syrpɑ'se], *v.t.* to surpass, to excel, to outdo, to exceed.

surpeuplé [syrpœ'ple], *a.* overpopulated.

surpeuplement [syrpœplə'mɑ̃], *n.m.* overpopulation, overcrowding.

surplis [syr'pli], *n.m. inv.* surplice.

surplomb [syr'plɔ̃], *n.m.* overhang (*of buildings*); **en surplomb,** overhanging.

surplomber [syrplɔ̃'be], *v.t., v.i.* to overhang.

surplus [syr'ply], *n.m. inv.* surplus, remainder, excess.

surpoids [syr'pwa], *n.m.* overweight, excess weight.

surprenant [syrprə'nɑ̃], *a.* surprising, astonishing.

surprendre [syr'prɑ̃ːdr], *v.t. irr.* (*conjug. like* PRENDRE) to surprise, to catch; to overhear; to entrap; to intercept. **se surprendre,** *v.r.* to surprise oneself; to catch oneself (*napping etc.*).

surprise [syr'priːz], *n.f.* surprise; amazement.

surproduction [syrprɔdyk'sjɔ̃], *n.f.* overproduction.

surréalisme [syrrea'lism], *n.m.* surrealism.

surréaliste [syrrea'list], *a.* and *n.* surrealist.

sursaut [syr'so], *n.m.* start, jump.

sursauter [syrso'te], *v.i.* to start up; *faire sursauter* (*quelqu'un*), to startle (someone).

surseoir [syr'swaːr], *v.t., v.i. irr.* to suspend, to delay, to postpone.

sursis [syr'si], *n.m.* delay, respite, reprieve.

surtaxe [syr'taks], *n.f.* surtax; surcharge.

surtaxer [syrtak'se], *v.t.* to overtax.

surtout [syr'tu], *adv.* above all, chiefly.—*n.m.* overcoat; centrepiece (*for table*).

surveillance [syrvɛ'jɑ̃ːs], *n.f.* supervision; surveillance.

surveillant [syrvɛ'jɑ̃], *n.m.* (*fem.* **-e**) inspector, superintendent; supervisor.

surveiller [syrvɛ'je], *v.t.* to superintend, to inspect; to watch, to supervise.

survenir [syrvə'niːr], *v.i. irr.* (*conjug. like* TENIR, *but with aux.* ÊTRE) to arrive *or* happen unexpectedly; to drop in.

survêtement [syrvɛt'mɑ̃], *n.m.* (*Spt.*) tracksuit.

survivant [syrvi'vɑ̃], *a.* surviving.—*n.m.* (*fem.* **-e**) survivor.

survivre [syr'viːvr], *v.i. irr.* (*conjug. like* VIVRE) to survive, to outlive someone (*à*). **se survivre,** *v.r.* to live *or* exist again.

survoler [syrvɔ'le], *v.t.* to fly over (*of aircraft*).

sus [sys], *prep.* upon; **en sus,** over and above. —*int.* courage! come on!

susceptibilité [syseptibili'te], *n.f.* susceptibility; irritability.

susceptible [sysɛp'tibl], *a.* susceptible, capable; likely to; touchy; irascible.

susciter [sysi'te], *v.t.* to raise up, to set up; to create; to arouse, to instigate.

suscription [syskrip'sjɔ̃], *n.f.* superscription, address.

susdit [sys'di], *a.* and *n.m.* (*fem.* **-e**) aforesaid.

suspect [sys'pɛkt, sys'pɛ], *a.* suspected, suspicious, suspect, doubtful.—*n.m.* suspect.

suspecter [syspɛk'te], *v.t.* to suspect.

suspendre [sys'pɑ̃ːdr], *v.t.* to suspend, to hang up; to delay, to defer.

suspendu [syspɑ̃'dy], *a.* suspended, hung up; in suspense.

suspens [sys'pɑ̃], *adv. phr.* **en suspens,** in suspense; (*person*) in doubt; (*thing*) in abeyance.

suspension [syspɑ̃'sjɔ̃], *n.f.* suspension, interruption; hanging-lamp.

suspicion [syspi'sjɔ̃], *n.f.* suspicion.

susurration [sysyra'sjɔ̃], *n.f.,* **susurrement** [sysyr'mɑ̃], *n.m.* susurration, whispering, murmur; rustling.

suttée [sy'te], **suttie** [sy'ti], *n.f.* suttee.

suture [sy'tyːr], *n.f.* suture; joint; stitching.

Suzanne [sy'zan], *f.* Susan.

suzerain [syz'rɛ̃], *a.* paramount, suzerain.—*n.m.* (*fem.* **-e**) suzerain, lord *or* lady paramount.

suzeraineté [syzrɛn'te], *n.f.* suzerainty.

svastika [zvasti'ka], *n.m.* swastika.

svelte [zvɛlt], *a.* slender, slim.

sveltesse [zvɛl'tɛs], *n.f.* slenderness, slimness.

sybarite [siba'rit], *a.* sybaritic.—*n.* sybarite, voluptuary.

sycomore [sikɔ'mɔːr], *n.m.* sycamore.

sycophante [sikɔ'fɑ̃ːt], *a.* sycophantic.—*n.m.* informer; hypocrite, impostor; sycophant, (*fam.*) toady.

syllabe [sil'lab], *n.f.* syllable.

syllabique [silla'bik], *a.* syllabic.

syllogisme [sillɔ'ʒism], *n.m.* syllogism.

sylphe [silf], *n.m.,* **sylphide** [sil'fid], *n.f.* sylph.

sylvain [sil'vɛ̃], *n.m.* sylvan.

sylvestre [sil'vɛstr], *a.* sylvan, growing in woods.

Sylvie [sil'vi], *f.* Sylvia.

symbole [sɛ̃'bɔl], *n.m.* symbol, sign, emblem; creed.

symbolique [sɛ̃bɔ'lik], *a.* symbolic, symbolical.

symboliser [sɛ̃bɔli'ze], *v.t.* to symbolize.

symbolisme [sɛ̃bɔ'lism], *n.m.* symbolism.

symétrie [sime'tri], *n.f.* symmetry.

symétrique [sime'trik], *a.* symmetrical.

symétriquement [simetrik'mɑ̃], *adv.* symmetrically.

sympathie [sɛ̃pa'ti], *n.f.* liking, fellow-feeling.

sympathique [sɛ̃pa'tik], *a.* congenial, likeable.

sympathisant

sympathisant [sɛ̃pati'zɑ̃], *a.* sympathizing.—*n.m.* (*Pol.*) fellow-traveller.
sympathiser [sɛ̃pati'ze], *v.i.* to get on well together.
symphonie [sɛ̃fo'ni], *n.f.* symphony.
symptomatique [sɛ̃ptɔma'tik], *a.* symptomatic.
symptôme [sɛ̃p'to:m], *n.m.* symptom; indication, sign; token.
synagogue [sina'gɔg], *n.f.* synagogue.
synchronisation [sɛ̃krɔniza'sjɔ̃], *n.f.* synchronization.
synchroniser [sɛ̃krɔni'ze], *v.t.* to synchronize.
syncope [sɛ̃'kɔp], *n.f.* syncope, swoon, fainting fit; (*Mus.*) syncopation.
syndic [sɛ̃'dik], *n.m.* syndic, trustee; assignee (*in bankruptcy*).
syndicalisme [sɛ̃dika'lism], *n.m.* **syndicalisme ouvrier**, trade-unionism.
syndicaliste [sɛ̃dika'list], *a.* and *n.* trade-unionist.
syndicat [sɛ̃di'ka], *n.m.* syndicate, trusteeship; **syndicat d'initiative**, tourists' information bureau; **syndicat ouvrier**, trade-union.
synonyme [sinɔ'nim], *a.* synonymous.—*n.m.* synonym.
syntaxe [sɛ̃'taks], *n.f.* syntax.
synthétique [sɛ̃te'tik], *a.* synthetic.
syriaque [si'rjak], *a.* Syriac.—*n.m.* Syriac (*language*).
Syrie [si'ri], **la**, *f.* Syria.
syrien [si'rjɛ̃], *a.* Syrian.—*n.m.* Syrian (*language*); (**Syrien**, *fem.* **-enne**) Syrian (*person*).
systématique [sistema'tik], *a.* systematic(al).
systématiquement [sistematik'mɑ̃], *adv.* systematically.
système [sis'tɛm], *n.m.* system, scheme, plan; device.

T

T, t [te], *n.m.* the twentieth letter of the alphabet.
t' [t], *elision* [TE].
ta [ta], [TON (1)].
tabac [ta'ba], *n.m.* tobacco; snuff.
tabatière [taba'tjɛːr], *n.f.* snuff-box.
tabernacle [tabɛr'nakl], *n.m.* tent; tabernacle.
table [tabl], *n.f.* table; board (*food, fare*); mess (*of officers etc.*); slab; face (*of anvil etc.*); table of contents etc.; **faire table rase**, to make a clean sweep; **mettre** or **dresser la table**, to lay the table.
tableau [ta'blo], *n.m.* (*pl.* **-eaux**) picture, painting, tableau; scene; description; list; blackboard.
tablée [ta'ble], *n.f.* company at table.
tablette [ta'blɛt], *n.f.* shelf; tablet; slab, bar (*of chocolate*); (*Pharm.*) lozenge; note-book.
tablier [ta'blje], *n.m.* apron (*in all senses*); chess- or draught-board.
tabou [ta'bu], *a.* and *n.m.* taboo.

tabouret [tabu'rɛ], *n.m.* stool, foot-stool.
tabourin [tabu'rɛ̃], *n.m.* chimney-cowl.
tabulateur [tabyla'tœːr], *n.m.* tabulator; (*Teleph.*) dial.
tachant [ta'ʃɑ̃], *a.* easily soiled.
tache [taʃ], *n.f.* spot, stain; (*fig.*) blot.
tâche [tɑːʃ], *n.f.* task, job.
tacher [ta'ʃe], *v.t.* to stain, to spot; (*fig.*) to taint.
tâcher [tɑ'ʃe], *v.i.* to try, to endeavour, to strive.
tacheter [taʃ'te], *v.t.* (*conjug. like* APPELER) to fleck, to speckle, to mottle.
tacite [ta'sit], *a.* tacit, implied.
tacitement [tasit'mɑ̃], *adv.* tacitly.
taciturne [tasi'tyrn], *a.* taciturn.
taciturnité [tasityrni'te], *n.f.* taciturnity.
tact [takt], *n.m.* feeling, touch; tact.
tacticien [takti'sjɛ̃], *n.m.* tactician.
tactile [tak'til], *a.* tactile.
tactilité [taktili'te], *n.f.* tactility.
tactique [tak'tik], *a.* tactical.—*n.f.* tactics; (*fig.*) stratagem, move.
taffetas [taf'ta], *n.m.* taffeta.
taie (1) [tɛ], *n.f.* **taie d'oreiller**, pillow-case.
taie (2) [tɛ], *n.f.* film, speck (*in the eye*).
taillade [tɑ'jad], *n.f.* slash, gash, cut.
taillader [tɑja'de], *v.t.* to slash, to cut, to gash.
taillant [tɑ'jɑ̃], *n.m.* edge (*of a knife etc.*).
taille [tɑːj], *n.f.* cutting, cut, fashion; edge (*of a sword*); height, stature; waist, figure; (*Hort.*) pruning; **de taille à**, quite capable of.
taillé [tɑ'je], *a.* cut, carved; well-built (*person*).
taille-crayon [tɑjkrɛ'jɔ̃], *n.m.* (*pl.* **-crayons**) pencil-sharpener.
taille-ongles [tɑj'ɔ̃:gl], *n.m. inv.* nail-clippers.
tailler [tɑ'je], *v.t.* to cut, to cut out; to carve; to hew; to prune; to sharpen; to shape; to deal (*cards*).
tailleur [tɑ'jœːr], *n.m.* tailor; cutter; hewer; (*woman's two-piece*) suit.
tailleuse [tɑ'jøːz], *n.f.* tailoress.
taillis [tɑ'ji], *n.m. inv.* copse; brushwood.
tain [tɛ̃], *n.m.* foil; silvering (*for mirrors*).
taire [tɛːr], *v.t. irr.* to say nothing of, to pass over in silence, to suppress, to keep dark. **se taire**, *v.r.* to be silent; to remain unsaid.
talc [talk], *n.m.* talc, talcum powder.
talent [ta'lɑ̃], *n.m.* talent; (*fig.*) ability.
talion [ta'ljɔ̃], *n.m.* talion, retaliation.
talisman [talis'mɑ̃], *n.m.* talisman.
taloche [ta'lɔʃ], *n.f.* cuff, thump, buffet.
talocher [talɔ'ʃe], *v.t.* to cuff, to box (*someone's*) ears.
talon [ta'lɔ̃], *n.m.* heel; counterfoil.
talonner [talɔ'ne], *v.t.* to be close on the heels of; to press hard, to spur.—*v.i.* (*Naut.*) to ground; (*Ftb.*) to heel out (*of the scrum*).
talonneur [talɔ'nœːr], *n.m.* (*Ftb.*) hooker.
talus [ta'ly], *n.m.* slope, ramp; embankment.
talutage [taly'ta:ʒ], *n.m.* sloping, embanking.
tamarin [tama'rɛ̃], *n.m.* tamarind.
tamaris [tama'ris], **tamarisc** [tama'risk], *n.m.* tamarisk.
tambour [tɑ̃'buːr], *n.m.* drum; drummer; embroidery frame; (*Anat.*) tympanum; **tambour de ville**, town crier.
tambourin [tɑ̃bu'rɛ̃], *n.m.* Provençal tabor.
tambourinage [tɑ̃buri'na:ʒ], *n.m.* drumming.
tambouriner [tɑ̃buri'ne], *v.t.* to advertise.—*v.i.* to drum, to tattoo.

tambour-major [tãburma'ʒɔːr], *n.m.* (*pl.* **tambours-majors**) drum-major.

tamis [ta'mi], *n.m. inv.* sieve, sifter, strainer.

tamisage [tami'zaːʒ], *n.m.* sifting, straining.

Tamise [ta'miːz], **la**, *f.* the Thames.

tamiser [tami'ze], *v.t.* to sift, to strain; to filter.

tamiseur [tami'zœːr], *n.m.* (*fem.* **-euse**) sifter.

tampon [tã'põ], *n.m.* stopper; plug; bung; buffer; pad (*used in engraving etc.*).

tamponnement [tãpɔn'mã], *n.m.* plugging, stopping; (*Rail.*) head-on collision.

tamponner [tãpɔ'ne], *v.t.* to plug, to stop up; to run into (*another train etc.*). **se tamponner**, *v.r.* to collide.

tan [tã], *a. inv.* tan(-coloured).—*n.m.* tan; tanner's bark.

tancer [tã'se], *v.t.* (*conjug. like* COMMENCER) to rate, to lecture, to scold.

tanche [tãːʃ], *n.f.* tench.

tandem [tã'dɛm], *n.m.* tandem.

tandis [tã'di] **que**, *conj. phr.* while; whereas.

tangage [tã'gaːʒ], *n.m.* pitching (*of ship, aeroplane*).

tangent [tã'ʒã], *a.* tangential.—*n.f.* (**-e**) tangent.

tangible [tã'ʒibl], *a.* tangible.

tangiblement [tãʒiblə'mã], *adv.* tangibly.

tangue [tãːg], *n.f.* slimy sand (*used as manure*).

tanguer [tã'ge], *v.i.* (*Naut.*) to pitch.

tanière [ta'njɛːr], *n.f.* den, hole, lair (*of beasts*).

tank [tãk], *n.m.* (*Mil.*) tank.

tannage [ta'naːʒ], *n.m.* tanning.

tannant [ta'nã], *a.* tanning; (*pop.*) tiresome, annoying.

tanné [ta'ne], *a.* tanned, sunburnt (*skin*); tawny.—*n.m.* tan (*colour*).

tanner [ta'ne], *v.t.* to tan; (*pop.*) to tease; to beat.

tannerie [tan'ri], *n.f.* tan-yard, tannery.

tanneur [ta'nœːr], *n.m.* tanner.

tant [tã], *adv.* so much, such; so many; as much, as many; to such a degree, so; so far; so long, as long; *tant bien que mal*, somehow or other, after a fashion; *tant pis*, too bad, never mind.

tantaliser [tãtali'ze], *v.t.* to tantalize.

tante [tãːt], *n.f.* aunt; (*pop.*) pawn-broker, 'uncle'.

tantôt [tã'to], *adv.* presently, by and by, anon; soon; a little while ago, just now; sometimes.

Tanzanie [tãza'ni], **la**, *f.* Tanzania.

taon [tã], *n.m.* ox-fly, gadfly, cleg.

tapage [ta'paːʒ], *n.m.* noise, uproar, row; (*colloq.*) show.

tapageur [tapa'ʒœːr], *a.* (*fem.* **-euse**) rackety, boisterous, noisy; flashy.—*n.m.* (*fem.* **-euse**) noisy person, blusterer.

tape [tap], *n.f.* rap, slap, tap, thump.

taper [ta'pe], *v.t.* to hit, to slap; to smack, to tap.—*v.i.* to hit, to stamp; to strum; to beat down (*of sun*).

tapinois [tapi'nwa], *only in* **en tapinois**, *adv. phr.* stealthily, slyly.

tapioca [tapjo'ka], *n.m.* tapioca.

tapir [ta'piːr], *n.m.* tapir (*animal*).

tapir (se) [sɔta'piːr], *v.r.* to squat, to crouch, to cower, to lurk.

tapis [ta'pi], *n.m.* carpet, rug; cover-cloth (*for tables etc.*).

tapis-brosse [tapi'brɔs], *n.m.* (*pl.* **-brosses**) door-mat.

tapisser [tapi'se], *v.t.* to hang with tapestry; to cover; to deck, to adorn; to paper; to carpet.

tapisserie [tapis'ri], *n.f.* tapestry, hangings; wallpaper; upholstery.

tapissier [tapi'sje], *n.m.* (*fem.* **-ière**) upholsterer; tapestry-worker.

tapoter [tapɔ'te], *v.t.* to pat, to tap; to strum.

taquin [ta'kɛ̃], *a.* teasing.—*n.m.* (*fem.* **-e**) tease, teasing person.

taquiner [taki'ne], *v.t.* to tease, to plague.

taquinerie [takin'ri], *n.f.* teasing; teasing disposition.

tard [taːr], *adv.* late.—*n.m.* late hour.

tarder [tar'de], *v.i.* to delay; to tarry, to loiter; to be long; (*impers.*) to long (*de*).

tardif [tar'dif], *a.* (*fem.* **-dive**) tardy, late; slow, belated; backward.

tardivement [tardiv'mã], *adv.* tardily, slowly, belatedly.

tare [taːr], *n.f.* tare; (*Comm.*) waste, damage; (*fig.*) blemish, defect.

taré [ta're], *a.* damaged, spoiled; disreputable.

tarentule [tarã'tyl], *n.f.* tarantula.

tarer [ta're], *v.t.* to injure, to damage, to spoil; (*Comm.*) to tare. **se tarer**, *v.r.* to spoil, to deteriorate.

targuer (se) [sɔtar'ge], *v.r.* to boast, to brag.

tarif [ta'rif], *n.m.* tariff, rate, scale of prices.

tarifer [tari'fe], *v.t.* to tariff; to price, to rate.

tarir [ta'riːr], *v.t.* to dry up; to exhaust.—*v.i.* to dry up; to be exhausted; to cease. **se tarir**, *v.r.* to dry up.

tarissable [tari'sabl], *a.* exhaustible.

tarissement [taris'mã], *n.m.* exhausting, drying up.

tartan [tar'tã], *n.m.* tartan, plaid.

tarte [tart], *n.f.* tart, flan.

tartelette [tar'tlɛt], *n.f.* tartlet.

tartine [tar'tin], *n.f.* slice of bread (*with butter, jam etc.*).

tartufe [tar'tyf], *n.m.* hypocrite.

tas [tã], *n.m. inv.* heap, pile; (*fig.*) lot, set (*of persons etc.*).

Tasmanie [tasma'ni], **la**, *f.* Tasmania.

tasmanien [tasma'njɛ̃], *a.* Tasmanian.—*n.m.* (**Tasmanien**, *fem.* **-enne**) Tasmanian (*person*).

tasse [taːs], *n.f.* cup.

tassement [tas'mã], *n.m.* settling, sinking, subsidence.

tasser [ta'se], *v.t.* to heap or pile up; to compress, to squeeze, to cram.—*v.i.* to grow thick. **se tasser**, *v.r.* to sink, to settle, to subside; to huddle together (*of persons*).

tâter [tɑ'te], *v.t.* to feel; to try, to taste; to sound, to test.—*v.i.* to taste, to try (*de or à*). **se tâter**, *v.r.* to examine oneself.

tatillon [tati'jõ], *a.* (*fem.* **-onne**) niggling, finical.

tâtonnement [tɑtɔn'mã], *n.m.* groping.

tâtonner [tɑtɔ'ne], *v.i.* to feel one's way, to grope.

tâtons (à) [atɑ'tõ], *adv. phr.* gropingly.

tatouage [ta'twaːʒ], *n.m.* tattooing.

tatouer [ta'twe], *v.t.* to tattoo.

taudis [to'di], *n.m.* hovel, slum, hole.

taupe [toːp], *n.f.* mole; moleskin.

taupier [to'pje], *n.m.* mole-catcher.
taupière [to'pjɛːr], *n.f.* mole-trap.
taupinière [topi'njɛːr], **taupinée** [topi'ne], *n.f.* mole-hill; hillock, knoll.
taure [toːr], *n.f.* heifer.
taureau [to'ro], *n.m.* (*pl.* **-eaux**) bull; (*Astron.*) Taurus.
taux [to], *n.m. inv.* price, rate; rate of interest.
taverne [ta'vɛrn], *n.f.* tavern, café, restaurant.
tavernier [tavɛr'nje], *n.m.* (*fem.* **-ière**) innkeeper.
taxation [taksɑ'sjɔ̃], *n.f.* taxation; fixing of prices.
taxe [taks], *n.f.* tax; duty, rate; fixing of prices; controlled price.
taxer [tak'se], *v.t.* to tax; to rate, to fix the price of; to accuse (*de*).
taxi [tak'si], *n.m.* taxi (-cab).
taxiphone [taksi'fon], *n.m.* public telephone (*box*).
Tchécoslovaquie [tʃekɔslɔva'ki], la, *f.* Czechoslovakia.
tchèque [tʃɛk], *a.* Czech.—*n.m.* Czech (*language*).—*n.* (**Tchèque**) Czech (*person*).
te [tə, t], *pron. obj.* *thee, you.
technicien [tɛkni'sjɛ̃], *n.m.* (*fem.* **-enne**) technician.
technique [tɛk'nik], *a.* technical.—*n.f.* technique.
techniquement [tɛknik'mã], *adv.* technically.
technologie [tɛknɔlɔ'ʒi], *n.f.* technology.
technologique [tɛknɔlɔ'ʒik], *a.* technological.
technologue [tɛknɔ'lɔg], *n.* technologist.
teck or **tek** [tɛk], *n.m.* teak, teak-wood.
teigne [tɛɲ], *n.f.* tinea (*moth*); tinea (*skin-disease, such as ringworm*).
teigneux [tɛ'ɲø], *a.* (*fem.* **-euse**) scurvy.—*n.m.* (*fem.* **-euse**) scurfy person.
teindre [tɛ̃ːdr], *v.t. irr.* (*conjug. like* CRAINDRE) to dye, to stain.
teint [tɛ̃], *n.m.* dye, colour; complexion; hue.
teinte [tɛ̃t], *n.f.* tint, colour, shade, hue; (*fig.*) smack, touch.
teinter [tɛ̃'te], *v.t.* to tint; to give a colour to.
teinture [tɛ̃'tyːr], *n.f.* dye; dyeing; colour, hue; (*Pharm.*) tincture.
teinturerie [tɛ̃tyr'ri], *n.f.* dyeing; dye-works; dry-cleaning.
teinturier [tɛ̃ty'rje], *n.m.* (*fem.* **-ière**) dyer; dry-cleaner.
tek [TECK].
tel [tɛl], *a.* (*fem.* **telle**) such; like, similar.—*pron. indef.* such a one; *M. un tel*, Mr. So-and-so.
télécommande [telekɔ'mãːd], *n.f.* remote control.
télécommunications [telekɔmynikɑ'sjɔ̃], *n.f. pl.* telecommunications.
télégramme [tele'gram], *n.m.* telegram.
télégraphe [tele'graf], *n.m.* telegraph.
télégraphie [telegra'fi], *n.f.* telegraphy; *télégraphie sans fil*, wireless telegraphy.
télégraphier [telegra'fje], *v.t., v.i.* to telegraph; to wire, to cable.
télégraphique [telegra'fik], *a.* telegraphic.
télégraphiste [telegra'fist], *n.* telegraphist.
téléguidé [telegi'de], *a.* guided; *engin téléguidé*, guided missile.
téléimprimeur [teleɛ̃pri'mœːr], **téléscripteur** [teleskrip'tœr], *n.m.* teleprinter.
télémètre [tele'mɛtr], *n.m.* rangefinder.

télépathie [telepa'ti], *n.f.* telepathy.
télépathique [telepa'tik], *a.* telepathic.
téléphérique [telefe'rik], *a.* and *n.m.* teleferic.
téléphone [tele'fon], *n.m.* telephone; *un coup de téléphone*, a telephone call.
téléphoner [telefo'ne], *v.t., v.i.* to telephone, to ring up.
téléphonique [telefo'nik], *a.* *cabine téléphonique*, call-box.
téléphoniste [telefo'nist], *n.* telephone operator.
télescope [telɛs'kɔp], *n.m.* telescope.
télescopique [telɛskɔ'pik], *a.* telescopic.
téléscripteur [teleskrip'tœːr], [TÉLÉIMPRIMEUR].
téléspectateur [telespɛkta'tœːr], *n.m.* (*fem.* **-trice**) televiewer.
téléviser [televi'ze], *v.t.* to televise.
téléviseur [televi'zœːr], *n.m.* television (receiving-)set.
télévision [televi'zjɔ̃], *n.f.* television.
tellement [tɛl'mã], *adv.* so, in such a manner; so much, so far.
téméraire [teme'rɛːr], *a.* rash, reckless.—*n.* reckless person, daredevil.
témérairement [temerɛr'mã], *adv.* rashly, recklessly.
témérité [temeri'te], *n.f.* temerity.
témoignage [temwa'naːʒ], *n.m.* testimony, evidence, witness; testimonial; (*fig.*) token, mark, proof.
témoigner [temwa'ɲe], *v.t.* to testify; to show, to prove, to be the sign of.—*v.i.* to testify, to give evidence (*de*).
témoin [te'mwɛ̃], *n.m.* witness, evidence, proof, mark; second (*in duels*).
tempe [tãːp], *n.f.* (*Anat.*) temple.
tempérament [tãpera'mã], *n.m.* constitution, temperament; temper; (*fig.*) moderation, compromise; *à tempérament*, by instalments.
tempérance [tãpe'rãːs], *n.f.* temperance.
température [tãpera'tyːr], *n.f.* temperature.
tempéré [tãpe're], *a.* temperate (*of climate*); limited, constitutional (*of governments*); restrained, sober (*of style*).
tempérer [tãpe're], *v.t.* (*conjug. like* CÉDER) to temper, to moderate, to allay, to assuage, to check. *se tempérer*, *v.r.* to become mild (*of the weather*).
tempête [tã'pɛːt], *n.f.* storm, tempest.
tempêter [tãpe'te], *v.i.* to storm, to bluster, to fume.
tempétueusement [tãpetɥøz'mã], *adv.* tempestuously, violently.
tempétueux [tãpe'tɥø], *a.* (*fem.* **-euse**) tempestuous, boisterous, stormy.
temple [tãːpl], *n.m.* temple; French Protestant church.
templier [tãpli'e], *n.m.* Knight-Templar.
temporaire [tãpɔ'rɛːr], *a.* temporary.
temporairement [tãpɔrɛr'mã], *adv.* temporarily, provisionally.
temporel [tãpɔ'rɛl], *a.* (*fem.* **-elle**) temporal.
temporisateur [tãpɔriza'tœːr], *a.* (*fem.* **-trice**) procrastinating, temporizing.—*n.m.* (*fem.* **-trice**) temporizer, procrastinator.
temporisation [tãpɔrizɑ'sjɔ̃], *n.f.* temporizing, procrastination.
temporiser [tãpɔri'ze], *v.i.* to temporize, to delay.

temps [tã], *n.m. inv.* time, while, period, term; occasion; season; weather; (*Gram.*) tense; *à temps,* in time; *avec le temps,* in course of time; *dans le temps,* formerly; *en temps et lieu,* in proper time and place.

tenable [tə'nabl], *a.* tenable; bearable.

tenace [tə'nas], *a.* tenacious, adhesive, sticky.

ténacité [tenasi'te], *n.f.* tenacity, toughness; retentiveness (*of memory*).

tenaille [tə'nɑːj], *n.f.* (*usu. in pl.*) pincers, nippers, pliers.

tenailler [tənɑ'je], *v.t.* to torture with red-hot pincers; (*fig.*) to torture.

tenant [tə'nã], *a. séance tenante,* during the sitting; forthwith, then and there.— *n.m.* holder (*at a tournament*); (*fig.*) champion, defender.

tendance [tã'dãːs], *n.f.* tendency; leaning, bent, inclination.

tendancieux [tãdã'sjø], *a.* (*fem.* **-euse**) tendentious; insinuating, suggestive.

tendeur [tã'dœːr], *n.m.* (*fem* **-euse**) spreader, layer, setter (*of snares*); wire-strainer.

tendoir [tã'dwaːr], *n.m.* clothes-line.

tendon [tã'dõ], *n.m.* tendon, sinew.

tendre (1) [tãːdr], *a.* tender, soft; delicate, sensitive; affectionate; moving, early, young, new.

tendre (2) [tãːdr], *v.t.* to stretch, to strain; to bend (*a bow etc.*); to spread, to lay, to set; to hold out; to pitch (*tents*); to hang (*tapestry etc.*).—*v.i.* to lead; to tend, to conduce.

tendrement [tãdrə'mã], *adv.* tenderly, affectionately.

tendresse [tã'drɛs], *n.f.* tenderness, fondness; (*pl.*) endearments.

tendron [tã'drõ], *n.m.* shoot (*of plants*).

tendu [tã'dy], *a.* stretched, held out; tight, tense; strained.

ténèbres [te'nɛːbr], *n.f.* (*used only in pl.*) darkness, night, gloom.

ténébreusement [tenebrøz'mã], *adv.* darkly gloomily; secretly.

ténébreux [tene'brø], *a.* (*fem.* **-euse**) dark, gloomy, overcast; obscure, mysterious.

teneur (1) [tə'nœːr], *n.f.* tenor, terms, text; purport.

teneur (2) [tə'nœːr], *n.m.* (*fem.* **-euse**) holder; *teneur de livres,* book-keeper.

ténia [te'nja], *n.m.* tapeworm.

tenir [tə'niːr], *v.t. irr.* to hold, to have hold of; to have, to possess; to seize; to occupy; to keep, to follow; to retain; to perform; to consider.—*v.i.* to hold; to adhere, to stick; to hold together; to cling; to prize (*à*); to be attached *or* related (*à*); to be contiguous; to depend, to result (*de*); to be held (*of fairs, markets, assemblies etc.*); to take after; to savour; to persist; to resist; to be anxious (*à*). **se tenir,** *v.r.* to hold fast, to remain; to adhere; to consider oneself; to contain oneself, to refrain.

tennis [te'nis], *n.m.* lawn-tennis.

tenon [tə'nõ], *n.m.* tenon; bolt (*of fire-arms*).

ténor [te'nɔːr], *n.m.* (*Mus.*) tenor.

tension [tã'sjõ], *n.f.* tension, strain; tenseness; (*Elec.*) voltage.

tentacule [tãta'kyl], *n.m.* tentacle, feeler.

tentant [tã'tã], *a.* tempting.

tentateur [tãta'tœːr], *a.* (*fem.* **-trice**) tempting.—*n.m.* (*fem.* **-trice**) tempter, temptress.

tentation [tãta'sjõ], *n.f.* temptation.

tentative [tãta'tiːv], *n.f.* attempt, trial, endeavour.

tente [tãːt], *n.f.* tent, pavilion; (*Naut.*) awning.

tenter [tã'te], *v.t.* to attempt, to try; to tempt.

tenture [tã'tyːr], *n.f.* hangings, tapestry; wall-paper; paper-hanging.

ténu [te'ny], *a.* tenuous, thin, slender.

tenue [tə'ny], *n.f.* holding (*of assemblies etc.*); session; attitude (*of a person*); behaviour, bearing; dress; keeping (*of books*); *grande tenue,* (*Mil.*) full dress; *petite tenue,* undress.

ténuité [tenɥi'te], *n.f.* tenuity, thinness; (*fig.*) insignificance.

tenure [tə'nyːr], *n.f.* tenure.

ter [tɛːr], *adv.* thrice; for the third time.

térébenthine [terebã'tin], *n.f.* turpentine.

térébinthe [tere'bɛ̃ːt], *n.m.* turpentine-tree, terebinth.

tergiversation [tɛrʒiversa'sjõ], *n.f.* tergiversation, evasion.

tergiverser [tɛrʒiver'se], *v.i.* to waver, to beat about the bush.

terme [tɛrm], *n.m.* term; termination, end; limit, boundary; time; three months; quarter's rent; expression; (*pl.*) state, conditions, terms; *avant terme,* prematurely.

terminaison [tɛrminɛ'zõ], *n.f.* termination, ending.

terminer [tɛrmi'ne], *v.t.* to bound, to limit; to terminate, to conclude. **se terminer,** *v.r.* to terminate; to be bounded.

terminus [tɛrmi'nys], *n.m.* terminus (*of railway*).

terne [tɛrn], *a.* dull, dim; wan; spiritless.

ternir [tɛr'niːr], *v.t.* to dull, to deaden; to tarnish. **se ternir,** *v.r.* to tarnish, to grow dull; to fade (*of colours*).

ternissure [tɛrni'syːr], *n.f.* tarnishing, fading; stain.

terrain [tɛ'rɛ̃], *n.m.* piece of ground; soil, earth; site; field, course.

terrassant [tɛra'sã], *a.* crushing (*news etc.*).

terrasse [tɛ'ras], *n.f.* terrace; flat roof, balcony.

terrassement [tɛras'mã], *n.m.* earthwork, embankment; ballasting.

terrasser [tɛra'se], *v.t.* to embank; to throw to the ground; to beat; to confound, to dismay.

terrassier [tɛra'sje], *n.m.* digger, excavator, navvy; earthwork contractor.

terre [tɛːr], *n.f.* earth; land; ground, soil; dominion, territory; grounds, estate, property; (*C*) farm.

terreau [tɛ'ro], *n.m.* (*pl.* **-eaux**) compost.

Terre-Neuve [tɛr'nœːv], *f.* Newfoundland.

terre-neuve [tɛr'nœːv], *n.m. inv.* Newfoundland (*dog*).

terrer [tɛ're], *v.t.* to earth up (*a tree etc.*). *v.i.* to burrow. **se terrer,** *v.r.* to go to ground.

terrestre [tɛ'rɛstr], *a.* terrestrial, earthly.

terreur [tɛ'rœːr], *n.f.* terror; awe, dread.

terreux [tɛ'rø], *a.* (*fem.* **-euse**) terreous, earthy; dirty; dull (*of colours*); ashen (*of the face*).

terrible [tɛ'ribl], *a.* terrible, dreadful; unmanageable (*of children*).

terriblement

terriblement [tɛriblə'mɑ̃], *adv.* terribly; (*colloq.*) with a vengeance.
terrier [tɛ'rje], *n.m.* burrow, hole; earth (*of fox*); terrier (*dog*).
terrifier [tɛri'fje], *v.t.* to terrify, to dismay.
terrine [tɛ'rin], *n.f.* earthen pan, dish; potted meat.
territoire [tɛri'twa:r], *n.m.* territory, district
territorial [tɛrito'rjal], *a.* (*m. pl.* **-aux**) territorial.
terroir [tɛ'rwa:r], *n.m.* soil, ground; *goût de terroir*, raciness (*of style*); native tang (*of wine*).
terroriser [tɛrɔri'ze], *v.t.* to terrorize.
terrorisme [tɛrɔ'rism], *n.m.* terrorism.
terroriste [tɛrɔ'rist], *n.m.* terrorist.
tertiaire [tɛr'sjɛ:r], *a.* tertiary.
tertre [tɛrtr], *n.m.*, knoll, hillock.
tes [te], [TON (1)].
tesson [tɛ'sɔ̃], *n.m.* potsherd, fragment of broken glass etc.
test [tɛst], *n.m.* shell; trial, test.
testacé [tɛsta'se], *a.* testaceous.—*n.m.* testacean.
testament [tɛsta'mɑ̃], *n.m.* will.
tester [tɛs'te], *v.t.* to test.—*v.i.* to make one's will.
testimonial [tɛstimɔ'njal], *a.* (*m. pl.* **-aux**) testifying, testimonial.
tétanos [teta'nɔs], *n.m.* tetanus, lock-jaw.
têtard [tɛ'ta:r], *n.m.* tadpole.
tête [tɛ:t], *n.f.* head; head-piece; face; beginning; top; van, vanguard; (*fig.*) brains, sense, judgment; presence of mind; *en tête*, in one's head; in front, ahead; *mal de tête*, headache; *tête de mort*, skull.
tête-à-tête [tɛta'tɛːt], *n.m. inv.* tête-à-tête, private interview *or* conversation; settee (*for two*).
téter [te'te], *v.t.* (*conjug. like* CÉDER) to suck.
têtière [tɛ'tjɛːr], *n.f.* infant's cap; head-stall (*of a bridle*); antimacassar.
tétin [te'tɛ̃], *n.m.* nipple, teat; breast.
téton [te'tɔ̃], *n.m.* teat; (*fam.*) breast.
tétrarque [te'trark], *n.m.* tetrarch.
tétras [te'tra], *n.m. inv.* (*Orn.*) grouse.
têtu [te'ty], *a.* headstrong, stubborn, obstinate.
teutonique [tøtɔ'nik], *a.* teutonic.
texte [tɛkst], *n.m.* text; theme, matter, subject; passage (*of Scripture*).
textile [tɛks'til], *a.* and *n.m.* textile.
textuel [tɛks'tɥɛl], *a.* (*fem.* **-elle**) textual, word for word.
textuellement [tɛkstɥɛl'mɑ̃], *adv.* textually.
texture [tɛks'ty:r], *n.f.* texture; disposition.
thaïlandais [taila'dɛ], *a.* Thai.—*n.m.* Thai (*language*); (**Thaïlandais,** *fem.* **-aise**) Thai (*person*).
Thaïlande [tai'lɑ̃:d], **la,** *f.* Thailand, Siam.
thé [te], *n.m.* tea; tea-party.
théâtral [tea'tral], *a.* (*m. pl.* **-aux**) theatrical.
théâtre [te'a:tr], *n.m.* theatre, playhouse; stage; plays (*collection*), scene; *coup de théâtre*, striking event.
théerie [te'ri], *n.f.* tea-plantation.
théière [te'jɛːr], *n.f.* teapot.
théisme [te'ism], *n.m.* theism.
thème [tɛ:m], *n.m.* topic, subject, theme; (*sch.*) prose, composition.
théodolite [teɔdɔ'lit], *n.m.* theodolite.
théologie [teɔlɔ'ʒi], *n.f.* theology; divinity.

théologien [teɔlɔ'ʒjɛ̃], *n.m.* theologian.
théorème [teɔ'rɛm], *n.m.* theorem.
théorie [teɔ'ri], *n.f.* theory, speculation.
théorique [teɔ'rik], *a.* theoretical.
théoriquement [teɔrik'mɑ̃], *adv.* theoretically.
théoriser [teɔri'ze], *v.t., v.i.* to theorize.
théoriste [teɔ'rist], *n.* theorist.
thérapie [tera'pi], *n.f.* therapy.
Thérèse [te'rɛːz], *f.* Theresa.
thermal [tɛr'mal], *a.* (*m. pl.* **-aux**) thermal; *eaux thermales*, hot springs.
thermomètre [tɛrmɔ'mɛtr], *n.m.* thermometer.
thermos [tɛr'mɔs], *n.m.* thermos (flask).
thermostat [tɛrmo'sta], *n.m.* thermostat.
thésauriser [tezɔri'ze], *v.t.* to treasure.—*v.i.* to hoard treasure.
thèse [tɛːz], *n.f.* thesis, proposition.
thibaude [ti'bo:d], *n.f.* hair-cloth, coarse drugget.
Thomas [tɔ'ma], *m.* Thomas.
thon [tɔ̃], *n.m.* tunny-fish.
thoracique [tɔra'sik], *a.* thoracic.
thorax [tɔ'raks], *n.m.* thorax, chest.
thrombose [trɔ̃'boːz], *n.f.* thrombosis.
thym [tɛ̃], *n.m.* thyme.
thyroïde [tirɔ'id], *a.* thyroid.
tiare [tja:r], *n.f.* tiara.
Tibet [ti'bɛ], *le m.* Tibet.
tibétain [tibe'tɛ̃], *a.* Tibetan.—*n.m.* Tibetan (*language*); (**Tibétain,** *fem.* **-aine**) Tibetan (*person*).
tibia [ti'bja], *n.m.* (*Anat.*) tibia, shin-bone.
tic [tik], *n.m.* tic, twitching; bad habit.
ticket [ti'kɛ], *n.m.* ticket (*for bus, underground etc., but not railways*).
tiède [tjɛd], *a.* lukewarm, tepid, mild; (*fig.*) indifferent.
tièdement [tjed'mɑ̃], *adv.* with indifference.
tiédeur [tje'dœːr], *n.f.* lukewarmness; (*fig.*) indifference.
tiédir [tje'diːr], *v.t.* to take the chill off, to tepefy.—*v.i.* to cool, to grow lukewarm.
tien [tjɛ̃], *pron. poss. m.* (*fem.* **tienne**) *thine, yours.—n.* (*pl.*) **les tiens,** your relations and friends.
tiens! [tjɛ̃], *imperative* [TENIR], *int.* well, hello! look here! here! really? you don't say so!
tierce (1) [tjɛrs], *n.f.* a third (*of time*); tierce (*at cards etc.*).
tiers [tjɛːr], *a.* (*fem.* **tierce** (2)) third.—*n.m.* third person, third party; (*fig.*) stranger; third part.
tige [tiːʒ], *n.f.* stem, stalk; trunk (*of tree*); straw (*of corn*); shank (*of a key, anchor etc.*); stock (*of a family*).
tignasse [ti'ɲas], *n.f.* old wig; (*pop.*) mop, shock (*of hair*).
tigre [tigr], *n.m.* (*fem.* **-esse**) tiger, tigress.
tigrer [ti'gre], *v.t.* to stripe, to spot, to speckle.
tillac [ti'jak], *n.m.* deck.
tilleul [ti'jœl], *n.m.* lime-tree, linden-tree.
timbale [tɛ̃'bal], *n.f.* kettledrum, timbal; metal cup *or* mug; kitchen-mould.
timbre [tɛ̃:br], *n.m.* bell, clock-chime; sound, tone; stamp; stamp-duty; postmark.
timbré [tɛ̃'bre], *a.* stamped; (*fam.*) cracked.
timbre-poste [tɛ̃brə'pɔst], *n.m.* (*pl.* **timbres-poste**) postage-stamp.

timbrer [tɛ̃′bre], *v.t.* to stamp; to stick a stamp on (*a letter*).

timide [ti′mid], *a.* shy, bashful, self-conscious; timid.

timidement [timid′mɑ̃], *adv.* shyly; timidly.

timidité [timidi′te], *n.f.* shyness, bashfulness; timidity.

timon [ti′mɔ̃], *n.m.* pole (*of a carriage, cart etc.*); shaft; beam (*of a plough*); (*Naut.*) helm, tiller; (*fig.*) direction, government.

timonerie [timɔn′ri], *n.f.* steerage, steering.

timonier [timɔ′nje], *n.m.* steersman, helmsman; wheel-horse.

timoré [timɔ′re], *a.* timorous, fearful.

Timothée [timɔ′te], *m.* Timothy.

tine [tin], *n.f.* tub, water-cask.

tintamarre [tɛ̃ta′maːr], *n.m.* hubbub, uproar, hurly-burly, din.

tintement [tɛ̃t′mɑ̃], *n.m.* ringing sound, tinkling; tolling; singing *or* buzzing (*in the ears etc.*).

tinter [tɛ̃′te], *v.t.* to ring, to toll; to sound (*a knell etc.*); (*Naut.*) to prop, to support.—*v.i.* to ring, to toll; to tinkle, to jingle; to tingle.

tintouin [tɛ̃′twɛ̃], *n.m.* (*fam.*) anxiety, trouble.

tique [tik], *n.f.* cattle-tick, dog-tick.

tiquer [ti′ke], *v.i.* to have a tic, to twitch.

tiqueté [tik′te], *a.* speckled, spotted.

tiqueture [tik′tyːr], *n.f.* mottling, speckles.

tir [tiːr], *n.m.* shooting; firing, fire; shooting-gallery, rifle-range.

tirade [ti′rad], *n.f.* passage (*of prose or verse*); tirade.

tirage [ti′raːʒ], *n.m.* drawing, hauling, towing; tow-path; (*fig.*) difficulties; working off; printing, circulation (*of newspaper*); drawing (*of a lottery*); focal length (*of camera*).

tiraillement [tirɑj′mɑ̃], *n.m.* pulling, hauling about; twinge, pain; (*fig.*) jarring, wrangling, vexation.

tirailler [tirɑ′je], *v.t.* to pull about; to tease, to pester.—*v.i.* to shoot wildly; to skirmish. **se tirailler**, *v.r.* to pull each other about.

tirailleur [tirɑ′jœːr], *n.m.* sharpshooter; skirmisher.

tirant [ti′rɑ̃], *n.m.* purse-string; boot-strap; (*Carp. etc.*) tie-beam; brace (*of a drum*); *tirant d'eau*, ship's draught.

tire [tiːr], *n.f.* pull.

tiré [ti′re], *a.* drawn; fatigued.—*n.m.* (*Comm.*) drawee (*of a bill*).

tire-bouchon [tirbu′ʃɔ̃], *n.m.* (*pl.* **-bouchons**) corkscrew; ringlet (*of hair*).

tire-bouton [tirbu′tɔ̃], *n.m.* (*pl.* **-boutons**) button-hook.

tire-d'aile (à) [atir′dɛl], *adv. phr.* at full speed (*of a bird flying*).

tire-larigot (à) [atirlari′go], *adv. phr.* (*fam.*) to one's heart's content.

tirelire [tir′liːr], *n.f.* money-box.

tirer [ti′re], *v.t.* to draw, to pull; to take out, to extract; to tap (*liquors*); to stretch, to tighten; to receive, to reap; to infer; to put on; to get; to shoot, to fire; (*Print.*) to print.—*v.i.* to draw, to pull; to fire; to tend, to border, to verge (*sur*). **se tirer**, *v.r.* to extricate oneself; to get out; to recover (*from illness*).

tiret [ti′re], *n.m.* hyphen, dash.

tiretaine [tir′tɛːn], *n.f.* linsey-woolsey.

tireur [ti′rœːr], *n.m.* (*fem.* **-euse**) one who draws; marksman, sharpshooter.

tiroir [ti′rwaːr], *n.m.* drawer (*in a table etc.*); slide, slide-valve (*steam engine*).

tisane [ti′zan], *n.f.* infusion of herbs etc.

tison [ti′zɔ̃], *n.m.* brand, fire-brand; (*fig.*) embers.

tisonner [tizɔ′ne], *v.t., v.i.* to poke (*the fire*).

tisonnier [tizɔ′nje], *n.m.* poker, fire-iron.

tissage [ti′saːʒ], *n.m.* weaving; cloth mill.

tisser [ti′se], *v.t.* to weave; *métier à tisser* weaving-loom.

tisserand [tis′rɑ̃], *n.m.* (*fem.* **-e**) weaver.

tissu [ti′sy], *a.* woven.—*n.m.* material, fabric; tissue.

tissure [ti′syːr], *n.f.* tissue, texture.

titan [ti′tɑ̃], *n.m.* Titan.

titanesque [tita′nɛsk], **titanique** [tita′nik], *a.* titanic.

titillant [titil′lɑ̃], *a.* titillating, tickling.

titillation [titillɑ′sjɔ̃], *n.f.* titillation, tickling.

titiller [titil′le], *v.t., v.i.* to titillate, to tickle.

titre [titr], *n.m.* title, style, denomination; title-page; head, heading; right, claim, reason; voucher; title-deed; *titre de circulation*, (railway) ticket *or* pass; *à bon titre* or *à juste titre*, deservedly, justly.

titrer [ti′tre], *v.t.* to give a title to.

titubant [tity′bɑ̃], *a.* staggering.

titubation [titybɑ′sjɔ̃], *n.f.* reeling, staggering.

tituber [tity′be], *v.i.* to stagger, to reel.

titulaire [tity′lɛːr], *a.* titular.—*n.* titular incumbent, holder, chief.

toast [tost], *n.m.* toast, health; toast(ed bread); *porter un toast* (*à quelqu'un*), to toast (*someone*).

toboggan [tɔbɔ′gɑ̃], *n.m.* toboggan.

toc [tɔk], *int.* tap, tap, rap.—*n.m.* rap, knock (*at a door etc.*).

tocsin [tɔk′sɛ̃], *n.m.* tocsin, alarm-bell.

toge [tɔːʒ], *n.f.* toga; (*fig.*) robe, gown (*of a judge etc.*).

Togo [tɔ′go], **le**, *m.* Togo.

togolais [tɔgɔ′lɛ], *a.* of Togo.—*n.m.* (**Togolais**, *fem.* **-aise**) native of Togo.

tohu-bohu [tɔybɔ′y], *n.m.* chaos; (*fig.*) confusion; jumble, hubbub.

toi [twa], *pron. pers.* *thou, *thee, you.

toile [twal], *n.f.* linen, cloth; canvas; sail; painting, picture; web; *toile cirée*, oilcloth; *toile d'araignée*, cobweb, spider's web.

toilette [twa′lɛt], *n.f.* doily; toilet-set; dressing-table, wash-stand; dress, attire; *cabinet de toilette*, dressing-room; *grande toilette*, full dress; *les toilettes*, toilets.

toise [twaːz], *n.f.* fathom; fathom-measure; (*fig.*) measure, standard.

toiser [twa′ze], *v.t.* to measure; to survey; (*fig.*) to eye from head to foot.

toiseur [twa′zœːr], *n.m.* measurer; quantity surveyor.

toison [twa′zɔ̃], *n.f.* fleece; (*fig.*) mop, thick head of hair.

toit [twa], *n.m.* roof, house-top; top, roof (*of a mine*); (*fig.*) house, home; *toit à cochons* pigsty.

toiture [twa′tyːr], *n.f.* roofing, roof.

tôle [toːl], *n.f.* sheet-iron; plate of steel; *tôle ondulée*, corrugated iron.

313

tolérable [tɔle'rabl], *a.* tolerable, bearable; middling.

tolérablement [tɔlerablə'mã], *adv.* tolerably.

tolérance [tɔle'rãːs], *n.f.* tolerance, toleration; endurance, forbearance; indulgence; deduction (*in coins*).

tolérant [tɔle'rã], *a.* tolerant.

tolérer [tɔle're], *v.t.* (*conjug. like* CÉDER) to tolerate, to allow; to endure, to bear; **to wink at.**

tomate [tɔ'mat], *n.f.* tomato.

tombal [tɔ̃'bal], *a.* (*m. pl.* **-aux**) pertaining to a tomb; *pierre tombale*, tombstone.

tombe [tɔ̃ːb], *n.f.* tomb, grave; tombstone.

tombeau [tɔ̃'bo], *n.m.* (*pl.* **-eaux**) tomb, grave; (*fig.*) sepulchre, death.

tombée [tɔ̃'be], *n.f.* fall (*of night etc.*).

tomber [tɔ̃'be], *v.i.* (*with aux.* ÊTRE) to fall, to fall down; to sink; to decay, to droop; to abate; to sag; to fall into; to meet, to light (upon) (*sur*); *laisser tomber*, to drop; *tomber amoureux* (*de*), to fall in love (with); *tomber bien* or *mal*, to come at the right *or* wrong moment; *tomber d'accord*, to agree; *tomber malade*, to fall ill.

tombereau [tɔ̃'bro], *n.m.* (*pl.* **-eaux**) tip-cart.

tombola [tɔ̃bɔ'la], *n.f.* tombola; raffle.

tome [toːm], *n.m.* volume, tome.

ton (1) [tɔ̃], *a. poss. m.* (*fem.* **ta**, *pl.* **tes**) *thy, your.

ton (2) [tɔ̃], *n.m.* tone; intonation, accent; tint; (*fig.*) manner, style; breeding; (*Mus.*) pitch, key.

tondaison [TONTE].

tondeur [tɔ̃'dœːr], *n.m.* (*fem.* **-euse**) shearer, clipper.—*n.f.* (**-euse**) shearing-machine, clipper; *tondeuse* (*de gazon*), lawn-mower.

tondre [tɔ̃ːdr], *v.t.* to shear, to clip, to crop; to cut, to mow, to trim.

tondu [tɔ̃'dy], *a.* shorn.

tonique [tɔ'nik], *a.* tonic; stressed.—*n.m.* (*Med.*) tonic.—*n.f.* (*Mus.*) keynote.

tonnage [tɔ'naːʒ], *n.m.* tonnage; displacement.

tonne [tɔn], *n.f.* tun (*wooden vessel*); ton (*20 cwt., approx. 1000 kil.*).

tonneau [tɔ'no], *n.m.* (*pl.* **-eaux**) tun (*cask*); tun (*measure*); ton [TONNE]; (*colloq.*) drunkard; *mettre un tonneau en perce*, to broach a cask; *tonneau percé*, (*fig.*) spendthrift.

tonnelier [tɔnə'lje], *n.m.* cooper.

tonnelle [tɔ'nɛl], *n.f.* arbour, bower.

tonnellerie [tɔnɛl'ri], *n.f.* cooperage.

tonner [tɔ'ne], *v.i.* to thunder; (*fig.*) to inveigh.

tonnerre [tɔ'nɛːr], *n.m.* thunder, thunderbolt; *coup* or *éclat de tonnerre*, clap of thunder.

tonsure [tɔ̃'syːr], *n.f.* tonsure.

tonsuré [tɔ̃sy're], *a.m.* tonsured, shaven.—*n.m.* cleric, priest.

tonte [tɔ̃ːt], **tondaison** [tɔ̃dɛ'zɔ̃], *n.f.* sheepshearing, clipping.

tonture [tɔ̃'tyːr], *n.f.* shearings, clippings; flock (*of cloth*); (*Naut.*) sheer.

top [tɔp], *n.m.* time signal; *les tops*, the pips.

topaze [tɔ'paːz], *n.f.* topaz.

toper [tɔ'pe], *v.i.* to agree; *tope là !* done! agreed!

topinambour [tɔpinã'buːr], *n.m.* Jerusalem artichoke.

topographe [tɔpɔ'graf], *n.m.* topographer.

topographie [tɔpɔgra'fi], *n.f.* topography.

topographique [tɔpɔgra'fik], *a.* topographical.

toquade or **tocade** [tɔ'kad], *n.f.* (*colloq.*) infatuation, whim, fad, craze.

toque [tɔk], *n.f.* toque; jockey's cap; magistrate's cap.

toqué [tɔ'ke], *a.* (*fam.*) cracked, touched; infatuated.

torche [tɔrʃ], *n.f.* torch, link; twist (*of straw etc.*); pad (*on head*).

torcher [tɔr'ʃe], *v.t.* to wipe, to clean; (*fig.*) to polish off. **se torcher**, *v.r.* to wipe oneself.

torchère [tɔr'ʃɛːr], *n.f.* torch-holder, tall candelabrum, hall-lamp.

torchis [tɔr'ʃi], *n.m.* cob, loam; *mur de torchis*, mud-wall.

torchon [tɔr'ʃɔ̃], *n.m.* duster, house-cloth, dish-cloth.

tordage [tɔr'daːʒ], *n.m.* twisting, twist.

tordeur [tɔr'dœːr], *n.m.* (*fem.* **-euse**) twister (*of wool etc.*); throwster (*of silk*).

tordoir [tɔr'dwaːr], *n.m.* mangle, wringer.

tordre [tɔrdr], *v.t.* to twist, to wring; to contort, to disfigure. **se tordre**, *v.r.* to twist; to writhe.

tordu [tɔr'dy], *a.* twisted, distorted.

toréador [tɔrea'dɔːr], *n.m.* toreador, bullfighter.

tornade [tɔr'nad], *n.f.* tornado.

torpédo [tɔrpe'do], *n.f.* (*Motor.*) open tourer.

torpeur [tɔr'pœːr], *n.f.* torpor.

torpide [tɔr'pid], *a.* torpid.

torpille [tɔr'piːj], *n.f.* torpedo (*numb-fish*); (*Navy, Av.*) torpedo.

torpiller [tɔrpi'je], *v.t.* to torpedo.

torpilleur [tɔrpi'jœːr], *n.m.* torpedo-boat.

torréfier [tɔre'fje], *v.t.* to torrefy, to roast (*coffee*).

torrent [tɔ'rã], *n.m.* torrent, stream; flood (*of tears etc.*); flow (*of words etc.*).

torrentiel [tɔrã'sjɛl], **torrentueux** [tɔrã'tɥø], *a.* (*fem.* **-elle, -euse**) torrential; impetuous.

torride [tɔ'rid], *a.* torrid.

tors [tɔr], *a.* (*fem.* **torse** (1) or **torte**) twisted, wreathed, contorted; wry, crooked.—*n.m.* twisting (*of ropes etc.*); torsion.

torsade [tɔr'sad], *n.f.* twisted fringe or cord; bullion (*on epaulets etc.*).

torse (2) [tɔrs], *n.m.* torso, trunk, bust.

torsion [tɔr'sjɔ̃], *n.f.* torsion, twisting.

tort [tɔːr], *n.m.* wrong, injustice; harm, injury, mischief, offence; prejudice, detriment; *à tort ou à raison*, rightly or wrongly; *avoir tort*, to be wrong.

torticolis [tɔrtikɔ'li], *n.m.* wryneck, stiffneck; crick (*in the neck*).

tortiller [tɔrti'je], *v.t.* to twist.—*v.i.* to wriggle, to shuffle; to prevaricate. **se tortiller**, *v.r.* to wriggle, to writhe.

tortionnaire [tɔrsjɔ'nɛːr], *n.m.* executioner, torturer.

tortu [tɔr'ty], *a.* crooked, tortuous; *jambes tortues*, bandy legs.

tortue [tɔr'ty], *n.f.* tortoise; *tortue de mer*, turtle.

tortueux [tɔr'tɥø], *a.* (*fem.* **-euse**) tortuous, winding, crooked; (*fig.*) artful, crafty.

torture [tɔr'ty:r], *n.f.* torture; the rack.

torturer [tɔrty're], *v.t.* to torture, to put on the rack.

tôt [to], *adv.* soon, quickly; early; *au plus tôt* or *le plus tôt possible*, as soon as possible; *tôt ou tard*, sooner or later.

total [tɔ'tal], *a.* (*m. pl.* **-aux**) total, whole, entire; utter.—*n.m.* whole, total, sum-total.

totalement [tɔtal'mɑ̃], *adv.* totally, wholly; utterly, completely.

totalisateur [tɔtaliza'tœ:r], *n.m.* calculating-machine; totalisator.

totaliser [tɔtali'ze], *v.t.* to tot up, to total up.

totalitaire [tɔtali'tɛ:r], *a.* totalitarian.

totalitarisme [tɔtalita'rism], *n.m.* totalitarianism.

totalité [tɔtali'te], *n.f.* totality, whole.

touage [twa:ʒ], *n.m.* towage, towing, warping.

toucan [tu'kɑ̃], *n.m.* toucan.

touchant [tu'ʃɑ̃], *a.* touching, moving, affecting.—*n.m.* the moving, affecting *or* impressive part.—*prep.* concerning, with regard to.

touche [tuʃ], *n.f.* touch; assay, trial; (*Paint. etc.*) manner, style; key (*of piano, typewriter etc.*); stop (*of organ*); (*Fishing*) nibble, bite; (*Fenc. etc.*) hit; drove of cattle; *pierre de touche*, touchstone.

touche-à-tout [tuʃa'tu], *a. inv.* meddling.—*n. inv.* meddler; Jack of all trades.

toucher [tu'ʃe], *v.t.* to touch; to handle, to feel, to finger; to assay, to try (*precious metals etc.*); to receive (*money*); to hit; to offend; to move, to affect; to whip, to drive (*animals*); to play on (*a musical instrument*); to express, to describe; to allude to; to concern, to regard; *toucher un chèque*, to cash a cheque.—*v.i.* to touch, to meddle (*à*); to reach; to play (*on a musical instrument*); to draw near, to be related, to be like; to concern; (*Naut.*) to go aground. **se toucher**, *v.r.* to touch, to touch each other; to be adjoining.—*n.m.* touch, feeling.

toue [tu], *n.f.* barge.

touée [tu'e], *n.f.* towing, warping; towline.

touer [tu'e], *v.t.* to tow, to warp.

toueur [tu'œːr], *n.m.* tower; tow-boat, tug.

touffe [tuf], *n.f.* tuft, clump, bunch, wisp.

touffer [tu'fe], *v.t.* to arrange in tufts.—*v.i.* to grow in a tuft or tufts.

touffu [tu'fy], *a.* tufted, bushy; leafy; full, thick; laboured (*of style*).

toujours [tu'ʒu:r], *adv.* always, ever, for ever; still; all the same, nevertheless, at least; *toujours est-il que . . .*, still, the fact remains that . . . .

toupet [tu'pɛ], *n.m.* tuft of hair; forelock; front, foretop (*on a horse*); (*colloq.*) effrontery, cheek, impudence.

toupie [tu'pi], *n.f.* top, spinning-top.

toupiller [tupi'je], *v.i.* to spin, to whirl round and round.

tour (1) [tu:r], *n.f.* tower; (*Chess*) rook, castle.

tour (2) [tu:r], *n.m.* turn, winding; revolution; circumference, circuit; twist, strain; tour, trip; trick; feat; *à tour de rôle*, in turn; *tour de force*, feat of strength; *tour de reins*, sprain in the back.

tour (3) [tu:r], *n.m.* lathe.

tourangeau [turɑ̃'ʒo], *a.* (*fem.* **-elle**, *m. pl.* **-eaux**) of Touraine.—*n.m.* (**Tourangeau**, *fem.* **-elle**) native of Touraine.

tourbe [turb], *n.f.* mob, rabble; peat, turf.

tourbeux [tur'bø], *a.* (*fem.* **-euse**) peaty.

tourbillon [turbi'jɔ̃], *n.m.* whirlwind; whirlpool, eddy; (*fig.*) hurly-burly, bustle.

tourbillonner [turbijo'ne], *v.i.* to whirl, to eddy; to swirl.

tourelle [tu'rɛl], *n.f.* turret; gun-turret; *tourelle de veille*, conning-tower.

touret [tu'rɛ], *n.m.* wheel (*of a lathe etc.*); angler's reel.

tourie [tu'ri], *n.f.* carboy.

tourillon [turi'jɔ̃], *n.m.* axle; axle-tree, arbor; spindle, pivot.

tourisme [tu'rism], *n.m.* touring, tourism.

touriste [tu'rist], *n.* tourist, tripper.

tourment [tur'mɑ̃], *n.m.* torment, torture; anguish, pain; agony of mind.

tourmente [tur'mɑ̃:t], *n.f.* tempest, storm; (*fig.*) disturbance, turmoil.

tourmenter [turmɑ̃'te], *v.t.* to torment, to torture, to rack; to distress, to harass; to worry; to jolt; to toss. **se tourmenter**, *v.r.* to be uneasy, to fret; to warp (*of wood*); to labour hard (*of a ship*).

tourmenteur [turmɑ̃'tœ:r], *a.* (*fem.* **-euse**) torturing, tormenting.—*n.m.* (*fem.* **-euse**) torturer, tormentor.

tournailler [turnɑ'je], *v.i.* (*colloq.*) to prowl round.

tournant [tur'nɑ̃], *a.* turning, winding; *plaque tournante*, turn-table; *pont tournant*, swing-bridge.—*n.m.* turn, turning, bend; street corner; (*fig.*) indirect means; turning-point.

tourné [tur'ne], *a.* turned, shaped; expressed; sour, spoilt; *avoir l'esprit mal tourné*, to be cross-grained.

tournebroche [turnə'brɔʃ], *n.m.* roasting-jack; turnspit.

tourne-disques [turnə'disk], *n.m. inv.* record-player.

tournedos [turnə'do], *n.m. inv.* fillet steak.

tournée [tur'ne], *n.f.* round, turn, visit, journey; circuit.

tournemain (en un) [ɑ̃nœ̃turnə'mɛ̃], *adv. phr.* in a trice.

tourner [tur'ne], *v.t.* to turn; to turn round, to revolve, to twirl; to wind; (*Cine.*) to shoot (*a film*); to convert; to interpret; to shape.—*v.i.* to turn, to turn round, to revolve; to turn out; to change; to ripen; to spoil, to curdle (*of liquids*). **se tourner**, *v.r.* to turn round; to turn; to change.

tournesol [turnə'sɔl], *n.m.* turnsole, sunflower; (*Chem.*) litmus.

tourneur [tur'nœ:r], *n.m.* turner.

tournevent [turnə'vɑ̃], *n.m.* cowl (*for chimney*).

tournevis [turnə'vis], *n.m.* screwdriver.

tourniole [tur'njɔl], *n.f.* whitlow.

tourniquet [turni'kɛ], *n.m.* turnstile; swivel; (*Surg.*) tourniquet.

tournoi [tur'nwa], *n.m.* tournament.

tournoiement [turnwa'mɑ̃], *n.m.* turning round, whirling, swirling; dizziness.

tournoyer [turnwa'je], *v.i.* (*conjug. like* EMPLOYER) to turn round and round, to wind; to eddy; (*fig.*) to beat about the bush, to shilly-shally.

tournure

tournure [tur'nyːr], *n.f.* turn, direction, course; figure, shape; (*fig.*) cast (*of mind, style etc.*); phrase, construction (*of language*); *les choses commencent à prendre une mauvaise tournure,* things are beginning to look bad.

tourte [turt], *n.f.* raised pie; big round loaf.

tourtereau [turtə'ro], *n.m.* (*pl.* **-eaux**) young turtle-dove; (*pl.*) (*fam.*) lovers.

tourterelle [turtə'rɛl], *n.f.* turtle-dove.

Toussaint [tu'sɛ̃], **la,** *f.* All Saints' Day.

tousser [tu'se], *v.i.* to cough.

tout [tu; *liaison-form,* tut], *a.* (*m. pl.* **tous**) all; whole, the whole of; every; each; any; *tous les jours,* every day; *toutes les fois que,* as often as, every time that; *tout le monde,* all the world, everybody.—*pron. indef.* (*m. pl. pronounced* tuːs) all, everything; (*pl.*) all men; *à tout prendre,* on the whole; *comme tout,* exceedingly, extremely; *du tout,* not at all; *en tout,* in all, on the whole.—*n.m.* whole, the whole; the chief point, only thing.—*adv.* wholly, entirely, quite, thoroughly; all, altogether; although, however, for all; *parler tout haut,* to speak aloud; *tout à coup,* suddenly; *tout à fait,* quite, entirely; *tout à l'heure,* just now; presently; *tout à vous,* sincerely yours; *tout beau* or *tout doux,* softly, gently, not so fast; *tout de bon,* in earnest; *tout de suite,* immediately; *tout nu,* stark naked.

toutefois [tut'fwa], *adv.* yet, nevertheless, however, still.

toute-puissance [tutpɥi'sɑ̃ːs], *n.f.* omnipotence, almighty power.

tout-puissant [tupɥi'sɑ̃], *a.* (*fem.* **toute-puissante**) almighty. — *n.m.* (**Tout-Puissant**) the Almighty.

toux [tu], *n.f. inv.* cough.

toxémie [tɔksɛ'mi], *n.f.* (*Med.*) toxaemia, blood poisoning.

toxique [tɔk'sik], *a.* toxic, poisonous.—*n.m.* poison.

tracas [tra'kɑ], *n.m.* bustle, turmoil, disturbance; worry, annoyance.

tracassement [trakas'mɑ̃], *n.m.* worrying.

tracasser [traka'se], *v.t.* to worry, to pester. **se tracasser,** *v.r.* to worry.

tracasserie [trakas'ri], *n.f.* worry, pestering, annoyance, vexation; (*pl.*) bickering.

tracassier [traka'sje], *a.* (*fem.* **-ière**) pestering, worrying, annoying; fussy; mischief-making.—*n.m.* (*fem.* **-ière**) pesterer, busybody; troublesome person, mischief-maker.

trace [tras], *n.f.* trace, track, footprint; spoor, trail; mark, impression, vestige; outline, sketch.

tracé [tra'se], *n.m.* outline, sketch (*of figure*); marking out; laying out (*of grounds etc.*); direction.

tracement [tras'mɑ̃], *n.m.* tracing, laying out (*of grounds, roads etc.*).

tracer [tra'se], *v.t.* (*conjug. like* COMMENCER) to trace, to draw, to trace out; to sketch; to portray; to lay out (*grounds, roads etc.*); (*fig.*) to set forth, to mark out.—*v.i.* to spread roots (*of trees*); to burrow (*of moles*).

trachée [tra'ʃe], *n.f.* trachea, air-vessel.

trachée-artère [traʃear'tɛːr], *n.f.* (*pl.* **trachées-artères**) trachea, windpipe.

tract [trakt], *n.m.* tract, leaflet (*for propaganda*).

tracteur [trak'tœːr], *n.m.* tractor, traction-engine.

traction [trak'sjɔ̃], *n.f.* traction; pulling; draught; *traction avant,* front-wheel drive.

tradition [tradi'sjɔ̃], *n.f.* tradition; (*Law*) delivery.

traditionnel [tradisjɔ'nɛl], *a.* (*fem.* **-elle**) traditional.

traducteur [tradyk'tœːr], *n.m.* (*fem.* **-trice**) translator.

traduction [tradyk'sjɔ̃], *n.f.* translation, (*sch.*) crib.

traduire [tra'dɥiːr], *v.t. irr.* (*conjug. like* CONDUIRE) to translate; to interpret, to construe; to convey, to express; to indicate, to denote.

traduisible [tradɥi'zibl], *a.* translatable.

trafic [tra'fik], *n.m.* traffic; trading, trade; dealings.

trafiquant [trafi'kɑ̃], *n.m.* (*fem.* **-e**) trafficker.

trafiquer [trafi'ke], *v.i.* to traffic, to trade, to deal (*de*).

tragédie [traʒe'di], *n.f.* tragedy.

tragédien [traʒe'djɛ̃], *n.m.* (*fem.* **-enne**) tragedian.

tragique [tra'ʒik], *a.* tragic, tragical.—*n.m.* tragedy, tragic art; tragic writer.

trahir [tra'iːr], *v.t.* to betray; to deceive; to divulge, to reveal. **se trahir,** *v.r.* to betray oneself; to betray each other.

trahison [trai'zɔ̃], *n.f.* treachery, treason, perfidy; breach of faith.

train [trɛ̃], *n.m.* pace, rate; train, suite, attendants; way, manner; noise, clatter, dust; carriage; quarters (*of a horse etc.*); (*Rail.*) train; *à fond de train,* at full speed; *être en train de faire quelque chose,* to be (in the act of) doing something; *train de maison,* style of living; *train de marchandises,* goods train; *train omnibus,* slow or stopping train.

traînage [trɛ'naːʒ], *n.m.* dragging, drawing; sledging, sleighing.

traînant [trɛ'nɑ̃], *a.* dragging, trailing (*dress*); drawling (*voice*); shuffling (*gait*).

traînard [trɛ'naːr], *n.m.* straggler, laggard, slow-coach.

traîne [trɛn], *n.f.* dragging, being dragged or drawn; train (*of a dress etc.*).

traîneau [trɛ'no], *n.m.* (*pl.* **-eaux**) sledge, sleigh; drag-net.

traînée [trɛ'ne], *n.f.* train (*of gunpowder etc.*); trail, track.

traîner [trɛ'ne], *v.t.* to drag, to draw; to track; to spin out, to drag out; to protract; to drawl; to put off.—*v.i.* to trail, to draggle, to lag; to droop; to languish, to flag; to lie about; to loiter, to linger, to be protracted. **se traîner,** *v.r.* to crawl along, to creep; to lag, to drag oneself along.

train-train [trɛ̃'trɛ̃], *n.m.* (*colloq.*) routine, regular course.

traire [trɛːr], *v.t. irr.* to milk; to draw (*milk*).

trait [trɛ], *n.m.* arrow, dart, bolt, shaft; thunderbolt; stroke, hit; trace (*of harness*); leash (*for dogs*); turn (*of the scale*); draught, gulp; dash (*of the pen etc.*); flash (*of light*); stroke, touch; trait, feature, lineament; act, deed; prime move (*at chess, draughts etc.*); *avoir trait à*, to have reference to; *boire à longs traits*, to drink long draughts of; *d'un seul trait*, at one gulp; *trait de génie*, stroke of genius, (*fam.*) brain-wave; *trait d'union*, hyphen.

traite [trɛt], *n.f.* stage, journey, stretch; milking; (*Comm.*) draft, bill; *traite des nègres*, slave-trade.

traité [trɛ'te], *n.m.* treatise, tract, dissertation; treaty; agreement.

traitement [trɛt'mã], *n.m.* treatment; (*Ind.*) processing; reception; salary, pay.

traiter [trɛ'te], *v.t.* to treat; (*Ind.*) to process; to entertain; to use, to behave to; to discuss, to handle; to call, to style; to negotiate; to execute, to do.—*v.i.* to treat, to negotiate.

traiteur [trɛ'tœːr], *n.m.* restaurant-keeper; caterer.

traître [trɛːtr], *a.* (*fem.* **-esse**) treacherous, perfidious.—*n.m.* (*fem.* **-esse**) treacherous person, traitor, traitress.

traîtreusement [trɛtrœz'mã], *adv.* treacherously.

traîtrise [trɛ'triːz], *n.f.* treachery.

trajectoire [traʒɛk'twaːr], *a.* and *n.f.* trajectory.

trajet [tra'ʒɛ], *n.m.* passage, journey, crossing, voyage; (*Med.*) course.

trame [tram], *n.f.* weft, woof; plot, conspiracy; course, progress, thread.

tramer [tra'me], *v.t.* to weave; (*fig.*) to plot, to contrive, to hatch.

tramontane [tramõ'tan], *n.f.* tramontane, north wind; north; North Star.

tramway [tra'mwɛ], *n.m.* tramcar.

tranchant [trã'ʃã], *a.* sharp, cutting; (*fig.*) trenchant, decisive; salient, prominent.—*n.m.* edge.

tranche [trãːʃ], *n.f.* slice, chop; slab; edge (*of a book*); *doré sur tranche*, gilt-edged (*of a book*); *tranche de lard*, rasher of bacon.

tranchée [trã'ʃe], *n.f.* trench, cutting; (*pl.*) colic.

trancher [trã'ʃe], *v.t.* to cut; to cut off; to slice; to decide, to determine, to settle.—*v.i.* to cut; to decide; to set up for; to affect; to be glaring (*of colours*).

tranchoir [trã'ʃwaːr], *n.m.* trencher, cutting-board.

tranquille [trã'kil], *a.* quiet, calm, tranquil, placid, peaceful; undisturbed (*in mind etc.*); *soyez tranquille*, set your mind at ease.

tranquillement [trãkil'mã], *adv.* peacefully, quietly.

tranquillisant [trãkili'zã], *a.* tranquillizing.—*n.m.* tranquillizer.

tranquilliser [trãkili'ze], *v.t.* to tranquillize, to make easy, to soothe. **se tranquilliser**, *v.r.* to become tranquil, to calm down.

tranquillité [trãkili'te], *n.f.* tranquillity, quiet, peace.

transaction [trãzak'sjõ], *n.f.* transaction, arrangement.

transalpin [trãzal'pɛ̃], *a.* transalpine.

transatlantique [trãzatlã'tik], *a.* transatlantic.—*n.m.* liner; deck-chair.

transborder [trãsbɔr'de], *v.t.* to tranship.

transbordeur [trãsbɔr'dœːr], *n.m.* transporter; *pont transbordeur*, transporter bridge.

transcendant [trãsã'dã], *a.* transcendent.

transcription [trãskrip'sjõ], *n.f.* transcription, transcript, copy.

transcrire [trã'skriːr], *v.t. irr.* (*conjug. like* ÉCRIRE) to transcribe, to copy out.

transe [trãːs], *n.f.* fright, apprehension; trance.

transférable [trãsfe'rabl], *a.* transferable.

transférer [trãsfe're], *v.t.* (*conjug. like* CÉDER) to transfer, to transport, to convey, to move.

transfert [trãs'fɛːr], *n.m.* transfer.

transfiguration [trãsfigyrɑ'sjõ], *n.f.* transfiguration.

transfigurer [trãsfigy're], *v.t.* to transfigure. **se transfigurer**, *v.r.* to be transfigured.

transformateur [trãsfɔrma'tœːr], *n.m.* (*Elec.*) transformer.

transformation [trãsfɔrmɑ'sjõ], *n.f.* transformation.

transformer [trãsfɔr'me], *v.t.* to transform; to change, to convert. **se transformer**, *v.r.* to be transformed.

transfuge [trãs'fyːʒ], *n.m.* deserter; fugitive; turncoat.

transgresser [trãsgrɛ'se], *v.t.* to transgress, to infringe, to contravene.

transgression [trãsgrɛ'sjõ], *n.f.* transgression.

transhumance [trãzy'mãːs], *n.f.* transhumance.

transi [trã'zi], *a.* chilled, benumbed.

transiger [trãzi'ʒe], *v.i.* (*conjug. like* MANGER) to compound, to compromise, to come to terms (*avec*).

transir [trã'ziːr], *v.t.* to chill, to benumb; to paralyse.—*v.i.* to be chilled; to be paralysed (*with fear etc.*).

transissement [trãzis'mã], *n.m.* chill, numbness; shivering (*with terror etc.*).

transistor [trãzis'tɔr], *n.m.* transistor.

transit [trã'zit], *n.m.* transit.

transitaire [trãzi'tɛːr], *a.* pertaining to the transit of goods.

transitif [trãzi'tif], *a.* (*fem.* **-tive**) transitive.

transition [trãzi'sjõ], *n.f.* transition.

transitoire [trãzi'twaːr], *a.* transitory.

translation [trãslɑ'sjõ], *n.f.* transfer(ring), relaying.

translucide [trãsly'sid], *a.* translucent.

translucidité [trãslysidi'te], *n.f.* translucence.

transmarin [trãsma'rɛ̃], *a.* transmarine, oversea.

transmetteur [trãsmɛ'tœːr], *n.m.* (*Rad.*) transmitter.

transmettre [trãs'mɛtr], *v.t. irr.* (*conjug. like* METTRE) to transmit, to convey, to send on; to transfer.

transmigration [trãsmigrɑ'sjõ], *n.f.* transmigration.

transmigrer [trãsmi'gre], *v.i.* to transmigrate.

transparence [trãspa'rãːs], *n.f.* transparency.

transparent [trãspa'rã], *a.* transparent.—*n.m.* paper ruled with black lines; transparency.

transpercer [trãspɛr'se], *v.t.* (*conjug. like* COMMENCER) to pierce through; to run through (*with a sword etc.*), to transfix.

transpiration [trãspirɑ'sjõ], *n.f.* perspiration, perspiring.

transpirer [trãspi're], *v.i.* to perspire; to ooze out; to transpire.

transplanter

transplanter [trăsplă′te], *v.t.* to transplant.

transport [trăs′pɔːr], *n.m.* carriage, conveyance; transport, removal; transfer, assignment; (*fig.*) rapture, ecstasy; transport-ship; *transport au cerveau*, stroke, fit of delirium.

transportation [trăsporta′sjõ], *n.f.* transportation.

transporté [trăspɔr′te], *n.m.* (*fem.* **-ée**) transported person, convict.

transporter [trăspɔr′te], *v.t.* to convey, to transport; to transfer; to banish; to enrapture. **se transporter**, *v.r.* to transport oneself, to go.

transporteur [trăspɔr′tœːr], *n.m.* carrier, conveyor.

transposer [trăspo′ze], *v.t.* to transpose.

transposition [trăspozi′sjõ], *n.f.* transposition.

transrhénan [trăsre′nă], *a.* from beyond the Rhine.

transsubstantiation [trăssybstãsja′sjõ], *n.f.* transubstantiation.

transvaser [trăsva′ze], *v.t.* to decant.

transversal [trăzvɛr′sal], *a.* (*m.pl.* **-aux**) transversal, transverse.

trapèze [tra′pɛːz], *n.m.* trapezium; trapeze.

trappe [trap], *n.f.* trap-door; trap, pitfall; curtain, register (*of chimney*).

trappeur [tra′pœːr], *n.m.* trapper.

trappiste [tra′pist], *a.* and *n.m.* Trappist.

trapu [tra′py], *a.* squat, dumpy, thick-set, stocky.

traquer [tra′ke], *v.t.* (*Hunt.*) to beat for game; to enclose, to encircle; to track down.

travail [tra′vaːj], *n.m.* (*pl.* **-aux**) labour, work; toil; travail; piece of work; workmanship; occupation; study; *cabinet de travail*, study (*room*); *travaux forcés*, hard labour.

travaillé [trava′je], *a.* worked, wrought; laboured, elaborate; labouring (*under*).

travailler [trava′je], *v.t.* to work, to work at; to do with care; to fashion; to till (*the ground*).—*v.i.* to labour, to work; to study; to strive; to ferment (*of wines*); to warp (*of wood*). **se travailler**, *v.r.* to torment oneself; to be overwrought.

travailleur [trava′jœːr], *a.* (*fem.* **-euse**) industrious, hard-working; painstaking.—*n.m.* (*fem.* **-euse**) workman, labourer; hard-working person.

travailliste [trava′jist], *a.* Labour, Socialist. —*n.* member of the Labour Party.

travée [tra′ve], *n.f.* (*Arch.*) bay; truss (*of bridges*); (*Av.*) rib (*of wing*).

travers [tra′vɛːr], *n.m.* breadth; fault, failing; oddity; (*Naut.*) side, broadside; *à travers*, across; *au travers de*, through; *de travers*, obliquely, awry, askew; *en travers*, across, crosswise; *à tort et à travers*, at random.

traverse [tra′vɛrs], *n.f.* cross-bar, cross-piece; cross-road, short cut; (*Rail.*) sleeper; (*pl.*) (*fig.*) setbacks.

traversée [travɛr′se], *n.f.* passage, crossing.

traverser [travɛr′se], *v.t.* to cross, to go over or through, to traverse, to get through or across; to run through (*with a sword etc.*); to lie across, to span; to intersect; to penetrate; to thwart.

traversier [travɛr′sje], *a.* (*fem.* **-ière**) cross-; that plies across.

traversin [travɛr′sɛ̃], *n.m.* bolster; (*Carp. etc.*) cross-beam; (*Naut.*) stretcher (*in boats*).

travesti [travɛs′ti], *a.* disguised; travestied, parodied.

travestir [travɛs′tiːr], *v.t.* to disguise, to travesty; (*fig.*) to misrepresent.

travestissement [travɛstis′mã], *n.m.* disguise; travesty.

trébuchant [treby′ʃã], *a.* of full weight (*of coins*); stumbling.

trébucher [treby′ʃe], *v.i.* to stumble, to slip; to err; (*fig.*) to turn the scale.

trébuchet [treby′ʃɛ], *n.m.* bird-trap; assay-balance.

tréfiler [trefi′le], *v.t.* to wire-draw.

trèfle [trefl], *n.m.* trefoil, clover; (*Cards*) clubs; *trèfle blanc*, shamrock.

tréfonds [tre′ʃõ], *n.m.* subsoil; (*fig.*) bottom; heart.

treillage [trɛ′jaːʒ], *n.m.* trellis(-work), lattice-work.

treille [trɛːj], *n.f.* vine-trellis; shrimp-net.

treillis [trɛ′j, ʃi], *n.m.* trellis, lattice; coarse canvas etc., sackcloth.

treizaine [trɛ′zɛn], *n.f.* baker's dozen.

treize [trɛːz], *a.* and *n.m.* thirteen; thirteenth.

treizième [trɛ′zjɛm], *a.* and *n.* thirteenth (part).

tréma [tre′ma], *n.m.* diaeresis.

tremblant [trã′blã], *a.* trembling, quivering; flickering (*of light etc.*).

tremble [trã:bl], *n.m.* aspen.

tremblé [trã′ble], *a.* wavy (*of lines*); shaky (*of writing*).

tremblement [trãblə′mã], *n.m.* trembling, shaking, quaking, trepidation, tremor; flickering (*of light*); (*Mus.*) tremolo; *tremblement de terre*, earthquake.

trembler [trã′ble], *v.i.* to tremble, to shake, to shiver; to quake; to fear; to flutter (*of wings*).

tremblotant [trãblo′tã], *a.* trembling, tremulous (*of sound etc.*); shivering, quivering, fluttering.

tremblotement [trãblot′mã], *n.m.* trembling, shivering.

trembloter [trãblo′te], *v.i.* to tremble (*of sound*); to quiver, to shiver; to flutter (*of wings*); to flicker (*of light*).

trémousser [tremu′se], *v.t.* to bestir, to move about, to flutter.—*v.i.* to shake, to stir. **se trémousser**, *v.r.* to flutter or frisk about; to bestir oneself.

trempage [trã′paːʒ], *n.m.* steeping, soaking; (*Print.*) wetting.

trempe [trã:p], *n.f.* temper (*of steel etc.*); (*fig.*) character, stamp, quality.

tremper [trã′pe], *v.t.* to soak, to steep, to wet, to drench; to temper (*iron, steel etc.*); to dilute (*wine etc.*).—*v.i.* to soak, to be steeped; to be implicated (*in a crime*).

tremplin [trã′plɛ̃], *n.m.* spring-board, diving board; trampoline.

trentaine [trã′tɛn], *n.f.* about thirty; age of thirty.

trente [trã:t], *a.* and *n.m.* thirty; thirtieth.

trentième [trã′tjɛm], *a.* and *n.* thirtieth (part).

trépan [tre'pɑ̃], n.m. trepan (instrument); trepanning.
trépaner [trepa'ne], v.t. to trepan.
trépas [tre'pɑ], n.m. inv. (poet.) decease, death.
trépassé [trepa'se], n.m. (fem. -ée) dead person.
trépasser [trepa'se], v.i. to depart this life, to pass away.
trépidant [trepi'dɑ̃], a. vibrating; (fig.) agitated, hectic.
trépidation [trepida'sjɔ̃], n.f. trepidation, trembling; agitation.
trépied [tre'pje], n.m. trivet; tripod.
trépignement [trepiɲ'mɑ̃], n.m. stamping (of feet).
trépigner [trepi'ɲe], v.i. to stamp, to stamp one's foot.
très [trɛ], adv. very; most; very much.
trésor [tre'zɔ:r], n.m. treasure; treasury; exchequer; thesaurus.
trésorerie [trezɔr'ri], n.f. treasury; treasurership.
trésorier [trezɔ'rje], n.m. treasurer; (Mil.) paymaster.
tressage [trɛ'sa:ʒ], n.m. plaiting, braiding.
tressaillement [trɛsaj'mɑ̃], n.m. start, bound, thrill, shudder; flutter.
tressaillir [trɛsa'jir], v.i. irr. (conjug. like ASSAILLIR) to start, to thrill; to quake, to tremble, to shudder.
tresse [trɛs], n.f. tress, plait (of hair); braid.
tresser [trɛ'se], v.t. to weave, to plait, to braid; to wreathe.
tréteau [tre'to], n.m. (pl. -eaux) trestle; (pl.) stage.
treuil [trœ:j], n.m. windlass; winch.
trêve [trɛ:v], n.f. truce.
tri [tri], n.m. sorting (of letters etc.).
triage [tri'ja:ʒ], n.m. picking, sorting; choice, selection.
triangle [tri'jɑ̃:gl], n.m. triangle.
triangulaire [trijɑ̃gy'lɛ:r], a. triangular.
tribord [tri'bɔ:r], n.m. (Naut.) starboard.
tribu [tri'by], n.f. tribe.
tribulation [tribyla'sjɔ̃], n.f. tribulation.
tribun [tri'bœ̃], n.m. tribune; (fig.) democratic leader.
tribunal [triby'nal], n.m. (pl. -aux) tribunal, bench; court of justice.
tribune [tri'byn], n.f. tribune (rostrum); hustings; gallery.
tribut [tri'by], n.m. tribute; grant, contribution; *duty; (fig.) debt.
tributaire [triby'tɛ:r], a. dependent (upon).—n.m. tributary.
tricher [tri'ʃe], v.t., v.i. to cheat, to trick.
tricherie [triʃ'ri], n.f. cheating, trick, trickery.
tricheur [tri'ʃœ:r], n.m. (fem. -euse) cheat, trickster.
tricolore [triko'lɔ:r], a. tricoloured.
tricorne [tri'kɔrn], a. three-cornered.—n.m. three-cornered hat.
tricot [tri'ko], n.m. knitting; jersey, jumper, (fam.) woolly; tricot de corps, vest.
tricotage [triko'ta:ʒ], n.m. knitting.
tricoter [triko'te], v.t., v.i. to knit.
trictrac [trik'trak], n.m. tric-trac (form of backgammon).
tricycle [tri'sikl], n.m. three-wheeled vehicle; tricycle.
trident [tri'dɑ̃], n.m. trident.

triennal [triɛ'nal], a. (m. pl. -aux) triennial.
trier [tri'je], v.t. to pick, to choose, to sort, to select; to marshal (trucks).
trieur [tri'jœ:r], n.m. (fem. -euse) sorter, picker.
trigonométrie [trigɔnɔme'tri], n.f. trigonometry.
trille [tri:j], n.m. quaver, trill.
triller [tri'je], v.t. to trill, to quaver.
trillion [tri'ljɔ̃], n.m. (since 1948 = 1 followed by 18 ciphers) trillion, one million billion(s); (Am.) quintillion.
trilogie [trilɔ'ʒi], n.f. trilogy.
trimbaler [trɛ̃ba'le], v.t. (fam.) to drag or lug about (parcels); to trail (children) about. **se trimbaler**, v.r. (pop.) to traipse round.
trimer [tri'me], v.i. (pop.) to drudge, to wear oneself out.
trimestre [tri'mɛstr], n.m. quarter (three months); quarter's pay; (Sch.) term.
trimestriel [trimɛstri'ɛl], a. (fem. -elle) quarterly.
tringle [trɛ̃:gl], n.f. rod.
Trinité [trini'te], n.f. Trinity; la Trinité, Trinity Sunday; l'Île de la Trinité, Trinidad.
trinquer [trɛ̃'ke], v.i. to clink glasses (before drinking); to drink to one another's health; (pop.) to suffer, to be hurt.
trio [tri'o], n.m. trio.
triomphal [triɔ̃'fal], a. (m. pl. -aux) triumphal.
triomphalement [triɔ̃fal'mɑ̃], adv. triumphantly.
triomphant [triɔ̃'fɑ̃], a. triumphant.
triomphe [tri'ɔ̃:f], n.m. triumph.
triompher [triɔ̃'fe], v.i. to triumph; to overcome; to exult; to excel.
triparti [tripar'ti], **tripartite** [tripar'tit], a. tripartite.
tripe [trip], n.f. tripe; imitation velvet, velveteen (also called tripe de velours).
triperie [trip'ri], n.f. tripe-shop.
triple [tripl], a. and n.m. treble, triple, three-fold.
tripler [tri'ple], v.t., v.i. to treble, to triple.
triplicata [triplika'ta], n.m. inv. triplicate.
tripode [tri'pɔd], a. and n.m. tripod.
tripot [tri'po], n.m. gambling-den; house of ill-fame.
tripotage [tripɔ'ta:ʒ], n.m. mess; underhand dealing; chore.
tripoter [tripɔ'te], v.t. to meddle with; to speculate in.—v.i. to make mischief, to mess about; to act in an underhand way.
tripoteur [tripɔ'tœ:r], n.m. (fem. -euse) mischief-maker, shady speculator.
trique [trik], n.f. (fam.) cudgel, stick, bludgeon.
trisaïeul [triza'jœl], n.m. (pl. -aïeuls) great-great-grandfather.
trisaïeule [triza'jœl], n.f. great-great-grandmother.
triste [trist], a. sorrowful, mournful, sad, melancholy, dejected; dull, dreary, dismal; poor, sorry (of persons); mean, paltry.
tristement [triste'mɑ̃], adv. sadly.
tristesse [tris'tɛs], n.f. sadness; melancholy; dreariness.
triton [tri'tɔ̃], n.m. triton, newt.
trivial [tri'vjal], a. (m. pl. -aux) vulgar, trifling; trite, hackneyed.—n.m. vulgarity.

trivialité [trivjali'te], *n.f.* vulgarity; triteness.
troc [trɔk], *n.m.* truck; barter; swop.
troène [trɔ'ɛn], *n.m.* privet.
troglodyte [trɔglɔ'dit], *n.m.* troglodyte.
trogne [trɔɲ], *n.f.* reddish *or* bloated face.
trognon [trɔ'nɔ̃], *n.m.* core (*of a pear or apple*); stump (*of a cabbage*); runt.
Troie [trwa], *f.* Troy.
trois [trwa], *a.* and *n.m. inv.* three; third.
troisième [trwa'zjɛm], *a.* third.—*n.* third.—*n.m.* third floor.
troisièmement [trwazjɛm'mã], *adv.* thirdly.
trombe [trɔ̃:b], *n.f.* waterspout.
tromblon [trɔ̃'blɔ̃], *n.m.* blunderbuss.
trombone [trɔ̃'bɔn], *n.m.* trombone; paper-clip (*of wire*).
trompe [trɔ̃:pe], *n.f.* *trump, horn; proboscis, trunk (*of elephants*).
tromper [trɔ̃'pe], *v.t.* to deceive, to impose upon; to delude; to cheat, to take in; to betray, to be unfaithful to (*wife, husband*). **se tromper**, *v.r.* to be mistaken, to make a mistake, to deceive oneself.
tromperie [trɔ̃'pri], *n.f.* cheat, fraud; illusion, delusion.
trompeter [trɔ̃pə'te], *v.t.* (*conjug. like* APPELER) to trumpet abroad.
trompette [trɔ̃'pɛt], *n.f.* trumpet.—*n.m.* trumpeter.
trompeur [trɔ̃'pœr], *a.* (*fem.* **-euse**) deceitful; false, misleading.—*n.m.* (*fem.* **-euse**) deceiver, cheat, impostor; betrayer.
trompeusement [trɔ̃pøz'mã], *adv.* deceitfully, deceptively.
tronc [trɔ̃], *n.m.* trunk, bole (*of tree*); stock; poor-box.
tronçon [trɔ̃'sɔ̃], *n.m.* broken piece, fragment, stump.
tronçonner [trɔ̃sɔ'ne], *v.t.* to cut into pieces.
trône [tro:n], *n.m.* throne.
trôner [tro'ne], *v.i.* to sit on a throne; (*fig.*) to lord it.
tronquer [trɔ̃'ke], *v.t.* to mutilate, to truncate; (*fig.*) to garble, to mangle.
trop [tro], *adv.* too much, too, over, too many; *de trop*, too much, too many; *être de trop*, to be in the way, not to be wanted; *par trop*, excessively.—*n.m.* excess, superfluity.
trophée [trɔ'fe], *n.m.* trophy.
tropical [trɔpi'kal], *a.* (*m. pl.* **-aux**) tropical.
tropique [trɔ'pik], *n.m.* tropic.
trop-plein [trɔ'plɛ̃], *n.m.* (*pl.* **-pleins**) overflow, waste; surplus, excess.
troquer [trɔ'ke], *v.t.* to truck, to barter, to exchange.
trot [tro], *n.m.* trot.
trotte-menu [trɔtmə'ny] *a. inv.* running with little steps, pitter-pattering.
trotter [trɔ'te], *v.i.* to trot; to run about, to toddle (*children*).
trotteur [trɔ'tœ:r], *n.m.* (*fem.* **-euse**) trotter. —*n.f.* (**-euse**) second(s) hand (*of watch*).
trottin [trɔ'tɛ̃], *n.m.* errand girl.
trottiner [trɔti'ne], *v.i.* to go at a jog-trot; to toddle along.
trottinette [trɔti'nɛt], *n.f.* (*child's*) scooter.
trottoir [trɔ'twa:r], *n.m.* foot-path, pavement, (*Am.*) sidewalk; *le bord du trottoir*, the kerb.
trou [tru], *n.m.* hole; gap; orifice, mouth; *boucher un trou*, to stop a gap, to pay a

debt; *trou d'air*, air pocket; *trou de la serrure*, keyhole; *trou du souffleur*, (*Theat.*) prompter's box.
troubadour [truba'du:r], *n.m.* troubadour.
troublant [tru'blã], *a.* disturbing, troubling.
trouble [trubl], *a.* thick, muddy, turbid, cloudy; dull.—*adv.* dimly, confusedly.—*n.m.* confusion, disorder, disturbance; perplexity, uneasiness; dispute, quarrel; (*pl.*) disturbances, dissensions.
trouble-fête [trublə'fɛ:t], *n.m. inv.* kill-joy.
troubler [tru'ble], *v.t.* to disturb, to make thick, to make muddy; to muddle, to turn; to confuse, to agitate; to perplex, to disconcert; to trouble; to interrupt; to ruffle, to annoy; to dim, to dull. **se troubler**, *v.r.* to grow thick, to become muddy; to be confused, to be disconcerted; to become cloudy; to become confused.
trouée [tru'e], *n.f.* opening, gap, breach; pass.
trouer [tru'e], *v.t.* to bore, to make a hole in. **se trouer**, *v.r.* to get holes in it.
trouille [tru:j], *n.f.* (*vulg.*) fear, funk.
troupe [tru:p], *n.f.* troop, band; crew, gang, set; company (*of actors*); flock, crowd; (*pl.*) troops, forces.
troupeau [tru'po], *n.m.* (*pl.* **-eaux**) flock, herd, drove.
troupier [tru'pje], *n.m.* soldier.
trousse [tru:s], *n.f.* bundle, truss; (*Surg.*) case of instruments; case for razors, toilet articles etc; *je suis à ses trousses*, I am after him.
troussé [tru'se], *a.* tucked up; *bien troussé*, well set up, neat, dapper.
trousseau [tru'so], *n.m.* (*pl.* **-eaux**) bunch (*of keys*); trousseau; outfit, kit.
trousser [tru'se], *v.t.* to tuck up, to turn up, to pin up; to truss; to dispatch (*business etc.*). **se trousser**, *v.r.* to tuck up one's clothes.
trouvaille [tru'va:j], *n.f.* godsend, windfall; find.
trouvé [tru've], *a.* found; *bien trouvé*, felicitous; *enfant trouvé*, foundling.
trouver [tru've], *v.t.* to find, to discover, to meet with, to hit upon; to detect; to find out; to deem, to judge; *trouver à dire* or *à redire à*, to find fault with; *trouver bon*, to think fit; *trouver mauvais*, to blame, to be displeased with; *vous trouvez?* you think so, do you? **se trouver**, *v.r.* to find oneself; to be, to exist; to feel; to prove, to turn out; *se trouver mal*, to faint.
truand [try'ã], *a.* vagrant.—*n.m.* (*fem.* **-e**) vagrant, beggar, tramp; crook.
truc (1) [tryk], *n.m.* knack, dodge, trick; (*Theat.*) machinery; (*pop.*) thing, thingummy, gadget.
truc (2) *or* **truck** [tryk], *n.m.* truck, bogie, (*Rail.*) open wagon.
trucheman *or* **truchement** [tryʃ'mã], *n.m.* interpreter; go-between.
truculent [tryky'lã], *a.* truculent.
truelle [try'ɛl], *n.f.* trowel; *truelle à poisson*, fish-slice.
truffe [tryf], *n.f.* truffle.
truie [trɥi], *n.f.* sow.
truite [trɥit], *n.f.* trout.
truité [trɥi'te], *a.* spotted, speckled.
trumeau [try'mo], *n.m.* (*pl.* **-eaux**) pier; pier-glass; leg of beef.

tsar [tsaːr], *n.m.* Tsar.
tsigane [TZIGANE].
tu [ty], *pron.* *thou, you.
tuant [tyˈɑ̃], *a.* killing, tiresome, laborious.
tube [tyb], *n.m.* tube, pipe; (*Anat.*) duct.
tuberculeux [tybɛrkyˈlø], *a.* (*fem.* **-euse**) tuberculous.
tuberculose [tybɛrkyˈloːz], *n.f.* tuberculosis.
tubulaire [tybyˈlɛːr], *a.* tubular.
tuer [tɥe], *v.t.* to kill, to slay; to slaughter, to butcher; to tire to death; to while away. **se tuer,** *v.r.* to kill oneself, to be killed; (*fig.*) to wear oneself out.
tuerie [tyˈri], *n.f.* slaughter, butchery; slaughter-house.
tue-tête (à) [atyˈtɛːt], *adv. phr.* at the top of one's voice.
tueur [tɥœːr], *n.m.* (*fem.* **-euse**) killer, thug.
tuile [tɥil], *n.f.* tile.
tuilerie [tɥilˈri], *n.f.* tile-works; **les Tuileries,** the Tuileries (*before 1871 a Royal palace, now a garden in Paris*).
tulipe [tyˈlip], *n.f.* tulip.
tulle [tyl], *n.m.* tulle, net.
tumeur [tyˈmœːr], *n.f.* tumour, swelling.
tumulte [tyˈmylt], *n.m.* tumult, uproar; hubbub.
tumultueux [tymylˈtɥø], *a.* (*fem.* **-euse**) tumultuous, riotous.
tunique [tyˈnik], *n.f.* tunic; envelope, film.
Tunisie [tyniˈzi], **la,** *f.* Tunisia.
tunisien [tyniˈzjɛ̃], *a.* Tunisian.—*n.m.* (**Tunisien,** *fem.* **-enne**) Tunisian (*person*).
tunnel [tyˈnɛl], *n.m.* tunnel.
turban [tyrˈbɑ̃], *n.m.* turban.
turbine [tyrˈbin], *n.f.* turbine.
turbopropulseur [tyrbopropylˈsœːr], *n.m.* turbo-prop(ulsor).
turboréacteur [tyrboreakˈtœːr], *n.m.* jet-engine; turbo-jet.
turbot [tyrˈbo], *n.m.* turbot.
turbulence [tyrbyˈlɑ̃ːs], *n.f.* turbulence.
turbulent [tyrbyˈlɑ̃], *a.* turbulent, boisterous; rowdy.
turc [tyrk], *a.* (*fem.* **turque**) Turkish.—*n.m.* Turkish (*language*); (**Turc,** *fem.* **Turque**) Turk.
turelure [tyrˈlyːr], *n.f.* fol-de-rol (*burden of a song*).
turf [tyrf], *n.m.* the turf, horse-racing.
turpitude [tyrpiˈtyd], *n.f.* turpitude, baseness, ignominy.
turque [TURC].
Turquie [tyrˈki], **la,** *f.* Turkey.
turquoise [tyrˈkwaːz], *a.* and *n.f.* turquoise.
tussor [tyˈsɔːr], *n.m.* tussore (*silk*).
tutelle [tyˈtɛl], *n.f.* tutelage, guardianship; (*Polit.*) trusteeship.
tuteur [tyˈtœːr], *n.m.* (*fem.* **tutrice**) guardian, trustee, protector.—*n.m.* (*Hort.*) stake.
tutoiement or **tutoîment** [tytwaˈmɑ̃], *n.m.* addressing a person as 'tu', 'theeing and thouing'.
tutoyer [tytwaˈje], *v.t.* (*conjug. like* EMPLOYER) to be on intimate terms with. **se tutoyer,** *v.r.* to be on familiar terms.
tutrice [tyˈtris], [TUTEUR].
tuyau [tɥiˈjo], *n.m.* (*pl.* **-aux**) pipe; tube; (chimney-)flue; shaft, funnel; stalk (*of corn*); nozzle (*of bellows etc.*); stem (*of a tobacco-pipe*); **tuyau d'arrosage,** garden-hose; **tuyau d'incendie,** fire-hose; **tuyau de poêle,** stove-pipe.
tuyautage [tɥijoˈtaːʒ], *n.m.* frilling, fluting; tubing.
tuyauter [tɥijoˈte], *v.t.* to goffer, to frill.
tuyauterie [tɥijoˈtri], *n.f.* system of pipes; plumbing; pipe-trade.
tympan [tɛ̃ˈpɑ̃], *n.m.* ear-drum, tympanum; tympan; spandrel.
type [tip], *n.m.* type; model, pattern; symbol, emblem; standard; (*Astron.*) plan, drawing; (*colloq.*) bloke, chap, fellow.
typhoïde [tifoˈid], *a.* typhoid.
typhon [tiˈfɔ̃], *n.m.* typhoon.
typhus [tiˈfyːs], *n.m.* typhus.
typique [tiˈpik], *a.* typical; characteristic.
typographe [tipoˈgraf], *n.m.* typographer.
typographie [tipograˈfi], *n.f.* typography.
tyran [tiˈrɑ̃], *n.m.* tyrant.
tyrannie [tiraˈni], *n.f.* tyranny.
tyrannique [tiraˈnik], *a.* tyrannical.
tyranniser [traniˈze], *v.t.* to tyrannize, to oppress.
tzar [TSAR].
tzigane or **tsigane** [tsiˈgan], *a.* and *n.* gipsy.

U

U, u [y], *n.m.* the twenty-first letter of the alphabet.
ubiquité [ybikɥiˈte], *n.f.* ubiquity.
Ukraine [yˈkrɛn], **l',** *f.* the Ukraine.
ukrainien [ykrɛˈnjɛ̃], *a.* Ukrainian.—*n.m.* (**Ukrainien,** *fem.* **-enne**) Ukrainian (*person*).
ulcère [ylˈsɛːr], *n.m.* ulcer.
ulcéré [ylseˈre], *a.* ulcerated; (*fig.*) embittered.
ulcérer [ylseˈre], *v.t.* (*conjug. like* CÉDER) to ulcerate; (*fig.*) to embitter, to incense.
ultérieur [ylteˈrjœːr], *a.* ulterior, further, later, subsequent.
ultérieurement [ylterjœrˈmɑ̃], *adv.* later on.
ultimatum [ultimaˈtɔm], *n.m.* ultimatum.
ultime [ylˈtim], *a.* last, final, ultimate.
ultra-sonore [yltrasoˈnɔːr], *a.* supersonic.
ultra-violet [yltravioˈlɛ], *a.* (*fem.* **-ette**) ultra-violet.
ululer [ylyˈle], *v.i.* to ululate, to hoot.
Ulysse [yˈlis], *m.* Ulysses.
umbre [ɔ̃ːbr], **omble** [ɔ̃ːbl], **ombre** [ɔ̃ːbr], *n.m.* grayling.
un [œ̃], *a.* and *art. indef.* (*fem.* **une**) one, the first; single; a, an; any, a certain.—*pron. indef.* one thing; one; *c'est tout un,* it is all one; *les uns disent oui, les autres disent non,* some say yes, others say no; *les uns et les autres,* all, all together; *l'un et l'autre,* both; *l'un ou l'autre,* the one or the other; *l'un vaut l'autre,* one is as good as the other; *un à un,* one by one.—*n.m.* one.
unanime [ynaˈnim], *a.* unanimous.
unanimement [ynanimˈmɑ̃], *adv.* unanimously.
unanimité [ynanimiˈte], *n.f.* unanimity.

321

uni [y'ni], *a.* united; smooth, even, level; uniform; plain, unaffected.

unicorne [yni'kɔrn], *n.m.* unicorn.

unième [y'njɛm], *a.* (*in compounds only*) first; *vingt et unième*, 21st.

unification [ynifika'sjɔ̃], *n.f.* unification.

unifier [yni'fje], *v.t.* to unify, to unite; to amalgamate.

uniforme [yni'fɔrm], *a.* uniform.—*n.m.* uniform, regimentals.

uniformément [yniforme'mɑ̃], *adv.* uniformly.

uniformité [yniformi'te], *n.f.* uniformity.

unilatéral [ynilate'ral], *a.* (*m. pl.* -aux) unilateral.

uniment [yni'mɑ̃], *adv.* evenly, smoothly; plainly.

union [y'njɔ̃], *n.f.* union; concord, agreement; mixture; marriage.

unique [y'nik], *a.* only, sole; single, unique, unparalleled; odd, singular; *fils unique*, only son; *sens unique*, one way (*street*).

uniquement [ynik'mɑ̃], *adv.* solely.

unir [y'niːr], *v.t.* to unite, to join; to smooth, to level; to pair. **s'unir**, *v.r.* to unite, to join together.

unisson [yni'sɔ̃], *n.m.* unison; (*fig.*) harmony, concert.

unité [yni'te], *n.f.* unity; unit; (*fig.*) concord, agreement.

univers [yni'vɛːr], *n.m. inv.* universe.

universalité [yniversali'te], *n.f.* universality; sum total, whole.

universel [yniver'sɛl], *a.* (*fem.* -elle) universal; residuary (*of legacies*).

universellement [yniversɛl'mɑ̃], *adv.* universally.

universitaire [yniversi'tɛːr], *a.* of the university, academic.—*n.* teacher, professor.

université [yniversi'te], *n.f.* university.

uranium [yra'njɔm], *n.m.* uranium.

urbain [yr'bɛ̃], *a.* urban.

urbanisme [yrba'nism], *n.m.* town-planning.

urbaniste [yrba'nist], *n.m.* town-planner.

urbanité [yrbani'te], *n.f.* urbanity.

urgence [yr'ʒɑ̃ːs], *n.f.* urgency; emergency; *d'urgence*, urgently, immediately.

urgent [yr'ʒɑ̃], *a.* urgent, pressing.

urinaire [yri'nɛːr], *a.* urinary.

urine [y'rin], *n.f.* urine.

uriner [yri'ne], *v.i.* to urinate, to make water.

urinoir [yri'nwaːr], *n.m.* (public) urinal.

urne [yrn], *n.f.* urn; *urne électorale*, ballot-box.

Ursule [yr'syl], *f.* Ursula.

urticaire [yrti'kɛːr], *n.f.* nettle-rash; urticaria.

Uruguay [yry'gɛ], *l'*, *m.* Uruguay.

uruguayen [yrygɛ'jɛ̃], *a.* Uruguayan.—*n.m.* (**Uruguayen**, *fem.* -enne) Uruguayan (*person*).

us [ys, yz], *n.m. pl. les us et coutumes*, the ways and customs.

usage [y'zaːʒ], *n.m.* custom, practice, usage; use; wear (*of clothes etc.*); *avoir de l'usage*, to have breeding; *hors d'usage*, out of use; *faire de l'usage* or *faire un bon usage*, to last or wear a long time.

usagé [yza'ʒe], *a.* used, worn, second-hand.

usager [yza'ʒe], *n.m.* user; *les usagers de la route*, road-users.

usé [y'ze], *a.* worn-out, threadbare; stale, trite, hackneyed.

user [y'ze], *v.t.* to use up, to consume; to wear out; to spend, to waste.—*v.i.* to make use of. **s'user**, *v.r.* to wear oneself out; to wear away.

usine [y'zin], *n.f.* works, mills, factory.

usinier [yzi'nje], *n.m.* manufacturer, mill-owner.

usité [yzi'te], *a.* used, usual, in common use.

ustensile [ystɑ̃'sil], *n.m.* utensil; tool, implement.

usuel [y'zɥɛl], *a.* (*fem.* -elle) usual, customary, ordinary.

usuellement [ysɥɛl'mɑ̃], *adv.* habitually, ordinarily.

usure [y'zyːr], *n.f.* usury, excessive interest; wear and tear.

usurier [yzy'rje], *a.* (*fem.* -ière) usurious.—*n.m.* (*fem.* -ière) usurer.

usurpateur [yzyrpa'tœːr], *a.* (*fem.* -trice) usurping.—*n.m.* (*fem.* -trice) usurper.

usurpation [yzyrpa'sjɔ̃], *n.f.* usurpation; encroachment.

usurper [yzyr'pe], *v.t.* to usurp; to encroach upon.

ut [yt], *n.m.* (*Mus.*) ut, do, the note C.

utérus [yte'rys], *n.m.* uterus, womb.

utile [y'til], *a.* useful, serviceable; advantageous, expedient, beneficial; *en temps utile*, in due or good time.—*n.m.* utility, usefulness.

utilement [ytil'mɑ̃], *adv.* usefully.

utilisation [ytiliza'sjɔ̃], *n.f.* use, utilization.

utiliser [ytili'ze], *v.t.* to use, to find use for, to employ.

utilité [ytili'te], *n.f.* utility, usefulness; benefit, profit, service, avail.

utopie [yto'pi], *n.f.* utopia.

utopique [yto'pik], *a.* utopian.

V

V, v [ve], *n.m.* the twenty-second letter of the alphabet.

vacance [va'kɑ̃ːs], *n.f.* vacancy; (*pl.*) vacation, holiday; recess (*of parliament etc.*).

vacant [va'kɑ̃], *a.* vacant; unoccupied, empty.

vacarme [va'karm], *n.m.* hubbub, uproar, fuss.

vacation [vaka'sjɔ̃], *n.f.* attendance, sitting (*of public officers etc.*); day's sale (*at auctions*); vacation (*of courts*).

vaccin [vak'sɛ̃], *n.m.* vaccine.

vaccination [vaksina'sjɔ̃], *n.f.* inoculation, vaccination.

vacciner [vaksi'ne], *v.t.* to inoculate, to vaccinate; to immunize.

vache [vaʃ], *n.f.* cow; cow-hide.

vacher [va'ʃe], *n.m.* (*fem.* -ère) cow-herd.

vacherie [va'ʃri], *n.f.* cow-house, byre.

vacillant [vasi'jɑ̃], *a.* vacillating, wavering, flickering; shaky, uncertain, unsteady.

vacillation [vasija'sjɔ̃], *n.f.* wobbling, flickering.

varier

vaciller [vasi'je], *v.i.* to vacillate; to waver, to stagger; to flicker (*of light etc.*).

vacuité [vakɥi'te], *n.f.* vacuity, emptiness.

vacuum [va'kɥɔm], *n.m.* vacuum.

va-et-vient [vae'vjɛ̃], *n.m. inv.* reciprocating motion, swing, see-saw motion, oscillation; (*fig.*) coming and going.

vagabond [vaga'bɔ̃], *a.* and *n.m.* (*fem.* **-e**) vagabond, vagrant.

vagabondage [vagabɔ̃'da:ʒ], *n.m.* vagrancy.

vagabonder [vagabɔ̃'de], *v.i.* to be a vagabond; to roam; (*fig.*) to flit from one thing to another.

vagin [va'ʒɛ̃], *n.m.* (*Anat.*) vagina.

vagir [va'ʒi:r], *v.i.* to wail, to pule (*of infants*).

vague (1) [vag], *n.f.* wave, billow.

vague (2) [vag], *a.* vague, indeterminate, uncertain; faint, indistinct, hazy; empty, vacant; *terres vagues*, waste-land; *terrain vague*, vacant site, piece of waste ground. —*n.m.* vagueness, looseness, uncertainty; empty space.

vaguement [vag'mɑ̃], *adv.* vaguely, dimly.

vaguer [va'ge], *v.i.* to ramble, to wander, to stray.

vaillamment [vaja'mɑ̃], *adv.* valiantly.

vaillance [va'jɑ̃:s], *n.f.* valour, bravery.

vaillant [va'jɑ̃], *a.* valiant, brave, gallant; stout (*heart*); *n'avoir pas un sou vaillant*, to be penniless.

vain [vɛ̃], *a.* vain, fruitless, ineffectual; empty, hollow, trifling; vainglorious; conceited; *en vain*, vainly, in vain.

vaincre [vɛ̃:kr], *v.t. irr.* to vanquish, to conquer, to overcome, to defeat; to outdo, to surpass; *se laisser vaincre*, to give way to, to yield.

vaincu [vɛ̃'ky], *a.* conquered, vanquished. —*n.m.* (*fem.* **-e**) conquered person, loser.

vainement [ven'mɑ̃], *adv.* vainly, in vain.

vainqueur [vɛ̃'kœ:r], *a.* conquering, victorious. —*n.m.* vanquisher, conqueror, victor; prize-winner.

vairon [vɛ'rɔ̃], *n.m.* minnow.

vaisseau [vɛ'so], *n.m.* (*pl.* **-eaux**) vessel, receptacle; ship; large covered space (*of a building*); (*Anat., Bot.*) vessel, tube, duct; (*pl.*) shipping.

vaisselle [vɛ'sɛl], *n.f.* plates and dishes; plate (*of gold or silver*); *faire la vaisselle*, to wash up.

val [val], *n.m.* (*pl.* **vals** or **vaux**) narrow valley, vale, dale.

valable [va'labl], *a.* valid, good.

valet [va'lɛ], *n.m.* footman, valet, manservant; knave (*at cards*); door-weight; holdfast; *valet de chambre*, valet; *valet de chiens*, whipper-in; *valet de ferme*, farm-worker.

valeter [val'te], *v.i.* (*conjug. like* APPELER) to cringe, to dance attendance.

valétudinaire [valetydi'nɛ:r], *a.* valetudinary. —*n.* valetudinarian, invalid.

valeur [va'lœ:r], *n.f.* value, worth, price; consideration; import, meaning; valour, bravery; (*pl.*) bills, paper, stocks, shares, securities.

valeureusement [valœrøz'mɑ̃], *adv.* bravely, courageously.

valeureux [valœ'rø], *a.* (*fem.* **-euse**) brave, courageous, gallant.

valide [va'lid], *a.* valid, good; healthy, able-bodied. —*n.* person in good health.

valider [vali'de], *v.t.* to make valid; to ratify, to validate.

validité [validi'te], *n.f.* validity; availability (*of a ticket*).

valise [va'li:z], *n.f.* suit-case; valise, portmanteau.

vallée [va'le], *n.f.* valley.

vallon [va'lɔ̃], *n.m.* small valley, vale, dale.

valoir [va'lwa:r], *v.t.v.i. irr.* to yield, to bring in; to procure, to furnish. —*v.i.* to be worth, to be as good as, to be equal to; to deserve, to merit; *autant vaut*, to all intents and purposes; *à valoir*, on account; *faire valoir son droit*, to assert one's right; *se faire valoir*, to boast; *vaille que vaille*, for better or worse; *valoir mieux*, to be better.

valse [vals], *n.f.* waltz.

valser [val'se], *v.i.* to waltz.

valve [valv], *n.f.* valve, clack, trap-door.

vampire [vɑ̃'pi:r], *n.m.* vampire.

van [vɑ̃], *n.m.* (*Agric.*) winnowing-basket.

vandale [vɑ̃'dal], *n.* vandal.

vandalisme [vɑ̃da'lism], *n.m.* vandalism.

vanille [va'ni:j], *n.f.* vanilla.

vanité [vani'te], *n.f.* vanity, conceit.

vaniteux [vani'tø], *a.* (*fem.* **-euse**) vainglorious, vain.

vannage [va'na:ʒ], *n.m.* winnowing.

vanne [van], *n.f.* sluice, sluice-gate.

vanneau [va'no], *n.m.* (*pl.* **-eaux**) lapwing, peewit.

vanner [va'ne], *v.t.* to winnow, to fan, to sift; (*pop.*) to tire out.

vannerie [van'ri], *n.f.* basket-making, basket-trade.

vanneur [va'nœ:r], *a.* (*fem.* **-euse**) winnowing. —*n.m.* (*fem.* **-euse**) winnower. —*n.f.* (-euse) winnowing-machine.

vannier [va'nje], *n.m.* (*fem.* **-iere**) basket-maker.

vannure [va'ny:r], *n.f.* chaff.

vantard [vɑ̃'ta:r], *a.* boasting, boastful, bragging. —*n.m.* (*fem.* **-e**) boaster, braggart.

vantardise [vɑ̃tar'di:z], *n.f.* boasting, bragging.

vanter [vɑ̃'te], *v.t.* to praise, to commend, to extol. **se vanter**, *v.r.* to boast, to pride oneself on (*de*).

vanterie [vɑ̃'tri], *n.f.* boasting, bragging.

va-nu-pieds [vany'pje], *n. inv.* ragamuffin.

vapeur [va'pœ:r], *n.f.* vapour; steam; haze, mist; *à la vapeur* or *à toute vapeur*, at full speed. —*n.m.* steamer, steamship.

vaporeux [vapɔ'rø], *a.* (*fem.* **-euse**) vaporous; steamy, hazy.

vaquer [va'ke], *v.i.* to be vacant; to attend, to devote oneself (*à*).

varech or **varec** [va'rɛk], *n.m.* sea-wrack, sea-weed.

variabilité [varjabili'te], *n.f.* variability, changeableness.

variable [va'rjabl], *a.* variable, fickle, unsettled. —*n.f.* (*Math.*) variable.

variant [va'rjɑ̃], *a.* variable, fickle. —*n.f.* (**-e**) variant (*reading* or *interpretation*).

variation [varja'sjɔ̃], *n.f.* variation.

varice [va'ris], *n.f.* varix varicose vein.

varier [va'rje], *v.t.* to vary, to change; to variegate. —*v.i.* to vary to be changeable; to disagree.

variété

variété [varje′te], *n.f.* variety, diversity, change; (*pl.*) miscellanea.

variole [va′rjɔl], *n.f.* smallpox.

Varsovie [varsɔ′vi], *f.* Warsaw.

vase (1) [vɑːz], *n.m.* vase, vessel.

vase (2) [vɑːz], *n.f.* slime, mud, mire, ooze.

vaseline [vaz′lin], *n.f.* petroleum jelly, Vaseline (*reg. trade mark*).

vaseux [va′zø], *a.* (*fem.* **-euse**) slimy, muddy, miry.

vasistas [vazis′tɑːs], *n.m. inv.* opening, fanlight (*over a door or a window*).

vassal [va′sal], *n.m.* (*fem.* **-e**, *m. pl.* **-aux**) vassal.

vaste [vast], *a.* vast, wide, spacious.

vastement [vastə′mã], *adv.* vastly, widely.

Vatican [vati′kã], **le**, *m.* the Vatican.

va-tout [va′tu], *n.m. inv.* one's all (*at cards*); *jouer son va-tout*, to stake one's all.

vaudeville [vod′vil], *n.m.* vaudeville; light form of comedy.

vau-l'eau (à) [avo′lo], *adv. phr.* with the current, down-stream; to rack and ruin.

vaurien [vo′rjɛ̃], *n.m.* (*fem.* **-enne**) good-for-nothing, scamp; rogue.

vautour [vo′tuːr], *n.m.* vulture.

vautre [voːtr], *n.m.* boar-hound.

vautrer (se) [savo′tre], *v.r.* to wallow; to sprawl.

veau [vo], *n.m.* (*pl.* **veaux**) calf; (*Cook.*) veal; calf-skin, calf-leather; (*fig.*) slow-witted fellow; *veau marin*, seal, seal-skin.

vedette [və′dɛt], *n.f.* vedette, mounted sentinel; scout; observation post, watch-tower; (*Theat.*) star.

végétal [veʒe′tal], *a.* (*m. pl.* **-aux**) vegetable. —*n.m.* (*pl.* **-aux**) vegetable, plant.

végétarien [veʒeta′rjɛ̃], *a.* and *n.m.* (*fem.* **-enne**) vegetarian.

végétation [veʒeta′sjɔ̃], *n.f.* vegetation; (*pl.*) adenoids.

végéter [veʒe′te], *v.i.* (*conjug. like* CÉDER) to vegetate.

véhémence [vee′mãːs], *n.f.* vehemence.

véhément [vee′mã], *a.* vehement, impetuous, hot, passionate.

véhiculaire [veiky′lɛːr], *a.* vehicular.

véhicule [vei′kyl], *n.m.* vehicle; medium.

veille [vɛːj], *n.f.* sleeplessness, watching; being awake; vigil; eve, day before; point, verge; (*pl.*) midnight work; *être à la veille de*, to be on the point of; *la veille de Noël*, Christmas Eve.

veillée [vɛ′je], *n.f.* time from supper to bed-time, evening (*in company*); sitting up to work etc. in company; night attendance (*upon a sick person*).

veiller [vɛ′je], *v.t.* to watch by, to nurse, to look after, to sit up with.—*v.i.* to sit up, to watch; to attend, to take care, to have an eye (*à*).

veilleur [vɛ′jœːr], *n.m.* (*fem.* **-euse**) watcher; *veilleur de nuit*, night-watchman.—*n.f.* (**-euse**) night-light.

veinard [vɛ′naːr], *a.* and *n.m.* (*fem.* **-e**) (*pop.*) lucky (person), lucky dog.

veine [vɛːn], *n.f.* vein; (*Geol. etc.*) seam; (*pop.*) good luck; *avoir de la veine*, to be in luck; *en veine de*, in the mood for; *un coup de veine*, a fluke.

veiné [vɛ′ne], *a.* veined, veiny.

veineux [vɛ′nø], *a.* (*fem.* **-euse**) veined, veiny; venous (*system, blood*).

vélin [ve′lɛ̃], *n.m.* vellum.

velléité [velei′te], *n.f.* passing fancy, mind, whim.

vélo [ve′lo], *n.m.* (*fam.*) bike.

vélocité [velosi′te], *n.f.* velocity.

vélodrome [velo′drɔm], *n.m.* cycle racing-track.

vélomoteur [velomo′tœːr], *n.m.* moped.

velours [və′luːr], *n.m.* velvet; *velours à côtes*, corduroy; *velours de coton*, velveteen.

velouté [vəlu′te], *a.* velvet, velvety, velvet-like; soft and smooth to the palate (*of wines*).—*n.m.* velvet-pile; softness; bloom (*of fruit*); smooth rich soup *or* sauce; *velouté de laine*, velours cloth.

velu [və′ly], *a.* hairy, shaggy, rough.—*n.m.* shagginess.

vélum [ve′lɔm], *n.m.* awning.

venaison [vənɛ′zɔ̃], *n.f.* venison.

vénal [ve′nal], *a.* (*m. pl.* **-aux**) venal, mercenary.

vénalité [venali′te], *n.f.* venality.

venant [və′nã], *a.* coming, thriving.—*n.m.* comer; *tout-venant*, unsorted (*of produce*).

vendable [vã′dabl], *a.* saleable, marketable.

vendange [vã′dãːʒ]. *n.f.* vintage, grape-gathering.

vendanger [vãdã′ʒe], *v.t.* (*conjug. like* MANGER) to gather in the grapes from; (*fig.*) to ravage, to spoil.—*v.i.* to pick (*the grapes*); (*fig.*) to make illicit profits.

vendangeur [vãdã′ʒœːr], *n.m.* (*fem.* **-euse**) vintager, grape-gatherer.

vendéen [vãde′ɛ̃], *a.* (*fem.* **-éenne**) Vendean.

vendetta [vãdɛ′ta], *n.f.* vendetta.

vendeur [vã′dœːr], *n.m.* (*fem.* **-euse**) vendor, seller, dealer; salesman, shop assistant.

vendre [vãːdr], *v.t.* to sell; (*fig.*) to betray; *à vendre*, for sale. **se vendre**, *v.r.* to sell oneself; to be sold; to go off (*well etc.*).

vendredi [vãdrə′di], *n.m.* Friday; *le Vendredi saint*, Good Friday.

vené [və′ne], *a.* high (*of meat*).

vénéneux [vene′nø], *a.* (*fem.* **-euse**) poisonous (*when eaten*).

vénérable [vene′rabl], *a.* a venerable.

vénération [venera′sjɔ̃], *n.f.* veneration.

vénérer [vene′re], *v.t.* (*conjug. like* CÉDER) to venerate, to hold in reverence.

vénerie [ven′ri], *n.f.* venery, hunting.

veneur [və′nœːr], *n.m.* huntsman.

Vénézuéla [venezɥe′la], **le**, *m.* Venezuela.

vénézuélien [venezɥe′ljɛ̃], *a.* (*fem.* **-enne**) Venezuelan.—*n.m.* (**Vénézuélien**, *fem.* **-enne**) Venezuelan (*person*).

vengeance [vã′ʒãːs], *n.f.* vengeance, revenge.

venger [vã′ʒe], *v.t.* (*conjug. like* MANGER) to revenge, to avenge. **se venger**, *v.r.* se *venger de quelqu'un*, to revenge oneself on someone.

vengeur [vã′ʒœːr], *a.* (*fem.* **-eresse**) revengeful, avenging.—*n.m.* (*fem.* **-eresse**) avenger, revenger.

véniel [ve′njɛl], *a.* (*fem.* **-elle**) venial.

venimeux [vəni′mø], *a.* (*fem.* **-euse**) communicating poison (*from outside*), venomous (*snake etc.*); (*fig.*) malignant, harmful.

324

venin [və'nɛ̃], *n.m.* venom, poison; (*fig.*) spite, malice.

venir [və'niːr], *v.i. irr.* (*conjug. like* TENIR, *but with aux.* ÊTRE) to come, to be coming; to arrive; to reach; to occur, to happen; to grow, to grow up; to thrive; to issue, to arise; to be descended; *d'où vient cela?* what is the cause of that? *en venir aux mains,* to come to blows; *faire venir le médecin,* to send for the doctor; *il va et vient,* he goes in and out; *je ne ferai qu'aller et venir,* I will not stay, I shall come straight back; *le voilà qui vient,* here he comes; *où voulez-vous en venir?* what are you getting at? *s'en venir,* to come away; *si ma lettre venait à se perdre,* if my letter should happen to go astray; *venir à bout de,* to master; *venir de,* to come from, (*followed by an infinitive,* to have just)—*je viens de le voir,* I have just seen him; *je venais de le quitter,* I had just left him).

Venise [və'niːz], *f.* Venice.

vent [vɑ̃], *n.m.* wind; breeze; breath, breathing; (*Med.*) (*pl.*) flatulence; (*Hunt.*) scent; (*fig.*) vanity, emptiness; *autant en emporte le vent,* all that is idle talk; *avoir vent de,* to get wind of; *coup de vent,* gust of wind; (*colloq.*) *dans le vent,* 'with it'; *en plein vent,* in the open air; *il fait du vent,* it is windy.

vente [vɑ̃ːt], *n.f.* sale; selling, auction; felling *or* cutting (*of timber*); *en vente,* for sale, on sale; *vente aux enchères,* sale by auction.

venter [vɑ̃'te], *v.i.* (*usu. impers.*) to blow, to be windy.

venteux [vɑ̃'tø], *a.* (*fem.* **-euse**) windy, gusty.

ventilateur [vɑ̃tila'tœːr], *n.m.* ventilator, fan, blower.

ventilation [vɑ̃tilɑ'sjɔ̃], *n.f.* ventilation, airing.

ventiler [vɑ̃ti'le], *v.t.* to ventilate, to air; (*fig.*) to discuss.

ventosité [vɑ̃tozi'te], *n.f.* flatulence.

ventouse [vɑ̃'tuːz], *n.f.* cupping-glass; vent, air-hole; sucker (*of leech*); nozzle (*of vacuum-cleaner*).

ventre [vɑ̃ːtr], *n.m.* belly, abdomen; stomach; womb; bowels, one's inside; bulge; *à plat ventre,* flat on one's face; *ventre à terre,* at full speed; *j'ai mal au ventre,* I have a stomach-ache.

ventrière [vɑ̃tri'ɛːr], *n.f.* abdominal belt; sling, brace; girth (*of horse*).

ventriloque [vɑ̃tri'lɔk], *n.* ventriloquist.

ventriloquie [vɑ̃trilɔ'ki], *n.f.* ventriloquy.

ventru [vɑ̃'try], *a.* big-bellied, corpulent; bulging.—*n.m.* (*fem.* **-e**) pot-bellied person.

venu [və'ny], *a.* come; done; come up, grown; *bien venu* [BIENVENU]; *enfant bien venu,* well-grown child; *mal venu,* unwelcome; open to censure.—*n.m.* (*fem.* **-e**) *le dernier venu,* the last arrival; *le premier venu* or *la première venue,* the first comer, anyone.—*n.f.* (**-e**) coming, arrival, advent; growth.

Vénus [ve'nys], *f.* Venus.

vêpres [veːpr], *n.f. pl.* vespers.

ver [vɛːr], *n.m.* worm; maggot, mite; moth; *mangé* or *rongé des vers,* worm-eaten; *nu comme un ver,* stark naked; *ver*

blanc, grub; *ver à soie,* silkworm; *ver luisant,* glow-worm; *ver solitaire,* tapeworm.

véracité [verasi'te], *n.f.* veracity.

véranda [verɑ̃'da], *n.f.* veranda.

verbal [vɛr'bal], *a.* (*m. pl.* **-aux**) verbal.

verbalement [verbal'mɑ̃], *adv.* verbally; (*colloq.*) by word of mouth.

verbaliser [vɛrbali'ze], *v.i.* to draw up a written statement.

verbe [vɛrb], *n.m.* verb; (*Theol.*) *le Verbe,* the Word.

verbeux [vɛr'bø], *a.* (*fem.* **-euse**) verbose.

verbiage [vɛr'bjaːʒ], *n.m.* verbiage.

verbosité [vɛrbozi'te], *n.f.* verbosity.

verdâtre [vɛr'dɑːtr], *a.* greenish.

verdelet [vɛr'dlɛ], *a.* (*fem.* **-ette**) greenish; tart (*of wine*); hale (*of old people*).

verdeur [vɛr'dœːr], *n.f.* greenness, sap (*of wood*); tartness, harshness (*of wine*); vigour; spryness (*of old people*); (*fig.*) crudeness (*of language*).

verdict [vɛr'dikt], *n.m.* verdict, finding.

verdier [vɛr'dje], *n.m.* greenfinch; verderer, ranger.

verdir [vɛr'diːr], *v.t.* to make *or* paint green. —*v.i.* to turn green.

verdoyant [vɛrdwa'jɑ̃], *a.* verdant, green.

verdoyer [vɛrdwa'je], *v.i.* (*conjug. like* EMPLOYER) to become green.

verdure [vɛr'dyːr], *n.f.* verdure; greenery; pot-herbs.

verdurier [vɛrdy'rje], *n.m.* (*fem.* **-ière**) greengrocer.

véreux [ve'rø], *a.* (*fem.* **-euse**) worm-eaten, maggoty; rotten; (*fig.*) suspect; insecure (*of bills etc.*).

verge [vɛːrʒ], *n.f.* rod, wand; shaft, pin; shank (*of an anchor etc.*); (C) yard (*measure*).

verger [vɛr'ʒe], *n.m.* orchard.

vergeté [vɛrʒə'te], *a.* streaky.

vergette [vɛr'ʒɛt], *n.f.* clothes-brush; bundle of rods, switch.

verglacé [vɛrgla'se], *a.* covered with glazed frost; icy.

verglas [vɛr'gla], *n.m.* thin coating of ice, frost after a thaw *or* rain; glazed frost.

vergne [vɛrɲ], **verne** [vɛrn], *n.m.* alder(-tree).

vergogne [vɛr'gɔɲ], *n.f.* shame; *sans vergogne,* shameless(ly).

vergue [vɛrg], *n.f.* yard (*for sail*).

véridicité [veridisi'te], *n.f.* veracity, truthfulness.

véridique [veri'dik], *a.* veracious, truthful.

vérificateur [verifika'tœːr], *n.m.* verifier, examiner, inspector; (*Eng.*) calipers, gauge; *vérificateur des comptes,* auditor.

vérification [verifika'sjɔ̃], *n.f.* verification, auditing, probate.

vérifier [veri'fje], *v.t.* to verify, to inspect, to examine, to audit; to prove.

vérin [ve'rɛ̃], *n.m.* (*Eng.*) jack.

véritable [veri'tabl], *a.* true, genuine, real; staunch, downright, thorough.

véritablement [veritablə'mɑ̃], *adv.* truly, in reality, indeed.

vérité [veri'te], *n.f.* truth, verity, truthfulness; *à la vérité,* indeed, it is true, I admit; *dire la vérité,* to speak the truth; *en vérité,* indeed, truly.

verjus [vɛr'ʒy], *n.m.* verjuice; sour grapes.

verjuté [vɛrʒy'te], *a.* sharp, tart, acid.

vermeil [vɛrˈmɛːj], *a.* (*fem.* **-eille**) vermilion, ruddy, rosy.—*n.m.* vermeil, silver-gilt.
vermicelle [vɛrmiˈsɛl], *n.m.* vermicelli.
vermiculaire [vɛrmikyˈlɛːr], *a.* vermicular, worm-shaped.
vermillon [vɛrmiˈjɔ̃], *a. inv.* and *n.m.* vermilion.
vermine [vɛrˈmin], *n.f.* vermin (*only insects such as fleas, lice etc.*); (*fig.*) rabble.
vermoulu [vɛrmuˈly], *a.* worm-eaten.
vermoulure [vɛrmuˈlyːr], *n.f.* worm-hole, rottenness caused by worms (*in wood*).
vermout(h) [vɛrˈmut], *n.m.* vermouth.
vernaculaire [vɛrnakyˈlɛːr], *a.* and *n.m.* vernacular.
vernal [vɛrˈnal], *a.* (*m. pl.* **-aux**) vernal, spring-like.
vernier [vɛrˈnje], *n.m.* vernier, sliding-scale.
vernir [vɛrˈniːr], *v.t.* to varnish; to glaze, to polish.
vernis [vɛrˈni], *n.m.* varnish, polish, glaze.
vernissage [vɛrniˈsaːʒ], *n.m.* varnishing; private view (*of art exhibition*).
vernisser [vɛrniˈse], *v.t.* to glaze (*pottery etc.*).
vérole [veˈrɔl], *n.f.* *petite vérole*, smallpox; *petite vérole volante*, chicken-pox.
véronal [veroˈnal], *n.m.* (*Chem.*) veronal, barbitone.
Véronique [veroˈnik], *f.* Veronica.
véronique [veroˈnik], *n.f.* veronica, speedwell.
verrat [vɛˈra], *n.m.* boar.
verre [vɛːr], *n.m.* glass; *verre à eau* or *verre gobelet*, tumbler; *verre à vin*, wine-glass; *verre de vin*, glass of wine.
verrerie [vɛˈri], *n.f.* glass-works; glass-ware.
verrier [vɛˈrje], *n.m.* glass-maker.
verrière [vɛˈrjɛːr], *n.f.* stained-glass window.
verroterie [veroˈtri], *n.f.* small glass-ware, glass beads.
verrou [vɛˈru], *n.m.* bolt.
verrouiller [veruˈje], *v.t.* to bolt. **se verrouiller**, *v.r.* to bolt oneself in.
verrue [vɛˈry], *n.f.* wart; *verrue plantaire*, verruca.
vers (1) [vɛːr], *n.m. inv.* verse, line (*of poetry*).
vers (2) [vɛːr], *prep.* towards, to; about; *vers (les) quatre heures*, about four o'clock.
versable [vɛrˈsabl], *a.* apt to overturn, liable to upset.
versage [vɛrˈsaːʒ], *n.m.* emptying, tipping; (*Agric.*) first ploughing (*of fallow land*).
versant (1) [vɛrˈsɑ̃], *a.* liable to be overturned.
versant (2) [vɛrˈsɑ̃], *n.m.* declivity, side, slope; watershed.
versatile [vɛrsaˈtil], *a.* inconstant, changeable.
versatilité [versatiliˈte], *n.f.* inconstancy.
verse (**à**) [aˈvɛrs], *adv.* abundantly; *il pleut à verse*, it is pouring with rain.
versé [vɛrˈse], *a.* spilt; well versed, conversant.
versement [vɛrsəˈmɑ̃], *n.m.* payment; deposit.
verser [vɛrˈse], *v.t.* to pour, to pour out; to discharge, to empty; to shed; to spill; to pay in, to deposit; to overturn, to upset; to lay (*corn*).—*v.i.* to overturn, to upset (*of vehicles*); to be laid (*of standing corn*).
verset [vɛrˈse], *n.m.* (*Bibl. etc.*) verse.

versificateur [vɛrsifikaˈtœːr], *n.m.* (*fem.* **-trice**) versifier.
versification [vɛrsifikaˈsjɔ̃], *n.f.* versification.
versifier [vɛrsiˈfje], *v.t., v.i.* to versify.
version [vɛrˈsjɔ̃], *n.f.* version; (*Sch.*) translation.
verso [vɛrˈso], *n.m.* verso, back, left-hand page.
vert [vɛːr], *a.* green; sharp, harsh (*of things*); tart (*of wine*); raw; sour; (*fig.*) vigorous, robust; spicy (*of stories*).—*n.m.* green, green colour; green food; sharpness (*of wine etc.*); (*Golf*) (putting-)green.
vert-de-gris [vɛrdəˈgri], *n.m.* verdigris.
vertèbre [vɛrˈtɛːbr], *n.f.* vertebra.
vertébré [vɛrteˈbre], *a.* and *n.m.* vertebrate.
vertement [vɛrtəˈmɑ̃], *adv.* sharply; harshly, severely.
vertical [vɛrtiˈkal], *a.* (*m. pl.* **-aux**) vertical.
verticalement [vɛrtikalˈmɑ̃], *adv.* vertically.
vertige [vɛrˈtiːʒ], *n.m.* dizziness, giddiness, vertigo; (*fig.*) madness, intoxication.
vertigineux [vɛrtiʒiˈnø], *a.* (*fem.* **-euse**) dizzy, giddy; (*fig.*) breath-taking.
vertigo [vɛrtiˈgo], *n.m.* staggers; (*fig.*) whim.
vertu [vɛrˈty], *n.f.* virtue, chastity; property, faculty, quality; efficacy, force.
vertueusement [vɛrtuøzˈmɑ̃], *adv.* virtuously.
vertueux [vɛrˈtɥø], *a.* (*fem.* **-euse**) virtuous, chaste.
verve [vɛrv], *n.f.* warmth, animation, verve, spirit, zest.
verveine [vɛrˈvɛːn], *n.f.* vervain, verbena.
vésicule [veziˈkyl], *n.f.* vesicle, bladder; *vésicule biliaire*, gall-bladder.
vespasienne [vɛspaˈzjɛn], *n.f.* public urinal; public convenience.
vessie [vɛˈsi], *n.f.* bladder.
veste [vɛst], *n.f.* jacket.
vestiaire [vɛsˈtjɛːr], *n.m.* cloakroom; changing-room; robing-room (*for judges*); hat-and-coat rack.
vestibule [vɛstiˈbyl], *n.m.* vestibule, lobby, hall.
vestige [vɛsˈtiːʒ], *n.m.* footprint, vestige, sign, mark; trace, remains.
veston [vɛsˈtɔ̃], *n.m.* jacket, lounge-coat; *complet veston*, lounge-suit.
Vésuve [veˈzyːv], le, *m.* Vesuvius.
vêtement [vɛtˈmɑ̃], *n.m.* garment; (*pl.*) dress, clothes; (*poet.*) raiment; *vêtements de dessous*, underwear.
vétéran [veteˈrɑ̃], *n.m.* veteran; (*Sch.*) boy who stays in a form a second year.
vétérinaire [veteriˈnɛːr], *a.* veterinary.—*n.m.* veterinary surgeon, vet.
vétille [veˈtiːj], *n.f.* trifle, bagatelle.
vétiller [vetiˈje], *v.i.* to trifle; to split hairs.
vétilleux [vetiˈjø], *a.* (*fem.* **-euse**) particular, finicky.
vêtir [vɛˈtiːr], *v.t. irr.* to clothe; to array, to dress; to put on. **se vêtir**, *v.r.* to dress oneself.
véto [veˈto], *n.m.* veto.
vêtu [vɛˈty], *a.* dressed, clothed, arrayed.
vétuste [veˈtyst], *a.* old, antiquated; dilapidated, worn out.
vétusté [vetysˈte], *n.f.* antiquity, old age, decay.

veuf [vœf], *a.* (*fem.* **veuve**) widowed.—*n.m.* widower.—*n.f.* (**veuve**) widow.
veule [vœ:l], *a.* feckless, weak, feeble.
veuvage [vœ'va:ʒ]. *n.m.* widowhood, widowerhood.
vexant [vɛk'sã], *a.* vexing, provoking.
vexer [vɛk'se], *v.t.* to vex, to plague, to annoy.
viable [vjabl], *a.* likely to live, viable; fit for traffic.
viaduc [vja'dyk], *n.m.* viaduct.
viager [vja'ʒe], *a.* (*fem.* **-ère**) for life, during life; *rente viagère*, life-annuity.
viande [vjã:d], *n.f.* meat; *menue viande*, fowl and game; *grosse viande*, butcher's meat.
vibrant [vi'brã], *a.* vibrating; vibrant, resonant.
vibration [vibrɑ'sjõ], *n.f.* vibration.
vibrer [vi'bre], *v.i.* to vibrate.
vicaire [vi'kɛːr], *n.m.* curate (*of a parish*).
vicariat [vika'rja], *n.m.*, **vicairie** [vikɛ'ri], *n.f.* curacy, chapel of ease.
vice [vis], *n.m.* fault, defect, flaw, blemish; vice, viciousness.
vice-amiral [visami'ral], *n.m.* (*pl.* **-aux**) vice-admiral; second ship of a fleet.
vice-roi [vis'rwa], *n.m.* (*pl.* **vice-rois**) viceroy.
vicié [vi'sje], *a.* vitiated, depraved, corrupted; foul (*of air etc.*).
vicier [vi'sje], *v.t.* to vitiate, to taint, to corrupt.
vicieusement [visjøz'mã], *adv.* viciously.
vicieux [vi'sjø], *a.* (*fem.* **-euse**) vicious; faulty, defective.
vicinal [visi'nal], *a.* (*m. pl.* **-aux**) local, connecting (*of roads*); *chemin vicinal*, by-road.
vicissitude [visisi'tyd], *n.f.* vicissitude, change.
vicomte [vi'kõ:t], *n.m.* viscount.
vicomtesse [vikõ'tɛs], *n.f.* viscountess.
victime [vik'tim], *n.f.* victim; sufferer; casualty.
Victoire [vik'twa:r], **Victoria** [viktɔ'rja], *f.* Victoria.
victoire [vik'twa:r], *n.f.* victory.
victorieux [viktɔ'rjø], *a.* (*fem.* **-euse**) victorious.
victuaille [vik'tɥa:j], *n.f.* (*colloq.*) provisions.
vidange [vi'dã:ʒ], *n.f.* emptying; draining off; night-soil; *tonneau en vidange*, broached cask.
vidanger [vidã'ʒe], *v.t.* (*conjug. like* MANGER) to empty, to clean out, to drain, to blow off.
vidangeur [vidã'ʒœ:r], *n.m.* scavenger.
vide [vid], *a.* empty; void, vacant, blank; destitute.—*n.m.* empty space, blank; vacuum; gap, hole; emptiness.—*adv. phr.* *à vide*, empty.
vidé [vi'de], *a.* emptied, exhausted.
vider [vi'de], *v.t.* to empty; to drain; to hollow out; to draw (*poultry*); to gut (*fish*); to vacate; to decide, to settle.
vie [vi], *n.f.* life; lifetime; existence, days; vitality; livelihood, living; food, subsistence; spirit, animation; noise; *être en vie*, to be alive; *le coût de la vie*, the cost of living; *niveau de vie*, standard of living.
vieil [vjɛj], [VIEUX].

vieillard [vjɛ'ja:r], *n.m.* old man.
vieille [vjɛj], [VIEUX].
vieillerie [vjɛj'ri], *n.f.* (*usu. pl.*) old things old clothes, old lumber, rubbish; obsolete ideas.
vieillesse [vjɛ'jɛs], *n.f.* old age; oldness.
vieillir [vjɛ'ji:r], *v.t.* to make old; to make look old.—*v.i.* to grow old; to become obsolete.
vieillissant [vjɛji'sã], *a.* growing old.
vieillot [vjɛ'jo], *a.* (*fem.* **-otte**) oldish.
vielle [vjɛl], *n.f.* *hurdy-gurdy.
Vienne [vjɛn], *f.* Vienna.
viennois [vjɛ'nwa], *a.* Viennese.—*n.m.* (**Viennois**, *fem.* **-oise**) Viennese (*person*).
vierge [vjɛrʒ], *a.* virgin, virginal, maiden; pure, untrodden; unwrought; free (*from*).— *n.f.* virgin, maid; (*Astron.*) Virgo.
Viet-Nam [vjɛt'nam], **le**, *m.* Vietnam.
vietnamien [vjɛtna'mjɛ̃], *a.* (*fem.* **-enne**) Vietnamese.—*n.m.* Vietnamese (*language*); (**Vietnamien**, *fem.* **-enne**) Vietnamese (*person*).
vieux [vjø], *a.* (*before a vowel or h mute*, **vieil**, *fem.* **vieille**) old, aged, advanced in years; ancient, venerable; *vieux jeu*, old-fashioned.—*n.m.* (*fem.* **vieille**) old man, old woman; *la retraite des vieux*, old-age pension; *mon vieux*, (a term of endearment) old friend, old chap.
vif [vif], *a.* (*fem.* **vive**) alive, live, living; quick; lively, brisk, sprightly, animated, fiery, mettlesome, ardent, eager; keen; sharp, violent (*of pain etc.*); bracing (*of air etc.*); vivid, bright (*of colours*).—*n.m.* the quick (*live flesh*); living person; *être pris sur le vif*, to be very lifelike; *piquer au vif*, to sting to the quick.
vif-argent [vifar'ʒã], *n.m.* quicksilver.
vigie [vi'ʒi], *n.f.* look-out man; look-out (*station* or *ship*); (*Rail.*) seat on the top of guard's van.
vigilance [viʒi'lã:s], *n.f.* vigilance.
vigilant [viʒi'lã], *a.* vigilant, watchful.
vigile [vi'ʒil], *n.f.* vigil, eve.
vigne [viɲ], *n.f.* vine; vineyard; *vigne vierge*, wild-grape, virginia-creeper.
vigneron [viɲə'rõ], *n.m.* (*fem.* **-onne**) vine-dresser, wine-grower.
vignette [vi'nɛt], *n.f.* vignette; (*pop.*) meadow-sweet.
vignoble [vi'nɔbl], *n.m.* vineyard.
vigoureusement [vigurøz'mã], *adv.* vigorously, energetically.
vigoureux [vigu'rø], *a.* (*fem.* **-euse**) vigorous, energetic; stout, stalwart.
vigueur [vi'gœ:r], *n.f.* vigour, strength; force, power, energy; *entrer en vigueur*, to come into force (*of laws etc.*).
vil [vil], *a.* vile, base, mean; abject, low; worthless; *à vil prix*, dirt cheap.
vilain [vi'lɛ̃], *a.* ugly; unsightly; pitiful; nasty; sordid, wretched; naughty (*of a child*); *un vilain tour*, a dirty trick; *vilain temps*, vile weather.—*n.m.* (*fem.* **-e**) *villein (*bondman*); nasty fellow; (*childish*) naughty boy *or* girl.
vilainement [vilɛn'mã], *adv.* uglily; basely shamefully, shabbily.
vilebrequin [vilbrə'kɛ̃], *n.m.* brace, wimble; (*Mech.*) crankshaft.
vilement [vil'mã], *adv.* vilely, basely.

327

vilenie

vilenie [vil′ni], *n.f.* nastiness, foulness; vile action; stinginess, meanness; (*pl.*) offensive words.

vileté [vil′te], *n.f.* cheapness, low price; vileness; mean action.

vilipender [vilipā′de], *v.t.* to vilify; to disparage.

villa [vil′la], *n.f.* villa.

village [vi′laːʒ], *n.m.* village.

villageois [vila′ʒwa], *a.* rustic.—*n.m.* (*fem.* -e) villager.

ville [vil], *n.f.* town, city; *être en ville*, to be out (*not at home*); *hôtel de ville*, town hall; *ville d'eaux*, spa.

villégiature [vileʒja′tyːr], *n.f.* sojourn in the country; *en villégiature*, staying in the country.

vin [vɛ̃], *n.m.* wine; *à bon vin point d'e-n seigne*, good wine needs no bush; *vin de Bordeaux rouge*, claret; *vin de marque*, vintage wine; *vin mousseux*, sparkling wine; *vin ordinaire*, dinner wine.

vinaigre [vi′nɛːgr], *n.m.* vinegar.

vinaigrer [vine′gre], *v.t.* to season with vinegar.

vindicatif [vɛ̃dika′tif], *a.* (*fem.* -tive) vindictive, revengeful.

vingt [vɛ̃], *a.* and *n.m. inv.* twenty, score; twentieth.

vingtaine [vɛ̃′tɛːn], *n.f.* a score, about twenty.

vingt-et-un [vɛ̃te′œ̃], *n.m.* vingt-et-un (*card game*).

vingtième [vɛ̃′tjɛːm], *a.* and *n.* twentieth.

vinicole [vini′kɔl], *a.* wine-growing, wine-producing.

viol [vjɔl], *n.m.* rape.

violateur [vjɔla′tœːr], *a.* (*fem.* -trice) violating, transgressing, infringing.—*n.m.* (*fem.* -trice) violator, infringer, breaker.

violation [vjɔla′sjɔ̃], *n.f.* violation, breach, infringement.

violâtre [vjɔ′lɑːtr], *a.* purplish.

viole [vjɔl], *n.f.* viol.

violemment [vjɔla′mã], *adv.* violently.

violence [vjɔ′lãːs], *n.f.* violence; (*Law*) duress; (*fig.*) stress, fury.

violent [vjɔ′lã], *a.* violent; strong (*of suspicion etc.*); (*colloq.*) excessive; *c'est par trop violent*, it really is too bad.

violenter [vjɔlã′te], *v.t.* to offer *or* do violence to, to force; to constrain; to violate.

violer [vjɔ′le], *v.t.* to violate; to outrage, to transgress.

violet [vjɔ′lɛ], *a.* (*fem.* -ette) violet-coloured, purple.—*n.m.* violet(-colour).—*n.f.* (-ette) (*Bot.*) violet.

violier [vjɔ′lje], *n.m.* wallflower, gillyflower.

violon [vjɔ′lɔ̃], *n.m.* violin, fiddle; violinist, fiddler; (*pop.*) lock-up, cells (*prison*).

violoncelle [vjɔlɔ̃′sɛl], *n.m.* violoncello, 'cello.

violoncelliste [vjɔlɔ̃se′list], *n.* violoncellist, 'cellist.

violoniste [vjɔlɔ′nist], *n.* violinist.

viorne [vjɔrn], *n.f.* viburnum.

vipère [vi′pɛːr], *n.f.* viper, adder.

virage [vi′raːʒ], *n.m.* turning, cornering; turn, bend, corner; (*Naut.*) tacking; *virage incliné*, bank; *virage en épingle à cheveux*, hair-pin bend.

virago [vira′go], *n.f.* virago, termagant.

virée [vi′re], *n.f.* turning; winding.

virement [vir′mã], *n.m.* turning; (*Naut.*) veering about, tacking; (*Book-keeping*) clearing, transfer; *banque de virement*, clearing-bank.

virer [vi′re], *v.t.* to transfer, to clear (*a sum of money*).—*v.i.* to turn, to turn about; (*Naut.*) to tack, to veer about.

vireux [vi′rø], *a.* (*fem.* -euse) poisonous, noxious, nauseous.

virginal [virʒi′nal], *a.* (*m. pl.* -aux) virginal, maidenly.

Virginie [virʒi′ni], *f.* Virginia; (*Geog.*) *La Virginie*, Virginia.

virginité [virʒini′te], *n.f.* virginity, maidenhood.

virgule [vir′gyl], *n.f.* comma; *point et virgule*, semi-colon.

viril [vi′ril], *a.* virile, male; manly.

virilement [viril′mã], *adv.* like a man; in a manly way.

virilité [virili′te], *n.f.* virility; manhood.

virole [vi′rɔl], *n.f.* ferrule.

virtuel [vir′tɥel], *a.* (*fem.* -elle) virtual; potentially.

virtuellement [virtɥel′mã], *adv.* virtually; potentially.

virtuose [vir′tɥoːz], *n.* virtuoso.

virtuosité [virtɥozi′te], *n.f.* virtuosity.

virulence [viry′lãːs], *n.f.* virulence.

virulent [viry′lã], *a.* virulent.

virus [vi′ryːs], *n.m.* virus.

vis [vis], *n.f. inv.* screw; *escalier à vis*, spiral staircase.

visa [vi′za], *n.m.* visa, signature, endorsement (*on passports etc.*).

visage [vi′zaːʒ], *n.m.* face, visage, countenance; aspect, look, air; *à deux visages*, double-faced; *à visage découvert*, openly, barefacedly; *avoir bon visage*, to look well.

vis-à-vis [viza′vi], *prep. phr.* opposite, over against; towards, in relation to; *vis-à-vis de l'église*, opposite the church.—*adv. phr.* opposite.—*n.m. inv.* vis-à-vis (in dancing etc.); person opposite (*at table etc.*).

viscère [vi′sɛːr], *n.m.* any of the viscera *or* vital organs.

viscosité [viskozi′te], *n.f.* viscosity, viscidity, stickiness.

visée [vi′ze], *n.f.* aim, end; design, plan.

viser [vi′ze], *v.t.* to aim at; to allude to; to pursue; to endorse.—*v.i.* to aim, to take aim; to aspire (*à*).

viseur [vi′zœːr], *n.m.* (*Phot.*) view-finder.

visibilité [vizibili′te], *n.f.* visibility.

visible [vi′zibl], *a.* visible; evident, manifest, obvious.

visiblement [viziblə′mã], *adv.* visibly, obviously.

visière [vi′zjɛːr], *n.f.* visor (*of a helmet*); peak (*of caps etc.*), eye-shade; sight (*on firearms*).

vision [vi′zjɔ̃], *n.f.* vision, sight; dream, phantom, fancy.

visionnaire [vizjɔ′nɛːr], *a.* visionary, fanciful. —*n.* seer; dreamer, visionary.

visite [vi′zit], *n.f.* visit; call; visitation (*of a bishop etc.*); examination, inspection; search; *droit de visite*, right of search; *faire la visite des bagages*, to examine luggage; *faire une visite* or *rendre visite*, to pay a visit.

visiter [vizi'te], *v.t.* to visit (*patients, clients etc.*); to go over (*cathedral etc.*); to search, to examine, to inspect.

visiteur [vizi'tœːr], *n.m.* (*fem.* **-euse**) visitor, caller; inspector, searcher.

vison [vi'zɔ̃], *n.m.* mink (*animal*).

visqueux [vis'kø], *a.* (*fem.* **-euse**) viscous, sticky; slimy; clammy.

visser [vi'se], *v.t.* to screw, to screw on, up *or* down. **se visser**, *v.r.* to fix or attach oneself firmly.

visserie [vi'sri], *n.f.* screws, nuts and bolts.

Vistule [vis'tyl], **la**, *f.* the Vistula.

visuel [vi'zɥɛl], *a.* (*fem.* **-elle**) visual.

vital [vi'tal], *a.* (*m. pl.* **-aux**) vital; (*fig.*) essential.

vitalement [vital'mɑ̃], *adv.* vitally.

vitalité [vitali'te], *n.f.* vitality.

vitamine [vita'min], *n.f.* vitamin.

vite [vit], *a.* swift, quick, speedy, rapid.—*adv.* quick, quickly, fast, rapidly, expeditiously; *vite !* quick! look sharp!

vitesse [vi'tɛs], *n.f.* quickness, rapidity, celerity, swiftness, speed; (*Motor.*) gear; *à grande or à toute vitesse*, at full speed; *boîte de vitesse*, gear-box; *changement de vitesse*, change of gear; *gagner (quelqu'un) de vitesse*, to outrun (someone).

Viti [vi'ti], **les Îles**, *f.pl.* the Fiji Islands.

viticole [viti'kɔl], *a.* pertaining to vine culture, viticultural.

viticulture [vitikyl'tyːr], *n.f.* vine-growing.

vitrage [vi'traːʒ], *n.m.* glazing; glass windows.

vitrail [vi'traːj], *n.m.* (*pl.* **-aux**) stained-glass window.

vitre [vitr], *n.f.* pane of glass; window.

vitré [vi'tre], *a.* glazed, of glass; (*Anat. etc.*) vitreous; *porte vitrée*, glass door.

vitrer [vi'tre], *v.t.* to furnish with glass windows, to glaze.

vitreux [vi'trø], *a.* (*fem.* **-euse**) vitreous, glassy.

vitrier [vitri'e], *n.m.* glass-maker; glazier.

vitrine [vi'trin], *n.f.* shop-window; show-case.

vitriol [vitri'ol], *n.m.* vitriol.

vitupération [vitypera'sjɔ̃], *n.f.* vituperation.

vitupérer [vitype're], *v.t.* (*conjug. like* CÉDER) to vituperate, to reprimand.

vivace [vi'vas], *a.* long-lived, perennial (*of plants*); inveterate, deep-rooted.

vivacité [vivasi'te], *n.f.* vivacity, liveliness, sprightliness; spirit, life, ardour.

vivant [vi'vɑ̃], *a.* living, alive; lively, animated; *langue vivante*, modern language; *portrait vivant*, lifelike portrait.—*n.m.* life, lifetime; *de son vivant*, in his lifetime. —*n.m.* (*fem.* **-e**) living person.

vivat! [vi'vat], *int.* and *n.m.* hurrah! huzza!

vivement [viv'mɑ̃], *adv.* quickly, briskly, sharply, vigorously; eagerly; keenly, acutely; smartly, angrily; spiritedly.

viveur [vi'vœːr], *n.m.* (*fem.* **-euse**) rake, gay dog, person who leads a fast life.

vivier [vi'vje], *n.m.* fish-pond.

vivifiant [vivi'fjɑ̃], *a.* vivifying, quickening; refreshing, invigorating.

vivifier [vivi'fje], *v.t.* to vivify, to quicken, to give life to; to enliven, to revive.

vivisection [vivisɛk'sjɔ̃], *n.f.* vivisection.

C) **vivoir** [vi'vwaːr], *n.m.* living-room.

vivoter [vivo'te], *v.i.* to live poorly, to rub along.

vivre [viːvr], *v.i. irr.* to live, to be alive; to subsist, to live on, to be maintained; to board, to take one's meals; to behave; to last; *vive la France !* long live France! *qui vive?* who goes there ? *il ne sait pas vivre*, he has no manners.—*n.m.* living, board, food; (*pl.*) provisions, victuals, rations.

vocable [vɔ'kabl], *n.m.* vocable, word, name.

vocabulaire [vɔkaby'lɛːr], *n.m.* vocabulary.

vocal [vɔ'kal], *a.* (*m. pl.* **-aux**) vocal.

vocation [vɔka'sjɔ̃], *n.f.* vocation, calling, call; inclination; bent, talent.

vociférant [vɔsife'rɑ̃], *a.* vociferous.

vociférer [vɔsife're], *v.t.* (*conjug. like* CÉDER) to vociferate, to bawl.

vœu [vø], *n.m.* (*pl.* **vœux**) vow; prayer, wish, desire; vote, suffrage.

vogue [vɔg], *n.f.* vogue, fashion; credit, craze; *avoir de la vogue*, to be in fashion.

voguer [vɔ'ge], *v.i.* to move forward by rowing (*of a galley etc.*); to sail, to float, to move along.

voici [vwa'si], *prep.* see here, behold; here is, here are, this is, these are; ago, past; *le voilà, me voici*, there he is, here I am; *monsieur que voici*, this gentleman; *voici trois mois que je suis à l'hôpital*, I have been in hospital for the past three months.

voilà [vwa'la], *prep.* there, behold, there now, there is, there are, that is; *ah ! vous voilà*, oh! there you are! *voilà une heure qu'il parle*, he has been speaking for an hour.

voile (1) [vwal], *n.m.* veil; (*fig.*) cover, mask, disguise, show, pretence.

voile (2) [vwal], *n.f.* sail; canvas; (*fig.*) ship; *faire voile*, to sail, to set sail.

voilé [vwa'le], *a.* rigged; veiled; clouded, dull, dim; (*wheel*) buckled, out of true.

voiler [vwa'le], *v.t.* to veil; to cover, to cloak, to blind, to disguise, to conceal; to buckle (*wheel*).—*v.i.* and **se voiler**, *v.r.* to wear a veil; to cloud over (*of the sky*); to buckle (*of a wheel*).

voilier [vwa'lje], *n.m.* sail-maker; sailing-ship.

voir [vwaːr], *v.t. irr.* to see; to behold; to witness; to look at, to observe, to view; to inspect, to superintend; to overlook; to visit; to frequent; to show, to let see; *voyons !* let us see! now then!—*v.i.* to see, to look, to watch; to have one's sight; *voir à or voir à ce que*, to see to it that. **se voir**, *v.r.* to see oneself; to see each other; to visit each other; to be obvious.

voire [vwaːr], *adv.* and even, and indeed.

voirie [vwa'ri], *n.f.* roads, system of roads; commission of public streets and highways; refuse-dump.

voisin [vwa'zɛ̃], *a.* bordering, adjacent, next; next door, neighbouring.—*n.m.* (*fem.* **-e**) neighbour.

voisinage

voisinage [vwazi'na:ʒ], *n.m.* neighbourhood; vicinity, proximity, nearness; neighbours.

voiturage [vwaty'ra:ʒ], *n.m.* carriage, cartage (*of goods etc.*).

voiture [vwa ty:r], *n.f.* vehicle, conveyance; carriage; coach; cart, car; cart-load; *descendre de voiture*, to alight from a carriage; *en voiture !* take your seats! *se promener en voiture* or *aller en voiture*, to drive; *voiture d'enfant*, perambulator, baby-carriage, (*fam.*) pram.

voiturer [vwaty're], *v.t.* to carry, to convey, to cart.

voiturier [vwaty'rje], *n.m.* carrier, carter.

voix [vwa], *n.f. inv.* voice; tone, sound; vote, suffrage; opinion, judgment; singer; *à demi-voix*, in a low voice; *à haute voix*, aloud; in a loud voice, loudly; *de vive voix*, by word of mouth.

vol (1) [vɔl], *n.m.* flying, soaring; flight; flock (*of birds*); spread (*of wings*); *au vol*, on the wing; *à vol d'oiseau*, as the crow flies.

vol (2) [vɔl], *n.m.* theft, robbery, stealing, larceny; stolen goods; *vol à l'étalage*, shoplifting; *vol avec effraction*, burglary.

volage [vɔ'la:ʒ], *a.* fickle, inconstant, flighty.

volaille [vɔ'la:j], *n.f.* poultry, fowls; *marchand de volaille*, poulterer.

volant [vɔ'lɑ̃], *a.* flying; loose, floating; movable, portable.—*n.m.* shuttlecock; flounce (*of a dress*); flywheel (*of machinery*); steering-wheel (*of a car*); sail (*of a windmill*).

volatil [vɔla'til], *a.* (*Chem.*) volatile; (*fig.*) volatile (*of temperament*).

volatile [vɔla'til], *a.* winged.—*n.m.* winged creature, bird.

vol-au-vent [vɔlo'vɑ̃], *n.m. inv.* vol-au-vent, puff-pie.

volcan [vɔl'kɑ̃], *n.m.* volcano.

volcanique [vɔlka'nik], *a.* volcanic, fiery.

volée [vɔ'le], *n.f.* flight (*of birds etc.*); flock, covey; brood; bevy; volley (*of guns*); shower (*of blows*); thrashing; peal (*of bells*); *à la volée*, flying, as it flies, in the air; (*fig.*) rashly, at random; *sonner à toute volée*, to ring a full peal; *volée d'escalier*, flight of stairs.

voler (1) [vɔ'le], *v.i.* to fly; to take wing, to soar; *entendre voler une mouche*, to hear a pin drop.

voler (2) [vɔ'le], *v.t.* to steal, to rob; to fleece, to plunder; (*fig.*) to embezzle, to usurp.—*v.i.* to steal.

volerie [vɔl'ri], *n.f.* robbery; pilfering.

volet [vɔ'lɛ], *n.m.* (window-)shutter; dovecot; (*Av.*) flap.

voleter [vɔl'te], *v.i.* (*conjug. like* APPELER) to flutter.

voleur [vɔ'lœːr], *n.m.* (*fem.* **-euse**) thief, robber; plunderer, extortioner; stealer; *au voleur !* stop thief!

volière [vɔ'ljɛːr], *n.f.* aviary, large bird-cage.

volontaire [vɔlɔ̃'tɛːr], *a.* voluntary, willing; intended, intentional; spontaneous; obstinate, wilful.—*n.* volunteer.

volontairement [vɔlɔ̃tɛr'mɑ̃], *adv.* voluntarily; wilfully.

volonté [vɔlɔ̃'te], *n.f.* will; (*pl.*) whims, caprices; *avoir de la bonne volonté*, to be willing; *à volonté*, at pleasure, at will; *dernières volontés*, last will and testament; *faire ses quatre volontés*, (*colloq.*)

to do as one pleases; *mauvaise volonté*, illwill; unwillingness.

volontiers [vɔlɔ̃'tje], *adv.* willingly, gladly, with pleasure.

volt [vɔlt], *n.m.* (*Elec.*) volt.

voltage [vɔl'ta:ʒ], *n.m.* voltage.

volte-face [vɔlt'fas], *n.f. inv.* turning round; *faire volte-face*, to face about; (*fig.*) to reverse one's opinions completely.

voltige [vɔl'ti:ʒ], *n.f.* slack-rope gymnastics, flying-trapeze exercises.

voltigeant [vɔlti'ʒɑ̃], *a.* fluttering, hovering.

voltigement [vɔltiʒ'mɑ̃], *n.m.* tumbling; fluttering.

voltiger [vɔlti'ʒe], *v.i.* (*conjug. like* MANGER) to flutter, to fly about, to hover.

voltigeur [vɔlti'ʒœːr], *n.m.* vaulter; light-infantry soldier, rifleman.

voltmètre [vɔlt'mɛtr], *n.m.* voltmeter.

volubilis [vɔlybi'lis], *n.m.* convolvulus.

volubilité [vɔlybili'te], *n.f.* volubility, fluency, glibness.

volume [vɔ'lym], *n.m.* volume; bulk, size mass.

volumineux [vɔlymi'nø], *a.* (*fem.* **-euse**) voluminous, bulky.

volupté [vɔlyp'te], *n.f.* voluptuousness, sensual pleasure.

voluptueux [vɔlyp'tɥø], *a.* (*fem.* **-euse**) voluptuous, sensual.—*n.m.* (*fem.* **-euse**) voluptuary.

volute [vɔ'ly:t], *n.f.* volute; scroll.

vomir [vɔ'mi:r], *v.t.* to vomit, to throw up, (*fig.*) to belch forth.—*v.i.* to vomit, to be sick.

vomissement [vɔmis'mɑ̃], *n.m.* vomit(ing).

vorace [vɔ'ras], *a.* voracious, ravenous.

voracité [vɔrasi'te], *n.f.* voracity.

vos [vo], [VOTRE].

votant [vɔ'tɑ̃], *n.m.* (*fem.* **-e**) voter.

vote [vɔt], *n.m.* vote; division, voting, poll.

voter [vɔ'te], *v.t., v.i.* to vote; to pass (*a bill*).

votif [vɔ'tif], *a.* (*fem.* **-tive**) votive.

votre [vɔtr], *a. poss.* (*pl.* **vos**) your.

vôtre [voːtr], *pron.poss.* (*m. sing.* **le vôtre**, *fem. sing.* **la vôtre**, *pl.* **les vôtres**) yours.— *n.* your own, your own property; (*pl.*) your relations, friends etc.; your pranks, tricks.

vouer [vwe], *v.t.* to devote, to dedicate; to vow, to swear. **se vouer**, *v.r.* to devote oneself.

vouloir [vu'lwaːr], *v.t. irr.* to want; to desire, to wish, to require; to consent; to please; to choose; to determine; to try, to attempt; to admit, to grant; to mean; *en vouloir à quelqu'un*, to bear someone a grudge; *oui, je (le) veux bien*, yes, I am willing; *que veut dire cela?* what does that mean? *que voulez-vous?* what do you want? what can I do for you ? what can you expect ? *veuillez me dire*, please tell me.—*n.m.* will; *bon vouloir*, goodwill, *mauvais vouloir*, illwill.

voulu [vu'ly], *a.* wished, desired, required, requisite; due, received; deliberate, studied.

vous [vu], *pron. pers.* you; to you.

voûte [vut], *n.f.* arch, vault; (*fig.*) roof, canopy; *clef de voûte*, keystone.

voûté [vu'te], *a.* vaulted, curved.

voûter [vu'te], *v.t.* to vault, to arch over; to bend. **se voûter**, *v.r.* to arch, to vault; to be bent, to stoop.

vouvoyer [vuvwa'je], *v.t.* (*conjug. like* EM-PLOYER) to say *vous* instead of *tu* when addressing somebody.
voyage [vwa'jaːʒ], *n.m.* travel; journey, voyage, trip; visit; (*pl.*) travels; *bon voyage!* pleasant journey to you! *être en voyage*, to be travelling.
voyager [vwaja'ʒe], *v.i.* (*conjug. like* MANGER) to travel, to journey.
voyageur [vwaja'ʒœːr], *a.* (*fem.* -euse) travelling; migrating; *commis voyageur*, commercial traveller; *oiseau voyageur*, migratory bird; *pigeon voyageur*, carrier pigeon.—*n.m.* (*fem.* -euse) traveller; passenger.
voyant [vwa'jɑ̃], *a.* gaudy, showy (*of colours*). —*n.m.* (*fem.* -e) seer, clairvoyant.
voyelle [vwa'jɛl], *n.f.* vowel.
voyou [vwa'ju], *n.m.* (*fam.*) guttersnipe, hooligan; loafer.
vrac (en) [ɑ̃'vrak], *adv. phr.* in bulk, loose, pell-mell.
vrai [vrɛ], *a.* true, real, genuine; right, proper, fit; downright, arrant.—*int.* truly, really, in truth!—*n.m.* truth; *à vrai dire*, to tell the truth, as a matter of fact.
vraiment [vrɛ'mɑ̃], *adv.* truly, in truth; indeed, really!
vraisemblable [vrɛsɑ̃'blablə], *a.* likely, probable.—*n.m.* probability, likelihood.
vraisemblance [vrɛsɑ̃'blɑːs], *n.f.* probability, likelihood, verisimilitude.
vrille [vriːj], *n.f.* gimlet, borer, piercer; (*Bot.*) tendril; (*Av.*) tail-spin.
vriller [vri'je], *v.t.* to bore.—*v.i.* to ascend spirally.
vrillette [vri'jɛt], *n.f.* death-watch beetle.
vrombir [vrɔ̃'biːr], *v.i.* to buzz, to hum, to whirr, to purr, to throb.
vu [vy], *a.* considered, regarded; seen, observed.—*prep.* considering, in view of.—*n.m.* sight, examination, inspection; (*Law*) preamble.—*conj. phr. vu que*, seeing that whereas.
vue [vy], *n.f.* sight, eyesight; eyes; view, survey, inspection; prospect; appearance; light, window; design; *à perte de vue*, as far as the eye can reach, out of sight; *à vue d'œil*, visibly.
Vulcain [vyl'kɛ̃], *m.* Vulcan.
vulcaniser [vylkani'ze], *v.t.* to vulcanize.
vulgaire [vyl'gɛːr], *a.* vulgar, common.—*n.m.* the common herd.
vulgairement [vylgɛr'mɑ̃], *adv.* vulgarly, commonly.
vulgariser [vylgari'ze], *v.t.* to popularize.
vulgarité [vylgari'te], *n.f.* vulgarity.
vulnérabilité [vylnerabili'te], *n.f.* vulnerability.
vulnérable [vylne'rablə], *a.* vulnerable.

W

W, w [dublə've], *n.m.* this twenty-third letter of the alphabet is used only in borrowed words.

wagon [va'gɔ̃], *n.m.* (*Rail.*) carriage, truck, van.
wagon-lit [vagɔ̃'li], *n.m.* (*pl.* **wagons-lits**) sleeping-car, sleeper.
wagonnet [vago'nɛ], *n.m.* tip-truck.
wallon [wa'lɔ̃], *a.* (*fem.* -onne) Walloon.—*n.m.* Walloon (*language*); (**Wallon**, *fem.* -onne) Walloon (*person*).
warrant [va'rɑ̃], *n.m.* warrant.
warranter [varɑ̃'te], *v.t.* to warrant, to guarantee, to certify.
water [wa'tɛr], les W.C. [lɛvɛ'se], *n.m. pl.* water-closet, lavatory, W.C.
watt [wat], *n.m.* (*Elec.*) watt.
wattman [wat'man], *n.m.* (*pl.* -men) tram-driver.
week-end [wik'ɛnd], *n.m.* (*pl.* **week-ends**) week-end.
whisky [wis'ki], *n.m.* whisky.
whist [wist], *n.m.* whist.
wigwam [wig'wam], *n.m.* wigwam.
wolfram [vɔl'fram], *n.m.* wolfram (*tungsten-ore*).

X

X, x [iks], *n.m.* the twenty-fourth letter of the alphabet; *rayons X*, X-rays.
xénophobe [kseno'fɔb], *a.* and *n.* xenophobe.
xérès [kse'rɛs], *n.m.* sherry (*wine*).
xylophone [ksilo'fɔn], *n.m.* (*Mus.*) xylophone.

Y

Y, y [i grɛk], *n.m.* the twenty-fifth letter of the alphabet.
y [il], *adv.* there; thither; within, at home; *ça y est!* that's it! *il y a*, there is, there are; *je l'y ai vu*, I saw him there; *j'y suis*, I follow you, I get you; *y compris*, included.—*pron.* by, for, in, at *or* to him, her, it *or* them.
yacht [jot, jak], *n.m.* yacht.
Yémen [je'mɛn], le, *m.* Yemen.
yéménite [jemə'nit], *a.* Yemeni.—*n.* (**Yémé-nite**) Yemeni (*person*).
yeuse [jøːz], *n.f.* ilex, holm-oak.
yeux [jøː], [ŒIL].
yodler [jo'dle], *v.i.* (*Mus.*) to yodel.
yogi or **yogui** [jo'gi], *n.m.* yogi.
yole [jɔl], *n.f.* yawl, gig.
yougoslave [jugɔs'lav], *a.* Yugoslav.—*n.m.* Yugoslav (*language*).—*n.* (**Yougoslave**) Yugoslav (*person*).
Yougoslavie [jugosla'vi], la, *f.* Yugoslavia.
youyou [ju'ju], *n.m.* dinghy.

Z

Z, z [zed], *n.m.* the twenty-sixth letter of the alphabet.
Zambie [zã'bi], **la,** *f.* Zambia.
zèbre [zɛbr], *n.m.* zebra.
zébré [ze'bre], *a.* striped like the zebra.
zèle [zɛːl], *n.m.* zeal, warmth, ardour, enthusiasm.
zélé [ze'le], *a.* zealous.
zélote [ze'lɔt], *n.m.* zealot.
zénith [ze'nit], *n.m.* zenith.
zéphire, zéphyr or **zéphyre** [ze'fiːr], *n.m.* zephyr, gentle breeze.
zéro [ze'ro], *n.m.* nought; zero (*of the thermometer*); (*fig.*) a mere cipher, nonentity.
zeste [zɛst], *n.m.* woody skin dividing sections of a walnut; peel (*of orange, lemon etc.*), rind; (*fig.*) straw, fig, nothing.
zézaiement or **zézayement** [zeze(j)'mã] *n.m.* lisping, lisp (*incorrect pronunciation of* [z] *instead of* [ʒ]).
zézayer [zeze'je], *v.i.* (*conjug. like* PAYER) to lisp.
zibeline [zi'blin], *n.f.* sable.
zigzag [zig'zag], *n.m.* zigzag; *éclair en zigzag,* forked lightning.
zinc [zɛ̃:g], *n.m.* zinc; (*slang*) bar or counter of public-house.
zingaro [zɛ̃ga'ro], *n.m.* (*pl.* **zingari**) gipsy.
zinguer [zɛ̃'ge], *v.t.* to cover with zinc; to zinc.
zizanie [ziza'ni], *n.f.* tare, *darnel; (*fig.*) discord, bickering.
zodiaque [zɔ'djak], *n.m.* zodiac.
zone [zoːn], *n.f.* zone, belt, area.
zoo [zo'o], *n.m.* (*fam.*) zoo.
zoologie [zɔɔlɔ'ʒi], *n.f.* zoology.
zoologique [zɔɔlɔ'ʒik], *a.* zoological.
zoologiste [zɔɔlɔ'ʒist], *n.* zoologist.
zouave [zwaːv], *n.m.* Zouave (*soldier*).
zut! [zyt], *int.* (*fam.*) (*to convey anger, scorn, disappointment, flat refusal*); *zut! zut alors! non, zut!* be blowed! no go! never! bother! dash it!

A

A, a (1) [ei]. première lettre de l'alphabet; (*Mus.*) la, *m.*; *a.m.*, du matin.
a (2) [ei, ə], **an** [æn, ən] (*before vowel*), *indef. art.* un, *m.*, une, *f.*; *a shilling a pound*, un shilling la livre; *three a day*, trois par jour.
aback [ə'bæk], *adv.* en arrière; (*fig.*) à l'improviste, au dépourvu.
abacus ['æbəkəs], *n.* (*pl.* **abaci** ['æbəkai]) (*Arch., Math.*) abaque, *m.*
abaft [ə'bɑ:ft], *adv.* sur l'arrière, en arrière.—*prep.* en arrière de, à l'arrière de.
abandon [ə'bændən], *v.t.* abandonner; délaisser, quitter; renoncer à, se désister de.—*n.* abandon, *m.*; désinvolture, *f.*
abandoned [ə'bændənd], *a.* abandonné; dépravé.
abandonment [ə'bændənmənt], *n.* abandonnement; délaissement; abandon, *m.*
abase [ə'beis], *v.t.* abaisser; ravaler.
abasement [ə'beismənt], *n.* abaissement; ravalement, *m.*; humiliation, *f.*
abash [ə'bæʃ], *v.t.* déconcerter, décontenancer; interdire, confondre.
abate [ə'beit], *v.t.* diminuer; rabattre; affaiblir, atténuer; amortir; calmer, apaiser. —*v.i.* diminuer; s'affaiblir; se calmer, s'apaiser (*temps etc.*); tomber, baisser, s'abattre (*vent etc.*).
abatement [ə'beitmənt], *n.* diminution, réduction, *f.*; rabais; affaiblissement, adoucissement; apaisement, *m.*
abbacy ['æbəsi], *n.* dignité d'abbé, *f.*
abbess ['æbes], *n.* abbesse, *f.*
abbey ['æbi], *n.* abbaye, *f.*
abbot ['æbət], *n.* abbé, supérieur (*d'abbaye*), *m.*
abbreviate [ə'bri:vieit], *v.t.* abréger; raccourcir.
abbreviation [əbri:vi'eiʃən], *n.* abréviation, *f.*
abdicate ['æbdikeit], *v.t.*, *v.i.* abdiquer.
abdication [æbdi'keiʃən], *n.* abdication, *f.*
abdomen [æb'doumən, 'æbdəmən], *n.* abdomen, bas-ventre, *m.*
abdominal [æb'dɔminəl], *a.* abdominal.
abduct [æb'dʌkt], *v.t.* détourner, enlever (*clandestinement* ou *par force*).
abduction [æb'dʌkʃən], *n.* abduction, *f.*, enlèvement (*de mineur etc.*), détournement, *m.*
abductor [æb'dʌktə], *n.* (*Anat.*) abducteur; (*Law*) ravisseur, *m.*
abed [ə'bed], *adv.* au lit, couché.
aberration [æbə'reiʃən], *n.* aberration, *f.*; éloignement, écart, égarement, *m.*; erreur (*de jugement*), *f.*
abet [ə'bet], *v.t.* soutenir, encourager (*à un crime*); *to aid and abet*, être le complice.
abetment [ə'betmənt], *abetting* [ə'betiŋ], *n.* encouragement (*à un crime*), *m.*
abettor [ə'betə], *n.* instigateur (*d'un crime*), *m.*; complice, *m.*, *f.*
abeyance [ə'beiəns], *n.* vacance; suspension, *f.*; *in abeyance*, en suspens; *to fall into abeyance*, tomber en désuétude.

abhor [əb'hɔ:], *v.t.* abhorrer, détester.
abhorrence [əb'hɔrəns], *n.* horreur, *f.*
abhorrent [əb'hɔrənt], *a.* odieux, répugnant (*à*).
abide [ə'baid], *v.t. irr.* attendre; supporter; subir, souffrir.—*v.i.* demeurer, rester; séjourner; durer; *to abide by* (*a decision etc.*), rester fidèle à; *to abide by* (*the laws etc.*), se conformer à.
abiding [ə'baidiŋ], *a.* constant, immuable.
ability [ə'biliti], *n.* capacité, *f.*; pouvoir; talent, *m.*; habileté, *f.*
abject ['æbdʒekt], *a.* abject, bas, vil.
abjection [æb'dʒekʃən], **abjectness** ['æbdʒektnis], *n.* abjection, misère, *f.*
abjectly ['æbdʒektli], *adv.* d'une manière abjecte.
abjure [æb'dʒuə], *v.t.* abjurer; renoncer à, renier.
ablative ['æblətiv], *a.* and *n.* (*Gram.*) ablatif, *m.*
ablaze [ə'bleiz], *a.* en feu, en flammes; (*fig.*) enflammé.
able [eibl], *a.* capable (*de*), à même (*de*); habile; *to be able to*, pouvoir.
able-bodied ['eiblbodid], *a.* fort, robuste, vigoureux.
ablution [ə'blu:ʃən], *n.* ablution, *f.*
ably ['eibli], *adv.* habilement, avec talent.
abnegation [æbni'geiʃən], *n.* abnégation, renonciation, *f.*; désaveu, *m.*
abnormal [æb'nɔ:məl], *a.* anormal.
abnormity [æb'nɔ:mæliti], *n.* anomalie; difformité, *f.*
abnormally [æb'nɔ:məli], *adv.* anormalement.
aboard [ə'bɔ:d], *adv.* à bord (*de*).
abode (1) [ə'boud], *n.* demeure, habitation, *f.*; séjour, *m.*
abode (2) [ə'boud], *past* and *p.p.* [ABIDE].
abolish [ə'bɔliʃ], *v.t.* abolir; supprimer.
abolishment [ə'bɔliʃmənt], **abolition** [æbə'liʃən], *n.* abolition, suppression, *f.*; abolissement, *m.*
abominable [ə'bɔminəbl], *a.* abominable, infâme, détestable.
abominably [ə'bɔminəbli], *adv.* abominablement.
abominate [ə'bɔmineit], *v.t.* abominer, détester.
abomination [əbɔmi'neiʃən], *n.* abomination, horreur, *f.*
aboriginal [æbə'ridʒinəl], *a.* aborigène, primitif.—*n.* aborigène, *m.*, *f.*
aborigine [æbə'ridʒini], *n.* aborigène, *m.*, *f.*
abortion [ə'bɔ:ʃən], *n.* avortement (*acte*); avorton (*embryon*), *m.*
abortive [ə'bɔ:tiv], *a.* abortif, manqué; avorté.
abortively [ə'bɔ:tivli], *adv.* avant terme; (*fig.*) sans résultat, sans succès.
abortiveness [ə'bɔ:tivnis], *n.* (*fig.*) insuccès, *m.*
abound [ə'baund], *v.i.* abonder (*de* ou *en*), regorger (*de*).

abounding

abounding [əˈbaundiŋ], *a.* abondant.
about [əˈbaut], *prep.* autour de; auprès de;
sur; vers; environ; touchant, au sujet de, à
l'égard de; à peu près; sur le point de; dans,
par; *about that*, là-dessus, à ce sujet;
about two o'clock, vers (les) deux heures;
what is it all about? de quoi s'agit-il ?—
adv. tout autour, à l'entour, à la ronde; çà
et là; *to be about to*, être sur le point de.
above [əˈbʌv], *prep.* au-dessus de, par-dessus;
en amont de; plus de; au delà de; *above
all*, surtout, par-dessus tout; *above board*,
ouvertement, franchement.—*adv.* en haut;
là-haut; au-dessus; ci-dessus.
abrasion [əˈbreiʒən], *n.* abrasion, écorchure, *f.*
abrasive [əˈbreisiv], *a.* and *n.* abrasif, *m.*
abreast [əˈbrest], *adv.* de front, à côté l'un de
l'autre; (*fig.*) de pair avec.
abridge [əˈbridʒ], *v.t.* abréger, raccourcir;
restreindre, priver; *abridged edition* (*of
book*), édition réduite, *f.*
abridgment [əˈbridʒmənt], *n.* abrégé, précis,
m.; réduction, diminution, *f.*
abroad [əˈbrɔːd], *adv.* à l'étranger; au loin, de
tous côtés; *to get abroad*, se répandre
(*nouvelles*).
abrogate [ˈæbrogeit], *v.t.* abroger.
abrogation [æbroˈgeiʃən], *n.* abrogation, *f.*
abrupt [əˈbrʌpt], *a.* brusque; brisé, saccadé;
précipité, soudain; abrupt, escarpé, à pic.
abruptly [əˈbrʌptli], *adv.* brusquement, tout
à coup.
abruptness [əˈbrʌptnis], *n.* précipitation; (*fig.*)
brusquerie, rudesse, *f.*; escarpement, *m.*
abscess [ˈæbses], *n.* abcès, dépôt, *m.*
abscond [əbˈskɔnd], *v.i.* se soustraire (*furtivement*) aux poursuites de la justice; disparaître; (*fam.*) décamper.
absconder [əbˈskɔndə], *n.* fugitif, *m.*; (*Law*)
contumace, *m., f.*
absence [ˈæbsəns], *n.* absence, *f.*; éloignement, *m.*; absence d'esprit, distraction, *f.*;
manque, *m.*
absent [ˈæbsənt], *a.* absent.—[æbˈsent], *v.r.*
to absent oneself, s'absenter.
absentee [æbsənˈtiː], *n.* absent, manquant, *m.*
absenteeism [æbsənˈtiːizm], *n.* absentéisme,
m.
absent-minded [ˈæbsəntˈmaindid], *a.* distrait.
absinthe [ˈæbsinθ], *n.* absinthe, *f.*
absolute [ˈæbsəluːt], *a.* absolu, illimité;
irrévocable (*décret*); véritable.
absolutely [æbsəˈluːtli], *adv.* absolument.
absolution [æbsəˈluːʃən], *n.* absolution;
(*R.-C. Ch.*) absoute, *f.*
absolve [əbˈzɔlv], *v.t.* absoudre (*de*); délier,
décharger, dégager, affranchir.
absorb [əbˈsɔːb], *v.t.* absorber; amortir (*un
choc*).
absorbent [əbˈsɔːbənt], *a.* and *n.* absorbant,
m.
absorption [əbˈsɔːpʃən], *n.* absorption, *f.*;
absorbement, amortissement, *m.*
abstain [əbˈstein], *v.i.* s'abstenir (*de*).
abstainer [əbˈsteinə], *n.* buveur d'eau, *m.*,
abstème, *m., f.*; *total abstainer*, personne
qui ne boit jamais d'alcool, *f.*
abstemious [əbˈstiːmiəs], *a.* tempérant,
sobre.
abstemiously [əbˈstiːmiəsli], *adv.* sobrement, avec modération.

abstemiousness [əbˈstiːmiəsnis], *n.* abstinence; modération, sobriété, *f.*
abstention [əbˈstenʃən], *n.* abstention, *f.*
abstinence [ˈæbstinəns], *n.* abstinence, *f.*
abstinent [ˈæbstinənt], *a.* abstinent, sobre.
abstract (1) [æbˈstrækt], *v.t.* soustraire,
dérober, détourner; faire abstraction de;
résumer, abréger.
abstract (2) [ˈæbstrækt], *a.* abstrait.—*n.*
abrégé, résumé, précis, *m.*; analyse, *f.*;
(*Comm.*) relevé, *m.*
abstracted [æbˈstræktid], *a.* séparé; distrait,
rêveur, pensif; soustrait, dérobé.
abstractedness [æbˈstræktidnis], *n.* caractère abstrait, *m.*; préoccupation, *f.*
abstraction [æbˈstrækʃən], *n.* soustraction,
distraction; abstraction; préoccupation, *f.*
abstractly [ˈæbstræktli], *adv.* abstractive-
ment, d'une manière abstraite.
abstruse [æbˈstruːs], *a.* caché; abstrus,
obscur.
absurd [əbˈsəːd], *a.* absurde.
absurdity [əbˈsəːditi], *n.* absurdité, *f.*
absurdly [əbˈsəːdli], *adv.* absurdement.
abundance [əˈbʌndəns], *n.* abondance,
grande quantité, *f.*; grand nombre, *m.*; (*fig.*)
prospérité, *f.*
abundant [əˈbʌndənt], *a.* abondant.
abundantly [əˈbʌndəntli], *adv.* abondamment, en abondance, à foison.
abuse (1) [əˈbjuːz], *v.t.* abuser de; maltraiter;
médire de; injurier, dire des injures à;
séduire.
abuse (2) [əˈbjuːs], *n.* abus, *m.*; insultes
injures, *f. pl.*
abuser [əˈbjuːzə], *n.* détracteur; séducteur;
trompeur, *m.*
abusive [əˈbjuːsiv], *a.* abusif; injurieux.
abusively [əˈbjuːsivli], *adv.* abusivement;
injurieusement.
abusiveness [əˈbjuːsivnis], *n.* langage injurieux *ou* grossier, *m.*
abut [əˈbʌt], *v.i.* aboutir (*à*); (*Build.*) s'appuyer
(*contre*).
abysmal [əˈbizməl], *a.* sans fond; (*ignorance*)
profonde.
abyss [əˈbis], *n.* abîme, gouffre, *m.*
Abyssinia [æbiˈsinjə]. l'Abyssinie, l'Éthiopie,
f.
Abyssinian [æbiˈsinjən], *a.* abyssinien.—*n.*
Abyssinien (*personne*), *m.*
acacia [əˈkeiʃə], *n.* acacia, *m.*
academic [ækəˈdemik], **academical** [ækə-
ˈdemikəl], *a.* académique, universitaire,
classique, scolaire.
academician [əkædəˈmiʃən], *n.* académicien, *m.*
academy [əˈkædəmi], *n.* académie (*société
savante*); école libre, *f.*, pensionnat, *m.*,
institution, *f.*
acanthus [əˈkænθəs], *n.* acanthe, *f.*
accede [ækˈsiːd], *v.i.* accéder consentir (*à*);
monter (*sur le trône*).
accelerate [ækˈseləreit], *v.t.* accélérer; hâter.
—*v.i.* s'accélérer.
acceleration [ækseləˈreiʃən], *n.* accélération, *f.*
accelerator [ækˈseləreitə], *n.* accélérateur,
m.
accent (1) [ækˈsent], *v.t.* accentuer.
accent (2) [ˈæksənt], *n.* accent, *m.*
accentuate [ækˈsentjueit], *v.t.* accentuer.

accept [ək'sept], *v.t.* accepter, agréer, admettre.

acceptability [əkseptə'biliti], **acceptableness** [ək'septəblnis], *n.* acceptabilité, *f.*; droit au bon accueil, *m.*

acceptable [ək'septəbl], *a.* acceptable; agréable.

acceptance [ək'septəns], *n.* acceptation, *f.*; accueil favorable, *m.*

acceptation [æksep'teiʃən], *n.* acception, *f.*, sens (*d'un mot*). *m.*

access ['ækses], *n.* accès, abord, *m.*; entrée, admission, *f.*

accessible [æk'sesibl], *a.* accessible, abordable.

accession [æk'seʃən], *n.* acquisition; augmentation, addition, *f.*, accroissement; avènement (*au trône etc.*), *m.*

accessory [æk'sesəri], *a.* accessoire.—*n.* accessoire (*chose*), *m.*; complice (*personne*), *m., f.*

accidence ['æksidəns], *n.* morphologie, *f.*; rudiments (*de grammaire*), *m. pl.*

accident ['æksidənt], *n.* accident, *m.*, avarie, *f.*, hasard; incident; malheur, *m.*

accidental [æksi'dentəl], *a.* accidentel, fortuit.

accidentally [æksi'dentəli], *adv.* accidentellement; par hasard.

acclaim [ə'kleim], *v.t.* acclamer, applaudir à; proclamer.—*n.* acclamation, *f.*

acclamation [æklə'meiʃən], *n.* acclamation, *f.*

acclimatation [əklaimə'teiʃən], **acclimation** [æklai'meiʃən], *n.* acclimatement, *m.*; acclimatisation, *f.*

acclimatization [əklaimətai'zeiʃən], *n.* acclimatation, *f.*

acclimatize [ə'klaimətaiz], *v.t.* acclimater; *to become acclimatized*, s'acclimater; s'accoutumer.

acclivity [ə'kliviti], *n.* montée, côte, rampe, *f.*

accolade [æko'leid], *n.* accolade, *f.*

accommodate [ə'komədeit], *v.t.* accommoder, ajuster; loger, recevoir; fournir; obliger (*par*), servir (*de*).

accommodating [ə'komədeitin], *a.* accommodant, obligeant; complaisant.

accommodation [əkomə'deiʃən], *n.* ajustement, accommodement, *m.*; complaisance, convenance, *f.*; logement, *m.*; facilités, *f.pl.*

accompaniment [ə'kʌmpnimənt], *n.* accompagnement, *m.*

accompanist [ə'kʌmpənist], *n.* (*Mus.*) accompagnateur, *m.*, accompagnatrice, *f.*

accompany [ə'kʌmpəni], *v.t.* accompagner; reconduire (*à sa voiture etc.*).

accomplice [ə'kʌmplis], *n.* complice, *m., f.*, compère, *m.*

accomplish [ə'kʌmpliʃ], *v.t.* accomplir, achever; effectuer; réaliser (*une prédiction etc.*).

accomplished [ə'kʌmpliʃt], *a.* accompli, achevé; parfait.

accomplishment [ə'kʌmpliʃmənt], *n.* accomplissement, *m.*; exécution, *f.*; (*usu. pl.*) arts d'agrément, talents, *m.pl.*

accord [ə'kɔːd], *v.t.* accorder, concéder.—*v.i.* s'accorder, être d'accord.—*n.* accord, consentement, *m.*; *of one's own accord*, de son propre gré, spontanément; *with one accord*, d'un commun accord.

accordance [ə'kɔːdəns], *n.* accord, rapport, *m.*; conformité, *f.*

according [ə'kɔːdin], *a.* conforme (*à*); *according as*, selon que, suivant que; *according to*, selon, suivant, conformément à, d'après.

accordingly [ə'kɔːdinli], *adv.* en conséquence; donc, aussi.

accordion [ə'kɔːdiən], *n.* accordéon, *m.*

accost [ə'kɔst], *v.t.* accoster, aborder.

account [ə'kaunt], *n.* compte; mémoire, rapport, exposé, compte rendu, *m.*; relation, *f.*, récit, *m.*; raison; cause; (*fig.*) considération, valeur, *f.*; cas, poids, *m.*; *by all accounts*, au dire de tout le monde; *current account*, compte courant; *on account of*, à cause de; *to keep accounts*, tenir les livres.—*v.t.* compter; estimer (*de*), regarder (*comme*), tenir (*pour*).—*v.i.* *to account for*, rendre compte de, expliquer; répondre de, rendre raison de.

accountable [ə'kauntəbl], *a.* responsable; comptable.

accountancy [ə'kauntənsi], *n.* comptabilité, *f.*

accountant [ə'kauntənt], *n.* comptable, agent comptable, *m.*; *chartered accountant*, expert comptable, *m.*

account-book [ə'kauntbuk], *n.* livre de comptes, *m.*

accoutre [ə'kuːtə], *v.t.* habiller, équiper; accoutrer (*un chevalier etc.*).

accoutrement [ə'kuːtəmənt], *n.* harnachement; équipement (*du soldat*), *m.*

accredit [ə'kredit], *v.t.* accréditer.

accretion [ə'kriːʃən], *n.* accroissement, *m.*

accrue [ə'kruː], *v.i.* provenir, résulter (*de*); s'accumuler.

accumulate [ə'kjuːmjuleit], *v.t.* accumuler, entasser; amonceler.—*v.i.* s'accumuler, s'amonceler.

accumulation [əkjuːmju'leiʃən], *n.* accumulation, *f.*; amoncellement, amas, entassement, *m.*

accumulative [ə'kjuːmjulətiv], *a.* (*chose*) qui s'accumule; (*personne*) qui accumule, thésauriseur.

accumulator [ə'kjuːmjuleitə], *n.* accumulateur, *m.*

accuracy ['ækjurisi], **accurateness** ['ækjuritnis], *n.* exactitude, justesse; précision, *f.*; soin, *m.*

accurate ['ækjurit], *a.* exact, juste, correct, précis.

accurately ['ækjuritli], *adv.* exactement, avec justesse.

accurateness [ACCURACY].

accursed [ə'kəːsid], *a.* maudit; détestable, exécrable.

accusation [ækju'zeiʃən], *n.* accusation, *f.*

accusative [ə'kjuːzətiv], *a.* and *n.* (*Gram.*), accusatif, *m.*

accusatory [ə'kjuːzətri], *a.* accusateur.

accuse [ə'kjuːz], *v.t.* accuser.

accuser [ə'kjuːzə], *n.* accusateur, *m.*

accustom [ə'kʌstəm], *v.t.* accoutumer, habituer.

ace [eis], *n.* as; (*fig.*) point, iota, *m.*; *within an ace of*, à deux doigts de.

acerb [ə'səːb], *a.* acerbe, aigre.

acerbity [ə'səːbiti], *n.* acerbité, aigreur; (*fig.*) âpreté, sévérité, *f.*

acetic [ə'siːtik, ə'setik], *a.* acétique.

acetylene [ə'setili:n], *n.* acétylène, *m.*
ache [eik], *n.* mal, *m.*; douleur, *f.*; *headache*, mal de tête; *toothache*, mal de dents.—*v.i.* faire mal; (*fig.*) souffrir (*de*); *my head aches*, j'ai mal à la tête.
achieve [ə'tʃi:v], *v.t.* exécuter, accomplir; remporter (*une victoire*); atteindre (*à*).
achievement [ə'tʃi:vmənt], *n.* exploit, fait d'armes; accomplissement, succès, *m.*; réalisation, *f.*
aching ['eikiŋ], *a.* endolori, douloureux; *an aching heart*, un cœur dolent.
acid ['æsid], *a. and n.* acide, *m.*; *acid drops*, bonbons acidulés, *m.pl.*
acidity [ə'siditi], *n.* acidité, *f.*
acknowledge [æk'nɔlidʒ], *v.t.* reconnaître; avouer, confesser; accuser réception de (*lettre*); répondre à.
acknowledgment [æk'nɔlidʒmənt], *n.* reconnaissance, *f.*; aveu; accusé de réception, *m.*; remerciements, *m.pl.*
acme ['ækmi], *n.* comble, faîte; apogée, *m.*
acolyte ['ækəlait], *n.* acolyte, *m.*
aconite ['ækənait], *n.* (*Bot.*) aconit, *m.*
acorn ['eikɔ:n], *n.* gland, *m.*
acoustic [ə'ku:stik], *a.* acoustique.—*n.* (*pl.*) acoustique, *f.*
acquaint [ə'kweint], *v.t.* informer (*de*); faire savoir à, faire part à; *to be acquainted with*, connaître, savoir.
acquaintance [ə'kweintəns], *n.* connaissance (*de*); personne de ma (sa *etc.*) connaissance, *f.*
acquainted [ə'kweintid], *a.* connu; instruit (*de*), familier (*avec*).
acquiesce [ækwi'es], *v.i.* acquiescer (*à*); accéder (*à*).
acquiescence [ækwi'esəns], *n.* acquiescement; consentement, *m.*
acquiescent [ækwi'esənt], *a.* résigné, soumis; consentant.
acquire [ə'kwaiə], *v.t.* acquérir, obtenir, gagner.
acquirement [ə'kwaiəmənt], *n.* acquisition; connaissance, *f.*
acquisition [ækwi'ziʃən], *n.* acquisition, *f.*
acquisitive [ə'kwizitiv], *a.* âpre au gain.
acquit [ə'kwit], *v.t.* régler (*une dette*); absoudre, acquitter (*un accusé*); s'acquitter (*d'un devoir*); *to acquit oneself well*, faire son devoir.
acquittal [ə'kwitəl], *n.* acquittement, *m.*
acre ['eikə], *n.* arpent, *m.*, acre, *f.*
acreage ['eikəridʒ], *n.* superficie, *f.*
acrid ['ækrid], *a.* âcre; (*fig.*) acerbe.
acridity [æ'kriditi], *n.* âcreté, *f.*
acrimonious [ækri'mouniəs], *a.* acrimonieux.
acrimoniously [ækri'mouniəsli], *adv.* avec aigreur, avec acrimonie.
acrimony ['ækriməni], *n.* acrimonie, aigreur, *f.*
acrobat ['ækrəbæt], *n.* acrobate, *m.*, *f.*
acrobatic [ækrə'bætik], *a.* acrobatique.—*n.* (*pl.*) acrobatie, *f.*
acropolis [ə'krɔpəlis], *n.* acropole, *f.*
across [ə'krɔs, ə'krɔ:s], *prep.* à travers, sur; *to come across*, rencontrer.—*adv.* à travers, en travers; de l'autre côté; *across the street*, de l'autre côté de la rue.
acrostic [ə'krɔstik], *n.* acrostiche, *m.*
act [ækt], *n.* acte, *m.*, loi; action, *f.*; *in the act*, sur le fait; *in the act of doing it*, en

train de le faire; *in the very act*, en flagrant délit.—*v.t.* jouer, représenter; feindre, contrefaire.—*v.i.* agir (*en, sur etc.*); se conduire; se comporter; opérer.
acting ['æktiŋ], *a.* qui agit; suppléant; (*Comm.*) gérant; *acting manager*, directeur gérant, *m.*—*n.* (*Theat.*) jeu, *m.*; (*fig.*) feinte, *f.*
action ['ækʃən], *n.* action, *f.*, fait; (*Law*) procès, *m.*; bataille, *f.*
actionable ['ækʃənəbl], *a.* actionnable, sujet à procès.
activate ['æktiveit], *v.t.* activer; rendre radioactif.
active ['æktiv], *a.* actif, agile, alerte.
actively ['æktivli], *adv.* activement.
activity [æk'tiviti], *n.* activité, *f.*
actor ['æktə], *n.* acteur, comédien, *m.*
actress ['æktris], *n.* actrice, comédienne, *f.*
actual ['æktjuəl], *a.* réel, véritable, effectif.
actuality [æktju'æliti], *n.* réalité, *f.*
actually ['æktjuəli], *adv.* réellement, en effet, positivement, véritablement; à vrai dire.
actuarial [æktju'ɛəriəl], *a.* actuariel.
actuary ['æktjuəri], *n.* actuaire, *m.*
actuate ['æktjueit], *v.t.* mettre en action; pousser, animer.
acuity [ə'kjuiti], *n.* acuité, *f.*
acumen [ə'kju:mən], *n.* finesse, pénétration, *f.*
acute [ə'kju:t], *a.* aigu, pointu, fin; (*fig.*) violent, poignant; perçant, pénétrant.
acutely [ə'kju:tli], *adv.* vivement; avec finesse.
acuteness [ə'kju:tnis], *n.* acuité; intensité; finesse, pénétration, *f.*
adage ['ædidʒ], *n.* adage, proverbe, *m.*
adamant ['ædəmənt], *a.* inflexible, intransigeant.—*n.* diamant, *m.*
adamantine [ædə'mæntain], *a.* adamantin, inflexible.
adapt [ə'dæpt], *v.t.* adapter, approprier, ajuster (*à*).
adaptability [ədæptə'biliti], *n.* faculté d'adaptation, souplesse, *f.*
adaptable [ə'dæptəbl], *a.* adaptable, qui peut s'adapter.
adapter [ə'dæptə], *n.* (*Elec.*) raccord, *m.*
add [æd], *v.t.* ajouter, joindre; additionner.
adder ['ædə], *n.* vipère, *f.*
addict ['ædikt], *n.* personne adonnée à (*stupéfiants etc.*), *f.*—[ə'dikt], *v.i.* s'adonner, se livrer (*à*).
addictedness [ə'diktidnis], **addiction** [ə'dikʃən], *n.* attachement, goût (*pour*), penchant (*à*), *m.*
addition [ə'diʃən], *n.* addition, *f.*; surcroît, supplément, accroissement, *m.*
additional [ə'diʃənəl], *a.* additionnel, supplémentaire, de plus.
additionally [ə'diʃənəli], *adv.* par addition, en sus, de plus, en outre.
addle [ædl], *v.t.* rendre couvi, corrompre; (*fig.*) brouiller (*le cerveau*).—*a.* or **addled** [ædld], couvi (*œuf*); pourri; (*fig.*) stérile.
addle-headed ['ædl'hedid], *a.* à cerveau vide, écervelé, à l'esprit brouillon.
address [ə'dres], *n.* adresse; habileté, dextérité; allocution, *f.*, discours; (*fig.*) abord, *m.*—*v.t.* adresser (*une lettre*); adresser la parole à, aborder (*quelqu'un*); (*Golf*) *to address the ball*, viser la balle.
addressee [ædre'si:], *n.* destinataire, *m.*, *f.*

adduce [ə'dju:s], *v.t.* alléguer; apporter, avancer, produire.

Adela ['ædilə]. Adèle, *f.*

Adelaide ['ædəleid]. Adélaïde, *f.*

adenoid ['ædinɔid], *a.* adénoïde.—*n.* (*pl.*) adénite, *f.*; végétations, *f. pl.*

adept [æ'dept], *a.* adepte, habile, versé (*dans*).—*n.* adepte, *m., f.*

adequacy ['ædikwəsi], **adequateness** ['ædikwitnis], *n.* juste proportion, suffisance, *f.*

adequate ['ædikwit], *a.* proportionné, suffisant (*à*), compétent.

adequately ['ædikwitli], *adv.* en juste proportion, suffisamment, convenablement.

adequateness [ADEQUACY].

adhere [əd'hiə], *v.i.* adhérer, s'attacher, s'en tenir (*à*).

adherence [əd'hiərəns], *n.* adhérence, *f.*, attachement, *m.*

adherent [əd'hiərənt], *n.* adhérent, *m.*

adhesion [əd'hi:ʒən], *n.* adhésion, *f.*

adhesive [əd'hi:siv], *a.* adhésif, tenace; gommé, agglutinant.

adieu [ə'dju:], *adv.* and *n.* adieu, *m.*; *to bid someone adieu*, faire ses adieux à quelqu'un.

adipose ['ædipous], *a.* adipeux.

adjacency [ə'dʒeisənsi], *n.* contiguïté, *f.*, voisinage, *m.*

adjacent [ə'dʒeisənt], *a.* adjacent, contigu (*à*), avoisinant.

adjectival [ædʒək'taivəl], *a.* comme adjectif.

adjectivally [ædʒək'taivəli], *adv.* adjectivement.

adjective ['ædʒəktiv], *a.* and *n.* adjectif, *m.*

adjoin [ə'dʒɔin], *v.t.* adjoindre, joindre; toucher, se joindre à.—*v.i.* se toucher, être contigu.

adjoining [ə'dʒɔiniŋ], *a.* adjacent, avoisinant, contigu (*à*).

adjourn [ə'dʒə:n], *v.t.* ajourner, différer, remettre.—*v.i.* s'ajourner, lever la séance.

adjournment [ə'dʒə:nmənt], *n.* ajournement, *m*; remise, *f.*

adjudge [ə'dʒʌdʒ], *v.t.* adjuger; juger, condamner; (*fig.*) estimer.

adjudicate [ə'dʒu:dikeit], *v.t.* adjuger; prononcer.

adjudication [ədʒu:di'keiʃən], *n.* jugement, *m.*; décision, *f.*, arrêt, *m.*

adjudicator [ə'dʒu:dikeitə], *n.* juge, arbitre, *m., f.*

adjunct ['ædʒʌŋkt], *a.* adjoint, accessoire.—*n.* accessoire; adjoint, *m.*

adjure [ə'dʒuə], *v.t.* adjurer.

adjust [ə'dʒʌst], *v.t.* ajuster, régler, arranger.

adjustable [ə'dʒʌstəbl], *a.* réglable.

adjustment [ə'dʒʌstmənt], *n.* ajustement, arrangement, accord, *m.*; mise au point, *f.*, réglage, *m.*

adjutant ['ædʒutənt], *n.* capitaine adjudant major; major de la garnison, *m.*

administer [əd'ministə], *v.t.* administrer, gérer, régir; faire prêter (*un serment*).

administrate [əd'ministreit], *v.t.* administrer; régir.

administration [ədminis'treiʃən], *n.* administration, *f.*, gouvernement, *m.*

administrative [əd'ministrətiv], *a.* administratif.

administrator [əd'ministreitə], *n.* administrateur; (*Law*) curateur, *m.*

admirable ['ædmərəbl], *a.* admirable.

admirably ['ædmərəbli], *adv.* admirablement, à ravir, à merveille.

admiral ['ædmərəl], *n.* amiral, *m.*; *rear-admiral*, contre-amiral, *m.*; *vice-admiral*, vice-amiral, *m.*

admiralty ['ædmərəlti], *n.* amirauté, *f.*; Ministère de la Marine (*en France*), *m.*; *Board of Admiralty*, conseil d'amirauté, *m.*; *First Lord of the Admiralty*, ministre de la marine, *m.*

admiration [ædmə'reiʃən], *n.* admiration, *f.*; étonnement, *m.*

admire [əd'maiə], *v.t.* admirer; aimer; s'étonner de.—*v.i.* s'étonner.

admirer [əd'maiərə], *n.* admirateur, *m.*, admiratrice, *f.*

admissible [əd'misibl], *a.* admissible.

admission [əd'miʃən], *n.* admission, entrée, *f.*; accès; aveu, *m.*, concession, *f.*

admit [əd'mit], *v.t.* admettre, laisser entrer; avouer, reconnaître; tolérer.—*v.i. to admit of*, comporter, permettre; souffrir.

admittance [əd'mitəns], *n.* accès, *m.*; admission, entrée, *f.*; *no admittance*, défense d'entrer.

admittedly [əd'mitidli], *adv.* de l'aveu général; il est vrai que.

admixture [əd'mikstʃə], *n.* mélange, *m.*

admonish [əd'mɔniʃ], *v.t.* avertir, exhorter; reprendre, réprimander.

admonishment [əd'mɔniʃmənt], **admonition** [ædmə'niʃən], *n.* admonition, *f.*, avertissement, *m.*; remontrance, réprimande, *f.*

ado [ə'du:], *n.* bruit, fracas, *m.*, façons, cérémonies, *f.pl.*, embarras, *m.*, peine, difficulté, *f.*; *much ado about nothing*, beaucoup de bruit pour rien; *without any more ado*, sans plus de façons.

adolescence [ædo'lesəns], *n.* adolescence, *f.*

adolescent [ædo'lesənt], *a.* and *n.* adolescent, *m.*

Adolphus [ə'dɔlfəs]. Adolphe, *m.*

adopt [ə'dɔpt], *v.t.* adopter.

adopted [ə'dɔptid], **adoptive** [ə'dɔptiv], *a.* adoptif, adopté, d'adoption.

adoption [ə'dɔpʃən], *n.* adoption, *f.*

adoptive [ADOPTED].

adorable [ə'dɔ:rəbl], *a.* adorable.

adorably [ə'dɔ:rəbli], *adv.* d'une manière adorable, adorablement.

adoration [ædo'reiʃən], *n.* adoration, *f.*

adore [ə'dɔ:], *v.t.* adorer.

adorer [ə'dɔ:rə], *n.* adorateur, *m.*

adoringly [ə'dɔ:riŋli], *adv.* avec adoration.

adorn [ə'dɔ:n], *v.t.* orner; parer, embellir; (*fig.*) faire l'ornement de.

adornment [ə'dɔ:nmənt], *n.* ornement, *m.*, parure; ornementation, *f.*

Adrian ['eidriən]. Adrien, *m.*

Adriatic Sea [eidri'ætik'si:]. la mer Adriatique, l'Adriatique, *f.*

adrift [ə'drift], *adv.* en *ou* à la dérive; à l'abandon.

adroit [ə'drɔit], *a.* adroit, habile.

adroitly [ə'drɔitli], *adv.* adroitement.

adroitness [ə'drɔitnis], *n.* adresse, dextérité, *f.*

adulate ['ædjuleit], *v.t.* aduler.

adulation [ædju'leiʃən], *n.* adulation, *f.*

adulatory ['ædjuleitəri], *a.* adulateur.

adult [ə'dʌlt, 'ædʌlt], *a.* and *n.* adulte, *m., f.*

337

adulterate

adulterate [ə'dʌltəreit], *v.t.* adultérer, frelater, falsifier, sophistiquer; (*fig.*) corrompre.

adulteration [ədʌltə'reiʃən], *n.* falsification, sophistication, *f.*, frelatage, *m.*

adulterator [ə'dʌltəreitə], *n.* frelateur, falsificateur, *m.*

adulterer [ə'dʌltərə], *n.* adultère, *m.*

adulteress [ə'dʌltəris], *n.* (femme) adultère, *f.*

adulterous [ə'dʌltərəs], *a.* adultère; (*fig.*) altéré, faux.

adultery [ə'dʌltəri], *n.* adultère, *m.*

advance [əd'vɑːns], *v.t.* avancer, faire avancer; élever, hausser, augmenter.—*v.i.* avancer, s'avancer, se porter en avant.—*n.* mouvement en avant, *m.*; avance (*de fonds*), *f.*; avancement, progrès, *m.*; **in advance,** d'avance.

advance-guard [əd'vɑːnsgɑːd], *n.* avant-garde, *f.*

advancement [əd'vɑːnsmənt], *n.* avancement, progrès, *m.*; (*Comm.*) avance, *f.*

advantage [əd'vɑːntidʒ], *n.* avantage; profit, intérêt, *m.*; **to have the advantage,** avoir le dessus; **to take advantage of,** profiter de; **to take advantage of someone's kindness,** abuser de la bonté de quelqu'un.

advantageous [ædvən'teidʒəs], *a.* avantageux (*à* ou *de*).

advantageously [ædvən'teidʒəsli], *adv.* avantageusement.

Advent ['ædvənt]. (*Eccles.*) l'Avent, *m.*

advent ['ædvənt], *n.* venue, *f.*

adventitious [ædven'tiʃəs], *a.* adventice, fortuit.

adventure [əd'ventʃə], *n.* aventure, entreprise hasardeuse, *f.*—*v.t.* aventurer, hasarder.—*v.i.* s'aventurer, se hasarder.

adventurer [əd'ventʃərə], *n.* aventurier, *m.*

adventuress [əd'ventʃəris], *n.* aventurière, *f.*

adventurous [əd'ventʃərəs], *a.* aventureux, hardi.

adventurously [əd'ventʃərəsli], *adv.* aventureusement.

adverb ['ædvəːb], *n.* adverbe, *m.*

adverbial [əd'vəːbjəl], *a.* adverbial.

adverbially [əd'vəːbjəli], *adv.* adverbialement.

adversary ['ædvəsəri], *n.* adversaire, *m.*, *f.*

adverse ['ædvəːs], *a.* adverse, contraire (*à*); défavorable.

adversely ['ædvəːsli], *adv.* d'une manière hostile, malheureusement.

adversity [əd'vəːsiti], *n.* adversité, *f.*

advert [əd'vəːt], *v.i.* faire allusion (*à*); parler (*de*).

advertise ['ædvətaiz], *v.t.* annoncer, faire annoncer, afficher, faire de la publicité pour.

advertisement [əd'vəːtizmənt], *n.* annonce (*journal*), publicité, réclame, *f.*; avis, *m.*; **classified advertisements,** petites annonces, *f.pl.*

advertiser ['ædvətaizə], *n.* personne qui fait des annonces, *f.*; journal d'annonces, *m.*

advertising ['ædvətaiziŋ], *n.* publicité, réclame, *f.*; **advertising agency,** agence de publicité, *f.*

advice [əd'vais], *n.* avis, conseil, *m.*; **if you take my advice,** si vous m'en croyez; **to take advice,** prendre conseil (*de*), consulter (*un médecin etc.*).

advisable [əd'vaizəbl], *a.* judicieux, convenable (*pour* ou *de*); opportun.

advisability [ədvaizə'biliti], *n.* convenance, utilité, opportunité, *f.*

advise [əd'vaiz], *v.t.* conseiller; donner avis (*de*); prévenir (*de*); annoncer.—*v.i.* délibérer, prendre conseil, consulter.

advisedly [əd'vaizidli], *adv.* avec réflexion, de propos délibéré.

adviser [əd'vaizə], *n.* conseiller, *m.*

advisory [əd'vaizəri], *a.* consultatif.

advocacy ['ædvəkəsi], *n.* profession d'avocat, défense, *f.*, plaidoyer, *m.*

advocate ['ædvəkit], *n.* avocat, défenseur; intercesseur, *m.*—['ædvəkeit], *v.t.* défendre, plaider; soutenir, appuyer, préconiser.

adze [ædz], *n.* herminette, doloire; aissette, *f.*—*v.t.* entailler à l'herminette, doler.

Aegean Sea [iː'dʒiːənsiː]. la mer Égée, *f.*

aegis ['iːdʒis], *n.* égide, *f.*

Aeneas [iː'niːəs]. Énée, *m.*

Aeneid [iː'niːiid]. l'Énéide, *f.*

aeon ['iːən], *n.* éternité, *f.*, éon, *m.*

aerate ['ɛəreit], *v.t.* aérer; gazéifier.

aeration [ɛə'reiʃən], *n.* aération, *f.*

aerial ['ɛəriəl], *a.* aérien.—*n.* antenne, *f.*

aerie, aery, eyrie, eyry ['ɛəri, 'iəri], *n.* aire, *f.*

aerobatics [ɛərə'bætiks], *n.pl.* acrobaties aériennes, *f.pl.*

aerodrome ['ɛərodroum], *n.* aérodrome, *m.*

aerodynamic ['ɛərodai'næmik], *a.* aérodynamique.—*n.* (*pl.*) aérodynamique, *f.*

aerolite ['ɛərolait], **aerolith** ['ɛəroliθ], *n.* aérolithe, bolide, *m.*

aeronaut ['ɛəronɔːt], *n.* aéronaute, *m.*, *f.*

aeronautic [ɛəro'nɔːtik], *a.* aéronautique.

aeroplane ['ɛəroplein], *n.* aéroplane, avion, *m.*

aerostat ['ɛərostæt], *n.* aérostat, *m.*

Aeschylus ['iːskiləs]. Eschyle, *m.*

Aesop ['iːsɔp]. Ésope, *m.*

aesthete ['iːsθiːt], *n.* esthète, *m.*, *f.*

aesthetic [iːs'θetik], **aesthetical** [iːs'θetikəl], *a.* esthétique.

aesthetically [iːs'θetikəli], *adv.* esthétiquement.

aestival [iːs'taivəl], *a.* estival.

aether [ETHER].

afar [ə'fɑː], *adv.* loin, de loin, au loin.

affability [æfə'biliti], **affableness** ['æfəblnis], *n.* affabilité, *f.*

affable ['æfəbl], *a.* affable, doux, gracieux.

affably ['æfəbli], *adv.* affablement, avec affabilité.

affair [ə'fɛə], *n.* affaire, *f.*

affect [ə'fekt], *v.t.* affecter; intéresser, toucher, émouvoir.

affectation [æfek'teiʃən], **affectedness** [ə'fektidnis], *n.* affectation, *f.*

affected [ə'fektid], *a.* disposé (*pour etc.*); affecté, précieux; maniéré, prétentieux (*style*).

affecting [ə'fektiŋ], *a.* touchant, émouvant, attendrissant.

affection [ə'fekʃən], *n.* affection, *f.*, amour; goût, attachement, penchant, *m.*; maladie, *f.*

affectionate [ə'fekʃənit], *a.* affectueux, affectionné.

affectionately [ə'fekʃənitli], *adv.* affectueusement.

affiance [ə'faiəns], *v.t.* fiancer.—*n.* fiançailles, *f.pl.*

affianced [ə'faiənst], *a.* fiancé.

affidavit [æfi'deivit], *n.* déclaration par écrit sous serment, attestation, *f.*

affiliate [ə'filieit], *v.t.* affilier; attribuer, rattacher (*à*).

affiliation [əfili'eiʃən], *n.* affiliation, *f.*

affinity [ə'finiti], *n.* affinité, *f.*

affirm [ə'fə:m], *v.t.* affirmer.

affirmation [æfə'meiʃən], *n.* affirmation, *f.*

affirmative [ə'fə:mətiv], *a.* affirmatif.—*n.* affirmative, *f.*

affirmatively [ə'fə:mətivli], *adv.* affirmativement.

affix [ə'fiks], *v.t.* apposer, attacher (*à*).

afflatus [ə'fleitəs], *n.* souffle, *m.*, inspiration, *f.*

afflict [ə'flikt], *v.t.* affliger (*de*); tourmenter.

afflicting [ə'fliktiŋ], *a.* affligeant.

affliction [ə'flikʃən], *n.* affliction; calamité, *f.*, malheur, *m.*

affluence ['æfluəns], *n.* opulence, affluence; abondance, *f.*, concours (*de personnes*), *m.*

affluent ['æfluənt], *a.* opulent, riche; affluent.

afford [ə'fɔ:d], *v.t.* donner, fournir, accorder; avoir les moyens de, pouvoir.

afforestation [əfɔris'teiʃən], *n.* boisement; reboisement, *m.*

affranchise [ə'fræntʃaiz], *v.t.* affranchir.

affray [ə'frei], *n.* bagarre, échauffourée, *f.*

affright [ə'frait], *v.t.* effrayer.

affront [ə'frʌnt], *n.* affront, *m.*, insulte, injure, *f.*, outrage, *m.*—*v.t.* affronter, offenser, insulter.

afield [ə'fi:ld], *adv.* aux champs, à la campagne; *to go far afield,* aller très loin.

afire [ə'faiə], *adv.* en feu.

aflame [ə'fleim], *adv.* en flammes.

afloat [ə'flout], *adv.* à flot; (*fig.*) en circulation.

afoot [ə'fut], *adv.* à pied; en marche, en route; (*fig.*) sur pied; en train.

afore [ə'fɔ:], *adv.* précédemment, auparavant; par devant.

aforementioned [ə'fɔ:menʃənd], *a.* mentionné plus haut, susdit, précité.

aforesaid [ə'fɔ:sed], *a.* susdit, ledit, susnommé.

aforethought [ə'fɔ:θɔ:t], *a. with malice aforethought,* avec intention criminelle.

afraid [ə'freid], *a.* effrayé, pris de peur; *I am afraid not,* je crains que non; *I am afraid she's gone,* je crains bien qu'elle ne soit partie; *to be afraid of,* avoir peur de.

afresh [ə'freʃ], *adv.* de nouveau, de plus belle.

Africa ['æfrikə]. l'Afrique, *f.*

African ['æfrikən], *a.* africain.—*n.* Africain (*personne*), *m.*

aft [ɑ:ft], *a.* arrière, de l'arrière.—*adv.* (*Naut.*) à l'arrière.

after ['ɑ:ftə], *a.* subséquent, ultérieur, futur; arrière.—*prep.* après; sur, à la suite de; selon, d'après.—*adv.* après, d'après, ensuite. —*conj.* après que.

aftercrop ['ɑ:ftəkrɔp], *n.* seconde récolte, *f.*; regain, *m.*

after-effects ['ɑ:ftərifekts], *n. pl.* suites, *f. pl.*, répercussion, *f.*

after-life ['ɑ:ftəlaif], *n.* suite de la vie, *f.*; au-delà, *m.*

aftermath ['ɑ:ftəmæθ], *n.* regain, *m.*; (*fig.*) suites, *f.pl.*

afternoon [ɑ:ftə'nu:n], *n.* après-midi, *m.* ou *f.*

afterthought ['ɑ:ftəθɔ:t], *n.* réflexion après coup, *f.*

afterward ['ɑ:ftəwəd], **afterwards** ['ɑ:ftə wədz], *adv.* après, ensuite, plus tard.

again [ə'gein], *adv.* encore; encore une fois, de nouveau; *again and again,* à plusieurs reprises; *as much again,* encore autant; *never again,* jamais plus.

against [ə'geinst], *prep.* contre; vis-à-vis; vers; pour.

agape [ə'geip], *adv.* bouche bée.

agate ['ægeit], *n.* agate, *f.*

Agatha ['ægəθə]. Agathe, *f.*

age [eidʒ], *n.* âge, *m.*; époque, *f.*; *of age,* majeur; *under age,* mineur; *Middle Ages,* moyen âge.—*v.t., v.i.* vieillir.

aged ['eidʒid, (*after prefix*) eidʒd], *a.* vieux, âgé; *middle-aged,* entre deux âges.

ageless ['eidʒlis], *a.* toujours jeune.

agency ['eidʒənsi], *n.* action, entremise; (*Comm.*) agence, *f.*

agenda [ə'dʒendə], *n.* ordre du jour; programme, *m.*

agent ['eidʒənt], *n.* représentant, agent, mandataire, *m.*

agglomerate [ə'glɔməreit], *v.t.* agglomérer.—*v.i.* s'agglomérer.—*a.* aggloméré.

agglomeration [əglɔmə'reiʃən], *n.* agglomération, *f.*

aggrandize [ə'grændaiz], *v.t.* agrandir.

aggrandizement [ə'grændizmənt], *n.* agrandissement, *m.*

aggravate ['ægrəveit], *v.t.* aggraver; exagérer; (*colloq.*) agacer, pousser à bout, exaspérer.

aggravation [ægrə'veiʃən], *n.* aggravation; circonstance aggravante, *f.*, agacement, *m.*

aggregate ['ægrigit], *a.* collectif, global, réuni. —*n.* masse, *f.*; ensemble, *m.*, somme totale, *f.*—['ægrigeit], *v.t.* rassembler.

aggregation [ægri'geiʃən], *n.* agrégation, *f.*, assemblage, *m.*

aggression [ə'greʃən], *n.* agression, *f.*

aggressive [ə'gresiv], *a.* agressif.

aggressiveness [ə'gresivnis], *n.* caractère agressif, *m.*

aggressor [ə'gresə], *n.* agresseur, *m.*

aggrieve [ə'gri:v], *v.t.* chagriner, affliger; blesser, léser.

aghast [ə'gɑ:st], *a.* consterné, ébahi, médusé, tout pantois.

agile ['ædʒail], *a.* agile, leste.

agility [ə'dʒiliti], *n.* agilité, *f.*

agio ['ædʒiou], *n.* prix du change, agio, *m.*

agiotage ['ædʒiotədʒ], *n.* agiotage, *m.*

agitate ['ædʒiteit], *v.t.* agiter, exciter; remuer, troubler.

agitation [ædʒi'teiʃən], *n.* agitation; discussion, *f.*, examen, *m.*

agitator ['ædʒiteitə], *n.* agitateur; meneur, *m.*

aglow [ə'glou], *a.* enflammé, resplendissant.

agnostic [æg'nɔstik], *a.* and *n.* agnosticiste, agnostique, *m.*, *f.*

agnosticism [æg'nɔstisizm], *n.* agnosticisme, *m.*

ago [ə'gou], *adv.* passé, il y a; *two days ago,* il y a deux jours.

agog [ə'gɔg], *adv.* excité, impatient, empressé; en train, en l'air; *to be all agog,* avoir la tête montée.

agonize ['ægənaiz], *v.t.* torturer, mettre au supplice.—*v.i.* souffrir l'agonie, être au supplice.

agonizing ['ægənaiziŋ], *a.* atroce, déchirant.
agony ['ægəni], *n.* douleur, angoisse, *f.,* paroxysme, *m.*
agrarian [ə'grɛəriən], *a.* agraire.
agree [ə'griː], *v.i.* s'accorder (*à* ou *avec*); être d'accord; consentir (*à*); convenir (*de*); être conforme (*à*).
agreeable [ə'griːəbl], *a.* agréable, aimable; conforme (*à*); consentant.
agreeably [ə'griːəbli], *adv.* agréablement; conformément (*à*).
agreed [ə'griːd], *a.* convenu, d'accord; *it's agreed,* c'est entendu.
agreement [ə'griːmənt], *n.* accord, *m.*; convention, *f.,* contrat, pacte, marché, *m.*; conformité, *f.*
agricultural [ægri'kʌltʃərəl], *a.* agricole, d'agriculture.
agriculture ['ægrikʌltʃə], *n.* agriculture, *f.*
agriculturist [ægri'kʌltʃərist], *n.* agriculteur, agronome, *m.*
aground [ə'graund], *adv.* échoué; à terre.
ague ['eigjuː], *n.* fièvre intermittente, *f.*
ahead [ə'hed], *adv.* en avant; (*fig.*) en tête; *go ahead !* en avant! vas-y! *straight ahead,* tout droit; *ahead of time,* en avance.
aid [eid], *v.t.* aider, assister; secourir; *to aid each other,* s'entr'aider.—*n.* aide, assistance, *f.*; secours, concours, subside, *m.*; *with the aid of,* à l'aide de.
aide-de-camp [eiddə'kɑ̃], *n.* aide de camp, *m.*
aigrette ['eigret], *n.* aigrette, *f.*
ail [eil], *v.t.* faire mal à; chagriner; *what ails him?* qu'est-ce qu'il a ?—*v.i.* être souffrant.
aileron ['eilerɔn], *n.* aileron, *m.*
ailing ['eiliŋ], *a.* souffrant, indisposé, mal portant.
ailment ['eilmənt], *n.* mal, malaise, *m.,* indisposition, *f.*
aim [eim], *v.t.* viser; diriger, lancer (*un coup etc.*).—*v.i.* viser (*à*); aspirer (*à*); avoir pour but (*de*).—*n.* point de mire, but, objet, dessein, *m.*; visée, *f.*; *to take aim at,* viser, coucher en joue.
aimless ['eimlis], *a.* sans but, sans objet.
air [ɛə], *n.* air; vent, *m.,* brise; (*fig.*) mine, expression, *f.*; *in the air,* en l'air; *in the open air,* en plein air.—*v.t.* aérer, donner de l'air à, mettre à l'air; sécher.
air-balloon ['ɛəbəluːn], *n.* ballon aérostatique, *m.*
airborne ['ɛəbɔːn], *a.* (*Av.*) aéroporté.
air-conditioned ['ɛəkəndiʃənd], *a.* climatisé.
air-conditioning ['ɛəkəndiʃəniŋ], *n.* climatisation, *f.*
air-cooling ['ɛəkuːliŋ], *n.* refroidissement par air, *m.*
aircraft ['ɛəkrɑːft], *n.* avion, *m.*; les avions, *m.pl.*
air-crew ['ɛəkruː], *n.* équipage (d'avion), *m.*
airfield ['ɛəfiːld], *n.* terrain d'aviation, *m.*
air-hostess ['ɛəhoustis], *n.* hôtesse de l'air, *f.*
airily ['ɛərili], *adv.* allègrement, légèrement.
airiness ['ɛərinis], *n.* situation aérée; (*fig.*) légèreté, vivacité, désinvolture, *f.*
airing ['ɛəriŋ], *n.* aérage, *m.,* exposition à l'air, *f.,* éventage, *m.*; promenade, *f.*
airlift ['ɛəlift], *n.* pont aérien, *m.*
air-line ['ɛəlain], *n.* ligne aérienne, *f.*
air-liner ['ɛəlainə], *n.* avion de ligne, *m.*
air-mail ['ɛəmeil], *n.* poste aérienne, *f.*

airman ['ɛəmən], *n.* aviateur, *m.*
air-mattress ['ɛəmætris], *n.* matelas à air, *m.*
air-pocket ['ɛəpɔkit], *n.* (*Av.*) trou d'air, *m.*
airport ['ɛəpɔːt], *n.* aéroport, *m.*
airship ['ɛəʃip], *n.* dirigeable, *m.*
airsickness ['ɛəsiknis], *n.* mal de l'air, *m.*
airstrip ['ɛəstrip], *n.* piste d'atterrissage, *f.*
airtight ['ɛətait], *a.* imperméable à l'air, hermétique.
airworthy ['ɛəwəːði], *a.* navigable.
airy ['ɛəri], *a.* ouvert à l'air; aérien, aéré; (*fig.*) léger, dégagé, gai, enjoué, insouciant; *air words,* paroles en l'air, *f.pl.*
aisle [ail], *n.* bas-côté, *m.,* nef latérale, *f.*
ajar [ə'dʒɑː], *a.* entr'ouvert, entrebâillé.
akimbo [ə'kimbou], *adv.* appuyé sur la hanche; *with one's arms akimbo,* les poings sur les hanches.
akin [ə'kin], *a.* allié (*à*); parent (*de*); (*fig.*) qui a rapport (*avec*).
alabaster ['æləbɑːstə], *a.* d'albâtre.—*n.* albâtre, *m.*
alack! [ə'læk], *int.* hélas!
alacrity [ə'lækriti], *n.* alacrité, *f.,* empressement, *m.,* promptitude, *f.*
Alan, Allan, Allen ['ælən]. Alain, *m.*
alarm [ə'lɑːm], *n.* alarme, alerte, *f.*; réveil (*réveille-matin*), *m.*—*v.t.* alarmer; effrayer, faire peur à.
alarm-bell [ə'lɑːmbel], *n.* cloche d'alarme, *f.,* tocsin, *m.*
alarm-clock [ə'lɑːmklɔk], *n.* réveille-matin, *m.*
alarming [ə'lɑːmiŋ], *a.* alarmant.
alarmingly [ə'lɑːmiŋli], *adv.* d'une manière alarmante.
alarmist [ə'lɑːmist], *n.* alarmiste, *m., f.*
alas! [ə'læs], *int.* hélas!
Albania [æl'beinjə]. l'Albanie, *f.*
Albanian [æl'beinjən], *a.* albanais.—*n.* Albanais (*personne*), *m.*
albatross ['ælbətrɔs], *n.* albatros, *m.*
*albeit [ɔːl'biːit], *conj.* quoique, bien que (*with subj.*).
albino [æl'biːnou], *a.* and *n.* albinos, *m., f.*
album ['ælbəm], *n.* album, *m.*
albumen [æl'bjuːmin], *n.* albumen; blanc d'œuf, *m.*; albumine, *f.*
albuminous [æl'bjuːminəs], *a.* albumineux.
alburnum [æl'bəːnəm], *n.* aubier, *m.*
alchemic [æl'kemik], **alchemical** [æl'kemikəl], *a.* alchimique.
alchemist ['ælkimist], *n.* alchimiste, *m.*
alchemistic [ælki'mistik], **alchemistical** [ælki'mistikəl], *a.* d'alchimiste, alchimique.
alchemy ['ælkimi], *n.* alchimie, *f.*
alcohol ['ælkəhɔl], *n.* alcool, *m.*
alcoholic [ælkə'hɔlik], *a.* and *n.* alcoolique, *m., f.*
alcoholism ['ælkəhɔlizm], *n.* alcoolisme, *m.*
Alcoran [ælko'rɑːn]. le Coran, le Koran.
alcove ['ælkouv], *n.* alcôve; niche, *f.,* enfoncement, *m.*
alder ['ɔːldə], *n.* aune, vergne, *m.*
alder-grove ['ɔːldəgrouv], *n.* aunaie, *f.*
alderman ['ɔːldəmən], *n.* (*pl.* -**men** [men]) conseiller municipal, alderman, échevin, *m.*
ale [eil], *n.* ale, bière, *f.*
ale-house ['eilhaus], *n.* taverne, *f.*
alembic [ə'lembik], *n.* alambic, *m.*
alert [ə'ləːt], *a.* alerte, vigilant, éveillé.—*n.* alerte, *f.*; *on the alert,* sur le qui-vive.

alertness [ə'lə:tnis], *n.* vigilance, promptitude, prestesse, *f.*

Alexander [ælig'zɑːndə]. Alexandre, *m.*

alexandrine [ælig'zɑːndrin], *n.* (*Pros.*) alexandrin, *m.*

alfresco [æl'freskou], *adv.* en plein air.

algebra ['ældʒəbrə], *n.* algèbre, *f.*

algebraic [ældʒə'breiik], **algebraical** [ældʒə'breiikəl], *a.* algébrique.

Algeria [æl'dʒiəriə]. l'Algérie, *f.*

Algerian [æl'dʒiəriən], *a.* algérien.—*n.* Algérien (*personne*), *m.*

Algiers [æl'dʒiəz]. Alger, *m.*

alias ['eiliəs], *n.* nom d'emprunt *ou* de rechange, *m.*—*adv.* dit, autrement nommé, alias.

alibi ['ælibai], *n.* alibi, *m.*

alien ['eiljən], *a.* étranger (à); éloigné (de).—*n.* étranger, *m.*

alienate ['eiljəneit], *v.t.* aliéner (de).

alienation [eiljə'neiʃən], *n.* aliénation, *f.*

alienist ['eiljənist], *n.* aliéniste, *m.*, *f.*

alight [ə'lait], *a.* allumé, embrasé.—*v.i.* descendre; mettre pied à terre; s'abattre (*oiseau etc.*); atterrir (*aviateur*), amerrir (*sur l'eau*).

align [ALINE].

alike [ə'laik], *adv.* également; de même, de la même manière; à la fois.—*a.* semblable, pareil; *to be alike,* se ressembler.

aliment ['ælimənt], *n.* aliment, *m.*

alimentary [æli'mentəri], *a.* alimentaire.

alimony ['æliməni], *n.* pension alimentaire, *f.*

aline, align [ə'lain], *v.t.* aligner; dresser.—*v.i.* s'aligner.

alinement, alignment [ə'lainmənt], *n.* alignement, *m.*

alive [ə'laiv], *a.* en vie, vivant; vif, éveillé; au monde; animé, sensible (à); *dead or alive,* mort ou vif; *to be alive with,* grouiller de, fourmiller de; *alive to,* sensible à; *while alive,* de son vivant.

alkali ['ælkəlai], *n.* alcali, *m.*

Alkoran [ALCORAN].

all [ɔːl], *a.* tout, tous; *all of you,* vous tous; *for all that,* malgré cela; *it is all the same to me,* cela m'est égal; *with all speed,* au plus vite, à toute vitesse.—*adv.* tout, entièrement; *all at once,* tout à coup, tout d'un coup; *all the better,* tant mieux; *not at all,* point du tout.—*n. and pron.* tout, *m.*; *above all,* surtout; *all but,* presque.

allay [ə'lei], *v.t.* apaiser, adoucir, calmer.

allegation [ælə'geiʃən], *n.* allégation, *f.*

allege [ə'ledʒ], *v.t.* alléguer, prétendre (*that, que*).

allegiance [ə'liːdʒəns], *n.* fidélité; obéissance, *f.*

allegorical [ælə'gɔrikəl], *a.* allégorique.

allegorically [ælə'gɔrikəli], *adv.* allégoriquement.

allegory ['æləgəri], *n.* allégorie, *f.*

allelujah [æli'luːjə], *n.* and *int.* alléluia, *m.*

allergic [ə'lə:dʒik], *a.* (*Med.*) allergique.

allergy ['ælədʒi], *n.* allergie, *f.*

alleviate [ə'liːvieit], *v.t.* alléger, soulager, adoucir.

alleviation [əliːvi'eiʃən], *n.* allégement, adoucissement, soulagement, *m.*

alley ['æli], *n.* ruelle (*d'une ville*); allée (*jardin*),

f.; *blind alley,* impasse, *f.*, cul de sac, *m.*

All Fools' Day [ɔːl'fuːlzdei]. le Ier avril.

alliance [ə'laiəns], *n.* alliance, *f.*

allied ['ælaid, ə'laid], *a.* allié; parent, voisin (*de*).

alligator ['æligeitə], *n.* alligator, caïman, *m.*

alliteration [əlitə'reiʃən], *n.* allitération, *f.*

alliterative [ə'litərətiv], *a.* allitératif.

allocate ['æləkeit], *v.t.* allouer, assigner.

allocation [ælo'keiʃən], *n.* allocation, *f.*

allot [ə'lɔt], *v.t.* assigner, donner en partage; répartir.

allotment [ə'lɔtmənt], *n.* partage, lot, lotissement, *m.*, portion; distribution, *f.*; lopin de terre, jardin ouvrier, *m.*

allow [ə'lau], *v.t.* permettre, autoriser; accorder, allouer; admettre, reconnaître; *to allow someone to do something,* permettre à quelqu'un de faire quelque chose.

allowable [ə'lauəbl], *a.* permis, admissible, légitime.

allowance [ə'lauəns], *n.* pension, rente; allocation; ration; remise, réduction; indulgence, indemnité, *f.*; *to make allowance for,* tenir compte de; *to put on short allowance,* rationner.

alloy [ə'lɔi], *n.* alliage, mélange, *m.*—*v.t.* allier; (*fig.*) altérer, diminuer, corrompre.

All Saints' Day [ɔːl'seintsdei]. la Toussaint, *f.*

All Souls' Day [ɔːl'soulzdei]. Jour des Morts, *m.*

allude [ə'ljuːd], *v.i.* faire allusion (à).

allure [ə'ljuə], *v.t.* amorcer, attirer, séduire, inviter (à).

allurement [ə'ljuəmənt], *n.* amorce, *f.*, appât, charme, attrait, *m.*

alluring [ə'ljuəriŋ], *a.* attrayant, séduisant.

alluringly [ə'ljuəriŋli], *adv.* d'une manière séduisante.

allusion [ə'ljuːʒən], *n.* allusion, *f.*

allusive [ə'ljuːsiv], *a.* allusif, plein d'allusions.

allusively [ə'ljuːsivli], *adv.* par allusion.

alluvia [ə'ljuːviə], *n.pl.* terres d'alluvion, *f.pl.*, alluvion, *f.*

alluvial [ə'ljuːviəl], *a.* alluvial, d'alluvion.

alluvium [ə'ljuːviəm], *n.* alluvion, *f.*

ally [ə'lai], *v.t.* allier.—*v.i.* s'allier (à ou avec).—['ælai, ə'lai], *n.* allié, confédéré, *m.*

almanac ['ɔːlmənæk], *n.* almanach, *m.*

almighty [ɔːl'maiti], *a.* tout-puissant; *the Almighty,* le Tout-Puissant.

almond ['ɑːmənd], *n.* amande, *f.*; *burnt almond,* praline, *f.*

almond-tree ['ɑːməndtriː], *n.* amandier, *m.*

almost ['ɔːlmoust], *adv.* presque, à peu près; *I almost fell,* j'ai failli tomber.

alms [ɑːmz], *n.* aumône, *f.*; *to give alms,* faire l'aumône.

alms-house ['ɑːmzhaus], *n.* maison de retraite, *f.*, asile, *m.*

aloe ['ælou], *n.* aloès, *m.*; *bitter aloes,* amer d'aloès, *m.*

aloft [ə'lɔft], *adv.* en haut, en l'air; (*Naut.*) dans la mâture.

alone [ə'loun], *a.* seul, solitaire; *leave me alone,* laissez-moi tranquille.

along [ə'lɔŋ], *adv.* and *prep.* le long de; *all along* (*time*), tout le temps; (*place*) tout le long du chemin; *along with,* avec; *come along,* venez donc; *get along with you,* allez-vous en, allez-vous promener.

alongside [ə'lɔŋsaid], *adv.* bord à bord; bord à quai.—*prep.* à côté de.
aloof [ə'luːf], *a.* distant.—*adv.* au loin, (*Naut.*) au large; éloigné, à l'écart; *to keep aloof,* se tenir à l'écart.
aloofness [ə'luːfnis], *n.* attitude distante, *f.*
aloud [ə'laud], *adv.* à haute voix, haut.
alpaca [æl'pækə], *n.* alpaga (*tissu*); alpaca (*animal*), *m.*
alphabet ['ælfəbet], *n.* alphabet; abécédaire (*livre d'enfant*), *m.*
alphabetic [ælfə'betik], **alphabetical** [ælfə'betikəl], *a.* alphabétique.
alphabetically [ælfə'betikəli], *adv.* alphabétiquement.
alpine ['ælpain], *a.* alpin; des Alpes, alpestre.
alpinist ['ælpinist], *n.* alpiniste, *m.*, *f.*
Alps [ælps]. les Alpes, *f. pl.*
already [ɔːl'redi], *adv.* déjà.
Alsatian [æl'seiʃən], *a.* alsacien.—*n.* (*chien*) chien-loup; (*personne*) Alsacien, *m.*
also ['ɔːlsou], *adv.* aussi, également.
altar ['ɔːltə], *n.* autel, *m.*; *high altar,* maître-autel, *m.*
altar-cloth ['ɔːltəklɔθ], *n.* nappe d'autel, *f.*
altar-screen ['ɔːltəskriːn], *n.* retable, *m.*
alter ['ɔːltə], *v.t.* changer, modifier; retoucher, corriger.—*v.i.* changer, se changer.
alteration [ɔːltə'reiʃən], *n.* changement, *m.*, modification, *f.*
altercation [ɔːltə'keiʃən], *n.* altercation, dispute, *f.*
alternate ['ɔːltəneit], *v.t.* alterner, faire alternativement.—*v.i.* alterner; se succéder; *alternating current,* courant alternatif, *m.*—[ɔːl'təːnit], *a.* alternatif; alternant; *alternate rhymes,* rimes croisées, *f. pl.*
alternately [ɔːl'təːnitli], *adv.* alternativement, tour à tour.
alternative [ɔːl'təːnətiv], *a.* alternatif.—*n.* alternative; autre solution, *f.*
alternatively [ɔːl'təːnətivli], *adv.* alternativement, tour à tour.
alternator ['ɔːltəneitə], *n.* (*Elec.*) alternateur, *m.*
although [ɔːl'ðou], *conj.* quoique, bien que (*with subj.*).
altimeter [ælti'miːtə], *n.* altimètre, *m.*
altitude ['æltitjuːd], *n.* altitude, élévation, hauteur, *f.*
alto ['æltou], *n.* alto, *m.*
altogether [ɔːltə'geðə], *adv.* tout à fait, entièrement.
altruistic [æltru'istik], *a.* altruiste.
alum ['æləm], *n.* alun, *m.*
aluminium [ælju'minjəm], *n.* aluminium, *m.*
always ['ɔːlweiz], *adv.* toujours.
*****amain** [ə'mein], *adv.* avec force, de toutes ses forces.
amalgam [ə'mælgəm], *n.* amalgame, *m.*
amalgamate [ə'mælgəmeit], *v.t.* amalgamer; (*Comm.*) fusionner.—*v.i.* s'amalgamer; (*Comm.*) fusionner.
amalgamation [əmælgə'meiʃən], *n.* amalgamation, *f.*; (*fig.*) amalgame, fusionnement, *m.*
amanuensis [əmænju'ensis], *n.* (*pl.* amanuenses** [əmænju'ensiːz]) secrétaire, *m.*, *f.*
amaranth ['æmərænθ], *n.* amarante, *f.*
amass [ə'mæs], *v.t.* amasser.
amateur ['æmətə:, 'æmətjuə], *n.* amateur, *m.*

amateurish [æmə'tə:riʃ, 'æmətjuəriʃ], *a.* d'amateur.
amateurism ['æmətə:rizm, 'æmətjuərizm], *n.* (*Spt.*) amateurisme, *m.*
amatory ['æmətəri], *a.* d'amour, amoureux.
amaze [ə'meiz], *v.t.* étonner, confondre, stupéfier; *to be amazed,* s'étonner.
amazement [ə'meizmənt], **amazedness** [ə'meizidnis], *n.* étonnement, *m.*, stupeur, stupéfaction, *f.*
amazing [ə'meiziŋ], *a.* étonnant.
Amazon ['æməzən], **the.** l'Amazone, *m.*
amazon ['æməzən], *n.* amazone, *f.*
ambassador [æm'bæsədə], *n.* ambassadeur, *m.*
ambassadress [æm'bæsədris], *n.* ambassadrice, *f.*
amber ['æmbə], *a.* d'ambre; *amber light* (*traffic*), feu orange, *m.*—*n.* ambre, *m.*
amber-coloured ['æmbəkʌləd], *a.* ambré.
ambergris ['æmbəgris], *n.* ambre gris, *m.*
ambidexter [æmbi'dekstə], *a.* and *n.* ambidextre, *m.*, *f.*
ambidextrous [æmbi'dekstrəs], *a.* ambidextre.
ambient ['æmbiənt], *a.* ambiant.
ambiguity [æmbi'gjuːiti], **ambiguousness** [æm'bigjuəsnis], *n.* ambiguïté; équivoque, *f.*
ambiguous [æm'bigjuəs], *a.* ambigu; équivoque; douteux.
ambiguously [æm'bigjuəsli], *adv.* ambigument, d'une manière équivoque.
ambit ['æmbit], *n.* tour, circuit, *m.*; (*fig.*) étendue, portée, *f.*
ambition [æm'biʃən], *n.* ambition, *f.*
ambitious [æm'biʃəs], *a.* ambitieux.
ambitiously [æm'biʃəsli], *adv.* ambitieusement.
amble [æmbl], *v.i.* aller (à) l'amble (*cheval*); (*fig.*) trottiner, aller son chemin, déambuler. —*n.* amble, *m.*
Ambrose ['æmbrouz]. Ambroise, *m.*
ambrosia [æm'brouziə], *n.* ambroisie, *f.*
ambulance ['æmbjuləns], *n.* ambulance, *f.*; hôpital militaire, *m.*
ambulant ['æmbjulənt], *a.* ambulant.
ambulatory ['æmbjulətri], *a.* ambulatoire.
ambuscade [æmbəs'keid], *n.* embuscade, *f.*; *to lay an ambuscade for,* dresser une embuscade à.—*v.t.* embusquer; mettre en embuscade.
ambush [æm'buʃ], *n.* embuscade, *f.*, guet-apens, *m.*—*v.t.* embusquer.
Amelia [ə'miːliə]. Amélie, *f.*
ameliorate [ə'miːljəreit], *v.t.* améliorer.—*v.i.* s'améliorer.
amelioration [əmiːljə'reiʃən], *n.* amélioration, *f.*
amen [aː'men], *int.* amen, ainsi soit-il.
amenable [ə'miːnəbl], *a.* responsable, comptable; docile, soumis, sujet (*à*).
amend [ə'mend], *v.t.* amender, corriger; réformer.—*v.i.* s'amender, se corriger.
amendment [ə'mendmənt], *n.* modification, *f.*, amendement, *m.*, amélioration, *f.*
amends [ə'mendz], *n. pl.* dédommagement, *m.*, compensation, réparation, *f.*; *to make amends for,* dédommager de, faire réparation de.
amenity [ə'miːniti, ə'meniti], *n.* aménité, *f.*, agrément, *m.*
America [ə'merikə]. l'Amérique, *f.*

American [ə'merikən], _a._ américain.—_n._ Américain (_personne_), _m._

amethyst ['æməθist], _n._ améthyste, _f._

amiability [eimjə'biliti], **amiableness** ['eimjəblnis], _n._ amabilité, _f._

amiable ['eimjəbl], _a._ aimable.

amiably ['eimjəbli], _adv._ aimablement, avec amabilité.

amicable ['æmikəbl], _a._ amical; _amicable settlement_, arrangement à l'amiable, _m._

amicably ['æmikəbli], _adv._ amicalement; à l'amiable.

amid [ə'mid], _prep._ au milieu de; parmi.

amidships [ə'midʃips], _adv._ (_Naut._) par le travers.

amidst [ə'midst], [AMID].

amiss [ə'mis], _adv._ mal, en mauvaise part; (_unseasonably_) mal à propos.

amity ['æmiti], _n._ amitié, _f._

ammeter ['æmitə], _n._ ampèremètre, _m._

ammonia [ə'mouniə], _n._ ammoniaque, _f._

ammunition [æmju'niʃən], _n._ munitions de guerre; cartouches, _f.pl._

amnesia [æm'ni:ziə], _n._ amnésie, _f._

amnesty ['æmnəsti], _n._ amnistie, _f._—_v.t._ amnistier.

amoeba [ə'mi:bə], _n._ (_pl._ **amoebae** [ə'mi:bai], **amoebas** [ə'mi:bəz]) amibe, _f._

amok [AMUCK].

among [ə'mʌŋ], **amongst** [ə'mʌŋst], _prep._ entre, parmi; au milieu de, chez, avec; _among other things_, entre autres choses; _from among_, d'entre.

amorous ['æmərəs], _a._ amoureux; porté à l'amour.

amorously ['æmərəsli], _adv._ amoureusement.

amorousness ['æmərəsnis], _n._ tempérament amoureux, _m._, tendance à l'amour, _f._

amorphous [ə'mɔ:fəs], _a._ amorphe.

amount [ə'maunt], _n._ montant, total, _m._, somme; quantité; (_fig._) valeur, _f._, résultat, _m._; _to the amount of_, jusqu'à concurrence de.—_v.i._ s'élever à, monter (_à_); revenir (_à_), se réduire (_à_); _that amounts to the same thing_, cela revient au même.

amour [ə'muə], _n._ intrigue amoureuse, _f._

ampere ['æmpeə], _n._ (_Elec._) ampère, _m._

amphibian [æm'fibiən], _n._ amphibie, _m._

amphibious [æm'fibiəs], _a._ amphibie.

amphitheatre [æmfi'θiətə], _n._ amphithéâtre, _m._

amphitheatrical [æmfiθi'ætrikəl], _a._ amphithéâtral, d'amphithéâtre.

amphora ['æmfərə], _n._ amphore, _f._

ample [æmpl], _a._ ample, large, abondant, copieux; très suffisant.

ampleness ['æmplnis], _n._ ampleur; grandeur, _f._

amplification [æmplifi'keiʃən], _n._ amplification, _f._

amplifier ['æmplifaiə], _n._ (_Rad._, _Tel._) amplificateur, _m._

amplify ['æmplifai], _v.t._ amplifier; exagérer.

amplitude ['æmplitju:d], _n._ amplitude, étendue, largeur, _f._

amply ['æmpli], _adv._ amplement.

amputate ['æmpjuteit], _v.t._ amputer.

amputation [æmpju'teiʃən], _n._ amputation, _f._

amuck [ə'mʌk], **amock**, **amok** [ə'mɔk], _adv._ _to run amuck_, devenir fou furieux.

amulet ['æmjulit], _n._ amulette, _f._

amuse [ə'mju:z], _v.t._ amuser, divertir; _to be amused at_, s'amuser _ou_ se divertir de.

amusement [ə'mju:zmənt], _n._ amusement, divertissement, _m._

amusing [ə'mju:ziŋ], _a._ amusant, divertissant.

amusingly [ə'mju:ziŋli], _adv._ d'une manière amusante.

Amy ['eimi]. Aimée, _f._

an [ʌ (ə)].

anachronism [ə'nækrənizm], _n._ anachronisme, _m._

anachronistic [ənækrə'nistik], _a._ anachronique.

anaconda [ænə'kɔndə], _n._ anaconda, eunecte, _m._

anaemia [ə'ni:miə], _n._ anémie, _f._

anaemic [ə'ni:mik], _a._ anémique.

anaesthesia [ænəs'θi:ziə], _n._ anesthésie, _f._

anaesthetic [ænəs'θetik], _a._ and _n._ anesthésique, _m._

anaesthetist [ə'ni:sθətist], _n._ anesthésiste, _m._, _f._

anaesthetize [ə'ni:sθətaiz], _v.t._ anesthésier.

anagram ['ænəgræm], _n._ anagramme, _f._

analgesia [ænæl'dʒiːziə], _n._ analgésie, analgie, _f._

analogical [ænə'lɔdʒikəl], _a._ analogique.

analogism [ə'nælədʒizm], _n._ (_Phil._) analogisme, _m._

analogous [ə'næləgəs], _a._ analogue.

analogy [ə'nælədʒi], _n._ analogie, _f._

analyse ['ænəlaiz], _v.t._ analyser, faire l'analyse de.

analysis [ə'nælisis], _n._ analyse, _f._

analyst ['ænəlist], _n._ analyste, _m._, _f._

analytic [ænə'litik], **analytical** [ænə'litikəl], _a._ analytique.

analytically [ænə'litikəli], _adv._ analytiquement.

anarchism ['ænəkizm], _n._ anarchisme, _m._

anarchist ['ænəkist], _a._ and _n._ anarchiste, _m._, _f._

anarchy ['ænəki], _n._ anarchie, _f._

anathema [ə'næθimə], _n._ anathème, _m._

anathematize [ə'næθimətaiz], _v.t._ anathématiser, frapper d'anathème; maudire.

anatomical [ænə'tɔmikəl], _a._ anatomique.

anatomically [ænə'tɔmikəli], _adv._ anatomiquement.

anatomist [ə'nætəmist], _n._ anatomiste, _m._, _f._

anatomize [ə'nætəmaiz], _v.t._ anatomiser.

anatomy [ə'nætəmi], _n._ anatomie, _f._

ancestor ['ænsəstə], _n._ aïeul, _m._

ancestors ['ænsəstəz], _n.pl._ ancêtres, pères, aïeux, _m.pl._

ancestral [æn'sestrəl], _a._ ancestral, d'ancêtres, de ses ancêtres; héréditaire.

ancestry ['ænsəstri], _n._ ancêtres, _m.pl._; race, origine, naissance, _f._, lignage, _m._

anchor ['æŋkə], _n._ ancre, _f._; _sheet-anchor_, maîtresse ancre, (_fig._) ancre de miséricorde; _to ride at anchor_, être à l'ancre; _to weigh anchor_, lever l'ancre.—_v.t._ mouiller, ancrer.—_v.i._ ancrer, s'ancrer, jeter l'ancre, mouiller; (_fig._) se fixer.

anchorage ['æŋkəridʒ], _n._ mouillage, ancrage _m._; retraite (_d'anachorète_), .

anchoret ['æŋkəret], **anchorite** ['æŋkərait], _n._ anachorète, ermite, _m._, _f._

anchovy [æn'tʃouvi, 'æntʃəvi], _n._ anchois, _m._

ancient ['einʃənt], a. ancien; antique.—n. ancien, m.; the Ancient of Days, l'Éternel, m.

anciently ['einʃəntli], adv. anciennement.

ancillary [æn'siləri], a. ancillaire, subordonné, auxiliare.

and [ænd], conj. et; and so on, et ainsi de suite; better and better, de mieux en mieux; carriage and pair, voiture à deux chevaux, f.; go and see, allez voir.

Andes ['ændiːz], the. les Andes, f.pl.

andiron ['ændaiən], n. landier; chenet, m.

Andrew ['ændruː]. André, m.

anecdote ['ænikdout], n. anecdote, f.

anecdotal [ænik'doutl], a. anecdotique.

anemone [ə'neməni], n. anémone, f.

*anent [ə'nent], prep. touchant, sur, à propos de.

aneroid ['ænərɔid], a. and n. anéroïde, m.

aneurism ['ænjurizm], n. anévrisme, m.

anew [ə'njuː], adv. de nouveau.

angel ['eindʒəl], n. ange, m.

Angela ['ændʒələ]. Angèle, f.

angelic [æn'dʒelik], angelical [æn'dʒelikəl], a. angélique.

angelica [æn'dʒelikə], n. angélique, f.

angelus ['ændʒələs], n. angélus, m.

anger ['æŋgə], n. colère, f.; emportement; courroux, m.—v.t. fâcher, irriter, mettre en colère.

angina [æn'dʒainə], n. (Path.) angine, f.

angle (1) [æŋgl], n. angle; coin, m.

angle (2) [æŋgl], v.i. pêcher à la ligne.

angled [æŋgld], a. à angles; right-angled, rectangulaire.

angler ['æŋglə], n. pêcheur à la ligne, m.; (Ichth.) baudroie, f.; crapaud de mer, m.

Anglican ['æŋglikən], a. anglican.—n. Anglican, m.

anglicism ['æŋglisizm], n. anglicisme, m.

anglicize ['æŋglisaiz], v.t. angliciser.

angling ['æŋgliŋ], n. pêche à la ligne, f.

anglophil(e) ['æŋglə(ə)il], n. anglophile, m.,f.

Anglo-Saxon ['æŋglo'sæksən], a. anglo-saxon.—n. Anglo-Saxon, m.

angrily ['æŋgrili], adv. en colère, avec colère.

angry ['æŋgri], a. en colère, fâché, irrité (contre ou de), courroucé; to be angry with, être en colère contre, en vouloir à.

anguish ['æŋgwiʃ], n. angoisse, douleur, f.—v.t. angoisser, navrer de douleur.

angular ['æŋgjulə], a. angulaire, angulé; anguleux; maigre, décharné.

angularity [æŋgju'læriti], n. angularité, f.

angularly ['æŋgjuləli], adv. angulairement.

anile ['einail], a. de vieille femme, débile.

aniline ['ænilain], n. (Chem.) aniline, f.

anility [ə'niliti], n. seconde enfance, f., radotage, m.

animadversion [ænimæd'vəːʃən], n. animadversion, censure, critique, f.

animadvert [ænimæd'vəːt], v.i. to animadvert upon, critiquer, censurer.

animal ['ænimǝl], a. and n. animal, m.

animalism ['ænimǝlizm], animality [æni'mælitij], n. animalité, f.

animalize ['ænimǝlaiz], v.t. animaliser.

animate ['ænimeit], v.t. animer (de).—['ænimit], a. animé.

animated ['ænimeitid], a. animé, vif.

animatedly ['ænimeitidli], adv. vivement.

animating ['ænimeitiŋ], a. qui anime, qui ranime.

animation [æni'meiʃən], n. animation, vivacité, vie, f.

animator ['ænimeitə], n. animateur, m.

animosity [æni'mositi], n. animosité, f.

animus ['æniməs], n. animosité, hostilité, f.; esprit (de), m.

anise ['ænis], n. anis, m.

aniseed ['ænisiːd], n. graine d'anis, f.

ankle [æŋkl], n. cheville du pied, f.

ankle-bone ['æŋklboun], n. astragale, m.

ankle-deep ['æŋkldiːp], adv. jusqu'aux chevilles.

Anna ['ænə]. Anne, f.

annalist ['ænəlist], n. annaliste, m., f.

annals ['ænəlz], n.pl. annales, f.pl.

Ann(e) [æn]. Anne, f.

anneal [ə'niːl], v.t. détremper; adoucir (acier etc.), recuire (verre).

annealing [ə'niːliŋ], n. recuite, f.

annex [ə'neks], v.t. annexer, joindre (à).— ['æneks], n. annexe, f.

annexation [ænek'seiʃən], n. annexation, f.

annexed [ə'nekst], a. ci-joint, annexé.

annihilate [ə'naiileit], v.t. anéantir, annihiler.

annihilation [ənaii'leiʃən], n. anéantissement, m., annihilation, f.

annihilator [ə'naiileitə], n. annihilateur, m.

anniversary [æni'vəːsəri], a. and n. anniversaire, m.

Anno Domini ['ænou'dominai], (abbr. A.D. [ei'diː]). l'an du Seigneur; l'an de grâce; ap. J.-C.

annotate ['ænoteit], v.t. annoter.

annotation [æno'teiʃən], n. annotation, f.

annotator ['ænoteitə], n. annotateur, m.

announce [ə'nauns], v.t. annoncer, proclamer.

announcement [ə'naunsmənt], n. annonce, f., avis, m.; lettre de faire-part, f.

announcer [ə'naunsə], n. annonciateur; (Theat.) compère, m., commère, f.; (Rad., Tel.) speaker, m., speakerine, f.

annoy [ə'nɔi], v.t. gêner; incommoder, ennuyer, importuner; contrarier, tracasser.

annoyance [ə'nɔiəns], n. ennui, désagrément, chagrin, m.; contrariété, f.

annoying [ə'nɔiiŋ], a. ennuyeux, contrariant, vexant.

annoyingly [ə'nɔiiŋli], adv. ennuyeusement.

annual ['ænjuəl], a. annuel.—n. annuaire, m.

annually ['ænjuəli], adv. annuellement, tous les ans.

annuitant [ə'njuːitənt], n. bénéficiaire d'une pension ou d'une rente viagère, m., f.

annuity [ə'njuːiti], n. annuité, rente annuelle, pension, f.; life annuity, rente viagère, f.

annul [ə'nʌl], v.t. annuler.

annular ['ænjulə], a. annulaire.

annulet ['ænjulit], n. annelet, filet, m.

annulment [ə'nʌlmənt], n. annulation, f.; decree of annulment, décret abolitif, m.

Annunciation [ənʌnsi'eiʃən], the. (Eccles.) l'Annonciation, f.

annunciation [ənʌnsi'eiʃən], n. annonce, proclamation, f., avis, m.

anode ['ænoud], n. (Elec.) anode, f.

anodyne ['ænədain], a. anodin, calmant.—n. anodin (remède), m.

anoint [ə'nɔint], v.t. oindre.

anointed [ə'nɔintid], a. oint; *the Lord's Anointed*, l'Oint du Seigneur, m.
anomalous [ə'nɔmələs], a. anomal, irrégulier.
anomaly [ə'nɔməli], n. anomalie, f.
anon [ə'nɔn], adv. tout à l'heure, bientôt; à l'instant.
anonymity [æno'nimiti], n. anonymat, m.
anonymous [ə'nɔniməs], a. anonyme.
anonymously [ə'nɔniməsli], adv. anonymement.
another [ə'nʌðə], a. and pron. autre, un autre; encore un; *one another*, l'un l'autre, les uns les autres.
answer ['ɑ:nsə], v.t. répondre; répondre à; satisfaire, suffire à.—v.i. faire réponse; répondre (de ou pour); raisonner; réussir.— n. réponse; solution (d'un problème), f.
answerable ['ɑ:nsərəbl], a. susceptible de réponse; responsable (for, de).
ant [ænt], n. fourmi, f.
antagonism [æn'tægənizm], n. antagonisme, m., opposition, f.
antagonist [æn'tægənist], n. antagoniste, m.,f.
antagonistic [æntægə'nistik], a. opposé (à); antagonique.
antagonize [æn'tægənaiz], v.t. eveiller l'antagonisme (de).
Antarctic [ænt'ɑ:ktik], a. antarctique.—n. Antarctique, m.
ant-eater ['ænti:tə], n. fourmilier, m.
antecedence [ænti'si:dəns], n. antériorité, f.
antecedent [ænti'si:dənt], a. and n. antécédent, m.
ante-chamber ['æntitʃeimbə], n. antichambre, f.
antediluvian [æntidi'lu:viən], a. and n. antédiluvien, m.
antelope ['æntiloup], n. antilope, f.
ante-meridiem [æntimə'ridiəm], (abbr. a.m. [ei'em]), adv. avant midi; *at II a.m.*, à onze heures du matin.
ante-natal ['ænti'neitəl], a. prénatal.
antenna [æn'tenə], n. (pl. antennae [æn'teni:]) antenne, f.
antepenult [æntipi'nʌlt], antepenultimate [æntipi'nʌltimit], a. and n. antépénultième, f.
anterior [æn'tiəriə], a. antérieur.
anteroom ['æntiru:m], n. antichambre, f.
anthem ['ænθəm], n. hymne (national), m.; antienne, f.
ant-hill ['ænthil], n. fourmilière, f.
anthology [æn'θɔlədʒi], n. anthologie, chrestomathie, f.
Anthony ['æntəni]. Antoine, m.
anthracite ['ænθrəsait], n. anthracite, m.
anthrax ['ænθræks], n. (Med.) anthrax, m.
anthropoid ['ænθrəpɔid], a. and n. anthropoïde, m.
anthropological [ænθrəpə'lɔdʒikəl], a. anthropologique.
anthropologist [ænθrə'pɔlədʒist], n. anthropologiste, anthropologue, m.,f.
anthropology [ænθrə'pɔlədʒi], n. anthropologie, f.
anti-aircraft [ænti'ɛəkrɑ:ft], a. contre-avion, antiaérien.
antibiotic [æntibai'ɔtik], a. and n. antibiotique, m.
antic ['æntik], n. bouffonnerie, farce, f.

Antichrist ['æntikraist], n. antéchrist, m.
antichristian ['ænti'kristjən], a. and n. antichrétien, m.
anticipate [æn'tisipeit], v.t. anticiper; prévenir, devancer; s'attendre à, prévoir, envisager; jouir d'avance de; se promettre.
anticipation [æntisi'peiʃən], n. anticipation, f.; avant-goût, m.; attente, f.
anticipatory [æn'tisipətri], a. par anticipation.
anticlerical [ænti'klerikəl], a. and n. anticlérical, m.
anticlericalism [ænti'klerikəlizm], n. anticléricalisme, m.
anti-climax [ænti'klaimæks], n. anticlimax, m.
anti-clockwise [COUNTER-CLOCKWISE].
anticyclone [ænti'saikloun], n. anticyclone, m.
anti-dazzle ['ænti'dæzl], a. anti-aveuglant; (Motor) *anti-dazzle head lights*, phares-code, m.pl.
antidote ['æntidout], n. antidote, contre-poison, m.
anti-freeze ['æntifri:z], n. anti-gel, m.
Antilles [æn'tili:z], the. les Antilles, f.pl.
antimacassar [æntimə'kæsə], n. têtière, f.
antimony ['æntiməni], n. antimoine, m.
antinomy [æn'tinəmi], n. antinomie, f.
antipathetic [æntipə'θetik], antipathetical [æntipə'θetikəl], a. antipathique.
antipathy [æn'tipəθi], n. antipathie, aversion, f.
antiphony [æn'tifəni], n. contre-chant, m.
antiphrasis [æn'tifrəsis], n. antiphrase, f.
antipodal [æn'tipədəl], a. antipodal.
antipodes [æn'tipədi:z], n. pl. antipodes, m.pl.
anti-pope ['æntipoup], n. antipape, m.
antiquarian [ænti'kwɛəriən], a. d'antiquaire; archéologique.—n. antiquaire, m.
antiquary ['æntikwəri], n. archéologue; antiquaire, m.
antiquated ['æntikweitid], a. vieilli, vétuste; suranné, démodé.
antique [æn'ti:k], a. antique, ancien.—n. the antique, l'antique, m.; *an antique*, un objet antique, une antiquité.
antiquity [æn'tikwiti], n. antiquité; ancienneté, f.
antirrhinum [ænti'rainəm], n. antirrhine, f.
anti-Semitism [ænti'semitizm], n. antisémitisme, m.
antiseptic [ænti'septik], a. and n. antiseptique, m.
anti-tank [ænti'tæŋk], a. anti-chars, m.
antithesis [æn'tiθisis], n. antithèse, f.
antithetic [ænti'θetik], antithetical [ænti'θetikəl], a. antithétique.
antler ['æntlə], n. andouiller, bois (de cerf), m.
Antony ['æntəni]. Antoine, m.
Antwerp ['æntwə:p]. Anvers, m.
anvil ['ænvil], n. enclume, f.; (fig.) *on the anvil*, sur le métier, en préparation.
anxiety [æŋ'zaiəti], n. anxiété, inquiétude, sollicitude, f.; désir, m.
anxious ['æŋkʃəs], a. inquiet, soucieux, plein de sollicitude (pour); désireux (de); *to be anxious to*, désirer vivement (de), tenir à.
anxiously ['æŋkʃəsli], adv. anxieusement, avec anxiété, avec inquiétude.

any ['eni], *a.* and *pron.* du, de la, etc.; en; aucun; quelque; n'importe lequel; *any man*, tout homme; *any others*, d'autres; *at any rate*, en tout cas; *I haven't any*, je n'en ai pas; *scarcely any*, presque pas.

anybody ['enibɔdi], **anyone** ['eniwʌn], *pron.* quelqu'un, chacun, qui que ce soit, n'importe qui, tout le monde; *I didn't see anybody*, je n'ai vu personne.

anyhow ['enihau], **anyway** ['eniwei], *adv.* de toute façon, de quelque manière que ce soit, en tout cas, quand même.

anyone [ANYBODY].

anything ['eniθiŋ], *pron.* quelque chose, *m.*, quoi que ce soit, n'importe quoi; *not to say anything*, ne rien dire.

anyway [ANYHOW].

anywhere ['eniwɛə], *adv.* quelque part, dans quelque endroit que ce soit, n'importe où; *not anywhere*, nulle part.

apace [ə'peis], *adv.* vite, à grands pas.

apanage, appanage ['æpənidʒ], *n.* apanage, *m.*

apart [ə'paːt], *adv.* à part; de côté, séparément.

apartheid [ə'paːtheit], *n.* (*en Afrique du Sud*) ségrégation, *f.*

apartment [ə'paːtmənt], *n.* chambre; pièce (*d'un appartement*), *f.*; logement; (*Am.*) appartement; (*pl.*) appartement, *m.*

apathetic [æpə'θetik], *a.* apathique.

apathy ['æpəθi], *n.* apathie, *f.*

ape [eip], *n.* singe, *m.*, guenon, *f.*—*v.t.* singer.

aperient [ə'piəriənt], **aperitive** [ə'peritiv], *a.* and *n.* laxatif, *m.*

aperture ['æpətjuə], *n.* ouverture, *f.*; orifice, *m.*

apex ['eipeks], *n.* (*pl.* **apices** ['eipisiːz], **apexes** ['eipeksiz]) sommet, *m.*, pointe, *f.*

aphorism ['æfərizm], *n.* aphorisme, *m.*

apiary ['eipiəri], *n.* rucher, *m.*

apiece [ə'piːs], *adv.* la pièce; par tête, par personne, chacun.

apish ['eipiʃ], *a.* de singe, simiesque; *apish trick*, singerie, *f.*

apocalypse [ə'pɔkəlips], *n.* apocalypse, *f.*

apocalyptic [əpɔkə'liptik], **apocalyptical** [əpɔkə'liptikəl], *a.* apocalyptique.

Apocrypha [ə'pɔkrifə], *n.pl.* les Apocryphes, *m.pl.*

apocryphal [ə'pɔkrifəl], *a.* apocryphe.

apogee ['æpədʒiː], *n.* apogée, *f.*

apologetic [əpɔlə'dʒetik], **apologetical** [əpɔlə'dʒetikəl], *a.* qui s'excuse, qui regrette; *he was quite apologetic about it*, il s'en excusa vivement.

apologetically [əpɔlə'dʒetikəli], *adv.* pour s'excuser, en s'excusant.

apologia [æpə'loudʒiə], *n.* apologie; justification, *f.*

apologist [ə'pɔlədʒist], *n.* apologiste, *m.*, *f.*

apologize [ə'pɔlədʒaiz], *v.i.* s'excuser, faire des excuses (*de* ou *auprès de*).

apologue ['æpəlɔg], *n.* apologue, *m.*

apology [ə'pɔlədʒi], *n.* excuses, *f.pl.*, apologie, *f.*

apoplectic [æpə'plektik], *a.* apoplectique; *apoplectic stroke*, coup de sang, *m.*

apoplexy ['æpəpleksi], *n.* apoplexie, *f.*; *a fit of apoplexy*, congestion cérébrale, *f.*

apostasy [ə'pɔstəsi], *n.* apostasie, *f.*

apostate [ə'pɔsteit], *a.* and *n.* apostat, *m.*

apostle [ə'pɔsl], *n.* apôtre, *m.*; *the Acts of the Apostles*, les actes des apôtres, *m.pl.*

apostolic [æpəs'tɔlik], **apostolical** [æpəs'tɔlikəl], *a.* apostolique.

apostrophe [ə'pɔstrəfi], *n.* apostrophe, *f.*

apostrophize [ə'pɔstrəfaiz], *v.t.* apostropher.

apothecary [ə'pɔθikəri], *n.* apothicaire; pharmacien, *m.*

apotheosis [əpɔθi'ousis], *n.* apothéose, *f.*

appal [ə'pɔːl], *v.t.* épouvanter, consterner.

appalling [ə'pɔːliŋ], *a.* épouvantable, effrayant.

appallingly [ə'pɔːliŋli], *adv.* épouvantablement.

appanage [APANAGE].

apparatus [æpə'reitəs], *n.* appareil, dispositif, *m.*

apparel [ə'pærəl], *v.t.* vêtir; parer.—*n.* habillement, vêtement, *m.*

apparent [ə'pærənt], *a.* évident, manifeste, apparent; *heir apparent*, héritier présomptif, *m.*

apparently [ə'pærəntli], *adv.* en apparence, apparemment.

apparition [æpə'riʃən], *n.* apparition, *f.*

appeal [ə'piːl], *v.i.* appeler, en appeler (*de*), faire appel (*à*); (*Law*) se pourvoir en cassation, réclamer (*contre* ou *à*); (*fig.*) attirer, séduire.—*n.* appel, attrait, *m.*; *Court of Appeal*, cour de cassation, *f.*

appealing [ə'piːliŋ], *a.* suppliant, attrayant, séduisant.

appear [ə'piə], *v.i.* paraître, apparaître; se montrer, se présenter (*à*).

appearance [ə'piərəns], *n.* apparition; apparence, figure, mine, *f.*, air, aspect, *m.*; (*Law*) comparution, *f.*; *at first appearance*, au premier abord, au premier coup d'œil.

appeasable [ə'piːzəbl], *a.* qu'on peut apaiser.

appease [ə'piːz], *v.t.* apaiser, pacifier.

appeasement [ə'piːzmənt], *n.* apaisement, adoucissement, *m.*; conciliation, *f.*

appellant [ə'pelənt], *a.* and *n.* (*Law*) appelant, *m.*

appellation [æpə'leiʃən], *n.* nom, *m.*, appellation, dénomination, *f.*

append [ə'pend], *v.t.* apposer, attacher (*à*).

appendage [ə'pendidʒ], *n.* accessoire, apanage, *m.*

appendant [ə'pendənt], *a.* accessoire, attaché, annexé (*à*).

appendicitis [əpendi'saitis], *n.* appendicite, *f.*

appendix [ə'pendiks], *n.* (*pl.* **appendixes** [ə'pendiksiz], **appendices** [ə'pendisiːz]) appendice, *m.*

appertain [æpə'tein], *v.i.* appartenir (*à*).

appetite ['æpitait], *n.* appétit; (*fig.*) désir, *m.*, soif, *f.*

appetize ['æpitaiz], *v.t.* mettre en appétit.

appetizer ['æpitaizə], *n.* apéritif, *m.*

appetizing ['æpitaiziŋ], *a.* appétissant.

applaud [ə'plɔːd], *v.t.*, *v.i.* applaudir (*à*).

applause [ə'plɔːz], *n.* applaudissements, *m.pl.*

apple [æpl], *n.* pomme, *f.*; *apple of the eye*, prunelle, *f.*

apple-pie ['æpl'pai], *n.* tourte aux pommes, *f.*

apple-sauce ['æpl'sɔːs], *n.* compote de pommes, *f.*

apple-tart ['æpl'taːt], *n.* tarte aux pommes, *f.*

apple-tree ['æpltriː], *n.* pommier, *m.*

appliance [ə'plaiəns], *n.* instrument, appareil, dispositif, *m.*

applicability [æplikə'biliti], **applicableness** ['æplikəblnis], *n.* applicabilité, *f.*

applicable ['æplikəbl], *a.* applicable.

applicant ['æplikənt], *n.* postulant, candidat; (*Law*) demandeur, *m.*

application [æpli'keiʃən], *n.* application; sollicitation, demande, *f.*; usage, *m.*; *for external application*, usage externe; *on application*, sur demande; *to make application to*, s'adresser à, faire une demande à.

apply [ə'plai], *v.t.* appliquer (*à*); *to apply the brake*, freiner; serrer le frein.—*v.i.* s'adresser (*à*); s'appliquer, être applicable; *to apply for* (*a job*), faire une demande (d'emploi); *to apply to*, s'adresser à *ou* chez.

appoint [ə'pɔint], *v.t.* arrêter, désigner, fixer; nommer; installer, équiper; *at the appointed hour*, à l'heure convenue; *a well-appointed house*, une maison bien installée.

appointment [ə'pɔintmənt], *n.* nomination, *f.*; décret, arrêt; établissement; emploi; rendez-vous, *m.*; convocation, *f.*

apportion [ə'pɔːʃən], *v.t.* partager, répartir, assigner.

apportionment [ə'pɔːʃənmənt], *n.* répartition, *f.*, partage, *m.*

apposite ['æpəzait], *a.* juste; à propos; approprié, convenable (*à*).

appositely ['æpəzaitli], *adv.* convenablement, justement, à propos.

appositeness ['æpəzaitnis], *n.* à-propos, *m.*, opportunité, *f.*

appraisal [APPRAISMENT].

appraise [ə'preiz], *v.t.* priser, évaluer, estimer.

appraisement [ə'preizmənt], **appraisal** [ə'preizəl], *n.* évaluation, estimation; expertise, *f.*

appraiser [ə'preizə], *n.* commissaire-priseur, expert, *m.*

appreciable [ə'priːʃəbl], *a.* appréciable, sensible.

appreciably [ə'priːʃəbli], *adv.* sensiblement.

appreciate [ə'priːʃieit], *v.t.* apprécier, estimer.—*v.i.* (*Comm. etc.*) augmenter de valeur.

appreciation [əpriːʃi'eiʃən], *n.* appréciation; hausse de valeur, *f.*

appreciative [ə'priːʃjətiv], *a.* appréciateur.

apprehend [æpri'hend], *v.t.* comprendre; prendre, saisir, arrêter, appréhender; craindre.

apprehension [æpri'henʃən], *n.* appréhension; arrestation, prise de corps; crainte, inquiétude, *f.*

apprehensive [æpri'hensiv], *a.* intelligent, prompt à saisir; appréhensif, inquiet.

apprentice [ə'prentis], *n.* apprenti, *m.*—*v.t.* mettre en apprentissage.

apprenticeship [ə'prentisʃip], *n.* apprentissage, *m.*

apprise [ə'praiz], *v.t.* prévenir; informer, instruire.

approach [ə'proutʃ], *n.* approche, *f.*; abord, accès; rapprochement, *m.*; (*Math.*) approximation, *f.*—*v.t.* approcher de, s'approcher de, aborder; (*fig.*) pressentir, tâter (*quelqu'un*).—*v.i.* approcher, s'approcher.

approachable [ə'proutʃəbl], *a.* abordable, accessible.

approbation [æpro'beiʃən], *n.* approbation, *f.*; *on approbation*, à condition, à l'essai.

appropriate [ə'prouprieit], *v.t.* approprier, affecter (*à*); s'approprier; s'emparer de.—[ə'proupriət], *a.* approprié; propre, convenable (*à*).

appropriately [ə'proupriətli], *adv.* à juste titre; convenablement.

appropriateness [ə'proupriətnis], *n.* convenance, *f.*, à-propos, *m.*, justesse, *f.*

appropriation [əproupri'eiʃən], *n.* application, destination, appropriation, *f.*; crédit (*budgétaire*), *m.*

approval [ə'pruːvəl], *n.* approbation, *f.*; *on approval*, à condition.

approve [ə'pruːv], *v.t.* approuver; trouver bon (*que, with subj.*).

approver [ə'pruːvə], *n.* approbateur, *m.*

approving [ə'pruːviŋ], *a.* approbateur, approbatif.

approvingly [ə'pruːviŋli], *adv.* avec approbation, d'un air approbateur.

approximate [ə'prɔksimeit], *v.t.* rapprocher.—*v.i.* se rapprocher (*de*).—[ə'prɔksimit], *a.* approximatif.

approximately [ə'prɔksimitli], *adv.* approximativement, à peu près.

approximation [əprɔksi'meiʃən], *n.* approximation, *f.*; rapprochement, *m.*

appulse [ə'pʌls], *n.* choc, *m.*

appurtenance [ə'pəːtinəns], *n.* appartenance, dépendance, *f.*; (*pl.*) accessoires, *m.pl.*

appurtenant [ə'pəːtinənt], *a.* appartenant (*à*), dépendant (*de*).

apricot ['eiprikɔt], *n.* abricot, *m.*

apricot-tree ['eiprikɔttriː], *n.* abricotier, *m.*

April ['eipril], *n.* avril, *m.*; *to make an April fool of*, donner un poisson d'avril à.

apron ['eiprən], *n.* tablier, *m.*; (*Av.*) aire de manœuvre *ou* d'atterrissage, *f.*

apron-stage ['eiprənsteidʒ], *n.* avant-scène, *f.*

apse [æps], **apsis** ['æpsis], *n.* (*pl.* **apses** ['æpsiːz], **apsides** [æp'saidiːz]) abside, *f.*; (*Astron.*) apside, *f.*

apt [æpt], *a.* sujet, enclin, porté (*à*); propre, convenable (*à*); capable; juste (*mot*).

aptitude ['æptitjuːd], **aptness** ['æptnis], *n.* aptitude, disposition, *f.*

aptly ['æptli], *adv.* à propos; convenablement.

aqua-fortis [ækwə'fɔːtis], *n.* eau-forte, *f.*

aquamarine [ækwəmə'riːn], *n.* aigue-marine, *f.*

aqua-regia [ækwə'riːdʒiə], *n.* eau régale, *f.*

aquarium [ə'kweəriəm], *n.* aquarium, *m.*

aquatic [ə'kwɔtik, ə'kwætik], *a.* aquatique.

aquatics [ə'kwætiks], **aquatic sports** [ə'kwætikspɔːts], *n.pl.* sports nautiques, *m.pl.*

aquavitae [ækwə'vaitiː], *n.* eau de vie, *f.*

aqueduct ['ækwidʌkt], *n.* aqueduc, *m.*

aqueous ['eikwiəs], *a.* aqueux.

aquiline ['ækwilain], *a.* aquilin, d'aigle.

Arab ['ærəb], *a.* arabe.—*n.* Arabe, *m.*, *f.*

arabesque [ærə'besk], *a.* and *n.* arabesque, *f.*

Arabia [ə'reibjə], l'Arabie, *f.*; *Saudi Arabia*, l'Arabie Séoudite.

Arabian [ə'reibiən], *a.* arabe.

Arabic ['ærəbik], *a.* arabe, arabique; *Arabic figures*, chiffres arabes, *m.pl.*—*n.* arabe (*langue*), *m.*
arable ['ærəbl], *a.* arable, labourable.
arbalest ['ɑːbəlest], *n.* arbalète, *f.*
arbiter ['ɑːbitə], *n.* arbitre, *m., f.*
arbitrament [ɑːˈbitrəmənt], *n.* arbitrage, *m.*, arbitration, *f.*; jugement, *m.*
arbitrarily ['ɑːbitrərəli], *adv.* arbitrairement.
arbitrary ['ɑːbitrəri], *a.* arbitraire.
arbitrate ['ɑːbitreit], *v.t., v.i.* arbitrer, décider.
arbitration [ɑːbiˈtreiʃən], *n.* arbitrage, *m.*
arbitrator ['ɑːbitreitə], *n.* arbitre, *m., f.*
arbour ['ɑːbə], *n.* berceau, *m.*, tonnelle, *f.*
arbutus [ɑːˈbjuːtəs], *n.* arbousier, *m.*
arc [ɑːk], *n.* arc, *m.*
arcade [ɑːˈkeid], *n.* arcade, *f.*; passage, *m.*
arch [ɑːtʃ], *a.* moqueur, malin, espiègle; grand, maître, archi-, insigne, fieffé.—*n.* arche, *f.*; arc, cintre, *m.*, voûte, *f.*; *pointed arch*, ogive, *f.*; *triumphal arch*, arc de triomphe.—*v.t.* voûter, cintrer, arquer.
archaeological [ɑːkiəˈlɔdʒikəl], *a.* archéologique.
archaeologist [ɑːkiˈɔlədʒist], *n.* archéologue, *m., f.*
archaeology [ɑːkiˈɔlədʒi], *n.* archéologie, *f.*
archaic [ɑːˈkeiik], *a.* archaïque.
archaism ['ɑːkeiizm], *n.* archaïsme, *m.*
archangel ['ɑːkeindʒəl], *n.* archange, *m.*
archbishop [ɑːtʃˈbiʃəp], *n.* archevêque, *m.*
archbishopric [ɑːtʃˈbiʃəprik], *n.* archevêché, *m.*
archdeacon [ɑːtʃˈdiːkən], *n.* archidiacre, *m.*
archduchess [ɑːtʃˈdʌtʃis], *n.* archiduchesse, *f.*
archduchy [ɑːtʃˈdʌtʃi], *n.* archiduché, *m.*
archduke [ɑːtʃˈdjuːk], *n.* archiduc, *m.*
archer ['ɑːtʃə], *n.* archer, *m.*; (*Astron.*) *the Archer*, Sagittaire, *m.*
archery ['ɑːtʃəri], *n.* tir à l'arc, *m.*
archetype ['ɑːkitaip], *n.* archétype; étalon (*mesure*), *m.*
archiepiscopal [ɑːkiəˈpiskəpəl], *a.* archiépiscopal.
archipelago [ɑːkiˈpeləgou], *n.* archipel, *m.*
architect ['ɑːkitekt], *n.* architecte; (*fig.*) artisan, *m.*
architectural [ɑːkiˈtektʃərəl], *a.* architectural.
architecture ['ɑːkitektʃə], *n.* architecture, *f.*
archives ['ɑːkaivz], *n. pl.* archives, *f.pl.*
archivist ['ɑːkivist], *n.* archiviste, *m., f.*
archly ['ɑːtʃli], *adv.* avec espièglerie, d'un air malin.
archness ['ɑːtʃnis], *n.* malice, espièglerie, *f.*
arc-lamp ['ɑːklæmp], *n.* lampe à arc, *f.*
Arctic ['ɑːktik], *a.* arctique.
ardent ['ɑːdənt], *a.* ardent; *ardent spirits*, spiritueux, *m.pl.*
ardently ['ɑːdəntli], *adv.* ardemment, avec ardeur.
ardour ['ɑːdə], *n.* ardeur, *f.*
arduous ['ɑːdjuəs], *a.* ardu, rude, pénible, difficile.
arduously ['ɑːdjuəsli], *adv.* difficilement, péniblement.
arduousness ['ɑːdjuəsnis], *n.* difficulté, *f.*
area ['ɛəriə], *n.* étendue; aire, surface, superficie; région, zone; courette d'entrée (*devant la maison*), *f.*; *area steps*, escalier de service, *m.*; *postal area*, zone postale, *f.*

arena [əˈriːnə], *n.* arène, *f.*
argent ['ɑːdʒənt], *a.* argenté.—*n.* (*Her.*) argent, *m.*
Argentina [ɑːdʒənˈtiːnə], l'Argentine, la République Argentine, *f.*
Argentine ['ɑːdʒəntain], *a.* argentin.—*n.* Argentin, *m.*; *the Argentine* [ARGENTINA].
Argentinian [ɑːdʒənˈtinjən], *a.* argentin.—*n.* Argentin (*personne*), *m.*
argil ['ɑːdʒil], *n.* argile, *f.*
argonaut ['ɑːgənɔːt], *n.* argonaute, *m.*
argosy ['ɑːgəsi], *n.* caraque, *f.*
argue ['ɑːgjuː], *v.t.* discuter; soutenir; (*fig.*) dénoter, indiquer, accuser.—*v.i.* argumenter (*contre*), raisonner (*sur*), discuter (*avec*); (*Law*) plaider.
argument ['ɑːgjumənt], *n.* argument, raisonnement, *m.*; discussion, dispute; thèse, *f.*; *for argument's sake*, à titre d'exemple.
argumentative [ɑːgjuˈmentətiv], *a.* raisonneur; disposé à argumenter.
aria ['ɑːriə], *n.* aria, *f.*
arid ['ærid], *a.* aride.
aridity [əˈriditi], **aridness** ['æridnis], *n.* aridité, *f.*
aright [əˈrait], *adv.* correctement; bien.
arise [əˈraiz], *v.i. irr.* (*conjug. like* RISE) se lever; s'élever; survenir, se présenter; provenir, résulter (*de*); *if the question arises*, le cas échéant.
aristocracy [ærisˈtɔkrəsi], *n.* aristocratie, *f.*
aristocrat ['æristəkræt], *n.* aristocrate, *m., f.*
aristocratic [æristəˈkrætik], *a.* aristocratique.
arithmetic [əˈriθmətik], *n.* arithmétique, *f.*, calcul, *m.*
arithmetical [æriˈθmetikəl], *a.* arithmétique.
arithmetically [æriˈθmetikəli], *adv.* arithmétiquement.
arithmetician [æriθməˈtiʃən], *n.* arithméticien, *m.*
ark [ɑːk], *n.* arche, *f.*; *Noah's ark*, l'arche de Noé.
arm [ɑːm], *n.* bras, *m.*; arme (*à feu*), *f.*; (*pl.*) (*Her.*) armes, armoiries, *f.pl.*; *arm in arm*, bras dessus bras dessous; *with arms folded*, les bras croisés; *with open arms*, à bras ouverts.—*v.t.* armer; donner des armes à.—*v.i.* armer; s'armer (*de*); prendre les armes.
armada [ɑːˈmɑːdə], *n.* armada, *f.*
armadillo [ɑːməˈdilou], *n.* tatou, *m.*
armament ['ɑːməmənt], *n.* armement, *m.*, armée, flotte, *f.*; *armaments race*, course aux armements, *f.*
armature ['ɑːmətjuə], *n.* armature, *f.*, induit, *m.*
arm-band ['ɑːmbænd], *n.* brassard, *m.*
arm-chair ['ɑːmtʃɛə], *n.* fauteuil, *m.*
Armenia [ɑːˈmiːniə], l'Arménie, *f.*
Armenian [ɑːˈmiːniən], *a.* arménien.—*n.* arménien (*langue*); Arménien (*personne*), *m.*
armful ['ɑːmful], *n.* brassée, *f.*
arm-hole ['ɑːmhoul], *n.* emmanchure, entournure, *f.*
armistice ['ɑːmistis], *n.* armistice, *m.*
armless ['ɑːmlis], *a.* sans bras.
armlet ['ɑːmlit], *n.* brassard; bracelet; petit bras (*de mer*), *m.*
armorial [ɑːˈmɔːriəl], *a.* armorial; *armorial bearings*, armoiries, *f.pl.*
armour ['ɑːmə], *n.* armure, *f.*; blindés, *m.pl.* —*v.t.* cuirasser, blinder.

ascetic

ascribable [ə'skraibəbl], *a.* attribuable, imputable.

ascribe [ə'skraib], *v.t.* attribuer, imputer (*à*).

aseptic [æ'septik], *a.* and *n.* aseptique, *m.*

asexual [æ'seksjuəl], *a.* asexué, asexuel.

ash (1) [æʃ], *a.* de frêne.—*n.* frêne (*arbre*); bâton, *m.*; **mountain-ash**, sorbier, *m.*

ash (2) [æʃ], *n.* cendre, *f.*; cendres, *f.pl.*

ashamed [ə'ʃeimd], *a.* honteux, confus; **to be ashamed of**, avoir honte de.

ash-bin, -pit ['æʃbin, -pit], *n.* cendrier, *m.*

ashcan ['æʃkæn], *n.* (*Am.*) boîte à ordures, *f.*

ashen (1) [æʃn], *a.* de frêne.

ashen (2) [æʃn], *a.* cendré; gris pâle.

ashore [ə'ʃɔː], *adv.* à terre; échoué (*navire*); **to go ashore**, débarquer.

ash-pit [ASH-BIN].

ashtray ['æʃtrei], *n.* cendrier, *m.*

Ash Wednesday [æʃ'wenzdi]. mercredi des Cendres, *m.*

ashy ['æʃi], *a.* cendré; gris pâle.

Asia ['eiʃə], l'Asie, *f.*

Asia Minor ['eiʃə'mainə]. l'Asie-Mineure, *f.*

Asiatic [eiʃi'ætik], **Asian** ['eiʃən], *a.* asiatique. —*n.* Asiatique (*personne*), *m.,f.*

aside [ə'said], *adv.* de côté; (*Theat.*) à part; à l'écart.—*n.* (*Theat.*) aparté, *m.*

asinine ['æsinain], *a.* d'âne; sot.

ask [ɑːsk], *v.t.* demander, prier (*de*); inviter (*à*); s'informer, se renseigner; poser (*une question*); **to ask in**, prier d'entrer; **to ask someone to do something**, demander à quelqu'un de faire quelque chose; **to ask to see**, demander à voir.

askance [ə'skɑːns], *adv.* de travers, obliquement.

askew [ə'skjuː], *adv.* de côté, de biais.

aslant [ə'slɑːnt], *adv.* obliquement, de biais, de côté, en travers.

asleep [ə'sliːp], *a.* endormi; **to be asleep**, dormir; **to fall asleep**, s'endormir.

asp (1) [æsp], **aspic** ['æspik], *n.* aspic, *m.*

asp (2) [æsp], **aspen** ['æspən], *n.* tremble, *m.*

asparagus [əs'pærəgəs], *n.* asperges, *f.pl.*

aspect ['æspekt], *n.* aspect, *m.*; exposition, *f.*; **to have a southern aspect**, être exposé au midi.

aspen ['æspən], *a.* de tremble.—*n.* [ASP (2)].

asperity [æs'periti], *n.* aspérité, âpreté, rudesse, *f.*

aspersion [æs'pɔːʃən], *n.* calomnie, *f.*; **to cast aspersions on**, répandre des calomnies sur.

asphalt ['æsfælt], *a.* d'asphalte.—*n.* asphalte, *m.*

asphyxia [æs'fiksiə], *n.* asphyxie, *f.*

asphyxiate [æs'fiksieit], *v.t.* asphyxier.

aspic [ASP (1)].

aspirant [ə'spaiərənt], *n.* aspirant, candidat, *m.*

aspirate ['æspireit], *v.t.* aspirer.—['æspirit] *a.* aspiré.

aspiration [æspi'reiʃən], *n.* aspiration, *f.*

aspire [ə'spaiə], *v.i.* aspirer (*à*), ambitionner.

aspirin ['æspirin], *n.* aspirine, *f.*

asquint [ə'skwint], *adv.* de travers, en louchant.

ass [æs], *n.* âne, *m.*; *he is a silly ass*, il est bête à manger du foin; *she-ass*, ânesse, *f.*; **to make an ass of oneself**, agir sottement; **young ass**, ânon, *m.*

assail [ə'seil], *v.t.* assaillir, attaquer.

assailant [ə'seilənt], *n.* assaillant, *m.*

assassin [ə'sæsin], *n.* assassin (*politique*), *m.*

assassinate [ə'sæsineit], *v.t.* assassiner.

assassination [əsæsi'neiʃən], *n.* assassinat, *m.*

assault [ə'sɔːlt], *n.* assaut, *m.*, attaque brusquée; (*Law*) tentative de voie de fait, *f.*; **assault and battery**, voies de fait, *f.pl.*; **indecent assault**, outrage aux mœurs, *m.* —*v.t.* assaillir, attaquer.

assay [ə'sei], *n.* épreuve, vérification, *f.*; essai, *m.*—*v.t.* essayer.

assemble [ə'sembl], *v.t.* assembler, réunir.— *v.i.* s'assembler, se réunir.

assembly [ə'sembli], *n.* assemblée, réunion, *f.*; assemblage (*d'une machine*), *m.*; **assembly line**, chaîne de montage, *f.*

assent [ə'sent], *v.i.* donner son assentiment (*à*), admettre.—*n.* assentiment, consentement, *m.*

assert [ə'sɔːt], *v.t.* affirmer, prétendre, soutenir; revendiquer, faire valoir (*ses droits etc.*).

assertion [ə'sɔːʃən], *n.* assertion, revendication, *f.*

assertive [ə'sɔːtiv], *a.* assertif.

assertively [ə'sɔːtivli], *adv.* d'un ton péremptoire.

assess [ə'ses], *v.t.* répartir, fixer; imposer; évaluer.

assessment [ə'sesmənt], *n.* imposition, répartition, assiette; évaluation, *f.*

assessor [ə'sesə], *n.* assesseur; répartiteur, *f.*

asset ['æset], *n.* avoir; avantage, *m.*

assets ['æsets], *n.pl.* actif, *m*; **assets and liabilities**, actif et passif, *m.*; **personal assets**, biens meubles, *m.pl.*; **real assets**, biens immobiliers, *m.pl.*

asseverate [ə'sevəreit], *v.t.* affirmer solennellement.

assiduity [æsi'djuːiti], *n.* assiduité, *f.*

assiduous [ə'sidjuəs], *a.* assidu.

assiduously [ə'sidjuəsli], *adv.* assidûment.

assign [ə'sain], *v.t.* assigner, attribuer; transférer (*à*).—*n.* (*Law*) ayant droit, *m.*

assignation [æsig'neiʃən], *n.* attribution, assignation, cession, *f.*; rendez-vous, *m.*

assignee [æsi'niː], *n.* cessionnaire, *m.,f.*; syndic (*de faillite*), *m.*

assimilate [ə'simileit], *v.t.* assimiler.—*v.i.* s'assimiler.

assimilation [əsimi'leiʃən], *n.* assimilation, *f.*

assist [ə'sist], *v.t.* aider; **to assist each other**, s'entr'aider.

assistance [ə'sistəns], *n.* assistance, aide, *f.*; secours, concours, *m.*

assistant [ə'sistənt], *a.* qui aide, auxiliaire.— *n.* aide; adjoint; commis (*dans une boutique*), *m.*; **assistant examiner**, examinateur adjoint, *m.*; **assistant manager**, sous-directeur, *m.*

assizes [ə'saiziz], *n. pl.* assises, *f.pl.*

associate [ə'souʃieit], *v.t.* associer (*avec* ou *à*). —*v.i.* s'associer (*avec* ou *à*); **to associate with**, fréquenter.—[ə'souʃiit], *a.* associé.— *n.* associé, *m.*; complice, *m.,f.*

association [əsousi'eiʃən], *n.* association, *f.*; souvenir, *m.*

assort [ə'sɔːt], *v.t.* assortir.

assorted [ə'sɔːtid], *a.* assorti.

assortment [ə'sɔːtmənt], *n.* assortiment, *m.*; classification, *f.*

assuage [ə'sweidʒ], v.t. adoucir, apaiser
calmer, soulager.—v.i. s'apaiser, se calmer.
assume [ə'sju:m], v.t. prendre sur soi,
s'arroger, s'attribuer; assumer (une responsabilité); supposer, présumer; se donner;
affecter.
assuming [ə'sju:miŋ], a. arrogant, présomptueux, prétentieux; assuming that, en
supposant que.
assumption [ə'sʌmpʃən], n. supposition;
prétention, f.; (Eccles.) the Assumption,
l'Assomption (de la Sainte Vierge), f.
assurance [ə'ʃuərəns], n. assurance, f.
assure [ə'ʃuə], v.t. assurer.
assuredly [ə'ʃuəridli], adv. assurément, à
coup sûr.
Assyria [ə'siriə]. l'Assyrie, f.
Assyrian [ə'siriən], a. assyrien.—n. assyrien
(langue); Assyrien (personne), m.
aster ['æstə], n. (Bot., Biol.) aster, m.
asterisk ['æstərisk], n. astérisque, m.
astern [ə'stə:n], adv. (Naut.) à l'arrière, sur
l'arrière; to go astern, culer.
asteroid ['æstərɔid], n. astéroïde, m.
asthma ['æsθmə], n. asthme, m.
asthmatic [æsθ'mætik], a. asthmatique.
astigmatism [ə'stigmətizm], n. astigmatisme,
m.
astir [ə'stə:], a. en mouvement, agité, en
émoi; debout.
astonish [ə'stɔniʃ], v.t. étonner.
astonishing [ə'stɔniʃiŋ], a. étonnant.
astonishment [ə'stɔniʃmənt], n. étonnement,
m.
astound [ə'staund], v.t. étonner, ébahir,
étourdir.
astounding [ə'staundiŋ], a. renversant,
abasourdissant.
astray [ə'strei], adv. égaré, (fig.) dévoyé; to
go astray, s'égarer.
astride [ə'straid], adv. à califourchon;
astride upon, à cheval sur.
astringent [ə'strindʒənt], a. and n. astringent, m.
astrologer [ə'strɔlədʒə], n. astrologue, m.,f.
astrology [ə'strɔlədʒi], n. astrologie, f.
astronaut ['æstrənɔ:t], n. astronaute, m.,f.
astronomer [ə'strɔnəmə], n. astronome, m.,f.
astronomical [æstrə'nɔmikəl], astronomical
[æstrə'nɔmikəl], a. astronomique.
astronomy [ə'strɔnəmi], n. astronomie, f.
astute [ə'stju:t], a. fin, avisé; rusé, astucieux.
astuteness [ə'stju:tnis], n. astuce, sagacité, f.
asunder [ə'sʌndə], adv. en deux.
asylum [ə'sailəm], n. asile, refuge; hospice, m.
at [æt], prep. à, en, dans; après; at first
d'abord; at hand, sous la main; at home,
chez soi; at last, enfin; at least, (quantity)
au moins; (fig.) du moins; at once, tout
de suite; à la fois; at school, à l'école;
at the same time, en même temps; at
work, à l'ouvrage.
atheism ['eiθiizm], n. athéisme, m.
atheist ['eiθiist], n. athée, m., f.
atheistic [eiθi'istik], a. athée, athéistique.
Athens ['æθənz]. Athènes, f.
athirst [ə'θə:st], a. altéré, assoiffé.
athlete ['æθli:t], n. athlète, m., f.
athletic [æθ'letik], a. athlétique.
athletics [æθ'letiks], n. pl. l'athlétisme, m.
Atlantic [ət'læntik], a. atlantique.—n.
l'(Océan) Atlantique, m.

atlas ['ætləs], n. atlas, m.
atmosphere ['ætməsfiə], n. atmosphère, f.
atmospheric [ætməs'ferik], atmospherical
[ætməs'ferikəl], a. atmosphérique.
atmospherics [ætməs'feriks], n.pl. (Rad.)
parasites, m.pl.
atoll ['ætɔl], n. atoll, attoll, m.
atom ['ætəm], n. atome, m.; atom bomb,
bombe atomique, f.
atomic [ə'tɔmik], a. atomique.
atomize ['ætəmaiz], v.t. pulvériser, vaporiser.
atomizer ['ætəmaizə], n. pulvérisateur, m.
atone [ə'toun], v.t., v.i. expier; racheter.
atonement [ə'tounmənt], n. expiation, f.
atop [ə'tɔp], adv. au sommet, en haut.
atrocious [ə'trouʃəs], a. atroce.
atrociously [ə'trouʃəsli], adv. atrocement.
atrocity [ə'trɔsiti], n. atrocité, f.
atrophy ['ætrəfi], n. atrophie, f.—v.t. atrophier.—v.i. s'atrophier.
attach [ə'tætʃ], v.t. attacher, lier (à).
attachable [ə'tætʃəbl], a. qu'on peut attacher.
attaché-case [ə'tæʃikeis], n. mallette, f.
attachment [ə'tætʃmənt], n. attachement, m.
attack [ə'tæk], v.t. attaquer.—n. attaque, f.,
accès, assaut, m.
attacker [ə'tækə], n. agresseur, m.
attain [ə'tein], v.t. atteindre, parvenir à.
attainable [ə'teinəbl], a. qu'on peut atteindre.
attainment [ə'teinmənt], n. acquisition, f.;
talent, m.; (pl.) connaissances, f.pl.
attaint [ə'teint], v.t. accuser; condamner;
flétrir, dégrader.
attempt [ə'tempt], v.t. tenter, essayer
tâcher (de).—n. tentative, f., essai, effort;
attentat, m.
attend [ə'tend], v.t. s'occuper de; soigner (un
malade); servir; assister (à).—v.i. faire
attention, écouter; assister (à); servir; s'appliquer (à).
attendance [ə'tendəns], n. service, m.;
assistance (à une réunion); présence; fréquentation (scolaire), f.; soins (pour un
malade), m.pl.
attendant [ə'tendənt], a. qui suit.—n. assistant, aide; serviteur, m.
attention [ə'tenʃən], n. attention, f.; (pl.)
soins, m.pl.
attentive [ə'tentiv], a. attentif (à), assidu
(auprès de).
attentively [ə'tentivli], adv. attentivement.
attest [ə'test], v.t. attester.
attic ['ætik], n. mansarde, f., grenier, m.
attire [ə'taiə], v.t. vêtir, parer.—n. vêtements
m.pl., costume, m.; parure, f., atours, m.pl.
attitude [ə'titju:d], n. attitude, pose, f.
attorney [ə'tə:ni], n. (Am.) avoué; mandataire, m.; power of attorney, procuration, f.
attorney-general [ə'tə:ni'dʒenərəl], n. pro-
cureur-général, m.
attract [ə'trækt], v.t. attirer.
attraction [ə'trækʃən], n. attraction, f.; (pl.)
attraits, appas, m.pl.
attractive [ə'træktiv], a. attrayant, séduisant;
attractif (de l'aimant etc.).
attractiveness [ə'træktivnis], n. attrait,
charme, m.
attributable [ə'tribjutəbl], a. attribuable.
attribute [ə'tribju:t], v.t. attribuer, imputer
(à).—['ætribju:t], n. attribut, m., qualité, f.

attrition [ə'triʃən], *n.* attrition, *f.*; *war of attrition*, guerre d'usure, *f.*

attune [ə'tjuːn], *v.t.* accorder.

auburn ['ɔːbən], *a.* châtain roux.

auction ['ɔːkʃən], *n.* enchère, *f.*—*v.t.* vendre aux enchères.

auctioneer [ɔːkʃə'niə], *n.* commissaire-priseur, *m.*

auction-room ['ɔːkʃənruːm], *n.* salle des ventes, *f.*

audacious [ɔː'deiʃəs], *a.* audacieux.

audaciously [ɔː'deiʃəsli], *adv.* audacieusement.

audacity [ɔː'dæsiti], *n.* audace, *f.*

audible ['ɔːdibl], *a.* qu'on peut entendre, audible; distinct, intelligible.

audibly ['ɔːdibli], *adv.* de manière à être entendu.

audience ['ɔːdjəns], *n.* auditoire, *m.*, assistance, audience, *f.*

audio-visual ['ɔːdjo'vizjuəl], *a.* audio-visuel.

audit ['ɔːdit], *v.t.* apurer, vérifier (*des comptes*).—*n.* apurement, *m.*, vérification de comptes, *f.*; *audit office*, cour des comptes, *f.*

audition [ɔː'diʃən], *n.* audition, *f.*—*v.t.* (*fam.*) auditionner.

auditor ['ɔːditə], *n.* vérificateur; expert comptable, *m.*

auger ['ɔːgə], *n.* tarière, *f.*

aught [ɔːt], *n.* quelque chose; quoi que ce soit, *m.*; *for aught I know*, pour autant que je sache.

augment [ɔːg'ment], *v.t.* augmenter, accroître.

augur ['ɔːgə], *v.t., v.i.* augurer, présager.—*n.* augure, *m.*

augury ['ɔːgjuri], *n.* augure, *m.*

August ['ɔːgəst]. août, *m.*; *in August*, en août.

august [ɔː'gʌst], *a.* auguste, imposant.

auk [ɔːk], *n.* (*Orn.*) pingouin, *m.*

aunt [aːnt], *n.* tante, *f.*

auntie ['aːnti], *n.* (*colloq.*) tata, *f.*

aura ['ɔːrə], *n.* exhalaison, *f.*, effluve, *m.*

aural ['ɔːrəl], *a.* de l'oreille.

Aurora [ɔː'rɔːrə], *n.* aurore, *f.*; *Aurora Borealis*, aurore boréale.

auspice ['ɔːspis], *n.* (*usu. in pl.*) auspice, *m.*

auspicious [ɔː'spiʃəs], *a.* de bon augure, propice.

auspiciously [ɔː'spiʃəsli], *adv.* sous d'heureux auspices.

austere [ɔːs'tiə], *a.* austère; âpre.

austerity [ɔːs'teriti], *n.* austérité, *f.*

Australasia [ɔːstrə'leiʃiə]. l'Australasie, *f.*

Australia [ɔːs'treiliə]. l'Australie, *f.*

Australian [ɔːs'treiliən], *a.* australien.—*n.* Australien (*personne*), *m.*

Austria ['ɔːstriə]. l'Autriche, *f.*

Austrian ['ɔːstriən], *a.* autrichien.—*n.* Autrichien (*personne*), *m.*

authentic [ɔː'θentik], *a.* authentique.

authentically [ɔː'θentikli], *adv.* authentiquement.

authenticate [ɔː'θentikeit], *v.t.* authentiquer, constater.

authenticated [ɔː'θentikeitid], *a.* authentique, avéré.

authenticity [ɔːθen'tisiti], *n.* authenticité, *f.*

author ['ɔːθə], *n.* auteur, *m.*

authoress ['ɔːθəris], *n.* femme auteur, femme écrivain, *f.*

authoritative [ɔː'θɔritətiv], *a.* d'autorité; autorisé; autoritaire, impérieux.

authority [ɔː'θɔriti], *n.* autorité; autorisation, *f.*, mandat, *m.*

authorization [ɔːθərai'zeiʃən], *n.* autorisation, *f.*

authorize ['ɔːθəraiz], *v.t.* autoriser.

authorship [ɔː'θəʃip], *n.* qualité d'auteur; (*colloq.*) paternité, *f.*

autobiographer [ɔːtəbai'ɔgrəfə], *n.* autobiographe, *m.*, *f.*

autobiography [ɔːtəbai'ɔgrəfi], *n.* autobiographie, *f.*

autocracy [ɔː'tɔkrəsi], *n.* autocratie, *f.*

autocrat ['ɔːtəkræt], *n.* autocrate, *m.*, *f.*

auto-cycle ['ɔːtosaikl], *n.* cyclomoteur, *m.*

autograph ['ɔːtəgraːf], *n.* autographe, *m.*—*v.t.* signer, autographier.

autogyro [ɔːto'dʒairou], *n.* autogyre, *m.*

automatic [ɔːtə'mætik], *a.* automatique.

automatically [ɔːtə'mætikli], *adv.* automatiquement; machinalement.

automation [ɔːtə'meiʃən], *n.* automation, *f.*

automaton [ɔː'tɔmətən], *n.* (*pl.* **automata** [ɔː'tɔmətə]) automate, *m.*

automobile ['ɔːtəməbiːl], *n.* (*Am.*) automobile, auto, voiture, *f.*

autonomous [ɔː'tɔnəməs], *a.* autonome.

autonomy [ɔː'tɔnəmi], *n.* autonomie, *f.*

autopsy ['ɔːtɔpsi, ɔː'tɔpsi], *n.* autopsie, *f.*

autumn ['ɔːtəm], *n.* automne, *m.* ou *f.*

autumnal [ɔː'tʌmnəl], *a.* automnal, d'automne.

auxiliary [ɔːg'ziljəri], *a. and n.* auxiliaire, *m.*

avail [ə'veil], *v.t., v.i.* profiter, servir; *to avail oneself of*, se servir de.—*n.* service, avantage, *m.*, utilité, *f.*; *of what avail is it?* à quoi bon?

available [ə'veiləbl], *a.* disponible; valable.

avalanche ['ævəlaːnʃ], *n.* avalanche, *f.*

avarice ['ævəris], *n.* avarice, *f.*

avaricious [ævə'riʃəs], *a.* avare, avaricieux.

avenge [ə'vendʒ], *v.t.* venger; *to avenge oneself*, se venger (*de* ou *sur*).

avenger [ə'vendʒə], *n.* vengeur, *m.*

avenging [ə'vendʒiŋ], *a.* vengeur.—*n.* vengeance, *f.*

avenue ['ævənjuː], *n.* avenue, *f.*

aver [ə'vəː], *v.t.* affirmer.

average ['ævəridʒ], *a.* commun, moyen.—*n.* moyenne, *f.*, prix moyen, terme moyen, *m.*; (*Naut.*) avarie, *f.*; *on an average*, en moyenne.—*v.t.* établir la moyenne de; atteindre une moyenne de.

averse [ə'vəːs], *a.* opposé (*à*), ennemi (*de*).

aversely [ə'vəːsli], *adv.* à contre-cœur.

aversion [ə'vəːʃən], *n.* répugnance, aversion, *f.*; *it is his pet aversion*, c'est sa bête noire.

avert [ə'vəːt], *v.t.* détourner, écarter.

aviary ['eiviəri], *n.* volière, *f.*

aviation [eivi'eiʃən], *n.* aviation, *f.*

aviator ['eivieitə], *n.* aviateur, *m.*

avid ['ævid], *a.* avide.

avidly ['ævidli], *adv.* avec avidité, avidement.

avoid [ə'void], *v.t.* éviter.

avoidable [ə'voidəbl], *a.* évitable.

avoidance [ə'voidəns], *n.* action d'éviter, *f.*

avoirdupois [ævədə'poiz], *n.* poids du commerce, *m.*

avow [ə'vau], *v.t.* avouer, confesser, déclarer.

avowal [ə'vauəl], *n.* aveu, *m.*

avowedly [ə'vauidli], *adv.* de son propre aveu.

await [ə'weit], *v.t.* attendre.

awake [ə'weik], *v.t. irr.* éveiller, réveiller.—*v.i.* s'éveiller, se réveiller.—*a.* éveillé; attentif.

awaken [ə'weikən], *v.t.* éveiller, réveiller.

awakening [ə'weiknin], *n.* réveil, *m.*

award [ə'wɔːd], *v.t.* décerner, adjuger.—*n.* décision, *f.*; jugement, *m.*; sentence; (*Sch.*) récompense, *f.*

aware [ə'weə], *a.* qui sait; instruit; *to be aware of*, savoir, avoir connaissance de; *not to be aware of*, ignorer.

awareness [ə'weənis], *n.* conscience, *f.*

away [ə'wei], *adv.* absent; loin, au loin; *away with you!* allez-vous en! *far away*, au loin; *right away*, immédiatement.

awe [ɔː], *n.* crainte, terreur, *f.*; respect, *m.*

awe-inspiring [ɔːinspaiərin], *a.* terrifiant.

awestruck [ɔːstrʌk], *a.* frappé de terreur.

awful [ɔːful], *a.* terrible, redoutable, effroyable; solennel; *what awful weather!* quel temps affreux!

awfully [ɔːfuli], *adv.* horriblement, terriblement; (*fam.*) diablement.

awhile [ə'wail], *adv.* un instant, un peu.

awkward [ɔːkwəd], *a.* gauche, maladroit; embarrassant.

awkwardly [ɔːkwədli], *adv.* gauchement, maladroitement.

awkwardness [ɔːkwədnis], *n.* gaucherie, maladresse, *f.*

awl [ɔːl], *n.* alène, *f.*; poinçon, *m.*

awning [ɔːnin], *n.* tente, banne, bâche, *f.*

awry [ə'rai], *a.* and *adv.* de travers.

axe [æks], *n.* hache, cognée, *f.*

axiom [æksiəm], *n.* axiome, *m.*

axiomatic [æksiə'mætik], *a.* axiomatique.

axis [æksis], *n.* (*pl.* **axes** [æksiːz]) axe, *m.*

axle [æksl], *n.* arbre, essieu, *m.*; (*Motor.*) *rear axle*, pont arrière, *m.*

ay, aye [ai], *adv.* oui, c'est vrai; *aye, aye! (Naut.)* bon quart!—*n.* *ayes and noes*, voix pour et contre, *f.pl.*

azalea [ə'zeiliə], *n.* (*Bot.*) azalée, *f.*

Azores [ə'zɔːz], **the.** les Açores, *f.pl.*

azote [ə'zout], *n.* (*Chem.*) azote, *m.*

azure [æʒuə, 'eiʒə], *a.* d'azur.—*n.* azur, *m.*

B

B, b [biː]. deuxième lettre de l'alphabet; (*Mus.*) si, *m.*

baa [baː], *v.i.* bêler.—*n.* bêlement, *m.*

babble [bæbl], *v.i.* babiller; gazouiller jaser; (*fig.*) murmurer (*ruisseau*).—*n.* babil, caquet; (*fig.*) murmure, *m.*, jaserie, *f.*

babbler [bæblə], *n.* babillard, *m.*

babbling [bæblin], *a.* babillard, bavard.

babe [beib], *n.* enfant nouveau-né, petit enfant, *m.*

Babel [beibəl]. Babel, *f.*

baboon [bə'buːn], *n.* babouin, *m.*

baby [beibi], *n.* bébé, *m.*; *baby grand (piano)*, piano à demi-queue, *m.*; *baby linen*, layette, *f.*

babyhood [beibihud], *n.* première enfance, *f.*

babyish [beibiiʃ], *a.* enfantin.

bacchanalia [bækə'neiliə], *n.pl.* bacchanales, *f.pl.*

bacchanalian [bækə'neiliən], *a.* bachique.—*n.* ivrogne, *m.*

bachelor [bætʃələ], *n.* célibataire, vieux garçon; bachelier (*ès lettres*), *m.*

back [bæk], *n.* dos, *m.*, reins, *m.pl.*; envers (*d'un tissu*); verso (*d'une page etc.*); fond (*d'une salle etc.*); (*Ftb.*) arrière; revers (*d'une colline etc.*); derrière (*d'une maison etc.*); dossier (*d'une chaise*), *m.*; *at the back of*, derrière; *back to back*, dos à dos; *on the back of* (*a letter etc.*), au verso.—*adv.* en arrière; de retour, rentré; *a few years back*, il y a quelques années; *to be back*, être de retour; *to call back*, rappeler; *to come back*, revenir.—*v.t.* soutenir (*Betting*) jouer (*un cheval*); faire reculer.—*v.i.* reculer.

backbite [bækbait], *v.t.* médire de, calomnier.

backbiting [bækbaitin], *n.* médisance, *f.*

backbone [bækboun], *n.* épine dorsale, *f.*

back-door [bæk'dɔː], *n.* porte de derrière, *f.*

backer [bækə], *n.* partisan, second; parieur pour, *m.*

back-fire [bæk'faiə], *v.i.* (*Motor.*) pétarader.

backgammon [bæk'gæmən], *n.* trictrac, *m.*

back-garden [bæk'gɑːdn], *n.* jardin de derrière, *m.*

background [bækgraund], *n.* arrière-plan, fond, *m.*

back-room [bæk'ruːm], *n.* chambre de derrière, *f.*

backside [bæk'said], *n.* (*pop.*) derrière, *m.*

backslide [bæk'slaid], *v.i.* retomber dans le vice ou le péché.

backstage [bæk'steidʒ], *adv.* derrière la scène; dans les coulisses.

backstairs [bæk'steəz], *n.* escalier de service, *m.*

backward [bækwəd], *a.* arriéré; en retard; en arrière; lent, tardif.

backward(s) [bækwəd(z)], *adv.* à reculons; en arrière; à la renverse.

backwoodsman [bækwudzmən], *n.* (*pl.* **-men** [men]) défricheur de forêts, *m.*

back-yard [bæk'jɑːd], *n.* cour de derrière, *f.*

bacon [beikən], *n.* lard, *m.*

bacterium [bæk'tiəriəm], *n.* (*pl.* **bacteria** [bæk'tiəriə]) bactérie, *f.*

bad [bæd], *a.* mauvais; méchant (*enfant etc.*); gâté (*aliment etc.*); malade; *that is too bad*, c'est trop fort.

badge [bædʒ], *n.* insigne, *m.*; plaque, *f.*; (*Mil.*) écusson; brassard, *m.*

badger [bædʒə], *n.* blaireau, *m.*—*v.t.* harceler.

badly [bædli], *adv.* mal; grièvement, fort, beaucoup.

badness [bædnis], *n.* méchanceté, *f.*; mauvais état, *m.*

baffle [bæfl], *v.t.* déjouer; confondre.

353

bag [bæg], *n.* sac; cornet (*papier*), *m.*; *game-bag*, gibecière, *f.*; *with bag and baggage*, avec armes et bagages.—*v.t.* mettre en sac; abattre (*du gibier*); (*colloq.*) s'emparer de; (*slang*) chiper.—*v.i.* bouffer (*pantalon*).

baggage ['bægidʒ], *n.* (*chiefly Am.*) bagages, *m.pl.*

bagpipes ['bægpaips], *n. pl.* cornemuse, *f.*

bail (1) [beil], *n.* caution, *f.*; *on bail*, sous caution.

bail (2), **bale** (1) [beil], *v.t.* écoper.

bailiff ['beilif], *n.* huissier, *m.*; *farm bailiff*, régisseur, *m.*

bait [beit], *v.t.* amorcer (*un hameçon*); (*fig.*) harceler, tourmenter.—*n.* amorce, *f.*; appât, leurre, *m.*

baize [beiz], *n.* serge, *f.*; *green baize*, tapis vert, *m.*

bake [beik], *v.t., v.i.* cuire au four.

bakehouse ['beikhaus], *n.* fournil, *m.*, boulangerie, *f.*

Bakelite ['beikəlait], *n.* bakélite (*reg. trade mark*), *f.*

baker ['beikə], *n.* boulanger, *m.*

bakery ['beikəri], *n.* boulangerie, *f.*

baking ['beikiŋ], *n.* cuisson; fournée, *f.*

balance ['bæləns], *n.* balance, *f.*; équilibre; balancier (*d'une pendule*), *m.*—*v.t.* équilibrer, balancer; *to balance up*, arrêter.

balance-sheet ['bælənsʃiːt], *n.* bilan, *m.*

balance-weight ['bælənsweit], *n.* contrepoids, *m.*

balcony ['bælkəni], *n.* balcon, *m.*

bald [bɔːld], *a.* chauve; (*fig.*) plat, sec (*style*).

baldly ['bɔːldli], *adv.* pauvrement, platement, sèchement.

baldness ['bɔːldnis], *n.* calvitie; (*fig.*) platitude, *f.*

bale (1) [BAIL (2)].

bale (2) [beil], *n.* balle, *f.*, ballot, *m.*—*v.t.* emballer.—*v.i. to bale out*, (*Av.*) sauter en parachute.

baleful ['beilful], *a.* sinistre, funeste.

balefully ['beilfuli], *adv.* d'une manière funeste.

balk, baulk [bɔːk], *n.* poutre, bille; (*Billiards*) ligne de départ, *f.*—*v.t.* frustrer, contrarier, déjouer.

Balkan ['bɔːlkən], *a.* balkanique.

Balkans ['bɔːlkənz], **the**, les Balkans, les États Balkaniques, *m.pl.*

ball (1) [bɔːl], *n.* balle; boule (*de neige*); pelote, *f.*, peloton (*de laine, de ficelle*); boulet (*de canon*), *m.*; (*Billiards*) bille; (*Cook.*) boulette, *f.*; ballon (*plein d'air*), *m.*; prunelle (*d'œil*), *f.*; *ball-point pen*, stylo à bille, *m.*

ball (2) [bɔːl], *n.* bal, *m.*; *fancy-dress ball*, bal masqué.

ballad ['bæləd], *n.* (*Mus.*) romance; ballade, *f.*

ballast ['bæləst], *n.* lest; (*Rail.*) ballast, *m.*; *in ballast*, sur lest.—*v.t.* lester; (*Rail.*) ensabler.

ballerina [bælə'riːnə], *n.* ballerine, *f.*

ballet ['bælei], *n.* ballet, *m.*

balloon [bə'luːn], *n.* ballon, aérostat, *m.*—*v.i.* se ballonner.

ballot ['bælət], *n.* boule, *f.*; bulletin, scrutin, *m.*; *by ballot*, au scrutin.—*v.i.* voter au scrutin.

ballot-box ['bælətbɔks], *n.* urne électorale, *f.*

ballot-paper ['bælətpeipə], *n.* bulletin de vote, *m.*

balm [bɑːm], *n.* baume, *m.*; mélisse, *f.*—*v.t.* parfumer.

balmy ['bɑːmi], *a.* embaumé, parfumé.

balsam ['bɔːlsəm], *n.* baume, *m.*

Baltic ['bɔːltik], **the**, la Baltique, *f.*

balustrade [bæləs'treid], *n.* balustrade, *f.*

bamboo [bæm'buː], *n.* bambou, *m.*

bamboozle [bæm'buːzl], *v.t.* (*colloq.*) tromper, duper, enjôler.

ban [bæn], *n.* ban, *m.*; interdiction, *f.*; (*Eccles.*) interdit, *m.*—*v.t.* interdire, proscrire.

banal [bə'næl, 'beinəl], *a.* banal.

banality [bə'næliti], *n.* banalité, *f.*

banana [bə'nɑːnə], *n.* banane, *f.*

banana-tree [bə'nɑːnətriː], *n.* bananier, *m.*

band (1) [bænd], *n.* bande, *f.*, lien; ruban, *m.*; raie, *f.*—*v.t.* bander.

band (2) [bænd], *n.* bande, troupe; (*Mil.*) musique, *f.*; orchestre, *m.*; *brass band*, fanfare, *f.*—*v.t.* liguer, réunir en troupe.—*v.i.* se liguer.

bandage ['bændidʒ], *n.* bandeau; (*Surg.*) bandage, pansement, *m.*

bandbox ['bændbɔks], *n.* carton (*de modiste*), *m.*

bandit ['bændit], *n.* bandit, *m.*

bandmaster ['bændmɑːstə], *n.* chef de musique, *m.*

bandoleer, bandolier [bændə'liə], *n.* bandoulière, *f.*

bandsman ['bændzmən], *n.* (*pl.* -men [men]) musicien, *m.*

bandstand ['bændstænd], *n.* kiosque à musique, *m.*

bandy ['bændi], *v.t.* renvoyer; échanger; se renvoyer; *to bandy words*, se renvoyer des paroles.—*v.i.* se disputer.

bandy-legged ['bændilegd], *a.* bancal.

bane [bein], *n.* poison; (*fig.*) fléau, *m.*

baneful ['beinful], *a.* pernicieux, funeste, nuisible.

bang [bæŋ], *n.* coup, grand bruit, *m.*, détonation, *f.*—*v.t.* frapper violemment, taper; *to bang a door*, claquer une porte.—*int.* pan! paf! boum!

bangle ['bæŋgl], *n.* porte-bonheur, bracelet, *m.*

banish ['bæniʃ], *v.t.* bannir, exiler.

banishment ['bæniʃmənt], *n.* bannissement, exil, *m.*

bank (1) [bæŋk], *n.* rivage, bord, *m.*; berge, rive; terrasse, *f.*; remblai, talus; banc (*de sable, de gazon etc.*), *m.*; digue, *f.*; carreau (*de mine*), *m.*—*v.t.* terrasser, remblayer.

bank (2) [bæŋk], *n.* (*Comm.*) banque, *f.*; *savings-bank*, caisse d'épargne, *f.*—*v.t.* encaisser (*de l'argent*).

banker ['bæŋkə], *n.* banquier, *m.*

banking ['bæŋkiŋ], *n.* banque, *f.*

bank-note ['bæŋknout], *n.* billet de banque, *m.*

bankrupt ['bæŋkrʌpt], *a.* failli, en faillite; (*fig.*) ruiné.—*v.t.* mettre en faillite, ruiner.—*n.* banqueroutier, failli, *m.*; *to go bankrupt*, faire faillite.

bankruptcy ['bæŋkrʌptsi], *n.* banqueroute, faillite, *f.*

banner ['bænə], *n.* bannière, *f.*

bannock ['bænək], *n.* (*grosse*) galette d'avoine *f.*

banns [bænz], *n.pl. banns of marriage*, bans de mariage, *m.pl.*

baste

banquet ['bæŋkwit], *n.* banquet; *festin, *m.*
banter ['bæntə], *v.t.* railler, badiner.—*n.* badinage, *m.*; raillerie, *f.*
baptism ['bæptizm], *n.* baptême, *m.*
baptismal [bæp'tizməl], *a.* baptismal.
baptist ['bæptist], *n.* baptiste, *m., f.*
baptize [bæp'taiz], *v.t.* baptiser.
bar (1) [bɑː], *n.* barre, *f.*; (*Law etc.*) barreau, parquet, *m.*; (*fig.*) barrière; buvette, *f.*, comptoir, bar (*de café, hôtel etc.*); (*Law*) banc des accusés, *m.*; (*Mus.*) mesure; tablette (*de chocolat*), *f.*; *to be called to the bar,* être reçu avocat.—*v.t.* barrer, empêcher; exclure.
bar (2) [BARRING].
barb [bɑːb], *n.* barbillon, dardillon (*hameçon*), *m.*; pointe (*flèche*); barbe, arête (*blé*), *f.*
Barbados [bɑː'beidɔs], la Barbade, *f.*
barbarian [bɑː'bɛəriən], *a.* and *n.* barbare, *m., f.*
barbaric [bɑː'bærik], *a.* barbare.
barbarism ['bɑːbərizm], *n.* barbarie, *f.*; (*Gram.*) barbarisme, *m.*
barbarity [bɑː'bæriti], *n.* barbarie, cruauté, *f.*
barbarous ['bɑːbərəs], *a.* barbare.
barbecue ['bɑːbəkjuː], *n.* grand gril; grand pique-nique (en plein air), *m.*—*v.t.* rôtir à la broche.
barbed [bɑːbd], *a.* barbelé; (*fig.*) acéré; *barbed wire,* fil de fer barbelé, *m.*
barbel ['bɑːbəl], *n.* (*Ichth.*) barbeau, *m.*
barber ['bɑːbə], *n.* coiffeur, *m.*
Barcelona [bɑːsə'lounə], Barcelone, *f.*
bard [bɑːd], *n.* barde, trouvère, *m.*
bare [bɛə], *a.* nu, découvert; (*fig.*) seul, simple; pauvre.—*v.t.* découvrir, dépouiller; mettre à nu.
bareback ['bɛəbæk], *adv.* à dos nu.
barefaced ['bɛəfeist], *a.* à visage découvert; éhonté, sans déguisement.
barefoot ['bɛəfut], *a.* nu-pieds, les pieds nus.
bareheaded ['bɛə'hedid], *a.* nu-tête, la tête nue.
barely ['bɛəli], *adv.* à peine; tout juste, simplement, seulement; pauvrement.
bareness ['bɛənis], *n.* nudité; misère, *f.*
bargain ['bɑːgin], *n.* marché, *m.*, affaire; occasion, *f.*; *into the bargain,* par-dessus le marché; *it is a bargain,* c'est convenu; *to strike a bargain,* conclure un marché.—*v.i.* marchander, faire marché.
barge [bɑːdʒ], *n.* chaland, *m.*; péniche, *f.*—*v.i. to barge into,* se heurter contre, bousculer.
bargee [bɑː'dʒiː], bargeman ['bɑːdʒmən] (*pl.* -men [men]), *n.* batelier, *m.*
baritone ['bæritoun], *a.* de baryton.—*n.* baryton, *m.*
bark (1) [bɑːk], *n.* écorce, *f.*; tan, *m.*
bark (2) [bɑːk], *n.* aboiement, *m.*—*v.i.* aboyer.
bark (3), barque [bɑːk], *n.* trois-mâts, *m.*
barking ['bɑːkiŋ], *n.* aboiement, *m.*
barley ['bɑːli], *n.* orge, *f.*
barmaid ['bɑːmeid], *n.* barmaid, *f.*
barman ['bɑːmən], *n.* (*pl.* -men [men]) barman, *m.*
barmy ['bɑːmi], *a.* (*colloq.*) fou, toqué.
barn [bɑːn], *n.* grange, *f.*; (*Am.*) étable, *f.*
barnacle ['bɑːnəkl], *n.* barnache (*oie*), *f.*; balane, anatife (*crustacé*), *m.*
barometer [bə'rɔmitə], *n.* baromètre, *m.*

barometric [bæro'metrik], *a.* barométrique.
baron ['bærən], *n.* baron, *m.*; *baron of beef,* double aloyau, *m.*
baroness ['bærənis], *n.* baronne, *f.*
baronet ['bærənet], *n.* baronnet, *m.*
baronial [bə'rouniəl], *a.* baronnial, seigneurial.
barony ['bærəni], *n.* baronnie, *f.*
barouche [bə'ruːʃ], *n.* calèche, *f.*
barque [BARK (3)].
barrack ['bærək], *n.* (*usu. in pl.*) caserne, *f.*; quartier (*pour la cavalerie*), *m.*
barrage ['bæridʒ, 'bærɑːʒ], *n.* barrage, *m.*
barrel ['bærəl], *n.* baril, *m.*; gonne, caque (*de poissons etc.*), *f.*; corps (*de pompe*); cylindre, tambour (*de machine*); canon (*de fusil*), *m.*—*v.t.* embariller, entonner, mettre en baril, encaquer.
barrel-organ ['bærələːgən], *n.* orgue de Barbarie, *m.*
barren ['bærən], *a.* stérile; infertile (*terre*).
barrenness ['bærənnis], *n.* stérilité, *f.*
barricade [bæri'keid], *n.* barricade, *f.*—*v.t.* barricader.
barrier ['bæriə], *n.* barrière, *f.*
barring ['bɑːriŋ], bar (2) [bɑː], *prep.* excepté, hormis, sauf.
barrister ['bæristə], *n.* avocat, *m.*
barrow (1) ['bærou], *n.* brouette, *f.*
barrow-boy ['bæroubɔi], *n.* (*fam.*) marchand des quatre saisons, *m.*
barter ['bɑːtə], *n.* échange, troc; trafic, *m.*—*v.t.* troquer, échanger.—*v.i.* échanger, faire échange.
basalt [bə'sɔːlt], *n.* basalte, *m.*
base (1) [beis], *a.* bas, vil, indigne, méprisable; illégitime (*enfant*); de mauvais aloi; non précieux, faux (*monnaie*).
base (2) [beis], *n.* base, *f.*, fondement; fond, *m.*—*v.t.* fonder (*sur*); asseoir (*l'impôt*).
baseball ['beisbɔːl], *n.* (*Spt.*) base-ball, *m.*
baseless ['beislis], *a.* sans fondement.
basely ['beisli], *adv.* bassement, lâchement.
basement ['beismənt], *n.* sous-sol, *m.*
baseness ['beisnis], *n.* bassesse, lâcheté, *f.*
bashful ['bæʃful], *a.* timide, intimidé.
bashfully ['bæʃfuli], *adv.* timidement, en rougissant.
bashfulness ['bæʃfulnis], *n.* timidité, fausse honte, *f.*
basic ['beisik], *a.* (*Chem.*) basique; de base.
basilica [bə'zilikə], *n.* basilique, *f.*
basilisk ['bæzilisk], *n.* basilic, *m.*
basin ['beisən], *n.* bassin; bol, *m.*; cuvette, *f.*
basis ['beisis], *n.* (*pl.* bases ['beisiːz]) base, *f.* fondement, *m.*
bask [bɑːsk], *v.i.* se chauffer.
basket ['bɑːskit], *n.* panier, *m.*, corbeille, *f.*
basket-ball ['bɑːskitbɔːl], *n.* (*Spt.*) basket-ball, (*fam.*) basket, *m.*
Basle [bɑːl]. Bâle, *f.*
bas-relief [bɑːrə'liːf], *n.* bas-relief, *m.*
bass (1) [beis], *n.* (*Mus.*) basse; basse-taille, *f.*; *double bass,* contre-basse, *f.*
bass (2) [bæs], *n.* (*Ichth.*) bar, *m.*; perche, *f.*
bassinet [bæsi'net], *n.* bercelonnette, *f.*, moïse, *m.*
bassoon [bə'suːn], *n.* basson, *m.*
bastard ['bæstəd], *a.* bâtard; (*fig.*) faux.—*n.* bâtard, *m.*, bâtarde, *f.*; (*pop.*) salaud, *m.*
baste [beist], *v.t.* arroser (*viande*); (*fig.*) bâtonner; (*Needlework*) bâtir.

bastion ['bæstiən], *n.* bastion, *m.*
bat (1) [bæt], *n.* (*Cricket*) batte, *f.*; *off his own bat*, de sa propre initiative.—*v.i.* être au guichet.
bat (2) [bæt], *n.* (*Zool.*) chauve-souris, *f.*
Batavian [bə'teiviən], *a.* batave.—*n.* Batave (*personne*), *m.*, *f.*
batch [bætʃ], *n.* fournée (*pain*); (*fig.*) troupe, bande, *f.*; tas; lot, *m.*
bate [beit], *v.t.* rabattre, rabaisser.
bath [bɑ:θ], *n.* bain, *m.*; baignoire, *f.*; *shower-bath*, douche, *f.*—*v.t.* donner un bain à, baigner.—*v.i.* prendre un bain.
bathe [beið], *v.t.* baigner; tremper, mouiller. —*v.i.* se baigner.—*n.* baignade, *f.*
bather ['beiðə], *n.* baigneur, *m.*, baigneuse, *f.*
bathing ['beiðiŋ], *n.* baignade, *f.*; bains, *m.pl.*
bathing-costume ['beiðiŋkɔstjum], *n.* costume de bain, maillot, *m.*
bathos ['beiθɔs], *n.* pathos, *m.*, enflure, *f.*
bath-room ['bɑ:θrum], *n.* salle de bain(s), *f.*
batman ['bætmən], *n.* (*pl.* **-men** [men]) ordonnance, brosseur, *m.*
baton ['bætən], *n.* bâton, *m.*; baguette, *f.*
batsman ['bætsmən], *n.* (*Cricket*) batteur, *m.*
battalion [bə'tæliən], *n.* bataillon, *m.*
batten ['bætən], *n.* volige, latte, *f.*—*v.t.* fermer; (*Carp.*) voliger.—*v.i.* s'engraisser.
batter ['bætə], *v.t.* battre en brèche; battre; délabrer, ébranler, démolir.—*n.* pâte, *f.*
battered ['bætəd], *a.* délabré.
battering-ram ['bætəriŋræm], *n.* bélier, *m.*
battery ['bætəri], *n.* batterie; (*Elec.*) pile, batterie, *f.*, accumulateur, *m.*; action de battre en brèche, *f.*; (*Law*) voies de fait, *f.pl.*
battle [bætl], *n.* bataille, *f.*, combat, *m.*; *pitched battle*, bataille rangée; *to give battle*, livrer bataille.—*v.i.* lutter, combattre; (*colloq.*) batailler.
battle-axe ['bætlæks], *n.* hache d'armes, *f.*
battledore ['bætldɔ:], *n.* raquette, *f.*
battle-dress ['bætldres], *n.* tenue de campagne, *f.*
battle-field ['bætlfi:ld], *n.* champ de bataille, *m.*
battlement ['bætlmənt], *n.* créneau, *m.*
battleship ['bætlʃip], *n.* cuirassé, *m.*
bauble [bɔ:bl], *n.* babiole, fanfreluche, *f.*; *fool's bauble*, marotte, *f.*
baulk [BALK].
bauxite ['bɔ:ksait, 'bouzait], *n.* bauxite, *f.*
Bavaria [bə'veəriə], la Bavière, *f.*
Bavarian [bə'veəriən], *a.* bavarois.—*n.* Bavarois (*personne*).
bawdy ['bɔ:di], *a.* obscène, paillard.
bawl [bɔ:l], *v.i.* crier, brailler.
bay (1) [bei], *a.* bai (*cheval*).
bay (2) [bei], *n.* baie, *f.*, golfe, *m.*; (*Arch.*) baie, *f.*
bay (3) [bei], *n.* (*Bot.*) baie, *f.*; laurier, *m.*
bay (4) [bei], *n.* abois, *m.pl.*; *at bay*, aux abois.—*v.i.* aboyer.
bayonet ['beiənit], *n.* baïonnette, *f.*—*v.t.* tuer *ou* percer à coups de baïonnette.
bay-window ['beiwindou], *n.* fenêtre en saillie *ou* à baie, *f.*
bazaar [bə'zɑ:], *n.* bazar, *m.*; vente de charité, *f.*
bazooka [bə'zu:kə], *n.* bazooka, *m.*
be [bi:], *v.i. irr.* être; exister; subsister; y

avoir, se trouver; avoir; faire; devoir, falloir; *be it so*, soit; *be that as it may*, quoi qu'il en soit; *how is it that . . .?* comment se fait-il que . . .? *I was to*, je devais; *to be better*, valoir mieux; se porter mieux; *to be mistaken*, se tromper; *to be right*, avoir raison.
beach [bi:tʃ], *n.* plage, grève, *f.*, rivage, *m.*— *v.t.* échouer.
beacon ['bi:kən], *n.* phare, fanal, *m.*; balise, *f.* —*v.t.* baliser, éclairer.
bead [bi:d], *n.* grain (*de chapelet, de bracelet, de collier*); globule, *m.*; *string of beads*, collier, chapelet, *m.*; *to tell one's beads*, égrener son chapelet.
beadle [bi:dl], *n.* bedeau; appariteur, *m.*
beagle [bi:gl], *n.* chien briquet, bigle, *m.*
beak [bi:k], *n.* bec, *m.*; bigorne (*enclume*), *f.*; (*Naut.*) éperon, *m.*
beaker ['bi:kə], *n.* gobelet, *m.*, coupe, *f.*
beakful ['bi:kful], *n.* becquée, *f.*
beam [bi:m], *n.* poutre, *f.*; timon (*charrue, voiture etc.*); rayon (*lumière*); large sourire (*de joie etc.*), *m.*—*v.t.* lancer, darder (*des rayons*).—*v.i.* rayonner.
beaming ['bi:miŋ], *a.* rayonnant, radieux.— *n.* rayonnement, *m.*
bean [bi:n], *n.* fève, *f.*; haricot; grain (*de café*), *m.*; *French beans*, haricots verts; *kidney beans*, haricots blancs.
bear (1) [beə], *n.* ours; (*St. Exch.*) joueur à la baisse, baissier, *m.*; *polar bear*, ours blanc.
bear (2) [beə], *v.t. irr.* porter, soutenir; endurer, supporter, souffrir, subir; avoir produire (*fruits etc.*); enfanter; donner naissance à; y tenir; remporter.—*v.i.* endurer, souffrir; porter, peser; avoir rapport (*à*); appuyer; porter (*sur*); rapporter.
bearable ['beərəbl], *a.* supportable.
beard [biəd], *n.* barbe, *f.*—*v.t.* braver, défier.
bearded ['biədid], *a.* barbu.
beardless ['biədlis], *a.* imberbe.
bearer ['beərə], *n.* porteur; (*Arch.*) support, *m.*
bearing ['beəriŋ], *n.* rapport; maintien, port, *m.*, conduite, relation, *f.*; aspect, *m.*, portée; face, *f.*; (*Arch.*) support; (*Mech.*) coussinet, *m.*; *ball-bearings*, roulement à billes, *m.*; *to take one's bearings*, s'orienter.
bearskin ['beəskin], *n.* (*Mil.*) bonnet d'oursin, *m.*
beast [bi:st], *n.* bête, *f.*; (*fig.*) animal, cochon, *m.*
beastliness ['bi:stlinis], *n.* saleté, saloperie, *f.*
beastly ['bi:stli], *a.* bestial; sale, malpropre, dégoûtant.
beat [bi:t], *v.t. irr.* battre; frapper; piler, broyer; l'emporter sur; fouetter (*pluie, neige etc.*); se frapper (*la poitrine etc.*); *beat it!* fiche-moi le camp! *that beats all*, cela dépasse tout; *to beat a retreat*, battre en retraite.—*v.i.* battre; être agité.—*n.* coup, battement; son; itinéraire, *m.*; ronde (*d'un agent de police*), *f.*, parcours (*facteurs etc.*), *m.*; (*Hunt.*) battue; (*Mus.*) mesure, *f.*, temps, *m.*; *beat of the drum*, batterie de tambour *f.*
beaten [bi:tn], *a.* battu.
beater ['bi:tə], *n.* batteur; (*Spt.*) rabatteur, *m.*; batte (*instrument*), *f.*
beating ['bi:tiŋ], *n.* battement, *m.*; rossée, *f.*; coups, *m.pl.*; batterie, *f.*; roulement (*tambour etc.*), *m.*

beau [bou], *n.* (*pl.* **beaux** [bouz]) petit-maître; prétendant (*amant*), *m.*
beauteous ['bjuːtiəs], *a.* (*Poet.*) beau.
beauteously ['bjuːtiəsli], *adv.* avec beauté.
beautiful ['bjuːtiful], *a.* très beau; (*colloq.*) magnifique.
beautifully ['bjuːtifuli], *adv.* admirablement.
beautify ['bjuːtifai], *v.t.* embellir, orner.—*v.i.* s'embellir.
beauty ['bjuːti], *n.* beauté (*personne et qualité*), *f.*
beauty-spot ['bjuːtispɔt], *n.* mouche, *f.*, grain de beauté; site pittoresque, *m.*
beaver ['biːvə], *n.* castor; chapeau de castor, *m.*
becalm [bi'kɑːm], *v.t.* *apaiser; calmer; abriter (*navire*).
because [bi'kɔz], *conj.* parce que; **because of,** à cause de.
beck (1) [bek], *n.* signe (*du doigt etc.*), *m.*—*v.i.* faire signe (*du doigt etc.*).
beck (2) [bek], *n.* ruisseau, *m.*
beckon ['bekən], *v.t.* faire signe à, appeler.—*v.i.* faire signe (*à*).
become [bi'kʌm], *v.t. irr.* (*conjug. like* COME) aller bien à, convenir à, être propre à.—*v.i.* devenir, commencer à être.
becoming [bi'kʌmiŋ], *a.* bienséant, convenable, qui va bien, attrayant.
becomingly [bi'kʌmiŋli], *adv.* avec bienséance.
bed [bed], *n.* lit, *m.*; couche; (*Geol.*) assise, *f.*; encaissement (*rue*); parterre, *m.*, plate-bande (*fleurs*), *f.*; carré, *m.*—*v.t.* coucher, mettre au lit; loger, fixer, enfoncer; parquer (*huîtres*).—*v.i.* coucher, se coucher.
bedaub [bi'dɔːb], *v.t.* barbouiller.
***bed-chamber** [BEDROOM].
bedclothes ['bedklouðz], *n.pl.* les draps et les couvertures, *m.pl.*
bedding ['bediŋ], *n.* literie; litière (*pour animaux*), *f.*
bedeck [bi'dek], *v.t.* parer (*de*).
***bedizen** [bi'daizn], *v.t.* attifer, parer.
bedraggle [bi'drægl], *v.t.* crotter, traîner dans la boue.
bedridden ['bedridn], *a.* alité.
bedroom ['bedruːm], ***bed-chamber** [bed tʃeimbə], *n.* chambre (à coucher), *f.*
bedside ['bedsaid], *n.* ruelle, *f.*, chevet, bord du lit, *m.*
bed-spread ['bedspred], *n.* couvrelit, dessus de lit, *m.*
bedstead ['bedsted], *n.* lit, bois de lit, *m.*; couchette, *f.*
bee [biː], *n.* abeille, *f.*; **to have a bee in one's bonnet,** avoir une araignée dans le plafond.
beech [biːtʃ], *n.* hêtre, *m.*
beef [biːf], *n.* bœuf (*viande*); *(pl.* **beeves** [biːvz]) bœuf (*animal*), *m.*
beef-steak ['biːf'steik], *n.* bifteck, *m.*
beehive ['biːhaiv], *n.* ruche, *f.*
bee-line ['biːlain], *n.* ligne droite, *f.*; **in a bee-line,** à vol d'oiseau; **to make a bee-line for,** se diriger tout droit vers.
Beelzebub [bi'elzəbʌb], Belzébuth, *m.*
beer [biə], *n.* bière, *f.*; **glass of beer,** bock, *m.*
beet [biːt], *n.* betterave, *f.*
beetle (1) [biːtl], *n.* coléoptère, scarabée, escarbot, *m.*

beetle (2) [biːtl], *n.* maillet, *m.*, mailloche; batte, *f.*, battoir (*de laveuse*), *m.*; hie, demoiselle (*d'un paveur*), *f.*; mouton (à enfoncer les pieux*), *m.*
beetle (3) [biːtl], *v.i.* surplomber.—*a.* en surplomb.
beetroot ['biːtruːt], *n.* betterave rouge, *f.*
beet-sugar ['biːtʃugə], *n.* sucre de betterave, *m.*
befall [bi'fɔːl], *v.t., v.i. irr.* (*conjug. like* FALL) arriver, survenir (à).
befit [bi'fit], *v.t.* convenir à.
befitting [bi'fitiŋ], *a.* convenable à.
before [bi'fɔː], *adv.* avant (*temps, ordre etc.*); auparavant, en avant; plus haut; jusqu'alors, naguère, jusqu'ici.—*prep.* devant (*endroit*); avant (*temps etc.*); **before going there,** avant d'y aller.—*conj.* avant que (*with subj.*).
beforehand [bi'fɔːhænd], *adv.* à l'avance, d'avance.
befriend [bi'frend], *v.t.* seconder, aider, secourir; devenir l'ami de (*quelqu'un*).
beg [beg], *v.t.* mendier (*demander l'aumône*); demander, prier (*de*).—*v.i.* mendier.
beget [bi'get], *v.t. irr.* engendrer; (*fig.*) produire, causer.
beggar ['begə], *n.* mendiant, *m.*, mendiante, *f.*; gueux, *m.*, gueuse, *f.*—*v.t.* appauvrir, ruiner; (*fig.*) épuiser.
beggarly ['begəli], *a.* chétif, pauvre, misérable.
beggary ['begəri], *n.* mendicité, misère, *f.*
begging ['begiŋ], *n.* mendicité, *f.*
begin [bi'gin], *v.t. irr.* commencer; entamer, débuter; se mettre à.—*v.i.* commencer (*by, with, par*); **begin afresh,** recommencez.
beginner [bi'ginə], *n.* commençant; débutant, *m.*
beginning [bi'giniŋ], *n.* commencement, début, *m.*, origine, *f.*
begone [bi'gɔn], *int.* va-t'en! allez-vous-en!
begonia [bi'gounjə], *n.* (*Bot.*) bégonia, *m.*
begrudge [bi'grʌdʒ], *v.t.* envier; refuser (*de*).
begrudgingly [bi'grʌdʒiŋli], *adv.* à contre-cœur.
beguile [bi'gail], *v.t.* tromper, séduire; (*fig.*) passer (*le temps*).
behalf [bi'hɑːf], *n.* faveur, part, *f.*; **on behalf of,** au nom de.
behave [bi'heiv], *v.i.* se comporter, se conduire; **well-behaved,** sage.
behaviour [bi'heivjə], *n.* conduite, tenue, *f.*; comportement, *m.*; manières, *f.pl.*
behead [bi'hed], *v.t.* décapiter.
behest [bi'hest], *n.* commandement, ordre, *m.*
behind [bi'haind], *adv.* derrière, par derrière, en arrière.—*prep.* derrière, en arrière de; après, en retard de.—*n.* (*colloq.*) derrière, *m.*
behindhand [bi'haindhænd], *a. and adv.* en arrière, en retard.
***behold** [bi'hould], *v.t. irr.* (*conjug. like* HOLD) voir, regarder.—*int.* voyez! voici! voilà!
beholden [bi'houldən], *a.* redevable (à).
behove [bi'houv], *v.i. impers.* incomber à; **it behoves,** il faut, il convient.
beige [beiʒ], *a.* and *n.* beige, *m.*
being ['biːiŋ], *n.* être, *m.*; existence, *f.*; **in being,** existant, vivant.—*pres.p.* [BE] étant; **for the time being,** pour le moment.
Beirut [bei'ruːt], Beyrouth, *m.*
belated [bi'leitid], *a.* attardé; tardif.

belch [beltʃ], *v.t.*, *v.i.* roter, éructer; *to belch forth*, vomir; *to belch out flames*, vomir des flammes.—*n.* rot, *m.*, éructation, *f.*
beleaguer [bi'li:gə], *v.t.* assiéger, investir.
belfry ['belfri], *n.* clocher, beffroi, *m.*
Belgian ['beldʒən], *a.* belge.—*n.* Belge (*personne*), *m.*, *f.*
Belgium ['beldʒəm]. la Belgique, *f.*
belie [bi'lai], *v.t.* démentir.
belief [bi'li:f], *n.* croyance, *f.*; credo, *m.*
believable [bi'li:vəbl], *a.* croyable.
believe [bi'li:v], *v.t.* croire.—*v.i.* croire (*en* ou *à*); *I believe not*, je crois que non, je ne le crois pas; *I believe so*, je crois que oui, je le crois.
believer [bi'li:və], *n.* croyant, *m.*
bell [bel], *n.* cloche, clochette, *f.*; grelot (*de chevaux etc.*), *m.*; sonnette (*de maison*), *f.*; timbre (*horloge, bicyclette*); (*Arch.*) vase, *m.*
belle [bel], *n.* belle, beauté, *f.*
bellicose ['belikous], *a.* belliqueux.
belligerent [bi'lidʒərənt], *a.* and *n.* belligérant, *m.*
bellow ['belou], *v.i.* beugler; mugir (*mer*); gronder (*tonnerre*).—*n.* beuglement, *m.*
bellows ['belouz], *n.pl.* soufflet, *m.*
bell-ringer ['belriŋə], *n.* sonneur, *m.*
bell-rope ['belroup], *n.* corde de cloche, *f.*
bell-tower ['beltauə], *n.* campanile; clocher, *m.*
belly ['beli], *n.* ventre, *m.*—*v.i.* bomber, s'enfler, se gonfler.
belong [bi'lɔŋ], *v.i.* appartenir, être (*à*).
belongings [bi'lɔŋiŋz], *n.pl.* effets, *m.pl.*, affaires, *f.pl.*
beloved [bi'lʌvd, bi'lʌvid], *a.* cher, chéri, bien-aimé.
below [bi'lou], *prep.* sous au-dessous de; en aval de.—*adv.* au-dessous, dessous, en bas; *here below*, ici-bas.
belt [belt], *n.* ceinture, *f.*; ceinturon; baudrier, *m.*; (*Mach.*) courroie, *f.*; *green belt*, zone verte, *f.*—*v.t.* ceindre, entourer.
bemoan [bi'moun], *v.t.* pleurer, déplorer.—*v.i.* gémir (*sur*).
bemuse [bi'mju:z], *v.t.* stupéfier.
bench [bentʃ], *n.* banc; gradin, *m.*; banquette, *f.*; établi (*de menuisier*); siège, tribunal, *m.*
bend [bend], *v.t. irr.* plier; courber, faire plier; incliner, tendre (*un arc*); fléchir (*le genou*); (*fig.*) appliquer.—*v.i.* plier, ployer; se courber, se pencher, s'incliner; s'appliquer (*à*); tourner; fléchir.—*n.* courbure, *f.*; coude, (*Motor.*) tournant, virage, *m.*
beneath [bi'ni:θ], *prep.* sous, au-dessous de.—*adv.* au-dessous, en bas.
Benedict ['benidikt]. Benoît, *m.*
benediction [beni'dikʃən], *n.* bénédiction, *f.*
benefaction [beni'fækʃən], *n.* bienfait, *m.*
benefactor ['benifæktə], *n.* bienfaiteur, *m.*
benefactress ['benifæktris], *n.* bienfaitrice, *f.*
benefice ['benifis], *n.* bénéfice, *m.*
beneficence [bə'nefisəns], *n.* bienfaisance, *f.*
beneficial [beni'fiʃəl], *a.* salutaire, avantageux.
beneficiary [beni'fiʃəri], *a.* and *n.* bénéficiaire, *m.*, *f.*
benefit ['benifit], *n.* bienfait, profit; bénéfice, *m.*; indemnité (*de chômage etc.*), *f.*—*v.t.* faire du bien à.—*v.i.* profiter.
Benelux ['benilʌks]. Bénélux, *m.*
benevolence [bə'nevələns], *n.* bienveillance, *f.*

benevolent [bə'nevələnt], *a.* bienveillant, bienfaisant.
benighted [bi'naitid], *a.* anuité, surpris par la nuit.
benign [bi'nain], *a.* bénin, *m.*, bénigne (*maladie, médecine etc.*), *f.*; bienfaisant (*personne*); doux, affable.
benignant [bi'nignənt], *a.* bon, bienveillant.
bent (1) [bent], *past* and *p.p.* [BEND].
bent (2) [bent], *a.* courbé, plié; *bent on*, résolu à.—*n.* penchant, *m.*, disposition, tendance, *f.*
benumb [bi'nʌm], *v.t.* engourdir.
benzene ['benzi:n], *n.* benzène, benzol, *m.*
benzine ['benzi:n], *n.* benzine, *f.*
bequeath [bi'kwi:ð], *v.t.* léguer.
bequest [bi'kwest], *n.* legs, *m.*
bereave [bi'ri:v], *v.t. irr.* priver (*de*).
bereavement [bi'ri:vmənt], *n.* privation, perte, *f.*; deuil, *m.*
beret ['berei], *n.* béret, *m.*
Bermuda(s) [bə:'mju:də(z)], (**the**). les (Îles) Bermudes, *f.pl.*
berry ['beri], *n.* baie, *f.*; grain, *m.*
berth [bə:θ], *n.* mouillage; lit, *m.*, couchette, *f.*; poste, *m.*, place, *f.*, emploi, *m.*—*v.t.* amarrer à quai.—*v.i.* mouiller.
Bertha ['bə:θə]. Berthe, *f.*
beseech [bi'si:tʃ], *v.t. irr.* supplier, implorer.
beset [bi'set], *v.t. irr.* (*conjug. like* SET) obséder, entourer, assaillir.
besetting [bi'setiŋ], *a.* habituel, obsesseur.
beside [bi'said], *prep.* à côté de, auprès de; hors, hormis, excepté.
besides [bi'saidz], *prep.* outre, hors, hormis, excepté.—*adv.* d'ailleurs, du reste, en outre, de plus.
besiege [bi'si:dʒ], *v.t.* assiéger.
besmear [bi'smiə], *v.t.* barbouiller; souiller.
besmirch [bi'smə:tʃ], *v.t.* tacher, salir.
besom ['bi:zəm], *n.* balai, *m.*
bespatter [bi'spætə], *v.t.* éclabousser, couvrir de boue.
bespeak [bi'spi:k], *v.t. irr.* (*conjug. like* SPEAK) commander; retenir; annoncer, dénoter, accuser.
best [best], *a.* and *n.* le meilleur, la meilleure, le mieux; *at best*, au mieux, tout au plus; *best man* (*at weddings*), garçon d'honneur, *m.*; *to do one's best*, faire de son mieux; *to have the best of it*, avoir le dessus; *to make the best of it*, tirer le meilleur parti; *to the best of my belief*, autant que je sache.—*adv.* le mieux.
bestial ['bestiəl], *a.* bestial, de bête.
bestir [bi'stə:], *v.t.* remuer, mettre en mouvement.
bestow [bi'stou], *v.t.* donner, accorder.
bestrew [bi'stru:], *v.t. irr.* (*conjug. like* STREW) joncher (*de*), parsemer (*de*).
bestride [bi'straid], *v.t. irr.* (*conjug. like* STRIDE) enjamber, enfourcher (*un cheval*); être à cheval sur.
bet [bet], *n.* pari, *m.*, gageure, *f.*—*v.t.*, *v.i.* parier.
betake [bi'teik], *v.r. irr.* (*conjug. like* TAKE) *to betake oneself to*, se mettre à, s'en aller à, avoir recours à.
bethink [bi'θiŋk], *v.t. irr.* (*conjug. like* THINK) s'aviser (*de*); *to bethink oneself of*, se rappeler.

Bethlehem ['beθlihem, 'beθliəm]. Bethléem, *m.*
betide [bi'taid], *v.t. woe betide you*, malheur à vous.—*v.i.* arriver, advenir.
***betimes** [bi'taimz], *adv.* de bonne heure.
betoken [bi'toukn], *v.t.* annoncer, présager.
betray [bi'trei], *v.t.* trahir; tromper; révéler; faire tomber, entraîner.
betrayal [bi'treiəl], *n.* trahison, perfidie, *f.*
betrayer [bi'treiə], *n.* traître, *m.*
betroth [bi'trouð], *v.t.* fiancer.
betrothal [bi'trouðəl], *n.* fiançailles, *f.pl.*
betrothed [bi'trouðd], *a.* and *n.* fiancé, *m.* fiancée, *f.*
better ['betə], *a.* meilleur; *to get the better of*, l'emporter sur.—*adv.* mieux; *better late than never*, mieux vaut tard que jamais; *better and better*, de mieux en mieux; *for better for worse*, vaille que vaille; *I had better*, je ferais mieux; *so much the better!* tant mieux!—*n.* meilleur; supérieur, *m.*—*v.t.* améliorer, avancer.
betterment ['betəmənt], *n.* amélioration, *f.*
betting ['betiŋ], *n.* paris, *m.pl.*
Betty ['beti]. Babette, *f.*
between [bi'twi:n], *prep.* entre.
***betwixt** [bi'twikst], *prep.* entre; *betwixt and between*, entre les deux.
bevel ['bevəl], *a.* de biais, en biseau.—*n.* fausse équerre (*outil*), *f.*—*v.t.* tailler en biseau.—*v.i.* biaiser.
beverage ['bevəridʒ], *n.* boisson, *f.*; *breuvage, *m.*
bevy ['bevi], *n.* volée; troupe, compagnie, *f.*
bewail [bi'weil], *v.t.* pleurer, lamenter.
bewailing [bi'weiliŋ], *n.* lamentation, *f.*
beware [bi'weə], *v.i.* se garder (*de*), prendre garde (*à*); se méfier (*de*).
bewilder [bi'wildə], *v.t.* égarer, embarrasser.
bewildering [bi'wildəriŋ], *a.* déroutant, ahurissant.
bewilderment [bi'wildəmənt], *n.* égarement, *m.*
bewitch [bi'witʃ], *v.t.* ensorceler.
bewitching [bi'witʃiŋ], *a.* enchanteur, séduisant.
beyond [bi'jɔnd], *prep.* par delà, au delà de; au-dessus de; outre, hors de.—*adv.* là-bas.—*n.* au-delà, *m.*
bias ['baiəs], *n.* and *adv.* de biais, de travers.—*n.* biais, *m.*, pente, *f.*; penchant, parti pris, préjugé, *m.*—*v.t.* décentrer (*boule*); faire pencher; prévenir; influencer.
biased ['baiəst], *a.* décentré; partial, prédisposé.
bib (1) [bib], *n.* bavette, *f.*
bib (2) [bib], *n.* tacaud (*poisson*), *m.*
Bible [baibl], *n.* Bible, *f.*
biblical ['biblikəl], *a.* biblique.
biceps ['baiseps], *n.* (*Anat.*) biceps, *m.*
bicker [bikə], *v.i.* se quereller, se chamailler.
bickering [bikəriŋ], *n.* bisbille, *f.*, querelles, *f.pl.*
bicycle ['baisikl], *n.* bicyclette, *f.*; (*pop.*) vélo, *m.*, bécane, *f.*
bid [bid], *v.t. irr.* ordonner, dire, commander (*de*); inviter (*à*); offrir, enchérir; *to bid good-bye to*, dire adieu à.—*n.* enchère, *f.*
bidder ['bidə], *n.* enchérisseur, acheteur, *m.*
bidding ['bidiŋ], *n.* commandement, ordre, *m.*; invitation, prière, *f.*; enchères, *f.pl.*

bide [baid], *v.t. irr. archaic except in to bide one's time*, attendre le bon moment.
biennial [bai'eniəl], *a.* biennal; (*Bot.*) bisannuel.
biennially [bai'eniəli], *adv.* tous les deux ans.
bier [biə], *n.* civière, *f.*, corbillard, *m.*
big [big], *a.* gros; grand, vaste; enceinte, grosse (*d'enfant*), pleine (*bête*); (*fig.*) fier, hautain.
bigamist ['bigəmist], *n.* bigame, *m.*, *f.*
bigamy ['bigəmi], *n.* bigamie, *f.*
bigness ['bignis], *n.* grosseur, grandeur, *f.*
bigot ['bigət], *n.* bigot, cagot, *m.*, fanatique, *m.*, *f.*
bigoted ['bigətid], *a.* bigot.
bigotry ['bigətri], *n.* bigoterie, *f.*, sectarisme, fanatisme, *m.*
bigwig ['bigwig], *n.* (*fam.*) gros bonnet, *m.*
bike [baik], *n.* (*colloq.*) vélo, *m.*, bécane, *f.*
bikini [bi'ki:ni], *n.* (*Cost.*) bikini, *m.*
bile [bail], *n.* bile, *f.*
bilge [bildʒ], *n.* (*Naut.*) sentine, *f.*; (*colloq.*) bêtises, *f.pl.*
bilge-water ['bildʒwɔ:tə], *n.* eau de la cale, *f.*
bilingual [bai'liŋgwəl], *a.* bilingue.
bilious ['biljəs], *a.* bilieux.
bill (1) [bil], *n.* bec (*d'oiseau*), *m.*
bill (2) [bil], *n.* hallebarde, *f.*
bill (3) [bil], *n.* mémoire, compte, *m.*; facture (*invoice*), note (*hôtels etc.*), addition (*restaurants*); (*Comm.*) note, *f.*; billet, effet, *m.*; (*Banking*) lettre de change, *f.*; (*Parl.*) projet de loi, *m.*; affiche, *f.*, placard, *m.*; *bill of fare*, menu, *m.*, carte, *f.*; *bill of health*, patente de santé, *f.*; *stick no bills!* défense d'afficher!
billet ['bilit], *n.* bûche, *f.*; (*Mil.*) billet de logement, *m.*—*v.t.*, *v.i.* loger chez l'habitant.
bill-hook ['bilhuk], *n.* serpe, *f.*, vouge, *m.*
billiard ['biljəd], *a.* de billard.
billiard-ball ['biljədbɔ:l], *n.* bille, *f.*
billiards ['biljədz], *n.pl.* billard, *m.*; *to play a game of billiards*, faire une partie de billard.
billiard-table ['biljədteibl], *n.* billard, *m.*
billion ['biljən], *n.* (*since 1948*) billion; (*Am.*) milliard, *m.*
billow ['bilou], *n.* grande vague, lame, *f.*—*v.i.* s'élever en vagues, rouler.
billowy ['biloui], *a.* houleux.
bill-sticker ['bilstikə], *n.* afficheur, colleur d'affiches, *m.*
billy-goat ['biligout], *n.* bouc, *m.*
bin [bin], *n.* huche, *f.*, bac; coffre, *m.*
binary ['bainəri], *a.* binaire.
bind [baind], *v.t. irr.* lier; obliger; resserrer; border (*chaussures etc.*); garrotter; serrer; rendre constipé; relier (*livres*); *to be bound to*, être tenu de.—*n.* (*pop.*) *that's a bind*, quelle scie!
binder ['baində], *n.* lieur; relieur, *m.*; bande, attache, *f.*
binding ['baindiŋ], *a.* obligatoire; (*Med.*) astringent.—*n.* reliure, *f.*; bandeau, galon, *m.*, bordure, *f.*
bindweed ['baindwi:d], *n.* liseron, *m.*
binge [bindʒ], *n.* (*pop.*) bombe, *f.*; *to be on the binge*, faire la bombe.
binoculars [bi'nɔkjuləz], *n.pl.* jumelles, *f.pl.*
binomial [bai'noumiəl], *a.* (*Alg.*) binôme.
biochemist [baio'kemist], *n.* biochimiste, *m.*
biochemistry [baio'kemistri], *n.* biochimie, *f.*

biographer [bai'ɔgrəfə], *n.* biographe, *m.*
biography [bai'ɔgrəfi], *n.* biographie, *f.*
biologist [bai'ɔlədʒist], *n.* biologiste, biologue, *m.*
biology [bai'ɔlədʒi], *n.* biologie, *f.*
biped ['baiped], *n.* bipède, *m.*
birch [bəːtʃ], *n.* bouleau, *m.*; verges, *f.pl.*; *silver birch*, bouleau blanc.—*v.t.* fouetter.
bird [bəːd], *n.* oiseau; (*fig.*) type, *m.*; (*pop.*) femme, fille, poule, *f.*; *little bird*, oiselet, *m.*
bird-cage ['bəːdkeidʒ], *n.* cage d'oiseau, *f.*
bird-lime ['bəːdlaim], *n.* glu, *f.*
bird's-eye view ['bəːdzai'vjuː], *n.* vue à vol d'oiseau, *f.*
bird's-nest ['bəːdznest], *n.* nid d'oiseau, *m.*
birth [bəːθ], *n.* naissance, *f.*; enfantement, *m.*; (*fig.*) origine, source, *f.*
birth-control ['bəːθkɔntroul], *n.* limitation des naissances, *f.*
birthday ['bəːθdei], *n.* anniversaire, *m.*
birthplace ['bəːθpleis], *n.* lieu de naissance, pays natal, *m.*
birth-rate ['bəːθreit], *n.* natalité, *f.*
birthright ['bəːθrait], *n.* droit d'aînesse, *m.*
Biscay ['biskei]. la Biscaye, *f.*; *the Bay of Biscay*, le Golfe de Gascogne, *m.*
biscuit ['biskit], *n.* biscuit, *m.*
bisect [bai'sekt], *v.t.* couper en deux.
bishop ['biʃəp], *n.* évêque; (*Chess*) fou, *m.*
bishopric ['biʃəprik], *n.* évêché, *m.*
bit (1) [bit], *n.* morceau, *m.*; pièce (*de monnaie*), *f.*; (*colloq.*) brin, bout, peu, *m.*; mèche (*outil*); (*Naut.*) bitte, *f.*; mors (*de bride*), *m.*
bit (2) [bit], *past* [BITE].
bitch [bitʃ], *n.* chienne; femelle (*in compounds*), *f.*
bite [bait], *n.* morsure; piqûre, *f.*; coup de dent, *m.*, bouchée; (*Fishing*) touche, *f.*—*v.t. irr.* mordre; piquer; ronger; (*fig.*) attraper, pincer, couper (*vent*).—*v.i.* mordre.
biting ['baitiŋ], *a.* mordant, piquant; coupant (*vent*).
bitter ['bitə], *a.* amer, acerbe; (*fig.*) acharné, mordant, aigre.—*n.* amer, *m.*
bitterly ['bitəli], *adv.* avec amertume; amèrement.
bittern ['bitən], *n.* butor, *m.*
bitterness ['bitənis], *n.* amertume, aigreur, âpreté, *f.*
bitumen [bi'tjuːmən], *n.* bitume, *f.*
bivouac ['bivuæk], *n.* bivouac, *m.*—*v.i.* bivouaquer.
blab [blæb], *v.i.* jaser, bavarder.—*n.* bavard, *m.*
black [blæk], *a.* noir; (*fig.*) obscur, sombre, triste.—*v.t.* noircir; cirer (*chaussures*).—*n.* noir, *m.*
black-ball ['blækbɔːl], *n.* boule noire, *f.*—*v.t.* rejeter au scrutin.
black-beetle ['blæk'biːtl], *n.* cafard, *m.*, blatte, *f.*
blackberry ['blækbəri], *n.* mûre (sauvage), *f.*
blackbird ['blækbəːd], *n.* merle, *m.*
blackboard ['blækbɔːd], *n.* tableau noir, *m.*
black-currant ['blæk'kʌrənt], *n.* cassis, *m.*
blacken ['blækən], *v.t., v.i.* noircir.
blackguard ['blægɑːd], *n.* polisson, gredin, vaurien, *m.*
blacking ['blækiŋ], *n.* cirage (*chaussures*); noircissement, *m.*
blackish ['blækiʃ], *a.* noirâtre.
blacklead [blæk'led], *n.* mine de plomb, *f.*

blackleg ['blækleg], *n.* (*Gambling*) escroc; (*Strikes*) renard, jaune, *m.*
blackmail ['blækmeil], *n.* chantage, *m.*—*v.t.* faire chanter.
blackmailer ['blækmeilə], *n.* maître-chanteur, *m.*
black-market [blæk'mɑːkit], *n.* marché noir, *m.*
blackness ['blæknis], *n.* noirceur, *f.*
black-out ['blækaut], *n.* extinction des lumières, *f.*; black-out, *m.*
blacksmith ['blæksmiθ], *n.* forgeron, *m.*
bladder ['blædə], *n.* vessie; (*Bot.*) vésicule, *f.*
blade [bleid], *n.* lame (*de couteau etc.*), *f.*; brin (*d'herbe*), *m.*; pelle (*d'un aviron*); pale (*d'hélice*), *f.*; (*fig.*) gaillard (*personne*), *m.*
blain [blein], *n.* pustule, *f.*
blame [bleim], *n.* blâme, *m.*; faute, *f.*—*v.t.* blâmer, s'en prendre à; censurer, reprocher.
blameless ['bleimlis], *a.* innocent, sans tache.
blanch [blɑːntʃ], *v.t.* blanchir; pâlir; faire pâlir; monder (*amandes*).—*v.i.* blanchir; pâlir.
blancmange [blə'mɔnʒ], *n.* blanc-manger, *m.*
bland [blænd], *a.* doux, aimable, affable.
blandish ['blændiʃ], *v.t.* caresser, flatter, cajoler.
blandishment ['blændiʃmənt], *n.* flatterie, *f.*
blank [blæŋk], *a.* blanc, en blanc; (*fig.*) vide, confus, déconcerté.—*n.* blanc; (*Lotteries*) billet blanc; (*fig.*) vide, *m.*, lacune, *f.*
blanket ['blæŋkit], *n.* couverture, *f.*
blare [blɛə], *v.t.* faire retentir.—*v.i.* sonner (*comme une trompette*), cuivrer.—*n.* sonnerie, *f.*
blaspheme [blæs'fiːm], *v.t., v.i.* blasphémer.
blasphemer [blæs'fiːmə], *n.* blasphémateur, *m.*
blasphemous ['blæsfəməs], *a.* blasphématoire.
blasphemy ['blæsfəmi], *n.* blasphème, *m.*
blast [blɑːst], *n.* vent, coup de vent; son (*d'un instrument à vent*), *m.*; explosion, *f.*—*v.t.* flétrir, brûler; détruire, ruiner; faire sauter.—*int.* sacrebleu!
blast-furnace ['blɑːstfəːnis], *n.* haut fourneau, *m.*
blasting ['blɑːstiŋ], *a.* destructeur.—*n.* coup de mine, *m.*, explosion, *f.*
blatant ['bleitənt], *a.* bruyant, criard.
blatantly ['bleitəntli], *adv.* avec une vulgarité criarde.
blaze (1) [bleiz], *n.* flamme; flambée, *f.*; feu; (*fig.*) éclat, *m.*; étoile (*de cheval*), *f.*—*v.t. to blaze a trail*, se frayer un chemin.—*v.i.* être en flammes; flamber, brûler.
blaze (2) [bleiz], **blazon** (1) ['bleizən], *v.t.* proclamer; *to blaze abroad*, répandre, crier par-dessus les toits.
blazing ['bleiziŋ], *a.* flambant; enflammé, embrasé; (*fig.*) brillant.
blazon (2) ['bleizən], *n.* blason, *m.*—*v.t.* blasonner.
bleach [bliːtʃ], *v.t., v.i.* blanchir; (*Hairdressing*) oxygéner.—*n.* agent de blanchiment, *m.*, eau de javel; (*Hairdressing*) oxygénée, *f.*
bleak [bliːk], *a.* ouvert, sans abri; froid; désert; triste, morne.
bleakness ['bliːknis], *n.* exposition découverte, *f.*; froid, *m.*; tristesse, *f.*; aspect morne, *m.*
blear [bliə], **bleary** ['bliəri], *a.* larmoyant.
bleat [bliːt], *v.i.* bêler.—*n.* bêlement, *m.*

bleed [bli:d], *v.t. irr.* saigner; (*colloq.*) débourser.—*v.i.* saigner; pleurer (*vignes etc.*).
bleeding ['bli:diŋ], *a.* saignant.—*n.* saignement, *m.*; (*Surg.*) saignée, *f.*
blemish ['blemiʃ], *v.t.* tacher, flétrir.—*n.* tache, flétrissure, *f.*, défaut, *m.*
blend [blend], *v.t.* mêler, mélanger; fondre.—*v.i.* se fondre, se marier (*à* ou *avec*).—*n.* mélange, *m.*
bless [bles], *v.t.* bénir; rendre heureux, réjouir.
blessed [blest, 'blesid], *a.* béni, saint; bienheureux.
blessedness ['blesidnis], *n.* béatitude, félicité, *f.*, bonheur, *m.*
blessing ['blesiŋ], *n.* bénédiction, *f.*; bonheur, bien, *m.*
blight [blait], *v.t.* flétrir (*vent*); brouir (*soleil*); (*fig.*) |frustrer, détruire.—*n.* brouissure (*des fleurs et des fruits*); rouille (*du blé etc.*); (*fig.*) flétrissure, *f.*
blind [blaind], *a.* aveugle; obscur; **blind alley,** impasse, *f.*; **blind in one eye,** borgne; **blind side,** côté faible, *m.*—*n.* store (*fenêtre*); abat-jour, *m.*; banne (*de boutique*); persienne (*à l'extérieur*), *f.*; (*fig.*) voile, *m.*; **Venetian blind,** jalousie, *f.*—*v.t.* aveugler; (*fig.*) éblouir.
blindfold ['blaindfould], *v.t.* bander les yeux à.—*a.* les yeux bandés.
blindly ['blaindli], *adv.* aveuglément.
blind-man's buff ['blaindmænz'bʌf], *n.* colin-maillard, *m.*
blindness ['blaindnis], *n.* cécité, *f.*; aveuglement, *m.*
blink [bliŋk], *v.i.* clignoter, cligner des yeux; vaciller (*lumière*).—*n.* clignotement, *m.*
blinker ['bliŋkə], *n.* œillère (*de cheval*), *f.*
bliss [blis], *n.* félicité, béatitude, *f.*
blissful ['blisful], *a.* bienheureux.
blister ['blistə], *n.* ampoule, bulle; cloque (*peinture*), *f.*—*v.t.* faire venir des ampoules à.—*v.i.* se couvrir d'ampoules; se cloquer (*peinture*).
blithe [blaið], **blithesome** ['blaiðsəm], *a.* gai, joyeux.
blitz [blits], *n.* bombardement aérien (*2me guerre mondiale*), *m.*
blizzard ['blizəd], *n.* tempête de neige, *f.*
bloat [blout], *v.t.* gonfler, bouffir, enfler.
bloater ['bloutə], *n.* hareng saur, *m.*
blob [blɔb], *n.* goutte (*d'eau*), *f.*; pâté (*d'encre*), *m.*; (*fam.*) bévue, *f.*
block [blɔk], *n.* bloc, *m.*, bille, *f.*; billot; (*fig.*) obstacle, *m.*; **block of houses,** pâté de maisons, *m.*; **block of flats,** immeuble, *m.*—*v.t.* bloquer; **to block up,** fermer, boucher.
blockade [blɔ'keid], *n.* blocus, *m.*—*v.t.* bloquer.
blockhead ['blɔkhed], *n.* imbécile, sot, *m.*
bloke [blouk], *n.* (*pop.*) type, *m.*
blond(e) [blɔnd], *a.* and *n.* blond, *m.*
blood [blʌd], *n.* sang, *m.*; (*fig.*) parenté, *f.*; tempérament, *m.*; race (*de cheval*), *f.*
blood-group ['blʌdgru:p], *n.* groupe sanguin, *m.*
bloodhound ['blʌdhaund], *n.* limier, *m.*
bloodless ['blʌdlis], *a.* exsangue; pâle.
bloodshed ['blʌdʃed], *n.* effusion de sang, *f.*
bloodshot ['blʌdʃɔt], *a.* injecté de sang.

bloodthirsty ['blʌdθə:sti], *a.* sanguinaire.
bloody ['blʌdi], *a.* sanglant, ensanglanté, sanguinaire.
bloom [blu:m], *n.* fleur, *f.*; duvet, velouté (*de fruit*), *m.*; (*Metal.*) loupe, *f.*—*v.i.* fleurir; (*fig.*) être éclatant.
blooming ['blu:miŋ], *a.* fleurissant; (*pop.*) sacré, satané.—*n.* floraison, *f.*
blossom ['blɔsəm], *n.* fleur, *f.*—*v.i.* fleurir; être en fleur; **to blossom out,** s'épanouir.
blossoming ['blɔsəmiŋ], *n.* floraison, *f.*
blot [blɔt], *n.* tache, *f.*; pâté (*d'encre*), *m.*—*v.t.* tacher, salir; faire un pâté sur; sécher (*avec papier buvard*); **to blot out,** rayer, effacer.—*v.i.* boire (*papier*).
blotch [blɔtʃ], *n.* pustule, tache, *f.*
blotchy ['blɔtʃi], *a.* tacheté.
blotting-paper ['blɔtiŋpeipə], *n.* papier buvard, *m.*
blouse [blauz], *n.* blouse; chemisette, *f.*; corsage, chemisier, *m.*
blow (1) [blou], *n.* coup, *m.*; **to come to blows,** en venir aux mains.
blow (2) [blou], *v.t. irr.* souffler; sonner (*un instrument à vent*); faire sauter (*plomb*); **to blow away,** chasser; **to blow out,** éteindre (*une lumière*); faire sauter (*la cervelle*); **to blow up,** faire sauter; gonfler (*un pneu*).—*v.i.* souffler; faire du vent; sauter (*plomb*); claquer (*ampoule électrique*); **to blow up,** sauter, éclater.
blow (3) [blou], *v.i.* s'épanouir (*fleurs*).
blower ['blouə], *n.* souffleur; rideau de cheminée, *m.*; (*pop.*) téléphone, *m.*
blow-lamp ['bloulæmp], *n.* lampe à souder, *f.*
blubber ['blʌbə], *n.* graisse de baleine, *f.*
bludgeon ['blʌdʒən], *n.* gourdin, *m.*; trique, *f.*
blue [blu:], *a.* bleu.—*n.* bleu; azur, *m.*—*v.t.* bleuir; (*slang*) gaspiller (*argent*).
blue-bell ['blu:bel], *n.* jacinthe des prés, *f.*
blueness ['blu:nis], *n.* couleur bleue, *f.*
blue-print ['blu:print], *n.* dessin négatif; (*fam.*) bleu, projet, *m.*
bluestocking ['blu:stɔkiŋ], *n.* bas bleu, *m.*
bluff (1) [blʌf], *a.* escarpé, accore; brusque (*personne*).—*n.* à-pic, *m.*, falaise, *f.*, escarpement, *m.*
bluff (2) [blʌf], *n.* bluff (*feinte*), *m.*—*v.t.* bluffer.
bluffness ['blʌfnis], *n.* rudesse, brusquerie, *f.*
bluish ['blu:iʃ], *a.* bleuâtre.
blunder ['blʌndə], *n.* bévue, étourderie, balourdise, *f.*—*v.t.* embrouiller.—*v.i.* faire une bévue.
blunderbuss ['blʌndəbʌs], *n.* tromblon, *m.*
blunderer ['blʌndərə], *n.* maladroit, étourdi, *m.*
blundering ['blʌndəriŋ], *a.* maladroit.
blunt [blʌnt], *a.* émoussé; (*fig.*) brusque, bourru.—*v.t.* émousser; épointer; (*fig.*) amortir.
bluntly ['blʌntli], *adv.* brusquement, carrément.
bluntness ['blʌntnis], *n.* état émoussé, *m.*; brusquerie, *f.*
blur [blə:], *v.t.* tacher, barbouiller; (*fig.*) brouiller.
blurt [blə:t], *v.t.* **to blurt out,** laisser échapper.
blush [blʌʃ], *v.i.* rougir.—*n.* rougeur, *f.*; **at the first blush,** au premier abord.
blushing ['blʌʃiŋ], *a.* rougissant.

bluster ['blʌstə], *v.i.* tempêter, crier (*contre*), fanfaronner.—*n.* fracas, tapage, *m.*, fanfaronnade, fureur (*d'une tempête*), *f.*

blusterer ['blʌstərə], *n.* fanfaron; *m.*, bravache, *m.*, *f.*

blustering ['blʌstəriŋ], *a.* orageux; bruyant; bravache.

boa ['bouə], *n.* boa, *m.*

boar [bɔː], *n.* verrat, *m.*; *wild boar*, sanglier, *m.*

board [bɔːd], *n.* planche, *f.*; écriteau, *m.*; table, pension, *f.*; conseil, *m.*, administration, *f.*; (*Bookb.*) carton; (*Tailors*) établi, (*Naut.*) bord; (*Chess*) échiquier, *m.*; *Board of Trade*, ministère du commerce, *m.*; *on board*, à bord.—*v.t.* planchéier; nourrir; (*Naut.*) aborder; *to board out*, mettre en pension.—*v.i.* se mettre en pension.

boarder ['bɔːdə], *n.* pensionnaire; interne, *m.*, *f.*

boarding ['bɔːdiŋ], *n.* planchéiage, plancher, *m.*; table, pension, *f.*; (*Naut.*) abordage, *m.*

boarding-house ['bɔːdiŋhaus], *n.* pension de famille, *f.*

boarding-school ['bɔːdiŋskuːl], *n.* pensionnat, internat, *m.*

boast [boust], *v.i.* se vanter, se glorifier.—*n.* vanterie, *f.*

boaster ['boustə], *n.* vantard, *m.*

boastful ['boustful], *a.* vantard.

boat [bout], *n.* bateau, canot, *m.*, barque, *f.*

boating ['boutiŋ], *n.* canotage, *m.*

boatman ['boutmən], *n.* batelier, *m.*

boatswain, bosun ['bousn], *n.* maître d'équipage, *m.*

bob [bɔb], *n.* (*Hairdressing*) perruque ronde; lentille (*d'un pendule*); secousse, *f.*; coup, *m.*, tape; petite révérence, *f.*—*v.t.* écourter (*la queue*); secouer, ballotter, balancer.—*v.i.* pendiller, osciller, s'agiter; *to bob up*, revenir à la surface.

bobbin ['bɔbin], *n.* bobine, *f.*

bode [boud], *v.t.*, *v.i.* présager; *to bode well (ill)*, être de bon (mauvais) augure.

bodice ['bɔdis], *n.* corsage, *m.*

bodiless ['bɔdilis], *a.* sans corps.

bodily ['bɔdili], *a.* corporel, matériel.—*adv.* corporellement; entièrement, en masse.

boding ['boudiŋ], *n.* présage, pressentiment, *m.*

bodkin ['bɔdkin], *n.* poinçon; passe-lacet, *m.*

body ['bɔdi], *n.* corps; fond; cœur, centre; gros (*d'une armée*), *m.*; bande, troupe; nef (*d'une église*); personne; sève (*de vin*), *f.*; carrosserie (*d'un véhicule*), *f.*; corsage (*d'une robe*), *m.*

body-guard ['bɔdigɑːd], *n.* garde du corps, *m.*

body-work ['bɔdiwəːk], *n.* carrosserie, *f.*

boffin ['bɔfin], *n.* (*fam.*) savant, inventeur, *m.*

bog [bɔg], *n.* marécage, *m.*, fondrière, *f.*; *to get bogged down*, s'embourber.

boggle [bɔgl], *v.i.* hésiter (*à*); reculer (*devant*).

boggy ['bɔgi], *a.* marécageux.

bogie ['bougi], *n.* (*Rail.*) bogie, *m.*

bogus ['bougəs], *a.* faux, simulé.

boil (1) [bɔil], *v.t.* faire bouillir; faire cuire à l'eau.—*v.i.* bouillir; bouillonner; *to boil over*, déborder.

boil (2) [bɔil], *n.* (*Med.*) furoncle, clou, *m.*

boiled [bɔild], *a.* bouilli, cuit à l'eau; *a boiled egg*, un œuf à la coque.

boiler ['bɔilə], *n.* chaudière, *f.*; réservoir à eau chaude, *m.*

boiler-house ['bɔiləhaus], *n.* salle des chaudières, *f.*

boiler-maker ['bɔiləmeikə], *n.* chaudronnier, *m.*

boiler-suit ['bɔiləsjuːt], *n.* bleus, *m.pl.*

boiling ['bɔiliŋ], *a.* en ébullition.—*n.* bouillonnement, *m.*

boisterous ['bɔistərəs], *a.* orageux, violent; bruyant, turbulent.

boisterously ['bɔistərəsli], *adv.* impétueusement; violemment; bruyamment.

boisterousness ['bɔistərəsnis], *n.* impétuosité, turbulence; violence, *f.*

bold [bould], *a.* hardi; audacieux, téméraire; impudent, effronté; saillant, net.

bold-faced ['bouldfeist], *a.* impudent, effronté.

boldly ['bouldli], *adv.* hardiment, intrépidement; impudemment.

boldness ['bouldnis], *n.* hardiesse, audace; assurance, effronterie, *f.*

bole [boul], *n.* tronc, fût (*d'un arbre*), *m.*

Bolivia [bə'liviə]. la Bolivie, *f.*

Bolivian [bə'liviən], *a.* bolivien.—*n.* Bolivien (*personne*), *m.*

bollard ['bɔləd], *n.* (*Naut.*) pieu d'amarrage, *m.*

Bolshevik ['bɔlʃivik], *a.* bolchevik.—*n.* Bolchevik, *m.*

Bolshevism ['bɔlʃivizm], *n.* bolchevisme, *m.*

bolster ['boulstə], *n.* traversin; coussin, *m.*—*v.t.* mettre un traversin sous; (*fig.*) appuyer, soutenir.

bolt [boult], *n.* verrou; pêne; (*Tech.*) boulon, *m.*, cheville, *f.*; (*fig.*) trait, *m.*, flèche; fuite, *f.*; *thunder-bolt*, éclair, *m.*—*v.t.* verrouiller; fermer au verrou; gober, avaler (*to swallow*).—*v.i.* décamper, filer; s'emporter, s'emballer (*cheval*).

bomb [bɔm], *n.* bombe, *f.*—*v.t.* bombarder.

bombard [bɔm'bɑːd], *v.t.* bombarder.

bombardier [bɔmbə'diə], *n.* bombardier, *m.*

bombardment [bɔm'bɑːdmənt], *n.* bombardement, *m.*

bombast ['bɔmbæst], *n.* emphase, enflure, *f.*, boursouflage, *m.*

bombastic [bɔm'bæstik], *a.* enflé, ampoulé.

bomber ['bɔmə], *n.* avion de bombardement, *m.*

bombing ['bɔmiŋ], *n.* bombardement, *m.*

bona fide [bounə'faidi], *a.* sérieux, de bonne foi.

bond [bɔnd], *n.* lien, *m.*; liaison, *f.*; engagement, *m.*; obligation, *f.*; (*Fin.*) bon, *m.*; *in bonds*, dans les fers.—*v.t.* entreposer; *bonded goods*, marchandises entreposées, *f.pl.*

bondage ['bɔndidʒ], *n.* esclavage, *m.*, servitude, *f.*

bond-holder ['bɔndhouldə], *n.* obligataire, *m.*, *f.*, porteur d'obligation, *m.*

bondman ['bɔndmən], **bondsman** ['bɔndzmən], *n.* (*pl.* **-men** [men]) serf, esclave, *m.*

bondwoman ['bɔndwumən], **bondswoman** ['bɔndzwumən], *n.* (*pl.* **-women** [wimin]) esclave, *f.*

bone [boun], *n.* os, *m.*; arête (*de poisson*); baleine (*whale bone*); ivoire (*des dents*), *f.*; (*pl.*) ossements, *m.pl.*; *bone of contention*, pomme de discorde, *f.*—*v.t.* désosser.

bonfire ['bɔnfaiə], *n.* feu de joie *ou* de jardin, *m.*

bonnet ['bɔnit], *n.* chapeau (*de femme*); bonnet (*d'un Écossais*); (*Motor.*) capot, *m.*

bonny ['bɔni], *a.* gentil, joli, joyeux, gai.

bonus ['bɔunəs], *n.* boni, *m.*; prime, *f.*

bony ['bɔuni], *a.* osseux; plein d'arêtes (*poisson*).

boo [bu:], *v.t.*, *v.i.* huer.—*n.* huée, *f.*—*int.* hou!

booby ['bu:bi], *n.* nigaud, benêt, *m.*

booby-trap ['bu:bitræp], *n.* attrape-nigaud, *m.*; (*Mil.*) mine-piège, *f.*

book [buk], *n.* livre, livret; registre; bouquin (*vieux livre*), *m.*; *exercise-book*, cahier, *m.* —*v.t.* retenir, réserver; enregistrer, inscrire.

bookbinder ['bukbaində], *n.* relieur, *m.*

bookbinding ['bukbaindiŋ], *n.* reliure, *f.*

book-case ['bukkeis], *n.* bibliothèque, *f.*

booking-office ['bukiŋɔfis], *n.* bureau d'enregistrement; guichet (*de gare etc.*), *m.*

bookish ['bukiʃ], *a.* studieux; livresque (*style*).

book-keeper ['bukki:pə], *n.* teneur de livres, *m.*

book-keeping ['bukki:piŋ], *n.* comptabilité, *f.*

booklover ['buklʌvə], *n.* bibliophile, *m.*, *f.*

bookseller ['bukselə], *n.* libraire, *m.*, *f.*

bookshelf ['bukʃelf], *n.* rayon (*de bibliothèque*), *m.*

book-shop ['bukʃɔp], (*Am.*) **book-store** ['bukstɔ:], *n.* librairie, *f.*

book-stall ['bukstɔ:l], *n.* (*Rail.*) bibliothèque, *f.*, étalage de livres, *m.*

boom [bu:m], *n.* (*Naut.*) bout-dehors, *m.*; chaîne (*des ports etc.*); (*Cine.*) perche, *f.*; grondement, retentissement, *m.*; (*fig., Comm.*) grande (et rapide) hausse, *f.*—*v.i.* gronder, retentir; (*Comm.*) être en hausse, prospérer.

boomerang ['bu:məræŋ], *n.* boumerang, *m.*

boon (1) [bu:n], *n.* bienfait, *m.*, faveur, *f.*; bien, avantage, *m.*

boon (2) [bu:n], *a.* gai, joyeux.

boor [buə], *n.* rustre, *m.*

boorish ['buəriʃ], *a.* rustre, grossier.

boost [bu:st], *v.t.* (*Am.*) pousser (*par derrière*); lancer; (*Elec.*) survolter.

boot (1) [bu:t], *n.* chaussure, bottine, botte, *f.*; coffre (*d'auto*), *m.*

boot (2) [bu:t], *n.* (*used only in*) *to boot*, en sus, par-dessus le marché.

booth [bu:ð], *n.* baraque, tente; cabine, *f.*

booty ['bu:ti], *n.* butin, *m.*

borax ['bɔ:ræks], *n.* borax, *m.*

border ['bɔ:də], *n.* bord, *m.*; bordure (*de vêtement etc.*); frontière (*d'un pays*), *f.*; (*Gard.*) parterre, *m.*, platebande, *f.*—*v.t.* border.—*v.i.* aboutir, toucher (*à*); avoisiner.

bordering ['bɔ:dəriŋ], *a.* contigu, voisin.

border-line ['bɔ:dəlain], *a.* indéterminé.—*n.* ligne de démarcation, *f.*

bore (1) [bɔ:], *v.t.* percer, forer; sonder, creuser; (*fig.*) ennuyer, embêter.—*v.i.* percer.—*n.* trou; calibre; (*fig.*) fâcheux (*personne*); ennui (*chose*); mascaret (*d'un fleuve*), *m.*

bore (2) [bɔ:], *past* [BEAR].

boredom ['bɔ:dəm], *n.* ennui, *m.*

born [bɔ:n], *a.* né; *to be born*, naître.

borough ['bʌrə], *n.* bourg, *m.*, ville, *f.*

borrow ['bɔrou], *v.t.* emprunter (*à*).

borrower ['bɔrouə], *n.* emprunteur, *m.*

bosh [bɔʃ], *n.* blague, farce, *f.*, bêtises, *f.pl.* galimatias, *m.*

bosom ['buzəm], *n.* sein; (*fig.*) cœur, *m.*

boss (1) [bɔs], *n.* bosse, *f.*; moyeu (*d'une roue*), *m.*

boss (2) [bɔs], *n.* patron, chef, contremaître, *m.*—*v.t.* diriger, contrôler; régenter.

bosun [BOATSWAIN].

botanic [bɔ'tænik], **botanical** [bɔ'tænikəl], *a.* botanique.

botanist ['bɔtənist], *n.* botaniste, *m.*, *f.*

botany ['bɔtəni], *n.* botanique, *f.*

botch [bɔtʃ], *n.* pustule, *f.*; (*fig.*) ravaudage, replâtrage, travail mal fait, *m.*—*v.t.* ravauder, replâtrer, saboter.

both [bouθ], *a.* and *pron.* tous les deux, tous deux, l'un et l'autre.—*conj.* tant, à la fois.

bother ['bɔðə], *v.t.* ennuyer, tracasser; (*colloq.*) embêter.—*n.* ennui, tracas, embêtement, *m.*

bottle [bɔtl], *n.* bouteille, *f.*; flacon; biberon (*d'enfant*), *m.*; botte (*de foin*), *f.*; *hot water bottle*, bouillotte, *f.*—*v.t.* mettre en bouteille.

bottle-neck ['bɔtlnek], *n.* goulot; embouteillage (*de circulation routière*), *m.*

bottling ['bɔtliŋ], *n.* mise en bouteilles, *f.*

bottom ['bɔtəm], *n.* fond; bas; dessous, pied; derrière, *m.*; base; (*Naut.*) carène, *f.*

bottomless ['bɔtəmlis], *a.* sans fond.

boudoir ['bu:dwa:], *n.* boudoir, *m.*

bough [bau], *n.* branche, *f.*, rameau, *m.*

boulder ['bouldə], *n.* grosse pierre, *f.* bloc, *m.*

bounce [bauns], *v.i.* sauter, (re)bondir; se vanter, poser.—*n.* saut, (re)bond, *m.*; vanterie, *f.*

bouncer ['baunsə], *n.* fanfaron, hâbleur, vantard, *m.*

bound (1) [baund], *n.* bond, saut *m.*—*v.i.* bondir, sauter.

bound (2) [baund], *n.* borne, limite, *f.*—*v.t.* borner, limiter.

bound (3) [baund], *a.* (*Naut.*) allant (*à*), en partance (*pour*).

bound (4) [baund], *past* and *p.p.* [BIND].

boundary ['baundri], *n.* limite, borne, frontière, *f.*

bounden ['baundən], *a.* obligatoire, impérieux.

boundless ['baundlis], *a.* sans bornes; illimité.

bounteous ['bauntiəs], **bountiful** ['bauntiful], *a.* libéral, généreux; abondant.

bounty ['baunti], *n.* bonté, générosité, libéralité, *f.*; don, *m.*

bouquet [bu'kei], *n.* bouquet, *m.*

bourne, **bourn** [bɔ:n], *n.* borne, frontière, limite, *f.*; terme, but, *m.*

bout [baut], *n.* tour, *m.*, partie, *f.*; accès, *m.*, crise, *f.*

bovine ['bouvain], *a.* bovin.

bow (1) [bau], *v.t.* courber, plier, fléchir, incliner.—*v.i.* se courber, s'incliner; saluer; se soumettre (*à*).—*n.* salut, *m.*, révérence, *f.*

bow (2) [bau], *n.* (*Naut.*) avant, bossoir, *m.*

bow (3) [bou], *n.* arc; archet (*de violon*); nœud (*rubans*), *m.*

bowels ['bauəlz], *n.pl.* entrailles, *f.pl.*, intestins, boyaux, *m.pl.*; (*fig.*); compassion, *f.*

bower ['bauə], *n.* berceau de verdure, *m.*, tonnelle, *f.*

bowl

bowl [boul], *n.* bol, vase, *m.*, coupe; jatte, *f.*; fourneau (*d'une pipe*), *m.*; boule (*sphère*), *f.*; (*pl.*) boules, *f.pl.*; **to play** (**at**) **bowls**, jouer aux boules.—*v.t.* rouler, faire rouler; (*Cricket*) lancer, bôler.

bow-legged ['bouleg(i)d], *a.* à jambes arquées, bancal.

bowler(-hat) ['boulə(hæt)], *n.* chapeau melon, *m.*

bowsprit ['bousprit], *n.* (*Naut.*) beaupré, *m.*

bow-tie ['bou'tai], *n.* nœud carré, *m.*

bow-window ['bou'windou], *n.* fenêtre en saillie, *f.*

box (1) [bɔks], *n.* boîte, *f.*; coffret (*petit*); coffre (*grand*), *m.*, caisse; malle; (*Theat.*) loge, *f.*; buis (*arbre*), *m.*—*v.t.* enfermer dans une boîte, emboîter, encaisser.

box (2) [bɔks], *v.t.* souffleter, gifler.—*v.i.* boxer.—*n.* soufflet, *m.*, gifle, *f.*

boxer ['bɔksə], *n.* boxeur, pugiliste, *m.*

boxing ['bɔksiŋ], *n.* la boxe, *f.*

box-office ['bɔksɔfis], *n.* (*Theat.*) bureau de location, *m.*

boy [bɔi], *n.* garçon, petit garçon; fils, *m.*

boycott ['bɔikɔt], *v.t.* boycotter.

boycotting ['bɔikɔtiŋ], *n.* boycottage, *m.*

boyhood ['bɔihud], *n.* enfance, adolescence, *f.*

boyish ['bɔiiʃ], *a.* puéril; d'enfant, enfantin.

boy scout ['bɔi'skaut], *n.* (jeune) éclaireur, scout, *m.*

bra [bra:], (*pop.*) [BRASSIÈRE].

brace [breis], *n.* couple (*gibier*); paire (*pistolets*), *f.*; vilebrequin (*outil*), *m.*; (*pl.*) bretelles, *f.pl.*—*v.t.* lier, serrer, attacher; (*fig.*) fortifier.

bracelet ['breislit], *n.* bracelet, *m.*

bracing ['breisiŋ], *a.* fortifiant, tonifiant.

bracken ['brækən], *n.* fougère, *f.*

bracket ['brækit], *n.* console, applique, *f.*, tasseau, *m.*; accolade, *f.*; bras (*pour une lampe etc.*), *m.*; (*Print.*) parenthèse, *f.*

brackish ['brækiʃ], *a.* saumâtre.

bradawl ['brædɔ:l], *n.* poinçon, *m.*

brag [bræg], *v.i.* se vanter.—*n.* fanfaronnade, vanterie, *f.*

braggart ['brægət], *n.* fanfaron, *m.*

braid [breid], *n.* tresse; soutache, ganse, *f.*; lacet; galon, *m.*—*v.t.* tresser, natter, soutacher.

braille [breil], *n.* braille, *m.*

brain [brein], *n.* cerveau (*organe*), *m.*; cervelle (*substance*), *f.*; (*fig.*) jugement, esprit, *m.*; tête, *f.*

brainless ['breinlis], *a.* sans cervelle; stupide.

brainy ['breini], *a.* intelligent.

braise [breiz], *v.t.* braiser.

brake (1) [breik], *n.* fourré, hallier, *m.*, fougère (*thicket*), *f.*

brake (2) [breik], *n.* frein; *m.*; **to put on the brake**, serrer le frein.—*v.t.*, *v.i.* freiner.

braking ['breikiŋ], *n.* freinage, *m.*

bramble ['bræmbl], *n.* ronce, *f.*

bran [bræn], *n.* son, *m.*

branch [bra:ntʃ], *n.* branche, *f.*, rameau, *m.*; succursale (*d'une banque etc.*), *f.*—*v.i.* **to branch off**, s'embrancher, bifurquer; **to branch out**, se ramifier.

brand [brænd], *n.* brandon, tison; fer chaud, stigmate, *m.*; flétrissure (*d'infamie*); (*Comm.*) marque, *f.*—*v.t.* marquer au fer chaud; flétrir; (*fig.*) stigmatiser (*de*).

brandish ['brændiʃ], *v.t.* brandir.

brand-new ['brænd'nju:], *a.* tout (flambant) neuf.

brandy ['brændi], *n.* eau-de-vie, *f.*, cognac, *m.*

brash [bræʃ], *a.* effronté, présomptueux.

brass [bra:s], *n.* cuivre jaune, laiton; (*fig.*) toupet, *m.*, effronterie, *f.*

brassière ['bræsjɛə], *n.* soutien-gorge, *m.*

brat [bræt], *n.* marmot, bambin, *m.*

bravado [brə'va:dou], *n.* bravade, *f.*

brave [breiv], *a.* courageux, brave, vaillant; (*fig.*) fameux, excellent.—*v.t.* braver, défier.

bravely ['breivli], *adv.* courageusement, bravement.

bravery ['breivəri], *n.* bravoure, *f.*, courage, *m.*

brawl [brɔ:l], *n.* dispute, rixe, querelle, *f.*; bruit, tapage, *m.*—*v.i.* brailler, disputer.

brawler ['brɔ:lə], *n.* tapageur; braillard, querelleur, *m.*

brawn [brɔ:n], *n.* pâté de cochon, fromage de tête, *m.*; (*fig.*) muscles, *m.pl.*

brawny ['brɔ:ni], *a.* charnu, musculeux.

bray (1) [brei], *v.t.* broyer, piler.

bray (2) [brei], *v.i.* braire (*ânes etc.*); (*fig.*) résonner.—*n.* braiment, *m.*

brazen ['breizən], *a.* d'airain; (*fig.*) effronté, impudent.—*v.t.* **to brazen it out**, payer d'effronterie.

brazen-faced ['breizənfeist], *a.* à front d'airain; effronté.

brazier ['breiziə], *n.* chaudronnier, *m.*

Brazil [brə'zil]. le Brésil, *m.*

Brazilian [brə'ziljən], *a.* brésilien.—*n.* Brésilien (*personne*), *m.*

brazil-nut [brə'zilnʌt], *n.* noix du Brésil, *f.*

breach [bri:tʃ], *n.* brèche, rupture; (*fig.*) violation, infraction, *f.*—*v.t.* battre en brèche.

bread [bred], *n.* pain, *m.*; **brown bread**, pain bis; **stale bread**, pain rassis.

breadcrumb ['bredkrʌm], *n.* miette, *f.*; (*pl.*) (*Cook.*) chapelure, *f.*, gratin, *m.*

breadth [bredθ], *n.* largeur, *f.*

bread-winner ['bredwinə], *n.* soutien de famille, *m.*

break [breik], *v.t. irr.* casser; briser; rompre; violer, enfreindre; ruiner; défricher (*terrain inculte*); (*fig.*) amortir (*un choc*); **to break through the sound barrier**, franchir le mur du son.—*v.i.* se casser, se briser, se rompre, casser, rompre; éclater (*tempête etc.*); (*Comm.*) faire faillite; poindre (*jour*); changer (*temps*); **to break away**, se détacher; (*Mil.*) rompre les rangs; (*Box.*) cesser le corps-à-corps; **to break down**, s'abattre, se délabrer, s'effondrer, s'écrouler; (*Motor.*) tomber en panne; défaillir, s'altérer (*santé*); fondre en larmes; **to break in**, envahir, pénétrer, entrer dans; **to break into**, entamer; éclater en; **to break loose**, s'échapper, s'évader; (*fig.*) s'émanciper; **to break off**, rompre, s'arrêter; **to break out**, éclater, se déclarer (*maladie*), jaillir, paraître, s'échapper; **to break up**, se disperser; entrer en vacances; **to break with**, rompre avec.—*n.* rupture, brisure, fracture; trouée, fente; (*fig.*) interruption, *f.*; changement (*de temps*); arrêt (*dans un voyage*), *m.*; (*Sch.*) récréation, *f.*; **break of day**, point du jour *m.*

breakage ['breikidʒ], *n.* rupture, cassure; (*Comm.*) casse, *f.*

breakdown ['breikdaun], *n.* (*Motor., Mech.*) panne; (*fig.*) débâcle, *f.*; **nervous breakdown**, dépression nerveuse, *f.*

breaker ['breikə], *n.* infracteur, briseur; violateur; brisant (*mer*), *m.*

breakfast ['brekfəst], *n.* petit déjeuner, *m.—v.i.* prendre le petit déjeuner.

breakwater ['breikwɔːtə], *n.* brise-lames, *m.*, digue, jetée, *f.*

bream [briːm], *n.* (*Ichth.*) brème, *f.*

breast [brest], *n.* sein, *m.*, poitrine, *f.*; (*fig.*) cœur, *m.*, âme, conscience, *f.*; poitrail (*d'un cheval*), *m.*

breastplate ['brestpleit], *n.* cuirasse, *f.*

breath [breθ], *n.* haleine, respiration, *f.*, souffle, *m.*; (*fig.*) vie, existence, *f.*; **to be out of breath**, être hors d'haleine *ou* tout essoufflé.

breathe [briːð], *v.t.* respirer, souffler; **to breathe in**, aspirer; **to breathe one's last**, rendre le dernier soupir; **to breathe out**, exhaler.—*v.i.* respirer; souffler, reprendre haleine.

breathing-space ['briːðiŋ'speis], *n.* temps de respirer, relâche, répit, *m.*

breathless ['breθlis], *a.* hors d'haleine, essoufflé, haletant.

breech [briːtʃ], *n.* culasse (*fusil*), *f.—v.t.* culotter.

breeches ['britʃiz], *n.pl.* culotte, *f.*

breed [briːd], *v.t. irr.* élever; faire naître.—*v.i.* multiplier, se reproduire.—*n.* race, *f.*

breeder ['briːdə], *n.* éleveur, *m.*

breeding ['briːdiŋ], *n.* élevage (*de bestiaux etc.*), *m.*; reproduction; éducation, *f.*; **good breeding**, politesse, *f.*, savoir-vivre, *m.*

breeze [briːz], *n.* (forte) brise, *f.*, vent assez fort, *m.*

breezy ['briːzi], *a.* frais; jovial.

brevity ['breviti], *n.* brièveté, concision, *f.*

brew [bruː], *v.t.* brasser; faire une infusion; (*fig.*) tramer, machiner.—*v.i.* faire de la bière; (*fig.*) se préparer, se tramer, couver.

brewer ['bruːə], *n.* brasseur, *m.*

brewery ['bruːəri], *n.* brasserie, *f.*

bribe [braib], *n.* présent (*dans le but de corrompre*); pot-de-vin, *m.—v.t.* gagner, corrompre, acheter.

bribery ['braibəri], *n.* corruption, *f.*

brick [brik], *a.* de briques, en briques.—*n.* brique, *f.*; (*fig.*) brave garçon, bon enfant, *m.*

brickbat ['brikbæt], *n.* briqueton, *m.*

brick-kiln ['brikkiln], *n.* four à briques, *m.*

bricklayer ['brikleiə], *n.* maçon, *m.*

bridal ['braidl], *a.* nuptial, de noces.—*n.* fête nuptiale, noce, *f.*

bride [braid], *n.* nouvelle mariée, mariée, *f.*

bridegroom ['braidgruːm], *n.* nouveau marié, *m.*

bridesmaid ['braidzmeid], *n.* demoiselle d'honneur, *f.*

bridge [bridʒ], *n.* pont, *m.*; passerelle (*de navire etc.*), *f.*; chevalet (*d'instrument à cordes*); dos (*du nez*); (*Cards*) bridge, *m.—v.t.* jeter un pont sur; (*fig.*) combler (*une lacune*).

bridge-head ['bridʒhed], *n.* tête de pont, *f.*, point d'appui, *m.*

Bridget ['bridʒit]. Brigitte, *f.*

bridle [braidl], *n.* bride, *f.*; (*fig.*) frein, *m.—v.t.* brider; (*fig.*) mettre un frein à.—*v.i.* redresser la tête, se rebiffer.

brief [briːf], *a.* bref, court; (*fig.*) concis.—*n.* abrégé; dossier, *m.—v.t.* confier une cause à; donner des instructions à.

brief-case ['briːfkeis], *n.* serviette, *f.*

briefly ['briːfli], *adv.* brièvement, en peu de mots.

brier ['braiə], *n.* bruyère, *f.*; églantier, *m.*; (*pl.*) ronces, *f.pl.*

brig [brig], *n.* (*Naut.*) brick, *m.*

brigade [bri'geid], *n.* brigade, *f.*

brigadier [brigə'diə], *n.* général de brigade, *m.*

brigand ['brigənd], *n.* brigand, *m.*

brigantine ['brigəntiːn], *n.* brigantin, *m.*

bright [brait], *a.* brillant; poli; clair, lumineux; éclatant, vif; (*fig.*) joyeux, intelligent.

brighten [braitn], *v.t.* faire briller; éclaircir, égayer; polir; (*fig.*) illustrer, embellir; dégourdir.—*v.i.* s'éclaircir; briller, étinceler.

brightly ['braitli], *adv.* brillamment, avec éclat.

brightness ['braitnis], *n.* brillant, *m.*; clarté, *f.*; éclat, *m.*; (*fig.*) joie, vivacité; intelligence, *f.*

brill [bril], *n.* (*Ichth.*) barbue, *f.*

brilliance ['briljəns], **brilliancy** ['briljənsi], *n.* lustre, éclat, *m.*

brilliant ['briljənt], *a.* brillant, éclatant.—*n.* brillant (*diamant*), *m.*

brilliantly ['briljəntli], *adv.* brillamment, avec éclat.

brim [brim], *n.* bord, *m.—v.i.* être plein jusqu'au bord; **brimming over**, débordant.

brimful ['brimful], *a.* rempli jusqu'au bord, tout plein.

brimstone ['brimstən], *n.* soufre, *m.*

brindle(d) [brindl(d)], *a.* tacheté, bringé.

brine [brain], *n.* saumure, *f.*

bring [briŋ], *v.t. irr.* apporter (*choses*); amener (*personnes et animaux*); conduire; porter (*to carry*); transporter; réduire (*to reduce*); (*fig.*) mettre; **to bring about**, amener, causer, opérer, provoquer; **to bring down**, descendre, abattre; **to bring forth**, produire, mettre au monde, mettre bas; **to bring forward**, amener, avancer; **to bring in**, faire entrer, rapporter; **to bring into play**, mettre en œuvre; **to bring off**, tirer d'affaire, sauver; conduire à bien, réussir; **to bring on**, amener, occasionner; **to bring to again**, faire reprendre connaissance à; **to bring together**, réunir, assembler, réconcilier; **to bring up**, nourrir, élever.

brink [briŋk], *n.* bord, *m.*

briny ['braini], *a.* saumâtre, salé; (*fig.*) amer.

brisk [brisk], *a.* vif; (*fig.*) animé, actif, gai, frais, dispos.

briskly ['briskli], *adv.* vivement.

briskness ['brisknis], *n.* vivacité; activité, *f.*

bristle [brisl], *n.* soie, *f.*; poil raide, *m.—v.i.* se hérisser (*de*); se raidir (*contre*).

bristling ['brisliŋ], **bristly** ['brisli], *a.* hérissé (*de*); (*Bot.*) poilu.

Britain ['britən]. la Grande-Bretagne, *f.*

Britannic [bri'tænik], *a.* (*rare*) britannique.

British ['britiʃ], *a.* britannique; **the British**, les Anglais, les Britanniques, *m.pl.*

Brittany ['britəni]. la Bretagne, *f*.
brittle [britl], *a*. fragile, cassant.
brittleness ['britlnis], *n*. fragilité, *f*.
broach [broutʃ], *n*. broche, *f*.—*v.t.* embrocher; mettre (*un tonneau*) en perce; introduire, entamer (*un sujet*).
broad [brɔːd], *a*. large, grand, gros, vaste; (*fig.*) libre, grossier, hardi; peu voilé (*allusion*); prononcé (*accent*).
broadcast ['brɔːdkaːst], *a*. à la volée; radiodiffusé.—*v.t.* semer (*du grain*) à la volée; répandre (*une nouvelle*); radiodiffuser.—*n.* émission, *f*.
broadcaster ['brɔːdkaːstə], *n*. speaker, *m*.
broadcasting ['brɔːdkaːstiŋ], *n*. radiodiffusion, *f*.; **broadcasting station**, poste émetteur, *m*.
broaden [brɔːdn], *v.t.* élargir.—*v.i.* s'élargir, s'étendre.
broadly ['brɔːdli], *adv.* largement.
broad-minded ['brɔːd'maindid], *a*. tolérant, à l'esprit large.
broadness ['brɔːdnis], *n*. largeur, *f*.; (*fig.*) grossièreté, *f*.
broadside ['brɔːdsaid], *n*. (*Naut.*) côté, flanc, *m*.; bordée, *f*.
brocade [bro'keid], *n*. brocart, *m*.
brogue (1) [broug], *n*. accent irlandais, *m*.
brogue (2) [broug], *n*. brogue (*chaussure*), *f*.
broil (1) [broil], *n*. querelle, *f*., tumulte, *m*.
broil (2) [broil], *v.t.* griller.—*v.i.* se griller.
broken ['broukən], *a*. cassé, brisé, rompu; (*fig.*) navré; entrecoupé, décousu (*discours etc.*); accidenté (*terrain*); interrompu (*sommeil*); délabré (*santé*).
broker ['broukə], *n*. courtier; brocanteur (*articles d'occasion*), *m*.; **ship-broker**, courtier maritime; **stockbroker**, agent de change, *m*.
brokerage ['broukəridʒ], *n*. courtage, *m*.
bromide ['broumaid], *n*. bromure, *m*.
bromine ['broumiːn, 'broumain], *n*. brome, *m*.
bronchia ['brɔŋkiə], *n.pl.* bronches, *f.pl.*
bronchial ['brɔŋkiəl], *a*. bronchial.
bronchitis [brɔŋ'kaitis], *n*. bronchite, *f*.
bronze [brɔnz], *n*. bronze, *m*.
bronzed [brɔnzd], *a*. bronzé, basané.
brooch [broutʃ], *n*. broche, *f*.
brood [bruːd], *v.i.* couver; **to brood over**, rêver à, ruminer.—*n.* couvée, *f*.
broody ['bruːdi], *a*. couveuse (*poule*); distrait (*personne*).
brook (1) [bruk], *n*. ruisseau, *m*.
brook (2) [bruk], *v.t.* (*always neg.*) souffrir; avaler, digérer.
broom [bruːm], *n*. balai; genêt (*plante*), *m*.
broth [brɔθ], *n*. bouillon, potage, *m*.
brother ['brʌðə], *n*. (*pl.* **brothers** ['brʌðəz], *rhet.* **brethren** ['breðrin]) frère, *m*.; **brother in arms**, frère d'armes; **foster-brother**, frère de lait.
brotherhood ['brʌðəhud], *n*. fraternité; confrérie, confraternité, *f*.
brother-in-law ['brʌðərinlɔː], *n*. beau-frère, *m*.
brotherly ['brʌðəli], *a*. fraternel.
brow [brau], *n*. front; sourcil; (*fig.*) sommet, *m*.
browbeat ['braubiːt], *v.t. irr.* (*conjug. like* BEAT) intimider, rudoyer.
brown [braun], *a*. brun; sombre, rembruni; châtain (*chevelure*); (*Cook.*) rissolé; **brown bread**, pain bis, *m*.; **brown study**, rêverie, *f*.; **brown sugar**, sucre brut, *m*.—

n. brun, *m*.—*v.t.* brunir; (*Cook.*) rissoler, faire dorer.
brownie ['brauni], *n*. jeannette, *f*.
brownish ['brauniʃ], *a*. brunâtre.
browse [brauz], *v.i.* brouter.
bruise [bruːz], *v.t.* meurtrir, contusionner; écraser, froisser.—*n*. meurtrissure, contusion, *f*.
brunette [bruː'net], *a*. and *n*. brune, *f*.
brunt [brʌnt], *n*. choc, *m*., violence, fureur, *f*.; **to bear the brunt of**, faire tous les frais de.
brush [brʌʃ], *n*. brosse, *f*.; balai; pinceau, *m*.; (*fig.*) escarmouche; queue (*d'un renard*), *f*.—*v.t.* brosser; balayer; (*fig.*) effleurer, raser.
brush-maker ['brʌʃmeikə], *n*. brossier, *m*.
brushwood ['brʌʃwud], *n*. broussailles, *f.pl.*, fourré, *m*.
brusque [brusk], *a*. brusque.
Brussels ['brʌslz]. Bruxelles, *f*; **Brussels sprouts**, choux de Bruxelles, *m.pl.*
brutal [bruːtl], *a*. brutal, cruel, inhumain.
brutality [bruː'tæliti], *n*. brutalité, cruauté, *f*.
brutally ['bruːtəli], *adv.* brutalement.
brute [bruːt], *a*. brut, insensible; sauvage; brutal (*animaux*).—*n*. animal, *m*., brute, bête, *f*., brutal, *m*.
bubble [bʌbl], *n*. bulle; (*fig.*) chimère, illusion; duperie, *f*.—*v.i.* bouillonner; pétiller (*vin*).
bubonic [bju'bɔnik], *a*. bubonique.
buccaneer [bʌkə'niə], *n*. boucanier, flibustier, *m*.
buck [bʌk], *n*. daim; chevreuil; mâle (*lièvre ou lapin*); (*fig.*) gaillard, beau, élégant, *m*.
bucket ['bʌkit], *n*. seau; baquet, *m*.
buckle [bʌkl], *n*. boucle, agrafe, *f*.—*v.t.* boucler, agrafer.—*v.i.* se boucler; se courber.
buckler ['bʌklə], *n*. bouclier, *m*.
buckram ['bʌkrəm], *n*. bougran, *m*.
buckwheat ['bʌkwiːt], *n*. sarrasin, blé noir, *m*.
bucolic [bju'kɔlik], *a*. bucolique.—*n*. poème bucolique, *m*.
bud [bʌd], *n*. bourgeon, bouton; (*fig.*) germe, *m*.—*v.t.* écussonner.—*v.i.* bourgeonner.
Buddha ['budə]. Bouddha, *m*.
Buddhism ['budizm], *n*. bouddhisme, *m*.
Buddhist ['budist], *n*. bouddhiste, *m*., *f*.
budge [bʌdʒ], *v.t.* bouger.—*v.i.* bouger, se remuer.
budgerigar [bʌdʒəri'gaː], *n*. (*Orn.*) perruche inséparable, *f*.
budget ['bʌdʒit], *n*. sac; (*Fin.*) budget, *m*.
buff [bʌf], *a*. de couleur chamois.—*n*. buffle, *m*., peau de buffle; couleur chamois, *f*.—*v.t.* polir au buffle.
buffalo ['bʌfəlou], *n*. buffle, *m*.
buffer ['bʌfə], *n*. tampon, amortisseur, *m*.
buffet (1) ['bʌfit], *n*. buffet (*sideboard*); ['bufei], buffet, *m*.
buffet (2) ['bʌfit], *v.t.* frapper à coups de poing, souffleter.—*v.i.* se battre à coups de poing.—*n*. soufflet, coup de poing, *m*.
buffoon [bʌ'fuːn], *n*. bouffon, *m*.
buffoonery [bʌ'fuːnəri], *n*. bouffonnerie, *f*.
bug [bʌg], *n*. punaise, *f*.
bugle [bjuːgl], *n*. cor de chasse; (*Mil.*) clairon, *m*.
bugler ['bjuːglə], *n*. clairon, *m*.
build [bild], *v.t. irr.* bâtir, faire bâtir, construire; (*fig.*) édifier, fonder, baser.—*n*. construction; forme, carrure, taille, *f*.

builder ['bildə], n. constructeur, entrepreneur de maçonnerie, m.

building ['bildiŋ], n. construction, f.; édifice, bâtiment, m.; *building society*, société immobilière, f.

bulb [bʌlb], n. bulbe, oignon, m.; cuvette (*de thermomètre*); poire (*en caoutchouc*); (*Elec.*) ampoule, lampe, f.

bulbous ['bʌlbəs], a. bulbeux.

Bulgaria [bʌl'gɛəriə]. la Bulgarie, f.

Bulgarian [bʌl'gɛəriən], a. bulgare.—n. bulgare (*langue*), m.; Bulgare (*personne*), m., f.

bulge [bʌldʒ], n. bombement, m., bosse, f.—v.t., v.i. faire saillie, bomber.

bulging ['bʌldʒiŋ], a. bombé.

bulk [bʌlk], n. volume, m., grosseur; masse, f., gros, m.; (*Naut.*) charge, f.; *in bulk*, en bloc, en gros.

bulkhead ['bʌlkhed], n. cloison étanche, f.

bulky ['bʌlki], a. gros, encombrant.

bull (1) [bul], n. taureau; (*St. Exch.*) haussier, m.

bull (2) [bul], n. bulle (*du Pape*), f.

bulldog ['buldɔg], n. bouledogue, m.

bulldozer ['buldouzə], n. bulldozer, m.

bullet ['bulit], n. balle, f.

bulletin ['bulətin], n. bulletin, communiqué, m.

bullet-proof ['bulitpru:f], a. à l'épreuve des balles.

bullfinch ['bulfintʃ], n. (*Orn.*) bouvreuil, m.

bullion ['buljən], n. or *ou* argent en lingots, m.

bullock ['bulək], n. bœuf, bouvillon, m.

bull's-eye ['bulzai], n. centre, noir (*d'une cible*); œil-de-bœuf (*fenêtre*), m.

bully ['buli], n. matamore, bravache, m.; brute, f.—v.t. malmener, intimider.—v.i. faire le matamore.

bulrush ['bulrʌʃ], n. (*Bot.*) jonc, m.

bulwark ['bulwək], n. rempart; (*Naut.*) pavois, m.

bumble-bee ['bʌmblbi:], n. bourdon, m.

bump [bʌmp], n. bosse, f.; heurt, cahot, coup, choc, m.—v.t. frapper, cogner.—v.i. se cogner, se heurter.

bumper ['bʌmpə], n. rasade, f., rouge-bord; (*Motor.*) pare-choc, m.

bumpkin ['bʌmpkin], n. rustre, lourdaud, m.

bumpy ['bʌmpi], a. cahoteux (*route*).

bun [bʌn], n. petit pain rond au lait; chignon (*coiffure*), m.

bunch [bʌntʃ], n. botte, f.; bouquet, m., gerbe (*de fleurs*); grappe (*de raisins*), f.; régime (*de bananes*); trousseau (*de clefs*), m.

bundle [bʌndl], n. paquet; ballot; faisceau; fagot (*de bois etc.*), m.; liasse (*de papiers*), f.—v.t. empaqueter.

bung [bʌŋ], n. bondon, tampon, m.—v.t. boucher.

bungalow ['bʌŋgəlou], n. maison sans étage, f.

bung-hole ['bʌŋhoul], n. bonde, f.

bungle [bʌŋgl], v.t. bousiller, gâcher, rater.—v.i. s'y prendre gauchement, faire de la mauvaise besogne.—n. bousillage; gâchis, m.

bungler ['bʌŋglə], n. maladroit, savetier, bousilleur, m.

bungling ['bʌŋgliŋ], a. maladroit, gauche.

bunion ['bʌnjən], n. oignon (*de pied*), m.

bunk [bʌŋk], n. (*Naut.*) couchette, f.

bunker ['bʌŋkə], n. soute (*à charbon*); (*Golf*) banquette, f.

bunting ['bʌntiŋ], n. étamine, f.; (*Orn.*) bruant, m.; (*fig.*) drapeaux, pavillons, m.pl.

buoy [bɔi], n. bouée, f.; *life-buoy*, bouée de sauvetage; *mooring buoy*, coffre d'amarrage, m.—v.t. *to buoy up*, soutenir sur l'eau; (*fig.*) encourager.

buoyancy ['bɔiənsi], n. légèreté, f.; élan, m.; vivacité, animation, f.

buoyant ['bɔiənt], a. léger, flottant; animé, vif.

burble [bə:bl], v.i. murmurer, bafouiller.—n. murmure, m.

burden [bə:dn], n. fardeau, m.; charge, f.; poids; refrain (*d'une chanson*), m.—v.t. charger.

burdensome ['bə:dnsəm], a. pesant, lourd; ennuyeux.

bureau [bjuə'rou], n. bureau, m.

bureaucracy [bjuə'rɔkrəsi], n. bureaucratie, f.

bureaucrat ['bjuərokræt], n. bureaucrate, m., f.

bureaucratic [bjuəro'krætik], a. bureaucratique.

burgess ['bə:dʒis], n. bourgeois, citoyen, électeur, m.

burgh ['bʌrə], n. (*Sc.*) bourg, m.

burglar ['bə:glə], n. cambrioleur, m.

burglary ['bə:gləri], n. vol avec effraction; cambriolage, m.

burgle ['bə:gl], v.t., v.i. cambrioler.

burgomaster ['bə:goma:stə], n. bourgmestre, m.

burial ['beriəl], n. enterrement, m., obsèques, f.pl.; inhumation, f.

burlesque [bə:'lesk], a. and n. burlesque, m.—v.t. parodier, travestir.

burliness ['bə:linis], n. grosseur, corpulence, f.

burly ['bə:li], a. de forte carrure.

Burma(h) ['bə:mə]. la Birmanie, f.

Burmese [bə:'mi:z], a. birman.—n. birman (*langue*); Birman (*personne*), m.

burn [bə:n], v.t. irr. brûler; cuire (*briques etc.*); incendier.—v.i. brûler; (*fig.*) brûler, être impatient de.—n. brûlure, f.

burner ['bə:nə], n. brûleur; bec (*de gaz etc.*), m.

burning ['bə:niŋ], a. en feu; brûlant, ardent. —n. brûlure, f.; incendie, m.

burnish ['bə:niʃ], v.t. brunir, polir.

burrow ['bʌrou], n. terrier, trou, m.—v.t. creuser.—v.i. se terrer; (*fig.*) se cacher.

bursar ['bə:sə], n. économe, intendant; trésorier; boursier, m.

bursary ['bə:səri], n. bourse (*d'études*), f.

burst [bə:st], v.t. irr. crever; faire éclater; fendre; rompre.—v.i. crever, éclater; sauter; jaillir; s'élancer; éclore (*bourgeon*); *to burst into tears*, fondre en larmes; *to burst out laughing*, éclater de rire.—n. éclat, éclatement, m., explosion; rupture, hernie, f.

bury ['beri], v.t. enterrer, ensevelir; (*fig.*) enfoncer; cacher.

bus [bʌs], n. autobus, m.

bus-conductor ['bʌskəndʌktə], n. receveur (d'autobus), m.

bush [buʃ], n. buisson; fourré, m.

bushel ['buʃl], n. boisseau, m.

bushy ['buʃi], a. buissonneux; touffu.

busily ['bizili], *adv.* activement; avec empressement.
business ['biznis], *n.* affaire, occupation, *f.*, devoir; état, métier, *m.*; affaires, *f.pl.*, commerce, *m.*; *what business is that of yours?* est-ce que cela vous regarde? *you have no business here*, vous n'avez que faire ici.
businesslike ['biznislaik], *a.* pratique, régulier, méthodique; franc, droit, sérieux.
buskin ['bʌskin], *n.* brodequin; *(fig.)* cothurne, *m.*
bust [bʌst], *n. (Sculp.)* buste, *m.*; gorge *(de femme)*; *(Art)* bosse, *f.*
bustard ['bʌstəd], *n. (Orn.)* outarde, *f.*
bustle [bʌsl], *n.* mouvement; bruit, *m.*, confusion, activité, agitation, *f.*—*v.i.* se remuer, s'empresser.
bustling ['bʌsliŋ], *a.* empressé, affairé, remuant; bruyant.
busy ['bizi], *a.* affairé, occupé, empressé, diligent.—*v.r. to busy oneself*, s'occuper.
busybody ['bizibɔdi], *n.* officieux, *m.*
but [bʌt], *conj.* mais, que; sauf que; qui ne; *but that*, sans que.—*adv.* ne . . . que; seulement; *all but*, presque.—*prep.* sans, excepté, à part.
butcher ['butʃə], *n.* boucher, *m.*; *butcher's shop*, boucherie, *f.*—*v.t.* égorger, massacrer.
butchery ['butʃəri], *n.* boucherie; tuerie, *f.*, massacre, carnage, *m.*
butler ['bʌtlə], *n.* maître d'hôtel, *m.*
butt (1) [bʌt], *n.* bout, *m.*; crosse *(d'un fusil)*; masse *(d'une queue de billard)*, *f.*
butt (2) [bʌt], *n.* cible, *f.*; *(fig.)* point de mire; plastron *(personne)*, *m.*
butt (3) [bʌt], *n.* coup de tête, *m.*—*v.t.* cosser, frapper de la tête *(animal)*.
butt (4) [bʌt], *n.* barrique, *f.*
butter ['bʌtə], *n.* beurre, *m.*—*v.t.* beurrer.
buttercup ['bʌtəkʌp], *n.* bouton d'or, *m.*
butter-dish ['bʌtədiʃ], *n.* beurrier, *m.*
butterfly ['bʌtəflai], *n.* papillon, *m.*
buttermilk ['bʌtəmilk], *n.* petit-lait, *m.*
buttery ['bʌtəri], *a.* de beurre, graisseux.—*n.* dépense, *f.*
buttock ['bʌtək], *n.* fesse; croupe *(de cheval)*; culotte *(de bœuf)*, *f.*
button ['bʌtn], *n.* bouton, *m.*—*v.t.* boutonner.—*v.i.* se boutonner.
buttonhole ['bʌtnhoul], *n.* boutonnière, *f.*—*v.t.* accrocher *(quelqu'un)*.
button-hook ['bʌtnhuk], *n.* tire-bouton, *m.*
buttress ['bʌtris], *n.* contrefort, éperon, *m.*; *flying-buttress*, arc-boutant, *m.*—*v.t.* arc-bouter.
buxom ['bʌksəm], *a.* plein de santé et d'entrain; rondelette et fraîche *(femme)*.
buy [bai], *v.t. irr.* acheter; prendre *(billet)*; corrompre, acheter *(quelqu'un)*; *to buy up*, accaparer.
buyer ['baiə], *n.* acheteur, acquéreur, *m.*
buying ['baiiŋ], *n.* achat, *m.*
buzz [bʌz], *v.i.* bourdonner.—*n.* bourdonnement; brouhaha *(de conversation)*, *m.*
buzzard ['bʌzəd], *n. (Orn.)* buse, *f.*
buzzer ['bʌzə], *n.* trompe, *f.*; vibreur, appel vibré, *m.*
by [bai], *prep.* par; de; à; sur; près de, auprès de, à côté de; en *(with participles)*; *by far*, de beaucoup; *by no means*, nullement; *by sight*, de vue.—*adv.* près; passé.

by-election ['baiilekʃən], *n.* élection partielle, *f.*
bygone ['baigɔn], *a.* passé, d'autrefois.
by-law ['bailɔ:], *n.* règlement local, *m.*
by-pass ['baipɑ:s], *n.* route d'évitement, déviation, *f.*—*v.t.* contourner, éviter *(une ville)*.
by-play ['baiplei], *n.* jeu de scène, jeu muet, *m.*
by-product ['baiprɔdʌkt], *n.* sous-produit, *m.*
byre ['baiə], *n.* étable à vaches, *f.*
bystander ['baistændə], *n.* spectateur, assistant, *m.*
byword ['baiwə:d], *n.* dicton, proverbe, *m.*; *(fig.)* risée, *f.*

C

C, c [si:]. troisième lettre de l'alphabet; *(Mus.)* ut, do, *m.*
cab [kæb], *n.* fiacre, taxi, *m.*
cabal [kə'bæl], *n.* cabale, *f.*—*v.i.* cabaler.
cabbage ['kæbidʒ], *n.* chou, *m.*
cabin ['kæbin], *n.* cabine, chambre *(pour officiers etc.)*; *(Av.)* carlingue; cabane, case, hutte, *f.*
cabin-boy ['kæbinbɔi], *n.* mousse, *m.*
cabinet ['kæbinit], *n.* meuble à tiroirs; classeur; cabinet; ministère, *m.*
cabinet-maker ['kæbinit'meikə], *n.* ébéniste, *m.*, *f.*
cable [keibl], *n.* câble; câblogramme, *m.*—*v.t.* câbler, télégraphier.
cablegram ['keiblgræm], *n.* câblogramme, *m.*
caboose [kə'bu:s], *n. (Naut.)* cuisine, cambuse, *f.*; *(Am. Rail.)* fourgon, *m.*
cackle [kækl], *n.* caquet, *m.*—*v.i.* caqueter; *(fig.)* ricaner, glousser; cacarder *(oie)*.
cackling ['kækliŋ], *n.* caquetage, *m.*
cactus ['kæktəs], *n.* cactus, *m.*
cad [kæd], *n.* goujat, *m.*; canaille, *f.*
cadaverous [kə'dævərəs], *a.* cadavéreux.
caddie ['kædi], *n. (Golf)* cadet, *m.*—*v.i.* servir de cadet.
caddy ['kædi], *n.* boîte à thé, *f.*
cadet [kə'det], *n.* cadet; élève-officier *(d'une école militaire ou d'une école navale)*, *m.*
cadge [kædʒ], *v.t., v.i.* colporter; quémander; écornifler.
cage [keidʒ], *n.* cage, *f.*—*v.t.* mettre en cage.
Cairo ['kaiərou]. le Caire, *m.*
cajole [kə'dʒoul], *v.t.* cajoler, enjôler.
cake [keik], *n.* gâteau, *m.*; masse, croûte *(matière solidifiée)*, *f.*; *cake of soap*, savonnette, *f.*—*v.i.* se cailler, se prendre, se coller.
calamitous [kə'læmitəs], *a.* calamiteux, désastreux, funeste.
calamity [kə'læmiti], *n.* calamité, *f.*, désastre, malheur, *m.*
calculate ['kælkjuleit], *v.t.* calculer; adapter; *(Am.)* penser, croire.
calculation [kælkju'leiʃən], *n.* calcul, compte, *m.*

caning

calculus ['kælkjuləs], *n.* (*Med.*) calcul; (*Math.*) calcul infinitésimal, *m.*
Caledonia [kæli'dəuniə]. la Calédonie, *f.*
calendar ['kæləndə], *n.* calendrier, *m.*; (*Law*) liste, *f.*
calender ['kæləndə], *n.* calandre, *f.*
calends ['kæləndz], *n.pl.* calendes, *f.pl.*
calf [kɑːf], *n.* (*pl.* **calves** [kɑːvz]) veau; mollet (*de la jambe*), *m.*
calibre ['kælibə], *n.* calibre; (*Tech.*) compas, *m.*
calibrate ['kælibreit], *v.t.* calibrer, graduer.
calico ['kælikou], *n.* calicot, *m.*; *printed calico*, indienne, *f.*
California [kæli'fɔːniə]. la Californie, *f.*
caliph ['keilif], *n.* calife, *m.*
calk [kɔːk], *v.t.* ferrer à glace (*cheval etc.*).
call [kɔːl], *n.* appel, cri, *m.*; voix, *f.*; (*Naut.*) sifflet, *m.*; (*fig.*) obligation, *f.*, devoir, *m.*; demande, invitation; visite, *f.*; coup de téléphone, *m.*; *within call*, à portée de voix.—*v.t.* appeler; nommer, qualifier (*de*); convoquer; rappeler; *to be called Peter*, s'appeler Pierre; *to call for*, demander, exiger; aller chercher; *to call in*, faire rentrer; *to call in a doctor*, faire venir un médecin; *to call off*, rappeler, rompre, décommander; *to call out*, appeler, crier; *to call to mind*, se rappeler; *to call up*, faire monter; réveiller; appeler sous les drapeaux, mobiliser.—*v.i.* appeler, crier; venir *ou* aller (*chez*), rendre visite (*à*); (*Naut.*) toucher (*à*); *to call at*, passer par, s'arrêter à; *to call on*, inviter, prier; rendre visite à; *to call upon*, faire appel (*à quelqu'un*).
call-box ['kɔːlbɔks], *n.* cabine téléphonique, *f.*
call-boy ['kɔːlbɔi], *n.* (*Theat.*) avertisseur, *m.*
caller ['kɔːlə], *n.* visiteur, *m.*; (*Teleph.*) celui *ou* celle qui appelle, *m.*, *f.*
calling ['kɔːliŋ], *n.* appel, *m.*; profession, vocation, *f.*, métier, état, *m.*
callipers ['kælipəz], *n.* compas de calibre, *m.*
callous ['kæləs], *a.* calleux, endurci; insensible.
callously ['kæləsli], *adv.* durement, impitoyablement.
callousness ['kæləsnis], *n.* insensibilité, *f.*, endurcissement, *m.*
callow ['kælou], *a.* sans plume; (*fig.*) jeune, novice.
call-up ['kɔːlʌp], *n.* (*Mil.*) appel sous les drapeaux, *m.*
calm [kɑːm], *a.* and *n.* calme, *m.*—*v.t.* calmer, apaiser.
calmly ['kɑːmli], *adv.* avec calme, tranquillement.
calorie ['kæləri], *n.* calorie, *f.*
calumniate [kə'lʌmnieit], *v.t.* calomnier.
calumnious [kə'lʌmniəs], *a.* calomnieux.
calumny ['kæləmni], *n.* calomnie, *f.*
calvary ['kælvəri], *n.* calvaire; chemin de la croix, *m.*
calve [kɑːv], *v.i.* vêler.
calves [CALF]
calyx ['keiliks, 'kæliks], *n.* calice, *m.*
cam [kæm], *n.* (*Mech.*) came, *f.*
camber ['kæmbə], *n.* cambrure, *f.*
Cambodia [kæm'boudiə]. le Cambodge, *m.*
Cambodian [kæm'boudiən], *a.* cambodgien. —*n.* cambodgien (*langue*); Cambodgien (*personne*), *m.*
cambric ['keimbrik], *n.* batiste, *f.*

camel ['kæməl], *n.* chameau, *m.*
camellia [kə'miːljə], *n.* camélia, *m.*
camel-hair ['kæməlhɛə], *n.* poil de chameau, *m.*
cameo ['kæmiou], *n.* camée, *m.*
camera ['kæmərə], *n.* appareil (photographique), *m.*; *cine-camera*, (ciné)caméra, *f.*
cameraman ['kæmərəmæn], *n.* (*pl.* **cameramen** ['kæmərəmen]) photographe (*de presse*); (*Cine. Tel.*) opérateur, cameraman, *m.*
camouflage ['kæmuflɑːʒ], *n.* camouflage, *m.* —*v.t.* camoufler.
camp [kæmp], *n.* camp, *m.*; *to break up a camp*, lever un camp; *to pitch a camp*, établir un camp.—*v.i.* camper.
campaign [kæm'pein], *n.* campagne, *f.*—*v.i.* faire campagne.
campaigner [kæm'peinə], *n.* vieux soldat, *m.*
campanile [kæmpə'niːli], *n.* campanile, *m.*
campanula [kæm'pænjulə], *n.* (*Bot.*) campanule, *f.*
camp-bed ['kæmpbed], *n.* lit de camp, *m.*
camper ['kæmpə], *n.* campeur, *m.*
camphor ['kæmfə], *n.* camphre, *m.*
camping ['kæmpiŋ], *n.* (*Mil.*) campement; camping, *m.*; *to go camping*, faire du camping.
can (1) [kæn], *n.* pot, broc, bidon, *m.*; boîte en fer blanc, *f.*—*v.t.* mettre en boîte.
can (2) [kæn], *v. aux. irr.* (*inf.* **to be able**) pouvoir (*to be able*); savoir (*to know how to*); *he can read*, il sait lire; *I can do it*, je peux *ou* je sais le faire.
Canada ['kænədə]. le Canada, *m.*
Canadian [kə'neidiən], *a.* canadien.—*n.* Canadien (*personne*), *m.*
canal [kə'næl], *n.* canal, *m.*
canary [kə'nɛəri], *n.* (*Orn.*) serin, *m.*
cancel ['kænsəl], *v.t.* annuler; effacer, biffer, rayer; oblitérer (*un timbre*); décommander; (*Comm.*) résilier.
cancellation [kænsə'leifən], *n.* annulation; résiliation, oblitération, *f.*
cancer ['kænsə], *n.* cancer, *m.*
cancerous ['kænsərəs], *a.* cancéreux.
candelabrum [kændi'lɑːbrəm], **candelabra** [kændi'lɑːbrə], *n.* candélabre, *m.*
candid ['kændid], *a.* sincère, franc.
candidate ['kændidit], *n.* aspirant, candidat, *m.*
candidature ['kændidit∫ə], *n.* candidature, *f.*
candidly ['kændidli], *adv.* franchement, de bonne foi.
candle [kændl], *n.* chandelle; bougie; (*fig.*) lumière, *f.*; (*Ch.*) cierge, *m.*
candle-grease ['kændlgriːs], *n.* suif, *m.*
Candlemas ['kændlməs]. la Chandeleur, *f.*
candlestick ['kændlstik], *n.* chandelier; bougeoir, *m.*
candour ['kændə], *n.* franchise, sincérité, bonne foi, *f.*
candy ['kændi], *n.* candi, *m.*; (*Am.*) bonbons, *m.pl.*
cane [kein], *n.* canne, *f.*; (*Agric.*) cep ,*m.*—*v.t.* donner des coups de canne à.
canine ['kænain, 'keinain], *a.* canin, de chien.
caning ['keiniŋ], *n.* coups de canne, *m.pl.*, râclée, *f.*

369

canister ['kænistə], *n.* boîte en fer blanc; boîte à thé, *f.*

canker ['kæŋkə], *n.* chancre; (*fig.*) ver rongeur; fléau, *m.*—*v.t.* ronger; (*fig.*) corrompre, empoisonner.—*v.i.* se ronger; (*fig.*) se gangrener, se corrompre.

canned [kænd], *a.* (*Am.*) conservé en boîtes (*fruits etc.*); (*Jam.*) enregistré (*musique*).

cannibal ['kænibəl], *n.* cannibale, anthropophage, *m., f.*

cannibalism ['kænibəlizm], *n.* cannibalisme, *m.*

cannon ['kænən], *n.* canon; (*Billiards*) carambolage, *m.*—*v.i.* caramboler.

cannonade [kænə'neid], *n.* cannonade, *f.*

cannon-ball ['kænənbɔ:l], *n.* boulet de canon, *m.*

canoe [kə'nu:], *n.* canoë, *m.*; périssoire; pirogue, *f.*

canoeist [kə'nu:ist], *n.* canoëiste, *m., f.*

canon ['kænən], *n.* chanoine; canon (*règle*), *m.*

canonical [kə'nɔnikl], *a.* canonique.

canonization [kænənai'zeiʃən], *n.* canonisation, *f.*

canonize ['kænənaiz], *v.t.* canoniser.

can-opener ['kænoupənə], *n.* (*Am.*) ouvre-boîte, *m.*

canopy ['kænəpi], *n.* dais; (*Arch.*) baldaquin, *m.*; voûte (*du ciel*), *f.*

cant (1) [kænt], *n.* cant, langage hypocrite, *m.*; afféterie; hypocrisie, *f.*—*v.i.* parler avec afféterie *ou* avec affectation.

cant (2) [kænt], *n.* (*Arch.*) pan coupé, *m.*—*v.t.* pousser, jeter de côté, incliner.

cantankerous [kæn'tæŋkərəs], *a.* acariâtre, revêche, bourru.

cantankerousness [kæn'tæŋkərəsnis], *n.* humeur acariâtre, *f.*

cantata [kæn'ta:tə], *n.* cantate, *f.*

canteen [kæn'ti:n], *n.* cantine, *f.*, restaurant; bidon (*boîte*), *m.*; **canteen of cutlery**, ménagère, *f.*

canter ['kæntə], *n.* petit galop, *m.*—*v.i.* aller au petit galop.

canticle ['kæntikl], *n.* cantique, *m.*

cantilever ['kæntili:və], *n.* (*Arch.*) encorbellement, modillon, *m.*

canto ['kæntou], *n.* chant, *m.*

canton ['kæntən], *n.* canton, *m.*

cantonment [kæn'tu:nmənt], *n.* cantonnement, *m.*

canvas ['kænvəs], *n.* toile, *f.*; tableau, *m.*, peinture; voile, toile à voiles, *f.*; **under canvas**, sous la tente.

canvass ['kænvəs], *n.* débat, *m.*, discussion; sollicitation de suffrages, *f.*—*v.t.* agiter, discuter; solliciter.—*v.i.* solliciter des suffrages; faire la place.

canvasser ['kænvəsə], *n.* agent électoral; (*Comm.*) représentant, *m.*

canvassing ['kænvəsiŋ], *n.* propagande électorale, *f.*; (*Comm.*) prospection, *f.*

canyon ['kænjən], *n.* gorge, *f.*, défilé, *m.*

cap [kæp], *n.* bonnet (*de femme*), *m.*; casquette (*d'homme*); barrette (*d'un cardinal*); capsule, amorce (*d'armes à feu*), *f.*; (*Phot.*) chapeau (*d'un objectif etc.*); capuchon (*d'un stylo*), *m.*—*v.t.* coiffer, couvrir; (*fig.*) couronner, surpasser.

capability [keipə'biliti], *n.* capacité, *f.*

capable ['keipəbl], *a.* capable; susceptible (*de*); compétent.

capacious [kə'peiʃəs], *a.* ample, vaste, spacieux.

capaciousness [kə'peiʃəsnis], *n.* capacité, étendue, *f.*

capacitate [kə'pæsiteit], *v.t.* rendre capable de.

capacity [kə'pæsiti], *n.* capacité, *f.*; *in the capacity of*, en qualité de.

cap-à-pie [kæpə'pi:], *adv.* de pied en cap.

caparison [kə'pærizn], *n.* caparaçon, *m.*—*v.t.* caparaçonner.

cape (1) [keip], *n.* cap, promontoire, *m.*

cape (2) [keip], *n.* pèlerine, cape (*manteau*), *f.*

caper (1) ['keipə], *n.* bond, entrechat, *m.*—*v.i.* cabrioler; bondir, sauter.

caper (2) ['keipə], *n.* (*Bot.*) câpre, *f.*

capillary [kə'piləri], *a.* capillaire.

capital ['kæpitl], *a.* capital; (*colloq.*) excellent; (*Print.*) majuscule.—*n.* capital, *m.*, capitaux, *m.pl.*; capitale (*ville*), *f.*; (*Comm.*) fonds; (*Arch.*) chapiteau, *m.*; (*Print.*) majuscule, *f.*

capitalism ['kæpitəlizm], *n.* capitalisme, *m.*

capitalist ['kæpitəlist], *n.* capitaliste, *m., f.*

capitalize ['kæpitəlaiz], *v.t.* capitaliser.

capitally ['kæpitəli], *adv.* principalement; admirablement, à merveille.

capitulate [kə'pitjuleit], *v.i.* capituler.

capitulation [kəpitju'leiʃən], *n.* capitulation, *f.*

capon ['keipən], *n.* chapon, *m.*

caprice [kə'pri:s], *n.* caprice, *m.*

capricious [kə'priʃəs], *a.* capricieux.

capriciously [kə'priʃəsli], *adv.* capricieusement.

capsize [kæp'saiz], *v.t.* faire chavirer.—*v.i.* chavirer (*bateau*).

capstan ['kæpstən], *n.* cabestan, *m.*

capsule ['kæpsju:l], *n.* capsule, *f.*

captain ['kæptin], *n.* capitaine, *m.*

caption ['kæpʃən], *n.* arrestation; saisie (*choses*), *f.*; en-tête (*d'un chapitre etc.*), *m.*, légende (*d'une photographie etc.*), *f.*; (*Cine.*) sous-titre, *m.*

captious ['kæpʃəs], *a.* insidieux, chicaneur.

captiousness ['kæpʃənnis], *n.* esprit de chicane; sophisme, *m.*

captivate ['kæptiveit], *v.t.* captiver; charmer, séduire.

captivating ['kæptiveitiŋ], *a.* enchanteur, séduisant.

captive ['kæptiv], *a.* captif.—*n.* captif, prisonnier, *m.*

captivity [kæp'tiviti], *n.* captivité, *f.*

capture ['kæptʃə], *n.* capture; prise, arrestation, *f.*—*v.t.* capturer, prendre, arrêter.

car [ka:], *n.* (*Motor.*) auto, voiture, *f.*; (*Rail.*) wagon; (*Lit.*) char, chariot, *m.*; nacelle (*d'un ballon*), *f.*; **dining-car**, wagon-restaurant, *m.*; **sleeping-car**, wagon-lit, *m.*

caramel ['kærəmel], *n.* caramel, *m.*

carat ['kærət], *n.* carat, *m.*

caravan [kærə'væn, 'kærəvæn], *n.* caravane; roulotte, *f.*

caravanserai [kærə'vænsərai], *n.* caravansérail, *m.*

caraway ['kærəwei], *n.* (*Bot.*) carvi, cumin des prés, *m.*

carbide ['ka:baid], *n.* carbure, *m.*

carbine ['ka:bain], *n.* carabine, *f.*

carbohydrate [ka:bou'haidreit], *n.* hydrate de carbone, *m.*

carbolic [kɑːˈbɔlik], a. phénique.
carbon [ˈkɑːbən], n. (Chem.) carbone; (Elec.) charbon, m.
carbonic [kɑːˈbɔnik], a. carbonique.
carboniferous [kɑːbəˈnifərəs], a. carbonifère.
carboy [ˈkɑːbɔi], n. tourie, bonbonne, f.
carbuncle [ˈkɑːbʌŋkl], n. escarboucle, f.; (Med.) charbon, furoncle, m.
carburation [kɑːbjuˈreiʃən], n. carburation, f.
carburettor [kɑːˈbjuˈreitə], n. carburateur, m.
carcase, carcass [ˈkɑːkəs], n. carcasse, f.; cadavre, m.
card [kɑːd], n. carte à jouer; fiche, carte; (Manuf.) carde, f.—v.t. carder.
cardboard [ˈkɑːdbɔːd], n. carton, m.
cardiac [ˈkɑːdiæk], a. cardiaque.
cardigan [ˈkɑːdigən], n. gilet de tricot, m.
cardinal [ˈkɑːdinl], a. cardinal, fondamental. —n. cardinal, m.
card-index [ˈkɑːdindeks], n. fichier, m.—v.t. encarter.
cardiograph [ˈkɑːdiogræf, -grɑːf], n. cardiographe, m.
card-sharper [ˈkɑːdʃɑːpə], n. grec, fileur de cartes, m.
card-table [ˈkɑːdteibl], n. table de jeu, f.
care [kɛə], n. soin; souci, m., sollicitude; précaution, attention, f.; care of (abbr. c/o), aux bons soins de chez; to take care of, avoir soin de, s'occuper de.—v.i. se soucier, s'inquiéter (de); I dont care! cela m'est égal! je m'en moque!
career [kəˈriə], n. carrière, course, f.—v.i. courir rapidement.
careerist [kəˈriərist], n. arriviste, m., f.
carefree [ˈkɛəfriː], a. libre de soucis; insouciant.
careful [ˈkɛəful], a. soigneux; attentif; prudent, économe; soucieux.
carefully [ˈkɛəfuli], adv. soigneusement, avec soin.
carefulness [ˈkɛəfulnis], n. attention, f.; soin, m.
careless [ˈkɛəlis], a. insouciant, nonchalant; négligent (de).
carelessly [ˈkɛəlisli], adv. nonchalamment, négligemment.
carelessness [ˈkɛəlisnis], n. insouciance, nonchalance; négligence, f.
caress [kəˈres], n. caresse, f.—v.t. caresser.
caretaker [ˈkɛəteikə], n. gardien, m., concierge, m., f.
cargo [ˈkɑːgou], n. cargaison, f., chargement, m.
cargo-boat [ˈkɑːgoubout], n. cargo, m.
Caribbean [kæriˈbiːən], a. antillais; Caribbean Sea, la mer des Antilles, f.—n. the Caribbean, les Antilles, f.pl.
caribou [kæriˈbuː], n. caribou, m.
caricature [ˈkærikəˈtjuə], n. caricature, charge, f.—v.t. caricaturer, faire la charge de.
carking [ˈkɑːkiŋ], a. cuisant (souci); rongeur.
carmine [ˈkɑːmain], a. and n. carmin, m.
carnage [ˈkɑːnidʒ], n. carnage, m.
carnal [kɑːnl], a. charnel.
carnally [ˈkɑːnəli], adv. charnellement.
carnation [kɑːˈneiʃən], n. (Bot.) œillet, incarnat, m., carnation (couleur), f.
carnival [ˈkɑːnivl], n. carnaval, m.

carnivorous [kɑːˈnivərəs], a. carnivore, carnassier.
carol [ˈkærəl], n. chanson, f., chant, m.; Christmas carol, noël, m.—v.i. chanter.
carousal [kəˈrauzəl], n. orgie, débauche, ripaille, f.; festin, m.
carouse [kəˈrauz], v.i. boire, faire la fête.
carp (1) [kɑːp], n. (Ichth.) carpe, f.
carp (2) [kɑːp], v.i. critiquer, chicaner (sur), censurer.
car-park [ˈkɑːpɑːk], n. parc de stationnement, m.
carpenter [ˈkɑːpintə], n. menuisier, charpentier, m.
carpentry [ˈkɑːpintri], n. grosse menuiserie, charpenterie, f.
carpet [ˈkɑːpit], n. tapis. m.; fitted carpet, moquette, f.—v.t. garnir de tapis, tapisser.
carpet-sweeper [ˈkɑːpitswiːpə], n. balai mécanique, m.
carping [ˈkɑːpiŋ], a. chicanier, pointilleux.
carpingly [ˈkɑːpiŋli], adv. en glosant; malignement.
carriage [ˈkæridʒ], n. voiture, f.; équipage; (Rail.) wagon, m., voiture, f.; port, factage (de paquets etc.); affût (de canon), m.; (Comm.) frais de transport, m.pl.; (fig.) maintien, m., tenue, démarche, f.
carriageway [ˈkæridʒwei], n. dual carriageway, route à double circulation, f.
carrier [ˈkæriə], n. camionneur; porteur, messager; (Cycl.) porte-bagages, m.; aircraft-carrier, porte-avions, m.inv.; carrier pigeon, pigeon voyageur, m.
carrion [ˈkæriən], n. charogne, f.
carrion-crow [ˈkæriənˈkrou], n. corbeau, m., corbine, f.
carrot [ˈkærət], n. carotte, f.
carry [ˈkæri], v.t. porter; emporter; rapporter (chien); mener, conduire, entraîner; faire voter, adopter; (Arith.) retenir; to carry away, emporter, enlever, emmener; to carry off, emporter, enlever, remporter; to carry on, poursuivre, continuer; to carry out, porter dehors; mettre à exécution; to carry through, mener à bonne fin. —v.i. porter (sons).
cart [kɑːt], n. charrette, f.; (Mil.) fourgon, m.; carriole (de paysan), f.—v.t. charrier, transporter, voiturer.
cartage [ˈkɑːtidʒ], n. charriage, transport, m.
carte [kɑːt], n. carte, f.; menu, m.
carter [ˈkɑːtə], n. charretier, roulier, voiturier, m.
cart-horse [ˈkɑːthɔːs], n. cheval de trait, m.
cartilage [ˈkɑːtilidʒ], n. cartilage, m.
cart-load [ˈkɑːtloud], n. charretée, f.
carton [ˈkɑːtən], n. carton, m.; petite boîte en carton, f.
cartoon [kɑːˈtuːn], n. carton, m.; (Polit.) caricature, f.; dessin humoristique; (Cine.) dessin animé, m.
cartoonist [kɑːˈtuːnist], n. caricaturiste, m., f.
cartridge [ˈkɑːtridʒ], n. cartouche, f.
cartridge-paper [ˈkɑːtridʒpeipə], n. (Ind.) papier à cartouche, m.
cartridge-pouch [ˈkɑːtridʒpautʃ], n. cartouchière, giberne, f.
cart-shed [ˈkɑːtʃed], n. hangar, m.
cartwright [ˈkɑːtrait], n. charron, m.
carve [kɑːv], v.t. sculpter, tailler; graver, ciseler; découper (viande etc.).

carver ['kɑːvə], *n.* découpeur; (*Art.*) sculpteur, graveur, ciseleur, *m.*

carving ['kɑːviŋ], *n.* découpage (*de viande*), *m.*; (*Art*) sculpture, gravure, ciselure, *f.*

cascade [kæs'keid], *n.* cascade, *f.*—*v.i.* tomber en cascade, cascader.

case (1) [keis], *n.* cas, état, *m.*; question; (*Law*) cause, affaire, *f.*; (*Med.*) malade, blessé, *m.*; *in any case,* en tout cas; *in case,* dans le cas où.

case (2) [keis], *n.* étui, fourreau, *m.*; caisse (*d'emballage*), *f.*; écrin (*à bijoux*), *m.*—*v.t.* enfermer; emballer; encaisser.

casemate ['keismeit], *n.* casemate, *f.*—*v.t.* casemater.

casement ['keismənt], *n.* châssis de fenêtre, *m.*

cash [kæʃ], *n.* argent, numéraire, *m.*; espèces (*argent*), *f.pl.*; *cash down,* argent comptant; *cash on delivery,* contre remboursement; *to pay cash,* payer en espèces; *to sell for cash,* vendre au comptant.—*v.t.* toucher, encaisser (*chèque, mandat-poste*); changer (*billet*); *to cash in on,* tirer profit de, tirer parti de.

cash-book ['kæʃbuk], *n.* livre de caisse, *m.*

cash-box ['kæʃbɔks], *n.* caisse, *f.*

cash-desk ['kæʃdesk], *n.* caisse, *f.*

cashier (1) [kæ'ʃiə], *n.* caissier, *m.*

cashier (2) [kæ'ʃiə], *v.t.* (*Mil.*) casser, dégrader.

cashmere ['kæʃmiə], *n.* cachemire, *m.*

cash-register ['kæʃredʒistə], *n.* caisse enregistreuse, *f.*

cask [kɑːsk], *n.* fût, baril, *m.*, barrique, *f.*, tonneau, *m.*

casket ['kɑːskit], *n.* écrin, *m.*, cassette, *f.*

Caspian (Sea) ['kæspiən(siː)], the. la mer Caspienne, *f.*

cassock ['kæsək], *n.* soutane, *f.*

cast [kɑːst], *v.t. irr.* jeter; se dépouiller de (*arbre, animal*); (*Metal.*) couler, fondre; (*Theat.*) distribuer les rôles; *to cast a glance at,* jeter un regard sur; *to cast aside,* mettre de côté, rejeter; *to cast down,* jeter par terre, abattre, décourager; *to cast its slough,* faire peau neuve; *to cast off,* rejeter, repousser, abandonner.—*v.i.* se jeter; se déjeter (*arbre*).—*a.* fondu.—*n.* coup, jet; moule, *m.*; (*Metal.*) fonte; (*Theat.*) distribution des rôles, *f.*; rôles, acteurs, *m.pl.*; (*fig.*) nuance, tournure, *f.*, air, caractère, *m.*; (*Sculp.*) statuette, figure, *f.*, plâtre, *m.*

castanet [kæstə'net], *n.* castagnette, *f.*

castaway ['kɑːstəwei], *a.* rejeté.—*n.* naufragé, *m.*

caste [kɑːst], *n.* caste, *f.*

castigate ['kæstigeit], *v.t.* châtier, punir; critiquer sévèrement.

castigation [kæsti'geiʃən], *n.* châtiment, *m.*, correction, discipline, *f.*

casting ['kɑːstiŋ], *n.* (*Metal.*) coulée, fonte, *f.*, moulage, *m.*; (*Theat.*) distribution des rôles, *f.*

cast-iron ['kɑːst'aiən], *a.* en fonte; (*fig.*) de fer, rigide.—*n.* fonte, *f.*

castle [kɑːsl], *n.* château, château fort, *m.*; (*Chess*) tour, *f.*; *castles in the air,* châteaux en Espagne.

castor ['kɑːstə], *n.* roulette (*de meuble*); poivrière, *f.*; (*pair of*) *castors,* huilier, *m.*

castor-oil ['kɑːstər'ɔil], *n.* huile de ricin, *f.*

castrate [kæs'treit], *v.t.* châtrer.

casual ['kæʒjuəl], *a.* fortuit, accidentel, casuel, de passage; insouciant.

casually ['kæʒjuəli], *adv.* fortuitement, par hasard; négligemment.

casualty ['kæʒjuəlti], *n.* accident; accidenté (*personne*), *m.*; (*pl.*) (*Mil.*) pertes, *f.pl.*

cat [kæt], *n.* chat; (*Mil., Navy*) fouet, martinet (à neuf queues), *m.*; *tom-cat,* matou, *m.*

catacombs ['kætəkuːmz], *n.pl.* catacombes, *f.pl.*

catalepsy ['kætəlepsi], *n.* catalepsie, *f.*

catalogue ['kætəlɔg], *n.* catalogue, *m.*, liste, *f.*

catamaran [kætəmə'ræn], *n.* catamaran, *m.*

catapult ['kætəpult], *n.* catapulte, *f.*; lance-pierre (*jouet*), *m.*

cataract ['kætərækt], *n.* cataracte, *f.*

catarrh [kə'tɑː], *n.* catarrhe, *m.*

catastrophe [kə'tæstrəfi], *n.* catastrophe, *f.*; désastre, *m.*

catch [kætʃ], *v.t. irr.* attraper, prendre, saisir; (*colloq.*) pincer; frapper (*l'œil etc.*); *to catch a cold,* s'enrhumer; *to catch on,* avoir du succès, réussir; *to catch up,* atteindre, rattraper.—*v.i.* s'accrocher (*à*), se prendre (*à*).—*n.* prise; attrape; (*fig.*) aubaine, belle affaire, *f.*; cliquet (*d'une roue*); crampon (*d'une porte*); mentonnet (*d'un loquet*), *m.*

catching ['kætʃiŋ], *a.* contagieux; communicatif (*rire*); facile à retenir (*air*).—*n.* prise, capture, *f.*

catechism ['kætəkizm], *n.* catéchisme, *m.*

categorical [kætə'gɔrikəl], *a.* catégorique.

categorically [kætə'gɔrikəli], *adv.* catégoriquement.

category ['kætəgəri], *n.* catégorie, *f.*

cater ['keitə], *v.i.* pourvoir (à).

caterer ['keitərə], *n.* pourvoyeur, fournisseur, *m.*

caterpillar ['kætəpilə], *n.* chenille, *f.*; *caterpillar tractor,* tracteur à chenilles, *m.*

cathedral [kə'θiːdrəl], *n.* cathédrale, *f.*

catholic ['kæθəlik], *a.* universel; éclectique; catholique.

catkin ['kætkin], *n.* (*Bot.*) chaton, *m.*

cattiness ['kætinis], **cattishness** ['kætiʃnis], *n.* méchanceté, sournoiserie, *f.*

cattish ['kætiʃ], **catty** ['kæti], *a.* méchant, sournois, rosse.

cattle [kætl], *n.* bétail, *m.*, bestiaux, *m.pl.*

Caucasus ['kɔːkəsəs], the. le Caucase, *m.*

cauldron ['kɔːldrən], *n.* chaudron, *m.*, chaudière, *f.*

cauliflower ['kɔliflauə], *n.* chou-fleur, *m.*

caulk [kɔːk], *v.t.* calfater (*navire*).

cause [kɔːz], *n.* raison, cause, *f.*, motif, sujet, *m.*—*v.t.* causer, être cause de; occasionner, provoquer (*un accident*).

causeway ['kɔːzwei], *n.* chaussée, *f.*

caustic ['kɔːstik], *a.* caustique, corrosif; (*fig.*) mordant.

cauterize ['kɔːtəraiz], *v.t.* cautériser.

cautery ['kɔːtəri], *n.* cautère, *m.*

caution ['kɔːʃən], *n.* avis (*avertissement*), *m.*; précaution, prévoyance, prudence; caution, garantie, *f.*—*v.t.* avertir, aviser (*de*); réprimander.

cautious ['kɔːʃəs], *a.* circonspect, prudent, en garde.

cautiously ['kɔːʃəsli], *adv.* avec précaution, prudemment.
cavalcade [kævəl'keid], *n.* cavalcade, *f.*
cavalier [kævə'liə], *a.* cavalier, désinvolte.—*n.* cavalier, *m.*
cavalry ['kævəlri], *n.* cavalerie, *f.*
cave [keiv], *n.* caverne, *f.*, antre, souterrain, *m.* —*v.t.* creuser.—*v.i.* **to cave in**, céder, s'affaisser, s'effondrer (*édifice*).
cavern ['kævən], *n.* caverne, *f.*
cavernous ['kævənəs], *a.* caverneux.
caviare [kævi'aː], *n.* caviar, *m.*
cavil ['kævil], *v.i.* chicaner (*sur*).
cavilling ['kæviliŋ], *a.* chicaneur.—*n.* chicanerie, *f.*
cavity ['kæviti], *n.* cavité, *f.*
cavort [kə'vɔːt], *v.i.* cabrioler.
caw [kɔː], *v.i.* croasser.
cawing ['kɔːiŋ], *n.* croassement, *m.*
cease [siːs], *v.t.* cesser; faire cesser.—*v.i.* cesser, discontinuer.
ceaseless ['siːslis], *a.* incessant, continuel.
ceaselessly ['siːslisli], *adv.* sans cesse.
Cecilia [sə'siliə]. Cécile, *f.*
cedar ['siːdə], *n.* cèdre, *m.*
cede [siːd], *v.t.*, *v.i.* (*Law*) céder.
cedilla [sə'dilə], *n.* (*Gram.*) cédille, *f.*
ceiling ['siːliŋ], *n.* plafond, *m.*
celebrate ['selibreit], *v.t.* célébrer, fêter.
celebrated ['selibreitid], *a.* célèbre, fameux.
celebration [seli'breiʃən], *n.* célébration, *f.*
celebrity [sə'lebriti], *n.* célébrité, *f.*
celerity [sə'leriti], *n.* célérité, vitesse, *f.*
celery ['seləri], *n.* céleri, *m.*
celestial [sə'lestjəl], *a.* céleste.
celibacy ['selibəsi], *n.* célibat, *m.*
celibate ['selibit], *a.* and *n.* célibataire, *m.*, *f.*
cell [sel], *n.* cellule, case; alvéole (*d'abeilles*), *f.*; compartiment; cachot; (*Elec.*) élément, *m.*, pile, *f.*
cellar ['selə], *n.* cave, *f.*; cellier, caveau, *m.*
'cello ['tʃelou], *n.* (*abbr.* of **violoncello**) violoncelle, *m.*
cellophane ['seləfein], *n.* cellophane, *f.*
celluloid ['seljuloid], *n.* celluloïd, celluloïde, *m.*
Celt [kelt, selt], *n.* Celte, *m.*, *f.*
Celtic ['keltik, 'seltik], *a.* celtique.
cement [si'ment], *n.* ciment, *m.*—*v.t.* cimenter; (*fig.*) consolider, fortifier.
cement-mixer [si'mentmiksə], *n.* bétonnière, *f.*
cemetery ['semətri], *n.* cimetière, *m.*
cenotaph ['senotæf, -taːf], *n.* cénotaphe, *m.*
censer ['sensə], *n.* encensoir, *m.*
censor ['sensə], *n.* censeur, *m.*—*v.t.* soumettre à des coupures; censurer.
censorious [sen'sɔːriəs], *a.* critique, hargneux.
censorship ['sensəʃip], *n.* censure, *f.*; fonctions de censeur, *f.pl.*
censure ['senʃə], *n.* censure, critique, *f.*, blâme, *m.*—*v.t.* censurer, critiquer, blâmer.
census ['sensəs], *n.* recensement, *m.*
cent [sent], *n.* cent; sou (*pièce de monnaie*), *m.*; **ten per cent**, dix pour cent.
centaur ['sentɔː], *n.* centaure, *m.*
centenarian [senti'nɛəriən], *n.* centenaire, *m.*, *f.*
centenary [sen'tiːnəri], *a.* and *n.* centenaire, *m.*
centennial [sen'teniəl], *a.* de cent ans, séculaire.

centesimal [sen'tesiməl], *a.* centésimal.—*n.* centième, *m.*
centigrade ['sentigreid], *a.* centigrade.
centipede ['sentipiːd], *n.* scolopendre, *f.*, mille-pattes, *m.*
central ['sentrəl], *a.* central; **central heating**, chauffage central, *m.*
centralization [sentrəlai'zeiʃən], *n.* centralisation, *f.*
centralize ['sentrəlaiz], *v.t.* centraliser.
centre ['sentə], *n.* centre; milieu; (*fig.*) foyer, *m.*—*v.t.* placer au centre; concentrer.—*v.i.* se concentrer.
centrifugal [sen'trifjugəl], *a.* centrifuge.
centripetal [sen'tripitl], *a.* centripète.
centuple ['sentjupl], *a.* and *n.* centuple, *m.*—*v.t.* centupler.
centurion [sen'tjuəriən], *n.* centurion, (*Bibl.*) centenier, *m.*
century ['sentʃuri], *n.* siècle, *m.*
ceramic [sə'ræmik], *a.* céramique.
ceramics [sə'ræmiks], *n.pl.* céramique, *f.*
cereal ['siəriəl], *a.* and *n.* céréale, *f.*
cerebral ['serəbrəl], *a.* cérébral.
ceremonial [seri'mouniəl], *a.* de cérémonie. —*n.* cérémonie, étiquette, *f.*; cérémonial, *m.*
ceremonially [seri'mouniəli], *adv.* rituellement.
ceremonious [seri'mouniəs], *a.* cérémonieux.
ceremoniously [seri'mouniəsli], *adv.* cérémonieusement.
ceremony ['seriməni], *n.* cérémonie, solennité, *f.*; **without ceremony**, sans façon.
cerise [sə'riːs], *a.* and *n.* cerise (*couler*), *m.*
certain ['səːtin], *a.* certain, sûr; **he is certain to do it**, il le fera certainement; **to make certain of something**, s'assurer de quelque chose.
certainly ['səːtinli], *adv.* certainement.
certainty ['səːtinti], *n.* certitude; chose certaine, *f.*
certificate [sə'tifikit], *n.* certificat; diplôme, brevet; concordat (*de faillite*); acte (*de naissance, de mariage* ou *de mort*), *m.*
certify ['səːtifai], *v.t.* certifier; notifier, donner avis à.
certitude ['səːtitjuːd], *n.* certitude, *f.*
cessation [se'seiʃən], *n.* cessation, suspension, *f.*
cession ['seʃən], *n.* cession, *f.*
cesspit ['sespit], **cesspool** ['sespuːl], *n.* puisard, *m.*, fosse d'aisances; (*fig.*) sentine, *f.*
Ceylon [si'lɔn]. le Ceylan, *m.*
Ceylonese [silo'niːz], *a.* cingalais.—*n.* Cingalais (*personne*).
chafe [tʃeif], *v.t.* échauffer, irriter; érailler (*un câble*).—*v.i.* frotter; s'user, s'érailler (*un câble*); s'irriter; s'enflammer.
chafer (1) ['tʃeifə], *n.* hanneton (*insecte*), *m.*
chafer (2) [tʃeifə], *n.* réchaud (*plat*), *m.*
chafing-dish ['tʃeifiŋdiʃ], *n.* réchaud (*de table*), *m.*
chaff [tʃaːf], *n.* menue paille; (*colloq.*) plaisanterie, raillerie, blague, *f.*—*v.t.* blaguer, taquiner, se moquer de.
chaffinch ['tʃæfintʃ], *n.* (*Orn.*) pinson, *m.*
chagrin ['ʃægriːn], *n.* chagrin; dépit, *m.*—*v.t.* chagriner, vexer.
chain [tʃein], *n.* chaîne; chaînée, *f.*—*v.t.* enchaîner.

chair [tʃɛə], n. chaise, f.; siège, m.; chaire (à l'université), f.; fauteuil (d'un président), m.; *arm-chair*, fauteuil; *deck-chair*, chaise longue, transat(lantique), m.; *rocking-chair*, fauteuil à bascule; *wheel-chair*, fauteuil roulant; *to be in the chair*, présider.

chairman ['tʃɛəmən], n. président, m.

chalice ['tʃælis], n. calice, m., coupe, f.

chalk [tʃɔːk], n. craie, f., calcaire; crayon (pour dessiner), m.—v.t. blanchir avec de la craie; marquer ou écrire à la craie.

chalk-pit ['tʃɔːkpit], n. carrière de craie, f.

chalky ['tʃɔːki], a. crayeux, crétacé, calcaire.

challenge ['tʃælindʒ], n. défi, cartel, m.; (fig.) provocation, demande; (Law) récusation, f.; (Mil.) qui-vive; (Spt.) challenge, m.—v.t. défier; contester; (Law) récuser.

challenger ['tʃælindʒə], n. auteur d'un cartel; provocateur, agresseur, champion; (Spt.) challenger, m.

chamber ['tʃeimbə], n. chambre; salle, pièce, f., cabinet, m.; (Artill.) âme, f.; (pl.) bureaux, m.pl., étude, f.

chamberlain ['tʃeimbəlin], n. chambellan; camérier (du Pape), m.

chamber-maid ['tʃeimbəmeid], n. femme de chambre, f.

chamber-music ['tʃeimbəmjuːzik], n. musique de chambre, f.

chameleon [kə'miːljən], n. caméléon, m.

chamfer ['tʃæmfə], n. chanfrein, m.—v.t. chanfreiner, biseauter.

chamois ['ʃæmwɑː], n. chamois, m.

chamois-leather ['ʃæmi'leðə], n. chamois, m., peau de chamois, f.

champ [tʃæmp], v.t. ronger, mâcher.—v.i. ronger son frein.

champagne [ʃæm'pein], n. champagne, vin de Champagne, m.

champion ['tʃæmpiən], n. champion, m.—v.t. soutenir, défendre.

championship ['tʃæmpiənʃip], n. championnat, m.

chance [tʃɑːns], a. accidentel, de hasard.—n. chance, f., hasard, sort, m.; *by chance*, par hasard; *to stand a chance of*, avoir des chances de.—v.t. risquer.—v.i. arriver par hasard, venir à.

chancel ['tʃɑːnsəl], n. sanctuaire, chœur, m.

chancellery ['tʃɑːnsələri], n. chancellerie, f.

chancellor ['tʃɑːnsələ], n. chancelier, m.

chancery ['tʃɑːnsəri], n. cour de la chancellerie, f.

chandelier [ʃændi'liə], n. lustre, m.

chandler ['tʃɑːndlə], n. marchand ou fabricant de chandelles, m.; *corn-chandler*, marchand de blé; *ship-chandler*, approvisionneur de navires, m.

change [tʃeindʒ], n. changement, m.; phase (de la lune); monnaie (espèces), f.; *change of life*, retour d'âge, m.; *changes of life*, vicissitudes, f.pl.; *for a change*, pour changer.—v.t. changer; modifier; donner la monnaie de.—v.i. changer (de); se renouveler (la lune); *to change for the better*, s'améliorer.

changeable ['tʃeindʒəbl], a. changeant, variable, inconstant.

changer ['tʃeindʒə], n. changeur, m.

channel [tʃænl], n. canal; lit (de rivière), m.; passe (de port), f.; (Naut.) détroit, m.; (fig.) voie, f., moyen, m., entremise, f.; *the Channel Islands*, les îles Anglo-normandes, f.pl.; *the English Channel*, la Manche, f.—v.t. creuser.

chant [tʃɑːnt], n. chant, plain-chant, m.—v.t., v.i. chanter.

chaos ['keiəs], n. chaos, m.

chaotic [kei'ɔtik], a. chaotique.

chap (1) [tʃæp], v.t. gercer.—v.i. gercer, se gercer.—n. gerçure, crevasse (dans la peau etc.), f.

chap (2) [tʃæp], n. garçon, gaillard, type, m.; *old chap*, (colloq.) mon vieux.

chap (3) [tʃæp], **chop** (1) [tʃɔp], n. mâchoire, bouche; bajoue (de cochon), f.

chapel [tʃæpl], n. chapelle, f.

chaperon ['ʃæpəroun], n. chaperon, m.—v.t. chaperonner.

chap-fallen ['tʃæpfɔːlən], a. (fam.) penaud, abattu, consterné.

chaplain ['tʃæplin], n. aumônier, m.

chaplet ['tʃæplit], n. chapelet, m., guirlande, f.

chapter ['tʃæptə], n. chapitre, m.

chapter-house ['tʃæptəhaus], n. chapitre, m.

char (1) [tʃɑː], v.t. carboniser.—v.i. se carboniser.

char (2) [tʃɑː], v.i. faire des ménages.—n. (pop. abbr. of CHARWOMAN) femme de ménage, f.

character ['kæriktə], n. caractère; (Theat.) rôle, personnage; genre, m., nature, qualité, réputation, f.; certificat (de mœurs); (fig.) personnage, type, m.; *a bad character*, un mauvais sujet; *he is quite a character*, c'est un vrai original; *out of character*, déplacé.

characteristic [kærikto'ristik], a. caractéristique.—n. trait caractéristique, m.

charade [ʃə'rɑːd], n. charade, f.

charcoal ['tʃɑːkoul], n. charbon de bois, m.

charge [tʃɑːdʒ], v.t. charger, accuser (de); faire payer; (fig.) adjurer; ordonner à.—v.i. (Mil.) charger.—n. charge, f.; prix, m.; garde, f.; soin; ordre, commandement; (Law) acte d'accusation, m., accusation, f.; mandement (d'un évêque); résumé (d'un juge), m.; (pl.) frais, dépens, m.pl.; *free of charge*, gratis; *the officer in charge*, l'officier commandant, m.; *to take charge of*, se charger de.

chargeable ['tʃɑːdʒəbl], a. à charge (à); accusable (de).

charger ['tʃɑːdʒə], n. grand plat; cheval de bataille; (Elec.) chargeur, m.

charily ['tʃɛərili], adv. avec précaution; frugalement.

chariot ['tʃæriət], n. char, chariot, m.

charioteer [tʃæriə'tiə], n. conducteur de chariot, m.

charitable ['tʃæritəbl], a. de charité; charitable.

charitably ['tʃæritəbli], adv. charitablement.

charity ['tʃæriti], n. charité, bienveillance; aumône, f.

charlatan ['ʃɑːlətən], n. charlatan, m.

charm [tʃɑːm], n. charme, m.; breloque (trinket), f., porte-bonheur, m. inv.; (pl.) attraits, m.pl.—v.t. charmer, enchanter.

charmer ['tʃɑːmə], n. enchanteur, charmeur, m.

charming ['tʃɑːmiŋ], a. enchanteur, charmant; ravissant.

charnel ['tʃɑːnəl], *a.* de charnier.
charnel-house ['tʃɑːnəlhaus], *n.* charnier, ossuaire, *m.*
chart [tʃɑːt], *n.* carte marine, *f.*—*v.t.* porter sur une carte.
charter ['tʃɑːtə], *n.* charte, *f.*, acte, *m.*; *on charter*, loué, affrété.—*v.t.* établir par un acte; (*Comm.*) fréter, affréter; *chartered accountant*, expert comptable, *m.*; *charter plane*, avion-taxi, *m.*
charwoman ['tʃɑːwumən], *n.* (*pl.* -women [wimin]) femme de journée, femme de ménage, *f.*
chary ['tʃɛəri], *a.* prudent, économe.
chase (1) [tʃeis], *n.* chasse; poursuite, *f.*—*v.t.* chasser, poursuivre; *to chase away*, chasser.
chase (2) [tʃeis], *v.t.* (*Metal.*) ciseler.
chasm [kæzm], *n.* abîme; chasme; vide énorme, *m.*, brèche, fissure, *f.*
chassis ['ʃæsi], *n.* (*Motor.*) châssis, *m.*
chaste [tʃeist], *a.* chaste, pudique; pur (*language*); de bon goût.
chasten [tʃeisn], *v.t.* châtier; purifier.
chastise [tʃæs'taiz], *v.t.* châtier.
chastisement ['tʃæstizmənt], *n.* châtiment, *m.*
chastity ['tʃæstiti], *n.* chasteté, pureté, *f.*
chasuble ['tʃæzjubl], *n.* chasuble, *f.*
chat [tʃæt], *n.* causerie; (*colloq.*) causette, *f.*, entretien, *m.*—*v.i.* causer, bavarder; (*colloq.*) faire la causette.
chattel [tʃætl], *n.* bien meuble, *m.*; *goods and chattels*, biens et effets, *m.pl.*
chatter ['tʃætə], *v.i.* jaser, bavarder; jacasser (*singes etc.*); babiller; claquer (*dents*).—*n.* caquetage, *m.*, jaserie, *f.*
chatterbox ['tʃætəbɔks], *n.* moulin à paroles, jaseur, babillard, *m.*
chattering ['tʃætəriŋ], *n.* jaserie, *f.*; claquement (*des dents*), *m.*
chatty ['tʃæti], *a.* causeur, bavard.
chauffeur ['ʃoufə, ʃou'fəː], *n.* chauffeur, *m.*
cheap [tʃiːp], *a.* (à) bon marché; peu coûteux; de peu de valeur; *dirt cheap*, pour rien, à vil prix.
cheapen ['tʃiːpən], *v.t.* faire baisser le prix de; *to cheapen oneself*, se déprécier.
cheaper ['tʃiːpə], *a.* (à) meilleur marché.
cheaply ['tʃiːpli], *adv.* à bon marché, à bon compte.
cheapness ['tʃiːpnis], *n.* bon marché, bas prix, *m.*
cheat [tʃiːt], *n.* fourberie, tromperie, *f.*; trompeur; (*Cards etc.*) tricheur, *m.*—*v.t.* tromper; (*Cards etc.*) tricher.
cheating ['tʃiːtiŋ], *n.* tromperie; (*Cards etc.*) tricherie, *f.*
check [tʃek], *v.t.* réprimer; arrêter; contenir; (*Comm.*) vérifier; enregistrer (*bagages etc.*); contrôler (*comptes*); (*Chess*) faire échec à.—*n.* échec, obstacle; (*Comm.*) bon; (*Am.*) [CHEQUE]; carreau, damier (*dessin*); (*Chess*) échec, *m.*
checking ['tʃekiŋ], *n.* répression, *f.*; contrôle, *m.*
checkmate ['tʃekmeit], *n.* échec et mat, *m.*—*v.t.* mettre échec et mat, mater.
cheek [tʃiːk], *n.* joue; bajoue (*cochon*); (*fig.*) impudence, *f.*, front, toupet, *m.*; *cheek by jowl*, côte à côte.—*v.t.* narguer.
cheek-bone ['tʃiːkboun], *n.* pommette, *f.*
cheeky ['tʃiːki], *a.* impudent, effronté.

cheep [tʃiːp], *n.* piaulement, *m.*—*v.i.* piauler.
cheer [tʃiə], *n.* chère (*aliment etc.*); gaieté, *f.*, courage, *m.*; acclamation, *f.*, applaudissement, hourra, vivat, *m.*—*v.t.* égayer, réjouir, animer; applaudir, acclamer.—*v.i.* se réjouir; applaudir.
cheerful ['tʃiəful], *a.* joyeux, gai; riant (*paysage etc.*).
cheerfully ['tʃiəfuli], *adv.* gaiement, joyeusement.
cheerfulness ['tʃiəfulnis], *n.* gaieté, allégresse, bonne humeur, *f.*
cheerily ['tʃiərili], *adv.* gaiement.
cheering ['tʃiəriŋ], *a.* consolant, encourageant.—*n.* applaudissements, *m.pl.*
cheerio! ['tʃiəriou], *int.* (*fam.*) (*good-bye*) à bientôt! (*when drinking*) à votre santé!
cheerless ['tʃiəlis], *a.* triste, morne.
cheery ['tʃiəri], *a.* gai, joyeux, réjoui.
cheese [tʃiːz], *n.* fromage, *m.*
cheese-paring ['tʃiːzpɛəriŋ], *n.*(*fig.*) économie de bouts de chandelle, *f.*
cheetah, chetah ['tʃiːtə], *n.* guépard, *m.*
chef [ʃef], *n.* chef (cuisinier), *m.*
chemical ['kemikəl], *a.* chimique.
chemically ['kemikli], *adv.* chimiquement.
chemicals ['kemikəlz], *n.pl.* produits chimiques, *m.pl.*
chemise [ʃi'miːz], *n.* chemise de femme, *f.*
chemist ['kemist], *n.* (*scientist*) chimiste, *m.*, *f.*; (*druggist*) pharmacien, *m.*; *chemist's shop*, pharmacie, *f.*
chemistry ['kemistri], *n.* chimie, *f.*
cheque [tʃek], *n.* chèque, *m.*; *crossed* or *open cheque*, chèque barré *ou* non barré.
cheque-book ['tʃekbuk], *n.* carnet de chèques, *m.*
cherish ['tʃeriʃ], *v.t.* chérir; soigner; nourrir, entretenir (*de l'espoir etc.*).
cherry ['tʃeri], *n.* cerise, *f.*
cherry-tree ['tʃeritriː], *n.* cerisier, *m.*
cherub ['tʃerəb], *n.* (*pl.* **cherubs** ['tʃerəbz], **cherubim** ['tʃerəbim]), chérubin, *m.*
cherubic [tʃə'ruːbik], *a.* de chérubin, angélique.
chess [tʃes], *n.* échecs, *m.pl.*
chess-board ['tʃesbɔːd], *n.* échiquier, *m.*
chessman ['tʃesmən], *n.* (*pl.* **chessmen** ['tʃesmen]) pièce, *f.*; *a set of chessmen*, un jeu d'échecs.
chest [tʃest], *n.* coffre, *m.*, caisse, *f.*; (*Anat.*) poitrine, *f.*; poitrail (*de cheval*), *m.*; *chest of drawers*, commode, *f.*
chestnut ['tʃesnʌt], *a.* châtain, marron (*couleur*); alezan (*cheval*).—*n.* marron, *m.*; châtaigne, *f.*
chestnut-tree ['tʃesnʌtriː], *n.* châtaignier (*Spanish chestnut*); marronnier (d'Inde) (*horse-chestnut*), *m.*
chevalier [ʃevə'liə], *n.* chevalier, *m.*
chevron ['ʃevrən], *n.* chevron, *m.*
chew [tʃuː], *v.t.* mâcher; (*fig.*) *to chew over*, ruminer.
chick [tʃik], *n.* poussin; (*fig.*) poulet, *m.*
chicken ['tʃikin], *n.* poussin; poulet, *m.*
chicken-hearted ['tʃikin'hɑːtid], *a.* peureux, poltron.
chicken-pox ['tʃikinpɔks], *n.* varicelle, *f.*
chickweed ['tʃikwiːd], *n.* mouron des oiseaux, *m.*

chicory ['tʃikəri], n. chicorée (*assaisonnement ou pour remplacer le café*); endive (*légume*), f.
chide [tʃaid], v.t. gronder, blâmer.
chief [tʃiːf], a. principal.—n. chef, m.; partie principale, f.; (*fam.*) **the chief**, le patron, m.
chiefly ['tʃiːfli], adv. surtout, principalement.
chieftain ['tʃiːftən], n. chef de clan, m.
chiffon ['ʃifɔn], n. chiffon, m.
chiffonier [ʃifə'niə], n. chiffonnier, m.
chilblain ['tʃilblein], n. engelure, f.
child [tʃaild], n. (pl. **children** ['tʃildrən]) enfant, m.,f.; **with child**, enceinte.
child-bed ['tʃaildbed], n. couches, f.pl.
child-birth ['tʃaildbəːθ], n. enfantement, m.
childhood ['tʃaildhud], n. enfance, f.
childish ['tʃaildiʃ], a. enfantin; puéril.
childishness ['tʃaildiʃnis], n. puérilité, f.; enfantillage, m.
Chile ['tʃili], le Chili, m.
Chilean ['tʃilien], a. chilien.—n. Chilien (*personne*), m.
chill [tʃil], a. froid; glacé.—n. froid; refroidissement, frisson, m.; **to catch a chill**, prendre froid.—v.t. refroidir; (*fig.*) glacer; décourager.
chilli ['tʃili], n. piment, m.
chilliness ['tʃilinis], n. froid, frisson, m.; froideur, f.
chilly ['tʃili], a. un peu froid (*chose*); frileux (*personne ou temps*).
chime [tʃaim], n. carillon, m.—v.t., v.i. carillonner.
chimera [kai'miərə], n. chimère, f.
chimney ['tʃimni], n. cheminée, f.
chimney-corner ['tʃimni'kɔːnə], n. coin du feu, m.
chimney-piece ['tʃimnipiːs], n. chambranle ou manteau de cheminée, m.; (*colloq.*) cheminée, f.
chimney-pot ['tʃimnipɔt], n. tuyau de cheminée, m.
chimney-sweep ['tʃimniswiːp], n. ramoneur, m.
chimpanzee [tʃimpæn'ziː], n. chimpanzé, m.
chin [tʃin], n. menton, m.
China ['tʃainə], la Chine, f.
china ['tʃainə], n. porcelaine, f.
Chinese [tʃai'niːz], a. chinois, de Chine.—n. chinois (*langue*); Chinois (*personne*), m.
chink [tʃiŋk], n. crevasse, fente, lézarde, f.; son, tintement; (*slang*) argent, m.—v.t. crevasser; faire sonner.—v.i. se fendiller; sonner.
chintz [tʃints], n. (*Tex.*) indienne, f.
chip [tʃip], n. copeau, fragment, éclat (*de bois*); (*Cards*) jeton, m.; (pl., *Cook.*) (pommes de terre) frites, f.pl.—v.t. tailler; railler.—v.i. s'écorner; s'écailler (*porcelaine etc.*).
chiropodist [ki'rɔpədist], n. pédicure, m.,f.
chirp [tʃəːp], v.i. pépier, gazouiller; crier (*insectes*).—n. gazouillement, pépiement; cri (*insectes*), m.
chirpy ['tʃəːpi], a. (*colloq.*) gai, réjoui.
chirrup ['tʃirəp], [CHIRP.]
chisel [tʃizl], n. ciseau, m.—v.t. ciseler.
chit [tʃit], n. marmot, bambin; billet (*lettre*), m.
chitchat ['tʃittʃæt], n. caquet, babillage, m.
chivalrous ['ʃivəlrəs], a. chevaleresque.
chivalry ['ʃivəlri], n. chevalerie, f.
chives [tʃaivz], n.pl. ciboulette, f.
chlorate ['klɔːreit], n. (*Chem.*) chlorate, m.

chlorinate ['klɔːrineit], v.t. verduniser (*eau potable*).
chlorine ['klɔːriːn], n. chlore, m.
chloroform ['klɔrəfɔːm], n. chloroforme, m.—v.t. chloroformer.
chlorophyll ['klɔrəfil], n. chlorophylle, f.
choc-ice ['tʃɔkais], n. chocolat glacé, m.
chock-full [tʃɔk'ful], (*fam.*) **chock-a-block** ['tʃɔkə'blɔk], a. plein comme un œuf, comble.
chocolate ['tʃɔkəlit], n. chocolat, m.
choice [tʃɔis], a. choisi; de choix; recherché; fin (*vin*).—n. choix, m.; élite, f.; assortiment, m.
choir ['kwaiə], n. chœur, m.
choke [tʃouk], v.t. étouffer, suffoquer; engorger.—v.i. s'engorger.—n. étranglement (*de voix*); (*Motor.*) starter, m.
choking ['tʃoukiŋ], a. étouffant.—n. étouffement, m., suffocation, f.
choky ['tʃouki], a. étouffant, suffoquant.
choler ['kɔlə], n. colère, bile, f.
cholera ['kɔlərə], n. choléra, m.
choleric ['kɔlərik], a. colérique, irascible.
choose [tʃuːz], v.t. irr. choisir; élire; préférer; vouloir.
chop (1) [CHAP.]
chop (2) [tʃɔp], v.t. couper en morceaux, hacher; trafiquer, troquer; **to chop down**, abattre.—v.i. trafiquer, troquer; (*Naut.*) tourner (*vent*); clapoter (*mer*); **to chop and change**, (*fig.*) girouetter.—n. tranche; côtelette (*de mouton*); (*colloq., pl.*) gueule, f.
chopper ['tʃɔpə], n. couperet, m.
chopping ['tʃɔpiŋ], n. coupe, action de couper, f.
choppy ['tʃɔpi], a. crevassé, haché; clapoteux (*mer*).
choral ['kɔːrəl], a. choral, en ou de chœur.
chord [kɔːd], n. corde, f.; (*Mus.*) accord, m.
chores [tʃɔːz], n.pl. corvées domestiques, f.pl.
chorister ['kɔristə], n. choriste, m.; enfant de chœur, m.,f.
chorus ['kɔːrəs], n. chœur; refrain, m.
Christ [kraist]. le Christ, m.
christen [krisn], v.t. baptiser.
Christendom ['krisndəm]. chrétienté, f.
christening ['krisniŋ], n. baptême, m.
Christian ['kristjən], a. and n. chrétien, m.; **Christian name**, prénom, m.
Christianity [kristi'æniti], n. christianisme, m.
Christmas ['krisməs]. Noël, m., la fête de Noël, f.; **Christmas carol**, chant de Noël, m.; **Christmas Eve**, la veille de Noël, f.
Christmas-box ['krisməsbɔks], n. étrennes, f.pl.
Christopher ['kristəfə]. Christophe, m.
chrome [kroum], n. bichromate de potasse, m.; **chrome leather**, cuir chromé, m.
chromium ['kroumiəm], n. chrome, m.
chronic ['krɔnik], a. chronique.
chronicle ['krɔnikl], n. chronique, f.
chronicler ['krɔniklə], n. chroniqueur, m.
chronological [krɔnə'lɔdʒikəl], a. chronologique.
chrysalis ['krisəlis], n. chrysalide, f.
chrysanthemum [kri'sænθəmʌm], n. chrysanthème, m.
chub [tʃʌb], n. (*Ichth.*) chabot, chevesne, m.
chubby ['tʃʌbi], a. joufflu; potelé (*mains*).

chuck (1) [tʃʌk], *n.* gloussement, *m.*—*v.i.* glousser.

chuck (2) [tʃʌk], *n.* petite tape sous le menton, *f.*

chuckle [tʃʌkl], *v.i.* rire tout bas, rire sous cape (*de*).—*n.* rire étouffé, gloussement, *m.*

chum [tʃʌm], *n.* copain, *m.*

chummy [tʃʌmi], *a.* intime.

chump [tʃʌmp], *n.* tronçon (*de bois*); (*colloq.*) idiot, *m.*; *chump chop,* côtelette de gigot, *f.*

chunk [tʃʌŋk], *n.* gros morceau, *m.*

church [tʃəːtʃ], *n.* église, *f.*; (*Protestant*) temple, *m.*

churchwarden [ˈtʃəːtʃˈwɔːdn], *n.* marguillier, *m.*

churchyard [ˈtʃəːtʃjɑːd], *n.* cimetière, *m.*

churl [tʃəːl], *n.* rustre, manant, ladre, *m.*

churlish [ˈtʃəːliʃ], *a.* grossier, rude, ladre.

churlishly [ˈtʃəːliʃli], *adv.* grossièrement.

churlishness [ˈtʃəːliʃnis], *n.* grossièreté, *f.*

churn [tʃəːn], *n.* baratte, *f.*; (*Rail.*) *milk churn,* bidon à lait, *m.*—*v.t.* baratter.

chute [ʃuːt], *n.* chute (*d'eau*); glissière, piste (*de luges*), *f.*

Cicero [ˈsisərou]. Cicéron, *m.*

cider [ˈsaidə], *n.* cidre, *m.*

cigar [siˈgɑː], *n.* cigare, *m.*

cigarette [sigəˈret], *n.* cigarette, *f.*

cinder [ˈsində], *n.* cendre, *f.*; (*pl.*) escarbilles (*de charbon*), *f.pl.*

Cinderella [sindəˈrelə]. Cendrillon, *f.*

cine-camera [ˈsinikæmərə], *n.* (ciné)caméra, *f.*

cinema [ˈsinimə], *n.* cinéma, *m.*

cinnamon [ˈsinəmən], *n.* cannelle, *f.*

cipher [ˈsaifə], *n.* zéro; chiffre, *m.*—*v.t., v.i.* chiffrer; calculer.

circle [səːkl], *n.* cercle, *m.*; (*fig.*) coterie, *f.*—*v.t.* entourer (*de*).—*v.i.* tournoyer.

circlet [ˈsəːklit], *n.* petit cercle, anneau, *m.*

circuit [ˈsəːkit], *n.* rotation, révolution, *f.*, tour; circuit, *m.*, circonférence; tournée (*de juge etc.*), *f.*

circuitous [səːˈkjuːitəs], *a.* détourné, sinueux.

circular [ˈsəːkjulə], *a.* circulaire.—*n.* circulaire, *f.*, bulletin, *m.*

circulate [ˈsəːkjuleit], *v.t.* mettre en circulation, faire circuler, répandre.—*v.i.* circuler.

circulating [ˈsəːkjuleitiŋ], *a.* circulant.

circulation [səːkjuˈleiʃən], *n.* circulation, *f.*; tirage (*d'un journal etc.*), *m.*

circumference [səːˈkʌmfərəns], *n.* circonférence, périphérie, *f.*

circumflex [ˈsəːkəmfleks], *a.* (*Gram.*) circonflexe.

circumlocution [səːkəmləˈkjuːʃən], *n.* circonlocution, *f.*

circumscribe [ˈsəːkəmskraib], *v.t.* circonscrire.

circumspect [ˈsəːkəmspekt], *a.* circonspect.

circumstance [ˈsəːkəmstæns], *n.* circonstance, *f.*; état, *m.*; (*pl.*) moyens, *m.pl.*; *in straitened circumstances,* dans la gêne; *in easy circumstances,* dans l'aisance; *under no circumstances,* en aucun cas.

circumstantial [səːkəmˈstænʃəl], *a.* circonstancié, minutieux; indirect (*témoignage*).

circumvent [səːkəmˈvent], *v.t.* circonvenir.

circumvention [səːkəmˈvenʃən], *n.* circonvention, *f.*

circus [ˈsəːkəs], *n.* cirque; rond-point (*de rues*), *m.*

cistern [ˈsistən], *n.* citerne, *f.*, réservoir, *m.*

citadel [ˈsitədl], *n.* citadelle, *f.*

citation [saiˈteiʃən], *n.* citation, *f.*

cite [sait], *v.t.* citer; sommer (*de*).

citizen [ˈsitizn], *n.* citoyen, bourgeois; habitant, *m.*

citron [ˈsitrən], *n.* cédrat, *m.*

city [ˈsiti], *n.* ville; cité, *f.*

civet [ˈsivit], *n.* civette, *f.*

civic [ˈsivik], *a.* civique.

civil [sivl], *a.* civil; municipal; honnête, poli; *civil servant,* fonctionnaire, *m.*; *in the Civil Service,* dans l'administration.

civilian [siˈviljən], *n.* bourgeois, civil, *m.*

civility [siˈviliti], *n.* civilité, politesse, *f.*

civilization [sivilaiˈzeiʃən], *n.* civilisation, *f.*

civilize [ˈsivilaiz], *v.t.* civiliser.

claim [kleim], *v.t.* demander, prétendre (*à*), réclamer; *civil servant,* revendiquer.—*n.* demande, *f.*; titre, droit, *m.*

claimant [ˈkleimənt], *n.* réclamateur, prétendant, *m.*

clam [klæm], *n.* peigne (*bivalve*), *m.*, palourde, *f.*

clamber [ˈklæmbə], *v.i.* grimper (*sur ou à*).

clammy [ˈklæmi], *a.* visqueux, pâteux; moite (*mains*).

clamorous [ˈklæmərəs], *a.* bruyant; criard.

clamour [ˈklæmə], *n.* clameur, *f.*, bruit, *m.*—*v.i.* crier, vociférer.

clamp [klæmp], *n.* crampon; (*Carp.*) serre-joints, *m.*—*v.t.* cramponner; serrer; entasser.

clan [klæn], *n.* clan, *m.*; clique, coterie, *f.*

clandestine [klænˈdestin], *a.* clandestin.

clang [klæŋ], *n.* cliquetis, son métallique, *m.*—*v.t.* faire résonner.—*v.i.* résonner.

clap [klæp], *n.* coup, *m.*; claque, *f.*; battement de mains; coup (*de tonnerre*), *m.*—*v.t.* claquer, frapper, battre (*mains, ailes etc.*); applaudir.—*v.i.* claquer *ou* battre des mains; applaudir.

clapper [ˈklæpə], *n.* applaudisseur; battant (*d'une cloche*); claquet (*d'un moulin*), *m.*

clapping [ˈklæpiŋ], *n.* battement des mains, *m.*, applaudissements, *m.pl.*

Clara [ˈklɛərə], **Clare** [klɛə]. Claire, *f.*

claret [ˈklærət], *n.* vin de Bordeaux rouge, *m.*

clarify [ˈklærifai], *v.t.* clarifier.—*v.i.* se clarifier.

clarinet [klæriˈnet], *n.* clarinette, *f.*

clarion [ˈklæriən], *n.* clairon, *m.*

clarity [ˈklæriti], *n.* clarté, *f.*

clash [klæʃ], *v.t.* faire résonner (*en frappant*); choquer, heurter.—*v.i.* résonner, se heurter; (*fig.*) être aux prises (*avec*), s'opposer.—*n.* fracas, choc, conflit; cliquetis (*d'armes etc.*), *m.*

clasp [klɑːsp], *n.* fermoir, *m.*; agrafe, *f.*; (*fig.*) embrassement, *m.*, étreinte, *f.*—*v.t.* agrafer; serrer, presser.

clasp-knife [ˈklɑːspnaif], *n.* couteau de poche, *m.*

class [klɑːs], *n.* classe, *f.*; (*Sch.*) cours; genre, *m.*, catégorie, *f.*—*v.t.* classer.

classic [ˈklæsik], *a.* and *n.* classique, *m*; *to study classics,* faire ses humanités *f.pl.*

classical [ˈklæsikəl], *a.* classique.

classification [klæsifiˈkeiʃən], *n.* classification, *f.*

classify ['klæsifai], *v.t.* classifier.
classroom ['klɑːsruːm], *n.* salle de classe, classe, *f.*
clatter ['klætə], *n.* bruit, tapage, fracas (*de ferraille etc.*), tintamarre, *m.*—*v.i.* faire du bruit, claquer.
clause [klɔːz], *n.* clause; proposition, *f.*
clavicle ['klævikl], *n.* (*Anat.*) clavicule, *f.*
claw [klɔː], *n.* griffe; (*Zool.*) serre; pince (*de crabes*), *f.*—*v.t.* griffer; déchirer; égratigner; (*fig.*) railler, gronder.
clay [klei], *n.* argile, terre glaise, glaise, *f.*—*v.t.* (*Agric.*) glaiser; terrer (*sucre*).
clayey ['kleii], *a.* argileux.
clean [kliːn], *a.* propre; blanc (*linge*); ciré (*chaussures*); (*fig.*) net, droit.—*adv.* entièrement, tout à fait, droit, raide.—*v.t.* nettoyer; décrotter, cirer (*chaussures*); écurer (*égouts, canaux etc.*).
cleaner ['kliːnə], *n.* nettoyeur (*personne*), *m.*
cleaning ['kliːniŋ], *n.* nettoyage, nettoiement, *m.*; **dry cleaning**, nettoyage à sec.
cleanliness ['klenlinis], **cleanness** ['kliːnnis], *n.* propreté; netteté, *f.*
cleanly ['klenli], *a.* propre; (*fig.*) pur.—['kliːnli], *adv.* proprement, nettement.
cleanness [CLEANLINESS].
cleanse [klenz], *v.t.* nettoyer; curer (*égouts etc.*); (*fig.*) purifier.
cleansing ['klenziŋ], *n.* nettoiement, nettoyage, *m.*; (*fig.*) purification, *f.*
clear [kliə], *a.* clair; net, évident; sûr; innocent, sans tache.—*adv.* clair, net; clarifier (*liquides*); faire évacuer (*salle etc.*); déblayer (*débris etc.*); gagner (*profit etc.*); (*Agric.*) défricher; (*fig.*) acquitter; (*Customs*) passer.—*v.i.* s'éclaircir; **to clear off**, s'en aller, filer; **to clear out**, se retirer; **to clear up**, élucider (*problème, mystère*); s'éclaircir, se rasséréner (*temps*).
clearance ['kliərəns], *n.* dégagement; déblaiement (*débris*), *m.*; levée (*du courrier*), *f.*; (*Naut.*) congé; (*Customs*) dédouanement, *m.*; **clearance sale**, solde, *m.*; liquidation, *f.*
clear-cut ['kliəkʌt], *a.* net, d'une grande netteté.
clear-headed ['kliə'hedid], *a.* à l'esprit clair.
clearing ['kliəriŋ], *n.* éclaircissement; débrouillement; acquittement; (*Customs*) dédouanement; défrichement (*de terrain*), *m.*; éclaircie (*de forêt*), *f.*; déblaiement (*débris*), *m.*
clearing-house ['kliəriŋhaus], *n.* (*Rail.*) bureau de liquidation, *m.*; (*Banking*) banque de virement, *f.*
clearly ['kliəli], *adv.* nettement, clairement, évidemment.
clearness ['kliənis], *n.* clarté, netteté, pureté, *f.*
cleavage ['kliːvidʒ], *n.* clivage, *m.*; fissure, scission, *f.*
cleave [kliːv], *v.t. irr.* fendre, se fendre; **in a cleft stick**, (*fig.*) dans une impasse.
clef [klef], *n.* (*Mus.*) clef, *f.*
cleft [kleft], *n.* fente, fissure, crevasse, *f.*
clemency ['klemənsi], *n.* clémence; douceur (*du temps*), *f.*
clement ['klemənt], *a.* doux, clément.
clench [klentʃ], *v.t.* river (*clous etc.*); serrer (*poing*).
Cleopatra [kliə'pætrə], Cléopâtre, *f.*
clergy ['klɜːdʒi], *n.* clergé, *m.*

clergyman ['klɜːdʒimən], *n.* (*pl.* **-men** [men]) ecclésiastique; (*R.-C. Ch.*) prêtre, abbé, curé; (*Protestant*) ministre, pasteur, *m.*
cleric ['klerik], *n.* ecclésiastique, prêtre, *m.*
clerical ['klerikəl], *a.* clérical; **clerical error**, faute de copiste, *f.*
clerk [klɑːk], *n.* (*Law*) clerc; (*Eccles.*) ecclésiastique; (*Comm.*) commis; (*Civil Service*) employé, *m.*
clerkship ['klɑːkʃip], *n.* place de clerc, place de commis, *f.*
clever ['klevə], *a.* adroit, habile, (*colloq.*) malin; intelligent; bien fait; (*Am.*) aimable; **to be clever at**, être fort en.
cleverly ['klevəli], *adv.* habilement, adroitement, avec adresse.
cleverness ['klevənis], *n.* habileté, dextérité, adresse; intelligence, *f.*
click [klik], *n.* faire tic-tac, cliqueter.—*n.* bruit sec, clic; cliquetis; déclic, *m.*
client ['klaiənt], *n.* client, *m.*
clientele [kliːɑ̃'tel], *n.* clientèle, *f.*
cliff [klif], *n.* falaise, *f.*; rocher escarpé, *m.*
climate ['klaimit], *n.* climat, *m.*
climatic [klai'mætik], *a.* climatique.
climax ['klaimæks], *n.* gradation, *f.*; (*fig.*) comble, apogée, *m.*
climb [klaim], *v.t.* escalader, gravir, monter.—*v.i.* grimper; monter (*sur*); (*fig.*) s'élever.—*n.* ascension, montée, *f.*
climber ['klaimə], *n.* grimpeur, *m.*; alpiniste, *m.*, *f.*; **social climber**, arriviste, *m.*, *f.*
clime [klaim], *n.* (*poet.*) climat; pays, *m.*
clinch [klintʃ], *v.t.* river (*clous*); **to clinch an argument**, confirmer un argument.—*n.* (*Box.*) corps à corps, *m.*
cling [kliŋ], *v.i. irr.* se cramponner, s'attacher, s'accrocher (*à*); coller (*à*) (*robe*).
clinic ['klinik], *a. and n.* clinique, *f.*
clinical ['klinikəl], *a.* clinique.
clink [kliŋk], *n.* tintement, cliquetis, *m.*—*v.t.* faire tinter.—*v.i.* tinter.
clinker ['kliŋkə], *n.* mâchefer, *m.*
clip [klip], *v.t.* couper (*à ciseaux*); tondre (*chiens, chevaux*); écorcher, estropier (*paroles*); contrôler (*billets*).—*n.* tonte, *f.*; pince-notes, *m.*
clipper ['klipə], *n.* rogneur; (*Naut.*) fin voilier, *m.*
clippers ['klipəz], *n.pl.* tondeuse, *f.*
clique [kliːk], *n.* coterie, *f.*
cloak [klouk], *n.* manteau; (*fig.*) voile, masque, prétexte, *m.*—*v.t.* couvrir d'un manteau, (*fig.*) masquer, voiler, cacher.
cloak-room ['kloukruːm], *n.* (*Rail.*) consigne, *f.*, (*Theat.*) vestiaire, *m.*
clock [klɔk], *n.* horloge (*grand*); pendule (*petit*), *f.*; **alarm clock**, réveille-matin, *m.*—*v.i.* (*Ind.*) **to clock in** or **out**, pointer à l'arrivée ou au départ.
clock-maker ['klɔkmeikə], *n.* horloger, *m.*
clockwise ['klɔkwaiz], *adv.* dans le sens des aiguilles d'une montre.
clockwork ['klɔkwɜːk], *a.* mécanique.—*n.* mouvement, mécanisme d'horlogerie; (*fig.*) travail régulier, *m.*
clod [klɔd], *n.* motte de terre, *f.*
clodhopper ['klɔdhɔpə], *n.* rustre; manant, *m.*
clog [klɔg], *n.* sabot, *m.*—*v.t.* obstruer.—*v.i.* se boucher, s'obstruer.

cloister ['klɔistə], n. cloître, m.
close (1) [klouz], v.t. fermer; clore, terminer.
—v.i. se fermer; clore, se terminer, conclure, finir.—n. fin, conclusion, clôture, f.
close (2) [klous], a. clos, bien fermé; serré; lourd (temps); (fig.) mystérieux.—adv. près; de près; **close by**, tout près; **close to**, près de.
close-fisted ['klous'fistid], a. avare.
closely ['klousli], adv. de près; étroitement; secrètement.
closeness ['klousnis], n. proximité; exactitude; lourdeur (temps); intimité, f.
closet ['klɔzit], n. cabinet; boudoir, m.; garde-robe, armoire, f.—v.t. **to be closeted with**, être en tête-à-tête avec.
close-up ['klousʌp], n. (Cine.) gros plan, m.
closing ['klouziŋ], a. dernier, final.—n. clôture, fermeture (de magasin); fin, conclusion, f.
closure ['klouʒə], n. clôture, fermeture, f.
clot [klɔt], n. grumeau, caillot, m.—v.i. se cailler, se figer.
cloth [klɔ:θ], n. drap (de laine ou tissu d'or ou d'argent), m.; toile (de lin), f.; **table-cloth**, nappe, f., tapis (de laine), m.
clothe [klouð], v.t. habiller, (re)vêtir.
clothes [klouðz], n.pl. habits, vêtements, m.pl., hardes, f.pl.; **bed-clothes**, draps et couvertures, m.pl.
clothing ['klouðiŋ], n. vêtement, habillement, m.; vêtements, m.pl.
cloud [klaud], n. nuage, m.; (poet.) nue; (fig.) nuée, f.; **every cloud has a silver lining**, après la pluie le beau temps; **to be under a cloud**, être mal vu du monde.—v.t. couvrir de nuages; obscurcir; (fig.) assombrir.—v.i. se couvrir (de nuages).
cloudburst ['klaudbə:st], n. trombe, rafale de pluie, f.
cloudless ['klaudlis], a. sans nuage.
cloudy ['klaudi], a. nuageux, couvert; trouble (liquides); (fig.) ténébreux.
clout [klaut], n. torchon, linge, m.; gifle, tape, f.—v.t. rapetasser; taper, souffleter.
clove [klouv], n. clou de girofle, m.; **clove of garlic**, gousse d'ail, f.
cloven [klouvn], a. fendu; fourchu; **to show the cloven foot**, laisser voir le bout de l'oreille.
clover ['klouvə], n. trèfle, m.
clown [klaun], n. rustre, manant; (Theat.) bouffon, clown, m.
cloy [klɔi], v.t. écœurer, rassasier.
club [klʌb], n. massue, f.; (Golf) club (instrument), m.; crosse, f.; cercle, club, m., association, f.; (Cards) trèfle, m.—v.t. frapper avec une massue.—v.i. se cotiser, s'associer.
club-foot ['klʌbfut], n. pied bot, m.
club-house ['klʌbhaus], n. cercle; pavillon (de golf etc.), m.
cluck [klʌk], v.i. glousser.
clucking ['klʌkiŋ], n. gloussement, m.
clue [klu:], n. fil, indice, signe, m.; idée, f.
clueless ['klu:lis], a. (fam.) **to be clueless**, ne savoir rien de rien.
clump [klʌmp], n. masse, f., gros bloc; (fig.) groupe, m.; **clump of trees**, bouquet d'arbres, m.
clumsily ['klʌmzili], adv. gauchement, maladroitement.

clumsiness ['klʌmzinis], n. gaucherie, maladresse, f.
clumsy ['klʌmzi], a. gauche, maladroit; mal fait (chose).
cluster ['klʌstə], n. grappe (de raisin), f.; bouquet (de fleurs); régime (de bananes); nœud (de diamants), m.—v.i. se former en grappes; se grouper.
clutch [klʌtʃ], v.t. saisir, empoigner.—n. griffe, serre, étreinte, f.; (Motor.) embrayage, m.; couvée (d'œufs), f.
clutter ['klʌtə], n. fracas, vacarme; encombrement, désordre, m.—v.t. **to clutter up**, encombrer.
coach [koutʃ], n. voiture, f., carrosse, m.; (Rail.) voiture, f., wagon; autocar, car; (Sch.) répétiteur; (Spt.) entraîneur, m.—v.t. entraîner; préparer aux examens.
coaching ['koutʃiŋ], n. (Spt.) entraînement (d'équipe), m.; (Sch.) répétitions, f.pl.
coachman ['koutʃmən], n. (pl. -men [men]) cocher, m.
coachwork ['koutʃwə:k], n. carrosserie, f.
coagulate [kou'ægjuleit], v.t. coaguler.—v.i. se coaguler.
coal [koul], n. charbon, m.; houille, f.; **live coal**, charbon ardent.—v.t. charbonner.—v.i. s'approvisionner de charbon (navire).
coal-cellar ['koulselə], n. cave à charbon, f.
coalesce [kouə'les], v.i. s'unir, se fondre, fusionner.
coal-field ['koulfi:ld], n. bassin houiller, m.
coalition [kouə'liʃən], n. coalition, f.
coal-mine ['koulmain], n. mine de charbon, houillère, f.
coal-miner ['koulmainə], n. mineur, m.
coal-scuttle ['koulskʌtl], n. seau à charbon, m.
coarse [kɔ:s], a. gros, grossier.
coarseness ['kɔ:snis], n. grossièreté, f.
coast [koust], n. côte, plage, f., rivage, littoral, m.—v.t. côtoyer.—v.i. côtoyer, suivre la côte; caboter; planer (oiseau); (Motor.) rouler au débrayé.
coastal ['koustəl], a. côtier.
coaster ['koustə], n. caboteur, m.
coast-guard ['koustga:d], n. garde-côte, m.
coast-line ['koustlain], n. littoral, m.
coat [kout], n. habit; enduit (de goudron etc.), m.; robe (de certains animaux); (Mil.) tunique; (Paint.) couche, f.; **coat of mail**, cotte de mailles, f.; **double breasted coat**, veston croisé, m.—v.t. revêtir; enduire (de).
coat-hanger ['kouthæŋə], n. cintre, m.; porte-vêtements, m. inv.
coax [kouks], v.t. amadouer, cajoler, flatter.
co-axial [kou'æksiəl], a. coaxial.
coaxing ['kouksiŋ], n. cajolerie, f., enjôlement, m.
cob [kɔb], n. bidet, goussant (cheval); épi (de maïs), m.
cobalt ['koubɔ:lt], n. cobalt, m.
cobble [kɔbl], v.t. saveter, raccommoder; paver en cailloutis.—n. galet rond, pavé m.
cobbler ['kɔblə], n. cordonnier, m.
cobnut ['kɔbnʌt], n. aveline, f.
cobra ['koubrə], n. cobra, m.
cobweb ['kɔbweb], n. toile d'araignée, f.
cocaine [ko'kein], n. cocaïne, f.
cochineal ['kɔtʃini:l], n. cochenille, f.

cock [kɔk], *n.* coq; mâle (*de petits oiseaux*); robinet (*tap*); chien (*de fusil*); tas, meulon (*de foin*), *m.*; **black-cock**, coq de bruyère, *m.*—*v.t.* relever; retrousser; armer (*fusil*); **cocked hat**, chapeau à cornes, *m.*

cockade [kɔ'keid], *n.* cocarde, *f.*

cock-a-doodle-doo ['kɔkədu:dl'du:], *n.* coquerico, cocorico, *m.*

cockatoo [kɔkə'tu:], *n.* kakatoès, cacatois, *m.*

cockatrice ['kɔkətri:s], *n.* basilic, *m.*

cockchafer ['kɔktʃeifə], *n.* hanneton, *m.*

cock-crow ['kɔkkrou], *n.* chant du coq; (*fig.*) point du jour, *m.*

cockerel ['kɔkərəl], *n.* jeune coq, *m.*

cock-eyed ['kɔkaid], *a.* de biais, de travers.

cockle [kɔkl], *n.* bucarde, *f.*

cock-pit ['kɔkpit], *n.* arène des combats de coqs; (*Av.*) carlingue, *f.*

cockroach ['kɔkroutʃ], *n.* blatte, *f.*

cockscomb ['kɔkskoum], *n.* crête de coq, *f.*; [COXCOMB].

cocksure ['kɔkʃuə], *a.* sûr et certain, outre-cuidant.

cocktail ['kɔkteil], *n.* cocktail, *m.*; **cocktail party**, cocktail.

cocky ['kɔki], *a.* effronté, suffisant.

coco ['koukou], *n.* coco, *m.*

cocoa ['koukou], *n.* cacao, *m.*

coconut, cocoa-nut ['koukənʌt], *n.* coco, *m.*, noix de coco, *f.*

cocoon [kə'ku:n], *n.* cocon, *m.*

cod [kɔd], *n.* morue, *f.*; cabillaud (*morue fraîche*), *m.*

coddle [kɔdl], *v.t.* mitonner; dorloter, choyer.

code [koud], *n.* code, *m.*—*v.t.* coder; chiffrer.

codicil ['kɔdisil], *n.* codicille, *f.*

codify ['kɔudifai], *v.t.* codifier.

cod-liver oil ['kɔdlivər'ɔil], *n.* huile de foie de morue, *f.*

co-education ['kouedju'keiʃən], *n.* enseigne-ment mixte, *m.*

co-educational ['kouedju'keiʃənəl], *a.* (*Sch.*) mixte.

coefficient [koui'fiʃənt], *n.* coefficient, *m.*

coerce [kou'ə:s], *v.t.* forcer, contraindre.

coercion [kou'ə:ʃən], *n.* coercition, contrainte, *f.*

coexist [kouig'zist], *v.i.* coexister.

coexistence [kouig'zistəns], *n.* coexistence, *f.*

coffee ['kɔfi], *n.* café, *m.*; **white coffee**, café au lait.

coffee-bean ['kɔfibi:n], *n.* grain de café, *m.*

coffee-house ['kɔfihaus], *n.* café, *m.*

coffee-mill ['kɔfimil], **coffee-grinder** ['kɔfi graində], *n.* moulin à café, *m.*

coffee-pot ['kɔfipɔt], *n.* cafetière, *f.*

coffer ['kɔfə], *n.* coffre; caisson; sas, *m.*

coffin ['kɔfin], *n.* cercueil, *m.*, bière, *f.*

cog [kɔg], *n.* dent, *f.*

cogency ['koudʒənsi], *n.* force, puissance, *f.*

cogent ['koudʒənt], *a.* puissant, fort.

cogged [kɔgd], *a.* denté, à dents.

cogitate ['kɔdʒiteit], *v.t.* penser (à.)—*v.i.* méditer, penser.

cogitation [kɔdʒi'teiʃən], *n.* réflexion, pensée, méditation, *f.*

cognate ['kɔgneit], *a.* de la même famille; analogue.

cognizance ['kɔgnizəns], *n.* connaissance, *f.*; (*Her.*) insigne, *m.*

cognomen [kɔg'noumən], *n.* surnom; nom de guerre, sobriquet, *m.*

cog-wheel ['kɔgwi:l], *n.* roue d'engrenage, *f.*

cohabit [kou'hæbit], *v.i.* cohabiter.

cohabitation [kouhæbi'teiʃən], *n.* cohabita-tion, *f.*

coherence [kou'hiərəns], *n.* cohésion, co-hérence, *f.*

coherent [kou'hiərənt], *a.* cohérent; con-séquent.

coherently [kou'hiərəntli], *adv.* d'une manière cohérente.

cohesion [kou'hi:ʒən], *n.* cohésion, *f.*

cohesive [kou'hi:siv], *a.* cohésif.

cohort ['kouhɔ:t], *n.* cohorte, *f.*

coil [kɔil], *n.* rouleau (*de cheveux etc.*); repli (*de serpents*), *m.*; (*Elec.*) bobine, *f.*—*v.t.* replier, enrouler.—*v.i.* se replier, s'enrouler.

coin [kɔin], *n.* pièce de monnaie, *f.*—*v.t.* monnayer; forger, fabriquer, inventer.

coinage ['kɔinidʒ], *n.* monnayage, *m.*, mon-naie; (*fig.*) fabrication, *f.*

coincide [kouin'said], *v.i.* s'accorder, coïn-cider (*avec*).

coincidence [kou'insidəns], *n.* coïncidence, *f.*

coincidental [kouinsi'dentl], *a.* de coïnci-dence.

coiner ['kɔinə], *n.* monnayeur; faux monna-yeur, *m.*

coition [kou'iʃən], *n.* coït, *m.*

coke [kouk], *n.* coke, *m.*

colander ['kʌləndə], *n.* passoire, *f.*

cold [kould], *a.* froid; **it is cold**, il fait froid; **to be cold** (*of people*), avoir froid.—*n.* froid; rhume (*maladie*), refroidissement; frisson (*sensation*), *m.*; **to catch cold**, s'enrhumer.

coldly ['kouldli], *adv.* froidement.

cole [koul], *n.* chou marin, *m.*

colic ['kɔlik], *n.* colique, *f.*

collaborate [kə'læbəreit], *v.i.* collaborer.

collaboration [kəlæbə'reiʃən], *n.* collabora-tion, *f.*

collaborator [kə'læbəreitə] *n.* collaborateur, *m.*

collapse [kə'læps], *v.i.* s'affaisser, s'écrouler, s'effondrer.—*n.* affaissement, *m.*, débâcle, *f.*

collapsible [kə'læpsibl], *a.* pliant, démontable.

collar ['kɔlə], *n.* collier (*de chien, de cheval, de décoration*); col (*de chemise*); collet (*de pardessus*), *m.*; collerette (*de dames*), *f.*—*v.t.* colleter, prendre au collet.

collar-bone ['kɔləboun], *n.* clavicule, *f.*

collar-stud ['kɔləstʌd], *n.* bouton de col, *m.*

collate [kə'leit], *v.t.* collationner, comparer.

collateral [kɔ'lætərəl], *a.* collatéral.

collation [kə'leiʃən], *n.* collation, *f.*; don, présent; repas froid, *m.*

colleague ['kɔli:g], *n.* collègue, confrère, *m.*

collect (1) [kə'lekt], *v.t.* recueillir; ramasser; collectionner; percevoir, encaisser (*impôts*); recouvrer (*dettes*); quêter; faire la levée (*du courrier*).—*v.i.* s'amasser.

collect (2) ['kɔlikt], *n.* collecte; (*courte*) prière, *f.*

collected [kə'lektid], *a.* rassemblé; (*fig.*) recueilli, calme, tranquille.

collection [kə'lekʃən], *n.* collection, *f.*; assem-blage, rassemblement, *m.*; collecte, quête; levée (*du courrier*), *f.*

collective [kə'lektiv], *a.* collectif.

collector [kə'lektə], *n.* collecteur; collectionneur; percepteur (*impôts*); quêteur (*aumône*); receveur (*douane*), *m.*

college ['kɔlidʒ], *n.* collège (d'Université), *m.*; école, *f.*

collide [kə'laid], *v.i.* se heurter.

collier ['kɔliə], *n.* mineur; (*Naut.*) (bateau) charbonnier, *m.*

colliery ['kɔljəri], *n.* houillère, mine de charbon, *f.*

collision [kə'liʒən], *n.* collision, *f.*, choc, *m.*

colloquial [kə'loukwiəl], *a.* de la conversation, familier; *colloquial French*, français parlé, *m.*

colloquialism [kə'loukwiəlizm], *n.* expression familière, *f.*

colloquy ['kɔləkwi], *n.* colloque, entretien, *m.*

collusion [kə'lu:ʒən], *n.* collusion, connivence, *f.*

Colombia [kə'lʌmbiə]. la Colombie, *f.*

colon (1) ['koulən], *n.* (*Anat.*) colon, *m.*

colon (2) ['koulən], *n.* (*Gram.*) deux points, *m.pl.*

colonel [kə:nl], *n.* colonel, *m.*

colonial [kə'lounjəl], *a.* colonial.

colonist ['kɔlənist], *n.* colon, *m.*

colonization [kɔlənai'zeiʃən], *n.* colonisation, *f.*

colonize ['kɔlənaiz], *v.t.* coloniser.

colony ['kɔləni], *n.* colonie, *f.*

Colorado-beetle ['kɔlərə:dou'bi:tl], *n.* doryphore, *m.*

colossal [kə'lɔsl], *a.* colossal.

Colosseum [kɔlə'si:əm]. Colisée, *m.*

colossus [kə'lɔsəs], *n.* (*pl.* colossi [kə'lɔsai], colossuses [kə'lɔsəsiz]) colosse, *m.*

colour ['kʌlə], *n.* couleur, *f.*; (*fig.*) prétexte, *m.*, apparence, *f.*; (*pl.*) (*Mil.*) drapeau; (*Navy*) pavillon, *m.*; *to be off colour*, être pâle, n'être pas bien en train; *with the colours*, sous les drapeaux.—*v.t.* colorer; colorier, enluminer (*gravure etc.*).—*v.i.* rougir (*personne*); se colorer (*chose*).

colour-blind ['kʌləblaind], *a.* daltonien.

colour-blindness ['kʌləblaindnis], *n.* daltonisme, *m.*

coloured ['kʌləd], *a.* coloré; colorié; de couleur.

colourful ['kʌləful], *a.* coloré, pittoresque.

colouring ['kʌləriŋ], *n.* coloris, *m.*; couleur, *f.*

colourless ['kʌləlis], *a.* sans couleur.

colt [koult], *n.* poulain; (*fig.*) novice, *m.*

Columbus [kə'lʌmbəs]. Colomb, *m.*

column ['kɔləm], *n.* colonne, *f.*

coma ['koumə], *n.* coma; assoupissement, *m.*

comb [koum], *n.* peigne, *m.*; étrille (*chevaux*); crête (*coq*), *f.*; rayon (*miel*) *m.*—*v.t.* peigner; étriller (*cheval*).

combat ['kɔmbæt], *n.* combat, *m.*—*v.t.*, *v.i.* combattre.

combatant ['kɔmbətənt], *n.* combattant, *m.*

combination [kɔmbi'neiʃən], *n.* combinaison; association, coalition, *f.*; concours (*de circonstances*), *m.*

combine [kəm'bain], *v.t.* combiner; réunir; allier.—*v.i.* se combiner; se coaliser (*avec*); s'unir (*à*); se syndiquer.—*v.t.* ['kɔmbain], *n.* (*Comm.*) cartel, *m.*

combine-harvester ['kɔmbain'ha:vistə], *n.* moissonneuse-batteuse, *f.*

combustion [kəm'bʌstʃən], *n.* combustion, *f.*

come [kʌm], *v.i. irr.* venir; arriver, parvenir; se présenter, advenir, se faire; devenir; *come in!* entrez! *come on!* allons! *to come back*, revenir; *to come down*, descendre; *to come for*, venir chercher; *to come forward*, s'avancer; *to come home*, rentrer; *to come in*, entrer; *to come off*, se détacher; *to come out*, sortir; *to come up*, monter.

comedian [kə'mi:diən], *n.* comédien, *m.*

comedy ['kɔmidi], *n.* comédie, *f.*

comeliness ['kʌmlinis], *n.* aspect gracieux, *m.*; agréments, *m.pl.*

comely ['kʌmli], *a.* avenant.

comer ['kʌmə], *n.* venant; venu, *m.*; *first comer*, premier venu; *newcomer*, nouveau venu.

comet ['kɔmit], *n.* comète, *f.*

comfort ['kʌmfət], *n.* réconfort; bien-être, agrément, confort, *m.*; aise(s); aisance, *f.*; *to take comfort*, se consoler.—*v.t.* réconforter, soulager; consoler.

comfortable ['kʌmfətəbl], *a.* à son aise; agréable, confortable.

comfortably ['kʌmfətəbli], *adv.* à son aise, confortablement.

comforter ['kʌmfətə], *n.* consolateur (*le Saint Esprit*); cache-nez (*foulard*), *m.*; tétine (*de bébé*), *f.*

comfortless ['kʌmfətlis], *a.* sans consolation; désolé, triste.

comic ['kɔmik], **comical** ['kɔmikəl], *a.* comique, drôle.

comically ['kɔmikli], *adv.* comiquement.

coming ['kʌmiŋ], *n.* venue; arrivée; approche, *f.*

comma ['kɔmə], *n.* virgule, *f.*; *inverted commas*, guillemets, *m.pl.*

command [kə'ma:nd], *n.* ordre, commandement; pouvoir, *m.*; autorité, *f.*—*v.t.* commander; posséder; inspirer (*respect*).

commandant ['kɔməndænt], *n.* commandant, *m.*

commandeer [kɔmən'diə], *v.t.* réquisitionner.

commander [kə'ma:ndə], *n.* commandant; commandeur (*décoration*); (*Navy*) capitaine (*de frégate etc.*), *m.*

commander-in-chief [kəma:ndərin'tʃi:f], *n.* généralissime, commandant en chef, *m.*

commanding [kə'ma:ndiŋ], *a.* commandant; imposant (*important*); qui domine (*surplombant*); impérieux (*de commandement*).

commandment [kə'ma:ndmənt], *n.* commandement (*de Dieu*), *m.*

commando [kə'ma:ndou], *n.* (*Mil.*) corps franc, commando, *m.*

commemorate [kə'meməreit], *v.t.* célébrer, solenniser; commémorer.

commemoration [kəmemə'reiʃən], *n.* célébration, commémoration, *f.*; souvenir, *m.*

commence [kə'mens], *v.t.*, *v.i.* commencer.

commencement [kə'mensmənt], *n.* commencement, début, *m.*

commend [kə'mend], *v.t.* confier (*à*); recommander; louer.

commendable [kə'mendəbl], *a.* louable.

commendation [kɔmen'deiʃən], *n.* éloge, *m.*, louange, *f.*

comment ['kɔment], *n.* commentaire, *m.*—*v.i.* commenter.

commentary ['kɔməntəri], *n.* commentaire, *m.*; *running commentary*, radio-reportage (*d'un match*), *m.*
commerce ['kɔmə:s], *n.* commerce, *m.*
commercial [kə'mə:ʃəl], *a.* commercial, de commerce; commerçant (*ville etc.*); *commercial traveller*, commis voyageur, *m.*— *n.* (*Tel.*) film publicitaire, *m.*
commingle [kə'miŋgl], *v.t.* mêler ensemble, mêler.—*v.i.* se mêler ensemble *ou* avec; se fondre (*dans* ou *en*).
commissariat [kɔmi'sɛəriət], *n.* commissariat, *m.*, intendance, *f.*
commission [kə'miʃən], *n.* commission, *f.*; (*Mil.*) brevet; (*Law*) mandat, *m.*—*v.t.* charger, commissionner.
commissionaire [kəmiʃə'nɛə], *n.* portier (*de magasin*); chasseur (*d'hôtel*); commissionnaire, *m.*
commissioner [kə'miʃənə], *n.* commissionnaire, *m.*
commit [kə'mit], *v.t.* commettre; confier, livrer, consigner; engager.
committee [kə'miti], *n.* comité, *m.*; (*Parl.*) commission, *f.*
commode [kə'moud], *n.* commode, *f.*
commodious [kə'moudjəs], *a.* spacieux.
commodity [kə'mɔditi], *n.* marchandise, denrée, *f.*, produit, *m.*
commodore ['kɔmədɔ:], *n.* (*Navy*) chef de division, *m.*; *air-commodore*, général de brigade, *m.*
common ['kɔmən], *a.* commun; ordinaire; vulgaire; (*fig.*) trivial; (*Mil.*) simple.—*n.* commune, *f.*; communal, *m.*; bruyère, lande, *f.*; *House of Commons*, Chambre des Communes, *f.*
commoner ['kɔmənə], *n.* bourgeois, roturier, *m.*
commonly ['kɔmənli], *adv.* ordinairement.
commonplace ['kɔmənpleis], *a.* banal, commun, trivial.—*n.* lieu commun, *m.*, banalité, *f.*
commonweal ['kɔmən'wi:l], *n.* le bien public, *m.*
commonwealth ['kɔmənwelθ], *n.* la chose publique, *f.*, l'État, *m.*; *the* (*British*) *Commonwealth*, le Commonwealth (britannique).
commotion [kə'mouʃən], *n.* secousse, agitation, *f.*, tumulte, *m.*
communal ['kɔmjunəl], *a.* communal.
commune (1) [kə'mju:n], *v.i.* parler, converser, s'entretenir (*avec*).
commune (2) ['kɔmju:n], *n.* commune, *f.*
communicate [kə'mju:nikeit], *v.t.* communiquer.—*v.i.* se communiquer.
communication [kəmju:ni'keiʃən], *n.* communication, *f.*
communion [kə'mju:njən], *n.* (*Eccles.*) communion, *f.*; commerce, *m.*
communiqué [kə'mju:nikei], *n.* communiqué, *m.*
Communism ['kɔmjunizm], *n.* communisme, *m.*
Communist ['kɔmjunist], *a.* and *n.* communiste, *m.*, *f.*
community [kə'mju:niti], *n.* communauté, société, *f.*
commutator ['kɔmjuteitə], *n.* commutateur, *m.*

compact (1) ['kɔmpækt], *n.* pacte, contrat; poudrier (*de dame*), *m.*
compact (2) [kəm'pækt], *a.* compact, serré, bien lié; concis.—*v.t.* rendre compact, unir.
companion [kəm'pænjən], *n.* compagnon, *m.*, compagne; dame *ou* demoiselle de compagnie (*to a lady*), *f.*; pendant (*mobilier*), *m.*
companionship [kəm'pænjənʃip], *n.* camaraderie; compagnie, *f.*
company ['kʌmpəni], *n.* compagnie; société, corporation; troupe (*acteurs*), *f.*; (*Naut.*) équipage, *m.*; *we have company today,* nous avons du monde aujourd'hui.
comparable ['kɔmpərəbl], *a.* comparable.
comparative [kəm'pærətiv], *a.* comparatif.
comparatively [kəm'pærətivli], *adv.* relativement, comparativement.
compare [kəm'pɛə], *v.t.* comparer.—*v.i.* être comparable à, rivaliser.
comparison [kəm'pærisən], *n.* comparaison, *f.*
compartment [kəm'pɑ:tmənt], *n.* compartiment, *m.*
compass ['kʌmpəs], *n.* compas; circuit, cercle, *m.*; boussole; portée (*atteinte*); étendue (*de la voix*), *f.*; *a pair of compasses*, un compas.—*v.t.* faire le tour de, entourer; accomplir; *to compass about*, environner.
compassion [kəm'pæʃən], *n.* compassion, pitié, *f.*
compassionate [kəm'pæʃənit], *a.* compatissant.
compatible [kəm'pætəbl], *a.* compatible (*avec*).
compatriot [kəm'pætriət], *n.* compatriote, *m.*, *f.*
compel [kəm'pel], *v.t.* contraindre, forcer (*de*), obliger (*à* ou *de*).
compelling [kəm'peliŋ], *a.* compulsif, irrésistible.
compensate ['kɔmpənseit], *v.t.* dédommager (*de*); compenser.—*v.i.* *to compensate for*, remplacer, racheter.
compensation [kɔmpən'seiʃən], *n.* dédommagement, *m.*; compensation, *f.*
compete [kəm'pi:t], *v.i.* concourir (*pour*), faire concurrence (*à*); disputer, rivaliser.
competence ['kɔmpitəns], *n.* capacité, aptitude; (*fig.*) aisance (*fortune*), *f.*
competent ['kɔmpitənt], *a.* compétent (*pour*), capable (*de*).
competently ['kɔmpitəntli], *adv.* avec compétence; suffisamment.
competition [kɔmpi'tiʃən], *n.* (*Comm.*) concurrence, *f.*; concours, *m.*
competitive [kəm'petitiv], *a.* compétitif, de concurrence; *competitive examination*, concours, *m.*
competitor [kəm'petitə], *n.* compétiteur, *m.*; (*Comm.*) concurrent, *m.*
compile [kəm'pail], *v.t.* compiler, composer.
complacent [kəm'pleisənt], *a.* suffisant, de suffisance.
complacently [kəm'pleisəntli], *adv.* avec un air *ou* ton suffisant.
complain [kəm'plein], *v.i.* se plaindre (*de*).
complaint [kəm'pleint], *n.* plainte; maladie, *f.*, mal (*illness*), *m.*; réclamation, *f.*; *to lodge a complaint*, porter plainte.
complaisance [kəm'pleisəns], *n.* complaisance, *f.*
complement ['kɔmplimənt], *n.* complément, *m.*

complementary [kɔmpli'mentəri], a. complémentaire.

complete [kəm'pli:t], a. complet, entier; achevé.—v.t. compléter, achever; (fig.) accomplir; remplir (une fiche).

completely [kəm'pli:tli], adv. complètement.

completion [kəm'pli:ʃən], n. achèvement, accomplissement, m., perfection, f.

complex ['kɔmpleks], a. and n. complexe, m.

complexion [kəm'plekʃən], n. teint, m., couleur, f.; caractère, m.; to put a different complexion on, présenter sous un autre jour.

complexity [kəm'pleksiti], n. complexité, f.

compliance [kəm'plaiəns], n. acquiescement, m.; obéissance, f.; in compliance with, conformément à.

complicate ['kɔmplikeit], v.t. compliquer; embrouiller.

complicated ['kɔmplikeitid], a. compliqué.

complication [kɔmpli'keiʃən], n. complication, f.

compliment ['kɔmplimənt], n. compliment, m.; (pl.) salutations, f.pl., hommages (à une dame), m.pl.—[kɔmpli'ment], v.t. complimenter, féliciter.

complimentary [kɔmpli'mentəri], a. flatteur; en hommage; complimentary ticket, billet de faveur, m.

comply [kəm'plai], v.i. se soumettre, se conformer; accéder (à).

component [kəm'pounənt], a. constituant, composant.—n. (Mech.) composant, m.

compose [kəm'pouz], v.t. composer; écrire; rédiger, arranger; calmer.

composed [kəm'pouzd], a. composé; calme.

composer [kəm'pouzə], n. auteur; (Mus.) compositeur, m.

composite ['kɔmpəzit] a. composé; (Arch.) composite.

composition [kɔmpə'ziʃən], n. composition; (Sch.) rédaction, f.; French composition, thème français, m.

compositor [kəm'pozitə], n. (Print.) compositeur, m.

compost ['kɔmpəst], n. compost, terreau, m.

composure [kəm'pouʒə], n. calme, m.

compound ['kɔmpaund], a. and n. composé, m.; compound interest, intérêts composés, m.pl.—[kəm'paund], v.t. composer; mêler, combiner; (Comm.) atermoyer.—v.i. s'arranger.

comprehend [kɔmpri'hend], v.t. comprendre.

comprehensible [kɔmpri'hensibl], a. compréhensible.

comprehension [kɔmpri'henʃən], n. compréhension, f.

comprehensive [kɔmpri'hensiv], a. étendu, compréhensif; comprehensive study, étude d'ensemble, f.

compress ['kɔmpres], n. compresse, f.—[kəm'pres], v.t. comprimer; (fig.) resserrer.

comprise [kəm'praiz], v.t. contenir, renfermer, comporter.

compromise ['kɔmprəmaiz], n. compromis, arrangement, m.—v.t. compromettre.—v.i. transiger.

compromising ['kɔmprəmaiziŋ], a. compromettant.

compulsion [kəm'pʌlʃən], n. contrainte, f.

compulsorily [kəm'pʌlsərili], adv. par force, forcément.

compulsory [kəm'pʌlsəri], a. forcé, obligatoire.

compute [kəm'pju:t], v.t. calculer, supputer.

computer [kəm'pju:tə], n. machine à calculer, f.; ordinateur, m.

comrade ['kɔmrid], n. camarade, compagnon, m.

comradeship ['kɔmridʃip], n. camaraderie, f.

concave ['kɔnkeiv], a. concave, creux.

conceal [kən'si:l], v.t. cacher; (fig.) dissimuler; celer ou céler (à).

concealment [kən'si:lmənt], n. dissimulation, f.; secret, mystère, m.; retraite, cachette, f.

concede [kən'si:d], v.t. concéder, accorder, admettre.—v.i. faire des concessions.

conceit [kən'si:t], n. suffisance, vanité, f.

conceited [kən'si:tid], a. suffisant, vaniteux.

conceivable [kən'si:vəbl], a. concevable, imaginable.

conceive [kən'si:v], v.t. concevoir; imaginer. —v.i. concevoir, devenir enceinte (femme).

concentrate ['kɔnsəntreit], v.t. concentrer.— v.i. se concentrer.

concentration [kɔnsən'treiʃən], n. concentration, f.

conception [kən'sepʃən], n. conception, idée, f.

concern [kən'sə:n], n. intérêt; soin, souci, m., anxiété; (Comm.) entreprise; (fig.) affaire, f. —v.t. concerner, regarder; intéresser; inquiéter.

concerning [kən'sə:niŋ], prep. touchant, concernant, en ce qui concerne, à l'égard de.

concert [kən'sə:t], v.t. concerter.—v.i. se concerter.—['kɔnsət], n. concert; accord, m.

concerto [kən'tʃə:tou], n. (Mus.) concerto, m.

concession [kən'seʃən], n. concession, f.

concessionary [kən'seʃənəri], a. concessionnaire.

conch [kɔŋk], n. conque, f.

conciliate [kən'silieit], v.t. concilier.

conciliation [kənsili'eiʃən], n. conciliation, f.

conciliator [kən'silieitə], n. conciliateur, m.

conciliatory [kən'siljətri], a. conciliant, conciliatoire.

concise [kən'sais], a. concis.

concisely [kən'saisli], adv. succinctement.

conclude [kən'klu:d], v.t. conclure; terminer; achever; estimer.

concluding [kən'klu:diŋ], a. final, dernier.

conclusion [kən'klu:ʒən], n. conclusion, fin; décision, f.

conclusive [kən'klu:siv], a. concluant; conclusif.

concoct [kən'kɔkt], v.t. confectionner; inventer, préparer; machiner (un plan), tramer.

concoction [kən'kɔkʃən], n. confection (d'un plat); potion; (fig.) machination (complot), f.

concord ['kɔŋkɔ:d], n. concorde, harmonie, f.; (Mus.) accord, m.

concourse ['kɔŋkɔ:s], n. concours, m., affluence, foule; réunion, f.

concrete ['kɔŋkri:t], a. concret.—n. béton; bétonnage, m.; reinforced concrete, béton armé.—v.t. bétonner.

concubine ['kɔŋkjubain], n. concubine, f.

concur [kən'kə:], v.i. s'accorder, être d'accord (avec).

concurrence [kən'kʌrəns], n. assentiment; concours, m.

concurrent

concurrent [kən'kʌrənt], *a.* qui concourt, qui s'accorde, concourant.
concurrently [kən'kʌrəntli], *adv.* concurremment.
concussion [kən'kʌʃən], *n.* secousse, *f.*; choc, *m.*; (*Med.*) commotion, *f.*
condemn [kən'dem], *v.t.* condamner (à); déclarer coupable; blâmer.
condemnation [kɔndem'neiʃən], *n.* condamnation, censure, *f.*, blâme, *m.*
condensation [kɔnden'seiʃən], *n.* condensation, *f.*
condense [kən'dens], *v.t.* condenser; (*fig.*) resserrer, abréger.
condenser [kən'densə], *n.* condenseur; (*Phys.*) condensateur, *m.*
condescend [kɔndə'send], *v.i.* condescendre, daigner (à).
condescension [kɔndə'senʃən], *n.* condescendance, *f.*; acte de condescendance, *m.*
condiment ['kɔndimənt], *n.* assaisonnement, condiment, *m.*
condition [kən'diʃən], *n.* condition, *f.*, état, *m.—v.t.* conditionner.
conditional [kən'diʃənəl], *a.* conditionnel.
conditionally [kən'diʃənəli], *adv.* conditionnellement.
condole [kən'doul], *v.i.* prendre part à la douleur (de), exprimer ses condoléances.
condolence [kən'douləns], *n.* condoléance, *f.*
condone [kən'doun], *v.t.* excuser, pardonner.
condor ['kɔndə], *n.* condor, *m.*
conduce [kən'dju:s], *v.i.* contribuer (à).
conducive [kən'dju:siv], *a.* qui contribue (à).
conduct ['kɔndʌkt], *n.* conduite; direction, *f.*; *safe conduct*, sauf-conduit, *m.*—[kən'dʌkt], *v.t.* conduire (à); diriger, mener.
conductor [kən'dʌktə], *n.* receveur (d'autobus); (*Am.*) (*Rail.*) chef de train; (*Mus.*) chef d'orchestre; (*Phys.*) conducteur, *m.*; *lightning-conductor*, paratonnerre, *m.*
conductress [kən'dʌktris], *n.* receveuse (d'autobus), *f.*
conduit ['kʌndit, 'kɔndit], *n.* conduit; tuyau, *m.*
cone [koun], *n.* cône; (*Bot.*) strobile, *m.*, pomme de pin, *f.*; *ice-cream cone*, cornet de glace, *m.*
confection [kən'fekʃən], *n.* bonbon, *m.*, friandise, *f.*
confectioner [kən'fekʃənə], *n.* confiseur, *m.*
confectionery [kən'fekʃənəri], *n.* confiserie, *f.*, bonbons, *m.pl.*
confederacy [kən'fedərəsi], *n.* confédération (d'États); ligue (de conspirateurs), *f.*
confederate [kən'fedərit], *a.* confédéré.—*n.* confédéré, *m.*, complice, *m.*, *f.*
confederation [kənfedə'reiʃən], *n.* confédération, *f.*
confer [kən'fə:], *v.t.* conférer, accorder.—*v.i.* conférer (de).
conference ['kɔnfərəns], *n.* conférence, *f.*, congrès, *m.*
confess [kən'fes], *v.t.* confesser, avouer.—*v.i.* se confesser.
confessed [kən'fest], *a.* reconnu, confessé, avoué.
confessedly [kən'fesidli], *adv.* de son propre aveu.
confession [kən'feʃən], *n.* confession, *f.*, aveu, *m.*
confessor [kən'fesə], *n.* confesseur, *m.*

confidant ['kɔnfidænt], *n.* confident, *m.*
confide [kən'faid], *v.t.* confier (à).—*v.i.* se confier, se fier (à).
confidence ['kɔnfidəns], *n.* confiance; hardiesse; assurance; confidence (*secret*), *f.*
confident ['kɔnfidənt], *a.* confiant, certain, sûr; assuré.
confidential [kɔnfi'denʃəl], *a.* de confiance (*personne*); confidentiel (*chose*).
confidentially [kɔnfi'denʃəli], *adv.* de confiance; confidentiellement.
confidently ['kɔnfidəntli], *adv.* avec confiance.
confine [kən'fain], *v.t.* confiner, enfermer; retenir; limiter; *to be confined* (*of woman*), faire ses couches, accoucher.—['kɔnfain], *n.* (*usu. in pl.*) confins, *m.pl.*; (*fig.*) limite, borne, *f.*
confinement [kən'fainmənt], *n.* emprisonnement, *m.*; (*Mil.*) arrêts, *m.pl.*; accouchement, *m.*, couches (*de femme*), *f.pl.*
confirm [kən'fə:m], *v.t.* confirmer; affermir.
confirmation [kɔnfə'meiʃən], *n.* confirmation, *f.*, affermissement, *m.*
confirmed [kən'fə:md], *a.* invétéré, fieffé, incorrigible.
confiscate ['kɔnfiskeit], *v.t.* confisquer.
confiscation [kɔnfis'keiʃən], *n.* confiscation, *f.*
conflagration [kɔnflə'greiʃən], *n.* conflagration, *f.*, incendie, *m.*
conflict ['kɔnflikt], *n.* conflit, *m.*; (*fig.*) lutte, contradiction, *f.*—[kən'flikt], *v.i.* s'entrechoquer, lutter (*contre*); être en conflit (*avec*).
conflicting [kən'fliktiŋ], *a.* en conflit, contradictoire.
confluence ['kɔnfluəns], *n.* confluent; concours, *m.*; (*Path.*) confluence, *f.*
conform [kən'fɔ:m], *v.t.* conformer.—*v.i.* se conformer.
conformity [kən'fɔ:miti], *n.* conformité, *f.*; *in conformity with*, conformément (à).
confound [kən'faund], *v.t.* confondre; (*fig.*) bouleverser; embarrasser; *confound it!* zut!
confounded [kən'faundid], *a.* maudit, sacré.
confoundedly [kən'faundidli], *adv.* terriblement, furieusement, diablement.
confront [kən'frʌnt], *v.t.* confronter; affronter, faire face à.
confuse [kən'fju:z], *v.t.* rendre confus, embrouiller; (*fig.*) déconcerter.
confused [kən'fju:zd], *a.* confus; embrouillé.
confusedly [kən'fju:zidli], *adv.* confusément.
confusion [kən'fju:ʒən], *n.* confusion, *f.*, désordre; (*fig.*) embarras, *m.*
confute [kən'fju:t], *v.t.* réfuter.
congeal [kən'dʒi:l], *v.t.* congeler, glacer, geler, figer.—*v.i.* se congeler, se geler, se figer.
congenial [kən'dʒi:niəl], *a.* de la même nature; sympathique (à ou *avec*); qui convient (à); *a congenial task*, une tâche agréable.
conger ['kɔŋgə], *n.* (*Ichth.*) congre, *m.*, anguille de mer, *f.*
congest [kən'dʒest], *v.t.* entasser; engorger; *to become congested*, se congestionner; s'embouteiller (*rues*).
congestion [kən'dʒestʃən], *n.* amoncellement, *m.*; (*Path.*) congestion, *f.*; encombrement (*des rues*), *m.*

conglomerate [kən'glɔməreit], *v.t.* conglomérer.—*v.i.* se conglomérer.—[kən'glɔmərit], *n.* (*Geol.*) conglomérat, *m.*
conglomeration [kɔnglɔmə'reiʃən], *n.* conglomération, *f.*
Congo ['kɔŋgou]. le Congo, *m.*
Congolese [kɔŋgo'liːz], *a.* congolais.—*n.* Congolais (*personne*).
congratulate [kən'grætjuleit], *v.t.* féliciter.
congratulation [kəngrætju'leiʃən], *n.* félicitation, *f.*
congregate ['kɔŋgrigeit], *v.t.* rassembler.—*v.i.* se rassembler.
congregation [kɔŋgri'geiʃən], *n.* (*Eccles.*) congrégation, *f.*, fidèles, *m.pl.*; assemblée, *f.*, auditoire, *m.*, assistance, *f.*
congress ['kɔŋgres], *n.* congrès, *m.*
congressional [kən'greʃənl], *a.* congressionnel.
congressman ['kɔŋgresmən], *n.* (*pl.* **-men** [men]) (*U.S.*) membre du Congrès, *m.*
conic ['kɔnik], conical ['kɔnikəl], *a.* conique.
conifer ['kounifə], *n.* conifère, *m.*
coniferous [ko'nifərəs], *a.* conifère.
conjecture [kən'dʒektʃə], *v.t.*, *v.i.* conjecturer.—*n.* conjecture, *f.*
conjugal ['kɔndʒugəl], *a.* conjugal.
conjugate ['kɔndʒugeit], *v.t.* conjuguer.
conjugation [kɔndʒu'geiʃən], *n.* conjugaison, *f.*
conjunction [kən'dʒʌŋkʃən], *n.* conjonction, *f.*
conjure ['kʌndʒə], *v.t.* ensorceler; escamoter; *to conjure up*, évoquer.
conjurer, conjuror ['kʌndʒərə], *n.* escamoteur, prestidigitateur, illusionniste, *m.*
conjuring ['kʌndʒəriŋ], *n.* prestidigitation, *f.*, escamotage, *m.*
connect [kə'nekt], *v.t.* lier, joindre, rattacher, unir (*à*); accoupler.—*v.i.* se lier; faire correspondance (*trains*).
connected [kə'nektid], *a.* joint, uni, lié; cohérent; en relations.
connection, connexion [kə'nekʃən], *n.* connexion, liaison, suite, *f.*; rapport, *m.*; (*Rail.*) correspondance, *f.*; (*Elec.*) contact, *m.*; (*Comm.*) clientèle, *f.*; (*pl.*) parents, *m.pl.*; *in connexion with*, à propos de.
connivance [kə'naivəns], *n.* connivence, *f.*
connive [kə'naiv], *v.i. to connive at*, fermer les yeux sur, être de connivence dans.
connoisseur [kɔnə'səː], *n.* connaisseur, *m.*
connubial [kə'njuːbiəl], *a.* conjugal.
conquer ['kɔŋkə], *v.t.* vaincre, dompter; conquérir.—*v.i.* vaincre, remporter la victoire.
conqueror ['kɔŋkərə], *n.* vainqueur, conquérant, *m.*
conquest ['kɔŋkwest], *n.* conquête, *f.*
conscience ['kɔnʃəns], *n.* conscience, *f.*; *conscience money*, restitution anonyme, *f.*
conscientious [kɔnʃi'enʃəs], *a.* consciencieux; de conscience; *conscientious objector*, objecteur de conscience, *m.*
conscientiously [kɔnʃi'enʃəsli], *adv.* consciencieusement.
conscious ['kɔnʃəs], *a.* conscient; *to be conscious*, avoir sa connaissance; *to be conscious of*, avoir conscience de.
consciously ['kɔnʃəsli], *adv.* sciemment, en connaissance de cause.

consciousness ['kɔnʃəsnis], *n.* conscience; connaissance, *f.*
conscript ['kɔnskript], *a.* and *n.* conscrit, *m.*—[kən'skript], *v.t.* enrôler (par la conscription).
conscription [kən'skripʃən], *n.* conscription, *f.*
consecrate ['kɔnsikreit], *v.t.* consacrer (*une église*); bénir (*pain*); sacrer (*évêque, roi*); *consecrated ground*, terre sainte, *f.*
consecration [kɔnsi'kreiʃən], *n.* consécration; canonisation, *f.*; sacre (*d'évêque, de roi etc.*), *m.*
consecutive [kən'sekjutiv], *a.* consécutif.
consent [kən'sent], *v.i.* consentir (*à*).—*n.* consentement; accord, *m.*
consequence ['kɔnsikwəns], *n.* conséquence, suite, *f.*, effet, *m.*; importance, *f.*
consequent ['kɔnsikwənt], *a.* résultant; (*Log.*) conséquent.—*n.* conséquent, *m.*
consequential [kɔnsi'kwenʃəl], *a.* conséquent, logique; (*fig.*) suffisant, important.
consequently ['kɔnsikwəntli], *adv.* and *conj.* par conséquent.
conservative [kən'səːvətiv], *a.* and *n.* conservateur, *m.*
conservatory [kən'səːvətri], *n.* conservatoire (*théâtre, musique*), *m.*; (*Hort.*) serre, *f.*
consider [kən'sidə], *v.t.* considérer, examiner; estimer.—*v.i.* considérer, réfléchir (*à*).
considerable [kən'sidərəbl], *a.* considérable, grand, important.
considerably [kən'sidərəbli], *adv.* considérablement.
considerate [kən'sidərit], *a.* modéré, indulgent; attentif, plein d'égards; prévenant.
consideration [kənsidə'reiʃən], *n.* considération, *f.*, examen, *m.*; égards, *m.pl.*; récompense, *f.*, dédommagement, *m.*; *to take into consideration*, tenir compte de.
considering [kən'sidəriŋ], *prep.* eu égard à, étant donné, vu.—*conj.* vu que, attendu que, étant donné que.
consign [kən'sain], *v.t.* consigner, livrer, confier (*à*); (*Comm.*) expédier.
consignment [kən'sainmənt], *n.* expédition, *f.*, envoi, *m.*
consist [kən'sist], *v.i.* consister (*en*); *to consist of*, se composer (*de*).
consistency [kən'sistənsi], *n.* consistance, suite, *f.*, esprit de suite; accord, *m.*, harmonie; stabilité, *f.*
consistent [kən'sistənt], *a.* consistant; compatible (*avec*), conséquent.
consistently [kən'sistəntli], *adv.* d'une manière conséquente, conséquemment.
consolation [kɔnsə'leiʃən], *n.* consolation, *f.*
console [kən'soul], *v.t.* consoler (*de*).
consolidate [kən'solideit], *v.t.* consolider.—*v.i.* se consolider; *consolidated annuities*, (*abbr.*) *consols*, consolidés, *m.pl.*
consolidation [kɔnsoli'deiʃən], *n.* consolidation, *f.*
consoling [kən'souliŋ], *a.* consolant, consolateur, *m.*
consonant ['kɔnsənənt], *a.* consonant, conforme (*à*).—*n.* (*Phon.*) consonne, *f.*
consort ['kɔnsɔːt], *n.* compagnon, compagne, *f.*; époux, *m.*, épouse, *f.*—[kən'sɔːt], *v.i.* s'associer (*à*); *to consort with*, fréquenter.

conspicuous [kənˈspikjuəs], *a.* bien visible, en évidence; remarquable, éminent.

conspicuously [kənˈspikjuəsli], *adv.* visiblement, manifestement, éminemment.

conspiracy [kənˈspirəsi], *n.* conspiration, conjuration, *f.*

conspirator [kənˈspirətə], *n.* conspirateur; conjuré, *m.*

conspire [kənˈspaiə], *v.i.* conspirer, comploter (*contre*); (*fig.*) se réunir (*pour*).

constable [ˈkʌnstəbl], *n.* gouverneur (*de château*); agent de police, *m.*; **chief constable**, commissaire de police, *m.*

constabulary [kənˈstæbjuləri], *n.* police; gendarmerie, *f.*

constancy [ˈkɔnstənsi], *n.* constance, fermeté, fidélité; régularité, *f.*

constant [ˈkɔnstənt], *a.* stable, constant, fidèle; continu.

constantly [ˈkɔnstəntli], *adv.* constamment, invariablement.

constellation [kɔnstəˈleiʃən], *n.* constellation, *f.*

consternation [kɔnstəˈneiʃən], *n.* consternation, *f.*, atterrement, *m.*

constipation [kɔnstiˈpeiʃən], *n.* constipation, *f.*

constituency [kənˈstitjuənsi], *n.* circonscription électorale, *f.*, électeurs, *m.pl.*

constituent [kənˈstitjuənt], *a.* constituant.— *n.* constituant; (*Polit.*) commettant, électeur, *m.*

constitute [ˈkɔnstitjuːt], *v.t.* constituer, faire.

constitution [kɔnstiˈtjuːʃən], *n.* constitution, *f.*, tempérament, *m.*

constitutional [kɔnstiˈtjuːʃənəl], *a.* constitutionnel.—*n.* promenade de santé, *f.*

constrain [kənˈstrein], *v.t.* contraindre, forcer; retenir; gêner.

constraint [kənˈstreint], *n.* contrainte, gêne, *f.*

constrict [kənˈstrikt], *v.t.* resserrer, étrangler; brider.

construct [kənˈstrʌkt], *v.t.* construire, bâtir.

construction [kənˈstrʌkʃən], *n.* construction, *f.*; bâtiment, *m.*; (*fig.*) interprétation, *f.*, sens, *m.*

constructive [kənˈstrʌktiv], *a.* constructif; implicite.

construe [kənˈstruː], *v.t.* traduire mot-à-mot; (*fig.*) expliquer, interpréter.

consul [ˈkɔnsəl], *n.* consul, *m.*

consular [ˈkɔnsjulə], *a.* consulaire.

consulate [ˈkɔnsjulit], **consulship** [ˈkɔnsəlʃip], *n.* consulat, *m.*

consult [kənˈsʌlt], *v.t.* consulter.—*v.i.* délibérer.

consultation [kɔnsəlˈteiʃən], *n.* consultation, délibération, *f.*

consume [kənˈsjuːm], *v.t.* consumer, dissiper, dévorer; gaspiller; consommer (*to use*).

consumer [kənˈsjuːmə], *n.* consommateur; abonné (*de gaz etc.*), *m.*; **consumer goods**, biens de consommation, *m.pl.*

consummate [ˈkɔnsəmeit], *v.t.* consommer, achever, accomplir.—[kənˈsʌmit], *a.* consommé, complet, achevé, fieffé.

consummation [kɔnsəˈmeiʃən], *n.* consommation, fin, *f.*; (*fig.*) comble, *m.*

consumption [kənˈsʌmpʃən], *n.* consommation; phtisie, consomption (*maladie*), *f.*

consumptive [kənˈsʌmptiv], *a.* poitrinaire, phtisique, tuberculeux.

contact [ˈkɔntækt], *n.* contact, rapport, *m.*—*v.t.* contacter, se mettre en relation avec, entrer en contact avec.

contagion [kənˈteidʒən], *n.* contagion, *f.*

contagious [kənˈteidʒəs], *a.* contagieux.

contain [kənˈtein], *v.t.* contenir; retenir, renfermer.

container [kənˈteinə], *n.* récipient, réservoir, *m.*; (*Comm.*) boîte, *f.*

contaminate [kənˈtæmineit], *v.t.* souiller, contaminer.

contamination [kəntæmiˈneiʃən], *n.* souillure, contamination, *f.*

contemplate [ˈkɔntəmpleit], *v.t.* contempler; méditer, projeter.—*v.i.* songer, méditer.

contemplation [kɔntəmˈpleiʃən], *n.* contemplation; méditation, *f.*; projet, *m.*

contemplative [kənˈtemplətiv], *a.* contemplatif; pensif.

contemporaneous [kəntempəˈreinjəs], *a.* contemporain.

contemporary [kənˈtempərəri], *a.* and *n.* contemporain, *m.*

contempt [kənˈtempt], *n.* mépris, dédain, *m.*

contemptible [kənˈtemptəbl], *a.* méprisable, à dédaigner.

contemptuous [kənˈtemptjuəs], *a.* méprisant, dédaigneux.

contend [kənˈtend], *v.i.* lutter, combattre; contester; prétendre (*que*).

contender [kənˈtendə], *n.* compétiteur, concurrent, *m.*

content (1) [kənˈtent], *a.* content, satisfait; *to be content with*, se contenter de.—*n.* contentement, *m.*—*v.t.* contenter, satisfaire.

content (2) [ˈkɔntent], *n.* contenu, *m.*; *table of contents*, table des matières, *f.*

contented [kənˈtentid], *a.* satisfait, content (*de*).

contentedly [kənˈtentidli], *adv.* avec contentement.

contention [kənˈtenʃən], *n.* dispute, lutte, *f.*, débat, *m.*; prétention, *f.*; *bone of contention*, pomme de discorde, *f.*

contentious [kənˈtenʃəs], *a.* contentieux, litigieux, querelleur.

contentiousness [kənˈtenʃəsnis], *n.* humeur querelleuse, *f.*

contentment [kənˈtentmənt], *n.* contentement, *m.*

conterminous [kənˈtəːminəs], *a.* limitrophe, voisin (*de*); attenant (*à*).

contest [ˈkɔntest], *n.* lutte, *f.*, combat; concours, *m.*—[kənˈtest], *v.t.*, *v.i.* contester, disputer.

contestant [kənˈtestənt], *n.* contestant, concurrent, *m.*

context [ˈkɔntekst], *n.* contexte, *m.*; *in this context*, à ce sujet.

contiguity [kɔntiˈgjuːiti], *n.* contiguïté, *f.*

contiguous [kənˈtigjuəs], *a.* contigu, attenant (*à*).

continence [ˈkɔntinəns], *n.* continence, chasteté; (*fig.*) retenue, *f.*

continent (1) [ˈkɔntinənt], *a.* continent, chaste; (*fig.*) modéré, retenu.

continent (2) [ˈkɔntinənt], *n.* continent, *m.*

continental [kɔntiˈnentl], *a.* and *n.* continental, *m.*

contingence [kənˈtindʒəns], **contingency** [kənˈtindʒənsi], *n.* éventualité, *f.* cas imprévu, *m.*

contingent [kən'tindʒənt], *a.* contingent, fortuit, imprévu.—*n.* (*Mil.*) contingent, *m.*

contingently [kən'tindʒəntli], *adv.* éventuellement, fortuitement.

continual [kən'tinjuəl], *a.* continuel.

continually [kən'tinjuəli], *adv.* continuellement.

continuance [kən'tinjuəns], *n.* continuation; durée, *f.*

continuation [kəntinju'eiʃən], *n.* continuation, durée, *f.*

continue [kən'tinju:], *v.t.* continuer; prolonger; reprendre; perpétuer.—*v.i.* continuer; demeurer; durer.

continued [kən'tinju:d], *a.* continu, suivi; à suivre (*feuilleton*); *to be continued,* à suivre.

continuity [kɒnti'nju:iti], *n.* continuité, *f.*

continuous [kən'tinjuəs], *a.* continu.

continuously [kən'tinjuəsli], *adv.* continûment, sans interruption.

contort [kən'tɔ:t], *v.t.* tordre, contourner, défigurer.

contorted [kən'tɔ:tid], *a.* tordu, contourné, défiguré.

contortion [kən'tɔ:ʃən], *n.* contorsion; (*Anat.*) luxation, *f.*

contortionist [kən'tɔ:ʃənist], *n.* contorsionniste, *m., f.*

contour ['kɒntuə], *n.* contour, tracé (*de niveau*), *m.*

contra ['kɒntrə], *prep.* contre; (*Comm.*) d'autre part.

contraband ['kɒntrəbænd], *a.* de contrebande.—*n.* contrebande, *f.*

contraception [kɒntrə'sepʃən], *n.* procédés anticonceptionnels, *m.pl.*

contraceptive [kɒntrə'septiv], *a.* anticonceptionnel.—*n.* procédé *ou* appareil anticonceptionnel, *m.*

contract [kən'trækt], *v.t.* contracter (*dans tous les sens*); abréger; (*fig.*) resserrer; rider, froncer (*les sourcils etc.*); prendre (*habitude*). —*v.i.* se contracter, se resserrer, se rétrécir; (*Comm.*) traiter (*pour*), contracter, entreprendre, soumissionner; *to contract out of something,* renoncer à *ou* se dégager de quelquechose par contrat.—['kɒntrækt], *n.* contrat; pacte, *m.*, convention; adjudication, *f.*

contractible [kən'træktəbl], *a.* contractile.

contraction [kən'trækʃən], *n.* contraction, *f.*, rétrécissement; raccourcissement; retrait (*métaux*), *m.*; (*Math.*) abréviation, *f.*

contractor [kən'træktə], *n.* contractant; entrepreneur (*constructeur*); fournisseur (*aux forces armées*); adjudicataire (*concesseur*), *m.*

contradict [kɒntrə'dikt], *v.t.* contredire, démentir.

contradiction [kɒntrə'dikʃən], *n.* contradiction, incompatibilité, *f.*, démenti (*négation*), *m.*

contradictory [kɒntrə'diktəri], *a.* contradictoire.

contralto [kən'træltou], *n.* (*Mus.*) contralto, contralte, *m.*

contrariety [kɒntrə'raiəti], *n.* contrariété, opposition, *f.*

contrarily ['kɒntrərili], *adv.* contrairement, en sens contraire.

contrary ['kɒntrəri], *a.* contraire, opposé; (*fam.*) [kən'trɛəri], contrariant (*personne*). —*n.* contraire, *m.*; *on the contrary,* au contraire.—*adv.* contrairement (*à*); à l'encontre (*de*).

contrast ['kɒntrɑ:st], *n.* contraste, *m.*—[kən 'trɑ:st], *v.t.* faire contraster; mettre en contraste.—*v.i.* contraster, faire contraste.

contravene [kɒntrə'vi:n], *v.t.* contrevenir à, enfreindre.

contravention [kɒntrə'venʃən], *n.* contravention, infraction, *f.*

contribute [kən'tribju:t], *v.t.* contribuer, payer.—*v.i.* contribuer (*à*).

contribution [kɒntri'bju:ʃən], *n.* contribution, *f.*

contributor [kən'tribjutə], *n.* contribuant; (*Journ.*) collaborateur, *m.*

contributory [kən'tribjutəri], *a.* contribuant.

contrite ['kɒntrait], *a.* contrit, pénitent.

contritely ['kɒntraitli], *adv.* avec contrition.

contriteness ['kɒntraitnis], **contrition** [kən 'triʃən], *n.* contrition, pénitence, *f.*

contrivance [kən'traivəns], *n.* invention; combinaison, idée, *f.*; artifice, *m.*

contrive [kən'traiv], *v.t.* inventer, imaginer; pratiquer, ménager.—*v.i.* s'arranger (*pour*), trouver moyen (*de*); parvenir (*à*).

contriver [kən'traivə], *n.* inventeur, *m.*, inventrice, *f.*

contriving [kən'traiviŋ], *a.* ingénieux.

control [kən'troul], *n.* autorité (*supérieure*); surveillance; (*Tech.*) commande, *f.*; *out of control,* désemparé; *remote control,* télécommande, *f.*—*v.t.* diriger, régler; gouverner, commander; *to control oneself,* se dominer, se retenir.

controller [kən'troulə], *n.* contrôleur, *m.*

controversial [kɒntrə'və:ʃəl], *a.* sujet à controverse, polémique.

controversy ['kɒntrəvə:si], *n.* controverse, polémique, *f.*; différend, *m.*

controvert ['kɒntrəvə:t], *v.t.* controverser, disputer.

contumacious [kɒntju'meiʃəs], *a.* obstiné, récalcitrant, opiniâtre; (*Law*) contumace.

contumaciousness [kɒntju'meiʃəsnis], **contumacy** ['kɒntjuməsi], *n.* obstination, opiniâtreté; (*Law*) contumace, *f.*

contumelious [kɒntju'mi:liəs], *a.* injurieux, outrageant.

contumely ['kɒntjuməli], *n.* injure, *f.*, outrage, *m.*, honte, *f.*

contuse [kən'tju:z], *v.t.* contusionner.

contusion [kən'tju:ʒən], *n.* contusion, meurtrissure, *f.*

conundrum [kə'nʌndrəm], *n.* énigme, devinette, *f.*

convalesce [kɒnvə'les], *v.i.* être en convalescence.

convalescence [kɒnvə'lesəns], *n.* convalescence, *f.*

convalescent [kɒnvə'lesənt], *a.* and *n.* convalescent, *m.*, convalescente, *f.*

convection [kən'vekʃən], *n.* convection, *f.*

convene [kən'vi:n], *v.t.* convoquer, réunir, assembler.—*v.i.* s'assembler, se réunir.

convenience [kən'vi:niəns], *n.* commodité, convenance, *f.*

convenient [kən'vi:niənt], *a.* commode, convenable.

conveniently [kən'viːniəntli], *adv.* commodément, convenablement, sans inconvénient.

convent ['kɔnvənt], *n.* couvent, *m.*

conventicle [kən'ventikl], *n.* conventicule, *m.*

convention [kən'venʃən], *n.* convention; assemblée, *f.*; (*pl.*) convenances, *f.pl.*

conventional [kən'venʃənəl], *a.* conventionnel, de convention.

conventual [kən'ventjuəl], *a.* conventuel.—*n.* conventuel, religieux, *m.*, religieuse, *f.*

converge [kən'vəːdʒ], *v.i.* converger.

conversant [kən'vəːsənt], *a.* versé (*dans*); familier (*avec*), au courant de.

conversation [kɔnvə'seiʃən], *n.* conversation, *f.*, entretien, *m.*

conversational [kɔnvə'seiʃənəl], *a.* de conversation.

conversationalist [kɔnvə'seiʃənəlist], *n.* causeur, *m.*

converse [kən'vəːs], *v.i.* causer, converser, s'entretenir.—['kɔnvəːs], *n.* entretien, *m.*, conversation; (*Math.*) réciproque, *f.*

conversely ['kɔnvəːsli], *adv.* réciproquement.

conversion [kən'vəːʃən], *n.* conversion, *f.*

convert [kən'vəːt], *v.t.* convertir, transformer; faire servir.—['kɔnvəːt], *n.* converti, *m.*, convertie, *f.*

converter [kən'vəːtə], *n.* convertisseur, *m.*

convertible [kən'vəːtibl], *a.* convertible (*chose*); convertissable (*personne*); (*Motor.*) décapotable.

convex ['kɔnveks], *a.* convexe.

convey [kən'vei], *v.t.* transporter (*marchandises etc.*); porter, conduire, amener; transmettre (*son etc.*); présenter (*remerciements etc.*); donner (*idée etc.*); communiquer (*nouvelle etc.*); céder (*propriété etc.*).

conveyable [kən'veiəbl], *a.* transportable; exprimable.

conveyance [kən'veiəns], *n.* transport, *m.*; transmission, *f.*; véhicule, *m.*; (*Law*) cession, *f.*

conveyor [kən'veiə], *n.* porteur, voiturier; (appareil) transporteur; conducteur (électrique), *m.*; *conveyor belt*, chaîne de montage, *f.*

convict [kən'vikt], *v.t.* condamner, déclarer coupable; convaincre (*quelqu'un de son erreur etc.*).—['kɔnvikt], *n.* forçat, *m.*

conviction [kən'vikʃən], *n.* conviction, persuasion; (*Law*) condamnation, *f.*

convince [kən'vins], *v.t.* convaincre, persuader.

convincing [kən'vinsiŋ], *a.* convaincant, persuasif.

convincingly [kən'vinsiŋli], *adv.* d'une manière convaincante.

convivial [kən'viviəl], *a.* joyeux, jovial.

conviviality [kənvivi'eliti], *n.* franche gaieté, *f.*; (*pl.*) joyeux repas, *m.pl.*

convocation [kɔnvə'keiʃən], *n.* convocation; (*Eccles.*) assemblée, *f.*, synode, *m.*

convoke [kən'vouk], *v.t.* convoquer, assembler.

convolvulus [kən'vɔlvjuləs], *n.* (*pl.* **convolvuli** [kən'vɔlvjulai]) volubilis, liseron, *m.*, belle-de-jour, *f.*

convoy ['kɔnvɔi], *n.* convoi, *m.*, escorte, *f.*

convulse [kən'vʌls], *v.t.* convulser; (*fig.*) ébranler, bouleverser.

convulsion [kən'vʌlʃən], *n.* convulsion; (*fig.*) commotion, *f.*

convulsive [kən'vʌlsiv], *a.* convulsif.

cony, coney ['kouni], *n.* lapin, *m.*

coo [kuː], *v.i.* roucouler.

cooing ['kuːiŋ], *n.* roucoulement, *m.*

cook [kuk], *n.* cuisinier, *m.*, cuisinière, *f.*; (*Naut.*) coq, *m.*; *head cook*, chef, *m.*—*v.t.* cuire, faire cuire.—*v.i.* cuire; faire la cuisine, cuisiner.

cooker ['kukə], *n.* cuisinière (*appareil*), *f.*; fruit à cuire, *m.*; *pressure cooker*, cocotteminute, *f.*

cookery ['kukəri], *n.* cuisine (*art*), *f.*

cooking ['kukiŋ], *n.* cuisine; cuisson, *f.*

cool [kuːl], *a.* frais, (*fig.*) calme, tranquille; peu gêné.—*n.* frais, *m.*, fraîcheur, *f.*—*v.t.* rafraîchir; refroidir; (*fig.*) calmer.—*v.i.* se refroidir; refroidir; *to cool down*, se calmer, s'apaiser.

cooling ['kuːliŋ], *a.* rafraîchissant, calmant; *cooling tower*, refroidisseur, *m.*

coolly ['kuːli], *adv.* fraîchement; (*fig.*) de sangfroid, tranquillement.

coolness ['kuːlnis], *n.* fraîcheur, *f.*, frais, *m.*; (*fig.*) froideur (*indifférence*), *f.*; sang-froid; sans-gêne (*insolence*), *m.*

coop [kuːp], *n.* cage à poules, mue, *f.*—*v.t.* mettre en mue; *to coop up*, enfermer étroitement, claquemurer.

cooper ['kuːpə], *n.* tonnelier, *m.*

co-operate [kou'ɔpəreit], *v.i.* coopérer, concourir (*à*).

co-operation [kouɔpə'reiʃən], *n.* coopération, *f.*; concours, *m.*

co-operative [kou'ɔpərətiv], *a.* coopérant, coopératif.

co-opt [kou'ɔpt], *v.t.* coopter.

co-ordinate [kou'ɔːdineit], *v.t.* coordonner.—[kou'ɔːdinit], *a.* du même rang, égal; (*Math.*) coordonné.

coot [kuːt], *n.* (*Orn.*) foulque, *f.*

cop [kɔp], *n.* cime, *f.*, sommet, *m.*; huppe, aigrette (*d'oiseau*), *f.*; (*slang*) flic (*agent de police*), *m.*

copartner [kou'pɑːtnə], *n.* associé, *m.*

copartnership [kou'pɑːtnəʃip], *n.* société en nom collectif, *f.*

cope (1) [koup], *n.* chaperon, *m.*, chape (*vêtement sacerdotal*), *f.*—*v.t.* couvrir, chaperonner.

cope (2) [koup], *v.i.* se débrouiller; *to cope with*, tenir tête à; venir à bout de.

Copenhagen [koupən'heigən], Copenhague, *f.*

copier ['kɔpiə], **copyist** ['kɔpiist], *n.* copiste, *m.*, *f.*; (*fig.*) imitateur, *m.*

coping ['koupiŋ], *n.* faîte (*d'un édifice*); couronnement (*d'un mur*), *m.*

copious ['koupiəs], *a.* abondant, copieux.

copiously ['koupiəsli], *adv.* copieusement, abondamment.

copiousness ['koupiəsnis], *n.* abondance, *f.*

copper ['kɔpə], *a.* de cuivre, en cuivre.—*n.* cuivre (rouge), *m.*; chaudière (*boiler*), *f.*; (*slang*) flic (*agent de police*), *m.*; (*pl.*) petite monnaie, *f.*—*v.t.* cuivrer; (*Naut.*) doubler en cuivre.

copper-beech ['kɔpə'biːtʃ], *n.* hêtre rouge, *m.*

copper-smith ['kɔpəsmiθ], *n.* chaudronnier, *m.*

coppice ['kɔpis], **copse** [kɔps], *n.* taillis, *m.*

copy ['kɔpi], *n.* copie, *f.*; exemple (*d'écriture*); exemplaire (*livre*); numéro (*journal*); modèle (*de dessin*), *m.*; rough copy. brouillon, *m.—v.t.* copier; imiter; *to copy out,* transcrire.

copy-book ['kɔpibuk], *n.* cahier d'écriture, *m.*

copyist [COPIER].

copyright ['kɔpirait], *n.* droits d'auteur, *m.pl.*; propriété littéraire, *f.*

coquet [ko'ket], *v.i.* faire des coquetteries (*à*); faire la coquette (*avec*).

coquette [ko'ket], *n.* coquette, *f.*

coquetry ['koukətri], *n.* coquetterie, *f.*

coquettish [ko'ketiʃ], *a.* coquet, en coquette; provocant (*sourire*).

coquettishly [ko'ketiʃli], *adv.* d'un air provocant.

coral ['kɔrəl], *a.* de corail.—*n.* corail, *m.*

cord [kɔːd], *n.* corde, *f.*, cordon; cordage, *m.*, ganse, *f.*; (*fig.*) lien, *m.—v.t.* corder.

cordial ['kɔːdiəl], *a.* cordial.—*n.* cordial, *m.*, liqueur, *f.*

cordiality [kɔːdi'æliti], *n.* cordialité, *f.*

cordially ['kɔːdiəli], *adv.* cordialement.

cordon ['kɔːdən], *n.* cordon, *m.—v.t. to cordon off,* isoler par un cordon (*de police*).

corduroy ['kɔːdjurɔi], *n.* velours à côtes, *m.*

core [kɔː], *n.* cœur; noyau (*d'un moule*); (*fig.*) milieu, centre, *m.*; (*Naut.*) âme (*de corde*), *f.*; trognon (*de pomme*), *m.—v.t.* vider (*une pomme*); creuser, évider (*un moule*).

co-respondent [kɔuris'pɔndənt], *n.* complice, *m.*, *f.*, co-défendeur (*en adultère*), *m.*

corgi, corgy ['kɔːgi], *n.* basset gallois, *m.*

cork [kɔːk], *n.* liège; bouchon (*à bouteille etc.*), *m.—v.t.* boucher.

corkscrew ['kɔːkskru], *n.* tire-bouchon, *m.*; *corkscrew staircase,* escalier en colimaçon, *m.*

cork-tipped [kɔːk'tipt], *a.* à bouts de liège (*cigarettes*).

corm [kɔːm], *n.* (*Bot.*) bulbe, *m.*

cormorant ['kɔːmərənt], *n.* cormoran; (*fig.*) rapace, affameur, *m.*

corn (1) [kɔːn], *n.* grain, *m.*; céréales, *f.pl.*; blé, *m.*; *Indian corn,* maïs, *m.—v.t.* saler (*bœuf*).

corn (2) [kɔːn], *n.* cor (au pied), *m.*

corn-chandler ['kɔːntʃɑːndlə], *n.* blatier, marchand de blé, *m.*

corn-crake ['kɔːnkreik], *n.* râle de genêt, *m.*

cornea ['kɔːniə], *n.* (*Anat.*) cornée, *f.*

corned beef ['kɔːnd'biːf], *n.* bœuf salé, bœuf de conserve, *m.*

corner ['kɔːnə], *n.* coin, angle, *m.*; encoignure, *f.*; (*fig.*) monopole, accaparement, *m.*; *blind corner,* tournant (*ou* virage) masqué, *m.—v.t.* (*Comm.*) accaparer; (*fig.*) pousser dans un coin, acculer.—*v.i.* prendre un virage, virer.

corner-stone ['kɔːnəstoun], *n.* pierre angulaire, *f.*

cornet ['kɔːnit], *n.* cornet (*à pistons*), *m.*

cornfield ['kɔːnfiːld], *n.* champ de blé, *m.*

cornflakes ['kɔːnfleiks], *n.pl.* paillettes de maïs, *f.pl.*

corn-flour ['kɔːnflauə], *n.* farine de maïs, *f.*

corn-flower ['kɔːnflauə], *n.* bluet, *m.*

cornice ['kɔːnis], *n.* corniche, *f.*

corn-poppy ['kɔːnpɔpi], *n.* coquelicot, *m.*

corollary [kə'rɔləri], *n.* corollaire, *m.*

coronation [kɔrə'neiʃən], *n.* couronnement, sacre, *m.*

coroner ['kɔrənə], *n.* coroner, *m.*

coronet ['kɔrənit], *n.* (petite) couronne, *f.*

corporal ['kɔːpərəl], *a.* corporel.—*n.* caporal (*infanterie*); brigadier (*cavalerie*), *m.*

corporate ['kɔːpərit], *a.* érigé en corporation; de corporation.

corporately ['kɔːpəritli], *adv.* collectivement.

corporation [kɔːpə'reiʃən], *n.* corporation, *f.*; conseil municipal, *m.*, municipalité (*d'une ville*), *f.*

corporeal [kɔː'pɔːriəl], *a.* corporel, matériel.

corps [kɔː], *n.inv.* corps, *m.*, formation, *f.*

corpse [kɔːps], *n.* cadavre, *m.*

corpulence ['kɔːpjuləns], corpulency ['kɔːpjulənsi], *n.* corpulence, *f.*, embonpoint, *m.*

corpulent ['kɔːpjulənt], *a.* corpulent, gros, gras.

corpuscle ['kɔːpʌsl], *n.* corpuscule, globule, *m.*

correct [kə'rekt], *a.* correct, exact, juste; (*fig.*) convenable, en règle; pur, bon (*style*); bien élevé (*personne*); comme il faut.—*v.t.* corriger, rectifier, reprendre; punir.

correction [kə'rekʃən], *n.* correction; punition, *f.*

correctly [kə'rektli], *adv.* correctement, exactement, justement.

correctness [kə'rektnis], *n.* exactitude, justesse; pureté (*de style*), *f.*

correlate ['kɔrileit], *v.t.* mettre en corrélation. —*v.i.* correspondre.

correlation [kɔri'leiʃən], *n.* corrélation, *f.*

correspond [kɔris'pɔnd], *v.i.* correspondre (*à ou avec*); répondre (*à*); s'accorder (*avec*); être conforme (*à*).

correspondence [kɔris'pɔndəns], *n.* correspondance, *f.*, rapport, *m.*

correspondent [kɔris'pɔndənt], *a.* conforme, qui se rapporte (*à*).—*n.* correspondant, *m.*

corridor ['kɔridɔː], *n.* corridor; couloir, *m.*

corroborate [kə'rɔbəreit], *v.t.* corroborer, confirmer.

corroboration [kərɔbə'reiʃən], *n.* corroboration, confirmation, *f.*; *in corroboration of,* à l'appui de.

corrode [kə'roud], *v.t.* corroder, ronger; (*fig.*) détruire.—*v.i.* se corroder.

corrosion [kə'rouʒən], *n.* corrosion; (*fig.*) destruction, *f.*

corrosive [kə'rouziv], *a.* corrosif; (*fig.*) rongeur.—*n.* corrosif, *m.*

corrugate ['kɔrugeit], *v.t.* rider, plisser, froncer; onduler; *corrugated iron,* tôle ondulée, *f.—v.i.* se plisser, se froncer.

corrupt [kə'rʌpt], *v.t.* corrompre.—*v.i.* se corrompre.—*a.* corrompu, dépravé, vicié.

corruption [kə'rʌpʃən], *n.* corruption; (*fig.*) altération (*d'un texte etc.*), *f.*

corruptive [kə'rʌptiv], *a.* corruptif.

corruptly [kə'rʌptli], *adv.* par corruption.

corsair ['kɔːseə], *n.* corsaire, *m.*

corset ['kɔːsit], *n.* corset, *m.*

corset-maker ['kɔːsitmeikə], *n.* corsetier, *m.* corsetière, *f.*

Corsica ['kɔːsikə], la Corse, *f.*

Corsican ['kɔːsikən], *a.* corse.—*n.* Corse (*personne*), *m.*, *f.*

corslet ['kɔːslit], *n.* corselet, *m.*

cortège [kɔː'teiʒ], *n.* cortège (*funèbre*), *m.*, procession; suite, *f.*

cortisone ['kɔːtizoun], *n.* cortisone, *f.*

coruscate ['kɔrəskeit], *v.i.* scintiller, briller.

corvette [kɔː'vet], *n.* (*Naut.*) corvette, *f.*

cosh [kɔʃ], *n.* matraque, *f.*—*v.t.* matraquer.

cosily ['kouzili], *adv.* à l'aise, bien au chaud, douillettement.

cosmetic [kɔz'metik], *a.* and *n.* cosmétique, *m.*

cosmic ['kɔzmik], **cosmical** ['kɔzmikəl], *a.* cosmique.

cosmopolitan [kɔzmo'pɔlitən], *a.* and *n.* cosmopolite, *m.*

cosmos ['kɔzmɔs], *n.* cosmos, *m.*

cosset ['kɔsit], *v.t.* dorloter, choyer.

cost [kɔst], *n.* prix; frais, *m.*, dépense, *f.*; (*Comm.*) coût, *m.*; (*Law*, *pl.*) dépens, *m.pl.*; *at any cost*, *at all costs*, à tout prix; *cost of living*, coût de la vie.—*v.i. irr.* coûter; *cost what it may*, coûte que coûte.

coster ['kɔstə], **costermonger** ['kɔstəmʌngə], *n.* marchand des quatre saisons, *m.*

costive ['kɔstiv], *a.* constipé.

costliness ['kɔstlinis], *n.* haut prix, prix élevé, *m.*

costly ['kɔstli], *a.* coûteux, de prix; somptueux.

costume ['kɔstjuːm], *n.* costume, *m.*

cosy ['kouzi], *a.* chaud, confortable, douillet; commode et petit (*appartement*).—*n.* (*tea*) *cosy*, couvre-théière, *m.*

cot [kɔt], *n.* cabane, chaumière, *f.*; bercail, parc (*à moutons*); petit lit, lit d'enfant, *m.*

coterie ['koutəri], *n.* coterie, clique, *f.*

cottage ['kɔtidʒ], *n.* chaumière; petite maison, villa, *f.*

cotton [kɔtn], *n.* coton, *m.*

cotton-mill ['kɔtnmil], *n.* filature de coton, *f.*

cotton-plant ['kɔtnplaːnt], *n.* cotonnier, *m.*

cotton-spinning ['kɔtnspiniŋ], *n.* filage du coton, *m.*

cotton-tree ['kɔtntriː], *n.* bombax, *m.*

cotton-wool ['kɔtn'wul], *n.* ouate, *f.*

couch [kautʃ], *n.* canapé, divan, *m.*—*v.t.* coucher; (*fig.*) rédiger, exprimer.—*v.i.* se coucher; se tapir.

cougar ['kuːgə], *n.* couguar, puma, *m.*

cough [kɔf], *n.* toux, *f.*; *whooping-cough*, coqueluche, *f.*—*v.i.* tousser.

coughing ['kɔfiŋ], *n.* toux, *f.*; *fit of coughing*, quinte de toux, *f.*

council ['kaunsil], *n.* conseil; (*Eccles.*) concile, *m.*

councillor ['kaunsilə], *n.* conseiller, *m.*

counsel ['kaunsəl], *n.* conseil, avis; dessein; avocat, *m.*—*v.t.* conseiller.

counsellor ['kaunsələ], *n.* conseiller; avocat, *m.*

count (1) [kaunt], *n.* comte (*titre*), *m.*

count (2) [kaunt], *n.* calcul, compte, total, *m.* —*v.t.* compter; (*fig.*) regarder, considérer; *to count on* or *upon*, compter sur.

countenance ['kauntinəns], *n.* figure, mine, *f.*, air, *m.*; (*fig.*) approbation, *f.*, appui, *m.*; *to give countenance to*, favoriser, encourager; *to keep one's countenance*, garder son sérieux; *to put out of countenance*, décontenancer.—*v.t.* appuyer, encourager, favoriser; être en faveur de.

counter ['kauntə], *n.* calculateur; compteur (*instrument*); (*Cards etc.*) jeton; comptoir (*de magasin*), *m.*—*adv.* contre, contrairement (*à*), à l'encontre (*de*).—*v.t.*, *v.i.* parer; contrer.

counteract [kauntə'rækt], *v.t.* contrecarrer, contre-balancer, neutraliser.

counteraction [kauntə'rækʃən], *n.* action contraire, opposition, résistance, *f.*

counter-clockwise ['kauntə'klɔkwaiz], **anti-clockwise** ['ænti'klɔkwaiz], *adv.* dans le sens contraire des aiguilles d'une montre.

counter-espionage ['kauntər'espiənɑːʒ], *n.* contre-espionnage, *m.*

counterfeit ['kauntəfiːt], *a.* contrefait, imité; faux.—*n.* contrefaçon; fausse pièce, fausse monnaie; imitation, *f.*—*v.t.* contrefaire, imiter; feindre.—*v.i.* feindre.

counterfoil ['kauntəfɔil], *n.* talon (*de registre*), *m.*, souche, *f.*

countermand [kauntə'mɑːnd], *v.t.* contremander.—*n.* contremandement, *m.*

counterpane ['kauntəpein], *n.* couvre-pied, couvre-lit, *m.*

counterpart ['kauntəpɑːt], *n.* contre-partie, *f.*; pendant, *m.*

countess ['kauntis], *n.* comtesse, *f.*

counting ['kauntiŋ], *n.* compte; dépouillement (*élections*), *m.*

counting-house ['kauntiŋhaus], *n.* bureau, comptoir, *m.*, caisse, *f.*

countless ['kauntlis], *a.* innombrable, sans nombre.

countrified ['kʌntrifaid], *a.* (devenu) campagnard *ou* provincial.

country ['kʌntri], *n.* pays, *m.*; contrée; région; campagne (*opposée à la ville*); province (*opposée à la capitale*); patrie (*fatherland*), *f.*; *across country*, à travers champs; *in open country*, en rase campagne; *in the country*, à la campagne.

countryman ['kʌntrimən], *n.* (*pl.* -men [men]) paysan, campagnard, *m.*; *fellow-countryman*, compatriote, *m.*

countryside ['kʌntrisaid], *n.* campagne, *f.*; paysage, *m.*

country-woman ['kʌntriwumən], *n.* (*pl.* -women [wimin]) paysanne, *f.*

county ['kaunti], *n.* comté, *m.*; *county council*, conseil général, *m.*; *county town*, chef-lieu, *m.*

couple [kʌpl], *n.* couple, *f.*; couple (*mâle et femelle*), *m.*—*v.t.* coupler, accoupler; atteler; joindre.—*v.i.* s'accoupler.

couplet ['kʌplit], *n.* couplet, distique, *m.*

coupling ['kʌpliŋ], *n.* accouplement, *m.*

coupon ['kuːpɔn], *n.* coupon; bon, *m.*

courage ['kʌridʒ], *n.* courage, *m.*

courageous [kə'reidʒəs], *a.* courageux.

courageously [kə'reidʒəsli], *adv.* courageusement.

courier ['kuriə], *n.* courrier, *m.*

course [kɔːs], *n.* cours, *m.*; carrière, voie, suite, *f.*; lit (*d'une rivière*); genre (*de vie*); service (*de repas*); courant (*durée*); (*Racing*) terrain de course; hippodrome, *m.*; (*Naut.*) route, *f.*; (*Med.*, *p.i.*) règles, *f.pl.*; *in due course*, en temps voulu; *of course*, naturellement, bien entendu.—*v.t.* courir; faire courir; chasser (*le lièvre*).—*v.i.* courir; circuler (*sang*).

courser ['kɔːsə], *n.* coureur, coursier, *m.*

---

cramped

court [kɔːt], *n.* cour, *f.*; tribunal, *m.*; impasse, *f.*, passage (*petite rue*); (*Ten.*) court, *m.*—*v.t.* faire sa cour à, courtiser; rechercher; briguer.
courteous [ˈkɔːtiəs], *a.* courtois, poli.
courteously [ˈkɔːtiəsli], *adv.* courtoisement, poliment.
courtesan [kɔːtiˈzæn], *n.* courtisane, *f.*
courtesy [ˈkɔːtəsi], *n.* courtoisie, politesse, *f.*
court-house [ˈkɔːthaus], *n.* palais de justice, *m.*
courtier [ˈkɔːtiə], *n.* courtisan, homme de cour, *m.*
courtliness [ˈkɔːtlinis], *n.* élégance, politesse, *f.*
courtly [ˈkɔːtli], *a.* poli, élégant, courtois.
court-martial [ˈkɔːtˈmɑːʃəl], *n.* conseil de guerre, *m.*—*v.t.* faire passer en conseil de guerre.
courtship [ˈkɔːtʃip], *n.* cour, *f.*
courtyard [ˈkɔːtjɑːd], *n.* cour (*de maison*), *f.*
cousin [kʌzn], *n.* cousin, *m.*
cove [kouv], *n.* anse, crique, *f.*
covenant [ˈkʌvənənt], *n.* convention, *f.*, pacte, contrat, *m.*—*v.t.* stipuler par contrat.—*v.i.* convenir (*de*), s'engager (*à*).
Coventry [ˈkʌvəntri, ˈkʌvəntri]. (*colloq.*) **to send to Coventry**, mettre en quarantaine.
cover [ˈkʌvə], *v.t.* couvrir; voiler, déguiser; cacher.—*n.* couverture; cloche (*d'un plat etc.*); enveloppe (*d'une lettre etc.*); housse (*d'une chaise*), *f.*; couvercle (*d'une casserole etc.*); couvert (*gibier*); (*fig.*) voile, abri, *m.*; **under cover of**, sous la protection de, à la faveur de.
covering [ˈkʌvəriŋ], *n.* couverture; enveloppe; housse (*de chaise*), *f.*; habits (*vêtements*), *m.pl.*; **covering letter**, lettre d'envoi, *f.*
coverlet [ˈkʌvəlit], *n.* couvre-pied, couvre-lit, *m.*
covert [ˈkʌvət], *a.* couvert, caché, secret.—*n.* couvert, abri; gîte, *m.*, tanière, *f.*
covertly [ˈkʌvətli], *adv.* secrètement, en cachette.
covet [ˈkʌvit], *v.t.* convoiter, désirer ardemment.
covetous [ˈkʌvitəs], *a.* avide, avaricieux, cupide.
covetously [ˈkʌvitəsli], *adv.* avec convoitise, avidement.
covetousness [ˈkʌvitəsnis], *n.* convoitise, cupidité, *f.*
covey [ˈkʌvi], *n.* compagnie (*de perdrix*), *f.*
cow (1) [kau], *n.* vache, *f.*
cow (2) [kau], *v.t.* intimider, dompter.
coward [ˈkauəd], *n.* lâche, poltron, *m.*, poltronne, *f.*
cowardice [ˈkauədis], **cowardliness** [ˈkauədlinis], *n.* couardise, poltronnerie, lâcheté, *f.*
cowardly [ˈkauədli], *a.* couard, lâche, poltron.—*adv.* lâchement.
cowboy [ˈkaubɔi], *n.* jeune vacher; (*Am.*) cowboy, *m.*
cower [ˈkauə], *v.i.* s'accroupir, se blottir, se tapir.
cowherd [ˈkauhəːd], *n.* vacher, *m.*
cowhide [ˈkauhaid], *n.* peau de vache, *f.*
cowl [kaul], *n.* capuchon; (*Naut., Av.*) capot; tabourin (*de cheminée*), *m.*
cow-shed [ˈkauʃed], *n.* vacherie, étable à vaches, *f.*

cowslip [ˈkauslip], *n.* primevère, *f.*, coucou, *m.*
coxcomb, cockscomb [ˈkɔkskoum], *n.* petit-maître, freluquet, fat, *m.*
coxswain [kɔksn], *n.* patron de chaloupe; (*Row.*) barreur, *m.*
coy [kɔi], *a.* timide, réservé.
coyly [ˈkɔili], *adv.* timidement, avec réserve.
coyness [ˈkɔinis], *n.* timidité, réserve, *f.*
coyote [kɔiˈjouti], *n.* loup de prairie, coyote, *m.*
cozen [kʌzn], *v.t.* duper, tromper.
crab [kræb], *n.* crabe, cancre; (*Astron.*) cancer, *m.*
crab-apple [ˈkræbæpl], *n.* pomme sauvage, *f.*
crabbed [kræbd], *a.* acariâtre, revêche, bourru.
crab-tree [ˈkræbtriː], *n.* pommier sauvage, *m.*
crabwise [ˈkræbwaiz], *adv.* comme un crabe, de biais.
crack [kræk], *v.t.* fendre; fêler (*porcelaine etc.*); gercer (*la peau etc.*); casser (*noix etc.*); faire claquer (*fouet*); faire sauter (*bouteille de vin*); faire, lâcher (*plaisanterie*); (*fig.*) rompre, briser.—*v.i.* se fendre, se lézarder; se gercer (*la peau etc.*); claquer (*fouet*); se fêler (*verre etc.*); muer (*la voix*).—*a.* fameux, d'élite; **to be a crack shot**, être un fin tireur.—*n.* fente, crevasse, fissure; détonation (*de fusil*); lézarde, fêlure (*verre*), *f.*; craquement (*bruit*); claquement (*d'un fouet*), *m.*; mue (*de la voix*); hâblerie (*boast*), *f.*
crack-brained [ˈkrækbreind], *a.* (*fam.*) timbré, fou.
cracked [krækd], *a.* fendu, fêlé; (*fig.*) timbré.
cracker [ˈkrækə], *n.* vantard; pétard (*feu d'artifice*); (*Am.*) biscuit, *m.*; **nut-crackers**, casse-noix, *m.inv.*
crackle [krækl], *v.i.* pétiller, craqueter, crépiter.
crackling [ˈkrækliŋ], *n.* pétillement, crépitement; (*fig.*) rissolé (*de rôti de porc*), *m.*
cracknel [ˈkræknəl], *n.* craquelin, croquignole, *f.*
cradle [kreidl], *n.* berceau; (*Naut.*) ber, *m.*—*v.t.* bercer; endormir (*en berçant*).
cradle-song [ˈkreidlsɔŋ], *n.* berceuse, *f.*
craft [krɑːft], *n.* métier (*trade*), *m.*; ruse, astuce (*cunning*); (*Naut.*) embarcation, *f.*, bâtiment, *m.*
craftily [ˈkrɑːftili], *adv.* sournoisement, avec ruse.
craftiness [ˈkrɑːftinis], *n.* artifice, *m.*, ruse, astuce, *f.*
craftsman [ˈkrɑːftsmən], *n.* (*pl.* **-men** [men]) artisan; artiste dans son métier, *m.*
craftsmanship [ˈkrɑːftsmənʃip], *n.* habileté technique, exécution, *f.*
crafty [ˈkrɑːfti], *a.* rusé, astucieux.
crag [kræg], *n.* rocher escarpé, rocher à pic, *m.*
craggy [ˈkrægi], *a.* rocailleux, escarpé, abrupt.
crake [kreik], *n.* (*Orn.*) râle, *m.*
cram [kræm], *v.t.* fourrer, remplir, bourrer; préparer, chauffer (*étudiants*).—*v.i.* se bourrer, s'empiffrer; (*fig.*) en conter, blaguer.
crammer [ˈkræmə], *n.* préparateur; (*colloq.*) colleur, *m.*
cramp [kræmp], *n.* crampe, *f.*; (*Tech.*) crampon, *m.*; (*fig.*) gêne, entrave, *f.*—*v.t.* cramponner; resserrer; (*fig.*) gêner, entraver, restreindre.
cramped [kræmpt], *a.* gêné; **to be cramped (for space)**, être très à l'étroit.

391

cranberry ['krænbəri], *n.* (*Bot.*) canneberge, *f.*

crane [krein], *n.* (*Orn., Tech.*) grue, *f.—v.t.* allonger, tendre (*le cou*).

cranial ['kreiniəl], *a.* crânien.

cranium ['kreiniəm], *n.* crâne, *m.*

crank [kræŋk], *n.* manivelle, *f.*; coude, *m.*; (*fig.*) maniaque, excentrique, *m., f.*, original (*personne*), *m.*

crankshaft ['kræŋkʃɑ:ft], *n.* arbre de manivelle; (*Motor.*) vilebrequin, *m.*

cranky ['kræŋki], *a.* capricieux, fantasque; impatient.

crannied ['krænid], *a.* crevassé, lézardé.

cranny ['kræni], *n.* crevasse, fente, lézarde, fissure, *f.*

crape [kreip], *n.* crêpe, *m.*

crash [kræʃ], *v.t.* fracasser, briser.—*v.i.* éclater, retentir; se tamponner (*deux autos etc.*).—*n.* fracas, grand bruit, *m.*; (*Motor.*) collision; (*fig.*) débâcle, ruine; faillite, *f.*

crash-helmet ['kræʃhelmit], *n.* casque, *m.*

crash-landing ['kræʃ'lændiŋ], *n.* (*Av.*) atterrissage brutal; crash, *m.*

crass [kræs], *a.* crasse, grossier, stupide.

crate [kreit], *n.* caisse à claire-voie, *f.—v.t.* emballer.

crater ['kreitə], *n.* cratère, *m.*

cravat [krə'væt], *n.* cravate, *f.*

crave [kreiv], *v.t.* implorer, solliciter; (*fig.*) soupirer après.

craven [kreivn], *a.* and *n.* lâche, poltron, *m.*

craving ['kreiviŋ], *n.* désir ardent, besoin impérieux, *m.*

crawfish [CRAYFISH].

crawl [krɔ:l], *v.i.* ramper, se traîner; **to crawl with**, grouiller de.—*n.* mouvement traînant; (*Swim.*) crawl, *m.*

crawling ['krɔ:liŋ], *a.* rampant; grouillant, fourmillant (*de*).

crayfish ['kreifiʃ], **crawfish** ['krɔ:fiʃ], *n.* écrevisse (*d'eau douce*), *f.*; **sea crayfish**, langouste, *f.*

crayon ['kreiən], *n.* crayon, pastel, fusain, *m.—v.t.* crayonner, dessiner au pastel.

craze [kreiz], *v.t.* craqueler (*porcelaine*); frapper de folie, rendre fou.—*n.* folie; (*fig.*) passion folle; toquade, *f.*

crazed [kreizd], *a.* craquelé (*porcelaine*); fou, dément.

crazily ['kreizili], *adv.* follement.

craziness ['kreizinis], *n.* délabrement, *m.*; démence, folie, *f.*

crazy ['kreizi], *a.* délabré; (*fam.*) fou, toqué.

creak [kri:k], *v.i.* crier, craquer, grincer.—*n.* cri, grincement, *m.*

creaking ['kri:kiŋ], *a.* qui crie, qui craque.—*n.* cri, grincement, *m.*

cream [kri:m], *n.* crème, *f.—v.i.* crémer, mousser.

cream-colour(ed) ['kri:mkʌlə(d)], *a.* crème.

creamery ['kri:məri], *n.* crémerie, *f.*

cream-jug ['kri:mdʒʌg], *n.* pot à crème, *m.*

creamy ['kri:mi], *a.* crémeux; de crème.

crease [kri:s], *n.* pli, faux pli, *m.—v.t.* faire des plis à, plisser, chiffonner, friper.—*v.i.* se plisser; se friper.

create [kri'eit], *v.t.* créer, faire naître; produire, engendrer, occasionner; faire.

creation [kri'eiʃən], *n.* création; nature, *f.*, univers, *m.*; dernière mode, *f.*

creative [kri'eitiv], *a.* créateur.

creator [kri'eitə], *n.* créateur, *m.*

creature ['kri:tʃə], *n.* créature, personne, *f.*, être; animal, *m.*

crèche [kreiʃ], *n.* crèche, *f.*

credence ['kri:dəns], *n.* créance, croyance, foi, *f.*; **to give credence to**, ajouter foi à.

credentials [kri'denʃəlz], *n.pl.* lettres de créance, *f.pl.*

credibility [kredi'biliti], *n.* crédibilité, *f.*

credible ['kredibl], *a.* croyable, digne de foi.

credibly ['kredibli], *adv.* d'une manière digne de foi; **to be credibly informed**, tenir de bonne source.

credit ['kredit], *n.* croyance, foi; (*fig.*) influence; réputation, *f.*; mérite, honneur; (*Comm.*) crédit, *m.*; **on credit**, à crédit; **to do credit to**, faire honneur à.—*v.t.* ajouter foi à, croire à; faire honneur à; (*Comm.*) faire crédit à.

creditable ['kreditəbl], *a.* honorable, estimable.

creditably ['kreditəbli], *adv.* honorablement.

creditor ['kreditə], *n.* créancier; (*Book-keeping*) créditeur, avoir, *m.*

credulity [kre'dju:liti], **credulousness** ['kredjuləsnis], *n.* crédulité, *f.*

credulous ['kredjuləs], *a.* crédule.

creed [kri:d], *n.* credo, *m.*; (*fig.*) profession de foi; croyance, foi, *f.*

creek [kri:k], *n.* crique, anse, *f.*

creel [kri:l], *n.* panier de pêche, *m.*

creep [kri:p], *v.i. irr.* se traîner, ramper, se glisser.

creeper ['kri:pə], *n.* reptile, *m.*; plante grimpante, *f.*; **tree creeper**, (*Orn.*) grimpereau, *m.*

creeping ['kri:piŋ], *a.* rampant, grimpant; qui fait frissonner.—*n.* fourmillement (*sensation*), *m.*

creepy ['kri:pi], *a.* horrifique, qui donne la chair de poule; rampant.

cremate [kri'meit], *v.t.* incinérer.

cremation [kri'meiʃən], *n.* crémation, incinération, *f.*

crematorium [kremə'tɔ:riəm], *n.* crématorium, *m.*

Creole ['kri:oul], *a.* créole.—*n.* Créole, *m., f.*

creosote ['kri:əsout], *n.* créosote, *f.*

crêpe [kreip], *n.* crêpe blanc (*ou* clair), *m.*

crescent ['kresənt], *a.* croissant.—*n.* croissant, *m.*, demi-lune; rue en demi-cercle, *f.*

cress [kres], *n.* cresson, *m.*

crest [krest], *n.* cimier, *m.*; crête (*d'un coq* ou *d'une montagne*), huppe (*d'un oiseau*); aigrette (*de paon*), *f.*; (*Her.*) écusson, *m.*; armoiries, *f.pl.*

crestfallen ['krestfɔ:lən], *a.* abattu, découragé, l'oreille basse.

Cretan ['kri:tən], *a.* crétois.—*n.* Crétois, *m.*

Crete [kri:t]. la Crète, la Candie, *f.*

crevasse [krə'væs], *n.* crevasse (*d'un glacier*), *f.—v.i.* se crevasser.

crevice ['krevis], *n.* crevasse, lézarde, fente (*mur*); fissure (*rocher*), *f.—v.t.* crevasser, lézarder, fissurer.

crew (1) [kru:], *n.* bande, troupe, *f.*; (*Naut.*) équipage, *m.*

crew (2) [kru:], *past* [CROW (2)].

crib [krib], *n.* lit d'enfant, *m.*; crèche, mangeoire, *f.*; (*colloq.*) livre de corrigés, *m.—v.t.* chiper; copier (*sur*).

crick [krik], *n.* crampe, *f.*, effort, torticolis, *m.* —*v.t.* **to crick one's neck**, se donner le torticolis.

cricket (1) ['krikit], *n.* (*Ent.*) grillon, *m.*

cricket (2) ['krikit], *n.* cricket (*jeu*), *m.*; (*colloq.*) **that's not cricket**, ça ne se fait pas, ce n'est pas loyal.

crier ['kraiə], *n.* crieur; huissier (*d'une cour*), *m.*

crime [kraim], *n.* crime, *m.*

Crimea [krai'miːə]. la Crimée, *f.*

criminal ['kriminl], *a.* and *n.* criminel, *m.*

criminologist [krimi'nɔlədʒist], *n.* criminaliste, *m.,f.*

criminology [krimi'nɔlədʒi], *n.* criminologie, *f.*

crimp [krimp], *v.t.* gaufrer; friser, boucler (*les cheveux*).

crimson [krimzn], *a.* and *n.* cramoisi; pourpre, *m.*—*v.t.* teindre en cramoisi.—*v.i.* devenir cramoisi.

cringe [krindʒ], *v.i.* faire des courbettes; s'humilier, ramper.

cringing ['krindʒiŋ], *a.* craintif; obséquieux. —*n.* basse servilité, *f.*

crinkle [kriŋkl], *v.t.* froisser; former en zigzag.—*v.i.* serpenter, aller en zigzag.—*n.* sinuosité, *f.*; pli, *m.*; fronce, *f.*

crinkly ['kriŋkli], *a.* ratatiné.

cripple [kripl], *n.* boiteux; estropié, *m.*—*v.t.* estropier; (*fig.*) paralyser.

crisis ['kraisis], *n.* (*pl.* **crises** ['kraisiːz]) crise, *f.*; dénouement, *m.*

crisp [krisp], *a.* croquant, croustillant (*pâtisserie etc.*); crépu, frisé (*cheveux*).—*v.t.* friser (*cheveux etc.*); crêper (*tissu*).—*v.i.* se crêper.

crispness ['krispnis], *n.* qualité de ce qui est croquant *ou* cassant; frisure; netteté (*style etc.*), *f.*

criss-cross ['kriskrɔs], *a.* entrecroisé, croisé, en croix.—*n.* entrecroisement, *m.*—*v.t.* entrecroiser.—*v.i.* s'entrecroiser.

criterion [krai'tiəriən], *n.* critérium, *m.*

critic ['kritik], *n.* critique; censeur, *m.*; **dramatic critic**, critique de théâtre.

critical ['kritikl], *a.* critique, (*fig.*) difficile, délicat.

critically ['kritikli], *adv.* d'une manière critique; avec soin; **critically ill**, dangereusement malade.

criticism ['kritisizm], *n.* critique, appréciation, censure, *f.*

criticize ['kritisaiz], *v.t.* critiquer, faire la critique de, censurer.—*v.i.* faire de la critique.

croak [krouk], *v.i.* coasser (*grenouille*); croasser (*freux*); (*fig.*) gronder, grogner.—*n.* coassement (*grenouille*); croassement (*freux*); (*fig.*) grognement, *m.*

croaker ['kroukə], *n.* grognon, *m.*; (*fig.*) pessimiste, *m., f.*

croaky ['krouki], *a.* enroué, rauque.

crochet ['krouʃei], *n.* ouvrage au crochet, *m.* —*v.t.*, *v.i.* broder au crochet.

crock [krɔk], *n.* cruche, *f.*; pot de terre, *m.*; (*fam.*) **old crock**, vieux clou, tacot (*bicyclette, auto etc.*); vieux débris, croulant (*personne*), *m.*

crockery ['krɔkəri], *n.* faïence, vaisselle, *f.*

crocodile ['krɔkədail], *n.* crocodile, *m.*; (*fig.*) procession, *f.*

crocus ['kroukəs], *n.* safran, crocus, *m.*

croft [krɔft], *n.* petit clos, *m.*, petite ferme, *f.*

crofter ['krɔftə], *n.* petit cultivateur, *m.*

crone [kroun], *n.* vieille femme, vieille, *f.*

crony ['krouni], *n.* vieux camarade; copain, compère, *m.*

crook [kruk], *n.* courbure; houlette (*de berger*); crosse (*d'évêque*), *f.*; (*fig.*) escroc (*personne*), *m.*; **by hook or by crook**, coûte que coûte, par un moyen ou par un autre.—*v.t.* courber; (*fig.*) pervertir.—*v.i.* se courber.

crook-backed ['krukbækt], *a.* bossu, voûté.

crooked ['krukid], *a.* courbé, crochu, tortueux; tortu; (*fig.*) malhonnête.

crookedly ['krukidli], *adv.* tortueusement, de travers.

crookedness ['krukidnis], *n.* nature tortueuse; difformité, *f.*; (*fig.*) travers, *m.*, perversité, *f.*

croon [kruːn], *v.i.* chantonner, fredonner.

crooner ['kruːnə], *n.* fredonneur, chanteur de charme, *m.*

crop [krɔp], *n.* récolte, moisson; cueillette (*de fruits*), *f.*; jabot (*d'un oiseau*), *m.*; coupe (*cheveux*), *f.*; **hunting-crop**, fouet (*de chasse*), *m.*; **second crop**, regain, *m.*—*v.t.* tondre; couper; écourter (*chevaux*); brouter (*l'herbe*).

crosier, crozier ['krouziə], *n.* crosse (*d'évêque*), *f.*

cross [krɔs], *a.* en travers, de travers; fâcheux, contraire; maussade, de mauvaise humeur, fâché.—*n.* croix, *f.*; (*fig.*) malheur, *m.*, traverse, *f.*; croisement (*dans la reproduction*), *m.*; **criss-cross**, croisé, en croix.— *v.t.* croiser; marquer d'une croix, barrer (*un chèque*); (*fig.*) franchir; contrarier; **to cross off** *ou* **out**, effacer, rayer, biffer; **to cross oneself**, faire le signe de la croix.—*v.i.* être mis en travers; faire la traversée; se croiser (*lettres*).

crossbow ['krɔsbou], *n.* arbalète, *f.*

cross-breed ['krɔsbriːd], *n.* race croisée, *f.*; métis, *m.*—*v.t.* croiser.

cross-country ['krɔs'kʌntri], *a.* à travers champs; (*Racing*) **cross-country running**, cross, *m.*

cross-examination ['krɔsigzæmi'neiʃən], *n.* contre-interrogatoire, *m.*

cross-examine ['krɔsig'zæmin], *v.t.* interroger; (*Law*) contre-interroger.

crossing ['krɔsiŋ], *n.* traversée (*de la mer*), *f.*; passage; carrefour, croisement (*de routes*); croisement (*animaux*), *m.*; **pedestrian crossing**, passage clouté.

crossly ['krɔsli], *adv.* de travers; avec mauvaise humeur.

crossness ['krɔsnis], *n.* mauvaise humeur, méchanceté, *f.*

cross-roads ['krɔsroudz], *n.pl.* carrefour, *m.*

crossword ['krɔswəːd], *n.* **crossword** (*puzzle*), mots croisés, *m.pl.*

crotchet ['krɔtʃit], *n.* lubie, *f.*, caprice, *m.*, marotte; (*Mus.*) noire, *f.*

crotchety ['krɔtʃiti], *a.* capricieux, d'humeur difficile.

crouch [krautʃ], *v.i.* se tapir, se blottir.

crouching ['krautʃiŋ], *a.* accroupi, tapi.

croup [kruːp], *n.* croupe (*animaux*), *f.*; croupion (*oiseaux*); (*Path.*) croup, *m.*

crow (1) [krou], *n.* corneille, *f.*; *as the crow flies*, à vol d'oiseau; *crow's nest*, (*Naut.*) hune, *f.*

crow (2) [krou], *v.i. irr.* chanter (*coq*).—*n.* chant du coq, *m.*

crow-bar ['kroubɑː], *n.* pince, *f.*; levier, *m.*

crowd [kraud], *n.* foule, cohue, *f.*—*v.t.* serrer, encombrer; presser.—*v.i.* se presser en foule, se serrer.

crown [kraun], *n.* couronne; crête, *f.*, sommet; écu (*pièce de monnaie*); fond (*d'un chapeau*), *m.*—*v.t.* couronner; combler.

crozier [CROSIER].

crucial ['kruːʃəl], *a.* crucial; (*fig.*) définitif, décisif.

crucible ['kruːsibl], *n.* creuset, *m.*

crucifix ['kruːsifiks], *n.* crucifix, *m.*

crucifixion [kruːsi'fikʃən], *n.* crucifiement, *m.*, crucifixion, *f.*

crucify ['kruːsifai], *v.t.* crucifier.

crude [kruːd], *a.* cru; (*fig.*) informe, indigeste; grossier; brut.

crudely ['kruːdli], *adv.* crûment.

crudeness ['kruːdnis], **crudity** ['kruːditi], *n.* crudité, nature informe, *f.*

cruel ['kruːəl], *a.* cruel.

cruelly ['kruːəli], *adv.* cruellement.

cruelty ['kruːəlti], *n.* cruauté, inhumanité, *f.*

cruet ['kruːit], *n.* burette, *f.*

cruet-stand ['kruːitstænd], *n.* huilier, *m.*

cruise ['kruːz], *n.* croisière, course, *f.*—*v.i.* croiser, faire la course; marauder (*taxi*).

cruiser ['kruːzə], *n.* croiseur, *m.*

crumb [krʌm], *n.* mie; miette, *f.*—*v.t.* émietter.

crumble [krʌmbl], *v.t.* émietter; (*fig.*) pulvériser, broyer.—*v.i.* s'émietter; tomber en poussière; *to crumble down*, tomber en ruine, s'écrouler.

crump [krʌmp], *n.* coup violent, *m.*; chute, *f.*

crumpet ['krʌmpit], *n.* sorte de petite crêpe, crêpe bretonne (*pour le thé*), *f.*

crumple [krʌmpl], *v.t.* chiffonner, froisser.—*v.i.* se rider, se chiffonner.

crunch [krʌntʃ], *v.t.* croquer; broyer, écraser.—*v.i.* crisser, s'écraser.—*n.* coup de dent; grincement; crissement, *m.*

crupper ['krʌpə], *n.* croupe; croupière, *f.*

crusade [kruː'seid], *n.* croisade, *f.*

crusader [kruː'seidə], *n.* croisé, *m.*

crush [krʌʃ], *n.* écrasement, choc, *m.*; foule, cohue, *f.*—*v.t.* écraser, broyer; froisser (*une robe*); (*fig.*) accabler, anéantir.—*v.i.* s'écraser.

crushing ['krʌʃiŋ], *a.* écrasant; (*fig.*) foudroyant.—*n.* broiement, écrasement, *m.*

crust [krʌst], *n.* croûte, *f.*, croûton, *m.*—*v.i.* s'encroûter.

crustily ['krʌstili], *adv.* d'une manière morose.

crusty ['krʌsti], *a.* couvert d'une croûte; (*fig.*) bourru, hargneux.

crutch [krʌtʃ], *n.* béquille, *f.*

crux [krʌks], *n.* nœud (*d'une question*), *m.*; crise, *f.*

cry [krai], *n.* cri, *m.*—*v.t.* crier.—*v.i.* pleurer; crier; s'écrier.

crying ['kraiiŋ], *n.* larmes, *f.pl.*, pleurs, *m.pl.*; cri, *m.*, cris, *m.pl.*

crypt [kript], *n.* crypte, *f.*

cryptic ['kriptik], *a.* secret; énigmatique.

crystal [kristl], *a.* de cristal.—*n.* cristal, *m.*

crystallize ['kristəlaiz], *v.t.* cristalliser.—*v.i.* se cristalliser; *crystallized fruits*, fruits glacés, *m.pl.*

cub [kʌb], *n.* petit (*d'une bête sauvage*); ourson (*ours*); lionceau (*lion*); louveteau (*loup*); renardeau (*renard*).

Cuba ['kjuːbə], le Cuba, *m.*

Cuban ['kjuːbən], *a.* cubain.—*n.* Cubain, *m.*

cubby-hole ['kʌbihoul], *n.* retraite, *f.*; placard, *m.*; niche, *f.*

cube [kjuːb], *n.* cube, *m.*

cubicle ['kjuːbikl], *n.* compartiment, *m.* cabine, *f.*

cubit ['kjuːbit], *n.* coudée, *f.*

cuckoo ['kukuː], *n.* coucou, *m.*

cucumber ['kjuːkʌmbə], *n.* concombre, *m.*

cud [kʌd], *n.* bol alimentaire, *m.*; *to chew the cud*, ruminer.

cuddle [kʌdl], *v.t.* serrer (tendrement) dans ses bras; étreindre.—*v.i.* s'étreindre (amoureusement); se blottir; se peloter.

cudgel ['kʌdʒəl], *n.* bâton, gourdin, *m.*—*v.t.* bâtonner.

cue [kjuː], *n.* queue de billard; (*Theat.*) réplique, *f.*; (*fig.*) avis, mot, indice, *m.*

cuff (1) [kʌf], *v.t.* souffleter, calotter, battre.—*n.* calotte, taloche, *f.*

cuff (2) [kʌf], *n.* manchette (*d'une manche*), *f.*; parement (*d'un pardessus*); poignet (*d'une robe*), *m.*

cuff-link ['kʌfliŋk], *n.* bouton de manchette, *m.*

cuirass [kwi'ræs], *n.* cuirasse, *f.*

cuirassier [kwi'ræsiə], *n.* cuirassier, *m.*

culinary ['kʌlinəri], *a.* de cuisine, culinaire.

cull [kʌl], *v.t.* recueillir, cueillir; (*fig.*) choisir.

culminate ['kʌlmineit], *v.i.* se terminer (*en*), finir (*par*); (*Astron.*) culminer.

culmination [kʌlmi'neiʃən], *n.* point culminant, apogée, *m.*; (*Astron.*) culmination, *f.*

culpable ['kʌlpəbl], *a.* coupable.

culprit ['kʌlprit], *n.* accusé; inculpé, *m.*; coupable, *m.*, *f.*

cult [kʌlt], *n.* culte, *m.*

cultivate ['kʌltiveit], *v.t.* cultiver.

cultivation [kʌlti'veiʃən], *n.* culture, *f.*

cultivator ['kʌltiveitə], *n.* cultivateur, *m.*

cultural ['kʌltʃərəl], *a.* agricole, cultural; culturel.

culture ['kʌltʃə], *n.* culture; (*fig.*) instruction, éducation, *f.*

cultured ['kʌltʃəd], *a.* cultivé.

culvert ['kʌlvəːt], *n.* ponceau, petit aqueduc, *m.*

cumber ['kʌmbə], *v.t.* embarrasser, encombrer (*de*).—*n.* embarras, obstacle, *m.*

cumbersome ['kʌmbəsəm], **cumbrous** ['kʌmbrəs], *a.* embarrassant, gênant.

cumulate ['kjuːmjuleit], *v.t.* accumuler, cumuler.

cunning ['kʌniŋ], *a.* fin, rusé, adroit, astucieux.—*n.* finesse, ruse, astuce, *f.*

cunningly ['kʌniŋli], *adv.* avec finesse, adroitement; par ruse.

cup [kʌp], *n.* tasse, coupe, *f.*; gobelet; (*Bot. etc.*) calice, *m.*; (*Med.*) ventouse, *f.*—*v.t.* (*Med.*) appliquer des ventouses à.

cupbearer ['kʌpbeərə], *n.* échanson, *m.*

cupboard ['kʌbəd], *n.* armoire (*pour vêtements etc.*), *f.*; placard (*dans un mur*), *m.*

cupidity [kjuː'piditi], *n.* cupidité, *f.*

cupola ['kjuːpələ], *n.* coupole, *f.*

cur [kəː], *n.* chien bâtard; roquet; (*fig.*) malotru, *m.*, vilaine bête, *f.*
curable ['kjuərəbl], *a.* guérissable.
curate ['kjuərit], *n.* vicaire, desservant, *m.*
curator [kjuə'reitə], *n.* administrateur; conservateur (*de musée*), *m.*
curb [kəːb], *n.* gourmette, *f.*; (*fig.*) frein, *m.*; [KERB].—*v.t.* gourmer; (*fig.*) réprimer, contenir, brider; freiner.
curd [kəːd], *n.* caillé, lait caillé, *m.*—*v.t.* cailler, figer.
curdle [kəːdl], *v.t.* cailler, figer.—*v.i.* se cailler, se figer.
cure [kjuə], *n.* guérison, *f.*; remède, *m.*; (*Eccles.*) cure, *f.*—*v.t.* guérir; sécher (*foin etc.*); mariner (*poisson etc.*); saler (*viande etc.*); (*fig.*) corriger.
curfew ['kəːfjuː], *n.* couvre-feu, *m.*
curio ['kjuəriou], *n.* curiosité, *f.*; bibelot, *m.*
curiosity [kjuəri'ositi], *n.* curiosité, *f.*
curious ['kjuəriəs], *a.* curieux; (*fig.*) remarquable, singulier.
curiously ['kjuəriəsli], *adv.* curieusement.
curl [kəːl], *n.* boucle (*de cheveux*); moue (*de lèvres*); spirale (*de fumée*); ondulation, *f.*—*v.t.* boucler, friser, (*fig.*) faire onduler.—*v.i.* friser; se replier (*serpent etc.*); s'entrelacer (*vignes etc.*); tourbillonner (*fumée*); onduler (*vagues*); **to curl up,** s'enrouler, se pelotonner (*chat*).
curled [kəːld], *a.* frisé.
curlew ['kəːljuː], *n.* (*Orn.*) courlis, *m.*
curly ['kəːli], *a.* frisé, bouclé.
curmudgeon [kəː'mʌdʒən], *n.* ladre, pingre; bourru, *m.*
currant ['kʌrənt], *n.* groseille (*à grappes*), *f.*; **black currant,** cassis, *m.*; (*dried*) **currants,** raisins de Corinthe, *m.pl.*
currant-bush ['kʌrəntbuʃ], *n.* groseillier, *m.*
currency ['kʌrənsi], *n.* circulation (*d'argent etc.*); monnaie, *f.*; cours; crédit, *m.*, vogue, *f.*
current ['kʌrənt], *a.* courant; actuel; admis, reçu; **current events,** actualités, *f.pl.*—*n.* courant; cours d'eau, *m.*
currently ['kʌrəntli], *adv.* couramment; généralement.
curriculum [kʌ'rikjuləm], *n.* (*Sch.*) programme, plan d'études, *m.*
currier ['kʌriə], *n.* corroyeur, *m.*
curry (1) ['kʌri], *v.t.* corroyer (*cuir*); étriller (*un cheval*); (*fig.*) rosser.
curry (2) ['kʌri], *v.t.* (*Cook.*) apprêter au cari. —*n.* cari, *m.*
curry-comb ['kʌrikoum], *n.* étrille, *f.*
curse [kəːs], *n.* malédiction, *f.*; (*fig.*) fléau, malheur, *m.*—*v.t.* maudire; (*fig.*) affliger.— *v.i.* jurer; (*colloq.*) sacrer.
cursed ['kəːsid], *a.* maudit, exécrable.
cursorily ['kəːsərili], *adv.* rapidement, superficiellement.
cursory ['kəːsəri], *a.* rapide, superficiel; général.
curt [kəːt], *a.* brusque, bref, sec.
curtail [kəː'teil], *v.t.* retrancher, raccourcir, abréger.
curtailment [kəː'teilmənt], *n.* raccourcissement, *m.*, réduction, *f.*
curtain ['kəːtn], *n.* rideau, *m.*; toile, *f.*—*v.t.* garnir de rideaux; (*fig.*) voiler.
curtly ['kəːtli], *adv.* brusquement, sèchement.

curtsy, or **curtsey** ['kəːtsi], *n.* révérence, *f.*— *v.i.* faire la révérence.
curve [kəːv], *n.* courbe, *f.*—*v.t.* courber; cintrer.—*v.i.* se courber.
curvet [kəː'vet], *v.i.* faire des courbettes; sauter, gambader.—*n.* courbette, *f.*
cushion ['kuʃən], *n.* coussin, *m.*; (*Billiards*) bande, *f.*—*v.t.* garnir de coussins; amortir.
custard ['kʌstəd], *n.* crème (au lait), *f.*; flan, *m.*
custodian [kʌs'toudiən], *n.* gardien; conservateur, *m.*
custody ['kʌstədi], *n.* garde; prison, détention, *f.*
custom ['kʌstəm], *n.* coutume, habitude, *f.*, usage, *m.*; pratique (*d'une boutique*), *f.*; achalandage (*d'un magasin*), *m.*; (*pl.*) douane, *f.*; droits (*taxes*), *m.pl.*
customarily ['kʌstəmərili], *adv.* ordinairement, d'habitude.
customary ['kʌstəməri], *a.* ordinaire, d'usage.
customer ['kʌstəmə], *n.* chaland, client, *m.*; pratique, *f.*; (*colloq.*) individu, *m.*
customs-officer ['kʌstəmzofisə], *n.* douanier, *m.*
cut [kʌt], *n.* coup, *m.*; coupure (*place cut open*); coupe (*de vêtements, cheveux, cartes à jouer*); taille (*forme*), façon, tournure (*silhouette*); (*Engr.*) gravure, planche, *f.*; chemin de traverse (*raccourci*); (*Ten. etc.*) coup tranchant, *m.*—*v.t. irr.* couper, trancher; fendre; rogner; se rogner (*les ongles*); piquer, percer; faire (*une dent*); **to cut down,** abattre; réduire; **to cut out,** tailler, découper; **to cut short,** abréger; interrompre, couper la parole à; **to be cut up,** être blessé; avoir de la peine.—*v.i.* couper; se couper; percer (*dent*).
cute [kjuːt], *a.* rusé, fin; (*Am.*) attirant (*enfant, fille*); amusant (*chose, truc*).
cuticle ['kjuːtikl], *n.* cuticule, *f.*
cutler ['kʌtlə], *n.* coutelier, *m.*
cutlery ['kʌtləri], *n.* coutellerie, *f.*
cutlet ['kʌtlit], *n.* côtelette; escalope, *f.*
cut-price ['kʌtprais], *n.* prix réduit, *m.*
cutter ['kʌtə], *n.* coupeur; coupoir (*outil*); (*Naut.*) cutter, cotre, *m.*
cutting ['kʌtiŋ], *a.* incisif; (*fig.*) piquant, tranchant, mordant.—*n.* incision; rognure (*morceau*); coupe (*bois, cartes, cheveux etc.*); (*Hort.*) bouture, *f.*
cyanide ['saiənaid], *n.* cyanure, *m.*
cycle [saikl], *n.* cycle, *m.*; bicyclette, *f.*, vélo, *m.*—*v.i.* aller à bicyclette.
cyclone ['saikloun], *n.* cyclone, *m.*
cygnet ['signit], *n.* jeune cygne, *m.*
cylinder ['silində], *n.* cylindre, *m.*
cymbal ['simbəl], *n.* cymbale, *f.*
cynic ['sinik], *n.* cynique; sceptique, *m., f.*
cynical ['sinikl], *a.* cynique.
cynically ['sinikli], *adv.* cyniquement.
cynicism ['sinisizm], *n.* cynisme, *m.*
cynosure ['sainəʃuə], *n.* (*fig.*) point de mire, *m.*
cypress ['saiprəs], *n.* cyprès, *m.*
Cyprian ['sipriən], *a.* cypriote.—*n.* Cypriote, *m., f.*
Cypriot ['sipriət], *n.* Cypriote, *m., f.*
Cyprus ['saiprəs], *n.* la Chypre, *f.*
cyst [sist], *n.* (*Anat. etc.*) kyste, *m.*
czar [TSAR].

Czech

Czech [tʃek], *a.* tchèque.—*n.* tchèque (*langue*), *m.*; Tchèque (*personne*), *m.*, *f.*
Chechoslovak [tʃekoˈslouvæk], *a.* tchécoslovaque.—*n.* tchécoslovaque (*langue*), *m.*; Tchécoslovaque (*personne*), *m.*, *f.*
Czechoslovakia [tʃekosloˈvækiə]. la Tchécoslovaquie, *f.*

D

D, d [di:]. quatrième lettre de l'alphabet; (*Mus.*) ré, *m.*
dab [dæb], *n.* coup léger, *m.*, tape; éclaboussure, tache, *f.*; (*slang*) adepte, *m.*; (*Ichth.*) limande, *f.*—*v.t.* toucher légèrement; éponger à petits coups.
dabble [dæbl], *v.t.* humecter; éclabousser.—*v.i.* barboter, patauger; **to dabble in**, se mêler de.
dace [deis], *n.* (*Ichth.*) vandoise, *f.*, dard, *m.*
dachshund ['dækshund], *n.* basset allemand, *m.*
dad [dæd], **daddy** ['dædi], *n.* papa, *m.*
dado ['deidou], *n.* lambris (*de mur*), *m.*
daffodil ['dæfədil], *n.* jonquille, *f.*, narcisse des prés, *m.*
daft [dɑ:ft], *a.* niais, sot, à moitié fou.
dagger ['dægə], *n.* poignard, *m.*, dague, *f.*
dahlia ['deiliə], *n.* (*Bot.*) dahlia, *m.*
daily ['deili], *a.* journalier, quotidien.—*n.* (*journal*) quotidien, *m.*; femme de ménage, *f.*—*adv.* journellement, tous les jours.
daintily ['deintili], *adv.* délicatement; avec délicatesse.
daintiness ['deintinis], *n.* délicatesse, *f.*, goût difficile, *m.*
dainty ['deinti], *a.* friand; délicat, difficile.—*n.* friandise, *f.*
dairy ['dɛəri], *n.* laiterie, *f.*
dairy-farm ['dɛərifɑ:m], *n.* ferme laitière, *f.*
dairy-man ['dɛərimən], *n.* (*pl.* -men [men]) nourrisseur; crémier, *m.*
dais [deis, 'deiis], *n.* estrade, *f.*
daisy ['deizi], *n.* marguerite, pâquerette, *f.*
dale [deil], *n.* vallon, *m.*; vallée, *f.*
dalliance ['dæliəns], *n.* folâtrerie, *f.*; badinage, *m.*; caresses, *f.pl.*
dally ['dæli], *v.i.* folâtrer, perdre son temps; tarder; (*fig.*) badiner (*avec*).
dam (1) [dæm], *n.* mère (*animaux*), *f.*
dam (2) [dæm], *n.* digue (*d'un canal*), *f.*; barrage (*d'une rivière*), *m.*—*v.t.* diguer, barrer.
damage ['dæmidʒ], *n.* dommage; tort, dégât; (*fig.*) préjudice, détriment, *m.*; (*pl.*) (*Law*) dommages-intérêts, *m.pl.*—*v.t.* endommager; avarier (*en transportant*); (*fig.*) faire tort à, nuire à.—*v.i.* s'endommager.
damask ['dæməsk], *n.* damas; damassé, *m.*
dame [deim], *n.* (*poet.*) dame, *f.*
damn [dæm], *v.t.* damner; (*fig.*) condamner, désapprouver.
damnation [dæm'neiʃən], *n.* damnation, *f.*
damnatory ['dæmnətəri], *a.* condamnatoire.
damned [dæmd], *a.* damné, maudit, exécrable.

damning ['dæmiŋ], *a.* écrasant (*témoignage*).
damp [dæmp], *a.* humide; moite; (*fig.*) triste, abattu.—*n.* or **dampness** ['dæmpnis], humidité; (*fig.*) tristesse, *f.*—*v.t.* rendre humide; (*fig.*) décourager.
damper ['dæmpə], *n.* éteignoir; (*Piano*) étouffoir; (*fig.*) rabat-joie, *m.*
***damsel** ['dæmzəl], *n.* jeune fille, demoiselle, *f.*
damson ['dæmzən], *n.* prune de Damas, *f.*
dance [dɑ:ns], *n.* danse, *f.*; bal, *m.*—*v.t.* danser; faire danser.—*v.i.* danser.
dancer ['dɑ:nsə], *n.* danseur, *m.*, danseuse, *f.*
dandelion ['dændilaiən], *n.* (*Bot.*) pissenlit, *m.*
dandle [dændl], *v.t.* dorloter, bercer.
dandruff ['dændrʌf], *n.* pellicules, *f.pl.*
dandy ['dændi], *n.* dandy, élégant, petit-maître, *m.*
Dane [dein], *n.* Danois (*personne*), *m.*
danger ['deindʒə], *n.* danger, péril, *m.*
dangerous ['deindʒərəs], *a.* dangereux.
dangerously ['deindʒərəsli], *adv.* dangereusement.
dangle [dæŋgl], *v.t.* laisser pendre, balancer.—*v.i.* pendiller, baller.
Danish ['deiniʃ], *a.* danois.—*n.* danois (*langue*), *m.*
dank [dæŋk], *a.* humide et froid.
Danube ['dænju:b], **the.** le Danube, *m.*
dapper ['dæpə], *a.* petit et vif, pimpant; soigné (*homme*).
dapple [dæpl], *v.t.* tacheter, pommeler.—*v.i.* se pommeler, se tacheter.—*a.* or **dappled** [dæpld], pommelé, truité, miroité.
dare [dɛə], *v.t.* défier; braver; provoquer.—*v.i.* oser; **I dare say!** sans doute; je le crois bien.
dare-devil ['dɛədevəl], *a.* and *n.* cassecou, *m.*
daring ['dɛəriŋ], *a.* audacieux, hardi, cassecou.—*n.* hardiesse, audace, *f.*
dark [dɑ:k], *a.* obscur, sombre, noir; foncé (*couleur*); brun, basané (*teint*); (*fig.*) secret, mystérieux.—*n.* ténèbres, *f.pl.*, obscurité, *f.*; *after dark*, à la nuit close.
darken ['dɑ:kən], *v.t.* obscurcir; brunir (*teint*) (*Paint.*) assombrir (*couleurs*).—*v.i.* s'obscurcir; s'assombrir.
darkening ['dɑ:kniŋ], *n.* obscurcissement, assombrissement, *m.*
darkness ['dɑ:knis], *n.* obscurité, *f.*, ténèbres, *f.pl.*, teint brun (*du visage*), *m.*
darling ['dɑ:liŋ], *a.* and *n.* chéri, mignon, bien-aimé, *m.*; **my darling**, (*colloq.*) mon ange, mon chou, *m.*, ma chérie, *f.*
darn [dɑ:n], *n.* reprise, *f.*—*v.t.* repriser.
darning ['dɑ:niŋ], *n.* reprise, *f.*
dart [dɑ:t], *n.* dard, trait, *m.*; fléchette, *f.*; élan soudain, *m.*—*v.t.* darder, lancer (*contre*).—*v.i.* se lancer, s'élancer (*sur*)
dash [dæʃ], *n.* choc, coup, *m.*; impétuosité, *f.*, entrain, cran; élan soudain; tiret; trait (*de plume*); (*fig.*) soupçon (*petite quantité*), *m.*—*v.t.* jeter; heurter; briser; abattre.—*v.i.* se briser; se précipiter.—*int.* zut!
dash-board ['dæʃbɔ:d], *n.* (*Motor.*) tableau de bord, *m.*
dashing ['dæʃiŋ], *a.* fougueux, brillant; pimpant, élégant.
dastard ['dæstəd], *n.* lâche ignoble, *m.*
dastardly ['dæstədli] *a.* lâche.

date (1) [deit], *n.* date, échéance, *f.*, millésime (*de pièce de monnaie*); (*Am. pop.*) rendez-vous, *m.*; *up to date*, à la page, à jour.—*v.t.* dater.—*v.i.* dater (*de*).

date (2) [deit], *n.* datte (*fruit*), *f.*

date-palm ['deitpɑ:m], *n.* dattier, *m.*

dative ['deitiv], *a.* and *n.* datif, *m.*

datum ['deitəm], *n.* (*pl.* **data** ['deitə]) donnée, *f.*

daub [dɔ:b], *v.t.* barbouiller, enduire; (*fig.*) déguiser (*de*).—*n.* barbouillage, *m.*; (*Paint.*) croûte, *f.*

daughter ['dɔ:tə], *n.* fille, *f.*

daughter-in-law ['dɔ:tərinlɔ:], *n.* belle-fille, bru, *f.*

daunt [dɔ:nt], *v.t.* effrayer, intimider, décourager.

dauntless ['dɔ:ntlis], *a.* intrépide.

dauphin ['dɔ:fin], *n.* dauphin, *m.*

David ['deivid], David, *m.*

davit ['dævit], *n.* (*Naut.*) bossoir, *m.*

dawdle [dɔ:dl], *v.i.* flâner, muser.

dawdler ['dɔ:dlə], *n.* flâneur, musard, *m.*

dawn [dɔ:n], *v.i.* poindre, paraître; (*fig.*) naître, percer.—*n.* aube, *f.*, point du jour, *m.*; aurore, *f.*

day [dei], *n.* jour, *m.*; journée (*de travail etc.*); (*fig.*) bataille, victoire, *f.*; *at the present day*, de nos jours; *every day*, tous les jours; *the day after*, le lendemain; *the day before*, la veille; *today*, aujourd'hui.

day-boarder ['deibɔ:də], *n.* demi-pensionnaire, *m.*, *f.*

day-book ['deibuk], *n.* journal, *m.*

day-boy ['deibɔi], **day-girl** ['deigə:l], *n.* externe, *m.*, *f.*

day-break ['deibreik], *n.* [DAWN].

daylight ['deilait], *n.* lumière du jour, *f.*

daze [deiz], *v.t.* éblouir; hébéter.—*n.* stupéfaction, *f.*; *in a daze*, hébété.

dazzle [dæzl], *v.t.* éblouir, aveugler.

dazzling ['dæzliŋ], *a.* éblouissant.

deacon ['di:kən], *n.* diacre, *m.*

dead [ded], *a.* mort; inanimé; inerte, insensible; éventé (*boisson alcoolique*); mat (*couleur*); au rebut (*lettres*); *dead drunk*, ivre-mort; *dead loss*, perte sèche, *f.*; (*fig.*) crétin (*personne*), *m.*; *dead march*, marche funèbre, *f.*; *dead stop*, halte subite, *f.* *dead weight*, poids mort, *m.*; *for a dead certainty*, à coup sûr.—*n.* cœur (*de l'hiver*), fort, *m.*; *at dead of night*, au plus profond de la nuit.

dead-beat ['ded'bi:t], *a.* éreinté, épuisé.

deaden [dedn], *v.t.* amortir; émousser (*les sens*); éventer (*boisson alcoolique*); assourdir (*son*).

dead-end ['ded'end], *n.* cul-de-sac, *m.*; impasse, *f.*

deadlock ['dedlɔk], *n.* situation sans issue; impasse, *f.*

deadly ['dedli], *a.* mortel, à mort; meurtrier.—*adv.* mortellement.

deadness ['dednis], *n.* mort, *f.*; (*fig.*) engourdissement, *m.*, froideur, *f.*

deaf [def], *a.* sourd; (*fig.*) insensible.

deafen [defn], *v.t.* rendre sourd, assourdir.

deafening ['defniŋ], *a.* assourdissant.

deaf-mute ['def'mju:t], *n.* sourd-muet, *m.*

deafness ['defnis], *n.* surdité, *f.*

deal (1) [di:l], *n.* quantité; (*Cards*) donne; affaire, *f.*, marché, *m.*; *a great* or *good*

deal, beaucoup (*de*); *by a good deal*, à beaucoup près.—*v.t. irr.* distribuer; répartir; (*Cards*) donner; porter, asséner (*coups*).—*v.i.* agir, traiter, en user (*avec*).

deal (2) [di:l], *n.* bois blanc, bois (de sapin), *m.*

dealer ['di:lə], *n.* marchand; (*Cards*) donneur, *m.*

dealing ['di:liŋ], *n.* conduite, *f.*; procédé, *m.*, affaire, *f.*; (*pl.*) relations, *f.pl.*, rapports, *m.pl.*

dean [di:n], *n.* doyen, *m.*

dear [diə], *a.* cher; précieux; (*fig.*) joli, gentil, charmant.—*adv.* cher; chèrement, beaucoup.—*n.* cher; cher ami, *m.*—*int. oh dear!* mon Dieu!

dearth [də:θ], *n.* disette, *f.*

death [deθ], *n.* mort, *f.*; (*poet.*) trépas; (*Law*) décès, *m.*

death-duties ['deθdju:tiz], *n.pl.* droits de succession, *m.pl.*

death-rate ['deθreit], *n.* taux de mortalité, *m.*

death-rattle ['deθrætl], *n.* râle, *m.*

death-throes ['deθθrouz], *n.* agonie, *f.*

debar [di'bɑ:], *v.t.* exclure, priver (*de*).

debase [di'beis], *v.t.* avilir, abaisser; abâtardir; (*Chem.*) adultérer; (*Coin.*) altérer.

debasement [di'beismənt], *n.* abaissement, avilissement, *m.*; (*Coin.*) altération, dépréciation, *f.*

debasing [di'beisiŋ], *a.* avilissant.

debatable [di'beitəbl], *a.* contestable.

debate [di'beit], *n.* débat, *m.*; discussion, *f.*—*v.t.* débattre, discuter, disputer.—*v.i.* délibérer (*sur*); contester (*avec*).

debauch [di'bɔ:tʃ], *n.* débauche, *f.*—*v.t.* débaucher, corrompre, pervertir.

debauchery [di'bɔ:tʃəri], *n.* débauche, *f.*

debenture [di'bentʃə], *n.* obligation, *f.*

debilitate [di'biliteit], *v.t.* débiliter, affaiblir, anémier.

debilitation [dibili'teiʃən], *n.* débilitation, *f.*, affaiblissement, *m.*

debility [di'biliti], *n.* débilité, faiblesse, *f.*

debit ['debit], *n.* débit, *m.*—*v.t.* débiter (*de*).

debonair [debə'nɛə], *a.* jovial; de caractère enjoué; élégant.

debouch [di'bu:ʃ], *v.i.* déboucher.

débris, debris ['debri:], *n.* débris, *m.pl.*

debt [det], *n.* dette, *f.*; dettes, *f.pl.*; créance, *f.*

debtor ['detə], *n.* débiteur, *m.*

debutante ['deibjutɑ:t], *n.* débutante (*à la cour*), *f.*

decade ['dekeid], *n.* décade; décennie, *f.*

decadence ['dekədəns], *n.* décadence, *f.*

decadent ['dekədənt], *a.* décadent.

decamp [di'kæmp], *v.i.* décamper; lever le camp.

decant [di'kænt], *v.t.* décanter, verser.

decanter [di'kæntə], *n.* carafe, *f.*

decapitate [di'kæpiteit], *v.t.* décapiter.

decapitation [dikæpi'teiʃən], *n.* décapitation, *f.*

decay [di'kei], *n.* décadence; pourriture; ruine; carie (*de dent*), *f.*—*v.i.* tomber en décadence; dépérir (*plante*); se carier (*dent*).

decease [di'si:s], *n.* (*Law*) décès, *m.*—*v.i.* décéder.

deceased [di'si:st], *a.* décédé, feu.—*n.* défunt, *m.*

deceit [di'si:t], *n.* supercherie, fourberie, tromperie, ruse, *f.*

deceitful

deceitful [di'si:tful], *a.* trompeur; décevant (*choses*).
deceive [di'si:v], *v.t.* tromper, abuser.
deceiver [di'si:və], *n.* imposteur, trompeur, *m.*
decelerate [di:'seləreit], *v.t., v.i.* ralentir.
December [di'sembə]. décembre, *m.*
decency ['di:sənsi], *n.* bienséance, *f.,* convenances, *f.pl.*; décence (*modestie*), *f.*
decennial [di'senjəl], *a.* décennal.
decent ['di:sənt], *a.* bienséant, décent; propre, convenable; gentil.
decently ['di:səntli], *adv.* décemment; convenablement.
decentralization ['di:sentrəlai'zeiʃən], *n.* décentralisation, *f.,* régionalisme, *m.*
decentralize [di:'sentrəlaiz], *v.t.* décentraliser.
deception [di'sepʃən], *n.* tromperie, fraude, duperie, *f.*
deceptive [di'septiv], *a.* trompeur.
decibel ['desibel], *n.* décibel, *m.*
decide [di'said], *v.t.* décider; décider de.—*v.i.* se décider.
decided [di'saidid], *a.* décidé, prononcé; positif; résolu.
decidedly [di'saididli], *adv.* décidément; positivement.
decimal ['desiməl], *a.* décimal; **decimal point**, virgule, *f.*—*n.* (fraction) décimale, *f.*
decimate ['desimeit], *v.t.* décimer.
decipher [di'saifə], *v.t.* déchiffrer.
decision [di'siʒən], *n.* décision; (*fig.*) résolution, fermeté, *f.*
decisive [di'saisiv], *a.* décisif; concluant.
decisively [di'saisivli], *adv.* décisivement.
deck [dek], *n.* (*Naut.*) pont; tillac (*navire marchand*); plan (*avion*), *m.*—*v.t.* parer (*de*); orner.
deck-chair ['dek'tʃeə], *n.* transat(lantique), *m.*
declaim [di'kleim], *v.t., v.i.* déclamer (*contre*).
declamatory [di'klæmətəri], *a.* déclamatoire.
declaration [deklə'reiʃən], *n.* déclaration; proclamation, *f.*
declare [di'kleə], *v.t.* déclarer; (*fig.*) annoncer, affirmer.—*v.i.* se déclarer, se prononcer (*pour*).
decline [di'klain], *v.t.* pencher, incliner; refuser.—*v.i.* pencher; décliner; baisser (*prix*).—*n.* déclin, *m.,* décadence; (*Path.*) maladie de langueur, *f.*
declutch [di'klʌtʃ], *v.i.* débrayer.
decode [di:'koud], *v.t.* déchiffrer.
decompose [di:kəm'pouz], *v.t.* décomposer.—*v.i.* se décomposer.
decompression [di:kəm'preʃən], *n.* décompression, *f.*
decontaminate [di:kən'tæmineit], *v.t.* désinfecter.
decontrol [di:kən'troul], *v.t.* rendre libre de nouveau, libérer (*prix, loyers etc.*).—*n.* libération (*prix, loyers etc.*), *f.*
decorate ['dekəreit], *v.t.* décorer, orner.
decoration [dekə'reiʃən], *n.* décoration, *f.*; ornement, *m.*
decorator ['dekəreitə], *n.* décorateur, *m.*
decorous ['dekərəs, di'kɔːrəs], *a.* bienséant, convenable.
decorously ['dekərəsli, di'kɔːrəsli], *adv.* convenablement.

decorum [di'kɔːrəm], *n.* bienséance, *f.,* décorum, *m.*
decoy [di'kɔi], *v.t.* leurrer, amorcer.—*n.* leurre; piège, *m.*
decrease ['di:kri:s], *n.* décroissement, *m.*; diminution; décrue (*eau*), *f.*—[di'kri:s], *v.t.* faire décroître.—*v.i.* diminuer; décroître.
decree [di'kri:], *n.* décret; (*Law*) arrêt, *m.*—*v.t.* arrêter, décréter.
decrepit [di'krepit], *a.* décrépit, caduc.
decry [di'krai], *v.t.* décrier, dénigrer.
dedicate ['dedikeit], *v.t.* dédier (*à*); consacrer (*à*).
dedication [dedi'keiʃən], *n.* dédicace, *f.*
deduce [di'dju:s], *v.t.* déduire, inférer (*de*).
deduct [di'dʌkt], *v.t.* déduire, rabattre.
deduction [di'dʌkʃən], *n.* déduction, *f.*
deed [di:d], *n.* action, *f.*; fait, exploit; (*Law*) titre, *m.*
deem [di:m], *v.t.* juger; penser, estimer.
deep [di:p], *a.* profond, extrême; foncé (*couleur*); grave (*son*); (*fig.*) rusé.—*n.* (*poet.*) océan, *m.*
deepen [di:pən], *v.t.* approfondir; assombrir. —*v.i.* devenir plus profond *ou* plus foncé.
deep-freeze ['di:p'fri:z], *n.* réfrigérateur à basse température, *m.*
deeply ['di:pli], *adv.* profondément; extrêmement.
deep-rooted ['di:p'ru:tid], **deep-seated** ['di:p'si:tid], *a.* profond, enraciné.
deer [diə], *n.* cervidé, *m.*; **fallow deer**, daim, *m.,* daine, *f.*; **red deer**, cerf, *m.*
deface [di'feis], *v.t.* défigurer; mutiler.
defamation [defə'meiʃən], *n.* diffamation, *f.*
defame [di'feim], *v.t.* diffamer.
default [di'fɔːlt], *n.* défaut, manque, *m.*; (*Law*) contumace, *f.*
defaulter [di'fɔːltə], *n.* délinquant; (*Mil.*) réfractaire; (*Law*) défaillant, *m.*
defeat [di'fi:t], *n.* défaite, déroute, *f.*—*v.t.* battre, vaincre; (*fig.*) annuler, déjouer.
defeatism [di'fi:tizm], *n.* défaitisme, *m.*
defeatist [di'fi:tist], *a.* and *n.* défaitiste, *m., f.*
defect [di'fekt], *n.* défaut, *m.*; imperfection, *f.*
defective [di'fektiv], *a.* défectueux, imparfait.
defence [di'fens], *n.* défense, *f.*
defend [di'fend], *v.t.* défendre (*de*), protéger (*contre*).
defender [di'fendə], *n.* défenseur, *m.*
defensible [di'fensəbl], *a.* défendable; (*fig.*) soutenable.
defensive [di'fensiv], *a.* défensif.—*n.* défensive, *f.*
defer [di'fə:], *v.t.* différer, remettre.—*v.i.* différer; déférer (*à*).
deference ['defərəns], *n.* déférence, *f.*
deferential [defə'renʃəl] *a.* de déférence, respectueux.
deferment [di'fə:mənt], *n.* (*Mil.*) sursis, *m.*
defiance [di'faiəns], *n.* défi, *m.*
defiant [di'faiənt], *a.* défiant.
deficiency [di'fiʃənsi], *n.* défaut, *m.*; insuffisance, *f.*
deficient [di'fiʃənt], *a.* défectueux; insuffisant.
deficit ['defisit], *n.* déficit, *m.*
defile (1) [di'fail], *n.* défilé, *m.*
defile (2) [di'fail], *v.t.* souiller; déshonorer.
define [di'fain], *v.t.* définir; déterminer.
definite ['definit], *a.* déterminé; (*Gram.*) défini.

definitely ['definitli], *adv.* absolument, nettement, d'une manière déterminée.
definition [defi'niʃən], *n.* définition, *f.*
deflate [di'fleit], *v.t.* dégonfler.
deflation [di'fleiʃən], *n.* dégonflement, *m.*; déflation monétaire, *f.*
deflect [di'flekt], *v.t.* faire dévier, détourner. —*v.i.* dévier.
deforestation [di:fɔris'teiʃən], *n.* déboisement, *m.*
deform [di'fɔ:m], *v.t.* déformer, défigurer.
deformation [di:fɔ:'meiʃən], *n.* déformation, *f.*
deformed [di'fɔ:md], *a.* difforme.
deformity [di'fɔ:miti], *n.* difformité; laideur, *f.*
defraud [di'frɔ:d], *v.t.* frauder.
defray [di'frei], *v.t.* défrayer; payer.
deft [deft], *a.* adroit, habile.
deftly ['deftli], *adv.* adroitement, lestement.
defunct [di'fʌŋkt], *a.* défunt, trépassé, décédé.—*n.* défunt, *m.*
defy [di'fai], *v.t.* défier, braver.
degeneracy [di'dʒenərəsi], **degeneration** [didʒenə'reiʃən], *n.* dégénérescence, *f.*
degenerate [di'dʒenərit], *a.* and *n.* dégénéré, *m.*—[di'dʒenəreit], *v.i.* dégénérer, s'abâtardir (*dans* ou *en*).
degradation [degrə'deiʃən], *n.* dégradation, *f.*; (*fig.*) avilissement, *m.*
degrade [di'greid], *v.t.* dégrader; (*fig.*) avilir.
degrading [di'greidiŋ], *a.* dégradant, avilissant.
degree [di'gri:], *n.* degré; rang, ordre, *m.*; qualité, *f.*; *university degree*, grade universitaire, *m.*
de-ice [di:'ais], *v.t.*, *v.i.* dégivrer.
deify ['di:ifai], *v.t.* déifier.
deign [dein], *v.t.*, *v.i.* daigner.
deity ['di:iti], *n.* divinité; (*Myth.*) déité, *f.*
dejected [di'dʒektid], *a.* abattu, triste.
dejection [di'dʒekʃən], *n.* abattement, *m.*
delay [di'lei], *n.* délai, retard, *m.*—*v.t.* différer; remettre.—*v.i.* tarder.
delegacy ['deligəsi], *n.* délégation, *f.*
delegate ['deligit], *n.* délégué, *m.*—['deligeit], *v.t.* déléguer.
delegation [deli'geiʃən], *n.* délégation, *f.*
delete [di'li:t], *v.t.* effacer, rayer, biffer.
deletion [di'li:ʃən], *n.* rature, *f.*, grattage, *m.*
deliberate [di'librit], *a.* délibéré, prémédité; réfléchi.—[di'libəreit], *v.i.* délibérer.
deliberately [di'libəritli], *adv.* à dessein; lentement.
deliberation [dilibə'reiʃən], *n.* délibération, *f.*
delicacy ['delikəsi], *n.* délicatesse; friandise (*a titbit*), *f.*
delicate ['delikit], *a.* délicat.
delicious [di'liʃəs], *a.* délicieux.
deliciously [di'liʃəsli], *adv.* délicieusement.
delight [di'lait], *n.* délices, *f.pl.*, plaisir, *m.*—*v.t.* plaire à, réjouir, enchanter; *to be delighted to*, être enchanté de.—*v.i.* se plaire à.
delightful [di'laitful], *a.* délicieux; charmant (*personne*).
delineate [di'linieit], *v.t.* esquisser, dessiner; (*fig.*) décrire.
delinquency [di'liŋkwənsi], *n.* délit, *m.*; *juvenile delinquency*, délinquance juvénile, *f.*

delinquent [di'liŋkwənt], *n.* délinquant, *m.*; *juvenile delinquent*, jeune délinquant.
delirious [di'liriəs], *a.* en délire; délirant.
delirium [di'liriəm], *n.* délire; (*fig.*) transport de joie, *m.*
deliver [di'livə], *v.t.* délivrer, sauver; distribuer (*lettres etc.*); remettre (*lettre, paquet etc.*); livrer (*marchandises*), prononcer (*un discours*); (faire) accoucher (*femme*).
deliverance [di'livərəns], *n.* délivrance, *f.*
deliverer [di'livərə], *n.* libérateur, sauveur, *m.*
delivery [di'livəri], *n.* délivrance, remise, *f.*; débit, *m.*, diction (*d'un discours*); livraison (*de marchandises*); distribution (*du courrier*), *f.*; (*Med.*) accouchement, *m.*; *payment on delivery*, livraison contre remboursement.
delivery-van [də'livərivæn], *n.* camion de livraison, *m.*; camionnette, *f.*
dell [del], *n.* vallon, *m.*
delta ['deltə], *n.* delta, *m.*
delude [di'lju:d], *v.t.* tromper, abuser.
deluge ['delju:dʒ], *n.* déluge, *m.*—*v.t.* inonder.
delusion [di'lju:ʒən], *n.* illusion, erreur, *f.*
delve [delv], *v.t.*, *v.i.* bêcher, creuser; (*fig.*) sonder.
demagnetize [di:'mægnitaiz], *v.t.* démagnétiser.
demagogue ['deməgɔg], *n.* démagogue, *m.*, *f.*
demand [di'mɑ:nd], *n.* exigence; réclamation; demande, requête, *f.*; *in great demand*, très demandé, très recherché; *on demand*, sur demande; *supply and demand*, l'offre et la demande, *f.*—*v.t.* exiger; réclamer; demander.
demarcation [di:mɑ:'keiʃən], *n.* démarcation, *f.*; *line of demarcation*, ligne de démarcation, *f.*
demean [di'mi:n], *v.i.* se comporter, se conduire; (*colloq.*) s'abaisser, se dégrader.
demeanour [di'mi:nə], *n.* conduite, *f.*, maintien, *m.*; tenue, *f.*
demented [di'mentid], *a.* fou, dément.
demi ['demi], *prep.* demi, à demi.
demigod ['demigɔd], *n.* demi-dieu, *m.*
demise [di'maiz], *n.* décès, *m.*, mort, *f.*—*v.t.* léguer; céder à bail.
demi-semiquaver ['demi'semikweivə], *n.* (*Mus.*) triple croche, *f.*
demister [di:'mistə], *n.* (*Motor.*) appareil antibuée, *m.*
demobilization [di:moubilai'zeiʃən], *n.* démobilisation, *f.*
demobilize [di:'moubilaiz], *v.t.* démobiliser.
democracy [di'mɔkrəsi], *n.* démocratie, *f.*
democrat ['deməkræt], *n.* démocrate, *m.*, *f.*
democratic [demə'krætik], *a.* démocratique.
democratically [demə'krætikəli], *adv.* démocratiquement.
demolish [di'mɔliʃ], *v.t.* démolir.
demolition [demə'liʃən], *n.* démolition, *f.*
demon ['di:mən], *n.* démon, diable, *m.*
demonstrate ['demənstreit], *v.t.* démontrer. —*v.i.* (*Polit.*) manifester.
demonstration [demən'streiʃən], *n.* démonstration; (*Polit.*) manifestation, *f.*
demonstrative [di'mɔnstrətiv], *a.* démonstratif.
demoralize [di:'mɔrəlaiz], *v.t.* démoraliser.
demote [di:'mout], *v.t.* (*Mil.*) réduire à un grade inférieur, rétrograder.
demur [di'mə:], *n.* hésitation, objection, *f.*—*v.i.* hésiter, temporiser.

demure

demure [di'mjuə], *a.* réservé, posé; d'une modestie affectée.

demurely [di'mjuəli], *adv.* d'un air posé; avec une modestie affectée.

den [den], *n.* antre; repaire (*de voleurs etc.*), *m.*; loge (*de ménagerie*), *f.*; (*fig.*) bouge, taudis; (*colloq.*) cabinet de travail, *m.*

denationalize [di:'næʃnəlaiz], *v.t.* dénationaliser.

denial [di'naiəl], *n.* déni, *m.*, dénégation, *f.*

denier [di'niə], *n.* (*Hosiery*) denier, *m.*; *a* **15-denier stocking**, un bas 15 deniers.

denigrate ['denigreit], *v.t.* noircir, dénigrer.

Denis [DENNIS].

denizen ['denizn], *n.* citoyen, habitant, *m.*

Denmark ['denma:k]. le Danemark, *m.*

Dennis [di'denis]. Denis, *m.*

denomination [dinɔmi'neiʃən], *n.* dénomination, *f.*; culte, *m.*, secte, *f.*

denominational [dinɔmi'neiʃənl], *a.* confessionnel (*école*).

denote [di'nout], *v.t.* dénoter, marquer, indiquer; signifier.

denounce [di'nauns], *v.t.* dénoncer.

dense [dens], *a.* dense, épais; compact; stupide.

densely ['densli], *adv.* en masse.

density ['densiti], *n.* densité, épaisseur, *f.*

dent [dent], *n.* renfoncement, *m.*, bosselure; coche, *f.*—*v.t.* bosseler, cabosser.

dental [dentl], *a.* dentaire; (*Phon.*) dental; *dental surgeon*, chirurgien dentiste, *m.*

dentifrice ['dentifris], *n.* dentrifrice, *m.*

dentist ['dentist], *n.* dentiste, *m.*, *f.*

dentistry ['dentistri], *n.* dentisterie, *f.*

denture ['dentʃə], *n.* dentier; (*fam.*) râtelier, *m.*

denude [di'nju:d], *v.t.* dénuder; (*fig.*) dénuer.

denunciation [dinʌnsi'eiʃən], *n.* dénonciation, *f.*

deny [di'nai], *v.t.* nier, démentir; (*Law*) dénier, renier; refuser.

deodorant [di:'oudərənt], **deodorizer** [di:'oudəraizə], *n.* désinfectant, désinfecteur, désodorisant, *m.*

depart [di'pa:t], *v.t.* quitter.—*v.i.* partir, s'en aller, se retirer, s'éloigner; (*fig.*) mourir.

departed [di'pa:tid], *a.* mort, défunt; passé, évanoui.—*n.* *the departed*, le défunt, *m.*, les trépassés, *m.pl.*

department [di'pa:tmənt], *n.* département, service; (*Polit.*) bureau; comptoir, rayon (*de boutique*), *m.*; *department store*, grand magasin, *m.*

departmental [di:pa:t'mentl], *a.* départemental.

departure [di'pa:tʃə], *n.* départ; éloignement, *m.*; déviation; (*fig.*) mort, *f.*

depend [di'pend], *v.i.* dépendre (*de*); compter (*sur*), se reposer (*sur*).

dependable [di'pendəbl], *a.* digne de confiance; sûr.

dependent [di'pendənt], *a.* dépendant; (*Law*) à la charge de; (*Gram.*) subordonné; *dependent relatives*, parents à charge, *m.pl.*

depict [di'pikt], *v.t.* peindre, dépeindre.

deplete [di'pli:t], *v.t.* amoindrir, épuiser.

deplorable [di'plɔ:rəbl], *a.* déplorable; pitoyable (*lamentable*).

deplore [di'plɔ:], *v.t.* déplorer.

deploy [di'plɔi], *v.t.* (*Mil.*) déployer.—*v.i.* se déployer.

depopulate [di:'pɔpjuleit], *v.t.* dépeupler.—*v.i.* se dépeupler.

deport [di'pɔ:t], *v.t.* déporter, expulser; *to deport oneself*, se comporter.

deportment [di'pɔ:tmənt], *n.* tenue, conduite, *f.*, manières, *f.pl.*

depose [di'pouz], *v.t.*, *v.i.* déposer (*de*).

deposit [di'pozit], *n.* dépôt; (*Banking*) versement; gage, nantissement, *m.*, arrhes, *f.pl.*, caution, *f.*; (*Geol.*) gisement, gîte, *m.*; *deposit account*, compte de dépôt, *m.*—*v.t.* déposer; verser.

deposition [depə'ziʃən, di:pə'ziʃən], *n.* déposition, *f.*; dépôt, *m.*

depositor [di'pozitə], *n.* (*Comm.*) déposant, *m.*

depository [di'pozitri], *n.* dépôt; garde-meubles, *m.*

depot ['depou], *n.* dépôt, *m.*; (*Am.*) ['di:pou], gare, *f.*

deprave [di'preiv], *v.t.* dépraver, corrompre.

depraved [di'preivd], *a.* dépravé, corrompu.

depravity [di'præviti], *n.* dépravation, *f.*

deprecate ['deprikeit], *v.t.* désapprouver, désavouer, s'opposer à.

deprecatingly ['deprikeitiŋli], *adv.* avec désapprobation.

deprecative ['deprikeitiv], **deprecatory** ['deprikeitəri], *a.* de déprécation.

depreciate [di'pri:ʃieit], *v.t.* déprécier.—*v.i.* se déprécier.

depreciation [dipri:ʃi'eiʃən], *n.* dépréciation, *f.*

depress [di'pres], *v.t.* baisser, abaisser; abattre; accabler, décourager.

depressed [di'prest], *a.* abattu; bas.

depression [di'preʃən], *n.* abaissement, *m.*; dépression; (*Comm.*) crise, *f.*

deprivation [depri'veiʃən], *n.* privation, perte, *f.*

deprive [di'praiv], *v.t.* priver (*de*); déposséder.

depth [depθ], *n.* profondeur, *f.*; enfoncement (*recoin*); fort (*des saisons*), *m.*; *in the depth of winter*, au cœur ou au plus fort de l'hiver, *m.*; *to get out of one's depth*, perdre pied.

depth-charge ['depθtʃa:dʒ], *n.* grenade sous-marine, *f.*

deputation [depju'teiʃən], *n.* députation, délégation, *f.*

depute [di'pju:t], *v.t.* députer, déléguer.

deputize ['depjutaiz], *v.i.* remplacer quelqu'un.

deputy ['depjuti], *n.* député, délégué; adjoint, *m.*

derail [di:'reil], *v.t.* (*Rail.*) dérailler.

derailment [di:'reilmənt], *n.* déraillement, *m.*

derange [di'reindʒ], *v.t.* déranger.

derangement [di'reindʒmənt], *n.* dérangement, *m.*

derelict ['derilikt], *a.* délaissé, abandonné.

deride [di'raid], *v.t.* tourner en dérision, se moquer de.

derision [di'riʒən], *n.* dérision, moquerie, *f.*

derisive [di'raisiv], *a.* dérisoire.

derivation [deri'veiʃən], *n.* dérivation; origine, *f.*

derivative [di'rivətiv], *n.* (*Gram.*) dérivé, *m.*

derive [di'raiv], *v.t.* dériver.—*v.i.* venir, dériver (*de*).

derogatory [di'rɔgətəri], *a.* péjoratif, dérogatoire, dérogeant (*à*).
derrick ['derik], *n.* grue, *f.*; derrick, *m.*
dervish ['dəːviʃ], *n.* derviche, *m.*
descend [di'send], *v.i.* descendre, tomber; s'abaisser; *to be descended from*, descendre de; *to descend upon*, tomber sur.
descendant [di'sendənt], *n.* descendant, *m.*
descendent [di'sendənt], *a.* descendant, qui descend, provenant (*de*).
descent [di'sent], *n.* descente; chute, pente; descendance, naissance, origine (*lignée*), *f.*
describe [dis'kraib], *v.t.* décrire, dépeindre, peindre.
description [dis'kripʃən], *n.* description; désignation (*d'une personne*), *f.*; (*Law*) signalement, *m.*; (*colloq.*) qualité, sorte, espèce, *f.*
descriptive [dis'kriptiv], *a.* descriptif.
descry [dis'krai], *v.t.* découvrir, apercevoir; aviser; reconnaître.
desecrate ['desəkreit], *v.t.* profaner.
desecration [desə'kreiʃən], *n.* profanation, *f.*
desert (1) [di'zəːt], *n.* mérite, *m.*; mérites, *m.pl.*
desert (2) ['dezət], *a.* désert; solitaire.—*n.* désert, *m.*; solitude, *f.*
desert (3) [di'zəːt], *v.t.* abandonner, déserter.
deserted [di'zəːtid], *a.* abandonné, désert.
deserter [di'zəːtə], *n.* déserteur, *m.*
desertion [di'zəːʃən], *n.* désertion, *f.*, abandon, *m.*
deserve [di'zəːv], *v.t.* mériter, être digne de.
deservedly [di'zəːvidli], *adv.* à bon droit, justement.
deserving [di'zəːviŋ], *a.* de mérite, méritoire.
desiccated ['desikeitid], *a.* desséché.
design [di'zain], *n.* dessein, projet; dessin (*drawing*); (*Manuf.*) modèle, *m.*; *by design*, à dessein.—*v.t.* projeter, se proposer de; dessiner.
designedly [di'zainidli], *adv.* à dessein.
designer [di'zainə], *n.* inventeur; auteur; architecte; dessinateur (*draughtsman*), *m.*
designing [di'zainiŋ], *a.* artificieux, intrigant.
designate ['dezigneit], *v.t.* désigner, nommer.—['dezignit], *a.* désigné, nommé.
desirable [di'zaiərəbl], *a.* désirable, à souhaiter.
desire [di'zaiə], *n.* désir, *m.*; prière, demande, *f.*—*v.t.* désirer, souhaiter; prier.
desirous [di'zaiərəs], *a.* désireux (*de*), empressé (*à*); *to be desirous of*, avoir envie de.
desist [di'zist], *v.i.* se désister, cesser (*de*).
desk [desk], *n.* pupitre (*école*); bureau (*meuble*), *m.*; caisse (*boutique*); chaire (*de professeur*), *f.*
desolate ['desəlit], *a.* désolé, inhabité, solitaire, dévasté.
desolation [desə'leiʃən], *n.* désolation, *f.*
despair [dis'pεə], *n.* désespoir, *m.*—*v.i.* désespérer (*de*).
despatch [DISPATCH].
desperado [despə'reidou, despə'rɑːdou], *n.* désespéré, *m.*
desperate ['despərit], *a.* désespéré; furieux, forcené; acharné, terrible.
desperately ['despəritli], *adv.* désespérément; (*fig.*) excessivement.

desperation [despə'reiʃən], *n.* désespoir, *m.*; fureur, *f.*, acharnement, *m.*
despicable ['dispikəbl], *a.* méprisable.
despise [dis'paiz], *v.t.* mépriser, dédaigner.
despite [dis'pait], *n.* (*Lit.*) dépit, *m.*—*prep.* en dépit de, malgré.
despoil [dis'pɔil], *v.t.* dépouiller.
despondency [dis'pɔndənsi], *n.* abattement, désespoir, *m.*
despondent [dis'pɔndənt], *a.* découragé, abattu.
despot ['despɔt], *n.* despote, *m.*, *f.*
despotic [des'pɔtik], *a.* despotique.
despotism ['despətizm], *n.* despotisme, *m.*
dessert [di'zəːt], *n.* dessert, *m.*
destination [desti'neiʃən], *n.* destination, *f.*
destine [destin], *v.t.* destiner, désigner.
destiny ['destini], *n.* destin, *m.*, destinée, *f.*
destitute ['destitjuːt], *a.* dépourvu, destitué; indigent.
destitution [desti'tjuːʃən], *n.* dénuement, abandon, *m.*, indigence, *f.*
destroy [dis'trɔi], *v.t.* détruire, ruiner.
destroyer [dis'trɔiə], *n.* (*Naut.*) contre-torpilleur, *m.*
destroying [dis'trɔiiŋ], *a.* destructeur, destructif.
destruction [dis'trʌkʃən], *n.* destruction, *f.*, anéantissement, *m.*; ruine, *f.*
destructive [dis'traktiv], *a.* destructeur; funeste, fatal (*à*).
desultorily ['desəltərili], *adv.* à bâtons rompus, sans suite.
desultory ['desəltəri], *a.* à bâtons rompus, décousu, sans suite.
detach [di'tætʃ], *v.t.* détacher (*de*); isoler; *to become detached*, se détacher.
detachable [di'tætʃəbl], *a.* démontable, détachable.
detached [di'tætʃt], *a.* détaché, isolé.
detachment [di'tætʃmənt], *n.* détachement, *m.*
detail ['diːteil], *n.* détail, *m.*—[di'teil], *v.t.* détailler; (*Mil.*) désigner (*pour*).
detain [di'tein], *v.t.* retenir; détenir; (*Law*) empêcher.
detect [di'tekt], *v.t.* découvrir; détecter.
detection [di'tekʃən], *n.* découverte, *f.*
detective [di'tektiv], *n.* agent de la (police de) sûreté, policier, détective, *m.*; *a detective story*, un roman policier.
detention [di'tenʃən], *n.* action de retenir; (*Law*) détention; (*Sch.*) consigne, *f.*
deter [di'təː], *v.t.* détourner, empêcher (*de*); dissuader (*de*).
detergent [di'təːdʒənt], *a.* and *n.* détersif, détergent, *m.*
deteriorate [di'tiəriəreit], *v.i.* se détériorer.
deterioration [ditiəriə'reiʃən], *n.* détérioration, *f.*; dépérissement, *m.*
determination [ditəːmi'neiʃən], *n.* détermination, décision, *f.*
determine [di'təːmin], *v.t.* déterminer, décider.—*v.i.* se déterminer, se décider, résoudre.
determined [di'təːmind], *a.* résolu, obstiné.
deterrent [di'terənt], *a.* préventif.—*n.* arme préventive, *f.*
detest [di'test], *v.t.* détester.
detestable [di'testəbl], *a.* détestable; (*fig.*) odieux.
detestation [diːtes'teiʃən], *n.* détestation, *f.*

dethrone [di'θroun], *v.t.* détrôner.
detonation [detə'neiʃən], *n.* détonation, *f.*
detonator ['detəneitə], *n.* détonateur, *m.*
detract [di'trækt], *v.t.* enlever, ôter (*à*); dénigrer.—*v.i.* déroger (*à*).
detriment ['detrimənt], *n.* détriment, préjudice, *m.*
detrimental [detri'mentl], *a.* préjudiciable, nuisible (*à*).
deuce [dju:s], *n.* (*Cards*) deux; (*Ten.*) à deux; à égalité; (*colloq.*) diable, diantre, *m.*
Deuteronomy [dju:tə'ronəmi]. Deutéronome, *m.*
devaluation [di:vælju'eiʃən], *n.* dévaluation, *f.*
devalue [di:'vælju], **devaluate** [di:'væljueit] *v.t.* dévaluer, déprécier.
devastate ['devəsteit], *v.t.* dévaster.
devastation [devəs'teiʃən], *n.* dévastation, *f.*
develop [di'veləp], *v.t.* développer.
developer [di'veləpə], *n.* (*Phot.*) révélateur, *m.*
development [di'veləpmənt], *n.* développement, *m.*
deviate ['di:vieit], *v.i.* dévier, se dévier; s'écarter (*de*).
deviation [di:vi'eiʃən], *n.* déviation, *f.*, écart, *m.*
device [di'vais], *n.* desscin, moyen, stratagème; dispositif, mécanisme, *m.*; devise (*motto*), *f.*
devil [devl], *n.* diable, démon, *m.*; **dare-devil**, téméraire, *m.*, *f.*—*v.t.* griller et poivrer; **devil-may-care**, étourdi, *m.*
devilish ['deviliʃ], *a.* maudit, diabolique.
devilment ['devilmənt], **devilry** ['devilri], *n.* diablerie, *f.*
devious ['di:viəs], *a.* détourné, écarté; (*fig.*) errant.
devise [di'vaiz], *v.t.* imaginer, inventer; tramer, machiner.
devitalize [di:'vaitəlaiz], *v.t.* dévitaliser.
devoid [di'void], *a.* exempt, dénué (*de*).
devote [di'vout], *v.t.* dévouer, consacrer (*à*).
devoted [di'voutid], *a.* dévoué, consacré.
devotee [devo'ti:], *n.* dévot; passionné, *m.*, fanatique, *m.*, *f.*
devotion [di'vouʃən], *n.* dévotion, *f.*; dévouement, *m.*
devour [di'vauə], *v.t.* dévorer.
devout [di'vaut], *a.* dévot, pieux, fervent.
devoutly [di'vautli], *adv.* dévotement.
dew [dju:], *n.* rosée, *f.*
dewdrop ['dju:drɔp], *n.* goutte de rosée, *f.*
dewlap ['dju:læp], *n.* fanon, *m.*
dewy ['dju:i], *a.* (couvert) de rosée.
dexterity [deks'teriti], *n.* dextérité, adresse, *f.*
dexterous ['dekstrəs], *a.* adroit; habile.
diabetes [daiə'bi:ti:z], *n.* diabète, *m.*
diabetic [daiə'betik], *a.* and *n.* diabétique, *m.*, *f.*
diabolic [daiə'bolik], **diabolical** [daiə'bolikl], *a.* diabolique.
diadem ['daiədem], *n.* diadème, *m.*
diæresis [dai'iərəsis], *n.* (*pl.* **diæreses** [dai'iərəsi:z]) tréma, *m.*
diagnose [daiəg'nouz], *v.t.* diagnostiquer.
diagnosis [daiəg'nousis], *n.* (*pl.* **diagnoses** [daiəg'nousi:z]) diagnose, *f.*; diagnostic, *m.*
diagonal [dai'ægənəl], *a.* diagonal.—*n.* diagonale, *f.*

diagram ['daiəgræm], *n.* diagramme, schéma, *m.*, épure, *f.*
diagrammatic [daiəgrə'mætik], *a.* schématique.
dial ['daiəl], *n.* cadran, *m.*; **sun-dial**, cadran solaire.—*v.t.* (*Teleph.*) composer (*un numéro*).
dialect ['daiəlekt], *n.* dialecte, patois; (*fig.*) langage, *m.*
dialogue ['daiəlɔg], *n.* dialogue; entretien, *m.*
diameter [dai'æmitə], *n.* diamètre, *m.*
diamond ['daiəmənd], *n.* diamant; (*Cards*) carreau, *m.*
diamond-cutter ['daiəməndkʌtə], *n.* lapidaire, *m.*
diamond-shaped ['daiəməndʃeipt], *a.* en losange.
Diana [dai'ænə]. (*Myth.*) Diane, *f.*
diaper ['daiəpə], *n.* linge ouvré, *m.*; (*Am.*) serviette hygiénique, couche (*d'enfant*), *f.*
diarrhoea [daiə'ri:ə], *n.* diarrhée, *f.*
diary ['daiəri], *n.* journal (particulier); agenda, *m.*
diatribe ['daiətraib], *n.* diatribe, *f.*
dice [dais], *n.pl.* dés, *m.pl.*—*v.i.* jouer aux dés.
dicky ['diki], *a.* (*fam.*) défectueux.
dictate [dik'teit], *v.t.* dicter.—*v.i.* commander (*à*).—['dikteit], *n.* précepte, ordre, *m.*
dictation [dik'teiʃən], *n.* dictée, *f.*
dictator [dik'teitə], *n.* dictateur, *m.*
dictatorial [diktə'tɔːriəl], *a.* dictatorial; impérieux.
dictatorship [dik'teitəʃip], *n.* dictature, *f.*
diction ['dikʃən], *n.* diction, *f.*; débit, *m.*
dictionary ['dikʃənri], *n.* dictionnaire, *m.*
dictum ['diktəm], *n.* (*pl.* **dicta** ['diktə]) dicton, *m.*
diddle [didl], *v.t.* (*colloq.*) duper, rouler.
die (1) [dai], *n.* (*pl.* **dies** [daiz]) coin (*pour estamper*).
die (2) [dai], *n.* (*pl.* **dice** [dais]) dé (*à jouer*), *m.*; (*fig.*) chance, *f.*
die (3) [dai], *v.i.* mourir; (*fig.*) s'éteindre; **to die down**, s'apaiser, se calmer; **to die of**, mourir de; **to die out**, s'éteindre, disparaître, s'oublier.
die-hard ['daihɑːd], *n.* intransigeant, *m.*
diet ['daiət], *n.* diète, *f.*, régime, *m.*; diète (*assemblée*), *f.*—*v.t.* mettre à la diète, mettre au régime.—*v.i.* faire diète, être au régime.
dietetics [daiə'tetiks], *n.pl.* diététique, *f.*
differ ['difə], *v.i.* différer (*de*); se quereller (*avec*).
difference ['difrəns], *n.* différence; dispute, *f.*; différend (*de valeur*), *m.*; **to split the difference**, partager le différend.
different ['difrənt], *a.* différent.
differentiate [difə'renʃieit], *v.t.* différencier, distinguer.
differently ['difrəntli], *adv.* différemment, autrement.
difficult ['difikəlt], *a.* difficile; malaisé.
difficulty ['difikəlti], *n.* difficulté; peine, *f.*, embarras; (*pl.*) embarras pécuniaire, *m.*
diffidence ['difidəns], *n.* défiance (*de soi*), modestie, timidité, *f.*
diffident ['difidənt], *a.* timide, hésitant.
diffidently ['difidəntli], *adv.* avec hésitation, timidement.
diffuse [di'fju:s], *a.* répandu, étendu; diffus, verbeux (*style*).—[di'fju:z], *v.t.* répandre.
diffusely [di'fju:sli], *adv.* diffusément.

dig [dig], *v.t. irr.* creuser; bêcher; piocher.—*v.i.* bêcher, piocher; faire des fouilles.—*n.* coup (*de coude*); (*colloq.*) coup de patte, *m.*

digest [di'dʒest], *v.t.* digérer (*aliment etc.*); résumer.—*v.i.* digérer.—['daidʒest], *n.* sommaire, abrégé, *m.*

digestion [di'dʒestʃən], *n.* digestion, *f.*

digestive [di'dʒestiv], *a.* and *n.* digestif, *m.*

digger ['digə], *n.* terrassier; mineur; fouilleur (*archéologue*); (*pop.*) Australien, *m.*

digging ['digiŋ], *n.* fouille, *f.*, creusement, *m.*; (*pl.*) (*pop.*) (*abbr.* **digs** [digz]) logement, *m.*

dignified ['dignifaid], *a.* plein de dignité, digne; noble.

dignify ['dignifai], *v.t.* honorer, élever, illustrer.

dignitary ['dignitri], *n.* dignitaire, *m.*, *f.*

dignity ['digniti], *n.* dignité, *f.*

digress [dai'gres], *v.i.* faire une digression; s'écarter (*de*).

digression [dai'greʃən], *n.* digression, *f.*

dike or **dyke** [daik], *n.* digue, *f.*, fossé, *m.*

dilapidated [di'læpideitid], *a.* délabré.

dilapidation [dilæpi'deiʃən], *n.* délabrement, *m.*

dilate [dai'leit], *v.t.* dilater, élargir, étendre.—*v.i.* se dilater.

dilatory ['dilətəri], *a.* négligent, lent.

dilemma [di'lemə, dai'lemə], *n.* dilemme; (*fig.*) embarras, *m.*; **on the horns of a dilemma**, enfermé dans un dilemme.

diligence ['dilidʒəns], *n.* diligence, assiduité, *f.*

diligent ['dilidʒənt], *a.* diligent, appliqué.

dilute [dai'lju:t, di'lju:t], *v.t.* délayer; diluer; couper (*vin*); (*fig.*) affaiblir.—*a.* dilué, mitigé.

dilution [dai'lju:ʃən, di'lju:ʃən], *n.* dilution (*liquides*), *f.*; délayement; (*fig.*) affaiblissement, *m.*

dim [dim], *a.* obscur, trouble; blafard; terne (*lumière*); indécis.—*v.t.* obscurcir; ternir.

dimension [di'menʃən, dai'menʃən], *n.* dimension, étendue, *f.*

dimensional [di'menʃənəl, dai'menʃənəl], *a.* dimensionnel; (*Cine.*) **three-dimensional** (**3-D**) **film**, film en relief, *m.*

diminish [di'miniʃ], *v.t.* diminuer; abaisser.—*v.i.* diminuer.

diminutive [di'minjutiv], *a.* diminutif, minuscule.

dimly ['dimli], *adv.* obscurément, indistinctement, faiblement, à peine; sans éclat.

dimness ['dimnis], *n.* obscurcissement, *m.*; obscurité; faiblesse (*de vue*), *f.*

dimple ['dimpl], *n.* fossette, *f.*—*v.i.* (*fig.*) se rider (*eau etc.*).

din [din], *n.* vacarme, tapage, fracas; cliquetis (*d'armes etc.*), *m.*

dine [dain], *v.i.* dîner (*de*).

diner ['dainə], *n.* dîneur, *m.*

dinghy ['diŋgi], *n.* (*Naut.*) youyou, canot, *m.*

dinginess ['dindʒinis], *n.* couleur terne, *f.*; aspect sale, *m.*

dingy ['dindʒi], *a.* terne; sale; défraîchi.

dining-car ['daininka:], *n.* wagon-restaurant, *m.*

dining-room ['dainiŋrum], *n.* salle à manger, *f.*

dinner ['dinə], *n.* dîner, *m.*

dinner-jacket ['dinədʒækit], *n.* smoking, *m.*

dint (1) [dint], *n.* force, *f.*, pouvoir, *m.*; **by dint of**, à force de.

dint (2) [dint], [DENT].

diocese ['daiəsis], *n.* diocèse, *m.*

dioxide [dai'ɔksaid], *n.* (*Chem.*) bioxyde, *m.*

dip [dip], *v.t.* plonger (*dans*); tremper, mouiller; (*Motor.*) mettre en code (*phares*).—*v.i.* plonger; **to dip into**, s'engager dans, feuilleter (*un livre*).—*n.* plongeon, *m.*, baignade, *f.*

diphtheria [dif'θiəriə], *n.* diphtérie, *f.*

diphthong ['difθɔŋ], *n.* diphtongue, *f.*

diploma [di'ploumə], *n.* diplôme, *m.*

diplomacy [di'plouməsi], *n.* diplomatie, *f.*

diplomat ['diploumæt], **diplomatist** [di'ploumətist], *n.* diplomate, *m.*, *f.*

diplomatic [diplo'mætik], *a.* diplomatique.

dip-stick ['dipstik], *n.* (*Motor.*) réglette-jauge, *f.*

dire ['daiə], *a.* terrible, affreux; cruel.

direct [di'rekt, dai'rekt], *a.* direct, droit; exprès, clair.—*adv.* (*colloq.*) directement.—*v.t.* diriger; ordonner, charger (*de*); indiquer, donner des renseignements à; **to direct a letter**, adresser une lettre.

direction [di'rekʃən], *n.* direction, *f.*; ordre, *m.*, instruction, *f.*; sens, côté, *m.*; adresse (*d'une lettre*), *f.*

directly [di'rektli], *adv.* directement, immédiatement; (*colloq.*) tout de suite; aussitôt que (*as soon as*).

director [di'rektə], *n.* directeur, administrateur, gérant; (*Cine.*) réalisateur, *m.*

directory [di'rektəri], *n.* directoire; (*Postal, Teleph.*) annuaire, *m.*

direful ['daiəful], *a.* terrible, affreux.

dirge [də:dʒ], *n.* chant funèbre, *m.*

dirt [də:t], *n.* saleté; crasse; boue, fange; ordure, *f.*

dirtily ['də:tili], *adv.* salement; (*fig.*) vilainement.

dirtiness ['də:tinis], *n.* saleté; (*fig.*) bassesse, *f.*

dirty ['də:ti], *a.* sale, malpropre, crasseux; (*fig.*) bas, vilain.—*v.t.* salir, crotter; (*fig.*) souiller.

disability [disə'biliti], *n.* incapacité, *f.*

disable [dis'eibl], *v.t.* rendre incapable, mettre hors d'état (*de*).

disabled [dis'eibld], *a.* hors de service; (*Mil.*) hors de combat; **disabled ex-service men**, mutilés de guerre, *m.pl.*

disadvantage [disəd'va:ntidʒ], *n.* désavantage, inconvénient, *m.*; perte, *f.*

disagree [disə'gri:], *v.i.* différer, ne pas s'accorder; **my dinner disagreed with me**, mon dîner m'a fait mal.

disagreeable [disə'gri:əbl], *a.* désagréable; fâcheux.

disagreeableness [disə'gri:əblnis], *n.* désagrément, *m.*, nature désagréable, *f.*

disagreeably [disə'gri:əbli], *adv.* désagréablement.

disagreement [disə'gri:mənt], *n.* différence, *f.*, désaccord; différend, *m.*; brouille, *f.*

disallow [disə'lau], *v.t.* désapprouver; refuser, défendre.

disappear [disə'piə], *v.i.* disparaître.

disappearance [disə'piərəns], *n.* disparition, *f.*

disappoint [disə'pɔint], *v.t.* désappointer, décevoir.

disappointing [disə'pɔintiŋ], *a.* décevant.

disappointment [disə'pɔintmənt], *n.* désappointement, *m.*; déception, *f.*; contretemps, *m.*

disapprobation [disæpro'beiʃən], **disapproval** [disə'pruːvəl], *n.* désapprobation, *f.*

disapprove [disə'pruːv], *v.t.* désapprouver.—*v.i.* **to disapprove of**, désapprouver.

disarm [dis'ɑːm], *v.t.* désarmer.

disarmament [dis'ɑːməmənt], *n.* désarmement, *m.*

disarrange [disə'reindʒ], *v.t.* déranger.

disarray [disə'rei], *v.i.* mettre en désarroi *ou* en désordre.—*n.* désarroi, désordre, *m.*

disaster [di'zɑːstə], *n.* désastre, malheur, *m.*

disastrous [di'zɑːstrəs], *a.* désastreux.

disavow [disə'vau], *v.t.* désavouer.

disband [dis'bænd], *v.t.* licencier, congédier; disperser.—*v.i.* se disperser.

disbelief [disbi'liːf], *n.* incrédulité, *f.*

disbelieve [disbi'liːv], *v.t.* ne pas croire, refuser de croire.

disbeliever [disbi'liːvə], *n.* incrédule, *m.*, *f.*

disc [DISK].

discard [dis'kɑːd], *v.t.* mettre de côté; congédier; écarter; éliminer; (*Cards*) faire son écart.—['diskɑːd], *n.* (*Cards*) écart, *m.*

discern [di'səːn, di'zəːn], *v.t.* discerner, distinguer.

discerning [di'səːniŋ, di'zəːniŋ], *a.* judicieux, éclairé, attentif.

discernment [di'səːnmənt, di'zəːnmənt], *n.* discernement, jugement, *m.*

discharge [dis'tʃɑːdʒ], *n.* déchargement, *m.*; décharge (*arme à feu etc.*); mise en liberté (*d'un prisonnier*), *f.*; accomplissement (*d'un devoir*), *m.*; réhabilitation (*d'un failli*); quittance (*récépissé*), *f.*; congé (*d'employé*); (*Mil.*) congé définitif; (*Med.*) écoulement, *m.*—*v.t.* décharger; congédier (*employé*); libérer (*de prison*); acquitter (*dette*); décharger (*arme à feu*); remplir (*devoir*); (*Mil.*, *Navy*) congédier; (*Law*) quitter.—*v.i.* suppurer (*blessure etc.*).

disciple [di'saipl], *n.* disciple, *m.*

disciplinarian [disipli'neəriən], *a.* disciplinaire.—*n.* personne rigide pour la discipline, *f.*

disciplinary ['disiplinəri], *a.* disciplinaire.

discipline ['disiplin], *n.* discipline, *f.*—*v.t.* discipliner.

disclaim [dis'kleim], *v.t.* désavouer, renier, nier.

disclose [dis'klouz], *v.t.* découvrir, révéler.

disclosure [dis'klouʒə], *n.* révélation, découverte, *f.*

discolour [dis'kʌlə], *v.t.* décolorer.

discomfort [dis'kʌmfət], *n.* incommodité, *f.*, inconfort, malaise, *m.*; gêne, *f.*

discompose [diskəm'pouz], *v.t.* déranger, troubler.

discomposure [diskəm'pouʒə], *n.* trouble, désordre, *m.*, agitation, *f.*

disconcert [diskən'səːt], *v.t.* déconcerter.

disconnect [diskə'nekt], *v.t.* désunir, séparer; (*Elec.*) débrancher; (*Mach.*) désembrayer.

disconnected [diskə'nektid], *a.* débrayé; déconnecté; (*fig.*) décousu.

disconsolate [dis'kɔnsəlit], *a.* inconsolable, désolé.

discontent [diskən'tent], *n.* mécontentement, *m.*

discontented [diskən'tentid], *a.* mécontent (*de*).

discontinue [diskən'tinjuː], *v.t.*, *v.i.* discontinuer; cesser de.

discord ['diskɔːd], *n.* discorde; (*Mus.*) dissonance, *f.*

discordant [dis'kɔːdənt], *a.* discordant; (*fig.*) en désaccord.

discount ['diskaunt], *n.* escompte; rabais, *m.* **at a discount**, au rabais, en baisse.—[dis'kaunt], *v.t.* escompter; (*fig.*) décompter, rabattre.—*v.i.* faire l'escompte.

discourage [dis'kʌridʒ], *v.t.* décourager, détourner.

discouragement [dis'kʌridʒmənt], *n.* découragement, *m.*

discouraging [dis'kʌridʒiŋ], *a.* décourageant.

discourse (1) ['diskɔːs], *n.* discours, entretien; (*fig.*) langage, propos, *m.*—[dis'kɔːs], *v.i.* discourir, s'entretenir, traiter (*de*).

discourteous [dis'kɔːtiəs], *a.* impoli.

discourtesy [dis'kɔːtisi], *n.* impolitesse, *f.*

discover [dis'kʌvə], *v.t.* découvrir; révéler, montrer.

discovery [dis'kʌvəri], *n.* découverte, *f.*

discredit [dis'kredit], *n.* discrédit, *m.*; honte, *f.*—*v.t.* ne pas croire; déshonorer.

discreditable [dis'kreditəbl], *a.* peu honorable; honteux.

discreet [dis'kriːt], *a.* discret, prudent, circonspect, sage.

discreetly [dis'kriːtli], *adv.* discrètement, sagement, prudemment.

discrepancy [dis'krepənsi], *n.* désaccord, *m.*

discretion [dis'kreʃən], *n.* discrétion, prudence, sagesse, *f.*; jugement, discernement, *m.*

discriminate [dis'krimineit], *v.t.* discriminer, distinguer.—*v.i.* faire des distinctions.

discriminating [dis'krimineitiŋ], *a.* discriminatoire, distinctif.

discrimination [diskrimi'neiʃən], *n.* discrimination, *f.*, discernement, *m.*

discuss [dis'kʌs], *v.t.* discuter, débattre.

discussion [dis'kʌʃən], *n.* discussion, *f.*, débat, *m.*

disdain [dis'dein], *n.* dédain, mépris, *m.*—*v.t.* dédaigner, mépriser.

disdainful [dis'deinful], *a.* dédaigneux, méprisant.

disease [di'ziːz], *n.* maladie, *f.*, mal; (*fig.*) vice, *m.*

diseased [di'ziːzd], *a.* malade; (*fig.*) dérangé.

disembark [disim'bɑːk], *v.t.*, *v.i.* débarquer.

disembarkation [disembɑː'keiʃən], *n.* débarquement, *m.*

disembodied [disim'bɔdid], *a.* désincarné.

disembowel [disim'bauəl], *v.t.* éventrer.

disengage [disin'geidʒ], *v.t.* dégager; (*Tech.*) débrayer.—*v.i.* se dégager.

disengaged [disin'geidʒd], *a.* dégagé; libre.

disentangle [disin'tæŋgl], *v.t.* démêler, débrouiller.

disentanglement [disin'tæŋglmənt], *n.* débrouillement, *m.*

disestablish [disis'tæbliʃ], *v.t.* séparer (*l'Église de l'État*).

disestablishment [disis'tæbliʃmənt], *n.* séparation de l'Église et de l'État, *f.*

disfavour [dis'feivə], *n.* défaveur, *f.*

disfigure [dis'figə], *v.t.* défigurer, enlaidir.

disfigurement [dis'figəmənt], *n.* action de défigurer; difformité, *f.*

disfranchisement [dis'fræntʃizmənt], *n.* privation *ou* perte de privilèges électoraux, *f.*

disgorge [dis'gɔ:dʒ], *v.t.* dégorger, rendre, vomir.—*v.i.* rendre gorge.

disgrace [dis'greis], *n.* disgrâce, honte, *f.,* déshonneur, *m.*—*v.t.* disgracier; déshonorer.

disgraceful [dis'greisful], *a.* honteux; déshonorant, ignoble.

disgracefully [dis'greisfuli], *adv.* honteusement.

disgruntled [dis'grʌntld], *a.* mécontent; de mauvaise humeur.

disguise [dis'gaiz], *n.* déguisement, travestissement; (*fig.*) masque, voile, *m.*—*v.t.* déguiser; (*fig.*) cacher, voiler.

disguised [dis'gaizd], *a.* déguisé.

disgust [dis'gʌst], *n.* dégoût, *m.,* aversion, *f.;* ennui, *m.*—*v.t.* dégoûter (*de*); écœurer.

disgusting [dis'gʌstiŋ], *a.* dégoûtant.

dish [diʃ], *n.* (*pl.* **dishes** ['diʃiz]) plat (*vaisselle*); mets (*aliment*), *m.;* (*pl.*) vaisselle, *f.*—*v.t.* dresser, servir, apprêter; (*colloq.*) enfoncer.

dish-cloth ['diʃklɔθ], *n.* torchon, *m.*

dishearten [dis'hɑ:tn], *v.t.* décourager.

disheartening [dis'hɑ:tniŋ], *a.* décourageant.

dishevel [di'ʃevəl], *v.t.* ébouriffer.

dishevelled [di'ʃevəld], *a.* dépeigné, ébouriffé.

dishonest [dis'ɔnist], *a.* malhonnête.

dishonestly [dis'ɔnistli], *adv.* malhonnêtement.

dishonesty [dis'ɔnisti], *n.* improbité, malhonnêteté, *f.*

dishonour [dis'ɔnə], *n.* déshonneur, *m.*—*v.t.* déshonorer; avilir; (*Comm.*) *dishonoured cheque,* chèque impayé, *m.*

dishonourable [dis'ɔnərəbl], *a.* sans honneur; honteux (*chose*).

dishonourably [dis'ɔnərəbli], *adv.* malhonnêtement.

disillusion [disi'lju:ʒən], *v.t.* désillusionner.—*n., also* **disillusionment** [disi'lju:ʒənmənt], désillusionnement, *m.*

disinclination [disinkli'neiʃən], *n.* éloignement, *m.;* aversion, *f.*

disinclined [disin'klaind], *a.* peu disposé.

disinfect [disin'fekt], *v.t.* désinfecter.

disinfectant [disin'fektənt], *n.* désinfectant, *m.*

disingenuous [disin'dʒenjuəs], *a.* sans franchise, de mauvaise foi, dissimulé.

disingenuously [disin'dʒenjuəsli], *adv.* de mauvaise foi.

disingenuousness [disin'dʒenjuəsnis], *n.* dissimulation, mauvaise foi, fausseté, *f.*

disinherit [disin'herit], *v.t.* déshériter.

disinheritance [disin'heritəns], *n.* déshéritement, *m.*

disintegrate [dis'intigreit], *v.t.* désagréger; désintégrer.—*v.i.* se désagréger, se désintégrer.

disintegration [disinti'greiʃən], *n.* désagrégation; désintégration, *f.*

disinter [disin'tə:], *v.t.* déterrer, exhumer.

disinterested [dis'intrəstid], *a.* désintéressé.

disjointed [dis'dʒɔintid], *a.* désarticulé, disloqué; (*fig.*) décousu, sans suite (*style etc.*).

disjointedly [dis'dʒɔintidli], *adv.* d'une manière décousue *ou* incohérente.

disk [disk], *n.* disque, *m.;* (*Med.*) *slipped disk,* hernie discale, *f.*

dislike [dis'laik], *v.t.* ne pas aimer; avoir du dégoût pour.—*n.* aversion, *f.;* dégoût, *m.*

dislocate ['dislokeit], *v.t.* disloquer, démettre; déboîter (*os etc.*).

dislodge [dis'lɔdʒ], *v.t.* déloger; déplacer.

disloyal [dis'lɔiəl], *a.* perfide, déloyal.

disloyalty [dis'lɔiəlti], *n.* défection (*de*), déloyauté, perfidie, *f.*

dismal ['dizməl], *a.* sombre, morne, triste.

dismally ['dizməli], *adv.* lugubrement, tristement.

dismantle [dis'mæntl], *v.t.* dévêtir; démonter (*machine*).

dismay [dis'mei], *n.* effroi, *m.,* terreur, épouvante, *f.*—*v.t.* effarer, épouvanter, consterner.

dismiss [dis'mis], *v.t.* renvoyer (*de*); congédier; quitter (*sujet etc.*); rejeter (*appel etc.*); chasser (*pensées etc.*).

dismissal [dis'misəl], *n.* renvoi; congé; (*Law*) acquittement, *m.*

dismount [dis'maunt], *v.t.* démonter.—*v.i.* descendre de cheval.

disobedience [disə'bi:diəns], *n.* désobéissance, *f.*

disobedient [disə'bi:diənt], *a.* désobéissant.

disobey [disə'bei], *v.t.* désobéir à.

disobliging [disə'blaidʒiŋ], *a.* désobligeant.

disorder [dis'ɔ:də], *n.* désordre, dérèglement, *m.;* maladie (*Med.*), *f.*—*v.t.* déranger, troubler.

disordered [dis'ɔ:dəd], *a.* en désordre, dérangé; malade.

disorderly [dis'ɔ:dəli], *a.* en désordre, déréglé; vicieux; tumultueux.

disorganization [disɔ:gəni'zeiʃən], *n.* désorganisation, *f.*

disorganize [dis'ɔ:gənaiz], *v.t.* désorganiser.

disown [dis'oun], *v.t.* désavouer, nier.

disparage [dis'pæridʒ], *v.t.* déprécier, ravaler, dénigrer.

disparagement [dis'pæridʒmənt], *n.* dénigrement, déshonneur, reproche, *m.;* honte, *f.,* tort, *m.*

disparaging [dis'pæridʒiŋ], *a.* dénigrant, injurieux.

disparagingly [dis'pæridʒiŋli], *adv.* avec mépris.

dispassionate [dis'pæʃənit], *a.* calme; impartial.

dispatch, despatch [dis'pætʃ], *v.t.* dépêcher, expédier; achever.—*n.* dépêche, *f.,* envoi, *m.;* promptitude, *f.;* **mentioned in dispatches,** cité à l'ordre du jour.

dispel [dis'pel], *v.t.* dissiper, chasser.

dispensary [dis'pensəri], *n.* dispensaire, *m.;* pharmacie, *f.*

dispensation [dispən'seiʃən], *n.* dispensation, *f.;* (*fig.*) bienfait, don, *m.*

dispense [dis'pens], *v.t.* distribuer, dispenser, administrer; (*Pharm.*) préparer (*médecine*); **to dispense with,** se passer de.

dispenser [dis'pensə], *n.* dispensateur, pharmacien, *m.*

dispersal [dis'pə:səl], *n.* dispersion, *f.*

disperse [dis'pə:s], *v.t.* disperser; dissiper.—*v.i.* se disperser.

dispirited [dis'piritid], *a.* découragé, abattu.

displace [dis'pleis], *v.t.* déplacer; destituer (*d'un emploi*).

displacement [dis'pleismənt], *n.* déplacement, *m.*

display [dis'plei], *n.* exposition, parade, *f.*; (*fig.*) étalage, *m.*—*v.t.* montrer, exposer, étaler.

displease [dis'pli:z], *v.t.* déplaire à; fâcher.

displeased [dis'pli:zd], *a.* mécontent, offensé (*de*).

displeasing [dis'pli:ziŋ], *a.* désagréable.

displeasure [dis'pleʒə], *n.* déplaisir; courroux, *m.*

disport [dis'pɔːt], *v.t.* **to disport oneself**, s'amuser, se divertir.

disposal [dis'pouzəl], *n.* disposition; vente, cession (*sale*), *f.*

dispose [dis'pouz], *v.t.* disposer; porter (*à croire*); **to dispose of**, céder, vendre, se défaire de, se débarrasser de.

disposition [dispə'ziʃən], *n.* disposition, *f.*; caractère, naturel, *m.*

dispossess [dispə'zes], *v.t.* déposséder (*de*).

disproportionate [disprə'pɔːʃənit], *a.* disproportionné.

disprove [dis'pruːv], *v.t.* réfuter.

dispute [dis'pjuːt], *n.* différend; conflit, *m.*; **beyond dispute**, sans contredit.—*v.t.* disputer, discuter.

disqualification [diskwɔlifi'keiʃən], *n.* incapacité, *f.*

disqualify [dis'kwɔlifai], *v.t.* rendre incapable (*de*).

disquiet [dis'kwaiət], *n.* inquiétude, *f.*

disregard [disri'gɑːd], *n.* insouciance, indifférence, *f.*—*v.t.* négliger, faire peu de cas de.

disrepair [disri'pɛə], *n.* délabrement, *m.*

disreputable [dis'repjutəbl], *a.* de mauvaise réputation; compromettant, déshonorant (*chose*).

disrepute [disri'pjuːt], *n.* discrédit, déshonneur, *m.*; mauvaise réputation, *f.*

disrespect [disris'pekt], *n.* manque de respect, irrespect, *m.*

disrespectful [disris'pektful], *a.* irrespectueux.

disrobe [dis'roub], *v.t.* déshabiller, dévêtir.—*v.i.* se déshabiller.

disrupt [dis'rʌpt], *v.t.* rompre.

dissatisfaction [dissætis'fækʃən], *n.* mécontentement, *m.*

dissatisfied [dis'sætisfaid], *a.* mécontent (*de*).

dissect [di'sekt], *v.t.* disséquer.

dissection [di'sekʃən], *n.* dissection, *f.*

dissemble [di'sembl], *v.t.* dissimuler, déguiser, cacher.—*v.i.* dissimuler, feindre.

disseminate [di'semineit], *v.t.* disséminer, répandre, propager.

dissension [di'senʃən], *n.* dissension, *f.*; **to sow dissension**, semer la zizanie.

dissent [di'sent], *n.* dissentiment, *m.*; (*Relig.*) dissidence, *f.*—*v.i.* différer (*de*); différer de sentiment (*avec*).

dissenter [di'sentə], *n.* dissident, *m.*, nonconformiste, *m.*, *f.*

disservice [di'səːvis], *n.* mauvais service, *m.*

dissever [di'sevə], *v.t.* séparer (*de*).

dissimilar [di'similə], *a.* dissemblable (*à*); différent (*de*).

dissimulate [di'simjuleit], *v.t.* dissimuler.

dissipate ['disipeit], *v.t.* dissiper.—*v.i.* se dissiper.

dissociate [di'souʃieit], *v.t.* désassocier, dissocier.

dissolute ['disəluːt], *a.* dissolu.

dissolve [di'zɔlv], *v.t.* dissoudre; désunir; supprimer; résoudre (*doute etc.*).—*v.i.* se dissoudre.

dissonance ['disənəns], *n.* dissonance; discordance, *f.*

dissuade [di'sweid], *v.t.* dissuader (*de*).

distaff ['distɑːf], *n.* quenouille, *f.*; **the distaff side**, le côté maternel.

distance ['distəns], *n.* distance, *f.*; éloignement, lointain, *m.*; (*fig.*) réserve, *f.*

distant ['distənt], *a.* éloigné, lointain; (*fig.*) réservé, froid.

distaste [dis'teist], *n.* dégoût, *m.*, aversion (*pour*), *f.*

distasteful [dis'teistful], *a.* désagréable, offensant.

distemper [dis'tempə], *n.* maladie (*de chien*); (*Paint.*) détrempe, *f.*—*v.t.* peindre en détrempe.

distend [dis'tend], *v.t.* étendre; dilater, enfler.—*v.i.* se détendre.

distil [dis'til], *v.t.*, *v.i.* distiller.

distillation [disti'leiʃən], *n.* distillation, *f.*

distiller [dis'tilə], *n.* distillateur, *m.*

distillery [dis'tiləri], *n.* distillerie, *f.*

distinct [dis'tiŋkt], *a.* distinct; exprès, clair, net.

distinction [dis'tiŋkʃən], *n.* distinction; (*Sch.*) mention, *f.*

distinctive [dis'tiŋktiv], *a.* distinctif.

distinctly [dis'tiŋktli], *adv.* distinctement, clairement; (*fig.*) indéniablement.

distinguish [dis'tiŋgwiʃ], *v.t.* distinguer (*de*).

distinguished [dis'tiŋgwiʃt], *a.* distingué; **a distinguished man**, un homme éminent.

distort [dis'tɔːt], *v.t.* tordre, contourner; décomposer (*les traits*); (*fig.*) torturer, défigurer.

distorted [dis'tɔːtid], *a.* tordu, décomposé; (*fig.*) torturé.

distortion [dis'tɔːʃən], *n.* contorsion, déformation, *f.*

distract [dis'trækt], *v.t.* distraire, détourner (*de*); tourmenter.

distracted [dis'træktid], *a.* bouleversé, fou, hors de soi.

distracting [dis'træktiŋ], *a.* atroce, déchirant, affolant.

distraction [dis'trækʃən], *n.* distraction, *f.*, trouble, *m.*, confusion; démence, folie, *f.*; **to drive to distraction**, mettre hors de soi.

distraught [dis'trɔːt], *a.* affolé, éperdu.

distress [dis'tres], *n.* détresse, affliction, peine, *f.*, chagrin, *m.*; misère (*pauvreté*), *f.*—*v.t.* affliger, désoler.

distressed [dis'trest], *a.* affligé, malheureux; dans la misère (*pauvre*).

distressing [dis'tresiŋ], *a.* affligeant, désolant, pénible.

distribute [dis'tribjuːt], *v.t.* distribuer.

distribution [distri'bjuːʃən], *n.* distribution, répartition, *f.*

district ['distrikt], *n.* contrée, région, *f.*, arrondissement, district; quartier (*de ville*); (*Postal*) secteur, *m.*

distrust [dis'trʌst], *n.* méfiance, *f.*—*v.t.* se méfier de.

distrustful [dis'trʌstful], *a.* défiant; méfiant, soupçonneux.

disturb [dis'tə:b], *v.t.* troubler; déranger.

disturbance [dis'tə:bəns], *n.* trouble, *m.*; confusion, émeute, *f.*; bruit, tapage; désordre, *m.*

disuse [dis'ju:s], *n.* désuétude, *f.*

disused [dis'ju:zd], *a.* hors d'usage.

ditch [ditʃ], *n.* fossé, *m.*—*v.t.* (*pop.*) abandonner.—*v.i.* creuser un fossé.

dither ['diðə], *n.* **to be all of a dither**, être tout agité.—*v.i.* trembler, trembloter, hésiter.

ditto ['ditou], *adv.* idem; (*Comm.*) dito.

ditty ['diti], *n.* chanson, chansonnette, *f.*

diurnal [dai'ə:nəl], *a.* journalier, du jour; (*Med.*) quotidien.

divan [di'væn], *n.* divan, *m.*

dive [daiv], *v.i.* plonger.—*n.* plongeon, *m.*; (*pop.*) boîte de nuit, *f.*

diver ['daivə], *n.* plongeur; plongeon (*oiseau*), *m.*

diverge [dai'və:dʒ], *v.i.* diverger (*de*).

divergent [dai'və:dʒənt], *a.* divergent.

diverse [dai'və:s], *a.* divers, varié.

diversify [dai'və:sifai], *v.t.* diversifier; varier (*couleurs*).

diversion [dai'və:ʃən], *n.* divertissement, amusement, *m.*; diversion, distraction, *f.*

diversity [dai'və:siti], *n.* diversité, variété, *f.*

divert [dai'və:t], *v.t.* divertir, réjouir; distraire, dévier, détourner (*de*).

diverting [dai'və:tiŋ], *a.* divertissant, amusant.

divest [di'vest, dai'vest], *v.t.* dépouiller (*de*).

divide [di'vaid], *v.t.* diviser; partager.—*v.i.* se diviser.

dividend ['dividend], *n.* dividende, *m.*

dividers [di'vaidəz], *n. pl.* compas à pointes sèches, *m.*

divine [di'vain], *a.* divin; (*fam.*) adorable.—*n.* théologien, ecclésiastique, *m.*—*v.t.* deviner, pressentir.

diving ['daiviŋ], *n.* plongement, plongeon, *m.*

diving-board ['daiviŋbɔ:d], *n.* plongeoir, *m.*

divinity [di'viniti], *n.* divinité; théologie, *f.*

divisible [di'vizibl], *a.* divisible.

division [di'viʒən], *n.* division, *f.*, partage, *m.*; scission, *f.*; vote, *m.*

divorce [di'vɔ:s], *n.* divorce, *m.*; séparation, *f.* —*v.t.* séparer, divorcer avec.—*v.i.* se séparer (*de*).

divorcee [divɔr'si:], *n.* divorcé, *m.*, divorcée, *f.*

divulge [dai'vʌldʒ, di'vʌldʒ], *v.t.* divulguer, publier.

dizziness ['dizinis], *n.* vertige, étourdissement, *m.*

dizzy ['dizi], *a.* étourdi; vertigineux (*élévation*).

do [du:], *v.t. irr.* faire; rendre (*service, justice etc.*); finir (*achever*); (*Cook.*) cuire; (*colloq.*) duper; *done!* c'est entendu! *done to a turn*, cuit à point; *he is done for*, c'en est fait de lui; *it can't be done*, pas moyen; *overdone*, trop cuit (*viande*); *to be doing well*, faire de bonnes affaires, réussir; *to do over*, enduire (*de*); couvrir (*de*); *to do up*, empaqueter, emballer, remettre en état, remettre à neuf; *underdone*, saignant (*viande*); *well done!* bravo! *what is to be done?* que faire?— *v.i.* se porter, se conduire; aller, convenir

(*faire l'affaire*); suffire (*répondre à un besoin*); finir (*terminer*); *how do you do?* comment allez-vous? *to do away with*, supprimer, se défaire de, faire disparaître; *to do by*, agir envers; *to do without*, se passer de.— *n.* duperie; soirée, réception, *f.*

docile ['dousail], *a.* docile.

docility [dou'siliti], *n.* docilité, *f.*

dock [dɔk], *v.t.* écourter; rogner (*comptes etc.*); (*Naut.*) mettre dans le bassin.—*v.i.* entrer aux docks.—*n.* bassin, dock, *m.*; (*Bot.*) patience, *f.*; (*Law*) banc des accusés, *m.*

docker ['dɔkə], *n.* déchargeur, docker, *m.*

docket ['dɔkit], *n.* étiquette, fiche, *f.*—*v.t.* étiqueter; enregistrer.

doctor ['dɔktə], *n.* docteur, médecin, *m.*— *v.t.* soigner, droguer; (*fig.*) altérer; frelater (*vin*).

doctrinaire [dɔktri'nɛə], *a.* doctrinaire.

doctrinal [dɔk'trainəl], *a.* doctrinal.

doctrine ['dɔktrin], *n.* doctrine, *f.*

document ['dɔkjumənt], *n.* document, titre, *m.*—*v.t.* munir de documents.

documentary [dɔkju'mentəri], *a.* justificatif, authentique.—*n.* (*Cine.*) documentaire, *m.*

documentation [dɔkjumen'teiʃən], *n.* documentation, *f.*

dodge [dɔdʒ], *v.t.* éviter; esquiver.—*v.i.* s'esquiver; (*fig.*) ruser, faire des détours.— *n.* tour, détour, *m.*; (*fig.*) ruse, ficelle, *f.*

dodger ['dɔdʒə], *n.* rusé, malin, finaud, *m.*

doe [dou], *n.* daine, *f.*

doer ['du:ə], *n.* faiseur; auteur, *m.*

doff [dɔf], *v.t.* tirer, enlever, ôter.

dog [dɔg], *n.* chien; (*facet.*) coquin, gaillard, *m.*; *lucky dog!* quel veinard!—*v.t.* suivre à la piste; harceler, épier.

dog-days ['dɔgdeiz], *n.pl.* canicule, *f.*

dogged ['dɔgid], *a.* obstiné; acharné.

doggedly ['dɔgidli], *adv.* avec acharnement.

doggedness ['dɔgidnis], *n.* obstination, *f.* acharnement, *m.*

doggerel ['dɔgərəl], *n.* vers burlesques, vers de mirliton, *m.pl.*

doggie ['dɔgi], *n.* (*Childish*) tou-tou, *m.*

doggo ['dɔgou], *adv.* **to lie doggo**, se tenir coi.

dogma ['dɔgmə], *n.* dogme, *m.*

dogmatic [dɔg'mætik], *a.* dogmatique.

dogmatism ['dɔgmətizm], *n.* dogmatisme, *m.*

doily ['dɔili], *n.* serviette de dessert, *f.* napperon, *m.*

doing ['du:iŋ], *n.* (*usu. in pl.*) faits, *m.pl.*; actions, *f.pl.*, exploits, *m.pl.*

dole [doul], *n.* aumône, *f.*, partage, *m.*; allocation de chômage, *f.*—*v.t.* **to dole out**, distribuer, répartir avec parcimonie.

doleful ['doulful], *a.* plaintif, lugubre.

doll [dɔl], *n.* poupée, *f.*—*v.r.* **to doll oneself up**, se pomponner.

dollar ['dɔlə], *n.* dollar, *m.*

dolphin ['dɔlfin], *n.* dauphin, *m.*

dolt [doult], *n.* lourdaud, sot, butor, *m.*

domain [do'mein], *n.* domaine, *m.*

dome [doum], *n.* dôme, *m.*

domestic [də'mestik], *a.* de famille; domestique (*animaux*).—*n.* domestique, *m. f.*, servante, *f.*

domesticate [də'mestikeit], *v.t.* domestiquer, apprivoiser; *fig.*) rendre casanier.

domesticated

domesticated [dəˈmestikeited], *a.* casanier (*personnes*); apprivoisé (*animaux*).

domicile [ˈdɔmisail, ˈdɔmisil], *n.* domicile, *m.*

dominance [ˈdɔminəns], *n.* dominance, *f.*

dominant [ˈdɔminənt], *a.* dominant.

dominate [ˈdɔmineit], *v.t.* dominer sur.—*v.i.* dominer; prévaloir, prédominer.

domination [dɔmiˈneiʃən], *n.* domination, *f.*

domineer [dɔmiˈniə], *v.i.* dominer (*sur*).

domineering [dɔmiˈniəriŋ], *a.* impérieux, autoritaire.

Dominican [doˈminikən], *a.* dominicain.—*n.* Dominicain (*personne*), *m.*; *Dominican nun*, Dominicaine, *f.*

dominie [ˈdɔmini], *n.* (Sc.) maître d'école, *m.*

dominion [doˈminiən], *n.* domination, autorité, *f.*; empire, *m.*; (*pl.*) états, *m.pl.*

domino [ˈdɔminou], *n.* domino (*capuchon, jeu*), *m.*

don [dɔn], *n.* don (*titre*); (*fig.*) grand seigneur; (*Univ.*) professeur d'université, *m.*—*v.t.* mettre, endosser.

donate [doˈneit], *v.t.* faire un don de.

donation [doˈneiʃən], *n.* donation, *f.*, don, *m.*

donkey [ˈdɔŋki], *n.* âne, baudet, *m.*

donor [ˈdounə], *n.* donateur, *m.*

doodle [duːdl], *v.i.* griffonner.—*n.* griffonnage, *m.*

doom [duːm], *v.t.* condamner (*à*); (*fig.*) destiner (*à*).—*n.* jugement; destin funeste, *m.*; perte, ruine, *f.*

doomsday [ˈduːmzdei], *n.* jour du jugement dernier, *m.*

door [dɔː], *n.* porte; portière (*d'une voiture*), *f.*; *folding-doors*, porte à deux battants; *next door*, à côté; *indoors*, à la maison; *out of doors*, dehors; *behind closed doors*, à huis clos.

door-bell [ˈdɔːbel], *n.* sonnette, *f.*

door-keeper [ˈdɔːkiːpə], *n.* concierge, portier (*d'une maison*); gardien (*des monuments publics*), *m.*

doorman [ˈdɔːmən], *n.* portier, *m.*

door-mat [ˈdɔːmæt], *n.* paillasson, *m.*

door-step [ˈdɔːstep], *n.* seuil de la porte, pas de (la) porte, *m.*

door-way [ˈdɔːwei], *n.* entrée, porte, *f.*

dope [doup], *n.* drogue, *f.*, narcotique, *m.*—*v.t.* droguer.

dormant [ˈdɔːmənt], *a.* dormant; assoupi.

dormer-window [ˈdɔːməwindou], *n.* lucarne, *f.*

dormitory [ˈdɔːmitri], *n.* dortoir, *m.*

dormouse [ˈdɔːmaus], *n.* (*pl.* **dormice** [ˈdɔːmais]) loir, *m.*

Dorothy [ˈdɔrəθi]. Dorothée, *f.*

dose [dous], *n.* dose, *f.*—*v.t.* médicamenter; doser.

dossier [ˈdɔsjei], *n.* dossier, *m.*

dot [dɔt], *n.* point, *m.*—*v.t.* marquer d'un point, marquer avec des points; (*Paint.*) pointiller.

dotage [ˈdoutidʒ], *n.* seconde enfance, *f.*, radotage, *m.*

dote [dout], *v.i.* radoter; raffoler (*de*).

double [dʌbl], *a.* double, en deux; *bent double*, voûté.—*n.* double, pendant, sosie; (*Mil.*) pas de course, *m.*—*adv.* double; au double; *to fold double*, plier en deux.—*v.t.* doubler; serrer (*poings*).—*v.i.* doubler;

user de ruse; *to double back*, revenir sur ses pas.

double-bed [ˈdʌblˈbed], *n.* lit à deux places, *m.*

double-breasted [ˈdʌblbrestid], *a.* croisé.

double-cross [ˈdʌblˈkrɔs], *v.t.* duper, tromper.

double-dealing [ˈdʌblˈdiːliŋ], *n.* duplicité, *f.*

double-decker [ˈdʌblˈdekə], *n.* autobus à impériale, *m.*

double-room [ˈdʌblˈruːm], *n.* chambre pour deux personnes, *f.*

doubt [daut], *n.* doute, *m.*; hésitation, *f.*; *beyond a doubt*, sans aucun doute.—*v.t.* douter de.—*v.i.* douter; soupçonner.

doubtful [ˈdautful], *a.* douteux, incertain.

doubtless [ˈdautlis], *adv.* sans doute.

dough [dou], *n.* pâte, *f.*

dough-nut [ˈdounʌt], *n.* pet de nonne, *m.*

doughty [ˈdauti], *a.* vaillant, preux.

dour [ˈduə], *a.* (Sc.) austère et froid.

douse [daus], *v.t.* plonger dans l'eau; éteindre.

dove [dʌv], *n.* colombe, *f.*; pigeon, *m.*

dove-cot(e) [ˈdʌvkɔt, ˈdʌvkout], *n.* colombier, *m.*

Dover [ˈdouvə]. Douvres, *m.*; *the Straits of Dover*, le Pas-de-Calais, *m.*

dowager [ˈdauədʒə], *n.* douairière, *f.*

dowdy [ˈdaudi], *a.f.* gauche et mal mise, mal fagotée.

dowel [ˈdauəl], *n.* (Carp.) goujon, *m.*

down (1) [daun], *n.* duvet (*poil follet*), *m.*; dune (*colline*), *f.*

down (2) [daun], *adv.* en bas; à bas; bas, à terre; tombé, apaisé (*vent*); couché (*soleil*); à plat (*pneu*); en baisse (*prix*); (*fig.*) sur le déclin; *to go down*, descendre.—*prep.* en bas de; vers le bas de.

downcast [ˈdaunkɑːst], *a.* abattu.

downfall [ˈdaunfɔːl], *n.* chute, *f.*; (*fig.*) débâcle, *f.*

downhill [ˈdaunhil], *a.* incliné; en pente.—[daunˈhil], *adv.* en descendant.

downpour [ˈdaunpɔː], *n.* averse, *f.*

downright [ˈdaunrait], *a.* direct; franc.—*adv.* net, tout à fait.

downstairs [daunˈstɛəz], *adv.* en bas (de l'escalier).

downtrodden [ˈdauntrɔdn], *a.* opprimé.

downward [ˈdaunwəd], *a.* de haut en bas, qui descend, descendant.—*adv.* (also **downwards** [ˈdaunwədz]) en bas, en descendant; en aval.

downy [ˈdauni], *a.* de duvet, duveteux.

dowry [ˈdauri], *n.* dot, *f.*

doze [douz], *v.i.* s'assoupir, sommeiller, être assoupi.—*n.* petit somme, *m.*

dozen [dʌzn], *n.* douzaine, *f.*

drab [dræb], *a.* gris sale, brun terne; (*fig.*) terne, décoloré.—*n.* (*fig.*) traînée (*femme*), *f.*

draft [drɑːft], *v.t.* dessiner, rédiger; (*Mil.*) détacher.—*n.* dessin (*esquisse*); brouillon (*projet*), *m.*; (*Comm.*) traite, *f.*; (*Mil.*) détachement, *m.*

drag [dræg], *v.t.* traîner, tirer; (*Naut.*) draguer; *to drag away from*, entraîner, arracher de; *to drag on*, entraîner; (*fig.*) traîner en longueur; *to drag out*, faire sortir de force.—*v.i.* se traîner; traîner; chasser (*ancre*).

draggle [drægl], *v.t.* traîner dans la boue.

drag-net [ˈdrægnet], *n.* seine, *f.*, chalut, *m.*

dragoman [ˈdrægomən], *n.* drogman, *m.*

dragon [ˈdrægən], *n.* dragon, *m.*

drill

dragon-fly ['drægənflai], *n.* demoiselle, libellule, *f.*, agrion, *m.*
dragoon [drə'guːn], *n.* (*Mil.*) dragon, *m.*— *v.t.* (*fig.*) forcer par des mesures violentes.
drain [drein], *v.t.* faire écouler; dessécher; drainer; (*fig.*) épuiser; vider (*verre etc.*).— *v.i.* s'écouler.—*n.* tranchée, *f.*, égout, *m.*
drainage ['dreinidʒ], **draining** ['dreiniŋ] *n.* écoulement; (*Agric.*) drainage, *m.*
draining-board ['dreiniŋbɔːd], *n.* égouttoir, *m.*
drake [dreik], *n.* canard, *m.*
dram [dræm], *n.* (*Pharm.*) drachme, *f.*
drama ['drɑːmə], *n.* drame; (*fig.*) théâtre, *m.*
dramatic [drə'mætik], **dramatical** [drə'mætikəl], *a.* dramatique.
dramatist ['drɑːmətist, 'dræmətist], *n.* auteur dramatique, *m.*, dramaturge, *m.,f.*
dramatize ['drɑːmətaiz, 'dræmətaiz], *v.t.* dramatiser.
drape [dreip], *v.t.* draper, tendre (*de*).—*n.* (*Am.*) rideau, *m.*
draper ['dreipə], *n.* drapier; marchand de drap *m.*
drapery ['dreipəri], *n.* draperie, *f.*
drastic ['dræstik], *a.* énergique, radical, brutal.
draught [drɑːft], *n.* tirage; trait; courant d'air; coup (*boisson*); dessin (*esquisse*); coup de filet (*de pêcheur*); tirant (*d'un navire*), *m.*; (*Med.*) potion, *f.*; (*pl.*) jeu de dames, *m.*
draught-board ['drɑːftbɔːd], *n.* damier, *m.*
draught-horse ['drɑːsthɔːs], *n.* cheval de trait, *m.*
draughtsman ['drɑːftsmən], *n.* (*pl.* -men [men]) dessinateur, *m.*
draughty ['drɑːfti], *a.* plein de courants d'air.
draw [drɔː], *v.t. irr.* tirer; traîner; dessiner (*tableau etc.*); toucher (*rations, appointements etc.*); arracher (*dent*); puiser (*eau etc.*); (*fig.*) attirer (*à* ou *sur*); **to draw lots for**, tirer au sort.—*v.i.* tirer; dégainer; dessiner (*au crayon*); (*Spt.*) faire partie nulle *ou* match nul.—*n.* tirage (*au sort*), *m.*; attraction; (*Spt.*) partie nulle, *f.*
drawback ['drɔːbæk], *n.* mécompte, désavantage, inconvénient, *m.*
drawbridge ['drɔːbridʒ], *n.* pont-levis, *m.*
drawer ['drɔːə], *n.* tireur (*d'un chèque*); puiseur (*d'eau*); tiroir (*meuble*); (*pl.*) caleçon (*vêtement*), *m.*; **chest of drawers**, commode, *f.*
drawing ['drɔːiŋ], *n.* tirage; dessin (*croquis*), *m.*
drawing-board ['drɔːiŋbɔːd], *n.* planche à dessin, *f.*
drawing-pin ['drɔːiŋpin], *n.* punaise (*pour le dessin*), *f.*
drawing-room ['drɔːiŋruːm], *n.* salon, *m.*; (*Court*) réception, *f.*
drawl [drɔːl], *v.i.* parler d'une voix traînante.—*n.* voix traînante, *f.*
drawling ['drɔːliŋ], *a.* traînant.
drawn [drɔːn], *a.* indécis, égal (*bataille etc.*); tiré, nu (*épée*); **drawn game**, partie nulle, *f.*
dray [drei], *n.* camion, haquet, *m.*
dread [dred], *a.* redoutable, terrible; auguste.—*n.* terreur, crainte, *f.*—*v.t.* craindre, redouter.

dreadful ['dredful], *a.* affreux, terrible, épouvantable.
dreadfully ['dredfuli], *adv.* terriblement, affreusement.
dream [driːm], *n.* songe, rêve, *m.*; **daydream**, rêverie, *f.*—*v.t. irr.* rêver.—*v.i.* rêver; (*fig.*) s'imaginer.
dreamer ['driːmə], *n.* rêveur, *m.*; (*fig.*) visionnaire, *m.,f.*
dreamy ['driːmi], *a.* rêveur; chimérique, visionnaire.
drear [driə], **dreary** ['driəri], *a.* triste, morne, lugubre.
drearily ['driərili], *adv.* tristement, lugubrement.
dreariness ['driərinis], *n.* tristesse, *f.*, aspect morne, *m.*
dredge (1) [dredʒ], *n.* drague, *f.*—*v.t., v.i.* draguer.
dredge (2) [dredʒ], *v.t.* saupoudrer (*de farine etc.*).
dredger (1) ['dredʒə], *n.* dragueur (*bateau*), *m.*
dredger (2) ['dredʒə], *n.* saupoudreuse, *f.*
dregs [dregz], *n.pl.* lie, *f.*
drench [drentʃ], *v.t.* tremper, mouiller (*de*); noyer (*de*).
dress [dres], *v.t.* habiller, vêtir, parer, orner; panser (*blessure etc.*); apprêter (*aliments etc.*); (*Mil.*) aligner; (*Navy*) pavoiser.—*v.i.* s'habiller; faire sa toilette; (*Mil.*) s'aligner.—*n.* habillement, *m.*; robe (*de femme*); mise, toilette; (*Mil.*) tenue, *f.*; **dress rehearsal**, répétition générale, *f.*; **evening dress**, tenue de soirée, *f.*
dress-circle ['dresəːkl], *n.* (*Theat.*) fauteuils de balcon, *m.pl.*
dresser ['dresə], *n.* habilleur (*personne*); dressoir (*de cuisine*), *m.*
dressing ['dresiŋ], *n.* toilette, *f.*, habillement; pansement (*de blessure etc.*); (*Cook.*) assaisonnement, *m.*; (*Agric.*) fumure, engrais, *m.*
dressing-case ['dresiŋkeis], *n.* mallette de toilette, *f.*
dressing-gown ['dresiŋgaun], *n.* robe de chambre, *f.*, peignoir, *m.*
dressing-room ['dresiŋruːm], *n.* cabinet de toilette, *m.*
dressing-table ['dresiŋteibl], *n.* coiffeuse, table de toilette, *f.*
dressmaker ['dresmeikə], *n.* couturière, *f.*
dressmaking ['dresmeikiŋ], *n.* confections pour dames, *f.pl.*, couture, *f.*
dressy ['dresi], *a.* élégant, chic, coquet (*personne*); habillé (*robe*).
dribble [dribl], *v.t.* laisser dégoutter, laisser tomber goutte à goutte; (*Ftb.*) dribbler.—*v.i.* tomber goutte à goutte, dégoutter; baver; (*Ftb.*) dribbler.
drier ['draiə], *comp. a.* [DRY].—*n.* [DRYER].
drift [drift], *n.* monceau; tourbillon, *m.*, rafale, *f.*; objet flottant, *m.*; (*fig.*) tendance; (*Naut.*) dérive, *f.*—*v.t.* chasser, pousser; amonceler.—*v.i.* dériver, aller à la dérive, flotter; s'amonceler, s'amasser.
drifter ['driftə], *n.* (*Naut.*) chalutier, *m.*
drill [dril], *n.* foret, *m.*, mèche, *f.*; (*Agric.*) sillon; (*Mil.*) exercice, *m.*, manœuvre, *f.*— *v.t.* forer, percer; (*Mil.*) exercer.—*v.i.* (*Mil.*) faire l'exercice.

409

drilling [ˈdriliŋ], n. forage; (Dent.) fraisage; (Mil.) exercice, m.

drink [driŋk], n. boisson; (fig.) ivresse (drunkenness), f.—v.t., v.i. irr. boire.

drinker [ˈdriŋkə], n. buveur; ivrogne, m.

drinking [ˈdriŋkiŋ], a. potable; à boire.—n. boire, m.; ivrognerie, f., alcoolisme, m.

drinking-fountain [ˈdriŋkiŋfauntin], n. fontaine publique, f.

drip [drip], v.t. faire dégoutter.—v.i. dégoutter, tomber goutte à goutte.—n. goutte, f.; égout, m.

dripping [ˈdripiŋ], n. graisse de rôti, f.; (pl.) gouttes, f.pl.

drive [draiv], v.t. irr. pousser; chasser; enfoncer (clou etc.); mener, conduire (voiture, cheval etc.); forcer, réduire (à); to drive away, chasser, éloigner; to drive back, repousser; to drive in, faire entrer, enfoncer; to drive out faire sortir, chasser.—v.i. conduire; aller en voiture; to drive at, tendre à, vouloir en venir à; to drive up, arriver (en voiture).—n. promenade ou course en voiture; grande avenue ou allée, f.

drivel [drivl], v.i. bave, f.—v.i. baver; (fig.) radoter.

driver [ˈdraivə], n. cocher (d'un carrosse); voiturier (d'une charrette); (Rail.) mécanicien; (Motor. etc.) chauffeur, conducteur, m.

driving [ˈdraiviŋ], n. action de conduire, f.; percement (d'un tunnel), m.

driving-licence [ˈdraiviŋlaisəns], n. permis de conduire, m.

driving-test [ˈdraiviŋtest], n. examen pour permis de conduire, m.

drizzle [drizl], v.i. bruiner.—n. bruine, pluie fine, f.

droll [droul], a. plaisant, drôle.

drollery [ˈdrouləri], n. plaisanterie, drôlerie, farce, f.

dromedary [ˈdrʌmədəri, ˈdrɔmədəri], n. dromadaire, m.

drone [droun], n. (Ent., Mus.) faux-bourdon; (fig.) frelon; fainéant (personne); bourdonnement (son), m.—v.i. bourdonner.

droning [ˈdrouniŋ], a. bourdonnant.—n. bourdonnement, m.

droop [druːp], v.t. laisser tomber, laisser pendre.—v.i. languir, se pencher, tomber, pencher; (fig.) s'affaiblir.

drooping [ˈdruːpiŋ], a. languissant, abattu; penché.—n. abattement, m., langueur, f.

drop [drɔp], n. goutte; chute (descente), f.; pendant (bijou), m.—v.t. laisser tomber; jeter (l'ancre); sauter (une maille); déposer (quelqu'un) quelque part; laisser échapper (prononcer); abandonner (lâcher).—v.i. tomber goutte à goutte; dégoutter (de); échapper (glisser); to drop behind, se laisser dépasser, rester en arrière; to drop in, entrer en passant; to drop out, se retirer.

dropsy [ˈdrɔpsi], n. hydropisie, f.

dross [drɔs], n. scorie, crasse, f.; (fig.) rebut, m.

drought [draut], n. sécheresse, f.

drove (1) [drouv], n. troupeau (en marche), m.; (fig.) foule (en marche), f.

drove (2) [drouv], past [DRIVE].

drover [ˈdrouvə], n. conducteur de bestiaux, bouvier, m.

drown [draun], v.t. noyer; (fig.) submerger; étouffer (bruit).—v.i. se noyer.

drowsily [ˈdrauzili], adv. comme endormi; (fig.) avec indolence.

drowsiness [ˈdrauzinis], n. assoupissement, m.

drowsy [ˈdrauzi], a. assoupi; somnolent; lourd, stupide.

drub [drʌb], v.t. rosser, battre.

drubbing [ˈdrʌbiŋ], n. volée (de coups), f.

drudge [drʌdʒ], n. homme (ou femme) de peine, souffre-douleur, m., f.—v.i. travailler sans relâche, peiner.

drudgery [ˈdrʌdʒəri], n. travail pénible, m.; corvée, vile besogne, f.

drug [drʌg], n. drogue, f.—v.t. droguer; (fig.) empoisonner.

drug-addict [ˈdrʌgædikt], n. toxicomane, m., f.

druggist [ˈdrʌgist], n. (Am.) pharmacien, m.

drug-store [ˈdrʌgstɔː], n. (Am.) pharmacie, f.

druid [ˈdruːid], n. druide, m.

drum [drʌm], n. tambour, m.; caisse, f.; tympan (de l'oreille), m.—v.t. (Mil.) to drum out, dégrader.—v.i. battre du tambour (sur); (fig.) tinter.

drum-major [ˈdrʌmmeidʒə], n. tambour-major, m.

drummer [ˈdrʌmə], n. tambour (homme), m.

drum-stick [ˈdrʌmstik], n. baguette de tambour, f.

drunk [drʌŋk], a. ivre, gris, soûl.

drunkard [ˈdrʌŋkəd], n. ivrogne, m.

drunkenness [ˈdrʌŋkənnis], n. ivresse; ivrognerie, f.

dry [drai], a. sec, desséché; aride; altéré; (fig.) caustique; ennuyeux.—v.t. sécher; dessécher.—v.i. sécher; to dry up, tarir; se taire.

dry-dock [ˈdraidɔk], n. bassin de radoub, m., cale sèche, f.

dryer, drier [ˈdraiə], n. (Ind. etc.) séchoir; (Paint.) siccatif, dessiccatif, m.; spin dryer, essoreuse (rotative), f.

dryness [ˈdrainis], n. sécheresse, aridité, f.

dry-shod [ˈdraiʃɔd], a. and adv. à pied sec.

dual [ˈdjuːəl], a. double; dual carriage-way, route à double circulation, f.—n. (Gram.) duel, m.

dub [dʌb], v.t. armer chevalier; (colloq.) qualifier, baptiser; (Cine.) doubler (film).

dubiety [djuˈbaiəti], **dubiousness** [ˈdjuːbiəsnis], n. doute, m., incertitude, f.

dubious [ˈdjuːbiəs], a. douteux, incertain.

dubiously [ˈdjuːbiəsli], adv. douteusement.

duchess [ˈdʌtʃis], n. duchesse, f.

duchy [ˈdʌtʃi], n. duché, m.

duck (1) [dʌk], n. cane, f.; canard; (colloq.) chou (mot tendre), m.

duck (2) [dʌk], n. (Box.) esquive, f.—v.t. plonger dans l'eau.—v.i. plonger; baisser la tête subitement; (Box.) esquiver.

duck (3) [dʌk], n. toile à voile, f.; (pl.) pantalon blanc, m.

ducking [ˈdʌkiŋ], n. plongeon; (Naut.) baptême de la ligne, m.

duckling [ˈdʌkliŋ], n. caneton, m.

duck-weed [ˈdʌkwiːd], n. lentille d'eau, f.

duct [dʌkt], n. conduit, f.; (Anat.) canal, m.

dudgeon [ˈdʌdʒən], n. colère, f.; in high dudgeon, fort en colère.

410

due [djuː], *a.* dû; convenable, propre, juste; (*Comm.*) échu; (*fig.*) requis, voulu; *to fall due*, échoir.—*n.* dû; (*pl.*) droit, impôt, *m.*, redevance, *f.*—*adv.* droit, directement.
duel ['djuːəl], *n.* duel, *m.*, (*fig.*) lutte, *f.*
duellist ['djuːəlist], *n.* duelliste, *m.*
duenna [djuːˈenə], *n.* duègne, *f.*
duet [djuːˈet], *n.* duo, *m.*
duke [djuːk], *n.* duc, *m.*
dukedom ['djuːkdəm], *n.* duché, *m.*; dignité de duc, *f.*
dull [dʌl], *a.* lourd, hébété, stupide (*personne*); lourd, gris, sombre (*temps*); sourd (*son*); triste (*morne*); émoussé (*moins aigu*); terne (*couleur*); ennuyeux.—*v.t.* hébéter; émousser (*rendre moins aigu*); ternir (*ôter l'éclat de*); engourdir (*de froid*).—*v.i.* s'hébéter; s'engourdir; s'émousser.
dullard ['dʌləd], *n.* âne, lourdaud (*personne*), *m.*
dullness ['dʌlnis], *n.* lenteur, *f.*; assoupissement, ennui; manque d'éclat, *m.*, faiblesse (*de son*), *f.*
dully ['dʌlli], *adv.* lourdement, tristement.
duly ['djuːli], *adv.* dûment, justement.
dumb [dʌm], *a.* muet, réduit au silence; (*Am.*) stupide.
dumb-bells ['dʌmbelz], *n.pl.* haltères, *m.pl.*
dumbfound [dʌmˈfaund], *v.t.* confondre, abasourdir, interdire.
dumbly ['dʌmli], *adv.* en silence.
dumbness ['dʌmnis], *n.* mutisme; (*fig.*) silence, *m.*
dumb-show ['dʌmʃou], *n.* pantomime, *f.*, jeu muet, *m.*
dummy ['dʌmi], *n.* muet, *m.*, muette, *f.*; mannequin, objet imité; (*fig.*) homme de paille; (*Cards*) mort, *m.*
dump [dʌmp], *v.t.* déposer, décharger, déverser.—*n.* tas; dépotoir, *m.*
dumpling ['dʌmplin], *n.* pâte cuite, *f.*
dumpy ['dʌmpi], *a.* trapu, gros et court.
dun (1) [dʌn], *a.* brun foncé; bai (*cheval*).
dun (2) [dʌn], *n.* créancier importun, *m.*—*v.t.* importuner.
dunce [dʌns], *n.* ignorant, âne, sot, *m.*
dune [djuːn], *n.* dune, *f.*
dung [dʌŋ], *n.* crotte, *f.*; crottin; (*Agric.*) fumier, *m.*
dung-cart ['dʌŋkaːt], *n.* tombereau à fumier, *m.*
dungeon ['dʌndʒən], *n.* cachot, *m.*
dunghill ['dʌŋhil], *n.* fumier, *m.*
duodenal [djuːoˈdiːnl], *a.* (*Anat.*) duodénal; *duodenal ulcer*, ulcère au duodénum, *m.*
dupe [djuːp], *n.* dupe, *f.*—*v.t.* duper, tromper.
duplicate ['djuːplikit], *a.* double.—*n.* double, duplicata, *m.*—['djuːplikeit], *v.t.* doubler; copier.
duplicity [djuːˈplisiti], *n.* duplicité, mauvaise foi, *f.*
durability [djuərəˈbiliti], **durableness** ['djuərəblnis], *n.* solidité, durabilité, *f.*
durable ['djuərəbl], *a.* durable.
duration [djuəˈreiʃən], *n.* durée, *f.*
during ['djuəriŋ], *prep.* pendant, durant.
dusk [dʌsk], *n.* crépuscule, *m.*; obscurité, *f.*
duskiness ['dʌskinis], *n.* obscurité, teinte sombre, *f.*
dusky ['dʌski], *a.* foncé, sombre; noiraud, noirâtre.
dust [dʌst], *n.* poussière; poudre, *f.*; (*fig.*)

cendres (des morts), *f.pl.*; *sawdust*, sciure, *f.*—*v.t.* épousseter.
dust-bin ['dʌstbin], *n.* boîte à ordures, poubelle, *f.*
dust-cart ['dʌstkaːt], *n.* tombereau, *m.*
duster ['dʌstə], *n.* torchon, chiffon, *m.*
dustman ['dʌstmən], *n.* (*pl.* -men [men]) boueur, *m.*
dusty ['dʌsti], *a.* poussiéreux, couvert de poussière; poudreux.
Dutch [dʌtʃ], *a.* hollandais, de Hollande.—*n.* hollandais (*langue*), *m.*; *the Dutch*, les Hollandais, *m.pl.*
Dutchman ['dʌtʃmən], *n.* (*pl.* -men [men]) Hollandais, *m.*
Dutchwoman ['dʌtʃwumən], *n.* (*pl.* -women [wimin]) Hollandaise, *f.*
duteous ['djuːtiəs], **dutiful** ['djuːtiful], *a.* obéissant, soumis.
dutifully ['djuːtifuli], *adv.* avec soumission, respectueusement.
duty ['djuːti], *n.* (*pl.* **duties** ['djuːtiz]) devoir; (*Customs*) droit; (*Mil. etc.*) service, *m.*; *on duty*, de service, de garde, en faction.
dwarf [dwoːf], *a. and n.* nain, *m.*, naine, *f.*—*v.t.* rapetisser; (*Hort.*) rabougrir.
dwell [dwel], *v.i. irr.* demeurer, habiter; rester; (*fig.*) *to dwell on*, insister sur.
dweller ['dwelə], *n.* habitant, *m.*, habitante, *f.*
dwelling ['dweliŋ], *n.* habitation, demeure, *f.*
dwindle [dwindl], *v.i.* diminuer, s'amoindrir; dépérir.
dye [dai], *v.t.* teindre.—*v.i.* teindre, se teindre.—*n.* teinture, teinte; couleur, nuance, *f.*; (*fig.*) caractère, *m.*
dyeing ['daiiŋ], *n.* teinture, *f.*
dyer ['daiə], *n.* teinturier, *m.*, teinturière, *f.*
dye-works ['daiwəːks], *n.pl.* teinturerie, *f.*
dying ['daiiŋ], *a.* mourant, moribond; suprême, dernier.
dyke [DIKE].
dynamic [daiˈnæmik], **dynamical** [daiˈnæmikəl], *a.* dynamique.
dynamics [daiˈnæmiks], *n.pl.* dynamique, *f.*
dynamite ['dainəmait], *n.* dynamite, *f.*—*v.t.* dynamiter.
dynamo ['dainəmou], *n.* dynamo, *f.*
dynasty ['dinəsti], *n.* dynastie, *f.*
dysentery ['disəntri], *n.* dysenterie, *f.*
dyspepsia [disˈpepsiə], *n.* dyspepsie, *f.*
dyspeptic [disˈpeptik], *a.* dyspepsique, dyspeptique.

E

E, e [iː]. cinquième lettre de l'alphabet; (*Mus.*) mi, *m.*
each [iːtʃ], *a.* chaque.—*pron.* chacun, *m.*, chacune, *f.*; *each other*, l'un l'autre, les uns les autres.
eager ['iːgə], *a.* vif, ardent (*à*); impatient (*de*); désireux; empressé (*à* ou *de*).
eagerly ['iːgəli], *adv.* ardemment; impatiemment.

eagerness ['i:gənis], *n.* ardeur, *f.*; empressement, *m.*

eagle [i:gl], *n.* aigle, *m.*, *f.*

eaglet ['i:glit], *n.* aiglon, *m.*

ear [iə], *n.* oreille, *f.*; épi (*de blé*), *m.—v.i.* monter en épi.

ear-ache ['iəreik], *n.* mal d'oreille, *m.*

ear-drum ['iədrʌm], *n.* tympan, tambour de l'oreille, *m.*

earl [ə:l], *n.* comte, *m.*

earldom ['ə:ldəm], *n.* comté, *m.*

earliness ['ə:linis], *n.* heure peu avancée; précocité (*de fruits*), *f.*

early ['ə:li], *a.* matinal; matineux (*personne*); ancien; précoce, hâtif (*fruit etc.*).—*adv.* de bonne heure, de bon matin, de grand matin; tôt.

ear-mark ['iəmɑːk], *v.t.* (*fig.*) réserver, mettre de côté.

earn [ə:n], *v.t.* gagner, acquérir; (*fig.*) mériter.

earnest (1) ['ə:nist], *a.* sérieux, empressé, sincère.

earnest (2) ['ə:nist], *n.* gage, *m.*, garantie, *f.*, arrhes, *f.pl.*

earnestly ['ə:nistli], *adv.* sérieusement, avec empressement.

earnestness ['ə:nistnis], *n.* ardeur, *f.*, empressement; sérieux, *m.*

earnings ['ə:ninz], *n.pl.* gain, *m.*; gages, *m.pl.*

ear-phones ['iəfounz], *n.pl.* casque, *m.*

ear-ring ['iərin], *n.* boucle d'oreille, *f.*

earth [ə:θ], *n.* terre, *f.*; terrier (*de renard etc.*), *m.—v.t.* enterrer, enfouir; couvrir de terre; (*Elec.*) joindre à la terre.

earthen ['ə:θən], *a.* de terre.

earthenware ['ə:θənwɛə], *n.* poterie, vaisselle de terre, faïence, *f.*

earthly ['ə:θli], *a.* terrestre.

earthquake ['ə:θkweik], *n.* tremblement de terre, *m.*

earthy ['ə:θi], *a.* de terre, terreux.

earwig ['iəwig], *n.* perce-oreille, *m.*

ease [i:z], *n.* aisance, aise; facilité; tranquillité, *f.*, repos; (*fig.*) abandon; soulagement (*de douleur*), *m.—v.t.* soulager, mettre à l'aise; (*fig.*) tranquilliser, calmer.

easel [i:zl], *n.* chevalet, *m.*

easily ['i:zili], *adv.* facilement, sans peine; aisément.

east [i:st], *a.* d'est, d'orient; oriental.—*n.* est, orient; levant, *m.*

Easter ['i:stə], *n.* Pâques, *m.*; (*Jewish*) Pâque, *f.*

easterly ['i:stəli], *a.* d'est.—*adv.* vers l'orient, vers l'est.

eastern ['i:stən], *a.* d'est, d'orient, oriental.

eastward ['i:stwəd], *adv.* vers l'est, vers l'orient.

easy ['i:zi], *a.* facile; aisé; confortable; tranquille; naturel (*style*); à l'aise; *easy chair*, fauteuil, *m.—adv.* doucement.

easy-going ['i:zigouin], *a.* accommodant, peu exigeant.

eat [i:t], *v.t.*, *v.i.* *irr.* manger; ronger (*corroder*); *to eat away*, consumer, ronger; *to eat up*, manger, achever de manger.

eatable ['i:təbl], *a.* mangeable, comestible.—*n.* comestible, *m.*; (*pl.*) vivres, *m.pl.*

eating ['i:tin], *n.* action de manger, *f.*; manger, *m.*

eaves [i:vz], *n.* avance du toit, *f.*; gouttières, *f.pl.*

eavesdrop ['i:vzdrɔp], *v.i.* écouter aux portes.

eavesdropper ['i:vzdrɔpə], *n.* écouteur aux portes, *m.*

ebb [eb], *v.i.* baisser; décliner, refluer, se retirer.—*n.* reflux; (*fig.*) déclin, *m.*, décadence, *f.*

ebb-tide ['ebtaid], *n.* jusant, *m.*

ebony ['ebəni], *a.* d'ébène.—*n.* ébène, *f.*, bois d'ébène, *m.*

ebony-tree ['ebənitri:], *n.* ébénier, *m.*

ebullience [i'bʌliəns], **ebulliency** [i'bʌliənsi], *n.* ébullition, effervescence, *f.*

ebullient [i'bʌliənt], *a.* en ébullition, bouillonnant; (*fig.*) exubérant, pétulant.

ebullition [ebə'liʃən], *n.* ébullition; (*fig.*) effervescence, *f.*, transport, *m.*

eccentric [ek'sentrik], *a.* excentrique; désaxé; (*fig.*) singulier.

eccentricity [eksen'trisiti], *n.* excentricité, *f.*

ecclesiastic [ikli:zi'æstik], *a.* and *n.* ecclésiastique, *m.*

echo ['ekou], *n.* écho, *m.—v.t.* répercuter; (*fig.*) répéter.—*v.i.* faire écho; retentir, résonner (*de*).

eclipse [i'klips], *n.* éclipse, *f.—v.t.* éclipser; (*fig.*) surpasser.—*v.i.* s'éclipser.

economic [i:kə'nɔmik], **economical** [i:kə'nɔmikəl], *a.* économique (*chose*); économe, ménager (*personne*).

economically [i:kə'nɔmikəli], *adv.* économiquement.

economics [i:kə'nɔmiks], *n.pl.* économie politique, *f.*

economist [i'kɔnəmist], *n.* économiste, *m.*, *f.*

economize [i'kɔnəmaiz], *v.t.* économiser.—*v.i.* user d'économie.

economy [i'kɔnəmi], *n.* économie, *f.*; système, *m.*; *planned economy*, économie planifiée.

ecstasy ['ekstəsi], *n.* extase, *f.*, transport, *m.*

ecstatic [eks'tætik], **ecstatical** [eks'tætikəl], *a.* extatique, d'extase.

Ecuador [ekwə'dɔ:], (la République de) l'Équateur, *f.*

Ecuadorean [ekwə'dɔːriən], *a.* équatorien.—*n.* Équatorien (*personne*), *m.*

eczema ['eksimə], *n.* eczéma, *m.*

eddy ['edi], *n.* remous (*eau*); tourbillon (*vent*), *m.—v.i.* tourbillonner.

Eden ['i:dən], Éden, *m.*

edge [edʒ], *n.* bord (*marge*); fil, tranchant (*de couteau etc.*), *m.*; lisière (*d'une forêt etc.*), *f.*; cordon (*d'une pièce de monnaie*), *m.*; tranche (*d'un livre*), *f.—v.t.* affiler, aiguiser; border (*entourer*).—*v.i.* *to edge away*, s'éloigner graduellement.

edged [edʒd], *a.* tranchant; bordé.

edgeways ['edʒweiz], **edgewise** ['edʒwaiz], *adv.* de côté, de champ.

edging ['edʒin], *n.* bordure, *f.*

edible ['edibl], *a.* comestible, bon à manger.

edict ['i:dikt], *n.* édit, *m.*

edifice ['edifis], *n.* édifice, *m.*

edify ['edifai], *v.t.* édifier.

Edinburgh ['edinbrə], Édimbourg, *m.*

edit ['edit], *v.t.* éditer, rédiger.

edition [i'diʃən], *n.* édition, *f.*

editor ['editə], *n.* compilateur, annotateur; (*Journ.*) rédacteur en chef, directeur, *m.*

editorial [edi'tɔːriəl], *a.* de rédacteur.—*n.* article de fond, éditorial, *m.*

412

electron

Edmund ['edmənd]. Edmond, m.
educate ['edjukeit], v.t. élever; instruire.
education [edju'keiʃən], n. éducation, f.;
enseignement, m.; instruction, f.
Edward ['edwəd]. Édouard, m.
eel [i:l], n. anguille, f.
eerie ['iəri], a. étrange, mystérieux.
eeriness ['iərinis], n. étrangeté surnaturelle,
f.
efface [i'feis], v.t. effacer.
effect [i'fekt], n. effet, m.; (pl.) effets, biens,
m.pl.; in effect, en effet; to carry into
effect, accomplir, exécuter, mettre à effet;
to no effect, en vain, sans résultat; to take
effect, faire son effet, opérer; (Law) entrer
en vigueur.—v.t. effectuer, exécuter, accomplir.
effective [i'fektiv], a. effectif; efficace.
effectively [i'fektivli], adv. effectivement;
efficacement.
effeminacy [i'feminəsi], n. mollesse, nature
efféminée, f.
effeminate [i'feminit], a. efféminé.
effervesce [efə'ves], v.i. être en effervescence; mousser (boisson).
effervescence [efə'vesəns], n. effervescence,
f.
effervescent [efə'vesənt], effervescing [efə
'vesiŋ], a. effervescent; mousseux; gazeux
(eau minérale).
effete [i'fi:t], a. usé; stérile, épuisé, caduc.
efficacious [efi'keiʃəs], a. efficace.
efficacy ['efikəsi], n. efficacité, f.
efficiency [i'fiʃənsi], n. efficacité; bonne condition, f.; (Mach.) rendement, m.
efficient [i'fiʃənt], a. efficace (remède);
capable, compétent (personne).
efficiently [i'fiʃəntli], adv. efficacement.
effigy ['efidʒi], n. effigie, f.
effloresce [eflo'res], v.i. s'effleurir.
efflorescence [eflo'resəns], n. efflorescence;
(Bot.) floraison, f.
efflorescent [eflo'resənt], a. efflorescent;
(Bot.) fleurissant.
effluvium [i'flu:viəm], n. (pl. effluvia [i'flu:
viə]) exhalaison, f., effluve, m.
effort ['efət], n. effort, m.
effortless ['efətlis], a. sans effort.
effrontery [i'frʌntəri], n. effronterie, f.
effulgence [i'fʌldʒəns], n. splendeur, f.,
éclat, m.
effulgent [i'fʌldʒənt], a. resplendissant,
éclatant.
effusion [i'fju:ʒən], n. effusion, f., épanchement, m.
effusive [i'fju:siv], a. expansif; (fig.) excessif,
exubérant.
egg [eg], n. œuf, m.; boiled egg, œuf à la
coque; fried egg, œuf sur le plat; hard-
boiled egg, œuf dur; new-laid egg, œuf
frais.—v.t. pousser (à).
egg-cup ['egkʌp], n. coquetier, m.
egg-shell ['egʃel], n. coquille d'œuf, f.
eglantine ['egləntain], n. églantier, m.;
églantine (fleur), f.
egoism ['egouizm], n. égoïsme, m.
egoist ['egouist], n. égoïste, m., f.
egotism ['egətizm], n. égotisme, culte du
moi, m.
egotist ['egətist], n. égotiste, m., f.
egregious [i'gri:dʒəs], a. insigne, énorme;
fameux.

egress ['i:gres], n. sortie, issue, f.
Egypt ['i:dʒipt]. l'Égypte, f.
Egyptian [i'dʒipʃən], a. égyptien.—n. Egyp-
tien (personne), m.
eider ['aidə], eider-duck ['aidədʌk], n.
eider, m.
eiderdown ['aidədaun], n. édredon, m.
eight [eit], a. huit.
eighteen ['ei'ti:n], a. dix-huit.
eighteenth ['ei'ti:nθ], a. dix-huitième; dix-
huit (roi etc.).—n. dix-huitième (fraction),
m.
eighth [eitθ], a. huitième; huit (roi etc.).—n.
huitième (fraction), m.; (Mus.) octave, f.
eightieth ['eitiiθ], a. quatre-vingtième.—n.
quatre-vingtième (fraction), m.
eighty ['eiti], a. quatre-vingts.
Eire ['eərə]. l'Irlande, f.
either ['aiðə, 'i:ðə], pron. l'un ou l'autre, m.,
l'une ou l'autre, f.; l'un d'eux, m., l'une
d'elles, f.; (used negatively) ni l'un ni l'autre,
m., ni l'une ni l'autre, f.—conj. ou, soit.—
adv. non plus.
ejaculate [i'dʒækjuleit], v.t. pousser (un cri).
—v.i. s'écrier; éjaculer.
ejaculation [idʒækju'leiʃən], n. cri, m.
exclamation; éjaculation, f.
eject [i'dʒekt], v.t. rejeter; émettre (flammes);
chasser, expulser.
ejection [i'dʒekʃən], ejectment [i'dʒekt
mənt], n. expulsion, éjection; (Law) éviction,
f.
eke [i:k], v.t. to eke out, allonger; suppléer à,
augmenter; ménager; to eke out a living,
se faire une maigre pitance.
elaborate [i'læbərit], a. élaboré, soigné;
compliqué.—[i'læbreit], v.t. élaborer.
elaboration [ilæbə'reiʃən], n. élaboration, f.
elapse [i'læps], v.i. s'écouler.
elastic [i'læstik], a. and n. élastique, m.
elasticity [elæs'tisiti], n. élasticité, f.
elate [i'leit], v.t. élever, exalter, transporter.
elation [i'leiʃən], n. transport de joie, m.,
exaltation, ivresse, f.
elbow ['elbou], n. coude, m.—v.t. coudoyer,
pousser du coude.
elder (1) ['eldə], n. sureau (arbre), m.
elder (2) ['eldə], a. aîné, plus âgé; plus
ancien.—n. aîné; ancien, m.
elderly ['eldəli], a. d'un certain âge.
eldest ['eldist], a. le plus âgé, l'aîné.
Eleanor ['elinə]. Éléonore, f.
elect [i'lekt], a. élu, choisi, nommé.—n. élu,
m.—v.t. élire, nommer, choisir; (fig.) se
décider à.
election [i'lekʃən], n. élection, f.
electioneer [ilekʃə'niə], v.i. solliciter des
votes, travailler les électeurs.
electioneering [ilekʃə'niəriŋ], n. manœuvres
électorales, f.pl.
elective [i'lektiv], a. électif; électoral.
elector [i'lektə], n. électeur, votant, m.
electric [i'lektrik], electrical [i'lektrikəl], a.
électrique; electric shock, secousse électrique, f.
electrician [elek'triʃən, ilek'triʃən], n. électricien, m.
electricity [elek'trisiti, ilek'trisiti], n. électricité, f.
electrify [i'lektrifai], v.t. électriser; électrifier.
electrocute [i'lektrokju:t], v.t. électrocuter.
electron [i'lektrən] n. électron m.

413

electronic [elek'trɔnik, ilek'trɔnik], *a.* électronique.

electronics [elek'trɔniks, ilek'trɔniks], *n.* électronique, *f.*

electro-plate [i'lektroupleit], *n.* argenture électrique, *f.*—*v.t.* plaquer, argenter.

elegance ['eligəns], *n.* élégance, *f.*

elegant ['eligənt], *a.* élégant, chic.—*n.* élégant, beau, *m.*

elegantly ['eligəntli], *adv.* élégamment.

elegiac [eli'dʒaiək], *a.* élégiaque.—*n.* vers élégiaque, *m.*

elegist ['elidʒist], *n.* poète élégiaque, *m.*

elegy ['elidʒi], *n.* élégie, *f.*

element ['elimənt], *n.* élément, *m.*; (*pl.*) rudiments, *m.pl.*

elemental [eli'mentl], **elementary** [eli'men tri], *a.* élémentaire.

elephant ['elifənt], *n.* éléphant, *m.*

elephantine [eli'fæntain], *a.* éléphantin.

elevate ['eliveit], *v.t.* élever; hausser, exalter, exciter.

elevation [eli'veiʃən], *n.* élévation; hauteur, altitude, *f.*

elevator [eli'veitə], *n.* (*Anat. etc.*) élévateur; (*Am.*) [LIFT].

eleven [i'levn], *a.* onze; *the eleven,* les apôtres, *m.pl.*; (*Spt.*) le onze, *m.*

eleventh [i'levnθ], *a.* onzième; onze (*roi etc.*). —*n.* onzième (*fraction*), *m.*

elf [elf], *n.* (*pl.* **elves** [elvz]) esprit follet, lutin, elfe, *m.*

elfin ['elfin], *a.* des lutins, des elfes.—*n.* gamin, bambin, *m.*

elicit [i'lisit], *v.t.* faire sortir, tirer (*de*); déduire, découvrir, faire avouer (*à*).

elide [i'laid], *v.t.* (*Gram.*) élider.—*v.i.* s'élider.

eligible ['elidʒibl], *a.* éligible; convenable (*pour*); acceptable.

eliminate [i'limineit], *v.t.* éliminer, supprimer.

eliminating [i'limineitiŋ], *a.* éliminateur, éliminatoire.

elimination [ilimi'neiʃən], *n.* élimination, *f.*

elision [i'liʒən], *n.* élision, *f.*

elixir [i'liksə], *n.* élixir, *m.*

Elizabeth [i'lizəbəθ]. Élisabeth, *f.*

elk [elk], *n.* (*Zool.*) élan, *m.*

ell [el], *n.* aune, *f.*

Ellen ['elin]. Hélène, *f.*

ellipse [i'lips], *n.* ellipse, *f.*

elliptic [i'liptik], **elliptical** [i'liptikəl], *a.* elliptique.

elm [elm], *n.* orme, *m.*

elocution [elo'kju:ʃən], *n.* élocution, diction, *f.*

elocutionist [elo'kju:ʃənist], *n.* déclamateur, *m.*

elongate ['i:lɔŋgeit], *v.t.* allonger, prolonger.

elongation [i:lɔŋ'geiʃən], *n.* allongement, prolongement, *m.*; (*Surg.*) élongation, *f.*

elope [i'loup], *v.i.* s'enfuir (*avec un amant*).

elopement [i'loupmənt], *n.* fuite, *f.*, enlèvement, *m.*

eloquence ['eləkwəns], *n.* éloquence, *f.*

eloquent ['eləkwənt], *a.* éloquent.

eloquently ['eləkwəntli], *adv.* éloquemment.

else [els], *adv.* autrement, ou bien, ailleurs.— *a.* autre; *anywhere else,* n'importe où ailleurs; *everything else,* tout le reste; *nobody else,* personne d'autre; *nothing*

else, rien d'autre; *someone* (*somebody*) *else,* quelqu'un d'autre.

elsewhere ['elsweə], *adv.* ailleurs, autre part.

Elsie ['elsi]. Élise, *f.*

elucidate [i'lju:sideit], *v.t.* expliquer, éclaircir, élucider.

elucidation [ilju:si'deiʃən], *n.* éclaircissement, *m.*, élucidation, explication, *f.*

elude [i'lju:d], *v.t.* éluder, éviter, échapper à.

elusion [i'lju:ʒən], *n.* subterfuge, *m.*, réponse évasive, *f.*

elusive [i'lju:siv], *a.* artificieux (*réponse*); fuyant, insaisissable (*personne*).

elves [ELF].

emaciate [i'meiʃieit], *v.t.* amaigrir.—*v.i.* maigrir, s'amaigrir.

emaciated [i'meiʃieitid], *a.* amaigri, maigre, décharné.

emaciation [imeiʃi'eiʃən], *n.* amaigrissement, *m.*, maigreur, *f.*

emanate ['eməneit], *v.i.* émaner.

emancipate [i'mænsipeit], *v.t.* affranchir, émanciper (*de*).

emancipation [imænsi'peiʃən], *n.* affranchissement, *m.*, émancipation, *f.*

emasculate [i'mæskjuleit], *v.t.* châtrer; (*fig.*) affaiblir, efféminer.

embalm [im'ba:m], *v.t.* embaumer.

embalmer [im'ba:mə], *n.* embaumeur, *m.*

embalming [im'ba:miŋ], *n.* embaumement, *m.*

embank [im'bæŋk], *v.t.* endiguer, remblayer; encaisser (*canal etc.*).

embankment [im'bæŋkmənt], *n.* levée, *f.*; terrassement, talus; (*Rail.*) remblai; quai (*rivière, canal*), *m.*

embarcation [EMBARKATION].

embargo [im'ba:gou], *n.* embargo, *m.*—*v.t.* mettre l'embargo sur; défendre, interdire.

embark [im'ba:k], *v.t.* embarquer.—*v.i.* s'embarquer (*sur*); (*fig.*) s'engager (*dans*).

embarkation or **embarcation** [emba:'kei ʃən], *n.* embarquement, *m.*

embarrass [im'bærəs], *v.t.* embarrasser, gêner.

embarrassment [im'bærəsmənt], *n.* embarras, *m.*; (*fig.*) perplexité; gêne (*manque d'argent*), *f.*

embassy ['embəsi], *n.* ambassade, *f.*

embellish [im'beliʃ], *v.t.* embellir, orner (*avec*).

embellishment [im'beliʃmənt] *n.* embellissement, ornement, *m.*

ember ['embə], *n.* braise, cendre ardente, *f.*

embezzle [im'bezl], *v.t.* détourner; s'approprier frauduleusement (*des fonds*).

embezzlement [im'bezlmənt], *n.* détournement, *m.*

embezzler [im'bezlə], *n.* détourneur (*de fonds*), *m.*

embitter [im'bitə], *v.t.* rendre amer; (*fig.*) empoisonner; aigrir.

emblazon [im'bleizn], *v.t.* blasonner (*de*); (*fig.*) publier, proclamer.

emblem ['embləm], *n.* emblème, *m.*; (*Her.*) devise, *f.*

embodiment [im'bɔdimənt], *n.* incarnation; personnification; (*Mil.*) incorporation, *f.*

embody [im'bɔdi], *v.t.* incarner; (*Mil. etc.*) incorporer (*dans*); (*fig.*) personnifier.

embolden [im'bouldn], *v.t.* enhardir.

emboss [im'bɔs]. *v.t.* bosseler, relever en bosse; gaufrer (*papier*).

encyclopaedic

embossing [im'bɔsiŋ], *n.* bosselage; gaufrage, *m.*

embrace [im'breis], *n.* embrassement, *m.*, étreinte, *f.*—*v.t.* embrasser, étreindre; (*fig.*) accepter; comprendre.

embrocation [embrə'keiʃən], *n.* embrocation, *f.*

embroider [im'brɔidə], *v.t.* broder.

embroidery [im'brɔidəri], *n.* broderie, *f.*

embroil [im'brɔil], *v.t.* brouiller, embrouiller.

embryo ['embriou], *n.* embryon, germe, *m.*

emend [i'mend], *v.t.* corriger; (*Law*) émender.

emendation [i:men'deiʃən], *n.* correction, émendation, *f.*

emerald ['emərəld], *n.* émeraude, *f.*

emerge [i'mə:dʒ], *v.i.* surgir; sortir (*de*); ressortir.

emergency [i'mə:dʒənsi], *n.* circonstance critique; crise, *f.*, cas imprévu, *m.*; *in case of emergency*, en cas d'urgence; *emergency exit*, sortie de secours, *f.*

emery ['eməri], *n.* émeri, *m.*; *emery cloth*, toile d'émeri, *f.*

emetic [i'metik], *n.* émétique, *m.*

emigrant ['emigrənt], *n.* émigrant; (*Fr. Hist.*) émigré, *m.*

emigrate ['emigreit], *v.i.* émigrer.

emigration [emi'greiʃən], *n.* émigration, *f.*

Emily ['emili], Émilie, *f.*

eminence ['eminəns], *n.* éminence, colline; (*fig.*) grandeur, distinction, *f.*

eminent ['eminənt], *a.* éminent; distingué, illustre.

eminently ['eminəntli], *adv.* éminemment, par excellence.

emissary ['emisəri], *n.* émissaire, messager, *m.*

emission [i'miʃən], *n.* émission, *f.*

emit [i'mit], *v.t.* jeter; exhaler, dégager; (*Fin.*) émettre.

emolument [i'mɔljumənt], *n.* (*usu. pl.*) émoluments, *m.pl.*, rémunération, *f.*; (*fig.*) profit, *m.*

emotion [i'mouʃən], *n.* émotion, *f.*

emotional [i'mouʃənəl], *a.* porté à l'émotion, émotif.

emperor ['empərə], *n.* empereur, *m.*

emphasis ['emfəsis], *n.* (*pl.* **emphases** ['emfəsi:z]) force, énergie, emphase, *f.*; accent, *m.*

emphasize ['emfəsaiz], *v.t.* appuyer sur; accentuer, souligner.

emphatic [im'fætik], *a.* fort, énergique; expressif; accentué, emphatique; (*fig.*) positif.

emphatically [im'fætikəli], *adv.* avec force, énergiquement; positivement.

empire ['empaiə], *n.* empire, *m.*

empiric [em'pirik], *n.* empirique; charlatan, *m.*—*a.* (*also* **empirical** [em'pirikəl]) empirique, guidé par l'expérience.

employ [im'plɔi], *v.t.* employer; se servir de. —*n.* emploi, *m.*; occupation, *f.*

employee [im'plɔii:], *n.* employé, *m.*

employer [im'plɔiə], *n.* patron; employeur, *m.*

employment [im'plɔimənt], *n.* emploi, *m.*, occupation, *f.*

emporium [em'pɔ:riəm], *n.* entrepôt; (*fam.*) grand magasin, *m.*

empower [em'pauə], *v.t.* autoriser (*à*), mettre à même (*de*).

empress ['empris], *n.* impératrice, *f.*

emptiness ['emptinis], *n.* vide, *m.*; (*fig.*) vanité, *f.*, néant, *m.*

empty ['empti], *a.* vide, à vide; désert (*rues etc.*); (*fig.*) vain, stérile.—*v.t.* vider, décharger.—*v.i.* se vider.

emu ['i:mju:], *n.* (*Orn.*) émeu, *m.*

emulate ['emjuleit], *v.t.* rivaliser avec; imiter.

emulation [emju'leiʃən], *n.* émulation, rivalité, *f.*

emulsion [i'mʌlʃən], *n.* émulsion, *f.*

enable [i'neibl], *v.t.* mettre à même (*de*); mettre en état (*de*); permettre (*de*).

enact [i'nækt], *v.t.* ordonner, arrêter; rendre (*loi*); jouer, faire (*un rôle*).

enactment [i'næktmənt], *n.* loi, ordonnance, *f.*, décret, *m.*

enamel [i'næml], *n.* émail, *m.*—*v.t.* émailler (*de*).—*v.i.* peindre en émail.

enamelling [i'næməliŋ], *n.* émaillure, *f.*; émaillage, *m.*

enamour [i'næmə], *v.t.* (*used now only in p.p.*) *to be enamoured of*, être épris de.

encamp [in'kæmp], *v.t.*, *v.i.* camper.

encase [in'keis], *v.t.* encaisser, enfermer.

enchain [in'tʃein], *v.t.* enchaîner.

enchant [in'tʃɑ:nt], *v.t.* enchanter; (*fig.*) charmer, ravir (*de*).

enchanter [in'tʃɑ:ntə], *n.* enchanteur, *m.*

enchanting [in'tʃɑ:ntiŋ], *a.* enchanteur, ravissant, charmant.

enchantment [in'tʃɑ:ntmənt], *n.* enchantement, charme, *m.*, fascination, *f.*

enchantress [in'tʃɑ:ntris], *n.* enchanteresse, *f.*

encircle [in'sə:kl], *v.t.* ceindre, entourer (*de*), encercler.

enclose [in'klouz], *v.t.* enclore; entourer, environner; renfermer; envoyer sous le même pli (*lettre etc.*).

enclosed [in'klouzd], *a.* entouré, environné; inclus, ci-inclus, sous ce pli (*paquet, lettre etc.*).

enclosure [in'klouʒə], *n.* clôture; enceinte (*espace clos*), *f.*; contenu (*objet renfermé*), *m.*

encomium [en'koumjəm], *n.* éloge, *m.*, louange, *f.*

encompass [in'kʌmpəs], *v.t.* entourer, environner; renfermer.

encore [ɔŋ'kɔ:], *n.* and *int.* bis.—*v.t.* bisser.

encounter [in'kauntə], *n.* rencontre, *f.*; combat, *m.*, lutte, *f.*—*v.t.* rencontrer, aborder; (*fig.*) éprouver, essuyer.

encourage [in'kʌridʒ], *v.t.* encourager.

encouragement [in'kʌridʒmənt], *n.* encouragement, *m.*

encroach [in'kroutʃ], *v.i.* empiéter (*sur*); abuser (*de*).

encroachment [in'kroutʃmənt], *n.* empiétement, *m.*, usurpation, *f.*

encumber [in'kʌmbə], *v.t.* encombrer, accabler, embarrasser (*de*); grever (*un héritage*).

encumbrance [in'kʌmbrəns], *n.* encombrement, embarras, *m.*; (*Law*) hypothèque, *f.*

encyclopaedia [insaiklə'pi:diə], *n.* encyclopédie, *f.*

encyclopaedic [insaiklə'pi:dik], *a.* encyclopédique.

end

end [end], *n.* fin; extrémité, *f.*, bout; but, objet; (*fig.*) dessein, *m.*, issue, *f.*; *at an end*, fini, terminé; *big end*, (*Motor.*) tête de bielle, *f.*; *from end to end*, d'un bout à l'autre; *in the end*, à la fin; *three days on end*, trois jours de suite; *to be at a loose end*, être désœuvré, se trouver sans avoir rien à faire; *to draw to an end*, tirer *ou* toucher à sa fin; *to make an end of*, en finir avec; *to make both ends meet*, joindre les deux bouts.—*v.t.* finir, terminer, achever.—*v.i.* finir, se terminer (*en*); cesser (*de*); aboutir (*à*).

endanger [in'deindʒə], *v.t.* mettre en danger, compromettre, risquer.

endear [in'diə], *v.t.* rendre cher (*à*).

endearing [in'diəriŋ], *a.* tendre, affectueux.

endearment [in'diəmənt], *n.* charme, *m.*; (*pl.*) caresses, *f.pl.*

endeavour [in'devə], *n.* effort, *m.*, tentative, *f.* —*v.i.* tâcher, essayer, tenter (*de*), chercher (*à*).

ending ['endiŋ], *n.* fin, conclusion; (*Gram.*) terminaison, *f.*

endive ['endiv], *n.* chicorée, *f.*

endless ['endlis], *a.* sans fin, éternel, perpétuel, interminable.

endlessly ['endlisli], *adv.* à l'infini, sans cesse.

endorse [in'dɔːs], *v.t.* endosser; viser (*passeport*); (*fig.*) sanctionner, approuver.

endorsement [in'dɔːsmənt], *n.* suscription, *f.*; (*Comm.*) endossement (*signature au dos*); visa (*de passeport*), *m.*; (*fig.*) sanction, *f.*

endow [in'dau], *v.t.* doter (*de*); (*fig.*) douer (*de*).

endowment [in'daumənt], *n.* dotation, *f.*

endurable [in'djuərəbl], *a.* supportable, endurable.

endurance [in'djuərəns], *n.* endurance; souffrance, patience, *f.*

endure [in'djuə], *v.t.* supporter, souffrir, endurer.—*v.i.* durer; endurer, souffrir.

enduring [in'djuəriŋ], *a.* endurant, qui endure, patient; durable, qui dure (*permanent*).

endways ['endweiz], **endwise** ['endwaiz], *adv.* debout, de champ; bout à bout (*horizontalement*).

enema ['enimə, i'niːmə], *n.* lavement, *m.*

enemy ['enəmi], *n.* ennemi, *m.*

energetic [enə'dʒetik], *a.* énergique.

energy ['enədʒi], *n.* énergie, *f.*

enervate ['enəveit], *v.t.* affaiblir, énerver.

enfeeble [in'fiːbl], *v.t.* affaiblir.

enfold [in'fould], *v.t.* envelopper.

enforce [in'fɔːs], *v.t.* donner de la force à; faire respecter; faire exécuter; forcer.

enforcement [in'fɔːsmənt], *n.* mise en vigueur, exécution, *f.*

enfranchise [in'fræntʃaiz], *v.t.* affranchir (*un esclave*); donner le droit de vote à.

enfranchisement [in'fræntʃizmənt], *n.* affranchissement, *m.*; admission au suffrage, *f.*

engage [in'geidʒ], *v.t.* engager; retenir, prendre (*réserver*); louer (*prendre à louage*); arrêter (*un marché*); occuper (*attention etc.*); (*fig.*) en venir aux mains avec.—*v.i.* s'engager (*à*); livrer combat.

engaged [in'geidʒd], *a.* fiancé (*futur époux*);

occupé (*pris par le travail*); pas libre (*téléphone, cabinets*); aux prises (*combat*).

engagement [in'geidʒmənt], *n.* engagement, *m.*; occupation, *f.*; fiançailles, *f.pl.*; combat, *m.*

engaging [in'geidʒiŋ], *a.* engageant, attrayant.

engender [in'dʒendə], *v.t.* engendrer, faire naître, causer.

engine [in'dʒin], *n.* machine, *f.*, moteur, *m.*; (*Rail.*) locomotive, *f.*; *fire-engine*, pompe à incendie, *f.*; *steam-engine*, machine à vapeur.

engine-driver ['endʒindraivə], *n.* (*Rail.*) mécanicien, *m.*

engineer [endʒi'niə], *n.* ingénieur, *m.*; (*Manuf.*) constructeur-mécanicien; (*Mil.*) soldat du génie; (*pl.*) le génie, *m.*

engineering [endʒi'niəriŋ], *n.* art de l'ingénieur, *m.*; *civil engineering*, génie civil, *m.*; *electrical engineering*, technique électrique, *f.*

England ['iŋglənd], *n.* l'Angleterre, *f.*

English ['iŋgliʃ], *a.* anglais; de l'Angleterre; *the English Channel*, la Manche, *f.*—*n.* anglais (*langue*), *m.*; *the English*, les Anglais, *m.pl.*

Englishman ['iŋgliʃmən], *n.* (*pl.* **-men** [men]) Anglais, *m.*

Englishwoman ['iŋgliʃwumən], *n.* (*pl.* **-women** [wimin]) Anglaise, *f.*

engrave [in'greiv], *v.t.* graver.

engraver [in'greivə], *n.* graveur, *m.*

engraving [in'greiviŋ], *n.* gravure; *copperplate engraving*, taille-douce, *f.*

engross [in'grous], *v.t.* grossoyer (*copier*); accaparer (*monopoliser*); absorber, occuper (*l'esprit*).

engulf [in'gʌlf], *v.t.* engouffrer; (*fig.*) engloutir.

enhance [in'haːns], *v.t.* enchérir, renchérir; (*fig.*) rehausser.

enhancement [in'haːnsmənt], *n.* hausse, *f.*; (*fig.*) rehaussement, *m.*

enigma [i'nigmə], *n.* énigme, *f.*

enigmatic [enig'mætik], **enigmatical** [enig'mætikəl], *a.* énigmatique, obscur.

enjoin [in'dʒɔin], *v.t.* enjoindre; prescrire (*à*).

enjoy [in'dʒɔi], *v.t.* jouir de, posséder; goûter; *to enjoy oneself*, s'amuser.

enjoyable [in'dʒɔiəbl], *a.* agréable.

enjoyment [in'dʒɔimənt], *n.* jouissance (*de*) *f.*; plaisir, *m.*

enkindle [in'kindl], *v.t.* enflammer; (*fig.*) exciter.

enlace [in'leis], *v.t.* enlacer.

enlarge [in'laːdʒ], *v.t.* agrandir, étendre, dilater.—*v.i.* grandir, s'agrandir.

enlargement [in'laːdʒmənt], *n.* agrandissement (*also Phot.*), *m.*; augmentation, *f.*

enlighten [in'laitn], *v.t.* éclairer; (*fig.*) éclaircir.

enlightenment [in'laitnmənt], *n.* éclaircissement, *m.*; lumières, *f.pl.*

enlist [in'list], *v.t.* enrôler, engager.—*v.i.* s'engager.

enlistment [in'listmənt], *n.* engagement, enrôlement, *m.*

enliven [in'laivn], *v.t.* égayer, animer.

enmity ['enmiti], *n.* inimitié; animosité, haine, hostilité, *f.*

ennoble [i'noubl], *v.t.* anoblir; (*fig.*) ennoblir.

ennoblement [i'noublmənt], *n.* anoblissement; (*fig.*) ennoblissement, *m.*

enormity [i'nɔːmiti], **enormousness** [i'nɔːməsnis], *n.* énormité, *f.*

enormous [i'nɔːməs], *a.* énorme; (*fig.*) atroce, monstrueux.

enormously [i'nɔːməsli], *adv.* énormément.

enough [i'nʌf], *a.* and *adv.* assez; *large enough*, assez grand; *more than enough*, plus qu'il n'en faut.

enquire [INQUIRE].

enrage [in'reidʒ], *v.t.* faire enrager; exaspérer.

enrapture [in'ræptʃə], *v.t.* transporter, ravir.

enrich [in'ritʃ], *v.t.* enrichir.

enrichment [in'ritʃmənt], *n.* enrichissement, *m.*

enrol [in'roul], *v.t.* enrôler, enregistrer, inscrire.—*v.i.* s'enrôler, se faire inscrire.

enrolment [in'roulmənt], *n.* enrôlement, *m.*, inscription, *f.*

ensconce [in'skɔns], *v.t.* cacher; *to ensconce oneself*, se cacher (*dans*), se blottir.

enshrine [in'ʃrain], *v.t.* enchâsser (*dans*).

enshroud [in'ʃraud], *v.t.* mettre dans un linceul; (*fig.*) couvrir.

ensign ['ensain, (R. *Navy*) 'ensin], *n.* enseigne, *f.*, drapeau; (*Mil.*) porte-drapeau (*personne*), *m.*

enslave [in'sleiv], *v.t.* asservir; (*fig.*) captiver.

ensnare [in'snɛə], *v.t.* prendre au piège; (*fig.*) attraper séduire.

ensue [in'sjuː], *v.i.* s'ensuivre.

ensuing [in'sjuːiŋ], *a.* suivant; prochain.

ensure [in'ʃuə], *v.t.* assurer; garantir.

entail [en'teil], *v.t.* substituer (*à*); (*fig.*) entraîner; impliquer.

entangle [in'tæŋgl], *v.t.* emmêler; enchevêtrer; empêtrer (*les pieds*); (*fig.*) embrouiller.

entanglement [in'tæŋglmənt], *n.* embrouillement, embarras, *m.*

enter ['entə], *v.t.* entrer dans, pénétrer; inscrire (*nom etc.*); enregistrer (*paquet*).—*v.i.* entrer; s'engager (*dans*).

enteritis [entə'raitis], *n.* entérite, *f.*

enterprise ['entəpraiz], *n.* entreprise, hardiesse, *f.*; esprit d'entreprise, *m.*

entertain [entə'tein], *v.t.* recevoir (*des invités*); divertir, amuser (*distraire*); concevoir (*idée etc.*); accepter (*proposition*).—*v.i.* recevoir (*invités*).

entertainer [entə'teinə], *n.* (*Theat. etc.*) diseur, *m.*, diseuse, *f.*, comique, *m.*, *f.*; hôte, *m.*, hôtesse, *f.*

entertainment [entə'teinmənt], *n.* hospitalité, *f.*; accueil (*reception*); festin, *m.*, fête, *f.*; divertissement, spectacle (*amusement*), *m.*

enthrall [in'θrɔːl], *v.t.* asservir, assujettir; (*fig.*) ravir.

enthuse [in'θjuːz], *v.i.* s'enthousiasmer de *ou* pour.

enthusiasm [in'θjuːziæzm], *n.* enthousiasme, *m.*

enthusiast [in'θjuːziæst], *n.* enthousiaste, *m.*, *f.*

enthusiastic [inθjuːzi'æstik], *a.* enthousiaste.

entice [in'tais], *v.t.* attirer; entraîner (*dans*); séduire (*à*).

enticement [in'taismənt], *n.* appât, charme, *m.*; tentation, *f.*

enticer [in'taisə], *n.* tentateur, séducteur, *m.*

enticing [in'taisiŋ], *a.* séduisant, attrayant, tentant.

entire [in'taiə], *a.* entier, complet.

entirely [in'taiəli], *adv.* entièrement, complètement, tout entier.

entirety [in'taiəti], *n.* totalité, intégrité, *f.*

entitle [in'taitl], *v.t.* intituler, appeler; donner droit à.

entity ['entiti], *n.* entité, *f.*, être de raison, *m.*

entomb [in'tuːm], *v.t.* ensevelir.

entrails ['entreilz], *n.pl.* entrailles, *f.pl.*

entrance (1) ['entrəns], *n.* entrée, *f.*; commencement, début (*de carrière*), *m.*; (*fig.*) initiation, *f.*

entrance (2) [in'trɑːns], *v.t.* extasier; ravir.

entrancing [in'trɑːnsiŋ], *a.* prenant; ravissant.

entrant ['entrənt], *n.* inscrit (*de concours*), *m.*; inscrite, *f.*; débutant (*dans une profession nouvelle*), *m.*, débutante, *f.*

entrap [in'træp], *v.t.* prendre au piège, attraper (*dans*).

entreat [in'triːt], *v.t.* supplier, prier instamment (*de*).

entreaty [in'triːti], *n.* prière; supplication; (*pl.*) sollicitation, *f.*, instances, *f.pl.*

entrust [in'trʌst], *v.t.* charger (*de*).

entry ['entri], *n.* entrée; inscription (*enregistrement*); (*Book-keeping*) écriture, *f.*, article, *m.*; (*Customs*) déclaration d'entrée, *f.*; *no entry*, sens interdit, passage interdit.

entwine [in'twain], *v.t.* enlacer, entortiller.—*v.i.* s'enlacer, s'entortiller.

enumerate [i'njuːməreit], *v.t.* énumérer, dénombrer.

enunciate [i'nʌnsieit], *v.t.* énoncer; prononcer.—*v.i.* articuler.

envelop [in'veləp], *v.t.* envelopper (*de ou dans*).

envelope ['enviloup, 'ɔnviloup], *n.* enveloppe, *f.*

envenom [in'venəm], *v.t.* envenimer; exaspérer (*aigrir*).

envious ['enviəs], *a.* envieux (*de*).

environ [in'vaiərən], *v.t.* environner (*de*).

environment [in'vaiərənmənt], *n.* milieu, entourage, environnement, *m.*

environs [in'vaiərənz], *n.pl.* environs, *m.pl.*

envisage [in'vizidʒ], *v.t.* envisager.

envoy ['envɔi], *n.* envoyé, *m.*

envy ['envi], *n.* envie, *f.*—*v.t.* envier, porter envie à.

epaulet(te) ['epɔːlet], *n.* épaulette, *f.*

ephemeral [i'femərəl], *a.* éphémère.

epic ['epik], *a.* épique; (*fig.*) légendaire.—*n.* épopée, *f.*, poème épique, *m.*

epicure ['epikjuə], *n.* gourmet, *m.*, gastronome, *m.*, *f.*

epidemic [epi'demik], *a.* épidémique.—*n.* épidémie, *f.*

epigram ['epigræm], *n.* épigramme, *f.*

epilepsy ['epilepsi], *n.* épilepsie, *f.*

epileptic [epi'leptik], *a.* and *n.* épileptique, *m.*, *f.*

epilogue ['epilɔg], *n.* épilogue, *m.*

episcopacy [i'piskəpəsi], *n.* épiscopat, *m.*

episcopal [i'piskəpəl], *a.* épiscopal.

episode ['episoud], *n.* épisode, *m.*

epistle [i'pisl], *n.* épître, *f.*

epitaph ['epitɑːf], *n.* épitaphe, *f.*

epithet ['epiθet], *n.* épithète, *f.*

epitome

epitome [i'pitəmi], *n.* épitomé, abrégé, précis, *m.*

epitomize [i'pitəmaiz], *v.t.* faire un abrégé de; être une image en petit de.

epoch ['i:pɔk], *n.* époque, *f.*

equable ['ekwəbl], *a.* uniforme, égal.

equal ['i:kwəl], *a.* égal; (*fig.*) impartial, juste; *equal to*, de force à, à la hauteur de.—*n.* égal, *m.*, égale, *f.*; (*pl.*) pareils, égaux, *m.pl.*—*v.t.* égaler, être égal à.

equality [i'kwɔliti], *n.* égalité, *f.*

equalize ['i:kwəlaiz], *v.t.* égaliser; compenser.

equally ['i:kwəli], *adv.* également, pareillement.

equanimity [i:kwə'nimiti], *n.* égalité d'âme, équanimité, *f.*

equation [i'kwei∫ən], *n.* équation, *f.*

equator [i'kweitə], *n.* équateur, *m.*

equatorial [ekwə'tɔːriəl], *a.* équatorial, de l'équateur.

equerry ['ekwəri], *n.* écuyer, *m.*

equestrian [i'kwestriən], *a.* équestre.—*n.* cavalier; (*Circus*) écuyer, *m.*

equilibrium [i:kwi'libriəm], *n.* équilibre, *m.*

equine ['i:kwain, 'ekwain], *a.* du cheval, équin.

equinox ['i:kwinɔks], *n.* équinoxe, *m.*

equip [i'kwip], *v.t.* équiper; (*Tech.*) outiller.

equipment [i'kwipmənt], *n.* équipement, matériel outillage, *m.*

equitable ['ekwitəbl], *a.* équitable, juste.

equity ['ekwiti], *n.* équité, justice, *f.*

equivalent [i'kwivələnt], *a.* équivalent (*à*); *to be equivalent to*, être équivalent à, équivaloir à.—*n.* équivalent, *m.*

equivocal [i'kwivəkl], *a.* équivoque, ambigu.

equivocate [i'kwivəkeit], *v.i.* user d'équivoque, équivoquer.

era ['iərə], *n.* ère, *f.*

eradicate [i'rædikeit], *v.t.* déraciner; (*fig.*) exterminer.

erase [i'reiz], *v.t.* raturer, effacer, rayer.

eraser [i'reizə], *n.* grattoir, *m.*, gomme à effacer, *f.*

erasure [i'reiʒə], *n.* grattage, *m.*, rature, *f.*

***ere** [eə], *conj.* avant que; plutôt que.—*prep.* avant.

erect [i'rekt], *a.* debout, droit, élevé.—*v.t.* ériger, dresser; (*fig.*) établir.

erection [i'rek∫ən], *n.* construction, érection, élévation; (*fig.*) fondation, *f.*

ermine ['ə:min], *a.* d'hermine.—*n.* hermine, *f.*

erode [i'roud], *v.t.* éroder, ronger.

erosion [i'rouʒən], *n.* érosion, *f.*

erotic [i'rotik], *a.* érotique.

err [ə:], *v.i.* s'écarter, s'égarer (*de*); (*fig.*) se tromper.

errand ['erənd], *n.* message, *m.*, commission, course, *f.*

errand-boy ['erəndbɔi], *n.* petit commissionnaire; saute-ruisseau (*de bureau*), chasseur (*dans un restaurant*), *m.*

erratic [i'rætik], *a.* erratique; errant, excentrique; irrégulier; inégal.

erroneous [i'rouniəs], *a.* erroné, faux.

erroneously [i'rouniəsli], *adv.* à faux, à tort.

error ['erə], *n.* erreur, faute, *f.*, écart, *m.*

erudite ['erudait], *a.* érudit, savant.

erudition [eru'di∫ən], *n.* érudition, *f.*

erupt [i'rʌpt], *v.i.* faire éruption (*volcan*); percer (*dent*).

eruption [i'rʌp∫ən], *n.* éruption, *f.*

erysipelas [eri'sipiləs], *n.* érysipèle, *m.*

escalade [eskə'leid], *n.* escalade, *f.*—*v.t.* escalader.

escalate ['eskəleit], *v.i.* escalader.

escalation [eskə'lei∫ən], *n.* escalade, *f.*

escalator ['eskəleitə], *n.* escalier roulant, *m.*

escapade [eskə'peid], *n.* escapade, *f.*

escape [is'keip], *n.* évasion; fuite (*gaz*); (*fig.*) délivrance, *f.*; *fire-escape*, échelle de sauvetage, *f.*; *to have a narrow escape*, l'échapper belle.—*v.t.* échapper à; éviter.—*v.i.* (s')échapper; s'évader (*de prison*).

escarpment [is'kɑ:pmənt], *n.* escarpement, talus, *m.*

eschew [is't∫u:], *v.t.* éviter; renoncer à.

escort [is'kɔ:t], *v.t.* escorter.—['eskɔ:t], *n.* escorte, *f.*; cavalier, *m.*

escutcheon [is'kʌt∫ən], *n.* écusson, *m.*

Eskimo ['eskimou], *a.* esquimau.—*n.* Esquimau (*personne*), *m.*

especial [is'pe∫əl], *a.* spécial, particulier.

especially [is'pe∫əli], *adv.* spécialement, surtout.

esplanade [esplə'neid], *n.* esplanade, promenade, *f.*

espouse [is'pauz], *v.t.* épouser; (*fig.*) adopter.

espy [is'pai], *v.t.* apercevoir, aviser, épier.

essay ['esei], *n.* essai; effort, *m.*; (*Sch.*) composition, dissertation, *f.*—[e'sei], *v.t.* essayer (*de*).

essence ['esəns], *n.* essence, *f.*

essential [i'sen∫əl], *a.* essentiel.—*n.* (*also pl.*) essentiel, *m.*

essentially [i'sen∫əli], *adv.* essentiellement.

establish [is'tæbli∫], *v.t.* établir, fonder; (*fig.*) confirmer; prouver.

establishment [is'tæbli∫mənt], *n.* établissement, *m.*; maison; (*fig.*) confirmation, *f.*

estate [is'teit], *n.* état, rang (*condition*), *m.*; propriété, *f.*, bien (*immeuble*), *m.*

estate-agent [is'teiteidʒənt], *n.* agent immobilier, *m.*

estate duty [is'teitdju:ti], *n.* droits de succession, *m.pl.*

esteem [is'ti:m], *n.* estime, considération, *f.*—*v.t.* estimer, regarder comme.

estimate ['estimit], *n.* évaluation, *f.*, calcul, devis, *m.*; (*fig.*) appréciation, *f.*—['estimeit] *v.t.* estimer, apprécier; évaluer, calculer.

Estonia [es'touniə]. l'Esthonie, *f.*

Estonian [es'touniən], *a.* esthonien.—*n.* esthonien (*langue*); Esthonien (*personne*), *m.*

estrange [is'treindʒ], *v.t.* aliéner, éloigner (*de*).

estrangement [is'treindʒmənt], *n.* aliénation, *f.*, éloignement, *m.*, brouille, *f.*

estuary ['estjuəri], *n.* estuaire, *m.*

etching ['et∫iŋ], *n.* gravure à l'eau-forte, *f.*

eternal [i'tə:nl], *a.* and *n.* éternel, *m.*

eternity [i'tə:niti], *n.* éternité, *f.*

ether ['i:θə], *n.* éther, *m.*

ethereal [i'θiəriəl], *a.* éthéré; céleste.

ethic ['eθik], **ethical** ['eθikəl], *a.* éthique; moral.

ethics ['eθiks], *n.pl.* morale, éthique, *f.*

Ethiopia [i:θi'oupiə]. l'Éthiopie, *f.*

Ethiopian [i:θi'oupiən], *a.* éthiopien.—*n.* Éthiopien (*personne*), *m.*

etiquette ['etiket], *n.* étiquette, *f.*, convenances, *f.pl.*

Etruria [i'truəriə]. l'Étrurie, *f.*

Etruscan [i'trʌskən], *a.* étrusque.—*n.* étrusque (*langue*); Étrusque (*personne*), *m., f.*
etymology [eti'mɒlədʒi], *n.* étymologie, *f.*
eucharist ['juːkərist], *n.* eucharistie, *f.*
eulogium [juː'loudʒiəm], **eulogy** ['juːlədʒi], *n.* éloge, panégyrique, *m.*
eulogize ['juːlədʒaiz], *v.t.* louer, faire l'éloge de.
eunuch ['juːnək], *n.* eunuque, *m.*
euphemism ['juːfimizm], *n.* euphémisme, *m.*
euphony ['juːfəni], *n.* euphonie, *f.*
Eurasian [juə'reiʒən], *a.* eurasien.—*n.* Eurasien (*personne*), *m.*
Europe ['juərəp]. l'Europe, *f.*
European [juərə'piːən], *a.* européen.—*n.* Européen (*personne*), *m.*
euthanasia [juːθə'neiziə], *n.* euthanasie, *f.*
evacuate [i'vækjueit], *v.t.* évacuer.
evacuation [ivækju'eiʃən], *n.* évacuation, *f.*
evade [i'veid], *v.t.* éluder, esquiver, éviter, se soustraire à; échapper à, déjouer (*la loi*).
evaluate [i'væljueit], *v.t.* évaluer.
evaporate [i'væpəreit], *v.t.* faire évaporer.—*v.i.* s'évaporer.
evaporation [ivæpə'reiʃən], *n.* évaporation, *f.*
evasion [i'veiʒən], *n.* subterfuge, *m.*; échappatoire, défaite, *f.*
eve [iːv], *n.* veille, *f.*; **on the eve of**, à la veille de.
even (1) [iːvn], *n.* (*Poet.*) soir, *m.*
even (2) [iːvn], *a.* égal; régulier (*respiration, pouls*); uni (*lisse*); de niveau (*avec*); pair (*numéro*).—*adv.* même, aussi bien; précisément.—*v.t.* égaler, égaliser; niveler.
evening ['iːvniŋ], *a.* du soir; **evening dress**, tenue de soirée, *f.*—*n.* soir, *m.*; soirée, *f.*; (*fig.*) déclin, *m.*
evenly ['iːvnli], *adv.* également; de niveau; (*fig.*) impartialement.
evenness ['iːvnnis], *n.* égalité; régularité; sérénité, *f.*
evensong ['iːvnsɒŋ], *n.* chant du soir, *m.*, vêpres, *m.pl.*
event [i'vent], *n.* événement, *m.*; issue, *f.*; **at all events**, en tout cas, dans tous les cas; **in the event of**, au cas où.
even-tempered ['iːvntempəd], *a.* calme, placide, égal.
eventful [i'ventful], *a.* mouvementé.
eventual [i'ventjuəl], *a.* éventuel, aléatoire; final, définitif.
eventually [i'ventjuəli], *adv.* finalement, à la fin, par la suite.
ever ['evə], *adv.* toujours; jamais; **ever since**, depuis; **for ever**, à jamais.
evergreen ['evəgriːn], *a.* toujours vert.—*n.* arbre toujours vert, *m.*
everlasting [evə'lɑːstiŋ], *a.* éternel, perpétuel.—*n.* éternité, *f.*; éternel, *m.*
everlastingly [evə'lɑːstiŋli], *adv.* éternellement.
evermore ['evəmɔː], *adv.* toujours; éternellement.
every ['evri], *a.* chaque, tout, tous les; **every one**, chacun, *m.*, chacune, *f.*, tous, *pl.*
everybody [EVERYONE].
everyday ['evridei], *a.* quotidien; ordinaire; de tous les jours.
everyone ['evriwʌn], **everybody** ['evribɒdi], *n.* tout le monde, *m.*
everything ['evriθiŋ], *n.* tout, *m.*
everywhere ['evriweə], *adv.* partout.

evict [i'vikt], *v.t.* évincer, expulser.
eviction [i'vikʃən], *n.* éviction, expulsion, *f.*
evidence ['evidəns], *n.* évidence; preuve, *f.*, témoignage; témoin (*personne*), *m.*—*v.t.* montrer, prouver, démontrer.
evident ['evidənt], *a.* évident, visible.
evidently ['evidəntli], *adv.* évidemment.
evil [iːvl], *a.* mauvais; malheureux, malfaisant, méchant (*esprit etc.*).—*n.* mal; malheur, *m.*, calamité, *f.*—*adv.* mal.
evil-doer ['iːvlduə], *n.* malfaiteur, méchant, *m.*
evil-speaking ['iːvlspiːkiŋ], *n.* médisance, *f.*
evince [i'vins], *v.t.* montrer, manifester, démontrer.
evoke [i'vouk], *v.t.* évoquer; susciter.
evolution [iːvə'luːʃən], *n.* évolution, *f.*
evolve [i'vɒlv], *v.t.* dérouler; développer.—*v.i.* se dérouler; se développer.
ewe [juː], *n.* brebis, *f.*
ewer ['juə], *n.* aiguière, *f.*, broc, *m.*
exact [ig'zækt], *v.t.* exiger, extorquer.—*a.* exact, précis.
exaction [ig'zækʃən], *n.* exaction, *f.*
exactitude [ig'zæktitjuːd], **exactness** [ig'zæktnis], *n.* exactitude, *f.*
exactly [ig'zæktli], *adv.* exactement, précisément, au juste; juste.
exaggerate [ig'zædʒəreit], *v.t.* exagérer.
exaggeration [igzædʒə'reiʃən], *n.* exagération, *f.*
exalt [ig'zɔːlt], *v.t.* exalter, élever; (*fig.*) louer.
exaltation [egzɔːl'teiʃən], *n.* exaltation, élévation, *f.*
examination [igzæmi'neiʃən], *n.* examen, *m.*; inspection, vérification, *f.*; (*Law*) interrogatoire (*de prisonniers*), *m.*; audition (*de témoins*), *f.*; **to pass an examination**, réussir à un examen; **to sit (for) an examination**, passer un examen.
examine [ig'zæmin], *v.t.* examiner; visiter; (*Law*) interroger.
examiner [ig'zæminə], *n.* examinateur; (*Law*) juge d'instruction, *m.*
example [ig'zɑːmpl], *n.* exemple, *m.*; **for example**, par exemple.
exasperate [ig'zɑːspəreit], *v.t.* exaspérer; irriter, aigrir.
exasperation [igzɑːspə'reiʃən], *n.* exaspération, irritation, *f.*
excavate ['ekskəveit], *v.t.* creuser, excaver.
excavation [ekskə'veiʃən], *n.* excavation, *f.*; fouilles, *f.pl.*
excavator ['ekskəveitə], *n.* piocheuse-défonceuse, *f.*
exceed [ik'siːd], *v.t.* excéder, dépasser; (*fig.*) surpasser.
exceeding [ik'siːdiŋ], *a.* grand, extrême.
exceedingly [ik'siːdiŋli], *adv.* très, fort, extrêmement.
excel [ik'sel], *v.t.* surpasser, l'emporter sur.—*v.i.* exceller, se distinguer (à).
excellence ['eksələns], *n.* excellence, supériorité, *f.*
excellent ['eksələnt], *a.* excellent.
excellently ['eksələntli], *adv.* excellemment, parfaitement.
except [ik'sept], *v.t.* excepter.—*prep.* excepté, à l'exception de, hors, sauf.—*conj.* à moins que, à moins de.
excepting [ik'septiŋ], *prep.* excepté, hormis.

exception [ik'sepʃən], *n.* exception; objection, *f.*; *to take exception to*, se formaliser de.

exceptionable [ik'sepʃənəbl], *a.* blâmable, à critiquer.

exceptional [ik'sepʃənəl], *a.* exceptionnel.

exceptionally [ik'sepʃənəli], *adv.* exceptionnellement.

excerpt ['eksə:pt], *n.* extrait, *m.*, citation, *f.*

excess [ik'ses], *n.* excès; excédent (*poids*), *m.*

excessive [ik'sesiv], *a.* excessif, extrême; immodéré.

excessively [ik'sesivli], *adv.* excessivement, à l'excès.

exchange [iks'tʃeindʒ], *n.* échange; (*Comm.*) change, *m.*; Bourse (*édifice*), *f.*; *bill of exchange*, lettre de change, *f.*; *rate of exchange*, taux du change, *m.*; *telephone exchange*, central téléphonique, *m.*—*v.t.* échanger, changer (*contre* ou *pour*).

exchequer [iks'tʃekə], *n.* trésor; Ministère des Finances, *m.*

excisable [ek'saizəbl], *a.* imposable; sujet aux droits de l'accise.

excise ['eksaiz], *n.* (*England*) excise, *f.*; (*France*) contributions indirectes, *f.pl.*, régie, *f.*

excise-man ['eksaizmən], *n.* (*pl.* **-men** [men]) préposé *ou* employé de la régie, *m.*

excitable [ik'saitəbl], *a.* excitable, impressionnable.

excite [ik'sait], *v.t.* exciter; irriter; émouvoir; (*fig.*) provoquer.

excitement [ik'saitmənt], *n.* émoi, *m.*, surexcitation; émotion, agitation, *f.*

exciting [ik'saitiŋ], *a.* émouvant, passionnant, palpitant.

exclaim [iks'kleim], *v.i.* s'écrier, se récrier, s'exclamer.

exclamation [eksklə'meiʃən], *n.* exclamation, *f.*, cri, *m.*

exclude [iks'klu:d], *v.t.* exclure (*de*); proscrire.

excluding [iks'klu:diŋ], *prep.* sans compter.

exclusion [iks'klu:ʒən], *n.* exclusion, *f.*

exclusive [iks'klu:siv], *a.* exclusif.

excommunicate [ekskə'mju:nikeit], *v.t.* excommunier.

excrement ['ekskrimənt], *n.* excrément, *m.*

excrescence [iks'kresəns], *n.* excroissance, *f.*

excruciate [iks'kru:ʃieit], *v.t.* tourmenter; torturer.

excruciating [iks'kru:ʃieitiŋ], *a.* atroce, affreux, horrible.

exculpate ['ekskʌlpeit], *v.t.* disculper, justifier.

excursion [iks'kə:ʃən], *n.* excursion, randonnée; (*fig.*) digression, *f.*

excusable [iks'kju:zəbl], *a.* excusable.

excuse [iks'kju:s], *n.* excuse, *f.*; prétexte, *m.*; *to find an excuse*, chercher des excuses; *to make excuses*, s'excuser.—[eks'kju:z], *v.t.* excuser, pardonner; *excuse me!* pardon! *to be excused from duty*, être exempt de service.

execrable ['eksikrəbl], *a.* exécrable.

execrate ['eksikreit], *v.t.* exécrer, maudire.

execute ['eksikju:t], *v.t.* exécuter, accomplir; remplir (*un ordre*); *to execute a deed*, signer un contrat.

execution [eksi'kju:ʃən], *n.* exécution, *f.*; accomplissement, supplice, *m.*

executioner [eksi'kju:ʃənə], *n.* bourreau, *m.*

executive [ig'zekjutiv], *a.* exécutif.—*n.* pouvoir exécutif; (*Comm.*) directeur, *m.*

executor [ig'zekjutə], *n.* exécuteur testamentaire, *m.*

exemplar [ig'zemplə], *n.* modèle, exemplaire, *m.*

exemplary [ig'zempləri], *a.* exemplaire; modèle.

exemplify [ig'zemplifai], *v.t.* démontrer par des exemples, illustrer; donner un exemple de.

exempt [ig'zempt, eg'zemt], *v.t.* exempter (*de*).—*a.* exempt.

exemption [ig'zempʃən], *n.* exemption, *f.*

exercise ['eksəsaiz], *n.* exercice; (*Sch.*) thème, devoir, *m.*—*v.t.* exercer; promener (*un chien*).—*v.i.* s'exercer; (*Mil.*) faire l'exercice.

exercise-book ['eksəsaizbuk], *n.* cahier (*de devoirs*), *m.*

exert [ig'zə:t], *v.t.* déployer; mettre en œuvre; exercer (*influence, pression etc.*); *to exert oneself*, faire des efforts (*pour*).

exertion [ig'zə:ʃən], *n.* effort, *m.*

exhale [eks'heil], *v.t.* exhaler, émettre.

exhaust [ig'zɔ:st], *v.t.* épuiser.—*n.* échappement, *m.*

exhausted [ig'zɔ:stid], *a.* épuisé.

exhaustion [ig'zɔ:stʃən], *n.* épuisement, *m.*

exhaustive [ig'zɔ:stiv], *a.* qui épuise; (*fig.*) complet.

exhaust-pipe [ig'zɔ:stpaip], *n.* (*Motor.*) tuyau d'échappement, *m.*

exhibit [ig'zibit], *v.t.* montrer; exposer; (*fig.*) exhiber.—*n.* objet exposé, *m.*

exhibition [eksi'biʃən], *n.* exposition; représentation, *f.*, spectacle, *m.*; (*Univ.*) bourse, *f.*

exhibitioner [eksi'biʃənə], *n.* (*Univ.*) boursier, *m.*

exhibitor [ig'zibitə], *n.* exposant, *m.*

exhilarate [ig'ziləreit], *v.t.* réjouir, égayer.

exhilarating [ig'ziləreitiŋ], *a.* qui égaye, réjouissant.

exhilaration [igzilə'reiʃən], *n.* réjouissance, gaieté, joie de vivre, *f.*

exhort [ig'zɔ:t], *v.t.* exhorter (*à*).

exhortation [egzɔ:'teiʃən], *n.* exhortation, *f.*

exhume [eks'hju:m], *v.t.* exhumer, déterrer.

exile ['eksail], *n.* exil; exilé (*personne*), *m.*—*v.t.* exiler.

exist [ig'zist], *v.i.* exister.

existence [ig'zistəns], *n.* existence, *f.*; être, *m.*

exit ['eksit], *n.* sortie, *f.*—*v.i.* (*Theat.*) il (elle) sort.

exodus ['eksədəs], *n.* exode, *m.*

exonerate [ig'zonəreit], *v.t.* décharger, exempter, exonérer, justifier.

exorbitant [ig'zɔ:bitənt], *a.* exorbitant, excessif, exagéré.

exotic [eg'zotik], *a.* exotique.

expand [iks'pænd], *v.t.* étendre, faire épanouir; amplifier; dilater (*gaz*).—*v.i.* se dilater; s'épanouir; se développer.

expanse [iks'pæns], *n.* étendue, *f.*

expansion [iks'pænʃən], *n.* expansion, *f.*

expatiate [eks'peiʃieit], *v.i.* s'étendre (*sur*).

expatriate [eks'peitrieit], *v.t.* expatrier, bannir.

expect [iks'pekt], *v.t.* attendre; s'attendre à, compter sur (*choses*); espérer; *she is expecting*, elle attend un bébé; *to know what to expect*, savoir à quoi s'en tenir.

expectant [iks'pektənt], *a.* expectant.
expectation [ekspek'teiʃən], *n.* attente, espérance; expectative; probabilité, *f.*
expedience [iks'piːdiəns], **expediency** [iks'piːdiənsi], *n.* convenance, utilité, opportunité, *f.*
expedient [iks'piːdiənt], *a.* convenable, à propos, utile, opportun.—*n.* expédient, *m.*
expedite ['ekspədait], *v.t.* expédier, hâter, accélerer.
expedition [ekspə'diʃən], *n.* expédition; promptitude, *f.*
expeditious [ekspi'diʃəs], *a.* expéditif, prompt.
expel [iks'pel], *v.t.* expulser, chasser; (*Sch.*) renvoyer.
expend [iks'pend], *v.t.* dépenser; (*fig.*) employer.
expenditure [iks'penditʃə], *n.* dépense, *f.*, dépenses, *f.pl.*; (*fig.*) sacrifice, *m.*
expense [iks'pens], *n.* dépense, *f.*; dépens; frais, *m.pl.*; **at any expense**, à tout prix; **incidental expenses**, faux frais; **to clear one's expenses**, faire ses frais.
expensive [iks'pensiv], *a.* coûteux, cher (*chose*); dépensier (*personne*).
expensively [iks'pensivli], *adv.* à grands frais.
experience [iks'piəriəns], *n.* expérience, *f.*; sentiment, *m.*—*v.t.* éprouver, faire l'expérience de.
experienced [iks'piəriənst], *a.* éprouvé, expérimenté.
experiment [iks'perimənt], *n.* expérience, *f.* —*v.i.* expérimenter.
experimental [eksperi'mentl], *a.* expérimental.
expert ['ekspəːt], *a.* expert, habile.—*n.* expert, *m.*
expiate ['ekspieit], *v.t.* expier.
expiation [ekspi'eiʃən], *n.* expiation, *f.*
expiration [ekspi'reiʃən], **expiry** [iks'paiəri], *n.* expiration; fin, *f.*, terme, *m.*
expire [iks'paiə], *v.i.* expirer, mourir.
explain [iks'plein], *v.t.* expliquer.—*v.i.* s'expliquer.
explanation [eksplə'neiʃən], *n.* explication, *f.*
explanatory [iks'plænətri], *a.* explicatif.
explicit [iks'plisit], *a.* explicite, formel; franc.
explode [iks'ploud], *v.t.* faire éclater; faire sauter (*mine*); (*fig.*) discréditer; **exploded theory**, théorie abandonnée, *f.*—*v.i.* éclater, sauter, faire explosion.
exploit ['eksplɔit], *n.* exploit, haut fait, *m.* —[iks'plɔit], *v.t.* exploiter.
exploitation [eksplɔi'teiʃən], *n.* exploitation, *f.*
exploration [eksplɔː'reiʃən], *n.* exploration, *f.*; (*fig.*) examen, *m.*
explore [iks'plɔː], *v.t.* explorer; (*fig.*) examiner.
explorer [iks'plɔːrə], *n.* explorateur, *m.*
explosion [iks'plouʒən], *n.* explosion, *f.*
explosive [iks'plousiv], *a.* and *n.* explosif, *m.*
exponent [eks'pounənt], *n.* (*Math.*) exposant; (*fig.*) représentant, *m.*
export ['ekspɔːt], *n.* exportation; marchandise exportée, *f.*—[eks'pɔːt], *v.t.* exporter, *f.*
expose [iks'pouz] *v.t.* exposer; (*fig.*) révéler, découvrir, démasquer.
expostulate [iks'pɔstjuleit], *v.i.* faire des remontrances (*à*).
exposure [iks'pouʒə], *n.* exposition (*aux*

intempéries, à un danger), *f.*; étalage (*de marchandises*); esclandre, *m.*; (*Phot.*) pose, *f.*; **to die of exposure**, mourir de froid.
expound [iks'paund], *v.t.* expliquer, exposer.
express [iks'pres], *a.* exprès; formel, explicite; **by express delivery**, par exprès.—*n.* exprès (*messager*); train express, *m.*—*v.t.* exprimer.
expression [iks'preʃən], *n.* expression, *f.*
expressive [iks'presiv], *a.* expressif.
expressly [iks'presli], *adv.* expressément, formellement.
expropriate [eks'prouprieit], *v.t.* exproprier.
expulsion [iks'pʌlʃən], *n.* expulsion, *f.*
expurgate ['ekspəːgeit], *v.t.* corriger, expurger (*livre*).
exquisite ['ekskwizit], *a.* exquis; vif, extrême (*douleur*); raffiné, délicat.
exquisitely ['ekskwizitli], *adv.* d'une manière exquise; parfaitement.
ex-service man [eks'səːvismən], *n.* (*pl.* -**men** [men]) ancien combattant, *m.*
extant [ek'stænt], *a.* qui existe encore.
extempore [eks'tempəri], *a.* improvisé.— *adv.* impromptu, sans préparation.
extemporize [eks'tempəraiz], *v.t.* improviser.
extend [iks'tend], *v.t.* étendre; prolonger; tendre (*la main*); **to extend a welcome**, souhaiter la bienvenue.—*v.i.* s'étendre; se prolonger (*temps*).
extension [iks'tenʃən], *n.* extension; étendue, prolongation (*de temps*), *f.*; (*Teleph.*) poste, *m.*
extensive [iks'tensiv], *a.* étendu, vaste; ample.
extensively [iks'tensivli], *adv.* d'une manière étendue; bien, très au loin.
extent [iks'tent], *n.* étendue, *f.*; (*fig.*) degré, point, *m.*; **to a certain extent**, jusqu'à un certain point; **to the extent of**, jusqu'à.
extenuate [eks'tenjueit], *v.t.* atténuer, amoindrir.
extenuating [eks'tenjueitiŋ], *a.* (*Law*) atténuant.
exterior [eks'tiəriə], *a.* extérieur, en dehors.— *n.* extérieur, *m.*
exterminate [iks'təːmineit], *v.t.* exterminer; extirper.
extermination [ikstəːmi'neiʃən], *n.* extermination, *f.*
external [eks'təːnl], *a.* extérieur; externe (*étudiant etc.*).
extinct [iks'tiŋkt], *a.* éteint; qui n'existe plus (*espèce etc.*); aboli.
extinguish [iks'tiŋgwiʃ], *v.t.* éteindre; (*fig.*) éclipser.
extinguisher [iks'tiŋgwiʃə], *n.* extincteur (*appareil*), *m.*
extirpate ['ekstəːpeit], *v.t.* extirper.
extol [iks'toul], *v.t.* exalter, vanter.
extort [iks'tɔːt], *v.t.* extorquer, arracher.
extortion [iks'tɔːʃən], *n.* extorsion, *f.*
extortionate [iks'tɔːʃənit], *a.* extorsionnaire, exorbitant.
extra ['ekstrə], *a.* en sus; supplémentaire; **extra charge**, prix en sus, supplément, *m.* —*n.* supplément; (*Cine.*) figurant, *m.*—*adv.* en sus, de plus; **extra strong**, extra-solide.
extract ['ekstrækt], *n.* extrait; concentré (*de viande etc.*), *m.*—[iks'trækt], *v.t.* extraire, tirer (*de*); arracher (*dent*) à.

extraction

extraction [iks'trækʃən], *n.* extraction; origine, *f.*

extraneous [eks'treinjəs], *a.* étranger (*à*); non-essentiel.

extraordinarily [iks'trɔːdnrili], *a.* extraordinairement.

extraordinary [iks'trɔːdnri], *a.* extraordinaire, rare.

extravagance [iks'trævəgəns], *n.* extravagance; prodigalité, *f.*, gaspillage, *m.*

extravagant [iks'trævəgənt], *a.* extravagant (*immodéré*); prodigue, dépensier; exorbitant (*prix*).

extravagantly [iks'trævəgəntli], *adv.* d'une manière extravagante.

extreme [iks'triːm], *a.* extrême.—*n.* extrémité, *f.*; extrême, *m.*

extremely [iks'triːmli], *adv.* extrêmement, au dernier degré.

extremist [iks'triːmist], *n.* extrémiste, *m.*, *f.*; ultra, *m.*

extremity [iks'tremiti], *n.* extrémité, *f.*, extrême; bout, comble, *m.*

extricate ['ekstrikeit], *v.t.* débarrasser, dégager; *to extricate oneself,* se tirer d'affaire.

extrovert ['ekstrəvəːt], *n.* extroverti, *m.*

exuberance [ig'zjuːbərəns], *n.* exubérance, surabondance, *f.*

exuberant [ig'zjuːbərənt], *a.* exubérant, surabondant.

exude [ek'sjuːd], *v.t.* faire exsuder.—*v.i.* exsuder.

exult [ig'zʌlt], *v.i.* se réjouir, exulter (*de*).

exultant [ig'zʌltənt], *a.* joyeux, triomphant.

exultation [egzʌl'teiʃən], *n.* triomphe, *m.*, exultation, *f.*

eye [ai], *n.* œil; trou (*d'une aiguille*); (*Bot.*) œil, bouton, *m.*; (*Needlework*) porte; (*fig.*) vue, *f.*; *black eye,* œil poché; *blind in one eye,* borgne; *in the twinkling of an eye,* en un clin d'œil; *to keep an eye on,* surveiller.—*v.t.* regarder; lorgner.

eyeball ['aibɔːl], *n.* bulbe de l'œil, *m.*

eyebrow ['aibrau], *n.* sourcil, *m.*

eyed [aid], *a.* *blue-eyed,* aux yeux bleus.

eyeglass ['aiglɑːs], *n.* monocle (*un seul verre*); lorgnon, pince-nez (*double*), *m.*

eye-hole ['aihoul], *n.* orbite; petit judas, *m.*

eyelash ['ailæʃ], *n.* cil, *m.*

eyelet ['ailit], *n.* œillet, *m.*

eyelid ['ailid], *n.* paupière, *f.*

eyesight ['aisait], *n.* vue, *f.*

eyesore ['aisɔː], *n.* chose qui blesse l'œil, *f.*, objet d'aversion, *m.*

eye-witness ['aiwitnis], *n.* témoin oculaire, *m.*

eyrie, eyry [AERIE].

F

F, f [ef]. sixième lettre de l'alphabet; (*Mus.*) fa, *m.*

fable [feibl], *n.* fable, *f.*, conte, *m.*

fabric ['fæbrik], *n.* construction, *f.*; édifice, ouvrage, *m.*; étoffe, *f.*; (*fig.*) système, *m.*

fabricate ['fæbrikeit], *v.t.* fabriquer, inventer, contrefaire.

fabrication [fæbri'keiʃən], *n.* fabrication, *f.*

fabulous ['fæbjuləs], *a.* fabuleux.

face [feis], *n.* figure, *f.*; visage, *m.*; face, surface (*des choses*); (*fig.*) apparence, *f.*, état, *m.*; mine, physionomie, *f.*; front (*insolence*), *m.*; façade, *f.*, devant (*front*), *m.*; facette (*d'un diamant*), *f.*; cadran (*de pendule*), *m.*; *face to face,* vis-à-vis; *to make faces at,* faire des grimaces à.—*v.t.* faire face à; affronter; mettre un revers à, parer (*vêtements*); revêtir (*mur etc.*); donner sur (*maison etc.*).—*v.i.* prendre un faux dehors; (*Mil.*) faire front; *face about!* volte-face!

facet ['fæsit], *n.* facette, *f.*—*v.t.* facetter.

facetious [fə'siːʃəs], *a.* facétieux.

facetiously [fə'siːʃəsli], *adv.* facétieusement, *f.*

facetiousness [fə'siːʃəsnis], *n.* plaisanterie, *f.*

facial ['feiʃəl], *a.* facial.

facile ['fæsail], *a.* facile; complaisant.

facility [fə'siliti], *n.* facilité, *f.*

facilitate [fə'siliteit], *v.t.* faciliter.

facing ['feisiŋ], *n.* parement (*de vêtements*); revers, *m.*

facsimile [fæk'simili], *n.* fac-similé, *m.*

fact [fækt], *n.* fait, *m.*; *as a matter of fact, in fact,* en effet; *in point of fact,* au fait; *matter-of-fact man,* homme positif, *m.*

faction ['fækʃən], *n.* faction; (*fig.*) discorde, dissension, *f.*

factor ['fæktə], *n.* agent; facteur, *m.*

factory ['fæktri], *n.* usine, fabrique, *f.*; (*obs.*), comptoir (*d'outre-mer*) *m.*

faculty ['fækəlti], *n.* faculté, *f.*, pouvoir, talent, *m.*

fad [fæd], *n.* marotte, manie, *f.*

fade [feid], *v.t.* flétrir, faire flétrir.—*v.i.* se faner, se flétrir; disparaître, périr.

fag [fæg], *v.t.* forcer à piocher; fatiguer, éreinter; *fagged out,* éreinté.—*v.i.* travailler dur, piocher (*à*).—*n.* fatigue, peine, corvée, *f.*; (*pop.*) cigarette, *f.*

fag-end ['fægend], *n.* (*pop.*) mégot (*de cigarette*), *m.*

faggot ['fægət], *n.* fagot, *m.*

fail [feil], *v.t.* manquer à, abandonner.—*v.i.* faillir; manquer (*to miss*); échouer (*ne pas réussir*); (*Comm.*) faire faillite.—*n.* manque, insuccès, *m.*

failing ['feiliŋ], *n.* défaut, *m.*, faute; (*Comm.*) faillite, *f.*—*prep.* à défaut de.

failure ['feiljə], *n.* manque, défaut (*want*); échec; insuccès, *m.*, affaire manquée, *f.*, fiasco, *m.*; chute (*d'une pièce etc.*); (*Comm.*) faillite, *f.*; *he is a failure,* c'est un raté.

*fain [fein], *adv.* avec plaisir, volontiers.

faint [feint], *a.* faible; affaibli; languissant; découragé; timide.—*v.i.* s'évanouir, défaillir.—*n.* évanouissement, *m.*

faint-hearted ['feinthɑːtid], *a.* timide, sans courage, découragé.

fainting ['feintiŋ], *n.* évanouissement, *m.*, défaillance, *f.*

faintly ['feintli], *adv.* faiblement; mollement.

faintness ['feintnis], *n.* faiblesse, *f.*

fair [fɛə], *a.* beau; favorable (*vent*); clair (*teint*); blond (*cheveux etc.*); juste, équitable (*fig.*) assez bon, passable; *fair play*, franc jeu, *m.*; *fair price*, juste prix, *m.*; *that is not fair* (*at games*), cela n'est pas de jeu.— *adv.* bien; de bonne foi, honorablement.—*n.* foire (*marché*), *f.*

fairly ['fɛəli], *adv.* bien; loyalement; doucement; avec justesse; de bonne foi; passablement, assez.

fairness ['fɛənis], *n.* beauté; couleur blonde (*des cheveux*); blancheur (*du teint*); équité, impartialité, *f.*

fairy ['fɛəri], *a.* des fées, féerique.—*n.* fée, *f.*

fairy-tale ['fɛəriteil], *n.* conte de fées, *m.*

faith [feiθ], *n.* foi, croyance; (*fig.*) fidélité, *f.*— *int.* ma foi! en vérité!

faithful ['feiθful], *a.* fidèle.

faithfully ['feiθfuli], *adv.* fidèlement; *yours faithfully* (*lettre d'affaires*), veuillez agréer mes salutations distinguées.

faithfulness ['feiθfulnis], *n.* fidélité, *f.*

faithless ['feiθlis], *a.* sans foi, infidèle.

faithlessness ['feiθlisnis], *n.* infidélité; déloyauté, *f.*

fake [feik], *v.t., v.i.* truquer, maquiller.

falcon ['fɔːlkən], *n.* faucon, *m.*

fall [fɔːl], *v.i. irr.* tomber; s'abaisser; baisser, diminuer; *to fall away from*, abandonner, quitter; *to fall back* tomber en arrière; (*Mil.*) reculer; *to fall down*, tomber par terre; *to fall for*, tomber amoureux de; *to fall for it*, s'y laisser prendre; *to fall in*, s'écrouler; (*Mil.*) se mettre en rangs, s'aligner; *to fall off*, tomber; diminuer; *to fall out*, tomber; se brouiller; (*Mil.*) *fall out!* rompez vos rangs! *to fall through*, échouer; *to fall to*, se mettre à; *to fall under*, être compris sous; tomber sous; *to fall upon*, tomber sur, attaquer; incomber à.—*n.* chute, *f.*; (*Am.*) automne, *m.* ou *f.*; tombée (*de la nuit*); baisse (*de prix*), *f.*; éboulement (*de terre*), *m.*; chute, cascade (*de rivières etc.*); décrue (*des eaux*); diminution (*de quantité*), *f.*

fallacy ['fæləsi], *n.* erreur, fausseté, illusion, *f.*

fallible ['fæləbl], *a.* faillible.

fall-out ['fɔːlaut], *n.* retombées radioactives, *f.pl.*

fallow ['fælou], *a.* en jachère; (*fig.*) inculte; fauve (*daim etc.*).—*n.* jachère, friche, *f.*

false [fɔːls], *a.* faux, perfide, déloyal; infidèle; prétendu; illégal (*détention*).

falsehood ['fɔːlshud], *n.* mensonge, *m.*

falsely ['fɔːlsli], *adv.* faussement.

falseness ['fɔːlsnis], *n.* fausseté; perfidie, *f.*

falsetto [fɔːl'setou], *n.* (*Mus.*) voix de fausset, *f.*

falsify ['fɔːlsifai], *v.t.* falsifier; fausser.

falter ['fɔːltə], *v.i.* hésiter; bégayer; chanceler.

faltering ['fɔːltəriŋ], *n.* hésitation, *f.*

fame [feim], *n.* gloire, renommée, *f.*

famed [feimd], *a.* renommé.

familiar [fə'miljə], *a.* familier, intime; de la famille; *to be familiar with*, être familier avec, connaître.—*n.* ami intime; esprit familier, *m.*

familiarity [fəmili'æriti], *n.* familiarité, *f.*

familiarly [fə'miliəli], *adv.* familièrement, sans cérémonie.

family ['fæmili], *a.* de famille, de la famille.— *n.* famille, *f.*

famine ['fæmin], *n.* famine, disette, *f.*

famished ['fæmiʃt], *a.* affamé.

famous ['feiməs], *a.* fameux, célèbre.

famously ['feiməsli], *adv.* fameusement; (*fig.*) prodigieusement.

fan [fæn], *n.* éventail; ventilateur; (*colloq.*) admirateur enthousiaste (*d'un artiste* ou *d'un sport*), *m.*—*v.t.* éventer; souffler (*feu*); (*Agric.*) vanner; (*fig.*) exciter, activer.

fanatic [fə'nætik], *a.* and *n.* fanatique, *m., f.*

fanatical [fə'nætikəl], *a.* fanatique.

fanaticism [fə'nætisizm], *n.* fanatisme, *m.*

fancied ['fænsid], *a.* imaginaire, imaginé; (*Turf*) bien coté (*cheval*).

fancier ['fænsiə], *n.* amateur (*de*), *m.*

fanciful ['fænsiful], *a.* fantasque, capricieux.

fancy ['fænsi], *a.* de fantaisie.—*n.* fantaisie, imagination; idée, *f.*, caprice, goût (*pour*), *m.*, envie (*de*), *f.*—*v.t.* s'imaginer, se figurer; avoir du goût pour.—*v.i.* s'imaginer, se figurer; *just fancy!* figurez-vous!

fancy-dress ['fænsidres], *n.* travesti, *m.*; *fancy-dress ball*, bal costumé, *m.*

fane [fein], *n.* temple, édifice sacré, *m.*

fanfare ['fænfɛə], *n.* fanfare, *f.*

fang [fæŋ], *n.* croc (*de chien*), *m.*; racine (*d'une dent*); défense (*de sanglier*); (*fig.*) griffe, *f.*

fantastic [fæn'tæstik], *a.* fantastique; fantasque (*personne*).

fantasy ['fæntəsi], *n.* fantaisie, *f.*

far [faː], *a.* (*comp.* **farther**, **further**; *superl.* **farthest**, **furthest**) lointain, éloigné, reculé; *the Far East*, l'extrême Orient, *m.* —*adv.* loin, au loin; bien, fort, beaucoup; *as far as*, aussi loin que, jusqu'à; *by far*, de beaucoup; *far and wide*, de tous côtés; *how far?* jusqu'où?

far-away ['faːrəwei], *a.* rêveur (*regard*); lointain.

farce [faːs], *n.* farce, *f.*

farcical ['faːsikl], *a.* burlesque; (*fig.*) drôle.

fare [fɛə], *v.i.* aller; se porter; se nourrir, vivre.—*n.* prix de la course; prix de la place, *m.*, place, *f.*; voyageur (*personne*), *m.*; chère (*aliment*), *f.*; *bill of fare*, menu, *m.*, carte du jour, *f.*; *return fare*, aller et retour, *m.*; *single fare*, billet simple, *m.*

farewell ['fɛəwel, fɛə'wel], *a.* d'adieu.—*n.* adieu, *m.*

far-fetched [faː'fetʃt], *a.* recherché; tiré par les cheveux.

farm [faːm], *n.* ferme, *f.*—*v.t.* affermer, prendre à ferme; exploiter.

farmer ['faːmə], *n.* fermier, métayer; cultivateur, *m.*

farm-house ['faːmhaus], *n.* ferme, *f.*

farming ['faːmiŋ], *n.* agriculture, exploitation agricole, *f.*

farm-yard ['faːmjaːd], *n.* basse-cour, *f.*

Faroe ['fɛərou] **Islands**. les îles Féroé, *f.pl.*

far-reaching ['faːˈriːtʃiŋ], *a.* d'une grande portée.

farrier ['færiə] *n.* maréchal ferrant, *m.*

farther [FURTHER].

farthest [FURTHERMOST].

fascinate ['fæsineit], *v.t.* fasciner, charmer, séduire.

fascinating ['fæsineitiŋ], *a.* fascinateur, enchanteur, séduisant.

fascination [fæsi'neiʃən], *n.* fascination, *f.*, charme, *m.*

fascism ['fæʃizm], *n.* fascisme, *m.*

fascist ['fæʃist], *a.* and *n.* fasciste, *m., f.*

fashion

fashion ['fæʃən], *n.* façon, forme; mode, *f.*; le grand monde, *m.*; *after a fashion*, tant bien que mal; *in fashion*, à la mode; *to set the fashion*, donner le ton.—*v.t.* façonner, former.

fashionable ['fæʃnəbl], *a.* à la mode, élégant, de bon ton, (*fam.*) chic.

fashionably ['fæʃnəbli], *adv.* à la mode, élégamment.

fast (1) [fɑːst], *n.* jeûne, *m.*—*v.i.* jeûner.

fast (2) [fɑːst], *a.* ferme, fixe (*solide*); fidèle (*constant*); bon teint (*couleur*); serré (*nœud*); (*Naut.*) amarré (*fixé*); bien fermé (*porte*); vite, rapide; en avance (*horloge etc.*); (*fig.*) dissolu; *to make fast*, assujettir, fermer (*porte, fenêtre*); (*Naut.*) amarrer.—*adv.* ferme (*stable*); vite, rapidement (*avec célérité*); fort (*pluie*); *to hold fast*, tenir bon; *to stand fast*, ne pas broncher.

fasten [fɑːsn], *v.t.* attacher; fixer; lier; fermer (*fenêtre, porte etc.*).—*v.i.* s'attacher (*à*); se fermer.

fastener ['fɑːsnə], **fastening** ['fɑːsniŋ], *n.* attache; agrafe (*de robe*); fermeture, *f.*

fastidious [fæs'tidiəs], *a.* difficile; dédaigneux; délicat; exigeant.

fastness ['fɑːstnis], *n.* fermeté; vitesse; place forte (*forteresse*); légèreté de conduite, *f.*

fat [fæt], *a.* gras; gros (*personne*); (*fig.*) riche, fertile.—*n.* gras, *m.*; graisse; (*fig.*) substance, *f.*; (*pl.*) matières grasses, *f.pl.*

fatal [feitl], *a.* fatal, funeste; mortel.

fatality [fə'tæliti], *n.* fatalité, *f.*; accident mortel, *m.*

fatally ['feitəli], *adv.* fatalement, mortellement.

fate [feit], *n.* destin, sort, *m.*

fated ['feitid], *a.* destiné.

fateful ['feitful], *a.* fatal; décisif.

fat-head ['fæthed], *n.* (*colloq.*) nigaud, *m.*

father ['fɑːðə], *n.* père, *m.*; (*pl.*) pères, ancêtres, aïeux, *m.pl.*; *godfather*, parrain, *m.*; *grandfather*, grand-père, *m.*; *stepfather*, beau-père, *m.*

father-in-law ['fɑːðərinlɔː], *n.* beau-père, *m.*

fatherland ['fɑːðəlænd], *n.* pays natal, *m.*, patrie, *f.*

fatherly ['fɑːðəli], *a.* paternel, de père.

fathom ['fæðəm], *n.* toise; (*Naut.*) brasse (= 6 pieds = 1 m. 829); (*fig.*) portée, profondeur, *f.*—*v.t.* sonder; (*fig.*) approfondir.

fatigue [fə'tiːg], *n.* fatigue; (*Mil.*) corvée, *f.*—*v.t.* fatiguer, lasser.

fatiguing [fə'tiːgiŋ], *a.* fatigant.—*pres.p.* fatiguant.

fatten [fætn], *v.t.* engraisser; (*fig.*) enrichir.

fattening ['fætniŋ], *a.* engraissant.—*n.* engraissement, *m.*

fatty ['fæti], *a.* graisseux.

fatuous ['fætjuəs], *a.* sot; béat.

fatuousness ['fætjuəsnis], *n.* fatuité, *f.*

fault [fɔːlt], *n.* faute, *f.*; défaut, vice, *m.*; (*Geol.*) faille, *f.*

faultless ['fɔːltlis], *a.* sans défaut, sans faute, impeccable.

faultlessly ['fɔːltlisli], *adv.* irréprochablement.

faultlessness ['fɔːltlisnis], *n.* perfection, *f.*

faulty ['fɔːlti], *a.* fautif, blâmable, défectueux.

favour ['feivə], *n.* faveur, *f.*, bonnes grâces, *f.pl.*; bienfait, *m.*; grâce (*permission*), *f.*; couleurs, faveurs (*rubans*), *f.pl.*; (*Comm.*) honorée, *f.*—*v.t.* favoriser, honorer (*de*).

favourable ['feivərəbl], *a.* favorable.

favourably ['feivərəbli], *adv.* favorablement.

favourite ['feivərit], *a.* favori, préféré.—*n.* favori, *m.*

fawn [fɔːn], *n.* faon, *m.*—*v.i. to fawn upon*, caresser, flatter.

fawning ['fɔːniŋ], *a.* flatteur, servile.—*n.* caresse, flatterie, *f.*

fear [fiə], *n.* crainte, peur; inquiétude, *f.*; *for fear of*, de peur de.—*v.t.* craindre, redouter, avoir peur de.—*v.i.* craindre, avoir peur.

fearful ['fiəful], *a.* craintif, timide; terrible; affreux, effrayant.

fearless ['fiəlis], *a.* sans peur, intrépide.

fearlessly ['fiəlisli], *adv.* sans crainte, avec intrépidité.

feasible ['fiːzəbl], *a.* faisable, praticable.

feast [fiːst], *n.* festin, *m.*; fête, *f.*; régal, *m.*—*v.t.* fêter, régaler.—*v.i.* faire festin, se régaler.

feat [fiːt], *n.* exploit, fait, haut fait, *m.*

feather ['feðə], *n.* plume; penne (*aile et queue d'oiseau*), *f.*; (*Mil.*) plumet, *m.*—*v.t.* orner d'une plume; *to feather one's nest*, faire sa pelote.

feature ['fiːtʃə], *n.* trait, *m.*; (*pl.*) visage, *m.* figure; (*fig.*) spécialité, *f.*

February ['februəri], *n.* février, *m.*

feckless ['feklis], *a.* faible, veule.

fecundity [fə'kʌnditi], *n.* fécondité, *f.*

federal ['fedərəl], *a.* fédéral.

federate ['fedərit], *a.* fédéré.—['fedəreit], *v.t.* fédérer.—*v.i.* se fédérer.

federation [fedə'reiʃən], *n.* fédération, *f.*

fee [fiː], *n.* honoraires, *m.pl.*, cachet, salaire; (*Eccles. etc.*) droit, *m.*

feeble [fiːbl], *a.* faible, débile.

feebleness ['fiːblnis], *n.* faiblesse, *f.*

feebly ['fiːbli], *adv.* faiblement.

feed [fiːd], *n.* nourriture; pâture, *f.*, pâturage (*pour bestiaux*), *m.*—*v.t. irr.* nourrir; donner à manger à; paître, faire paître (*bestiaux*); (*pop.*) *to be fed up*, en avoir marre.—*v.i.* se nourrir; paître (*animaux*).

feed-back ['fiːdbæk], *n.* (*Rad.*) rétro-action, *f.*

feeding ['fiːdiŋ], *n.* nourriture; pâture (*pour bestiaux*), *f.*

feeding bottle ['fiːdiŋbɔtl], *n.* biberon, *m.*

feel [fiːl], *v.t. irr.* tâter, toucher, sentir; éprouver; *to feel one's way*, avancer à tâtons.—*v.i.* sentir, se sentir; se trouver; *to feel cold*, avoir froid; *to feel like doing something*, avoir envie de faire quelque chose.—*n.* toucher; attouchement; tact, *m.*

feeler ['fiːlə], *n.* antenne (*d'insecte*), *f.*; (*fig.*) ballon d'essai, *m.*

feeling ['fiːliŋ], *a.* tendre, touchant.—*n.* toucher; sentiment, *m.*, sensibilité, émotion, *f.*

feet [FOOT].

feign [fein], *v.t.* feindre, simuler.—*v.i.* feindre, faire semblant (*de*).

feigned [feind], *a.* feint, simulé.

feint [feint], *n.* feinte, *f.*—*v.i.* feinter.

felicitate [fi'lisiteit], *v.t.* féliciter.

felicitation [filisi'teiʃən], *n.* félicitation, *f.*

felicity [fi'lisiti], *n.* félicité, *f.*, bonheur, *m.*

fell (1) [fel], *v.t.* abattre, assommer, terrasser

424

fell (2) [fel], *past* [FALL].
fellow ['felou], *n.* compagnon, camarade, confrère; associé, membre; pendant, pareil (*choses*); (*colloq.*) garçon; individu, type, *m.*; *good fellow*, brave type.
fellow-citizen ['felou'sitizn], *n.* concitoyen, *m.*
fellow-countryman ['felou'kʌntrimən], *n.* (*pl.* -**men** [men]) compatriote, *m.*
fellow-feeling ['felou'fi:liŋ], *n.* sympathie, *f.*
fellowship ['felouʃip], *n.* société, association; camaraderie, *f.*
fellow-traveller ['felou'trævlə], *n.* compagnon de voyage; (*Polit.*) sympathisant communiste, communisant, *m.*
felon ['felən], *a.* félon, traître.—*n.* criminel, *m.*
felony ['feləni], *n.* crime, *m.*
felt (1) [felt], *n.* feutre, chapeau de feutre, *m.*; *roofing felt*, carton bitumé, *m.*
felt (2) [felt], *past* [FEEL].
female ['fi:meil], *a.* féminin, de femme; femelle (*animaux*); *a female friend*, une amie.—*n.* femme; jeune personne; femelle (*animaux*), *f.*
feminine ['feminin], *a.* féminin.
fen [fen], *n.* marais, marécage, *m.*
fence [fens], *n.* clôture, enceinte; palissade, barrière; (*Turf*) haie; (*Spt.*) escrime (*à l'épée*); (*fig.*) défense, *f.*; (*slang*) receleur (*d'objets volés*), *m.*; *to sit on the fence*, (*fig.*) ne pas s'engager, ménager la chèvre et le chou.—*v.t.* enclore, mettre une clôture à, palissader; (*fig.*) protéger.—*v.i.* faire des armes.
fencing ['fensiŋ], *n.* (*Spt.*) escrime; enceinte, clôture, *f.*
fencing-master ['fensiŋmɑ:stə],' *n.* maître d'armes, *m.*
fend [fend], *v.t. to fend off*, parer.—*v.i. to fend for oneself*, se débrouiller, veiller à ses intérêts.
fender ['fendə], *n.* garde-feu, *m.*; (*Naut.*) défense, *f.*; (*Am. Motor.*) pare-boue, *m.*
ferment ['fə:mənt], *n.* ferment, *m.*; fermentation, *f.*—[fə:'ment], *v.t.* faire fermenter.—*v.i.* fermenter.
fermentation [fə:mən'teiʃən], *n.* fermentation, *f.*
fern [fə:n], *n.* fougère, *f.*
ferocious [fə'rouʃəs], *a.* féroce.
ferociously [fə'rouʃəsli], *adv.* avec férocité.
ferocity [fə'rɔsiti], *n.* férocité, *f.*
ferret ['ferit], *n.* furet, *m.*—*v.t.* fureter; *to ferret out*, dépister, dénicher.
ferrule ['feru:l], *n.* virole (*anneau*), *f.*
ferry ['feri], *v.t.* passer en bac.—*n.* bac, passage, *m.*; *air-ferry*, avion transbordeur, *m.*
ferry-boat ['feribout], *n.* bac, bateau transbordeur de trains, *m.*
fertile ['fə:tail], *a.* fertile, fécond.
fertility [fə'tiliti], *n.* fertilité, fécondité, *f.*
fertilize ['fə:tilaiz], *v.t.* fertiliser.
fertilizer ['fə:tilaizə], *n.* fertilisant, engrais, *m.*
fervent ['fə:vənt], *a.* ardent, fervent, vif.
fervently ['fə:vəntli], *adv.* ardemment, avec ferveur.
fester ['festə], *v.i.* s'ulcérer; (*fig.*) se corrompre.—*n.* abcès, *m.*, pustule, *f.*
festival ['festivl], *a.* de fête, joyeux.—*n.* fête, *f.*; (*Mus., Theat.*) festival, *m.*
festive ['festiv], *a.* de fête, joyeux.

festivity [fes'tiviti], *n.* fête, *f.*; réjouissances, *f.pl.*
festoon [fes'tu:n], *n.* feston, *m.*—*v.t.* festonner (*de*).
fetch [fetʃ], *v.t.* chercher, aller chercher; apporter (*choses*); amener (*personnes etc.*); rapporter (*prix*).—*n.* ruse, *f.*; tour, *m.*
fête [feit], *n.* fête, *f.*—*v.t.* fêter.
fetlock ['fetlok], *n.* fanon (de cheval), *m.*
fetter ['fetə], *v.t.* entraver, enchaîner.
fetters ['fetəz], *n.pl.* (*fig.*) fers, *m.pl.*, chaînes; entraves (*de cheval*), *f.pl.*
fettle [fetl], *v.t.* arranger, préparer.—*n.* bon état, *m.*
feud [fju:d], *n.* querelle; vendetta, *f.*
feudal ['fju:dl], *a.* féodal.
feudalism ['fju:dlizm], *n.* féodalité, *f.*
fever ['fi:və], *n.* fièvre, *f.*
feverish ['fi:vəriʃ], *a.* fiévreux; (*fig.*) fébrile.
few [fju:], *a.* peu de; *a few*, quelques.—*n.* peu de gens, *m.pl.*; *a few*, quelques-uns, *m.pl.*, quelques-unes, *f.pl.*
fewer ['fju:ə], *a.* moins (*de*); moins nombreux.
fiasco [fi'æskou], *n.* fiasco, four, *m.*
fib [fib], *n.* petit mensonge, *m.*—*v.i.* mentir.
fibber ['fibə], *n.* menteur, *m.*
fibre ['faibə], *n.* fibre, *f.*
fibrositis [faibrə'saitis], *n.* (*Med.*) cellulite, *f.*
fibrous ['faibrəs], *a.* fibreux.
fickle [fikl], *a.* volage, inconstant.
fickleness ['fiklnis], *n.* inconstance, légèreté, *f.*
fiction ['fikʃən], *n.* fiction, *f.*; *works of fiction*, romans, *m.pl.*
fictitious [fik'tiʃəs], *a.* fictif, imaginaire; (*fig.*) faux, factice.
fiddle [fidl], *n.* violon; (*pej.*) crincrin, *m.*; (*pop.*) resquille, combine, *f.*—*v.i.* jouer du violon; (*fig.*) niaiser (*baguenauder*); (*pop.*) resquiller.
fiddler ['fidlə], *n.* joueur de violon; ménétrier, *m.*
fiddlesticks! ['fidlstiks], *int.* bah! quelle blague!
fidelity [fi'deliti], *n.* fidélité, *f.*
fidget ['fidʒit], *n.* agitation, *f.*; être remuant (*personne*), *m.*—*v.i.* se remuer, s'agiter.
fidgety ['fidʒiti], *a.* remuant, agité; ennuyeux (*gênant*).
field [fi:ld], *n.* champ; pré, *m.*, prairie; (*Mil.*) campagne, *f.*; champ de bataille, *m.*; (*Turf etc.*) courants, *m.pl.*; *in the scientific field*, dans le domaine des sciences.—*v.t.* (*Cricket*) arrêter (*une balle*); réunir (*équipe*).—*v.i.* (*Cricket*) tenir le champ.
field-day ['fi:lddei], *n.* (*Mil.*) jour de manœuvres; (*fig.*) jour de grand succès, *m.*
field-marshal ['fi:ldmɑ:ʃl], *n.* maréchal, *m.*
fiend [fi:nd], *n.* démon, *m.*
fiendish ['fi:ndiʃ], *a.* diabolique, infernal.
fierce [fiəs], *a.* féroce, farouche, furieux.
fiercely ['fiəsli], *adv.* férocement, furieusement.
fierceness ['fiəsnis], *n.* violence, fureur, brutalité, *f.*; (*fig.*) acharnement, *m.*
fieriness ['faiərinis], *n.* fougue, ardeur, *f.*
fiery ['faiəri], *a.* de feu; (*fig.*) ardent, fougueux.
fife [faif], *n.* fifre, *m.*
fifteen [fif'ti:n], *a.* and *n.* quinze, *m.*
fifteenth [fif'ti:nθ], *a.* quinze (*jour du mois, roi etc.*).—*n.* quinzième (*fraction*), *m.*

fifth

fifth [fifθ], *a.* cinquième; cinq (*jour du mois, roi etc.*); **Charles the Fifth,** Charles-Quint.—*n.* cinquième (*fraction*), *m.*; (*Mus.*) quinte, *f.*

fiftieth [ˈfiftiəθ], *a.* cinquantième.—*n.* cinquantième (*fraction*), *m.*

fifty [ˈfifti], *a.* and *n.* cinquante, *m.*; **about fifty,** une cinquantaine.

fig [fig], *n.* figue, *f.*; figuier (*arbre*), *m.*

fight [fait], *v.t. irr.* se battre avec, combattre; livrer (*une bataille*).—*v.i.* se battre; combattre (*avec*).—*n.* combat, *m.*, bataille; (*fig.*) lutte, *f.*

fighter [ˈfaitə], *n.* combattant; (*pej.*) batailleur; (*Av.*) chasseur, *m.*

fighting [ˈfaitiŋ], *n.* combat, *m.*; lutte, *f.*

figment [ˈfigmənt], *n.* fiction, invention, *f.*

figurative [ˈfigjuərətiv], *a.* figuré; figuratif.

figuratively [ˈfigjuərətivli], *adv.* au figuré; figurativement.

figure [ˈfigə], *n.* figure; taille, tournure (*d'une personne*), *f.*; dessin (*sur un tissu*); (*Arith.*) chiffre, *m.*; **figure of speech,** figure de rhétorique, métaphore; (*fam.*) façon de parler, *f.*; **to cut a figure,** faire figure. —*v.t.* figurer, former; façonner; (*fig.*) imaginer; **to figure out,** calculer.—*v.i.* figurer.

figure-head [ˈfigəhed], *n.* (*Naut.*) figure de proue, *f.*; (*fig.*) homme de paille; prête-nom, *m.*

Fiji [ˈfiːdʒi]; **the Fiji Islands.** les îles Fidji *ou* Viti, *f.pl.*

filament [ˈfiləmənt], *n.* filament, *m.*

filbert [ˈfilbət], *n.* aveline, grosse noisette, *f.*

filch [filtʃ], *v.t.* escamoter, filouter, chiper.

file [fail], *n.* lime (*outil*), liasse, *f.*, dossier, classeur (*de papiers*), *m.*; liste; collection (*de journaux*); (*Mil.*) file; (*Theat. etc.*) queue, *f.*; **card-index file,** fichier, *m.*—*v.t.* limer, affiler; mettre en liasse; (*Law*) déposer (*une requête etc.*); **to file away,** classer.—*v.i.* (*Mil.*) marcher à la file; **to file off** or **past,** défiler.

filial [ˈfiliəl], *a.* filial.

filibuster [ˈfilibʌstə], *n.* flibustier, *m.*

filing [ˈfailiŋ], *n.* limage, *m.*; mise en liasse, *f.*, classement, *m.*; (*pl.*) limaille, *f.*

filing-cabinet [ˈfailiŋkæbinit], *n.* cartonnier, classeur, *m.*

fill [fil], *v.t.* emplir, remplir; combler (*jusqu'au bord*); occuper; rassasier; **to fill a tooth,** plomber une dent.—*v.i.* se remplir, s'emplir. —*n.* suffisance, *f.*; (*colloq.*) **one's fill,** tout son soûl.

fillet [ˈfilit], *n.* bandeau; filet (*de poisson*), *m.*

filling [ˈfiliŋ], *a.* qui remplit; rassasiant.

filling-station [ˈfiliŋˈsteiʃən], *n.* poste d'essence, *m.*

filly [ˈfili], *n.* pouliche, *f.*

film [film], *n.* taie (*devant les yeux*), pellicule; (*Anat.*) tunique, *f.*; (*fig.*) nuage, voile, *m.*; (*Phot.*) pellicule, couche sensible, *f.*; (*Cine.*) film, *m.*; **film script,** scénario, script, *m.*; **film star,** vedette de cinéma, *f.*—*v.t.* couvrir d'une tunique, d'une pellicule etc.; filmer, mettre à l'écran.—*v.i.* tourner un film.

film-strip [ˈfilmstrip], *n.* film fixe, *m.*

filter [ˈfiltə], *n.* filtre, *m.*—*v.t.* filtrer.

filter-tip [ˈfiltəˈtip], *n.* bout filtrant, *m.*

filth [filθ], *n.* ordure saleté; (*fig.*) corruption, *f.*

filthy [ˈfilθi], *a.* sale, immonde;(*fig.*) obscène, infect.

fin [fin], *n.* nageoire, *f.*; aileron (*de requin*), *m.*; (*Naut., Av.*) dérive; (*Motor.*) ailette (*de radiateur*), *f.*

final [fainl], *a.* final, dernier; décisif.—*n.* (*Spt.*) finale, *f.*

finally [ˈfainəli], *adv.* enfin, finalement; définitivement.

finance [fiˈnæns, faiˈnæns], *n.* finance, *f.*

financial [fiˈnænʃəl], *a.* financier.

financier [fiˈnænsiə], *n.* financier, *m.*

finch [fintʃ], *n.* (*Orn.*) pinson, *m.*

find [faind], *v.t. irr.* trouver; estimer; (*Law*) déclarer (*coupable*); prononcer (*un verdict*); (*fig.*) pourvoir; **to find out,** trouver, découvrir, inventer, résoudre; démasquer; **to find out about,** se renseigner sur; découvrir la vérité de.—*n.* découverte, trouvaille, *f.*

finding [ˈfaindiŋ], *n.* (*Law*) verdict, *m.*

fine (1) [fain], *n.* amende, *f.*—*v.t.* mettre à l'amende.

fine (2) [fain], *a.* fin; raffiné; subtil; beau (*à voir*); (*fig.*) bon, accompli; (*colloq.*) fameux; **it is fine,** il fait beau (*temps*).

fine arts [fainˈɑːts], *n.pl.* beaux arts, *m.pl.*

finely [ˈfainli], *adv.* fin, délicatement; élégamment; (*colloq.*) bien; (*iron.*) joliment.

fineness [ˈfainnis], *n.* finesse, délicatesse, *f.*

finery [ˈfainəri], *n.* parure, *f.*, beaux habits, *m.pl.*

finesse [fiˈnes], *n.* finesse, *f.*

finger [ˈfiŋgə], *n.* doigt, *m.*; (*fig.*) main, *f.*—*v.t.* toucher, manier.—*v.i.* (*Mus.*) doigter.

fingering [ˈfiŋgəriŋ], *n.* maniement; (*Mus.*) doigté, *m.*

finger-nail [ˈfiŋgəneil], *n.* ongle de la main, *m.*

finger-print [ˈfiŋgəprint], *n.* empreinte digitale, *f.*

finger-stall [ˈfiŋgəstɔːl], *n.* doigtier, *m.*

finical [ˈfinikl], **finicking** [ˈfinikiŋ], (*colloq.*) **finicky** [ˈfiniki], *a.* précieux, méticuleux, vétilleux.

finish [ˈfiniʃ], *v.t.* finir, terminer; achever; (*Tech.*) usiner.—*v.i.* cesser, finir, prendre fin.—*n.* fini, *m.*; (*fig.*) fin; (*Spt.*) arrivée, *f.*

finished [ˈfiniʃt], *a.* fini; (*fig.*) parfait.

finishing [ˈfiniʃiŋ], *a.* dernier; (*Spt.*) **finishing line,** ligne d'arrivée, *f.*

finite [ˈfainait], *a.* fini; borné.

Finland [ˈfinlənd], *n.* la Finlande, *f.*

Finn [fin], *n.* Finlandais, Finnois, *m.*

Finnish [ˈfiniʃ], *a.* finlandais.—*n.* finnois (*langue*), *m.*

fir [fəː], *n.* sapin; bois de sapin, *m.*

fir-cone [ˈfəːkoun], *n.* pomme de pin, *f.*

fire [faiə], *n.* feu; incendie (*accidentel*), *m.*; (*fig.*) ardeur, *f.*; **fire!** au feu! **to be on fire,** être en feu; **to catch fire,** prendre feu; **to hang fire,** faire long feu; **to miss fire,** rater; **to set on fire, to set fire to,** mettre le feu à.—*v.t.* mettre le feu à; embraser, incendier; tirer (*fusil*); (*pop.*) renvoyer.—*v.i.* prendre feu; tirer; (*Motor.*) donner; **fire!** (*Mil.*) feu!

fire-alarm [ˈfaiərəlɑːm], *n.* avertisseur d'incendie, *m.*

fire-arms [ˈfaiərɑːmz], *n.pl.* armes à feu, *f.pl.*

426

fire-brigade ['faiəbrigeid], *n.* (corps de) sapeurs pompiers, *m.*

fire-engine ['faiərendʒin], *n.* pompe à incendie, *f.*

fire-escape ['faiəriskeip], *n.* échelle de sauvetage, *f.*

fire-extinguisher ['faiərikstiŋgwiʃə], *n.* extincteur, *m.*

fire-fly ['faiəflai], *n.* luciole, *f.*

fire-guard ['faiəga:d], *n.* garde-feu, *m.*

fireman ['faiəmən], *n.* (*pl.* -men [men]) pompier, *m.*

fireplace ['faiəpleis], *n.* cheminée, *f.*, foyer, âtre, *m.*

fireproof ['faiəpru:f], *a.* incombustible, ignifuge.

fireside ['faiəsaid], *n.* coin du feu; (*fig.*) foyer domestique, *m.*

fire-station ['faiəsteiʃən], *n.* caserne de pompiers, *f.*

fireworks ['faiəwə:ks], *n.pl.* feu d'artifice, *m.*

firing ['faiəriŋ], *n.* action d'incendier, *f.*; chauffage (*heating*), *m.*; cuisson (*de poterie etc.*), *f.*; combustible (*fuel*); (*Mil.*) feu, tir, *m.*, fusillade, *f.*

firm [fə:m], *a.* ferme, solide; constant.—*n.* maison de commerce, raison sociale, firme, *f.*

firmament ['fə:məmənt], *n.* firmament, *m.*

firmly ['fə:mli], *adv.* fermement, solidement.

firmness ['fə:mnis], *n.* fermeté, solidité, *f.*

first [fə:st], *a.* premier; (*in compounds*) unième; **twenty-first**, vingt et unième.—*n.* (le) premier, *m.*, (la) première, *f.*—*adv.* premièrement; **at first**, d'abord.

first-aid ['fə:st'eid], *n.* premiers secours, *m.pl.*; **first-aid post**, poste de secours, *m.*

first-born ['fə:stbɔ:n], *a.* premier-né, aîné.

first-class ['fə:st'kla:s], **first-rate** ['fə:st'reit], *a.* de premier ordre; de premier choix; (*colloq.*) de première force; **first-class compartment**, compartiment de première classe, *m.*

firth [fə:θ], *n.* (*Sc.*) estuaire, *m.*

fiscal ['fiskəl], *a.* fiscal.

fiscally ['fiskəli], *adv.* fiscalement.

fish [fiʃ], *n.* poisson, *m.*; **a pretty kettle of fish**, un beau gâchis; **a queer fish**, un drôle de type.—*v.t.* pêcher.—*v.i.* pêcher; **to fish for**, pêcher; (*fig.*) rechercher, quêter.

fish-bone ['fiʃboun], *n.* arête, *f.*

fisher ['fiʃə], **fisherman** ['fiʃəmən] (*pl.* -men [men]), *n.* pêcheur, *m.*

fishery ['fiʃəri], *n.* pêche; pêcherie, *f.*

fish-hook ['fiʃhuk], *n.* hameçon.

fishing ['fiʃiŋ], *n.* pêche, *f.*; **to go fishing**, aller à la pêche.

fishing-boat ['fiʃiŋbout], *n.* bateau de pêche, *m.*

fishing-rod ['fiʃiŋrɔd], *n.* canne à pêche, *f.*

fish-knife ['fiʃnaif], *n.* couteau à poisson, *m.*

fishmonger ['fiʃmʌŋgə], *n.* marchand de poisson, *m.*

fish-slice ['fiʃslais], *n.* truelle à poisson, *f.*

fishy ['fiʃi], *a.* de poisson, poissonneux; qui sent le poisson; (*slang*) louche, véreux.

fission ['fiʃən], *n.* (*Biol.*) fissiparité, *f.*; (*Phys.*) fission, désintégration, *f.*; **nuclear fission**, fission nucléaire.

fissure ['fiʃə], *n.* fissure, fente, *f.*

fist [fist], *n.* poing, *m.*

fisted ['fistid], *a.* **close-fisted**, avare, dur à la détente.

fisticuffs ['fistikʌfs], *n.pl.* coups de poing, *m.pl.*

fit (1) [fit], *n.* accès (*de colère etc.*), *m.*; attaque (*de maladie*); convulsion, *f.*; **by fits and starts**, à bâtons rompus, par accès.

fit (2) [fit], *a.* propre, bon, convenable (*à*); juste, à propos; capable (*de*); en bonne santé, en forme; **to think fit**, juger convenable, juger bon.—*n.* ajustement (*de vêtements*), *m.*; (*fig.*) coupe, forme, *f.*—*v.t.* convenir à; aller à (*vêtements*); habiller; adapter, ajuster; **to fit out**, équiper, monter, armer (*un navire*).—*v.i.* convenir; s'adapter (*à*), aller bien (*vêtements*); **to fit in with**, s'accorder avec.

fitful ['fitful], *a.* agité; capricieux; irrégulier.

fitfully ['fitfuli], *adv.* par boutades; irrégulièrement.

fitly ['fitli], *adv.* à propos, convenablement.

fitness ['fitnis], *n.* convenance, *f.*; à-propos, *m.*; **physical fitness**, bonne forme, *f.*

fitter ['fitə], *n.* ajusteur; (*Dress.*) essayeur, *m.*

fitting ['fitiŋ], *a.* convenable, à propos, juste. —*n.* ajustement, essayage, *m.*, (*pl.*) garniture, *f.*

five [faiv], *a.* and *n.* cinq, *m.*

fix [fiks], *v.t.* fixer, attacher, arrêter, établir; (*colloq.*) réparer.—*v.i.* se fixer.—*n.* difficulté, impasse, *f.*, embarras, *m.*

fixation [fik'seiʃən], *n.* fixation, *f.*

fixed [fikst], *a.* fixe, fixé.

fixedly ['fiksidli], *adv.* fixement.

fixture ['fikstʃə], *n.* meuble à demeure, *m.*, agencements fixes, *m.pl.*; match, engagement (*prévu, annoncé*), *m.*

fizzy ['fizi], *a.* gazeux (*limonade etc.*), mousseux (*vin*).

flabby ['flæbi], *a.* flasque; mollasse (*personne*).

flag (1) [flæg], *v.i.* pendre mollement; se relâcher, faiblir; s'affaisser.

flag (2) [flæg], *n.* drapeau, (*Naut.*) pavillon; iris (*plante*); carreau, *m.*, dalle (*pierre*), *f.*— *v.t.* paver, daller; pavoiser.

flag-day ['flægdei], *n.* jour de quête, *m.*

flag-officer ['flægɔfisə], *n.* chef d'escadre, *m.*

flagon ['flægən], *n.* flacon, *m.*; burette (*d'église*), *f.*

flagrancy ['fleigrənsi], *n.* énormité, notoriété.

flagrant ['fleigrənt], *a.* flagrant, notoire, énorme.

flag-ship ['flægʃip], *n.* vaisseau amiral, *m.*

flagstaff ['flægsta:f], *n.* mât de pavillon, *m.*

flagstone ['flægstoun], *n.* dalle, *f.*

flail [fleil], *n.* fléau, *m.*

flair [fleə], *n.* perspicacité, *f.*, flair, *m.*; aptitude (*à*), *f.*

flake [fleik], *n.* flocon, *m.*; écaille; étincelle, *f.* —*v.t.* former en flocons, écailler.—*v.i.* s'écailler.

flaky ['fleiki], *a.* floconneux; écaillé; feuilleté (*pâtisserie*).

flame [fleim], *n.* flamme, *f.*; feu, *m.*—*v.i.* flamber.

flaming ['fleimiŋ], *a.* flamboyant, flambant; (*fig.*) violent, ardent; (*pop.*) sacré.

flamingo [flə'miŋgou], *n.* (*Orn.*) flamant, *m.*

flan [flæn], *n.* flan, *m.*

Flanders ['fla:ndəz]. la Flandre, *f.*

flange

flange [flændʒ], n. bride, f., rebord (*d'un tube etc.*); (*Tech.*) boudin (*de roue*), m.; (*Motor.*) ailette, collerette, f.

flank [flæŋk], n. flanc; côté, m.—v.t. flanquer (*de*); (*Mil.*) prendre en flanc.—v.i. border.

flannel [flænl], a. de flanelle.—n. flanelle, f.; (*pl.*) pantalon de flanelle, m.

flap [flæp], v.t. frapper légèrement; battre, agiter.—v.i. battre légèrement (*fig., pop.*) s'affoler.—n. battement (*d'aile*); claquement (*de voile*); petit coup (*de la main*), m.; tape, f.; battant (*d'une table etc.*), m.; patte (*d'une poche*), f.; pan (*d'un habit*); rabat (*d'une enveloppe*); (*fig., pop.*) affolement, m.

flare [fleə], v.i. flamboyer; s'évaser (*jupe*); **to flare up**, flamber; (*fig.*) se mettre en colère.—n. flamme, f.; (*Av.*) brûlot, m.

flash [flæʃ], n. éclair, éclat, jet de lumière; (*fig.*) trait; (*Mil.*) écusson, m.—v.t. faire jaillir, lancer.—v.i. luire, éclater, étinceler.

flashy [flæʃi], a. voyant, clinquant; superficiel.

flask [flɑːsk], n. flacon, m., gourde, f.

flat [flæt], a. plat; étendu (*à terre*); éventé (*vin etc.*); (*Comm.*) languissant; (*Mus.*) bémol; grave (*son*); (*fig.*) net, clair; fade, insipide (*goût*).—n. surface plane, f.; étage (*d'une maison*), appartement, m.; (*Mus.*) bémol; (*Theat.*) châssis, m.

flat-iron [flætaiən], n. fer à repasser, m.

flatly [flætli], adv. à plat; (*fig.*) nettement, clairement.

flatten [flætn], v.t. aplatir, aplanir; éventer (*boisson alcoolique*); (*fig.*) abattre, attrister; (*Mus.*) rendre grave.—v.i. s'aplatir; s'éventer (*boisson alcoolique*).

flatter [flætə], v.t. flatter.

flatterer [flætərə], n. flatteur, m.

flattering [flætəriŋ], a. flatteur.

flattery [flætəri], n. flatterie, f.

flatulence [flætjuləns], n. flatuosité; flatulence, f.

flatulent [flætjulənt], a. flatueux.

flaunt [flɔːnt], v.t. faire parade de, étaler, déployer.—v.i. se pavaner, parader, flotter.—n. étalage, m., parade, f.

flavour [fleivə], n. saveur, f.; goût, fumet (*de viande*); arome (*de thé, café etc.*); bouquet (*de vin*), m.—v.t. donner du goût, un arome etc. à, assaisonner (*de*).

flavouring [fleivəriŋ], n. assaisonnement, m.

flaw [flɔː], n. défaut, m.; fêlure; brèche, fente; paille (*de pierres précieuses*), f.

flawless [flɔːlis], a. parfait, sans défaut.

flax [flæks], a. de lin.—n. lin, m.

flaxen [flæksən], a. de lin; blond filasse (*cheveux*).

flay [flei], v.t. écorcher.

flaying [fleiiŋ], n. écorchement, m.

flea [fliː], n. puce, f.

fleck [flek], n. tache, moucheture, marque, f.—v.t. moucheter, tacheter (*de*).

fledg(e)ling [fledʒliŋ], n. oisillon, m.

flee [fliː], v.t. irr. fuir, éviter.—v.i. s'enfuir, se réfugier.

fleece [fliːs], n. toison, f.—v.t. tondre; (*fig.*) écorcher, plumer.

fleecy [fliːsi], a. laineux, (*fig.*) floconneux.

fleet (1) [fliːt], n. flotte, f.; **the Home Fleet**, la flotte métropolitaine.

fleet (2) [fliːt], a. vite, rapide, leste.

fleeting [fliːtiŋ], a. fugitif, passager.

Fleming [flemiŋ], n. Flamand, m.

Flemish [flemiʃ], a. flammand.—n. flamand (*langue*), m.

flesh [fleʃ], n. chair; viande (*meat*), f.; **in the flesh**, en chair et en os; **to put on flesh**, s'empâter, prendre de l'embonpoint.—v.t. (*Hunt.*) acharner; écharner (*peaux*).

fleshy [fleʃi], a. charnu.

flex (1) [fleks], n. fil électrique, m.

flex (2) [fleks], v.t. fléchir.

flexibility [fleksi'biliti], n. flexibilité, souplesse, f.

flexible [fleksibl], a. flexible, souple.

flick [flik], n. petit coup (*de fouet, de torchon*), m.; chiquenaude, f.; (*pl.*) (*pop.*) ciné, m.—v.t. effleurer; donner une chiquenaude à.

flicker [flikə], v.i. trembloter, vaciller (*lumière*); ciller (*paupières*).

flickering [flikəriŋ], a. vacillant, clignotant.—n. trémoussement; clignement, m.; vacillation, f.

flight [flait], n. vol, m., volée (*d'oiseaux etc.*); fuite, f.; (*fig.*) élan, m.; (*Av.*) escadrille, f.; **flight of stairs**, escalier, m.; **flight of steps**, perron, m.; **in flight**, en déroute.

flightiness [flaitinis], n. légèreté, étourderie, f.

flighty [flaiti], a. étourdi, léger; volage.

flimsiness [flimzinis], n. légèreté; (*fig.*) mesquinerie, f.

flimsy [flimzi], a. mollasse, léger, sans consistance.

flinch [flintʃ], v.i. reculer, céder.

fling [fliŋ], v.t. irr. jeter, lancer.—n. coup (*lancé*), m.; ruade (*de cheval*), f.; pas seul (*danse écossaise*); (*fig.*) essai; trait, coup de patte, m., raillerie, f.

flint [flint], n. silex, m., pierre à briquet; (*fig.*) roche, dureté, f.

flip [flip], n. petit coup, m., chiquenaude, f.; flip (*boisson*), m.

flippancy [flipənsi], n. ton léger; bavardage, m.

flippant [flipənt], a. léger; désinvolte; cavalier (*manières, mine*).

flipper [flipə], n. nageoire, f.

flirt [fləːt], v.i. faire la coquette, flirter (*femme*); conter fleurette (*homme*).—n. coquette, f.

flirtation [fləː'teiʃən], n. coquetterie, f.; flirt, m.

flit [flit], v.i. fuir, voltiger; (*Sc.*) déménager.—n. **to do a moonlight flit**, déménager à la cloche de bois.

float [flout], v.t. faire flotter, (*fig.*) lancer.—v.i. flotter, surnager; **to float on one's back**, faire la planche.—n. train (*bois*); flotteur; char (*carnaval*), m.

floating [floutiŋ], a. flottant; **floating capital**, fonds de roulement, m.; **floating dock**, bassin à flot, m.

flock [flɔk], n. troupeau, m.; bande, troupe, f.; ouailles (*paroissiens*), f.pl.; flocon, m., bourre (*de laine etc.*), f.—v.i. s'attrouper, s'assembler.

floe [flou], n. nappe de glaçons flottants; banquise, f.

flog [flɔg], v.t. fouetter, flageller; (*pop.*) bazarder.

flogging [flɔgiŋ], n. fouet, m.; flagellation, f.

flood [flʌd], *n.* déluge, *m.*; inondation, crue, *f.*; (*fig.*) cours d'eau, torrent, *m.*; marée, *f.*—*v.t.* inonder, submerger, noyer.

flood-light ['flʌdlait], *n.* projecteur, *m.*—*v.t.* illuminer (*un monument*) avec des projecteurs.

flood-tide ['flʌdtaid], *n.* marée montante, *f.*

floor [flɔː], *n.* plancher; carreau, parquet (*pavage*); étage (*storey*), *m.*—*v.t.* planchéier, parqueter; (*fig.*) terrasser, réduire au silence.

flooring ['flɔːriŋ], *n.* plancher, parquet, *m.*

flop [flɔp], *int.* plouf!—*n.* (*Theat.*) four, *m.*

floral ['flɔːrəl, 'flɔːrəl], *a.* floral; **floral games**, jeux floraux, *m.pl.*

Florence ['flɔrəns]. Florence, *f.*

florid ['flɔrid], *a.* fleuri.

Florida ['flɔridə]. la Floride, *f.*

florist ['flɔrist], *n.* fleuriste, *m., f.*

floss [flɔs], *n.* bourre (*de soie*), *f.*; (*Metal.*) floss; (*Bot.*) duvet, *m.*

flotilla [flo'tilə], *n.* flottille, *f.*

flounder (1) ['flaundə], *n.* (*Ichth.*) flet, petit flétan, *m.*

flounder (2) ['flaundə], *v.i.* se débattre; patauger.

flour ['flauə], *n.* farine; fécule (*des pommes de terre etc.*), *f.*

flourish ['flʌriʃ], *n.* éclat, *m.*; fleur de rhétorique, *f.*; panache (*manières, geste*); moulinet, tour, *m.*; (*Mus.*) fioriture; fanfare (*trompettes*), *f.*—*v.t.* fleurir; parafer; brandir (*épée etc.*).—*v.i.* fleurir; venir bien (*plantes*); prospérer.

flourishing ['flʌriʃiŋ], *a.* florissant.

flout [flaut], *v.t.* railler; se moquer de.—*n.* moquerie, raillerie, *f.*

flow [flou], *v.i.* s'écouler, couler; monter (*marée*); (*fig.*) découler (*de*).—*n.* écoulement; flux; (*fig.*) épanchement, *m.*

flower ['flauə], *n.* fleur; (*fig.*) élite, *f.*—*v.i.* fleurir, être en fleur.

flower-bed ['flauəbed], *n.* plate-bande, *f.*, parterre, *m.*

flowered ['flauəd], *a.* figuré; fleuri; **double flowered**, à fleurs doubles.

flower-garden ['flauəgɑːdn], *n.* jardin d'agrément, *m.*

flower-pot ['flauəpɔt], *n.* pot à fleurs, *m.*

flowing ['flouiŋ], *a.* coulant; (*fig.*) naturel.—*n.* cours, écoulement, *m.*

flown [floun], *a.* envolé; **high-flown**, gonflé, outré (*style*).

flu [fluː], (*colloq.*) [INFLUENZA].

fluctuate ['flʌktjueit], *v.i.* balancer, flotter, varier.

fluctuating ['flʌktjueitiŋ], *a.* flottant; incertain; variable.

fluctuation [flʌktju'eiʃən], *n.* fluctuation, *f.*; (*fig.*) balancement, doute, *m.*

flue [fluː], *n.* tuyau de cheminée; carneau (*d'un fourneau*), *m.*

fluency ['fluːənsi], *n.* facilité (*de parole*), *f.*

fluent ['fluːənt], *a.* coulant, courant; facile.

fluently ['fluːəntli], *adv.* couramment, avec facilité.

fluff [flʌf], *n.* duvet, *m.*, peluches, *f.pl.*

fluid ['fluːid], *a.* and *n.* fluide, liquide, *m.*

fluke [fluːk], *n.* patte (*d'ancre*), *f.*; carrelet (*poisson*), *f.*; (*fig.*) coup de raccroc, *m.*

flunkey ['flʌŋki], *n.* laquais, (*colloq.*) sycophante, *m.*

flurry ['flʌri], *n.* agitation, *f.*, désordre, émoi, *m.*—*v.t.* agiter, ahurir.

flush [flʌʃ], *a.* frais, plein de vigueur; à fleur, au ras (*de niveau*); **flush with the ground**, à ras de terre.—*n.* rougeur, *f.*; transport, *m.*; chasse d'eau, *f.*; (*Cards*) flush, *m.*—*v.t.* faire rougir; laver à grande eau; (*Hunt.*) lever; (*fig.*) animer.—*v.i.* rougir; partir tout à coup.

fluster ['flʌstə], *v.t.* déconcerter, agiter, ahurir.—*n.* agitation, *f.*

flute [fluːt], *n.* flûte, *f.*

fluted ['fluːtid], *a.* cannelé.

flutter ['flʌtə], *n.* trémoussement, émoi, *m.*; agitation, *f.*; battement d'ailes, *m.*—*v.t.* mettre en désordre, agiter, ahurir.—*v.i.* battre des ailes; agiter; palpiter.

flux [flʌks], *n.* flux, courant; (*Metal.*) fondant, *m.*

fly (1) [flai], *n.* (*pl.* **flies** [flaiz]) (*Ent.*) mouche, *f.*

fly (2) [flai], *v.t. irr.* faire voler; fuir, éviter.—*v.i.* voler, s'envoler, se sauver, prendre la fuite, fuir. s'enfuir; **to fly into a passion**, s'emporter, se mettre en colère; **to fly over**, survoler.—*a.* (*pop.*) malin.

flyer ['flaiə], *n.* aviateur, *m.*

flying ['flaiiŋ], *a.* volant; **flying squad**, brigade mobile, *f.*

flying-boat ['flaiiŋbout], *n.* hydravion, *m.*

flying-buttress ['flaiiŋbʌtris], *n.* arc-boutant, *m.*

fly-over ['flaiouvə], *n.* enjambement, *m.*

fly-paper ['flaipeipə], *n.* papier tue-mouches, *m.*

fly-past ['flaipɑːst], *n.* défilé aérien, *m.*

foal [foul], *n.* poulain, *m.*, pouliche, *f.*—*v.i.* pouliner, mettre bas.

foam [foum], *n.* écume; bave; mousse, *f.*—*v.i.* écumer; moutonner (*mer*); baver (*animaux*).

foaming ['foumiŋ], *a.* écumant.

fob [fɔb], *n.* gousset (*de pantalon*), *m.*—*v.t.* (*fam.*) **to fob someone off with something**, refiler quelque chose à quelqu'un.

fo'c's'le [fouksl], [FORECASTLE].

focus ['foukəs], *n.* (*pl.* **foci** ['fousai], **focuses** ['foukəsiz]) foyer, *m.*—*v.t.* mettre au point.

fodder ['fɔdə], *n.* fourrage, *m.*, pâture, *f.*; **cannon-fodder**, chair à canon, *f.*

foe [fou], *n.* ennemi, adversaire, *m.*

fog [fɔg], *n.* brouillard, *m.*; (*fig.*) perplexité, *f.*; **sea fog**, brume, *f.*

fog-bound ['fɔgbaund], *a.* enveloppé de brouillard; arrêté par le brouillard.

foggy ['fɔgi], *a.* brumeux; (*fig.*) sombre; **it is foggy**, il fait du brouillard.

fogy, fogey ['fougi], *n.* ganache, vieille perruque, *f.*

foil [fɔil], *n.* feuille de métal, *f.*; tain (*de miroir*), *m.*; défaite, *f.*, échec (*check*); contraste, repoussoir (*set off*); (*Fenc.*) fleuret, *m.*—*v.t.* déjouer, faire échouer; frustrer.

fold (1) [fould], *v.t.* plier, ployer; envelopper; serrer; **to fold one's arms**, croiser les bras. —*n.* pli, repli, *m.*; **threefold**, triple; **twofold**, double.

fold (2) [fould], *n.* parc (*à moutons*), *m.*, bergerie, *f.*—*v.t.* **to fold sheep**, parquer des moutons.

folder ['fouldə], *n.* chemise (*à documents*), *f.*; dépliant, prospectus, *m.*

folding ['fouldiŋ], *a.* pliant; brisé, à deux battants (*porte*).

foliage ['fouliidȝ], *n.* feuillage, *m.*

folio ['fouliou], *n.* in-folio, *m.*; page, *f.*, folio, *m.*

folk(s) [fouk(s)], *n.* (*pl.*) gens, *m.pl.*, *f.pl.*, personnes, *f.pl.*

folklore ['fouklɔ:], *n.* folklore, *m.*, légendes, traditions populaires, *f.pl.*

folk-song ['fouksɔŋ], *n.* chanson populaire, *f.*

follow ['folou], *v.t.* suivre; poursuivre; observer, imiter; exercer (*une profession*).—*v.i.* s'ensuivre, résulter; *as follows*, comme suit.

follower ['folouə], *n.* suivant; partisan; compagnon; (*colloq.*) amoureux, *m.*

following ['folouiŋ], *a.* suivant.—*n.* suite, *f.*, parti, *m.*

folly ['foli], *n.* folie, sottise, bêtise, *f.*

foment [fo'ment], *v.t.* fomenter.

fond [fond], *a.* passionné (*pour*); fou (*de*); indulgent (*pour*); doux, cher (*espoir*); vain, sot; *to be (passionately) fond of*, aimer (à la folie).

fondle [fondl], *v.t.* câliner, caresser.

fondly ['fondli], *adv.* tendrement.

fondness ['fondnis], *n.* tendresse; affection, *f.*; penchant, goût, *m.*

font [font], *n.* fonts baptismaux, *m.pl.*

food [fu:d], *n.* nourriture, *f.*, aliment. *m.*; vivres, *m.pl.*; denrées, *f.pl.*; pâture (*pour animaux*), *f.*

food-stuffs ['fu:dstʌfs], *n.pl.* comestibles, *m.pl.*

fool [fu:l], *n.* sot; insensé, imbécile, niais, *m.*; dupe, *f.*, fou (*bouffon*), *m.*; *to make a fool of*, se moquer de; *to make a fool of oneself*, se rendre ridicule, se faire moquer de soi.—*v.t.* duper; (*colloq.*) se moquer de.—*v.i.* faire la bête; *you are fooling*, vous plaisantez; vous blaguez.

foolery ['fu:ləri], *n.* folie, sottise; niaiserie, *f.*

foolhardy ['fu:lha:di], *a.* téméraire.

foolish ['fu:liʃ], *a.* sot, insensé, bête, ridicule.

foolishly ['fu:liʃli], *adv.* follement, sottement.

foolishness ['fu:liʃnis], *n.* folie, sottise, *f.*

foolproof ['fu:lpru:f], *a.* indéréglable.

foot [fut], *n.* (*pl.* **feet** [fi:t]) pied, *m.*; patte (*d'insectes etc.*); base (*de colonne*), *f.*; bas (*d'une page*), *m.*; (*Mil.*) infanterie, *f.*; *on foot*, à pied.

football ['futbɔ:l], *n.* ballon; football (*jeu*), *m.*

foot-bridge ['futbridȝ], *n.* passerelle, *f.*

footfall ['futfɔ:l], *n.* pas, bruit de pas, *m.*

foothold ['futhould], *n.* prise pour le pied, *f.*; (*fig.*) point d'appui, *m.*

footing ['futiŋ], *n.* pied, point d'appui; établissement, *m.*; position, *f.*; *on an equal footing*, sur un pied d'égalité.

footlights ['futlaits], *n.pl.* (*Theat.*) rampe, *f.*

footman ['futmən], *n.* (*pl.* **-men** [men]) laquais, valet de pied, *m.*

footnote ['futnout], *n.* note au bas de la page, apostille, *f.*

foot-path ['futpa:θ], *n.* sentier; trottoir (*de rue*), *m.*

foot-print ['futprint], *n.* empreinte du pied, *f.*

foot-soldier ['futsouldȝə], *n.* fantassin, *m.*

footstep ['futstep], *n.* pas, *m.*; trace, *f.*; vestige, *m.*

footstool ['futstu:l], *n.* tabouret, *m.*

footwear ['futweə], *n.* chaussures, *f.pl.*

fop [fop], *n.* fat, *m.*

foppery ['fopəri], *n.* affectation, fatuité, *f.*

foppish ['fopiʃ], *a.* affecté, sot, fat.

for [fɔ:], *prep.* pour, par; de, à, vers, pendant; depuis; en place de, en lieu de; en faveur de; à cause de, pour le compte de; malgré; pour avoir; pour que (*with subj.*).—*conj.* car.

forage ['foridȝ], *n.* fourrage, *m.*—*v.i.* fourrager.

****forasmuch** [fɔrəz'mʌtʃ], *conj.* **forasmuch as**, d'autant que, vu que.

foray ['forei], *n.* incursion, razzia, *f.*, raid, *m.*

forbear (1) [FOREBEAR].

forbear (2) [fɔ:'bɛə], *v.t. irr.* cesser; épargner; supporter.—*v.i.* s'abstenir, se garder (*de*).

forbearance [fɔ:'bɛərəns], *n.* patience; indulgence, *f.*

forbid [fə'bid], *v.t. irr.* défendre, interdire (*de*); empêcher (*de*); *God forbid!* à Dieu ne plaise!

forbidding [fə'bidiŋ], *a.* rebutant, repoussant.

force [fɔ:s], *n.* force; violence; efficacité; valeur, *f.*; (*Mil.*) forces, *f.pl.*, armée, *f.*; *in force*, (*Law*) en vigueur.—*v.t.* forcer, contraindre (*à* ou *de*); violenter.

forced [fɔ:st], *a.* forcé, contraint; guindé (*style*).

forcedly ['fɔ:sidli], *adv.* de force.

forceps ['fɔ:seps], *n.pl.* (*Surg.*) pince, *f.*, forceps, *m.*

forcible ['fɔ:sibl], **forceful** ['fɔ:sful], *a.* fort; énergique.

forcibly ['fɔ:sibli], *adv.* par force; fortement.

ford [fɔ:d], *n.* gué, *m.*—*v.t.* passer à gué, guéer.

fore! (1) [fɔ:], *int.* (*Golf*) gare devant!

fore (2) [fɔ:], *a.* antérieur; de devant; (*Naut.*) de misaine; *fore and aft*, (*Naut.*) de l'avant à l'arrière.—*adv.* d'avance; (*Naut.*) de l'avant.

forearm (1) [fɔ:r'a:m], *v.t.* prémunir.

forearm (2) ['fɔ:ra:m], *n.* avant-bras, *m.*

forebear ['fɔ:bɛə], *n.* aïeul, ancêtre, *m.*

forebode [fɔ:'boud], *v.t.* présager, prédire; pressentir.

foreboding [fɔ:'boudiŋ], *n.* présage, pressentiment, *m.*

forecast ['fɔ:ka:st], *n.* prévoyance, prévision, *f.*; pronostic, *m.*; *weather forecast*, prévisions météorologiques, *f.pl.*—*v.t.* prévoir; pronostiquer.

forecastle [fouksl, 'fɔ:ka:sl], *n.* gaillard d'avant, *m.*

fore-court ['fɔ:kɔ:t], *n.* avant-cour, *f.*

forefather ['fɔ:fa:ðə], *n.* aïeul, ancêtre, *m.*

forefinger ['fɔ:fiŋgə], *n.* index, *m.*

forego [fɔ:'gou], *v.t.* précéder, aller devant.

foregone [fɔ:'gɔn], *a.* prévu, résolu, décidé d'avance.

foreground ['fɔ:graund], *n.* premier plan, *m.*

forehead ['forid], *n.* front, *m.*

foreign ['forin], *a.* étranger; *Foreign Office*, Ministère des Affaires Étrangères, *m.*

foreigner ['forinə], *n.* étranger, *m.*

foreland ['fɔ:lənd], *n.* promontoire, cap, *m.*

foreleg ['fɔ:leg], *n.* patte de devant, *f.*

forelock ['fɔ:lɔk], *n.* goupille, *f.*; toupet, *m.*

foreman ['fɔ:mən], *n.* (*pl.* **-men** [men]) chef (*d'un jury*); contremaître; chef d'atelier *ou* d'équipe; brigadier, *m.*

foremast ['fɔ:ma:st], *n.* mât de misaine, *m.*

foremost ['fɔːmoust], *a.* premier; en tête, au premier rang; *first and foremost*, tout d'abord.
forenoon ['fɔːnuːn], *n.* matin, *m.*, matinée, *f.*
forensic [fɔ'rensik], *a.* **forensic medicine**, médecine légale, *f.*
forerunner ['fɔːrʌnə], *n.* précurseur, *m.*
foresee [fɔː'siː], *v.t. irr. (conjug. like* SEE) prévoir.
foreseeable [fɔː'siːəbl], *a.* prévisible.
foreshore ['fɔːʃɔː], *n.* plage, *f.*
foreshorten [fɔː'ʃɔːtn], *v.t. (Paint.)* dessiner en raccourci.
foreshortening [fɔː'ʃɔːtniŋ], *n.* raccourci, *m.*
foresight ['fɔːsait], *n.* prévoyance, *f.*; guidon *(d'arme à feu)*, *m.*; *lack of foresight*, imprévoyance, *f.*
forest ['fɔrist], *a.* de forêt, forestier.—*n.* forêt, *f.*
forestall [fɔː'stɔːl], *v.t.* anticiper, devancer.
forester ['fɔristə], *n.* garde forestier; habitant d'une forêt, *m.*
forestry ['fɔristri], *n.* sylviculture, *f.*
foretaste ['fɔːteist], *n.* avant-goût, *m.*; anticipation, *f.*
foretell [fɔː'tel], *v.t. irr. (conjug. like* TELL) prédire.
forethought ['fɔːθɔːt], *n.* prévoyance, prescience, *f.*
forewarn [fɔː'wɔːn], *v.t.* prévenir, avertir.
foreword ['fɔːwəːd], *n.* préface, *f.*; avant-propos, *m.*
forfeit ['fɔːfit], *a.* confisqué; *(fig.)* perdu.—*n.* amende *(à payer)*; forfaiture, confiscation, *f.*; *(Games)* gage, *m.*—*v.t.* forfaire *(à)*; confisquer; perdre.
forfeiture ['fɔːfitʃə], *n.* forfaiture, confiscation; perte, déchéance, *f.*
forgather [fɔː'gæðə], *v.i.* s'assembler, se réunir.
forge [fɔːdʒ], *n.* forge, *f.*—*v.t.* forger; contrefaire *(monnaie etc.)*, fabriquer *(document etc.)*.—*v.i.* commettre un faux; *to forge ahead*, pousser de l'avant.
forger ['fɔːdʒə], *n.* faussaire; faux-monnayeur, *m.*
forgery ['fɔːdʒəri], *n.* falsification; contrefaçon, *f.*; faux, *m.*
forget [fə'get], *v.t., v.i. irr.* oublier.
forgetful [fə'getful], *a.* oublieux.
forgetfulness [fə'getfulnis], *n.* oubli, manque de mémoire, *m.*; négligence, *f.*
forget-me-not [fə'getminɔt], *n.* myosotis, *m.*
forgive [fə'giv], *v.t. irr. (conjug. like* GIVE) pardonner, faire grâce de; pardonner à.
forgiveness [fə'givnis], *n.* pardon, *m.*; clémence, grâce, *f.*
forgiving [fə'giviŋ], *a.* clément, miséricordieux.
forgo [fɔː'gou], *v.t. irr. (conjug. like* GO) renoncer à, s'abstenir de, se refuser à.
fork [fɔːk], *n.* fourchette; fourche; bifurcation *(de rues)*; pointe *(d'une flèche etc.)*, *f.*; zigzag *(d'éclair)*, *m.*—*v.t.* enlever avec une fourche.—*v.i.* fourcher; bifurquer.
forked [fɔːkt], *a.* fourchu; *(Bot.)* bifurqué.
forlorn [fə'lɔːn], *a.* abandonné, désespéré, délaissé.
forlornness [fə'lɔːnnis], *n.* délaissement, abandon; état désespéré, *m.*
form [fɔːm], *n.* forme, figure; formalité, *f.*; banc *(siège)*, *m.*; *(Sch.)* classe, *f.*; gîte *(de lièvre)*;

imprimé *(fiche)*, *m.*—*v.t.* former, faire; façonner.—*v.i.* se former; se gîter *(lièvres)*.
formal ['fɔːməl], *a.* formel; pointilleux; affecté, cérémonieux, formaliste.
formality [fɔː'mæliti], *n.* formalité, cérémonie, *f.*
formally ['fɔːməli], *adv.* avec formalité, en forme, formellement.
formation [fɔː'meiʃən], *n.* formation, *f.*; ordre, *m.*
formative ['fɔːmətiv], *a.* formatif, formateur, plastique.
former ['fɔːmə], *a.* précédent, passé; ancien; premier *(de deux)*.—*pron.* celui-là, celle-là. —*n.* moule, *m.*
formerly ['fɔːməli], *adv.* autrefois, auparavant; jadis.
formidable ['fɔːmidəbl], *a.* formidable, redoutable.
formless ['fɔːmlis], *a.* informe, sans forme.
Formosa [fɔː'mouzə], Formose, *f.*
formula ['fɔːmjulə], *n. (pl.* **formulæ** ['fɔː mjul(a)iː]) formule, *f.*
forsake [fə'seik], *v.t. irr.* délaisser, abandonner.
forsaking [fə'seikiŋ], *n.* délaissement, abandon, *m.*
***forsooth** [fə'suːθ], *adv.* en vérité, ma foi.
forswear [fɔː'swɛə], *v.t. irr. (conjug. like* SWEAR) abjurer, répudier.—*v.i.* se parjurer.
fort [fɔːt], *n.* fort, *m.*, forteresse, *f.*
forth [fɔːθ], *adv.* en avant; au dehors; *and so forth*, et ainsi de suite.
forthcoming [fɔːθ'kʌmiŋ], *a.* tout prêt, prêt à paraître; prochain, à venir.
forthright ['fɔːθrait], *a.* franc, carré, brutal.
forthwith [fɔːθ'wið], *adv.* incontinent, aussitôt, sur-le-champ, tout de suite.
fortieth ['fɔːtiəθ], *a.* quarantième.—*n.* quarantième *(fraction)*, *m.*
fortification [fɔːtifi'keiʃən], *n.* fortification, *f.*
fortify ['fɔːtifai], *v.t.* fortifier; munir *(de)*.
fortifying ['fɔːtifaiiŋ], *a. (fig.)* réconfortant, fortifiant.
fortitude ['fɔːtitjuːd], *n.* force d'âme, *f.*, courage, *m.*
fortnight ['fɔːtnait], *n.* quinze jours, *m.pl.*, quinzaine, *f.*
fortnightly ['fɔːtnaitli], *a.* bimensuel.—*adv.* tous les quinze jours.
fortress ['fɔːtris], *n.* forteresse, place forte, *f.*
fortuitous [fɔː'tjuːitəs], *a.* fortuit.
fortuitously [fɔː'tjuːitəsli], *adv.* fortuitement, par hasard.
fortunate ['fɔːtʃənit, 'fɔːtjunit], *a.* heureux, fortuné.
fortunately ['fɔːtʃənitli], *adv.* heureusement.
fortune ['fɔːtʃən], *n.* fortune, *f.*, sort *(lot)*, destin, *m.*; *by good fortune*, par bonheur.
fortune-hunter ['fɔːtʃənhʌntə], *n.* aventurier, coureur de dots, *m.*
fortune-teller ['fɔːtʃəntelə], *n.* diseur de bonne aventure, *m.*
forty ['fɔːti], *a.* quarante; *she must be nearly forty*, elle doit friser la quarantaine.
forward ['fɔːwəd], *a.* avancé; *(fig.)* empressé *(de)*, ardent *(à)*; précoce *(fruits etc.)*; présomptueux.—*n. (Ftb.)* avant, *m.*—*adv.* en avant; en évidence.—*v.t.* avancer, hâter; *(Comm.)* envoyer, expédier; faire suivre *(lettre)*.

forwardness

forwardness ['fɔːwədnis], *n.* empressement; progrès, *m.*; précocité (*fruits etc.*); hardiesse; effronterie, *f.*
fossil ['fɔsil], *a. and n.* fossile, *m.*
foster ['fɔstə], *v.t.* élever, nourrir; (*fig.*) encourager.
foster-brother ['fɔstəbrʌðə], *n.* frère de lait, *m.*
foster-child ['fɔstətʃaild], *n.* nourrisson, *m.*
foster-father ['fɔstəfɑːðə], *n.* père nourricier, *m.*
foster-mother ['fɔstəmʌðə], *n.* mère nourricière, *f.*
foster-sister ['fɔstəsistə], *n.* sœur de lait, *f.*
foul [faul], *a.* sale, malpropre, immonde, trouble, bourbeux (*eau*); grossier (*langage*); *by fair means or foul,* de gré ou de force; *foul air,* air vicié, *m.*; *foul play,* trahison, *f.*—*n.* (*Spt.*) coup-bas, *m.*—*v.t.* salir, souiller, troubler; encrasser (*arme à feu*); (*Naut.*) aborder; s'engager (*cordes*).
foully ['faulli], *adv.* salement, honteusement.
foul-mouthed ['faulmauðd], *a.* grossier.
foulness ['faulnis], *n.* saleté, impureté; turpitude, noirceur, *f.*
found (1) [faund], *past and p.p.* [FIND].
found (2) [faund], *v.t.* fonder, établir; fondre (*to cast*).
foundation [faun'deiʃən], *n.* fondement, *m.*, fondation; (*fig.*) base, source, *f.*
founder (1) ['faundə], *n.* fondateur, auteur; (*Metal.*) fondeur, *m.*
founder (2) ['faundə], *v.t.* surmener (*un cheval*).—*v.i.* (*Naut.*) sombrer, couler bas; broncher (*un cheval*); (*fig.*) échouer.
foundered ['faundəd], *a.* courbatu (*cheval*); sombré (*navire*).
foundling ['faundliŋ], *n.* enfant trouvé, *m.*
foundry ['faundri], *n.* fonderie, *f.*
fount [faunt], *n.* fontaine, (*fig.*) cause, source, *f.*
fountain ['fauntin], *n.* fontaine, source, *f.*; jet d'eau, *m.*
fountain-head ['fauntinhed], *n.* source, origine, *f.*
fountain-pen ['fauntinpen], *n.* stylo, *m.*
four [fɔː], *a. and n.* quatre, *m.*; *carriage and four,* voiture à quatre chevaux, *f.*; *on all fours,* à quatre pattes.
four-engined ['fɔːrendʒind], *a.* (*Av.*) quadrimoteur.
four-fold ['fɔːfould], *a.* quatre fois, quatre fois autant, quadruple.
four-footed ['fɔːfutid], *a.* quadrupède, à quatre pieds.
fourteen ['fɔːtiːn], *a. and n.* quatorze, *m.*
fourteenth ['fɔːtiːnθ], *a.* quatorzième; quatorze (*date; rois etc.*).—*n.* quatorzième (*fraction*), *m.*
fourth [fɔːθ], *a.* quatrième; quatre (*date, roi etc.*).—*n.* quart (*fraction*), *m.*; (*Mus.*) quarte, *f.*
fowl [faul], *n.* oiseau, *m.*, poule (*hen*); (*Cook.*) volaille, *f.*
fowler ['faulə], *n.* oiseleur, *m.*
fowl-house ['faulhaus], *n.* poulailler, *m.*
fowling-piece ['fauliŋpiːs], *n.* fusil de chasse, *m.*
fox [fɔks], *n.* (*pl.* **foxes** ['fɔksiz]) renard; (*fig.*) rusé, *m.*
foxglove ['fɔksglʌv], *n.* digitale, *f.*
foxy ['fɔksi], *a.* de renard, rusé; roux (*red*).
fraction ['frækʃən], *n.* fraction, *f.*

fractious ['frækʃəs], *a.* revêche, maussade, hargneux, de mauvaise humeur.
fracture ['fræktʃə], *n.* fracture, cassure, *f.*—*v.t.* casser, rompre; (*Surg.*) fracturer.
fragile ['frædʒail], *a.* fragile.
fragility [frə'dʒiliti], *n.* fragilité, *f.*
fragment ['frægmənt], *n.* fragment, éclat, *m.*
fragrance ['freigrəns], *n.* odeur suave, *f.* parfum, *m.*
fragrant ['freigrənt], *a.* odoriférant, parfumé.
frail [freil], *a.* frêle, fragile, faible.—*n.* cabas, panier d'emballage, *m.*
frailty ['freilti], *n.* faiblesse, fragilité, *f.*
frame [freim], *n.* charpente, *f.*; châssis (*de fenêtre etc.*), chambranle (*de porte*), *m.*; (*fig.*) forme, *f.*; cadre (*de tableau etc.*), *m.*; disposition (*d'esprit*), *f.*—*v.t.* former, construire; encadrer; inventer.
framer ['freimə], *n.* encadreur; (*fig.*) auteur (*d'un projet*), *m.*
France [frɑːns]. la France, *f.*
Frances ['frɑːnsis]. Françoise, *f.*
franchise ['fræntʃaiz], *n.* franchise, *f.*, droit de vote, *m.*
Francis ['frɑːnsis]. François, Francis, *m.*
Franciscan [fræn'siskən], *a. and n.* Franciscain, *m.*
frank [fræŋk], *a.* franc, sincère, libéral; libre.—*v.t.* affranchir.
frankincense ['fræŋkinsens], *n.* encens, *m.*
frankly ['fræŋkli], *adv.* franchement.
frankness ['fræŋknis], *n.* franchise, sincérité, *f.*
frantic ['fræntik], *a.* frénétique, forcené, furieux.
frantically ['fræntikəli], *adv.* follement, avec frénésie.
fraternal [frə'təːnəl], *a.* fraternel.
fraternity [frə'təːniti], *n.* fraternité, confrérie, *f.*
fraud [frɔːd], *n.* imposteur (*personne*), *m.*; (*also* **fraudulence** ['frɔːdjuləns]) fraude, supercherie, *f.*, dol, *m.*
fraudulent ['frɔːdjulənt], *a.* frauduleux, de mauvaise foi.
fraught [frɔːt], *a.* rempli, plein (*de*); riche fertile (*en*).
fray (1) [frei], *n.* échauffourée, mêlée, bagarre, *f.*
fray (2) [frei], *v.t.* érailler, effilocher.—*v.i.* s'érailler.
fraying ['freiiŋ], *n.* éraillure, *f.*
freak [friːk], *n.* caprice, *m.*; bizarrerie, *f.*; monstre, *m.*; bigarrure, *f.*—*v.t.* bigarrer, tacheter (*de*).
freakish ['friːkiʃ], *a.* bizarre, fantasque, capricieux.
freckle ['frekl], *n.* tache de rousseur, tache de son, *f.*—*v.t.* tacheter.
Frederick ['fredrik]. Frédéric, *m.*
free [friː], *a.* libre; exempt; sincère, franc; gratuit; aisé, dégagé; *delivered free,* rendu franco à domicile; *free and easy,* sans façon.—*adv.* gratis.—*v.t.* délivrer, libérer.
freebooter ['friːbuːtə], *n.* maraudeur; flibustier, *m.*
freedman ['friːdmən], *n.* (*pl.* **-men** [men]) affranchi, *m.*
freedom ['friːdəm], *n.* liberté; indépendance; aisance; bourgeoisie (*d'une ville*), *f.*

432

freehold ['fri:hould], *n.* propriété foncière libre, *f.*

free-holder ['fri:houldə], *n.* propriétaire foncier, *m.*

freely ['fri:li], *adv.* librement, sans contrainte, gratuitement; libéralement.

freeman ['fri:mən], *n.* (*pl.* **-men** [men]) citoyen, homme libre, *m.*

freemason ['fri:meisn], *n.* franc-maçon, *m.*

freemasonry ['fri:meisnri], *n.* franc-maçonnerie, *f.*

freestone ['fri:stoun], *n.* pierre de taille, *f.*

freestyle ['fri:stail], *n.* nage libre, *f.*

freethinker ['fri:'θiŋkə], *n.* esprit fort, libre penseur, *m.*

free-trade ['fri:'treid], *n.* libre-échange, *m.*; *free-trade area,* zone de libre-échange, *f.*

free-trader ['fri:'treidə], *n.* libre-échangiste, *m.,f.*

freeze [fri:z], *v.t. irr.* geler; (*Fin.*) bloquer (*prix, salaires*).—*v.i.* se geler, se glacer.

freezing ['fri:ziŋ], *a.* glacial.—*n.* congélation, *f.*; (*Fin.*) blocage, *m.*

freight [freit], *n.* cargaison, *f.*, chargement; fret (*cost*), *m.*—*v.t.* fréter.

French [frentʃ], *a.* français; *French window,* porte-fenêtre, *f.*—*n.* français (*langue*), *m.*; *the French,* les Français, *m.pl.*

Frenchman ['frentʃmən], *n.* (*pl.* **-men** [men]) Français, *m.*

Frenchwoman ['frentʃwumən], *n.* (*pl.* **-women** [wimin]) Française, *f.*

frenzy ['frenzi], *n.* frénésie, *f.*; délire, *m.*

frequence ['fri:kwəns], **frequency** ['fri:kwənsi], *n.* fréquence; répétition fréquente, *f.*; *V.H.F.,* modulation de fréquence, *f.*

frequent ['fri:kwənt], *a.* fréquent, très répandu; rapide (*pouls*).—[fri'kwent], *v.t.* fréquenter; hanter.

frequently ['fri:kwəntli], *adv.* fréquemment, souvent.

fresco ['freskou], *n.* fresque, *f.*

fresh [freʃ], *a.* frais; récent, nouveau; (*fig.*) vigoureux; novice, vert; *fresh water,* eau douce, *f.*

freshen ['freʃən], *v.t.* rafraîchir.—*v.i.* se rafraîchir.

freshly ['freʃli], *adv.* fraîchement; récemment, depuis peu.

freshman ['freʃmən], *n.* (*pl.* **-men** [men]) étudiant de première année, bizuth, *m.*

freshness ['freʃnis], *n.* fraîcheur; (*fig.*) nouveauté, *f.*

freshwater ['freʃwɔ:tə], *a.* d'eau douce *ou* de rivière.

fret [fret], *n.* fermentation; (*fig.*) agitation de l'âme, *f.*—*v.t.* frotter (*contre*); ronger, écorcher (*excorier*); chagriner, irriter; découper.—*v.i.* se chagriner, s'inquiéter; s'user, s'érailler.

fretful ['fretful], *a.* chagrin, maussade; agité, inquiet.

fretfulness ['fretfulnis], *n.* mauvaise humeur, irritation, *f.*

fretsaw ['fretsɔ:], *n.* scie à découper, *f.*

fretwork ['fretwə:k], *n.* ouvrage à claire-voie; découpage, *m.*

friable ['fraiəbl], *a.* friable.

friar ['fraiə], *n.* moine, *m.*

friction ['frikʃən], *n.* frottement, *m.*; (*Med.*) friction, *f.*

Friday ['fraid(e)i]. vendredi, *m.*; *Good Friday,* vendredi saint.

friend [frend], *n.* ami, *m.*, amie, *f.*

friendless ['frendlis], *a.* sans ami, délaissé.

friendliness ['frendlinis], *n.* bienveillance, *f.*

friendly ['frendli], *a.* d'ami, amical; bienveillant (*pour*).

friendship ['frendʃip], *n.* amitié, *f.*

frieze [fri:z], *a.* de frise.—*n.* frise, *f.*

frigate ['frigit], *n.* frégate, *f.*

fright [frait], *n.* effroi, *m.*, épouvante, frayeur, *f.*

frighten [fraitn], *v.t.* épouvanter, effrayer, faire peur à.

frightful ['fraitful], *a.* épouvantable, effroyable, affreux.

frightfulness ['fraitfulnis], *n.* horreur, frayeur, *f.*

frigid ['fridʒid], *a.* froid, glacial.

frigidity [fri'dʒiditi], **frigidness** ['fridʒidnis], *n.* frigidité, froideur, *f.*

frill [fril], *n.* volant, *m.*, ruche, *f.*, jabot (*de chemise*), *m.*; *without frills,* sans façons.—*v.t.* plisser, froncer; rucher.

fringe [frindʒ], *n.* frange; crépine, *f.*; bord, *m.*; bordure, *f.*; effilé, *m.*—*v.t.* franger, border.

frippery ['fripəri], *n.* parure sans valeur, *f.*; clinquant, *m.*

frisk [frisk], *n.* gambade, *f.*—*v.i.* sautiller, gambader, frétiller.

friskiness ['friskinis], *n.* folâtrerie, gaieté, vivacité, *f.*

frisky ['friski], *a.* vif, enjoué, folâtre; fringant (*cheval*).

fritter ['fritə], *n.* (*Cook.*) beignet, *m.*—*v.t.* couper en morceaux, morceler; *to fritter away* (*one's time ou money*), gaspiller *ou* dissiper (*son temps ou son argent*).

frivolity [fri'voliti], *n.* frivolité, *f.*

frivolous ['frivələs], *a.* frivole.

frivolousness ['frivələsnis], *n.* frivolité, *f.*

frizz [friz], **frizzle** [frizl], *v.t.* friser, crêper.—*v.i.* frisotter (*cheveux*).—*n.* frisure, *f.*

frizzy ['frizi], *a.* frisottant, crêpé.

fro [frou], *adv.* en s'éloignant; *to go to and fro,* aller et venir.

frock [frok], *n.* robe d'enfant, robe, *f.*; froc (*de moine*), *m.*

frock-coat ['frokkout], *n.* redingote, *f.*

frog [frog], *n.* grenouille, *f.*

frogman ['frogmən], *n.* (*pl.* **-men** [men]) homme-grenouille, *m.*

frolic ['frolik], *n.* espièglerie, *f.*, ébats, *m.pl.*, gambades, *f.pl.*—*v.i.* folâtrer, gambader.

frolicsome ['froliksəm], *a.* folâtre, espiègle.

from [from], *prep.* de; depuis, dès, à partir de; par (*à cause de*); d'après (*selon*); par suite de, en conséquence de (*en raison de*); de la part de (*comme représentant de*); *as from,* à partir de (*telle ou telle date*); *from above,* d'en haut; *from afar,* de loin; *from behind,* de derrière; *from hence,* d'ici; *from thence,* de là; *from . . . till,* depuis . . . jusqu'à; *from you,* de votre part.

front [frʌnt], *n.* devant, *m.*; face, façade (*d'un édifice*); audace, *f.*, front, *m.*—*v.t.* faire face à; s'opposer à; donner sur.

frontage ['frʌntidʒ], *n.* façade, devanture (*de magasin*), *f.*

front-door ['frʌnt'dɔ:], *n.* porte d'entrée, *f.*

frontier ['frʌntiə], a. and n. frontière, f.
frontispiece ['frʌntispiːs], n. frontispice, m.
frost [frɔst], n. gelée, f., gel, m.; **glazed frost**, verglas, m.; **ground frost**, gelée blanche; **hoar-frost**, givre, m.—v.t. glacer; damasquiner.
frost-bite ['frɔstbait], n. gelure, froidure, f.
frosted ['frɔstid], a. givré; dépoli (verre).
frosty ['frɔsti], a. de gelée; glacé; (fig.) froid.
froth [frɔθ], n. écume; mousse (de boisson), f.
—v.i. écumer; mousser.
frothy ['frɔθi], a. écumeux; écumant; mousseux; (fig.) vain, frivole.
frown [fraun], n. froncement de sourcil, m.—
v.i. froncer les sourcils; être contraire (à); (fig.) **to frown upon**, désapprouver.
frowning ['frauniŋ], a. rechigné, renfrogné; (fig.) menaçant.
frowzy ['frauzi], a. sale, malpropre.
frozen [frouzn], a. glacé, gelé; (Fin.) bloqué.
fructify ['frʌktifai], v.t. fertiliser, féconder.—
v.i. fructifier.
frugal [fruːgl], a. frugal, économe, ménager.
frugality [fruːˈgæliti], n. économie, frugalité, f.
fruit [fruːt], a. à fruit, fruitier.—n. fruit, m.; fruits, m.pl.; (fig.) avantage, profit, m.; **first fruits**, prémices, f.pl.
fruiterer ['fruːtərə], n. fruitier, m.
fruitful ['fruːtful], a. fertile; (fig.) fécond.
fruitfully ['fruːtfuli], adv. fertilement, abondamment.
fruitfulness ['fruːtfulnis], n. fertilité; (fig.) fécondité, f.
fruition [fruːˈiʃən], n. jouissance, réalisation, f.
fruitless ['fruːtlis], a. stérile; (fig.) infructueux, inutile.
frump [frʌmp], n. femme désagréable et mal habillée, f.
frustrate [frʌsˈtreit], v.t. frustrer, rendre inutile, déjouer.
frustration [frʌsˈtreiʃən], n. frustration, f., insuccès, m.
fry (1) [frai], n. fretin, frai (petits poissons), m.
fry (2) [frai], n. (Cook.) friture, f.—v.t. frire, faire frire, sauter; **fried eggs**, œufs au plat, m.pl.—v.i. frire.
frying-pan ['fraiiŋpæn], n. poêle à frire, f.
fuchsia ['fjuːʃə], n. fuchsia, m.
fuddle [fʌdl], v.t. griser; hébéter.—v.i. se griser.
fudge [fʌdʒ], int. bah!—n. blague, faribole, f.; fondant américain (bonbon), m.
fuel ['fjuəl], n. combustible; (fig.) aliment, m.
fuel-oil ['fjuəlɔil], n. mazout, m.
fugitive ['fjuːdʒitiv], a. fugitif; fuyard, passager.—n. fugitif, transfuge, déserteur; (Mil.) fuyard, m.
fugue [fjuːg], n. (Mus.) fugue, f.
fulcrum ['fʌlkrəm], n. (pl. fulcra ['fʌlkrə]) point d'appui, m.
fulfil [fulˈfil], v.t. accomplir, réaliser; satisfaire.
fulfilment [fulˈfilmənt], n. exécution, f., accomplissement, m.
full [ful], a. plein, rempli; comble, replet; gras; entier, complet; ample; (fig.) repu; (Gram.) **full stop**, point, m.; **full up!** (autobus etc.) complet!—adv. tout à fait, entièrement; parfaitement.—n. plein; comble, m., satiété, f.; soûl, m.

full-back ['fulbæk], n. (Ftb. etc.) arrière, m.
full-blown ['fulbloun], a. épanoui; (fig.) dans tout son éclat.
full-bodied ['fulbɔdid], a. gros, replet; corsé (vin).
fuller ['fulə], n. foulon, m.
full-faced ['fulˈfeist], a. au visage plein.
full-length ['fulˈleŋθ], a. en pied (portrait).
fullness ['fulnis], n. plénitude, abondance; ampleur, f.
fully ['fuli], adv. pleinement, entièrement, tout à fait; parfaitement.
fulmar ['fulmə], n. (Orn.) fulmar, m.
fulminate ['fʌlmineit], v.t., v.i. fulminer.
fulsome ['fulsəm], a. excessif, écœurant, servile; gonflé (style).
fumble [fʌmbl], v.t. manier maladroitement.
—v.i. farfouiller; tâtonner.
fumbler ['fʌmblə], n. maladroit, m.
fume [fjuːm], n. fumée, vapeur; (fig.) colère, f.—v.t. fumer.—v.i. fumer, s'exhaler; (fig.) être en colère.
fumigate ['fjuːmigeit], v.t. fumiger; désinfecter.
fun [fʌn], n. amusement, m., plaisanterie, drôlerie, f.
function ['fʌŋkʃən], n. fonction, f., métier, m.; cérémonie, réception, f.—v.i. fonctionner, marcher.
fund [fʌnd], n. fonds, m.; caisse, f.
fundamental [fʌndəˈmentl], a. fondamental.
—n.(pl.) principe fondamental, m.
funeral ['fjuːnərəl], a. funèbre, funéraire.—
n. enterrement, convoi funèbre, m.; funérailles, obsèques, f.pl.
funereal [fjuːˈniəriəl], a. funèbre; lugubre.
fungus ['fʌŋgəs], n. (pl. fungi ['fʌndʒai]) champignon; (Med.) fongus, m.
funk [fʌŋk], n. peur, f.—v.t. éviter, avoir peur de.
funnel [fʌnl], n. entonnoir; tuyau, m.; cheminée (de bateau à vapeur), f.
funny ['fʌni], a. amusant, drôle, comique; bizarre.
fur [fəː], n. fourrure, f.; gibier à poil; (fig.) dépôt, m., incrustation, f.—v.t. fourrer, garnir de fourrure.—v.i. s'incruster, s'encrasser (la langue).
furbish ['fəːbiʃ], v.t. fourbir.
furious ['fjuəriəs], a. furieux, acharné.
furiously ['fjuəriəsli], adv. avec fureur, avec acharnement.
furl [fəːl], v.t. (Naut.) ferler, serrer.
furlong ['fəːlɔŋ], n. furlong (le huitième d'un mille anglais, 201 mètres), m.
furlough ['fəːlou], n. (Mil.) congé, m.
furnace ['fəːnis], n. fournaise, f.; fourneau (d'une forge); foyer (de locomotive), m.; **blast-furnace**, haut fourneau, m.
furnish ['fəːniʃ], v.t. fournir, garnir, pourvoir (de); meubler.
furnisher ['fəːniʃə], n. fournisseur, marchand de meubles, m.
furnishing ['fəːniʃiŋ], n. ameublement, m., garniture, f.
furniture ['fəːnitʃə], n. meubles, m.pl. mobilier, ameublement; équipage, m.; **a piece of furniture**, un meuble.
furrier ['fʌriə], n. fourreur, pelletier, m.
furrow ['fʌrou], n. sillon, f.; ride; rainure, f.
—v.t. sillonner, rider (la figure).
furry ['fəːri], a. fourré.

further ['fə:ðə], v.t. avancer; faciliter, favoriser, seconder.—a. (also **farther** ['fɑ:ðə]) plus éloigné, ultérieur; autre, nouveau; *further end*, extrémité, f.—adv. (also **farther** ['fɑ:ðə]) plus loin; de plus, en outre, davantage, encore; ultérieurement; au delà.

furtherance ['fə:ðərəns], n. avancement; progrès, m.

furthermore ['fə:ðəmɔ:], adv. de plus, en outre, d'ailleurs.

furthermost ['fə:ðəmoust], **furthest** ['fə:ðist], **farthest** ['fɑ:ðist], a. le plus éloigné; le plus reculé.—adv. and n. le plus loin.

furtive ['fə:tiv], a. furtif.

furtively ['fə:tivli], adv. furtivement, à la dérobée.

fury ['fjuəri], n. furie, fureur, f.; acharnement, m.

furze [fə:z], n. ajonc, genêt épineux, m.

fuse [fju:z], v.t. fondre, liquéfier.—v.i. se fondre.—n. mèche, fusée, f.; (Elec.) fusible, plomb, m.; *the fuse has gone*, le plomb a sauté.

fuselage ['fju:zilə:ʒ, 'fju:zilidʒ], n. fuselage, m.

fuse-wire ['fju:zwaiə], n. fil fusible, m.

fusible ['fju:zibl], a. fusible.

fusilier [fju:zi'liə], n. fusilier, m.

fusillade [fju:zi'leid], n. fusillade, f.

fusion ['fju:ʒən], n. fusion, f.

fuss [fʌs], n. fracas, embarras, m., façons, f.pl.

fussily ['fʌsili], adv. avec embarras.

fussy ['fʌsi], a. qui fait des embarras; affairé.

fustian ['fʌstjən], n. futaine, f.; (fig.) galimatias, m.

fusty ['fʌsti], a. qui sent le renfermé ou le moisi.

futile ['fju:tail], a. futile, vain, frivole.

futility [fju:'tiliti], n. futilité, f.

future ['fju:tʃə], a. futur, à venir.—n. avenir; (Gram.) futur, m.

fuzz [fʌz], n. bourre, f., duvet (de couverture); flou (de photographie), m.

fuzzy ['fʌzi], a. duveteux, floconneux; bouffant, moutonné (cheveux); flou (photographie).

G

G, g [dʒi:]. septième lettre de l'alphabet; (Mus.) sol, m.

gab [gæb], n. faconde, f., bagout, m.; *to have the gift of the gab*, (colloq.) avoir la langue bien pendue.

gabardine [GABERDINE].

gabble [gæbl], v.i. parler très vite, bredouiller; caqueter, jacasser.—n. bredouillement; caquet, m.

gaberdine, gabardine [gæbə'di:n], n. gabardine, f.

gable [geibl], n. pignon, gable, m.

gadfly ['gædflai], n. taon, m.

gadget ['gædʒit], n. instrument, accessoire; truc, machin, m.

gaff [gæf], n. gaffe, f.—v.t. gaffer (poisson).

gag [gæg], n. bâillon, m.; (Theat.) plaisanterie, f.; (Cine.) gag, m.—v.t. bâillonner.

gage [geidʒ], n. gage, m., assurance, f.

gaggle [gægl], n. troupeau d'oies, m.

gaiety ['geiəti], n. gaieté, f.; éclat, m.

gaily ['geili], adv. gaiement, joyeusement.

gain [gein], n. gain, profit, avantage, m.—v.t. gagner, acquérir; remporter (victoire); atteindre.—v.i. avancer (montre etc.).

gainings ['geiniŋz], n.pl. gains, profits, m.pl.

gainsay ['geinsei, gein'sei], v.t. contredire.

gait [geit], n. démarche, allure, f.

gaiter ['geitə], n. guêtre, f.

gala ['geilə, 'gɑ:lə], n. gala, m.; fête, f.

galaxy ['gæləksi], n. voie lactée, galaxie, f.; (fig.) assemblage brillant, m.

gale [geil], n. coup de vent, m., tempête, f.

Galilee ['gælili:]. la Galilée, f.

gall [gɔ:l], n. fiel, m.; écorchure (plaie); noix de galle, galle (d'arbres etc.); (fig.) rancune, f., chagrin, m.—v.t. écorcher; (fig.) fâcher.

gallant ['gælənt], a. brave, intrépide; [gə'lænt] galant.—n. brave; preux; [gə'lænt] galant; amant, m.

gallantry ['gæləntri], n. vaillance; galanterie, f.

gall-bladder ['gɔ:lblædə], n. vésicule bilaire, f.

galleon ['gæliən], n. galion, m.

gallery ['gæləri], n. galerie, f.; (Theat.) balcon, m.; (Parl.) tribune publique, f.

galley ['gæli], n. galère (Naut.) cuisine, f.

galley-slave ['gælisleiv], n. galérien, m.

Gallic ['gælik], a. gaulois.

galling ['gɔ:liŋ], a. irritant, vexant.

gallon ['gælən], n. gallon (quatre litres et demi), m.

gallop ['gæləp], n. galop, m.—v.i. galoper, aller au galop.

gallows ['gælouz], n. potence, f.

galvanize ['gælvənaiz], v.t. galvaniser.

Gambia ['gæmbiə], n. la Gambie, f.

gamble [gæmbl], v.i. jouer de l'argent.

gambler ['gæmblə], n. joueur, m.

gambling ['gæmbliŋ], n. jeu, m.

gambol [gæmbl], n. gambade, f.; ébats, m.pl.—v.i. gambader, folâtrer.

game (1) [geim], a. estropié (jambe, bras etc.).

game (2) [geim], a. courageux.—n. jeu, m., partie, f.; *drawn game*, partie nulle; *to make game of*, se moquer de.—v.i. jouer de l'argent.

game (3) [geim], n. gibier, m.

game-bag ['geimbæg], n. carnassière, f.

game-keeper ['geimki:pə], n. garde-chasse, m.

gamester ['geimstə], n. joueur, m.

gammon ['gæmən], n. quartier de lard fumé, m.—v.t. saler et fumer (jambon).

gamut ['gæmət], n. (Mus.) gamme, f.

gander ['gændə], n. jars, m.

gang [gæŋ], n. bande, troupe, brigade, équipe (d'ouvriers), f.

ganger ['gæŋə], n. chef d'équipe; cantonnier, m.

Ganges ['gændʒi:z]. le Gange, m.

gangrene ['gæŋgri:n], n. gangrène, f.

gangster ['gæŋstə], n. (Am.) bandit, gangster, m.

gangway ['gæŋwei], n. passage, m.; (Naut.) passerelle (pour débarquer), coupée, f.

gannet ['gænit], n. (Orn.) fou, m.

gaol

gaol [JAIL].

gap [gæp], *n.* brèche, ouverture, *f.*, trou, *m.*; (*fig.*) lacune; trouée (*dans une forêt*), *f.*

gape [geip], *v.i.* bâiller; s'entr'ouvrir (*porte etc.*); (*fig.*) bayer; **to gape at**, regarder bouche bée.—*n.* bâillement, *m.*

gaping ['geipiŋ], *a.* béant.—*n.* bâillement, *m.*

garage ['gæra:ʒ], *n.* garage, *m.*—*v.t.* garer.

garb [ga:b], *n.* costume, habit, habillement, *m.*

garbage ['ga:bidʒ], *n.* entrailles, issues; (*Am.*) ordures, *f.pl.*

garble [ga:bl], *v.t.* mutiler, tronquer (*citation etc.*), altérer.

garden [ga:dn], *n.* jardin, *m.*—*v.i.* jardiner.

garden-city ['ga:dn'siti], *n.* cité-jardin, *f.*

gardener ['ga:dnə], *n.* jardinier, *m.*

gardenia [ga:'di:njə], *n.* gardenia, *m.*

gardening ['ga:dniŋ], *n.* jardinage, *m.*

gargle [ga:gl], *v.i.* se gargariser.—*n.* gargarisme, *m.*

gargoyle ['ga:goil], *n.* gargouille, *f.*

garish ['gɛəriʃ], *a.* éclatant, voyant.

garland ['ga:lənd], *n.* guirlande, *f.*—*v.t.* enguirlander.

garlic ['ga:lik], *n.* ail, *m.*

garment ['ga:mənt], *n.* vêtement, *m.*

garner ['ga:nə], *n.* grenier, *m.*—*v.t.* mettre en grenier, engranger; (*fig.*) amasser.

garnet ['ga:nit], *n.* grenat, *m.*

garnish ['ga:niʃ], *v.t.* garnir, orner de.—*n.* garniture, *f.*

garret ['gærət], *n.* galetas, *m.*, mansarde, soupente, *f.*

garrison ['gærisən], *n.* garnison, *f.*—*v.t.* mettre garnison dans; mettre en garnison.

garrotte [gə'rɔt], *n.* garrotte, *f.*—*v.t.* garrotter.

garrulity [gə'ru:liti], *n.* garrulité, loquacité, *f.*

garrulous ['gæruləs], *a.* babillard, loquace.

garter ['ga:tə], *n.* jarretière, *f.*; (*Am.*) support-chaussette, *m.*

gas [gæs], *n.* (*pl.* gases ['gæsiz]) gaz, *m.*; **laughing gas**, gaz hilarant.—*v.t.* gazer; intoxiquer par un gaz.

gas-cooker ['gæs'kukə], *n.* réchaud à gaz, four à gaz, *m.*

gaseous ['geisiəs], *a.* gazeux.

gash [gæʃ], *n.* balafre, estafilade, entaille, *f.*—*v.t.* balafrer, taillader.

gas-holder ['gæshouldə], gasometer [gæ'sɔmitə], *n.* gazomètre, *m.*

gas-mask ['gæsma:sk], *n.* masque à gaz, *m.*

gasometer [GAS-HOLDER].

gasp [ga:sp], *v.i.* respirer avec peine.—*n.* respiration haletante, *f.*; sursaut (*de surprise*), soupir convulsif, *m.*

gasping ['ga:spiŋ], *a.* haletant.—*n.* respiration haletante, *f.*

gas-stove ['gæsstouv], *n.* fourneau à gaz, *m.*

gastric ['gæstrik], *a.* gastrique.

gastronomy [gæs'trɔnəmi], *n.* gastronomie, *f.*

gate [geit], *n.* porte; barrière (*de péage*); grille (*en fer forgé*), *f.*

gate-keeper ['geitki:pə], *n.* portier; (*Rail.*) garde-barrière, *m.*

gate-post ['geitpoust], *n.* montant de porte, *m.*

gateway ['geitwei], *n.* porte, porte cochère, *f.*; portail (*grand*); guichet (*petit*), *m.*

gather ['gæðə], *v.t.* ramasser; assembler; recueillir (*réunir*); cueillir (*fruits etc.*); (*fig.*)

conclure; (*Dress.*) froncer.—*v.i.* se rassembler, se réunir, s'assembler; s'amasser.—*n.* pli, froncis, *m.*

gatherer ['gæðərə], *n.* cueilleur; percepteur (*des contributions directes*); vendangeur (*de raisins*), *m.*

gathering ['gæðəriŋ], *n.* rassemblement, *m.*; assemblée, réunion; perception (*des contributions directes*); récolte (*de fruits etc.*), *f.*; (*Dress.*) froncis; (*Med.*) abcès, *m.*

gaudiness ['gɔ:dinis], *n.* faste, faux brillant, *m.*

gaudy ['gɔ:di], *a.* éclatant; criard, fastueux, de mauvais goût.

gauge [geidʒ], *v.t.* jauger, mesurer; (*fig.*) juger.—*n.* jauge, mesure, *f.*; calibre, *m.*; (*Rail.*) voie, *f.*

Gaul [gɔ:l]. la Gaule, *f.*

Gauls [gɔ:lz], **the.** les Gaulois, *m.pl.*

gaunt [gɔ:nt], *a.* maigre, décharné.

gauntlet ['gɔ:ntlit], *n.* gantelet, *m.*

gauze [gɔ:z], *n.* gaze, *f.*

gawk [gɔ:k], *n.* sot, maladroit, *m.*

gawky ['gɔ:ki], *a.* dégingandé.

gay [gei], *a.* gai, réjoui, joyeux; pimpant.

gayety [GAIETY].

gayly [GAILY].

gaze [geiz], *v.i.* regarder fixement.—*n.* regard fixe *ou* attentif, *m.*

gazelle [gə'zel], *n.* gazelle, *f.*

gazette [gə'zet], *n.* gazette, *f.*; bulletin officiel, *m.*—*v.t.* publier *ou* annoncer dans le journal officiel.

gazetteer [gæzi'tiə], *n.* dictionnaire géographique; gazetier, *m.*

gear [giə], *n.* appareil, attirail; harnais (*d'un cheval*), *m.*; (*colloq.*) vêtements; (*Naut.*) apparaux, *m.pl.*; (*Mach.*) engrenage, *m.*; (*Motor.*) vitesse, *f.*; (*Motor.*) **bottom, first** or **low gear**, première, *f.*; **neutral gear**, point mort, *m.*; **in top gear**, en prise.

gear-box ['giəbɔks], *n.* boîte de changement de vitesse, *f.*

geese [GOOSE].

gelatine ['dʒeləti:n], *n.* gélatine, *f.*

gelatinous [dʒe'lætinəs], *a.* gélatineux.

gelding ['geldiŋ], *n.* cheval hongre, *m.*

gem [dʒem], *n.* pierre précieuse, *f.*, joyau, *m.*

gender ['dʒendə], *n.* genre, *m.*

genealogical [dʒi:niə'lɔdʒikl], *a.* généalogique.

genealogist [dʒi:ni'ælədʒist], *n.* généalogiste, *m.*, *f.*

genealogy [dʒi:ni'ælədʒi], *n.* généalogie, *f.*

general ['dʒenərəl], *a.* général, commun.—*n.* général, *m.*

generalize ['dʒenrəlaiz], *v.t.* généraliser.

generally ['dʒenrəli], *adv.* en général, ordinairement, généralement.

generate ['dʒenəreit], *v.t.* produire, engendrer.

generation [dʒenə'reiʃən], *n.* génération, famille; production, *f.*; âge, *m.*

generator ['dʒenəreitə], *n.* générateur, *m.*; **electricity generator**, génératrice, *f.*

generic [dʒə'nerik], generical [dʒe'nerikəl], *a.* générique.

generosity [dʒenə'rɔsiti], *n.* générosité, magnanimité, libéralité, *f.*

generous ['dʒenərəs], *a.* généreux; (*fig.*) abondant, riche (*en*).

gimmick

generously [ˈdʒenərəsli], *adv.* généreuse-ment.

genesis [ˈdʒenəsis], *n.* genèse, *f.*

genetics [dʒəˈnetiks], *n.* génétique, *f.*

Geneva [dʒəˈniːvə]. Genève, *f.*

genial [ˈdʒiːniəl], *a.* bon; affable; cordial, joyeux.

geniality [dʒiːniˈæliti], *n.* bonne humeur, nature sympathique, gaieté, *f.*, entrain, *m.*

genially [ˈdʒiːniəli], *adv.* avec bonté, d'un air affable.

genie [ˈdʒiːni], *n.* (*Myth.*) génie, djinn, *m.*

genitive [ˈdʒenitiv], *n.* (*Gram.*) génitif, *m.*

genius [ˈdʒiːniəs], *n.* génie, *m.*

Genoa [ˈdʒenouə]. Gênes, *f.*

genteel [dʒenˈtiːl], *a.* (*now often iron.*) de bon ton, comme il faut, distingué.

gentility [dʒenˈtiliti], *n.* bon ton, *m.*, distinction, *f.*

gentle [dʒentl], *a.* doux, aimable; paisible; modéré (*pente etc.*).

gentlefolk [ˈdʒentlfouk], *n.pl.* personnes de bon ton, *f.pl.*, gens comme il faut, *m.pl.*

gentleman [ˈdʒentlmən], *n.* (*pl.* **gentlemen** [-men]) monsieur; homme comme il faut, galant homme, homme bien né, *m.*

gentlemanly [ˈdʒentlmənli], *a.* distingué, de bon ton, comme il faut.

gentleness [ˈdʒentlnis], *n.* douceur, bonté, *f.*

gentlewoman [ˈdʒentlwumən], *n.* (*pl.* **-women** [wimin]) dame *ou* jeune fille de bonne famille, *f.*

gently [ˈdʒentli], *adv.* doucement.

genuine [ˈdʒenjuin], *a.* pur, vrai, véritable, authentique, naturel; sincère.

genuinely [ˈdʒenjuinli], *adv.* purement, sincèrement, authentiquement.

genuineness [ˈdʒenjuinnis], *n.* authenticité; sincérité, *f.*

genus [ˈdʒiːnəs], *n.* (*pl.* **genera** [ˈdʒenərə]) genre, *m.*

Geoffrey [ˈdʒefri]. Geoffroi, *m.*

geographer [dʒiˈɔgrəfə], *n.* géographe, *m.*, *f.*

geographical [dʒiəˈgræfikl], *a.* géographique.

geography [dʒiˈɔgrəfi], *n.* géographie, *f.*

geology [dʒiˈɔlədʒi], *n.* géologie, *f.*

geometry [dʒiˈɔmitri], *n.* géométrie, *f.*

George [dʒɔːdʒ]. Georges, *m.*

geranium [dʒəˈreiniəm], *n.* (*Bot.*) géranium, *m.*

germ [dʒəːm], *n.* germe, *m.*

German [ˈdʒəːmən], *a.* allemand.—*n.* allemand (*langue*); Allemand (*personne*), *m.*

Germany [ˈdʒəːməni]. l'Allemagne, *f.*

germinate [ˈdʒəːmineit], *v.t.* germer; pousser.

gesticulate [dʒesˈtikjuleit], *v.i.* gesticuler.

gesticulation [dʒestikjuˈleiʃən], *n.* gesticulation, *f.*

gesture [ˈdʒestʃə], *n.* geste, *m.*, action, *f.*—*v.i.* gesticuler.

get [get], *v.t. irr.* (se) procurer, acquérir, obtenir; recevoir; remporter (*to gain*); gagner (*to earn*); avoir; acheter (*to buy*); arriver à, atteindre (*to reach*); aller chercher (*to fetch*); trouver (*to find*); faire, se faire (*to induce, make, cause etc.*); attraper, s'attirer (*to catch etc.*); **to get hold of**, s'emparer de, saisir, obtenir.—*v.i.* se mettre (*en*); devenir, se faire (*to become*); aller (*to go*); **to get about**, sortir, prendre de l'exercice; **to get at**, arriver à; attaquer; atteindre; **to get away**, s'en aller, se

sauver, échapper (*à*); **to get back**, revenir, regagner; recouvrer; **to get in**, entrer, faire entrer, rentrer; **to get off**, s'en tirer, s'échapper; descendre; ôter, enlever; **to get on**, avancer, réussir, faire des progrès; monter sur; **to get out**, sortir, s'en tirer, faire sortir; **to get over**, passer, surmonter, vaincre; se consoler de; **to get rid of**, se débarrasser de; **to get through**, passer par, parcourir; réussir (*à un examen*); **to get up**, se lever, monter, faire monter, lever; préparer.

gewgaw [ˈgjuːgɔː], *n.* babiole, bagatelle, *f.*, colifichet, *m.*

geyser [ˈgiːzə], *n.* chauffe-bain; (*Geol.*) geyser, *m.*

Ghana [ˈgɑːnə]. le Ghana, *m.*

Ghanaian [gɑːˈneiən], *a.* du Ghana.—*n.* citoyen(ne) du Ghana, *m.*, *f.*

ghastliness [ˈgɑːstlinis], *n.* pâleur, *f.*; aspect effrayant, *m.*

ghastly [ˈgɑːstli], *a.* pâle, pâle comme la mort; horrible, affreux.

gherkin [ˈgəːkin], *n.* cornichon, *m.*

ghetto [ˈgetou], *n.* ghetto, *m.*

ghost [goust], *n.* revenant, fantôme, spectre, *m.*; ombre, *f.*; **the Holy Ghost**, le Saint-Esprit.

ghostly [ˈgoustli], *a.* spirituel; de spectre.

ghoul [guːl], *n.* goule, *f.*

ghoulish [ˈguːliʃ], *a.* de goule.

ghyll [GILL (2)].

giant [ˈdʒaiənt], *a.* de géant.—*n.* géant, *m.*

gibber [ˈdʒibə], *v.i.* baragouiner.

gibberish [ˈdʒibəriʃ], *n.* baragouin, charabia, *m.*

gibbet [ˈdʒibit], *n.* potence, *f.*, gibet, *m.*

gibe [dʒaib], *v.t.*, *v.i.* railler, se moquer (*de*).—*n.* sarcasme, *m.*; raillerie, moquerie, *f.*

giblets [ˈdʒiblits], *n.pl.* abatis, *m.pl.*

giddily [ˈgidili], *adv.* étourdiment, à l'étourdie.

giddiness [ˈgidinis], *n.* vertige, *m.*; (*fig.*) étourderie, *f.*

giddy [ˈgidi], *a.* étourdi; (*fig.*) volage; vertigineux; **I feel giddy**, la tête me tourne; **that makes me feel giddy**, cela me donne le vertige.

gift [gift], *n.* don, présent, cadeau; (*fig.*) talent, *m.*; **Christmas gifts**, étrennes, *f.pl.*—*v.t.* douer, doter (*de*).

gifted [ˈgiftid], *a.* doué, de talent.

gigantic [dʒaiˈgæntik], *a.* gigantesque, de géant.

giggle [gigl], *v.i.* rire nerveusement, rire un peu bêtement.—*n.* ricanement, petit rire bête, *m.*

gild [gild], *v.t.* dorer; (*fig.*) embellir.

gilding [ˈgildin], *n.* dorure, *f.*

Giles [dʒailz]. Gilles, *m.*

gill (1) [gill], *n.* (*usu. pl.*) ouïe (*de poisson*), *f.*

gill (2), **ghyll** [gill], *n.* ravin boisé; ruisseau (*du ravin*), *m.*

gill (3) [dʒil], *n.* treize centilitres, *m.pl.*

***gillyflower** [ˈdʒiliflauə], *n.* giroflée, *f.*

gilt [gilt], *a.* doré.—*n.* dorure, *f.*

gilt-edged [ˈgiltedʒd], *a.* **gilt-edged securities**, valeurs de tout repos, *f.pl.*

gimcrack [ˈdʒimkræk], *n.* pacotille, camelote, *f.*

gimlet [ˈgimlit], *n.* vrille, *f.*

gimmick [ˈgimik], *n.* machin; tour (*artifice*), *m.*

437

gin (1) [dʒin], n. trébuchet, piège, m.

gin (2) [dʒin], n. genièvre, gin (*liquor*), m.

ginger ['dʒindʒə], n. gingembre; (*fam.*) poil de carotte (*personne aux cheveux roux*), m.

gingerbread ['dʒindʒəbred], n. pain d'épice, m.

gingerly ['dʒindʒəli], adv. tout doucement, délicatement.

gipsy, gypsy ['dʒipsi], n. bohémien, tzigane, m., bohémienne, f.

giraffe [dʒi'rɑːf], n. girafe, f.

gird (1) [gəːd], v.t. *irr.* ceindre (*de*); entourer (*de*).

gird (2) [gəːd], v.i. to gird at, railler.

girder ['gəːdə], n. poutre, solive, traverse, f.

girdle [gəːdl], n. ceinture, f.; ceinturon, m.; gaine, f.—v.t. ceinturer.

girl [gəːl], n. fille, jeune fille; jeune personne f.

girlish ['gəːliʃ], a. de jeune fille.

girth [gəːθ], n. sangle, f.; tour, m., circonférence, f.

gist [dʒist], n. fond, fin mot; point principal, m., substance (*d'un discours*), f.

give [giv], v.t. *irr.* donner; livrer, rendre, accorder; faire (*réponse, crédit, compliment, amitiés etc.*); remettre; porter (*un coup etc.*); pousser (*un gémissement etc.*); émettre (*un son*); to give away, donner; trahir; to give up, abandonner, renoncer à.—v.i. céder; plier (*se courber*); prêter (*s'allonger*); give and take, donnant donnant; to give in, céder; to give oneself up, se rendre; to give way, céder, se relâcher.

given [givn], a. adonné, porté (*à*); donné; given these difficulties, étant donné ces difficultés.

giver ['givə], n. donneur, m.

gizzard ['gizəd], n. gésier, m.

glacial ['gleiʃəl], a. glacial, glaciaire.

glacier ['glæsiə], n. glacier, m.

glad [glæd], a. content, aise, bien aise; heureux (*de*).

gladden [glædn], v.t. réjouir.

glade [gleid], n. clairière, percée, f.

gladiator ['glædieitə], n. gladiateur, m.

gladiolus ['glædi'ouləs], n. (*pl.* gladioli [glædi'oulai]) glaïeul, m.

gladly ['glædli], adv. volontiers, avec plaisir.

glamorous ['glæmərəs], a. charmeur, ensorcelant.

glamour ['glæmə], n. charme, prestige, éclat, m.

glance [glɑːns], n. ricochet, coup en biais; regard, coup d'œil, m.—v.i. jeter un coup d'œil (*sur*); étinceler; to glance off, ricocher.

gland [glænd], n. (*Anat.*) glande, f.

glare [gleə], n. éclat, m., lueur, f.; regard irrité *ou* farouche, m.—v.i. éblouir; luire; regarder d'un air furieux.

glaring ['gleəriŋ], a. voyant, éblouissant; choquant; manifeste.

glass [glɑːs], n. de verre.—n. (*pl.* glasses ['glɑːsiz]) verre, m.; vitre (*de fenêtre*), f.; (*pl.*) lunettes, f. pl.; cut glass, cristal taillé, m.; field-glasses, jumelles, f.pl.; looking-glass, miroir, m.; magnifying glass, loupe, f.; stained glass, vitraux, m.pl.; (*weather-*)glass, baromètre, m.

glass-maker ['glɑːsmeikə], n. verrier, m.

glass-ware ['glɑːsweə], n. verrerie, f.

glassy ['glɑːsi], a. vitreux, transparent.

glaze [gleiz], v.t. vitrer; vernir.

glazier ['gleiziə], n. vitrier, m.

glazing ['gleiziŋ], n. vitrage (*de fenêtres*); vernissage (*de peintures*), m.

gleam [gliːm], n. rayon, m., lueur, f.—v.i. briller, luire (*de*).

gleaming ['gliːmiŋ], a. miroitant, luisant.

glean [gliːn], v.t. glaner.

gleaner ['gliːnə], n. glaneur, m.

glebe [gliːb], n. glèbe, terre, f., sol, m.

glee [gliː], n. joie, gaieté, f.

gleeful ['gliːful], a. joyeux, gai.

glen [glen], n. vallon, ravin, m.

glib [glib], a. coulant, délié, volubile.

glibly ['glibli], adv. avec volubilité; douce-reusement.

glide [glaid], v.i. couler, glisser; se glisser (*dans*).—n. glissade, f.; (*Av.*) vol plané, m.

glider ['glaidə], n. (*Av.*) planeur, m.

glimmer ['glimə], n. lueur, f., faible rayon, m.—v.i. entre-luire, luire faiblement; poindre (*l'aube*).

glimpse [glimps], n. coup d'œil, m., vue rapide, f.; to catch a glimpse of, entrevoir.

glint [glint], n. trait de lumière, m., lueur, f.—v.i. luire par moments.

glisten [glisn], glister ['glistə], glitter ['glitə], v.i. reluire, scintiller, chatoyer.—n. éclat, lustre, m.

gloaming ['gloumiŋ], n. crépuscule, m.

gloat [glout], v.i. dévorer *ou* couver des yeux; (*fig.*) se régaler de.

global ['gloubl], a. global; global war, conflit mondial, m.

globe [gloub], n. globe, m.

globule ['glɔbjuːl], n. globule, m.

gloom [gluːm], gloominess ['gluːminis], n. obscurité, f., ténèbres, f.pl.; (*fig.*) tristesse, f.

gloomily ['gluːmili], adv. obscurément; d'un air triste, lugubrement.

gloomy ['gluːmi], a. sombre, obscur; morne, triste.

glorify ['glɔːrifai], v.t. glorifier.

glorious ['glɔːriəs], a. glorieux; illustre, superbe.

glory ['glɔːri], n. gloire; (*Paint.*) auréole, f.—v.i. se glorifier (*de*).

gloss [glɔs], n. lustre; apprêt, m.; (*fig.*) glose, f., commentaire, m.—v.i. gloser, interpréter; lustrer; to gloss over, glisser sur.

glossary ['glɔsəri], n. glossaire, m.

glossiness ['glɔsinis], n. lustre, brillant, glacé, m.

glossy ['glɔsi], a. lustré, brillant, luisant.

glove [glʌv], n. gant, m.

glover ['glʌvə], n. gantier, m.

glow [glou], v.i. brûler (*de*); briller; (*fig.*) s'échauffer.—n. lueur rouge, f.; (*fig.*) feu, éclat, m., splendeur, f.

glowing ['glouiŋ], a. embrasé; ardent, chaleureux.

glow-worm ['glouwəːm], n. ver luisant, m.

glue [gluː], n. colle-forte, f.—v.t. coller.

glum [glʌm], a. maussade, de mauvaise humeur, morne.

glut [glʌt], v.t. gorger, rassasier; engorger (*le marché*).—n. surabondance, f., excès, m.

glutton [glʌtn], n. gourmand, goinfre, m.

grab

gluttonous ['glʌtənəs], a. gourmand, glouton, vorace.

gluttony ['glʌtəni], n. gloutonnerie, f.

glycerine ['glisəri:n], n. glycérine, f.

gnarled [nɑ:ld], a. noueux.

gnash [næʃ], v.t. grincer.—v.i. grincer des dents.

gnashing ['næʃiŋ], n. grincement, m.

gnat [næt], n. cousin, moucheron, m.

gnaw [nɔ:], v.t. ronger.

gnawing ['nɔ:iŋ], a. rongeant, rongeur.—n. rongement, m.

gnome [noum], n. gnome, m.

gnu [nu:], n. gnou, m.

go [gou], v.i. irr. aller, se rendre; marcher, passer; s'en aller, partir (to leave); disparaître; devenir (to become); to go astray, s'égarer; to go away, s'en aller, partir; to go back, retourner, s'en retourner, reculer; to go backward, aller à reculons, reculer; to go down, descendre; se coucher (soleil); tomber; to go off, partir (fusil); s'en aller; to go on, aller, avancer, continuer; se passer; to go through, passer par, traverser; subir, souffrir; to go to sleep, s'endormir; to go without, se passer de; to let go, lâcher prise.—n. mode, vogue, f.; (fig.) entrain, coup, essai, m.

goad [goud], n. aiguillon, m.—v.t. aiguillonner; (fig.) stimuler.

goal [goul], n. but; terme, m.

goal-keeper ['goulki:pə], n. (Ftb.) gardien de but, m.

goat [gout], n. chèvre, f.; he-goat, bouc, m.

gobble [gɔbl], v.t. gober, avaler.—v.i. glouglouter (dindon).

goblet ['gɔblit], n. gobelet, m.

goblin ['gɔblin], n. lutin, m.

God [gɔd], n. Dieu, m.

god [gɔd], n. dieu, m.

godchild ['gɔdtʃaild], n. filleul, m., filleule, f.

goddaughter ['gɔddɔ:tə], n. filleule, f.

goddess ['gɔdis], n. déesse, f.

godfather ['gɔdfɑ:ðə], n. parrain, m.

Godfrey ['gɔdfri]. Godefroi, m.

godless ['gɔdlis], a. athée, impie.

godliness ['gɔdlinis], n. piété, f.

godly ['gɔdli], a. pieux, dévot.

godmother ['gɔdmʌðə], n. marraine, f.

godsend ['gɔdsend], n. aubaine, trouvaille, f.

godson ['gɔdsʌn], n. filleul, m.

godspeed ['gɔd'spi:d], n. succès, m.

goffer ['gɔfə], v.t. gaufrer.

goggle [gɔgl], v.i. rouler de gros yeux; goggle eyes, des yeux en boules de loto, m.pl.

goggles [gɔglz], n.pl. lunettes (protectrices), f.pl.

going ['gouiŋ], n. marche, démarche, allée, f.; départ, m.

goitre ['gɔitə], n. (Med.) goitre, m.

gold [gould], n. or.—a. d'or, en or.—n. or, m.

golden ['gouldn], a. d'or.

goldfinch ['gouldfintʃ], n. chardonneret, m.

goldfish ['gouldfiʃ], n. poisson rouge, m.

goldsmith ['gouldsmiθ], n. orfèvre, m.

golf [gɔlf, gɔf], n. golf, m.

golf-club ['gɔlfklʌb], n. club de golf (société ou instrument), m.

golf-course ['gɔlfkɔ:s], n. terrain de golf, m.

gondola ['gɔndələ], n. gondole; nacelle (de ballon), f.

gondolier [gɔndə'liə], n. gondolier, m.

gone [gɔːn, gɔn], a. allé, parti; perdu, disparu; passé, écoulé; adjugé (aux enchères).

gong [gɔŋ], n. gong; timbre (d'une horloge), m.

good [gud], a. bon; de bien, honnête; convenable, avantageux; valide, solide; (colloq.) sage; good luck, bonheur, m., bonne chance, f.; to make good, exécuter; compenser, indemniser; assurer.—n. bien, bon, avantage, profit, m.; for good (and all), pour (tout) de bon; what's the good of? à quoi bon? (pl.) effets, biens, m.pl., marchandises, f.pl.—adv. bien.—int. bon! bien! c'est très bien!

good-bye! [gud'bai], int. adieu! good-bye for the present, au revoir.

good-for-nothing [gudfə'nʌθiŋ], n. vaurien, m.

Good Friday [gud'fraid(e)i]. vendredi saint, m.

good-humoured ['gud'hju:məd], a. de bonne humeur, enjoué, gai.

good-natured ['gud'neitʃəd], a. d'un bon naturel, bon, bienveillant.

goodness ['gudnis], n. bonté; probité, f.; thank goodness! Dieu merci!

goodwill [gud'wil], n. bienveillance, bonne volonté, bonté; (Comm.) clientèle, f.

goose [gu:s], n. (pl. geese [gi:s]) oie, f.; (fig.) imbécile, nigaud, m.

gooseberry ['guzbri], n. groseille à maquereau, f.

gooseberry-bush ['guzbribuʃ], n. groseillier, m.

goose-flesh ['gu:sfleʃ], n. chair de poule, f.

gore [gɔ:], n. sang, sang caillé, m.—v.t. donner un coup de corne à.

gorge [gɔ:dʒ], n. gorge, f.; gosier, m.—v.t. gorger, avaler, rassasier.—v.i. se gorger (de).

gorgeous ['gɔ:dʒəs], a. magnifique, splendide, fastueux.

gorilla [gə'rilə], n. gorille, m.

gorse [gɔ:s], n. ajonc, m.

gory ['gɔ:ri], a. sanglant, couvert de sang.

gosling ['gɔzliŋ], n. oison, m.

gospel ['gɔspəl], n. évangile, m.

gossamer ['gɔsəmə], n. fil de la Vierge, m.

gossip ['gɔsip], n. commère, f., causeur (personne), m.; causerie, f., commérage, m.—v.i. bavarder, faire des commérages.

gossip-writer ['gɔsipraitə], n. (Journ.) échotier, m.

Goth [gɔθ], n. Goth; (fig.) barbare, m.

Gothic ['gɔθik], a. gothique, ogival.

gouge [gaudʒ], n. gouge, f.—v.t. gouger; to gouge out, arracher (l'œil etc.).

gourd [guəd], n. gourde, calebasse, f.

gout [gaut], n. goutte, f.

gouty ['gauti], a. goutteux.

govern ['gʌvən], v.t. gouverner, régir, diriger.

governess ['gʌvənis], n. institutrice, gouvernante, f.

government ['gʌvənmənt], n. gouvernement, m., administration, f., régime, m.

governor ['gʌvənə], n. gouverneur, gouvernant; directeur (d'une institution); (Mech.) régulateur, m.

gown [gaun], n. robe, f.; dressing-gown, peignoir, m., robe de chambre, f.; night-gown, chemise de nuit, f.

grab [græb], v.t. empoigner, saisir (d'un geste brusque).

439

grace

grace [greis], *n.* grâce; faveur, *f.*; pardon; (*Mus.*) agrément; bénédicité (*avant le repas*) *m.*; grâces (*après le repas*), *f.pl.*—*v.t.* orner, embellir; illustrer, honorer (*de*).

graceful ['greisful], *a.* gracieux, bien fait, élégant.

gracefully ['greisfuli], *adv.* gracieusement, élégamment.

gracefulness ['greisfulnis], *n.* grâce, *f.*

graceless ['greislis], *a.* sans grâce; dépravé.

gracious ['greiʃəs], *a.* gracieux, clément, bon, favorable, bénin.

graciously ['greiʃəsli], *adv.* gracieusement, avec bonté, favorablement.

graciousness ['greiʃəsnis], *n.* bonté, grâce, *f.*

grade [greid], *n.* grade; degré, rang, *m.*—*v.t.* classer; calibrer; graduer.

grading ['greidiŋ], *n.* classement; calibrage, *m.*; graduation, *f.*

gradient ['greidiənt], *n.* (*Rail.*) rampe, inclinaison, *f.*

gradual ['grædjuəl], *a.* graduel, par degrés, gradué.

gradually ['grædjuəli], *adv.* graduellement, par degrés, peu à peu.

graduate ['grædjueit], *v.t.* graduer.—*v.i.* être reçu à un examen d'enseignement supérieur. —['grædjuit], *n.* gradué, *m.*

graduation [grædju'eiʃən], *n.* graduation; (*Univ.*) remise d'un diplôme, *f.*

graft (1) [graːft], *v.t.* greffer, enter (*sur*).—*n.* greffe, *f.*

graft (2) [graːft], *n.* (*colloq.*) corruption, *f.*

grafting ['graːftiŋ], *n.* greffe, *f.*

grafting-knife ['graːftiŋnaif], *n.* greffoir, *m.*

grain [grein], *n.* grain, *m.*; céréales; fibres (*de bois*), *f.pl.*; *against the grain*, contre le fil, (*fig.*) à contre-cœur, à rebrousse-poil.

gram, gramme [græm], *n.* gramme, *m.*

grammar ['græmə], *n.* grammaire, *f.*

grammar-school ['græməskuːl], *n.* lycée, collège, *m.*

grammatical [grə'mætikəl], *a.* grammatical; de grammaire.

gramophone ['græməfoun], *n.* gramophone; phonographe, *m.*

grampus ['græmpəs], *n.* épaulard, *m.*

granary ['grænəri], *n.* grenier, *m.*

grand [grænd], *a.* grand, magnifique, sublime, grandiose; *grand (piano)*, piano à queue, *m.*

grandchild ['græntʃaild], *n.* (*pl.* **grandchildren** ['græntʃildrən]) petit-fils, *m.*, petite-fille, *f.*

granddaughter ['grændɔːtə], *n.* petite-fille, *f.*

grandee [græn'diː], *n.* grand d'Espagne, *m.*

grandeur ['grændjə], *n.* grandeur, *f.*, éclat, *m.*

grandfather ['grænfaːðə], *n.* grand-père, *m.*

grandiloquence [græn'diləkwəns], *n.* langage pompeux, *m.*; emphase, grandiloquence, *f.*

grandiloquent [græn'diləkwənt], *a.* pompeux, enflé, grandiloquent.

grandly ['grændli], *adv.* grandement, avec éclat.

grandmother ['grænmʌðə], *n.* grand-mère, *f.*

grandson ['grænsʌn], *n.* petit-fils, *m.*

grandstand ['grændstænd], *n.* tribune, *f.*

grange [greindʒ], *n.* manoir (avec ferme), *m.*

granite ['grænit], *n.* granit, *m.*

grant [graːnt], *v.t.* accorder, concéder; convenir, avouer, admettre.—*n.* aide, bourse; concession, *f.*

granulate ['grænjuleit], *v.t.* grener, granuler. —*v.i.* se granuler.

granule ['grænjuːl], *n.* granule, *m.*

grape [greip], *n.* grain de raisin, *m.*; (*pl.*) raisins, *m.pl.*; *a bunch of grapes*, une grappe de raisin.

grape-fruit ['greipfruːt], *n.* pamplemousse, *m.*

grape-shot ['greipʃɔt], *n.* mitraille, *f.*

graph [graːf], *n.* (*Math.*) courbe, *f.*; graphique, *m.*—*v.t.* graphiquer.

graphic ['græfik], *a.* graphique, pittoresque.

graph-paper ['graːfpeipə], *n.* papier quadrillé, *m.*

graphite ['græfait], *n.* graphite, *m.*

grapnel ['græpnəl], *n.* grappin, *m.*

grapple ['græpl], *n.* grappin, *m.*; lutte, *f.*— *v.t.* accrocher; grappiner.—*v.i.* en venir aux prises; lutter (*contre*).

grasp [graːsp], *v.t.* empoigner, saisir, serrer; embrasser; vouloir se saisir de.—*n.* prise, étreinte, poignée; (*fig.*) portée; compréhension, *f.*; *within one's grasp*, à la portée de la main.

grasping ['graːspiŋ], *a.* avide, cupide, avare.

grass [graːs], *n.* herbe, *f.*; gazon, herbage, *m.*

grasshopper ['graːshɔpə], *n.* sauterelle, *f.*

grassy ['graːsi], *a.* herbeux, couvert de gazon, verdoyant.

grate [greit], *n.* grille, *f.*; foyer (*âtre*), *m.*— *v.t.* râper; frotter.—*v.i.* crisser (*sur* ou *contre*).

grateful ['greitful], *a.* reconnaissant; (*fig.*) agréable.

gratefully ['greitfuli], *adv.* avec reconnaissance; (*fig.*) agréablement.

grater ['greitə], *n.* râpe, *f.*

gratification [grætifi'keiʃən], *n.* satisfaction, *f.*; plaisir, *m.*; gratification, récompense, *f.*

gratify ['grætifai], *v.t.* satisfaire, faire plaisir à; récompenser.

gratifying ['grætifaiiŋ], *a.* agréable; (*fig.*) flatteur.

grating ['greitiŋ], *a.* grinçant, discordant, choquant, désagréable.—*n.* grille, *f.*, grillage; grincement (*bruit*), *m.*

gratis ['greitis], *adv.* gratuitement, gratis pour rien.

gratitude ['grætitjuːd], *n.* gratitude, reconnaissance, *f.*

gratuitous [grə'tjuːitəs], *a.* gratuit; (*fig.*) volontaire; bénévole.

gratuitously [grə'tjuːitəsli], *adv.* gratuitement; (*fig.*) sans motif.

gratuity [grə'tjuːiti], *n.* don, présent, *m.* gratification, *f.*; pourboire, *m.*

grave (1) [greiv], *n.* tombe, fosse, *f.*; tombeau, *m.*

grave (2) [greiv], *a.* grave, sérieux.

grave (3) [greiv], *v.t.* graver, tailler, ciseler.

grave-digger ['greivdigə], *n.* fossoyeur, *m.*

gravel ['grævl], *n.* gravier, sable, *m.*—*v.t.* sabler.

gravely ['greivli], *adv.* gravement, sérieusement.

graven [greivn], *a.* gravé, taillé, ciselé.

graver ['greivə], *n.* graveur; burin (*instrument*), *m.*

gravity ['græviti], *n.* gravité, *f.*, air sérieux, *m.*; pesanteur, *f.*

gravy ['greivi], *n.* jus (*de viande*), *m.*; sauce, *f.*

gray (*Am.*) [GREY].

440

grayling ['greiliŋ], n. (Ichth.) ombre, m.
graze [greiz], v.t. effleurer, raser, frôler; érafler, écorcher (la peau).—v.i. paître, brouter.—n. écorchure, éraflure, f.
grease [gri:s], n. graisse, f.—v.t. graisser.
greasiness ['gri:sinis, 'gri:zinis], n. état graisseux, m.; (fig.) onctuosité, f.
greasy ['gri:si, 'gri:zi], a. gras, graisseux; (fig.) onctueux.
great [greit], a. grand; considérable; important, principal; gros (de); **a great deal (of), a great many (of),** beaucoup (de).
great-coat ['greitkout], n. pardessus, m.; (Mil.) capote, f.
great-grandparents ['greitgrændpɛərənts], n.pl. arrière-grands-parents, m.pl.
greatly ['greitli], adv. grandement, fort, beaucoup, de beaucoup.
greatness ['greitnis], n. grandeur; sublimité; force, f.
Grecian ['gri:ʃən], a. grec, de Grèce.—n. Helléniste, m., f.
Greece [gri:s]. la Grèce, f.
greed [gri:d], **greediness** ['gri:dinis], n. cupidité, avidité; gourmandise, f.
greedily ['gri:dili], adv. avidement.
greedy ['gri:di], a. cupide, avide; glouton.
Greek [gri:k], a. grec, de Grèce.—n. grec (langue); Grec (personne), m.
green [gri:n], a. vert; (fig.) frais, nouveau; novice.—n. vert, m.; verdure, f.; gazon, m.; (pl.) légumes verts, m.pl.
greenfinch ['gri:nfintʃ], n. verdier, m.
greengage ['gri:ngeidʒ], n. reine-claude, f.
greengrocer ['gri:ngrousə], n. fruitier, marchand de légumes, m.
greenhorn ['gri:nhɔ:n], n. blanc-bec, niais, m.
greenhouse ['gri:nhaus], n. serre, f.
greenish ['gri:niʃ], a. verdâtre.
Greenland ['gri:nlənd]. le Groenland, m.
greet [gri:t], v.t. saluer, accueillir.
greeting ['gri:tiŋ], n. salutation, f., salut, m.; (pl.) compliments, m.pl.
gregarious [gri'gɛəriəs], a. grégaire.
Gregory ['gregəri]. Grégoire, m.
grenade [grə'neid], n. grenade, f.
grenadier [grenə'diə], n. grenadier, m.
grey [grei], a. gris.
greyhound ['greihaund], n. lévrier, m.
greyish ['greiiʃ], a. grisâtre.
grid [grid], **gridiron** ['gridaiən], n. gril, m.
grief [gri:f], n. douleur, tristesse, peine, f.; chagrin, m.
grievance ['gri:vəns], n. grief, m.; injustice, f.
grieve [gri:v], v.t. chagriner, attrister, faire de la peine à.—v.i. se chagriner, s'affliger.
grievous ['gri:vəs], a. lourd, douloureux, grave, affligeant; atroce.
grievously ['gri:vəsli], adv. grièvement, cruellement.
grill [gril], v.t. griller, faire griller.—n. gril, m.; grillade; viande grillée, f.
grim [grim], a. farouche, féroce; lugubre, effrayant; sinistre.
grimace [gri'meis], n. grimace; (pl.) grimacerie, f.—v.i. grimacer.
grime [graim], n. saleté, noirceur, f.
grimly ['grimli], adv. d'un air farouche ou sinistre.
grimness ['grimnis], n. air renfrogné, air farouche, m.

grimy ['graimi], a. sale, noirci, encrassé.
grin [grin], n. grimace, f., ricanement, m.—v.i. ricaner, grimacer.
grind [graind], v.t. irr. moudre; broyer; aiguiser, repasser (couteau etc.); grincer (dents); (fig.) opprimer.
grinder ['graində], n. repasseur, émouleur, broyeur, m.; dent molaire, f.
grinding ['graindiŋ], n. broiement, grincement (des dents etc.); repassage (de couteaux), m.; (fig.) oppression, f.
grindstone ['graindstoun], n. meule, f.
grip [grip], n. prise, étreinte, f., serrement, m.—v.t. empoigner, saisir, serrer.
gripe [graip], v.t. saisir; opprimer; donner la colique à.—v.i. avoir la colique.—n. saisine; (pl.) colique, f.
griping ['graipiŋ], a. (fig.) cuisant, affreux; avare (pingre).—n. colique, f.
grisly ['grizli], a. hideux, affreux, horrible.
grist [grist], n. blé à moudre, m., mouture, f.; (fig.) gain, profit, m.
gristle [grisl], n. cartilage, m.
grit [grit], n. grès, sable; (fig.) courage, m.
gritty ['griti], a. graveleux.
grizzled [grizld], a. grison, grisâtre.
grizzly ['grizli], a. grisâtre; **grizzly bear,** ours gris d'Amérique, m.
groan [groun], n. gémissement, grognement, m.—v.i. gémir, grogner.
grocer ['grousə], n. épicier, m.
grocery ['grousəri], n. épicerie, f.
groggy ['grogi], a. gris, pochard; titubant; aux jambes faibles (cheval).
groin [groin], n. aine; (Arch.) arête, f.
groom [gru:m], n. palefrenier, valet d'écurie, m.—v.t. panser; **well-groomed,** bien soigné, m.
groove [gru:v], n. rainure, rayure, cannelure; (fig.) ornière (rut), f.—v.t. creuser, canneler.
grope [group], v.i. tâtonner.
gropingly ['groupiŋli], adv. à tâtons.
gross [grous], a. gros; grossier, rude; (Comm.) brut; (fig.) flagrant, énorme.—n. gros, m., grosse; masse, f.
grossly ['grousli], adv. grossièrement; d'une manière flagrante.
grossness ['grousnis], n. grossièreté; énormité, f.
grotto ['grotou], n. grotte, f.
grotesque [gro'tesk], a. grotesque.
ground (1) [graund], past and p.p. [GRIND] and a. broyé, moulu; aiguisé (affilé).
ground (2) [graund], n. terre, f.; terrain (plot); sol (soil), m.; fond (de tableau, de dessin textile etc.); (fig.) fondement, sujet, motif, m., cause, f.; (pl.) terrains, m.pl., sédiment, marc de café, m.—v.t. fonder, baser, établir, appuyer (sur).—v.i. échouer.
grounded ['graundid], a. fondé, établi; **well-grounded,** bien fondé.
ground-floor ['graund'flɔ:], n. rez-de-chaussée, m.
groundless ['graundlis], a. sans fondement.
groundlessly ['graundlisli], adv. sans fondement.
group [gru:p], n. groupe, peloton, m.—v.t. grouper.
grouping ['gru:piŋ], n. groupement, m.
grouse (1) [graus], n. (Orn.) tétras; coq de bruyère, m.
grouse (2) [graus], v.i. grogner, grincher.

grove

grove [grouv], *n.* bocage, bosquet, *m.*
grovel [grɔvl], *v.i.* ramper, se vautrer.
grovelling [ˈgrɔvliŋ], *a.* rampant, abject, vil.
—*n.* bassesse, *f.*
grow [grou], *v.t. irr.* cultiver.—*v.i.* croître,
pousser; s'accroître; devenir, se faire (*to
become*); **to grow up,** croître, grandir,
arriver à maturité.
grower [ˈgrouə], *n.* cultivateur, producteur, *m.*
growing [ˈgrouiŋ], *a.* croissant.—*n.* croissance; culture, *f.*
growl [graul], *v.i.* grogner, gronder.—*n.*
grognement, grondement, *m.*
grown-up [ˈgrounʌp], *a.* fait, grand.—*n.*
adulte, *m., f.*
growth [grouθ], *n.* croissance, *f.*; produit
cru, *m.*, récolte (*produce*), *f.*; (*fig.*) progrès,
m.
grub [grʌb], *n.* larve, *f.*, ver blanc, *m.*—*v.t.*
défricher, fouiller.—*v.i.* bêcher, creuser.
grubby [ˈgrʌbi], *a.* véreux; (*fig.*) sale.
grudge [grʌdʒ], *n.* rancune, animosité, *f.*; **to
bear a grudge against,** en vouloir à.—
v.t. donner à contre-cœur.
grudgingly [ˈgrʌdʒiŋli], *adv.* à contre-cœur;
de mauvaise grâce.
gruel [ˈgruːəl], *n.* gruau, *m.*
gruesome [ˈgruːsəm], *a.* macabre, horrible,
lugubre.
gruff [grʌf], *a.* bourru, rude, rébarbatif.
grumble [grʌmbl], *v.i.* se plaindre, grogner
grommeler (*contre* ou *de*).
grumbler [ˈgrʌmblə], *n.* grondeur, grogneur
m.
grumbling [ˈgrʌmbliŋ], *n.* grognement, *m.*
grunt [grʌnt], *v.i.* grogner.—*n.* grognement,
m.
guarantee [gærənˈtiː], *n.* garant, *m.*, caution,
garantie, *f.*—*v.t.* garantir.
guard [gɑːd], *n.* garde; défense, protection, *f.*;
garde (*personne*), *m.*; (*Rail.*) conducteur, chef
de train, *m.*—*v.t.* garder, défendre, protéger, veiller sur.—*v.i.* se garder, se prémunir (*contre*).
guarded [ˈgɑːdid], *a.* prudent, circonspect;
réservé.
guardedly [ˈgɑːdidli], *adv.* avec circonspection, avec réserve.
guardian [ˈgɑːdjən], *a.* gardien, tutélaire.—*n.*
gardien; tuteur (*de jeunes*), *m.*
guardianship [ˈgɑːdjənʃip], *n.* tutelle, protection, *f.*
guard-room [ˈgɑːdrum], *n.* corps de garde,
m., salle de police, *f.*
Guatemala [gwætəˈmɑːlə]. le Guatemala, *m.*
gudgeon [ˈgʌdʒən], *n.* goujon; (*Mech.*)
tourillon, *m.*; (*fig.*) dupe, *f.*
guess [ges], *v.t., v.i.* deviner, conjecturer.—
n. conjecture, *f.*
guest [gest], *n.* invité, convive, *m., f.*;
hôte, *m.*
guffaw [gəˈfɔː], *n.* gros rire, *m.*—*v.i.* pouffer
de rire.
guidance [ˈgaidəns], *n.* conduite, direction, *f.*
guide [gaid], *n.* guide, conducteur, *m.*;
Girl Guide, éclaireuse, *f.*—*v.t.* conduire,
guider; diriger; *guided missile* (*Mil.*)
engin téléguidé, *m.*
guild [gild], *n.* corporation, guilde, *f.*
guildhall [ˈgildhɔːl], *n.* hôtel de ville, *m.*
guile [gail], *n.* astuce, *f.*, artifice, *m.*
guilt [gilt], *n.* culpabilité, *f.*

guiltily [ˈgiltili], *adv.* criminellement.
guiltless [ˈgiltlis], *a.* innocent.
guilty [ˈgilti], *a.* coupable; **the guilty
party,** le coupable; **to find guilty,** (*Law*)
déclarer coupable; **to plead guilty,**
s'avouer coupable.
Guinea [ˈgini]. la Guinée, *f.*
guinea [ˈgini], *n.* guinée, *f.*
guinea-fowl [ˈginifaul], *n.* pintade, *f.*
guinea-pig [ˈginipig], *n.* cochon d'Inde, *m.*
guise [gaiz], *n.* guise, façon, apparence, *f.*;
costume, *m.*, dehors, *m.pl.*
guitar [giˈtɑː], *n.* guitare, *f.*
gulf [gʌlf], *n.* golfe; (*fig.*) gouffre, *m.*
gull [gʌl], *n.* mouette, *f.*, goéland; (*fig.*)
jobard, *m.*—*v.t.* duper, flouer.
gullet [ˈgʌlit], *n.* gosier, *m.*
gullible [ˈgʌlibl], *a.* crédule.
gully [ˈgʌli], *n.* ravin, *m.*
gulp [gʌlp], *v.t.* avaler, gober.—*n.* goulée,
gorgée, *f.*, trait, *m.*; **at a gulp,** d'un trait.
gum [gʌm], *n.* gomme; (*Anat.*) gencive, *f.*
gumboil [ˈgʌmbɔil], *n.* abcès aux gencives, *m.*
gumption [ˈgʌmpʃən], *n.* (*colloq.*) sens
pratique, *m.*, jugeotte, *f.*
gum-tree [ˈgʌmtriː], *n.* gommier, *m.*; (*fig.*)
up a gum-tree, dans le pétrin.
gun [gʌn], *n.* canon, *m.*; pièce d'artillerie,
bouche à feu, *f.*; fusil (non rayé); (*Am.*)
revolver, *m.*; **machine-gun,** mitrailleuse
f.
gunboat [ˈgʌnbout], *n.* canonnière, *f.*
guncarriage [ˈgʌnkæridʒ], *n.* affût (de
canon), *m.*
gunnel [GUNWALE].
gunner [ˈgʌnə], *n.* canonnier, servant, artilleur, *m.*
gunnery [ˈgʌnəri], *n.* artillerie, *f.*; tir au
canon, *m.*
gunpowder [ˈgʌnpaudə], *n.* poudre à canon, *f.*
gunshot [ˈgʌnʃɔt], *n.* portée de fusil (*distance*),
f.; coup de canon (*décharge*); coup de feu
(*blessure*), *m.*
gunwale [gʌnl], *n.* (*Naut.*) plat-bord, *m.*
gurgle [gəːgl], *v.i.* faire glouglou; gargouiller.
gush [gʌʃ], *n.* jaillissement, *m.*; effusion, *f.*,
jet; débordement (*de sentiments*), *m.*—*v.i.*
jaillir; (*fig.*) être sentimental à l'excès.
gusher [ˈgʌʃə], *n.* (*Min.*) puits jaillissant, *m.*
gushing [ˈgʌʃiŋ], *a.* jaillissant; bouillonnant;
(*fig.*) expansif, empressé.
gusset [ˈgʌsit], *n.* gousset, *m.*
gust [gʌst], *n.* coup de vent, *m.*, bouffée,
rafale, *f.*
gusty [ˈgʌsti], *a.* orageux, venteux.
gut [gʌt], *n.* boyau, intestin, *m.*; corde à
boyau (*fabriqué*), *f.*; (*pl.*) (*fam.*) intestins,
m.pl.; ventre; courage, cran, *m.*—*v.t.*
éventrer, vider; (*fig.*) détruire.
gutter [ˈgʌtə], *n.* gouttière (*d'une maison*), *f.*;
ruisseau, caniveau (*dans la rue*), *m.*—*v.i.*
couler.
guttersnipe [ˈgʌtəsnaip], *n.* gamin, voyou, *m.*
guttural [ˈgʌtərəl], *a.* guttural.
guy [gai], *n.* épouvantail, *m.*; (*Naut.*) corde
soutien, *f.*, guide; (*Am.*) type, individu, *m.*
Guyana [giˈɑːnə, gaiˈɑːnə]. la Guyane, *f.*
guzzle [gʌzl], *v.t., v.i.* bouffer (*aliment*),
lamper (*boisson*).
gym [dʒim], [GYMNASIUM].
gymkhana [dʒimˈkɑːnə], *n.* gymkhana, *m.*
gymnasium [dʒimˈneiziəm], *n.* gymnase, *m.*

442

hand

gymnast ['dʒimnæst], *n.* gymnaste, *m., f.*
gymnastic [dʒim'næstik], *a.* gymnastique.—
n.(pl.) gymnastique, *f.*
gypsum ['dʒipsəm], *n.* gypse, *m.*
gypsy [GIPSY].
gyrate [dʒai'reit], *v.i.* tournoyer.
gyration [dʒai'reiʃən], *n.* mouvement giratoire, *m.*

H

H, h [eitʃ]. huitième lettre de l'alphabet, *m.*
ou *f.; H-bomb,* [HYDROGEN].
haberdasher ['hæbədæʃə], *n.* mercier, *m.*
haberdashery ['hæbədæʃəri], *n.* mercerie, *f.*
habit ['hæbit], *n.* habitude, coutume, *f.; (pl.)*
mœurs, *f.pl.; riding-habit,* amazone, *f.;*
to be in the habit of, avoir coutume de.—
v.t. vêtir.
habitable ['hæbitəbl], *a.* habitable.
habitation [hæbi'teiʃən], *n.* habitation, demeure, *f.*
habitual [hə'bitjuəl], *a.* habituel.
habitually [hə'bitjuəli], *adv.* habituellement,
d'habitude.
habituate [hə'bitjueit], *v.t.* habituer, accoutumer.
hack (I) [hæk], *v.t.* hacher, couper; ébrécher;
(fig.) massacrer, écorcher.
hack (2) [hæk], *n.* cheval de louage, *m.;* rosse
(cheval sans force), f.; (fig.) écrivassier à
gages, *m.*
hackney ['hækni], *n. hackney-carriage,*
fiacre, *m.*
hackneyed ['hæknid], *a.* banal, rebattu;
hackneyed phrase, cliché, *m.*
haddock ['hædək], *n. (Ichth.)* aiglefin, *m.*
Hades ['heidiːz]. les Enfers, *m.pl.*
haemoglobin [hiːmə'gloubin], *n.* hémoglobine, *f.*
haemorrhage ['heməridʒ], *n.* hémorrhagie, *f.*
haft [haːft], *n.* manche, *m.,* poignée, *f.*
hag [hæg], *n.* vieille sorcière; *(pop.)* vieille
fée, *f.*
haggard ['hægəd], *a.* hagard, farouche, égaré.
haggle [hægl], *v.i.* marchander.
Hague [heig], The. La Haye, *f.*
hail (I) [heil], *n.* grêle, *f.—v.i.* grêler.
hail (2) [heil], *n.* salut, appel, *m.—int.* salut!
—*v.t.* saluer; *(Naut.)* héler; *to hail a
taxi,* héler *ou* appeler un taxi; *to hail
from,* venir de.
hailstone ['heilstoun], *n.* grêlon, *m.*
hailstorm ['heilstɔːm], *n.* tempête de grêle, *f.*
hair [heə], *n.* cheveu *(a single hair), m.;*
cheveux, *m.pl.,* chevelure *(head of hair), f.;*
poil *(on the body, on animals etc.),* crin
(horsehair), m.; soies *(bristles), f.pl.; to do
one's hair,* se coiffer; *to split hairs,*
chicaner sur les mots.
hair-brush ['heəbrʌʃ], *n.* brosse à cheveux, *f.*
hair-cut ['heəkʌt], *n.* coupe de cheveux, *f.*
hairdresser ['heədresə], *n.* coiffeur, *m.*
hairless ['heəlis], *a.* chauve, sans cheveux;
sans poil *(animal).*

hair-net ['heənet], *n.* résille, *f.*
hairy ['heəri], *a.* velu, chevelu, poilu.
Haiti [hai'iːti]. Haïti, *m.* ou *f.*
Haitian [hai'iːʃən], *a.* haïtien.—*n.* Haïtien
(personne), m.
hake [heik], *n. (Ichth.)* merluche, *f., (fam.)*
colin, *m.*
halberd ['hælbəd], *n.* hallebarde, *f.*
hale [heil], *a.* robuste, sain, bien portant; *to
be hale and hearty,* avoir bon pied, bon
œil.
half [haːf], *a.* demi.—*n. (pl.* halves [haːvz])
moitié, *f.,* demi, *m., half an hour,* une
demi-heure, *f.; (pop.) not half!* tu parles!
—*adv.* à demi, à moitié.
half-back ['haːfbæk], *n. (Ftb.)* demi, *m.*
half-brother ['haːfbrʌðə], *n.* demi-frère,
frère utérin, frère consanguin, *m.*
half-caste ['haːfkaːst], *n.* métis, *m.*
half-fare ['haːffeə], *n.* demi-place, *f.,* demi-
tarif, *m.*
half-holiday ['haːf'hɔlidi], *n.* demi-congé, *m.*
half-pay ['haːf'pei], *n.* demi-solde, *f.*
half-time ['haːf'taim], *n. (Spt.)* la mi-temps, *f.*
half-way ['haːf'wei], *adv.* à mi-chemin; *half-
way up the hill,* à mi-côte.
half-witted ['haːf'witid], *a.* niais, sot, idiot.
half-year ['haːf'jiə], *n.* semestre, *m.*
halibut ['hælibət], *n. (Ichth.)* flétan, *m.*
hall [hɔːl], *n.* salle, *f.;* vestibule *(entrance-
hall);* château, manoir *(seat);* réfectoire
(dining-hall); hôtel de ville *(town hall), m.;*
hall porter, concierge, *m.*
hall-mark ['hɔːlmaːk], *n.* poinçon de contrôle, *m.—v.t.* contrôler.
hallo! [hə'lou], *int.* holà! hé!
hallow ['hælou], *v.t.* sanctifier, consacrer.
hallucinate [hə'ljuːsineit], *v.i.* halluciner.
hallucination [həljuːsi'neiʃən], *n.* hallucination; *(fig.)* déception, illusion, *f.*
halo ['heilou], *n. (Astron.)* halo, *m.; (Paint.
etc.)* auréole, *f.*
halt (I) [hɔːlt], *n.* halte, *f.;* arrêt; clochement,
m.—v.i. faire halte.—*int.* halte-là!
*halt (2) [hɔːlt], *a.* boiteux, estropié.
halter ['hɔːltə], *n.* licou, *m.,* longe *(à cheval);*
corde *(du gibet), f.*
halve [haːv], *v.t.* diviser en deux.
ham [hæm], *n.* jambon; *jarret *(humain), m.*
hamlet ['hæmlit], *n.* hameau, *m.*
hammer ['hæmə], *n.* marteau, *m.; to bring
under the hammer,* mettre aux enchères.—*v.t.* marteler, forger.
—*v.i.* marteler.
hammock ['hæmək], *n.* hamac, *m.*
hamper (I) ['hæmpə], *n.* panier, *m.,* manne, *f.*
hamper (2) ['hæmpə], *v.t.* empêtrer, embarrasser, gêner.
hamstring ['hæmstriŋ], *n.* tendon du jarret,
m.—v.t. irr. (conjug. like STRING) couper le
jarret à; *(fig.)* couper les moyens à.
hand [hænd], *n.* main; palme *(mesure de 4
pouces);* signature; écriture *(calligraphie), f.;*
(Cards) jeu, *m.;* aiguille *(d'une montre etc.),
f.;* ouvrier, employé, *m.; at hand,* sous la
main; *off-hand,* sur-le-champ; *second-
hand,* d'occasion.—*v.t.* passer, donner,
remettre; donner la main à; conduire,
guider; *to hand about* or *round,* faire
passer de main en main, faire circuler; *to
hand down,* transmettre; *to hand over,*
remettre, céder.

443

handbag ['hændbæg], *n.* sac à main, *m.*
hand-bell ['hændbel], *n.* sonnette, clochette, *f.*
handbook ['hændbuk], *n.* manuel; guide, *m.*
handcuff ['hændkʌf], *n.* menotte, *f.*—*v.t.* mettre les menottes à.
handful ['hændful], *n.* poignée, *f.*; (*fig.*) petit nombre, peu, *m.*
handicap ['hændikæp], *n.* handicap, *m.*—*v.t.* handicaper.
handicraft ['hændikrɑːft], *n.* métier, travail manuel, *m.*
handiwork ['hændiwəːk], *n.* ouvrage, travail manuel, *m.*
handkerchief ['hæŋkətʃif], *n.* mouchoir, *m.*
handle [hændl], *n.* manche, *m.*; poignée (*d'une epée etc.*), *f.*; bouton (*d'une porte*), *m.*; anse (*d'une cruche*); queue (*d'une poêle*), *f.*; **starting handle**, (*Motor.*) manivelle (de mise en marche),*f.*—*v.t.* manier; toucher à, manipuler.
handle-bar ['hændlbɑː], *n.* guidon (*de bicyclette*), *m.*
handling ['hændliŋ], *n.* maniement, traitement, *m.*
handmaid ['hændmeid], *n.* servante, *f.*
handrail ['hændreil], *n.* garde-fou, *m.*, rampe, main courante, *f.*
handshake ['hændʃeik], *n.* poignée de main, *f.*, serrement de main, *m.*
handsome ['hænsəm], *a.* beau, élégant; (*fig.*) gracieux.
handsomely ['hænsəmli], *adv.* joliment, élégamment; généreusement.
handwriting ['hændraitiŋ], *n.* écriture, *f.*
handy ['hændi], *a.* adroit (*personne*); commode; à portée de la main.
hang [hæŋ], *v.t. irr.* pendre, suspendre; accrocher (*à*); tendre, tapisser (*de*); laisser pendre, pencher, baisser (*la tête etc.*); poser (*portes etc.*); **hang it!** fichtre! **go and be hanged**, va-t'en au diable! *to hang fire*, faire long feu; (*fig.*) vaciller.—*v.i.* pendre, être suspendu; s'accrocher, se pendre; baisser, se pencher (*à*); *to hang about*, rôder autour de; *to hang over*, être suspendu sur, surplomber.
hangar ['hæŋə], *n.* (*Av.*) hangar, *m.*
hang-dog ['hæŋdɔg], *n.* **hang-dog look**, mine patibulaire, *f.*
hanger-on ['hæŋə'rɔn], *n.* dépendant, parasite, *m.*
hanging ['hæŋiŋ], *a.* suspendu.—*n.* suspension, pendaison; pose (*papier de tenture*), *f.*; collage, *m.*; (*pl.*) tapisserie, tenture, *f.*
hangman ['hæŋmən], *n.* (*pl.* **-men** [men]) bourreau, *m.*
hank [hæŋk], *n.* poignée, *f.*, écheveau, *m.*
hanker ['hæŋkə], *v.i. to hanker after*, désirer ardemment.
hankering ['hæŋkəriŋ], *n.* grande envie, *f.*, vif désir, *m.*
haphazard [hæp'hæzəd], *a.* au petit bonheur, fortuit.—*n.* hasard, sort, *m.*
haply ['hæpli], *adv.* par hasard; peut-être.
happen [hæpn], *v.i.* arriver, advenir, se passer; se trouver par hasard.
happily ['hæpili], *adv.* heureusement, par bonheur.
happiness ['hæpinis], *n.* bonheur, *m.*
happy ['hæpi], *a.* heureux, content.
harass ['hærəs], *v.t.* harasser, harceler.

harbinger ['hɑːbindʒə], *n.* avant-coureur, précurseur, *m.*
harbour ['hɑːbə], *n.* port, havre; (*fig.*) refuge, asile, gîte, *m.*—*v.t.* héberger, recéler, donner asile à; (*fig.*) entretenir, nourrir.—*v.i.* se réfugier.
hard [hɑːd], *a.* dur, ferme; (*fig.*) malaisé, difficile; pénible, rude, rigoureux; dur à la détente (*pingre*); **hard frost**, forte gelée, *f.*; **hard labour**, travaux forcés, *m.pl.*; **hard up**, à court (d'argent).—*adv.* dur, rudement, péniblement; fort, ferme.
harden [hɑːdn], *v.t.* durcir; (*fig.*) endurcir (*à*).—*v.i.* s'endurcir, devenir dur.
hardening ['hɑːdniŋ], *n.* durcissement; (*fig.*) endurcissement, *m.*; trempe (*d'acier*), *f.*
hardihood ['hɑːdihud], *n.* hardiesse, audace, intrépidité, *f.*
hardily ['hɑːdili], *adv.* durement, hardiment.
hardiness ['hɑːdinis], *n.* hardiesse, *f.*; tempérament robuste, *m.*; (*fig.*) effronterie, assurance, *f.*
hardly ['hɑːdli], *adv.* durement, rudement, mal; à peine, guère (*presque pas*); **hardly ever**, presque jamais.
hardness ['hɑːdnis], *n.* dureté, solidité; difficulté; crudité (*d'eau*), *f.*
hardship ['hɑːdʃip], *n.* fatigue, peine, privation, *f.*; (*pl.*) épreuves, souffrances, *f.pl.*
hardware ['hɑːdwɛə], *n.* quincaillerie, *f.*
hardy ['hɑːdi], *a.* hardi, courageux; fort; de pleine terre (*plantes*).
hare [hɛə], *n.* lièvre, *m.*
hare-brained ['hɛəbreind], *a.* écervelé, étourdi.
hare-lip ['hɛəlip], *n.* bec-de-lièvre, *m.*
hark [hɑːk], *v.i.* écouter, prêter l'oreille.—*int.* écoutez!
harlequin ['hɑːlikwin], *n.* arlequin *m.*
harm [hɑːm], *n.* tort, dommage, mal, *m.*—*v.t.* nuire à, faire du mal à.
harmful ['hɑːmful], *a.* nuisible, malfaisant, nocif.
harmless ['hɑːmlis], *a.* innocent, inoffensif.
harmonic [hɑː'mɔnik], *a.* harmonique; harmonieux.—*n.*(*pl.*) harmonique, *f.*
harmonious [hɑː'mouniəs], *a.* harmonieux; mélodieux.
harmonize ['hɑːmənaiz], *v.t.* rendre harmonieux, accorder, harmoniser.—*v.i.* s'harmoniser; (*fig.*) s'accorder.
harmony ['hɑːməni], *n.* harmonie, *f.*; accord, *m.*
harness ['hɑːnis], *n.* harnais, harnachement, *m.*—*v.t.* harnacher; atteler (*à une voiture*).
harp [hɑːp], *n.* harpe, *f.*; **Jew's harp**, guimbarde, *f.*—*v.i.* jouer de la harpe; *to harp on one string*, rabâcher toujours la même chose.
harpist ['hɑːpist], *n.* harpiste, *m.*, *f.*
harpoon [hɑː'puːn], *n.* harpon, *m.*—*v.t.* harponner.
harpsichord ['hɑːpsikɔːd], *n.* clavecin, *m.*
harridan ['hæridən], *n.* chipie, mégère, *f.*
harrow ['hærou], *n.* herse, *f.*—*v.t.* herser; (*fig.*) torturer.
harrowing ['hærouiŋ], *a.* navrant.—*n.* hersage; (*fig.*) déchirement, *m.*
Harry ['hæri], Henri, *m.*
harry ['hæri], *v.t.* harceler; piller.
harsh [hɑːʃ], *a.* âpre, rude, dur; discordant.
harshly ['hɑːʃli], *adv.* durement, sévèrement.

444

harshness ['hɑːʃnis], *n.* âpreté; discordance, *f.*

hart [hɑːt], *n.* cerf, *m.*

harum-scarum ['hɛərəm'skɛərəm], *a.* écervelé, étourdi.

harvest ['hɑːvist], *n.* moisson (*de blé*); récolte (*de fruits etc.*); vendange (*de raisins*), *f.*—*v.t.* moissonner; récolter; vendanger.

hash [hæʃ], *n.* hachis, *m.*—*v.t.* hacher, hacher menu; (*fig.*) plagier.

hasp [hæsp, hɑːsp], *n.* loquet, *m.*

hassock ['hæsək], *n.* coussin (*pour les genoux* ou *les pieds*), *m.*

haste [heist], *n.* hâte, précipitation, *f.*, emportement, *m.*; diligence, *f.*; *in haste*, à la hâte; *to make haste*, se hâter, se dépêcher.—*v.i.* or **hasten** [heisn], se hâter, se dépêcher, s'empresser.

hasten [heisn], *v.t.* hâter, dépêcher.

hastily ['heistili], *adv.* à la hâte; brusquement.

hastiness ['heistinis], *n.* hâte, précipitation, *f.*; emportement, *m.*

hasty ['heisti], *a.* rapide, précipité; inconsidéré, emporté.

hat [hæt], *n.* chapeau, *m.*; *bowler-hat*, chapeau melon; *felt hat*, feutre, *m.*; *soft felt hat*, chapeau mou; *straw hat*, chapeau de paille; *top hat*, chapeau haut de forme.

hatch (1) [hætʃ], *n.* (*pl.* **hatches** ['hætʃiz]) couvée (*de poulets*); éclosion (*d'œufs*); porte coupée (*dans le mur*); (*Naut.*) écoutille, *f.*; (*pl.*) panneaux des écoutilles, *m.pl.*—*v.t.* couver (*incuber*); faire éclore; (*fig.*) tramer, produire.—*v.i.* éclore.

hatch (2) [hætʃ], *v.t.* hacher (*un dessin*).

hatchet ['hætʃit], *n.* cognée, hachette, hache, *f.*

hate [heit], *n.* haine, *f.*—*v.t.* haïr, détester.

hateful ['heitful], *a.* odieux, détestable.

hatred ['heitrid], *n.* haine, *f.*

hat-stand ['hætstænd], *n.* porte-chapeaux, *m. inv.*

hatter ['hætə], *n.* chapelier, *m.*

haughtily ['hɔːtili], *adv.* hautainement, avec arrogance.

haughtiness ['hɔːtinis], *n.* arrogance, *f.*

haughty ['hɔːti], *a.* hautain, arrogant.

haul [hɔːl], *n.* tirage, remorquage; coup de filet, *m.*—*v.t.* tirer, remorquer, haler; charrier, transporter.

haulage ['hɔːlidʒ], *n.* camionnage, roulage; remorquage, *m.*

haulier ['hɔːljə], *n.* camionneur, *m.*

haunch [hɔːntʃ], *n.* hanche (*d'un animal*), *f.*, cuissot (*de venaison*), *m.*

haunt [hɔːnt], *n.* retraite, *f.*; repaire (*de voleurs etc.*), *m.*—*v.t.* hanter, fréquenter; (*fig.*) obséder.

Havana [hə'vænə]. la Havane, *f.*

have [hæv], *v.t.* and *aux. irr.* avoir; tenir, posséder; contenir; prendre; faire; *I had rather*, j'aimerais mieux; *I have it*, j'y suis; *to have to*, devoir, falloir, avoir à.

haven [heivn], *n.* havre, port; (*fig.*) asile, *m.*

haversack ['hævəsæk], *n.* (*Mil.*) musette, *f.*; havresac, *m.*

havoc ['hævɒk], *n.* dégât, ravage, *m.*

hawk [hɔːk], *n.* faucon, *m.*—*v.t.* chasser au faucon; colporter (*vendre*).

hawker ['hɔːkə], *n.* colporteur, *m.*

hawser ['hɔːzə], *n.* haussière, *f.*, grelin, *m.*

hawthorn ['hɔːθɔːn], *n.* aubépine, *f.*

hay [hei], *n.* foin, *m.*

hay-fever ['hei'fiːvə], *n.* rhume des foins, *m.*

hay-making ['heimeikiŋ], *n.* fenaison, *f.*

hayrick ['heirik], **haystack** ['heistæk], *n.* meule de foin, *f.*

hazard ['hæzəd], *n.* hasard, danger, risque, *m.*—*v.t.* hasarder, risquer.—*v.i.* se hasarder, s'aventurer.

hazardous ['hæzədəs], *a.* hasardeux, risqué, dangereux.

haze [heiz], *n.* petite brume; (*fig.*) obscurité, *f.*

hazel [heizl], *a.* noisette.—*n.* noisetier, coudrier, *m.*

hazel-nut ['heizlnʌt], *n.* noisette, *f.*

hazily ['heizili], *adv.* indistinctement.

hazy ['heizi], *a.* brumeux; *to have hazy notions*, avoir des idées vagues.

he [hiː], *pron.* il, celui, lui; *he and I*, lui et moi; *he that* or *he who*, celui qui.

he- [hiː], *pref.* mâle.

head [hed], *a.* premier, principal, en chef.—*n.* tête, *f.*; chef, avant, *m.*; proue (*de navire*), *f.*; haut bout (*d'une table*); chevet (*d'un lit*), *m.*; chute (*d'eau*), *f.*; pièces (*de gibier*), *f.pl.*; source (*d'une rivière*), *f.*; (*fig.*) sujet, chapitre, *m.*—*v.t.* conduire, diriger.—*v.i.* *to head for*, (*Naut.*) mettre le cap sur; se diriger vers, s'avancer vers.

headache ['hedeik], *n.* mal de tête, *m.*, migraine, *f.*

head-dress ['heddres], *n.* coiffure, *f.*

heading ['hediŋ], *n.* titre, en-tête, *m.*

headland ['hedlənd], *n.* cap, promontoire, *m.*

head-light ['hedlait], *n.* (*Motor.*) phare, *m.*

headline ['hedlain], *n.* (*Journ.*) titre, sous-titre, *m.*

headlong ['hedlɒŋ], *adv.* la tête la première. (*fig.*) tête baissée.—*a.* précipité, irréfléchi.

headmaster ['hed'mɑːstə], *n.* principal, directeur, proviseur, *m.*

head-mistress ['hed'mistris], *n.* directrice, *f.*

head-phone ['hedfoun], *n.* (*Teleph.*) écouteur, *m.*

head-quarters ['hed'kwɔːtəz], *n.pl.* quartier général, *m.*

headstone ['hedstoun], *n.* pierre tombale, *f.*

headstrong ['hedstrɒŋ], *a.* opiniâtre, obstiné, entêté.

headway ['hedwei], *n.* progrès, *m.*; *to make headway*, avancer, progresser.

heady ['hedi], *a.* capiteux (*boisson*).

heal [hiːl], *v.t.* guérir; (*fig.*) apaiser.—*v.i.* guérir, se guérir; se cicatriser.

healing ['hiːliŋ], *a.* curatif; (*fig.*) salutaire.—*n.* guérison, *f.*

health [helθ], *n.* santé, *f.*; toast, *m.*; *National Health Service*, sécurité sociale, *f.*; *bill of health*, patente de santé, *f.*

healthily ['helθili], *adv.* en santé; sainement.

healthy ['helθi], *a.* bien portant, en bonne santé; sain, salubre.

heap [hiːp], *n.* tas, monceau, amas, *m.*—*v.t.* entasser, amonceler.

hear [hiə], *v.t. irr.* entendre; entendre dire; écouter (*faire attention à*); (*fig.*) apprendre; *to hear it said*, entendre dire.—*v.i.* entendre; entendre parler; écouter; recevoir des nouvelles, avoir des nouvelles (*de*); *hear! hear!* très bien! bravo!

hearing ['hiəriŋ], *n.* ouïe (*sens auditif*); audition (*de témoins*), *f.*; **hard of hearing,** dur d'oreille; **within hearing,** à portée de la voix.
hearken ['hɑːkn], *v.i.* écouter.
hearsay ['hiəsei], *n.* ouï-dire, *m.*
hearse [həːs], *n.* corbillard, *m.*
heart [hɑːt], *n.* cœur; (*fig.*) courage; centre, *m.*
heart-attack ['hɑːtətæk], *n.* crise cardiaque, *f.*
heart-breaking ['hɑːtbreikiŋ], *a.* qui fend le cœur, navrant.
heart-broken ['hɑːtbroukən], *a.* qui a le cœur brisé.
heartburn ['hɑːtbəːn], *n.* brûlures d'estomac, aigreurs, *f.pl.*
hearten [hɑːtn], *v.t.* encourager, animer.
heart-failure ['hɑːtfeiljə], *n.* arrêt du cœur *m.*
heartfelt ['hɑːtfelt], *a.* qui vient du cœur.
hearth [hɑːθ], *n.* âtre, foyer, *m.*
heartily ['hɑːtili], *adv.* cordialement, de bon cœur; de bon appétit (*manger*).
heartiness ['hɑːtinis], *n.* cordialité; vigueur (*de l'appétit*), *f.*
heartless ['hɑːtlis], *a.* sans cœur, sans pitié.
hearty ['hɑːti], *a.* sincère, cordial; abondant, bon (*repas*).
heat [hiːt], *n.* chaleur; (*fig.*) ardeur; colère (*courroux*); (*Racing*) épreuve, *f.—v.t.* chauffer, échauffer.—*v.i.* s'échauffer.
heated ['hiːtid], *a.* chaud; échauffé; animé.
heath [hiːθ], *n.* bruyère, lande; brande (*plante*), *f.*
heathen [hiːðn], *a.* and *n.* païen, *m.*
heather ['heðə], *n.* bruyère, brande, *f.*
heating ['hiːtiŋ], *n.* chauffage, *m.*
heave [hiːv], *n.* effort (*pour soulever*), *m.*, secousse, *f.*; soulèvement, *m.—v.t.* irr. lever; élever; soulever; pousser (*un soupir*).—*v.i.* se soulever; palpiter, battre (*sein, cœur etc.*).
heaven [hevn], *n.* ciel, *m.*, cieux, *m.pl.*
heavenly ['hevnli], *a.* céleste, divin.
heavily ['hevili], *adv.* pesamment, lourdement; fortement.
heaviness ['hevinis], *n.* pesanteur, lourdeur; (*fig.*) tristesse, *f.*
heavy ['hevi], *a.* lourd, pesant; (*fig.*) gros; triste.
Hebrew ['hiːbruː], *a.* hébreu, *m.*; hébraïque, *f.—n.* hébreu (*langue*); Hébreu, Juif (*personne*), *m.*
heckle [hekl], *v.t.* embarrasser de questions, harasser (*en public*).
hectic ['hektik], *a.* hectique; agité, fiévreux.
hedge [hedʒ], *n.* haie, *f.—v.t.* entourer d'une haie.—*v.i.* (*fig.*) éviter de se compromettre.
hedgehog ['hedʒhɔg], *n.* hérisson, *m.*
hedge-sparrow ['hedʒspærou], *n.* mouchet, *m.*, fauvette d'hiver, *f.*
heed [hiːd], *n.* attention, *f.*, soin, *m.—v.t.* faire attention à, prendre garde à, écouter.
heedless ['hiːdlis], *a.* étourdi, inattentif, insouciant.
heedlessly ['hiːdlisli], *adv.* négligemment; étourdiment.
heel [hiːl], *n.* talon, *m.*; **to be down at heel,** traîner la savate; **to cool one's heels,** faire antichambre.—*v.i.* **to heel over,** (*Naut.*) donner de la bande.
hefty ['hefti], *a.* (*fam.*) solide, costaud.

heifer ['hefə], *n.* génisse, *f.*
height [hait], *n.* hauteur, élévation; taille, *f.*; (*fig.*) comble, faîte, *m.*; **the height of summer,** le cœur *ou* le fort de l'été.
heighten [haitn], *v.t.* rehausser, relever.
heinous ['heinəs], *a.* atroce.
heir [ɛə], *n.* héritier, *m.*
heiress ['ɛəris], *n.* héritière, *f.*
heirloom ['ɛəluːm], *n.* meuble *ou* bijou (de famille), *m.*
Helen ['helin]. (*Myth.*) Hélène, *f.*
helicopter ['helikɔptə], *n.* hélicoptère, *m.*
helium ['hiːliəm], *n.* (*Chem.*) hélium, *m.*
hell [hel], *n.* enfer, *m.*
hellish ['heliʃ], *a.* infernal, d'enfer.
hello! [he'lou], **hullo!** [hʌ'lou], *int.* holà! allô! (*au téléphone*); tiens! (*surprise*).
helm (1) [helm], *n.* (*Naut.*) gouvernail, timon, *m.*, barre, *f.*
helm (2) [helm], *n.* (*poet.*) heaume (*casque*), *m.*
helmet ['helmit], *n.* casque, *m.*
helmsman ['helmzmən], *n.* (*pl.* -**men** [men]) timonier, *m.*
help [help], *n.* secours, *m.*; aide, assistance, *f.*; remède (*recours*), *m.*; **help!** au secours!— *v.t.* aider, secourir, assister; servir (*à table*); empêcher (*prevent*); éviter (*avoid*); **help yourself** (*at table*), servez-vous; **how can I help it?** que voulez-vous que j'y fasse? **how can it be helped?** qu'y faire? **I can't help it,** je n'y puis rien; **I cannot help saying,** je ne puis m'empêcher de dire.— *v.i.* aider, servir, contribuer.
helper ['helpə], *n.* aide, *m.f.*
helpful ['helpful], *a.* utile; secourable.
helpless ['helplis], *a.* faible, impuissant; sans appui.
helplessly ['helplisli], *adv.* faiblement; sans ressource.
helter-skelter ['heltə'skeltə], *adv.* pêle-mêle; en pagaille.
helve [helv], *n.* manche, *m.*
hem [hem], *n.* ourlet, bord, *m.—v.t.* ourler, border; **to hem in,** entourer.
hemisphere ['hemisfiə], *n.* hémisphère, *m.*
hemlock ['hemlɔk], *n.* ciguë, *f.*
hemorrhage [HAEMORRHAGE].
hemp [hemp], *n.* (*Bot.*) chanvre, *m.*; (*fig.*) corde, *f.*
hen [hen], *n.* poule; femelle (*d'oiseau*), *f.*
hence [hens], *adv.* d'ici; de là, ainsi (*pour cela*); désormais (*temps*).
henceforth ['hensfɔːθ], **henceforward** [hens'fɔːwəd], *adv.* désormais, dorénavant, à l'avenir.
henchman ['hentʃmən], *n.* (*pl.* -**men** [men]) écuyer, valet; (*fig.*) partisan, *m.*
hen-house ['henhaus], *n.* poulailler, *m.*
hen-pecked ['henpekt], *a.* gouverné par sa femme.
Henry ['henri]. Henri, *m.*
her [həː], *pers. pron.* elle, la, lui.—*poss. a.* son, sa, ses.—*dem. pron.* celle, *f.*
herald ['herəld], *n.* héraut; (*fig.*) avant-coureur, précurseur, *m.—v.t.* annoncer.
heraldry ['herəldri], *n.* science héraldique, *f.*, blason, *m.*
herb [həːb], *n.* herbe, *f.*; **pot-herbs,** herbes potagères, *f.pl.*; **sweet herbs,** fines herbes, *f.pl.*
herbaceous [həː'beiʃəs], *a.* herbacé.
herbage ['həːbidʒ], *n.* herbage, *m.*

herbalist ['hə:bəlist], *n.* herboriste, *m.*, *f.*
Hercules ['hə:kjuli:z], Hercule, *m.*
herd [hə:d], *n.* troupeau, *m.*, troupe, *f.*—*v.t.* garder.—*v.i.* vivre en troupeau.
herdsman ['hə:dzmən], *n.* (*pl.* **-men** [men]) bouvier, *m.*
here [hiə], *adv.* ici; voici, que voici; *here!* présent! *here and there*, çà et là; *here they are*, les voici; *I am here*, me voici; *this one here*, celui-ci.
hereafter [hiər'ɑːftə], *adv.* désormais; dans la vie à venir.—*n.* l'au-delà, *m.*
hereby [hiə'bai], *adv.* par ce moyen, par là.
hereditary [hi'reditəri], *a.* héréditaire.
heredity [hi'rediti], *n.* hérédité, *f.*
heresy ['herisi], *n.* hérésie, *f.*
heretic ['heritik], *n.* hérétique, *m.*, *f.*
heretical [hi'retikəl], *a.* hérétique.
heretofore ['hiətufɔ:], *adv.* jadis, jusqu'ici.
hereupon [hiərə'pɔn], *adv.* là-dessus.
herewith [hiə'wið], *adv.* ci-joint.
heritage ['heritidʒ], *n.* héritage, *m.*
hermetic [hə:'metik], *a.* hermétique.
hermetically [hə:'metikli], *adv.* hermétiquement.
hermit ['hə:mit], *n.* ermite, *m.*
hero ['hiərou], *n.* (*pl.* **heroes** ['hiərouz]) héros, *m.*
heroic [hi'rouik], **heroical** [-əl], *a.* héroïque.
heroine ['herouin], *n.* héroïne, *f.*
heroism ['herouizm], *n.* héroïsme, *m.*
heron ['herən], *n.* héron, *m.*
herring ['heriŋ], *n.* hareng, *m.*; *red herring*, hareng saur; (*fig.*) diversion, *f.*
hers [hə:z], *pron.* le sien, *m.*, la sienne, *f.*, les siens, *m.pl.*, les siennes, *f.pl.*; *a friend of hers*, une de ses amies, *f.*
herself [hə:'self], *pron.* elle-même, elle; (*reflexive*) se; *by herself*, toute seule.
hesitant ['hezitənt], *a.* hésitant.
hesitate ['heziteit], *v.i.* hésiter.
hesitation [hezi'teiʃən], *n.* hésitation, *f.*
heterodox ['hetərədɔks], *a.* hétérodoxe.
heterogeneous [hetərə'dʒi:niəs], *a.* hétérogène.
hew [hju:], *v.t. irr.* tailler, couper.
hewer ['hjuə], *n.* tailleur (*de pierre*); piqueur (*de charbon*); fendeur (*de bois*), *m.*
hexagon ['heksəgən], *n.* hexagone, *m.*
heyday ['heidei], *n.* beaux jours, *m.pl.*
hiatus [hai'eitəs], *n.* hiatus, *m.*; (*fig.*) lacune, *f.*
hibernate ['haibəneit], *v.i.* hiverner, hiberner.
hiccough, hiccup ['hikʌp], *n.* hoquet, *m.*—*v.i.* avoir le hoquet.
hidden [hidn], *a.* caché, secret; (*fig.*) occulte.
hide (1) [haid], *n.* peau, *f.*, cuir, *m.*
hide (2) [haid], *v.t. irr.* cacher; enfouir (*en terre*); *hide-and-seek*, cache-cache, *m.*—*v.i.* se cacher, se tenir caché.
hideous ['hidiəs], *a.* hideux, affreux.
hiding (1) ['haidiŋ], *n.* (*colloq.*) rossée, raclée, *f.*; *to give someone a good hiding*, tanner le cuir à quelqu'un.
hiding (2) ['haidiŋ], *n. in hiding*, caché; *hiding-place*, cachette, *f.*
hie [hai], *v.i.* se hâter, se rendre (*à*).
hierarchy ['haiərɑ:ki], *n.* hiérarchie, *f.*
high [hai], *a.* haut, élevé; (*fig.*) grand; sublime; fier, altier; faisandé (*gibier*); avancé (*viande*); *from on high*, d'en haut; *high road*, grand-route, *f.*; *high street*, grand-

rue, *f.*; *it is high time*, il est grand temps.
—*adv.* haut, hautement; grandement; fort; *to run high*, s'échauffer (*sentiments*).
highbrow ['haibrau], *a.* and *n.* (*fam.*) intellectuel, *m.*
higher ['haiə], *comp. a.* plus haut, plus élevé; supérieur.
highest ['haiist], *superl. a.* le plus haut, le plus élevé; *at the highest*, au comble.
high-flown ['haifloun], *a.* enflé; ampoulé (*style*).
high-handed ['hai'hændid], *a.* arbitraire, tyrannique.
Highland ['hailənd], *a.* de la Haute Écosse.
highland ['hailənd], *a.* des montagnes.
Highlander ['hailəndə], *n.* montagnard de l'Écosse, *m.*
Highlands ['hailəndz], **the.** les hautes terres d'Écosse, *f.pl.*, la haute Écosse, *f.*
highlands ['hailəndz], *n.pl.* pays montagneux, *m.*
highlight ['hailait], *n.* point culminant, (*fam.*) clou, *m.*
highly ['haili], *adv.* hautement; fortement.
Highness ['hainis], *n.* Altesse (*titre*), *f.*
highness ['hainis], *n.* hauteur, *f.*
high-pitched ['haipitʃt], *a.* aigu (*son*).
high-sounding ['haisaundiŋ], *a.* pompeux; ronflant (*style*).
high-spirited ['haispiritid], *a.* fougueux, plein de cœur.
highway ['haiwei], *n.* grand chemin, *m.*, grand-route, *f.*
highwayman ['haiweimən], *n.* (*pl.* **-men** [men]) voleur de grand chemin, *m.*
hike [haik], *n.* excursion à pied, *f.*—*v.i.* aller à pied, vagabonder; faire des excursions à pied.
hiker ['haikə], *n.* touriste à pied, *m.*, *f.*
hilarious [hi'leəriəs], *a.* gai, joyeux.
hilarity [hi'læriti], *n.* hilarité, *f.*
hill [hil], *n.* colline, montagne, *f.*, coteau, *m.*, butte; côte, *f.*
hillock ['hilək], *n.* monticule, *m.*, butte, *f.*
hilly ['hili], *a.* montagneux, accidenté.
hilt [hilt], *n.* poignée, garde, *f.*
him [him], *pers. pron.* le, lui.—*dem. pron.* celui.
himself [him'self], *pron.* lui-même, lui; (*reflexive*) se; *by himself*, tout seul.
hind (1) [haind], *n.* (*Zool.*) biche, *f.*
hind (2) [haind], *a.* de derrière, postérieur, arrière.
hinder ['hində], *v.t.* empêcher; gêner, embarrasser, retarder.
hindrance ['hindrəns], *n.* empêchement, obstacle, *m.*
Hindu [hin'du:], *a.* hindou.—*n.* Hindou, *m.*
hinge [hindʒ], *n.* gond, *m.*; paumelle; charnière (*butt-hinge*), *f.*; (*fig.*) pivot, *m.*
hint [hint], *n.* insinuation, allusion, *f.*; (*fig.*) soupçon, *m.*; conseils, *m.pl.*; *broad hint*, allusion évidente; *to take the hint*, comprendre à demi-mot.—*v.i.* donner à entendre (*à*), insinuer, suggérer.
hip [hip], *n.* hanche, *f.*
hippopotamus [hipə'pɔtəməs], *n.* (*pl.* **hippopotami** [hipə'pɔtəmai], **hippopotamuses** [hipə'pɔtəməsəz]) hippopotame, *m.*
hire ['haiə], *n.* louage, prix de louage; salaire *m.*, gages, *m.pl.*; *for hire*, à louer, libre (*taxi*).—*v.t.* louer; engager, employer.
hireling ['haiəliŋ], *a.* and *n.* mercenaire, *m.*

hire-purchase ['haiə'pəːtʃəs], *n.* vente à tempérament, location-vente, *f.*

hirsute ['həːsjuːt], *a.* velu, hirsute.

his [hiz], *a.* son, sa, ses.—*pron.* le sien, *m.*, la sienne, *f.*, les siens, *m.pl.*, les siennes, *f.pl.*; *a friend of his*, un de ses amis; *it is his*, c'est à lui.

hiss [his], *v.t.*, *v.i.* siffler.—*n.* sifflement; sifflet, *m.*

hissing ['hisiŋ], *a.* sifflant.—*n.* sifflement, *m.*

historian [his'tɔːriən], *n.* historien, *m.*

historic [his'tɔrik], **historical** [his'tɔrikəl], *a.* historique.

history ['histəri], *n.* histoire, *f.*

hit [hit], *v.t. irr.* frapper, heurter; atteindre (*le but*); donner (*un coup*); toucher.—*v.i.* frapper, heurter (*contre*).—*n.* coup, *m.*; chance, trouvaille; (*fig.*) invention, *f.*; (*Theat.*) succès, *m.*

hitch [hitʃ], *v.t.* accrocher, attacher; (*Naut.*) nouer, amarrer.—*n.* accroc, *m.*; entrave, *f.*; empêchement; (*Naut.*) nœud, *m.*

hitch-hike ['hitʃhaik], *v.i.* faire de l'auto-stop.

hither ['hiðə], *adv.* ici; *hither and thither*, çà et là.

hitherto [hiðə'tuː], *adv.* jusqu'ici.

hive [haiv], *n.* ruche, *f.*; (*fig.*) essaim (*swarm*), *m.*

hoard [hɔːd], *n.* monceau, amas (*secret*) trésor, *m.*—*v.t.* amasser, accumuler.—*v.i.* thésauriser.

hoarding ['hɔːdiŋ], *n.* accumulation, *f.*; panneau-réclame, *m.*

hoar-frost ['hɔːfrɔst], *n.* gelée blanche, *f.*, givre, *m.*

hoarse [hɔːs], *a.* enroué, rauque.

hoary ['hɔːri], *a.* blanc; aux cheveux gris *ou* blancs.

hoax [houks], *n.* mystification, *f.*; mauvais tour (*brimade*); canard (*fausse nouvelle*), *m.* —*v.t.* mystifier; attraper.

hob [hɔb], *n.* plaque (*de l'âtre*), *f.*

hobble [hɔbl], *v.t.* entraver.—*v.i.* clocher, clopiner; aller clopin clopant.—*n.* clochement, *m.*, difficulté, *f.*; embarras, *m.*; entrave, *f.*

hobby ['hɔbi], *n.* marotte (*manie*), distraction, *f.*, passe-temps, *m.*

hobby-horse ['hɔbihɔːs], *n.* cheval de bois, dada, *m.*

hobgoblin [hɔb'gɔblin], *n.* lutin, *m.*

hobnob ['hɔbnɔb], *v.i.* trinquer ensemble.

hobo ['houbou], *n.* (*Am.*) chemineau, *m.*

hock [hɔk], *n.* jarret (*d'un cheval*); vin du Rhin, *m.*

hockey ['hɔki], *n.* hockey, *m.*

hockey-stick ['hɔkistik], *n.* crosse de hockey, *f.*

hoe [hou], *n.* houe, binette, *f.*; *Dutch hoe*, sarcloir, *m.*—*v.t.*, *v.i.* houer; biner, sarcler.

hog [hɔg], *n.* cochon; goret; (*Comm.*) porc, pourceau; (*fam.*) glouton, *m.*

hogshead ['hɔgzhed], *n.* muid, *m.*; barrique de 240 litres (*tonneau*), *f.*

hoist [hɔist], *v.t.* hisser; guinder (*avec un treuil*); lever; arborer (*un drapeau*).—*n.* grue, *f.*, palan, *m.*

hold [hould], *n.* prise, *f.*; soutien (*appui*), *m.*; garde (*custody*); place forte (*forteresse*); (*Naut.*) cale, *f.*; *to take hold of*, prendre, saisir; *to let go one's hold*, lâcher prise.— *v.t. irr.* tenir, retenir; arrêter; garder, maintenir; occuper, avoir; contenir (*to contain*);

regarder comme; célébrer; *to hold back*, retenir, cacher; *to hold fast*, tenir ferme, tenir bon; *to hold off*, tenir à distance; *to hold over*, remettre, ajourner; *to hold up*, lever, soulever, soutenir; arrêter, retarder. —*v.i.* tenir; se maintenir, durer; supporter; adhérer (*à*); rester; s'arrêter; être vrai; *hold on*, arrêtez! (*Teleph.*) ne quittez pas! *hold tight !* ne lâchez pas! *to hold back*, se tenir en arrière, hésiter; *to hold fast*, tenir ferme; *to hold forth*, haranguer, pérorer; *to hold on*, s'accrocher à; persévérer, poursuivre.

hold-all ['houldɔːl], *n.* enveloppe de voyage, *f.*

holder ['houldə], *n.* personne qui tient, *f.*; (*Spt.*) tenant, locataire, *m.*; poignée, anse, *f.*, manche, *m.*, (*in compound words*) porte-; (*Fin.*) titulaire, *m.*

holding ['houldiŋ], *n.* possession, tenure; ferme, *f.*

hold-up ['houldʌp], *n.* arrêt de la circulation, *m.*; panne, *f.*; hold-up, *m.*

hole [houl], *n.* trou; antre, *m.*, caverne, *f.*; orifice, *m.*, ouverture, *f.*

holiday ['hɔlidei], *a.* de fête, de congé; de vacances.—*n.* fête, *f.*, jour de fête, jour férié, (*Sch. etc.*) congé, *m.*, (*pl.*) vacances, *f.pl.*; *bank-holiday*, fête légale; *on holiday*, en vacance(s).

holiness ['houlinis], *n.* sainteté, *f.*

Holland ['hɔlənd]. la Hollande, *f.*

hollow ['hɔlou], *a.* creux; vide; sourd (*son*).— *n.* creux, *m.*, cavité, *f.*; bas-fond, *m.*—*v.t.* creuser, évider.

holly ['hɔli], *n.* houx, *m.*

hollyhock ['hɔlihɔk], *n.* rose trémière, *f.*

holster ['houlstə], *n.* fonte (*de selle*), *f.*; étui (*de revolver*), *m.*

holy ['houli], *a.* saint, sacré; bénit; *Holy Ghost*, le Saint-Esprit; *Holy Land*, la Terre Sainte; *holy water*, eau bénite, *f.*; *Holy Week*, la semaine sainte, *f.*

homage ['hɔmidʒ], *n.* hommage, *m.*

home [houm], *a.* de la maison, domestique; (*fig.*) qui porte (*coup*).—*n.* foyer domestique, chez-soi; logis, *m.*, maison, *f.*, intérieur, *m.*; (*fig.*) demeure, *f.*; pays, *m.*, patrie (*pays natal*), *f.*; *at home*, chez soi, à la maison; *Home Office*, Ministère de l'Intérieur, *m.*; *to make oneself at home*, faire comme chez soi.—*adv.* chez soi, au logis, à la maison; dans son pays; (*fig.*) directement; *to bring home to*, faire admettre à; *homing pigeon*, pigeon voyageur, *m.*

home-coming ['houmkʌmiŋ], *n.* retour au foyer, *m.*

homeland ['houmlænd], *n.* patrie, *f.*; pays natal, *m.*

homeliness ['houmlinis], *n.* caractère domestique, *m.*; simplicité; rusticité, *f.*

homely ['houmli], *a.* du ménage; simple, sans façon; (*Am.*) laid.

Homer ['houmə]. Homère, *m.*

home-sick ['houmsik], *a.* qui a le mal du pays, nostalgique.

home-sickness ['houmsiknis], *n.* mal du pays, *m.*, nostalgie, *f.*

homestead ['houmsted], *n.* manoir, *m.*, ferme, *f.*

homeward(s) ['houmwəd(z)], *adv.* vers la maison; vers son pays.

homework ['houmwəːk], *n.* devoirs, *m.pl.*
homicide ['homisaid], *n.* homicide, *m.*
homogeneous [homə'dʒiːniəs], *a.* homogène.
homosexual [houmo'seksjuəl], *a.* and *n.* homosexuel, *m.*
Honduran [hon'djuərən], *a.* hondurien.—*n.* Hondurien (*personne*), *m.*
Honduras [hon'djuərəs]. l'Honduras, *m.*
hone [houn], *n.* pierre à aiguiser. *f.*—*v.t.* aiguiser.
honest ['onist], *a.* honnête, loyal, probe, de bonne foi, sincère; **honest man**, homme de bien, honnête homme, *m.*
honestly ['onistli], *adv.* honnêtement, sincèrement.
honesty ['onisti], *n.* honnêteté, probité, bonne foi, sincérité, *f.*
honey ['hʌni], *n.* miel, *m.*; (*fig.*) (*Am.*) chérie, *f.*, ange, *m.*
honeycomb ['hʌnikoum], *n.* rayon de miel, *m.*
honeymoon ['hʌnimuːn], *n.* lune de miel, *f.*
honeysuckle ['hʌnisʌkl], *n.* chèvrefeuille, *m.*
honorary ['onərəri], *a.* honoraire.
honour ['onə], *n.* honneur, *m.*; (*fig.*) dignité, estime, *f.*—*v.t.* honorer (*de*); faire honneur à; faire bon accueil à (*une facture*).
honourable ['onərəbl], *a.* honorable, d'honneur.
hood [hud], *n.* capuchon, *m.*; coiffe; capote (*de voiture*), *f.*; (*Am. Motor.*) [BONNET].
hoodwink ['hudwiŋk], *v.t.* bander les yeux à; (*fig.*) tromper.
hoof [huːf, huf], *n.* (*pl.* **hooves** [huːvz]) sabot, *m.*
hook [huk], *n.* crochet, croc; hameçon (*pour pêcher*), *m.*; faucille (*sickle*), *f.*; **hook and eye**, agrafe et porte, *f.*—*v.t.* accrocher; agrafer; attraper.
hooked [hukt], *a.* crochu, recourbé; aquilin (*nez*).
hooligan ['huːligən], *n.* voyou, *m.*
hooliganism ['huːligənizm], *n.* voyouterie, *f.*
hoop [huːp], *n.* cercle; cerceau, *m.*; huppe (*d'oiseau*); jante (*de roue*), *f.*; panier (*de robe*); (*Croquet*) arceau, *m.*—*v.t.* cercler; (*fig.*) entourer.
hoot [huːt], *v.t.*, *v.i.* hululer (*hibou*); huer; (*Motor.*) klaxonner.
hooter ['huːtə], *n.* (*colloq.*) sirène d'usine, *f.* klaxon, *m.*
hop (1) [hop], *n.* saut, sautillement; bal populaire, *m.*—*v.i.* sauter, sautiller; (*pop.*) to **hop it**, ficher le camp.
hop (2) [hop], *n.* (*Bot.*) houblon, *m.*
hop-field ['hopfiːld], *n.* houblonnière, *f.*
hopscotch ['hopskotʃ], *n.* marelle, *f.*
hope [houp], *n.* espérance, *f.*, espoir, *m.*, attente, *f.*—*v.t.* espérer, s'attendre à.—*v.i.* espérer.
hopeful ['houpful], *a.* plein d'espérance; qui promet beaucoup; encourageant.
hopefully ['houpfuli], *adv.* avec espoir, avec confiance; si tout va bien.
hopeless ['houplis], *a.* vain (*effort*); non valable (*excuse*); inextricable (*difficulté*); inconsolable (*douleur*); irrémédiable (*mal*); inutile (*négociation*); incorrigible (*personne*); désespéré (*situation*).
hopelessly ['houplisli], *adv.* sans espoir.
hopper ['hopə], *n.* trémie (*d'un moulin*), *f.*; (*Agric.*) semoir, *m.*

horizon [hə'raizən], *n.* horizon, *m.*
horizontal [hori'zontl], *a.* horizontal.
hormone ['hoːmoun], *n.* hormone, *f.*
horn [hoːn], *a.* de corne.—*n.* corne, *f.*; bois (*de cerf*), *m.*; coupe (*à boire*); (*Ent.*) antenne *f.*; (*Mus.*) cor, cornet, *m.*
hornet ['hoːnit], *n.* frelon, *m.*
horrible ['horibl], *a.* horrible, affreux.
horribly ['horibli], *adv.* horriblement, affreusement.
horrid ['horid], *a.* affreux, horrible.
horrific [ho'rifik], *a.* horrifique.
horrify ['horifai], *v.t.* horrifier.
horror ['horə], *n.* horreur, *f.*
horse [hoːs], *n.* cheval, *m.*, chevaux, *m.pl.*; (*Mil.*) cavalerie, *f.*; chevalet (*pour scier*), séchoir (*pour le linge*), *m.*
horseback ['hoːsbæk], *n.* dos de cheval, *m.*; **on horseback**, à cheval.
horseblock ['hoːsblok], *n.* montoir, *m.*
horse-chestnut ['hoːs'tʃesnʌt], *n.* marron d'Inde; marronnier d'Inde (*arbre*), *m.*
horse-dealer ['hoːsdiːlə], *n.* maquignon, *m.*
horse-doctor ['hoːsdoktə], *n.* vétérinaire, *m.*
horse-fly ['hoːsflai], *n.* taon, *m.*
horseman ['hoːsmən], *n.* (*pl.* **-men** [men]) cavalier; écuyer, *m.*
horsemanship ['hoːsmənʃip], *n.* équitation, *f.*; manège, *m.*
horse-play ['hoːsplei], *n.* jeu de mains, *m.*
horse-power ['hoːspauə], *n.* cheval-vapeur, *m.*
horseshoe ['hoːsʃuː], *a.* en fer à cheval.—*n.* fer de cheval; fer à cheval, *m.*
horsewhip ['hoːswip], *n.* cravache, *f.*—*v.t.* cravacher.
horticulture ['hoːtikʌltʃə], *n.* horticulture, *f.*
hose [houz], *n.* bas, *m.pl.*; tuyau d'arrosage, boyau, *m.*
hosiery ['houʒəri], *n.* bonneterie, *f.*
hospitable ['hospitəbl], *a.* hospitalier.
hospital ['hospitl], *n.* hôpital, *m.*, infirmerie, *f.*; hospice, *m.*
hospitality [hospi'tæliti], *n.* hospitalité, *f.*
host [houst], *n.* hôte; hôtelier, aubergiste, *m.*; armée, foule; (*R.-C. Ch.*) hostie, *f.*
hostage ['hostidʒ], *n.* otage, *m.*
hostel ['hostəl], *n.* hôtel ou foyer pour les étudiants etc. *m.*; **youth hostel**, auberge de la jeunesse, *f.*
hostess ['houstis, 'houstes], *n.* hôtesse, *f.*
hostile ['hostail], *a.* hostile, ennemi; (*fig.*) opposé (*à*).
hostility [hos'tiliti], *n.* hostilité, *f.*
hot [hot], *a.* chaud, ardent; brûlant, piquant, épicé (*plat, sauce*); (*fig.*) vif, violent, échauffé; **boiling hot**, tout bouillant; **to be hot**, avoir chaud (*personne*), faire chaud (*temps*), être chaud (*chose*).
hotbed ['hotbed], *n.* couche, *f.*
hotel [ho'tel], *n.* hôtel, *m.*
hot-headed ['hot'hedid], *a.* violent, fougueux.
hot-house ['hothaus], *n.* serre, *f.*
hotly ['hotli], *adv.* avec chaleur, avec acharnement.
hotness ['hotnis], *n.* chaleur, *f.*; (*fig.*) passion, violence, *f.*
hot-water-bottle [hot'woːtəbotl], *n.* bouillotte, *f.*
hough [hok], *n.* jarret (*d'animal*), *m.*
hound [haund], *n.* chien de chasse, *m.*—*v.t.* chasser; (*fig.*) traquer; exciter.

hour ['auə], *n.* heure, *f.*; *an hour ago*, il y a une heure; *an hour and a half*, une heure et demie; *a quarter of an hour*, un quart d'heure; *half an hour*, une demi-heure.

hourly ['auəli], *a.* continuel, d'heure en heure, à l'heure.—*adv.* d'heure en heure.

house [haus], *n.* maison, *f.*, logis, *m.*, demeure, habitation, *f.*; ménage (*household*), *m.*; famille; (*Parl.*) chambre; (*Theat.*) salle, *f.*; *a country-house*, une maison de campagne; *a nobleman's house*, un hôtel; *house full*, (*Theat.*) salle comble; *public house*, café, *m.*, brasserie, *f.*—[hauz], *v.t.* loger, héberger; garer (*une voiture*); rentrer (*blé etc.*); faire rentrer (*bestiaux etc.*).

house-agent ['hauseidʒənt], *n.* agent de location, agent immobilier, *m.*

house-breaker ['hausbreikə], *n.* cambrioleur (*voleur*); démolisseur (*ouvrier*), *m.*

house-breaking ['hausbreikiŋ], *n.* vol avec effraction, *m.*

household ['haushould], *a.* de ménage, domestique.—*n.* maison, *f.*, ménage, *m.*, famille, *f.*

householder ['haushouldə], *n.* chef de famille, chef de maison, *m.*

housekeeper ['hauski:pə], *n.* femme de charge, ménagère, *f.*; concierge, *m.*, *f.*

housekeeping ['hauski:piŋ], *n.* ménage, *m.*

housemaid ['hausmeid], *n.* bonne à tout faire, *f.*

house-surgeon ['haussə:dʒən], *n.* interne (en chirurgie), *m.*

housewife ['hauswaif], *n.* ménagère, *f.*

housework ['hauswə:k], *n.* travaux ménagers, *m.pl.*; *to do the housework*, faire le ménage.

housing ['hauziŋ], *n.* logement, *m.*; rentrée, *f.*, rentrage, *m.*; (*Tech.*) enchâssure, *f.*

hovel [hɔvl], *n.* appentis, *m.*, bicoque, *f.*, taudis, *m.*, masure, *f.*

hover ['hɔvə], *v.i.* planer; hésiter.

how [hau], *adv.* comment, de quelle façon; combien; comme, que; *how are you?* comment allez-vous? *how far*, jusqu'où; *how many, how much*, combien de; *how old are you?* quel âge avez-vous?

however [hau'evə], *conj.* cependant, pourtant, du reste, d'ailleurs, toutefois.—*adv.* de quelque manière que; quelque . . . que; *however rich he may be*, quelque riche qu'il soit, tout riche qu'il est; *however that may be*, quoi qu'il en soit.

howl [haul], *n.* hurlement, cri; mugissement, *m.*—*v.i.* hurler, crier; mugir.

howler ['haulə], *n.* faute grossière, bévue, *f.*

howling ['hauliŋ], *a.* hurlant; *a howling success*, un succès fou.—*n.* hurlement, *m.*

hoyden ['hɔidn], *n.* garçon manqué (*se dit d'une jeune fille*), *m.*

hub [hʌb], *n.* moyeu, *m.*; (*fig.*) centre, *m.*

hubbub ['hʌbʌb], *n.* vacarme, brouhaha, tintamarre, *m.*

hub-cap ['hʌbkæp], *n.* (*Motor.*) enjoliveur, *m.*

huddle [hʌdl], *v.t.* entasser pêle-mêle, (*fig.*) brouiller, confondre ensemble.—*v.i.* se mêler, se presser les uns contre les autres; (*fig.*) se confondre.—*n.* tas confus, fouillis, méli-mélo, ramassis, *m.*

hue [hju:], *n.* couleur, teinte, nuance; huée;

clameur, *f.*; *to raise a hue and cry after*, crier haro sur, élever un tollé contre.

huff [hʌf], *n.* emportement, accès de colère, *m.*—*v.t.* froisser; (*Draughts*) souffler.—*v.i.* se gonfler, se mettre en colère.

hug [hʌg], *v.t.* embrasser, étreindre; étouffer (*en serrant*).—*n.* embrassement, *m.*, étreinte, *f.*

huge [hju:dʒ], *a.* vaste, immense, énorme.

hulk [hʌlk], *n.* carcasse (*d'un navire*), *f.*, ponton; (*pl.*) bagne, *m.*

hulking ['hʌlkiŋ], *a.* gros, lourd.

hull [hʌl], *n.* coque (*d'un navire*); cosse, gousse (*de pois, fèves etc.*); écale (*de noix*), *f.*—*v.t.* écaler (*noix*); écosser (*fèves*).

hullo [HELLO].

hum [hʌm], *n.*, *v.i.* fredonner (*personne*), bourdonner (*abeilles*); *to hum and ha(w)*, bredouiller.—*n.* bourdonnement; brouhaha (*de conversation*), *m.*

human ['hju:mən], *a.* humain.

humane [hju:'mein], *a.* humain, compatissant.

humanist ['hju:mənist], *n.* humaniste, *m.*, *f.*

humanity [hju:'mæniti], *n.* humanité, *f.*

humanly ['hju:mənli], *adv.* humainement.

humble [hʌmbl], *a.* humble; modeste.—*v.t.* humilier, abaisser, mortifier.

humble-bee ['hʌmblbi:], *n.* bourdon, *m.*

humbly ['hʌmbli], *adv.* humblement, avec humilité; modestement.

humbug ['hʌmbʌg], *n.* blague, farce, *f.*, charlatanisme; blagueur, farceur, charlatan, *m.*

humdrum ['hʌmdrʌm], *a.* monotone, assommant.

humid ['hju:mid], *a.* humide.

humidity [hju:'miditi], *n.* humidité, *f.*

humiliate [hju:'milieit], *v.t.* humilier, abaisser.

humiliating [hju:'milieitiŋ], *a.* humiliant.

humiliation [hju:mili'eiʃən], *n.* humiliation, *f.*

humility [hju:'militi], *n.* humilité, *f.*

humming ['hʌmiŋ], *n.* bourdonnement, fredonnement; (*fig.*) murmure, *m.*

humming-bird ['hʌmiŋbə:d], *n.* oiseau-mouche, colibri, *m.*

humorist ['hju:mərist], *n.* humoriste, *m.*, *f.*, personne spirituelle, *f.*

humorous ['hju:mərəs], *a.* humoristique; plaisant, drôle, comique.

humour ['hju:mə], *n.* humeur, disposition, *f.*; humour, *m.*—*v.t.* complaire à, laisser faire.

hump [hʌmp], *n.* bosse, *f.*; *to have the hump*, (*slang*) être maussade.

humpbacked ['hʌmpbækt], *a.* bossu.

hunch [hʌntʃ], *n.* gros morceau (*de pain, de fromage*) *m.*; bosse (*du dos*); (*fig., fam.*) idée, *f.*, soupçon, *m.*; *to have a hunch that*, soupçonner que.

hunchback ['hʌntʃbæk], *n.* bossu, *m.*

hundred ['hʌndrəd], *a.* cent.—*n.* cent, *m.*; centaine, *f.*; canton, district, *m.*

hundredth ['hʌndrətθ], *a.* centième.—*n.* centième (*fraction*), *m.*

hundredweight ['hʌndrədweit], *n.* quintal, *m.*

Hungarian [hʌŋ'gɛəriən], *a.* hongrois.—*n.* hongrois (*langue*); Hongrois (*personne*), *m.*

Hungary ['hʌŋgəri], la Hongrie, *f.*

hunger ['hʌŋgə], *n.* faim, *f.*—*v.i.* avoir faim; être affamé (*de*).

hungrily ['hʌŋgrili], *adv.* avidement.

hungry ['hʌŋgri], a. affamé, qui a faim; maigre (terre etc.); **to be hungry**, avoir faim.

hunk [hʌŋk], n. gros morceau (de gâteau, de fromage), m.

hunt [hʌnt], v.t. chasser à courre; (fig.) poursuivre, chercher.—v.i. chasser, aller à la chasse.—n. chasse à courre, f.

hunter ['hʌntə], n. chasseur; cheval de chasse, m.

hunting ['hʌntiŋ], n. chasse; (fig.) recherche, f.

huntress ['hʌntris], n. chasseuse; (poet.) chasseresse, f.

huntsman ['hʌntsmən], n. (pl. -men [men]) veneur, piqueur, m.

hurdle [hə:dl], n. claie, f.; (Spt.) obstacle, m., haie, f.; **hurdle-race**, course de haies, f.

hurdy-gurdy ['hə:di'gə:di], n. vielle, f.

hurl [hə:l], v.t. lancer (avec force), précipiter, jeter.

hurly-burly ['hə:li'bə:li], n. tintamarre, brouhaha, tohu-bohu, m.

hurrah [hu'rɑ:], hurray [hu'rei], n. hourra, m.

hurricane ['hʌrikən], n. ouragan, m.

hurried ['hʌrid], a. précipité, pressé; fait à la hâte.

hurriedly ['hʌridli], adv. précipitamment, à la hâte.

hurry ['hʌri], n. hâte, précipitation, f.; (fig.) tumulte, m., confusion, f.; **to be in a hurry**; être pressé.—v.t. hâter, presser, précipiter.—v.i. se hâter, se dépêcher, se presser.

hurt [hə:t], n. mal, m., blessure, f.; (fig.) tort, m.—v.t. irr. faire mal à, (fig.) nuire à, offenser, blesser; **to hurt oneself**, se faire du mal.—v.i. faire du mal; faire mal.

hurtful ['hə:tful], a. nuisible (à).

hurtle [hə:tl], v.t. lancer.—v.i. se précipiter; se heurter.

husband ['hʌzbənd], n. mari, époux, m.—v.t. ménager, économiser.

husbandman ['hʌzbəndmən], n. (pl. -men [men]) laboureur, cultivateur, m.

husbandry ['hʌzbəndri], n. agriculture, industrie agricole; économie, f.

hush [hʌʃ], n. silence, calme, m.—int. chut! paix!—v.t. taire, faire taire; (fig.) calmer.—v.i. se taire, faire silence.

husk [hʌsk], n. cosse, gousse (de pois etc.), f.; brou, m., écale (de noix); balle, pellicule (de grain), f.

huskiness ['hʌskinis], n. enrouement (de la voix), m.

husky ['hʌski], a. cossu; rauque, enroué (voix); (colloq.) costaud, fort.—n. chien esquimau, m.

hussar [hu'zɑ:] n. hussard, m.

hussy ['hʌsi], n. friponne, coquine, f.

hustle [hʌsl], v.t. bousculer, presser, pousser. —v.i. se presser, se dépêcher.

hut [hʌt], n. hutte, cabane, f. (Mil.) baraque, f.

hutch [hʌtʃ], n. huche, f.; clapier (de lapin), m.

hyacinth ['haiəsinθ], n. (Bot.) jacinthe, f.

hybrid ['haibrid], a. and n. hybride, m.

hydrangea [hai'dræn(d)ʒə, hai'dreindʒə], n. (Bot.) hortensia, m.

hydrant ['haidrənt], n. prise d'eau, f.; **fire hydrant**, bouche d'incendie, f.

hydraulic [hai'drɔ:lik], a. hydraulique.

hydrochloric [haidrə'klɔrik], a. (acide) chlorhydrique.

hydrogen ['haidridʒən], n. hydrogène, m.; **hydrogen bomb** or (fam.) **H-bomb**, bombe à hydrogène, bombe H, f.

hydrophobia [haidro'foubiə], n. hydrophobie, rage, f.

hyena [hai'i:nə], n. hyène, f.

hygiene ['haidʒi:n], n. hygiène, f.

hygienic [hai'dʒi:nik], a. hygiénique.

hymn [him], n. (Eccles.) hymne, m. ou f., cantique, m.

hymn-book ['himbuk], hymnal [himnl], n. hymnaire, m.

hyperbola [hai'pə:bələ], n. (Geom.) hyperbole, f.

hyperbole [hai'pə:bəli], n. (Gram.) hyperbole, f.

hyphen ['haifən], n. trait d'union, m.

hypnosis [hip'nousis], n. hypnose, f.

hypnotism ['hipnotizm], n. hypnotisme, m.

hypnotist ['hipnotist], n. hypnotiste, m., f.

hypocrisy [hi'pɔkrisi], n. hypocrisie, f.

hypocrite ['hipəkrit], n. hypocrite, m., f.

hypocritical [hipə'kritikl], a. hypocrite.

hypothesis [hai'pɔθisis], n. (pl. hypotheses [hai'pɔθisi:z]) hypothèse, f.

hysteria [his'tiəriə], n., hysterics [his'teriks], n.pl. crise de nerfs, attaque de nerfs, f.

hysterical [his'terikəl], a. hystérique.

I

I (1), i [ai]. neuvième lettre de l'alphabet, m.

I (2) [ai], pron. je; moi.

ibex ['aibeks], n. bouquetin, m.

ibis ['aibis], n. (Orn.) ibis, m.

ice [ais], n. glace, f.—v.t. glacer (gâteau); frapper (vin).—v.i. (Av.) **to ice up**, givrer.

ice-axe ['aisæks], n. piolet, m.

iceberg ['aisbə:g], n. iceberg, m.

ice-bound ['aisbaund], a. pris dans ou bloqué par les glaces.

ice-box ['aisbɔks], n. glacière, f.

ice-breaker ['aisbreikə], n. brise-glace, m.

ice-cream ['ais'kri:m], n. glace, f.

iced [aist], a. glacé; frappé (vin etc.); **iced lolly**, sucette, f.

ice-floe ['aisflou], n. banc de glace, m.

Iceland ['aislənd], l'Islande, f.

Icelander ['aisləndə], n. Islandais, m.

Icelandic [ais'lændik], a. islandais, d'Islande.

icicle ['aisikl], n. petit glaçon, m.

icing ['aisiŋ], n. glacé; frappage (de vin), m.

icon ['aikɔn], n. icone, f.

icy ['aisi], a. glacé, glacial; **icy road**, route verglacée, f.

idea [ai'diə], n. idée, f.

ideal [ai'diəl], a. and n. idéal, m.

idealism [ai'diəlizm], n. idéalisme, m.

idealist [ai'diəlist], n. idéaliste, m., f.

ideally [ai'diəli], adv. idéalement.

identical [ai'dentikl], a. identique.

identification [aidentifi'keiʃən], n. identification, f.

identify [ai'dentifai], *v.t.* identifier (*avec*); reconnaître.
identity [ai'dentiti], *n.* identité, *f.*
idiocy ['idiəsi], *n.* idiotie, *f.*
idiom ['idiəm], *n.* idiome; idiotisme, *m.*
idiomatic [idiə'mætik], *a.* idiomatique.
idiot ['idiət], *n.* idiot, *m.*; imbécile, *m., f.*
idiotic [idi'ɔtik], *a.* idiot, d'imbécile.
idle [aidl], *a.* oisif, paresseux (*indolent*); désœuvré (*inactif*); en chômage (*personne sans travail*), en repos (*machine*); (*fig.*) inutile, frivole; **idle fellow**, fainéant, paresseux, *m.*; **idle talk**, balivernes, *f.pl.*—*v.t.* **to idle away**, perdre, gaspiller.—*v.i.* ne rien faire, faire le paresseux, fainéanter; (*Motor.*) tourner au ralenti.
idleness ['aidlnis], *n.* paresse; oisiveté; (*fig.*) inutilité, *f.*; désœuvrement, *m.*
idler ['aidlə], *n.* oisif, fainéant, paresseux, *m.*
idly ['aidli], *adv.* dans l'oisiveté en paresseux; inutilement.
idol [aidl], *n.* idole, *f.*
idolater [ai'dɔlətə], **idolatress** [ai'dɔlətris], *n.* idolâtre, *m., f.*
idolatry [ai'dɔlətri], *n.* idolâtrie, *f.*
idolize ['aidəlaiz], *v.t.* idolâtrer.
idyllic [ai'dilik, i'dilik], *a.* idyllique.
if [if], *conj.* si, quand, quand même; **even if**, même si, quand même; **if necessary**, s'il le faut, au besoin; **if not**, sinon, si ce n'est.
igloo ['iglu:], *n.* hutte de neige, *f.*; igloo (*des Esquimaux*), *m.*
ignite [ig'nait], *v.t.* allumer.—*v.i.* prendre feu.
ignition [ig'niʃən], *n.* ignition, *f.*; (*Motor.*) allumage, *m.*; **ignition key**, clé de contact, *f.*
ignoble [ig'noubl], *a.* roturier; ignoble.
ignominious [ignə'miniəs], *a.* ignominieux.
ignominy ['ignəmini], *n.* ignominie, *f.*
ignoramus [ignə'reiməs], *n.* ignorant, (*fam.*) âne bâté, *m.*
ignorance ['ignərəns], *n.* ignorance, *f.*
ignorant ['ignərənt], *a.* ignorant.
ignore [ig'nɔ:], *v.t.* feindre d'ignorer; ne tenir aucun compte de.
ill [il], *a.*; malade (*santé*); mauvais, méchant.—*n.* mal, *m.*—*adv.* mal; peu; **it ill becomes you**, il vous sied mal.
ill-bred ['il'bred], *a.* mal élevé.
illegal [i'li:gəl], *a.* illégal; illicite.
illegible [i'ledʒibl], *a.* illisible.
illegitimate [ilə'dʒitimit], *a.* illégitime; naturel (*enfant*).
ill-fated ['il'feitid], *a.* infortuné, malheureux.
ill-feeling ['il'fi:liŋ], *n.* ressentiment, *m.*
ill-gotten ['il'gɔtn], *a.* mal acquis.
ill-health ['il'helθ], *n.* mauvaise santé, *f.*
illicit [i'lisit], *a.* illicite.
ill-informed [ilin'fɔ:md], *a.* mal renseigné.
illiteracy [i'litərəsi], *n.* analphabétisme, *m.*
illiterate [i'litərit], *a.* and *n.* illettré, *m.*
ill-mannered ['il'mænəd], *a.* malappris.
ill-natured ['il'neitʃəd], *a.* méchant, d'un mauvais naturel.
illness ['ilnis], *n.* maladie, indisposition, *f.*
illogical [i'lɔdʒikl], *a.* illogique peu logique.
ill-tempered ['il'tempəd], *a.* maussade, de mauvaise humeur.
ill-treat ['il'tri:t], *v.t.* maltraiter.
illuminate [i'lju:mineit], *v.t.* illuminer, éclairer; enluminer (*un livre*).
illumination [ilju:mi'neiʃən], *n.* illumination; enluminure (*de livres etc.*), *f.*

illusion [i'lu:ʒən, i'lju:ʒən], *n.* illusion, *f.*
illustrate ['iləstreit], *v.t.* illustrer; (*fig.*) expliquer; orner, embellir.
illustration [iləs'treiʃən], *n.* illustration; explication, *f.*; éclaircissement, *m.*
illustrative [i'lʌstrətiv], *a.* explicatif.
illustrious [i'lʌstriəs], *a.* illustre, célèbre.
ill-will ['il'wil], *n.* mauvais vouloir, *m.*; rancune, *f.*
I'm [aim] (=**I am**) [BE].
image ['imidʒ], *n.* image, *f.*; (*fig.*) portrait, *m.*
imagery ['imidʒri], *n.* images, *f.pl.*; langage figuré, *m.*
imaginable [i'mædʒinəbl], *a.* imaginable.
imaginary [i'mædʒinəri], *a.* imaginaire.
imagination [imædʒi'neiʃən], *n.* imagination; conception, idée, *f.*
imagine [i'mædʒin], *v.t.* imaginer; s'imaginer, se figurer.
imbecile ['imbisi:l], *a.* and *n.* faible d'esprit, *m., f.*
imbecility [imbi'siliti], *n.* faiblesse d'esprit, *f.*
imbibe [im'baib], *v.t.* imbiber, absorber; (*fig.*) puiser.
imbue [im'bju:], *v.t.* imprégner, teindre; (*fig.*) pénétrer, douer (*de*).
imbued [im'bju:d], *a.* imbu, pénétré (*de*).
imitate ['imiteit], *v.t.* imiter.
imitation [imi'teiʃən], *n.* imitation; (*Comm.*) contrefaçon, *f.*
imitative ['imitətiv], *a.* imitatif, imitateur.
immaculate [i'mækjulit], *a.* sans tache, immaculé.
immaterial [imə'tiəriəl], *a.* immatériel; peu important.
immature [imə'tjuə], *a.* pas mûr; prématuré.
immeasurable [i'meʒərəbl], *a.* infini; incommensurable.
immeasurably [i'meʒərəbli], *adv.* outre mesure, infiniment.
immediate [i'mi:djit], *a.* immédiat; urgent, très pressé (*sur enveloppe*).
immediately [i'mi:djitli], *adv.* immédiatement, tout de suite, sur-le-champ.—*conj.* aussitôt que, dès que.
immense [i'mens], *a.* immense.
immensely [i'mensli], *adv.* immensément.
immensity [i'mensiti], *n.* immensité, *f.*
immerse [i'mə:s], *v.t.* plonger, immerger.
immigrant ['imigrənt], *a.* and *n.* immigrant, *m.*
immigrate ['imigreit], *v.i.* immigrer.
immigration [imi'greiʃən], *n.* immigration, *f.*
imminent ['iminənt], *a.* imminent.
immobilize [i'moubilaiz], *v.t.* immobiliser.
immodest [i'mɔdist], *a.* immodeste, peu modeste, impudique.
immoral [i'mɔrl], *a.* immoral; dissolu.
immorality [imə'ræliti], *n.* immoralité, *f.*
immortal [i'mɔ:tl], *a.* immortel.
immortality [imɔ:'tæliti], *n.* immortalité, *f.*
immortalize [i'mɔ:təlaiz], *v.t.* immortaliser, rendre immortel.
immovable [i'mu:vəbl], *a.* fixe, immuable, inébranlable.
immutable [i'mju:təbl], *a.* immuable.
imp [imp], *n.* diablotin, petit démon; petit diable (*gamin*), *m.*
impact ['impækt], *n.* choc, impact, *m.*—[im'pækt], *v.t.* serrer, encastrer.
impair [im'pɛə], *v.t.* altérer, affaiblir.

impale [im'peil], *v.t.* empaler.
impalpable [im'pælpəbl], *a.* impalpable; intangible.
impart [im'pɑːt], *v.t.* accorder, donner; communiquer.
impartial [im'pɑːʃl], *a.* impartial, désintéressé.
impartially [im'pɑːʃəli], *adv.* impartialement.
impassable [im'pɑːsəbl], *a.* impraticable, infranchissable.
impassioned [im'pæʃənd], *a.* passionné.
impassive [im'pæsiv], *a.* impassible, insensible.
impatience [im'peiʃəns], *n.* impatience, *f.*
impatient [im'peiʃənt], *a.* impatient; (*fig.*) emporté.
impatiently [im'peiʃəntli], *adv.* impatiemment.
impeach [im'piːtʃ], *v.t.* accuser; attaquer.
impeachment [im'piːtʃmənt], *n.* mise en accusation; accusation, *f.*
impeccable [im'pekəbl], *a.* impeccable.
impecunious [impi'kjuːniəs], *a.* besogneux.
impede [im'piːd], *v.t.* empêcher; retarder gêner.
impediment [im'pedimənt], *n.* empêchement, obstacle, *m.*; (*fig.*) difficulté, *f.*
impel [im'pel], *v.t.* pousser (à); forcer (de).
impelling [im'peliŋ], *a.* impulsif, moteur.
impend [im'pend], *v.i.* être suspendu sur, menacer; être imminent.
impending [im'pendiŋ], *a.* imminent, menaçant.
impenetrable [im'penitrəbl], *a.* impénétrable; (*fig.*) insensible.
impenitent [im'penitənt], *a.* impénitent.
imperative [im'perətiv], *a.* impératif; (*fig.*) obligatoire.—*n.* (*Gram.*) impératif, *m.*
imperceptible [impə'septibl], *a.* imperceptible, insensible.
imperceptibly [impə'septibli], *adv.* imperceptiblement.
imperfect [im'pəːfikt], *a.* imparfait; incomplet; (*Gram.*) imparfait.—*n.* (*Gram.*) imparfait, *m.*
imperfection [impə'fekʃən], *n.* imperfection, *f.*
imperfectly [im'pəːfiktli], *adv.* imparfaitement.
imperial [im'piəriəl], *a.* impérial; (*fig.*) princier.
imperil [im'peril], *v.t.* mettre en danger, hasarder.
imperious [im'piəriəs], *a.* impérieux.
imperishable [im'periʃəbl], *a.* impérissable.
impersonal [im'pəːsənəl], *a.* impersonnel.
impersonate [im'pəːsəneit], *v.t.* personnifier; (*Theat.*) représenter, jouer le rôle de.
impertinence [im'pəːtinəns], *n.* impertinence, insolence, *f.*
impertinent [im'pəːtinənt], *a.* impertinent, insolent; hors de propos.
impertinently [im'pəːtinəntli], *adv.* d'un ton insolent; mal à propos.
imperturbable [impə'təːbəbl], *a.* imperturbable.
impervious [im'pəːviəs], *a.* imperméable, impénétrable; (*fig.*) inaccessible.
impetuous [im'petjuəs], *a.* impétueux.
impetus ['impitəs], *n.* impulsion, *f.*; élan, essor, *m.*

impinge [im'pindʒ], *v.i.* se heurter (à ou *contre*); empiéter (*sur*).
impious ['impiəs], *a.* impie.
impiously ['impiəsli], *adv.* en impie, avec impiété.
impish ['impiʃ], *a.* espiègle, malicieux.
implacable [im'plækəbl], *a.* implacable, acharné.
implant [im'plɑːnt], *v.t.* implanter; (*fig.*) imprimer, inculquer.
implement ['implimənt], *n.* outil; instrument; ustensile, *m.*—['impliment], *v.t.* exécuter; accomplir.
implicate ['implikeit], *v.t.* impliquer.
implication [impli'keiʃən], *n.* implication, *f.*; *by implication,* implicitement.
implicit [im'plisit], *a.* implicite; (*fig.*) aveugle.
implied [im'plaid], *a.* implicite, tacite.
implore [im'plɔː], *v.t.* implorer, conjurer, supplier (*de*).
imply [im'plai], *v.t.* impliquer, signifier, vouloir dire; donner à entendre (*suggérer*).
impolite [impə'lait], *a.* impoli.
impoliteness [impə'laitnis], *n.* impolitesse, *f.*
import [im'pɔːt], *n.* portée, signification, *f.*, sens, *m.*; importance; (*Comm.*) importation, *f.*—[im'pɔːt], *v.t.* importer; introduire; signifier.
importance [im'pɔːtəns], *n.* importance, *f.*
important [im'pɔːtənt], *a.* important.
importer [im'pɔːtə], *n.* importateur, *m.*
importunate [im'pɔːtjunit], *a.* importun; pressant.
importune [impɔː'tjuːn], *v.t.* importuner.
impose [im'pouz], *v.t.* imposer.—*v.i.* en imposer (à).
imposing [im'pouziŋ], *a.* imposant.
imposition [impə'ziʃən], *n.* impôt (*taxe*), *m.*; imposture (*tromperie*), *f.*; (*Sch.*) pensum, *m.*
impossibility [imposi'biliti], *n.* impossibilité, *f.*
impossible [im'posibl], *a.* impossible.
impostor [im'postə], *n.* imposteur, *m.*
imposture [im'postʃə], *n.* imposture, tromperie, *f.*
impotence ['impotəns], **impotency** ['impotənsi], *n.* impuissance, *f.*
impotent ['impotənt], *a.* impuissant, faible.
impound [im'paund], *v.t.* mettre en fourrière; (*fig.*) enfermer, confisquer.
impoverish [im'povəriʃ], *v.t.* appauvrir.
impracticable [im'præktikəbl], *a.* impossible, impraticable; intraitable (*personne*).
imprecation [impra'keiʃən], *n.* imprécation, *f.*
impregnable [im'pregnəbl], *a.* imprenable; (*fig.*) inébranlable.
impregnate [im'pregneit], *v.t.* imprégner (*de*); féconder.
impress [im'pres], *v.t.* imprimer (à); faire bien comprendre (*quelque chose à quelqu'un*); pénétrer (*de*); impressionner.
impression [im'preʃən], *n.* impression, empreinte; (*fig.*) idée, *f.*
impressive [im'presiv], *a.* impressionnant, frappant, touchant, émouvant.
impressiveness [im'presivnis], *n.* force, puissance, grandeur, *f.*
imprint [im'print], *v.t.* imprimer, empreindre.—['imprint], *n.* empreinte, *f.*

imprison

imprison [im'prizn], *v.t.* emprisonner, enfermer.

imprisonment [im'priznmənt] *n.* emprisonnement, *m.*, détention, *f.*

improbability [improbə'biliti], *n.* improbabilité; invraisemblance, *f.*

improbable [im'probəbl], *a.* improbable, invraisemblable.

impromptu [im'promptju:], *a.* impromptu, improvisé.—*adv.* par improvisation, impromptu.

improper [im'propə], *a.* inconvenant; peu propre (*à*), impropre (*langage*).

improperly [im'propəli], *adv.* d'une manière peu convenable; à tort, mal à propos.

impropriety [imprə'praiəti], *n.* inconvenance (*de conduite*); impropriété (*de langage*), *f.*

improve [im'pru:v], *v.t.* améliorer, perfectionner (*invention etc.*); faire avancer; utiliser; bonifier (*terre etc.*); embellir (*rendre plus beau*); exploiter (*cultiver*).—*v.i.* s'améliorer; se perfectionner; se bonifier (*vin etc.*); faire des progrès; (*Comm.*) hausser; augmenter de prix; *to improve upon*, améliorer, perfectionner, surpasser.

improvement [im'pru:vmənt], *n.* amélioration, *f.*; perfectionnement; progrès, avancement (*en connaissances*), *m.*

improvident [im'providənt], *a.* imprévoyant.

improvisation [imprəvai'zeiʃən], *n.* improvisation, *f.*

improvise ['imprəvaiz], *v.t.* improviser.

imprudence [im'pru:dəns], *n.* imprudence, *f.*

imprudent [im'pru:dənt], *a.* imprudent.

imprudently [im'pru:dəntli], *adv.* imprudemment.

impudence ['impjudəns], *n.* impudence, effronterie, *f.*

impudent ['impjudənt], *a.* impudent, effronté.

impudently ['impjudəntli], *adv.* impudemment, effrontément.

impugn [im'pju:n], *v.t.* attaquer, contester; (*fig.*) mettre en doute.

impulse ['impʌls], **impulsion** [im'pʌlʃən], *n.* impulsion, *f.*, mouvement; (*fig.*) élan, *m.*; *sudden impulse*, coup de tête, *m.*

impulsive [im'pʌlsiv], *a.* impulsif, primesautier.

impulsively [im'pʌlsivli], *adv.* par impulsion, par un mouvement involontaire.

impunity [im'pju:niti], *n.* impunité, *f.*; *with impunity*, impunément.

impure [im'pjuə], *a.* impur; impudique.

impurity [im'pjuəriti], *n.* impureté; impudicité, *f.*

imputation [impju'teiʃən], *n.* imputation, accusation, *f.*

impute [im'pju:t], *v.t.* imputer, attribuer (*à*).

in [in], *prep.* en, dans; à; par; pour; sur; avec, chez, parmi (*en compagnie de*); *he will do it in one hour*, il fera cela en une heure; *he will start in one hour*, il partira dans une heure; *in bed*, au lit; *in England*, en Angleterre; *in Japan*, au Japon; *in Paris*, à Paris; *in spite of*, malgré; *in spring*, au printemps; *in summer (autumn, winter)*, en été (automne, hiver); *in the morning*, le matin; *in the U.S.A.*, aux États-Unis; *one in ten*, un sur dix; *to be clothed in*, être vêtu de.—*adv.* dedans, au dedans, rentré; chez soi, à la maison, y (*at home*); élu (*vainqueur aux élections*); au pouvoir (*parti politique*); *all in*, tout compris. —*n. to know all the ins and outs of a matter*, connaître les tenants et les aboutissants d'une affaire.

inability [inə'biliti], *n.* impuissance, incapacité, *f.*

inaccessible [inæk'sesibl], *a.* inaccessible; inabordable (*à*).

inaccuracy [in'ækjurəsi], *n.* inexactitude, *f.*

inaccurate [in'ækjurit], *a.* inexact.

inaction [in'ækʃən], *n.* inaction, inertie, *f.*

inactive [in'æktiv], *a.* inactif; inerte (*choses*).

inactivity [inæk'tiviti], *n.* inactivité, *f.*

inadequacy [in'ædikwəsi], *n.* insuffisance, imperfection, *f.*

inadequate [in'ædikwit], *a.* insuffisant; imparfait, défectueux, incomplet.

inadequately [in'ædikwitli], *adv.* insuffisamment.

inadmissible [inad'misibl], *a.* inadmissible.

inadvertence [inad'və:təns], **inadvertency** [inad'və:tənsi], *n.* inadvertance, *f.*

inadvertent [inad'və:tənt], *a.* négligent, inattentif.

inadvertently [inad'və:təntli], *adv.* par inadvertance.

inalienable [in'eiliənbl], *a.* inaliénable; inséparable.

inane [i'nein], *a.* vide; (*fig.*) inepte, absurde.

inanimate [in'ænimit], *a.* inanimé; mort.

inanition [inə'niʃən], *n.* inanition, *f.*

inanity [i'næniti], *n.* inanité, *f.*

inapplicable [in'æplikabl], *a.* inapplicable.

inappreciable [inə'pri:ʃiəbl], *a.* inappréciable, insensible.

inappropriate [inə'proupriit], *a.* peu propre, qui ne convient pas.

inapt [in'æpt], *a.* inapte, impropre, peu propre (*à*).

inarticulate [ina:'tikjulit], *a.* inarticulé, qui s'exprime peu clairement.

inartistic [ina:'tistik], *a.* peu artistique.

inasmuch [inəz'mʌtʃ], *adv.* vu que, attendu que, d'autant que.

inattention [inə'tenʃən], *n.* inattention; distraction, *f.*

inattentive [inə'tentiv], *a.* inattentif, distrait; négligent.

inattentively [inə'tentivli], *adv.* sans attention, négligemment.

inaudible [in'o:dibl], *a.* imperceptible, qu'on ne peut entendre.

inaudibly [in'o:dibli], *adv.* à ne pouvoir être entendu.

inaugural [in'o:gjurəl], *a.* inaugural.

inaugurate [in'o:gjureit], *v.t.* inaugurer.

inauspicious [ino:'spiʃəs], *a.* malheureux, peu propice.

inauspiciously [ino:'spiʃəsli], *adv.* sous de mauvais auspices.

inborn ['inbo:n], **inbred** ['inbred], *a.* inné, naturel.

incalculable [in'kælkjuləbl], *a.* incalculable.

incapable [in'keipəbl], *a.* incapable (*de*).

incapacitate [inkə'pæsiteit], *v.i.* rendre incapable (*de*).

incarcerate [in'ka:səreit], *v.t.* incarcérer, mettre en prison.

incarnate [in'ka:nit], *a.* incarné.

incautious [in'ko:ʃəs], *a.* inconsidéré, imprudent.

454

incendiarism [in'sendjərizm] *n.* crime d'incendie, *m.*

incendiary [in'sendjəri], *a.* and *n.* incendiaire, *m., f.*

incense ['insens], *n.* encens, *m.*—[in'sens], *v.t.* irriter, exaspérer (*contre*).

incentive [in'sentiv], *a.* excitant, stimulant.—*n.* motif, stimulant, encouragement, *m.*

inception [in'sepʃən], *n.* commencement, *m.*

incessant [in'sesənt], *a.* incessant; continuel.

incest ['insest], *n.* inceste, *m.*

inch [intʃ], *n.* pouce (2·539 *centimètres*), *m.*

incident ['insidənt], *a.* qui arrive; particulier. —*n.* incident, événement, *m.*

incidental [insi'dentl], *a.* fortuit, accidentel; accessoire; *incidental expenses*, faux frais, *m.pl.*

incidentally [insi'dentli], *adv.* fortuitement, par hasard; soit dit en passant.

incinerate [in'sinəreit], *v.t.* incinérer.

incipient [in'sipiənt], *a.* naissant, qui commence.

incise [in'saiz], *v.t.* inciser, graver.

incision [in'siʒən], *n.* incision, *f.*

incisive [in'saisiv], *a.* incisif.

incite [in'sait], *v.t.* inciter, stimuler; encourager (*à*).

incitement [in'saitmənt], *n.* encouragement, motif, stimulant, *m.*

incivility [insi'viliti], *n.* incivilité, impolitesse, *f.*

inclemency [in'klemənsi], *n.* inclémence, *f.*; intempéries, *f.pl.*, rigueur (*du temps etc.*), *f.*

inclement [in'klemənt], *a.* inclément; rigoureux.

inclination [inkli'neiʃən], *n.* inclinaison, pente; inclination (*de la tête* ou *du corps*), *f.*; penchant, goût (*disposition*), *m.*

incline ['inklain], *n.* pente; (*Rail.*) rampe, *f.* —[in'klain], *v.t.* incliner, (faire) pencher; (*fig.*) porter, disposer (*à*).—*v.i.* incliner, s'incliner, pencher; (*fig.*) être porté (*à*).

inclined [in'klaind], *a.* incliné; enclin (*à*); porté, disposé (*à*).

include [in'klu:d], *v.t.* comprendre, renfermer.

included [in'klu:did], *a.* compris, y compris.

including [in'klu:diŋ], *prep.* comprenant, y compris.

inclusion [in'klu:ʒən], *n.* inclusion, *f.*

inclusive [in'klu:siv], *a.* inclusif; qui renferme, qui comprend; *inclusive of*, y compris.

incoherence [inko'hiərəns], *n.* incohérence, *f.*

incoherent [inko'hierənt], *a.* incohérent.

incombustible [inkəm'bʌstibl], *a.* incombustible.

income ['inkəm], *n.* revenu, *m.*; *private income*, rente, *f.*, rentes, *f.pl.*

income-tax ['inkəmtæks], *n.* impôt sur le revenu, *m.*

incommode [inkə'moud], *v.t.* incommoder, gêner, déranger.

incommodious [inkə'moudjəs], *a.* incommode.

incomparable [in'kɔmprəbl], *a.* incomparable.

incompatible [inkəm'pætibl], *a.* incompatible.

incompetence [in'kɔmpitəns], *n.* incompétence, insuffisance; incapacité *f.*

incompetent [in'kɔmpitənt], *a.* incompétent, incapable.

incompetently [in'kɔmpitəntli], *adv.* avec incompétence.

incomplete [inkəm'pli:t], *a.* imparfait, inachevé, incomplet.

incompletely [inkəm'pli:tli], *adv.* incomplètement, imparfaitement.

incomprehensibility [inkɔmprihensi'biliti], *n.* incompréhensibilité, *f.*

incomprehensible [inkɔmpri'hensibl], *a.* incompréhensible.

inconceivable [inkən'si:vəbl], *a.* inconcevable.

inconclusive [inkən'klu:siv], *a.* qui n'est pas concluant.

incongruity [inkɔŋ'gru:iti], *n.* désaccord, *m.*, incongruité; inconvenance, *f.*

incongruous [in'kɔŋgruəs], *a.* incongru, inconvenant, (*fig.*) disparate.

inconsequence [in'kɔnsikwəns], *n.* inconséquence; fausse déduction, *f.*

inconsequent [in'kɔnsikwənt], *a.* inconséquent.

inconsiderable [inkən'sidərəbl], *a.* petit, insignifiant; de peu d'importance.

inconsiderate [inkən'sidərit], *a.* inconsidéré, irréfléchi; sans égards pour les autres.

inconsistency [inkən'sistənsi], *n.* inconséquence; contradiction, *f.*

inconsistent [inkən'sistənt], *a.* incompatible (*avec*), contradictoire (*à*); inconséquent.

inconsistently [inkən'sistəntli], *adv.* avec un manque de continuité.

inconspicuous [inkən'spikjuəs], *a.* peu apparent, peu remarquable; discret.

inconstancy [in'kɔnstənsi], *n.* inconstance, *f.*; caractère changeant, *m.*

inconstant [in'kɔnstənt], *a.* inconstant, volage, changeant.

incontestable [inkən'testəbl], *a.* incontestable, irrécusable.

incontrovertible [inkɔntrə'və:tibl], *a.* incontestable, indisputable.

inconvenience [inkən'vi:niəns], *n.* inconvénient; embarras, dérangement, *m.*—*v.t.* déranger, incommoder, gêner.

inconvenient [inkən'vi:niənt], *a.* incommode, gênant.

inconveniently [inkən'vi:niəntli], *adv.* incommodément mal.

incorporate [in'kɔ:pəreit], *v.t.* incorporer, former en société.—*v.i.* s'incorporer.

incorrect [inkə'rekt], *a.* incorrect, inexact.

incorrectly [inkə'rektli], *adv.* incorrectement; inexactement.

incorrectness [inkə'rektnis], *n.* incorrection; inexactitude, *f.*

incorrigible [in'kɔridʒibl], *a.* incorrigible.

incorrupt [inkə'rʌpt], *a.* incorrompu, pur, intègre.

incorruptible [inkə'rʌptibl], *a.* incorruptible.

increase [in'kri:s], *v.t.* augmenter, agrandir, accroître.—*v.i.* croître, s'accroître; augmenter.—['inkri:s], *n.* augmentation (*de prix*), *f.*, accroissement (*de vitesse*); (*fig.*) produit, *m.*; crue (*de rivière*), *f.*

increasing [in'kri:siŋ], *a.* croissant.

increasingly [in'kri:siŋli], *adv.* de plus en plus.

incredible [in'kredibl], *a.* incroyable.

incredibly [in'kredibli], *adv.* incroyablement, d'une manière incroyable.
incredulity [inkrə'dju:liti], *n.* incrédulité, *f.*
incredulous [in'kredjuləs], *a.* incrédule.
increment ['inkrimənt], *n.* augmentation, *f.*; produit, *m.*
incriminate [in'krimineit], *v.t.* incriminer.
incubate ['inkjubeit], *v.t.* couver.
incubation [inkju'beiʃən], *n.* incubation, *f.*
incubator ['inkjubeitə], *n.* couveuse artificielle, *f.*
incubus ['inkjubəs], *n.* incube, cauchemar; (*fig.*) grand poids, *m.*
inculcate ['inkʌlkeit], *v.t.* inculquer (*à*).
incumbent [in'kʌmbənt], *a.* couché (*sur*); imposé, obligatoire; *to be incumbent on*, incomber à; *to feel it incumbent on one to do*, se faire un devoir de.—*n.* titulaire, bénéficier, *m.*
incur [in'kə:], *v.t.* encourir (*blâme*), s'attirer (*colère*); faire (*dettes*).
incurable [in'kjuərəbl], *a.* incurable, inguérissable.—*n.* incurable, *m.*, *f.*
incursion [in'kə:ʃən], *n.* incursion, irruption, *f.*
indebted [in'detid], *a.* endetté; redevable (*de*).
indebtedness [in'detidnis], *n.* dette, obligation, *f.*
indecency [in'di:sənsi], *n.* indécence, *f.*
indecent [in'di:sənt], *a.* indécent.
indecently [in'di:səntli], *adv.* indécemment.
indecision [indi'siʒən], *n.* irrésolution, *f.*
indecisive [indi'saisiv], *a.* peu décisif, indécis.
indecorous [in'dekərəs], *a.* inconvenant.
indecorousness [in'dekərəsnis], **indecorum** [indi'ko:rəm], *n.* manque de décorum, *m.*, inconvenance, *f.*
indeed [in'di:d], *adv.* en effet, en vérité; vraiment; à dire vrai, à la vérité.—*int.* vraiment! allons donc!
indefatigable [indi'fætigəbl], *a.* infatigable.
indefensible [indi'fensibl], *a.* indéfendable, inexcusable.
indefinable [indi'fainəbl], *a.* indéfinissable.
indefinite [in'definit], *a.* indéfini, vague.
indefinitely [in'definitli], *adv.* indéfiniment, vaguement.
indelible [in'delibl], *a.* indélébile, ineffaçable.
indelibly [in'delibli], *adv.* d'une manière indélébile, ineffaçablement.
indelicacy [in'delikəsi], *n.* indélicatesse, grossièreté, inconvenance, *f.*
indelicate [in'delikit], *a.* indélicat, grossier, inconvenant.
indemnify [in'demnifai], *v.t.* dédommager, indemniser (*de*).
indemnity [in'demniti], *n.* dédommagement, *m.*; indemnité, *f.*
indent [in'dent], *v.t.* denteler; ébrécher, échancrer.—*v.i. to indent for*, réquisitionner.—*n.* dentelure, bosselure, *f.*
indented [in'dentid], *a.* dentelé; échancré.
indenture [in'dentʃə], *n.* titre; (*esp. pl.*) contrat d'apprentissage, *m.*—*v.t.* mettre en apprentissage.
independence [indi'pendəns], **independency** [indi'pendənsi], *n.* indépendance, *f.*
independent [indi'pendənt], *a.* indépendant; libre.
independently [indi'pendəntli], *adv.* indépendamment; dans l'indépendance.
indescribable [indi'skraibəbl], *a.* indicible, indescriptible.

indestructible [indi'strʌktibl], *a.* indestructible.
index ['indeks], *n.* (*pl.* **indexes** ['indeksiz], **indices** ['indisi:z]) indice, signe, indicateur; index (*d'un livre*), *m.*; aiguille (*d'une montre etc.*), *f.*; (*Anat.*) index, doigt indicateur; (*Math.*) exposant, *m.*
India ['indjə]. l'Inde, *f.*
Indian ['indjən], *a.* indien; des Indiens; de l'Inde, des Indes; *Indian corn*, maïs, *m.*—*n.* Indien (*personne*), *m.*; *Red Indian*, Peau-Rouge, *m.*, *f.*
india-rubber ['indjə'rʌbə], *n.* caoutchouc, *m.*
indicate ['indikeit], *v.t.* indiquer.
indication [indi'keiʃən], *n.* indication, *f.* signe, indice, *m.*
indicative [in'dikətiv], *a.* and *n.* indicatif, *m.*
indicator ['indikeitə], *n.* indicateur, *m.*
indict [in'dait], *v.t.* inculper, mettre en accusation.
indictment [in'daitmənt], *n.* accusation; mise en accusation, *f.*
Indies ['indiz],'the. les Indes, *f.pl.*; *the West Indies*, les Antilles, *f.pl.*
indifference [in'difrəns], *n.* indifférence, apathie, *f.*
indifferent [in'difrənt], *a.* indifférent; impartial; passable, médiocre.
indifferently [in'difrəntli], *adv.* indifféremment; médiocrement.
indigence ['indidʒəns], *n.* indigence, *f.*
indigent ['indidʒənt], *a.* nécessiteux, indigent.
indigenous [in'didʒinəs], *a.* du pays, indigène.
indigestible [indi'dʒestibl], *a.* indigeste.
indigestion [indi'dʒestʃən], *n.* indigestion, dyspepsie, *f.*
indignant [in'dignənt], *a.* indigné (*de*); plein d'indignation.
indignantly [in'dignəntli], *adv.* avec indignation.
indignation [indig'neiʃən], *n.* indignation, *f.*
indignity [in'digniti], *n.* indignité, *f.*; outrage, affront, *m.*
indigo ['indigou], *n.* indigo, *m.*
indirect [indi'rekt], *a.* indirect; (*fig.*) oblique, insidieux.
indiscreet [indis'kri:t], *a.* indiscret, irréfléchi, imprudent.
indiscreetly [indis'kri:tli], *adv.* indiscrètement.
indiscretion [indis'kreʃən], *n.* indiscrétion, imprudence, *f.*
indiscriminate [indis'kriminit], *a.* confus, sans distinction; aveugle.
indiscriminately [indis'kriminitli], *adv.* sans distinction, à tort et à travers, aveuglément.
indispensable [indis'pensəbl], *a.* indispensable, nécessaire.
indispose [indis'pouz], *v.t.* indisposer (*contre*), déranger, détourner (*de*).
indisposed [indis'pouzd], *a.* souffrant.
indisposition [indispə'ziʃən], *n.* indisposition, *f.*; malaise, *m.*
indisputable [indis'pju:təbl], *a.* incontestable, indiscutable.
indisputably [indis'pju:təbli], *adv.* incontestablement.
indissoluble [indi'sɔljubl], *a.* indissoluble.
indistinct [indis'tiŋkt], *a.* indistinct, confus, imprécis, vague.

infiltrate

indistinctly [indis'tiŋktli], *adv.* indistincte-ment, confusément, vaguement.
indistinguishable [indis'tiŋgwiʃəbl], *a.* in-distinct, imperceptible.
indite [in'dait], *v.t.* rédiger.
individual [indi'vidjuəl], *a.* individuel; seul, unique.—*n.* individu, particulier, *m.*
individuality [individju'æliti], *n.* individua-lité, personnalité, *f.*
individually [indi'viduəli], *adv.* individuelle-ment.
indivisible [indi'vizibl], *a.* indivisible.
indoctrinate [in'dɔktrineit], *v.t.* instruire; endoctriner.
indolence ['indələns], *n.* indolence, paresse, *f.*
indolent ['indələnt], *a.* indolent, paresseux.
indolently ['indələntli], *adv.* indolemment, nonchalamment.
indomitable [in'dɔmitəbl], *a.* indomptable.
Indonesia [indo'ni:ziə]. l'Indonésie, *f.*
Indonesian [indo'ni:ziən], *a.* indonésien.—*n.* indonésien (*langue*); Indonésien (*personne*), *m.*
indoors [in'dɔ:z], *adv.* à la maison, au dedans.
indubitable [in'dju:bitəbl], *a.* indubitable, incontestable.
induce [in'dju:s], *v.t.* porter, persuader, induire, pousser (*à*); amener, causer, pro-duire.
inducement [in'dju:smənt], *n.* raison, tenta-tion, *f.*, motif, mobile, *m.*
induction [in'dʌkʃən], *n.* installation; induc-tion, *f.*
indulge [in'dʌldʒ], *v.t.* satisfaire; avoir trop d'indulgence pour; (*fig.*) flatter, caresser (*une espérance etc.*).—*v.i.* se laisser aller, se livrer à, s'abandonner (*à*).
indulgence [in'dʌldʒəns], *n.* faveur, *f.*, plaisir, agrément, *m.*; (*R.-C. Ch.*) indul-gence, *f.*
indulgent [in'dʌldʒənt], *a.* indulgent, facile, complaisant.
industrial [in'dʌstriəl], *a.* industriel, de l'industrie.
industrialist [in'dʌstriəlist], *n.* industriel, *m.*
industrious [in'dʌstriəs], *a.* travailleur; dili-gent, laborieux.
industriously [in'dʌstriəsli], *adv.* assidûment, diligemment.
industry ['indəstri], *n.* travail, *m.*, diligence, assiduité, *f.*; (*fig.*) empressement, *m.*; industrie (*production*), *f.*
inebriate [i'ni:brieit], *v.t.* enivrer.—[i'ni:briit], *a.* enivré.—*n.* ivrogne, *m.*, *f.*
inebriation [ini:bri'eiʃən], **inebriety** [ini'braiəti], *n.* ivresse, ébriété, *f.*
inedible [in'edibl], *a.* immangeable; non comestible.
ineffable [in'efəbl], *a.* ineffable.
ineffaceable [ini'feisəbl], *a.* ineffaçable, in-délébile.
ineffective [ini'fektiv], *a.* inefficace, sans effet.
ineffectual [ini'fektjuəl], *a.* inefficace, inutile, vain; incapable.
ineffectually [ini'fektjuəli], *adv.* inutilement, sans effet.
inefficacious [inefi'keiʃəs], *a.* inefficace.
inefficiency [ini'fiʃənsi], *n.* inefficacité, in-capacité, incompétence, *f.*
inefficient [ini'fiʃənt], *a.* inefficace; incapable.

ineligible [in'elidʒibl], *a.* inéligible; peu propre (*à*).
inept [in'ept], *a.* inepte, sot, absurde, peu propre (*à*).
inequality [ini'kwɔliti], *n.* inégalité, dis-parité, *f.*
inert [i'nə:t], *a.* inerte.
inertia [i'nə:ʃə], *n.* inertie, inactivité, *f.*
inestimable [in'estiməbl], *a.* inestimable; incalculable.
inevitable [in'evitəbl], *a.* inévitable; fatal.
inevitably [in'evitəbli], *adv.* inévitablement.
inexact [inig'zækt], *a.* inexact.
inexcusable [iniks'kju:zəbl], *a.* inexcusable, sans excuse.
inexhaustible [inig'zɔ:stibl], *a.* inépuisable.
inexorable [in'eksərəbl], *a.* inexorable, inflexible.
inexpedient [iniks'pi:d,ənt], *a.* inopportun, mal à propos.
inexpensive [iniks'pensiv], *a.* peu coûteux, bon marché.
inexperience [iniks'piəriəns], *n.* inexpérience, *f.*
inexperienced [iniks'piəriənst], *a.* inexpéri-menté, sans expérience.
inexplicable [in'eksplikəbl], *a.* inexplicable.
inexpressible [iniks'presibl], *a.* inexprimable, indicible.
inextricable [in'ekstrikəbl], *a.* inextricable.
infallible [in'fælibl], *a.* infaillible, imman-quable.
infamous ['infəməs], *a.* infâme.
infamy ['infəmi], *n.* infamie, *f.*
infancy ['infənsi], *n.* première enfance, *f.*, bas âge, *m.*
infant ['infənt], *a.* en bas âge, dans l'enfance, petit; (*fig.*) naissant, qui commence.—*n.* enfant en bas âge, nourrisson, bébé; (*Law*) mineur, *m.*
infantile ['infəntail], *a.* enfantin, d'enfant.
infantry ['infəntri], *n.* infanterie, *f.*
infant-school ['infənt'sku:l], *n.* école mater-nelle, *f.*
infatuate [in'fætjueit], *v.t.* infatuer, entêter, affoler; *to become infatuated with*, s'engouer de, s'amouracher de.
infatuation [infætju'eiʃən], *n.* engouement, *m.*; infatuation; (*fam.*) toquade, *f.*
infect [in'fekt], *v.t.* infecter (*de*).
infection [in'fekʃən], *n.* infection, contagion, *f.*
infectious [in'fekʃəs], *a.* infect; contagieux, infectieux.
infectiousness [in'fekʃəsnis], *n.* nature con-tagieuse, contagion, *f.*
infer [in'fə:], *v.t.* inférer; (*fig.*) supposer.
inference ['infərəns], *n.* conséquence, conclu-sion, déduction, *f.*
inferior [in'fiəriə], *a.* inférieur; subordonné.—*n.* inférieur, *m.*
inferiority [infiəri'ɔriti], *n.* infériorité, *f.*
infernal [in'fə:nəl], *a.* infernal, d'enfer; (*fig.*) diabolique.
inferno [in'fə:nou], *n.* enfer; brasier, *m.*
infest [in'fest], *v.t.* infester.
infidel ['infidəl], *a.* and *n.* infidèle; incrédule, *m.*, *f.*
infidelity [infi'deliti], *n.* infidélité; déloyauté (*d'un serviteur*), *f.*
infiltrate ['infiltreit], *v.i.* s'infiltrer (*dans*); pénétrer.

457

infinite

infinite ['infinit], *a.* and *n.* infini, *m.*
infinitely ['infinitli], *adv.* infiniment, à l'infini; fort.
infinitive [in'finitiv], *a.* and *n.* infinitif, *m.*
infinity [in'finiti], *n.* infinité; immensité, *f.*
infirm [in'fə:m], *a.* infirme, faible; (*fig.*) inconstant, irrésolu.
infirmary [in'fə:məri], *n.* hôpital, *m.*, infirmerie, *f.*
infirmity [in'fə:miti], *n.* infirmité, faiblesse, *f.*
inflame [in'fleim], *v.t.* enflammer; (*fig.*) exciter.—*v.i.* s'enflammer.
inflammable [in'flæməbl], *a.* inflammable.
inflammation [inflə'meiʃən], *n.* inflammation, fluxion, *f.*
inflammatory [in'flæmətri], *a.* inflammatoire; (*fig.*) incendiaire.
inflate [in'fleit], *v.t.* enfler, gonfler.
inflated [in'fleitid], *a.* enflé, gonflé; exagéré; boursouflé (*style*).
inflation [in'fleiʃən], *n.* enflure, *f.*, gonflement, *m.*; inflation (*monétaire*), *f.*
inflect [in'flekt], *v.t.* fléchir; varier, moduler (*la voix*).
inflection [in'flekʃən], *n.* inflexion, modulation, *f.*
inflexible [in'fleksibl], *a.* inflexible.
inflict [in'flikt], *v.t.* infliger, faire (*une peine*).
infliction [in'flikʃən], *n.* infliction; (*fig.*) peine, *f.*
influence ['influəns], *n.* influence (*sur*), *f.*, empire, *m.*—*v.t.* influencer; influer (*sur*).
influential [influ'enʃəl], *a.* influent, qui a de l'influence.
influenza [influ'enzə], *n.* influenza, grippe, *f.*
influx ['inflʌks], *n.* affluence; invasion; embouchure, *f.*
inform [in'fə:m], *v.t.* informer, instruire, renseigner, avertir; faire savoir à; *to inform against*, dénoncer.
informal [in'fə:məl], *a.* sans cérémonie, simple.
informality [infə:'mæliti], *n.* manque de cérémonie, *m.*; simplicité, *f.*
informally [in'fə:məli], *adv.* sans cérémonie; sans façon.
informant [in'fə:mənt], *n.* correspondant; informateur, *m.*
information [infə'meiʃən], *n.* renseignements, *m.pl.*; *piece of information*, renseignement, avis, *m.*, nouvelle, *f.*; savoir, *m.*; (*Law*) dénonciation, *f.*
informative [in'fə:mətiv], *a.* instructif; éducatif.
informer [in'fə:mə], *n.* délateur, dénonciateur, *m.*
infraction [in'frækʃən], *n.* infraction, contravention, *f.*
infra-red [infrə'red], *a.* infra-rouge.
infrequent [in'fri:kwənt], *a.* rare.
infringe [in'frindʒ], *v.t.* enfreindre, violer, transgresser.
infringement [in'frindʒmənt], *n.* infraction, violation; contrefaçon (*d'un brevet*), *f.*
infuriate [in'fjuərieit], *v.t.* rendre furieux.
infuriated [in'fjuərieitid], *a.* furieux, en fureur.
infuse [in'fju:z], *v.t.* infuser; faire infuser; macérer; (*fig.*) inspirer (à).
infusion [in'fju:ʒən], *n.* infusion, *f.*
ingenious [in'dʒi:niəs], *a.* ingénieux, habile.

ingeniously [in'dʒi:niəsli], *adv.* ingénieusement; spirituellement.
ingeniousness [in'dʒi:niəsnis], **ingenuity** [indʒi'nju:iti], *n.* ingéniosité, habileté, *f.*
ingenuous [in'dʒenjuəs], *a.* ingénu; naïf; candide.
ingenuously [in'dʒenjuəsli], *adv.* ingénument, naïvement.
ingenuousness [in'dʒenjuəsnis], *n.* ingénuité, naïveté, *f.*
inglorious [in'glɔ:riəs], *a.* obscur; inconnu; honteux.
ingloriously [in'glɔ:riəsli], *adv.* sans gloire; honteusement.
ingoing ['ingouiŋ], *a.* entrant, nouveau.—*n.* entrée, *f.*
ingot ['ingət], *n.* lingot, *m.*
ingrained [in'greind], *a.* encrassé; (*fig.*) enraciné, invétéré.
ingratiate [in'greiʃieit], *v.t.* insinuer (*dans*); *to ingratiate oneself with*, s'insinuer dans les bonnes grâces de.
ingratitude [in'grætitju:d], *n.* ingratitude, *f.*
ingredient [in'gri:diənt], *n.* ingrédient; élément, *m.*
ingrowing ['ingrouiŋ], *a.* incarné (*ongle*).
inhabit [in'hæbit], *v.t.* habiter; habiter (*dans*).
inhabitable [in'hæbitəbl], *a.* habitable.
inhabitant [in'hæbitənt], *n.* habitant, *m.*
inhabited [in'hæbitid], *a.* habité.
inhalation [inhə'leiʃən], *n.* inhalation; inspiration, *f.*
inhale [in'heil], *v.t.* aspirer; respirer, humer.
inherent [in'hiərənt], *a.* inhérent, naturel (à).
inherit [in'herit], *v.t.* hériter (*de*).—*v.i.* hériter.
inheritance [in'heritəns], *n.* héritage, patrimoine, *m.*
inhibit [in'hibit], *v.t.* arrêter, empêcher interdire.
inhibition [inhi'biʃən], *n.* interdiction; (*Psych.*) inhibition, *f.*
inhospitable [in'hɔspitəbl], *a.* inhospitalier.
inhuman [in'hju:mən], *a.* inhumain; dénaturé; cruel.
inhumanity [inhju'mæniti], *n.* inhumanité; brutalité, *f.*
inhumation [inhju'meiʃən], *n.* inhumation, *f.*, enterrement, *m.*
inimical [i'nimikl], *a.* hostile, ennemi; contraire (à).
inimitable [i'nimitəbl], *a.* inimitable.
iniquitous [i'nikwitəs], *a.* inique, injuste.
iniquity [i'nikwiti], *n.* iniquité, *f.*
initial [i'niʃəl], *a.* initial; premier.—*n.* initiale, *f.*—*v.t.* mettre ses initiales à; parafer.
initially [i'niʃəli], *adv.* au commencement.
initiate [i'niʃieit], *v.t.* initier (à ou *dans*); amorcer, commencer.
initiation [iniʃi'eiʃən], *n.* initiation, *f.*
initiative [i'niʃiətiv], *n.* initiative, *f.*
inject [in'dʒekt], *v.t.* injecter; faire une piqûre.
injection [in'dʒekʃən], *n.* injection; (*Med.*) piqûre, *f.*
injudicious [indʒu'diʃəs], *a.* peu judicieux malavisé, imprudent.
injudiciously [indʒu'diʃəsli], *adv.* peu judicieusement, imprudemment.
injunction [in'dʒʌŋkʃən], *n.* injonction; recommandation, *f.*

injure ['indʒə], *v.t.* nuire à, faire tort à, léser; endommager (*to damage*); faire mal à, blesser.

injured ['indʒəd], *a.* offensé; blessé; *the injured*, les blessés, les accidentés, *m.pl.*

injurious [in'dʒuəriəs], *a.* nuisible, préjudiciable (*à*).

injuriously [in'dʒuəriəsli], *adv.* à tort.

injury ['indʒəri], *n.* tort, mal; dégât, dommage (*à des marchandises*), *m.*; (*Med.*) lésion, blessure, *f.*

injustice [in'dʒʌstis], *n.* injustice, *f.*

ink [iŋk], *n.* encre, *f.*; *Indian ink*, encre de Chine.—*v.t.* tacher *ou* barbouiller d'encre.

inkling ['iŋkliŋ], *n.* soupçon, vent (*d'une affaire*), *m.*

inkstand ['iŋkstænd], *n.* encrier de bureau, *m.*

ink-well ['iŋkwel], *n.* encrier, *m.*

inky ['iŋki], *a.* d'encre; taché d'encre.

inlaid [in'leid], *a.* incrusté, marqueté.

inland ['inlənd], *a.* intérieur, de l'intérieur.—*n.* intérieur (*d'un pays*), *m.*

inlay ['inlei], *n.* marqueterie, incrustation, *f.*—[in'lei], *v.t. irr.* (*conjug. like* LAY) marqueter, incruster.

inlet ['inlit], *n.* entrée, *f.*, passage, *m.*, voie, *f.*; petit bras de mer, *m.*

inmate ['inmeit], *n.* habitant, *m.*, locataire (*dans une maison*); interne, pensionnaire (*dans une maison de santé*), *m.*, *f.*

inmost ['inmoust], *a.* le plus profond, le plus secret.

inn [in], *n.* auberge, *f.*; hôtel, *m.*; hôtellerie, *f.*; *to put up at an inn*, descendre à une auberge.

innate [i'neit], *a.* inné; foncier.

innavigable [i'nævigəbl], *a.* innavigable.

inner ['inə], *a.* intérieur, de l'intérieur; (*fig.*) interne, secret.

innermost ['inəmoust], *a.* le plus intérieur, le plus reculé.

innkeeper ['inki:pə], *n.* aubergiste, *m.*, *f.*, hôtelier, *m.*

innocence ['inəsəns], *n.* innocence, *f.*

innocent ['inəsənt], *a.* innocent; permis, légitime.

innocently ['inəsəntli], *adv.* innocemment.

innocuous [i'nɔkjuəs], *a.* innocent, inoffensif.

innovate ['inoveit], *v.i.* innover.

innovation [ino'veiʃən], *n.* innovation, *f.*, changement, *m.*

innuendo [inju'endou], *n.* insinuation, allusion malveillante, *f.*

innumerable [i'nju:mərəbl], *a.* innombrable, sans nombre.

inoculate [i'nɔkjuleit], *v.t.* inoculer, vacciner.

inoculation [inɔkju'leiʃən], *n.* inoculation, *f.*, vaccin, *m.*

inodorous [in'oudərəs], *a.* inodore.

inoffensive [ino'fensiv], *a.* inoffensif.

inopportune [in'ɔpətju:n], *a.* inopportun, intempestif, mal à propos.

inopportunely [in'ɔpətju:nli], *adv.* inopportunément, mal à propos.

inordinate [i'nɔ:dinit], *a.* démesuré, immodéré.

inordinately [i'nɔ:dinitli], *adv.* démesurément, immodérément.

inorganic [inɔ:'gænik], *a.* inorganique.

inquest ['inkwest], *n.* enquête (*après une mort subite*), *f.*

inquire [in'kwaiə], *v.t.* demander.—*v.i.* s'enquérir, s'informer (*de*); s'adresser (*à* ou *chez*).

inquiring [in'kwaiəriŋ], *a.* investigateur, curieux.

inquiry [in'kwaiəri], *n.* demande, investigation, recherche, *f.*; (*pl.*) informations, *f.pl.* renseignements, *m.pl.*, (*Law*) enquête, *f.*

inquisition [inkwi'ziʃən], *n.* recherche, investigation; (*R.-C. Ch.*) inquisition, *f.*

inquisitive [in'kwizitiv], *a.* curieux.

inroad ['inroud], *n.* incursion, invasion, *f.*; (*fig.*) empiétement (*sur*), *m.*

insalubrious [insə'lju:briəs], *a.* insalubre.

insane [in'sein], *a.* fou, aliéné; dérangé; (*fig.*) insensé.

insanitary [in'sænitəri], *a.* insalubre, malsain.

insanity [in'sæniti], *n.* folie, démence, *f.*

insatiable [in'seiʃəbl], *a.* insatiable.

insatiate [in'seiʃiit], *a.* insatiable; inassouvi.

inscribe [in'skraib], *v.t.* inscrire; dédier (*à*).

inscription [in'skripʃən], *n.* inscription, *f.*; titre (*title*), *m.*; dédicace (*dedication*), *f.*

inscrutable [in'skru:təbl], *a.* inscrutable, impénétrable.

insect ['insekt], *n.* insecte, *m.*

insecticidal [in'sektisaidl], *a.* insecticide.

insecticide [in'sektisaid], *n.* insecticide, *m.*

insecure [insi'kjuə], *a.* en danger; chanceux, hasardeux; peu sûr, mal assuré.

insecurely [insi'kjuəli], *adv.* sans sûreté, en danger.

insecurity [insi'kjuəriti], *n.* manque de sûreté; danger, péril, *m.*; incertitude, *f.*

insensible [in'sensibl], *a.* imperceptible; insignifiant; inconscient (*unconscious*); sans connaissance.

insensibly [in'sensibli], *adv.* insensiblement, peu à peu.

insensitive [in'sensitiv], *a.* insensible.

inseparable [in'sepərəbl], *a.* inséparable.

insert [in'sə:t], *v.t.* insérer, faire insérer (*dans*).

insertion [in'sə:ʃən], *n.* insertion; interpolation, *f.*

inshore [in'ʃɔ:], *a.* and *adv.* près du rivage.

inside ['insaid], *a.* intérieur, d'intérieur.—*n.* dedans, intérieur, *m.*; *inside out*, à l'envers; [in'said] entrailles, *f.pl.*—[in'said], *adv.* à l'intérieur, en dedans.—[in'said], *prep.* en, dans, à l'intérieur de.

insidious [in'sidiəs], *a.* insidieux, captieux, perfide.

insight ['insait], *n.* perspicacité, pénétration, *f.*

insignia [in'signiə], *n.pl.* insignes, *m.pl.*

insignificance [insig'nifikəns], *n.* insignifiance, *f.*, peu d'importance, *m.*

insignificant [insig'nifikənt], *a.* insignifiant.

insincere [insin'siə], *a.* peu sincère, faux, hypocrite.

insincerely [insin'siəli], *adv.* de mauvaise foi, hypocritement.

insincerity [insin'seriti], *n.* manque de sincérité, *m.*, fausseté, *f.*

insinuate [in'sinjueit], *v.t.* insinuer, glisser (*dans*); donner à entendre.—*v.i.* s'insinuer, se glisser (*dans*).

insinuation [insinju'eiʃən], *n.* insinuation, *f.*

insipid [in'sipid], *a.* insipide, fade.

insipidity [insi'piditi], *n.* insipidité, fadeur, *f.*

insist [in'sist], *v.i.* insister (*sur* ou *à*); persister; vouloir absolument.

insistence [in'sistəns], *n.* insistance, *f.*

459

insistent [in'sistənt], *a.* insistant.
insobriety [inso'braiəti], *n.* intempérance, *f.*
insolence ['insələns], *n.* insolence; effronterie, *f.*
insolent ['insələnt], *a.* insolent.
insolently ['insələntli], *adv.* insolemment.
insoluble [in'sɔljubl], *a.* insoluble.
insolvency [in'sɔlvənsi], *n.* insolvabilité, faillite, *f.*
insolvent [in'sɔlvənt], *a.* insolvable, en faillite.
insomnia [in'sɔmniə], *n.* insomnie, *f.*
insomuch [inso'mʌtʃ], *adv.* au point (*que*), à un tel point (*que*), tellement (*que*).
inspect [in'spekt], *v.t.* inspecter, examiner, visiter.
inspection [in'spekʃən], *n.* inspection, revue, *f.*, contrôle, examen, *m.*; surveillance, *f.*
inspector [in'spektə], *n.* inspecteur, *m.*
inspiration [inspi'reiʃən], *n.* inspiration, *f.*; encouragement, *m.*
inspire [in'spaiə], *v.t.* inspirer, souffler (*dans*); animer (*de*).—*v.i.* aspirer.
inspiring [in'spaiəriŋ], *a.* inspirateur; qui donne du courage; qui élève l'esprit.
inspirit [in'spirit], *v.t.* animer, encourager.
instability [instə'biliti], *n.* instabilité, *f.*
install [in'stɔ:l], *v.t.* installer; monter (*appareil, machine*).
installation [instə'leiʃən], *n.* installation, *f.*; montage (*de machine, équipement*), *m.*
instalment [in'stɔ:lmənt], *n.* installation, *f.*; (*Comm.*) accompte, versement (*partiel*); épisode (*de feuilleton*), *m.*
instance ['instəns], *n.* requête, demande, *f.*; exemple, *m.*, occasion, *f.*, cas, *m.*; *for instance*, par exemple; *in the first instance*, en premier lieu.—*v.t.* citer comme exemple.
instant ['instənt], *n.* instant, *m.*, pressant, immédiat; courant (*mois*).—*n.* instant, moment, *m.*
instantaneous [instən'teiniəs], *a.* instantané.
instantaneously [instən'teiniəsli], *adv.* instantanément.
instantly ['instəntli], *adv.* à l'instant; tout de suite; sur-le-champ.
instead [in'sted], *adv.* à la place, en; *instead of*, au lieu de.
instep ['instep], *n.* cou-de-pied, *m.*
instigate ['instigeit], *v.t.* exciter, inciter, pousser (*à*).
instigation [insti'geiʃən], *n.* instigation, *f.*
instil [in'stil], *v.t.* instiller; (*fig.*) inspirer (*à*).
instillation [insti'leiʃən], *n.* instillation; (*fig.*) inspiration, *f.*
instinct ['instiŋkt], *n.* instinct, *m.*
instinctive [in'stiŋktiv], *a.* instinctif; (*fig.*) spontané.
instinctively [in'stiŋktivli], *adv.* d'instinct, instinctivement.
institute [in'stitju:t], *n.* institut, *m.*—*v.t.* instituer, établir; intenter (*un procès*).
institution [insti'tju:ʃən], *n.* institution, *f.*, établissement, *m.*
instruct [in'strʌkt], *v.t.* instruire, enseigner; charger (*de*).
instruction [in'strʌkʃən], *n.* instruction, *f.*, enseignement, *m.*
instructive [in'strʌktiv], *a.* instructif.
instructor [in'strʌktə], *n.* (*Mil.*) instructeur; précepteur, *m.*

instructress [in'strʌktris], *n.* préceptrice, monitrice, *f.*
instrument ['instrumənt], *n.* instrument; (*fig.*) agent, *m.*
instrumental [instru'mentl], *a.* instrumental; *to be instrumental in*, contribuer à.
insubordinate [insə'bɔ:dinit], *a.* insubordonné; indocile.
insubordination [insəbɔ:di'neiʃən], *n.* insubordination; insoumission, *f.*
insufferable [in'sʌfərəbl], *a.* insupportable intolérable.
insufficiency [insə'fiʃənsi], *n.* insuffisance, *f.*
insufficient [insə'fiʃənt], *a.* insuffisant.
insufficiently [insə'fiʃəntli], *adv.* insuffisamment.
insular ['insjulə], *a.* insulaire; (*fig.*) borné, rétréci.
insularity [insju'læriti], *n.* insularité, *f.*
insulate ['insjuleit], *v.t.* isoler; calorifuger.
insulation [insju'leiʃən], *n.* isolement, *m.*; (*Phys.*) isolation, *f.*
insulator ['insjuleitə], *n.* isolateur, isoloir, *m.*
insulin ['insjulin], *n.* insuline, *f.*
insult [in'sʌlt], *v.t.* insulter, faire insulte à, injurier.—['insʌlt], *n.* insulte, injure, *f.*, affront, *m.*
insulting [in'sʌltiŋ], *a.* insultant, outrageux, injurieux.
insultingly [in'sʌltiŋli], *adv.* insolemment, injurieusement.
insuperable [in'sju:pərəbl], *a.* insurmontable, invincible.
insupportable [insə'pɔ:təbl], *a.* insupportable, intolérable.
insuppressible [insə'presibl], *a.* irrépressible, irrésistible, inextinguible (*rire*).
insurance [in'ʃuərəns], *n.* assurance, *f.*; *fire-insurance*, assurance contre l'incendie; *life-insurance*, assurance sur la vie; (*fig.*) garantie, *f.*
insure [in'ʃuə], *v.t.* assurer, faire assurer; (*fig.*) garantir.
insurgent [in'sə:dʒənt], *a.* and *n.* insurgé, *m.*
insurmountable [insə'mauntəbl], *a.* insurmontable, infranchissable.
insurrection [insə'rekʃən], *n.* insurrection, *f.* soulèvement, *m.*
intact [in'tækt], *a.* intact, indemne.
intangible [in'tændʒibl], *a.* intangible.
integer ['intədʒə], *n.* entier, nombre entier, *m.*
integral ['intəgrəl], *a.* intégral; *an integral part*, une partie intégrante.—*n.* totalité, *f.*, tout, *m.*
integrate ['intigreit], *v.t.* compléter, rendre entier.
integrity [in'tegriti], *n.* intégrité, probité, *f.*
intellect ['intilekt], *n.* intelligence, *f.*, esprit, *m.*
intellectual [inti'lektjuəl], *a.* intellectuel; intelligent.—*n.* intellectuel, *m.*
intellectually [inti'lektjuəli], *adv.* intellectuellement.
intelligence [in'telidʒəns], *n.* intelligence, *f.*, esprit; renseignement, avis, *m.*; nouvelle, *f.*
intelligent [in'telidʒənt], *a.* intelligent.
intelligently [in'telidʒəntli], *adv.* intelligemment, avec intelligence.
intelligibility [intelidʒi'biliti], *n.* intelligibilité, clarté, *f.*
intelligible [in'telidʒibl], *a.* intelligible.

intemperance [in'tempərəns], *n.* intempérance, *f.*
intemperate [in'tempərit], *a.* démesuré, immodéré; intempérant; violent, emporté (*langage*).
intend [in'tend], *v.t.* se proposer de, avoir l'intention de, compter, vouloir; destiner (*à*); vouloir dire.
intended [in'tendid], *a.* projeté; intentionnel; *to be intended for*, être destiné à.
intense [in'tens], *a.* intense, véhément; (*fig.*) opiniâtre, très sérieux; vif, fort, aigu (*douleur etc.*).
intensely [in'tensli], *adv.* avec intensité, vivement, fortement.
intenseness [in'tensnis], **intensity** [in'tensiti], *n.* intensité; force, violence, *f.*
intensify [in'tensifai], *v.t.* rendre plus vif, intensifier.
intensive [in'tensiv], *a.* intensif.
intent [in'tent], *a.* attentif, absorbé (*par*); déterminé (*à*); fixe (*regard*).—*n.* dessein, but; sens, *m.*, intention, portée, *f.*; *to all intents and purposes*, à tous égards.
intention [in'tenʃən], *n.* intention, *f.*; dessein, but, *m.*
intentional [in'tenʃənəl], *a.* intentionnel, fait à dessein.
intentionally [in'tenʃənəli], *adv.* avec intention, à dessein, exprès.
intently [in'tentli], *adv.* attentivement.
intentness [in'tentnis], *n.* attention, force d'application, *f.*
inter [in'tə:], *v.t.* enterrer, inhumer, ensevelir.
intercede [intə'si:d], *v.t.* intercéder (*auprès de*).
intercept [intə'sept], *v.t.* intercepter; arrêter; (*fig.*) surprendre.
interchange [intə'tʃeindʒ], *v.t.* échanger.— ['intətʃeindʒ], *n.* échange, *m.*, succession; (*fig.*) variété, *f.*
intercourse ['intəkɔ:s], *n.* commerce, *m.*, relations, *f.pl.*, rapports, *m.pl.*
interdict [intə'dikt], *v.t.* interdire, interdire à, défendre à.—['intədikt], *n.* or **interdiction** [intə'dikʃən], interdit, *m.*, défense, interdiction, *f.*
interest ['intrəst], *v.t.* intéresser; *to be interested in*, s'intéresser à.—*n.* intérêt, *m.*; protection, *f.*, crédit, *m.*
interested ['intrəstid], *a.* intéressé.
interesting ['intrəstiŋ], *a.* intéressant.
interfere [intə'fiə], *v.i.* intervenir, se mêler (*de*); *to interfere with*, se mêler de, gêner, contrarier, déranger.
interference [intə'fiərəns], *n.* intervention, *f.*; (*Rad.*) brouillage, *m.*
interim ['intərim], *a.* provisoire.—*n.* intérim, intervalle, *m.*; *in the interim*, en attendant.
interior [in'tiəriə], *a.* and *n.* intérieur, *m.*; *interior angle*, angle interne, *m.*
interject [intə'dʒekt], *v.t.* interjecter; s'écrier (*en conversation*).
interjection [intə'dʒekʃən], *n.* interjection, *f.*
interlace [intə'leis], *v.t.* entrelacer.
interlacing [intə'leisiŋ], *n.* entrelacement, *m.*
interleave [intə'li:v], *v.t.* interfolier (*de*).
interloper ['intəloupə], *n.* intrus, *m.*
interlude ['intəlu:d], *n.* intermède, *m.*
intermediary [intə'mi:diəri], *a.* and *n.* intermédiaire, *m.*

intermediate [intə'mi:djit], *a.* intermédiaire, moyen.
interment [in'tə:mənt], *n.* enterrement, *m.*, inhumation, *f.*
interminable [in'tə:minəbl], *a.* interminable.
intermingle [intə'miŋgl], *v.t.* entremêler.— *v.i.* s'entremêler.
intermission [intə'miʃən], *n.* interruption momentanée, *f.*; relâche, intervalle; (*Cine.*) entr'acte, *m.*
intermittent [intə'mitənt], *a.* intermittent.
intermittently [intə'mitəntli], *adv.* par intervalles.
intern [in'tə:n], *v.t.* interner.
internal [in'tə:nl], *a.* interne, intérieur.
international [intə'næʃənl], *a.* international. —*n.* (joueur) international, *m.*
internecine [intə'ni:sain], *a.* meurtrier.
internee [intə:'ni:], *n.* interné, *m.*
internment [in'tə:nmənt], *n.* internement, *m.*; *internment camp*, camp de concentration, camp de prisonniers, *m.*
interplanetary [intə'plænətəri], *a.* interplanétaire.
interpolate [in'tə:poleit], *v.t.* interpoler; intercaler.
interpose [intə'pouz], *v.t.* interposer.—*v.i.* s'interposer, intervenir.
interpret [in'tə:prit], *v.t.* interpréter; expliquer.
interpretation [intə:pri'teiʃən], *n.* interprétation, *f.*
interpreter [in'tə:pritə], *n.* interprète, *m.*, *f.*
interracial [intə'reiʃəl], *a.* interracial.
interrogate [in'terəgeit], *v.t.* interroger questionner.
interrogation [interə'geiʃən], *n.* interrogation, question, *f.*
interrogative [intə'rɔgətiv], *a.* interrogatif interrogateur.
interrupt [intə'rʌpt], *v.t.* interrompre.
interruption [intə'rʌpʃən], *n.* interruption, *f.*; (*fig.*) obstacle, *m.*
intersect [intə'sekt], *v.t.* entrecouper; (*Geom.*) couper.—*v.i.* (*Geom.*) se couper, se croiser.
intersection [intə'sekʃən], *n.* intersection, *f.*
intersperse [intə'spə:s], *v.t.* entremêler (*de*); parsemer (*de*).
interstice [in'tə:stis], *n.* interstice, intervalle, *m.*
intertwine [intə'twain], *v.t.* entrelacer.—*v.i.* s'entrelacer.
interval ['intəvəl], *n.* intervalle (*Theat.*) entr'acte, *m.*; (*Ftb.*) mi-temps, *f.*
intervene [intə'vi:n], *v.i.* intervenir, s'interposer; survenir, arriver (*événements*); s'écouler (*temps*).
intervening [intə'vi:niŋ], *a.* intervenant (*personnes*); intermédiaire (*espace, endroits, temps etc.*).
intervention [intə'venʃən], *n.* intervention, *f.*
interview ['intəvju:], *n.* entrevue; (*Journ.*) interview, *f.*—*v.t.* avoir une entrevue avec; (*Journ.*) interviewer.
interviewer ['intəvju:ə], *n.* interviewer, *m.*
interweave [intə'wi:v], *v.t.* irr. (*conjug. like* WEAVE) entrelacer; entremêler.
intestate [in'testit], *a.* intestat.
intestine [in'testin], *a.* and *n.* intestin, *m.*
intimacy ['intiməsi], *n.* intimité, *f.*
intimate ['intimit], *a.* intime, lié.—['intimeit], *v.t.* donner à entendre; intimer (*à*).

intimately ['intimitli], *adv.* intimement.
intimation [inti'meiʃən], *n.* avis, *m.*, indication, *f.*
intimidate [in'timideit], *v.t.* intimider.
intimidation [intimi'deiʃən], *n.* intimidation, *f.*
into ['intu], *prep.* dans, en, à, entre.
intolerable [in'tɔlərəbl], *a.* intolérable, insupportable.
intolerance [in'tɔlərəns], *n.* intolérance, *f.*
intolerant [in'tɔlərənt], *a.* intolérant.
intonation [intou'neiʃən], *n.* intonation, *f.*
intone [in'toun], *v.t.*, *v.i.* psalmodier; entonner.
intoxicant [in'tɔksikənt], *n.* boisson alcoolique, *f.*
intoxicate [in'tɔksikeit], *v.t.* enivrer (*de*).
intoxicated [in'tɔksikeitid], *a.* ivre; (*fig.*) enivré (*de*).
intoxicating [in'tɔksikeitiŋ], *a.* enivrant.
intoxication [intɔksi'keiʃən], *n.* ivresse, *f.*; (*fig.*) enivrement, *m.*
intractability [intræktə'biliti], *n.* naturel intraitable, *m.*, indocilité, *f.*
intractable [in'træktəbl], *a.* intraitable, indocile.
intransigence [in'trænsidʒəns, in'trɑːnsidʒəns], *n.* intransigeance, *f.*
intransigent [in'trænsidʒənt, in'trɑːnsidʒənt], *a.* intransigeant.
intransitive [in'trænsitiv, in'trɑːnsitiv], *a.* intransitif.
intrepid [in'trepid], *a.* intrépide.
intricacy ['intrikəsi], *n.* embrouillement, *m.*; complication, *f.*, dédale, *m.*
intricate ['intrikit], *a.* embrouillé; embarrassé; obscur; compliqué.
intrigue [in'triːg], *n.* intrigue, *f.*—*v.t.* intriguer.—*v.i.* intriguer, s'intriguer.
intriguing [in'triːgiŋ], *a.* intrigant, qui excite la curiosité.
intrinsic [in'trinsik], **intrinsical** [in'trinsikəl], *a.* intrinsèque.
introduce [intrə'djuːs], *v.t.* introduire, faire entrer; présenter (*personnes*), faire connaître (*à*).
introduction [intrə'dʌkʃən], *n.* introduction; présentation; recommandation (*par lettre*), *f.*; avant-propos (*de livre*), *m.*
introductory [intrə'dʌktəri], *a.* introductoire, préliminaire.
introspection [intro'spekʃən], *n.* introspection, *f.*
introspective [intro'spektiv], *a.* introspectif; qui s'analyse.
introvert [in'trovəːt], *n.* introverti, *m.*
intrude [in'truːd], *v.i.* s'introduire, se faufiler, se fourrer; *to intrude on*, importuner, déranger.
intruder [in'truːdə], *n.* intrus, *m.*
intrusion [in'truːʒən], *n.* intrusion, importunité; (*fig.*) usurpation, *f.*, empiètement, *m.*
intuition [intju'iʃən], *n.* intuition, *f.*
intuitive [in'tjuːitiv], *a.* intuitif, d'intuition.
inundate ['inʌndeit], *v.t.* inonder (*de*).
inundation [inʌn'deiʃən], *n.* inondation, *f.*, débordement, *m.*
inure [i'njuə], *v.t.* habituer, endurcir, rompre.
invade [in'veid], *v.t.* envahir.
invader [in'veidə], *n.* envahisseur, *m.*
invading [in'veidiŋ], *a.* envahissant; d'invasion.

invalid ['invəliːd], *a.* malade, infirme; [in'vælid], (*Law*) invalide, de nul effet.—*n.* malade, *m.*, *f.*, personne malade, *f.*—*v.t.* to *invalid out* (*of the army*), réformer.
invalidate [in'vælideit], *v.t.* invalider, casser.
invaluable [in'væljuəbl], *a.* inestimable, sans prix.
invariable [in'vɛəriəbl], *a.* invariable, constant, uniforme.
invariably [in'vɛəriəbli], *adv.* invariablement; constamment.
invasion [in'veiʒən], *n.* invasion, *f.*, envahissement, *m.*; (*fig.*) violation, *f.*
invective [in'vektiv], *n.* invective, *f.*
inveigh [in'vei], *v.i.* invectiver (*contre*).
inveigle [in'viːgl, in'veigl], *v.t.* séduire, attirer, entraîner.
invent [in'vent], *v.t.* inventer.
invention [in'venʃən], *n.* invention, *f.*
inventive [in'ventiv], *a.* inventif.
inventor [in'ventə], *n.* inventeur, *m.*
inventory ['invəntri], *n.* inventaire, *m.*
inverse [in'vəːs], *a.* inverse.
inversely [in'vəːsli], *adv.* en sens inverse, inversement.
inversion [in'vəːʃən], *n.* inversion, *f.*
invert [in'vəːt], *v.t.* tourner sens dessus dessous, renverser.
invertebrate [in'vəːtibrit], *a.* and *n.* invertébré, *m.*
invest [in'vest], *v.t.* vêtir, revêtir (*de*); (*Mil.*) investir, bloquer; placer (*argent*).
investigate [in'vestigeit], *v.t.* rechercher, examiner; enquêter sur.
investigation [investi'geiʃən], *n.* investigation, recherche, enquête, *f.*
investigator [in'vestigeitə], *n.* investigateur, *m.*; *private investigator*, détective privé, *m.*
investment [in'vestmənt], *n.* placement (*d'argent*); (*Mil.*) investissement, *m.*
investor [in'vestə], *n.* actionnaire, *m.*, *f.*, personne qui place ses fonds, *f.*
inveterate [in'vetərit], *a.* invétéré, enraciné; acharné.
invidious [in'vidiəs], *a.* odieux; désagréable, ingrat (*tâche*).
invigorate [in'vigəreit], *v.t.* fortifier; donner de la vigueur à.
invigorating [in'vigəreitiŋ], *a.* fortifiant, vivifiant, tonifiant.
invincible [in'vinsibl], *a.* invincible.
inviolable [in'vaiələbl], *a.* inviolable.
inviolate [in'vaiəlit], *a.* inviolé, pur, intact.
invisible [in'vizibl], *a.* invisible.
invitation [invi'teiʃən], *n.* invitation, *f.*
invite [in'vait], *v.t.* inviter, engager (*à*); (*fig.*) appeler, provoquer.
inviting [in'vaitiŋ], *a.* attrayant, appétissant, tentant.
invoice ['invɔis], *n.* facture, *f.*—*v.t.* facturer.
invoke [in'vouk], *v.t.* invoquer.
involuntarily [in'vɔləntərili], *adv.* involontairement.
involuntary [in'vɔləntəri], *a.* involontaire.
involve [in'vɔlv], *v.t.* envelopper (*to envelop*); compromettre, impliquer, entraîner (*to entail*); comprendre, renfermer (*to comprise*); embarrasser, entortiller (*to entangle*).
involved [in'vɔlvd], *a.* embrouillé, entortillé, compliqué.
invulnerable [in'vʌlnərəbl], *a.* invulnérable.

inward ['inwəd], *a.* intérieur, interne.—*adv.* (*also* **inwards** ['inwədz]) en dedans, intérieurement.

inwardly ['inwədli], *adv.* intérieurement, intimement.

iodine ['aiədiːn, 'aiədain], *n.* iode, *m.*

ion ['aiən], *n.* ion, *m.*

ionosphere [ai'ɒnəsfiə], *n.* ionosphère, *f.*

iota [ai'outə], *n.* iota; rien, *m.*

Iran [i'rɑːn], l'Iran, *m.*

Iranian [i'reiniən, ai'reiniən], *a.* iranien, *m.*—*n.* Iranien (*personne*), *m.*

Iraq, Irak [i'rɑːk], l'Irak, *m.*

Iraqi [i'rɑːki], *a.* irakien.—*n.* Irakien (*personne*), *m.*

irascible [i'ræsibl], *a.* irascible.

irate [ai'reit], *a.* courroucé, irrité.

ire ['aiə], *n.* colère, *f.*, courroux, *m.*

Ireland ['aiələnd], l'Irlande, *f.*

Irene [ai'riːni, ai'riːn], Irène, *f.*

iridescent [iri'desənt], *a.* iridescent, irisé; chatoyant.

iris ['aiəris], *n.* (*pl.* **irises** ['aiərisiz]) iris, *m.*

Irish ['aiəriʃ], *a.* irlandais.—*n.* irlandais (*langue*), *m.*; **the Irish**, les Irlandais, *m.pl.*

Irishman ['aiəriʃmən], *n.* (*pl.* **-men** [men]) Irlandais, *m.*

Irishwoman ['aiəriʃwumən], *n.* (*pl.* **-women** [wimin]) Irlandaise, *f.*

irk [əːk], *v.t.* peiner, affliger; ennuyer.

irksome ['əːksəm], *a.* pénible, ennuyeux, ingrat.

iron ['aiən], *a.* de fer, en fer.—*n.* fer, *m.*; **cast iron**, fonte, *f.*; **corrugated iron**, tôle ondulée, *f.*; **sheet-iron**, tôle, *f.*; **wrought iron**, fer forgé.—*v.t.* repasser (*linge etc.*).

ironic [ai'rɒnik], **ironical** [ai'rɒnikəl], *a.* ironique.

ironing ['aiəniŋ], *a.* à repasser.—*n.* repassage, *m.*

ironing-board ['aiəniŋbɔːd], *n.* planche à repasser, *f.*

ironmonger ['aiənmʌŋgə], *n.* quincaillier, *m.*

ironmongery ['aiənmʌŋgəri], *n.* quincaillerie, *f.*

iron-ore ['aiənɔː], *n.* minerai de fer, *m.*

iron-works ['aiənwəːks], *n.pl.* forges, *f.pl.*; usine métallurgique, *f.*

irony ['aiərəni], *n.* ironie, *f.*

irradiate [i'reidieit], *v.t.* rayonner sur; éclairer.—*v.i.* rayonner.

irrational [i'ræʃənl], *a.* irraisonnable, déraisonnable; (*Math.*) irrationnel.

irreclaimable [iri'kleiməbl], *a.* incorrigible, invétéré.

irreconcilable [irekən'sailəbl], *a.* irréconciliable (*avec*); incompatible (*avec*); implacable.

irrecoverable [iri'kʌvərəbl], *a.* irrécouvrable; irréparable.

irredeemable [iri'diːməbl], *a.* irrachetable; irrémédiable.

irreducible [iri'djuːsibl], *a.* irréductible.

irreformable [iri'fɔːməbl], *a.* inaltérable, irréformable.

irrefutable [i'refjutəbl], *a.* irréfutable.

irregular [i'regjulə], *a.* irrégulier, anormal; déréglé.

irregularity [iregju'læriti], *n.* irrégularité, *f.*, dérèglement, *m.*

irregularly [i'regjuləli], *adv.* irrégulièrement.

irrelevant [i'reləvənt], *a.* hors de propos, non pertinent; inapplicable (*à*).

irreligious [iri'lidʒəs], *a.* irréligieux.

irremediable [iri'miːdiəbl], *a.* irrémédiable, sans remède.

irremovable [iri'muːvəbl], *a.* inébranlable, immuable; inamovible.

irreparable [i'repərəbl], *a.* irréparable.

irreplaceable [iri'pleisəbl], *a.* irremplaçable.

irrepressible [iri'presibl], *a.* irrépressible; inextinguible (*rire*).

irreproachable [iri'proutʃəbl], *a.* irréprochable, sans tache.

irresistible [iri'zistibl], *a.* irrésistible.

irresolute [i'rezoljuːt], *a.* irrésolu, indécis.

irresolutely [i'rezoljuːtli], *adv.* irrésolument, avec hésitation.

irresolution [irezo'ljuːʃən], **irresoluteness** [i'rezoljuːtnis], *n.* irrésolution, indécision, *f.*

irrespective [iris'pektiv], *a.* indépendant (*de*), sans égard (*pour*); **irrespective of**, indépendamment de.

irrespectively [iris'pektivli], *adv.* indépendamment (*de*), sans égard (*pour*).

irresponsibility [irisponsi'biliti], *n.* irresponsabilité, étourderie, *f.*

irresponsible [iris'ponsibl], *a.* irresponsable; irréfléchi, étourdi.

irretrievable [iri'triːvəbl], *a.* irréparable, irrémédiable.

irreverence [i'revərəns], *n.* irrévérence, *f.*, manque de respect, *m.*

irreverent [i'revərənt], *a.* irrévérencieux.

irrevocable [i'revəkəbl], *a.* irrévocable.

irrigate ['irigeit], *v.t.* arroser, irriguer.

irrigation [iri'geiʃən], *n.* arrosement, *m.* irrigation, *f.*

irritability [irito'biliti], *n.* irritabilité, *f.*

irritable ['iritəbl], *a.* irritable.

irritate ['iriteit], *v.t.* irriter; **to be irritated**, s'irriter.

irritation [iri'teiʃən], *n.* irritation, *f.*

irruption [i'rʌpʃən], *n.* irruption, *f.*

Isabel ['izəbel], **Isabella** [izə'belə]. Isabelle, *f.*

island ['ailənd], *n.* île, *f.*; refuge (*au centre de la rue*), *m.*

islander ['ailəndə], *n.* insulaire, *m.*, *f.*

isle [ail], *n.* île, *f.*

islet ['ailit], *n.* îlot, *m.*

isobar ['aisobɑː], *n.* isobare, *f.*

isolate ['aisəleit], *v.t.* isoler.

isolated ['aisəleitid], *a.* isolé, seul.

isolation [aisə'leiʃən], *n.* isolement, *m.*

isosceles [ai'sɒsiliːz], *a.* isocèle, isoscèle.

Israel ['izreil], l'Israel, *m.*

Israeli [iz'reili], *a.* israélien.—*n.* Israélien (*personne*), *m.*

issue ['isjuː, 'iʃjuː], *n.* issue, sortie (*egress*), *f.*; écoulement (*d'eau etc.*), *m.*; distribution (*envoi*); émission (*de billets de banque, timbres-poste*); publication (*de livres etc.*), *f.*; résultat (*conséquence*), *m.*; enfants, *m.pl.*; (*Law*) question, *f.*; **at issue**, en question.—*v.t.* publier; expédier, distribuer; émettre (*billets de banque*).—*v.i.* sortir, jaillir (*de*); (*fig.*) provenir.

isthmus ['isməs], *n.* isthme, *m.*

it [it], *pron.* il, *m.*, elle, *f.*; (*accusatif*) le, *m.*, la, *f.*; (*datif*) lui; (*impersonnel*) il, ce, cela.

Italian [i'tæliən], *a.* italien.—*n.* italien (*langue*); Italien (*personne*), *m.*

italic [i'tælik], *a.* italique.—*n.* (*pl.*) italiques, *m.pl.*

italicize [i'tælisaiz], *v.t.* mettre *ou* imprimer en italiques.

Italy ['itəli]. l'Italie, *f.*

itch [itʃ], *n.* démangeaison; gale (*maladie*), *f.*—*v.i.* démanger.

item ['aitəm], *n.* article; détail, *m.*, rubrique, *f.*; **item of news**, nouvelle, *f.*—*adv.* item, de plus.

itinerant [i'tinərənt], *a.* ambulant.

itinerary [i'tinərəri], *n.* itinéraire, *m.*

its [its], *poss. a.* son, *m.*, sa, *f.*; ses, *m.pl.*

itself [it'self], *pron.* lui, *m.*, elle, *f.*, soi, lui-même, *m.*, elle-même, *f.*, soi-même, *m.*; (*reflexive*) se.

ivory ['aivəri], *a.* d'ivoire.—*n.* ivoire, *m.*

ivy ['aivi], *n.* lierre, *m.*

J

J, j [dʒei]. dixième lettre de l'alphabet, *m.*

jabber ['dʒæbə], *v.i.* jaboter, baragouiner.—*n.* bavardage, baragouinage, *m.*

jack [dʒæk], *n.* chevalet (*de scieur*); cric (*pour auto*); (*Cards*) valet; (*Bowls*) cochonnet, *m.*—*v.t.* **to jack up**, soulever avec un cric.

jackal ['dʒækɔːl], *n.* chacal, *m.*

jackanapes ['dʒækəneips], *n.* singe; fat, *m.*

jackass ['dʒækæs], *n.* âne, baudet, bourriquet; (*fig.*) idiot, *m.*

jackdaw ['dʒækdɔː], *n.* choucas, *m.*

jacket ['dʒækit], *n.* veste, *f.*; veston, *m.*; (*Tech.*) chemise, enveloppe, jaquette, *f.*

jack-in-the-box ['dʒækinðəbɔks], *n.* boîte à surprise, *f.*

jack-tar ['dʒæk'tɑː], *n.* marin, *m.*

jade (1) [dʒeid], *n.* rosse; haridelle; (*fig.*) coquine (*femme*), *f.*—*v.t.* surmener, harasser, éreinter.

jade (2) [dʒeid], *n.* (*Min.*) jade, *m.*

jaded ['dʒeidid], *a.* surmené, éreinté.

jagged ['dʒægid], **jaggy** ['dʒægi], *a.* dentelé, ébréché.

jaguar ['dʒægjuə], *n.* jaguar, *m.*

jail [dʒeil], *n.* prison, geôle, *f.*

jailer ['dʒeilə], *n.* geôlier, *m.*

jam [dʒæm], *n.* confitures, *f.pl.*; encombrement, embouteillage (*de circulation*), *m.*—*v.t.* serrer, presser, bloquer; (*Rad.*) brouiller.—*v.i.* se coincer.

jamming ['dʒæmiŋ], *n.* coincement; (*Rad.*) brouillage, *m.*

Jamaica [dʒə'meikə]. la Jamaïque, *f.*

Jamaican [dʒə'meikən], *a.* jamaïquain.—*n.* Jamaïquain (*personne*), *m.*

James [dʒeimz]. Jacques, *m.*

Jane [dʒein]. Jeanne, *f.*

jangle ['dʒæŋgl], *v.t.* choquer avec bruit; (*fig.*) agacer (*nerfs*).—*v.i.* faire un bruit de ferraille.

janitor ['dʒænitə], *n.* portier, concierge, *m.*

January ['dʒænjuəri]. janvier, *m.*

Japan [dʒə'pæn]. le Japon, *m.*

japan [dʒə'pæn], *n.* laque, vernis, *m.*—*v.t.* laquer; vernir.

Japanese [dʒæpə'niːz], *a.* japonais.—*n.* japonais (*langue*); Japonais (*personne*), *m.*

jar (1) [dʒɑː], *v.t.* remuer, secouer; ébranler.—*v.i.* être discordant (*instrument de musique*); heurter, s'entrechoquer (*être en conflit*); jurer (*couleurs*); (*fig.*) se disputer.—*n.* son discordant, choc, *m.*; querelle, *f.*

jar (2) [dʒɑː], *n.* jarre, cruche (*faïence*), *f.*, bocal (*verre*), *m.*

jargon ['dʒɑːgən], *n.* jargon, *m.*

jarring ['dʒɑːriŋ], *a.* discordant; en conflit.—*n.* son discordant, *m.*; querelles, *f.pl.*

jasmine ['dʒæzmin], *n.* jasmin, *m.*

jasper ['dʒæspə], *n.* jaspe, *m.*

jaundice ['dʒɔːndis], *n.* jaunisse, *f.*

jaundiced ['dʒɔːndist], *a.* qui a la jaunisse; (*fig.*) prévenu (*contre*).

jaunt [dʒɔːnt], *n.* petite promenade *ou* excursion, *f.*—*v.i.* faire une petite promenade *ou* excursion.

jauntily ['dʒɔːntili], *adv.* avec insouciance, légèrement.

jauntiness ['dʒɔːntinis], *n.* légèreté, *f.*, enjouement, *m.*

jaunty ['dʒɔːnti], *a.* léger, enjoué, sémillant.

javelin ['dʒævəlin], *n.* javeline, *f.*, javelot, *m.*

jaw [dʒɔː], *n.* mâchoire, *f.*; (*fig.*, *pl.*) portes, *f.pl.*; bras, *m.pl.*, étreintes, *f.pl.*

jawbone ['dʒɔːboun], *n.* mâchoire, *f.*

jay [dʒei], *n.* geai, *m.*

jay-walker ['dʒeiwɔːkə], *n.* piéton distrait, *m.*

jazz [dʒæz], *n.* jazz, *m.*

jealous ['dʒeləs], *a.* jaloux.

jealously ['dʒeləsli], *adv.* jalousement; par jalousie.

jealousy ['dʒeləsi], *n.* jalousie, *f.*

jean [dʒiːn], *n.* coutil, treillis; (*pl.*) pantalon (*de coutil*), *m.*

jeep [dʒiːp], *n.* jeep, *f.*

jeer [dʒiə], *n.* raillerie, moquerie, *f.*—*v.t.* railler, huer, se moquer de.—*v.i.* railler, se moquer, goguenarder.

jeering ['dʒiəriŋ], *a.* railleur, moqueur, goguenard.—*n.* raillerie, moquerie, *f.*

jeeringly ['dʒiəriŋli], *adv.* en raillant, d'un ton moqueur.

jelly ['dʒeli], *n.* gelée, *f.*

jelly-fish ['dʒelifiʃ], *n.* méduse, *f.*

jennet ['dʒenit], *n.* genet (*d'Espagne*), *m.*

jeopardize ['dʒepədaiz], *v.t.* hasarder, risquer, mettre en danger.

jeopardy ['dʒepədi], *n.* danger, hasard, *m.*

jerk [dʒəːk], *n.* saccade, secousse, *f.*—*v.t.* donner une poussée à; jeter.

jerkily ['dʒəːkili], *adv.* par saccades.

jerkin ['dʒəːkin], *n.* pourpoint; paletot (*de cuir*), *m.*

jerky ['dʒəːki], *a.* saccadé; irrégulier.

jersey ['dʒəːzi], *n.* vareuse de laine, *f.*, maillot, tricot, *m.*

jest [dʒest], *n.* plaisanterie, facétie, *f.*, bon mot, *m.*; geste (*objet de rire*), *f.*—*v.i.* plaisanter (*de* ou *avec*), badiner (*sur*).

jester ['dʒestə], *n.* plaisant, railleur; bouffon, fou, *m.*

jesting ['dʒestiŋ], *a.* pour rire, badin.—*n.* raillerie, plaisanterie, *f.*, badinage, *m.*

jestingly ['dʒestiŋli], *adv.* en plaisantant, pour rire.

Jesuit ['dʒezjuit], *n.* Jésuite, *m.*

Jesus ['dʒiːzəs]. Jésus, *m.*
jet [dʒet], *n.* jet, jet d'eau; (*Min.*) jais, *m.*; **jet engine,** turbo-réacteur, *m.*; **jet plane,** avion à réaction, *m.*—*v.i.* s'élancer; gicler.
jet-black ['dʒet'blæk], *a.* noir comme du jais.
jetsam ['dʒetsəm], *n.* marchandise jetée à la mer, *f.*, épaves, *f.pl.*
jettison ['dʒetisən], *n.* jet à la mer, *m.*—*v.t.* jeter par-dessus bord.
jetty ['dʒeti], *n.* jetée, *f.*
Jew [dʒuː], *n.* Juif, *m.*
jewel ['dʒuːəl], *n.* joyau, bijou, *m.*, pierre précieuse, *f.*; (*pl.*) pierreries, *f.pl.*; rubis (*de montre*), *m.pl.*—*v.t.* orner de bijoux.
jeweller ['dʒuːələ], *n.* joaillier, bijoutier, *m.*
jewellery ['dʒuːəlri], *n.* joaillerie, bijouterie, *f.*
Jewess ['dʒuːis], *n.* Juive, *f.*
Jewish ['dʒuːiʃ], *a.* juif, des Juifs.
Jewry ['dʒuːri], *n.* Juiverie, *f.*
jib [dʒib], *n.* (*Naut.*) foc, *m.*—*v.i.* reculer; regimber.
jiffy ['dʒifi], *n.* **in a jiffy,** en un clin d'œil.
jig [dʒig], *n.* gigue (*danse*), *f.*, gabarit, *m.*—*v.i.* danser la gigue.
jilt [dʒilt], *n.* coquette, *f.*—*v.t.* planter là; abandonner, (*fam.*) plaquer (*un amoureux*).
jingle ['dʒiŋgl], *n.* tintement (*de cloches*); cliquetis (*de verres, métaux etc.*), *m.*—*v.t.* faire tinter, faire cliqueter.—*v.i.* tinter (*grelots etc.*); s'entrechoquer (*verres etc.*).
jingo ['dʒiŋgou], *n.* chauvin, *m.*; **by jingo!** par exemple!
jingoism ['dʒiŋgouizm], *n.* chauvinisme, *m.*
jinx [dʒiŋks], *n.* porte-guigne, *m.*
Joan [dʒoun]. Jeanne, *f.*; **Joan of Arc,** Jeanne d'Arc.
job [dʒɔb], *n.* travail, ouvrage, *m.*; tâche, pièce; besogne, affaire, *f.*; emploi, *m.*; **job lot,** solde, *m.*, occasion, *f.*; **that's just the job,** cela fait juste l'affaire.—*v.t.* louer; tripoter.—*v.i.* travailler à la tâche; (*Comm.*) agioter, spéculer.
jobber ['dʒɔbə], *n.* ouvrier à la tâche; (*Comm.*) agioteur, coulissier; exploiteur, *m.*
jobbing ['dʒɔbiŋ], *a.* **jobbing gardener,** jardinier à la journée, *m.*—*n.* ouvrage à la tâche; (*Comm.*) agiotage; tripotage, *m.*
jockey ['dʒɔki], *n.* jockey, *m.*
jocose [dʒo'kous], *a.* plaisant, jovial.
jocular ['dʒɔkjulə], *a.* plaisant, facétieux.
jocularly ['dʒɔkjuləli], *adv.* facétieusement.
jocund ['dʒɔkənd], *a.* joyeux, enjoué, gai.
jog [dʒɔg], *v.t.* pousser d'un coup de coude; secouer, cahoter; (*fig.*) rafraîchir (*la mémoire*).—*v.i.* se mouvoir; marcher lentement; **to jog along,** aller doucement.—*n.* secousse légère, *f.*, cahot; coup de coude, *m.*; **jog trot,** petit trot, *m.*
John [dʒɔn]. Jean, *m.*; **Johnnie,** (*colloq.*) Jeannot, *m.*
join [dʒɔin], *v.t.* joindre, unir; associer (à); rejoindre (*rattraper*); relier (*rues etc.*); **will you join us?** voulez-vous être des nôtres?—*v.i.* se joindre, s'unir; s'inscrire; s'associer; prendre part (à).
joiner ['dʒɔinə], *n.* menuisier, *m.*
joinery ['dʒɔinəri], *n.* menuiserie, *f.*
joint [dʒɔint], *a.* commun, ensemble, réuni.—*n.* jointure, *f.*, joint, *m.*; pièce, *f.*; rôti (*de viande*), *m.*; phalange (*du doigt*); charnière (*de porte*); soudure; (*Anat.*) articulation, *f.*; (*Bot.*) nœud, *m.*; (*slang*) boîte, *f.*; **out of**

joint, disloqué, (*fig.*) dérangé; **to put one's arm out of joint,** se démettre le bras.—*v.t.* couper aux jointures; joindre.
jointed ['dʒɔintid], *a.* articulé, jointé; séparé.
jointly ['dʒɔintli], *adv.* conjointement.
joint-stock ['dʒɔintstɔk], *n.* capital, fonds commun, *m.*; **joint-stock bank,** banque par actions, *f.*; **joint-stock company,** société anonyme, *f.*
joist [dʒɔist], *n.* solive, poutre, poutrelle, *f.*
joke [dʒouk], *n.* bon mot, mot pour rire, *m.*, plaisanterie, (*fam.*) blague, *f.*; **a practical joke,** une farce, un mauvais tour; **to crack a joke,** dire un bon mot.—*v.t.* plaisanter sur, railler de.—*v.i.* plaisanter, badiner; rire de.
joker ['dʒoukə], *n.* plaisant, farceur; (*Cards*) joker, *m.*
joking ['dʒoukiŋ], *n.* plaisanterie, farce, *f.*
jokingly ['dʒoukiŋli], *adv.* en plaisantant, pour rire.
jollification [dʒɔlifi'keiʃən], *n.* partie de plaisir, *f.*
jollity ['dʒɔliti], *n.* joie, gaieté, *f.*
jolly ['dʒɔli], *a.* gai, joyeux, gaillard, réjoui.
jolt [dʒoult], *n.* cahot, choc, *m.*—*v.t.* cahoter.—*v.i.* faire des cahots.
Jonah ['dʒounə]. Jonas, *m.*—*n.* porte-malheur, *m.*
jonquil ['dʒɔŋkwil], *n.* (*Bot.*) jonquille, *f.*
Jordan ['dʒɔːdən]. le Jourdain (*rivière*), *m.*; la Jordanie (*pays*), *f.*
Jordanian [dʒɔː'deiniən], *a.* jordanien.—*n.* Jordanien (*personne*), *m.*
jostle [dʒɔsl], *v.t.* pousser, bousculer; (*Spt.*) gêner (*un concurrent*).—*v.i.* jouer des coudes.
jot [dʒɔt], *n.* iota, brin, *m.*—*v.t.* **to jot down,** noter, prendre note de.
journal ['dʒəːnəl], *n.* journal, *m.*; revue, *f.*
journalism ['dʒəːnəlizm], *n.* journalisme, *m.*
journalist ['dʒəːnəlist], *n.* journaliste, *m.*, *f.*
journey ['dʒəːni], *n.* voyage; trajet (*distance*), *m.*; **a pleasant journey to you!** bon voyage! **on the journey,** en route; **to go on a journey,** faire un voyage.—*v.i.* voyager.
journeyman ['dʒəːnimən], *n.* (*pl.* -men [men]) garçon, ouvrier, *m.*
joust [dʒaust, dʒuːst], *n.* joute, *f.*—*v.i.* jouter.
Jove [dʒouv]. Jupiter, *m.*; **by Jove!** bigre! mâtin!
jovial ['dʒouviəl], *a.* joyeux, gai.
joviality [dʒouvi'æliti], *n.* humeur joviale, jovialité, *f.*
jowl [dʒaul], *n.* joue; hure (*de saumon*), *f.*; **cheek by jowl,** côte à côte.
joy [dʒɔi], *n.* joie, *f.*; **to wish someone joy,** féliciter quelqu'un.—*v.i.* se réjouir (*de ou avec*).
joyful ['dʒɔiful], *a.* joyeux.
joyfully ['dʒɔifuli], *adv.* joyeusement.
joyfulness ['dʒɔifulnis], *n.* allégresse, joie, *f.*
joyous ['dʒɔiəs], *a.* joyeux.
jubilant ['dʒuːbilənt], *a.* réjoui; jubilant.
jubilation [dʒuːbi'leiʃən], *n.* réjouissances de triomphe, *f.pl.*, jubilation, *f.*
jubilee ['dʒuːbiliː], *n.* jubilé, *m.*
Judaea [dʒuː'diə]. la Judée, *f.*
Judaism ['dʒuːdeiizm], *n.* judaïsme, *m.*

465

judge [dʒʌdʒ], *n.* juge; (*fig.*) connaisseur, *m.*; *to be a judge of*, se connaître à *ou* en.— *v.t.* juger; discerner, considérer.

judgment ['dʒʌdʒmənt], *n.* jugement; arrêt, *m.*, sentence, *f.*; (*fig.*) avis, sens, *m.*, opinion, *f.*

judicature ['dʒuːdikətʃə], *n.* judicature, justice; cour de justice, *f.*

judicial [dʒuːʹdiʃl], *a.* judiciaire, juridique.

judicious [dʒuːʹdiʃəs], *a.* judicieux, prudent.

judiciously [dʒuːʹdiʃəsli], *adv.* judicieusement.

judo ['dʒuːdou], *n.* jiu-jitsu, (*fam.*) judo, *m.*

jug [dʒʌg], *n.* broc, *m.*; cruche, *f.*; *water jug*, pot à eau, *m.*—*v.t.* faire un civet de (*lièvre*); *jugged hare*, civet de lièvre, *m.*

juggle [dʒʌgl], *v.t.* jouer, duper, escamoter.— *v.i.* faire des tours de passe-passe; (*fig.*) escamoter.—*n.* jonglerie, *f.*; escamotage, tour de passe-passe, *m.*

juggler ['dʒʌglə], *n.* jongleur; escamoteur; (*fig.*) charlatan, *m.*

juggling ['dʒʌgliŋ], *n.* jonglerie, *f.*, escamotage, *m.*

jugular ['dʒʌgjulə], *a.* and *n.* jugulaire, *f.*

juice [dʒuːs], *n.* jus; suc, *m.*

juicy ['dʒuːsi], *a.* juteux; succulent.

ju-jitsu [dʒuːʹdʒitsu], *n.* jiu-jitsu, *m.*

jukebox ['dʒuːkbɔks], *n.* phonographe à sous, jukebox, *m.*

Julian ['dʒuːliən]. Julien, *m.*

Juliet ['dʒuːliət]. Juliette, *f.*

July [dʒuʹlai]. juillet, *m.*

jumble [dʒʌmbl], *v.t.* jeter pêle-mêle, mêler ensemble, confondre.—*n.* pêle-mêle, mélimélo, *m.*, confusion, *f.*; *jumble-sale*, vente de charité, *f.*

jump [dʒʌmp], *n.* saut, bond; sursaut; obstacle (à sauter), *m.*; *high jump*, saut en hauteur; *long jump*, saut en longueur.— *v.t* sauter, franchir d'un bond; sauter de; faire sauter; (*fam.*) *to jump the queue*, resquiller (dans une queue).—*v.i.* sauter; se jeter, se précipiter (*sur*); *to jump at*, accepter avec empressement.

jumper (1) ['dʒʌmpə], *n.* sauteur, *m.*

jumper (2) ['dʒʌmpə], *n.* chandail, jersey, jumper, *m.*

jumpy ['dʒʌmpi], *a.* nerveux.

junction ['dʒʌŋkʃən], *n.* jonction, *f.*; (*Rail.*) embranchement, *m.*

juncture ['dʒʌŋktʃə], *n.* jointure, *f.*; moment critique, *m.*

June [dʒuːn]. juin, *m.*

jungle [dʒʌŋgl], *n.* jungle, *f.*; fourré, *m.*

junior ['dʒuːniə], *a.* jeune, cadet.—*n.* cadet, inférieur en âge, *m.*

juniper ['dʒuːnipə], *n.* genièvre, *m.*

junk (1) [dʒʌŋk], *n.* jonque (*navire*), *f.*

junk (2) [dʒʌŋk], *n.* objets de rebut, *m.pl.*

junket ['dʒʌŋkit], *n.* lait caillé, *m.*; jonchée (*fromage*), talmouse (*gâteau*), *f.*—*v.t.* régaler. —*v.i.* se régaler.

jurisdiction [dʒuəris'dikʃən], *n.* juridiction, *f.*

jurisprudence [dʒuəris'pruːdəns], *n.* jurisprudence, *f.*

jurist ['dʒuərist], *n.* juriste, *m.*, *f.*

juror ['dʒuərə], *n.* juré, *m.*

jury ['dʒuəri], *n.* jury, *m.*

juryman ['dʒuərimən], *n.* (*pl.* **-men** [men]) juré, *m.*

just [dʒʌst], *a.* juste, équitable.—*adv.* juste, justement, précisément; tout, tout juste, seulement, un peu; *he has just gone out*, il vient de sortir; *just now*, à l'instant, tout à l'heure; *just so*, précisément.

justice ['dʒʌstis], *n.* justice, *f.*; juge (*magistrat*), *m.*; *Justice of the Peace*, juge de paix; *to do justice to*, (*fig.*) faire honneur à (*un repas etc.*).

justifiable [dʒʌsti'faiəbl], *a.* justifiable, légitime.

justification [dʒʌstifi'keiʃən], *n.* justification, *f.*

justify ['dʒʌstifai], *v.t.* justifier, autoriser, permettre; *to feel justified in*, se croire autorisé à, croire devoir.

justly ['dʒʌstli], *adv.* exactement, justement; à bon droit.

jut [dʒʌt], *v.i.* avancer, faire saillie.

jute [dʒuːt], *n.* jute, *m.*

jutting ['dʒʌtiŋ], *a.* en saillie, saillant.

juvenile ['dʒuːvənail], *a.* jeune; juvénile, de jeunesse; *juvenile delinquent*, jeune délinquant, *m.*—*n.* jeune, *m.*, *f.*; adolescent, *m.*

juxtaposition [dʒʌkstəpə'ziʃən], *n.* juxtaposition, *f.*; *in juxtaposition*, juxtaposé.

K

K, k [kei]. onzième lettre de l'alphabet, *m.*

kale, kail [keil], *n.* (*Sc.*) chou, *m.*; *sea-kale*, chou marin.

kaleidoscope [kə'laidəskoup], *n.* kaléidoscope, *m.*

kangaroo [kæŋgə'ruː], *n.* kangourou, *m.*

Katharine, Katherine ['kæθərin]. Catherine, *f.*

keel [kiːl], *n.* quille; carène, *f.*

keen [kiːn], *a.* affilé, aigu, aiguisé; (*fig.*) vif, ardent; amer, mordant (*acerbe*); pénétrant, perçant (*brisant la surface de*); dévorant (*appétit*).

keenly ['kiːnli], *adv.* vivement, ardemment, âprement.

keenness ['kiːnnis], *n.* finesse (*de tranchant*); (*fig.*) subtilité; vivacité, ardeur, *f.*, empressement; mordant (*de troupes*), *m.*, âpreté (*du froid*), *f.*

keep [kiːp], *v.t. irr.* tenir, retenir, garder; maintenir, conserver (*ne pas perdre*); avoir (*volaille etc.*); entretenir (*subvenir aux besoins de*); nourrir (*avoir en pension*); avoir à son service; (*fig.*) observer; célébrer, fêter; garantir, protéger; remplir; continuer; *keep it up!* continuez! *to keep away*, éloigner, tenir éloigné; *to keep back*, retenir, garder, tenir en réserve; retarder; *to keep from*, préserver de, empêcher de; *to keep in*, tenir enfermé, retenir; *to keep on*, continuer; *to keep out*, ne pas admettre, écarter, éloigner; *to keep to*, s'en tenir à; *to keep up*, tenir levé, soutenir; continuer; entretenir.—*v.i.* se tenir; rester, demeurer (*ne pas cesser d'être*); se garder, se conserver (*durer*); (*fig.*) se garder, s'abstenir; *to keep away*, se tenir éloigné; *to keep back*, se tenir en arrière; *to keep (doing, saying, telling etc.)*, ne pas cesser de; *to keep silent*, se taire; *to keep up with*, aller de pair avec.—*n.* donjon, réduit (*forteresse*), *m.*; nourriture, *f.*, entretien (*subsistance*), *m.*

keeper [ˈkiːpə], *n.* garde; gardien; surveillant, *m.*

keeping [ˈkiːpiŋ], *n.* garde, surveillance; conservation; (*fig.*) harmonie, *f.*

keepsake [ˈkiːpseik], *n.* souvenir, *m.*

keg [keg], *n.* caque (*de hareng*), *f.*, petit baril, *m.*

ken [ken], *n.* vue; portée, *f.*

kennel [ˈkenl], *n.* chenil, *m.*; niche, *f.*

Kenya [ˈkenjə]. le Kénya, *m.*

kept [kept], *a.* entretenu.—*p.p.* [KEEP].

kerb [kəːb], *n.* bordure (*de trottoir*), margelle (*de puits*), *f.*

kerb-stone [ˈkəːbstoun], *n.* bordure (*de trottoir*), *f.*, parement, *m.*

*kerchief [ˈkəːtʃif], *n.* fichu, *m.*

kernel [ˈkəːnl], *n.* graine, amande, *f.*, pignon (*de pomme de pin*); noyau (*de drupe*); (*fig.*) fond, essentiel, *m.*

kerosene [ˈkerosiːn], *n.* kérosène; pétrole lampant, *m.*

kestrel [ˈkestrəl], *n.* crécerelle, *f.*

ketch [ketʃ], *n.* (*Naut.*) quaiche, *f.*; ketch, *m.*

kettle [ketl], *n.* bouilloire, *f.*; chaudron (*bassine à confitures*), *m.*; *a pretty kettle of fish*, un beau gâchis.

kettledrum [ˈketldrʌm], *n.* timbale, *f.*

key [kiː], *n.* clef, clé, *f.*; (*Arith. etc.*) corrigé; (*Mus.*) ton, *m.*; touche (*sur le piano etc.*), *f.*; *under lock and key*, sous clef.

key-board [ˈkiːbɔːd], *n.* clavier, *m.*

keyhole [ˈkiːhoul], *n.* trou de la serrure, *m.*

key-note [ˈkiːnout], *n.* tonique; (*fig.*) idée maîtresse, *f.*

key-stone [ˈkiːstoun], *n.* clef de voûte, *f.*

khaki [ˈkɑːki], *n.* kaki, *m.*

khan [kɑːn], *n.* kan, khan, *m.*

kick [kik], *n.* coup de pied; recul (*d'un fusil*), *m.*; ruade (*d'animal*), *f.*; (*Ftb.*) *free kick*, coup franc, *m.*—*v.t.* donner un coup de pied à; frapper ou pousser du pied; (*Ftb.*) botter; *to kick out*, chasser à coups de pied; *to kick up a row*, faire du tapage.—*v.i.* donner des coups de pied; ruer, regimber (*animal*); reculer (*fusil*).

kick-off [ˈkikɔf], *n.* (*Ftb.*) coup d'envoi, *m.*

kid [kid], *a.* de chevreau; *kid gloves*, gants de chevreau, *m.pl.*—*n.* chevreau, *m.*; (*colloq.*) enfant, gosse, *m.*—*v.t.* (*fam.*) en conter à; *no kidding !* sans blague!

kidnap [ˈkidnæp], *v.t.* enlever.

kidney [ˈkidni], *n.* rein; rognon (*d'animal*), *m.*

kidney-bean [ˈkidniˈbiːn], *n.* haricot, *m.*

kill [kil], *v.t.* tuer; faire mourir; abattre (*assassiner*).

killer [ˈkilə], *n.* tueur, *m.*

killing [ˈkiliŋ], *a.* mortel; assommant (*travail*). —*n.* tuerie, boucherie, *f.*, massacre, *m.*

kiln [kiln], *n.* four, *m.*

kilogramme [ˈkiləgræm], *n.* kilogramme, *m.*

kilometre [ˈkiləmiːtə], *n.* kilomètre, *m.*

kilowatt [ˈkiləwɔt], *n.* kilowatt, *m.*

kin [kin], *n.* parenté, *f.*; parent, allié, *m.*; *next of kin*, le plus proche parent.

kind [kaind], *a.* bon, bienveillant, bienfaisant; obligeant, complaisant (*accommodant*); *my kind regards to him*, faites-lui toutes mes amitiés; *will you be so kind as to*, voulez-vous avoir la bonté de.—*n.* genre, *m.*, sorte, espèce, *f.*; *in kind*, en nature.

kindergarten [ˈkindəgɑːtn], *n.* école maternelle, *f.*

kindhearted [ˈkaindˈhɑːtid], *a.* bon, bienveillant.

kindle [kindl], *v.t.* allumer, enflammer; (*fig.*) éveiller, exciter.—*v.i.* s'allumer, s'enflammer.

kindliness [ˈkaindlinis], *n.* bienveillance, bonté, *f.*

kindly [ˈkaindli], *a.* bon, bienveillant, favorable.—*adv.* avec bienveillance.

kindness [ˈkaindnis], *n.* bienveillance, bonté, *f.*; bienfait, *m.*

kindred [ˈkindrid], *a.* de même nature.—*n.* parenté, *f.*; parents, *m.pl.*

kinema [ˈkinimə], [CINEMA].

king [kiŋ], *n.* roi, *m.*; (*Draughts*) dame, *f.*

kingdom [ˈkiŋdəm], *n.* royaume; (*fig.*) empire; (*Nat. Hist.*) règne, *m.*; *the United Kingdom*, le Royaume-Uni.

kingfisher [ˈkiŋfiʃə], *n.* (*Orn.*) martin-pêcheur, *m.*

kingly [ˈkiŋli], *a.* de roi, royal.

kink [kiŋk], *n.* nœud; (*colloq.*) point faible, défaut, *m.*

kinsman [ˈkinzmən], *n.* (*pl.* -**men** [men]) parent, allié, *m.*

kiosk [ˈkiɔsk], *n.* kiosque, *m.*; *telephone kiosk*, cabine téléphonique, *f.*

kirk [kəːk], *n.* église d'Écosse, *f.*

kiss [kis], *n.* baiser, *m.*—*v.t.*, *v.i.* embrasser; *to kiss (each other)*, s'embrasser.

kit [kit], *n.* petit équipement, *m.*, effets, *m.pl.*; trousse, *f.*; outils (*d'un ouvrier*), *m.pl.*

kit-bag [ˈkitbæg], *n.* sac, *m.*

kitchen [ˈkitʃin], *n.* cuisine, *f.*

kitchen-garden [ˈkitʃiŋgɑːdn], *n.* jardin potager, *m.*

kitchen-utensils [ˈkitʃinjuːtenslz], *n.pl.* batterie de cuisine, *f.*

kite [kait], *n.* milan (*oiseau*); cerf-volant (*jouet*), *m.*

kith [kiθ], *n.* *kith and kin*, parents et amis, *m.pl.*

kitten [kitn], *n.* chaton, petit chat, *m.*

knack [næk], *n.* adresse, *f.*, tour de main, *m.*

knapsack [ˈnæpsæk], *n.* havresac, *m.*

knave [neiv], *n.* fripon, coquin; (*Cards*) valet, *m.*

knavery [ˈneivəri], *n.* friponnerie, coquinerie, *f.*

knavish [ˈneiviʃ], *a.* fripon; malin.

knead [niːd], *v.t.* pétrir.

knee [niː], *n.* genou, *m.*

knee-breeches [ˈniːbritʃiz], *n.pl.* culotte courte, *f.*

knee-cap [ˈniːkæp], *n.* genouillère; (*Anat.*) rotule, *f.*

kneel [niːl], *v.i. irr.* s'agenouiller.

knell [nel], *n.* glas, *m.*

knickers [ˈnikəz], *n.* culotte (*de femme*), *f.*

knick-knack [ˈniknæk], *n.* brimborion, *m.*, babiole, *f.*; colifichet, bibelot, *m.*

knife [naif], *n.* (*pl.* **knives** [naivz]) couteau, *m.*; (*Tech.*) coupoir; (*Surg.*) scalpel, bistouri, *m.*; *carving-knife*, couteau à découper, *m.*; *pen-knife*, canif, *m.*—*v.t.* poignarder.

knife-grinder

knife-grinder ['naifgraində], *n.* rémouleur, *m.*

knight [nait], *n.* chevalier; (*Chess*) cavalier, *m.*—*v.t.* créer chevalier.

knighthood ['naithud], *n.* chevalerie, *f.*

knightly ['naitli], *a.* chevaleresque, de chevalier.

knit [nit], *v.t.* tricoter; froncer (*les sourcils*); (*fig.*) joindre, attacher, lier.

knitting ['nitiŋ], *n.* tricot, *m.*

knitting-needle ['nitiŋni:dl], *n.* aiguille à tricoter, *f.*

knives [KNIFE].

knob [nɔb], *n.* bosse, *f.*; bouton (*de porte*), *m.*

knock [nɔk], *v.t.* frapper, heurter, cogner; *to knock about*, bousculer, malmener; *to knock down*, renverser, assommer; adjuger (*aux enchères*).—*v.i. to knock about*, rouler sa bosse, aller de par le monde; *to knock off*, cesser le travail.—*n.* coup, choc; cognement, *m.*

knocker ['nɔkə], *n.* marteau (*de porte*), *m.*

knocking ['nɔkiŋ], *n.* coups, *m.pl.*

knoll [nəul], *n.* monticule, tertre, *m.*, butte, *f.*

knot [nɔt], *n.* nœud; groupe (*de personnes etc.*), *m.*; (*fig.*) difficulté, *f.*, embarras, *m.*—*v.t.* nouer; lier; (*fig.*) embrouiller.—*v.i.* faire des nœuds; se nouer.

knotted ['nɔtid], *a.* noueux.

knotty ['nɔti], *a.* noueux; (*fig.*) dur (*difficile*); embrouillé, compliqué.

know [nəu], *v.t. irr.* savoir, apprendre (*to learn*); connaître (*to be acquainted with*); reconnaître (*to recognize*); *to know by heart*, savoir par cœur; *to know by sight*, connaître de vue; *to know some-one*, connaître quelqu'un; *to know some-thing*, savoir quelque chose.—*n. to be in the know*, être dans le secret.

know-how ['nouhau], *n.* savoir-faire, *m.*

knowing ['nouiŋ], *a.* intelligent, instruit; fin, malin.

knowingly ['nouiŋli], *adv.* sciemment; avec ruse.

knowledge ['nɔlidʒ], *n.* connaissance, science, *f.*; savoir, *m.*; *not to my knowledge*, pas que je sache; *without my knowledge*, à mon insu.

knowledgeable ['nɔlidʒəbl], *a.* bien informé.

knuckle [nʌkl], *n.* jointure, articulation du doigt, *f.*; jarret (*de viande*), *m.*—*v.i. to knuckle under*, se soumettre, mettre les pouces.

knuckle-bone ['nʌklbəun], *n.* osselet, *m.*

Korea [kə'ri:ə]. la Corée, *f.*

Korean [kə'ri:ən], *a.* coréen.—*n.* coréen (*langue*); Coréen (*personne*), *m.*

Kuwait [ku'weit]. le Koweit, *m.*

L

L, l [el]. douzième lettre de l'alphabet *m.*

la [lɑ:], *n.* (*Mus.*) la, *m.*

lab [læb], *n.* (*fam.*) labo, *m.*

label [leibl], *n.* étiquette, *f.*; (*Ind.*) label, *m.*—*v.t.* étiqueter; (*fig.*) désigner sous le nom de.

laboratory [lə'bɔrətəri, 'læbrətəri], *n.* laboratoire, *m.*

laborious [lə'bɔ:riəs], *a.* laborieux, pénible.

laboriously [lə'bɔ:riəsli], *adv.* laborieusement, péniblement.

labour ['leibə], *n.* travail, labeur, *m.*, peine, *f.*; ouvrage (*piece of work*); travail d'enfant (*accouchement*), *m.*; *hard labour*, travaux forcés, *m.pl.*; *manual labour*, main-d'œuvre, *f.*; *the Labour Party*, le parti travailliste.—*v.t.* travailler; (*fig.*) élaborer.—*v.i.* travailler; souffrir, peiner; chercher (*à*), s'efforcer (*de*); *to labour under a delusion*, être dans l'erreur.

labourer ['leibərə], *n.* manœuvre, homme de peine, *m.*

labour-exchange ['leibəriks'tʃeindʒ], *n.* bureau de placement (*municipal* ou *d'état*), *m.*

labour-saving ['leibəseiviŋ], *a.* labour-saving device, économiseur de travail, *m.*

Labrador ['læbrədɔ:]. le Labrador, *m.*

labrador ['læbrədɔ:], *n.* chien de Labrador, *m.*

laburnum [lə'bə:nəm], *n.* faux ébénier; cytise, *m.*

labyrinth ['læbirinθ], *n.* labyrinthe, *m.*

lace [leis], *n.* dentelle, *f.*, point, galon; lacet (*cordon*); ruban (*bande*), *m.*; *boot-lace*, lacet de bottine.—*v.t.* lacer (*ses souliers*); garnir de dentelle, galonner (*orner de dentelle*); (*fig.*) orner.

lacerate ['læsəreit], *v.t.* déchirer, lacérer.

laceration [læsə'reiʃən], *n.* déchirure, lacération, *f.*

lachrymose ['lækrimous], *a.* larmoyant.

lacing ['leisiŋ], *n.* lacement, *m.*

lack [læk], *n.* manque, besoin, défaut, *m.*; *for lack of*, faute de.—*v.t.* manquer de.—*v.i.* manquer.

lackey ['læki], *n.* laquais, *m.*

lacking ['lækiŋ], *a.* manquant (*de*), dépourvu (*de*).

laconic [lə'kɔnik], *a.* laconique.

lacquer ['lækə], *n.* laque, *m.*

lad [læd], *n.* garçon, jeune homme; gaillard, *m.*

ladder ['lædə], *n.* échelle, *f.*; démaillage (*d'un bas*) *m.*; *ladder-proof*, indémaillable (*bas*).—*v.t.* démailler (*un bas*).

lade [kid], *v.t.* (*Naut.*) charger.

laden [leidn], *a.* chargé.

lading ['leidiŋ], *n.* chargement, *m.*; *bill of lading*, connaissement, *m.*

ladle [leidl], *n.* louche, cuiller à pot, *f.*

lady ['leidi], *n.* (*pl.* ladies ['leidiz]) dame, *f.*; *young lady*, demoiselle, *f.*

lady-bird ['leidibə:d], *n.* coccinelle, bête à bon Dieu, *f.*

lady-killer ['leidikilə], *n.* bourreau des cœurs, *m.*

lady-like ['leidilaik], *a.* de dame, comme il faut, qui a l'air distingué.

lag [læg], *v.i.* se traîner; traîner (*choses*).—*n.* retard, *m.*

laggard ['lægəd], *n.* traînard, lambin, *m.*

lager ['lɑ:gə], *n.* bière blonde (allemande), *f.*

lagoon [lə'gu:n], *n.* lagune, *f.*

lair [lɛə], *n.* repaire, antre, *m.*

laird [lɛəd], *n.* (*Sc.*) propriétaire, châtelain, *m.*

laity ['leiiti], *n.* laïques, *m.pl.*

lake [leik], *n.* lac, *m.*; laque (*couleur*), *f.*
lamb [læm], *n.* agneau, *m.*—*v.i.* agneler.
lambkin ['læmkin], *n.* agnelet, petit agneau, *m.*
lame [leim], *a.* boiteux, estropié (*infirme*); (*fig.*) défectueux, imparfait; *a lame excuse*, une piètre excuse; *a lame man*, un boiteux.—*v.t.* estropier.
lamely ['leimli], *adv.* en boitant; (*fig.*) imparfaitement, mal.
lameness ['leimnis], *n.* claudication, *f.*; clochement, boitement, *m.*; (*fig.*) faiblesse (*d'une excuse*), *f.*
lament [lə'ment], *v.t.* se lamenter sur, pleurer; s'affliger de.—*v.i.* se lamenter, pleurer.—*n.* lamentation, complainte, plainte, *f.*
lamentable ['læməntəbl], *a.* lamentable, pitoyable.
lamentation [læmən'teiʃən], *n.* lamentation, plainte, jérémiade, *f.*
lamented [lə'mentid], *a.* regretté (*feu*).
lamp [læmp], *n.* lampe; lanterne (*carrosse etc.*); (*fig.*) lumière, *f.*; *street-lamp*, réverbère, *m.*
lampoon [læm'puːn], *n.* satire, *f.*, libelle, *m.*
lamp-post ['læmppoust], *n.* lampadaire, *m.*
lamp-shade ['læmpʃeid], *n.* abat-jour, *m.*
lance [lɑːns], *n.* lance, *f.*—*v.t.* percer d'un coup de lance; (*Surg.*) donner un coup de lancette à, percer.
lance-corporal ['lɑːns'kɔːpərəl], *n.* soldat de première classe, *m.*
lancer ['lɑːnsə], *n.* lancier, *m.*
lancet ['lɑːnsit], *n.* lancette; (*Arch.*) ogive, *f.*
land [lænd], *n.* terre, *f.*; pays (*territoire*); (*Law*) bien-fonds, *m.*; *Holy Land*, la Terre Sainte.—*v.t.* mettre à terre, prendre (*poisson*); débarquer.—*v.i.* débarquer (*à* ou *sur*), aborder; (*fig.*) arriver; (*Av.*) atterrir.
landed ['lændid], *a.* foncier; territorial.
landing ['lændiŋ], *n.* palier (*d'escalier*); (*Naut.*) débarquement; (*Av.*) atterrissage, *m.*
landing-ground ['lændiŋgraund], *n.* terrain d'atterrissage, *m.*
landing-stage ['lændiŋsteidʒ], *n.* débarcadère, *m.*
landing-strip ['lændiŋstrip], *n.* piste d'atterrissage, *f.*
landlady ['lændleidi], *n.* propriétaire (*d'une maison*), logeuse (*d'un meuble*); aubergiste, hôtesse (*d'une auberge*), *f.*
landlord ['lændlɔːd], *n.* propriétaire; hôte, hôtelier, aubergiste (*d'une auberge*), *m.*
landlubber ['lændlʌbə], *n.* marin d'eau douce, *m.*
landmark ['lændmɑːk], *n.* borne, limite, *f.*; point de repère, *m.*
landowner ['lændounə], *n.* propriétaire foncier, *m.*
landscape ['lændskeip], *n.* paysage, *m.*; vue, *f.*
landscape-garden ['lændskeip'gɑːdən], *n.* jardin paysager, *m.*
land-tax ['lændtæks], *n.* impôt foncier, *m.*
lane [lein], *n.* ruelle, *f.*; passage, *m.*; voie (*d'autoroute*), *f.*; chemin vicinal (*de campagne*), *m.*
language ['læŋgwidʒ], *n.* langage, *m.*, langue, expression, *f.*; *modern languages*, langues vivantes, *f.pl.*
languid ['læŋgwid], *a.* languissant.

languish ['læŋgwiʃ], *v.i.* languir.
languishing ['læŋgwiʃiŋ], *a.* languissant, langoureux.
languor ['læŋgə], *n.* langueur, *f.*
laniard [LANYARD].
lank [læŋk], *a.* efflanqué; maigre; décharné; fluet, grêle.
lanky ['læŋki], *a.* grand et maigre; *lanky fellow*, grand flandrin, *m.*
lantern ['læntən], *n.* lanterne, *f.*; (*Mil.*) falot; (*Naut.*) fanal, phare, *m.*; *Chinese lantern*, lanterne vénitienne; *dark lantern*, lanterne sourde; *lantern-jaws*, joues creuses, *f.pl.*
lanyard ['lænjəd], *n.* (*Naut.*) ride, *f.*; (*Artill.*) (cordon) tire-feu, *m.*
Laos [laus]. le Laos, *m.*
Laotian ['lauʃən], *a.* laotien.—*n.* laotien (*langue*); Laotien (*personne*), *m.*
lap (1) [læp], *n.* pan (*de manteau etc.*); giron, *m.*; (*fig.*) genoux, *m.pl.*; sein; (*Racing*) tour de piste, *m.*; *in the lap of*, au sein de.—*v.i.* se replier.
lap (2) [læp], *v.t.* (*Racing*) prendre un tour (*à*).
lap (3) [læp], *v.t.* laper (*boire*).—*v.i.* laper; clapoter (*vagues*).
lap-dog ['læpdɔg], *n.* bichon, petit chien, *m.*
lapel [lə'pel], *n.* revers (*d'habit*), *m.*
lapidary ['læpidəri], *a.* and *n.* lapidaire, *m.*—*v.t.* lapider.
lapidation [læpi'deiʃən], *n.* lapidation, *f.*
Lapland ['læplænd]. la Laponie, *f.*
Laplander ['læpləndə], *n.* Lapon, *m.*
Lapp [læp], *a.* lapon.—*n.* lapon (*langue*); Lapon (*personne*), *m.*
lapse [læps], *n.* cours, laps (*temps*), *m.*; faute, erreur, *f.*; manquement, écart, manque (*divergence*), *m.*—*v.i.* s'écouler; tomber, faillir, manquer (*à*).
lapsed [læpst], *a.* périmé; caduc (*contrat, testament*).
lapwing ['læpwiŋ], *n.* vanneau, *m.*
larceny ['lɑːsəni], *n.* larcin, vol, *m.*
larch [lɑːtʃ], *n.* (*Bot.*) mélèze, *m.*
lard [lɑːd], *n.* saindoux, *m.*—*v.t.* larder (*de*).
larder ['lɑːdə], *n.* garde-manger, *m.*
large [lɑːdʒ], *a.* grand, gros; étendu, considérable; fort; *as large as life*, grandeur nature; *at large*, en liberté, libre; en général.
largely ['lɑːdʒli], *adv.* amplement, largement; au long, en grande partie.
largeness ['lɑːdʒnis], *n.* grandeur, étendue, ampleur, *f.*
largess(e) ['lɑːdʒes], *n.* largesse, libéralité, *f.*
lark [lɑːk], *n.* alouette; (*fig.*) escapade, *f.*
larkspur ['lɑːkspəː], *n.* pied-d'alouette, *m.*
larva ['lɑːvə], *n.* (*pl.* **larvae** ['lɑːviː]) larve, *f.*
laryngitis [lærin'dʒaitis], *n.* laryngite, *f.*
larynx ['læriŋks], *n.* (*pl.* **larynges** ['lærindʒiːz]) larynx, *m.*
lascar ['læskə], *n.* matelot indien, *m.*
lascivious [lə'siviəs], *a.* lascif.
lash [læʃ], *n.* coup de fouet; (*fig.*) coup, trait, *m.*; *eyelash* [EYE].—*v.t.* cingler, fouetter; châtier; lier, attacher (*to tie*).
lashing ['læʃiŋ], *a.* cinglant, fouettant.—*n.* coups de fouet, *m.pl.*; (*Naut.*) ligne d'amarrage, *f.*
lass [læs], *n.* (*Sc.*) jeune fille, *f.*
lassitude ['læsitjuːd], *n.* lassitude, *f.*

last

last (I) [lɑːst], a. dernier, passé; *last but one*, avant-dernier; *last night*, hier soir; *last week*, la semaine dernière; *the last time*, la dernière fois; *this day last week*, il y a aujourd'hui huit jours.—n. bout, m., fin, f.; *at last*, à la fin, enfin; *to the last*, jusqu'au bout, jusqu'à la fin.—v.i. durer.

last (2) [lɑːst], n. forme (*pour chaussures*), f.

lasting ['lɑːstiŋ], a. durable, permanent.

lastly ['lɑːstli], adv. en dernier lieu, enfin.

latch [lætʃ], n. loquet m.—v.t. fermer au loquet.

latchkey ['lætʃkiː], n. passe-partout, m. clef de la maison, f.

late [leit], a. tard; en retard; tardif (*fruits, légumes etc.*); avancé (*heure*); ancien, ex-(*autrefois*); feu (*décédé*); récent, dernier (*depuis peu*); *the late king*, feu le roi; *to be late*, être en retard.—adv. tard; sur la fin; récemment, depuis peu; *at latest*, au plus tard; *better late than never*, mieux vaut tard que jamais; *of late*, récemment; *to be getting late*, (*impers.*) se faire tard.

lately ['leitli], adv. dernièrement, récemment.

lateness ['leitnis], n. retard, m.; heure avancée, f., temps avancé, m.; tardiveté, f.

latent ['leitənt], a. caché, secret, latent.

later ['leitə], a. postérieur, ultérieur.—adv. plus tard.

lateral ['lætərəl] a. de côté, latéral.

latest ['leitist], a. dernier; *at the latest*, au plus tard.

lath [lɑːθ], n. latte, f.

lathe [leið], n. tour, m.

lather ['lɑːðə, lɑːðə], n. mousse; (*fig.*) écume, f.—v.t. savonner; (*colloq.*) rosser.

Latin ['lætin], a. latin.—n. latin (*langue*), m.

Latin-American [lætinə'merikən], a. latino-américain.—n. Latino-Américain (*personne*), m.

latish ['leitiʃ], a. un peu tard, un peu en retard.—adv. un peu tard.

latitude ['lætitjuːd], n. latitude; étendue (*breadth*), f.

latter ['lætə], a. dernier; moderne, récent; *the latter*, ce dernier, celui-ci, m.

lattice ['lætis], n. treillis, treillage, m.

Latvia ['lætviə]. la Lettonie, f.

Latvian ['lætviən], a. lette, letton.—n. lette, letton (*langue*), m.; Lette, m., f., Letton, m. (*personne*).

laud [lɔːd], v.t. louer, célébrer.

laudable ['lɔːdəbl], a. louable, digne de louanges.

laugh [lɑːf], n. rire, m., risée (*moquerie*), f.; *loud laugh*, gros rire, éclat de rire, m.—v.i. rire; *to burst out laughing*, éclater de rire; *to laugh at*, se moquer de.

laughable ['lɑːfəbl], a. risible.

laughing ['lɑːfiŋ], a. rieur, enjoué; *it is no laughing matter*, il n'y a pas de quoi rire.

laughing-stock ['lɑːfiŋstɔk], n. risée, f.

laughingly ['lɑːfiŋli], adv. en riant.

laughter ['lɑːftə], n. rire, m., rires, m.pl.; risée, moquerie, f.; *burst of laughter*, éclat de rire, m.

launch [lɔːntʃ], v.t. lancer; mettre à la mer.—v.i. se lancer, se jeter.—n. lancement, m.; chaloupe (*bateau*), vedette, f.

launching ['lɔːntʃiŋ], n. (*Naut.*) mise à l'eau,

f., lancement, m.; *launching pad*, piste de lancement, f.

launder ['lɔːndə] v.t. blanchir; lessiver (*linge*).

launderette [lɔːndə'ret], n. laverie automatique. f.

laundress ['lɔːndris], n. blanchisseuse, f.

laundromat ['lɔːndrəmæt], (*Am.*) [LAUNDERETTE].

laundry ['lɔːndri], n. buanderie; blanchisserie, f.; linge à blanchir, m.

laurel ['lerəl], n. laurier, m.

lava ['lɑːvə], n. lave, f.

lavatory ['lævət(ə)ri], n. water-clo et, m., les lavabos, les water, m.pl.

lavender ['lævində], n. lavande, f.

lavish ['læviʃ], a. prodigue.—v.t. prodiguer.

lavishly ['læviʃli], adv. prodigalement.

lavishness ['læviʃnis], n. prodigalité, f.

law [lɔː], n. loi, f.; droit, m.; *Law Courts*, Palais de Justice, m.

lawful ['lɔːful], a. légitime, licite, permis.

lawfully ['lɔːfuli], adv. légitimement.

lawless ['lɔːlis], a. sans loi; (*fig.*) sans rrein, déréglé.

lawlessness ['lɔːlisnis], n. désordre, m., licence, f.

lawn (I) [lɔːn], n. pelouse. f.

lawn (2) [lɔːn], n. linon (*tissu*), m.

lawn-mower ['lɔːnmouə], n. tondeuse de gazon, f.

lawsuit ['lɔːsjuːt], n. procès, m.

lawyer ['lɔːjə], n. homme de loi; avocat; avoué (*solicitor*); notaire (*notary*), m.

lax [læks], a. lâche, mou, flasque; (*fig.*) relâché, négligent.

laxative ['læksətiv], a. and n. laxatif, m.

laxity ['læksiti], laxness ['læksnis], n. relâchement, m.; flaccidité, f.; manque d'exactitude, m.

lay (I) [lei], *past* [LIE (2)].

lay (2) [lei], v.t. irr. placer, mettre, poser; coucher, étendre (*de tout son long*); faire; parier (*pari*); pondre (*œuf*); tendre, dresser (*piège*); abattre (*poussière*); calmer, apaiser (*rendre tranquille*); *to lay aside*, mettre de côté; *to lay claim to*, prétendre à; *to lay down*, mettre bas, poser (*principe*); *to lay down one's life for*, donner sa vie pour; *to lay hold of*, s'emparer de; *to lay in*, faire provision de; *to lay on*, appliquer, (*fam.*) arranger; *to lay out*, arranger; ensevelir (*cadavre*); disposer (*jardin etc.*); *to lay siege to*, assiéger; *to lay up*, mettre do côté, faire garder la chambre à; *to lay waste*, dévaster.—v.i. pondre (*œufs*).

lay (3) [lei], n. lai, m., chanson, f., chant, m.

lay (4) [lei], a. lai, laïque.

layer ['leiə], n. couche, f., lit (*strate*), m.; (*Geol.*) assise; (*Hort.*) marcotte, f.; provin (*de vigne*), m.; marcotter (*poule*), f.

laying ['leiiŋ], n. mise, pose; ponte (*d'œufs*), f.

layman ['leimən], n. (*pl.* -men [men]) laïque, profane, séculier, m.

lay-out ['leiaut], n. dessin, tracé, m.; disposition, f.

Lazarus ['læzərəs]. Lazare, m.

laze [leiz], v.i. *to laze about*, baguenauder.

lazily ['leizili], adv. lentement, en paresseux.

laziness ['leizinis], n. paresse, oisiveté, f.

lazy ['leizi], a. paresseux, indolent; *lazy fellow*, fainéant, m.

470

lea [li:], *n.* (*poet.*) prairie, *f.*

lead (1) [led], *n.* plomb (*métal*), *m.*; (*Naut.*) sonde; (*Print.*) interligne; mine de plomb (*pour des crayons*), *f.*; **blacklead**, mine de plomb.

lead (2) [li:d], *v.t. irr.* mener, guider, conduire; porter, faire, induire (*à*); entraîner (*à ou dans*); **to lead astray**, égarer; **to lead back**, ramener, reconduire; **to lead in**, introduire; **to lead out**, emmener; **to lead someone to believe**, faire croire à quelqu'un; **to lead up to**, amener.—*v.i.* conduire, mener; (*Spt.*) jouer le premier. —*n.* conduite, direction, *f.*, commandement, *m.*; laisse (*chien*), *f.*; (*Spt.*) début; (*Theat.*) premier rôle, *m.*, vedette, *f.*; (*Elec.*) conducteur, *m.*

leader ['li:də], *n.* conducteur, guide, chef, meneur; (*Journ.*) article de fond, éditorial; (*Polit.*) chef de parti, leader, *m.*

leadership ['li:dəʃip], *n.* conduite, direction, *f.*; qualités de chef, *f.pl.*

leading ['li:diŋ], *a.* premier, principal; **leading article**, article de fond, *m.*—*n.* conduite, direction, *f.*

leaf [li:f], *n.* (*pl.* **leaves** [li:vz]) feuille, *f.*, feuillet (*livre etc.*); battant (*porte*), *m.*; rallonge (*table*), *f.*; **to turn over a new leaf**, (*fig.*) changer de conduite; **to turn over the leaves of**, feuilleter.

leaflet ['li:flit], *n.* feuillet, imprimé, prospectus, *m.*

leafy ['li:fi], *a.* feuillu, couvert de feuilles.

league [li:g], *n.* ligue; lieue (*3 miles*), *f.*

leak [li:k], *n.* fuite, perte d'eau; (*Naut.*) voie d'eau, *f.*; **to spring a leak**, (*Naut.*) faire eau.—*v.i.* fuir, couler, faire eau; prendre l'eau (*chaussures*); **to leak out**, s'éventer.

leakage ['li:kidʒ], *n.* coulage, *m.*; fuite, *f.*

leaky ['li:ki], *a.* qui coule; (*Naut.*) qui fait eau.

lean (1) [li:n], *a.* et *n.* maigre, *m.*

lean (2) [li:n], *v.t. irr.* appuyer, faire pencher, incliner.—*v.i.* s'appuyer, s'incliner, se pencher; **to lean back against**, s'adosser à; **to lean out**, se pencher au dehors.

leaning ['li:niŋ], *a.* penché.—*n.* penchant, *m.*; (*fig.*) tendance, *f.*

leanness ['li:nnis], *n.* maigreur, *f.*

lean-to ['li:ntu:], *n.* appentis, *m.*

leap [li:p], *n.* saut, bond, *m.*—*v.t. irr.* sauter, franchir.—*v.i.* sauter, bondir; s'élancer, se précipiter.

leap-frog ['li:pfrɔg], *n.* saute-mouton, *m.*

leap-year ['li:pjiə], *n.* année bissextile, *f.*

learn [lə:n], *v.t. irr.* apprendre.—*v.i.* apprendre, s'instruire.

learned ['lə:nid], *a.* savant, instruit, érudit; **learned man**, savant, *m.*; **learned profession**, profession libérale, *f.*

learner ['lə:nə], *n.* élève, commençant, apprenti, *m.*; **learner driver**, élève chauffeur, *m.*

learning ['lə:niŋ], *n.* science, instruction, *f.*, savoir, *m.*, connaissances, *f.pl.*; érudition, *f.*

lease [li:s], *n.* bail, *m.*—*v.t.* louer, donner à bail; prendre à bail.

leasehold ['li:should], *a.* à bail.—*n.* tenure par bail, *f.*

leash [li:ʃ], *n.* laisse, *f.*—*v.t.* mener en laisse, attacher.

least [li:st], *a.* le moindre, le plus petit.—*adv.* le moins; **at least**, au moins, du moins; **not in the least**, point du tout, nullement.

leather ['leðə], *a.* de cuir.—*n.* cuir, *m.*; **upper leather**, empeigne, *f.*—*v.t.* (*colloq.*) étriller, rosser.

leave [li:v], *n.* permission, *f.*, congé; adieu, *m.*; **on leave**, en congé (*un mois ou plus*), en permission (*moins d'un mois*); **with your leave**, avec votre permission.—*v.t. irr.* laisser; quitter, partir de (*s'en aller de*); cesser (*de*); **he left the house**, il quitta la maison, il partit de la maison; **he left the pen on the table**, il laissa le stylo sur la table; **to be left**, rester; **to leave about**, laisser traîner; **to leave alone**, laisser tranquille; **to leave off**, cesser (*de*); **to leave out**, supprimer, omettre, oublier. —*v.i.* partir, quitter; cesser.

leaven [levn], *n.* levain, *m.*—*v.t.* faire lever.

leaves [LEAF].

leave-taking ['li:vteikiŋ], *n.* adieux, *m.pl.*

leavings ['li:viŋz], *n.pl.* restes, *m.pl.*

Lebanese ['lebəni:z], *a.* libanais.—*n.* Libanais (*personne*), *m.*

Lebanon ['lebənən]. le Liban, *m.*

lecherous ['letʃərəs], *a.* lascif, libertin, lubrique.

lecherousness ['letʃərəsnis], **lechery** ['letʃəri], *n.* lasciveté, *f.*

lectern ['lektə:n], *n.* lutrin, *m.*

lecture ['lektʃə], *n.* conférence (*sur*), leçon (*de*), *f.*; (*fig.*) sermon, *m.*, semonce, *f.*—*v.t.* faire un cours à; (*fig.*) sermonner, semoncer. —*v.i.* faire un cours (*de*), faire une conférence (*sur*).

lecturer ['lektʃərə], *n.* conférencier; maître de conférences, *m.*

lecture-room ['lektʃəru:m], *n.* salle de conférences, *f.*

ledge [ledʒ], *n.* rebord, bord, *m.*; (*Arch.*) saillie, *f.*

ledger ['ledʒə], *n.* grand livre, *m.*

lee [li:], *a.* sous le vent.—*n.* (*Naut.*) côté sous le vent, *m.*

leech [li:tʃ], *n.* sangsue, *f.*

leek [li:k], *n.* poireau, *m.*

leer [liə], *n.* œillade, *f.*; regard de côté, *m.*— *v.i.* lorgner.

lees [li:z], *n.pl.* lie, *f.*

leeward ['lu:əd], *a.* and *adv.* (*Naut.*) sous le vent.

lee-way ['li:wei], *n.* dérive; (*fig.*) marge, *f.*

left (1) [left], *past* and *p.p.* [LEAVE].

left (2) [left], *a.* and *n.* gauche, *f.*; **on the left**, à gauche.

left-handed ['left'hændid], *a.* gaucher; à gauche (*vis*); (*fig.*) gauche.

left-overs ['leftouvəz], *n.pl.* restes (*d'un repas*), *m.pl.*

leg [leg], *n.* jambe; patte (*d'oiseau, d'insecte etc.*); tige (*bottines*); cuisse (*volaille*), *f.*; pied (*meuble*); gigot (*mouton*); trumeau (*bœuf*), *m.*; branche (*compas*), *f.*; **to pull someone's leg**, se moquer de quelqu'un.

legacy ['legəsi], *n.* legs, *m.*

legal ['li:gl], *a.* légal, judiciaire, juridique.

legality [li:'gæliti], *n.* légalité, *f.*

legalize ['li:gəlaiz], *v.t.* légaliser, (*fig.*) autoriser.

legally ['li:gəli], *adv.* légalement.

legation [li:'geiʃən], *n.* légation, *f.*

legend ['ledʒənd], *n.* légende, *f.*

legendary ['ledʒəndri], *a.* légendaire, fabuleux.

legged [legd, 'legid], *a.* à jambes, à pieds;

leggings

four-legged, à quatre pattes; ***two-legged***, à deux jambes, bipède.
leggings ['leginz], *n.pl.* jambières, guêtres, *f.pl.*
legibility [ledʒi'biliti], *n.* lisibilité, netteté d'écriture, *f.*
legible ['ledʒibl], *a.* lisible.
legion ['liːdʒən], *n.* légion, *f.*; ***the Foreign Legion***, la Légion (étrangère).
legislate ['ledʒisleit], *v.t.* légiférer, faire des lois.
legislation [ledʒis'leiʃən], *n.* législation, *f.*
legislative ['ledʒislətiv], *a.* législatif.
legitimate [lə'dʒitimit], *a.* légitime; juste, correct.
leisure ['leʒə], *n.* loisir, *m.*; ***at leisure***, de loisir; ***at one's leisure***, à loisir; ***you are at leisure to come or not***, il vous est loisible de venir ou non.
leisurely ['leʒəli], *a.* sans hâte, mesuré.—*adv.* à loisir.
lemon ['lemən], *n.* citron, limon, *m.*
lemonade [lemə'neid], *n.* limonade, *f.*
lemon squash ['lemən'skwɔʃ], *n.* citronnade, *f.*
lemon-squeezer ['lemən'skwiːzə], *n.* presse-citrons, *m.inv.*
lemon-tree ['lemən'triː], *n.* citronnier, *m.*
lend [lend], *v.t. irr.* prêter; (*fig.*) donner.
lender ['lendə], *n.* prêteur, *m.*
lending ['lendiŋ], *n.* prêt, *m.*; ***lending library***, bibliothèque de prêt, *f.*
length [leŋθ], *n.* longueur; étendue, *f.*; degré, point (*extrémité*), *m.*; durée (*temps*), *f.*; ***at full length***, tout au long (*non abrégé*); en toutes lettres (*mots*); de tout son; long (*personnes*); ***at great length***, longuement; ***at length***, enfin; ***full length***, de grandeur nature; ***two feet in length***, deux pieds de longueur ou de long.
lengthen ['leŋθn], *v.t.* allonger, étendre; prolonger (*temps*).—*v.i.* s'allonger, s'étendre; se prolonger (*temps*); (*colloq.*) rallonger (*journées etc.*).
lengthening ['leŋθniŋ], *n.* allongement, *m.*; prolongation (*de temps*), *f.*; accroissement (*des journées*), *m.*
lengthways ['leŋθweiz], **lengthwise** ['leŋθwaiz], *adv.* en longueur, en long.
lengthy ['leŋθi], *a.* un peu long, ennuyeux.
leniency ['liːniənsi], *n.* douceur, clémence, indulgence (*pour*), *f.*
lenient ['liːniənt], *a.* doux, indulgent (*à, envers ou pour*).
leniently ['liːniəntli], *adv.* avec douceur, avec indulgence.
lens [lenz], *n.* (*pl.* **lenses** ['lenziz]) (*Opt.*) lentille, loupe, *f.*
Lent [lent], le carême, *m.*
lentil ['lentil], *n.* lentille, *f.*
leonine ['liːənain], *a.* de lion, léonin.
leopard ['lepəd], *n.* léopard, *m.*
leper ['lepə], *n.* lépreux, *m.*
leprosy ['leprəsi], *n.* lèpre, *f.*
leprous ['leprəs], *a.* lépreux.
less [les], *a.* moindre, plus petit, inférieur; ***to grow less***, diminuer.—*adv.* moins; ***less and less***, de moins en moins; ***no less***, rien moins, pas moins; ***so much the less***, d'autant moins; ***the less . . . the more . . .***, moins . . . plus . . .—*n.* moins; moindre, *m.*
essee [le'siː], *n.* locataire à bail, *m., f.*

lessen [lesn], *v.t.* diminuer, amoindrir, rapetisser, rabaisser (*to lower*); ralentir (*la vitesse*).—*v.i.* diminuer, s'amoindrir.
lesser ['lesə], *a.* moindre, plus petit.
lesson [lesn], *n.* leçon, *f.*
lest [lest], *conj.* de peur que, de crainte que (*followed by* ne *with subj.*).
let (1) [let], *v.t. irr.* laisser, permettre à (*donner la permission à*); souffrir que (*with subjunctive*); faire (*causer*); louer (*maison*); ***let him come***, qu'il vienne; ***let me see***, voyons; ***let us go***, allons; ***to let alone***, laisser tranquille; ***to let down***, descendre, faire descendre, baisser, rabattre; ***to let fall***, laisser tomber; ***to let go***, lâcher; ***to let in***, faire entrer; ***to let know***, faire savoir à; ***to let off***, laisser échapper; tirer (*arme à feu*); ***to let out***, faire sortir, laisser sortir; élargir (*vêtements*).
let (2) [let], *n.* empêchement; obstacle, délai, *m.*; (*Tennis*) (balle) à remettre.
lethal [liːθl], *a.* mortel, fatal.
lethargic [le'θɑːdʒik], *a.* léthargique.
lethargy ['leθədʒi], *n.* léthargie, *f.*
letter ['letə], *n.* lettre, *f.*; (*pl., fig.*) belles-lettres, *f.pl.*; ***registered letter***, lettre recommandée.
letter-box ['letəbɔks], *n.* boîte aux lettres, *f.*
letter-card ['letəkɑːd], *n.* carte-lettre, *f.*
lettered ['letəd], *a.* lettré, savant.
lettering ['letəriŋ], *n.* titre, *m.*
letting ['letiŋ], *n.* louage, *m.*; ***letting out***, location, *f.*; agrandissement (*de vêtement*), *m.*
lettuce ['letis], *n.* laitue, *f.*
let-up ['letʌp], *n.* diminution, *f.*
Levant [lə'vænt], **the.** le Levant, *m.*
Levantine [li'væntain], *a.* du Levant, levantin.—*n.* Levantin (*personne*), *m.*; levantine (*soie*), *f.*
level [levl], *a.* de niveau (*avec*), au niveau (*de*); uni (*surface*); égal (*à*); ***level crossing***, passage à niveau, *m.*—*n.* niveau, *m.*, surface unie, *f.*; ***at ministerial level***, à l'échelon ministériel.—*v.t.* aplanir, niveler, mettre de niveau; braquer, pointer (*arme à feu*); porter (*coup*).—*v.i.* viser, mettre en joue, pointer.
level-headed ['levlhedid], *a.* équilibré, de sens rassis.
levelling ['levliŋ], *n.* nivellement; pointage (*de fusil*), *m.*
lever ['liːvə], *n.* levier, *m.*; ***hand-lever***, manette, *f.*
leveret ['levərit], *n.* levraut, *m.*
levity ['leviti], *n.* légèreté, *f.*; manque de sérieux, *m.*
levy ['levi], *n.* levée; perception (*d'impôts*), *f.*—*v.t.* lever; imposer (*amende etc.*).
lewd [ljuːd], *a.* impudique, lascif.
lexicon ['leksikn], *n.* lexique, dictionnaire, *m.*
liability [laiə'biliti], *n.* responsabilité; tendance, *f.*; danger, *m.*; (*Comm.*) engagements, *m.pl.*, passif, *m.*; ***assets and liabilities***, actif et passif, *m.*
liable ['laiəbl], *a.* sujet (*à*), exposé (*à*), responsable (*de*).
liar ['laiə], *n.* menteur, *m.*
libel [laibl], *n.* libelle, écrit diffamatoire, *m.*—*v.t.* diffamer.
libellous ['laibələs], *a.* diffamatoire.
liberal ['libərəl], *a.* libéral, généreux; prodigue, abondant.—*n.* (*Polit.*) Libéral, *m.*
liberality [libə'ræliti], *n.* libéralité, *f.*

liberate ['libəreit], v.t. libérer, rendre libre; délivrer (de).
liberation [libə'reiʃən], n. mise en liberté, f., élargissement (de prisonniers); affranchissement, m.; libération, délivrance, f.
liberator ['libəreitə], n. libérateur, m.
Liberia [lai'biəriə]. le Libéria, m.
Liberian [lai'biəriən], a. libérien.—n. Libérien (personne), m.
liberty ['libəti], n. liberté, f.; privilèges, m.pl., franchises, f.pl.
librarian [lai'brεəriən], n. bibliothécaire, m.,f.
library ['laibrəri], n. bibliothèque, f.; film library, cinémathèque, f.; record library, discothèque, f.
Libya ['libiə]. la Lybie, f.
Libyan ['libiən], a. libyen.—n. Libyen (personne), m.
lice [LOUSE].
licence ['laisəns], n. licence, liberté; permission, f., permis; certificat; (fig.) dérèglement, m.; autorisation (de prédicateur), f.; brevet (de libraire), m.; (Comm.) patente, f.; driving licence, permis de conduire; gun-licence, permis de port d'armes; permis de chasse; marriage-licence, dispense de bans, f.
license ['laisəns], v.t. autoriser, accorder un permis à.
licensed ['laisənst], a. autorisé; breveté; (Comm.) patenté.
licentious [lai'senʃəs], a. licencieux.
lichen ['laikən], n. lichen, m.
lick [lik], v.t. lécher, laper (boire); (slang) rosser (battre).—n. coup de langue, m.
licking ['likiŋ], n. (slang) coups, m.pl., raclée, f.
licorice [LIQUORICE].
lid [lid], n. couvercle, m.; paupière (d'œil), f.
lie (1) [lai], n. mensonge; démenti, m.; to give the lie to, donner un démenti à; white lie, mensonge pieux.—v.i. mentir.
lie (2) [lai], v.i. irr. être couché, se coucher; reposer, être, être situé, se trouver; s'appuyer (se soutenir); rester (to remain); consister; here lies, ci-gît; lie down! (à un chien) couchez! lie to lie about (objets), traîner çà et là; to lie down, se coucher, se reposer.—n. gisement, m., position, situation, f.
lieutenant [lef'tenənt], n. lieutenant, m.
life [laif], n. (pl. lives [laivz]) vie, f.; homme vivant, m.; personne; (fig.) vie, âme, vivacité, f., entrain; mouvement; (Paint. etc.) naturel, m.; a double life, une vie double; for life, à vie, à perpétuité; from life, d'après nature; high life, le grand monde, m.; never in my life, jamais de ma vie; pension for life, pension viagère, f.; prime of life, fleur de l'âge, f.; single life, célibat, m.; to come to life, s'animer.
life-belt ['laifbelt], n. ceinture de sauvetage, f.
life-boat ['laifbout], n. canot de sauvetage, m.
life-buoy ['laifbɔi], n. bouée de sauvetage, f.
lifeguard ['laifgɑːd], n. garde du corps, m.; (pl.) les Gardes du corps, m.pl.; sauveteur, m.
life-insurance ['laifinʃuərəns], n. assurance sur la vie, f.
lifeless ['laiflis], a. sans vie, inanimé.
lifelike ['laiflaik], a. comme un être vivant, d'après nature, vivant.

lifelong ['laiflɔŋ], a. de toute la vie.
life-size ['laifsaiz], a. de grandeur nature.
lifetime ['laiftaim], n. vie, f., vivant, m.; in his or her lifetime, de son vivant.
lift [lift], n. action de lever, élévation, f., effort; coup de main (aide); monte-charge (machine); ascenseur, m.—v.t. lever, soulever, hausser, soupeser (évaluer le poids de); (fig.) élever, relever.
lift-man ['liftmən], n. (pl. -men [men]) liftier, m.
light (1) [lait], n. lumière, f., jour (du soleil); clair (de la lune etc.), m.; clarté (de l'œil etc.), lueur, f.; (fig.) aspect, point de vue, m.; electric light, éclairage à l'électricité, m.; it is light, il fait jour; light and shade, clair-obscur, m.; traffic lights, feux de circulation, m.pl.; will you give me a light? voulez-vous me donner du feu?—v.t. irr. allumer; illuminer, éclairer (fenêtres etc.).—v.i. to light up, briller, s'enflammer.
light (2) [lait], v.i. to light upon, descendre ou tomber sur.
light (3) [lait], a. léger; (fig.) gai, frivole; clair (couleur etc.); blond (teint).
lighten (1) [laitn], v.t. éclairer, illuminer.—v.i. éclairer; faire des éclairs.
lighten (2) [laitn], v.t. soulager, alléger (adoucir).
lightening ['laitniŋ], n. éclaircissement; allègement; soulagement, m.
lighter ['laitə], n. allumeur; briquet (pour cigarettes), m.; (Naut.) allège, gabare, f., chaland, m.
light-hearted [lait'hɑːtid], a. gai, réjoui.
light-heartedness [lait'hɑːtidnis], n. enjouement, m., gaieté, f.
lighthouse ['laithaus], n. phare, m.
lighting ['laitiŋ], n. éclairage, m.; lighting-up time, heure d'éclairage, f.
lightly ['laitli], adv. légèrement, à la légère; lestement, facilement, aisément; gaiement.
lightness ['laitnis], n. légèreté, f.
lightning ['laitniŋ], n. éclair, m., les éclairs, m.pl.; foudre, f.; flash of lightning, éclair.
lightning-conductor ['laitniŋkən'dʌktə], n. paratonnerre, m.
lights [laits], n.pl. mou (d'animal), m.
lightship ['laitʃip], n. bateau-feu, m.
like (1) [laik], a. semblable, tel, pareil; même, égal, *vraisemblable; as like as not, probablement; that is something like! à la bonne heure! to be like, ressembler à; to feel like doing something, avoir envie de faire quelque chose; what is he like? comment est-il?—prep. comme, semblable à, pareil à.—n. chose pareille, f., pareil, m.; même chose, f.; the likes of you, les gens de votre sorte, m.pl., f.pl.
like (2) [laik], v.t. aimer, aimer bien, trouver bon, trouver bien; vouloir (bien), désirer, être bien aise (de); as you like, comme il vous plaira, comme vous voudrez.—n. goût, m.; préférence, f.; everyone has his likes and dislikes, chacun son goût.
likeable ['laikəbl], a. sympathique, aimable.
likelihood ['laiklihud], n. probabilité, vraisemblance, f.
likely ['laikli], a. probable, vraisemblable.—adv. probablement, vraisemblablement.

473

liken

liken [laikn], *v.t.* comparer (*à* ou *avec*).
likeness ['laiknis], *n.* ressemblance, *f.*; portrait, *m.*
likewise ['laikwaiz], *adv.* également, pareillement, de même, aussi.
liking ['laikiŋ], *n.* gré, goût, penchant, *m.*, inclination; amitié, *f.*
lilac ['lailək], *n.* lilas, *m.*
lily ['lili], *n.* lis, *m.*; *lily of the valley*, muguet, *m.*
limb [lim], *n.* membre (*du corps*); (*colloq.*) enfant terrible, *m.*; grosse branche (*d'arbre*), *f.*
limber (1) ['limbə], *a.* souple, flexible; (*fig.*) agile.—*v.i.* *to limber up*, se chauffer les muscles.
limber (2) ['limbə], *n.* avant-train, *m.*
limbo ['limbou], *n.* limbes, *m.pl.*
lime (1) [laim], *n.* (*Bot.*) lime, limette, *f.*; *lime-juice*, jus de limette, *m.*; *lime-tree*, tilleul (*linden*); limettier, *m.*
lime (2) [laim], *n.* chaux; glu (*pour prendre des oiseaux*), *f.*
limelight ['laimlait], *n.* (*Theat.*) les feux de la lampe, *m.pl.*; *to be in the limelight*, être en évidence.
limestone ['laimstoun], *n.* pierre à chaux, *f.*; (*Geol.*) calcaire, *m.*
limit ['limit], *n.* limite, borne, *f.*; (*fam.*) *that's the limit!* ça c'est le comble!—*v.t.* limiter, borner, restreindre.
limitation [limi'teiʃən], *n.* limitation, restriction, *f.*
limited ['limitid], *a.* limité, borné; (*Comm.*) anonyme.
limitless ['limitlis], *a.* sans limite.
limp [limp], *a.* mou, flasque, sans consistance.—*v.i.* boiter.
limpet ['limpit], *n.* lépas, *m.*, patelle, *f.*
limpid ['limpid], *a.* limpide.
linden [lindn], *n.* (*Bot.*) tilleul, *m.*
line (1) [lain], *n.* ligne, corde, *f.*, cordeau (*ficelle*), *m.*; file, *f.*, alignement (*rang*) trait (*écrit*), *m.*; raie (*bande*), *f.*; contour (*profil*), *m.*; ride (*pli du visage*); (*Rail.*) voie; lignée, race (*descendance*), *f.*; (*fig.*) genre (*d'affaires etc.*); (*Pros.*) vers; mot, petit mot (*lettre brève*), *m.*; limite (*de territoire*), *f.*; *air-line*, ligne aérienne; (*Teleph.*) *hold the line!* ne quittez pas! *it is hard lines*, c'est dur; *not in my line*, pas de mon ressort.—*v.t.* ligner, régler; *to line up*, aligner.
line (2) [lain], *v.t.* doubler (*vêtement*); garnir (*de*); border (*de*).
lineage ['liniədʒ], *n.* lignée, race, famille, *f.*
lineal ['liniəl], *a.* linéal.
lineally ['liniəli], *adv.* en ligne directe.
linear ['liniə], *a.* linéaire.
linen ['linin], *a.* de toile.—*n.* toile, toile de lin, *f.*, lin; linge (*habits*), *m.*
liner (2) ['lainə], *n.* (*Naut.*) paquebot de ligne, transatlantique, *m.*
linesman ['lainzmən], *n.* (*pl.* **-men** [men]) (*Ftb.*) arbitre de touche, *m.*
linger ['liŋgə], *v.i.* traîner, tarder; hésiter.
lingering ['liŋgəriŋ], *a.* qui traîne, lent; languissant.—*n.* retard, *m.*, lenteur; hésitation, *f.*
lingo ['liŋgou], *n.* (*slang*) jargon, *m.*; langue, *f.*
linguist ['liŋgwist], *n.* linguiste, *m.*, *f.*
liniment ['linimənt], *n.* liniment, *m.*
lining ['lainiŋ], *n.* doublure; garniture (*de*

vêtement); coiffe (*de chapeau*), *f.*; (*Build.*) revêtement, *m.*
link [liŋk], *n.* chaînon, anneau; (*fig.*) lien; trait d'union, *m.*; *cuff-links*, boutons de manchettes, *m.pl.*—*v.t.* lier, relier (*avec.*); enchaîner (*dans*); unir.—*v.i.* s'allier (*à*).
links [liŋks], *n.pl.* *golf-links*, terrain de golf, *m.*
linnet ['linit], *n.* linotte, *f.*
linoleum [li'nouljəm], *n.* linoléum, *m.*
linotype ['lainotaip], *n.* linotype, *f.*
linseed ['linsi:d], *n.* graine de lin, *f.*; *linseed-oil*, huile de lin, *f.*
lint [lint], *n.* charpie, *f.*
lintel [lintl], *n.* linteau, *m.*
lion ['laiən], *n.* lion, *m.*; (*fig.*) célébrité, *f.*; *lion's cub*, lionceau, *m.*
lioness ['laiənes], *n.* lionne, *f.*
lion-tamer ['laiənteimə], *n.* dompteur de lions, *m.*
lip [lip], *n.* lèvre; babine (*de certains animaux*), *f.*; bord (*de choses*), *m.*; (*fig.*) impertinence, *f.*
lipstick ['lipstik], *n.* bâton de rouge, *m.*
liquefy ['likwifai], *v.t.* liquéfier.—*v.i.* se liquéfier.
liqueur [li'kjuə], *n.* liqueur, *f.*
liquid ['likwid], *a.* liquide; doux, coulant.—*n.* liquide, *m.*
liquidate ['likwideit], *v.t.* liquider.
liquidation [likwi'deiʃən], *n.* liquidation, *f.*, acquittement (*d'une dette*), *m.*
liquor ['likə], *n.* (*Chem.*) liqueur, solution; (*Am.*) boisson alcoolique, *f.*; (*Am.*) *hard liquor*, alcool, *m.*
liquorice ['likəris], *n.* réglisse, *f.*
Lisbon ['lizbən]. Lisbonne, *f.*
lisp [lisp], *v.t.*, *v.i.* dire (θ, δ) au lieu de (s, z); (*colloq.*) susurrer, zozoter.
lissom [lism], *a.* souple, leste.
list (1) [list], *n.* liste, *f.*, rôle, *m.*; *Army List*, annuaire de l'armée, *m.*—*v.t.* enrôler, enregistrer.
list (2) [list], *v.i.* (*Naut.*) donner de la bande.—*n.* (*Naut.*) bande, *f.*
listen [lisn], *v.i.* écouter.
listener ['lisnə], *n.* auditeur, *m.*
listless ['listlis], *a.* apathique.
listlessness ['listlisnis], *n.* apathie, *f.*
lists [lists], *n. pl.* lice, arène (*arena*), *f.*
litany ['litəni], *n.* litanie, *f.*
literal ['litərəl], *a.* littéral.
literally ['litərəli], *adv.* littéralement, à la lettre.
literary ['litərəri], *a.* littéraire; lettré (*personne*).
literature ['litəritʃə], *n.* littérature, *f.*
lithe [laið], *a.* pliant, flexible, souple.
lithograph ['liθogra:f], *n.* lithographie, *f.*
lithographer [li'θogrəfə], *n.* lithographe, *m.*, *f.*
Lithuania [liθju'einiə]. la Lituanie, la Lithuanie, *f.*
Lithuanian [liθju'einiən], *a.* lituanien, lithuanien.—*n.* lituanien, lithuanien (*langue*); Lituanien, Lithuanien (*personne*), *m.*
litigant ['litigənt], *n.* plaideur, *m.*
litigate ['litigeit], *v.t.* plaider, disputer.—*v.i.* être en procès.
litigation [liti'geiʃən], *n.* litige; procès, *m.*
litre ['li:tə], *n.* litre, *m.*
litter ['litə], *n.* litière, civière (*véhicule*), *f.*; ordures, *f.pl.*, détritus, *m.pl.*; (*fig.*) fouillis, désordre, *m.*; portée (*d'animal*), *f.*—*v.t.*

joncher; jeter çà et là; (*fig.*) mettre en désordre; mettre bas (*animal*); salir; *to litter down* (*of horse*), faire la litière à.

litter-bin ['litəbin], *n.* boîte à ordures, *f.*

little [litl], *a.* petit; minime, exigu; mesquin; *little one*, enfant, *m.*, *f.*, petit, *m.*—*n.* peu, *m.*; *to think little of*, faire peu de cas de.—*adv.* peu, un peu, pas beaucoup, peu de chose, peu de; *a little*, un peu; *as little as possible*, le moins possible; *little by little*, petit à petit, peu à peu; *little or none*, peu ou point.

littleness ['litlnis], *n.* petitesse, *f.*

liturgy ['litədʒi], *n.* liturgie, *f.*

live (1) [liv], *v.t.* mener (une vie).—*v.i.* vivre; résider, demeurer, habiter; *long live the Queen!* vive la Reine! *to live by*, vivre de; *to live down a scandal*, faire oublier un scandale avec le temps; *to live on*, se nourrir de.

live (2) [laiv], *a.* en vie, vivant; ardent, vif (*charbons*); *live rail*, rail conducteur, *m.*; *livestock*, bétail, *m.*; *live wire*, fil sous tension, *m.*

lived [livd], *a.* de vie; *long-lived*, qui vit longtemps, de longue vie.

livelihood ['laivlihud], *n.* vie, subsistance, *f.*; gagne-pain, *m.*

liveliness ['laivlinis], *n.* vivacité, gaieté, *f.*

livelong ['livlɔŋ], *a.* durable, long, sans fin; *the livelong day*, toute la sainte journée.

lively ['laivli], *a.* vif, gai, enjoué, animé; vivant (*endroit*).

liven [laivn], *v.t. to liven up*, animer.

liver (1) ['livə], *n. fast liver*, viveur, noceur, *m.*

liver (2) ['livə], *n.* (*Anat.*) foie, *m.*

livery ['livəri], *n.* livrée (*de chevaux*), *f.*

lives [LIFE].

livestock ['laivstɔk], [LIVE (2)].

livid ['livid], *a.* livide, blême.

living ['liviŋ], *a.* en vie, vivant; vif.—*n.* vie, subsistance, existence, *f.*; genre de vie, *m.*, chère, *f.*; (*Eccles.*) bénéfice, *m.*, cure, *f.*

living-room ['liviŋrum], *n.* salle de séjour, *f.*

lizard ['lizəd], *n.* lézard, *m.*

llama ['lɑːmə], *n.* lama, *m.*

lo! [lou], *int.* voici! voilà! voyez! regardez!

load [loud], *n.* charge, *f.*, fardeau; (*fig.*) chargement, *m.*; charretée (*cartful*), *f.*—*v.t.* charger; (*fig.*) combler, accabler (*de*).

loaf [louf], *n.* (*pl.* **loaves** [louvz]) pain (*long*), *m.*; miche (*rond*), *f.*—*v.i.* flâner, fainéanter; *to loaf about town*, battre le pavé.

loafer ['loufə], *n.* fainéant, batteur de pavé, *m.*

loam [loum], *n.* terre grasse, *f.*

loamy ['loumi], *a.* glaiseux.

loan [loun], *n.* emprunt; prêt, *m.*; *to raise a loan*, faire un emprunt.—*v.t.* prêter.

loath [louθ], *a.* fâché, peiné; *to be loath to*, faire à contre-cœur.

loathe [louð], *v.t.* détester.

loathing ['louðiŋ], *n.* dégoût, *m.*, aversion, *f.*

loathsome ['louðsəm], *a.* dégoûtant, odieux.

loaves [LOAF].

lobby ['lɔbi], *n.* couloir, *m.*; salle d'attente (*vestibule*); (*Theat.*) entrée, *f.*—*v.t.*, *v.i.* (*Polit.*) faire les couloirs.

lobe [loub], *n.* lobe, *m.*

lobelia [lo'biːliə], *n.* lobélie, *f.*

lobster ['lɔbstə], *n.* homard, *m.*

local ['loukəl], *a.* local; topographique.

locality [lo'kæliti], *n.* localité, *f.*

localize ['loukəlaiz], *v.t.* localiser.

locally ['loukəli], *adv.* localement.

locate [lo'keit], *v.t.* placer, localiser; repérer.

location [lo'keiʃən], *n.* situation, *f.*, emplacement, *m.*; location, *f.*; (*Cine.*) extérieurs, *m.pl.*

loch [lɔx], *n.* (*Sc.*) lac, *m.*

lock [lɔk], *n.* serrure; écluse (*de canal*); platine (*de fusil*); mèche, boucle (*de cheveux*), *f.*; flocon (*de laine*), *m.*; (*pl.*) cheveux, *m.pl.*; *dead-lock*, impasse, *f.*; *padlock*, cadenas, *m.*—*v.t.* fermer à clef; accrocher (*roues etc.*); *to lock in*, enfermer; *to lock up*, serrer, enfermer, mettre en prison.—*v.i.* fermer à clef.

locker ['lɔkə], *n.* armoire, *f.*; coffre, *m.*

locket ['lɔkit], *n.* médaillon, *m.*

lock-jaw ['lɔkdʒɔː], *n.* trisme, tétanos, *m.*

locksmith ['lɔksmiθ], *n.* serrurier, *m.*

locomotion [loukə'mouʃən], *n.* locomotion, *f.*

locomotive [loukə'moutiv], *a.* locomotif.—*n.* locomotive, *f.*

locust (1) ['loukəst], *n.* sauterelle d'Orient, *f.*, criquet, *m.*

locust (2) ['loukəst], *n.* caroubier (*plante*), *m.*; *locust-tree*, robinier, *m.*

lodge [lɔdʒ], *n.* loge (*de concierge*), *f.*; pavillon, *m.*; maisonnette (*de garde*), *f.*—*v.t.* loger; abriter; enfoncer (*mettre dans*); déposer (*placer*); implanter (*dans le cœur*); interjeter (*appel*); *to lodge a complaint*, porter plainte.—*v.i.* loger, se loger; s'arrêter, se fixer.

lodger ['lɔdʒə], *n.* locataire; pensionnaire, *m.*, *f.*

lodging ['lɔdʒiŋ], *n.* logement; appartement, *m.*; *to live in furnished lodgings*, loger en garni *ou* en meublé.

lodging-house ['lɔdʒiŋhaus], *n.* hôtel garni, hôtel meublé, *m.*

loft [lɔft], *n.* grenier, *m.*; tribune, *f.*; pigeonnier, *m.*

loftily ['lɔftili], *adv.* haut, avec hauteur, pompeusement.

loftiness ['lɔftinis], *n.* élévation; hauteur, fierté, pompe; sublimité, *f.*

lofty ['lɔfti], *a.* haut, élevé; altier; sublime (*style*).

log [lɔg], *n.* bûche, *f.*; (*Naut.*) loch, *m.*; *to sleep like a log*, dormir comme une souche.

loganberry ['lougənberi], *n.* ronce-framboise, *f.*

logarithm ['lɔgəriðm], *n.* logarithme, *m.*

log-book ['lɔgbuk], *n.* journal *ou* livre de bord; (*Motor.*) carnet de route, *m.*

loggerhead ['lɔgəhed], *n.* lourdaud, *m.*; *to be at loggerheads*, être aux prises *ou* à couteaux tirés.

logic ['lɔdʒik], *n.* logique, *f.*

logical ['lɔdʒikəl], *a.* logique, de la logique.

loin [lɔin], *n.* longe (*de veau*), *f.*; filet (*de mouton*), *m.*; (*pl.*) reins, lombes, *m.pl.*

loiter ['lɔitə], *v.t.* perdre, gaspiller.—*v.i.* flâner, traîner, s'amuser en chemin.

loiterer ['lɔitərə], *n.* musard, flâneur, *m.*

loitering ['lɔitəriŋ], *n.* flânerie, *f.*

loll [lɔl], *v.t.* laisser pendre (*la langue*).—*v.i.* s'étaler, se pencher; pendre (*la langue*).

lolling ['lɔliŋ], *a.* étendu, étalé.
lollipop ['lɔlipɔp], *n.* sucre d'orge, *m.*, sucette, *f.*
lolly ['lɔli], *n.* (*fam.*) sucette; (*slang*) galette (*argent*), *f.*
London ['lʌndən]. Londres, *m.* ou *f.*
Londoner ['lʌndənə], *n.* Londonien, *m.*
lone [loun], *a.* isolé, solitaire; délaissé.
loneliness ['lounlinis], *n.* solitude, *f.*; isolement, *m.*
lonely ['lounli], *a.* isolé; délaissé.
long (1) [lɔŋ], *v.i.* avoir bien envie, brûler (*de*); (*impers.*) tarder (*de*).
long (2) [lɔŋ], *a.* long; étendu, prolongé, allongé; *a long time,* longtemps, depuis longtemps, pendant longtemps; *in the long run,* à la longue; *to be three feet long,* avoir trois pieds de long, être long de trois pieds.—*n. the long and the short of,* le fort et le faible de.—*adv.* long; longtemps, longuement; depuis longtemps; pendant longtemps; durant; *all night long,* tout le long de la nuit; *before long,* bientôt, avant peu, sous peu; *how long have you been here?* combien de temps y a-t-il que vous êtes ici? *long ago,* il y a longtemps, depuis longtemps; *not long after,* peu de temps après; *so long as,* tant que.
longer ['lɔŋgə], *a.* plus long.—*adv.* plus longtemps; de plus.
longing ['lɔŋiŋ], *n.* désir ardent, *m.*, envie, *f.*
longitude ['lɔndʒitjuːd], *n.* longitude, *f.*
long-sighted ['lɔŋsaitid], *a.* presbyte; (*fig.*) clairvoyant; *I am long-sighted,* j'ai la vue longue.
look [luk], *v.i.* regarder (*d'une fenêtre*); sembler, avoir l'air, paraître; donner sur (*maison etc.*); *look out!* attention! gare! *to look after,* soigner, s'occuper de; *to look away,* détourner ses regards; *to look back,* regarder en arrière; *to look down upon,* mépriser; *to look for,* chercher; *to look forward to,* attendre avec impatience; *to look in,* faire une petite visite, dire un petit bonjour à; *to look into,* examiner; *to look like,* ressembler à; *to look on,* regarder, considérer; *to look over,* jeter un coup d'œil sur, examiner.—*n.* regard, air, *m.*, apparence, mine, *f.*; coup d'œil, *m.*
looker-on ['lukərɔn], *n.* spectateur, *m.*
looking ['lukiŋ], *a.* à l'air . . . ; à la mine . . . ; *good-looking,* beau.
looking-glass ['lukiŋglɑːs], *n.* miroir, *m.*, glace, *f.*
look-out ['lukaut], *n.* guet, *m.*, vigilance, vue, *f.*; (*Mil.*) guetteur, *m.*; (*Naut.*) vigie, *f.*; *to keep a look-out,* avoir l'œil au guet.
loom [luːm], *n.* métier à tisser, *m.*—*v.i.* apparaître indistinctement, surgir.
looming ['luːmiŋ], *a.* vague, estompé.
loop [luːp], *n.* boucle; bride (*pour bouton*), *f.*; (*Av.*) looping, *m.*
loop-hole ['luːphoul], *n.* meurtrière (*pour bouton*), *f.*; (*fig.*) échappatoire, *f.*, faux-fuyant, *m.*
loose [luːs], *a.* délié, défait; branlant; (*fig.*) relâché, lâche (*mœurs*); vague; licencieux; libre; *loose cash,* menue monnaie, *f.—n. on the loose,* dissolu, dissipé.—*v.t.* délier, lâcher, (*fig.*) déchaîner.
loosely ['luːsli], *adv.* librement, négligemment; licencieusement.

loosen [luːsn], *v.t.* délier, détacher, défaire; desserrer; ébranler.—*v.i.* se délier; se défaire; se desserrer.
looseness ['luːsnis], *n.* état desserré, relâchement; caractère vague, *m.*
loot [luːt], *n.* butin; pillage, *m.*—*v.t.* piller.
looter ['luːtə], *n.* pillard, *m.*
lop [lɔp], *v.t.* élaguer, ébrancher.
lopsided ['lɔpsaidid], *a.* qui penche trop d'un côté, déjeté.
loquacious [lo'kweiʃəs], *a.* loquace.
lord [lɔːd], *n.* seigneur; (*fig.*) maître; lord (*titre anglais*); Monseigneur (*à un prince, noble, évêque etc.*), *m.*; *Our Lord,* notre Seigneur; *the Lord's Prayer,* l'oraison dominicale, *f.*; *the year of our Lord,* l'an de grâce, *m.*—*v.t. to lord it over,* dominer, faire le maître.
lordliness ['lɔːdlinis], *n.* hauteur, *f.*, orgueil, *m.*
lordling ['lɔːdliŋ], *n.* petit seigneur; hobereau, *m.*
lordly ['lɔːdli], *a.* de seigneur, noble; hautain, fier.
lore [lɔː], *n.* savoir, *m.*; science, *f.*
lorry ['lɔri], *n.* camion, *m.*
lose [luːz], *v.t. irr.* perdre; égarer; *to lose one's temper,* s'emporter; *to lose one's way,* s'égarer; *to lose sight of,* perdre de vue.—*v.i.* perdre (*de valeur*); retarder (*horloge etc.*).
loss [lɔs], *n.* perte, *f.*; (*Hunt.*) défaut, *m.*; extinction (*de voix*), *f.*; *at a loss,* dans l'embarras; *dead loss,* perte sèche.
lost [lɔst], *a.* perdu; égaré (*fourvoyé*); abîmé (*endommagé*).
lot [lɔt], *n.* sort, destin, *m.*, part; quantité, *f.*; tas (*de personnes*); lot (*à une vente*), *m.*; *a lot of,* beaucoup de; *to draw* ou *cast lots,* tirer au sort.
lotion ['louʃən], *n.* lotion, *f.*
lottery ['lɔtəri], *n.* loterie, *f.*
loud [laud], *a.* haut; fort, grand; bruyant, retentissant; tapageur (*tumultueux*); criard (*couleurs*).
loudly ['laudli], *adv.* haut, fort, à haute voix; avec grand bruit, à grands cris.
loudness ['laudnis], *n.* force, *f.*, grand bruit, éclat, *m.*
loud-speaker [laud'spiːkə], *n.* (*Rad.*) haut-parleur, *m.*
Louisa [lu'iːzə], **Louise** [lu'iːz]. Louise, *f.*
lounge [laundʒ], *v.i.* flâner; être couché *ou* étendu *ou* appuyé paresseusement (*sur*).—*n.* promenoir; sofa (*canapé*); petit salon; hall (*d'hôtel*), *m.*; *lounge jacket,* veston, *m.*; *lounge suit,* complet veston, *m.*
lounger ['laundʒə], *n.* flâneur, *m.*
lour, lower (1) ['lauə], *v.i.* froncer les sourcil ; s'assombrir, s'obscurcir (*du temps*); *the sky lours,* le temps se couvre.
louring, lowering (1) ['lauəriŋ], *a.* couvert, sombre; (*fig.*) menaçant.
louse [laus], *n.* (*pl.* **lice** [lais]) pou, *m.*
lousy ['lauzi], *a.* pouilleux; (*fig.*) bas, vil, sale.
lout [laut], *n.* rustre, butor, *m.*
loutish ['lautiʃ], *a.* rustre.
lovable ['lʌvəbl], *a.* digne d'être aimé; aimable.
love [lʌv], *n.* amour, *m.*, affection; amitié, *f.*; ami (*mot tendre*), *m.*; (*Ten.*) zéro, rien, *m.*; *my love to all,* mes

amitiés à tous; *to be in love with*, être amoureux de.

love-affair ['lʌvəfɛə], *n.* amourette, *f.*

love-letter ['lʌvletə], *n.* billet doux, *m.*

loveliness ['lʌvlinis], *n.* amabilité; beauté, *f.*, charme, *m.*

lovely ['lʌvli], *a.* charmant, ravissant, séduisant, gracieux.

lover ['lʌvə], *n.* amant, amoureux; amateur (*de*), *m.*

lovesick ['lʌvsik], *a.* en mal d'amour.

loving ['lʌviŋ], *a.* aimant, affectueux, affectionné, tendre; d'amour (*choses*); *loving kindness*, bonté, miséricorde, *f.*

low (1) [lou], *a.* bas; petit; peu élevé, vulgaire; profond (*révérence*); (*fig.*) lent (*fièvre*); abattu (*humeur*); *at low water*, à marée basse; *in a low voice*, d'une voix basse. —*adv.* bas, en bas; à voix basse; profondément (*révérence*).

low (2) [lou], *v.i.* beugler.

low-brow ['loubrau], *a.* peu intellectuel.—*n.* philistin, *m.*

lower (1) [LOUR].

lower (2) ['louə], *a.* plus bas, inférieur; bas.— *v.t.* baisser, abaisser; descendre; rabaisser humilier; diminuer, affaiblir.

lower-class ['louəklɑ:s], *n.* peuple, *m.*

lowering (1) [LOURING].

lowering (2) ['louəriŋ], *n.* abaissement, *m.*, diminution, *f.*

lowest ['louist], *a.* le plus bas, le dernier.

lowing ['louiŋ], *n.* mugissement, beuglement, *m.*

lowliness ['loulinis], *n.* humilité, *f.*

lowly ['louli], *a.* humble.—*adv.* humblement.

lowness ['lounis], *n.* situation basse, petitesse; faiblesse (*santé*); dépression (*prix*), *f.*; abaissement (*température*); abattement (*humeur*), découragement, *m.*; vulgarité, *f.*

loyal ['lɔiəl], *a.* fidèle, loyal.

loyalty ['lɔiəlti], *n.* fidélité, *f.*

lozenge ['lɔzindʒ], *n.* pastille, *f.*; (*Geom., Her. etc.*) losange, *m.*

lubber ['lʌbə], *n.* lourdaud, *m.*; *land-lubber*, marin d'eau douce, *m.*

lubricant ['lu:brikənt] *n.* lubrifiant, *m.*

lubricate ['lu:brikeit], *v.t.* lubrifier.

lubrication [lu:bri'keiʃən], *n.* lubrication, *f.*

lucid ['lu:sid], *a.* lucide; limpide, transparent.

lucidity [lu:'siditi], **lucidness** ['lu:sidnis], *n.* transparence, limpidité, lucidité, *f.*

luck [lʌk], *n.* chance, fortune, *f.*, bonheur, *m.*; *by good luck*, par bonheur; *by ill luck*, par malheur; *good luck*, bonne chance.

luckily ['lʌkili], *adv.* heureusement, par bonheur.

lucky ['lʌki], *a.* heureux; *to be lucky*, avoir de la chance; porter bonheur (*chose*).

lucrative ['lu:krətiv], *a.* lucratif.

lucre ['lu:kə], *n.* lucre, *m.*

Lucy ['lu:si], Lucie, *f.*

ludicrous ['lu:dikrəs], *a.* risible, comique, ridicule.

luggage ['lʌgidʒ], *n.* bagage, *m.*, bagages *m.pl.*; *left-luggage office*, consigne, *f.*

lugubrious [lu'gju:briəs], *a.* lugubre.

lukewarm ['lu:kwɔ:m], *a.* tiède; (*fig.*) peu zélé.

lull [lʌl], *v.t.* bercer, endormir; calmer.—*v.i.* se calmer, s'apaiser.—*n.* moment de calme, *m.*; (*Naut.*) accalmie, *f.*

lullaby ['lʌləbai], *n.* berceuse, *f.*

lumbago [lʌm'beigou], *n.* lumbago, *m.*

lumber ['lʌmbə], *n.* vieilleries, *f.pl.*; (*Am.*) bois de charpente, *m.*—*v.t.* entasser sans ordre; remplir de fatras.—*v.i.* se traîner lourdement.

lumbering ['lʌmbəriŋ], *a.* lourd, encombrant.

lumberjack ['lʌmbədʒæk], *n.* bûcheron, *m.*

luminous ['lju:minəs], *a.* lumineux.

lump [lʌmp], *n.* masse, *f.*; morceau, bloc (*piece*), *m.*—*v.t.* prendre en bloc; réunir ensemble.

lumpish ['lʌmpiʃ], *a.* gros, lourd, pesant.

lumpy ['lʌmpi], *a.* grumeleux.

lunacy ['lu:nəsi], *n.* aliénation mentale, *f.*

lunar ['lu:nə], *a.* lunaire.

lunatic ['lu:nətik], *a.* de fou, d'aliéné.—*n.* aliéné; fou, *m.*, folle, *f.*

lunatic-asylum ['lu:nətikəsailəm], *n.* asile d'aliénés, *m.*

lunch [lʌntʃ], *n.* déjeuner (*vers midi*), *m.*— *v.i.* déjeuner.

lung [lʌŋ], *n.* (*usu. in pl.*) poumon; mou (*de veau*), *m.*; *iron lung*, poumon d'acier.

lunge [lʌndʒ], *n.* (*Fenc.*) botte, *f.*, coup droit, *m.*—*v.i.* porter une botte.

lupin ['lju:pin], *n.* (*Bot.*) lupin, *m.*

lurch [lə:tʃ], *n.* embardée, *f.*, cahot; (*fig.*) embarras, *m.*; *to leave in the lurch*, planter là.—*v.i.* faire une embardée (*navire*).

lure [ljuə], *n.* leurre, appât, piège; (*fig.*) attrait, *m.*—*v.t.* leurrer, attirer, séduire.

lurid ['ljuərid], *a.* sombre, blafard; sensationnel.

lurk [lə:k], *v.i.* être aux aguets; se tenir caché.

luscious ['lʌʃəs], *a.* délicieux, savoureux; liquoreux (*vin*).

lusciousness ['lʌʃəsnis], *n.* nature succulente, douceur extrême; volupté, *f.*

lush [lʌʃ], *a.* luxuriant.

lust [lʌst], *n.* luxure, *f.*; désir lascif, *m.*; (*fig.*) convoitise, *f.*—*v.i.* désirer immodérément; *to lust after*, convoiter.

lustily ['lʌstili], *adv.* vigoureusement.

lustre ['lʌstə], *n.* brillant, lustre; (*fig.*) éclat, *m.*, splendeur, *f.*

lustrous ['lʌstrəs], *a.* brillant, lustré.

lusty ['lʌsti], *a.* vigoureux, robuste, fort.

lute [lju:t], *n.* luth, *m.*

Luxembourg ['lʌksəmbə:g]. le Luxembourg (*Duché*), *m.*

luxuriance [lʌg'zjuəriəns], *n.* exubérance, surabondance, luxuriance, *f.*

luxuriant [lʌg'zjuəriənt], *a.* exubérant, surabondant, luxuriant.

luxurious [lʌg'zjuəriəs], *a.* de luxe, somptueux, luxueux.

luxuriously [lʌg'zjuəriəsli], *adv.* avec luxe, somptueusement.

luxuriousness [lʌg'zjuəriəsnis], *n.* somptuosité, *f.*

luxury ['lʌkʃəri], *n.* luxe, *m.*, exubérance, *f.*; fin morceau; objet de luxe, *m.*

lying ['laiiŋ], *a.* menteur; mensonger (*choses*). —*n.* mensonge, *m.*

lymph [limf], *n.* lymphe, *f.*; vaccin, *m.*

lynch [lintʃ], *v.t.* lyncher (*exécuter sommairement*).

lynx [liŋks], *n.* lynx, *m.*

lyre ['laiə], *n.* lyre, *f.*
lyric ['lirik], *a.* lyrique.—*n.* poème lyrique, *m.*; (*pl.*) paroles (*d'une chanson*), *f.pl.*
lyrical ['lirikəl], *a.* lyrique.

M

M, m [em]. treizième lettre de l'alphabet, *m.*
macadam [mə'kædəm], *n.* macadam, *m.*
macaroni [mækə'rouni], *n.* macaroni, *m.*
macaroon [mækə'ru:n], *n.* macaron, *m.*
mace [meis], *n.* masse (*de cérémonie*), *f.*
mace-bearer ['meisbeərə], *n.* massier, *m.*
Macedonia [mæsə'douniə]. la Macédoine, *f.*
Macedonian [mæsə'douniən], *a.* macédonien.
—*n.* Macédonien (*personne*), *m.*
macerate ['mæsəreit], *v.t.* macérer.
machine [mə'ʃi:n], *n.* machine, *f.*; (*fig.*) instrument; appareil (*avion*), *m.*
machine-gun [mə'ʃi:ngʌn], *n.* mitrailleuse, *f.*
machinery [mə'ʃi:nəri], *n.* mécanique, *f.*, mécanisme, *m.*; machines, *f.pl.*
machine-tool [mə'ʃi:ntu:l], *n.* machine-outil, *f.*
mackerel ['mækərəl], *n.* maquereau, *m.*
mackintosh ['mækintoʃ], *n.* imperméable, *m.*
mad [mæd], *a.* fou, aliéné, insensé; affolé; furieux (*déchaîné*); enragé (*animal*).
Madagascan [mædə'gæskən], *a.* malgache.— *n.* Malgache (*personne*), *m.*, *f.*
Madagascar [mædə'gæskə]. Madagascar, *m.*
madam ['mædəm], *n.* madame, *f.*
madcap ['mædkæp], *a.* étourdi, fou.—*n.* fou, *m.*
madden [mædn], *v.t.* rendre fou; faire enrager.
maddening ['mædniŋ], *a.* à rendre fou, enrageant.
madder ['mædə], *n.* garance, *f.*
made [meid], *a.* fait, confectionné; *self-made man*, fils de ses œuvres, *m.*; *made up*, inventé (*histoire*); maquillé (*visage*).
Madeira [mə'diərə]. Madère, *f.*—*n.* madère (*vin*), *m.*
madly ['mædli], *adv.* follement, furieusement.
madman ['mædmən], *n.* (*pl.* -men [men]) aliéné, fou, *m.*
madness ['mædnis], *n.* démence, fureur, folie; rage (*d'animal*), *f.*
Madonna [mə'dɔnə]. la Madone, *f.*
maelstrom ['meilstroum, 'meilstrəm], *n.* (*Geog.*) maelstrom; (*fig.*) tourbillon, *m.*
magazine [mægə'zi:n], *n.* magasin (*boutique*; *aussi chargeur d'arme à feu*); magazine, *m.*, revue (*périodique*), *f.*
magenta [mə'dʒentə], *a. and n.* magenta (*couleur*), *m.*
maggot ['mægət], *n.* larve, *f.*, ver, asticot, *m.*
magic ['mædʒik], *a.* magique.—*n.* magie, *f.*
magical ['mædʒikəl], *a.* magique.
magician [mə'dʒiʃən], *n.* magicien, *m.*
magisterial [mædʒis'tiəriəl], *a.* de maître; magistral.
magistrate ['mædʒistreit], *n.* magistrat, *m.*; *examining magistrate*, juge d'instruc-

tion, *m.*; *police court magistrate*, juge de paix, *m.*
magnanimity [mægnə'nimiti], *n.* magnanimité, *f.*
magnanimous [mæg'næniməs], *a.* magnanime.
magnate ['mægneit], *n.* magnat; grand; (*colloq.*) gros bonnet, *m.*
magnesia [mæg'ni:ʃə], *n.* magnésie, *f.*
magnesium [mæg'ni:ziəm], *n.* magnésium, *m.*
magnet ['mægnit], *n.* aimant, *m.*
magnetic [mæg'netik], *a.* aimanté; magnétique; (*fig.*) attirant.
magnetism ['mægnitizm], *n.* magntéisme, *m.*; (*Elec.*) aimantation, *f.*
magnetize ['mægnitaiz], *v.t.* aimanter; (*fig.*) magnétiser.
magneto [mæg'ni:tou], *n.* magnéto, *f.*
magnificence [mæg'nifisəns], *n.* magnificence, *f.*
magnificent [mæg'nifisənt], *a.* magnifique, superbe.
magnify ['mægnifai], *v.t.* magnifier, augmenter, grossir; (*fig.*) exalter.
magnifying ['mægnifaiiŋ], *a.* qui grossit; *magnifying-glass*, loupe, *f.*
magnitude ['mægnitju:d], *n.* grandeur, importance, *f.*
magnolia [mæg'nouliə], *n.* (*Bot.*) magnolia, magnolier, *m.*
magpie ['mægpai], *n.* pie, *f.*
mahogany [mə'hɔgəni], *n.* acajou, bois d'acajou, *m.*
maid [meid], *n.* fille, jeune fille; vierge (*virgin*); bonne, servante, domestique, *f.*; *chambermaid*, fille de chambre; *kitchen-maid*, fille de cuisine; *maid of all work*, bonne à tout faire; *maid of honour*, demoiselle d'honneur, *f.*
maiden [meidn], *a.* de fille, de jeune fille; virginal; (*fig.*) pur, neuf; *maiden aunt*, tante non mariée, *f.*; *maiden name*, nom de jeune fille, *m.*; *maiden speech*, premier discours (*d'un nouveau membre du Parlement*), *m.*; *maiden voyage*, premier voyage, *m.*—*n.* jeune fille, fille, *f.*
maidenly ['meidnli], *a.* de jeune fille; modeste, chaste.
mail (1) [meil], *n.* mailles (*armure*), *f.pl.*
mail (2) [meil], *n.* courrier, *m.*, dépêches (*lettres*), *f.pl.*—*v.t.* (*Am.*) mettre à la poste.
mail-bag ['meilbæg], *n.* sac postal, *m.*
mail-train ['meiltrein], *n.* train-postal, *m.*
maim [meim], *v.t.* mutiler, estropier.
main (1) [mein], *a.* principal, premier; grand; important, essentiel.—*n.* gros, *m.*, plus grande partie, *f.*; principal océan, *m.*; *in the main*, pour la plupart, en général.
main (2) [mein], *n.* force, *f.*
main-deck ['meindek], *n.* premier pont, *m.*
mainland ['meinlənd], *n.* continent, *m.*
mainly ['meinli], *adv.* principalement, surtout.
mainmast ['meinmɑ:st], *n.* grand mât, *m.*
mainstay ['meinstei], *n.* soutien, *m.*
maintain [men'tein], *v.t.* maintenir; soutenir, alléguer; conserver; entretenir, nourrir (*subvenir aux besoins de*).
maintenance ['meintənəns], *n.* maintien, soutien; entretien, *m.*
maize [meiz], *n.* maïs, *m.*

manganese

majestic [mə'dʒestik], *a.* majestueux.
majesty ['mædʒəsti], *n.* majesté, *f.*; **His** or **Her Majesty**, Sa Majesté.
major ['meidʒə], *a.* plus grand, majeur.—*n.* commandant, *m.*; (*Law*) personne majeure, *f.*; **drum-major**, tambour-major, *m.*; **sergeant-major**, adjudant, *m.*
Majorca [mə'jɔːkə]. Majorque, *f.*
majority [mə'dʒɔriti], *n.* majorité, *f.*
make [meik], *v.t. irr.* faire; créer, façonner, fabriquer, confectionner; rendre (*faire devenir*); forcer, contraindre (*obliger*); amasser, gagner (*argent*); **to make a mistake**, se tromper; **to make a noise**, faire du bruit; **to make believe**, faire accroire à; **to make fun of**, se moquer de; **to make good**, soutenir; réparer/dédommager de; **to make it up**, se raccommoder; **to make known**, faire connaître, faire savoir à; **to make out**, comprendre, déchiffrer, distinguer; **to make over to**, céder à; **to make sure of**, s'assurer de; **to make up**, compléter, inventer (*histoire*); arranger (*querelle*); régler (*comptes*); **to make up for**, suppléer à; rattraper (*temps*); **to make up one's mind**, se décider.—*v.i.* se diriger (*vers*); contribuer (*à*); faire (*comme si*); **to make believe**, faire semblant; **to make of**, comprendre; **to make off**, se sauver; **to make up**, se maquiller; **to make up for**, suppléer à; dédommager de, compenser.—*n.* façon, forme, tournure; fabrication, *f.*
make-believe ['meikbiliːv], *n.* feinte, *f.*, semblant, *m.*
maker ['meikə], *n.* créateur, auteur; faiseur; (*Comm.*) fabricant, *m.*
makeshift ['meikʃift], *n.* pis aller, expédient, *m.*
make-up ['meikʌp], *n.* contexture, *f.*; maquillage (*du visage*), *m.*
make-weight ['meikweit], *n.* supplément; (*fig.*) remplissage, *m.*
making ['meikiŋ], *n.* création; façon, fabrication, construction; confection (*de vêtements*), *f.*
maladjusted [mælə'dʒʌstid], *a.* inadapté.
maladjustment [mælə'dʒʌstmənt], *n.* inadaptation, *f.*
maladministration [mælədminis'treiʃən], *n.* mauvaise administration, *f.*
malady ['mælədi], *n.* maladie, *f.*
malaria [mə'lɛəriə], *n.* malaria, *f.*, paludisme, *m.*
Malay [mə'lei], *a.* malais.—*n.* malais (*langue*); Malais (*personne*), *m.*
Malaysia [mə'leiziə]. la Malaisie, *f.*
Malaysian [mə'leiziən], *a.* malais.—*n.* Malais (*personne*), *m.*
malcontent ['mælkəntent], *a.* and *n.* mécontent, *m.*
male [meil], *a.* mâle; masculin.—*n.* mâle, *m.*
malediction [mæli'dikʃən], *n.* malédiction, *f.*
malefactor ['mælifæktə], *n.* malfaiteur, *m.*
malevolence [mə'levələns], *n.* malveillance, *f.*
malevolent [mə'levələnt], *a.* malveillant.
Mali ['mɑːli]. le Mali, *m.*
malice ['mælis], *n.* malice; malveillance, méchanceté; rancune, *f.*; **to bear malice**, vouloir du mal à, garder rancune à.
malicious [mə'liʃəs], *a.* malicieux, méchant.
maliciously [mə'liʃəsli], *adv.* méchamment.

maliciousness [mə'liʃəsnis], *n.* malice, malveillance, *f.*
malign [mə'lain], *a.* malin; méchant.—*v.t.* diffamer, noircir.
malignant [mə'lignənt], *a.* malin, méchant.
malignantly [mə'lignəntli], *adv.* malignement, méchamment.
malignity [mə'ligniti], *n.* malignité, malveillance, *f.*
malinger [mə'liŋgə], *v.i.* (*Mil.*) faire le malade; tirer au flanc.
mall (1) [mɔːl], *n.* gros maillet, *m.*
mall (2) [mæl], *n.* mail (*rue*), *m.*
mallard ['mæləd], *n.* (*Orn.*) canard sauvage, *m.*
malleability [mæliə'biliti], *n.* malléabilité, *f.*
malleable ['mæliəbl], *a.* malléable.
mallet ['mælit], *n.* maillet, *m.*; tapette, *f.*
mallow ['mæloul], *n.* (*Bot.*) mauve, *f.*
malmsey ['mɑːmzi], *n.* malvoisie, *f.*
malnutrition [mælnju'triʃən], *n.* sous-alimentation, *f.*
malpractice [mæl'præktis], *n.* malversation *f.*, méfait, *m.*
malt [mɔːlt], *n.* malt, *m.*—*v.t.* malter.
Malta ['mɔːltə]. Malte, *f.*
Maltese [mɔːl'tiːz], *a.* maltais.—*n.* Maltais (*personne*), *m.*
maltreat [mæl'triːt], *v.t.* maltraiter.
maltreatment [mæl'triːtmənt], *n.* mauvais traitement, *m.*
mammal ['mæməl], *n.* mammifère, *m.*
mammoth ['mæməθ], *n.* mammouth, *m.*
man [mæn], *n.* (*pl.* **men** [men]) homme; domestique, valet (*servant*), *m.*; (*Chess*) pièce, *f.*; (*Draughts*) pion, *m.*; **the man in the street**, l'homme de la rue, le grand public; **well, my man!** eh bien! mon brave!—*v.t.* garnir d'hommes; armer (*pompe, bateau*).
manacle ['mænəkl], *v.t.* mettre les menottes à.—*n.* (*pl.*) menottes, *f.pl.*
manage ['mænidʒ], *v.t.* diriger, mener, conduire; arranger (*choses*); gouverner, administrer, gérer; ménager (*habilement*); manier, dompter (*cheval*).—*v.i.* s'arranger (*pour*), parvenir à; venir à bout (*de*).
manageable ['mænidʒəbl], *a.* traitable, maniable.
management ['mænidʒmənt], *n.* conduite, administration; (*Comm.*) gestion (*direction*), *f.*; artifice, savoir-faire (*manège*), *m.*
manager ['mænidʒə], *n.* directeur, administrateur; (*Comm.*) gérant; (*Theat.*) régisseur; (*Spt.*) manager, *m.*
manageress [mænidʒə'res], *n.* directrice, gérante, *f.*
Manchuria [mæn'tʃuəriə]. la Mandchourie, *f.*
Manchu(rian) [mæn'tʃu(əriən)], *a.* mandchou.—*n.* mandchou (*langue*); Mandchou (*personne*), *m.*
mandarin ['mændərin], *n.* mandarin, *m.*; mandarine (*orange*), *f.*
mandate ['mændeit], *n.* commandement, mandat; ordre, *m.*
mandatory ['mændətəri], *a.* and *n.* mandataire, *m.*
mandolin ['mændəlin], *n.* mandoline, *f.*
mane [mein], *n.* crinière, *f.*
manfully ['mænfuli], *adv.* en homme, virilement, vaillamment.
manganese ['mæŋgəniːz], *n.* manganèse, *m.*

mange

mange [meindʒ], *n.* gale (*d'animaux*), *f.*

manger ['meindʒə], *n.* mangeoire, crèche, *f.*

mangle [mæŋgl], *v.t.* déchirer, mutiler; calandrer (*linge*).—*n.* calandre, *f.*

mango ['mæŋgou], *n.* (*Bot.*) mangue, *f.*; manguier (*arbre*), *m.*

mangrove ['mæŋgrouv], *n.* (*Bot.*) mangle, *f.*; manglier, manguier (*arbre*), *m.*

mangy ['meindʒi], *a.* galeux.

man-handle ['mænhændl], *v.t.* manutentionner; (*fig.*) maltraiter.

man-hole ['mænhoul], *n.* bouche d'égout, *f.*

manhood ['mænhud], *n.* virilité, *f.*; âge viril, *m.*; nature humaine, *f.*

mania ['meiniə], *n.* folie, rage, manie, *f.*

maniac ['meiniæk], *a.* furieux, fou.—*n.* fou furieux, fou, *m.*; (*fig.*) maniaque, *m.*, *f.*

maniacal [mə'naiəkl], *a.* furieux, fou.

manicure ['mænikjuə], *n.* soin des ongles, *m.*—*v.t.* soigner les ongles.

manicurist ['mænikjuərist], *n.* manucure, *m.*, *f.*

manifest ['mænifest], *v.t.* manifester, témoigner, montrer; *to manifest a cargo*, déclarer une cargaison.—*a.* manifeste, évident.—*n.* manifeste, *m.*

manifestation [mænifes'teiʃən], *n.* manifestation, *f.*

manifesto [mæni'festou], *n.* manifeste, *m.*

manifold ['mænifould], *a.* divers, multiple; varié.

manikin ['mænikin], *n.* bout d'homme, mannequin, homuncule, *m.*

Manila [mə'nilə], Manille, *f.*

manipulate [mə'nipjuleit], *v.t.* manipuler.

mankind [mæn'kaind], *n.* genre humain, *m.*, l'humanité, *f.*

manlike ['mænlaik], *a.* d'homme, viril; mâle; hommasse (*femme*).

manliness ['mænlinis], *n.* caractère viril, *m.*

manly ['mænli], *a.* d'homme, viril, mâle.

manna ['mænə], *n.* manne, *f.*

mannequin ['mænikin], *n.* (*Dress.*) mannequin, *m.*; *mannequin parade*, défilé de mannequins, *m.*

manner ['mænə], *n.* manière, *f.*, air; genre, *m.*, sorte, façon, espèce; coutume, habitude, *f.*; (*pl.*) mœurs, *f.pl.*, politesse, *f.*; *after the manner of*, à la manière de, d'après; *all manner of things*, toutes sortes de choses, *f.pl.*; *in the same manner as*, de même que.

mannerism ['mænərizm], *n.* air maniéré, maniérisme; tic, *m.*

mannerly ['mænəli], *a.* poli.

manning ['mæniŋ], *n.* armement, équipement, *m.*

mannish ['mæniʃ], *a.* hommasse.

manœuvre [mə'nuːvə], *n.* manœuvre, *f.*—*v.t.*, *v.i.* manœuvrer.

manor ['mænə], *n.* seigneurie, *f.*; manoir, château seigneurial, *m.*

manorial [mə'nɔːriəl], *a.* seigneurial.

man-power ['mænpauə], *n.* main d'œuvre, *f.*

manse [mæns], *n.* presbytère, *m.*

mansion ['mænʃən], *n.* château *m.* (*à la campagne*); hôtel particulier (*en ville*), *m.*

manslaughter ['mænslɔːtə], *n.* (*Law*) homicide involontaire, *m.*

mantel [mæntl], **mantelpiece** ['mæntlpiːs], *n.* manteau *ou* dessus de cheminée, *m.*, cheminée, *f.*

mantilla [mæn'tilə], *n.* mantille, *f.*

mantis ['mæntis], *n.* (*Ent.*) mante, *f.*; *praying mantis*, mante religieuse.

mantle [mæntl], *n.* manteau, *m.*—*v.t.* couvrir, voiler.

manual ['mænjuəl], *a.* manuel, de la main.—*n.* manuel (*livre*); (*Organ*) clavier, *m.*

manufacture [mænju'fæktʃə], *n.* manufacture, confection, fabrication, *f.*; (*pl.*) produits manufacturés, *m.pl.*—*v.t.* manufacturer, fabriquer.

manufacturer [mænju'fæktʃərə], *n.* fabricant, industriel, *m.*

manure [mə'njuə], *n.* engrais, fumier, *m.*—*v.t.* engraisser, fumer.

manuscript ['mænjuskript], *a.* and *n.* manuscrit, *m.*

Manx [mæŋks], *a.* de l'île de Man, mannois; *Manx cat*, chat sans queue, *m.*

many ['meni], *a.* beaucoup (*de*), bien (*des*); nombreux; plusieurs, maint; *as many as*, autant que, jusqu'à (*devant un numéro*); *how many?* combien? *many a time*, maintes fois; *so many*, tant, tant de; *too many*, trop, trop de.—*n.* *the many*, la multitude, la foule, *f.*

many-coloured ['menikʌləd], *a.* multicolore.

many-sided ['menisaidid], *a.* polygone; (*fig.*) complexe.

map [mæp], *n.* carte, carte géographique, *f.*; *map of a town*, plan d'une ville, *m.*; *map of the world*, mappemonde, *f.*—*v.t.* faire une carte *ou* un plan de, tracer.

maple [meipl], *n.* érable, *m.*

mar [mɑː], *v.t.* gâter, défigurer; (*fig.*) troubler.

marathon ['mærəθən], *n.* marathon, *m.*

marauder [mə'rɔːdə], *n.* maraudeur, malandrin, *m.*

marauding [mə'rɔːdiŋ], *n.* maraude, *f.* maraudage, *m.*

marble [mɑːbl], *a.* de marbre.—*n.* marbre, *m.*; bille (*jouet*), *f.*

marbled [mɑːbld], *a.* marbré.

marbling ['mɑːbliŋ], *n.* marbrure, *f.*

March [mɑːtʃ], *n.* mars (*mois*), *m.*

march (1) [mɑːtʃ], *n.* (*Mil.*) marche, *f.*; (*fig.*) progrès, *m.*; *march past*, défilé, *m.*—*v.t.* mettre en marche; emmener.—*v.i.* marcher, se mettre en marche; (*fig.*) avancer; *to march past*, défiler devant.

march (2) [mɑːtʃ], *n.* frontière, *f.*

marching ['mɑːtʃiŋ], *a.* de marche.—*n.* marche, *f.*

marchioness [mɑːʃə'nes], *n.* marquise, *f.*

mare [mɛə], *n.* jument, *f.*

Margaret ['mɑːgərit], Marguerite, *f.*

margarine ['mɑːgəriːn, 'mɑːdʒəriːn], *n.* margarine, *f.*

margin ['mɑːdʒin], *n.* marge (*de papier etc.*), *f.*; bord (*de rivière, de lac*), *m.*—*v.t.* border.

marginal ['mɑːdʒinəl], *a.* en marge; marginal.

marigold ['mærigould], *n.* (*Bot.*) souci, *m.*

marine [mə'riːn], *a.* marin, de mer; naval.—*n.* fusilier marin, *m.*; *tell that to the marines*, allez conter cela à d'autres.

mariner ['mærinə], *n.* marin, *m.*

maritime ['mæritaim], *a.* maritime, *f.*

Mark [mɑːk], Marc, *m.*

mark (1) [mɑːk], *n.* marque, *f.*, signe, *m.*; em-

480

preinte; (*fig.*) distinction, importance, *f.*; témoignage (*d'estime*), *m.*; (*Sch.*) note, *f.*, point, *m.*; cible (*but*); croix (*signature*), *f.* —*v.t.* marquer, remarquer; (*Sch.*) noter; (*fig.*) observer, faire attention à.

mark (2) [maːk], *n.* marc (*pièce de monnaie*), *m.*

marked [maːkt], *a.* marqué, évident; prononcé (*accent*).

marker ['maːkə], *n.* marqueur; jeton (*au jeu*); signet (*de livre*), *m.*

market ['maːkit], *n.* marché, *m.*; halle, *f.*; débit (*vente*); cours (*prix*); (*Comm.*) débouché, *m.*—*v.t.* acheter au marché; vendre au marché.

market-garden ['maːkit'gaːdn], *n.* jardin maraîcher, *m.*

market-gardener ['maːkit'gaːdnə], *n.* maraîcher, *m.*

marking ['maːkiŋ], *n.* marquage, *m.*

marking-ink ['maːkiŋiŋk], *n.* encre à marquer, *f.*

marksman ['maːksmən], *n.* (*pl.* **-men** [men]) bon tireur, *m.*

marksmanship ['maːksmənʃip], *n.* adresse au tir, *f.*

marl [maːl], *n.* marne, *f.*—*v.t.* marner.

marline-spike ['maːlinspaik], *n.* épissoir, *m.*

marmalade ['maːməleid], *n.* confiture d'oranges, *f.*

marmoset ['maːməzet], *n.* ouistiti, *m.*

marmot ['maːmət], *n.* marmotte, *f.*

maroon (1) [mə'ruːn], *n.* nègre marron, *m.*—*v.t.* abandonner dans une île déserte.

maroon (2) [mə'ruːn], *a.* and *n.* marron pourpré (*couleur*), *m.*

marquee [maː'kiː], *n.* grande tente, *f.*

marquess, marquis ['maːkwis], *n.* marquis, *m.*

marquetry ['maːkətri], *n.* marqueterie, *f.*

marquis [MARQUESS].

marriage ['mæridʒ], *n.* mariage, *m.*; noces (*fêtes*), *f.pl.*

marriageable ['mæridʒəbl], *a.* mariable, nubile.

married ['mærid], *a.* marié; conjugal.

marrow ['mærou], *n.* moelle; (*fig.*) essence, *f.*; *vegetable marrow*, courgette, *f.*

marry ['mæri], *v.t.* marier (*donner* ou *unir en mariage*); se marier avec, épouser (*prendre pour époux*).—*v.i.* se marier.

Marseilles [maː'seilz]. Marseille, *f.*

marsh [maːʃ], *n.* marais, *m.*

marshal ['maːʃl], *n.* maréchal.—*v.t.* ranger; mettre en ordre; classer.

marsh-mallow ['maːʃ'mælou], *n.* (*Bot.*) guimauve, *f.*; bonbon à la guimauve, *m.*

marshy ['maːʃi], *a.* marécageux.

mart [maːt], *n.* marché, entrepôt, *m.*

marten [maːtn], *n.* martre, *f.*; *beech marten*, fouine, *f.*

Martha ['maːθə]. Marthe, *f.*

martial ['maːʃl], *a.* martial; de guerre, de bataille; guerrier, belliqueux.

martin ['maːtin], *n.* martin, martinet, *m.*

martinet [maːti'net], *n.* officier strict sur la discipline, *m.*

Martinmas ['maːtinmæs]. la Saint-Martin, *f.*

martyr ['maːtə], *n.* martyr, *m.*—*v.t.* martyriser.

martyrdom ['maːtədəm], *n.* martyre, *m.*

martyrize ['maːtəraiz], *v.t.* (*fam.*) faire souffrir, martyriser.

marvel [maːvl], *n.* merveille, *f.*—*v.i.* s'émerveiller, s'étonner.

marvellous ['maːv(i)ləs], *a.* merveilleux, étonnant.

marvellously ['maːv(i)ləsli], *adv.* à merveille.

Marxism ['maːksizm], *n.* Marxisme, *m.*

Marxist ['maːksist], *a.* marxiste.—*n.* Marxiste, *m., f.*

Mary ['mɛəri]. Marie, *f.*

marzipan [maːzi'pæn], *n.* massepain, *m.*

mascot ['mæskət], *n.* mascotte, *f.*

masculine ['mæskjulin], *a.* mâle, d'homme; (*Gram.*) masculin; hommasse (*femme*).—*n.* masculin, *m.*

mash [mæʃ], *n.* mélange, *m.*, pâte, bouillie; mâche (*pour bestiaux*); pâtée (*pour chien, volaille*), *f.*—*v.t.* broyer; mélanger; (*Brewing*) brasser; *mashed potatoes*, purée de pommes de terre, *f.*

mask [maːsk], *n.* masque; loup (*de soie, de velours*), *m.*—*v.t.* masquer; déguiser.—*v.i.* se masquer.

mason [meisn], *n.* maçon, *m.*; *freemason*, franc-maçon, *m.*

masonic [mə'sɔnik], *a.* maçonnique.

masonry ['meisənri], *n.* maçonnerie, *f.*; *freemasonry*, franc-maçonnerie, *f.*

masquerade [mæskə'reid], *n.* mascarade *f.* —*v.i.* se masquer; *to masquerade as*, se faire passer pour.

mass (1) [mæs], *n.* masse, *f.*; amas, gros, *m.*; multitude, foule (*de gens*), *f.*—*v.i.* se masser; s'amonceler (*nuages*).

mass (2) [mæs, maːs], *n.* (*R.-C. Ch.*) messe, *f.*

massacre ['mæsəkə], *n.* massacre, *m.*—*v.t.* massacrer.

massive ['mæsiv], *a.* massif.

mass-meeting ['mæs'miːtiŋ], *n.* assemblée en masse, *f.*, grand meeting, *m.*

mast [maːst], *n.* mât, *m.*; (*pl.*) mâts, *m.pl.*, mâture, *f.*; *half-mast*, à mi-mât, en berne.

master ['maːstə], *n.* maître, directeur, chef; (*Naut.*) patron, maître (*d'un navire*); patron (*d'ouvriers*); (*Sch. etc.*) maître d'école, professeur; (*fig.*) possesseur, *m.*—*v.t.* maîtriser, surmonter, dompter, vaincre; se rendre maître de; l'emporter sur.

masterful ['maːstəful], *a.* de maître, impérieux, dominateur.

master-key ['maːstəkiː], *n.* passe-partout, *m.*

masterly ['maːstəli], *a.* de maître; magistral.

master-mind ['maːstəmaind], *n.* esprit supérieur, *m.*

masterpiece ['maːstəpiːs], *n.* chef-d'œuvre, *m.*

master-stroke ['maːstəstrouk], **master-touch** ['maːstətʌtʃ], *n.* coup de maître, *m.*

mastery ['maːstəri], *n.* empire, pouvoir, *m.*; supériorité, maîtrise, *f.*

masticate ['mæstikeit], *v.t.* mâcher.

mastication [mæsti'keiʃən], *n.* mastication, *f.*

mastiff ['mæstif], *n.* mâtin, *m.*

mastitis [mæs'taitis], *n.* mastite, *f.*

mastodon ['mæstədon], *n.* mastodonte, *m.*

mastoid ['mæstɔid], *a.* mastoïde.

mat [mæt], *n.* natte, *f.*; dessous de lampe, *m.*; *door-mat*, paillasson, *m.*; *table-mat*, dessous de plat, *m.*—*v.t.* natter, tresser.

match (1) [mætʃ], *n.* pareil, pendant, égal (*semblable*); mariage; parti (*futur époux*), *m.*; lutte (*concours*), *f.*; (*Spt.*) match, *m.*, partie; course, *f.*; **to be a bad match**, aller mal ensemble (*choses*); **to be more than a match for**, être trop fort pour; **to make a good match**, faire un bon mariage.—*v.t.* assortir, appareiller, égaler, apparier (*deux choses*); se mesurer avec (*opposer*).—*v.i.* s'assortir, être pareil.

match (2) [mætʃ], *n.* allumette, *f.*

match-box ['mætʃbɔks], *n.* boîte d'allumettes *ou* à allumettes, *f.*

matchless ['mætʃlis], *a.* incomparable, sans pareil.

match-maker (1) ['mætʃmeikə], *n.* marieur, *m.*

match-maker (2) ['mætʃmeikə], *n.* fabricant d'allumettes, *m.*

mate (1) [meit], *n.* camarade, compagnon, *m.*, compagne, *f.*; second (*de marine marchande*), *m.*—*v.t.* égaler, assortir, apparier; tenir compagnie avec; accoupler (*oiseaux*).—*v.i.* s'accoupler (*animaux*).

mate (2) [meit], *n.* (*Chess*) mat, *m.*—*v.t.* mater.

material [mə'tiəriəl], *a.* matériel; important. —*n.* matière; étoffe, *f.*, tissu (*textile*); matériel (*réserves*), *m.*; (*pl.*) matériaux, *m.pl.*; **raw material**, matière première.

materialism [mə'tiəriəlizm], *n.* matérialisme, *m.*

materialist [mə'tiəriəlist], *n.* matérialiste, *m.*, *f.*

materialistic [mətiəriə'listik], *a.* matérialiste.

materialize [mə'tiəriəlaiz], *v.t.* matérialiser. —*v.i.* se réaliser; se concrétiser.

materially [mə'tiəriəli], *adv.* matériellement; essentiellement.

maternal [mə'tə:nl], *a.* maternel.

maternity [mə'tə:niti], *n.* maternité, *f.*

mathematics [mæθə'mætiks], *n.pl.* mathématiques, *f.pl.*

Matilda [mə'tildə]. Mathilde, *f.*

matins ['mætinz], *n.pl.* matines, *f.pl.*

matriarch ['meitria:k], *n.* matriarche, *f.*

matricide ['mætrisaid], *n.* matricide (*crime*), *m.*; matricide (*criminel*), *m.*, *f.*

matrimonial [mætri'mouniəl], *a.* conjugal.

matrimony ['mætriməni], *n.* mariage, *m.*, vie conjugale, *f.*

matron ['meitrən], *n.* matrone, mère de famille; infirmière en chef, *f.*

matronly ['meitrənli], *a.* de matrone; d'un certain âge; respectable.

matt [mæt], *a.* mat.

matter ['mætə], *n.* matière; chose, affaire, *f.*; fond; sujet; (*Med.*) pus, *m.*; (*fig.*) importance, *f.*; **as a matter of fact**, le fait est que; **what is the matter?** Nothing, qu'y a-t-il? Il n'y a rien; **what is the matter with you?** Nothing, qu'avez-vous? Je n'ai rien.—*v.imp.* importer; **it doesn't matter**, n'importe; **it doesn't matter very much**, ce n'est pas grand'chose; **it matters little**, peu importe; **what matter?** qu'importe?

matter-of-fact ['mætərəvfækt], *a.* pratique, positif.

Matthew ['mæθju]. Mathieu, *m.*

mattock ['mætək], *n.* pioche, *f.*

mattress ['mætris], *n.* matelas, *m.*

mature [mə'tjuə], *a.* mûr, mûri.—*v.t.* mûrir, faire mûrir.—*v.i.* mûrir; (*Comm.*) échoir.

maturity [mə'tjuəriti], *n.* maturité; (*Comm.*) échéance, *f.*

matutinal [mætju'tainl], *a.* matutinal, du matin.

Maud [mɔ:d]. Madelon, *f.*

maudlin ['mɔ:dlin], *a.* pleurard, pleur-nichard.

maul [mɔ:l], *n.* maillet, *m.*—*v.t.* rosser, rouer de coups.

maul-stick ['mɔ:lstik], *n.* (*Paint.*) appui-main, *m.*

Mauritania [mɔri'teiniə]. la Mauritanie, *f.*

Mauritanian [mɔri'teiniən], *a.* mauritanien. —*n.* Mauritanien (*personne*), *m.*

Mauritian [mɔ'riʃən], *a.* mauritien.—*n.* Mauritien (*personne*), *m.*

Mauritius [mɔ'riʃəs]. l'Île Maurice, *f.*

mausoleum [mɔ:sə'li:əm], *n.* mausolée, *m.*

mauve [mouv], *a.* mauve.

maw [mɔ:], *n.* jabot (*d'oiseau*), *m.*; caillette (*de ruminant*), *f.*

mawkish ['mɔ:kiʃ], *a.* fade, insipide; sotte-ment sentimental.

maxim ['mæksim], *n.* maxime, *f.*

maximum ['mæksiməm], *n.* (*pl.* **maxima** ['mæksimə]) maximum, *m.*

May [mei]. mai (*mois*), *m.*

may [mei], *v.aux. irr.* pouvoir, être autorisé à; **he may go**, il peut sortir; **it may be that**, il se peut que (*with subj.*); **it might be**, cela se pourrait; **maybe**, peut-être; **may I?** puis-je? **one might as well**, autant vaudrait; **that may be**, cela se peut; **that might be**, cela pourrait être; **you might have gone there**, vous auriez pu y aller.

may-blossom ['meiblɔsəm], *n.* aubépine, *f.*

May-day ['meidei], *n.* premier mai, *m.*

mayor [mɛə], *n.* maire, *m.*

maze [meiz], *n.* labyrinthe, dédale; (*fig.*) embarras, *m.*

mazy ['meizi], *a.* sinueux; (*fig.*) compliqué.

mazurka [mə'zə:kə], *n.* mazurka, *f.*

me [mi:], *pron.* me, moi.

mead [mi:d], *n.* hydromel; (*poet.*) pré (*champ*), *m.*

meadow ['medou], *n.* pré, *m.*, prairie, *f.*

meagre ['mi:gə], *a.* maigre; pauvre.

meagreness ['mi:gənis], *n.* maigreur; pau-vreté, *f.*

meal (1) [mi:l], *n.* repas, *m.*

meal (2) [mi:l], *n.* farine, *f.*

mealy ['mi:li], *a.* farineux, poudreux.

mealy-mouthed ['mi:limauθd], *a.* doucereux.

mean (1) [mi:n], *a.* bas, méprisable, vil, abject; médiocre (*de peu de valeur*); mes-quin; pauvre, humble; sordide; avare; **a mean trick**, un vilain tour.

mean (2) [mi:n], *a.* moyen.—*n.* milieu, moyen terme, *m.*; (*Math.*) moyenne, *f.*; **golden mean**, le juste milieu.

mean (3) [mi:n], *v.t. irr.* signifier, vouloir dire, entendre; se proposer de, avoir l'inten-tion de, vouloir (*to intend*); destiner (*pour ou de*); **do you mean it?** êtes-vous sérieux? **what does that word mean?** que veut dire ce mot? **what do you mean?** que voulez-vous dire?—*v.i.* vouloir, entendre; **to mean well**, avoir de bonnes intentions.

melt

meander [mi'ændə], n. détour, méandre, m.,
sinuosité, f.—v.i. serpenter.
meandering [mi'ændəriŋ], a. onduleux,
sinueux, tortueux.
meaning ['mi:niŋ], a. significatif; à intentions; well-meaning, bien intentionné.—
n. signification, f., sens, m.; intention, f.,
dessein, m.; pensée (idée), f.; double
meaning, double sens.
meaningless ['mi:niŋlis], a. qui n'a pas de
sens, dénué de sens.
meanly ['mi:nli], adv. bassement; vilement,
abjectement; pauvrement; médiocrement.
meanness ['mi:nnis], n. bassesse; pauvreté,
mesquinerie; médiocrité, f.
means [mi:nz], n. moyen, m., voie, f.; moyens,
m.pl., fortune, f., ressources, f.pl.
meantime ['mi:ntaim], meanwhile ['mi:n
wail], n. and adv. in the meantime, dans
l'intervalle, en attendant, cependant, sur ces
entrefaites.
measles [mi:zlz], n.pl. rougeole, f.; German
measles, rubéole, f.
measurable ['meʒərəbl], a. mesurable.
measure ['meʒə], n. mesure; (fig.) capacité,
portée, f.; (Parl.) projet de loi, m.; assise (de
charbon), f.—v.t. mesurer; arpenter (terre);
prendre mesure à (une personne pour vêtements); (fig.) considérer, toiser, métrer; this
measures ten feet, ceci a dix pieds de
longueur.
measured ['meʒəd], a. mesuré; égal, cadencé.
measurement ['meʒəmənt], n. mesurage;
arpentage (de terre), m.; mesure, dimension,
f.
meat [mi:t], n. viande; nourriture, f., aliment
(manger), m.
meat-safe ['mi:tseif], n. garde-manger, m.
meaty ['mi:ti], a. charnu; (fig.) bien rempli.
Mecca ['mekə]. la Mecque, f.
mechanic [mi'kænik], n. artisan, ouvrier
mécanicien, m.; garage mechanic,
garagiste, m.
mechanical [mi'kænikəl], a. mécanique;
d'ouvrier; machinal (fait sans intelligence).
mechanically [mi'kænikli], adv. mécaniquement; machinalement (sans intelligence).
mechanics [mi'kæniks], n.pl. mécanique, f.
mechanism ['mekənizm], n. mécanisme, m.
mechanization [mekənai'zeiʃən], n. mécanisation, f.
mechanize ['mekənaiz], v.t. mécaniser;
mechanized farming, motoculture, f.;
mechanized army, armée motorisée, f.
medal [medl], n. médaille, f.
medallion [mi'dæljən], n. médaillon, m.
medallist ['medlist], n. médaillé (honoré), m.
meddle [medl], v.i. se mêler (de), toucher (à),
s'immiscer (dans).
meddler ['medlə], n. intrigant; officieux, m.
meddlesome ['medlsəm], meddling
['medliŋ], a. intrigant; officieux.
mediaeval [medi'i:vəl], a. du moyen âge.
medial ['mi:diəl], a. moyen; (Gram.) médial.
mediate ['mi:dieit], v.i. s'entremettre; s'interposer (dans).
mediation [mi:di'eiʃən], n. médiation, entremise, f.
mediator ['mi:dieitə], n. médiateur, m.
medical ['medikəl], a. médical; de médecine
(école); en médecine (étudiant); medical

officer, officier sanitaire, m.; to take
medical advice, consulter un médecin.
medicament [me'dikəmənt], n. médicament,
m.
medicinal [mə'disinl], a. médicinal.
medicine ['medsin], n. médecine, f., médicament; (fig.) remède, m.
medicine-chest ['medsintʃest], n. pharmacie, f.
medicine-man ['medsinmæn], n. sorcier, m.
mediocre ['mi:dioukə], a. médiocre.
mediocrity [mi:di'ɔkriti], n. médiocrité, f.
meditate ['mediteit], v.t. se proposer de,
projeter.—v.i. méditer (sur.).
meditation [medi'teiʃən], n. méditation, f.
Mediterranean [meditə'reiniən], a. méditerrané; méditerranéen.—n. la Méditerranée, f.
medium ['mi:djəm], a. moyen.—n. (pl.
media ['mi:diə], mediums ['mi:djəmz])
milieu, moyen, m.; voie, entremise; (Math.)
moyenne proportionnelle, f.; agent intermédiaire; (Spiritualism) médium, m.
medlar ['medlə], n. nèfle (fruit), f.; néflier
(arbre), m.
medley ['medli], a. mêlé, hétéroclite.—n.
mélange, m.; confusion, f.; (Mus.) pot
pourri, m.
medulla [mi'dʌlə], n. médulle, moelle, f.
meed [mi:d], n. récompense; part (portion), f.
meek [mi:k], a. doux, humble, soumis.
meekly ['mi:kli], adv. avec douceur; humblement.
meekness ['mi:knis], n. douceur; humilité, f.
meet (1) [mi:t], v.t. irr. rencontrer, aller à la
rencontre de; trouver, recevoir (atteindre);
faire la connaissance de; faire face à, affronter (braver); se présenter devant (paraître
devant); faire honneur à (dette); (fig.) satisfaire, remplir (demande).—v.i. se rencontrer; se voir; se réunir, s'assembler; se
joindre (s'unir); to meet half-way, se
faire des concessions mutuelles.—n. rendez-
vous de chasse, m.
meet (2) [mi:t], a. propre, convenable.
meeting ['mi:tiŋ], n. rencontre; entrevue;
assemblée, réunion, f., meeting, m.; séance
(session), f.; confluent (rivières), m.; jonction
(routes), f.
megaton ['megətʌn], n. mégatonne, f.
melancholy ['melənkəli], a. mélancolique,
triste, affligeant.—n. mélancolie, tristesse, f.
mellifluous [mə'lifluəs], a. mielleux, doucereux.
mellow ['melou], a. mûr, fondant (fruit);
moelleux, doux; gris (à moitié ivre); meuble
(terre).—v.t. mûrir, faire mûrir; ameublir
(terre); (fig.) adoucir.—v.i. mûrir; devenir
meuble (terre); (fig.) s'adoucir.
mellowness ['melounis], n. maturité, f.;
moelleux, m.; (fig.) douceur, f.
melodious [mə'loudiəs], a. mélodieux.
melodiously [mə'loudiəsli], adv. mélodieusement.
melodrama ['melədrɑ:mə], n. mélodrame,
m.
melodramatic [melədrə'mætik], a. mélodramatique.
melody ['melədi], n. mélodie, f., air, m.
melon ['melən], n. melon, m.
melt [melt], v.t. fondre, faire fondre; (fig.)
attendrir.—v.i. fondre, se fondre; (fig.)
s'attendrir.

483

melting ['meltiŋ], a. qui fond; fondant (*fruit*); (*fig.*) attendrissant.—n. fusion, fonte, *f.*; attendrissement, *m.*
melting-pot ['meltiŋpɔt], n. creuset, *m.*
member ['membə], n. membre; (*Parl.*) député, *m.*
membered ['membəd], a. membré; qui a des membres; *large-membered*, membru.
membership ['membəʃip], n. les membres d'une société etc., *m.pl.*
membrane ['membrein], n. membrane, *f.*
memento [mə'mentou], n. souvenir, mémento, *m.*
memoir ['memwɑː], n. mémoire, *m.*
memorable ['memərəbl], a. mémorable.
memorandum [memə'rændəm], n. (*pl.* **memoranda** [memə'rændə]) note, *f.*, mémorandum; (*Comm.*) bordereau, *m.*
memorial [mi'mɔːriəl], a. commémoratif.—n. souvenir, mémoire; monument commémoratif, *m.*; requête, pétition, *f.*
memorize ['meməraiz], v.t. apprendre par cœur.
memory ['meməri], n. mémoire, *f.*; (*colloq.*) souvenir, *m.*; *in memory of*, en souvenir de; *to the best of my memory*, autant qu'il m'en souvient.
men [MAN].
menace ['menəs], n. menace, *f.*—v.t. menacer.
menagerie [mə'nædʒəri], n. ménagerie, *f.*
mend [mend], v.t. raccommoder, réparer; corriger, améliorer; *to mend one's ways*, rentrer dans le bon chemin.—v.i. s'améliorer, se corriger; se rétablir (*santé*); se remettre au beau (*temps*).
mendacious [men'deiʃəs], a. mensonger.
mendacity [men'dæsiti], n. mensonge, *m.*; duplicité, *f.*
mendicant ['mendikənt], a. and n. mendiant, *m.*
mendicity [men'disiti], n. mendicité, *f.*
mending ['mendiŋ], n. raccommodage; reprisage (*des bas*), *m.*; réparation, *f.*
menial ['miːniəl], a. de domestique; (*fig.*) servile.—n. domestique, *m.*, *f.*; (*fig.*) valet, laquais, *m.*
meningitis [menin'dʒaitis], n. méningite, *f.*
mental [mentl], a. mental; *a mental case*, un aliéné.
mentality [men'tæliti], n. mentalité, *f.*; esprit, *m.*
mention ['menʃən], n. mention, indication, *f.*—v.t. dire, faire mention de, mentionner, parler de; citer; *don't mention it!* il n'y a pas de quoi! *not to mention*, sans compter.
menu ['menju], n. menu, *m.*, carte, *f.*
mercantile ['məːkəntail], a. marchand, de commerce, commerçant; *mercantile marine*, marine marchande, *f.*
mercenary ['məːsənri], a. mercenaire, vénal.—n. mercenaire, *m.*
merchandise ['məːtʃəndaiz], n. marchandise, *f.*
merchant ['məːtʃənt], a. marchand; commercial.—n. négociant, commerçant; marchand en gros, *m.*
merchantman ['məːtʃəntmən] (*pl.* **-men** [men]), **merchant-ship** ['məːtʃəntʃip], n. navire marchand, *m.*
merchant-service ['məːtʃənt'səːvis], n. marine marchande, *f.*

merciful ['məːsiful], a. miséricordieux.
merciless ['məːsilis], a. sans pitié, impitoyable.
mercurial [məː'kjuəriəl], a. de Mercure; de mercure; (*fig.*) mercuriel, vif.
mercury ['məːkjuəri], n. mercure, *m.*
mercy ['məːsi], n. miséricorde; pitié; grâce, indulgence (*pardon*), *f.*; *for mercy's sake*, par grâce; *recommendation to mercy*, recours en grâce, *m.*; *sisters of mercy*, sœurs de charité, *f.pl.*
mere (1) [miə], n. lac, étang, *m.*
mere (2) [miə], a. pur, simple, seul, rien que.
merely ['miəli], adv. simplement, seulement, rien que.
meretricious [meri'triʃəs], a. d'un éclat factice (*style*).
merge [məːdʒ], v.t. fondre, amalgamer, absorber.—v.i. se perdre (*dans*).
merger ['məːdʒə], n. fusion, *f.*
meridian [mə'ridiən], a. méridien; de midi.—n. méridien; (*fig.*) apogée, *m.*
merino [mə'riːnou], n. mérinos, *m.*
merit ['merit], n. mérite, *m.*—v.t. mériter.
meritorious [meri'tɔːriəs], a. méritoire (*choses*); méritant (*personnes*).
meritoriously [meri'tɔːriəsli], adv. d'une manière méritoire.
mermaid ['məːmeid], n. sirène, *f.*
merrily ['merili], adv. joyeusement, gaiement.
merriment ['merimənt], n. gaieté, réjouissance, *f.*
merry ['meri], a. joyeux, gai, plaisant; un peu gris; *to make merry*, se réjouir, se divertir.
merry-go-round ['merigouraund], n. chevaux de bois, *m.pl.*; manège, *m.*
merry-making ['merimeikiŋ], n. réjouissance, fête, *f.*, divertissement, *m.*
mesh [meʃ], n. maille, *f.*; engrenage, *m.*
mesmerism ['mezmərizm], n. mesmérisme, magnétisme animal, *m.*
mesmerize ['mezməraiz], v.t. magnétiser; hypnotiser.
mess (1) [mes], n. gâchis, *m.*; saleté, *f.*; *to be in a fine mess*, être dans de beaux draps; *what a mess!* quel gâchis!—v.t. salir.—v.i. faire du gâchis.
mess (2) [mes], n. mets, plat; (*Mil.*) mess, *m.*; *mess tin*, gamelle (individuelle), *f.*—v.t. donner à manger à.—v.i. manger; manger ensemble.
message ['mesidʒ], n. message, *m.*, commission, *f.*
messenger ['mesəndʒə], n. messager; commissionnaire; coursier (*dans un bureau*); (*fig.*) avant-coureur, *m.*
Messiah [mə'saiə], n. Messie, *m.*
messmate ['mesmeit], n. camarade de table, *m.*
messy ['mesi], a. sale; graisseux, salissant.
metabolism [mə'tæbolizm], n. métabolisme, *m.*
metal [metl], n. métal; cailloutis, empierrement (*pour routes*); (*Rail.*) rail, *m.*
metalled [metld], a. empierré.
metallic [mə'tælik], a. métallique.
metallurgy [me'tælədʒi], n. métallurgie, *f.*
metamorphosis [metə'mɔːfəsis], n. métamorphose, *f.*
metaphor ['metəfə], n. métaphore, *f.*
metaphysical [metə'fizikl], a. métaphysique.

milkmaid

metaphysics [metə'fiziks], *n.pl.* métaphysique, *f.*

mete [mi:t], *v.t.* mesurer; *to mete out*, distribuer, décerner (*prix*); assigner (*punitions*).

meteor ['mi:tiə], *n.* météore, *m.*

meteoric [mi:ti'ɔrik], *a.* météorique.

meteorite ['mi:tiərait], *n.* météorite, *m.* ou *f.*

meteorological [mi:tiərə'lɔdʒikl], *a.* météorologique.

meteorologist [mi:tiə'rɔlədʒist], *n.* météorologiste, *m., f.*

meteorology [mi:tiə'rɔlədʒi], *n.* météorologie, *f.*

meter ['mi:tə], *n.* mesureur; compteur (*de gaz*), *m.*

method ['meθəd], *n.* méthode, *f.*; procédé, *m.*; modalité; (*fig.*) manière, *f.*, ordre, *m.*

methodical [mə'θɔdikəl], *a.* méthodique.

methylate ['meθileit], *v.t.* méthyler; *methylated spirit*, alcool à brûler, *m.*

meticulous [mə'tikjuləs], *a.* méticuleux.

meticulousness [mə'tikjuləsnis], *n.* méticulosité, *f.*

metre ['mi:tə], *n.* mètre; (*Pros.*) vers, *m.*, mesure, *f.*

metric ['metrik], *a.* métrique.

metrical ['metrikl], *a.* métrique; en vers.

metropolis [mə'trɔpəlis], *n.* capitale, métropole, *f.*

metropolitan [metrə'pɔlitən], *a.* de la capitale, métropolitain.

mettle [metl], *n.* courage, cœur, *m.*; fougue, ardeur, vivacité, *f.*; caractère, *m.*; *to put someone on his mettle*, piquer quelqu'un d'honneur.

mettled [metld], **mettlesome** ['metlsəm], *a.* fougueux, ardent, vif.

mew (1) [mju:], *n.* mue, cage, *f.*; (*pl.*) écuries, *f.pl.*; impasse, ruelle (*derrière les grandes maisons de ville*), *f.*—*v.t.* enfermer (*emprisonner*).—*v.i.* changer.

mew (2) [mju:], *v.i.* miauler (*chat*).

mew (3) [mju:], *n.* (*Orn.*) mouette, *f.*

mewing ['mju:iŋ], *n.* miaulement (*de chat*), *m.*

Mexican ['meksikn], *a.* mexicain.—*n.* Mexicain (*personne*), *m.*

Mexico ['meksikou]. le Mexique (*pays*); *Mexico City*, Mexico, *m.*

miasma [mi'æzmə], *n.* (*pl.* **miasmata** [mi'æzmətə]) miasme, *m.*

mica ['maikə], *n.* mica, *m.*

mice [MOUSE].

Michael [maikl]. Michel, *m.*

Michaelmas ['miklməs]. la Saint-Michel, *f.*

microbe ['maikroub], *n.* microbe, *m.*

microphone ['maikrəfoun], *n.* microphone, *m.*

microscope ['maikrəskoup], *n.* microscope, *m.*

microscopic [maikrə'skɔpik], *a.* microscopique.

mid [mid], *a.* du milieu, moyen.—*prep.* au milieu de.

mid-air [mid'ɛə], *n.* milieu de l'air, haut des airs, *m.*; *in mid-air*, entre ciel et terre.

midday ['middei], *a.* de midi.—*n.* midi, *m.*

middle [midl], *a.* du milieu, central; moyen; *Middle Ages*, Moyen Âge, *m.*; *middle class*, bourgeoisie, *f.*; *middle course*, moyen terme, *m.*—*n.* milieu, centre, *m.*; ceinture, *f.*

middle-aged ['midleidʒd], *a.* entre deux âges.

middle-man ['midlmæn], *n.* (*pl.* **-men** [men]) intermédiaire, tiers, *m.*

middling ['midliŋ], *a.* médiocre, passable, assez bien (*santé*); (*Comm.*) bon, ordinaire.

midget ['midʒit], *n.* nain, nabot, *m.*

midland ['midlənd], *a.* de l'intérieur, du centre.

Mid-Lent ['mid'lent], mi-carême, *f.*

midnight ['midnait], *a.* de minuit.—*n.* minuit, *m.*

midriff ['midrif], *n.* diaphragme, *m.*

midshipman ['midʃipmən], *n.* (*pl.* **-men** [men]) aspirant de marine, *m.*

midships ['midʃips], [AMIDSHIPS].

midst [midst], *n.* milieu; (*fig.*) fort, sein, cœur, *m.*—*prep.* au milieu de, parmi.

midstream ['midstri:m], *n.* milieu du courant; milieu du fleuve, *m.*

midsummer ['midsʌmə], *n.* milieu de l'été, cœur de l'été, *m.*; *Midsummer Day*, la Saint-Jean, *f.*

midway ['midwei], *a.* and *adv.* à mi-chemin; à mi-côte (*d'une colline*).

midwife ['midwaif], *n.* (*pl.* **midwives** ['midwaivz]) sage-femme, accoucheuse, *f.*

midwifery ['midwifri], *n.* obstétrique, *f.*

midwinter ['midwintə], *n.* fort de l'hiver, *m.*

mien [mi:n], *n.* mine, *f.*, air, *m.*

might (1) [mait], *past* [MAY].

might (2) [mait], *n.* force, puissance, *f.*

mightily ['maitili], *adv.* fortement, vigoureusement; extrêmement.

mighty ['maiti], *a.* fort, puissant; grand, important.—*adv.* fort, très, extrêmement.

mignonette [minjə'net], *n.* réséda, *m.*

migraine ['mi:grein], *n.* (*Med.*) migraine, *f.*

migrate [mai'greit], *v.i.* émigrer.

migration [mai'greiʃən], *n.* migration, *f.*

migratory ['maigrətəri], *a.* migratoire; migrateur.

milch [miltʃ], *a.* à lait, laitière.

mild [maild], *a.* doux; léger (*boisson, tabac etc.*); bénin.

mildew ['mildju:], *n.* rouille, moisissure, *f.*, taches d'humidité, *f.pl.*—*v.t.* gâter par l'humidité; souiller, tacher.

mildly ['maildli], *adv.* doucement, avec douceur; modérément.

mildness ['maildnis], *n.* douceur, *f.*

mile [mail], *n.* mille, *m.*

mileage ['maildʒ], *n.* distance en milles, *f.*; prix par mille, *m.*

milestone ['mailstoun], *n.* borne milliaire, borne kilométrique, *f.*

militant ['militənt], *a.* militant.—*n.* activiste, *m., f.*

militarism ['militərizm], *n.* militarisme, *m.*

military ['militəri], *a.* militaire.—*n. the military*, les militaires, *m.pl.*, la troupe, *f.*

militate ['militeit], *v.i.* militer (*contre*).

militia [mi'liʃə], *n.* milice, *f.*

milk [milk], *n.* lait, *m.*; *milk and water*, lait coupé; (*fig.*) fade, insipide, sans caractère; *skim milk*, lait écrémé; *to come home with the milk*, rentrer à la première heure.—*v.t.* traire.

milk-can ['milkkæn], *n.* pot au lait, *m.*

milkiness ['milkinis], *n.* nature laiteuse; (*fig.*) douceur, *f.*

milkmaid ['milkmeid], *n.* laitière, *f.*

485

milkman ['milkmən], *n.* (*pl.* -men [men]) laitier, *m.*

milk-pail ['milkpeil], *n.* seau à lait, *m.*

milksop ['milksɔp], *n.* (*colloq.*) poule mouillée, *f.*

milky ['milki], *a.* laiteux; **Milky Way**, voie lactée, *f.*

mill [mil], *n.* moulin, *m.*; filature, fabrique (*usine*), *f.*—*v.t.* moudre; (*Coin.*) estamper.—*v.i.* fourmiller (*foule*).

millenary ['milənəri], *a.* millénaire.

millennium [mi'leniəm], *n.* millénaire, *m.*, mille ans; les temps messianiques, *m.pl.*

miller ['milə], *n.* meunier, *m.*

millet ['milit], *n.* millet, mil, *m.*

millimetre ['milimi:tə], *n.* millimètre, *m.*

milliner ['milinə], *n.* marchande de modes; modiste, *f.*

millinery ['milinri], *n.* modes, *f.pl.*

million ['miljən], *n.* million, *m.*

millionaire [miljə'nɛə], *n.* millionnaire, *m.*, *f.*

millstone ['milstoun], *n.* meule de moulin, *f.*

mime [maim], *n.* mime.—*v.t.* mimer (*une scène*).—*v.i.* jouer par gestes.

mimic ['mimik], *a.* imitateur, mimique; imitatif (*animaux*).—*n.* mime, imitateur, *m.* —*v.t.* contrefaire, imiter.

mimicry ['mimikri], *n.* mimique, imitation, *f.*

minatory ['minətəri], *a.* menaçant.

mince [mins], *v.t.* hacher menu.—*v.i.* marcher à petits pas; minauder (*parler d'une façon affectée*).—*n.* hachis, haché, *m.*

mincemeat ['minsmi:t], *n.* hachis, *m.*; pâte d'épices, *f.*, mincemeat, *m.*

mince-pie ['mins'pai], *n.* tartelette au mincemeat, *f.*

mincing ['minsiŋ], *a.* affecté, minaudier.

mind [maind], *n.* esprit, *m.*, intelligence; envie, *f.*, désir (*inclination*), *m.*; pensée, *f.*, avis (*opinion*); souvenir (*mémoire*), *m.*—*v.t.* songer à, faire attention à; regarder à (*s'occuper de*); se défier de (*se douter de*); obéir à, écouter (*se soumettre à*); soigner, garder (*veiller sur*); surveiller, observer (*étudier*); **mind your own business**, mêlez-vous de ce qui vous regarde; **never mind**, peu importe, tant pis.

minded ['maindid], *a.* disposé, enclin.

mindful ['maindful], *a.* attentif (*à*), soigneux (*de*); qui se souvient (*de*).

mindfulness ['maindfulnis], *n.* attention, *f.*

mindless ['maindlis], *a.* inattentif (*à*); sans esprit.

mine (1) [main], *pron.poss.* le mien, *m.*, la mienne, *f.*; les miens, *m.pl.*, les miennes, *f.pl.*—*a.* à moi; **a friend of mine**, un de mes amis.

mine (2) [main], *n.* mine, *f.*—*v.t.* miner, saper.

mine-layer ['mainleiə], *n.* (*Navy*) mouilleur de mines, *m.*

miner ['mainə], *n.* mineur, *m.*

mineral ['minərəl], *a.* and *n.* minéral, *m.*

mineralogy [minə'rælədʒi], *n.* minéralogie, *f.*

mine-sweeper ['mainswi:pə], *n.* (*Navy*) dragueur de mines, *m.*

mingle [miŋgl], *v.t.* mélanger, mêler.—*v.i.* se mêler, se mélanger (*avec, dans* ou *en*).

mingling ['miŋgliŋ], *n.* mélange, *m.*

miniature ['mini(ə)tʃə], *a.* en miniature.—*n.* miniature, *f.*

minim ['minim], *n.* goutte, *m.*; (*Mus.*) blanche, *f.*

minimum ['miniməm], *n.* (*pl.* minima ['minimə]) minimum, *m.*

mining ['mainiŋ], *a.* des mines; de mineur, minier.—*n.* travail dans les mines, *m.*

minion ['minjən], *n.* favori, *m.*, favorite, *f.*

minister ['ministə], *n.* ministre; (*Eccles.*) pasteur, *m.*—*v.t.* administrer; fournir.—*v.i.* servir (*à*); (*Eccles.*) officier à.

ministerial [minis'tiəriəl], *a.* de ministère, ministériel.

ministration [minis'treiʃən], *n.* ministère; service, *m.*

ministry ['ministri], *n.* ministère, département, *m.*

mink [miŋk], *n.* vison, *m.*

minnow ['minou], *n.* vairon, *m.*

minor ['mainə], *a.* moindre; secondaire; (*Mus.*, *Geog. etc.*) mineur.—*n.* mineur, *m.*

Minorca [mi'nɔ:kə], Minorque, *f.*

minority [mai'nɔriti], *n.* minorité, *f.*

minster ['minstə], *n.* cathédrale, église abbatiale, *f.*

minstrel ['minstrəl], *n.* ménestrel; (*fam.*) poète, musicien, chanteur, *m.*

mint (1) [mint], *n.* menthe, *f.*; **peppermint**, menthe poivrée.

mint (2) [mint], *n.* **The Mint**, la Monnaie, *f.* —*v.t.* monnayer, frapper; (*fig.*) forger.

mintage ['mintidʒ], *n.* objet monnayé, *m.*

minting ['mintiŋ], *n.* monnayage, *m.*

minuet [minju'et], *n.* menuet, *m.*

minus ['mainəs], *prep.* moins; sans (*n'ayant pas de*).—*n.* moins, *m.*

minute (1) [mai'nju:t], *a.* menu, minuscule, très petit; minutieux.

minute (2) ['minit], *n.* minute, *f.*; instant; moment, *m.*; note, *f.*; (*pl.*) procès-verbal, compte-rendu (*d'une réunion*), *m.*—*v.t.* minuter, prendre note de.

minute-book ['minitbuk], *n.* journal, *m.*

minute-hand ['minithænd], *n.* grande aiguille, *f.*

minutely [mai'nju:tli], *adv.* minutieusement; exactement; en détail.

minuteness [mai'nju:tnis], *n.* petitesse; exactitude, *f.*; détails minutieux, *m.pl.*

minx [miŋks], *n.* coquine, friponne, *f.*

miracle ['mirəkl], *n.* miracle, *m.*

miraculous [mi'rækjuləs], *a.* miraculeux.

mirage [mi'rɑ:ʒ], *n.* mirage, *m.*

mire ['maiə], *n.* boue, bourbe, fange, vase, *f.*

miry ['maiəri], *a.* fangeux, bourbeux.

mirror ['mirə], *n.* miroir, *m.*, glace, *f.*; **driving-mirror**, rétroviseur, *m.*—*v.t.* refléter.

mirth [mə:θ], *n.* gaieté, hilarité, *f.*, rire, *m.*

mirthful ['mə:θful], *a.* gai, joyeux.

misadventure [misəd'ventʃə], *n.* mésaventure, *f.*, contretemps, *m.*

misanthropist [mi'sænθrəpist], *n.* misanthrope, *m.*, *f.*

misanthropy [mi'sænθrəpi], *n.* misanthropie, *f.*

misapplication [misæpli'keiʃən], *n.* mauvaise application, *f.*

misapply [misə'plai], *v.t.* mal appliquer, détourner (*fonds etc.*).

misapprehend [misæpri'hend], *v.t.* comprendre mal.

misapprehension [misæpri'henʃən], *n.* malentendu, *m.*, méprise, *f.*

misappropriate [misə'prouprieit], *v.t.* détourner.

misappropriation [misəproupri'eiʃən], *n.* détournement, mauvais emploi, *m.*

misbehave [misbi'heiv], *v.i.* se conduire mal.

misbehaviour [misbi'heivjə], *n.* mauvaise conduite, *f.*

miscalculate [mis'kælkjuleit], *v.t.* calculer mal.

miscalculation [miskælkju'leiʃən], *n.* calcul erroné; mécompte, *m.*

miscarriage [mis'kæridʒ], *n.* insuccès, coup manqué, *m.*; fausse couche (*de femme*), *f.*

miscarry [mis'kæri], *v.i.* manquer, échouer; faire une fausse couche (*femme*).

miscellaneous [misi'leinjəs], *a.* varié, divers; général; *miscellaneous news,* faits divers, *m.pl.*

miscellany [mi'seləni], *n.* (*pl.* **miscellanies** [mi'seləniz]) mélange, *m.*; mélanges (*livre*), *m.pl.*

mischance [mis'tʃɑːns], *n.* malheur, accident, *m.*, mésaventure, infortune, *f.*

mischief ['mistʃif], *n.* mal, dommage, dégât, tort, *m.*

mischief-maker ['mistʃifmeikə], *n.* brouillon, *m.*

mischievous ['mistʃivəs], *a.* méchant, malicieux; malfaisant, mauvais, nuisible (*chose*); espiègle (*enfant*).

mischievously ['mistʃivəsli], *adv.* méchamment.

mischievousness ['mistʃivəsnis], *n.* méchanceté; espièglerie (*d'enfant*), *f.*

misconceive [miskən'siːv], *v.t., v.i.* mal concevoir, juger mal.

misconception [miskən'sepʃən], *n.* malentendu, *m.*

misconduct [mis'kɔndʌkt], *n.* mauvaise conduite, *f.*—[miskən'dʌkt], *v.t.* conduire mal; *to misconduct oneself,* se conduire mal.

misconstruction [miskən'strakʃən], *n.* fausse interprétation, *f.*, contresens, *m.*

misconstrue [miskən'struː], *v.t.* mal interpréter.

miscount [mis'kaunt], *v.t.* compter mal.—*v.i.* faire une erreur de compte.—*n.* mécompte, *m.*

miscreant ['miskriənt], *n.* mécréant, *m;* (*fig.*) misérable, *m., f.*

misdeal [mis'diːl], *v.t.* maldonner.—*n.* maldonne, *f.*

misdeed [mis'diːd], *n.* méfait, *m.*

misdemean [misdə'miːn], *v.r. to misdemean oneself,* se comporter mal.

misdemeanour [misdə'miːnə], *n.* délit, crime, *m.*, offense, *f.*

misdirect [misdi'rekt], *v.t.* mal diriger, renseigner mal; mettre une fausse adresse à (*lettre*).

misdoing [mis'duːiŋ], *n.* méfait, *m.*

miser ['maizə], *n.* avare, *m., f.*

miserable ['mizərəbl], *a.* misérable, pitoyable, malheureux; mesquin (*piètre*).

miserliness ['maizəlinis], *n.* avarice, *f.*

miserly ['maizəli], *a.* d'avare, avare, sordide.

misery ['mizəri], *n.* misère, *f.;* (*fig.*) tourment; supplice, *m.; to put out of misery,* mettre fin aux souffrances (*de*).

misfire [mis'faiə], *v.i.* rater; (*Motor.*) avoir des ratés.—*n.* raté d'allumage, *m.*

misfit ['misfit], *n.* vêtement manqué; inadapté (*personne*), *m.*

misfortune [mis'fɔːtʃən], *n.* malheur, *m.*, infortune, *f.*

misgiving [mis'givin], *n.* pressentiment, soupçon, doute, *m.*; inquiétude, *f.*

misgovern [mis'gʌvən], *v.t.* gouverner mal.

misgovernment [mis'gʌvənmənt], *n.* mauvais gouvernement, *m.*

misguided [mis'gaidid], *a.* malencontreux; peu judicieux; dévoyé.

mishandle [mis'hændl], *v.t.* manier mal, malmener.

mishap [mis'hæp], *n.* contretemps, malheur, *m.*, mésaventure, *f.*

misinform [misin'fɔːm], *v.t.* mal renseigner.

misinterpret [misin'tə:prit], *v.t.* interpréter mal.

misjudge [mis'dʒʌdʒ], *v.t.* juger mal, méjuger.

mislay [mis'lei], *v.t. irr.* (*conjug. like* LAY) égarer.

mislead [mis'liːd], *v.t. irr.* (*conjug. like* LEAD) égarer; induire en erreur, fourvoyer; tromper.

misleading [mis'liːdiŋ], *a.* trompeur.

mismanage [mis'mænidʒ], *v.t.* diriger mal. —*v.i.* s'y prendre mal, s'arranger mal (*pour*).

mismanagement [mis'mænidʒmənt], *n.* mauvaise administration, *f.*

misnomer [mis'noumə], *n.* faux nom, *m.*

misogynist [mi'sodʒinist], *n.* misogyne, *m.*

misogyny [mi'sodʒini], *n.* misogynie, *f.*

misplace [mis'pleis], *v.t.* mal placer; déplacer.

misprint ['misprint], *n.* faute d'impression, *f.* —[mis'print], *v.t.* imprimer incorrectement.

mispronounce [misprə'nauns], *v.t.* prononcer mal.

mispronunciation [misprənʌnsi'eiʃən], *n.* prononciation incorrecte, *f.*

misquote [mis'kwout], *v.t.* citer à faux.

misread [mis'riːd], *v.t. irr.* (*conjug. like* READ) mal lire, mal interpréter.

misrepresent [misrepri'zent], *v.t.* représenter mal, dénaturer.

misrepresentation [misreprizen'teiʃən], *n.* faux rapport, *m.*

misrule [mis'ruːl], *n.* désordre; mauvais gouvernement, *m.*

miss (1) [mis], *n.* mademoiselle, demoiselle, *f.*

miss (2) [mis], *n.* manque, *m.*; perte (*privation*); erreur (*méprise*), *f.*; coup manqué, *m.* —*v.t.* manquer; omettre; s'apercevoir de l'absence de, regretter vivement, ne plus trouver; *I miss my friend very much,* mon ami me manque beaucoup.—*v.i.* manquer; ne pas réussir, échouer, se tromper; *to be missing,* être absent, manquer.

missal [misl], *n.* missel, *m.*

misshapen [mis'ʃeipən], *a.* difforme.

missile ['misail], *a.* de jet, de trait.—*n.* projectile, *m.*; *guided missile,* engin téléguidé, *m.*

missing ['misiŋ], *a.* absent, perdu, disparu.

mission ['miʃən], *n.* mission, *f.*

missionary ['miʃənəri], *a.* des missions.—*n.* missionnaire, *m., f.*

missive ['misiv], *a.* missive.—*n.* missive, lettre, *f.*

misspell [mis'spel], *v.t. irr.* (*conjug. like* SPELL) épeler mal.

misspelling [mis'speliŋ], *n.* faute d'ortho-graphe, *f.*

misspend [mis'spend], *v.t. irr. (conjug. like* SPEND*)* employer mal; gaspiller.

misstate [mis'steit], *v.t.* rapporter incorrecte-ment.

misstatement [mis'steitmənt], *n.* rapport erroné, *m.*

mist [mist], *n.* brume; buée *(sur une glace), f.*; *Scotch mist*, bruine, *f.*—*v.t.* couvrir *(une glace)* de buée.—*v.i.* se couvrir de buée.

mistake [mis'teik], *v.t. irr. (conjug. like* TAKE*)* se tromper de *ou* sur, se méprendre à *ou* sur; prendre *(pour)*.—*v.i.* se tromper, se méprendre, s'abuser.—*n.* erreur, méprise, faute; bévue *(erreur grossière), f.*; *to make a mistake*, se tromper.

mistaken [mis'teikən] *a.* qui se trompe; faux, erroné *(chose).*

mistimed [mis'taimd], *a.* inopportun.

mistletoe ['misltou], *n.* gui, *m.*

mistress ['mistris], *n.* maîtresse; patronne; institutrice *(d'école primaire), f.*; *head-mistress*, directrice, *f.*

mistrust [mis'trʌst], *n.* méfiance, *f.*, soupçon, *m.*—*v.t.* se méfier de, soupçonner.

mistrustful [mis'trʌstful], *a.* méfiant.

misty ['misti], *a.* brumeux; vaporeux *(lumière); (fig.)* confus.

misunderstand [misʌndə'stænd], *v.t. irr. (conjug. like* STAND*)* mal comprendre, entendre mal, se méprendre sur.

misunderstanding [misʌndə'stændiŋ], *n.* malentendu *(manque de compréhension), m.*; mésintelligence *(querelle), f.*

misuse [mis'ju:s], *n.* abus, *m.*—[mis'ju:z], *v.t.* mésuser de; maltraiter *(faire du mal à).*

mite (1) [mait], *n. (Zool.)* mite, *f.*

mite (2) [mait], *n.* denier *(argent); (fig.)* rien, *m.*, obole, *f.*; *(fam.)* petit gosse, *m.*

mitigate ['mitigeit], *v.t.* mitiger, adoucir, modérer.

mitigating ['mitigeitiŋ], *a.* adoucissant, atténuant.

mitigation [miti'geiʃən], *n.* mitigation, *f.*, adoucissement, *m.*

mitre ['maitə], *n.* mitre, *f.*

mitten [mitn], *n.* mitaine, *f.*

mix [miks], *v.t.* mêler, mélanger; couper *(boissons); to mix up*, mêler, embrouiller, confondre.—*v.i.* se mélanger, se mêler *(de)*; s'associer *(à).*

mixed [mikst], *a.* mélangé, mêlé *(de)*; mixte.

mixture ['mikstʃə], *n.* mélange, *m.*; *(Pharm.)* potion, mixture, *f.*

mix-up ['miksʌp], *n.* confusion, *f.*, embrouil-lement, *m.*; *(pop.)* pagaïe, *f.*

mizzen [mizn], *n.* artimon, *m.*

mizzen-mast ['miznmɑ:st], *n.* mât d'artimon, *m.*

moan [moun], *n.* gémissement, *m.*, plainte; *(fig.)* lamentation, *f.*—*v.t.* gémir de *ou* sur; se lamenter sur.—*v.i.* gémir; *(fig.)* se la-menter; *(pop.)* grognonner.

moat [mout], *n.* fossé, *m.*, douve, *f.*

mob [mɔb], *n.* foule; populace, canaille, *f.*—*v.t.* houspiller, malmener; assiéger.

mobile ['moubail], *a.* mobile.

mobility [mou'biliti], *n.* mobilité; légèreté *(inconstance), f.*

mobilization [moubilai'zeiʃən], *n.* mobilisa-tion, *f.*

mobilize ['moubailaiz], *v.t.* mobiliser.

mock [mɔk], *v.t.* se moquer de; narguer.—*v.i.* railler.—*a.* dérisoire; faux, simulé *(false).*

mocker ['mɔkə], *n.* moqueur, *m.*

mockery ['mɔkəri], *n.* moquerie, *f.*

mocking-bird ['mɔkiŋbə:d], *n.* oiseau moqueur, *m.*

mode [moud], *n.* mode, façon, manière, *f.*

model [mɔdl], *n.* modèle; mannequin, *m.*—*v.t.* modeler; *(Cloth.)* présenter des vête-ments *(défilé de mannequins).*

moderate ['mɔdərit], *a.* modéré; modique, ordinaire, passable, médiocre.—['mɔdəreit], *v.t.* modérer, adoucir, tempérer.—*v.i.* se modérer.

moderately ['mɔdəritli], *adv.* modérément, passablement.

moderation [mɔdə'reiʃən], *n.* modération, *f.*

moderator ['mɔdəreitə], *n.* modérateur, *m.*

modern ['mɔdən], *a. and n.* moderne, *m., f.*; *modern languages*, langues vivantes, *f.pl.*

modernize ['mɔdənaiz], *v.t.* moderniser.

modest ['mɔdist], *a.* modeste; pudique; modéré *(demandes etc.).*

modesty ['mɔdisti], *n.* modestie, *f.*

modicum ['mɔdikəm], *n.* petite portion, *f.*

modification [mɔdifi'keiʃən], *n.* modifica-tion, *f.*

modify ['mɔdifai], *v.t.* modifier.

modulate ['mɔdjuleit], *v.t.* moduler.

modulation [mɔdju'leiʃən], *n.* modulation, *f.*

Mohair ['mouheə], *n.* poil de chèvre angora, mohair, *m.*

Mohammed [mo'hæməd]. Mahomet, *m.*

Mohammedan [mo'hæmədən], *a.* mahomé-tan.—*n.* Mahométan, *m.*

mohammedanism [mo'hæmədənizm], *n.* mahométisme, *m.*

moist [mɔist], *a.* moite, humide.

moisten [mɔisn], *v.t.* humecter; mouiller.

moisture ['mɔistʃə], **moistness** ['mɔistnis], *n.* moiteur, humidité, *f.*

molasses [mo'læsiz], *n.pl.* mélasse, *f.*

mole (1) [moul], *n.* taupe *(animal), f.*

mole (2) [moul], *n.* tache, *f.*, grain de beauté *(sur la peau), m.*

mole (3) [moul], *n.* môle *(jetée), m.*

molecular [mo'lekjulə], *a.* moléculaire.

molecule ['mɔlikju:l], *n.* molécule *f.*

mole-hill ['moulhil], *n.* taupinière, *f.*

moleskin ['moulskin], *n.* peau de taupe, molesquine, *f.*, velours de coton, *m.*

molest [mo'lest], *v.t.* molester; vexer.

mollify ['mɔlifai], *v.t.* amollir; adoucir.

molten ['moultən], *a.* fondu.

moment ['moumənt], *n.* moment, instant, *m.*; *(fig.)* importance, *f.*; *at the present moment*, actuellement; *at this moment*, en ce moment; *not for a moment*, pour rien au monde; *of no moment*, d'aucune importance; *the moment that*, dès que, aussitôt que.

momentarily ['mouməntərili], *adv.* momen-tanément.

momentary ['mouməntəri], *a.* momentané.

momentous [mo'mentəs], *a.* important, d'une importance capitale.

momentum [mo'mentəm], *n. (Phys.)* force vive; vitesse acquise, *f.*; élan, *m.*

monarch ['mɔnək], *n.* monarque, *m.*

monarchy ['mɔnəki], *n.* monarchie, *f.*

monastery ['mɔnəstri], *n.* monastère, *m.*

monastic [mə'næstik], *a.* monastique.

monasticism [mə'næstisizm], *n.* monachisme, *m.*

Monday ['mʌndi], lundi, *m.*

monetary ['mʌnətəri], *a.* monétaire.

money ['mʌni], *n.* argent, *m.*; monnaie, *f.*, espèces (*pièces*), *f.pl.*; *made of money*, cousu d'or; *ready money*, argent comptant; *to make money*, gagner de l'argent.

money-box ['mʌniboks], *n.* tirelire, *f.*

money-changer ['mʌnitʃeindʒə], *n.* changeur, *m.*

moneyed ['mʌnid], *a.* riche.

money-grubber ['mʌnigrʌbə], *n.* grippe-sou, *m.*

money-lender ['mʌnilendə], *n.* prêteur d'argent, *m.*

money-market ['mʌnimɑːkit], *n.* bourse, *f.*

money-order ['mʌniɔːdə], *n.* mandat, *m.*

Mongol ['mɔŋgɔl], *a.* mongol.—*n.* Mongol (*personne*), *m.*

Mongolia [mɔŋ'goulia]. la Mongolie, *f.*

Mongolian [mɔŋ'goulian], *a.* mongol.—*n.* mongol (*langue*); Mongol (*personne*), *m.*

mongrel ['mʌŋgrəl], *a.* métis.—*n.* métis, *m.* métisse, *f.*

monitor ['mɔnitə], *n.* moniteur, *m.*

monk [mʌŋk], *n.* moine, *m.*

monkey ['mʌŋki], *n.* singe, *m.*; guenon, *f.*

monkey-wrench ['mʌŋkirentʃ], *n.* clé anglaise, *f.*

monocle ['mɔnəkl], *n.* monocle, *m.*

monogram ['mɔnəgræm], *n.* monogramme, *m.*

monologue ['mɔnələg], *n.* monologue, *m.*

monoplane ['mɔnəplein], *n.* monoplan, *m.*

monopoly [mə'nɔpəli], *n.* monopole, accaparement, *m.*

monorail ['mɔnəreil], *n.* monorail, *m.*

monotonous [mə'nɔtənəs], *a.* monotone.

monotonously [mə'nɔtənəsli], *adv.* avec monotonie.

monotony [mə'nɔtəni], *n.* monotonie, *f.*

monsoon [mɔn'suːn], *n.* mousson, *f.*

monster ['mɔnstə], *n.* monstre, *m.*

monstrosity [mɔn'strɔsiti], *n.* monstruosité, *f.*

monstrous ['mɔnstrəs], *a.* monstrueux; prodigieux.

month [mʌnθ], *n.* mois, *m.*; *calendar month*, mois civil; *the day of the month*, le quantième du mois, *m.*

monthly ['mʌnθli], *a.* mensuel, de tous les mois.—*n.* (*fam.*) revue mensuelle, *f.*—*adv.* tous les mois, par mois.

monument ['mɔnjumənt], *n.* monument, *m.*

monumental [mɔnju'mentl], *a.* monumental.

moo [muː], *v.i.* meugler, bugler.—*n.* meuglement, *m.*

mood [muːd], *n.* humeur, *f.*; (*Gram. etc.*) mode, *m.*

moody ['muːdi], *a.* de mauvaise humeur, triste.

moon [muːn], *n.* lune, *f.*; *by the light of the moon*, au clair de la lune.—*v.i.* muser; *to moon about*, flâner.

moonbeam ['muːnbiːm], *n.* rayon de lune, *m.*

moonlight ['muːnlait], *n.* clair de lune, *m.*

moonlit ['muːnlit], *a.* éclairé par la lune.

moonshine ['muːnʃain], *n.* clair de lune, *m.*; (*fig.*) chimères, *f.pl.*

moonstrike ['muːnstraik], *n.* alunissage, *m.*

moonstruck ['muːnstrʌk], *a.* lunatique.

Moor [muə], *n.* Maure, *m.*, *f.*

moor (1) [muə], *n.* lande, bruyère, *f.*; marais, *m.*

moor (2) [muə], *v.t.* amarrer.—*v.i.* s'amarrer.

moor-hen ['muəhen], *n.* poule d'eau, *f.*

moorings ['muəriŋz], *n.* amarres, *f.pl.*, mouillage, *m.*

moorland ['muələnd], *n.* lande, bruyère, *f.*, marais, *m.*

moose [muːs], *n.* élan du Canada, *m.*

moot [muːt], *v.t.* discuter, débattre, controverser.—*a. moot point*, question discutable, *f.*

mop [mɔp], *n.* balai à laver, *m.*—*v.t.* nettoyer avec un balai, éponger; *to mop one's face*, s'éponger la figure.

mope [moup], *v.i.* s'ennuyer; être hébété.

moping ['moupiŋ], *a.* triste, hébété.

moral ['mɔrəl], *a.* moral.—*n.* morale, moralité, *f.*; (*pl.*) mœurs, *f.pl.*

morale [mɔ'rɑːl], *n.* moral (*de militaires etc.*), *m.*

morality [mə'ræliti], *n.* morale; moralité, *f.*

moralize ['mɔrəlaiz], *v.i.* moraliser.

morally ['mɔrəli], *adv.* moralement.

morass [mə'ræs], *n.* marais, *m.*, fondrière, *f.*

morbid ['mɔːbid], *a.* maladif, malsain, morbide.

morbidly ['mɔːbidli], *adv.* morbidement.

morbidness ['mɔːbidnis], *n.* état maladif, état morbide, *m.*

more [mɔː], *a.* and *adv.* plus; plus de; plus nombreux; encore; davantage; *more and more*, de plus en plus; *more than*, plus que, plus de (*suivi d'un nombre*); *no more*, pas davantage; *no more of that!* arrêtez cela! *once more*, encore une fois; *some more*, encore un peu, davantage.

moreover [mɔː'rouvə], *adv.* de plus, d'ailleurs, en outre.

moribund ['mɔribʌnd], *a.* moribond.

Mormon ['mɔːmən], *a.* mormon.—*n.* Mormon (*personne*), *m.*

morn [mɔːn], *n.* (*poet.*) matin, *m.*, aurore, *f.*

morning ['mɔːniŋ], *a.* du matin.—*n.* matin, *m.*, matinée, *f.*; *good morning*, bonjour; *in the morning*, le matin; *the next morning*, le lendemain matin.

Moroccan [mə'rɔkən], *a.* marocain.—*n.* Marocain (*personne*), *m.*

Morocco [mə'rɔkou]. le Maroc, *m.*

morocco-leather [mə'rɔkou'leðə], *n.* maroquin, *m.*

moron ['mɔːrɔn], *n.* crétin, idiot, *m.*

morose [mə'rous], *a.* morose.

morphia ['mɔːfiə], **morphine** ['mɔːfiːn], *n.* morphine, *f.*

morrow ['mɔrou], *n.* (*poet.*) demain, lendemain, *m.*; *tomorrow*, demain.

morsel [mɔːsl], *n.* morceau, *m.*

mortal [mɔːtl], *a.* mortel, funeste (*fatal*); des mortels, humain (*terrestre*); à outrance, à mort (*combat*); *any mortal thing*, n'importe quoi.—*n.* mortel, *m.*

mortality [mɔː'tæliti], *n.* mortalité; humanité, *f.*

mortally ['mɔːtəli], *adv.* mortellement, à mort.

mortar ['mɔːtə], *n.* mortier, *m.*

mortgage ['mɔːgidʒ], *n.* hypothèque, *f.*—
v.t. hypothéquer.

mortician [mɔːˈtiʃən], *n.* (*Am.*) entrepreneur
de pompes funèbres, *m.*

mortification [mɔːtifiˈkeiʃən], *n.* mortification; (*Path.*) gangrène, *f.*

mortify ['mɔːtifai], *v.t.* mortifier; (*Path.*)
faire gangrener.—*v.i.* se gangrener.

mortise ['mɔːtis], *n.* mortaise, *f.*—*v.t.* mor-
taiser.

mortuary ['mɔːtjuəri], *a.* mortuaire.—*n.*
morgue, *f.*, dépôt mortuaire, *m.*

mosaic [moˈzeiik], *a.* and *n.* mosaïque, *f.*

Moscow ['mɔskou]. Moscou, *m.*

Moses ['mouziz]. Moïse, *m.*

Moslem ['mazlim, 'mɔzləm], *a.* musulman.—
n. Musulman (*personne*), *m.*

mosque [mɔsk], *n.* mosquée, *f.*

mosquito [mɔsˈkiːtou], *n.* moustique, *m.*

mosquito-net [mɔsˈkiːtounet], *n.* moustiquaire, *f.*

moss ['mɔs], *n.* mousse, *f.*; marais, *m.*; *peat-
moss*, tourbière, *f.*

moss-grown ['mɔsgroun], **mossy** ['mɔsi], *a.*
couvert de mousse, moussu.

moss-rose ['mɔsrouz], *n.* rose moussue, *f.*

most [moust], *a.* le plus; le plus grand; *most
men*, la plupart des hommes; *the most
part*, la plus grande partie.—*adv.* le plus,
plus; très, fort; *a most valuable book*,
un livre des plus précieux; *most likely*,
très probablement.—*n.* la plupart, *f.*; le
plus grand nombre, *m.*

mostly ['moustli], *adv.* pour la plupart; le
plus souvent; principalement.

mote [mout], *n.* grain de poussière, *m.*; paille
(*dans l'œil*), *f.*

motel ['moutel], *n.* motel, *m.*

motet [mouˈtet], *n.* (*Mus.*) motet, *m.*

moth [mɔθ], *n.* (*Ent.*) lépidoptère; papillon de
nuit, *m.*; phalène; mite (*de vêtements*), *f.*

moth-eaten ['mɔθiːtn], *a.* mité.

mother ['mʌðə], *a.* mère; maternel; métropolitain (*église*); *mother tongue*, langue
maternelle, *f.*—*n.* mère; bonne mère, bonne
femme (*terme familier*), *f.*; *stepmother*,
belle-mère, *f.*—*v.t.* servir de mère à;
adopter; enfanter (*quelque chose*).

mother-country ['mʌðəkʌntri], *n.* mère
patrie, *f.*

mother-in-law ['mʌðərinlɔː], *n.* belle-mère,
f.

motherly ['mʌðəli], *a.* maternel, de mère.—
adv. maternellement, en mère.

mother-of-pearl [mʌðərəvˈpəːl], *n.* nacre, *f.*

motion ['mouʃən], *n.* mouvement; signe
(*signal*), *m.*; motion, proposition (*à une
réunion*); (*Med.*) selle, *f.*—*v.t.* faire signe (*à*).

motionless ['mouʃənlis], *a.* immobile.

motivate ['moutiveit], *v.t.* motiver (*une
action*).

motive ['moutiv], *a.* moteur, qui fait mouvoir;
motive power, force motrice, *f.*—*n.* motif,
mobile, *m.*

motley ['mɔtli], *a.* bigarré, mélangé.

motor ['moutə], *n.* moteur, *m.*—*v.i.* aller *ou*
voyager en auto.

motor-boat ['moutəbout], *n.* canot automobile, *m.*

motor-car ['moutəkaː], *n.* automobile, auto,
voiture, *f.*

motor-cycle ['moutəsaikl], *n.* motocyclette, *f.*

motoring ['moutəriŋ], *n.* automobilisme, *m.*

motorist ['moutərist], *n.* automobiliste, *m.*, *f.*

motorway ['moutəwei], *n.* autoroute, *f.*

mottle [mɔtl], *v.t.* madrer; marbrer.

motto ['mɔtou], *n.* (*pl.* **mottoes** ['mɔtouz])
devise, *f.*

mould (1) [mould], *n.* moisi (*mousse*); terreau
(*humus*), *m.*—*v.i.* se moisir.

mould (2) [mould], *n.* moule, *m.*, forme, *f.*—
v.t. mouler; (*fig.*) pétrir.

moulder ['mouldə], *v.i.* se réduire en poudre
ou en poussière.

mouldiness ['mouldinis], *n.* moisissure, *f.*

moulding ['mouldiŋ], *n.* moulure, *f.*

mouldy ['mouldi], *a.* moisi.

moult [moult], *v.i.* muer.

moulting ['moultiŋ], *n.* mue, *f.*

mound [maund], *n.* butte, *f.*, tertre, *m.*;
(*Fort.*) remparts, *m.pl.*

mount [maunt], *n.* mont, *m.*, montagne;
monture (*cheval*); (*Turf*) monte, *f.*; (*Phot.*)
carton, *m.*—*v.t.* monter, monter sur.—*v.i.*
monter, s'élever; monter à cheval.

mountain ['mauntin], *a.* de montagne, des
montagnes, montagnard, montagneux (*paysage*).—*n.* montagne, *f.*

mountaineer [maunti'niə], *n.* montagnard,
m.; alpiniste, *m.*, *f.*

mountaineering [maunti'niəriŋ], *n.* alpinisme, *m.*

mountainous ['mauntinəs], *a.* montagneux,
de montagnes; (*fig.*) énorme.

mountebank ['mauntibæŋk], *n.* charlatan, *m.*

mounted ['mauntid], *a.* monté, à cheval;
(*Phot.*) collé.

mounting ['mauntiŋ], *n.* montage, *m.*, monture, *f.*; (*Phot.*) collage, *m.*

mourn [mɔːn], *v.t.* pleurer, déplorer.—*v.i.*
pleurer, se lamenter.

mourner ['mɔːnə], *n.* personne affligée, *f.*;
pleureur (*professionnel*), *m.*, personne qui suit
le convoi, *f.*

mournful ['mɔːnful], *a.* triste, lugubre.

mourning ['mɔːniŋ], *a.* affligé, triste; de
deuil.—*n.* affliction, lamentation, *f.*; deuil
(*vêtements*), *m.*

mouse [maus], *n.* (*pl.* **mice** [mais]) souris, *f.*;
field-mouse, mulot, *m.*

mouse-trap ['maustræp], *n.* souricière, *f.*

moustache [məˈstaːʃ], *n.* moustache, *f.*

mousy ['mausi], *a.* gris (*couleur*); timide.

mouth [mauθ], *n.* (*pl.* **mouths** [mauðz])
bouche; gueule (*de bête sauvage*); embouchure (*de rivière*); ouverture, entrée, *f.*,
orifice (*donnant accès*); goulot (*d'une bouteille*), *m.*; *by word of mouth*, de vive voix.
—[mauð], *v.t.*, *v.i.* crier.

mouthed [mauðd], *a.* *foul-mouthed*, mal
embouché; *mealy-mouthed*, doucereux.

mouthful ['mauθful], *n.* bouchée, gorgée (*de
vin*), *f.*

mouthpiece ['mauθpiːs], *n.* embouchure, *f.*;
(*fig.*) interprète, porte-parole, *m.*

movable ['muːvəbl], *a.* mobile.—*n.* meuble,
m.

move [muːv], *v.t.* remuer; déplacer; mouvoir,
faire mouvoir, mettre en mouvement; faire
marcher, faire aller; transporter (*marchandises etc.*); (*fig.*) émouvoir, toucher; exciter,
pousser (*à*); proposer (*que*); (*Chess*) jouer;
to move forward, avancer; *to move out*,
déloger, sortir.—*v.i.* bouger, se remuer,

mouvoir, se déplacer; se mettre en mouvement, aller, partir, marcher, s'avancer; s'ébranler (*armée*); déménager (*changer de résidence*); (*Chess*) jouer; *move on!* circulez! *to move aside*, s'écarter; *to move away*, s'éloigner; *to move back*, reculer, se reculer; *to move in*, emménager; *to move off*, s'éloigner, s'en aller; *to move on*, avancer; *to move out*, sortir, déménager.—*n.* mouvement; coup; (*Chess*) trait, *m.*; *masterly move*, coup de maître; *to be on the move*, être en mouvement, se remuer; *to get a move on*, se presser; *to make a move*, se préparer à partir.

movement ['muːvmənt], *n.* mouvement, *m.*

mover ['muːvə], *n.* moteur; mobile, *m.*; force motrice, *f.*; auteur d'une proposition, *m.*

movie ['muːvi], *n.* (*Am.*) film, *m.*; *the movies*, le cinéma, *m.*

moving ['muːviŋ], *a.* mouvant, mobile; (*fig.*) émouvant.—*n.* mouvement; déménagement (*de mobilier*); déplacement (*changement de place*), *m.*

movingly ['muːviŋli], *adv.* d'une manière émouvante.

mow [mou], *v.t. irr.* faucher; tondre.

mower ['mouə], *n.* faucheur (*personne*), *m.*; faucheuse, tondeuse (*machine*), *f.*

Mr. ['mistə], Monsieur (*abbr.* M.).

Mrs. ['misiz], Madame (*abbr.* Mme.).

much [mʌtʃ], *adv.* beaucoup, bien, fort, très; *as much*, autant; *how much?* combien (*de*)? *much more*, bien plus; *nothing much*, pas grand'chose; *pretty much*, à peu près; *so much*, tant; *so much more*, d'autant plus; *so much the better*, tant mieux; *to make much of*, faire grand cas de; *too much*, trop (*de*).

muck [mʌk], *n.* fumier (*engrais*), *m.*; fange (*boue*); (*fig.*) saleté, *f.*—*v.t.* fumer; salir.

muckiness ['mʌkinis], *n.* saleté, ordure, *f.*

mucky ['mʌki], *a.* sale, malpropre.

mucous ['mjuːkəs], *a.* muqueux; *mucous membrane*, muqueuse, *f.*

mucus ['mjuːkəs], *n.* mucus, *m.*; mucosité, *f.*

mud [mʌd], *n.* boue, bourbe, vase, *f.*, limon, *m.*

mudguard ['mʌdgɑːd], *n.* garde-boue, *m.*

muddle [mʌdl], *v.t.* brouiller; troubler; gâcher.—*v.i.* faire du gâchis.—*n.* confusion, *f.*, désordre, gâchis, *m.*

muddled [mʌdld], *a.* troublé; hébété.

muddler ['mʌdlə], *n.* brouillon, *m.*

muddy ['mʌdi], *a.* boueux, bourbeux; crotté.

muff [mʌf], *n.* manchon, *m.*

muffle [mʌfl], *v.t.* emmitoufler, affubler; assourdir (*cloche*); voiler (*tambour*).—*n.* moufle, *f.*

muffler ['mʌflə], *n.* cache-nez, *m.*

mug [mʌg], *n.* pot, *m.*, tasse; (*slang*) gueule, binette, *f.*; (*colloq.*) imbécile, *m., f.*

muggy ['mʌgi], *a.* humide, lourd.

mulberry ['mʌlbəri], *n.* mûre, *f.*; *mulberry-tree*, mûrier, *m.*

mulch [mʌltʃ], *n.* paillis, *m.*—*v.t.* pailler, fumer.

mule [mjuːl], *n.* mulet, *m.*, mule, *f.*

mulish ['mjuːliʃ], *a.* de mulet; (*fig.*) têtu.

mull [mʌl], *n.* gâchis, *m.*—*v.t.* faire chauffer et épicer; *mulled wine*, vin chaud épicé.

multicoloured ['mʌltikʌləd], *a.* multicolore.

multifarious [mʌltiˈfɛəriəs], *a.* varié, divers, multiplié.

multi-millionaire ['mʌltimiljəˈnɛə], *n.* milliardaire, *m., f.*

multiple ['mʌltipl], *a. and n.* multiple, *m.*; *multiple store*, maison à succursales, *f.*

multiplication [mʌltipliˈkeiʃən], *n.* multiplication, *f.*

multiplicity [mʌltiˈplisiti], *n.* multiplicité, *f.*

multiply ['mʌltiplai], *v.t.* multiplier.—*v.i.* multiplier, se multiplier.

multitude ['mʌltitjuːd], *n.* multitude, *f.*

multitudinous [mʌltiˈtjuːdinəs], *a.* très nombreux, innombrable.

mum (1) [mʌm], *a.* muet.—*int.* bouche close! chut!

mum (2) [mʌm], *n.* (*fam.*) maman, *f.*

mumble [mʌmbl], *v.i.* marmotter.

mumbler ['mʌmblə], *n.* marmotteur, *m.*

mummer ['mʌmə], *n.* mime (*acteur*), *m.*

mummify ['mʌmifai], *v.t.* momifier.

mummy (1) ['mʌmi], *n.* momie, *f.*

mummy (2), **mummie** ['mʌmi], *n.* (*fam.*) maman, *f.*

mumps [mʌmps], *n.pl.* (*Med.*) oreillons, *m.pl.*

munch [mʌntʃ], *v.t., v.i.* mâcher, croquer.

mundane ['mʌndein], *a.* mondain.

municipal [mjuˈnisipl], *a.* municipal.

municipality [mjunisiˈpæliti], *n.* municipalité, *f.*

munificence [mjuˈnifisəns], *n.* munificence, *f.*

munificent [mjuˈnifisənt], *a.* libéral, généreux.

munition [mjuˈniʃən], *n.* munitions (*de guerre*), *f.pl.*—*v.t.* approvisionner. |

mural ['mjuərəl], *a.* mural.—*n.* peinture murale, *f.*

murder ['məːdə], *n.* meurtre, homicide, *m.*; *wilful murder*, meurtre avec préméditation, assassinat, *m.*—*v.t.* assassiner, tuer; (*fig.*) écorcher (*une langue etc.*).

murderer ['məːdərə], *n.* meurtrier, assassin, *m.*

murderess ['məːdəris], *n.* meurtrière, *f.*

murdering ['məːdəriŋ], *a.*, **murderous** ['məːdərəs], *a.* meurtrier, assassin.

murkiness ['məːkinis], *n.* obscurité, *f.*

murky ['məːki], *a.* sombre, obscur, ténébreux.

murmur ['məːmə], *n.* murmure, *m.*—*v.i.* murmurer.

murmuring ['məːməriŋ], *a.* murmurant, murmurateur.—*n.* murmure, *m.*, murmures, *m.pl.*

muscle [mʌsl], *n.* muscle, *m.*

muscular ['mʌskjulə], *a.* musculaire (*force*); musculeux (*membres*).

Muse [mjuːz], *n.* muse, *f.*

muse [mjuːz], *v.i.* méditer (*sur*) rêver (*à*).—*n.* muse, rêverie, méditation, *f.*

museum [mjuˈziːəm], *n.* musée, *m.*

mushroom ['mʌʃrum], *n.* champignon, *m.*

music ['mjuːzik], *n.* musique, *f.*

musical ['mjuːzikəl], *a.* musical; (*fig.*) harmonieux, mélodieux; qui aime la musique.

musician [mjuˈziʃən], *n.* musicien, *m.*

music-stand ['mjuːzikstænd], *n.* pupitre à musique, *m.*

music-stool ['mjuːzikstuːl], *n.* tabouret de piano, *m.*

musing ['mjuːziŋ], *n.* méditation; (*pl.*) rêverie, *f.*

musk [mʌsk], *n.* musc, *m.*
musket ['mʌskit], *n.* fusil, mousquet, *m.*
musketeer [mʌski'tiə], *n.* mousquetaire, *m.*
musketry ['mʌskitri], *n.* mousqueterie, *f.*, tir, *m.*
musky ['mʌski], *a.* musqué, parfumé de musc.
Muslim ['mʌzlim], [MOSLEM].
muslin ['mʌzlin], *a.* de mousseline.—*n.* mousseline, *f.*
mussel ['mʌsl], *n.* moule, *f.*
must (1) [mʌst], *v. aux.* falloir; devoir; *I must do it*, il faut que je le fasse; *you must know*, vous devez savoir.
must (2) [mʌst], *n.* moût (*de vin*), *m.*
mustard ['mʌstəd], *n.* moutarde, *f.*
muster ['mʌstə], *n.* appel, *m.*, revue, *f.*; rassemblement, *m.*; troupe, bande, *f.*; contrôles (*liste*), *m.pl.*—*v.t.* faire l'appel de; passer en revue; réunir, rassembler; se procurer; *to muster up courage*, prendre son courage à deux mains.—*v.i.* s'assembler, se réunir.
mustiness ['mʌstinis], *n.* moisi, *m.*
musty ['mʌsti], *a.* moisi; qui sent le renfermé.
mutability [mju:tə'biliti], *n.* mutabilité, *f.*
mutation [mju:'teiʃən], *n.* mutation, *f.*
mute [mju:t], *a. and n.* muet, *m.*—*v.t.* amortir (*les cordes d'un violon etc.*).
mutely ['mju:tli], *adv.* en silence.
mutilate ['mju:tileit], *v.t.* mutiler, estropier.
mutilated ['mju:tileitid], *a.* mutilé.
mutilation [mju:ti'leiʃən], *n.* mutilation, *f.*
mutineer [mju:ti'niə], *n.* révolté, rebelle, mutin, *m.*
mutinous ['mju:tinəs], *a.* rebelle, mutiné, mutin.
mutinously ['mju:tinəsli], *adv.* séditieusement.
mutiny ['mju:tini], *n.* mutinerie, sédition, révolte, *f.*—*v.i.* se mutiner, s'insurger.
mutter ['mʌtə], *v.t.*, *v.i.* marmotter.—*n.* marmottement, *m.*
muttering ['mʌtəriŋ], *a.* marmotteur, murmurant.—*n.* murmure, marmottement, marmottage, *m.*
mutton [mʌtn], *n.* mouton (*viande*), *m.*; *leg of mutton*, gigot, *m.*
mutton-chop ['mʌtn'tʃɔp], *n.* côtelette de mouton, *f.*
mutual ['mju:tjuəl], *a.* mutuel, réciproque; *mutual friend*, ami commun, *m.*
mutually ['mju:tjuəli], *adv.* mutuellement.
muzzle [mʌzl], *n.* museau (*d'animal*), *m.*; bouche, gueule (*de canon*), *f.*; bout (*de fusil etc.*), *m.*; muselière (*pour chien*), *f.*—*v.t.* museler.
muzzy ['mʌzi], *a.* brouillé, confus.
my [mai], *poss. a.* mon, *m.*, ma, *f.*, mes, *pl.*
myopic [mai'ɔpik], *a.* myope.
myriad ['miriəd], *a.* (*poet.*) innombrable.—*n.* myriade, *f.*
myrrh [mə:], *n.* myrrhe, *f.*
myrtle [mə:tl], *n.* myrte, *m.*
myself [mai'self], *pron.* me; moi-même; moi; *I consider myself*, je me crois.
mysterious [mis'tiəriəs], *a.* mystérieux.
mysteriously [mis'tiəriəsli], *adv.* mystérieusement.
mystery ['mistəri], *n.* mystère, *m.*
mystic ['mistik], *a. and n.* (*Theol.*) mystique, *m.*, *f.*

mysticism ['mistisizm], *n.* mysticisme, *m.*
mystify ['mistifai], *v.t.* envelopper de mystère, mystifier.
mystique [mis'ti:k], *n.* mystique, *f.*
myth [miθ], *n.* mythe, *m.*
mythical ['miθikl], *a.* mythique.
mythology [mi'θɔlədʒi], *n.* mythologie, *f.*

N

N, n [en]. quatorzième lettre de l'alphabet, *m.* ou *f.*
nab [næb], *v.t.* happer, saisir, pincer.
nag (1) [næg], *n.* bidet, petit cheval, *m.*
nag (2) [næg], *v.t.*, *v.i.* gronder, chamailler, criailler.
nagging ['nægiŋ], *a.* querelleur (*personne*); agaçant (*sensation*).
nail [neil], *n.* clou; ongle (*de griffes, de doigts*), *m.*—*v.t.* clouer; clouter.
nail-brush ['neilbrʌʃ], *n.* brosse à ongles, *f.*
naïve [nai'i:v], *a.* naïf, ingénu.
naked ['neikid], *a.* nu, à nu; à découvert, ouvert (*sans protection*); dégarni (*sans meubles*); *stark naked*, tout nu.
nakedness ['neikidnis], *n.* nudité, *f.*
name [neim], *n.* nom; (*fig.*) renom, *m.*, renommée, réputation, *f.*; *Christian name*, nom de baptême, prénom, *m.*; *maiden name*, nom de jeune fille; *what is your name?* comment vous appelez-vous?—*v.t.* nommer, appeler; désigner; *to be named*, s'appeler, se nommer.
named [neimd], *a.* nommé, désigné.
nameless ['neimlis], *a.* sans nom, anonyme; inconnu.
namely ['neimli], *adv.* à savoir, c'est-à-dire.
namesake ['neimseik], *n.* homonyme, *m.*
nanny ['næni], *n.* bonne d'enfant; (*childish*) nounou, *f.*
Napoleon [nə'pouljən]. Napoléon, *m.*
narcissus [naː'sisəs], *n.* narcisse, *m.*
narcotic [naː'kɔtik], *a. and n.* narcotique, *m.*
narrate [næ'reit], *v.t.* raconter, narrer.
narration [næ'reiʃən], *n.* narration, *f.*, récit, *m.*
narrative ['nærətiv], *a.* narratif.—*n.* récit, narré, *m.*
narrator [nə'reitə], *n.* narrateur, *m.*
narrow ['nærou], *a.* étroit, resserré; à l'étroit, gêné; rétréci, limité, borné (*esprit*); *to have a narrow escape*, l'échapper belle, (*pl.*) détroit, pas, *m.*—*v.t.* rétrécir, resserrer, limiter, borner.—*v.i.* se rétrécir, se resserrer.
narrowly ['nærouli], *adv.* étroitement, à l'étroit; de près.

narrow-minded ['nærou'maindid], *a.* à l'esprit étroit.
narrowness ['nærounis], *n.* étroitesse, *f.*
nasal [neizl], *a.* nasal, du nez.
nascent ['næsənt], *a.* naissant.
nastily ['nɑ:stili], *adv.* salement, malproprement.
nastiness ['nɑ:stinis], *n.* saleté; grossièreté, *f.*
nasturtium [nəs'tə:ʃəm], *n.* capucine, *f.*
nasty ['nɑ:sti], *a.* sale, malpropre; (*fig.*) méchant, vilain; dégoûtant.
natal [neitl], *a.* natal, de naissance.
nation ['neiʃən], *n.* nation, *f.*
national ['næʃənl], *a.* national; *national anthem*, hymne national, *m.*; *national debt*, dette publique, *f.*; *national insurance*, assurances sociales, *f.pl.*
nationalism ['næʃnəlizm], *n.* nationalisme, *m.*
nationality [næʃə'næliti], *n.* nationalité, *f.*
nationalization [næʃnəlai'zeiʃən], *n.* nationalisation (*d'une industrie*); (*Am.*) naturalisation (*d'une personne*), *f.*
nationalize ['næʃnəlaiz], *v.t.* nationaliser.
native ['neitiv], *a.* natif, naturel; indigène (*personne* ou *plante*); maternel (*langue etc.*); *native land*, patrie, *f.—n.* natif (*d'une ville*); habitant (*d'une île*); naturel (*de tribu sauvage*); indigène (*des pays d'outremer*), *m.*; *a native of England*, Anglais de naissance, *m.*; *a native of Paris*, natif de Paris.
nativity [nə'tiviti], *n.* nativité; naissance, *f.*
natty ['næti], *a.* pimpant, propret, coquet.
natural ['nætʃərəl], *a.* naturel; réel; naïf, simple; (*Mus.*) bécarre.
naturalist ['nætʃərəlist], *n.* naturaliste, *m., f.*
naturalization [nætʃərəlai'zeiʃən], *n.* naturalisation, *f.*
naturally ['nætʃərəli], *adv.* naturellement.
nature ['neitʃə], *n.* nature, *f.*; naturel (*disposition*), *m.*
naught [nɔ:t], *n.* néant, rien; (*Arith.*) zéro, *m.*; *to come to naught*, échouer.
naughtily ['nɔ:tili], *adv.* par méchanceté.
naughtiness ['nɔ:tinis], *n.* méchanceté, *f.*
naughty ['nɔ:ti], *a.* méchant, vilain.
nausea ['nɔ:ziə], *n.* nausée, *f.*
nauseating ['nɔ:zieitiŋ], *a.* nauséabond, dégoûtant, écœurant.
nautical ['nɔ:tikl], *a.* nautique; marin (*milles etc.*).
naval [neivl], *a.* naval; maritime; de la marine (*de guerre*); *naval officer*, officier de marine, *m.*
nave (1) [neiv], *n.* nef (*d'église*), *f.*
nave (2) [neiv], *n.* moyeu (*de roue*), *m.*
navel [neivl], *n.* nombril, *m.*
navigable ['nævigəbl], *a.* navigable.
navigate ['nævigeit], *v.t.* gouverner.—*v.i.* naviguer.
navigation [nævi'geiʃən], *n.* navigation, *f.*
navigator ['nævigeitə], *n.* navigateur, *m.*
navvy ['nævi], *n.* terrassier, *m.*
navy ['neivi], *n.* marine de guerre, *f.*; *Merchant Navy*, marine marchande.
navy blue ['neivi'blu:], *a.* and *n.* bleu marine, *m.inv.*
*****nay** [nei], *adv.* non; bien plus; et même, qui plus est; *to say nay*, refuser.
Neapolitan [niə'pɔlitən], *a.* napolitain, de Naples.—*n.* Napolitain (*personne*), *m.*
neap tide ['ni:p'taid], *n.* marée de morte eau, *f.*

near [niə], *a.* proche, rapproché; chiche (*parcimonieux*); cher (*bien-aimé*); fidèle (*intime*); de gauche (*left*).—*adv.* près, près de, de près; presque.—*prep.* près de, auprès de.—*v.t., v.i.* s'approcher de.
nearby ['niəbai], *a.,* [niə'bai], *adv.* tout près, tout proche.
nearly ['niəli], *adv.* de près; à peu près; presque; *he was nearly drowned*, il faillit se noyer.
nearness ['niənis], *n.* proximité; parcimonie (*avarice*), *f.*
neat [ni:t], *a.* propre, soigné, net; simple et élégant; pur, sec (*sans mélange*).
neatly ['ni:tli], *adv.* proprement; nettement adroitement (*habilement*).
neatness ['ni:tnis], *n.* propreté, netteté, *f.*
nebula ['nebjulə], *n.* (*Astron.*) nébuleuse, *f.*
nebulous ['nebjuləs], *a.* nébuleux.
necessaries ['nesəsəriz], *n.pl.* nécessaire, *m.*
necessarily ['nesəsərili], *adv.* nécessairement forcément.
necessary ['nesəsri], *a.* nécessaire.
necessitate [ni'sesiteit], *v.t.* nécessiter.
necessitous [ni'sesitəs], *a.* nécessiteux, dans le besoin.
necessity [ni'sesiti], *n.* nécessité, *f.*; besoin (*indigence*), *m.*; *of necessity*, nécessairement, forcément.
neck [nek], *n.* cou; goulot (*de bouteille etc.*); manche (*de violon*); collet (*de viande*), *m.*; encolure (*d'une robe*), langue (*de terre*), *f.*; *stiff neck*, torticolis, *m.*
neckerchief ['nekətʃif], *n.* foulard (*d'homme*), fichu (*de femme*), *m.*
necklace ['neklis], *n.* collier, *m.*
neck-tie ['nektai], *n.* cravate, *f.*
necromancy ['nekrəmænsi], *n.* nécromancie, *f.*
necropolis [ni'krɔpəlis], *n.* nécropole, *f.*
nectar ['nektə], *n.* nectar, *m.*
nectarine ['nektərin], *n.* brugnon, *m.*
need [ni:d], *n.* besoin, *m.*; nécessité; indigence, *f.*; *if need be*, le cas échéant; *in case of need*, au besoin; *to be in need*, être dans la misère; *to be in need of* or *to have need of*, avoir besoin de.—*v.t.* avoir besoin de; exiger.—*v.i.* avoir besoin; devoir, avoir (*à*); (*impers.*) falloir, être nécessaire.
needful ['ni:dful], *a.* nécessaire; *the needful*, le nécessaire, *m.*
needle [ni:dl], *n.* aiguille, *f.*
needless ['ni:dlis], *a.* inutile.
needlework ['ni:dlwə:k], *n.* ouvrage à l'aiguille, *m.*; (*Sch.*) couture, *f.*
*****needs** [ni:dz], *adv.* (*used only with* must) nécessairement, absolument; *I must needs*, il faut absolument que je (*with subj.*).
needy ['ni:di], *a.* indigent, nécessiteux.
ne'er [nɛə], (*poet.*) [NEVER].
nefarious [ni'fɛəriəs], *a.* abominable, infâme.
negation [ni'geiʃən], *n.* négation, *f.*
negative ['negətiv], *a.* négatif.—*n.* négative, *f.*; (*Phot.*) cliché, négatif, *m.—v.t.* rejeter.
neglect [ni'glekt], *n.* négligence, *f.*; oubli, *m.* —*v.t.* négliger.
neglected [ni'glektid], *a.* négligé.
neglectful [ni'glektful], *a.* négligent.
negligence ['neglidʒəns], *n.* négligence, *f.*
negligent ['neglidʒənt], *a.* négligent.

negligible

negligible ['neglidʒibl], *a.* négligeable.
negotiable [ni'gouʃiəbl], *a.* négociable.
negotiate [ni'gouʃieit], *v.t., v.i.* négocier.
negotiation [nigouʃi'eiʃən], *n.* négociation, *f.*
negotiator [ni'gouʃieitə], *n.* négociateur, *m.*
Negress ['ni:gres], *n. (sometimes pej.)* noire, *f.*
Negro ['ni:grou], *n.* noir, *m.*
neigh [nei], *v.i.* hennir.—*n.* hennissement, *m.*
neighbour ['neibə], *n.* voisin; *(Bibl.)* prochain, *m.*
neighbourhood ['neibəhud], *n.* voisinage, *m.*; alentours, environs, *m.pl.*; quartier, *m.*
neighbouring ['neibəriŋ], *a.* voisin.
neighbourly ['neibəli], *a.* de voisin, de bon voisin.
neighing ['neiiŋ], *n.* hennissement, *m.*
neither ['naiðə, 'ni:ðə], *a. and pron.* ni l'un ni l'autre, *m.*—*conj.* ni; non plus; *neither ... nor*, ni ... ni.—*adv.* du reste, d'ailleurs.
Nemesis ['nemisis], *n.* némésis, *f.*
neolithic [ni:ə'liθik], *a.* néolithique.
neon ['ni:ɔn], *a. neon light*, lampe au néon, *f.*—*n. (Chem.)* néon, *m.*
Nepal [nə'pɔ:l], *n.* le Népal, *m.*
Nepalese [nepə'li:z], *a.* népalais.—*n.* Népalais *(personne)*, *m.*
nephew ['nefju, 'nevju], *n.* neveu, *m.*
nepotism ['nepətizm], *n.* népotisme, *m.*
Nero ['niərou], Néron, *m.*
nerve [nə:v], *n.* nerf; *(fig.)* courage, *m.*; audace, *f.*; *(pop.)* toupet, *m.*
nerve-cell ['nə:vsel], *n.* cellule nerveuse, *f.*
nerveless ['nə:vlis], *a.* sans nerf; *(fig.)* sans vigueur.
nerve-racking ['nə:vrækiŋ], *a.* horripilant, énervant.
nervous ['nə:vəs], *a.* nerveux *(physiquement)*; timide, craintif *(moralement)*; *nervous breakdown*, dépression nerveuse, *f.*
nervousness ['nə:vəsnis], *n.* inquiétude, timidité; nervosité, *f.*
nest [nest], *n.* nid, *m.*; nichée *(couvée d'oiseaux)*, *f.*; *(fig.)* repaire, *m.*; *nest of tables*, table gigogne, *f.*—*v.i.* nicher, faire un nid.
nestle [nesl], *v.i.* nicher, se nicher.
nestling ['nesliŋ], *n.* petit oiseau encore au nid, béjaune, *m.*
net [net], *a.* net; pur.—*n.* filet, rets, *m.*; résille *(à cheveux)*, *f.*; tulle *(tissu)*, *m.*—*v.t.* prendre dans un filet; *(Comm.)* rapporter net.
nether ['neðə], *a.* bas, inférieur.
Netherlands ['neðələndz], the. les Pays-Bas, *m.pl.*
nethermost ['neðəmoust], *a.* le plus bas.
netting ['netiŋ], *n.* filet, réseau; grillage *(de fil de fer)*, *m.*
nettle [netl], *n.* ortie, *f.*—*v.t.* piquer, agacer, irriter.
nettlerash ['netlræʃ], *n.* urticaire, *f.*
network ['netwə:k], *n.* réseau, enchevêtrement, *m.*
neuralgia [nju'rældʒə], *n.* névralgie, *f.*
neuritis [nju'raitis], *n.* névrite, *f.*
neurosis [nju'rousis], *n.* névrose, *f.*
neurotic [nju'rɔtik], *a. and n.* névrosé, *m.*, neurotique, *m., f.*
neuter ['nju:tə], *a.* and *n.* neutre, *m.*
neutral ['nju:trəl], *a.* neutre; indifférent.—*n. (Motor.)* point-mort, *m.*
neutrality [nju'træliti], *n.* neutralité; indifférence, *f.*

neutralize ['nju:trəlaiz], *v.t.* neutraliser.
neutron ['nju:trɔn], *n.* neutron, *m.*
never ['nevə], *adv.* jamais; ne ... jamais; *never mind!* peu importe!
nevermore [nevə'mɔ:], *adv.* ne ... jamais plus, ne ... plus jamais.
nevertheless [nevəðə'les], *conj.* néanmoins, cependant, pourtant.
new [nju:], *a.* neuf *(qui n'a pas servi)*; nouveau *(récemment acquis, différent)*; frais, récent *(arrivé depuis peu)*; *brand-new*, flambant neuf, tout battant neuf; *New Year's Day*, le jour de l'an, *m.*
new-born ['nju:bɔ:n], *a.* nouveau-né; *new-born daughters*, filles nouveau-nées, *f.pl.*
new-comer ['nju:kʌmə], *n.* nouveau venu, *m.*
Newfoundland ['nju:fəndlænd, nju:'faundlənd]. la Terre-Neuve, *f.*—*n.* terre-neuve *(chien)*, *m.*
New Guinea [nju:'gini]. la Nouvelle-Guinée, *f.*
new-laid ['nju:leid], *a.* frais *(œuf)*.
newly ['nju:li], *adv.* nouvellement, fraîchement, récemment, de nouveau.
newness ['nju:nis], *n.* nouveauté, *f.*
New Orleans [nju:'ɔ:liənz]. la Nouvelle-Orléans, *f.*
news [nju:z], *n.* nouvelle, *f.*, nouvelles, *f.pl.*; *(Rad., Tel.)* bulletin d'informations, *m.*
news-agent ['nju:zeidʒənt], *n.* marchand de journaux, *m.*
newspaper ['nju:speipə], *n.* journal, *m.*
newt [nju:t], *n.* triton, *m.*, salamandre, *f.*
New Zealand [nju:'zi:lənd]. la Nouvelle-Zélande, *f.*—*a.* néo-zélandais.
New Zealander [nju:'zi:ləndə], *n.* Néo-Zélandais, *m.*
next [nekst], *a.* voisin, le plus voisin; le plus près; de côté; prochain *(dans l'avenir)*; suivant *(dans le passé)*; premier *(à la suite de)*.—*adv.* après, ensuite, puis; *what next?* et après? ensuite?—*prep. next to*, à côté de.
nib [nib], *n.* bec *(de stylo)*, *m.*; pointe *(d'outil)*, *f.*
nibble [nibl], *v.t.* mordiller, grignoter; mordre à *(l'hameçon)*; brouter *(l'herbe etc.)*.—*n.* grignotement, *m.*; touche *(du poisson)*, *f.*
Nicaragua [nikə'rægjuə]. le Nicaragua, *m.*
Nicaraguan [nikə'rægjuən], *a.* nicaraguayen.—*n.* Nicaraguayen *(personne)*, *m.*
nice [nais], *a.* bon, agréable, friand; *(colloq.)* délicat, gentil, aimable, charmant, propre; exact, difficile, exigeant *(délicat)*; *a nice child*, un enfant gentil, *m.*
nicely ['naisli], *adv.* bien, agréablement; délicatement; gentiment, aimablement; joliment; d'une manière recherchée.
nicety ['naisəti], *n. (pl. niceties* ['naisətiz]) délicatesse, finesse, *f.*; soin scrupuleux, *m.*; précision; exactitude, *f.*; *(pl.)* subtilités, finesses, *f.pl.*
niche [nitʃ], *n.* niche, *f.*
Nicholas ['nikələs]. Nicolas, *m.*
nick [nik], *n.* moment précis, *m.*; encoche, entaille *(coupure)*, *f.*; *(Print.)* cran, *m.*; *in the nick of time*, fort à propos, à point nommé.
nickel [nikl], *n.* nickel, *m.*; *(Am.)* pièce de cinq cents, *f.*
nickname ['nikneim], *n.* sobriquet, surnom, *m.*—*v.t.* donner un sobriquet à.
nicotine ['nikəti:n], *n.* nicotine, *f.*

niece [niːs], *n.* nièce, *f.*
nifty ['nifti], *a.* (*fam.*) pimpant.
Niger ['naidʒə], the. le Niger, *m.*
Nigeria [nai'dʒiəriə]. le Nigéria, *m.*
Nigerian [nai'dʒiəriən], *a.* nigérien.—*n.* Nigérien (*personne*), *m.*
niggard ['nigəd], *a.* and *n.* avare, ladre, *m.*
niggardliness ['nigədlinis], *n.* mesquinerie, ladrerie, *f.*
niggardly ['nigədli], *a.* mesquin, ladre, chiche.—*adv.* avec avarice, en avare.
niggle [nigl], *v.i.* tatillonner; fignoler.
nigh [nai], *adv.* près; presque; *to draw nigh*, approcher, s'approcher (*de*).
night [nait], *n.* nuit, *f.*; soir, *m.*; *first night*, première, *f.*
night-club ['naitklʌb], *n.* boîte de nuit, *f.*
night-dress ['naitdres], *n.* chemise de nuit, *f.*
night-fall ['naitfɔːl], *n.* tombée de la nuit, *f.*
nightie ['naiti], *colloq. abbr.* [NIGHT-DRESS].
nightingale ['naitiŋgeil], *n.* rossignol, *m.*
night-light ['naitlait], *n.* veilleuse, *f.*
nightly ['naitli], *a.* nocturne, de nuit.—*adv.* chaque nuit, toutes les nuits; tous les soirs.
nightmare ['naitmeə], *n.* cauchemar, *m.*
night-time ['naittaim], *n.* nuit, *f.*; *in the night-time*, pendant la nuit.
night-watchman ['nait'wɔtʃmən], *n.* (*pl.* -men [men]) veilleur de nuit, *m.*
nihilism ['naiilizm], *n.* nihilisme, *m.*
nil [nil], *n.* rien, néant, zéro, *m.*
Nile [nail], the. le Nil, *m.*
nimble [nimbl], *a.* agile, léger, leste.
nimbly ['nimbli], *adv.* agilement, lestement.
nine [nain], *a.* and *n.* neuf, *m.*
ninefold ['nainfould], *a.* neuf fois autant.
ninepins ['nainpinz], *n.pl.* quilles, *f.pl.*; jeu de quilles, *m.*
nineteen [nain'tiːn], *a.* and *n.* dix-neuf, *m.*
nineteenth [nain'tiːnθ], *a.* dix-neuvième; dix-neuf (*du mois ou souverains*).—*n.* dix-neuvième (*fraction*), *m.*
ninetieth ['naintiiθ], *a.* quatre-vingt-dixième. —*n.* quatre-vingt-dixième (*fraction*), *m.*
ninety ['nainti], *a.* and *n.* quatre-vingt-dix, *m.*
ninny ['nini], *n.* nigaud, niais, *m.*
ninth [nainθ], *a.* neuvième; neuf (*du mois ou souverains*).—*n.* neuvième (*fraction*), *m.*
nip [nip], *n.* pincement, *m.*, pince, *f.*, serrement, *m.*; morsure; (*Hort.*) brûlure (*par le froid*), *f.*—*v.t.* pincer; mordre; (*Hort.*) brûler (par le froid); *to nip off*, couper, enlever le bout de.
nipper ['nipə], *n.* pince, *f.*; (*colloq.*) gamin, gosse, *m.*; (*pl.*) pincettes, pinces, *f.pl.*
nipple [nipl], *n.* mamelon, bout de sein, *m.*
nippy ['nipi], *a.* preste, rapide; perçant (*froid*).
nit [nit], *n.* lente, *f.*
nitrate ['naitreit], *n.* nitrate, *m.*
nitre ['naitə], *n.* nitre, *m.*
nitric ['naitrik], *a.* nitrique, azotique.
nitrogen ['naitrədʒən], *n.* azote, *m.*
nitwit ['nitwit], *n.* imbécile, *m.*
no [nou], *a.* and *adv.* non, pas, ne . . . pas de ne . . . point de; pas un, nul, aucun.—*n.* non, *m.*
Noah ['nouə]. Noé, *m.*
nob [nɔb], *n.* (*colloq.*) caboche, *f.*; gros bonnet, *m.*
nobility [no'biliti], *n.* noblesse, *f.*
noble [noubl], *a.* noble; illustre, grand; généreux.—*n.* noble, *m.*

nobleman ['noublmən], *n.* (*pl.* -men [men]) noble, gentilhomme, *m.*
nobly ['noubli], *adv.* noblement; superbement.
nobody ['noubədi], *pron.* personne, *m.*; *I know nobody*, je ne connais personne; *nobody else*, personne d'autre.—*n.* zéro, inconnu, *m.*
nocturnal [nɔk'təːnl], *a.* nocturne, de nuit.
nod [nɔd], *n.* signe de tête, *m.*; inclination de tête, *f.*—*v.i.* faire un signe de tête; s'incliner; sommeiller (*s'assoupir*).
noggin ['nɔgin], *n.* petit pot (*en étain*), *m.*
noise [nɔiz], *n.* bruit; tapage, fracas, vacarme; tintement (*de cloche*) bourdonnement (*d'insectes etc.*); (*fig.*) éclat, *m.*—*v.t.* ébruiter, publier, répandre.
noiseless ['nɔizlis], *a.* sans bruit; silencieux.
noiselessly ['nɔizlisli], *adv.* sans bruit.
noisily ['nɔizili], *adv.* bruyamment.
noisome ['nɔisəm], *a.* malsain, infect, nuisible.
noisy ['nɔizi], *a.* bruyant; turbulent (*enfants*).
nomad ['noumæd], *n.* nomade, *m.*
nomadic [no'mædik], *a.* nomade.
nominal ['nɔminl], *a.* nominal; de nom; *nominal roll*, état nominatif, *m.*
nominally ['nɔminəli], *adv.* de nom; nominalement.
nominate ['nɔmineit], *v.t.* nommer; désigner; présenter, proposer (*un candidat etc.*).
nomination [nɔmi'neiʃən], *n.* nomination; présentation, *f.*
nominative ['nɔminətiv], *a.* au nominatif, nominatif.—*n.* (*Gram.*) nominatif, *m.*
nominee [nɔmi'niː], *n.* personne nommée, *f.*
nonagenarian [nounədʒi'neəriən], *a.* and *n.* nonagénaire, *m.*, *f.*
non-aggression [nɔnə'greʃən], *n.* non-agression, *f.*
non-alcoholic [nɔnælkə'hɔlik], *a.* non-alcoolique.
non-attendance [nɔnə'tendəns], *n.* absence, *f.*
nonchalance ['nɔnʃələns], *n.* nonchalance, *f.*
non-combatant [nɔn'kʌmbətənt, nɔn'kɔmbətənt], *a.* and *n.* non-combattant, *m.*
non-commissioned [nɔnkə'miʃənd], *a.* sans brevet; *non-commissioned officer*, sous-officier, *m.*
non-committal [nɔnkə'mitl], *a.* qui n'engage à rien, diplomatique.
nonconformist [nɔnkən'fɔːmist], *a.* and *n.* dissident, nonconformiste, *m.*, *f.*
nondescript [nɔn'diskript], *a.* indéfinissable, quelconque.—*n.* chose sans nom, chose indéfinissable, *f.*
none [nʌn], *a.* and *pron.* nul, *m.*, nulle, *f.*, aucun, *m.*, aucune, *f.*; pas un, *m.*, pas une, *f.*, personne, *m.*—*adv.* pas, point; néant (*sur des bordereaux*).
nonentity [nɔ'nentiti], *n.* néant, *m.*; (*fig.*) nullité, *f.*, zéro, *m.*
nonesuch ['nʌnsʌtʃ], *a.* sans pareil, non-pareil.
non-existent [nɔnig'zistənt], *a.* qui n'existe pas.
non-intervention ['nɔnintə'venʃən], *n.* non-intervention, *f.*
non-observance ['nɔnəb'zəːvəns], *n.* inobservation, *f.*
non-payment ['nɔn'peimənt], *n.* non-payement, *m.*

nonplussed ['nɔn'plʌst], *a.* embarrassé, dé-routé.

nonsense ['nɔnsəns], *n.* non-sens, *m.*; sottise, absurdité, *f.*; **nonsense!** allons donc! quelle sottise!

nonsensical [nɔn'sensikl], *a.* vide de sens, absurde.

non-skid ['nɔn'skid], *a.* antidérapant.

non-stop ['nɔn'stɔp], *a.* and *adv.* sans arrêt.

noodle [nu:dl], *n.* nigaud, benêt, sot, *m.*; (*pl.*) (*Cook.*) nouilles, *f.pl.*

nook [nuk], *n.* recoin, réduit, *m.*

noon [nu:n], *n.* midi, *m.*

noonday ['nu:ndei], *a.* de midi.—*n.* midi, *m.*

noontide ['nu:ntaid], *n.* heure de midi, *f.*, midi, *m.*

noose [nu:s], *n.* nœud coulant, lacet, *m.*

nor [nɔ:], *conj.* ni; ni . . . ne.

norm [nɔ:m], *n.* norme, *f.*

normal [nɔ:ml], *a.* normal.

normally ['nɔ:məli], *adv.* normalement.

Norman ['nɔ:mən], *a.* normand.—*n.* Nor-mand (*personne*).

Normandy ['nɔ:məndi]. la Normandie, *f.*

north [nɔ:θ], *a.* du nord, septentrional.—*n.* nord, septentrion, *m.*—*adv.* au nord.

north-east [nɔ:θ'i:st], *n.* nord-est, *m.*

northerly ['nɔ:ðəli], *a.* septentrional, du nord. —*adv.* au nord, vers le nord.

northern ['nɔ:ðən], *a.* du nord; **northern lights,** aurore boréale, *f.*

northerner ['nɔ:ðənə], *n.* habitant du nord, *m.*

north-west [nɔ:θ'west], *n.* nord-ouest, *m.*

Norway ['nɔ:wei]. la Norvège, *f.*

Norwegian [nɔ:'wi:dʒən], *a.* norvégien.—*n.* norvégien (*langue*); Norvégien (*personne*), *m.*

nose [nouz], *n.* nez; museau (*d'animal*); odorat (*flair*), *m.*; **Roman nose,** nez aquilin; **to blow one's nose,** se moucher; **to put someone's nose out of joint,** supplanter quelqu'un; **to turn up one's nose at,** faire fi de; **turned-up nose,** nez retroussé.—*v.t.* flairer.—*v.i.* **to nose about,** fureter.

nose-bag ['nouzbæg], *n.* musette (*de cheval etc.*), *f.*

nose-dive ['nouzdaiv], *v.i.* (*Av.*) piquer du nez.—*n.* piqué, *m.*

nosegay ['nouzgei], *n.* bouquet, *m.*

nostalgia [nɔs'tældʒiə], *n.* nostalgie, *f.*, mal du pays, *m.*

nostril ['nɔstril], *n.* narine, *f.*; naseau (*de cheval etc.*), *m.*

nosy ['nouzi], *a.* (*pop.*) fouinard.

not [nɔt], *adv.* non; ne . . . pas, ne . . . point, pas, non pas; **not at all,** point du tout; **why not?** pourquoi pas?

notability [nouta'biliti], *n.* notabilité, *f.*

notable ['noutabl], *a.* notable, insigne; remarquable.—*n.* notable, *m.*, *f.*

notably ['noutabli], *adv.* notamment (*particu-lièrement*).

notary ['noutəri], *n.* notaire, *m.*

notation [no'teiʃən], *n.* notation, *f.*

notch [nɔtʃ], *n.* encoche, entaille, brèche, *f.*—*v.t.* entailler, ébrécher.

note [nout], *n.* note, marque, *f.*, signe, *m.*; lettre, *f.*; billet, *m.*; marque (*distinction*), *m.*; **bank-note,** billet de banque; **to take a note of,** prendre note de.—*v.t.* noter; remarquer.

notebook ['noutbuk], *n.* carnet, *m.*

noted ['noutid], *a.* distingué (*personne*); célèbre (*chose*).

notepaper ['noutpeipə], *n.* papier à lettres, *m.*

noteworthy ['noutwə:ði], *a.* remarquable.

nothing ['nʌθiŋ], *n.* rien, néant, *m.*; **a mere nothing,** un zéro.—*pron.* (ne) . . . rien; **good-for-nothing,** bon à rien, *m.*; **nothing at all,** rien du tout; **to do noth-ing but,** ne faire que.—*adv.* en rien, nulle-ment, aucunement.

nothingness ['nʌθiŋnis], *n.* néant, rien, *m.*

notice ['noutis], *n.* connaissance; attention, *f.*; préavis, *m.*; notice (*article dans un journal*); (*Law*) notification; annonce (*dans un journal*); affiche (*avis placardé*), *f.*; **a week's notice,** un préavis de huit jours; **at short notice,** à court délai; **to give notice,** avertir, donner congé; **to take notice of,** faire attention à, remarquer; **until further notice,** jusqu'à nouvel ordre.—*v.t.* prendre connaissance de, remarquer, s'apercevoir de.

noticeable ['noutisəbl], *a.* perceptible.

noticeably ['noutisəbli], *adv.* perceptible-ment, sensiblement.

notice-board ['noutisbɔ:d], *n.* écriteau, *m.*

notification [noutifi'keiʃən], *n.* notification, *f.*, avis, avertissement, *m.*

notify ['noutifai], *v.t.* faire savoir, notifier.

notion ['nouʃən], *n.* notion, idée, *f.*

notoriety [noutə'raiəti], *n.* notoriété, *f.*

notorious [no'tɔ:riəs], *a.* notoire.

notwithstanding [nɔtwið'stændiŋ], *prep.* malgré, nonobstant.—*adv.* néanmoins.

noun [naun], *n.* nom, substantif, *m.*

nourish ['nʌriʃ], *v.t.* nourrir; (*fig.*) entretenir.

nourishing ['nʌriʃiŋ], *a.* nourrissant, nutritif.

nourishment ['nʌriʃmənt], *n.* nourriture, alimentation, *f.*

Nova Scotia ['nouvə'skouʃə]. la Nouvelle-Écosse, *f.*

novel [nɔvl], *a.* nouveau, original.—*n.* roman, *m.*

novelist ['nɔvəlist], *n.* romancier, *m.*

novelty ['nɔvəlti], *n.* nouveauté, *f.*

November [no'vembə]. novembre, *m.*

novercal [no'və:kl], *a.* de marâtre.

novice ['nɔvis], *n.* novice, *m.*, *f.*

novitiate [nə'viʃiit], *n.* noviciat, *m.*

now [nau], *adv.* maintenant, à présent, actuellement; alors, or, donc (*raisonnement*); **now and then,** de temps en temps; **now . . . now,** tantôt . . . tantôt; **now then!** eh bien!

nowadays ['nauədeiz], *adv.* aujourd'hui, de nos jours.

nowhere ['nouweə], *adv.* nulle part.

nowise ['nouwaiz], *adv.* en aucune manière.

noxious ['nɔkʃəs], *a.* nuisible.

nozzle [nɔzl], *n.* nez; bec, bout; (*Motor. etc.*) ajutage, *m.*; lance (*de tuyau*), *f.*

nuclear ['nju:kliə], *a.* nucléaire; **nuclear fission,** fission de l'atome, *f.*; **nuclear war,** guerre atomique, *f.*

nucleus ['nju:kliəs], *n.* noyau, *m.*

nude [nju:d], *a.* and *n.* nu, *m.*

nudge [nʌdʒ], *n.* coup de coude, *m.*—*v.t.* donner un coup de coude à, pousser du coude.

nugget ['nʌgit], *n.* pépite (*d'or*), *f.*

nuisance ['nju:səns], *n.* peste, plaie, *f.*, fléau; (*Law*) dommage, *m.*

null [nʌl], *a.* nul; *null and void*, nul et non avenu.
nullify [ˈnʌlifai], *v.t.* annuler.
nullity [ˈnʌliti], *n.* nullité, *f.*
numb [nʌm], *a.* engourdi, transi.—*v.t.* engourdir (*par*).
number [ˈnʌmbə], *n.* nombre; chiffre (*de o à 9*); numéro (*d'une série*), *m.*; livraison (*de publications*), *f.*; (*fig., pl.*) nombres, *m.pl.*; *a number of*, plusieurs, une foule de (*gens*); *cardinal, ordinal, odd, or even number*, nombre cardinal, ordinal, impair *ou* pair.—*v.t.* compter; numéroter (*en série*).
numberless [ˈnʌmbəlis], *a.* innombrable.
number-plate [ˈnʌmbəpleit], *n.* (*Motor.*) plaque d'immatriculation, *f.*
numbness [ˈnʌmnis], *n.* engourdissement, *m.*
numeral [ˈnjuːmərəl], *a.* numéral.—*n.* lettre numérale, *f.*, chiffre, *m.*
numerical [njuˈmerikl], *a.* numérique.
numerous [ˈnjuːmərəs], *a.* nombreux.
numskull [ˈnʌmskʌl], *n.* benêt, idiot, *m.*
nun [nʌn], *n.* religieuse, (*fam.*) nonne, *f.*
nunnery [ˈnʌnəri], *n.* couvent (de religieuses), *m.*
nuptial [ˈnʌpʃəl], *a.* nuptial, de noces.
nuptials [ˈnʌpʃəlz], *n.pl.* noces, *f.pl.*
nurse [nəːs], *n.* bonne d'enfant, *f.*; garde-malade, *m., f.*; infirmier, *m.*, infirmière, *f.* (*à l'hôpital*); *wet nurse*, nourrice, *f.*—*v.t.* nourrir, élever; soigner, garder (*les malades*).
nurse-maid [ˈnəːsmeid], *n.* bonne d'enfant, *f.*
nursery [ˈnəːsəri], *n.* chambre d'enfants; (*Hort.*) pépinière, *f.*; *nursery rhyme*, chanson d'enfants, *f.*
nursery-man [ˈnəːsərimən], *n.* (*pl.* -men [men]) pépiniériste, *m.*
nursery-school [ˈnəːsərisku:l], *n.* école maternelle, *f.*
nursing-home [ˈnəːsiŋhoum], *n.* clinique, maison de santé, *f.*
nurture [ˈnəːtʃə], *n.* nourriture; éducation, *f.* —*v.t.* nourrir; élever.
nut [nʌt], *n.* noix (*du noyer etc.*); noisette (*du noisetier*), *f.*; (*Tech.*) écrou, *m.*
nut-brown [ˈnʌtbraun], *a.* châtain.
nut-cracker [ˈnʌtkrækə], *n.* casse-noix (*oiseau*), *m.*; (*pl.*) casse-noisettes, *m.pl.*
nutmeg [ˈnʌtmeg], *n.* muscade, *f.*
nutrient [ˈnjuːtriənt], *a.* nourrissant.
nutrition [njuˈtriʃən], *n.* nutrition; alimentation, *f.*
nutritious [njuˈtriʃəs], *a.* nourrissant, nutritif.
nutshell [ˈnʌtʃel], *n.* coquille de noix, *f.*
nut-tree [ˈnʌttriː], *n.* noisetier, *m.*
nutty [ˈnʌti], *a.* qui a un goût de noisette; (*pop.*) fêlé, toqué.
nylon [ˈnailən], *n.* nylon, *m.*
nymph [nimf], *n.* nymphe, *f.*

O

O, o [ou]. quinzième lettre de l'alphabet, *m.*
oaf [ouf], *n.* idiot, *m.*
oafish [ˈoufiʃ], *a.* stupide, idiot.

oak [ouk], *n.* chêne; bois de chêne, *m.*
oak-apple [ˈoukæpl], *n.* pomme de chêne, *f.*
oak-tree [ˈouktriː], *n.* chêne, *m.*
oar [ɔː], *n.* aviron, *m.*, rame, *f.*
oarsman [ˈɔːzmən], *n.* (*pl.* -men [men]) rameur, *m.*
oasis [ouˈeisis], *n.* (*pl.* **oases** [ouˈeisiːz]) oasis, *f.*
oat [out], [OATS].
oatcake [ˈoutkeik], *n.* galette d'avoine, *f.*
oaten [outn], *a.* d'avoine.
oath [ouθ], *n.* serment; juron, *m.*; *on oath*, sous serment; *to take an oath*, prêter serment.
oatmeal [ˈoutmiːl], *n.* farine d'avoine, *f.*
oats [outs], *n.pl.* avoine, *f.*
obduracy [ˈɔbdjurəsi], *n.* endurcissement, entêtement, *m.*
obdurate [ˈɔbdjurit], *a.* endurci; obstiné, opiniâtre; impénitent.
obedience [oˈbiːdjəns], *n.* obéissance, soumission, *f.*
obedient [oˈbiːdjənt], *a.* obéissant, soumis.
obediently [oˈbiːdjəntli], *adv.* avec obéissance.
obeisance [oˈbeisəns], *n.* révérence, *f.*
obelisk [ˈɔbəlisk], *n.* obélisque, *m.*
obese [oˈbiːs], *a.* obèse.
obesity [oˈbiːsiti], *n.* obésité, *f.*
obey [oˈbei], *v.t.* obéir à.—*v.i.* obéir.
obfuscate [ˈɔbfʌskeit], *v.t.* offusquer, obscurcir.
obituary [oˈbitjuəri], *a.* obituaire; nécrologique.—*n.* nécrologie, *f.*
object (1) [ˈɔbdʒikt], *n.* objet; but (*fin*), *m.*; considération, *f.*; (*Gram.*) régime, *m.*
object (2) [əbˈdʒekt], *v.t.* objecter.—*v.i.* s'opposer (à).
objection [əbˈdʒekʃən], *n.* objection, *f.*; obstacle, *m.*; (*Racing*) contestation, *f.*
objectionable [əbˈdʒekʃənəbl], *a.* déplaisant; inadmissible.
objective [əbˈdʒektiv], *a.* objectif.—*n.* objectif, but, *m.*
objectively [əbˈdʒektivli], *adv.* objectivement.
oblation [oˈbleiʃən], *n.* oblation, offrande, *f.*
obligation [ɔbliˈgeiʃən], *n.* obligation, *f.*; engagement, *m.*
obligatory [əˈbligətəri], *a.* obligatoire.
oblige [əˈblaidʒ], *v.t.* obliger; faire plaisir à.
obliging [əˈblaidʒiŋ], *a.* obligeant.
oblique [oˈbliːk], *a.* oblique; indirect.
obliterate [əˈblitəreit], *v.t.* effacer, oblitérer.
obliteration [əblitəˈreiʃən], *n.* oblitération, *f.*
oblivion [əˈbliviən], *n.* oubli, *m.*; *act of oblivion*, loi d'amnistie, *f.*
oblivious [əˈbliviəs], *a.* oublieux (*de*).
oblong [ˈɔblɔŋ], *a.* oblong.—*n.* rectangle, *m.*
obnoxious [ɔbˈnɔkʃəs], *a.* odieux, désagréable, déplaisant.
oboe [ˈoubou], *n.* hautbois, *m.*
obscene [ɔbˈsiːn], *a.* obscène, sale.
obscenity [ɔbˈseniti], *n.* obscénité, *f.*
obscure [əbˈskjuə], *a.* obscur; (*fig.*) caché.—*v.t.* obscurcir; voiler (*lumière*).
obscurely [əbˈskjuəli], *adv.* obscurément.
obscurity [əbˈskjuəriti], *n.* obscurité, *f.*
obsequies [ˈɔbsikwiz], *n.pl.* obsèques, *f.pl.*
obsequious [ɔbˈsiːkwiəs], *a.* obséquieux.
obsequiousness [ɔbˈsiːkwiəsnis], *n.* soumission obséquieuse, *f.*

497

observance

observance [əb'zəːvəns], *n.* observance; pratique, observation, *f.*
observant [əb'zəːvənt], *a.* observateur.
observation [ɔbzə'veiʃən], *n.* observation, *f.*
observatory [əb'zəːvətri], *n.* observatoire, *m.*
observe [əb'zəːv], *v.t.* observer; remarquer; faire remarquer.
observer [əb'zəːvə], *n.* observateur, *m.*
obsess [əb'ses], *v.t.* obséder.
obsessed [əb'sest], *a.* obsédé.
obsession [əb'seʃən], *n.* obsession, *f.*
obsolete ['ɔbsəliːt], *a.* vieilli, suranné; tombé en désuétude.
obstacle ['ɔbstəkl], *n.* obstacle, *m.*
obstetrics [ɔb'stetriks], *n.pl.* obstétrique, *f.*
obstinacy ['ɔbstinəsi], *n.* obstination, opiniâtreté, *f.*; entêtement (*de caractère*), *m.*
obstinate ['ɔbstinit], *a.* obstiné, opiniâtre, entêté; têtu (*enfant*).
obstinately ['ɔbstinitli], *adv.* obstinément.
obstreperous [əb'strepərəs], *a.* turbulent, tapageur; récalcitrant.
obstruct [əb'strʌkt], *v.t.* empêcher, retarder; obstruer, encombrer, boucher.
obstruction [əb'strʌkʃən], *n.* empêchement, obstacle, *m.*; (*Med., Polit.*) obstruction, *f.*; encombrement (*circulation*), *m.*
obstructive [əb'strʌktiv], *a.* qui empêche; (*Med.*) obstructif.
obtain [əb'tein], *v.t.* obtenir, gagner; se procurer.—*v.i.* prévaloir.
obtainable [əb'teinəbl], *a.* qu'on peut obtenir, procurable.
obtrude [əb'truːd], *v.t.* imposer.—*v.i.* s'introduire de force; être importun.
obtrusive [əb'truːsiv], *a.* importun.
obtuse [əb'tjuːs], *a.* obtus; émoussé; stupide.
obtuseness [əb'tjuːsnis], *n.* (*fig.*) stupidité, *f.*
obverse ['ɔbvəːs], *n.* face, *f.*, avers, obvers (*de médaille etc.*), *m.*
obviate ['ɔbvieit], *v.t.* éviter, obvier à.
obvious ['ɔbviəs], *a.* évident, clair.
obviously ['ɔbviəsli], *adv.* évidemment.
occasion [ə'keiʒən], *n.* occasion, rencontre; raison, cause, *f.*; besoin (*nécessité*), *m.*—*v.t.* occasionner, causer.
occasional [ə'keiʒənəl], *a.* occasionnel, fortuit.
occasionally [ə'keiʒənəli], *adv.* quelquefois, de temps en temps.
occident ['ɔksidənt], *n.* occident, *m.*
occidental [ɔksi'dentl], *a.* occidental.
occult [ə'kʌlt], *a.* occulte.
occupant ['ɔkjupənt], *n.* occupant, *m.*; locataire (*de chambre louée*); titulaire (*d'un poste*), *m., f.*
occupation [ɔkju'peiʃən], *n.* occupation, *f.*; emploi, métier, *m.*; possession, *f.*
occupier ['ɔkjupaiə], *n.* occupant, *m.*; locataire (*de chambre louée*), *m., f.*, habitant, *m.*
occupy ['ɔkjupai], *v.t.* occuper; employer; habiter (*une maison*).
occur [ə'kəː], *v.i.* arriver, avoir lieu, se produire; venir à l'esprit; *it occurred to me that*, l'idée m'est venue que.
occurrence [ə'kʌrəns], *n.* occurrence, rencontre, *f.*, événement, *m.*
ocean ['ouʃən], *a.* de l'océan.—*n.* océan, *m.*
oceanic [ousi'ænik], *a.* océanique.
ochre ['oukə], *n.* ocre, *f.*
o'clock [ə'klɔk], [CLOCK].
octagon ['ɔktəgən], *n.* octogone, *m.*

octagonal [ɔk'tægənəl], *a.* octogone, octogonal.
octane ['ɔktein], *n.* octane, *m.*; *high-octane fuel*, supercarburant, *m.*
octave ['ɔktiv], *n.* (*Mus., Eccles.*) octave, *f.*
octavo [ɔk'teivou], *n.* in-octavo, *m.*
octet(te) [ɔk'tet], *n.* (*Mus.*) octuor, *m.*
October [ɔk'toubə], octobre, *m.*
octogenarian [ɔktoudʒi'nɛəriən], *a.* and *n.* octogénaire, *m., f.*
octopus ['ɔktəpəs], *n.* pieuvre, *f.*
ocular ['ɔkjulə], *a.* oculaire.
oculist ['ɔkjulist], *n.* oculiste, *m.*
odd [ɔd], *a.* impair; de surplus; d'appoint (*argent*); dépareillé (*article isolé d'une collection*); étrange, singulier, bizarre; *odd moments*, moments perdus, *m.pl.*; *odd number*, nombre impair, *m.*
oddity ['ɔditi], *n.* bizarrerie, *f.*; original (*personne*), *m.*
odd-looking ['ɔdlukiŋ], *a.* à la mine bizarre.
oddly ['ɔdli], *adv.* étrangement; bizarrement.
oddments ['ɔdmənts], *n.pl.* bric-à-brac, *m.*, fins de séries, *f.pl.*
odds [ɔdz], *n.pl.* inégalité, *f.*; (*fig.*) avantage, *m.*, supériorité, *f.*; chances, *f.pl.*; *it makes no odds*, cela ne fait rien; *odds and ends*, petits bouts, *m.pl.*; *to be at odds with*, être mal avec.
ode [oud], *n.* ode, *f.*
odious ['oudiəs], *a.* odieux.
odium ['oudiəm], *n.* détestation, *f.*
odorous ['oudərəs], *a.* odorant.
odour ['oudə], *n.* odeur, *f.*, parfum, *m.*; *in bad odour*, en mauvaise odeur.
odourless ['oudəlis], *a.* sans odeur.
o'er ['ɔːə], (*poet.*) [OVER].
of [ɔv], *prep.* de; d'entre.
off [ɔf, ɔːf], *adv.* au loin, à distance; d'ici; rompu, enlevé; fini; fermé (*électricité etc.*); qui n'est plus frais (*aliments*); *day off*, jour de congé, *m.*; *fifty yards off*, à cinquante pas; *I am off*, je m'en vais; *off and on*, de temps à autre; *time off*, temps libre, *m.*; *to be well off*, être dans l'aisance.—*a. off day*, jour de congé, *m.*; *off side*, côté droit, hors montoir; (*Ftb.*) hors-jeu; *off white*, blanc teinté.—*prep.* de, de dessus; éloigné de; (*Naut.*) au large de.
offal [ɔfl], *n.* issues, *f.pl.*; abats, *m.pl.*; rebut, *m.*
offence [ə'fens], *n.* agression; offense; injure; violation (*d'une loi etc.*), *f.*, délit, crime, *m.*
offend [ə'fend], *v.t.* offenser, outrager, blesser; violer (*transgresser*).—*v.i.* déplaire (à); commettre une offense.
offender [ə'fendə], *n.* offenseur, *m.*; (*Law*) délinquant, *m.*
offensive [ə'fensiv], *a.* offensant, désagréable; choquant; offensif (*attaquant*).—*n.* offensive, *f.*
offensively [ə'fensivli], *adv.* d'une manière offensante; offensivement.
offensiveness [ə'fensivnis], *n.* nature offensante, *f.*
offer ['ɔfə], *v.t.* offrir, présenter, proposer à.—*v.i.* s'offrir, se présenter à; essayer de.—*n.* offre, *f.*
offering ['ɔfəriŋ], *n.* offrande, *f.*; sacrifice, *m.*
off-hand ['ɔf'hænd], *adv.* au premier abord; sans réflexion, sur-le-champ; cavalière-

498

ment.—*a.* brusque, cavalier; impromptu, improvisé.

off-handed [ˈɔfˈhændid], *a.* sans façon, sans gêne.

off-handedness [ˈɔfˈhændidnis], *n.* sans-façon, sans-gêne, *m.*

office [ˈɔfis], *n.* bureau (*immeuble*), *m.*, agence, *f.*; cabinet (*du directeur*), *m.*; étude (*d'avoué etc.*), *f.*; office, emploi; ministère, *m.*, charge, *f.*, fonctions, *f.pl.*; (*pl.*) devoirs (*services*), *m.pl.*; place, *f.*; office (*d'une maison*), *m.*

officer [ˈɔfisə], *n.* officier; fonctionnaire (*du gouvernement*); agent (*de police*), *m.*; *non-commissioned officer*, sous-officier, *m.*—*v.t.* fournir des officiers à; encadrer.

official [əˈfiʃəl], *a.* officiel.—*n.* fonctionnaire; employé, *m.*

officialdom [əˈfiʃəldəm], *n.* bureaucratie, *f.*

officially [əˈfiʃəli], *adv.* officiellement.

officiate [əˈfiʃieit], *v.i.* officier, desservir.

officious [əˈfiʃəs], *a.* officieux; importun.

officiousness [əˈfiʃəsnis], *n.* zèle officieux, *m.*

offing [ˈɔfiŋ], *n.* (*Naut.*) *in the offing*, au large; (*fig.*) en perspective.

offset [ˈɔfset], *v.t.* (*Comm.*) compenser; (*Tech.*) désaxer, décaler.

offshoot [ˈɔfʃuːt], *n.* rejeton, *m.*

offspring [ˈɔfspriŋ], *n.* enfants, descendants, *m.pl.*; (*fig.*) fruit, produit, *m.*

often [ˈɔfn], **oft* [ɔft], **oftentimes* [ˈɔfn taimz], **oft-times* [ˈɔfttaimz], *adv.* souvent, maintes fois.

ogle [ougl], *v.t.* lorgner; lancer des œillades à.—*n.* œillade, *f.*

ogler [ˈouglə], *n.* lorgneur, *m.*

ogling [ˈougliŋ], *n.* lorgnerie, *f.*, œillades, *f.pl.*

ogre [ˈougə], *n.* ogre, *m.*

ogress [ˈougris], *n.* ogresse, *f.*

oh! [ou], *int.* oh! hélas!

ohm [oum], *n.* (*Elec.*) ohm, *m.*

oil [ɔil], *n.* huile, *f.*; (*crude*) *oil*, pétrole (brut), *m.*; *fuel oil*, mazout, *m.*; *paraffin oil*, pétrole (lampant), *m.*—*v.t.* huiler; graisser; (*fig.*) délier (*la langue*).

oilcake [ˈɔilkeik], *n.* tourteau, *m.*

oil-can [ˈɔilkæn], *n.* burette, *f.*

oil-cloth [ˈɔilklɔθ], *n.* toile cirée, *f.*

oil-field [ˈɔilfiːld], *n.* gisement pétrolifère, *m.*

oiliness [ˈɔilinis], *n.* onctuosité, nature huileuse, *f.*

oil-lamp [ˈɔillæmp], *n.* lampe à huile *ou* à pétrole, *f.*

oil-painting [ˈɔilpeintiŋ], *n.* peinture à l'huile, *f.*

oilskin [ˈɔilskin], *n.* toile cirée vernie, *f.*

oil-stove [ˈɔilstouv], *n.* réchaud à pétrole, *m.*

oil-tanker [ˈɔiltæŋkə], *n.* (*Naut.*) pétrolier; (*Motor.*) camion-citerne, *m.*

oil-well [ˈɔilwel], *n.* puits de pétrole, *m.*

oily [ˈɔili], *a.* huileux; (*fig.*) oléagineux, onctueux.

ointment [ˈɔintmənt], *n.* onguent, *m.*, pommade, *f.*

old [ould], *a.* vieux; âgé; ancien, antique; *how old are you?* quel âge avez-vous? *old man* (*chap, boy*), mon vieux mon brave; *to grow old*, vieillir.

olden [ˈouldən], *a.* vieux, ancien; *in olden times*, au temps jadis.

old-fashioned [ould'fæʃənd] *a.* démodé, suranné.

oldish [ˈouldiʃ], *a.* un peu vieux, vieillot.

old-maid [ˈouldmeid], *n.* vieille fille, *f.*

oleaginous [ouliˈædʒinəs], *a.* oléagineux.

oleander [ouliˈændə], *n.* (*Bot.*) laurier-rose, oléandre, *m.*

oligarchy [ˈɔligaːki], *n.* oligarchie, *f.*

olive [ˈɔliv], *n.* olive, *f.*, olivier (*arbre*), *m.*

Oliver [ˈɔlivə]. Olivier, *m.*

Olympian [oˈlimpiən], *a.* olympien.

Olympic [oˈlimpik], *a.* olympique; *the Olympic Games*, les jeux olympiques, *m.pl.*

Olympus [oˈlimpəs]. Olympe, *m.*

omega [ˈoumigə], *n.* oméga, *m.*

omelet(te) [ˈɔmlit], *n.* omelette, *f.*

omen [ˈoumən], *n.* augure, *m.*

ominous [ˈɔminəs], *a.* de mauvais augure, sinistre; menaçant.

ominously [ˈɔminəsli], *adv.* de mauvais augure.

omission [oˈmiʃən], *n.* omission, *f.*

omit [oˈmit], *v.t.* omettre; oublier.

omnipotence [ɔmˈnipətəns], *n.* omnipotence, toute-puissance, *f.*

omnipotent [ɔmˈnipətənt], *a.* tout-puissant, omnipotent.

omniscient [ɔmˈnisiənt], *a.* omniscient.

omnivorous [ɔmˈnivərəs], *a.* omnivore.

on [ɔn], *prep.* sur, dessus; à; de; en, dans; lors de, après; *on foot*, à pied; *on Monday*, lundi; *on purpose*, à dessein, exprès; *on the whole*, en somme.—*adv.* dessus; en avant, avant, avancé; toujours (*continuation*); de suite (*succession*); *and so on*, et ainsi de suite; *on and on*, sans cesse, interminablement; *play on*, continuez de jouer; *read on*, lisez toujours.

once [wʌns], *adv.* une fois, une seule fois; autrefois, jadis (*anciennement*); *at once*, sur-le-champ, tout de suite; *once upon a time there was*, il était une fois.

one [wʌn], *a.* un; seul, unique; un certain.—*n.* un, *m.*, une, *f.*—*pron.* on, l'on; vous (*accusatif*); celui, *m.*, celle, *f.*; quelqu'un; un homme, *m.*, une femme, *f.*

one-armed [ˈwʌnaːmd], *a.* manchot.

one-eyed [ˈwʌnaid], *a.* borgne.

onerous [ˈɔnərəs], *a.* onéreux.

onerousness [ˈɔnərəsnis], *n.* poids, *m.*, charge, *f.*

oneself [wʌnˈself], *pron.* soi, soi-même; (*reflexive*) se.

one-sided [ˈwʌnˈsaidid], *a.* à un côté, à une face; (*fig.*) partial, unilatéral.

one-sidedness [ˈwʌnˈsaididnis], *n.* partialité, *f.*

one-way [ˈwʌnwei], *a.* *one-way street*, rue à sens unique, *f.*; *one-way ticket*, billet simple, *m.*

onion [ˈʌnjən], *n.* oignon, *m.*; *spring onion*, ciboule, *f.*

onion-bed [ˈʌnjənbed], *n.* oignonnière, *f.*

onlooker [ˈɔnlukə], *n.* spectateur, *m.*

only [ˈounli], *a.* seul; unique; *only child*, enfant unique, *m.*, *f.*—*adv.* seulement; rien que; uniquement; ne . . . que.—*conj.* mais.

onset [ˈɔnset], *n.* assaut, *m*, attaque, charge, *f.*

onslaught [ˈɔnslɔːt], *n.* attaque, *f.*; assaut, *m.*

onus [ˈounəs], *n.* charge, responsabilité, obligation, *f.*

onward

onward ['ɔnwəd], *a.* en avant; avancé, progressif.—*adv.* or **onwards** ['ɔnwədz], en avant.
onyx ['ɔniks], *n.* onyx, *m.*
ooze [uːz], *n.* limon, *m.*—*v.i.* suinter, filtrer; (*fig.*) s'ébruiter.
oozing ['uːziŋ], *n.* suintement; (*fig.*) ébruitement, *m.*
oozy ['uːzi], *a.* vaseux, limoneux.
opal [oupl], *n.* opale, *f.*
opaque [o'peik], *a.* opaque; (*fig.*) épais.
opaqueness [o'peiknis], *n.* opacité, *f.*
open ['oupən], *v.t.* ouvrir; déboucher (*une bouteille*); (*fig.*) expliquer; commencer, entamer; révéler; décacheter (*une lettre*); défaire (*un colis*); inaugurer.—*v.i.* s'ouvrir; commencer.—*a.* ouvert, découvert, à découvert, nu, à nu; franc, sincère; libre; (*fig.*) clair; *in the open (air)*, en plein air; *on the open sea*, en pleine mer.
opener ['oupnə], *n.* ouvreur, *m.*; *tin-opener*, ouvre-boîte, *m.*
open-handed ['oupən'hændid], *a.* libéral, généreux.
open-hearted ['oupən'hɑːtid], *a.* franc.
opening ['oupniŋ], *a.* qui commence, d'inauguration; *the opening chapter*, le premier chapitre.—*n.* ouverture, embrasure, *f.*; commencement, début, *m.*; chance; éclaircie (*dans une forêt etc.*), *f.*
openly ['oupənli], *adv.* ouvertement; franchement.
open-minded ['oupən'maindid], *a.* sans parti pris, large, à l'esprit ouvert.
open-mouthed ['oupən'mauðd], *a.* bouche béante, bouche bée.
openness ['oupənnis], *n.* franchise, sincérité, candeur, *f.*
opera ['ɔpərə], *n.* opéra, *m.*
opera-glass ['ɔprəglɑːs], *n.* lorgnette, *f.*; (*pl.*) jumelles, *f.pl.*
opera-hat ['ɔprəhæt], *n.* claque, *m.*
opera-house ['ɔprəhaus], *n.* opéra, *m.*
operate ['ɔpəreit], *v.t.* opérer, effectuer.—*v.i.* opérer, agir; (*Fin.*) spéculer; *to operate on someone for appendicitis*, opérer quelqu'un de l'appendicite.
operatic [ɔpə'rætik], *a.* d'opéra.
operation [ɔpə'reiʃən], *n.* opération, action, *f.*
operative ['ɔpərətiv], *a.* actif, efficace; des ouvriers.—*n.* artisan, ouvrier, *m.*
operator ['ɔpəreitə], *n.* opérateur, *m.* *telephone operator*, téléphoniste, *m., f.*; *wireless operator*, radio, *m.*
operetta [ɔpə'retə], *n.* opérette, *f.*
opiate ['oupiit], *a.* opiacé.—*n.* opiat, *m.*
opinion [ə'pinjən], *n.* opinion, *f.*, avis, sentiment, *m.*; idée, pensée; (*Law*) consultation, *f.*; *in my opinion*, à mon avis.
opinionated [ə'pinjəneitid], *a.* opiniâtre, têtu, imbu de ses opinions.
opium ['oupjəm], *n.* opium, *m.*
opossum [o'pɔsəm], *n.* opossum, *m.*; sarigue, *f.*
opponent [ə'pounənt], *n.* opposant, *m.*, adversaire, *m., f.*
opportune ['ɔpətjuːn], *a.* opportun, à propos.
opportunely ['ɔpətjuːnli], *adv.* à propos.
opportunity [ɔpə'tjuːniti], *n.* occasion, *f.*
oppose [ə'pouz], *v.t.* opposer; s'opposer à.
opposite ['ɔpəzit], *a.* opposé; vis-à-vis, contraire (à), en face.—*n.* opposé, contre-pied,

m.—*adv.* vis-à-vis, en face.—*prep.* en face de, vis-à-vis de.
opposition [ɔpə'ziʃən], *n.* opposition, résistance; concurrence (*rivalité*), *f.*; obstacle, *m.*
oppress [ə'pres], *v.t.* opprimer; accabler.
oppression [ə'preʃən], *n.* oppression, *f.*
oppressive [ə'presiv], *a.* accablant, oppressif; lourd.
oppressiveness [ə'presivnis], *n.* caractère oppressif, *m.*, lourdeur, *f.*
oppressor [ə'presə], *n.* oppresseur, *m.*
opprobrious [ə'proubriəs], *a.* infamant; injurieux.
opprobrium [ə'proubriəm], *n.* opprobre, *m.*
opt [ɔpt], *v.i.* opter.
optic ['ɔptik], **optical** ['ɔptikəl], *a.* optique; d'optique.
optician [ɔp'tiʃən], *n.* opticien, *m.*
optimism ['ɔptimizm], *n.* optimisme, *m.*
optimist ['ɔptimist], *n.* optimiste, *m., f.*
optimistic [ɔpti'mistik], *a.* optimiste.
option ['ɔpʃən], *n.* option, *f.*, choix, *m.*
optional ['ɔpʃənəl], *a.* facultatif.
opulence ['ɔpjuləns], *n.* opulence, *f.*
opulent ['ɔpjulənt], *a.* opulent.
or [ɔː], *conj.* ou; (*negatively*) ni; *or else*, ou bien, autrement.
oracle ['ɔrəkl], *n.* oracle, *m.*
oracular [ə'rækjulə], *a.* d'oracle; (*fig.*) dogmatique.
oral ['ɔːrəl], *a.* oral.
orally ['ɔːrəli], *adv.* oralement; par la bouche.
orange ['ɔrindʒ], *n.* orange; couleur orange, *f.*
orangery ['ɔrindʒəri], *n.* orangerie, *f.*
orange-tree ['ɔrindʒtriː], *n.* oranger, *m.*
orang-outang [o'ræŋuˈtæŋ], *n.* orang-outang, *m.*
oration [o'reiʃən], *n.* allocution, *f.*, discours, *m.*; *funeral oration*, oraison funèbre, *f.*
orator ['ɔrətə], *n.* orateur, *m.*
oratorical [ɔrə'tɔrikəl], *a.* oratoire.
oratorio [ɔrə'tɔːriou], *n.* oratorio, *m.*
oratory ['ɔrətri], *n.* art oratoire, *m.*, éloquence, *f.*; oratoire (*chapelle*), *m.*
orb [ɔːb], *n.* globe; corps sphérique; orbe, *m.*
orbit ['ɔːbit], *n.* orbe, *m.*; (*Anat., Astron.*) orbite, *f.*
orchard ['ɔːtʃəd], *n.* verger, *m.*
orchestra ['ɔːkistrə], *n.* orchestre, *m.*
orchestral [ɔː'kestrəl], *a.* d'orchestre, orchestral.
orchid ['ɔːkid], *n.* orchidée, *f.*
ordain [ɔː'dein], *v.t.* ordonner, décréter.
ordeal [ɔː'diːəl], *n.* dure épreuve, *f.*
order ['ɔːdə], *n.* ordre; règlement, *m.*; décoration (*insigne*); (*Mil.*) consigne; classe, *f.*, rang, *m.*; commande (*de marchandises*), *f.*; mandat (*de payer*), *m.*; *in order that*, afin que; *in order to*, afin de; *postal order*, mandat-poste, *m.*—*v.t.* ordonner; régler; diriger (*administrer*); commander; prescrire (*médecine*).
ordering ['ɔːdəriŋ], *n.* disposition, *f.*, arrangement, *m.*
orderliness ['ɔːdəlinis], *n.* bon ordre, *m.*, méthode, *f.*
orderly ['ɔːdəli], *a.* en bon ordre, méthodique, rangé.—*n.* (*Mil.*) planton, *m.*
ordinal ['ɔːdinl], *a.* ordinal.
ordinance ['ɔːdinəns], *n.* ordonnance, *f.*

500

ordinarily ['ɔːdinrili], *adv.* ordinairement, d'ordinaire.
ordinary ['ɔːdinri], *a.* ordinaire; moyen.—*n.* ordinaire, *m.*; table d'hôte, *f.*
ordination [ɔːdi'neiʃən], *n.* ordination, *f.*
ordnance ['ɔːdnəns], *n.* artillerie, *f.*; *ordnance map*, carte d'état major, *f.*
ore [ɔː], *n.* minerai, *m.*
organ ['ɔːgən], *n.* (*Anat. etc.*) organe; (*Mus.*) orgue, *m.*
organic [ɔː'gænik], *a.* organique; des organes.
organism ['ɔːgənizm], *n.* organisme, *m.*
organist ['ɔːgənist], *n.* organiste, *m.*, *f.*
organization [ɔːgənai'zeiʃən], *n.* organisation; œuvre, *f.*
organize ['ɔːgənaiz], *v.t.* organiser; aménager.
organizer ['ɔːgənaizə], *n.* organisateur, *m.*
orgy ['ɔːdʒi], *n.* orgie, *f.*
orient ['ɔːriənt], *n.* orient, *m.*
Oriental [ɔːri'entl], *a.* oriental, d'Orient.—*n.* natif de l'Orient, oriental, *m.*
orifice ['ɔrifis], *n.* orifice, *m.*, ouverture, *f.*
origin ['ɔridʒin], *n.* origine, source; provenance, *f.*
original [ə'ridʒinl], *a.* original, inédit (*nouveau*); primitif (*sens des mots etc.*).—*n.* original, *m.*
originality [əridʒi'næliti], *n.* originalité, *f.*
originally [ə'ridʒinəli], *adv.* originairement; originalement.
originate [ə'ridʒineit], *v.t.* faire naître, produire; (*fig.*) inventer.—*v.i.* tirer son origine (*de*), provenir de.
originator [ə'ridʒineitə], *n.* initiateur, auteur, *m.*
oriole ['ɔːrioul], *n.* (*Orn.*) loriot, *m.*
orison ['ɔrizn], *n.* oraison, prière, *f.*
Orkneys ['ɔːkniz], the. les Orcades, *f.pl.*
ornament ['ɔːnəmənt], *n.* ornement, *m.*—*v.t.* orner, décorer (*de*).
ornamental [ɔːnə'mentl], *a.* ornemental, d'ornement; d'agrément.
ornate [ɔː'neit], *a.* orné, élégant, paré.
ornately [ɔː'neitli], *adv.* avec ornement.
ornithologist [ɔːni'θɔlədʒist], *n.* ornithologiste, ornithologue, *m.*, *f.*
ornithology [ɔːni'θɔlədʒi], *n.* ornithologie, *f.*
orphan ['ɔːfən], *n.* a. and *n.* orphelin, *m.*
orphanage ['ɔːfənidʒ], *n.* état d'orphelin; orphelinat, *m.*
orthodox ['ɔːθədɔks], *a.* orthodoxe.
orthodoxy ['ɔːθədɔksi], *n.* orthodoxie, *f.*
orthographic [ɔːθə'græfik], *a.* orthographique.
orthography [ɔː'θɔgrəfi], *n.* orthographe, orthographie, *f.*
orthop(a)edic [ɔːθə'piːdik], *a.* orthopédique.
orthop(a)edist [ɔːθə'piːdist], *n.* orthopédiste, *m.*
orthop(a)edy ['ɔːθəpiːdi], *n.* orthopédie, *f.*
oscillate ['ɔsileit], *v.i.* osciller; (*fig.*) balancer, vaciller.
oscillation [ɔsi'leiʃən], *n.* oscillation, *f.*
oscillatory ['ɔsileitəri], *a.* oscillatoire.
osier ['ouʒiə], *n.* osier, *m.*
osier-bed ['ouʒiəbed], *n.* oseraie, *f.*
osprey ['ɔsprei], *n.* (*Orn.*) orfraie, *f.*
osseous ['ɔsiəs], *a.* osseux.
ossicle ['ɔsikl], *n.* ossicule, osselet, *m.*
ossification [ɔsifi'keiʃən], *n.* ossification, *f.*
ossify ['ɔsifai], *v.t.* ossifier.—*v.i.* s'ossifier.
ostensible [ɔs'tensibl], *a.* prétendu.

ostensibly [ɔs'tensibli], *adv.* en apparence.
ostentation [ɔsten'teiʃən], *n.* ostentation, *f.*, faste, *m.*
ostentatious [ɔsten'teiʃəs], *a.* pompeux, fastueux.
osteopath ['ɔstiopæθ], *n.* ostéopathe, *m.*
ostler ['ɔslə], *n.* garçon d'écurie, *m.*
ostracism ['ɔstrəsizm], *n.* ostracisme, *m.*
ostracize ['ɔstrəsaiz], *v.t.* frapper d'ostracisme, exiler.
ostrich ['ɔstritʃ], *n.* autruche, *f.*
other ['ʌðə], *a.* autre; *every other day*, tous les deux jours; *other people*, d'autres, autrui.—*pron.* autre; autrui; *all the others*, tous les autres.
otherwise ['ʌðəwaiz], *adv.* autrement; sans quoi.
otter ['ɔtə], *n.* loutre, *f.*
ought [ɔːt], *v.aux.* devoir; falloir; *you ought to do it*, vous devriez le faire; *you ought to have seen*, il aurait fallu voir.
ounce (1) [auns], *n.* once (*poids*), *f.*
ounce (2) [auns], *n.* (*Zool.*) once, *f.*
our ['auə], *a.poss.* notre, *sing.*, nos, *pl.*
ours ['auəz], *pron.* le nôtre, *m.*, la nôtre, *f.*, les nôtres, *pl.*; à nous.
ourselves [auə'selvz], *pron.* nous-mêmes; nous.
oust [aust], *v.t.* évincer, déloger.
out [aut], *adv.* hors, dehors; sorti (*pas chez soi*); découvert, exposé (*dévoilé*); éteint (*feu etc.*); épuisé, fini (*tout vendu* ou *tout consumé*), jusqu'au bout; haut, à haute voix (*parler*); dans l'erreur (*pas exact*); publié, paru (*livre*); épanoui (*fleur*).—*a.* externe.
outbid [aut'bid], *v.t. irr.* (*conjug. like* BID) enchérir sur, surenchérir.
outboard ['autbɔːd], *a.* *outboard motor-boat*, hors-bord, *m.*
outbreak ['autbreik], *n.* éruption, explosion; épidémie, *f.*
outburst ['autbəːst], *n.* explosion, *f.*, transport, éclat, *m.*
outcast ['autkɑːst], *a.* expulsé, proscrit, rejeté.—*n.* proscrit, banni, paria, *m.*
outcome ['autkʌm], *n.* résultat, *m.*
outcry ['autkrai], *n.* clameur, *f.*, tollé, *m.*
outdated [aut'deitid], *a.* démodé.
outdo [aut'duː], *v.t. irr.* (*conjug. like* DO) surpasser, exceller.
outdoor ['autdɔː], *a.* en plein air; externe.
outdoors [aut'dɔːz], *adv.* en plein air; hors de la maison.
outer ['autə], *a.* extérieur, du dehors, externe.
outermost ['autəmoust], *a.* le plus extérieur.
outfit ['autfit], *n.* attirail, équipement; trousseau, *m.*
outfitter ['autfitə], *n.* confectionneur et chemisier, *m.*
outflank [aut'flæŋk], *v.t.* déborder, tourner.
outgoing ['autgouiŋ], *a.* sortant, qui sort.—*n.* (*pl.*) dépenses, *f.pl.*
outgrow [aut'grou], *v.t.irr.* (*conjug. like* GROW) dépasser, surpasser.
outgrowth ['autgrouθ], *n.* excroissance; conséquence, *f.*
outhouse ['authaus], *n.* hangar, *m.*; dépendance, *f.*
outing ['autiŋ], *n.* excursion, promenade, *f.*
outlandish [aut'lændiʃ], *a.* étranger; bizarre; retiré.
outlast [aut'lɑːst], *v.t.* survivre à.

outlaw

outlaw ['autlɔ:], *n.* proscrit, *m.—v.t.* mettre hors la loi, proscrire.
outlay ['autlei], *n.* dépense, *f.*, débours, *m.pl.*
outlet ['autlit], *n.* issue, sortie, *f.*; (*Comm.*) débouché, *m.*
outline ['autlain], *n.* contour; profil, *m.*, ébauche, *f.—v.t.* esquisser.
outlive [aut'liv], *v.t.* survivre à.
outlook ['autluk], *n.* vue, perspective, *f.*
outlying ['autlaiiŋ], *a.* éloigné, détaché.
outnumber [aut'nʌmbə], *v.t.* surpasser en nombre.
out-of-date [autəv'deit], *a.* démodé, dépassé.
outpost ['autpoust], *n.* avant-poste, *m.*
outpour [aut'pɔ:], *v.t.* épancher, verser à flots.
outpouring ['autpɔ:riŋ], *n.* effusion, *f.*, épanchement, *m.*
outrage ['autreidʒ], *n.* outrage, *m.—v.t.* outrager.
outrageous [aut'reidʒəs], *a.* outrageux, outrageant.
outrageousness [aut'reidʒəsnis], *n.* nature outrageante, énormité, *f.*
outright ['autrait], *adv.* complètement; carrément (*à cœur ouvert*).
outrun [aut'rʌn], *v.t. irr.* (*conjug. like* RUN) dépasser à la course, gagner de vitesse.
outset ['autset], *n.* début, commencement, *m.*; *at the very outset*, dès l'origine.
outshine [aut'ʃain], *v.t. irr.* (*conjug. like* SHINE) surpasser en éclat, éclipser.
outside ['autsaid], *a.* extérieur, externe, du dehors.—*n.* dehors, extérieur, *m.*—[aut'said], *adv.* en dehors, à l'extérieur.— [aut'said], *prep.* hors de, à l'extérieur de.
outsider [aut'saidə], *n.* étranger; (*Racing*) outsider, *m.*
outsize ['autsaiz], *a.* de grande taille, hors série.
outskirts ['autskə:ts], *n.pl.* bords, *m.pl.*; lisière (*d'un bois*), banlieue, *f.*, faubourg (*d'une ville*), *m.*
outspoken [aut'spoukən], *a.* franc, clair, carré.
outstanding [aut'stændiŋ], *a.* saillant, remarquable, excellent; non payé; en suspens (*affaires*).
outstretched [aut'stretʃt], *a.* étendu, déployé, tendu.
outstrip [aut'strip], *v.t.* devancer, distancer.
outward ['autwəd], *a.* extérieur, du dehors, externe; superficiel.—*adv.* or *outwards* ['autwədz], à l'extérieur; au dehors, extérieurement; en partance.
outwardly ['autwədli], *adv.* extérieurement, à l'extérieur; (*fig.*) en apparence.
outweigh [aut'wei], *v.t.* peser plus que; l'emporter sur.
outwit [aut'wit], *v.t.* surpasser en finesse, duper.
oval [ouvl], *a.* and *n.* ovale, *m.*
ovary ['ouvəri], *n.* ovaire, *m.*
ovation [o'veiʃən], *n.* ovation, *f.*
oven [ʌvn], *n.* four, *m.*
over ['ouvə], *prep.* sur; par-dessus; au-dessus de; de l'autre côté de (*en face*); pendant (*au cours de*); *over there*, là-bas. —*adv.* d'un côté à l'autre; par-dessus, au-dessus; trop (*à l'excès*); plus de (*excédant*);

de reste (*surplus inemployé*); fini, terminé, fait; passé.
overact [ouvər'ækt], *v.t.* outrer, exagérer.
overall ['ouvərɔ:l], *a.* total.—*n.* blouse, *f.*; tablier, *m.*; (*pl.*) salopette, combinaison, *f.*
overawe [ouvər'ɔ:], *v.t.* intimider, imposer à.
overbalance [ouvə'bæləns], *v.t.* l'emporter sur.—*v.i.* perdre l'équilibre.
overbearing [ouvə'bɛəriŋ], *a.* impérieux, autoritaire.
overboard ['ouvəbɔ:d], *adv.* par-dessus bord.
overburden [ouvə'bə:dn], *v.t.* surcharger; accabler (*de*).
overcast ['ouvəka:st], *a.* couvert, nuageux.
overcharge [ouvə'tʃɑ:dʒ], *v.t.* surcharger; faire payer trop cher.—*n.* prix excessif, *m.*
overcoat ['ouvəkout], *n.* pardessus, *m.*
overcome [ouvə'kʌm], *v.t. irr.* (*conjug. like* COME) surmonter, vaincre, accabler.— *v.i.* l'emporter.
over-confident ['ouvə'kɔnfidənt], *a.* trop confiant; présomptueux, téméraire.
overcrowd [ouvə'kraud], *v.t.* encombrer à l'excès, trop remplir.
overcrowding [ouvə'kraudiŋ], *n.* surpeuplement, *m.*
overdo [ouvə'du:], *v.t. irr.* (*conjug. like* DO) exagérer, outrer; faire trop cuire; harasser.
overdone [ouvə'dʌn], *a.* trop cuit; (*fig.*) exagéré.
overdose ['ouvədous], *n.* dose trop forte, *f.*
overdraw [ouvə'drɔ:], *v.t. irr.* (*conjug. like* DRAW) excéder; *to overdraw one's account*, tirer à découvert; tirer un chèque sans provision.
overdue [ouvə'dju:], *a.* en retard.
overestimate [ouvər'estimeit], *v.t.* évaluer trop haut.
overflow [ouvə'flou], *v.t.* inonder.—*v.i.* déborder, se déborder.—['ouvəflou], *n.* inondation, *f.*, débordement, *m.*
overflowing [ouvə'flouiŋ], *a.* qui déborde, trop plein.—*n.* débordement, *m.*
overgrown [ouvə'groun], *a.* couvert (*d'herbes, ronces*); trop grand, énorme.
overhang ['ouvəhæŋ], *n.* surplomb, *m.*— [ouvə'hæŋ], *v.t. irr.* (*conjug. like* HANG) pencher sur, surplomber; faire saillie.
overhanging ['ouvəhæŋiŋ], *a.* en surplomb.
overhaul [ouvə'hɔ:l], *v.t.* examiner, revoir; réviser, vérifier, démonter.—['ouvəhɔ:l], *n.* examen détaillé, *m.*
overhead [ouvə'hed], *adv.* par-dessus la tête, en haut.—*a.* aérien (*fil etc.*).—['ouvəhedz], *n.* (*pl.*) (*Comm.*) frais généraux, *m.pl.*
overhear [ouvə'hiə], *v.t. irr.* (*conjug. like* HEAR) entendre par hasard.
overheat [ouvə'hi:t], *v.t.* surchauffer.
overjoyed [ouvə'dʒɔid], *a.* transporté de joie, ravi.
overland ['ouvəlænd], *a.* and *adv.* par voie de terre.
overlap [ouvə'læp], *v.t.* recouvrir.—['ouvəlæp], *n.* recouvrement, *m.*
overlapping [ouvə'læpiŋ], *n.* recouvrement, chevauchement, *m.*
overload [ouvə'loud], *v.t.* surcharger, surmener.
overlook [ouvə'luk], *v.t.* donner sur, dominer; surveiller (*diriger*); fermer les yeux sur (*passer sur*); oublier, négliger.

padding

overlooking [ouvə'lukiŋ], *a.* donnant (*sur*).
overmuch ['ouvəmʌtʃ], *a.* excessif.—*n.* trop, *m.*—*adv.* par trop, excessivement.
overnight [ouvə'nait], *adv.* durant la nuit; hier soir; du jour au lendemain.
overpay [ouvə'pei], *v.t. irr.* (*conjug. like* PAY) payer trop.
overpower [ouvə'pauə], *v.t.* vaincre; accabler (*de*).
overpowering [ouvə'pauəriŋ], *a.* accablant, écrasant.
overproduction [ouvəprə'dʌkʃən], *n.* surproduction, *f.*
overrate [ouvə'reit], *v.t.* estimer trop haut.
overreach [ouvə'ri:tʃ], *v.t.* tromper.—*v.i.* forger (*chevaux*); *to overreach oneself*, trop présumer de ses forces.
override [ouvə'raid], *v.t. irr.* (*conjug. like* RIDE) surmener, outrepasser.
overrule [ouvə'ru:l], *v.t.* dominer; (*Law*) rejeter.
overrun [ouvə'rʌn], *v.t. irr.* (*conjug. like* RUN) envahir, faire une irruption dans; infester (*de*).—*v.i.* déborder.
oversea ['ouvəsi:], **overseas** ['ouvəsi:z, ouvə'si:z], *a. and adv.* d'outre-mer.
oversee [ouvə'si:], *v.t. irr.* (*conjug. like* SEE) surveiller.
overseer ['ouvəsiə], *n.* surveillant; contre-maître (*d'usine etc.*), *m.*
overshadow [ouvə'ʃædou], *v.t.* ombrager; éclipser.
overshoes ['ouvəʃu:z], *n.pl.* caoutchoucs, *m.pl.*
overshoot [ouvə'ʃu:t], *v.t. irr.* (*conjug. like* SHOOT) dépasser.
oversight ['ouvəsait], *n.* inadvertance, *f.*, oubli, *m.*
oversleep [ouvə'sli:p], *v.i. irr.* (*conjug. like* SLEEP) dormir au delà de son heure.
overstate [ouvə'steit], *v.t.* exagérer.
overstatement [ouvə'steitmənt], *n.* exagération, *f.*
overstep [ouvə'step], *v.t.* dépasser.
overt ['ouvə:t], *a.* ouvert, manifeste.
overtake [ouvə'teik], *v.t. irr.* (*conjug. like* TAKE) rattraper; doubler, dépasser.
overtax [ouvə'tæks], *v.t.* surtaxer, surcharger.
overthrow [ouvə'θrou], *v.t. irr.* (*conjug. like* THROW) renverser; défaire, détruire.— ['ouvəθrou], *n.* renversement, *m.*, défaite; destruction, *f.*
overtime ['ouvətaim], *n.* heures supplémentaires, *f.pl.*
overtop [ouvə'tɔp], *v.t.* s'élever au-dessus de, dépasser.
overture ['ouvətjuə], *n.* ouverture; offre, *f.*
overturn [ouvə'tə:n], *v.t.* renverser; bouleverser.—*v.i.* verser.
overweening [ouvə'wi:niŋ], *a.* présomptueux, outrecuidant.
overweight ['ouvəweit], *n.* excédent, *m.*
overwhelm [ouvə'welm], *v.t.* accabler (*de*); combler (*de*) (*bontés etc.*).
overwhelming [ouvə'welmiŋ], *a.* accablant, écrasant.
overwork [ouvə'wə:k], *v.t.* surcharger de travail, surmener.—*n.* travail excessif; surmenage, *m.*
ovoid ['ouvoid], *a.* ovoïde.
owe [ou], *v.t.* devoir; être redevable à . . . de.

owing ['ouiŋ], *a.* dû (*à*); *owing to*, à cause de, grâce à.
owl [aul], *n.* hibou, *m.*; chouette, *f.*
owlet ['aulit], *n.* jeune hibou, *m.*
own (1) [oun], *a.* propre (*à soi*); *my own money*, mon propre argent; *to hold one's own*, se maintenir.—*v.t.* posséder, être propriétaire de (*avoir*).
own (2) [oun], *v.t.* avouer, confesser.
owner ['ounə], *n.* possesseur, *m.*, propriétaire, *m., f.*
ownership ['ounəʃip], *n.* propriété, *f.*
ox [ɔks], *n.* (*pl.* **oxen** ['ɔksən]) bœuf, *m.*
oxalic [ɔk'sælik], *a.* oxalique.
ox-fly ['ɔksflai], *n.* taon, *m.*
oxide ['ɔksaid], *n.* oxyde, *m.*
oxidization [ɔksidai'zeiʃən], *n.* oxydation, calcination, *f.*
oxidize ['ɔksidaiz], *v.t.* oxyder; calciner.
oxyacetylene [ɔksiə'setili:n], *a.* oxyacétylénique.
oxygen ['ɔksidʒən], *n.* oxygène, *m.*
oxygenate ['ɔksidʒəneit], *v.t.* oxygéner.
oxygenous [ɔk'sidʒənəs], *a.* d'oxygène.
oyster ['ɔistə], *n.* huître, *f.*
oyster-bed ['ɔistəbed], *n.* banc d'huîtres, *m.*
ozone [ou'zoun], *n.* ozone, *m.*

P

P, p [pi:]. seizième lettre de l'alphabet, *m.*
pabulum ['pæbjuləm], *n.* aliment, *m.*, nourriture, *f.*
pace [peis], *n.* pas, *m.*; allure (*de cheval*), *f.*; train, *m.*; vitesse, *f.*; *to put someone through his paces*, mettre quelqu'un à l'épreuve.—*v.t.* arpenter; (*Spt.*) entraîner.—*v.i.* aller au pas, marcher.
pacific [pə'sifik], *a.* pacifique, paisible.—*n.* the Pacific (*Ocean*), le Pacifique, l'océan Pacifique, *m.*
pacification [pæsifi'keiʃən], *n.* pacification, *f.*
pacifier ['pæsifaiə], *n.* pacificateur, *m.*
pacifism ['pæsifizm], *n.* pacifisme, *m.*
pacifist ['pæsifist], *n.* pacifiste, *m., f.*
pacify ['pæsifai], *v.t.* pacifier, apaiser.
pack [pæk], *n.* paquet, ballot, *m.*; meute (*chiens de chasse*), *f.*; jeu (*de cartes*), *m.*—*v.t.* emballer, empaqueter.—*v.i.* s'assembler; se grouper; faire sa malle.
package ['pækidʒ], *n.* colis, paquet, *m.*
packer ['pækə], *n.* emballeur, *m.*
packet ['pækit], *n.* paquet; paquebot (*bateau*), *m.*
pack-horse ['pækhɔ:s], *n.* cheval de bât, *m.*
pack-ice ['pækais], *n.* glace de banquise, *f.*, pack, *m.*
packing ['pækiŋ], *n.* emballage, *m.*
pact [pækt], *n.* pacte, *m.*
pad [pæd], *n.* tampon; coussinet, *m.*; *writing-pad*, sous-main, bloc de papier, *m.*—*v.t.* ouater; rembourrer.—*v.i.* aller à pied.
padding ['pædiŋ], *n.* ouate, bourre, *f.*

paddle

paddle [pædl], *n.* pagaie; aube (*de roue*), *f.* —*v.t.* pagayer.—*v.i.* patauger.
paddle-boat ['pædlbout], *n.* bateau à aubes, *m.*
paddock ['pædək], *n.* enclos, pré, pâturage, *m.*
padlock ['pædlɔk], *n.* cadenas, *m.*—*v.t.* cadenasser, fermer au cadenas.
paean ['pi:ən], *n.* péan, *m.*
pagan ['peigən], *a.* and *n.* païen, *m.*
paganism ['peigənizm], *n.* paganisme, *m.*
page (1) [peidʒ], *n.* page (*garçon*), *m.*
page (2) [peidʒ], *n.* page (*de livre*), *f.*
pageant ['pædʒənt], *n.* spectacle pompeux, cortège *ou* spectacle historique, *m.*
pageantry ['pædʒəntri], *n.* pompe, *f.*, faste, apparat, *m.*
pagoda [pə'goudə], *n.* pagode, *f.*
paid [peid], *a.* payé, acquitté; affranchi (*lettres*).
pail [peil], *n.* seau, *m.*
pailful ['peilful], *n.* (plein) seau, *m.*
pain [pein], *n.* douleur; peine (*effort*), *f.*; **on pain of**, sous peine de; **to take pains**, se donner de la peine.—*v.t.* faire mal à; (*fig.*) faire de la peine à; affliger.
painful ['peinful], *a.* douloureux, pénible.
painless ['peinlis], *a.* sans douleur, indolore.
painstaking ['peinzteikiŋ], *a.* soigneux, assidu.
paint [peint], *n.* couleur; peinture, *f.*; fard (*pour le visage*), *m.*—*v.t.* peindre; farder (*le visage*).—*v.i.* peindre; se farder.
painter (1) ['peintə], *n.* peintre, *m.*
painter (2) ['peintə], *n.* (*Naut.*) amarre, *f.*
painting ['peintiŋ], *n.* peinture, *f.*; tableau (*picture*), *m.*
pair [pɛə], *n.* paire, *f.*; couple (*époux etc.*), *m.*—*v.t.* accoupler.—*v.i.* s'accoupler.
Pakistan [pɑ:ki'stɑ:n], le Pakistan, *m.*
Pakistani [pɑ:ki'stɑ:ni], *a.* pakistanais.—*n.* Pakistanais (*personne*), *m.*
pal [pæl], *n.* (*colloq.*) camarade, copain, *m.*
palace ['pælis], *n.* palais, *m.*; **archbishop's palace**, archevêché, *m.*; **bishop's palace**, évêché, *m.*
palatable ['pælətəbl], *a.* agréable au goût, bon.
palate ['pælit], *n.* palais; (*fig.*) goût, *m.*
palatial [pə'leiʃl], *a.* du palais, palatial; grandiose.
palaver [pə'lɑ:və], *n.* palabre (*chez certains peuples primitifs*), *f.*; verbiage, *m.*; flagornerie, *f.*—*v.i.* palabrer, faire des phrases.
pale (1) [peil], *a.* pâle, blême; (*fig.*) blafard (*lumière*).—*v.i.* pâlir; (*fig.*) s'éclipser.
pale (2) [peil], *n.* pieu, palis, *m.*; limites (*bornes*), *f.pl.*; **beyond the pale**, au ban de la société.
pale-faced ['peilfeist], *a.* au teint pâle.
paleness ['peilnis], *n.* pâleur, *f.*
Palestine ['pælistain], la Palestine, *f.*
Palestinian [pælis'tiniən], *a.* palestinien.
palette ['pælit], *n.* palette, *f.*
palfrey ['pɔːlfri], *n.* palefroi, *m.*
paling ['peiliŋ], *n.* palissade, *f.*
palisade [pæli'seid], *n.* palissade, *f.*—*v.t.* palissader.
palish ['peiliʃ], *a.* un peu pâle, pâlot.
pall [pɔːl], *n.* poêle; (*fig.*) drap mortuaire;

voile (*de fumée etc.*), *m.*—*v.i.* devenir fade, s'affadir.
pallet ['pælit], *n.* grabat, *m.*, paillasse, *f.*
palliate ['pælieit], *v.t.* pallier.
palliation [pæli'eiʃən], *n.* palliation, *f.*
palliative ['pæliətiv], *a.* and *n.* palliatif, *m.*
pallid ['pælid], *a.* pâle, blême, blafard.
pallor ['pælə], *n.* pâleur, *f.*
palm (1) [pɑːm], *n.* paume (*de main*), *f.*—*v.t.* **to palm off** (*something on someone*), passer, refiler (*quelque chose à quelqu'un*).
palm (2) [pɑːm], *n.* palmier (*arbre*), *m.*; palme (*rameau*), *f.*; **Palm Sunday**, dimanche des Rameaux, *m.*
palmist ['pɑːmist], *n.* chiromancien, *m.*
palmistry ['pɑːmistri], *n.* chiromancie, *f.*
palmy ['pɑːmi], *a.* beau, glorieux, heureux.
palpable ['pælpəbl], *a.* palpable; manifeste.
palpitate ['pælpiteit], *v.i.* palpiter.
palpitation [pælpi'teiʃən], *n.* palpitation, *f.*
palsied ['pɔːlzid], *a.* frappé de paralysie, paralytique.
palsy ['pɔːlzi], *n.* paralysie, *f.*
palter ['pɔːltə], *v.i.* tergiverser, biaiser.
paltriness ['pɔːltrinis], *n.* mesquinerie, *f.*
paltry ['pɔːltri], *a.* mesquin, misérable.
pamper ['pæmpə], *v.t.* choyer, dorloter.
pamphlet ['pæmflit], *n.* brochure, *f.*; (*pej.*) pamphlet, *m.*
pamphleteer [pæmfli'tiə], *n.* auteur de brochures, *m.*; (*pej.*) pamphlétaire, *m.*, *f.*
pan [pæn], *n.* casserole, *f.*, poêlon, *m.*; **frying-pan**, poêle, *f.*
panacea [pænə'si:ə], *n.* panacée, *f.*
Panama ['pænəmɑ:], le Panama, *m.*
Panamanian [pænə'meiniən], *a.* panamanien.—*n.* Panamanien (*personne*), *m.*
pancake ['pænkeik], *n.* crêpe, *f.*
pancreas ['pænkriəs], *n.* (*Anat.*) pancréas, *m.*
pandemonium [pændi'mouniəm], *n.* pandémonium, *m.*
pander ['pændə], *v.i.* se prêter à, se faire complaisant pour.
pane [pein], *n.* carreau, *m.*, vitre, *f.*
panegyric [pæni'dʒirik], *a.* de panégyrique.—*n.* panégyrique, *m.*
panegyrist [pæni'dʒirist], *n.* panégyriste, *m.*, *f.*
panel [pænl], *n.* panneau, *m.*; liste (*de juré etc.*), *f.*; **instrument panel**, tableau de manœuvre, *m.*—*v.t.* diviser en panneaux; lambrisser.
panelling ['pæniliŋ], *n.* panneaux, *m.pl.* lambrissage, *m.*
pang [pæŋ], *n.* angoisse, vive douleur, *f.*, serrement de cœur, *m.*
panic ['pænik], *a.* panique.—*n.* panique; terreur panique, *f.*—*v.i.* s'affoler.
pannier ['pæniə], *n.* panier, *m.*, hotte, *f.*
panoply ['pænəpli], *n.* panoplie, armure complète, *f.*
panorama [pænə'rɑ:mə], *n.* panorama, *m.*
panoramic [pænə'ræmik], *a.* panoramique.
pansy ['pænzi], *n.* (*Bot.*) pensée, *f.*
pant [pænt], *n.* palpitation, *f.*, halètement, *m.* —*v.i.* haleter, palpiter, panteler.
pantechnicon [pæn'teknikn], *n.* garde-meuble, *m.*; voiture de déménagement, *f.*
pantheism ['pænθiizm], *n.* panthéisme, *m.*
pantheist ['pænθiist], *n.* panthéiste, *m.*, *f.*
pantheistic [pænθi'istik], *a.* panthéistique.
panther ['pænθə], *n.* panthère, *f.*

pantile ['pæntail], *n.* tuile faîtière *ou* flamande, *f.*

pantomime ['pæntəmaim], *n.* pantomime, *f.*

pantomimic [pæntə'mimik], *a.* pantomime.

pantry ['pæntri], *n.* office, *f.*, garde-manger, *m.*

pants [pænts], *n.pl.* (*colloq.*) caleçon; (*Am.*) pantalon, *m.*

pap [pæp], *n.* mamelle; bouillie (*aliment*), *f.*

papacy ['peipəsi], *n.* papauté, *f.*

papal ['peipəl], *a.* papal, du pape.

paper ['peipə], *a.* de papier.—*n.* papier, *m.*; feuille de papier, *f.*; journal; papier-monnaie, *m.*; billets, *m.pl.*; mémoire, *m.*, étude (*article*); composition (*d'examen*), *f.*; (*pl.*) papiers, *m.pl.*; dossier, *m.*; *blotting-paper*, papier buvard; *brown paper*, papier gris.—*v.t.* tapisser (de papier).

paper-back ['peipəbæk], *n.* livre broché, *m.*

paper-clip ['peipəklip], *n.* attache, *f.*, trombone (*de fil*), *m.*

paper-hanger ['peipəhæŋə], *n.* colleur de papier, *m.*

paper-knife ['peipənaif], *n.* coupe-papier, *m.*

paper-maker ['peipəmeikə], *n.* fabricant de papier, *m.*

paper-mill ['peipəmil], *n.* papeterie, *f.*

paper-trade ['peipətreid], *n.* papeterie, *f.*

papism ['peipizm], *n.* papisme, *m.*

papist ['peipist], *n.* papiste, *m.*, *f.*

Papua ['pɑ:puə], *n.* la Papouasie, *f.*

Papuan [pə'puən], *a.* papou.—*n.* Papou (*personne*), *m.*

papyrus [pə'paiərəs], *n.* (*pl.* **papyri** [pə'paiərai]) papyrus, *m.*

par [pɑ:], *n.* pair, *m.*, égalité, (*Golf*) normale, *f.*; *at par*, au pair.

parable ['pærəbl], *n.* parabole, *f.*

parabola [pə'ræbələ], *n.* (*Math.*) parabole, *f.*

parachute ['pærə'ʃu:t], *n.* parachute, *m.*—*v.t.*, *v.i.* parachuter.

parachutist ['pærə'ʃu:tist], *n.* parachutiste, *m.*, *f.*

parade [pə'reid], *n.* parade, *f.*; étalage, *m.*; esplanade, *f.*; (*Mil.*) rassemblement, *m.*; procession, *f.*—*v.t.* faire parade de.—*v.i.* faire de la parade; (*Mil.*) parader.

paradise ['pærədais], *n.* paradis, *m.*

paradox ['pærədɒks], *n.* paradoxe, *m.*

paradoxical [pærə'dɒksikl], *a.* paradoxal.

paraffin ['pærəfin], *n.* (*Chem.*) paraffine, *f.*; *paraffin (oil)*, pétrole (lampant), *m.*

paragon ['pærəgən], *n.* parangon; modèle, *m.*

paragraph ['pærəgrɑ:f], *n.* paragraphe; alinéa, *m.*—*v.t.* diviser en paragraphes.

Paraguay ['pærəgwai], le Paraguay, *m.*

Paraguayan [pærə'gwaiən], *a.* paraguayen.—*n.* Paraguayen (*personne*), *m.*

parakeet ['pærəki:t], *n.* (*Orn.*) perruche, *f.*

parallel ['pærəlel], *a.* parallèle; (*fig.*) semblable, pareil.—*n.* ligne parallèle, *f.*, parallèle, *m.*; (*fig.*) comparaison, *f.*—*v.t.* mettre en parallèle; (*fig.*) comparer (*à*); être pareil (*à*).

parallelism ['pærəlelizm], *n.* parallélisme, *m.*; (*fig.*) comparaison, *f.*

parallelogram [pærə'leləgræm], *n.* parallélo-gramme, *m.*

paralyse ['pærəlaiz], *v.t.* paralyser.

paralysis [pə'rælisis], *n.* paralysie, *f.*

paralytic [pærə'litik], *a.* and *n.* paralytique, *m.*, *f.*

paramount ['pærəmaunt], *a.* souverain, suprême; *of paramount importance*, d'une importance capitale.—*n.* souverain, seigneur, *m.*

paramour ['pærəmuə], *n.* amant, *m.*, maî-tresse, *f.*

parapet ['pærəpit], *n.* (*Fort.*) parapet; garde-fou (*sur un pont etc.*), *m.*

paraphernalia [pærəfə'neiliə], *n.pl.* (*Law*) biens paraphernaux, *m.pl.*; équipage, attirail, *m.*

paraphrase ['pærəfreiz], *n.* paraphrase, *f.*—*v.t.* paraphraser.

parasite ['pærəsait], *n.* parasite, *m.*

parasitic [pærə'sitik], **parasitical** [pærə'sitikl], *a.* parasite, parasitique.

parasol ['pærə'sɒl], *n.* ombrelle, *f.*, parasol, *m.*

paratrooper ['pærətru:pə], *n.* (soldat) para-chutiste, *m.*

parcel ['pɑ:sl], *n.* colis, paquet; lot, *m.*—*v.t.* morceler, diviser, partager; empaqueter.

parch [pɑ:tʃ], *v.t.* brûler, dessécher (*par la chaleur*).—*v.i.* se brûler; se dessécher.

parchment ['pɑ:tʃmənt], *n.* parchemin, *m.*

pardon [pɑ:dn], *n.* pardon, *m.*; (*Law*) grâce, *f.*; *I beg your pardon?* plaît-il? pardon? comment?—*v.t.* pardonner (*quelque chose à quelqu'un*); *pardon me!* pardon! permettez!

pardonable ['pɑ:dnəbl], *a.* excusable, par-donnable (*acte*); digne de pardon (*personne*).

pare [pɛə], *v.t.* peler (*fruits etc.*); éplucher; rogner (*ongles etc.*).

parent ['pɛərənt], *a.* mère.—*n.* père, *m.*, mère, *f.*; (*pl.*) parents, les père et mère, *m.pl.*

parentage ['pɛərəntidʒ], *n.* parentage, *m.*; extraction, *f.*

parental [pə'rentl], *a.* des parents, du père, de la mère; paternel, maternel.

parenthesis [pə'renθisis], *n.* (*pl.* **paren-theses** [pə'renθisi:z]) parenthèse, *f.*

parenthetic [pærən'θetik], **parenthetical** [pærən'θetikl], *a.* entre parenthèses.

pariah ['pæriə], *n.* paria, *m.*

paring ['pɛəriŋ], *n.* rognage; épluchage, *m.*

paring-knife ['pɛəriŋ'naif], *n.* tranchet, *m.*

parish ['pæriʃ], *a.* de la commune; com-munal, vicinal (*routes, impôts etc.*); (*Eccles.*) de la paroisse, paroissial.—*n.* (*Eccles.*) paroisse; (*civil*) commune, *f.*

parishioner [pə'riʃənə], *n.* paroissien, *m.*

Parisian [pə'riziən], *a.* de Paris, parisien.—*n.* Parisien (*personne*), *m.*

parity ['pæriti], *n.* parité; égalité (*de rang etc.*), *f.*

park [pɑ:k], *n.* parc, *m.*—*v.t.* parquer, garer.—*v.i.* stationner.

parking ['pɑ:kiŋ], *n.* stationnement, parcage, *m.*

parlance ['pɑ:ləns], *n.* parler, langage, *m.*; *in common parlance*, dans le langage ordinaire.

parley ['pɑ:li], *n.* pourparlers, *m.pl.*—*v.i.* être *ou* entrer en pourparlers (*avec*); (*Mil.*) parlementer.

parliament ['pɑ:ləmənt], *n.* parlement, *m.*; (*France*) les Chambres, *f.pl.*

parliamentary [pɑ:lə'mentəri], *a.* parlemen-taire, du parlement.

parlour ['pɑ:lə], *n.* petit salon; parloir (*de couvent ou école*), *m.*

parlous ['pɑ:ləs], *a.* alarmant, précaire.

505

parochial [pə'roukiəl], *a.* communal; (*Eccles.*) paroissial.

parody ['pærədi], *n.* parodie, *f.*—*v.t.* parodier.

parole [pə'roul], *n.* parole (d'honneur), *f.*

paroxysm ['pærəksizm], *n.* paroxysme, accès, *m.*

parquet ['pɑːkei, pɑː'ket], *n.* parquet, *m.*—*v.t.* parqueter.

parquetry ['pɑːkitri], *n.* parqueterie, *f.*

parricidal [pæri'saidl], *a.* parricide.

parricide ['pærisaid], *n.* parricide (*crime*), *m.*; parricide (*personne*), *m.*, *f.*

parrot ['pærət], *n.* (*Orn.*) perroquet, *m.*

parry ['pæri], *v.t.* parer, détourner; (*fig.*) éviter.

parse [pɑːz], *v.t.* analyser (grammaticalement).

parsimonious [pɑːsi'mouniəs], *a.* parcimonieux; pingre.

parsimony ['pɑːsiməni], *n.* parcimonie, épargne, *f.*

parsley ['pɑːsli], *n.* (*Bot.*) persil, *m.*

parsnip ['pɑːsnip], *n.* (*Bot.*) panais, *m.*

parson [pɑːsn], *n.* curé; (*Protestant*) pasteur, *m.*

parsonage ['pɑːsnidʒ], *n.* presbytère, *m.*, cure, *f.*

part [pɑːt], *n.* partie; part, portion, *f.*; (*Theat.*) rôle; parti (*dans une dispute etc.*), *m.*; région (*de ville, pays etc.*), *f.*, quartier (*de ville*); (*pl.*) talent, *m.*; **spare parts**, pièces de rechange, *f.pl.*—*v.t.* partager; séparer (*de*).—*v.i.* se séparer (*de*); se quitter; se rompre (*câble*).

partake [pɑː'teik], *v.t.*, *v.i. irr.* (*conjug. like* TAKE) prendre part à, participer à.

partaker [pɑː'teikə], *n.* participant, *m.*

partial [pɑː'fl], *a.* partial (*prévenu*), injuste; partiel (*en partie*).

partiality [pɑːfi'æliti], *n.* partialité (*favoritisme*), *f.*; (*fig.*) goût, *m.*

partially ['pɑːfəli], *adv.* partialement (*injustement*); en partie.

participant [pɑː'tisipənt], *a. and n.* participant, *m.*

participate [pɑː'tisipeit], *v.i.* participer (*à*).

participation [pɑːtisi'peifən], *n.* participation, *f.*

participle ['pɑːtisipl], *n.* participe, *m.*

particle ['pɑːtikl], *n.* particule, molécule, parcelle, *f.*; atome, *m.*

particular [pə'tikjulə], *a.* particulier, spécial; méticuleux, pointilleux; exigeant (*difficile*), —*n.* particularité, *f.*, détail, *m.*; (*pl.*) renseignements, *m.pl.*; signalement, *m.*

particularity [pətikju'læriti], *n.* particularité, *f.*; détail, *m.*

particularize [pə'tikjuləraiz], *v.t.* particulariser.—*v.i.* préciser.

particularly [pə'tikjuləli], *adv.* particulièrement; principalement, surtout.

parting ['pɑːtin], *a.* de séparation; d'adieu; dernier.—*n.* séparation; raie (*cheveux*), *f.*

partisan [pɑːti'zæn], *n.* partisan, *m.*

partition [pɑː'tifən], *n.* partage (*division*), *m.*; cloison (*dans une pièce etc.*), *f.*—*v.t.* partager, diviser.

partitive ['pɑːtitiv], *a. and n.* partitif, *m.*

partly ['pɑːtli], *adv.* en partie, partiellement.

partner ['pɑːtnə], *n.* (*Comm.*) associé; (*Dancing*) danseur, cavalier, *m.*; (*Cards, Spt.*) partenaire, *m.*, *f.*—*v.t.* s'associer à;

(*Spt.*) être le partenaire de; mener (*une femme en dansant*).

partnership ['pɑːtnəfip], *n.* association, *f.*

partridge ['pɑːtridʒ], *n.* (*Orn.*) perdrix, *f.*; **young partridge**, perdreau, *m.*

part-time ['pɑːttaim], *a. and n.* (emploi) à temps partiel, *m.*; **to be on part-time**, être en chômage partiel.

party ['pɑːti], *n.* parti (*politique*), *m.*; partie (*de plaisir*), *f.*; (*fig.*) réunion; réception, *f.*, groupe, *m.*; **to give a party**, recevoir du monde, donner une soirée.

party-wall ['pɑːtiwoːl], *n.* mur mitoyen, *m.*

pasha ['pɑːfə], *n.* pacha, *m.*

pass [pɑːs], *v.t.* passer; passer par, passer devant; dépasser; devancer; faire passer; prononcer (*sur*); voter (*un projet de loi etc.*); **to pass an examination**, être reçu *ou* réussir à un examen.—*v.i.* passer, se passer, s'écouler (*temps*); mourir; (*Exam.*) être reçu; (*Ftb.*) faire une passe; (*fig.*) arriver; **to pass away**, disparaître, mourir; **to pass out**, sortir; (*fig.*) s'évanouir.—*n.* passage, défilé, *m.*; gorge, *f.*, col; permis; laissez-passer, *m.*, permission; (*Ftb.*) passe, *f.*; (*fig.*) point, état, *m.*, extrémité, *f.*

passable ['pɑːsəbl], *a.* praticable; navigable (*fleuve etc.*); passable.

passage ['pæsidʒ], *n.* passage, *m.*, traversée, *f.*; (*Arch.*) couloir, corridor, *m.*

pass-book ['pɑːsbuk], *n.* livre de compte, carnet de banque, *m.*

passenger ['pæsindʒə], *n.* voyageur; passager (*par mer ou avion*), *m.*

passer-by ['pɑːsə'bai], *n.* (*pl.* **passers-by** ['pɑːsəz'bai]) passant, *m.*

passing ['pɑːsin], *a.* passager, éphémère, fugitif.—*adv.* extrêmement, éminemment.—*n.* passage; écoulement (*de temps*); (*fig.*) trépas (*mort*), *m.*

passion ['pæfən], *n.* passion; colère, *f.*, emportement, *m.*

passionate ['pæfənit], *a.* passionné, ardent; irascible.

passionately ['pæfənitli], *adv.* à la passion; à la folie, passionnément.

passion-flower ['pæfənflauə], *n.* passiflore, fleur de la passion, *f.*

passion-play ['pæfənplei], *n.* mystère (de la Passion), *m.*

Passion Week ['pæfənwiːk]. semaine de la Passion, *f.*

passive ['pæsiv], *a. and n.* passif, *m.*

passiveness ['pæsivnis], *n.* passivité, inertie, *f.*

pass-key ['pɑːskiː], *n.* passe-partout, *m.*

Passover ['pɑːsouvə]. la Pâque, *f.*

passport ['pɑːspoːt], *n.* passeport, *m.*

password ['pɑːswəːd], *n.* mot de passe; mot d'ordre, *m.*

past [pɑːst], *a.* passé; ancien; dernier (*récent*).—*prep.* au-delà de; près de; sans, hors de; plus de (*âge*); **past three o'clock**, trois heures passées.—*n.* passé, *m.*

paste [peist], *n.* colle (*glu*); pâte (*pour pâtisseries*), *f.*; stras (*faux diamant*), *m.*—*v.t.* coller; **to paste up**, afficher.

pastel ['pæstəl], *n.* pastel, *m.*

pastern ['pæstən], *n.* paturon, *m.*

pasteurize ['pɑːstjuəraiz], *v.t.* pasteuriser (*lait*).

pastille [pæs'tiːl], *n.* pastille, *f.*

pastime ['pɑːstaim], *n.* passe-temps, amusement, *m.*, distraction, *f.*

pastor ['pɑːstə], *n.* (*literal and fig.*) pasteur; (*literal*) berger, *m.*

pastoral ['pɑːstərəl], *a.* pastoral.—*n.* pastorale, églogue, *f.*

pastry ['peistri], *n.* pâtisserie, *f.*

pastry-cook ['peistrikuk], *n.* pâtissier, *m.*

pasture ['pɑːstʃə], *n.* pâture, *f.*, herbage; pâturage (*champ etc.*), *m.*—*v.t.* faire paître.—*v.i.* paître.

pasty ['peisti], *a.* pâteux.—['pɑːsti], *n.* pâté, *m.*

pat [pæt], *a.* and *adv.* à propos, tout juste.—*n.* petite tape; caresse, *f.*; rond de beurre, *m.*—*v.t.* taper, tapoter, caresser.

patch [pætʃ], *n.* pièce; mouche (*pour le visage*), *f.*; morceau (*de terre*); pan (*de ciel*), *m.*; tache (*de couleur*), *f.*—*v.t.* rapiécer, raccommoder; arranger.

patching ['pætʃiŋ], *n.* rapiéçage, ravaudage, *m.*

patchwork ['pætʃwəːk], *n.* mélange, *m.*, mosaïque, *f.*

patchy ['pætʃi], *a.* inégal.

pate [peit], *n.* (*colloq.*) caboche, tête, *f.*

patent ['peitənt, 'pætənt], *a.* breveté; (*fig.*) patent, apparent, évident.—*n.* lettres patentes, *f.pl.*, brevet d'invention, *m.*—*v.t.* breveter.

patentee [peitən'tiː], *n.* breveté, *m.*

paternal [pə'təːnl], *a.* paternel.

paternally [pə'təːnəli], *adv.* paternellement.

paternity [pə'təːniti], *n.* paternité, *f.*

paternoster ['pætə'nɒstə], *n.* patenôtre, *f.*, pater, *m.*

path [pɑːθ], *n.* sentier, chemin, *m.*; allée (*dans un jardin*), *f.*

pathless ['pɑːθlis], *a.* sans chemin frayé; (*fig.*) inconnu.

pathetic [pə'θetik], *a.* and *n.* pathétique, *m.*

pathfinder ['pɑːθfaində], *n.* pionnier, éclaireur, *m.*

pathological [pæθə'lɒdʒikl], *a.* pathologique.

pathologist [pə'θɒlədʒist], *n.* pathologiste, *m.*, *f.*

pathology [pə'θɒlədʒi], *n.* pathologie, *f.*

pathos ['peiθɒs], *n.* pathétique, *m.*

pathway ['pɑːθwei], *n.* sentier; trottoir (*de rue*); accotement (*de route*), *m.*

patience ['peiʃəns], *n.* patience; (*Cards*) réussite, *f.*

patient ['peiʃənt], *a.* patient, endurant.—*n.* malade, *m.*, *f.*; patient; client (*de médecin*), *m.*

patiently ['peiʃəntli], *adv.* patiemment.

patriarch ['peitriɑːk], *n.* patriarche, *m.*

patriarchal [peitri'ɑːkl], *a.* patriarcal.

Patrick [pætrik]. Patrice, *m.*

patrimony ['pætriməni], *n.* patrimoine, *m.*

patriot ['peitriət, 'pætriət], *n.* patriote, *m.*, *f.*

patriotic [peitri'ɒtik], *a.* patriotique (*chose*); patriote (*personne*).

patriotism ['peitriətizm], *n.* patriotisme, *m.*

patrol [pə'troul], *n.* patrouille, ronde, *f.*—*v.t.* faire la patrouille dans.—*v.i.* patrouiller; faire une ronde.

patron ['peitrən], *n.* patron; protecteur; (*Comm.*) client, *m.*; pratique, *f.*

patronage ['pætrənidʒ], *n.* patronage, *m.*, protection, *f.*

patroness ['peitrənes], *n.* patronne, protec-

trice; dame patronnesse (*d'œuvre de bienfaisance*), *f.*

patronize ['pætrənaiz], *v.t.* protéger, patronner; fréquenter (*un magasin*); traiter avec condescendance.

patronizing ['pætrənaiziŋ], *a.* protecteur; **patronizing tone**, ton de condescendance, *m.*

patronymic [pætrə'nimik], *a.* patronymique. —*n.* nom patronymique, *m.*

patten ['pætən], *n.* patin, socque; (*Arch.*) soubassement, *m.*

patter ['pætə], *v.i.* frapper à petits coups, crépiter; trottiner.

pattering ['pætəriŋ], *n.* grésillement; bruit de petits coups, *m.*

pattern ['pætən], *n.* modèle (*pour*); patron (*à couper*); échantillon (*morceau de tissu etc.*); dessin (*de décoration*); exemple, *m.*

patty ['pæti], *n.* petit pâté, *m.*; bouchée (à la reine), *f.*

paucity ['pɔːsiti], *n.* petit nombre, *m.*, disette (*de*), *f.*

Paul [pɔːl]. Paul, *m.*

Paula ['pɔːlə]. Paule, *f.*

paunch [pɔːntʃ], *n.* panse, *f.*, ventre, *m.*

paunchy ['pɔːntʃi], *a.* pansu.

pauper ['pɔːpə], *n.* indigent, *m.*

pauperism ['pɔːpərizm], *n.* paupérisme, *m.*

pauperize ['pɔːpəraiz], *v.t.* réduire à l'indigence.

pause [pɔːz], *n.* pause, *f.*; moment de silence; intervalle, *m.*—*v.i.* faire une pause, s'arrêter.

pave [peiv], *v.t.* paver (*de*); **to pave the way for**, frayer le chemin à ou pour.

pavement ['peivmənt], *n.* trottoir (*bord de rue*); dallage; pavé (*de marbre etc.*), *m.*

paver ['peivə], **paviour** ['peivjə], *n.* paveur, *m.*

pavilion [pə'viljən], *n.* pavillon, *m.*, tente, *f.*

paving ['peiviŋ], *n.* pavage, *m.*

paw [pɔː], *n.* patte; (*facet.*) main, *f.*—*v.t.* manier, tripoter (*manier*); **to paw the ground**, piaffer.

pawn (1) [pɔːn], *n.* (*Chess*) pion, *m.*

pawn (2) [pɔːn], *v.t.* engager, mettre en gage. —*n.* gage, *m.*

pawnbroker ['pɔːnbroukə], *n.* prêteur sur gage, *m.*

pawnshop ['pɔːnʃɒp], *n.* mont-de-piété, *m.*

pay [pei], *n.* paie, *f.*; salaire (*ouvrier*), traitement (*fonctionnaire*), *m.*, gages (*domestique*), *m.pl.*; (*Mil.*) solde (*officier*), *f.*, prêt (*soldat*), *m.*—*v.t. irr.* payer, acquitter, s'acquitter de; faire (*compliments etc.*); rendre (*honneur*); **carriage paid**, port payé; **to pay a visit to**, faire une visite à.—*v.i.* payer; rapporter.

payable ['peiəbl], *a.* payable; **payable to bearer**, au porteur; **payable to order**, à l'ordre de.

payee [pei'iː], *n.* porteur, *m.*, bénéficiaire, *m.*, *f.*

payer ['peiə], *n.* payeur, *m.*

pay-load ['peiloud], *n.* (*Av.*) poids utile, *m.*

paymaster ['peimɑːstə], *n.* payeur; trésorier, *m.*

payment ['peimənt], *n.* payement, paiement, versement, *m.*

pea [piː], *n.* pois, *m.*; **green peas**, petits pois, *m.pl.*; **sweet pea**, pois de senteur.

peace [piːs], *n.* paix, *f.*

peaceable ['piːsəbl], *a.* pacifique.
peaceably ['piːsəbli], *adv.* en paix; avec calme.
peaceful ['piːsful], *a.* paisible; tranquille, calme.
peacefully ['piːsfuli], *adv.* paisiblement, tranquillement.
peacefulness ['piːsfulnis], *n.* tranquillité, *f.*, calme, *m.*
peaceless ['piːslis], *a.* sans paix, agité.
peacemaker ['piːsmeikə], *n.* pacificateur, *m.*
peach [piːtʃ], *n.* pêche, *f.*
peach-tree ['piːtʃtriː], *n.* pêcher, *m.*
peacock ['piːkɔk], *n.* paon, *m.*
pea-green ['piːgriːn], *a.* and *n.* vert pois.
pea-hen ['piːhen], *n.* paonne, *f.*
peak [piːk], *n.* cime (*de montagne*), *f.*; pic, sommet, *m.*; visière (*d'une casquette*), *f.*
peaked [piːkt], *a.* à pic, à pointe; à visière.
peal [piːl], *n.* carillon (*de cloches*); coup, bruit, grondement (*de tonnerre etc.*); éclat (*de rire*), *m.*—*v.i.* carillonner; retentir, résonner; gronder.
peanut ['piːnʌt], *n.* arachide, cacahuète, *f.*
pea-pod ['piːpɔd], *n.* cosse de pois, *f.*
pear [pɛə], *n.* poire, *f.*
pearl [pəːl], *n.* perle, *f.*; *mother-of-pearl*, nacre, *f.*—*v.t.*, *v.i.* perler.
pearl-oyster ['pəːlɔistə], *n.* huître perlière, *f.*
pearly ['pəːli], *a.* de perle, perlé.
pear-tree ['pɛətriː], *n.* poirier, *m.*
peasant ['pezənt], *n.* paysan, *m.*
peasantry ['pezəntri], *n.* paysans, *m.pl.*
pea-soup ['piːsuːp], *n.* purée de pois, *f.*
peat [piːt], *n.* tourbe, *f.*
peat-bog ['piːtbɔg], **peat-moss** ['piːtmɔs], *n.* tourbière, *f.*
pebble [pebl], *n.* caillou, galet (*de plage*), *m.*
pebbly ['pebli], *a.* caillouteux.
peccadillo [pekə'dilou], *n.* peccadille, *f.*
peck (1) [pek], *n.* picotin (*d'avoine etc.*), *m.*
peck (2) [pek], *n.* coup de bec (*d'oiseau*), *m.*—*v.t.* becqueter; *a hen-pecked husband*, un mari mené par sa femme.
pectoral ['pektərəl], *a.* and *n.* pectoral, *m.*
peculation [pekju'leiʃən], *n.* péculat, *m.*
peculator ['pekjuleitə], *n.* concussionnaire, *m.*, *f.*
peculiar [pi'kjuːliə], *a.* particulier, propre; singulier, bizarre.
peculiarity [pikjuli'æriti], *n.* singularité, particularité, *f.*
peculiarly [pi'kjuːliəli], *adv.* particulièrement, singulièrement.
pecuniary [pi'kjuːniəri], *a.* pécuniaire.
pedagogic(al) [pedə'gɔdʒik(l)], *a.* pédagogique.
pedagogue ['pedəgɔg], *n.* pédagogue, *m.*, *f.*
pedal [pedl], *n.* pédale, *f.*—*v.i.* pédaler.
pedant ['pedənt], *n.* pédant, *m.*
pedantic [pi'dæntik], *a.* pédant (*personne*), pédantesque (*choses*).
pedantry ['pedəntri], *n.* pédantisme, *m.*, pédanterie, *f.*
peddle [pedl], *v.t.* colporter.—*v.i.* faire le colportage.
peddler [PEDLAR].
pedestal ['pedistl], *n.* piédestal, socle, *m.*
pedestrian [pə'destriən], *a.* à pied, pédestre; (*fig.*) prosaïque.—*n.* piéton, marcheur, *m.*
pedigree ['pedigriː], *n.* généalogie; origine, *f.*; arbre généalogique, *m.*
pediment ['pedimənt], *n.* (*Arch.*) fronton, *m.*

pedlar ['pedlə], *n.* colporteur, *m.*
pedometer [pə'dɔmitə], *n.* podomètre, *m.*
peel [piːl], *n.* pelure; écorce (*d'orange etc.*), *f.*—*v.t.* peler; éplucher.—*v.i.* se peler; s'écailler.
peep [piːp], *n.* coup d'œil furtif, *m.*; pointe (*du jour*), *f.*—*v.i.* regarder à la dérobée; paraître, poindre.
peeper ['piːpə], *n.* curieux, *m.*
peep-hole ['piːphoul], *n.* judas, *m.*
peeping-Tom ['piːpin'tɔm], *n.* voyeur, *m.*
peer (1) [piə], *v.i.* scruter du regard.
peer (2) [piə], *n.* pair; (*fig.*) égal, pareil, *m.*
peerage ['piəridʒ], *n.* pairie, *f.*; les pairs, *m.pl.*
peeress ['piəris], *n.* pairesse, *f.*
peerless ['piəlis], *a.* incomparable; sans pareil.
peerlessly ['piəlisli], *adv.* incomparablement.
peerlessness ['piəlisnis], *n.* supériorité incomparable, *f.*
peevish ['piːviʃ], *a.* irritable, maussade.
peevishly ['piːviʃli], *adv.* maussadement, avec mauvaise humeur.
peevishness ['piːviʃnis], *n.* maussaderie, humeur acariâtre, *f.*
peewit [PEWIT].
peg [peg], *n.* cheville; patère (*à chapeau etc.*), *f.*; fausset (*de tonneaux*), piquet (*de tente*), *m.*; *clothes-peg*, pince à linge, *f.*—*v.t.*, *v.i.* cheviller.
pejorative [pə'dʒɔrətiv, 'piːdʒərətiv], *a.* péjoratif.
Pekinese [piːki'niːz], *a.* pékinois.—*n.* (épagneul) pékinois; Pékinois (*personne*), *m.*
Peking [piː'kin], Pékin, *m.*
Pekingese [piːkin'iːz], [PEKINESE].
pelican ['pelikən], *n.* pélican, *m.*
pellet ['pelit], *n.* boulette, *f.*; grain de plomb, *m.*
pellicle ['pelikl], *n.* pellicule, *f.*
pell-mell ['pel'mel], *adv.* pêle-mêle.
pellucid [pə'ljuːsid], *a.* transparent, clair, pellucide.
pelmet ['pelmit], *n.* lambrequin, *m.*
pelt (1) [pelt], *v.t.* assaillir, battre.
pelt (2) [pelt], *n.* peau, *f.*—*v.t.* écorcher.
pelting ['peltin], *a.* battant (*pluie*).—*n.* attaque, *f.*; assaut, *m.*; grêle (*de pierres*), *f.*
pelvic ['pelvik], *a.* pelvien.
pelvis ['pelvis], *n.* bassin, *m.*
pemmican ['pemikən], *n.* conserve de viande, *f.*; pemmican, *m.*
pen [pen], *n.* plume, *f.*; parc, enclos (*bestiaux etc.*); poulailler (*pour volaille*), *m.*; *fountain-pen*, stylo, *m.*—*v.t.* écrire; rédiger; parquer, enfermer (*bétail*).
penal [piːnl], *a.* pénal, passible d'une amende; *penal servitude*, travaux forcés, *m.pl.*
penalize ['piːnəlaiz], *v.t.* infliger une peine à (*quelqu'un*); (*Spt.*) pénaliser.
penalty ['penlti], *n.* peine; pénalité, amende, *f.*; (*Ftb.*) penalty, *m.*
penance ['penəns], *n.* pénitence, *f.*
pence [PENNY].
pencil [pensl], *n.* crayon, *m.*—*v.t.* dessiner *ou* écrire au crayon.
pencil-case ['penslkeis], *n.* porte-crayon, *m.*
pencil-sharpener ['pensl'ʃɑːpnə], *n.* taille-crayon, *m.*
pendant ['pendənt], *n.* pendant, *m.*; pendeloque, *f.*; pendentif, *m.*

pendent ['pendənt], *a.* pendant; suspendu.
pending ['pendiŋ], *a.* pendant, non décidé; en cours.—*prep.* en attendant.
pendulum ['pendjuləm], *n.* pendule, balancier, *m.*
penetrable ['penitrəbl], *a.* pénétrable, sensible, *m.*
penetrate ['penitreit], *v.t., v.i.* pénétrer (*dans*).
penetrating ['penitreitiŋ], *a.* pénétrant, perçant; clairvoyant, perspicace.
penetration [peni'treiʃən], *n.* pénétration, *f.*
penguin ['pengwin], *n.* manchot, *m.*
pen-holder ['penhouldə], *n.* porte-plume, *m.*
penicillin [peni'silin], *n.* pénicilline, *f.*
peninsula [pi'ninsjulə], *n.* péninsule, presqu'île, *f.*
peninsular [pi'ninsjulə], *a.* péninsulaire.
penitence ['penitəns], *n.* pénitence, *f.,* repentir, *m.*
penitent ['penitənt], *a.* pénitent, repentant.
penitentiary [peni'tenʃəri], *a.* pénitentiaire. —*n.* pénitencier, *m.;* (*Am.*) prison, *f.*
penknife ['pennaif], *n.* canif, *m.*
pennant ['penənt], *n.* (*Naut.*) flamme, *f.*
penniless ['penilis], *a.* sans le sou, sans ressources.
penny ['peni], *n.* (*pl.* **pence** [pens], *of a sum,* or **pennies** [peniz], *of a number of coins*) penny, *m.*
pension ['penʃən], *n.* pension; pension de retraite, retraite (*d'officiers etc.*), *f.*—*v.t.* **to pension off,** mettre à la retraite.
pensioner ['penʃənə], *n.* pensionnaire, *m., f.;* (*Mil.*) invalide, *m.*
pensive ['pensiv], *a.* pensif, préoccupé, rêveur.
pensively ['pensivli], *adv.* d'un air pensif.
pensiveness ['pensivnis], *n.* air pensif, air préoccupé, *m.*
pent [pent], *a.* **pent up,** enfermé, (*fig.*) étouffé, refoulé.
pentagon ['pentəgən], *n.* pentagone, *m.*
Pentecost ['pentikɔst], Pentecôte, *f.*
penthouse ['penthaus], *n.* appartement sur toit; appentis, *m.*
penultimate [pe'nʌltimit], *a.* pénultième, avant-dernier.
penurious [pi'njuəriəs], *a.* avare; ladre; pauvre (*choses*).
penury ['penjuəri], *n.* pénurie, *f.*
peony ['pi:əni], *n.* pivoine, *f.*
people [pi:pl], *n.* peuple, *m.,* nation, *f.,* gens, *m.pl.;* on, monde, *m.,* personnes (*en général*), *f.pl.*—*v.t.* peupler (*de*).
pepper ['pepə], *n.* poivre, *m.*—*v.t.* poivrer; (*fig.*) cribler de coups.
pepper-caster ['pepə'kɑ:stə], *n.* poivrière, *f.*
peppercorn ['pepəkɔ:n], *n.* grain de poivre, *m.*
peppermint ['pepəmint], *n.* menthe poivrée, *f.*
peppery ['pepəri], *a.* poivré; (*fig.*) irritable.
per [pə:], *prep.* par; le, *m.,* la, *f.,* les, *pl.; three francs per pound,* trois francs la livre.
perambulate [pə'ræmbjuleit], *v.t.* parcourir.
perambulation [pəræmbju'leiʃən], *n.* parcours, *m.;* promenade, *f.*
perambulator [pə'ræmbjuleitə], *n.* voiture d'enfant, *f.*
perceive [pə'si:v], *v.t.* apercevoir (*visuellement*), s'apercevoir de (*se rendre compte de*).

percentage [pə'sentidʒ], *n.* pourcentage, *m.*
perceptibility [pəsepti'biliti], *n.* perceptibilité, *f.*
perceptible [pə'septibl], *a.* perceptible, sensible.
perceptibly [pə'septibli], *adv.* perceptiblement, sensiblement.
perception [pə'sepʃən], *n.* perception, sensibilité; découverte, *f.*
perceptive [pə'septiv], *a.* perceptif.
perch (1) [pə:tʃ], *n.* perche (*poisson*), *f.*
perch (2) [pə:tʃ], *n.* perchoir (*à poules etc.*), *m.* —*v.t., v.i.* percher.
percolate ['pə:kəleit], *v.t., v.i.* filtrer, passer.
percolation [pə:kə'leiʃən], *n.* filtration, infiltration, *f.*
percolator ['pə:kəleitə], filtre (à café), *m.*
percussion [pə'kʌʃən], *n.* percussion, *f.*
percussion-cap [pə'kʌʃənkæp], *n.* capsule, *f.*
perdition [pə'diʃən], *n.* perdition, ruine, *f.*
peregrinate ['perigrineit], *v.i.* voyager.
peregrination [perigri'neiʃən], *n.* pérégrination, *f.,* voyage à l'étranger, *m.*
peremptorily [pə'remptərili], *adv.* péremptoirement, absolument, formellement.
peremptory [pə'remptəri], *a.* péremptoire, absolu.
perennial [pə'reniəl], *a.* vivace (*plantes*); (*fig.*) éternel.—*n.* plante vivace, *f.*
perfect (1) ['pə:fikt], *a.* parfait; achevé.— [pə'fekt], *v.t.* rendre parfait, perfectionner; achever.
perfect (2) ['pə:fikt], *n.* (*Gram.*) parfait, *m.*
perfection [pə'fekʃən], *n.* perfection, *f.*
perfectly ['pə:fiktli], *adv.* parfaitement.
perfidious [pə'fidiəs], *a.* perfide.
perfidiousness [pə'fidiəsnis], **perfidy** ['pə:fidi], *n.* perfidie, *f.*
perforate ['pə:fəreit], *v.t.* perforer, percer.
perforation [pə:fə'reiʃən], *n.* percement, *m.,* perforation; dentelure (*de timbre-poste*), *f.*
perforce [pə'fɔ:s], *adv.* forcément, de force.
perform [pə'fɔ:m], *v.t.* exécuter, accomplir, (*Theat.*) jouer.—*v.i.* jouer un rôle.
performance [pə'fɔ:məns], *n.* accomplissement; ouvrage, *m.,* œuvre (*chose achevée*), *f.;* (*Mach.*) fonctionnement, *m.;* (*Theat.*) représentation; (*Mus.*) exécution; (*Spt.*) performance, *f.*
performer [pə'fɔ:mə], *n.* (*Theat.*) acteur, *m.,* actrice, *f.;* (*Mus.*) artiste, *m., f.*
perfume ['pə:fjum], *n.* parfum, *m.*—[pə'fju:m], *v.t.* parfumer (*de*).
perfumery [pə'fju:məri], *n.* parfumerie, *f.*
perfunctorily [pə'fʌŋktərili], *adv.* par manière d'acquit; tant bien que mal.
perfunctory [pə'fʌŋktəri], *a.* de pure forme; négligent.
perhaps [pə'hæps], *adv.* peut-être; *perhaps not,* peut-être que non; *perhaps so,* peut-être que oui.
peril ['peril], *n.* péril, danger, *m.*
perilous ['periləs], *a.* périlleux, dangereux.
perilously ['periləsli], *adv.* périlleusement, *f.*
perimeter [pə'rimitə], *n.* périmètre, *m.*
period ['piəriəd], *n.* période, *f.,* temps, *m.,* durée; époque; fin, *f.,* terme (*conclusion*); (*Am.*) point (*ponctuation*), *m.;* (*Rhet. etc.*) phrase, *f.;* (*pl.*) (*Physiol.*) règles, *f.pl.*
periodic [piəri'ɔdik], *a.* périodique.
periodical [piəri'ɔdikl], *a.* and *n.* périodique, *m.*

periodically

periodically [piəri'odikli], adv. périodiquement.
peripatetic [peripə'tetik], a. péripatéticien.
periphery [pə'rifəri], n. périphérie, f.
periphrasis [pə'rifrəsis], n. (pl. periphrases [pə'rifrəsi:z]) périphrase, f.
periscope ['periskoup], n. périscope, m.
perish ['periʃ], v.i. périr (de), mourir; dépérir.
perishable ['periʃəbl], a. périssable.
peritonitis [perita'naitis], n. péritonite, f.
*periwig ['periwig], n. perruque, f.
periwinkle ['periwiŋkl], n. (Bot.) pervenche, f.; bigorneau (mollusque), m.
perjure ['pə:dʒə], v.t. to perjure oneself, se parjurer.
perjurer ['pə:dʒərə], n. parjure, m., f.
perjury ['pə:dʒəri], n. parjure; (Law) faux témoignage, faux serment, m.; wilful perjury, parjure prémédité.
perk [pə:k], v.i. to perk up, se ranimer, se raviver.—n. (pl.) (fam.) [PERQUISITE].
perky ['pə:ki], a. déluré; outrecuidant.
permanency ['pə:mənənsi], permanence ['pə:mənəns], n. permanence, f.
permanent ['pə:mənənt], a. permanent; en permanence.
permanently ['pə:mənəntli], adv. en permanence.
permeable ['pə:miəbl], a. perméable.
permeate ['pə:mieit], v.t. pénétrer.
permissible [pə'misibl], a. permis.
permission [pə'miʃən], n. permission, f., permis, m.
permissive [pə'misiv], a. qui permet; toléré.
permit [pə'mit], v.t. permettre (à quelqu'un de . . .).—['pə:mit], n. permis, m.
permutation [pə:mju'teiʃən], n. permutation, f.
pernicious [pə'niʃəs], a. pernicieux.
perniciously [pə'niʃəsli], adv. pernicieusement.
peroration [perə'reiʃən], n. péroraison, f.
peroxide [pə'rɔksaid], n. peroxyde, m.—v.t. oxygéner (cheveux).
perpendicular [pə:pən'dikjulə], a. and n. perpendiculaire, f.
perpendicularly [pə:pən'dikjuləli], adv. perpendiculairement.
perpetrate ['pə:pitreit], v.t. commettre; (Law) perpétrer.
perpetration [pə:pi'treiʃən], n. exécution; (Law) perpétration, f.
perpetrator ['pə:pitreitə], n. auteur (d'un crime), m.
perpetual [pə'petjuəl], a. perpétuel.
perpetually [pə'petjuəli], adv. perpétuellement.
perpetuate [pə'petjueit], v.t. perpétuer.
perpetuation [pəpetju'eiʃən], n. perpétuation, f.
perpetuity [pə:pi'tju:iti], n. perpétuité, f.
perplex [pə'pleks], v.t. embarrasser.
perplexed [pə'plekst], a. perplexe, embarrassé.
perplexing [pə'pleksiŋ], a. embarrassant.
perplexity [pə'pleksiti], n. perplexité, f.
perquisite ['pə:kwizit], n. émolument casuel, m.
perry ['peri], n. poiré, m.
persecute ['pə:sikju:t], v.t. persécuter.
persecuting ['pə:sikju:tiŋ], a. persécuteur.
persecution [pə:si'kju:ʃən], n. persécution, f.

persecutor ['pə:sikjutə], n. persécuteur, m.
perseverance [pə:si'viərəns], n. persévérance, f.
persevere [pə:si'viə], v.i. persévérer (à ou dans).
persevering [pə:si'viəriŋ], a. persévérant.
perseveringly [pə:si'viəriŋli], adv. avec persévérance.
Persia ['pə:ʃə]. la Perse, f.
Persian ['pə:ʃən], a. de Perse, persan.—n. perse (langue); Persan (personne), m.; the Persian Gulf, le Golfe Persique.
persist [pə'sist], v.i. persister (dans ou à); continuer.
persistence [pə'sistəns], n. persistance, f.
persistent [pə'sistənt], a. persistant; opiniâtre.
person ['pə:sən], n. personne, f.; personnage, caractère, m.; (pl.) personnes, f.pl., gens, m.pl., f.pl.; young persons, les jeunes gens.
personage ['pə:sənidʒ], n. personnage, m.
personal ['pə:sənl], a. personnel.
personality [pə:sə'næliti], n. personnalité, f.
personally ['pə:sənli], adv. personnellement.
personate ['pə:səneit], v.t. se faire passer pour; représenter, contrefaire.
personification [pəsɔnifi'keiʃən], n. personnification, f.
personify [pə'sɔnifai], v.t. personnifier.
personnel [pə:sə'nel], n. personnel, m.
perspective [pə'spektiv], a. perspectif.—n. perspective, f.
perspicacious [pə:spi'keiʃəs], a. pénétrant, perspicace; perçant (la vision).
perspicacity [pə:spi'kæsiti], n. perspicacité, f.
perspicuity [pə:spi'kju:iti], n. clarté, f.
perspicuous [pə'spikjuəs], a. clair, net.
perspiration [pə:spi'reiʃən], n. transpiration, sueur, f.
perspire [pə'spaiə], v.i. transpirer, suer.
persuade [pə'sweid], v.t. persuader; to persuade from, dissuader de.
persuasion [pə'sweiʒən], n. persuasion, f.
persuasive [pə'sweisiv], a. persuasif.
persuasiveness [pə'sweisivnis], n. force persuasive, f.
pert [pə:t], a. mutin, hardi; impertinent, insolent (effronté).
pertain [pə'tein], v.i. appartenir.
pertinacious [pə:ti'neiʃəs], a. obstiné, opiniâtre.
pertinacity [pə:ti'næsiti], n. obstination, f.
pertinence ['pə:tinəns], n. convenance, f.
pertinent ['pə:tinənt], a. pertinent, convenable.
pertly ['pə:tli], adv. impertinemment, insolemment.
pertness ['pə:tnis], n. impertinence, f.
perturb [pə'tə:b], v.t. agiter, troubler.
perturbation [pə:tə'beiʃən], n. agitation, f.
perturbed [pə'tə:bd], a. troublé, inquiet.
Peru [pə'ru:]. le Pérou, m.
perusal [pə'ru:zl], n. lecture, f.
peruse [pə'ru:z], v.t. lire attentivement.
Peruvian [pə'ru:viən], a. péruvien, du Pérou.—n. Péruvien (personne), m.
pervade [pə'veid], v.t. pénétrer dans; se répandre dans, remplir.
pervading [pə'veidiŋ], a. all-pervading, dominant.
perverse [pə'və:s], a. pervers.

physiology

perversely [pə'vəːsli], adv. avec perversité.
perverseness [pə'vəːsnis], perversity [pə'vəː siti], n. perversité, f.
perversion [pə'vəːʃən], n. perversion, f.
pervert [pə'vəːt], v.t. pervertir; fausser, dénaturer.—['pəːvəːt], n. perverti, m.
perverted [pə'vəːtid], a. perverti.
pervious ['pəːviəs], a. perméable, pénétrable.
pessimism ['pesimizm], n. pessimisme, m.
pessimist ['pesimist], n. pessimiste, m., f.
pessimistic [pesi'mistik], a. pessimiste.
pest [pest], n. peste, f.
pester ['pestə], v.t. tourmenter, ennuyer.
pestilence ['pestiləns], n. peste, pestilence, f.
pestilent ['pestilənt], a. pestilentiel, contagieux.
pestilential [pesti'lenʃl], a. pestilentiel.
pet (1) [pet], a. favori; pet aversion, bête noire, f.—n. chéri, m., chérie, f., favori, m., favorite, f.; animal familier; enfant gaté, m.—v.t. choyer, dorloter; (Am.) caresser.
pet (2) [pet], n. accès d'humeur, m.
petal [petl], n. pétale, m.
Peter ['piːtə]. Pierre, m.
peter out [piːtə'raut], v.i. (colloq.) s'épuiser; tomber à l'eau (projet), flancher (machine).
petition [pi'tiʃən], n. pétition, f.—v.t. pétitionner.
petitioner [pi'tiʃənə], n. (Law) requérant, m.; pétitionnaire, m., f.
petrel ['petrəl], n. (Orn.) pétrel, m.
petrifaction [petri'fækʃən], n. pétrification, f.
petrify ['petrifai], v.t. pétrifier.—v.i. se pétrifier.
petrol ['petrəl], n. essence, f.; petrol station, poste d'essence, m.
petrol-can ['petrəlkæn], n. bidon d'essence, m.
petroleum [pi'trouliəm], n. pétrole, m., huile de pétrole, f.
petticoat ['petikout], n. jupon, m.
pettifogging ['petifɔgiŋ], a. avocassier, chicaneur; chicanier (méthodes etc.).
pettiness ['petinis], n. petitesse, mesquinerie, f.
petty ['peti], a. petit; mesquin, chétif; (Law) inférieur.
petty-officer ['peti'ɔfisə], n. (Navy) officier marinier, m.
petulance ['petjuləns], n. irritabilité, f.
petulant ['petjulənt], a. irritable.
pew [pjuː], n. banc d'église, m.
pewit ['piːwit], n. (Orn.) vanneau, m.
pewter ['pjuːtə], n. étain, potin, m.; vaisselle d'étain, f.
phalanx ['fælæŋks], n. (pl. phalanges [fə'lændʒiːz]) phalange, f.
phantom ['fæntəm], n. fantôme, m.
Pharaoh ['fɛərou], m. Pharaon, m.
Pharisee ['færisiː], n. Pharisien, m.
pharmaceutical [fɑːmə'sjuːtikəl], a. pharmaceutique.
pharmacy ['fɑːməsi], n. pharmacie, f.
phase [feiz], n. phase, f.
pheasant ['fezənt], n. faisan, m.
phenomenal [fi'nɔmənəl], a. phénoménal.
phenomenon [fi'nɔmənən], n. (pl. phenomena [fi'nɔmənə]) phénomène, m.
phew! [fjuː], int. pouf!
phial ['faiəl], n. fiole, f.
philanthropic [filən'θrɔpik], a. philanthropique.

philanthropist [fi'lænθrəpist], n. philanthrope, m., f.
philanthropy [fi'lænθrəpi], n. philanthropie, f.
philatelist [fi'lætəlist], n. philatéliste, m., f.
philharmonic [filhɑː'mɔnik], a. philharmonique.
Philip ['filip]. Philippe, m.
Philippine ['filipiːn], a. philippine.
Philippines ['filipiːnz], the, les Philippines, f.pl.
Philistine ['filistain], a. philistin.—n. Philistin (personne), m.
philologist [fi'lɔlədʒist], n. philologue, m., f.
philology [fi'lɔlədʒi], n. philologie, f.
philosopher [fi'lɔsəfə], n. philosophe, m., f.
philosophical [filə'sɔfikl], a. philosophique; philosophe (personnes).
philosophize [fi'lɔsəfaiz], v.i. philosopher.
philosophy [fi'lɔsəfi], n. philosophie, f.; natural philosophy, la physique, f.
philter, philtre ['filtə], n. philtre, m.
phlegm [flem], n. flegme, m.
phlegmatic [fleg'mætik], a. flegmatique.
phobia ['foubiə], n. phobie, f.
Phoebe ['fiːbi]. Phébé, f.
Phoenician [fi'niʃən], a. phénicien.—n. Phénicien (personne), m.
phoenix ['fiːniks], n. phénix, m.
phone [foun], (colloq.) [TELEPHONE].
phonetic [fə'netik], a. phonétique.
phonetics [fə'netiks], n.pl. phonétique, f.
phoney ['founi], a. (colloq.) faux, factice.—n. charlatan, m.
phonic ['fɔnik], a. phonique.
phosphate ['fɔsfeit], n. phosphate, m.
phosphor ['fɔsfə], n. phosphore, m.
phosphoric [fɔs'fɔrik], a. phosphorique.
phosphorus ['fɔsfərəs], n. phosphore, m.
photo ['foutou], (colloq.) [PHOTOGRAPH].
photogenic [foutə'dʒenik], a. photogénique.
photograph ['foutəgrɑːf, 'foutəgræf], n. photographie, (colloq.) photo, f.—v.t. photographier.
photographer [fə'tɔgrəfə], n. photographe, m., f.
photographic [foutə'græfik], a. photographique.
photography [fə'tɔgrəfi], n. photographie, f.
photostat ['foutəstæt], n. appareil photostat, m.
phrase [freiz], n. phrase, locution, f.—v.t. exprimer, nommer; (Mus.) phraser.
phraseology [freizi'ɔlədʒi], n. phraséologie, f.
phrenetic [fre'netik], a. fou, frénétique.
phrenologist [fre'nɔlədʒist], n. phrénologiste, phrénologue, m., f.
phrenology [fre'nɔlədʒi], n. phrénologie, f.
physic ['fizik], n. médecine, f.—v.t. médicamenter; purger.
physical ['fizikəl], a. physique; physical training, éducation physique, f.
physically ['fizikəli], adv. physiquement.
physician [fi'ziʃən], n. médecin, m.
physicist ['fizisist], n. physicien, m.
physics ['fiziks], n.pl. physique, f.
physiognomy [fizi'ɔnəmi, fizi'ɔgnəmi], n. physionomie, f.
physiological [fiziə'lɔdʒikl], a. physiologique.
physiology [fizi'ɔlədʒi], n. physiologie, f.

511

physiotherapy [fizio'θerəpi], *n.* physio-thérapie, *f.*
physique [fi'zi:k], *n.* physique, *m.*
pianist ['piənist], *n.* pianiste, *m., f.*
piano ['pjænou, 'pjɑ:nou], **pianoforte** [-'fɔ:ti], *n.* piano, *m.*; **grand piano**, piano à queue; **to play (on) the piano**, jouer du piano.
pick [pik], *n.* pic, *m.*, pioche (*outil*), *f.*; choix, *m.—v.t.* piquer; cueillir; choisir, trier; ronger (*un os*); chercher (*querelle*); voler à la tire (*dans une poche*); crocheter (*une serrure*); **to pick up**, ramasser, relever.
pickaback ['pikəbæk], *adv.* sur le dos.
pickaxe ['pikæks], *n.* pioche, *f.*
picked [pikt], *a.* d'élite, choisi.
picker ['pikə], *n.* cueilleur, *m.*
picket ['pikit], *n.* piquet, jalon; petit poste, *m.* —*v.t.* former en piquet; guetter (*grévistes* etc.).
pickle [pikl], *n.* saumure, marinade, *f.*; (*pl.*) conserves au vinaigre, *f.pl.—v.t.* conserver au vinaigre, mariner; saler.
pickled [pikld], *a.* mariné, conservé au vinaigre; (*pop.*) ivre.
pickpocket ['pikpɔkit], *n.* voleur à la tire, *m.*
pick-up ['pikʌp], *n.* ramassage, *m.*; reprise (*de machine, des affaires*), *f.*; pick-up (*tourne-disque*), *m.*
picnic ['piknik], *n.* pique-nique, *m.—v.i.* faire un pique-nique.
pictorial [pik'tɔ:riəl], *a.* illustré; de peintre.
pictorially [pik'tɔ:riəli], *adv.* avec illustra-tions.
picture ['piktʃə], *n.* tableau, *m.*; peinture; (*fig.*) image, *f.*; **the pictures**, le cinéma.— *v.t.* peindre; (*fig.*) dépeindre, représenter.
picturesque [piktʃə'resk], *a.* pittoresque.
pie [pai], *n.* pâté (*de viande*), *m.*; tourte (*de fruit*), *f.*; (*colloq.*) **as easy as pie**, simple comme bonjour; **to eat humble pie**, avaler des couleuvres.
piebald ['paibɔ:ld], *a.* pie (*cheval*).
piece [pi:s], *n.* pièce (*grand*), *f.*; morceau (*petit*); fragment, bout, *m.*; **a piece of furniture**, un meuble; **a piece of news**, une nouvelle; **to break to pieces**, mettre en pièces; **to take to pieces**, démonter.— *v.t.* rapiécer.
piecemeal ['pi:smi:l], *adv.* par morceaux, peu à peu.
pied [paid], *a.* bariolé, bigarré; pie (*cheval*).
pie-dish ['paidiʃ], *n.* tourtière, terrine, *f.*
pier [piə], *n.* jetée, *f.*; ponton (*de rivière*), *m.*; pile (*d'un pont*), *f.*
pierce [piəs], *v.t.* percer, pénétrer.
pierced [piəst], *a.* à jour (*ouvrage*), *m.*
piercing ['piəsiŋ], *a.* perçant; pénétrant.
pier-glass ['piəgla:s], *n.* trumeau, *m.*
piety ['paiəti], *n.* piété, *f.*
pig [pig], *n.* cochon, porc, pourceau, *m.*; **to buy a pig in a poke**, acheter chat en poche.
pigeon ['pidʒin], *a.* timide, craintif.—*n.* pigeon, *m.*; **carrier-pigeon**, pigeon voya-geur.
pigeon-hole ['pidʒinhoul], *n.* boulin, *m.*; case (*à papiers* etc.), *f.*; **set of pigeon-holes**, casier, *m.—v.t.* classer.
piggery ['pigəri], *n.* étable à cochons, *f.*
piggy ['pigi], **piglet** ['piglit], *n.* porcelet, goret, *m.*

pigheaded ['pighedid], *a.* têtu, stupide.
pig-iron ['pigaiən], *n.* gueuse, *f.*
pigment ['pigmənt], *n.* couleur, *f.*, pigment, *m.*
pigmy [PYGMY].
pigsty ['pigstai], *n.* porcherie, *f.*
pigtail ['pigteil], *n.* queue (*de cheveux*), *f.*
pigtailed ['pigteild], *a.* à queue.
pike [paik], *n.* pique (*arme*), *f.*; brochet (*poisson*), *m.*
pilchard ['piltʃəd], *n.* (*Ichth.*) pilchard, *m.*
pile [pail], *n.* tas, monceau; (*fig.*) (*Build.*) édifice, bâtiment; pieu (*poteau*); poil (*de tissu*), *m.*; **atomic pile**, pile atomique, *f.*; **funeral pile**, bûcher, *m.—v.t.* entasser, empiler, amonceler.—*v.i.* **to pile up**, s'empiler, s'entasser.
piles [pailz], *n.pl.* (*Path.*) hémorroïdes, *f.pl.*
pilfer ['pilfə], *v.t.* dérober, chiper.—*v.i.* dérober.
pilferer ['pilfərə], *n.* chapardeur, chipeur, *m.*
pilfering ['pilfəriŋ], *n.* petit vol, larcin, *m.*
pilgrim ['pilgrim], *n.* pèlerin, *m.*
pilgrimage ['pilgrimidʒ], *n.* pèlerinage, *m.*
pill [pil], *n.* pilule, *f.*
pillage ['pilidʒ], *n.* pillage, saccagement, *m.— v.t.* saccager, piller.
pillar ['pilə], *n.* pilier, *m.*, colonne, *f.*; (*fig.*) soutien, *m.*
pillar-box ['piləbɔks], *n.* boîte aux lettres, *f.*
pillion ['piljən], *n.* coussinet (*de cheval*), *m.*; siège, *m.* (ou selle, *f.*) arrière (*de moto-cyclette*); **to ride pillion**, monter en croupe, monter derrière.
pillory ['piləri], *n.* pilori, *m.—v.t.* pilorier, mettre au pilori.
pillow ['pilou], *n.* oreiller, *m.—v.t.* reposer, coucher.
pillow-case ['piloukeis], **pillow-slip** ['pilou slip], *n.* taie d'oreiller, *f.*
pilot ['pailət], *n.* pilote, *m.*; **test pilot**, pilote d'essais.—*v.t.* piloter, servir de pilote à.
pilotage ['pailotidʒ], *n.* pilotage, *m.*
pimpernel ['pimpənel], *n.* pimprenelle, *f.*, mouron, *m.*
pimple [pimpl], *n.* bouton, *m.*
pimply ['pimpli], *a.* bourgeonné, pustuleux.
pin [pin], *n.* épingle; cheville (*de bois*), *f.*; (*fig.*) rien, *m.—v.t.* épingler, attacher; cheviller.
pinafore ['pinəfɔ:], *n.* tablier (*d'enfant*), *m.*
pincers ['pinsəz], *n.pl.* pince, *f.*, tenailles, *f.pl.*
pinch [pintʃ], *n.* pincée (*de sel* etc.); prise (*de tabac*), *f.*; (*fig.*) embarras, *m.*; **at a pinch**, à la rigueur, au besoin.—*v.t.* pincer; serrer, gêner (*habits*); (*pop.*) chiper (*voler*); pincer (*arrêter*).—*v.i.* pincer; se gêner.
pinching ['pintʃiŋ], *a.* pressant, piquant (*froid*).—*n.* pincement, *m.*
pin-cushion ['pinkuʃən], *n.* pelote, *f.*
pine (1) [pain], *n.* pin (*arbre*); bois de pin, *m.*
pine (2) [pain], *v.i.* languir; **to pine after**, soupirer après.
pineapple ['painæpl], *n.* ananas, *m.*
ping [piŋ], *n.* sifflement (*de balle de fusil*), *m.— v.i.* siffler.
ping-pong ['piŋpɔŋ], *n.* ping-pong, *m.*
pinion ['pinjən], *n.* aileron, bout d'aile, *m.— v.t.* couper le bout de l'aile à; lier.
pink (1) [piŋk], *a.* couleur de rose, rose.—*n.* œillet (*fleur*); rose (*couleur*), *m.*; **in the pink of condition**, en excellente condition;

(*colloq.*) *to be in the pink*, se porter à merveille.

pink (2) [piŋk], *v.i.* cliqueter (*moteur*).
pinnace ['pinəs], *n.* pinasse, *f.*
pinnacle ['pinəkl], *n.* pinacle, *m.*
pin-point ['pinpoint], *v.t.* indiquer exactement.
pin-pricks ['pinpriks], *n.pl.* coups d'épingles, *m.pl.*
pint [paint], *n.* pinte (*un demi-litre*), *f.*
pintail ['pinteil], *n.* (*Orn.*) pilet, *m.*
pioneer [paiə'niə], *n.* pionnier, *m.*
pious ['paiəs], *a.* pieux.
piously ['paiəsli], *adv.* pieusement.
pip [pip], *n.* pépin (*de fruit*); (*Rad.*) top, *m.*— *v.i.* piauler (*oiseaux*).
pipe [paip], *n.* tuyau, conduit, *m.*; pipe (*à fumer, à vin etc.*), *f.*; (*Mus.*) pipeau, chalumeau, *m.*—*v.i.* jouer du chalumeau, siffler; (*pop.*) *pipe down!* boucle-la!
pipe-line ['paiplain], *n.* canalisation, *f.*, oléoduc, pipe-line, *m.*
piper ['paipə], *n.* joueur de flûte etc., *m.*
piping ['paipiŋ], *a.* qui joue du chalumeau, sifflant; flûté (*la voix*).—*n.* tubulure, *f.*, tuyautage, *m.*
pipit ['pipit], *n.* (*Orn.*) pipit, *m.*
pippin ['pipin], *n.* reinette, *f.*
piquancy ['pi:kənsi], *n.* goût piquant, *m.*
piquant ['pi:kənt], *a.* piquant.
pique [pi:k], *n.* pique, brouillerie, *f.*
piquet [pi'ket], *n.* (*Cards*) piquet, *m.*
piracy ['pairəsi], *n.* piraterie; (*fig.*) contrefaçon, *f.*, plagiat, *m.*
pirate ['pairit], *n.* pirate; (*fig.*) contrefacteur, *m.*
piratical [pai'rætikl], *a.* de pirate; (*fig.*) de contrefaçon.
pirouette [piru'et], *n.* pirouette, *f.*
pish! [piʃ], *int.* bah!
piss [pis], *v.i.* (*vulg.*) pisser.—*n.* urine, *f.*
pistol [pistl], *n.* pistolet, *m.*
piston ['pistən], *n.* piston, *m.*
piston-ring ['pistənriŋ], *n.* segment de piston, *m.*
piston-rod ['pistənrɔd], *n.* tige de piston, *f.*
pit [pit], *n.* fosse; (*fig.*) cavité, *f.*; (*Theat.*) parterre; (*Mining*) puits; creux (*de l'estomac*), *m.*; aisselle (*du bras*), *f.*—*v.t.* creuser; marquer de petits creux.
pitch (1) [pitʃ], *n.* jet, lancement (*de caillou, balle*); (*Naut.*) tangage; point, degré, *m.*; pente (*de toit etc.*), *f.*; (*Mus.*) ton, diapason, *m.*; *to play pitch-and-toss*, jouer à pile ou face.—*v.t.* jeter, lancer; établir (*fixer*); dresser (*une tente*).—*v.i.* (*Naut.*) tanguer, plonger; tomber, se jeter.
pitch (2) [pitʃ], *n.* poix, *f.*; *pitch dark*, noir comme dans un four.
pitched [pitʃt], *a.* rangé; *pitched battle*, bataille rangée, *f.*
pitcher ['pitʃə], *n.* cruche, *f.*
pitchfork ['pitʃfɔ:k], *n.* fourche, *f.*
pitching ['pitʃiŋ], *n.* plongement (*de véhicules*); (*Naut.*) tangage, *m.*
pitch-pine ['pitʃpain], *n.* pin à trochets, pitchpin, *m.*
piteous ['pitiəs], *a.* piteux; pitoyable (*digne de pitié*).
piteously ['pitiəsli], *adv.* piteusement.
piteousness ['pitiəsnis], *n.* état piteux, *m.*; tristesse, *f.*

pitfall ['pitfɔ:l], *n.* trappe, *f.*, piège, *m.*
pith [piθ], *n.* moelle; vigueur, énergie, *f.*; essentiel, *m.*
pithily ['piθili], *adv.* fortement, vigoureusement.
pithy ['piθi], *a.* plein de moelle; (*fig.*) substantiel, concis.
pitiable ['pitiəbl], *a.* pitoyable, à faire pitié.
pitiful ['pitiful], *a.* pitoyable.
pitifully ['pitifuli], *adv.* pitoyablement.
pitiless ['pitilis], *a.* impitoyable, sans pitié.
pitilessly ['pitilisli], *adv.* impitoyablement, sans pitié.
pitman ['pitmən], *n.* (*pl.* **-men** [men]) mineur, *m.*
pittance ['pitəns], *n.* pitance, *f.*
pitted ['pitid], *a.* grêlé (*de petite vérole*).
pity ['piti], *n.* pitié, *f.*; dommage (*regret*), *m.*; *what a pity!* quel dommage!—*v.t.* avoir pitié de, plaindre.
pityingly ['pitiiŋli], *adv.* avec pitié.
pivot ['pivət], *n.* pivot, *m.*
placable ['plækəbl], *a.* facile à apaiser.
placard ['plækɑ:d], *n.* placard, *m.*, affiche, pancarte, *f.*—*v.t.* afficher, placarder (*de*).
placate [plə'keit], *v.t.* apaiser.
place [pleis], *n.* lieu, endroit, *m.*, localité; place (*siège etc.*); position, *f.*, rang (*classe*), *m.*; demeure, résidence (*chez soi*), *f.*; emploi (*profession*), *m.*; *come to my place*, venez chez moi; *to take place*, avoir lieu; *out of place*, déplacé, inopportun.—*v.t.* placer, mettre.
placid ['plæsid], *a.* placide, tranquille, calme.
plagiarism ['pleidʒiərizm], *n.* plagiat, *m.*
plagiarist ['pleidʒiərist], *n.* plagiaire, *m.*, *f.*
plagiarize ['pleidʒiəraiz], *v.t.* plagier.
plague [pleig], *n.* peste; (*fig.*) plaie, *f.*, fléau, *m.*—*v.t.* (*fig.*) tourmenter.
plaice [pleis], *n.* carrelet, *m.*; plie franche, *f.*
plaid [plæd], *n.* (*Sc.*) plaid; tartan, *m.*
plain [plein], *a.* uni, plat; simple, sans façon; ordinaire; sans attraits (*mine*); évident (*qui saute aux yeux*); franc (*sincère*); *in plain clothes*, en civil; *plain cooking*, cuisine bourgeoise *ou* au naturel, *f.*—*n.* plaine, *f.*— *adv.* simplement; franchement.
plainly ['pleinli], *adv.* bonnement; distinctement; franchement.
plainness ['pleinnis], *n.* simplicité; clarté; sincérité, *f.*
plain-speaking ['plein'spi:kiŋ], *n.* franchise, *f.*
plain-spoken ['plein'spoukn], *a.* franc, clair, explicite.
plaint [pleint], *n.* plainte, *f.*
plaintiff ['pleintif], *n.* plaignant, *m.*
plaintive ['pleintiv], *a.* plaintif.
plaintively ['pleintivli], *adv.* d'une voix plaintive.
plaintiveness ['pleintivnis], *n.* ton plaintif, *m.*
plait [plæt], *n.* natte, tresse (*de cheveux*), *f.*; pli, *m.*—*v.t.* tresser, natter (*cheveux*); plisser.
plaited ['plætid], *a.* tressé (*cheveux*); plissé.
plan [plæn], *n.* plan; dessein, projet; système, *m.*—*v.t.* tracer un plan de; (*fig.*) projeter.
plane (1) [plein], *n.* (*Geom.*) plan; (*Carp.*) rabot; (*colloq.*) avion, *m.*—*v.t.* raboter, aplanir.
plane (2) [plein], **plane-tree** ['pleintri:], *n.* platane, *m.*
planet ['plænit], *n.* planète, *f.*

planetarium

planetarium [plæni'tɛəriəm], *n.* planéta-rium, *m.*
planetary ['plænitəri], *a.* planétaire.
planing ['pleiniŋ], *n.* rabotage, *m.*
plank [plæŋk], *n.* planche, *f.*, madrier; (*Naut.*) bordage, *m.—v.t.* planchéier; (*Naut.*) border.
plankton ['plæŋktən], *n.* plancton, *m.*
planner ['plænə], *n.* auteur d'un plan, *m.*; *town-planner*, urbaniste, *m.*
planning ['plæniŋ], *n.* tracé d'un plan, *m.*; planification; (*fig.*) invention, *f.*; *town-planning*, urbanisme, *m.*
plant [plɑːnt], *n.* plante, *f.*; (*Tech.*) matériel, *m.—v.t.* planter; (*fig.*) poser.
plantain ['plæntin], *n.* plantain, *m.*
plantation [plɑːn'teiʃən], *n.* plantation, *f.*
planter ['plɑːntə], *n.* planteur, colon, *m.*
planting ['plɑːntiŋ], *n.* plantage, *m.*, planta-tion, *f.*
plasma ['plæzmə], *n.* plasma (du sang), *m.*
plaster ['plɑːstə], *n.* plâtre; (*Pharm.*) em-plâtre, *m.*; *sticking plaster*, sparadrap, *m.—v.t.* plâtrer.
plasterer ['plɑːstərə], *n.* plâtrier, *m.*
plastering ['plɑːstəriŋ], *n.* plâtrage, *m.*
plastic ['plæstik], *a.* plastique.—*n.* (*pl.*) plas-tiques, *m.pl.*
plat [PLAIT].
Plate [pleit], **the River.** le Rio de la Plata, *m.*
plate [pleit], *n.* assiette; (*Metal.*, *Phot.*) plaque, *f.—v.t.* plaquer (*de*); laminer; étamer (*une glace*).
plateau ['plætou, plə'tou], *n.* plateau, *m.*
plated ['pleitid], *a.* plaqué.
plateful ['pleitful], *n.* assiettée, *f.*
plate-glass ['pleitglɑːs], *n.* glace sans tain, *f.*
plate-layer ['pleitleiə], *n.* (*Rail.*) poseur de rails, *m.*
plate-rack ['pleitræk], *n.* porte-assiettes, *m.*
platform ['plætfɔːm], *n.* plateforme; estrade, *f.*; (*Rail.*) quai, *m.*
plating ['pleitiŋ], *n.* placage, *m.*; *armour-plating*, blindage, *m.*
platinum ['plætinəm], *n.* platine, *m.*
platitude ['plætitjuːd], *n.* platitude, *f.*
Plato ['pleitou] Platon, *m.*
platoon [plə'tuːn], *n.* (*Mil.*) section, *f.*
platter ['plætə], *n.* écuelle, *f.*; (*Am.*) plat, *m.*
platypus ['plætipəs], *n.* ornithor(h)ynque, *m.*
plaudit ['plɔːdit], *n.* applaudissement, *m.*
plausible ['plɔːzibl], *a.* plausible; spécieux.
play [plei], *n.* jeu, *m.*; récréation (*d'enfants*), *f.*; essor (*champ libre*); badinage, *m.*; (*Mus.*) exécution; (*Theat.*) comédie, pièce, *f.*; *fair play*, franc jeu.—*v.t.* jouer, jouer à; faire jouer (*une machine etc.*); représenter, faire (*une pièce, un rôle etc.*); (*Mus.*) jouer de.—*v.i.* jouer; folâtrer (*s'amuser*).
play-bill ['pleibil], *n.* affiche de théâtre, *f.*
player ['pleiə], *n.* joueur; (*Theat.*) acteur, *m.*, actrice, *f.*; artiste, *m., f.*
playfellow ['pleifelou], **playmate** ['plei-meit], *n.* camarade de jeu, *m., f.*
playful ['pleiful], *a.* folâtre, badin.
playfully ['pleifuli], *adv.* en badinant.
playfulness ['pleifulnis], *n.* badinage, enjoue-ment, *m.*
playground ['pleigraund], *n.* cour de récréa-tion, *f.*
playhouse ['pleihaus], *n.* théâtre, *m.*
plaything ['pleiθiŋ], *n.* jouet, joujou, *m.*

playtime ['pleitaim], *n.* récréation, *f.*
playwright ['pleirait], *n.* auteur dramatique, *m.*, dramaturge, *m., f.*
plea [pliː], *n.* procès, *m.*, cause, *f.*; prétexte, *m.*, excuse, *f.*
plead [pliːd], *v.t., v.i.* plaider.
pleasant ['plezənt], *a.* agréable, charmant.
pleasantly ['plezəntli], *adv.* agréablement.
pleasantness ['plezəntnis], *n.* agrément, charme, *m.*
pleasantry ['plezəntri], *n.* plaisanterie, *f.*
please [pliːz], *v.t.* plaire à; *to be pleased*, être content.—*v.i.* plaire (*à*); (*impers.*) il plaît; *as you please*, comme vous voudrez; *if I please*, si cela me plaît; (*if you*) *please*, s'il vous plaît.
pleased [pliːzd], *a.* charmé, content (*de*); satisfait (*de choses*).
pleasing ['pliːziŋ], *a.* agréable, charmant.
pleasurable ['pleʒərəbl], *a.* agréable.
pleasure ['pleʒə], *n.* plaisir; gré (*will*), *m.*
pleasure-ground ['pleʒəgraund], *n.* parc, jardin d'agrément, *m.*
pleat [pliːt], *n.* plissé, *m.—v.t.* plisser.
plebeian [plə'biːən], *a.* and *n.* plébéien, *m.*
pledge [pledʒ], *n.* gage; nantissement, *m.*; (*Law*) caution, *f.—v.t.* engager; garantir.
plenary ['pliːnəri], *a.* plein, complet, entier.
plenipotentiary [plenipo'tenʃəri], *a.* and *n.* plénipotentiaire, *m.*
plenitude ['plenitjuːd], *n.* plénitude, *f.*
plenteous ['plentiəs], *a.* abondant.
plenteously ['plentiəsli], *adv.* abondamment.
plentiful ['plentiful], *a.* abondant.
plenty ['plenti], *n.* abondance, *f.*; *plenty of*, beaucoup de.
plethora ['pleθərə], *n.* pléthore, *f.*
pleurisy ['pluərəsi], *n.* pleurésie, *f.*
pliable ['plaiəbl], *a.* pliable, flexible.
pliancy ['plaiənsi], *n.* flexibilité, *f.*
pliant ['plaiənt], *a.* pliant, flexible.
pliers ['plaiəz], *n.pl.* pinces, *f.pl.*
plight [plait], *n.* état, *m.*, condition; situation difficile, *f.—v.t.* engager.
plinth [plinθ], *n.* plinthe, *f.*
plod [plɔd], *v.i.* marcher péniblement; (*fig.*) peiner, travailler assidûment.
plodder ['plɔdə], *n.* piocheur, *m.*
plodding ['plɔdiŋ], *a.* laborieux, piocheur.—*n.* travail pénible, *m.*
plop [plɔp], *adv., n.* and *int.* plouf, flac, pouf, *m.*
plot [plɔt], *n.* complot; petit terrain, *m.*; intrigue (*d'une pièce etc.*), *f.*; *building-plot*, lotissement, *m.—v.t.* comploter; (*Surv.*) faire le plan de.—*v.i.* comploter.
plotter ['plɔtə], *n.* conspirateur, comploteur, *m.*
plotting ['plɔtiŋ], *n.* complots, *m.pl.*; (*Surv.*) action de rapporter, *f.*
plough [plau], *n.* charrue, *f.*; *the Plough*, le Chariot, *m.*, la Grande-Ourse, *f.—v.t.* labourer; (*fig.*) sillonner.—*v.i.* labourer.
ploughing ['plauiŋ], *n.* labourage, *m.*
ploughman ['plaumən], *n.* (*pl.* -men [men]) laboureur, *m.*
ploughshare ['plauʃeə], *n.* soc de charrue, *m.*
plover ['plʌvə], *n.* (*Orn.*) pluvier, vanneau, *m.*
pluck [plʌk], *v.t.* cueillir (*fleurs, fruits etc.*); plumer (*volaille*); épiler (*sourcils*).—*n.* cœur, courage, *m.*
pluckily ['plʌkili], *adv.* courageusement.

514

plucky ['plʌki], *a.* courageux.
plug [plʌg], *n.* tampon, bouchon, *m.*; bonde (*de tonneau*); (*Elec.*) prise de courant; (*Teleph.*) fiche, *f.*; *sparking plug*, bougie (d'allumage), *f.—v.t.* tamponner, boucher.
plum [plʌm], *n.* prune, *f.*
plumage ['plu:midʒ], *n.* plumage, *m.*
plumb [plʌm], *a.* droit, vertical.—*adv.* à plomb; (*Am., colloq.*) complètement.—*v.t.* plomber; (*Naut.*) sonder.—*n.* plomb, *m.*
plumber ['plʌmə], *n.* plombier, *m.*
plumbing ['plʌmiŋ], *n.* plomberie; tuyauterie, *f.*
plumb-line ['plʌmlain], *n.* fil à plomb, *m.*
plume [plu:m], *n.* plume, *f.*; plumet, *m.—v.t.* plumer.
plummet ['plʌmit], *n.* plomb, *m.*
plump (1) [plʌmp], *a.* dodu, potelé, gras.
plump (2) [plʌmp], *adv.* tout d'un coup; droit.—*v.i.* *to plump for*, donner tous ses votes pour.
plumpness ['plʌmpnis], *n.* embonpoint, *m.*, rondeur, *f.*
plum-tree ['plʌmtri:], *n.* prunier, *m.*
plunder ['plʌndə], *v.t.* piller, dépouiller.—*n.* butin (*chose pillée*); pillage (*acte de piller*), *m.*
plunderer ['plʌndərə], *n.* pillard, *m.*
plunge [plʌndʒ], *v.t.* plonger, précipiter.—*v.i.* plonger; se précipiter.—*n.* plongeon, *m.*
plural ['pluərəl], *a.* and *n.* pluriel, *m.*
plus [plʌs], *prep.* (*Math.*) plus.—*a.* positif.—*n.* plus, *m.—adv.* et davantage.
plush [plʌʃ], *n.* peluche, *f.*
plutocrat ['plu:tokræt], *n.* ploutocrate, *m.*, *f.*
plutocratic [plu:to'krætik], *a.* ploutocratique.
plutonium [plu'tounjəm], *n.* plutonium, *m.*
pluvial ['plu:viəl], *a.* pluvial.
ply (1) [plai], *v.t.* manier (*fortement*); exercer, employer; presser (*quelqu'un de prendre quelque chose*).—*v.i.* travailler; faire le service.
ply (2) [plai], *n.* pli (*de tissu*); fil (*de laine*); toron (*de corde*), *m.*
plywood ['plaiwud], *n.* contre-plaqué, *m.*
pneumatic [nju'mætik], *a.* pneumatique.
pneumonia [nju'mounia], *n.* pneumonie, *f.*
poach (1) [poutʃ], *v.t.* braconner, voler.—*v.i.* braconner.
poach (2) [poutʃ], *v.t.* pocher (*œufs*).
poacher ['poutʃə], *n.* braconnier, *m.*
poaching ['poutʃiŋ], *n.* braconnage, *m.*
pock [pok], *n.* pustule (*de petite vérole*), *f.*
pocket ['pokit], *n.* poche, *f.*; gousset (*du gilet*), *m.*; blouse (*de billard*), *f.—v.t.* empocher, mettre en poche.
pocket-book ['pokitbuk], *n.* portefeuille (*pour l'argent*); livre de poche; calepin (*carnet*), *m.*
pocketful ['pokitful], *n.* pleine poche, *f.*
pocket-knife ['pokitnaif], *n.* couteau de poche, canif, *m.*
pocket-money ['pokitmʌni], *n.* argent de poche, *m.*
pod [pod], *n.* cosse, gousse, *f.—v.t.* écosser.
podgy ['podʒi], *a.* gras, potelé.
poem ['pouim], *n.* poème, *m.*
***poesy** ['pouizi], *n.* poésie, *f.*
poet ['pouit], *n.* poète, *m.*
poetaster ['poui'tæstə], *n.* rimailleur, *m.*
poetess ['poui'tes], *n.* poétesse, *f.*
poetic [pou'etik], **poetical** [pou'etikəl], *a.* poétique.

poetry ['pouitri], *n.* poésie, *f.*
poignancy ['poinjənsi], *n.* piquant, *m.*; nature poignante, *f.*
poignant ['poinjənt], *a.* piquant, vif, poignant.
poignantly ['poinjəntli], *adv.* d'une manière piquante.
point [point], *n.* point (*endroit*), *m.*; pointe (*bout aiguisé etc.*), *f.*; (*Compass*) quart de vent; (*Spt.*) point; (*fig.*) but; (*pl.*) (*Rail.*) aiguillage, *m.*; *decimal point*, virgule, *f.*; *in point of fact*, en effet; *not to the point*, hors de propos; *that is not the point*, ce n'est pas là la question; *to make a point of*, se faire un devoir de; *to the point*, à propos.—*v.t.* aiguiser, tailler (*affiler*); indiquer; pointer (*fusils etc.*); (*Build.*) jointoyer; *to point out*, signaler; faire remarquer.—*v.i.* se tourner (*vers*); tomber en arrêt (*chiens*); *to point at*, montrer du doigt, indiquer.
point-blank ['point'blæŋk], *adv.* à bout portant; à brûle-pourpoint, carrément.
pointed ['pointid], *a.* pointu; (*fig.*) mordant.
pointedly ['pointidli], *adv.* d'une manière piquante.
pointer ['pointə], *n.* index; chien d'arrêt, *m.*
pointing ['pointiŋ], *n.* (*Build.*) jointoiement, *m.*
pointless ['pointlis], *a.* sans pointe; (*fig.*) inutile, plat.
pointsman ['pointsmən], *n.* (*pl.* **-men** [men]) (*Rail.*) aiguilleur, *m.*
poise [poiz], *n.* poids, équilibre, *m.—v.t.* balancer, tenir en équilibre.
poison [poizn], *n.* poison, *m.—v.t.* empoisonner.
poisoner ['poizna], *n.* empoisonneur, *m.*
poisoning ['poizniŋ], *n.* empoisonnement, *m.*
poisonous ['poiznas], *a.* vénéneux (*plante*); venimeux (*serpent etc.*); toxique (*gaz*).
poke (1) [pouk], *n.* coup de coude *ou* de poing, *m.—v.t.* fourrer; pousser (*des doigts*); remuer, fourgonner (*le feu*); *to poke fun at*, se moquer de.—*v.i.* *to poke about*, tâtonner.
poke (2) [pouk], *n.* *sac, *m.*; poche, *f.*
poker ['pouka], *n.* tisonnier, *m.*
poky ['pouki], *a.* (*colloq.*) petit, mesquin.
Poland ['pouland]. la Pologne, *f.*
polar ['poulə], *a.* polaire.
Pole [poul], *n.* Polonais (*personne*), *m.*
pole (1) [poul], *n.* perche, *f.*; bâton (*de rideau*); timon (*d'une voiture*); échalas (*de vignes etc.*); mât (*de drapeau etc.*); poteau (*télégraphique*), *m.*
pole (2) [poul], *n.* (*Astron., Geog.*) pôle, *m.*
poleaxe ['poulæks], *n.* hache d'armes, *f.*; assommoir, merlin, *m.—v.t.* assommer.
polecat ['poulkæt], *n.* putois, *m.*
polemics [pə'lemiks], *n.pl.* polémique, *f.*
pole-star ['poulsta:], *n.* étoile polaire, *f.*
pole-vault ['poulvo:lt], *n.* saut à la perche, *m.*
police [pə'li:s], *n.* police, *f.*; *county police*, gendarmerie, *f.*; *police-court*, tribunal de simple police, *m.*; *police-station*, commissariat *ou* poste de police.—*v.t.* policer.
policeman [pə'li:smən], *n.* (*pl.* **-men** [men]) agent de police, gardien de la paix, *m.*
policewoman [pə'li:swumən], *n.* (*pl.* **-women** [wimin]) femme agent, *f.*
policy ['polisi], *n.* politique, *f.*; plan, *m.*; *insurance policy*, police d'assurance, *f.*

515

poliomyelitis

poliomyelitis ['pouliomaiə'laitis], (fam.) polio ['pouliou], n. poliomyélite, f.

Polish ['pouliʃ], a. polonais.—n. polonais (langue), m.

polish ['poliʃ], v.t. polir; vernir (meubles); cirer (chaussures).—v.i. se polir.—n. poli, m.; (fig.) élégance, f.; floor polish, cire à parquet, f. shoe polish, cirage, m.

polished ['poliʃt], a. poli.

polisher ['poliʃə], n. polisseur; polissoir (outil), m.; floor polisher, cireur de parquet, m.

polite [pə'lait], a. poli, élégant, complaisant (pour).

politely [pə'laitli], adv. poliment.

politeness [pə'laitnis], n. politesse, f.

politic ['politik], a. politique.

political [pə'litikl], a. politique.

politically [pə'litikli], adv. politiquement.

politician [poli'tiʃən], n. homme politique; (pej.) politicien, m.

politics ['politiks], n.pl. politique, f.

poll [poul], n. (Anat.) *tête; liste électorale; élection, f., scrutin; sondage (de l'opinion publique), m.—v.t. étêter (arbres); voter; obtenir (un certain nombre de votes).

pollen ['polən], n. pollen, m.

pollination [poli'neiʃən], n. pollination, f.

polling ['poulin], n. élection, f.; polling-booth, bureau de scrutin, m.

pollute [pə'lju:t], v.t. polluer, souiller (de).

pollution [pə'lju:ʃən], n. pollution, souillure, f.

polo ['poulou], n. polo, m.

polygamist [po'ligəmist], n. polygame, m., f.

polygamy [po'ligəmi], n. polygamie, f.

polyglot ['poliglot], a. and n. polyglotte, m., f.

polygon ['poligən], n. polygone, m.

Polynesia [poli'ni:ziə], la Polynésie, f.

polypus ['polipəs], n. polype, m.

polytechnic [poli'teknik], a. polytechnique. —n. école d'arts et métiers, f.

pomade [pə'meid], n. pommade, f.

pomegranate ['pomgrænit], n. grenade, f.; pomegranate tree, grenadier, m.

pommel [paml], v.t. battre, rosser.—n. pommeau (d'une selle, d'une epée etc.), m.

pomp [pomp], n. pompe, f., éclat, faste, m.

Pompey ['pompi]. Pompée, m.

pompon ['pompon], n. pompon, m.

pomposity [pom'positi], n. pompe, f.

pompous ['pompəs], a. pompeux, fastueux.

pompously ['pompəsli], adv. pompeusement.

pond [pond], n. étang, vivier, m.; mare (pool), f.

ponder ['pondə], v.t. peser, considérer, réfléchir à.—v.i. méditer.

ponderous ['pondərəs], a. lourd, pesant.

ponderously ['pondərəsli], adv. pesamment.

pontiff ['pontif], n. pontife, m.

pontificate [pon'tifikeit], n. pontificat, m.—v.i. pontifier.

Pontius Pilate ['pontʃəs'pailət]. Ponce Pilate, m.

pontoon [pon'tu:n], n. ponton, m.; (Cards) vingt-et-un, m.

pony ['pouni], n. poney, petit cheval, m.

poodle [pu:dl], n. caniche, m.

pooh! [pu:], int. bah! allons donc!

pooh-pooh ['pu:'pu:]. v.t. tourner en ridicule.

pool [pu:l], n. étang, m., mare; piscine (pour

nager); (Cards, Billiards etc.) poule; mise en commun, f.—v.t. mettre en commun.

poop[[pu:p], n. dunette, poupe, f.

poor [puə], a. pauvre, indigent; malheureux (sans joie); triste (de pauvre qualité); mauvais (pas bon).

poor-box ['puəboks], n. tronc des pauvres, m.

*poor-house ['puəhaus], n. asile des indigents, m.

*poor-law ['puələ:], n. loi sur l'assistance publique, f.

poorly ['puəli], a. indisposé, souffrant.—adv. pauvrement, mal, tristement.

poorness ['puənis], n. pauvreté; médiocrité, f.

pop (1)[[pop], n. petit bruit vif et sec, m.; (colloq.) boisson pétillante, f.—v.t. pousser, fourrer ou mettre subitement.—v.i. entrer ou sortir subitement.—int. crac! pan!

pop (2) [pop], n. (Am., colloq.) papa, m.

pop (3) [pop], a. and n. (colloq.) (musique) populaire, f.; the pops, les chansons en vogue, f.pl.

Pope [Poup], n. Pape, m.

popedom ['poupdəm], n. papauté, f.

popery ['poupəri], n. papisme, m.

popish ['poupiʃ], a. papiste; de papiste (choses).

poplar ['poplə], n. (Bot.) peuplier, m.

poplin ['poplin], n. popeline, f.

poppet ['popit], n. poupée, marionnette, f.

poppy ['popi], n. pavot (cultivé); coquelicot (sauvage), m.

populace ['popjuləs], n. populace, f.

popular ['popjulə], a. populaire; en vogue.

popularity [popju'læriti], n. popularité, f.

popularize ['popjuləraiz], v.t. populariser.

popularly ['popjuləli], adv. populairement.

populate ['popjuleit], v.t. peupler.

population [popju'leiʃən], n. population, f.

populous ['popjuləs], a. populeux.

porcelain ['po:slin], n. porcelaine, f.

porch [po:tʃ], n. porche, m.

porcupine ['po:kjupain], n. porc-épic, m.

pore (1) [po:], n. pore, m.

pore (2) [po:], v.i. regarder avec grande attention; to pore over, dévorer (un livre).

pork [po:k], n. porc, m.

pork-butcher ['po:kbutʃə], n. charcutier, m.; pork-butcher's shop, charcuterie, f.

porker ['po:kə], n. porc d'engrais, cochon, m.

pork-pie ['po:k'pai], n. pâté de porc, m.

pornography [po:'nogrəfi], n. pornographie, f.

porous ['po:rəs], a. poreux.

porphyry ['po:firi], n. porphyre, m.

porpoise ['po:pəs], n. marsouin, m.

porridge ['poridʒ], n. bouillie, f.

porringer ['porindʒə], n. bol à bouillie, m.

port (1) [po:t], n. port (ville maritime), m.

port (2) [po:t], n. (Naut.) bâbord, m.

port (3) [po:t], n. porto (vin), m.

portable ['po:təbl], a. portatif, transportable.

portal [po:tl], n. portail, m.

portcullis [po:t'kalis], n. herse, f.

portend [po:'tend], v.t. présager, augurer.

portent ['po:tənt], n. mauvais augure, m.

portentous [po:'tentəs], a. de mauvais augure.

porter ['po:tə], n. commissionnaire; concierge (de maison); porteur (de rue); (Rail.) porteur, m.

porterage ['po:təridʒ], n. port; factage, m.

portfolio ['pɔːt'fouliou], *n.* carton, *m.*; serviette, *f.*; (*Polit.*) portefeuille, *m.*
port-hole ['pɔːthoul], *n.* sabord, *m.*
portico ['pɔːtikou], *n.* portique, *m.*
portion ['pɔːʃən], *n.* partie, part; dot (*de mariage*), *f.*—*v.t.* partager; doter (*pour le mariage*).
portliness ['pɔːtlinis], *n.* corpulence, *f.*
portly ['pɔːtli], *a.* d'un port majestueux; corpulent.
portmanteau [pɔːt'mæntou], *n.* valise, *f.*
portrait ['pɔːtrit], *n.* portrait, *m.*
portray [pɔː'trei], *v.t.* peindre; (*fig.*) dépeindre, décrire.
Portugal ['pɔːtʃug(ə)l]. le Portugal, *m.*
Portuguese [pɔːtʃu'giːz], *a.* portugais.—*n.* portugais (*langue*); Portugais (*personne*), *m.*
pose [pouz], *v.t.* embarrasser, confondre; poser (*une question*).—*v.i.* poser (*avec affectation*).—*n.* pose, *f.*
poser ['pouzə], *n.* question embarrassante, *f.*
poseur [pou'zəː], *n.* poseur, *m.*
position [pə'ziʃən], *n.* situation, position, *f.*
positive ['pozitiv], *a.* positif; absolu, sûr; décisif.—*n.* positif, *m.*
positively ['pozitivli], *adv.* positivement; absolument.
positiveness ['pozitivnis], *n.* nature positive, *f.*
*****posse** ['posi], *n.* détachement (d'agents de police), *m.*; foule (*de civils*), *f.*
possess [pə'zes], *v.t.* posséder; avoir; jouir de.
possession [pə'zeʃən], *n.* possession, *f.*
possessive [pə'zesiv], *a.* possessif.
possessor [pə'zesə], *n.* possesseur, *m.*
*****posset** ['posit], *n.* lait caillé au vin, *m.*
possibility [posi'biliti], *n.* possibilité, *f.*; moyen (*façon*), *m.*
possible ['posibl], *a.* possible.
possibly ['posibli], *adv.* peut-être.
post (1) [poust], *n.* emploi, *m.*; (*Mil.*) poste; courrier (*livraison de lettres*), *m.*; (*Post-office*) poste, *f.*—*v.t.* mettre à la poste; (*Mil. etc.*) poster, affecter.
post (2) [poust], *n.* poteau (*en bois*); montant (*de porte*), *m.*—*v.t.* afficher.
postage ['poustidʒ], *n.* port de lettre, port, affranchissement, *m.*
postage-stamp ['poustidʒstæmp], *n.* timbre-poste, *m.*
postal ['poustəl], *a.* postal; *postal order*, mandat-poste, *m.*
postcard ['poustkɑːd], *n.* carte postale, *f.*
postdate [poust'deit], *v.t.* postdater.
poster ['poustə], *n.* affiche, *f.*, placard, *m.*
posterior [pos'tiəriə], *a.* postérieur.
posterity [pos'teriti], *n.* postérité, *f.*
postern ['poustəːn], *a.* de derrière.—*n.* poterne, *f.*
post-haste ['poust'heist], *adv.* en grande hâte.
posthumous ['postjuməs], *a.* posthume.
posthumously ['postjuməsli], *adv.* après décès.
postillion [pos'tiliən], *n.* postillon, *m.*
postman ['poustmən], *n.* (*pl.* -men [men]) facteur, *m.*
postmark ['poustmɑːk], *n.* cachet de la poste, *m.*
postmaster ['poustmɑːstə], *n.* receveur des postes, *m.*
post meridiem ['poustmə'ridiəm], (*abbr.*

p.m. ['piː'em]) *adv.* de l'après-midi, du soir.
post-mortem [poust'mɔːtəm], *adv.* après décès.—*n.* autopsie, *f.*
post-office ['poustɔfis], *n.* bureau de poste, *m.*, poste, *f.*
postpone [poust'poun], *v.t.* ajourner, différer, remettre.
postponement [poust'pounmənt], *n.* ajournement, *m.*, remise, *f.*
postscript ['poustskript], (*abbr.* **P.S.** ['piː'es]) *n.* post-scriptum, *m.*
postulate ['postjuleit], *v.t.* postuler.
posture ['postʃə], *n.* posture, pose, *f.*
post-war [poust'wɔː], *a.* d'après guerre.
posy ['pouzi], *n.* petit bouquet, *m.*
pot [pot], *n.* pot, *m.*; marmite, *f.*; *pots and pans*, batterie de cuisine, *f.*—*v.t.* empoter, mettre en pot.
potable ['poutəbl], *a.* potable.
potash ['potæʃ], *n.* potasse, *f.*
potassium [pə'tæsiəm], *n.* potassium, *m.*
potato [pə'teitou], *n.* (*pl.* **potatoes** [pə'teitouz]) pomme de terre, *f.*
pot-bellied ['potbelid], *a.* pansu, ventru.
potency ['poutənsi], *n.* puissance, force, *f.*
potent ['poutənt], *a.* puissant, fort; (*fig.*) efficace.
potentate ['poutənteit], *n.* potentat, *m.*
potential [pə'tenʃəl], *a.* potentiel, latent.—*n.* (*Elec. etc.*) potentiel, *m.*
potful ['potful], *n.* potée, *f.*
*****pother** ['poðə], *n.* tumulte; bruit, *m.*
pot-hole ['pothoul], *n.* (*Geol.*) marmite torrentielle; (*Motor.*) flache, *f.*
pot-holer ['pothoulə], *n.* spéléologue, *m.*, *f.*
pot-holing ['pothoulin], *n.* spéléologie, *f.*
pothook ['pothuk], *n.* crémaillère, *f.*
potion ['pouʃən], *n.* potion, *f.*; breuvage, *m.*
pot-luck ['pot'lʌk], *n.* fortune du pot, *f.*
pot-shot ['potʃot], *n.* coup tiré au petit bonheur, *m.*
*****pottage** ['potidʒ], *n.* potage (épais), *m.*
potted ['potid], *a.* en pot, en terrine; *potted meat*, conserve de viande, *f.*
potter ['potə], *n.* potier, *m.*—*v.i.* *to potter about*, s'amuser à des riens.
pottery ['potəri], *n.* poterie, *f.*
potting ['potin], *a.* *potting shed*, serre, resserre, *f.*—*n.* (*Hort.*) mise en pot, *f.*
pouch [pautʃ], *n.* poche, *f.*, petit sac, *m.*; blague (*à tabac*), *f.*
poulterer ['poultərə], *n.* marchand de volailles, *m.*
poultice ['poultis], *n.* cataplasme, *m.*—*v.t.* mettre un cataplasme à.
poultry ['poultri], *n.* volaille, *f.*
pounce [pauns], *v.i.* fondre (*sur*).
pound [paund], *n.* livre; livre sterling; fourrière (*clôture*), *f.*—*v.t.* broyer; (*Metal.*) bocarder.
poundage ['paundidʒ], *n.* commission de tant par livre, *f.*
pounding ['paundin], *n.* broiement; (*Metal.*) bocardage, *m.*
pour [pɔː], *v.t.* verser.—*v.i.* couler; pleuvoir à verse (*pluie*).
pouring ['pɔːrin], *a.* torrentiel (*pluie*).
pout [paut], *v.i.* bouder, faire la moue.—*n.* bouderie, moue, *f.*
pouting ['pautin], *a.* qui fait la moue; boudeur.

517

poverty ['pɔvəti], *n.* pauvreté, misère, indigence, *f.*

poverty-stricken ['pɔvətistrikn], *a.* réduit à la misère, indigent.

powder ['paudə], *n.* poudre, *f.*; *face-powder*, poudre de riz; *gunpowder*, poudre à canon; *tooth-powder*, poudre dentifrice.—*v.t.* réduire en poudre; poudrer (*les cheveux*); (*Cook.*) saupoudrer; *to powder one's face*, se poudrer.

powder-compact ['paudəkɔmpækt], *n.* poudrier (*de dame*), *m.*

powdered ['paudəd], *a.* pulvérisé; poudré (*cheveux*).

powder-puff ['paudəpʌf], *n.* houppe, *f.*, pompon, *m.*

powdery ['paudəri], *a.* poudreux; friable.

power ['pauə], *n.* pouvoir, *m.*; force (*physique*); autorité, puissance (*morale*), *f.*; *the Great Powers*, les grandes puissances, *f.pl.*; *to be in power*, être au pouvoir.

powerful ['pauəful], *a.* puissant, fort.

powerfully ['pauəfuli], *adv.* puissamment, fortement.

powerless ['pauəlis], *a.* impuissant, faible.

power-station ['pauəsteiʃən], *n.* usine génératrice, centrale électrique, *f.*

pox [pɔks], *n.* vérole, *f.*; *chicken-pox*, varicelle, *f.*; *small-pox*, petite vérole, variole, *f.*

practicability [præktikə'biliti], *n.* possibilité, praticabilité, *f.*

practicable ['præktikəbl], *a.* praticable.

practical ['præktikl], *a.* pratique; *practical joke*, mauvaise farce, *f.*

practically ['præktikli], *adv.* en pratique; à peu près.

practice ['præktis], *n.* pratique, habitude, *f.*, usage, exercice, *m.*; clientèle (*de médecin, d'avocat etc.*); intrigue, *f.*

practise ['præktis], *v.t.* pratiquer, mettre en pratique; exercer, pratiquer (*une profession etc.*); (*Mus.*) étudier.—*v.i.* (*Mus.*) étudier; s'exercer (*à*); exercer, faire de la clientèle (*médecin*).

practised ['præktist], *a.* exercé (*à*); versé (*dans*); habile.

practising ['præktisiŋ], *a.* praticien, exerçant.

practitioner [præk'tiʃənə], *n.* praticien, *m.*; *general practitioner*, médecin ordinaire, *m.*; *medical practitioner*, médecin, *m.*

pragmatic [præg'mætik], **pragmatical** [præg'mætikəl], *a.* pragmatique; officieux; infatué de soi.

pragmatism ['prægmətizm], *n.* pragmatisme, *m.*

prairie ['preəri], *n.* prairie, savane, *f.*

praise [preiz], *n.* louange, *f.*, éloge, *m.*—*v.t.* louer, faire l'éloge de; vanter.

praiseworthy ['preizwə:ði], *a.* louable, digne d'éloges.

pram [præm], *n.* voiture d'enfant, *f.*

prance [prɑ:ns], *v.i.* fringuer (*cheval*).

prancing ['prɑ:nsiŋ], *a.* fringant.

prank [præŋk], *n.* escapade, niche, *f.*, tour, *m.*

prate [preit], *v.i.* jaser, babiller, bavarder (*de*).

prating ['preitiŋ], *a.* bavard, babillard.

pratingly ['preitiŋli], *adv.* en bavard, en babillard.

prattle [prætl], *v.i.* babiller, jaser, caqueter.—*n.* babil, caquetage, bavardage, *m.*

prattler ['prætlə], *n.* bavard, babillard, *m.*

prattling ['prætliŋ], *n.* bavardage, caquet, *m.*

prawn [prɔ:n], *n.* crevette rouge; salicoque, *f.*

pray [prei], *v.t.* prier, supplier.—*v.i.* prier.

prayer [preə], *n.* prière, supplication; (*Law*) demande, *f.*; *the Lord's Prayer*, l'oraison dominicale, *f.*

prayer-book ['preəbuk], *n.* livre de prières, *m.*; liturgie, *f.*

preach [pri:tʃ], *v.t.*, *v.i.* prêcher.

preacher ['pri:tʃə], *n.* prédicateur, *m.*

preaching ['pri:tʃiŋ], *n.* prédication, *f.*

preamble [pri:'æmbl], *n.* préambule, *m.*

prearrange [pri:ə'reindʒ], *v.t.* arranger d'avance.

prebendary ['prebəndəri], *n.* chanoine, prébendier, *m.*

precarious [pri'keəriəs], *a.* précaire.

precariously [pri'keəriəsli], *adv.* précairement.

precariousness [pri'keəriəsnis], *n.* nature précaire; incertitude, *f.*

precaution [pri'kɔ:ʃən], *n.* précaution, *f.*

precautionary [pri'kɔ:ʃənri], *a.* de précaution.

precede [pri'si:d], *v.t.* précéder.

precedence ['presidəns], *n.* préséance, *f.*; *to have* or *take precedence over*, avoir le pas sur.

precedent (1) [pri'si:dənt], **preceding** [pri'si:diŋ] *a.* précédent.

precedent (2) ['presidənt], *n.* précédent, *m.*

precept ['pri:sept], *n.* précepte, *m.*

precinct ['pri:siŋkt], *n.* limite, borne, enceinte, *f.*

precious ['preʃəs], *a.* précieux; affecté; (*fam.*) fameux, fichu.

preciously ['preʃəsli], *adv.* précieusement; (*fam.*) fameusement, diablement.

preciousness ['preʃəsnis], *n.* haute valeur, *f.*

precipice ['presipis], *n.* précipice, *m.*

precipitate (1) [pri'sipitit], *a.* précipité.—*n.* (*Chem.*) précipité, *m.*

precipitate (2) [pri'sipiteit], *v.t.* précipiter.—*v.i.* se précipiter.

precipitation [prisipi'teiʃən], *n.* précipitation, *f.*

precipitous [pri'sipitəs], *a.* escarpé, abrupt.

precipitously [pri'sipitəsli], *adv.* à pic, en précipice; (*fig.*) précipitamment.

precise [pri'sais], *a.* précis, exact; formaliste, pointilleux, scrupuleux.

precisely [pri'saisli], *adv.* précisément.

precision [pri'siʒən], *n.* précision, exactitude, *f.*

preclude [pri'klu:d], *v.t.* exclure; empêcher (*mettre obstacle à*).

preclusion [pri'klu:ʒən], *n.* exclusion, *f.*

precocious [pri'kouʃəs], *a.* précoce.

precociousness [pri'kouʃəsnis], *n.* précocité, *f.*

preconceived ['pri:kən'si:vd], *a.* formé d'avance; *preconceived idea*, idée préconçue, *f.*

precursor [pri'kə:sə], *n.* précurseur, avant-coureur, *m.*

predatory ['predətəri], *a.* de rapine, de proie, pillard, rapace.

predecease ['pri:di'si:s], *v.t.* prédécéder.

predestinate [pri:'destineit], **predestine** [pri:'destin], *v.t.* prédestiner.

predestination [priːdestiˈneiʃən], n. prédestination, f.

predetermine [priːdiˈtəːmin], v.t. prédéterminer, arrêter d'avance.

predicament [priˈdikəmənt], n. état, m., position difficile, situation fâcheuse; catégorie, f., ordre, m.

predicate [ˈpredikit], n. prédicat, attribut, m.

predict [priˈdikt], v.t. prédire.

prediction [priˈdikʃən], n. prédiction, prévision, f.

predilection [priːdiˈlekʃən], n. prédilection, f.

predispose [priːdisˈpouz], v.t. prédisposer.

predisposition [priːdispəˈziʃən], n. prédisposition, f.

predominance [priˈdɔminəns], n. prédominance, f., ascendant, m.

predominant [priˈdɔminənt], a. prédominant.

predominantly [priˈdɔminəntli], adv. d'une manière prédominante.

predominate [priˈdɔmineit], v.i. prédominer, prévaloir.

pre-eminence [priːˈeminəns], n. prééminence, supériorité, f.

pre-eminent [priːˈeminənt], a. prééminent.

pre-eminently [priːˈeminəntli], adv. par excellence.

preen [priːn], v.t lisser, nettoyer (ses plumes); to preen oneself, se piquer.

pre-engage [priːinˈgeidʒ], v.t. engager d'avance.

pre-exist [priːigˈzist], v.i. préexister.

pre-existence [priːigˈzistəns], n. préexistence, f.

prefabricate [priːˈfæbrikeit], v.t. préfabriquer.

preface [ˈprefis], n. préface, f.; avant-propos, m.—v.t. faire une préface à.

prefect [ˈpriːfekt], n. préfet (Sch.) surveillant, m.

prefer [priˈfəː], v.t. préférer, aimer mieux; avancer, élever (aux honneurs); porter (une accusation).

preferable [ˈprefərəbl], a. préférable (à).

preferably [ˈprefərəbli], adv. préférablement, de préférence.

preference [ˈprefərəns], n. préférence, f.

preferential [prefəˈrenʃl], a. préférentiel.

preferment [priˈfəːmənt], n. avancement, m., promotion, f.

prefix [ˈpriːfiks], n. (Gram.) préfixe, m.

pregnancy [ˈpregnənsi], n. grossesse, f.

pregnant [ˈpregnənt], a. enceinte, grosse; (fig.) gros, plein (de); fertile, fécond (en).

prehensile [priˈhensail], a. préhensile.

prehistoric [priːhisˈtɔrik], a. préhistorique.

prejudge [priːˈdʒʌdʒ], v.t. juger d'avance.

prejudice [ˈpredʒudis], v.t. prévenir, nuire à (faire du tort à).—n. prévention, f., préjugé; préjudice, tort (détriment), m.

prejudiced [ˈpredʒudist], a. prévenu.

prejudicial [predʒuˈdiʃl], a. préjudiciable, nuisible (à).

prelate [ˈprelit], n. prélat, m.

preliminary [priˈliminəri], a. and n. préliminaire, m.

prelude [ˈpreljuːd], n. prélude, m.

premature [ˈpremətjuə], a. prématuré.

prematurely [preməˈtjuəli], adv. prématurément.

premeditate [priˈmediteit], v.t. préméditer.

premeditated [priˈmediteitid], a. prémédité.

premeditation [primediˈteiʃən], n. préméditation, f.

premier [ˈpriːmiə, ˈpremiə], a. premier (de rang).—n. premier ministre, m.

premise [ˈpremis], n. (Log.) prémisse, f.

premises [ˈpremisiz], n.pl. lieux, m.pl.; établissement, local, m.

premium [ˈpriːmiəm], n. prime, f.; prix, m.

premonition [priːməˈniʃən], n. avertissement; pressentiment, m.

prenatal [priːˈneitl], a. prénatal.

preoccupied [priːˈɔkjupaid], a. préoccupé.

preordain [priːɔːˈdein], v.t. ordonner ou arranger d'avance.

prep [prep], n. (Sch. fam. abbr. preparation) étude, f.; devoirs, m.pl.

prepaid [priːˈpeid], a. affranchi, franc de port.—adv. franco.

preparation [prepəˈreiʃən], n. préparation, f.; préparatifs, apprêts (de voyage etc.), m.pl.

preparatory [priˈpærətri], a. préparatoire.

prepare [priˈpɛə], v.t. préparer.—v.i. se préparer, s'apprêter (à).

preparedness [priˈpɛə(ri)dnis], n. état de préparation, m.

prepay [priːˈpei], v.t. irr (conjug. like PAY) payer d'avance; affranchir (lettres).

prepayment [priːˈpeimənt], n. payement d'avance; affranchissement (de lettres), m.

preponderance [priˈpɔndərəns], n. prépondérance, f.

preponderant [priˈpɔndərənt], a. prépondérant.

preponderate [priˈpɔndəreit], v.i. avoir la prépondérance, l'emporter (sur).

preposition [prepəˈziʃən], n. préposition, f.

prepossessing [priːpəˈzesiŋ], a. prévenant, engageant.

preposterous [priˈpɔstərəs], a. absurde, déraisonnable.

preposterously [priˈpɔstərəsli], adv. absurdement, déraisonnablement.

prerogative [priˈrɔgətiv], n. prérogative, f.

Presbyterian [prezbiˈtiəriən], a. and n. presbytérien, m.

Presbyterianism [prezbiˈtiəriənizm], n. presbytérianisme, m.

presbytery [ˈprezbitəri], n. presbytère, m.

prescience [ˈpreʃiəns], n. prescience, f.

prescribe [priˈskraib], v.t. prescrire; (Med.) ordonner.—v.i. (Med.) faire une ordonnance.

prescription [priˈskripʃən], n. (Law) prescription; (Med.) ordonnance, f.

presence [ˈprezəns], n. présence, f.; air, maintien, m., mine (aspect), f.; personnage supérieur, m.; presence of mind, présence d'esprit.

present [ˈprezənt], a. présent; actuel; at the present moment, à présent, actuellement; to be present at, assister à.—n. présent; cadeau, don, m.; for the present, pour le moment.—[priˈzent], v.t. présenter, offrir (à).

presentable [priˈzentəbl], a. présentable.

presentation [prezənˈteiʃən], n. présentation, f.; don, m.

presentiment

presentiment [pri'zentimənt], *n.* pressentiment, *m.*

presently ['prezəntli], *adv.* tout à l'heure, bientôt.

preservation [prezə'veiʃən], *n.* salut, *m.*, conservation; préservation (*de*), *f.*

preservative [pri'zɔ:vətiv], *a.* and *n.* préservateur, préservatif, *m.*

preserve [pri'zɔ:v], *n.* confiture, *f.*, conserves, *f.pl.*; réserve, chasse réservée, *f.*—*v.t.* conserver (*de*); conserver; confire (*fruits etc.*); *preserved fruits*, fruits confits, *m.pl.*; *preserved meat*, conserves de viande, *f.pl.*

preserver [pri'zɔ:və], *n.* sauveur; conservateur, *m.*; *life preserver*, porte-respect, *m.*

preside [pri'zaid], *v.i.* présider (*à*).

presidency ['prezidənsi], *n.* présidence, *f.*

president ['prezidənt], *n.* président, *m.*; *vice-president*, vice-président, *m.*

presidential [prezi'denʃəl], *a.* présidentiel; de président.

presiding [pri'zaidiŋ], *a.* présidant.

press (1) [pres], *v.t.* presser; serrer, étreindre; satiner (*papier*); pressurer (*fruits*); repasser (*vêtements*); (*fig.*) insister sur.—*v.i.* presser, pousser; avancer; se presser.—*n.* presse, pression, *f.*; pressoir (*à fruits etc.*), *m.*; armoire à linge, *f.*; *the press*, la presse.

press (2) [pres], *v.t.* enrôler (*marins*) de force.

press-agency ['preseidʒənsi], *n.* agence de presse, *f.*

press-cutting ['preskʌtiŋ], *n.* coupure de journal, *f.*

pressed [prest], *a.* satiné; *hard pressed*, serré de près; aux abois; *pressed for time*, très pressé.

*****press-gang** ['presgæŋ], *n.* (*Naut.*) presse, *f.*

pressing ['presiŋ], *a.* urgent, pressant.

pressman ['presmən], *n.* (*pl.* **-men** [men]) journaliste, reporter, *m.*

pressure ['preʃə], *n.* pression; tension; urgence, *f.*; poids (*lourdeur*), *m.*; *blood pressure*, tension artérielle.

pressure-cooker ['preʃəkukə], *n.* autoclave; auto-cuiseur, *m.*, cocotte-minute, *f.*

pressure-gauge ['preʃəgeidʒ], *n.* manomètre *m.*

pressurize ['preʃəraiz], *v.t.* pressuriser.

prestige [pres'ti:ʒ], *n.* prestige, *m.*

presumably [pri'zju:məbli], *adv.* probablement.

presume [pri'zju:m], *v.t.* présumer; supposer.—*v.i.* présumer; se permettre, avoir l'audace (*de*), prendre la liberté (*de*); *to presume upon*, présumer trop de.

presuming [pri'zju:miŋ], *a.* présomptueux, indiscret.

presumption [pri'zʌmpʃən], *n.* présomption, *f.*

presumptive [pri'zʌmptiv], *a.* présumé; (*Law*) présomptif.

presumptuous [pri'zʌmptjuəs], *a.* présomptueux.

presumptuousness [pri'zʌmptjuəsnis], *n.* présomption, *f.*

presuppose [pri:sə'pouz], *v.t.* présupposer.

pretence [pri'tens], *n.* prétexte, *m.*, simulation; prétention, *f.*; *to make a pretence of*, faire semblant de; *under false pretences*, par des moyens frauduleux.

pretend [pri'tend], *v.t.* prétexter; feindre.—*v.i.* prétendre (*à*); feindre (*de*), faire semblant (*de*).

pretended [pri'tendid], *a.* prétendu, soi-disant.

pretender [pri'tendə], *n.* prétendant, *m.*

pretension [pri'tenʃən], *n.* prétention, *f.*

pretentious [pri'tenʃəs], *a.* prétentieux, ambitieux.

pretentiousness [pri'tenʃəsnis], *n.* air prétentieux, *m.*, prétention, *f.*

preternatural [pri:tə'nætʃərəl], *a.* surnaturel, contre nature.

pretext ['pri:tekst], *n.* prétexte, faux semblant, *m.*; *under the pretext of*, sous prétexte de.

prettily ['pritili], *adv.* joliment, gentiment.

prettiness ['pritinis], *n.* gentillesse, *f.*, agrément, *m.*

pretty ['priti], *a.* joli, gentil.—*adv.* assez; passablement; *pretty much*, presque, à peu près.

prevail [pri'veil], *v.i.* prévaloir, l'emporter (*sur*); réussir (*avoir du succès*); dominer.

prevailing [pri'veiliŋ], *a.* dominant, régnant, général.

prevalence ['prevələns], *n.* influence, prédominance; fréquence, durée (*de temps, maladie etc.*), *f.*

prevalent ['prevələnt], *a.* régnant, dominant, général.

prevaricate [pri'værikeit], *v.i.* équivoquer; tergiverser, mentir.

prevarication [priværi'keiʃən], *n.* tergiversation, *f.*

prevaricator [pri'værikeitə], *n.* chicaneur, menteur, *m.*

prevent [pri'vent], *v.t.* empêcher, détourner (*de*); prévenir.

preventable [pri'ventəbl], *a.* évitable.

prevention [pri'venʃən], *n.* empêchement, *m.*

preventive [pri'ventiv], *a.* préventif.—*n.* préservatif, *m.*

preview ['pri:vju:], *n.* avant-première, *f.*

previous ['pri:viəs], *a.* antérieur, préalable.

previously ['pri:viəsli], *adv.* antérieurement, auparavant.

previousness ['pri:viəsnis], *n.* antériorité, priorité; (*colloq.*) anticipation, *f.*

prey [prei], *n.* proie, *f.*; *to be a prey to*, être en proie à.—*v.i. to prey on*, faire sa proie de; tourmenter, obséder (*l'esprit*).

price [prais], *n.* prix, *m.*; *at any price*, à tout prix; *cost price*, prix coûtant; *market price*, prix courant.—*v.t.* tarifer, mettre un prix à.

priceless ['praislis], *a.* sans prix, inappréciable; impayable (*plaisanterie etc.*).

price-list ['praislist], *n.* tarif, *m.*

prick [prik], *n.* piqûre; pointe, *f.*; (*fig.*) aiguillon (*stimulant*); remords, *m.*—*v.t.* piquer; dresser (*les oreilles*); aiguillonner (*stimuler*); (*fig.*) exciter, tourmenter de remords.

pricker ['prikə], *n.* poinçon, *m.*, pointe, *f.*

pricking ['prikiŋ], *a.* qui pique, piquant.—*n.* piqûre, *f.*; picotement (*sensation*), *m.*

prickle [prikl], *n.* aiguillon, piquant, *m.*; épine, *f.*—*v.t.* piquer.

prickly ['prikli], *a.* piquant, épineux, hérissé.

pride [praid], *n.* orgueil, *m.*, fierté; bande (*de lions*), *f.*—*v.r. to pride oneself on*, se piquer de, s'enorgueillir de.

prier ['praiə], *n.* curieux, *m.*

priest [priːst], n. prêtre, m.
priestess ['priːstes], n. prêtresse, f.
priesthood ['priːsthuːd], n. prêtrise, f., sacerdoce, clergé, m.
priestly ['priːstli], a. de prêtre, sacerdotal.
prig [prig], n. faquin, fat; pédant, m.
priggish ['prigiʃ], a. suffisant, pédant.
priggishly['prigiʃli], adv. avec suffisance.
prim [prim], a. affecté, précieux, collet monté.
primacy ['praiməsi], n. primauté, f.
primal ['praiməl], a. primitif; principal.
primarily ['praimərili], adv. dans le principe.
primary ['praiməri], a. primitif, premier; principal; (Sch.) primaire, élémentaire.
primate ['praimit], n. primat, m.
prime [praim], a. premier, principal; de premier rang, de première qualité; *prime minister*, premier ministre, m.—n. aube, f.; commencement; printemps, m.; fleur, élite, f., choix (*mieux*), m.; première jeunesse, f.; *prime of life*, fleur de l'âge, f. —v.t. amorcer (*fusils*); (Paint.) imprimer.
primer ['praimə], n. premier livre (*de lecture etc.*); (R.-C. Ch.) livre d'heures, m.
primeval [prai'miːvəl], a. primitif, primordial.
priming ['praimiŋ], n. amorçage, m.; amorce (*d'un fusil*); (Paint.) impression, f.
primitive ['primitiv], a. and n. primitif, m.
primitiveness ['primitivnis], n. caractère primitif, m.
primly ['primli], adv. d'un air collet monté.
primness ['primnis], n. afféterie, f.
primogeniture [praimou'dʒenitjuə], n. primogéniture, f.
primordial [prai'mɔːdiəl], a. primordial.
primrose ['primrouz], n. primevère, f.
prince [prins], n. prince, m.
princeliness ['prinslinis], n. caractère de prince, m.
princely ['prinsli], a. de prince, princier; magnifique.—adv. en prince, en princesse, magnifiquement.
princess [prin'ses], n. princesse, f.
principal ['prinsipl], a. principal, premier, en chef.—n. partie principale, f., chef; directeur, patron; proviseur (*d'un lycée*), m.; directrice, f.
principality [prinsi'pæliti], n. principauté, f.
principally ['prinsipli], adv. principalement, surtout.
principle ['prinsipl], n. principe, m.
principled ['prinsipld], a. qui a des principes.
print [print], v.t. imprimer; faire une empreinte sur; (Phot. etc.) tirer; *printed matter*, imprimé(s), m. (pl.).—n. empreinte (*de pas etc.*), impression; estampe, gravure; indienne (*tissu*); (Phot.) épreuve, f.; (Print.) caractère, m.
printer ['printə], n. imprimeur, typographe, m.
printing ['printiŋ], n. impression (*tirage*); imprimerie (*art etc.*), f.
printing-machine ['printiŋmə'ʃiːn], n. presse mécanique, f.
printing-press ['printiŋpres], n. presse à imprimer, f.
prior ['praiə], a. antérieur.—adv. antérieurement (*à*), avant.—n. prieur, m.
prioress ['praiəris], n. prieure, f.
priority [prai'ɔriti], n. priorité, f.

priory ['praiəri], n. prieuré, m.
prise [praiz], n. levier, m.—v.t. *to prise open*, ouvrir avec un levier.
prism [prizm], n. prisme, m.
prismatic [priz'mætik], prismatical [priz'mætikəl], a. prismatique.
prison [prizn], n. prison, f.
prisoner ['priznə], n. prisonnier, m.; (Law) *prisoner (at the bar)*, accusé, prévenu, m.
prison-van ['priznvæn], n. voiture cellulaire, f.
pristine ['pristain], a. primitif, premier.
privacy ['praivəsi, 'privəsi], n. retraite, solitude, intimité, f.
private ['praivit], a. particulier, personnel, privé; confidentiel, secret; (Law) à huis clos.—n. (Mil.) simple soldat, m.
privateer [praivə'tiə], n. corsaire, m.
privately ['praivitli], adv. en particulier; en secret; (Law) à huis clos.
privation [prai'veiʃən], n. privation, f.
privet ['privit], n. (Bot.) troène, m.
privilege ['privilidʒ], n. privilège, m., (Law) immunité, f.—v.t. privilégier.
privileged ['privilidʒd], a. privilégié.
privily ['privili], adv. secrètement, en secret.
privy ['privi], a. privé, secret; caché; *Privy Council*, conseil privé, m.
prize [praiz], n. prise (*ce qu'on prend*), f.; prix (*récompense*); lot (*dans une loterie*), m.—v.t. priser, estimer.
prize-giving ['praizgiviŋ], n. distribution des prix, f.
prize-winner ['praizwinə], n. lauréat, gagnant, m.
pro [prou], prep. pour; *pros and cons*, le pour et le contre.
probability [prɔbə'biliti], n. probabilité, vraisemblance, f.
probable ['prɔbəbl], a. probable; vraisemblable.
probably ['prɔbəbli], adv. probablement.
probate ['proubeit], n. vérification (*d'un testament*), f.
probation [prə'beiʃən], n. probation, épreuve, f.; (Univ. etc.) examen, stage, m.; *on probation*, (Law) sous surveillance de la police.
probationary [prə'beiʃənəri], a. d'épreuve; de probation.
probationer [prə'beiʃənə], n. aspirant, m., stagiaire; novice, m., f.
probe [proub], n. sonde, f., stylet, m.—v.t. sonder; (fig.) examiner à fond.
probing ['proubiŋ], a. pénétrant (*question*).
probity ['proubiti], n. probité, f.
problem ['prɔbləm], n. problème, m.
problematic [prɔbli'mætik], problematical [prɔbli'mætikəl], a. problématique.
proboscis [prə'bɔsis], n. (pl. probosces [prə'bɔsiːz]) trompe, f., (facet.) nez, m.
procedure [prə'siːdʒə], n. procédé, m., procédure, f.
proceed [prə'siːd], v.i. procéder, avancer, continuer son chemin; provenir (*de*); se mettre (*à*).
proceeding [prə'siːdiŋ], n. procédé, m.; manière d'agir, f.; (pl.) démarches, f.pl., faits, actes, m.pl.
proceeds ['prousiːdz], n.pl. produit, montant, m.

521

process ['prouses], *n.* procédé; processus; cours, *m.*, marche, suite (*du temps*), *f.*—*v.t.* (*Ind.*) traiter.

procession [prə'seʃən], *n.* procession, *f.*, cortège, *m.*

processional [prə'seʃənəl], *a.* processionnel. —*n.* hymne processionnel, *m.*

proclaim [prə'kleim], *v.t.* proclamer, déclarer, publier.

proclamation [prɔklə'meiʃən], *n.* proclamation, publication, déclaration; ordonnance, *f.*

proclivity [prə'kliviti], *n.* penchant, *m.*, inclination (*à*), *f.*

procrastinate [pro'kræstineit], *v.t.* remettre. —*v.i.* retarder.

procrastination [prokræsti'neiʃən], *n.* retardement, délai, *m.*

procrastinator [pro'kræstineitə], *n.* temporiseur, *m.*

procreate ['proukrieit], *v.t.* procréer.

procreation [proukri'eiʃən], *n.* procréation, *f.*

procreative ['proukrieitiv], *a.* procréateur, productif.

proctor ['prɔktə], *n.* (*Univ.*) censeur; (*Law*) procureur, *m.*

procurable [prə'kjuərəbl], *a.* qu'on peut se procurer.

procuration [prɔkju'reiʃən], *n.* gestion des affaires d'autrui; (*Law*) procuration, *f.*

procurator ['prɔkjureitə], *n.* agent d'affaires; (*Law*) procurateur, *m.*

procure [prə'kjuə], *v.t.* procurer, faire avoir, se procurer.

prod [prɔd], *v.t.* pousser du doigt *ou* du bout d'un bâton; piquer; (*fig.*) aiguillonner.—*n.* coup de pointe, *m.*

prodigal ['prɔdigl], *a.* and *n.* prodigue, *m.*, *f.*

prodigality ['prɔdi'gæliti], *n.* prodigalité, *f.*

prodigious [prə'didʒəs], *a.* prodigieux.

prodigy ['prɔdidʒi], *n.* prodige, *m.*, *f.*

produce ['prɔdjuːs], *n.* produit, *m.*—[prə'djuːs], *v.t.* produire; exhiber, montrer; (*Geom.*) prolonger; (*Theat.*) mettre en scène.

producer [prə'djuːsə], *n.* producteur; (*Theat.*) metteur en scène, *m.*

producible [prə'djuːsibl], *a.* productible.

product ['prɔdʌkt], *n.* produit, *m.*; *by-product*, sous-produit, *m.*

production [prə'dʌkʃən], *n.* production, *f.*; (*Chem. etc.*) produit, *m.*; (*Theat.*) mise en scène, *f.*

productive [prə'dʌktiv], *a.* productif; fécond.

productivity [prɔdʌk'tiviti], *n.* productivité, *f.*

profanation [prɔfə'neiʃən], *n.* profanation, *f.*

profane [prə'fein], *a.* profane.—*v.t.* profaner.

profanely [prə'feinli], *adv.* d'une manière profane.

profaner [prə'feinə], *n.* profanateur, *m.*

profanity [prə'fæniti], *n.* conduite profane, impiété, *f.*; langage profane, *m.*

profess [prə'fes], *v.t.* professer, faire profession de, déclarer.

professed [prə'fest], *a.* déclaré, de profession.

professedly [prə'fesidli], *adv.* ouvertement; de profession.

profession [prə'feʃən], *n.* profession, *f.*; état, métier (*emploi*), *m.*

professional [prə'feʃənəl], *a.* de sa profession, professionnel; *professional man*, homme qui exerce une carrière libérale, *m.*—*n.*

homme du métier, homme de l'art; (*Spt.*) professionnel, *m.*

professionalism [prə'feʃənəlizm], *n.* caractère professionnel; (*Spt.*) professionnalisme, *m.*

professionally [prə'feʃənəli], *adv.* par profession; en homme du métier.

professor [prə'fesə], *n.* professeur (d'université), *m.*

professorial [prɔfe'sɔːriəl], *a.* de professeur, professoral.

professorship [prə'fesəʃip], *n.* professorat, *m.*, chaire, *f.*

proffer ['prɔfə], *n.* offre, *f.*—*v.t.* offrir, proposer.

proficiency [prə'fiʃənsi], *n.* capacité, *f.*; talent, *m.*, compétence, *f.*

proficient [prə'fiʃənt], *a.* versé, fort, compétent.

profile ['proufail], *n.* profil, *m.*; *in profile*, de profil.

profit ['prɔfit], *n.* profit, bénéfice, rapport; (*fig.*) avantage, *m.*—*v.t.* profiter à, faire du bien à; avantager.—*v.i.* profiter (*de*).

profitable ['prɔfitəbl], *a.* profitable, avantageux.

profitably ['prɔfitəbli], *adv.* avantageusement, avec profit.

profiteer [prɔfi'tiə], *n.* profiteur, *m.*—*v.i.* faire des bénéfices excessifs.

profitless ['prɔfitlis], *a.* sans profit, inutile.

profligacy ['prɔfligəsi], *n.* dérèglement, *m.*, dissolution, *f.*, libertinage, *m.*

profligate ['prɔfligit], *a.* débauché, dissolu, libertin.—*n.* libertin, mauvais sujet, *m.*

profound [prə'faund], *a.* profond; approfondi.

profoundly [prə'faundli], *adv.* profondément.

profundity [prə'fʌnditi], *n.* profondeur, *f.*

profuse [prə'fjuːs], *a.* prodigue; abondant, excessif (*choses*).

profusely [prə'fjuːsli], *adv.* profusément, à profusion.

profuseness [prə'fjuːsnis], **profusion** [prə'fjuːʒən], *n.* profusion, prodigalité, abondance, *f.*

progenitor [prou'dʒenitə], *n.* aïeul, ancêtre, *m.*

progeny ['prɔdʒəni], *n.* postérité, *f.*, descendants, *m.pl.*

prognostic [prɔg'nɔstik], *a.* pronostique.—*n.* pronostic, *m.*

prognosticate [prɔg'nɔstikeit], *v.t.* pronostiquer.

prognostication [prɔgnɔsti'keiʃən], *n.* pronostic, *m.*

programme ['prougræm], *n.* programme, *m.*

progress ['prougres], *n.* progrès, avancement, cours, *m.*; marche, *f.*; voyage (*de cérémonie*), *m.*—[prə'gres], *v.i.* s'avancer, faire des progrès, avancer.

progression [prə'greʃən], *n.* progression, *f.*

progressive [prə'gresiv], *a.* and *n.* progressif, *m.*; (*Polit.*) progressiste, *m.*, *f.*

progressiveness [prə'gresivnis], *n.* marche progressive, *f.*

prohibit [prə'hibit], *v.t.* prohiber, défendre, interdire (*à*); *smoking prohibited*, défense de fumer.

prohibition [prouhi'biʃən], *n.* prohibition, défense, *f.*

prohibitive [prə'hibitiv], **prohibitory** [prə'hibitri], *a.* prohibitif (*mœurs*); *prohibitive price*, prix exorbitant, *m.*

project ['prɔdʒekt], *n.* projet, dessein, *m.*—[prə'dʒekt], *v.t.* projeter.—*v.i.* avancer, faire saillie.

projectile [prə'dʒektail], *n.* projectile, *m.*

projecting [prə'dʒektiŋ], *a.* saillant, en saillie.

projection [prə'dʒekʃən], *n.* projection, saillie, *f.*; (*Arch.*) ressaut, *m.*

projector [prə'dʒektə], *n.* homme à projets, projeteur; projecteur (*lumière*); (*Cine.*) appareil de projection, *m.*

proletarian [prouli'tɛəriən], *a.* and *n.* prolétaire, *m., f.*

proletariat [prouli'tɛəriət], *n.* prolétariat, *m.*

prolific [prə'lifik], *a.* prolifique; fécond, fertile.

prolix ['prouliks], *a.* prolixe.

prolixity [prə'liksiti], **prolixness** ['prouliks nis], *n.* prolixité, *f.*

prologue ['proulɔg], *n.* prologue, *m.*

prolong [prə'lɔŋ], *v.t.* prolonger; retarder, différer (*remettre*); *to be prolonged*, se prolonger.

prolongation [proulɔŋ'geiʃən], *n.* prolongement, *m.*; prolongation (*du temps etc.*), *f.*

promenade [prɔmə'nɑːd], *n.* promenade; esplanade (*au bord de la mer*), *f.*—*v.i.* se promener, se faire voir.

promenader [prɔmə'nɑːdə], *n.* promeneur, *m.*

prominence ['prɔminəns], *n.* proéminence; (*fig.*) distinction, *f.*

prominent ['prɔminənt], *a.* proéminent, saillant; prononcé (*remarquable*); (*fig.*) éminent, distingué.

prominently ['prɔminəntli], *adv.* en saillie; d'une manière frappante.

promiscuity [prɔmis'kjuːiti], **promiscuousness** [prə'miskjuəsnis], *n.* mélange confus, *m.*; promiscuité, *f.*

promiscuous [prə'miskjuəs], *a.* sans distinction de sexe, promiscu; mêlé, confus, sans ordre.

promiscuously [prə'miskjuəsli], *adv.* confusément; en commun, en promiscuité.

promise ['prɔmis], *n.* promesse; (*fig.*) espérance, *f.*—*v.t., v.i.* promettre.

promising ['prɔmisiŋ], *a.* prometteur, qui promet; qui donne des espérances.

promissory ['prɔmisəri], *a.* qui contient une promesse; *promissory note*, billet à ordre, *m.*

promontory ['prɔməntri], *n.* promontoire, *m.*

promote [prə'mout], *v.t.* servir, avancer; promouvoir; encourager; *to promote a company*, lancer une société anonyme.

promoter [prə'moutə], *n.* promoteur, protecteur, instigateur; (*Comm.*) lanceur d'affaires, *m.*

promotion [prə'mouʃən], *n.* promotion, *f.*, avancement, *m.*

prompt [prɔmpt], *v.t.* exciter, porter, pousser; inspirer, suggérer; (*Theat.*) souffler.—*a.* prompt, empressé.

prompter ['prɔmptə], *n.* souffleur, *m.*; *prompter's box*, trou du souffleur, *m.*

promptitude ['prɔmptitjuːd], **promptness** ['prɔmptnis], *n.* promptitude, *f.*, empressement, *m.*

promptly ['prɔmptli], *adv.* promptement, avec empressement.

promptness [PROMPTITUDE].

promulgate ['prɔmɔlgeit], *v.t.* promulguer.

promulgation [prɔmɔl'geiʃən], *n.* promulgation, *f.*

promulgator ['prɔmɔlgeitə], *n.* promulgateur, *m.*

prone [proun], *a.* penché, incliné; couché, étendu; (*fig.*) disposé, porté (*à*).

proneness ['prounnis], *n.* disposition, inclination, *f.*, penchant, *m.*

prong [prɔŋ], *n.* fourchon, *m.*, dent, *f.*

pronged [prɔŋd], *a.* à fourchons, à dents.

pronoun ['prounaun], *n.* pronom, *m.*

pronounce [prə'nauns], *v.t.* prononcer; déclarer, annoncer, dire.

pronounceable [prə'naunsəbl], *a.* prononçable.

pronouncement [prə'naunsmənt], *n.* prononcement, *m.*, déclaration, *f.*

pronunciation [prənʌnsi'eiʃən], *n.* prononciation, *f.*, accent, *m.*

proof [pruːf], *a. proof against*, résistant à, à l'épreuve de; *waterproof*, imperméable.—*n.* preuve; épreuve, *f.*

proofless ['pruːflis], *a.* sans preuve.

proof-sheet ['pruːfʃiːt], *n.* (*Print.*) épreuve, *f.*

prop [prɔp], *n.* étai, étançon; (*Hort.*) tuteur, échalas; (*fig.*) appui, soutien; (*Theat.*) (*fam.*) accessoire, *m.*—*v.t.* étayer; appuyer, soutenir; (*Hort.*) échalasser.

propaganda [prɔpə'gændə], *n.* propagande, *f.*

propagandist [prɔpə'gændist], *n.* propagandiste, *m., f.*

propagate ['prɔpəgeit], *v.t.* propager; (*fig.*) répandre; créer, enfanter (*des êtres*).—*v.i.* se propager.

propagation [prɔpə'geiʃən], *n.* propagation, *f.*

propagator ['prɔpəgeitə], *n.* propagateur, *m.*

propel [prə'pel], *v.t.* pousser en avant, faire marcher, propulser.

propeller [prə'pelə], *n.* hélice, *f.*; propulseur, moteur, *m.*

propelling [prə'peliŋ], *a.* propulseur, moteur; *propelling force*, force motrice, *f.*

propensity [prə'pensiti], *n.* penchant, *m.*, tendance, *f.*

proper ['prɔpə], *a.* propre, particulier; convenable, à propos (*comme il faut*); juste, exact (*correct*).

properly ['prɔpəli], *adv.* proprement, comme il faut.

property ['prɔpəti], *n.* propriété, *f.*; bien, *m.*, biens, *m.pl.*; qualité, *f.*; (*Theat., Cine.*) accessoire, *m.*

property-tax ['prɔpətitæks], *n.* impôt foncier, *m.*

prophecy ['prɔfisi], *n.* prophétie, *f.*

prophesy ['prɔfisai], *v.t.* prophétiser, prédire.

prophet ['prɔfit], *n.* prophète, *m.*

prophetess ['prɔfites], *n.* prophétesse, *f.*

prophetic [prə'fetik], **prophetical** [prə'feti kəl], *a.* prophétique.

propinquity [prə'piŋkwiti], *n.* proximité, *f.*; parenté (*de personnes*), *f.*

propitiate [prə'piʃieit], *v.t.* rendre propice.

propitiation [prəpiʃi'eiʃən], *n.* propitiation, *f.*

propitiator [prə'piʃieitə], *n.* propitiateur, *m.*

propitiatory [prə'piʃiətri], *a.* and *n.* propitiatoire, *m.*

propitious [prə'piʃəs], *a.* propice, favorable.

523

propitiousness [prə'piʃəsnis], *n.* nature propice, *f.*
proportion [prə'pɔːʃən], *n.* proportion; partie; portion, *f.*; *in proportion as*, à mesure que.—*v.t.* proportionner.
proportional [prə'pɔːʃənəl], *a.* en proportion; proportionnel.
proportionate [prə'pɔːʃənit], *a.* proportionné.
proposal [prə'pouzl], *n.* proposition; demande en mariage, *f.*
propose [prə'pouz], *v.t.* proposer; offrir; *to propose a toast*, porter un toast.—*v.i.* se proposer; faire une demande en mariage.
proposer [prə'pouzə], *n.* auteur d'une proposition, *m.*
proposition [prɔpə'ziʃən], *n.* proposition; affaire, *f.*
propound [prə'paund], *v.t.* proposer, exposer, mettre en avant.
proprietary [prə'praiətri], *a.* de propriété.—*n.* actionnaires, *m.pl.*
proprietor [prə'praiətə], *n.* propriétaire, *m.*
proprietress [prə'praiətris], *n.* propriétaire, maîtresse, *f.*
propriety [prə'praiəti], *n.* convenance, propriété, *f.*
propulsion [prə'pʌlʃən], *n.* propulsion, *f.*; *jet propulsion*, propulsion à réaction.
prorogation [prourə'geiʃən], *n.* prorogation, *f.*
prorogue [prə'roug], *v.t.* proroger.
prosaic [pro'zeiik], *a.* prosaïque.
proscenium [pro'siːniəm], *n.* proscenium, *m.*, avant-scène, *f.*
proscribe [pro'skraib], *v.t.* proscrire.
proscription [pro'skripʃən], *n.* proscription, *f.*
prose [prouz], *n.* prose, *f.*, (*Sch.*) thème, *m.*
prosecute ['prɔsikjuːt], *v.t.* poursuivre; revendiquer (*ses droits etc.*).
prosecution [prɔsi'kjuːʃən], *n.* poursuite, *f.*, procès criminel, *m.*; *witness for the prosecution*, témoin à charge, *m.*
prosecutor ['prɔsikjuːtə], *n.* poursuivant, plaignant, *m.*; *public prosecutor*, procureur de la république, *m.*
prosecutrix ['prɔsikjuːtriks], *n.* poursuivante, plaignante, *f.*
proselyte ['prɔsəlait], *n.* prosélyte, *m.*, *f.*
proselytism ['prɔsəlitizm], *n.* prosélytisme, *m.*
proselytize ['prɔsəlitaiz], *v.t.* convertir.—*v.i.* faire des prosélytes.
prose-writer ['prouzraitə], *n.* prosateur, *m.*
prosily ['prouzili], *adv.* prosaïquement, ennuyeusement.
prosiness ['prouzinis], *n.* prosaïsme, *m.*; verbosité, *f.*
prosody ['prɔsədi], *n.* prosodie, *f.*
prospect ['prɔspekt], *n.* vue; perspective, *f.*; (*fig.*) espoir; avenir, *m.*—[prə'spekt], *v.i.* faire des recherches (*minerai, pétrole etc.*), prospecter.
prospective [prə'spektiv], *a.* en perspective; à venir.
prospectively [prə'spektivli], *adv.* pour l'avenir.
prospector [prə'spektə], *n.* explorateur; *orpailleur, *m.*
prospectus [prə'spektəs], *n.* prospectus, *m.*

prosper ['prɔspə], *v.t.* faire prospérer, favoriser.—*v.i.* prospérer, réussir.
prosperity [prɔs'periti], *n.* prospérité, *f.*
prosperous ['prɔspərəs], *a.* prospère; florissant (*affaires*); (*fig.*) heureux; favorable.
prostitute ['prɔstitjuːt], *n.* prostituée, *f.*—*v.t.* prostituer.
prostitution [prɔsti'tjuːʃən], *n.* prostitution, *f.*
prostrate [prɔs'treit], *v.t.* coucher, prosterner; (*fig.*) renverser; *to prostrate oneself before*, se prosterner devant.— ['prɔstrit], *a.* prosterné; (*fig.*) abattu.
prostration [prɔs'treiʃən], *n.* prosternation, *f.*; (*fig.*) abattement, *m.*
prosy ['prouzi], *a.* ennuyeux, fastidieux.
protagonist [prou'tægənist], *n.* protagoniste, *m.*
protect [prə'tekt], *v.t.* protéger, défendre; garantir, abriter (*contre le temps etc.*); sauvegarder (*intérêts*).
protection [prə'tekʃən], *n.* protection, défense; garantie, *f.*, abri (*contre le temps etc.*), *m.*; (*Law*) sauvegarde, *f.*
protectionism [prə'tekʃənizm], *n.* protectionnisme, *m.*
protectionist [prə'tekʃənist], *a.* and *n.* protectionniste, *m.*, *f.*
protective [prə'tektiv], *a.* protecteur.
protector [prə'tektə], *n.* protecteur, *m.*
protectorate [prə'tektərit], *n.* protectorat, *m.*
protectress [prə'tektris], *n.* protectrice, *f.*
protein ['proutiːn], *n.* protéine, *f.*
protest ['proutest], *n.* protestation, *f.*; (*Comm.*) protêt, *m.*—[prə'test], *v.t.*, *v.i.* protester.
Protestant ['prɔtistənt], *a.* and *n.* protestant, *m.*
Protestantism ['prɔtistəntizm], *n.* protestantisme, *m.*
protestation [prɔtes'teiʃən], *n.* protestation, *f.*
protester [prə'testə], *n.* personne qui fait faire un protêt, *f.*
protocol ['proutəkɔl], *n.* protocole, *m.*
proton ['prouton], *n.* proton, *m.*
prototype ['proutətaip], *n.* prototype, *m.*
protract [prə'trækt], *v.t.* prolonger, traîner en longueur.
protraction [prə'trækʃən], *n.* prolongation, *f.*
protractor [prə'træktə], *n.* rapporteur (*instrument*), *m.*
protrude [prə'truːd], *v.t.* pousser en avant, faire sortir.—*v.i.* s'avancer, faire saillie.
protruding [prə'truːdiŋ], *a.* en saillie, saillant.
protrusion [prə'truːʒən], *n.* saillie, *f.*
protuberance [prə'tjuːbərəns], *n.* protubérance, *f.*
protuberant [prə'tjuːbərənt], *a.* protubérant.
proud [praud], *a.* fier (*de*); orgueilleux.
proudly ['praudli], *adv.* fièrement, orgueilleusement.
provable ['pruːvəbl], *a.* prouvable, démontrable.
prove [pruːv], *v.t.* prouver, démontrer; mettre à l'épreuve, éprouver (*la qualité de*); vérifier (*testament etc.*).—*v.i.* se montrer, se révéler.
proved [pruːvd], *a.* prouvé, démontré, reconnu.
provender ['prɔvəndə], *n.* fourrage, *m.*, nourriture (*d'animaux*), *f.*

proverb ['prɔvə:b], n. proverbe, m.
proverbial [prə'və:biəl], a. proverbial.
provide [prə'vaid], v.t. pourvoir, fournir, munir; préparer (à); stipuler.—v.i. pourvoir.
provided [prə'vaidid], a. pourvu.—conj. *provided that*, pourvu que (*with subj.*).
providence ['prɔvidəns], n. providence (*divine*); prévoyance (*humaine*), f.
provident ['prɔvidənt], a. prévoyant; économe.
providential [prɔvi'denʃəl], a. providentiel, de la providence.
providently ['prɔvidəntli], adv. avec prévoyance.
provider [prə'vaidə], n. pourvoyeur, fournisseur, m.
province ['prɔvins], n. province, f.; (*fig.*) département, ressort, m.
provincial [prə'vinʃəl], a. provincial, de province.—n. provincial, m.
provincialism [prə'vinʃəlizm], n. provincialisme, m.
proving ['pru:viŋ], n. vérification, mise à l'épreuve, f.
provision [prə'viʒən], n. action de pourvoir; stipulation; (*Law*) disposition (*d'un projet de loi etc.*), f.; (*pl.*) vivres, comestibles, m.pl.—v.t. approvisionner.
provisional [prə'viʒənəl], a. provisoire.
provision-dealer [prə'viʒəndi:lə], n. marchand de comestibles, m.
proviso [prə'vaizou], n. condition, clause conditionnelle, f.
provisory [prə'vaizəri], a. provisoire, conditionnel.
provocation [prɔvə'keiʃən], n. provocation, f.
provocative [prə'vɔkətiv], a. provocant, provocateur.
provoke [prə'vouk], v.t. provoquer; inciter; fâcher, irriter.
provoker [prə'voukə], n. provocateur, m.
provoking [prə'voukiŋ], a. provocant; ennuyeux, fâcheux, agaçant.
provokingly [prə'voukiŋli], adv. d'une manière provocante *ou* contrariante.
provost ['prɔvəst], n. prévôt; (*Univ.*) principal; (*Sc.*) maire, m.
prow [prau], n. proue, f.
prowess ['prauis], n. bravoure, prouesse, f.
prowl [praul], n. action de rôder, f.—v.i. rôder.
prowler ['praulə], n. rôdeur, m.
proximate ['prɔksimit], a. proche, immédiat.
proximity [prɔk'simiti], n. proximité, f.
proximo ['prɔksimou], adv. du mois prochain.
proxy ['prɔksi], n. mandataire, m., f., délégué, m.; procuration (*chose*), f.; *by proxy*, par procuration.
prude [pru:d], n. prude, mijaurée, f.
prudence ['pru:dəns], n. prudence, f.
prudent ['pru:dənt], a. prudent, sage.
prudential [pru:'denʃəl], a. de prudence, dicté par la prudence.
prudently ['pru:dəntli], adv. prudemment, sagement.
prudery ['pru:dəri], n. pruderie, f.
prudish ['pru:diʃ], a. prude, de prude.
prudishly ['pru:diʃli], adv. avec pruderie.
prune [pru:n], n. pruneau, m.—v.t. élaguer, tailler, émonder.
prunella [pru'nelə], n. prunelle, f.

pruning ['pru:niŋ], n. taille, f., élagage, m.
pruning-shears ['pru:niŋʃiəz], n.pl. sécateur, m., cisailles, f.pl.
prurience ['pruəriəns], **pruriency** ['pruəriənsi], n. démangeaison, f.
prurient ['pruəriənt], a. qui démange.
Prussia ['prʌʃə], la Prusse, f.
Prussian ['prʌʃən], a. prussien.—n. Prussien (*personne*), m.
prussic ['prʌsik], a. prussique.
pry [prai], v.t. soulever avec un levier.—v.i. fureter; fouiller (*dans*); *to pry into*, se mêler de.—n. regard scrutateur, regard indiscret, m.
prying ['praiiŋ], a. scrutateur, curieux.—n. curiosité, f.
psalm [sɑ:m], n. psaume, m.
psalmist ['sɑ:mist], n. psalmiste, m.
psalmody ['sɑ:mədi], n. psalmodie, f.
psalter ['sɔ:ltə], n. psautier, m.
pseudonym ['sju:dənim], n. pseudonyme, m.
pshaw! [pʃɔ:], int. bah! fi donc!
psychiatric [saiki'ætrik], a. psychiatrique.
psychiatrist [sai'kaiətrist], n. psychiatre, m., f.
psychiatry [sai'kaiətri], n. psychiatrie, f.
psychic(al) ['saikik(l)], a. psychique.
psycho-analyse [saikou'ænəlaiz], v.t. psychanalyser.
psycho-analysis [saikouə'næləsis], n. psychanalyse, f.
psycho-analyst [saikou'ænəlist], n. psychanalyste, m., f.
psychological [saikə'lɔdʒikl], a. psychologique.
psychologist [sai'kɔlədʒist], n. psychologiste, psychologue, m.
psychology [sai'kɔlədʒi], n. psychologie, f.
psychopath ['saikopæθ], n. psychopathe, m., f.
psychosis [sai'kousis], n. psychose, f.
ptarmigan ['tɑ:migən], n. lagopède, m.
ptomaine ['toumein], n. ptomaïne, f.; *ptomaine poisoning*, intoxication alimentaire, f.
puberty ['pju:bəti], n. puberté, f.
pubescence [pju'besəns], n. pubescence, f.
pubescent [pju'besənt], a. pubescent.
public ['pʌblik], a. and n. public, m.
publican ['pʌblikən], n. cafetier, patron de bistro(t); (*Bibl.*) publicain, m.
publication [pʌbli'keiʃən], n. publication, f.
public-house ['pʌblik'haus], n. café, m., brasserie, f., bistro(t), m.
publicist ['pʌblisist], n. publiciste, journaliste; publicitaire, m., f.
publicity [pʌb'lisiti], n. publicité; réclame, f.
publicize ['pʌblisaiz], v.t. faire connaître au public.
publicly ['pʌblikli], adv. publiquement; en public.
publish ['pʌbliʃ], v.t. publier; éditer.
publisher ['pʌbliʃə], n. éditeur, m.; *bookseller and publisher*, libraire-éditeur, m.
puce [pju:s], a. puce.
puck (1) [pʌk], n. lutin, m.
puck (2) [pʌk], n. (*Spt.*) palet de hockey (sur glace), m.
pucker ['pʌkə], v.t. rider, plisser; (*Dress.*) faire goder.—v.i. goder.—n. ride; (*Dress.*) poche, f.; mauvais pli, m.
puckering ['pʌkəriŋ], n. froncement, m.
puckish ['pʌkiʃ], a. malicieux; de lutin.

pudding ['pudiŋ], *n.* pudding, pouding, *m.*; *black pudding*, boudin (noir), *m.*
puddle [pʌdl], *n.* flaque (d'eau), mare, *f.—v.t.* troubler, rendre bourbeux.
puerile ['pjuərail], *a.* puéril.
puerility [pjuə'riliti], *n.* puérilité, *f.*
puff [pʌf], *n.* souffle (*d'haleine*), *m.*; bouffée (*de vent, fumée etc.*), *f.*; feuilleté (*pâtisserie*), *m.*; houppe à poudrer (*de dames*), *f.*; bouillon (*de robes*); puff, *m.*, réclame tapageuse, *f.—v.t.* souffler, bouffir (*les joues*), gonfler; (*fig.*) faire mousser (*publicité*).*—v.i.* souffler, boursoufler, bouffir, bouffer, se gonfler; haleter.
puffin [pʌfin], *n.* (*Orn.*) macareux, *m.*
puffiness ['pʌfinis], *n.* boursouflure, enflure, *f.*
puff-pastry ['pʌfpeistri], *n.* pâte feuilletée, *f.*
puffy ['pʌfi], *a.* bouffi, gonflé.
pug [pʌg], *n.* carlin (*chien*), *m.*
pugilism ['pju:dʒilizm], *n.* pugilat, *m.*, boxe, *f.*
pugilist ['pju:dʒilist], *n.* boxeur, pugiliste, *m.*
pugilistic [pjudʒi'listik], *a.* de pugilat.
pugnacious [pʌg'neiʃəs], *a.* querelleur; batailleur.
pugnaciously [pʌg'neiʃəsli], *adv.* d'un air batailleur.
pugnacity [pʌg'næsiti], *n.* pugnacité, *f.*
pug-nose ['pʌgnouz], *n.* nez épaté, *m.*
puke [pju:k], *v.i.* vomir.
pule [pju:l], *v.i.* piauler.
puling ['pju:liŋ], *n.* cri; piaulement, *m.*
pull [pul], *v.t.* tirer; arracher; presser (*la détente*); *to pull a wry face*, faire la grimace; *to pull down*, abattre, démolir; *to pull off*, arracher, enlever; *to pull up*, hisser; déraciner; arrêter.—*v.i.* ramer (*tirer la rame*); *to pull in*, s'arrêter; *to pull round*, se remettre; *to pull through*, guérir, s'en tirer; *to pull up*, s'arrêter.—*n.* action de tirer, traction, *f.*; coup (d'aviron), effort, *m.*; secousse, *f.*; (*fig.*) avantage, *m.*; *hard pull*, rude effort.
pullet ['pulit], *n.* poulette, *f.*
pulley ['puli], *n.* poulie, *f.*
pullover ['pulouvə], *n.* pull-over, *m.*
pulmonary ['pʌlmənəri], *a.* pulmonaire.
pulp [pʌlp], *n.* pulpe; pâte (*papier*), *f.—v.t.* réduire en pâte.
pulpiness ['pʌlpinis], *n.* nature pulpeuse, *f.*
pulpit ['pulpit], *n.* chaire, *f.*
pulpous ['pʌlpəs], **pulpy** ['pʌlpi], *a.* pulpeux.
pulsate [pʌl'seit], *v.i.* battre; palpiter.
pulsation [pʌl'seiʃən], *n.* pulsation, *f.*
pulsatory ['pʌlsətri], *a.* pulsatoire.
pulse [pʌls], *n.* pouls, *m.*; pulsation, *f.*; plantes légumineuses, *f.pl.*
pulverization [pʌlvərai'zeiʃən], *n.* pulvérisation, *f.*
pulverize ['pʌlvəraiz], *v.t.* pulvériser.
puma ['pju:mə], *n.* puma, couguar, *m.*
pumice ['pʌmis], *n.* pierre ponce, *f.*
pump [pʌmp], *n.* pompe, *f.*; escarpin (*chaussure*), *m.—v.t.* pomper; (*fig.*) sonder; *to pump up*, gonfler (*pneu*).—*v.i.* pomper.
pumpkin ['pʌmpkin], *n.* citrouille, courge, *f.*, potiron, *m.*
pump-room ['pʌmpru:m], *n.* buvette, *f.*
pun [pʌn], *n.* calembour, jeu de mots, *m.—v.i.* faire des calembours.
punch (1) [pʌntʃ], *n.* emporte-pièce; (*Print.*) poinçon, *m.—v.t.* percer, poinçonner.

punch (2) [pʌntʃ], *n.* coup de poing, *m.—v.t.* donner un coup de poing à.
punch (3) [pʌntʃ], *n.* punch (*boisson*), *m.*
punch-bowl ['pʌntʃboul], *n.* bol à punch, *m.*
puncheon ['pʌntʃən], *n.* poinçon, *m.*, pièce (de vin), *f.*
punctilio [pʌŋk'tiliou], *n.* exactitude scrupuleuse, *f.*, point d'étiquette, *m.*
punctilious [pʌŋk'tiliəs], *a.* pointilleux.
punctiliousness [pʌŋk'tiliəsnis], *n.* exactitude scrupuleuse, pointillerie, *f.*
punctual ['pʌŋktjuəl], *a.* ponctuel, exact.
punctuality [pʌŋktju'æliti], *n.* ponctualité, exactitude, *f.*
punctually ['pʌŋktjuəli], *adv.* ponctuellement, exactement.
punctuate ['pʌŋktjueit], *v.t.* ponctuer.
punctuation [pʌŋktju'eiʃən], *n.* ponctuation, *f.*
puncture ['pʌŋktʃə], *n.* piqûre; crevaison (*d'un pneu*), *f.—v.t.* piquer; crever (*pneu*).
pundit ['pʌndit], *n.* pandit, *m.*
pungency ['pʌndʒənsi], *n.* âcreté; aigreur, *f.*
pungent ['pʌndʒənt], *a.* âcre; piquant, mordant.
pungently ['pʌndʒəntli], *adv.* avec causticité.
puniness ['pju:ninis], *n.* petitesse, nature chétive, *f.*
punish ['pʌniʃ], *v.t.* punir, corriger; malmener.
punishable ['pʌniʃəbl], *a.* punissable.
punishment ['pʌniʃmənt], *n.* punition; peine, *f.*, châtiment, *m.*; *capital punishment*, peine capitale.
punitive ['pju:nitiv], *a.* punitif.
punnet ['pʌnit], *n.* maniveau, *m.*
punt [pʌnt], *n.* bachot, *m.—v.i.* conduire un bachot (*à la perche*).
puny ['pju:ni], *a.* petit, chétif.
pup [pʌp], *n.* petit chien, petit; (*pej.*) freluquet, fat, *m.*
pupil (1) ['pju:pil], *n.* élève, *m.*, *f.*
pupil (2) ['pju:pil], *n.* pupille (*de l'œil*), *f.*
pupilary ['pju:piləri], *a.* pupillaire.
puppet ['pʌpit], *n.* marionnette, *f.*; *glove puppet*, marionnette à gaine; *puppet government*, gouvernement fantoche, *m.*
puppet-show ['pʌpitʃou], *n.* (spectacle de) marionnettes, *f.pl.*
puppy ['pʌpi], *n.* petit chien; (*fig.*) fat, freluquet, *m.*
purblind ['pə:blaind], *a.* myope.
purchase ['pə:tʃis], *n.* achat, *m.*, acquisition, emplette; (*Mech.*) prise, *f.—v.t.* acheter, acquérir.
purchase-deed ['pə:tʃisdi:d], *n.* contrat d'achat, *m.*
purchaser ['pə:tʃisə], *n.* acquéreur, acheteur, *m.*
purchasing ['pə:tʃisiŋ], *n.* achat, *m.*; *purchasing power*, pouvoir d'achat, *m.*
pure [pjuə], *a.* pur; *pure-bred*, de race.
purely ['pjuəli], *adv.* purement.
pureness ['pjuənis], *n.* pureté, *f.*
purgation [pə'geiʃən], *n.* purgation, *f.*
purgative ['pə:gətiv], *a.* and *n.* purgatif, *m.*
purgatorial [pə:gə'tɔ:riəl], *a.* du purgatoire.
Purgatory ['pə:gətəri], *n.* purgatoire, *m.*
purge [pə:dʒ], *v.t.* purger; purifier, épurer.—*n.* purgation, purge, *f.*; (*Polit.*) nettoyage, *m.*

purification [pjuərifi'keiʃən], *n.* purification; épuration, *f.*

purifier ['pjuərifaiə], *n.* purificateur, *m.*

purify ['pjuərifai], *v.t.* purifier.—*v.i.* se purifier.

purist ['pjuərist], *n.* puriste, *m., f.*

Puritan ['pjuəritən], *n.* puritain, *m.*

puritan ['pjuəritən], *a.* puritain.

puritanical [pjuəri'tænikl], *a.* de puritain, puritain.

Puritanism ['pjuəritənizm], *n.* puritanisme, *m.*

purity ['pjuəriti], *n.* pureté, *f.*

purl [pə:l], *v.i.* engrêler (*dentelle*).—*v.i.* murmurer, gazouiller.—*n.* engrêlure (*de dentelle*), *f.*; doux murmure; gazouillement, *m.*

purlieu ['pə:lju:], *n.* alentours, environs, *m.pl.*

purloin [pə'lɔin], *v.t.* dérober, voler.

purple [pə:pl], *a.* violet, mauve; pourpre.—*n.* pourpre, mauve (*couleur*), *m.*; pourpre (*teinture etc.*), *f.*—*v.t.* teindre en pourpre, empourprer, rougir.

purport ['pə:pət], *n.* sens, *m.*, teneur, portée, *f.*—[pə'pɔ:t], *v.t.* tendre à montrer, signifier, vouloir dire.

purpose ['pə:pəs], *n.* but, objet, *m.*, fin, *f.*, dessein, *m.*, intention, *f.*; *on purpose*, exprès, à dessein; *to answer one's purpose*, faire son affaire.—*v.t., v.i.* se proposer, avoir l'intention (*de*).

purposely ['pə:pəsli], *adv.* à dessein, exprès.

purr [pə:], *v.i.* ronronner.

purring ['pə:riŋ], *a.* qui fait ronron.—*n.* ronron, *m.*

purse [pə:s], *n.* porte-monnaie, *m.*; bourse, *f.*; (*Am.*) sac à main, *m.*—*v.t.* plisser, froncer (*les sourcils etc.*).

purser ['pə:sə], *n.* commissaire (*de navire*); (*Mining*) agent comptable, *m.*

pursuance [pə'sju:əns], *n.* poursuite, conséquence, *f.*; *in pursuance of*, conformément à.

pursuant [pə'sju:ənt], *a.* en conséquence (*de*), conforme (*à*).

pursue [pə'sju:], *v.t.* poursuivre; suivre, chercher.

pursuer [pə'sju:ə], *n.* poursuivant, *m.*

pursuit [pə'sju:t], *n.* poursuite, recherche; occupation, *f.*; (*pl.*) travaux, *m.pl.*

purulence ['pjuəruləns], **purulency** ['pjuə rulənsi], *n.* purulence, *f.*

purulent ['pjuərulənt], *a.* purulent.

purvey [pə'vei], *v.t.* fournir, approvisionner; procurer.

purveyor [pə'veiə], *n.* pourvoyeur, fournisseur, *m.*

pus [pʌs], *n.* pus, *m.*

push [puʃ], *v.t.* pousser; (*fig.*) presser, importuner; *to push back*, repousser, faire reculer; *to push down*, faire tomber, renverser.—*v.i.* pousser; faire un effort; *to push off*, pousser au large; *to push on*, pousser en avant.—*n.* impulsion, poussée, *f.*; effort, *m.*; extrémité, *f.*

pushing ['puʃiŋ], *a.* entreprenant.

pusillanimity [pju:silə'nimiti], *n.* pusillanimité, *f.*

pusillanimous [pju:si'læniməs], *a.* pusillanime.

puss [pus], *n.* (*colloq.*) minet, *m.*, minette, *f.*

pustule ['pʌstju:l], *n.* pustule, *f.*

put [put], *v.t. irr.* mettre, poser, placer; proposer (*solution etc.*); lancer (*poids etc.*); *to put about*, gêner; *to put aside*, mettre de côté; *to put back*, replacer, remettre; *to put by*, mettre de côté; *to put forward*, mettre en avant; *to put off*, ôter; remettre; *to put on*, mettre (*vêtements*); *to put on the light*, allumer; *to put out*, mettre dehors; éteindre (*feu etc.*); *to put up*, installer; loger, caser (*dans un hôtel etc.*).—*v.i.* aller; germer, pousser; (*Naut.*) se mettre; *to put in*, entrer au port; *to put up*, loger (*à ou chez*), descendre (*à*); *to put up with*, supporter.

putrefaction [pju:tri'fækʃən], *n.* putréfaction, *f.*

putrefy ['pju:trifai], *v.t.* putréfier.—*v.i.* se putréfier.

putrid ['pju:trid], *a.* putride.

putridity [pju:'triditi], *n.* putridité, *f.*

putt [pʌt], *v.t.* (*Golf*) poter.

putter ['pʌtə], *n.* (*Golf*) poteur, *m.*

putting ['putiŋ], *n.* action du mettre, mise, *f.*

putty ['pʌti], *n.* mastic, *m.*

puzzle [pʌzl], *n.* (*fig.*) énigme, *f.*; jeu de patience, casse-tête (*jouet*), *m.*; *crossword puzzle*, mots croisés, *m.pl.*—*v.t.* intriguer, embarrasser; *to puzzle one's brains*, se creuser la tête.

pygmean [pig'miən], *a.* de pygmée.

pygmy ['pigmi], *n.* pygmée, *m.*

pyjamas [pi'dʒɑ:məz], *n.pl.* pyjama, *m.*

pylon ['pailən], *n.* pylône, *m.*

pyramid ['piræmid], *n.* pyramide, *f.*

pyramidal [pi'ræmidl], *a.* pyramidal.

pyre ['paiə], *n.* bûcher, *m.*

Pyrenees [pirə'ni:z], the. les Pyrénées, *f.pl.*

pyrethrum [pai'ri:θrəm], *n.* (*Bot.*) pyrèthre, *m.*

pyrotechnic [paiərou'teknik], **pyrotechnical** [paiərou'teknikəl], *a.* pyrotechnique, pyrique.

pyrotechnics [paiərou'tekniks], *n.pl.* pyrotechnie, *f.*

pyrotechnist [paiərou'teknist], *n.* artificier, *m.*

python ['paiθən], *n.* python, *m.*

pyx [piks], *n.* ciboire, *m.*

Q

Q, q [kju:]. dix-septième lettre de l'alphabet, *m.*

quack [kwæk], *a.* de charlatan.—*n.* charlatan; couac, cri du canard, *m.*—*v.i.* crier (comme les canards *etc.*).

quackery ['kwækəri], *n.* charlatanisme, *m.*

Quadragesima [kwodrə'dʒesimə]. Quadragésime, *f.*

quadrangle ['kwodræŋgl], *n.* quadrilatère carré, *m.*; (*Univ.*) cour d'honneur, *f.*

quadrant ['kwodrənt], *n.* quart de cercle, *m.*

quadratic [kwod'rætik], *a.* du second degré.

quadrennial [kwod'reniəl], *a.* quadriennal.

quadrennially [kwod'reniəli], *adv.* tous les quatre ans.

527

quadrilateral [kwɔdri'lætərəl], a. quadri-
latéral.—n. quadrilatère, m.
quadrille [kwə'dril], n. quadrille, m.; contredanse, f.
quadroon [kwə'druːn], n. quarteron, m.
quadruped ['kwɔdruped], n. quadrupède, m.
quadruple ['kwɔdrupl], a. and n. quadruple,
m.—v.t. quadrupler.
quadruplet ['kwɔdruplit], n. quadruplette, f.;
(pl.) (colloq.) quads [kwɔdz], quadruplés,
m.pl.
quaff [kwæf], v.t. boire à grands traits.
quaffer ['kwæfə], n. buveur, m.
quagmire ['kwægmaiə], n. fondrière, f.
quail (1) [kweil], v.i. perdre courage, fléchir.
quail (2) [kweil], n. (Orn.) caille, f.
quaint [kweint], a. singulier, bizarre; pittoresque.
quaintly ['kweintli], adv. singulièrement,
bizarrement.
quaintness ['kweintnis], n. bizarrerie, originalité, f.
quake [kweik], v.i. trembler; branler.—n.
tremblement, m.
Quaker ['kweikə], n. Quaker, m.
Quakerism ['kweikərizm], n. Quakerisme,
m.
quaking ['kweikiŋ], a. tremblant.—n. tremblement, m.; terreur, f.
qualifiable ['kwɔlifaiəbl], a. qualifiable.
qualification [kwɔlifi'keiʃən], n. qualification, qualité; aptitude, f.; talent, m.; réserve,
restriction, f.; (pl.) qualités, f.pl., titres,
m.pl.
qualified ['kwɔlifaid], a. qui a les qualités
requises (pour), propre (à); qualified
teacher, professeur diplômé, m.
qualify ['kwɔlifai], v.t. rendre capable (de);
autoriser (à); modérer.—v.i. se préparer (à).
qualifying ['kwɔlifaiiŋ], a. qualificatif.
quality ['kwɔliti], n. qualité, f.; (colloq.)
talent, m.
qualm [kwɑːm], n. nausée, f.; (fig.) scrupule,
m.
qualmish ['kwɑːmiʃ], a. qui a mal au cœur.
quandary ['kwɔndəri], n. embarras, m.,
impasse, f.
quantitative ['kwɔntitətiv], a. quantitatif.
quantity ['kwɔntiti], n. quantité, f.; grand
nombre, m.
quantum ['kwɔntəm], n. montant, quantum,
m.
quarantine ['kwɔrəntiːn], n. quarantaine, f.
—v.t. mettre en quarantaine.
quarrel ['kwɔrəl], n. querelle, dispute,
brouille, f.—v.i. se quereller, se brouiller.
quarreller ['kwɔrələ], n. querelleur, m.
quarrelling ['kwɔrəliŋ], n. querelle; dispute,
f.
quarrelsome ['kwɔrəlsəm], a. querelleur.
quarrelsomeness ['kwɔrəlsəmnis], n. humeur
querelleuse, f.
quarry (1) ['kwɔri], n. carrière, f.—v.t. tirer
d'une carrière.
quarry (2) ['kwɔri], n. (Hunt.) curée; proie,
f.
quarrying ['kwɔriiŋ], n. extraction d'une
carrière, f.
quarryman ['kwɔrimən], n. (pl. -men [men])
carrier, m.
quart [kwɔːt], n. quart de gallon (1·14 litre), m.
quarter ['kwɔːtə], n. quart; quart de quintal

(12·70 kg.); quartier (de ville, de la lune, de
mouton etc.), m.; partie, région (d'un pays),
f.; côté (direction); trimestre (de l'année), m.;
hanche (de navire), f.; (pl.) logement; (Mil.)
quartier, m.; to come to close quarters
en venir aux mains.—v.t. diviser en quatre;
(Mil.) caserner; loger (dans une maison);
(Her.) écarteler.
quarter-day ['kwɔːtədei], n. jour du terme, m.
quarter-deck ['kwɔːtədek], n. gaillard d'arrière, m.
quartering ['kwɔːtəriŋ], n. division en quatre
parties, f.; (Mil.) logement; (Her.) écartèlement, m.
quarterly ['kwɔːtəli], a. trimestriel.—adv.
par trimestre, tous les trois mois.
quartermaster ['kwɔːtəmɑːstə], n. (Navy)
maître timonier; (Mil.) officier d'approvisionnement, m.
quartet [kwɔː'tet], n. quatuor, m.
quarto ['kwɔːtou], a. and n. in-quarto, m.
quartz [kwɔːts], n. quartz, m.
quash [kwɔʃ], v.t. écraser; (fig.) dompter;
(Law) annuler, casser.
quasi ['kweisai], adv. quasi.
quatrain ['kwɔtrein], n. quatrain, m.
quaver ['kweivə], n. tremblement de la voix,
trille, m.; (Mus.) croche, f.—v.i. trembler;
(Mus.) faire des trilles.
quavering ['kweivəriŋ], a. tremblant, chevrotant.—n. trille, tremolo; tremblement de
voix, m.
quay [kiː], n. quai, m.
quayage ['kiːidʒ], n. quayage, m.
queen [kwiːn], n. reine; (Cards etc.) dame, f.
queen-bee ['kwiːnbiː], n. reine-abeille, f.
queen-like ['kwiːnlaik], queenly ['kwiːnli],
adv. de reine, digne d'une reine.
queen-mother [kwiːn'mʌðə], n. reine-
mère, f.
queer [kwiə], a. bizarre, étrange, drôle.
queerly ['kwiəli], adv. étrangement, bizarrement.
queerness ['kwiənis], n. étrangeté, bizarrerie,
f.; malaise, m.
quell [kwel], v.t. réprimer, dompter.
quench [kwentʃ], v.t. éteindre; étancher;
étouffer (élan etc.); to quench one's
thirst, étancher sa soif, se désaltérer.
quenchable ['kwentʃəbl], a. extinguible.
quenchless ['kwentʃlis], a. inextinguible.
querulous ['kweruləs], a. plaintif, maussade.
querulousness ['kweruləsnis], n. humeur
chagrine, f.
query ['kwiəri], n. question, f.; point d'interrogation, m.—v.t. mettre en doute.—v.i.
questionner.
quest [kwest], n. enquête; recherche, f.; in
quest of, à la recherche de.
question ['kwestʃən], n. question, interrogation, demande, f.; sujet (problème), m.;
(Parl.) interpellation, f.; out of the question, absolument impossible; that is not
the question, il ne s'agit pas de cela; to
ask a question, poser une question.—v.t.
questionner, interroger; mettre en doute.—
v.i. se demander (si).
questionable ['kwestʃənəbl], a. contestable,
douteux, incertain; suspect, équivoque.
questioner ['kwestʃənə], n. questionneur, m.
questioning ['kwestʃəniŋ], n. questions, f.pl.,
interrogation, f.

rabbet-plane

question-master [ˈkwestʃənmɑːstə], *n.* (*Rad.*, *Tel.*) meneur de débats, *m.*
questionnaire [kwestʃəˈnɛə], *n.* questionnaire, *m.*
queue [kjuː], *n.* queue, *f.*—*v.i.* faire la queue.
quibble [ˈkwibl], *n.* argutie, chicane, *f.*—*v.i.* ergoter, chicaner.
quibbler [ˈkwiblə], *n.* ergoteur, chicaneur, *m.*
quick [kwik], *a.* vite, rapide, prompt; agile, leste; vif (*vivant*); (*fig.*) fin.—*adv.* vite, promptement, lestement.—*n.* vif, *m.*; chair vive, *f.*; **stung to the quick**, piqué au vif; (*collect.*) **the quick**, les vivants, *m.pl.*
quicken [ˈkwikən], *v.t.* animer, vivifier; raviver, accélérer, hâter.—*v.i.* prendre vie, s'animer.
quickening [ˈkwikəniŋ], *a.* vivifiant, qui ranime.
quicklime [ˈkwiklaim], *n.* chaux vive, *f.*
quickly [ˈkwikli], *adv.* vite; promptement; bientôt.
quickness [ˈkwiknis], *n.* vitesse; promptitude; activité; pénétration; fréquence (*du pouls*), *f.*
quicksand [ˈkwiksænd], *n.* sable mouvant, *m.*
quickset [ˈkwikset], *a.* vive; **quickset hedge**, haie vive, *f.*—*n.* plante vive, *f.*
quicksilver [ˈkwiksilvə], *n.* vif-argent, mercure, *m.*
quicksilvered [ˈkwiksilvəd], *a.* étamé.
quicksilvering [ˈkwiksilvəriŋ], *n.* étamage, *m.*
quick-tempered [ˈkwikˈtempəd], *a.* emporté, vif, colérique.
quick-witted [ˈkwikˈwitid], *a.* à l'esprit vif.
quid [kwid], *n.* chique;‖ (*slang*) livre sterling, *f.*
quidnunc [ˈkwidnʌŋk], *n.* curieux, colporteur de nouvelles, *m.*
quiescence [kwiˈesəns], *n.* quiétude, tranquillité, *f.*, repos, *m.*
quiescent [kwiˈesənt], *a.* paisible, en repos, tranquille.
quiet [ˈkwaiət], *a.* tranquille, calme; paisible, silencieux; (*fig.*) modeste; **be quiet!** silence! taisez-vous! **to keep quiet**, se tenir tranquille, rester tranquille.—*n.* tranquillité, quiétude, *f.*; repos, calme, *m.*—*v.t.* (*also* **quieten**) [ˈkwaiətn]) tranquilliser, apaiser, calmer.—*v.i.* **to quiet(en) down**, s'apaiser, se calmer.
quieten, *v.t.*, *v.i.* [QUIET].
quieting [ˈkwaiətiŋ], *a.* calmant, tranquillisant.
quietly [ˈkwaiətli], *adv.* tranquillement; doucement; en silence, sans bruit, discrètement, sans éclat.
quietness [ˈkwaiətnis], *n.* tranquillité, *f.*; calme, repos, *m.*
quietude [ˈkwaiitjuːd], *n.* quiétude, tranquillité, *f.*
quietus [kwaiˈiːtəs], *n.* repos, *m.*; mort, *f.*; (*fig.*) coup de grâce, *m.*; décharge, quittance, *f.*
quill [kwil], *n.* (tuyau de) plume; plume d'oie (*pour écrire*), *f.*; piquant (*de porc-épic*), *m.*—*v.t.* tuyauter, rucher.
quilling [ˈkwiliŋ], *n.* tuyautage, *m.*, ruche, *f.*
quilt [kwilt], *n.* édredon, *m.*, courtepointe, *f.* —*v.t.* piquer.
quilting [ˈkwiltiŋ], *n.* piqué; piquage, *m.*
quince [kwins], *n.* coing; cognassier (*arbre*), *m.*
quinine [kwiˈniːn], *n.* quinine, *f.*

Quinquagesima [kwiŋkwəˈdʒesimə]. Quinquagésime, *f.*
quinquennial [kwiŋˈkwenjəl], *a.* quinquennial.
quinquina [kiŋˈkiːnə], *n.* quinquina, *m.*
quinsy [ˈkwinzi], *n.* angine, *f.*
quint [kwint], *n.* quinte, *f.*
quintal [ˈkwintl], *n.* quintal, *m.*
quintessence [kwinˈtesəns], *n.* quintessence, *f.*
quintet [kwinˈtet], *n.* quintette, *m.*
quintuple [ˈkwintjupl], *a.* quintuple.—*v.t.* quintupler.
quintuplets [ˈkwintjuplits], (*colloq.*) **quins** [kwinz], *n.pl.* quintuplés, *m.pl.*
quip [kwip], *n.* mot piquant, sarcasme, *m.*—*v.t.* railler.
quire [ˈkwaiə], *n.* main (*de papier*), *f.*
quirk [kwəːk], *n.* sarcasme, *m.*, pointe; subtilité (*chicane*), *f.*
quit [kwit], *v.t.* *irr.* quitter, abandonner; **notice to quit**, congé, *m.*—*a.* quitte; **to get quit of**, se débarrasser de.
quite [kwait], *adv.* tout à fait, entièrement, complètement, tout; bien, parfaitement; assez.
quits [kwits], *a.* quitte.
quiver [ˈkwivə], *n.* carquois, *m.*—*v.i.* trembler, frissonner; palpiter (*la chair*); frémir.
quivering [ˈkwivəriŋ], *n.* tremblement, frissonnement; battement des paupières, *m.*
Quixote [ˈkwiksət], **Don.** Don Quichotte, *m.*
quixotic [kwikˈsotik], *a.* de Don Quichotte; extravagant, exalté.
quiz [kwiz], *n.* plaisanterie, devinette, *f.*; persifleur, railleur, *m.*; **radio quiz**, jeu radiophonique, *m.*—*v.t.* railler, persifler; lorgner (*to stare at*).
quizzical [ˈkwizikəl], *a.* railleur; risible.
quizzing [ˈkwiziŋ], *n.* raillerie, *f.*, persiflage, *m.*; lorgnerie, *f.*
quodlibet [ˈkwodlibet], *n.* quolibet, *m.*, subtilité, *f.*
quoin [koin], *n.* coin, *m.*
quoit [koit], *n.* palet, *m.*
quondam [ˈkwondəm], *a.* ci-devant, ancien.
quorum [ˈkwoːrəm], *n.* nombre suffisant, quorum, *m.*
quota [ˈkwoutə], *n.* quote-part, *f.*
quotable [ˈkwoutəbl], *a.* citable.
quotation [kwoˈteiʃən], *n.* citation; (*Comm.*) cote, *f.*; (*St. Exch.*) cours, *m.*
quote [kwout], *v.t.* citer; alléguer; (*Comm.*) coter.
quotidian [kwoˈtidiən], *a.* quotidien, journalier.
quotient [ˈkwouʃənt], *n.* quotient, *m.*

R

R, r [ɑː]. dix-huitième lettre de l'alphabet, *m.*
rabbet [ˈræbət], *n.* feuillure, rainure, *f.*—*v.t.* faire une rainure à.
rabbet-plane [ˈræbətplein], *n.* guillaume, *m.*

529

rabbi ['ræbai], *n.* rabbin, *m.*; *chief rabbi*, grand rabbin.
rabbit ['ræbit], *n.* lapin, *m.*; *young rabbit*, lapereau, *m.*
rabble [ræbl], *n.* foule; populace, canaille, *f.*
rabid ['ræbid], *a.* féroce; furieux; enragé (*chien*).
rabies ['reibi:z], *n.* rage, hydrophobie, *f.*
raccoon [RACOON].
race (1) [reis], *n.* (*Biol.*) race, *f.*
race (2) [reis], *n.* (*Spt.*) course, *f.*; raz, raz de marée (*courant*), *m.*—*v.i.* courir vite, courir, lutter de vitesse; *to go racing*, aller aux courses.
race-course ['reiskɔ:s], *n.* champ de courses, hippodrome, *m.*
race-horse ['reishɔ:s], *n.* cheval de course, *m.*
racer ['reisə], *n.* coureur; cheval de course, *m.*
race-track ['reistræk], *n.* piste, *f.*
racial ['reiʃəl], *a.* de (la) race, ethnique.
raciness ['reisinis], *n.* piquant, *m.*, verve, *f.*
racing ['reisiŋ], *a.* de course.—*n.* les courses, *f.pl.*
racing-car ['reisiŋka:], *n.* automobile de course, *f.*
racism ['reisizm], *n.* racisme, *m.*
rack [ræk], *n.* râtelier (*dans une écurie etc.*); chevalet (*instrument de tension*), *m.*; roue (*instrument de supplice*); (*Tech.*) crémaillère, *f.*; *luggage-rack*, (*Rail.*) filet, *m.*—*v.t.* mettre à la torture; (*fig.*) tourmenter; *to rack one's brains*, se creuser la cervelle.
racket ['rækit], *n.* fracas, tapage, tintamarre, caquet, *m.*; (*Ten.*) raquette; escroquerie, supercherie, combine, *f.*
rackety ['rækiti], *a.* tapageur.
racking ['rækiŋ], *a.* de torture; atroce (*douleur*).
racoon [rə'ku:n], *n.* raton laveur, *m.*
racy ['reisi], *a.* (*fig.*) vif, piquant, plein de verve (*style etc.*).
radar ['reida:], *n.* radar, *m.*
radiance ['reidiəns], **radiancy** ['reidiənsi], *n.* rayonnement, éclat, *m.*, splendeur, *f.*
radiant ['reidiənt], *a.* rayonnant (*de*); radieux, éclatant.
radiantly ['reidiəntli], *adv.* en rayonnant, splendidement.
radiate ['reidieit], *v.t.* émettre comme des rayons.—*v.i.* rayonner (*de*).
radiation [reidi'eiʃən], *n.* rayonnement, *m.*, radiation, *f.*
radiator ['reidieitə], *n.* radiateur, *m.*
radical ['rædikəl], *a.* radical; fondamental.—*n.* radical, *m.*
radicalism ['rædikəlizm], *n.* radicalisme, *m.*
radically ['rædikəli], *adv.* radicalement, essentiellement.
radio ['reidiou], *n.* radio, la T.S.F., *f.*
radioactive [reidiou'æktiv], *a.* radio-actif.
radioactivity ['reidiouæk'tiviti], *n.* radio-activité, *f.*
radio-control ['reidioukən'troul], *n.* téléguidage, *m.*—*v.t.* téléguider.
radiogram ['reidiougræm], *n.* combiné radio-électrophone, *m.*
radiography [reidi'ɔgrəfi], *n.* radiographie, *f.*
radish ['rædiʃ], *n.* radis, *m.*; *horse-radish*, raifort, *m.*
radium ['reidiəm], *n.* radium, *m.*
radius ['reidiəs], *n.* rayon, *m.*

radix ['reidiks], *n.* (*pl.* **radices** ['reidisi:z]) racine; base, *f.*
raffle [ræfl], *n.* loterie, tombola, *f.*—*v.t.* mettre en tombola.
raft [ra:ft], *n.* radeau; train de bois, *m.*
rafter ['ra:ftə], *n.* chevron, *m.*
raftered ['ra:ftəd], *a.* à chevrons.
rafting ['ra:ftiŋ], *n.* flottage en train, *m.*
raftsman ['ra:ftsmən], *n.* flotteur, *m.*
rag [ræg], *n.* chiffon (*nettoyage etc.*); haillon, *m.*, guenille, loque (*de vêtement*), *f.*; (*Sch.*) chahut, *m.*; brimade, *f.*—*v.t.* (*Sch.*) chahuter, brimer.
ragamuffin ['rægəmʌfin], *n.* gueux, polisson, va-nu-pieds, *m.*
rage [reidʒ], *n.* rage, fureur, *f.*, emportement, *m.*; furie, manie, *f.*; *it's all the rage*, cela fait fureur.—*v.i.* être furieux, être en fureur, s'emporter; (*fig.*) sévir.
ragged ['rægid], *a.* en haillons, déguenillé (*personnes*); en lambeaux, déchiré (*choses*).
raggedness ['rægidnis], *n.* délabrement, déguenillement, *m.*; guenilles, *f.pl.*
raging ['reidʒiŋ], *a.* furieux, en fureur; déchaîné, acharné, violent (*tempête, guerre etc.*).—*n.* fureur, violence, *f.*
ragman ['rægmən], *n.* (*pl.* **-men** [men]) chiffonnier, *m.*
rag-time ['rægtaim], *n.* (*Mus.*) musique syncopée, *f.*
raid [reid], *n.* incursion, *f.*; raid, coup de main, *m.*; *air raid*, raid aérien.—*v.t.* faire une incursion dans; piller; bombarder.
raider ['reidə], *n.* maraudeur; commando, *m.*
rail (1) [reil], *n.* barre, *f.*, barreau (*bois, métal etc.*), *m.*; rampe (*d'escalier*), *f.*; parapet (*de pont etc.*); (*Rail.*) rail, *m.*—*v.t.* enclore, griller.
rail (2) [reil], *v.i. to rail at*, criailler, invectiver.
railer ['reilə], *n.* criailleur, médisant, *m.*
railing (1) ['reiliŋ], *n.* grille, *f.*, garde-fou, *m.*
railing (2) ['reiliŋ], *n.* injures, invectives, *f.pl.*
raillery ['reiləri], *n.* raillerie, *f.*
railway ['reilwei], *n.* chemin de fer, *m.*, voie ferrée, *f.*
railwayman ['reilweimən], *n.* (*pl.* **-men** [men]) employé des chemins de fer, cheminot, *m.*
raiment ['reimənt], *n.* vêtement, *m.*
rain [rein], *n.* pluie, *f.*—*v.t.* faire pleuvoir.—*v.i.* pleuvoir; *it is pouring with rain*, il pleut à verse.
rainbow ['reinbou], *n.* arc-en-ciel, *m.*
raincoat ['reinkout], *n.* imperméable, *m.*
rainfall ['reinfɔ:l], *n.* pluie annuelle, pluie tombée, *f.*
rain-gauge ['reingeidʒ], *n.* pluviomètre, *m.*
rainy ['reini], *a.* pluvieux.
raise [reiz], *v.t.* lever; élever; hausser (*prix etc.*); soulever (*élever à une petite hauteur etc.*); cultiver (*légumes*); augmenter, accroître (*ajouter à*); faire naître (*soupçons*); pousser (*un cri*); faire lever (*pâte*); se procurer (*argent*); faire (*un emprunt etc.*).
raised [reizd], *a.* levé; en relief.
raisin [reizn], *n.* raisin sec, *m.*
raising ['reiziŋ], *n.* augmentation, *f.*, accroissement, *m.*; levée (*d'impôts, de troupes, de sièges etc.*), *f.*; élevage (*de bestiaux*), *m.*; culture (*de plantes etc.*), *f.*

rake (1) [reik], *n.* (*Hort.*) râteau.—*v.t.* (*Agric.*) râteler; (*Hort.*) ratisser; ramasser (*rassembler*); (*Mil.*) enfiler.

rake (2) [reik], *n.* roué (*libertin*), *m.*

raking ['reikiŋ], *a.* d'enfilade.—*n.* (*Hort.*) ratissage; (*Agric.*) râtelage, *m.*

rakish ['reikiʃ], *a.* dissolu; élancé (*navire*).

rakishness ['reikiʃnis], *n.* libertinage; air crâne, *m.*

rally ['ræli], *v.t.* rallier, rassembler.—*v.i.* se rallier, se rassembler; (*fig.*) se remettre.—*n.* ralliement, *m.*

Ralph [reif, rælf]. Raoul, *m.*

ram [ræm], *n.* bélier; mouton, *m.*—*v.t.* enfoncer; pilonner, tasser (*terre etc.*); bourrer (*dans un canon*).

ramble ['ræmbl], *n.* excursion à pied, grande promenade; (*fig.*) divagation, *f.*—*v.i.* errer, se promener; errer çà et là; (*fig.*) divaguer.

rambler ['ræmblə], *n.* excursionniste (à pied), *m.*; (*Hort.*) rosier grimpant, *m.*

rambling ['ræmbliŋ], *a.* errant, vagabond; (*fig.*) décousu, incohérent.—*n.* excursions, promenades à l'aventure; (*fig.*) divagations, *f.pl.*

ramification [ræmifi'keiʃən], *n.* ramification, *f.*

ramify ['ræmifai], *v.i.* se ramifier.

rammer ['ræmə], *n.* pilon, *m.*

ramp [ræmp], *n.* rampe, montée; (*fam.*) escroquerie, *f.*

rampant ['ræmpənt], *a.* dominant, violent; effréné; (*Her.*) rampant.

rampart ['ræmpɑ:t], *n.* rempart, *m.*

ramrod ['ræmrɔd], *n.* baguette (*de fusil*), *f.*; écouvillon (*de canon*), *m.*; **stiff as a ramrod**, droit comme un piquet.

ramshackle ['ræmʃækl], *a.* qui tombe en ruines, délabré.

rancid ['rænsid], *a.* rance.

rancidity [ræn'siditi], rancidness ['rænsidnis], *n.* rancidité, *f.*

rancorous ['ræŋkərəs], *a.* rancunier, haineux.

rancour ['ræŋkə], *n.* haine, rancune, *f.*

Randolph ['rændɔlf]. Rodolphe, *m.*

random ['rændəm], *a.* fait au hasard.—*n.* hasard, *m.*; **at random**, au hasard.

range [reindʒ], *n.* rangée, *f.*, rang (*file*), *m.*; chaîne (*de montagnes etc.*); étendue, portée, *f.*, fourneau; tir (*armes à feu*), *m.*; gamme (*de couleurs*), *f.*—*v.t.* ranger, arranger; aligner (*avec*); parcourir.—*v.i.* s'aligner; être rangé.

range-finder ['reindʒfaində], *n.* télémètre, *m.*

ranger ['reindʒə], *n.* garde-forestier, *m.*

rank (1) [ræŋk], *n.* rang, ordre, *m.*, classe, *f.*; (*Mil.*) grade; (*fig.*) haut rang, *m.*; station de taxis, *f.*—*v.t.* ranger, classer.—*v.i.* se ranger, être classé; occuper un rang.

rank (2) [ræŋk], *a.* luxuriant; (*fig.*) rude; extrême; fétide (*odeur*).

rankle [ræŋkl], *v.i.* s'envenimer, s'enflammer.

rankness ['ræŋknis], *n.* surabondance; grossièreté; rancidité, *f.*

ransack ['rænsæk], *v.t.* saccager, piller; fouiller.

ransacking ['rænsækiŋ], *n.* pillage, *m.*

ransom ['rænsəm], *n.* rançon, *f.*—*v.t.* rançonner.

rant [rænt], *n.* déclamation extravagante, *f.*—*v.i.* extravaguer; tempêter.

ranter ['ræntə], *n.* déclamateur, énergumène, *m.*

ranting ['ræntiŋ], *a.* d'énergumène, extravagant.

ranunculus [rə'nʌŋkjuləs], *n.* (*Bot.*) renoncule, *f.*

rap [ræp], *n.* tape, *f.*, petit coup sec, *m.*—*v.t.* *v.i.* frapper.

rapacious [rə'peiʃəs], *a.* rapace.

rapaciously [rə'peiʃəsli], *adv.* avec rapacité.

rapaciousness [rə'peiʃəsnis], rapacity [rə'pæsiti], *n.* rapacité, *f.*

rape (1) [reip], *n.* (*Poet.*) rapt, enlèvement; (*Law*) viol, *m.*—*v.t.* enlever de force; violer.

rape (2) [reip], *n.* (*Agric.*) colza, *m.*, navette, *f.*

rapid ['ræpid], *a.* and *n.* rapide, *m.*

rapidity [rə'piditi], rapidness ['ræpidnis], *n.* rapidité, *f.*

rapidly ['ræpidli], *adv.* rapidement.

rapier ['reipiə], *n.* rapière, *f.*

rapine ['ræpain], *n.* rapine, *f.*

rapt [ræpt], *a.* ravi, extasié; profond (*attention*).

rapture ['ræptʃə], *n.* ravissement, transport, *m.*, extase, *f.*

rapturous ['ræptʃərəs], *a.* ravissant; joyeux.

rapturously ['ræptʃərəsli], *adv.* avec transport.

rare [rɛə], *a.* rare; clairsemé; à moitié cru (*viande*).

rarefaction [rɛəri'fækʃən], *n.* raréfaction, *f.*

rarefy ['rɛərifai],{*v.t.* raréfier.—*v.i.* se raréfier.

rarely ['rɛəli], *adv.* rarement.

rareness ['rɛənis], rarity ['rɛəriti], *n.* rareté, *f.*

rascal ['rɑ:skl], *n.* coquin, fripon, gredin, *m.*

rascality [rɑ:s'kæliti], *n.* friponnerie, gredinerie, coquinerie, *f.*

rascally ['rɑ:skəli], *a.* coquin, fripon.

rase [RAZE].

rash (1) [ræʃ], *a.* téméraire; irréfléchi, imprudent.

rash (2) [ræʃ], *n.* éruption, *f.*

rasher ['ræʃə], *n.* tranche, *f.*

rashly ['ræʃli], *adv.* témérairement; imprudemment.

rashness ['ræʃnis], *n.* témérité; précipitation, imprudence, *f.*

rasp [rɑ:sp], *n.* râpe, *f.*—*v.t.* râper; râcler; écorcher (*surface, peau*).—*v.i.* grincer, crisser.

raspberry ['rɑ:zbəri], *n.* framboise, *f.*

raspberry-bush ['rɑ:zbəribuʃ], *n.* framboisier, *m.*

rasping ['rɑ:spiŋ], *a.* grinçant, âpre, rauque (*voix*).—*n.* râpage; crissement, *m.*

rat [ræt], *n.* rat, *m.*; **to smell a rat**, se douter de quelque chose.

ratchet ['rætʃit], *n.* cliquet, *m.*, dent d'engrenage, *f.*

ratchet-brace ['rætʃitbreis], ratchet-jack ['rætʃitdʒæk], *n.* vilbrequin à cliquet, *m.*

rate (1) [reit], *n.* prix, *m.*; raison, proportion, *f.*; taux (*argent, population*); cours (*de change*); degré, rang, ordre, *m.*; vitesse; taxe, *f.*, impôt (*taxe municipale*), *m.*; **at any rate**, en tout cas; **first-rate**, de première classe.—*v.t.* évaluer; classer; taxer; faire une estimation; regarder (*comme*).—*v.i.* **to rate as**, être classé comme.

rate (2) [reit], *v.t.* gronder.

rateable

rateable ['reitəbl], *a.* imposable; *rateable value*, valeur locative imposable (*d'un immeuble*), *f.*
rate-payer ['reitpeiə], *n.* contribuable, *m.*, *f.*
rather ['rɑːðə], *adv.* plutôt; un peu, quelque peu (*légèrement*); assez, passablement (*suffisamment*).
ratification [rætifi'keiʃən], *n.* ratification, *f.*
ratify ['rætifai], *v.t.* ratifier, approuver.
ratifying ['rætifaiiŋ], *a.* ratificatif.
rating (1) ['reitiŋ], *n.* estimation, évaluation; répartition d'impôt, *f.*; (*Navy*) matelot, *m.*
rating (2) ['reitiŋ], *n.* gronderie, *f.*
ratio ['reiʃiou], *n.* proportion, raison, *f.*, rapport, *m.*
ration ['ræʃən], *n.* ration, *f.*—*v.t.* rationner.
ration-book ['ræʃənbuk], *n.* carte d'alimentation, *f.*
rationing ['ræʃəniŋ], *n.* rationnement, *m.*
rational ['ræʃənl], *a.* raisonnable, rationnel.
rationalism ['ræʃnəlizm], *n.* rationalisme, *m.*
rationalist ['ræʃnəlist], *n.* rationaliste, *m.*, *f.*
rationalize ['ræʃnəlaiz], *v.t.* rationaliser.
rationally ['ræʃnəli], *adv.* raisonnablement, rationnellement.
rattan [rə'tæn], *n.* rotin, *m.*
ratten [rætn], *v.t.* intimider; saboter.
rattle [rætl], *v.t.* faire claquer, faire sonner; secouer (*chaînes etc.*).—*v.i.* faire un bruit sec, cliqueter, crépiter.—*n.* bruit; cliquetis (*de métaux*); râle (*à la gorge*); hochet (*jouet*), *m.*; crécelle, *f.*
rattlesnake ['rætlsneik], *n.* serpent à sonnettes, crotale, *m.*
rattling ['rætliŋ], *a.* bruyant; (*fig.*) excellent. —*n.* bruit, cliquetis, *m.*
rat-trap ['rættræp], *n.* ratière, *f.*
raucous ['rɔːkəs], *a.* rauque.
ravage ['rævidʒ], *n.* ravage, *m.*—*v.t.* ravager.
ravager ['rævidʒə], *n.* ravageur, dévastateur, *m.*
rave [reiv], *v.i.* être en délire; (*fig.*) extravaguer.
ravel [rævl], *v.t.* embrouiller, entortiller.—*v.i.* s'embrouiller, s'entortiller.
raven (1) [reivn], *n.* (*Orn.*) corbeau, *m.*
raven (2) [rævn], *v.t.* dévorer.
ravenous ['rævənəs], *a.* dévorant, vorace.
ravenously ['rævənəsli], *adv.* avec voracité.
ravenousness ['rævənəsnis], *n.* voracité, rapacité, *f.*
ravine [rə'viːn], *n.* ravin, *m.*
raving ['reiviŋ], *a.* en délire, délirant; furieux, fou.—*n.* délire, *m.*
ravish ['ræviʃ], *v.t.* ravir; enlever; (*fig.*) transporter.
ravisher ['ræviʃə], *n.* ravisseur, *m.*
ravishing ['ræviʃiŋ], *a.* ravissant.
raw [rɔː], *a.* cru; vif, écorché (*égratigné etc.*); (*fig.*) sans expérience, novice; pur (*alcool*); brut (*cuir etc.*); froid et humide (*temps*); *raw materials*, matières premières, *m.pl.*
raw-boned ['rɔːbound], *a.* maigre, décharné.
rawness ['rɔːnis], *n.* crudité, *f.*; froid humide (*du temps*), *m.*; (*fig.*) inexpérience, *f.*
ray (1) [rei], *n.* rayon, *m.*
ray (2) [rei], *n.* (*Ichth.*) raie, *f.*
rayless ['reilis], *a.* sans rayon, sans lumière.
Raymond ['reimənd], Raymond, *m.*
rayon ['reiən], *n.* rayonne, *f.*
raze [reiz], *v.t.* raser, effleurer; rayer, effacer (*supprimer*); abattre, détruire (*édifice*).

razor ['reizə], *n.* rasoir, *m.*; *safety razor*, rasoir de sûreté.
razor-bill ['reizəbil], *n.* petit pingouin, *m.*
re [riː, rei], *prep.* au sujet de, à propos de.
reach [riːtʃ], *n.* portée, atteinte; étendue (*capacité*), *f.*; bief (*de canal*), *m.*—*v.t.* atteindre, toucher; passer, donner (*rendre*); arriver à, parvenir à (*accomplir*).—*v.i.* s'étendre de . . . à.
reachable ['riːtʃəbl], *a.* qu'on peut atteindre.
react [ri'ækt], *v.i.* réagir (*sur*).
reaction [ri'ækʃən], *n.* réaction, *f.*
reactionary [ri'ækʃənəri], *a. and n.* réactionnaire, *m.*, *f.*
reactor [ri'æktə], *n.* réacteur, *m.*
read [riːd], *v.t. irr.* lire; faire la lecture de; (*fig.*) étudier.—*v.i.* lire; faire la lecture; se lire.
readable ['riːdəbl], *a.* lisible; qui se lit avec plaisir.
readableness ['riːdəblnis], *n.* lisibilité, *f.*
readdress [riːə'dres], *v.t.* faire suivre (*lettre*).
reader ['riːdə], *n.* lecteur; (*Print.*) correcteur; liseur (*amateur de lecture*); (*Sch.*) livre de lecture, *m.*
readily ['redili], *adv.* tout de suite, promptement; volontiers (*de bon gré*), avec plaisir.
readiness ['redinis], *n.* empressement, *m.*, promptitude; facilité; bonne volonté (*complaisance*), *f.*
reading ['riːdiŋ], *n.* lecture; variante (*textuelle*), leçon; hauteur (*de baromètre*), *f.*
reading-book ['riːdiŋbuk], *n.* livre de lecture, *m.*
reading-desk ['riːdiŋdesk], *n.* pupitre, *m.*
reading-lamp ['riːdiŋlæmp], *n.* lampe de travail, *f.*
reading-room ['riːdiŋruːm], *n.* salle de lecture, *f.*
readjust [riːə'dʒʌst], *v.t.* rajuster, rectifier.
readjustment [riːə'dʒʌstmənt], *n.* rajustement, *m.*
ready ['redi], *a.* prêt, prompt; facile; vif (*qui comprend vite*); *ready money*, argent comptant, *m.*
ready-made ['redimeid], *a.* tout fait, confectionné.
ready-reckoner ['redi'reknə], *n.* barème, *m.*
ready-witted ['redi'witid], *a.* à l'esprit vif.
reaffirm [riːə'fəːm], *v.t.* réaffirmer.
reafforestation [riːəfɔris'teiʃən], *n.* reboisement, *m.*
real ['riːəl], *a.* réel; vrai, véritable; effectif; (*Law*) immeuble, immobilier.
realism ['riːəlizm], *n.* réalisme, *m.*
realist ['riːəlist], *n.* réaliste, *m.*, *f.*
realistic [riːə'listik], *a.* réaliste.
reality [ri'æliti], *n.* réalité, *f.*; réel, *m.*
realizable ['riːəlaizəbl], *a.* réalisable.
realization [riːəlai'zeiʃən], *n.* réalisation; conception nette, *f.*
realize ['riːəlaiz], *v.t.* réaliser; effectuer; se rendre compte de, bien comprendre; se figurer; rapporter (*somme*).
really ['riːəli], *adv.* réellement, en effet, effectivement; vraiment.—*int.* en vérité! à vrai dire!
realm [relm], *n.* royaume, *f.*; domaine, *m.*
realty ['riːəlti], *n.* biens immeubles, *m.pl.*
ream [riːm], *n.* rame (*de papier*), *f.*

reap [ri:p], *v.t.*, *v.i.* moissonner; (*fig.*) recueillir.

reaper ['ri:pə], *n.* moissonneur, *m.*

reaping ['ri:piŋ], *n.* moisson, *f.*

reaping-machine ['ri:piŋməʃi:n], *n.* moissonneuse, *f.*

reappear [ri:ə'piə], *v.i.* reparaître, réapparaître.

reappearance [ri:ə'piərəns], *n.* réapparition; rentrée (*d'acteur*), *f.*

reappoint [ri:ə'pɔint], *v.t.* réintégrer; renommer.

reappointment [ri:ə'pɔintmənt], *n.* réintégration, *f.*

rear (1) [riə], *a.* situé à l'arrière; postérieur; *rear wheel*, roue arrière, *f.*—*n.* dernier rang, *m.*; arrière-garde, *f.*; derrière (*d'édifice etc.*), *m.*; *to bring up the rear*, fermer la marche.

rear (2) [riə], *v.t.* élever.—*v.i.* se cabrer.

rear-admiral ['riərædmərəl], *n.* contre-amiral, *m.*

re-arm [ri:'a:m], *v.t.*, *v.i.* réarmer.

re-armament [ri:'a:məmənt], *n.* réarmement, *m.*

rearwards ['riəwədz], *adv.* à l'arrière.

reascend [ri:ə'send], *v.t.*, *v.i.* remonter.

reason [ri:zn], *n.* raison, *f.*; raisonnement, *m.*; *the reason why*, la raison pour laquelle; *that stands to reason*, cela va sans dire; *to have reason to believe*, avoir lieu de croire.—*v.t.*, *v.i.* raisonner.

reasonable ['ri:znəbl], *a.* raisonnable; modéré.

reasonableness ['ri:znəblnis], *n.* raison, modération, *f.*

reasonably ['ri:znəbli], *adv.* raisonnablement.

reasoner ['ri:zənə], *n.* raisonneur, logicien, *m.*

reasoning ['ri:zəniŋ], *n.* raisonnement, *m.*

reassemble [ri:ə'sembl], *v.t.* rassembler.—*v.i.* se rassembler.

reassert [ri:ə'sə:t], *v.t.* affirmer de nouveau.

reassess [ri:ə'ses], *v.t.* réévaluer.

reassessment [ri:ə'sesmənt], *n.* réimposition; réévaluation, *f.*

reassign [ri:ə'sain], *v.t.* réassigner.

reassignment [ri:ə'sainmənt], *n.* réassignation, *f.*

reassume [ri:ə'sju:m], *v.t.* réassumer; reprendre (*position*).

reassurance [ri:ə'ʃuərəns], *n.* action de rassurer; (*Comm.*) réassurance, *f.*

reassure [ri:ə'ʃuə], *v.t.* rassurer; (*Comm.*) réassurer.

rebate ['ri:beit], *n.* rabais, *m.*, remise, *f.*—[ri'beit], *v.t.* diminuer, rabattre.

rebel [rebl], *n.* rebelle, *m.*, *f.*, révolté, *m.*—[ri'bel], *v.i.* se révolter, se soulever (*contre*).

rebellion [ri'beljən], *n.* rébellion, *f.*

rebellious [ri'beljəs], *a.* rebelle.

rebelliously [ri'beljəsli], *adv.* en rebelle.

rebelliousness [ri'beljəsnis], *n.* rébellion, *f.*

rebirth [ri:'bə:θ], *n.* renaissance, *f.*

reborn [ri:'bɔ:n], *a.* né de nouveau; réincarné.

rebound ['ri:baund], *n.* rebondissement, contre-coup, *m.*—[ri'baund], *v.i.* rebondir.

rebuff [ri'bʌf], *n.* rebuffade, *f.*, échec, *m.*—*v.t.* rebuter, repousser.

rebuild [ri:'bild], *v.t.* irr. (*conjug. like* BUILD) rebâtir, reconstruire.

rebuke [ri'bju:k], *n.* réprimande, *f.*, reproche, *m.*—*v.t.* réprimander, reprendre, censurer.

rebus ['ri:bəs], *n.* rébus, *m.*

rebut [ri'bʌt], *v.t.* rebuter, repousser, réfuter.

recalcitrant [ri'kælsitrənt], *a.* récalcitrant, insoumis, réfractaire.

recall [ri'kɔ:l], *n.* rappel, *m.*; révocation, *f.*; *beyond recall*, irrévocablement.—*v.t.* rappeler; se rappeler (*se souvenir de*).

recant [ri'kænt], *v.t.* rétracter, désavouer, abjurer.—*v.i.* se rétracter.

recantation [ri:kæn'teiʃən], *n.* rétractation, palinodie, *f.*

recapitulate [ri:kə'pitjuleit], *v.t.* récapituler.

recapitulation [ri:kəpitju'leiʃən], *n.* récapitulation, *f.*

recapture [ri:'kæptʃə], *n.* reprise, *f.*—*v.t* reprendre.

recast [ri:'ka:st], *v.t.* irr. (*conjug. like* CAST) refondre; (*Theat.*) faire une nouvelle distribution des rôles.

recede [ri'si:d], *v.i.* se retirer (*de*); s'éloigner.

receding [ri'si:diŋ], *a.* fuyant (*le front*), effacé (*menton*).

receipt [ri'si:t], *n.* reçu, *m.*, quittance, *f.*, acquit, *m.*; réception (*le fait de recevoir*); (*pl.*) recette, *f.*, recettes, *f.pl.*; récépissé, *m.*—*v.t.* acquitter.

receive [ri'si:v], *v.t.* recevoir, accepter; accueillir; recéler (*biens volés*).

receiver [ri'si:və], *n.* receveur; receleur (*d'objets volés*); liquidateur (*faillite*); (*Teleph.*) récepteur, *m.*

receiving [ri'si:viŋ], *n.* réception, *f.*; recel (*d'objets volés*), *m.*

recent [ri'sənt], *a.* récent, frais, nouveau.

recently ['ri:səntli], *adv.* récemment, depuis peu.

receptacle [ri'septkl], *n.* réceptacle; récipient, *m.*

reception [ri'sepʃən], *n.* réception, *f.*; accueil, *m.*

receptionist [ri'sepʃənist], *n.* réceptionniste, *m.*, *f.*

receptive [ri'septiv], *a.* réceptif (*esprit*).

recess [ri'ses], *n.* enfoncement, *m.*, niche, *f.*; recoin, *m.*; vacances, *f.pl.*

recession [ri'seʃən], *n.* retraite, *f.*; désistement (*d'une revendication*), *m.*; (*St. Exch.*) baisse, *f.*

recidivist [ri'sidivist], *n.* récidiviste, *m.*, *f.*

recipe ['resipi], *n.* (*Cook.*) recette, *f.*

recipient [ri'sipiənt], *n.* personne qui reçoit, *f.*; destinataire (*de lettre*), *m.*, *f.*; (*Chem.*) récipient, *m.*

reciprocal [ri'siprəkl], *a.* réciproque.

reciprocate [ri'siprəkeit], *v.t.* échanger; répondre à.—*v.i.* alterner; se succéder.

reciprocation [risiprə'keiʃən], **reciprocity** [resi'prositi], *n.* réciprocité, *f.*

recital [ri'saitl], *n.* récit, *m.*; narration, énumération, *f.*; (*Mus.*) récital, *m.*

recitation [resi'teiʃən], *n.* récitation, *f.*

recitative [resitə'ti:v], *n.* récitatif, *m.*

recite [ri'sait], *v.t.* réciter, faire le récit de; raconter.

reciter [ri'saitə], *n.* récitateur; diseur, narrateur, *m.*

reck [rek], *v.i.* se soucier de.

reckless ['reklis], *a.* insouciant (*de*); téméraire, insensé.

recklessly ['reklisli], *adv.* témérairement, avec insouciance.

recklessness ['reklisnis], *n.* insouciance, témérité, *f.*

reckon [rekn], *v.t.* compter, calculer; regarder, évaluer (*comme*).—*v.i.* compter; *to reckon on*, compter sur; *to reckon with*, tenir compte de.

reckoner ['reknə], *n.* calculateur, chiffreur, *m.*; *ready-reckoner*, barême, *m.*

reckoning ['reknin], *n.* compte, calcul; écot, *m.*, note (*dans un hôtel*); addition (*dans un restaurant*); (*Naut.*) estime, *f.*

reclaim [ri'kleim], *v.t.* réformer, corriger; ramener (*de*); réclamer, revendiquer (*ses droits*); défricher (*terre*).

reclaimable [ri'kleiməbl], *a.* corrigible; cultivable, défrichable (*terre*).

reclaiming [ri'kleimin], **reclamation** [reklə'meiʃən], *n.* défrichement (*de terre*), *m.*; réforme, correction (*de criminels*), *f.*

recline [ri'klain], *v.i.* s'appuyer, se reposer, se coucher.

reclining [ri'klainin], *a.* incliné, appuyé, couché.

reclothe [ri'klouð], *v.t.* rhabiller.

recluse [ri'kluːs], *a.* reclus; solitaire, retiré.— *n.* reclus, *m.*

reclusion [ri'kluːʒən], *n.* réclusion, *f.*

recognition [rekəg'niʃən], *n.* reconnaissance, *f.*

recognizable [rekəg'naizəbl], *a.* reconnaissable.

recognizance [ri'kɔgnizəns], *n.* reconnaissance; (*Law*) obligation contractée, *f.*

recognize ['rekəgnaiz], *v.t.* reconnaître.

recoil [ri'kɔil], *n.* recul; contre-coup, *m.*; (*fig.*) répugnance, *f.*—*v.i.* reculer; retomber.

recollect [rekə'lekt], *v.t.* se souvenir de, se rappeler.

recollection [rekə'lekʃən], *n.* souvenir, *m.*; mémoire, *f.*

recommence [riːkə'mens], *v.t., v.i.* recommencer.

recommend [rekə'mend], *v.t.* recommander.

recommendation [rekəmen'deiʃən], *n.* recommandation; apostille (*d'une pétition*), *f.*

recompense ['rekəmpens], *n.* récompense, *f.*; dédommagement, *m.*—*v.t.* récompenser (*de*); dédommager (*de*); compenser, réparer.

reconcilable [rekən'sailəbl], *a.* réconciliable; conciliable (*avec*) (*choses*).

reconcile ['rekənsail], *v.t.* réconcilier (*avec*); habituer, accoutumer (*familiariser*); *to reconcile oneself to*, se résigner à.

reconciliation [rekənsili'eiʃən], *n.* réconciliation; conciliation (*de choses*); (*Bibl.*) expiation, *f.*

recondite [ri'kɔndait, 'rekəndait], *a.* secret, abstrus, profond, mystérieux.

recondition [riːkən'diʃən], *v.t.* remettre à neuf, refaire.

reconnaissance [ri'kɔnisəns], *n.* reconnaissance, *f.*

reconnoitre [rekə'nɔitə], *v.t.* reconnaître.— *v.i.* faire une reconnaissance.

reconsider [riːkən'sidə], *v.t.* considérer de nouveau; revenir sur (*une décision*).

reconsideration [riːkənsidə'reiʃən], *n.* reconsidération, *f.*

reconstitute [riː'kɔnstitjuːt], *v.t.* reconstituer.

reconstruct [riːkən'strʌkt], *v.t.* reconstruire.

reconstruction [riːkən'strʌkʃən], *n.* reconstruction, *f.*

record ['rekɔːd], *n.* registre, *m.*, archives, *f.pl.*; disque (*de phonographe*); (*Spt.*) record; dossier, *m.*; *keeper of the records*, archiviste, *m., f.*; *long-playing record*, disque longue durée, *m*; *public records*, archives, *f.pl.*; *record library*, discothèque, *f.*; greffe, *m.*—[ri'kɔːd], *v.t.* enregistrer; graver, imprimer (*dans l'esprit etc.*); mentionner (*fait historique*).

recorder [ri'kɔːdə], *n.* enregistreur, archiviste; greffier; (*Law*) officier judiciaire d'une ville; (*Mus.*) flageolet, *m.*; *tape recorder*, magnétophone, *m.*

recording [ri'kɔːdin], *n.* enregistrement, *m.*

recount (1) [ri'kaunt], *v.t.* raconter.

recount (2) [ri'kaunt], *v.t.* recompter.— ['riːkaunt], *n.* nouvelle addition des voix (*aux élections*), *f.*

recoup [ri'kuːp], *v.t.* rembourser, dédommager (*de*).

recourse [ri'kɔːs], *n.* recours, *m.*

recover (1) [ri'kʌvə], *v.t.* recouvrer, retrouver; réparer (*perte*).—*v.i.* se rétablir, guérir; se remettre (*d'une maladie*); se relever (*d'une perte*).

recover (2) [riː'kʌvə], *v.t.* recouvrir; regarnir.

recovery [ri'kʌvəri], *n.* recouvrement, *m.*; guérison, *f.*; rétablissement, *m.*; (*Econ.*) reprise, *f.*; *past recovery*, incurable, sans remède.

recreant ['rekriənt], *a. and n.* lâche, infidèle, *m., f.*, apostat, *m.*

re-create [riːkri'eit], *v.t.* recréer.

recreation [rekri'eiʃən], *n.* récréation, *f.*, divertissement, *m.*

recriminate [ri'krimineit], *v.i.* récriminer (*contre*).

recrimination [rikrimi'neiʃən], *n.* récrimination, *f.*

recriminatory [ri'kriminətri], *a.* récriminatoire.

recrudescence [riːkru'desəns], *n.* recrudescence, *f.*

recruit [ri'kruːt], *n.* recrue, *f.*, conscrit, *m.*— *v.t.* rétablir, réparer (*restaurer*); (*Mil.*) recruter.—*v.i.* se recruter, se remettre.

recruiting [ri'kruːtin], **recruitment** [ri'kruːtmənt], *n.* recrutement, *m.*; *recruiting-officer*, officier de recrutement, *m.*

rectangle ['rektæŋgl], *n.* rectangle, *m.*

rectangular [rek'tæŋgjulə], *a.* rectangulaire, rectangle, à angle droit.

rectifiable ['rektifaiəbl], *a.* rectifiable.

rectification [rektifi'keiʃən], *n.* rectification, *f.*

rectifier ['rektifaiə], *n.* rectificateur; (*Elec.*) redresseur, *m.*

rectify ['rektifai], *v.t.* rectifier; redresser.

rectilineal [rekti'liniəl], *a.* rectiligne.

rectitude ['rektitjuːd], *n.* rectitude, droiture, *f.*

rector ['rektə], *n.* (*Ch. of England*) prêtre; (*R.-C.*) curé; (*Univ. etc.*) recteur, principal, *m.*

rectorial [rek'tɔːriəl], *a.* rectoral.

rectorship ['rektəʃip], *n.* rectorat, *m.*

rectory ['rektəri], *n.* cure, *f.*, presbytère, *m.*

recumbent [ri'kʌmbənt], *a.* couché, étendu; appuyé (*sur*).

recuperate [ri'ku:pəreit], *v.t.* recouvrer, récupérer.—*v.i.* se rétablir, se remettre, reprendre ses forces.

recuperation [riku:pə'reiʃən], *n.* recouvrement; rétablissement (*personne*), *m.*

recur [ri'kə:], *v.i.* revenir; se reproduire.

recurrence [ri'kʌrəns], *n.* retour, *m.*

recurrent [ri'kʌrənt], **recurring** [ri'kə:riŋ], *a.* périodique; (*Anat. etc.*) récurrent.

red [red], *a.* rouge; roux (*cheveux*); vermeil (*lèvres etc.*); **red lead**, minium, *m.*; **red-letter day**, jour de fête, *m.*—*n.* rouge, *m.*

redbreast ['redbrest], *n.* rouge-gorge, *m.*

redden [redn], *v.t., v.i.* rougir.

reddish ['rediʃ], *a.* rougeâtre, roussâtre.

redeem [ri'di:m], *v.t.* racheter; (*Fin.*) rembourser, amortir; retirer (*objets mis en gage*); (*fig.*) réparer.

redeemable [ri'di:məbl], *a.* rachetable.

redeemer [ri'di:mə], *n.* rédempteur, *m.*

redeeming [ri'di:miŋ], *a.* qui rachète.

redemption [ri'dempʃən], *n.* rédemption, *f.*; (*Fin.*) amortissement; rachat (*de billets*), *m.*

red-hot ['redhɔt], *a.* tout rouge, chauffé au rouge, ardent (*charbon*).

redirect [ri:di'rekt], *v.t.* faire suivre (*lettre*).

rediscover [ri:dis'kʌvə], *v.t.* redécouvrir.

redistribution [ri:distri'bju:ʃən], *n.* nouvelle distribution, répartition, *f.*

redness ['rednis], *n.* rougeur; rousseur (*de cheveux*), *f.*

redolence ['redoləns], *n.* parfum, *m.*; senteur, *f.*

redolent ['redolənt], *a.* qui a un parfum de; **redolent of . . .**, qui sent le . . .

redouble [ri:'dʌbl], *v.t., v.i.* redoubler.

redoubt [ri'daut], *n.* redoute, *f.*

redoubtable [ri'dautəbl], *a.* redoutable.

redound [ri'daund], *v.i.* contribuer (*à, en*), résulter (*pour*), rejaillir (*sur*).

redpole, redpoll ['redpoul], *n.* (*pop.*) linotte, *f.*

redraft [ri:'drɑ:ft], *n.* nouveau dessin, *m.*; (*Comm.*) retraite, *f.*—*v.t.* rédiger de nouveau.

redress [ri'dres], *v.t.* redresser, corriger, réparer.—*n.* redressement, *m.*, réparation, *f.*; remède, *m.*

redshank ['redʃæŋk], *n.* (*Orn.*) chevalier, *m.*, gambette, *f.*

Redskin ['redskin], *n.* Peau-Rouge, *m., f.*

red-tape ['red'teip], *n.* bolduc, *m.*; (*fig.*) routine administrative, *f.*

reduce [ri'dju:s], *v.t.* réduire (*à* ou *en*); maigrir (*chair*); dégrader (*abaisser*); **a person in reduced circumstances**, une personne tombée dans la gêne.—*v.i.* maigrir.

reduction [ri'dʌkʃən], *n.* réduction, *f.*; **a reduction in prices**, une baisse des prix, *f.*; **reduction to the ranks**, cassation, *f.*

redundance [ri'dʌndəns], **redundancy** [ri'dʌndənsi], *n.* redondance, *f.*

redundant [ri'dʌndənt], *a.* redondant, superflu.

re-echo [ri:'ekou], *v.t.* répéter.—*v.i.* retentir.—*n.* écho répété, *m.*

reed [ri:d], *n.* roseau; chalumeau, *m.*; (*Mus.*) anche, *f.*

reed-pipe ['ri:dpaip], *n.* chalumeau, pipeau, *m.*

reedy ['ri:di], *a.* couvert de roseaux; flûtée (*voix*).

reef (1) [ri:f], *n.* récif, écueil, *m.*

reef (2) [ri:f], *n.* ris (*de voile*), *m.*—*v.t.* prendre un ris dans.

reef-knot ['ri:fnɔt], *n.* nœud plat, *m.*

reek [ri:k], *n.* fumée, *f.*, relent, *m.*—*v.i.* fumer; exhaler; **reeking with**, tout fumant de; **to reek of**, puer, empester.

reel (1) [ri:l], *n.* dévidoir, *m.*; bobine (*de coton*), *f.*; (*Angling*) moulinet, *m.*; (*Cine.*) bobine, bande, *f.*; **newsreel**, les actualités, *f.pl.*—*v.t.* **to reel off**, dévider, débiter.—*v.i.* tournoyer, chanceler, trébucher.

reel (2) [ri:l], *n.* branle écossais (*danse*), *m.*

re-elect [ri:i'lekt], *v.t.* réélire.

re-election [ri:i'lekʃən], *n.* réélection, *f.*

re-embark [ri:əm'bɑ:k], *v.t.* rembarquer.—*v.i.* se rembarquer.

re-embarkation [ri:emba'keiʃən], *n.* rembarquement, *m.*

re-embody [ri:əm'bɔdi], *v.t.* réincorporer.

re-enact [ri:i'nækt], *v.t.* remettre en vigueur (*une loi*); reconstituer (*un crime*).

re-enactment [ri:i'næktmənt], *n.* remise en vigueur; reconstitution, *f.*

re-engage [ri:in'geidʒ], *v.t.* rengager.

re-enlist [ri:in'list], *v.t., v.i.* (se) rengager.

re-enter [ri:'entə], *v.t., v.i.* rentrer.

re-entrant [ri:'entrənt], *a.* and *n.* rentrant, *m.*

re-establish [ri:is'tæbliʃ], *v.t.* rétablir.

re-establishment [ri:is'tæbliʃmənt], *n.* rétablissement, *m.*

re-examine [ri:ig'zæmin], *v.t.* examiner de nouveau, revoir.

re-export [ri:iks'pɔ:t], *v.t.* réexporter.

refashion [ri:'fæʃən], *v.t.* refaçonner.

refasten [ri:'fa:sn], *v.t.* rattacher; ragrafer.

refection [ri'fekʃən], *n.* repas, *m.*, collation, *f.*

refectory [ri'fektəri], *n.* réfectoire, *m.*

refer [ri'fə:], *v.t.* renvoyer, rapporter; adresser (*à*); remettre à la décision de.—*v.i.* se référer, se rapporter, avoir rapport (*à*); s'en rapporter, se référer (*personnes*); s'adresser (*à*).

referee [refə'ri:], *n.* arbitre, *m., f.*—*v.t., v.i.* (*Spt.*) arbitrer.

reference ['refərəns], *n.* renvoi; rapport (*respect*), *m.*; allusion, *f.*; renseignements, *m.pl.*, références (*de bonne vie et mœurs*), *f.pl.*; (*Comm.*) référence, *f.*; **book of reference**, ouvrage à consulter, *m.*; **with reference to**, au sujet de; **to make reference to**, faire allusion à.

referendum [refə'rendəm], *n.* référendum, *m.*

refill [ri:'fil], *v.t.* remplir.—*v.i.* (*Motor.*) faire le plein (*d'essence*).—['ri:fil], *n.* objet (*feuilles, pile, ampoule*) de rechange; (*Motor.*) plein (*d'essence*), *m.*

refine [ri'fain], *v.t.* épurer (*liquides*); (*Metal.*) affiner, raffiner (*sucre etc.*); (*fig.*) purifier.

refined [ri'faind], *a.* raffiné; pur, délicat (*goût*).

refinement [ri'fainmənt], *n.* raffinage (*de sucre*); (*Metal.*) affinage, *m.*; épuration (*de liquides*); (*fig.*) délicatesse, *f.*

refinery [ri'fainəri], *n.* raffinerie (*de sucre*); (*Metal.*) affinerie, *f.*

refit [ri:'fit], *v.t.* réparer; (*Naut.*) radouber.—['ri:fit], *n.* réparation; (*Naut.*) refonte, *f.*

reflect [ri'flekt], *v.t.* réfléchir; faire rejaillir sur; refléter.—*v.i.* réfléchir; **to reflect upon**, réfléchir à, méditer sur.

reflected [ri'flektid], *a.* réfléchi.

reflection [REFLEXION].
reflective [ri'flektiv], *a.* réfléchissant; méditatif.
reflector [ri'flektə], *n.* réflecteur; (*Cycl., Motor.*) catadioptre, *m.*
reflex ['ri:fleks], *a.* réfléchi; (*Paint.*) reflété; (*Physiol. etc.*) réflexe.—*n.* (*Paint.*) reflet; (*Physiol.*) réflexe, *m.*
reflexion [ri'flek∫ən], *n.* réflexion, *f.*; reflet (*lumière etc.*), *m.*; censure, *f.*; blâme, *m.*
reflexive [ri'fleksiv], *a.* réfléchi.
reform [ri'fɔ:m], *n.* réforme, *f.*—*v.t.* réformer; corriger.—*v.i.* se réformer, se corriger.
re-form [ri:'fɔ:m], *v.t.* reformer.—*v.i.* se reformer.
reformation [refə'mei∫ən], *n.* réformation; réforme, *f.*; *the Reformation*, (*Hist.*) la Réforme.
re-formation [ri:fɔ:'mei∫ən], *n.* formation nouvelle, *f.*
reformer [ri'fɔ:mə], *n.* réformateur, *m.*
refract [ri'frækt], *v.t.* réfracter.
refraction [ri'fræk∫ən], *n.* réfraction, *f.*
refractive [ri'fræktiv], *a.* réfractif; réfringent.
refractory [ri'fræktri], *a.* indocile, récalcitrant, intraitable, rebelle; (*Chem. etc.*) réfractaire; rétif (*cheval*).
refrain [ri'frein], *v.i.* se retenir, s'abstenir (*de*).—*n.* refrain, *m.*
refresh [ri'fre∫], *v.t.* rafraîchir; délasser, restaurer; *to refresh oneself*, se rafraîchir.
refreshing [ri'fre∫iŋ], *a.* rafraîchissant; réparateur, qui repose.
refreshment [ri'fre∫mənt], *n.* rafraîchissement, *m.*; *refreshment-bar*, buvette, *f.*; *refreshment-car*, wagon-restaurant, *m.*; *refreshment-room*, buffet, *m.*
refrigerate [ri'fridʒəreit], *v.t.* réfrigérer, frigorifier.
refrigeration [rifridʒə'rei∫ən], *n.* réfrigération, *f.*
refrigerator [ri'fridʒəreitə], *n.* réfrigérateur; (*fam.*) Frigidaire (*marque déposée*), *m.*
refuel [ri:'fjuəl], *v.i.* (*Av.*) faire le plein (d'essence).
refuge ['refju:dʒ], *n.* refuge (*contre*), *m.*; *to take refuge*, se réfugier.
refugee [refju'dʒi:], *n.* réfugié, *m.*
refulgence [ri'fʌldʒəns], *n.* éclat, *m.*, splendeur, *f.*
refulgent [ri'fʌldʒənt], *a.* éclatant.
refund [ri'fʌnd], *v.t.* rembourser, rendre.—['ri:fʌnd], *n.* remboursement, *m.*
refurnish [ri:'fə:ni∫], *v.t.* remeubler.
refusal [ri'fju:zl], *n.* refus, *m.*
refuse ['refju:s], *n.* rebut, *m.*, ordures (*ménagères, de marché*), *f.pl.*; *refuse dump*, voirie, *f.*—[ri'fju:z], *v.t.* refuser; rejeter.—*v.i.* refuser.
refute [ri'fju:t], *v.t.* réfuter.
regain [ri'gein], *v.t.* regagner, reprendre.
regal [ri:gl], *a.* royal.
regale [ri'geil], *v.t.* régaler.—*v.i.* se régaler.
regally ['ri:gəli], *adv.* royalement, en roi.
regard [ri'gɑ:d], *n.* égard, *m.*; considération, *f.*; respect (*estime*), *m.*; (*pl.*) amitiés, *f.pl.*, compliments, *m.pl.*; *out of regard for*, par égard pour; *with regard to*, quant à.—*v.t.* regarder; considérer; *as regards*, quant à.

regarding [ri'gɑ:diŋ], *prep.* quant à, concernant.
regardless [ri'gɑ:dlis], *a.* peu soigneux (*de*); sans égard (*pour*); *regardless of*, sans se soucier de.
regatta [ri'gætə], *n.* régate(s), *f.*(*pl.*).
regency ['ri:dʒənsi], *n.* régence, *f.*
regenerate [ri'dʒenərət], *a.* régénéré.—[ri'dʒenəreit], *v.t.* régénérer.
regenerating [ri'dʒenəreitiŋ], *a.* régénérateur.
regeneration [ridʒenə'rei∫ən], *n.* régénération, *f.*
regent ['ri:dʒənt], *n.* régent, *m.*
regicide ['redʒisaid], *n.* régicide (*crime*), *m.*; régicide (*personne*), *m.*, *f.*
régime [rei'ʒi:m], *n.* (*Polit.*) régime, *m.*
regimen ['redʒimən], *n.* (*Gram., Med.*) régime, *m.*
regiment ['redʒimənt], *n.* régiment, *m.*
regimental [redʒi'mentl], *a.* du régiment, de régiment.
regimentation [redʒimen'tei∫ən], *n.* enrégimentation, *f.*
Reginald ['redʒinəld]. Renaud, *m.*
region ['ri:dʒən], *n.* région, *f.*
regional ['ri:dʒənl], *a.* régional.
register ['redʒistə], *n.* registre, *m.*; liste électorale (*de votants*), *f.*—*v.t.* enregistrer; recommander (*lettre, paquet*); déclarer (*naissance*); immatriculer (*voiture*); déposer (*marque de fabrique etc.*).
registrar ['redʒistrɑ:], *n.* (*Law*) greffier; (*Univ.*) secrétaire et archiviste; officier de l'état civil (*de naissances etc.*), *m.*
registration [redʒis'trei∫ən], *n.* enregistrement; chargement (*de lettres*); dépôt (*d'une marque de fabrique etc.*), *m.*; immatriculation (*de véhicule*); inscription (*des bagages*), *f.*; *registration number*, (*Motor.*) numéro minéralogique, *m.*
registry ['redʒistri], *n.* enregistrement; (*Law*) greffe, *m.*
registry-office ['redʒistri'ɔfis], *n.* bureau de l'état civil, *m.*
regret [ri'gret], *n.* regret, *m.*—*v.t.* regretter (*de*), avoir du regret (*à*).
regretful [ri'gretful], *a.* plein de regrets; regrettable.
regretfully [ri'gretfuli], *adv.* avec regret, à regret.
regrettable [ri'gretəbl], *a.* fâcheux, regrettable.
regular ['regjulə], *a.* régulier; réglé; en règle; ordinaire (*normal*); (*fig.*) franc, fieffé.
regularity [regju'læriti], *n.* régularité, *f.*
regularly ['regjuləli], *adv.* régulièrement.
regulate ['regjuleit], *v.t.* régler; diriger.
regulation [regju'lei∫ən], *a.* réglementaire.—*n.* règlement, *m.*
regulator ['regjuleitə], *n.* régulateur, *m.*
rehabilitate [ri:hə'biliteit], *v.t.* réhabiliter.
rehabilitation [ri:həbili'tei∫ən], *n.* réhabilitation, *f.*
rehearsal [ri'hə:sl], *n.* récit, *m.*; (*Theat.*) répétition, *f.*; *dress rehearsal*, répétition générale.
rehearse [ri'hə:s], *v.t.* (*Theat.*) répéter; (*fig.*) raconter (*narrer*).
rehouse [ri:'hauz], *v.t.* reloger.
reign [rein], *n.* règne, *m.*—*v.i.* régner.

reigning ['reiniŋ], *a.* régnant; (*fig.*) dominant (*prevailing*).
reimburse [ri:im'bə:s], *v.t.* rembourser.
reimbursement [ri:im'bə:smənt], *n.* remboursement, *m.*
rein [rein], *n.* rêne, *f.*—*v.t.* conduire à la bride, gouverner, brider; contenir.
reincarnation [ri:inka:'neiʃən], *n.* réincarnation, *f.*
reindeer ['reindiə], *n.* renne, *m.*
reinforce [ri:in'fɔ:s], *v.t.* renforcer; *reinforced concrete*, béton armé, *m.*
reinforcement [ri:in'fɔ:smənt], *n.* renforcement; (*Mil.*) renfort, *m.*
reinstall [ri:in'stɔ:l], *v.t.* réinstaller.
reinstate [ri:in'steit], *v.t.* rétablir.
reinstatement [ri:in'steitmənt], *n.* rétablissement, *m.*
reintroduce [ri:intrə'dju:s], *v.t.* introduire de nouveau, réintroduire.
reinvest [ri:in'vest], *v.t.* replacer.
reinvigorate [ri:in'vigəreit], *v.t.* ranimer.
reissue [ri:'isju:], *v.t.* émettre de nouveau; rééditer (*livre*).—*n.* nouvelle émission; nouvelle édition, *f.*
reiterate [ri:'itəreit], *v.t.* réitérer.
reiteration [ri:itə'reiʃən], *n.* réitération, *f.*
reiterative [ri:'itərətiv], *a.* réitératif.
reject [ri'dʒekt], *v.t.* rejeter.—['ri:dʒekt], *n.* pièce de rebut, *f.*
rejection [ri'dʒekʃən], *n.* rejet, *m.*
rejoice [ri'dʒɔis], *v.t.* réjouir.—*v.i.* se réjouir (*de*).
rejoicing [ri'dʒɔisiŋ], *n.* réjouissance, joie, *f.*
rejoin [ri'dʒɔin], *v.t.* rejoindre.—[ri'dʒɔin], *v.i.* répliquer, répondre.
rejoinder [ri'dʒɔində], *n.* repartie; (*Law*) réplique, *f.*
rejuvenate [ri'dʒu:vəneit], *v.t.* rajeunir.
rejuvenation [ridʒu:və'neiʃən], *n.* rajeunissement, *m.*
rekindle [ri:'kindl], *v.t.* rallumer.
relapse ['ri'læps], *n.* rechute, *f.*—*v.i.* retomber (*dans*); récidiver (*criminel*).
relate [ri'leit], *v.t.* raconter; rapporter.—*v.i.* se rapporter, avoir rapport (*à*).
related [ri'leitid], *a.* ayant rapport; parent (*de*); allié (*à*) (*par mariage etc.*).
relating [ri'leitiŋ], *a.* relatif, qui se rapporte (*à*).
relation [ri'leiʃən], *n.* relation, *f.*, rapport; récit (*narration*); parent (*de la famille*); allié (*par mariage*), *m.*; (*pl.*) relations, *f.pl.*, rapports (*contact*), *m.pl.*
relationship [ri'leiʃənʃip], *n.* parenté, *f.*; rapport, *m.*
relative ['relətiv], *a.* relatif (*à*).—*n.* parent; (*Gram.*) relatif, *m.*
relatively ['relətivli], *adv.* relativement.
relativity [relə'tiviti], *n.* relativité, *f.*
relax [ri'læks], *v.t.* relâcher, détendre.—*v.i.* se relâcher; se détendre; se délasser.
relaxation [ri:læk'seiʃən], *n.* relâchement, relâche, *m.*, détente, *f.*; (*Med.*) repos, *m.*
relaxing [ri'læksiŋ], *a.* relâchant; énervant, débilitant (*climat*).
relay ['ri:lei], *n.* relais, *m.*—*v.t.* relayer.
re-lay [ri:'lei], *v.t.* poser de nouveau.
release [ri'li:s], *v.t.* relâcher, élargir (*un prisonnier*); décharger (*de*); déclencher.—*n.* élargissement, *m.*; délivrance; décharge

(*d'une obligation*); (*Cine.*) sortie (*d'un film*), *f.*; déclenchement (*de ressort etc.*), *m.*
relegate ['reləgeit], *v.t.* reléguer.
relegation [relə'geiʃən], *n.* relégation, *f.*
relent [ri'lent], *v.i.* s'amollir, s'attendrir; se repentir (*regretter*).
relenting [ri'lentiŋ], *n.* attendrissement, *m.*
relentless [ri'lentlis], *a.* inflexible, impitoyable.
relentlessly [ri'lentlisli], *adv.* impitoyablement.
relentlessness [ri'lentlisnis], *n.* rigueur, dureté, *f.*
relevance ['reləvəns], **relevancy** ['reləvənsi], *n.* relation, *f.*, rapport, *m.*; pertinence, convenance, *f.*, à-propos, *m.*
relevant ['reləvənt], *a.* relatif, applicable (*à*); à propos, pertinent.
reliable [ri'laiəbl], *a.* digne de confiance; sûr, exact, bien fondé (*renseignement*).
reliability [rilaiə'biliti], *n.* crédibilité, véracité; sûreté, *f.*
reliance [ri'laiəns], *n.* confiance, *f.*
relic ['relik], *n.* relique (*de saint* ou *martyr*), *f.*; (*pl.*) restes (*d'un être*); vestiges (*du passé*), *m.pl.*
relief [ri'li:f], *n.* soulagement (*de douleur etc.*); secours (*aide*), *m.*; (*Mil.*) relève, *f.*; (*Sculp. etc.*) relief, *m.*; *relief train*, train supplémentaire, *m.*
relieve [ri'li:v], *v.t.* soulager, adoucir; délivrer (*de*); secourir, aider (*assister*); (*Mil.*) relever (*sentinelle*).
religion [ri'lidʒən], *n.* religion, *f.*
religious [ri'lidʒəs], *a.* religieux; de religion.
religiously [ri'lidʒəsli], *adv.* religieusement.
relinquish [ri'liŋkwiʃ], *v.t.* abandonner; renoncer à.
relinquishment [ri'liŋkwiʃmənt], *n.* abandon, *m.*; renonciation, *f.*
reliquary ['relikwəri], *n.* reliquaire, *m.*
relish ['reliʃ], *n.* goût, *m.*, saveur, *f.*; (*Cook.*) assaisonnement, *m.*—(*fig.*) charme; appétit, *m.*—*v.t.* goûter, savourer; relever le goût de.
relive [ri:'liv], *v.t.* revivre.
reload [ri:'loud], *v.t.* recharger.
reluctance [ri'lʌktəns], *n.* répugnance, *f.*
reluctant [ri'lʌktənt], *a.* qui a de la répugnance,à, qui agit à contre-cœur; peu disposé (*à*).
reluctantly [ri'lʌktəntli], *adv.* à contre-cœur.
rely [ri'lai], *v.i.* compter (*sur*), avoir confiance (*en*).
remain [ri'mein], *v.i.* rester, demeurer.
remainder [ri'meində], *n.* reste, *m.*
remaining [ri'meiniŋ], *a.* de reste, restant.
remains [ri'meinz], *n.pl.* restes; débris, *m.pl.*; *mortal remains*, dépouille mortelle, *f.*
remake [ri:'meik], *v.t. irr.* (*conjug. like* MAKE) refaire.
remand [ri'ma:nd], *v.t.* renvoyer à une autre audience.—*n.* renvoi à une autre audience, *m.*
remark [ri'ma:k], *n.* remarque, *f.*—*v.t.* remarquer, observer; faire remarquer, faire observer (*à une personne*).
remarkable [ri'ma:kəbl], *a.* remarquable.
remarkably [ri'ma:kəbli], *adv.* remarquablement.
remarriage [ri:'mæridʒ], *n.* remariage, *m.*
remarry [ri:'mæri], *v.t.* épouser de nouveau.—*v.i.* se remarier.

remedial [ri'mi:djəl], *a.* réparateur; (*Med.*) curatif.

remedy ['remədi], *n.* remède; (*Law*) recours, *m.*—*v.t.* remédier à, porter remède à.

remember [ri'membə], *v.t.* se souvenir de, se rappeler; reconnaître (*de vue*).

remembrance [ri'membrəns], *n.* souvenir, *m.*, mémoire, *f.*

remind [ri'maind], *v.t.* rappeler à, faire souvenir (*à . . . de*), faire penser à.

reminder [ri'maində], *n.* mémento, *m.*

reminisce [remi'nis], *v.i.* raconter ses souvenirs.

reminiscence [remi'nisəns], *n.* réminiscence, *f.*

reminiscent [remi'nisənt], *a.* qui rappelle.

remiss [ri'mis], *a.* négligent.

remission [ri'miʃən], *n.* rémission, *f.*, pardon; relâchement (*détente*), *m.*; remise (*de dette, peine*), *f.*

remit [ri'mit], *v.t.* relâcher (*détendre*); remettre (*amende etc.*).—*v.i.* se relâcher, se calmer; diminuer.

remittance [ri'mitəns], *n.* remise, *f.*; envoi de fonds, *m.*

remittent [ri'mitənt], *a.* (*Path.*) rémittent.

remnant ['remnənt], *n.* reste; coupon, bout (*de tissu*), *m.*; (*pl.*) restes, débris, *m.pl.*

remodel [ri:'mɔdl], *v.t.* remodeler.

remonstrance [ri'mɔnstrəns], *n.* remontrance, *f.*

remonstrate ['remənstreit], *v.i.* remontrer.

remorse [ri'mɔːs], *n.* remords, *m.*

remorseful [ri'mɔːsful], *a.* rempli de remords.

remorseless [ri'mɔːslis], *a.* sans remords, impitoyable.

remorselessness [ri'mɔːslisnis], *n.* cruauté, inhumanité, *f.*

remote [ri'mout], *a.* éloigné, lointain; reculé (*époque*); distant (*personne*).

remotely [ri'moutli], *adv.* de loin; faiblement.

remoteness [ri'moutnis], *n.* éloignement, *m.*; réserve (*attitude*), *f.*

remould [ri:'mould], *v.t.* mouler de nouveau.

remount [ri:'maunt], *v.t., v.i.* remonter.—*n.* remonte, *f.*

removable [ri'mu:vəbl], *a.* transportable; (*fig.*) amovible (*fonctionnaire etc.*).

removal [ri'mu:vl], *n.* éloignement, départ; transport; déménagement (*de meubles*); déplacement, *m.*; révocation (*de ses fonctions*), *f.*

remove [ri'mu:v], *n.* degré (*parenté*), *m.*; distance, *f.*—*v.t.* éloigner; déplacer (*bouger*); transporter; déménager (*meubles*); ôter, enlever (*emporter*); renvoyer (*de ses fonctions*).—*v.i.* s'éloigner, se déplacer; déménager (*changer de domicile*).

removed [ri'mu:vd], *a.* éloigné; **first cousin once removed**, cousin issu de germains, *m.*

remover [ri'mu:və], *n.* déménageur, *m.*; **nail-varnish remover**, dissolvant (pour ongles), *m.*

remunerate [ri'mju:nəreit], *v.t.* rémunérer.

remuneration [rimju:nə'reiʃən], *n.* rétribution, rémunération, *f.*

remunerative [ri'mju:nərətiv], *a.* rémunérateur; (*Law*) rémunératoire.

rename [ri:'neim], *v.t.* renommer.

rend [rend], *v.t. irr.* déchirer; (*fig.*) fendre.

render ['rendə], *v.t.* rendre; interpréter, traduire; (*Cook.*) fondre (*graisse etc.*).

rendering ['rendəriŋ], *n.* traduction, interprétation, *f.*

renegade ['renigeid], *n.* renégat, *m.*

renew [ri'nju:], *v.t.* renouveler; renouer (*connaissance*).

renewal [ri'nju:əl], *n.* renouvellement, *m.*; **renewal of subscription**, réabonnement, *m.*

renounce [ri'nauns], *v.t.* renoncer (*à*); renier.

renouncement [ri'naunsmənt], *n.* renoncement, *m.*, renonciation, *f.*

renovate ['renəveit], *v.t.* renouveler; rajeunir.

renovation [renə'veiʃən], *n.* rénovation, *f.*

renovator ['renəveitə], *n.* rénovateur, *m.*

renown [ri'naun], *n.* renommée, *f.*, renom, *m.*

renowned [ri'naund], *a.* renommé.

rent (1) [rent], *n.* déchirure, fente, *f.*; accroc (*de vêtements*), *m.*

rent (2) [rent], *n.* loyer (*de maison ou d'appartement*); fermage (*de ferme*), *m.*; (*pl.*) rentes, *f.pl.*, revenu, *m.*; **ground-rent**, rente foncière, *f.*—*v.t.* louer, prendre à ferme, donner à ferme.—*v.i.* se louer.

rent (3) [rent], *past* and *p.p.* [REND].

rental [rentl], *n.* valeur locative, *f.*

rent-free ['rentfri:], *a.* exempt de loyer.

renunciation [rinʌnsi'eiʃən], *n.* renonciation, *f.*, renoncement, *m.*

reoccupation [ri:ɔkju'peiʃən], *n.* réoccupation, *f.*

reoccupy [ri:'ɔkjupai], *v.t.* réoccuper.

reopen [ri:'oupən], *v.t.* rouvrir.—*v.i.* rentrer (*écoles, tribunaux etc.*).

reopening [ri:'oupniŋ], *n.* réouverture; rentrée (*d'écoles etc.*), *f.*

reorganization [ri:ɔ:gənai'zeiʃən], *n.* réorganisation, *f.*

reorganize [ri:'ɔ:gənaiz], *v.t.* réorganiser.

rep (1) [rep], *a.* de reps.—*n.* reps (*tissu*), *m.*

rep (2) [rep], [REPERTORY].

rep (3) [rep], [REPRESENTATIVE].

repaint [ri:'peint], *v.t.* repeindre.

repair (1) [ri'pɛə], *v.t.* réparer; raccommoder (*vêtements etc.*); (*fig.*) rétablir.—*n.* réparation, *f.*; raccommodage (*de vêtements etc.*); **to keep in repair**, entretenir.

repair (2) [ri'pɛə], *n.* séjour (*retraite*), *m.*—*v.i.* aller; se rendre (*à*).

repairer [ri'pɛərə], *n.* réparateur; raccommodeur (*de vêtements*), *m.*

reparable ['repərəbl], *a.* réparable.

reparation [repə'reiʃən], *n.* réparation (*d'une offense*), *f.*

repartee [repɑ:'ti:], *n.* repartie, riposte, *f.*

repast [ri'pɑ:st], *n.* repas, *m.*

repatriate [ri'pætrieit], *v.t.* rapatrier.

repay [ri'pei], *v.t. irr.* (*conjug. like* PAY) rembourser; (*fig.*) valoir la peine (*de*).

repayment [ri:'peimənt], *n.* remboursement, *m.*

repeal [ri'pi:l], *v.t.* révoquer; abroger (*loi etc.*).—*n.* révocation; abrogation (*de loi*), *f.*

repeat [ri'pi:t], *v.t.* répéter, réitérer; réciter (*par cœur*); bis (*après vers de chanson etc.*).—*n.* répétition; (*Mus.*) reprise, *f.*

repeated [ri'pi:tid], *a.* répété, réitéré.

repeatedly [ri'pi:tidli], *adv.* à plusieurs reprises; souvent, bien des fois.

repeating [ri'pi:tiŋ], *a.* qui répète; à répétition.

repel [ri'pel], *v.t.* repousser; combattre.
repellent [ri'pelənt], *a.* répulsif, répugnant.—*n.* répulsif; (*Med.*) révulsif, *m.*
repent [ri'pent], *v.t.* se repentir de.—*v.i.* se repentir.
repentance [ri'pentəns], *n.* repentir, *m.*
repentant [ri'pentənt], *a.* répentant.
repercussion [ri:pə'kʌʃən], *n.* répercussion, *f.*
repertory ['repətri], *n.* répertoire, *m.*; *repertory theatre,* (*fam.*) *rep,* troupe à demeure, *f.*
repetition [repi'tiʃən], *n.* répétition; (*Mus.*) reprise, *f.*
repetitive [ri'petitiv], *a.* qui se répète.
repine [ri'pain], *v.i.* murmurer (*contre*); se plaindre (*de*).
repining [ri'painiŋ], *a.* disposé à se plaindre, mécontent.—*n.* plainte, *f.,* regret, *m.*
replace [ri:'pleis], *v.t.* replacer; remplacer (*substituer*).
replacement [ri:'pleismənt], *n.* remplacement, *m.*
replant [ri:'plɑ:nt], *v.t.* replanter.
replay ['ri:plei], *n.* match rejoué *m.*—[ri:'plei], *v.t., v.i.* rejouer.
replenish [ri'pleniʃ], *v.t.* remplir (*de*).—*v.i.* se remplir.
replenishment [ri'pleniʃmənt], *n.* remplissage, *m.*
replete [ri'pli:t], *a.* plein, rempli (*de*).
repletion [ri'pli:ʃən], *n.* plénitude; (*Med.*) réplétion, *f.*
replica ['replikə], *n.* double, *m.,* copie, *f.*
reply [ri'plai], *n.* réponse; (*Law*) réplique, *f.* —*v.t., v.i.* répondre, répliquer.
repopulate [ri:'pɔpjuleit], *v.t.* repeupler.
report [ri'pɔ:t], *v.t.* rapporter, raconter, dire; rendre compte de; signaler; dénoncer (à *la police*); *to report oneself,* se présenter à.—*n.* rapport; bruit, ouï-dire (*rumeur*); compte rendu, procès-verbal (*de réunion etc.*); (*Sch.*) bulletin; coup (*de fusil*), *m.*; réputation (*renom*), *f.*
reporter [ri'pɔ:tə], *n.* rapporteur; reporter (*journaliste*), *m.*
reporting [ri'pɔ:tiŋ], *n.* reportage, *m.*
repose [ri'pouz], *v.t.* reposer.—*v.i.* se reposer. —*n.* repos, *m.*
repository [ri'pɔzitri], *n.* dépôt, *m.*
repossess [ri:pə'zes], *v.t.* rentrer en possession de.
reprehend [repri'hend], *v.t.* réprimander, censurer, blâmer (*de*).
reprehensible [repri'hensibl], *a.* répréhensible, blâmable.
represent [repri'zent], *v.t.* représenter.
representation [reprizen'teiʃən], *n.* représentation, *f.*
representative [repri'zentətiv], *a.* représentatif, qui représente.—*n.* représentant; (*Comm.*) (*fam. abbr.* **rep**) agent, *m.*
repress [ri'pres], *v.t.* réprimer.
repression [ri'preʃən], *n.* répression, *f.*
repressive [ri'presiv], *a.* répressif.
reprieve [ri'pri:v], *n.* sursis; répit, *m.*—*v.t.* accorder un sursis à; commuer (*une peine*), grâcier.
reprimand ['reprimɑ:nd], *n.* réprimande *f.* —[repri'mɑ:nd], *v.t.* réprimander.
reprint ['ri:print], *n.* réimpression, *f.*—[ri:'print], *v.t.* réimprimer.
reprisal [ri'praizl], *n.* représailles, *f.pl.*

reproach [ri'proutʃ], *n.* reproche; opprobre (*honte*), *m.*; *above reproach,* irréprochable. —*v.t.* reprocher.
reprobate ['reprəbit], *n.* vaurien, *m.*
reprobation [reprə'beiʃən], *n.* réprobation, *f.*
reproduce [ri:prə'dju:s], *v.t.* reproduire.—*v.i.* se reproduire.
reproduction [ri:prə'dʌkʃən], *n.* reproduction, *f.*
reproductive [ri:prə'dʌktiv], *a.* reproducteur.
reproof [ri'pru:f], *n.* reproche, *m.,* réprimande, *f.*
reprove [ri'pru:v], *v.t.* blâmer; censurer.
reproving [ri'pru:viŋ], *a.* réprobateur.
reprovingly [ri'pru:viŋli], *adv.* d'un air *ou* ton réprobateur.
reptile ['reptail], *a.* reptile; (*fig.*) rampant, vil.—*n.* reptile, *m.*
reptilian [rep'tiliən], *a.* reptilien.
republic [ri'pʌblik], *n.* république, *f.*
republican [ri'pʌblikən], *a.* and *n.* républicain, *m.*
republication [ri:pʌbli'keiʃən], *n.* nouvelle édition, réimpression (*de livre*), *f.*
republish [ri:pʌbliʃ], *v.t.* republier, rééditer.
repudiate [ri'pju:dieit], *v.t.* répudier.
repudiation [ripju:di'eiʃən], *n.* répudiation, *f.*
repugnance [ri'pʌgnəns], *n.* répugnance, *f.*
repugnant [ri'pʌgnənt], *a.* répugnant.
repulse [ri'pʌls], *v.t.* repousser, rebuter.—*n.* échec, refus, *m.,* rebuffade, *f.*; *to meet with a repulse,* essuyer un échec.
repulsion [ri'pʌlʃən], *n.* répulsion, *f.*
repulsive [ri'pʌlsiv], *a.* rebutant; repoussant (*forbidding*).
repulsiveness [ri'pʌlsivnis], *n.* caractère repoussant, *m.*
repurchase [ri:'pɔ:tʃis], *v.t.* racheter.—*n.* rachat; (*Law*) réméré, *m.*
reputable ['repjutəbl], *a.* honourable, de bonne réputation, considéré.
reputably ['repjutəbli], *adv.* honorablement.
reputation [repju'teiʃən], *n.* réputation, *f.*
repute [ri'pju:t], *v.t.* (*usu. pass.*) réputer, estimer.—*n.* réputation, *f.,* renom, *m.*
reputed [ri'pju:tid], *a.* réputé, censé, qui passe pour.
request [ri'kwest], *n.* demande, prière; (*Law*) requête, *f.*; *request stop,* arrêt facultatif (*autobus*), *m.*—*v.t.* demander; prier.
requiem ['rekwiem], *n.* requiem, *m.*
require [ri'kwaiə], *v.t.* exiger, requérir; avoir besoin de (*manquer de*); (*impers.*) falloir.
requirement [ri'kwaiəmənt], *n.* exigence, nécessité, *f.,* besoin, *m.*; condition requise, *f.*
requisite ['rekwizit], *a.* requis, exigé, nécessaire.—*n.* qualité *ou* condition requise; chose requise, *f.*
requisition [rekwi'ziʃən], *n.* réquisition, *f.*— *v.t.* réquisitionner.
requital [ri'kwaitl], *n.* récompense, *f.*
requite [ri'kwait], *v.t.* récompenser; rendre la pareille à; payer de retour.
reredos ['riədɔs], *n.* retable, *m.*
rescind [ri'sind], *v.t.* rescinder, annuler.
rescue ['reskju:], *n.* délivrance, *f.*; sauvetage, *m.*; *to the rescue,* au secours!—*v.t.* sauver, délivrer (*de*).
rescuer ['reskju:ə], *n.* sauveteur, libérateur, *m.*
research [ri'sə:tʃ], *n.* recherche, *f.*—*v.i.* faire des recherches.

reseat [ri:'si:t], *v.t.* rasseoir.
resemblance [ri'zembləns], *n.* ressemblance, *f.*; (*fig.*) rapport, *m.*
resemble [ri'zembl], *v.t.* ressembler (*à*); *to resemble each other*, se ressembler.
resent [ri'zent], *v.t.* ressentir, se ressentir de; s'offenser de; prendre en mauvaise part.
resentful [ri'zentful], *a.* rancunier.
resentfully [ri'zentfuli], *adv.* avec ressentiment.
resentment [ri'zentmənt], *n.* ressentiment, *m.*, rancœur, *f.*
reservation [rezə'veiʃən], *n.* réserve, restriction, arrière-pensée, *f.*; (*Am.*) terrain réservé, *m.*; réservation, location (*place assise*), *f.*
reserve [ri'zə:v], *n.* réserve; retenue, prudence; arrière-pensée, *f.*—*v.t.* réserver.
reserved [ri'zə:vd], *a.* réservé.
reservedly [ri'zə:vidli], *adv.* avec réserve.
reservist [ri'zə:vist], *n.* réserviste, *m.*, *f.*
reservoir ['rezəvwɑ:], *n.* réservoir, *m.*
reset [ri:'set], *v.t. irr.* (*conjug. like* SET) poser *ou* fixer de nouveau; (*Print.*) composer de nouveau; (*Surg.*) remettre.
resetting [ri:'setiŋ], *n.* remontage (*de pierre précieuse*), *m.*; (*Print.*) recomposition, *f.*
resettle [ri:'setl], *v.t.* rétablir.—*v.i.* s'établir de nouveau.
resettlement [ri:'setlmənt], *n.* rétablissement, *m.*
reshape [ri:'ʃeip], *v.t.* reformer; remanier.
reside [ri'zaid], *v.i.* résider, demeurer.
residence ['rezidəns], *n.* résidence, demeure, *f.*; *board* (*and*) *residence*, la table et le logement.
resident ['rezidənt], *a.* résidant; interne (*de la maison*).—*n.* habitant; résident, *m.*
residential [rezi'denʃl], *a.* résidentiel.
residual [ri'zidjuəl], *a.* résiduel.
residuary [ri'zidjuəri], *a.* de résidu, de reste; universel (*légataire*).
residue ['rezidju:], *n.* reste, (*Chem.*) résidu; reliquat (*de dette*), *m.*
resign [ri'zain], *v.t.* donner sa démission de; renoncer à; *to be resigned to* or *resign oneself to*, se résigner à.—*v.i.* donner sa démission, démissionner (*de*).
resignation [rezig'neiʃən], *n.* résignation; cession; démission (*de ses fonctions*), *f.*
resigned [ri'zaind], *a.* résigné; démissionnaire (*d'un poste*).
resilience [ri'ziliəns], **resiliency** [ri'ziliənsi], *n.* rebondissement, *m.*; élasticité, *f.*
resilient [ri'ziliənt], *a.* rebondissant.
resin ['rezin], *n.* résine; colophane (*pour violons*), *f.*
resist [ri'zist], *v.t.* résister à.—*v.i.* résister.
resistance [ri'zistəns], *n.* résistance, *f.*
resistant [ri'zistənt], *a.* résistant.
re-sole [ri:'soul], *v.t.* ressemeler.
resolute ['rezəlju:t], *a.* déterminé, résolu.
resolutely ['rezəlju:tli], *adv.* résolument.
resoluteness ['rezəlju:tnis], *n.* résolution, fermeté, *f.*
resolution [rezə'lju:ʃən], *n.* résolution; décision (*d'assemblée*), *f.*
resolve [ri'zɔlv], *n.* résolution, *f.*—*v.t.* résoudre; fondre (*liquéfier*); éclaircir, dissiper (*doutes etc.*); déterminer, décider (*assemblée*). —*v.i.* se résoudre, se décider; se fondre (*se dissoudre*).

resolved [ri'zɔlvd], *a.* résolu.
resolvent [ri'zɔlvənt], *n.* (*Med.*) résolvant, *m.*
resonance ['rezənəns], *n.* résonance, *f.*
resonant ['rezənənt], *a.* résonnant, sonore.
resort [ri'zɔ:t], *n.* ressource, *f.*, recours; séjour, rendezvous (*endroit*); (*Law*) ressort, *m.*; *seaside resort*, station balnéaire, plage, *f.*—*v.i.* recourir, avoir recours (*à*); se rendre, aller (*à*).
resound [ri'zaund], *v.i.* résonner, retentir.
resounding [ri'zaundiŋ], *a.* retentissant.—*n.* retentissement, *m.*
resource [ri'sɔ:s], *n.* ressource, *f.*
resourceful [ri'sɔ:sful], *a.* plein de ressources.
respect [ri'spekt], *n.* respect, *m.*, estime, *f.*; égard, *m.*; (*pl.*) respects, hommages, *m.pl.*; *in every respect*, sous tous les rapports; *in respect of*, à l'égard de.—*v.t.* respecter, considérer, avoir égard à.
respectability [rispektə'biliti], *n.* honorabilité, *f.*; convenances, *f.pl.*; bienséance, *f.*
respectable [ri'spektəbl], *a.* respectable, honorable; comme il faut, convenable.
respectably [ri'spektəbli], *adv.* comme il faut, très bien.
respectful [ri'spektful], *a.* respectueux.
respectfully [ri'spektfuli], *adv.* avec respect; *yours respectfully* (*à un supérieur hiérarchique*), veuillez agréer, Monsieur, l'assurance de mes sentiments respectueux.
respecting [ri'spektiŋ], *prep.* à l'égard de, quant à, touchant.
respective [ri'spektiv], *a.* respectif, relatif.
respectively [ri'spektivli], *adv.* respectivement.
respiration [respi'reiʃən], *n.* respiration, *f.*
respirator ['respireitə], *n.* respirateur, *m.*
respiratory ['respirətri], *a.* respiratoire.
respire [ri'spaiə], *v.t.*, *v.i.* respirer.
respite ['respit], *n.* répit, relâche; (*Law*) sursis, *m.*
resplendence [ri'splendəns], *n.* éclat, *m.*, splendeur, *f.*
resplendent [ri'splendənt], *a.* resplendissant (*de*).
respond [ri'spɔnd], *v.i.* répondre (*à*).
respondent [ri'spɔndənt], *n.* répondant; (*Law*) défendeur, *m.*
response [ri'spɔns], *n.* réponse, *f.*; (*fig.*) écho; (*Eccles.*) répons, *m.*
responsibility [risɔnsi'biliti], *n.* responsabilité, *f.*
responsible [ri'spɔnsibl], *a.* chargé (*de*), responsable (*de*); digne de confiance.
responsive [ri'spɔnsiv], *a.* sensible, facile à émouvoir.
rest (1) [rest], *n.* repos, *m.*; (*Mus.*) pause, *f.*; appui (*soutien*), *m.*; *at rest*, en repos.—*v.t.* reposer; faire reposer; (*fig.*) fonder.—*v.i.* se reposer; s'appuyer; *it rests with me to...*, c'est à moi de...; *to rest assured*, être assuré.
rest (2) [rest], *n.* reste, restant, *m.*; les autres, *m.pl.*—*v.i.* demeurer, rester.
restart [ri:'stɑ:t], *v.t.*, *v.i.* recommencer.
restaurant ['restɔrɑ̃:], *n.* restaurant, *m.*
restful ['restful], *a.* qui donne du repos, paisible.
resting ['restiŋ], *a.* couché, se reposant; appuyé, s'appuyant.—*n.* repos, *m.*
resting-place ['restiŋpleis], *n.* lieu de repos, gîte, *m.*

restitution [resti'tju:ʃən], *n.* restitution, *f.*
restive ['restiv], *a.* rétif; inquiet.
restiveness ['restivnis], *n.* naturel rétif, *m.*; nervosité, *f.*
restless ['restlis], *a.* sans repos; inquiet; agité.
restlessly ['restlisli], *adv.* sans repos.
restlessness ['restlisnis], *n.* agitation; insomnie, *f.*
restock [ri:'stɔk], *v.t.* repeupler (*chasse réservée*); regarnir (*boutique*), réassortir.
restoration [restə'reiʃən], *n.* restauration, *f.*; rétablissement, *m.*; restitution (*après une perte injuste*), *f.*
restorative [ri'stɔːrətiv], *a.* and *n.* fortifiant, *m.*
restore [ri'stɔː], *v.t.* restituer, rendre (*redonner*); ramener (*personne*); restaurer (*bâtiment etc.*); remettre (*replacer*); rétablir.
restorer [ri'stɔːrə], *n.* restaurateur, *m.*
restrain [ri'strein], *v.t.* retenir, contenir; **to restrain from,** empêcher de; **to restrain oneself,** se contraindre, se contenir.
restraining [ri'streiniŋ], *a.* qui restreint, restrictif.
restraint [ri'streint], *n.* contrainte; gêne, *f.*
restrict [ri'strikt], *v.t.* restreindre.
restriction [ri'strikʃən], *n.* restriction, *f.*
restrictive [ri'striktiv], *a.* restrictif.
result [ri'zʌlt], *n.* résultat, *m.*; **as a result of,** par suite de.—*v.i.* résulter; **to result in,** aboutir à.
resultant [ri'zʌltənt], *a.* résultant.—*n.* résultante, *f.*
resume [ri'zju:m], *v.t.* reprendre, renouer, continuer.
resumption [ri'zʌmpʃən], *n.* reprise, *f.*
resurface [ri:'səːfis], *v.t.* remettre en état (*route*).—*v.i.* remonter à la surface.
resurgence [ri:'səːdʒəns], *n.* résurrection, *f.*
resurrect [rezə'rekt], *v.t.* ranimer, ressusciter.
resurrection [rezə'rekʃən], *n.* résurrection, *f.*
resuscitate [ri'sʌsiteit], *v.t.* ressusciter.
resuscitation [risʌsi'teiʃən], *n.* résurrection; renaissance (*des arts etc.*); (*Med.*) ressuscitation, *f.*
retail ['ri:teil], *a.* en détail; **retail price,** prix de détail *m.*—*n.* détail, *m.*, vente au détail, *f.*—[ri'teil], *v.t.* vendre en détail, détailler; (*fig.*) débiter; colporter (*nouvelles*).
retailer [ri'teilə], *n.* détaillant; colporteur (*de nouvelles*), *m.*
retain [ri'tein], *v.t.* retenir; engager (*en payant des arrhes*).
retainer [ri'teinə], *n.* serviteur, dépendant, *m.*; honoraires donnés d'avance (*acompte*), *m.pl.*
retaining [ri'teiniŋ], *a.* qui retient; **retaining wall,** mur de soutènement, *m.*
retake [ri:'teik], *v.t. irr.* (*conjug. like* TAKE) reprendre; (*Cine.*) retourner (*un plan*).
retaking [ri:'teikiŋ], *n.* reprise, *f.*
retaliate [ri'tælieit], *v.i.* rendre la pareille à.
retaliation [ritæli'eiʃən], *n.* représailles, *f.pl.*
retaliatory [ri'tæliətəri], *a.* de représailles.
retard [ri'tɑːd], *v.t.* retarder.
retch [ri:tʃ], *v.i.* avoir des haut-le-cœur.
retching ['ri:tʃiŋ], *n.* haut-le-cœur, *m.*
retell [ri:'tel], *v.t. irr.* (*conjug. like* TELL) redire, répéter.
retention [ri'tenʃən], *n.* conservation; (*Med.*) rétention, *f.*

retentive [ri'tentiv], *a.* qui retient; tenace, fidèle (*la mémoire*).
retentiveness [ri'tentivnis], *n.* pouvoir de rétention, *m.*; fidélité (*de la mémoire*), *f.*
reticence ['retisəns], *n.* réticence, *f.*
reticent ['retisənt], *a.* réservé, taciturne.
reticular [re'tikjulə], *a.* réticulaire.
reticulate [re'tikjulit], *a.* réticulé.
retina ['retinə], *n.* rétine, *f.*
retinue ['retinju:], *n.* suite, *f.*; cortège, *m.*
retire [ri'taiə], *v.t.* retirer.—*v.i.* se retirer, prendre sa retraite.
retired [ri'taiəd], *a.* retiré, retraité (*qui a pris sa retraite*); ancien (*qui n'exerce plus cette profession*); **on the retired list,** en retraite.
retirement [ri'taiəmənt], *n.* retraite; (*fig.*) solitude, *f.*
retiring [ri'taiəriŋ], *a.* réservé, timide, modeste; sortant (*d'un emploi*).
retort (1) [ri'tɔːt], *n.* réplique, riposte, *f.*—*v.i.* riposter, répliquer.
retort (2) [ri'tɔːt], *n.* (*Chem.*) cornue, *f.*
retouch [ri'tʌtʃ], *v.t.* retoucher.
retrace [ri'treis], *v.t.* (*Paint.*) retracer; **to retrace one's steps,** revenir sur ses pas, rebrousser chemin.
retract [ri'trækt], *v.t.* rétracter.—*v.i.* se rétracter, se dédire.
retractable [ri'træktebl], *a.* (*Av.*) escamotable.
retransmit [ri:træns'mit], *v.t.* retransmettre.
retread [ri:'tred], *v.t.* (*Motor.*) rechaper (*pneu*).—['ri:tred], *n.* pneu rechapé, *m.*
retreat [ri'tri:t], *n.* retraite, *f.*—*v.i.* se retirer (*à ou dans*); (*Mil.*) battre en retraite.
retreating [ri'tri:tiŋ], *a.* qui bat en retraite; fuyant (*le front*).
retrench [ri'trentʃ], *v.t.* retrancher.—*v.i.* se retrancher.
retrenchment [ri'trentʃmənt], *n.* retranchement, *m.*
retribution [retri'bju:ʃən], *n.* récompense, rétribution, *f.*; (*fig.*) châtiment, *m.*, vengeance, *f.*
retrievable [ri'tri:vəbl], *a.* recouvrable (*argent*); réparable (*perte*).
retrieve [ri'tri:v], *v.t.* rétablir; réparer (*chose brisée*); recouvrer (*chose perdue*); rapporter (*chien*).
retriever [ri'tri:və], *n.* chien rapporteur, *m.*
retroaction [ri:trou'ækʃən], *n.* rétroaction, *f.*
retroactive [ri:trou'æktiv], *a.* rétroactif.
retrograde ['retrogreid], *a.* rétrograde.
retrogression [retro'greʃən], *n.* rétrogression, rétrogradation, *f.*
retrogressive [retro'gresiv], *a.* rétrogressif.
retrospect ['retrospekt], *n.* regard jeté en arrière, *m.*; revue, *f.*; **in retrospect,** en rétrospective.
retrospective [retro'spektiv], *a.* rétrospectif; (*Law*) rétroactif.
retrospectively [retro'spektivli], *adv.* rétrospectivement; (*Law*) rétroactivement.
retroversion [retro'vəːʃən], *n.* renversement, *m.*
retrovert [retro'vəːt], *v.t.* renverser.
return [ri'təːn], *v.t.* rendre; renvoyer; rembourser (*argent etc.*); rapporter (*intérêt*); (*Comm.*) rendre compte; élire (*candidat*); **he was returned,** il fut élu.—*v.i.* revenir; retourner; rentrer.—*n.* retour, rentrée, *f.*; renvoi, *m.*; remise en place (*chose déplacée*), *f.*; profit, *m.*; restitution, *f.*; remboursement,

m.; élection, *f.*; rapport, relevé, état (*impôts etc.*); bilan (*de banque*); (*pl.*) produit, *m.*; *by return of post*, par retour du courrier; *in return for*, en retour de; *nil return*, état néant; *on sale or return*, en dépôt; *return journey*, retour; *return match*, revanche, *f.*; *return ticket*, billet d'aller et retour, *m.*

returnable [ri'təːnəbl], *a.* restituable.
reunion [riːˈjuːniən], *n.* réunion, *f.*
reunite [riːjuˈnait], *v.t.* réunir.—*v.i.* se réunir.
rev [rev], *n.* (*colloq., Motor.*) tour, *m.*—*v.t. to rev the engine*, faire s'emballer le moteur.
   —*v.i.* s'emballer.
reveal [ri'viːl], *v.t.* révéler.
reveille [ri'væli], *n.* réveil, *m.*
revel [revl], *n.* (*pl.*) divertissements, *m.pl.*—*v.i.* se réjouir, se divertir; *to revel in*, se délecter à.
revelation [revəˈleiʃən], *n.* révélation, *f.*; *Book of Revelation*, Apocalypse, *f.*
reveller ['revələ], *n.* joyeux convive, *m.*
revelry ['revəlri], *n.* réjouissances, *f.pl.*, joyeux ébats, *m.pl.*
revenge [ri'vendʒ], *n.* vengeance; (*Spt.*) revanche, *f.*—*v.t.* venger; se venger de; *to revenge oneself on*, se venger de.
revengeful [ri'vendʒful], *a.* vindicatif.
revengefully [ri'vendʒfuli], *adv.* par vengeance.
revenue ['revənjuː], *n.* revenu; (*State*) fisc, trésor, *m.*; *revenue-officer*, officier de la douane, *m.*
reverberate [ri'vəːbəreit], *v.t.* réverbérer; renvoyer (*son, chaleur etc.*).—*v.i.* se répercuter.
reverberation [rivəːbəˈreiʃən], *n.* réverbération (*de chaleur*); répercussion, *f.*
revere [ri'viə], *v.t.* révérer, vénérer.
reverence ['revərəns], *n.* révérence, *f.*
reverend ['revərənd], *a.* révérend (*titre ecclésiastique*).
reverent ['revərənt], *a.* révérencieux.
reverently ['revərəntli], *adv.* avec révérence.
reverie ['revəri], *n.* rêverie, *f.*
reversal [ri'vəːsl], *n.* annulation; cassation, *f.*
reverse [ri'vəːs], *a.* contraire, opposé.—*n.* revers, *m.*; défaite, *f.*; *quite the reverse*, tout le contraire (*de*); *the reverse way*, en sens inverse.—*v.t.* renverser; appliquer en sens inverse; (*Law*) infirmer, casser.—*v.i.* (*Motor.*) faire marche *ou* machine en arrière.
reversed [ri'vəːst], *a.* renversé; inverse.
reversible [ri'vəːsibl], *a.* révocable, réversible, à double face (*tissu*).
reversion [ri'vəːʃən], *n.* réversion, *f.*
revert [ri'vəːt], *v.i.* revenir (*sur*).
revertible [ri'vəːtibl], *a.* réversible.
revetment [ri'vetmənt], *n.* revêtement, *m.*
revictual [riːˈvitl], *v.t.* ravitailler.
revictualling [riːˈvitliŋ], *n.* ravitaillement, *m.*
review [ri'vjuː], *n.* revue, revision; critique; revue, *f.*, périodique, *m.*—*v.t.* revoir, reviser; passer en revue; analyser, critiquer (*livre etc.*).
reviewer [ri'vjuːə], *n.* critique, *m., f.*
revile [ri'vail], *v.t.* injurier, insulter, outrager.
revilement [ri'vailmənt], *n.* injure, insulte, *f.*
reviling [ri'vailiŋ], *a.* diffamatoire, outrageant.
   —*n.* insultes, injures, *f.pl.*
revisal [ri'vaizl], *n.* revision, *f.*
revise [ri'vaiz], *v.t.* revoir, reviser, réviser.

reviser [ri'vaizə], *n.* personne qui revoit, *f.*, reviseur, *m.*
revision [ri'viʒən], *n.* revision, révision, *f.*
revisit [riːˈvizit], *v.t.* revisiter, retourner voir.
revitalize [riːˈvaitəlaiz], *v.t.* revivifier.
revival [ri'vaivl], *n.* rétablissement, *m.*; renaissance (*des arts*); reprise (*d'une pièce*), *f.*; réveil (*religieux*), *m.*
revive [ri'vaiv], *v.t.* ressusciter; raviver.—*v.i.* se ranimer; renaître (*arts etc.*).
revivify [ri'vivifai], *v.t.* revivifier.
revocable ['revəkəbl], *a.* révocable.
revocation [revəˈkeiʃən], *n.* révocation, *f.*
revoke [ri'vouk], *v.t.* révoquer.—*v.i.* (*Cards*) renoncer.—*n.* (*Cards*) renonce, *f.*
revolt [ri'voult], *n.* révolte, *f.*—*v.i.* se révolter, se soulever.
revolting [ri'voultiŋ], *a.* révoltant.
revolution [revəˈljuːʃən], *n.* révolution, *f.*; tour (*de roue*), *m.*
revolutionary [revəˈljuːʃənəri], *a.* and *n.* révolutionnaire, *m., f.*
revolve [ri'vɔlv], *v.t.* tourner; retourner, repasser, rouler (*dans l'esprit*).—*v.i.* tourner; (*fig.*) retourner, revenir.
revolver [ri'vɔlvə], *n.* revolver, *m.*
revolving [ri'vɔlviŋ], *a.* tournant.
revue [ri'vjuː], *n.* (*Theat.*) revue, *f.*
revulsion [ri'vʌlʃən], *n.* révulsion, *f.*
reward [ri'wɔːd], *n.* récompense, *f.*; prix, *m.*—*v.t.* récompenser (*de*).
rewind [riːˈwaind], *v.t. irr.* (*conjug. like* WIND) rebobiner (*soie etc.*); remonter (*montre, horloge*); rembobiner (*film*).
rewrite [riːˈrait], *v.t. irr.* (*conjug. like* WRITE) récrire.
rhapsody ['ræpsədi], *n.* rapsodie, *f.*
Rheims [riːmz]. Reims, *m.*
Rhenish ['reniʃ], *a.* du Rhin.—*n.* vin du Rhin, *m.*
rheostat ['riːostæt], *n.* rhéostat, *m.*
rhesus ['riːsəs], *n.* (*Med.*) rhésus.
rhetoric ['retərik], *n.* rhétorique, *f.*
rhetorical [ri'tɔrikl], *a.* de rhétorique; *rhetorical question*, question de pure forme, *f.*
rheum [ruːm], *n.* rhume, catarrhe, *m.*
rheumatic [ruːˈmætik], *a.* rhumatismal; *rheumatic fever*, rhumatisme articulaire aigu, *m.*
rheumatism ['ruːmətizm], *n.* rhumatisme, *m.*
rheumatoid ['ruːmətɔid], *a.* rhumatoïde; *rheumatoid arthritis*, rhumatisme articulaire, *m.*
Rhine [rain]. the. le Rhin, *m.*
Rhineland ['rainlænd]. la Rhénanie, *f.*
Rhinelander ['rainlændə], *n.* Rhénan, *m.*
rhinoceros [rai'nɔsərəs], *n.* rhinocéros, *m.*
Rhodesia [rou'diːziə]. la Rhodésie, *f.*
Rhodesian [rou'diːziən], *a.* rhodésien.—*n.* Rhodésien (*personne*), *m.*
rhododendron [roudə'dendrən], *n.* rhododendron, *m.*
rhombus ['rɔmbəs], *n.* losange, *m.*
Rhone [roun]. le Rhône, *m.*
rhubarb ['ruːbɑːb], *n.* rhubarbe, *f.*
rhyme [raim], *n.* rime, *f.*; (*pl.*) vers, *m.pl.*—*v.t., v.i.* rimer; rimailler.
rhythm [riðm], *n.* rythme, *m.*; cadence, *f.*
rhythmical [ˈriðmikl], *a.* rythmique.
rhythmically [ˈriðmikli], *adv.* avec rythme.
rib [rib], *n.* côte; baleine (*de parapluie*), *f.*

ribald ['ribəld], *a*. grossier, obscène.

ribaldry ['ribəldri], *n*. obscénités, *f.pl.*

ribbed [ribd], *a*. à côtes.

ribbon ['ribən], *n*. ruban; cordon (*de médaille*); lambeau (*morceau de tissu déchiré*), *m.*

rice [rais], *n*. riz, *m*.; *rice-field*, rizière, *f.*

rich [ritʃ], *a*. riche; fertile, fécond (*terre*); de haut goût (*fort assaisonné*); voyant (*couleur*); (*fig.*) délicieux, généreux (*vin*); *the rich*, les riches, *m.pl.*; *to grow rich*, s'enrichir.

riches ['ritʃiz], *n.pl.* richesse, *f.*

richly ['ritʃli], *adv*. richement; grandement; (*fam.*) joliment.

richness ['ritʃnis], *n*. richesse; fécondité, *f.*; haut goût, *m.*

rick [rik], *n*. meule, *f.*

rickets ['rikits], *n.pl.* rachitis, rachitisme, *m.*

rickety ['rikiti], *a*. (*fig.*) boiteux (*meuble*).

rickshaw ['rikʃɔː], *n*. pousse-pousse, *m.*

ricochet ['rikəʃei], *n*. ricochet, *m.—v.i.* ricocher.

rid [rid], *v.t. irr.* délivrer, débarrasser; *to get rid of*, se débarrasser de.

riddance ['ridəns], *n*. débarras, *m.*

riddle (1) [ridl], *n.* énigme, *f.*

riddle (2) [ridl], *v.t.* cribler.—*n.* crible, *m.*

ride [raid], *v.t. irr.* monter, être monté sur; mener, conduire; faire (*une distance précise*). —*v.i.* monter (*à cheval, à bicyclette etc.*), aller, venir, être *ou* se promener (*à cheval, à bicyclette, en voiture etc.*); être monté (*sur*); flotter, voguer (*sur*); être (à l'ancre); *to ride away*, partir, s'en aller; *to ride back*, revenir, s'en retourner.—*n.* promenade, course (*à cheval, en voiture, à bicyclette etc.*), *f.*; trajet, *m.*; allée cavalière (*sentier dans un bois etc.*), *f.*

rider ['raidə], *n*. cavalier, *m.*, cavalière, *f.*; écuyer, *m.*, écuyère (*de cirque*), *f.*; jockey; codicille (*document*), *m.*

riderless ['raidəlis], *a.* sans cavalier.

ridge [ridʒ], *n.* sommet (*pic*), *m.*, cime; chaîne (*de montagnes*); arête, crête (*d'une montagne*) *f.*; faîte (*de toit*); (*Agric.*) sillon, billon, *m.—v.t.* sillonner.

ridicule ['ridikjuːl], *n.* ridicule, *m.—v.t.* tourner en ridicule, ridiculiser.

ridiculous [ri'dikjuləs], *a.* ridicule.

ridiculously [ri'dikjuləsli], *adv.* ridiculement.

riding (1) ['raidiŋ], *n.* promenade à cheval, *f.*, exercice à cheval, *m.*, équitation, *f.*; (*Naut.*) mouillage, *m.*

riding (2) ['raidiŋ], *n.* (*Yorkshire*) arrondissement, *m.*

riding-habit ['raidiŋhæbit], *n.* amazone, *f.*

riding-hood ['raidiŋhud], *n.* capuchon, *m.*; *Little Red Riding Hood*, le petit Chaperon rouge.

rife [raif], *a.* abondant, répandu; *to be rife*, régner (*tumulte etc.*), courir (*bruit*).

riff-raff ['rifræf], *n.* racaille, canaille, *f.*

rifle (1) [raifl], *v.t.* piller, dévaliser.

rifle (2) [raifl], *v.t.* rayer (*armes à feu*).—*n.* fusil (rayé), *m.*, carabine, *f.*; *rifle-gallery* or *-range*, tir, *m.*; *rifle-practice* or *-shooting*, tir au fusil, tir à la carabine, *m.*; *rifle-shot*, coup de fusil, *m.*

rifleman ['raiflmən], *n.* (*pl.* **-men** [men]) carabinier, *m.*

rifling (1) ['raifliŋ], *n.* pillage.

rifling (2) ['raifliŋ], *n.* rayage (*de fusils*), *m.*

rift [rift], *n.* fente; éclaircie (*aux nuages*), *f.*

rig [rig], *n.* gréement; accoutrement (*vêtements*), *m.—v.t.* équiper, gréer; (*fig.*) accoutrer, attifer.

rigged [rigd], *a.* gréé.

rigging ['rigiŋ], *n.* gréement, *m.*, agrès, *m.pl.*

right [rait], *a.* droit; direct, en ligne droite; vrai, véritable; bon, propre, convenable; juste, correct; en règle; *all right!* c'est bien! *that is right*, c'est cela; *the right man*, l'homme qu'il faut; *the right road*, le bon chemin; *to be right*, avoir raison; être juste (*compte*); *to put right*, mettre en bon ordre, arranger.—*adv.* droit, tout droit; justement (*avec justice*); comme il faut, bien (*correctement*); tout à fait (*entièrement*); fort (*beaucoup*); très.—*n.* droit, *m.*, justice, raison, *f.*; côté droit, *m.*, droite, *f.*; *on* or *to the right*, à droite; *right of way*, droit de passage; *to put* or *set to rights*, arranger, mettre en ordre.—*v.t.* redresser, corriger (*choses*).—*v.i.* se redresser se relever.

righteous ['raitʃəs], *a.* juste, droit.

righteously ['raitʃəsli], *adv.* justement.

righteousness ['raitʃəsnis], *n.* droiture, vertu, *f.*

rightful ['raitful], *a.* légitime, véritable.

right-handed ['raithændid], *a.* droitier.

rightly ['raitli], *adv.* bien; à juste titre; comme il faut (*convenablement*); juste (*exactement*).

rightness ['raitnis], *n.* rectitude; droiture; justesse, *f.*

rigid ['ridʒid], *a.* rigide, raide.

rigidity [ri'dʒiditi], *n.* rigidité; raideur, *f.*

rigidly ['ridʒidli], *adv.* rigidement; avec raideur.

rigmarole ['rigməroul], *n.* galimatias, *m.*

rigor ['rigə, 'raigə], *n.* (*Path.*) rigidité, *f.*

rigorous ['rigərəs], *a.* rigoureux.

rigorously ['rigərəsli], *adv.* rigoureusement, avec rigueur, à la rigueur.

rigour ['rigə], *n.* rigueur, *f.*

rile [rail], *v.t.* (*colloq.*) faire enrager, agacer.

rill [ril], *n.* petit ruisseau, *m.*

rim [rim], *n.* bord, rebord, *m.*; jante (*de roue*), *f.*

rime [raim], *n.* givre, *m.*; gelée blanche, *f.*

rimless ['rimlis], *a.* sans monture (*lunettes*).

rind [raind], *n.* écorce, peau, pelure; croûte (*de fromage*); couenne (*de lard*), *f.*

ring (1) [riŋ], *n.* anneau, *m.*, bague (*pour le doigt etc.*), *f.*; cercle, rond, *m.*; arène (*pour se battre*), *f.*; ring (*pour la boxe*), *m.*; (*fig.*) bande, clique, *f.*; (*Comm.*) syndicat, *m.—v.t.* mettre un anneau à; entourer.

ring (2) [riŋ], *v.t. irr.* sonner, faire sonner; *to ring someone up*, téléphoner à quelqu'un.—*v.i.* sonner; retentir (*de*); tinter (*aux oreilles*), *m.*; sonnerie, *f.*; *there's a ring at the door*, on sonne.

ring-dove ['riŋdʌv], *n.* pigeon ramier, *m.*

ringer ['riŋə], *n.* sonneur, *m.*

ringing ['riŋiŋ], *n.* son (*de cloche*), *m.*; sonnerie, *f.*; tintement, retentissement, *m.*

ringleader ['riŋliːdə], *n.* meneur, chef de bande, *m.*

ringlet ['riŋlit], *n.* boucle (*de cheveux*), *f.*

ring-road ['riŋroud], *n.* route de ceinture, *f.*

ringworm ['riŋwəːm], *n.* herpès tonsurant, *m.*

543

rink [riŋk], *n.* patinoire (*de glace*), *f.*; skating (*pour patinage à roulettes*), *m.*

rinse [rins], *v.t.* rincer.

riot ['raiət], *n.* émeute, *f.*; vacarme, tumulte (*bruit*), *m.*; (*fig.*) festins, *m.pl.*—*v.i.* faire une émeute.

rioter ['raiətə], *n.* émeutier; tapageur, *m.*

riotous ['raiətəs], *a.* séditieux, tumultueux.

rip (1) [rip], *v.t.* fendre, déchirer; *to rip open*, ouvrir.—*n.* déchirure, *f.*

rip (2) [rip], *n.* (*slang*) vaurien, polisson, *m.*

ripe [raip], *a.* mûr.

ripen ['raipən], *v.t.* mûrir, faire mûrir.—*v.i.* mûrir, venir à maturité.

ripeness ['raipnis], *n.* maturité, *f.*

ripening ['raipniŋ], *n.* maturation, *f.*

ripple [ripl], *v.t.* rider.—*v.i.* se rider; onduler. —*n.* ride (*d'eau*), *f.*

rippling ['ripliŋ], *n.* clapotis, murmure, *m.*

rip-roaring ['riprɔːriŋ], *a.* tumultueux; robuste; épatant.

rise [raiz], *v.i. irr.* se lever, se relever (*après une chute, un malheur etc.*); s'élever, monter; se dresser (*montagne etc.*); s'augmenter, hausser (*prix*); aller en montant (*rue*); se soulever (*rébellion*); ressusciter (*les morts*); prendre sa source (*en ou dans*).—*n.* lever, *m.*; montée (*de colline etc.*); crue (*des eaux*); hausse (*de prix*), augmentation; source, origine, *f.*

riser ['raizə], *n.* marche (*d'escalier*), *f.*; *early riser*, personne matinale, *f.*

risible ['rizibl], *a.* rieur.

rising ['raiziŋ], *a.* levant; montant (*marée*); (*fig.*) naissant; qui a de l'avenir (*qui promet*). —*n.* lever (*du lit, du soleil*), *m.*; montée (*de colline*); crue (*des eaux*); clôture (*d'assemblée*); résurrection, *f.*; soulèvement, *m.*, insurrection, *f.*

risk [risk], *n.* risque, *m.*—*v.t.* risquer.

risky ['riski], *a.* risqué, hasardeux.

rite [rait], *n.* rite, *m.*; cérémonie, *f.*

ritual ['ritjuəl], *a. ou* liturgique.—*n.* rituel, *m.*

rival [raivl], *a. and n.* rival, *m.*—*v.t.* rivaliser avec.

rivalry ['raivlri], *n.* rivalité, *f.*

rive [raiv], *v.t. irr.* fendre.—*v.i.* se fendre.

river ['rivə], *a.* de rivière, fluvial.—*n.* fleuve (*qui débouche dans la mer*), *m.*; (*autrement*) rivière, *f.*; *down the river*, en aval; *up the river*, en amont.

riverside ['rivəsaid], *a.* au bord de l'eau.—*n.* bord de l'eau, *m.*

rivet ['rivit], *n.* rivet, *m.*; attache (*de porcelaine*), *f.*—*v.t.* river, riveter; (*fig.*) fixer.

riveting ['rivitiŋ], *n.* rivetage, *m.*

rivulet ['rivjulit], *n.* ruisseau, *m.*

roach [routʃ], *n.* (*Ichth.*) gardon, *m.*

road [roud], *n.* route, *f.*, chemin, *m.*; chaussée; rue (*en ville*); (*Naut.*) rade, *f.*; *by-road*, chemin détourné; *carriage-road*, route carrossable; *cross-roads*, carrefour, *m.*; *high road*, grand-route, *f.*; *roads and bridges*, ponts et chaussées, *m.pl.*

road-hog ['roudhɔg], *n.* (*Motor.*) chauffard, *m.*

road-house ['roudhaus], *n.* auberge, hôtellerie, *f.*

road-map ['roudmæp], *n.* carte routière, *f.*

road-mender ['roudmendə], *n.* cantonnier, *m.*

road-metal ['roudmetl], *n.* cailloutis, empierrement, *m.*

roadside ['roudsaid], *n.* bord de la route, *m.*; *by the roadside*, au bord de la route.

roadstead ['roudsted], *n.* rade, *f.*

roadway ['roudwei], *n.* chaussée; voie (*de pont*), *f.*

roadworthy ['roudwəːði], *a.* (*Motor.*) en état de marche.

roam [roum], *v.t.* rôder dans *ou* parmi.—*v.i.* errer, rôder.

roan [roun], *a.* rouan.

roar [rɔː], *n.* rugissement (*de lion etc.*); mugissement (*de la mer etc.*); éclat (*de rire*); grondement (*de tonnerre etc.*), *m.*—*v.i.* rugir (*lion etc.*); mugir (*mer etc.*); gronder (*tonnerre, canon etc.*); (*colloq.*) vociférer; *to roar with laughter*, rire aux éclats.

roaring ['rɔːriŋ], *a.* rugissant, mugissant; *to do a roaring trade*, faire des affaires d'or.

roast [roust], *v.t.* rôtir; faire rôtir; torréfier (*café*); (*Metal.*) griller.—*v.i.* rôtir; griller. —*a.* rôti; *roast beef*, rosbif, *m.*; *roast pork*, rôti de porc, *m.*

roaster ['roustə], *n.* rôtisseur (*personne*), *m.*; rôtissoire (*chose*), *f.*

roasting ['roustiŋ], *a.* brûlant.—*n.* (*Metal.*) grillage, *m.*; torréfaction (*de café*), *f.*

rob [rɔb], *v.t.* voler; piller; priver (*de*).

robber ['rɔbə], *n.* voleur, *m.*

robbery ['rɔbəri], *n.* vol, *m.*

robe [roub], *n.* robe, *f.*—*v.t.* vêtir (d'une robe); revêtir (*de*).

robin ['rɔbin], **robin-redbreast** [rɔbin'red brest], *n.* (*Orn.*) rouge-gorge, *m.*

robot ['roubɔt], *n.* automate, robot, *m.*

robust [ro'bʌst], *a.* robuste, vigoureux.

robustness [ro'bʌstnis], *n.* robustesse, vigueur, *f.*

rock (1) [rɔk], *n.* rocher, roc, *m.*; (*Geol.*) roche, *f.*; sucre d'orge (*bonbon*), *m.*

rock (2) [rɔk], *v.t.* balancer; bercer, remuer.— *v.i.* se balancer; branler, trembler.

rockery ['rɔkəri], *n.* jardin de rocaille, *m.*

rocket ['rɔkit], *n.* fusée, *f.*; *rocket-launcher*, lance-fusée, *m.*—*v.i.* monter en flèche (*prix*).

rockiness ['rɔkinis], *n.* nature rocailleuse, *f.*

rocking ['rɔkiŋ], *n.* balancement; bercement, *m.*

rocking-chair ['rɔkiŋtʃɛə], *n.* chaise à bascule, *f.*

rocking-horse ['rɔkiŋhɔːs], *n.* cheval à bascule, *m.*

rock-salt ['rɔksɔːlt], *n.* sel gemme, *m.*

rocky ['rɔki], *a.* rocailleux, rocheux.

rod [rɔd], *n.* verge; baguette; tringle (*à rideaux etc.*); canne à pêche; perche (= 5·0291 *metres*); bielle (*de piston*), *f.*

rodent ['roudənt], *n.* (*Zool.*) rongeur, *m.*

rodeo [ro'deiou], *n.* rodéo, *m.*

roe (1) [rou], *n.* œufs (de poisson), *m.pl.*

roe (2) [rou], *n.* chevreuil, *m.*, chevrette, *f.*

roebuck ['roubʌk], *n.* chevreuil, *m.*

Roger ['rɔdʒə]. Roger, *m.*

rogue [roug], *n.* coquin, fripon, fourbe, *m.*

roguery ['rougəri], *n.* coquinerie, friponnerie, fourberie, *f.*

roguish ['rougiʃ], *a.* coquin, fripon; (*facet.*) espiègle.

roguishly ['rougiʃli], *adv.* en fripon, en fourbe; (*facet.*) avec espièglerie.

roister ['rɔistə], *v.i.* faire du tapage.
roisterer ['rɔistərə], *n.* tapageur, *m.*
roistering ['rɔistəriŋ], *a.* tapageur, bruyant.
—*n.* tapage, *m.*
role [roul], *n.* rôle, *m.*
roll [roul], *n.* rouleau; roulement (*acte de rouler quelque chose*); roulis (*de navire*); petit pain; roulement (*de tambour*); rôle (*liste*), *m.*; (*pl.*) rôles, *m.pl.*; annales, archives, *f.pl.*—*v.t.* rouler; passer au rouleau (*gazon, gravier etc.*); (*Metal.*) laminer.—*v.i.* rouler, se rouler; tourner; (*Naut.*) avoir du roulis.
roll-call ['roulkɔ:l], *n.* appel, *m.*
roller ['roulə], *n.* rouleau; cylindre, *m.*
roller-skate ['rouləskeit], *n.* patin à roulettes, *m.*
rollicking ['rɔlikiŋ], *a.* folâtre, joyeux.
rolling ['rouliŋ], *n.* roulement; roulis (*de navire*); (*Metal.*) laminage, *m.*; **rolling stock**, matériel roulant, *m.*
rolling-pin ['rouliŋpin], *n.* rouleau, *m.*
Roman ['roumən], *a.* romain; aquilin (*nez*).—*n.* Romain (*personne*), *m.*
Romance [ro'mæns], *a.* roman; **Romance languages**, langues romanes, *f.pl.*
romance [ro'mæns], *n.* roman de chevalerie, *m.*; histoire romanesque; (*Mus.*) romance; (*fam.*) amourette, aventure, *f.*—*v.i.* inventer à plaisir, exagérer, broder.
romanesque [roumə'nesk], *a.* (*Arch.*) roman.
Romania [ro'meiniə], [RUMANIA].
romantic [ro'mæntik], *a.* romanesque; romantique (*paysage, style etc.*).
romanticism [ro'mæntisizm], *n.* romantisme, *m.*
romanticist [ro'mæntisist], *n.* romantique, *m., f.*
Rome [roum]. Rome, *f.*
romp [rɔmp], *n.* gamine, garçonnière (*jeune fille*), *f.*; jeu violent, tapage, *m.*—*v.i.* jouer rudement, folâtrer.
rompers ['rɔmpəz], *n.pl.* barboteuse, *f.*
romping ['rɔmpiŋ], *n.* jeux rudes, *m.pl.*
roof [ru:f], *n.* toit; palais (*de la bouche*), *m.*—*v.t.* couvrir d'un toit; couvrir.
roofing ['ru:fiŋ], *n.* toiture, *f.*
roof-rack ['ru:fræk], *n.* (*Motor.*) galerie, *f.*
rook (1) [ruk], *n.* freux, *m.*, (*pop.*) corneille, *f.*; (*slang*) tricheur, *m.*—*v.t., v.i.* (*slang*) friponner, filouter.
rook (2) [ruk], *n.* (*Chess*) tour, *f.*
rookery ['rukəri], *n.* colonie de freux, *f.*
rookie ['ruki], *n.* (*Mil. slang*) bleu, *m.*
room [ru:m], *n.* place, *f.*; espace, *m.*; chambre, salle, pièce (*d'appartement*), *f.*
roomful ['ru:mful], *n.* chambrée, *f.*
roominess ['ru:minis], *n.* nature spacieuse, grandeur, *f.*
roomy ['ru:mi], *a.* spacieux, vaste.
roost [ru:st], *n.* juchoir, perchoir, *m.*—*v.i.* se jucher.
rooster ['ru:stə], *n.* coq, *m.*
root [ru:t], *n.* racine, *f.*; (*fig.*) source, *f.*—*v.t.* **to root out**, déraciner, extirper.
rooted ['ru:tid], *a.* enraciné; (*fig.*) invétéré.
rooting ['ru:tiŋ], *n.* enracinement, *m.*; **rooting out**, arrachement, *m.*, extirpation, *f.*
rope [roup], *n.* corde, *f.*; (*Naut.*) cordage, *m.*; (*Mount.*) cordée, *f.*; **a piece of rope**, un bout de filin.—*v.t.* attacher avec une

corde; lier.—*v.i.* filer (*vin etc.*); (*Mount.*) s'encorder.
rope-walker ['roupwɔ:kə], *n.* funambule, *m., f.*
ropiness ['roupinis], *n.* viscosité, *f.*
ropy ['roupi], *a.* qui file, filant, visqueux.
rosary ['rouzəri], *n.* chapelet, *m.*
rose (1) [rouz], *n.* rose; (*Tech.*) pomme d'arrosoir; (*Arch.*) rosace, *f.*
rose (2) [rouz], *past* [RISE].
roseate ['rouziit], *a.* rosé.
rose-bed ['rouzbed], *n.* massif de rosiers, *m.*
rosebud ['rouzbʌd], *n.* bouton de rose, *m.*
rose-bush ['rouzbuʃ], *n.* rosier, *m.*
rose-garden ['rouzgɑ:dn], *n.* roseraie, *f.*
rosemary ['rouzməri], *n.* romarin, *m.*
rosette [ro'zet], *n.* rosette, *f.*
rose-window ['rouzwindou], *n.* rosace, *f.*
rosin ['rɔzin], *n.* colophane, *f.*
rosiness ['rouzinis], *n.* couleur rose, *f.*
rostrum ['rɔstrəm], *n.* (*Rom. Hist.*) rostres, *m.pl.*; tribune (*estrade*), *f.*
rosy ['rouzi], *a.* de rose, rose, rosé, vermeil.
rot [rɔt], *n.* pourriture; (*colloq.*) blague, *f.*—*v.t.* pourrir, faire pourrir; carier (*dent*).—*v.i.* pourrir, se pourrir; se carier (*dent*).
rota ['routə], *n.* **by rota**, à tour de rôle.
rotary ['routəri], *a.* rotatif, rotatoire.
rotate [ro'teit], *v.t., v.i.* tourner.
rotation [ro'teiʃən], *n.* rotation, succession, *f.*; **rotation of crops**, assolement, *m.*
rote [rout], *n.* routine, *f.*; **by rote**, par cœur.
rotten [rɔtn], *a.* pourri; carié (*dent*); gâté (*œuf*).
rottenness ['rɔtnnis], *n.* pourriture; carie (*des dents*), *f.*
rotter ['rɔtə], *n.* (*fam.*) sale type, *m.*
rotting ['rɔtiŋ], *a.* qui pourrit; qui se carie.—*n.* putréfaction, *f.*
rotund [ro'tʌnd], *a.* rond, arrondi.
rotundity [ro'tʌnditi], *n.* rondeur, rotondité, *f.*
rouble [ru:bl], *n.* rouble, *m.*
rouge [ru:ʒ], *n.* rouge, fard, *m.*
rough [rʌf], *a.* rude; hérissé; raboteux (*chemin*); grosse, houleuse (*mer*); orageux (*temps*); âpre (*goût*); dépoli (*verre*); grossier (*manières*); approximatif (*pas exact*); **rough-and-ready**, fait à la va-vite; **rough copy** or **draft**, brouillon, *m.*; **rough estimate**, appréciation en gros, *f.*—*adv.* brutalement, rudement.—*n.* voyou, polisson, *m.*; **rough-and-tumble**, mêlée, bousculade, *f.*
roughcast ['rʌfkɑ:st], *v.t.* ébaucher; (*Build.*) crépir.—*n.* ébauche, *f.*; (*Build.*) crépi, *m.*
roughen [rʌfn], *v.t.* rendre rude.
rough-hewn ['rʌfhju:n], *a.* ébauché.
rough-house ['rʌfhaus], *n.* (*fam.*) chahut, *m.*
roughly ['rʌfli], *adv.* rudement; grossièrement; à peu près.
roughness ['rʌfnis], *n.* aspérité, rudesse; apreté (*au goût*); agitation (*de la mer*); grossièreté (*de manières*), *f.*; mauvais état (*de rue*), *m.*
round [raund], *a.* rond; circulaire; en rond.—*adv.* en rond; à la ronde; tout autour, à l'entour; **to go round**, faire le tour de.—*prep.* autour de.—*n.* rond, cercle; tour (*petite promenade*), *m.*; rouelle (*de bœuf etc.*); salve (*d'applaudissements*), *f.*; (*Artill.*) coup de canon, *m.*; ronde (*de veilleurs, police etc.*); (*Golf*) tournée, *f.*; (*Box.*) round, *m.*; **round**

545

roundabout

of ammunition, cartouche, *f.*—*v.t.* arrondir; entourer, faire le tour de (*faire un cercle*); doubler (*cap*); *to round off*, arrondir, finir, compléter; *to round up*, rassembler (*bestiaux etc.*); faire une rafle.—*v.i.* s'arrondir.

roundabout ['raundəbaut], *a.* détourné; indirect.—*n.* manège; (*Motor.*) rondpoint, *m.*

rounded ['raundid], *a.* arrondi.

*roundelay ['raundəlei], *n.* rondeau, *m.*

rounders ['raundəz], *n.pl.* balle au camp, *f.*

roundish ['raundiʃ], *a.* arrondi; rondelet (*personne*).

roundly ['raundli], *adv.* en rond; (*fig.*) rondement.

roundness ['raundnis], *n.* rondeur; (*fig.*) franchise, *f.*; (*Comm.*) livreur, *m.*

roundsman ['raundzmən], *n.* (*pl.* **-men** [men]); (*pl.* **-men** [men]); livreur, *m.*

round-up ['raundʌp], *n.* rassemblement (*de bétail*), *m.*; rafle (*de criminels*), *f.*

roup [ruːp], *n.* pépie (*maladie de volaille*), *f.*

rouse [rauz], *v.t.* éveiller, (*fig.*) réveiller, exciter.

rout [raut], *n.* cohue; déroute (*d'une armée*), *f.*—*v.t.* mettre en déroute.

route [ruːt], *n.* itinéraire, parcours, *m.*—*v.t.* router (*circulation, colis etc.*).

route-map ['ruːtmæp], *n.* carte routière, *f.*

routine [ruː'tiːn], *n.* routine, *f.*

rove [rouv], *v.i.* rôder, courir.

rover ['rouvə], *n.* rôdeur, vagabond; pirate; (*Scouting*) éclaireur chevalier, *m.*

roving ['rouviŋ], *a.* errant, vagabond.

row (1) [rau], *n.* tapage, vacarme, *m.*; querelle, scène, *f.*

row (2) [rou], *n.* rang, *m.*, rangée, file; colonne (*de chiffres*), *f.*

row (3) [rou], *n.* promenade en bateau, *f.*—*v.t.* (*Naut.*) faire aller à la rame.—*v.i.* ramer; (*Naut.*) nager.

rowan ['rauən], *n.* (*Sc.*) sorbier des oiseaux, *m.*

rowdy ['raudi], *a.* tapageur.—*n.* voyou, gredin, *m.*

rowdyism ['raudiizm], **rowdiness** ['raudinis], *n.* tapage, *m.*

rower ['rouə], *n.* rameur *m.* (*Naut.*) nageur, *m.*

rowing ['rouiŋ], *n.* canotage, *m.*

rowing-boat ['rouiŋbout], *n.* bateau à rames, *m.*

rowlock ['rʌlək], *n.* tolet, *m.*, dame, *f.*

royal ['rɔiəl], *a.* royal, de roi.

royalist ['rɔiəlist], *a. and n.* royaliste, *m.*, *f.*

royally ['rɔiəli], *adv.* royalement, en roi.

royalty ['rɔiəlti], *n.* royauté; (*usu. pl.*) commission, *f.*, droit d'auteur, *m.*

rub [rʌb], *v.t.*, *v.i.* frotter; (*Med.*) frictionner.—*n.* frottement; coup de brosse, *m.*; (*fig.*) difficulté, *f.*, obstacle, *m.*

rubber (1) ['rʌbə], *n.* frotteur; frottoir (*chose*), *m.*; (*pl.*) (*Am.*) caoutchoucs (*chaussures*), *m.pl.*; **indiarubber**, caoutchouc, *m.*, gomme (à effacer), *f.*

rubber (2) ['rʌbə], *n.* (*Cards*) rob, *m.*

rubber-stamp ['rʌbəstæmp], *n.* tampon; (*fig.*) béni-oui-oui, *m.*—*v.t.* ratifier.

rubbing ['rʌbiŋ], *n.* frottement; frottage, *m.*; (*Med.*) friction, *f.*

rubbish ['rʌbiʃ], *n.* débris, *m.pl.*; ordures, *f.pl.*; fatras (*sottises*), *m.*

rubbish-bin ['rʌbiʃbin], *n.* poubelle, *f.*

rubbish-cart ['rʌbiʃkaːt], *n.* tombereau, *m.*

rubbish-dump ['rʌbiʃdʌmp], *n.* dépotoir, *m.*

rubbishy ['rʌbiʃi], *a.* de rebut, sans valeur.

rubble ['rʌbl], *n.* blocaille, *f.*, moellons; décombres, *m.pl.*

rubicund ['ruːbikənd], *a.* rubicond.

rubric ['ruːbrik], *n.* rubrique, *f.*

ruby ['ruːbi], *a.* de rubis, vermeil.—*n.* rubis, *m.*; teinte rouge, *f.*, incarnat, *m.*

ruck [rʌk], *n.* peloton (*de coureurs, cyclistes*), *m.*

rucksack ['rʌksæk], *n.* sac à dos, *m.*

ruction ['rʌkʃən], *n.* (*colloq.*) bagarre, dispute, *f.*

rudder ['rʌdə], *n.* gouvernail, *m.*

ruddiness ['rʌdinis], *n.* rougeur, *f.*

ruddy ['rʌdi], *a.* rouge, au teint vermeil; (*slang*) sacré.

rude [ruːd], *a.* grossier, impoli; (*fig.*) rude, violent.

rudely ['ruːdli], *adv.* grossièrement; rudement.

rudeness ['ruːdnis], *n.* rudesse; grossièreté; insolence; violence, *f.*

rudiment ['ruːdimənt], *n.* rudiment, *m.*

rudimentary [ruːdi'mentri], *a.* rudimentaire.

rue [ruː], *v.t.* se repentir de, regretter.

rueful ['ruːful], *a.* triste; lamentable.

ruefully ['ruːfuli], *adv.* tristement, déplorablement.

ruff [rʌf], *n.* fraise, collerette, *f.*

ruffian ['rʌfiən], *n.* bandit, *m.*; brute, *f.*

ruffianism ['rʌfiənizm], *n.* brutalité, *f.*

ruffianly ['rʌfiənli], *a.* de brigand, brutal.

ruffle [rʌfl], *n.* manchette, ruche, *f.*—*v.t.* froncer (*le front etc.*); froisser (*sentiments*); ébouriffer (*les cheveux*).

rug [rʌg], *n.* couverture, *f.*; tapis, *m.*

rugby ['rʌgbi], *n.* (*Spt.*) rugby, *m.*

rugged ['rʌgid], *a.* rude; raboteux; âpre; bourru (*personne*).

ruggedness ['rʌgidnis], *n.* rudesse, âpreté, *f.*

ruin ['ruːin], *n.* ruine; perte, *f.*—*v.t.* ruiner.

ruination [ruːi'neiʃən], *n.* perte, *f.*

ruinous ['ruːinəs], *a.* ruineux; en ruine.

ruinously ['ruːinəsli], *adv.* ruineusement.

rule [ruːl], *n.* règle, *f.*; règlement; gouvernement, empire (*domination*), *m.*; (*Law*) ordonnance, *f.*; *as a rule*, en général, d'ordinaire.—*v.t.* régler, diriger; gouverner; régir; (*Law*) décider.—*v.i.* gouverner; (*Law*) décider; *to rule over*, régner sur.

ruler ['ruːlə], *n.* gouvernant, souverain, *m.*; règle (*instrument*), *f.*

ruling ['ruːliŋ], *a.* dominant, régnant, dirigeant.—*n.* (*Law*) ordonnance de juge, décision, *f.*

rum (1) [rʌm], *a.* drôle, (*colloq.*) cocasse.

rum (2) [rʌm], *n.* rhum, *m.*

Rumania [ruː'meinjə], la Roumanie, *f.*

Rumanian [ruː'meinjən], *a.* roumain.—*n.* roumain (*langue*); Roumain (*personne*), *m.*

rumba ['rʌmbə], *n.* rumba, *f.*

rumble [rʌmbl], *v.i.* gronder, gargouiller.

rumbling ['rʌmbliŋ], *a.* qui gronde; qui gargouille.—*n.* grondement; gargouillement, *m.*

rumbustious [rʌm'bʌstjəs], *a.* (*fam.*) turbulent, tapageur.

ruminant ['ruːminənt], *a. and n.* ruminant, *m.*

ruminate ['ruːmineit], *v.i.* ruminer.

rumination [ruːmi'neiʃən], *n.* rumination, *f.*

sack

rummage ['rʌmidʒ], *v.t.*, *v.i.* fouiller.—*n.* remue-ménage, *m.*

rummage-sale ['rʌmidʒseil], *n.* vente d'objets usagés, *f.*

rumour ['ruːmə], *n.* rumeur, *f.*; bruit, *m.*—*v.t.* faire courir le bruit de.

rump [rʌmp], *n.* croupe; culotte (*de viande*), *f.*; croupion (*de volaille*), *m.*

rumple [rʌmpl], *v.t.* chiffonner, froisser.—*n.* pli, *m.*, froissure, *f.*

rumpus ['rʌmpəs], *n.* (*colloq.*) boucan, tapage, *m.*

run [rʌn], *v.t. irr.* courir; encourir; faire courir, faire marcher, conduire (*machines*); pousser, enfoncer, diriger, exploiter, tenir; *to run down*, dénigrer (*décrier*); (*Hunt.*) forcer; *to run for*, courir chercher; *to run in*, enfoncer; arrêter, coffrer; (*Motor.*) roder; *to run out*, faire sortir; épuiser; *to run over*, (*Motor.*) écraser (*personne, animal*); *to run up*, monter en courant.—*v.i.* courir; accourir (*s'approcher*); se sauver (*s'échapper*); s'étendre; fuir (*bateau*); couler (*liquide*); se fondre (*couleurs*); fondre (*se dissoudre*); être (*exister*); courir, circuler; faire le service (*autobus etc.*); marcher, être en marche (*mécanisme*); s'écouler (*temps*); pleurer (*les yeux*); rouler (*avancer en tournant*); devenir; filer (*navire etc.*); suppurer (*ulcère etc.*); monter (*somme*); (*Am.*) se présenter (*aux élections*); *to run about*, courir çà et là; *to run after*, chercher; *to run against*, courir contre; *to run aground*, échouer; *to run at*, attaquer; *to run away*, se sauver, s'emballer (*cheval*); s'écouler (*liquide etc.*); *to run down*, descendre en courant, aller, venir, couler (*liquide*); s'arrêter (*mécanisme*); *to run from*, s'enfuir de; *to run in*, entrer, entrer précipitamment; *to run out*, courir dehors; fuir; se terminer, expirer, tirer à sa fin; descendre (*marée*); *to run over*, déborder (*liquide etc.*); *to run through*, passer à travers de, parcourir; gaspiller; *to run up*, courir en haut, monter; *to run up to*, s'élever à, monter à.—*n.* course (*action de courir*), *f.*; cours (*série*); trajet, voyage, *m.*; durée, *f.*, succès (*vogue*), *m.*; irruption (*dans une banque etc.*), *f.*; commun (*généralité*), *m.*; *in the long run*, à la longue, à la fin.

runaway ['rʌnəwei], *a.* emballé (*cheval*).—*n.* fuyard; fugitif, déserteur, *m.*

rung (1) [rʌŋ], *n.* échelon (*d'échelle*); bâton (*de chaise etc.*), *m.*

rung (2) [rʌŋ], *p.p.* [RING (2)].

runner ['rʌnə], *n.* coureur; messager, courrier; (*Bot.*) rejeton, *m.*; *scarlet runner*, haricot d'Espagne, *m.*

running ['rʌniŋ], *a.* courant; de suite (*consécutivement*).—*n.* course, *f.*; écoulement (*d'eau*), *m.*

runt [rʌnt], *n.* bétail petit *ou* chétif; (*fig.*) avorton, nain, *m.*

runway ['rʌnwei], *n.* (*Av.*) piste d'envol, *f.*

rupee [ruːˈpiː], *n.* roupie, *f.*

rupture ['rʌptʃə], *n.* rupture; (*Med.*) hernie, *f.*—*v.t.* rompre.—*v.i.* se rompre.

rural ['ruərəl], *a.* champêtre, rural, rustique.

ruse [ruːz], *n.* ruse, *f.*, stratagème, *m.*

rush (1) [rʌʃ], *n.* (*Bot.*) jonc, *m.*

rush (2) [rʌʃ], *n.* ruée, *f.*, mouvement précipité, *m.*; foule, presse (*gens*), *f.*—*v.t.* en-traîner brusquement; dépêcher; envahir.—*v.i.* se jeter, se ruer, se précipiter (*sur*).

rushing ['rʌʃiŋ], *a.* impétueux.—*n.* élan, *m.*, précipitation, *f.*

rusk [rʌsk], *n.* biscotte, *f.*

russet ['rʌsit], *a.* roussâtre.—*n.* roux, *m.*; reinette grise (*pomme*), *f.*

Russia ['rʌʃə], la Russie, *f.*

Russian ['rʌʃən], *a.* russe, de Russie.—*n.* russe (*langue*), *m.*; Russe (*personne*), *m.*, *f.*

rust [rʌst], *n.* rouille, *f.*—*v.i.* se rouiller.

rustic ['rʌstik], *a.* rustique, champêtre.—*n.* rustre, paysan, *m.*

rusticate ['rʌstikeit], *v.t.* reléguer à la campagne; (*Univ.*) renvoyer temporairement.—*v.i.* se retirer à *ou* habiter la campagne.

rustication [rʌstiˈkeiʃən], *n.* villégiature, *f.*; (*Univ.*) renvoi temporaire, *m.*

rusticity [rʌsˈtisiti], *n.* simplicité, rusticité, *f.*

rustiness ['rʌstinis], *n.* rouille, *f.*

rustle [rʌsl], *v.t.* (*Am.*) voler (*du bétail*).—*v.i.* bruire, frémir; faire frou-frou (*robe*); *to rustle against*, frôler.—*n.* frôlement; bruissement; frou-frou (*de robe*), *m.*

rustler ['rʌslə], *n.* (*Am.*) voleur de bétail, *m.*

rustless ['rʌstlis], *a.* inoxydable.

rustling ['rʌsliŋ], *a.* qui fait frou-frou, frémissant.—*n.* (*Am.*) vol de bétail, *m.*

rusty ['rʌsti], *a.* rouillé; roux (*couleur*).

rut [rʌt], *n.* ornière (*de route*), *f.*—*v.t.* sillonner d'ornières.

ruthless ['ruːθlis], *a.* impitoyable, insensible.

ruthlessly ['ruːθlisli], *adv.* sans pitié, sans merci.

ruthlessness ['ruːθlisnis], *n.* cruauté, inhumanité, *f.*

Rwanda ['rwʌndə]. le Rwanda, le Ruanda, *m.*

rye [rai], *n.* seigle, *m.*

rye-grass ['raigrɑːs], *n.* ivraie, *f.*, ray-grass, *m.*

S

S, s [es]. dix-neuvième lettre de l'alphabet, *m.*

Saar [sɑː]. la Sarre, *f.*

Sabbath ['sæbəθ], *n.* (*Jews*) sabbat; dimanche; (*fig.*) repos, *m.*

sabbatic [səˈbætik], **sabbatical** [səˈbætikəl], *a.* sabbatique, du sabbat.

sable [seibl], *a.* de zibeline, de martre; (*Her.*) de sable.—*n.* martre, zibeline, *f.*; (*Her.*) sable, *m.*

sabot ['sæbou], *n.* sabot, *m.*

sabotage ['sæbətɑːʒ], *n.* sabotage, *m.*—*v.t.* saboter.

saboteur [sæbəˈtəː], *n.* saboteur, *m.*

sabre ['seibə], *n.* sabre, *m.*—*v.t.* sabrer.

sac [sæk], *n.* (*Anat.*) sac, *m.*; bourse, *f.*

saccharine ['sækərin], *n.* saccharine, *f.*

sacerdotal [sæsəˈdoutl], *a.* sacerdotal.

sack (1) [sæk], *n.* sac, *m.*; *to get the sack*, (*colloq.*) être renvoyé; *to give the sack to*, renvoyer, congédier.—*v.t.* (*colloq.*) congédier.

sack (2) [sæk], *n.* sac, saccagement (*d'une ville*), *m.*—*v.t.* saccager, mettre à sac.

547

sackcloth ['sækkləθ], *n.* toile à sac, *f.*
sackful ['sækful], *n.* sac plein, *m.*, sachée, *f.*
sacking (I) ['sækiŋ], *n.* toile à sac, *f.*
sacking (2) ['sækiŋ], *n.* sac, saccagement (*de ville*), *m.*
sacrament ['sækrəmənt], *n.* sacrement, *m.*
sacramental [sækrə'mentl], *a.* sacramentel.
sacred ['seikrid], *a.* sacré; saint (*histoire etc.*); (*fig.*) inviolable.
sacredly ['seikridli], *adv.* saintement; religieusement.
sacredness ['seikridnis], *n.* sainteté, *f.*, caractère sacré, *m.*
sacrifice ['sækrifais], *v.t., v.i.* sacrifier.—*n.* sacrifice, *m.*; victime, *f.*
sacrificer ['sækrifaisə], *n.* sacrificateur, *m.*
sacrificial [sækri'fiʃl], *a.* des sacrifices, sacrificatoire.
sacrilege ['sækrilidʒ], *n.* sacrilège, *m.*
sacrilegious [sækri'lidʒəs], *a.* sacrilège.
sacrilegiously [sækri'lidʒəsli], *adv.* d'une manière sacrilège.
sacrilegiousness [sækri'lidʒəsnis], *n.* caractère sacrilège, *m.*
sacristy ['sækristi], *n.* sacristie, *f.*
sacrosanct ['sækrosæŋkt], *a.* sacro-saint.
sad [sæd], *a.* triste; pitoyable, déplorable; cruel (*perte*).
sadden ['sædn], *v.t.* attrister.—*v.i.* s'attrister.
saddle [sædl], *n.* selle, *f.*; *pack-saddle*, bât, *m.*; *side-saddle*, selle d'amazone.—*v.t.* seller; charger, accabler.
saddle-bag ['sædlbæg], *n.* sacoche, *f.*
saddle-bow ['sædlbou], *n.* arçon, *m.*
saddler ['sædlə], *n.* sellier, *m.*
saddle-room ['sædlru:m], *n.* sellerie, *f.*
saddlery ['sædləri], *n.* sellerie, *f.*
sadism ['seidizm], *n.* sadisme, *m.*
sadist ['seidist], *n.* sadique, *m., f.*
sadistic [sə'distik], *a.* sadique.
sadly ['sædli], *adv.* tristement; mal, beaucoup, grandement.
sadness ['sædnis], *n.* tristesse, *f.*
safe [seif], *a.* sauf, en sûreté; à l'abri (*de*); sûr; *safe and sound*, sain et sauf.—*n.* coffre-fort (*pour l'argent*); garde-manger (*pour aliments*), *m.*
safe-conduct ['seif'kɔndʌkt], *n.* sauf-conduit, *m.*
safeguard ['seifgɑːd], *n.* sauvegarde, *f.*—*v.t.* sauvegarder.
safe-keeping ['seif'kiːpiŋ], *n.* bonne garde, sûreté, *f.*
safely ['seifli], *adv.* sain et sauf; en sûreté.
safety ['seifti], *a.* de sûreté.—*n.* sûreté, *f.*, salut, *m.*
safety-catch ['seiftikætʃ], *n.* cran de sûreté, cran d'arrêt, *m.*
safety-lamp ['seiftilæmp], *n.* lampe de sûreté, *f.*
safety-match ['seiftimætʃ], *n.* allumette suédoise, *f.*
safety-pin ['seiftipin], *n.* épingle de sûreté, *f.*
safety-valve ['seiftivælv], *n.* soupape de sûreté, *f.*
saffron ['sæfrən], *a.* couleur safran; de safran. —*n.* safran, *m.*
saffrony ['sæfrəni], *a.* safrané.
sag [sæg], *v.i.* plier, ployer, s'affaisser; se relâcher (*câble*).
saga ['sɑːgə], *n.* saga, *f.*

sagacious [sə'geiʃəs], *a.* sagace; intelligent (*animal*).
sagaciously [sə'geiʃəsli], *adv.* avec sagacité.
sagaciousness [sə'geiʃəsnis], **sagacity** [sə'gæsiti], *n.* sagacité, *f.*
sage (I) [seidʒ], *a.* sage, prudent.—*n.* sage, *m.*
sage (2) [seidʒ], *n.* sauge (*herbes*), *f.*
sagely ['seidʒli], *adv.* sagement, prudemment.
sagging ['sægiŋ], *a.* affaissé, fléchi, ployé.— *n.* courbure, *f.*, affaissement, *m.*; baisse (*de prix*), *f.*
sago ['seigou], *n.* sagou; sagouier, sagoutier (*arbre*), *m.*
sagy ['seidʒi], *a.* qui a un goût de sauge.
Sahara [sə'hɑːrə], *the.* le Sahara, *m.*
said [sed], *a.* dit, susdit (SAY).
sail [seil], *n.* voile, *f.*; (*collect.*) voiles, *f.pl.*, voilure; aile (*de moulin à vent*); course *ou* promenade à la voile (*sur l'eau*), *f.*—*v.t.* naviguer (*sur*), voguer (*sur ou dans*).—*v.i.* faire voile; cingler, naviguer; mettre à la voile, appareiller.
sailable ['seiləbl], *a.* navigable.
sail-cloth ['seilklɔθ], *n.* toile à voiles, *f.*
sailing ['seiliŋ], *a.* à voiles.—*n.* navigation, *f.*; appareillage, *m.*; partance (*départ*), *f.*
sailing-boat ['seiliŋbout], *n.* bateau à voiles, *m.*
sailing-ship ['seiliŋʃip], *n.* bâtiment à voiles voilier, *m.*
sail-maker ['seilmeikə], *n.* voilier, *m.*
sailor ['seilə], *n.* marin, matelot, *m.*
saint [seint] *strong form*, [sənt] *weak form*, *n.* saint, *m.*, sainte, *f.*; *All Saints' Day*, la Toussaint, *f.*
saintliness ['seintlinis], *n.* sainteté, *f.*
saintly ['seintli], *a.* saint; de saint, vénérable.
sake [seik], *n.* (*used only with* FOR); *art for art's sake*, l'art pour l'art; *for God's sake*, pour l'amour de Dieu; *for the sake of appearances*, pour sauver les apparences; *for the sake of health*, pour cause de santé; *for your sake*, par égard pour vous.
sal [sæl], *n.* sel, *m.*
salaam [sə'lɑːm], *n.* salamalec, *m.*
salad ['sæləd], *n.* salade, *f.*
salad-bowl ['sælədboul], *n.* saladier, *m.*
salad-oil ['sælədoil], *n.* huile de table, *f.*
salamander ['sæləmændə], *n.* salamandre, *f.*
salaried ['sælərid], *a.* qui touche des appointements.
salary ['sæləri], *n.* appointements, *m.pl.*; traitement (*de fonctionnaire*), *m.*
sale [seil], *n.* vente; mise en vente, *f.*; *for sale*, à vendre; *on sale*, en vente; *private sale*, vente à l'amiable; *sale by auction*, vente aux enchères; *to put up for sale*, mettre en vente.
saleable ['seiləbl], *a.* vendable; de bonne vente.
sale-room ['seilruːm], *n.* salle des ventes, *f.*
salesman ['seilzmən], *n.* (*pl.* -men [men]) vendeur, marchand; courtier de commerce, *m.*
Salic ['sælik], *a.* salique.
salient ['seiliənt], *a.* and *n.* saillant, *m.*
saliently ['seiliəntli], *adv.* d'une manière saillante.
salify ['sælifai], *v.t.* salifier.
saline ['seilain], *a.* salin.
saliva [sə'laivə], *n.* salive, *f.*

salivate ['sæliveit], *v.t.* faire saliver.
sallow ['sælou], *a.* jaunâtre, jaune, blême.
sallowness ['sælounis], *n.* teint blême, *m.*
sally ['sæli], *n.* sortie; (*fig.*) excursion; saillie (*d'esprit*), *f.—v.i.* sortir, faire une sortie.
salmon ['sæmən], *n.* saumon, *m.*
salmon-trout ['sæməntraut], *n.* truite saumonée, *f.*
saloon [sə'luːn], *n.* (grand) salon, *m.*, salle; (*Am.*) buvette, *f.*, bar, *m.*; conduite-intérieure (*voiture*), *f.*
salsify ['sælsifi], *n.* (*Bot.*) salsifis, *m.*
salt [sɔːlt], *a.* salé; de sel.—*n.* sel, *m.*; **Epsom salts**, sels anglais, *m.pl.—v.t.* saler.
salt-cellar ['sɔːltselə], *n.* salière, *f.*
salted ['sɔːltid], *a.* salé; (*fig.*) aguerri.
salter ['sɔːltə], *n.* saunier; saleur, *m.*
salting ['sɔːltiŋ], *n.* salaison, *f.*, salage, *m.*
saltish ['sɔːltiʃ], *a.* un peu salé, saumâtre.
saltless ['sɔːltlis], *a.* sans sel; (*fig.*) insipide.
salt-marsh ['sɔːltmɑːʃ], *n.* marais salant, *m.*
salt-mine ['sɔːltmain], *n.* mine de sel, *f.*
saltness ['sɔːltnis], *n.* salure, *f.*
saltpetre [sɔːlt'piːtə], *n.* salpêtre, *m.*
saltpetre-works [sɔːlt'piːtəwəːks], *n.pl.* salpêtrière, *f.*
saltpetrous [sɔːlt'petrəs], *a.* salpêtreux.
salt-water ['sɔːltwɔːtə], *n.* eau de mer, *f.*
salty ['sɔːlti], *a.* salé; qui a un goût de sel.
salubrious [sə'ljuːbriəs], *a.* salubre, sain.
salubriously [sə'ljuːbriəsli], *adv.* d'une manière salubre.
salubrity [sə'ljuːbriti], *n.* salubrité, *f.*
salutary ['sæljutəri], *a.* salutaire.
salutation [sælju'teiʃən], *n.* salut, *m.*, salutation, *f.*
salute [sə'ljuːt], *n.* salut, *m.*, salutation, salve (*de fusils*), *f.—v.t.* saluer.
Salvador ['sælvədɔː], **El.** le Salvador, *m.*
Salvadorean [sælvə'dɔːriən], *a.* salvadorègne. —*n.* Salvadorègne (*personne*), *m.*, *f.*
salvage ['sælvidʒ], *n.* sauvetage, *m.*, objets sauvés, *m.pl.*; (*Ind.*) récupération, *f.—v.t.* récupérer; relever (*navire*).
salvage-money ['sælvidʒmani], *n.* prix *ou* droit de sauvetage, *m.*
salvage-vessel ['sælvidʒvesl], *n.* navire de relevage, *m.*
salvation [sæl'veiʃən], *n.* salut, *m.*; *Salvation Army*, Armée du Salut, *f.*
salve [sælv, sɑːv], *n.* onguent; (*fig.*) remède, baume, *m.—*[sælv], *v.t.* remédier à; (*Naut.*) sauver, sauveter.
salver ['sælvə], *n.* plateau, *m.*
salvo ['sælvou], *n.* réserve, restriction; salve (*d'artillerie*), *f.*
Samaritan [sə'mæritən], *a.* samaritain.—*n.* Samaritain (*personne*), *m.*
same [seim], *a.* même.—*n.* le même, *m.*, la même; même chose, *f.*; ledit, *m.*, ladite, *f.*, lesdits, *m.pl.*, lesdites, *f.pl.*; *all the same*, néanmoins, quand même; *it is all the same*, c'est égal; *just the same*, tout de même; *much about the same*, à peu près de même; *the same to you*, et vous de même.
sameness ['seimnis], *n.* identité; uniformité, *f.*
sample [sɑːmpl], *n.* échantillon, *m.—v.t.* échantillonner; déguster (*vin*).
sampler ['sɑːmplə], *n.* modèle, (*Needlework*) canevas, *m.*

sampling ['sɑːmpliŋ], *n.* échantillonnage, *m.*; gustation (*des mets*), *f.*
sanatorium [sænə'tɔːriəm], *n.* sanatorium, *m.*
sanctification [sæŋktifi'keiʃən], *n.* sanctification, *f.*
sanctified ['sæŋktifaid], *a.* sanctifié, saint.
sanctify ['sæŋktifai], *v.t.* sanctifier.
sanctimonious [sæŋkti'mouniəs], *a.* papelard, béat, hypocrite.
sanctimoniously [sæŋkti'mouniəsli], *adv.* d'un air béat.
sanctimoniousness [sæŋkti'mouniəsnis], *n.* dévotion affectée; cagoterie, *f.*
sanction ['sæŋkʃən], *n.* sanction, autorité, *f.— v.t.* sanctionner, autoriser.
sanctity ['sæŋktiti], *n.* sainteté, *f.*
sanctuary ['sæŋktjuəri], *n.* sanctuaire, asile, refuge, *m.*
sanctum ['sæŋktəm], *n.* sanctuaire; (*colloq.*) cabinet de travail, *m.*, retraite, *f.*
sand [sænd], *n.* sable; sablon (*sable fin*), *m.*; (*pl.*) plage, *f.*, bord de la mer, *m.—v.t.* sabler.
sandal [sændl], *n.* sandale, *f.*; santal, *m.*
sandbag ['sændbæg], *n.* sac de terre, *m.*
sand-bank ['sændbæŋk], *n.* banc de sable, *m.*
sand-drift ['sænddrift], *n.* amas de sable, *m.*
sand-eel ['sændiːl], *n.* lançon, *m.*, équille, *f.*
sand-glass ['sændglɑːs], *n.* sablier, *m.*
sand-martin ['sændmɑːtin], *n.* hirondelle de rivage, *f.*
sand-paper ['sændpeipə], *n.* papier de verre, *m.—v.t.* passer au papier de verre.
sand-pit ['sændpit], *n.* sablière, sablonnière, *f.*
sand-shoes ['sændʃuːz], *n.pl.* espadrilles, *f.pl.*
sandstone ['sændstoun], *n.* grès, *m.*
sand-storm ['sændstɔːm], *n.* ouragan de sable, *m.*
sandwich ['sændwitʃ], *n.* sandwich, *m.*
sandwich-man ['sændwitʃmæn], *n.* (*pl.* -men* [men]) homme-sandwich, homme-affiche, *m.*
sandy ['sændi], *a.* sablonneux, de sable; d'un blond ardent, roux (*couleur*).
sane [sein], *a.* sain, sain d'esprit.
sanguinary ['sæŋgwinəri], *a.* sanguinaire.
sanguine ['sæŋgwin], *a.* sanguin; plein de confiance, confiant.
sanguineness ['sæŋgwinnis], *n.* confiance, assurance, *f.*
sanitary ['sænitəri], *a.* sanitaire, hygiénique; *sanitary towel*, serviette hygiénique, *f.*
sanitation [sæni'teiʃən], *n.* assainissement, *m.*
sanity ['sæniti], *n.* état sain, jugement sain, *m.*
Sanskrit ['sænskrit], *a.* and *n.* sanscrit, *m.*
Santa Claus ['sæntə'klɔːz], *n.* Père Noël, *m.*
sap (1) [sæp], *n.* sève, *f.*
sap (2) [sæp], *n.* (*Mil.*) sape, *f.—v.t.* saper.
sapience ['seipiəns], *n.* sagesse, *f.*
sapient ['seipiənt], *a.* sage.
sapless ['sæplis], *a.* sans sève; sec, desséché.
sapling ['sæpliŋ], *n.* jeune arbre, baliveau, *m.*
saponaceous [sæpə'neiʃəs], *a.* saponacé.
saponify [sə'pɔnifai], *v.t.* saponifier.—*v.i.* se saponifier.
sapper ['sæpə], *n.* sapeur, *m.*
sapphic ['sæfik], *a.* and *n.* (*Pros.*) saphique, *m.*
sapphire ['sæfaiə], *n.* saphir, *m.*
sappiness ['sæpinis], *n.* abondance de sève, *f.*
sappy ['sæpi], *a.* plein de sève.
saraband ['særəbænd], *n.* sarabande, *f.*

Saracen ['særəsn], *a.* sarrasin.—*n.* Sarrasin, *m.*
sarcasm ['sɑːkæzm], *n.* sarcasme, *m.*
sarcastic [sɑː'kæstik], *a.* sarcastique.
sarcastically [sɑː'kæstikəli], *adv.* d'une manière *ou* d'un ton sarcastique.
sarcophagus [sɑː'kofəgəs], *n.* sarcophage, *m.*
sardine [sɑː'diːn], *n.* sardine, *f.*
Sardinia [sɑː'dinjə], la Sardaigne, *f.*
Sardinian [sɑː'dinjən], *a.* sarde.—*n.* Sarde (*personne*), *m., f.*
sardonic [sɑː'donik], *a.* sardonique.
sarong [sə'roŋ], *n.* pagne, *m.*, jupe (*malaisien*), *f.*
sarsaparilla [sɑːsəpə'rilə], *n.* salsepareille, *f.*
sash (1) [sæʃ], *n.* ceinture; écharpe (*décoration*), *f.*
sash (2) [sæʃ], *n.* châssis (*de fenêtre*), *m.*
sash-window ['sæʃwindou], *n.* fenêtre à guillotine, *f.*
sassafras ['sæsəfræs], *n.* (*Bot.*) sassafras, *m.*
Satan ['seitən]. Satan, *m.*
satanic [sə'tænik], **satanical** [sə'tænikəl], *a.* satanique.
satchel [sætʃl], *n.* sacoche, *f.*; sac d'écolier, cartable, *m.*
sate [seit], *v.t.* rassasier (*de*), assouvir.
satellite ['sætəlait], *n.* satellite, *m.*
satiate ['seiʃieit], *v.t.* rassasier (*de*).
satiated ['seiʃieitid], *a.* rassasié (*de*); gorgé.
satiety [sə'taiəti], *n.* satiété, *f.*
satin ['sætin], *a.* de satin.—*n.* satin, *m.*
satin-wood ['sætinwuːd], *n.* bois de citronnier, *m.*
satire ['sætaiə], *n.* satire, *f.*
satiric [sə'tirik], **satirical** [sə'tirikəl], *a.* satirique.
satirist ['sætirist], *n.* satirique, *m., f.*
satirize ['sætiraiz], *v.t.* satiriser.
satisfaction [sætis'fækʃən], *n.* satisfaction; réparation (*récompense*), *f.*
satisfactorily [sætis'fæktərili], *adv.* d'une manière satisfaisante.
satisfactory [sætis'fæktri], *a.* satisfaisant.
satisfy ['sætisfai], *v.t.* satisfaire; satisfaire à; acquitter (*dette*); assouvir (*passion*); rassasier (*de*) (*appétit*); **to be satisfied that,** être persuadé, être convaincu que; **to be satisfied with,** être satisfait de, être content de.—*v.i.* satisfaire, donner satisfaction.
satisfying ['sætisfaiiŋ], *a.* satisfaisant; nourrissant (*nourriture*).
saturate ['sætʃureit], *v.t.* saturer.
saturation [sætʃu'reiʃən], *n.* saturation, *f.*
Saturday ['sætədei], samedi, *m.*
Saturn ['sætən]. Saturne, *m.*
Saturnalia [sætə'neiliə]. saturnales, *f.pl.*
saturnine ['sætənain], *a.* sombre, taciturne.
satyr ['sætə], *n.* satyre, *m.*
sauce [sɔːs], *n.* sauce; (*fig.*) insolence, impertinence, *f.*—*v.t.* assaisonner; flatter (*le goût*); (*fig.*) dire des impertinences à.
sauce-boat ['sɔːsbout], *n.* saucière, *f.*
saucer ['sɔːsə], *n.* soucoupe, *f.*; **flying saucer,** soucoupe volante.
saucepan ['sɔːspən], *n.* casserole, *f.*
saucily ['sɔːsili], *adv.* insolemment.
sauciness ['sɔːsinis], *n.* insolence, impertinence, *f.*
saucy ['sɔːsi], *a.* insolent, impertinent.
Saudi Arabia ['saudiə'reibiə]. l'Arabie Séoudite, *f.*
sauerkraut ['sauəkraut], *n.* choucroute, *f.*

saunter ['sɔːntə], *v.i.* flâner.—*n.* flânerie, *f.*
saunterer ['sɔːntərə], *n.* flâneur, *m.*
sauntering ['sɔːntəriŋ], *a.* de flâneur.—*n.* flânerie, *f.*
sausage ['sosidʒ], *n.* saucisse (*à cuire*), *f.*; saucisson (*salami etc.*), *m.*
sausage-meat ['sosidʒmiːt], *n.* chair à saucisse, *f.*
sausage-roll ['sosidʒ'roul], *n.* friand, *m.*
savage ['sævidʒ], *a.* sauvage; féroce.—*n.* sauvage, *m., f.*—*v.t.* attaquer, mordre (*bête*).
savagely ['sævidʒli], *adv.* sauvagement, en sauvage; d'une manière féroce.
savageness ['sævidʒnis], *n.* férocité, brutalité; sauvagerie, *f.*
savagery ['sævidʒəri], *n.* férocité, barbarie, *f.*
savannah [sə'vænə], *n.* savane, prairie, *f.*
save; [seiv], *v.t.* sauver (*de*); épargner (*argent etc.*); mettre de côté, économiser.—*v.i.* économiser, faire des économies.—*n.* (*Spt.*) arrêt, *m.*—*prep.* hormis, excepté, sauf.
saver ['seivə], *n.* sauveur, libérateur, *m.*; économe (*ménager*), *m., f.*
saving ['seiviŋ], *a.* économe, ménager.—*n.* épargne; économie, *f.*; salut, *m.*
savings-bank ['seiviŋzbæŋk], *n.* caisse d'épargne, *f.*
saviour ['seivjə], *n.* sauveur, *m.*
savour ['seivə], *n.* saveur, *f.*; goût, *m.*, odeur, *f.*—*v.t.* goûter, savourer.—*v.i.* avoir du goût; sentir.
savouriness ['seivərinis], *n.* goût agréable, *m.*, saveur, *f.*
savoury ['seivəri], *a.* savoureux, appétissant. —*n.* plat épicé, *m.*
saw (1) [sɔː], *past* [SEE].
saw (2) [sɔː], *n.* scie, *f.*—*v.t., v.i. irr.* scier.
saw (3) [sɔː], *n.* adage, dicton (*proverbe*), *m.*
sawdust ['sɔːdʌst], *n.* sciure (*de bois*), *f.*
saw-mill ['sɔːmil], *n.* scierie, *f.*
sawyer ['sɔːjə], *n.* scieur, scieur de long, *m.*
saxifrage ['sæksifreidʒ], *n.* (*Bot.*) saxifrage, *f.*
Saxon ['sæksən], *a.* saxon, de Saxe.—*n.* saxon (*langue*); Saxon (*personne*), *m.*
saxophone ['sæksəfoun], *n.* saxophone, *m.*
say [sei], *v.t. irr.* dire; parler, répéter, réciter; *I say!* dites donc! *that is to say,* c'est-à-dire; *they say,* on dit.—*n.* dire, mot, ce qu'on a à dire, *m.*
saying ['seiiŋ], *n.* mot, proverbe, dicton, *m.*; sentence, maxime, *f.*
scab [skæb], *n.* croûte (*sur blessure etc.*); gale (*de mouton etc.*), *f.*
scabbard ['skæbəd], *n.* fourreau, *m.*
scabbiness ['skæbinis], *n.* état galeux, *m.*
scabby ['skæbi], *a.* couvert de croûtes; galeux.
scabious ['skeibiəs], *a.* scabieux.—*n.* scabieuse (*plante*), *f.*
scaffold ['skæfəld], *n.* échafaud, *m.*—*v.t.* échafauder.
scaffolding ['skæfəldiŋ], *n.* échafaudage, *m.*
scald [skɔːld], *n.* brûlure, *f.*—*v.t.* échauder, ébouillanter.
scalding ['skɔːldiŋ], *n.* échaudage, *m.*
scalding-hot ['skɔːldiŋ'hot], *a.* tout bouillant.
scale (1) [skeil], *n.* échelle; (*Mus.*) gamme, *f.* —*v.t.* escalader.
scale (2) [skeil], *n.* écaille (*de poisson*), *f.*
scale (3) [skeil], *n.* bassin, plateau (*balance*), *m.*; *scales* or *pair of scales,* balance, *f.*

scholar

scale-maker ['skeilmeikə], *n.* balancier, *m.*

scalene ['skeili:n], *a.* scalène.

scaliness ['skeilinis], *n.* nature écailleuse, *f.*

scaling (1) ['skeiliŋ], *n.* escalade (*montagnes*), *f.*

scaling (2) ['skeiliŋ], *n.* écaillage (*peintures*), *m.*

scallop ['skoləp], *n.* coquille Saint-Jacques; coquille; dentelure, *f.*, feston, *m.*—*v.t.* denteler; (*Needlework*) festonner.

scalp [skælp], *n.* cuir chevelu, *m.*, chevelure, *f.*, scalpe; (*fig.*) front, *m.*, tête, *f.*—*v.t.* scalper.

scalpel ['skælpəl], *n.* (*Surg.*) scalpel, *m.*

scaly ['skeili], *a.* écaillé; (*Bot.*) écailleux.

scamp [skæmp], *n.* chenapan, vaurien, *m.*; *young scamp*, petit polisson, *m.*—*v.t.* bâcler.

scamper ['skæmpə], *v.i.* courir, s'enfuir.—*n.* course rapide, *f.*

scampi ['skæmpi], *n.pl.* langoustine, *f.*

scan [skæn], *v.t.* scruter; (*Pros.*) scander; (*Rad.*) balayer.

scandal [skændl], *n.* scandale, *m.*; honte; médisance, *f.*

scandalize ['skændəlaiz], *v.t.* scandaliser; choquer; calomnier.

scandal-monger ['skændlmʌŋgə], *n.* médisant, *m.*

scandalous ['skændələs], *a.* scandaleux; honteux.

Scandinavia [skændi'neivjə], la Scandinavie, *f.*

Scandinavian [skændi'neivjən], *a.* scandinave.—*n.* Scandinave (*personne*), *m.*, *f.*

scanner ['skænə], *n.* scrutateur, *m.*; *radar scanner*, déchiffreur de radar, *m.*

scanning ['skæniŋ], *n.* examen minutieux, *m.*; (*Pros.*) scansion, *f.*; (*Rad.*) balayage, *m.*

scansion ['skænʃən], *n.* scansion, *f.*

scant [skænt], *a.* rare; rétréci; faible; peu de.

scantily ['skæntili], *adv.* faiblement, d'une manière insuffisante.

scantiness ['skæntinis], *n.* insuffisance (*de vivres etc.*); faiblesse (*de poids*), *f.*

scantling ['skæntliŋ], *n.* échantillon, *m.*; (*Carp.*) volige, *f.*, équarrissage, *m.*

scanty ['skænti], *a.* rétréci, faible, peu abondant, insuffisant; clairsemé (*cheveux*).

scapegoat ['skeipgout], *n.* bouc émissaire; (*fig.*) souffre-douleur, *m.*

scapegrace ['skeipgreis], *n.* vaurien, mauvais sujet, *m.*

scapement ['skeipmənt], *n.* échappement, *m.*

scapula ['skæpjulə], *n.* (*Anat.*) omoplate, *f.*

scapular ['skæpjulə], *a.* scapulaire.

scapulary ['skæpjuləri], *n.* (*R.-C. Ch.*) scapulaire, *m.*

scar [ska:], *n.* cicatrice, balafre, *f.*—*v.t.* cicatriser; balafrer.

scarab ['skærəb], **scarabaeus** [skærə'bi:əs], *n.* scarabée, *m.*

scaramouch ['skærəmu:ʃ], *n.* scaramouche, *m.*

scarce [skeəs], *a.* rare; *to make oneself scarce*, disparaître, décamper, filer.

scarcely ['skeəsli], *adv.* à peine, presque pas, guère.

scarcity ['skeəsiti], *n.* rareté; disette (*famine*), *f.*

scare [skeə], *n.* panique, frayeur subite, *f.*—*v.t.* effrayer, épouvanter, effaroucher.

scarecrow ['skeəkrou], *n.* épouvantail, *m.*

scarf [ska:f], *n.* (*pl.* **scarfs** [ska:fs], **scarves** [ska:vz]) écharpe, *f.*; cache-nez, *m.inv.*; foulard, *m.*

scarifier ['skærifaiə], *n.* scarificateur, *m.*

scarify ['skærifai], *v.t.* scarifier (*peau*), ameublir (*terre*).

scarlatina [ska:lə'ti:nə], *n.* (fièvre) scarlatine, *f.*

scarlet ['ska:lit], *a.* and *n.* écarlate, *f.*; *scarlet fever*, fièvre scarlatine, *f.*; *scarlet runner*, haricot d'Espagne, *m.*

scarp [ska:p], *n.* (*Fort.*) escarpe, *f.*—*v.t.* escarper.

scarves [SCARF].

scatheless ['skeiðlis], *a.* sans dommage, sain et sauf.

scathing ['skeiðiŋ], *a.* acerbe, cinglant, cassant.

scatter ['skætə], *v.t.* disperser, dissiper; répandre, éparpiller.—*v.i.* se disperser, se répandre.

scattered ['skætəd], *a.* dispersé, éparpillé, épars.

scattering ['skætəriŋ], *n.* éparpillement; petit nombre, *m.*

scavenge ['skævindʒ], *v.t.* ébouer, balayer.

scavenger ['skævindʒə], *n.* boueur; balayeur, *m.*

scavenging ['skævindʒiŋ], *n.* ébouage, balayage, *m.*

scene [si:n], *n.* scène; (*Theat.*) scène, décoration, *f.*; décor; (*fig.*) théâtre, *m.*; *behind the scenes*, dans la coulisse; *scene-shifter*, machiniste, *m.*,

scenery ['si:nəri], *n.* scène; (*fig.*) vue, perspective, *f.*, paysage, *m.*; (*Theat.*) décors, *m.pl.*

scenic ['si:nik], *a.* scénique.

scent [sent], *n.* odeur, senteur, *f.*, parfum; odorat; flair, nez (*de chien*), *m.*; voie (*de cerf*); (*fig.*) piste (*traces*), *f.*—*v.t.* parfumer (*de*); sentir, flairer (*animal*).

scent-bottle ['sentbotl], *n.* flacon de parfum, *m.*

scentless ['sentlis], *a.* sans odeur, inodore.

scent-spray ['sentsprei], *n.* vaporisateur, *m.*

sceptic ['skeptik], *n.* sceptique, *m.*, *f.*

sceptical ['skeptikl], *a.* sceptique.

scepticism ['skeptisizm], *n.* scepticisme, *m.*

sceptre ['septə], *n.* sceptre, *m.*

sceptred ['septəd], *a.* portant le sceptre.

schedule ['ʃedju:l, (*Am.*) 'skedju:l], *n.* liste, *f.*, inventaire; (*Comm.*) bilan; (*Law*) bordereau, *m.*—*v.t.* enregistrer, inventorier.

scheme [ski:m], *n.* arrangement, *m.*, combinaison, *f.*; projet, système, *m.*—*v.t.* projeter, combiner.—*v.i.* faire des projets; (*fig.*) intriguer.

schemer ['ski:mə], *n.* faiseur de projets; (*fig.*) intrigant, *m.*

scheming ['ski:miŋ], *a.* à projets; intrigant.—*n.* projets *m.pl.*, intrigues, *f.pl.*

schism [sizm], *n.* schisme, *m.*

schismatic [siz'mætik], *n.* schismatique, *m.*, *f.*

schizophrenia [skitso'fri:niə], *n.* (*Med.*) schizophrénie, *f.*

schizophrenic [skitso'fri:nik], *a.* and *n.* schizophrène, *m.*, *f.*

scholar ['skolə], *n.* écolier; érudit, savant (*learned person*), *m.*; *day scholar*, externe, *m.*, *f.*

scholarly ['skɔləli], *a.* d'érudit, savant.
scholarship ['skɔləʃip], *n.* érudition, *f.*, savoir, *m.*; (*Univ. etc.*) bourse, *f.*
scholastic [skɔ'læstik], *a.* and *n.* scolastique, *m.*, *f.*
scholasticism [skɔ'læstisizm], *n.* scolastique, *f.*
school [sku:l], *n.* école; bande, troupe (*de baleines etc.*), *f.*; *at school*, en classe, à l'école; *boarding-school*, pension, *f.*, pensionnat, *m.*; *primary school*, école primaire; *grammar school*, collège, lycée, *m.*; *infant-school*, école maternelle.—*v.t.* instruire, enseigner; réprimander.
schooled [sku:ld], *a.* formé, entraîné, dressé.
schooling ['sku:liŋ], *n.* instruction; réprimande, *f.*
schoolmaster ['sku:lmɑːstə], *n.* instituteur, professeur, *m.*
schoolmistress ['sku:lmistris], *n.* maîtresse d'école, institutrice, *f.*
schooner ['sku:nə], *n.* (*Naut.*) goélette, *f.*
sciatic [sai'ætik], *a.* sciatique.
sciatica [sai'ætikə], *n.* sciatique, *f.*
science ['saiəns], *n.* science, *f.*
scientific [saiən'tifik], *a.* scientifique.
scientist ['saiəntist], *n.* homme de science, savant, *m.*
Scilly Isles ['siliailz], *the*, les Sorlingues, *f.pl.*
scimitar ['simitə], *n.* cimeterre, *m.*
scintillant ['sintilənt], *a.* scintillant.
scintillate ['sintileit], *v.i.* scintiller.
scintillation [sinti'leiʃən], *n.* scintillation, *f.*, scintillement, *m.*
scion ['saiən], *n.* (*Bot.*) scion; (*fig.*) rejeton, *m.*
scission ['siʃən], *n.* scission, *f.*
scissors ['sizəz], *n.pl.* ciseaux, *m.pl.*
scoff [skɔf], *n.* moquerie, *f.*, sarcasme, *m.*—*v.t.* se moquer de, bafouer.—*v.i.* railler.
scoffer ['skɔfə], *n.* moqueur, railleur, *m.*
scoffing ['skɔfiŋ], *a.* moqueur.—*n.* moquerie, dérision, *f.*
scoffingly ['skɔfiŋli], *adv.* par moquerie, en dérision.
scold [skould], *v.t.* gronder, criailler (*après*).—*v.i.* gronder.
scolding ['skouldiŋ], *a.* bougon.—*n.* semonce, *f.*
sconce [skɔns], *n.* candélabre (*fixé au mur*), *m.*; bobèche (*de bougeoir*), *f.*
scone [skɔn, skoun], *n.* petite galette (ronde), *f.*
scoop [sku:p], *n.* grande cuiller; (*Naut.*) écope; (*Journ. slang*) nouvelle à sensation, *f.*—*v.t.* vider, creuser; (*Naut.*) écoper.
scooter ['sku:tə], *n.* patinette, *f.*; scooter, *m.*
scope [skoup], *n.* portée, étendue; visée; liberté, *f.*
scorch [skɔːtʃ], *v.t.* brûler, roussir, griller.—*v.i.* se brûler.
scorching ['skɔːtʃiŋ], *a.* brûlant, très chaud.
score [skɔː], *n.* entaille, coche, *f.*; compte; vingt, *m.*, vingtaine, *f.*; (*Games*) nombre de points; (*fig.*) motif, *m.*, raison, cause; (*Mus.*) partition, *f.*; *on what score?* à quel titre?—*v.t.* entailler, marquer; rayer; (*Mus.*) orchestrer; *to score out*, rayer, biffer (*texte*).—*v.i.* marquer des points.
scorer ['skɔːrə], *n.* marqueur, *m.*
scoring ['skɔːriŋ], *n.* (*Games etc.*) marque; (*Mus.*) orchestration, *f.*
scorn [skɔːn], *v.t.* mépriser; dédaigner.—*v.i.* mépriser; dédaigner (*de*); *to scorn to fly*,

dédaigner de fuir.—*n.* mépris, dédain, *m.* dérision, *f.*
scornful ['skɔːnful], *a.* méprisant, dédaigneux.
scornfully ['skɔːnfuli], *adv.* dédaigneusement, avec dédain.
scornfulness ['skɔːnfulnis], *n.* caractère dédaigneux, *m.*
scorpion ['skɔːpjən], *n.* scorpion, *m.*
Scot [skɔt], *n.* Écossais, *m.*
Scotch [skɔtʃ], *a.* écossais (*but used* ONLY *in certain fixed expressions, which include the following*) *Scotch terrier*, terrier griffon, *m.*; *Scotch* (*whisky*), whisky écossais, *m.*; [SCOTS].
scotch [skɔtʃ], *v.t.* entailler; enrayer (*roue*); (*fig.*) annuler.
scot-free [skɔt'friː], *a.* sans frais; (*fig.*) sain et sauf, indemne.
Scotland ['skɔtlənd]. l'Écosse, *f.*
Scots [skɔts], **Scottish** ['skɔtiʃ], *a.* écossais; *Scots Law*, droit écossais, *m.*
Scotsman ['skɔtsmən], *n.* (*pl.* **-men** [men]) Écossais, *m.*
Scotswoman ['skɔtswumən], *n.* (*pl.* **-women** [winin]) Écossaise, *f.*
Scottish [SCOTS].
scoundrel ['skaundrəl], *n.* gredin, coquin, scélérat, *m.*
scour (1) ['skauə], *v.t.* nettoyer, récurer, purger, écurer.—*v.i.* écurer; nettoyer.
scour (2) ['skauə], *v.t.* parcourir.—*v.i.* courir.
scourer ['skauərə], *n.* récureur, nettoyeur, *m.*
scourge [skəːdʒ], *n.* fouet; (*fig.*) fléau, *m.*—*v.t.* fouetter, flageller; (*fig.*) châtier.
scourger ['skəːdʒə], *n.* châtieur; (*Eccles. Hist.*) flagellant, *m.*
scourging ['skəːdʒiŋ], *n.* flagellation, *f.*
scouring ['skauəriŋ], *n.* récurage; nettoyage, *m.*
scout [skaut], *n.* éclaireur; scout, *m.*; (*Naut.*) vedette, *f.*; (*Av.*) avion de chasse, *m.*—*v.t.* repousser avec mépris.—*v.i.* aller en éclaireur.
scowl [skaul], *v.i.* se re(n)frogner, froncer le sourcil.—*n.* re(n)frognement, froncement de sourcil, *m.*
scowling ['skauliŋ], *a.* re(n)frogné, menaçant.
scrag [skræg], *n.* corps décharné, squelette, *m.*; *scrag-end*, bout saigneux (*de viande*), *m.*
scragginess ['skræginis], *n.* état raboteux, *m.*; maigreur, *f.*
scraggy ['skrægi], *a.* noueux, rugueux; rabougri.
scramble [skræmbl], *v.t.* (*Teleg.*) brouiller (*message*); *scrambled eggs*, œufs brouillés, *m.pl.*—*v.i.* grimper; se battre, se disputer.—*n.* mêlée, lutte, *f.*
scrap (1) [skræp], *n.* morceau, fragment, bout, *m.*; (*pl.*) bribes, *f.pl.*; restes, *m.pl.*—*v.t.* mettre au rebut.
scrap (2) [skræp], *n.* (*slang*) bagarre, rixe, *f.*
scrap-book ['skræpbuk], *n.* album, *m.*
scrape [skreip], *v.t.* gratter, érafler, râcler; décrotter (*bottes etc.*); (*Cook.*) ratisser; *to scrape together*, amasser petit à petit.—*v.i.* gratter; (*fam.*) râcler (*jouer du violon*); *to scrape through*, passer de justesse; *to bow and scrape*, faire des salamalecs.—*n.* grattage, *m.*; (*fig.*) difficulté, mauvaise affaire, *f.*

scraper ['skreipə], *n.* grattoir; râcloir, *m.*; (*Agric.*) ratissoire, *f.*; décrottoir (*pour chaussures*), *m.*

scrap-heap ['skræphi:p], *n.* tas de ferraille, *m.*

scraping ['skreipiŋ], *n.* grattage, *m.*; ratissure (*de légumes*), *f.*; **with much bowing and scraping**, avec force révérences.

scrap-iron ['skræpaiən], *n.* ferraille, *f.*

scratch [skrætʃ], *n.* égratignure, *f.*; coup de griffe *ou* d'ongle, *m.*; raie, rayure (*sur une surface polie*), *f.—v.t.* gratter; rayer (*surface polie*).—*v.i.* gratter; (*Spt.*) renoncer à concourir.

scratcher ['skrætʃə], *n.* égratigneur; grattoir (*instrument*), *m.*

scratching ['skrætʃiŋ], *n.* grattage, *m.*; égratignure; rayure, *f.*

scrawl [skrɔ:l], *n.* griffonnage, *m.*, pattes de mouche, *f.pl.—v.t., v.i.* griffonner.

scrawler ['skrɔ:lə], *n.* griffonneur, *m.*

scrawny ['skrɔ:ni], *a.* décharné, émacié.

scream [skri:m], *n.* cri perçant, *m.—v.i.* crier, pousser des cris.

screamer ['skri:mə], *n.* crieur, *m.*

screaming ['skri:miŋ], *a.* perçant; qui crie.— *n.* cris, *m.pl.*

screech [skri:tʃ], *n.* cri perçant, *m.—v.i.* crier.

screech-owl [skri:tʃaul], *n.* effraie, chouette, *f.*

screen [skri:n], *n.* écran; paravent (*pliant*); rideau (*d'arbres etc.*), *m.*; (*fig.*) voile, *f.*, abri, *m.*; défense, *f.—v.t.* mettre à couvert; abriter (*contre*).

screw [skru:], *a.* à hélice.—*n.* vis; hélice (*de navire etc.*), *f.—v.t.* visser; (*fig.*) serrer (*presser*); pressurer (*opprimer*).—*v.i.* se visser.

screw-bolt ['skru:boult], *n.* boulon à vis, *m.*

screw-cap ['skru:kæp], *n.* couvercle à vis, *m.*

screw-driver ['skru:draivə], *n.* tournevis, *m.*

screw-nail ['skru:neil], *n.* vis à bois, *f.*

screw-nut ['skru:nʌt], *n.* écrou, *m.*

screw-wrench ['skru:rentʃ], *n.* clef anglaise, *f.*

scribble [skribl], *n.* griffonnage; barbouillage, *m.—v.t., v.i.* griffonner.

scribbler ['skriblə], *n.* griffonneur; gratte-papier, *m.*

scribe [skraib], *n.* scribe; écrivain, *m.—v.t.* (*Carp.*) tracer.

scrimmage ['skrimidʒ], *n.* lutte; rixe; (*Ftb.*) mêlée, *f.*

scrip [skrip], *n.* petit sac; (*Comm.*) titre *ou* certificat provisoire, *m.*

script [skript], *n.* manuscrit; (*Cine.*) scénario, *m.*

scriptural ['skriptʃuərəl], *a.* de l'Écriture Sainte, biblique, scriptural.

Scripture ['skriptʃə], *n.* l'Écriture Sainte, *f.*

script-writer ['skriptraitə], *n.* (*Cine.*) scénariste, *m., f.*

scrofula ['skrɔfjulə], *n.* scrofule, *f.*

scrofulous ['skrɔfjuləs], *a.* scrofuleux.

scroll [skroul], *n.* rouleau, *m.*

scrounge [skraundʒ], *v.t., v.i.* (*slang*) chiper, chaparder, grapiller; **to scrounge on someone**, vivre aux crochets de quelqu'un.

scrounger ['skraundʒə], *n.* chapardeur, *m.*

scrub [skrʌb], *v.t., v.i.* frotter fort; laver, récurer.—*n.* broussailles, *f.pl.*; maquis, *m.*

scrubbing ['skrʌbiŋ], *n.* frottage, récurage, *m.*

scrubbing-brush ['skrʌbiŋbrʌʃ], *n.* brosse de cuisine, *f.*

scrubby ['skrʌbi], *a.* rabougri, chétif, mal rasé.

scruff [skrʌf], *n.* nuque, *f.*

scruple [skru:pl], *n.* scrupule, *m.—v.i.* se faire scrupule (*de*), hésiter (*à*).

scrupulous ['skru:pjuləs], *a.* scrupuleux.

scrupulously ['skru:pjuləsli], *adv.* scrupuleusement.

scrupulousness ['skru:pjuləsnis], *n.* scrupule, doute, *m.*

scrutator [skru:'teitə], *n.* scrutateur, *m.*

scrutineer [skru:ti'niə], *n.* pointeur (*de votes*); scrutateur, *m.*

scrutinize ['skru:tinaiz], *v.t.* scruter, examiner à fond.

scrutinizing ['skru:tinaiziŋ], *a.* scrutateur, inquisiteur.

scrutiny ['skru:tini], *n.* enquête rigoureuse, vérification, *f.*

scud [skʌd], *n.* léger nuage, *m.*; course rapide, *f.—v.i.* s'enfuir; courir (*nuages*).

scuffle [skʌfl], *n.* bagarre, rixe, mêlée, *f.— v.i.* se battre; traîner les pieds.

scull [skʌl], *n.* rame; godille, *f.—v.i.* ramer.

scullery ['skʌləri], *n.* arrière-cuisine, laverie, *f.*; **scullery maid**, laveuse de vaisselle, *f.*

sculptor ['skʌlptə], *n.* sculpteur, *m.*

sculpture ['skʌlptʃə], *n.* sculpture, *f.—v.t.* sculpter.

scum [skʌm], *n.* écume, *f.*; (*fig.*) rebut (*ordures*), *m.*; lie, *f.—v.t.* écumer.

scupper ['skʌpə], *n.* (*Naut.*) dalot, *m.—v.t.* saborder.

scurf [skə:f], *n.* pellicules (*des cheveux*), *f.pl.*

scurfy ['skə:fi], *a.* pelliculeux (*cheveux*).

scurrility [skʌ'riliti], **scurrilousness** ['skʌriləsnis], *a.* grossièreté, *f.*

scurrilous ['skʌriləs], *a.* grossier, ordurier.

scurry ['skʌri], *n.* débandade, *f.*; tourbillon (*de poussière, de neige etc.*), *m.—v.i.* se hâter.

scurvily ['skə:vili], *adv.* bassement, vilement.

scurviness ['skə:vinis], *n.* état scorbutique, *m.*; (*fig.*) bassesse; mesquinerie (*avarice*), *f.*

scurvy ['skə:vi], *a.* scorbutique; (*fig.*) vil, vilain.—*n.* scorbut, *m.*

scut [skʌt], *n.* couette (*de lièvre etc.*), *f.*

scutcheon ['skʌtʃən], [ESCUTCHEON].

scuttle (1) [skʌtl], *n.* panier; seau à charbon, *m.*

scuttle (2) [skʌtl], *n.* (*Naut.*) hublot, *m.*; écoutille, *f.—v.t.* saborder.

scuttle (3) [skʌtl], *v.i.* aller à pas précipités.

scuttling ['skʌtliŋ], *n.* en fuite, qui détale.— *n.* sabordage, *m.*

scythe [saið], *n.* faux, *f.—v.t.* faucher.

sea [si:], *a.* de mer, marin, maritime.—*n.* mer; lame; (*fig.*) multi.ude, *f.*, déluge, *m.*; **at sea**, en mer; **heavy sea**, mer houleuse; **in the open sea**, en pleine mer, au grand large.

seaboard ['si:bɔ:d], *n.* littoral, rivage, *m.*, côte, *f.*

sea-borne ['si:bɔ:n], *a.* transporté par mer.

sea-calf ['si:ka:f], *n.* veau marin, *m.*

sea-cow ['si:kau], *n.* lamantin, *m.*

sea-dog ['si:dɔg], *n.* loup de mer (*marin*), *m.*

seafarer ['si:fɛərə], *n.* homme de mer, marin, *m.*

seafaring ['si:fɛəriŋ], *a.* marin; **seafaring man**, marin, *m.*

sea-front ['si:frʌnt], *n.* esplanade, *f.*, bord de mer, *m.*

sea-gauge ['siːgeidʒ], *n.* tirant d'eau, *m.*
sea-going ['siːgouiŋ], *a.* de haute mer.
sea-gull ['siːgʌl], *n.* mouette, *f.*, goéland, *m.*
sea-horse ['siːhɔːs], *n.* morse, *m.*
sea-kale ['siːkeil], *n.* chou marin, *m.*
seal (1) [siːl], *n.* cachet; sceau (*officiel*), *m.*; (*Law*) scellés, *m.pl.*; **Privy Seal**, petit sceau.—*v.t.* cacheter; (*Law*) sceller; (*Customs*) plomber.
seal (2) [siːl], *n.* phoque, *m.*
sea-legs ['siːlegz], *n.pl.* pied marin, *m.*
sea-level ['siːlevəl], *n.* niveau de la mer, *m.*
sealing ['siːliŋ], *n.* action de sceller, *f.*
sealing-wax ['siːliŋwæks], *n.* cire à cacheter, *f.*
sea-lion ['siːlaiən], *n.* lion de mer, *m.*, otarie, *f.*
seam [siːm], *n.* (*Dress.*) couture; (*Mining*) couche; (*Geol.*) veine, *f.*—*v.t.* coudre; couturer.
seaman ['siːmən], *n.* (*pl.* **-men** [men]) marin, matelot, homme de mer, *m.*
seamanship ['siːmənʃip], *n.* matelotage, *m.*
seamless ['siːmlis], *a.* sans couture.
seamstress ['siːmstris], [SEMPSTRESS].
seamy ['siːmi], *a.* plein de coutures; **the seamy side of life**, les dessous de la vie, *m.pl.*
sea-nymph ['siːnimf], *n.* néréide, *f.*
seaplane ['siːplein], *n.* hydravion, *m.*
seaport ['siːpɔːt], *n.* port de mer, *m.*
sear [siə], *a.* séché, fané, flétri.—*v.t.* brûler; cautériser; faner.
search [səːtʃ], *n.* recherche; (*Law*) perquisition; (*Customs*) visite, *f.*—*v.t.* chercher, examiner, fouiller; (*Law*) faire une perquisition chez; (*Customs*) visiter.—*v.i.* chercher; fouiller.
searcher ['səːtʃə], *n.* chercheur, *m.*
searching ['səːtʃiŋ], *a.* scrutateur, pénétrant; vif, perçant (*vent*).
searchingly ['səːtʃiŋli], *adv.* minutieusement.
searchlight ['səːtʃlait], *n.* projecteur, *m.*
search-party ['səːtʃpɑːti], *n.* expédition de secours, *f.*
search-warrant ['səːtʃwɔrənt], *n.* mandat de perquisition, *m.*
sea-route ['siːruːt], *n.* voie de mer, *f.*
seascape ['siːskeip], *n.* (*Paint.*) marine, *f.*
sea-scout ['siːskaut], *n.* (boy-)scout marin, *m.*
sea-shell ['siːʃel], *n.* coquillage, *m.*
seashore ['siːʃɔː], *n.* bord de la mer, rivage, *m.*, côte, *f.*
sea-sick ['siːsik], *a.* qui a le mal de mer.
sea-sickness ['siːsiknis], *n.* mal de mer, *m.*
seaside ['siːsaid], *n.* bord de la mer, *m.*
season [siːzn], *n.* saison, *f.*; (*fig.*) temps, moment opportun, *m.*—*v.t.* assaisonner (*de*); sécher (*bois*); (*fig.*) accoutumer (*à*).—*v.i.* s'acclimater; se sécher (*bois*).
seasonable ['siːznəbl], *a.* de saison; (*fig.*) à propos, opportun, convenable.
seasonably ['siːznəbli], *adv.* à propos.
seasonal ['siːznəl], *a.* des saisons; saisonnier.
seasoned [siːznd], *a.* assaisonné (*viande*); (*fig.*) endurci, aguerri, acclimaté.
seasoning ['siːzniŋ], *n.* assaisonnement, *m.*; séchage (*du bois*), *m.*
season-ticket ['siːzn'tikit], *n.* carte d'abonnement, *f.*
seat [siːt], *n.* siège; banc, *m.*; banquette (*dans un véhicule*); (*fig.*) place; demeure (*château*), *f.*; théâtre (*de guerre*); fond (*de pantalon*), *m.*;

take your seats, please! en voiture!—*v.t.* asseoir; faire asseoir; placer.
seated ['siːtid], *a.* assis, placé.
sea-wall ['siːwɔːl], *n.* digue, chaussée, *f.*
seaward ['siːwəd], *a.* tourné vers la mer.—*adv.* vers la mer.
seaweed ['siːwiːd], *n.* algue, *f.*, goémon, varech, *m.*
seaworthiness ['siːwəːðinis], *n.* navigabilité (*navire*), *f.*
seaworthy ['siːwəːði], *a.* en bon état (de navigation).
secant ['siːkənt], *a.* sécant.—*n.* sécante, *f.*
secede [si'siːd], *v.i.* se séparer (*de*).
seceder [si'siːdə], *n.* scissionnaire, *m.*, *f.*; dissident, *m.*
secession [si'seʃən], *n.* sécession, séparation, *f.*
seclude [si'kluːd], *v.t.* séparer; éloigner.
secluded [si'kluːdid], *a.* retiré, isolé, solitaire.
seclusion [si'kluːʒən], *n.* retraite, solitude, *f.*
second ['sekənd], *a.* second, deuxième; deux (*du mois*); inférieur; **on second thoughts**, à la réflexion.—*n.* témoin, second (*dans un duel*), *m.*; seconde (*temps*), *f.*—*v.t.* seconder, aider; appuyer (*une motion*); [si'kɔnd] détacher (*fonctionnaire*).
secondary ['sekəndri], *a.* secondaire; accessoire.
seconder ['sekəndə], *n.* personne qui appuie, *f.*
second-hand ['sekənd'hænd], *a.* and *adv.* d'occasion.
secondly ['sekəndli], *adv.* secondement; en second lieu.
second-rate ['sekəndreit], *a.* de second ordre.
secrecy ['siːkrəsi], *n.* secret, *m.*; discrétion, *f.*
secret ['siːkrit], *a.* secret; retiré (*maison etc.*).—*n.* secret, *m.*
secretarial [sekrə'tεəriəl], *a.* de secrétaire.
secretariat [sekrə'tεəriæt], *n.* secrétariat, *m.*
secretary ['sekrətri], *n.* secrétaire, *m.*, *f.*
secretaryship ['sekrətriʃip], *n.* secrétariat, *m.*
secrete [si'kriːt], *v.t.* cacher; (*Physiol.*) sécréter.
secretion [si'kriːʃən], *n.* sécrétion, *f.*
secretive ['siːkrətiv], *a.* réservé; dissimulé.
secretiveness ['siːkrətivnis], *n.* caractère cachottier, *m.*
secretly ['siːkrətli], *adv.* en secret; intérieurement.
sect [sekt], *n.* secte, *f.*
sectarian [sek'tεəriən], *a.* de sectaire.—*n.* sectaire, *m.*, *f.*
sectarianism [sek'tεəriənizm], *n.* esprit de secte, sectarisme, *m.*
section ['sekʃən], *n.* section; coupe, *f.*, profil, *m.*; (*Mil.*) groupe de combat, *m.*
sectional ['sekʃənəl], *a.* en coupe; en sections.
sector ['sektə], *n.* secteur, *m.*
secular ['sekjulə], *a.* temporel; laïque; séculaire (*année*).
secularity [sekju'læriti], **secularness** ['sekjulənis], *n.* sécularité, mondanité, *f.*
secularization [sekjulərai'zeiʃən], *n.* sécularisation, *f.*
secularize ['sekjuləraiz], *v.t.* séculariser.
secure [si'kjuə], *a.* dans la sécurité, en sûreté; sûr, assuré (*chose*); bien fermé.—*v.t.* mettre en sûreté; assurer (*garantir*); s'assurer de; fermer; barrer (*attacher fortement*); (*fig.*) affermir.
securely [si'kjuəli], *adv.* en sûreté; sûrement; fortement.

secureness [si'kjuənis], *n.* sécurité, *f.*
security [si'kjuəriti], *n.* sécurité, sûreté; garantie, *f.*; (*pl.*) titres, *m.pl.*, valeurs, *f.pl.*; (*Law*) caution, *f.*
sedan-chair [si'dæn'tʃɛə], *n.* chaise à porteurs, *f.*
sedate [si'deit], *a.* posé, calme, rassis.
sedately [si'deitli], *adv.* posément, avec calme.
sedateness [si'deitnis], *n.* calme, *m.*
sedative ['sedətiv], *a.* and *n.* sédatif, *m.*
sedentary ['sedntri], *a.* sédentaire; inactif.
sedge [sedʒ], *n.* laîche, *f.*, jonc, *m.*
sediment ['sedimənt], *n.* sédiment, dépôt, *m.*
sedition [si'diʃən], *n.* sédition, *f.*
seditious [si'diʃəs], *a.* séditieux.
seditiousness [si'diʃəsnis], *n.* esprit séditieux, *m.*
seduce [si'djuːs], *v.t.* séduire.
seducer [si'djuːsə], *n.* séducteur, *m.*
seducing [si'djuːsiŋ], *a.* séduisant.
seduction [si'dʌkʃən], *n.* séduction, *f.*
seductive [si'dʌktiv], *a.* séducteur, séduisant.
sedulity [si'djuːliti], sedulousness ['sedjuləsnis], *n.* assiduité, diligence, *f.*
sedulous ['sedjuləs], *a.* assidu, diligent, zélé.
sedulously ['sedjuləsli], *adv.* assidûment, diligemment, avec application.
sedulousness [SEDULITY].
see (1) [siː], *n.* siège épiscopal, évêché; archevêché (*d'un archevêque*), *m.*; **the Holy See**, le Saint-Siège, *m.*
see (2) [siː], *v.t. irr.* voir; comprendre; accompagner, conduire.—*v.i.* voir; s'occuper (*de*); *I will see to it*, j'y veillerai.
seed [siːd], *n.* semence; graine (*de légumes*); (*fig.*) race, *f.*; *to run to seed*, monter en graine.—*v.t.* ensemencer; (*Spt.*) trier.—*v.i.* grener.
seed-bed ['siːdbed], *n.* semis, *m.*
seed-cake ['siːdkeik], *n.* gâteau à l'anis, *m.*
seedling ['siːdliŋ], *n.* semis, sauvageon, *m.*
seedsman ['siːdzmən], *n.* (*pl.* -men [men]) grainetier, *m.*
seed-time ['siːdtaim], *n.* semailles, *f.pl.*
seedy ['siːdi], *a.* râpé, usé (*vêtement*); souffrant; miteux.
seeing ['siːiŋ], *n.* vue; vision, *f.*—*conj. phr.* *seeing that*, vu que, puisque.
seek [siːk], *v.t. irr.* chercher; poursuivre, en vouloir à (*la vie etc.*).—*v.i.* chercher.
seeker ['siːkə], *n.* chercheur, *m.*
seeking ['siːkiŋ], *n.* recherche, poursuite, *f.*
seem [siːm], *v.i.* sembler, paraître, avoir l'air (*de*).
seeming ['siːmiŋ], *a.* apparent, spécieux.—*n.* semblant, *m.*, apparence, *f.*, dehors, *m.*
seemingly ['siːmiŋli], *adv.* en apparence, apparemment.
seemliness ['siːmlinis], *n.* bienséance; convenance, *f.*
seemly ['siːmli], *a.* bienséant, convenable; joli.—*adv.* convenablement.
seep [siːp], *v.i.* s'infiltrer, suinter.
seer ['siːə], *n.* prophète, voyant, *m.*
seesaw ['siːsɔː], *n.* bascule, balançoire, *f.*, va-et-vient, *m.*—*v.i.* faire la bascule.
seethe [siːð], *v.t.* faire bouillir.—*v.i.* bouillir, bouillonner.
segment ['segmənt], *n.* segment, *m.*
segregate ['segrigeit], *v.t.* séparer.—*v.i.* se diviser.

segregation [segri'geiʃən], *n.* séparation, ségrégation, *f.*
seize [siːz], *v.t.* saisir; se saisir de, s'emparer de; (*Naut.*) amarrer.—*v.i.* (*Mech.*) gripper, caler; se coincer.
seizure ['siːʒə], *n.* saisie, prise de possession; (*Path.*) attaque, *f.*
seldom ['seldəm], *adv.* rarement.
select [si'lekt], *a.* choisi; d'élite.—*v.t.* choisir.
selection [si'lekʃən], *n.* choix, *m.*
selectness [si'lektnis], *n.* excellence, *f.*
selector [si'lektə], *n.* (*Spt.*) sélectionneur, *m.*
self [self], *pron.* (*pl.* selves [selvz]) même, soi-même; (*reflexively*) se.—*n.* le moi, individu, *m.*, personne, *f.*
self-assertion ['selfə'səːʃən], *n.* caractère impérieux, *m.*, outrecuidance, *f.*
self-assertive ['selfə'səːtiv], *a.* autoritaire, outrecuidant.
self-centred ['self'sentəd], *a.* égocentrique.
self-confidence ['self'kɒnfidəns], *n.* confiance en soi-même, assurance, *f.*
self-confident ['self'kɒnfidənt], *a.* sûr de soi-même.
self-conscious ['self'kɒnʃəs], *a.* embarrassé, intimidé; gêné.
self-consciousness ['self'kɒnʃəsnis], *n.* embarras, *m.*, gêne, *f.*
self-contained ['selfkən'teind], *a.* indépendant; avec entrée particulière (*appartement*).
self-control ['selfkən'troul], *n.* sang-froid, *m.*; maîtrise de soi, *f.*
self-defence ['selfdi'fens], *n.* défense personnelle; légitime défense, *f.*
self-denial ['selfdi'naiəl], *n.* abnégation, *f.*; désintéressement, *m.*
self-denying ['selfdi'naiiŋ], *a.* qui fait abnégation de soi.
self-educated ['self'edjukeitid], *a.* autodidacte.
self-esteem ['selfi'stiːm], *n.* amour-propre, *m.*
self-evident ['self'evidənt], *a.* évident en soi, qui saute aux yeux.
self-governed ['self'gʌvənd], *a.* indépendant autonome.
self-government ['self'gʌvənmənt], *n.* autonomie, *f.*
self-help ['self'help], *n.* efforts personnels, *m.pl.*
self-importance ['selfim'pɔːtəns], *n.* suffisance, vanité, *f.*
self-important ['selfim'pɔːtənt], *a.* plein de soi, suffisant.
self-inflicted ['selfin'fliktid], *a.* volontaire.
selfish ['selfiʃ], *a.* égoïste.
selfishly ['selfiʃli], *adv.* en égoïste, d'une manière égoïste.
selfishness ['selfiʃnis], *n.* égoïsme, *m.*
selfless ['selflis], *a.* désintéressé.
self-made ['self'meid], *a.* qui s'est fait ce qu'il est; *he is a self-made man*, il est fils de ses œuvres.
self-opinioned ['selfə'pinjənd], self-opinionated ['selfə'pinjəneitid], *a.* entêté.
self-possessed ['selfpə'zest], *a.* calme; maître de soi.
self-possession ['selfpə'zeʃən], *n.* sang-froid, aplomb, *m.*
self-praise ['self'preiz], *n.* éloge de soi-même, *m.*
self-preservation ['selfprezə'veiʃən], *n.* conservation de soi-même, *f.*

555

self-propelled ['selfprə'peld], *a.* autopropulsé.

self-registering ['self'redʒistriŋ], *a.* à registre, enregistreur.

self-reliance ['selfri'laiəns], *n.* confiance en soi, indépendance, *f.*

self-respect ['selfris'pekt], *n.* respect de soi-même, amour-propre, *m.*; dignité, *f.*

self-righteous ['self'raitʃəs], *a.* pharisaïque.

self-sacrifice ['self'sækrifais], *n.* sacrifice de soi-même, *m.*, abnégation, *f.*

self-same ['selfseim], *a.* absolument le même.

self-satisfied ['self'sætisfaid], *a.* content de soi.

self-seeking ['self'si:kiŋ], *a.* égoïste.

self-service ['self'sə:vis], *n.* libre service, self-service, *m.*

self-starter ['self'sta:tə], *n.* démarreur automatique, *m.*

self-styled ['self'staild], *a.* soi-disant, prétendu.

self-sufficiency ['selfsə'fiʃənsi], *n.* suffisance; indépendance, *f.*

self-sufficient ['selfsə'fiʃənt], *a.* suffisant; indépendant.

self-supporting ['selfsə'pɔ:tiŋ], *a.* qui subsiste par ses propres moyens.

self-taught ['self'tɔ:t], *a.* autodidacte.

self-will ['self'wil], *n.* obstination, opiniâtreté, *f.*

self-willed ['self'wild], *a.* obstiné, opiniâtre.

sell [sel], *v.t. irr.* vendre.—*v.i.* se vendre; *to be sold out of an article*, avoir tout vendu, ne plus avoir d'un article.—*n.* attrape, *f.*

seller ['selə], *n.* vendeur, *m.*, vendeuse, *f.*

selling ['seliŋ], *n.* vente, *f.*; *selling off*, liquidation, *f.*

seltzer ['seltsə], **seltzer water** ['seltsə'wɔ:tə], *n.* eau de Seltz, *f.*

selvedge ['selvidʒ], *n.* lisière, *f.*

selves [SELF].

semaphore ['seməfɔ:], *n.* sémaphore, *m.*

semblance ['sembləns], *n.* semblant, *m.*, apparence, *f.*

semi ['semi], *pref.* semi, demi, à demi, à moitié.

semibreve ['semibri:v], *n.* (*Mus.*) ronde, *f.*

semi-circle ['semisə:kl], *n.* demi-cercle, *m.*

semicolon ['semi'koulən], *n.* point-virgule, *m.*

semi-detached ['semidi'tætʃt], *a.* *semi-detached houses*, maisons jumelles, *f.pl.*

semi-final ['semifainl], *n.* demi-finale, *f.*

seminary ['seminəri], *n.* séminaire, *m.*; institution (*école*), *f.*

semi-official ['semiə'fiʃl], *a.* demi-officiel, officieux.

semiquaver ['semikweivə], *n.* (*Mus.*) double croche, *f.*

semitone ['semitoun], *n.* (*Mus.*) demi-ton, semi-ton, *m.*

semolina [semə'li:nə], *n.* semoule, *f.*

sempstress ['sempstris, 'semstris], *n.* couturière, *f.*

senate ['senit], *n.* sénat, *m.*

senator ['senitə], *n.* sénateur, *m.*

senatorial [seni'tɔ:riəl], *a.* sénatorial.

send [send], *v.t. irr.* envoyer, faire parvenir; expédier (*marchandises*); *to send away*, renvoyer, congédier; *to send back*, renvoyer; *to send for*, envoyer chercher, faire venir; *to send forth*, lancer, émettre; *to*

send in, faire entrer; *to send on*, faire suivre (*lettres etc.*).—*v.i.* envoyer.

sender ['sendə], *n.* envoyeur; (*Comm.*) expéditeur, *m.*

Senegal ['senigɔ:l]. le Sénégal, *m.*

Senegalese [senigə'li:z], *a.* sénégalais.—*n.* Sénégalais (*personne*), *m.*

senile ['si:nail], *a.* de vieillard, sénile.

senility [sə'niliti], *n.* sénilité, *f.*

senior ['si:njə], *a.* aîné; ancien; plus ancien, supérieur.—*n.* aîné; ancien; doyen, *m.*

seniority [si:ni'ɔriti], *n.* priorité d'âge; ancienneté, *f.*

senna ['senə], *n.* séné, *m.*

sensation [sen'seiʃən], *n.* sensation, *f.*

sensational [sen'seiʃənl], *a.* à sensation, à effet.

sensationalism [sen'seiʃənlizm], *n.* recherche du sensationnel, *f.*

sense [sens], *n.* sens; bon sens, sens commun; sentiment, *m.*; signification, *f.*

senseless ['senslis], *a.* sans connaissance, insensible; insensé, absurde (*pas raisonnable*).

senselessly ['senslisli], *adv.* d'une manière insensée; sottement.

senselessness ['senslisnis], *n.* sottise, absurdité, *f.*

sensibility [sensi'biliti], *n.* sensibilité, *f.*; sentiment, *m.*

sensible ['sensibl], *a.* sensé, raisonnable (*intelligent*); sensible (*de*); en pleine connaissance.

sensibly ['sensibli], *adv.* sensiblement; sensément, sagement (*avec intelligence*).

sensitive ['sensitiv], *a.* sensible (*à*); sensitif, impressionnable; susceptible (*ombrageux*).

sensitiveness ['sensitivnis], **sensitivity** [sensi'tiviti], *n.* sensibilité; susceptibilité (*facilité à se vexer etc.*), *f.*

sensitized ['sensitaizd], *a.* (*Phot.*) sensible (*papier*).

sensory ['sensəri], *a.* sensoriel, des sens.

sensual ['sensjuəl], *a.* sensuel; des sens.

sensualist ['sensjuəlist], *n.* sensualiste, *m.*, *f.*, sensuel, *m.*

sensuality [sensju'æliti], *n.* sensualité, *f.*

sentence ['sentəns], *n.* phrase; maxime, *f.*; jugement, arrêt, *m.*, sentence, *f.*—*v.t.* prononcer une sentence *ou* un jugement (*contre*), condamner.

sententious [sen'tenʃəs], *a.* sentencieux.

sententiousness [sen'tenʃəsnis], *n.* caractère sentencieux, *m.*

sentient ['senʃənt], *a.* sensible.

sentiment ['sentimənt], *n.* sentiment; avis, *m.*, pensée, *f.*

sentimental [senti'mentl], *a.* sentimental.

sentimentality [sentimen'tæliti], *n.* sensiblerie, sentimentalité, *f.*

sentinel ['sentinl], **sentry** ['sentri], *n.* sentinelle, *f.*, factionnaire, *m.*

sentry-box ['sentriboks], *n.* guérite, *f.*

separable ['sepərəbl], *a.* séparable, divisible.

separate ['sepərit], *a.* séparé; disjoint, désuni.—['sepəreit], *v.t.* séparer; disjoindre, désunir.—*v.i.* se séparer; se disjoindre.

separately ['sepəritli], *adv.* séparément, à part.

separation [sepə'reiʃən], *n.* séparation; désunion, *f.*

sepia ['si:pjə], *n.* sépia (*couleur*); seiche (*poisson*), *f.*

settle

sepoy ['si:pɔi], n. cipaye, m.
September [sep'tembə]. septembre, m.
septennial [sep'teniəl], a. septennal.
septennially [sep'teniəli], adv. tous les sept ans.
septic ['septik], a. septique; infecté (blessure).
septuagenarian [septjuədʒə'neəriən], a. and n. septuagénaire, m., f.
Septuagesima [septjuə'dʒesimə]. Septuagésime, f.
sepulchral [si'pʌlkrəl], a. sépulcral.
sepulchre ['sepəlkə], n. sépulcre, m.
sepulture ['sepəltʃə], n. sépulture; inhumation, f.
sequel ['si:kwəl], n. suite, conséquence, f.
sequence ['si:kwəns], n. suite, série; succession; (Cine.) séquence, f.
sequester [si'kwestə], v.t. séquestrer.
sequestered [si'kwestəd], a. retiré, écarté; (Law) en séquestre.
sequestrate ['si:kwəstreit, si'kwestreit], v.t. séquestrer.
sequestration [si:kwəs'treiʃən], n. séquestre, m.; retraite, f., isolement (personne), m.
sequestrator ['si:kwəstreitə], n. (Law) séquestre, m.
sequin ['si:kwin], n. sequin, m.
seraglio [se'rɑ:ljou], n. sérail, m.
seraph ['serəf], n. (pl. seraphim ['serəfim]) séraphin, m.
seraphic [sə'ræfik], a. séraphique.
Serbia ['sə:biə]. la Serbie, f.
Serbian ['sə:biən], a. serbe.—n. serbe (langue), m.; Serbe (personne), m., f.
sere [SEAR].
serenade [serə'neid], n. sérénade, f.—v.t. donner une sérénade à.
serene [si'ri:n], a. serein, calme; sérénissime (titre).
serenely [si'ri:nli], adv. avec sérénité.
sereneness [si'ri:nnis], serenity [si'reniti], n. sérénité, f., calme, m.
serf [sə:f], n. serf, m.
serfdom ['sə:fdəm], n. servage, m.
serge [sə:dʒ], n. serge, f.
sergeant, serjeant ['sɑ:dʒənt], n. sergent (infanterie); maréchal des logis (cavalerie, artillerie); brigadier (police), m.
sergeant-major ['sɑ:dʒənt'meidʒə], n. adjudant, m.
serial ['siəriəl], a. paraissant par numéros ou par livraisons; serial (story), (roman-) feuilleton, m.
serially ['siəriəli], adv. par numéros.
seriatim [siəri'eitim], adv. par série; successivement.
series ['siəri:z], n. série, suite, succession, f.
serious ['siəriəs], a. sérieux; grave.
seriously ['siəriəsli], adv. sérieusement; gravement.
seriousness ['siəriəsnis], n. sérieux, m.; gravité, f.
serjeant [SERGEANT].
sermon ['sə:mən], n. sermon, m.
sermonize ['sə:mənaiz], v.t. prêcher; sermonner.
sermonizer ['sə:mənaizə], n. sermonneur, m.
serpent ['sə:pənt], n. serpent, m.
serpentine ['sə:pəntain], a. serpentin, sinueux.—n. (Min.) serpentine, f.
serrate ['sereit], a. en scie, dentelé; serraté.

serration [se'reiʃən], n. dentelure, f.
serried ['serid], a. compact, serré.
serum ['siərəm], n. sérum, m.
servant ['sə:vənt], n. serviteur, m., servante, f.; employé (de compagnies etc.), m.; domestique, m.; ordonnance (d'officier), m., f.; civil servant, fonctionnaire, m., f.
serve [sə:v], v.t. servir; servir à, être bon à; faire (apprentissage); desservir (localité); signifier (une assignation); it serves him right, c'est bien fait.—v.i. servir; être au service; suffire.—n. (fam.) (Ten.) service, m.
server ['sə:və], n. servant; (Ten.) serveur; (Eccles.) acolyte, m.
service ['sə:vis], n. service; (fig.) avantage, m.; utilité; signification (d'assignation); (Mil.) arme, f.—v.t. (Motor.) entretenir, réparer.
serviceable ['sə:visəbl], a. utile (à), avantageux, de bon usage.
serviceableness ['sə:visəblnis], n. utilité, f.
service-station ['sə:vissteiʃən], n. station-service, f.
serviette [sə:vi'et], n. serviette de table, f.
servile ['sə:vail], a. servile; asservi.
servility [sə:'viliti], n. servilité, bassesse, f.
serving ['sə:viŋ], a. servant, qui sert.
servitude ['sə:vitju:d], n. servitude, f., asservissement, m.; penal servitude, travaux forcés, m.pl.
sesame ['sesəmi], n. sésame, m.
session ['seʃən], n. session, séance, f.; (pl.) assises, f.pl.
set [set], v.t. irr. poser, opposer (sceau, signature), mettre, placer, poster; planter (fleurs); fixer; ajuster, arranger (régler); affûter (outil); donner (exemple); (Mus.) mettre en musique; remettre (os); sertir (pierre précieuse); dresser, tendre (piège); déployer (voiles); (Print.) composer; to set aside, mettre de côté; to set at ease, mettre à l'aise; to set back, reculer; to set forth, énoncer; to set forward, avancer; to set off, faire ressortir (faire valoir); to set up, ériger, établir (fonder).—v.i. se fixer; diriger, porter (vers ou à); se coucher (soleil); prendre (confitures etc.); to set about, commencer, se mettre à; to set out, partir, se mettre en route; to set up (dans un commerce etc.), s'établir.—a. mis, posé, placé; serti (pierre précieuse); prêt, arrêté, fixe; réglé; d'apparat, préparé (discours); all set? ça y est?—n. collection, f., ensemble, assortiment, m., série, f., jeu; service (de porcelaine etc.), m.; parure (de pierres précieuses); mise en plis (cheveux), f.; (Theat.) décor; groupe, m.
set-back ['setbæk], n. recul, échec, m.
set-square ['setskweə], n. équerre, f.
settee [se'ti:], n. canapé, m., causeuse, f.
setter ['setə], n. chien d'arrêt, m.; bone-setter, rebouteur, rebouteux, m.
setting ['setiŋ], n. mise, pose, f.; coucher (du soleil etc.), m.; décor (naturel ou de théâtre), m.; (Mus.) mise en musique, f.; remboîtement (d'os), m.; monture (de pierre précieuse), f.
settle (1) [setl], v.t. fixer; établir; décider, arrêter; assigner (des biens à); coloniser (un pays); accommoder; payer, régler (dettes).—v.i. s'établir, se fixer; se marier; se calmer (devenir tranquille); se poser (oiseau); s'ar-

557

settle

ranger (*avec*); **to settle down**, se fixer, s'établir; **to settle down to**, s'appliquer à.
settle (2) [setl], *n.* banc (à dossier), *m.*
settled [setld], *a.* établi; calme, tranquille.
settlement ['setlmənt], **settling** ['setliŋ], *n.* établissement, arrangement; dépôt (*au fond des liquides*); accord, contrat, *m.*; colonisation; colonie, *f.*; règlement, solde (*des comptes*); (*Build.*) tassement, *m.*
settler ['setlə], *n.* colon, immigrant, *m.*
set-up ['setʌp], *n.* organisation, *f.*
seven ['sevən], *a. and n.* sept, *m.*
sevenfold ['sevənfould], *a.* septuple.—*adv.* sept fois.
seventeen [sevən'tiːn], *a. and n.* dix-sept, *m.*
seventeenth [sevən'tiːnθ], *a.* dix-septième; dix-sept (*des rois etc.*).—*n.* dix-septième (*fraction*), *m.*
seventh ['sevənθ], *a.* septième; sept (*des rois etc.*).—*n.* septième (*fraction*), *m.*; (*Mus.*) septième, *f.*
seventieth ['sevəntiiθ], *a.* soixante-dixième.—*n.* soixante-dixième (*fraction*), *m.*
seventy ['sevənti], *a. and n.* soixante-dix, *m.*
sever ['sevə], *v.t.* séparer, diviser (*de*); disjoindre; couper.—*v.i.* se séparer (*de*).
several ['sevrəl], *a.* plusieurs, divers; distinct, respectif.
severally ['sevrəli], *adv.* séparément, individuellement.
severance ['sevərəns], *n.* séparation, disjonction; rupture, *f.*
severe [si'viə], *a.* sévère; rigoureux, rude (*temps etc.*); violent, aigu, vif (*douleur etc.*).
severity [si'veriti], *n.* sévérité; rigueur, *f.*
sew [sou], *v.t. irr.* coudre; brocher (*livre*).
sewage ['sjuːidʒ], *n.* eaux d'égout, *f.pl.*
sewer (1) ['souə], *n.* couseur, *m.*
sewer (2) ['sjuːə], *n.* égout, *m.*
sewerage ['sjuːəridʒ], *n.* système d'égouts, *m.*, égouts, *m.pl.*
sewing ['souiŋ], *n.* couture, *f.*; **sewing-machine**, machine à coudre, *f.*
sex [seks], *n.* sexe, *m.*
sexagenarian [seksədʒə'neəriən], *a. and n.* sexagénaire, *m., f.*
Sexagesima [seksə'dʒesimə], Sexagésime, *f.*
sexennial [sek'seniəl], *a.* sexennal.
sexennially [sek'seniəli], *adv.* tous les six ans.
sextant ['sekstənt], *n.* sextant, *m.*
sextet [seks'tet], *n.* (*Mus.*) sextuor, *m.*
sexton ['sekstən], *n.* sacristain; fossoyeur, *m.*
sextuple ['sekstjupl], *a. and n.* sextuple, *m.*
sexual ['seksjuəl], *a.* sexuel.
sexuality [seksju'æliti], *n.* sexualité, *f.*
shabbily ['ʃæbili], *adv.* mal, pauvrement (*mis* ou *vêtu*); (*fig.*) mesquinement.
shabbiness ['ʃæbinis], *n.* état râpé (*de vêtements*), *m.*; (*fig.*) mesquinerie, *f.*
shabby ['ʃæbi], *a.* râpé; mal vêtu, mal mis; (*fig.*) mesquin, ignoble.
shackle [ʃækl], *v.t.* enchaîner; (*fig.*) entraver.
shackles [ʃæklz], *n.pl.* fers, *m.pl.*, chaînes; (*fig.*) entraves, *f.pl.*
shad [ʃæd], *n.* alose (*poisson*), *f.*
shade [ʃeid], *n.* ombre, *f.*; ombrage (*d'arbre etc.*); abat-jour (*de lampe etc.*); garde-vue (*pour les yeux*), *m.*; nuance (*couleur*), *f.*; (*pl.*) enfers (*où vivent les immortels*), *m.pl.*; **in the shade**, à l'ombre.—*v.t.* ombrager (*de*); obscurcir; abriter (*protéger*), (*Paint.*) ombrer, nuancer; hachurer (*une carte*).

shaded ['ʃeidid], *a.* à l'ombre; ombragé (*de*); (*Paint.*) ombré.
shadiness ['ʃeidinis], *n.* ombrage, *m.*, ombre; (*fig.*) nature suspecte, *f.*
shading ['ʃeidiŋ], *n.* ombres, nuances; hachures, *f.pl.*
shadow ['ʃædou], *n.* ombre, *f.*—*v.t.* ombrager; filer, espionner (*suivre de près*).
shadowing ['ʃædouiŋ], *n.* espionnage, *m.*, filature, *f.*
shadowy ['ʃædoui], *a.* ombragé; sombre (*morne*); vague, chimérique (*irréel*).
shady ['ʃeidi], *a.* ombragé, ombreux; sombre (*noir*); (*colloq.*) louche (*malhonnête*).
shaft [ʃɑːft], *n.* flèche, *f.*, dard, trait; brancard (*de charette*); manche (*d'outil, d'arme*); puits (*de mine*); (*Mach.*) arbre, *m.*
shag [ʃæg], *n.* poil rude; caporal (*tabac*); cormoran huppé (*oiseau*), *m.*
shagginess ['ʃæginis], *n.* état poilu, état hérissé, *m.*
shaggy ['ʃægi], *a.* poilu, velu; raboteux (*pays*).
shagreen [ʃə'griːn], *a.* de peau de chagrin.—*n.* peau de chagrin, *f.*
shah [ʃɑː], *n.* shah, *m.*
shake [ʃeik], *n.* secousse, *f.*; serrement, *m.*; poignée (de main), *f.*; hochement (de tête), *m.*—*v.t. irr.* secouer, branler, agiter; ébranler, faire trembler; **to shake hands with**, serrer la main à.—*v.i.* trembler (*de*); s'agiter, branler; chanceler (*sur ses jambes*).
shakedown ['ʃeikdaun], *n.* lit improvisé, *m.*
shakily ['ʃeikili], *adv.* en branlant; à pas chancelants.
shaking ['ʃeikiŋ], *n.* secousse, *f.*, ébranlement, tremblement; ballottement (*à cheval*), *m.*
shako ['ʃækou], *n.* shako, *m.*
shaky ['ʃeiki], *a.* branlant; (*fig.*) peu solide; faible, chancelant (*personne*).
shale [ʃeil], *n.* argile schisteuse, *f.*
shall [ʃæl], *v.aux. irr.* (*used as sign of the future*) **I shall go**, j'irai; devoir; vouloir; **shall I go?** dois-je aller? voulez-vous que j'aille? **but he shall**, mais je l'y forcerai; **but I shall not**, mais je n'en ferai rien.
shallop ['ʃæləp], *n.* chaloupe, péniche, pinasse, *f.*
shallot [ʃə'lɔt], *n.* échalote, *f.*
shallow ['ʃælou], *a.* peu profond; (*fig.*) superficiel, léger, borné.
shallowness ['ʃælounis], *n.* peu de profondeur; esprit borné, *m.*
sham [ʃæm], *a.* feint, simulé; faux, factice.—*n.* feinte, *f.*, prétexte, *m.*; imposture, frime, *f.*—*v.t.* feindre, simuler; faire le, la ou les.—*v.i.* feindre, faire semblant; jouer la comédie.
shamble [ʃæmbl], *v.i.* marcher en traînant les pieds.
shambles [ʃæmblz], *n.pl.* abattoir, *m.*; (*fig.*) scène de carnage; une belle pagaille, *f.*
shambling ['ʃæmbliŋ], *a.* traînant.
shame [ʃeim], *n.* honte; ignominie (*déshonneur*), *f.*; opprobre, *m.*; **what a shame!** quel dommage!—*v.t.* faire honte à.
shamefaced ['ʃeimfeist], *a.* honteux, confus.
shamefacedly ['ʃeim'feisidli], *adv.* d'un air penaud.
shamefacedness ['ʃeimfeistnis], *n.* mauvaise honte; timidité, *f.*
shameful ['ʃeimful], *a.* honteux; déshonnête.

shamefulness ['ʃeimfulnis], *n.* honte, ignominie, *f.*
shameless ['ʃeimlis], *a.* éhonté, effronté, impudent.
shamelessly ['ʃeimlisli], *adv.* sans honte, effrontément.
shamelessness ['ʃeimlisnis], *n.* effronterie, impudence, *f.*
shammer ['ʃæmə], *n.* simulateur, *m.*
shampoo [ʃæm'pu:], *v.t.* frictionner; nettoyer (*la tête*).—*n.* shampooing, *m.*
shamrock ['ʃæmrɔk], *n.* trèfle (d'Irlande), *m.*
shank [ʃæŋk], *n.* jambe, *f.*
shanty ['ʃænti], *n.* cabane, bicoque, hutte, *f.*
shanty-town ['ʃæntitaun], *n.* bidonville, *m.*
shape [ʃeip], *n.* forme, figure; tournure, taille (*de personne*); façon, coupe (*de vêtement*), *f.*—*v.t.* former, façonner; modeler (*sur*).
shapeless ['ʃeiplis], *a.* informe, sans forme.
shapelessness ['ʃeiplisnis], *n.* absence de forme, difformité, *f.*
shapeliness ['ʃeiplinis], *n.* beauté de forme, *f.*, galbe, *m.*
shapely ['ʃeipli], *a.* bien fait, beau.
share (1) [ʃɛə], *n.* soc (*de charrue*), *m.*
share (2) [ʃɛə], *n.* part, portion; (*St. Exch.*) action, *f.*; **preference share**, action privilégiée.—*v.t.*, *v.i.* partager; prendre part à; avoir part à.
shareholder ['ʃɛəhouldə], *n.* actionnaire, *m.,f.*
sharer ['ʃɛərə], *n.* participant; (*Law*) partageant, *m.*
sharing ['ʃɛəriŋ], *n.* partage, *m.*
shark [ʃɑːk], *n.* requin; (*fig.*) escroc, filou (*personne*), *m.*
sharp [ʃɑːp], *a.* tranchant, affilé, qui coupe bien; pointu, aigu; saillant (*angle*); (*fig.*) vif, intelligent, pénétrant, perçant; anguleux (*traits*); piquant, aigre (*goût etc.*); rusé (*astucieux*); (*Mus.*) dièse; **sharp practice**, filouterie, rouerie, *f.*—*adv.* précise (*l'heure*); **at four o'clock sharp**, à quatre heures précises; **look sharp!** faites vite!—*n.* (*Mus.*) dièse, *m.*
sharpen ['ʃɑːpən], *v.t.* affiler, aiguiser; tailler en pointe, tailler (*crayon etc.*); (*fig.*) rendre vif.
sharper ['ʃɑːpə], *n.* aigrefin, escroc, chevalier d'industrie, *m.*
sharply ['ʃɑːpli], *adv.* rudement, vivement; nettement.
sharpness ['ʃɑːpnis], *n.* tranchant (*d'une lame*), *m.*; pointe (*acuité*); acidité (*de fruit*); violence (*de douleur etc.*); âpreté (*de langage etc.*); netteté (*de contour etc.*), *f.*; esprit éveillé (*d'enfants etc.*), *m.*
sharp-sighted ['ʃɑːp'saitid], *a.* à la vue perçante.
sharp-witted ['ʃɑːp'witid], *a.* à l'esprit délié.
shatter ['ʃætə], *v.t.* fracasser, briser en pièces.—*v.i.* se briser, se fracasser.
shave [ʃeiv], *v.t.* raser; faire la barbe à; effleurer (*friser*); (*Tech.*) planer.—*v.i.* se raser, se faire la barbe; **to have a close shave**, l'échapper belle; **to have a shave**, se raser, se faire raser.
shaving ['ʃeiviŋ], *n.* action de raser, *f.*; copeau (*de bois*), *m.*
shaving-brush ['ʃeiviŋbrʌʃ], *n.* blaireau, *m.*
shaving-cream ['ʃeiviŋkri:m], *n.* crème à raser, *f.*

shaving-soap ['ʃeiviŋsoup], *n.* savon pour la barbe, *m.*
shawl [ʃɔːl], *n.* châle, *m.*
she [ʃiː], *pron.* elle; femelle (*de certains animaux*), *f.*
sheaf [ʃiːf], *n.* (*pl.* **sheaves** [ʃiːvz]) gerbe, *f.*; faisceau (*de flèches*), *m.*—*v.t.* engerber, mettre en gerbe.
shear [ʃiə], *v.t. irr.* tondre.
shearer ['ʃiərə], *n.* tondeur, *m.*; tondeuse (*machine*), *f.*
shearing ['ʃiəriŋ], *n.* tonte, tondaison, *f.*
shears [ʃiəz], *n.pl.* grands ciseaux, *m.pl.*; cisailles (*pour haie, pour métal*), *f.pl.*
she-ass ['ʃiːæs], *n.* ânesse, *f.*
sheath [ʃiːθ], *n.* (*pl.* **sheaths** [ʃiːðz]) gaine, *f.*; fourreau (*à épée*); étui (*à ciseaux etc.*); (*Ent.*) élytre, *m.*
sheathe [ʃiːð], *v.t.* mettre dans le fourreau, rengainer; envelopper; revêtir (*de*).
sheaves [SHEAF].
she-cat ['ʃiːkæt], *n.* chatte, *f.*
shed (1) [ʃed], *n.* hangar; (*Build.*) atelier, *m.*; **cow-shed**, étable (à vaches), *f.*; **lean-to shed**, appentis, *m.*
shed (2) [ʃed], *v.t. irr.* répandre, verser; se dépouiller de, perdre (*feuilles etc.*); jeter (*animal*).
shedding ['ʃediŋ], *n.* effusion (*de sang*); perte (*feuilles etc.*), *f.*
sheen [ʃiːn], *n.* éclat, lustre, brillant, *m.*
sheep [ʃiːp], *n.inv.* mouton, *m.*; (*fig.*) brebis, *f.*; **black sheep**, brebis galeuse; **lost sheep**, brebis égarée.
sheep-dip ['ʃiːpdip], *n.* bain parasiticide, *m.*
sheep-dog ['ʃiːpdɔg], *n.* chien de berger, *m.*
sheep-fold ['ʃiːpfould], *n.* bergerie, *f.*, bercail, *m.*
sheepish ['ʃiːpiʃ], *a.* penaud, bête, niais.
sheepishly ['ʃiːpiʃli], *adv.* d'un air penaud.
sheep-pen ['ʃiːppen], *n.* parc à moutons, *m.*
sheep-shearing ['ʃiːpʃiəriŋ], *n.* tonte, *f.*
sheepskin ['ʃiːpskin], *n.* peau de mouton; basane (*cuir*), *f.*
sheer (1) [ʃiə], *a.* pur; escarpé, à pic (*rocher*); **sheer force**, pure force, *f.*; **sheer nonsense**, pure sottise, *f.*—*adv.* tout droit; tout à fait.
sheer (2) [ʃiə], *n.* (*Naut.*) tonture; embardée, *f.*—*v.i.* faire des embardées; **to sheer off**, pousser au large, s'esquiver.
sheet [ʃiːt], *n.* drap, *m.*; feuille (*de papier ou métal*); nappe (*d'eau etc.*); (*Naut.*) écoute (*corde*), *f.*; **winding-sheet**, linceul, *m.*
sheet-anchor ['ʃiːtæŋkə], *n.* ancre de miséricorde; (*fig.*) ancre de salut, *f.*
sheet-iron ['ʃiːtaiən], *n.* tôle, *f.*
sheet-lightning ['ʃiːt'laitniŋ], *n.* éclair en nappe, *m.*
sheikh [ʃeik], *n.* cheik, *m.*
shelf [ʃelf], *n.* (*pl.* **shelves** [ʃelvz]) planche, *f.*; rayon (*de bibliothèque*), *m.*; tablette, *f.*; écueil (*dans la mer*), *m.*; **set of shelves**, étagères, *f.pl.*
shell [ʃel], *n.* coque (*d'œuf, fruits etc.*); coquille (*œuf vide*); cosse (*de petits pois etc.*); écaille (*d'huître, de tortue*); carapace (*de homard*), *f.*; (*Artill.*) obus; (*fig.*) extérieur, *m.*—*v.t.* écaler (*noisette etc.*); écosser (*petits pois etc.*); égrener (*graine*); (*Mil.*) bombarder.
shell-fish ['ʃelfiʃ], *n.* coquillage, mollusque, *m.*, crustacés, *m.pl.*

shelling ['ʃeliŋ], *n.* écossage; égrenage; (*Mil.*) bombardement, *m.*

shell-proof ['ʃelpruːf], *a.* blindé.

shelter ['ʃeltə], *n.* abri, couvert; (*fig.*) asile, *m.*; *to take shelter*, s'abriter.—*v.t.* abriter; protéger.—*v.i.* s'abriter.

sheltered ['ʃeltəd], *a.* abrité.

shelve [ʃelv], *v.t.* mettre sur un rayon; (*fig.*) enterrer.—*v.i.* aller en pente.

shelves [SHELF].

shelving ['ʃelviŋ], *a.* en pente, incliné.

shepherd ['ʃepəd], *n.* berger, pâtre; (*fig.*) pasteur, *m.*—*v.t.* piloter, guider.

shepherdess ['ʃepədes], *n.* bergère, *f.*

sherbet ['ʃəːbət], *n.* sorbet, *m.*

sheriff ['ʃerif], *n.* shérif; (*Am.*) chef de l'administration de la justice (d'un comté), *m.*

sherry ['ʃeri], *n.* vin de Xérès, *m.*

shield [ʃiːld], *n.* bouclier; écran protecteur; (*Her.*) écu, écusson, *m.*—*v.t.* défendre de, protéger contre.

shift [ʃift], *n.* changement; expédient, *m.*, ressource, *f.*; détour, faux-fuyant (*artifice*), *m.*; *chemise de femme*; équipe, journée (*d'ouvriers*), *f.*—*v.t.*, *v.i.* changer; changer de place; (*fig.*) trouver des expédients; *to shift for oneself*, se débrouiller.

shiftiness ['ʃiftinis], *n.* manque de franchise, *m.*

shifting ['ʃiftiŋ], *a.* changeant; *shifting sand*, sable mouvant, *m.*—*n.* changement; déplacement (*de cargaison etc.*), *m.*

shiftless ['ʃiftlis], *a.* sans initiative; sans énergie; paresseux.

shifty ['ʃifti], *a.* plein d'expédients; *he is a shifty customer*, c'est un roublard.

shilling ['ʃiliŋ], *n.* shilling, *m.*

shilly-shally ['ʃili'ʃæli], *n.* irrésolution, *f.*—*v.i.* hésiter, être irrésolu.

shimmer ['ʃimə], *n.* lueur, *f.*—*v.i.* miroiter.

shin [ʃin], *n.* devant de la jambe; jarret (*de bœuf*), *m.*

shin-bone ['ʃinboun], *n.* tibia, *m.*

shindy ['ʃindi], *n.* tapage, *m.*

shine [ʃain], *v.i.* *irr.* luire; reluire; briller.—*n.* brillant, éclat, lustre, *m.*

shingle (1) [ʃiŋgl], *n.* bardeau (*pour toiture*), *m.*; coiffure à la garçonne, *f.*

shingle (2) [ʃiŋgl], *n.* galets, cailloux (*au bord de la mer*), *m.*

shingles [ʃiŋglz], *n.pl.* (*Med.*) zona, *m.*

shingly ['ʃiŋgli], *a.* couvert de galets.

shining ['ʃainiŋ], *a.* luisant, brillant.

shiny ['ʃaini], *a.* luisant, reluisant.

ship [ʃip], *n.* navire; vaisseau, bâtiment, *m.*—*v.t.* embarquer; expédier (*marchandises*); armer (*avirons*).—*v.i.* s'embarquer.

shipboard ['ʃipbɔːd], *n.* bord de navire, *m.*

shipbuilder ['ʃipbildə], *n.* constructeur de navires, *m.*

shipbuilding ['ʃipbildiŋ], *n.* construction navale, *f.*

ship-chandler ['ʃip'tʃaːndlə], *n.* fournisseur de navires, *m.*

shipmate ['ʃipmeit], *n.* camarade de bord, *m.*

shipment ['ʃipmənt], *n.* chargement, *m.*

shipowner ['ʃipounə], *n.* armateur, *m.*

shipper ['ʃipə], *n.* expéditeur, *m.*

shipping ['ʃipiŋ], *a.* maritime.—*n.* vaisseaux, navires, *m.pl.*; navigation; marine marchande; mise à bord (*chargement*), *f.*

ship's-boat ['ʃips'bout], *n.* chaloupe, *f.*

ship's-carpenter ['ʃips'kaːpintə], *n.* charpentier du bord, *m.*

shipshape ['ʃipʃeip], *a.* en ordre, bien arrangé.

shipwreck ['ʃiprek], *n.* naufrage, *m.*—*v.t.* faire faire naufrage à; *to be shipwrecked*, faire naufrage.

shipwrecked ['ʃiprekt], *a.* naufragé.

shipwright ['ʃiprait], *n.* constructeur de navires, *m.*

shipyard ['ʃipjaːd], *n.* chantier naval, *m.*

shire ['ʃaiə], *n.* comté, *m.*

shirk [ʃəːk], *v.t.* éviter, éluder.—*v.i.* finasser; tirer au flanc.

shirker ['ʃəːkə], *n.* carottier; flanchard, *m.*

shirt [ʃəːt], *n.* chemise (*d'homme*), *f.*; *shirt-collar*, col de chemise, *m.*; *shirt-front*, devant de chemise, plastron, *m.*

shiver (1) ['ʃivə], *v.t.* briser en morceaux, fracasser.—*v.i.* se briser en morceaux.—*n.* fragment, morceau, éclat, *m.*

shiver (2) ['ʃivə], *v.i.* grelotter (*de froid*); frissonner (*de peur*).—*n.* frisson, tremblement, *m.*

shivering ['ʃivəriŋ], *a.* frissonnant.—*n.* frissonnement, frisson, *m.*

shoal [ʃoul], *n.* banc (*de poissons*), *m.*; (*fig.*) foule, *f.*; bas-fond, haut-fond (*de la mer*), *m.*; *in shoals*, en foule.

shock (1) [ʃɔk], *n.* choc, *m.*; (*Elec.*) secousse, *f.*—*v.t.* choquer, heurter; scandaliser.

shock (2) [ʃɔk], *n.* moyette (*de blé*); tignasse (*de cheveux*), *f.*

shock-absorber ['ʃɔkəbsɔːbə], *n.* (*Motor.*) amortisseur, *m.*

shocking ['ʃɔkiŋ], *a.* choquant, affreux, dégoûtant.

shockingly ['ʃɔkiŋli], *adv.* affreusement.

shod [ʃɔd], *a.* ferré (*cheval*); chaussé (*personne*).

shoddy ['ʃɔdi], *a.* d'effilochage; de pacotille. —*n.* drap de laine d'effilochage, *m.*

shoe [ʃuː], *n.* soulier, *m.*; chaussure, *f.*; fer (*à cheval*); sabot (*en bois*), *m.*—*v.t.* *irr.* chausser; ferrer (*cheval etc.*).

shoe-black ['ʃuːblæk], *n.* cireur, *m.*

shoe-horn ['ʃuːhɔːn], *n.* chausse-pied, *m.*

shoeing ['ʃuːiŋ], *n.* ferrage, *m.*

shoeing-smith ['ʃuːiŋsmiθ], *n.* maréchal ferrant, *m.*

shoe-lace ['ʃuːleis], *n.* lacet de chaussure, *m.*

shoemaker ['ʃuːmeikə], *n.* cordonnier, *m.*

shoe-making ['ʃuːmeikiŋ], *n.* cordonnerie, *f.*

shoe-polish ['ʃuːpɔliʃ], *n.* cirage, *m.*

shoot [ʃuːt], *v.t.* *irr.* tirer, lancer, darder; décharger, tirer un coup (*de fusil etc.*); atteindre (*une cible*); tuer (*faire mourir*); fusiller; descendre (*rapides etc.*); *to shoot a film*, tourner un film; *to shoot oneself*, se tuer.—*v.i.* tirer; chasser (*gibier*); (*fig.*) s'élancer; filer (*étoile etc.*); pousser (*plante etc.*).—*n.* rejeton, *m.*, pousse (*plante*), *f.*; sarment (*de vigne*); dépôt de décombres (*ordures*), *m.*

shooter ['ʃuːtə], *n.* tireur, *m.*

shooting ['ʃuːtiŋ], *a.* lancinant (*douleur*); *shooting star*, étoile filante, *f.*—*n.* tir (*de fusil*), *m.*; chasseau fusil, *f.*; élancement (*de douleur*), *m.*; pousse (*de plante*); décharge (*des ordures*), *f.*; (*Cine.*) tournage (*de film*), *m.*

shooting-brake ['ʃuːtiŋbreik], *n.* (*Motor.*) canadienne, *f.*

shooting-gallery [ˈʃuːtiŋgæləri], *n.* tir, stand, *m.*

shop [ʃɔp], *n.* boutique (*petit*), *f.*, magasin (*grand*); atelier (*de fabrication*), *m.*—*v.i.* faire des emplettes; *to go shopping*, aller faire des courses.

shop-assistant [ˈʃɔpəsistənt], *n.* vendeur, *m.*, vendeuse, commise, *f.*

shopkeeper [ˈʃɔpkiːpə], *n.* marchand, *m.*

shoplifter [ˈʃɔpliftə], *n.* voleur à l'étalage, *m.*

shoplifting [ˈʃɔpliftiŋ], *n.* vol à l'étalage, *m.*

shopper [ˈʃɔpə], *n.* acheteur, client, *m.*

shopping-centre [ˈʃɔpiŋsentə], *n.* quartier commerçant, *m.*

shop-soiled [ˈʃɔpsɔild], *a.* défraîchi.

shop-steward [ˈʃɔpstjuəd], *n.* responsable syndical, délégué ouvrier, *m.*

shop-walker [ˈʃɔpwɔːkə], *n.* chef de rayon; inspecteur de magasin, *m.*

shop-window [ˈʃɔpˈwindou], *n.* devanture, vitrine, *f.*, étalage, *m.*

shore [ʃɔː], *n.* rivage, bord, *m.*, plage, côte, *f.*—*v.t.* étayer, étançonner.

short [ʃɔːt], *a.* court; bref; passager (*temps*); petit (*taille*); insuffisant; croquant (*pâte*); brusque (*bourru*); *short circuit*, court-circuit, *m.*; *short story*, conte, *m.*, nouvelle, *f.*; *to cut the matter short*, pour en finir.—*adv.* court, vivement, brusquement; *it falls far short of it*, il s'en faut de beaucoup.

shortbread [ˈʃɔːtbred], *n.* (gâteau) sablé, *m.*

short-circuit [ˈʃɔːtˈsəːkit], *v.t.* mettre en court-circuit.

shortcoming [ˈʃɔːtkʌmiŋ], *n.* défaut, *m.*, insuffisance, *f.*

shorten [ʃɔːtn], *v.t.* raccourcir; abréger.—*v.i.* (se) raccourcir.

shortening [ˈʃɔːtniŋ], *n.* raccourcissement, *m.*

shorthand [ˈʃɔːthænd], *n.* sténographie, *f.*

short-handed [ˈʃɔːtˈhændid], *a.* à court de personnel.

shorthand-typist [ˈʃɔːthændˈtaipist], *n.* sténodactylographe, (*fam.*) sténodactylo, *f.*

short-lived [ˈʃɔːtˈlivd], *a.* qui vit peu de temps, éphémère.

shortly [ˈʃɔːtli], *adv.* bientôt, sous peu; brièvement.

shortness [ˈʃɔːtnis], *n.* courte durée, *f.*; peu d'étendue, *m.*; petitesse (*de taille*), *f.*

shorts [ˈʃɔːts], *n.pl.* culotte courte, *f.*, caleçon court, slip; short, *m.*

short-sighted [ˈʃɔːtˈsaitid], *a.* myope; (*fig.*) peu prévoyant.

short-sightedness [ˈʃɔːtˈsaitidnis], *n.* myopie, *f.*; (*fig.*) manque de prévoyance, *m.*

short-tempered [ˈʃɔːtˈtempəd], *a.* vif, pétulant, brusque.

short-winded [ˈʃɔːtˈwindid], *a.* à l'haleine courte; poussif (*cheval*).

shot (1) [ʃɔt], *past* and *p.p.* [SHOOT].

shot (2) [ʃɔt], *a.* chatoyant; *shot silk*, soie gorge-de-pigeon, *f.*—*n.* coup de fusil, coup; trait (*d'arc*), *m.*; balle (*de fusil*), *f.*, boulet (*de canon*); plomb (*de fusil de chasse*), *m.*; (*Artill.*) charge; portée (*étendue*), *f.*; tireur (*personne*); (*Ftb.*) coup au but, *m.*; (*Med.*) injection; (*Cine.*) prise, *f.*; *at a shot*, d'un seul coup; *like a shot*, comme un trait; *to be a good shot*, être bon tireur; *to fire a shot*, tirer un coup de feu.

shot-gun [ˈʃɔtgʌn], *n.* fusil de chasse, *m.*

should [ʃud], *v.aux.* (*past of* **shall**, *used as sign of the conditional*) *I should speak*, je parlerais; (= *ought to*, *conditional tense of* **devoir**) *you should see it*, vous devriez le voir.

shoulder [ˈʃouldə], *n.* épaule; (*Tech.*) languette, *f.*; *round shoulders*, dos rond, *m.*—*v.t.* charger sur les épaules; se charger de; porter (*armes*).

shoulder-blade [ˈʃouldəbleid], *n.* omoplate, *f.*

shout [ʃaut], *v.t.*, *v.i.* crier, huer, pousser des cris; vociférer.—*n.* cri, *m.*; acclamations, *f.pl.*; éclat (*de rire*), *m.*

shouting [ˈʃautiŋ], *n.* acclamation, *f.*, cris, *m.pl.*

shove [ʃʌv], *v.t.* pousser; *to shove away*, repousser, éloigner.—*v.i.* pousser.—*n.* coup, *m.*, poussée, *f.*

shovel [ˈʃʌvl], *n.* pelle, *f.*—*v.t.* ramasser avec la pelle, pelleter.

shovelful [ˈʃʌvlful], *n.* pelletée, *f.*

show [ʃou], *v.t. irr.* montrer, faire voir, exposer à la vue; manifester, témoigner, démontrer; indiquer; expliquer; *to show in*, faire entrer; *to show off*, faire valoir.—*v.i.* paraître, se montrer; se faire remarquer; *to show off*, poser, se donner des airs.—*n.* apparence, *f.*; étalage, *m.*, parade, *f.*; spectacle, concours, *m.*; exposition, *f.*

show-case [ˈʃoukeis], *n.* montre, vitrine, *f.*

shower [ˈʃauə], *n.* ondée (*légère*); averse (*grosse*); pluie, grêle (*de coups, pierres etc.*); douche, *f.*—*v.t.* inonder (*de pluie*); (*fig.*) verser.

shower-bath [ˈʃauəbɑːθ], *n.* douche, *f.*, bain-douche, *m.*

showery [ˈʃauəri], *a.* pluvieux.

show-ring [ˈʃouriŋ], *n.* arène de vente, *f.*

show-room [ˈʃouruːm], *n.* salle d'exposition, *f.*

showy [ˈʃoui], *a.* voyant, prétentieux, criard.

shrapnel [ˈʃræpnəl], *n.* éclats d'obus, *m.pl.*

shred [ʃred], *n.* lambeau, bout, brin, *m.*; *to tear to shreds*, déchirer en lambeaux.—*v.t.* déchiqueter; râper grossièrement.

shrew [ʃruː], *n.* mégère, femme acariâtre, *f.*

shrewd [ʃruːd], *a.* sagace, fin, perspicace.

shrewdly [ˈʃruːdli], *adv.* avec sagacité, avec pénétration, finement.

shrewdness [ˈʃruːdnis], *n.* sagacité, pénétration, finesse, *f.*

shrewish [ˈʃruːiʃ], *a.* acariâtre.

shrewishly [ˈʃruːiʃli], *adv.* en mégère.

shrewishness [ˈʃruːiʃnis], *n.* humeur acariâtre, *f.*

shriek [ʃriːk], *n.* cri perçant, *m.*—*v.t.* crier.—*v.i.* jeter un cri aigu.

shrieking [ˈʃriːkiŋ], *n.* cris stridents, *m.pl.*

shrift [ʃrift], *n.* confession, *f.*; (*fig.*) *short shrift*, très court délai, *m.*

shrill [ʃril], *a.* aigu, perçant; aigre (*voix*).

shrillness [ˈʃrilnis], *n.* son aigu, ton aigu, *m.*

shrilly [ˈʃrilli], *adv.* d'un ton aigu.

shrimp [ʃrimp], *n.* crevette (*grise*), *f.*

shrine [ʃrain], *n.* châsse, *f.*; tombeau, *m.*; chapelle (*d'un saint*), *f.*

shrink [ʃriŋk], *v.t. irr.* rétrécir, faire rétrécir.—*v.i.* rétrécir, se rétrécir; se retirer; reculer, se tasser; se ratatiner; se tasser (*en vieillissant*).

shrinkage [ˈʃriŋkidʒ], *n.* rétrécissement, *m.*, contraction, *f.*

shrinking ['ʃriŋkiŋ], *n.* rétrécissement, *m.*; action de reculer, *f.*
*****shrive** [ʃraiv], *v.t. irr.* confesser.
shrivel [ʃrivl], *v.t.* faire ratatiner, faire recroqueviller, rider, racornir.—*v.i.* se ratatiner, se recroqueviller.
shroud [ʃraud], *n.* linceul, suaire, *m.*; (*Naut., pl.*) haubans, *m.pl.*—*v.t.* (*fig.*) abriter, couvrir.
Shrovetide ['ʃrouvtaid], les jours gras, *m.pl.*; *Shrove Tuesday*, mardi-gras, *m.*
shrub [ʃrʌb], *n.* arbuste, arbrisseau, *m.*
shrubbery ['ʃrʌbəri], *n.* plantation d'arbrisseaux, *f.*
shrubby ['ʃrʌbi], *a.* plein d'arbrisseaux, touffu.
shrug [ʃrʌg], *n.* haussement d'épaules, *m.*—*v.t.* hausser; *to shrug one's shoulders*, hausser les épaules.
shudder ['ʃʌdə], *v.i.* frissonner, frémir (*de*).—*n.* frissonnement, frémissement, *m.*
shuffle [ʃʌfl], *v.t.* mêler; (*Cards*) battre.—*v.i.* traîner les pieds; battre les cartes; tergiverser (*équivoquer*).
shuffling ['ʃʌfliŋ], *a.* chicaneur, biaiseur; traînant (*allure*).—*n.* marche traînante, *f.*; (*Cards*) battement des cartes, *m.*; (*fig.*) chicane, *f.*
shun [ʃʌn], *v.t.* éviter, fuir.
shunt [ʃʌnt], *v.t.* garer (*train*); détourner.
shunting ['ʃʌntiŋ], *n.* changement de voie, garage, *m.*
shut [ʃʌt], *v.t. irr.* fermer; enfermer; *to shut off*, intercepter, couper (*vapeur etc.*); *to shut out*, exclure; *to shut up*, fermer, enfermer; condamner (*porte etc.*); faire taire.—*v.i.* fermer, se fermer; *shut up!* taisez-vous!
shutter ['ʃʌtə], *n.* volet, contrevent (*à l'extérieur de la fenêtre*), *m.*
shuttle [ʃʌtl], *n.* navette; vanne, *f.*
shuttle-cock ['ʃʌtlkɔk], *n.* volant, *m.*
shuttle-service ['ʃʌtləːvis], *n.* navette, *f.*
shy (1) [ʃai], *a.* réservé, timide, honteux.—*v.i.* être ombrageux, faire un écart (*cheval*).
shy (2) [ʃai], *v.t.* jeter, lancer.—*n.* coup (*de pierre etc.*); essai, *m.*; *to have a shy at*, s'essayer à (*faire quelque chose*).
shyly ['ʃaili], *adv.* timidement, avec réserve.
shyness ['ʃainis], *n.* timidité, retenue, réserve; fausse honte, *f.*
Siam [sai'æm], le Siam, *m.*
Siamese [saiə'miːz], *a.* siamois.—*n.* siamois (*langue*); Siamois (*personne*), *m.*
Siberia [sai'biəriə], la Sibérie, *f.*
Siberian [sai'biəriən], *a.* sibérien.—*n.* Sibérien (*personne*), *m.*
sibilant ['sibilənt], *a.* sifflant.—*n.* lettre sifflante, *f.*
siccative ['sikətiv], *a.* and *n.* siccatif, *m.*
Sicilian [si'siliən], *a.* sicilien.—*n.* Sicilien (*personne*), *m.*
Sicily ['sisili], la Sicile, *f.*
sick [sik], *a.* malade; qui a des nausées, qui a mal au cœur; *sick headache*, migraine, *f.*; *sick man* or *woman*, malade, *m.*, *f.*; *sick of*, dégoûté de; *to be sea-sick*, avoir le mal de mer; *to be sick*, vomir.
sick-bed ['sikbed], *n.* lit de douleur, *m.*
sicken [sikn], *v.t.* rendre malade; (*fig.*) lasser, dégoûter.—*v.i.* tomber malade.

sickening ['sikniŋ], *a.* écœurant; (*fig.*) dégoûtant.
sickle [sikl], *n.* faucille, *f.*
sick-leave ['sikliːv], *n.* congé de convalescence, *m.*
sickliness ['siklinis], *n.* mauvaise santé, *f.*
sick-list ['siklist], *n.* rôle des malades, *m.*
sickly ['sikli], *a.* maladif; affadissant, affadi (*goût etc.*).
sickness ['siknis], *n.* maladie, *f.*; nausées, *f.pl.*
sick-nurse ['siknəːs], *n.* garde-malade, *f.*
sick-room ['sikruːm], *n.* chambre de malade, *f.*
side [said], *a.* de côté; latéral; indirect.—*n.* côté; flanc; bord; versant (*de montagne*); parti (*Spt.*) camp, *m.*; *by his side*, à côté de lui; *side by side*, côte à côte; *this side up* (*caisses*), dessus; *to take sides*, prendre parti; *wrong side out*, à l'envers.—*v.i.* to *side with*, se ranger du côté de.
sideboard ['saidbɔːd], *n.* buffet, *m.*
sided ['saidid], *a.* à côtés, à faces; *two-sided*, à deux faces.
side-door ['saiddɔː], *n.* porte latérale, *f.*
side-line ['saidlain], *n.* occupation secondaire, *f.*
sidelong ['saidlɔŋ], *a.* and *adv.* de côté.
side-show ['saidʃou], *n.* spectacle forain, *m.*
sidesman ['saidzmən], *n.* (*pl.* **-men** [men]) (*Eccles.*) marguillier, *m.*
side-track ['saidtræk], *v.t.* garer (*train*); (*fig.*) semer (*quelqu'un*).
sidewalk ['saidwɔːk], *n.* (*Am.*) trottoir (*de rue*), *m.*
sideways ['saidweiz], *adv.* de côté; obliquement.
siding ['saidiŋ], *n.* voie d'évitement, voie de garage, *f.*
sidle [saidl], *v.i.* marcher de côté; s'insinuer.
siege [siːdʒ], *n.* siège, *m.*; *to lay siege to*, mettre le siège devant, faire le siège de, assiéger.
Sienna [si'enə], Sienne, *f.*
sierra [si'eərə], *n.* sierra, *f.*
Sierra Leone [si'eərəli'oun], le Sierra-Leone, *m.*
siesta [si'estə], *n.* sieste, *f.*
sieve [siv], *n.* tamis (*fin*); crible (*grand*), *m.*
sift [sift], *v.t.* tamiser; cribler; sasser (*farine*); (*fig.*) examiner.
sifting ['siftiŋ], *n.* tamisage; (*fig.*) examen minutieux, *m.*
sigh [sai], *n.* soupir, *m.*—*v.i.* soupirer; *to sigh after*, soupirer après; *to sigh over*, gémir sur.
sighing ['saiiŋ], *n.* soupirs, *m.pl.*
sight [sait], *n.* vue, vision, *f.*; regard, *m.*, yeux, *m.pl.*; guidon, *m.*, hausse (*armes à feu*), *f.*; spectacle, *m.*; *a sight better*, beaucoup mieux; *at first sight*, à première vue; *by sight*, de vue; *in sight*, en vue; *out of sight*, hors de vue; *second sight*, clairvoyance, *f.*; *to catch sight of*, apercevoir; *to come in sight*, apparaître.—*v.t.* apercevoir.
sighted ['saitid], *a.* en vue; qui voit, voyant; *long-sighted*, presbyte; *short-sighted*, myope; (*fig.*) peu clairvoyant.
sightliness ['saitlinis], *n.* beauté, *f.*
sight-reading ['saitriːdiŋ], *n.* (*Mus.*) déchiffrement, *m.*

sight-seeing ['saitsiːiŋ], *n.* *to go sight-seeing*, aller voir les curiosités.

sight-seer ['saitsiːə], *n.* touriste, *m.*, *f.*, visiteur (*d'une ville*), *m.*

sign [sain], *n.* signe; indice, *m.*; enseigne (*panneau*), *f.*—*v.t.*, *v.i.* signer.

signal ['signəl], *a.* signalé, insigne.—*n.* signal; signe; (*Rail.*) sémaphore, *m.*; (*pl.*) (*Mil.*) les transmissions, *f.pl.*—*v.t.* signaler, faire signe à.—*v.i.* signaler; donner un signal.

signal-box ['signəlbɔks], *n.* poste à signaux, *m.*

signalman ['signəlmən], *n.* (*pl.* -men [men]) (*Rail.*) signaleur, *m.*

signaller ['signələ], *n.* signaleur, *m.*

signally ['signəli], *adv.* remarquablement.

signatory ['signətəri], *a.* and *n.* signataire, *m.*, *f.*

signature ['signətʃə], *n.* signature, *f.*

sign-board ['sainbɔːd], *n.* enseigne, *f.*

signet ['signit], *n.* sceau; cachet, *m.*

signet-ring ['signitriŋ], *n.* chevalière, *f.*

significance [sig'nifikəns], *n.* signification, *f.*, sens, *m.*; importance, *f.*

significant [sig'nifikənt], *a.* significatif.

signification [signifi'keiʃən], *n.* signification, *f.*

signify ['signifai], *v.t.* vouloir dire, signifier; faire connaître; importer.

sign-post ['sainpoust], *n.* poteau indicateur, *m.*

silence ['sailəns], *n.* silence, *m.*; *silence !* (*notice*), défense de parler.—*v.t.* réduire au silence, faire taire.

silent ['sailənt], *a.* silencieux; peu loquace (*qui ne parle pas beaucoup*); muet (*lettre, film*).

silently ['sailəntli], *adv.* silencieusement, en silence; sans bruit.

Silesia [sai'liːʃə, sai'liːsiə]. la Silésie, *f.*

silex ['saileks], *n.* silex, *m.*

silhouette [silu'et], *n.* silhouette, *f.*

silica ['silikə], *n.* silice, *f.*

silicon ['silikən], *n.* silicium, *m.*

silicosis [sili'kousis], *n.* (*Med.*) silicose, *f.*

silk [silk], *a.* de soie, en soie.—*n.* soie, *f.*; (*pl.*) soieries, *f.pl.*

silken ['silkən], *a.* de soie; soyeux.

silkiness ['silkinis], *n.* nature soyeuse, *f.*

silkworm ['silkwəːm], *n.* ver à soie, *m.*

silky ['silki], *a.* de soie, soyeux.

sill [sil], *n.* seuil (*d'une porte*); rebord (*d'une fenêtre*), *m.*

silliness ['silinis], *n.* sottise, niaiserie, *f.*

silly ['sili], *a.* and *n.* sot, nigaud, niais, *m.*; *silly ass*, imbécile, *m.*; *silly thing*, sottise, *f.*; nigaud (*personne*).

silt [silt], *v.t.* envaser.—*v.i.* s'envaser.—*n.* vase, *f.*, limon, *m.*

silting ['siltiŋ], *n.* envasement, *m.*

silver ['silvə], *a.* d'argent; argenté (*couleur*); argentin (*son*).—*n.* argent, *m.*; monnaie d'argent; argenterie (*vaisselle*), *f.*—*v.t.* argenter; étamer (*miroir*).

silver-gilt ['silvəgilt], *n.* argent doré, vermeil, *m.*

silvering ['silvəriŋ], *n.* argenture, *f.*; étamage (*de miroirs*), *m.*

silver-plated ['silvə'pleitid], *a.* argenté, en plaqué.

silversmith ['silvəsmiθ], *n.* orfèvre, *m.*

silvery ['silvəri], *a.* d'argent; argenté (*couleur*); argentin (*son*).

similar ['similə], *a.* semblable, pareil; similaire (*de nature*).

similarity [simi'læriti], *n.* ressemblance, similitude; similarité (*de nature*), *f.*

similarly ['similəli], *adv.* pareillement, d'une manière semblable.

simile ['simili], *n.* comparaison, *f.*

similitude [si'militjuːd], *n.* similitude, *f.*

simmer ['simə], *v.i.* bouillir lentement, mijoter.

simmering ['siməriŋ], *n.* mijotement, *m.*

simnel ['simnəl], *n.* gâteau de Pâques *ou* de la mi-carême, *m.*

simper ['simpə], *n.* sourire niais, *m.*—*v.i.* sourire niaisement, minauder.

simpering ['simpəriŋ], *a.* minaudier.—*n.* minauderie, *f.*

simperingly ['simpəriŋli], *adv.* en minaudant.

simple [simpl], *a.* simple; *as simple as ABC*, simple comme bonjour.—*n.* simple, *m.*

simple-hearted ['simpl'hɑːtid], **simple-minded** ['simplmaindid], *a.* simple, ingénu, naïf.

simpleness ['simplnis], *n.* simplicité, *f.*

simpleton ['simpltən], *n.* niais, nigaud, *m.*

simplicity [sim'plisiti], *n.* simplicité, *f.*

simplification ['simplifi'keiʃən], *n.* simplification, *f.*

simplify ['simplifai], *v.t.* simplifier.

simply ['simpli], *adv.* simplement (*sans complexité*); tout bonnement (*et rien de plus*).

simulate ['simjuleit], *v.t.* feindre, simuler.

simulation [simju'leiʃən], *n.* simulation, *f.*

simulator ['simjuleitə], *n.* simulateur, *m.*

simultaneous [siməl'teinjəs], *a.* simultané.

simultaneously [siməl'teinjəsli], *adv.* simultanément.

sin [sin], *n.* péché, *m.*; (*fig.*) offense, *f.*—*v.i.* pécher.

since [sins], *conj.* puisque (*parce que*); depuis que (*temps*).—*prep.* depuis; *since then*, depuis lors.—*adv.* depuis; *ever since*, depuis ce temps-là; *long since*, il y a longtemps.

sincere [sin'siə], *a.* sincère.

sincerely [sin'siəli], *adv.* sincèrement; *yours sincerely* (*lettre amicale mais sans intimité*), veuillez croire, cher Monsieur, à mes sentiments les meilleurs.

sincerity [sin'seriti], *n.* sincérité, bonne foi, *f.*

sine [sain], *n.* (*Trig.*) sinus, *m.*

sinecure ['sainəkjuə], *n.* sinécure, *f.*

sinew ['sinjuː], *n.* tendon, (*colloq.*) nerf, *m.*

sinewy ['sinjuːi], *a.* tendineux; (*fig.*) nerveux, vigoureux.

sinful ['sinful], *a.* pécheur, coupable.

sinfully ['sinfuli], *adv.* d'une manière coupable, en pécheur.

sinfulness ['sinfulnis], *n.* culpabilité, iniquité, *f.*

sing [siŋ], *v.t.*, *v.i.* *irr.* chanter; célébrer (*louer*); siffler (*vent*); *to make someone sing small*, rabattre le caquet à quelqu'un.

Singapore [siŋə'pɔː]. Singapour, *m.*

singe [sindʒ], *v.t.* flamber; roussir (*vêtements etc.*); (*Tech.*) griller.—*n.* légère brûlure, *f.*

singeing ['sindʒiŋ], *n.* flambage; (*Tech.*) grillage, *m.*

singer ['siŋə], *n.* chanteur, *m.*; cantatrice (*professionnelle*), *f.*

singing ['siŋiŋ], *a.* qui chante; chanteur (*oiseau*).—*n.* chant; bourdonnement (*dans les oreilles*), *m.*

single [siŋgl], *a.* seul, simple, unique; particulier (*individuel*); singulier (*combat*); non marié, célibataire; **single bedroom**, chambre à un lit, *f.*; **single man**, célibataire, garçon, *m.*; **single** (*ticket*), billet simple, *m.*; **single woman**, femme non mariée, fille, *f.*—*n.* (*pl.*) (*Ten.*) partie simple, *f.*—*v.t.* choisir; **to single out**, choisir, distinguer de la foule.

single-handed ['siŋgl'hændid], *adv.* tout seul, sans aide.

single-hearted ['siŋgl'hɑ:tid], *a.* sincère, honnête.

singleness ['siŋglnis], *n.* sincérité, simplicité, *f.*

singlet ['siŋglit], *n.* maillot fin, *m.*

single-track ['siŋgltræk], *a.* (*Rail.*) à voie unique; (*Cine.*) à simple piste.

singly ['siŋgli], *adv.* seulement; séparément; individuellement, un à un.

singsong ['siŋsɔŋ], *n.* chant monotone, *m.*

singular ['siŋgjulə], *a.* singulier; étrange (*bizarre*); simple (*pas complexe*), (*Gram.*)—*n.* singulier, *m.*

singularity [siŋgju'læriti], *n.* singularité, *f.*

singularly ['siŋgjuləli], *adv.* singulièrement.

sinister ['sinistə], *a.* sinistre; (*Her.*) sénestre.

sink [siŋk], *n.* évier (*de cuisine*); égout (*conduit*), *m.*; **a sink of iniquity**, un cloaque d'iniquité.—*v.t. irr.* faire tomber au fond, enfoncer; couler (*navire*); creuser (*puits etc.*); placer (*argent*) à fonds perdu; amortir (*dette*).—*v.i.* aller au fond, tomber au fond; s'enfoncer; sombrer, couler (*navire*); décliner, s'affaiblir (*santé etc.*); baisser (*prix etc.*); être abattu (*âme, cœur etc.*); descendre, se coucher (*soleil etc.*); dégénérer (*en*).

sinker ['siŋkə], *n.* plomb (*de ligne de pêche*), *m.*

sinking ['siŋkiŋ], *a.* qui coule (*navire*).—*n.* foncement (*de puits etc.*); tassement (*de fondements*); affaissement (*santé*); placement à fonds perdu (*d'argent*); amortissement (*d'une dette*); engloutissement (*de navire*), *m.*

sinking-fund ['siŋkiŋfʌnd], *n.* fonds, *m.*, *ou* caisse d'amortissement (*d'une dette publique*), *f.*

sinless ['sinlis], *a.* sans péché, innocent; pur.

sinner ['sinə], *n.* pécheur, *m.*, pécheresse, *f.*

sinuous ['sinjuəs], *a.* sinueux.

sinus ['sainəs], *n.* (*Anat.*) sinus, *m.*

sip [sip], *n.* petit coup, *m.*, petite gorgée, *f.*—*v.t., v.i.* boire à petit coups, siroter.

siphon ['saifən], *n.* siphon, *m.*—*v.t.* siphonner.

sir [sə:], *n.* monsieur, *m.*

sire ['saiə], *n.* père; sire (*à un roi*), *m.*; (*pl.*) pères, aïeux, *m.pl.*; **grand-sire**, grand-père, *m.*

siren ['saiərən], *n.* sirène, *f.*

Sirius ['siriəs]. (*Astron.*) Sirius, *m.*

sirloin ['sə:lɔin], *n.* aloyau; faux-filet, *m.*

sirocco [si'rɔkou], *n.* siroco, *m.*

siskin ['siskin], *n.* (*Orn.*) tarin, *m.*

sissy ['sisi], *n.* (*colloq.*) poule mouillée, *f.*

sister ['sistə], *n.* sœur; du même gabarit (*navire*).—*n.* sœur; (*Med.*) infirmière-major, *f.*

sisterhood ['sistəhud], *n.* communauté de sœurs, *f.*, sœurs, *f.pl.*

sister-in-law ['sistərinlɔ:], *n.* belle-sœur, *f.*

sisterly ['sistəli], *a.* de sœur, en sœur.

sit [sit], *v.t. irr.* asseoir; se tenir sur (*cheval*).—*v.i.* s'asseoir (*acte*); être assis (*attitude*); siéger, tenir séance, se réunir (*assemblée, cour, juge etc.*); couver (*poule etc.*), percher (*oiseau*); poser (*pour un portrait*); **to sit down**, s'asseoir; **to sit up**, se tenir droit; veiller (*s'abstenir du sommeil*).

sit-down strike ['sitdaunstraik], *n.* grève sur le tas, *f.*

site [sait], *n.* situation, *f.*, emplacement (*de bâtiment*); site (*paysage*), *m.*—*v.t.* placer.

sitfast ['sitfɑ:st], *n.* (*Vet.*) cor, durillon, *m.*

sitter ['sitə], *n.* personne assise, *f.*; (*Paint.*) modèle, *m.*

sitting ['sitiŋ], *a.* assis; en séance (*cour etc.*); perché (*oiseau*); qui couve (*poule*).—*n.* séance; audience (*d'une cour*); couvaison (*des œufs*); place (*réservée*); (*Paint.*) séance, *f.*

sitting-room ['sitiŋru:m], *n.* petit salon, *m.*

situate (1) ['sitjueit], *v.t.* situer.

situate (2) ['sitjuit], **situated** ['sitjueitid], *a.* situé; (*Law*) sis.

situation [sitju'eiʃən], *n.* situation, position, *f.*, état, *m.*; place, *f.*, emploi, *m.*

six [siks], *a.* and *n.* six, *m.*

sixteen ['siks'ti:n], *a.* and *n.* seize, *m.*

sixteenth [siks'ti:nθ], *a.* seizième; seize (*rois etc.*).—*n.* seizième (*fraction*), *m.*

sixth [siksθ], *a.* sixième; six (*rois etc.*).—*n.* sixième (*fraction*), *m.*; (*Mus.*) sixte, *f.*; **sixth form**, (*Sch.*) la classe de première, *f.*

sixthly ['siksθli], *adv.* sixièmement.

sixtieth ['sikstiiθ], *a.* soixantième.—*n.* soixantième (*fraction*), *m.*

sixty ['siksti], *a.* and *n.* soixante, *m.*; **about sixty**, une soixantaine (*de*), *f.*

sizable ['saizəbl], *a.* d'une bonne grosseur.

size (1) [saiz], *n.* grandeur, dimension, taille (*physique*); grosseur, *f.*, volume (*espace occupé*); calibre (*de cartouche*); format (*de livre ou de papier*), *m.*; encolure (*de chemise*); pointure (*de gant, de chaussure etc.*), *f.*; effectif (*d'école, de classe*), *m.*; (*Comm.*) numéro, *m.*—*v.t.* classer, ranger (*par grosseur, par taille*); **to size up**, juger.

size (2) [saiz], *n.* colle, *f.*, encollage, *m.*—*v.t.* coller, encoller.

sized [saizd], *a.* de grosseur; de taille.

sizzle [sizl], *n.* grésillement, *m.*—*v.i.* grésiller.

skate (1) [skeit], *n.* (*Ichth.*) raie, *f.*

skate (2) [skeit], *n.* patin, *m.*; **roller skate**, patin à roulettes.—*v.i.* patiner.

skater ['skeitə], *n.* patineur, *m.*

skating ['skeitiŋ], *n.* patinage, *m.*

skating-rink ['skeitiŋriŋk], *n.* patinoire, *f.*

skein [skein], *n.* écheveau, *m.*

skeleton ['skelətən], *n.* squelette, *m.*; (*Tech.*) charpente, carcasse, *f.*

skeleton-key ['skelətən'ki:], *n.* passe-partout, *m.inv.*, crochet, *m.*

sketch [sketʃ], *n.* esquisse, *f.*, croquis, *m.*, ébauche (*Theat.*) saynète, *f.*; (*fig.*) aperçu, *m.*—*v.t.* esquisser, ébaucher.

sketch-book ['sketʃbuk], *n.* cahier de croquis, *m.*

sketchily ['sketʃili], *adv.* incomplètement.

sketchy ['sketʃi], *a.* d'esquisse, ébauché; rudimentaire.

skew [skju:], *a.* oblique, en biais.

skewer ['skju:ə], *n.* brochette, *f.*—*v.t.* embrocher.

ski [ski:], *n.* ski, *m.*—*v.i.* faire du ski.

skid [skid], *n.* (*Motor.*) dérapage (*de*), *m.*, embardée, *f.*; (*Av.*) patin, *m.*—*v.i.* déraper (*bicyclette* ou *véhicule*).

skier ['ski:ə], *n.* skieur, *m.*

skiff [skif], *n.* esquif, *m.*

ski-ing ['ski:iŋ], *n.* le ski, *m.*

skilful ['skilful], *a.* adroit, habile.

skilfully ['skilfuli], *adv.* adroitement, habilement.

ski-lift ['ski:lift], *n.* remonte-pentes, *m.inv.*

skill [skil], *n.* habileté, dextérité, adresse, *f.*

skilled [skild], *a.* habile, adroit; *skilled labour*, main-d'œuvre spécialisée, *f.*; *skilled workman*, ouvrier qualifié, *m.*

skim [skim], *v.t.* écumer; écrémer (*lait*); (*fig.*) raser, effleurer.

skimp [skimp], *v.t.* lésiner; bâcler (*travail*).

skimpy ['skimpi], *a.* mesquin, chiche, étriqué.

skin [skin], *n.* peau, *f.*; *banana skin*, pelure de banane, *f.*; *to escape by the skin of one's teeth*, l'échapper belle; *wet to the skin*, trempé jusqu'aux os.—*v.t.* écorcher (*personne* ou *animal*); peler, éplucher (*fruits etc.*); (*fig.*) écorcher, plumer.

skin-deep ['skindi:p], *a.* superficiel, peu profond.

skinflint ['skinflint], *n.* pince-maille, grigou, ladre, *m.*

skinless ['skinlis], *a.* sans peau.

skinner ['skinə], *n.* écorcheur; pelletier (*marchand*), *m.*

skinny ['skini], *a.* maigre, décharné.

skip [skip], *n.* saut, bond, *m.*—*v.t.* sauter; passer (*en lisant*).—*v.i.* sauter, sautiller, gambader.

skipper ['skipə], *n.* patron (*de navire marchand*); (*Spt.*) chef d'équipe, *m.*

skipping ['skipiŋ], *n.* action de sauter, *f.*; saut à la corde, *m.*

skipping-rope ['skipiŋroup], *n.* corde à sauter, *f.*

skirmish ['skə:miʃ], *n.* escarmouche, *f.*—*v.i.* escarmoucher.

skirmisher ['skə:miʃə], *n.* tirailleur, *m.*

skirmishing ['skə:miʃiŋ], *n.* escarmouches, *f.pl.*

skirt [skə:t], *n.* pan (*d'un habit*), *m.*; jupe (*de robe*); (*pl.*) lisière, extrémité, *f.*, bord (*de forêt etc.*), *m.*; *outskirts*, bords, faubourgs, *m.pl.*—*v.t.* border; longer (*rivière etc.*).

skirting ['skə:tiŋ], **skirting-board** ['skə:tiŋbɔ:d], *n.* bord, *m.*, bordure; (*Arch.*) plinthe, *f.*

skit [skit], *n.* parodie, *f.*

skittish ['skitiʃ], *a.* capricieux, volage.

skittishly ['skitiʃli], *adv.* capricieusement.

skittishness ['skitiʃnis], *n.* légèreté, inconstance, *f.*

skittle [skitl], *n.* quille, *f.*

skittle-alley ['skitl'æli], *n.* jeu de quilles, *m.*

skulk [skʌlk], *v.i.* se cacher; rôder (*autour de*).

skull [skʌl], *n.* crâne, *m.*

skull-cap ['skʌlkæp], *n.* calotte, *f.*

skunk [skʌŋk], *n.* putois d'Amérique, *m.*

sky [skai], *n.* ciel, *m.*

sky-blue ['skaiblu:], *a.* bleu ciel, azuré.

sky-high ['skai'hai], *a.* qui touche aux cieux; *to blow up sky-high*, faire sauter jusqu'aux cieux; (*fig.*) tancer vertement.

skylark ['skaila:k], *n.* alouette (des champs), *f.*—*v.i.* (*fig.*) faire des farces.

skylarking ['skaila:kiŋ], *n.* farces, *f.pl.*

skylight ['skailait], *n.* châssis vitré, *m.* lucarne faîtière, *f.*

sky-line ['skailain], *n.* horizon, *m.*

sky-scraper ['skaiskreipə], *n.* gratte-ciel, *m.*

slab [slæb], *n.* dalle, plaque, table; tablette (*de chocolat*); dosse, *f.*

slack [slæk], *a.* lâche; faible, mou; détendu (*corde*); négligent; *business is slack*, les affaires ne vont pas; *the slack season*, la morte-saison, *f.*—*n.* menu charbon; mou (*de corde*); (*Eng.*) jeu; (*pl.*) pantalon, *m.*

slacken ['slækən], *v.t.* relâcher, détendre; affaiblir (*la rigueur*); ralentir (*vitesse*).—*v.i.* se relâcher, se détendre; se ralentir; diminuer; tomber.

slackening ['slækniŋ], *n.* relâchement, *m.*

slacker ['slækə], *n.* paresseux, *m.*

slacking ['slækiŋ], *n.* paresse, *f.*

slackly ['slækli], *adv.* mollement, lâchement; négligemment.

slackness ['slæknis], *n.* relâchement, *m.*; négligence, nonchalance (*morale*), *f.*

slag [slæg], *n.* scorie, *f.*; mâchefer, *m.*

slag-heap ['slæghi:p], *n.* crassier, *m.*

slake [sleik], *v.t.* éteindre (*chaux*); *to slake one's thirst*, se désaltérer.

slam [slæm], *v.t.* fermer avec violence, claquer.—*v.i.* se fermer avec bruit.—*n.* (*Cards*) vole, *f.*, chelem, *m.*

slander ['sla:ndə], *n.* calomnie; (*Law*) diffamation, *f.*—*v.t.* calomnier; (*Law*) diffamer.

slanderer ['sla:ndərə], *n.* calomniateur; (*Law*) diffamateur, *m.*

slanderous ['sla:ndərəs], *a.* calomnieux; (*Law*) diffamatoire.

slang [slæŋ], *n.* argot, *m.*, langue verte, *f.*

slangy ['slæŋi], *a.* d'argot, argotique.

slant [sla:nt], *v.t.* incliner.—*v.i.* incliner; être de biais, biaiser.—*n.* inclinaison, pente, *f.*; *on the slant*, en écharpe, en biais.

slanting ['sla:ntiŋ], *a.* oblique; en écharpe (*coup d'épée etc.*).

slantingly ['sla:ntiŋli], **slantwise** ['sla:ntwaiz], *adv.* obliquement, en biais.

slap [slæp], *n.* tape, *f.*; soufflet (*sur la figure*), *m.*—*v.t.* souffleter, donner une fessée à (*un enfant*).—*adv.* tout droit, en plein.

slapdash ['slæpdæʃ], *adv.* à la six-quatre-deux, n'importe comment.—*a.* fait à la hâte.

slap-happy ['slæp'hæpi], *a.* toqué.

slapstick ['slæpstik], *n.* (*Theat., Cine.*) *slapstick comedy* (*fam.*), tarte à la crème, *f.*

slash [slæʃ], *n.* taillade; balafre (*sur la figure*), *f.*—*v.t.* taillader; balafrer (*la figure*).—*v.i.* frapper.

slashing ['slæʃiŋ], *a.* mordant, cinglant.

slate [sleit], *n.* ardoise, *f.*—*v.t.* couvrir d'ardoises; (*colloq.*) tancer.

slate-coloured ['sleitkʌləd], *a.* ardoisé, gris d'ardoise.

slate-pencil ['sleitpensl], *n.* crayon d'ardoise, *m.*

slater ['sleitə], *n.* couvreur en ardoise, *m.*

slating ['sleitiŋ], *n.* toiture en ardoise; (*colloq.*) semonce, *f.*

slattern ['slætən], *n.* femme malpropre, souillon, *f.*

slatternly ['slætənli], *a.* négligent, malpropre, mal soigné.

slaty ['sleiti], *a.* schisteux, d'ardoise; ardoisé (*couleur*).

slaughter ['slɔːtə], *n.* tuerie, boucherie, *f.*, massacre; abattage (*des animaux*), *m.—v.t.* massacrer; abattre (*animaux*).

slaughterer ['slɔːtərə], *n.* abatteur, *m.*

slaughter-house ['slɔːtəhaus], *n.* abattoir, *m.*

Slav [slɑːv], *a.* slave.—*n.* Slave (*personne*), *m.*, *f.*

slave [sleiv], *n.* esclave, *m.*, *f.—v.i.* travailler comme un esclave, peiner.

slave-driver ['sleivdraivə], *n.* (*fig.*) maître sévère et cruel, *m.*

slaver (1) ['sleivə], *n.* négrier, bâtiment négrier, *m.*

slaver (2) ['slævə], *v.i.* baver (*sur*).—*n.* bave, salive, *f.*

slavery ['sleivəri], *n.* esclavage, *m.*

slave-trade ['sleivtreid], *n.* traite des noirs, *f.*

slavish ['sleiviʃ], *a.* d'esclave; servile (*imitation etc.*).

slavishly ['sleiviʃli], *adv.* en esclave; servilement.

slavishness ['sleiviʃnis], *n.* servilité, *f.*

Slavonic [slə'vɔnik], *a.* slave.—*n.* slave (*langues*), *m.*

slay [slei], *v.t. irr.* tuer.

slayer ['sleiə], *n.* tueur (*de*), meurtrier, *m.*

slaying ['sleiiŋ], *n.* tuerie, *f.*

sledge [sledʒ], *n.* traîneau, *m.—v.i.* (*also to go sledging*) se promener en traîneau.

sledge-hammer ['sledʒhæmə], *n.* marteau à deux mains, *m.*

sleek [sliːk], *a.* lisse, luisant, poli; (*fig.*) doucereux, onctueux.

sleekness ['sliːknis], *n.* luisant, *m.*; (*fig.*) douceur, onctuosité, *f.*

sleep [sliːp], *n.* sommeil, *m.*; *beauty sleep*, sommeil avant minuit; *sound sleep*, profond sommeil; *to go to sleep*, s'endormir; *to put a dog to sleep*, tuer un chien.—*v.t. irr.* dormir.—*v.i.* dormir, coucher (*à, chez* ou *dans*).

sleeper ['sliːpə], *n.* dormeur, *m.*; (*Rail.*) traverse, *f.*; (*colloq.*) wagon-lit, *m.*

sleepily ['sliːpili], *adv.* d'un air endormi.

sleepiness ['sliːpinis], *n.* assoupissement, *m.*

sleeping ['sliːpiŋ], *a.* endormi; dormant.—*n.* sommeil, repos, *m.*; *sleeping pills* or *tablets*, somnifère, *m.*

sleeping-bag ['sliːpiŋbæg], *n.* sac de couchage, *m.*

sleeping-berth ['sliːpiŋbəːθ], *n.* couchette, *f.*

sleeping-car ['sliːpiŋkɑː], *n.* wagon-lit, *m.*

sleeping-draught ['sliːpiŋdrɑːft], *n.* somnifère, *m.*

sleeping-partner ['sliːpiŋ'pɑːtnə], *n.* associé commanditaire, *m.*

sleepless ['sliːplis], *a.* sans sommeil.

sleeplessness ['sliːplisnis], *n.* insomnie, *f.*

sleep-walker ['sliːpwɔːkə], *n.* somnambule, *m.*, *f.*

sleepy ['sliːpi], *a.* qui a envie de dormir; soporifique (*somnifère*); *to feel sleepy*, avoir sommeil.

sleepy-head ['sliːpihed], *n.* paresseux, *m.*

sleet [sliːt], *n.* neige fondue, *f.*; grésil, *m.*

sleeve [sliːv], *n.* manche, *f.*

sleeveless ['sliːvlis], *a.* sans manches.

sleigh [slei], *n.* traîneau, *m.*

sleight [slait], *n.* habileté, *f.*, escamotage, *m.*; *sleight of hand*, tour de passe-passe, *m.*

slender ['slendə], *a.* mince; élancé; svelte (*taille*); (*fig.*) léger; chétif, maigre.

slenderness ['slendənis], *n.* minceur, légèreté; modicité, *f.*

sleuth(-hound) ['sluːθ(haund)], *n.* (chien) limier; (*fig.*) détective, *m.*

slice [slais], *n.* tranche; écumoire (*ustensile*), *f.*; *fish-slice*, truelle, *f.*; *slice of bread and jam*, tartine de confiture, *f.—v.t.* couper en tranches.

slick [slik], *a.* adroit.

slickness ['sliknis], *n.* adresse, habileté, *f.*

slide [slaid], *n.* glissoire, glissade, *f.*; *lantern-slide*, diapositive, vue fixe, *f.—v.t. irr.* glisser; tirer (*de*).—*v.i.* glisser; couler.

slide-rule ['slaidruːl], *n.* règle à calcul, *f.*

sliding ['slaidiŋ], *a.* glissant; à coulisse.—*n.* glissade, *f.*, glissement, *m.*

sliding-door ['slaidiŋ'dɔː], *n.* porte à coulisse, *f.*

sliding-scale ['slaidiŋ'skeil], *n.* (*Econ.*) échelle mobile, *f.*

slight [slait], *a.* mince, léger; insignifiant; *not in the slightest*, pas le moins du monde.—*n.* manque d'égards; affront, *m.*, insulte, *f.—v.t.* traiter sans égards; mépriser.

slightingly ['slaitiŋli], *adv.* avec mépris, avec dédain.

slightly ['slaitli], *adv.* légèrement, un peu.

slightness ['slaitnis], *n.* minceur; légèreté, *f.*

slim [slim], *a.* svelte, mince; (*colloq.*) rusé.—*v.i.* s'amincir.

slime [slaim], *n.* vase, *f.*, limon, *m.*, bave (*de colimaçon*), *f.*

sliminess ['slaiminis], *n.* viscosité, *f.*

slimness ['slimnis], *n.* sveltesse, taille mince, *f.*

slimy ['slaimi], *a.* vaseux, limoneux; visqueux, gluant; (*fam.*) obséquieux.

sling [sliŋ], *n.* fronde; bretelle (*de fusil*); écharpe (*pour un membre cassé*), *f.—v.t. irr.* lancer (*avec une fronde*); suspendre (*fusil etc.*).

slinger ['sliŋə], *n.* frondeur, *m.*

slink [sliŋk], *v.i. irr.* s'esquiver, se dérober.

slip [slip], *v.t.* glisser, couler; perdre; lâcher; filer (*câble*); pousser (*verrou*); *to slip in*, introduire; *to slip off*, enlever, ôter; *to slip on*, passer, mettre.—*v.i.* glisser, couler (*nœud*); patiner (*roues*); (*fig.*) faire un faux pas; *to slip away*, s'esquiver; *to slip down*, tomber; *to slip in*, se faufiler, entrer furtivement; *to slip up*, (*fam.*) se tromper.—*n.* glissade; combinaison (*sous-vêtement*); laisse (*à chien*), *f.*; engobe (*céramique*); (*Hort.*) scion, *m.*; cale (*de port etc.*); faute d'étourderie, *f.*, lapsus, *m.*; *pillow-slip*, taie d'oreiller, *f.*; *slip of paper*, bout de papier, *m.*; *slip of the pen*, erreur de plume, *f.*; *to give someone the slip*, planter quelqu'un là; *to make a slip*, faire un faux pas.

slip-knot ['slipnɔt], *n.* nœud coulant, *m.*

slipper ['slipə], *n.* pantoufle, *f.*

slippered ['slipəd], *a.* en pantoufles.

slipperiness ['slipərinis], *n.* nature glissante; volubilité (*de la langue*), *f.*

slippery ['slipəri], *a.* glissant; incertain, peu sûr; peu stable; matois, rusé; *slippery customer*, rusé compère, *m.*

slipshod ['slipʃɔd], *a.* (*fig.*) négligé; décousu (*style*).

slipstream ['slipstri:m], *n.* sillage, *m.*
slipway ['slipwei], *n.* cale, *f.*
slit [slit], *v.t. irr.* fendre.—*v.i.* se fendre.—*n.* fente, fissure, *f.*
slither ['sliðə], *v.i.* glisser; ramper (*reptile*).
sliver ['slivə, 'slaivə], *n.* éclat, *m.*, tranche, *f.*, ruban, *m.*
slobber ['slɔbə], *v.i.* baver.
sloe [slou], *n.* (*Bot.*) prunelle, *f.*
sloe-tree ['sloutri:], *n.* prunellier, *m.*
slogan ['slougən], *n.* mot d'ordre, *m.*, devise, *f.*, slogan, *m.*
sloop [slu:p], *n.* sloop, aviso, *m.*
slop [slɔp], *n.* (*usu. in pl.*) rinçures, *f.pl.*—*v.t.* répandre, renverser.
slop-basin ['slɔpbeisn], **slop-bowl** ['slɔp boul], *n.* bol à rinçures (*de thé*), *m.*
slope [sloup], *n.* pente, *f.*; talus, versant, *m.*— *v.t.* couper en biais; taluter.—*v.i.* pencher, aller en pente, incliner.
sloping ['sloupiŋ], *a.* de biais, en pente.
sloppiness ['slɔpinis], *n.* état détrempé, *m.*; mollesse (*personne*), *f.*
sloppy ['slɔpi], *a.* bourbeux, humide; (*fig.*) mou.
slot [slɔt], *n.* rainure, mortaise, fente; barre de bois, *f.*
sloth (1) [slouθ], *n.* paresse, fainéantise, *f.*
sloth (2) [slouθ], *n.* (*Zool.*) paresseux, aï, *m.*
slothful ['slouθful], *a.* paresseux, fainéant.
slot-machine ['slɔtməʃi:n], *n.* distributeur automatique, *m.*
slouch [slautʃ], *n.* démarche molle *ou* lourde, *f.*; lourdaud (*personne*), *m.*—*v.i.* marcher lourdement; *to slouch along*, marcher d'un pas traînant.
slouching ['slautʃiŋ], *a.* lourd et gauche.
slough [slau], *n.* bourbier, *m.*, fondrière; dépouille (*de serpent*), *f.*
Slovak ['slouvæk], *a.* slovaque.—*n.* Slovaque (*personne*), *m., f.*
sloven [slʌvn], *n.* sans-soin, mal-soigné, *m.*
Slovene ['slouvi:n], *n.* Slovène (*personne*), *m., f.*
Slovenian [slo'vi:niən], *a.* slovène.
slovenliness ['slʌvnlinis], *n.* malpropreté, saleté, négligence, *f.*
slovenly ['slʌvnli], *a.* mal soigné, mal peigné, débraillé.
slow [slou], *a.* lent, tardif; lourd (*pesant*); en retard (*montre etc.*).—*adv.* lentement.— *v.t.* ralentir.—*v.i.* se ralentir.
slowly ['slouli], *adv.* lentement, tardivement.
slowness ['slounis], *n.* lenteur; paresse; lourdeur (*pesanteur*), *f.*; retard (*de montre etc.*), *m.*
slow-worm ['slouwə:m], *n.* orvet, *m.*
sludge [slʌdʒ], *n.* boue, vase, *f.*; cambouis, *m.*
slug [slʌg], *n.* limace, *f.*; lingot (*de fusil*), *m.*
sluggard ['slʌgəd], *n.* paresseux, *m.*
sluggish ['slʌgiʃ], *a.* paresseux, indolent, lourd; lent (*ruisseau*).
sluggishly ['slʌgiʃli], *adv.* paresseusement, lourdement.
sluggishness ['slʌgiʃnis], *n.* paresse; lenteur (*de ruisseau*), *f.*
sluice [slu:s], *n.* écluse; bonde (*dans un étang*), *f.*—*v.t.* lâcher par une écluse; inonder d'eau.
sluice-gate ['slu:sgeit], *n.* vanne, *f.*
slum [slʌm], *n.* taudis, *m.*, (*pl.*) bas quartiers, *m.pl.*; *slum-clearance*, lutte contre les taudis, *f.*

slumber ['slʌmbə], *n.* sommeil, *m.*—*v.i.* sommeiller, dormir.
slumberer ['slʌmbərə], *n.* dormeur, *m.*
slumbering ['slʌmbəriŋ], *a.* endormi, assoupi. —*n.* sommeil, assoupissement, *m.*
slump [slʌmp], *v.i.* s'enfoncer soudainement. —*n.* baisse subite; crise, *f.*
slur [slə:], *n.* tache; (*Mus.*) liaison, *f.*; *to cast a slur upon*, flétrir, dénigrer.—*v.t.* tacher, salir; (*Mus.*) lier; *to slur over*, glisser sur.
slurred [slə:d], *a.* (*Mus.*) coulé; brouillé (*paroles*).
slurring ['slə:riŋ], *n.* (*Mus.*) liaison, *f.*
slush [slʌʃ], *n.* boue, fange; neige à moitié fondue, *f.*
slut [slʌt], *n.* saligaude, souillon, *f.*
sly [slai], *a.* sournois, rusé; *on the sly*, en sourdine; *sly dog*, fin matois, *m.*
slyly ['slaili], *adv.* avec ruse, sournoisement.
slyness ['slainis], *n.* ruse, finesse, nature sournoise, *f.*
smack (1) [smæk], *n.* claquement (*de fouet*), *m.*; claque (*de la main*); gifle (*sur la figure*), *f.*; gros baiser, *m.*—*adv.* *smack in the middle*, en plein milieu.—*v.t.* faire claquer (*fouet, les lèvres*); donner une claque à.
smack (2) [smæk], *n.* (*fig.*) saveur, *f.*—*v.i. to smack of*, sentir (*le, la etc.*).
smack (3) [smæk], *n.* bateau de pêche, *m.*
smacking ['smækiŋ], *n.* claquement, *m.*; fessée, *f.*
small [smɔ:l], *a.* petit; fin, menu; (*fig.*) chétif, mince, pauvre; modeste, peu considérable; *small arms*, armes portatives, *f.pl.*; *small fry*, menu fretin, *m.*; *small letters*, minuscules, *f.pl.*—*n.* partie mince, *f.*; *small of the back*, chute des reins, *f.*
smallish ['smɔ:liʃ], *a.* un peu petit, un peu menu.
smallness ['smɔ:lnis], *n.* petitesse, *f.*; peu d'importance, *m.*
smallpox ['smɔ:lpɔks], *n.* petite vérole, *f.*
smarmy ['smɑ:mi], *a.* (*pop.*) mielleux.
smart [smɑ:t], *a.* piquant, cuisant, vif; vigoureux, rude; intelligent, éveillé; beau, élégant, pimpant, chic; *look smart!* dépêchez-vous! *smart Aleck*, finaud, *m.*— *n.* douleur aiguë, vive douleur, cuisson, *f.*— *v.i.* cuire, éprouver une vive douleur.
smarten [smɑ:tn] (**up**), *v.t.* animer; *to smarten oneself up*, se faire beau, s'attifer.
smarting ['smɑ:tiŋ], *a.* cuisant, poignant.—*n.* douleur cuisante, *f.*
smartly ['smɑ:tli], *adv.* lestement, vivement; habilement; vigoureusement, rudement; élégamment.
smartness ['smɑ:tnis], *n.* force, vigueur; élégance, *f.*, éclat (*de vêtements*), *m.*; finesse (*astuce*), *f.*
smash [smæʃ], *v.t.* briser, écraser; (*fig.*) ruiner.—*v.i.* se briser.—*n.* fracas, *m.*; (*Fin.*) déconfiture, faillite, banqueroute; (*Rail.*) catastrophe, *f.*—*adv. to go smash*, faire faillite.
smashing ['smæʃiŋ], *a.* (*pop.*) formidable, épatant.
smattering ['smætəriŋ], *n.* connaissances superficielles, *f.pl.*
smear [smiə], *v.t.* enduire; (*fig.*) salir.—*n.* tache, *f.*; (*fig.*) calomnie, atteinte à la réputation, *f.*

smell [smel], *n.* odeur, *f.*; odorat (*sens*); flair (*de chien*), *m.—v.t., v.i. irr.* sentir; flairer (*chien*).
smelly ['smeli], *a.* malodorant.
smelt (1) [smelt], *n.* (*Ichth.*) éperlan, *m.*
smelt (2) [smelt], *v.t.* fondre.
smelting ['smeltiŋ], *n.* fonte, *f.*
smile [smail], *n.* sourire, *m.—v.i.* sourire.
smiling ['smailiŋ], *a.* souriant; riant (*paysage etc.*).
smilingly ['smailiŋli], *adv.* en souriant.
smirch [smə:tʃ], *v.t.* souiller, salir.—*n.* tache, *f.*
smirk [smə:k], *v.i.* minauder.—*n.* sourire affecté, *m.*
smirking ['smə:kiŋ], *a.* affecté, minaudier.
smite [smait], *v.t. irr.* frapper; détruire; châtier; (*fig.*) charmer.
smith [smiθ], *n.* forgeron, *m.*
smithereens [smiðə'ri:nz], *n.pl.* **to smash to smithereens**, mettre en miettes.
smithy ['smiði], *n.* forge, *f.*
smock [smɔk], *n.* blouse, *f.*
smog [smɔg], *n.* brouillard épais et enfumé, *m.*
smoke [smouk], *n.* fumée, *f.—v.t., v.i.* fumer.
smokeless ['smouklis], *a.* sans fumée.
smoker ['smoukə], *n.* fumeur (*personne*), *m.*
smoke-stack ['smoukstæk], *n.* cheminée, *f.*
smokiness ['smoukinis], *n.* état enfumé, *m.*
smoking ['smoukiŋ], *a.* fumant.—*n.* habitude de fumer, *f.*; **no smoking**, défense de fumer.
smoky ['smouki], *a.* qui fume, plein de fumée.
smooth [smu:ð], *a.* uni; égal (*régulier*); doux (*non âpre*); poli, lisse (*verni*); plat (*mer*); doucereux (*personne*).—*v.t.* polir; adoucir; aplanir, unir; dérider (*le front*); lisser (*les cheveux*).
smooth-faced ['smu:ðfeist], *a.* imberbe.
smoothing-iron ['smu:ðiŋaiən], *n.* fer à repasser, *m.*
smoothly ['smu:ðli], *adv.* uniment; sans difficulté; doucement.
smoothness ['smu:ðnis], *n.* égalité, douceur, *f.*; calme (*de la mer*), *m.*
smooth-tongued ['smu:ð'tʌŋd], *a.* mielleux, doucereux.
smother ['smʌðə], *v.t.* suffoquer, étouffer.
smothering ['smʌðəriŋ], *a.* étouffant, suffocant.—*n.* étouffement, *m.*
smoulder ['smouldə], *v.i.* brûler sans fumée ni flamme; (*fig.*) couver.
smouldering ['smouldəriŋ], *a.* qui couve.
smudge [smʌdʒ], *v.t.* barbouiller, noircir.—*n.* barbouillage, *m.*, tache, *f.*
smudgy ['smʌdʒi], *a.* barbouillé; taché.
smug [smʌg], *a.* suffisant, content de soi.
smuggle [smʌgl], *v.t.* passer en contrebande.—*v.i.* faire la contrebande.
smuggled [smʌgld], *a.* de contrebande.
smuggler ['smʌglə], *n.* contrebandier, *m.*
smuggling ['smʌgliŋ], *n.* contrebande, fraude, *f.*
smugness ['smʌgnis], *n.* suffisance, *f.*
smut [smʌt], *n.* tache de suie; (*fig.*) saleté (*grivoiserie*), *f.—v.t.* noircir.
smuttiness ['smʌtinis], *n.* noirceur; (*fig.*) saleté, *f.*
smutty ['smʌti], *a.* noir; (*fig.*) obscène, grivois.
snack [snæk], *n.* morceau; casse-croûte, *m.*

snack-bar ['snækbɑ:], *n.* snack-bar, *m.*
snaffle [snæfl], *n.* mors de bridon, filet, *m.—*
snag [snæg], *n.* (*fig.*) obstacle caché, *m.*
snail [sneil], *n.* escargot, limaçon, colimaçon, *m.*
snail's-pace ['sneilzpeis], *n.* pas de tortue, *m.*
snake [sneik], *n.* serpent, *m.—v.i.* (*Naut.*) serpenter.
snap [snæp], *v.t.* saisir; happer; casser, rompre, éclater; faire claquer (*fouet etc.*); fermer avec un bruit sec; dire d'un ton sec.—*v.i.* tâcher de mordre *ou* de happer; se casser, se rompre; craquer; **to snap at**, (*fam.*) brusquer.—*a.* imprévu.—*n.* coup de dent, *m.*; cassure, *f.*; claquement (*de fouet etc.*); bruit sec; fermoir (*de sac à main*); biscuit craquant, *m.*; vivacité, *f.*
snapdragon ['snæpdrægən], *n.* muflier, *m.*
snappy ['snæpi], *a.* vif; **make it snappy!** dépêchez-vous!
snapshot ['snæpʃɔt], *n.* (*colloq.* **snap** [snæp]) instantané, *m.*
snare [snɛə], *n.* lacet, collet; (*fig.*) piège, *m.—v.t.* prendre (au piège).
snarl [snɑ:l], *v.i.* grogner; montrer les dents.—*n.* grognement, *m.*
snarling ['snɑ:liŋ], *a.* hargneux.—*n.* grognement, *m.*
snatch [snætʃ], *v.t.* saisir; **to snatch at**, chercher à saisir; **to snatch from**, arracher à; **to snatch up**, empoigner.—*n.* **by snatches**, à bâtons rompus; **snatches of conversation**, des bribes de conversation, *f.pl.*
sneak [sni:k], *v.t.* chiper.—*v.i.* s'en aller furtivement; (*Sch.*) cafarder, moucharder.—*n.* pleutre, pied-plat; cafard, *m.*
sneaking ['sni:kiŋ], *a.* rampant, servile; furtif, inavoué.
sneer [sniə], *n.* rire *ou* sourire moqueur, sarcasme, ricanement, *m.—v.i.* ricaner, se moquer (*de*).
sneering ['sniəriŋ], *a.* ricaneur, moqueur.—*n.* ricanement, *m.*
sneeringly ['sniəriŋli], *adv.* en ricanant.
sneeze [sni:z], *n.* éternuement, *m.—v.i.* éternuer.
sneezing ['sni:ziŋ], *n.* éternuement, *m.*
sniff [snif], *v.t.* flairer.—*v.i.* renifler.—*n.* reniflement, *m.*
snigger ['snigə], *v.i.* rire du bout des lèvres, ricaner.—*n.* rire en dessous, *m.*
snip [snip], *n.* coup de ciseaux, *m.*; (*pop.*) certitude, *f.—v.t.* couper (*d'un coup de ciseaux*).
snipe [snaip], *n.* bécassine, *f.—v.i.* (*Shooting*) canarder.
sniper ['snaipə], *n.* tireur embusqué, franc-tireur, *m.*
snippet ['snipit], *n.* petit morceau, *m.*
snivel [snivl], *v.i.* être morveux; (*fig.*) pleurnicher.
sniveller ['snivlə], *n.* pleurnicheur, *m.*
snivelling ['snivliŋ], *a.* morveux; (*fig.*) pleurnicheur.—*n.* pleurnicherie, *f.*
snob [snɔb], *n.* poseur; fat, snob, *m.*
snobbery ['snɔbəri], *n.* snobisme, *m.*
snobbish ['snɔbiʃ], *a.* affecté, poseur, prétentieux.
snobbishness ['snɔbiʃnis], *n.* snobisme, *m.*
snoop [snu:p], *v.i.* fureter.
snooper ['snu:pə], *n.* fureteur, *m.*

snooze [snuːz], *n.* somme, *m.*—*v.i.* sommeiller.
snore [snɔː], *v.i.* ronfler.—*n.* ronflement, *m.*
snoring [ˈsnɔːriŋ], *n.* ronflement, *m.*
snort [snɔːt], *v.i.* renâcler, s'ébrouer (*cheval*); ronfler.
snorting [ˈsnɔːtiŋ], *n.* ronflement, *m.*
snot [snɒt], *n.* (*vulg.*) morve, *f.*
snotty [ˈsnɒti], *a.* (*vulg.*) morveux.
snout [snaut], *n.* museau; mufle (*de taureau*); groin (*de cochon*), *m.*
snow [snou], *n.* neige, *f.*—*v.i.* neiger, tomber de la neige.
snowball [ˈsnoubɔːl], *n.* boule de neige, *f.*
snow-capped [ˈsnoukæpt], *a.* couronné de neige.
snow-drift [ˈsnoudrift], *n.* congère, *f.*, amas de neige, *m.*
snowdrop [ˈsnoudrɒp], *n.* perce-neige, *m.*
snowflake [ˈsnoufleik], *n.* flocon de neige, *m.*
snow-man [ˈsnoumæn], *n.* (*pl.* -men [men]) bonhomme de neige, *m.*
snow-plough [ˈsnouplau], *n.* chasse-neige, *m.*
snow-shoe [ˈsnouʃuː], *n.* raquette, *f.*
snow-storm [ˈsnoustɔːm], *n.* tempête de neige, *f.*
Snow White [ˈsnouˈwait]. Blanche-Neige, *f.*
snow-white [ˈsnouwait], *a.* blanc comme la neige.
snowy [ˈsnoui], *a.* de neige; neigeux.
snub [snʌb], *n.* rebuffade, *f.*; affront, *m.*—*v.t.* rabrouer, rembarrer.
snub-nosed [ˈsnʌbnouzd], *a.* au nez camus.
snuff (1) [snʌf], *n.* tabac (à priser), *m.*; *pinch of snuff*, prise de tabac, *f.*
snuff (2) [snʌf], *n.* lumignon (*de mèche*), *m.*—*v.t.* moucher (*chandelle*).
snuff-box [ˈsnʌfbɒks], *n.* tabatière, *f.*
snuffle [ˈsnʌfl], *n.* reniflement, *m.*—*v.i.* nasiller, renifler.
snuffling [ˈsnʌfliŋ], *a.* nasillard.—*n.* nasillement, *m.*
snug [snʌg], *a.* confortable, commode et agréable, où l'on est bien; gentil; serré, compact; *we are very snug here*, nous sommes on ne peut mieux ici.
snuggery [ˈsnʌgəri], *n.* endroit petit et commode (*où l'on se sent chez soi*), *m.*
snuggle [ˈsnʌgl], *v.t.* serrer.—*v.i.* se serrer.
snugly [ˈsnʌgli], *adv.* commodément, à son aise.
snugness [ˈsnʌgnis], *n.* confort, bien-être, *m.*
so [sou], *adv. and conj.* ainsi, de cette manière, comme cela, comme ça (*de cette façon*); de même, de la même manière, tel (*pareillement*); si, tellement, tant (*à tel point*); aussi, donc (*alors*); *and so on*, et ainsi de suite; *be it so*, soit! *how so?* comment cela? *is that so?* vraiment? *just so!* parfaitement! *Mr. So-and-So*, Monsieur un tel; *or so*, environ, à peu près; *so as to*, de manière à; *so that*, de sorte que.
soak [souk], *v.t.* tremper; (*colloq.*) estamper.—*v.i.* tremper, s'infiltrer.
soaking [ˈsoukiŋ], *a.* qui trempe.—*n.* trempée (*de pluie*), *f.*
soap [soup], *n.* savon, *m.*—*v.t.* savonner.
soap-bubble [ˈsoupbʌbl], *n.* bulle de savon, *f.*
soap-flakes [ˈsoupfleiks], *n.pl.* savon en paillettes, *m.*
soap-suds [ˈsoupsʌdz], *n.pl.* eau de savon, *f.*

soar [sɔː], *v.i.* prendre l'essor, s'élever; *to soar over*, planer sur.
soaring [ˈsɔːriŋ], *a.* qui s'élève; (*fig.*) élevé.—*n.* essor, élan, *m.*
sob [sɒb], *v.i.* sangloter.—*n.* sanglot, *m.*
sobbing [ˈsɒbiŋ], *n.* sanglots, *m.pl.*
sober [ˈsoubə], *a.* qui n'a pas bu, qui n'est pas ivre; sobre, tempéré; grave, sérieux; sensé; calme, posé, rassis.—*v.t.* dégriser; (*fig.*) calmer.—*v.i. to sober up*, se désenivrer.
soberly [ˈsoubəli], *adv.* sobrement; raisonnablement.
soberness [ˈsoubənis], **sobriety** [səˈbraiəti], *n.* sobriété, tempérance; gravité, *f.*
so-called [ˈsoukɔːld], *a.* soi-disant, prétendu.
soccer [ˈsɒkə], *n.* (*fam.*) football, *m.*
sociability [souʃəˈbiliti], *n.* sociabilité, *f.*
sociable [ˈsouʃəbl], *a.* sociable.
social [ˈsouʃəl], *a.* social.
socialism [ˈsouʃəlizm], *n.* socialisme, *m.*
socialist [ˈsouʃəlist], *a. and n.* socialiste, *m., f.*
socially [ˈsouʃəli], *adv.* socialement.
society [səˈsaiəti], *n.* société, *f.*; la société, *f.*; le monde, *m.*
sociology [sousiˈɒlədʒi], *n.* sociologie, *f.*
sock [sɒk], *n.* chaussette; semelle (*intérieure*), *f.*
socket [ˈsɒkit], *n.* emboîture; orbite (*de l'œil*), *f.*; trou, *m.*, cavité; douille (*d'outil etc.*), *f.*
Socrates [ˈsɒkrətiːz]. Socrate, *m.*
sod [sɒd], *n.* gazon, *m.*; motte de gazon, *f.*
soda [ˈsoudə], *n.* soude, *f.*; *baking soda*, bicarbonate de soude, *m.*
soda-water [ˈsoudəwɔːtə], *n.* eau de Seltz, *f.*, soda, *m.*
sodden [ˈsɒdn], *a.* imprégné d'eau, détrempé; pâteux (*pain*); abruti (*d'alcool*).
sodium [ˈsoudiəm], *n.* (*Chem.*) sodium, *m.*
sodomy [ˈsɒdəmi], *n.* sodomie, *f.*
sofa [ˈsoufə], *n.* canapé, *m.*
soft [sɒft], *a.* mou, mol, mollet; délicat, doux, facile, pas résistant; tendre; efféminé; faible; sot, niais (*Gram.*) doux; *soft fruits*, fruits rouges, *m.pl.*—*adv.* mollement, doucement.—*int.* doucement! tout doux!
soften [ˈsɒfn], *v.t.* amollir, ramollir; adoucir, apaiser; affaiblir; attendrir (*cœur*).—*v.i.* s'amollir, se ramollir; s'affaiblir; s'attendrir (*cœur*).
softener [ˈsɒfnə], *n.* chose qui amollit, *f.*
softening [ˈsɒfniŋ], *n.* amollissement; affaiblissement; attendrissement (*du cœur*), *m.*
soft-headed [ˈsɒftˈhedid], *a.* niais; sot.
soft-hearted [ˈsɒftˈhɑːtid], *a.* tendre, compatissant.
softly [ˈsɒftli], *adv.* mollement; doucement; tendrement.
softness [ˈsɒftnis], *n.* mollesse; faiblesse; niaiserie; douceur, *f.*
soggy [ˈsɒgi], *a.* détrempé; pâteux (*pain*).
soil (1) [sɔil], *n.* sol, terrain, terroir, *m.*, terre, *f.*
soil (2) [sɔil], *n.* tache, souillure, *f.*—*v.t.* salir, souiller.
sojourn [ˈsɒdʒən], *n.* séjour, *m.*—*v.i.* séjourner.
sojourning [ˈsɒdʒəniŋ], *n.* séjour, *m.*
solace [ˈsɒlis], *n.* consolation, *f.*, soulagement, *m.*—*v.t.* consoler (*de*).
solar [ˈsoulə], *a.* solaire, du soleil.
solder [ˈsɒ(l)də], *n.* soudure, *f.*—*v.t.* souder.
soldering [ˈsɒ(l)dəriŋ], *n.* soudure, *f.*; soudage (*action*), *m.*; *soldering-iron*, fer à souder, *m.*

569

soldier

soldier ['souldʒə], *n.* soldat, militaire, *m.*; ***foot-soldier***, fantassin, *m.*; ***private soldier***, simple soldat.—*v.i.* servir comme soldat.

soldierly ['souldʒəli], *a.* de soldat, militaire, martial.

soldiery ['souldʒəri], *n.* troupes, *f.pl.*, soldats, *m.pl.*

sole (1) [soul], *a.* seul, unique.

sole (2) [soul], *n.* plante (*du pied*); semelle (*de soulier, d'outil etc.*), *f.*—*v.t.* ressemeler.

sole (3) [soul], *n.* (*Ichth.*) sole, *f.*

solecism ['sɔlisizm], *n.* solécisme, *m.*

solely ['soulli], *adv.* seulement, uniquement.

solemn ['sɔləm], *a.* solennel.

solemnity [sə'lemniti], *n.* solennité, *f.*

solemnization [sɔləmnai'zeiʃən], *n.* solennisation; célébration solennelle, *f.*

solemnize ['sɔləmnaiz], *v.t.* solenniser, célébrer.

solemnly ['sɔləmli], *adv.* solennellement.

solenoid ['sɔlinɔid], *n.* (*Elec.*) solénoïde, *m.*

solicit [sə'lisit], *v.t.* solliciter.

solicitation [səlisi'teiʃən], *n.* sollicitation, *f.*

solicitor [sə'lisitə], *n.* (*Law*) avoué et notaire, *m.*

solicitous [sə'lisitəs], *a.* désireux; ***solicitous about***, soigneux, attentif à.

solicitude [sə'lisitju:d], *n.* sollicitude, *f.*

solid ['sɔlid], *a.* solide, massif.—*n.* solide, *m.*

solidarity [sɔli'dæriti], *n.* solidarité, *f.*

solidification [səlidifi'keiʃən], *n.* solidification, *f.*

solidify [sə'lidifai], *v.t.* solidifier.—*v.i.* se solidifier.

solidity [sə'liditi], **solidness** ['sɔlidnis], *n.* solidité, *f.*

solidly ['sɔlidli], *adv.* solidement.

soliloquize [sə'liləkwaiz], *v.i.* faire un soliloque.

soliloquy [sə'liləkwi], *n.* soliloque, *m.*

soling ['soulin], *n.* ressemelage, *m.*

solitary ['sɔlitəri], *a.* solitaire, retiré, isolé; seul.

solitude ['sɔlitju:d], *n.* solitude, *f.*

solo ['soulou], *n.* solo, *m.*

soloist ['soulouist], *n.* soliste, *m., f.*

Solomon ['sɔləmən]. Salomon, *m.*

solstice ['sɔlstis], *n.* solstice, *m.*

solubility [sɔlju'biliti], *n.* solubilité, *f.*

soluble ['sɔljubl], *a.* soluble.

solution [sə'lju:ʃən], *n.* solution, *f.*

solvable ['sɔlvəbl], *a.* soluble.

solve [sɔlv], *v.t.* résoudre, expliquer, éclaircir.

solvency ['sɔlvənsi], *n.* (*Fin.*) solvabilité, *f.*

solvent ['sɔlvənt], *a.* dissolvant; (*Comm.*) solvable.—*n.* dissolvant, *m.*

Somali [so'mɑ:li], *a.* somali.—*n.* somali (*langue*); Somali (*personne*), *m.*

Somalia [so'mɑ:liə]. la Somalie, *f.*

Somaliland [so'mɑ:lilænd]. la Somalie, *f.*

sombre ['sɔmbə], *a.* sombre.

sombrely ['sɔmbəli], *adv.* sombrement.

some [sʌm], *a.* quelque, *m., f.*, quelques, *pl.*; un certain, *m.*, certains, *m.pl.*, plusieurs, *pl.*; du, *m.*, de la, *f.*, de l', *m., f.*, des, *pl.*, de; quelconque; un *certain* nombre de, un peu de, une partie de.—*adv.* à peu près, environ, quelque.—*pron.* quelques-uns, *m.pl.*, quelques-unes, *f.pl.*; les uns, *m.pl.*, les unes, *f.pl.*, . . . les autres, *pl.*; en.

somebody ['sʌmbədi], **someone** ['sʌmwʌn], *pron.* quelqu'un, *m.*, quelqu'une, *f.*, on; ***somebody else***, quelqu'un d'autre, quelque autre, un autre.

somehow ['sʌmhau], *adv.* d'une manière ou d'une autre, de façon ou d'autre.

someone [SOMEBODY].

somersault ['sʌməsɔ:lt], *n.* saut périlleux, *m.*, culbute, *f.*

something ['sʌmθiŋ], *n.* and *pron.* quelque chose (*de*), *m.*; ***something else***, autre chose, *f.*—*adv.* un peu, quelque peu, tant soit peu.

sometime ['sʌmtaim], *adv.* autrefois, jadis; ***sometime or other***, tôt ou tard.—*a.* ancien.

sometimes ['sʌmtaimz], *adv.* quelquefois, parfois; tantôt.

somewhat ['sʌmwɔt], *adv.* quelque peu, un peu; assez.—*n.* un peu, quelque peu, tant soit peu.

somewhere ['sʌmwɛə], *adv.* quelque part; ***somewhere else***, ailleurs.

somnambulist [sɔm'næmbjulist], *n.* somnambule, *m., f.*

somniferous [sɔm'nifərəs], *a.* somnifère.

somnolence ['sɔmnələns], *n.* somnolence, *f.*

somnolent ['sɔmnələnt], *a.* somnolent.

son [sʌn], *n.* fils; (*fig.*) descendant, *m.*

sonata [sə'nɑ:tə], *n.* sonate, *f.*

song [sɔŋ], *n.* chanson, *f.*; chant, *m.*; (*fig.*) ballade, *f.*; ***a mere song***, un rien, *m.*, une bagatelle, *f.*

songster ['sɔŋstə], *n.* chanteur; oiseau chanteur, *m.*

songstress ['sɔŋstris], *n.* chanteuse, *f.*

song-thrush ['sɔŋθrʌʃ], *n.* grive chanteuse, *f.*

song-writer ['sɔŋraitə], *n.* chansonnier, *m.*

son-in-law ['sʌninlɔ:], *n.* gendre, *m.*

sonnet ['sɔnit], *n.* sonnet, *m.*

sonny ['sʌni], *n.* (*fam.*) mon petit, mon fiston, *m.*

sonorous ['sɔnərəs], *a.* sonore.

soon [su:n], *adv.* bientôt; tôt (*de bonne heure*); ***as soon as***, aussitôt que, dès que; ***how soon?*** quand? ***see you soon!*** à bientôt; ***so soon***, si tôt; ***too soon***, trop tôt.

sooner ['su:nə], *adv.* plus tôt (*de meilleure heure*); plutôt (*mieux*); ***no sooner said than done***, aussitôt dit, aussitôt fait; ***sooner or later***, tôt ou tard; ***sooner than***, plutôt que.

soonest ['su:nist], *adv.* le plus tôt.

soot [sut], *n.* suie, *f.*

soothe [su:ð], *v.t.* apaiser, calmer; (*fig.*) charmer.

soothing ['su:ðiŋ], *a.* calmant, consolant; flatteur.

soothingly ['su:ðiŋli], *adv.* d'un ton doux.

soothsay ['su:θsei], *v.i.* prophétiser, prédire.

soothsayer ['su:θseiə], *n.* devin, *m.*, devineresse, *f.*; prophète, *m.*

sooty ['suti], *a.* de suie, fuligineux; plein *ou* couvert de suie.

sop [sɔp], *n.* morceau (de pain) trempé; (*fig.*) pot-de-vin (*pourboire*), *m.*—*v.t.* tremper.

Sophia [sə'faiə]. Sophie, *f.*

sophism ['sɔfizm], *n.* sophisme, *m.*

sophist ['sɔfist], *n.* sophiste, *m., f.*

sophisticate [sə'fistikeit], *v.t.* sophistiquer, falsifier.

sophisticated [sə'fistikeitid], *a.* falsifié; blasé (*personne*).

sophistication [səfisti'keiʃən], *n.* sophistication, falsification, *f.*

sophistry ['sofistri], *n.* sophismes, *m.pl.*

Sophocles ['sofəkli:z]. Sophocle, *m.*

soporific [sopə'rifik], *a.* and *n.* soporifique, *m.*

sopping ['sopiŋ] (wet), *a.* trempé.

soprano [sə'pra:nou], *n.* soprano, *m.*, *f.*

sorcerer ['so:sərə], *n.* sorcier, magicien, *m.*

sorceress ['so:səris], *n.* sorcière, magicienne, *f.*

sorcery ['so:səri], *n.* sorcellerie, magie, *f.*

sordid ['so:did], *a.* sordide, sale; bas, vil.

sordidly ['so:didli], *adv.* sordidement.

sordidness ['so:didnis], *n.* sordidité, *f.*

sore [so:], *a.* douloureux, endolori, sensible; (*fig.*) rude; fâché; *sore throat*, mal à la gorge, *m.*—*n.* plaie, *f.*

sorely ['so:li], *adv.* gravement, fortement, cruellement, rudement.

soreness ['so:nis], *n.* douleur; sensation pénible, *f.*

sorrel ['sorəl], *a.* saure; alezan.—*n.* oseille, *f.*; alezan (*cheval*), *m.*

sorrily ['sorili], *adv.* misérablement, pauvrement.

sorrow ['sorou], *n.* chagrin, *m.*, douleur; peine, tristesse, *f.*—*v.i.* être affligé.

sorrowful ['sorouful], *a.* triste, affligé.

sorrowfully ['sorofuli], *adv.* tristement.

sorrowing ['sorouiŋ], *a.* affligé.

sorry ['sori], *a.* fâché, désolé (*de*); triste, pauvre, méchant, pitoyable; *I am sorry for you*, je vous plains; *I am sorry to say that . . .*, je regrette d'avoir à dire que . . .; *sorry!* pardon!

sort (1) [so:t], *n.* sorte, *f.*, genre, *m.*, espèce; manière, façon, *f.*; *nothing of the sort*, pas du tout.

sort (2) [so:t], *v.t.* assortir, classer, distribuer; trier (*lettres etc.*).

sorted ['so:tid], *a.* assorti; trié, arrangé, séparé.

sorter ['so:tə], *n.* trieur, *m.*

sortie ['so:ti], *n.* (*Mil.*) sortie, *f.*; (*Av.*) vol, *m.*

sorting ['so:tiŋ], *n.* triage, tri; assortiment (*classement*), *m.*

so-so ['sou'sou], *a.* comme ci comme ça, (*fam.*) couci-couça.

sot [sot], *n.* ivrogne, *m.*, *f.*

sottish ['sotiʃ], *a.* hébété, abruti.

sough [sau, sʌf], *v.i.* murmurer, soupirer (*vent*).

soughing ['sauiŋ], *n.* bruissement, murmure, *m.*

soul [soul], *n.* âme, *f.*; (*fig.*) être; principe (*essence*), *m.*; *All Souls' Day*, le jour des morts, *m.*

soulful ['soulful], *a.* sentimental.

soulfully ['soulfuli], *adv.* avec expression; avec sentiment.

soulless ['soullis], *a.* sans âme; abrutissant.

sound (1) [saund], *n.* détroit (*goulet*), *m.*; (*Surg.*) sonde, *f.*—*v.t.* sonder (*les profondeurs etc.*); (*Surg.*) ausculter.

sound (2) [saund], *a.* en bon état, sain; (*fig.*) solide; profond (*sommeil*); valide, bien fondé; *safe and sound*, sain et sauf.

sound (3) [saund], *v.t.* faire sonner; proclamer.—*v.i.* sonner; retentir, résonner (*de*); sembler.—*n.* son, bruit, *m.*; *to break the*

sound barrier, (*Av.*) franchir le mur du son.

sounding (1) ['saundiŋ], *n.* sondage, *m.*; (*Surg.*) auscultation, *f.*

sounding (2) ['saundiŋ], *a.* résonnant, retentissant; (*fig.*) pompeux.—*n.* retentissement, résonnement, *m.*

sounding-balloon ['saundiŋbə'lu:n], *n.* (*Meteor.*) ballon sonde, *m.*

sounding-lead ['saundiŋled], *n.* plomb de sonde, *m.*

sounding-line ['saundiŋlain], *n.* ligne de sonde, *f.*

soundless ['saundlis], *a.* sans bruit, muet.

soundly ['saundli], *adv.* vigoureusement, rudement, ferme, bien; sainement, solidement; profondément (*sommeil*).

soundness ['saundnis], *n.* bon état, *m.*; force, vigueur (*physique*); droiture (*morale*), *f.*

sound-proof ['saundpru:f], *a.* insonore.

sound-track ['saundtræk], *n.* (*Cine.*) piste sonore, *f.*

sound-wave ['saundweiv], *n.* onde sonore, *f.*

soup [su:p], *n.* potage, *m.*, soupe, *f.*; (*colloq.*) *to be in the soup*, être dans le pétrin.

soup-ladle ['su:pleidl], *n.* louche, *f.*

soup-tureen ['su:ptju'ri:n], *n.* soupière, *f.*

sour [sauə], *a.* aigre, acide; tourné (*lait*); (*fig.*) âpre.—*v.t.* aigrir; (*fig.*) empoisonner. —*v.i.* s'aigrir.

source [so:s], *n.* source, *f.*

souring ['sauəriŋ], *n.* aigrissement, *m.*

sourish ['sauəriʃ], *a.* suret, aigrelet.

sourly ['sauəli], *adv.* avec aigreur; (*fig.*) aigrement, âprement.

sourness ['sauənis], *n.* aigreur, acidité; (*fig.*) âpreté, *f.*

souse [saus], *v.t.* tremper; faire mariner.—*n.* marinade, *f.*

south [sauθ], *a.* sud, du sud, du midi, méridional.—*n.* sud, midi, *m.*—*adv.* vers le midi, vers le sud, au sud; *South Africa*, l'Afrique du Sud, *f.*; *South America*, l'Amérique du Sud, *f.*

south-east ['sauθ'i:st], *a.* sud-est, du sud-est.—*n.* sud-est, *m.*—*adv.* vers le sud-est.

south-easter ['sauθ'i:stə], *n.* vent du sud-est, *m.*

south-easterly ['sauθ'i:stəli], **south-eastern** ['sauθ'i:stn], *a.* du sud-est.

southerly ['sʌðəli], **southern** ['sʌðən], *a.* du sud, du midi, méridional.

southerner ['sʌðənə], *n.* méridional, *m.*; (*Am.*) sudiste, *m.*, *f.*

southernmost ['sʌðənmost], *a.* à l'extrême sud.

southward ['sauθwəd], *adv.* vers le sud, au sud.

south-west ['sauθ'west], *a.* sud-ouest, du sud-ouest.—*n.* sud-ouest, *m.*—*adv.* vers le sud-ouest.

southwester [sau'westə], [sou'WESTER].

south-westerly ['sauθ'westəli], **south-western** ['sauθ'westən], *a.* du sud-ouest, sud-ouest.

souvenir ['su:vəniə], *n.* souvenir, *m.*

sou'wester, southwester [sau'westə], *n.* vent du sud-ouest; suroît (*coiffure*), *m.*

sovereign ['sovrin], *a.* and *n.* souverain, *m.*

sovereignty ['sovrinti], *n.* souveraineté, *f.*

Soviet ['souviet], *n.* Soviet, *m.*; *the Soviet Union*, l'Union Soviétique, *f.*

sow (1) [sau], *n.* truie; gueuse (*de fer*), *f.*

sow (2) [sou], *v.t. irr.* semer.—*v.i.* semer, faire les semailles.

sower ['souə], *n.* semeur, *m.*

sowing ['souiŋ], *n.* semailles, *f.pl.*, ensemencement, *m.*

soya-bean ['sɔiə'bi:n], *n.* soya, soja, *m.*

spa [spɑ:], *n.* source minérale; ville d'eaux, *f.*

space [speis], *n.* espace, *m.*, étendue; place, *f.*; intervalle, *m.*—*v.t.* (*Print.*) espacer.

space-ship ['speisʃip], *n.* astronef, *m.*

space-suit ['speissju:t], *n.* combinaison spatiale, *f.*

space-travel ['speistrævl], *n.* astronautique, *f.*, voyages interplanétaires, *m.pl.*

space-traveller ['speistrævlə], *n.* astronaute, cosmonaute, *m.*, *f.*

spacing ['speisiŋ], *n.* espacement; (*Print.*) interligne, *m.*

spacious ['speiʃəs], *a.* spacieux, vaste.

spaciously ['speiʃəsli], *adv.* spacieusement; amplement.

spaciousness ['speiʃəsnis], *n.* vaste étendue, *f.*

spade [speid], *n.* bêche, pelle (*d'enfant*), *f.*; (*Cards*) pique, *m.*

spadeful ['speidful], *n.* pelletée, *f.*

Spain [spein]. l'Espagne, *f.*

span [spæn], *n.* empan, *m.*; envergure (*d'ailes*), *f.*; moment, instant, *m.*—*v.t.* mesurer; embrasser; traverser.

spangle [spæŋgl], *n.* paillette, *f.*—*v.t.* pailleter (*de*).

Spaniard ['spænjəd], *n.* Espagnol, *m.*

spaniel ['spænjəl], *n.* épagneul, *m.*

Spanish ['spæniʃ], *a.* espagnol, d'Espagne.— *n.* espagnol (*langue*), *m.*

spank [spæŋk], *v.t.* fesser.—*n.* (*also* spanking (1) ['spæŋkiŋ]) fessée, *f.*

spanking (2) ['spæŋkiŋ], *a.* vigoureux; rapide (*pas*).

spanner ['spænə], *n.* clef à écrous, *f.*; adjustable spanner, clef anglaise, *f.*

spar [spɑ:], *n.* perche, *f.*, poteau; (*Naut.*) espar; (*Box.*) combat d'entraînement, *m.*— *v.i.* faire un assaut amical (*de boxe ou de paroles*); se disputer.

spare [speə], *v.t.* épargner; ménager, économiser (*dépenser avec précaution*); se passer de (*se priver de*); donner, céder; prêter.—*a.* disponible, de reste (*superflu*); libre (*temps*); (*Motor. etc.*) de rechange; modique, faible, pauvre; maigre, sec (*taille*).

spareness ['speənis], *n.* maigreur, *f.*

spare-rib ['speə'rib], *n.* côte de porc, *f.*

sparing ['speəriŋ], *a.* économe, ménager, frugal, sobre (*de*); parcimonieux.

sparingly ['speəriŋli], *adv.* frugalement, avec parcimonie; économiquement.

sparingness ['speəriŋnis], *n.* frugalité, épargne, parcimonie, *f.*

spark [spɑ:k], *n.* étincelle; (*fig.*) lueur, *f.*— *v.i.* produire des étincelles.

sparking-plug ['spɑ:kiŋplʌg], *n.* (*Motor.*) bougie (d'allumage), *f.*

sparkle [spɑ:kl], *n.* étincellement, éclat, *m.*; vivacité (*d'esprit*), *f.*—*v.i.* étinceler, scintiller; pétiller (*boisson*).

sparkling ['spɑ:kliŋ], *a.* étincelant; mousseux (*boisson*).

sparling ['spɑ:liŋ], *n.* (*Ichth.*) éperlan, *m.*

sparrow ['spærou], *n.* moineau, passereau, *m.*

sparrow-hawk ['spærouhɔ:k], *n.* épervier, *m.*

sparse [spɑ:s], *a.* épars; éparpillé, clairsemé.

sparsely ['spɑ:sli], *adv.* d'une manière éparse, de loin en loin.

sparseness ['spɑ:snis], *n.* rareté, *f.*; éparpillement, *m.*

Sparta ['spɑ:tə]. Sparte, *f.*

Spartan ['spɑ:tən], *a.* spartiate.—*n.* Spartiate (*personne*), *m.*, *f.*

spasm [spæzm], *n.* spasme, accès, *m.*

spasmodic [spæz'mɔdik], spasmodical [spæz'mɔdikəl], *a.* spasmodique.

spasmodically [spæz'mɔdikəli], *adv.* par à-coups.

spastic ['spæstik], *a.* spasmodique.—*n.* paraplégique, *m.*, *f.*

spat (1) [spæt], *past* and *p.p.* [SPIT].

spat (2) [spæt], *n.* guêtre de ville, *f.*

spate [speit], *n.* crue (*de rivière*); (*fig.*) affluence, *f.*

spatter ['spætə], *v.t.* éclabousser (*de*).

spatula ['spætjulə], *n.* spatule, *f.*

spavin ['spævin], *n.* éparvin, *m.*

spawn [spɔ:n], *n.* frai, *m.*; (*fig.*) race, engeance, *f.*—*v.t.* (*fig.*) engendrer.—*v.i.* frayer; (*fig.*) naître.

spawning-ground ['spɔ:niŋgraund], *n.* frayère, *f.*

speak [spi:k], *v.t. irr.* parler; dire; (*Naut.*) héler; to speak one's mind, dire sa pensée.—*v.i.* parler; causer (*avec*); faire un discours (*en public*); dire; so to speak, pour ainsi dire; to speak out, parler à haute voix; to speak up, parler plus fort.

speaker ['spi:kə], *n.* personne qui parle, *f.*; orateur; (*Parl.*) président; (*Rad.* = loud-speaker) haut-parleur, *m.*

speaking ['spi:kiŋ], *a.* parlant, qui parle.—*n.* parole, *f.*, langage, discours, *m.*

speaking-tube ['spi:kiŋtju:b], *n.* tuyau *ou* tube acoustique, *m.*

spear [spiə], *n.* lance, *f.*—*v.t.* percer d'un coup de lance; harponner (*poisson etc.*).

spear-head ['spiəhed], *n.* fer de lance, *m.*; (*Mil.*) avancée, pointe, *f.*

spearman ['spiəmən], *n.* (*pl.* -men [men]) lancier, *m.*

spearmint ['spiəmint], *n.* menthe verte, *f.*

special ['speʃl], *a.* spécial, exprès; extraordinaire.

specialist ['speʃəlist], *n.* spécialiste, *m.*, *f.*

speciality [speʃi'æliti], specialty ['speʃəlti], *n.* spécialité, *f.*

specialization [speʃəlai'zeiʃən], *n.* spécialisation, *f.*

specialize ['speʃəlaiz], *v.i.* se spécialiser.

specially ['speʃəli], *adv.* particulièrement, surtout.

specie ['spi:ʃi], *n.* espèces, *f.pl.*, numéraire, *m.*

species ['spi:ʃi:z], *n.* espèce, *f.*; (*fig.*) genre, *m.*, sorte, *f.*

specific [spi'sifik], *a.* spécifique; précis.

specification [spesifi'keiʃən], *n.* spécification; description précise (*de brevet d'invention*), *f.*

specify ['spesifai], *v.t.* spécifier, déterminer; fixer d'avance (*une heure*).

specimen ['spesimən], *n.* spécimen, modèle, échantillon, *m.*

specious ['spi:ʃəs], *a.* spécieux, captieux.

speciousness ['spi:ʃəsnis], *n.* spéciosité, apparence plausible, *f.*

speck [spek], *n.* petite tache, marque, *f.*, point; grain (*de poussière*), *m.*—*v.t.* tacher, marquer.

speckle [spekl], *v.t.* tacheter, marqueter, moucheter (*de*).—*n.* moucheture (*peau d'animal*), *f.*

speckled [spekld], *a.* tacheté, marqueté, moucheté.

spectacle ['spektəkl], *n.* spectacle, *m.*; (*pl.*) lunettes, *f.pl.*

spectacle-case ['spektəklkeis], *n.* étui à lunettes, *m.*

spectacle-maker ['spektəklmeikə], *n.* lunetier, *m.*

spectacular [spek'tækjulə], *a.* théâtral, impressionnant.

spectator [spek'teitə], *n.* spectateur, *m.*; (*pl.*) assistants, *m.pl.*

spectral ['spektrəl], *a.* de spectre, spectral.

spectre ['spektə], *n.* spectre, fantôme, *m.*

spectroscope ['spektrəskoup], *n.* spectroscope, *m.*

spectrum ['spektrəm], *n.* (*pl.* **spectra** ['spektrə]) spectre, *m.*

speculate ['spekjuleit], *v.i.* spéculer (*sur*), méditer (*sur*).

speculation [spekju'leiʃən], *n.* spéculation, méditation, *f.*

speculative ['spekjulətiv], *a.* spéculatif, contemplatif; (*Comm.*) spéculateur.

speculatively ['spekjulətivli], *adv.* en théorie.

speculator ['spekjuleitə], *n.* spéculateur, *m.*

speech [spi:tʃ], *n.* parole, *f.*; discours, *m.*, allocution (*public*); langue (*parler*), *f.*; ***extempore speech***, improvisation, *f.*; (*Parl.*) ***maiden speech***, discours de début.

speech-day ['spi:tʃdei], *n.* (*Sch.*) distribution des prix, *f.*

speechless ['spi:tʃlis], *a.* sans voix; muet, interdit.

speechlessness ['spi:tʃlisnis], *n.* mutisme, *m.*

speed [spi:d], *n.* vitesse, rapidité, célérité; hâte, diligence, promptitude, *f.*; (*fig.*) succès, *m.*; ***God-speed!*** bon succès! bonne chance!—*v.t. irr.* expédier, hâter; faire réussir (*faciliter*).—*v.i.* se hâter, se dépêcher.

speed-boat ['spi:dbout], *n.* motoglisseur, *m.*; hors-bord, *m.inv.*

speedily ['spi:dili], *adv.* vite, en toute hâte.

speediness ['spi:dinis], *n.* célérité, hâte, *f.*

speed-limit ['spi:dlimit], *n.* limitation de vitesse, *f.*

speedometer [spi:'dɔmitə], *n.* indicateur de vitesse, tachymètre, *m.*

speedwell ['spi:dwel], *n.* (*Bot.*) véronique, *f.*

speedy ['spi:di], *a.* rapide, vite, prompt.

spell (1) [spel], *n.* temps, *m.*, période, *f.*; tour (*de service*), *m.*

spell (2) [spel], *n.* charme, *m.*—*v.t.*, *v.i. irr.* épeler (*nommer les lettres*); orthographier (*écrire correctement*); signifier.

spell-bound ['spelbaund], *a.* charmé, fasciné.

speller ['spelə], *n.* personne qui orthographie *ou* qui épèle, *f.*

spelling ['speliŋ], *n.* orthographe; épellation, *f.*

spelling-bee ['speliŋbi:], *n.* concours orthographique, *m.*

spelling-book ['speliŋbuk], *n.* abécédaire, syllabaire, *m.*

spelter ['speltə], *n.* zinc, *m.*

spend [spend], *v.t. irr.* dépenser; gaspiller,

perdre (*prodiguer*); passer (*temps*).—*v.i.* dépenser; se perdre (*se dissiper*); se consumer.

spending ['spendiŋ], *n.* action de dépenser, dépense, *f.*

spendthrift ['spendθrift], *n.* prodigue, *m.*, *f.*, dissipateur, *m.*

spent [spent], *a.* épuisé; mort (*balle etc.*).

sperm [spə:m], *n.* sperme; frai (*poisson etc.*); blanc de baleine, *m.*

spew [spju:], *v.t.*, *v.i.* vomir.

spewing ['spju:iŋ], *n.* vomissement, *m.*

sphere ['sfiə], *n.* sphère, *f.*

spherical ['sferikl], *a.* sphérique.

spherics ['sferiks], *n.pl.* théorie de la sphère, *f.*

spheroid ['sfiərɔid], *n.* sphéroïde, *m.*

sphinx [sfiŋks], *n.* (*pl.* **sphinxes** ['sfiŋksiz]) sphinx, *m.*

spice [spais], *n.* épice, *f.*—*v.t.* épicer (*de*).

spiciness ['spaisinis], *n.* goût épicé, *m.*

spick-and-span ['spikənd'spæn], *a.* tiré à quatre épingles; bien astiqué.

spicy ['spaisi], *a.* épicé, aromatique, parfumé.

spider ['spaidə], *n.* araignée, *f.*

spigot ['spigət], *n.* fausset; (*Am., Sc.*) robinet, *m.*

spike [spaik], *n.* pointe, *f.*; clou à grosse tête (*de métal*), *m.*; cheville (*de bois*), *f.*; ***marline-spike***, épissoir, *m.*—*v.t.* clouer; hérisser.

spiked [spaikt], *a.* à pointes, barbelé.

spikenard ['spaikna:d], *n.* nard indien, *m.*

spiky ['spaiki], *a.* à pointe aiguë; armé de pointes.

spill (1) [spil], *v.t. irr.* répandre, verser; renverser.—*v.i.* se verser, se répandre.—*n.* culbute (*renversement*), *f.*

spill (2) [spil], *n.* allumette de papier, allumette en copeau, *f.*

spin [spin], *v.t. irr.* filer; faire tourner.—*v.i.* filer (*aller vite*); tourner.—*n.* tournoiement, *m.*; (*Av.*) vrille, *f.*; (*Motor.*) tour, *m.*; promenade, *f.*

spinach ['spinidʒ], *n.* épinards, *m.pl.*

spinal [spainl], *a.* spinal; ***spinal column***, colonne vertébrale, *f.*

spindle [spindl], *n.* fuseau; pivot; (*Mach.*) essieu; (*Tech.*) axe, *m.*

spindleful ['spindlful], *n.* fusée, *f.*

spindle-legs ['spindllegz], **spindle-shanks** ['spindlʃæŋks], *n.pl.* jambes de fuseau, *f.pl.*

spindrift ['spindrift], *n.* embrun, *m.*

spine [spain], *n.* épine dorsale; (*Bot.*) épine, *f.*

spineless ['spainlis], *a.* sans épines; (*fig.*) mou, flasque, invertébré.

spinet ['spinit, spin'net], *n.* épinette, *f.*

spinner ['spinə], *n.* fileur, *m.*

spinney ['spini], *n.* petit bois, bosquet, *m.*

spinning ['spiniŋ], *a.* tournoyant, tournant.—*n.* filage (*processus*), *m.*; filature (*art*), *f.*; tournoiement, *m.*

spinning-machine ['spiniŋmə'ʃi:n], *n.* machine à filer, *f.*

spinning-mill ['spiniŋmil], *n.* filature, *f.*

spinning-top ['spiniŋtɔp], *n.* toupie, *f.*

spinning-wheel ['spiniŋwi:l], *n.* rouet, *m.*

spinous ['spainəs], *a.* épineux.

spinster ['spinstə], *n.* fille non mariée, célibataire, *f.*

spinsterhood ['spinstəhud], *n.* célibat, *m.*

spiny ['spaini], *a.* épineux, couvert d'épines; (*fig.*) difficile.

spiraea [spai'ri:ə], *n.* (*Bot.*) spirée, *f.*
spiral ['spaiərəl], *a.* spiral; en colimaçon
(*escalier*).—*n.* spirale, *f.*—*v.i.* monter en
spirale.
spirally ['spaiərəli], *adv.* en spirale.
spire ['spaiə], *n.* aiguille, flèche, *f.*
spirit (1) ['spirit], *n.* esprit, *m.*, âme, *f.*, fantôme, spectre (*apparition*), *m.*—*v.t.* **to
spirit away**, faire disparaître.
spirit (2) ['spirit], **spiritedness** ['spiritidnis],
n. (*fig.*) ardeur, force, vigueur, *f.*, feu, élan,
entrain, *m.*; fougue (*d'un cheval*); verve,
bonne humeur, *f.*, entrain, courage, *m.*—*v.t.*
animer, encourager.
spirit (3) ['spirit], *n.* (*sing.* or *pl.*) spiritueux,
m. inv.; liqueur spiritueuse *ou* alcoolique, *f.*;
esprit (*de vin etc.*), *m.*; **methylated spirit**,
alcool à brûler, *m.*
spirited ['spiritid], *a.* animé, plein de cœur,
plein de vivacité; vif, plein de verve; fougueux (*cheval*).
spiritedly ['spiritidli], *adv.* avec ardeur,
chaleureusement, avec force, avec entrain.
spiritedness [SPIRIT (2)].
spirit-lamp ['spiritlæmp], *n.* lampe à alcool,
f.
spiritless ['spiritlis], *a.* sans vigueur, mou,
énervé; sans courage; abattu (*découragé*).
spirit-level ['spiritlevl], *n.* niveau à bulle
d'air, *m.*
spiritual ['spiritjuəl], *a.* spirituel.—*n.* chant
religieux (*des Noirs*), *m.*
spiritualism ['spiritjuəlizm], *n.* spiritisme
(*communication avec les esprits*), *m.*
spiritualist ['spiritjuəlist], *n.* spirite (*adepte
du spiritisme*), *m.*, *f.*
spiritualize ['spiritjuəlaiz], *v.t.* spiritualiser.
spirituous ['spiritjuəs], *a.* spiritueux.
spiry ['spaiəri], *a.* en flèche, élancé.
spit (1) [spit], *n.* broche; profondeur de
bêche (*plongée dans la terre*), *f.*—*v.t.* embrocher, mettre à la broche.
spit (2) [spit], *n.* crachat, *m.*, salive, *f.*—*v.t.*
irr. cracher.—*v.i.* cracher (*sur ou à*).
spite [spait], **spitefulness** ['spaitfulnis], *n.*
dépit, *m.*; rancune, malveillance, *f.*; **in
spite of**, en dépit de, malgré; **out of spite**,
par dépit; **to have a spite against**, en
vouloir à.—*v.t.* vexer, blesser, contrarier.
spiteful ['spaitful], *a.* rancunier, malveillant,
vindicatif.
spitefully ['spaitfuli], *adv.* par dépit, par
rancune.
spitefulness [SPITE].
spitfire ['spitfaiə], *n.* rageur, *m.*
spitter ['spitə], *n.* cracheur, *m.*
spitting ['spitiŋ], *n.* crachement, *m.*
spittle [spitl], *n.* salive, *f.*; (*colloq.*) crachat, *m.*
splash [splæʃ], *v.t.* éclabousser.—*v.i.* éclabousser; clapoter (*vagues*); patauger.—*n.*
éclaboussure, *f.*; clapotement, clapotis (*des
vagues*); flac (*bruit*), *m.*
splashing ['splæʃiŋ], *n.* éclaboussement (*acte*),
m.; éclaboussure (*ce qui rejaillit*), *f.*
splashy ['splæʃi], *a.* éclaboussé, bourbeux.
splay [splei], *v.t.* évaser; (*Arch.*) ébraser;
épauler (*cheval*).—*n.* écartement; (*Arch.*)
ébrasement, *m.*
splay-footed ['spleifutid], *a.* aux pieds plats
et tournés en dehors.
spleen [spli:n], *n.* rate, *f.*; (*fig.*) fiel, *m.*,
animosité, *f.*; spleen, *m.*, mélancolie, *f.*

splendid ['splendid], *a.* resplendissant,
somptueux, magnifique.
splendidly ['splendidli], *adv.* avec éclat,
magnifiquement.
splendour ['splendə], *n.* splendeur, *f.*, éclat,
m.
splenetic [splə'netik], *a.* splénétique, atrabilaire.
splice [splais], *n.* épissure, *f.*, raccordement,
m.—*v.t.* épisser; (*Carp.*) joindre.
splint [splint], *n.* éclisse, attelle, *f.*—*v.t.*
éclisser.
splinter ['splintə], *n.* éclat, éclat de bois, *m.*—
v.t. briser en éclats.—*v.i.* voler en éclats.
splintery ['splintəri], *a.* plein d'éclats, esquil-
leux.
split [split], *a.* fendu; **split personality**,
dédoublement de la personnalité, *m.*; **split
pin**, goupille, *f.*—*n.* fente; (*fig.*) scission, *f.*
—*v.t. irr.* fendre; diviser, partager.—*v.i.* se
fendre; se quereller.
split-second ['splitsekənd], *a.* ultra-rapide.
splitting ['splitiŋ], *n.* fendage, *m.*; **splitting
of the atom**, fission de l'atome, *f.*
splotch [splɔtʃ], *n.* grosse tache, *f.*, barbouillage, *m.*
splutter ['splʌtə], *v.i.* bredouiller, cracher
(*plume* ou *graisse*).—*n.* or **spluttering**
['splʌtəriŋ], bredouillement, crachage, *m.*
spoil [spɔil], *v.t. irr.* gâter, abîmer; dépouiller
(*de*); ravager (*piller*).—*v.i.* se gâter, s'abîmer.
—*n.* butin, *m.*, dépouille, *f.*, pillage, *m.*
spoiled [spɔild], *a.* gâté.
spoiler ['spɔilə], *n.* personne qui gâte, *f.*;
spoliateur (*pilleur*), *m.*
spoiling ['spɔiliŋ], *n.* action de gâter; avarie, *f.*
spoil-sport ['spɔilspɔ:t], *n.* trouble-fête, *m.*
spoke [spouk], *n.* rais, rayon, *m.*
spoke-shave ['spoukʃeiv], *n.* (*Carp.*) plane, *f.*
spokesman ['spouksmən] (*pl.* **-men** [men]),
spokeswoman ['spoukswumən] (*pl.*
-women [wimin]), *n.* porte-parole, *m.inv.*
spoliate ['spoulieit], *v.t.* spolier, piller.
spoliation [spouli'eiʃən], *n.* spoliation, *f.*
sponge [spʌndʒ], *n.* éponge, *f.*; (*Artill.*)
écouvillon, *m.*—*v.t.* éponger; (*Artill.*)
écouvillonner.—*v.i.* **to sponge on**, vivre
aux dépens de.
sponge-cake ['spʌndʒkeik], *n.* gâteau de
Savoie, *m.*
sponger ['spʌndʒə], *n.* pique-assiette, parasite, *m.*
sponginess ['spʌndʒinis], *n.* nature spon-
gieuse, *f.*
sponging ['spʌndʒiŋ], *n.* épongement, *m.*;
(*fig.*) écorniflerie, *f.*
spongy ['spʌndʒi], *a.* spongieux.
sponsor ['spɔnsə], *n.* parrain, *m.*, marraine, *f.*;
garant (*qui cautionne*), *m.*—*v.t.* répondre
pour; parrainer.
sponsorship ['spɔnsəʃip], *n.* parrainage, *m.*
spontaneity [spɔntə'ni:iti], *n.* spontanéité, *f.*
spontaneous [spɔn'teiniəs], *a.* spontané.
spontaneously [spɔn'teiniəsli], *adv.* spontanément.
spool [spu:l], *n.* bobine, *f.*
spoon [spu:n], *n.* cuiller, cuillère, *f.*
spoonbill ['spu:nbil], *n.* (*Orn.*) palette, *f.*
spoonful ['spu:nful], *n.* cuillerée, *f.*
spoor [spuə], *n.* trace, *f.*, empreintes, *f.pl.*
sporadic [spə'rædik], *a.* sporadique.
spore [spɔ:], *n.* spore, *f.*

sport [spɔ:t], *n.* jeu, divertissement, amusement, *m.*; moquerie, raillerie, *f.*; jouet; sport, *m.*—*v.t.* faire parade de.—*v.i.* se divertir, s'amuser.

sporting ['spɔ:tiŋ], *a.* de sport; sportif.

sportive ['spɔ:tiv], *a.* badin, folâtre.

sportively ['spɔ:tivli], *adv.* en badinant.

sportiveness ['spɔ:tivnis], *n.* folâtrerie, *f.*

sportsman ['spɔ:tsmən], *n.* (*pl.* **-men** [men]) sportif, sportsman, *m.*

sportsmanship ['spɔ:tsmənʃip], *n.* sportivité, *f.*

spot [spɔt], *n.* tache, *f.*; endroit, lieu, *m.*; **on the spot**, sur place, sur-le-champ.—*v.t.* tacheter, moucheter; tacher; (*fam.*) repérer; (*colloq.*) observer.

spot-check ['spɔt'tʃek], *n.* contrôle-surprise, *m.*

spotless ['spɔtlis], *a.* sans tache; (*fig.*) immaculé, pur, irréprochable.

spotlessness ['spɔtlisnis], *n.* pureté, *f.*

spotted ['spɔtid], *a.* tacheté, moucheté; truité.

spotter ['spɔtə], *n.* (*Mil. Av.*) observateur, *m.*

spotty ['spɔti], *a.* couvert de taches, moucheté, tacheté.

spouse [spauz], *n.* époux, *m.*, épouse, *f.*; mari, *m.*, femme, *f.*

spout [spaut], *n.* tuyau, *m.*; gouttière (*de maison*), *f.*; bec (*de cruche etc.*), *m.*—*v.i.* jaillir; (*fam.*) déclamer.

spouter ['spautə], *n.* (*fam.*) déclamateur, *m.*

spouting ['spautiŋ], *n.* jaillissement, *m.*; déclamation, *f.*

sprain [sprein], *n.* entorse, foulure, *f.*—*v.t.* fouler; se faire une entorse à.

sprat [spræt], *n.* esprot, sprat, *m.*

sprawl [sprɔ:l], *v.i.* s'étendre, s'étaler.

spray [sprei], *n.* branche, ramille (*d'arbrisseau etc.*), *f.*; embrun, *m.*; poussière (*d'eau*), *f.*; vaporisateur, *m.*—*v.t.* pulvériser, vaporiser, asperger.

spread [spred], *v.t. irr.* étendre, déployer; répandre; couvrir (*table*); mettre (*nappe*); tendre (*voiles etc.*).—*v.i.* s'étendre, se déployer; se répandre, se propager.—*n.* étendue; envergure (*ailes*), *f.*; (*fam.*) festin (*banquet*), *m.*

spreading ['sprediŋ], *a.* étendu, qui se répand.

spree [spri:], *n.* (*colloq.*) bamboche, bombe, *f.*

sprig [sprig], *n.* brin, *m.*, brindille; pointe (*clou*), *f.*

sprightliness ['spraitlinis], *n.* vivacité, *f.*, entrain, *m.*

sprightly ['spraitli], *a.* enjoué, vif, animé, gai.

spring [spriŋ], *v.t. irr.* (*Naut.*) **to spring a leak,** faire une voie d'eau; **to spring upon,** présenter à l'improviste . . . à.—*v.i.* bondir, s'élancer; jaillir (*sourdre*); pousser, naître (*se développer*); paraître, poindre (*jour*); provenir, découler, descendre (*avoir pour ancêtres*).—*n.* saut, bond, élan; ressort (*élasticité*), *m.*; source; cause, origine, *f.*; printemps, *m.*; (*pl.*) suspension (*de voiture*), *f.*

spring-board ['spriŋbɔ:d], *n.* tremplin, *m.*

springiness ['spriŋinis], *n.* élasticité, *f.*

springlike ['spriŋlaik], *a.* printanier.

spring-tide ['spriŋtaid], *n.* grande marée, *f.*

springy ['spriŋi], *a.* élastique.

sprinkle [spriŋkl], *v.t.* répandre; arroser (*de*), asperger (*de*) (*eau bénite*); saupoudrer (*de*).

sprinkler ['spriŋklə], *n.* (*Eccles.*) aspersoir, *m.*; (*Hort.*) arroseuse à jet tournant, *f.*

sprinkling ['spriŋkliŋ], *n.* arrosage, *m.*; (*Eccles.*) aspersion, *f.*; (*fig.*) petit nombre, *m.*

sprint [sprint], *n.* sprint, *m.*—*v.i.* courir à toute vitesse.

sprinter ['sprintə], *n.* coureur de vitesse, sprinter, *m.*

sprite [sprait], *n.* esprit follet, lutin, *m.*

sprout [spraut], *n.* pousse, *f.*, jet, rejeton, *m.*; *Brussels sprouts,* choux de Bruxelles, *m.pl.*—*v.i.* pousser, bourgeonner (*plantes*).

sprouting ['sprautiŋ], *n.* germination, *f.*

spruce (I) [spru:s], *a.* paré, bien mis, pimpant. —*v.t.* attifer.

spruce (2) [spru:s], *n.* sapin (*arbre*), *m.*

spry [sprai], *a.* alerte, plein d'entrain.

spunk [spʌŋk], *n.* amadou; (*colloq.*) cœur, courage, *m.*

spur [spə:], *n.* éperon; ergot (*de coq etc.*); (*fig.*) aiguillon, stimulant, *m.*—*v.t.* éperonner; stimuler.

spurious ['spjuəriəs], *a.* faux, falsifié.

spuriousness ['spjuəriəsnis], *n.* fausseté, *f.*

spurn [spə:n], *v.t.* repousser, écarter (*du pied*); mépriser.—*n.* mépris, dédain, *m.*

spurred [spə:d], *a.* éperonné.

spurt [spə:t], *v.t.* faire jaillir.—*v.i.* s'élancer; (*Spt.*) démarrer.—*n.* jaillissement; (*fig.*) effort soudain; (*Spt.*) démarrage, *m.*

sputnik ['spʌtnik, 'sputnik], *n.* spoutnik, *m.*

sputter ['spʌtə], *v.i.* cracher; bredouiller.—*n.* salive, *f.*

sputtering ['spʌtəriŋ], *n.* bredouillement, *m.*

sputum ['spju:təm], *n.* crachat, *m.*

spy [spai], *n.* espion, *m.*—*v.t.* scruter; apercevoir.—*v.i.* épier, espionner.

spy-glass ['spaiglɑ:s], *n.* longue-vue, *f.*

spying ['spaiiŋ], *n.* espionnage, *m.*

spy-ring ['spairiŋ], **spy-system** ['spaisistəm] *n.* espionnage, *m.*

squabble [skwɔbl], *n.* dispute, querelle, *f.*— *v.i.* se chamailler.

squabbler ['skwɔblə], *n.* querelleur, *m.*

squad [skwɔd], *n.* (*Mil.*) peloton, *m.*; (*Rail.*) brigade; équipe (*de sauvetage etc.*), *f.*

squadron ['skwɔdrən], *n.* (*Mil.*) escadron, *m.*; (*Av.*) escadrille; (*Naut.*) escadre, *f.*

squadron-leader ['skwɔdrənli:də], *n.* (*Av.*) commandant, *m.*

squalid ['skwɔlid], *a.* malpropre, sale.

squalidness [SQUALOR].

squall [skwɔ:l], *n.* cri; coup de vent, *m.*, bourrasque, rafale (*de vent*), *f.*—*v.i.* crier, brailler.

squalling ['skwɔ:liŋ], *a.* criard, braillard.— *n.* criaillerie, *f.*

squally ['skwɔ:li], *a.* à grains, à rafales.

squalor ['skwɔlə], **squalidness** ['skwɔlidnis], *n.* malpropreté, *f.*

squamous ['skweiməs], *a.* squameux; écailleux.

squander ['skwɔndə], *v.t.* dissiper, gaspiller.

squanderer ['skwɔndərə], *n.* gaspilleur, *m.*, prodigue, *m.*, *f.*

squandering ['skwɔndəriŋ], *n.* gaspillage, *m.*

square [skwɛə], *a.* carré; soldé (*comptes etc.*); (*fig.*) équitable, juste; de superficie (*mesure*). —*n.* carré; carreau (*de verre etc.*), *m.*; **case** (*d'échiquier*); place (*dans une ville*); place d'armes (*de ville de garnison*), *f.*, parvis (*devant une église*), *m.*—*v.t.* carrer; (*Carp.*)

équarrir; balancer (*comptes*); (*fig.*) régler, ajuster.—*v.i.* cadrer, s'accorder (*avec*).

square-built ['skwɛəbilt], *a.* aux épaules carrées.

squarely ['skwɛəli], *adv.* carrément; (*fig.*) justement.

squareness ['skwɛənis], *n.* forme carrée, *f.*

squaring ['skwɛəriŋ], *n.* équarrissage, *m.*; **squaring of the circle**, quadrature du cercle, *f.*

squarish ['skwɛəriʃ], *a.* à peu près carré.

squash [skwɔʃ], *v.t.* écraser, aplatir; (*fig.*) rembarrer (*personne*).—*n.* écrasement (*aplatissement*), *m.*; foule serrée (*de gens*), *f.*; **lemon squash**, citronnade, *f.*

squashy ['skwɔʃi], *a.* mou et humide.

squat [skwɔt], *a.* accroupi, blotti; trapu, ramassé (*courtaud*).—*v.i.* s'accroupir; se blottir; (*Am.*) s'établir (sans droit).

squatter ['skwɔtə], *n.* personne accroupie, *f.*; colon (*sans droit*), *m.*

squatting ['skwɔtiŋ], *n.* accroupissement, *m.*

squaw [skwɔ:], *n.* femme peau-rouge, *f.*

squawk [skwɔ:k], *n.* cri rauque; couac, *m.*—*v.i.* pousser des cris rauques.

squeak [skwi:k], *n.* petit cri aigu, *m.*—*v.i.* pousser des cris aigus; jurer (*instrument de musique*).

squeaking ['skwi:kiŋ], *a.* criard; qui jure (*instrument de musique*).

squeal [skwi:l], *v.i.* pousser des cris perçants.—*n.* cri perçant, *m.*

squeamish ['skwi:miʃ], *a.* qui se soulève (*l'estomac*); trop délicat, difficile (*scrupuleux*).

squeamishly ['skwi:miʃli], *adv.* avec dégoût.

squeamishness ['skwi:miʃnis], *n.* délicatesse exagérée, *f.*, goût difficile, *m.*

squeeze [skwi:z], *n.* compression; cohue, *f.*—*v.t.* serrer, presser; *to squeeze money out of*, extorquer de l'argent à; *to squeeze out*, exprimer; *to squeeze through*, forcer à travers.—*v.i.* *to squeeze through*, se forcer à travers.

squeezing ['skwi:ziŋ], *n.* étreinte, compression, *f.*; serrement (*de la main*), *m.*

squelch [skweltʃ], *v.t.* écraser, aplatir.

squib [skwib], *n.* pétard, *m.*; (*fig.*) satire, *f.*

squill [skwil], *n.* scille (*plante*), *f.*

squint [skwint], *a.* louche.—*n.* regard louche, *m.*—*v.i.* loucher.

squinting ['skwintiŋ], *a.* louche.—*n.* action de loucher, *f.*, strabisme, *m.*

squire ['skwaiə], *n.* écuyer; châtelain; cavalier servant (*d'une dame*), *m.*—*v.t.* escorter (*une dame*).

squireen [skwaiə'ri:n], *n.* hobereau, *m.*

squirm [skwə:m], *v.i.* se tortiller, se tordre (*de douleur ou d'embarras*).

squirrel ['skwirəl], *n.* écureuil, *m.*

squirt [skwə:t], *n.* seringue, *f.*—*v.t.* seringuer, faire jaillir.—*v.i.* jaillir.

stab [stæb], *n.* coup de poignard, de couteau etc., *m.*—*v.t.* poignarder.

stabbing ['stæbiŋ], *a.* lancinant.—*n.* coup de poignard, *m.*

stability [stə'biliti], *n.* stabilité, solidité; (*fig.*) fermeté, *f.*

stabilization [steibilai'zeiʃən], *n.* stabilisation, *f.*

stabilize ['steibilaiz], *v.t.* stabiliser.

stable (1) [steibl], *a.* stable, fixe, solide; (*fig.*) constant.

stable (2) [steibl], *n.* écurie, *f.*—*v.t.* loger (*chevaux*); établer (*bétail*).

stable-boy ['steiblbɔi], **stableman** ['steibl mən] (*pl.* **-men** [men]), *n.* garçon d'écurie, *m.*

stabling ['steibliŋ], *n.* écuries (*pour chevaux*) étables (*pour bétail*), *f.pl.*

staccato [stə'kɑ:tou], *a.* saccadé.—*adv.* en staccato.

stack [stæk], *n.* souche (*d'une cheminée*); pile *f.*, tas (*de charbon, de bois*), *m.*; meule (*de foin etc.*), *f.*—*v.t.* empiler (*bois*); emmeuler (*foin etc.*).

stacking ['stækiŋ], *n.* emmeulage, empilage entassement, *m.*

stack-yard ['stækjɑ:d], *n.* cour de ferme, *f.*

stadium ['steidiəm], *n.* stade, *m.*

staff [stɑ:f], *n.* (*pl.* **staves** [steivz]) bâton, bourdon (*de pèlerin*), *m.*; hampe (*à drapeau*), *f.*; (*pl.* **staffs**) corps, personnel; (*Mil.*) état-major, *m.*; *to be on the staff*, être attaché à, faire partie du personnel de.—*v.t.* fournir le personnel de.

staff-officer ['stɑ:fɔfisə], *n.* officier d'état-major, *m.*

stag [stæg], *n.* cerf, *m.*

stag-beetle ['stægbi:tl], *n.* (*Ent.*) cerf-volant lucane, *m.*

stage [steidʒ], *n.* estrade (*dans une salle*); (*Theat.*) scène, *f.*; (*fig.*) théâtre, *m.*; étape (*voyage*), *f.*; (*fig.*) degré, *m.*, phase, période, *f.*—*v.t.* *to stage a play*, monter une pièce.

stage-coach ['steidʒkoutʃ], *n.* diligence, *f.*

stage-door ['steidʒ'dɔ:], *n.* entrée des artistes, *f.*

stage-effect ['steidʒifekt], *n.* effet scénique, *m.*

stage-hand ['steidʒhænd], *n.* machiniste, *m.*

stage-manager ['steidʒ'mænidʒə], *n.* régisseur, *m.*

stage-properties ['steidʒ'prɔpətiz], *n.pl.* accessoires de théâtre, *m.pl.*

stage-set ['steidʒset], *n.* décor, *m.*

stagger ['stægə], *v.t.* faire chanceler; (*fig.*) étonner; échelonner (*heures, vacances etc.*). —*v.i.* chanceler.

staggering ['stægəriŋ], *a.* chancelant; incertain.—*n.* chancellement; échelonnage, *m.*

stagnancy ['stægnənsi], **stagnation** [stæg 'neiʃən], *n.* stagnation, *f.*

stagnant ['stægnənt], *a.* stagnant; (*fig.*) inactif, mort.

stagnate [stæg'neit], *v.i.* être stagnant.

stagnation [STAGNANCY].

staid [steid], *a.* posé, sérieux, grave.

staidness ['steidnis], *n.* gravité, *f.*

stain [stein], *n.* tache; (*Paint.*) teinte; (*fig.*) honte, *f.*, opprobre (*disgrâce*), *m.*—*v.t.* tacher (*de*); (*fig.*) souiller; (*Dyeing*) teindre. —*v.i.* se tacher.

stained [steind], *a.* taché; (*fig.*) souillé; (*Dyeing*) teint; *stained glass*, vitrail, *m.*

stainer ['steinə], *n.* teinturier, *m.*

staining ['steiniŋ], *n.* teinture, *f.*

stainless ['steinlis], *a.* sans tache; inoxydable (*acier*).

stair [stɛə], *n.* marche, *f.*; degré; (*pl.*) escalier, *m.*

staircase ['stɛəkeis], *n.* escalier, *m.*; cage d'escalier, *f.*; *back-staircase*, escalier de service; *moving staircase*, escalier roulant.

stair-rod ['stɛərɔd], *n.* tringle (de tapis) d'escalier, *f.*

stake [steik], *n.* pieu, poteau, bûcher (*de martyre*); (*Cards etc.*) enjeu, *m.* mise, *f.* —*v.t.* parier, gager; hasarder (*risquer*); **to stake out**, jalonner.

stalactite ['stælɔktait], *n.* stalactite, *f.*

stalagmite ['stælɔgmait], *n.* stalagmite, *f.*

stale [steil], *a.* vieux, rassis (*pain*); (*fig.*) suranné, passé, usé.

stalemate ['steilmeit], *v.t.* (*Chess*) faire pat.— *n.* pat, *m.*; (*fig.*) impasse, *f.*

staleness ['steilnis], *n.* vieillesse, *f.*; état rassis (*pain*), *m.*; banalité, *f.*

stalk [stɔ:k], *n.* tige; queue (*de fleur*), *f.*; trognon (*de chou*), *m.*; démarche fière (*allure*), *f.*—*v.t.* chasser à l'affût.—*v.i.* marcher fièrement.

stalker ['stɔ:kə], *n.* chasseur à l'affût, *m.*

stalking ['stɔ:kiŋ], *n.* (*Hunt.*) chasse à l'affût, *f.*

stall (1) [stɔ:l], *n.* stalle (*d'église* ou *d'écurie*), étable (*à bétail*); écurie (*à chevaux*); échoppe, boutique, *f.*, étalage; (*Theat.*) fauteuil d'orchestre, *m.*

stall (2) [stɔ:l], *v.t.*, *v.i.* caler (*machine*).

stallion ['stæljən], *n.* étalon, *m.*

stalwart ['stɔ:lwət], *a.* vigoureux, robuste; vaillant.

stamen ['steimen], *n.* (*Bot.*) étamine, *f.*

stamina ['stæminə], *n.* vigueur, résistance, *f.*

stammer ['stæmə], *v.t.*, *v.i.* bégayer, balbutier.—*n.* bégaiement, *m.*

stammerer ['stæmərə], *n.* bègue, *m.*, *f.*

stammering ['stæməriŋ], *a.* bègue.—*n.* bégaiement, *m.*

stamp [stæmp], *v.t.* frapper du pied; piétiner; empreindre, imprimer; contrôler (*garantir*); estamper (*pièce de monnaie*); timbrer (*documents, lettres etc.*); (*Metal.*) bocarder, estampiller (*marchandises*); affranchir (*payer d'avance*); poinçonner (*billet*).—*v.i.* trépigner, frapper du pied.—*n.* estampe (*outil*), *f.*; coin, poinçon, *m.*; empreinte, marque (*impression*), *f.*; poinçon de contrôle (*sur l'or*); timbre (*sur documents*); (*Metal.*) bocard, *m.*; (*Comm.*) estampille (*sur marchandises*), *f.*; (*fig.*) caractère, *m.*, trempe, *f.*; coup de pied, trépignement; timbre-poste, *m.*; **rubber stamp**, tampon, *m.*

stamp-collecting ['stæmpkəlektiŋ], *n.* philatélie, *f.*

stamp-collector ['stæmpkə'lektə], *n.* philatéliste, *m.*, *f.*

stamp-duty ['stæmp'dju:ti], *n.* droit de timbre, *m.*

stampede [stæm'pi:d], *n.* débandade, panique, *f.*—*v.i.* fuir en désordre.

stamping ['stæmpiŋ], *n.* contrôlage (*garantie*); timbrage (*Metal.*) bocardage; piétinement, trépignement (*des pieds*), *m.*

stamp-machine ['stæmpmə'ʃi:n], *n.* distributeur automatique de timbres-poste, *m.*

stanch [sta:ntʃ], **staunch** [stɔ:ntʃ], *a.* solide, ferme; (*fig.*) sûr, dévoué.—*v.t.* étancher.

stanchion ['sta:nʃən], *n.* étançon, étai, *m.*

stanchness ['sta:ntʃnis], **staunchness** ['stɔ:ntʃnis], *n.* fermeté; constance, dévotion, *f.*

stand [stænd], *v.t. irr.* mettre debout, placer, poser; endurer, souffrir, supporter, soutenir; subir; résister à; payer (*à boire*).—*v.i.* se tenir; rester debout; se soutenir (*difficilement*); se placer, se mettre (*prendre place*);

être debout; se trouver, être (*bâtiment*); se maintenir (*ne pas lâcher pied*); se présenter (*comme candidat*); **stand by!** attention! **to stand aside**, se tenir à l'écart; **to stand by**, assister à (*être présent*); défendre, s'en tenir à (*un avis etc.*); se tenir prêt; **to stand down**, se retirer; **to stand firm**, tenir ferme, tenir bon; **to stand for**, soutenir, signifier; **to stand in for someone**, remplacer quelqu'un; **to stand out**, se dessiner (*être en relief*); résister; **to stand still**, s'arrêter, se tenir tranquille; **to stand up**, se lever.—*n.* arrêt, *m.*, halte, pause, *f.*; stand, étalage (*exposition etc.*); socle (*à vases etc.*), *m.*; (*fig.*) cessation, résistance, *f.*

standard ['stændəd], *a.* type, standard, normal; étalon; au titre (*argent*); classique (*livre*); (*Hort.*) en plein vent (*arbre*), sur tige (*roses*); régulateur (*prix*).—*n.* étendard, (*Naut.*) pavillon; étalon (*de poids et mesures*); titre (*d'or et d'argent*); (*fig.*) type, modèle; (*Hort.*) arbre en plein vent, *m.*

standard-bearer ['stændədbɛərə], *n.* porte-étendard, *m.*

standardization [stændədai'zeiʃən], *n.* étalonnage, *m.*; (*Comm.*) standardisation, *f.*

standardize ['stændədaiz], *v.t.* étalonner, standardiser.

stand-by ['stændbai], *n.* appui, soutien, *m.*, ressource, *f.*

stand-in ['stændin], *n.* remplaçant, *m.*

standing ['stændiŋ], *a.* stagnant; fixe; debout, sur pied (*non abattu*); (*fig.*) invariable.—*n.* position, *f.*; rang, *m.*; durée, date, *f.*, service, *m.*

stand-offish [stænd'ɔfiʃ], *a.* réservé, distant.

stand-point ['stændpoint], *n.* point de vue, *m.*

standstill ['stændstil], *n.* arrêt, *m.*

stand-to ['stænd'tu:], *n.* (*Mil.*) alerte, *f.*

stanza ['stænzə], *n.* stance, strophe, *f.*

staple (1) [steipl], *a.* établi; principal.—*n.* denrée principale (*marchandises*), *f.*; (*fig.*) fond, *m.*

staple (2) [steipl], *n.* agrafe; gâche (*de serrure*) *f.*—*v.t.* agrafer.

stapler ['steiplə], *n.* agrafeuse (*machine*), *f.*

star [sta:], *n.* étoile, *f.*, astre, *m.*; (*Theat. Cine.*) vedette, *f.*—*v.t.* étoiler, parsemer d'étoiles; avoir comme vedettes.—*v.i.* tenir le premier rôle.

starboard ['sta:bəd], *n.* tribord, *m.*

starch [sta:tʃ], *n.* amidon, *m.*; fécule (*aliment*); (*fig.*) raideur, *f.*—*v.t.* empeser.

starchiness ['sta:tʃinis], *n.* raideur, *f.*

starchy ['sta:tʃi], *a.* féculent; empesé; (*fig.*) guindé.

stare [stɛə], *v.t.* dévisager.—*v.i.* regarder fixement; ouvrir de grands yeux (*être ébahi*).—*n.* regard fixe; regard ébahi, *m.*

starfish ['sta:fiʃ], *n.* étoile de mer, *f.*

star-gazer ['sta:geizə], *n.* astrologue, *m.*, *f.*; rêveur, *m.*

staring ['stɛəriŋ], *a.* voyant, tranchant (*couleur etc.*).

stark [sta:k], *adv.* tout, tout à fait.—*a.* raide; stérile (*paysage*).

starless ['sta:lis], *a.* sans étoiles.

starling ['sta:liŋ], *n.* étourneau, sansonnet, *m.*

starlit ['sta:lit], *a.* étoilé.

starry ['sta:ri], *a.* étoilé; (*fig.*) étincelant; **starry-eyed**, peu pratique.

start

start [stɑːt], *v.t.* commencer; faire lever (*gibier*); faire partir; mettre en marche (*machine*).—*v.i.* tressaillir (*de* ou *à*); partir (*s'en aller*); commencer, débuter; sursauter (*faire un bond*).—*n.* tressaillement; saut, bond; commencement, début; départ, *m.*; **to wake with a start**, se réveiller en sursaut.

starter ['stɑːtə], *n.* starter (*de course*); (*Motor.*) démarreur, *m.*

starting ['stɑːtiŋ], *n.* tressaillement; départ; commencement, début, *m.*; mise en marche (*de moteur etc.*), *f.*

starting-handle ['stɑːtiŋhændl], *n.* (*Motor.*) manivelle, *f.*

starting-point ['stɑːtiŋpɔint], *n.* point de départ, *m.*

starting-post ['stɑːtiŋpoust], *n.* poteau de départ, *m.*

startle [stɑːtl], *v.t.* faire tressaillir, effrayer.

startling ['stɑːtliŋ], *a.* étonnant, saisissant.

starvation [stɑːˈveiʃən], *n.* inanition, faim, *f.*

starve [stɑːv], *v.t.* faire mourir de faim; affamer.—*v.i.* mourir de faim.

starveling ['stɑːvliŋ], *n.* affamé, meurt-de-faim, *m.*

starving ['stɑːviŋ], *a.* affamé, mourant de faim.

state [steit], *n.* état, *m.*, condition, *f.*; état (*organisme politique*); rang (*classe*), *m.*; pompe, *f.*, apparat (*pompe*), *m.*; **the** (*United*) **States**, les États-Unis, *m.pl.*—*v.t.* énoncer, déclarer.

state-controlled ['steitkənˈtrould], *a.* étatisé.

statecraft ['steitkrɑːft], *n.* politique, *f.*

stated ['steitid], *a.* réglé, fixe.

stateless ['steitlis], *a.*; **stateless person**, apatride, *m.*, *f.*

stateliness ['steitlinis], *n.* majesté, grandeur, *f.*

stately ['steitli], *a.* imposant, majestueux, noble.—*adv.* majestueusement, avec dignité.

statement ['steitmənt], *n.* exposé, énoncé, rapport, *m.*; déclaration, *f.*

statesman ['steitsmən], *n.* (*pl.* **-men** [men]) homme d'État, *m.*

statesmanlike ['steitsmənlaik], *a.* d'homme d'État.

statesmanship ['steitsmənʃip], *n.* science du gouvernement, politique, *f.*

static ['stætik], **statical** ['stætikəl], *a.* statique.

station ['steiʃən], *n.* station, *f.*; rang (*classe*), *m.*; position; (*Rail.*) gare, *f.*; (*Mil.*) poste, *m.*, garnison, *f.*—*v.t.* placer; (*Mil.*) poster.

stationary ['steiʃənəri], *a.* stationnaire; fixe.

stationer ['steiʃənə], *n.* papetier, *m.*

stationery ['steiʃənəri], *n.* papeterie, *f.*

station-master ['steiʃənmɑːstə], *n.* chef de gare, *m.*

statistic [stəˈtistik], **statistical** [stəˈtistikəl], *a.* statistique.

statistician [stætisˈtiʃən], *n.* statisticien, *m.*

statistics [stəˈtistiks], *n.pl.* statistique, *f.*

statuary ['stætjuəri], *n.* statuaire, *f.*

statue ['stætjuː], *n.* statue, *f.*

statuesque [stætjuˈesk], *a.* plastique.

stature ['stætʃə], *n.* stature, taille, *f.*

status ['steitəs], *n.* statut légal, *m.*; condition, *f.*, rang, *m.*

statute ['stætjuːt], *n.* statut, *m.*, loi, *f.*

statutory ['stætjutəri], *a.* réglementaire, statutaire.

staunch [STANCH].

stave [steiv], *n.* douve (*de baril*); (*Mus.*) portée, *f.*; verset (*de psaume*), *m.*—*v.t. irr.* crever; défoncer (*baril*); **to stave off**, chasser, repousser, éloigner, écarter, prévenir (*danger*).

staves [STAFF].

stay [stei], *v.t.* arrêter; apaiser (*sa faim*); étayer, accoter (*appuyer*).—*v.i.* rester; demeurer (*séjourner*); descendre; attendre. —*n.* séjour; (*Law*) sursis; soutien, appui (*aide*), *m.*

stay-at-home ['steiəthoum], *a.* and *n.* casanier, *m.*

stead [sted], *n.* lieu, *m.*, place, *f.*

steadfast ['stedfəst], *a.* ferme, constant, stable.

steadfastly ['stedfəstli], *adv.* fermement, avec constance.

steadfastness ['stedfəstnis], *n.* fermeté, constance, *f.*

steadily ['stedili], *adv.* fermement, avec persistance.

steadiness ['stedinis], *n.* fermeté; assurance, *f.*

steady ['stedi], *a.* ferme, assuré; posé (*sérieux*); régulier.—*adv.* doucement.—*v.t.* affermir; assujettir (*fixer*); calmer.

steak [steik], *n.* tranche (*de viande*), *f.*; entrecôte, *m.*; **fillet steak**, bifteck dans le filet, *m.*

steal [stiːl], *v.t. irr.* voler, dérober.—*v.i.* se dérober, se glisser furtivement, aller ou venir à la dérobée.

stealer ['stiːlə], *n.* voleur, *m.*

stealing ['stiːliŋ], *n.* vol, *m.*

stealth [stelθ], *n.* **by stealth**, à la dérobée, furtivement.

stealthily ['stelθili], *adv.* à la dérobée, furtivement, à pas de loup.

stealthy ['stelθi], *a.* dérobé, furtif.

steam [stiːm], *n.* vapeur, *f.*—*v.t.* (*Cook.*) cuire à la vapeur.—*v.i.* jeter de la vapeur; fumer.

steamboat ['stiːmbout], *n.* bateau à vapeur, *m.*

steam-engine ['stiːmendʒin], *n.* machine à vapeur, *f.*

steamer ['stiːmə], *n.* vapeur, steamer, *m.*

steam-gauge ['stiːmgeidʒ], *n.* manomètre, *m.*

steaming ['stiːmiŋ], *a.* fumant.

steam-pipe ['stiːmpaip], *n.* tuyau de vapeur, *m.*

steam-roller ['stiːmroulə], *n.* rouleau compresseur, *m.*—*v.t.* (*fig.*) écraser.

steamship ['stiːmʃip], *n.* vapeur, *m.*

steam-whistle ['stiːmwisl], *n.* sifflet à vapeur, *m.*

steamy ['stiːmi], *a.* humide.

steed [stiːd], *n.* (*poet*) coursier, *m.*

steel [stiːl], *a.* d'acier, en acier.—*n.* acier; fusil (*pour aiguiser un couteau*); (*fig.*) fer, *m.* —*v.t.* acérer, garnir d'acier; (*fig.*) fortifier.

steel-clad ['stiːlklæd], *a.* revêtu d'acier, bardé de fer.

steeliness ['stiːlinis], *n.* dureté d'acier; (*fig.*) dureté, *f.*

steel-plated ['stiːlpleitid], *a.* cuirassé.

steel-works ['stiːlwəːks], *n.pl.* aciérie, *f.*

steely ['stiːli], *a.* d'acier; (*fig.*) dur, de fer.

steelyard ['sti:lja:d], *n.* romaine, *f.*

steep (1) [sti:p], *a.* escarpé, à pic; raide (*escalier*).—*n.* pente rapide, *f.*; escarpement, *m.*

steep (2) [sti:p], *v.t.* tremper; (*fig.*) saturer (*de*).

steeping ['sti:piŋ], *n.* trempage, *m.*

steeple [sti:pl], *n.* clocher, *m.*

steeplechase [sti:pltʃeis], *n.* course au clocher, *f.*, steeplechase, *m.*

steepled [sti:pld], *a.* à clocher.

steeple-jack ['sti:pldʒæk], *n.* réparateur de clochers *ou* de cheminées, *m.*

steeply ['sti:pli], *adv.* en pente rapide.

steepness ['sti:pnis], *n.* raideur, pente rapide, *f.*

steer [stiə], *n.* bouvillon, jeune bœuf, *m.*—*v.t.* gouverner; diriger; (*Motor. etc.*) conduire. —*v.i.* se diriger.

steerage ['stiəridʒ], *n.* timonerie, *f.*; l'avant; logement des passagers de troisième classe, *m.*

steering ['stiəriŋ], *n.* direction; (*Motor.*) conduite, *f.*

steering-wheel ['stiəriŋwi:l], *n.* volant, *m.*

steersman ['stiəzmən], *n.* (*pl.* -men [men]) timonier, *m.*

stellar ['stelə], *a.* stellaire.

stem [stem], *n.* tige; queue (*d'une fleur etc.*); (*fig.*) souche (*d'une famille*), *f.*—*v.t.* refouler (*courant*); (*fig.*) résister à.—*v.i.* **to stem from**, être issu de.

stench [stentʃ], *n.* puanteur, *f.*

stencil ['stensil], *n.* patron, pochoir, stencil *m.*—*v.t.* tracer au patron, tirer au stencil.

sten-gun ['stengʌn], *n.* fusil mitrailleur, *m.*

stenographer [ste'nɔgrəfə], *n.* sténographe *m., f.*

stenography [ste'nɔgrəfi], *n.* sténographie, *f.*

stentorian [sten'tɔ:riən], *a.* de stentor.

step [step], *v.t.* mesurer en comptant les pas, arpenter.—*v.i.* faire un pas, marcher pas à pas; marcher, aller; monter (*dans*); descendre (*de*); **to step aside**, s'écarter; **to step back**, reculer; **to step forward**, s'avancer; **to step on**, fouler; **to step over**, enjamber.—*n.* pas; degré, *m.*, marche (*d'escalier*), *f.*; échelon (*d'échelle*); marchepied (*de voiture ou de bicyclette*), *m.*; (*fig.*) démarche; (*pl.*) échelle, *f.*

stepbrother ['stepbrʌðə], *n.* beau-frère, *m.*

stepchild ['steptʃaild], *n.* beau-fils, *m.*, belle-fille, *f.*

stepfather ['stepfɑ:ðə], *n.* beau-père, *m.*

Stephen [sti:vn]. Étienne, *m.*

stepmother ['stepmʌðə], *n.* belle-mère; marâtre, *f.*

steppe [step], *n.* steppe (*plaine*), *f.*

stepping ['stepiŋ], *n.* marche, allure, *f.*

stepping-stone ['stepiŋstoun], *n.* (*pl.*) pierres de gué, *f.pl.*; (*fig.*) introduction, *f.*

stepsister ['stepsistə], *n.* belle-sœur, *f.*

stereoscopic [stiəriə'skɔpik], *a.* stéréoscopique.

stereotype ['stiəriətaip], *a.* stéréotypé; cliché. —*n.* stéréotypage; (*fig.*) cliché, *m.*—*v.t.* clicher; stéréotyper.

stereotyped ['stiəriətaipt], *a.* (*usu. fig.*) stéréotypé.

sterile ['sterail], *a.* stérile.

sterility [stə'riliti], *n.* stérilité, *f.*

sterilization [sterilai'zeiʃən], *n.* stérilisation, *f.*

sterilize ['sterilaiz], *v.t.* stériliser.

sterling ['stə:liŋ], *a.* sterling; (*fig.*) vrai, de bon aloi.

stern (1) [stə:n], *a.* sévère, dur; rigoureux.

stern (2) [stə:n], *n.* (*Naut.*) arrière, *m.*

sternly ['stə:nli], *adv.* sévèrement, durement.

sternmost ['stə:nmoust], *a.* le dernier.

sternness ['stə:nnis], *n.* sévérité, austérité, *f.*

stethoscope ['steθəskoup], *n.* stéthoscope, *m.*

stevedore ['sti:vədɔ:], *n.* arrimeur; déchargeur, *m.*

stew [stju:], *n.* étuvée, *f.*, ragoût (*de viande*); (*fig.*) embarras, *m.*, confusion, *f.*; **Irish stew**, ragoût de mouton.—*v.t.* étuver; mettre en ragoût, faire un ragoût de.—*v.i.* cuire à l'étuvée; (*fig.*) cuire dans sa peau.

steward ['stjuəd], *n.* intendant, régisseur (*d'une propriété*); économe (*de collège*); commissaire (*de bal etc.*); (*Naut.*) steward, *m.*; **steward's room**, cambuse, *f.*

stewardess ['stjuədis], *n.* femme de chambre (de bord), stewardesse, *f.*

stewardship ['stjuədʃip], *n.* intendance; (*fig.*) administration, *f.*

stewed [stju:d], *a.* étuvé, en ragoût; en compote.

stew-pan ['stju:pæn], *n.* casserole, *f.*

stew-pot ['stju:pɔt], *n.* cocotte, *f.*, faitout, *m.*

stick (1) [stik], *n.* bâton, *m.*; canne (*pour marcher*), *f.*; (*Av.*) manche; chapelet (*de bombes*), *m.*

stick (2) [stik], *v.t. irr.* percer, piquer; enfoncer; coller; **stick no bills**, défense d'afficher.—*v.i.* se coller, s'attacher; rester (*demeurer*); **to stick close**, ne pas quitter; **to stick out**, faire saillie; persister; **to stick to**, s'en tenir à; **to stick up**, se dresser.

stickiness ['stikinis], *n.* viscosité, *f.*

sticking-plaster ['stikiŋ'plɑ:stə], *n.* taffetas d'Angleterre, *m.*

stickle [stikl], *v.i.* tenir beaucoup (*à*); se disputer.

stickleback ['stiklbæk], *n.* épinoche, *f.*

stickler ['stiklə], *n.* partisan, *m.*; rigoriste, *m., f.*

sticky ['stiki], *a.* gluant, collant; (*fig.*) difficile (*personne*).

stiff [stif], *a.* raide, rigide, tenace; dur, ferme (*non fluide*); opiniâtre (*entêté*); gêné (*contraint*); courbatu (*muscles*); affecté, guindé (*style*).

stiffen [stifn], *v.t.* raidir; (*fig.*) endurcir.— *v.i.* se raidir; (*fig.*) s'endurcir.

stiffening ['stifniŋ], *n.* raidissement; soutien (*appui*), *m.*

stiffly ['stifli], *adv.* avec raideur; obstinément.

stiff-neck ['stifnek], *n.* torticolis, *m.*

stiff-necked ['stifnekt], *a.* opiniâtre, entêté.

stiffness ['stifnis], *n.* raideur; gêne (*contrainte*); opiniâtreté (*entêtement*), *f.*; (*fig.*) air guindé, *m.*

stifle [staifl], *v.t., v.i.* étouffer, suffoquer.—*n.* (*Vet.*) grasset, *m.*

stifling ['staifliŋ], *a.* étouffant, suffocant. —*n.* suffocation, *f.*

stigma ['stigmə], *n.* stigmate, *m.*, flétrissure, *f.*

stigmatize ['stigmətaiz], *v.t.* stigmatiser, flétrir.

stile [stail], *n.* échallier, échalis, *m.*
stiletto [sti'letou], *n.* stylet, *m.*; ***stiletto heels***, talons aiguille, *m.pl.*
still (1) [stil], *a.* silencieux; tranquille, calme, paisible, en repos; immobile; non mousseux (*vin*).—*adv.* encore, toujours; cependant, néanmoins (*malgré tout*).—*v.t.* calmer, apaiser.
still (2) [stil], *n.* alambic, *m.*
still-born ['stilbɔ:n], *a.* mort-né.
stillness ['stilnis], *n.* tranquillité, *f.*, calme, *m.*
still-room ['stilru:m], *n.* distillerie, *f.*, laboratoire, *m.*
stilt [stilt], *n.* échasse, *f.*; pilotis, pieu (*de pont etc.*), *m.*
stilted ['stiltid], *a.* guindé, pompeux.
stimulant ['stimjulənt], *n.* stimulant, *m.*
stimulate ['stimjuleit], *v.t.* stimuler; (*fig.*) exciter.
stimulating ['stimjuleitiŋ], *a.* stimulant.
stimulation [stimju'leiʃən], *n.* stimulation, *f.*
stimulus ['stimjuləs], *n.* stimulant, aiguillon, stimulus, *m.*
sting [stiŋ], *n.* aiguillon; dard (*d'ortie etc.*), *m.*; piqûre; (*fig.*) pointe, *f.*—*v.t. irr.* piquer; (*fig.*) irriter.
stingily ['stindʒili], *adv.* chichement, mesquinement.
stinginess ['stindʒinis], *n.* mesquinerie, ladrerie, *f.*
stinging ['stiŋiŋ], *a.* piquant; cinglant.—*n.* piqûre, *f.*
stingy ['stindʒi], *a.* avare, mesquin, ladre, chiche.
stink [stiŋk], *n.* puanteur, mauvaise odeur, *f.*—*v.i. irr.* puer; sentir mauvais.
stinking ['stiŋkiŋ], *a.* puant.
stint [stint], *v.t.* limiter, restreindre; ***to stint oneself***, se priver (*de*).—*n.* limite, borne, portion; besogne, *f.*
stipend ['staipend], *n.* traitement (*d'ecclésiastique ou de magistrat*), *m.*
stipendiary [sti'pendiəri], *a.* appointé.
stipple [stipl], *v.t.* pointiller.
stippling ['stipliŋ], *n.* pointillage (*processus*); pointillé (*résultat*), *m.*
stipulate ['stipjuleit], *v.i.* stipuler (*de ou que*).
stipulation [stipju'leiʃən], *n.* stipulation, condition, *f.*
stipulator ['stipjuleitə], *n.* partie stipulante, *f.*
stir [stə:], *v.t.* remuer; (*fig.*) agiter; ***to stir the fire***, attiser le feu.—*v.i.* remuer, se remuer, bouger.—*n.* remuement, bruit, *m.*; agitation, *f.*
stirring ['stə:riŋ], *a.* remuant; émouvant (*histoire etc.*).—*n.* agitation, *f.*
stirrup ['stirəp], *n.* étrier, *m.*
stirrup-cup ['stirəpkʌp], *n.* coup de l'étrier, *m.*
stirrup-leather ['stirəp'leðə], *n.* étrivière, *f.*
stitch [stitʃ], *n.* point, *m.*; maille (*en tricot*), *f.*; (*Med.*) point de suture, *m.*; ***a stitch in time saves nine***, un point à temps en épargne cent.—*v.t.* piquer, coudre; brocher (*livres*); (*Med.*) suturer.
stitched [stitʃt], *a.* piqué, broché (*livre*).
stitching ['stitʃiŋ], *n.* couture, *f.*; brochage (*de livre*), *m.*; (*Med.*) suture, *f.*
stoat [stout], *n.* hermine d'été, *f.*
stock (1) [stɔk], *a.* courant, habituel.—*n.* souche (*d'arbre, famille etc.*), *f.*; cep (*de vigne*);1 bloc (*de bois etc.*), *m.*; monture (*de fusil*); (*Hort.*) ente (*pour greffer*), *f.*; (*Cook.*) consommé, *m.*; (*fig.*) race, famille, *f.*; approvisionnement, stock (*réserve*), assortiment (*sélection*), *m.*; (*pl.*) fonds, fonds publics, *m.pl.*, rentes, actions, *f.pl.*; (*Shipbuilding*) chantier, *m.*, cale de construction, *f.*; ceps (*punition*), *m.pl.*; ***rolling stock***, matériel roulant, *m.*; ***to take stock of***, faire l'inventaire de.—*v.t.* pourvoir (*de*); stocker (*magasin*); meubler (*ferme*); empoissonner (*vivier*).
stock (2) [stɔk], *n.* (*Bot.*) giroflée, *f.*
stockade [stɔ'keid], *n.* palissade, *f.*—*v.t.* palissader.
stock-book ['stɔkbuk], *n.* livre de magasin, magasinier, *m.*
stock-breeder ['stɔkbri:də], *n.* éleveur, *m.*
stock-breeding ['stɔkbri:diŋ], *n.* élevage, *m.*
stockbroker ['stɔkbroukə], *n.* agent de change, *m.*
stock-exchange ['stɔkikstʃeindʒ], *n.* bourse; compagnie des agents de change, *f.*
stockholder ['stɔkhouldə], *n.* actionnaire, *m.*, *f.*, rentier, *m.*
stocking ['stɔkiŋ], *n.* bas, *m.*
stockpile ['stɔkpail], *n.* stocks de réserve, *m.pl.*—*v.t.*, *v.i.* stocker.
stock-still ['stɔk'stil], *a.* immobile.—*adv.* sans bouger.
stock-taking ['stɔkteikiŋ], *n.* inventaire, *m.*
stocky ['stɔki], *a.* trapu.
stodgy ['stɔdʒi], *a.* pâteux, lourd.
stoic ['stouik], *n.* stoïcien, *m.*
stoic ['stouik], **stoical** ['stouikəl], *a.* stoïcien; (*fig.*) stoïque.
stoicism ['stouisizm], *n.* stoïcisme, *m.*
stoke [stouk], *v.t.* chauffer; tisonner (*le feu*).
stoker ['stoukə], *n.* chauffeur, *m.*
stoking ['stoukiŋ], *n.* chauffage, *m.*, chauffe, *f.*
stole (1) [stoul], *n.* étole; (*Cost.*) écharpe, *f.*
stole (2) [stoul], *past* [STEAL].
stolen ['stoulən], *a.* volé, dérobé.
stolid ['stɔlid], *a.* lourd, impassible.
stolidity [stə'liditi], **stolidness** ['stɔlidnis], *n.* flegme, *m.*
stomach ['stʌmək], *n.* estomac; (*euph.*) ventre; appétit, *m.*—*v.t.* avaler; endurer.
stomach-ache ['stʌməkeik], *n.* mal à l'estomac, *m.*, colique, *f.*
stone [stoun], *a.* de pierre, en pierre; de grès (*céramique*).—*n.* pierre, *f.*; caillou (*galet*); noyau (*de fruits*); pépin (*de raisins*); (*Path.*) calcul; (*Weight*) stone (*kg.* 6·348), *m.*—*v.t.* lapider; ôter les noyaux de (*fruits*).
stone-blind ['stounblaind], *a.* complètement aveugle.
stone-cold ['stounkould], *a.* complètement froid.—*adv.* complètement.
stone-dead ['stoun'ded], *a.* raide mort.
stone-deaf ['stoundef], *a.* complètement sourd.
stone-fruit ['stounfru:t], *n.* fruit à noyau, *m.*
stone-mason ['stounmeisən], *n.* maçon, marbrier (*pour tombes*), *m.*
stone's-throw ['stounzθrou], *n.* jet de pierre, *m.*
stoneware ['stounwɛə], *n.* grès, *m.*, poterie de grès, *f.*
stonework ['stounwə:k], *n.* maçonnerie, *f.*
stoniness ['stouninis], *n.* nature pierreuse; (*fig.*) dureté, *f.*
stoning ['stouniŋ], *n.* lapidation, *f.*

strangely

stony ['stouni], a. de pierre; pierreux (plein de pierres); (fig.) insensible; **stony-hearted**, au cœur de pierre.

stook [stu:k], n. tas de gerbes, m.—v.t. mettre en gerbes.

stool [stu:l], n. tabouret; escabeau, m.

stoop [stu:p], v.i. se pencher, se baisser; se voûter (fig.) s'abaisser.—n. inclination, f.; (fig.) abaissement, m.

stooping ['stu:piŋ], a. penché, courbé.

stop [stɔp], n. halte; pause, f.; obstacle; (Organ) jeu, registre; arrêt (de trains etc.), m.; (Gram.) **full stop**, point, m.—v.t. arrêter, empêcher; couper (le souffle); suspendre (paiement etc.); retenir (la paye); (Mus.) presser; (Gram.) ponctuer; boucher (trou etc.); stopper (machine); plomber (dent).—v.i. s'arrêter; stopper.

stopcock ['stɔpkɔk], n. robinet d'arrêt, m.

stop-gap ['stɔpgæp], n. bouche-trou, m.

stoppage ['stɔpidʒ], n. interruption, halte, f.; arrêt (d'un train etc.), m.; obstruction; retenue (de salaire), f.; chômage (arrêt de travail); plombage (de dent), m.

stopper ['stɔpə], n. bouchon (en verre), m.—v.t. boucher.

stopping ['stɔpiŋ], n. arrêt; plombage (de dent), m.; matière à plomber, f.

stop-watch ['stɔpwɔtʃ], n. chronomètre, m.

storage ['stɔ:ridʒ], n. emmagasinage, m., accumulation, f.

store [stɔ:], n. provision, f.; approvisionnement, m., réserve, f.; magasin, m., boutique, f.; (fig.) fonds, trésor, m.; **in store**, en réserve; **to lay in a store of**, faire une provision de.—v.t. pourvoir, munir, approvisionner (de); enrichir (l'esprit).

store-house ['stɔ:haus], n. magasin, entrepôt, dépôt, m.

store-keeper ['stɔ:ki:pə], n. garde-magasin; marchand (boutiquier), m.

store-room ['stɔ:ru:m], n. dépôt, office, m.; réserve, f.

storey, story (1) ['stɔ:ri], n. étage, m.

storied (1) ['stɔ:rid], a. à étage.

storied (2) ['stɔ:rid], a. orné d'inscriptions etc.

stork [stɔ:k], n. cigogne, f.

storm [stɔ:m], n. orage, m., tempête, f.—v.t. donner à l'assaut à, prendre d'assaut.—v.i. faire de l'orage; (fig.) tempêter, s'emporter.

storm-bell ['stɔ:mbel], n. tocsin, m.

storm-cloud ['stɔ:mklaud], n. nuée, f.

storminess ['stɔ:minis], n. état orageux, m.

storming ['stɔ:miŋ], n. assaut, m., prise d'assaut; (fig.) rage, f.

stormy ['stɔ:mi], a. orageux, à l'orage; **stormy petrel**, pétrel, m.

story (1) [STOREY].

story (2) ['stɔ:ri], n. histoire, f., récit; conte (littéraire); mensonge (tromperie), m.

story-book ['stɔ:ribuk], n. livre de contes, m.

story-teller ['stɔ:ritelə], n. conteur (narrateur); menteur (trompeur), m.

stout [staut], a. fort; gros, corpulent; (fig.) brave, courageux.—n. stout, m., bière brune forte (boisson), f.

stoutly ['stautli], adv. vigoureusement, fort et ferme.

stoutness ['stautnis], n. embonpoint, m., corpulence; (fig.) fermeté, f.

stove (1) [stouv], past and p.p. [STAVE].

stove (2) [stouv], n. poêle; fourneau (de cuisine), m.

stow [stou], v.t. mettre en place; (Naut.) arrimer; **to stow away**, emmagasiner.

stowage ['stouidʒ], n. mise en place, f., (Naut.) arrimage, m.

stowaway ['stouəwei], n. passager clandestin m.—v.i. s'embarquer clandestinement.

straddle ['strædl], v.t. enfourcher.—v.i. écarter les jambes, marcher les jambes écartées.

strafe [stra:f], v.t. mitrailler, bombarder.

straggle ['strægl], v.i. s'écarter; marcher à la débandade.

straggler ['stræglə], n. rôdeur; (Mil.) traînard, m.

straggling ['strægliŋ], a. séparé; éparpillé (disséminé).

straight [streit], a. droit; (fig.) équitable, juste.—adv. droit, tout droit, directement; **straight away**, sur-le-champ, tout de suite.

straight-edge ['streitedʒ], n. règle à araser, f.

straighten [streitn], v.t. rendre droit, redresser; ajuster (habits); mettre en ordre (affaires, maison).

straight-faced ['streit'feisd], a. imperturbable.

straightforward [streit'fɔ:wəd], a. droit, direct; (fig.) franc; simple (problème).

straightforwardly [streit'fɔ:wədli], adv. avec droiture; (colloq.) carrément.

straightforwardness [streit'fɔ:wədnis], n. droiture, franchise, f.

straightness ['streitnis], n. ligne directe; droiture, f.

straightway ['streitwei], adv. sur-le-champ, à l'instant.

strain (1) [strein], v.t. tendre; forcer (contraindre); se fouler (muscles); filtrer, passer (liquide).—v.i. s'efforcer; se filtrer (liquide).—n. grand effort, m., tension; entorse, foulure (de muscles), f.; ton; chant, m.

strain (2) [strein], n. race, lignée, f.

strained [streind], a. forcé, pas naturel (langage etc.); tendu.

strainer ['streinə], n. passoire, f.

straining ['streiniŋ], n. tension, f., grand effort, m., exagération, f.; filtrage (d'un liquide), m.

strait [streit], a. étroit, serré; strict.—n. (usu. pl.) (Geog.) détroit, m.; (pl.) gêne, difficulté, f., embarras, m.

straiten [streitn], v.t. rétrécir (resserrer); (fig.) gêner.

strait-laced ['streitleist], a. lacé étroitement; (fig.) sévère, prude.

straitness ['streitnis], n. étroitesse, f.

strait-waistcoat ['streitweiskout], strait-jacket ['streitdʒækit], n. camisole de force, f.

strand (1) [strænd], n. plage, grève, f.—v.t. jeter à la côte, échouer.—v.i. échouer.

strand (2) [strænd], n. cordon (de corde), m.

stranded ['strændid], a. échoué; (fig.) dans l'embarras.

stranding ['strændiŋ], n. échouement, échouage, m.

strange [streindʒ], a. étrange, singulier, bizarre.

strangely ['streindʒli], adv. étrangement, singulièrement.

strangeness ['streindʒnis], *n.* étrangeté, bizarrerie, *f.*

stranger ['streindʒə], *n.* étranger, inconnu, *m.*

strangle [stræŋgl], *v.t.* étrangler.

strangler ['stræŋglə], *n.* étrangleur, *m.*

strangling ['stræŋgliŋ], *n.* étranglement, *m.*

strangulation [stræŋgju'leiʃən], *n.* strangulation, *f.*

strap [stræp], *n.* courroie, *f.*; lien, *m.*, bande (*de fer*), *f.*—*v.t.* attacher avec une courroie; lier.

strapper ['stræpə], *n.* grand gaillard, *m.*

strapping ['stræpiŋ], *a.* bien découplé, bien bâti.

stratagem ['strætədʒəm], *n.* stratagème, *m.*

strategic [strə'ti:dʒik], **strategical** [strə'ti:dʒikəl], *a.* stratégique.

strategist ['strætədʒist], *n.* stratégiste, *m.*, *f.*

strategy ['strætədʒi], *n.* stratégie, *f.*

stratify ['strætifai], *v.t.* stratifier.

stratocruiser ['stræto'kru:zə], *n.* avion stratosphérique, *m.*

stratosphere ['strætəsfiə], *n.* stratosphère, *f.*

stratum ['stra:təm], *n.* (*pl.* **strata** ['stra:tə]) couche, *f.*

straw [strɔ:], *a.* de paille.—*n.* paille, *f.*; *it's the last straw*, c'est le comble.—*v.t.* rempailler (*chaise*).

strawberry ['strɔ:bəri], *n.* fraise, *f.*; fraisier (*plante*), *m.*

straw-coloured ['strɔ:kʌləd], *a.* jaune-paille.

straw-mat ['strɔ:'mæt], *n.* paillasson, *m.*

stray [strei], *v.i.* s'égarer, errer, vaguer; s'écarter (*de*).—*a.* égaré; (*fig.*) fortuit.—*n.* épave, *f.*; *waifs and strays*, des épaves, *f.pl.*

straying ['streiiŋ], *n.* égarement, *m.*

streak [stri:k], *n.* raie, bande, *f.*; *streak of lightning*, éclair, *m.*—*v.t.* rayer, strier; barioler, bigarrer.—*v.i.* filer.

streaked [stri:kt], *a.* rayé (*de*); bariolé, bigarré.

streaky ['stri:ki], *a.* rayé; veiné (*marbre*); entrelardé (*viande*).

stream [stri:m], *n.* courant; cours d'eau, *m.*, rivière, *f.*; ruisseau, *m.*; (*fig.*) cours; jet (*de lumière etc.*); torrent (*de paroles etc.*), *m.*; *to go down stream*, aller en aval; *to go up stream*, aller en amont.—*v.i.* couler; ruisseler (*sang etc.*); rayonner (*lumière*).

streamer ['stri:mə], *n.* banderole; (*Naut.*) flamme, *f.*; (*pl.*) serpentins (*de papier*), *m.pl.*

streamlet ['stri:mlit], *n.* petit ruisseau; ru, *m.*

stream-line ['stri:mlain], *n.* fil de l'eau, *m.* —*v.t.* caréner; (*fig.*) moderniser.

stream-lined ['stri:mlaind], *a.* **stream-lined body**, carrosserie carénée, *f.*; **stream-lined car**, voiture aérodynamique, *f.*

street [stri:t], *n.* rue, *f.*

street-door ['stri:t'dɔ:], *n.* porte sur la rue, *f.*

street-lamp ['stri:tlæmp], *n.* réverbère, *m.*

street-sweeper ['stri:tswi:pə], *n.* balayeur de rue (*personne*), *m.*; balayeuse (*machine*), *f.*

strength [streŋθ], *n.* force, *f.*, forces, *f.pl.*; (*Build.*) solidité, *f.*; (*Mil.*) effectif, *m.*

strengthen [streŋθn], *v.t.* fortifier, affermir, raffermir; (*Mil.*) renforcer.—*v.i.* se fortifier, s'affermir; se raffermir.

strengthener ['streŋθnə], *n.* (*Med.*) fortifiant, *m.*

strengthening ['streŋθniŋ], *a.* fortifiant.

strenuous ['strenjuəs], *a.* énergique, vif, ardent, vigoureux.

strenuously ['strenjuəsli], *adv.* avec zèle, ardemment; vigoureusement.

strenuousness ['strenjuəsnis], *n.* zèle, *m.*, ardeur; vigueur, *f.*

streptococcus [strepto'kɔkəs], *n.* streptocoque, *m.*

streptomycin [strepto'maisin], *n.* streptomycine, *f.*

stress [stres], *n.* force, emphase, *f.*, poids; (*Gram.*) accent, *m.*; violence (*du temps*); (*Mech.*) tension, *f.*—*v.t.* appuyer sur, accentuer.

stretch [stretʃ], *v.t.* tendre (*un élastique*); étendre; déployer (*ailes*); élargir; forcer (*faire violence à*); (*fig.*) exagérer.—*v.i.* s'étendre; s'étirer; se déployer; s'élargir; prêter (*gants, tissu*).—*n.* étendue, tension, extension; section (*de route*), *f.*; (*fig.*) effort, *m.*; *at a stretch*, d'un trait.

stretcher ['stretʃə], *n.* brancard, *m.*, civière; baguette (*à gants*), *f.*, tendeur (*à chaussures*), *m.*

stretcher-bearer ['stretʃəbɛərə], *n.* brancardier, *m.*

stretching ['stretʃiŋ], *n.* élargissement, *m.*; tension, *f.*

strew [stru:], *v.t. irr.* répandre, parsemer, semer.

strewing ['stru:iŋ], *n.* jonchée, *f.*

striate ['straiit], **striated** [strai'eitid], *a.* strié.

striation [strai'eiʃən], *n.* striure, *f.*

stricken [strikn], *p.p.* [STRIKE].—*a.* affligé; (*Med.*) atteint (*de*).

strict [strikt], *a.* exact, strict, précis; rigide; sévère.

strictly ['striktli], *adv.* strictement, formellement; *strictly speaking*, rigoureusement parlant.

strictness ['striktnis], *n.* exactitude, rigueur; sévérité, *f.*

stricture ['striktʃə], *n.* censure, critique, *f.*; (*Med.*) étranglement, *m.*

stride [straid], *n.* grand pas, *m.*, enjambée, *f.* —*v.i. irr.* marcher à grands pas *ou* à grandes enjambées.

strident ['straidənt], *a.* strident.

strife [straif], *n.* lutte, querelle, dispute, *f.*

strike [straik], *v.t. irr.* frapper; battre, cogner; asséner, porter (*un coup*); sonner (*l'heure*); rendre (*muet etc.*); établir (*l'équilibre*); allumer (*allumette*); faire (*marché etc.*); amener (*drapeau*); plier (*tente*); *to strike down*, abattre; *to strike off*, retrancher, effacer.—*v.i.* frapper; toucher; échouer (*heurter un écueil etc.*); heurter, donner (*contre*); sonner (*pendule etc.*); (*Hort.*) prendre racine; faire grève, se mettre en grève (*ouvriers*); *to strike out*, se lancer; (*Mus.*) *to strike up*, commencer à jouer.— *n.* grève (*d'ouvriers*), *f.*; *sit-down strike*, débrayage, *m.*; *stay-in-strike*, grève sur le tas.

striker ['straikə], *n.* frappeur, *m.*; gréviste (*ouvrier en grève*), *m.*,*f.*; percuteur (*de fusil*), *m.*

striking ['straikiŋ], *a.* frappant, saisissant; remarquable.—*n.* frappement, *m.*; frappe; sonnerie (*de pendule*), *f.*

strikingly ['straikiŋli], *adv.* d'une manière frappante.

style

string [striŋ], n. ficelle, corde, f., fil; cordon, lacet (de chaussures etc.); chapelet (d'oignons etc.), m.; corde (de violon); bride (de bonnet etc.); (fig.) suite, série, f.; **the strings**, les instruments à cordes (d'un orchestre), m.pl.—v.t. irr. garnir de cordes; enfiler (grains etc.); (Mus.) accorder.

stringed [striŋd], a. à cordes (instrument de musique).

stringency ['strindʒənsi], n. rigueur, f.

stringent ['strindʒənt], a. rigoureux, strict.

stringy ['striŋi], a. fibreux; filandreux (viande).

strip [strip], n. bande, f., ruban; lambeau, m., langue (de terre), f.—v.t. dépouiller (de); dévaliser (voler); déshabiller (dévêtir); **to strip off**, se dépouiller de.—v.i. se déshabiller.

stripe [straip], n. raie; barre, bande; marque (cicatrice), f.; (Mil.) chevron, galon, m.—v.t. rayer, barrer.

striped [straipt], striped ['straipi], a. rayé, à raies, zébré.

stripling ['stripliŋ], n. adolescent, m.

strive [straiv], v.i. irr. s'efforcer (de), faire des efforts (pour), se débattre; se disputer (rivaliser).

striving ['straiviŋ], n. lutte, f., efforts, m.pl.

stroke [strouk], n. coup; trait; trait de plume; coup d'aviron, m.; brassée (de la nage), course (de piston), f.; (Med.) coup de sang, m., attaque, f.; chef de nage (de bateau à rames), m.; **at a stroke**, d'un coup, d'un trait.—v.t. caresser.

stroking ['stroukiŋ], n. caresses, f.pl.

stroll [stroul], n. (courte) promenade, f., tour, m., flânerie, f.—v.i. errer, flâner.

stroller ['stroulə], n. flâneur, m.

strong [stroŋ], a. fort, solide; (fig.) vigoureux, résolu; **strong light**, vive lumière, f.

strong-box ['stroŋbɒks], n. coffre-fort, m.

stronghold ['stroŋhould], n. forteresse, f., fort, m.

strongly ['stroŋli], adv. fortement, fermement.

strong-room ['stroŋru:m], n. cave aux coffres-forts, f.

strontium ['strɒnʃiəm], n. strontium, m.

strop [strɒp], n. cuir à rasoir, m.—v.t. repasser, affiler.

strophe ['stroufi, 'strɒfi], n. stance, strophe, f.

structural ['strʌktʃərəl], a. de structure, structural.

structure ['strʌktʃə], n. construction, structure, f.; édifice, m.; facture (de pièce, de poème), f.

struggle [strʌgl], n. lutte, f., effort, m.—v.i. lutter, se débattre.

struggling ['strʌgliŋ], n. lutte, f.; effort, m.

strum [strʌm], v.t. tapoter, taper (sur).

strumming ['strʌmiŋ], n. tapotage, m.

strut [strʌt], n. démarche fière, f.; (Carp. etc.) étai, m.—v.i. se pavaner, se carrer.

strychnine ['strikni:n], n. strychnine, f.

stub [stʌb], n. souche, f.; bout, m.

stubble [stʌbl], n. chaume, m.

stubborn ['stʌbən], a. obstiné, opiniâtre.

stubbornness ['stʌbənnis], n. opiniâtreté, f.

stubby ['stʌbi], a. trapu (taille).

stucco ['stʌkou], n. stuc, m.

stud (1) [stʌd], n. bouton de chemise; clou, m.—v.t. clouter; parsemer (de).

stud (2) [stʌd], n. écurie, f.; **stud-farm**, haras, m.

student ['stju:dənt], n. étudiant, m., élève, m., f.

studied ['stʌdid], a. étudié (style etc.); prémédité (calculé).

studio ['stju:diou], n. atelier; (Cine., Rad.) studio, m.

studious ['stju:diəs], a. studieux; diligent.

studiously ['stju:diəsli], adv. studieusement.

studiousness ['stju:diəsnis], n. application, f.

study ['stʌdi], n. étude, f.; soin, m., application (attention), f.; cabinet d'étude (pièce), m.; **to be in a brown study**, être dans la lune.—v.t. étudier, s'occuper de.—v.i. étudier, travailler.

stuff [stʌf], n. étoffe, f., tissu, m.; (fig.) matière, f.; fatras (bêtises), m.—v.t. rembourrer; bourrer (remplir); boucher (trou); (Taxidermy) empailler; (Cook.) farcir.—v.i. se bourrer; se gorger.

stuffing ['stʌfiŋ], n. bourre (substances), f.; rembourrage (opération), m.; (Cook.) farce, f.; (Taxidermy) empaillage, m.

stuffy ['stʌfi], a. privé d'air, renfermé; **to be stuffy**, sentir le renfermé; (fig.) avoir des préjugés.

stultify ['stʌltifai], v.t. rendre nul; contredire (démentir); **to stultify oneself**, se rendre ridicule.

stumble [stʌmbl], v.i. trébucher, broncher; (fig.) faire un faux pas, faillir.—n. faux pas, m.

stumbling ['stʌmbliŋ], a. trébuchant.—n. trébuchement, m.

stumbling-block ['stʌmbliŋblɒk], n. pierre d'achoppement, f.

stump [stʌmp], n. tronçon, m., souche, f.; chicot (de dent); trognon (de chou); moignon (de membre), m.; (Drawing) estompe, f.

stumpy ['stʌmpi], a. trapu (personne).

stun [stʌn], v.t. étourdir.

stunning ['stʌniŋ], a. étourdissant; (slang) épatant.

stunt (1) [stʌnt], v.t. rabougrir.

stunt (2) [stʌnt], n. tour de force, m.; réclame, f.

stunted ['stʌntid], a. rabougri.

stupefaction [stju:pi'fækʃən], n. stupéfaction, f.

stupefy ['stju:pifai], v.t. hébéter, abrutir; stupéfier.

stupefying ['stju:pifaiiŋ], a. stupéfiant.

stupendous [stju'pendəs], a. prodigieux, foudroyant.

stupid ['stju:pid], a. stupide, sot, bête.

stupidity [stju'piditi], n. stupidité, bêtise, f.

stupidly ['stju:pidli], adv. stupidement.

stupor ['stju:pə], n. stupeur, f.

sturdy ['stə:di], a. vigoureux, fort, robuste; hardi.

sturgeon ['stə:dʒən], n. esturgeon, m.

stutter ['stʌtə], v.t., v.i. bégayer.

stutterer ['stʌtərə], n. bègue, m., f.

stuttering ['stʌtəriŋ], n. bégaiement, m.

sty (1) [stai], n. étable (à cochons), f.

sty (2), stye [stai], n. orgelet (à l'œil), m.

Stygian ['stidʒiən], a. stygien.

style [stail], n. style; (fig.) genre, m., manière, f.; titre, m.; raison sociale (d'une compagnie), f.; **to live in style**, avoir un train de maison.—v.t. appeler, qualifier de.

stylish

stylish ['stailiʃ], *a.* élégant, de bon ton.
stylus ['stailəs], *n.* style, *m.*
styptic ['stiptik], *a.* and *n.* (*Med.*) styptique, *m.*
suave [swɑːv], *a.* suave.
suavity ['swɑːviti], *n.* suavité, *f.*
subaltern ['sʌbəltən], *a.* subalterne.—*n.* (sous-)lieutenant, *m.*
subconscious [sʌb'kɔnʃəs], *a.* and *n.* (*Psych.*) subconscient, *m.*
subconsciously [sʌb'kɔnʃəsli], *adv.* inconsciemment.
subdivide [sʌbdi'vaid], *v.t.* subdiviser.
subdue [səb'djuː], *v.t.* subjuguer; dompter, étouffer; *subdued light,* demi-jour, *m.*
sub-editor [sʌb'editə], *n.* secrétaire de la rédaction, *m.*, *f.*
subject ['sʌbdʒikt], *a.* assujetti, soumis; sujet (*à*), exposé (*à*).—*n.* sujet, *m.*; (*Sch.*) matière, *f.*; particulier, *m.*, personne, *f.*— [səb'dʒekt], *v.t.* assujettir, soumettre; rendre sujet (*à*), exposer (*à*).
subjection [səb'dʒekʃən], *n.* sujétion, *f.*
subjective [səb'dʒektiv], *a.* subjectif.
subjectively [səb'dʒektivli], *adv.* subjectivement.
subject-matter ['sʌbdʒiktmætə], *n.* sujet, *m.* matière, *f.*
subjugate ['sʌbdʒugeit], *v.t.* subjuguer.
subjunctive [səb'dʒʌŋktiv], *a.* and *n.* (*Gram.*) subjonctif, *m.*
sublet [sʌb'let], *v.t. irr.* (*conjug. like* LET) sous-louer.
sub-lieutenant [sʌblef'tenənt], *n.* (*Navy*) enseigne, *m.*
sublimate ['sʌblimeit], *v.t.* sublimer.
sublime [sə'blaim], *a.* and *n.* sublime, *m.*
sublimeness [sə'blaimnis], *n.* sublimité, *f.*; sublime, *m.*
sub-machine-gun [sʌbmə'ʃiːngʌn], *n.* mitraillette, *f.*
submarine ['sʌbməriːn], *a.* and *n.* sous-marin, *m.*
submerge [səb'məːdʒ], *v.t.* submerger.—*v.i.* plonger.
submission [səb'miʃən], *n.* soumission; résignation, déférence, *f.*
submissive [səb'misiv], *a.* soumis (*à*); docile.
submit [səb'mit], *v.t.* soumettre (*à*).—*v.i.* se soumettre (*à*).
subnormal [sʌb'nɔːml], *a.* sous-normal.
subordinate [sə'bɔːdinit], *a.* subordonné (*à*).—*n.* subordonné, *m.*—[sə'bɔːdineit], *v.t.* subordonner (*à*).
subordination [səbɔːdi'neiʃən], *n.* subordination, *f.*; rang inférieur, *m.*
suborn [sə'bɔːn], *v.t.* suborner.
subpoena [sʌb'piːnə], *n.* (*Law*) citation, assignation, *f.*—*v.t.* citer, assigner.
subscribe [səb'skraib], *v.t.* souscrire.—*v.i.* souscrire (*à* ou *pour*); s'abonner (*à un journal*).
subscriber [səb'skraibə], *n.* abonné (*à un journal*), *m.*
subscription [səb'skripʃən], *n.* souscription, *f.*; abonnement (*à un journal etc.*), *m.*
subsection ['sʌbsekʃən], *n.* subdivision, *f.*
subsequent ['sʌbsikwənt], *a.* subséquent, postérieur.
subsequently ['sʌbsikwəntli], *adv.* ensuite, après.

subservient [səb'səːvjənt], *a.* subordonné (*à*); qui contribue à; obséquieux.
subserviently [səb'səːvjəntli], *adv.* en sous-ordre, utilement; servilement.
subside [səb'said], *v.i.* s'affaisser (*être accablé*); baisser, s'abaisser, se calmer, s'apaiser (*s'adoucir*); se taire (*personne*); *to subside into,* se changer en.
subsidence ['sʌbsidəns, səb'saidəns], *n.* affaissement, *m.*; (*fig.*) baisse (*rivière*), *f.*
subsidiary [səb'sidjəri], *a.* subsidiaire (*à*).— *n.* auxiliaire, *m.*; filiale (*compagnie*), *f.*
subsidize ['sʌbsidaiz], *v.t.* subventionner.
subsidy ['sʌbsidi], *n.* subvention, *f.*
subsist [səb'sist], *v.i.* subsister, exister.
subsistence [səb'sistəns], *n.* subsistance, *f.*; entretien, *m.*; existence, *f.*
subsistent [səb'sistənt], *a.* existant, qui existe.
subsoil ['sʌbsɔil], *n.* sous-sol, *m.*
sub-species ['sʌbspiːʃiːz], *n.* sous-espèce, *f.*
substance ['sʌbstəns], *n.* substance, *f.*; fond (*l'essentiel*), *m.*; biens (*richesses*), *m.pl.*
substantial [səb'stænʃl], *a.* substantiel, réel, solide; aisé (*riche*).
substantially [səb'stænʃəli], *adv.* solidement, fortement, considérablement.
substantiate [səb'stænʃieit], *v.t.* établir, confirmer.
substantive ['sʌbstəntiv], *a.* indépendant; (*Gram.*) substantif.—*n.* (*Gram.*) substantif, *m.*
substitute ['sʌbstitjuːt], *v.t.* substituer (*à*).— *n.* substitut, remplaçant, *m.*
substitution [sʌbsti'tjuːʃən], *n.* substitution, *f.*
substratum [sʌb'strɑːtəm], *n.* (*pl.* **substrata** [sʌb'strɑːtə]) substratum, substrat, *m.*, couche inférieure, *f.*; (*Agric.*) sous-sol, *m.*
subtenant ['sʌbtenənt], *n.* sous-locataire, *m.*, *f.*
subterfuge ['sʌbtəfjuːdʒ], *n.* subterfuge, faux-fuyant, *m.*
subterranean [sʌbtə'reiniən], *a.* souterrain.
sub-title ['sʌbtaitl], *n.* sous-titre, *m.*
subtle [sʌtl], *a.* subtil, rusé; fin.
subtlety ['sʌtlti], *n.* subtilité, finesse, *f.*
subtly ['sʌtli], *adv.* subtilement.
subtract [səb'trækt], *v.t.* défalquer; (*Arith.*) soustraire.
subtraction [səb'trækʃən], *n.* (*Arith.*) soustraction, *f.*
suburb ['sʌbəːb], *n.* faubourg, *m.*, (*pl.*) alentours, environs, *m.pl.*, banlieue, *f.*; *garden suburb,* cité-jardin, *f.*
suburban [sə'bəːbən], *a.* de la banlieue, suburbain.
subvention [səb'venʃən], *n.* subvention, *f.*
subversive [səb'vəːsiv], *a.* subversif.
subway ['sʌbwei], *n.* passage souterrain; (*Am.*) métro, *m.*
succeed [sək'siːd], *v.t.* succéder à, suivre; *to succeed each other,* se succéder.—*v.i.* succéder (*à*); hériter (*une propriété*); parvenir (*à*), réussir (*avoir du succès*).
succeeding [sək'siːdiŋ], *a.* suivant (*dans le passé*); à venir, futur (*à l'avenir*); successif (*consécutif*).
success [sək'ses], *n.* succès, *m.*; *I wish you success!* bonne chance!
successful [sək'sesful], *a.* heureux; couronné de succès, réussi, victorieux; *to be successful,* réussir.

584

successfully [sək'sesfuli], *adv.* heureusement, avec succès.
succession [sək'seʃən], *n.* succession, suite, *f.*;
avènement (*au trône etc.*), *m.*; postérité
(*descendance*), *f.*; **in succession**, successivement, de suite.
successive [sək'sesiv], *a.* successif, consécutif.
successor [sək'sesə], *n.* successeur, *m.*
succinct [sək'siŋkt], *a.* succinct, concis.
succinctly [sək'siŋktli], *adv.* avec concision.
succinctness [sək'siŋktnis], *n.* concision,
brièveté, *f.*
succour ['sʌkə], *v.t.* secourir, aider.—*n.*
secours, *m.*, aide, *f.*
succulent ['sʌkjulənt], *a.* succulent, plein de
jus.
succumb [sə'kʌm], *v.i.* succomber (à).
such [sʌtʃ], *a.* tel, pareil, semblable; **he is
such a bore**, il est si ennuyeux; **such a
one**, un tel, *m.*, une telle, *f.*; **such a one as**,
tel que; **such as it is**, tel quel, *m.*, telle
quelle, *f.*; **such as you**, tel que vous.
suchlike ['sʌtʃlaik], *a.* semblable, pareil; de
ce genre.
suck [sʌk], *v.t., v.i.* sucer; têter (*à la mamelle*);
aspirer.
sucker ['sʌkə], *n.* suceur; (*fig.*) gobeur, *m.*
sucking ['sʌkiŋ], *a.* qui suce, aspirant.—*n.*
sucement, *m.*, succion, *f.*
sucking-pig ['sʌkiŋpig], *n.* cochon de lait, *m.*
suckle [sʌkl], *v.t.* allaiter, nourrir.
suction ['sʌkʃən], *n.* succion, aspiration, *f.*
Sudan [su'dæn, su'dɑːn], le Soudan, *m.*
Sudanese [sudə'niːz], *a.* soudanais.—*n.*
Soudanais (*personne*), *m.*
sudden [sʌdn], *a.* subit, soudain; (*fam.*) **all
of a sudden**, tout à coup.
suddenly ['sʌdnli], *adv.* subitement, soudain,
tout à coup.
suddenness ['sʌdnnis], *n.* soudaineté, *f.*
Sudetenland [su'deitnlænd], les Sudètes,
m.pl.
suds [sʌdz], **soap-suds** ['soupsʌdz], *n.pl.* eau
de savon, lessive, *f.*
sue [sjuː], *v.t.* poursuivre (en justice).—*v.i.*
implorer.
suède [sweid], *n.* daim (*chaussures*); suède
(*gants*), *m.*
suet ['sjuːit], *n.* graisse de bœuf, *f.*
suffer ['sʌfə], *v.t.* souffrir; supporter, endurer,
subir (*éprouver*); laisser, permettre (*autoriser*).—*v.i.* souffrir (*de*); **to suffer for**,
porter la peine de.
sufferable ['sʌfərəbl], *a.* supportable, tolérable.
sufferance ['sʌfərəns], *n.* tolérance, *f.*
sufferer ['sʌfərə], *n.* victime (*de*), *f.*; patient,
m.
suffering ['sʌfəriŋ], *a.* souffrant.—*n.* souffrance, douleur, *f.*
suffice [sə'fais], *v.t.* suffire à, satisfaire.—*v.i.*
suffire.
sufficiency [sə'fiʃənsi], *n.* suffisance; aisance
(*financière*), *f.*
sufficient [sə'fiʃənt], *a.* suffisant, assez.
sufficiently [sə'fiʃəntli], *adv.* suffisamment,
assez.
suffix ['sʌfiks], *n.* suffixe, *m.*
suffocate ['sʌfəkeit], *v.t., v.i.* suffoquer,
étouffer, asphyxier.
suffocating ['sʌfəkeitiŋ], *a.* suffocant, étouffant, asphyxiant.

suffocation [sʌfə'keiʃən], *n.* suffocation,
asphyxie, *f.*
suffrage ['sʌfridʒ], *n.* suffrage, *m.*
suffuse [sə'fjuːz], *v.t.* répandre, couvrir (*de*);
répandre sur; se répandre sur.
suffusion [sə'fjuːʒən], *n.* épanchement, *m.*,
suffusion, *f.*
sugar ['ʃugə], *n.* sucre, *m.*; **barley sugar**,
sucre d'orge; **brown sugar** or **moist
sugar**, cassonade, *f.*; **castor sugar**, sucre
en poudre; **granulated sugar**, sucre
cristallisé; **lump sugar**, sucre cassé.—*v.t.*
sucrer; (*fig.*) adoucir.
sugar-basin ['ʃugəbeisn], *n.* sucrier, *m.*
sugar-beet ['ʃugəbiːt], *n.* betterave à sucre, *f.*
sugar-cane ['ʃugəkein], *n.* canne à sucre, *f.*
sugared ['ʃugəd], *a.* sucré; (*fig.*) doux.
sugar-loaf ['ʃugəlouf], *n.* pain de sucre, *m.*
sugar-refinery ['ʃugəri'fainəri], *n.* raffinerie
de sucre, *f.*
sugary ['ʃugəri], *a.* sucré; trop sucré.
suggest [sə'dʒest], *v.t.* suggérer; inspirer.
suggestion [sə'dʒestʃən], *n.* suggestion; proposition, idée; nuance, *f.*
suggestive [sə'dʒestiv], *a.* suggestif.
suicidal [sjuːi'saidl], *a.* de suicide; fatal.
suicide ['sjuːisaid], *n.* suicide (*acte*); suicidé
(*personne*), *m.*; **to commit suicide**, se
suicider.
suit [sjuːt], *n.* suite, collection complète, *f.*,
assortiment, *m.*; (*Cards*) couleur; sollicitation, prière; recherche en mariage; (*Law*)
instance, *f.*, procès, *m.*; **suit (of clothes)**,
complet (*d'homme*), tailleur (*de femme*), *m.*—
v.t. adapter; convenir à, aller à; plaire à
—*v.i.* s'accorder (*de*).
suitability [sjuːtə'biliti], *n.* convenance, *f.*
suitable ['sjuːtəbl], *a.* convenable (à); à
propos.
suitably ['sjuːtəbli], *adv.* convenablement.
suite [swiːt], *n.* suite, *f.*, ensemble, *m.*; **suite
of rooms**, appartement, *m.*; **suite of
furniture**, ameublement complet, *m.*
suitor ['sjuːtə], *n.* prétendant (*amoureux*);
(*Law*) plaideur, *m.*
sulk [sʌlk], *v.i.* bouder, faire la mine.
sulkily ['sʌlkili], *adv.* en boudant, en faisant
la mine.
sulkiness ['sʌlkinis], **sulking** ['sʌlkiŋ], *n.*
bouderie, *f.*
sulks [sʌlks], *n.pl.* mauvaise humeur, bouderie, *f.*
sulky ['sʌlki], *a.* boudeur.
sullen ['sʌlən], *a.* maussade, morose, renfrogné.
sullenly ['sʌlənli], *adv.* maussadement, d'un
air renfrogné.
sullenness ['sʌlənnis], *n.* air maussade, *m.*
sully ['sʌli], *v.t.* souiller, ternir (*de*).
sulphate ['sʌlfeit], *n.* sulfate, *m.*
sulphide ['sʌlfaid], *n.* sulfure, *m.*
sulphite ['sʌlfait], *n.* sulfite, *m.*
sulphonamide [sʌl'founəmaid], *n.* sulfa-
mide, *f.*
sulphur ['sʌlfə], *n.* soufre, *m.*
sulphuric [sʌl'fjuərik], *a.* sulfurique.
sulphurous [sʌl'fjuərəs], *a.* sulfureux.
sultan ['sʌltən], *n.* sultan, *m.*
sultana [sʌl'tɑːnə], *n.* sultane, *f.*; (*pl.*) raisins
de Smyrne, *m.pl.*
sultriness ['sʌltrinis], *n.* chaleur étouffante, *f.*

sultry

sultry ['sʌltri], *a.* d'une chaleur étouffante, étouffant, suffocant; (*fam.*) épicé, salé (*histoire etc.*); *it is very sultry*, il fait très lourd.

sum [sʌm], *n.* somme (*d'argent*), *f.*; (*Arith.*) problème, calcul, *m.*; *the four sums*, les quatre opérations, *f.pl.*—*v.t.* *to sum up*, additionner, faire l'addition de; (*fig.*) récapituler.

summarily ['sʌmərili], *adv.* sommairement.

summarize ['sʌməraiz], *v.t.* résumer sommairement.

summary ['sʌməri], *a.* sommaire, prompt.— *n.* sommaire, résumé, *m.*

summer ['sʌmə], *a.* d'été, estival—*n.* été, *m.*; *in summer*, en été.

summer-house ['sʌməhaus], *n.* pavillon, *m.*

summing-up ['sʌmiŋ'ʌp], *n.* résumé, *m.*

summit ['sʌmit], *n.* sommet, *m.*, cime, *f.*; (*fig.*) comble, *m.*

summon ['sʌmən], *v.t.* convoquer (*un rassemblement etc.*); sommer (*ordonner*); (*Law*) citer en justice; assigner (*témoins*).

summons ['sʌmənz], *n.* sommation (*commandement*); convocation, *f.*; appel (*invitation*), *m.*; (*Law*) citation, *f.*, mandat de comparution, *m.*—*v.t.* assigner, citer (en justice), appeler à comparaître.

sump [sʌmp], *n.* (*Mining*) puisard; (fond de) carter (*de voiture*), *m.*

sumptuous ['sʌmptjuəs], *a.* somptueux.

sumptuously ['sʌmptjuəsli], *adv.* somptueusement.

sun [sʌn], *n.* soleil, *m.*—*v.t.* exposer au soleil.

sun-bath ['sʌnbɑ:θ], *n.* bain de soleil, *m.*

sun-bathe ['sʌnbeið], *v.i.* prendre des bains de soleil.

sunbeam ['sʌnbi:m], *n.* rayon de soleil, *m.*

sun-blind ['sʌnblaind], *n.* store, *m.*

sunburn ['sʌnbə:n], *n.* hâle; coup de soleil, *m.*

sunburnt ['sʌnbə:nt], *a.* hâlé; basané.

Sunday ['sʌndi], *n.* dimanche, *m.*

sunder ['sʌndə], *v.t.* séparer; couper en deux.

sundial ['sʌndaiəl], *n.* cadran solaire, *m.*

sundries ['sʌndriz], *n.pl.* choses diverses, *f.pl.*

sundry ['sʌndri], *a.* divers.

sun-flower ['sʌnflauə], *n.* tournesol, *m.*

sunken ['sʌnkən], *a.* enfoncé; cave (*joues*); creux (*yeux*).

sunless ['sʌnlis], *a.* sans soleil.

sunlight ['sʌnlait], *n.* lumière du soleil, *f.*

sunlit ['sʌnlit], *a.* ensoleillé.

sunny ['sʌni], *a.* ensoleillé; (*fig.*) heureux; *it is sunny*, il fait du soleil.

sunrise ['sʌnraiz], *n.* lever du soleil, *m.*

sunset ['sʌnset], *n.* coucher du soleil, *m.*

sunshade ['sʌnʃeid], *n.* parasol, *m.*, ombrelle *f.*

sunshine ['sʌnʃain], *n.* soleil, *m.*, clarté du soleil, *f.*

sunstroke ['sʌnstrouk], *n.* coup de soleil, *m.* insolation, *f.*

sup [sʌp], *n.* (*Sc.*) petit coup, *m.*, gorgée, *f.*— *v.t.* boire à petits coups.—*v.i.* souper.

super ['sju:pə], *a.* (*slang*) *it is super*, c'est sensass (sensationnel).

superable ['sju:pərəbl], *a.* surmontable.

superabundance [sju:pərə'bʌndəns], *n.* surabondance, *f.*

superannuate [sju:pər'ænjueit], *v.t.* mettre à la retraite.

superannuated [sju:pər'ænjueitid], *a.* mis à la retraite, en retraite (*personne*); démodé.

superannuation [sju:pərænju'eiʃən], *n.* mise à la retraite, retraite, *f.*; *superannuation fund*, caisse de retraites, *f.*

superb [sju'pə:b], *a.* superbe.

superbly [sju'pə:bli], *adv.* superbement.

supercilious [sju:pə'siliəs], *a.* hautain, arrogant.

superciliously [sju:pə'siliəsli], *adv.* avec hauteur.

superciliousness [sju:pə'siliəsnis], *n.* hauteur; arrogance, *f.*

superficial [sju:pə'fiʃl], *a.* superficiel; de superficie (*mesure*).

superficiality [sju:pəfiʃi'æliti], *n.* caractère superficiel, *m.*

superficially [sju:pə'fiʃəli], *adv.* superficiellement.

superfine ['sju:pəfain], *a.* superfin; (*Comm.*) surfin.

superfluity [sju:pə'flu:iti], *n.* superfluité, *f.*; superflu, *m.*

superfluous [sju'pə:fluəs], *a.* superflu, inutile.

superhuman [sju:pə'hju:mən], *a.* surhumain.

superimpose [sju:pərim'pouz], *v.t.* superposer, surimposer.

superintend [sju:pərin'tend], *v.t.* surveiller.

superintendent [sju:pərin'tendənt], *n.* chef; directeur, inspecteur, surintendant; commissaire de police, *m.*

superior [sju'piəriə], *a.* and *n.* supérieur, *m.*

superiority [sjupiəri'oriti], *n.* supériorité, *f.*

superlative [sju'pə:lətiv], *a.* suprême; (*Gram.*) superlatif.—*n.* (*Gram.*) superlatif, *m.*

superman ['sju:pəmæn], *n.* (*pl.* **-men** [men]) surhomme, *m.*

supernatural [sju:pə'nætʃərəl], *a.* and *n.* surnaturel, *m.*

supernumerary [sju:pə'nju:mərəri], *a.* surnuméraire.—*n.* surnuméraire; (*Theat.*) figurant, *m.*

superscribe [sju:pə'skraib], *v.t.* mettre une adresse, une suscription *ou* une inscription à.

superscription [sju:pə'skripʃən], *n.* suscription; inscription; (*Coin.*) légende, *f.*; entête (*de lettre*), *m.*

supersede [sju:pə'si:d], *v.t.* remplacer.

superseded [sju:pə'si:did], *a.* démodé, périmé.

supersonic [sju:pə'sonik], *a.* (*onde*) ultrasonore; (*Av.*) supersonique.

superstition [sju:pə'stiʃən], *n.* superstition, *f.*

superstitious [sju:pə'stiʃəs], *a.* superstitieux.

superstructure [sju:pə'strʌktʃə], *n.* superstructure, *f.*

super-tax ['sju:pətæks], *n.* surtaxe, *f.*

supervene [sju:pə'vi:n], *v.i.* survenir.

supervention [sju:pə'venʃən], *n.* survenance, *f.*

supervise ['sju:pəvaiz], *v.t.* surveiller.

supervision [sju:pə'viʒən], *n.* surveillance; inspection, *f.*

supervisor ['sju:pəvaizə], *n.* surveillant, *m.*

supine [sju'pain], *a.* couché sur le dos; (*fig.*) nonchalant.—['sju:pain], *n.* (*Gram.*) supin, *m.*

supper ['sʌpə], *n.* souper, *m.*; *supper-time*, heure du souper, *f.*

supplant [sə'plɑ:nt], *v.t.* supplanter.

supple [sʌpl], *a.* souple, flexible.

supplement ['sʌpli'ment], *v.t.* suppléer à; compléter.—['sʌplimənt] *n.* supplément, *m.*

supplementary [sʌpli'mentəri], *a.* supplémentaire.

suppleness ['sʌplnis], *n.* souplesse, *f.*

suppliant ['sʌpliənt], *a.* and *n.* suppliant, *m.*

supplicate ['sʌplikeit], *v.t.* supplier, implorer.

supplication [sʌpli'keiʃən], *n.* supplication, prière, *f.*

supplier [sə'plaiə], *n.* pourvoyeur; fournisseur, *m.*

supply [sə'plai], *n.* fourniture; provision, *f.* approvisionnement (*réserve*), *m.*; (*Elec.*) alimentation, *f.*; (*Mil., pl.*) vivres (*ravitaillement*); (*Parl.*) subsides, *m.pl.*—*v.t.* fournir; pourvoir à, subvenir à (*besoins*), ravitailler.

support [sə'pɔ:t], *v.t.* soutenir, supporter; entretenir (*faire vivre*); appuyer (*aider*).—*n.* appui, soutien; support (*physique*); entretien (*des dépendants*), *m.*

supportable [sə'pɔ:təbl], *a.* supportable.

supporter [sə'pɔ:tə], *n.* adhérent, partisan; appui, soutien; (*Spt.*) supporter; (*Her.*) support, *m.*

suppose [sə'pouz], *v.t.* supposer, s'imaginer; *to be supposed to* (**know**), être censé (savoir); *suppose we go*, si nous y allions.

supposed [sə'pouzd], *a.* présumé; prétendu, soi-disant; censé.

supposedly [sə'pouzidli], *adv.* censément.

supposing [sə'pouzin], *conj.* supposons, supposé (*que*).

supposition [sʌpə'ziʃən], *n.* supposition, *f.*

suppress [sə'pres], *v.t.* supprimer; réprimer (*révolte etc.*); étouffer; *a suppressed laugh*, un rire étouffé.

suppression [sə'preʃən], *n.* suppression; répression; dissimulation (*de la vérité*), *f.*

suppressor [sə'presə], *n.* (*Rad., Tel.*) dispositif anti-parasites, *m.*

suppurate ['sʌpjureit], *v.i.* suppurer.

suppuration [sʌpju'reiʃən], *n.* suppuration, *f.*

supremacy [sju'preməsi], *n.* suprématie, *f.*

supreme [sju'pri:m], *a.* suprême.

supremely [sju'pri:mli], *adv.* suprêmement.

surcharge ['sə:tʃa:dʒ], *n.* surcharge, surtaxe, *f.*

sure [ʃuə], *a.* sûr, certain; assuré; *to be sure!* certainement! bien sûr! *to be sure to,* ne pas manquer de.—*adv.* sûrement, à coup sûr.

sure-footed [ʃuə'futid], *a.* au pied sûr.

surely ['ʃuəli], *adv.* sûrement, assurément, à coup sûr.

sureness ['ʃuənis], *n.* certitude, sûreté, *f.*

surety ['ʃuəti], *n.* certitude (*véracité*); sûreté, sécurité (*garantie*), *f.*; (*Law*) garant, *m.*

surf [sə:f], *n.* ressac, *m.*, brisants sur la plage, *m.pl.*

surface ['sə:fis], *n.* surface, *f.*

surfeit ['sə:fit], *n.* rassasiement, *m.*; *to have a surfeit of,* être rassasié de.

surf-riding ['sə:fraidiŋ], *n.* sport de l'aquaplane, planking, surf, *m.*

surge [sə:dʒ], *n.* houle, lame de fond, *f.*—*v.i.* s'enfler, s'élever.

surgeon ['sə:dʒən], *n.* chirurgien, *m.*

surgery ['sə:dʒəri], *n.* chirurgie (*art*), *f.*; dispensaire; cabinet (*de consultations*), *m.*

surgical ['sə:dʒikl], *a.* chirurgical.

surliness ['sə:linis], *n.* morosité, *f.*

surly ['sə:li], *a.* morose; hargneux (*chien*).

surmise ['sə:maiz], *n.* soupçon, *m.*, conjecture, *f.*—[sə'maiz], *v.t.* soupçonner, conjecturer.

surmount [sə'maunt], *v.t.* surmonter.

surmountable [sə'mauntəbl], *a.* surmontable.

surname ['sə:neim], *n.* nom de famille, *m.*

surpass [sə'pɑ:s], *v.t.* surpasser, l'emporter sur.

surpassable [sə'pɑ:səbl], *a.* qu'on peut surpasser.

surpassing [sə'pɑ:siŋ], *a.* éminent, supérieur, rare.

surplice ['sə:plis], *n.* surplis, *m.*

surplus ['sə:pləs], *a.* de surplus.—*n.* surplus, *m.*; *surplus stock,* solde, *m.*

surprise [sə'praiz], *n.* surprise, *f.*; étonnement, *m.*—*v.t.* surprendre, étonner.

surprising [sə'praiziŋ], *a.* surprenant, étonnant.

surrealism [sə'ri:əlizm], *n.* surréalisme, *m.*

surrender [sə'rendə], *n.* reddition, capitulation, *f.*; abandon (*d'un titre, d'un droit*), *m.*; (*Law*) cession, *f.*—*v.t.* rendre; (*fig.*) abandonner, livrer (*personne etc.*); (*Law*) céder.—*v.i.* se rendre.

surreptitious [sʌrəp'tiʃəs], *a.* subreptice, clandestin; frauduleux.

surreptitiously [sʌrəp'tiʃəsli], *adv.* subrepticement.

surround [sə'raund], *n.* encadrement (*de porte, de fenêtre*), *m.*—*v.t.* entourer, environner (*de*), (*Mil.*) cerner.

surrounding [sə'raundiŋ], *a.* environnant, d'alentour.—*n.* (*pl.*) alentours, environs, *m.pl.*, entourage, milieu, *m.*

surtax ['sə:tæks], *n.* surtaxe, *f.*

survey ['sə:vei], *n.* vue, *f.*, coup d'œil, *m.*; inspection (*examen*); expertise (*évaluation*), *f.*; arpentage (*de terrain etc.*); (*Ordnance*) levé topographique, *m*; *aerial survey,* levé aérophotogrammétrique, *m.*—[sə'vei], *v.t.* arpenter (*terrain*); (*Ordnance*) lever le plan de; (*fig.*) examiner, contempler.

surveying [sə'veiiŋ], *n.* arpentage, levé de plans, *m.*

surveyor [sə'veiə], *n.* inspecteur, arpenteur (*de terrain*); agent voyer (*ponts et chaussées*), *m.*

survival [sə'vaivl], *n.* survivance; survie, *f.*

survive [sə'vaiv], *v.t.* survivre à.—*v.i.* survivre.

surviving [sə'vaiviŋ], *a.* survivant.

survivor [sə'vaivə], *n.* survivant, *m.*

Susan [su:zn]. Suzanne, *f.*

susceptibility [səsepti'biliti], *n.* susceptibilité; sensibilité, *f.*

susceptible [sə'septibl], *a.* susceptible (*de*).

suspect ['sʌspekt], *a.* and *n.* suspect, *m.*—[sə'spekt], *v.t., v.i.* soupçonner.

suspend [sə'spend], *v.t.* suspendre; cesser (*payements*).

suspender [sə'spendə], *n.* (*pl.*) jarretelles (*pour bas*); (*Am.*) bretelles (*pour pantalon*), *f.pl.*

suspense [sə'spens], *n.* suspens, doute, *m.*

suspension [sə'spenʃən], *n.* suspension, *f.*

suspicion [sə'spiʃən], *n.* soupçon, *m.*

suspicious [sə'spiʃəs], *a.* soupçonneux; suspect, louche (*équivoque*).

suspiciously [sə'spiʃəsli], *adv.* avec méfiance; d'une manière suspecte.

suspiciousness [sə'spiʃəsnis], *n.* caractère soupçonneux, *m.*, défiance, méfiance, *f.*
sustain [sə'stein], *v.t.* soutenir, supporter; éprouver, essuyer (*perte*).
sustaining [sə'steiniŋ], *a.* fortifiant, nourrissant.
sustenance ['sʌstinəns], *n.* nourriture, *f.*, aliments, *m.pl.*; entretien, *m.*, subsistance, *f.*
suzerain ['sjuːzərein], *a.* and *n.* suzerain, *m.*
suzerainty ['sjuːzəreinti], *n.* suzeraineté, *f.*
swab [swɔb], *n.* torchon; (*Naut.*) faubert; tampon (*de coton hydrophile*). *m.*—*v.t.* fauberter; nettoyer.
swaddle [swɔdl], *v.t.* emmailloter.
swaddling ['swɔdliŋ], *n.* emmaillotement, *m.*; *swaddling-clothes*, maillot, *m.*
swag [swæg], *n.* (*slang*) butin; (*Australia*) baluchon, *m.*
swagger ['swægə], *v.i.* faire le rodomont; se donner des airs, se vanter.
swaggerer ['swægərə], *n.* fanfaron, *m.*
swaggering ['swægəriŋ], *a.* de fanfaron.—*n.* fanfaronnade, *f.*
swagman ['swægmən], *n.* (*pl.* **-men** [men]) (*Australia*) chemineau, *m.*
swain [swein], *n.* (*poet.*) berger, jeune paysan, *m.*
swallow (1) ['swɔlou], *v.t.* avaler; engloutir (*faire disparaître*); consumer; (*fig.*) gober. —*n.* (*pop.*) avaloir, gosier (*gorge*), *m.*; gorgée (*ce qu'on avale*), *f.*
swallow (2) ['swɔlou], *n.* hirondelle (*oiseau*), *f.*
swallow-dive ['swɔloudaiv], *n.* (*Swim.*) saut de l'ange, *m.*
swallower ['swɔlouə], *n.* avaleur, *m.*
swallow-tail ['swɔlouteil], *a.* en queue d'aronde.—*n.* habit à queue de morue, *m.*
swamp [swɔmp], *n.* marais, marécage, *m.*—*v.t.* submerger; faire couler (*bateau*).
swampy ['swɔmpi], *a.* marécageux.
swan [swɔn], *n.* cygne, *m.*
swank [swæŋk], *n.* pose; (*pop.*) épate, *f.*—*v.i.* (*pop.*) crâner, poser; faire du chiqué.
swanky ['swæŋki], *a.* chic, rupin.
swap [swɔp], *v.t.* (*colloq.*) échanger, troquer. —*n.* troc, échange, *m.*
sward [swɔːd], *n.* (*poet.*) gazon, *m.*, pelouse, *f.*
swarm [swɔːm], *n.* essaim (*d'abeilles*), *m.*— *v.i.* essaimer; (*fig.*) accourir en foule.
swarming ['swɔːmiŋ], *n.* essaimage, *m.*
swarthiness ['swɔːðinis], *n.* teint basané, *m.*
swarthy ['swɔːði], *a.* basané, hâlé.
swashbuckler ['swɔʃbʌklə], *n.* fanfaron, matamore, *m.*
swastika ['swɔstikə], *n.* croix gammée, *f.*
swat [swɔt], *v.t.* écraser, tuer (*mouche*).
swath [swɔːθ], *n.* andain, *m.*, fauchée, *f.*
swathe [sweið], *v.t.* emmailloter.
sway [swei], *v.t.* manier, porter; balancer (*agiter*); (*fig.*) diriger (*gouverner*); influencer (*l'opinion*).—*v.i.* se balancer.—*n.* empire, *m.*; domination (*règne*), *f.*
swaying ['sweiiŋ], *n.* balancement, *m.*; oscillation, *f.*
swear [sweə], *v.t. irr.* faire prêter serment à (*témoins etc.*); prêter (*serment*); *to swear at*, injurier.—*v.i.* jurer; prêter serment.
swearer ['sweərə], *n.* jureur, *m.*
swearing ['sweəriŋ], *n.* serments; jurons (*gros mots*), *m.pl.*; *swearing in*, prestation de serment, assermentation (*de juges etc.*), *f.*

swear-word ['sweəwɔːd], *n.* juron, gros mot, *m.*
sweat [swet], *n.* sueur, transpiration, *f.*—*v.t.* faire suer.—*v.i.* suer, transpirer.
sweater ['swetə], *n.* chandail, tricot, pull-over (*vêtement*), *m.*
sweatiness ['swetinis], *n.* sueur, *f.*, état de sueur, *m.*
sweating ['swetiŋ], *a.* en sueur; tout en sueur. —*n.* moiteur; fatigue, *f.*
sweaty ['sweti], *a.* en sueur.
Swede [swiːd], *n.* Suédois (*personne*), *m.*
swede [swiːd], *n.* (*Bot.*) rutabaga, *m.*
Sweden [swiːdn], la Suède, *f.*
Swedish ['swiːdiʃ], *a.* suédois, de Suède.—*n.* suédois (*langue*), *m.*
sweep [swiːp], *v.t. irr.* balayer; ramoner (*cheminée*); draguer (*rivière*).—*v.i.* passer rapidement.—*n.* coup de balai; ramoneur (*de cheminées*), *m.*; étendue, portée (*distance*), courbe, *f.*; (*fig.*) sweepstake, *m.*; *to make a clean sweep of*, faire table rase de.
sweeper ['swiːpə], *n.* balayeur; ramoneur (*de cheminées*), *m.*
sweeping ['swiːpiŋ], *a.* rapide, irrésistible; (*fig.*) général.—*n.* balayage; ramonage (*de cheminées*), *m.*; (*pl.*) balayures, ordures, *m.pl.*
sweepstake ['swiːpsteik], *n.* poule, *f.*; sweepstake, *m.*
sweet [swiːt], *a.* doux, sucré; parfumé (*odeur*); (*Mus.*) suave, mélodieux; frais (*poisson etc.*); (*fig.*) joli, charmant.—*n.* chose douce, *f.*; (*pl.*) entremets, sucreries, *f.pl.*; chéri, *m.*
sweetbread ['swiːtbred], *n.* ris de veau *ou* d'agneau, *m.*
sweeten [swiːtn], *v.t.* sucrer; purifier (*salle, l'air etc.*); (*fig.*) adoucir.
sweetener ['swiːtnə], *n.* adoucissant, *m.*
sweetening ['swiːtniŋ], *n.* adoucissement, *m.*
sweetheart ['swiːthɑːt], *n.* amoureux; amant; bon ami, *m.*
sweetly ['swiːtli], *adv.* doucement, gentiment; mélodieusement.
sweetmeat ['swiːtmiːt], *n.* sucrerie, *f.*, bon-bon, *m.*
sweetness ['swiːtnis], *n.* douceur; fraîcheur; mélodie, *f.*; (*fig.*) charme, *m.*
sweet-pea ['swiːt'piː], *n.* pois de senteur, *m.*
sweet-shop ['swiːtʃɔp], *n.* confiserie, *f.*
sweet-william ['swiːt'wiljəm], *n.* œillet de poète, *m.*
swell [swel], *v.t. irr.* enfler, gonfler; aggraver; augmenter (*ajouter à*).—*v.i.* enfler, s'enfler, se gonfler; grossir, croître (*multiplier*); (*fig.*) bouffir (*d'orgueil, de colère etc.*).—*a.* (*colloq.*) à la mode, chic; épatant.—*n.* élévation, montée, *f.*; renflement (*de son*), *m.*; houle (*de mer*), *f.*; (*colloq.*) rupin, élégant, *m.*
swelling ['sweliŋ], *a.* grandissant (*qui augmente*).—*n.* enflure; bouffissure (*pathologique*), *f.*; gonflement (*protubérance*), *m.*, crue (*de rivière*), *f.*; soulèvement (*des vagues*); (*fig.*) mouvement, transport (*de colère etc.*), *m.*
swelter ['sweltə], *v.i.* étouffer de chaleur; *it is sweltering hot*, il fait une chaleur étouffante.
swerve [swəːv], *v.i.* s'écarter, se détourner, faire un écart (*cheval*), faire une embardée (*voiture*).
swerving ['swəːviŋ], *n.* écart, *m.*, déviation, embardée (*de voiture*), *f.*

swift [swift], *a.* vite; rapide, prompt.—*n.* (*Orn.*) martinet, *m.*

swift-footed ['swift'futid], *a.* rapide à la course; au pied léger.

swiftly ['swiftli], *adv.* vite, rapidement.

swiftness ['swiftnis], *n.* rapidité, vitesse, *f.*

swig [swig], *v.t., v.i.* (*pop.*) boire à longs traits. —*n.* long trait (*d'alcool*), *m.*

swill [swil], *v.t.* laver, rincer; boire avidement.—*v.i.* boire; (*colloq.*) s'enivrer.—*n.* lavure de vaisselle, lavure, *f.*; grand coup (*d'alcool*), *m.*

swim [swim], *v.t. irr.* traverser à la nage.— *v.i.* nager; flotter, surnager; (*fam.*) tourner (*la tête*); être inondé (de) (*être submergé*).— *n.* nage, *f.*; *in the swim*, à la page.

swimmer ['swimə], *n.* nageur, *m.*

swimming ['swimiŋ], *n.* natation (*sport*); nage (*action*), *f.*; (*fam.*) étourdissement (*de tête*), *m.*; *by swimming*, à la nage.

swimming-baths ['swimiŋbɑ:θz], **swimming-pool** ['swimiŋpu:l], *n.* piscine, *f.*

swimmingly ['swimiŋli], *adv.* à merveille.

swim-suit ['swimsju:t], *n.* maillot de bain, *m.*

swindle [swindl], *v.t.* escroquer.—*n.* escroquerie, *f.*

swindler ['swindlə], *n.* escroc, filou, *m.*

swindling ['swindliŋ], *n.* escroquerie, *f.*

swine [swain], *n.inv.* cochon, pourceau, porc; (*pop.*) salaud, *m.*

swing [swiŋ], *v.t. irr.* balancer; brandir (*une arme etc.*).—*v.i.* se balancer; osciller; pendiller, être suspendu.—*n.* oscillation (*mouvement*), *f.*; balancement, *m.*; balançoire (*siège*), *f.*; (*Mus.*) swing, *m.*; *in full swing*, en pleine activité.

swing-door ['swiŋ'dɔ:], *n.* porte battante, *f.*

swinging ['swiŋiŋ], *n.* balancement, *m.*, oscillation, *f.*

swipe [swaip], *n.* taloche, *f.*—*v.t.* donner une taloche à; (*fam.*) chiper.

swirl [swə:l], *v.i.* tourbillonner.—*n.* remous, *m.*

swish [swiʃ], *v.t.* cingler, fouetter.—*v.i.* siffler, bruire.

Swiss [swis], *a.* helvétique, suisse.—*n.* Suisse (*personne*), *m.*, Suissesse, *f.*

switch [switʃ], *n.* badine, houssine, gaule; (*Rail.*) aiguille, *f.*; (*Elec.*) commutateur, interrupteur, *m.*—*v.t.* houspiller, cingler; (*Rail.*) aiguiller; changer (*de*); *to switch off*, couper; *to switch on*, ouvrir.—*v.i. to switch off*, couper le courant; *to switch on*, mettre le courant.

switchboard ['switʃbɔ:d], *n.* standard (téléphonique), *m.*; *switchboard operator*, standardiste, *m., f.*

Switzerland ['switsələnd]. la Suisse, *f.*

swivel [swivl], *n.* émerillon; pivot, *m.*—*v.i.* pivoter.

swoon [swu:n], *v.i.* s'évanouir.—*n.* evanouissement, *m.*

swoop [swu:p], *v.i.* fondre (*sur*).—*n. at one (fell) swoop*, d'un seul coup (*fatal*).

sword [sɔ:d], *n.* épée, *f.*

sword-bearer ['sɔ:dbɛərə], *n.* porte-épée, *m.*

sword-fish ['sɔ:dfiʃ], *n.* espadon, *m.*

swordsman ['sɔ:dzmən], *n.* (*pl.* **-men** [men]) tireur, homme d'épée, *m.*

swordstick ['sɔ:dstik], *n.* canne à épée, *f.*

sworn [swɔ:n], *a.* juré; (*Law*) assermenté; acharné (*ennemi*).

swot [swɔt], *v.i.* (*Sch. slang*) piocher, bûcher.— *n.* bûcheur, *m.*

sycamore ['sikəmɔ:], *n.* sycomore, *m.*

sycophancy ['sikəfənsi], *n.* adulation, *f.*

sycophant ['sikəfənt], *n.* adulateur, *m.*

sycophantic [sikə'fæntik], *a.* adulateur.

syllabic [si'læbik], *a.* syllabique.

syllable ['siləbl], *n.* syllabe, *f.*

syllabus ['siləbəs], *n.* résumé; sommaire, programme (*surtout d'études scolaires*), *m.*

syllogism ['silədʒizm], *n.* syllogisme, *m.*

sylph [silf], *n.* sylphe, *m.*

sylvan ['silvən], *a.* sylvestre, des bois, champêtre, agreste.

symbol [simbl], *n.* symbole, *m.*

symbolic [sim'bɔlik], **symbolical** [sim'bɔlikl], *a.* symbolique.

symbolism ['simbəlizm], *n.* symbolisme, *m.*

symbolize ['simbəlaiz], *v.t., v.i.* symboliser.

symmetrical [si'metrikl], *a.* symétrique.

symmetry ['simitri], *n.* symétrie, *f.*

sympathetic [simpə'θetik], *a.* sympathique (*nerf*); compatissant.

sympathize ['simpəθaiz], *v.i.* sympathiser (*avec*); compatir (*à*).

sympathizer ['simpəθaizə], *n.* sympathisant, *m.*

sympathy ['simpəθi], *n.* sympathie; compréhension, *f.*; condoléances, *f.pl.*

symphony ['simfəni], *n.* symphonie, *f.*

symposium [sim'pouzjəm], *n.* (*fig.*) recueil d'articles (*sur un seul sujet*), *m.*

symptom ['simptəm], *n.* symptôme, *m.*

symptomatic [simptə'mætik], *a.* symptomatique.

synagogue ['sinəgɔg], *n.* synagogue, *f.*

synchromesh ['siŋkromeʃ], *a.* and *n.* synchromesh, *m.*

synchronise ['siŋkrənaiz], *v.i.* synchroniser (*avec*).

syncopate ['siŋkəpeit], *v.t.* syncoper.

syndic ['sindik], *n.* syndic, *m.*

syndicate ['sindikit], *n.* syndicat, *m.*—['sindi keit], *v.t.* syndiquer.—*v.i.* se syndiquer.

synod ['sinəd], *n.* synode, *m.*

synonym ['sinənim], *n.* synonyme, *m.*

synonymous [si'nɔniməs], *a.* synonyme.

synopsis [si'nɔpsis], *n.* (*pl.* **synopses** [si'nɔp si:z]) sommaire, *m.*

syntax ['sintæks], *n.* syntaxe, *f.*

synthesis ['sinθisis], *n.* (*pl.* **syntheses** ['sin θisi:z]) synthèse, *f.*

synthesize ['sinθisaiz], *v.t.* synthétiser.

synthetic [sin'θetik], *a.* synthétique.

synthetically [sin'θetikli], *adv.* synthétiquement.

Syria ['siriə]. la Syrie, *f.*

Syriac ['siriæk], *a.* syriaque.—*n.* syriaque (*langue*), *m.*

Syrian ['siriən], *a.* syrien.—*n.* syrien (*langue*); Syrien (*personne*), *m.*

syringe ['sirindʒ], *n.* seringue, *f.*—*v.t.* seringuer.

syrup ['sirəp], *n.* sirop, *m.*

syrupy ['sirəpi], *a.* sirupeux.

system ['sistəm], *n.* système, régime; réseau (*ferroviaire*), *m.*

systematic [sistə'mætik], *a.* systématique.
systematically [sistə'mætikli], *adv.* systématiquement.
systematize ['sistəmətaiz], *v.t.* systématiser.

T

T, t [ti:]. vingtième lettre de l'alphabet, *m.*; **T-square**, té à dessin, *m.*
tab [tæb], *n.* étiquette; patte, *f.*, écusson, *m.*
tabby ['tæbi], *a.* tacheté, moucheté.—*n.* chat moucheté, rayé *ou* tigré, *m.*
tabernacle ['tæbənækl], *n.* tabernacle, *m.*
table [teibl], *n.* table, *f.*; **to be seated at table**, être attablé; **to clear the table**, desservir; **to lay the table**, mettre le couvert; **to sit down to table**, se mettre à table.—*v.t.* déposer (*un projet de loi*).
table-cloth ['teiblkləθ], *n.* nappe, *f.*
table-linen ['teibllinin], *n.* linge de table, *f.*
tablespoon ['teiblspu:n], *n.* cuiller à soupe, *f.*
tablespoonful ['teiblspu:nful], *n.* grande cuillerée, *f.*
tablet ['tæblit], *n.* tablette, *f.*; (*Med.*) comprimé, *m.*
taboo [tə'bu:], *a.* and *n.* tabou, *m.*
tabulate ['tæbjuleit], *v.t.* cataloguer.
tacit ['tæsit], *a.* tacite, implicite.
tacitly ['tæsitli], *adv.* tacitement, implicitement.
taciturn ['tæsitə:n], *a.* taciturne.
Tacitus ['tæsitəs]. (*L. Lit.*) Tacite, *m.*
tack [tæk], *n.* petit clou, *m.*, broquette; (*Naut.*) amure, *f.*—*v.t.* clouer; (*Needlework*) bâtir, faufiler.—*v.i.* (*Naut.*) virer vent devant.
tackiness ['tækinis], *n.* viscosité, *f.*
tacking ['tækiŋ], *n.* cloutage, *m.*; (*Needlework*) faufilure, *f.*; (*Naut.*) virement de bord, louvoyage, *m.*
tackle [tækl], *n.* attirail; (*Naut.*) palan; (*Spt.*) plaquage, *m.*; (*fig.*) ustensiles, *m.pl.*; **fishing-tackle**, articles de pêche, *m.pl.*—*v.t.* empoigner; (*Ftb.*) plaquer; (*fig.*) attaquer (*travail etc.*).
tacky ['tæki], *a.* collant, visqueux, gluant.
tact [tækt], *n.* toucher; (*fig.*) tact, savoir-faire, *m.*
tactful ['tæktful], *a.* plein de tact.
tactical ['tæktikl], *a.* tactique.
tactician [tæk'tiʃən], *n.* tacticien, *m.*
tactics ['tæktiks], *n.pl.* tactique, *f.*
tactile ['tæktail], *a.* tactile.
tactless ['tæktlis], *a.* sans tact, sans savoir-faire.
tadpole ['tædpoul], *n.* têtard, *m.*
taffeta ['tæfitə], *n.* taffetas, *m.*
taffrail ['tæfreil], *n.* couronnement (*de la poupe*), *f.*
tag [tæg], *n.* ferret, fer, bout ferré, *m.*; étiquette (*fiche*), *f.*; dicton, *m.*—*v.t.* ferrer (*cordon*); (*fig.*) coudre (*à*).
tail [teil], *n.* queue; (*fig.*) extrémité, *f.*; bout; pan (*d'habit*), *m.*; pile (*de pièce de monnaie*), *f.*; empennage (*d'avion*), *m.*—*v.t.* couper la queue (*d'un animal*); ôter les queues (*de fruits*); (*fam.*) filer (*criminels etc.*).
tail-coat ['teilkout], *n.* habit, *m.*
tailed [teild], *a.* à queue.
tailless ['teillis], *a.* sans queue, anoure.
tail-light ['teillait], *n.* feu arrière, *m.*
tailor ['teilə], *n.* tailleur, *m.*
tailor-made ['teilə'meid], *a.* and *n.* tailleur, *m.*
tail-plane ['teilplein], *n.* (*Av.*) stabilisateur, *m.*
taint [teint], *v.t.* corrompre, gâter.—*v.i.* se corrompre; se gâter (*viande*).—*n.* souillure, corruption; tache (*du péché*), *f.*
take [teik], *v.t.* *irr.* prendre; mener (*quelqu'un*); conduire (*personne en voiture*); porter (*chose*); emmener (*quelqu'un*); enlever (*voler*); soustraire (*retrancher*); saisir; accepter; (*fig.*) supposer; profiter de (*une occasion*); contenir (*avoir de la place pour*); faire (*une promenade etc.*); avoir (*vengeance etc.*); retenir (*chambre etc.*); suivre (*une route etc.*); mettre (*temps*); **to take advantage of**, profiter de; **to take away**, emmener (*personne*), emporter (*choses*), ôter (*retirer*); desservir (*le couvert etc.*); dérober (*voler*); **to take back**, reprendre, remporter; **to take down**, descendre; rabattre (*humilier*); démolir (*maison*); prendre note de (*inscrire*); **to take heed**, prendre garde (*à*); **to take in**, faire entrer; comprendre (*consister en*); recevoir, recevoir chez soi (*loger*); tromper, duper; faire sa provision de (*vivres etc.*); **to take off**, enlever, ôter, retirer (*vêtement*); caricaturer (*imiter*); **to take out**, faire sortir, sortir (*chose*); promener (*personne*); arracher (*dents*); ôter, enlever (*taches etc.*); **to take over**, se charger de, prendre la succession de (*affaires*); **to take up**, monter, faire monter, soulever (*lever*); ramasser (*relever*); commencer, entamer, aborder (*des études etc.*); occuper (*temps*).—*v.i.* réussir (*avoir du succès*); prendre (*feu etc.*); **to take after**, ressembler à; (*Av.*) **to take off**, décoller; (*fam.*) **to take on**, se lamenter, s'affliger; **to take up with**, s'associer à.—*n.* prise, pêche, quantité (*de poissons*); (*Cine.*) prise de vue, *f.*
take-in ['teikin], *n.* duperie, attrape, *f.*
take-off ['teikɔ:f], *n.* caricature, charge, *f.*; (*Av.*) décollage, *m.*
take-over ['teikouvə], *n.* (*Fin.*) rachat (*d'entreprise*), *m.*; **take-over bid**, offre de rachat, *f.*
taking ['teikiŋ], *a.* attrayant, séduisant; (*colloq.*) contagieux (*maladie*).—*n.* prise; arrestation, *f.*; (*pl.*) recettes (*argent*), *f.pl.*
talc [tælk], *n.* talc, *m.*
talcum powder ['tælkəm'paudə], *n.* talc, *m.*
tale [teil], *n.* conte, récit, *m.*; histoire, *f.*
talent ['tælənt], *n.* talent, *m.*
talented ['tæləntid], *a.* de talent, habile, bien doué.
talisman ['tælizmən], *n.* talisman, *m.*
talk [tɔ:k], *v.t.* parler, dire; **to talk over** cajoler (*quelqu'un*); discuter (*quelque chose*).—*v.i.* parler (*de*); converser, causer; bavarder, jaser (*babiller*); **to talk at**, haranguer.—*n.* entretien, *m.*, propos, *m.pl.*, conversation; causerie (*intime*), *f.*; bavardage, bruit (*racontar*), *m.*; **small talk**, banalités, *f.pl.*
talkative ['tɔ:kətiv], *a.* causeur, bavard.

talker ['tɔːkə], n. causeur, parleur, m.
talking ['tɔːkiŋ], a. causeur, bavard.—n. conversation, causerie, f.
tall [tɔːl], a. grand (personne); haut (chose).
tallboy ['tɔːlbɔi], n. chiffonnier, m.; (haute) commode-secrétaire, f.
tallness ['tɔːlnis], n. grande taille, hauteur, f.
tallow ['tælou], n. suif, m.
tallow-candle ['tælou'kændl], n. chandelle, f.
tally ['tæli], n. taille; entaille, marque; étiquette (à bagages), f.—v.i. s'accorder; to tally with, s'accorder avec, correspondre à.
tally-ho! [tæli'hou], int. (Hunt.) taïaut!
Talmud ['tælmʌd], n. talmud, m.
talon ['tælən], n. serre, griffe, f.
tambourine [tæmbə'riːn], n. tambour de basque, m.
tame [teim], a. apprivoisé; domestique; (fig.) insipide.—v.t. apprivoiser; dompter (dominer).
tamely ['teimli], adv. avec soumission; sans cœur.
tameness ['teimnis], n. apprivoisement, m., domesticité; soumission; (fig.) faiblesse (de style etc.), f.
tamer ['teimə], n. dompteur (de bête sauvage) m.
taming ['teimiŋ], n. apprivoisement, m.
tamp [tæmp], v.t. bourrer, tamponner.
tamper ['tæmpə], v.i. to tamper with, se mêler (de); expérimenter (avec); jouer avec; fausser (serrure etc.).
tampering ['tæmpəriŋ], n. menées secrètes, f.pl.
tan [tæn], n. tan; tanné (couleur); hâle (de la peau), m.—v.t. tanner; bronzer (la peau).
tandem ['tændəm], n. tandem (bicyclette), m.
tang [tæŋ], n. goût, m., saveur, f.
tangent ['tændʒənt], n. tangente, f.
tangerine [tændʒə'riːn], n. mandarine, f.
tangible ['tændʒibl], a. tangible, palpable.
Tangier(s) [tæn'dʒiə(z)]. Tanger, m.
tangle [tæŋgl], n. enchevêtrement, m.—v.t. embrouiller, enchevêtrer.
tangled [tæŋgld], a. embrouillé.
tango ['tæŋgou], n. tango, m.
tank [tæŋk], n. réservoir; (Mil.) char (d'assaut), m.
tankard ['tæŋkəd], n. chope, f.
tanker ['tæŋkə], n. bateau citerne, m.
tanner ['tænə], n. tanneur, m.
tannery ['tænəri], n. tannerie, f.
tanning ['tæniŋ], n. tannage, m.; (fam.) rossée, f.
tantalize ['tæntəlaiz], v.t. tantaliser, tourmenter.
tantalizing ['tæntəlaiziŋ], a. tentant, torturant.
tantamount ['tæntəmaunt], a. équivalent (à).
tantrum ['tæntrəm], n. mauvaise humeur, f.
Tanzania [tænzə'niːə]. la Tanzanie, f.
tap (1) [tæp], n. robinet (bain); comptoir (bar), m.; cannelle (de baril), f.; taraud (outil), m.; on tap, en perce.—v.t. tirer (liquide); mettre en perce (baril); inciser (arbre); tarauder (vis etc.); (Surg.) faire la ponction à.
tap (2) [tæp], n. tape, f., petit coup (à la porte etc.), m.—v.t. taper, frapper doucement.—v.i. taper, frapper.
tape [teip], n. ruban (de fil), m.; ganse (sur habit); bande (magnétique), f.; red tape, (fig.) routine administrative, f.

tape-measure ['teipmeʒə], n. mètre ruban, m.
taper ['teipə], n. bougie effilée, f.; (Eccles.) cierge, m.
tape-recorder ['teiprikɔːdə], n. magnétophone, m.
tape-recording ['teiprikɔːdiŋ], n. enregistrement magnétique, m.
tapering ['teipəriŋ], a. effilé.
tapestry ['tæpistri], n. tapisserie, f.
tape-worm ['teipwəːm], n. ver solitaire, m.
tapioca [tæpi'oukə], n. tapioca, m.
tapir ['teipiə], n. tapir, m.
tappet ['tæpit], n. taquet (de soupape), m.
tapping (1) ['tæpiŋ], n. taraudage (de vis), m.; mise en perce (de baril); incision (d'arbre); (Surg.) ponction, f.
tapping (2) ['tæpiŋ], n. tapotement, m.
tar [tɑː], n. goudron; loup de mer (matelot), m.—v.t. goudronner.
tarantella [tærən'telə], n. tarentelle (danse), f.
tarantula [tə'ræntjulə], n. tarentule, f.
tardily ['tɑːdili], adv. tardivement, lentement.
tardiness ['tɑːdinis], n. lenteur; tardiveté (de fruit), f.
tardy ['tɑːdi], a. lent; en retard, tardif.
tare (1) [tɛə], n. tare (poids), f.
tare (2) [tɛə], n. (Script.) ivraie; (pl.) (Agric.) vesce, f.
target ['tɑːgit], n. cible, f.; but, objectif, m.
tariff ['tærif], n. tarif, m.
tarmac ['tɑːmæk], n. macadam, m.; (Av.) piste d'envol, f.—v.t. goudronner.
tarn [tɑːn], n. petit lac (de montagne), m.
tarnish ['tɑːniʃ], v.t. ternir; (fig.) souiller, flétrir.—v.i. se ternir.
tarpaulin [tɑː'pɔːlin], n. (Naut.) prélart, m., bâche, toile goudronnée, f.
tarry (1) ['tɑːri], a. goudronneux, bitumeux.
tarry (2) ['tæri], v.i. rester, tarder.
tart (1) [tɑːt], n. tarte, tourte, f.
tart (2) [tɑːt], a. acide, âcre; (fig.) aigre.
tartan ['tɑːtən], n. tartan, m.
tartar ['tɑːtə], n. (Chem.) tartre, m.
tartaric [tɑː'tærik], a. tartrique.
tartish ['tɑːtiʃ], a. aigrelet.
tartly ['tɑːtli], adv. avec aigreur; (fig.) vertement, sévèrement.
tartness ['tɑːtnis], n. acidité; (fig.) aigreur, f.
task [tɑːsk], n. tâche, f.; devoir (leçon); pensum (punition), m.; to take to task, réprimander, semoncer.
taskmaster ['tɑːskmɑːstə], n. chef de corvée, m.
Tasmania [tæz'meinjə]. la Tasmanie, f.
Tasmanian [tæz'meinjən], a. tasmanien.—n. Tasmanien (personne), m.
tassel [tæsl], n. gland, m.
taste [teist], v.t. goûter; (fig.) savourer, éprouver.—v.i. goûter (de); avoir un goût (de).—n. goût; soupçon (trace), m.
tasteful ['teistful], a. de bon goût.
tastefully ['teistfuli], adv. avec goût.
tasteless ['teistlis], a. fade, insipide.
tastelessly ['teistlisli], adv. insipidement, fadement.
taster ['teistə], n. dégustateur, m.
tasting ['teistiŋ], n. dégustation, f.
tasty ['teisti], a. (colloq.) de bon goût; savoureux.

tatter

tatter ['tætə], *n.* haillon, lambeau, *m.*, guenille, *f.*

tattered ['tætəd], *a.* déguenillé, en haillons (*personne*); en lambeaux, tout déchiré (*vêtements etc.*).

tatting ['tætiŋ], *n.* frivolité (*dentelle*), *f.*

tattle [tætl], *n.* babil, caquet, *m.*—*v.i.* bavarder.

tattler ['tætlə], *n.* babillard, bavard, *m.*

tattling ['tætliŋ], *a.* babillard, bavard.

tattoo [tə'tu:], *v.t.* tatouer.—*n.* tatouage, *m.*; (*Mil.*) fête militaire, *f.*

taunt [tɔ:nt], *n.* injure, *f.*, taxe; (*fig.*) reproche amer, *m.* —*v.t.* tancer, reprocher à, injurier.

tauntingly ['tɔ:ntiŋli], *adv.* injurieusement.

Taurus ['tɔ:rəs]. (*Astron.*) le Taureau, *m.*

taut [tɔ:t], *a.* raide, tendu; enflé (*voile*).

tautology [tɔ:'tɔlədʒi], *n.* tautologie, *f.*

tavern ['tævən], *n.* taverne, *f.*; cabaret, *m.*

tawdry ['tɔ:dri], *a.* criard, de mauvais goût, prétentieux.

tawny ['tɔ:ni], *a.* fauve.

tawse [tɔ:z], *n.* martinet, *m.*

tax [tæks], *n.* impôt, *m.*, taxe; (*fig.*) contribution, *f.*; **income-tax**, impôt sur le revenu; **purchase tax**, taxe de luxe; **tax evasion**, fraude fiscale, *f.*; **surtax**, surtaxe, *f.*—*v.t.* imposer, taxer; (*fig.*) accuser (*de*).

taxable ['tæksəbl], *a.* imposable.

taxation [tæk'seiʃən], *n.* taxation, *f.*

tax-free ['tæks'fri:], *a.* exempt d'impôts.

taxi ['tæksi], *n.* taxi, *m.*

tax-payer ['tækspeiə], *n.* contribuable, *m.f.*

tea [ti:], *n.* thé, *m.*; tisane (*infusion*), *f.*; goûter (*repas*), *m.*

tea-caddy ['ti:kædi], *n.* boîte à thé, *f.*

tea-cake ['ti:keik], *n.* brioche, *f.*

teach [ti:tʃ], *v.t. irr.* enseigner, instruire; apprendre (*à*).—*v.i.* enseigner, professer.

teachable ['ti:tʃəbl], *a.* disposé à apprendre, docile; enseignable (*chose*).

teacher ['ti:tʃə], *n.* maître, instituteur; professeur (*de lycée*), *m.*

tea-chest ['ti:tʃest], *n.* caisse à thé, *f.*

teaching ['ti:tʃiŋ], *n.* enseignement, *m.*

tea-cup ['ti:kʌp], *n.* tasse à thé, *f.*

teak [ti:k], *n.* (*Bot.*) teck, tek, *m.*

teal [ti:l], *n.* (*Orn.*) sarcelle, *f.*

team [ti:m], *n.* attelage, *m.*, (*Spt.*) équipe, *f.*

teapot ['ti:pɔt], *n.* théière, *f.*

tear (1) [tiə], *n.* larme, *f.*, pleur, *m.*

tear (2) [tɛə], *v.t. irr.* déchirer; (*fig.*) arracher; **to tear asunder**, déchirer en deux.—*v.i.* se déchirer.—*n.* déchirure, *f.*; **wear and tear**, usure, *f.*

tear-drop ['tiədrɔp], *n.* larme, *f.*

tearful ['tiəful], *a.* tout en larmes.

tearfully ['tiəfuli], *adv.* les larmes aux yeux.

tearing ['tɛəriŋ], *n.* déchirement, *m.*

tease [ti:z], *v.t.* taquiner, tourmenter; carder (*laine*).—*n.* taquin, *m.*

tea-service ['ti:sə:vis], *n.* service à thé, *m.*

teasing ['ti:ziŋ], *a.* taquin.—*n.* taquinerie, *f.*

teaspoon ['ti:spu:n], *n.* cuiller à thé, *f.*

teaspoonful ['ti:spu:nful], *n.* petite cuillerée, *f.*

tea-strainer ['ti:streinə], *n.* passe-thé, *m.*

teat [ti:t], *n.* mamelon, tétin, *m.*; tette, *f.*

tea-table ['ti:teibl], *n.* table à thé, *f.*

tea-time ['ti:taim], *n.* l'heure du thé, *f.*

tea-tray ['ti:trei], *n.* plateau à thé, *m.*

tea-urn ['ti:ə:n], *n.* fontaine à thé, *f.*

technical ['teknikl], *a.* technique, de l'art; **technical school**, école professionnelle, *f.*

technicality [tekni'kæliti], *n.* caractère technique; terme technique (*mot*), *m.*; (*fig.*) formalité, *f.*

technically ['teknikli], *adv.* techniquement.

technician [tek'niʃən], *n.* technicien, *m.*

technique [tek'ni:k], *n.* technique, *f.*

technologist [tek'nɔlədʒist], *n.* technologue, *m.f.*

technology [tek'nɔlədʒi], *n.* technologie, *f.*

teddy ['tedi], *n.* **teddy bear**, ours en peluche, *m.*

tedious ['ti:diəs], *a.* ennuyeux, fatigant.

tedium ['ti:diəm], *n.* ennui, *m.*

tee [ti:], *n.* dé (*au golf*), *m.*

teem [ti:m], *v.i.* être fécond (*en*); **to teem with**, abonder en.

teeming ['ti:miŋ], *a.* fécond, fertile, surabondant (*de*).

teenager ['ti:neidʒə], *n.* adolescent, *m.*

teens [ti:nz], *n.pl.* l'âge de treize à dix-neuf ans, *m.*; **to be in one's teens**, n'avoir pas vingt ans.

teeth [TOOTH].

teethe [ti:ð], *v.i.* faire ses dents.

teething ['ti:ðiŋ], *n.* dentition, *f.*

teetotal [ti:'toutl], *a.* de tempérance.

teetotal(l)er [ti:'toutlə], *n.* buveur d'eau, *m.*

teetotalism [ti:'toutəlizm], *n.* abstinence de boissons alcooliques, *f.*

telegram ['teligræm], *n.* télégramme, *m.*, dépêche, *f.*

telegraph ['teligrɑ:f, -græf], *n.* télégraphe, *m.*; **telegraph office**, bureau télégraphique, *m.*—*v.t.*, *v.i.* télégraphier.

telegraphic [teli'græfik], *a.* télégraphique.

telegraphist [ti'legrəfist], *n.* télégraphiste, *m.f.*

telegraph-post ['teligrɑ:fpoust], **telegraph-pole** ['teligrɑ:fpoul], *n.* poteau télégraphique, *m.*

telegraph-wire ['teligrɑ:fwaiə], *n.* fil télégraphique, *m.*

telegraphy [ti'legrəfi], *n.* télégraphie, *f.*; **wireless telegraphy**, télégraphie sans fil.

telepathy [ti'lepəθi], *n.* télépathie, *f.*

telephone ['telifoun], *n.* téléphone, *m.*; **telephone exchange**, central téléphonique, *m.*—*v.t.*, *v.i.* téléphoner.

telephonic [teli'fɔnik], *a.* téléphonique.

telephonist [ti'lefənist], *n.* téléphoniste, *m.f.*

teleprinter ['teliprintə], *n.* téléimprimeur, télétype, *m.*

telescope ['teliskoup], *n.* (*Astron.*) télescope, *m.*; longue vue, *f.*

telescopic [teli'skɔpik], *a.* télescopique.

televiewer ['telivju:ə], *n.* téléspectateur, *m.*

televise ['telivaiz], *v.t.* téléviser.

television [teli'viʒən], *n.* télévision, *f.*; **television-set**, téléviseur, appareil de télévision, *m.*

tell [tel], *v.t. irr.* dire; faire part de; raconter (*réciter*); montrer, indiquer (*expliquer*); révéler, dévoiler; énumérer (*compter*); avouer (*confesser*); reconnaître (*à*); savoir (*deviner*).—*v.i.* dire; faire son effet, porter (*influer*); juger (*interpréter*).

teller ['telə], *n.* diseur; raconteur; (*Am.*, *Sc.*) caissier (*de banque*); (*Parl.*) scrutateur, *m.*

592

telling ['teliŋ], *a.* qui porte; expressif.—*n.* récit, *m.*, narration, *f.*

tell-tale ['telteil], *a.* rapporteur; (*fig.*) révélateur.—*n.* rapporteur, *m.*

temerity [ti'meriti], *n.* témérité, *f.*

temper ['tempə], *n.* tempérament, *m.*, disposition; humeur; colère (*rage*), *f.*; sangfroid (*équanimité*), *m.*; trempe (*d'acier etc.*), *f.*; **to lose one's temper**, se mettre en colère.—*v.t.* tempérer (*de*); détremper (*couleurs*); tremper (*acier etc.*); (*fig.*) adoucir.

temperament ['tempərəmənt], *n.* tempérament, *m.*

temperamental [tempərə'mentl], *a.* capricieux, instable.

temperance ['tempərəns], *n.* tempérance, *f.*

temperate ['tempərit], *a.* modéré; tempéré (*climat*).

temperature ['tempritʃə], *n.* température, *f.*

tempest ['tempist], *n.* tempête, *f.*

tempestuous [tem'pestjuəs], *a.* orageux, tempétueux.

templar ['templə], *n.* templier, *m.*

temple [templ], *n.* temple, *m.*; (*Anat.*) tempe, *f.*

templet ['templit], *n.* patron, gabarit, *m.*

temporal ['tempərəl], *a.* temporel; (*Anat.*) temporal.

temporarily ['tempərərili], *adv.* temporairement.

temporary ['tempərəri], *a.* temporaire, provisoire.

temporization [tempərai'zeiʃən], *n.* temporisation, *f.*

temporize ['tempəraiz], *v.i.* temporiser.

tempt [tempt], *v.t.* tenter (*de*); pousser (*à*).

temptation [temp'teiʃən], *n.* tentation, *f.*

tempter ['temptə], *n.* tentateur, *m.*

tempting ['temptiŋ], *a.* tentant; séduisant, attrayant; appétissant (*nourriture*).

temptress ['temptris], *n.* tentatrice, *f.*

ten [ten], *a.* dix.—*n.* dix, *m.*; une dizaine (*dix environ*), *f.*

tenable ['tenəbl], *a.* soutenable.

tenacious [ti'neiʃəs], *a.* tenace.

tenaciously [ti'neiʃəsli], *adv.* d'une manière tenace, obstinément.

tenacity [ti'næsiti], *n.* ténacité, *f.*

tenancy ['tenənsi], *n.* location, *f.*

tenant ['tenənt], *n.* locataire, *m.*, *f.*

tench [tentʃ], *n.* (*Ichth.*) tanche, *f.*

tend [tend], *v.t.* garder, soigner.—*v.i.* tendre (*à*); se diriger vers.

tendency ['tendənsi], *n.* tendance, disposition, *f.*

tender (1) ['tendə], *n.* offre (*proposition*); (*Comm.*) soumission, *f.*; **legal tender**, monnaie légale, *f.*—*v.t.* offrir.—*v.i.* **to tender for**, soumissionner pour.

tender (2) ['tendə], *n.* (*Naut.*) allège, *f.*; (*Rail.*) tender, *m.*

tender (3) ['tendə], *a.* tendre; sensible (*vulnérable*).

tender-hearted ['tendə'ha:tid], *a.* sensible, au cœur tendre.

tenderly ['tendəli], *adv.* tendrement.

tenderness ['tendənis], *n.* tendresse; sensibilité (*vulnérabilité*); sollicitude, *f.*

tendon ['tendən], *n.* tendon, *m.*

tendril ['tendril], *n.* (*Bot.*) vrille, *f.*

tenement ['tenimənt], *n.* habitation, maison, *f.*

tenet ['ti:nit, 'tenit], *n.* principe, *m.*

tenfold ['tenfould], *a.* décuple.—*adv.* dix fois.

tennis ['tenis], *n.* tennis; *jeu de paume, *m.*

tennis-court ['teniskɔ:t], *n.* court de tennis, tennis; *jeu de paume, *m.*

tennis-racket ['tenisrækit], *n.* raquette de tennis, *f.*

tenor ['tenə], *n.* (*Mus.*) ténor, *m.*

tense (1) [tens], *n.* (*Gram.*) temps, *m.*

tense (2) [tens], *a.* tendu, raide.

tensile ['tensail], *a.* ductile (*métal*).

tension ['tenʃən], *n.* tension, *f.*

tent [tent], *n.* tente, *f.*; **bell-tent**, tente conique.

tentacle ['tentəkl], *n.* tentacule, *m.*

tentative ['tentətiv], *a.* tentatif, d'essai.

tentatively ['tentətivli], *adv.* en guise d'essai.

tenter-hook ['tentəhuk], *n.* clou à crochet, *m.*; **to be on tenter-hooks**, être sur des épines.

tenth [tenθ], *a.* dixième; dix (*du mois, roi etc.*). —*n.* dixième (*fraction*), *m.*; (*Eccles.*) dîme, *f.*

tenuous ['tenjuəs], *a.* délié, mince, ténu.

tenure ['tenjuə], *n.* tenure, *f.*

tepid ['tepid], *a.* tiède.

tercentenary [tə:sen'ti:nəri], *a.* de trois siècles.—*n.* tricentenaire, *m.*

term [tə:m], *n.* terme, *m.*; limite; (*Law*) session, *f.*; (*Sch.*) trimestre, *m.*; (*pl.*) conditions, *f.pl.*; prix, *m.*—*v.t.* nommer, appeler.

termagant ['tə:məgənt], *n.* mégère, *f.*

terminable ['tə:minəbl], *a.* terminable.

terminal ['tə:minl], *a.* terminal.—*n.* (*Elec.*) borne, *f.*; **air terminal**, gare aérienne, aérogare, *f.*

terminate ['tə:mineit], *v.t.* terminer, finir.

termination [tə:mi'neiʃən], *n.* fin, terminaison, *f.*

terminology [tə:mi'nɔlədʒi], *n.* terminologie, *f.*

terminus ['tə:minəs], *n.* terminus (*gare*), *m.*; tête de ligne, *f.*

tern [tə:n], *n.* sterne, *m.*, hirondelle de mer, *f.*

ternary ['tə:nəri], *a.* ternaire.

terrace ['teris], *n.* terrasse, *f.*

terraced ['terist], *a.* étagé en terrasse.

terra-cotta ['terə'kɔtə], *n.* terre cuite, *f.*

terra firma ['terə'fə:mə], *n.* terre ferme, *f.*

terrestrial [tə'restriəl], *a.* terrestre.

terrible ['teribl], *a.* terrible.

terribly ['teribli], *adv.* terriblement; (*colloq.*) diablement.

terrier ['teriə], *n.* terrier, chien terrier, *m.*

terrific [tə'rifik], *a.* terrible, épouvantable; (*fam.*) formidable.

terrify ['terifai], *v.t.* terrifier.

territorial [teri'tɔ:riəl], *a.* territorial.

territory ['teritəri], *n.* territoire, *m.*

terror ['terə], *n.* terreur, *f.*; effroi, *m.*

terrorism ['terərizm], *n.* terrorisme, *m.*

terrorist ['terərist], *n.* terroriste, *m.*, *f.*

terrorize ['terəraiz], *v.t.* terroriser.

terse [tə:s], *a.* net, concis; bien tourné, élégant.

tersely ['tə:sli], *adv.* nettement; d'une manière concise.

terseness ['tə:snis], *n.* netteté, *f.*

tertian ['tə:ʃən], *a.* tierce.

tertiary ['tə:ʃəri], *a.* tertiaire.

tessellated ['tesə'leitid], *a.* tessellé.

test

test [test], *n.* épreuve, *f.*; test; essai, *m.*; pierre de touche, *f.*—*v.t.* éprouver, mettre à l'épreuve, tester; (*Metal.*) coupeller.
testament ['testəmənt], *n.* testament, *m.*
testator [tes'teitə], *n.* testateur, *m.*
testicle ['testikl], *n.* testicule, *m.*
testify ['testifai], *v.t.* témoigner; (*Law*) déposer (*de*).—*v.i.* (*Law*) déposer.
testimonial [testi'mouniəl], *n.* témoignage; certificat, témoignage d'estime, *m.*
testimony ['testiməni], *n.* témoignage, *m.*
testiness ['testinis], *n.* humeur, irritabilité, *f.*
testing ['testiŋ], *n.* épreuve, *f.*, essai, *m.*
test-tube ['testtju:b], *n.* éprouvette, *f.*
testy ['testi], *a.* irritable, susceptible.
tetanus ['tetənəs], *n.* tétanos, *m.*
tether ['teðə], *n.* longe, *f.*; *to be at the end of one's tether*, être à bout de forces.—*v.t.* mettre à l'attache, attacher (*à*).
tetrahedron [tetrə'hi:drən], *n.* tétraèdre, *m.*
tetrarch ['tetra:k], *n.* tétrarque, *m.*
Teuton ['tju:tən], *a.* teuton.—*n.* Teuton (*personne*), *m.*
Teutonic [tju:'tɔnik], *a.* teutonique.
text [tekst], *n.* texte, *m.*
text-book ['tekstbuk], *n.* manuel, livre de classe, *m.*
textile ['tekstail], *a.* textile.—*n.* tissu, textile, *m.*, étoffe, *f.*
textual ['tekstjuəl], *a.* textuel.
texture ['tekstʃə], *n.* tissu, *m.*; contexture (*d'écrits etc.*), *f.*
Thai [tai], *a.* thaïlandais.—*n.* thaïlandais (*langue*); Thaïlandais (*personne*), *m.*
Thailand ['tailænd]. la Thaïlande, *f.*, le Siam, *m.*
Thames [temz], **the.** la Tamise, *f.*
than [ðæn], *conj.* que; de (*between more or less and a number*); que de (*before an infinitive*).
thank [θæŋk], *v.t.* remercier (*de*); rendre grâces à.
thankful ['θæŋkful], *a.* reconnaissant (*de*).
thankfully ['θæŋkfuli], *adv.* avec reconnaissance.
thankfulness ['θæŋkfulnis], *n.* reconnaissance, *f.*
thankless ['θæŋklis], *a.* ingrat; oublié (*non reconnu*).
thanklessness ['θæŋklisnis], *n.* ingratitude, *f.*
thank-offering ['θæŋkɔfəriŋ], *n.* sacrifice d'actions de grâces, *m.*
thanks [θæŋks], *n.pl.* remercîments, remerciements, *m.pl.*, grâces, *f.pl.*
thanksgiving ['θæŋksgiviŋ], *n.* actions de grâces, *f.pl.*
that [ðæt], *dem.a.* (*pl.* those [ðouz]) ce, cet, *m.*, cette, *f.*; (*emphatically*) ce . . . -là, cet . . . -là, *m.*, cette . . . -là, *f.*—*dem.pron.* celui-là, *m.*, celle-là (*that one*), *f.*; cela, (*colloq.*) ça, *m.*—*rel.pron.* qui, que, lequel, *m.*, laquelle, *f.*, lesquels, *m.pl.*, lesquelles, *f.pl.*—*conj.* que.
thatch [θætʃ], *n.* chaume, *m.*—*v.t.* couvrir de chaume.
thatcher ['θætʃə], *n.* couvreur en chaume, *m.*
thaw [θɔ:], *n.* dégel, *m.*—*v.t.* dégeler; (*fig.*) fondre, attendrir.—*v.i.* dégeler, se dégeler; (*fig.*) fondre, s'attendrir.
the [ðə], *def. art.* le, l', *m.*, la, l', *f.*, les, *pl.* (*before vowel* [ði])
theatre ['θiətə], *n.* théâtre, *m.*
theatrical [θi:'ætrikl], *a.* de théâtre, théâtral.
theatricals [θi:'ætriklz], *n.pl.* spectacle, *m.*

*thee [ði:], *pron.* (*also Poet.*) toi; te.
theft [θeft], *n.* vol, *m.*; *petty theft*, larcin, *m.*
their [ðeə], *poss.a.* leur, leurs, *pl.*
theirs [ðeəz], *poss.pron.* le leur, *m.*, la leur, *f.*, les leurs, *pl.*, à eux, *m.pl.*, à elles, *f.pl.*
theism ['θi:izm], *n.* théisme, *m.*
theist ['θi:ist], *n.* théiste, *m.*, *f.*
theistic [θi:'istik], *a.* théiste.
them [ðem], *pron.* eux, *m.pl.*, elles, *f.pl.*; (*obj.*) les; (*dat.*) leur, *pl.*
theme [θi:m], *n.* thème, sujet, *m.*
theme-song ['θi:msɔŋ], *n.* chanson leit-motif, *f.*
themselves [ðem'selvz], *pron.* eux-mêmes, *m.pl.*, elles-mêmes, *f.pl.*; (*reflexive*) se, *pl.*
then [ðen], *adv.* alors; ensuite, puis (*après*); dans ce cas (*puisqu'il en est ainsi*); donc; *but then*, par contre; *by then*, alors, déjà; *now and then*, de temps en temps.—*conj.* donc.
thence [ðens], *adv.* de là, en; dès lors.
thenceforth [ðens'fɔ:θ], thenceforward [ðens'fɔ:wəd], *adv.* dès lors, depuis lors, à partir de ce moment-là.
theocracy [θi:'ɔkrəsi], *n.* théocratie, *f.*
theocratic [θi:ə'krætik], *a.* théocratique.
theodolite [θi:'ɔdəlait], *n.* théodolite, *m.*
theologian [θi:ə'loudʒiən], *n.* théologien, *m.*
theological [θi:ə'lɔdʒikl], *a.* théologique.
theology [θi:'ɔlədʒi], *n.* théologie, *f.*
theorem ['θi:ərəm], *n.* théorème, *m.*
theoretic [θi:ə'retik], theoretical [θi:ə'reti kəl], *a.* théorique.
theorist ['θi:ərist], theorizer ['θi:əraizə], *n.* théoricien, *m.*
theorize ['θi:əraiz], *v.i.* théoriser.
theory ['θi:əri], *n.* théorie, *f.*
therapeutic [θerə'pju:tik], *a.* thérapeutique.
therapeutics [θerə'pju:tiks], *n.pl.* thérapeutique, *f.*
therapist ['θerəpist], *n.* praticien, *m.*
therapy ['θerəpi], *n.* thérapie, *f.*
there [ðeə], *adv.* là, y; (*impers.*) il; en cela; voilà; *here and there*, çà et là; *over there*, là-bas; *there and then*, séance tenante; *there he comes!* le voilà qui vient! *there is* or *there are*, il y a.
thereabout [ðeərə'baut], thereabouts [ðeərə 'bauts], *adv.* par là, près de là; à peu près, environ (*plus ou moins*).
thereafter [ðeər'a:ftə], *adv.* après, d'après cela, ensuite.
thereat [ðeər'æt], *adv.* par là, à cet endroit; (*fig.*) là-dessus, à cela.
thereby [ðeə'bai], *adv.* par là, par ce moyen.
therefore ['ðeəfɔ:], *adv.* donc, par conséquent.
therefrom [ðeə'frɔm], *adv.* de là, en.
therein [ðeər'in], *adv.* là-dedans, en cela; y.
thereof [ðeər'ɔv], *adv.* en, de cela.
thereon [ðeər'ɔn], *adv.* là-dessus.
Theresa [tə'ri:zə]. Thérèse, *f.*
thereto [ðeə'tu:], thereunto [ðeər'ʌntu], *adv.* y, à cela; à quoi.
thereupon [ðeərə'pɔn], *adv.* là-dessus, sur cela, sur ce.
therewith [ðeə'wið], *adv.* avec cela, de cela, en.
therm [θə:m], *n.* thermie, *f.*
thermal ['θə:məl], *a.* thermal.
thermometer [θə'mɔmitə], *n.* thermomètre, *m.*

594

thermometrical [θə:mo'metrikl], *a.* thermométrique.
thermonuclear [θə:mo'nju:kliə], *a.* thermonucléaire.
thermos ['θə:mɔs], *a.* (*reg. trade mark*) *thermos flask*, bouteille Thermos *ou* isolante, *f.*
thermostat ['θə:məstæt], *n.* thermostat, *m.*
these [ðiːz], *a.* ces, ces . . . -ci, *pl.*—*pron.* ceux-ci, *m.pl.*, celles-ci, *f.pl.*
thesis ['θiːsis], *n.* thèse, *f.*
Thespian ['θespiən], *a.* tragique, de la tragédie.
thew [θjuː], *n.* tendon, muscle, nerf, *m.*
they [ðei], *pron.* ils, eux, *m.pl.*, elles, *f.pl.*; (*followed by a relative*) ceux, *m.pl.*, celles, *f.pl.*; (*impers.*) on (*les gens*); *they say*, on dit.
thick [θik], *a.* épais; gros (*tuyau*); fort, solide (*porte etc.*); trouble (*boisson*); dru, serré (*touffu*); indistinct (*prononciation*); (*fam.*) intime.—*n.* fort, *m.*; *in the thick of*, au (plus) fort de.—*adv.* (*also* **thickly** ['θikli]) épais; dru (*vite*); en foule (*l'un après l'autre*).
thicken [θikn], *v.t.* épaissir; lier (*sauce*).—*v.i.* s'épaissir; augmenter; se lier (*sauce*).
thickening ['θikniŋ], *n.* épaississement, *m.*; liaison (*d'une sauce*), *f.*
thicket ['θikit], *n.* fourré, hallier, taillis, *m.*
thick-headed ['θik'hedid], *a.* sot, bête, stupide.
thickly [THICK].
thickness ['θiknis], *n.* épaisseur; consistance (*composition*), *f.*
thick-set ['θikset], *a.* touffu; trapu (*personne*).
thick-skinned ['θik'skind], *a.* (*fig.*) peu sensible.
thief [θiːf], *n.* (*pl.* **thieves** [θiːvz]) voleur; larron, *m.*
thieve [θiːv], *v.i.* voler.
thieving ['θiːviŋ], *n.* vol, larcin, *m.*, rapine, *f.*
thievish ['θiːviʃ], *a.* adonné au vol; voleur.
thievishly ['θiːviʃli], *adv.* en voleur; par le vol.
thievishness ['θiːviʃnis], *n.* penchant au vol, *m.*, habitude du vol, *f.*
thigh [θai], *n.* cuisse, *f.*
thigh-bone ['θaiboun], *n.* fémur, *m.*
thimble [θimbl], *n.* dé, *m.*
thimbleful ['θimblful], *n.* un plein dé, *m.*
thin [θin], *a.* mince; maigre (*décharné*); élancé, délié (*svelte*); peu nombreux (*gens*); clair; clairsemé, rare (*arbres etc.*); grêle, faible (*son etc.*).—*adv.* d'une manière éparse, clair.—*v.t.* amincir, allonger (*sauce etc.*); éclaircir; raréfier.
*thine [ðain], *pron.* le tien, *m.*, la tienne, *f.*, les tiens, *m.pl.*, les tiennes, *f.pl.*; à toi.
thing [θiŋ], *n.* chose, *f.*, objet, *m.*, affaire, *f.*; être, *m.*; (*pl.*) affaires, *f.pl.*, effets, *m.pl.*
think [θiŋk], *v.t. irr.* penser; croire (*tenir pour vrai*); imaginer, songer (*avoir l'idée*); trouver, juger (*considérer*).—*v.i.* penser; croire; s'imaginer; songer (*à*); s'aviser (*de*); avoir une idée *ou* opinion (*de*); *to think over*, réfléchir à; *to think up*, inventer.
thinker ['θiŋkə], *n.* penseur, *m.*
thinking ['θiŋkiŋ], *a.* pensant, qui pense, réfléchi.—*n.* pensée, *f.*; jugement, avis, *m.*
thinly ['θinli], *adv.* légèrement (*vêtu*); clairsemé, de loin en loin (*répandu*).
thinness ['θinnis], *n.* ténuité; fluidité; rareté,

f., petit nombre (*quantité*), *m.*; maigreur (*du corps*), *f.*
thin-skinned ['θin'skind], *a.* à la peau mince; (*fig.*) irritable, chatouilleux, susceptible.
third [θə:d], *a.* troisième; trois (*mois, roi etc.*). —*n.* tiers (*fraction*), *m.*; (*Mus.*) tierce, *f.*
thirdly ['θə:dli], *adv.* troisièmement.
thirst [θə:st], *n.* soif, *f.*; *to quench one's thirst*, se désaltérer.—*v.i.* avoir soif (*de*).
thirstily ['θə:stili], *adv.* avidement.
thirstiness ['θə:stinis], *n.* soif, *f.*
thirsty ['θə:sti], *a.* qui a soif; altéré.
thirteen [θə:'tiːn], *a.* and *n.* treize, *m.*
thirteenth [θə:'tiːnθ], *a.* treizième; treize (*rois etc.*).—*n.* treizième (*fraction*), *m.*
thirtieth ['θə:tiiθ], *a.* trentième; trente (*du mois*).—*n.* trentième (*fraction*), *m.*
thirty ['θə:ti], *a.* and *n.* trente, *m.*
this [ðis], *a.* (*pl.* **these** [ðiːz]) ce, cet, *m.*, cette, *f.*; ce . . . -ci, cet . . . -ci, *m.*; cette . . . -ci, *f.*—*pron.* celui-ci, *m.*, celle-ci (*this one*), *f.*; ceci, *m.*
thistle [θisl], *n.* (*Bot.*) chardon, *m.*
thistly ['θisli], *a.* plein de chardons.
thither ['ðiðə], *adv.* là, y; *hither and thither*, çà et là.
thong [θɔŋ], *n.* courroie, lanière, sangle, *f.*
thoracic [θɔ'ræsik], *a.* thoracique.
thorax ['θɔ:ræks], *n.* thorax, *m.*
thorn [θɔ:n], *n.* épine, *f.*
thorn-bush ['θɔ:nbuʃ], *n.* buisson épineux, *m.*
thorny ['θɔ:ni], *a.* épineux.
thorough ['θʌrə], *a.* entier, complet; achevé, parfait; vrai (*véritable*).
thoroughbred ['θʌrəbred], *a.* pur sang (*cheval*); (*colloq.*) consommé.
thoroughfare ['θʌrəfɛə], *n.* voie de passage, *f.*, passage, *m.*; artère, *f.*; *no thoroughfare*, passage interdit.
thoroughgoing ['θʌrəgouiŋ], *a.* résolu; achevé, consommé.
thoroughly ['θʌrəli], *adv.* tout à fait, entièrement; à fond.
thoroughness ['θʌrənis], *n.* caractère achevé, *m.*, perfection, *f.*
thorough-paced ['θʌrəpeist], *a.* achevé, franc, fieffé.
those [ðouz], *a.* ces; ces . . . -là, *pl.*—*pron.* ceux-là, *m.pl.*, celles-là, *f.pl.*
*thou [ðau], *pron.* tu; *than thou*, que toi.
though [ðou], *conj.* quoique, bien que (*with subj.*); quand même (*même si*).—*adv.* cependant, pourtant.
thought (1) [θɔ:t], *past and p.p.* [THINK].
thought (2) [θɔ:t], *n.* pensée; idée, *f.*; sentiment (*opinion*), *m.*
thoughtful ['θɔ:tful], *a.* pensif, réfléchi; rêveur, méditatif; inquiet (*troublé*); attentif, soucieux (*prévenant*).
thoughtfully ['θɔ:tfuli], *adv.* pensivement, avec attention.
thoughtfulness ['θɔ:tfulnis], *n.* méditation, *f.*, recueillement, *m.*; sollicitude, prévenance (*attentions*), *f.*
thoughtless ['θɔ:tlis], *a.* irréfléchi, insouciant.
thoughtlessly ['θɔ:tlisli], *a.* avec insouciance; sans réfléchir.
thoughtlessness ['θɔ:tlisnis], *n.* insouciance, négligence, *f.*
thousand ['θauzənd], *a.* mille; mil (*dates*).— *n.* mille; millier, *m.*, (*pl.*) milliers, *m.pl.*

thousandth ['θauzəndθ], *a.* millième.—*n.* millième (*fraction*), *m.*

thraldom ['θrɔːldəm], *n.* esclavage, asservissement, *m.*

thrall [θrɔːl], *n.* esclave, *m., f.*; esclavage, *m.*

thrash [θræʃ], *v.t.* battre, rosser (*quelqu'un*); [THRESH].

thrasher ['θræʃə], [THRESHER].

thrashing ['θræʃiŋ], *n.* rossée, *f.*; [THRESHING].

thrashing machine [THRESHING MACHINE].

thread [θred], *n.* fil; filet (*de vis*), *m.*—*v.t.* enfiler; traverser (*faire son chemin à travers*).

threadbare ['θredbɛə], *a.* râpé; (*fig.*) rebattu.

threat [θret], *n.* menace, *f.*

threaten [θretn], *v.t.* menacer (*de*).

threatening ['θretniŋ], *a.* menaçant; de menaces.—*n.* menaces, *f.pl.*

threateningly ['θretniŋli], *adv.* avec menaces; d'un air menaçant.

three [θriː], *a.* and *n.* trois, *m.*

three-cornered ['θriːkɔːnəd], *a.* à trois cornes; *three-cornered hat*, tricorne, *m.*

threefold ['θriːfould], *a.* triple.

three-master ['θriːmɑːstə], *n.* trois-mâts, *m.*

three-ply ['θriːplai], *a.* à trois épaisseurs; *three-ply wood*, contreplaqué, *m.*

threescore ['θriːskɔː], *a.* soixante.—*n.* soixantaine, *f.*

thresh [θreʃ], *v.t.* (*Agric.*) battre (*en grange*).

thresher ['θreʃə], *n.* batteur en grange, *m.*

threshing ['θreʃiŋ], *n.* (*Agric.*) battage, *m.*

threshing machine ['θreʃiŋməˈʃiːn], *n.* batteuse, *f.*

threshold ['θreʃould], *n.* seuil; (*fig.*) début, *m.*

thrift [θrift], *n.* épargne, économie, *f.*

thriftily ['θriftili], *adv.* avec économie.

thriftiness [THRIFT].

thriftless ['θriftlis], *a.* dépensier, prodigue.

thriftlessly ['θriftlisli], *adv.* en prodigue, follement.

thriftlessness ['θriftlisnis], *n.* prodigalité, *f.*, gaspillage, *m.*

thrifty ['θrifti], *a.* ménager, économe, frugal.

thrill [θril], *v.t.* faire frissonner, faire tressaillir (*de*).—*v.i.* frémir, tressaillir (*de*).—*n.* tressaillement, frisson, *m.*

thriller ['θrilə], *n.* (*fam.*) roman *ou* film à sensation, *m.*

thrilling ['θriliŋ], *a.* saisissant, poignant, palpitant.

thrive [θraiv], *v.i. irr.* prospérer; réussir.

thriving ['θraiviŋ], *a.* florissant, vigoureux.

throat [θrout], *n.* gorge, *f.*; gosier, *m.*

throaty ['θrouti], *a.* guttural (*voix*).

throb [θrɔb], *v.i.* battre; palpiter.—*n.* battement, *m.*

throbbing ['θrɔbiŋ], *a.* palpitant, vibrant; lancinant (*douleur*).—*n.* battement; ronflement (*de moteur*), *m.*

throes [θrouz], *n. pl.* douleurs, angoisses, *f.pl.*

thrombosis [θrɔmˈbousis], *n.* thrombose, *f.*

throne [θroun], *n.* trône, *m.*

throng [θrɔŋ], *n.* foule, multitude, *f.*—*v.t.* remplir.—*v.i.* accourir en foule, se presser.

thronged [θrɔŋd], *a.* serré (*personnes*); comble (*salle*).

throstle [θrɔsl], *n.* (*Orn.*) grive chanteuse, *f.*

throttle [θrɔtl], *v.t.* étrangler; étouffer.—*n.* gosier; (*Motor. etc.*) papillon, *m.*

through [θruː], *prep.* à travers; au travers de;

par; dans; par suite de (*à cause de*).—*n.* direct (*train, billet etc.*).—*adv.* directement, droit (*sans s'arrêter*); de part en part; d'un bout à l'autre (*dans toute sa longueur*); jusqu'à la fin, jusqu'au bout; complètement; *to be wet through*, être trempé jusqu'aux os; *to fall through*, manquer, échouer (*projet*); *to go through with* (*something*), *to see* (*something*) *through*, mener (quelque chose) à bonne fin.

throughout [θruːˈaut], *prep.* dans tout, par tout.—*adv.* d'un bout à l'autre; entièrement.

throw [θrou], *v.t. irr.* jeter; lancer; renverser; tordre (*soie*); démonter, désarçonner (*cavalier*); *to throw aside*, jeter de côté; *to throw away*, jeter, rejeter; gaspiller; *to throw off*, se défaire de, ôter (*vêtements*).—*n.* jet, coup; (*fig.*) élan, *m.*

thrower ['θrouə], *n.* jeteur, lanceur, *m.*

thrush [θrʌʃ], *n.* (*Orn.*) grive, *f.*

thrust [θrʌst], *v.t.* pousser, enfoncer, fourrer; presser.—*v.i.* porter une botte *ou* un coup (*à*); se fourrer.—*n.* coup, *m.*; (*Fenc.*) botte; (*Arch. etc.*) poussée, *f.*

thud [θʌd], *n.* bruit sourd; son mat, *m.*—*v.i.* faire un bruit sourd.

thug [θʌg], *n.* bandit, *m.*

thumb [θʌm], *n.* pouce, *m.*—*v.t.* manier gauchement; feuilleter; salir (avec les pouces).

thumbnail ['θʌmneil], *a.* en raccourci, minuscule.

thumb-screw ['θʌmskruː], *n.* vis à ailettes, *f.*; poucettes (*supplice*), *f.pl.*

thumbstall ['θʌmstɔːl], *n.* poucier, doigtier, *m.*

thump [θʌmp], *v.t.* frapper du poing, cogner.—*n.* coup, *m.*, bourrade, *f.*

thunder ['θʌndə], *n.* tonnerre, *m.*; (*fig.*) foudre, *f.*—*v.i.* tonner; (*fig.*) fulminer.

thunderbolt ['θʌndəboult], *n.* foudre, *f.*

thunder-clap ['θʌndəklæp], *n.* coup de tonnerre, *m.*

thundering ['θʌndəriŋ], *a.* tonnant, foudroyant; (*colloq.*) énorme.

thunderous ['θʌndərəs], *a.* orageux; à tout rompre (*applaudissements*).

thunderstorm ['θʌndəstɔːm], *n.* orage (accompagné de tonnerre), *m.*

thunderstruck ['θʌndəstrʌk], *a.* foudroyé; (*fig.*) atterré.

thundery ['θʌndəri], *a.* orageux.

Thursday ['θəːzd(ɔ)i], jeudi, *m.*

thus [ðʌs], *adv.* ainsi; *thus far*, jusqu'ici.

thwack [θwæk], *n.* coup, *m.*—*v.t.* frapper, rosser, battre.

thwacking ['θwækiŋ], *n.* roulée de coups, raclée, *f.*

thwart [θwɔːt], *v.t.* traverser; (*fig.*) contrarier.—*adv.* en travers.—*n.* banc de rameurs, *m.*

*thy [ðai], *poss.a.* (*also poet.*) ton, *m.*, ta, *f.*, tes, *pl.*

thyme [taim], *n.* thym, *m.*

thyroid ['θairɔid], *a.* thyroïde.

*thyself [ðaiˈself], *pron.* (*also poet.*) toi-même, toi; (*reflexive*) te.

tiara [tiˈɑːrə], *n.* tiare, *f.*

Tibet [tiˈbet], le Tibet, *m.*

Tibetan [tiˈbetn], *a.* tibétain.—*n.* tibétain (*langue*); Tibétain (*personne*), *m.*

tin-plate

tibia ['tibiə], *n.* (*Anat.*) tibia (*os de la jambe*), *m.*

tic [tik], *n.* tic, *m.*

tick (1) [tik], *n.* tic-tac (*bruit*), *m.*; marque, *f.* —*v.t.* marquer; **to tick off**, pointer.—*v.i.* faire tic-tac, battre (*horloges etc.*).

tick (2) [tik], *n.* coutil (*de matelas*), *m.*

ticket ['tikit], *n.* billet; ticket, *m.*; étiquette, *f.*; **return ticket**, billet d'aller et retour; **season ticket**, carte d'abonnement, *f.*; **single ticket**, billet simple.—*v.t.* étiqueter, numéroter.

ticket-collector ['tikitkəlektə], *n.* contrôleur, *m.*

ticket-office ['tikitɔfis], *n.* bureau des billets, guichet, *m.*

ticking (1) ['tikiŋ], *n.* tic-tac, battement (*de montre etc.*), *m.*

ticking (2) ['tikiŋ], *n.* coutil, *m.*, toile à matelas, *f.*

tickle [tikl], *v.t.*, *v.i.* chatouiller.

tickling ['tikliŋ], *n.* chatouillement, *m.*

ticklish ['tikliʃ], *a.* chatouilleux; critique, délicat.

tidal [taidl], *a.* de marée; **tidal harbour**, port à marée, *m.*; **tidal wave**, raz de marée, *m.*

tide [taid], *n.* marée, *f.*; courant (*flot*), *m.*; (*fig.*) époque, *f.*

tidily ['taidili], *adv.* proprement, en bon ordre.

tidiness ['taidinis], *n.* propreté, netteté, *f.*, bon ordre, *m.*

tidings ['taidiŋz], *n.pl.* nouvelles, *f.pl.*

tidy ['taidi], *a.* rangé, bien arrangé, en ordre, propre, net.—*v.t.* mettre en ordre; ranger; arranger (*papiers etc.*).

tie [tai], *v.t.* lier, attacher; nouer, faire (*un nœud*).—*v.i.* se lier, se nouer; être à égalité. —*n.* lien; nœud (*knot*); cordon (*de chaussure*), *m.*; cravate; (*Mus.*) liaison; (*Games*) partie nulle, *f.*

tier [tiə], *n.* rang, *m.*; rangée, *f.*

tierce [tiəs], *n.* (*Cards*) tierce, *f.*

tiff [tif], *n.* petite querelle, pique, *f.*

tiffany ['tifəni], *n.* gaze de soie (*tissu*), *f.*

tiger ['taigə], *n.* tigre, *m.*

tiger-lily ['taigəlili], *n.* (*Bot.*) lis tigré, *m.*

tiger-moth ['taigəmɔθ], *n.* arctie, *f.*

tight [tait], *a.* serré; raide, tendu (*corde*); trop étroit (*vêtements*); imperméable; **air-tight** or **water-tight**, imperméable à l'air *ou* à l'eau.

tighten [taitn], *v.t.* serrer; tendre (*contraindre*); (*fig.*) resserrer.

tight-fisted ['tait'fistid], *a.* serré, ladre.

tightly ['taitli], *adv.* ferme, fortement; étroitement serré.

tightness ['taitnis], *n.* raideur; étroitesse (*des vêtements*), *f.*

tight-rope ['taitroup], *n.* corde raide, *f.*; **tight-rope walker**, funambule, danseur de corde, *m.*

tights [taits], *n.pl.* collant, maillot, *m.*

tigress ['taigris], *n.* tigresse, *f.*

tile [tail], *n.* tuile, *f.*; carreau (*for flooring*), *m.* —*v.t.* couvrir de tuiles; carreler (*une pièce*).

tiler ['tailə], *n.* couvreur (en tuiles), *m.*

tile-works ['tailwə:ks], *n.* tuilerie, *f.*

till (1) [til], *prep.* jusqu'à.—*conj.* jusqu'à ce que (*with subj.*).

till (2) [til], *n.* caisse, *f.*

till (3) [til], *v.t.* labourer, cultiver.

tillable ['tiləbl], *a.* labourable.

tillage ['tilidʒ], *n.* labourage, *m.*

tiller (1) ['tilə], *n.* laboureur, *m.*

tiller (2) ['tilə], *n.* (*Naut.*) barre du gouvernail, *f.*

tilt (1) [tilt], *n.* bâche, banne (*toile*), *f.*

tilt (2) [tilt], *n.* joute; inclinaison, *f.*—*v.t.* incliner, faire pencher.—*v.i.* jouter; incliner, pencher.

tilth [tilθ], *n.* labourage, *m.*, culture, *f.*

timber ['timbə] *n.* bois de construction, *m.*— *v.t.* boiser.

timbering ['timbəriŋ], *n.* boisage, *m.*

timber-work ['timbəwə:k], *n.* charpente, *f.*

timbrel ['timbrəl], *n.* tambour de basque, tambourin, *m.*

time [taim], *n.* temps, *m.*; saison, époque, *f.*; terme (*période*), *m.*; heure (*de la journée*), *f.*; moment, *m.*; occasion; fois (*répétition*); époque, *f.*, siècle (*d'histoire*), *m.*; mesure, *f.*; (*Drilling*) pas, *m.*; **at times**, parfois, de temps à autre; **in no time**, en un clin d'œil; **in time**, à temps; (*Mus.*) en mesure.—*v.t.* faire à propos; fixer l'heure de; (*Spt.*) chronométrer; **ill-timed**, inopportun; **well-timed**, opportun, à propos.

time-bomb ['taimbɔm], *n.* bombe à retardement, *f.*

time-fuse ['taimfju:z], *n.* fusée à temps, *f.*

time-honoured ['taimɔnəd], *a.* vénérable; séculaire.

time-keeper ['taimki:pə], *n.* surveillant, contrôleur, *m.*

time-lag ['taimlæ:g], *n.* décalage, retard, *m.*

timeliness ['taimlinis], *n.* opportunité, *f.*, à-propos, *m.*

timely ['taimli], *a.* opportun, à propos.

time-piece ['taimpi:s], *n.* pendule, *f.*

time-sheet ['taimʃi:t], *n.* feuille de présence, *f.*

timetable ['taimteibl], *n.* indicateur, horaire; (*Sch.*) emploi du temps, *m.*

time-worn ['taimwɔ:n], *a.* usé par le temps.

timid ['timid], *a.* timide, craintif, peureux.

timidity [ti'miditi], *n.* timidité, *f.*

timing ['taimiŋ], *n.* ajustement, règlement; réglage (*de montre etc.*), *m.*

timorous ['timərəs], *a.* timoré, timide.

timorously ['timərəsli], *adv.* craintivement.

timorousness ['timərəsnis], *n.* timidité, *f.*

tin [tin], *n.* étain, *m.*; boîte (*de conserve*), *f.*— *v.t.* étamer.

tincture ['tiŋktʃə], *n.* teinture, *f.*, extrait, *m.*; (*fig.*) nuance, *f.*—*v.t.* teindre (*de*).

tinder ['tində], *n.* am adou, *m.*

tinder-box ['tindəbɔks], *n.* boîte à amadou, *f.*, briquet à silex, *m.*

tinfoil ['tinfɔil], *n.* feuille d'étain, *f.*

tinge [tindʒ], *n.* teinte, nuance, *f.*; soupçon (*goût*), *m.*—*v.t.* teindre.

tingle [tiŋgl], *v.i.* tinter; picoter, cuire (*douleur*).

tingling ['tiŋgliŋ], *n.* tintement (*son*); picotement, *m.*

tinker ['tiŋkə], *n.* rétameur, *m.*—*v.t.* rétamer; raccommoder.

tinkle [tiŋkl], *v.t.* faire tinter.—*v.i.* tinter.—*n.* tintement, *m.*

tinkling ['tiŋkliŋ], *n.* tintement, *m.*

tinny ['tini], *a.* qui abonde en étain; grêle (*son*).

tin-plate ['tinpleit], *n.* fer-blanc, *m.*

tinsel

tinsel ['tinsəl], *a.* de clinquant; (*fig.*) faux.—*n.* clinquant; (*fig.*) faux éclat, *m.*

tinsmith ['tinsmiθ], *n.* ferblantier, *m.*

tint [tint], *n.* teinte, nuance, *f.*—*v.t.* teinter, nuancer (*de*).

tin-tack ['tintæk], *n.* semence étamée, *f.*

tinware ['tinweə], *n.* ferblanterie, *f.*

tiny ['taini], *a.* tout petit, minuscule.

tip (1) [tip], *n.* bout, *m.*; extrémité, pointe, *f.*—*v.t.* garnir le bout.

tip (2) [tip], *n.* tape (*coup léger*), *f.*; pourboire (*gratuity*); dépotoir (*débris*); (*Spt.*) tuyau, *m.*—*v.t.* donner un pourboire à; décharger (*véhicule*); (*Spt.*) tuyauter.

tippet ['tipit], *n.* pèlerine, palatine (*fourrure*), *f.*

tipple [tipl], *v.i.* boire, pinter.—*n.* boisson, *f.*

tippler ['tiplə], *n.* buveur, *m.*

tippling ['tipliŋ], *n.* ivrognerie, *f.*

tipstaff ['tipstɑːf], *n.* huissier, *m.*

tipster ['tipstə], *n.* (*Spt.*) tuyauteur, *m.*

tipsy ['tipsi], *a.* gris, ivre.

tiptoe ['tiptou], *n.* pointe du pied, *f.*; *on tiptoe*, sur la pointe des pieds.

tip-top ['tiptɔp], *a.* (*colloq.*) excellent.—*n.* comble, sommet, *m.*

tirade [ti'reid, tai'reid], *n.* tirade, diatribe, *f.*

tire ['taiə], *v.t.* lasser, fatiguer; ennuyer (*moralement*).—*v.i.* se fatiguer, se lasser.

tired ['taiəd], *a.* las, fatigué; ennuyé.

tiredness ['taiədnis], *n.* fatigue, lassitude, *f.*

tiresome ['taiəsəm], *a.* fatigant; ennuyeux (*assommant*).

tiresomeness ['taiəsəmnis], *n.* nature fatigante, *f.*; ennui, *m.*

tiro [TYRO].

tissue ['tiʃjuː, 'tisjuː], *n.* tissu, *m.*—*v.t.* tisser, broder.

tissue-paper ['tiʃjuːpeipə], *n.* papier de soie, *m.*

tit (1) [tit], *n.* mésange (*oiseau*), *f.*

tit (2) [tit], *n.* *tit for tat*, un prêté pour un rendu.

titanic [tai'tænik], *a.* titanique, titanesque.

titbit ['titbit], *n.* morceau friand, *m.*

tithe [taið], *n.* dîme, *f.*, dixième, *m.*—*v.t.* dîmer.

titillate ['titileit], *v.t., v.i.* chatouiller, titiller.

titillation [titi'leiʃən], *n.* titillation, *f.*, chatouillement, *m.*

titlark ['titlɑːk], *n.* alouette des prés, *f.*

title [taitl], *n.* titre; (*fig.*) droit, document, *m.*—*v.t.* titrer, qualifier (*de*).

titled [taitld], *a.* titré.

title-deed ['taitldiːd], *n.* titre (de propriété), *m.*

title-page ['taitlpeidʒ], *n.* titre, *m.*

titmouse ['titmaus], *n.* (*pl.* **titmice** ['titmais]) mésange, *f.*

titter ['titə], *v.i.* rire tout bas.—*n.* petit rire étouffé, *m.*

tittle [titl], *n.* point, iota, *m.*

tittle-tattle ['titltætl], *n.* caquetage, bavardage, *m.*—*v.i.* jaser, bavarder.

titular ['titjulə], *a.* titulaire.

titulary ['titjuləri], *a.* de titre.—*n.* titulaire, *m., f.*

to [tu], *prep.* à, de (*before infinitive*); pour, afin de (*dans le but de*); à (*un endroit*); en (*before names of countries of the feminine gender and those of the masculine gender beginning with a vowel*); dans (*followed by* le, la, *etc.*); vers (*un endroit*); contre (*pari*); près de (*cour royale etc.*); outre, en addition à (*en plus de*);

pour (*faire quelque chose*); en comparaison de, auprès de (*à côté de*); jusqu'à (*telle ou telle limite*); envers (*à l'égard de*).

toad [toud], *n.* crapaud, *m.*

toadish ['toudiʃ], *a.* de crapaud.

toadstool ['toudstuːl], *n.* champignon vénéneux, *m.*

toady ['toudi], *n.* flagorneur, *m.*—*v.t.* flagorner, aduler.

toadyism ['toudiizm], *n.* flagornerie, servilité, *f.*

toast [toust], *n.* rôtie, tranche de pain grillée, *f.*; toast (*bu à la santé de quelqu'un*), *m.*—*v.t.* rôtir, griller; porter un toast à.

toaster ['toustə], *n.* grille-pain, *m.inv.*

toasting-fork ['toustiŋfɔːk], *n.* fourchette à rôties, *f.*

toast-master ['toustmɑːstə], *n.* préposé aux toasts, *m.*

toast-rack ['toustræk], *n.* porte-rôties, porte-toasts, *m.inv.*

tobacco [tə'bækou], *n.* tabac, *m.*

tobacco-box [tə'bækoubɔks], *n.* boîte à tabac, *f.*

tobacco-jar [tə'bækoudʒɑː], *n.* pot à tabac, *m.*

tobacconist [tə'bækənist], *n.* marchand de tabac, *m.*; *tobacconist's shop*, bureau de tabac, *m.*

tobacco-pouch [tə'bækoupautʃ], *n.* blague à tabac, *f.*

toboggan [tə'bɔgən], *n.* toboggan, *m.*; luge, *f.*—*v.t.* luger.

tocsin ['tɔksin], *n.* tocsin, *m.*

today [tə'dei], *adv.* aujourd'hui.

toddle [tɔdl], *v.i.* trottiner.

toddler ['tɔdlə], *n.* tout petit enfant, *m.*

to-do [tə'duː], *n.* tapage, éclat, *m.*, (*fam.*) histoire, *f.*

toe [tou], *n.* orteil, doigt de pied; devant du sabot, *m.,* pince (*de cheval*), *f.*; bout (*de bas*), *m.*

toe-nail ['touneil], *n.* ongle de pied, *m.*

toffee, toffy ['tɔfi], *n.* caramel au beurre, *m.*

toga ['tougə], *n.* toge, *f.*

together [tə'geðə], *adv.* ensemble, à la fois, en même temps (*simultanément*); de concert (*entre eux*); de suite (*consécutivement*).

Togo ['tougou]. le Togo, *m.*

Togolese [tougo'liːz], *a.* togolais.—*n.* Togolais (*personne*), *m.*

toil [tɔil], *n.* travail dur, labeur, *m.*; peine, *f.*; (*pl.*) piège, *m.*—*v.i.* travailler fort, se fatiguer.

toiler ['tɔilə], *n.* travailleur, *m.*

toilet ['tɔilit], *n.* toilette, *f.*; les toilettes (*dans les hôtels etc.*), *f.pl.*

toiling ['tɔiliŋ], *n.* travail, labeur, *m.*, peine, *f.*

toilsome ['tɔilsəm], *a.* pénible, laborieux, fatigant.

toilsomeness ['tɔilsəmnis], *n.* difficulté, *f.*

token ['toukən], *n.* marque, *f.*; gage (*témoignage*); jeton (*jeux de cartes, téléphone etc.*), *m.*; *book token*, bon de livre, *m.*; *token strike*, grève d'avertissement, *f.*

tolerable ['tɔlərəbl], *a.* tolérable, passable (*assez bon*).

tolerably ['tɔlərəbli], *adv.* passablement, assez.

tolerance ['tɔlərəns], *n.* tolérance, *f.*

tolerant ['tɔlərənt], *a.* tolérant.

tolerate ['tɔləreit], *v.t.* tolérer; supporter.
toleration [tɔlə'reiʃən], *n.* tolérance, *f.*
toll (1) [toul], *n.* péage; droit; octroi (*impôt municipal*), *m.*
toll (2) [toul], *n.* tintement, glas (*de cloche*), *m.* —*v.t., v.i.* sonner, tinter (*cloche*).
toll-bar ['toulbɑ:], **toll-gate** ['toulgeit], *n.* barrière de péage, *f.*
toll-bridge ['toulbridʒ], *n.* pont à péage, *m.*
toll-gatherer ['toulgæðərə], *n.* péager, *m.*
toll-house ['toulhaus], *n.* bureau de péage, *m.*
tolling ['touliŋ], *n.* tintement, *m.*
tomahawk ['tɔməhɔ:k], *n.* tomahawk, *m.*; hache de guerre, *f.*
tomato [tə'mɑ:tou], *n.* tomate, *f.*
tomb [tu:m], *n.* tombeau, *m.*; tombe, *f.*
tomboy ['tɔmbɔi], *n.* garçon manqué, *m.*
tombstone ['tu:mstoun], *n.* pierre tombale, *f.*
tom-cat ['tɔmkæt], *n.* matou, *m.*
tome [toum], *n.* tome, volume, *m.*
tomfool [tɔm'fu:l], *n.* sot, bête, niais, *m.*
tomfoolery [tɔm'fu:ləri], *n.* sottise, bêtise, niaiserie, *f.*
tommy-gun ['tɔmigʌn], *n.* mitraillette, *f.*
tomorrow [tə'mɔrou], *adv.* demain.
tomtit ['tɔmtit], *n.* (*Orn.*) mésange bleue, *f.*
tom-tom ['tɔmtɔm], *n.* tam-tam, *m.*
ton [tʌn], *n.* tonne (*poids*), *f.*, tonneau (*capacité*), *m.*
tone [toun], *n.* ton; accent, timbre (*de voix*), *m.*—*v.t.* donner le ton à, régler; (*Mus.*) accorder; (*Phot.*) virer; *to tone down*, adoucir, pallier.
toneless ['tounlis], *a.* sans éclat, sans chaleur (*voix*).
tongs [tɔŋz], *n.pl.* pincettes; (*Tech.*) tenailles, pinces, *f.pl.*
tongue [tʌŋ], *n.* langue, *f.*; *to hold one's tongue*, se taire.
tongued [tʌŋd], *a.* à langue.
tongue-tied ['tʌŋtaid], *a.* qui a la langue liée; (*fig.*) réduit au silence, muet.
tonic ['tɔnik], *a.* and *n.* (*Med.*) tonique, fortifiant, *m.*
tonight [tə'nait], *n.* cette nuit, *f.*, ce soir, *m.*
tonnage ['tʌnidʒ], *n.* tonnage, *m.*
tonsil [tɔnsl], *n.* (*Anat.*) amygdale, *f.*
tonsil(l)itis [tɔnsi'laitis], *n.* amygdalite, *f.*
tonsure ['tɔnʃə], *n.* tonsure, *f.*—*v.t.* tonsurer.
too [tu:], *adv.* trop, par trop; aussi, de même, également (*pareillement*); d'ailleurs, de plus; *too much* or *too many*, trop.
tool [tu:l], *n.* outil, instrument; (*fig.*) agent, *m.*
tool-chest ['tu:ltʃest], *n.* boîte à outils, *f.*
tooth [tu:θ], *n.* (*pl.* teeth [ti:θ]) dent, *f.*; *set of teeth*, râtelier, *m.*; *wisdom tooth*, dent de sagesse.—*v.t.* denteler.
toothache ['tu:θeik], *n.* mal de dents, *m.*
toothbrush ['tu:θbrʌʃ], *n.* brosse à dents, *f.*
toothed [tu:θt], *a.* à dents; (*Tech.*) denté.
toothless ['tu:θlis], *a.* sans dents, édenté.
tooth-paste ['tu:θpeist], *n.* pâte dentifrice, *f.*, dentifrice, *m.*
tooth-pick ['tu:θpik], *n.* cure-dents, *m.inv.*
tooth-powder ['tu:θpaudə], *n.* poudre dentifrice, *f.*
toothsome ['tu:θsəm], *a.* agréable au goût, savoureux, friand.
toothsomeness ['tu:θsəmnis], *n.* goût agréable, *m.*
top (1) [tɔp], *a.* premier, principal, extrême.—*n.* haut, sommet, *m.*; cime (*de montagne etc.*),

f.; faîte (*d'édifice*), *m.*; (*Naut.*) hune, *f.*; dessus (*de table*), *m.*—*v.t.* couronner, surmonter (*de*).
top (2) [tɔp], *n.* toupie (*jouet*), *f.*
topaz ['toupæz], *n.* topaze, *f.*
top-boots ['tɔpbu:ts], *n.pl.* bottes à revers, *f.pl.*
top-coat ['tɔpkout], *n.* pardessus, *m.*
tope (1) [toup], *v.i.* (*colloq.*) pinter, boire.
tope (2) [toup], *n.* chien de mer, *m.*
toper ['toupə], *n.* ivrogne, *m.*, *f.*
top-hat ['tɔp'hæt], *n.* chapeau haut de forme, *m.*
topic ['tɔpik], *n.* matière, *f.*, sujet, *m.*
topical ['tɔpikl], *a.* d'actualité; (*Med.*) topique.
topmast ['tɔpmɑ:st], *n.* mât de hune, *m.*
topmost ['tɔpmoust], *a.* le plus haut, le plus élevé.
top-sail [tɔpsl], *n.* hunier, *m.*
topographer [tə'pɔgrəfə], *n.* topographe, *m.*
topographic [tɔpə'græfik], **topographical** [tɔpə'græfikəl], *a.* topographique.
topography [tə'pɔgrəfi], *n.* topographie, *f.*
topple [tɔpl], *v.i.* tomber, dégringoler.
topsy-turvy ['tɔpsi'tə:vi], *adv.* sens dessus dessous.
torch [tɔ:tʃ], *n.* torche, *f.*, flambeau, *m.*, lampe de poche, *f.*
torch-bearer ['tɔ:tʃbɛərə], *n.* porte-flambeau, *m.*
toreador [tɔriə'dɔ:], *n.* toréador, *m.*
torment (1) ['tɔ:ment], *n.* tourment, *m.*, torture, *f.*, supplice, *m.*
torment (2) [tɔ:'ment], *v.t.* tourmenter, torturer.
tormentor [tɔ:'mentə], *n.* tourmenteur, bourreau, *m.*
tornado [tɔ:'neidou], *n.* tornade, *f.*, ouragan, cyclone, *m.*
torpedo [tɔ:'pi:dou], *n.* torpille, *f.*—*v.t.* torpiller.
torpedo-boat [tɔ:'pi:doubout], *n.* torpilleur, *m.*
torpid ['tɔ:pid], *a.* engourdi, torpide, inerte.
torpor ['tɔ:pə], *n.* torpeur, apathie, *f.*
torrefaction [tɔri'fækʃən], *n.* torréfaction, *f.*
torrefy ['tɔrifai], *v.t.* torréfier.
torrent ['tɔrənt], *n.* torrent, *m.*
torrential [tɔ'renʃl], *a.* torrentiel.
torrid ['tɔrid], *a.* brûlant, torride.
torridness ['tɔridnis], **torridity** [tɔ'riditi], *n.* chaleur brûlante, *f.*
torsion ['tɔ:ʃən], *n.* torsion, *f.*
torso ['tɔ:sou], *n.* torse, *m.*
tortoise ['tɔ:təs], *n.* tortue, *f.*
tortoise-shell ['tɔ:təsʃel], *a.* d'écaille.—*n.* écaille de tortue, écaille, *f.*
tortuous ['tɔ:tjuəs], *a.* tortueux, sinueux.
tortuousness ['tɔ:tjuəsnis], *n.* tortuosité, *f.*
torture ['tɔ:tʃə], *n.* torture, *f.*; supplice, *m.*—*v.t.* torturer; (*fig.*) faire souffrir.
torturer ['tɔ:tʃərə], *n.* bourreau, *m.*
toss [tɔs], *n.* jet, lancement, *m.*; *to win the toss*, gagner (à pile *ou* face).—*v.t.* lancer *ou* jeter (*en l'air*); ballotter; secouer.—*v.i.* s'agiter.
tossing ['tɔsiŋ], *n.* secousse, *f.*; ballottement; hochement, *m.*
toss-up ['tɔsʌp], *n.* coup de pile ou face, *m.*
total [toutl], *a.* total, complet, entier.—*n.* total, montant, *m.*, somme, *f.*—*v.t.* se monter à.

599

totalitarian

totalitarian [toutæli'tɛəriən], *a.* (*Polit.*) totalitaire.

totalitarianism [toutæli'tɛəriənizm], *n.* totalitarisme, *m.*

totality [tou'tæliti], *n.* totalité, *f.*, montant, tout, *m.*

totalizator ['toutəlaizeitə], *n.* totalisateur, *m.*

totally ['toutəli], *adv.* totalement, tout à fait, entièrement.

totem ['toutəm], *n.* totem, *m.*

totter ['tɔtə], *v.i.* chanceler; (*fig.*) vaciller, trembler.

tottering ['tɔtəriŋ], *a.* chancelant, tremblant. —*n.* chancellement, *m.*

tottery ['tɔtəri], *a.* chancelant.

touch [tʌtʃ], *v.t.* toucher; toucher à (*s'ingérer dans*); (*fig.*) émouvoir (*attendrir*); **to touch up,** retoucher.—*v.i.* toucher; se toucher; **to touch at,** aborder à (*navire*); **to touch upon,** effleurer, (*fig.*) faire allusion à.—*n.* le toucher (*sens tactile*); attouchement (*contact*), *m.*; légère attaque (*d'une maladie*), *f.*; (*fig.*) soupçon (*trace*), *m.*; **it was touch and go,** il s'en est fallu de bien peu; **to get in touch with,** se mettre en rapports, entrer en contact avec; **to keep in touch with,** garder le contact avec.

touchiness ['tʌtʃinis], *n.* irascibilité, *f.*

touching ['tʌtʃiŋ], *a.* touchant, émouvant.— *prep.* concernant, au sujet de.

touch-line ['tʌtʃlain], *n.* (*Ftb.*) ligne de touche, *f.*

touchstone ['tʌtʃstoun], *n.* pierre de touche, *f.*

touch-wood ['tʌtʃwud], *n.* amadou, *m.*

touchy ['tʌtʃi], *a.* irritable, susceptible.

tough [tʌf], *a.* dur, raide, résistant; coriace (*viande*); fort (*solide*); difficile.

toughen ['tʌfn], *v.t.* durcir.—*v.i.* s'endurcir.

toughish ['tʌfiʃ], *a.* un peu dur.

toughly ['tʌfli], *adv.* durement; vigoureusement.

toughness ['tʌfnis], *n.* raideur; dureté, nature coriace (*viande etc.*); (*fig.*) difficulté, *f.*

tour ['tuə], *n.* tour, voyage, *m.*; randonnée, tournée, *f.*—*v.t.*, *v.i.* visiter (*un pays*); voyager dans (*un pays*); excursionner.

tourism ['tuərizm], *n.* tourisme, *m.*

tourist ['tuərist], *n.* touriste, *m.*, *f.*, voyageur, *m.*; **tourist agency,** bureau de tourisme, *m.*

tournament ['tuənəmənt], *n.* tournoi; concours, *m.*

tourniquet ['tuənikei], *n.* garrot, *m.*

tousle [tauzl], *v.t.* tirailler, chiffonner; **tousled hair,** cheveux ébouriffés, *m.pl.*

tout [taut], *v.i.* racoler.—*n.* racoleur, *m.*

touting ['tautiŋ], *n.* racolage, *m.*

tow [tou], *n.* filasse, étoupe (*chanvre*); remorque, *f.*; **in tow,** à la remorque.—*v.t.* remorquer, touer, haler.

towage ['touidʒ], *n.* remorquage, touage, halage, *m.*

toward, towards [tu'wɔːd(z)], *prep.* vers, envers; du côté de; à l'égard de (*par respect pour*); sur, environ, vers (*l'heure*).

tow-boat ['toubout], *n.* remorqueur, *m.*

towel ['tauəl], *n.* essuie-mains, *m.inv.*, serviette, *f.*

towelling ['tauəliŋ], *n.* toile pour serviettes, *f.*; tissu-éponge, *m.*

tower ['tauə], *n.* tour, *f.*—*v.i.* s'élever (*au-dessus de*), dominer.

towering ['tauəriŋ], *a.* élevé; dominant; violent.

towing ['touiŋ], *n.* remorque, *f.*; halage (*sur canal*), *m.*

towing-boat ['touiŋbout], *n.* [TOW-BOAT].

tow(ing)-line ['tou(iŋ)lain], **tow(ing)-rope** ['tou(iŋ)roup], *n.* cable de remorque, *m.*, remorque, *f.*

tow(ing)-path ['tou(iŋ)pɑːθ], *n.* chemin de halage, *m.*

town [taun], *n.* ville, *f.*

town clerk ['taun'klɑːk], *n.* secrétaire de, mairie, *m.*

town council ['taun'kaunsl], *n.* conseil municipal, *m.*

town councillor ['taun'kaunsilə], *n.* conseiller municipal, *m.*

town hall ['taun'hɔːl], *n.* hôtel de ville, *m.*, mairie, *f.*

town planning ['taun'plæniŋ], *n.* urbanisme, *m.*

townsfolk [TOWNSPEOPLE].

township ['taunʃip], *n.* commune, *f.*

townsman ['taunzmən], *n.* (*pl.* **-men** [men]) habitant de la ville, bourgeois, *m.*

townspeople ['taunzpiːpl], *n.* (*pl.*), **townsfolk** ['taunzfouk], *n.* habitants (de la ville), citadins, *m.pl.*

tow-rope [TOW(ING)-LINE].

toxic ['tɔksik], *a.* toxique.

toxicology [tɔksi'kɔlədʒi], *n.* toxicologie, *f.*

toy [tɔi], *n.* jouet, joujou, *m.*—*v.i.* jouer; folâtrer, s'amuser (*avec*).

trace (1) [treis], *n.* trace, *f.*; tracé (*calque*), *m.*—*v.t.* tracer; calquer (*dessin*); suivre la trace de (*to track*); (*fig.*) remonter à l'origine de.

trace (2) [treis], *n.* (*usu. pl.*) traits (*harnais*), *m.pl.*

traceable ['treisəbl], *a.* que l'on peut tracer.

tracer ['treisə], *n.* traceur; traçoir (*instrument*), *m.*

tracery ['treisəri], *n.* (*Arch.*) réseau, *m.*

trachea [trə'kiːə], *n.* (*Anat.*) trachée-artère, *f.*

tracing ['treisiŋ], *n.* tracé, tracement; calque, *m.*; **tracing-paper,** papier à calquer, *m.*

track [træk], *n.* (*Spt.*) piste, *f.*, chemin (*route*), *m.*; (*Hunt.*) piste; (*Rail.*) voie; (*Astron.*) orbite, *f.*, sillage (*de bateau*), *m.*; **beaten track,** sentier battu, *m.*; (*Cine.*) **sound track,** bande sonore, *f.*—*v.t.* suivre à la piste; haler, remorquer.

tracker ['trækə], *n.* traqueur, *m.*

tracking ['trækiŋ], *n.* action de suivre à la trace, *f.*

trackless ['træklis], *a.* sans trace; sans chemins.

tract [trækt], *n.* étendue; contrée; brochure (*petit livre*), *f.*

tractable ['træktəbl], *a.* traitable, maniable.

tractile ['træktail], *a.* ductile.

traction ['trækʃən], *n.* traction, tension, *f.*

traction-engine ['trækʃənendʒin], *n.* locomotive routière, *f.*

tractor ['træktə], *n.* tracteur, *m.*

trade [treid], *n.* commerce, trafic, négoce; métier, *m.*, profession (*vocation*), *f.*; **Board of Trade,** Ministère du Commerce, *m.*; **free trade,** libre-échange, *m.* (*Comm.*) **trade name,** marque déposée, *f.*—*v.i.* trafiquer, faire le commerce (*de*).

trade-mark ['treidmɑːk], *n.* marque de fabrique, *f.*

trader ['treidə], *n.* négociant, *m.*

tradesman ['treidzmən], *n.* (*pl.* **-men** [men]) marchand, boutiquier (*détaillant*); fournisseur, *m.*

trade(s)-union ['treid(z)'juːnjən], *n.* syndicat ouvrier, *m.*

trade-unionism ['treid'juːnjənizm], *n.* syndicalisme, *m.*

trade-unionist ['treid'juːnjənist], *n.* syndicaliste, *m.*, *f.*

trade-winds ['treidwindz], *n.pl.* vents alizés, *m.pl.*

trading ['treidiŋ], *a.* marchand, de commerce.—*n.* négoce, commerce, *m.*

tradition [trə'diʃən], *n.* tradition, *f.*

traditional [trə'diʃənəl], *a.* traditionnel.

traduce [trə'djuːs], *v.t.* diffamer, calomnier.

traducer [trə'djuːsə], *n.* calomniateur, *m.*

traffic ['træfik], *n.* trafic; commerce, négoce, *m.*; circulation (*de voitures*), *f.*; (*Rail.*) mouvement, *m.*; *traffic jam*, embouteillage, *m.*—*v.i.* trafiquer, commercer.

trafficker ['træfikə], *n.* trafiquant, *m.*

traffic-light ['træfiklait], *n.* feu, *m.*

tragedian [trə'dʒiːdiən], *n.* auteur tragique; tragédien, *m.*

tragedy ['trædʒədi], *n.* tragédie, *f.*

tragic ['trædʒik], **tragical** ['trædʒikəl], *a.* tragique.

tragi-comedy ['trædʒi'kɔmidi], *n.* tragi-comédie, *f.*

tragi-comical ['trædʒi'kɔmikəl], *a.* tragi-comique.

trail [treil], *n.* traînée; (*Hunt.*) piste, *f.*—*v.t.* suivre à la piste; traîner (*tirer après soi*).—*v.i.* traîner.

trailer ['treilə], *n.* remorque (*bicyclette, camion etc.*); (*Am.*) roulotte, caravane; (*Cine.*) bande de lancement, *f.*

train [trein], *n.* (*Rail.*) train, *m.*; suite, *f.* cortège (*personnel*), *m.*; série, *f.*, enchaînement (*succession*), *m.*; traînée (*de poudre à canon*); queue, traîne (*de robe*), *f.*; *breakdown train*, train de secours, *m.*; *excursion train*, train de plaisir.—*v.t.* former; exercer, instruire; dresser, entraîner (*cheval etc.*).—*v.i.* s'entraîner.

train-bearer ['treinbɛərə], *n.* porte-queue, *m.*

trainee [trei'niː], *n.* stagiaire, *m.*, *f.*

trainer ['treinə], *n.* dresseur; entraîneur, *m.*

training ['treiniŋ], *n.* éducation, instruction, *f.*; dressage (*de cheval*); entraînement (*de cheval de course*), *m.*

training-ship ['treiniŋʃip], *n.* vaisseau-école, *m.*

trait [trei], *n.* trait, *m.*

traitor ['treitə], *n.* traître, *m.*

traitorous ['treitərəs], *a.* traître, perfide.

traitorously ['treitərəsli], *adv.* en traître, perfidement.

traitress ['treitris], *n.* traîtresse, *f.*

trajectory [trə'dʒektəri], *n.* trajectoire, *f.*

tram(-car) ['træm(kɑː)], *n.* tramway, *m.*

trammel ['træml], *n.* tramail (*filet*), *m.*; entrave (*de cheval*), *f.*—*v.t.* entraver, empêtrer (*de*).

tramp [træmp], *v.t.* faire à pied, faire.—*v.i.* aller à pied, marcher lourdement.—*n.* randonnée (*à pied*), *f.*; bruit de pas (*marche pesante*); vagabond, *m.*

trample [træmpl], *v.t.* fouler (*aux pieds*).

trampling ['træmpliŋ], *n.* piétinement, bruit de pas, *m.*

trance [trɑːns], *n.* extase; (*Path.*) catalepsie, *f.*

tranquil ['træŋkwil], *a.* tranquille.

tranquillity [træŋ'kwiliti], *n.* tranquillité, *f.*, calme, *m.*

tranquillize ['træŋkwilaiz], *v.t.* tranquilliser, calmer.

tranquillizer ['træŋkwilaizə], *n.* calmant, *m.*

transact [træn'zækt], *v.t.* traiter, expédier.

transaction [træn'zækʃən], *n.* transaction, affaire, *f.*

transactor [træn'zæktə], *n.* négociateur, *m.*

transalpine [træn'zælpain], *a.* transalpin.

transatlantic [trænzət'læntik], *a.* transatlantique.

transcend [træn'send], *v.t.* dépasser, surpasser.

transcendence [træn'sendəns], **transcendency** [træn'sendənsi], *n.* excellence, transcendance, *f.*

transcendent [træn'sendənt], *a.* transcendant.

transcendental [trænsen'dentl], *a.* transcendantal.

transcribe [træn'skraib], *v.t.* transcrire, copier.

transcriber [træn'skraibə], *n.* copiste, *m.*, *f.*, transcripteur, *m.*

transcript ['trænskript], *n.* copie, *f.*

transcription [træn'skripʃən], *n.* transcription, *f.*

transept ['trænsept], *n.* transept, *m.*

transfer [træns'fəː], *v.t.* transporter; (*Law*) transférer.—['trænsfəː], *n.* copie, *f.*; (*Law*) transfert, *m.*

transferable ['trænsfərəbl], *a.* transférable, transmissible.

transference ['trænsfərəns], *n.* transfert, *m.*

transfiguration [trænsfigjuːreiʃən], *n.* transfiguration, transformation, *f.*

transfigure [træns'figə], *v.t.* transfigurer.

transfix [træns'fiks], *v.t.* transpercer.

transform [træns'fɔːm], *v.t.* transformer, changer (*en*).—*v.i.* se transformer (*en*).

transformation [trænsfə'meiʃən], *n.* transformation, *f.*, changement, *m.*; *transformation scene*, changement à vue, *m.*

transformer [træns'fɔːmə], *n.* transformateur, *m.*

transfuse [træns'fjuːz], *v.t.* transfuser.

transfusion [træns'fjuːʒən], *n.* transfusion, *f.*

transgress [træns'gres, trænz'gres], *v.t.* transgresser, enfreindre.—*v.i.* transgresser, pécher.

transgression [træns'greʃən], *n.* transgression, infraction, *f.*

transgressor [træns'gresə], *n.* pécheur, *m.* pécheresse, *f.*

tranship [træn'ʃip], *v.t.* transborder.

transience ['trænziəns], *n.* nature transitoire, courte durée, *f.*

transient ['trænziənt], *a.* passager, transitoire.

transistor [træn'zistə], *n.* transistor, transistron, *m.*

transit ['trænzit], *n.* passage, *m.*; *in transit* en transit.

transition [træn'ziʃən], *n.* transition, *f.*

transitional [træn'ziʃənəl], *a.* de transition.

transitive ['trænzitiv], *a.* qui passe; (*Gram.*) transitif.

transitoriness

transitoriness ['trænzitərinis], *n.* nature transitoire, courte durée, *f.*

transitory ['trænzitəri], *a.* transitoire, passager.

translatable [træns'leitəbl], *a.* traduisible.

translate [træns'leit], *v.t.* traduire; transférer (*évêque*).

translation [træns'leiʃən], *n.* traduction; translation (*d'un évêque*), *f.*

translator [træns'leitə], *n.* traducteur, *m.*

translucent [trænz'lju:sənt], *a.* translucide.

transmarine [trænzmə'ri:n], *a.* d'outremer.

transmigrate ['trænzmaigreit], *v.i.* passer d'un corps dans un autre; émigrer.

transmigration [trænzmai'greiʃən], *n.* transmigration; métempsyc(h)ose (*des âmes*), *f.*

transmissible [trænz'misibl], *a.* transmissible.

transmission [trænz'miʃən], *n.* transmission, *f.*

transmit [trænz'mit], *v.t.* transmettre, envoyer; (*Rad.*) émettre.

transmitter [trænz'mitə], *n.* (*Rad.*) émetteur, *m.*

transmutable [trænz'mju:təbl], *a.* transmuable.

transmutation [trænzmju'teiʃən], *n.* transmutation, *f.*; changement (*de couleur*), *m.*

transmute [trænz'mju:t], *v.t.* transmuer, convertir.

transom ['trænsəm], *n.* traverse (*de fenêtre*), imposte, *f.*

transparency [træns'pɛərənsi], *n.* transparence, *f.* (*Phot.*) diapositive, *f.*

transparent [træns'pɛərənt], *a.* transparent.

transparently [træns'pɛərəntli], *adv.* avec transparence; évidemment.

transpire [træns'paiə, trænz'paiə], *v.i.* transpirer; (*fig.*) avoir lieu, arriver.

transplant [træns'plɑ:nt, trænz'plɑ:nt], *v.t.* transplanter; (*fig.*) déplacer.

transplanting [træns'plɑ:ntiŋ, trænz'plɑ:ntiŋ], *n.* transplantation, *f.*

transport ['trænspɔ:t], *n.* transport, *m.*—[træns'pɔ:t], *v.t.* transporter; déporter (*forçat*).

transportation [trænspɔ:'teiʃən], *n.* transport, *m.*; déportation (*des forçats*), *f.*

transporter [træns'pɔ:tə], *n.* entrepreneur de transports; (pont) transbordeur, *m.*

transporting [træns'pɔ:tiŋ], *a.* ravissant, transportant.

transposal [træns'pouzl], *n.* transposition, *f.*

transpose [trænz'pouz], *v.t.* transposer.

transubstantiation [trænsəbstænʃi'eiʃən], *n.* transsubstantiation, *f.*

Transvaal ['trænzvɑ:l], **the.** le Transvaal, *m.*

transversal [trænz'və:sl], *a.* transversal.

transversely [trænz'və:sli], *adv.* en travers.

transverse [trænz'və:s], *a.* transverse, transversal.

trap [træp], *n.* trappe, *f.*, piège, *m.*; carriole (*véhicule*), *f.*—*v.t.* prendre au piège, attraper.

trap-door ['træpdɔ:], *n.* trappe, *f.*

trapeze [trə'pi:z], *n.* trapèze, *m.*

trapper ['træpə], *n.* trappeur, *m.*

trappings ['træpiŋz], *n.pl.* harnais, *m.*; (*fig.*) parure, *f.*, atours, *m.pl.*

traps [træps], *n.pl.* bagages, *m.pl.*

trash [træʃ], *n.* rebut, *m.*; camelote, *f.*; fatras (*écrits*), *m.*

trashy ['træʃi], *a.* de rebut, sans valeur.

travel [trævl], *v.t.* parcourir; faire (*distance etc.*).—*v.i.* voyager, être en voyage.—*n.* voyage, *m.*

traveller ['trævlə], *n.* voyageur; (*Comm.*) commis voyageur, *m.*; *traveller's cheque,* chèque de voyage, *m.*

travelling ['trævliŋ], *a.* voyageur, de voyage; ambulant (*itinérant*); *travelling expenses,* frais de déplacement, *m.pl.*; *travelling-case,* nécessaire de voyage, *m.*—*n.* voyage, *m.*, voyages, *m.pl.*

travelogue ['trævələg], *n.* film de tourisme, *m.*

traverse ['trævəs], *a.* oblique.—*n.* traverse, *f.* —*v.t.* traverser; (*Law*) nier.

travesty ['trævəsti], *n.* travestissement, *m.*; parodie, *f.*—*v.t.* travestir, parodier.

trawl [trɔ:l], *n.* chalut (*filet*), *m.*—*v.i.* pêcher au chalut.

trawler ['trɔ:lə], *n.* chalutier, *m.*

trawling ['trɔ:liŋ], *n.* pêche au chalut, *f.*

tray [trei], *n.* plateau, *m.*

treacherous ['tretʃərəs], *a.* traître, perfide.

treacherously ['tretʃərəsli], *adv.* en traître.

treachery ['tretʃəri], *n.* trahison, perfidie, *f.*

treacle [tri:kl], *n.* mélasse, *f.*

tread [tred], *v.t. irr.* fouler, écraser.—*v.i.* mettre le pied, marcher (*sur*); se poser (*pieds*).—*n.* pas, *m.*; marche (*d'escalier*), *f.*

treading ['trediŋ], *n.* pas, *m.*; marche, *f.*; foulage (*de raisins etc.*), *m.*

treadle [tredl], *n.* marche; pédale, *f.*

treadmill ['tredmil], *n.* *moulin de discipline, *m.*

treason [tri:zn], *n.* trahison, *f.*; *high treason,* lèse-majesté, *f.*

treasonable ['tri:znəbl], *a.* de trahison.

treasonably ['tri:znəbli], *adv.* par trahison, traîtreusement.

treasure ['treʒə], *n.* trésor, *m.*—*v.t.* garder, priser.

treasurer ['treʒərə], *n.* trésorier, *m.*

treasure-trove ['treʒətrouv], *n.* trésor trouvé, *m.*

treasury ['treʒəri], *n.* trésor, trésor public, *m.*, finances, *f.pl.*, trésorerie, *f.*

treat [tri:t], *n.* régal, festin, *m.*, (*fig.*) plaisir, *m.*—*v.t.* traiter (*de*).—*v.i.* traiter (*de*); négocier.

treatise ['tri:tis], *n.* traité (*de* ou sur), *m.*

treatment ['tri:tmənt], *n.* traitement, *m.*

treaty ['tri:ti], *n.* traité, *m.*

treble [trebl], *a.* triple; (*Mus.*) de dessus, soprano.—*n.* triple; (*Mus.*) dessus, soprano, *m.*—*v.t., v.i.* tripler.

trebling ['trebliŋ], *n.* triplement, *m.*

trebly ['trebli], *adv.* triplement, trois fois.

tree [tri:], *n.* arbre; embauchoir (*pour botte*), *m.*; (*fig.*) croix, *f.*

trefoil ['tri:foil], *n.* trèfle, *m.*

trellis ['trelis], *n.* treillis, treillage, *m.*

trellised ['trelist], *a.* treillissé.

tremble [trembl], *v.i.* trembler.

trembling ['trembliŋ], *a.* tremblant, tremblotant.—*n.* tremblement, *m.*

tremendous [tri'mendəs], *a.* terrible, épouvantable.

tremendously [tri'mendəsli], *adv.* terriblement.

tremor ['tremə], *n.* tremblement, *m.*; secousse, *f.*

tremulous ['tremjuləs], *a.* tremblant, (*fig.*) craintif.

tremulously ['tremjuləsli], *adv.* en tremblant, en tremblotant.

tremulousness ['tremjuləsnis], *n.* tremblotement, *m.*

trench [trentʃ], *n.* fossé, *m.*, tranchée; rigole (*entre sillons etc.*), *f.*—*v.t.* creuser.

trenchancy ['trentʃənsi], *n.* causticité, *f.*

trenchant ['trentʃənt], *a.* tranchant, caustique.

trencher ['trentʃə], *n.* tranchoir, tailloir, *m.*

trencherman ['trentʃəmən], *n.* (*pl.* -**men** [men]) gros mangeur, *m.*

trend [trend], *n.* direction, tendance, *f.*—*v.i.* se diriger, tendre (*vers*).

trepan [trə'pæn], *n.* (*Surg.*) trépan, *m.*—*v.t.* trépaner.

trepanning [trə'pæniŋ], *n.* trépanation *f.*

trepidation [trepi'deiʃən], *n.* trépidation, *f.*

trespass ['trespəs], *n.* violation de propriété, *f.*, délit, *m.*; (*Scripture*) offense, *f.*—*v.i.* violer la propriété; empiéter (*sur*); (*Scripture*) pécher; transgresser.

trespasser ['trespəsə], *n.* violateur du droit de propriété; (*Scripture*) pécheur, *m.*, pécheresse, *f.*

tress [tres], *n.* tresse, boucle, *f.*

trestle [tresl], *n.* tréteau, *m.*

trestle-bed ['treslbed], *n.* lit de sangle, *m.*

triad ['traiæd], *n.* triade, *f.*

trial ['traiəl], *a.* d'essai.—*n.* expérience, épreuve, *f.*, essai; (*Law*) procès, *m.*

triangle ['traiæŋgl], *n.* triangle, *m.*

triangular [trai'æŋgjulə], *a.* triangulaire.

tribal [traibl], *a.* tribal.

tribe [traib], *n.* tribu, peuplade; (*fig.*) race, *f.*

tribulation [tribju'leiʃən], *n.* tribulation, *f.*

tribunal [trai'bju:nl], *n.* tribunal, *m.*

tribune ['tribju:n], *n.* (*Rom. Hist.*) tribun, *m.*; tribune (*estrade*), *f.*

tributary ['tribjutəri], *a.* tributaire.—*n.* tributaire; affluent (*rivière*), *m.*

tribute ['tribju:t], *n.* tribut; (*fig.*) hommage, *m.*

trice (1) [trais], *n. in a trice*, en un clin d'œil.

trice (2) [trais], *v.t.* (*Naut.*) hisser.

trick [trik], *n.* tour, artifice, *m.*; (*Cards*) levée; ruse, finesse, *f.*; tic (*habitude*), *m.*; *nasty trick*, vilain tour; *to play someone a trick*, faire une niche *ou* jouer un tour à quelqu'un.—*v.t.* duper; tricher (*en jouant*); *to trick out*, parer, orner.

trickery ['trikəri], *n.* tromperie, fourberie, tricherie, *f.*

trickish ['trikiʃ], *a.* trompeur, fourbe, fin.

trickle [trikl], *v.i.* suinter, dégoutter.

trickling ['trikliŋ], *n.* écoulement, *m.*

trickster ['trikstə], *n.* fourbe, escroc, *m.*

tricky ['triki], *a.* fourbe, rusé; (*fig.*) compliqué; délicat (*à manier*).

tricolour ['traikʌlə], *n.* drapeau tricolore, *m.*

tricoloured ['traikʌləd], *a.* tricolore.

tricycle ['traisikl], *n.* tricycle, *m.*

trident ['traidənt], *n.* trident, *m.*

tried [traid], *a.* éprouvé.

triennial [trai'eniəl], *a.* triennal.—*n.* (*Bot.*) plante triennale, *f.*

triennially [trai'eniəli], *adv.* tous les trois ans.

trier ['traiə], *n.* (*Law*) juge; arbitre, *m.*; (*fig.*) épreuve, pierre de touche, *f.*

trifle [traifl], *n.* bagatelle; (*Cook.*) sorte de charlotte russe, *f.*—*v.i.* badiner; *to trifle with*, plaisanter avec, se moquer de.

trifler ['traiflə], *n.* personne frivole, *f.*

trifling ['traifliŋ], *a.* de rien, insignifiant, frivole.—*n.* frivolité, *f.*, badinage, *m.*

trigamy ['trigəmi], *n.* trigamie, *f.*

trigger ['trigə], *n.* détente, *f.*

trigonometry [trigə'nomətri], *n.* trigonométrie, *f.*

trilateral [trai'lætərəl], *a.* trilatéral.

trill [tril], *n.* trille, *m.*—*v.i.* triller.

trillion ['triljən], *n.* (*since* 1948) trillion; (*before* 1948) quintillion, *m.*

trilogy ['trilədʒi], *n.* trilogie, *f.*

trim [trim], *a.* soigné, coquet, bien mis, bien arrangé.—*n.* bon ordre, *m.*; assiette (*de bateau*), *f.*; orientement (*des voiles*); arrimage (*de cale*), *m.*—*v.t.* arranger, mettre en ordre; garnir, parer (*de*); émonder, tailler (*couper*); (*Naut.*) arrimer (*cargaison*); orienter (*voiles*).—*v.i.* (*Polit. slang*) balancer entre deux partis.

trimly ['trimli], *adv.* bien, gentiment, proprement.

trimmer ['trimə], *n.* (*Polit.*) opportuniste, *m.*, *f.*; (*Naut.*) soutier, *m.*

trimming ['trimiŋ], *n.* garniture; semonce; (*pl.*) parure (*de viande*), *f.*

trimness ['trimnis], *n.* air soigné, bon ordre, *m.*

Trinidad ['trinidæd]. (Île de la) Trinité, *f.*

Trinity ['triniti], *n.* Trinité, *f.*

trinket ['triŋkit], *n.* petit bijou, *m.*, breloque, *f.*

trinomial [trai'noumiəl], *a.* and *n.* trinôme, *m.*

trio ['tri:ou], *n.* trio, *m.*

trip [trip], *v.t.* renverser, faire tomber.—*v.i.* trébucher, faire un faux pas; fourcher (*la langue*); courir légèrement.—*n.* croc-en-jambe, faux pas, *m.*; excursion, *f.*, tour, voyage, *m.*

tripe [traip], *n.* tripes, *f.pl.*

triple [tripl], *a.* triple.—*v.t.* tripler.

triplet ['triplit], *n.* (*Pros.*) tercet; (*Mus.*) triolet, *m.*; (*pl.*) triplés, *m.pl.*

triplicate ['triplikit], *a.* triplé.—*n.* triplicata (*copie*), *f.*

tripod ['traipod], *n.* trépied, *m.*

tripper ['tripə], *n.* (*colloq.*) excursionniste, *m.*, *f.*

tripping ['tripiŋ], *a.* agile, léger.—*n.* croc en jambe, faux pas, *m.*; erreur, *f.*; pas léger, *m.*

trireme ['trairi:m], *n.* trirème, *f.*

trisect [trai'sekt], *v.t.* couper en trois.

trisyllabic [traisi'læbik], *a.* trissyllabe.

trisyllable [trai'siləbl], *n.* trissyllabe, *m.*

trite [trait], *a.* usé, banal, rebattu.

triteness ['traitnis], *n.* nature banale, trivialité, *f.*

Triton ['traitən]. Triton, *m.*

triumph ['traiəmf], *n.* triomphe, *m.*—*v.i.* triompher.

triumphal [trai'ʌmfl], *a.* triomphal.

triumphant [trai'ʌmfənt], *a.* triomphant.

triumphantly [trai'ʌmfəntli], *adv.* en triomphe.

triumvir [trai'ʌmvə], *n.* triumvir, *m.*

triumvirate [trai'ʌmvərit], *n.* triumvirat, *m.*

trivet ['trivit], *n.* trépied, *m.*

trivial

trivial ['triviəl], *a.* banal, insignifiant, sans importance.
triviality [trivi'æliti], *n.* insignifiance; banalité, *f.*
troat [trout], *n.* bramement, *m.*—*v.t.* bramer, raire (*cerf*).
trochaic [tro'keiik], *a.* trochaïque.
trochee ['trouki], *n.* trochée, *m.*
Trojan ['troudʒən], *a.* troyen.—*n.* Troyen, *m.*
troll [troul], *v.t.* rouler, tourner.
trolley, trolly ['trɔli], *n.* fardier, chariot; (*Elec.*) trolley, *m.*; **dinner trolley**, table roulante, *f.*
trolley-bus ['trɔlibʌs], *n.* trolleybus, *m.*
trollop ['trɔləp], *n.* souillon, *f.*
trombone [trɔm'boun], *n.* trombone, *m.*
troop [tru:p], *n.* troupe, bande, *f.*—*v.i.* s'attrouper, s'assembler.
trooper ['tru:pə], *n.* (*Mil.*) soldat à cheval, cavalier, *m.*
trophy ['troufi], *n.* trophée, *m.*
tropic ['trɔpik], *n.* tropique, *m.*
tropical ['trɔpikəl], *a.* tropical, des tropiques.
trot [trɔt], *n.* trot, *m.*—*v.i.* trotter, aller au trot; trottiner (*enfant*).
troth [trouθ], *n.* foi, *f.*; **by my troth!** ma foi!
trotter ['trɔtə], *n.* cheval de trot, trotteur, *m.*; (*pl.*) pieds de mouton, pieds de cochon, *m.pl.*
trotting ['trɔtiŋ], *a.* trotteur.—*n.* trot, *m.*
troubadour ['tru:bəduə], *n.* troubadour, *m.*
trouble ['trʌbl], *v.t.* agiter; troubler, déranger (*gêner*); tourmenter, affliger (*faire souffrir*); inquiéter (*préoccuper*).—*v.i.* s'inquiéter, se donner la peine (*de*).—*n.* trouble, *m.*; peine (*effort*), affliction, *f.*, souci, chagrin (*tristesse*); ennui (*difficulté*), *m.*; **it is not worth the trouble**, ce n'est pas la peine.
troubled ['trʌbld], *a.* inquiet, agité; trouble (*eau etc.*).
troublesome ['trʌblsəm], *a.* ennuyeux, incommode; fatigant, fâcheux.
troublesomeness ['trʌblsəmnis], *n.* ennui, embarras, *m.*, gêne, *f.*
*troublous ['trʌbləs], *a.* troublé, agité, orageux.
trough [trɔf], *n.* auge, huche, *f.*; (*Cook.*) pétrin; auget, abreuvoir (*pour boire*), *m.*
trounce [trauns], *v.t.* rosser, étriller.
trouncing ['traunsiŋ], *n.* raclée, *f.*, étrillage, *m.*
trouser-press ['trauzəpres], *n.* presse-pantalon, *m.*
trousers ['trauzəz], *n.pl.* pantalon, *m.*
trousseau ['tru:sou], *n.* trousseau, *m.*
trout [traut], *n.* truite, *f.*
trowel ['trauəl], *n.* truelle, *f.*
Troy [trɔi], Troie, *f.*
troy-weight ['trɔiweit], *n.* troy (*poids de douze onces à la livre*), *m.*
truant ['tru:ənt], *n.* fainéant, vagabond, *m.*; **to play truant**, faire l'école buissonnière.
truce [tru:s], *n.* trêve, *f.*
truck [trʌk], *n.* fardier, chariot (*charrette*); (*Am.*) camion; (*Rail.*) wagon, *m.*—*v.t.* troquer.
truckle ['trʌkl], *n.* roulette, *f.*—*v.i.* ramper s'abaisser (*devant*).
truckle-bed ['trʌklbed], *n.* grabat, *m.*
truckling ['trʌkliŋ], *n.* soumission, *f.*, abaissement, *m.*

truculence ['trʌkjuləns], *n.* férocité, truculence, *f.*
truculent ['trʌkjulənt], *a.* brutal, féroce, farouche.
trudge [trʌdʒ], *n.* marche pénible, *f.*—*v.i.* clopiner, marcher péniblement.
true [tru:], *a.* vrai, véritable; fidèle (*véridique*); exact (*juste*); loyal (*honnête*); droit (*vertueux*); **to come true**, se réaliser.—*int.* c'est vrai! c'est juste!—*adv.* juste (*précisément*).—*v.t.* ajuster.
true-bred ['tru:bred], *a.* de bonne race, pur sang; (*fig.*) accompli.
true-hearted ['tru:'hɑ:tid], *a.* au cœur sincère.
trueness ['tru:nis], *n.* fidélité; justesse, *f.*
truffle ['trʌfl], *n.* truffe, *f.*; **to stuff with truffles**, truffer.
truism ['tru:izm], *n.* truisme, *m.*
truly ['tru:li], *adv.* vraiment, véritablement.
trump [trʌmp], *n.* trompe, trompette, *f.*; (*Cards.*) atout, *m.*—*v.t.* jouer atout, couper.
trumpery ['trʌmpəri], *a.* sans valeur, mesquin.—*n.* rebut, *m.*, blague, *f.*
trumpet ['trʌmpit], *n.* trompette, *f.*—*v.t.* proclamer.—*v.i.* barrir (*éléphant*).
trumpet-call ['trʌmpitkɔ:l], *n.* coup de trompette, *m.*
trumpeter ['trʌmpitə], *n.* trompette, *m.*
truncate [trʌŋ'keit], *v.t.* tronquer.
truncheon ['trʌntʃən], *n.* bâton, *m.*; matraque, *f.*
trundle [trʌndl], *v.t.* rouler.
trunk [trʌŋk], *n.* tronc, *m.*; malle (*boîte*); trompe (*d'éléphant etc.*), *f.*; (*Sculp.*) torse, *m.*
trunk-call ['trʌŋkkɔ:l], *n.* (*Teleph.*) appel interurbain, *m.*
trunk-road ['trʌŋkroud], *n.* route à grande circulation, *f.*
trunnion ['trʌnjən], *n.* tourillon, *m.*
truss [trʌs], *n.* botte (*de foin etc.*), *f.*; paquet; (*Surg.*) bandage herniaire, *m.*—*v.t.* trousser (*une poule*); lier (*foin*).
trust [trʌst], *n.* confiance (*en*), *f.*; dépôt, *m.*; garde (*charge*), *f.*; crédit; (*Law*) fidéicommis; (*Comm.*) trust, syndicat, *m.*—*v.t.* se fier à, se confier à; faire crédit à (*en matière d'argent*).—*v.i.* avoir confiance (*en ou dans*); s'attendre (à).
trust-deed ['trʌstdi:d], *n.* acte fiduciaire, *m.*
trusted ['trʌstid], *a.* de confiance.
trustee [trʌs'ti:], *n.* gardien, *m.*, dépositaire; (*Law*) fidéicommissaire, *m.*, *f.*
trusteeship [trʌs'ti:ʃip], *n.* administration; tutelle, *f.*, (*Law*) fidéicommis, *m.*
trustiness ['trʌstinis], *n.* fidélité, loyauté, *f.*
trusting ['trʌstiŋ], *a.* plein de confiance.
trustworthiness ['trʌstwə:ðinis], *n.* fidélité (*personne*); exactitude (*des nouvelles etc.*), *f.*
trustworthy ['trʌstwə:ði], *a.* digne de confiance; exact (*nouvelles*).
trusty ['trʌsti], *a.* sûr, fidèle, loyal.
truth [tru:θ], *n.* vérité, *f.*, vrai, *m.*; **to tell the truth . . .**, à vrai dire . . .
truthful ['tru:θful], *a.* véridique, vrai.
truthfully ['tru:θfuli], *adv.* véridiquement, avec vérité.
truthfulness ['tru:θfulnis], *n.* véracité, *f.*
try [trai], *v.t.* essayer, mettre à l'épreuve; tenter (*se prêter à*); (*Law*) juger.—*v.i.* essayer, tâcher (*de*).—*n.* essai, *m.*

604

trying ['traiiŋ], a. difficile, pénible.
*tryst [traist], n. rendez-vous, m.
Tsar [zɑː], n. Tsar, m.
Tsarina [zɑːˈriːnə], n. Tsarine, f.
tsetse ['tsetsi], n. mouche tsé-tsé, f.
tub [tʌb], n. cuve, f., baquet; bain (moderne), m.—v.t. encuver; (Gard.) encaisser.
tuba ['tjuːbə], n. tuba, m.; contrebasse à vent, f.
tubby ['tʌbi], a. gros, obèse.
tube [tjuːb], n. tube; (Anat.) conduit, canal; (Rail.) métro, m.; inner tube, chambre à air, f.
tuber ['tjuːbə], n. tubercule, m.
tubercular [tjuˈbəːkjulə], a. tuberculeux.
tuberculosis [tjubəːkjuˈlousis], n. tuberculose, f.
tuberose ['tjuːbərous], a. tubéreux.—n. tubéreuse, f.
tuberous ['tjuːbərəs], a. tubéreux.
tubular ['tjuːbjulə], a. tubulaire.
tuck [tʌk], n. pli, m.—v.t. plisser; serrer; retrousser.
tucker ['tʌkə], n. chemisette, collerette, f.
Tuesday ['tjuːzd(e)i]. mardi, m.; Shrove Tuesday, mardi gras.
tuft [tʌft], n. touffe (d'herbe ou de cheveux); huppe (d'oiseau), f.
tufted ['tʌftid], a. touffu; huppé (oiseau).
tug [tʌg], v.t. tirer avec effort; remorquer (to tow).—n. tiraillement; remorqueur (bateau), m.
tuition [tjuˈiʃən], n. instruction, f., enseignement, m.
tulip ['tjuːlip], n. tulipe, f.
tulle [tjuːl], n. tulle, m.
tumble ['tʌmbl], n. culbute, chute, f.—v.t. culbuter.—v.i. tomber; rouler (descendre en roulant); dégringoler (se tourner).
tumbledown ['tʌmbldaun], a. croulant, délabré.
tumbler ['tʌmblə], n. verre sans pied; gobelet; culbutant (pigeon), m.
tumblerful ['tʌmbləful], n. plein un grand verre, m.
tumbril ['tʌmbril], tumbrel ['tʌmbrəl], n. tombereau, m.
tumefaction [tjuːmiˈfækʃən], n. tuméfaction, f.
tumefy ['tjuːmifai], v.t. tuméfier.—v.i. se tuméfier.
tumid ['tjuːmid], a. enflé, gonflé; (fig.) boursouflé.
tumidity [tjuˈmiditi], tumidness ['tjuːmidnis], n. enflure; (fig.) turgescence, f.
tumour ['tjuːmə], n. tumeur, f.
tumular ['tjuːmjulə], a. en monticule.
tumult ['tjuːmʌlt], n. tumulte; trouble, m.
tumultuous [tjuˈmʌltjuəs], a. tumultueux, turbulent, agité.
tumultuousness [tjuˈmʌltjuəsnis], n. turbulence, f.
tun [tʌn], n. tonneau, fût, m.; cuve, f.
tunable ['tjuːnəbl], a. accordable.
tundra ['tʌndrə], n. toundra, f.
tune [tjuːn], n. air; accord, m.; (fig.) harmonie, humeur, f.; in tune, d'accord; out of tune, faux.—v.t. accorder, mettre d'accord. —v.i. (Rad.) to tune in, accrocher (un poste).
tuneful ['tjuːnful], a. harmonieux, mélodieux.

tuneless ['tjuːnlis], a. discordant.
tuner ['tjuːnə], n. accordeur, m.
tungsten ['tʌŋstən], n. tungstène, m.
tunic ['tjuːnik], n. tunique, f.
tuning ['tjuːniŋ], n. accord, m., action d'accorder, f.
tuning-fork ['tjuːniŋfɔːk], n. diapason, m.
tuning-hammer ['tjuːniŋhæmə], n. accordoir, m.
Tunisia [tjuˈniziə]. la Tunisie, f.
Tunisian [tjuˈniziən], a. tunisien.—n. Tunisien (personne), m.
tunnel [tʌnl], n. tunnel, passage souterrain, m. —v.t. percer un tunnel dans.
tunnelling ['tʌnəliŋ], n. construction de tunnels, f.
tunny ['tʌni], n. (Ichth.) thon, m.
turban ['təːbən], n. turban, m.
turbid ['təːbid], a. trouble, bourbeux.
turbidity [təːˈbiditi], turbidness ['təːbidnis], n. état bourbeux, état trouble, m.
turbine ['təːbin, 'təːbain], n. turbine, f.
turbo-prop ['təːboprɔp], a. (Av.) à turbo-propulseur.
turbot ['təːbət], n. turbot, m.
turbulence ['təːbjuləns], turbulency ['təːbjulənsi], n. turbulence, f., tumulte, m.
turbulent ['təːbjulənt], a. tumultueux, turbulent.
turbulently ['təːbjuləntli], adv. tumultueusement.
tureen [tjuˈriːn], n. soupière, f.
turf [təːf], n. gazon, m.; motte de gazon; tourbe (combustible), f.; (fig.) turf, m.—v.t. gazonner.
turfing ['təːfiŋ], n. gazonnement, m.
turf-moss ['təːfmɔs], turf-pit ['təːfpit], n. tourbière, f.
turfy ['təːfi], a. gazonné; tourbeux.
turgid ['təːdʒid], a. gonflé; boursouflé.
turgidity [təˈdʒiditi], turgidness ['təːdʒidnis], n. turgescence; (fig.) emphase (de style), f.
Turk [təːk], n. Turc (personne), m.
Turkey ['təːki]. la Turquie, f.
turkey ['təːki], n. dindon, m.; hen-turkey, dinde, f.
Turkish ['təːkiʃ], a. de Turquie, turc.—n. turc (langue), m.
turmoil ['təːmɔil], n. tumulte, m., agitation, f.
turn [təːn], v.t. tourner, faire tourner; faire pencher (la balance); retourner (vêtement etc.); changer, convertir (transformer); traduire (en une autre langue); soulever (l'estomac); émousser (le tranchant); (fig.) rouler (dans la tête); to turn aside, détourner, écarter (de); to turn away, renvoyer, congédier; to turn back, faire retourner; to turn down, rabattre (un col); refuser; to turn in, tourner en dedans; to turn into, changer en; to turn off, couper (vapeur), fermer (robinet); to turn on, donner (vapeur), ouvrir (robinet); to turn out, mettre dehors; éteindre (lumière); to turn over, retourner, feuilleter (pages d'un livre); to turn tail, prendre la fuite; to turn up, retrousser.—v.i. tourner, se tourner; se retourner (vers); se détourner (s'écarter); se changer (en); devenir, se faire; to turn back, rebrousser chemin; to turn from, s'éloigner de; to turn in, se coucher (aller au lit); to turn round, tourner, se

tourner, se retourner; *to turn to*, s'adresser à; *to turn up*, se retrousser; arriver (*se passer*).—*n.* tour; coude, détour (*tournant*); service; changement, *m.*; occasion; tournure (*d'esprit*), *f.*; trait (*de balance*), *m.*; *a bad turn*, un mauvais tour; *a good turn*, un service; *by turns*, *in turns*, à tour de rôle.

turncoat ['təːnkout], *n.* renégat, *m.*

turn-cock ['təːnkɔk], *n.* fontainier, *m.*

turner ['təːnə], *n.* tourneur, *m.*

turnery ['təːnəri], *n.* art du tourneur, *m.*

turning ['təːniŋ], *n.* tournant (*de route etc.*); (*Carp.*) tournage, *m.*

turning-lathe ['təːniŋleið], *n.* tour, *m.*

turning-point ['təːniŋpɔint], *n.* point décisif, moment critique, *m.*

turnip ['təːnip], *n.* navet, *m.*

turnkey ['təːnkiː], *n.* guichetier, porte-clefs, *m.*

turn-out ['təːnaut], *n.* équipage, *m.*; tenue, *f.*

turn-over ['təːnouvə], *n.* chiffre d'affaires; chausson (*pâte*), *m.*

turnpike ['təːnpaik], *n.* barrière de péage, *f.*, tourniquet, *m.*

turnspit ['təːnspit], *n.* tournebroche, *m.*

turnstile ['təːnstail], *n.* tourniquet, *m.*

turn-table ['təːnteibl], *n.* plaque tournante; platine, *f.*

turn-up ['təːnʌp], *n.* revers (*de pantalon*), *m.*

turpentine ['təːpəntain], *n.* térébenthine, *f.*

turpitude ['təːpitjuːd], *n.* turpitude, *f.*

turquoise ['təːkwɔiz], *n.* turquoise, *f.*

turret ['tʌrit], *n.* tourelle, *f.*

turreted ['tʌritid], *a.* garni de tourelles.

turtle [təːtl], *n.* tortue de mer, *f.*; *to turn turtle*, chavirer (*bateau*), capoter (*voiture*).

turtle-dove ['təːtldʌv], *n.* tourterelle, *f.*

Tuscan ['tʌskən], *a.* toscan.—*n.* Toscan (*personne*), *m.*

Tuscany ['tʌskəni], la Toscane, *f.*

tush! [tʌʃ], *int.* bah! fi donc!

tusk [tʌsk], *n.* défense (*d'éléphant*), *f.*; croc (*dent*), *m.*

tussle [tʌsl], *n.* lutte, bagarre, *f.*

tut! [tʌt], *int.* bah! allons donc!

tutelage ['tjuːtilidʒ], *n.* tutelle, *f.*

tutor ['tjuːtə], *n.* précepteur (*dans une famille*); (*Univ.*) maître-assistant, *m.*—*v.t.* instruire, enseigner.

tutorial [tjuːˈtɔːriəl], *a.* de précepteur.

tutoring ['tjuːtəriŋ], *n.* instruction, *f.*

tutorship ['tjuːtəʃip], *n.* préceptorat, *m.*

twaddle [twɔdl], *n.* bavardage, caquetage, *m.*

*twain [twein], *a.* and *n.* deux, *m.*

twang [twæŋ], *n.* son sec (*d'une corde qui vibre*); accent nasillard (*voix*), *m.*—*v.t.* faire résonner, faire vibrer.—*v.i.* résonner, nasiller.

tweak [twiːk], *v.t.* pincer (*en tordant*).

tweezers ['twiːzəz], *n.pl.* pinces à épiler (*pour poils*), *f.pl.*

twelfth [twelfθ], *a.* douzième; douze (*du mois, des rois etc.*), *m.*; *Twelfth Night*, jour des Rois, *m.*—*n.* douzième (*fraction*), *m.*

twelve [twelv], *a.* and *n.* douze, *m.*; *twelve o'clock*, midi (*noon*), minuit (*midnight*), *m.*

twelvemonth ['twelvmʌnθ], *n.* an, *m.*, année, *f.*

twentieth ['twentiəθ], *a.* vingtième; vingt (*du mois etc.*).—*n.* vingtième (*fraction*), *m.*

twenty ['twenti], *a.* and *n.* vingt, *m.*

twenty-first ['twentiˈfəːst], *a.* vingt et unième; vingt et un (*du mois etc.*).

twice [twais], *adv.* deux fois.

twig [twig], *n.* brindille, ramille, *f.*

twilight ['twailait], *a.* crépusculaire.—*n.* crépuscule, *m.*

twill [twil], *n.* étoffe croisée, *f.*

twin [twin], *a.* jumeau; jumelé; (*Bot.*) double, géminé.—*n.* jumeau, *m.*, jumelle, *f.*

twine [twain], *n.* ficelle, *f.*—*v.t.* retordre; enlacer.—*v.i.* s'entrelacer, s'enrouler.

twinge [twindʒ], *n.* élancement; remords (*de conscience*), *m.*—*v.i.* élancer; (*fig.*) torturer.

twinkle [twiŋkl], *v.i.* étinceler.

twinkling ['twiŋkliŋ], *a.* étincelant, scintillant.—*n.* scintillement, clignotement (*des yeux*), *m.*; *in the twinkling of an eye*, en un clin d'œil.

twirl [twəːl], *v.t.* faire tournoyer; friser (*favoris*).—*v.i.* tournoyer, tourner rapidement.—*n.* tournoiement, *m.*; pirouette, *f.*

twist [twist], *v.t.* tordre; tortiller, retordre; cercler, entourer; enlacer (*entortiller*); (*fig.*) pervertir (*dénaturer*).—*v.i.* se tordre, s'entrelacer, s'enlacer, s'enrouler.—*n.* cordon, *m.*, corde, *f.*; tortillon (*de papier*), *m.*; carotte (*de tabac*), *f.*

twisted ['twistid], *a.* tordu; (*fig.*) perverti, défiguré, dénaturé.

twisting ['twistiŋ], *a.* tortueux.—*n.* tordage; tortillement, *m.*

twitch [twitʃ], *n.* saccade, *f.*; tic (*contraction spasmodique*); tiraillement (*de douleur*), *m.*—*v.t.* tirer brusquement; crisper.—*v.i.* se contracter nerveusement.

twitching ['twitʃiŋ], *n.* saccade, crispation (*des muscles etc.*), *f.*; tiraillement (*de douleur*), *m.*

twitter ['twitə], *v.t.*, *v.i.* gazouiller.—*n.* gazouillement, *m.*

two [tuː], *a.* and *n.* deux, *m.*

two-edged ['tuːedʒd], *a.* à deux tranchants.

twofold ['tuːfould], *a.* double.—*adv.* doublement, deux fois.

two-stroke ['tuːstrouk], *a.* à deux temps.

tycoon [taiˈkuːn], *n.* taïcoun; (*fam.*) brasseur d'affaires, manitou, *m.*

type [taip], *n.* type; (*Print.*) caractère; (*pop.*) type, *m.*—*v.t.* [TYPEWRITE].

typewrite ['taiprait], *v.t.* écrire à la machine, dactylographier, taper.

typewriter ['taipraitə], *n.* machine à écrire, *f.*

typewritten ['taipritn], *a.* tapé à la machine.

typhoid ['taifɔid], *a.* typhoïde.

typhoon [taiˈfuːn], *n.* typhon, *m.*, trombe, *f.*

typhus ['taifəs], *n.* typhus, *m.*

typical ['tipikl], *a.* typique.

typically ['tipikli], *adv.* d'une manière typique.

typify ['tipifai], *v.t.* symboliser.

typing ['taipiŋ], *n.* dactylographie, (*fam.*) dactylo, *f.*

typist ['taipist], *n.* dactylographe, (*fam.*) dactylo, *m.*, *f.*

typography [taiˈpɔgrəfi], *n.* typographie, *f.*

tyrannical [tiˈrænikl], *a.* tyrannique.

tyrannically [tiˈrænikli], *adv.* tyranniquement.

tyrannize ['tirənaiz], *v.i.* faire le tyran; *to tyrannize over*, tyranniser.

tyranny ['tirəni], n. tyrannie, f.
tyrant ['taiərənt], n. tyran, m.
tyre ['taiə], n. pneu (de roue), m.
tyro ['taiərou], n. novice, débutant, m.
Tzar [TSAR].

U

U, u [ju:]. vingt et unième lettre de l'alphabet, m.
ubiquitous [ju'bikwitəs], a. omniprésent.
ubiquity [ju'bikwiti], n. ubiquité, f.
udder ['ʌdə], n. mamelle, f., pis, m.
ugh! [u:x, u:h, ʌx, uf], int. pouah!
ugliness ['ʌglinis], n. laideur, f.
ugly ['ʌgli], a. laid, vilain.
Ukraine [ju'krein], the. l'Ukraine, f.
Ukrainian [ju'kreiniən], a. ukrainien.—n. Ukrainien (personne), m.
ukulele [ju:kə'leili], n. ukulélé, m.
ulcer ['ʌlsə], n. ulcère, m.
ulcerate ['ʌlsəreit], v.t. ulcérer.—v.i. s'ulcérer.
ulcerated ['ʌlsəreitid], a. ulcéré.
ulceration [ʌlsə'reiʃən], n. ulcération, f.
ulcerous ['ʌlsərəs], a. ulcéreux.
ullage ['ʌlidʒ], n. vidange, f.
ulterior [ʌl'tiəriə], a. ultérieur; *without ulterior motive*, sans arrière-pensée.
ultimate ['ʌltimit], a. dernier; extrême.
ultimately ['ʌltimitli], adv. finalement, à la fin.
ultimatum [ʌlti'meitəm], n. (pl. **ultimata** [ʌlti'meitə]) ultimatum, m.
ultimo ['ʌltimou], adv. (abbr. **ult.** [ʌlt]) du mois dernier.
ultra ['ʌltrə], n. ultra, m.
ultramarine [ʌltrəmə'ri:n], a. d'outremer.—n. outremer, m.
ululate ['ju:ljuleit], v.i. ululer.
Ulysses [ju:'lisi:z]. Ulysse, m.
umber ['ʌmbə], n. (Paint.) terre d'ombre, f.
umbilical [ʌm'bilikl], a. ombilical.
umbrage ['ʌmbridʒ], n. ombrage, m.
umbrella [ʌm'brelə], n. parapluie, m.; *umbrella-stand*, porte-parapluies, m.inv.
umpire ['ʌmpaiə], n. arbitre, m.—v.t., v.i. arbitrer.
unabashed [ʌnə'bæʃt], a. sans être confus.
unabated [ʌnə'beitid], a. sans diminution.
unable [ʌn'eibl], a. incapable (de); *to be unable to*, ne pas pouvoir.
unabridged [ʌnə'bridʒd], a. non abrégé; en entier.
unacceptable [ʌnək'septəbl], a. inacceptable.
unaccommodating [ʌnə'kɔmədeitiŋ], a. peu accommodant.
unaccompanied [ʌnə'kʌmpənid], a. seul, sans suite.
unaccountable [ʌnə'kauntəbl], a. inexplicable, inconcevable.
unaccountably [ʌnə'kauntəbli], adv. inconcevablement.
unaccustomed [ʌnə'kʌstəmd], a. inaccoutumé (à); peu habitué.

unacknowledged [ʌnək'nɔlidʒd], a. non reconnu; sans réponse (lettre).
unacquainted [ʌnə'kweintid], a. étranger (à); peu familier (avec).
unadopted [ʌnə'dɔptid], a. non adopté.
unadorned [ʌnə'dɔ:nd], a. sans ornement.
unadulterated [ʌnə'dʌltəreitid], a. pur, non frelaté.
unadvisable [ʌnəd'vaizəbl], a. peu sage, inopportun.
unadvised [ʌnəd'vaizd], a. malavisé; imprudent (rash).
unadvisedly [ʌnəd'vaizidli], adv. inconsidérément.
unaffected [ʌnə'fektid], a. sans affectation; insensible (peu ému).
unaffectedly [ʌnə'fektidli], adv. sans affectation.
unafraid [ʌnə'freid], a. sans peur.
unaided [ʌn'eidid], a. seul, sans aide.
unallayed [ʌnə'leid], a. non apaisé.
unallowable [ʌnə'lauəbl], a. non permis; inadmissible.
unalloyed [ʌnə'lɔid], a. pur, sans alliage, sans mélange.
unalterable [ʌn'ɔ:ltərəbl], a. inaltérable, invariable.
unalterably [ʌn'ɔ:ltərəbli], adv. immuablement.
unambitious [ʌnæm'biʃəs], a. sans ambition.
unanimity [ju:nə'nimiti], n. unanimité, f.
unanimous [ju'næniməs], a. unanime.
unanimously [ju'næniməsli], adv. unanimement, à l'unanimité.
unanswerable [ʌn'ɑ:nsərəbl], a. incontestable.
unanswered [ʌn'ɑ:nsəd], a. sans réponse.
unappeasable [ʌnə'pi:zəbl], a. implacable.
unappetizing [ʌn'æpitaiziŋ], a. peu appétissant.
unappreciated [ʌnə'pri:ʃieitid], a. inapprécié.
unapproachable [ʌnə'proutʃəbl], a. inaccessible, inabordable.
unarmed [ʌn'ɑ:md], a. sans armes.
unascertainable [ʌnæsə'teinəbl], a. qu'on ne peut constater.
unashamed [ʌnə'ʃeimd], a. sans honte.
unasked [ʌn'ɑ:skt], a. sans être invité; spontané.—adv. spontanément.
unaspiring [ʌnə'spaiəriŋ], a. sans ambition.
unassailable [ʌnə'seiləbl], a. hors d'atteinte; inattaquable, irréfutable.
unassisted [ʌnə'sistid], a. sans aide.
unassuming [ʌnə'sju:miŋ], a. sans prétention, modeste.
unattached [ʌnə'tætʃt], a. sans être attaché (à); en disponibilité.
unattainable [ʌnə'teinəbl], a. inaccessible.
unattended [ʌnə'tendid], a. seul, sans suite.
unattested [ʌnə'testid], a. non attesté.
unattractive [ʌnə'træktiv], a. peu attrayant, sans attrait.
unauthenticated [ʌnɔ:'θentikeitid], a. dont l'authenticité n'est pas prouvée.
unauthorized [ʌn'ɔ:θəraizd], a. sans autorisation; illicite, illégal (chose).
unavailable [ʌnə'veiləbl], a. non valable; inutilisable (billet); indisponible (fonds, personne); qu'on ne peut se procurer (chose).
unavailing [ʌnə'veiliŋ], a. inutile, inefficace.
unavenged [ʌnə'vendʒd], a. impuni, non vengé.

unavoidable [ʌnəˈvɔidebl], *a.* inévitable.
unavoidably [ʌnəˈvɔidəbli], *adv.* inévitablement.
unaware [ʌnəˈwɛə], *a.* ignorant; *to be unaware of,* ignorer.
unawares [ʌnəˈwɛəz], *adv.* à l'improviste; à son insu (*sans s'en rendre compte*); *to be taken unawares,* être pris au dépourvu.
unbalanced [ʌnˈbælənst], *a.* mal équilibré.
unbearable [ʌnˈbɛərəbl], *a.* insupportable, intolérable.
unbearably [ʌnˈbɛərəbli], *adv.* insupportablement.
unbeatable [ʌnˈbiːtəbl], *a.* invincible.
unbeaten [ʌnˈbiːtn], *a.* invaincu.
unbecoming [ʌnbiˈkʌmiŋ], *a.* peu convenable, malséant; qui ne va pas bien (*vêtement*).
unbecomingly [ʌnbiˈkʌmiŋli], *adv.* d'une manière peu séante.
unbefitting [ʌnbiˈfitiŋ], *a.* qui ne convient pas, peu propre.
unbeknown [ʌnbiˈnoun], *a.* inconnu; *unbeknown to me,* à mon insu.
unbelief [ʌnbiˈliːf], *n.* incrédulité, incroyance, *f.*
unbelievable [ʌnbiˈliːvəbl], *a.* incroyable.
unbeliever [ʌnbiˈliːvə], *n.* incrédule; sceptique, *m., f.*
unbelieving [ʌnbiˈliːviŋ], *a.* incrédule; sceptique.
unbend [ʌnˈbend], *v.t. irr.* (*conjug. like* BEND) détendre, relâcher; débander (*l'arc*); (*fig.*) délasser (*l'esprit*).—*v.i.* se détendre.
unbending [ʌnˈbendiŋ], *a.* inflexible.
unbiased [ʌnˈbaiəst], *a.* sans prévention, impartial.
unbidden [ʌnˈbidn], *a.* sans être invité.
unbind [ʌnˈbaind], *v.t. irr.* (*conjug. like* BIND) délier, détacher.
unbleached [ʌnˈbliːtʃt], *a.* écru.
unblemished [ʌnˈblemiʃt], *a.* sans tache.
unblushing [ʌnˈblʌʃiŋ], *a.* qui ne rougit point, éhonté, sans vergogne.
unblushingly [ʌnˈblʌʃiŋli], *adv.* sans rougir.
unbolt [ʌnˈboult], *v.t.* tirer les verrous de, ouvrir.
unborn [ʌnˈbɔːn], *a.* encore à naître; futur, à venir (*chose*).
unbosom [ʌnˈbuzm], *v.t. to unbosom oneself,* ouvrir son cœur.
unbound [ʌnˈbaund], *a.* délié; non relié (*livre*).
unbounded [ʌnˈbaundid], *a.* illimité, infini.
unbreakable [ʌnˈbreikəbl], *a.* incassable.
unbridled [ʌnˈbraidld], *a.* débridé; (*fig.*) effréné.
unbroken [ʌnˈbroukn], *a.* non rompu; continu (*ininterrompu*); indompté (*non vaincu*); intact (*non violé*); non dressé (*animal*).
unbrotherly [ʌnˈbrʌðəli], *a.* peu fraternel.
unbuckle [ʌnˈbakl], *v.t.* déboucler.
unburden [ʌnˈbəːdn], *v.t.* décharger; *to unburden oneself,* ouvrir son cœur.
unburied [ʌnˈberid], *a.* sans sépulture.
unbusinesslike [ʌnˈbiznislaik], *a.* peu pratique.
unbutton [ʌnˈbatn], *v.t.* déboutonner.
uncalled [ʌnˈkɔːld], *a.* sans être appelé; *uncalled for,* sans être demandé; gratuit (*superflu*); peu convenable (*mal élevé*); non mérité (*injuste*).

uncanny [ʌnˈkæni], *a.* mystérieux, surnaturel.
uncared-for [ʌnˈkɛədfɔː], *a.* négligé.
unceasing [ʌnˈsiːsiŋ], *a.* incessant, sans cesse.
unceasingly [ʌnˈsiːsiŋli], *adv.* continuellement, sans cesse.
uncensored [ʌnˈsensəd], *a.* non expurgé.
unceremonious [ʌnseriˈmouniəs], *a.* peu cérémonieux; sans façon.
unceremoniously [ʌnseriˈmouniəsli], *adv.* sans cérémonie, sans façon.
uncertain [ʌnˈsəːtin], *a.* incertain, peu sûr.
uncertainty [ʌnˈsəːtinti], *n.* incertitude, *f.*
uncertificated [ʌnsəˈtifikətid], *a.* non diplômé (*instituteur*).
unchain [ʌnˈtʃein], *v.t.* déchaîner.
unchallenged [ʌnˈtʃælindʒd], *a.* indisputé.
unchangeable [ʌnˈtʃeindʒəbl], *a.* inaltérable, immuable.
unchanged [ʌnˈtʃeindʒd], *a.* inchangé, toujours le même.
unchanging [ʌnˈtʃeindʒiŋ], *a.* invariable, constant.
uncharitable [ʌnˈtʃæritəbl], *a.* peu charitable.
uncharitableness [ʌnˈtʃæritəblnis], *n.* manque de charité, *m.*
uncharitably [ʌnˈtʃæritəbli], *adv.* sans charité.
uncharted [ʌnˈtʃɑːtid], *a.* inexploré.
unchaste [ʌnˈtʃeist], *a.* incontinent, impudique.
unchecked [ʌnˈtʃekt], *a.* non réprimé, sans frein; non vérifié.
unchivalrous [ʌnˈʃivlrəs], *a.* peu chevaleresque.
unchristian [ʌnˈkristiən], *a.* peu chrétien.
uncircumcised [ʌnˈsəːkəmsaizd], *a.* incirconcis.
uncivil [ʌnˈsivil], *a.* malhonnête, impoli.
uncivilized [ʌnˈsivilaizd], *a.* peu civilisé, barbare.
uncivilly [ʌnˈsivili], *adv.* malhonnêtement, impoliment.
unclaimed [ʌnˈkleimd], *a.* non réclamé.
unclasp [ʌnˈklɑːsp], *v.t.* dégrafer, défaire.
unclassified [ʌnˈklæsifaid], *a.* non classé.
uncle [ʌŋkl], *n.* oncle, *m.*; (*slang*) **at uncle's,** chez ma tante (*le prêteur sur gage*).
unclean [ʌnˈkliːn], *a.* malpropre, sale; impudique (*obscène*); impur.
uncleanliness [ʌnˈklenlinis], **uncleanness** [ʌnˈkliːnnis], *n.* saleté; (*fig.*) impureté, *f.*
unclench [ʌnˈklentʃ], *v.t.* ouvrir, desserrer.
uncloak [ʌnˈklouk], *v.t.* dévoiler.
unclose [ʌnˈklouz], *v.t.* ouvrir.
unclosed [ʌnˈklouzd], *a.* non fermé, ouvert.
unclothe [ʌnˈklouð], *v.t.* déshabiller.
unclothed [ʌnˈklouðd], *a.* déshabillé, nu.
unclouded [ʌnˈklaudid], *a.* sans nuage, serein.
uncock [ʌnˈkok], *v.t.* désarmer (*fusil etc.*).
uncoil [ʌnˈkɔil], *v.t.* dérouler.—*v.i.* se dérouler.
uncombed [ʌnˈkoumd], *a.* mal peigné, ébouriffé.
uncomfortable [ʌnˈkʌmfətəbl], *a.* peu confortable, incommode; gêné (*personne*).
uncomfortably [ʌnˈkʌmfətəbli], *adv.* peu confortablement; mal à l'aise.
uncommitted [ʌnkəˈmitid], *a.* non commis; non engagé, libre.

uncommon [ʌn'kɔmən], *a.* peu commun; rare.

uncommonly [ʌn'kɔmənli], *adv.* rarement; infiniment (*singulièrement*).

uncommunicative [ʌnkə'mjuːnikətiv], *a.* peu communicatif, réservé.

uncomplaining [ʌnkəm'pleiniŋ], *a.* sans plainte, résigné.

uncomplainingly [ʌnkəm'pleiniŋli], *adv.* sans se plaindre, sans plainte.

uncompleted [ʌnkəm'pliːtid], *a.* inachevé, incomplet.

uncomplimentary [ʌnkɔmpli'mentəri], *a.* peu flatteur.

uncompromising [ʌn'kɔmprəmaiziŋ], *a.* peu accommodant, intransigeant.

unconcern [ʌnkən'səːn], *n.* insouciance, indifférence, *f.*

unconcerned [ʌnkən'səːnd], *a.* indifférent, insouciant.

unconcernedly [ʌnkən'səːnidli], *adv.* avec indifférence.

unconditional [ʌnkən'diʃənl], *a.* sans conditions, absolu.

unconditionally [ʌnkən'diʃənəli], *adv.* sans condition.

unconfined [ʌnkən'faind], *a.* libre; illimité.

unconfinedly [ʌnkən'fainidli], *adv.* sans limite.

unconfirmed [ʌnkən'fəːmd], *a.* non confirmé.

uncongenial [ʌnkən'dʒiːniəl], *a.* désagréable; peu sympathique.

unconnected [ʌnkə'nektid], *a.* détaché, sans rapport (*avec*); décousu (*style*).

unconquerable [ʌn'kɔŋkərəbl], *a.* invincible.

unconquered [ʌn'kɔŋkəd], *a.* insoumis.

unconscionable [ʌn'kɔnʃənəbl], *a.* déraisonnable.

unconscionably [ʌn'kɔnʃənəbli], *adv.* déraisonnablement.

unconscious [ʌn'kɔnʃəs], *a.* ignorant (*de*); sans connaissance, insensible.—*n.* inconscient, *m.*

unconsciously [ʌn'kɔnʃəsli], *adv.* à son insu.

unconsciousness [ʌn'kɔnʃəsnis], *n.* inconscience, *f.*; évanouissement, *m.*

unconsecrated [ʌn'kɔnsikreitid], *a.* non consacré.

unconsidered [ʌnkən'sidəd], *a.* inconsidéré.

unconstitutional [ʌnkɔnsti'tjuːʃənl], *a.* inconstitutionnel.

unconstrained [ʌnkən'streind], *a.* sans contrainte; aisé (*style*).

unconstraint [ʌnkən'streint], *n.* aisance, *f.*

uncontaminated [ʌnkən'tæmineitid], *a.* sans souillure.

uncontested [ʌnkən'testid], *a.* incontesté.

uncontrollable [ʌnkən'trouləbl], *a.* irrésistible; fou (*rire*).

uncontrollably [ʌnkən'trouləbli], *adv.* irrésistiblement.

uncontrolled [ʌnkən'trould], *a.* irrésistible.

unconventional [ʌnkən'venʃənl], *a.* peu conventionnel.

unconverted [ʌnkən'vəːtid], *a.* inconverti.

unconvinced [ʌnkən'vinst], *a.* non convaincu.

unconvincing [ʌnkən'vinsiŋ], *a.* peu convaincant.

uncooked [ʌn'kukt], *a.* non cuit, cru.

uncork [ʌn'kɔːk], *v.t.* déboucher.

uncorrupted [ʌnkə'rʌptid], *a.* non corrompu (*par*); intègre.

uncouple [ʌn'kʌpl], *v.t.* découpler; débrayer.

uncouth [ʌn'kuːθ], *a.* bizarre; grossier; gauche.

uncouthly [ʌn'kuːθli], *adv.* rudement; gauchement.

uncover [ʌn'kʌvə], *v.t.* découvrir.

uncovered [ʌn'kʌvəd], *a.* découvert.

uncreasable [ʌn'kriːsəbl], *a.* infroissable.

uncritical [ʌn'kritikl], *a.* sans discernement.

uncrowned [ʌn'kraund], *a.* non couronné.

unction ['ʌŋkʃən], *n.* onction, *f.*

unctuous ['ʌŋktjuəs], *a.* onctueux.

unctuously ['ʌŋktjuəsli], *adv.* onctueusement.

uncultivated [ʌn'kʌltiveitid], *a.* inculte.

uncultured [ʌn'kʌltʃəd], *a.* sans culture.

uncurl [ʌn'kəːl], *v.t.* dérouler; défriser (*cheveux*).—*v.i.* se dérouler; se défriser (*cheveux*).

uncustomary [ʌn'kʌstəməri], *a.* inaccoutumé.

uncut [ʌn'kʌt], *a.* non coupé; entier; non entamé (*pain etc.*).

undamaged [ʌn'dæmidʒd], *a.* non endommagé; intact (*réputation*).

undated [ʌn'deitid], *a.* sans date.

undaunted [ʌn'dɔːntid], *a.* intrépide.

undeceive [ʌndi'siːv], *v.t.* désabuser, détromper.

undecided [ʌndi'saidid], *a.* indécis.

undecipherable [ʌndi'saifərəbl], *a.* indéchiffrable.

undefeated [ʌndi'fiːtid], *a.* invaincu.

undefended [ʌndi'fendid], *a.* sans défense, non défendu; sans défenseur (*accusé*).

undefiled [ʌndi'faild], *a.* sans tache, immaculé.

undefinable [ʌndi'fainəbl], *a.* indéfinissable.

undefined [ʌndi'faind], *a.* indéfini.

undelivered [ʌndi'livəd], *a.* non délivré.

undemonstrative [ʌndi'mɔnstrətiv], *a.* peu démonstratif, réservé.

undeniable [ʌndi'naiəbl], *a.* incontestable.

undenominational [ʌndinɔmi'neiʃənl], *a.* laïque (*école*).

under ['ʌndə], *a.* de dessous, inférieur; sous, subalterne, subordonné (*rang*).—*prep.* sous; au-dessous de (*inférieur à etc.*); dans, en (*en état de*); avec, à (*ayant*); *to be under obligations to*, avoir des obligations à; *to be under way* (*ship*), être en marche; *under age*, mineur; *under consideration*, à l'examen; *under cover of*, sous prétexte de; *under discussion*, en discussion; *under the breath*, à demi-voix; *under these circumstances*, dans ces circonstances.—*adv.* dessous, au-dessous; *see under*, voyez ci-dessous.

under-carriage ['ʌndəkæridʒ], *n.* (*Av.*) train d'atterrissage, *m.*

underclothes ['ʌndəklouðz], *n.pl.* sous-vêtements, *m.pl.*

undercurrent ['ʌndəkʌrənt], *n.* courant inférieur, *m.*

undercut (1) ['ʌndəkʌt], *n.* filet (*de bœuf*), *m.*

undercut (2) [ʌndə'kʌt], *v.t. irr.* (*conjug. like* CUT) vendre meilleur marché.

under-developed [ʌndədi'veləpt], *a.* sous-développé.

under-dog ['ʌndədɔg], *n.* opprimé, *m.*

underdone [ʌndə'dʌn], *a.* peu cuit, saignant.

under-estimate [ˌʌndərˈestimeit], *v.t.* sous-estimer.

under-exposed [ˌʌndəriksˈpouzd] *a.* (*Phot.*) sous-exposé.

underfelt [ˈʌndəfelt], *n.* thibaude, *f.*

underfoot [ˌʌndəˈfut], *adv.* sous les pieds.

undergo [ˌʌndəˈgou], *v.t. irr.* (*conjug. like* GO) subir; supporter, endurer.

undergraduate [ˌʌndəˈgrædjuət] *n.* étudiant, *m.*

underground [ˈʌndəgraund], *a.* souterrain; clandestin.—*n.* (*Rail.*) métro, *m.*—[ˌʌndə'graund], *adv.* sous terre.

undergrowth [ˈʌndəgrouθ], *n.* broussailles, *f.pl.*

underhand [ˈʌndəhænd], *a.* clandestin; sournois (*personne*).—[ˌʌndə'hænd], *adv.* sous main; en cachette.

underline [ˌʌndəˈlain], *v.t.* souligner.

underling [ˈʌndəliŋ], *n.* subalterne, *m.*, *f.*

underlying [ˌʌndəˈlaiiŋ], *a.* fondamental.

under-manned [ˌʌndəˈmænd], *a.* à court de personnel.

undermentioned [ˌʌndəˈmenʃənd], *a.* ci-dessous.

undermine [ˌʌndəˈmain], *v.t.* miner; (*fig.*) détruire.

undermost [ˈʌndəmoust], *a.* le plus bas.

underneath [ˌʌndəˈniːθ], *prep.* sous, au-dessous de.—*adv.* dessous, au-dessous, par-dessous, en dessous.

under-nourished [ˌʌndəˈnʌriʃt], *a.* sous-alimenté.

underpaid [ˌʌndəˈpeid], *a.* mal payé.

underpants [ˈʌndəpænts], *n.pl.* caleçons, *m.pl.*

under-privileged [ˌʌndəˈprivilidʒd], *a.* non privilégié.

under-production [ˌʌndəprəˈdʌkʃən], *n.* sous-production, *f.*

underrate [ˌʌndəˈreit], *v.t.* sous-estimer, déprécier.

under-ripe [ˌʌndəˈraip], *a.* pas assez mûr, vert.

under-secretary [ˈʌndəsekrətəri], *n.* sous-secrétaire, *m.*, *f.*

under-side [ˈʌndəsaid], *n.* dessous, *m.*

undersigned [ˈʌndəsaind], *a.* and *n.* sous-signé, *m.*

undersized [ˌʌndəˈsaizd], *a.* au-dessous de la moyenne.

understand [ˌʌndəˈstænd], *v.t. irr.* (*conjug. like* STAND) entendre, comprendre; apprendre, entendre dire (*être informé de*); s'entendre (*à* ou *en*) (*savoir faire*).—*v.i.* comprendre.

understandable [ˌʌndəˈstændəbl], *a.* intelligible; compréhensible.

understanding [ˌʌndəˈstændiŋ], *n.* entendement, *m.*, intelligence; compréhension; entente (*accord*), *f.*

understudy [ˈʌndəstʌdi], *n.* doublure, *f.*

undertake [ˌʌndəˈteik], *v.t. irr.* (*conjug. like* TAKE) entreprendre, se charger (*de*); s'engager (*à*); promettre (*de*).

undertaker [ˈʌndəteikə], *n.* entrepreneur des pompes funèbres, *m.*

undertaking [ˌʌndəˈteikiŋ], *n.* entreprise, *f.*

undertone [ˈʌndətoun], *n.* ton bas, *m.*; *in an undertone*, à voix basse.

underwear [ˈʌndəwɛə], *n.* sous-vêtements, *m.pl.*

underworld [ˈʌndəwəːld], *n.* enfer, *m.*; (*fig.*) bas-fonds (*des criminels*), *m.pl.*

underwrite [ˌʌndəˈrait], *v.t. irr.* (*conjug. like* WRITE) souscrire; (*Insurance*) assurer.

underwriter [ˈʌndəraitə], *n.* assureur, *m.*

undeserved [ˌʌndiˈzəːvd], *a.* immérité, non mérité.

undeservedly [ˌʌndiˈzəːvidli], *adv.* à tort, injustement.

undesirable [ˌʌndiˈzaiərəbl], *a.* peu désirable.

undetected [ˌʌndiˈtektid], *a.* non découvert, inaperçu.

undetermined [ˌʌndiˈtəːmind], *a.* indéterminé, indéfini.

undeterred [ˌʌndiˈtəːd], *a.* sans être découragé.

undeveloped [ˌʌndiˈveləpt], *a.* non développé.

undies [ˈʌndiz], *n.pl.* (*fam.*) lingerie, *f.*

undigested [ˌʌndiˈdʒestid], *a.* non digéré.

undignified [ʌnˈdignifaid], *a.* sans dignité.

undiluted [ˌʌndaiˈljuːtid], *a.* non dilué.

undiminished [ˌʌndiˈminiʃt], *a.* non diminué.

undiplomatic [ˌʌndiploˈmætik], *a.* peu diplomatique.

undisciplined [ʌnˈdisiplind], *a.* indiscipliné.

undisclosed [ˌʌndisˈklouzd], *a.* non révélé, caché.

undiscovered [ˌʌndisˈkʌvəd], *a.* non découvert.

undisguised [ˌʌndisˈgaizd], *a.* sans déguisement.

undismayed [ˌʌndisˈmeid], *a.* sans peur, sans terreur.

undisputed [ˌʌndisˈpjuːtid], *a.* incontesté.

undistinguished [ˌʌndisˈtiŋgwiʃt], *a.* (*fig.*) sans distinction.

undisturbed [ˌʌndisˈtəːbd], *a.* tranquille, calme.

undivided [ˌʌndiˈvaidid], *a.* sans partage, tout entier.

undo [ʌnˈduː], *v.t. irr.* (*conjug. like* DO) défaire; délier, détacher (*dénouer*); ruiner, perdre (*détruire*).

undoing [ʌnˈduːiŋ], *n.* ruine, perte, *f.*

undone [ʌnˈdʌn], *a.* ruiné, perdu; défait, délié.

undoubted [ʌnˈdautid], *a.* incontestable, certain.

undoubtedly [ʌnˈdautidli], *adv.* sans aucun doute.

undress [ʌnˈdres], *v.t.* déshabiller.—*v.i.* se déshabiller.—*n.* (*Mil.*) petite tenue, *f.*

undressed [ʌnˈdrest], *a.* déshabillé.

undrinkable [ʌnˈdriŋkəbl], *a.* imbuvable, non potable.

undue [ʌnˈdjuː], *a.* non dû; excessif.

undulate [ˈʌndjuleit], *v.i.* onduler, ondoyer.

undulating [ˈʌndjuleitiŋ], *a.* accidenté (*terrain*).

undulation [ˌʌndjuˈleiʃən], *n.* ondulation, *f.*

unduly [ʌnˈdjuːli], *adv.* indûment; à tort; trop.

undying [ʌnˈdaiiŋ], *a.* impérissable, immortel.

unearned [ʌnˈəːnd], *a.* qu'on n'a pas gagné; immérité; *unearned income*, rentes, *f.pl.*

unearth [ʌnˈəːθ], *v.t.* déterrer.

unearthly [ʌnˈəːθli], *a.* surnaturel; (*colloq.*) infernal.

uneasily [ʌnˈiːzili], *adv.* mal à son aise; difficilement, péniblement, avec gêne.

uneasiness [ʌn'iːzinis], *n.* malaise, *m.*, peine; inquiétude (*d'esprit*), *f.*

uneasy [ʌn'iːzi], *a.* inquiet, gêné.

uneatable [ʌn'iːtəbl], *a.* immangeable.

uneconomical [ʌniːkə'nɔmikl], *a.* non économique.

uneducated [ʌn'edjukeitid], *a.* sans éducation.

unemotional [ʌni'mouʃənl], *a.* peu impressionnable; peu émotif.

unemployed [ʌnim'plɔid], *a.* sans travail, inoccupé; (*fig.*) inactif, oisif.—*n.pl. the unemployed*, les sans-travail, les chômeurs, *m.pl.*

unemployment [ʌnim'plɔimənt], *n.* manque de travail, chômage, *m.*

unencumbered [ʌnin'kʌmbəd], *a.* non embarrassé (*de*); non hypothéqué (*biens*).

unending [ʌn'endiŋ], *a.* interminable.

unendurable [ʌnin'djuərəbl], *a.* insupportable, intolérable.

un-English [ʌn'iŋgliʃ], *a.* non anglais; indigne d'un Anglais.

unenlightened [ʌnin'laitnd], *a.* peu éclairé.

unenterprising [ʌn'entəpraiziŋ], *a.* peu entreprenant.

unenthusiastic [ʌninθjuːzi'æstik], *a.* peu enthousiaste.

unenviable [ʌn'enviəbl], *a.* peu enviable.

unequal [ʌn'iːkwəl], *a.* inégal; au-dessous (*de*); *unequal to the task*, pas à la hauteur de la tâche.

unequalled [ʌn'iːkwəld], *a.* sans égal, sans pareil.

unequivocal [ʌni'kwivəkl], *a.* non équivoque.

unequivocally [ʌni'kwivəkli], *adv.* sans équivoque.

unerring [ʌn'əːriŋ], *a.* infaillible, sûr.

uneven [ʌn'iːvn], *a.* inégal; raboteux (*terrain*).

unevenly [ʌn'iːvinli], *adv.* inégalement.

unevenness [ʌn'iːvinnis], *n.* inégalité, *f.*

uneventful [ʌni'ventful], *a.* sans incidents, monotone.

unexaggerated [ʌnig'zædʒəreitid], *a.* nullement exagéré.

unexciting [ʌnik'saitiŋ], *a.* peu intéressant.

unexpected [ʌniks'pektid], *a.* inopiné, inattendu; imprévu.

unexpectedly [ʌniks'pektidli], *adv.* à l'improviste.

unexpired [ʌniks'paiəd], *a.* non expiré.

unexplained [ʌniks'pleind], *a.* sans explication, inexpliqué.

unexploded [ʌniks'ploudid], *a.* non éclaté.

unexplored [ʌniks'plɔːd], *a.* inexploré.

unexposed [ʌniks'pouzd], *a.* non exposé.

unextinguished [ʌniks'tiŋgwiʃt], *a.* non éteint.

unfading [ʌn'feidiŋ], *a.* (*fig.*) impérissable, immortel.

unfailing [ʌn'feiliŋ], *a.* inépuisable; infaillible (*certain*).

unfair [ʌn'fɛə], *a.* injuste; (*Spt.*) pas de jeu.

unfairly [ʌn'fɛəli], *adv.* injustement.

unfairness [ʌn'fɛənis], *n.* injustice, *f.*

unfaithful [ʌn'feiθful], *a.* infidèle.

unfaithfulness [ʌn'feiθfulnis], *n.* infidélité, *f.*

unfaltering [ʌn'fɔːltəriŋ], *a.* ferme, assuré; résolu (*actions etc.*).

unfamiliar [ʌnfə'miljə], *a.* peu familier (*avec*); peu connu.

unfashionable [ʌn'fæʃənəbl], *a.* démodé.

unfasten [ʌn'fɑːsn], *v.t.* ouvrir, détacher, défaire.

unfathomable [ʌn'fæðəməbl], *a.* insondable.

unfavourable [ʌn'feivərəbl], *a.* peu favorable.

unfed [ʌn'fed], *a.* mal nourri.

unfeeling [ʌn'fiːliŋ], *a.* insensible, dur, cruel.

unfeigned [ʌn'feind], *a.* vrai, sincère.

unfeignedly [ʌn'feinidli], *adv.* sincèrement.

unfelt [ʌn'felt], *a.* qu'on ne sent pas.

unfenced [ʌn'fenst], *a.* sans clôture.

unfetter [ʌn'fetə], *v.t.* ôter les fers à; (*fig.*) délivrer.

unfettered [ʌn'fetəd], *a.* libre, sans entraves.

unfilial [ʌn'filiəl], *a.* peu filial.

unfinished [ʌn'finiʃt], *a.* inachevé.

unfit [ʌn'fit], *a.* peu propre; impropre (*à*); incapable (*de*); en mauvaise santé.

unfitting [ʌn'fitiŋ], *a.* inconvenant.

unfix [ʌn'fiks], *v.t.* détacher.

unfixed [ʌn'fikst], *a.* mobile; indécis.

unflagging [ʌn'flægiŋ], *a.* infatigable.

unfledged [ʌn'fledʒd], *a.* sans plumes; (*fig.*) novice.

unflinching [ʌn'flintʃiŋ], *a.* ferme, déterminé.

unfold [ʌn'fould], *v.t.* déplier, déployer; révéler.—*v.i.* se déployer, se dévoiler.

unforeseen [ʌnfɔː'siːn], *a.* imprévu.

unforgettable [ʌnfə'getəbl], *a.* inoubliable.

unforgiving [ʌnfə'giviŋ], *a.* implacable.

unforgotten [ʌnfə'gɔtn], *a.* pas oublié.

unfortified [ʌn'fɔːtifaid], *a.* non fortifié, ouvert.

unfortunate [ʌn'fɔːtʃənit], *a.* infortuné, malheureux.

unfortunately [ʌn'fɔːtʃənitli], *adv.* malheureusement.

unfounded [ʌn'faundid], *a.* sans fondement.

unframed [ʌn'freimd], *a.* sans cadre.

unfrequented [ʌnfri'kwentid], *a.* peu fréquenté, solitaire.

unfriendliness [ʌn'frendlinis], *n.* disposition peu amicale, *f.*

unfriendly [ʌn'frendli], *a.* peu amical (*personne*); malveillant (*chose*).

unfrock [ʌn'frɔk], *v.t.* défroquer.

unfruitful [ʌn'fruːtful], *a.* infertile, stérile.

unfulfilled [ʌnful'fild], *a.* non accompli.

unfurl [ʌn'fɔːl], *v.t.* déferler, déployer.

unfurnished [ʌn'fəːniʃt], *a.* non meublé.

ungainly [ʌn'geinli], *a.* maladroit.

ungenerous [ʌn'dʒenərəs], *a.* peu généreux.

ungentlemanliness [ʌn'dʒentlmənlinis], *n.* impolitesse, *f.*

ungentlemanly [ʌn'dʒentlmənli], *a.* de mauvais ton.

ungodliness [ʌn'gɔdlinis], *n.* impiété, *f.*

ungodly [ʌn'gɔdli], *a.* impie.

ungovernable [ʌn'gʌvənəbl], *a.* ingouvernable; effréné.

ungraceful [ʌn'greisful], *a.* peu gracieux.

ungracious [ʌn'greiʃəs], *a.* peu gracieux, déplaisant.

ungrammatical [ʌngrə'mætikl], *a.* incorrect.

ungrateful [ʌn'greitful], *a.* ingrat (*envers*).

ungratefully [ʌn'greitfuli], *adv.* avec ingratitude.

ungrudging [ʌn'grʌdʒiŋ], *a.* de bon cœur.

ungrudgingly [ʌn'grʌdʒiŋli], *adv.* volontiers, de bon cœur.

unguarded [ʌn'gɑːdid], *a.* sans défense; imprudent, irréfléchi (*inconsidéré*).

unguardedly

unguardedly [ʌn'gɑ:didli], adv. imprudemment.

unguent ['ʌŋgwənt], n. onguent, m.

unhallowed [ʌn'hæloud], a. non sanctifié.

unhampered [ʌn'hæmpəd], a. non embarrassé (par).

***unhand** [ʌn'hænd], v.t. lâcher.

unhappily [ʌn'hæpili], adv. malheureusement.

unhappiness [ʌn'hæpinis], n. malheur, m.

unhappy [ʌn'hæpi], a. malheureux.

unharmed [ʌn'hɑ:md], a. sain et sauf.

unharness [ʌn'hɑ:nis], v.t. déharnacher; dételer (d'une charrette).

unhatched [ʌn'hætʃt], a. non éclos.

unhealthy [ʌn'helθi], a. insalubre, malsain; maladif (personne).

unheard [ʌn'hə:d], a. sans être entendu; *unheard of*, inconnu, inouï (extraordinaire).

unheeded [ʌn'hi:did], a. inaperçu, négligé.

unheedful [ʌn'hi:dful], **unheeding** [ʌn 'hi:diŋ], a. insouciant; inattentif.

unhesitating [ʌn'heziteitiŋ], a. sans hésitation; résolu.

unhesitatingly [ʌn'heziteitiŋli], adv. sans hésiter.

unhewn [ʌn'hju:n], a. brut; non taillé.

unhinge [ʌn'hindʒ], v.t. démonter.

unhitch [ʌn'hitʃ], v.t. décrocher; dételer (cheval).

unholy [ʌn'houli], a. profane, impie.

unhook [ʌn'huk], v.t. décrocher; dégrafer (vêtements).

unhoped [ʌn'houpt], a. inattendu; *unhoped for*, inespéré.

unhorse [ʌn'hɔ:s], v.t. désarçonner, démonter.

unhurried [ʌn'hʌrid], a. lent, sans précipitation.

unhurt [ʌn'hə:t], a. sain et sauf, sans blessures.

unhygienic [ʌnhai'dʒi:nik], a. peu hygiénique.

unicorn ['ju:nikɔ:n], n. licorne, f.

unidentified [ʌnai'dentifaid], a. non identifié.

unification [ju:nifi'keiʃən], n. unification, f.

uniform ['ju:nifɔ:m], a. and n. uniforme, m.

uniformity [ju:ni'fɔ:miti], n. uniformité, f.

uniformly ['ju:nifɔ:mli], adv. uniformément.

unify ['ju:nifai], v.t. unifier.

unilateral [ju:ni'lætərəl], a. unilatéral.

unimaginable [ʌni'mædʒinəbl], a. inimaginable, inconcevable.

unimaginative [ʌni'mædʒinətiv], a. peu imaginatif.

unimpaired [ʌnim'pɛəd], a. inaltéré, intact.

unimpeachable [ʌnim'pi:tʃəbl], a. irréprochable.

unimpeded [ʌnim'pi:did], a. sans empêchement.

unimportance [ʌnim'pɔ:təns], n. peu d'importance, m., insignifiance, f.

unimportant [ʌnim'pɔ:tənt], a. sans importance, insignifiant.

unimpressed [ʌnim'prest], a. sans être ému.

unimpressive [ʌnim'presiv], a. peu frappant.

uninformed [ʌnin'fɔ:md], a. non informé; ignorant.

uninhabitable [ʌnin'hæbitəbl], a. inhabitable.

uninhabited [ʌnin'hæbitid], a. inhabité.

uninitiated [ʌni'niʃieitid], a. non initié.

uninjured [ʌn'indʒəd], a. sain et sauf, sans blessures.

uninspired [ʌnin'spaiəd], a. non inspiré, terne.

uninspiring [ʌnin'spaiəriŋ], a. banal.

unintelligible [ʌnin'telidʒibl], a. inintelligible.

unintentional [ʌnin'tenʃənl], a. sans intention, involontaire.

unintentionally [ʌnin'tenʃənli], adv. fait sans le vouloir, sans intention.

uninterested [ʌn'intristid], a. non intéressé, indifférent.

uninteresting [ʌn'intristiŋ], a. peu intéressant.

uninterrupted [ʌnintə'rʌptid], a. ininterrompu.

uninvited [ʌnin'vaitid], a. sans invitation.

uninviting [ʌnin'vaitiŋ], a. peu attrayant; peu appétissant (nourriture).

union ['ju:niən], n. union, f.; *trade(s)-union*, syndicat ouvrier, syndicat (corporatif), m.

unique [ju'ni:k], a. unique.

uniquely [ju'ni:kli], adv. d'une manière unique.

unison ['ju:nizn], n. unisson, m.; *in unison*, à l'unisson.

unit ['ju:nit], n. unité, f., bloc, élément, m.

unite [ju'nait], v.t. unir (à ou avec); joindre, réunir (efforts etc.).—v.i. s'unir, se réunir; se joindre (à ou avec).

united [ju'naitid], a. uni; réuni; joint; *the United Kingdom*, le Royaume-Uni, m.; *the United States*, les États-Unis, m.pl.

unity ['ju:niti], n. unité; union, f.

universal [ju:ni'və:sl], a. universel.

universally [ju:ni'və:səli], adv. universellement.

universe ['ju:nivə:s], n. univers, m.

university [ju:ni'və:siti], n. université, f.; *university degree*, grade universitaire, m.

unjust [ʌn'dʒʌst], a. injuste, inique.

unjustly [ʌn'dʒʌstli], adv. injustement.

unjustifiable [ʌn'dʒʌstifaiəbl], a. injustifiable.

unjustified [ʌn'dʒʌstifaid], a. sans justification.

unkind [ʌn'kaind], a. désobligeant; peu aimable; cruel.

unkindliness [ʌn'kaindlinis], n. désobligeance; malveillance, f.

unkindly [ʌn'kaindli], a. peu propice, défavorable.—adv. sans bienveillance; cruellement, mal.

unkindness [ʌn'kaindnis], n. manque d'amabilité, m., désobligeance; cruauté, dureté, f.

unknowingly [ʌn'nouiŋli], adv. sans le savoir, à son insu.

unknown [ʌn'noun], a. inconnu; *unknown to me* (without my knowledge), à mon insu.

unlace [ʌn'leis], v.t. délacer, détacher.

unladylike [ʌn'leidilaik], a. peu digne d'une dame, de mauvais ton.

unlatch [ʌn'lætʃ], v.t. lever le loquet de, ouvrir.

unlawful [ʌn'lɔ:ful], a. illégal; illicite.

unlawfully [ʌn'lɔ:fuli], adv. illégalement; illicitement.

unleash [ʌn'li:ʃ], v.t. lâcher (chien).

unleavened [ʌn'levənd], a. sans levain; (*Scripture*) azyme.
unless [ʌn'les], conj. à moins que . . . ne (*with subjunctive*); à moins de (*followed by infinitive*); si . . . ne . . . pas (*followed by indicative*); si ce n'est, excepté que.
unlicensed [ʌn'laisənst], a. non autorisé; (*Comm.*) non patenté.
unlike [ʌn'laik], a. différent (*de*); qui ne ressemble pas (*à*).
unlikelihood [ʌn'laiklihud], n. invraisemblance, improbabilité, f.
unlikely [ʌn'laikli], a. improbable, invraisemblable, peu sûr.
unlimited [ʌn'limitid], a. illimité.
unlined [ʌn'laind], a. non doublé.
unlink [ʌn'liŋk], v.t. défaire, détacher.
unload [ʌn'loud], v.t. décharger; désarmer (*fusil*).
unlock [ʌn'lɔk], v.t. ouvrir.
unlooked-for [ʌn'luktfɔ:], a. inattendu, imprévu.
unloose [ʌn'lu:s], v.t. délier, détacher.
unloved [ʌn'lʌvd], a. pas aimé.
unluckily [ʌn'lʌkili], adv. malheureusement, par malheur.
unlucky [ʌn'lʌki], a. malheureux, infortuné; sinistre, de mauvais augure, de mauvais présagé.
unmade [ʌn'meid], a. défait; pas fait (*lit*); non empierré (*route*).
unmanageable [ʌn'mænidʒəbl], a. ingouvernable; rebelle.
unmanliness [ʌn'mænlinis], n. conduite indigne d'un homme, lâcheté, f.
unmanly [ʌn'mænli], a. indigne d'un homme, lâche; mou, efféminé.
unmannerliness [ʌn'mænəlinis], n. grossièreté, impolitesse, f.
unmannerly [ʌn'mænəli], a. grossier, mal appris, impoli.
unmarked [ʌn'mɑːkt], a. non marqué (*de*); inaperçu.
unmarketable [ʌn'mɑːkitəbl], a. invendable.
unmarried [ʌn'mærid], a. célibataire; *unmarried man*, célibataire, m.; *unmarried woman*, demoiselle, vieille fille, f.
unmask [ʌn'mɑːsk], v.t. démasquer; (*fig.*) dévoiler.
unmastered [ʌn'mɑːstəd], a. indompté.
unmatched [ʌn'mætʃt], a. dépareillé; (*fig.*) sans pareil.
unmentionable [ʌn'menʃənəbl], a. dont on ne parle pas.
unmerciful [ʌn'məːsiful], a. impitoyable, cruel.
unmercifully [ʌn'məːsifuli], adv. impitoyablement, sans pitié.
unmerited [ʌn'meritid], a. immérité.
unmindful [ʌn'maindful], a. peu soucieux (*de*).
unmistakable [ʌnmis'teikəbl], a. évident, clair.
unmistakably [ʌnmis'teikəbli], adv. évidemment, clairement.
unmitigated [ʌn'mitigeitid], a. non adouci; (*colloq.*) fieffé (*gredin etc.*).
unmolested [ʌnmə'lestid], a. sans être molesté.
unmotherly [ʌn'mʌðəli], a. peu maternel.
unmounted [ʌn'mauntid], a. à pied (*sans cheval*); non collé (*photographie etc.*).

unmourned [ʌn'mɔːnd], a. sans être pleuré.
unmoved [ʌn'muːvd], a. immobile; (*fig.*) non ému.
unmusical [ʌn'mjuːzikl], a. peu harmonieux; pas musicien (*personne*).
unmuzzle [ʌn'mʌzl], v.t. démuseler.
unnamed [ʌn'neimd], a. innommé; anonyme.
unnatural [ʌn'nætʃrəl], a. contre nature; dénaturé (*personne*).
unnavigable [ʌn'nævigəbl], a. innavigable.
unnecessarily [ʌn'nesəsərili], adv. sans nécessité, inutilement; par trop.
unnecessary [ʌn'nesəsəri], a. peu nécessaire, inutile.
unneighbourly [ʌn'neibəli], a. peu obligeant; de mauvais voisin.
unnerve [ʌn'nəːv], v.t. énerver; (*fig.*) décourager.
unnoticed [ʌn'noutist], a. inaperçu, inobservé.
unnumbered [ʌn'nʌmbəd], a. innombrable.
unobjectionable [ʌnəb'dʒekʃənəbl], a. irrécusable.
unobliging [ʌnə'blaidʒiŋ], a. désobligeant.
unobservant [ʌnəb'zəːvənt], a. peu observateur.
unobserved [ʌnəb'zəːvd], a. inaperçu.
unobtainable [ʌnəb'teinəbl], a. impossible à obtenir.
unobtrusive [ʌnəb'truːsiv], a. réservé, discret.
unobtrusively [ʌnəb'truːsivli], adv. sans importunité, avec modestie.
unoccupied [ʌn'ɔkjupaid], a. inoccupé; libre, disponible (*temps etc.*); inhabité (*maison*).
unofficial [ʌnə'fiʃl], a. non officiel.
unofficially [ʌnə'fiʃəli], adv. non officiellement.
unopened [ʌn'oupənd], a. fermé; non décacheté (*lettre etc.*).
unopposed [ʌnə'pouzd], a. sans opposition.
unorganized [ʌn'ɔːgənaizd], a. non organisé.
unoriginal [ʌnə'ridʒinəl], a. peu original.
unorthodox [ʌn'ɔːθədɔks], a. peu orthodoxe.
unostentatious [ʌnɔsten'teiʃəs], a. sans faste; modeste.
unostentatiously [ʌnɔsten'teiʃəsli], adv. sans ostentation.
unpack [ʌn'pæk], v.t. déballer (*marchandises*); dépaqueter (*paquets*).
unpacking [ʌn'pækiŋ], n. déballage; dépaquetage (*de petits paquets*), m.
unpaid [ʌn'peid], a. non payé, sans paye.
unpalatable [ʌn'pælətəbl], a. désagréable (au goût).
unparalleled [ʌn'pærəleld], a. sans pareil; sans précédent.
unpardonable [ʌn'pɑːdnəbl], a. impardonnable.
unparliamentary [ʌnpɑːli'mentəri], a. peu parlementaire.
unpatriotic [ʌnpætri'ɔtik], a. peu patriotique (*sentiment*); peu patriote (*personne*).
unpaved [ʌn'peivd], a. non pavé.
unperturbed [ʌnpə'təːbd], a. peu ému, impassible.
unphilosophical [ʌnfilə'sɔfikl], a. peu philosophique.
unpick [ʌn'pik], v.t. découdre.
unpicked [ʌn'pikt], a. non cueilli; décousu (*couture*).

613

unpin

unpin [ʌn'pin], v.t. défaire.
unpitied [ʌn'pitid], a. qu'on ne plaint pas.
unpitying [ʌn'pitiiŋ], a. sans pitié, impitoyable.
unplayable [ʌn'pleiəbl], a. injouable.
unpleasant [ʌn'plezənt], a. déplaisant, fâcheux.
unpleasantly [ʌn'plezəntli], adv. désagréablement.
unpleasantness [ʌn'plezəntnis], n. désagrément, m.
unploughed [ʌn'plaud], a. non labouré.
unpoetical [ʌnpo'etikl], a. peu poétique.
unpolished [ʌn'pɔliʃt], a. non poli; mat (or etc.); non ciré (chaussures); dépoli (verre); (fig.) grossier.
unpolluted [ʌnpə'lju:tid], a. non souillé; pur.
unpopular [ʌn'pɔpjulə], a. impopulaire.
unpopularity [ʌnpɔpju'læriti], n. impopularité, f.
unpractical [ʌn'præktikl], a. peu pratique.
unpractised [ʌn'præktist], a. inexpérimenté.
unprecedented [ʌn'presidəntid], a. sans précédent.
unprejudiced [ʌn'predʒudist], a. sans préjugés, impartial.
unpremeditated [ʌnpri'mediteitid], a. inopiné, improvisé, sans préméditation.
unprepared [ʌnpri'pɛəd], a. non préparé; to be unprepared for, ne pas s'attendre à.
unpreparedness [ʌnpri'pɛəridnis], n. manque de préparation, m.
unprepossessing [ʌnpri:pə'zesiŋ], a. peu engageant.
unprincipled [ʌn'prinsipld], a. sans principes, sans mœurs.
unproductive [ʌnprə'dʌktiv], a. improductif; stérile (terre).
unproductiveness [ʌnprə'dʌktivnis], n. stérilité, f.
unprofessional [ʌnprə'feʃənəl], a. contraire aux règles d'une profession.
unprofitable [ʌn'prɔfitəbl], a. peu lucratif, sans profit; inutile.
unprofitably [ʌn'prɔfitəbli], adv. inutilement, sans profit.
unpronounceable [ʌnprə'naunsəbl], a. imprononçable.
unpropitious [ʌnprə'piʃəs], a. peu propice (à).
unprotected [ʌnprə'tektid], a. sans protection, sans défense; à découvert.
unprovided [ʌnprə'vaidid], a. dépourvu, dénué (de); we were unprovided for that, nous ne nous attendions pas à cela.
unprovoked [ʌnprə'voukt], a. sans provocation; an unprovoked insult, une insulte gratuite.
unpublished [ʌn'pʌbliʃt], a. inédit.
unpunished [ʌn'pʌniʃt], a. impuni.
unqualified [ʌn'kwɔlifaid], a. incapable (de), incompétent; (fig.) sans réserve; (Law) inhabile (à); non autorisé (médecins etc.).
unquenchable [ʌn'kwentʃəbl], a. inextinguible.
unquestionable [ʌn'kwestʃənəbl], a. incontestable, indubitable.
unquestionably [ʌn'kwestʃənəbli], adv. incontestablement; sans contredit.
unravel [ʌn'rævl], v.t. démêler, débrouiller. —v.i. se démêler, se débrouiller, s'effiler.
unreadable [ʌn'ri:dəbl], a. illisible.

unreadily [ʌn'redili], adv. lentement, à contre-cœur.
unreadiness [ʌn'redinis], n. manque de préparation ou de bonne volonté, m.
unready [ʌn'redi], a. mal préparé; lent.
unreal [ʌn'riːəl], a. irréel; chimérique, imaginaire.
unrealistic [ʌnriːə'listik], a. peu réaliste.
unreality [ʌnri'æliti], n. défaut de réalité, m.
unrealizable [ʌn'riːəlaizəbl], a. irréalisable.
unreasonable [ʌn'riːznəbl], a. déraisonnable; exorbitant.
unreasonableness [ʌn'riːznəblnis], n. déraison; absurdité, extravagance (de demande), f.
unreasonably [ʌn'riːznəbli], adv. sans raison, à l'excès.
unrecognizable [ʌn'rekəgnaizəbl], a. méconnaissable.
unrecognized [ʌn'rekəgnaizd], a. sans être reconnu; (fig.) méconnu (non apprécié).
unrecompensed [ʌn'rekəmpenst], a. sans récompense.
unreconciled [ʌn'rekənsaild], a. irréconcilié.
unrecorded [ʌnri'kɔ:did], a. non enregistré.
unredeemable [ʌnri'di:məbl], a. irrachetable.
unredeemed [ʌnri'di:md], a. non racheté.
unrefined [ʌnri'faind], a. non raffiné, brut; (fig.) grossier.
unregistered [ʌn'redʒistəd], a. non enregistré; non recommandé (lettre etc.).
unrelated [ʌnri'leitid], a. sans rapport (avec); who is unrelated to, qui n'est pas parent de.
unrelenting [ʌnri'lentiŋ], a. inflexible, implacable.
unreliable [ʌnri'laiəbl], a. peu sûr; sur qui ou sur quoi l'on ne peut compter.
unrelieved [ʌnri'liːvd], a. non soulagé; sans relief.
unremitting [ʌnri'mitiŋ], a. incessant, infatigable.
unremunerative [ʌnri'mju:nərətiv], a. peu rémunérateur, peu lucratif.
unrepentant [ʌnri'pentənt], a. impénitent.
unrepresented [ʌnrepri'zentid], a. non représenté.
unrequited [ʌnri'kwaitid], a. sans être récompensé; qui n'est pas payé de retour (amour).
unreserved [ʌnri'zə:vd], a. sans réserve; absolu (total).
unreservedly [ʌnri'zə:vidli], adv. sans réserve.
unresisting [ʌnri'zistiŋ], a. qui ne résiste pas, soumis.
unresolved [ʌnri'zɔlvd], a. non résolu; irrésolu, indécis (personne).
unresponsive [ʌnris'pɔnsiv], a. peu sensible; froid.
unrest [ʌn'rest], n. inquiétude, agitation, f.
unrestrained [ʌnri'streind], a. non restreint; non réprimé; effréné, déréglé.
unrestricted [ʌnri'striktid], a. sans restriction.
unretentive [ʌnri'tentiv], a. peu tenace; peu fidèle (la mémoire).
unrevenged [ʌnri'vendʒd], a. non vengé.
unrevised [ʌnri'vaizd], a. non revu, non revisé.
unrewarded [ʌnri'wɔ:did], a. sans récompense.

unrewarding [ʌnri'wɔːdiŋ], a. peu rémunérateur.
unrig [ʌn'rig], v.t. dégréer.
unrighteous [ʌn'raitʃəs], a. injuste, inique.
unrighteousness [ʌn'raitʃəsnis], n. injustice, iniquité, f.
unripe [ʌn'raip], a. pas mûr, vert; (fig.) prématuré.
unrivalled [ʌn'raivəld], a. sans rival, sans égal.
unroll [ʌn'roul], v.t. dérouler, déployer.—v.i. se dérouler, se déployer.
unruffled [ʌn'rʌfld], a. tranquille, calme.
unruly [ʌn'ruːli], a. indiscipliné, insoumis, turbulent.
unsaddle [ʌn'sædl], v.t. desseller; débâter (âne); désarçonner (cavalier).
unsafe [ʌn'seif], a. peu sûr, dangereux, hasardeux.
unsaleable [ʌn'seiləbl], a. invendable.
unsalted [ʌn'sɔːltid], a. non salé, sans sel.
unsanctified [ʌn'sæŋktifaid], a. non consacré, profane.
unsatisfactorily [ʌnsætis'fæktərili], adv. d'une manière peu satisfaisante.
unsatisfactory [ʌnsætis'fæktəri], a. peu satisfaisant.
unsatisfied [ʌn'sætisfaid], a. peu satisfait.
unsavouriness [ʌn'seivərinis], n. insipidité, fadeur, f.; mauvais goût, m.
unsavoury [ʌn'seivəri], a. sans saveur, insipide; repoussant (désagréable).
unscarred [ʌn'skaːd], a. sans cicatrices.
unscathed [ʌn'skeiðd], a. sans blessures, sain et sauf.
unscholarly [ʌn'skɔləli], a. illettré, ignorant.
unscientific [ʌnsaiən'tifik], a. peu scientifique.
unscientifically [ʌnsaiən'tifikli], adv. peu scientifiquement.
unscrew [ʌn'skruː], v.t. dévisser.
unscrupulous [ʌn'skruːpjuləs], a. peu scrupuleux.
unscrupulously [ʌn'skruːpjuləsli], adv. sans scrupule.
unscrupulousness [ʌn'skruːpjuləsnis], n. manque de scrupule, m.
unseal [ʌn'siːl], v.t. décacheter; desceller.
unsealed [ʌn'siːld], a. décacheté, ouvert.
unseasonable [ʌn'siːznəbl], a. mal à propos; indu (heure); pas de saison (temps).
unseat [ʌn'siːt], v.t. renverser; désarçonner (d'un cheval); (Polit.) invalider.
unseaworthy [ʌn'siːwəːði], a. incapable de tenir la mer, innavigable.
unsecured [ʌnsi'kjuəd], a. sans garantie; mal fermé (porte).
unseeing [ʌn'siːiŋ], a. aveugle.
unseemliness [ʌn'siːmlinis], n. inconvenance, f.
unseemly [ʌn'siːmli], a. inconvenant; indécent.
unseen [ʌn'siːn], a. sans être vu, invisible.
unselfish [ʌn'selfiʃ], a. désintéressé.
unserviceable [ʌn'səːvisəbl], a. inutile, bon à rien.
unsettle [ʌn'setl], v.t. déranger; (fig.) troubler.
unsettled [ʌn'setld], a. mal fixé, mal établi; incertain (temps etc.); irrésolu (personne); dérangé, troublé (esprit); variable, changeant (inconstant).

unshackled [ʌn'ʃækld], a. sans entraves, libre.
unshaken [ʌn'ʃeikn], a. inébranlable, ferme.
unshapely [ʌn'ʃeipli], a. difforme, informe.
unshaved [ʌn'ʃeivd], **unshaven** [ʌn'ʃeivn], a. non rasé.
unsheathe [ʌn'ʃiːð], v.t. dégainer.
unship [ʌn'ʃip], v.t. débarquer; démonter (gouvernail etc.); désarmer (avirons).
unshod [ʌn'ʃɔd], a. sans chaussures; déferré (cheval).
unshorn [ʌn'ʃɔːn], a. non tondu.
unshrinkable [ʌn'ʃriŋkəbl], a. irrétrécissable.
unsightliness [ʌn'saitlinis], n. laideur, f.
unsightly [ʌn'saitli], a. laid, déplaisant.
unsigned [ʌn'saind], a. non signé.
unsisterly [ʌn'sistəli], a. peu digne d'une sœur.
unskilful [ʌn'skilful], a. inhabile, maladroit.
unskilled [ʌn'skild], a. inexpérimenté (dans); non qualifié; **unskilled labour**, travail de manœuvre, m.; main-d'œuvre non spécialisée, f.
unsociable [ʌn'souʃəbl], a. insociable.
unsoiled [ʌn'sɔild], a. sans tache.
unsold [ʌn'sould], a. invendu.
unsoldierly [ʌn'souldʒəli], a. indigne d'un soldat.
unsolicited [ʌnsə'lisitid], a. sans être sollicité.
unsolved [ʌn'sɔlvd], a. non résolu.
unsophisticated [ʌnsə'fistikeitid], a. qui n'est pas frelaté; pur, vrai.
unsought [ʌn'sɔːt], a. non recherché; spontané.
unsound [ʌn'saund], a. défectueux, malsain; faux, erroné; mal établi (crédit); vicieux, pas sain (cheval); **of unsound mind**, non sain d'esprit.
unsparing [ʌn'spɛəriŋ], a. libéral, prodigue; impitoyable (sans pitié).
unsparingly [ʌn'spɛəriŋli], adv. avec prodigalité; impitoyablement.
unspeakable [ʌn'spiːkəbl], a. inexprimable; indicible; ignoble, sans nom.
unspecified [ʌn'spesifaid], a. non spécifié.
unspoiled [ʌn'spɔild], a. non corrompu; bien élevé (enfant).
unspoken [ʌn'spoukn], a. non prononcé; tacite.
unsportsmanlike [ʌn'spɔːtsmənlaik], a. indigne d'un chasseur ou d'un sportsman.
unspotted [ʌn'spɔtid], a. sans tache.
unstable [ʌn'steibl], a. irrésolu; inconstant; (Mech.) instable.
unstained [ʌn'steind], a. sans tache.
unstamped [ʌn'stæmpt], a. non timbré, sans timbre.
unsteadily [ʌn'stedili], adv. en chancelant; d'une manière irrégulière.
unsteadiness [ʌn'stedinis], n. instabilité, irrésolution, f.
unsteady [ʌn'stedi], a. chancelant; mal assuré, irrésolu, inconstant, irrégulier (conduite).
unstinted [ʌn'stintid], a. non restreint, abondant.
unstop [ʌn'stɔp], v.t. déboucher, ouvrir.
unstrengthened [ʌn'streŋθənd], a. non renforcé.
unstressed [ʌn'strest], a. inaccentué, atone.
unsubdued [ʌnsəb'djuːd], a. indompté.
unsubmissive [ʌnsəb'misiv], a. insoumis.

unsubmissiveness [ʌnsəb'misivnis], *n.* insoumission, *f.*
unsubstantial [ʌnsəb'stænʃl], *a.* peu substantiel; peu solide; (*fig.*) immatériel; chimérique.
unsuccessful [ʌnsək'sesful], *a.* qui n'a pas réussi, sans succès.
unsuccessfully [ʌnsək'sesfuli] *adv.* sans succès.
unsuitable [ʌn'sjuːtəbl], *a.* peu convenable, peu propre (*à*).
unsuited [ʌn'sjuːtid], *a.* peu fait (*pour*), peu convenable (*à*).
unsullied [ʌn'sʌlid], *a.* sans souillure, sans tache.
unsung [ʌn'sʌŋ], *a.* non célébré.
unsupervised [ʌn'sjuːpəvaizd], *a.* non surveillé.
unsupported [ʌnsə'pɔːtid], *a.* non soutenu; (*fig.*) sans appui.
unsuppressed [ʌnsə'prest], *a.* mal contenu.
unsure [ʌn'ʃuə], *a.* peu sûr.
unsurpassed [ʌnsə'pɑːst], *a.* non surpassé, sans égal.
unsuspected [ʌnsə'spektid], *a.* insoupçonné; non suspect.
unsuspecting [ʌnsə'spektiŋ], sans soupçon, confiant.
unsuspicious [ʌnsə'spiʃəs], *a.* sans méfiance, confiant.
unsustained [ʌnsə'steind], *a.* non soutenu.
unswayed [ʌn'sweid], *a.* qui ne se laisse pas influencer.
unswerving [ʌn'swəːviŋ], *a.* qui ne s'écarte pas, inébranlable.
unsymmetrical [ʌnsi'metrikl], *a.* asymétrique.
unsympathetic [ʌnsimpə'θetik], *a.* froid, peu compatissant.
unsystematic [ʌnsisti'mætik], *a.* peu systématique.
untainted [ʌn'teintid], *a.* non corrompu; frais (*viande*).
untamable [ʌn'teiməbl], *a.* indomptable.
untamed [ʌn'teimd], *a.* indompté; non apprivoisé.
untapped [ʌn'tæpt], *a.* inexploité (*ressources*).
untarnished [ʌn'tɑːniʃt], *a.* non terni.
untaught [ʌn'tɔːt], *a.* ignorant, illettré.
untaxed [ʌn'tækst], *a.* exempt d'impôts.
unteachable [ʌn'tiːtʃəbl], *a.* incapable d'apprendre.
untearable [ʌn'tɛərəbl], *a.* indéchirable.
untempered [ʌn'tempəd], *a.* non trempé (*métal*).
untenable [ʌn'tenəbl], *a.* insoutenable.
untended [ʌn'tendid], *a.* non gardé.
untested [ʌn'testid], *a.* non essayé.
unthanked [ʌn'θæŋkt], *a.* sans être remercié.
unthinking [ʌn'θiŋkiŋ], *a.* inconsidéré, étourdi.
unthinkingly [ʌn'θiŋkiŋli], *adv.* sans y penser.
untidily [ʌn'taidili], *adv.* sans ordre, sans soin.
untidiness [ʌn'taidinis], *n.* désordre, *m.*
untidy [ʌn'taidi], *a.* en désordre; négligé.
untie [ʌn'tai], *v.t.* délier, dénouer; défaire (*nœud*).
until [ən'til], *prep.* jusqu'à; avant.—*conj.* jusqu'à ce que, avant que.
untilled [ʌn'tild], *a.* inculte, en friche.
untimeliness [ʌn'taimlinis], *n.* inopportunité, *f.*

untimely [ʌn'taimli], *a.* prématuré, inopportun.—*adv.* avant terme, prématurément.
untiring [ʌn'taiəriŋ], *a.* infatigable.
untiringly [ʌn'taiəriŋli], *adv.* sans relâche.
***unto** [ʹʌntu], *prep.* [TO].
untold [ʌn'tould], *a.* non raconté, non exprimé; sans nombre; inouï.
untouchable [ʌn'tʌtʃəbl], *a.* and *n.* hors caste, paria, intouchable, *m.*, *f.*
untouched [ʌn'tʌtʃt], *a.* non touché; (*fig.*) non ému (*de*).
untoward [ʌn'tɔːd, ʌn'touəd], *a.* insoumis, indocile (*rebelle*); fâcheux.
untraceable [ʌn'treisəbl], *a.* introuvable.
untrained [ʌn'treind], *a.* inexpérimenté (*inexpert*); indiscipliné; non dressé (*animal*).
untrammelled [ʌn'træməld], *a.* sans entraves.
untranslatable [ʌntrɑːns'leitəbl], *a.* intraduisible.
untravelled [ʌn'trævld], *a.* peu connu (*terre*); qui n'a pas voyagé (*personne*).
untried [ʌn'traid], *a.* non essayé; qui n'a pas encore été jugé.
untrimmed [ʌn'trimd], *a.* sans garniture; non émondé (*arbre*).
untrodden [ʌn'trɔdn], *a.* non frayé; immaculé (*neige*).
untroubled [ʌn'trʌbld], *a.* calme, tranquille.
untrue [ʌn'truː], *a.* faux; inexact (*nouvelle etc.*); déloyal (*à*).
untrustworthiness [ʌn'trʌstwəːðinis], *n.* inexactitude, fausseté, *f.*
untrustworthy [ʌn'trʌstwəːði], *a.* indigne de confiance; inexact, mensonger (*nouvelle etc.*).
untruth [ʌn'truːθ], *n.* contre-vérité, fausseté, *f.*
untruthful [ʌn'truːθful], *a.* menteur; mensonger (*nouvelle etc.*); perfide, faux, déloyal (*traître*).
untruthfulness [ʌn'truːθfulnis], *n.* fausseté, *f.*
untutored [ʌn'tjuːtəd], *a.* peu instruit, ignorant.
untwine [ʌn'twain], *v.t.* détordre; dérouler.
untwist [ʌn'twist], *v.t.* détordre, détortiller, défaire.
unused (1) [ʌn'juːzd], *a.* non employé, inutilisé; inusité (*mot*).
unused (2) [ʌn'juːst], *a.* inaccoutumé; *unused to*, inaccoutumé à.
unusual [ʌn'juːʒuəl], *a.* peu commun, rare.
unusually [ʌn'juːʒuəli], *adv.* rarement, extraordinairement.
unutterable [ʌn'ʌtərəbl], *a.* inexprimable, indicible.
unuttered [ʌn'ʌtəd], *a.* non prononcé.
unvanquished [ʌn'væŋkwiʃt], *a.* indompté.
unvaried [ʌn'vɛərid], *a.* uniforme.
unvarnished [ʌn'vɑːniʃt], *a.* non verni; (*fig.*) simple, naturel.
unvarying [ʌn'vɛəriiŋ], *a.* invariable, uniforme.
unveil [ʌn'veil], *v.t.* dévoiler; découvrir.
unventilated [ʌn'ventileitid], *a.* mal aéré.
unversed [ʌn'vəːst], *a.* peu versé (*dans*).
unvisited [ʌn'vizitid], *a.* non visité, peu fréquenté.
unwarily [ʌn'wɛərili], *adv.* sans précaution imprudemment.

unwariness [ʌn'wɛərinis], *n.* imprévoyance, imprudence, *f.*

unwarlike [ʌn'wɔːlaik], *a.* pacifique, peu belliqueux.

unwarrantable [ʌn'wɔrəntəbl], *a.* injustifiable.

unwarrantably [ʌn'wɔrəntəbli], *adv.* inexcusablement.

unwarranted [ʌn'wɔrəntid], *a.* non garanti; *an unwarranted insult*, une insulte gratuite.

unwary [ʌn'wɛəri], *a.* inconsidéré, imprudent.

unwashed [ʌn'wɔʃt], *a.* non lavé, sale, malpropre.

unwavering [ʌn'weivəriŋ], *a.* résolu, inébranlable.

unwearable [ʌn'wɛərəbl], *a.* qu'on ne peut plus porter.

unwearied [ʌn'wiərid], *a.* non lassé, infatigable.

unwelcome [ʌn'welkəm], *a.* importun; fâcheux.

unwell [ʌn'wel], *a.* indisposé, souffrant, mal portant.

unwept [ʌn'wept], *a.* non pleuré, non regretté.

unwholesome [ʌn'houlsəm], *a.* malsain, insalubre.

unwieldy [ʌn'wiːldi], *a.* lourd, pesant, difficile à manier.

unwilling [ʌn'wiliŋ], *a.* peu disposé, mal disposé; *to be unwilling to*, n'être pas disposé à.

unwillingly [ʌn'wiliŋli], *adv.* à contre-cœur, sans le vouloir.

unwillingness [ʌn'wiliŋnis], *n.* mauvaise volonté, *f.*

unwind [ʌn'waind], *v.t. irr. (conjug. like* WIND) dévider; dérouler; *(fig.)* débrouiller. —*v.i.* se dévider.

unwise [ʌn'waiz], *a.* peu sage, malavisé, insensé.

unwisely [ʌn'waizli], *adv.* peu sagement, imprudemment.

unwished (for) [ʌn'wiʃt(fɔː)], *a.* non souhaité.

unwitnessed [ʌn'witnist], *a.* sans témoin, non certifié.

unwitting [ʌn'witiŋ], *a.* inconscient.

unwittingly [ʌn'witiŋli], *adv.* sans le savoir, inconsciemment.

unwomanly [ʌn'wumənli], *a.* indigne d'une femme.

unwonted [ʌn'wountid], *a.* inaccoutumé, rare.

unworkable [ʌn'wəːkəbl], *a.* impraticable.

unworked [ʌn'wəːkt], *a.* inexploité *(mine etc.).*

unworn [ʌn'wɔːn], *a.* non usé, non usagé.

unworthily [ʌn'wəːðili], *adv.* indignement, sans le mériter.

unworthiness [ʌn'wəːðinis], *n.* indignité, *f.*

unworthy [ʌn'wəːði], *a.* indigne *(de)*, sans mérite.

unwrap [ʌn'ræp], *v.t.* défaire, désenvelopper.

unwrinkle [ʌn'riŋkl], *v.t.* dérider.

unwrinkled [ʌn'riŋkld], *a.* sans rides, uni.

unwritten [ʌn'ritn], *a.* non écrit; *(fig.)* oral, traditionnel.

unyielding [ʌn'jiːldiŋ], *a.* qui ne cède pas, inflexible.

unyoke [ʌn'jouk], *v.t.* ôter le joug à, dételer.

up [ʌp], *adv.* au haut, en haut, haut; en l'air; levé, sur pied *(pas au lit)*; sur l'horizon; debout *(pas assis)*; en révolte, en insurrection; fini *(expiré)*; élevé *(prix)*; en hausse *(valeurs de Bourse)*; *it is up to us to do it*, c'est à nous de le faire; *road up*, rue barrée; *to be up to*, être au courant de; *to make up to*, faire des avances à; *up and down*, en haut et en bas, çà et là, de long en large, de haut en bas; *up there*, là-haut; *up to*, jusqu'à la hauteur de; *up to date*, à la dernière mode; à jour; *up to now*, jusqu'ici; *up to then*, jusque-là; *what's up? (colloq.)* qu'est-ce qu'il y a donc?—*prep.* en haut de, au haut de; en montant; *up hill* or *up stream*, en amont. —*n.* haut, *m.*; *the ups and downs*, les hauts et les bas, *m.pl.*

upbraid [ʌp'breid], *v.t.* reprocher à; réprouver.

upbraiding [ʌp'breidiŋ], *n.* reproche, *m.*

upcast [ʌp'kɑːst], *n.* jet; coup, *m.*

upheaval [ʌp'hiːvl], *n.* soulèvement, *m.*

uphill ['ʌphil], *a.* qui monte; *(fig.)* ardu, pénible.—[ʌp'hil], *adv.* en côte, en montant.

uphold [ʌp'hould], *v.t. irr. (conjug. like* HOLD) soutenir, maintenir.

upholster [ʌp'houlstə], *v.t.* tapisser.

upholsterer [ʌp'houlstərə], *n.* tapissier, *m.*

upholstery [ʌp'houlstəri], *n.* tapisserie, *f.*

upkeep ['ʌpkiːp], *n.* entretien, *m.*

upland ['ʌplənd], *a.* élevé, des hautes terres.

uplands ['ʌpləndz], *n.pl.* terrain élevé, haut pays, *m.*, hautes terres, *f.pl.*

uplift [ʌp'lift], *v.t.* lever, élever, soulever. —['ʌplift], *n. (fig.)* inspiration, *f.*

uplifting [ʌp'liftiŋ], *n.* soulèvement, *m.*

upon [ə'pɔn], *prep.* sur; *upon pain of*, sous peine de.

upper ['ʌpə], *a.* supérieur, d'en haut, de dessus, au-dessus; haut; *the Upper House* la Chambre Haute; *upper circle*, troisièmes loges, *f.pl.*; *upper deck*, pont supérieur, *m.*; *upper hand*, dessus, *m.*, supériorité, *f.*

uppermost ['ʌpəmoust], *a.* le plus élevé; *(fig.)* le plus fort.

uppers ['ʌpəz], *n.pl.* empeignes *(de chaussures)*, *f.pl.*; *(fam.)* *to be on one's uppers*, être dans la débine.

Upper Volta ['ʌpə'vɔltə]. la Haute Volta, *f.*

uppish ['ʌpiʃ], *a.* fier, arrogant.

uppishness ['ʌpiʃnis], *n.* fierté, arrogance, *f.*

upraise [ʌp'reiz], *v.t.* soulever, élever.

upright ['ʌprait], *a.* droit, debout; d'aplomb, vertical; *(fig.)* honnête *(intègre).*—*adv.* tout droit.—*n.* montant, *m.*

uprightness ['ʌpraitnis], *n.* droiture, intégrité, *f.*

uprising [ʌp'raiziŋ], *n.* lever; soulèvement, *m.*

uproar ['ʌprɔː], *n.* tumulte, désordre; tapage, *m.*

uproarious [ʌp'rɔːriəs], *a.* bruyant; tumultueux.

uproariously [ʌp'rɔːriəsli], *adv.* avec un grand vacarme.

uproot [ʌp'ruːt], *v.t.* déraciner, extirper.

uprooting [ʌp'ruːtiŋ], *n.* déracinement, *m.*

upset [ʌp'set], *v.t. irr. (conjug. like* SET) renverser; *(fig.)* bouleverser.—*v.i.* se renverser;

verser (*véhicules*).—['ʌpset], *n.* bouleversement, *m.*
upshot ['ʌpʃɔt], *n.* résultat, *m.*, fin, *f.*, fin
mot, *m.*
upside-down ['ʌpsaid'daun], *adv.* sens dessus
dessous.
upstairs ['ʌpstɛəz], *a.* d'en haut.—[ʌp'stɛəz],
adv. en haut.
upstanding [ʌp'stændiŋ], *a.* droit, debout.
upstart ['ʌpstɑːt], *n.* parvenu, nouveau riche,
m.
upsurge [ʌp'səːdʒ], *n.* poussée, *f.*
upward ['ʌpwəd], *a.* dirigé en haut; ascendant.—*adv.* or **upwards** ['ʌpwədz], en
haut; en montant; *upwards of*, plus de.
Ural ['juərəl] **Mountains.** les Monts Ourals,
m.pl.
uranium [ju'reiniəm], *n.* uranium, *m.*
urban ['əːbən], *a.* urbain.
urbane [əː'bein], *a.* qui a de l'urbanité, poli.
urbanely [əː'beinli], *adv.* avec urbanité.
urbanity [əː'bæniti], *n.* urbanité, *f.*
urbanize ['əːbənaiz], *v.t.* urbaniser.
urchin ['əːtʃin], *n.* gamin, polisson; (*colloq.*)
mioche, gosse, *m.*; *sea-urchin*, oursin, *m.*
urge [əːdʒ], *v.t.* presser; pousser, exciter,
porter (*à*); alléguer (*insister sur*); *to urge
on*, pousser en avant.—*n.* impulsion;
poussée, *f.*
urgency ['əːdʒənsi], *n.* urgence, *f.*
urgent ['əːdʒənt], *a.* urgent, instant.
urgently ['əːdʒəntli], *adv.* avec urgence,
instamment.
urging ['əːdʒiŋ], *n.* sollicitation, *f.*
uric ['juərik], *a.* urique.
urinal ['juərinl], *n.* urinoir; (*Med.*) urinal, *m.*;
vespasienne (*urinoir public*), *f.*
urinate ['juərineit], *v.i.* uriner.
urine ['juərin], *n.* urine, *f.*
urn [əːn], *n.* urne; fontaine (*à thé, à café etc.*), *f.*
Ursula ['əːsjulə], Ursule, *f.*
Uruguay ['juərugwai]. l'Uruguay, *m.*
Uruguayan [juəru'gwaiən], *a.* uruguayen.—
n. Uruguayen (*personne*), *m.*
us [ʌs], *pron.* nous; *for us Frenchmen*, pour
nous autres Français.
usable ['juːzəbl], *a.* utilisable, employable.
usage ['juːzidʒ], *n.* usage, *m.*
use [juːs], *n.* usage, emploi, *m.*; utilité, *f.*,
avantage, profit, *m.*; habitude, *f.*; (*Law*)
usufruit, *m.*; *it is of no use*, cela ne sert à
rien; *of use*, utile; *to make use of*, se
servir de; *what is the use of that?* à
quoi sert cela?—[juːz], *v.t.* user de, faire
usage de, employer, se servir de; utiliser;
consommer.
used [juːzd], *a.* usité (*mot etc.*), d'occasion
(*voiture*); *very little used*, qui a peu servi,
presque neuf (*vêtement etc.*).—[juːst] *to be*
or *get used to*, s'accoutumer à, s'habituer
à.—[juːst], *v. aux. in the expression used to
(followed by inf.) usu. translated by the Imp.
Tense in French; he used to admire*, il
admirait.
useful ['juːsful], *a.* utile.
usefully ['juːsfuli], *adv.* utilement, avec profit.
usefulness ['juːsfulnis], *n.* utilité, *f.*
useless ['juːslis], *a.* inutile; vain.
uselessly ['juːslisli], *adv.* inutilement.
uselessness ['juːslisnis], *n.* inutilité, *f.*
usher ['ʌʃə], *n.* huissier (*de cour de justice*);

sous-maître, *m.*—*v.t.* faire entrer, introduire
(*dans*); (*fig.*) annoncer.
usherette [ʌʃə'ret], *n.* (*Cine.*) ouvreuse, *f.*
usual ['juːʒuəl], *a.* usuel, ordinaire, habituel,
accoutumé; d'usage; *as usual*, comme
d'habitude.
usually ['juːʒuəli], *adv.* ordinairement, d'ordinaire, d'habitude.
usurer ['juːʒərə], *n.* usurier, *m.*
usurious [juː'ʒuəriəs], *a.* usuraire.
usurp [juː'zəːp], *v.t.* usurper.
usurpation [juːzə'peiʃən], *n.* usurpation, *f.*
usurper [juː'zəːpə], *n.* usurpateur, *m.*
usury ['juːʒəri], *n.* usure, *f.*
utensil [ju'tensil], *n.* ustensile, *m.*
uterine ['juːtərain], *a.* utérin.
uterus ['juːtərəs], *n.* utérus, *m.*
utilitarian [juːtili'tɛəriən], *a.* utilitaire.
utilitarianism [juːtili'tɛəriənizm], *n.* utili-
tarisme, *m.*
utility [juː'tiliti], *n.* utilité, *f.*
utilizable ['juːtilaizəbl], *a.* utilisable.
utilization [juːtilai'zeiʃən], *n.* utilisation, *f.*
utilize ['juːtilaiz], *v.t.* utiliser.
utmost ['ʌtmoust], *a.* extrême, le dernier, le
plus haut, le plus grand; le plus élevé (*prix
etc.*).—*n.* extrême, comble, *m.*; *to do one's
utmost*, faire tout son possible (*pour*).
Utopia [juː'toupiə]. Utopie, *f.*
Utopian [juː'toupiən], *a.* d'utopie, utopique.
utter (1) ['ʌtə], *a.* entier, complet; absolu;
le plus profond (*extrême*); vrai; fieffé (*véritable*).
utter (2) ['ʌtə], *v.t.* pousser; proférer, prononcer; dire; émettre (*fausse monnaie*).
utterable ['ʌtərəbl], *a.* exprimable.
utterance ['ʌtərəns], *n.* énonciation, prononciation, parole, expression, *f.*
utterer ['ʌtərə], *n.* personne qui prononce, *f.*;
émetteur (*de fausse monnaie*), *m.*
utterly ['ʌtəli], *adv.* tout à fait, entièrement.
uttermost ['ʌtəmoust], *a.* extrême; le plus
reculé.
uvula ['juːvjulə], *n.* (*Anat.*) luette, uvule, *f.*
uvular ['juːvjulə], *a.* uvulaire.
uxorious [ʌk'sɔːriəs], *a.* uxorieux, esclave de
sa femme.
uxoriousness [ʌk'sɔːriəsnis], *n.* complaisance
excessive pour sa femme, *f.*

V

V, v [viː]. vingt-deuxième lettre de l'alphabet,
m.
vacancy ['veikənsi], *n.* vacance, place vacante,
f.; vide, *m.*; lacune (*trou*), *f.*
vacant ['veikənt], *a.* vacant, vide; libre
(*inoccupé*); vide d'expression (*regard perdu*).
vacate [və'keit], *v.t.* laisser vacant, quitter.
vacation [və'keiʃən], *n.* vacation, *f.*, vacances,
f.pl.
vaccinate ['væksineit], *v.t.* vacciner.
vaccination [væksi'neiʃən], *n.* vaccination,
vaccine, *f.*
vaccine ['væksiːn], *a.* de vache.—*n.* vaccin, *m.*

vacillate ['væsileit], v.i. vaciller; (fig.) hésiter.
vacillating ['væsileitiŋ], a. vacillant, indécis.
vacillation [væsi'leiʃən], n. vacillation, indécision, f.
vacuity [və'kju:iti], n. vide, m.; vacuité, f.
vacuous ['vækjuəs], a. vide; (fig.) bête.
vacuum ['vækjuəm], n. vide, m.
vacuum-cleaner ['vækjuəm'kli:nə], n. aspirateur, m.
vade-mecum ['veidi'mi:kəm], n. vademecum, m.
vagabond ['vægəbɔnd], a. errant, vagabond. —n. vagabond, m.
vagary ['veigəri], n. caprice, m., lubie, boutade, f.
vagina [və'dʒainə], n. (Anat.) vagin, m.
vagrancy ['veigrənsi], n. vagabondage, m.
vagrant ['veigrənt], a. vagabond, errant.—n. vagabond, mendiant, m.
vague [veig], a. vague.
vaguely ['veigli], adv. vaguement.
vagueness ['veignis], n. vague, m.
vain [vein], a. vain; faux (creux); vaniteux, glorieux (fier); in vain, en vain.
vainglorious [vein'glɔ:riəs], a. vain, vaniteux.
vainglory [vein'glɔ:ri], n. vaine gloire, gloriole, f.
vainly ['veinli], adv. en vain, vainement.
vainness ['veinnis], n. vanité, f.
valance ['væləns], n. frange de lit, f.
vale [veil], n. (poet.) vallon, m., vallée, f.
valedictory [væli'diktəri], a. d'adieu.—n. discours d'adieu, m.
valet ['vælit], n. valet de chambre, m.
valetudinarian [vælitju:di'neəriən], a. and n. valétudinaire, m., f.
valiant ['væliənt], a. vaillant, valeureux.
valiantly ['væliəntli], adv. vaillamment.
valid ['vælid], a. valide, valable.
validate ['vælideit], v.t. valider, rendre valable.
validity [və'liditi], validness ['vælidnis], n. validité, f.
validly ['vælidli], adv. validement.
validness [VALIDITY].
valise [və'li:z], n. valise, f.; sac de voyage, m.
valley ['væli], n. vallée, f., vallon, m.
valorous ['vælərəs], a. valeureux.
valour ['vælə], n. valeur, vaillance, f.
valuable ['væljuəbl], a. précieux.
valuation [vælju'eiʃən], n. évaluation, f.
valuator ['væljueitə], n. estimateur, m.
value ['vælju:], n. valeur, f.; prix, m.—v.t. évaluer, estimer.
valued ['vælju:d], a. estimé, apprécié.
valueless ['væljulis], a. sans valeur.
valuer ['væljuə], n. estimateur, commissaire-priseur, m.
valve [vælv], n. soupape; valve; (Rad.) lampe, f.
valved [vælvd], a. à soupape; (Bot.) valvé, à valves.
valvular ['vælvjulə], a. (Med.) valvulaire.
vamp [væmp], n. empeigne; enjôleuse, femme fatale, f.—v.t. (fig.) raccommoder, rapiécer; (Mus.) improviser.
vampire ['væmpaiə], n. vampire, m.
van [væn], n. camionnette, voiture (de déménagement), f.; (Rail. etc.) fourgon, m.; avant-garde (précurseur), f.

vandal [vændl], n. vandale, m., f.
vandalism ['vændəlizm], n. vandalisme, m.
vane [vein], n. girouette, f.
vanguard ['vænga:d], n. avant-garde, f.
vanilla [və'nilə], n. vanille, f.
vanish ['væniʃ], v.i. s'évanouir, disparaître.
vanishing-point ['væniʃiŋpɔint], n. point de fuite, m.
vanity ['væniti], n. vanité, f.
vanquish ['væŋkwiʃ], v.t. vaincre.
vanquisher ['væŋkwiʃə], n. vainqueur, m.
vantage ['va:ntidʒ], n. avantage, m., supériorité, f.
vapid ['væpid], a. fade, insipide; éventé (boisson alcoolique).
vapidity [væ'piditi], vapidness ['væpidnis], n. fadeur, insipidité, f.
vaporization [veipərai'zeiʃən], n. vaporisation, f.
vaporize ['veipəraiz], v.t. vaporiser.—v.i. se vaporiser.
vaporous ['veipərəs], a. vaporeux.
vapour ['veipə], n. vapeur; (fig.) fumée, f.
vapourish ['veipəriʃ], vapoury ['veipəri], a. vaporeux.
variability [veəriə'biliti], variableness ['veəriəblnis], n. variabilité; inconstance, f.
variable ['veəriəbl], a. variable; inconstant.
variance ['veəriəns], n. désaccord, m.
variation [veəri'eiʃən], n. variation, f., changement, m.
varicose ['værikous], a. variqueux; varicose vein, varice, f.
varied ['veərid], a. varié, divers.
variegate ['veərigeit], v.t. varier; nuancer.
variegated ['veərigeitid], a. varié, bigarré; (Bot.) panaché.
variegation [veəri'geiʃən], n. bigarrure, f.
variety [və'raiəti], n. variété, diversité, f.
various ['veəriəs], a. divers, différent.
variously ['veəriəsli], adv. diversement.
varnish ['va:niʃ], n. vernis, m.—v.t. vernir; vernisser (poterie etc.).
varnisher ['va:niʃə], n. vernisseur, m.
varnishing ['va:niʃiŋ], n. vernissure, f.; vernissage, m.
vary ['veəri], v.t. varier; diversifier.—v.i. varier, changer.
varying ['veəriiŋ], a. changeant, qui varie, divers.
vascular ['væskjulə], a. vasculaire.
vase [va:z], n. vase, m.
vaseline ['væsəli:n], n. (reg. trade mark) vaseline, f.
vassal [væsl], n. vassal, m.
vassalage ['væsəlidʒ], n. vasselage, m.; (fig.) servitude, f.
vast [va:st], a. vaste, immense.—n. immensité, f.
vastly ['va:stli], adv. immensément, excessivement.
vastness ['va:stnis], n. vaste étendue, grandeur, f.
vat [væt], n. cuve, f.
vatful ['vætful], n. cuvée, f.
Vatican ['vætikən], n. le Vatican, m.
vaudeville ['voudəvil], n. vaudeville, m.
vault [vɔ:lt], n. voûte, cave, f.; caveau (lieu de sépulture); saut (bond), m.—v.t. voûter.—v.i. sauter.
vaulted ['vɔ:ltid], a. voûté, en voûte.

619

vaulter ['vɔːltə], *n.* voltigeur, sauteur, *m.,* acrobate, *m., f.*
vaulting ['vɔːltiŋ], *n.* construction de voûtes, *f.*; voûtes, *f.pl.*; voltige (*acrobatie*), *f.*
vaunt [vɔːnt], *n.* vanterie, *f.—v.t.* vanter élever jusqu'aux nues.
vaunter ['vɔːntə], *n.* vantard, *m.*
vaunting ['vɔːntiŋ], *a.* plein de jactance.
vauntingly ['vɔːntiŋli], *adv.* avec jactance.
veal [viːl], *n.* veau, *m.*
vedette [və'det], *n.* vedette, *f.*
veer [viə], *v.t.* virer (*bateau*).—*v.i.* tourner, changer de direction; virer (*bateau*).
vegetable ['vedʒitəbl], *a.* végétal.—*n.* végétal, légume, *m.*
vegetal ['vedʒitl], *a.* végétal.
vegetarian [vedʒi'tɛəriən], *a.* and *n.* végétarien, *m.*
vegetate ['vedʒiteit], *v.i.* végéter.
vegetation [vedʒi'teiʃən], *n.* végétation, *f.*
vegetative ['vedʒitətiv], *a.* végétatif, végétant.
vehemence ['viːiməns], *n.* véhémence; (*fig.*) ardeur, *f.*
vehement ['viːimənt], *a.* véhément, impétueux.
vehemently ['viːiməntli], *adv.* avec véhémence, impétueusement.
vehicle ['viːikl], *n.* véhicule, *m.,* voiture, *f.*
veil [veil], *n.* voile, *m.*; voilette (*de dame*), *f.—v.t.* voiler; (*fig.*) déguiser.
vein [vein], *n.* veine; (*fig.*) humeur, *f.—v.t.* veiner.
veined [veind], **veiny** ['veini], *a.* veiné.
vellum ['veləm], *n.* vélin, *m.*
velocity [və'lɔsiti], *n.* vélocité, vitesse, rapidité, *f.*
velvet ['velvit], *a.* de velours; (*Bot.*) velouté.—*n.* velours, *m.*
velveteen [velvə'tiːn], *n.* velours de coton, *m.*
velvety ['velviti], *a.* velouté.
venal ['viːnl], *a.* vénal.
venality [viː'næliti], *n.* vénalité, *f.*
vend [vend], *v.t.* vendre (*petits articles*).
vendee [ven'diː], *n.* acheteur, *m.*
vendetta [ven'detə], *n.* vendetta, *f.*
vendible ['vendibl], *a.* vendable.
vendor ['vendə], *n.* vendeur, *m.*
veneer [və'niə], *n.* feuille (*de bois etc.*); plaque, *f.*; (*fig.*) vernis, *m.—v.t.* plaquer (*de*).
veneering [və'niəriŋ], *n.* placage, *m.*
venerable ['venərəbl], *a.* vénérable.
venerableness ['venərəblnis], *n.* caractère vénérable, *m.*
venerate ['venəreit], *v.t.* vénérer.
veneration [venə'reiʃən], *n.* vénération, *f.*
venerator ['venəreitə], *n.* vénérateur, *m.*
venery ['venəri], *n.* chasse, vénerie, *f.*
Venetian [və'niːʃən], *a.* vénitien, de Venise; *Venetian blind,* jalousie, *f.*; *Venetian shutter,* persienne, *f.—n.* Vénitien (*personne*), *m.*
Venezuela [venə'zweilə]. le Vénézuéla, *m.*
Venezuelan [venə'zweilən], *a.* vénézuélien.—*n.* Vénézuélien (*personne*), *m.*
vengeance ['vendʒəns], *n.* vengeance, *f.*; *with a vengeance,* furieusement, à outrance.
vengeful ['vendʒful], *a.* vindicatif.
venial ['viːniəl], *a.* véniel, pardonnable.
veniality [viːni'æliti], *n.* vénialité, *f.*

Venice ['venis]. Venise, *f.*
venison ['venizn], *n.* venaison, *f.*
venom ['venəm], *n.* venin, *m.*
venomous ['venəməs], *a.* venimeux (*animal*); vénéneux (*plante*); (*fig.*) méchant.
venous ['viːnəs], *a.* veineux.
vent [vent], *v.t.* donner issue à, exhaler, décharger.—*n.* issue, *f.,* passage, cours; trou de fausse (*de baril*); soupirail (*pour l'air*), *m.*; *to give vent to,* donner libre cours à.
ventilate ['ventileit], *v.t.* ventiler; aérer, (*fig.*) discuter.
ventilation [venti'leiʃən], *n.* ventilation, *f.*; *ventilation shaft,* puits d'aérage, *m.*
ventilator ['ventileitə], *n.* ventilateur, *m.*
ventral ['ventrəl], *a.* ventral.
ventricle ['ventrikl], *n.* ventricule, *m.*
ventriloquism [ven'triləkwizm], *n.* ventriloquie, *f.*
ventriloquist [ven'triləkwist], *n.* ventriloque, *m., f.*
venture ['ventʃə], *n.* aventure, entreprise, *f.* —*v.t.* aventurer, risquer.—*v.i.* oser, se hasarder, s'aventurer; s'aviser de (*se permettre*).
venturer ['ventʃərə], *n.* personne aventureuse, *f.*
venturesome ['ventʃəsəm], *a.* aventureux, audacieux.
venue ['venjuː], *n.* juridiction, *f.*; lieu de réunion, *m.*
Venus ['viːnəs]. Vénus, *f.*
veracious [və'reiʃəs], *a.* véridique.
veracity [və'ræsiti], *n.* véracité, *f.*
veranda, verandah [və'rændə], *n.* véranda, *f.*
verb [vəːb], *n.* verbe, *m.*
verbal ['vəːbəl], *a.* verbal, littéral.
verbally ['vəːbəli], *adv.* verbalement, mot à mot.
verbatim [vəː'beitim], *adv.* mot pour mot.
verbena [vəː'biːnə], *n.* verveine, *f.*
verbiage ['vəːbiidʒ], *n.* verbiage, *m.*
verbose [vəː'bous], *a.* verbeux, diffus, prolixe.
verbosity [vəː'bɔsiti], *n.* verbosité, *f.*
verdant ['vəːdənt], *a.* verdoyant, vert.
verdict ['vəːdikt], *n.* verdict; (*fig.*) arrêt, *m.*
verdigris ['vəːdigriːs], *n.* vert-de-gris, *m.*
verdure ['vəːdjə], *n.* verdure, *f.*
verge (I) [vəːdʒ], *n.* bord, *m.,* bordure; lisière (*de forêt etc.*); verge (*baguette*), *f.*; *on the verge of setting out,* à la veille de partir. —*v.i.* pencher (*vers*); *to verge on,* toucher à.
verger ['vəːdʒə], *n.* bedeau, huissier à verge, *m.*
verification [verifi'keiʃən], *n.* vérification, *f.*
verifier ['verifaiə], *n.* vérificateur, *m.*
verify ['verifai], *v.t.* vérifier.
***verily** ['verili], *adv.* en vérité, vraiment.
verisimilar [veri'similə], *a.* vraisemblable.
verisimilitude [verisi'militjuːd], *n.* vraisemblance, *f.*
veritable ['veritəbl], *a.* véritable.
verity ['veriti], *n.* vérité, *f.*
vermicelli [vəːmi'seli], *n.* vermicelle, *m.*
vermicule [vəː'mikjuːl], *n.* vermisseau, *m.*
vermilion [vəː'miljən], *a.* vermeil.—*n.* vermillon, *m.*
vermin ['vəːmin], *n.* vermine, *f.*
verminous ['vəːminəs], *a.* vermineux.

vernacular [və'nækjulə], *a.* du pays, indigène. —*n.* langue vernaculaire, *f.*

vernal ['və:nəl], *a.* printanier.

veronica [və'rɔnikə], *n.* véronique, *f.*

versatile ['və:sətail], *a.* qui a des connaissances variées; qui se plie à tout.

versatility [və:sə'tiliti], *n.* souplesse, faculté d'adaptation, *f.*

verse [və:s], *n.* vers, *m.*, poésie; strophe (*stance*), *f.*

versed [və:st], *a.* versé (*dans*).

versification [və:sifi'keiʃən], *n.* versification, *f.*

versifier ['və:sifaiə], *n.* versificateur, rimailleur, *m.*

versify ['və:sifai], *v.t.* mettre en vers.—*v.i.* versifier.

version ['və:ʃən], *n.* version, *f.*

versus ['və:səs], *prep.* contre.

vertebra ['və:tibrə], *n.* (*pl.* **vertebræ** ['və:ti bri]) vertèbre, *f.*

vertebral ['və:tibrəl], *a.* vertébral.

vertebrate ['və:tibrit], *a.* and *n.* vertébré, *m.*

vertex ['və:teks], *n.* (*pl.* **vertices** ['və:tisi:z]) sommet, zénith, *m.*

vertical ['və:tikl], *a.* vertical.

vertically ['və:tikli], *adv.* verticalement.

vertiginous [və:'tidʒinəs], *a.* vertigineux.

vertigo ['və:tigou], *n.* vertige, *m.*

verve [və:v], *n.* verve, *f.*

very ['veri], *a.* vrai, même, véritable.—*adv.* fort, bien, très.

vesper ['vespə], *n.* étoile du soir, *f.*; soir *m.*; (*pl.*) vêpres, *f.pl.*

vessel [vesl], *n.* vase; vaisseau, bâtiment, navire, *m.*

vest [vest], *n.* tricot de corps; (*Am.*) gilet, *m.*—*v.t.* vêtir, revêtir; investir (*de*).—*v.i.* échoir (*à*).

vestal [vestl], *a.* vestale, de Vesta; (*fig.*) chaste.—*n.* vestale, *f.*

vestibule ['vestibju:l], *n.* vestibule, *m.*

vestige ['vestidʒ], *n.* vestige, *m.*, trace, *f.*

vestment ['vestmənt], *n.* vêtement (de cérémonie), *m.*; chasuble, *f.*

vestry ['vestri], *n.* sacristie, *f.*

vesture ['vestʃə], *n.* vêtements, *m.pl.*

Vesuvius [vi'su:vjəs]. le Vésuve, *m.*

vetch [vetʃ], *n.* vesce, *f.*

veteran ['vetərən], *a.* vieux, ancien, expérimenté.—*n.* vétéran, *m.*

veterinary ['vetərinri], *a.* vétérinaire; *veterinary surgeon*, vétérinaire, *m.*, *f.*

veto ['vi:tou], *n.* veto, *m.*—*v.t.* mettre son veto à, interdire.

vex [veks], *v.t.* fâcher, vexer, contrarier.

vexation [vek'seiʃən], *n.* vexation, contrariété, *f.*, chagrin, *m.*

vexatious [vek'seiʃəs], *a.* vexatoire; irritant, fâcheux, ennuyeux.

vexatiousness [vek'seiʃəsnis], *n.* caractère vexatoire, *m.*

vexed [vekst], *a.* vexé, fâché; (*fig.*) épineux (*question*).

vexing ['veksiŋ], *a.* contrariant, vexant, ennuyeux.

via ['vaiə], *prep.* par, par voie de, via.

viability [vaiə'biliti], *n.* viabilité, *f.*

viable ['vaiəbl], *a.* viable.

viaduct ['vaiədʌkt], *n.* viaduc, *m.*

vial ['vaiəl], *n.* fiole, *f.*

viands ['vaiəndz], *n. pl.* aliments, *m.pl.*; mets, *m.*

viaticum [vai'ætikəm], *n.* viatique, *m.*

vibrate [vai'breit], *v.t.* faire vibrer.—*v.i.* vibrer, osciller.

vibration [vai'breiʃən], *n.* vibration, oscillation, *f.*

vibrating [vai'breitiŋ], **vibratory** ['vaibrə təri], *a.* vibrant, vibratoire.

vicar ['vikə], *n.* (*Engl. Ch.*) pasteur; (*R.-C. Ch.*) curé (*de paroisse*), *m.*; *vicar-general*, vicaire, *m.*

vicarage ['vikəridʒ], *n.* cure, *f.*, presbytère, *m.*

vicarial [vi'kɛəriəl], *a.* de la cure, du curé.

vicarious [vi'kɛəriəs], *a.* vicarial, de vicaire; (*fig.*) de substitution.

vicariously [vi'kɛəriəsli], *adv.* par délégation, par substitution.

vice (1) [vais], *n.* vice, défaut, *m.*; *vice squad*, brigade de mœurs, *f.*

vice (2) [vais], *n.* (*Tech.*) étau, *m.*

vice-admiral [vais'ædmirəl], *n.* vice-amiral, *m.*

vice-chancellor ['vaist'ʃɑ:nsələ], *n.* vice-chancelier; (*Univ.*) recteur, *m.*

vice-president ['vaisprezidənt], *n.* vice-président, *m.*

viceroy ['vaisrɔi], *n.* vice-roi, *m.*

vicinity [vi'siniti], *n.* voisinage, *m.*, proximité, *f.*, alentours, *m.pl.*

vicious ['viʃəs], *a.* vicieux; haineux.

viciously ['viʃəsli], *adv.* vicieusement; rageusement.

viciousness ['viʃəsnis], *n.* nature vicieuse, *f.*, vice, *m.*

vicissitude [vi'sisitju:d], *n.* vicissitude, *f.*

victim ['viktim], *n.* victime, *f.*

victimization [viktimai'zeiʃən], *n.* tyrannisation, *f.*

victimize ['viktimaiz], *v.t.* exercer des représailles contre, tromper.

victor ['viktə], *n.* vainqueur, *m.*

victorious [vik'tɔ:riəs], *a.* victorieux, de victoire.

victoriously [vik'tɔ:riəsli], *adv.* victorieusement, en vainqueur.

victory ['viktəri], *n.* victoire, *f.*

victual [vitl], *v.t.* approvisionner, ravitailler.

victualler ['vitlə], *n.* pourvoyeur, fournisseur (de vivres), *m.*; *licensed victualler*, débitant de boissons, *m.*

victualling ['vitliŋ], *n.* ravitaillement, *m.*

victuals [vitlz], *n.pl.* vivres, *m.pl.*, provisions, *f.pl.*

vie [vai], *v.i.* rivaliser, lutter (*de*); le disputer (*à*).

Vienna [vi'enə]. Vienne, *f.*

Viennese [vi:ə'ni:z], *a.* viennois.—*n.* Viennois (*personne*), *m.*

Vietnam [vjet'næm]. le Vietnam, *m.*

Vietnamese [vjetnə'mi:z], *a.* vietnamien.—*n.* Vietnamien (*personne*), *m.*

view [vju:], *n.* vue, perspective, scène, *f.*; regard (*coup d'œil*); aperçu, examen (*exposé*), *m.*; intention, *f.*, dessein, *m.*; opinion, pensée, *f.*; *in view of*, en considération de; *on view*, ouvert au public; *with a view to*, en vue de.—*v.t.* regarder; considérer; examiner, inspecter; explorer.

viewer ['vju:ə], *n.* spectateur; téléspectateur, *m.*

viewing ['vju:iŋ], *n.* examen, *m.*, inspection, *f.*

view-point ['vju:pɔint], n. point de vue, m.
vigil ['vidʒil], n. veille, veillée, (*Eccles.*) vigile, f.
vigilance ['vidʒiləns], n. vigilance, f.
vigilant ['vidʒilənt], a. vigilant, éveillé.
vigilantly ['vidʒiləntli], adv. avec vigilance.
vigorous ['vigərəs], a. vigoureux.
vigorously ['vigərəsli], adv. vigoureusement.
vigorousness ['vigərəsnis], **vigour** ['vigə], n. vigueur, f.
vile [vail], a. vil, abject, bas; détestable.
vileness ['vailnis], n. bassesse, f.
vilification [vilifi'keiʃən], n. diffamation, f.
vilifier ['vilifaiə], n. diffamateur, m.
vilify ['vilifai], v.t. vilipender, dénigrer.
villa ['vilə], n. villa, maison de campagne, f.
village ['vilidʒ], n. village, m.
villager ['vilidʒə], n. villageois, m.
villain ['vilən], n. scélérat, gredin; (*Theat.*) traître, m.
villainous ['vilənəs], a. vil, infâme.
villainy ['viləni], n. scélératesse, vilenie, f.
vindicate ['vindikeit], v.t. soutenir, défendre, justifier; venger.
vindication [vindi'keiʃən], n. défense, justification, f.
vindicator ['vindikeitə], n. défenseur, m.
vindictive [vin'diktiv], a. vindicatif.
vindictively [vin'diktivli], adv. d'une manière vindicative.
vindictiveness [vin'diktivnis], n. esprit de vengeance, m.
vine [vain], n. vigne, f.
vine-dresser ['vaindresə], n. vigneron, m.
vinegar ['vinigə], n. vinaigre, m.
vine-grower ['vaingrouə], n. viticulteur, m.
vine-growing ['vaingrouiŋ], n. viticulture, f.
vine-harvest ['vainhɑ:vist], n. vendange, f.
vine-prop ['vainprɔp], n. échalas, m.
vinery ['vainəri], n. serre à vignes, f.
vineyard ['vinjəd], n. vigne, f.; vignoble, m.
vinicultural [vini'kaltʃərəl], a. vinicole.
viniculture ['vinikaltʃə], n. viniculture, f.
vinous ['vainəs], a. vineux.
vintage ['vintidʒ], n. vendange; vinée, récolte de vin (*cueillette*), f.; vendanges (*temps de la récolte*), f.pl.; **a vintage wine**, un vin de marque, m.
vintager ['vintidʒə], n. vendangeur, m.
vintner ['vintnə], n. négociant en vins, m.
viny ['vaini], a. de vigne, de raisin; de vignoble.
viola (1) [vi'oulə], n. (*Mus.*) alto, m.; **viola player**, altiste, m., f.
viola (2) ['vaiələ], n. (*Bot.*) violette, f.
violate ['vaiəleit], v.t. violer, faire violence à; outrager.
violation [vaiə'leiʃən], n. violation, infraction, f., viol (*d'une femme*), m.
violator ['vaiəleitə], n. violateur, m.
violence ['vaiələns], n. violence, f.; **with violence** (*of robbery*), à main armée.
violent ['vaiələnt], a. violent; atroce (*douleur*).
violently ['vaiələntli], adv. violemment, avec violence.
violet ['vaiəlit], n. violette (*plante*), f.; violet (*couleur*), a.
violin [vaiə'lin], n. violon, m.
violinist [vaiə'linist], n. violoniste, m., f.
violist [vi'oulist], n. altiste, violiste, m., f.

violoncellist [vaiələn'tʃelist], n. violoncelliste, m., f.
violoncello [vaiələn'tʃelou], n. violoncelle, m.
viper ['vaipə], n. vipère, f.
viperish ['vaipəriʃ], **viperous** ['vaipərəs], a. de vipère; (*fig.*) venimeux.
virago [vi'rɑ:gou], n. virago, mégère, f.
virgin ['və:dʒin], a. vierge; virginal, de vierge.—n. vierge, f.
virginal ['və:dʒinəl], a. virginal, de vierge.
virginia-creeper [və'dʒinjə'kri:pə], n. vigne vierge, f.
virginity [və'dʒiniti], n. virginité, f.
viridity [vi'riditi], n. verdeur, fraîcheur, f.
virile ['virail], a. viril, mâle.
virility [vi'riliti], n. virilité, nature virile, f.
virtual ['və:tjuəl], a. virtuel; de fait.
virtually ['və:tjuəli], adv. virtuellement, de fait.
virtue ['və:tju:], n. vertu; (*fig.*) valeur, f. mérite, m.
virtuosity [və:tju'ositi], n. virtuosité, f.
virtuoso [və:tju'ousou], n. (*pl.* **virtuosi** [və:tju'ousi]) virtuose, m., f.
virtuous ['və:tjuəs], a. vertueux.
virtuously ['və:tjuəsli], adv. vertueusement.
virtuousness ['və:tjuəsnis], n. vertu, f.
virulence ['viruləns], n. virulence, f.
virulent ['virulənt], a. virulent.
virus ['vaiərəs], n. virus, m.
visa ['vi:zə], n. visa, m.—v.t. viser.
visage ['vizidʒ], n. visage, m., figure, f.
viscera ['visərə], n.pl. viscères, m.pl.
viscid ['visid], a. visqueux.
viscosity [vis'kositi], n. viscosité, f.
viscount ['vaikaunt], n. vicomte, m.
viscountess ['vaikauntis], n. vicomtesse, f.
viscountship ['vaikauntʃip], **viscounty** ['vaikaunti], n. vicomté, f.
viscous ['viskəs], a. visqueux, glutineux.
visibility [vizi'biliti], n. visibilité, f.
visible ['vizibl], a. visible; clair.
visibly ['vizibli], adv. visiblement, à vue d'œil.
vision ['viʒən], n. vision, vue, f.
visionary ['viʒənəri], a. and n. visionnaire, m., f.
visit ['vizit], n. visite, f.; séjour (*a stay*), m.—v.t. visiter, aller, rendre visite à; **I visit the theatre twice a week**, je vais au théâtre deux fois par semaine.—v.i. faire des visites.
visitant ['vizitənt], n. visiteur, m.
visitation [vizi'teiʃən], n. inspection; épreuve, f.
visiting ['viziting], a. en visite, de visite.—n. visites, f.pl.
visitor ['vizitə], n. visiteur; (*official*) inspecteur, m.; **she has visitors**, elle a du monde.
visor ['vaizə], n. visière, f.
vista ['vistə], n. vue, perspective, f.
Vistula ['vistjulə], the. la Vistule, f.
visual ['viʒuəl], a. visuel.
visualize ['viʒuəlaiz], v.t. se représenter.
vital [vaitl], a. vital, de vie; (*fig.*) essentiel.
vitality [vai'tæliti], n. vitalité, f.
vitalize ['vaitəlaiz], v.t. vivifier; (*fig.*) animer.
vitally ['vaitəli], adv. vitalement.
vitals [vaitlz], n.pl. parties vitales, f.pl.
vitamin ['vitəmin], n. vitamine, f.

vitiate ['viʃieit], v.t. vicier; (fig.) corrompre.
vitiation [viʃi'eiʃən], n. viciation; (fig.) corruption, f.
vitreous ['vitriəs], a. vitreux; (Anat.) vitré.
vitrify ['vitrifai], v.t. vitrifier.—v.i. se vitrifier.
vitriol ['vitriəl], n. vitriol, m.
vitriolic [vitri'ɔlik], a. vitriolique.
vituperate [vi'tju:pəreit], v.t. vilipender, injurier.
vituperation [vitju:pə'reiʃən], n. reproches, m.pl., invectives, f.pl.
vituperative [vi'tju:pərətiv], a. injurieux, hargneux.
vivacious [vi'veiʃəs], a. vif, vivace, animé.
vivaciously [vi'veiʃəsli], adv. vivement, avec vivacité.
vivaciousness [vi'veiʃəsnis], n. vivacité, f.; vivacity [vi'væsiti], n. vivacité, f.
vivary ['vivəri], n. vivier, m.
vivid ['vivid], a. vif, frappant.
vividly ['vividli], adv. d'une manière frappante, avec éclat.
vividness ['vividnis], n. vivacité, f., éclat, m.
vivification [vivifi'keiʃən], n. vivification, f.
vivify ['vivifai], v.t. vivifier.
vivifying ['vivifaiiŋ], a. vivifiant.
viviparous [vi'vipərəs], a. vivipare.
vivisection [vivi'sekʃən], n. vivisection, f.
vivisector [vivi'sektə], n. vivisecteur, m.
vixen ['viksən], n. renarde (bête); mégère (femme), f.
vixenish ['viksəniʃ], a. de mégère, méchante.
viz. [viz] (usu. read namely), adv. à savoir.
vizier [vi'ziə], n. vizir, m.
vocabulary [vo'kæbjuləri], n. vocabulaire, m.
vocal [voukl], a. vocal, de la voix.
vocalist ['voukəlist], n. chanteur, m., chanteuse, f.
vocalize ['voukəlaiz], v.t., v.i. vocaliser.
vocally ['voukəli], adv. par la voix, vocalement.
vocation [vo'keiʃən], n. vocation; profession, f.
vocational [vo'keiʃənəl], a. professionnel.
vocative ['vɔkətiv], n. vocatif, m.
vociferate [və'sifəreit], v.t., v.i. vociférer.
vociferation [vəsifə'reiʃən], n. vocifération, f.
vociferous [və'sifərəs], a. qui vocifère, bruyant.
vociferously [və'sifərəsli], adv. en vociférant.
vodka ['vɔdkə], n. vodka, f.
vogue [voug], n. vogue, f.
voice [vɔis], n. voix, f.; at the top of one's voice, à tue-tête.—v.t. publier; exprimer.
void [vɔid], a. vide, vacant; (Law) nul, de nul effet.—n. vide, espace vide, m.—v.t. vider; (Law) annuler.
voidable ['vɔidəbl], a. annulable.
volatile ['vɔlətail], a. volatil; qui vole, volant; inconstant (volage).
volatility [vɔlə'tiliti], n. volatilité, f.
volcanic [vɔl'kænik], a. volcanique.
volcano [vɔl'keinou], n. volcan, m.
vole [voul], n. campagnol, m.
volition [və'liʃən], n. volition, volonté, f.
volley ['vɔli], n. décharge, salve (de mousqueterie); volée (de canon), f.—v.t. (Ten.) renvoyer (la balle) de volée.
volt [voult], n. (Elec.) volt, m.

voltage ['voultidʒ], n. voltage, m.
volte-face ['vɔltfɑːs], n. volte-face, f.
volubility [vɔlju'biliti], n. volubilité, f.
voluble ['vɔljubl], a. délié (langue); facile (débit).
volubly ['vɔljubli], adv. avec volubilité.
volume ['vɔljum], n. volume; tome (livre), m.
voluminous [və'lju:minəs], a. volumineux.
voluminously [və'lju:minəsli], adv. d'une manière volumineuse.
voluminousness [və'lju:minəsnis], n. grosseur, f.
voluntarily ['vɔləntərili], adv. volontairement, spontanément.
voluntariness ['vɔləntərinis], n. spontanéité, f.
voluntary ['vɔləntəri], a. volontaire, spontané; libre; intentionnel.—n. (Mus.) improvisation, f.
volunteer [vɔlən'tiə], n. volontaire, m., f.—v.t. offrir volontairement.—v.i. offrir ses services; s'engager comme volontaire.
voluptuary [və'lʌptjuəri], n. voluptueux, épicurien, m.
voluptuous [və'lʌptjuəs], a. voluptueux.
voluptuously [və'lʌptjuəsli], adv. voluptueusement.
voluptuousness [və'lʌptjuəsnis], n. volupté, f.
volute [və'lju:t], n. volute, f.
voluted [və'lju:tid], a. voluté.
volution [və'lju:ʃən], n. spirale, f.
vomit ['vɔmit], v.t., v.i. vomir.—n. vomissement, m.
voodoo ['vu:du:], n. vaudou, m.
voracious [və'reiʃəs], a. vorace.
voraciously [və'reiʃəsli], adv. avec voracité.
voraciousness [və'reiʃəsnis], n. voracité, f.; voracity [və'ræsiti], n. voracité, f.
vortex ['vɔ:teks], n. (pl. vortices ['vɔ:tisi:z]) tourbillon, m.
vortical ['vɔ:tikl], a. tourbillonnant, en tourbillon.
votaress ['voutəris], n. adoratrice, f.
votary ['voutəri], n. adorateur; (fig.) admirateur, m.
vote [vout], n. vote, m.; voix, f.—v.t., v.i. voter.
voter ['voutə], n. votant, m.
voting ['voutiŋ], n. vote, m.; voting-paper, bulletin de vote, m.
votive ['voutiv], a. votif, voué.
vouch [vautʃ], v.t. attester; affirmer.—v.i. témoigner (de), répondre (de).
voucher ['vautʃə], n. garant, m., garantie; pièce justificative, f.; luncheon voucher, bon de repas, m.
vouchsafe [vautʃ'seif], v.t. daigner, accorder.
vow [vau], n. vœu, m.—v.t. vouer.—v.i. faire un vœu; jurer.
vowel ['vauəl], n. voyelle, f.
voyage ['vɔiidʒ], n. voyage (par mer), m.
voyager ['vɔiidʒə], n. voyageur, passager, m.
vulcanite ['vʌlkənait], n. caoutchouc vulcanisé, m., ébonite, f.
vulcanize ['vʌlkənaiz], v.t. vulcaniser.
vulgar ['vʌlgə], a. vulgaire, commun.
vulgarism ['vʌlgərizm], n. expression vulgaire, f.
vulgarity [vʌl'gæriti], n. vulgarité, grossièreté, f.; mauvais goût, m.
vulgarize ['vʌlgəraiz], v.t. vulgariser.

623

vulnerability

vulnerability [vʌlnərə'biliti], *n.* vulnérabilité, *f.*
vulnerable ['vʌlnərəbl], *a.* vulnérable.
vulpine ['vʌlpain], *a.* de renard; (*fig.*) rusé.
vulture ['vʌltʃə], *n.* vautour, *m.*

W

W, w ['dʌbəlju:]. vingt-troisième lettre de l'alphabet, *m.*
wad [wɔd], *n.* bourre (*armes à feu etc.*), *f.*; tampon, paquet (*faisceau*), *m.—v.t.* bourrer (*armes à feu etc.*); ouater (*vêtement etc.*).
wadded ['wɔdid], *a.* ouaté (*de*).
wadding ['wɔdiŋ], *n.* bourre (*armes à feu*); ouate (*rembourrage*), *f.*
waddle [wɔdl], *v.i.* se dandiner.
waddling ['wɔdliŋ], *n.* dandinement, *m.*
wade [weid], *v.t.* traverser à gué.—*v.i.* marcher (dans l'eau *ou* dans la vase).
wafer ['weifə], *n.* pain à cacheter, *m.*; gaufrette; (*R.-C. Ch.*) hostie, *f.*
waffle [wɔfl], *n.* gaufre, *f.*
waffle-iron ['wɔflaiən], *n.* gaufrier, *m.*
waft [wɔft], *v.t.* porter, transporter; faire flotter.
wag [wæg], *n.* badin, plaisant, farceur, *m.—v.t.* remuer, agiter.—*v.i.* s'agiter, remuer, se mouvoir.
wage [weidʒ], *v.t.* faire.—*n.* [WAGES].
wager ['weidʒə], *n.* gageure, *f.*, pari, *m.—v.t.* gager, parier.
wages ['weidʒiz], *n.pl.* gages (*de serviteur*), *m.pl.*; salaire, *m.*, paye (*d'ouvrier*), *f.*
waggery ['wægəri], *n.* espièglerie, plaisanterie, *f.*
waggish ['wægiʃ], *a.* badin, malin, facétieux.
waggishness ['wægiʃnis], *n.* badinage, *m.*, espièglerie, *f.*
waggle [wægl], *v.t.* remuer.—*v.i.* frétiller.
waggon, wagon ['wægən], *n.* charrette, *f.*, chariot; (*Mil.*) caisson, fourgon; (*Rail.*) wagon, *m.*
wagtail ['wægteil], *n.* hochequeue, *m.*
waif [weif], *n.* épave, *f.*
wail [weil], *v.t.* pleurer. lamenter.—*v.i.* pleurer, gémir, se lamenter.—*n.* (*also* **wailing** ['weiliŋ]) cri, *m.*, lamentation, plainte, *f.*
wain [wein], *n.* charrette, *f.*
wainscot ['weinzkət], *n.* lambris, *m.*, boiserie, *f.*
waist [weist], *n.* ceinture, taille, *f.*
waistband ['weistbænd], *n.* ceinture (*de pantalon etc.*), *f.*
waistcoat ['weis(t)kout], *n.* gilet, *m.*
wait [weit], *v.t.* attendre.—*v.i.* attendre; servir (*à table etc.*).—*n.* embuscade, *f.*, guet-apens, *m.*; attente, *f.*
waiter ['weitə], *n.* garçon, *m.*
waiting ['weitiŋ], *n.* attente, *f.*; service (*attentions*), *m.*; **no waiting**, stationnement interdit, *m.*
waiting-maid ['weitiŋmeid], **waiting-woman** ['weitiŋwumən] (*pl.* **-women**

[wimin]), *n.* femme de chambre; cameriste (*de princesse etc.*), *f.*
waiting-room ['weitiŋru:m], *n.* salle d'attente, *f.*
waitress ['weitris], *n.* servante, fille de service, *f.*
waits [weits], *n.pl.* chanteurs de noëls, *m.pl.*
waive [weiv], *v.t.* écarter, mettre de côté; abandonner, renoncer.
wake (1) [weik], *v.t. irr.* éveiller, réveiller.—*v.i.* veiller (*ne pas se coucher*); se réveiller (*de sommeil*).—*n.* fête de village, *f.*
wake (2) [weik], *n.* sillage (*de navire*), *m.*; (*fig.*) suite, *f.*
wakeful ['weikful], *a.* éveillé; vigilant.
wakefulness ['weikfulnis], *n.* insomnie, *f.*
waken ['weikən], *v.t.* éveiller, réveiller.—*v.i.* s'éveiller, se réveiller.
waking ['weikiŋ], **wakening** ['weikniŋ], *a.* éveillé.—*n.* réveil, *m.*
wale [weil], *n.* marque (*de fouet*); côte (*de tissu*); (*pl.*) (*Naut.*) préceinte, *f.*
Wales [weilz]. le Pays de Galles, *m.*
walk [wɔ:k], *v.t.* parcourir, traverser à pied; faire à pied (*distance etc.*); mettre au pas (*cheval*).—*v.i.* marcher; aller à pied; se promener (*pour le plaisir*); aller au pas (*cheval*); **to walk over**, traverser *ou* parcourir à pied.—*n.* marche; promenade, *f.*, tour, *m.*; allée (*sentier*); démarche, allure, *f.*; pas (*de cheval*), *m.*; (*fig.*) sphère, *f.*, chemin, *m.*; **at a walk**, au pas.
walker ['wɔ:kə], *n.* promeneur, marcheur; piéton, *m.*
walkie-talkie ['wɔ:ki'tɔ:ki], *n.* (*fam.*) émetteur-récepteur portatif, *m.*
walking ['wɔ:kiŋ], *a.* ambulant; de marche.—*n.* la marche; promenade à pied, *f.*
walking-stick ['wɔ:kiŋstik], *n.* canne, *f.*
walk-over ['wɔ:kouvə], *n.* (*Spt.*) **to have a walk-over**, remporter une victoire facile, gagner sans concurrent.
wall [wɔ:l], *n.* muraille, *f.*, mur, *m.*, paroi, *f.*, espalier (*à fruits*), *m.—v.t.* entourer de murailles; **to wall up**, murer.
wallet ['wɔlit], *n.* portefeuille, *f.*
wall-eye ['wɔ:lai], *n.* œil vairon, *m.*
wallflower ['wɔ:lflauə], *n.* giroflée jaune, ravenelle, *f.*
wall-fruit ['wɔ:lfru:t], *n.* fruit d'espalier, *m.*
walling ['wɔ:liŋ], *n.* muraillement, *m.*; murs, *m.pl.*
wallop ['wɔləp], *v.t.* rosser.
walloping ['wɔləpiŋ], *n.* rossée, volée de coups, roulée, *f.*
wallow ['wɔlou], *v.i.* se vautrer, se rouler.
wall-paper ['wɔ:lpeipə], *n.* papier peint, *m.*
walnut ['wɔ:lnʌt], *n.* noix, *f.*; noyer (*bois*), *m.*
walnut-tree ['wɔ:lnʌttri:], *n.* noyer, *m.*
walrus ['wɔ:lrəs], *n.* morse, cheval marin, *m.*
Walter ['wɔ:ltə]. Gauthier, *m.*
waltz [wɔ:l(t)s], *n.* valse, *f.—v.i.* valser.
waltzer ['wɔ:l(t)sə], *n.* valseur, *m.*
waltzing ['wɔ:l(t)siŋ], *n.* valse, *f.*
wan [wɔn], *a.* blême, pâle, pâlot.
wand [wɔnd], *n.* baguette, *f.*
wander ['wɔndə], *v.i.* errer; divaguer (*l'esprit*); délirer.
wanderer ['wɔndərə], *n.* vagabond, *m.*
wandering ['wɔndəriŋ], *a.* errant, vagabond; nomade (*tribu etc.*); (*fig.*) distrait.—*n.* course errante, divagation, *f.*; délire, *m.*

wanderlust ['wɔndəlʌst], *n.* manie des voyages, *f.*

wane [wein], *n.* déclin, *m.*; (*fig.*) décadence, *f.* —*v.i.* décroître (*lune*); (*fig.*) décliner.

wanly ['wɔnli], *adv.* avec pâleur.

wanness ['wɔnnis], *n.* pâleur, *f.*

want [wɔnt], *n.* besoin; manque, défaut (*absence*), *m.*; indigence, misère (*pauvreté*), *f.*; **for want of,** faute de.—*v.t.* avoir besoin de; manquer de; vouloir, désirer (*avoir envie de*); demander (*réclamer*).—*v.i.* manquer (*de*).

wanting ['wɔntiŋ], *a.* qui manque, manquant.

wanton ['wɔntən], *a.* folâtre (*capricieux*); licencieux, libertin (*impudique*); gratuit (*sans cause*).—*n.* débauchée, *f.*—*v.i.* folâtrer.

wantonly ['wɔntənli], *adv.* en folâtrant; gratuitement.

wantonness ['wɔntənnis], *n.* légèreté, *f.*; libertinage, *m.*

war [wɔ:], *n.* guerre, *f.*—*v.i.* faire la guerre (*à*), lutter (*contre*).

warble [wɔ:bl], *v.t., v.i.* gazouiller; (*fig.*) chanter.

warbler ['wɔ:blə], *n.* oiseau chanteur, *m.*; fauvette (*oiseau*), *f.*

warbling ['wɔ:bliŋ], *a.* mélodieux.—*n.* gazouillement, *m.*

ward [wɔ:d], *n.* pupille, *m.*, *f.*; tutelle (*protection*); garde (*de serrure*); salle (*d'hôpital*), *f.*; arrondissement (*de ville*), *m.*—*v.i.* **to ward off,** parer, détourner.

warden ['wɔ:dn], *n.* gardien; gouverneur, recteur (*d'université*); directeur (*de collège*), conservateur (*de jardin public*), *m.*

warder ['wɔ:də], *n.* gardien de prison, *m.*

wardress ['wɔ:dris], *n.* gardienne de prison, *f.*

wardrobe ['wɔ:droub], *n.* garde-robe, armoire (*meuble*), *f.*

ward-room ['wɔ:dru:m], *n.* (*Naut.*) carré des officiers, *m.*

ware [wɛə], *n.* (*collect.*) articles fabriqués, *m.pl.*; (*pl.*) marchandises, *f.pl.*

warehouse ['wɛəhaus], *n.* magasin; entrepôt, *m.*—*v.t.* emmagasiner.

warehousing ['wɛəhauziŋ], *n.* emmagasinage, *m.*

warfare ['wɔ:fɛə], *n.* la guerre, *f.*; les opérations, *f.pl.*

warily ['wɛərili], *adv.* prudemment, avec circonspection.

wariness ['wɛərinis], *n.* prudence, circonspection, *f.*

warlike ['wɔ:laik], *a.* guerrier, martial, belliqueux.

warlock ['wɔ:lɔk], *n.* sorcier, *m.*

warm [wɔ:m], *a.* chaud; (*fig.*) zélé, ardent; chaleureux (*accueil*).—*v.t.* chauffer; réchauffer (*ce qui s'était refroidi*); (*fig.*) échauffer.—*v.i.* chauffer, se chauffer, (*fig.*) s'animer.

warming ['wɔ:miŋ], *n.* chauffage, *m.*

warming-pan ['wɔ:miŋpæn], *n.* bassinoire, *f.*

warmly ['wɔ:mli], *adv.* chaudement; (*fig.*) vivement.

war-monger ['wɔ:mʌŋgə], *n.* belliciste, *m.*, *f.*

warmth [wɔ:mθ], *n.* chaleur; (*fig.*) ardeur, *f.*

war-office ['wɔ:rɔfis], *n.* ministère de la guerre, *m.*

warn [wɔ:n], *v.t.* avertir, prévenir (*de*); **to warn against,** mettre en garde contre.

warning ['wɔ:niŋ], *n.* avertissement, avis, *m.*

warp [wɔ:p], *n.* chaîne (*tissage*), *f.*—*v.t.* ourdir (*tissage*); faire déjeter (*bois*); (*Naut.*) touer; (*fig.*) fausser, pervertir.—*v.i.* se déjeter, se déformer; gauchir; (*fig.*) dévier (*de*).

warping ['wɔ:piŋ], *n.* ourdissage (*tissage*); déjettement, gauchissement (*de bois*), *m.*

warrant ['wɔrənt], *n.* autorisation, garantie, *f.*; ordre, mandat; mandat d'amener, *m.*; (*fig.*) justification, *f.*—*v.t.* garantir, autoriser.

warrant-officer ['wɔrəntɔfisə], *n.* (*Mil.*) adjudant; (*Naut.*) premier maître, *m.*

warrantor ['wɔrəntə], *n.* (*Law*) garant, *m.*

warranty ['wɔrənti], *n.* garantie, *f.*

warren ['wɔrən], *n.* garenne, *f.*

warrior ['wɔriə], *n.* guerrier, soldat, *m.*

Warsaw ['wɔ:sɔ:], Varsovie, *f.*

wart [wɔ:t], *n.* verrue, *f.*, poireau, *m.*

warted ['wɔ:tid], **warty** ['wɔ:ti], *a.* couvert de verrues; (*Bot.*) verruqueux.

wary ['wɛəri], *a.* avisé, prudent; défiant.

wash [wɔʃ], *n.* blanchissage, *m.*, lessive (*de linge*), *f.*; (*Paint.*) lavis; sillage (*de navire*), *m.*—*v.t.* blanchir (*linge*); (*fig.*) mouiller, laver.—*v.i.* se laver; faire la lessive (*blanchisseuse etc.*); **to wash up,** faire la vaisselle.

washable ['wɔʃəbl], *a.* lavable.

washer ['wɔʃə], *n.* laveur, *m.*; machine à laver; (*Tech.*) rondelle, *f.*

washer-woman ['wɔʃəwumən], *n.* (*pl.* **-women** [wimin]) blanchisseuse, *f.*

wash-hand basin ['wɔʃhændbeisn], *n.* cuvette, *f.*

wash-house ['wɔʃhaus], *n.* lavoir, *m.*, buanderie, *f.*

washing ['wɔʃiŋ], *n.* lavage; blanchissage (*du linge*), *m.*

washing-machine ['wɔʃiŋməʃi:n], *n.* machine à laver, *f.*

wash-leather ['wɔʃlɛðə], *n.* peau de chamois, *f.*

wash-stand ['wɔʃstænd], *n.* toilette, *f.*; lavabo (*petit*), *m.*

wash-tub ['wɔʃtʌb], *n.* baquet, *m.*

washy ['wɔʃi], *a.* humide, mouillé; (*fig.*) fade.

wasp [wɔsp], *n.* guêpe, *f.*; **wasps' nest,** guêpier, *m.*

waspish ['wɔspiʃ], *a.* irascible, irritable.

waspishness ['wɔspiʃnis], *n.* humeur irascible, *f.*

wastage ['weistidʒ], *n.* gaspillage, *m.*

waste [weist], *a.* de rebut; sans valeur; perdu (*inemployé*), *f.*; inculte (*terre*).—*n.* perte (*mauvais emploi*), *f.*; déchet (*à nettoyer*); gaspillage; rebut, *m.*; terre inculte, *f.*—*v.t.* gaspiller; perdre (*employer mal*); gâcher (*faire sans soin*); ravager, dévaster (*piller*).—*v.i.* s'user, s'épuiser; **to waste away,** dépérir, maigrir.

waste-book ['weistbuk], *n.* brouillard, *m.*

wasteful ['weistful], *a.* dissipateur, prodigue.

wastefulness ['weistfulnis], *n.* prodigalité, perte, *f.*, gaspillage, *m.*

waste-paper ['weist'peipə], *n.* papier de rebut, *m.*

waste-paper basket ['weistpeipə'bɑ:skit], *n.* corbeille à papier, *f.*

waste-pipe ['weistpaip], *n.* tuyau de dégagement; écoulement, *m.*

waster ['weistə], **wastrel** ['weistril] *n.* prodigue, *m.*, *f.*, gaspilleur, *m.*

wasting ['weistiŋ], *a.* qui épuise.—*n.* dépérissement, *m.*, consumption (*du corps*), *f.*

watch [wɔtʃ], *n.* montre; veille (*nocturne*); vigilance (*attention*); garde, *f.*; (*Naut.*) quart, *m.*—*v.t.* veiller sur, surveiller, regarder, épier.—*v.i.* veiller (*ne pas dormir*); prendre, garde (*faire attention*); monter la garde; (*Naut.*) faire le quart.

watch-dog ['wɔtʃdɔg], *n.* chien de garde, *m.*

watcher ['wɔtʃə], *n.* surveillant, veilleur, *m.*

watch-fire ['wɔtʃfaiə], *n.* feu de bivouac, *m.*

watchful ['wɔtʃful], *a.* vigilant, attentif.

watchfulness ['wɔtʃfulnis], *n.* vigilance, *f.*

watching ['wɔtʃiŋ], *n.* surveillance, *f.*

watch-maker ['wɔtʃmeikə], *n.* horloger, *m.*

watch-making ['wɔtʃmeikiŋ], *n.* horlogerie, *f.*

watchman ['wɔtʃmən], *n.* (*pl.* **-men** [men]) gardien; veilleur de nuit, *m.*

watch-tower ['wɔtʃtauə], *n.* tour de guet, *f.*

watchword ['wɔtʃwəːd], *n.* mot d'ordre, *m.*

water ['wɔːtə], *a.* d'eau, à eau; aquatique. —*n.* eau; marée (*flux*), *f.*, (*fig.*) ordre, rang, *m.*; *drinking water*, eau potable; *fresh water*, eau douce (*pas salée*).—*v.t.* arroser; donner à boire à, abreuver (*animal*); mettre de l'eau dans, couper (*diluer*); moirer (*étoffe*).

water-bottle ['wɔːtəbɔtl], *n.* carafe, *f.*; (*Mil. etc.*) bidon, *m.*; bouillotte (*pour chauffer le lit*), *f.*

water-carrier ['wɔːtəkæriə], *n.* porteur d'eau; broc (*à eau*), *m.*

water-cart ['wɔːtəkɑːt], *n.* voiture d'arrosage, *f.*

water-closet ['wɔːtəklɔzit], *n.* toilettes, *f.pl.*, cabinet d'aisances, *m.*

water-colour ['wɔːtəkʌlə], *n.* aquarelle, *f.*

watercress ['wɔːtəkres], *n.* cresson, cresson de fontaine, *m.*

water-cure ['wɔːtəkjuə], *n.* hydrothérapie, *f.*

watered ['wɔːtəd], *a.* arrosé; moiré (*étoffe*).

waterfall ['wɔːtəfɔːl], *n.* cascade; chute d'eau, *f.*

water-fowl ['wɔːtəfaul], *n.* oiseau aquatique, *m.*

waterfront ['wɔːtəfrʌnt], *n.* les quais, *m.pl.*, port, *m.*

water-hen ['wɔːtəhen], *n.* poule d'eau, *f.*

wateriness ['wɔːtərinis], *n.* aquosité, *f.*

watering ['wɔːtəriŋ], *n.* arrosage (*plantes*), *m.*; irrigation (*terre*), *f.*; abreuvage (*animaux*); moirage (*étoffe*), *m.*

watering-can ['wɔːtəriŋkæn], *n.* arrosoir, *m.*

watering-place ['wɔːtəriŋpleis], *n.* ville d'eaux, station thermale, *f.*; abreuvoir (*pour animaux*), *m.*

water-jug ['wɔːtədʒʌg], *n.* pot à eau, *m.*

water-level ['wɔːtəlevl], *n.* niveau d'eau, *m.*

water-lily ['wɔːtəlili], *n.* nénuphar, *m.*

water-line ['wɔːtəlain], *n.* ligne de flottaison, *f.*

water-logged ['wɔːtəlɔgd], *a.* envahi par les eaux.

watermark ['wɔːtəmɑːk], *n.* étiage (*de rivière*); filigrane (*sur papier*), *m.*

water-melon ['wɔːtəmelən], *n.* melon d'eau, *m.*, pastèque, *f.*

water-mill ['wɔːtəmil], *n.* moulin à eau, *m.*

water-pipe ['wɔːtəpaip], *n.* tuyau d'eau, *m.*

water-plant ['wɔːtəplɑːnt], *n.* plante aquatique, *f.*

water-polo ['wɔːtəpoulou], *n.* polo nautique, *m.*

water-power ['wɔːtəpauə], *n.* force hydraulique, *f.*

water-pressure ['wɔːtəpreʃə], *n.* pression d'eau, *f.*

waterproof ['wɔːtəpruːf], *a.* and *n.* imperméable, *m.*—*v.t.* rendre imperméable, cirer (*un tissu*).

water-rat ['wɔːtəræt], *n.* rat d'eau, *m.*

water-rate ['wɔːtəreit], *n.* taux d'abonnement aux eaux de la ville, *m.*

watershed ['wɔːtəʃed], *n.* versant, *m.*

waterspout ['wɔːtəspaut], *n.* trombe, *f.*; tuyau de descente, *m.*

water-tank ['wɔːtətæŋk], *n.* réservoir à eau, *m.*, citerne, *f.*

water-tight ['wɔːtətait], *a.* étanche.

water-works ['wɔːtəwəːks], *n.pl.* établissement pour la distribution des eaux, *m.*, machine hydraulique, *f.*

watery ['wɔːtəri], *a.* aqueux; mouillé, plein d'eau; (*poet.*) humide.

watt [wɔt], *n.* (*Elec.*) watt, *m.*

wattage ['wɔtidʒ], *n.* (*Elec.*) wattage, *m.*

wattle [wɔtl], *n.* claie (*d'osier etc.*), *f.*—*v.t.* clayonner.

wave [weiv], *n.* vague, *f.*, flot, *m.*, lame, ondulation; (*poet.*) onde, *f.*; signe (*de la main*), *m.*; *permanent wave*, permanente, indéfrisable, *f.*; *long waves*, (*Rad.*) grandes ondes, *f.*; *short waves*, petites ondes, ondes courtes, *f.pl.*—*v.t.* agiter, faire signe de (*la main*); onduler (*cheveux*).—*v.i.* ondoyer, onduler, flotter; faire signe (*à*).

waved [weivd], *a.* ondulé.

wave-length ['weivleŋθ], *n.* longueur d'onde, *f.*

waver ['weivə], *v.i.* hésiter, vaciller, balancer.

waverer ['weivərə], *n.* personne indécise, *f.*, esprit vacillant, *m.*

wavering ['weivəriŋ], *a.* indécis, vacillant, irrésolu.—*n.* hésitation, indécision, *f.*

waving ['weiviŋ], *n.* ondoiement, *m.*, ondulation (*blé etc.*), *f.*; geste (*de la main*), *m.*

wavy ['weivi], *a.* ondoyant, onduleux.

wax [wæks], *n.* cire; poix (*de cordonnier*); (*colloq.*) colère, *f.*—*v.t.* cirer, enduire de cire. —*v.i.* croître (*lune*), s'accroître; devenir.

wax-candle ['wæks'kændl], *n.* bougie, *f.*

waxen [wæksn], *a.* de cire; cireux.

wax-taper ['wæks'teipə], *n.* rat de cave; (*Eccles.*) cierge, *m.*

waxwing ['wækswiŋ], *n.* (*Orn.*) jaseur, *m.*

waxwork ['wækswəːk], *n.* ouvrage de cire, *m.*; (*pl.*) figures de cire, *f.*, *pl.*

waxy ['wæksi], *a.* cireux; (*colloq.*) en colère.

way [wei], *n.* chemin, *m.*, route, voie, *f.*; passage; côté, sens, *m.*, direction; manière, façon, mode, *f.*; moyen, *m.*, méthode, *f.*; état (*condition*), *m.*; *a long way off*, loin, très loin; *by a long way* (*by far*), de beaucoup; *by the way*, à propos.

way-bill ['weibil], *n.* feuille de route, *f.*

wayfarer ['weifeərə], *n.* voyageur, *m.*

wayfaring ['weifeəriŋ], *a.* qui voyage.

waylay [wei'lei], *v.t.* guetter, guetter au passage.

wayside ['weisaid], *a.* au bord de la route.— *n.* bord de la route, *m.*

wayward ['weiwəd], *a.* capricieux, entêté.

waywardness ['weiwədnis], *n.* humeur capricieuse, *f.*

we [wi:], *pron.* nous; (*indef.*) on; *we Frenchmen,* nous autres Français.

weak [wi:k], *a.* faible, infirme, débile.

weaken ['wi:kn], *v.t.* affaiblir; atténuer.—*v.i.* s'affaiblir.

weakening ['wi:kniŋ], *n.* affaiblissement, *m.*

weakling ['wi:kliŋ], *n.* être faible, faiblard, *m.*

weakly ['wi:kli], *a.* faible; infirme, débile.— *adv.* faiblement, sans force.

weak-minded ['wi:k'maindid], *a.* d'esprit faible.

weakness ['wi:knis], *n.* faiblesse; débilité, *f.*; (*fig.*) faible, *m.*

weak-spirited ['wi:k'spiritid], *a.* mou, sans courage.

weal [wi:l], *n.* bien, bien-être, bonheur, *m.*; marque (*sur la peau*), *f.*

wealth [welθ], *n.* richesse, *f.*, richesses, *f.pl.*; profusion, *f.*

wealthy ['welθi], *a.* riche, opulent.

wean [wi:n], *v.t.* sevrer; (*fig.*) détacher.

weaning ['wi:niŋ], *n.* sevrage, *m.*

weanling ['wi:nliŋ], *n.* enfant *ou* animal en sevrage, *m.*

weapon [wepn], *n.* arme, *f.*

wear [wɛə], *v.t. irr.* porter (*habits*); mettre (*enfiler*); *to wear out,* user, (*fig.*) épuiser, lasser.—*v.i.* s'user (*s'élimer*); se porter (*habits*); (*fig.*) se conserver.—*n.* usage (*port*), *m.*; usure (*élimage*), *f.*

wearable ['wɛərəbl], *a.* mettable.

wearied ['wiərid], *a.* fatigué, las; (*fig.*) ennuyé.

wearily ['wiərili], *adv.* péniblement, d'un air las.

weariness ['wiərinis], *n.* fatigue, lassitude, *f.*; (*fig.*) ennui, *m.*

wearisome ['wiərisəm], *a.* ennuyeux; lassant.

wearisomeness ['wiərisəmnis], *n.* nature ennuyeuse, *f.*

weary ['wiəri], *a.* fatigué, las, ennuyé; ennuyeux (*chose*).—*v.t.* lasser, fatiguer; ennuyer.

weasel ['wi:zl], *n.* belette, *f.*

weather ['weðə], *a.* du côté du vent.—*n.* temps, *m.*; (*fig.*) tempête, *f.*—*v.t.* résister à (*tempête etc.*); (*fig.*) tenir tête à.

weather-beaten ['weðəbi:tn], *a.* battu par la tempête; (*fig.*) fatigué; hâlé.

weathercock ['weðəkɔk], *n.* girouette, *f.*

weather-glass ['weðəglɑ:s], *n.* baromètre, *m.*

weather-proof ['weðəpru:f], *a.* à l'épreuve du (*mauvais*) temps, imperméable.

weather-report ['weðəripɔ:t], *n.* bulletin météorologique, *m.*

weather-ship ['weðəʃip], *n.* navire météorologique, *m.*

weave [wi:v], *n.* (*Tex.*) tissage, *m.*—*v.t., v.i. irr.* tisser; tresser (*entrelacer*).

weaver ['wi:və], *n.* tisserand, *m.*

weaving ['wi:viŋ], *n.* tissage, *m.*

web [web], *n.* tissu, *m.*; sangle (*pour selle*); toile (*d'araignée*), *f.*

webbed [webd], **webby** ['webi], *a.* palmé.

webbing ['webiŋ], *n.* sangles (*de chaise, lit etc.*), *f.pl.*

web-footed ['webfutid], *a.* palmipède.

wed [wed], *v.t.* épouser, se marier avec.—*v.i.* se marier.

wedded ['wedid], *a.* marié (*à*); conjugal.

wedding ['wediŋ], *a.* de noces, de mariage.— *n.* noce, *f.*, noces, *f.pl.*, mariage, *m.*

wedding-ring ['wediŋriŋ], *n.* alliance, *f.*

wedge [wedʒ], *n.* coin, *m.*; cale (*pour tenir immobile*), *f.*—*v.t.* serrer; caler; coincer.

wedge-shaped ['wedʒʃeipt], *a.* en forme de coin, cunéiforme.

wedlock ['wedlɔk], *n.* mariage, *m.*

Wednesday ['wenzd(e)i]. mercredi, *m.*; *Ash Wednesday,* mercredi des Cendres.

weed [wi:d], *n.* mauvaise herbe, *f.*; *widow's weeds,* vêtements de deuil, *m.pl.*—*v.t.* sarcler; (*fig.*) nettoyer; *to weed out,* extirper.

weeder ['wi:də], *n.* sarcleur (*personne*); sarcloir (*outil*), *m.*

weeding ['wi:diŋ], *n.* sarclage, *m.*

weed-killer ['wi:dkilə], *n.* herbicide, *m.*

weedy ['wi:di], *a.* plein de mauvaises herbes; (*fig.*) chétif.

week [wi:k], *n.* semaine, *f.*; *this day week,* d'aujourd'hui en huit (*avenir*); il y a huit jours (*passé*).

weekday ['wi:kdei], *n.* jour ouvrable, jour de semaine, *m.*

week-end ['wi:k'end], *n.* fin de la semaine, *f.*, week-end, *m.*

weekly ['wi:kli], *a.* de la semaine; hebdomadaire (*revue*).—*n.* hebdomadaire, *m.*—*adv.* par semaine, tous les huit jours.

weep [wi:p], *v.t., v.i. irr.* pleurer; *to weep bitterly,* pleurer à chaudes larmes.

weeping ['wi:piŋ], *a.* qui pleure, éploré; (*Bot.*) pleureur; *weeping-willow,* saule pleureur, *m.*—*n.* pleurs, *m.pl.*, larmes, *f.pl.*

weever ['wi:və], *n.* (*Ichth.*) vive, *f.*

weevil ['wi:vl], *n.* charançon, *m.*

weft [weft], *n.* trame, *f.*

weigh [wei], *v.t.* peser; (*fig.*) juger; (*Naut.*) lever (*l'ancre*).—*v.i.* peser.

weigh-bridge ['weibridʒ], *n.* pont à bascule, *m.*

weighing ['weiiŋ], *n.* pesage, *m.*; *weighing-machine,* bascule, *f.*

weight [weit], *n.* poids, *m.*; *atomic weight,* masse atomique, *f.*

weighted ['weitid], *a.* chargé (*de*).

weightily ['weitili], *adv.* pesamment.

weightless ['weitlis], *a.* sans poids.

weightlessness ['weitlisnis], *n.* apesanteur, *f.*

weighty ['weiti], *a.* pesant, lourd; (*fig.*) important.

weir [wiə], *n.* barrage, déversoir, *m.*

weird [wiəd], *a.* fantastique, étrange.

weirdness ['wiədnis], *n.* étrangeté, magie, *f.*

welcome ['welkəm], *a.* bienvenu, agréable (*chose*); libre (*à profiter de quelque chose*).— *n.* bienvenue, *f.*, accueil, *m.*; *to bid (someone) welcome,* souhaiter la bienvenue à (quelqu'un).—*int.* soyez le bienvenu.—*v.t.* souhaiter la bienvenue à, bien accueillir.

weld [weld], *v.t.* souder; (*fig.*) unir.—*n.* soudure, *f.*

welder ['weldə], *n.* soudeur, *m.*

welding ['weldiŋ], *n.* soudure, *f.*

welfare ['welfɛə], *n.* bien-être, bien, *m.*; *Welfare State,* état providence, *m.*

well (1) [wel], *n.* puits, *m.*; (*fig.*) source, *f.*; *ink-well,* encrier, *m.*—*v.i.* jaillir (*de*).

well (2) [wel], *a.* bien, en bonne santé; bon, heureux (*fortuné*); utile, profitable; *to get well,* se rétablir; *well off,* aisé (*riche*).—

adv. bien; très, fort; comme il faut; *well!* eh bien! *well done!* très bien! bravo! *well, I never!* pas possible!

well-being ['wel'biːiŋ], *n.* bien-être, *m.*

well-informed ['welin'fɔːmd], *a.* instruit; bien renseigné.

wellingtons ['weliŋtənz], *n.pl.* demi-bottes, *f.pl.*

well-known ['welnoun], *a.* bien connu, célèbre.

well-meaning ['wel'miːniŋ], *a.* bien intentionné.

well-meant ['wel'ment], *a.* fait à bonne intention.

well-nigh ['welnai], *adv.* presque.

well-timed ['wel'taimd], *a.* à propos, fait à propos.

well-to-do ['weltə'duː], *a.* très aisé, cossu.

well-wisher ['welwiʃə], *n.* ami, partisan, *m.*

Welsh [welʃ], *a.* gallois, du pays de Galles.— *n.* gallois *(langue)*, *m.*; *the Welsh*, les Gallois, *m.pl.*

Welshman ['welʃmən], *n.* (*pl.* **-men** [men]) Gallois, *m.*

welt [welt], *n.* bordure *(de gant)*; trépointe *(de semelle)*, *f.*

welter ['weltə], *n.* confusion, *f.*—*v.i.* se vautrer, se rouler.

wen [wen], *n.* loupe, *f.*; goitre, *m.*

wench [wentʃ], *n.* donzelle; (*pej.*) souillon, *f.*

wend [wend], *v.t.*, *v.i.* aller; *to wend one's way*, se diriger (*vers*).

wer(e)wolf ['wəːwulf], *n.* loup-garou, *m.*

west [west], *a.* de l'ouest, occidental.—*n.* ouest, occident, couchant, *m.*—*adv.* à l'ouest.

westerly ['westəli], *a.* d'ouest.—*adv.* vers l'ouest.

western ['westən], *a.* de l'ouest, occidental, ouest, d'occident; à l'ouest *(vue)*.—*n.* (*Cine.*) western, *m.*

westward ['westwəd], *adv.* à l'ouest.

wet [wet], *a.* mouillé, humide; pluvieux *(temps)*; *it is wet*, il pleut; *to get wet*, se mouiller; *wet through*, mouillé jusqu'aux os, trempé.—*n.* humidité; pluie, *f.* —*v.t. irr.* mouiller, humecter; arroser.

wetness ['wetnis], *n.* humidité, *f.*; état pluvieux, *m.*

wetting ['wetiŋ], *n.* trempage, *m.*

whack [hwæk], *n.* grand coup, *m.*; *(fam.)* part, *f.*—*v.t.* frapper, battre.

whale [hweil], *n.* baleine, *f.*

whalebone ['hweilboun], *n.* baleine, *f.*

whale-oil ['hweiloil], *n.* huile de baleine, *f.*

whaler ['hweilə], *n.* baleinier, *m.*

wharf [hwɔːf], *n.* (*pl.* **wharfs** [hwɔːfs], **wharves** [hwɔːvz]) quai, embarcadère, débarcadère; entrepôt *(pour marchandises)*, *m.*

what [hwɔt], *a.* quel, *m.*, quelle, *f.*, quels, *m.pl.*, quelles, *f.pl.*—*pron.rel.* ce qui, ce que; qui, que; quoi.—*inter. pron.* qu'est-ce qui? que? qu'est-ce que? quoi? *what!* comment!

whatever [hwɔt'evə], **whatsoever** [hwɔtsou'evə], *pron.* and *a.* quoi que ce soit; quelque … que; tout ce qui, tout ce que *(all that)*.

whatnot ['hwɔtnɔt], *n.* étagère, *f.*

whatsoever [WHATEVER].

wheat [hwiːt], *n.* blé, froment, *m.*

wheaten ['hwiːtn], *a.* de froment.

wheedle [hwiːdl], *v.t.* cajoler, câliner.

wheedling ['hwiːdliŋ], *a.* cajoleur, câlin.—*n.* cajolerie, câlinerie, *f.*

wheel [hwiːl], *n.* roue, *f.*; volant *(pour conduire)*; rouet *(pour filer)*, *m.*; révolution, *f.*, tour, cercle *(rotation)*; soleil *(feu d'artifice)*, *m.*; *driving wheel*, roue motrice, *f.*; *fly-wheel*, volant, *m.*—*v.t.* rouler, faire tourner; brouetter; voiturer.—*v.i.* rouler *(sur des roues)*; tourner, se tourner *(en cercle)*; tournoyer *(pirouetter)*; *(Mil.)* faire une conversion; *to wheel round*, faire volte-face.

wheel-barrow ['hwiːlbærou], *n.* brouette, *f.*

wheel-chair ['hwiːltʃɛə], *n.* voiture de malade, *f.*, fauteuil roulant, *m.*

wheeled [hwiːld], *a.* à roues.

wheeling ['hwiːliŋ], *n.* (*Mil.*) conversion, *f.*; tournoiement *(d'oiseau)*, *m.*

wheelwright ['hwiːlrait], *n.* charron, *m.*

wheeze [hwiːz], *v.i.* siffler en respirant.

wheezing ['hwiːziŋ], *n.* sifflement, *m.*

wheezy ['hwiːzi], *a.* poussif, asthmatique.

whelk [hwelk], *n.* buccin, *m.*

whelp [hwelp], *n.* petit *(d'un fauve)*. *m.*—*v.i.* mettre bas.

when [hwen], *conj.* quand, lorsque; que, où; *the day when I saw him*, le jour où je l'ai vu.—*inter. adv.* quand est-ce que? quand?

whence [hwens], *adv.* d'où.

whenever [hwen'evə], **whensoever** [hwen sou'evə], *adv.* toutes les fois que, quand, à n'importe quel moment que.

where [hwɛə], *adv.* où; là où.

whereabouts ['hwɛərəbauts], *adv.* où à peu près.—*n.* *to know someone's whereabouts*, savoir où est quelqu'un.

whereas [hwɛər'æz], *adv.* au lieu que, tandis que; *(Law)* vu que.

whereat [hwɛər'æt], *adv.* à quoi, de quoi; sur quoi.

whereby [hwɛə'bai], *adv.* par lequel, par où.

wherefore ['hwɛəfɔː], *adv.* pourquoi, c'est pourquoi.

wherein [hwɛər'in], *adv.* en quoi, dans lequel, où.

whereof [hwɛər'ɔv], *adv.* dont, de quoi, duquel.

whereon [hwɛər'ɔn], **whereupon** ['hwɛərə 'pɔn], *adv.* sur quoi, sur lequel; là-dessus.

wheresoever [hwɛəsou'evə], [WHEREVER].

wherever [hwɛər'evə], *adv.* partout où, n'importe où.

wherewith [hwɛə'wið], *adv.* avec quoi; de quoi.

wherewithal [hwɛəwið'ɔːl], *n.* *to find the wherewithal to …*, trouver les moyens de … *ou* l'argent pour ….

wherry ['hweri], *n.* bachot, *m.*

whet [hwet], *v.t.* aiguiser, affiler; *(fig.)* stimuler.—*n.* aiguisement, repassage; *(fig.)* stimulant, *m.*

whether ['hweðə], *conj.* soit que; si, que; *whether … or*, soit … soit, si … ou, que … ou.

whetstone ['hwetstoun], *n.* pierre à aiguiser, *f.*

whey [hwei], *n.* petit lait, *m.*

which [hwitʃ], *a.* quel, *m.*, quelle, *f.*, quels, *m.pl.*, quelles, *f.pl.*; lequel, *m.*, laquelle, *f.* lesquels, *m.pl.*, lesquelles, *f.pl.*—*rel. pron.*

whose

qui, que, lequel, *m.*, laquelle, *f.*, lesquels, *m.pl.*, lesquelles, *f.pl.*; ce qui, ce que (*that which*), *m.*

whichever [hwitʃ′evə], *pron.* lequel, *m.*, laquelle, *f.*, lesquels, *m.pl.*, lesquelles, *f.pl.*; quelque . . . que; *whichever you buy*, n'importe lequel que vous achetiez.

whiff [hwif], *n.* bouffée, haleine, *f.*—*v.t.* lancer en bouffées.

while [hwail], *n.* temps, *m.*; *a little while ago*, il y a peu de temps; *it is not worth while*, cela n'en vaut pas la peine.—*v.t.* passer, faire passer; *to while away the time*, tuer le temps.—(*also* **whilst** [hwailst]), *conj.* pendant que (*au cours de*); tandis que (*par contraste*); tant que (*tout le temps que*); en, tout en (*suivi d'un participe présent*).

whilst [WHILE].

whim [hwim], *n.* caprice, *m.*

whimper [′hwimpə], *v.i.* pleurnicher.

whimpering [′hwimpəriŋ], *a.* pleurnicheur, geignard.—*n.* pleurnichement, *m.*

whimsical [′hwimzikl], *a.* fantasque; capricieux.

whimsically [′hwimzikli], *adv.* capricieusement, fantasquement.

whin [hwin], *n.* ajonc, genêt épineux, *m.*

whine [hwain], *v.i.* se plaindre, geindre, pleurnicher.—*n.* pleurnichement, *m.*

whining [′hwainiŋ], *a.* plaintif, dolent.—*n.* gémissement, geignement, *m.*; (*fig.*) plaintes, *f.pl.*

whinny [′hwini], *v.i.* hennir.—*n.* hennissement, *m.*

whip [hwip], *n.* fouet, *m.*; cravache (*de cavalier*), *f.*; (*Parl.*) secrétaire d'un parti, appel fait aux membres d'un parti, *m.*—*v.t.* fouetter; (*fig.*) battre.

whip-cord [′hwipkɔːd], *n.* fouet; (*Tex.*) fil à fouet, *m.*

whip-hand [′hwiphænd], *n.* dessus, avantage, *m.*

whip-lash [′hwiplæʃ], *n.* mèche (de fouet), *f.*

whipper-in [′hwipər′in], *n.* piqueur, *m.*

whipper-snapper [′hwipəsnæpə], *n.* petit bout d'homme, *m.*

whippet [′hwipit], *n.* lévrier (de course), *m.*

whipping [′hwipiŋ], *n.* coups de fouet, *m.pl.*

whipping-top [′hwipiŋtɔp], *n.* sabot, *m.*

whir(r) [hwəː], *v.i.* tourner avec bruit; vrombir.—(*also* **whirring** [′hwəːriŋ]), *n.* bruissement, ronronnement, *m.*

whirl [hwəːl], *v.t.* faire tourner, faire tournoyer.—*v.i.* tournoyer, tourbillonner; pirouetter.—*n.* tournoiement; tourbillon (*de poussière etc.*), *m.*

whirligig [′hwəːligig], *n.* tourniquet, *m.*; pirouette, *f.*

whirlpool [′hwəːlpuːl], *n.* tourbillon (d'eau), *m.*

whirlwind [′hwəːlwind], *n.* tourbillon, cyclone, *m.*

whirring [WHIR(R)].

whisk [hwisk], *n.* vergette, époussette, verge (*à œufs etc.*), *f.*—*v.t.* épousseter; fouetter (*crème*); battre (*œufs*).—*v.i.* passer rapidement.

whiskered [′hwiskəd], *a.* à favoris; à moustaches (*animal*).

whiskers [′hwiskəz], *n.* favoris, *m.pl.*; moustache (*de chat etc.*), *f.*

whisky, whiskey [′hwiski], *n.* whisky, *m.*

whisper [′hwispə], *n.* chuchotement, *m.*—*v.t.* chuchoter, dire à l'oreille.—*v.i.* chuchoter, parler tout bas.

whispering [′hwispəriŋ], *n.* chuchotement, *m.*

whist [hwist], *n.* whist, *m.*

whistle [hwisl], *n.* sifflet; coup de sifflet; sifflement (*du vent*); (*colloq.*) gosier, bec (*gorge*), *m.*—*v.t., v.i.* siffler.

whistler [′hwislə], *n.* siffleur, *m.*

whistling [′hwisliŋ], *a.* sifflant.—*n.* sifflement, coup de sifflet, *m.*

whit [hwit], *n.* iota, point, atome, brin, *m.*

white [hwait], *a.* blanc; (*fig.*) sans tache, pur.—*n.* blanc; aubier (*de bois*), *m.*

whitebait [′hwaitbeit], *n.* blanchaille, *f.*

whiten [hwaitn], *v.t.* blanchir; (*Build.*) badigeonner.—*v.i.* blanchir.

whiteness [′hwaitnis], *n.* blancheur; pâleur, *f.*

whitening [′hwaitniŋ], *n.* action de blanchir, *f.*; [WHITING (1)].

whitewash [′hwaitwɔʃ], *n.* blanc de chaux, *m.*—*v.t.* blanchir à la chaux; badigeonner.

whither [′hwiðə], *adv.* où, par où.

whithersoever [hwiðəsou′evə], *adv.* n'importe où.

whiting (1) [′hwaitiŋ], **whitening** [′hwaitniŋ], *n.* blanc d'Espagne, *m.*

whiting (2) [′hwaitiŋ], *n.* (*Ichth.*) merlan, *m.*

whitish [′hwaitiʃ], *a.* blanchâtre.

whitlow [′hwitlou], *n.* panaris, *m.*

Whitsun [′hwitsən], *a.* de la Pentecôte; *Whitsunday*, le dimanche de la Pentecôte.

Whitsuntide [′hwitsəntaid]. Pentecôte, *f.*

whiz(z) [hwiz], *v.i.* siffler.

whizzing [′hwiziŋ], *n.* sifflement, *m.*

who [huː], *pron.* (*rel.*) qui; lequel; (*inter.*) qui? qui est-ce qui?

whodunit [huː′dʌnit], *n.* (*colloq.*) roman policier, *m.*

whoever [huː′evə], *pron.* qui, quiconque; qui que ce soit; celui qui.

whole [houl], *a.* tout, entier, tout entier, complet; intégral; bien portant; en grains (*non moulu*).—*n.* tout, ensemble; total, montant, *m.*; somme, totalité, *f.*; *on the whole*, en somme, dans l'ensemble.

whole-hearted [houl′haːtid], *a.* sincère.

whole-heartedly [houl′haːtidli], *adv.* sincèrement.

wholesale [′houlseil], *a.* en gros.—*n.* vente en gros, *f.*

wholesome [′houlsəm], *a.* sain, salubre; salutaire; utile.

wholesomeness [′houlsəmnis], *n.* salubrité, nature salutaire, *f.*

wholly [′houlli], *adv.* entièrement, complètement, tout à fait.

whom [huːm], *pron.* (*rel.*) que, lequel; (*inter.*) qui? qui est-ce que?

whomsoever [huːmsou′evə], *pron.* qui que ce soit que.

whoop [huːp], *n.* huée, *f.*; cri (*de guerre*), *m.*—*v.t., v.i.* huer, crier.

whooping [′huːpiŋ], *n.* huées, *f.pl.*

whooping-cough [′huːpiŋkɔf], *n.* coqueluche, *f.*

whopper [′hwɔpə], *n.* (*slang*) chose énorme, *f.*; mensonge énorme, *m.*; bourde, *f.*

whose [huːz], *pron.* (*rel.*) dont, de qui; duquel, *m.*, de laquelle, *f.*, desquels, *m.pl.*, desquelles, *f.pl.*; (*inter.*) à qui?

whosoever [hu:sou'evə], *pron.* qui que ce soit qui.
why [hwai], *adv.* pourquoi?—*int.* eh bien, mais! tiens!
wick [wik], *n.* mèche, *f.*
wicked ['wikid], *a.* méchant, malin.
wickedly ['wikidli], *adv.* méchamment.
wickedness ['wikidnis], *n.* méchanceté, perversité, *f.*
wicker ['wikə], *a.* d'osier, en osier.—*n.* osier, *m.*
wicker-work ['wikəwə:k], *n.* clayonnage, *m.*; vannerie, *f.*
wicket ['wikit], *n.* guichet, *m.*
wide [waid], *a.* large, grand, ample, vaste, immense (*d'étendue*); ***three feet wide***, large de trois pieds; ***to open wide***, ouvrir tout grand.—*adv.* loin, au loin, largement; ***far and wide***, partout; ***wide apart***, écarté, espacé.
wide-awake ['waidə'weik], *a.* bien éveillé.
widely ['waidli], *adv.* au loin, loin; grandement; largement; ***widely known***, bien connu.
widen [waidn], *v.t.* élargir, étendre.—*v.i.* s'élargir, s'étendre.
wideness ['waidnis], *n.* largeur, étendue, *f.*
widening ['waidniŋ], *n.* élargissement, *m.*
wide-spread ['waidspred], *a.* répandu; général, universel.
widow ['widou], *n.* veuve, *f.*
widowed ['widoud], *a.* veuf, veuve; (*fig.*) privé (*de*).
widower ['widouə], *n.* veuf, *m.*
widowhood ['widouhud], *n.* veuvage, *m.*
width [widθ], *n.* largeur, étendue, *f.*
wield [wi:ld], *v.t.* manier, tenir.
wife [waif], *n.* (*pl.* **wives** [waivz]) femme, épouse, *f.*
wifely ['waifli], **wife-like** ['waiflaik], *a.* de femme, d'épouse, conjugal.
wig [wig], *n.* perruque, *f.*
wig-maker ['wigmeikə], *n.* perruquier, *m.*
wigged [wigd], *a.* à perruque, portant perruque.
wigging ['wigiŋ], *n.* (*colloq.*) savon, *m.*, semonce, *f.*
wiggle [wigl], *v.t.* agiter.—*v.i.* se dandiner.
wild [waild], *a.* sauvage; farouche (*non apprivoisé*); effaré, déréglé (*désordonné*); furieux (*de rage*); insensé, extravagant (*fou*); étrange, bizarre (*baroque*); ***wild beast***, fauve, *m.*; ***wild boar***, sanglier, *m.*; ***wild cat***, chat sauvage, *m.*—*n.*(*pl.*) désert, lieu sauvage, *m.*
wilderness ['wildənis], *n.* lieu désert, *m.*
wildfire ['waildfaiə], *n.* feu grégeois, *m.*; ***like wildfire***, comme l'éclair.
wildly ['waildli], *adv.* d'une manière farouche, d'un air effaré; étourdiment, follement; à tort et à travers.
wildness ['waildnis], *n.* état sauvage; dérèglement, désordre, *m.*, turbulence, licence, *f.*
wile [wail], *n.* (*usu. pl.*) artifice, *m.*, ruse, *f.*
wilful ['wilful], *a.* opiniâtre; obstiné, volontaire, prémédité.
wilfully ['wilfuli], *adv.* opiniâtrement; à dessein.
wilfulness ['wilfulnis], *n.* obstination, opiniâtreté, *f.*
will [wil], *n.* volonté, *f.*; vouloir; bon plaisir, gré (*inclination*); (*Law*) testament, *m.*—

v.t. vouloir, ordonner; léguer (*par testament*).—*v. aux. irr.*, *when used to indicate the future it is not translated*; ***he will come***, il viendra; *when used emphatically it is translated by* ***vouloir***; *I will not do it*, je ne veux pas le faire.
William ['wiljəm]. Guillaume, *m.*
willing ['wiliŋ], *a.* bien disposé; de bonne volonté; ***to be willing***, vouloir bien, être disposé (*à*).
willingly ['wiliŋli], *adv.* volontiers.
willingness ['wiliŋnis], *n.* bonne volonté, *f.*, bon vouloir, *m.*; complaisance, *f.*
will-o'-the-wisp [wiləðə'wisp], *n.* feu follet, *m.*
willow ['wilou], *n.* saule, *m.*
willy-nilly ['wili'nili], *adv.* bon gré mal gré.
wily ['waili], *a.* rusé, fin, astucieux.
win [win], *v.t. irr.* gagner (*bataille, argent etc.*); remporter (*prix, victoire etc.*).—*v.i.* gagner; remporter la victoire, triompher.
wince [wins], *v.i.* sourciller, tressaillir (*de douleur*).—*n.* tressaillement, *m.*
winch [wintʃ], *n.* manivelle, *f.*, treuil (*cabestan*), *m.*
wind (1) [wind], *n.* vent; souffle, *m.*, respiration, haleine (*breath*), *f.*; (*Med.*) vents, *m.pl.* flatuosité, *f.*—*v.t.* faire perdre haleine à essouffler (*cheval*).
wind (2) [waind], *v.t. irr.* enrouler (*en peloton*); dévider (*soie etc.*); ***to wind up***, remonter (*pendule etc.*); terminer (*négociations*); (*Comm.*) liquider.—*v.i.* tourner; se rouler, s'enrouler, s'enlacer; faire un détour; serpenter (*route, rivière*).
wind-bag ['windbæg], *n.* (*fig.*) moulin à paroles, *m.*
winded ['windid], *a.* hors d'haleine, essoufflé; ***long-winded***, de longue haleine.
winder ['waində], *n.* dévidoir (*appareil*); remontoir (*de montre*), *m.*
windfall ['windfɔ:l], *n.* (*fig.*) bonne aubaine, *f.*
wind-gauge ['windgeidʒ], *n.* anémomètre, *m.*
winding ['waindiŋ], *a.* sinueux, tortueux; en spirale (*escalier*).—*n.* sinuosité, *f.*; (*Elec.*) enroulement, *m.*
winding-sheet ['waindinʃi:t], *n.* linceul, *m.*
wind-jammer ['winddʒæmə], *n.* (*Naut.*) voilier, *m.*
windlass ['windləs], *n.* treuil; (*Naut.*) guindeau, cabestan, *m.*
windmill ['windmil], *n.* moulin à vent, *m.*
window ['windou], *n.* fenêtre; glace (*de train, voiture etc.*); montre, vitrine, *f.*, étalage (*de magasin*), *m.*; (*pl.*) vitraux (*d'église*), *m.pl.*
window-box ['windoubɔks], *n.* jardinière, *f.*
window-cleaner ['windoukli:nə], *n.* laveur de carreaux, *m.*
window-dresser ['windoudresə], *n.* étalagiste, *m.*, *f.*
window-dressing ['windoudresiŋ], *n.* art de l'étalage; (*fam.*) trompe-l'œil, *m.*
window-frame ['windoufreim], *n.* châssis de fenêtre, *m.*
window-pane ['windoupein], *n.* carreau, *m.*
window-shopping ['windouʃɔpiŋ], *n.* lèche-vitrine, *m.*
window-shutter ['windouʃʌtə], *n.* volet; contrevent, *m.*
window-sill ['windousil], *n.* rebord *ou* appui de fenêtre, *m.*
windpipe ['windpaip], *n.* trachée-artère, *m.*

windscreen ['windskri:n], *n. (Motor.)* pare-brise, *m.*
wind-sock ['windsɔk], *n. (Av.)* manche à air, *f.*
wind-tunnel ['windtʌnl], *n. (Av.)* tunnel aérodynamique, *m.*
windward ['windwəd], *adv.* au vent.—*n.* côté du vent, *m.*
windy ['windi], *a.* du vent; venteux; *it is windy,* il fait du vent.
wine [wain], *n.* vin, *m.*—*v.t. to wine and dine,* fêter.
wine-bibber ['wainbibə], *n.* buveur, *m.,* ivrogne, *m., f.*
wine-bin ['wainbin], *n.* porte-bouteilles, *m.*
wine-cellar ['wainselə], *n.* cave, *f.*
wineglass ['waingla:s], *n.* verre à vin, *m.*
wine-growing ['waingrouin], *a.* viticole.—*n.* viticulture, *f.*
wine-merchant ['wainmə:tʃənt], *n.* négociant en vins, *m.*
wine-press ['wainpres], *n.* pressoir, *m.*
wine-tasting ['wainteistin], *n.* dégustation de vins, *f.*
wine-waiter ['wainweitə], *n.* sommelier, *m.*
wing [win], *n.* aile, *f. (Av.)* escadre; *(Theat.) (pl.)* coulisse, *f.; on the wing,* au vol.—*v.t.* blesser à l'aile.
winged [wind], *a.* ailé; *(fig.)* rapide; blessé à l'aile.
winger ['winə], *n. (Ftb.)* ailier, *m.*
wing-span ['winspæn], *n.* envergure, *f.*
wink [wink], *n.* clin d'œil, *m.,* œillade, *f.*—*v.i.* cligner de l'œil; clignoter *(lumière).*
winking ['winkin], *a.* clignotant.—*n.* clignotement; clignement d'œil, *m.*
winkle [winkl], *n. (Ichth.)* bigorneau, *m.*
winner ['winə], *n.* gagnant; vainqueur *(d'une course etc.),* m.
winning ['winin], *a.* gagnant; *(fig.)* attrayant, séduisant.—*n. (pl.)* gain, *m.*
winning-post ['wininpoust], *n.* poteau d'arrivée, but, *m.*
winnow ['winou], *v.t.* vanner.
winter ['wintə], *a.* d'hiver.—*n.* hiver, *m.; in winter,* en hiver.—*v.i.* hiverner, passer l'hiver *(à).*
wintry ['wintri], *a.* d'hiver, hivernal; *(fig.)* glacial.
wipe [waip], *v.t.* essuyer; *to wipe off,* effacer; *to wipe up,* nettoyer.
wiper ['waipə], *n. windscreen wiper,* essuie-glace, *m.*
wire ['waiə], *n.* fil métallique, fil de fer, *m.;* dépêche *(télégramme),* f.; *barbed wire,* fil de fer barbelé.—*v.t.* attacher *ou* lier avec du fil de métal; griller; *(fig.)* télégraphier.
wire-cutters ['waiəkʌtəz], *n.pl.* cisailles coupe-fil, *f.pl.*
wire-haired ['waiəhɛəd], *a.* à poil dur *(chien).*
wireless ['waiəlis], *a.* sans fil.—*n.* radio, T.S.F., *f.; wireless set,* poste de T.S.F., *m.,* radio, *f.*
wire-netting ['waiə'netin], *n.* grillage, treillis métallique, *m.*
wire-rope ['waiə'roup], *n.* câble métallique, *m.*
wiring ['waiərin], *n. (Elec.)* canalisation, *f.;* câblage, *m.*
wiry ['waiəri], *a. (fig.)* nerveux, souple.
wisdom ['wizdəm], *n.* sagesse; prudence, *f.*
wise [waiz], *a.* sage, sensé, prudent.—*n.* manière, façon, sorte, guise, *f.*

wise-crack ['waizkræk], *n.* bon mot, *m.*
wisely ['waizli], *adv.* sagement; prudemment.
wish [wiʃ], *n.* souhait, désir, *m.,* envie, *f.*—*v.t., v.i.* souhaiter, désirer, vouloir; *I wish I could,* je voudrais pouvoir; *I wish I were . . .,* je voudrais être . . .; *to wish well to,* vouloir du bien à.
wish-bone ['wiʃboun], *n.* lunette, fourchette, *f.*
wishful ['wiʃful], *a.* désireux *(de).*
wishy-washy ['wiʃi'wɔʃi], *a.* faible, pauvre.
wisp [wisp], *n.* bouchon de paille etc., *m.;* mèche *(de cheveux), f.*
wistaria [wis'tɛəriə], *n.* glycine, *f.*
wistful ['wistful], *a.* désireux; d'envie, de regret, pensif *(air, regard, sourire).*
wistfully ['wistfuli], *adv.* d'un air de vague regret.
wit [wit], *n.* esprit; entendement, jugement; *(fig.)* bel esprit; *(pl.)* esprit, *m.,* raison, tête, *f.,* sens, bon sens, *m.; to be at one's wits' end,* ne savoir que faire.—*v.t.* savoir; *to wit,* c'est-à-dire.
witch [witʃ], *n.* sorcière, magicienne, *f.*
witchcraft ['witʃkra:ft], *n.* sorcellerie, magie noire, *f.*
witch-hazel ['witʃheizl], *n. (Bot.)* hamamélis, *m.*
with [wið], *prep.* avec; de, par *(au moyen de);* à, au, à la, aux *(in descriptive phrases);* chez, parmi *(en compagnie de);* auprès de *(de l'avis de);* malgré *(en dépit de); angry with,* fâché contre.
withal [wið'ɔ:l], *adv.* avec tout cela, en outre.
withdraw [wið'drɔ:], *v.t. irr. (conjug. like* DRAW) retirer; rappeler; éloigner *(de).*—*v.i.* se retirer, s'éloigner *(de).*
withdrawal [wið'drɔ:əl] *n.* retraite *(des vaincus), f.;* retrait *(enlèvement), m.*
wither ['wiðə], *v.i.* se flétrir, se faner.
withering ['wiðərin], *a.* écrasant *(sarcastique).*
withers ['wiðəz], *n.pl.* garrot *(de cheval), m.*
withhold [wið'hould], *v.t. irr. (conjug. like* HOLD) retenir; refuser.
within [wið'in], *prep.* dans, en; à moins de *(pas plus de);* *within a pound or so,* à une livre près; *within reach of,* à portée de.—*adv.* en dedans, à l'intérieur; à la maison, chez soi.
without [wið'aut], *prep.* sans *(manquant de).*—*conj.* à moins que, sans que *(unless).*—*adv.* en dehors, au dehors.
withstand [wið'stænd], *v.t. irr. (conjug. like* STAND) résister à, combattre.
withy [wiði], *a.* d'osier.—*n.* osier, *m.*
witless ['witlis], *a.* sans esprit; sot.
witness ['witnis], *n.* témoin; témoignage *(preuve), m.*—*v.t.* témoigner; être témoin de.—*v.i.* témoigner, porter témoignage.
witticism ['witisizm], *n.* bon mot, *m.*
wittily ['witili], *adv.* spirituellement, avec esprit.
wittiness ['witinis], *n.* esprit, caractère spirituel, *m.*
wittingly ['witinli], *adv.* sciemment, à dessein.
witty ['witi], *a.* spirituel; plaisant *(facétieux).*
wives [WIFE].
wizard ['wizəd], *n.* sorcier, magicien, *m.*
wizened ['wizənd], *a.* ratatiné, ridé.
wobble [wɔbl], *v.i.* vaciller, ballotter.

wobbling ['wɔbliŋ], *a.* vacillant, branlant.— *n.* vacillation, *f.*; dandinement, *m.*

wobbly ['wɔbli], *a.* branlant, vacillant.

woe [wou], *n.* (*fig.*) peine, douleur, *f.*; malheur, *m.*

woebegone ['woubigɔn], **woeful** ['wouful], *a.* triste, malheureux, abattu.

woefully ['woufuli], *adv.* tristement.

wolf [wulf], *n.* (*pl.* **wolves** [wulvz]) loup, *m.*; *she-wolf*, louve, *f.*

wolf-cub ['wulfkʌb], *n.* louveteau, *m.*

wolf-dog ['wulfdɔg], *n.* chien-loup, *m.*

wolfish ['wulfiʃ], *a.* de loup; (*fig.*) rapace.

wolves [WOLF].

woman ['wumən], *n.* (*pl.* **women** ['wimin]) femme, *f.*

woman-hater ['wumənheitə], *n.* misogyne, *m.*

womanhood ['wumənhud], *n.* état de femme, *m.*

womankind ['wumənkaind], *n.* le sexe féminin, *m.*; les femmes, *f.pl.*

womanly ['wumənli], *a.* de femme.

womanliness ['wumənlinis], *n.* fémininité, *f.*

womb [wu:m], *n.* (*Anat.*) matrice, *f.*; (*fig.*) sein, *m.*, flancs, *m.pl.*

women [WOMAN].

wonder ['wʌndə], *n.* étonnement, *m.*, surprise; merveille (*spectacle etc.*), *f.*, miracle, prodige, *m.*—*v.i.* s'étonner, être étonné; se demander; *to wonder whether*, se demander si.

wonderful ['wʌndəful], *a.* étonnant, merveilleux.

wonderfully ['wʌndəfuli], *adv.* étonnamment, merveilleusement.

wonderment ['wʌndəmənt], *n.* étonnement, *m.*

wondrous ['wʌndrəs], *a.* merveilleux.

wondrously ['wʌndrəsli], *adv.* merveilleusement.

wont [wount], *a.* *to be wont to*, avoir l'habitude de.—*n.* coutume, habitude, *f.*

wonted ['wountid], *a.* accoutumé, habituel.

woo [wu:], *v.t.* faire la cour à; courtiser.

wood [wud], *n.* bois (*matériel ou forêt*), *m.*

woodbine ['wudbain], *n.* chèvrefeuille, *m.*

woodcock ['wudkɔk], *n.* bécasse, *f.*

woodcut ['wudkʌt], *n.* gravure sur bois, *f.*

wood-cutter ['wudkʌtə], *n.* bûcheron, *m.*

wooded ['wudid], *a.* boisé.

wooden [wudn], *a.* de bois, en bois; (*fig.*) gauche (*mouvement etc.*).

woodland ['wudlənd], *a.* des bois, sylvestre. —*n.* pays boisé, bois, *m.*

woodman ['wudmən], *n.* (*pl.* **-men** [men]) garde forestier; bûcheron, *m.*

wood-nymph ['wudnimf], *n.* nymphe des bois, dryade, *f.*

woodpecker ['wudpekə], *n.* pic, *m.*; *green woodpecker*, pivert, *m.*

wood-pigeon ['wudpidʒin], *n.* pigeon ramier, *m.*

wood-pulp ['wudpʌlp], *n.* pâte de bois, *f.*

wood-wind ['wudwind], *n.* (*Mus.*) les bois, *m.pl.*

woodwork ['wudwə:k], *n.* boiserie; menuiserie; charpente, *f.*

wood-worm ['wudwə:m], *n.* artison, *m.*

woody ['wudi], *a.* boisé; ligneux.

wood-yard ['wudjɑ:d], *n.* chantier, *m.*

wooer ['wu:ə], *n.* amoureux, prétendant, *m.*

woof [wu:f], *n.* trame, *f.*; tissu (*texture*), *m.*

wooing ['wu:iŋ], *n.* cour, *f.*

wool [wul], *n.* laine, *f.*

woollen ['wulən], *a.* de laine, à laine.—*n.*(*pl.*) tissus de laine, *m.pl.*, laines, *f.pl.*, lainages, *m.pl.*; *woollen-cloth*, drap, *m.*; *woollen-draper*, marchand de draps, *m.*; *woollen-goods*, (*fam.*) *woollies*, lainages, *m.pl.*

woolliness ['wulinis], *n.* nature laineuse; (*fig.*) imprécision, *f.*

woolly ['wuli], *a.* laineux.

Woolsack ['wulsæk], *n.* sac de laine (*siège du Lord Chancellor*), *m.*

word [wə:d], *n.* mot, *m.*; parole (*prononcée*), *f.*; avis, *m.*, nouvelle (*communication*), *f.*; *by word of mouth*, de vive voix; *in a word*, en un mot; *not a word !* bouche close!— *v.t.* exprimer; énoncer; rédiger (*télégramme*).

word-book ['wə:dbuk], *n.* vocabulaire, lexique, *m.*

wordiness ['wə:dinis], *n.* prolixité, verbosité, *f.*

wording ['wə:diŋ], *n.* expression, *f.*; énoncé (*d'un problème*), *m.*

wordy ['wə:di], *a.* verbeux, diffus.

work [wə:k], *v.t.* travailler; façonner (*ouvrager*); se frayer (*un chemin*); payer (*son passage*) en travaillant; broder (*coudre*); faire aller, manœuvrer (*machine etc.*); exploiter (*mine etc.*); *to work off*, user; *to work oneself up*, s'exciter; *to work out*, résoudre (*problème*).—*v.i.* travailler; fonctionner, marcher, aller, jouer; opérer, avoir de l'effet (*agir*); *to work loose*, se desserrer.— *n.* travail; ouvrage, *m.*, besogne (*tâche*); (*fig.*) affaire; (*Lit.*) œuvre, *f.*; (*pl.*) mécanisme (*de moteur*), *m.*; manœuvres (*d'une machine*), *f.*; (*Ind.*) fabrique, usine, *f.*; (*Fort.*) travaux, *m.pl.*; mouvement (*de montre*), *m.*; *road works ahead*, attention, travaux! *to be out of work*, chômer.

workable ['wə:kəbl], *a.* réalisable; exploitable (*mine etc.*).

workaday ['wə:kədei], *a.* de tous les jours.

work-bench ['wə:kbentʃ], *n.* établi, *m.*

work-box ['wə:kbɔks], *n.* boîte à ouvrage, *f.*

worker ['wə:kə], *n.* travailleur; ouvrier; employé, *m.*

workhouse ['wə:khaus], *n.* maison des pauvres, *f.*; hospice, *m.*

working ['wə:kiŋ], *a.* qui travaille, ouvrier; de travail (*vêtements*); *hard-working*, laborieux; *in working order*, en état de fonctionnement; *working capital*, capital d'exploitation, *m.*; *working man*, ouvrier, *m.*—*n.* travail, *m.*; marche, *f.*; fonctionnement, jeu (*de machine*), *m.*; opération; exploitation (*de mine etc.*), *f.*

working-class ['wə:kiŋ'klɑ:s], *n.* classe ouvrière, *f.*

working-day ['wə:kiŋ'dei], *n.* jour ouvrable, *m.*

workman ['wə:kmən], *n.* (*pl.* **-men** [men]) ouvrier, artisan, *m.*

workmanlike ['wə:kmənlaik] *a.* bien fait, bien travaillé.

workmanship ['wə:kmənʃip], *n.* ouvrage, travail, *m.*

work-room ['wə:kru:m], **work-shop** ['wə:kʃɔp], *n.* atelier, *m.*

world [wə:ld], *n.* monde; l'univers; (*fig*) monde, *m.*, vie, *f.*; *all the world over*

writing-desk

dans le monde entier; *a world of good*, un bien infini; *the first world war*, la première guerre mondiale.

worldliness ['wəːldlinis], *n.* mondanité; frivolité, *f.*

worldly ['wəːldli], *a.* mondain, du monde.

worldwide ['wəːldwaid], *a.* universel, répandu partout.

worm [wəːm], *n.* ver, *m.*; chenille, larve, *f.*; filet *(de vis)*, *m.—v.t.* miner; *to worm oneself into*, s'insinuer, se faufiler dans.

worm-cast ['wəːmkaːst], *n.* déjection de ver (de terre), *f.*

worm-eaten ['wəːmiːtn], *a.* rongé des vers, vermoulu.

worm-screw ['wəːmskruː], *n.* tire-bourre, *m.*

wormwood ['wəːmwud], *n.* armoise amère, *f.*; *(fig.)* fiel, *m.*

worried ['wʌrid], *a.* tourmenté, harassé, ennuyé.

worry ['wʌri], *n.* ennui, tracas, souci, *m.—v.t.* tourmenter, tracasser.—*v.i.* tracasser; *don't worry!* soyez tranquille!

worse [wəːs], *a.* pire; plus mauvais; plus malade, plus mal *(santé).—n.* pire; plus mauvais, *m.—adv.* plus mal, pis; *far worse*, bien pis, bien pire; *so much the worse*, tant pis.

worsen [wəːsn], *v.i.* empirer.

worsening ['wəːsniŋ], *n.* aggravation, *f.*

worship ['wəːʃip], *n.* culte, *m.*, adoration, *f.*; honneur *(titre)*, *m.—v.t.*, *v.i.* adorer.

worshipful ['wəːʃipful], *a.* honorable.

worshipper ['wəːʃipə], *n.* adorateur, *m.*

worst [wəːst], *a.* le plus mauvais, le pire.—*adv.* le pis, le plus mal.—*n.* le plus mauvais, le pire, le pis.—*v.t.* battre, vaincre, défaire.

worsted ['wustid], *a.* de laine peignée.—*n.* laine peignée, *f.*

worth [wəːθ], *a.* qui vaut, valant; qui mérite *(digne)*; qui est riche de *(qui possède)*; *to be worth doing*, valoir la peine de faire.—*n.* valeur, *f.*; prix, *m.*; *for all one's worth*, de toutes ses forces.

worthily ['wəːðili], *adv.* dignement.

worthiness ['wəːðinis], *n.* mérite, *m.*

worthless ['wəːθlis], *a.* sans valeur, qui ne vaut rien; *worthless fellow*, vaurien, *m.*

worth-while ['wəːθ'hwail], *a.* qui vaut la peine *(de)*.

worthy ['wəːði], *a.* digne, honorable; *(colloq.)* brave.—*n.* *(colloq.)* brave homme; homme illustre, *m.*

would [wud], *v.aux. past* and *cond.* [WILL]. *When used emphatically would is translated by vouloir.*

would-be ['wudbiː], *a.* prétendu, soi-disant.

wound (1) [waund], *past* and *p.p.* [WIND (2)].

wound (2) [wuːnd], *n.* blessure; plaie, *f.—v.t.* blesser.

wounded ['wuːndid], *a.* blessé.

woven ['wouvn], *a.* tissé.

wrack [ræk], *n.* varech, *m.*; ruine, *f.*, débris, *m.*

wraith [reiθ], *n.* revenant, *m.*

wrangle [ræŋgl], *n.* dispute, querelle, *f.—v.i.* se disputer, se quereller.

wrangling ['ræŋgliŋ], *n.* dispute, *f.*, chamailleries, *f.pl.*

wrap [ræp], *v.t.* enrouler, envelopper.—*n.* châle, peignoir, *m.*

wrapper ['ræpə], *n.* enveloppe; toile d'emballage *(pour paquets)*; bande *(pour journal)*; couverture *(de livre)*, *f.*

wrapping ['ræpiŋ], *n.* enveloppe, couverture, *f.*; *wrapping-paper*, papier d'emballage, *m.*

wrath [rɔːθ], *n.* courroux, *m.*, colère, *f.*

wrathful ['rɔːθful], *a.* courroucé.

wreak [riːk], *v.t.* exécuter, satisfaire.

wreath [riːθ], *n.* guirlande, *f.*, feston, *m.*; couronne *(d'épouse etc.)*, *f.*

wreathe [riːð], *v.t.* entrelacer, tresser *(de).—v.i.* s'entrelacer, s'enrouler.

wreathed [riːðd], *a.* entrelacé.

wreck [rek], *n.* naufrage; navire naufragé, *m.*, épave; *(fig.)* ruine, *f.—v.t.* faire faire naufrage à; *(fig.)* ruiner.

wreckage ['rekidʒ], *n.* débris de naufrage, *m.*, épaves, *f.pl.*

wrecked [rekt], *a.* naufragé; ruiné.

wrecker ['rekə], *n.* pilleur d'épaves, naufrageur, *m.*

wren [ren], *n.* *(Orn.)* roitelet, *m.*

wrench [rentʃ], *n.* torsion, *f.*, arrachement, *m.*; entorse *(des muscles)*; clef *(outil)*, *f.—v.t.* arracher *(à* ou *de)*; se fouler *(cheville etc.)*.

wrest [rest], *v.t.* arracher *(à)*.

wrestle [resl], *v.i.* lutter.

wrestler ['reslə], *n.* lutteur, *m.*

wrestling ['resliŋ], *n.* lutte, *f.*; catch, *m.*; *all-in wrestling*, lutte libre.

wretch [retʃ], *n.* malheureux, *m.*; misérable *(scélérat)*, *m.*, *f.*; *poor wretch*, pauvre diable, *m.*

wretched ['retʃid], *a.* malheureux, misérable; vilain, triste; pitoyable, à faire pitié.

wretchedly ['retʃidli], *adv.* malheureusement, misérablement; d'une manière pitoyable.

wretchedness ['retʃidnis], *n.* misère, pauvreté, *f.*

wriggle [rigl], *v.i.* se tortiller, se remuer.

wriggling ['rigliŋ], *n.* tortillement, *m.*

wring [riŋ], *v.t. irr.* tordre; arracher *(à)*; presser, serrer *(étreindre)*.

wringer ['riŋə], *n.* essoreuse *(à linge)*, *f.*

wringing ['riŋiŋ], *a.* *wringing wet*, trempé jusqu'aux os *(personne)*; mouillé à tordre *(vêtement)*.

wrinkle [riŋkl], *n.* ride *(à la figure etc.)*, *f.*; pli, faux pli *(de vêtement)*; *(slang)* tuyau *(renseignement)*, *m.—v.t.* rider; plisser; *to wrinkle one's brow*, froncer les sourcils. —*v.i.* se rider.

wrinkled [riŋkld], *a.* ridé; *(Bot.)* plissé.

wrist [rist], *n.* poignet, *m.*

wristband ['ristbænd], *n.* poignet, *m.*

wrist-watch ['ristwɔtʃ], *n.* montre-bracelet, *f.*

writ [rit], *n.* exploit, mandat, *m.*, ordonnance; *(Parl.)* lettre de convocation, *f.*

write [rait], *v.t.*, *v.i. irr.* écrire; *to write off*, *(Comm.)* passer au compte des profits et pertes.

write-off ['raitɔf], *n.* annulation; non-valeur *(personne)*, *f.*

writer ['raitə], *n.* écrivain; *(Comm.)* commis aux écritures, *m.*

writhe [raið], *v.i.* se tordre *(de douleur)*; se crisper.

writing ['raitiŋ], *n.* écriture *(calligraphie)*, *f.*; écrit *(chose écrite)*; *(fig.)* ouvrage, document, *m.*; inscription, *f.*; *in writing*, par écrit.

writing-case ['raitiŋkeis], *n.* papeterie, *f.*

writing-desk ['raitiŋdesk], *n.* pupitre, bureau, secrétaire, *m.*

writing-paper ['raitiŋpeipə], *n.* papier à écrire, *m.*

writing-table ['raitiŋteibl], *n.* table à écrire, *f.*

written [ritn], *a.* écrit, par écrit.

wrong [rɔŋ], *a.* faux, erroné, inexact (*pas vrai*); mal, mauvais; *to be wrong*, avoir tort (*personne*), n'être pas à l'heure, aller mal (*montre*); *what's wrong with you?* qu'avez-vous? *wrong number*, (*Teleph.*) mauvais numéro, *m.*; *wrong side*, envers, *m.*; *wrong side up*, sens dessus dessous.— *adv.* mal, à tort, à faux.—*n.* mal, *m.*, injustice, *f.*, tort; dommage, *m.*—*v.t.* faire du tort à, nuire à.

wrongdoer ['rɔŋduə], *n.* pervers, méchant, *m.*

wrongdoing ['rɔŋduiŋ], *n.* le mal, *m.*

wrongful ['rɔŋful], *a.* injuste.

wrongfully ['rɔŋfuli], *adv.* à tort, injustement.

wrongly ['rɔŋli], *adv.* mal, à tort; *rightly or wrongly*, à tort ou à raison.

wroth [rouθ], *a.* (*poet.*) en colère, irrité, courroucé.

wrought [rɔːt], *a.* travaillé; façonné; ouvré (*tissu*); *wrought iron*, fer forgé, *m.*

wry [rai], *a.* de travers, tordu, tors; *to pull a wry face*, faire la grimace.

X

X, x [eks]. vingt-quatrième lettre de l'alphabet; X, dix, *m.*

Xerxes ['zəːksiːz]. Xerxès, *m.*

Xmas ['krisməs]. (*abbr.* CHRISTMAS) Noël, *m.*

X-ray ['eksrei], *a.* radiographique; *X-ray photograph*, radiographie, *f.*—*n.* (*pl.*) rayons X, *m.pl.*—*v.t.* radiographier.

xylophone ['zailəfoun], *n.* xylophone; (*slang*) claquebois, *m.*

Y

Y, y [wai]. vingt-cinquième lettre de l'alphabet; (I')i grec, *m.*

yacht [jɔt], *n.* yacht, *m.*

yacht-club ['jɔtklʌb], *n.* cercle nautique, *m.*

yachting ['jɔtiŋ], *n.* yachting, *m.*

yachtsman ['jɔtsmən], *n.* (*pl.* -men [men]) yachtman, *m.*

yak [jæk], *n.* (*Zool.*) ya(c)k, *m.*

yam [jæm], *n.* igname, *f.*

yank [jæŋk], *v.t.* (*fam.*) tirer brusquement.

Yankee ['jæŋki], *n.* Yankee, Américain, *m.*

yap [jæp], *v.i.* japper, aboyer.—*n.* jappement, *m.*

yard (1) [jɑːd], *n.* cour, *f.*, préau, *m.*

yard (2) [jɑːd], *n.* (*Naut.*) vergue, *f.*; (*Measure*) yard (*mètre* 0·914383), *m.*

yard-arm ['jɑːdɑːm], *n.* bout de vergue, *m.*

yarn [jɑːn], *n.* fil (*Naut.*) fil de caret; récit, conte (*histoire*), *m.*

yawl [jɔːl], *n.* (*Naut.*) sloop, *m.*; (*Row.*) yole de mer, *f.*

yawn [jɔːn], *n.* bâillement, *m.*—*v.i.* bâiller.

yawning ['jɔːniŋ], *a.* qui bâille; (*fig.*) béant.

*****ye** [jiː], *pron.pl.* vous.

yea [jei], *adv.* oui; vraiment, en vérité.—*n.* vote affirmatif, *m.*

year [jiə], *n.* an (*unité de temps*), *m.*; année (*particulière*), *f.*; *every year*, tous les ans; *four times a year*, quatre fois par an; *new year*, nouvel an; *next year*, l'an prochain.

year-book ['jiəbuk], *n.* annuaire, *m.*

yearling ['jiəliŋ], *a.* âgé d'un an.—*n.* poulain, *m.*, *ou* pouliche, *f.*, d'un an.

yearly ['jiəli], *a.* annuel.—*adv.* tous les ans.

yearn [jəːn], *v.i. to yearn after*, soupirer après; *to yearn to do something*, brûler de faire quelque chose.

yearning ['jəːniŋ], *n.* désir ardent, *m.*

yeast [jiːst], *n.* levure, *f.*

yell [jel], *n.* hurlement, *m.*—*v.i.* hurler, pousser des hurlements.

yelling ['jeliŋ], *n.* hurlements, *m.pl.*

yellow ['jelou], *a.* jaune; (*slang*) poltron.—*n.* jaune, *m.*—*v.t.*, *v.i.* jaunir.

yellow-hammer ['jelouhæmə], *n.* (*Orn.*) bruant jaune, *m.*

yellowish ['jelouiʃ], *a.* jaunâtre.

yellowness ['jelounis], *n.* couleur jaune, *f.*

yelp [jelp], *v.i.* glapir, japper.

yelping ['jelpiŋ], *n.* glapissement, jappement, *m.*

Yemen ['jemən]. le Yémen, *m.*

Yemeni ['jeməni], *a.* yémenite.—*n.* Yémenite (*personne*), *m.*, *f.*

yeoman ['joumən], *n.* (*pl.* -men [men]) fermier-propriétaire, *m.*

yeomanry ['joumənri], *n.* fermiers-propriétaires, *m.pl.*

yes [jes], *adv.* oui; si (*in reply to a negative*).

yes-man ['jesmæn], *n.* (*pl.* -men [men]) (*pop.*) Béni-oui-oui, *m.*

yesterday ['jestəd(e)i], *adv.* and *n.* hier, *m.*; *the day before yesterday*, avant-hier; *yesterday evening*, hier soir.

yet [jet], *conj.* pourtant, cependant, tout de même.—*adv.* encore, déjà; *as yet*, jusqu'ici; *not yet*, pas encore.

yew [juː], *n.* (*Bot.*) if, *m.*

yield [jiːld], *v.t.* produire, rapporter; livrer, céder (*au vainqueur*); *to yield up*, rendre.— *v.i.* se rendre, céder (*à*); consentir (*à*).—*n.* rendement, produit, rapport, *m.*

yielding ['jiːldiŋ], *a.* complaisant, facile.—*n.* reddition; soumission, *f.*

yoke [jouk], *n.* joug; attelage, *m.*, paire; palanche (*pour seaux*), *f.*; (*Dress.*) empiècement, *m.*—*v.t.* atteler, accoupler.

yokel [joukl], *n.* rustre, campagnard, *m.*

yolk [jouk], *n.* jaune (*d'œuf*), *m.*

*****yonder** ['jɔndə], *adv.* là, là-bas.—*a. yonder castle*, ce château-là.

*****yore** [jɔː], *adv.* autrefois, jadis.

you [juː], *pron.* vous; (*to a child, relative, pet etc.*) tu, te, toi; (*indef.*) on.

young [jʌŋ], *a.* jeune; novice, neuf, inexpérimenté (*non éprouvé*); (*fig.*) naissant; *young folks* or *young people*, jeunes gens, *m.pl.*; *young lady*, demoiselle, *f.*—*n.pl.* les jeunes, les jeunes gens; les petits, *m.pl.*; *with young*, pleine (*animal*).

younger ['jʌŋgə], *a.* plus jeune; cadet (*de deux frères etc.*).
youngest ['jʌŋgist], *a.* le plus jeune.
youngish ['jʌŋiʃ], *a.* assez jeune.
youngster ['jʌŋstə], *n.* jeune homme; gamin, mioche, *m.*, gosse, *m.*, *f.*
your [jɔ:], *a.* votre, (*pl.*) vos; (*to a child, relative, pet etc.*) ton, ta, tes; (*indef.*) son, sa, ses.
yours [jɔ:z], *pron.* le vôtre, *m.*, la vôtre, *f.*, les vôtres, *pl.*; à vous (*your property*); de vous (*by you*); (*to a child, relative, pet etc.*) le tien, la tienne, les tiens, les tiennes; à toi (*your property*); de toi (*by you*).
yourself [jɔ:'self], *pron.* (*pl.* **yourselves** [jɔ:'selvz]) vous-même, toi-même; (*pl.*) vous-mêmes; (*reflexive*) vous, te.
youth [ju:θ], *n.* jeunesse, adolescence, *f.*; jeune homme, adolescent (*personne*), *m.*; (*fig.*) jeunes gens, *m.pl.*
youthful ['ju:θful], *a.* jeune; de jeunesse.
youthfulness ['ju:θfulnis], *n.* jeunesse, *f.*
Yugoslav ['ju:go'slɑ:v], *a.* yougoslave.—*n.* Yougoslave (*personne*), *m.*, *f.*
Yugoslavia [ju:go'slɑ:vjə]. la Yougoslavie, *f.*
****Yule** [ju:l], **Yule-tide** ['ju:ltaid], *n.* Noël, *m.*, fête de Noël, *f.*
Yule-log ['ju:llɔg], *n.* bûche de Noël, *f.*

Z

Z, z [zed, (*Am.*) zi:]. vingt-sixième lettre de l'alphabet, *m.*

Zambesi [zæm'bi:zi]. le Zambèze, *m.*
Zambia ['zæmbjə]. la Zambie, *f.*
zany ['zeini], *n.* zani, bouffon, *m.*
zeal [zi:l], *n.* zèle, *m.*
zealot ['zelət], *n.* zélateur, *m.*, fanatique, *m.*, *f.*
zealous ['zeləs], *a.* zélé, zélateur.
zealously ['zeləsli], *adv.* avec zèle.
zebra ['zi:brə], *n.* zèbre, *m.*; ***zebra crossing***, passage clouté, *m.*
zenith ['zeniθ], *n.* zénith; (*fig.*) apogée, *m.*
zephyr ['zefə], *n.* zéphyr, zéphire, Zéphyre, *m.*
zero ['ziərou], *n.* zéro; (*fig.*) rien, *m.*; ***zero hour***, l'heure H, *f.*
zest [zest], *n.* goût, *m.*, saveur, *f.*; zeste (*d'orange, de citron*); (*fig.*) entrain, *m.*, verve, *f.*
Zeus [zju:s]. (*Myth.*) Zeus, *m.*
zigzag ['zigzæg], *a.* en zigzag.—*n.* zigzag, *m.* —*v.i.* aller en zigzag, zigzaguer.
zinc [ziŋk], *n.* zinc, *m.*—*v.t.* zinguer.
zinnia ['zinjə], *n.* (*Bot.*) zinnia, *m.*
Zion ['zaiən]. Sion, *m.*
zip [zip], *n.* sifflement (*de balle*), *m.*; énergie, verve, *f.*—*v.t.* siffler; ***zip fastener***, fermeture à glissière, *f.*
zither ['ziðə], *n.* cithare, *f.*
zodiac ['zoudiæk], *n.* zodiaque, *m.*
zone [zoun], *n.* zone, *f.*
zoo [zu:], *n.* jardin zoologique, (*fam.*) zoo, *m.*
zoological [zouə'lɔdʒikl], *a.* zoologique; ***zoological gardens***, jardin zoologique, *m.*
zoologist [zou'ɔlədʒist], *n.* zoologiste, zoologue, *m.*, *f.*
zoology [zou'ɔlədʒi], *n.* zoologie, *f.*
zoom [zu:m], *n.* bourdonnement, ronflement, *m.*—*v.i.* vrombir.
Zulu ['zu:lu:], *a.* zoulou.—*n.* Zoulou, *m.*

French Verbs

1. All verbs not marked *irr.* in the French-English section of the Dictionary are either
   (a) regular, and conjugated like AIMER, FINIR or VENDRE according to their ending
   (see below) or
   (b) anomalous, and conjugated like the verb in that group to which the user is referred.
2. The Imperfect Indicative, Conditional, Imperative, and Imperfect Subjunctive are not given
   and may be assumed to be formed as follows:
   Imperfect Indicative: by substituting for the final *-ons* of 1st Person Plural, Present Indicative
   the endings *-ais, -ais, -ait, -ions, -iez, -aient* (except *être: j'étais*).
   Conditional: by substituting for the endings of the Future those of the Imperfect Indicative
   given above.
   Imperative: (a) 2nd Person Singular, 1st and 2nd Person Plural, by using these forms of

Infinitive	Participles	Present Indicative	Past Historic
REGULAR VERBS First Conjugation Infinitive in *-er*			
aim-*er*	aim-*ant* aim-*é*	aim-*e* aim-*es* aim-*e* aim-*ons* aim-*ez* aim-*ent*	aim-*ai* aim-*as* aim-*a* aim-*âmes* aim-*âtes* aim-*èrent*
Second Conjugation Infinitive in *-ir*			
fin-*ir*	fin-*issant* fin-*i*	fin-*is* fin-*is* fin-*it* fin-*issons* fin-*issez* fin-*issent*	fin-*is* fin-*is* fin-*it* fin-*îmes* fin-*îtes* fin-*irent*
Third Conjugation Infinitive in *-re*			
vend-*re*	vend-*ant* vend-*u*	vend-*s* vend-*s* vend vend-*ons* vend-*ez* vend-*ent*	vend-*is* vend-*is* vend-*it* vend-*îmes* vend-*îtes* vend-*irent*
ANOMALOUS VERBS			
amener	amenant amené	amène amènes amène amenons amenez amènent	amenai . . . amenâmes . . .
appeler	appelant appelé	appelle appelles appelle appelons appelez appellent	appelai . . . appelâmes . . .
assiéger	assiégeant assiégé	assiège assièges assiège assiégeons assiégez assiègent	assiégeai . . . assiégeâmes . . .

the Present Indicative without pronouns (*-er* verbs drop the final *s* of the 2nd Person Singular).

    (*b*) 3rd Person Singular and Plural by using these forms of the Present Subjunctive.

Imperfect Subjunctive: from the 2nd Person Singular of the Past Historic by adding *-se, -ses, -ˆt, -sions, -siez, -sent.*

3. Exceptions to the above rules are indicated in footnotes.
4. Compound verbs (e.g. DEVENIR, REVENIR, etc.) are given only where they differ from the simple form (e.g. VENIR).
5. Defective verbs are marked † and all existing forms are given.

Future	Present Subjunctive	English
aimer-*ai* aimer-*as* aimer-*a* aimer-*ons* aimer-*ez* aimer-*ont*	aim-*e* aim-*es* aim-*e* aim-*ions* aim-*iez* aim-*ent*	to like, to love
finir-*ai* finir-*as* finir-*a* finir-*ons* finir-*ez* finir-*ont*	fini-*sse* fini-*sses* fini-*sse* fini-*ssions* fini-*ssiez* fini-*ssent*	to finish
vendr-*ai* vendr-*as* vendr-*a* vendr-*ons* vendr-*ez* vendr-*ont*	vend-*e* vend-*es* vend-*e* vend-*ions* vend-*iez* vend-*ent*	to sell
amènerai... amènerons...	amène amènes amène amenions ameniez amènent	to bring
appellerai... appellerons ...	appelle appelles appelle appelions appeliez appellent	to call
assiégerai ... assiégerons ...	assiège assièges assiège assiégions assiégiez assiègent	to besiege

French Verbs

Infinitive	Participles	Present Indicative	Past Historic
battre	battant battu	bats bats bat battons battez battent	battis . . . battîmes . . .
céder	cédant cédé	cède cèdes cède cédons cédez cèdent	cédai . . . cédâmes . . .
commencer	commençant commencé	commence commences commence commençons commencez commencent	commençai commenças commença commençâmes commençâtes commencèrent
dépecer	dépeçant dépecé	dépèce dépèces dépèce dépeçons dépecez dépècent	dépeçai dépeças dépeça dépeçâmes dépeçâtes dépecèrent
employer[1]	employant employé	emploie emploies emploie employons employez emploient	employai . . . employâmes . . .
manger	mangeant mangé	mange manges mange mangeons mangez mangent	mangeai mangeas mangea mangeâmes mangeâtes mangèrent
payer[1]	(See footnote)		
rapiécer	rapiéçant rapiécé	rapièce rapièces rapièce rapiéçons rapiécez rapiècent	rapiéçai rapiéças rapiéça rapiéçâmes rapiéçâtes rapiécèrent
rompre	rompant rompu	romps romps rompt rompons rompez rompent	rompis . . . rompîmes . . .

IRREGULAR VERBS

† absoudre	absolvant absous, *m.*, absoute, *f.*	absous absous absout absolvons absolvez absolvent	

[1] All verbs in *-oyer* and *-uyer* change *y* to *i* before a mute *e*.   With verbs in *-ayer*, *y* or *i* may

638

Future	Present Subjunctive	English
battrai . . . battrons . . .	batte . . . battions . . .	to beat
céderai . . . céderons . . .	cède cèdes cède cédions cédiez cèdent	to yield
commencerai . . . commencerons . . .	commence . . . commencions . . .	to begin
dépècerai . . . dépècerons . . .	dépèce dépèces dépèce dépecions dépeciez dépècent	to cut up
emploierai . . . emploierons . . .	emploie emploies emploie employions employiez emploient	to employ, to use
mangerai . . . mangerons . . .	mange . . . mangions . . .	to eat
		to pay (for)
rapiécerai . . . rapiécerons . . .	rapièce rapièces rapièce rapiécions rapiéciez rapiècent	to patch
romprai . . . romprons . . .	rompe . . . rompions . . .	to break
absoudrai . . . absoudrons . . .	absolve . . . absolvions . . .	to absolve

be used. With *grasseyer* y is always used.

French Verbs

Infinitive	Participles	Present Indicative	Past Historic
† accroire	(used only in the infinitive in the phrase '*faire accroire*', to make one		
acquérir	acquérant acquis	acquiers acquiers acquiert acquérons acquérez acquièrent	acquis... acquîmes...
† advenir	advenant advenu	il advient	il advint
aller[1]	allant allé	vais vas va allons allez vont	allai... allâmes...
assaillir	assaillant assailli	assaille... assaillons...	assaillis... assaillîmes...
asseoir	asseyant *or* assoyant assis	assieds[2] assieds assied asseyons asseyez asseyent	assis... assîmes...
avoir[3]	ayant eu	ai as a avons avez ont	eus... eûmes...
boire	buvant bu	bois bois boit buvons buvez boivent	bus... bûmes...
bouillir	bouillant bouilli	bous bous bout bouillons bouillez bouillent	bouillis... bouillîmes...
† braire[4]	brayant brait	il brait ils braient	
† bruire[5]	bruissant bruit	il bruit ils bruissent	
† choir	chu	chois chois choit	chus... chûmes...
† clore	clos	clos clos clôt closent	

[1] 2nd pers. sing. Imperative: *va*.
[2] The forms in *-oi* (or *-eoi*) (same conjugation as *prévoir*) are accepted by the Académie Française but considered as familiar or even vulgar.

Future	Present Subjunctive	English
believe)		
acquerrai... acquerrons...	acquière acquières acquière acquérions acquériez acquièrent	to acquire
il adviendra	il advienne	to happen
irai... irons...	aille ailles aille allions alliez aillent	to go
assaillirai... assaillirons...	assaille... assaillions...	to assault
assiérai... or assoirai... assiérons... or assoirons...	asseye[2]... asseyions...	to set to seat
aurai... aurons...	aie aies ait ayons ayez aient	to have
boirai... boirons...	boive boives boive buvions buviez boivent	to drink
bouillirai... bouillirons...	bouille... bouillions...	to boil
il braira ils brairont		to bray
		to rustle
cherrai... or choirai... cherrons... or choirons...		to fall
clorai... clorons...	close... closions...	to close

---

[3] Imperative: *aie, ayons, ayez.*
[4] Imperfect Indicative: *il brayait, ils brayaient.*
[5] Imperfect Indicative: *il bruissait, ils bruissaient* or *il bruyait, ils bruyaient.*

French Verbs

Infinitive	Participles	Present Indicative	Past Historic
conclure	concluant conclu	conclus, -s, -t concluons...	conclus... conclûmes...
conduire	conduisant conduit	conduis, -s, -t conduisons...	conduisis... conduisîmes...
confire	confisant confit	confis, -s, -t confisons...	confis... confîmes...
connaître	connaissant connu	connais connais connaît connaissons connaissez connaissent	connus... connûmes...
coudre	cousant cousu	couds... cousons...	cousis... cousîmes...
courir	courant couru	cours,-s,-t courons...	courus... courûmes...
craindre	craignant craint	crains,-s,-t craignons...	craignis... craignîmes...
croire	croyant cru	crois crois croit croyons croyez croient	crus... crûmes...
croître	croissant crû, *m.*, crue, *f.*	croîs croîs croît croissons croissez croissent	crûs... crûmes...
cueillir	cueillant cueilli	cueille... cueillons...	cueillis... cueillîmes...
† déchoir[1]	déchu	déchois déchois déchoit déchoyons déchoyez déchoient	déchus... déchûmes...
devoir	devant dû, *m.*, due, *f.*, dus, *m.pl.*	dois dois doit devons devez doivent	dus... dûmes...
dire	disant dit	dis dis dit disons dites disent	dis... dîmes...
† échoir	échéant échu	il échoit ils échoient	il échut ils échurent

[1] No Imperfect Indicative.

Future	Present Subjunctive	English
conclurai... conclurons...	conclue... concluions...	to conclude
conduirai... conduirons...	conduise... conduisions...	to lead to drive
confirai... confirons...	confise... confisions...	to preserve
connaîtrai... connaîtrons...	connaisse... connaissions...	to know
coudrai... coudrons...	couse... cousions...	to sew
courrai... courrons...	coure... courions...	to run
craindrai... craindrons...	craigne... craignions...	to fear
croirai... croirons...	croie croies croie croyions croyiez croient	to believe
croîtrai... croîtrons...	croisse... croissions...	to grow
cueillerai... cueillerons...	cueille... cueillions...	to gather
décherrai... décherrons...	déchoie déchoies déchoie déchoyions déchoyiez déchoient	to fall to lose
devrai... devrons...	doive doives doive devions deviez doivent	to owe to have to
dirai... dirons...	dise... disions...	to say
il échoira or écherra ils échoiront or écherront	il échoie or échée ils échéent	to fall due

French Verbs

Infinitive	Participles	Present Indicative	Past Historic
écrire	écrivant écrit	écris,-s,-t écrivons...	écrivis... écrivîmes...
envoyer	envoyant envoyé	envoie envoies envoie envoyons envoyez envoient	envoyai... envoyâmes...
être[1]	étant été	suis es est sommes êtes sont	fus... fûmes...
† faillir	faillant failli	faut[2]	faillis[3]... faillîmes...
faire	faisant fait	fais fais fait faisons faites font	fis... fîmes...
† falloir[4]	fallu	il faut	il fallut
† férir[5]	féru		
† forfaire (à)	forfait		
† frire	frit	fris fris frit	
fuir	fuyant fui	fuis fuis fuit fuyons fuyez fuient	fuis... fuîmes...
† gésir[6]	gisant	gît gisons gisez gisent	
haïr	haïssant haï	hais,-s,-t haïssons...	haïs... haïmes[7]...
lire	lisant lu	lis,-s,-t lisons...	lus... lûmes...
luire	luisant lui	luis,-s,-t luisons...	luis... luîmes...
maudire	conjugated like the regular verbs in -ir, e.g. finir, except for the past		
médire (de)	médisant médit	médis... médisons...	médis... médîmes...

[1] Imperfect Indic.: *j'étais*; Imperative: *sois, soyons, soyez*.
[2] Only in the phrase *le cœur me faut*.
[3] In current usage followed by an infinitive, *e.g. il faillit tomber*, he nearly fell.
[4] Imperfect Indic.: *il fallait*.

Future	Present Subjunctive	English
écrirai... écrirons...	écrive... écrivions...	to write
enverrai... enverrons...	envoie envoies envoie envoyions envoyiez envoient	to send
serai... serons...	sois sois soit soyons soyez soient	to be
faudrai *or* faillirai		to fail
ferai... ferons...	fasse... fassions...	to make, to do
il faudra	il faille	to be necessary
		to strike
		to be false (to)
frirai... frirons...		to fry
fuirai... fuirons...	fuie... fuyions...	to flee
		to lie
haïrai... haïrons...	haïsse... haïssions...	to hate
lirai... lirons...	lise... lisions...	to read
luirai... luirons...	luise... luisions...	to gleam
participle (*maudit*).		to curse
médirai... médirons...	médise... médisions...	to speak ill of

[5] The infinitive is used only in the phrase *sans coup férir*, without striking a blow. *Féru* is adjectival only (*féru d'amour*, lovesick).
[6] The Imperfect Indic., *je gisais*, etc., is used.
[7] The plural is written without a circumflex: *haïmes, haïtes*.

French Verbs

Infinitive	Participles	Present Indicative	Past Historic
mettre	mettant mis	mets,-s,-t mettons...	mis... mîmes...
moudre	moulant moulu	mouds mouds moud moulons moulez moulent	moulus... moulûmes...
mourir	mourant mort	meurs meurs meurt mourons mourez meurent	mourus... mourûmes...
mouvoir	mouvant [1]mû, *m.*, mue, *f.*, mus, *m.pl.*	meus meus meut mouvons mouvez meuvent	mus... mûmes...
naître	naissant né	nais nais naît naissons naissez naissent	naquis... naquîmes...
nuire (à)	nuisant nui	nuis,-s,-t nuisons...	nuisis... nuisîmes...
† oindre[2]	oint		
† ouïr[3]	oyant ouï		ouïs... ouïmes...
ouvrir	ouvrant ouvert	ouvre... ouvrons...	ouvris... ouvrîmes...
† paître	paissant	pais pais paît paissons paissez paissent	
plaire	plaisant plu	plais plais plaît plaisons plaisez plaisent	plus... plûmes...
† pleuvoir	pleuvant plu	il pleut	il plut
† poindre	poignant point	il point	
pourvoir	pourvoyant pourvu	pourvois,-s,-t pourvoyons,-yez,-ient	pourvus... pourvûmes...

[1] The past part. of *émouvoir* is *ému*, and of *promouvoir*, *promu* (no circumflex on the *u* of the masculine sing.).

Future	*Present Subjunctive*	*English*
mettrai... mettrons...	mette... mettions...	to put
moudrai... moudrons...	moule... moulions...	to grind
mourrai... mourrons...	meure meures meure mourions mouriez meurent	to die
mouvrai... mouvrons...	meuve meuves meuve mouvions mouviez meuvent	to move
naîtrai... naîtrons...	naisse... naissions...	to be born
nuirai... nuirons...	nuise... nuisions...	to harm
oindrai...		to anoint
ouïrai... ouïrons...		to hear
ouvrirai... ouvrirons...	ouvre... ouvrions...	to open
paîtrai... paîtrons...	paisse... paissions...	to graze
plairai... plairons...	plaise... plaisions...	to please
il pleuvra	il pleuve	to rain
il poindra ils poindront		to dawn to sting
pourvoirai... pourvoirons...	pourvoie... pourvoyions...	to provide

[2] Imperfect Indic.: *je oignais*.
[3] This verb is seldom used other than in the infinitive and in the compound tenses.

647

French Verbs

Infinitive	Participles	Present Indicative	Past Historic
pouvoir	pouvant pu	peux *or* puis peux peut pouvons pouvez peuvent	pus... pûmes...
prendre	prenant pris	prends prends prend prenons prenez prennent	pris... prîmes...
prévoir	prévoyant prévu	prévois,-s,-t prévoyons, -yez, -ient	prévis... prévîmes...
recevoir	recevant reçu	reçois reçois reçoit recevons recevez reçoivent	reçus... reçûmes...
résoudre	résolvant résolu *or* résous	résous résous résout résolvons résolvez résolvent	résolus... résolûmes...
rire	riant ri	ris,-s,-t rions...	ris... rîmes...
savoir[1]	sachant su	sais,-s,-t savons...	sus... sûmes...
sentir	sentant senti	sens,-s,-t sentons...	sentis... sentîmes...
† seoir	seyant	il sied ils siéent	
suffire	suffisant suffi	suffis,-s,-t suffisons...	suffis... suffîmes...
suivre	suivant suivi	suis,-s,-t suivons...	suivis... suivîmes...
surseoir[2]	sursoyant sursis	sursois,-s,-t sursoyons, -yez, -ient	sursis... sursîmes...
taire	conjug. like *plaire* except that there is no circumflex on the *i* of the 3rd		
tenir[3]	tenant tenu	tiens tiens tient tenons tenez tiennent	tins tins tint tînmes tîntes tinrent
† traire	trayant trait	trais,-s,-t trayons...	

[1] Imperative: *sache, sachons, sachez.*
[2] The Past Historic and the Imperfect Indicative are seldom used.

Future	Present Subjunctive	English
pourrai... pourrons...	puisse... puissions...	to be able
prendrai... prendrons...	prenne... prenions...	to take
prévoirai... prévoirons...	prévoie... prévoyions...	to foresee
recevrai... recevrons...	reçoive reçoives reçoive recevions receviez reçoivent	to receive
résoudrai... résoudrons...	résolve... résolvions...	to resolve
rirai... rirons...	rie... riions...	to laugh
saurai... saurons...	sache... sachions...	to know
sentirai... sentirons...	sente... sentions...	to feel to smell
il siéra ils siéront	il siée ils siéent	to become to suit
suffirai... suffirons...	suffise... suffisions...	to suffice
suivrai... suivrons...	suive... suivions...	to follow
surseoirai... surseoirons...	sursoie... sursoyions...	to delay to suspend
Pers. Sing. Pres. Indic.: *il tait.*		to keep silent about
tiendrai... tiendrons...	tienne tiennes tienne tenions teniez tiennent	to hold
trairai... trairons...	traie... trayions...	to milk

Imperfect Subjunctive: *tinsse, -es, tînt, tinssions, -iez, -ent.*

French Verbs

Infinitive	Participles	Present Indicative	Past Historic
vaincre	vainquant vaincu	vaincs vaincs vainc vainquons vainquez vainquent	vainquis... vainquîmes...
valoir	valant valu	vaux, -x, -t valons...	valus... valûmes...
vêtir	vêtant vêtu	vêts, vêts, vêt vêtons...	vêtis... vêtîmes...
vivre	vivant vécu	vis,-s,-t vivons...	vécus... vécûmes...
voir	voyant vu	vois,-s,-t voyons, -yez, -ient	vis... vîmes...
vouloir[1]	voulant voulu	veux veux veut voulons voulez veulent	voulus... voulûmes...

[1] Imperative: *veuille, veuillons, veuillez.*

Future	Present Subjunctive	English
vaincrai... vaincrons...	vainque... vainquions...	to conquer
vaudrai... vaudrons...	[2]vaille... valions...	to be worth
vêtirai... vêtirons...	vête... vêtions...	to clothe
vivrai... vivrons...	vive... vivions...	to live
verrai... verrons...	voie... voyions...	to see
voudrai... voudrons...	veuille... voulions...	to be willing to want, to wish

[2] *prévaloir: prévale, prévalions.*

English Verbs

All verbs not marked *irr.* in the English-French section of the Dictionary come in one of the following categories:

(*a*) Regular verbs, conjugated like WORK or LIVE.

(*b*) Verbs ending in -*y* preceded by one or more consonants, e.g. DENY, REPLY, IMPLY, conjugated like CARRY (i.e. the *y* changes to *i* in the Past Tense and Past Participle).

(*c*) Verbs ending in a single consonant preceded by one or more vowels (but not a diphthong, e.g. WAIT, or a double vowel, e.g. SEEM), which are monosyllabic or in which the stress falls on the last syllable, conjugated like DROP and PREFER (i.e. the final consonant is doubled in the Past Tense and Past Participle).

N.B.   Apart from those which are irregular, all verbs ending in -*l* preceded by one or more vowels (but not a diphthong, e.g. SAIL, or a double vowel, e.g. PEEL) double the *l* in the Past Tense and Past Participle even if the stress does not fall on the last syllable, e.g. IMPERIL, DIAL.

* = obsolete.   *A = obsolete, but still used adjectivally.   † = becoming obsolete.

Infinitive	*Past Tense*	*Past Participle*	*French*
REGULAR VERBS (*a*)			
work	worked	worked	travailler
live	lived	lived	vivre
REGULAR VERBS (*b*)			
carry	carried	carried	porter
REGULAR VERBS (*c*)			
drop	dropped	dropped	laisser tomber
prefer	preferred	preferred	préférer
imperil	imperilled	imperilled	hasarder
dial	dialled	dialled	composer un numéro
IRREGULAR VERBS			
abide	abode	abode	demeurer
awake	awoke	awoken *or* awakened	éveiller
be *Pres. Indic.* am, art, is, are	was, were	been	être
bear	bore	borne *or* born[1]	porter
beat	beat	beaten	battre
beget	begot *begat	begotten	engendrer
begin	began	begun	commencer
bend	bent	bent	courber
bereave	bereaved *or* bereft	bereaved *or* bereft	priver (de)
beseech	besought	besought	supplier
bid	bade *or* bid	bidden *or* bid	ordonner

[1] *born* = né; *borne* = porté.

Infinitive	Past Tense	Past Participle	French
bind	bound	bound *A bounden[1]	lier
bite	bit	bitten	mordre
bleed	bled	bled	saigner
blow	blew	blown	souffler
break	broke	broken	casser
breed	bred	bred	élever
bring	brought	brought	apporter
build	built	built	construire
burn	burnt *or* burned	burnt *or* burned	brûler
burst	burst	burst	éclater
buy	bought	bought	acheter
Pres. Indic. can	could	——	pouvoir
cast	cast	cast	jeter
catch	caught	caught	attraper
choose	chose	chosen	choisir
cleave (*v.t.*)	cleft *clove	cleft *A cloven[2]	fendre
cling	clung	clung	s'attacher
come	came	come	venir
cost	cost	cost	coûter
creep	crept	crept	ramper
crow	crowed *or* †crew	crowed	chanter (coq)
cut	cut	cut	couper
deal	dealt	dealt	distribuer
dig	dug	dug	creuser
do	did	done	faire
draw	drew	drawn	tirer, dessiner
dream	dreamt *or* dreamed	dreamt *or* dreamed	rêver
drink	drank	drunk *A drunken[3]	boire
drive	drove	driven	conduire

[1] It is his *bounden* duty.   [2] *Cloven* hoof.   [3] A *drunken* brawl.

English Verbs

Infinitive	Past Tense	Past Participle	French
dwell	dwelt	dwelt	demeurer
eat	ate	eaten	manger
fall	fell	fallen	tomber
feed	fed	fed	nourrir
feel	felt	felt	sentir
fight	fought	fought	combattre
find	found	found	trouver
flee	fled	fled	fuir
fling	flung	flung	lancer
fly	flew	flown	voler
forbear	forbore	forborne	s'abstenir
forbid	forbade *or* forbad	forbidden	interdire
forget	forgot	forgotten	oublier
forsake	forsook	forsaken	abandonner
freeze	froze	frozen	geler
get	got	got *or* gotten[1]	obtenir, devenir
gird	girded *or* girt	girded *or* girt	ceindre
give	gave	given	donner
go	went	gone	aller
grind	ground	ground	moudre
grow	grew	grown	croître, devenir
hang[2]	hung	hung	pendre
have *Pres. Indic.* have, hast, has	had	had	avoir
hear	heard	heard	entendre
heave	heaved *or* hove	heaved *or* hove	soulever
hew	hewed	hewn *or* hewed	tailler
hide	hid	hidden	cacher
hit	hit	hit	frapper

[1] Ill-*gotten* gains; *gotten* is common in American usage.
[2] To suspend. In the meaning 'to execute by hanging', the verb is regular.

Infinitive	Past Tense	Past Participle	French
hold	held	held	tenir
hurt	hurt	hurt	blesser
keep	kept	kept	garder
kneel	knelt	knelt	s'agenouiller
know	knew	known	savoir
lay	laid	laid	poser
lead	led	led	conduire
lean	leant *or* leaned	leant *or* leaned	pencher
leap	leapt *or* leaped	leapt *or* leaped	sauter
learn	learnt *or* †learned	learnt *or* †learned	apprendre
leave	left	left	laisser, quitter
lend	lent	lent	prêter
let	let	let	laisser
lie[1]	lay	lain	être couché
light	lit *or* lighted	lit *or* lighted	allumer
lose	lost	lost	perdre
make	made	made	faire
Pres. Indic. may	might	—	pouvoir (permission, probabilité)
mean	meant	meant	signifier
meet	met	met	rencontrer
mow	mowed	mowed *or* mown	faucher
pay	paid	paid	payer
put	put	put	mettre
quit	quitted *or* quit	quitted *or* quit	quitter
read	read	read	lire
rend	rent	rent	déchirer
rid	rid	rid	débarrasser
ride	rode	ridden	aller à cheval
ring[2]	rang	rung	sonner

[1] To recline. In the meaning 'to be untruthful', the verb is regular.
[2] (Of a bell). In the meaning 'to put a ring round', the verb is regular.

English Verbs

Infinitive	Past Tense	Past Participle	French
rise	rose	risen	se lever
rive	rived	riven *or* rived	fendre
run	ran	run	courir
saw	sawed	sawn	scier
say	said	said	dire
see	saw	seen	voir
seek	sought	sought	chercher
sell	sold	sold	vendre
send	sent	sent	envoyer
set	set	set	placer
sew	sewed	sewn *or* sewed	coudre
shake	shook	shaken	secouer
Pres. Indic. shall[1]	should[1]	——	——
shear	sheared	shorn *or* sheared	tondre
shed	shed	shed	verser
shine	shone	shone	briller
shoe	shod	shod	chausser
shoot	shot	shot	tirer (au fusil)
show	showed	shown *or* showed	montrer
shrink	shrank	shrunk *A shrunken	rétrécir
shrive	shrove	shriven	se confesser
shut	shut	shut	fermer
sing	sang	sung	chanter
sink	sank	sunk *A sunken[2]	sombrer
sit	sat	sat	être assis
slay	slew	slain	tuer
sleep	slept	slept	dormir
slide	slid	slid	glisser
sling	slung	slung	lancer

[1] Used as auxiliaries only.   [2] *Sunken* cheeks.

Infinitive	Past Tense	Past Participle	French
slink	slunk	slunk	s'esquiver
slit	slit	slit	fendre
smell	smelt or smelled	smelt or smelled	sentir
smite	smote	smitten	frapper
sow	sowed	sown or sowed	semer
speak	spoke *spake	spoken	parler
speed	sped or speeded	sped or speeded	se hâter
spell	spelt or spelled	spelt or spelled	épeler
spend	spent	spent	dépenser
spill	spilt or spilled	spilt or spilled	verser
spin	spun	spun	filer
spit[1]	spat	spit	cracher
split	split	split	fendre
spoil	spoilt or spoiled	spoilt or spoiled	gâter
spread	spread	spread	s'étendre
spring	sprang	sprung	s'élancer
stand	stood	stood	être debout
stave	staved or stove	staved or stove	crever
steal	stole	stolen	voler
stick	stuck	stuck	coller
sting	stung	stung	piquer
stink	stank	stunk	puer
strew	strewed	strewed *A strewn	répandre
stride	strode	stridden	marcher à grands pas
strike	struck	struck *A stricken[2]	frapper
string	strung	strung	ficeler
strive	strove	striven	s'efforcer
swear	swore	sworn	jurer
sweep	swept	swept	balayer

[1] To expectorate. In the meaning 'to put on a spit', the verb is regular.
[2] *Stricken* in years.

English Verbs

Infinitive	Past Tense	Past Participle	French
swell	swelled	swollen *or* swelled	enfler
swim	swam	swum	nager
swing	swung	swung	se balancer
take	took	taken	prendre
teach	taught	taught	enseigner
tear	tore	torn	déchirer
tell	told	told	dire
think	thought	thought	penser
thrive	thrived *or* throve	thrived *or* thriven	prospérer
throw	threw	thrown	jeter
thrust	thrust	thrust	lancer
tread	trod	trodden	fouler
wake	woke *or* waked	waked *or* woken	éveiller
wear	wore	worn	porter (vêtements)
weave	wove	woven	tisser
weep	wept	wept	pleurer
wet	wetted *or* wet	wetted *or* wet	mouiller
will	would	——	vouloir
win	won	won	gagner
wind	wound	wound	enrouler
wring	wrung	wrung	tordre
write	wrote	written	écrire